THE YEAR'S WORK 2009

The Year's Work in English Studies Volume 90

Covering work published in 2009

Edited by
WILLIAM BAKER
and
KENNETH WOMACK
with associate editors

OLGA FISCHER
MARY SWAN
ANNALIESE CONNOLLY
KIRSTIE BLAIR
CHRIS HOPKINS
THERESA SAXON
JAMES DECKER
PAUL SHARRAD

Published for
THE ENGLISH ASSOCIATION
by

OXFORD
UNIVERSITY PRESS

OXFORD
UNIVERSITY PRESS
Great Clarendon Street, Oxford OX2 6DP, UK
Oxford University Press is a department of the University of Oxford.
It furthers the University's objective of excellence in research, scholarship,
and education by publishing worldwide in
Oxford New York
Athens Auckland Bangkok Bogotá Buenos Aires Cape Town
Chennai Dar es Salaam Delhi Florence Hong Kong Istanbul Karachi
Kolkata Kuala Lumpur Madrid Melbourne Mexico City Mumbai Nairobi
Paris São Paulo Shanghai Taipei Tokyo Toronto Warsaw

First published 2011

British Library Cataloguing in Publication Data
Data available
ISSN 0084-4144
ISBN 9780199642892
1 3 5 7 9 10 8 6 4 2
Typeset by Cepha Imaging Pvt. Ltd., Bangalore, India
Printed in Great Britain on acid-free paper by the MPG Books Group

The English Association

The object of The English Association is to promote the knowledge and appreciation of English language and its literatures.

The Association pursues these aims by creating opportunities of co-operation among all those interested in English; by furthering the recognition of English as essential in education; by discussing methods of English teaching; by holding lectures, conferences, and other meetings; by publishing several journals, books, and leaflets; and by forming local branches overseas and at home. English Association Fellowships recognize distinction and achievement in the field of English worldwide.

Publications

The Year's Work in English Studies. An annual narrative bibliography which aims to cover all work of quality in English studies published in a given year. Published by Oxford University Press.

The Year's Work in Critical and Cultural Theory. An annual narrative bibliography which aims to provide comprehensive cover of all work of quality in critical and cultural theory published in a given year. Published by Oxford University Press.

Essays and Studies. A well-established series of annual themed volumes edited each year by a distinguished academic.

English. This internationally-known journal of the Association is aimed at teachers of English in universities and colleges, with articles on all aspects of literature and critical theory, an extensive reviews section and original poetry. Four issues per year. Published by Oxford University Press.

Use of English. The longest-standing journal for English teachers in schools and colleges. Three issues per year.

English 4–11. Designed and developed by primary English specialists to give practical help to primary and middle school teachers. Three issues per year.

English Association Studies. A new monograph series published in association with Liverpool University Press.

Issues in English. Occasional pamphlet series.

Membership

Membership information can be found at http://www.le.ac.uk/engassoc or please write to The English Association, University of Leicester, University Road, Leicester LE1 7RH, UK or email: engassoc@le.ac.uk.

The Year's Work in English Studies

Subscriptions for Volume 90

Institutional (combined rate to both *The Year's Work in English Studies* and *The Year's Work in Critical and Cultural Theory*) print and online: £340.00/$605.00/€510.00. *Institutional* (*The Year's Work in English Studies* only) print and online: £233.00/$436.00/€350.00.

Please note: £/€ rates apply in Europe, US$ elsewhere. All prices include postage, and for subscribers outside the UK delivery is by Standard Air. There may be other subscription rates available. For a complete listing, please visit www.ywes.oxfordjournals.org/oup_journals/ywes/access_purchase/price_list.html.

Online Access

For details please email Oxford University Press Journals Customer Services on: jnls.cust.serv@oup.com.

Order Information

Full prepayment, in the correct currency, is required for all orders. Orders are regarded as firm and payments are not refundable. Subscriptions are accepted and entered on a complete volume basis. Claims cannot be considered more than FOUR months after publication or date of order, whichever is later. All subscriptions in Canada are subject to GST. Subscriptions in the EU may be subject to European VAT. If registered, please supply details to avoid unnecessary charges. For subscriptions that include online versions, a proportion of the subscription price may be subject to UK VAT.

Methods of payment. (i) Cheque (payable to Oxford University Press, Cashiers Office, Great Clarendon Street, Oxford OX2 6DP, UK) in GB£ Sterling (drawn on a UK bank), US$ Dollars (drawn on a US bank), or EU€ Euros. (ii) Bank transfer to Barclays Bank Plc, Oxford Group Office, Oxford (bank sort code 20-65-18) (UK), overseas only Swift code BARC GB 22 (GB£ Sterling to account no. 70299332, IBAN GB89BARC20651870299332; US$ Dollars to account no. 66014600, IBAN GB27BARC20651866014600; EU€ Euros to account no. 78923655, IBAN GB16BARC20651878923655). (iii) Credit card (Mastercard, Visa, Switch or American Express).

Back Issues

The current plus two back volumes are available from Oxford University Press. Previous volumes can be obtained from the Periodicals Service Company, 11 Main Street, Germantown, NY 12526, USA. Email: psc@periodicals.com; tel: +1 (518) 537 4700; fax: +1 (518) 537 5899.

Further information. Journals Customer Service Department, Oxford University Press, Great Clarendon Street, Oxford OX2 6DP, UK. Email: jnls.cust.serv@oup.com; tel (and answerphone outside normal working hours): +44 (0) 1865 353907; fax: +44 (0) 1865 353485. *In the US, please contact:* Journals Customer Service Department, Oxford University Press, 2001 Evans Road, Cary, NC 27513, USA. Email: jnlorders@oup.com; tel (and answerphone outside normal working hours): 800 852 7323 (toll-free in USA/Canada); fax: 919 677 1714. *In Japan, please contact:* Journals Customer Services, Oxford Journals, Oxford University Press, Tokyo, 4-5-10-8F Shiba, Minato-ku, Tokyo 108-8386, Japan. Email: custserv.jp@oup.com; Tel: +81 3 5444 5858; Fax: +81 3 3454 2929.

The Year's Work in English Studies (ISSN 0084 4144) is published annually by Oxford University Press, Oxford, UK. Annual subscription price is £340.00/$605.00/ €510.00. *The Year's Work in English Studies* is distributed by Mercury International, 365 Blair Road, Avenel, NJ 07001, USA. Periodicals postage paid at Rahway, NJ and at additional entry points.

US Postmaster: send address changes to *The Year's Work in English Studies*, c/o Mercury International, 365 Blair Road, Avenel, NJ 07001, USA.

The Table of Contents email alerting service allows anyone who registers their email address to be notified via email when new content goes online. Details are available at http://ywes.oxfordjournals.org/cgi/alerts/etoc.

Permissions

For permissions requests, please visit www.oxfordjournals.org/permissions.

Advertising

Inquiries about advertising should be sent to Oxford Journals Advertising, Oxford University Press, Great Clarendon Street, Oxford, OX2 6DP, UK. Email: jnlsadvertising@oup.com; tel: +44 (0) 1865 354767; fax: +44 (0) 1865 353774.

Disclaimer

Statements of fact and opinion in the articles in *The Year's Work in English Studies* are those of the respective authors and contributors and not of the English Association or Oxford University Press. Neither Oxford University Press nor the English Association make any representation, express or implied, in respect of the accuracy of the material in this journal and cannot accept any legal responsibility or liability for any errors or omissions that may be made.

Contents

Abbreviations

1. Journals, Series and Reference Works

19	*Interdisciplinary Studies in the Long Nineteenth Century*
1650–1850	*1650–1850 Ideas, Aesthetics, and Inquiries in the Early Modern Era*
A&D	*Art and Design*
A&E	*Anglistik und Englischunterricht*
AAA	*Arbeiten aus Anglistik und Amerikanistik*
AAAJ	*Accounting, Auditing and Accountability Journal*
AAR	*African American Review*
ABäG	*Amsterdamer Beiträge zur Älteren Germanistik*
ABC	*American Book Collector*
ABELL	*Annual Bibliography of English Language and Literature*
ABM	*Antiquarian Book Monthly Review*
ABQ	*American Baptist Quarterly*
ABR	*American Benedictine Review* (now *RBR*)
ABSt	*A/B: Auto/Biography Studies*
AC	*Archeologia Classica*
Academy Forum	*Academy Forum*
AcadSF	*Academia Scientiarum Fennica*
ACar	*Analecta Cartusiana*
ACF	*Annuli, Facolta di Lingue e Litterature Straniere di Ca'Foscari*
ACH	*Australian Cultural History*
ACLALSB	*ACLALS Bulletin*
ACM	*Aligarh Critical Miscellany*
ACR	*Australasian Catholic Record*
ACS	*Australian-Canadian Studies: A Journal for the Humanities and Social Sciences*
Acta	*Acta* (Binghamton, NY)
Adaptation	*Adaptation*
AdI	*Annali d'Italianistica*
ADS	*Australasian Drama Studies*
AEB	*Analytical and Enumerative Bibliography*
Æstel	*Æstel*
AF	*Anglistische Forschungen*
AfricanA	*African Affairs*
AfrSR	*African Studies Review*
AfT	*African Theatre*
AgeJ	*Age of Johnson: A Scholarly Annual*
Agenda	*Agenda*
Agni	*Agni Review*
AGP	*Archiv für Geschichte der Philosophie*
Ahornblätter	*Ahornblätter: Marburger Beiträge zur Kanada-Forschung*
AH	*Art History*

AHR	*American Historical Review*
AHS	*Australian Historical Studies*
AI	*American Imago*
AICRJ	*American Indian Culture and Research Journal*
AILA	*Association Internationale de Linguistique Appliqué*
AIQ	*American Indian Quarterly*
AJ	*Art Journal*
AJGLL	*American Journal of Germanic Linguistics and Literatures*
AJIS	*Australian Journal of Irish Studies*
AJL	*Australian Journal of Linguistics*
AJP	*American Journal of Psychoanalysis*
AJPH	*Australian Journal of Politics and History*
AJS	*American Journal of Semiotics*
AKML	*Abhandlungen zur Kunst-, Musik- and Literaturwis-senschaft*
AL	*American Literature*
ALA	*African Literature Association Annuals*
ALASH	*Acta Linguistica Academiae Scientiarum Hungaricae*
Albion	*Albion*
AlexS	*Alexander Shakespeare*
ALH	*Acta Linguistica Hafniensia; International Journal of Linguistics*
Alif	*Journal of Comparative Poetics* (Cairo, Egypt)
ALitASH	*Acta Literaria Academiae Scientiarum Hungaricae*
Allegorica	*Allegorica*
ALN	*American Literary Nationalism Newsletter*
ALR	*American Literary Realism, 1870–1910*
ALS	*Australian Literary Studies*
ALT	*African Literature Today*
Alternatives	*Alternatives*
AmasJ	*Amerasian Journal*
AmDram	*American Drama*
Americana	*Americana*
AmerP	*American Poetry*
AmerS	*American Studies*
AmLH	*American Literary History*
AmLS	*American Literary Scholarship: An Annual*
AMon	*Atlantic Monthly*
AmPer	*American Periodicals*
AmRev	*Americas Review: A Review of Hispanic Literature and Art of the USA*
Amst	*Amerikastudien/American Studies*
AN	*Acta Neophilologica*
Anaïs	*Anaïs*
AnBol	*Analecta Bollandiana*
ANCH	*American Nineteenth Century History*
ANF	*Arkiv för Nordisk Filologi*
Angelaki	*Angelaki*
Anglia	*Anglia: Zeitschrift für Englische Philologie*
Anglistica	*Anglistica*
Anglistik	*Anglistik: Mitteilungen des Verbandes Deutscher Anglisten*
AnH	*Analecta Husserliana*
AnL	*Anthropological Linguistics*
AnM	*Annuale Mediaevale*
Ann	*Annales: Économies, Sociétés, Civilisations*

ANQ	*ANQ: A Quarterly Journal of Short Articles, Notes and Reviews* (formerly *American Notes and Queries*)
AntColl	*Antique Collector*
Anthurium	*Anthurium: A Caribbean Studies Journal*
AntigR	*Antigonish Review*
Antipodes	*Antipodes: A North American Journal of Australian Literature*
ANStu	*Anglo-Norman Studies*
ANZSC	*Australian and New Zealand Studies in Canada*
ANZTR	*Australian and New Zealand Theatre Record*
APBR	*Atlantic Provinces Book Review*
APL	*Antwerp Papers in Linguistics*
AppLing	*Applied Linguistics*
APR	*American Poetry Review*
AQ	*American Quarterly*
Aquarius	*Aquarius*
AR	*Antioch Review*
ArAA	*Arbeiten aus Anglistik und Amerikanistik*
ARAL	*Annual Review of Applied Linguistics*
Arcadia	*Arcadia*
Archiv	*Archiv für das Stadium der Neueren Sprachen und Literaturen*
ARCS	*American Review of Canadian Studies*
ArdenS	*Arden Shakespeare*
ArielE	*Ariel: A Review of International English Literature*
Arion	*Arion: A Journal of the Humanities and the Classics*
ArkQ	*Arkansas Quarterly: A Journal of Criticism*
ArkR	*Arkansas Review: A Journal of Criticism*
ArQ	*Arizona Quarterly*
ARS	*Augustan Reprint Society*
ARSR	*Australian Religion Studies Review*
ArtB	*Art Bulletin*
Arth	*Arthuriana*
ArthI	*Arthurian Interpretations*
ArthL	*Arthurian Literature*
Arv	*Arv: Nordic Yearbook of Folklore*
AS	*American Speech*
ASch	*American Scholar*
ASE	*Anglo-Saxon England*
ASInt	*American Studies International*
ASoc	*Arts in Society*
Aspects	*Aspects: Journal of the Language Society* (University of Essex)
AspectsAF	*Aspects of Australian Fiction*
ASPR	*Anglo-Saxon Poetic Records*
ASSAH	*Anglo-Saxon Studies in Archaeology and History*
Assaph	*Assaph: Studies in the Arts (Theatre Studies)*
Assays	*Assays: Critical Approaches to Medieval and Renaissance Texts*
ASUI	*Analele Stiintifice ale Universitatii 'Al.I. Cuza' din lasi (Serie Noua), e. Lingvistica*
AteneaPR	*Atenea: A Bilingual Journal of the Humanities and Social Science*
Atlantis	*Atlantis: A Journal of the Spanish Association for Anglo-American Studies*
ATQ	*American Transcendental Quarterly: A Journal of New England Writers*

ATR	*Anglican Theological Review*
AuBR	*Australian Book Review*
AuFolk	*Australian Folklore*
AuFS	*Australian Feminist Studies*
AuHR	*Australian Humanities Review*
AuJL	*Australian Journal of Linguistics*
AUMLA	*Journal of the Australasian Universities Language and Literature Association*
Aurealis	*Australian Fantasy and Science Fiction Magazine*
AuS	*Australian Studies*
AuSA	*Australian Studies* (Australia)
AusCan	*Australian-Canadian Studies*
AusPl	*Australian Playwrights*
AusRB	*Australians' Review of Books*
AustrianS	*Austrian Studies*
AuVSJ	*Australasian Victorian Studies Journal*
AuWBR	*Australian Women's Book Review*
AvC	*Avalon to Camelot*
AY	*Arthurian Yearbook*
BakhtinN	*Bakhtin Newsletter*
BALF	*Black American Literature Forum*
BandL	*Borrowers and Lenders: The Journal of Shakespeare and Appropriation*
BAReview	*British Academy Review*
BARS Bulletin	*British Association for Romantic Studies Bulletin & Review*
BAS	*British and American Studies*
BASAM	*BASA Magazine*
BathH	*Bath History*
BaylorJ	*Baylor Journal of Theatre and Performance*
BayreuthAS	*Bayreuth African Studies*
BB	*Bulletin of Bibliography*
BBCS	*Bulletin of the Board of Celtic Studies*
BBCSh	*BBC Shakespeare*
BBN	*British Book News*
BBSIA	*Bulletin Bibliographique de la Société Internationale Arthurienne*
BC	*Book Collector*
BCan	*Books in Canada*
BCMA	*Bulletin of Cleveland Museum of Art*
BCS	*B.C. Studies*
BDEC	*Bulletin of the Department of English* (Calcutta)
BDP	*Beiträge zur Deutschen Philologie*
Belfagor	*Belfagor: Rassegna di Varia Umanità*
Believer	*Believer*
Bell	*Belgian Essays on Language and Literature*
BEPIF	*Bulletin des Itudes Portugaises et Brésiliennes*
BFLS	*Bulletin de la Faculté des Lettres de Strasbourg*
BGDSL	*Beiträge zur Geschichte der Deutschen Sprache and Literatur*
BH	*Book History*
BHI	*British Humanities Index*
BHL	*Bibliotheca Hagiographica Latina Antiquae et Mediae Aetatis*
BHM	*Bulletin of the History of Medicine*
BHR	*Bibliothèque d'Humanisme et Renaissance*
BHS	*Bulletin of Hispanic Studies*

BI	*Books at Iowa*
Biblionews	*Biblionews and Australian Notes and Queries: A Journal for Book Collectors*
Bibliotheck	*Bibliotheck: A Scottish Journal of Bibliography and Allied Topics*
Biography	*Biography: An Interdisciplinary Quarterly*
BioL	*Biolinguistics*
BIS	*Browning Institute Studies: An Annual of Victorian Literary and Cultural History*
BJA	*British Journal of Aesthetics*
BJCS	*British Journal of Canadian Studies*
BJDC	*British Journal of Disorders of Communication*
BJECS	*British Journal for Eighteenth-Century Studies*
BJHP	*British Journal for the History of Philosophy*
BJHS	*British Journal for the History of Science*
BJJ	*Ben Jonson Journal*
BJL	*Belgian Journal of Linguistics*
BJPS	*British Journal for the Philosophy of Science*
BJRL	*Bulletin of the John Rylands* (University Library of Manchester)
BJS	*British Journal of Sociology*
Blake	*Blake: An Illustrated Quarterly*
BLE	*Bulletin de Littérature Ecclésiastique*
BLJ	*British Library Journal*
BLR	*Bodleian Library Record*
BMC	*Book and Magazine Collector*
BMJ	*British Medical Journal*
BN	*Beiträge zur Namenforschung*
BNB	*British National Bibliography*
BoH	*Book History*
Bookbird	*Bookbird*
Borderlines	*Borderlines*
Boundary	*Boundary 2: A Journal of Postmodern Literature and Culture*
BP	*Banasthali Patrika*
BPMA	*Bulletin of Philadelphia Museum of Art*
BPN	*Barbara Pym Newsletter*
BQ	*Baptist Quarterly*
BRASE	*Basic Readings in Anglo-Saxon England*
BRH	*Bulletin of Research in the Humanities*
Brick	*Brick: A Journal of Reviews*
BRMMLA	*Bulletin of the Rocky Mountain Modern Language Association*
BRONZS	*British Review of New Zealand Studies*
BS	*Bronte Studies*
BSAL	*Beckford Society Annual Lecture*
BSANZB	*Bibliographical Society of Australia and New Zealand Bulletin*
BSE	*Brno Studies in English*
BSEAA	*Bulletin de la Société d'Études Anglo-Américaines des XVIIe et XVIIIe Siècles*
BSJ	*Baker Street Journal: An Irregular Quarterly of Sherlockiana*
BSLP	*Bulletin de la Société de Linguistique de Paris*
BSNotes	*Browning Society Notes*
BSRS	*Bulletin of the Society for Renaissance Studies*
BSSA	*Bulletin de la Société de Stylistique Anglaise*
BST	*Brontë Society Transactions*
BSUF	*Ball State University Forum*

BTHGNewsl	*Book Trade History Group Newsletter*
BTLV	*Bijdragen tot de Taal-, Land- en Volkenhunde*
Bul	*Bulletin (Australia)*
Bullán	*Bullán*
BunyanS	*Bunyan Studies*
BuR	*Bucknell Review*
BurlM	*Burlington Magazine*
BurnsC	*Burns Chronicle*
BWPLL	*Belfast Working Papers in Language and Linguistics*
BWVACET	*Bulletin of the West Virginia Association of College English Teachers*
ByronJ	*Byron Journal*
CABS	*Contemporary Authors Bibliographical Series*
CahiersE	*Cahiers Élisabéthains*
CAIEF	*Cahiers de l'Association Internationale des Études Françaises*
Caliban	*Caliban* (Toulouse, France)
Callaloo	*Callaloo*
CalR	*Calcutta Review*
CamObsc	*Camera Obscura: A Journal of Feminism and Film Theory*
CamR	*Cambridge Review*
CanD	*Canadian Drama/L'Art Dramatique Canadienne*
CanJL	*Canadian Journal of Linguistics*
C&L	*Christianity and Literature*
C&Lang	*Communication and Languages*
C&M	*Classica et Medievalia*
CanL	*Canadian Literature*
CAnn	*Carlyle Annual*
CanPo	*Canadian Poetry*
CapR	*Capilano Review*
CARA	*Centre Aixois de Recherches Anglaises*
Carib	*Carib*
Caribana	*Caribana*
CaribW	*Caribbean Writer*
CarR	*Caribbean Review*
Carrell	*Carrell: Journal of the Friends of the University of Miami Library*
CASE	*Cambridge Studies in Anglo-Saxon England*
CathHR	*Catholic Historical Review*
CatR	*Catalan Review*
CaudaP	*Cauda Pavonis*
CBAA	*Current Bibliography on African Affairs*
CBEL	*Cambridge Bibliography of English Literature*
CCL	*Canadian Children's Literature*
CCor	*Cardiff Corvey: Reading the Romantic Text*
CCRev	*Comparative Civilizations Review*
CCS	*Comparative Critical Studies*
CCrit	*Comparative Criticism: An Annual Journal*
CCTES	*Conference of College Teachers of English Studies*
CCV	*Centro de Cultura Valenciana*
CDALB	*Concise Dictionary of American Literary Biography*
CDCP	*Comparative Drama Conference Papers*
CDIL	*Cahiers de l'Institut de Linguistique de Louvain*
CdL	*Cahiers de Lexicologie*
CDS	*Critical Discourse Studies*

CE	*College English*
CEA	*CEA Critic*
CEAfr	*Cahiers d'Études Africaines*
CE&S	*Commonwealth Essays and Studies*
CentR	*Centennial Review*
Cervantes	*Cervantes*
CF	*Crime Factory*
CFM	*Canadian Fiction Magazine*
CFS	*Cahiers Ferdinand de Saussure: Revue de Linguistique Générale*
CH	*Computers and the Humanities*
Chapman	*Chapman*
Chasqui	*Chasqui*
ChauR	*Chaucer Review*
ChauS	*Chaucer Studion*
ChauY	*Chaucer Yearbook*
ChE	*Changing English*
ChH	*Church History*
ChildL	*Children's Literature: Journal of Children's Literature Studies*
ChiR	*Chicago Review*
ChLB	*Charles Lamb Bulletin*
CHLSSF	*Commentationes Humanarum Litterarum Societatis Scientiarum Fennicae*
CHR	*Camden History Review*
ChRC	*Church History and Religious Culture*
CHum	*Computers and the Humanities*
CI	*Critical Idiom*
CILT	*Amsterdam Studies in the Theory and History of the Language Sciences IV: Current Issues in Linguistic Theory*
Cinéaste	*Cinéaste*
CinJ	*Cinema Journal*
CIQ	*Colby Quarterly*
CISh	*Contemporary Interpretations of Shakespeare*
Cithara	*Cithara: Essays in the Judaeo Christian Tradition*
CJ	*Classical Journal*
CJE	*Cambridge Journal of Education*
CJH	*Canadian Journal of History*
CJIS	*Canadian Journal of Irish Studies*
CJL	*Canadian Journal of Linguistics*
CJR	*Christian–Jewish Relations*
CK	*Common Knowledge*
CL	*Comparative Literature* (Eugene, OR)
CLAJ	*CLA Journal*
CLAQ	*Children's Literature Association Quarterly*
ClarkN	*Clark Newsletter: Bulletin of the UCLA Center for Seventeenth- and Eighteenth-Century Studies*
ClassW	*Classical World*
CLC	*Columbia Library Columns*
CLE	*Children's Literature in Education*
CLet	*Confronto Letterario*
CLIN	*Cuadernos de Literatura*
ClioI	*Clio: A Journal of Literature, History and the Philosophy of History*
CLLT	*Corpus Linguistics and Linguistic Theory*
CLQ	*Colby Library Quarterly*

CLS	*Comparative Literature Studies*
Clues	*Clues: A Journal of Detection*
CMCS	*Cambridge Medieval Celtic Studies*
CML	*Classical and Modern Literature*
CN	*Chaucer Newsletter*
CNIE	*Commonwealth Novel in English*
CogLing	*Cognitive Linguistics*
Cognition	*Cognition*
Cog&Em	*Cognition and Emotion*
ColB	*Coleridge Bulletin*
ColF	*Columbia Forum*
Collections	*Collections*
CollG	*Colloquia Germanica*
CollL	*College Literature*
Colloquy	*Colloquy: Text Theory Critique*
Com	*Commonwealth*
Comitatus	*Comitatus: A Journal of Medieval and Renaissance Studies*
Commentary	*Commentary*
Comparatist	*Comparatist: Journal of the Southern Comparative Literature Association*
ComparativeCS	*Comparative Critical Studies*
CompD	*Comparative Drama*
CompLing	*Contemporary Linguistics*
ConcordSaunterer	*Concord Saunterer: Annual Journal of the Thoreau Society*
Configurations	*Official Journal of the Society for Literature, Science and the Arts*
ConfLett	*Confronto Letterario*
ConL	*Contemporary Literature*
Connotations	*Connotations*
ConnR	*Connecticut Review*
Conradian	*Conradian*
Conradiana	*Conradiana: A Journal of Joseph Conrad Studies*
ContempR	*Contemporary Review*
ConTR	*Contemporary Theatre Review*
Coppertales	*Coppertales: A Journal of Rural Arts*
Cosmos	*Cosmos*
Costume	*Journal of the Costume Society*
CP	*Concerning Poetry*
CQ	*Cambridge Quarterly*
CR	*Critical Review*
CRCL	*Canadian Review of Comparative Literature*
CRev	*Chesterton Review*
CRevAS	*Canadian Review of American Studies*
Crit	*Critique: Studies in Modern Fiction*
CritI	*Critical Inquiry*
Criticism	*Criticism: A Quarterly for Literature and the Arts*
Critique	*Critique* (Paris)
CritQ	*Critical Quarterly*
CritT	*Critical Texts: A Review of Theory and Criticism*
CrM	*Critical Mass*
CRNLE	*CRNLE Reviews Journal*
Crossings	*Crossings*
CRUX	*CRUX: A Journal on the Teaching of English*
CS	*Critical Survey*

CSA	*Carlyle Studies Annual*
CSASE	*Cambridge Studies in Anglo-Saxon England*
CSCC	*Case Studies in Contemporary Criticism*
CSELT	*Cambridge Studies in Eighteenth-Century Literature and Thought*
CSLBull	*Bulletin of the New York C.S. Lewis Society*
CSLL	*Cardozo Studies in Law and Literature*
	Critical Studies in Media Communication
CSML	*Cambridge Studies in Medieval Literature*
CSNCLC	*Cambridge Studies in Nineteenth-Century Literature and Culture*
CSPC	*Cambridge Studies in Paleography and Codicology*
CSR	*Cambridge Studies in Romanticism*
CSRev	*Christian Scholar's Review*
CStA	*Carlyle Studies Annual* (previously CAnn)
CTC	
CTR	*Canadian Theatre Review*
Cuadernos	*Cuadernos de Literatura Infantil y Juvenil*
CulC	*Cultural Critique*
CulS	*Cultural Studies*
CulSR	*Cultural Studies Review*
CUNY	*CUNY English Forum*
CultGeo	*Cultural Geographies*
Current Writing	*Current Writing: Text and Reception in Southern Africa*
CV2	*Contemporary Verse 2*
CVE	*Cahiers Victoriens et Edouardiens*
CW	*Current Writing: Text and Perception in Southern Africa*
CWAAS	*Transactions of the Cumberland and Westmorland Antiquarian and Archaeological Society*
CWS	*Canadian Woman Studies*
Cycnos	
DA	*Dictionary of Americanisms*
DAE	*Dictionary of American English*
DAEM	*Deutsches Archiv für Erforschung des Mittelalters*
DAI	*Dissertation Abstracts International*
DAL	*Descriptive and Applied Linguistics*
D&CN&Q	*Devon and Cornwall Notes and Queries*
D&S	*Discourse and Society*
Daphnis	*Daphnis: Zeitschrift für Mittlere Deutsche Literatur*
DC	*Dickens Companions*
DerbyM	*Derbyshire Miscellany*
Descant	*Descant*
DFS	*Dalhousie French Studies*
DHLR	*D.H. Lawrence Review*
DHS	*Dix-huitième Siècle*
Diac	*Diacritics*
Diachronica	*Diachronica*
Dialogue	*Dialogue: Canadian Philosophical Review*
Dickensian	*Dickensian*
DicS	*Dickinson Studies*
Dictionaries	*Dictionaries: Journal of the Dictionary Society of North America*
Dionysos	*Dionysos*
Discourse	*Discourse*
DisS	*Discourse Studies*

DLB — *Dictionary of Literary Biography*
DLN — *Doris Lessing Newsletter*
DM — *Dublin Magazine*
DMT — *Durham Medieval Texts*
DNB — *Dictionary of National Biography*
DOE — *Dictionary of Old English*
Dolphin — *Dolphin: Publications of the English Department* (University of Aarhus)
DOST — *Dictionary of the Older Scottish Tongue*
DownR — *Downside Review*
DPr — *Discourse Processes*
DQ — *Denver Quarterly*
DQR — *Dutch Quarterly Review of Anglo-American Letters*
DQu — *Dickens Quarterly*
DR — *Dalhousie Review*
Drama — *Drama: The Quarterly Theatre Review*
DrS — *Dreiser Studies*
DS — *Deep South*
DSA — *Dickens Studies Annual*
DSNA — *DSNA Newsletter*
DubJJJ — *Dublin James Joyce Journal*
DU — *Der Deutschunterricht: Beiträge zu Seiner Praxis und Wissenschaftlichen Grundlegung*
DUJ — *Durham University Journal*
DVLG — *Deutsche Viertejahrsschrift für Literaturwissenschaft und Geistesgeschichte*
DWPELL — *Dutch Working Papers in English Language and Linguistics*
EA — *Études Anglaises*
EAL — *Early American Literature*
E&D — *Enlightenment and Dissent*
E&S — *Essays and Studies*
E&Soc — *Economy and Society*
EarT — *Early Theatre*
EAS — *Early American Studies*
EASt — *Englisch Amerikanische Studien*
EBST — *Edinburgh Bibliographical Society Transactions*
EC — *Études Celtiques*
ECan — *Études Canadiennes/Canadian Studies*
ECCB — *Eighteenth Century: A Current Bibliography*
ECent — *Eighteenth Century: Theory and Interpretation*
ECF — *Eighteenth-Century Fiction*
ECI — *Eighteenth-Century Ireland*
ECIntell — *East-Central Intelligencer*
ECLife — *Eighteenth-Century Life*
ECN — *Eighteenth-Century Novel*
ECon — *L'Époque Conradienne*
ECr — *L'Esprit Créateur*
ECS — *Eighteenth-Century Studies*
ECSTC — *Eighteenth-Century Short Title Catalogue*
ECW — *Essays on Canadian Writing*
ECWomen — *Eighteenth-Century Women: Studies in their Lives, Work, and Culture*
EDAMN — *EDAM Newsletter*

EDAMR	*Early Drama, Art, and Music Review*
EDH	*Essays by Divers Hands*
EdL	*Études de Lettres*
EdN	*Editors' Notes: Bulletin of the Conference of Editors of Learned Journals*
EDSL	*Encyclopedic Dictionary of the Sciences of Language*
EEMF	*Early English Manuscripts in Facsimile*
EF	*Études Francaises*
EHL	*English Historical Linguistics*
EHR	*English Historical Review*
EI	*Études Irlandaises* (Lille)
EIC	*Essays in Criticism*
EinA	*English in Africa*
EiP	*Essays in Poetics*
EIRC	*Explorations in Renaissance Culture*
Éire	*Éire-Ireland*
EiTET	*Essays in Theatre/Études Théâtrales*
EIUC	
EJ	*English Journal*
EJES	*European Journal of English Studies*
EL	*Études lawrenciennes*
ELangT	*ELT Journal: An International Journal for Teachers of English to Speakers of Other Languages*
ELet	*Esperienze Letterarie: Rivista Trimestrale di Critica e Cultura*
ELH	*English Literary History*
ELing	*English Linguistics*
ELL	*English Language and Linguistics*
ELN	*English Language Notes*
ELR	*English Literary Renaissance*
ELS	*English Literary Studies*
ELT	*English Literature in Transition*
ELWIU	*Essays in Literature* (Western Illinois University)
EM	*English Miscellany*
Embl	*Emblematica: An Interdisciplinary Journal of English Studies*
EMD	*European Medieval Drama*
EME	*Early Modern Europe*
EMedE	*Early Medieval Europe* (online)
EMLS	*Early Modern Literary Studies* (online)
EMMS	*Early Modern Manuscript Studies*
EMS	*English Manuscript Studies, 1100–1700*
EMu	*Early Music*
EMW	*Early Modern Englishwomen*
Encult	*Enculturation: Cultural Theories and Rhetorics*
Encyclia	*Encyclia*
English	*English: The Journal of the English Association*
EnT	*English Today: The International Review of the English Language*
EONR	*Eugene O'Neill Review*
EPD	*English Pronouncing Dictionary*
ER	*English Review*
ERLM	*Europe-Revue Littéraire Mensuelle*
ERR	*European Romantic Review*
ES	*English Studies*

ESA	*English Studies in Africa*
ESC	*English Studies in Canada*
ESQ	*ESQ: A Journal of the American Renaissance*
ESRS	*Emporia State Research Studies*
EssaysMedSt	*Essays in Medieval Studies*
EST	*Eureka Street*
Estudios Ingleses	*Estudios Ingleses de la Universidad Complutense*
ET	*Elizabethan Theatre*
Etropic	*Etropic*
EurekaStudies	*Eureka Studies*
EuroS	*European Studies: A Journal of European Culture, History and Politics*
EWhR	*Edith Wharton Review*
EWIP	*Edinburgh University, Department of Linguistics, Work in Progress*
EWN	*Evelyn Waugh Newsletter*
EWPAL	*Edinburgh Working Papers in Applied Linguistics*
EWW	*English World-Wide*
Excavatio	*Excavatio*
Exemplaria	*Exemplaria*
Exit	
Expl	*Explicator*
Extrapolation	*Extrapolation: A Journal Science Fiction and Fantasy*
FC	*Feminist Collections: A Quarterly of Women's Studies Resources*
FCEMN	*Mystics Quarterly* (formerly *Fourteenth-Century English Mystics Newsletter*)
FCS	*Fifteenth-Century Studies*
FDT	*Fountainwell Drama Texts*
FemR	*Feminist Review*
FemSEL	*Feminist Studies in English Literature*
FemT	*Feminist Theory*
FFW	*Food and Foodways*
FH	*Die Neue Gesellschaft/Frankfurter Hefte*
Fiction International	*Fiction International*
FilmJ	*Film Journal*
FilmQ	*Film Quarterly*
FilmS	*Film Studies*
Fiveb	*Fivebells*
FiveP	*Five Points: A Journal of Literature and Art* (Atlanta, GA)
FJS	*Fu Jen Studies: Literature and Linguistics* (Taipei)
FLH	*Folia Linguistica Historica*
Florilegium	*Florilegium: Carleton University Annual Papers on Classical Antiquity and the Middle Ages*
FLS	*Foreign Literature Studies* (Central China Normal University, Wuhan, People's Republic of China)
FMLS	*Forum for Modern Language Studies*
FNS	*Frank Norris Studies*
Folklore	*Folklore*
FoLi	*Folia Linguistica*
Forum	*Forum*
FranS	*Franciscan Studies*
FreeA	*Free Associations*
FrontenacR	*Revue Frontenac*

Frontiers	*Frontiers: A Journal of Women's Studies*
FS	*French Studies*
FSt	*Feminist Studies*
FT	*Fashion Theory*
FuL	*Functions of Language*
Futures	*Futures*
GAG	*Göppinger Arbeiten zur Germanistik*
GaR	*Georgia Review*
GBB	*George Borrow Bulletin*
GBK	*Gengo Bunka Kenkyu: Studies in Language and Culture*
GEGHLS	*George Eliot–George Henry Lewes Studies*
GeM	*Genealogists Magazine*
Genders	*Genders*
Genre	*Genre*
GER	*George Eliot Review*
Gestus	*Gestus: A Quarterly Journal of Brechtian Studies*
Gettysburg Review	*Gettysburg Review*
GG@G	*Generative Grammar in Geneva* (online)
GHJ	*George Herbert Journal*
GissingJ	*Gissing Journal*
GJ	*Gutenberg-Jahrbuch*
GL	*General Linguistics*
GL&L	*German Life and Letters*
GlasR	*Glasgow Review*
Glossa	*Glossa: An International Journal of Linguistics*
GLQ	*A Journal of Lesbian and Gay Studies* (Duke University)
GLS	*Grazer Linguistische Studien*
GPQ	*Great Plains Quarterly*
GR	*Germanic Review*
Gramma	*Gramma: Journal of Theory and Criticism*
Gramma/TTT	*Tijdschrift voor Taalwetenschap*
GrandS	*Grand Street*
Granta	*Granta*
Greyfriar	*Greyfriar Siena Studies in Literature*
GRM	*Germanisch-Romanische Monatsschrift*
Grove	*The Grove: Working Papers on English Studies*
GSE	*Gothenberg Studies in English*
GSJ	*Gaskell Society Journal*
GSN	*Gaskell Society Newsletter*
GURT	*Georgetown University Round Table on Language and Linguistics*
HamS	*Hamlet Studies*
H&T	*History and Theory*
HardyR	*Hardy Review*
Harvard Law Review	*Harvard Law Review*
Haskins Soc Jnl	*Haskins Society Journal*
HatcherR	*Hatcher Review*
HazlittR	*The Hazlitt Review*
HBS	*Henry Bradshaw Society*
HC	*Hollins Critic*
HCM	*Hitting Critical Mass: A Journal of Asian American Cultural Criticism*
HE	*History of Education*

HEAT	*HEAT*
Hecate	*Hecate: An Interdisciplinary Journal of Women's Liberation*
HEdQ	*History of Education Quarterly*
HEI	*History of European Ideas*
HeineJ	*Heine Jahrbuch*
HEL	*Histoire Épistémologie Language*
Helios	*Helios*
HEng	*History of the English Language*
Hermathena	*Hermathena: A Trinity College Dublin Review*
HeroicA	*Heroic Age: A Journal of Early Medieval Northwestern Europe*
HeyJ	*Heythrop Journal*
HFR	*Hayden Ferry Review*
HistJ	*Historical Journal*
History	*History: The Journal of the Historical Association*
HistR	*Historical Research*
HJEAS	*Hungarian Journal of English and American Studies*
HJR	*Henry James Review* (Baton Rouge, LA)
HL	*Historiographia Linguistica*
HLB	*Harvard Library Bulletin*
HLQ	*Huntingdon Library Quarterly*
HLSL	(online)
HNCIS	*Harvester New Critical Introductions to Shakespeare*
HNR	*Harvester New Readings*
HOPE	*History of Political Economy*
HopRev	*Hopkins Review*
HPT	*History of Political Thought*
HQ	*Hopkins Quarterly*
HR	*Harvard Review*
HRB	*Hopkins Research Bulletin*
HSci	*History of Science*
HSE	*Hungarian Studies in English*
HSELL	*Hiroshima Studies in English Language and Literature*
HSJ	*Housman Society Journal*
HSL	*University of Hartford Studies in Literature*
HSN	*Hawthorne Society Newsletter*
HSSh	*Hungarian Studies in Shakespeare*
HSSN	*Henry Sweet Society Newsletter*
HT	*History Today*
HTR	*Harvard Theological Review*
HudR	*Hudson Review*
HumeS	*Hume Studies*
HumLov	*Humanistica Lovaniensia: Journal of Neo-Latin Studies*
Humor	*Humor: International Journal of Humor Research*
HUSL	*Hebrew University Studies in Literature and the Arts*
HWJ	*History Workshop*
HWS	*History Workshop Series*
Hypatia	*Hypatia*
IAL	*Issues in Applied Linguistics*
IAN	*Izvestiia Akademii Nauk SSSR* (Moscow)
I&C	*Ideology and Consciousness*
I&P	*Ideas and Production*
ICAME	*International Computer Archive of Modern and Medieval English*
ICS	*Illinois Classical Studies*

IEEETrans	*IEEE Transactions on Professional Communications*
IF	*Indogermanische Forschungen*
IFR	*International Fiction Review*
IGK	*Irland: Gesellschaft and Kultur*
IJAES	*International Journal of Arabic-English Studies*
IJAL	*International Journal of Applied Linguistics*
IJB	*International Journal of Bilingualism*
IJBEB	*International Journal of Bilingual Education & Bilingualism*
IJCL	*International Journal of Corpus Linguistics*
IJCT	*International Journal of the Classical Tradition*
IJECS	*Indian Journal for Eighteenth-Century Studies*
IJES	*Indian Journal of English Studies*
IJL	*International Journal of Lexicography*
IJPR	*International Journal for Philosophy of Religion*
IJSL	*International Journal of the Sociology of Language*
IJSS	*Indian Journal of Shakespeare Studies*
IJWS	*International Journal of Women's Studies*
ILR	*Indian Literary Review*
ILS	*Irish Literary Supplement*
ILStud	*Interdisciplinary Literary Studies: A Journal of Criticism and Theory*
Imaginaires	*Imaginaires*
Imago	*Imago: New Writing*
IMB	*International Medieval Bibliography*
Imprimatur	*Imprimatur*
Indexer	*Indexer*
IndH	*Indian Horizons*
IndL	*Indian Literature*
InG	*In Geardagum: Essays on Old and Middle English Language and Literature*
Inklings	*Inklings: Jahrbuch für Literatur and Ästhetik*
Ioc	*Index to Censorship*
Inquiry	*Inquiry: An Interdisciplinary Journal of Philosophy*
Interactions	*Interactions: Aegean Journal of English and American Studies*
InteractionsAJ	*Interactions: Aegean Journal of English and American Studies/ Ege Ingiliz ve Amerikan Incelemeleri Dergisi*
Interlink	*Interlink*
Interpretation	*Interpretation*
Intertexts	*Intertexts*
Interventions	*Interventions: The International Journal of Postcolonial Studies*
IowaR	*Iowa Review*
IPrag	*Intercultural Pragmatics*
IRAL	*IRAL: International Review of Applied Linguistics in Language Teaching*
Iris	*Iris: A Journal of Theory on Image and Sound*
IS	*Italian Studies*
ISh	*Independent Shavian*
ISJR	*Iowa State Journal of Research*
Island	*Island Magazine*
Islands	*Islands*
Isle	*Interdisciplinary Studies in Literature and Environment*
ISR	*Irish Studies Review*
IUR	*Irish University Review: A Journal of Irish Studies*
JAAC	*Journal of Aesthetics and Art Criticism*

JAAR	*Journal of the American Academy of Religion*
Jacket	*Jacket*
JADT	*Journal of American Drama and Theatre*
JAF	*Journal of American Folklore*
JafM	*Journal of African Marxists*
JAIS	*Journal of Anglo-Italian Studies*
JAL	*Journal of Australian Literature*
JamC	*Journal of American Culture*
JAmH	*Journal of American History*
JAmS	*Journal of American Studies*
JAP	*Journal of Analytical Psychology*
JAPC	*Journal of Asian Pacific Communication*
JArabL	*Journal of Arabic Literature*
JAS	*Journal of Australian Studies*
JASAL	*Journal of the Association for the Study of Australian Literature*
JAStT	*Journal of American Studies of Turkey*
JBeckS	*Journal of Beckett Studies*
JBS	*Journal of British Studies*
JBSSJ	*Journal of the Blake Society at St James*
JCAKSU	*Journal of the College of Arts* (King Saud University)
JCanL	*Journal of Canadian Literature*
JCC	*Journal of Canadian Culture*
JCERL	*Journal of Classic and English Renaissance Literature*
JCF	*Journal of Canadian Fiction*
JCGL	*Journal of Comparative Germanic Linguistics*
JChL	*Journal of Child Language*
JChLS	*Journal of Children's Literature Studies*
JCL	*Journal of Commonwealth Literature*
JCP	*Journal of Canadian Poetry*
JCPCS	*Journal of Commonwealth and Postcolonial Studies*
JCSJ	*John Clare Society Journal*
JCSR	*Journal of Canadian Studies/Revue d'Études Canadiennes*
JCSt	*Journal of Caribbean Studies*
JDECU	*Journal of the Department of English* (Calcutta University)
JDHLS	*Journal of D.H. Lawrence Studies* (formerly *The Journal of the D.H. Lawrence Society*)
JDJ	*John Donne Journal*
JDN	*James Dickey Newsletter*
JDTC	*Journal of Dramatic Theory and Criticism*
JEBS	*Journal of the Early Book Society*
JECS	*Journal of Eighteenth-Century British Studies (formerly British Journal ...[BJECS])*
JEDRBU	*Journal of the English Department* (Rabindra Bharati University)
JEEBS	
JEGP	*Journal of English and Germanic Philology*
JEH	*Journal of Ecclesiastical History*
JELL	*Journal of English Language and Literature*
JEMCS	*Journal of Early Modern Cultural Studies*
JEn	*Journal of English* (Sana'a University)
JEngL	*Journal of English Linguistics*
JENS	*Journal of the Eighteen Nineties Society*
JEP	*Journal of Evolutionary Psychology*

JEPNS	*Journal of the English Place-Name Society*
JES	*Journal of European Studies*
JETS	*Journal of the Evangelical Theological Society*
JFR	*Journal of Folklore Research*
JGE	*Journal of General Education*
JGenS	*Journal of Gender Studies*
JGH	*Journal of Garden History*
JGL	*Journal of Germanic Linguistics*
JGN	*John Gower Newsletter*
JH	*Journal of Homosexuality*
JHI	*Journal of the History of Ideas*
JHLP	*Journal of Historical Linguistics and Philology*
JHP	*Journal of the History of Philosophy*
JHPrag	*Journal of Historical Pragmatics*
JHSex	*Journal of the History of Sexuality*
JHu	*Journal of Humanities*
JHuP	*Journal of Humanistic Psychology*
JIEP	*Journal of Indo-European Perspectives*
JIES	*Journal of Indo-European Studies*
JIL	*Journal of Irish Literature*
JIPA	*Journal of the International Phonetic Association*
JIWE	*Journal of Indian Writing in English*
JIWS	*Journal of International Women's Studies*
JJ	*Jamaica Journal*
JJA	*James Joyce Annual*
JJB	*James Joyce Broadsheet*
JJLS	*James Joyce Literary Supplement*
JJQ	*James Joyce Quarterly*
JKS	*Journal of Kentucky Studies*
JL	*Journal of Linguistics*
JLC THEMA	*Journal of Language and Contact*
JLH	*Journal of Library History, Philosophy and Comparative Librarianship*
JLLI	*Journal of Logic, Language and Information*
JLP	*Journal of Linguistics and Politics*
JLS	*Journal of Literary Semanitcs*
JLT	*Journal of Literary Theory*
JLSP	*Journal of Language and Social Psychology*
JLVSG	*Journal of the Longborough Victorian Studies Group*
JmedL	
JMemL	*Journal of Memory and Language*
JMEMS	*Journal of Medieval and Early Modern Studies*
JMGS	*Journal of Modern Greek Studies*
JMH	*Journal of Medieval History*
JMJS	*Journal of Modern Jewish Studies*
JML	*Journal of Modern Literature*
JMMD	*Journal of Multilingual and Multicultural Development*
JMMLA	*Journal of the Midwest Modern Language Association*
JModH	*Journal of Modern History*
JMRS	*Journal of Medieval and Renaissance Studies*
JMS	*Journal of Men's Studies*
JNLH	*Journal of Narrative and Life History*
JNPH	*Journal of Newspaper and Periodical History*

JNT	*Journal of Narrative Theory* (formerly *Technique*)
JNZL	*Journal of New Zealand Literature*
JNZS	*Journal of New Zealand Studies*
Jouvert	*Jouvert: A Journal of Postcolonial Studies*
JoyceSA	*Joyce Studies Annual*
JP	*Journal of Philosophy*
JPC	*Journal of Popular Culture*
JPCL	*Journal of Pidgin and Creole Languages*
JPhon	*Journal of Phonetics*
JPJ	*Journal of Psychology and Judaism*
JPolR	*Journal of Politeness Research: Language, Behavior, and Culture*
JPrag	*Journal of Pragmatics*
JPRAS	*Journal of Pre-Raphaelite and Aesthetic Studies*
JPsyR	*Journal of Psycholinguistic Research*
Jpub	
JPW	*Journal of Postcolonial Writing*
JQ	*Journalism Quarterly*
JR	*Journal of Religion*
JRAHS	*Journal of the Royal Australian Historical Society*
JRH	*Journal of Religious History*
JRMA	*Journal of the Royal Musical Association*
JRMMRA	*Journal of the Rocky Mountain Medieval and Renaissance Association (see also Quidditas)*
JRSA	*Journal of the Royal Society of Arts*
JRT	*Journal of Religion and Theatre*
JRUL	*Journal of the Rutgers University Libraries*
JSA	*Journal of the Society of Archivists*
JSaga	*Journal of the Faculty of Liberal Arts and Science* (Saga University)
JSAS	*Journal of Southern African Studies*
JScholP	*Journal of Scholarly Publishing*
JSem	*Journal of Semantics*
JSoc	*Journal of Sociolinguistics*
JSP	*Journal of Scottish Philosophy*
JSPNS	
JSSE	*Journal of the Short Story in English*
JSTWS	*Journal of the Sylvia Townsend Warner Society*
JTheoS	*Journal of Theological Studies*
JVC	*Journal of Victorian Culture*
JWCI	*Journal of the Warburg and Courtauld Institutes*
JWH	*Journal of Women's History*
JWIL	*Journal of West Indian Literature*
JWMS	*Journal of the William Morris Society*
JWSL	*Journal of Women's Studies in Literature*
KanE	*Kansas English*
Ka Mate Ka Ora	*Ka Mate Ka Ora: A New Zealand Journal of Poetry and Poetics*
KanQ	*Kansas Quarterly*
KB	*Kavya Bharati*
KCLMS	*King's College London Medieval Series*
KCS	*Kobe College Studies* (Japan)
KDNews	*Kernerman Dictionary News*
KJ	*Kipling Journal*
KN	*Kwartalnik Neoflologiczny* (Warsaw)

KompH	*Komparatistische Hefte*
Kotare	*Kotare: New Zealand Notes and Queries*
KPR	*Kentucky Philological Review*
KR	*Kenyon Review*
KSJ	*Keats-Shelley Journal*
KSMB	*Keats-Shelley Memorial Bulletin*
KSR	*Keats-Shelley Review*
Kuka	*Kuka: Journal of Creative and Critical Writing* (Zaria, Nigeria)
Kunapipi	*Kunapipi*
KWS	*Key-Word Studies in Chaucer*
L&A	*Literature and Aesthetics*
L&B	*Literature and Belief*
L&C	*Language and Communication*
L&E	*Linguistics and Education: An International Research Journal*
Landfall	*Landfall: A New Zealand Quarterly*
L&H	*Literature and History*
L&IC	*Language & Intercultural Communication*
L&L	*Language and Literature*
L&LC	*Literary and Linguistic Computing*
L&M	*Literature and Medicine*
L&P	*Literature and Psychology*
L&S	*Language and Speech*
L&T	*Literature and Theology: An Interdisciplinary Journal of Theory and Criticism*
L&U	*Lion and the Unicorn: A Critical Journal of Children's Literature*
Lang&S	*Language and Style*
LangCog	*Language and Cognition*
LangF	*Language Forum*
LangQ	*USF Language Quarterly*
LangR	*Language Research*
LangS	*Language Sciences*
Language	*Language* (Linguistic Society of America)
LanM	*Les Langues Modernes*
La Revue LISA	*La Revue LISA*
LATR	*Latin American Theatre Review*
LaTrobe	*La Trobe Journal*
LawL	*Law and Literature*
LawLi	*Law and the Literary Imagination*
LB	*Leuvense Bijdragen*
LBR	*Luso-Brazilian Review*
LCrit	*Literary Criterion* (Mysore, India)
LCUT	*Library Chronicle* (University of Texas at Austin)
LDOCE	*Longman Dictionary of Contemporary English*
LeedsSE	*Leeds Studies in English*
LeF	*Linguistica e Filologia*
Legacy	*Legacy: A Journal of Nineteenth-Century American Women Writers*
Le Journal	*Le Journal*
Lemuria	*Lemuria: A Half-Yearly Research Journal of Indo-Australian Studies*
L'EpC	*L'Epoque Conradienne*
LeS	*Lingua e Stile*
Lexicographica	*Lexicographica: International Annual for Lexicography*
Lexicography	*Lexicography*
LFQ	*Literature/Film Quarterly*

LH	*Library History*
LHY	*Literary Half-Yearly*
LI	*Studies in the Literary Imagination*
Library	*Library*
Library Review	*Library Review*
LibrQ	*Library Quarterly*
LIN	*Linguistics in the Netherlands*
LinC	*Languages in Contrast*
LingA	*Linguistic Analysis*
Ling&P	*Linguistics and Philosophy*
Ling&Philol	*Linguistics and Philology*
LingB	*Linguistische Berichte*
LingI	*Linguistic Inquiry*
LingInv	*Lingvisticæ Investigationes*
LingP	*Linguistica Pragensia*
LingRev	*Linguistic Review*
Lingua	*Lingua: International Review of General Linguistics*
Linguistics	*Linguistics*
LinguisticT	
Linguistique	*La Linguistique*
LiNQ	*Literature in Northern Queensland*
LiRevALSC	*Literary Imagination: The Review of the Association of Literary Scholars and Critics*
LIT	*LIT: Literature, Interpretation, Theory*
LitComp	*Literature Compass (also LiteratureC previously)*
LitH	*Literary Horizons*
LitI	*Literary Imagination: The Review of the Association of Literary Scholars and Critics*
LitR	*Literary Review: An International Journal of Contemporary Writing*
LittPrag	*Litteraria Pragensia: Studies in Literature and Culture*
LJCS	*London Journal of Canadian Studies*
LJGG	*Literaturwissenschaftliches Jahrbuch im Aufrage der Görres-Gesellschaft*
LJHum	*Lamar Journal of the Humanities*
LMag	*London Magazine*
LockeN	*Locke Newsletter*
LocusF	*Locus Focus*
Logos	*Logos: A Journal of Catholic Thought and Culture*
LongR	*Long Room: Bulletin of the Friends of the Library* (Trinity College, Dublin)
Lore&L	*Lore and Language*
LP	*Lingua Posnaniensis*
LPLD	*Liverpool Papers in Language and Discourse*
LPLP	*Language Problems and Language Planning*
LR	*Les Lettres Romanes*
LRB	*London Review of Books*
LSE	*Lund Studies in English*
LSLD	*Liverpool Studies in Language and Discourse*
LSoc	*Language in Society*
LSp	*Language and Speech*
LST	*Longman Study Texts*
LTM	*Leeds Texts and Monographs*

LTP	*LTP: Journal of Literature Teaching Politics*
LTR	*London Theatre Record*
LuK	*Literatur und Kritik*
Lumen	*Lumen*
LVC	*Language Variation and Change*
LW	*Life Writing*
LWU	*Literatur in Wissenschaft und Unterricht*
M&Lang	*Mind and Language*
MÆ	*Medium Ævum*
MAEL	*Macmillan Anthologies of English Literature*
MaComere	*MaComère: Journal of the Association of Caribbean Women Writers and Scholars*
Magistra	*Magistra: A Women's Spirituality in History*
MagL	*Magazine Littéraire*
Mana	*Mana*
MAS	*Modern Asian Studies*
M&H	*Medievalia et Humanistica*
M&L	*Music and Letters*
M&N	*Man and Nature/L'Homme et la Nature: Proceedings of the Canadian Society for Eighteenth-Century Studies*
M&Sym	*Metaphor and Symbol*
M&T	
Manuscripta	*Manuscripta*
MAR	*Mid-American Review*
Margin	*Margin: Life and Letters in Early Australia*
MarkhamR	*Markham Review*
Matatu	*Matatu*
Matrix	*Matrix*
MBL	*Modern British Literature*
MC&S	*Media, Culture and Society*
MCI	*Modern Critical Interpretations*
MCJNews	*Milton Centre of Japan News*
McNR	*McNeese Review*
MCRel	*Mythes, Croyances et Religions dans le Monde Anglo-Saxon*
MCV	*Modern Critical Views*
MD	*Modern Drama*
ME	*Medieval Encounters*
Meanjin	*Meanjin*
MED	*Middle English Dictionary*
MedFor	*Medieval Forum* (online)
MedHis	*Media History*
Mediaevalia	*Mediaevalia: An Interdisciplinary Journal of Medieval Studies Worldwide*
MedPers	*Medieval Perspectives*
MELUS	*MELUS: The Journal of the Society of Multi-Ethnic Literature of the United States*
Meridian	*Meridian*
MES	*Medieval and Early Modern English Studies*
MESN	*Mediaeval English Studies Newsletter*
MET	*Middle English Texts*
Met&Sym	
METh	*Medieval English Theatre*
MFF	*Medieval Feminist Forum* (formerly *Medieval Feminist Newsletter*)

MFN	*Medieval Feminist Newsletter* (now *Medieval Feminist Forum*)
MFS	*Modern Fiction Studies*
MH	*Malahat Review*
MHL	*Macmillan History of Literature*
MHLS	*Mid-Hudson Language Studies*
MichA	*Michigan Academician*
MiltonQ	*Milton Quarterly*
MiltonS	*Milton Studies*
MinnR	*Minnesota Review*
MissQ	*Mississippi Quarterly*
MissR	*Missouri Review*
Mittelalter	*Das Mittelalter: Perspektiven Mediavistischer Forschung*
MJLF	*Midwestern Journal of Language and Folklore*
ML	*Music and Letters*
MLAIB	*Modern Language Association International Bibliography*
MLing	*Modèles Linguistiques*
MLJ	*Modern Language Journal*
MLN	*Modern Language Notes*
MLQ	*Modern Language Quarterly*
MLR	*Modern Language Review*
MLRev	*Malcolm Lowry Review*
MLS	*Modern Language Studies*
MMD	*Macmillan Modern Dramatists*
MMG	*Macmillan Master Guides*
MMisc	*Midwestern Miscellany*
MOCS	*Magazine of Cultural Studies*
ModA	*Modern Age: A Quarterly Review*
ModCult	*Modernist Cultures*
ModET	*Modern English Teacher*
ModM	*Modern Masters*
ModSp	*Moderne Sprachen*
Mo/Mo	*Modernism/Modernity* (also M/M previously)
Monist	*Monist*
MonSP	*Monash Swift Papers*
Month	*Month: A Review of Christian Thought and World Affairs*
MOR	*Mount Olive Review*
Moreana	*Moreana: Bulletin Thomas More* (Angers, France)
Mosaic	*Mosaic: A Journal for the Interdisciplinary Study of Literature*
Moving Worlds	*Moving Worlds*
MoyA	*Moyen Age*
MP	*Modern Philology*
MPHJ	*Middlesex Polytechnic History Journal*
MPR	*Mervyn Peake Review*
MPsych	*Media Psychology*
MQ	*Midwest Quarterly*
MQR	*Michigan Quarterly Review*
MR	*Massachusetts Review*
MRDE	*Medieval and Renaissance Drama in England*
MRTS	*Medieval and Renaissance Texts and Studies*
MS	*Mediaeval Studies*
MSC	*Malone Society Collections*
MSE	*Massachusetts Studies in English*
MSEx	*Melville Society Extracts*

MSh	*Macmillan Shakespeare*
MSNH	*Mémoires de la Société Néophilologique de Helsinki*
MSpr	*Moderna Språk*
MSR	*Malone Society Reprints*
MSSN	*Medieval Sermon Studies Newsletter*
MT	*Musical Times*
MTJ	*Mark Twain Journal*
Multilingua	*Multilingua: Journal of Cross-Cultural and Interlanguage Communication*
MusR	*Music Review*
MW	*Muslim World* (Hartford, CT)
MWQ	*Mid-West Quarterly*
MysticsQ	*Mystics Quarterly*
Mythlore	*Mythlore: A Journal of J.R.R. Tolkein, C.S. Lewis, Charles Williams, and the Genres of Myth and Fantasy Studies*
NA	*Nuova Antologia*
Names	*Names: Journal of the American Name Society*
NAmR	*North American Review*
N&F	*Notes & Furphies*
N&Q	*Notes and Queries*
Narrative	*Narrative*
Navasilu	*Navasilu*
NB	*Namn och Bygd*
NCaS	*New Cambridge Shakespeare*
NCBEL	*New Cambridge Bibliography of English Literature*
NCC	*Nineteenth-Century Contexts*
NCE	*Norton Critical Editions*
NCFS	*Nineteenth-Century French Studies*
NCI	*New Critical Idiom*
NCLE	*Nineteenth-Century Literature in English*
NConL	*Notes on Contemporary Literature*
NCP	*Nineteenth-Century Prose*
NCS	*New Clarendon Shakespeare*
NCSR	*New Chaucer Society Readings*
NCSTC	*Nineteenth-Century Short Title Catalogue*
NCStud	*Nineteenth-Century Studies*
NCT	*Nineteenth-Century Theatre*
NDQ	*North Dakota Quarterly*
Nebula	*Nebula*
NegroD	*Negro Digest*
NELS	*North Eastern Linguistic Society*
Neoh	*Neohelicon*
Neophil	*Neophilologus*
NEQ	*New England Quarterly*
NERMS	*New England Review*
NewA	*New African*
NewBR	*New Beacon Review*
NewC	*New Criterion*
New Casebooks	*New Casebooks: Contemporary Critical Essays*
NewComp	*New Comparison: A Journal of Comparative and General Literary Studies*
NewF	*New Formations*
NewHibR	*New Hibernian Review*

NewHR	*New Historical Review*
NewR	*New Republic*
NewSt	*Newfoundland Studies*
NewV	*New Voices*
Nexus	*The International Henry Miller Journal*
NF	*Neiophilologica Fennica*
NfN	*News from Nowhere*
NF&LS	*Newfoundland and Labrador Studies*
NFS	*Nottingham French Studies*
NGC	*New German Critique*
NGS	*New German Studies*
NH	*Northern History*
NHR	*Nathaniel Hawthorne Review*
NIS	*Nordic Irish Studies*
NJES	*Nordic Journal of English Studies*
NJL	*Nordic Journal of Linguistics*
NL	*Nouvelles Littéraires*
NLAN	*National Library of Australia News*
NL<	*Natural Language and Linguistic Theory*
NLH	*New Literary History: A Journal of Theory and Interpretation*
NLitsR	*New Literatures Review*
NLR	*New Left Review*
NLS	*Natural Language Semantics*
NLWJ	*National Library of Wales Journal*
NM	*Neuphilologische Mitteilungen*
NMAL	*NMAL: Notes on Modern American Literature*
NMer	*New Mermaids*
NMIL	*Notes on Modern Irish Literature*
NML	*New Medieval Literatures*
NMS	*Nottingham Medieval Studies*
NMW	*Notes on Mississippi Writers*
NN	*Nordiska Namenstudier*
NNER	*Northern New England Review*
Nomina	*Nomina: A Journal of Name Studies Relating to Great Britain and Ireland*
NoP	*Northern Perspective*
NOR	*New Orleans Review*
Nordlit	*Nordlit: Arbeidstidsskrift i litteratur og kultur*
NorfolkA	*Norfolk Archaeology*
NortonCE	*Norton Critical Edition*
Novel	*Novel: A Forum on Fiction*
Novitas-ROYAL	*Research on Youth and Language*
NOWELE	*North-Western European Language Evolution*
NPEC	*New Perspectives on the Eighteenth Century*
NPS	*New Penguin Shakespeare*
NR	*Nassau Review*
NRF	*La Nouvelle Revue Française*
NRRS	*Notes and Records of the Royal Society of London*
NS	*Die neuren Sprachen*
NSS	*New Swan Shakespeare*
NTQ	*New Theatre Quarterly*
NTU	*NTU: Studies in Language and Literature*

NVSAWC	*Newsletter of the Victorian Studies Association of Western Canada*
NwJ	*Northward Journal*
NWR	*Northwest Review*
NWRev	*New Welsh Review*
NYH	*New York History*
NYLF	*New York Literary Forum*
NYRB	*New York Review of Books*
NYT	*New York Times*
NYTBR	*New York Times Book Review*
NZB	*New Zealand Books*
NZJAS	*New Zealand Journal of Asian Studies*
NZListener	*New Zealand Listener*
NZW	*NZWords*
OA	*Oxford Authors*
OB	*Ord och Bild*
Obsidian	*Obsidian II: Black Literature in Review*
OBSP	*Oxford Bibliographical Society Publications*
OED	*Oxford English Dictionary*
OEDNews	*Oxford English Dictionary News*
OENews	*Old English Newsletter*
OELH	*Oxford English Literary History*
OET	*Oxford English Texts*
OH	*Over Here: An American Studies Journal*
OHEL	*Oxford History of English Literature*
OhR	*Ohio Review*
OL	
OLR	*Oxford Literary Review*
OnCan	*Onomastica Canadiana*
OPBS	*Occasional Papers of the Bibliographical Society*
OpenGL	*Open Guides to Literature*
OpL	*Open Letter*
OPL	*Oxford Poetry Library*
OPLiLL	*Occasional Papers in Linguistics and Language Learning*
OPSL	*Occasional Papers in Systemic Linguistics*
OralT	*Oral Tradition*
Orbis	*Orbis*
OrbisLit	*Orbis Litterarum*
OS	*Oxford Shakespeare*
OSS	*Oxford Shakespeare Studies*
OT	*Oral Tradition*
Outrider	*Outrider: A Publication of the Wyoming State Library*
Overland	*Overland*
PA	*Présence Africaine*
PAAS	*Proceedings of the American Antiquarian Society*
PacStud	*Pacific Studies*
Paideuma	*Paideuma: A Journal Devoted to Ezra Pound Scholarship*
PAJ	*Performing Art Journal*
P&C	*Pragmatics and Cognition*
P&CT	*Psychoanalysis and Contemporary Thought*
P&L	*Philosophy and Literature*
P&P	*Past and Present*
P&R	*Philosophy and Rhetoric*

P&SC	*Philosophy and Social Criticism*
P&MS	
PAns	*Partial Answers*
PAPA	*Publications of the Arkansas Philological Association*
Papers	*Papers: Explorations into Children's Literature*
PAPS	*Proceedings of the American Philosophical Society*
PAR	*Performing Arts Resources*
Parabola	*Parabola: The Magazine of Myth and Tradition*
Paragraph	*Paragraph: The Journal of the Modern Critical Theory Group*
Parergon	*Parergon: Bulletin of the Australian and New Zealand Association for Medieval and Renaissance Studies*
ParisR	*Paris Review*
Parnassus	*Parnassus: Poetry in Review*
PastM	*Past Masters*
PaterN	*Pater Newsletter*
PAus	*Poetry Australia*
PBA	*Proceedings of the British Academy*
PBerLS	*Proceedings of the Berkeley Linguistics Society*
PBSA	*Papers of the Bibliographical Society ofAmerica*
PBSC	*Papers of the Biographical Society of Canada*
PCL	*Perspectives on Contemporary Literature*
PCLAC	*Proceedings of the California Linguistics Association Conference*
PCLS	*Proceedings of the Comparative Literature Symposium* (Lubbock, TX)
PCP	*Pacific Coast Philology*
PCRev	*Popular Culture Review*
PCS	*Penguin Critical Studies*
PEAN	*Proceedings of the English Association North*
PE&W	*Philosophy East and West: A Quarterly of Asian and Comparative Thought*
PELL	*Papers on English Language and Literature* (Japan)
Pequod	*Pequod: A Journal of Contemporary Literature and Literary Criticism*
Performance	*Performance*
PerfR	*Performance Review*
Peritia	*Peritia: Journal of the Medieval Academy of Ireland*
Perspicuitas	*Perspicuitas: Internet-Periodicum für Mediävistische Sprach-, Literature- und Kulturwissenschaft*
Persuasions	*Persuasions: Journal of the Jane Austen Society of North America*
Persuasions On-Line	*The Jane Austen Journal On-Line*
Philament	*Philament: Online Journal of the Arts and Culture Phonology*
Philosophy	*Philosophy*
PhilRev	*Philosophical Review: A Quarterly Journal*
PhiN	*Philologie im Netz*
PHist	*Printing History*
Phonetica	*Phonetica: International Journal of Speech Science*
Phonology	*Phonology*
PHOS	*Publishing History Occasional Series*
PhRA	*Philosophical Research Archives*
PhT	*Philosophy Today*
PiL	*Papers in Linguistics*

PIMA	*Proceedings of the Illinois Medieval Association*
PinterR	*Pinter Review*
PJCL	*Prairie Journal of Canadian Literature*
PLL	*Papers on Language and Literature*
PLPLS	*Proceedings of the Leeds Philosophical and Literary Society, Literary and Historical Section*
PM	*Penguin Masterstudies*
PMHB	*Pennsylvania Magazine of History and Biography*
PMLA	*Publications of the Modern Language Association of America*
PMPA	*Proceedings of the Missouri Philological Association*
PNotes	*Pynchon Notes*
PNR	*Poetry and Nation Review*
PoeS	*Poe Studies*
Poetica	*Poetica: Zeitschrift fur Sprach- und Literaturwissenschaft* (Amsterdam)
PoeticaJ	*Poetica: An International Journal of Linguistic-Literary Studies* (Tokyo)
Poetics	*Poetics: International Review for the Theory of Literature*
Poétique	*Poétique: Revue de Théorie et d'Analyse Littéraires*
Poetry	*Poetry* (Chicago)
PoetryCR	*Poetry Canada Review*
PoetryNZ	*Poetry New Zealand*
PoetryR	*Poetry Review*
PoetryW	*Poetry Wales*
POMPA	*Publications of the Mississippi Philological Association*
PostS	*Past Script: Essays in Film and the Humanities*
PoT	*Poetics Today*
PP	*Penguin Passnotes*
PP	*Philologica Pragensia*
PPA	*Philosophical Perspectives Annual*
PPMRC	*Proceedings of the International Patristic, Mediaeval and Renaissance Conference*
PPR	*Philosophy and Phenomenological Research*
PQ	*Philological Quarterly*
PQM	*Pacific Quarterly* (Moana)
PR	*Partisan Review*
Pragmatics	*Pragmatics: Quarterly Publication of the International Pragmatics Association*
PrairieF	*Prairie Fire*
Praxis	*Praxis: A Journal of Cultural Criticism*
PRep	
Prépub	*(Pré)publications*
PRev	*Powys Review*
PRIA	*Proceedings of the Royal Irish Academy*
PRIAA	*Publications of the Research Institute of the Abo Akademi Foundation*
PRMCLS	*Papers from the Regional Meetings of the Chicago Linguistics Society*
Prospects	*Prospects: An Annual Journal of American Cultural Studies*
Prospero	*Prospero: Journal of New Thinking in Philosophy for Education*
Proteus	*Proteus: A Journal of Ideas*
Proverbium	*Proverbium*

PrS	*Prairie Schooner*
PSt	*Prose Studies*
PsyArt	*Psychological Study of the Arts* (hyperlink journal)
PsychR	*Psychological Reports*
PTBI	*Publications of the Sir Thomas Browne Institute*
PubH	*Publishing History*
PULC	*Princeton University Library Chronicle*
PURBA	*Panjab University Research Bulletin (Arts)*
PVR	*Platte Valley Review*
PWC	*Pickering's Women's Classics*
PY	*Phonology Yearbook*
QDLLSM	*Quaderni del Dipartimento e Lingue e Letterature Straniere Moderne*
QE	*Quarterly Essay*
QI	*Quaderni d'Italianistica*
QJS	*Quarterly Journal of Speech*
QLing	*Quantitative Linguistics*
QQ	*Queen's Quarterly*
QR	*Queensland Review*
QRFV	*Quarterly Review of Film and Video*
Quadrant	*Quadrant* (Sydney)
Quarendo	*Quarendo*
Quarry	*Quarry*
Quidditas	*Journal of the Rocky Mountain Medieval and Renaissance Association*
QWERTY	*QWERTY: Arts, Littératures, et Civilisations du Monde Anglophone*
RadP	*Radical Philosophy*
RAL	*Research in African Literatures*
RALS	*Resources for American Literary Study*
Ramus	*Ramus: Critical Studies in Greek and Roman Literature*
R&C	*Race and Class*
R&L	*Religion and Literature*
Raritan	*Raritan: A Quarterly Review*
Rask	*Rask: International tidsskrift for sprog og kommunikation*
RaVoN	*Romanticism and Victorianism on the Net*
RB	*Revue Bénédictine*
RBPH	*Revue Belge de Philologie et d'Histoire*
RBR	*Rare Book Review* (formerly *ABR*)
RCEI	*Revista Canaria de Estudios Ingleses*
RCF	*Review of Contemporary Fiction*
RCPS	*Romantic Circles Praxis Series* (online)
RDN	*Renaissance Drama Newsletter*
RE	*Revue d'Esthétique*
Reader	*Reader: Essays in Reader-Oriented Theory, Criticism, and Pedagogy*
ReAL	*Re: Artes Liberales*
REALB	*REAL: The Yearbook of Research in English and American Literature* (Berlin)
ReAr	*Religion and the Arts*
RecBucks	*Records of Buckinghamshire*
RecL	*Recovery Literature*
REPCS	*Review of Education, Pedagogy and Cultural Studies*

RECTR	*Restoration and Eighteenth-Century Theatre Research*
RedL	*Red Letters: A Journal of Cultural Politics*
REED	*Records of Early English Drama*
REEDN	*Records of Early English Drama Newsletter*
ReFr	*Revue Française*
Reinardus	*Reinardus*
REL	*Review of English Literature* (Kyoto)
RELC	*RELC Journal: A Journal of Language Teaching and Research in Southeast Asia*
Ren&R	*Renaissance and Reformation*
Renascence	*Renascence: Essays on Values in Literature*
RenD	*Renaissance Drama*
Renfor	*Renaissance Forum* (online)
RenP	*Renaissance Papers*
RenQ	*Renaissance Quarterly*
Rep	*Representations*
RePublica	*RePublica*
RES	*Review of English Studies*
Restoration	*Restoration: Studies in English Literary Culture, 1660–1700*
Rev	*Review* (Blacksburg, VA)
RevAli	*Revista Alicantina de Estudios Ingleses*
Revels	*Revels Plays*
RevelsCL	*Revels Plays Companion Library*
RevelsSE	*Revels Student Editions*
Revista Canaria	*Revista Canaria De Estudios Ingleses*
RevR	*Revolution and Romanticism, 1789–1834*
RFEA	*Revue Française d'Études Américaines*
RFR	*Robert Frost Review*
RG	*Revue Générale*
RH	*Recusant History*
Rhetorica	*Rhetorica: A Journal of the History of Rhetoric*
Rhetorik	*Rhetorik: Ein Internationales Jahrbuch*
RhetR	*Rhetoric Review*
RHist	*Rural History*
RHL	*Revue d'Histoire Littéraire de la France*
RHT	*Revue d'Histoire du Théâtre*
RIB	*Revista Interamericana de Bibliografia: Inter-American Reviews of Bibliography*
Ricardian	*Ricardian: Journal of the Richard III Society*
RJ	*Richard Jefferies Society Newsletter*
RJES	*Romanian Journal of English Studies*
RL	*Rereading Literature*
RLAn	*Romance Languages Annual*
RLC	*Revue de Littérature Comparée*
RL&C	*Research on Language and Computation*
RLing	*Rivista di Linguistica*
RLit	*Russian Literature*
RLM	*La Revue des Lettres Modernes: Histoire des Idées des Littératures*
RLMC	*Rivista di Letterature Moderne e Comparate*
RLT	*Russian Literature Triquarterly*
RM	*Rethinking Marxism*
RMR	*Rocky Mountain Review of Language and Literature*

RM	*Renaissance and Modern Studies*
RMSt	*Reading Medieval Studies*
ROA	*Rutgers Optimality Archive*
Romania	*Romania*
Romanticism	*Romanticism*
RomN	*Romance Notes*
RomQ	*Romance Quarterly*
ROMRD	
RomS	*Romance Studies*
RomText	*Romantic Textualities: Literature and Print Culture, 1780–1840 (formerly Cardiff Corvey)*
RoN	*Romanticism on the Net* (now *Romanticism and Victorianism on the Net*)
ROO	*Room of One's Own: A Feminist Journal of Literature and Criticism*
RORD	*Research Opportunities in Renaissance Drama*
RPT	*Russian Poetics in Translation*
RQ	*Riverside Quarterly*
RR	*Romanic Review*
RRDS	*Regents Renaissance Drama Series*
RRestDS	*Regents Restoration Drama Series*
RS	*Renaissance Studies*
RSQ	*Rhetoric Society Quarterly*
RSV	*Rivista di Studi Vittoriani*
RUO	*Revue de l'Université d'Ottawa*
RUSEng	*Rajasthan University Studies in English*
RuskN	*Ruskin Newsletter*
RUUL	*Reports from the Uppsala University Department of Linguistics*
R/WT	*Readerly/Writerly Texts*
SAC	*Studies in the Age of Chaucer*
SAD	*Studies in American Drama, 1945–Present*
SAF	*Studies in American Fiction*
Saga-Book	*Saga-Book (Viking Society for Northern Research)*
Sagetrieb	*Sagetrieb: A Journal Devoted to Poets in the Pound–H.D. Williams Tradition*
SAIL	*Studies in American Indian Literatures: The Journal of the Association for the Study of American Indian Literatures*
SAJL	*Studies in American Jewish Literature*
SAJMRS	*South African Journal of Medieval and Renaissance Studies*
Sal	*Salmagrundi: A Quarterly of the Humanities and Social Sciences*
SALALS	*Southern African Linguistics and Applied language Studies*
SALCT	*SALCT: Studies in Australian Literature, Culture and Thought*
S&P	*Script and Print (formerly BSANZB, Bibliographical Society of Australia and New Zealand Bulletin)*
S&Prag	*Semantics and Pragmatics*
S&S	*Sight and Sound*
SAntS	*Studia Anthroponymica Scandinavica*
Salt	*Salt: An International Journal of Poetry and Poetics*
SAP	*Studia Anglica Posnaniensia*
SAQ	*South Atlantic Quarterly*
SAR	*Studies in the American Renaissance*
SARB	*South African Review of Books*
SARev	*South Asian Review*

Sargasso	*Sargasso*
SASLC	*Studies in Anglo-Saxon Literature and Culture*
SatR	*Saturday Review*
SB	*Studies in Bibliography*
SBHC	*Studies in Browning and his Circle*
SC	*Seventeenth Century*
Scan	*Scandinavica: An International Journal of Scandinavian Studies*
ScanS	*Scandinavian Studies*
SCC&HTLJ	*Santa Clara Computer and High Technology Law Journal*
SCel	*Studia Celtica*
SCER	*Society for Critical Exchange Report*
Schuylkill	*Schuylkill: A Creative and Critical Review* (Temple University)
Scintilla	*Scintilla: Annual Journal of Vaughan Studies and New Poetry*
SCJ	*Sixteenth Century Journal*
SCL	*Studies in Canadian Literature*
ScLJ	*Scottish Literary Journal: A Review of Studies in Scottish Language and Literature*
ScLJ(S)	*Scottish Literary Journal Supplement*
SCLOP	*Society for Caribbean Linguistics Occasional Papers*
SCN	*Seventeenth-Century News*
ScotL	*Scottish Language*
ScotLR	*Scottish Literary Review*
ScottN	*Scott Newsletter*
SCR	*South Carolina Review*
Screen	*Screen* (London)
SCRev	*South Central Review*
Scriblerian	*Scriblerian and the Kit Cats: A Newsjournal Devoted to Pope, Swift, and their Circle*
Scripsi	*Scripsi*
Scriptorium	*Scriptorium: International Review of Manuscript Studies*
ScTh	*Scottish Journal of Theology*
SD	*Social Dynamics*
SDR	*South Dakota Review*
SECC	*Studies in Eighteenth-Century Culture*
SECOLR	*SECOL Review: Southeastern Conference on Linguistics*
SED	*Survey of English Dialects*
SEDERI	*Journal of the Spanish Society for Renaissance Studies (Sociedad Española de Estudios Renacentistas Ingleses)*
SEEJ	*Slavic and East European Journal*
SEL	*Studies in English Literature, 1500–1900* (Rice University)
Selim	*SELIM: Journal of the Spanish Society for Medieval English Language and Literature*
SELing	*Studies in English Linguistics* (Tokyo)
SELit	*Studies in English Literature* (Tokyo)
SELL	*Studies in English Language and Literature*
Sem	*Semiotica: Journal of the International Association for Semiotic Studies*
SEMC	*Studies in Early Medieval Coinage*
Semiosis	*Semiosis: Internationale Zeitschrift für Semiotik und Ästhetik*
SER	*Studien zur Englischen Romantik*
Seven	*Seven: An Anglo-American Literary Review*
SF&R	*Scholars' Facsimiles and Reprints*
SFic	*Science Fiction: A Review of Speculative Literature*

SFNL	*Shakespeare on Film Newsletter*
SFQ	*Southern Folklore Quarterly*
SFR	*Stanford French Review*
SFS	*Science-Fiction Studies*
SH	*Studia Hibernica* (Dublin)
Shakespeare	
ShakB	*Shakespeare Bulletin*
ShakS	*Shakespeare Studies* (New York)
Shandean	*Shandean*
Sh&Sch	*Shakespeare and Schools*
ShawR	*Shaw: The Annual of Bernard Shaw Studies*
Shenandoah	*Shenandoah*
SherHR	*Sherlock Holmes Review*
ShIntY	*Shakespeare International Yearbook*
Shiron	*Shiron*
ShJE	*Shakespeare Jahrbuch* (Weimar)
ShJW	*Deutsche Shakespeare-Gesellschaft West Jahrbuch* (Bochum)
ShLR	*Shoin Literary Review*
ShN	*Shakespeare Newsletter*
ShortS	
SHPBBS	*Studies in the History of Philosophy of Biological and Biomedical Sciences*
SHPS	*Studies in the History and Philosophy of Science*
SHR	*Southern Humanities Review*
ShS	*Shakespeare Survey*
ShSA	*Shakespeare in Southern Africa*
ShStud	*Shakespeare Studies* (Tokyo)
SHW	*Studies in Hogg and his World*
ShY	*Shakespeare Yearbook*
SiAF	*Studies in American Fiction*
SiCS	*Sino-Christian Studies: An International Journal of the Bible, Theology, and Philosophy*
SIcon	*Studies in Iconography*
SidJ	*Sidney Journal*
SidN	*Sidney Newsletter and Journal*
Signs	*Signs: Journal of Women in Culture and Society*
SiHoLS	*Studies in the History of the Language Sciences*
SIL	*Studies in Literature*
SiMed	*Studies in Medievalism*
SIM	*Studies in Music*
SiP	*Shakespeare in Performance*
SIP	*Studies in Philology*
SiPr	*Shakespeare in Production*
SiR	*Studies in Romanticism*
SJC	
SJS	*San José Studies*
SL	*Studia Linguistica*
SLang	*Studies in Language*
SLCS	*Studies in Language Companion Series*
SLI	*Studies in the Literary Imagination*
SLJ	*Southern Literary Journal*
SLJH	*Sri Lanka Journal of the Humanities*
SLRev	*Stanford Literature Review*

SLSc	*Studies in the Linguistic Sciences*
SMART	*Studies in Medieval and Renaissance Teaching*
SmAx	*Small Axe: A Caribbean Journal of Criticism*
SMC	*Studies in Medieval Culture*
SMed	*Studi Medievali*
SMELL	*Studies in Medieval English Language and Literature*
SMLit	*Studies in Mystical Literature* (Taiwan)
SMRH	*Studies in Medieval and Renaissance History*
SMRT	*Studies in Medieval and Renaissance Teaching*
SMS	*Studier i Modern Språkvetenskap*
SMy	*Studia Mystica*
SN	*Studia Neophilologica*
SNNTS	*Studies in the Novel* (North Texas State University)
SO	*Shakespeare Originals*
SOA	*Sydsvenska Ortnamnssällskapets Årsskrift*
SoAR	*South Atlantic Review*
SoC	*Senses of Cinema* (online)
Sociocrit	*Sociocriticism*
Socioling	*Sociolinguistica*
SocN	*Sociolinguistics*
SocSem	*Social Semiotics*
SocT	*Social Text*
SohoB	*Soho Bibliographies*
SoQ	*Southern Quarterly*
SoR	*Southern Review* (Baton Rouge, LA)
SoRA	*Southern Review* (Adelaide)
SoSt	*Southern Studies: An Interdisciplinary Journal of the South*
Soundings	*Soundings: An Interdisciplinary Journal*
Southerly	*Southerly: A Review of Australian Literature*
SovL	*Soviet Literature*
SP	*Studies in Philology*
SPAN	*SPAN: Newsletter of the South Pacific Association for Commonwealth Literature and Language Studies*
SPAS	*Studies in Puritan American Spirituality*
SPC	*Studies in Popular Culture*
Spectrum	*Spectrum*
Speculum	*Speculum: A Journal of Medieval Studies*
SpeechComm	*Speech Communication*
SPELL	*Swiss Papers in English Language and Literature*
Sphinx	*Sphinx: A Magazine of Literature and Society*
Spiritus	*Spiritus: A Journal of Christian Spirituality*
SpM	*Spicilegio Moderno*
SpNL	*Spenser Newsletter*
Sport	*Sport*
Sprachwiss	*Sprachwissenschalt*
SpringE	*Spring: The Journal of the e.e. cummings Society*
SPub	*Studies in Publishing*
SPWVSRA	*Selected Papers from the West Virginia Shakespeare and Renaissance Association*
SQ	*Shakespeare Quarterly*
SR	*Sewanee Review*
SRen	*Studies in the Renaissance*
SRSR	*Status Report on Speech Research* (Haskins Laboratories)

SSEL	*Stockholm Studies in English*
SSELER	*Salzburg Studies in English Literature: Elizabethan and Renaissance*
SSELJDS	*Salzburg Studies in English Literature: Jacobean Drama Studies*
SSELPDPT	*Salzburg Studies in English Literature: Poetic Drama and Poetic Theory*
SSELRR	*Salzburg Studies in English Literature: Romantic Reassessment*
SSEng	*Sydney Studies in English*
SSF	*Studies in Short Fiction*
SSILA Newsletter	*Newsletter of the Society for the Study of the Indigenous Languages of the Americas*
SSL	*Studies in Scottish Literature*
SSLA	*Studies in Second Language Acquisition*
SPap	*Sydney Papers*
SSR	*Scottish Studies Review*
SSt	*Spenser Studies*
SStud	*Swift Studies: The Annual of the Ehrenpreis Center*
Staffrider	*Staffrider*
StaffordS	*Staffordshire Studies*
STAH	*Strange Things Are Happening*
StCH	*Studies in Church History*
STGM	*Studien und Texte zur Geistegeschichte des Mittelalters*
StHR	*Stanford Historical Review*
StHum	*Studies in the Humanities*
StIn	*Studi Inglesi*
StLF	*Studi di Letteratura Francese*
STP	*Studies in Theatre and Performance*
StQ	*Steinbeck Quarterly*
StrR	*Structuralist Review*
StTCL	*Studies in Twentieth-Century Literature*
StTW	*Studies in Travel Writing*
StudiesAmNaturalism	*Studies in American Naturalism*
StudUBBPhil	*Studia Universitatis Babeş-Bolyai Philologia*
StudWF	*Studies in Weird Fiction*
STUF	*Sprachtypologie und Universalienforschung*
Style	*Style* (De Kalb, IL)
SUAS	*Stratford-upon-Avon Studies*
SubStance	*SubStance: A Review of Theory and Literary Criticism*
SUS	*Susquehanna University Studies*
SussexAC	*Sussex Archaeological Collections*
SussexP&P	*Sussex Past & Present*
SVEC	*Studies on Voltaire and the Eighteenth Century*
SWPLL	*Sheffield Working Papers in Language and Linguistics*
SWR	*Southwest Review*
SwR	*Swansea Review: A Journal of Criticism*
Sycamore	*Sycamore*
Symbolism	*Symbolism: An International Journal of Critical Aesthetics*
Synthese	*An International Journal for Epistemology, Methodology and Philosophy of Science*
TA	*Theatre Annual*
Tabu	*Bulletin voor Taalwetenschap, Groningen*
Takahe	*Takahe*
Talisman	*Talisman*

TC	*Textual Cultures: Texts, Contexts, Interpretation*
T&C	*Text and Context*
T&L	*Translation and Literature*
T&P	*Text and Performance*
T&S	*Theology and Sexuality*
T&T	*Text & Talk*
TAPS	*Transactions of the American Philosophical Society*
TCBS	*Transactions of the Cambridge Bibliographical Society*
TCE	*Texas College English*
TCL	*Twentieth-Century Literature*
TCS	*Theory, Culture and Society: Explorations in Critical Social Science*
TCWAAS	*Transactions of the Cumberland and Westmorland Antiquarian and Archaeological Society*
TD	*Themes in Drama*
TDR	*Drama Review*
TEAMS	*Consortium for the Teaching of the Middle Ages*
TEAS	*Twayne's English Authors Series*
Telos	*Telos: A Quarterly Journal of Post-Critical Thought*
TennEJ	*Tennessee English Journal*
TennQ	*Tennessee Quarterly*
TennSL	*Tennessee Studies in Literature*
TeReo	*Te Reo: Journal of the Linguistic Society of New Zealand*
TSLL	*Texas Studies in Language and Literature*
Text	*Text: Transactions of the Society for Textual Scholarship*
Textus	*Textus, English Studies in Italy*
TH	*Texas Humanist*
THA	*Thomas Hardy Annual*
Thalia	*Thalia: Studies in Literary Humor*
ThC	*Theatre Crafts*
Theater	*Theater*
TheatreS	*Theatre Studies*
Theoria	*Theoria: A Journal of Studies in the Arts, Humanities and Social Sciences* (Natal)
THES	*Times Higher Education Supplement*
Thesis	*Thesis Eleven*
THIC	*Theatre History in Canada*
THJ	*Thomas Hardy Journal*
ThN	*Thackeray Newsletter*
ThoreauQ	*Thoreau Quarterly: A Journal of Literary and Philosophical Studies*
Thought	*Thought: A Review of Culture and Ideas*
Thph	*Theatrephile*
ThreR	*Threepenny Review*
ThS	*Theatre Survey: The American Journal of Theatre History*
THSJ	*Thomas Hardy Society Journal*
THSLC	*Transactions of the Historic Society of Lancashire and Cheshire*
THStud	*Theatre History Studies*
ThTop	*Theatre Topics*
THY	*Thomas Hardy Yearbook*
TiLSM	*Trends in Linguistics: Studies and Monographs*
Tip	*Theory in Practice*
Tirra Lirra	*Tirra Lirra: The Quarterly Magazine for the Yarra Valley*

TJ	*Theatre Journal*
TJS	*Transactions* (Johnson Society)
TJAAWP	*Text: Journal of the Australian Association of Writing Programs*
TkR	*Tamkang Review*
TL	*Theoretical Linguistics*
TLJ	*The Linguistics Journal*
TLR	*Linguistic Review*
TLS	*Times Literary Supplement*
TMLT	*Toronto Medieval Latin Texts*
TN	*Theatre Notebook*
TNWSECS	*Transactions of the North West Society for Eighteenth Century Studies*
Torre	*Torre*
TP	*Terzo Programma*
TPLL	*Tilbury Papers in Language and Literature*
TPQ	*Text and Performance Quarterly*
TPr	*Textual Practice*
TPS	*Transactions of the Philological Society*
TR	*Theatre Record*
Traditio	*Traditio: Studies in Ancient and Medieval History, Thought, and Religion*
Transition	*Transition*
TRB	*Tennyson Research Bulletin*
TRHS	*Transactions of the Royal Historical Society*
TRI	*Theatre Research International*
TriQ	*TriQuarterly*
Trivium	*Trivium*
Tropismes	*Tropismes*
TSAR	*Toronto South Asian Review*
TSB	*Thoreau Society Bulletin*
TSLang	*Typological Studies in Language*
TSLL	*Texas Studies in Literature and Language*
TStud	*Tolkien Studies*
TSWL	*Tulsa Studies in Women's Literature*
TTR	*Trinidad and Tobago Review*
TUSAS	*Twayne's United States Authors Series*
TWAS	*Twayne's World Authors Series*
TWBR	*Third World Book Review*
TWQ	*Third World Quarterly*
TWR	*Thomas Wolfe Review*
Txt	*Text: An Interdisciplinary Annual of Textual Studies*
TYDS	*Transactions of the Yorkshire Dialect Society*
Typophiles	*Typophiles* (New York)
UCrow	*Upstart Crow*
UCTSE	*University of Cape Town Studies in English*
UCWPL	*UCL Working Papers in Linguistics*
UDR	*University of Drayton Review*
UE	*Use of English*
UEAPL	*UEA Papers in Linguistics*
UES	*Unisa English Studies*
Ufahamu	*Ufahamu*
ULR	*University of Leeds Review*
UMSE	*University of Mississippi Studies in English*

Untold	*Untold*
UOQ	*University of Ottawa Quarterly*
URM	*Ultimate Reality and Meaning: Interdisciplinary Studies in the Philosophy of Understanding*
USSE	*University of Saga Studies in English*
UtopST	*Utopian Studies*
UTQ	*University of Toronto Quarterly*
UWR	*University of Windsor Review*
VCT	*Les Voies de la Création Théâtrale*
VEAW	*Varieties of English around the World*
Verbatim	*Verbatim: The Language Quarterly*
VIA	*VIA: The Journal of the Graduate School of Fine Arts* (University of Pennsylvania)
Viator	*Viator: Medieval and Renaissance Studies*
Views	*Viennese English Working Papers*
VIJ	*Victorians Institute Journal*
VLC	*Victorian Literature and Culture*
VN	*Victorian Newsletter*
Voices	*Voices*
VP	*Victorian Poetry*
VPR	*Victorian Periodicals Review*
VQR	*Virginia Quarterly Review*
VR	*Victorian Review*
VS	*Victorian Studies*
VSB	*Victorian Studies Bulletin*
VWB	*Virginia Woolf Bulletin*
VWM	*Virginia Woolf Miscellany*
WAJ	*Women's Art Journal*
WAL	*Western American Literature*
W&I	*Word and Image*
W&L	*Women and Literature*
W&Lang	*Women and Language*
Wasafiri	*Wasafiri*
WascanaR	*Wascana Review*
WBEP	*Wiener Beiträge zur Englischen Philologie*
WC	*World's Classics*
WC	*Wordsworth Circle*
WCR	*West Coast Review*
WCSJ	*Wilkie Collins Society Journal*
WCWR	*William Carlos Williams Review*
Wellsian	*Wellsian: The Journal of the H.G. Wells Society*
WEn	*World Englishes*
Westerly	*Westerly: An Annual Review*
WestHR	*West Hills Review: A Walt Whitman Journal*
WF	*Western Folklore*
WHASN	*W.H. Auden Society Newsletter*
WHR	*Western Humanities Review*
WI	*Word and Image*
WLA	*Wyndham Lewis Annual*
WL&A	*War Literature, and the Arts: An International Journal of the Humanities*
WLT	*World Literature Today*
WLWE	*World Literature Written in English*

WMQ	*William and Mary Quarterly*
WoHR	*Women's History Review*
WolfenbütteleB	*Wolfenbüttele Beiträge: Aus den Schätzen der Herzog August Bibliothek*
Women	*Women: A Cultural Review*
WomGY	*Women in German Yearbook*
WomHR	*Women's History Review*
WorcesterR	*Worcester Review*
WORD	*WORD: Journal of the International Linguistic Association*
WPW	*Working Papers on the Web*
WQ	*Wilson Quarterly*
WRB	*Women's Review of Books*
WS	*Women's Studies: An Interdisciplinary Journal*
WSIF	*Women's Studies: International Forum*
WSJour	*Wallace Stevens Journal*
WSR	*Wicazo Sa Review*
WstA	*Woolf Studies Annual*
WTJ	*Westminster Theological Journal*
WTW	*Writers and their Work*
WVUPP	*West Virginia University Philological Papers*
WW	*Women's Writing*
WWR	*Walt Whitman Quarterly Review*
XUS	*Xavier Review*
YCC	*Yearbook of Comparative Criticism*
YeA	*Yeats Annual*
YER	*Yeats Eliot Review*
YES	*Yearbook of English Studies*
YEuS	*Yearbook of European Studies/Annuaire d'Études Européennes*
YFS	*Yale French Studies*
Yiddish	*Yiddish*
YJC	*Yale Journal of Criticism: Interpretation in the Humanities*
YLS	*Yearbook of Langland Studies*
YM	*Yearbook of Morphology*
YNS	*York Note Series*
YPL	*York Papers in Linguistics*
YR	*Yale Review*
YREAL	*The Yearbook of Research in English and American Literature*
YULG	*Yale University Library Gazette*
YWES	*Year's Work in English Studies*
ZAA	*Zeitschrift für Anglistik and Amerikanistik*
ZCP	*Zeitschrift für celtische Philologie*
ZDA	*Zeitschrift für deutsches Altertum und deutsche Literatur*
ZDL	*Zeitschrift für Dialektologie und Linguistik*
ZGKS	*Zeitschrfit für Gesellschaft für Kanada-Studien*
ZGL	*Zeitschrift für germanistische Linguistik*
ZPSK	*Zeitschrift für Phonetik Sprachwissenshaft und Kommunikationsforschung*
ZSpr	*Zeitschrift für Sprachwissenshaft*
ZVS	*Zeitschrift für vergleichende Sprachforschung*

Volume numbers are supplied in the text, as are individual issue numbers for journals that are not continuously paginated through the year.

2. Publishers

AAAH	Acta Academiae Åboensis Humaniora, Åbo, Finland
AAH	Australian Academy of Humanities
A&B	Allison & Busby, London
A&R	Angus & Robertson, North Ryde, NSW, Australia
A&U	Allen & Unwin (now Unwin Hyman)
A&UA	Allen & Unwin, North Sydney, NSW, Australia
A&W	Almqvist & Wiksell International, Stockholm, Sweden
AarhusUP	Aarhus UP, Aarhus, Denmark
ABC	ABC Enterprises
ABC CLIO	ABC CLIO Reference Books, Santa Barbara, CA
Abbeville	Abbeville Press, New York, NY
ABDO	Association Bourguignonne de Dialectologie et d'Onomastique, Dijon, France
AberdeenUP	Aberdeen UP, Aberdeen
Abhinav	Abhinav Publications, New Delhi, India
Abingdon	Abingdon Press, Nashville, TN
ABL	Armstrong Browning Library, Waco, TX
Ablex	Ablex Publishing, Norwood, NJ
Åbo	Åbo Akademi, Åbo, Finland
Abrams	Harry N. Abrams, New York, NY
Academia	Academia Press, Melbourne, VIC, Australia
Academic	Academic Press, London and Orlando
Academy	Academy Press, Dublin, Eire
AcademyC	Academy Chicago Publishers, Chicago, IL
AcademyE	Academy Editions, London
Acadiensis	Acadiensis Press, Fredericton, NB, Canada
ACarS	Association for Caribbean Studies, Coral Gables, FL
ACC	Antique Collectors' Club, Woodbridge, Suffolk
ACCO	ACCO, Leuven, Belgium
ACLALS	Association for Commonwealth Literature and Language Studies, Canberra, ACT, Australia
ACMRS	Arizona Center for Medieval and Renaissance Studies
ACP	Another Chicago Press, Chicago, IL
ACS	Association for Canadian Studies, Ottawa, ON, Canada
Adam Hart	Adam Hart Publishers, London
Adam Matthew	Adam Matthew, Suffolk
Addison-Wesley	Addison-Wesley, Wokingham, Berkshire
ADFA	Australian Defence Force Academy, Department of English
Adosa	Adosa, Clermont-Ferrand, France
AEMS	American Early Medieval Studies
AF	Akademisk Forlag, Copenhagen, Denmark
Affiliated	Affiliated East–West Press, New Delhi, India
AFP	Associated Faculty Press, New York, NY
Africana	Africana Publications, New York, NY
A–H	Amold-Heinemann, New Delhi, India
Ahriman	Ahriman-Verlag, Freiburg im Breisgau, Germany
AIAS	Australian Institute of Aboriginal Studies, Canberra, ACT, Australia
Ajanta	Ajanta Publications, Delhi, India
AK	Akadémiai Kiadó, Budapest, Hungary
ALA	ALA Editions, Chicago, IL
Al&Ba	Allen & Bacon, Boston, MA
Albatross	Albatross Books, Sutherland, NSW, Australia

Albion	Albion, Appalachian State University, Boone, NC
Alderman	Alderman Press, London
Aldwych	Aldwych Press
AligarhMU	Aligarh Muslim University, Uttar Pradesh, India
Alioth	Alioth Press, Beaverton, OR
Allen	W.H. Allen, London
Allied Publishers	Allied Indian Publishers, Lahore and New Delhi, India
Almond	Almond Press, Sheffield
AM	Aubier Montaigne, Paris, France
AMAES	Association des Médiévistes Angliciste de l'Enseignement Supérieur, Paris, France
Amate	Amate Press, Oxford
AmberL	Amber Lane, Oxford
Amistad	Amistad Press, New York, NY
AMP	Aurora Metro Press, London
AMS	AMS Press, New York, NY
AMU	Adam Mickiewicz University, Posnan, Poland
Anansi	Anansi Press, Toronto, ON, Canada
Anderson-Lovelace	Anderson-Lovelace, Los Altos Hills, CA
Anma Libri	Anma Libri, Saratoga, CA
Antipodes	Antipodes Press, Plimmerton, New Zealand
Anvil	Anvil Press Poetry, London
APA	APA, Maarssen, The Netherlands
APH	Associated Publishing House, New Delhi, India
API	API Network, Perth, WA, Australia
APL	American Poetry and Literature Press, Philadelphia, PA
APP	Australian Professional Publications, Mosman, NSW, Australia
Applause	Applause Theatre Book Publishers
Appletree	Appletree Press, Belfast
APS	American Philosophical Society, Philadelphia, PA
Aquarian	Aquarian Press, Wellingborough, Northants
ArborH	Arbor House Publishing, New York, NY
Arcade	Arcade Publishing, New York, NY
Archon	Archon Books, Hamden, CT
ArchP	Architectural Press Books, Guildford, Surrey
Ardis	Ardis Publishers, Ann Arbor, MI
Ariel	Ariel Press, London
Aristotle	Aristotle University, Thessaloniki, Greece
Ark	Ark Paperbacks, London
Arkona	Arkona Forlaget, Aarhus, Denmark
Arlington	Arlington Books, London
Arnold	Edward Arnold, London
ArnoldEJ	E.J. Arnold & Son, Leeds
ARP	Australian Reference Publications, N. Balwyn, VIC, Australia
Arrow	Arrow Books, London
Arsenal	Arsenal Pulp Press
Artmoves	Artmoves, Parkdale, VIC, Australia
ASAL	Association for the Study of Australian Literature
ASB	Anglo-Saxon Books, Middlesex
ASchP	Australian Scholarly Publishing, Melbourne, VIC, Australia
ASECS	American Society for Eighteenth-Century Studies, c/o Ohio State University, Columbus, OH

Ashfield	Ashfield Press, London
Ashgate	Ashgate, Brookfield, VT
Ashton	Ashton Scholastic
Aslib	Aslib, London
ASLS	Association for Scottish Literary Studies, Aberdeen
Asmara	Audio Visual Institute of Eritrea (AVIE)
ASP	Australian Scholarly Publishing
AStP	Aboriginal Studies Press, Canberra, ACT, Australia
ASU	Arizona State University, Tempe, AZ
Atheneum	Atheneum Publishers, New York, NY
Athlone	Athlone Press, London
Atlantic	Atlantic Publishers, Darya Ganj, New Delhi, India
Atlas	Atlas Press, London
Attic	Attic Press, Dublin, Eire
AuBC	Australian Book Collector
AucklandUP	Auckland UP, Auckland, New Zealand
AUG	Acta Universitatis Gothoburgensis, Sweden
AUP	Associated University Presses, London and Toronto
AUPG	Academic & University Publishers, London
Aurum	Aurum Press, London
Auslib	Auslib Press, Adelaide, SA, Australia
AUU	Acta Universitatis Umensis, Umeå, Sweden
AUUp	Acta Universitatis Upsaliensis, Uppsala, Sweden
Avebury	Avebury Publishing, Aldershot, Hampshire
Avero	Avero Publications, Newcastle upon Tyne
A-V Verlag	A-V Verlag, Franz Fischer, Augsburg, Germany
AWP	Africa World Press, Trenton, NJ
Axelrod	Axelrod Publishing, Tampa Bay, FL
BA	British Academy, London
BAAS	British Association for American Studies, c/o University of Keele
Bagel	August Bagel Verlag, Dusseldorf, Germany
Bahri	Bahri Publications, New Delhi, India
Bamberger	Bamberger Books, Flint, MI
B&B	Boydell & Brewer, Woodbridge, Suffolk
B&J	Barrie & Jenkins, London
B&N	Barnes & Noble, Totowa, NJ
B&O	Burns & Oates, Tunbridge Wells, Kent
B&S	Michael Benskin and M.L. Samuels, Middle English Dialect Project, University of Edinburgh
BAR	British Archaelogical Reports, Oxford
Barn Owl	Barn Owl Books, Taunton, Somerset
Barnes	A.S. Barnes, San Diego, CA
Barr Smith	Barr Smith Press, Barr Smith Library, University of Adelaide
Bath UP	Bath UP, Bath
Batsford	B.T. Batsford, London
Bayreuth	Bayreuth African Studies, University of Bayreuth, Germany
BBC	BBC Publications, London
BClarkL	Bruccoli Clark Layman Inc./Manly Inc.
BCP	Bristol Classical Press, Bristol
Beacon	Beacon Press, Boston, MA
Beck	Verlag C.H. Beck oHG, Munich, Germany
Becket	Becket Publications, London

Beckford Society	Beckford Society, UK
Belin	Éditions Belin, Paris, France
Belknap	Belknap Press, Cambridge, MA
Belles Lettres	Société d'Édition les Belles Lettres, Paris, France
Bellew	Bellew Publishing, London
Bellflower	Belflower Press, Case University, Cleveland, OH
Benjamins	John Benjamins, Amsterdam, The Netherlands
BenjaminsNA	John Benjamins North America, Philadelphia, PA
BennC	Bennington College, Bennington, VT
Berg	Berg Publishers, Oxford
BFI	British Film Institute, London
BGUP	Bowling Green University Popular Press, Bowling Green, OH
BibS	Bibliographical Society, London
BilinguaGA	Bilingua GA Editions
Bilingual	Bilingual Press, Arizona State University, Tempe, AZ
Bingley	Clive Bingley, London
Binnacle	Binnacle Press, London
Biografia	Biografia Publishers, London
Birkbeck	Birkbeck College, University of London
Bishopsgate	Bishopsgate Press, Tonbridge, Kent
BL	British Library, London
Black	Adam & Charles Black, London
Black Cat	Black Cat Press, Blackrock, Eire
Blackie	Blackie & Son, Glasgow
Black Moss	Black Moss, Windsor, ON, Canada
Blackstaff	Blackstaff Press, Belfast
Black Swan	Black Swan, Curtin, UT
Blackwell	Basil Blackwell, Oxford
BlackwellR	Blackwell Reference, Oxford
Blackwood	Blackwood, Pillans & Wilson, Edinburgh
Bl&Br	Blond & Briggs, London
Blandford	Blandford Press, London
Blaue Eule	Verlag die Blaue Eule, Essen, Germany
Bloodaxe	Bloodaxe Books, Newcastle upon Tyne
Bloomsbury	Bloomsbury Publishing, London
Blubber Head	Blubber Head Press, Hobart, TAS, Australia
BM	Bobbs-Merrill, New York, NY
BMP	British Museum Publications, London
Bodleian	Bodleian Library, Oxford
Bodley	Bodley Head, London
Bogle	Bogle L'Ouverture Publications, London
BoiseSUP	Boise State UP, Boise, ID
Book Enclave	Book Enclave, Shanti Nagar, Jaipur, India
Book Guild	Book Guild, Lewes, E. Sussex
BookplateS	Bookplate Society, Edgbaston, Birmingham
Booksplus	Booksplus Nigeria Limited, Lagos, Nigeria
Boombana	Boombana Press, Brisbane, QLD, Australia
Borealis	Borealis Press, Ottawa, ON, Canada
Borgo	Borgo Press, San Bernardino, CA
BostonAL	Boston Athenaeum Library, Boston, MA
Bouma	Bouma's Boekhuis, Groningen, The Netherlands
Bowker	R.R. Bowker, New Providence, NJ
Boyars	Marion Boyars, London and Boston, MA

Boydell	Boydell Press, Woodbridge, Suffolk
Boyes	Megan Boyes, Allestree, Derbyshire
Br&S	Brandl & Schlesinger
Bran's Head	Bran's Head Books, Frome, Somerset
Braumüller	Wilhelm Braumüller, Vienna, Austria
Breakwater	Breakwater Books, St John's, NL, Canada
Brentham	Brentham Press, St Albans, Hertfordshire
Brepols	Brepols, Turnhout, Belgium
Brewer	D.S. Brewer, Woodbridge, Suffolk
Brewin	Brewin Books, Studley, Warwicks
Bridge	Bridge Publishing, S. Plainfield, NJ
Brill	E.J. Brill, Leiden, Belgium
BrillA	Brill Academic Publishers
Brilliance	Brilliance Books, London
Broadview	Broadview, London, ON and Lewiston, NY
Brookside	Brookside Press, London
Browne	Sinclair Browne, London
Brownstone	Brownstone Books, Madison, IN
BrownUP	Brown UP, Providence, RI
Brynmill	Brynmill Press, Harleston, Norfolk
BSA	Bibliographical Society of America
BSB	Black Swan Books, Redding Ridge, CT
BSP	Black Sparrow Press, Santa Barbara, CA
BSU	Ball State University, Muncie, IN
BuckUP	Bucknell UP, Lewisburg, PA
Bulzoni	Bulzoni Editore, Rome, Italy
BUP	Birmingham University Press
Burnett	Burnett Books, London
Buske	Helmut Buske, Hamburg, Germany
Butterfly	Butterfly Books, San Antonio, TX
BWilliamsNZ	Bridget Williams Books, Wellington, New Zealand
CA	Creative Arts Book, Berkeley, CA
CAAS	Connecticut Academy of Arts and Sciences, New Haven, CT
CAB International	Centre for Agriculture and Biosciences International, Wallingford, Oxfordshire
Cadmus	Cadmus Editions, Tiburon, CA
Cairns	Francis Cairns, University of Leeds
Calaloux	Calaloux Publications, Ithaca, NY
Calder	John Calder, London
CALLS	Centre for Australian Language and Literature Studies, English Department, University of New England, Armidale, NSW, Australia
Cambria	Cambria Press, Amherst, NY
CambridgeSP	Cambridge Scholars Publishing, Newcastle upon Tyne, United Kingdom
Camden	Camden Press, London
CamdenH	Camden House (an imprint of Boydell and Brewer), Rochester, NY
C&G	Carroll & Graf, New York, NY
C&W	Chatto & Windus, London
Canongate	Canongate Publishing, Edinburgh
Canterbury	Canterbury Press, Norwich
Canterbury UP	Canterbury University Press, Christchurch, New Zealand

Cape	Jonathan Cape, London
Capra	Capra Press, Santa Barbara, CA
Carcanet	Carcanet New Press, Manchester, Lancashire
Cardinal	Cardinal, London
CaribB	Caribbean Books, Parkersburg, IA
CarletonUP	Carleton UP, Ottawa, ON, Canada
Carucci	Carucci, Rome, Italy
Cascadilla	Cascadilla Press, Somerville, MA
Cass	Frank Cass, London
Cassell	Cassell, London
Cavaliere Azzurro	Cavaliere Azzurro, Bologna, Italy
Cave	Godfrey Cave Associates, London
CBA	Council for British Archaeology, London
CBS	Cambridge Bibliographical Society, Cambridge
CCEUCan	Centre for Continuing Education, University of Canterbury, Christchurch, New Zealand
CCCP	Critical, Cultural and Communications Press, Nottingham
CCP	Canadian Children's Press, Guelph, ON, Canada
CCS	Centre for Canadian Studies, Mount Allison University, Sackville, NB, Canada
CDSH	Centre de Documentation Sciences Humaines, Paris, France
CENS	Centre for English Name Studies, University of Nottingham
Century	Century Publishing, London
Ceolfrith	Ceolfrith Press, Sunderland, Tyne and Wear
CESR	Société des Amis du Centre d'Études Supérieures de la Renaissance, Tours, France
CETEDOC	Library of Christian Latin Texts
CFA	Canadian Federation for the Humanities, Ottawa, ON, Canada
CG	Common Ground
CH	Croom Helm, London
C–H	Chadwyck–Healey, Cambridge
Chambers	W. & R. Chambers, Edinburgh
Champaign	Champaign Public Library and Information Center, Champaign, IL
Champion	Librairie Honoré Champion, Paris, France
Chand	S. Chand, Madras, India
Chaucer	Chaucer Press
ChelseaH	Chelsea House Publishers, New York, New Haven, and Philadelphia
ChLitAssoc	Children's Literature Association
Christendom	Christendom Publications, Front Royal, VA
Chronicle	Chronicle Books, London
Chrysalis	Chrysalis Press
ChuoUL	Chuo University Library, Tokyo, Japan
Churchman	Churchman Publishing, Worthing, W. Sussex
Cistercian	Cistercian Publications, Kalamazoo, MI
CL	City Lights Books, San Francisco, CA
CLA	Canadian Library Association, Ottawa, ON, Canada
Clarendon	Clarendon Press, Oxford
Claridge	Claridge, St Albans, Hertfordshire
Clarion	Clarion State College, Clarion, PA
Clark	T. & T. Clark, Edinburgh
Clarke	James Clarke, Cambridge

Classical	Classical Publishing, New Delhi, India
CLCS	Centre for Language and Communication Studies, Trinity College, Dublin, Eire
ClogherHS	Clogher Historical Society, Monaghan, Eire
CLUEB	Cooperativa Libraria Universitaria Editrice, Bologna, Italy
Clunie	Clunie Press, Pitlochry, Tayside
CMAP	Caxton's Modem Arts Press, Dallas, TX
CMERS	Center for Medieval and Early Renaissance Studies, Binghamton, NY
CML	William Andrews Clark Memorial Library, Los Angeles, CA
CMST	Centre for Medieval Studies, University of Toronto, ON, Canada
Coach House	Coach House Press, Toronto, ON, Canada
Colleagues	Colleagues Press, East Lansing, MI
Collector	Collector, London
College-Hill	College-Hill Press, San Diego, CA
Collins	William Collins, London
CollinsA	William Collins (Australia), Sydney, NSW, Australia
Collins & Brown	Collins & Brown, London
ColUP	Columbia UP, New York, NY
Comedia	Comedia Publishing, London
Comet	Comet Books, London
Compton	Compton Press, Tisbury, Wiltshire
Constable	Constable, London
Contemporary	Contemporary Books, Chicago, IL
Continuum	Continuum Publishing, New York, NY
Copp	Copp Clark Pitman, Mississauga, ON, Canada
Corgi	Corgi Books, London
CorkUP	Cork UP, Eire
Cormorant	Cormorant Press, Victoria, BC
Cornford	Cornford Press, Launceston, TAS, Australia
CornUP	Cornell UP, Ithaca, NY
Cornwallis	Cornwallis Press, Hastings, E. Sussex
Coronado	Coronado Press, Lawrence, KS
Cosmo	Cosmo Publications, New Delhi, India
Coteau	Coteau Books, Regina, SK, Canada
Cowley	Cowley Publications, Cambridge, MA
Cowper	Cowper House, Pacific Grove, CA
CPP	Canadian Poetry Press, London, Ontario, ON, Canada
CQUP	Central Queensland UP, Rockhampton, QLD, Australia
Crabtree	Crabtree Press, Sussex
Craftsman House	Craftsman House, The Netherlands
Craig Pottoon	Craig Pottoon Publishing, New Zealand
Crawford	Crawford House Publishing, Hindmarsh, SA
Creag Darach	Creag Durach Publications, Stirling
CreativeB	Creative Books, New Delhi, India
Cresset	Cresset Library, London
CRNLE	Centre for Research in the New Literatures in English, Adelaide, SA, Australia
Crossing	Crossing Press, Freedom, CA
Crossroad	Crossroad Publishing, New York, NY
Crown	Crown Publishers, New York, NY
Crowood	Crowood Press, Marlborough, Wiltshire

CSAL	Centre for Studies in Australian Literature, University of Western Australia, Nedlands, WA, Australia
CSLI	Center for the Study of Language and Information, Stanford University, CA
CSP	Canadian Scholars' Press, Toronto, ON, Canada
CSU	Cleveland State University, Cleveland, OH
CTHS	Éditions du Comité des Travaux Historiques et Scientifiques, Paris, France
CUAP	Catholic University of America Press, Washington, DC
Cuff	Harry Cuff Publications, St John's, NL, Canada
CULouvain	Catholic University of Louvain, Belgium
CULublin	Catholic University of Lublin, Poland
CUP	Cambridge UP, Cambridge, New York, and Melbourne
Currency	Currency Press, Paddington, NSW, Australia
Currey	James Currey, London
Cushing	Cushing Memorial Library & Archives
CV	Cherry Valley Edition, Rochester, NY
CVK	Cornelson-Velhagen & Klasing, Berlin, Germany
CWU	Carl Winter Universitätsverlag, Heidelberg, Germany
Da Capo	Da Capo Press, New York
Dacorum	Dacorum College, Hemel Hempstead, Hertfordshire
Daisy	Daisy Books, Peterborough, Cambridgeshire
Dalkey	Dalkey Archive Press, Elmwood Park, IL
D&C	David & Charles, Newton Abbot, Devon
D&H	Duncker & Humblot, Berlin, Germany
D&M	Douglas & McIntyre, Vancouver, BC, Canada
D&S	Duffy and Snellgrove, Polts Point, NSW, Australia
Dangaroo	Dangaroo Press, Mundelstrup, Denmark
Daniel	Daniel & Daniel Publishers Inc., CA
DavidB	David Brown Books
Dawson	Dawson Publishing, Folkestone, Kent
DawsonsPM	Dawsons Pall Mall
DBAP	Daphne Brasell Associates Press
DBP	Drama Book Publishers, New York, NY
Deakin UP	Deakin UP, Geelong, VIC, Australia
De Boeck	De Boeck-Wesmael, Brussels, Belgium
Dee	Ivan R. Dee Publishers, Chicago, IL
De Graaf	De Graaf, Nierwkoup, The Netherlands
Denoël	Denoël S.A.R.L., Paris, France
Dent	J.M. Dent, London
DentA	Dent, Ferntree Gully, VIC, Australia
Depanee	Depanee Printers and Publishers, Nugegoda, Sri Lanka
Deutsch	André Deutsch, London
Didier	Éditions Didier, Paris, France
Diesterweg	Verlag Moritz Diesterweg, Frankfurt am Main, Germany
Dim Gray Bar Press	Dim Gray Bar Press
Doaba	Doaba House, Delhi, India
Dobby	Eric Dobby Publishing, St Albans
Dobson	Dobson Books, Durham
DodoP	Dodo Press, Gloucester
Dolmen	Dolmen Press, Portlaoise, Eire
Donald	John Donald, Edinburgh
Donker	Adriaan Donker, Johannesburg, South Africa

Dorset	Dorset Publishing
Doubleday	Doubleday, London and New York
Dove	Dove, Sydney, NSW, Australia
Dovecote	Dovecote Press, Wimborne, Dorset
Dovehouse	Dovehouse Editions, Canada
Dover	Dover Publications, New York, NY
Drew	Richard Drew, Edinburgh
Droste	Droste Verlag, Düsseldorf, Germany
Droz	Librairie Droz SA, Geneva, Switzerland
DublinUP	Dublin UP, Dublin, Eire
Duckworth	Gerald Duckworth, London
Duculot	J. Duculot, Gembloux, Belgium
DukeUP	Duke UP, Durham, NC
Dundurn	Dundurn Press, Toronto and London, ON, Canada
Duquesne	Duquesne UP, Pittsburgh, PA
Dutton	E.P. Dutton, New York, NY
DWT	Dr Williams's Trust, London
EA	English Association, London
EAS	English Association Sydney Incorporated
Eason	Eason & Son, Dublin, Eire
East Bay	East Bay Books, Berkeley, CA
Ebony	Ebony Books, Melbourne, SA, Australia
Ecco	Ecco Press, New York, NY
ECNRS	Éditions du Centre National de la Recherche Scientifique, Paris, France
ECW	ECW Press, Downsview, Ontario, ON, Canada
Eden	Eden Press, Montreal and St Albans, VT
EdinUP	Edinburgh UP, Edinburgh
Edizioni	Edizioni del Grifo
Educare	Educare, Burnwood, VIC, Australia
EEM	East European Monographs, Boulder, CO
Eerdmans	William Eerdmans, Grand Rapids, MI
EETS	Early English Text Society, c/o Exeter College, Oxford
1890sS	Eighteen-Nineties Society, Oxford
Eihosha	Eihosha, Tokyo, Japan
Elephas	Elephas Books, Kewdale, WA, Australia
Elibank	Elibank Press, Wellington, New Zealand
Elm Tree	Elm Tree Books, London
Ember	Ember Press, Brixham, South Devon
EMSH	Editions de la Maison des Sciences de l'Homme, Paris, France
Enitharmon	Enitharmon Press, London
Enzyklopädie	Enzyklopädie, Leipzig, Germany
EONF	Eugene O'Neill Foundation, Danville, CA
EPNS	English Place-Name Society, Beeston, Nottingham
EPURE	Editions et Presses universitaires de Reims, France
Epworth	Epworth Press, Manchester
Eriksson	Paul Eriksson, Middlebury, VT
Erlbaum	Erlbaum Associates, NJ
Erskine	Erskine Press, Harleston, Norfolk
EscutchP	Escutcheon Press
ESI	Edizioni Scientifiche Italiane, Naples, Italy
ESL	Edizioni di Storia e Letteratura, Rome, Italy
EUFS	Editions Universitaires Fribourg Suisse, Switzerland

EUL	Edinburgh University Library, Edinburgh
Europa	Europa Publishers, London
Evans	M. Evans, New York, NY
Exact Change	Exact Change, Boston, MA
Exeter UP	Exeter UP, Devon
Exile	Exile Editions, Toronto, ON, Canada
Eyre	Eyre Methuen, London
FAB	Free Association Books, London
Faber	Faber & Faber, London
FAC	Federation d'Activites Culturelles, Paris, France
FACP	Fremantle Arts Centre Press, Fremantle, WA, Australia
Falcon Books	Falcon Books, Eastbourne
FALS	Foundation for Australian Literary Studies, James Cook University of North Queensland, Townsville, QLD, Australia
F&F	Fels & Firn Press, San Anselmo, CA
F&S	Feffer & Simons, Amsterdam, The Netherlands
Farrand	Farrand Press, London
Fay	Barbara Fay, Stuttgart, Germany
F–B	Ford–Brown, Houston, TX
FCP	Four Courts Press, Dublin, Eire
FDUP	Fairleigh Dickinson UP, Madison, NJ
FE	Fourth Estate, London
Feminist	Feminist Press, New York, NY
FictionColl	Fiction Collective, Brooklyn College, Brooklyn, NY
Field Day	Field Day, Derry
Fifth House	Fifth House Publications, Saskatoon, Saskatchewan
FILEF	FILEF Italo–Australian Publications, Leichhardt, NSW, Australia
Fine	Donald Fine, New York, NY
Fink	Fink Verlag, Munich, Germany
Five Leaves	Five Leaves Publications, Nottingham
Flamingo	Flamingo Publishing, Newark, NJ
Flammarion	Flammarion, Paris, France
FlindersU	Flinders University of South Australia, Bedford Park, SA, Australia
Floris	Floris Books, Edinburgh
FlorSU	Florida State University, Tallahassee, FL
FOF	Facts on File, New York, NY
Folger	Folger Shakespeare Library, Washington, DC
Folio	Folio Press, London
Fontana	Fontana Press, London
Footprint	Footprint Press, Colchester, Essex
FordUP	Fordham UP, New York, NY
Foris	Foris Publications, Dordrecht, The Netherlands
Forsten	Egbert Forsten Publishing, Groningen, The Netherlands
Fortress	Fortress Press, Philadelphia, PA
Francke	Francke Verlag, Berne, Switzerland
Franklin	Burt Franklin, New York, NY
FreeP	Free Press, New York, NY
FreeUP	Free UP, Amsterdam, The Netherlands
Freundlich	Freundlich Books, New York, NY
Frommann-Holzboog	Frommann-Holzboog, Stuttgart, Germany
FS&G	Farrar, Straus & Giroux

FSP	Five Seasons Press, Madley, Hereford
FW	Fragments West/Valentine Press, Long Beach, CA
FWA	Fiji Writers' Association, Suva, Fiji
FWP	Falling Wall Press, Bristol
Gale	Gale Research, Detroit, MI
Galilée	Galilée, Paris, France
Gallimard	Gallimard, Paris, France
G&G	Grevatt & Grevatt, Newcastle upon Tyne
G&M	Gill & Macmillan, Dublin, Eire
Garland	Garland Publishing, New York, NY
Gasson	Roy Gasson Associates, Wimbourne, Dorset
Gateway	Gateway Editions, Washington, DC
GE	Greenwich Exchange, UK
GIA	GIA Publications, USA
Girasole	Edizioni del Girasole, Ravenna, Austria
GL	Goose Lane Editions, Fredericton, NB
GlasgowDL	Glasgow District Libraries, Glasgow
Gleerup	Gleerupska, Lund, Sweden
Gliddon	Gliddon Books Publishers, Norwich
Gloger	Gloger Family Books, Portland, OR
GMP	GMP Publishing, London
GMSmith	Gibbs M. Smith, Layton, UT
Golden Dog	Golden Dog, Ottawa, ON, Canada
Gollancz	Victor Gollancz, London
Gomer	Gomer Press, Llandysul, Dyfed
GothU	Gothenburg University, Gothenburg, Sweden
Gower	Gower Publishing, Aldershot, Hants
GRAAT	Groupe de Recherches Anglo-Américaines de Tours
Grafton	Grafton Books, London
GranB	Granary Books, New York, NY
Granta	Granta Publications, London
Granville	Granville Publishing, London
Grasset	Grasset & Fasquelle, Paris, France
Grassroots	Grassroots, London
Graywolf	Graywolf Press, St Paul, MI
Greenhalgh	M.J. Greenhalgh, London
Greenhill	Greenhill Books, London
Greenwood	Greenwood Press, Westport, CT
Gregg	Gregg Publishing, Surrey
Greville	Greville Press, Warwick
Greymitre	Greymitre Books, London
GroC	Grolier Club, New York, NY
Groos	Julius Groos Verlag, Heidelberg, Switzerland
Grove	Grove Press, New York, NY
GRP	Greenfield Review Press, New York, NY
Grüner	B.R. Grüner, Amsterdam, The Netherlands
Gruyter	Walter de Gruyter, Berlin, Germany
Guernica	Guernica Editions, Montreal, QC, Canada
Guilford	Guilford, New York, NY
Gulmohar	Gulmohar Press, Islamabad, Pakistan
Haggerston	Haggerston Press, London
HakluytS	Hakluyt Society, c/o British Library, London
Hale	Robert Hale, London

Hall	G.K. Hall, Boston, MA
Halstead	Halstead Press, Rushcutters Bay, NSW, Australia
HalsteadP	Halstead Press, c/o J. Wiley & Sons, Chichester, W. Sussex
Hambledon	Hambledon Press, London
H&I	Hale & Iremonger, Sydney, NSW, Australia
H&L	Hambledon and London
H&M	Holmes & Meier, London and New York
H&S	Hodder & Stoughton, London
H&SNZ	Hodder & Stoughton, Auckland, New Zealand
H&W	Hill & Wang, New York, NY
Hansib	Hansib Publishing, London
Harbour	Harbour Publishing, Madeira Park, BC
Harman	Harman Publishing House, New Delhi, India
Harper	Harper & Row, New York, NY
Harrap	Harrap, Edinburgh
HarrV	Harrassowitz Verlag, Wiesbaden, Germany
HarvardUP	Harvard UP, Cambridge, MA
Harwood	Harwood Academic Publishers, Langhorne, PA
Hatje	Verlag Gerd Hatje, Germany
HBJ	Harcourt Brace Jovanovich, New York and London
HC	HarperCollins, London
HCAus	HarperCollins Australia, Pymble, NSW, Australia
Headline	Headline Book Publishing, London
Heath	D.C. Heath, Lexington, MS
HebrewUMP	Hebrew University Magnes Press
Heinemann	William Heinemann, London
HeinemannA	William Heinemann, St Kilda, VIC, Australia
HeinemannC	Heinemann Educational Books, Kingston, Jamaica
HeinemannNg	Heinemann Educational Books, Nigeria
HeinemannNZ	Heinemann Publishers, Auckland (now Heinemann Reed)
HeinemannR	Heinemann Reed, Auckland, New Zealand
Helm	Christopher Helm, London
HelmI	Helm Information
Herbert	Herbert Press, London
Hermitage	Hermitage Antiquarian Bookshop, Denver, CO
Hern	Nick Hern Books, London
Hertfordshire	Hertfordshire Publications
Heyday	Heyday Books, Berkeley, CA
HH	Hamish Hamilton, London
Hilger	Adam Hilger, Bristol
HM	Harvey Miller, London
HMSO	HMSO, London
Hodder, Moa, Beckett	Hodder, Moa, Beckett, Milford, Auckland, New Zealand
Hodge	A. Hodge, Penzance, Cornwall
Hogarth	Hogarth Press, London
HongKongUP	Hong Kong UP, Hong Kong
Horsdal & Schubart	Horsdal & Schubart, Victoria, BC, Canada
Horwood	Ellis Horwood, Hemel Hempstead, Hertfordshire
HoughtonM	Houghton Mifflin, Boston, MA
Howard	Howard UP, Washington, DC
HREOC	Human Rights and Equal Opportunity Commission, Commonweath of Australia, Canberra, ACT, Australia

HRW	Holt, Reinhart & Winston, New York, NY
Hudson	Hudson Hills Press, New York, NY
Hueber	Max Hueber, Ismaning, Germany
HUL	Hutchinson University Library, London
HullUP	Hull UP, University of Hull
Humanities	Humanities Press, Atlantic Highlands, NJ
Humanities-Ebooks	Humanities Ebooks, Penrith
Huntington	Huntington Library, San Marino, CA
Hurst	C. Hurst, Covent Garden, London
Hutchinson	Hutchinson Books, London
HW	Harvester Wheatsheaf, Hemel Hempstead, Hertfordshire
HWWilson	H.W. Wilson, New York, NY
Hyland House	Hyland House Publishing, VIC, Australia
HyphenP	Hyphen Press, London
IA	Imprint Academic
IAAS	Indian Institute of Advanced Studies, Lahore and New Delhi
Ian Henry	Ian Henry Publications, Hornchurch, Essex
IAP	Irish Academic Press, Dublin
Ibadan	Ibadan University Press
IBK	Innsbrucker Beiträge zur Kulturwissenschaft, University of Innsbruck, Austria
ICA	Institute of Contemporary Arts, London
IHA	International Hopkins Association, Waterloo, ON, Canada
IJamaica	Institute of Jamaica Publications, Kingston, Jamaica
Imago	Imago Imprint, New York, NY
Imperial WarMuseum	Imperial War Museum Publications, London
IndUP	Indiana UP, Bloomington, IN
Inkblot	Inkblot Publications, Berkeley, CA
IntUP	International Universities Press, New York, NY
Inventions	Inventions Press, London
IonaC	Iona College, New Rochelle, NY
IowaSUP	Iowa State UP, Ames, IA
IOWP	Isle of Wight County Press, Newport, Isle of Wight
IP	In Parenthesis, London
Ipswich	Ipswich Press, Ipswich, MA
IrishAP	Irish Academic Press, Dublin, Eire
ISI	ISI Press, Philadelphia, PA
Italica	Italica Press, New York, NY
IULC	Indiana University Linguistics Club, Bloomington, IN
IUP	Indiana University of Pennsylvania Press, Indiana, PA
Ivon	Ivon Publishing House, Bombay, India
Jacaranda	Jacaranda Wiley, Milton, QLD, Australia
JadavpurU	Jadavpur University, Calcutta, India
James CookU	James Cook University of North Queensland, Townsville, QLD, Australia
Jarrow	Parish of Jarrow, Tyne and Wear
JBPC	John Benjamins Publishing Company, Amsterdam, The Netherlands
Jesperson	Jesperson Press, St John's, NL, Canada
JHall	James Hall, Leamington Spa, Warwickshire
JHUP	Johns Hopkins UP, Baltimore, MD
JIWE	JIWE Publications, University of Gulbarga, India

JLRC	Jack London Research Center, Glen Ellen, CA
J-NP	Joe-Noye Press
Jonas	Jonas Verlag, Marburg, Germany
Joseph	Michael Joseph, London
Journeyman	Journeyman Press, London
JPGM	J. Paul Getty Museum
JT	James Thin, Edinburgh
Junction	Junction Books, London
Junius-Vaughan	Junius-Vaughan Press, Fairview, NJ
Jupiter	Jupiter Press, Lake Bluff, IL
JyväskyläU	Jyväskylä University, Jyväskylä, Finland
Kaibunsha	Kaibunsha, Tokyo, Japan
K&N	Königshausen & Neumann, Würzburg, Germany
K&W	Kaye & Ward, London
Kangaroo	Kangaroo Press, Simon & Schuster (Australia), Roseville, NSW, Australia
Kansai	Kansai University of Foreign Studies, Osaka, Japan
Kardo	Kardo, Coatbridge, Scotland
Kardoorair	Kardoorair Press, Adelaide, SA, Australia
Karia	Karia Press, London
Karnak	Karnak House, London
Karoma	Karoma Publishers, Ann Arbor, MI
Katha	Katha, New Delhi, India
KC	Kyle Cathie, London
KCL	King's College London
KeeleUP	Keele University Press
Kegan Paul	Kegan Paul International, London
Kenkyu	Kenkyu-Sha, Tokyo, Japan
Kennikat	Kennikat Press, Port Washington, NY
Kensal	Kensal Press, Oxford
KentSUP	Kent State University Press, Kent, OH
KenyaLB	Kenya Literature Bureau, Nairobi, Kenya
Kerosina	Kerosina Publications, Worcester Park, Surrey
Kerr	Charles H. Kerr, Chicago, IL
Kestrel	Viking Kestrel, London
K/H	Kendall/Hunt Publishing, Dubuque, IA
Kingsley	J. Kingsley Publishers, London
Kingston	Kingston Publishers, Kingston, Jamaica
Kinseido	Kinseido, Tokyo, Japan
KITLV	KITLV Press, Leiden, The Netherlands
Klostermann	Vittorio Klostermann, Frankfurt am Main, Germany
Kluwer	Kluwer Academic Publications, Dordrecht, The Netherlands
Knopf	Alfred A. Knopf, New York, NY
Knowledge	Knowledge Industry Publications, White Plains, NY
Kraft	Kraft Books, Ibadan, Nigeria
Kraus	Kraus International Publications, White Plains, NY
KSUP	Kent State UP, Kent OH
LA	Library Association, London
LACUS	Linguistic Association of Canada and the United States, Chapel Hill, NC
Lake View	Lake View Press, Chicago, IL
LAm	Library of America, New York, NY
Lancelot	Lancelot Press, Hantsport, NS

Landesman	Jay Landesman, London
L&W	Lawrence & Wishart, London
Lane	Allen Lane, London
Lang	Peter D. Lang, Frankfurt am Main and Berne
Latimer	Latimer Trust
Learning Media	Learning Media Ltd, Wellington, New Zealand
LehighUP	Lehigh University Press, Bethlehem, PA
LeicAE	University of Leicester, Department of Adult Education
LeicsCC	Leicestershire County Council, Libraries and Information Service, Leicester
LeicUP	Leicester UP, Leicester
LeidenUP	Leiden UP, Leiden, The Netherlands
Leopard's Head	Leopard's Head Press, Oxford
Letao	Letao Press, Albury, NSW, Australia
LeuvenUP	Leuven UP, Leuven, Belgium
Lexik	Lexik House, Cold Spring, NY
Lexington	Lexington Publishers
LF	LiberFörlag, Stockholm, Sweden
LH	Lund Humphries Publishers, London
Liberty	Liberty Classics, Indianapolis, IN
Libris	Libris, London
LibrU	Libraries Unlimited, Englewood, CO
Liffey	Liffey Press, Dublin, Eire
Liguori	Liguori, Naples, Italy
Limelight	Limelight Editions, New York, NY
Lime Tree	Lime Tree Press, Octopus Publishing, London
LincolnUP	Lincoln University Press, NB, Canada
LINCOM	LINCOM Europa, Munich, Germany
LIT	Lit Verlag
LITIR	LITIR Database, University of Alberta, AB, Canada
LittleH	Little Hills Press, Burwood, NSW, Australia
Liveright	Liveright Publishing, New York, NY
LiverUP	Liverpool UP, Liverpool
Livre de Poche	Le Livre de Poche, Paris, France
Llanerch	Llanerch Enterprises, Lampeter, Dyfed
Locust Hill	Locust Hill Press, West Cornwall, CT
Loewenthal	Loewenthal Press, New York, NY
Longman	Pearson Longman Wesley, Harlow, Essex
LongmanC	Longman Caribbean, Harlow, Essex
LongmanF	Longman, France
LongmanNZ	Longman, Auckland, New Zealand
Longspoon	Longspoon Press, University of Alberta, Edmonton, AB, Canada
Lovell	David Lovell Publishing, Brunswick, VIC, Australia
Lowell	Lowell Press, Kansas City, MS
Lowry	Lowry Publishers, Johannesburg, South Africa
LSUP	Louisiana State UP, Baton Rouge, LA
L3	L3: Liege Language and Literature, University of Liege, Belgium
LundU	Lund University, Lund, Sweden
LUP	Loyola UP, Chicago, IL
Lutterworth	Lutterworth Press, Cambridge
Lymes	Lymes Press, Newcastle, Staffordshire
Lythrum	Lythrum Press, Adelaide, SA, Australia

MAA	Medieval Academy of America, Cambridge, MA
Macleay	Macleay Press, Paddington, NSW, Australia
Macmillan	Macmillan Publishers, London
MacmillanC	Macmillan Caribbean
Madison	Madison Books, Lanham, MD
Madurai	Madurai University, Madurai, India
Maecenas	Maecenas Press, Iowa City, IA
Magabala	Magabala Books, Broome, WA
Magnes	Magnes Press, The Hebrew University, Jerusalem, Israel
Mainstream	Mainstream Publishing, Edinburgh
MaIP	Marymount Institute Press, Tsehai Publishers, Los Angeles, CA
Maisonneuve	Maisonneuve Press, Washington, DC
Malone	Malone Society, c/o King's College, London
Mambo	Mambo Press, Gweru, Zimbabwe
ManCASS	Manchester Centre for Anglo-Saxon Studies, University of Manchester
M&E	Macdonald & Evans, Estover, Plymouth, Devon
M&S	McClelland & Stewart, Toronto, ON, Canada
Maney	W.S. Maney & Sons, Leeds
Mango	Mango Publishing, London, United Kingdom
Manohar	Manohar Publishers, Darya Gan, New Delhi
Mansell	Mansell Publishing, London
Manufacture	La Manufacture, Lyons, France
ManUP	Manchester UP, Manchester
Mardaga	Mardaga
Mariner	Mariner Books, Boston, MA
MarquetteUP	Marquette UP, Milwaukee, WI
Marvell	Marvell Press, Calstock, Cornwall
MB	Mitchell Beazley, London
McDougall, Littel	McDougall, Littel, Evanston, IL
McFarland	McFarland, Jefferson, NC
McG-QUP	McGill-Queen's UP, Montreal, QC, Canada
McGraw-Hill	McGraw-Hill, New York, NY
McIndoe	John McIndoe, Dunedin, New Zealand
McPheeG	McPhee Gribble Publishers, Fitzroy, VIC, Australia
McPherson	McPherson, Kingston, NY
MCSU	Maria Curie Skłodowska University, Lublin, Poland
ME	M. Evans, New York, NY
Meany	P.D. Meany Publishing, Port Credit, ON, Canada
Meckler	Meckler Publishing, Westport, CT
MelboumeUP	Melbourne UP, Carlton South, VIC, Australia
Mellen	Edwin Mellen Press, Lewiston, NY
MellenR	Mellen Research UP
Menzies	Menzies Centre for Australian Studies
MercerUP	Mercer UP, Macon, GA
Mercury	Mercury Press, Stratford, ON, Canada
Merlin	Merlin Press, London
Methuen	Methuen, London
MethuenA	Methuen Australia, North Ryde, NSW, Australia
MethuenC	Methuen, Toronto, ON, Canada
Metro	Metro Publishing, Auckland, New Zealand
Metzler	Metzler, Stuttgart, Germany

MGruyter	Mouton de Gruyter, Berlin, New York, and Amsterdam
MH	Michael Haag, London
MHRA	Modern Humanities Research Association, London
MHS	Missouri Historical Society, St Louis, MO
MI	Microforms International, Pergamon Press, Oxford
Micah	Micah Publications, Marblehead, MA
MichSUP	Michigan State UP, East Lansing, MI
MidNAG	Mid-Northumberland Arts Group, Ashington, Northumbria
Miegunyah	Miegunyah Press, Carlton, VIC, Australia
Mieyungah	Mieyungah Press, Melbourne University Press, Carlton South, VIC, Australia
Milestone	Milestone Publications, Horndean, Hampshire
Millennium	Millennium Books, E.J. Dwyer, Newtown, Australia
Millstream	Millstream Books, Bath
Milner	Milner, London
Minuit	Éditions de Minuit, Paris, France
MIP	Medieval Institute Publications, Western Michigan University, Kalamazoo, MI
MITP	Massachusetts Institute of Technology Press, Cambridge, MA
MLA	Modern Language Association of America, New York, NY
MIM	Multilingual Matters, Clevedon, Avon
MLP	Manchester Literary and Philosophical Society, Manchester
MnaN	Mkuki na Nyota Publishers, Dar es Salaam, Tanzania
Modern Library	Modern Library (Random House), New York, NY
Monarch	Monarch Publications, Sussex
Moonraker	Moonraker Press, Bradford-on-Avon, Wiltshire
Moorland	Moorland Publishing, Ashbourne, Derby
Moreana	Moreana, Angers, France
MorganSU	Morgan State University, Baltimore, MD
Morrow	William Morrow, New York, NY
Mosaic	Mosaic Press, Oakville, ON, Canada
Motilal	Motilal Books, Oxford
Motley	Motley Press, Romsey, Hampshire
Mouton	Mouton Publishers, New York and Paris
Mowbray	A.R. Mowbray, Oxford
MR	Martin Robertson, Oxford
MRS	Medieval and Renaissance Society, North Texas State University, Denton, TX
MRTS	MRTS, Binghamton, NY
MSUP	Memphis State UP, Memphis, TN
MtAllisonU	Mount Allison University, Sackville, NB, Canada
MTP	Museum Tusculanum Press, University of Copenhagen, Denmark
Mulini	Mulini Press, ACT, Australia
Muller	Frederick Muller, London
MULP	McMaster University Library Press
Murray	John Murray, London
Mursia	Ugo Mursia, Milan, Italy
NAL	New American Library, New York, NY
Narr	Gunter Narr Verlag, Tübingen, Germany
Nathan	Fernand Nathan, Paris, France
NBB	New Beacon Books, London
NBCAus	National Book Council of Australia, Melbourne, VIC, Australia

NCP	New Century Press, Durham
ND	New Directions, New York, NY
NDT	Nottingham Drama Texts, c/o University of Nottingham
NEL	New English Library, London
NELM	National English Literary Museum, Grahamstown, S. Africa
Nelson	Nelson Publishers, Melbourne, VIC, Australia
NelsonT	Thomas Nelson, London
New Endeavour	New Endeavour Press
NeWest	NeWest Press, Edmonton, AB, Canada
New Horn	New Horn Press, Ibadan, Nigeria
New Island	New Island Press
NewIssuesP	New Issues Press, Western Michigan University, MI
NH	New Horizon Press, Far Hills, NJ
N-H	Nelson-Hall, Chicago, IL
NHPC	North Holland Publishing, Amsterdam and New York
NicV	Nicolaische Verlagsbuchhandlung, Berlin, Germany
NIE	La Nuova Italia Editrice, Florence, Italy
Niemeyer	Max Niemeyer, Tübingen, Germany
Nightwood	Nightwood Editions, Toronto, ON, Canada
NIUP	Northern Illinois UP, De Kalb, IL
NLA	National Library of Australia
NLB	New Left Books, London
NLC	National Library of Canada, Ottawa, ON, Canada
NLP	New London Press, Dallas, TX
NLS	National Library of Scotland, Edinburgh
NLW	National Library of Wales, Aberystwyth, Dyfed
Nodus	Nodus Publikationen, Münster, Germany
Northcote	Northcote House Publishers, Plymouth
NortheastemU	Northeastern University, Boston, MA
NorthwesternUP	Norhwestem UP, Evanston, IL
Norton	W.W. Norton, New York and London
NorUP	Norwegian University Press, Oslo, Norway
Novus	Novus Press, Oslo, Norway
NPF	National Poetry Foundation, Orono, ME
NPG	National Portrait Gallery, London
NPP	North Point Press, Berkeley, CA
NSP	New Statesman Publishing, New Delhi, India
NSU Press	Northern States Universities Press
NSWUP	New South Wales UP, Kensington, NSW, Australia
NT	National Textbook, Lincolnwood, IL
NUC	Nipissing University College, North Bay, ON, Canada
NUP	National University Publications, Millwood, NY
NUSam	National University of Samoa
NUU	New University of Ulster, Coleraine
NWAP	North Waterloo Academic Press, Waterloo, ON, Canada
NWP	New World Perspectives, Montreal, QC, Canada
NYPL	New York Public Library, New York, NY
NYUP	New York UP, New York, NY
OakK	Oak Knoll Press, New Castle, DE
O&B	Oliver & Boyd, Harlow, Essex
Oasis	Oasis Books, London
OBAC	Organization of Black American Culture, Chicago, IL
OberlinCP	Oberlin College Press, Oberlin, OH

Oberon	Oberon Books, London
O'Brien	O'Brien Press, Dublin, Eire
OBS	Oxford Bibliographical Society, Bodleian Library, Oxford
Octopus	Octopus Books, London
OdenseUP	Odense UP, Odense, Denmark
OE	Officina Edizioni, Rome, Italy
OEColl	Old English Colloquium, Berkeley, CA
Offord	John Offord Publications, Eastbourne, E. Sussex
OhioUP	Ohio UP, Athens, OH
Oldcastle	Oldcastle Books, Harpenden, Hertfordshire
Olms	Georg Ohms, Hildesheim, Germany
Olschki	Leo S. Olschki, Florence, Italy
O'Mara	Michael O'Mara Books, London
Omnigraphics	Omnigraphics, Detroit, MI
Oneworld	Oneworld Classics, Surrey
Open Books	Open Books Publishing, Wells, Somerset
Open Court	Open Court Publishing, IL
OpenUP	Open UP, Buckingham and Philadelphia
OPP	Oxford Polytechnic Press, Oxford
Orbis	Orbis Books, London
OregonSUP	Oregon State UP, Corvallis, OR
Oriel	Oriel Press, Stocksfield, Northumberland
Orient Longman	Orient Longman, India
OrientUP	Oriental UP, London
OriginalNZ	Original Books, Wellington, New Zealand
ORP	Ontario Review Press, Princeton, NJ
Ortnamnsarkivet	Ortnamnsarkivet i Uppsala, Sweden
Orwell	Orwell Press, Southwold, Suffolk
Oryx	Oryx Press, Phoenix, AR
OSUP	Ohio State UP, Columbus, OH
Other	Otherland, Kingsbury, VIC, Australia
OTP	Oak Tree Press, London
OUCA	Oxford University Committee for Archaeology, Oxford
OUP	Oxford UP, Oxford
OUPAm	Oxford UP, New York, NY
OUPAus	Oxford UP, Melbourne, VIC, Australia
OUPC	Oxford UP, Toronto, ON, Canada
OUPI	Oxford UP, New Delhi, India
OUPNZ	Oxford UP, Auckland, New Zealand
OUPSA	Oxford UP Southern Africa, Cape Town, South Africa
Outlet	Outlet Book, New York, NY
Overlook	Overlook Press, New York, NY
Owen	Peter Owen, London
Owl	Owl
Pace UP	Pace University Press, New York, NY
Pacifica	Press Pacifica, Kailua, Hawaii, HI
Paget	Paget Press, Santa Barbara, CA
PAJ	PAJ Publications, New York, NY
Paladin	Paladin Books, London
Palgrave	Palgrave, NY
Pan	Pan Books, London
PalMac	Palgrave Macmillan, Hampshire, UK
PanAmU	Pan American University, Edinburgh, TX

P&C	Pickering & Chatto, London
Pandanus	Pandanus Press, Canberra, ACT, Australia
Pandion	Pandion Press, Capitola, CA
Pandora	Pandora Press, London
Pan Macmillan	Pan Macmillan Australia, South Yarra, VIC, Australia
Pantheon	Pantheon Books, New York, NY
ParagonH	Paragon House Publishers, New York, NY
Parnassus	Parnassus Imprints, Hyannis, MA
Parousia	Parousia Publications, London
Paternoster	Paternoster Press, Carlisle, Cumbria
Patten	Patten Press, Penzance
Paulist	Paulist Press, Ramsey, NJ
Paupers	Paupers' Press, Nottingham
Pavilion	Pavilion Books, London
PBFA	Provincial Booksellers' Fairs Association, Cambridge
PCP	Playwrights Canada Press, ON, Canada
Peachtree	Peachtree Publishers, Atlanta, GA
Pearson	David Pearson, Huntingdon, Cambridge
Peepal Tree	Peepal Tree Books, Leeds
Peeters	Peeters Publishers and Booksellers, Leuven, Belgium
Pelham	Pelham Books, London
Pembridge	Pembridge Press, London
Pemmican	Pemmican Publications, Winnipeg, MB, Canada
PencraftI	Pencraft International, Ashok Vihar II, Delhi, India
Penguin	Penguin Books, Harmondsworth, Middlesex
PenguinA	Penguin Books, Ringwood, VIC, Australia
PenguinNZ	Penguin Books, Auckland, New Zealand
Penkevill	Penkevill Publishing, Greenwood, FL
Pentland	Pentland Press, Ely, Cambridge
Penumbra	Penumbra Press, Moonbeam, Ontario, ON, Canada
People's	People's Publications, London
Pergamon	Pergamon Press, Oxford
Permanent	Permanent Press, Sag Harbor, NY
Permanent Black	Permanent Black, Delhi, India
Perpetua	Perpetua Press, Oxford
Petton	Petton Books, Oxford
Pevensey	Pevensey Press, Newton Abbot, Devon
PH	Prentice-Hall, Englewood Cliffs, NJ
Phaidon	Phaidon Press, London
PHI	Prentice-Hall International, Hemel Hempstead, Hertfordshire
PhilL	Philosophical Library, New York, NY
Phillimore	Phillimore, Chichester
Phoenix	Phoenix
Piatkus	Piatkus Books, London
Pickwick	Pickwick Publications, Allison Park, PA
Pilgrim	Pilgrim Books, Norman, OK
PIMS	Pontifical Institute of Mediaeval Studies, Toronto, ON, Canada
Pinter	Frances Pinter Publishers, London
Plains	Plains Books, Carlisle
Plenum	Plenum Publishing, London and New York
Plexus	Plexus Publishing, London
Pliegos	Editorial Pliegos, Madrid, Spain
Ploughshares	Ploughshares Books, Watertown, MA

PlovdivUP	Plovdiv University Press, Bulgaria
Pluto	Pluto Press, London
PML	Pierpont Morgan Library, New York, NY
Polity	Polity Press, Cambridge
Polygon	Polygon, Edinburgh
Polymath	Polymath Press, TAS, Australia
Poolbeg	Poolbeg Press, Swords, Dublin, Eire
Porcepic	Press Porcepic, Victoria, BC, Canada
Porcupine	Porcupine's Quill, ON, Canada
PortN	Port Nicholson Press, Wellington, NZ
Potter	Clarkson N. Potter, New York, NY
Power	Power Publications, University of Sydney, NSW, Australia
PPUBarcelona	Promociones y Publicaciones Universitarias, Barcelona, Spain
Praeger	Praeger, New York, NY
Prakash	Prakash Books, India
Prestel	Prestel Verlag, Germany
PrestigeB	Prestige Books, New Delhi, India
Primavera	Edizioni Primavera, Gunti Publishing, Florence, Italy
Primrose	Primrose Press, Alhambra, CA
PrincetonUL	Princeton University Library, Princeton, NJ
PrincetonUP	Princeton UP, Princeton, NJ
Printwell	Printwell Publishers, Jaipur, India
Prism	Prism Press, Bridport, Dorset
PRO	Public Record Office, London
Profile	Profile Books, Ascot, Berks
ProgP	Progressive Publishers, Calcutta, India
PSUP	Pennsylvania State UP, University Park, PA
Pucker	Puckerbrush Press, Orono, ME
PUF	Presses Universitaires de France, Paris, France
PULM	Presses Universitaires de la Mediterranee, Université Paul-Valéry - Montpellier III, France
PUPV	Publications de l'université Paul-Valéry, Montpellier 3, France
PurdueUP	Purdue UP, Lafayette, IN
Pushcart	Pushcart Press, Wainscott, NY
Pustet	Friedrich Pustet, Regensburg, Germany
Putnam	Putnam Publishing, New York, NY
PWP	Poetry Wales Press, Ogmore by Sea, mid-Glamorgan
QED	QED Press, Ann Arbor, MI
Quarry	Quarry Press, Kingston, ON, Canada
Quartet	Quartet Books, London
Quaternary	The Quaternary Institute
Quirk	Quirk Books
QUT	Queensland University of Technology, QLD, Australia
RA	Royal Academy of Arts, London
Rainforest	Rainforest Publishing, Faxground, NSW, Australia
Rampant Lions	Rampant Lions Press, Cambridge
R&B	Rosenklide & Bagger, Copenhagen, Denmark
R&L	Rowman & Littlefield, Totowa, NJ
Randle	Ian Randle, Kingston, Jamaica
RandomH	Random House, London and New York
RandomHAus	Random House Australia, VIC, Australia
RandomHNZ	Random House New Zealand Limited, Auckland, New Zealand

Ravan	Ravan Press, Johannesburg, South Africa
Ravette	Ravette, London
Ravi Dayal	Ravi Dayal Publishers, New Delhi, India
Rawat	Rawat Publishing, Jaipur and New Delhi, India
Reaktion	Reaktion Books, London
Rebel	Rebel Press, London
Red Kite	Red Kite Press, Guelph, ON, Canada
Red Rooster	Red Rooster Press, Hotham Hill, VIC, Australia
Red Sea	Red Sea Press, NJ
Reed	Reed Books, Port Melbourne, VIC, Australia
Reed NZ	Reed Publishing NZ Ltd., Auckland, New Zealand
Reference	Reference Press, Toronto, ON, Canada
Regents	Regents Press of Kansas, Lawrence, KS
Reichenberger	Roswitha Reichenberger, Kessel, Germany
Reinhardt	Max Reinhardt, London
Remak	Remak, Alblasserdam, The Netherlands
RenI	Renaissance Institute, Sophia University, Tokyo, Japan
Research	Research Publications, Reading
RETS	Renaissance English Text Society, Chicago, IL
RH	Ramsay Head Press, Edinburgh
RHS	Royal Historical Society, London
RIA	Royal Irish Academy, Dublin, Eire
RiceUP	Rice UP, Houston, TX
Richarz	Hans Richarz, St Augustin, Germany
RICL	Research Institute for Comparative Literature, University of Alberta, AB, Canada
Rivers Oram	Rivers Oram Press, London
Rizzoli	Rizzoli International Publications, New York, NY
RobartsCCS	Robarts Centre for Canadian Studies, York University, North York, ON, Canada
Robinson	Robinson Publishing, London
Robson	Robson Books, London
Rodopi	Rodopi, Amsterdam, The Netherlands
Roebuck	Stuart Roebuck, Suffolk
RoehamptonI	Roehampton Institute London
Ronsdale	Ronsdale Press
Routledge	Routledge, London and New York
Royce	Robert Royce, London
RS	Royal Society, London
RSC	Royal Shakespeare Company, London
RSL	Royal Society of Literature, London
RSVP	Research Society for Victorian Periodicals, University of Leicester
RT	RT Publications, London
Running	Running Press, Philadelphia, PA
Russell	Michael Russell, Norwich
RutgersUP	Rutgers UP, New Brunswick, NJ
Ryan	Ryan Publishing, London
SA	Sahitya Akademi, New Delhi, India
Sage	Sage Publications, London
SAI	Sociological Abstracts, San Diego, CA
Salamander	Salamander Books, London
Salem	Salem Press, Englewood Cliffs, NJ

S&A	Shukayr and Akasheh, Amman, Jordan
S&D	Stein & Day, Briarcliff Manor, NJ
S&J	Sidgwick & Jackson, London
S&M	Sun & Moon Press, Los Angeles, CA
S&P	Simon & Piere, Toronto, ON, Canada
S&S	Simon & Schuster, New York and London
S&W	Secker & Warburg, London
Sangam	Sangam Books, London
Sangsters	Sangsters Book Stores, Kingston, Jamaica
SAP	Scottish Academic Press, Edinburgh
Saros	Saros International Publishers
Sarup	Sarup & Sons, New Delhi, India
SASSC	Sydney Association for Studies in Society and Culture, University of Sydney, NSW, Australia
Saur	Bowker-Saur, Sevenoaks, Kent
Savacou	Savacou Publications, Kingston, Jamaica
S-B	Schwann-Bagel, Düsseldorf, Germany
ScanUP	Scandinavian University Presses, Oslo, Norway
Scarecrow	Scarecrow Press, Metuchen, NJ
Schäuble	Schäuble Verlag, Rheinfelden, Germany
Schmidt	Erich Schmidt Verlag, Berlin, Germany
Schneider	Lambert Schneider, Heidelberg, Germany
Schocken	Schocken Books, New York, NY
Scholarly	Scholarly Press, St Clair Shores, MI
ScholarsG	Scholars Press, GA
Schöningh	Ferdinand Schöningh, Paderborn, Germany
Schwinn	Michael Schwinn, Neustadt, Germany
SCJP	Sixteenth-Century Journal Publications
Scolar	Scolar Press, Aldershot, Hampshire
SCP	Second Chance Press, Sag Harbor, NY
Scribe	Scribe Publishing, Colchester
Scribner	Charles Scribner, New York, NY
SDSU	Department of English, South Dakota State University, SD
Seafarer	Seafarer Books, London
Seaver	Seaver Books, New York, NY
Segue	Segue, New York, NY
Semiotext(e)	Semiotext(e), Columbia University, New York, NY
SePA	Self-Publishing Association
Seren Books	Seren Books, Bridgend, mid-Glamorgan
Serpent's Tail	Serpent's Tail Publishing, London
Sessions	William Sessions, York
Seuil	Éditions du Seuil, Paris, France
7:84 Pubns	7:84 Publications, Glasgow
Severn	Severn House, Wallington, Surrey
SF&R	Scholars' Facsimiles and Reprints, Delmar, NY
SH	Somerset House, Teaneck, NJ
Shalabh	Shalabh Book House, Meerut, India
ShAP	Sheffield Academic Press
Shaun Tyas	Paul Watkins Publishing, Donington, Lincolnshire
Shearsman	Shearsman Books, Exeter
Shearwater	Shearwater Press, Lenah Valley, TAS, Australia
Sheba	Sheba Feminist Publishers, London

Sheed&Ward	Sheed & Ward, London
Sheldon	Sheldon Press, London
SHESL	Société d'Histoire et d'Épistemologie des Sciences du Langage, Paris, France
Shinozaki	Shinozaki Shorin, Tokyo, Japan
Shinshindo	Shinshindo Publishing, Tokyo, Japan
Shire	Shire Publications, Princes Risborough, Buckinghamshire
Shoal Bay Press	Shoal Bay Press, New Zealand
Shoe String	Shoe String Press, Hamden, CT
SHP	Shakespeare Head Press
SIAS	Scandinavian Institute of African Studies, Uppsala, Sweden
SIL	Summer Institute of Linguistics, Academic Publications, Dallas, TX
SIUP	Southern Illinois University Press, IL
Simon King	Simon King Press, Milnthorpe, Cumbria
Sinclair-Stevenson	Sinclair-Stevenson, London
SingaporeUP	Singapore UP, Singapore
Sismel	Società Internazionale per lo Studio del Medioevo Latino. Published by Edizione del Galluzo, Florence, Italy
SIUP	Southern Illinois UP, Carbondale, IL
SJSU	San Jose State University, San Jose, CA
Skilton	Charles Skilton, London
Skoob	Skoob Books, London
Slatkine	Éditions Slatkine, Paris, France
Slavica	Slavica Publishers, Columbus, OH
Sleepy Hollow	Sleepy Hollow Press, Tarrytown, NY
SLG	SLG Press, Oxford
Smith Settle	Smith Settle, W. Yorkshire
SMUP	Southern Methodist UP, Dallas, TX
Smythe	Colin Smythe, Gerrards Cross, Buckinghamshire
SNH	Société Néophilologique de Helsinki, Finland
SNLS	Society for New Language Study, Denver, CO
SOA	Society of Authors, London
Soho	Soho Book, London
SohoP	Soho Press, New York, NY
Solaris	Solaris Press, Rochester, MI
SonoNis	Sono Nis Press, Victoria, BC
Sorbonne	Publications de la Sorbonne, Paris, France
SorbonneN	Publications du Conseil Scientifique de la Sorbonne Nouvelle, Paris, France
Souvenir	Souvenir Press, London
SPA	SPA Books
SPACLALS	South Pacific Association for Commonwealth Literature and Language Studies, Wollongong, NSW, Australia
Spaniel	Spaniel Books, Paddington, NSW, Australia
SPCK	SPCK, London
Spectrum	Spectrum Books, Ibadan, Nigeria
Split Pea	Split Pea Press, Edinburgh
Spokesman	Spokesman Books, Nottingham
Spoon River	Spoon River Poetry Press, Granite Falls, MN
SRC	Steinbeck Research Center, San Jose State University, San Jose, CA

SRI	Steinbeck Research Institute, Ball State University, Muncie, IN
SriA	Sri Aurobindo, Pondicherry, India
Sri Satguru	Sri Satguru Publications, Delhi, India
SSA	John Steinbeck Society of America, Muncie, IN
SSAB	Sprakförlaget Skriptor AB, Stockholm, Sweden
SSNS	Scottish Society for Northern Studies, Edinburgh
StanfordUP	Stanford UP, Stanford, CA
Staple	Staple, Matlock, Derbyshire
Starmont	Starmont House, Mercer Island, WA
Starrhill	Starrhill Press, Washington, DC
Station Hill	Station Hill, Barrytown, NY
Stauffenburg	Stauffenburg Verlag, Tübingen, Germany
StDL	St Deiniol's Library, Hawarden, Clwyd
Steel Rail	Steel Rail Publishing, Ottawa, ON, Canada
Steele Roberts	Steele Roberts Publishing Ltd, Wellington, New Zealand
Steiner	Franz Steiner, Wiesbaden, Germany
Sterling	Sterling Publishing, New York, NY
SterlingND	Sterling Publishers, New Delhi, India
Stichting	Stichtig Neerlandistiek, Amsterdam, The Netherlands
St James	St James Press, Andover, Hampshire
St Martin's	St Martin's Press, New York, NY
StMut	State Mutual Book and Periodical Source, New York, NY
Stockwell	Arthur H. Stockwell, Ilfracombe, Devon
Stoddart	Stoddart Publishing, Don Mills, ON, Canada
StPB	St Paul's Bibliographies, Winchester, Hampshire
STR	Society for Theatre Research, London
Strauch	R.O.U. Strauch, Ludwigsburg, Germany
Streamline	Streamline Creative, Auckland, New Zealand
Stree	Stree/Bhatkal, Kolkata, India
Studio	Studio Editions, London
Stump Cross	Stump Cross Books, Stump Cross, Essex
Sud	Sud, Marseilles, France
Suhrkamp	Suhrkamp Verlag, Frankfurt am Main, Germany
Summa	Summa Publications, Birmingham, AL
SUNYP	State University of New York Press, Albany, NY
SUP	Sydney University Press, NSW, Australia
Surtees	R.S. Surtees Society, Frome, Somerset
SusquehannaUP	Susquehanna UP, Selinsgrove, PA
SussexAP	Sussex Academic Press, Sydney, NSW, Australia
SussexUP	Sussex UP, University of Sussex, Brighton
Sutton	Alan Sutton, Stroud, Gloucester
SVP	Sister Vision Press, Toronto, ON, Canada
S–W	Shepheard–Walwyn Publishing, London
Swallow	Swallow Press, Athens, OH
SWG	Saskatchewan Writers Guild, Regina, SK, Canada
Sybylla	Sybylla Feminist Press
SydneyUP	Sydney UP, Sydney, NSW, Australia
SyracuseUP	Syracuse UP, Syracuse, NY
Tabb	Tabb House, Padstow, Cornwall
Taishukan	Taishukan Publishing, Tokyo, Japan
Talonbooks	Talonbooks, Vancouver, BC, Canada
TamilU	Tamil University, Thanjavur, India

T&F	Taylor & Francis Books
T&H	Thames & Hudson, London
Tantivy	Tantivy Press, London
Tarcher	Jeremy P. Tarcher, Los Angeles, CA
Tartarus	Tartarus Press
Tate	Tate Gallery Publications, London
Tavistock	Tavistock Publications, London
Taylor	Taylor Publishing, Bellingham, WA
TaylorCo	Taylor Publishing, Dallas, TX
TCG	Theatre Communications Group, New York, NY
TCP	Three Continents Press, Washington, DC
TCUP	Texas Christian UP, Fort Worth, TX
TEC	Third Eye Centre, Glasgow
Tecumseh	Tecumseh Press, Ottawa, ON, Canada
Telos	Telos Press, St Louis, MO
TempleUP	Temple UP, Philadelphia, PA
TennS	Tennyson Society, Lincoln
TexA&MUP	Texas A&MUP, College Station, TX
Text	Text Publishing, Melbourne, VIC, Australia
TextileB	Textile Bridge Press, Clarence Center, NY
TexTULib	Friends of the University Library, Texas Tech University, Lubbock, TX
The Smith	The Smith, New York, NY
Thimble	Thimble Press, Stroud, Gloucester
Thoemmes	Thoemmes Press, Bristol
Thornes	Stanley Thornes, Cheltenham
Thorpe	D.W. Thorpe, Port Melbourne, VIC, Australia
Thorsons	Thorsons Publishers, London
Times	Times of Gloucester Press, Gloucester, ON, Canada
TMP	Thunder's Mouth Press, New York, NY
Tombouctou	Tombouctou Books, Bolinas, CA
Totem	Totem Books, Don Mills, ON, Canada
Toucan	Toucan Press, St Peter Port, Guernsey
Touzot	Jean Touzot, Paris, France
TPF	Trianon Press Facsimiles, London
Tragara	Tragara Press, Edinburgh
Transaction	Transaction Publishers, New Brunswick, NJ
Transcendental	Transcendental Books, Hartford, CT
Transworld	Transworld, London
TrinityUP	Trinity UP, San Antonio, TX
Tsar	Tsar Publications, Canada
TTUP	Texas Technical University Press, Lubbock, TX
Tuckwell	Tuckwell Press, East Linton
Tuduv	Tuduv, Munich, Germany
TulaneUP	Tulane UP, New Orleans, LA
TurkuU	Turku University, Turku, Finland
Turnstone	Turnstone Press, Winnipeg, MB, Canada
Turtle Island	Turtle Island Foundation, Berkeley, CA
Twayne	Twayne Publishing, Boston, MA
UAB	University of Aston, Birmingham
UAdelaide	University of Adelaide, Australia
UAlaP	University of Alabama Press, Tuscaloosa, AL
UAlbertaP	University of Alberta Press, Edmonton, AB, Canada

UAntwerp	University of Antwerp, The Netherlands
UArizP	University of Arizona Press, Tucson, AZ
UArkP	University of Arkansas Press, Fayetteville, AR
UAthens	University of Athens, Greece
UBarcelona	University of Barcelona, Spain
UBCP	University of British Columbia Press, Vancouver, BC, Canada
UBergen	University of Bergen, Norway
UBrno	J.E. Purkyne University of Brno, Czechoslovakia
UBrussels	University of Brussels, Belgium
UCalgaryP	University of Calgary Press, AB, Canada
UCalP	University of California Press, Berkeley, CA
UCAP	University of Central Arkansas Press, Conway, AR
UCapeT	University of Cape Town Press, South Africa
UChicP	University of Chicago Press, IL
UCDubP	University College Dublin Press, Eire
UCL	University College London Press
UCopenP	University of Copenhagen Press, Denmark
UDelP	University of Delaware Press, Newark, DE
UDijon	University of Dijon, France
UDur	University of Durham, Durham, UK
UEA	University of East Anglia, Norwich
UErlangen-N	University of Erlangen-Nuremberg, Germany
UEssex	University of Essex, Colchester
UExe	University of Exeter, Devon
UFlorence	University of Florence, Italy
UFlorP	University of Florida Press, FL
UFR	Université François Rabelais, Tours, France
UGal	University College, Galway, Eire
UGeoP	University of Georgia Press, Athens, Greece
UGhent	University of Ghent, Belgium
UGlasP	University of Glasgow Press
UHawaiiP	University of Hawaii Press, Honolulu, HI
UHertP	University of Hertfordshire Press
UHuelva	Universidad de Huelva Publicaciones, Spain
UIfeP	University of Ife Press, Ile-Ife, Nigeria
UIllp	University of Illinois Press, Champaign, IL
UInnsbruck	University of Innsbruck, Austria
UIowaP	University of Iowa Press, Iowa City, IA
UKanP	University of Kansas Press, Lawrence, KS
UKL	University of Kentucky Libraries, Lexington, KY
ULavalP	Les Presses de l'Université Laval, Quebec, QC, Canada
ULiège	University of Liège, Belgium
ULilleP	Presses Universitaires de Lille, France
ULondon	University of London
Ulster	University of Ulster, Coleraine
U/M	Underwood/Miller, Los Angeles, CA
UMalta	University of Malta, Msida, Malta
UManitobaP	University of Manitoba Press, Winnipeg, MB, Canada
UMassP	University of Massachusetts Press, Amherst, MA
Umeå	Umeå Universitetsbibliotek, Umeå, Sweden
UMichP	University of Michigan Press, Ann Arbor, MI
UMinnP	University of Minnesota Press, Minneapolis, MN
UMirail-ToulouseP	University of Mirail-Toulouse Press, France

UMIRes	UMI Research Press, Ann Arbor, MI
UMissP	University of Missouri Press, Columbia, MO
UMontP	Montpellier University Press, France
UMP	University of Mississippi Press, Lafayette, MS
UMysore	University of Mysore, India
UNancyP	Presses Universitaires de Nancy, France
UNCP	University of North Carolina Press, Chapel Hill, NC
Undena	Undena Publications, Malibu, CA
UNDP	University of Notre Dame Press, Notre Dame, IN
UNebP	University of Nebraska Press, Lincoln, NE
UNevP	University of Nevada Press, Reno, NV
UNewE	University of New England, Armidale, NSW, Australia
UnEWE, CALLS	University of New England, Centre for Australian Language and Literature Studies, NSW, Australia
Ungar	Frederick Ungar, New York, NY
Unicopli	Edizioni Unicopli, Milan, Italy
UnisaP	University of South Africa Press, Muckleneuk, South Africa
Unity	Unity Press, Hull
UnityP	Unity Press Woollahra, NSW, Australia
Universa	Uilgeverij Universa, Wetteren, Belgium
UNMP	University of New Mexico Press, Albuquerque, NM
UNorthTP	University of North Texas Press, TX
UNott	University of Nottingham
UNSW	University of New South Wales, NSW, Australia
Unwin	Unwin Paperbacks, London
Unwin Hyman	Unwin Hyman, London
UOklaP	University of Oklahoma Press, Norman, OK
UOslo	University of Oslo, Norway
UOtagoP	University of Otago Press, Dunedin, New Zealand
UOttawaP	University of Ottawa Press, ON, Canada
UPA	UP of America, Lanham, MD
UParis	University of Paris, France
UPColorado	UP of Colorado, Niwot, CO
UPennP	University of Pennsylvania Press, Philadelphia, PA
UPFlorida	University Press of Florida, FL
UPittP	University of Pittsburgh Press, Pittsburgh, PA
UPKen	University Press of Kentucky, Lexington, KY
UPMissip	UP of Mississippi, Jackson, MS
UPN	Université de Paris Nord, Paris, France
UPNE	UP of New England, Hanover, NH
Uppsala	Uppsala University, Uppsala, Sweden
UProvence	University of Provence, Aix-en-Provence, France
UPSouth	University Press of the South, NO
UPSouthDen	University Press of Southern Denmark
UPValéry	University Paul Valéry, Montpellier, France
UPVirginia	UP of Virginia, Charlottesville, VA
UQDE	University of Queensland, Department of English, QLD, Australia
UQP	University of Queensland Press, St Lucia, QLD, Australia
URouen	University of Rouen, Mont St Aignan, France
URP	University of Rochester Press
USalz	Institut für Anglistik and Amerikanstik, University of Salzburg, Austria

USantiago	University of Santiago, Spain
USCP	University of South Carolina Press, Columbia, SC
USFlorP	University of South Florida Press, Florida, FL
USheff	University of Sheffield
Usher	La Casa Usher, Florence, Italy
USPacific	University of the South Pacific, Institute of Pacific Studies, Suva, Fiji
USQ, DHSS	University of Southern Queensland, Department of Humanities and Social Sciences, QLD, Australia
USydP	University of Sydney Press, Sydney, NSW, Australia
USzeged	University of Szeged, Hungary
UtahSUP	Utah State UP, Logan, UT
UTampereP	University of Tampere Press, Knoxville, TN
UTas	University of Tasmania, Hobart, TAS, Australia
UTennP	University of Tennessee Press, Knoxville, TN
UTexP	University of Texas Press, Austin, TX
UTorP	University of Toronto Press, Toronto, ON, Canada
UTours	Université de Tours, France
UVerm	University of Vermont, Burlington, VT
UVict	University of Victoria, Victoria, BC
UWalesP	University of Wales Press, Cardiff
UWAP	University of Western Australia Press, Nedlands, WA, Australia
UWarwick	University of Warwick, Coventry
UWashP	University of Washington Press, Seattle, WA
UWaterlooP	University of Waterloo Press, Waterloo, ON, Canada
UWI	University of the West Indies, St Augustine, Trinidad
UWIndiesP	University of West Indies Press, Mona, Jamaica
UWiscM	University of Wisconsin, Milwaukee, WI
UWiscP	University of Wisconsin Press, Madison, WI
UWoll	University of Wollongong, NSW, Australia
UYork	University of York, York
Valentine	Valentine Publishing and Drama, Rhinebeck, NY
V&A	Victoria and Albert Museum, London
VanderbiltUP	Vanderbilt UP, Nashville, TE
V&R	Vandenhoeck & Ruprecht, Göttingen, Germany
Van Gorcum	Van Gorcum, Assen, The Netherlands
Vantage	Vantage Press, New York, NY
Variorum	Variorum, Ashgate Publishing, Hampshire
Vehicule	Vehicule Press, Montreal, QC, Canada
Vendome	Vendome Press, New York, NY
Verdant	Verdant Publications, Chichester
Verso	Verso Editions, London
VictUP	Victoria UP, Victoria University of Wellington, New Zealand
Vieweg	Vieweg Braunschweig, Wiesbaden, Germany
Vikas	Vikas Publishing House, New Delhi, India
Viking	Viking Press, New York, NY
VikingNZ	Viking, Auckland, New Zealand
Virago	Virago Press, London
Vision	Vision Press, London
VLB	VLB Éditeur, Montreal, QC, Canada
VP	Vulgar Press, Carlton North, VIC, Australia
VR	Variorum Reprints, London
Vrin	J. Vrin, Paris, France

VUP	Victoria University Press, Wellington, New Zealand
VUUP	Vrije Universiteit UP, Amsterdam, The Netherlands
Wakefield	Wakefield Press
W&B	Whiting & Birch, London
W&N	Weidenfeld & Nicolson, London
Water Row	Water Row Press, Sudbury, MA
Watkins	Paul Watkins, Stanford, Lincsolnshire
WB	Wissenschaftliche Buchgesellschaft, Darmstadt, Germany
W/B	Woomer/Brotherson, Revere, PA
Weaver	Weaver Press
Webb&Bower	Webb & Bower, Exeter
Wedgestone	Wedgestone Press, Winfield, KS
Wedgetail	Wedgetail Press, Earlwood, NSW, Australia
WesleyanUP	Wesleyan UP, Middletown, CT
West	West Publishing, St Paul, MN
WHA	William Heinemann Australia, Port Melbourne, VIC, Australia
Wheatsheaf	Wheatsheaf Books, Brighton
Whiteknights	Whiteknights Press, University of Reading, Berkshire
White Lion	White Lion Books, Cambridge
Whitston	Whitston Publishing, Troy, NY
Whittington	Whittington Press, Herefordshire
WHP	Warren House Press, Sale, Cheshire
Wiener	Wiener Publishing, New York, NY
Wildwood	Wildwood House, Aldershot, Hampshire
Wiley	John Wiley, Chichester, New York and Brisbane
Wilson	Philip Wilson, London
Winter	Carl Winter Universitätsverlag, Heidelberg, Germany
Winthrop	Winthrop Publishers, Cambridge, MA
WIU	Western Illinois University, Macomb, IL
WL	Ward Lock, London
WLUP	Wilfrid Laurier UP, Waterloo, ON, Canada
WMP	World Microfilms Publications, London
WMU	Western Michigan University, Kalamazoo, MI
Woeli	Woeli Publishing Services
Wolfhound	Wolfhound Press, Dublin, Eire
Wombat	Wombat Press, Wolfville, NS
Wo-No	Wolters-Noordhoff, Groningen, The Netherlands
Woodstock	Woodstock Books, Oxford
Woolf	Cecil Woolf, London
Words	Words, Framfield, E. Sussex
WP	Women's Press, London
WPC	Women's Press of Canada, Toronto, ON, Canada
WSUP	Wayne State UP, Detroit, MI
WUS	Wydawnictwo Uniwersytetu Slaskiego, Katowice, Poland
WVT	Wissenschaftlicher Verlag Trier, Germany
WVUP	West Virginia UP, Morgantown, WV
W-W	Williams-Wallace, Toronto, ON, Canada
WWU	Western Washington University, Bellingham, WA
Xanadu	Xanadu Publications, London
XLibris	XLibris Corporation
YaleUL	Yale University Library Publications, New Haven, CT
YaleUP	Yale UP, New Haven, CO and London
Yamaguchi	Yamaguchi Shoten, Kyoto, Japan

YMP	York Medieval Press
YorkP	York Press, Fredericton, NB, Canada
Younsmere	Younsmere Press, Brighton
Zed	Zed Books, London
Zell	Hans Zell, East Grinstead, W. Sussex
Zena	Zena Publications, Penrhyndeudraeth, Gwynedd
Zephyr	Zephyr Press, Somerville, MA
Zomba	Zomba Books, London
Zwemmer	A. Zwemmer, London

3. Acronyms

AAVE	African-American Vernacular English
AmE	American English
AusE	Australian English
BrE	British English
DP	Determiner Phrase
ECP	Empty Category Principle
EFL	English as a Foreign Language
EIL	English as an International Language
ELF	English as a Lingua Franca
ELT	English Language Teaching
eModE	early Modern English
ENL	English as a Native Language
EPNS	English Place-Name Society
ESL	English as a Second Language
ESP	English for Special Purposes
HPSG	Head-driven Phrase Structure Grammar
LF	Logical Form
LFG	Lexical Functional Grammar
ME	Middle English
MED	*Middle English Dictionary*
NZE	New Zealand English
ODan	Old Danish
OE	Old English
OED	*Oxford English Dictionary*
OF	Old French
ON	Old Norse
OT	Optimality Theory
PDE	Present-Day English
PF	Phonological Form
PP	Prepositional Phrase
SABE	South African Black English
SAE	South African English
SingE	Singapore English
TESOL	Teaching English to Speakers of other Languages
TMA	Tense, Mood and Aspect
UG	Universal Grammar

Preface

The Year's Work in English Studies is a narrative bibliography that records and evaluates scholarly writing on English language and on literatures written in English. It is published by Oxford University Press on behalf of the English Association.

The Editors and the English Association are pleased to announce that this year's Beatrice White Prize has been awarded to Penny Granger for *The N-Town Play: Drama and Liturgy in Medieval East Anglia* (Boydell & Brewer; ISBN 9 7818 4384 1890).

The authors of *YWES* attempt to cover all significant contributions to English studies. Writers of articles can assist this process by sending offprints to the journal, and editors of journals that are not readily available in the UK are urged to join the many who send us complete sets of current and back issues. These materials should be addressed to The Editors, *YWES*, The English Association, University of Leicester, University Road, Leicester LEI 7RH, UK.

Our coverage of articles and books is greatly assisted by the Modern Language Association of America, who annually supply proofs of their *International Bibliography* in advance of the publication of each year's coverage.

The views expressed in *YWES* are those of its individual contributors and are not necessarily shared by the Editors, Associate Editors, the English Association, or Oxford University Press.

We wish to thank Michele Kennedy at Penn State Altoona for her kindness, professionalism, and unwavering support.

The Editors

I

English Language

VERENA HASER, ANITA AUER, BERT BOTMA,
MARION ELENBAAS, WIM VAN DER WURFF,
BEÁTA GYURIS, JULIE COLEMAN, EDWARD CALLARY,
LIESELOTTE ANDERWALD, ANNE SCHRÖDER,
MARCUS CALLIES AND ROCÍO MONTORO

This chapter has twelve sections: 1. General; 2. History of English Linguistics; 3. Phonetics and Phonology; 4. Morphology; 5. Syntax; 6. Semantics; 7. Lexicography, Lexicology, and Lexical Semantics; 8. Onomastics; 9. Dialectology and Sociolinguistics; 10. New Englishes and Creolistics; 11. Pragmatics and Discourse Analysis; 12. Stylistics. Section 1 is by Verena Haser; section 2 is by Anita Auer; section 3 is by Bert Botma; sections 4 and 5 are by Marion Elenbaas and Wim van der Wurff; section 6 is by Beáta Gyuris; section 7 is by Julie Coleman; section 8 is by Edward Callary; section 9 is by Lieselotte Anderwald; section 10 is by Anne Schröder; section 11 is by Marcus Callies; section 12 is by Rocío Montoro.

1. General

Two important collections of papers concerned with linguistic evolution have been published in 2009. Both of them grew out of a conference on the topic held in 2006. The first volume, *The Prehistory of Language*, edited by Rudolf Botha and Chris Knight, offers a collection of fifteen cutting-edge articles from a wide range of disciplines, including not only linguistics, but also anthropology, cognitive science, psychology, evolutionary biology, and artificial intelligence. All chapters are well written and most of them present fresh perspectives on the evolutionary trajectory of human language. The introductory chapter by Rudolf Botha (pp. 1–11) is particularly helpful in highlighting a number of apparently contradictory positions that emerge from the individual contributions. As emphasized in the introduction, the various contributors bring a very broad range of perspectives and a no less diverse panoply of methodologies to bear on the key issues at stake. Among those issues, the social context of language development takes pride of place in a

The Year's Work in English Studies, Volume 90 (2011)
doi:10.1093/ywes/mar001

number of contributions. For example, both Robin Dunbar's paper ('Why Only Humans Have Language', pp. 12–36) and Luc Steels's article ('Is Sociality a Crucial Prerequisite for the Emergence of Language?', pp. 36–57) highlight what the authors perceive as the social preconditions for linguistic evolution. Dunbar offers a very intriguing account of his hypothesis that language developed primarily for the purpose of strengthening social relations, rather than for communicating information. According to Dunbar, language evolved when group size became too large, and consequently, individuals could no longer use grooming behaviour for establishing bonds with all other group members. A different way of establishing and fostering social relations was needed—in this way, language developed essentially as a substitute for grooming. Furthermore, language is essentially an offshoot of early forms of music-like 'chorusing' behaviour that fulfilled the function of social bonding in early human societies. Luc Steels provides another intriguing discussion of possible social prerequisites for language evolution; he stresses the importance of co-operation, the ability to engage in perspective reversal, and the willingness to be truthful as key conditions for the emergence of language. As suggested by a number of experiments surveyed by the author, this essentially social behaviour is the *sine qua non* for language evolution. The relationship between music and language is the focus of Steven Mithen's contribution ('Holistic Communication and the Co-evolution of Language and Music', pp. 58–76), who offers arguments in favour of the view that the proto-language of our ancestors was music-like. In a similar vein, Ian Cross and Ghofur Eliot Woodruff ('Music as a Communicative Medium', pp. 77–98) propose that language and music both developed from a communicative system which combined language-like and music-like elements. John Odling-Smee and Kevin Laland in their paper on 'Cultural Niche Construction' (pp. 99–121) approach the social underpinnings of language from a different perspective than the previously mentioned authors, emphasizing the function of language as a means of communicating to the young important skills for survival. Three chapters investigate the topic of linguistic evolution from primatological perspectives. Sonia Ragir and Sue Savage-Rumbaugh's contribution 'Playing with Meaning' (pp. 122–41) elucidates the link between social play and language. David Leavens, Timothy Racine, and William Hopkins ('The Ontogeny and Phylogeny of Non-Verbal Deixis', pp. 142–65) and Simone Pika and John Mitani ('The Directed Scratch: Evidence for a Referential Gesture in Chimpanzees', pp. 166–80), respectively, concentrate on deixis in great apes. Great apes develop deictic gestures even when not specifically trained to do so. With deixis as one of the principal manifestations of the ability to draw someone's attention to a particular point in space, the capacity for joint attention may turn out to be part and parcel of our language faculty. According to Pika and Mitani, the directed scratch gestures found in chimpanzees constitute the origin of symbolic gestures. On the basis of evidence from a broad range of disciplines including psycholinguistics, language acquisition, and primatology, Maggie Tallerman's paper elaborates on 'The Origins of the Lexicon' (pp. 181–200). A number of chapters present a generativist view of language evolution. Following Eric Reuland ('Language: Symbolization and Beyond', pp. 201–24), the emergence of recursion has substantially changed communicative signs, resulting in 'desymbolization' as the pivotal feature of human language (i.e., the loss of a transparent link between form and meaning). How the study of historical syntax can bear on the issue of language origins is addressed by Elly van Gelderen in 'Grammaticalization from a Biolinguistic Perspective' (pp. 225–43). She assumes that the evolution of syntax has parallels in diachronic syntactic change and child language acquisition. Against the backdrop of the Minimalist Program, the author sketches the changes that mark the crucial developments leading up to human syntax. The relevance of recursion to human language and human thinking takes centre stage in Frederick Coolidge and Thomas Wynn's contribution ('Recursion, Phonological Storage Capacity, and the Evolution of Modern Speech', pp. 244–54). Of particular interest is their suggestion that recursion might be indispensable for symbolic cognition. Bart de Boer ('Why Women Speak Better Than Men', pp. 255–65) explores the topic of language evolution from an acoustic and articulatory perspective, comparing among other things the female and the male vocal tract with regard to their suitability for producing speech. The final chapter, by Wendy Wilkins ('Mosaic Neurobiology and Anatomical Plausibility', pp. 266–86), emphasizes the importance of anatomically plausible hypotheses about language evolution.

The companion volume to the above-mentioned book, *The Cradle of Language*, also edited by Chris Knight and Rudolf Botha, zooms in on the origins of language in Africa. Many chapters in this collection do not focus on language as such, but rather deal more generally with the topic of human origins. The common thread that runs through several contributions is that the hypothesized revolution that gave rise to modern humans cannot be traced to one particular mutation.

Crosslinguistic Approaches to the Psychology of Language, edited by Jiansheng Guo, Elena Lieven, Nancy Budwig, Susan Ervin-Tripp, Keiko Nakamura, and Seyda Özcliskan offers a very broad conspectus of 'Research in the Tradition of Dan Isaac Slobin' (as the subtitle suggests). Dedicated to the groundbreaking work of Dan Slobin, the collection encompasses forty contributions by well-known (psycho)linguists. The book falls into four parts. Part I, 'Language Learning in Crosslinguistic Perspective', comprises papers covering a wide range of topics, from the acquisition of animal terms ('Alligators All Around: The Acquisition of Animal Terms in English and Russian' by Jean Berko Gleason, Brenda Caldwell Philips, and Richard Ely, pp. 17–26), to home-sign in the US, China, and Turkey ('Making Language Around the Globe' by Susan Goldin-Meadow, Asli Özyürek, Burcu Sancar, and Carolyn Mylander, pp. 27–40), and the 'One-to-One Mapping between Temporal and Spatial Relations (by Richard Weist, pp. 69–80). A paper by Heike Behrens on 'Direction and Perspective in German Child Language' (pp. 55–68) focuses on deictic verbal particles in German language acquisition, raising the question whether Slobin's assumption is correct that the existence of such particles attunes children to deixis. Other contributions in this section are concerned with 'Transitivity and the Grammar of Accusing, Commanding, and Perspective-Sharing in Toddler's Peer Disputes' (by Amy Kyratzis, pp. 41–54), 'English and Turkish Character Introductions in Elicited

Narrative' (by Aylin C. Küntay and Dilara Kochas, pp. 81–92), the acquisition of noun class prefixes in Sesotho ('Revisiting the Acquisition of Sesotho Noun Class Prefixes', by Katherine Demuth and David Ellis, pp. 93–104), and 'Dialogic Priming and the Acquisition of Argument Marking in Korean' (by Patricia Clancy, pp. 105–20). Part II features eleven chapters concerned with 'Narratives and their Development'. Many papers in this section concentrate on the encoding of motion events in different languages, a topic that has been a principal focus of Slobin's own research. Contributors to this section include Keiko Nakamura, Ageliki Nicolopoulou, Raphale Berthele, and Lourdes de León, to name but a few. Part III casts its net wider, discussing 'Theoretical Perspectives on Language Development, Language Change, and Typology'. The authors of the various papers discuss a plethora of issues including the question whether apes can learn grammar (by Talmy Givón and Sue Savage Rumbaugh, pp. 299–310), grammaticalization (by Joan Bybee, pp. 333–44), the relation between 'Child Language, Aphasia and General Psycholinguistics' (by Lise Menn, pp. 375–88), and Universal Grammar (by Robert van Valin, pp. 311–20). Again, motion events figure prominently in a number of chapters, for example in the contribution by Wany Sampaio, Chris Sinha, and Vera da Silva Sinha on 'Mixing and Mapping: Motion, Path, and Manner in Amondawa' (pp. 427–42). Part IV, on 'Language and Cognition: Universals and Typological Comparisons', contains eight fascinating chapters, including a contribution by Penelope Brown and Stephen Levinson on 'Language as Mind Tools: Learning How to Think through Speaking', who revisit Slobin's take on linguistic relativism against the backdrop of data from the acquisition of spatial language in Tzeltal. Another very interesting paper—Dedre Gentner and Melissa Bowerman's account of 'The Typological Prevalence Hypothesis' (pp. 465–80)—is concerned with the question why particular spatial categories pose greater difficulties in language acquisition than others. Slobin's 'thinking for speaking' notion is echoed and taken up in many chapters, for example in David McNeill's 'Imagery for Speaking' (pp. 517–30), and Stéphanie Pourcel's 'Relativistic Application of Thinking for Speaking' (pp. 493–504). Taken together, the chapters in this volume offer a stimulating point of entry into major themes of research in linguistic typology and language acquisition.

Cedric Boeckx's *Language in Cognition: Uncovering Mental Structures and the Rules behind Them* is a sustained argument in favour of the Chomskian view of mind and language. Designed as a textbook, the work is well written and accessible, drawing on a wide range of evidence supporting the Chomskian account, such as research on language acquisition and aphasia. The book covers key ideas that pervade generativist thought—UG, modularity, mentalism, the computational theory of mind, etc. The final chapter takes up issues such as the relation between mind and brain and the evolution of the human mind. In general, the author sets out his generativist view of linguistics and his computationalist view of cognitive science with admirable clarity.

A diametrically opposed view of cognitive science is represented by what has come to be known as the embodied cognition approach. In 2009 a range of interesting publications has emerged out of this budding research area. According to the embodied cognition view, affordances of objects figure importantly in language comprehension (the term 'affordances' refers to the types of interaction that are possible between particular objects and particular agents/bodies, for example a stool affords sitting for a human body, but not for an elephant; a chair does not afford swimming). According to the 'Indexical Hypothesis', language is comprehended by indexing words to (perceptual symbols for) things in one's environment. Language users extract affordances from these perceptual symbols and integrate them in such a way that they square with the possibilities and limits of human action. The major finding of a series of experiments conducted by Arthur Glenberg, Raymond Becker, Susann Klötzer, Lidia Kolanko, Silvana Müller, and Mike Rinck (*LangCog* 1[2009] 113–35) is to have shown that even purely momentary ('episodic') affordances contribute to language comprehension. More specifically, the authors show that knowledge about the spatial location of objects (which is part of the knowledge how to successfully interact with objects) plays a role in the comprehension of sentences dealing with these objects. In their experiments, subjects had to determine whether a sentence related to normal or odd objects (*The apple has a stem* vs. *The apple has an antenna*). The relevant objects were located on the left or the right of a response box. The response key was also located either on the left or the right of the box. The experiments highlighted an 'action-sentence-compatibility effect': Pressing the 'normal' key was easier (as reflected in response latencies) when the key was located at the side where the object was located. This compatibility effect emerged not only for sentences specifying actions (*Touch the apple at the stem*), but also for sentences specifying states of the relevant objects (*The apple has a stem*). Indeed, the effect was equally pronounced for both types of sentence. Furthermore, it could also be observed after the named objects were removed; the effect, however, dissolved when the subjects were no longer required to move in order to respond. The experiments cast new light on human 'embodied' language comprehension.

Proponents of the embodied framework have repeatedly pointed out the role of gesture in communication. One particular type of gesturing—spatial mapping—is the focus of a paper by Sarah Taub, Dennis Galvan, and Pilar Pinar (*CogLing* 20[2009] 71–92) on 'The Role of Gesture in Crossmodal Typological Studies'. Spatial mapping refers to the process of mentally projecting entities onto the space surrounding language users, with the speaker's body or hands signalling the shape of the entities referred to and sketching their movements. These movements represent the movements or shape of the real entities involved in an analogue fashion, i.e. by means of similarity. The authors investigate spatial mapping in English, Spanish, and ASL, focusing on the expression of motion events. Their study shows that once spatial mapping is taken into consideration, the well-known typological differences between these languages with regard to the expression of motion events tend to become insignificant. While Spanish speakers tend to verbally encode less path information than speakers of English and ASL, these differences are levelled out once the information conveyed via spatial mapping is integrated into our analysis. Another important finding is that particular types of spatial elements tend to be primarily encoded lexically (figure and ground), while other types, such as path information, tend to be communicated via spatial mapping.

The Anatomy of Meaning: Speech, Gesture, and Composite Utterances by Nick Enfield is concerned with speech-with-gesture combinations. Most of the chapters in the book are revisions of previously published work. The first chapter offers a number of succinct examples illustrating the composite nature of meaning. The author favours a modality-independent account of gesture, which allows us to identify functional equivalents of gestures across different types of composite utterances, including those types of composite utterances that do not involve visible gestures (e.g. telephone conversations). Furthermore, major emphasis should be placed on the idea that a gesture has meaning only as part of a more encompassing utterance complex. Enfield proposes what he calls an enchronic perspective on speech-with-gesture, i.e. a type of account that focuses on neighbouring moments in a larger communicative sequence. The book falls into three major parts. Following the introductory chapter, the first part (chapters 2–4) is concerned with deictic components of speech-with-gesture composites; the second part (chapters 5–7) investigates illustrative gestures such as virtual kinship diagrams drawn in the air. Chapter 2 discusses pointing carried out with the help of language, more specifically demonstrative pronouns in Lao. In contrast to traditional views of demonstrative semantics, Enfield's analysis shows that Lao demonstratives do not encode distance information. Much as other notions typically associated with demonstratives, such as the (in)visibility of the referent object, this kind of information may figure importantly in the use of demonstratives. However, neither distance information nor information about the visibility of the referent is part of the meaning of demonstratives. Rather, a dynamic and context-bound conception of what constitutes here-space, in conjunction with systematic pragmatic contrasts between the two determiners (captured in terms of informativeness scales) can account for the observed range of uses of these terms. Thus, the meaning of demonstratives is significantly enriched by markedness relations contracted between the individual members of the demonstrative paradigm. In a similar vein, systematic contrasts can be observed between different types of bodily pointing, such as lip-pointing (dealt with in chapter 3), small finger-pointing, and big finger-pointing (dealt with in chapter 4), which goes to show that gestures have their own grammar in the sense of participating in a system of meaningful contrasts. Part II is concerned with the ways in which gestures can create models of artefacts (in the cases investigated by Enfield, fish traps), as well as be used to visualize abstract relationships. Enfield shows that the spaces created via gestures are virtually real—even to the extent that these virtual creations may have to be 'edited' in various ways by their creators—for example the virtual diagrams created through gestures may have to be revised. A major insight to be gleaned from Enfield's studies is that gestures may display linear segmentation and combinatorial properties.

Gestural language essentially makes use of the space around the human body to convey information. How language users communicate spatial information has long been a major focus of research in psycholinguistics. To date, however, attention has largely been devoted to monologue contexts, with very little research investigating the use of spatial language in dialogue. The collection of thirteen papers on *Spatial Language and Dialogue*, edited by

Kenny Coventry, Thora Tenbrink, and John Bateman, is designed to redress this imbalance. Following a succinct introduction by the editors (pp. 1–8), the paper by Matthew Watson, Martin Pickering, and Holly Branigan ('Why Dialogue Methods are Important for Investigating Spatial Language', pp. 8–22) offers a conspectus of research on dialogue inspired by the 'Interactive Alignment Model of Dialogue', elucidating how this model bears on research on spatial language. The authors present experiments which show that the study of spatial language in a dialogic context is an important extension of previous research on spatial language, which was typically limited to monologue paradigms. Michael Schober examines 'Spatial Dialogue between Partners with Mismatched Abilities' (pp. 23–39). His main finding is that high-ability subjects are able to take their low-ability interlocutor's perspective. High-ability partners quickly notice and adapt to their interlocutor's level of ability. As a counterpoint to the preceding papers, Constanze Vorwerg emphasizes the role of 'Consistency in Successive Spatial Utterances' (pp. 40–55), showing that the tendency to adapt to one's interlocutor's perspective is counterbalanced by the tendency to remain consistent with one's own choice of reference frame. Anna Filipi and Roger Wales, in 'An Interactionally Situated Analysis of what Prompts Shift in the Motion Verbs *Come* and *Go* in a Map Task' (pp. 56–68), investigate the use of motion verbs in an interactional context. Their paper presents an approach to deixis which assumes that the 'origo' shifts as speakers shift spatial location and perspective or topic, attaching great importance to the social context of deixis and the idea that indexicality cannot be adequately explained unless speaker attitudes to the referent and their interlocutors are taken into consideration. The authors show that shifts in the use of motion verbs reflects a shift in spatial perspective. Analysis of the data also reveals that such shifts play a role in grounding information between interlocutors (for example *come* may serve to signal 'shared arrival points', p. 68). The concepts of proximity and distalness that are invoked to explain these shifts are rather different from the concrete spatial notions traditionally held to underlie the use of deictics (for example proximity is recast as familiarity or shared knowledge). Luc Steels and Martin Loetzsch's 'Perspective Alignment in Spatial Language' (pp. 70–88) examines spatial language in dialogue from the perspective of robotic research. They propose that in virtue of being embodied, agents take a particular spatial perspective and that communicating about space is impossible without considering one's interlocutor's perspective. Furthermore, perspective alignment presupposes the ability to see where one's interlocutor is located as well as the ability to carry out the so-called 'Egocentric Perspective Transform'—a function carried out by the parietal-temporal-occipital junction. The Egocentric Perspective Transform allows interlocutors to project themselves into their interlocutor's perspective. Another important result of their study is that perspective alignment becomes easier once one's interlocutor's perspective is marked as egocentric or allocentric. Laura Carlson and Patrick Hill investigate 'Spatial Descriptions across Various Dialogue Contexts' (pp. 89–103), looking at the factors that determine which type of spatial description is selected in cases where several alternatives are available. Two potential factors that spring to mind are, firstly, salience of the reference objects used to locate a particular target object (e.g. *The glass is behind the book*, where the book is the reference object, and the glass is the target object), and secondly, the extent to which the spatial relation between reference object and target object exemplifies a prototypical spatial relation. The authors suggest that both of these principles work in combination, influencing subjects' choice of spatial relations. Thora Tenbrink (pp. 104–18) offers a 'Contrastive Linguistic Analysis of Spatial Reference', comparing English and German. Barbara Tversky, Julie Heiser, Paul Lee, and Marie-Paule Daniel ('Explanations in Gesture, Diagram, and Word', pp. 119–31) contrast three different means of solving spatial tasks (language, gesture, diagrams), assessing their relative merits and disadvantages as well as the common structure underlying all three types of explanation. Timo Sowa and Ipke Wachsmuth ('A Computational Model for the Representation and Processing of Shape in Coverbal Iconic Gestures', pp. 132–46) put forward a classification of gestures that relate to shape. Kristina Striegnitz, Paul Tepper, Andrew Lovett, and Justine Cassell in 'Knowledge Representation for Generating Locating Gestures in Route Directions' (pp. 147–65) examine feedback strategies in route descriptions. Philippe Muller and Laurent Prévot are concerned with 'Grounding Information in Route Explanation Dialogues'. Finally, Shi Hui and Thora Tenbrink's 'Telling Rolland Where to Go' (pp. 177–90) examines route descriptions as used in communication between robots and human beings.

We end this year's review with a completely different topic: online corpora. *Exploring English with Online Corpora: An Introduction* by Wendy Anderson and John Corbett is a primer for everyone interested in online corpora for English. The authors offer a highly readable introduction to topics such as the interpretation of corpus data in terms of statistical analysis. Separate chapters are devoted to the study of lexis, grammar, discourse, and pronunciation with the help of corpora. The book is rounded off by a chapter focusing, *inter alia*, on how to derive contextual information from a corpus, and the final chapter addresses the use of corpora for English language teaching (for some more detail see also section 5(a) below).

2. History of English Linguistics

The number of publications on the history of English linguistics in the year 2009 reflects the increasing popularity and interest in this particular field of research. One important contribution is the volume *Current Issues in Late Modern English*, edited by Ingrid Tieken-Boon van Ostade and Wim van der Wurff. This volume contains papers presented at the Third International Conference on lModE, held at the University of Leiden (The Netherlands) in August 2007. Joan C. Beal's paper 'Three Hundred Years of Prescriptivism (and Counting)' (pp. 35–55) critically traces the development of prescriptivism from the eighteenth century up to the present day. While the eighteenth-century grammarian Robert Lowth (1710–87) has been portrayed as the epitome of prescriptivism by twentieth-century linguists, recent detailed studies of his work have shown that his comments on language usage were a lot more nuanced, and also less prescriptive, than was generally believed.

The texts that were most successful during the late nineteenth and early twentieth century 'were those that steered a middle path between prescription and description' (p. 39), for example H.W. Fowler's *Modern English Usage* [1926]. Beal illustrates that even nowadays manuals of usage are much in demand, as for instance Truss's *Eats, Shoots and Leaves: The Zero Tolerance Guide to Punctuation* [2003], which are concerned with teaching 'correct' language use. This leads to the conclusion that now, as in eighteenth-century England, there is 'a market for prescriptive texts amongst those who wish to climb the social ladder and succeed in business' (p. 47). Robin Straaijer's contribution, 'Deontic and Epistemic Modals as Indicators of Prescriptive and Descriptive Language in the Grammars by Joseph Priestley and Robert Lowth' (pp. 57–87), is also concerned with the prescriptivism-descriptivism dichotomy. The two grammarians Priestley and Lowth have become strongly associated with these opposed approaches to grammar writing, namely Priestley as the descriptivist and Lowth as the prescriptivist. Straaijer investigates the grammarians' use of modal verbs in 'the metalanguage of their grammars' (p. 61) in order to draw conclusions about the prescriptive and/or descriptive nature of the works. The deontic modal auxiliaries (*ought to*, *must*, *should*, would) are considered indicative of the prescriptive approach, the deontic modal *cannot* as proscriptive language and the epistemic modals *may* and *might* as indicative of descriptivism. The grammars under investigation are Joseph Priestley's *Rudiments of English Grammar* (editions from 1761 and 1768) and Robert Lowth's *Short Introduction to English Grammar* (editions of 1762 and 1763), both the main texts of the grammars and the footnotes. As the results of the study are not statistically significant, Straaijer concludes that the outcome, which indicates that Priestley is the more descriptive grammarian, ought to be considered as supplementing results from traditional approaches that establish where a grammar is situated on the prescriptivism–descriptivism continuum. The paper ' "Telling People How To Speak": Rhetorical Grammars and Pronouncing Dictionaries' (pp. 89–116) by Raymond Hickey closely studies the works by the elocutionists Thomas Sheridan (1719–88; Irish) and John Walker (1732–1807; English) in order to shed light on ongoing phonological change during the eighteenth century as well as on the effect that their works had on English and its development during the nineteenth and twentieth centuries. With the social developments that took place in eighteenth-century England, the mastery of the standard form of English was considered to conceal any traces of social and/or regional origin. Hickey's study shows that even though Sheridan and Walker were highly regarded in the lModE period (1700–1900) and though they influenced the work of later elocutionists, the strictures put forward by Sheridan and Walker did not have an effect on the way in which standard BrE was later pronounced. Carol Percy's 'Periodical Reviews and the Rise of Prescriptivism: The *Monthly* (1749–1844) and *Critical Review* (1756–1817) in the Eighteenth Century' (pp. 117–50) shows that not only the grammarians' approach to cite the 'best writers' in order to illustrate appropriate language use had an influence on the rise of prescriptivism but also that reviews, which also exemplified 'bad grammar with quotations from contemporary authors' (p. 118), must have contributed to the linguistic insecurity that existed around the 1750s. Percy illustrates how reviewers humiliated authors for using erroneous and non-codified standard language. She concludes that it is not clear whether the reviewers' comments had an effect on language users. However, as Percy notes, '[i]t is not surprising that publishers in the early 1760s facilitated the fixing and dissemination of grammatical standards by providing readers with an increasing choice of English grammars' (p. 138). The paper by María Esther Rodríguez-Gil and Nuria Yáñez-Bouza, 'The ECEG-Database: A Bio-Bibliographical Approach to the Study of Eighteenth-Century English Grammars' (pp. 153–82), introduces the new database of Eighteenth-Century English Grammars (ECEG) by describing the context, methodology, and contents of the database. This tool, which consisted 'of 330 English grammars written by 279 different authors in the time-span 1700–1800' (p. 174) and has been extended since, will probably not only be of great use to scholars of eighteenth-century grammatical tradition but will also be of interest for scholars of literary and historical studies. In her article '"With a Concise Historical Account of the Language": Outlines of the History of English in Eighteenth-Century Dictionaries' (pp. 183–208), Alicia Rodríguez-Álvarez investigates fifteen dictionaries (three from the seventeenth and twelve from the eighteenth century) with respect to the historical accounts of the English language contained in the prefaces of these works. The study reveals that the English histories in the dictionaries have many features in common such as the organization of the information, the periodization of the history, the emphasis on and pride in its Germanic lineage as well as the Germanic character that the English language retained. The author observes that many of these accounts strongly rely on earlier accounts. The similarities thus inevitably give the impression of 'a sense of conformity to certain common notions about the writing of historical accounts of English' (p. 204). Charlotte Brewer's study is concerned with 'The *Oxford English Dictionary*'s Treatment of Female-Authored Sources of the Eighteenth Century' (pp. 209–38). The author provides a critical history of the composition of the *Dictionary* and notices that the *OED Online* still contains many variations, both with respect to periods and also the types of source; for instance, the 'most quoted authors were those of the late-nineteenth-century literary canon', poetic sources were preferred to prose, the eighteenth century appears to be under-quoted, and male authors were quoted in higher numbers than female authors (pp. 212–13). Brewer raises the question of whether these variations may be seen as a reflection of the nature of the English language or whether they instead mirror the lexicographers' assumptions about language. Her study of the representation of eighteenth-century female writers reveals that Frances Burney (1752–1840), Maria Edgeworth (1768–1849), and Ann Radcliffe (1764–1823) received most attention in terms of *OED* quotations whereas interesting usages by other significant writers such Anna Letitia Barbauld (b. 1743) were not recorded in the *OED*. Brewer concludes that there is still need for a more balanced representation of quotations by male and female writers in the *OED*. The *OED* also features in Lynda Mugglestone's 'Living History: Andrew Clark, the *OED* and the Language of the First World War' (pp. 239–61). The main aim of the *OED* was, from the beginning, to record the English language on historical principles, and the lexicographers were thus expected to apply a descriptive, evidence-based approach rather than to serve as critics and to judge or evaluate. In her paper, Mugglestone shows that the lexicographers Craigie and Onion, who edited the 1933 *Supplement*, acted as critics rather than as neutral historians in selecting certain usages and quotations while rejecting others. The study on the lexicographers' choices is based on material collected by the scholar, classicist, and rector Andrew Clark, who was one of the voluntary contributors to the *OED*. During the First World War Clark had written more than seventy notebooks on 'Words in War-Time' and over ninety volumes of a war diary that recorded language change as well as Clark's image of history, with a particular focus on the ordinary and everyday, and which was made available to the *OED* after Clark's death. These sources were scrutinized by the *OED* editors and many of the usages that Clark found were 'deliberately marginalized in the historical record of English constructed by Craigie and Onions in 1933' (p. 253). The contribution by Manfred Markus, which focuses on 'Joseph Wright's *English Dialect Dictionary* and its Sources' (pp. 263–82), does not only shed light on the way in which Wright dealt with sources, i.e. their number and validity, but also provides a picture of the general interest in dialects in the nineteenth century. The study reveals that both the (eighty) glossaries published by the *English Dialect Society* and Wright's *EDD* have their merits as well as disadvantages. While the glossaries that Wright used as a source for the *EDD* contain many folkloristic expressions, idiomatic phrases, and dialect sayings, the scholarly ambition and the linguistic value is limited. Wright did not only rely on the glossaries but also used other written sources such as manuscripts, published books, and works of general reference. The *EDD Online*, which is currently being prepared by scholars from the University of Innsbruck (Austria), will allow a closer inspection of all the sources that Wright included in his work. The eighteenth-century Quaker grammarian Lindley Murray (1745–1826) and his use of epistolary formulae, and in particular the use of the term *friend*, are under investigation in Lyda Fens-de Zeeuw's 'Plain Speech in Lindley Murray's Letters: Peculiar or Polite?' (pp. 391–408). By comparing the use of epistolary formulae in selected eighteenth-century correspondence to Murray's epistolary use, Fens-de Zeeuw draws the conclusion that the use of the formulae varied considerably among eighteenth-century letter-writers. As for the word *friend*, it expressed positive politeness in a rather neutral way in Murray's letters. The use of this particular word ensured that all his correspondents, whether they were Quakers and not, felt equal.

The article 'Learning and Virtue: English Grammar and the Eighteenth-Century Girls' School' by Carol Percy, which appeared in the volume *Educating the Child in Enlightenment Britain: Beliefs, Cultures, Practices* (edited by Mary Hilton and Jill Shefrin, pp. 77–98), provides very good insight into the multiple objectives of teaching grammar to girls as well as the roles of women teachers in this process and their 'image management . . . in a climate of social anxiety' (p. 78). The first part of the paper, 'The Georgian Woman Schoolteacher', discusses the multiple images of the female schoolteacher as well as contemporary debates on girls' education with respect to their later roles in life. The second part, 'Vernacular Grammar', is concerned with the reasons for teaching English grammar. Apart from being 'a fundamental as well as a common subject of study' (p. 81), Percy notes that learning grammar (a) was considered a class marker and it therefore conveyed social capital alongside moral and intellectual instruction, (b) was encouraged as 'the key to good writing' (p. 83), and (c) functioned as a basic tool for learning other languages. Also, the author notes that many teachers correlated grammar with industriousness, which was furthermore associated with children's virtue and moral education. The next part, 'Women Teachers of Grammars', focuses on the impact of teaching grammar at girls' schools, which is illustrated by many examples in both theory and practice. In the final part, 'Girls' Learning and Virtue: A Public Demonstration', Percy illustrates how public competitions were used as testing grounds for contemporary debates regarding 'the intellectual capacities of males and females' or 'the merits of home and school education' (p. 96). All in all, this paper is extremely informative with respect to the role (as well as the authority) of women teachers and also the position of women in society when they had mastered grammar. The female grammarian Ellenor Fenn and her approach to teaching English grammar is the focus of Karlijn Navest's 'Reading Lessons for "Baby Grammarians": Lady Ellenor Fenn and the Teaching of English Grammar' (in Styles and Arizpe, eds., *Acts of Reading: Teachers, Text and Childhood*, pp. 73–86). Ellenor Fenn (1744–1813) is known as the author of grammar books, such as *The Child's Grammar* [1798], *The Mother's Grammar* [1798], and *Parsing Lessons for Elder Pupils* [1798], as well as books that teach reading skills, as for example the *Spelling Book* [1787] and *The Infant's Friend* (2 volumes, [1797]). By way of example, Navest convincingly shows that Fenn aimed at using spelling books (including reading lessons) for teaching children the rudiments of grammar as well, for example to practice parsing with older children by using the reading lessons. Even though other grammar books such as Dilworth's *New Guide to the English Tongue* [1740] contain a spelling section alongside a grammar section, Fenn appears to be the first to have combined the instruction of reading and grammar from a didactic point of view.

Eighteenth-century grammarians also feature in two papers published in Arja Nurmi, Minna Nevala, and Minna Palander-Colin, eds., *The Language of Daily Life in England (1400–1800)* (see also section 9). Mikko Laitinen's 'Singular *You Was/Were* Variation and English Normative Grammars in the Eighteenth Century' (pp. 199–217) investigates the sociolinguistic mechanisms that are in operation when the *you was* variant was established as a non-standard form and the *you were* variation as a standard and high-prestige variant. The study, which is based on eighteenth-century correspondence, reveals that *you was* is particularly frequently used in the middle of the eighteenth century and then makes way for *you were*. The gradual decline of *you was* can be observed at the same time as the variant became a socially stigmatized linguistic marker, as reflected in the comments made by normative grammarians. Moreover, Laitinen observes that this linguistic change is led by men. The contribution by Anni Sairio, 'Methodological and Practical Aspects of Historical Network Analysis: A Case Study of the Bluestocking Letters' (pp. 107–35), is concerned with Elizabeth Montagu's Bluestocking network. Sairio proposes a network strength scale (NSS), the scores of which she compares to the use of pied-piping and preposition stranding in the correspondence of the network. As preposition stranding had been under censure since the late seventeenth century and pied-piping was considered the more agreeable variant, the use of these two variants correlated with the network ties can show whether any of the variants were preferred depending on the closeness to/distance from other network members. In fact, Sairio's study shows that preposition stranding was the preferred variant in Elizabeth Montagu's correspondence when there were strong network ties with the recipient and the recipient was socially below her. Conversely, pied-piping was the favoured variant 'when the recipients were her social superiors' (p. 131) (for both articles see also section 9). Sairio's research on the *Language and Letters of the Bluestocking Network: Sociolinguistic Issues in Eighteenth-Century Epistolary English* was also published as a monograph in 2009. The first two parts of the book introduce the theoretical frameworks, the methods applied, and the material: the Bluestocking Corpus, which consists of 218 letters and covers the period 1738–78. The third part of the book focuses on syntactic processes, in particular (a) the progressive and (b) preposition stranding versus pied-piping. As regards the progressive, which, according to Svenja Kranich [2008] had taken on an increasingly aspectual function in the course of the eighteenth century, Sairio notes that the corpus 'does not attest to particular changes in progress when it comes to the development of the progressive in the eighteenth century' (p. 189). It can, however, be noted that Elizabeth Montagu's letters to friends contain the progressive a lot more frequently, as reflected by the stronger network ties. In the case of preposition stranding versus pied-piping, Sairio observes that Elizabeth's Montagu's choice of preposition stranding was not controlled by sociolinguistic variables and/or social network ties. Instead, it appears that the developments can be connected 'to the broader contemporary trends of prescriptivism and the appreciation of polite learning and refinement' (p. 213). The main focus in Sairio's monograph is on epistolary spelling (Part IV), in which she discusses the spelling of preterites and past participles as well as auxiliary verbs. In the eighteenth century, epistolary spelling differed from that found in printed material, which means that a dual standard of spelling existed at the time. Sairio is concerned with the development of the Bluestocking spelling habits over time, in particular whether prescriptive grammars, sociolinguistic variables, or social networks had any effect on the observed trends. All in all, the study reveals that gender, register, and social rank were significant variables in the choice of linguistic variants whereas social network ties appeared to have little or no influence. This monograph may be seen as an important contribution to the language of letters in eighteenth-century England.

Another monograph that is concerned with language use in the eighteenth century is Anita Auer's *The Subjunctive in the Age of Prescriptivism: English and German Developments during the Eighteenth Century*. As the title indicates, it is a study of the inflectional subjunctive and its development in both English and German, of which only the English part will be discussed here. The approach adopted by Auer is to compare a precept corpus, which consists of metalinguistic comments by eighteenth-century grammarians on the subjunctive mood, to a so-called practice corpus, i.e. actual use of the subjunctive during the period 1710–1900. The systematic analysis of the subjunctive in the precept corpus reveals that eighteenth-century grammarians did not at all agree on the system of moods and the existence of the subjunctive mood in this system. This disagreement is also reflected in the individual accounts of the subjunctive, which Auer analysed with respect to morphology, syntax, and semantics. As regards the status of the subjunctive, from 1755 onwards more and more grammarians commented on the decline of the inflectional subjunctive and also advocated the revival of its usage. In their accounts the grammarians associated the use of the subjunctive with the educated language of 'polite' London society. As regards the investigation of the 'practice corpus', Auer analyses the subjunctive against indicative and modal auxiliary use over the period 1650–1990 in the multi-genre corpus ARCHER. This part of the study reveals that the subjunctive form declines between 1650 and 1749, followed by a rise between 1750 and 1850, and then a severe drop in frequency between 1850 and 1990. As for the increase in frequency during 1750–1850, the author tentatively concludes that prescriptivism might have had an effect on the revival of the inflectional subjunctive (see also below, section 5(b)).

The textbook *Introduction to Late Modern English* by Ingrid Tieken-Boon van Ostade also discusses Late Modern English grammars and grammarians. In fact, chapter 5 of the textbook is concerned with grammar-related issues such as sociolinguistic stereotypes and markers, grammar strictures versus actual usage, and the normative grammarians' influence. Tieken-Boon van Ostade illustrates these topics with existing studies on, for instance, the subjunctive mood, the use of *will* and *shall*, and the counterfactual perfect infinitive. Most of these studies investigated the relationship between grammarians' precepts and a possible influence on actual language usage. All in all, the textbook is very accessible for university students. The book draws on recent research in the field of sociohistorical linguistics and corpus linguistics and it provides research questions that encourage readers to work with databases such as Eighteenth Century Collections Online (ECCO) and the Proceedings of the Old Bailey.

The year 2009 also saw the reissuing of H.W. Fowler's *Dictionary of Modern English Usage: The Classic First Edition* (first published in 1926), which contains a new introduction and notes by David Crystal. Fowler's *Modern English Usage* is probably the best-known usage guide of the English language and it has had an enormous effect on attitudes to the English language since it was first published. The 2009 edition is valuable because of David Crystal's contribution. The introduction contains a history of the *Modern English Usage*, whose account is embedded in the contemporary (linguistic) climate. Importantly, Crystal sheds light on consistency problems in Fowler's work and also discusses topics such as Fowler's style and pedantry as well as Fowler's status. Crystal's 'Notes on the Entries', which can be found at the end of the book, may be seen as an update to Fowler's entries in terms of actual language usage (including Google search results) as well as a critical apparatus, for example with respect to the historical development of selected words or word forms. 'Henry Fowler and his Eighteenth-Century

Predecessors' is the title of an interesting and timely article by Ingrid Tieken-Boon van Ostade (*HLSL* 9[2009]), in which she traces the approach that Fowler took in his *Dictionary* back to the eighteenth century. A systematic comparison between Fowler's usage guide, Baker's *Reflections on the English Language* [1770], and Lowth's *Short Introduction to English Grammar* [1762] reveals a number of similarities between the three works, such as similar strictures, criticism of the best authors, middle-class readership, and popularity. The study concludes that the three authors created their works independently of each other. The similarities in the three works may thus be explained by the fact that Baker, Lowth, and Fowler aimed to give guidance in linguistic matters, which they tackled in the same way.

3. Phonetics and Phonology

A long-standing generalization in English phonology has been that NN compounds are regularly fore-stressed (e.g. *RAdio station*), while phrases are regularly end-stressed (e.g. *blue BOOK*). The former is usually captured by the Compound Stress Rule, which states that compounds have fore-stress unless the rightmost element is branching (as in *government WORking party*, but not e.g. *ENgine-oil waste*), a regularity that is paralleled in single morphemes such as *semiNOla* (vs. *NIGHtingale*). Forms which violate this generalization (e.g. *apple PIE*, *Madison ROAD*), according to this view, are not compounds but phrases. This account of English compound and phrasal stress dates back at least as far as Bloomfield. 'Bloomfield was wrong' is the shortest sentence in Heinz J. Giegerich's 'The English Compound Stress Myth' (*WS* 2[2009] 1–17). Contrary to Bloomfield, and contrary to the consensus in the phonological literature since, Giegerich argues that forms like *apple pie* and *Madison Road* are best treated as compounds, and that their end-stress is not exceptional but instead a property of 'a reasonably well defined class of attribute-head NNs' (p. 1). He goes on to show that the Compound Stress Rule is also unable to handle the range of stress patterns found in larger compounds, e.g. *sand-stone WALL* (vs. *government WORking party*) and *OWL nest-box* (vs. *ENgine-oil waste*). As Giegerich observes, the 'stress mess' (p. 14) in compounds is parallelled by non-compound nouns. English nouns of Germanic origin have fore-stress while non-Germanic nouns have end-stress (e.g. *kangaROO*), or have lost their end-stress in favour of fore-stress (e.g. *virTUE* > *VIRtue*).

Another article that questions a long-held idea is Peter Schrijver's 'Celtic Influence on Old English: Phonological and Phonetic Evidence' (*ELL* 13[2009] 193–211). The traditional view is that the influence of Celtic on OE was limited to a handful of loanwords. However, if the original Celtic population shifted to speaking OE, one would also expect to find traces of phonological influence. According to Schrijver, such traces can be found in the highly similar vowel changes that are found in OE dialects. These changes, Schrijver argues, cannot be explained in terms of contact between the speakers of these dialects, but they rather suggest a common substrate language; more specifically, they suggest a language shift by a non-Anglo-Saxon population to Anglo-Saxon. Schrijver argues that the substrate language in question is more likely to have been Irish Celtic than British Celtic or British Latin. Another possible influence of Celtic on OE phonology is discussed by Stephen Laker, in 'An Explanation for the Early Phonemicisation of a Voice Contrast in English Fricatives' (*ELL* 13[2009] 213–26). Traditionally, the development of phonemic voiced fricatives has been attributed to the influence of French, to the degemination of intervocalic voiceless fricatives, and to the apocope of final vowels (or to a combination of these factors). Laker argues that a simpler explanation for the emergence of a voicing contrast in OE is through language contact with Celtic. Further support for the influence of Celtic phonology on OE can be found in Stephen Laker's dissertation, which I hope to discuss in next year's volume.

To what extent do listeners make use of universal preferences which are not directly reflected in their native language? In their article 'Listeners' Knowledge of Phonological Universals: Evidence from Nasal Clusters' (*Phonology* 26[2009] 75–108), Iris Berent, Tracy Lennertz, Paul Smolensky, and Vered Vaknin-Nusbaum address this question in relation to the perception of initial nasal clusters such as *md* by English listeners. Such clusters are absent from English and from many other languages, presumably because they have a falling sonority slope; *md* is typologically more marked than a nasal cluster with rising sonority, such as *ml*. On the basis of experimental evidence, the authors do indeed find evidence for the relative markedness of *md*. Their results show that nasal-initial clusters with falling sonority are more likely to be misperceived as disyllabic by English listeners, i.e. with an intervening epenthetic vowel, and to be misjudged as identical to their epenthetic counterparts. The results further show that onsets with falling sonority are reproduced less accurately than those with rising sonority, suggesting that their encoding is less faithful. Berent et al. conclude from this that English speakers possess phonological knowledge which cannot be explained purely from their linguistic experience, but which is fully expected on the basis of universal grammar. One possible formalization of this knowledge, favoured by the authors, is in terms of Optimality-theoretic markedness constraints.

A phonological topic which continues to be of interest is /r/-liaison. This is for a good reason, because, as Jose Mompeán and Pilar Mompeán-Guillamón note in '/r/-Liaison in English: An Empirical Study' (*CogLing* 20[2009] 733–76), theirs is the first study to investigate whether /r/-liaison in non-rhotic dialects is conditioned by sociolinguistic, phonetic, and usage-based factors. One of the authors' findings is that the relatively low rate of occurrence of intrusive /r/ (in relation to linking /r/) shows that the former continues to be stigmatized. The authors relate this to the observation that educated speakers are more conscious of spelling, and so tend to avoid producing sounds which are not reflected in the orthography. The study further shows that there are no speakers who produce linking /r/ and intrusive /r/ whenever the appropriate phonological context is met. The authors also observe that there are no significant differences in /r/-liaison usage between men and women. This is perhaps somewhat surprising, since their study suggests at the same time that a high rate of occurrence of intrusive /r/ is related to less prestigious lects.

With regard to possible phonetic conditioning, the authors observe that /r/-liaison is not affected by the quality of the preceding vowel, but is less frequent when the syllable already contains an /r/, as in *a* [r]*oa*[r] *of laughter*. Finally, with regard to usage-based factors, this study shows a higher frequency of /r/-liaison in contexts with a high degree of entrenchment or repeated use, i.e. in constructions such as compounds (e.g. *Fa*[r] *East*), collocations (e.g. *fo*[r] *example*), and root-affix combinations (e.g. *colou*[r]*ing*).

In 'Exploring the Role of Token Frequency in Phonological Change: Evidence of TH-Fronting in East-Central Scotland' (*ELL* 13[2009] 33–55), Lynn Clark and Graeme Trousdale focus on the gradual spread of TH-fronting (i.e. /θ/ > /f/) in west Fife. (The same change is found in other non-standard varieties of English.) The authors stress the need to integrate lexical frequency into a more general theory of language use. While their data fail to show a large correlation between token frequency and TH-fronting, Clark and Trousdale do observe a number of other significant factors. These include word class (names and ordinals are more resistant to TH-fronting than other lexical items), position in the syllable (/f/ is more likely to occur in non-initial position), priming (TH-fronting is more likely to occur after another /f/), and, most of all, the social structure of the group of speakers being investigated. Interestingly, Clark and Trousdale observe that one class of items which consistently fails to undergo TH-fronting is that of *–thing* compounds (e.g. *something*, *anything*), which display lenition to [h], glottal stop, or zero instead. The authors speculate that this lenition is due to lexicalization, which leads to a greater entrenchment of *–thing* compounds as units. This may account for the observation that these items are resistant to TH-fronting.

In Chloe R. Marshall and Heather K.J. van der Lely's 'Effects of Word Position and Stress on Onset Cluster Production: Evidence from Typical Development, Specific Language Impairment, and Dyslexia' (*Language* 85[2009] 39–57), the authors investigate whether children with specific language impairment (SLI) and children with dyslexia show differences in phonological development. The authors use a non-word repetition task for this in which they manipulate the phonological context of onset clusters (initial vs. medial, stressed vs. unstressed position). Previous studies have shown that the initial position of words is a psycholinguistically strong position, while stressed syllables are phonetically strong. The results of Marshall and van der Lely's study show that impaired children have greater difficulty reproducing medial clusters than initial ones, but that only the dyslexic children show less accuracy in the repetition of unstressed clusters. The latter result is important, since it suggests that the phonological deficits underlying SLI and dyslexia are different, and also that structural position and stress are independent elements in phonological development.

Another developmental study that appeals to the notion of 'strength' is Daniel A. Dinnsen and Ashley W. Farris-Trimble's 'Developmental Shifts in Phonological Strength Relations' (in Nasukawa and Backley, eds., *Strength Relations in Phonology*, pp. 113–48). Dinnsen and Farris-Trimble point out that adult languages exhibit an implicational relationship in that whenever a phonological contrast is permitted in a weak position (e.g. the syllable coda), it is also permitted in a strong position (e.g. the syllable onset), but not vice versa. The authors observe that this relationship does not hold in child language. In their corpus of English child language data, one of the children, for example, replaces initial fricatives by stops (e.g. [dæntə] 'Santa'), but retains the contrast between stops and fricatives in final position (e.g. [but] 'boot' vs. [mauθ] 'mouse'). Such data present a 'prominence paradox' and cast doubt on the claim that adult grammars and child grammars are governed by the same grammatical principles (the so-called 'continuity hypothesis'). The authors solve this paradox by introducing two types of violable prominence constraints, InitialProm and FinalProm, which favour prominence in initial and in final position respectively. They assume that the default state is one in which FinalProm is ranked higher than InitialProm. The change from child grammar to adult grammar then involves the re-ranking of these constraints, leading to a shift in the distribution of contrasts from final to initial position. Dinnsen and Farris-Trimble speculate that this re-ranking is triggered by changes in the size and the organization of the lexicon. In the same volume we find Bert Botma and Colin J. Ewen's 'Against Rhymal Adjuncts: The Syllabic Affiliation of English Postvocalic Consonants' (pp. 221–50). In this article, the authors attempt to extend their analysis of words like *field* and *shoulder*, where /l/ arguably occupies the specifier position of the syllable onset, to /n/ and /s/, in words like *paint* and *feast*. These sounds form a natural class to the extent that when they occur as the first element of a consonant cluster, they allow a preceding vowel length contrast. That is, English has such contrasts as *build* vs. *field*, *mint* vs. *paint*, and *fist* vs. *feast*, but not *think* vs. **theenk* or *frisk* vs. **freesk*. Botma and Ewen argue that this difference is difficult to account for if /l, n, s/ occupied the syllable coda.

Moving on to the world of textbooks, Bruce Hayes's *Introductory Phonology* offers an introduction to the field that is very much in the tradition of the *Sound Pattern of English*. Hayes devotes much space to features and rules, which provides readers with a solid foundation and leaves them well equipped to tackle more advanced, theoretically oriented material. In the latter part of the book Hayes deals with such topics as syllables, tone, diachrony, and phonological productivity. A particularly attractive feature of the book is the problem sets at the end of each chapter. These offer an excellent illustration of the kinds of questions that phonologists attempt to answer.

While Hayes's book presupposes some background in linguistics, Chris McCully's *The Sound Structure of English: An Introduction* is aimed at beginning students of English linguistics. The author offers an accessible and hands-on introduction to the articulatory properties of English sounds, but on the whole the book's focus is more phonological than phonetic. McCully provides a detailed discussion of patterns of vowel allophony, consonant allophony, and syllable structure, with data drawn from various dialects of English. The chapters on syllable structure anticipate the author's Optimality-theoretic perspective, which concludes the book.

We end this review by mentioning two new textbooks on phonetics. Both make for interesting reading, as they combine excellent coverage of the basic issues with the authors' respective theoretical perspectives. Ken Lodge's *A Critical Introduction to Phonetics* not only offers a thorough treatment of such aspects as articulation, transcription, and acoustics, but also stresses the fundamentally continuous nature of the speech stream. From this viewpoint, segments are a convenient but not always appropriate idealization. Accordingly, Lodge also devotes ample discussion to prosodic aspects of speech.

While Lodge's examples are drawn from a wide variety of languages, Richard Ogden's *An Introduction to English Phonetics* focuses on examples from around the English-speaking world, which he uses to introduce the core areas of phonetics. An important and attractive feature of the book is that the data are drawn from naturally occurring conversational English. Another is that Ogden discusses the relevance of such aspects as semantics, morphology, sociolinguistics, and conversational interaction to phonetic analysis—topics which have received little attention in earlier phonetics textbooks.

Finally, if this year's crop of books seems rather small, it may be worth noting that Cambridge University Press has reissued a number of older monographs on phonetics and phonology, copies of which are printed on demand. Phonologists will be happy to hear that this includes Ian Maddieson's *Patterns of Sounds*, originally published back in 1984.

4. Morphology

James and Juliette Blevins have edited *Analogy in Grammar: Form and Acquisition*, another witness to the resurgence of interest in the role of analogy in language. In all the papers morphological issues occupy centre stage, though some also consider syntax and phonology. The editors' 'Introduction: Analogy in Grammar' (pp. 1–12) gives a broad overview of the notion, its history, the different types that can be distinguished and the reasons for the neglect of analogy in generative work. Raphael Finkel and Gregory Stump contribute 'Principal Parts and Degrees of Paradigmatic Transparency' (pp. 13–53), taking a quantitative approach to the issue of how the realization of cells in an inflectional paradigm can be predicted from other cells. An information-theoretical approach to the same issue is taken in 'Parts and Wholes: Implicative Patterns in Inflectional Paradigms' by Farrell Ackerman, James Blevins, and Robert Malouf (pp. 54–82), who obtain results supporting use of the Word and Paradigm model of morphology. The empirical data in both articles come from heavily inflected languages, but it should be possible to apply their methods to OE and reconstructed pre-OE, potentially also yielding insights into diachronic change in paradigm make-up and organization. Specifically concerned with change is Andrew Wedel in 'Resolving Pattern Conflict: Variation and Selection in Phonology and Morphology' (pp. 83–100). An important role in his model is played by the notion of similarity-biased error, with repeated (small) errors causing a shift in the degrees of entrenchment of forms and patterns, as demonstrated through computer simulations of the learning of abstract morphological patterns. Lou-Ann Gerken, Rachel Wilson, Rebecca Gómez, and Erika Nurmsoo investigate 'The Relation between Linguistic Analogies and Lexical Categories' (pp. 101–17), the central question being to what extent learners use analogy to decide whether a given and—to them—new word form is part of a specific paradigm (and therefore a specific lexical category). Various psycholinguistic tests suggest that learners make use of analogy only if there are several clues that the new form is indeed part of the paradigm. Andrea Krott's 'The Role of Analogy for Compound Words' (pp. 118–36) reviews work on the selection of linking elements, speed of recognition, and interpretation of compounds. In all of these, analogy tends to be based on a compound's 'constituent families', i.e. the sets of compounds with the same modifier or head as the compound that is being tested. Interestingly, children tend to attach greater weight to head families and adults to modifier families. In 'Morphological Analogy: Only a Beginning' (pp. 137–63), John Goldsmith sketches a model of morphological learning based on the information-technological notion of Minimum Description Length. Royal Skousen 'Expand[s] Analogical Modeling into a General Theory of Language Prediction' (pp. 164–84); he proposes that apparent rules should be attributed to the workings of analogy, with the choice of exemplars being governed by principled criteria (ruling out, for example, an analogy like *buy~bought = try~X*). Adam Albright's 'Modeling Analogy as Probabilistic Grammar' (pp. 185–213) also addresses the problem of restricting possible analogical inferences, arguing that the job can be done by combining rewrite rules in the classical format (i.e. A -> B/ C _ D) with a probabilistic component. Finally, Petar Milin, Victor Kuperman, Alexander Kostić, and Harald Baayen contribute 'Words and Paradigms Bit by Bit: An Information-Theoretic Approach to the Processing of Inflection and Derivation' (pp. 214–52), arguing that paradigmatic structure influences lexical processing (both of inflected and derived forms), using results from lexical decision and word-naming experiments. Altogether, these papers clearly bring out the increasing importance of formal modelling and quantification in analogy research land.

There is a second edition of the textbook *English Words: History and Structure* by Donka Minkova and Robert Stockwell. There has been some updating and streamlining, but the basics remain unchanged. The book still deals with the classical component of English vocabulary and in the process provides a good introduction to morphological analysis. There are chapters on methods of creating new words, the historical background and layering of English vocabulary, morphological concepts and techniques, assimilation and weakening/strengthening, deletion rules, etymology, semantic change, and the pronunciation of classical words in English. An appendix lists 422 classical morphemes commonly found in English, with their meanings, examples, and source languages. A website has useful exercises for each chapter and answers to these (locked to students). All the material is presented in a clear and highly accessible manner and is informed throughout by the massive amounts of scholarship and experience that the two authors bring to the task.

Ryuichi Hotta's book *The Development of the Nominal Plural Forms in Early Middle English*, a revised version of his doctoral dissertation, investigates the diachronic development and geographical distribution of different nominal plural forms in early ME. Hotta approaches the subject from three theoretical perspectives, introduced in chapter 1: he takes a dialectological approach, using the *Linguistic Atlas of Early Middle English* (*LAEME*), and also makes use of the lexical diffusion model and of contact linguistics. Chapter 2 offers a preliminary discussion in the form of a review of earlier studies on the subject and a comparison of nominal plural systems and their development in other Germanic languages. Chapter 3 analyses data drawn from late OE and ME texts, showing that both the development of individual items and the reorganization of the plural system as a whole were motivated both by cross-dialectal contact and by independent developments in each dialect. Chapter 4 contextualizes this by discussing examples from different versions of five texts: *Lambeth Homilies*, *The Owl and the Nightingale*, *Ancrene Wisse/Riwle*, *Poema Morale*, and *The Peterborough Chronicle*. Chapter 5 takes a theoretical viewpoint, and applies the model of lexical diffusion to the early ME plural system. Hotta finds that the development of nominal plural forms in this period is characterized by different types of diffusion which are shared cross-dialectally and by 'some irregular behaviours of individual speakers, sites and dialects' (pp. 131–2). Chapter 6 investigates a number of possible language-internal motivations for the developments in the nominal plural system. The language-internal factors (phonetic, morphological, syntactic, and semantic) are shown to be relatively weak, in that they underlie the developments, but do not determine them. In chapter 7, Hotta argues that language contact with ON in late OE and early ME was responsible for the development of the nominal plural forms. In addition, he argues that the spread of the plural *–s* ending from the Northeast to the Southwest was the result of dialect contact. Chapter 8 presents the conclusions.

Britta Mondorf's *More Support for* More-*Support: The Role of Processing Constraints on the Choice between Synthetic and Analytic Comparative Forms* offers by far the most comprehensive account of the linguistic factors constraining the comparative alternation. Mondorf aims to prove what she terms the *more*-support hypothesis, which states that '[i]n cognitively more demanding environments which require an increased processing load, language users tend to make up for the additional effort by resorting to the analytic (*more*) rather than the synthetic (*–er*) comparative' (p. 6). On the basis of an in-depth synchronic and diachronic corpus study, Mondorf examines the linguistic determinants constraining the comparative alternation. She shows that phonological complexity leads to the use of the analytic variant: it is used as a strategy to avoid stress clashes (*a more bitter taste* vs. *a bitterer taste*), haplology (*more bitter* vs. *bitterer*) and less optimal coda-onset sequences (*more co.rrupt* vs. *corrup.ter*). Looking at morphological complexity, Mondorf finds that disyllabic morphologically complex adjectives in <-l, le> (e.g. *awful*) allow only the analytic variant (**awfuller*). With regard to lexical complexity, Mondorf demonstrates that longer adjectives (measured by the number of syllables), as well as less frequent, less entrenched adjectives, and compound adjectives (*more old-fashioned* vs. *older-fashioned*) favour the *more*-variant in order to reduce the processing cost. Syntactic complexity is also shown to trigger the use of the analytic comparative, which is favoured when the adjective selects a complement and when the adjective occurs in predicative position. The *more*-variant can also facilitate processing in cases of semantic complexity, such as when the adjective has an abstract or a figurative meaning, and when the adjective is weakly gradable. In the field of pragmatics, the analytic comparative can be used to create end-weight, which Mondorf links to its ability to add intensity or emphasis. The diachronic development of the comparative alternation also receives detailed attention. Mondorf shows that it is characterized by a functional specialization whereby the analytic comparative is used in cognitively complex structures from the onset, whereas the synthetic comparative is used in easy-to-process structures. A close look at the differences between comparative formation in BrE and AmE reveals that AmE uses fewer comparative forms than BrE, especially with adjectives occurring in cognitively complex environments.

Lieselotte Anderwald's *The Morphology of English Dialects: Verb-Formation in Non-Standard English* is a corpus-based study of past-tense formation in non-standard varieties of English. Most of the data are drawn from the *Freiburg English Dialect corpus* (FRED), which allows for quantitative analyses across BrE dialects. The descriptive overview in chapter 1 is followed by a review of a number of past-tense theories in chapter 2, which shows that different theories sometimes make different predictions concerning weak (regular) versus strong (irregular) past-tense formation in non-standard varieties of English. Having reviewed the morphological theories, Anderwald chooses to adopt a model that combines natural morphology and the network model. Chapter 3 examines the characteristics of the English verb system, and provides an overview of the pervasive patterns in non-standard paradigms. Chapter 4 shows that in non-standard English, unlike in StE, some very high-frequency verbs (Anderwald discusses *sell* and *know*) are affected by the trend to regularize strong past-tense forms. Chapter 5 discusses the non-standard strong verbs *drink*, *see*, *do*, and *eat*, which have two-part paradigms rather than three-part paradigms as in StE. The pattern PRES ≠ PAST = PPL has a more prominent role in non-standard English than in StE and in this respect non-standard systems are claimed to be more natural than the standard system, because they involve more levelling. Chapter 6 examines the non-standard strong verbs *come* and *run*, which have a one-part paradigm and are therefore maximally levelled. Anderwald shows that their paradigms are remarkably stable, due to a number of historical coincidences. Overall, the non-standard past-tense forms are historically attested forms that persist in the language. The concluding chapter (chapter 7) summarizes the findings. Anderwald's study convincingly demonstrates that the non-standard English past-tense system is simpler and therefore generally more economical than the StE counterpart.

Finally on inflexional matters, it is not commonly realized that English has an inflexional prefix, but Michael Montgomery traces its development and twentieth-century use in 'Historical and Comparative Perspectives on *A*-Prefixing in the English of Appalachia' (*AS* 84[2009] 5–26). He reviews its history (attributing its presence in AmE to eighteenth-century BrE) and then presents data from a corpus of interviews done in the period 1939–84, enabling him to confirm several grammatical and phonological constraints on the use of the prefix proposed in earlier work that was based on a much smaller data-set.

The derivational harvest contains just a few items this year. Ingo Plag and Harald Baayen discuss 'Suffix Ordering and Morphological Processing'

(*Language* 85[2009] 109–52). Using examples from English, they argue for a processing-driven account of ordering regularities but, unlike earlier work along these lines, also point at the important role of lexical storage. A formalization of their findings is offered and some attention is also paid to the fact that suffix combinations strongly tend to be acyclic (making words like *fearlessnesslessness* very odd), a fact for which they propose a functional processing explanation. Mark Baker and Nadya Vinokurova write 'On Agent Nominalizations and Why They are Not Like Event Nominalizations' (*Language* 85[2009] 517–56). They show that, in English and other languages, derived forms like *finding* can have certain clausal properties (for example allowing adverbs, voice markers, aspect, and negation), but that forms like *finder* cannot. Their explanation for this is structural: agentive nominalizers combine directly with a bare VP (making them similar to the head of VoiceP in clausal syntax). Daniel García Velasco, 'Conversion in English and its Implications for Functional Discourse Grammar' (*Lingua* 119[2009] 1164–85), argues that the process of conversion in English, which is understood as innovative coinage, is essentially similar to lexical flexibility, by which lexemes are underspecified for lexical category in the lexicon and only acquire full meaning once they are inserted in a syntactic slot.

As editors Rochelle Lieber and Pavol Štekauer point out in their introduction (pp. 3–18) to *The Oxford Handbook of Compounding*, studying compounds is like the parable of the blind men and the elephant, with some men even doubting that there is an elephant at all. This does not prevent the editors from demonstrating the (partial) usefulness of several phonological, syntactic, and morphological criteria for defining and identifying compounds and previewing the remainder of the book. Part I contains fifteen further chapters, some describing properties of compounds but most approaching them from a specific general theory of language or morpho-syntax. Stanislav Kavka writes about 'Compounding and Idiomatology' (pp. 19–33); Sergio Scalise and Antonietta Bisetto contribute 'The Classification of Compounds' (pp. 34–53); Pius ten Hacken describes 'Early Generative Approaches' (pp. 54–77); Rochelle Lieber takes 'A Lexical Semantic Approach to Compounding (pp. 78–104); Ray Jackendoff considers 'Compounding in the Parallel Architecture and Conceptual Semantics' (pp. 105–28); Heidi Harley looks at 'Compounding in Distributed Morphology' (pp. 129–44); Anna Maria Di Sciullo asks 'Why are Compounds a Part of Human Language? A View from Asymmetry Theory' (pp. 145–77); Heinz Giegerich presents 'Compounding and Lexicalism' (pp. 178–200); Geert Booij writes 'Compounding and Construction Morphology' (pp. 201–16); Joachim Grzega looks at 'Compounding from an Onomasiological Perspective' (pp. 217–32); Liesbet Heyvaert contributes 'Compounding in Cognitive Linguistics' (pp. 233–54); Christina Gagné writes on 'Psycholinguistic Perspectives' (pp. 255–71); Pavol Štekauer explores the 'Meaning Predictability of Novel Context-Free Compounds' (pp. 272–97); Ruth Berman investigates 'Children's Acquisition of Compound Constructions' (pp. 298–322); and Dieter Kastovsky presents 'Diachronic Perspectives' (pp. 323–40). This is followed by a typological Part II, occupying about half of the book: after a chapter on the 'Typology of Compounds' by Laurie Bauer (pp. 343–56), there are seventeen chapters on compounds in specific languages, eight Indo-European and eleven from other language families. In her chapter on compounds in English (pp. 357–69), Rochelle Lieber discusses the different types, their internal structure, and their interpretation. We also mention here Robert Kirchner and Elena Nicoladis's 'A Level Playing-Field: Perceptibility and Inflection in English Compounds' (*CanJL* 54[2009] 91–116), where the authors show that inside English compounds *-ing* is freely allowed, *-s* is not uncommon, and *-ed* is generally excluded. They attribute this to a difference in perceptibility of these three affixes, casting this in an OT framework.

In his study *Productivity in English Word-Formation: An Approach to N+N Compounding*, Jesús Fernández-Domínguez critically scrutinizes the phenomenon of morphological productivity, which is the property of word-formation processes whereby new words are created to satisfy a naming need. He does so by examining a very productive word-formation type, N+N compounding, using a corpus compiled from the *BNC Sampler* with the help of *Wordsmith Tools* (Scott 2004). The study is motivated by the fact that most existing models of productivity measurement are based on affixation, ignoring other word-formation processes. Fernández-Domínguez seeks to establish to what extent N+N compounding requires a new model of productivity measurement. The introductory chapter is followed by chapter 2, which discusses the main properties of compounds and compounding, such as the high productivity of compounding, which poses difficulties when distinguishing compounds from phrases. Chapter 3 focuses on morphological productivity, an important but elusive concept in the study of morphology. The author provides an overview of processes and concepts that are generally brought into relation with productivity. He also addresses the 'crucial dilemma' (p. 53) of whether productivity is a theoretical primitive or an epiphenomenon and concludes it is the latter. Chapter 4 reviews existing models of productivity measurement and applies them to N+N compounding. Using the concept of profitability, i.e. actual utilization in performance, Fernández-Domínguez presents an alternative model for productivity measurement, which also pays attention to poorly productive processes. Chapter 5 concludes the study, providing conclusions as well as directions for further research into morphological productivity.

We finish with three clearly diachronic pieces. Michiko Ogura, in 'The Interchangeability of the Endings *-ende* and *-enne* in Old and Early Middle English' (*ES* 90[2009] 721–34), finds that the interchange of *-ende* and *-enne* on present participles and inflected infinitives occurred in late OE, which allowed the appearance of the variant forms of present participles as well as the subsequent development of the *-ing* form in ME. Simon Horobin's 'Traditional English? Chaucerian Methods of Word-Formation' (*NM* 110[2009] 141–57) argues that Chaucer made use of traditional methods of word-formation, including affixation, conversion, and compounding, to produce new and innovative formations, such as *unloven* 'to stop loving', *assure* as a noun (instead of *assuraunce*) and *lette-game* 'spoilsport'. Carola Trips has written *Lexical Semantics and Diachronic Morphology: The Development of* -hood, -dom, *and* -ship *in the History of English*. Her main argument is that all three elements have undergone a development from independent lexical item to element in a compound to suffix. Detailed corpus data for the entire history of English are presented to back up this claim. The cause of the development, Trips argues, lies in semantic change. In particular, the elements became generalized in meaning, losing their association with persons and being increasingly used also in connection with abstract entities. This change, and the attendant increase in token frequency of the three elements, triggered morphologization. Like Lieber and Štekauer above, Trips notes the difficulty of demarcating the difference between compounding and derivation, but suggests that suffixes show greater productivity and a more abstract semantics.

5. Syntax

(a) Modern English

We start with an excellent introduction to syntactic analysis, Peter Culicover's *Natural Language Syntax*. It has chapters dealing with syntactic categories, the basic structure of the clause, phrasal categories, sentence meaning and the lexicon, non-canonical argument realizations (as in passives, causatives, null arguments), raising and control, predication, A-bar phenomena, binding and sentence fragments (a topic usually shunned in introductory works). Each of these chapters describes the basic facts and problems, outlines how they can be analysed in general terms, and then goes into more depth by showing how specific issues have been addressed in earlier and more recent work. The later sections in each chapter are labelled as being more advanced, as are some of the Problems and Research questions in each chapter, thus making it possible to use the book either for undergraduate or graduate teaching. In approach, the book follows mainstream generative ideas, but its main objective is clearly not to present a specific version of generative theory but to make the student see how syntactic facts and puzzles can and have been tackled. Not surprisingly, in doing so Culicover regularly draws on the theory that he and Ray Jackendoff presented in their 2005 *Simpler Syntax* (see *YWES* 88[2009] 32). In particular, the level of Conceptual Structure plays a prominent role in several of the analyses described.

Undergraduates doing linguistics and English language at Lancaster University are no doubt very familiar with the 700-page book *English Language: Description, Variation and Context*, edited by Jonathan Culpeper, Francis Katamba, Paul Kerswill, Ruth Wodak, and Tony McEnery. Its thirty-nine chapters, each ten to fifteen pages long, are all written by linguists who work—or used to work—at Lancaster, who introduce students to all the different areas of language study. Grouped into six parts (structure, history, regional and social variation, styles and genre, communication and interaction, learning and teaching) they range from phonetics, phonology, word structure, grammar (three chapters on this), semantics, pragmatics via standardization, the history of English spelling, phonological change, lexical change, semantic change, discourse types, language in specific registers, stylistics, to conversation analysis, politeness phenomena, gender in language, language acquisition, language in education, and TESOL (and a few more).

The material is presented in very accessible fashion, and there is an abundance of tables, diagrams, and examples, and boxed sections contain more advanced materials. In a useful concluding chapter, Charles Alderson and Jonathan Culpeper present 'Reflections' on 'Studying the English Language' (pp. 659–66), including a justification for the choice of topics, thoughts on the nature of linguistic evidence and analysis as well as some predictions for English language studies in the future. This looks like a fine textbook; it would also be possible to use individual chapters as basic introductions to materials and approaches in the subject areas covered. But in doing so, it has to be realized that the emphasis tends to be on language used in and for communication, rather than language as an object with formal properties.

Caroline Coffin, Jim Donohue, and Sarah North have written a textbook introducing students to functional systemic grammar (FSG): *Exploring English Grammar: From Formal to Functional*. After an introductory chapter, there are four chapters showing how traditional grammatical analysis is carried out and how it can be used to advantage in analysing the meanings of texts; the chapters focus on texts containing procedures, descriptions, accounts of events in the past, and predictions/hypotheses. Chapter 6 builds on this communicative groundwork to advance to FSG proper. The remaining chapters deal with the well-known FSG concepts of genre, ideational meaning, the interpersonal dimension, and coherence/cohesiveness. Each chapter abounds with texts, worked examples, and activities, giving the student hands-on practice with the theory. We particularly admire the way a sensible balance is struck between the use of traditional grammatical notions and the explanation of FSG-specific methods and analyses.

More pocket guide than textbook is *The Basics of English Usage* by Wynford Hicks. Aimed at those that sometimes wonder—or worry—about correct or appropriate usage in matters of spelling, grammar, vocabulary, and punctuation, it provides practical explanation and advice about each of these areas. The section on grammar—a bit less than half of the work and also containing advice on stylistic issues—is arranged along alphabetical lines, with entries on, for example, adjectives (where a very brief description is followed by the advice to avoid—at least in formal writing—the use of a superlative when comparing two things or people), back-formation (where words like *reminisce* are said to be good examples of the flexibility of English, in spite of objections by pedants), *between* (where *between you and I* is said to be wrong), and some 200 or 300 further items. The approach is traditional and the advice given varies between the neutral, the positive, and (more often) the condemnatory, though the tone is light throughout.

Fundamental issues in language are addressed in Thomas Berg's *Structure in Language: A Dynamic Perspective* (some of which could have been discussed in sections 4 and 5(b) as well). Defining structure as the process of building units and focusing on this process as taking place during language processing, Berg explores the way it operates at the levels of phonology, morphology, and syntax. After an introductory chapter, he examines in detail the constituent structure and branching direction of each of these levels in English. For syntax, he shows amongst other things that there is very strong evidence for a VP in English, coming not only from the classical constituency tests (each of which he subjects to some critical discussion) but also from psycholinguistic experiments. The predominant branching direction is rightward, which has certain processing benefits, in particular in complex clauses. Morphology too is predominantly right-branching, as Berg establishes by analysing large numbers of affixed words and compounds, using various criteria to decide their directionality. In a later chapter, a similar exercise is carried out on OE data. At that stage, Berg argues, the VP was less articulated and less strongly established (a possibility fully allowed within his overall theory, which recognizes scales of strength and activation). Evidence for this comes from the fact that there are often elements intervening between object and verb, that there was a certain amount of *pro*-drop (hence utterances without fully elaborated clausal structure), that the pre-modals could function as main verbs (hence being part of a simpler hierarchical structure than in PDE), and that there was less subordination in OE than in PDE. Moreover, in OE syntax as well as morphology, there is greater incidence of left-branching, which suggests that there has been diachronic change. Further chapters consider cross-linguistic variation in structure activation, the acquisition of structure, the loss of structure in aphasia, and possible differences in structure between speech, writing, and typing. Altogether, this book clearly casts a wide net, bringing up many interesting ideas and analyses but also raising the question of how these findings can be integrated with other work on these topics.

Another fundamental question about language is whether languages can differ in their degree of complexity. The claim that they can is controversial but is nevertheless made, defended, and elaborated on in the volume *Language Complexity as an Evolving Variable*, edited by Geoffrey Sampson, David Gil, and Peter Trudgill. In the first chapter, Geoffrey Sampson writes about 'A Linguistic Axiom Challenged' (pp. 1–18), sketching the evolution of the idea that all languages are equal in complexity, distinguishing various possible interpretations of this axiom and then presenting evidence against it, coming from language history, individual differences between speakers, differences between older and younger speakers, and differences between different language types. His conclusion is that the axiom is a 'melting iceberg' (p. 18). Most—though not all—of the following seventeen chapters support this conclusion, providing more detailed evidence for it, some impressive in its numerical scope. A point demonstrated in several chapters is that no trade-off relation between, for example, simple morphology and complex syntax can be assumed. We summarize here only the papers that include (more than passing) discussion of English; however, all of them are thought-provoking.

In 'Between Simplification and Complexification: Non-Standard Varieties of English around the World' (pp. 64–79), Benedikt Szmrecsanyi and Bernd Kortmann use a list of seventy-six variable morpho-syntactic features to show that traditional vernaculars (e.g. Northern and East Anglian English in England) have more ornamental complexity and irregularity than high-contact varieties (e.g. Scottish and Irish English, but also colloquial American and Australian English), while L2 varieties (e.g. East African and Hongkong English) tend to have more transparent grammatical marking than either of these two (see also section 9 below). Peter Trudgill focuses on 'Sociolinguistic Typology and Complexification' (pp. 98–109), arguing that irregular, less transparent, and more redundant forms are prone to be created in small and isolated communities of speakers, as in the case of traditional English dialects. On the basis of this, he suggests that language in the past may well have been considerably more complex than today. 'Individual Differences in Processing Complex Grammatical Structures' are explored by Ngoni Chipere (pp. 178–91), who finds that there is a clear correlation between English native speakers' level of academic ability and their recall and comprehension of sentences with complex NPs, such as *Tom knows that the fact that flying planes low is dangerous excites the pilot*. Liljana Progovac contributes 'Layering of Grammar: Vestiges of Protosyntax in Present-Day Languages' (pp. 203–12). Building on her earlier work (see *YWES* 87[2008] 50), she proposes that unembedded small clauses such as *John a doctor?!*, *Everybody out!* and *Case closed* represent fossilized survivals of linguistic structures in human protolanguage; she demonstrates that the structures in question are less complex than those in modern languages (in having no movement, functional projections, or embedding). Eugénie Stapert asks, 'Universals in Language or Cognition? Evidence from English Language Acquisition and from Pirahã' (pp. 230–42). The starting point is Pirahã, an Amazonian language, which famously appears not to have sentential embedding. English clearly does, for example with mental verbs like *think*, *know*, and *believe*. However, Stapert argues that such verbs in English child speech and colloquial adult speech are often part of routinized chunks which are adverbial in nature. The difference from Pirahã may then be that some adult speakers of English sometimes engage in more complex forms of cognition, leading to use of unambiguous embedding structures. That Pirahã also had these at an earlier stage in its history is suggested by the shape of some of its suffixes. For John Hawkins, problems in defining and operationalizing the notion of complexity suggest that we should turn to 'An Efficiency Theory of Complexity and Related Phenomena' (pp. 252–68); using his well-known theory of word order and processing (which allows for trade-off effects), he shows how performance (dis)preferences for certain complex orders in English as compared with other languages can be predicted.

On the theoretical front, minimalism continues to attract attention. In *Bare Syntax*, Cedric Boeckx embarks on an ambitious project to unify different types of locality found in the grammar of human language and to derive them from underlying (minimalist) principles. After sketching the basics of minimalist thinking, he presents his main ideas on how the locality of selection and the locality of long-distance dependencies can be brought together. He then goes on to address in more detail the role of Merge, the nature of cartographies, and the proper analysis of island effects. Data from English play an important role in the argument, but there is also a very generous helping of other languages. However, the overall aim is clearly to shed light on the nature of grammar (in particular, its hows and whys) rather than on the nature of specific types of data.

Other authors proposing minimalist analyses include Fabian Heck, who argues in 'On Certain Properties of Pied-Piping' (*LingI* 40[2009] 75–111) that pied-piping is not the effect of *wh*-feature percolation but of Agree and proposes a detailed account of pied-piping restrictions within this framework.

In a more general generative vein, much work over the past decade has argued that that the CP should be split into a number of different functional categories, an idea first put forward by Luigi Rizzi in 1997 (see *YWES* 78[2000] 21–2). But two articles this year argue that perhaps the idea is not so good after all; both are in the collection *Dislocated Elements in Discourse: Syntactic, Semantic, and Pragmatic Perspectives*, edited by Benjamin Shaer, Philippa Cook, Werner Frey, and Claudia Maienborn (more on this at the end of this subsection, where we discuss dislocation generally). Nicholas Sobin investigates 'Echo Questions and Split CP' (pp. 95–113). He points out that a major feature of echo questions is that they have a 'frozen' CP area, so that an utterance like *Did Mary meet Mozart?* can be echo-questioned only by *Did Mary meet WHO?*, not by *WHO did Mary meet?* or *Mary met WHO?*. This is easily stated in the unsplit CP analysis but requires all kinds of stipulations, depending on the specifics of the sentence type, if CP is split. Other arguments for an unsplit CP are given by Frederick Newmeyer in 'On Split CPs and the "Perfectness" of Language' (pp. 114–40). He argues that some of the explanatory work done by the split CP hypothesis is already done by independent principles (e.g. the utterance **He's a man liberty to whom we could never grant* violates both the nested-dependency constraint and the adjacency requirement for relative clauses and head nouns), and also shows, using facts involving focus and topic, that there is a general absence of correlation between the function and position of elements, thus casting doubt on the basic idea underlying the split CP hypothesis and also Chomsky's recent suggestion that movement is triggered by interpretative features of constituents.

While work on English syntactic analysis and theory has never stood still, researchers nowadays also have to make sure they are up-to-date on the corpora that are available for their work. A lot of useful information about corpus creation and new individual corpora can be found in *Creating and Digitizing Language Corpora* edited by Joan Beal, Karen Corrigan, and Hermann Moisl. Volume 1 is devoted to *Synchronic Databases*, most of them being 'unconventional' in not representing finite and/or balanced amounts of standard language in different—preponderantly written—registers. In their introduction, 'Taming Digital Voices and Text: Models and Methods for Handling Unconventional Synchronic Corpora' (pp. 1–16), the editors address issues that inevitably arise in planning and constructing such corpora. In the other eight papers in the volume, corpus creators describe their work. Thus, Jean Anderson, Dave Beavan, and Christian Kay discuss their 'SCOTS: Scottish Corpus of Texts and Speech' (pp. 17–34). Lieselotte Anderwald and Susanne Wagner contribute 'FRED—The Freiburg English Dialect Corpus: Applying Corpus-Linguistic Research Tools to the Analysis of Dialect Data' (pp. 35–53). Sjef Barbiers, Leonie Cornips, and Jan Pieter Kunst describe 'The Syntactic Atlas of the Dutch Dialects (SAND): A Corpus of Elicited Speech and Text as an Online Dynamic Atlas' (pp. 54–90), of importance not only because of its scope and size but also because its innovative methodology is inspiring similar projects in other countries. Penelope Gardner-Chloros, Melissa Moyer, and Mark Sebba contribute 'Coding and Analysing Multilingual Data: The LIDES Project' (pp. 91–120), a corpus initiative based on CHILDES methodology. Jeffrey Kallen and John Kirk write about the creation of 'ICE-Ireland: Local Variations on Global Standards' (pp. 121–62), highlighting issues concerning funding, regional differentiation, text selection, and copyright as well as describing some initial results obtained by exploring the corpus. Brian MacWhinney describes 'The TalkBank Project' (pp. 163–80), whose aim is to make available recordings and transcriptions of naturalistic human (and animal) communication; this wide remit necessitates careful planning of transcription and coding practices. Mark Sebba and Susan Dray write about their work in 'Developing and Using a Corpus of Written Creole' (pp. 181–204), specifically Jamaican Creole, with data coming from Britain as well as Jamaica. Finally, Sali Tagliamonte in 'Representing Real Language: Consistency, Trade-Offs and Thinking Ahead!' (pp. 205–40) describes the methods that she has used in converting the audio files from her various UK-based fieldwork projects into usable corpora.

A somewhat more diffuse (though no less interesting) collection of corpus articles is *Contemporary Corpus Linguistics* edited by Paul Baker. After his useful introduction (pp. 1–8), which provides a brief but sensible update on the current status of corpus work, there are sixteen chapters by different authors on the way corpora can contribute to the study of all kinds of topics, including metaphor, critical discourse analysis, stylistics, lexical patterning, patterns in speech, linguistic variation, dictionaries, second language teaching, translation, and on the more technical issues of software development and corpus-building. There is relatively little on straightforward syntax but this, we feel, may not be a bad thing for corpus linguistics, since the field may have been in danger of becoming dominated by this area.

An excellent resource for those who, like us, use online corpora of PDE in their teaching to undergraduates is *Exploring English with Online Corpora: An Introduction* by Wendy Anderson and John Corbett. The first chapter sketches some background to corpus use and creation and introduces the five online corpora that most of the following chapters draw on: the BNC; the Corpus of Contemporary American English; the TIME corpus (these first three all available on the invaluable website of Mark Davies); the Michigan Corpus of Academic Spoken English; and the Scottish Corpus of Texts and Speech. Chapter 2 provides material and concepts for interpreting corpus data, and the following four chapters deal with the corpus exploration of lexis, grammar, discourse, pronunciation. Chapter 7 alerts readers to the need to contextualize corpus texts, in terms of various sociolinguistic categories. The final chapter offers ideas on corpora in teaching and on future developments in online corpora. An appendix describes several more corpora that are available online and the book ends with a brief glossary of technical terms. The individual chapters abound with practical demonstrations and there are also Tasks (mostly corpus searches) for the students to carry out. Altogether, our verdict is: highly recommended.

From these more general materials, we turn to NPs and their elements. Leszek Berezowski's well-argued *The Myth of the Zero Article* takes an original approach to the topic of article absence in some (predicative) NPs in PDE. Rather than regarding this as a phenomenon where an element is missing, Berezowski proposes that it involves contexts where use of the article has not yet grammaticalized, thus representing a case of incomplete grammaticalization. The relevant contexts are identified as cases where there is only one salient 'role holder' available, as in the case of NPs headed by words like *king*, *president*, *chairman*, or *geometrical mean*. Chapter 1 traces the development of the notion of zero article; chapter 2 surveys the contexts in English where no article is used; chapter 3 deals with earlier theoretical accounts of the phenomenon; chapter 4 looks at the grammaticalization of articles (not in the history of English, but cross-linguistically); chapter 5 develops the notion of role holders; and chapter 6 presents corpus data for the different types of predicative NP heads that promote article-less-ness (or: which have not yet been affected by the process of grammaticalization). The final chapter presents the general conclusions and calls for further study of mass nouns and indefinite plurals from the same perspective.

There is a special issue of *Transactions of the Philological Society* on 'History and Structure in the English Noun Phrase' this year. In it, Freek van de Velde's answer to the question 'Do We Need the Category of Postdeterminer in the NP?' (*TPS* 107[2009] 293–321) is negative. While some grammars put quantifiers, numerals, and certain adjectives in this position, Van de Velde argues that it has been misused to classify words that are undergoing a diachronic shift from adjective to determiner. The examples he considers include the possessive pronouns (which used to freely co-occur with determiners), the word *such* (still adjective-like in many respects) and the items *same* (which often occurs without a determiner) and *other* (which often merges with the word *an* to yield determiner-like *another*). P.H. Matthews writes 'On the Microsyntax of Attributive Adjectives' (*TPS* 107[2009] 358–75). Taking issue with the idea that multiple adjectives must be either co-ordinated or structurally stacked, he considers cases where two adjectives seem to form a unit, as in *a tiny little bird* or *a fine old mess*, and compares them with other adjective-adjective sequences. Also concerned with adjective sequences is Robert Truswell's 'Attributive Adjectives and Nominal Templates' (*LingI* 40[2009] 525–33). The author reports that data obtained using Google show many exceptions to the rather rigid order of adjectives proposed in the cartographic project, corresponding to an equally rigid order of elements in the clausal domain. His conclusion is that the attempt to find similarity between nominal and clausal structure is misguided.

That it is possible to compare 'The English Genitive and Double Case' as found in Old Georgian is shown by John Payne (*TPS* 107[2009] 322–57). Rejecting the idea that possessive's is a clitic, he argues that it is an affix that can be passed from an NP to the rightmost element of the NP, leading to double case forms like *me's* in *the girl who invited me's mother*. The analysis that he develops predicts that phrasal genitives with a plural head noun should be impossible when the plural is regular (as in **the queens of England's*) but allowed when the plural is irregular (as in *the women next door's*). A small corpus study largely confirms this, though (plural) proper names form an exception, perhaps because they function as atomic units. Moving on to personal pronouns, Mark Balhorn reports on 'The Epicene Pronoun in Contemporary Newspaper Prose' (*AS* 84[2009] 391–413). After reviewing earlier work and opinions on the use of epicene *they* as in *A criminal is a criminal no matter what they wear*, he presents and analyses newspaper data, paying attention to various factors, including sex of the writer and syntactic form of the antecedent. Among the results is the finding that the epicene is used less often when the antecedent is a gender-stereotyped profession like *the CEO* or *the doctor*—these show greater amounts of *he or she*, perhaps as a result of conscious striving for PC. Carlos Acuña-Fariña, 'Aspects of the Grammar of Close Apposition and the Structure of the Noun Phrase' (*ELL* 13[2009] 453–81), provides an analysis of close appositives (e.g. *the poet Burns*) as an instance of inchoate NP structure, which is not fully elaborated because of a lack of strong functional pressure.

Auxiliaries matter too this year, especially the modal kind. Peter Collins has written *Modals and Quasi-Modals in English*, a corpus-based study of (the meanings of) modals (e.g. *can*, *may*, *will*, *shall*, *must*) and quasi-modals (e.g. *be able to*, *be going to*, *be supposed to*) in contemporary BriE, AmE, and AusE. Chapter 1 introduces the corpora that were used for the study and offers a preview of the findings. The study provides evidence that stylistic factors are at play in developments of modals and quasi-modals. For example, the use (and growth) of quasi-modals is most evident in speech, whereas the use of modals can be linked most clearly to written language. This stylistic difference is shown to interact with region: it is most clearly marked in AmE and least clearly marked in BrE. Chapter 2 provides the theoretical preliminaries, defining and examining the properties of modal and quasi-modal auxiliaries. Quasi-modals are distinguished from modals on the basis of the criteria grammaticalization, idiomaticity, and semantic relatedness to a central modal auxiliary. Chapters 3–5 deal with different groupings of modal auxiliaries, based on their semantics. Chapter 3 concentrates on the (quasi-)modals of necessity and obligation, which can be subdivided according to modal strength: the strong forms *must*, *have to*, *have got to*, *need*, *need to*, *be bound to*, and *be to*; and the medium-strength forms *should*, *ought to*, *had better*, and *be supposed to*. Chapter 4 examines *can/could*, *may/might*, and *be able to*, the (quasi–)modals of possibility, permission, and ability. It reports some striking regional differences, with *may* being more popular in BrE (ICE-GB corpus) than in AmE (C-US) and AusE (ICE-AUS), and with *might* being less popular in AmE than in the other two varieties. Chapter 5 examines the (quasi–)modals of predication and volition *will/would*, *shall*, *be going to*, *want to*, and *be about to*. One of the findings is that the volitional quasi-modal *want to* may be challenging the volitional modal *will*. Chapter 6 offers a summary of the findings. The overall picture that emerges from Collins's corpus study of modals and quasi-modals is that AmE is innovative, BrE is conservative and AusE is somewhere in between. Some of this material can also be found in the same author's 'The English Modals and Semi-Modals: Regional and Stylistic Variation' (in Nevalainen et al., eds. *The Dynamics of Linguistic Variation: Corpus Evidence on English Past and Present*, pp. 129–45). Modals in American journalistic writing are investigated in Neil Millar's 'Modal Verbs in TIME: Frequency Changes 1923–2006' (*IJCL* 14[2009] 191–220), which reveals an overall growth rather than a decline in the use of (semi–)modals.

Göran Kjellmer, '"How Do I Be Positive?" On Factors Promoting DO-Support of *Be*' (*NM* 110[2009] 73–84), shows that analogy and co-ordination with lexical verbs are the main operative factors in the use of DO-support with *be* in contexts other than imperatives. Rena Torres Cacoullos and James A. Walker look at 'The Present of the English Future: Grammatical Variation and Collocations in Discourse' (*Language* 85[2009] 321–54). Using a multivariate approach, they argue that the use of *will*, *be going to*, and the simple present tense with future meaning is not regulated by general principles but that each form occupies several niches, as a result of historical grammaticalization patterns. For example, use of *going to* is favoured in interrogatives and in complement clauses, while *will* tends to occur with indefinite adverbials and in the matrix of *if*-sentences.

Moving on to complements, Silke Höche's study *Cognate Object Constructions in English: A Cognitive-Linguistic Account* provides an in-depth description of English cognate object constructions (COCs) such as *He grinned his evil grin* and offers a cognitive-linguistic analysis of these constructions. Höche's study comprises twelve chapters: chapter 1 is introductory; chapters 2 and 3 have a summarizing function, with chapter 2 presenting an overview of existing treatments of COCs and chapter 3 introducing Cognitive Linguistics. Höche's comprehensive overview of existing treatments of COCs (chapter 2) makes clear that a crucial issue in the description and analysis of COCs is how cognate objects (COs) differ from other kinds of objects. Previous accounts therefore discuss the precise status of the cognate object as well as the semantics of COCs. With regard to the latter, Höche argues in chapter 4 that COs can be both resultative and eventive, which results in the polysemous nature of COCs. The conceptual content of COCs and the form of COCs receive a cognitive-linguistic description: the overlap in conceptual content of the verb and CO in a COC are argued to have an intensifying effect and COs are taken to be arguments (not adjuncts) of their verb. Chapter 5 outlines a possible usage-based network of constructions that specifies subtypes of COCs, motivated by the verbs that are most strongly associated with these subtypes. Chapter 6 focuses on the transitivity of COCs and argues that they elaborate or restructure the participant order, 'bringing about a change of energetic characteristics of the event' (p. 179). Chapter 7 discusses the aspectual characteristics of COs and COCs and shows that COs have a telic effect: they provide an event boundary when the verb of the COC expresses an unbounded event. Chapter 8 examines the make-up of COs, discussing the types of determiner COs can combine with and the modification patterns found in COs. Chapters 9 and 10 contrast COCs with apparently similar constructions: the verb + adverb construction (VAC) in chapter 9, the light verb construction (LVC) in chapter 10. The data are collected from the BNC, and occurrences of COCs and VACs with the verbs *live*, *die*, and *smile* are sparse, which hampers an adequate comparative analysis. As for the comparison of COCs and LVCs (chapter 10), both constructions allow the inclusion of modification material and represent a bounded event. The constructions show differences in meaning, notably the spread of semantic content across the construction's elements: in LVCs, the semantic content is located in the object, whereas in COCs the semantic content is spread out evenly across the verb and the object. Chapter 11 explores collocational and idiomatic COCs and examines the distribution of these COC types across different registers. COCs generally occur mostly in written language (e.g. fiction), and when they are found in casual speech they are often collocational or idiomatic. Chapter 12 concludes this thorough study on a fascinating construction.

Evelien Keizer, 'Verb-Preposition Constructions in FDG' (*Lingua* 119[2009] 1186–1211), accounts for English verb-preposition constructions (e.g. *The lights went out*, *Pete switched off the lights*) by distinguishing three predication frames: the 'composite predicate frame', the 'resultative frame', and the 'verb + prepositional complement frame'. Erica J. Benson, 'Everyone Wants *In*: *Want* + Prepositional Adverb in the Midland and Beyond' (*JEngL* 37[2009] 28–60), finds a wider than expected regional distribution of forms of *want* + prepositional adverb (e.g. *I can move if you want by*), as well as differences in acceptability of different forms. In the Midland, which shows the greatest concentration of use, variation is found across styles rather than across social variables, arguing that a change from below is spreading *want* + prepositional adverb beyond the Midlands.

We have seen two items on adverbs and adjuncts. Josef Bayer's 'Nominal Negative Quantifiers as Adjuncts' (*JCGL* 12[2009] 5–30) discusses the negative polarity use of the negative quantifier *nothing* in English, German, Dutch, and Italian, which emerges when *nothing* occurs as a non-argument. In Ignacio Palacios Martinez's '"Quite frankly, I'm not quite sure that it is quite the right colour": A Corpus-Based Study of the Syntax and Semantics of *Quite* in Present-Day English' (*ES* 90[2009] 180–213), the intensifying adverb *quite* is shown, among other things, to be very frequent (especially in spoken British English) and to function either as an amplifier or a compromiser.

We have reached complex sentences. Timothy Osborne, 'Comparative Coordination vs. Comparative Subordination' (*NL<* 27[2009] 427–54), gives a theory-neutral (surface) syntactic account of comparatives in English and German, arguing that the syntax of *than*-phrase comparatives is a combination of co-ordination and subordination, and that the choice relies on the notion of functional equivalence. Patrick Duffley and Rafika Abida investigate 'Complementation with Verbs of Choice in English' (*CanJL* 54[2009] 1–26). They explain the choice between infinitive and gerund after the verbs *prefer*, *choose*, *elect*, *select*, *pick*, and *opt* by appealing to semantic properties of these verbs in combination with the semantics of infinitive and gerund. Pieter A.M. Seuren and Camiel Hamans, 'Semantic Conditioning of Syntactic Rules: Evidentiality and Auxiliation in English and Dutch' (*FoLi* 43[2009] 135–69), show that, in English and Dutch, lexical evidential meaning is a clear determinant for the induction of syntactic auxiliation, as illustrated in examples such as *John is likely to win the race* versus **John is probable to win the race*. Lieven Vandelanotte and Kristin Davidse, in 'The Emergence and Structure of *Be Like* and Related Quotatives: A Constructional Account' (*CogLing* 20[2009] 777–807), argue that the syntactic structure of innovative quotatives such as *be like*, *be all*, and *go* in English contains a quotative/reporting clause (*I'm like*, *He went*) that takes the quoted clause as its complement. An van Linden and Kristin Davidse, in 'The Clausal Complementation Deontic-Evaluative Adjectives in Extraposition Constructions: A Synchronic-Diachronic Approach' (*FoLi* 43[2009]

171–211), show that importance-adjectives and appropriateness-adjectives in extraposition constructions had a common start as mandative complement-taking predicates and still show constructional analogy.

Susanna Lyne has chosen a long title for '*Her daughter's Being Taken into Care* or *Her Daughter Being Taken . . . ?*: Genitive and Common-Case Marking of Subjects of Verbal Gerund Clauses in Present-Day English' (in Nevalainen et al., eds., pp. 311–33). As a follow-up to her 2006 study of pronominal subjects of gerunds (see *YWES* 87[2008] 54) and drawing on data from the BNC, she shows that genitive marking of a non-pronominal subject is rare and virtually limited to formal texts. Within that register, the choice is partly determined by some of the well-known factors favouring use of the genitive in general (e.g. animacy and relative shortness of the NP). In 'This Construction Looks Like a Copy Is Optional' (*LingI* 40[2009] 343–6), Idan Landau compares the following two similar constructions, *Mary seems/looks/appears like/as if her job is going well* and *Sheryl thought about/of Tim that the police would never catch him*, concluding that they cannot be conflated and proposing that they have different predicate types. Glyn Hicks has studied an old chestnut, '*Tough*-Constructions and their Derivation' (*LingI* 40[2009] 535–66), but comes up with a new idea for the analysis of sentences like *John was tough to please*: first there is A-bar movement of a complex null operator (inside the infinitival clause) and then there is A-movement into the matrix surface position. Various recalcitrant problems surrounding this construction are argued to follow from this account.

We have seen little on non-argumental clauses. Göran Kjellmer, in 'Is There a Relative Adverb *There* in Modern English?' (*ES* 90[2009] 328–32), concludes on the basis of corpus and internet data that relative *there* in ModE (e.g. *A place there we wanted to eat*) seems to be used by '*some* speakers *some* of the time' (p. 332). Ivano Caponigro and Lisa Pearl argue for 'The Nominal Nature of *Where*, *When*, and *How*: Evidence from Free Relatives' (*LingI* 40[2009] 155–64). Their starting point is sentences like *Lily adores where/the place that this very tree grows* and *Lily napped where/in the place that this very tree grows*. After developing their analysis (in which these *wh*-elements are base-generated as complement to a preposition, which can be silent), they show that it can also be extended to interrogative clauses. That there are more relatives than one might suspect is argued by Boban Arsenijević in 'Clausal Complementation as Relativization' (*Lingua* 119[2009] 39–50). He argues that finite complement clauses of cognition and utterance verbs (e.g. *believe* and *ask* respectively) are best analysed as a special type of relative clause whose relativization site is the force projection. Liliane Haegeman's 'The Movement Analysis of Temporal Adverbial Clauses' (*ELL* 13[2009] 385–408) provides additional empirical evidence for this analysis, in which they are derived by *wh*-movement of an operator (e.g. *when*) to the left periphery.

We finish with various phenomena and processes at the clausal level. Pam Peters examines 'Patterns of Negation: The Relationship between NO and NOT in Regional Varieties of English' (in Nevalainen et al., eds., pp. 147–62). Usefully distinguishing between *no* used as a negative reply, as part of a fixed collocation (e.g. *no doubt, no idea*) and as a productive premodifier in a NP, she shows that, in BrE, AmE, AusE, and NZE corpus data, high levels of *no* (of all types) go together with high levels of *not*, casting doubt on the idea of direct competition between the two forms, and that the highest levels of productive *no* (and the lowest of formulaic *no*) are found in NZE, in particular in the register of fiction. Robert D. Borsley, 'On So-Called Transitive Expletives in Belfast English' (*ELL* 13[2009] 409–31), analyses sentences like *There shouldn't anybody say that* in terms of underspecified lexical descriptions, using the model of HPSG. In Belfast English, expletive *there* not only occurs in the extra lexical description of *be*, but also in that of modals and *have* (and *seem* and *likely*) (see also section 9 below). Elena Seoane, 'Syntactic Complexity, Discourse Status and Animacy as Determinants of Grammatical Variation in Modern English' (*ELL* 13[2009] 365–84), contradicts the widely held belief that animacy strongly influences the choice between active and (long) passive: Seoane's corpus results show that the choice of the long passive over the active is not determined by the relative animacy of the passive subject and the *by*-phrase.

In the introduction to the volume on dislocated elements that they have edited (from which we discussed the papers by Sobin and Newmeyer above), Benjamin Shaer, Philippa Cook, Werner Frey, and Claudia Maienborn discuss 'Dislocation: Concepts, Questions, Goals' (in Shaer et al., eds., pp. 1–27). They provide a useful review of the different types of preposing and postposing that have been distinguished, the theoretical issues that they raise for analyses of clausal structure, and the meanings that they convey, followed by a brief summary of the articles that follow. One of these is 'Periphery Effects and the Dynamics of Tree Growth' (pp. 141–70), where Ruth Kempson, Jieun Kiaer, and Ronnie Cann demonstrate how various types of dislocation in various languages including English can be analysed within the model of Dynamic Syntax, which aims to reflect the step-by-step process of tree construction as a sentence is being parsed. In 'Noncanonical Word Order and the Distribution of Inferable Information in English' (pp. 232–54), Betty Birner shows how the use of non-canonical word orders systematically correlates with the information status of elements, as expressed by the features hearer old/new and discourse old/new. She proposes that inferable information (derivable from relations like part-whole, type-subtype and spatial proximity) may represent the combination of hearer-new and discourse-old—though, as she acknowledges, further work is needed to establish what the explanatory benefits of this idea could be. In 'Fronted Quantificational Adverbs' (pp. 312–27; see also section 6 below), Ariel Cohen examines the interpretative difference between sentences like *Often a politician is crooked* and *A politician is often crooked*, interestingly linking it to the different intonation patterns for such fronted and non-fronted adverbs. A rather extreme form of dislocation would be when the relevant element is syntactically not part of the sentence in which it occurs. That this is possible is argued by Liliane Haegeman in 'Parenthetical Adverbials: The Radical Orphanage Approach (originally published in 1991, but reprinted in Shaer et al., eds., on pp. 331–47), who advances several pieces of evidence appearing to show that adverbial clauses as in *I've lost my money, if you want to know* are not linked with the syntactic structure of the matrix clause. In a 'Postscript: Problems and Solutions for Orphan Analyses' (pp. 348–65), Liliane Haegeman, Benjamin Shaer, and Werner Frey consider the way sequence of tenses, illocutionary subordination, and verb-second operate in such adverbial clauses, reaching the conclusion that these apparent problems for an orphan analysis can all be solved. Further detail on how the orphan analysis could work for left-dislocated elements is given by Benjamin Shaer in 'German and English Left-Peripheral Elements and the "Orphan" Analysis of Non-Integration' (pp. 366–97). After demonstrating in detail that such elements fail to interact syntactically with elements in the matrix clause, he sketches a model of how they are integrated in the sentence at the discourse level, using Segmented Discourse Representation Theory in doing so.

Klaus Fischer examines 'Cleft Sentences: Form, Function, and Translation' (*JGL* 21[2009] 167–91), comparing the frequencies, syntax, semantics, and stylistic properties of clefts in English and German and making the general point that full understanding can only be achieved if structural analysis is complemented with analysis at the level of parole. Andreea S. Calude and Steven Miller's squib 'Are Clefts Contagious in Conversation?' (*ELL* 13[2009] 127–32) presents corpus evidence (drawn from a corpus of conversation excerpts in NZE) that if one speaker uses a cleft, other speakers are likely to do so as well.

Niina Ning Zhang considers 'The Syntax of *Same* and ATB Constructions' (*CanJL* 54[2009] 367–99). After proposing an analysis of *same*, she argues that in sentences like *The same man Mary helped and John ruined*, the traditional assumption of across-the-board movement from both conjuncts is incorrect. Instead, she proposes that there is movement from the first conjunct only, the second conjunct containing a *pro* form. Kyle Johnson argues that 'Gapping is Not (VP-) Ellipsis' (*LingI* 40[2009] 289–328), though conceding that pseudo-gapping (as in *Some have served mussels to Sue while others have swordfish*) is. Gapping, however (as in *Some have served mussels to Sue and others swordfish*) is a special instance of across-the-board movement, for which he proposes a specific analysis.

Donna Jo Napoli and Jack Hoeksema, 'The Grammatical Versatility of Taboo Terms' (*SLang* 33[2009] 612–43; see also *YWES* 89[2010] 57), argue that the grammar recognizes taboo terms by their pragmatic import, since they easily occur in different syntactic contexts, despite having a disparate semantics. In 'Scope Inversion' (*UCWPL* 21[2009] 261–305), Ad Neeleman and Hans van de Koot make two claims: one is that LF encodes where scope relations diverge from surface scope (rather than being a full representation of scope), the other is that whereas overt scope-shifting involves movement, covert scope-shifting involves percolation of a scope-marking index.

(b) Early Syntax

Paola Crisma and Giuseppe Longobardi have edited *Historical Syntax and Linguistic Theory*, a collection of articles based on talks given at the ninth DiGS conference, held in 2006. In their introduction, 'Change, Relatedness, and Inertia in Historical Syntax' (pp. 1–13), the editors sketch the implications for historical change of the notions E-language and I-language (one of them being that languages may be expected to be rather stable, or 'inert'), and provide an overview of what historical syntax can and should do. We review in this subsection those articles directly analysing English data but would recommend reading of the entire volume to those wishing to stay abreast of recent generative thinking about syntactic change. Elly van Gelderen's chapter, 'Feature Economy in the Linguistic Cycle' (pp. 93–109), advances the idea that formal economy can lead to change; examples come from changes in relative markers in ME and the development of *after* into a subordinator (from fronted PP *after that*, in which *that* had a rather bland and generalized meaning). We also note the same author's related piece on 'Renewal in the Left Periphery: Economy and the Complementiser Layer' (*TPS* 107[2009] 131–95), where she shows how elements that are frequently fronted, such as *wh*-items or certain adverbials, can be subsequently reinterpreted as being in COMP, through principles like 'head preference'. Among the examples dealt with here is the development of the words *whether* (from argument to complementizer) and *that* (from demonstrative to complementizer).

If we take the title of this subsection, Early Syntax, literally, there is also a need for us to report on work done in the field of language evolution. Twenty-three papers dealing with this topic, but also with the nature of language and its connections with other mental capacities in humans and animals, are found in the volume *Of Minds and Language: A Dialogue with Noam Chomsky in the Basque Country*, edited by Massimo Piattelli-Palmarini, Juan Uriagereka, and Pello Salaburu. Two of the papers are by Chomsky himself, the 'Opening Remarks' (pp. 13–43), in which he sketches the antecedents and development of the Minimalist Program, and the 'Conclusion' (pp. 379–409), in which he responds to and makes connections between many of the ideas put forward in the other papers. These other papers are all written by people with an interest in biolinguistics, working in the fields of cognitive biology, evolution theory, brain science, and of course linguistics; among the linguists contributing are Cedric Boeckx, Wolfram Hinzen, James Higginbotham, Luigi Rizzi, Juan Uriagereka, Lila Gleitman, Janet Dean Fodor, Thomas Bever, and Itziar Laka. Since much of the material is programmatic and searching rather than argumentative, and also goes well beyond the boundaries of narrow syntax, it is not possible here to summarize the individual articles. But we can say that together they form a rich collection of work being carried out at the frontiers of understanding in this area. Technical detail is eschewed as much as possible, reflecting the origins of most of the papers in oral presentations for a fairly mixed audience, and all papers contain a (slightly edited) transcription of the ensuing discussion.

On the topic of early language in Africa, there is *The Cradle of Language*, edited by Rudolf Botha and Chris Knight, which explores all kinds of aspects of the emergence of human language some 200,000 years ago. As a consequence, a wide variety of subjects is addressed, with many of the papers focusing on fossil, genetic, and archaeological data and their relevance for language origin. Of the more syntacticky papers, we mention Rudolf Botha's 'Theoretical Underpinnings of Inferences about Language Evolution: The Syntax Used at Blombos Cave' (pp. 93–111), which cautions against speculative conclusions about early syntax on the basis of early artefacts; James Hurford and Dan Dediu's 'Diversity in Languages, Genes, and the

Language Faculty' (pp. 167–88), which cautions against the common assumption that language arose through one single event, at one time, in one place; Michael Cysouw and Bernard Comrie's 'How Varied Typologically are the Languages of Africa?', which uses data from the World Atlas of Language Structures to show that it is not possible (yet) to demonstrate deep chronological layering by examining present-day typological characteristics of languages, partly because of the apparent ease with which such features can diffuse across space.

Volume 2 of *Creating and Digitizing Language Corpora*, edited by Joan Beal, Karen Corrigan, and Hermann Moisl, is devoted to *Diachronic Databases*. After an introduction by the editors (pp. 1–15), nine newly created corpora with a historical dimension are described, eight of them being focused on English. Will Allen, Joan Beal, Karen Corrigan, Warren Maguire, and Hermann Moisl describe 'A Linguistic "Time Capsule": The Newcastle Electronic Corpus of Tyneside English' (pp. 16–48), in which are amalgamated the materials from the Tyneside Linguistic Survey of the 1960s–1970s and the Phonological Variation and Change materials from the 1990s, resulting in a geographically well delimited corpus with historical depth (generally known now among socio- and geo-linguists by the affectionate name NECTE). Another non-conventional corpus is described by Susan Fitzmaurice in 'Questions of Standardization and Representativeness in the Development of Social Networks-Based Corpora: The Story of the Network of Eighteenth-Century English Texts' (pp. 49–81). Since inclusion of texts is based on the criterion of the author having had social connections with Joseph Addison, this is an ideal resource for detailed study of the social network-language relation in this period. Elizabeth Gordon, Margaret Maclagan, and Jennifer Haye's 'The ONZE Corpus' (pp. 82–104) is about the Origins of New Zealand English Corpus, which—again through amalgamation of materials from diverse sources—contains recordings from 1946 onwards. Raymond Hickey contributes 'Tracking Dialect History: A Corpus of Irish English' (pp. 105–26), a searchable digital collection of some ninety, mainly literary, texts written in Irish English from the early fourteenth century to the twentieth. For Scottish, there is now 'The Manuscript-Based Diachronic Corpus of Scottish Correspondence' (CSC; pp. 127–47), a 500,000-word corpus covering the period 1400–1800, created and described here by Anneli Meurman-Solin. In 'Historical Sociolinguistics: The Corpus of Early English Correspondence' (pp. 148–71), Helena Raumolin-Brunberg and Terttu Nevalainen describe the work of their team on the original 2.7 million-word correspondence corpus (created in the 1990s; covering the period 1410–1680) and some of the extensions that they are working on now. The latter include a fully parsed version of the corpus using similar methodology as in 'The York-Toronto-Helsinki Parsed Corpus of Old English Prose', described by Ann Taylor (pp. 196–227). This 1.5 million-word fully annotated corpus contains all OE prose texts that are of syntactic interest (so excluding very short, list-like, and similar materials). With the materials that already exist for ME and EModE, and further work in progress, the historical syntax of English is thus receiving yet another strong boost. In the same spirit, we welcome Linda van Bergen and David Denison's 'A Corpus of Late

Eighteenth-Century Prose' (pp. 228–46). Bridging part of the gap between the Helsinki and Brown families of corpora, the corpus contains about 300,000 words of unpublished letters from the period 1760–1790.

We also welcome yet another introduction to the history of English this year: Dan McIntyre's *History of English: A Resource Book for Students*. The work has four sections: one dealing with the external history of English (i.e. the various invasions and their linguistic consequences, dialect divisions, processes of standardization, the spread of English, etc.); one describing the linguistic properties of the language at its various stages (including the basics of OE and ME spelling and pronunciation, OE grammar, changes in vocabulary, some changes in pronunciation and grammar, properties of New Englishes, etc.; for the latter see also section 9 below); one entitled 'Exploration', which contains exercises involving (short) texts, sets of words, or sentences, interspersed with some further explanation of linguistic processes; and a final section containing nine pieces of further reading on a variety of topics (four to eight pages long), taken from introductory works on (English) historical linguistics, all briefly introduced and followed by some questions for discussion. The book also has a brief glossary and some annotated suggestions for further study. Altogether, this looks to us like a useful addition to the range of materials now available for first-year modules on the subject. It assumes little or no prior knowledge in the reader—thus, a description of the Great Vowel Shift is preceded by a three-page explanation of basic phonetics (pp. 54–7). However, that section is immediately followed by some discussion of the uniformitarian principle, as applied not only to linguistic but also to sociolinguistic processes and phenomena. The material is presented in a way that should make it accessible to all students, and there is enough of it to ensure that they will emerge from the book with a decent knowledge of the basic facts in the history of English and a good awareness of how processes of linguistic change relate to changes in society. It may also be useful to mention here Eric Haeberli's 'Histories of English' (*Diachronica* 26[2009] 103–16), a review of three general histories of English published in 2006, containing valuable general reflection on this type of work.

Jeremy Smith's *Old English: A Linguistic Introduction* does exactly and professionally what it says in the title. After providing some (pre–)historical background to the emergence of English, the author gives a basic description of phonetic, syntactic, and morphological concepts, as applicable to OE; an introduction to the properties of OE using a passage from the *Dream of the Rood*; an account of the spellings and sounds of OE; a chapter on the OE lexicon; one on OE syntax; and one on inflexional morphology. Each chapter has a few exercises and there are several texts, with notes, to apply the knowledge acquired. The overall approach is traditional and the work should appeal to both teachers and students.

Moving further on, we were happy to see that there is now also an Edinburgh textbook on the most recent historical period: Ingrid Tieken-Boon van Ostade's *An Introduction to Late Modern English* (already briefly discussed above in section 2). As the author writes in her introductory note, 'Late Modern English (1700–1900) is currently receiving a lot of scholarly attention' (p. ix). Her textbook is therefore a welcome introduction to the language of the

Georgian, Regency, and Victorian periods. Chapter 1 provides a general introduction to the language of the lModE period, which is shown to be unstable and not a uniform variety, despite the fact that lModE comes at the end of the standardization process and despite the influence of prescriptivism. The variable and unstable nature of lModE is illustrated in the chapters that follow. Chapter 2 focuses on pronunciation, discussing evidence of how people spoke in the lModE period and showing that there was a rise of a prestigious form of speech in the course of the nineteenth century. Chapter 3 concentrates on spelling and demonstrates that there were two spelling systems (public and private) in the eighteenth century, which by the end of this century had merged. Chapter 4 makes use of the *OED* to trace developments in the lModE lexicon triggered by new developments in science, culture, and technology. Chapter 5 discusses the relationship between actual usage and the grammatical norms formulated by grammarians and enforced by prescriptivists. Chapter 6 applies the social network model to a number of lModE networks, clarifying linguistic changes and the language of women, which is often closer to the standard than that of men. Chapter 7 looks at a number of different lModE text types, including letters, journals, wills, and recipes, stressing the importance of studying the specific language of different text types, as it can illuminate the complex linguistic developments that took place in the lModE period. Each chapter concludes with helpful suggestions for further reading as well as a set of research questions, which will steer students of lModE in the direction of interesting research topics and will guide them through the increasing number of tools and resources for this period of English.

And there is more for lModE from Ingrid Tieken-Boon van Ostade: together with Wim van der Wurff she has edited the volume *Current Issues in Late Modern English*, which contains papers from the Third Late Modern English conference (3LModE). The editors' introduction, 'Papers from 3LModE: An Introduction' (pp. 9–31), provides a brief history of work on late Modern English and presents an overview of the papers included in the volume. The third part of the volume ('Studies in Grammar and Lexis') contains two papers on grammatical issues. The first of these is Günter Rohdenburg's paper 'Grammatical Divergence between British and American English in the Nineteenth and Early Twentieth Centuries' (pp. 301–329), which 'surveys a number of largely neglected grammatical changes involving the areas of nominal and sentential complementation' (p. 301). Rohdenburg finds no evidence for colonial lag: British and American English share the same set of developments, and there is a tendency towards the use of simpler variants, which is more advanced in American English than in British English. The second paper in 'Studies in Grammar and Lexis' to deal with grammar is Svenja Kranich's paper 'Interpretative Progressives in Late Modern English' (pp. 331–357), which investigates a function of the progressive that became more common in the course of the Late Modern English period, namely the function of marking a subjective interpretation of the speaker. In the fourth part of the volume ('Studies on Letters'), we come across Tony Fairman's paper *She has Four and Big Agane: Ellipses and Prostheses in Mechanically Schooled Writing in England, 1795–1834* (pp. 409–429), which discusses the question of whether writers apply ellipsis or prosthesis and why they make a particular choice, focusing on non-finite and verbless clauses. For several of the other papers in this volume, see section 2.

Tim William Machan's *Language Anxiety: Conflict and Change in the History of English* does in-depth sociohistorical linguistics without counting. Its main thesis is that anxiety about language, language choice, and language change always goes hand in hand with—and often displaces—anxiety about issues other than language, such as social relations, politics, religion, and the economy. The first chapter sketches the general framework; chapter 2 surveys a number of prominent changes in the history of English and the social meanings that have been attached to them; chapter 3 discusses the way language change has been represented in myth and in literature, with the Tower of Babel looming large but lesser-known ideologies also popping up, such as those associated with the creation of artificial languages like Esperanto and, our personal favourite, Volapük; chapter 4 examines how governments have responded to contact between English and other languages; chapter 5 deals with standardization and codification, through grammars and dictionaries, of different varieties of English; and chapter 6 is a summing up, advocating that social, political, or economic anxieties should trigger examination of the real issues rather than being displaced towards language. This is an impressive book making a persuasive case, with a wealth of evidence being presented from many domains.

The extent and nature of Celtic influence in the shaping of English is fully discussed in *English and Celtic in Contact* by Markku Filppula, Juhani Klemola, and Heli Paulasto. The authors review a great deal of earlier work, provide new data, and propose new analyses for well-known data. Part I focuses on Celtic influence in medieval English, first outlining the historical background of the contact situation and then considering possible cases of Celtic influence on English in this period. The cases are mainly grammatical in nature (involving, for example, the use of the possessive pronoun to express inalienable possession, the difference between the *b*-forms and the *s*-forms of the verb *to be* in OE, the northern subject rule, the emergence of periphrastic *do* and rise of the progressive). Part II focuses on the modern age, i.e. on the special features of the various regional Celtic Englishes that may be due to the Celtic substratum. Among the syntactic features discussed here are the use of the definite article, the form and meaning of the perfect, inversion in indirect questions, and the use of focusing constructions. Overall, the authors clearly favour Celtic explanations for historical developments in English, but this does not prevent them from setting out all the evidence and the different views that can be and have been taken. We feel this is a timely publication, which provides a state-of-the-art report on a topic on which a great amount of work has been done but which is seldom discussed systematically in general works on the history of English. There is also an *English Language and Linguistics* special issue on 'Re-evaluating the Celtic hypothesis' (*ELL* 13[2009]). The details of this, and of further work on this topic, are discussed in section 9 below.

Since it contains numerous diachronic observations, we also discuss here *One Language, Two Grammars? Differences between British and American English*, edited by Günter Rohdenburg and Julia Schlüter, which is a collection of papers on syntactic and morphological differences between BrE and AmE. The focus of comparative studies of BrE and AmE has often been on differences in pronunciation and vocabulary, underestimating grammatical differences ('accent divides, syntax unites'). In their introduction (pp. 1–12), the editors recognize that the grammars of BrE and AmE 'differ in many more ways than have so far been discovered' (p. 1). They point out that the availability of large computerized corpora allows for a much better systematic comparison of BrE and AmE than was hitherto possible. The papers included in the volume are strongly data-driven and study a range of examples of immediately competing grammatical alternatives. The programmatic chapter 1 (pp. 13–37), by Marianne Hundt, demonstrates that long-term diachronic changes in BrE and AmE cannot simply be reduced to the dichotomy 'colonial lag' vs. 'colonial innovation'. Chapter 2 (pp. 38–59), by Peter Erdmann, shows that compound verbs such as *to baby-sit* and *to pinpoint* are more productive in AmE than in BrE. In chapter 3 (pp. 60–85), Magnus Levin shows that the regularization of preterite and past participle forms (e.g. *burned* vs. *burnt*) has progressed considerably further in AmE than in BrE, the latter showing more variation between the regular and irregular forms. Chapter 4 (pp. 86–107), by Britta Mondorf, shows that AmE uses more analytic comparative adjectives than BrE, and overall uses fewer comparatives (synthetic and analytic) than BrE (see also section 4 above). In chapter 5 (pp. 108–129), Julia Schlüter shows that the Principle of Rhythmic Alternation determines the choice between past participle variants (e.g. *lighted* vs. *lit*) and between pre- and post-determiner position of *quite* in BrE as well as in AmE. Chapter 6 (pp. 130–148), by Eva Berlage, discusses the influence of functional constraints on the distribution and historical development of pre- and postpositional *notwithstanding* in BrE and AmE. In chapter 7 (pp. 149–165), David Denison focuses on the patterns *substitute* NEW *for* OLD (standard pattern) and *substitute* OLD *with* NEW (*replace*-like pattern), and the recent British usage *substitute* OLD *for* NEW. Chapter 8 (pp. 166–181), by Günter Rohdenburg, demonstrates that the tendency for reflexive verb uses (e.g. *to shave oneself*) to be replaced by non-reflexive uses (e.g. *to shave*), attested in BrE and AmE, is accelerated in AmE. In chapter 9 (pp. 182–193), Douglas Biber, Jack Grieve, and Gina Iberri-Shea investigate diachronic trends in the structure of NPs in BrE and AmE. Chapter 10 (pp. 194–211), by Günter Rohdenburg, describes a number of British–American contrasts in the area of nominal (and prepositional) complementation. Chapter 11 (pp. 212–227), by Uwe Vosberg, explores differences between BrE and AmE in the distribution of *to*-infinitival complements and *–ing* complements. In chapter 12 (pp. 228–245), Johan Elsness shows that the decline of the present perfect (and the rise of the preterite) has progressed further in AmE than in BrE. Chapters 13–15, by Göran Kjellmer (pp. 246–256), William Crawford (pp. 257–276), and Julia Schlüter (pp. 277–305) respectively, focus on the use of the subjunctive in English. Chapter 16 (pp. 306–323), by D.J. Allerton, investigates the structure, functions and frequencies of different types of tag-questions in BrE and AmE. In chapter 17 (pp. 324–340), Karin Aijmer focuses on the use of the adverb *sure* in AmE, where it is much more frequent than in BrE. Chapter 18 (pp. 341–363) is another programmatic chapter in which Gunnel Tottie advances further cases showing that the grammatical differences between BrE and AmE are greater than previously thought. Chapter 19 (pp. 364–423), by the editors, provides an outlook in the form of over forty pilot studies of different grammatical phenomena that show divergent usage in BrE and AmE.

We now turn to individual elements of the clause, beginning with nominals. Rhona Alcorn, in 'Grammatical Person and the Variable Syntax of Old English Personal Pronouns' (*ELL* 13[2009] 433–51), shows that the special placement of OE personal pronouns to the left of the governing preposition correlates with narrative mode and positioning of the preposition relative to the main verb. Juan Kristin Davidse contributes '*Complete* and *Sort of*: From Identifying to Intensifying?' (*TPS* 107[2009] 262–92), studying the development of these two items from ME onwards. *Contra* suggestions in earlier work, she finds that they have acquired intensifying meaning through different routes, with *complete* going from descriptive to emphasizing and *sort of* from quantifying to intensifying. Victorina González-Díaz examines 'Little Old Problems: Adjectives and Subjectivity in the English NP' (*TPS* 107[2009] 376–402), comparing the ways in which the adjectives *little* and *old* have over time acquired subjective-affective meanings and the relation between such meanings and position (leftmost or rightmost in the premodifying string). Tine Breban, 'Structural Persistence: A Case Based on the Grammaticalization of English Adjectives of Difference' (*ELL* 13[2009] 77–96), argues on the basis of a case study into the development of adjectives of difference (e.g. *other*, *different*, *various*) that grammaticalization processes involve, apart from lexical persistence, structural persistence as well. Benedikt Szmrecsanyi and Lars Hinrichs have investigated 'Probabilistic Determinants of Genitive Variation in Spoken and Written English: A Multivariate Comparison across Time, Space, and Genres' (in Nevalainen et al., eds., pp. 291–309). Using various AmEng and BrEng corpora, the authors find that, since the 1960s, the *s*-genitive has increased in frequency in written news texts, making this register similar to spoken English. However, they go on to show that the factors determining the choice between genitive and *of*-phrase (such as possessor animacy and thematicity) have very different strengths in the two registers, suggesting that the diachronic change in newspaper English is not one of colloquialization but one of economization, with journalists increasingly striving to create compact NPs and hence using genitives rather than *of*-phrases. Edward Keenan has written 'Linguistic Theory and the Historical Creation of English Reflexives' (in Crisma and Longobardi, eds., pp. 17–40). He explains the gradual obligatorification of the *self*-forms to denote reflexivity by appealing to several general principles, including inertia (seen, for example, in the continuation of possessive *his own* even after *self* had spread to other reflexive contexts), decay (of the contrastive meaning originally expressed by *self*) and anti-synonymy (causing *him* and *himself* to become subject to different licensing requirements). Changes in the determiner system are addressed in Akira Watanabe's 'A Parametric Shift in the D-System in Early Middle English: Relativization, Articles, Adjectival Inflection, and Indeterminates' (in Crisma and Longobardi, eds., pp. 358–74). It is argued that certain D-features went from being formal to semantic in ME; from this, the following changes are derived: the end to the use of *wh*-forms to express indeterminate meaning (as in OE *gehwa* 'every'); the loss of *swa*-relatives (as in OE *swa hwylce swa* 'whichever'); and the loss of the relative use of the demonstratives.

Kiriko Sato's study *The Development from Case-Forms to Prepositional Constructions in Old English Prose* aims to answer the question of whether there was a significant change in the use of case forms, on the one hand, and of prepositional constructions, on the other, in contexts where both types were possible. To this end, Sato examines early OE prose texts (*Parker Chronicle*, Boethius' *Consolation of Philosophy*, and *Bede's Ecclesiastical History of the English People*) and later OE prose texts (Ælfric's *Catholic Homilies*, Ælfric's *Lives of the Saints*, and Wulfstan's *Homilies*). For each of these six prose texts, discussed in chapters 1–6, Sato investigates the chronological development of the functions for which case forms and prepositional constructions overlapped in OE: (1) instrumentality/manner, (2) accompaniment, (3) point of time, (4) duration of time, (5) origin, (6) specification, and (7) dative absolute constructions. She also considers stylistic factors, such as preferences of individual authors and Latin influence and rhythm. In chapter 7, Sato summarizes her findings, which are that case forms and prepositional constructions are competing with each other in early OE (with case forms being slightly more frequent than prepositional constructions in this period), and that case forms are becoming much less common in later OE, where prepositional constructions predominate. In parallel with this general tendency, prepositional constructions increase in proportion for the first five functions (instrumentality/manner, accompaniment, point of time, duration of time, and origin). In a number of the texts studied, stylistic factors, especially Latin influence, were also found to play a role in the choice between case forms and prepositional constructions.

There are several items in the area of tense, mood, aspect, and auxiliaries. Anita Auer has investigated *The Subjunctive in the Age of Prescriptivism*. Using the ARCHER corpus and a self-compiled corpus of poetry, she is able to show that, after a decline in the seventeenth century, the subjunctive became more prominent again in English in the second half of the eighteenth century and the beginning of the nineteenth century, especially in stylistically more elevated texts. On the basis of a study of what English grammars of the period have to say about the subjunctive, she suggests that this reversal may be due to grammars advocating use of the subjunctive—even though its exact meaning and distribution is not always fully grasped. Auer relates these findings to the ongoing process of standardization, viewed as in Einar Haugen's well-known model involving the selection, codification, elaboration, and acceptance of norms (see also section 2 above).

Marianne Hundt and Nicholas Smith, 'The Present Perfect in British and American English: Has There Been any Change, Recently?' (*ICAME* 33[2009] 45–64), present corpus evidence that the present perfect has decreased somewhat (in favour of the simple past) in BrE as well as AmE, suggesting 'relatively stable regional variation rather than ongoing change' (p. 57). Göran Kjellmer, 'On the Old English Nonoccurring Auxiliary' (*SN* 81[2009] 24–32), suggests that the phenomenon of a 'non-occurring' auxiliary in OE ((*beon*/*weorðan*/*habban*) + participle) is a manifestation of a more general Germanic tendency made possible by various contextual factors. Mark Sundaram, in 'Anterior Future Constructions and the Structure of Old English Narratives' (*NM* 110[2009] 267–81), shows that anterior future constructions in OE (notably the preterite forms of the modals *willan* and **sculan*) play a role in structuring narratives, controlling tempo, rhythm and other expressive effects, and as such function as important pragmatic markers.

Developments affecting *have* are studied in Heidi Quinn's 'Downward Reanalysis and the Rise of Stative HAVE *got*' (in Crisma and Longobardi, eds., pp. 212–30). Quinn argues that stative *have*, as in *They have one horse*, was originally a functional element (just like *be*), but was then re-analysed as a lexical verb which underwent movement to a functional head; the word *got* is a spelled-out copy of moved *have*. Peter Petré and Hubert Cuykens develop an account for the loss of OE *weorðan* in 'Constructional Change in Old and Middle English Copular Constructions and its Impact on the Lexicon' (*FLH* 30[2009] 311–66). Using a Radical Construction Grammar framework, they first describe the typical complement of this verb as denoting a property that is unstable in time. When the *be*-passive became fully grammaticalized in English, a growing split took place between resultatives and property-ascribing constructions. However, *weorðan* persisted in its established patterns, where the two were not differentiated. Hence it started sounding archaic and declined. This case, the authors argue, therefore provides an illustration of how changes in higher-level schemata can force a concrete verb to either adapt its patterning (going along with the change) or lose out (as happened to *weorðan*). Dirk Noël and Johan van der Auwera, in 'Revisiting *be supposed to* from a Diachronic Constructionist Perspective' (*ES* 90[2009] 599–623), show that the diachronic origin of deontic *be supposed to*, which they consider to be an evidential nominative and infinitive (NCI) construction, is a passive of volitive/deontic *suppose*, arguing in favour of a developmental path volition > obligation. Lucía Loureiro-Porto writes 'More on the Idiosyncrasy of Dan Michel's *Ayenbite of Inwit*: *Behove* as a (Modal) Verb of Necessity' (*FLH* 30[2009] 247–69). She shows that the very high frequency of *behove*, in the basic meaning 'need', in this fourteenth-century work is unparalleled elsewhere. Not unexpectedly given its high frequency, it shows some signs of incipient grammaticalization (as seen in its frequent use with a bare infinitive). Its heavy use is not due to lack of other words with the required senses and sub-senses because, semantically, it overlaps with *need* and *tharf*. The author instead suggests that there may have been direct or indirect influence from Dutch, whose cognate *hoeven* is frequent and has the same meaning as English *behove*. Failure of subject–verb agreement is the topic of Kleanthes Grohmann and Richard Ingham's 'Expletive *pro* and Misagreement in Late Middle English' (in Crisma and Longobardi, eds., pp. 311–28). The phenomena they try to explain are the occurrence in late ME of sentences like *There are three men* alongside *There is three men*, as well as sentences lacking expletive *it* (as in *This year was ordained that*...). Their account postulates the existence in late ME of an empty singular expletive *pro*[3sg], introduced when it became obligatory to project [Spec,TP].

On complements, Inés Lareo and Isabel Moskowich consider '*Make* plus Adjective in Eighteenth-Century Science and Fiction: Some Issues Made

Public' (*ES* 90[2009] 345–62), showing that complex predicates of the type *make* + adjective are more frequently employed by eighteenth-century fiction writers than by eighteenth-century science writers, which suggests, as expected, that these collocations are more commonly used in colloquial language. Inés Lareo on her own has looked at '*Make*-Collocations in Nineteenth-Century Scientific English' (*SN* 81[2009] 1–16), exploring the (frequent) use of *make*-collocations with nouns (e.g. *make a profit*) and presenting a semantic and syntactic analysis of corpus data.

Erik Smitterberg contributes 'The Progressive and Phrasal Verbs: Evidence of Colloquialization in Nineteenth-Century English?' (in Nevalainen et al., eds., pp. 269–89). Data show a split between informal, speech-based registers and more literate ones, with the latter being stable over time but the former showing an increase in the frequency of progressives and phrasal verbs. Smitterberg concludes from this that the process of colloquialization, posited to explain certain late twentieth-century developments (including the continued rise of progressives and phrasal verbs), was already operative in the nineteenth century. Kiriko Sato, 'The Absolute Participle Construction in Old English: Ælfric's Exploitation of the Latinate Syntax in his Vernacular Prose' (*ES* 90[2009] 2–16), argues that Ælfric's use of the absolute participle should be regarded as an adaptation of Latin syntax, rather than as a literal translation, as is the case for literally translated texts.

On adverbs, there is Tine Defour's '"*And so now*...": The Grammaticalisation and (Inter)Subjectification of *Now*' (in Nevalainen et al., eds., pp. 17–36), which traces how the word *now* developed from temporal to textual and (inter)personal marker in texts from the OE period up to the eighteenth century. She notes that its propositional meaning made it an ideal candidate for such processes of grammaticalization and subjectification, which already started in the earliest materials. In 'Multal Adverbs in Nineteenth-Century English' (*SN* 81[2009] 121–44), Erik Smitterberg examines how the distribution of different types of multal adverbs (e.g. *a great deal*) in nineteenth-century English is influenced by extra-linguistic and linguistic factors (such as gender of the writer and the construction modified by the multal adverb respectively).

Complex sentences have inspired several items. Cristina Suárez-Gómez, 'On the Syntactic Differences between OE Dialects: Evidence from the Gospels' (*ELL* 13[2009] 57–75), examines the existence of variation in the syntax of relative constructions in three versions of the Gospels from late OE, representing West Saxon, Northumbrian, and Mercian dialects, focusing on the distribution of relativizers and the position of the relative clause. In 'Pressing *-Ing* into Service: *I don't want you coming around here any more*' (in Nevalainen et al., eds., pp. 85–97), Michael Wherrity and Solveig Granath investigate the recent rise in frequency of the verb *want* followed by an *ing*-clause. Using data from the *Guardian–Observer* archive for the period 1990–2004, they show that this usage has undergone a 50 per cent increase, mainly in negative clauses and performing a number of pragmatic functions, all deriving from its basic meaning of expressing ongoing action in a vivid manner. Kristin Killie and Toril Swan, in 'The Grammaticalization and Subjectification of Adverbial *–ing* Clauses (Converb Clauses) in English' (*ELL*

13[2009] 337–63), make the controversial claim that the development of converb clauses, which are argued to have emerged from reinterpretation and from participial relative clauses, is an instance of grammaticalization.

Junichi Toyota, 'Fossilisation of Passive in English: Analysis of Passive Verbs' (*ES* 90[2009] 476–97), looks at the synchronic and diachronic grammatical characteristics of the 'passive verbs' *aggrieve*, *cloister*, *repute*, and *re-incarnate*, which among other things tend to have an animate subject, whereas the subject of a normal passive tends to be inanimate. Anne Breitbarth, 'A Hybrid Approach to Jespersen's Cycle in West Germanic' (*JCGL* 12[2009] 81–114), proposes that the change from Stage I (*ne* V) to Stage II (*ne* V *not*) of Jespersen's cycle in West Germanic is the result of a shift in the licensing conditions of *n*-indefinites (e.g. *no one*). Gunnel Tottie and Sebastian Hoffmann's 'Tag Questions in English: The First Century' (*JEngL* 37[2009] 130–61) argues that the rise of the single sentence negator *not* is the most important factor in the emergence of canonical tag questions (e.g. *It is cold, isn't it?*) in the sixteenth century.

And then there was word order. In 'Many Small Catastrophes: Gradualism in a Microparametric Perspective' (in Crisma and Longobardi, eds., pp. 75–90), Marit Westergaard sheds light on the loss of verb-second in ME by presenting data from dialects of Norwegian. In those, verb-second appears to be variable, but close analysis reveals that there are in fact categorical rules, relating to the nature of the subject, the verb, and the initial element. Hence what looks like free variation actually results from the setting of various micro-parameters. In a closely related piece, 'Word Order in Old and Middle English: The Role of Information Structure and First Language Acquisition' (*Diachronica* 26[2009] 65–102), the same author considers the OE and ME loss of verb-second in more detail, arguing that it is indeed possible to distinguish several successive verb-second grammars, slightly differing from each other in the nature of their fronting operations. Bettelou Los, 'The Consequences of the Loss of Verb-Second in English: Information Structure and Syntax in Interaction' (*ELL* 13[2009] 97–125), shows that the loss of verb-second in ME, resulting in a rigid subject-verb-object syntax, disrupted information structure, and argues that syntax and information structure are autonomous, because the syntactic change ran its course despite 'the havoc caused at the I[nformation]S[tructure] level' (p. 98).

The ME change from OV to VO order features prominently in 'The Return of the Subset Principle' by Theresa Biberauer and Ian Roberts (in Crisma and Longobardi, eds., pp. 58–74). They argue that, with empirical evidence for certain subtypes of OV order becoming less robust, the subset principle would lead to the abandonment, firstly, of the option of VP-pied-piping (which, roughly speaking, had produced OXV orders) and, subsequently, of the option of fronting objects that were not negative. In both cases there was a change from a wider grammar to a narrower one (from OV + OXV to only OV; and from OV with all Os to OV with negative Os only), making it indeed likely that the subset principle played some role in the development. Javier Pérez-Guerra and David Tizón-Couto write 'On Left Dislocation in the Recent History of English: Theory and Data Hand in Hand' (in Shaer et al., eds., pp. 31–48). Using corpus data, they show that the frequency of sentences such as *This paper, I have not checked it yet* has declined drastically since the late ME period, thus confirming the idea that (written) English has come to favour syntactic integration of clausal elements. They also report that left-dislocated elements tend to be long (seven to eight words on average), their use thus going against the principle of end-weight.

6. Semantics

Mouton's new series, The Expression of Cognitive Categories, which is concerned with the ways some of the very basic cognitive categories are expressed in various human languages, intended primarily for students and non-experts in the relevant fields, continued with two new volumes in 2009. In the first one, *The Expression of Possession*, edited by William McGregor, the possessive relation is defined as a 'relational concept that potentially covers a wide range of conceptual relations between entities, including, for human beings, between persons and their body-parts and products, between persons and their kin, between persons and their representations . . . between persons and their material belongings, between persons and things that they have usership-rights to or control over, between persons and cultural and intellectual products, and so on' (p. 1). Unfortunately, the contributions to this volume fail to represent the variety of perspectives that made the first volume of the series so useful for the intended audience. The very brief introduction by the editor is restricted to providing basic definitions (for example the list of the three general types of possessive constructions, attributive, predicative, external, that can be found in human languages), and overviews of the rest of the papers, all empirical studies on various languages. Among the contributions with relevance to English, 'English Possessives as Reference-Point Constructions and their Function in the Discourse' (pp. 13–50), by Peter Willemse, Kristin Davidse and Liesbet Heyvaert, argues that a binary distinction between considering possessum referents of possessive NPs in English as *given* vs. *new* does not capture their discourse status, and proposes to introduce a continuum of discourse statuses. Jan Rijkhoff, 'On the Co-Variation between Form and Function of Adnominal Possessive Modifiers in Dutch and English' (pp. 51–106), looks at adnominal possessive modifiers of common nouns denoting concrete objects introduced by *van* 'of' in Dutch and *of* in English, analyses the functions of these possessives within his layered model of the NP (Rijkhoff 2002), and describes the grammatical parameters with respect to which adnominal possessives vary, concluding that the constructions do not serve a unique modifying function in either language.

The editors of the second title in the series, *The Expression of Time*, Wolfgang Klein and Ping Li, have managed to find the right balance between papers concerned with the theoretical modelling of the expression of time in natural language and case studies based on empirical investigations. The chapter 'Concepts of Time' (pp. 5–38), written by the first editor, reviews some of the most important notions of time in philosophy, physics, biology, psychology, culture, and language, three recurrent themes in talking about time (i.e. the relation between time and change, the units of time, the relation of time and the observer), while also reviewing the properties of the basic time structure used in the expression of temporal relations (normally expressed by grammatical categories and simple adverbs) and their extensions into more differentiated time structures. The section 'How Time is Encoded' (pp. 39–81), also the work of Wolfgang Klein, reviews the most important properties of six of the most widespread devices human languages use to encode time in natural language: tense, (grammatical) aspect, *Aktionsarten* (lexical aspect), temporal adverbials, particles, and discourse principles, pointing out some problems with traditional definitions and making suggestions for their amendment. A further important contribution to the volume, 'Tenses in Compositional Semantics' (pp. 129–66), by Arnim von Stechow, explains how the interpretation of tense and aspect is captured in formal semantic theories. The remaining papers represent the empirical strand: Jürgen Bohnemeyer, 'Temporal Anaphora in a Tenseless Language' (pp. 83–128), reviews the means by which time is expressed in a tenseless language (Yucatec Maya); Yasuhiro Shirai addresses the question of how the expression of temporality is acquired ('Temporality in First and Second Language Acquisition', pp. 167–93); Christiane von Stutterheim, Mary Carroll, and Wolfgang Klein discuss 'New Perspectives in Analyzing Aspectual Distinctions' (pp. 195–216), based on experimental data; and Carol J. Madden and Todd R. Ferretti report on a study of the contribution of verb aspect to the representation of situations with psycholinguistic methods ('Verb Aspect and Situation Representation', pp. 217–40). The volume closes with a paper illustrating yet another perspective from which expressions of temporality can be studied: Ping Li and Xiaowei Zhao's discussion of 'Computational Modeling of the Expression of Time' (pp. 241–71).

Several further publications are concerned with the study of tenses in natural languages, as well as their interactions with aspect and modality. *Representing Time: An Essay on Temporality as Modality*, by K.M. Jaszczolt, is 'a philosophical-semantic, as well as a linguistic-semantic enquiry into the concept of time and its linguistic representation' (p. 4), addressing the questions of how human beings conceptualize time, whether these concepts are primitive or built up from some more basic constituents, what the semantics of expressions with temporal reference is, and why the availability of forms for expressing different tenses varies in human languages. The enquiry begins in chapter 1 with a review of various philosophical positions about the way time is conceptualized, and a summary of the author's basic assumptions for theorizing about time, which include the distinction between real (metaphysical) time and internal (psychological) time and the assumption that real time does not flow, the flow is part of human experience. In chapter 2 the author goes on to argue against considering time a primitive concept and a primitive semantic notion, proposing instead, given that temporality is underlyingly detachment from certainty, that it can be traced back to epistemic commitment/possibility, that is, to modality. If temporality is a form of epistemic commitment, what kind of unit is it a commitment to? This is the question addressed in chapter 3, which concludes that it cannot be an event but a construct called 'merged proposition' (a post-Gricean pragmatically assembled proposition), which 'reflects the representation of a state of affairs by a model speaker, as recovered by a model addressee in the process of conversation or other linguistic interaction' (p. 114), as proposed in the Default Semantics framework of Jaszczolt (2005). The way the above assumptions lead to capturing utterance meaning is then illustrated in chapter 4 by giving semantic/conceptual representations for utterances containing expressions with future, present, and past time reference in Default Semantics.

The Semantics of the Future, by Bridget Copley, follows the contemporary formal semantics tradition in providing a formal, compositional interpretation to sentences that are used to express a high degree of certainty about the future, concentrating primarily on English data. More specifically, she relies closely on Angelika Kratzer's (1991) theory on modality (which was in turn inspired by David Lewis's publications), providing the logical representations of natural language sentences in a version of Irene Heim and Angelika Kratzer's (1998) extensional framework that is complemented with worlds and times in a truly Montagovian fashion. The first chapter introduces the central assumptions and the formal tools used in what follows, and provides a background to modality, which the author considers essential for talking about the future. Chapter 2 investigates the semantics of *futurates*, sentences that can be used to refer to the future in spite of having no specifically future inflectional morphology, like those with a present continuous or simple present verb form in English. These are claimed to introduce a presupposition that there is an entity (the director) that can see to it that the eventuality described by the proposition either takes place or does not take place, and assert that the director is committed to making the eventuality happen. Chapter 3 is devoted to the discussion of *will* and *going to* and their close relatives, pointing out similarities between them and the two subtypes of futurates. The author argues for the presence of modal and aspectual components in the meaning of all the above constructions, claiming that their meaning involves an aspectual operator on top of a bouletic-inertial modal. Chapter 4 takes a look at the semantics of conditionals containing *will*, *going to* and the futurates, arguing for a distinction between two types of conditionals according to the temporal interpretation of their antecedents and consequents.

Text, Time, and Context, edited by Richard P. Meier, Helen Aristar-Dry, and Emilie Destruel, is a collection of the most influential papers written by the eminent semanticist Carlota S. Smith, who made significant contributions to the study of English syntax, child language development, the syntax and semantics of tense and aspect, and discourse interpretation. The collection, which was planned by the author herself before her death in 2007, contains publications from the last two strands of her research, grouped into five sections: 'Aspect', 'Tense', 'The Acquisition of Tense', 'Discourse Structure and Discourse Modes', and 'Context and Interpretation'. Given the significance of the individual papers to the cross-linguistic study of tense, aspect, and discourse, as well as the informed introductions to the sections written by outstanding scholars of the relevant areas (including Manfred Krifka, Jacqueline Guéron, Richard P. Meier, Barbara H. Partee, and Helen Aristar-Dry), which put Carlota S. Smith's research into the perspective of previous and subsequent developments as well as summarizing the insights of the papers included, the collection is bound to become an important resource material for graduate students and scholars alike.

Many journal articles address temporal, aspectual issues and their interactions with modality. Gerhard Schaden, 'Present Perfects Compete' (*Ling&P* 32[2009] 115–41), argues for a pragmatically based explanation for the reduced distribution of the present perfect in English and Spanish, and that of the simple past in French and German. Peter Hallmann, 'Proportions in Time: Interactions of Quantification and Aspect (*NLS* 17[2009] 29–61), studies the interaction of proportional quantification and progressive aspect, and Douglas J. Wulf discusses 'Two New Challenges for the Modal Account of the Progressive' (*NLS* 17[2009] 205–18). Valentine Hacquard, 'On the Interaction of Aspect and Modal Auxiliaries' (*Ling&P* 32[2009] 279–315), explores why in certain environments some modals seem to not merely express a possibility, but rather implicate the realization of their complement, which is responsible for the apparent contradictoriness of *Yesterday, Jane was able to swim across Lake Balaton, but she didn't*, which contrasts with the acceptable example *In her twenties, Jane was able to swim across Lake Balaton, though she never did*.

It is widely known that the analysis of modality is one of the success stories of formal semantics due to seminal work by logician-philosophers Saul Kripke and Jaakko Hintikka in the 1950s and semanticist Angelika Kratzer in the 1970s. Quite aptly, therefore, *Modality* by Paul Portner figures as volume 1 of the new Oxford Surveys in Semantics and Pragmatics. In a careful and transparent step-by-step fashion the author takes us through the various models, introducing problem sets and formal tools for handling them. In addition to an introduction, the book contains four chapters, devoted to 'Modal Logic', 'Major Linguistic Theories of Modality', 'Sentential Modality', and 'Modality and Other Intensional Categories'. Classical notions like 'possible worlds' and 'accessibility relations' are introduced in specific subsections. Different approaches to modality, such as the ones rooted in dynamic logic, cognitive linguistics, and functionalism, are discussed. Modal categories are studied in their interaction with tense, aspect, and evidentiality, as well as sentence mood and performativity. The sections on 'Subjectivity and Intersubjectivity' and 'Relativism' promise to be of value to philosophically minded readers. The individual chapters are nicely linked through look-ahead sections, and a sixteen-page bibliography provides useful further orientation.

We turn now to noun phrase semantics. *Quantificational Topics: A Scopal Treatment of Exceptional Wide Scope Phenomena*, by Cornelia Endriss, is concerned with the derivation of the wide-scope readings of quantifiers in non-opaque contexts as in *Anne has read every book that* ***some teacher*** *recommended* and in *If* ***some relative*** *of Paul dies, he will inherit a fortune*. The central claims of the author are that exceptional wide scope is genuine wide scope and that it is due to the topical status of the quantificational DPs concerned. The ingredients for proving the above claims are introduced in a step-wise fashion. First the definition of sentence topic and the various strategies of topic marking are reviewed, together with the types of DPs that can be marked as topical. Next, it is shown that exceptional wide scope is independent of the specific-nonspecific distinction, and different from apparent wide- or narrow-scope readings, thus proving the first hypothesis of the work. It is then argued, on the basis of the fact that only emphatic indefinites seem to support genuine wide-scope readings, that exceptional wide scope is restricted to topical indefinites, and the emphasis is a way of signalling topicality, which brings us to the proof of the second hypothesis. The exceptional wide-scope interpretations of topical DPs are then derived as follows. Utterances containing the latter are used to perform two speech-acts: the first one is a frame-setting (topic-establishing) act, in the course of which a sensible representative of the entire quantifier is selected that can stand proxy for the quantifier, followed by the usual assertive act, in the course of which the comment part of the sentence is applied to the discourse referent corresponding to the topic. The topical quantifier necessarily takes wide scope over all operators in the comment part because the Frame-Setting act happens first. The account is extended to embedded topic-comment structures and to functional topics. Adrian Brasoveanu and Donka F. Farkas are concerned with the same problem in 'Exceptional Scope as Discourse Reference to Quantificational Dependencies' (in Bosch et al., eds., *Logic, Language, and Computation*, pp. 165–79), where they claim exceptional scope readings (of universal and existential DPs) can have two sources: discourse anaphora to particular sets of entities and quantificational dependencies between these entities that restrict the domain of quantification of the two universal determiners and the indefinite article, or non-local accommodation of the discourse referent that restricts the quantificational domain of the indefinite article. More studies on quantifiers can be found in the journals. Josef Bayer's 'Nominal Negative Quantifiers as Adjuncts' (*JCGL* 12[2009] 5–30) analyses an exceptional, non-argumental use of the negative quantifier *nothing*, as in *my dentist's chair looks nothing like that*, arguing that the adjunct *nothing* encodes both (the feature of) sentential negation and a NPI. In 'Branching Quantification vs. Two-Way Quantification' (*JSem* 26[2009] 367–92), Nina Gierasimczuk and Jakub Szymanik call into question Jaakko Hintikka's (1973) claim that natural language sentences like *Some villager of every relative and some relative of every townsman hate each other* are not to be expressed with linear formulae, and propose a linear representation, also claimed to be supported by experimental data. Martin Hackl, in 'On the Grammar and Processing of Proportional Quantifiers: Most versus More Than Half (*NLS* 17[2009] 63–98), argues against the accepted view in Generalized Quantifier Theory that the interpretation of *most* or relations between sets in general are semantic primitives, proposing instead that the proportional quantifier *most* is a superlative expression composed of a degree function *many* and a degree quantifier *–est*, based on the cross-linguistic inventory of proportional quantifiers and experimental studies of verification procedures triggered by *most* and *more than half*. Another study in experimental semantics, 'The Logical Syntax of Number Words: Theory, Acquisition and Processing' (*Cognition* 111[2009] 24–45), by Julien Musolino, discusses the interpretations of sentences containing two numerals or a numeral and a quantifier by adults and preschool children, showing that the independently motivated, linguistically based processing model of Bart Geurts (2003) accounts for the differences between the two groups. The logical properties of quantificational expressions are studied by Jakub Szymanik in 'The Computational Complexity of Quantified Reciprocals' (in Bosch et al., eds., pp. 139–52), and by Richard Zuber in 'A Semantic Constraint on Binary Determiners' (*Ling&P* 32[2009] 95–114). Ariel Cohen, in 'Fronted Quantificational Adverbs' (in Shaer et al., eds., pp. 312–27; and see also section 5(a) above), looks at the effect of fronting the quantificational adverb in English on truth-conditions, as in *Usually/Often, officers accompany ballerinas*, arguing that fronting marks the adverbs as Background, which does not effect the truth-conditions of adverbs with absolute readings but it does affect the so-called relative readings of those that have one. In 'No Alternative to Alternatives' (*JSem* 26[2009] 1–48), the same author argues, in opposition to recent proposals claiming the opposite, that the concept of the focus semantic value introduced by Mats Rooth (1985) to the semantic analysis of focus cannot be dispensed with, illustrating the claim by showing that the relative readings of quantificational sentences that have them can be captured using semantic values triggered by alternatives to the focus, background marking, and the world of evaluation.

In 'Less Form—More Meaning: Why Bare Singular Nouns are Special' (*Lingua* 119[2009] 280–95), Henriëtte de Swart and Joost Zwarts study a number of constructions where nominals can appear without an article in languages like English, which include bare location (*in town*), bare co-ordination (*mother and daughter*), bare predication (*Anne is head of department*), bare reduplication (*page for page*), and bare incorporation (*berry picking*). The special meaning effects can be characterized in terms of stereotypicality, and are accounted for in terms of BiOT. In 'Number-Neutral Bare Plurals and the Multiplicity Implicature' (*Ling&P* 32[2009] 353–407), Eytan Zweig is concerned with the interpretation of bare plurals on which these constituents function similarly to indefinites. In these constructions, as in *John owns rare Amazonian parrots*, the 'more than one' meaning is claimed not to be part of the denotation of the bare plural but to arise as a scalar implicature.

Harry C. Bunt's *Mass Terms and Model Theoretic Semantics* [1985] was reissued in paperback in 2009. The work, which has been extensively cited since its first publication, studies the formal semantic properties of mass terms in a framework referred to by the author as two-level model-theoretic semantics, based on an extension of classical set theory called Ensemble Theory. The first part of the book is devoted to the model-theoretic semantics of mass terms, including a discussion of their syntactic properties, a review of their previous semantic treatments, desiderata for a theory capable of handling the problems faced by the latter, an informal introduction to Ensemble Theory, the definition of a formal language in which ensemble concepts are used, a discussion of the theoretical status of semantic representations and that of the two-level model theoretic semantics, and, finally, a discussion of how English expressions containing count terms as well as mass terms can be translated into the formal language previously defined. In the two-level model-theoretic semantics advocated by the author, the denotations are assigned to natural language expressions in two stages: the analysis of the logical semantic aspects of a natural language expression is followed by the analysis of its referential semantic aspects in relation to a model of a certain domain of discourse. Each stage of the analysis results in a representation in a formal language, the relation between which is defined by model-theoretic interpretation rules, where the expressions of the representation language at the referential level serve as interpretations of those of the other representation language. Part II of the book is devoted to the discussion of the formal properties of Ensemble Theory. A contemporary study, 'The Interpretation of Functional Heads: Using Comparatives to Explore the Mass/Count Distinction' (*JSem* 26[2009] 217–52) by Alan C. Bale and David Barner, points out that no current theory can explain the fact that all words that can be used in both mass and count syntax always denote individuals when used in count syntax but never denote individuals when used in mass syntax, and that some mass nouns can denote individuals while others cannot.

Many studies investigate the interpretation of proper names, of other referring expressions, as well as that of pronouns and anaphors. In 'Proper Names and Indexicals Trigger Rigid Presuppositions' (*JSem* 26[2009] 253–315), Emar Maier provides a hybrid analysis of proper names and indexicals combining insights from the competing theories of referentialism and descriptivism, in the framework of Layered Discourse Representation Theory. Stavroula Glezakos takes a new look at the role of descriptions in the course of referring with public proper names in 'Public Proper Names and Idiolectal Identifying Descriptions' (*Ling&P* 32[2009] 317–26). In 'Processing Definite Determiners: Formal Semantics meets Experimental Results' (in Bosch et al., eds., pp. 242–56), Peter Bosch looks at experiments of online comprehension testing the meaning of the English definite determiner, and argues for an incremental variant of current formal semantics to account for the data. Anders J. Schoubye's 'Descriptions, Truth Value Intuitions, and Questions' (*Ling&P* 32[2009] 583–617) considers the reasons for the existence of conflicting intuitions regarding the truth values of statements with non-referring definites, and argues that the intuitions of falsity, which proponents of the Russellian quantificational analysis of definites often appeal to, result from evaluating sentences in relation to specific questions in context. Ping Chen, in 'Aspects of Referentiality' (*JPrag* 41[2009] 1657–74), distinguishes between three kinds of referentiality (semantic, pragmatic, and discourse thematic), and investigates their expression in English and Chinese. The nature and mechanisms of reference is the topic of Torben Thrane's *Referential-Semantic analysis: Aspects of a Theory of Linguistic Reference*, first published in 1980 and now reissued in paperback. In 'Making a Pronoun: Fake Indexicals as Windows into the Properties of Pronouns' (*LingI* 40[2009] 187–237), Angelika Kratzer proposes a novel theory of referential and bound pronouns where the semantics of pronominal features determines the make-up of a pronoun at the beginning of a syntactic derivation.

Negation in Gapping, by Sophie Repp, is concerned with the syntactic, semantic, and prosodic properties of gapping sentences (a type of ellipsis which in English and other head-initial languages elides the finite verb in the second conjunct) that contain a negative marker in the second conjunct which is not present in the first one. The author proposes that such structures can be interpreted in three different ways. On the 'distributed-scope readings', the second conjunct is interpreted as negative, just like the first one, as in *Pete hasn't got a video and John _ a DVD*, provided the two conjuncts are realized as two intonational phrases, the verb is de-accented, and the contrast pairs are highlighted by accents. According to the 'wide-scope reading', the negation scopes over the whole co-ordination, as in *Pete didn't clean the whole flat and John _ laze around all afternoon*, provided it is pronounced as a single intonational phrase, without a pause between the conjuncts. On the 'narrow-scope reading', only the first conjunct is interpreted as negative, as in *Pete wasn't called by Vanessa and John only _ by Jessie*. After providing a thorough overview of some relevant data (from different languages) and theories on gapping, the author looks individually at the three interpretations outlined above, aiming to discover their sources, also on the basis of intensive cross-linguistic comparisons. She finds that apart from intonational properties, the factors that influence the interpretation of the negation include the content of the gap (finite main verb, finite modal/auxiliary, etc.), the type of co-ordinator used, the presence of semantic operators in the second clause (*only*, even), and the type of negation (propositional vs. speech-act level) involved. In the course of these investigations, Repp makes a proposal on the syntactic analysis of gapping and investigates the semantic roles negation can have in the clause.

In 'Contrast as Denial in Multi-Dimensional Semantics' (*JSem* 41[2009] 1707–26) by Jennifer Spenader and Emar Maier, contrastive statements are claimed to be a subtype of denials targeting a specific type of information. The authors model the context change caused by these constructions in a novel, multidimensional framework, i.e. Layered Discourse Representation Theory (Bart Geurts and Emar Maier 2003), which can incorporate non-monotonic context-change potentials necessary to account for denial. Still on the topic of information structuring, 'Multiple Focus' by Sigrid Beck and Shravan Vasishth (*JSem* 26[2009] 159–84) presents the negative results of an experimental investigation into whether multiple-focus configurations (that is, two nested focus-sensitive operators and two foci supposed to associate with those operators) are considered interpretable, which confirms Mats Rooth's (1992) predictions.

On the semantics of adjectives, Marcin Morzycki's 'Degree Modification of Gradable Nouns: Size Adjectives and Adnominal Degree Morphemes' (*NLS* 17[2009] 175–203), examines a variety of degree modification in which a gradable predicate is provided by a noun, and an adjective that normally expresses size characterizes the degree to which the gradable predicate holds, as in *Gladys is a big stamp-collector*. Morzycki argues for a compositional semantics for degree readings of size adjectives in which they are a kind of adnominal counterpart of measure phrases in AP. In 'Degree Structure as Trope Structure: A Trope-Based Analysis of Positive and Comparative Adjectives' (*Ling&P* 32[2009] 51–94), Friderike Moltmann offers an analysis of adjectives in terms of tropes, that is, particularized properties.

Moving on to adjectives characterizing subjective evaluation, Peter Lasersohn's 'Relative Truth, Speaker Commitment, and Control of Implicit Arguments' (*Synthese* 166[2009] 359–74) offers independent motivation for relativist semantic theories proposed first to account for cases of faultless disagreement (cf. Lasersohn 2005, among others) as opposed to theories using hidden indexicals on the basis of the interpretation of predicates of personal taste in certain attitude contexts (*John considers/believes the licorice to be tasty*) and presuppositional constructions (*John recognizes that licorice is tasty*). In 'Judgment Ascriptions' (*Ling&P* 32[2009] 327–52) Kjell Johan Sæbø shows that there are propositional attitude verbs in various languages that require that their complement contains some subjective predicate, illustrated by the contrast between *#Homer finds Bart gay* and *Homer found himself great*. He argues for an analysis according to which the role of these verbs is to set the judge, without assuming a judge index or judge argument. A unified semantics for *de dicto*, de re, and *de se* belief reports is offered by Emar Maier in 'Presupposing Acquaintance: A Unified Semantics for *De Dicto*, *De Re* and *De Se* Belief Reports' (*Ling&P* 32[2009] 429–74).

In 'Speaker-Oriented Adverbs' (*NL<* 27[2009] 497–544), Thomas Ernst presents an account of the ordering of speaker-oriented adverbs (*honestly*, *unfortunately*, *probably*) with respect to each other and negation, arguing that the data are derivable on the basis of a distinction between subjective and objective modification and the fact that these adverbs are positive polarity items presenting the speaker's subjective commitment to the truth of the proposition expressed by the sentence. In 'Between Being Wise and Acting Wise: A Hidden Conditional in Some Constructions with Propensity Adjectives' (*JL* 45[2009] 363–93), David Y. Oshima proposes an analysis of three constructions in Sign-Based Construction Grammar, which he claims to have an identical semantics: the subject-oriented adverb construction (*Wisely, John left early*), the 'Adj+to Inf' construction (*John was wise to leave early*), and the 'Adj+of NP' construction (*It was wise of John to leave early*).

Turning now to *real* conditionals, in 'Conditionals and Indexical Relativism' (*Synthese* 166[2009] 333–57), Brian Weatherson argues for an approach to indicative conditionals that is based on the assumption that the proposition (semantically) expressed by an utterance of a conditional is a function of (among other things) the speaker's context and the assessor's context, which implies that a single utterance may be correctly assessed as true by one assessor and false by another. Luis Alonso-Ovalle studies the interpretation of disjunctive counterfactual conditionals like *If we had had good weather this summer or the sun had grown cold, we would have had a bumper crop* in 'Counterfactuals, Correlatives, and Disjunction' (*Ling&P* 32[2009] 207–44), arguing that their natural interpretation can be derived formally if disjunctions introduce propositional alternatives in the semantic derivation (as suggested by independently motivated proposals about the semantics of *or*), and by treating conditionals as correlative constructions, again proposed independently in the literature. Ana Arregui takes a fresh look at the role of similarity in the semantic analysis of counterfactuals ('Similarity in Counterfactuals', *Ling&P* 32[2009] 245–78). She proposes that, as opposed to the theories of David Lewis (1973) and Robert Stalnaker (1968), where counterfactuals of the form *if A, would B* are true iff the A-worlds globally most similar to the actual one are also B-worlds, one should take a local approach to similarity (so that only particular features of the world 'count') and tie the evaluation of similarity to the interaction of the semantics of tense and the modal meaning of *would*.

Given the unfailing interest of semanticists in the interpretation of conditionals, which the above high-quality papers also testify to, the reviewer can only welcome the publication of a paperback reissue of the collection *On Conditionals* from 1986, edited by Elizabeth Closs Traugott, Alice ter Meulen, Judy Snitzer Reilly, and Charles A. Ferguson, which contains some of the most authoritative studies on the subject, written by Jon Barwise, P.N. Johnson-Laird, Bernard Comrie, Tanya Reinhart, Alice ter Meulen, Frank Veltman, Ernest W. Adams, Samuel Fillerbaum, Johan van der Auwera, John Haiman, Ekkehard König, Joseph Greenberg, Martin B. Harris, Melisse Bowerman, Judy Snitzer Reilly, Niroko Akatsuka, Cecilia E. Ford, and Sandra A. Thompson, a must-read for anyone intending to embark on a serious study of conditionals from a cognitive, philosophical, linguistic, or AI point of view.

The collection *Theory and Evidence in Semantics*, edited by Erhard Hinrichs and John Nerbonne, contains the written versions of the talks presented at a workshop organized in honour of the sixtieth birthday of the eminent semanticist David Dowty. The range of topics addressed includes many that Dowty has made significant contributions to, including the extension of the programme of logic-based semantics to the lexical domain, investigations on the division of labour between semantics and pragmatics, methodological issues on the nature of compositionality, and the use of categorial grammar to offer solutions to various linguistics problems. In '*know-how*: A Compositional Approach' (pp. 183–213) Craige Roberts proposes a compositional account of constructions containing verbs that take infinitival question complements like *Lingens doesn't know how to get out of the library*. Manfred Krifka, 'Approximate Interpretations of Number Words: A Case for Strategic Communication' (pp. 109–31), puts forth a pragmatic explanation for why round numbers such as 100 receive an approximate interpretation but numbers like 103 receive a more precise interpretation, placing the issue within the context of strategic communication. Chris Barker's 'Reconstruction as Delayed Evaluation' (pp. 1–28) shows that that the fully compositional account of scope and binding proposed in Chris Barker and Chung-Chieh Shan (2006) can account for the interpretation of structures like *[Which of his$_i$ relatives] does everyone$_i$ love _?*, which can only be explained in derivational syntactic theories if the bracketed material is assumed to reconstruct to the position of the gap. Pauline Jacobson, in 'Do Representations Matter or Do Meanings Matter: The Case of Antecedent Containment' (pp. 81–107), argues, based on data with Antecedent Contained Deletion (ACD) against the need for an immediate level of semantic representations, as in *Mary voted for every candidate that Bill will*, and develops a variable-free, directly compositional account of ACD in the framework of Combinatory Categorial Grammar. Peter Lasersohn's 'Compositional Interpretation in which the Meanings of Complex Expressions Are Not Computable from the Meanings of their Parts' (pp. 133–58), argues for a view of compositionality according to which it simply requires the existence of a homomorphism from syntax to semantics, as opposed to the interpretation (often attributed to the concept in the literature) that the compositionality of meanings amounts to the computability of the meanings of complex constituents on the basis of the meanings of the parts.

Several other important topics for natural language semantics have only been represented by one paper each. Itamar Francez offers a new analysis of existential sentences (of the form *There be NP NP*) in 'Existentials, Predication, and Modification' (*Ling&P* 32[2009] 1–50). In 'A Theory of Individual-Level Predicates Based on Blind Mandatory Scalar Implicatures' (*NLS* 17[2009] 245–97), Giorgio Magri defends the idea of an implicature-based theory of individual-level predicates. 'Generics and the Ways of Normality' (*Ling&P* 31[2009] 629–48), by Bernhard Nickel, argues for a so-called inquiry-based view of characterizing generic statements such as *Ravens are black*, according to which they are about what is normal, captured in terms of our investigative aims and the intrinsic properties of the objects concerned, which is contrasted to the so-called majority-based views. In 'What Man Does' (*Ling&P* 31[2009] 671–724), Eric McCready provides a discussion and formal account of the meaning and use of the English particle *man*, which is claimed to express an emotional attitude and intensification in sentence-initial position (e.g. *Man, it's hot!*), and to strengthen the action performed by the sentence in sentence-final position (*It's hot, man!*). Kjell Johan Sæbø, 'Possession and Pertinence: The Meaning of *Have*' (*NLS* 17[2009] 369–97), offers a new analysis of sentences where *have* embeds a small clause, as in *Shrek has a donkey for a friend.* Jeroen Groenendijk proposes a semantics for a language of propositional logic in 'Inquisitive Semantics: Two Possibilities for Disjunction' (in Bosch et al., eds., pp. 80–94), whose significance lies in its applicability in modelling the semantics of interrogatives in natural language. A unified logical framework where the contributions of propositional content and illocutionary force can be represented simultaneously, thus providing a general semantic theory of natural languages, was the aim of Daniel Vanderveken's two-volume work *Meaning and Speech Acts* that appeared in 1990–1; it has now been reissued in paperback and still provides compulsory, albeit not easy, reading for students interested in formal ways of capturing illocutionary meaning.

As the discussion so far has probably indicated already, the reliance on data collected by experimental methods as a means of supporting theoretical approaches to semantics has become the norm rather than the exception. The list of additional studies on experimental semantics includes 'Perspective-Shifting with Appositives and Expressives', by Jesse A. Harris and Christopher Potts (*Ling&P* 32[2009] 523–52), which presents two experiments and novel corpus studies on the availability of non-speaker-oriented readings of appositives and expressives. The authors argue for the systematicity of non-speaker-oriented readings and for an account based on pragmatically mediated perspective shifting, instead of binding by higher operators such as attitude predicates. Andrea Gualmini and Bernhard Schwarz consider two semantic learnability problems that have featured prominently in the literature on language acquisition in 'Solving Learnability Problems in the Acquisition of Semantics' (*JSem* 26[2009] 185–215), while Anastasia Conroy, Eri Takahashi, Jeffrey Lidz, and Colin Phillips look at two puzzles that have been discussed widely in the literature in relation to children's application of Principle B, a constraint that prohibits local antecedents for pronouns in 'Equal Treatment for All Antecedents: How Children Succeed with Principle B' (*LingI* 40[2009] 446–86).

7. Lexicography, Lexicology, and Lexical Semantics

The most significant publication on the historical study of dictionaries this year was A.P. Cowie's edited collection, *The Oxford History of English Lexicography*. The first volume considers general-purpose dictionaries, including bilingual as well as monolingual dictionaries of English, and the second volume covers specialized dictionaries. Cowie's surpasses earlier histories of English lexicography in a number of respects: it is international in its coverage, it is written by a range of specialists and practising lexicographers, and it doesn't tell a distorting single story of the history of lexicography. It is particularly useful to see the development of monolingual dictionaries discussed alongside advances in bilingual and polyglot lexicography, and it is not unusual that several chapters offer usefully different perspectives on the same publication or issue. Cowie's introductions to each volume provide an invaluable overview in their own right, by drawing together developments observed across periods and dictionary types. Perhaps one of the benefits of so expansive an account of the history of lexicography is that it draws attention to types of dictionary that are not included in the volume, such as dictionaries for children, dictionaries focusing on a particular author (such as Shakespeare) or works (such as the Bible), dictionaries of euphemism and taboo, dictionaries of African American English, dictionaries of political movements (such as feminism), rhyming dictionaries, concise dictionaries (other than American college dictionaries), and so on. The history of lexicography is not yet told in full, but Cowie's volumes provide a considerably firmer foundation for future work. A further contribution to the development of historical dictionary research is provided in 'Forensic Dictionary Analysis: Principles and Practice' (*IJL* 22[2009] 1–22), in which Julie Coleman and Sarah Ogilvie argue that dictionary historians must subject lexicographers' accounts of their methodologies to evidence-based analysis. They also evaluate some of the statistical methods that have been used for this purpose. Cowie's chapters are arranged broadly chronologically, which reveals some interesting interrelationships; they will be discussed below by topic, interspersed with this year's other publications in the same area. The chapters in Cowie are particularly valuable in that they are written with a broad readership in mind. For example, Hans Sauer's 'Glosses, Glossaries, and Dictionaries in the Medieval Period' (vol. 1, pp. 17–40) is not written merely for an audience of medievalists: it explains the periodization of the history of English and also the relationship between English and other languages used in England during the medieval period. It also discusses why and how manuscripts were glossed. Four main types of glossary were produced during the medieval period: *glossae collectae*, providing a key to the vocabulary of specific texts; alphabetical glossaries, offering the same vocabulary reordered for wider application; class glossaries, in which vocabulary was arranged semantically;

and derivational glossaries, where words were grouped by their etymological relationships. Noel Osselton's 'The Early Development of the English Monolingual Dictionary (Seventeenth and Early Eighteenth Centuries)' (vol. 1, pp. 131–54) argues that this period spans the emergence of a distinctive and stable type of reference work that would be recognizable to modern readers. He charts three stages in this development: the hard-word dictionaries of the first half of the seventeenth century, the encyclopaedic dictionaries of the later seventeenth century, and the universal dictionaries of the early eighteenth century, which aimed to include even the most basic words of English.

Lisa Berglund discusses reviewers' suspicion that respectful plagiarism underlay a female lexicographer's work in 'Fossil Fish: Preserving Samuel Johnson within Hester Lynch Piozzi's *British Synonymy*' (*Dictionaries* 30[2009] 96–107). Although the friendship between Piozzi (also known as Mrs Thrale) and Johnson was both well known and valuable to her in her other publications, Piozzi distanced herself from Johnson when she turned to lexicography. In 'Johnson's Prescriptive Labels—a Reassessment' (*Dictionaries* 30[2009] 108–18), Kate Wild argues that Johnson's prescriptivism has been overstated by dictionary historians. She finds that labels such as *proper*, *improper*, and *ludicrous* are not always used prescriptively. Chris P. Pearce considers 'Samuel Johnson's Use of Scientific Sources in the *Dictionary*' (*Dictionaries* 30[2009] 119–29), with reference to Johnson's annotations on an interleaved copy of the first edition. In a brief treatment of 'Dr. Johnson and the American Vocabulary' (*Dictionaries* 30[2009] 130–5), Richard W. Bailey finds that Nathan Bailey's *Dictionarium Britannicum* [1736], provided a better coverage of Americanisms than Johnson did, even though Bailey was one of his sources. Allan Reddick discusses 'Johnson and Richardson' (in Cowie, ed., vol. 1, pp. 155–81), arguing that Johnson was revolutionary in considering the meaning of words according to their usage, although he did so without reference to historical development. Richardson objected to Johnson's emphasis on context and to his division of citations under separate definitions for a single headword: 'in the Etymology of each word must be found [its] single intrinsic meaning' (quoted p.173).

In addition to reviewing existing scholarship, Lynda Mugglestone has the difficult task of finding something new to say about the first edition of 'The *Oxford English Dictionary*' (in Cowie, ed., vol. 1, pp. 230–59). She does so by placing the Philological Society's desire to better Johnson's work in the context of earlier proposals and requests that someone should undertake the same task, and by paying close attention to annotated proofs of the dictionary. David Micklethwait takes 'A Further Trip over the Tramlines' (*Dictionaries* 30[2009] 18–21), and argues that Onions and Craigie were wrong to remove tramlines (||, used to mark non-naturalized words) from the 1933 Supplement because their task was to produce a supplement to a main work that included them. Charlotte Brewer discusses 'The *OED* Supplements' (in Cowie, ed., vol. 1, pp. 260–78), focusing particularly on Robert Burchfield's reported and actual revisions to the dictionary. Edmund Wiener's 'The Electronic *OED*: The Computerization of a Historical Dictionary' (in Cowie, ed., vol. 1, pp. 378–409) charts more recent developments motivated both by the need for modernization and the desire to extend and protect copyright. He provides an interesting account of the computerization as well as the editing process, offering an insight into the technical and practical challenges involved. John Considine's '"Rippe, Rippe You Kitchinstuffe Wrangler": Nashe and a Ghost Word in *OED*' (*N&Q* 56[2009] 619–21) demonstrates that two later writers and an *OED* editor were misled by Nashe's use of *rip*. Considine also examines claims that the *OED*'s citation evidence distorts its record of the English language, and explores whether alternative quotation evidence would have presented a different account, in 'Literary Classics in *OED* Citation Evidence' (*RES* 60[2009] 620–38). Charlotte Brewer looks at the *OED*'s changing treatment of one literary author in 'The *OED* as "Literary Instrument": Its Treatment Past and Present of the Vocabulary of Virginia Woolf' (*N&Q* 56[2009] 430–44). With reference to citations in a 2006 book on the history of art, Rodney Stenning Edgecombe offers 'Two Ante-Datings for Words in the *OED*' (*N&Q* 56[2009] 270), apparently without referring back to their original context. Carole Hough reports the discovery of 'Field-Names Antedating the *OED* entries for *Courtin* and *Cot-Garth*' (*N&Q* 56[2009] 346–7). *Cot-garth* 'a small enclosure attached to a cottage' is antedated by 263 years, to 1613; *Courtin* 'a yard for cattle' by nineteen years to 1775. Michael Adams discusses 'The Period Dictionaries' that arose from the *OED* project (in Cowie, ed., vol. 1, pp. 326–52), treating in their chronological order *The Early Modern English Dictionary* (never published), *The Middle English Dictionary* (published, after false starts, 1952–2001), and *The Old English Dictionary* (1986–). Accounts by Carole Hough and Patrick Hanks of, respectively, 'Dictionaries of Place-Names' and 'Dictionaries of Personal Names' (in Cowie, ed., vol. 2, pp. 94–121, 122–48) are both introduced with an account of the history of naming patterns. Hough's chapter contextualizes a variety of variable place-name dictionaries with reference to publications arising from the English Place-Name Survey. With no comparable modern authority in his field, Hanks spends more time on the history of the lexicographic tradition.

Sidney Landau discusses 'Major American Dictionaries' (in Cowie, ed., vol. 1, pp. 182–229). Although earlier American dictionaries are acknowledged, the chapter focuses on Webster and later dictionaries based on his. Landau also covers Funk and Wagnalls' dictionaries, the *World Book Dictionary* [1963] and *The Random House Dictionary of the English Language* [1966, 1987] in some detail. Cynthia L. Hallen and Dallin J. Bailey provide a list of entries that were unique to or amended in the '1844 Addenda to Noah Webster's *American Dictionary of the English Language (ADEL)*' (*Dictionaries* 30[2009] 22–94). The brief introduction does not explain what function this list might serve, and no analysis is offered. Sidney Landau discusses 'The American Collegiate Dictionary' (in Cowie, ed., vol. 2, pp. 361–4), among 'Dictionaries Specialized According to Users and Uses'. Although this type of dictionary arose in response to an unprecedented growth in higher education, they are a clear development from the American dictionaries discussed in volume 1.

Richard W. Bailey considers the history of dictionaries of Americanisms, along with dictionaries of English used in South Asia, South Africa, Australia and New Zealand, Canada, and Ireland, in his chapter on 'National and Regional Dictionaries of English' (in Cowie, ed., vol. 1, pp. 279–301). A historical account of 'Dictionaries of Scots', the earliest of which date from the

1590s, is provided by Margaret Dareau and Iseabail Macleod (in Cowie, ed., vol. 1, pp. 302–25), and 'Dictionaries of Caribbean English' are surveyed by Jeannette Allsopp (in Cowie, ed., vol. 1, pp. 353–77). Robert Penhallurick provides a historical account of 'Dialect Dictionaries' (in Cowie, ed., vol. 2, pp. 290–313), describing the forebears and context of Wright's *English Dialect Dictionary*, and moving on to consider his twentieth-century successors.

Julie Coleman's 'Slang and Cant Dictionaries' (in Cowie, ed., vol. 2, pp. 314–36) emphasizes the difficulty of determining what is or is not a slang dictionary, let alone determining what is or is not slang.

Werner Hüllen's 'Dictionaries of Synonyms and Thesauri' (in Cowie, ed., vol. 2, pp. 25–46) ranges across monolingual, bilingual, and polyglot works that organize vocabulary primarily by meaning, placing them in the context of the development of the relevant dictionary traditions. Hüllen's *Networks and Knowledge in Roget's Thesaurus from Ancient to Medieval* collects some earlier publications on topical dictionaries, focusing specifically on Roget's *Thesaurus* in its linguistic, philosophical, and historical context, and considering its influence on the treatment of other languages. The volume offers some interesting insights into how new words were inserted into the structure in later editions of Roget's work. *Negro*, for example, was categorized under 'sensation' as a person characterized by 'blackness' in the first edition of 1852, with some synonymous words listed under 'slave'. Although the vocabulary was expanded in later editions, the assumptions underlying the original classification remained unchallenged. Thesauruses modelled on Roget's structure are found in German, French, and Italian.

In 'Scientific and Technical Dictionaries' (in Cowie, ed., vol. 2, pp. 47–93), Michael Rand Hoare provides a fascinating account of some 2,000 works barely noticed by dictionary historians. His subsections on dictionaries of particular disciplines, such as astronomy, chemistry, mathematics, law, and music, provide a glimpse of much work that remains to be done. Elizabeth Knowles's 'Dictionaries of Quotations' (in Cowie, ed., vol. 2, pp. 245–68) concentrates on the earlier history of this particular genre, beginning with Edward Bysshe's *The Art of English Poetry* [1702]. Hilary Nesi's 'Dictionaries in Electronic Form' (in Cowie, ed., vol. 2, pp. 458–78) spans the use of computers in lexicography, handheld electronic dictionaries, dictionaries on disk, on the internet, and on mobile phones.

Learners' dictionaries have also received a great deal of coverage this year. Janet Bately's 'Bilingual and Multilingual Dictionaries of the Renaissance and Early Seventeenth Century' (in Cowie, ed., vol. 1, pp. 41–64) explains that humanist lexicographers looked to the Continent for their sources rather than building on the insular tradition. The first bi-directional bilingual dictionary including English was published in 1644. Monique C. Cormier covers 'Bilingual Dictionaries of the Late Seventeenth and Eighteenth Centuries' (in Cowie, ed., vol. 1, pp. 65–85), emphasizing the relationship between the decline of Latin as the lingua franca and the consequent need for dictionaries of modern languages. Subsections focus on English–Latin, English–French, English–Spanish, English–German, and English–Dutch dictionaries from the period. Carla Marello's 'Bilingual Dictionaries of the Nineteenth and Twentieth Centuries' (in Cowie, ed., vol. 1, pp. 86–104) includes the same subsections, but adds English–Greek and English–Italian, as well as discussing the development of bilingualized learners' dictionaries. Donna M.T. Cr. Farino and George Durman provide an account of 'Bilingual Dictionaries of English and Russian in the Eighteenth to the Twentieth Centuries' (in Cowie, ed., vol. 1, pp. 105–28), which appear to have originated largely independently of other bilingual English dictionaries. A.P. Cowie looks back to these bi- and multilingual dictionaries as well as to the earliest monolingual English dictionaries in 'The Earliest Foreign Learners' Dictionaries' (in Cowie, ed., vol. 2, pp. 385–411), but begins his own account with Simeon Potter's *English Vocabulary for Foreign Students* [1930]. He discusses, in particular, the vocabulary control movement, grammar, phraseology, and collocation. Learners' dictionaries also bulk large in Cowie's second volume, with Thierry Fontenelle's 'Linguistic Research and Learners' Dictionaries: The *Longman Dictionary of Contemporary English*' and Rosamund Moon's 'The Cobuild Project' (pp. 412–35 and 436–57) each concentrating on the contributions of a single influential publishing house.

Concentrating on other learners' aspects, Joan C. Beal ('Pronouncing Dictionaries—I. Eighteenth and Early Nineteenth Centuries', in Cowie, ed., vol. 2, pp. 149–75) and Beverley Collins and Inger M. Mees ('Pronouncing Dictionaries—II. Mid-Nineteenth Century to the Present Day', vol. 2, pp. 176–218) consider both specialized dictionaries of pronunciation and the treatment of pronunciation in general dictionaries. Pronunciation dictionaries originated with the sense that some accents were more prestigious, and therefore more advantageous, than others, but by the later period they tended to be produced with non-native learners in mind. Robert Allen's 'Dictionaries of Usage' (in Cowie, ed., vol. 2, pp. 339–60) offers an account of another group of dictionaries designed for those who wished to obscure their lowly origins or acquire native-speaker fluency.

Thomas Herbst and Michael Klotz consider 'Syntagmatic and Phraseological Dictionaries' (in Cowie, ed., vol. 2, pp. 219–44), including dictionaries of catchphrases, proverbs, and idioms, as well as EFL dictionaries of phrasal verbs, valency, and collocation. Marta Dick-Bursztyn explores 'The Lexicographic Representation of Grammar—The Significance of Exhaustive Grammatical Information from the Perspective of Active and Passive Dictionary Use' (in Górecka-Smolińska et al., eds., *Historical Semantics Brought to the Fore*, pp. 9–16), with particular reference to learners' dictionaries. In the same volume, Doroto Osuchowska looks at Oxford's children's dictionaries in 'The Stories behind Words: The Issue of Etymologising in British Dictionaries for Young Learners' (pp. 117–27). Osuchowska also provides an 'Interim Report on Research into the College Students' Use of Dictionaries in Text Production' (in Kleparski et al., eds., *Old Pitfalls, Changing Attitudes and New Vistas*, pp. 115–24), finding that using dictionaries does enlarge students' vocabularies. Conversely, Robert Lew and Joanna Doroszewska find that providing animated pictures to illustrate definitions has an adverse effect on vocabulary retention, in 'Electronic Dictionary Entries with Animated Pictures: Lookup Preferences and Word Retention' (*IJL* 22[2009] 239–57).

In 'The Electronic Dictionary for Writing: A Solution or a Problem?' (*IJL* 22[2009] 23–54), Y.V. Chon reports that limited knowledge of L2 words can create additional challenges for dictionary users, but that they overcome these difficulties in a number of fruitful ways. Anna Włodarczyk-Stachurska makes 'Some Remarks on Selected Currents in the Field of EFL Lexicography' (in Kleparski et al., eds., pp. 147–55), and concludes that recent developments have shown a greater awareness of learners' needs and difficulties. Crayton Walker discusses 'The Treatment of Collocation by Learners' Dictionaries, Collocational Dictionaries and Dictionaries of Business English' (*IJL* 22[2009] 281–99). In 'What is a Dictionary? A View from Chomskyan Linguistics' (*IJL* 22[2009] 399–421), Pius ten Hacken takes the contentious position that dictionaries should be evaluated with regard to the success of their presentation of information rather than by reference to completeness and accuracy.

This year's publications in lexicology frequently made the welcome observation that a diachronic perspective can often offer more useful information for analysis than a narrowly focused synchronic approach. Studies of individual words and groups of words are considered chronologically here. Joseph P. McGowan argues that OE *þyrs* has been too narrowly defined, in 'Giants and Snake-Charmers: OE *þyrs*' (*N&Q* 56[2009) 487–90). Lucía Loureiro-Porto's *The Semantic Predecessors of* Need *in the History of English (c750–1710)* observes that the current modal use of *need* cannot be fully understood without reference to its unusual historical evolution, in that it did not develop from a preterite-present form in OE. With careful reference to corpus evidence for impersonality, grammaticalization, and modality, Loureiro-Porto explores why and how *need* survived where competitor forms such as, *tharf*, *betharf*, *behove*, and the less frequent French loan *mister*, fell from use. Distinguishing between *need* v.1 'to compel; to force' and *need* v.2 'to be necessary', Loureiro-Porto finds that OE tended to use *tharf* modally, while early ME preferred *behove*, and the period from late ME onwards used *need* with the highest frequency. Although *behove* became more frequent in the intervening period, *need* proved to be a good semantic substitute for the various senses of *tharf*. These three more frequently used verbs are the only ones to show evidence of grammaticalization.

Allison Burkette describes the use of textual and picture questions to elicit accurate information about the distribution and use of terms referring to wardrobes, chests of drawers, and other furniture for storing clothes in American English, in 'The Lion, the Witch, and the Armoire: Lexical Variation in Case Furniture Terms' (*AS* 84[2009] 315–39). Inside the wardrobe, Angelina Rusinek writes 'On the Non-Exclusiveness of Semantic Changes in the Category Clothes' (in Kleparski et al., eds., pp. 90–7), arguing that changes in the field of CLOTHES have often interacted with changes in HUMAN BEING.

Michael Adams's *Slang: The People's Poetry* was the most significant of the publications on contemporary lexis this year. It is structured around four main themes: a consideration of what slang is, the social dynamics of slang, aesthetic dimensions of slang, and cognitive aspects of slang. Adams takes his examples largely from contemporary American slang, including *mongo* 'a discarded item salvaged for re-use', *hang* 'to hang out (in company or alone)', and *bash the bishop* '(of a male) to masturbate'. Adams takes issue with the position that a term can only qualify as slang if it is used in opposition to a standard synonym, and argues that reference to context is necessary to determine whether or not a term is slang. The chapter on cognitive aspects of slang is particularly interesting, and starts from the proposition that the unusual use of words stimulates the brain. Wayne Glowka, Grant Barrett, David K. Barnhart, Megan Melançon, and Megan Salter look at words coined or disseminated during the 2008 presidential campaign in 'Among the New Words' (*AS* 84[2009] 83–102). These include *dap*, fist-bump, and numerous terms formed on Obama's surname, such as *Obamafy*, Obamakin, and *Obamanation*. With a particular focus on eponyms, Eve Konieczna asks 'Why Does "Obamaphilia" Win out over "The Love for Barack Obama"? A Few Remarks on Nonce-Formations and Neologisms in Polish and English Language Mass Media' (in Kleparski et al., eds., pp. 67–76). Grant Barrett considers the semantic development of *jack* in 'Among the New Words' (*AS* 84[2009] 340–9), finding that many uses are parallel with those of *jerk*. 'On Selected Aspects of Human *Otherness* in Language: A Cognitive Account of Appellative Exonyms in English and Polish' (in Górecka-Smolińska et al., eds., pp. 91–8), by Marcin Kudła, looks at names used to describe outsiders. Four main groups emerge: those referring to outsiders by their clothes, by their food, by their language, or by their personal names. Kudła returns to the subject of food-based terms for outsiders in 'On the Edibility of Aliens: The Case of *Sauerkrauts*, *Kapuśniaks* and *Potato-Heads*' (in Kleparski et al., eds., pp. 83–9).

This year's most significant publication on figurative language was Kathryn Allan's *Metaphor and Metonymy: A Diachronic Approach*. Allan argues that although metaphor and metonymy have been treated as marginal ornamental features of language, they are actually fundamental to our understanding and expression of the world around us. Synchronic approaches are faced with the problem of having to distinguish, largely subjectively, between more or less active metaphors, but the advantage of Allan's diachronic perspective is that it necessitates a pragmatic approach based on the data available. Allan takes her data from the *Historical Thesaurus of English* section on INTELLIGENCE, in full awareness of the limitations of using data originally drawn from the *OED*, and uses cognitive linguistics, theories of child language acquisition, historical evidence, and lexical case studies to explore metaphor and metonymy within her field. She finds that clear A > B mappings of source and target are problematic from a historical perspective and that metaphor and metonymy are often intertwined. Beata Kopecka also argues, in 'On the Interlocking Nature of Metaphor and Metonymy: A Case Study of Body Parts and Proper Names' (in Górecka-Smolińska et al., eds., pp. 79–89), that these two strategies of mental conceptualization frequently interact. In the same volume, Robert Kiełtyka provides 'A Panchronic Account of Canine Verbal Zoosemy' (pp. 25–36), by discussing animal names transferred to human referents. In 'On Morphology-Semantics Interface' (in Kleparski et al., eds., pp. 51–9), Kiełtyka looks particularly at the effect of the use of diminutive animal names. Agnieska Uberman finds that it is useful to teach learners the connotations of colour terms, in 'On Metaphorics and Symbolism of Colour Terms' (in Kleparski et al., eds., pp. 141–6).

Philip Durkin's *The Oxford Guide to Etymology* provides a useful introduction to the principles and processes of etymology, remaining clear and comprehensible at all times without in any way obscuring the intricacies of its subject-matter. Its scope is broader than the title suggests, in that it also covers aspects of morphology, semantics, metaphor, phonology, and onomastics, on the grounds that all are fundamental to the practice of etymology. A glossary of terms is provided, although each term is also carefully explained and exemplified on first use. Durkin assumes a background in historical linguistics, and suggests additional reading for those that need it. Chapter and subsection summaries are a helpful way of ensuring that the reader is able to see the argument behind the detailed examples, and the use of questions in headings is also useful in this respect. Durkin has also, clearly, thought carefully about how to engage his readers with the subject accessibly: he doesn't consider sound changes until chapter 7, for example. The adoption of lexicographer's lower-case for cited terms even when they occurred at the beginning of sentences was less helpful for me, in that the apparent typos interrupted my focus. Readers might have been trusted to deduce that these terms should not always be capitalized. That minor caveat aside, Durkin's *Guide* will be invaluable for historical linguists and their students alike, as well as for students of the *OED*. It is illuminated by engaging examples of word-history, such as the origins of *meticulous* in Latin *metus* 'fear', of *bureau* in a type of cloth, of *milliner* in Milan, and in the merging of two OE verbs to form ModE *melt*: one meaning 'to become liquid' and the other 'to make liquid'. Anatoly Liberman's chapter on 'English Etymological Dictionaries' (in Cowie, ed., vol. 2, pp. 269–89) offers a detailed account of a number of etymological dictionaries, though without a clear explanation of how the line is to be drawn between etymological and general dictionaries.

A number of articles deal with specific etymologies. Andrew Breeze provides 'A Welsh Etymology for *Eskibah* in *Ancrene Wisse*' (*N&Q* 56[2009] 332–3), arguing that it should be interpreted as 'little brush'. William Sayers offers French *cele* and an English gerundial suffix as the origins of *ceiling* in 'The Etymology and Early History of *Ceiling*' (*N&Q* 56[2009] 496–9). Sayers also finds 'Two Etymologies: *Inkle* and *Natty*' (*N&Q* 56[2009] 350–4) in Middle French *encol-* and English *natter* or Irish *nathach*, respectively. He argues that etymologists have paid insufficient attention to the language of crafts and trades in both cases. John Considine's 'Early Uses and Etymology of *Blotto*' (*AS* 84[2009] 72–82) traces the origins of this word to the Western Front in the First World War, where the erratic behaviour of delivery riders on tricycles manufactured by the Blotto Frères company offers a likely source for this word.

Moving to less etymological word studies, Grzegorz. A. Kleparski asks 'What's in the Name of *Helga*, *Guido* and *Sandomierz*-Loving *Czesiek*? With Special Reference to the Evaluative Load of *Dutch* in English' (in Kleparski et al., eds., pp. 15–28), and finds that references to Dutchness generally bear negative connotations in English. Kleparski also writes 'On Sound Symbolism: A Pilot Study of Pejorative Load of Selected English Phoneme Clusters' (in Górecka-Smolińska et al., eds., pp. 57–64). It covers five initial phoneme clusters, grouping some different sounds together, such as /fa/ /fr/ /fo/, which are held to connote motion, stealth, deception, cowardice, and weakness. Unconvincing examples include *fabulous*, *factitious*, *fox*, *forge*, *frame*, and *fragile*. Ewa Konieczna works towards 'De-obscuring the Language: Folk-Etymology in Modern English and Polish' (in Górecka-Smolińska et al., eds., pp. 71–8) by applying a panchronic view to Lise Winer's typology.

Modern English loanwords were also the focus of a number of shorter studies this year. Albert J. Schütz's '*Webster's Third* and the Pronunciation of Hawaiian Loanwords in English: A Different View of *Usage*' (*Dictionaries* 30[2009] 1–17) argues that a representation of the closest approximation to standard Hawaiian pronunciation consonant with English phonology should always be offered unless another pronunciation is well established in English. David Nash's 'Australian Aboriginal Words in Dictionaries: A Reaction' (*IJL* 22[2009] 179–88) and R.M.W. Dixon's 'Australian Aboriginal Words in Dictionaries: Response to Nash' (*IJL* 22[2009] 189–90) examine some contentious assertions regarding the *OED*'s treatment of words borrowed from the Australian languages. In 'Words Escape Us' (*NZW* 13[2009] 1–2), Joan Metge reflects on the frequency with which Maori words are used, unglossed, in New Zealand writing and speech, and suggests that the adoption of Maori terms is one way in which the politically dominant group seeks to make NZE distinctive. John MacAlister discusses a related issue in 'Investigating the Changing Use of Te Reo' (*NZW* 13[2009] 3–4), where he reports on a longitudinal study demonstrating that English speakers are becoming more familiar with a range of Maori words, particularly those relating to social culture. Tony Deverson discusses the issues of national and ethnic identity involved in 'Recognising New Zealandisms' (*NZW* 13[2009] 5–7).

8. Onomastics

For onomastic publication 2009 was a good year. A number of books appeared in addition to the usual journals and anthologies. Most of the books were, as usual, on aspects of toponymy rather than personal names. I will first consider the reference books which appeared in 2009, then proceed to the area place-name studies and close with the major articles of the year.

From its title and subtitle, Patricia Roberts Clark's *Tribal Names of the Americas: Spelling Variants and Alternative Forms, Cross-Referenced* would appear to be a most welcome compilation of the names used over the years to designate families, tribes, totems, gens, and other subgroupings of Native Americans. Roberts, a reference archivist in the Southwest Collection/Special Collections Library at Texas Tech University in Lubbock with years of previous experience with Native American languages and tribal groupings while working in the Los Angeles Public Library's central office, has amassed (and that is the only word that comes close to describing the contents of this volume) thousands of names applied to Native American groups which have appeared in documents over the past half-millennium plus. The need for a reference such as this has been painfully obvious for more than a century. (With publications such as this, essentially a collation and alphabetical organization of such a large number of names, publishers usually state the number of entries, at least in general terms; curiously, McFarland has apparently not done so. My rough estimate is that Roberts has included between 40,000 and 50,000 names, drawn almost exclusively from federal government publications. To have included names from locally produced sources, manuscripts, diaries, and the like would have tripled or quadrupled the number of entries, so vast has been the variety of recordings of the names.) When I, therefore, saw the announcements of the publication of this book, I thought this would be a welcome addition to the onomastic reference shelf. Unfortunately, my enthusiasm was short-lived. The book is difficult to use, many of the references appear to be ad hoc, and the cross-references, so highly touted in the promotional materials, often lead nowhere and are occasionally inaccurate. Since this is a suggestive report rather than a full review I will mention only two of the more obvious examples of the book's difficulty of use and confusing organization. The indispensable multi-volume *Handbook of North American Indians* is abbreviated *Hdbk* plus the appropriate volume number, except for one: volume 8, dealing with California, is given its own abbreviation, CA-8, with no explanation. As an example where Roberts is incorrect in her reported relationships, she claims that Saukies, a seventeenth-century recording for the Sauk, a tribe primarily of north-western Illinois and southern Wisconsin, is a variant of Sauk (which it is), a tribe of Washington state (which it is not). In short, this volume contains a great deal of serious, potentially very valuable scholarship but unfortunately misused and misdirected.

On a more positive note, Adrian Room, arguably the world's foremost scholarly compiler of names and author of many onomastic references, including *A Dictionary of Pseudonyms, Place-Name Changes 1900–1991*, and *Placenames of the World*, returned in 2009 with *Alternate Names of Places*, a compendium of some 7,000 names, primarily those of populated places, although some rivers, mountains, and even ice shelves are included, from around the world, which appear in variant spellings or in entirely different forms. These are all 'formal' names in that they appear on official documents. Nicknames are not included, so there is no listing for Cincinnati, alternatively known as 'Porkopolis', or Florida, 'The Sunshine State'. Many of the alternative names, probably most, are exonyms, names imposed by those from outside the entity being named, Bombay for Mumbai, Japan for Nihon. Room's book is filled with the kind of information we find both illuminating and edifying. We learn that the aboriginal name for Australia's Ayers Rock is *Uluru*; we follow the name changes of *Petrograd* to *Leningrad* to *St Petersburg*, and we gain an understanding of why the name *Macedonia* is unacceptable to Greece but *The Former Yugoslav Republic of Macedonia* is not. Politics and onomastics are rarely separate. Room has included an interesting appendix of some of the better-known place names in English as they appear in languages of several language families, all of linguistic as well as onomastic interest: French (Golden Horn = Corne D'Or), German (Baltic Sea = Ostsee), Turkish

(Morocco = Fas), Finnish (United States = Yhdysvallat), Polish (Italy = Włochy), Welsh (English Channel = Môr Udd).

At least one popularizing (not popular—there are important differences) onomastics book appeared in 2009. In *Lost States*, Michael Trinklein looks at some seventy-five land areas that have been proposed—more or less seriously—as states of the American union. While this does not pretend to be a 'scholarly' book in the traditional sense, its discussions are drawn from existing scholarly works and would be of interest to many history and geography buffs. It would also provide a valuable service in introducing onomastics to a wider audience. Our interest of course is in the names proposed for the suggested but unrealized future states of America. Each of the names contributes to a better understanding of the times and motivations of the name creators. The process began early. Shortly after the American Revolution, when the fledgling United States doubled in size with territory gained from Britain's losses, Thomas Jefferson, the first US Secretary of State, proposed that the newly acquired Northwest Territory be divided in up to ten new states, which he suggested—in a odd mix of classical morphemes, Native American names, and honorary names—be called Illinoia, Michigania, Washington, Saratoga, Pelisipia, Polypotamia, Metropotamia, Assenisipia, Sylvania, and Chersonesus. (I didn't know that last one, either; it is Greek for 'peninsula', and Jefferson chose Chersonesus to name that part of the area which is now the state of Michigan; quite appropriate as it turns out since Michigan is indeed a peninsula or rather two peninsulas: the upper part of Michigan, the part abutting Wisconsin, is known as the UP or the Upper Peninsula.) Other names offering insights into aspects of American history, major or minor, include Vandalia, the name proposed for the fourteenth English colony in North America; Jacinto, named for the battle of San Jacinto, which made possible American control of the Southwest and California, seriously considered in the 1860s as the name of the new state comprised of what is now north and east Texas; and Deseret, taken from the Book of Mormon, meaning 'honeybee' and proposed by Brigham Young as the name of the area that became the state of Utah.

Of state or area place-name books, one of the more enduring is Roberta C. Cheney's *Names on the Face of Montana*, first published in 1971. So much has been learned about the history, etymology, and socio-political dynamics of place-naming in the intervening forty years that this volume, exemplary for its day, was long overdue for not only a minor updating but a thorough rewriting. A new volume, which necessarily begins with Cheney, Aarstad et al., *Montana Place Names*, was published by the Montana Historical Society in 2009. This book is a collaborative effort by four historians and archivists, who apparently wrote the individual entries in their own areas of specialization. Since, despite its size, Montana has fewer known and named places than many other areas, the authors include some 1,200 Montana names. (Most state place-name books contain twice or even three times that number.) The entries include discussions of names along with related historical, cultural, and social information of cities and towns, geographic names such as those of mountains and valleys, parks, battlefields, reservations, and sites listed on the National Register of Historic Places. Each entry is keyed to one of twenty-four colour maps which allow for easy geographic orientation, while the period pictures bring to vivid life the communities and features which Montanans found useful to name. The Montana Historical Society has made the entire text available online. It can be accessed at mtplacenames.org. To my knowledge this is the first onomastics book to be made available electronically at the same time it was published in a print edition.

With few exceptions, onomastics, and in particular toponymy, has remained at a rather primitive level; it has been restricted largely to basic data collection and generally avoided theoretical discussions. (There are no even remotely agreed-upon taxonomies for either personal or geographic names.) There are, however, some signs that this unfortunate situation may be changing. The 2009 book with the greatest potential for moving onomastics in a more theoretical direction is *Critical Toponymies: The Contested Politics of Place Naming*, a collection of essays edited by Lawrence D. Berg, of the University of British Columbia, and Jani Vuolteenaho, of the University of Helsinki. It is, however, likely to get little exposure and to languish on the fringes of onomastics because the publisher (Ashgate) does not have a major publicity or distribution practice in many parts of the world and the price ($115) is prohibitive for all but the best-endowed research libraries. The volume brings together thirteen essays by cultural geographers and others, all of which bear on the notion that place-naming is power *par excellence*, and as Kearns and Berg put it 'rather than being entities *in* the landscape, names are a constitutive component of landscape itself' (p. 154). Some sense of the nature of the essays included can be gathered from their titles (themselves political and social acts of naming). Those of greatest interest to English-speaking readers include 'Naming the Past: The Significance of Commemorative Street Names', 'The Aloha State: Place Names and the Anti-Conquest of Hawai'i', and 'Proclaiming Place: Towards a Geography of Place Name Pronunciation'. Two of the chapters deal with the politics of the name of Martin Luther King, Jr., a topic of onomastic interest and debate for more than fifty years. These are 'Street Names as Memorial Arenas: The Reputational Politics of Commemorating Martin Luther King, Jr., in a Georgia County' and 'Virtual Place Naming, Internet Domains, and the Politics of Misdirection: The Case of www.martinlutherking.org'. These essays are provocative forays into the historical and contemporary use of place names both as shields and swords and as tools in fashioning and refashioning landscapes. One would hope that this volume becomes widely known and frequently cited. It has potential for influencing the direction of onomastics.

The Place-Names of Leicestershire, part 4: *Gartree Hundred*, by Barrie Cox, is volume 84 of the Survey of English Place-Names sponsored by the English Place-Name Society. A 'Hundred' was an administrative subdivision of a shire or county in much of western Europe (especially the Germanic-speaking areas) until quite recently, and remains—somewhat archaically—in Australia today. The origin of the word, outside of obviously relating to a hundred of something, is obscure, but the entity remained an important part of English government for better than a thousand years. The English Place-Name Society began publishing these remarkable surveys of place names in 1924, and this volume continues the traditions of authority and reliability established by those which preceded it. Characterized by impeccable scholarship lightly worn, and consistent with other volumes in the place-name series, Cox opens with a consideration of the name *Gartree* itself (origin uncertain but likely related to the senses 'spear' or 'tree', which appear as 'Gardena' in the Beowulf manuscript and first noted as *Geretrev* in the Domesday Book of 1086) and proceeds to a consideration of the names of the fifty-plus parishes comprising Gartree Hundred. An especially valuable feature is Cox's seventy-five-page appendix of elements found in the place names of Gartree Hundred, from *abbat* and *abbaye* 'an abbey' through *gāra* (ModE 'gore') to *yoman* 'an attendant or assistant to a governmental official or royal'. These entries provide a great deal of information regarding the sources and constructions of English place names, giving etymologies, glosses, and examples found in Gartree Hundred. For instance, and to give but one example from many dozens of how onomastics can inform studies of PDE, the element *hovel* occurs in more than a dozen place names in Gartree Hundred with the apparent meaning 'a shed or rack upon which grain is stacked'. The meaning of the word has wandered quite far from this sense in the past millennium.

For its size and relatively small population, the island nation of Jamaica has more than its share of unusual place names, such as *Half-a-Bottle*, *District of Look Behind*, and *Slippery Gut*. In *Jamaican Place Names*, historian B.W. Higman and geographer B.J. Hudson, using maps drawn over the past 300 years, discuss several thousand Jamaican names, concentrating on those which are characteristic of the naming patterns of the island over that time. Somewhat surprisingly, since it had such an extensive history of European colonization, 'the truly common place names of Jamaica, the ones . . . that give the Jamaican settlement a particular character . . . [are not] derived from personal names or transferred from other places . . . [but] are associated with sentiment' (p. 61): names such as *Fellowship*, *Content*, and *Rest and be Thankful*. The surprising etymologies are here (*Montego Bay*, for all its exotic allure, derives from Spanish *manteca* 'lard, hog fat') as well as names from words which have developed characteristic Jamaican senses (a *pen* may be the residence of a wealthy merchant, a *crawl* 'corral' may be an area where food is grown, and a *cockpit* is a depression among steep hills). Unlike most place-name books, this volume is not arranged alphabetically (although a complete name index is provided); rather, it is organized thematically. Two introductory chapters are followed by 'Common Names', 'Topographical Names', 'Hydrological Names', 'Coastal Names', 'Enterprise Names', 'Settlement Names', and 'Route Names'.

Before turning to onomastic articles I want to mention and praise the special issue of *Onomastica Canadiana* edited by Benoît Leblanc, entitled *Onomastic Encounters: From Children's Literature to Theology* since it addresses a recurring problem in onomastics: how to improve the image of name studies in educational institutions and how to attract young members to the field. This issue contains six essays on a variety of onomastic topics, all written by students. Unfortunately, they are all in French and therefore a review would be inappropriate for this venue. However, the existence of this collection should be noted and should provide inspiration for senior onomasts to make renewed efforts to engage and encourage students to become involved in onomastics, surely the most interdisciplinary of all studies. And we should all be grateful to Professor Leblanc and to the Canadian Society for the Study of Names for their part in underwriting this worthy endeavour.

A sub-field of onomastics which is extremely difficult to characterize since there is no generally (or even partially) recognized, much less accepted, definition of its parameters is that of 'literary onomastics', a term coined, if my memory serves, by Grace Alvarez-Altman in the 1970s as a cover term for names which are created or adopted by writers of creative literature. Serious study of authors' use of names in fiction has been hindered by the fact that, while its worth has rarely been questioned, no one is really sure just what it is and just what it covers. Does it more appropriately belong to literary criticism or to onomastics? Should names in literature be seen as windows into the interpretation of the text (in other words as an arm of literary criticism) or should they be viewed as objects unto themselves and therefore as falling into the domain of onomastics? Tatyana Hramova confronts this and several other issues in 'What's in Literary Onomastics?' (*OnCan* 91[2009] 11–22). After a historical introduction, Hramova discusses the authorial uses of names and concludes with two answers to the problems mentioned above: one dealing with how one might approach the how and why of authors' choices of names in literature, the other with the area properly included by the term 'literary onomastics'. As to the first problem, Hramova says 'literary onomastics should deal with the name as a part of language, literature and a particular text, discussing the ways in which it correlates with them and the referent'. And as to the second, 'Literary onomastics can . . . be defined as an interdisciplinary area that analyses proper names in literature using methods of linguistics and literary criticism, but also address[ing] a wide scope of questions concerning the usage and functions of names in literature . . .' (p. 19). This is a thoughtful, provocative, and informative essay sure to spur discussion of the boundaries between the literary uses of names and their inherent characteristics.

It is always gratifying to encounter names in areas where heretofore they have been of minimal concern or treated casually as merely adjuncts to 'significant' areas of linguistics or other disciplines. The past several years have seen names used in wider and more significant ways in pragmatics, discourse, and discussions of speech-acts than previously. A particularly striking article is Michael Adams's 'Power, Politeness, and the Pragmatics of Nicknames' (*Names* 57[2009] 81–91), which looks at the roles of nicknames as pragmatic objects of locutionary, illocutionary, and perlocutionary discourse. As Adams states, 'a theory of nicknames and nicknaming depends on the pragmatics of nicknames and the politeness structures implicated in them, rather than conventional logico-semantic accounts of names' leading to 'iterations of "naming contracts" between named and namer, such that nicknames are politically focusing social objects' (p. 81). Articles such as this point out not only the possible uses of names in linguistic and social theory but also their primacy in providing windows of opportunity to see the dynamics of both language and society.

For the past several years Marc Picard, of Concordia University in Montreal, Canada, has been exploring the origins and histories of (largely

North American) surnames through the opportunities made possible by genealogical websites, which have proliferated in the past several decades. Especially useful are those such as Genealogy.com and Rootsweb.com, which are professionally moderated. Picard's work has provided valuable insights into the changes in the form(s) of names as they pass from one cultural-linguistic group to another. In his comprehensive *Dictionary of American Family Names* [OUP, 2003], Patrick Hanks lists some 1,300 names whose origin is problematic, either unidentified or unclassified. Of these, Picard, in a recently released book published by VDM of Saarbrücken, has identified the origins of about 95 per cent, using genealogical databases available online, a remarkable achievement. In an overview of the tremendous potential that genealogical sites hold for onomastics, Picard, in 'Genealogical Evidence and the Americanization of European Family Names' (*Names* 57[2009] 30–51), lists and glosses several hundred Americanized names which have been changed, either in minor ways such as altered spellings, or radical alterations and reinterpretations, morphologically or semantically based. Picard has salvaged the names from the 'origin unknown', 'origin unclear', or 'origin disputed' categories. Among the names of the former group (minor alterations) would be *Deshane* from *Duchêne* and *Peckenpaugh* from *Beckenback*. Among those with more significant changes in form are *Shelnutt* from German *Schildknecht* (literally 'shield servant') and *Tyo* from French *Taillon* 'tailor'.

Kenneth Tucker, a statistician at Carleton University, Ottawa, Canada, continued his investigations into long-term trends in naming in the English-speaking world with the article 'Increased Competition and Reduced Popularity: US Given Name Trends of the Twentieth and Early Twenty-First Centuries' (*Names* 57[2009] 52–62). Using data available on the Social Security Administration website (erroneously referred to as the Social Security Agency) Tucker lists and plots on log-linear graphs the most popular names given to males and to females by decade from 1880 through 2006, the most recent year for which information was available, seeking trends and looking 'to understand the laws that parents implicitly obey in the everyday practice of naming a baby' (p. 52). In 2006 the ten most popular boys' names (encompassing in total just under 10 per cent of all boys' names) were (in order of popularity) Jacob, Michael, Joshua, Ethan, Matthew, Daniel, Christopher, Andrew, Anthony, and William. For girls, the top ten names (comprising less than 8 per cent of the population) were Emily, Emma, Madison, Isabella, Ava, Abigail, Olivia, Hannah, Sophia, and Samantha. It has long been known that traditionally boys' names are relatively stable and the most popular of these account for a large percentage of all names while the most popular girls' names are more varied. Tucker's data show that this pattern is changing; the names given to both genders are becoming more varied, with the trend being especially noticeable in the naming of boys. In 1880, for instance, John, the most popular boy's name, accounted for more than 8 per cent of all names, while in 2006 the most popular boy's name, Jacob, accounted for just 1 per cent. Similarly, in 1880, Mary, the most popular girls' name, accounted for more than 7 per cent of the population but in 2006 the most popular girl's name, Emily, accounted for 1 per cent. More generally, in the 1880s the 100 most popular male names accounted for nearly 75 per cent of all names but by 2006 this had fallen to 50 per cent. Girls' names trended in the same direction; in the 1880s the 100 most popular names accounted for 70 per cent of all names and by 2006 for only 36 per cent. Tucker's conclusion is apt: 'What we see for both males and females is a striking reduction in the frequency of the most popular given name. Whereas in 1880 names like *John* and *Mary* dominated the selection, later they were displaced not by a new name but by a set of new names, all of roughly the same frequency' (p. 55).

The study of nicknames, especially public and self-chosen nicknames, has long been a staple of onomastics, from the names of entertainers to baseball players to outlaws and other social misfits (think 'Duke' Ellington, 'Babe' Ruth', and 'Pretty Boy' Floyd). Ernest L. Able, in 'Women Who Fight' (*Names* 57[2009] 141–61), looks at the public nicknames of some 400 female boxers. Three main categories evolved; the two most common stemmed from the apparent paradox of female boxers attempting to retain femininity in a sport which emphasizes violence and masculinity. Nicknames emphasizing power and combativeness (about 45 per cent of the total) included 'The Assassin', 'Bonecrusher', 'Merciless', and 'Fists of Fury'. Those emphasizing femininity (also about 45 per cent) included 'All American Girl', 'Dakota Princess', 'Baby Doll', and 'Sweet Tea'.

9. Dialectology and Sociolinguistics

In the area of sociolinguistics, we note the publication of only a few textbooks this year, unlike many previous years. We have received only two new editions of old favourites. Raj Mesthrie, Joan Swann, Ana Deumert, and William L. Leap have been working on the second edition of their *Introducing Sociolinguistics* which we praised in its first edition for being less Anglocentric than other textbooks, and the same can of course still be said for the second edition. Unfortunately the authors do not provide us with a preface making clear what they have changed, and why. The text seems to be slightly rewritten in places, there are some new sub-chapters, and some mistakes have been rectified, but these changes only add up to minor changes. Much the same can be said for a revised (in fact, the third) edition of another classic, Jack Chambers's *Sociolinguistic Theory*, which is also noteworthy for being the only edition of a textbook we have come across in recent years that has actually become shorter rather than longer. The reader is hard pushed to find evidence of the 'new material that [was] warranted' (preface); indeed the only sub-chapter that has been added are two pages on the 'Decline of Briticisms in Canadian English', and we can only wonder what made the author delete two sections on Baghdad Arabic, one of the few glimpses outside the Anglo-American area that this book affords. Still, this is the only sociolinguistic book we are aware of that even begins to discuss the 'Adaptive Significance of Language Variation' in biological terms. If you do not mind the strongly positivist stance Chambers takes here, or if you need a textbook to argue *against*, this might still be the introduction to classical variationist sociolinguistics for you. Variationist sociolinguistics is largely coterminous with *Quantitative Methods in Sociolinguistics*, and this just happens to be the next textbook on our desk, thoroughly new, written by Ronald K.S. Macaulay. Or perhaps we should say booklet, since the text is just over 100 pages long. This book is a wonderful read and comes across as very personal; thus, at the beginning we encounter the author as a young lad, sitting in the library, reading Labov. It is both a reminder to all active sociolinguists to pay attention to questions of methodology as well as a hands-on introduction for students to conduct their own research in a responsible and reflective way. Macaulay looks at the (traditional) social categories that are usually distinguished in variationist research and then discusses the nature of the data, and problems in collecting the data and in tabulating the results; he presents several methods of analysis, and compares the methodology of some individual studies (from Labov's New York study (1966) to his own, Macaulay 2005) in a critical and thought-provoking way.

We must also record here the publication of yet another NEW book, *The New Sociolinguistics Reader* edited by Nikolas Coupland and Adam Jaworski. We are reminded of the same editors' *Sociolinguistics: A Reader and Coursebook* from 1997, but the copyright page assures us that this year's reader is indeed an original product. Be that as it may, we will still compare the two, but it has to be said that not much has remained the same, warranting the label NEW for this reader. Each part of the *New Sociolinguistics Reader* contains an introduction by the editors, providing background information to the field, and a brief discussion of the individual contributions. The contributions are well chosen and emphasize the state of the art, although some classics have been retained. Part I looks at 'Language Variation' and has extracts from Walt Wolfram, William Labov, Peter Trudgill, Sali Tagliamonte, James and Lesley Milroy, Deborah Cameron, Jenny Cheshire, and Penny Eckert, giving a good (and up-to-date) overview of the field. Part II is completely new and concentrates on 'Language, Gender and Sexuality', and in its length (with seven chapters) pays tribute to the importance of this new field that has established itself over the last fifteen years or so. Contributions are perhaps not quite as representative as the ones for Part I; they include studies on dominance, fraternity men, nerd girls, and drag queens (all articles have appeared before, and have been reviewed in earlier *YWES* chapters). Part III is revamped from the earlier edition where it was called 'Stylistic Variation'; it is now 'Style, Stylization and Identity', and in this terminological shift already indicates the development this field has undergone. Apart from the introductory classic on 'audience design' (by Allan Bell), all other contributions are new. They discuss crossing, metacultural performance, and global hip-hop. Part IV deals with 'Language Attitudes, Ideologies and Stances' (we will come back to the last of these terms in a moment), and here we find a selection of readings from folk linguistics to the German spelling reform. Part V, on 'Multilingualism, Code-Switching and Diglossia', contains nine chapters, only two of which were included before (Joshua Fishman on ethnicity, and Susan Gal on language change in Oberwart). Added are introductions to code-switching, bilingual conversation, language rights, language death, and globalization. The final part, VI, is entitled 'Language, Culture and Interaction' and moves to a more ethnographically informed sociolinguistics.

Texts included emphasize the performance aspect of communication, be this in the form of ritual insults (the classic from Labov), humour, small talk, tourist–host encounters, sign language, or sociolinguistics in later modernity. As the editors write, this section of the reader would lend itself well to cross-referenced reading with any of the earlier parts, 'to take stock of... what Sociolinguistics is delivering... in terms of insights about the language/society interface' (p. 581). And perhaps this is the claim that this reader achieves overall: it gives a wide-ranging overview of some classics, but certainly covers the broad field of sociolinguistics that is presented by research today. Still, this in a way complements the 1997 reader, so keep the first version on your shelf!

Another reader has gone into a second edition, Alessandro Duranti's *Linguistic Anthropology: A Reader* (the first edition was from 2001). New chapters on ethnicity (much needed!), hip hop, language change, multi-media, and sexuality (among others a very interesting contribution by Don Kulick on the word 'No' (pp. 423–503)) have brought this reader up to date and should make it of interest to sociolinguists as well. Instead of growing longer, some old classics had to make room for the new arrivals, though. We were a bit sorry to see Dell Hymes's 'Communicative Competence' go, as well as Benjamin Lee Whorf's 'The Relation of Habitual Thought and Behaviour to Language'. If you feel the same, simply hold on to the first edition.

Stance is the term we wanted to come back to, and Alexandra Jaffe has edited a volume of papers with just this title: *Stance: Sociolinguistic Perspectives*. Particularly relevant for English sociolinguistics are the introduction by the editor, the discussion by Barbara Johnstone on 'Stance, Style, and the Linguistic Individual' (chapter 2), and the contribution by Scott F. Kiesling on 'Style as Stance: Stance as the Explanation for Patterns of Sociolinguistic Variation' (chapter 8). Johnstone illustrates 'how repeated patterns of stancetaking can come together as a style associated with a particular individual' (p. 29), in this case Barbara Jordan, who ultimately uses stance-taking to create rhetorical credibility. Similarly, Scott Kiesling argues that stances, through repetition, become associated with identities (in specific situations), and are thus what underlies the sociolinguistic concept of 'style'.

Speaking of identity, John Edwards has written a monograph on *Language and Identity*, specifically investigating the relationship of the individual and the group, be it national, religious, or gender-based. From a discussion of the role of language in national identity, it is only a short step to investigate the use of language planning (the last chapter in this book), and the 'Ecology of Language' is also dealt with in passing, in particular understood here as the preservation of linguistic diversity. Edwards's chapters on dialects (chapters 3 and 4) and on gender are thoughtful introductions to the complex and difficult interaction between language and identity. For example, he takes perception seriously and reminds us that 'the power of perception creates its own reality', so that, for example, 'dialects broadly viewed as inferior *are*, for all practical intents and purposes, inferior' (p. 5). But what really sets this book apart from others is the discussion of language and religion since the link is usually not made. Here, Edwards links the ancient argument over the one original language to a discourse just as ancient, namely on language and identity, which is at times amusing, but he also discusses the strong links between religion and language for the Celtic languages, where all amusement vanishes in the historical tracing of the Northern Ireland conflict, to mention but one. In this book, Edwards has included a few study questions after each chapter (of the type 'Why has language always been considered a central pillar of nationalism?') that summarize his main arguments, and in this way this book might be suitable as a textbook at undergraduate level if you have dedicated students that do not mind densely written, but very insightful, texts.

On a very different tack, from decades of work in dialectology William A. Kretzschmar Jr. has contributed what is probably the most interesting book of the year with *The Linguistics of Speech*. Kretzschmar argues firmly in favour of taking empirical results of language use (*parole*, not *langue*) seriously (this already tells you that this book is not primarily written for dialectologists, but for a much wider audience), in a way as an antidote to decades of structuralism, yet firmly based on Saussure's ideas of *parole*. The recurring results from Kretzschmar's atlas studies, but also from sociolinguistics, perceptual dialectology, and corpus linguistics suggest asymptotic curves as the ordering principle behind most of the data. This means that typically a small number of variants are extraordinarily frequent, whereas there is a wide range of equally infrequent other options (often known as the long tail). Kretzschmar claims that 'at any given time, we always see much more variety in language behavior than might have been predicted by a structural approach in which speakers are assumed to share some unitary fixed system' (p. 172), which he links to the conception of 'Speech as a Complex System' (his chapter 6), the central chapter of this book, where he characterizes speech as a non-linear system with the property of scaling, as well as areas of emergent order. This has important implications for dialectology, sociolinguistics, and corpus linguistics, as well as theories of language change (and probably beyond); for example minority variants can get recycled, they can serve to distinguish speech communities (in terms of frequency, not categorically), they can characterize individuals' variability with regard to different situations, interlocutors, etc., and perhaps a more detailed knowledge of these structures of speech can serve to inform lay notions of appropriateness (as opposed to the ideology of correctness). Food for much thought, if not your next study, and we are certain we haven't heard the last from Kretzschmar on this topic yet. (A-curves will reappear in some detailed studies below.)

Benedikt Szmrecsanyi and Bernd Kortmann are some of the most prolific writers this year. Their main strands of argumentation are represented in their contribution 'Between Simplification and Complexification: Non-Standard Varieties of English around the World' (in Sampson et al., eds., pp. 64–79). The authors distinguish different kinds of complexity: the endearingly termed 'ornamental rule complexity' (for complex features that do not seem to have a clear function), 'L2 acquisition difficulty', 'grammaticity' (i.e. redundant grammatical marking), and 'irregularities', and they find that in varieties of English around the world, it is the language type rather than geographical region that seems to be the best determiner of a variety's structure, such that 'L2 varieties are least complex and most transparent, while traditional, low-contact L1 vernaculars are most complex and least transparent' (p. 75) (see also section 5(a) above). Maybe we would have guessed this without the intricate statistical modelling, but the surprising result is that, *pace* John McWhorter, English-based pidgins and creoles 'turn out not to be any less ornamental than high-contact L1 varieties of English' (p. 76). In the same collection, Peter Trudgill links 'Sociolinguistic Typology and Complexification' (pp. 98–109). Trudgill's main claim here is that 'certain types of social factors may determine linguistic complexity, in particular the degree of contact, dense vs. loose social networks, and the community size. Trudgill here uses just one of Szmrecsanyi and Kortmann's criteria of complexity, i.e. L2-acquisition difficulty. Trudgill links high contact with simplification, defining simplification as (a) regularization, (b) increased transparency, and (c) loss of redundancy, embodied by (c1) loss of morphological categories and (c2) reduction of repetition of information. (You can see that discussions of simplicity can themselves become quite complex.) Again all this is rather obvious if you think about it, so the interesting twist is to discuss 'complexification': if language contact leads to simplification, in which circumstances can we observe the emergence of more complex structures? And Trudgill's answer is: in small, tight-knit, isolated communities, since these are 'more able, because of their network structures, to push through, enforce, and sustain linguistic changes which would have a much smaller chance of success in larger, more fluid communities' (p. 102), and he provides some innovative variants from traditional (low-contact) dialects of English that support his point.

Besides (and in conjunction with) 'complexity', another catchphrase this year must be 'vernacular universals', promoted in particular by the volume *Vernacular Universals and Language Contact: Evidence from Varieties of English and Beyond* edited by Markku Filppula, Juhani Klemola, and Heli Paulasto. Amongst other things, this line of research inspired by functional typology seems to have led to an almost inflationary terminology on –'versals' (we have so far met with 'Angloversals', 'typoversals', 'phyloversals', 'varioversals', and 'areoversals', and we wouldn't be surprised if there are more). Almost all the contributions here are relevant. Where they are clearly regional, they will be discussed further below. In a general vein, J.K. Chambers discusses 'Cognition and the Linguistic Continuum from Vernacular to Standard' (pp. 19–32) on the basis of the (rather contentious) claim that 'dialects become more complex as they become more standard or literary' (p. 19)—surely a claim that was already rebuked by Trudgill above, but upheld by Chambers on the reasoning that 'cognitive cost is involved in some kinds of linguistic complexity', making vernacular dialects 'cognitively more efficacious' (p. 20). In particular, expletive *there*-constructions (extremely frequently used with singular verbs, notwithstanding the nominal subject following the verb) serve to support Chambers's point, and he claims that the cognitive cost involved in this 'look-ahead mechanism' is cross-linguistically supported. (It has to be said, though, that this phenomenon is so frequent even in the spoken standard that naming it a *vernacular* universal is probably a misnomer.) Peter Trudgill reacts to this more strongly in 'Vernacular Universals and the Sociolinguistic Typology of English Dialects' (pp. 304–22), claiming that 'the search for vernacular universals [as envisaged by Chambers] . . . has ultimately been in vain' (pp. 304–5), mainly because the koinéized urban non-standard varieties of either Britain or North America taken as the basis for Chambers's putative vernacular universals are typologically not distinct from StE. Good examples would be third-person marking, irregular forms of *be* (Trudgill rejects the term 'default singular' for being Standard-centred, and the term 'non-concord' as well), and irregular verbs. In line with his other contribution this year, Trudgill advocates distinguishing this general English from low-contact traditional dialects, where we can observe weird and wonderful developments of complexification—see above.

Szmrecsanyi and Kortmann (also in Filppula et al., eds., pp. 33–53) look at many more non-standard features, seventy-six to be exact, in their contribution on 'Vernacular Universals and Angloversals in a Typological Perspective'. Here, they try to determine on the basis of the *Handbook* data whether any of these are truly Angloversals (a quick look at typological data shows that they cannot be truly universal, *pace* Chambers). Arguing from a position in typology, these authors are able to qualify some of Chambers's claims showing that what has been proposed as vernacular universals (conjugation regularization, default singulars, see Chambers above, multiple negation, and copula absence) are, at best, vernacular universals of English, and indeed in many cases, of the Americas only, which in a way justifies the proliferation of terminology mentioned above as necessary 'for achieving descriptive and explanatory accuracy' (p. 49). A similar topic is discussed by the same authors in *Lingua* (119[2009] 1643–63), where they investigate 'The Morphosyntax of Varieties of English Worldwide: A Quantitative Perspective' and again find the most striking typological differences between L1-varieties on the one hand, and pidgins and creoles on the other. More specifically, multi-dimensional scaling, cluster analysis, and principal component analysis reveal two axes of differentiation: morphosyntactic complexity and analyticity, along which the variety types differ. These two features are also discussed by Benedikt Szmrecsanyi alone in 'Typological Parameters of Intralingual Variability: Grammatical Analyticity Versus Syntheticity in Varieties of English' (*LVC* 21[2009] 319–53) across a wide range of corpus materials (BNC, Brown family, Switchboard, FRED, and ICE family) for English. Resonating with results from the *Handbook* material reported above, Szmrecsanyi finds that low-contact varieties are more synthetic than high-contact varieties, L1-varieties are more synthetic than L2-varieties, and non-Southeast Asian varieties are more synthetic than Southeast Asian ones, but interestingly there does not seem to be a trade-off between syntheticity and analyticity. Rather, grammatical marking as such, be it synthetic or analytic, seems to vary with the absence of such marking.

Back to the collection in Filppula et al., eds., Daniel Schreier restricts himself to just two features and asks, 'How Diagnostic are English Universals?' (pp. 57–79). He discusses in particular consonant cluster reduction (CCR) in varieties of English around the world, and default singulars (despite Trudgill's cautioning), here the variation between *was* and *were*. CCR seems to be a truly universal feature and as such carries little diagnostic worth for English varieties (since all of them have CCR, including the standard, it cannot serve to distinguish much *per se*), but Schreier finds significant quantitative and qualitative differences and posits 'contact-sensitivity' as the underlying reason for these differences. Similarly, levelling to *was* seems to be particularly frequent in transplanted varieties of English, cautiously supporting Chambers's impression that this might be a universal of English(es).

Terttu Nevalainen adds a historical perspective and investigates 'Number Agreement in Existential Constructions: A Sociolinguistic Study of Eighteenth-Century English' (in Filppula et al., eds., pp. 80–102) since by this period *there*-existentials actually dominate over constructions without a dummy subject. Although default singulars decline over time, they are much more frequent in the past tense (*there was*) than in the present tense, and are used much more frequently by women than by men, which might be an indication that the development of notional concord (the standard pattern) may have been a change from above, led by men with access to formal education. Default singulars are also the topic of Sali Tagliamonte's chapter, entitled 'There *Was* Universals; Then There *Weren't*: A Comparative Sociolinguistic Perspective on "Default Singulars"' (in Filppula et al., eds., pp. 103–29). Comparing data across thirteen different locales of the English-speaking world, Tagliamonte finds that even for the purported universal (read: Angloversal) of 'default singulars', the frequencies as well as the constraint hierarchies differ in rather unpredictable ways across speech communities, which leads her to conclude that 'the constraint exists nearly everywhere, but the ranking order fluctuates' (p. 129). Indeed, as the title indicates, at one moment the universals are there, the next they disappear...

Peter Siemund, again from a standpoint in typology, discusses 'Linguistic Universals and Vernacular Data' (in Filppula et al., eds., pp. 323–48) more generally and points out that some areas of functional typology have not been systematically applied to the study of vernaculars yet, although they might carry great potential. Thus, the study of grammaticalization processes could 'offer a window into the past and the future' (p. 330), or one could explore in more detail the idea that language contact could lead to 'contact-induced grammaticalisation' (p. 332), as perhaps in the case of the Irish English *after*-perfect. (Pietsch's study on the medial-object perfect discussed below will take up this idea again.) Finally in this collection, Sarah G. Thomason asks, 'Why Universals VERSUS Contact-Induced Change?' (pp. 349–64), in a way following on from Siemund, since, as she argues, 'many linguistic changes involve both kinds of process' (p. 349). In an interesting twist, the reverse also holds, such that different causes (such as structure-internal drift, dialect contact, or language contact) can lead to the same type of change, so that what looks like an Angloversal might actually be due to different causes in different localities! Thomason also has some examples that cannot be plausibly explained as simplifying (or complicating), throwing into relief some of Trudgill's claims above.

From a different perspective, Verena Haser and Bernd Kortmann discuss 'Agreement in English Dialects' (in Dufter et al., eds., *Describing and Modeling Variation in Grammar*, pp. 271–96), specifically again *was*/*were*-generalization, which they try to analyse in a model of construction grammar. Curiously, although the authors constantly speak of the 'stages' and 'development' of these constructions (out of the standard, or out of each other), this does not seem to mean actual historical development, of which no actual account is given here.

A very different kind of comparative analysis is presented by April McMahon, who discusses 'Perspectives on Weakness from English /r/' (in Minkova, ed., *Phonological Weakness in English: From Old to Present-Day English*, pp. 99–115), arguing that the historical development of R-loss still constitutes 'the major dividing line' between varieties of English, both within Great Britain and world-wide, as shown by multi-dimensional calculations of phonetic distances between varieties.

The new field of historical sociolinguistics is well represented this year, and one such study (Nevalainen's) has already been mentioned above. One area where the rise of historical sociolinguistics is also noticeable is in overview books. Thus, Joan C. Beal and Philip A. Shaw have updated Charles Barber's *The English Language: A Historical Introduction*, where the sociolinguistic slant is now observable everywhere. Thus, mechanisms of language change in chapter 2 now include a discussion of different kinds of prestige, as well as an illustration of how changes in the social structure can lead to linguistic change. The most rewriting must have gone into the last parts of the book, dealing with EModE and Late ModE (a chapter that used to be called 'English in the Scientific Age'). Here in particular the readers will note Joan Beal's influence: the chapter on Late ModE reads like a short version of her monograph *English in Modern Times 1700–1945* from 2004 (which is a recommendation, not a criticism).

A new introductory book in Routledge's 'Resource Book' format is Dan McIntyre's *History of English: A Resource Book for Students*; like its predecessors divided into sections A to D, with the A section giving the reader a broad overview, B going into details, in this case tracing linguistic (and extra-linguistic) developments, C exploring sample problems, and D providing excerpts for reading by other authors—curiously mainly other introductory books, but perhaps they can be considered classics (e.g. Baugh and Cable's *History*). Different from other histories, McIntyre integrates insights from sociolinguistics everywhere, although curiously he reifies dialects consistently and speaks of 'dialects meeting, coming into contact etc.', rather than their speakers. Varieties dealt with in more detail are AmE and Early AAE, AusE, IndE, West African pidgins and creoles, and Tok Pisin, most of them surely unexpected in a history of the English language. What is also quite modern about this history is the weight it gives to the periods after ME: the process of standardization, the periods of colonialism and imperialism, and 'Moves towards Present Day English' are all given equal room here, also indicating the advent of Late ModE (although it is not called this here) and beyond in historical linguistics—hurrah! (For more information, see also section 5(b) above.)

In a more traditional vein, Ans van Kemenade and Bettelou Los have edited *The Handbook of the History of English*. Although this handbook does include a chapter on 'Historical Sociolinguistics and Language Change' by Terttu Nevalainen (pp. 558–88), the handbook as a whole is much less informed by recent developments in sociolinguistics, and the remaining chapters (where they deal with language change, rather than dialectology) are written from more traditional, mostly structuralist, perspectives, so that Nevalainen's chapter feels almost like just a token reference. It has to be said, though, that Nevalainen does a brilliant job of introducing the new subdiscipline of historical sociolinguistics in thirty pages, and this could well become the new reference introduction to this approach. She covers real-time changes, variation across genres, studies of social networks, the social and regional embedding of changes, sex and prestige differences, and even discusses vernacular universals (yes, they really are everywhere this year!). Some varieties are also covered in this handbook; apart from the expected sections on 'Old English Dialectology' by Richard Hogg, and on 'Early Middle English Dialectology' by Margaret Laing and Roger Lass, we find a chapter on Early AAE (by Shana Poplack), one on British dialects (by Sali Tagliamonte), one on Celtic Englishes (by Markku Filppula), and one on global English (by Suzanne Romaine), which constitutes a slightly different choice from McIntyre above (all clearly regional contributions are discussed in a little more detail below).

The rise of Late ModE as a period worth 'serious' study is also documented by the publication of a new monograph in Edinburgh's little textbook series: Ingrid Tieken-Boon van Ostade's *An Introduction to Late Modern English*. Tieken gives an overview of the pronunciation of the period (or rather, what the—sometimes conflicting—evidence of pronunciation is, and how to deal with it responsibly), the spelling systems, where she also discusses 'Spelling as a Social Phenomenon', dictionary-making, grammar-writing, and grammar writers, where she also deals with some 'Sociolinguistic Stereotypes and Markers' and how they were dealt with in typical grammar books of the time. The most sociolinguistic part of this book must surely be chapter 6 on 'Language and Social Networks' (pp. 100–17), where the social network of Dr Johnson is scrutinized, whereas the last chapter, on the 'Language of Letters and other Text Types', includes far fewer insights into the social distribution of language (although cookbooks, for one, were clearly targeted at different classes of readers, and buyers, and some of this is reflected in the language employed). Much more could have been made of the sample analyses Tieken presents, but then this is a rather short book which might serve as inspiration for further research (for more information, see also section 5(b)).

Going further back in time, Arja Nurmi, Minna Nevala, and Minna Palander-Collin have edited a collection of papers dealing with *The Language of Daily Life in England (1400–1800)*, mainly based on the Corpus of Early English Correspondence in Helsinki. Particularly interesting for historical sociolinguistics is Anni Sairio's contribution on 'Methodological and Practical Aspects of Historical Network Analysis: A Case Study of the Bluestocking Letters' (pp. 107–35), where she correlates network strength with grammatical features like preposition stranding vs. pied-piping (apparently, the eighteenth-century Bluestocking Elizabeth Montague tended to avoid preposition stranding with her social superiors). Also very relevant is Terttu Nevalainen's study of 'Grasshoppers and Blind Beetles: Caregiver Language in Early Modern English Correspondence' (pp. 138–64). Here, Nevalainen compares linguistic features in child-directed letters by Katherine Paston with inter-adult communication and finds that 'many of them must be a direct continuation of the caregiver language Katherine Paston used when her son was young' (p. 159), such as the pronoun *thou*, use of the lexemes *son* or *child*, but also giving direct orders, or showing appreciation. Helena Raumolin-Brunberg finds 'Lifespan Changes in the Language of Three Early Modern Gentlemen' (pp. 165–96), in particular in early seventeenth-century changes such as the possessive *my/thy* (as opposed to *mine/thine*), 3sg *–s* (as opposed to *–th*), affirmative and negative *do*, and the use of the subject relative *who*. This questions one of the main assumptions of sociolinguistic apparent time studies, viz. the stability of adult vernaculars. (Although it has to be said, as Guy Bailey has shown, that longitudinal change, if anything, accelerates synchronic trends but typically does not revert them or swerve off in different directions, and this, very roughly, is also what Raumolin-Brunberg's data show.) Harking back to the typologically inspired discussion of 'default singulars' above (however faulty the term itself might be), Mikko Laitinen looks at 'Singular YOU WAS/WERE variation and English Normative Grammars in the Eighteenth Century' (pp. 199–217) and finds that with the decline of *thou*, *you was* was introduced as the singular form, at least temporarily. This development peaked in the early eighteenth century but then became a stigmatized marker, helped if not caused by comments in normative grammars, in particular Bishop Lowth's one. Interestingly, both changes (the rise of *you was*, and the decline of it) are led by men, a rather rare sight in historical (and synchronic) sociolinguistics, suggesting that access to education may again have been a decisive factor.

Historical dialectology may soon have a new resource to work with, if the report by Alexander Onysko, Manfred Markus, and Reinhard Heuberger on work on 'Joseph Wright's "English Dialect Dictionary" in Electronic Form: A Critical Discussion of Selected Lexicographic Parameters and Query Options' (in Renouf and Kehoe, eds., *Corpus Linguistics: Refinements and Reassessments*, pp. 201–19) is anything to go by. On the other hand, there have been several announcements before, and yet the project still seems to be ongoing—some reasons why this is not as straightforward as one might perhaps think are not only the sheer volume of the original, but also the complex structure of individual entries (which varies across entries, forcing the team to manually edit them), the complex and fuzzy layers of dialect attribution (on the county, regional, or national level), and the inclusion of usage labels and comments beside the (often extensive) citations, all of which the team has tried to preserve in the electronic version.

Moving to more regional studies, we will begin our overview with studies concentrating on the Celtic Englishes. As mentioned above, Markku Filppula presents 'The Making of Hiberno-English and Other "Celtic Englishes"' (in van Kemenade et al., eds., pp. 507–36), but perhaps this title is a bit of a misnomer. Filppula does give the usual story of early and modern contact between English and Celtic, but most of this chapter is concerned with an enumeration of purported contact features of the Celtic Englishes; he looks at common features first, and then at divergent features. Another historical overview in the other already mentioned handbook is provided by Robert D. King, who sees the introduction of English to 'Wales and Ireland' as the 'First

Steps' (in Kachru et al., eds., *The Handbook of World Englishes*, pp. 30–40), i.e. in the development from English as a regional language to what we now call 'World Englishes'. However, this overview is not only short and non-technical, which might actually be a positive thing for an introductory text; the list of distinctive features King provides is also couched in pseudo-terms that are not encountered in the relevant literature (e.g. 'foregrounding' for the phenomenon of verb-fronting in Welsh, or the term 'interrogatories' for 'interrogatives'), making this rather useless as an introduction. In the same collection, we also find an article by Fiona Douglas on 'English in Scotland' (pp. 41–57) which can be taken much more seriously. Douglas traces the early ascent of *Inglis*, the process of Anglicization, the present-day continuum situation, and then gives a good brief overview of at least some of the phonetic and morphosyntactic features of this variety.

In considerably more detail, Karen P. Corrigan (in the universals debate mentioned above) discusses 'Irish Daughters of Northern British Relatives: Internal and External Constraints on the System of Relativization in South Armagh English (SArE)' (in Filppula et al., eds., pp. 133–62). Comparing data from up to sixty years ago with data from today, Corrigan finds that the frequency of zero-relatives has decreased, and that overall typological constraints (such as the Accessibility Hierarchy), or, generally speaking, matters of complexity, are the best predictor of the actual relativization strategies used.

Raymond Hickey deals with the well-known phenomenon of lenition in 'Weak Segments in Irish English'—the title probably caused by the title of the collection, *Phonological Weakness in English: From Old to Present-Day English* edited by Donka Minkova (pp. 116–29). Hickey identifies alveolars as a preferred site for lenitions, and discusses 'various types of lenition' in Irish English such as /t/-tapping, frication of /t/ (to an apical fricative), and even removals of the oral gesture altogether (as /sɪh/ for /sɪt/), or segment deletion, resulting in /sɪ/.

Lukas Pietsch discusses 'Hiberno-English Medial-Object Perfects Reconsidered: A Case of Contact-Induced Grammaticalization' (*SIL* 33[2009] 528–68) on the basis of historical corpus material, where he argues that since medial object constructions can both be found in earlier forms of English and in Celtic, a convincing analytic compromise would be considering the emergence of this feature in Irish English as just that, 'contact-induced grammaticalization' (in other words, a source construction in English grammaticalizes along familiar paths, triggered by the presence of the same or a very similar construction in Irish Gaelic), in this way overcoming the dichotomy of 'substrate' vs. 'retentionist' theories for this phenomenon.

Robert D. Borsley takes issue with Alison Henry and Siobhán Cottell 'On So-Called Transitive Expletives in Belfast English' (*ELL* 13[2009] 409–31). Henry and Cottell argued two years ago in the same journal that in Belfast English [BE], expletive *there* can be used in transitive constructions (*there shouldn't anybody say that*). Borsley shows that the constraints are slightly different: 'what distinguishes BE from SE [StE] is not what verbs may follow the associate of the expletive but what elements may precede it' (p. 409), i.e.

modals, *have*, *seem*, and perhaps more marginally, *likely* (see also section 5(a) above).

Moving to Scotland, Remco Knooihuizen discovers 'Shetland Scots as a New Dialect: Phonetic and Phonological Considerations' (*ELL* 13[2009] 483–501), supporting Robert McColl Millar's analysis from last year of this dialect as the product of new dialect formation resulting from a Norn substrate and thus a non-native variety of Scots, and massive in-migration from the Scottish mainland with several immigrant dialects. Robert McColl Millar himself moves to the mainland and discusses 'The Origins of the Northern Scots Dialects' (in Dossena and Lass, eds., *Studies in English and European Historical Dialectology*, pp. 191–208), a dialect area so far little described (but cf. McColl Millar's own contribution from a year ago, *Northern and Insular Scots*) in the very north-east of Scotland, and characterized by a much stronger influence of Gaelic than the more southern Scottish varieties. In fact, the author speculates that 'mass bilingualism rather than rapid change towards Scots would have been the northern route' (p. 197). In addition to this substrate influence, however, he proposes that 'something else has happened to these Northern dialects' (p. 191), i.e. perhaps koinéization in contact with Dutch and Low German settlers, but as he—rather pessimistically—concedes, 'when we look back seven or eight hundred years . . . any hope of precise assignment of origin is lost' (p. 206).

Drawing on data from part of the north-east, Jennifer Smith, Mercedes Durham, and Liane Fortune discuss 'Universals and Dialect-Specific Pathways of Acquisition: Caregivers, Children, and T/D Deletion' (*LVC* 21[2009] 69–95) in data from Buckie, where the following phonological segment places the strongest constraint on t/d-deletion, whereas the morpho-syntactic constraint is not (yet) relevant for the children studied. Slightly further south, Lynn Clark and Graeme Trousdale are 'Exploring the Role of Token Frequency in Phonological Change: Evidence from TH-Fronting in East-Central Scotland' (*ELL* 13[2009] 33–55), where this change is 'complicated in this community [i.e. the Isle of Fife] by the existence of certain local variants which are lexically restricted' (p. 33). A multi-variate study reveals that token frequency of the individual lexemes has the weakest effect, after friendship group membership, preceding /f/, syllable structure, and the type of the lexical item.

Nicholas Brownless moves our interest to Welsh English in his historical investigation of 'Welsh English in English Civil War Pamphlets' (in Dossena and Lass, eds., pp. 209–31)—admittedly a highly stereotypical depiction of mock-Welsh features in the early seventeenth century that served to denigrate the Welsh monarchist cause. Linking linguistic features with the depiction of stock characters on stage, Brownless finds stereotypical features like plosive devoicing (*prittish* for *British*), fricative substitution (*tink* for *think*), and the substitution of affricates by fricatives (*shentleman* for *gentleman*) in the orthographic representation of (purported) Welsh characters; particularly striking in terms of morphology is the use of *her* as an unmarked pronoun (all persons, all numbers, all cases), but perhaps what is more striking still is the lack of any other morphosyntactic features that we perhaps have come to expect from Welsh English (e.g. periphrastic *do*, habitual *–s*, lack of subject–verb concord). Of course, these linguistic traits served to characterize Welsh English as 'the dialect of borderland rustics and bumpkins' (p. 229) and for this reason cannot be taken as an accurate depiction of historical Welsh English.

Linking the Celtic Englishes with English English dialects (and indeed beyond), Markku Filppula, Juhani Klemola, and Heli Paulasto are 'Digging for Roots: Universals and Contact in Regional Varieties of English' (in Filppula et al., eds., pp. 231–61). They compare three features that have been linked with Celtic roots: the absence of plural marking with nouns of measurement (*two pintØ*), non-standard use of the definite article (*she went to the hospital*), and a wider use of the progressive with stative verbs (*were you understanding it?*) across English English dialects (Klemola's Survey of English Dialects Recordings), Welsh English dialects (Paulasto's Welsh corpus) and Irish English dialects (Filppula's south Ireland corpus). These traditional dialects are compared with educated ('standard') national varieties (in Britain, India, Singapore, the Philippines, and East Africa—a slightly curious choice that may have been due to sheer constraints on the availability of corpus materials). The authors find that absence of plural marking is highest in traditional English dialects, and at best marginal in educated (world-wide) varieties. A wider use of the definite article, on the other hand, characterizes Irish English, probably through substrate influence, and is also quite frequent in India and East Africa. Wider use of the progressive, finally, seems to be rapidly spreading into all the global standard varieties investigated here. Again, it is most frequent in Irish English, India, and East Africa (indeed, it is a stereotypical feature of IndEn, where it may have been caused by similar Hindi constructions) and may be developing into a general imperfective marker.

The 'Celtic Hypothesis' is also discussed at length this year in a special issue of *English Language and Linguistics* (13:ii[2009]) edited by Markku Filppula and Juhani Klemola. The Celtic Hypothesis extends beyond the Celtic Englishes and investigates substrate (i.e. early Celtic contact) influence on English in general, and the editors have collected a number of high-profile researchers for in-depth studies that make for very thought-provoking (and controversial) reading. In this vein, John McWhorter argues, in 'What Else Happened to English? A Brief for the Celtic Hypothesis' (*ELL* 13[2009] 163–91), that periphrastic *do* in English is almost unparalleled in any other language (family), except Celtic, and concludes that it 'is virtually impossible to deny' borrowing from Brythonic Celtic, establishing a 'direct line of influence from [historical] Celtic to English' (p. 186). Peter Schrijver similarly argues for early substratum 'Celtic Influence on Old English: Phonological and Phonetic Evidence' (*ELL* 13[2009] 193–211), which, he claims, changed the OE sound system from the common West Germanic one. In a similar vein, Stephen Laker gives 'An Explanation for the Early Phonemicisation of a Voice Contrast in English Fricatives' (*ELL* 13[2009] 213–26); according to him, this phonemicization of earlier allophonic variation is due to contact with Brittonic, 'and language shift would have led directly to the phonemicisation' (p. 213). Angelika Lutz, in 'Celtic Influence on Old English and West Germanic' (*ELL* 13[2009] 227–49), finds that also the twofold paradigm of *to be* in OE is probably due to large-scale language shift by speakers of British Celtic, which had a similar formal and functional distinction. Erich Poppe focuses on the English identity of reflexives and identifiers in 'Standard Average European and the Celticity of English Intensifiers and Reflexives: Some Considerations and Implications' (*ELL* 13[2009] 251–66). Poppe's argument is that English here (again) patterns with the Celtic languages, and that both are clearly different from Standard Average European. Markku Filppula deals with another un-Germanic English topic in 'The Rise of *It*-Clefting in English: Areal-Typological and Contact-Linguistic Considerations' (*ELL* 13[2009] 267–93), where he shows that *it*-clefts rise in frequency and grammaticalize until ME, and are chronologically preceded by clefts in Celtic, which again would be an argument for early substratum influence. In 'Traces of Historical Infinitive in English Dialects and their Celtic Connections' (*ELL* 13[2009] 295–308), Juhani Klemola discusses unusual adverb+infinitive constructions in Midlands dialects (e.g. *away to go* 'away he went', or *out to come* 'come out!'), which he links to similar uses of the 'historic infinitive' in British Celtic languages. Finally, Theo Vennemann in 'Celtic Influence in English? Yes and No' (*ELL* 13[2009] 309–34), links early Celtic influence to the (again typologically unusual, or at least un-Germanic) English short response sentences to yes/no-questions (*yes, he does*), which, he claims, were carried into the language by speakers of Insular Celtic shifting to Anglo-Saxon. (Only slightly begging the question why this answer strategy does not show in English roughly until Shakespeare's time.)

Moving to present-day dialects now, on a quite general note David Britain asks 'One Foot in the Grave? Dialect Death, Dialect Contact, and Dialect Birth in England' (*IJSL* 196/7[2009] 121–55), claiming that despite massive processes of dialect contact and levelling, 'the attrition process has not led to a widespread shift toward RP or standard English' (p. 121), but new socially and regionally based koinéized varieties are emerging. This does not mean a homogenization of the speech community, however: 'local social or demographic developments can provoke specific local outcomes of radical contact' (p. 149).

Isabelle Buchstaller and Alexandra D'Arcy postulate 'Localized Globalization: A Multi-Local, Multivariate Investigation of Quotative *Be Like*' (*JSoc* 13[2009] 291–331), where they compare our favourite sociolinguistic feature of recent years in AmE (based on the Switchboard Corpus from the mid-1990s) with material from Derby and Newcastle from a similar period. They find that not all features of this quotative are taken over in the process of 'weak transfer' from AmE into BrE: quotative *be like* is preferred for reported thoughts, for first person subjects and for mimetic effect both in England and in North America, but the English speakers disprefer the historic present, and in England this construction is used most by (working-class) men. In this way, globalization can go hand in hand with local reinterpretation. (We will come back to the quotative marker below.)

Northern (English) English is the topic of Julia Fernández Cuesta and María Nieves Rodríguez Ledesma, who trace 'The Northern Echo: Continuities in Contemporary Northern English' (in Dossena and Lass, eds., pp. 157–89). Based mainly on the SED, the authors investigate the regional distribution of five phonological and five morphological features (the vowel before <mb,nd,ng>; reflexes of OE /a:/ and ME /o:/, plosives vs. affricates in lexemes such as *kirk* vs. *church*, or *sic* vs. *such*; the initial sibilant in *shall*, should; the form of the demonstrative, personal pronouns, the present tense inflections, the form of the present participle, and the use of zero genitives). They find that especially the phonological features have persisted, whereas in the realm of morphology, especially the old forms of the demonstrative and the 3sg feminine pronoun seem to be recessive. Interestingly, with regard to almost every feature Lancashire has a dubious status, and as a rule does not conform to the northern pattern, supporting its special status historically.

Moving to (present-day) northeast, Michael Pearce draws 'A Perceptual Dialect Map of North East England' (*JEngL* 37[2009] 162–92) based on responses by informants from the area. His cumulated maps reveal three broad areas that are distinguished: a 'Northern sector' around Newcastle and Tyneside ('Geordie'), a central sector around Durham and Sunderland, and a southern sector including Middlesbrough, Hartlepool, and Darlington, roughly conforming to 'objective' dialect boundaries.

Judith Broadbent contributes an intriguing study of the non-existent form *amn't*, or in other words 'The *Amn't* Gap: The View from West Yorkshire' (*JLing* 45[2009] 251–84), where she argues that this perceived gap is not a real gap. Instead, based on historical dialect data, Broadbent claims that the orthographic representation of *aren't I* should be *amn't I*, where the phonological forms /a:nt/ or /a:t/ have arisen out of secondary contractions which are quite common in Yorkshire (as *shun't* for *shouldn't*) and can be traced back to nineteenth-century English. Another typical feature of the area is definite article reduction, and Sali A. Tagliamonte and Rebecca V. Roeder investigate this in 'Variation in the English Definite Article: Socio-Historical Linguistics in t' Speech Community' (*JSoc* 13[2009] 435–71), where they discover 'a rich system of variability between the standard forms as well as reduced and zero variants' (p. 435). Interestingly, the apparent time analysis suggests that this may be a feature characterized by age-grading—it is associated in particular with younger and older speakers, with a noticeable dip for the middle-aged, and in particular with men, which might even suggest that these speakers (younger men) use this feature 'to affirm a positive new attitude toward local identity' (p. 462) in the context of a new pride in being northern. An interesting secondary result is that article reduction and zero forms (deletion) should probably be treated as separate phenomena, since zero has its own pattern of use.

Linking Northumbria and Yorkshire, Joan C. Beal applies the new theory of enregisterment to the historical evolution of two northern identities in 'Enregisterment, Commodification, and Historical Context: "Geordie" Versus "Sheffieldish"' (*AS* 84[2009] 138–56). Her analysis of nineteenth-century texts shows that urban dialects were early on associated with iconic working-class figures (i.e. enregistered), and that 'features that were actually more widespread in the north of England and in Scotland were "claimed" as unique to each of these new urban dialects'. In this way 'a repertoire of features emerged that continues to be cited and indeed used by speakers and writers today... often in performative contexts' (p. 138). However, Tyneside ('Geordie') identity is commodified in various ways, whereas Sheffield is not (there are no mugs, dialect birth certificates, or tea towels), which Beal links to a higher awareness of Geordie distinctiveness (or third-order indexicality in Michael Silverstein's framework), as well as 'branding' of Geordie identity. (We will also come back to enregisterment.) In a different contribution, Joan C. Beal also claims that '"You're not from New York City, you're from Rotherham": Dialect and Identity in British Indie Music' (*JEngL* 37[2009] 223–40). Beal here investigates lyrics by the Sheffield band the Arctic Monkeys, who avoid American pronunciations and instead use 'features of local accent and dialect to index values such as authenticity and independence from the corporate machine' (p. 223). High-school girls from the north-west are investigated by Emma Moore and Robert Podesva in 'Style, Indexicality, and the Social Meaning of Tag Questions' (*LSoc* 38[2009] 447–85). They show that several features correlate with the Community of Practice of these girls. The more 'burnout' girls use more vernacular forms, and the more 'jock' girls often use co-operative overlap. In this way, the girls employ tag questions to construct 'distinct group styles' (p. 464).

Moving to London now, Jenny Cheshire and Sue Fox discuss '*Was*/*Were* Variation: A Perspective from London' (*LVC* 21[2009] 1–38), where a mixed system (generalization of *was* in positive contexts, *weren't* in negative clauses) is on the increase in outer London (as in much of the rest of Britain, or indeed the English-speaking world—see above!), whereas in the ethnically mixed inner-London borough of Hackney the situation is more diverse, and generalization both to negative *wasn't* and *weren't* occurs, among other things also depending on ethnic group. In the same speech community, David Britain and Sue Fox discuss a phonotactic issue in 'The Regularization of the Hiatus Resolution System in British English: A Contact-Induced "Vernacular Universal?"' (in Filppula et al., eds., pp. 177–205). In Britain (the country, not the linguist), the traditional strategies (linking /j/, linking /w/ or linking or intrusive /r/, or the indefinite article *an*) are typologically rather unusual, and they seem to be giving way, at least in the speech of adolescents from east London, to glottal stops, a development led by Bangladeshi boys. In this way, Britain and Fox argue, 'contact may well be crucial to the very emergence of widely distributed non-standard forms' (p. 199), at the same time giving rise to typologically unmarked solutions. Talking of ethnic adolescents, we must mention here Ben Rampton's argument in favour of 'Interactional Ritual and Not Just Artful Performance in Crossing and Stylization' (*LSoc* 38[2009] 149–76). *Pace* Nikolas Coupland, Rampton claims that stylization does not always include a notion of performance—indeed, a performance of 'other-ethnic styles could actually be quite risky' (p. 150) in the adolescents he studied; Ervin Goffman's notion of 'interactional ritual' may actually work better descriptively here. In particular, Rampton found that stylized Asian English occurred 'in a greeting, an apology, demand for remediation', whereas crossing into British Creole was used in 'expressions of annoyance and of admiration' (p. 161). Similarly, another group of adolescents used stylized Cockney and RP ('posh') 'at ritually sensitive moments' (humiliation by a teacher, impending separation from their friends, etc.), where a notion of performance would be 'insufficient to do justice to the subtlety of these processes' (p. 170).

Across the Atlantic, CanE serves as the basis for Rena Torres Cacoullos and James A. Walker's study 'On the Persistence of Grammar in Discourse Formulas: A Variationist Study of *That*' (*Linguistics* 47[2009] 1–43), in particular of the variation between complementizer *that* and zero. A multi-variate analysis reveals that *that* is absent in particular when the two clauses behave more like a single proposition, for example especially if the matrix clause contains *think/know/say/tell*, probably a more general finding that extends beyond CanE. Charles Boberg reports on 'The Emergence of a New Phoneme: Foreign (a) in Canadian English' (*LVC* 21[2009] 355–80), i.e. in loanwords like *drama* or *pasta*, where traditionally /ae/ was preferred in CanE, but in a new development, 'younger speakers adopt... American /ah/ variants' (p. 355). In this process, Boberg finds a third, intermediate variant in around 20 per cent of all cases 'which may constitute a new low-central vowel phoneme' (p. 355) in CanE.

Sandra Clarke and Philip Hiscock discover 'Hip-Hop in a Post-Insular Community: Hybridity, Local Language, and Authenticity in an Online Newfoundland Rap Group' (*JEngL* 37[2009] 241–61). They investigate an adolescent white hip-hop group who used vernacular Newfoundland English, but whose authenticity was quickly contested. In contrast to Beal above, Clarke and Hiscock claim that here parody was involved in the overuse (and wrong use) of local features, or, as they call it, 'strategic inauthenticity', making fun of traditional Newfoundland speakers of Irish ancestry.

Linking Britain and America, differences between these two standard reference varieties of English are very well documented this year, thanks in great part to the publication of Günter Rohdenburg and Julia Schlüter's edited volume *One Language, Two Grammars?*. Contributors include the crème de la crème of corpus linguistics, and the facets of language investigated span compound verbs, verb paradigms, comparatives, the phonology–grammar interface, prepositions, argument structures, reflexives, noun phrase modifications, nominal complements, non-finite complements, choice of tenses, the subjunctive, tag questions, and adverbs, probably as complete a list of differences as has ever been produced. All, or almost all, contributions are based on careful corpus work, mostly on a new version of ARCHER, but documentation in the *OED* also plays a role, as do some newspaper corpora, the BNC, the incomplete ANC, and the Longman Corpus. All studies are clearly relevant as background reading for more sociolinguistically inspired work, but are not sociolinguistic or dialectological *per se*, and for this reason will not be discussed here in detail. If you want a quick overview, Marianne Hundt's introductory chapter on '*Colonial Lag, Colonial Innovation* or Simply *Language Change*?' (pp. 13–37) is highly recommended. More details of this volume can be found in section 5(b) above.

Not directly visible from the title, *Change in Contemporary English: A Grammatical Study*, co-authored by Geoffrey Leech, Marianne Hundt, Christian Mair, and Nicholas Smith, is also to a large degree concerned with differences between BrE and AmE, in this case arrived at on the basis of the Brown family of corpora. In this way, Leech et al. is complementary to

Rohdenburg and Schlüter above, since the materials used are different (the Brown family of corpora plays virtually no role in Rohdenburg and Schlüter), hardly any of the topics and, except for Hundt, none of the authors overlap either. The chapters in this book very much concentrate on observable change in the VP. Thus there are chapters on the subjunctive, the modal auxiliaries and semi-modals, the progressive (still on the rise), the passive, expanded predicates, and non-finite clauses, and only one chapter on the NP. The summary 'Linguistic and other Determinants of Change' (pp. 236–72) is particularly interesting, as the authors here quite daringly posit several general trends for recent changes in English grammar, one of them 'Americanization'. Again, this monograph is a must-read in background information for any dialectologist interested in non-standard variation, but is neither sociolinguistic nor dialectological itself, and for this reason we leave it at this shortish notice. (More details can be found in sections 11 and 12 below.)

A historical overview of 'English in North America' is provided by Edgar W. Schneider (in Kachru et al., eds., pp. 58–73), who points out that despite the status of being an inner-circle variety, and indeed the one hegemonic variety today, viewing it in the context of 'World Englishes' 'makes sense, given that . . . AmE . . . went through the same process of linguistic and cultural appropriation that has shaped other postcolonial varieties' (p. 58), especially koinéization during its rapid expansion westward. Schneider traces the division into dialect areas to the settlement patterns, presents the study of AmE in lexicography, dialectology, and sociolinguistics, and also gives a few examples of 'The Growing Impact of AmE on Other World Englishes', which makes this a very readable (and student-friendly) short introduction to AmE. David Eddington and Michael Taylor discuss 'T-Glottalization in American English' (*AS* 84[2009] 298–314), a feature better known from England, but especially in word-final position also encountered in the US. The authors find that glottal stops are particularly frequent before front vowels, replacing intervocalic taps in this position especially for younger (female) speakers, and are more frequently encountered in the western US. In other words, this may be a feature undergoing change.

And yes, we are coming back to our favourite quotative with Federica Barbieri's overview study of 'Quotative *be like* in American English' (*EWW* 30[2009] 68–90), where she compares the diachronic development of *be like* (as opposed to *go*, *say*, and the new *be all*) over the last ten years or so. She finds that today, *be like* is the most popular marker for speakers under 40, and that these speakers (who were teenagers in 1995) have even increased their use. Overall, Barbieri concludes, *be like* is a change in progress, rather than a phenomenon of age-grading, and probably here to stay. In a way continuing from this quotative, Anna Marie Trester looks at the 'Discourse Marker "Oh" as a Means for Realizing the Identity Potential of Constructed Dialogue in Interaction' (*JSoc* 13[2009] 147–68). Although based on the speech of only one informant, Trester claims that *oh* is used more for introducing speech than thought, and used more for introducing the speech of others than of oneself. It also indicates a difference in footing, or stance, and can be employed both for uni-directional double voicing (where the speaker's and the other's discourses run in the same direction), and for vari-directional voicing, where a conflict exists. In this way, *oh* can be used to display and to evaluate information in quite a complementary way to *be like*.

Kathryn Campbell-Kibler continues her investigation of the variable (ING) in 'The Nature of Sociolinguistic Perception' (*LVC* 21[2009] 135–56), concentrating on the level of 'intelligence/education' indexed by this stereotypical feature. Based on matched-guised perception studies she can show that '(ING) impacts social perception variably' (p. 135). Campbell-Kibler claims that 'speakers were heard as less educated/intelligent when they used *–in*, but this effect is driven by reactions to speakers heard as aregional [e.g. as not coming from the south] and not as working-class' (p. 135).

Dealing with what must be the most northern US American dialect, Thomas Purnell, Eric Raimy, and Joseph Salmons, in 'Defining Dialect, Perceiving Dialect, and New Dialect Formation: Sarah Palin's Speech' (*JEngL* 37[2009] 331–55), discuss the frequent mis-classification in the media of Sarah Palin as a speaker from the Upper Midwest. In particular, they investigate G-dropping, her vowels, and final /z/-devoicing and conclude that the perception may be due to her actual use of some salient Midwestern features, even though they may not be very frequent. Ultimately, this can be explained with the settlement pattern of Alaska, since the area Palin comes from was indeed settled mainly from the Upper Midwest.

On a more historical note, and much further east, Adrian Pablè tries to 'Reconstruct . . . the History of Two Colonial New England Terms of Address: *Goodman* and *Goodwife*' (in Dossena and Lass, eds., pp. 233–52). These address terms were brought from England, but underwent a significant shift in usage, from the English application to artisans, to designating 'highly respectable and well-to-do members of the community' in America (p. 238), promoted though not exclusively used by (and to) Puritans, no doubt helped by the folk-etymology of *good* + *man* (or *woman*). Although their occurrence is usually only noted for New England, where they are documented until the early eighteenth century, these terms are also occasionally found in the southern states.

Dale F. Coye discusses present-day 'Dialect Boundaries in New Jersey' (*AS* 84[2009] 414–52) based on a questionnaire study of phonological, lexical, and grammatical items. Coye finds that in many cases 'the dialect differences [today] match those in existence for many generations, with a north-south division clearly evident' (p. 414), for example in the terms *water ice*/*Italian ice*, *sub(marine)*/*hoagie*, *dresser*/*bureau*, or the acceptance of positive *anymore* (only in the south). In other cases, the influence of New York is clearly noticeable (in the vowels of *gone* and *on*, the spread of *wait on line*, and /r/-less *forward*), or is even an obstacle to more nationwide trends, such as the retention of pronunciations without /l/ in *calm* or *almond*, or the pronunciation of *human*, *hurry*, or *Florida*. Interestingly, none of the college and high-school students from the New York subregion report non-rhoticity, perhaps because of the stigma associated with this feature. Quite the opposite is true for the speakers studied by Kara Becker in '/R/ and the Construction of Place Identity on New York City's Lower East Side' (*JSoc* 13[2009] 634–58). Becker claims that non-rhoticity, probably one of the most heavily stereotyped features of New York City speech, is 'imbued with local social meaning' in this part of New York, which shows up in the fact that when talk turns on neighbourhood topics, non-rhoticity increases, giving speakers the opportunity to present themselves as 'authentic neighbourhood residents' (as opposed to more gentrified newcomers).

Moving south a little, Barbara Johnstone (in a similar vein to Beal above for Newcastle and Sheffield in England) looks at 'Pittsburghese Shirts: Commodification and the Enregisterment of an Urban Dialect' (*AS* 84[2009] 157–75), and claims that these material artefacts are strong evidence of local dialect awareness and actually contribute to the creation and focusing of a Pittsburgh dialect. In sum, Johnstone argues that these shirts (and other artefacts) 'put local speech on display; they imbue local speech with value; they standardize local speech; and they link local speech with particular social meaning' (p. 159).

Applying the concept of enregisterment to a locality in Michigan, Kathryn Remlinger examines 'Everyone Up Here: Enregisterment and Identity in Michigan's Keweenaw Peninsula' (*AS* 84[2009] 118–37). Here, Copper Country English has been recognized and 'normed' as the local dialect indexing local identity. Contributing to this study, Kathryn Remlinger, Joseph Salmons, and Luanne von Schneidemesser, in 'Revised Perceptions: Changing Dialect Perceptions in Wisconsin and Michigan's Upper Peninsula' (*AS* 84[2009] 176–91), investigate the rise in awareness of regional differences in this area, which they link to the economic transition from agriculture (and mining) to tourism. This change seems to have brought about third-order indexicality (or enregisterment) and a switch from ethnic (German immigrant-derived) to local identity for features such as TH-stopping, or the use of *once* or *yet* (*get me a beer once*), as well as a number of dialect words.

Erica J. Benson claims that 'Everyone Wants In: *Want* + Prepositional Adverb in the Midland and Beyond' (*JEngL* 37[2009] 28–60) is undergoing change and is spreading outward from the Midland area, where it originated. Her questionnaire study reveals that these constructions also show high acceptability ratings in the north, and the south, and that it does not show social stratification.

Michael B. Montgomery provides some 'Historical and Comparative Perspectives on *A*-Prefixing in the English of Appalachia' (*AS* 84[2009] 5–26), a stereotypical feature of this region that is a grammatical relic of an early ME preposition and the present participle. Montgomery suggests that southern English dialects may have been the source for this feature and investigates the phonological and syntactic constraints of its occurrence today: *a*-prefixing is prohibited before an unstressed syllable or an initial vowel, before a true gerund and after a preposition, although Montgomery can show that these constraints are not categorical—there are a few counterexamples. Appalachia is also investigated more critically by Sarah Hamilton and Kirk Hazen, who conduct 'Dialect Research in Appalachia: A Family Case Study' (*West Virginia History* 3[2009] 81–111), where they compare the dialect features of family members who migrated to northern cities for a considerable length of time (and then returned) to those who stayed in West Virginia, and find that those migrants that feel the most connected with home use vernacular variants much like the non-migrants, although all over phonological variants were more likely to persist than morphosyntactic ones.

On a lexical subject, Allison Burkette looks at 'The Lion, the Witch, and the Armoire: Lexical Variation in Case Furniture Terms' (*AS* 84[2009] 315–39) in the atlas material LAMSAS and LAGS, as well as her own study based on line-drawings of the objects in question. Burkette finds A-curves (see Kretzschmar above) for the items for 'wardrobe' (mostly called *wardrobe*, *chifforobe*, or indeed *armoire*), 'dresser' (mostly called *bureau*, *dresser*, or *chest of drawers*), 'dresser with mirror' (called *dresser* or *vanity*) and 'chest on chest' (also called *dresser*, *chest of drawers*, or *chest*) (see also section 7 above).

A southern stereotype is under investigation in 'Articulation Rate Across Dialect, Age, and Gender' (*LVC* 21[2009] 233–56) by Ewa Jacewicz, Robert A. Fox, Caitlin O'Neill, and Joseph Salmons, and the authors find that, apart from within-speaker factors, region also plays a role, and indeed speech tempo (both in reading and in informal talk) is significantly lower in speakers from North Carolina than in speakers from Wisconsin; in addition, younger speakers talked more quickly than older speakers, but differences between genders were only small. Wendy Baker, David Eddington, and Lyndsey Nay investigate 'Dialect Identification: The Effects of Region of Origin and Amount of Experience' (*AS* 84[2009] 48–71), based on Utahn speech, where they find that both elements of familiarity with the dialect in question are good predictors of dialect identification.

Shana Poplack gives a historical overview of 'How English Became African American English' (in Kemenade and Los, eds., pp. 452–76), but the choice of author for this topic already indicates a heavy slant towards the neo-Anglicist camp, and indeed Poplack uses the space of this chapter to defend her (and Sali Tagliamonte's) project of reconstructing earlier stages of AAE by employing data from present-day relic areas—a project that has met with considerable criticism from the creolist, but also the dialectological camp (see any earlier *YWES*). Indeed it has to be said that the creolist hypothesis is not really given fair treatment here, and as a general overview this chapter can thus only have limited value. Jennifer Bloomquist examines 'Dialect Differences in Central Pennsylvania: Regional Dialect Use and Adaptation by African Americans in the Lower Susquehanna Valley' (*AS* 84[2009] 27–47), in particular the use (or non-use) of local regional dialect vocabulary and syntax by members of the African American speech community. Bloomquist finds that urban African Americans actually 'report MORE usage of regional syntactic patterns' than their more rural counterparts, and are at least passively familiar with local dialect words, calling into question some generalizations on the current supra-regionalization of urban AAVE. Tyler Kendall and Walt Wolfram discuss 'Local and External Language Standards in African American English' (*JEngL* 37[2009] 305–30). They find that their speakers under investigation, community leaders in rural southern communities, do not styleshift between sociolinguistic interviews and public settings: 'there is no appreciable difference in the use of vernacular features' (p. 310), which the authors link to the fact that these public settings here are still very local.

Mary Elizabeth Kohn and Hannah Askin Franz discover 'Localized Patterns for Global Variants: The Case of Quotative Systems of African American and Latino Speakers' (*AS* 84[2009] 259–97) in North Carolina. In all communities, quotative *be like* patterns in the same way as for white speakers (i.e. reporting thought and, more marginally, direct speech, with a preference for first-person subjects for Latino speakers, and a more equal distribution between first- and third-person subjects for African Americans), whereas gender seems more locally determined.

Jennifer Renn and J. Michael Terry deal with 'Operationalizing Style: Quantifying the Use of Style Shift in the Speech of African American Adolescents' (*AS* 84[2009] 367–90) by observing 108 sixth-grade students across two levels of formality. They compare calculations based on the complete set of features with calculations based just on a subset of features AAVE is known for (specifically NG-fronting, copula absence, modal absence, absence of 3rd sg –s, multiple negation and the use of *ain't*). Also for the reduced subset, the authors finds that 'speakers used significantly more AAVE features in the informal context' (p. 383), validating the use of just the subset.

To conclude this overview, let us briefly look at some studies concentrating on gender this year. Pia Pichler investigates *Talking Young Femininities*, in particular three groups of 15–17-year-old friends from different social and ethnic backgrounds: one group of Bangladeshi girls in the East End of London, one group of white girls from the same area, and one group of middle-class girls from a private school in the West End. Pichler finds that these girls share some topics they talk about, but differ in the 'discursive and interactive construction of identities'. Thus, the middle-class girls adopt a rather mild anti-school stance because this is 'cool' (Pichler speaks of a 'tame non-conformity' that consciously distances them from what they see as elite, sheltered upper-middle-class identities); interestingly, the middle-class girls are the only group that explicitly talks about social class. The working-class group, on the other hand, surprisingly frequently talk about their mothers, and Pichler identifies a 'balancing of teenage voices of adventure and rebellion with positions which show that the girls have appropriated their mothers'... voices' (p. 246), in this way distancing themselves from more stereotypical pictures of working-class teenage femininities (such as the teenage mother, the school drop-out, or the vandalizing truant). The Bangladeshi girls 'frequently adopt the most pronounced anti-school and truanting stances', approaching most what we know from US-American studies as 'burnout' behaviour, accomplishing 'toughness' as a result. This is particularly noteworthy for being in stark opposition to the stereotype of the 'timid, quiet, and studious Asian girl' (p. 246). Not surprisingly, talk about sex is also highly distinct between the groups. The middle-class girls talk about sex in a mostly impersonal, 'cool' way, showing themselves knowledgeable, but without self-disclosure. The white working-class girls talk about sex the most, trying to 'balance the strong pro-sex norms they experience in their peer group with their own needs, anxieties/concerns and pleasures' (p. 15), ultimately presenting themselves as self-determined. The Bangladeshi girls talk about sex mostly by teasing each other and boasting, playing a 'bad girl' persona off a non-sexual 'good girl' identity. Pichler claims that in this group, the opposing identities are in addition culture-specific, 'one celebrating sexual experience as a essential part of British adolescence, the other celebrating female premarital chastity, linked . . . to their Bangladeshi community and . . . "religion"' (p. 16). Nevertheless, the girls ultimately align themselves with the dominant discourse on respectability, which for the Asian girls means Muslim Bangladeshi norms, including an acceptance of a modified version of arranged marriage.

Pia Pichler is also one of the editors of a collection of essays on gender, *Gender and Spoken Interaction* (the other editor being Eva Eppler). In it, Deborah Cameron discusses 'Theoretical Issues for the Study of Gender and Spoken Interaction' (pp. 1–17), cautioning readers not to overstate the shifts of the 'postmodern turn' and likewise cautioning them that the social constructivist method also contains significant problems, not only the problem of how to warrant claims about the data but also the danger of going 'too' local, and losing sight of larger social structures. Linking gender and (pre–)adolescence, Janet Maybin discusses 'Airhostess Legs and Jealous Husbands: Explorations of Gender and Heterosexuality in 10–11-Year-Olds' Conversations' (pp. 42–62), who can switch between innocent children and the discourse of sexually more knowledgeable adolescents; reassuringly, perhaps (at least for their parents), for these children 'sexuality is very much a public affair with the peer group providing resources, stage and audience' (p. 58) to experiment and play with. Pia Pichler herself takes up a topic from her book mentioned above, the self-positioning of rather privileged upper-middle-class girls, in '"All I've gotta do is wank on about some bollocky poem": Cool and Socially Aware Positions in the Talk of Private School Girls' (pp. 87–114), who are quite aware of their privileged positions, and use coolness to detach themselves from what they see as 'sheltered' (and socially unaware) identities of other schoolgirls around them 'without aligning themselves with stereotypes of tough working-classness' (p. 97). Siân Preece shifts the emphasis to young men, more specifically '"A Group of Lads, Innit?": Performances of Laddish Masculinity in British Higher Education' (pp. 115–38), where a group of ethnic male first-year students adopt a 'laddish' position (including the ability to intimidate others, be tough, and 'have a laugh' rather than attend to academic work) to compensate for their rather marginalized state in this institution as 'non-traditional' students. This topic is taken up in her book-length study on *Posh Talk: Language and Identity in Higher Education*, but expanded, since here she does not only deal with 'Multilingual Masculinities in the Classroom' (chapter 4) and 'Multilingual Masculinities in Lecturer/Student Interactions' (chapter 7) but also with the feminine counterparts (chapters 5 and 7). Like her essay above, this monograph draws heavily on data collected in an academic writing programme at the pseudonymed Millennium University in London. In contrast to the 'lads', the female first-year students made much more use of the peer group to exchange their experiences of the transition from late adolescence to early adulthood, of the conflict between their family and peers, and new demands by the university: 'how to fit in and not stand out socially or academically' (p. 107).

Finally for this section, Cecilia E. Ford studies *Women Speaking Up: Getting and Using Turns in Workplace Meetings* [2008], to some degree countering the stereotype of the silenced, dominated woman in the workplace. Instead, on the basis of videotaped business meetings, Ford can show how the women under investigation communicate effectively: 'women are competent at initiating turns in the meetings' (p. 90); they are 'treated as consequential, individuals whose expertise and whose challenges warrant and receive serious responses and expansions' (p. 118), and they 'successfully initiate and expand turns that deliver disaffiliative actions' (p. 119), in sum, providing 'evidence for women's observable competence at speaking in such contexts' (p. 165).

10. New Englishes and Creolistics

A number of books dealing with English as a world language have been published this year, notably the paperback edition of *The Handbook of World Englishes*, edited by Braij B. Kachru, Yamuna Kachru, and Cecil L. Nelson. This edition is an exact replica of the hardback edition published in 2006 and was therefore discussed in detail in an earlier volume (*YWES* 87[2008] 119). This year has also seen the second edition of Jennifer Jenkins's *World Englishes: A Resource Book for Students*, a textbook designed for classroom use. The new edition has basically kept the structure and content of the first edition, published in 2003 (*YWES* 84[2005] 86), with a few additions and minor changes. Thus the first section still introduces key topics in World Englishes, including historical and political issues and the debate on theories of the genesis of pidgins and creoles, while the second section concerns itself with the development of New Englishes, standardization, and the characteristics of pidgin and creole languages; the third section explores current debates such as the 'English Only movement' in the US, the sociolinguistics of London Jamaican, the teaching and testing of English world-wide, and the discussion of English as a 'killer language'. The discussion of Asian Englishes in this section, however, has seen the addition of an Expanding Circle variety, China English, and thus has a wider coverage than the equivalent chapter in the previous edition of this book. The final section has kept the form of a reader, presenting text extracts from seminal papers by well-known authors such as Chinua Achebe, David Crystal, David Graddol, Lesley Milroy, Alastair Pennycook, Henry Widdowson, and many more. This last section has been slightly updated, especially in the 'issues to consider' sections which follow each text extract, and with a rearrangement in the sections dealing with ELF, which now include a text by Barbara Seidlhofer, and the ones addressing attitudes to local norms and the future of English world-wide. With its many original examples, student activities, study questions, sample analyses, and suggestions for further reading this accessible textbook is likely to remain one of the main sources for beginning students of World Englishes.

Hans-Georg Wolf and Frank Polzenhagen's *World Englishes: A Cognitive Sociolinguistic Approach* obviously aims at an entirely different readership. Using African varieties of English as a test case, the authors explore the field of New Englishes within the framework of cognitive sociolinguistics, a newly established field of research within cognitive linguistics, making a contribution to the theoretical discussion of the study of World Englishes in general. This is particularly thoroughly done in the first chapter of the book, which extensively compares and discusses different traditional and more recent theoretical and practical approaches to New Englishes. The book is definitely not an easy read and the theoretical claims made are perhaps not always conclusively supported by empirical evidence, but it is certainly worthwhile trying to follow the authors' line of argument, which provides ample food for thought as well as interesting insights into intercultural communication in English.

A rather different approach is taken in Phyllis Ghim-Lian Chew's *Emergent Lingua Francas and World Orders: The Politics and Place of English as a World Language*. According to the author, 'lingua francas are best studied not as individual languages per se but as part of broad sociolinguistic contexts' (p. xiii) and this is what the books aims to do, by linking the study of English as a world language to the development of other lingua francas and the phenomenon of 'world order', defined in the first chapter as a framework which humans need in order to organize and make sense of the age they live in. The next chapter introduces Chew's spiral and cyclical model of evolving world orders and lingua francas and emphasizes the importance of a diachronic perspective in the study of world languages. The model implies historical change and posits a connection between language and evolution. The following three chapters deal with the concept of liminality as the transition zone between two different phases of development or 'the buffer between the two world orders' (p. 61). Liminality includes qualities such as instability, fluidity, mobility, and temporality. A liminal period is thus one of change and indeterminacy, and Chew claims that in the present liminal period, English is connected to the discussions of globalism, as was Arabic to the discussion of nation states in the Middle Ages. The next three chapters each present a detailed case study: the progression from multilingualism to monolingualism in Singapore in chapter 6, the succession of different world orders in China, which is seen 'as a microcosm of the world at large' (p. 175), in chapter 7, followed by an in-depth discussion of the Min language spoken on the south-east coast of the People's Republic of China in chapter 8. This leads to the final and summarizing chapter and the discussion of 'the place of English in the world today'. This last chapter also touches upon issues of language and identity and educational implications. In sum, the book links the development of English as a world-wide lingua franca to other lingua francas such as Latin, Arabic, Kiswahili, and Chinese, highlighting similarities through the spiral model presented.

Thomas Hoffmann and Lucia Siebers, eds., *World Englishes: Problems, Properties and Prospects*, contains a collection of articles first presented at the thirteenth annual conference of the International Association of World Englishes (IAWE) at Regensburg in 2007. The contributions with a more general focus on World Englishes will be discussed here, while papers dealing with particular regions and individual varieties of English will be referred to in the sections below. The volume features five articles with innovative and interdisciplinary approaches to New Englishes: Salikoko S. Mufwene discusses 'The Indigenization of English in North America' (pp. XX), taking up the concept of ecology from biology and pointing out universal developments in language contact situations. Margie Berns, Jennifer Jenkins, Marko Modiano,

Barbara Seidlhofer, and Yasukata Yano highlight five different 'Perspectives on English as a Lingua Franca' discussing the relationship between World Englishes and English as an international lingua franca. Stephanie Hackert presents a 'Discourse-Historical Approach to the English Native Speaker' and discusses the ownership of the English language. In her contribution, 'World Englishes and Peace Sociolinguistics: Towards a Common Goal of Linguistic Understanding', Patricia Friedrich argues that language plays an important role in promoting peace. Jill Hallett's article, 'New Voices in the Canon: The Case for Including World Englishes in Literature', combines linguistic and literary studies and investigates the use of linguistic markers in African American literary texts. The volume also includes four articles pursuing a comparative approach to New Englishes: Bernd Kortmann and Benedikt Szmrecsanyi's 'World Englishes between Simplification and Complexification' offers support for the claim that the degree of morpho-syntactic simplification correlates with the level of language contact, by comparing corpus data from various linguistic corpora as well as the data collected for the *Handbook of Varieties of English* (Kortmann et al. 2004, see *YWES* 85[2006] 86–7). In her contribution 'Global Feature—Local Norms? A Case Study on the Progressive Passive', Marianne Hundt compares the use of the progressive passive in Inner Circle (British, New Zealand, and Australian English) and Outer Circle (Indian, Philippine, Hong Kong, and Singapore English) varieties of English on the basis of various ICE corpora. 'The Shared Core of the Perfect across English: A Corpus-Based Analysis' by Bertus van Rooy also uses three ICE corpora to contrast the semantics of the perfect in British, East African, and Hong Kong English. Finally, Thomas Biermeier presents 'Word-Formation in New Englishes. Properties and Trends', comparing eight varieties (British, Indian, Singapore, Philippine, Kenyan, Tanzanian, New Zealand and Jamaican English) on the basis of quantitative and qualitative analyses of the respective ICE sub-corpora.

A number of articles published elsewhere also deal with comparative approaches to World Englishes. Nadja Nesselhauf, for instance, compares the use of competing collocations in the ICE corpora of Kenyan, Indian, Singaporean, and Jamaican English to their use in the *International Corpus of Learner English*, in her paper 'Co-Selection Phenomena across New Englishes: Parallels (and Differences) to Foreign Learner Varieties' (*EWW* 30[2009] 1–26). Joybrato Mukherjee and Stefan Th. Gries investigate 'Collostructional Nativisation in New Englishes: Verb Construction Associations in the International Corpus of English' (*EWW* 30:[2009] 27–51). They examine three varieties of English (Hong Kong, Indian, and Singapore English) and show that the evolutionary stage of a variety correlates with its structural nativization at the level of verb complementation. Peter Collins reports on findings from a study based on eight ICE sub-corpora (Great Britain, Australia, New Zealand, the Philippines, Singapore, Hong Kong, India, Kenya) and comparable corpus data representing AmE. He investigates two complementary trends in the development of 'Modals and Quasi-Modals in World Englishes' (*WEn* 28[2009] 281–92), i.e. the declining use of the former correlating to a rise of the latter. As he is able to show in some detail, among the Inner Circle varieties, AmE seems to be most advanced with regard to this development, and the Southeast Asian varieties the most advanced among the Outer Circle varieties. Benedikt Szmrecsanyi and Bernd Kortmann investigate 'The Morphosyntax of Varieties of English Worldwide: A Quantitative Perspective' (*Lingua* 119[2009] 1643–63) and demonstrate using the database of the *Handbook of Varieties of English* (Kortmann et al. [2004]) that typological differences seem to exist between English L1 vernaculars and pidgins and creoles. Devyani Sharma, however, argues that research on 'Typological Diversity in New Englishes' (*EWW* 30[2009] 170–95) should always 'include an assessment of the grammatical conditioning of features and a comparison with the relevant substrates' (p. 170). By comparing the use of three putative English universals (i.e. past tense omission, over-extension of the progressive, copula omission) in IndE and SingE she shows that similarity at the surface may actually be explained by the substrate system or by substrate–superstrate interactions. Politeness strategies and the performance of leadership across diverse cultures are compared in 'Politeness and Leadership Discourse in New Zealand and Hong Kong: A Cross-Cultural Case Study of Workplace Talk' (*JPolR* 5[2009] 131–57) by Stephanie Schnurr and Angela Chan. Augustin Simo Bobda investigates 'The Meaning of English Words across Cultures, with a Focus on Cameroon and Hong Kong' (*JMMD* 30:v[2009] 375–89), confirming that cultural background knowledge is essential for interpreting the lexical meaning of words. Finally, Richard Xiao presents results from an impressive and detailed study, which compares 141 linguistic features in five ICE sub-corpora (from Great Britain, Hong Kong, India, the Philippines, and Singapore) along twelve registers, applying Douglas Biber's multidimensional analysis (MDA) approach, in his article 'Multidimensional Analysis and the Study of World Englishes' (*WEn* 28[2009] 421–50).

Daniel Schreier, in 'Assessing the Status of Lesser-Known Varieties of English' (*EnT* 97, 25:i[2009] 19–24), takes St Helenian English as a test case and challenges existing models for the classification of World Englishes, as the consideration of structural factors, on the one hand, and historical and social ones, on the other, may produce different results for individual varieties, especially for the lesser-known ones. Schreier therefore argues that more fine-grained analyses and models for the description of World Englishes are needed. Eric Anchimbe believes that 'Revisiting the Notion of Maturation in New Englishes' (*WEn* 28[2009] 336–51) is necessary in order to re-evaluate the status of these varieties. They should not be seen as sociohistorically less developed types of English which still need to advance towards a higher level, but rather as independent varieties, appropriately reflecting the sociolinguistic needs and ecological make-up of the societies in which they have developed. In his programmatic article '"World English" and the Latin Analogy: Where We Get it Wrong' (*EnT* 98, 25:ii[2009] 49–54) Kanavillil Rajagopalan claims that the comparison between Latin and English continues to be made, and points out that 'the Latin analogy is deceptive and misleading' (p. 52), primarily because (unlike speakers of Latin in the Middle Ages) in the age of globalization speakers of English world-wide are constantly in contact, which will, he believes, ultimately prevent it from developing into mutually unintelligible languages. Finally, in their article 'The Karmic Cycle of World

Englishes: Some Futuristic Constructs' (*WEn* 28[2009] 1–14) Yamuna Kachru and Larry E. Smith give an overview of past developments and current points of discussion of the spread of English world-wide.

A large number of publications focus on ELF, EIL, and ELT. For instance, the papers in *English as an International Language: Perspectives and Pedagogical Issues*, edited by Farzad Sharifian, reconsider and expand on well-established issues in the debate. The volume is structured in four main parts, each of which considers one of the major sub-themes in the field. Thus, the papers by Adrian Holiday, Sadia Ali, and Marko Modiano in Part I deal with the 'Native/Non-Native Divide: Politics, Policies and Practices' and the criticisms frequently voiced in this context, taking into consideration both Gulf Corporation Council Countries (e.g. Saudi Arabia, Kuwait, Bahrain, Qatar) and the current status of English in the European Union. Part II is concerned with 'EIL, Attitudes and Identity(ies)' and contains three papers on the pedagogical model of the native speaker, linking it to self-perception and identity construction and issues of intelligibility. In Part III, three further contributions reconsider issues revolving around 'EIL, Teacher Education and Language Testing: Gaps and Challenges', which include a consideration of how far research into World Englishes and EIL has been taken into consideration in teacher education, or the contribution of call centres, for example in India, as well as the stigmatization of some varieties of English. Finally, five papers are grouped together in Part IV, re-examining 'The Scope of EIL: Widening, Tightening and the Emerging Themes'. This collection is an excellent overview of the state of the art in EIL research, and at the same time it opens up new perspectives and paths for research.

Christiane M. Bongartz and Joybrato Mukherjee have edited a special issue of *Anglistik* (20:ii[2009]) dedicated to non-native Englishes, containing three papers on more general aspects of ELF, EIL, and ELT. Thus, Friederike Klippel's contribution on 'Teaching English as a Foreign Language: New Approaches and Challenges' (*Anglistik* 20:ii[2009] 13–25) reconsiders the development of ELT in Germany and the way new challenges are currently researched. Stavroula Tsiplakou argues in 'English in Cyprus: Outer or Expanding Circle?' (*Anglistik* 20:ii[2009] 75–87) that this variety should not be classified as belonging to the Outer Circle. Finally, 'English in Academia: Does Nativeness Matter?' by Ute Römer (*Anglistik* 20:ii[2009] 89–100) uses corpora to show that the 'native academic writer does not seem to exist' (p. 99) and that, in fact, experience in academic writing plays a more important role than native-speaker competence.

A number of articles in volume 28:ii of *World Englishes* are dedicated to the World English (WE) paradigm and ELF research and are therefore concerned with fundamental issues in these approaches. They are introduced by Barbara Seidlhofer and Margie Berns in 'Perspectives on English as a Lingua Franca: Introduction' (*WEn* 28[2009] 190–1). Jennifer Jenkins discusses various aspects of 'English as a Lingua Franca: Interpretations and Attitudes' (*WEn* 28[2009] 200–7), and Barbara Seidlhofer focuses more specifically on 'Common Ground and Different Realities: World Englishes and English as a Lingua Franca' (*WEn* 28[2009] 236–45), pointing out the many issues both have in common. Anne Pakir's 'English as a Lingua Franca: Analyzing Research

Frameworks in International English, World Englishes, and ELF' (*WEn* 28[2009] 224–35) deals with definitions of the term lingua franca and the use of English both as international and as national lingua franca. Yasukata Yano also highlights some central questions for the ELF/ELT debate in 'English as an International Lingua Franca: From Societal to Individual' (*WEn* 28[2009] 246–55). These include the native/non-native speaker divide and the question of regional standards; she asks whether 'It is possible to think of English for Specific Cultures (ESC)...?' (p. 253). Margie Berns turns our attention to Europe and thus to the supreme example of English in the Expanding Circle in her contribution 'English as Lingua Franca and English in Europe' (*WEn* 28[2009] 192–9), as does Angelika Breiteneder in 'English as Lingua Franca in Europe: An Empirical Perspective' (*WEn* 28[2009] 256–69). Breiteneder presents results from an exploratory study on the deletion of third person singular *–s*, based on the Vienna–Oxford International Corpus of English (VOICE). Marko Modiano also discusses 'Inclusive/Exclusive? English as a Lingua Franca in the European Union' (*WEn* 28[2009] 208–23), linking ELT in Europe to language ideologies and globalization.

Mario Saraceni is concerned with 'Relocating English: Towards a New Paradigm for English in the World' (*L&IC* 9[2009] 175–86), contending that academic discourse on the pluri-centricity of the English language has so far had little impact on the practices of ELT; he believes that this can only be remedied if English is not taught as a foreign but as an additional language, reflecting 'the cultural relocation of English that is taking place in the real world, a relocation from Anglo-American cultures to global and local ones' (p. 184). Will Baker investigates 'The Cultures of English as a Lingua Franca' (*TQ* 43[2009] 567–92) on the basis of a qualitative study conducted at a university in Thailand, which attempts to investigate students' notions of 'the cultures of English'.

We now come to the survey of individual varieties and we will start, as in previous years, with those of the southern hemisphere. We welcome the publication of a very interesting and useful collection edited by Pam Peters, Peter Collins, and Adam Smith. *Comparative Studies in Australian and New Zealand English: Grammar and Beyond* contains nineteen corpus-based papers on various morphological, syntactic, and pragmatic aspects of AusE and NZE. The volume features three articles in the first section focusing on morphology. Pam Peters's contribution, 'Irregular Verbs. Regularization and Ongoing Variability', investigates regional differences in the use of variable verb forms in AusE, NZE and BrE; she conclusively shows that 'the two southern hemisphere varieties... pattern together in contrast to BrE in their tolerance of non-standard past forms in the *ring*, *shrink*, *spring* set, and in their greater use of the nonstandardized *–t* suffix for the past forms of verbs such as *burn*, *leap*, *spell*' (p. 27). Heidi Quinn compares the distribution of 'Pronoun Forms', in AusE, NZE, AmE, and BrE, trying to identify regional differences in the use of case forms, for example I/me, he/him etc., and of second person plural variants. Dianne Bardsley and Jane Simpson compare 'Hypocoristics in New Zealand and Australian English', and show that 'similarities in settlement history and in the economic basis for settlement... and the long interchange between New Zealand and Australia have led to similar patterns of word creation' (p. 65), although AusE seems to exhibit a greater use of hypocoristics in *–o*. The second section of the volume comprises five papers dealing with verbs and verb phrases: Peter Collins presents a comparative study of 'Modals and Quasi-Modals', in AusE, NZE, BrE, and AmE and argues that a decline of modals can be linked to a rise in the use of quasi-modals. This diachronic change is exhibited on a continuum from the most advanced stage in AmE to the least advanced in BrE and NZE, with AusE falling in between. The distribution of 'The Perfect and the Preterite in Australian and New Zealand English', is the topic of Johan Elsness's contribution; he shows that both varieties are closer to BrE norms than to AmE ones but that AusE seems to be developing in the direction of the AmE model. When it comes to 'The Progressive' in these four varieties, Peter Collins's study shows that NZE and AusE are in fact more advanced than AmE and BrE with regard to the increased use of this verb form, with AusE outstripping NZE. Pam Peters compares 'The Mandative Subjunctive in Spoken English' in AusE, NZE, BrE, SingE, and Philippine English and shows that this verb form 'remains a formal construction by its limited frequency and restricted contexts of use (mostly written) [in BrE]; whereas in AusE and NZE, as well as SingE, it is also found in several kinds of public speech' (p. 136). Finally, Adam Smith analyses 'Light Verbs in Australian, New Zealand and British English', with regard to regional and register differences in their use. Light verbs appear to be more frequent in spoken than in written registers of all three varieties; NZE and AusE seem to be more innovative than BrE in extending the senses of light verbs in colloquial usages.

The next section of the collection deals with nouns and noun phrases. The first paper, by Adam Smith, looks at 'Non-Numerical Quantifiers', in AusE, NZE, and BrE and finds, for example, *loads of* to be much more frequent in BrE, whereas *heaps of* seems to be more frequent in AusE and NZE. The second paper, 'From Chairman to Chairwoman to Chairperson: Exploring the Move from Sexist Usages to Gender Neutrality', by Janet Holmes, Robert Sigley, and Agnes Terraschke, examines BrE, AmE, AusE, and NZE with regard to terms referring to women and men. This diachronic study shows that 'references to women more than doubled between 1961 and 1991, and then ebbed again in the late 1990s, at least in Australia and New Zealand' (p. 201), and that this increase can be correlated with a decrease in references to men. More recently AusE seems to exhibit a move towards gender-neutral forms for occupational terms referring to women, while in NZE and BrE terms for women tend to be linguistically marked. Section IV, on clauses and sentences, starts with an article by Marianne Hundt on 'Concord with Collective Nouns and New Zealand English'. Her investigation of this syntactic variable does not 'provide evidence of substantial regional differences between AusE and NZE nor between the southern hemisphere varieties and BrE, not even at the level of individual nouns. Instead, language internal variation seems to dominate the picture' (p. 218). '*No* in the Lexicogrammar of English' is analysed in AusE, NZE, and BrE by Pam Peters and Yasmin Funk; they conclude that 'the two southern hemisphere varieties are . . . on opposite sides of the cusp in lexicogrammatical terms' (p. 238), because NZE seems to be more conservative than AusE with regard to the replacement of *no*-negation by *not*-negation, and the use of *no* in reaction signals and in boilerplate. Kate Kearns investigates 'Zero Complementizer, Syntactic Context, and Regional Variety'. Her study of the alternation between *that* and zero complementizer in BrE, AmE, NZE, and AusE shows that zero complementation is more frequent in AusE and NZE in overall terms and that differences also occur with regard to different syntactic constructions. Kearns claims that 'the general factor of adjacency between the embedded clause and a potential zero-licensing lexical head is a weaker inhibitor of zero in the AusE and NZE data than in the AmE and BrE data' (p. 260). Christian Mair's contribution, 'Infinitival and Gerundial Complements', presents empirical findings on three different patterns of non-finite clause complementation, which exhibit only negligible differences between BrE, AusE, and NZE and thus illustrate that with regard to this aspect of syntax the southern hemisphere varieties seem to be little influenced by AmE syntax. Peter G. Peterson investigates 'Commas and Connective Adverbs', and presents a change in the use of the adverbs *however*, *therefore*, and *thus*, increasingly used as a syntactic link introducing a second main clause within a single orthographic sentence. According to Peterson's findings, this development seems to be more advanced in AusE and NZE than in BrE and AmE. In the final section of the volume, four contributions deal with discourse phenomena. Peter Collins reports on the findings of a study of five 'Information-Packaging Constructions', which are investigated across a range of registers in AusE, NZE, BrE, and AmE. AusE and NZE seem to follow BrE patterns more closely than AmE ones; the latter variety is apparently leading a change towards reversed pseudo-cleft constructions at the expense of the *it*-cleft. With regard to the support of dummy *it* and *there*, NZE seems to be even more conservative than BrE. The analysis of '*Like* and other Discourse Markers', in AusE and NZE by Jim Miller shows that *like* serves various discourse functions and that differences between the two southern hemisphere varieties are minimal with regard to this aspect of discourse. In their contribution, Jean Mulder, Sandra A. Thompson and Cara Pentry Williams provide strong evidence that 'Final *But* in Australian English Conversation' has established itself as a distinctive feature of AusE and is indeed indexical of 'Australianness'. The final chapter of this section is on 'Swearing', often claimed to be a characteristic feature of AusE and NZE and, as this corpus-based study reveals, certainly an important feature of these two varieties. However the authors of this paper, Keith Allan and Kate Burridge, doubt whether a systematic comparison of these two varieties with other varieties of English would actually uncover more differences than similarities between NZE and AusE on the one hand and, for example, AmE and BrE on the other. All in all, this comprehensive volume brings together different studies of aspects of AusE and NZE, which have—as Peter Collins points out in the 'Prologue'—only recently come into focus, with the advent of corpora of AusE and NZE. Moreover, the findings of these individual studies enable wider explorations of the developmental status and the question of the endo-normativity of AusE and NZE, as Pam Peters points out in her 'Epilogue'. The book impresses by the quality of the individual papers and the well-thought-out structure and is therefore highly recommended to everyone interested in World Englishes in general and in southern hemisphere varieties in particular.

In another article comparing southern hemisphere varieties of English, Joseph Sowa discusses '"Sweet As!": The Intensifier *as* in New Zealand and Australian English' (*EnT* 98, 25:ii[2009] 58–61) and investigates the use of A as a post-modifying intensifier on Australian and New Zealand websites. He finds evidence for an increase in productivity of this construction, which may also be used with adverbial function, as in *It drove me home sweet as*. In addition, Pam Peters describes 'Australian English as a regional epicenter' (in Hoffmann and Siebers, eds., pp. 107–24), showing that lexical innovations and morphological particularities, such as hypocoristics, have had an influence on the development of the neighbouring variety, NZE. Laura Thompson, Catherine J. Watson, and Donna Stark (in Hoffmann and Siebers, eds., pp. 125–40) demonstrate that differences between the vowel system of the Niuean variety of NZE and that of general NZE are subtle but nevertheless may be an expression of identity.

Two papers by Carolin Biewer investigate South Pacific Englishes: In 'Modals and Semi-Modals of Obligation and Necessity in South Pacific Englishes' (*Anglistik* 20[2009] 41–55), the author compares the expression of obligation and necessity in Fiji English, Samoan English, and Cook Islands English with AmE, BrE and NZE, on the basis of newspapers downloaded from the internet. Her results suggest that Cook Islands English follows NZE patterns most closely, while Samoan English and Fiji English resemble AmE with regard to a number of features. She investigates Fiji English in greater detail in 'Passive Constructions in Fiji English: A Corpus-Based Study' (in Jucker et al., eds., *Corpora: Pragmatics and Discourse*, pp. 361–77), which is based on ICE-GB, ICE-NZ, and a preliminary version of ICE-Fiji. Focusing on *get*-passives and *be*-passives, her results show that Fiji English resembles the other two varieties with regard to the frequency of *be*-passives, but seems to exhibit a lower number of agentive or long passives; the number of uses of *get*-passives in Fiji English is lower than in NZE, but higher than for BrE.

The bulk of this year's publications on individual varieties of English is concerned with Asian varieties of English. There is an entire volume of *AILA* dedicated to the topic of 'Multilingual, Globalizing Asia: Implications for Policy and Education' (*AILA* 22[2009]), edited by Lisa Lim and Ee-Ling Low. In addition, Lisa Lim and Nikolas Gisborne have edited a special issue on the typology of Asian Englishes (*EWW* 30:ii[2009]), providing an overview of the topic and of the contributions to follow in their introductory paper 'The Typology of Asian Englishes: Setting the Agenda' (*EWW* 30[2009] 123–32). Similarly, Umberto Ansaldo discusses 'The Asian Typology of English: Theoretical and Methodological Considerations' (*EWW* 30[2009] 133–48) in terms of an evolutionary and ecological perspective, which is reminiscent of Salikoko Mufwene's theory of language ecology and selection from a feature pool (cf. e.g. *YWES* 82[2003] 85). Taking Singlish as a case in point, Ansaldo concludes that many so-called Asian varieties of English might in fact rather be typologically classified as Asian language varieties with English influences, because 'morphological reduction is not necessarily an instance of simplification or faulty acquisition, but rather a reflection of typological traits of isolating languages (where present) which win in the competition and selection process' (p. 145). Lisa Lim argues along similar lines in 'Revisiting English Prosody: (Some) New Englishes as Tone Languages?' (*EWW* 30[2009] 218–39). As she points out, due to the typological make-up of their substrate languages and thus to their language ecology, some Asian varieties of English have their own prosodic system and need to be considered as tone languages. She illustrates this using Singapore and Hong Kong English as examples. These results can be related to those presented in Priyankoo Sarmah, Divya Verma Gogoi, and Caroline Wiltshire's investigation of 'Thai English: Rhythm and Vowels' (*EWW* 30[2009] 196–217). The authors collected data from twelve Thai speakers of English. As their analyses reveal, Thai English, as an Expanding Circle and L2 variety of English, is distinct from New Englishes such as SingE and Hong Kong English, partly because of rhythmic characteristics transferred from the Thai language, which lead to a stress-timed rather than a syllable-timed rhythm.

With *Contact Languages: Ecology and Evolution in Asia* Umberto Ansaldo presents us with yet another very interesting account of language contact, ecology, and language evolution, focusing on Monsoon Asia, a region stretching 'from the South China Sea to the eastern half of the Indian Ocean, including the Indonesian archipelago' (p. 6). Clearly set in Mufwene's conceptual framework of language ecology, the book explores the interaction between a society and the grammatical structures evolving in the formation of contact languages. The theoretical backdrop of the book is outlined in the introductory chapter, which is followed by a historical description of the language ecology of Monsoon Asia in chapter 2. Chapter 3 focuses on the sociolinguistic ecologies of Southeast Asia, particularly the roles of Malay and Portuguese, as well as the evolution of vernacular varieties in the region. In chapter 4, major theoretical concepts relating to the study of language contact in general are reconsidered. This leads to an evaluation in chapter 5 of the contribution language contact studies can make to general linguistics. The author claims that, generally speaking, theories of language are grounded on wrong assumptions, such as monolingualism, despite the fact that 'tutored, normative acquisition in a monolingual setting is not the norm in the history of the world, where multilingual practices and informal transmission of language have by far been prevalent in many of the world's societies' (p. 118). These theoretical considerations are followed by three chapters which present in-depth accounts of the evolution of contact languages in Sri Lanka, Southeast Asia, and Southern China respectively. The book closes with a chapter which summarizes the main findings and highlights further theoretical implications. This book is a valuable theoretical contribution to the study of language contact and contact language formation. Although the only variety of English discussed is actually China Coast Pidgin English, it provides important information for anyone interested in language variation and language creativity in this region of Asia and in the interplay of social and ecological factors in the creation of new grammars and mixed codes.

In the field of South Asian Englishes, two new monographs deal with IndE. *Contemporary Indian English: Variation and Change* by Andreas Sedlatschek is a comprehensive corpus-based description of IndE, which impresses the reader with a wealth of information on the lexical, morphological, and grammatical characteristics of this variety of English. The study is based on two corpora: a micro-corpus of 180,000 words specifically collected and designed for the purposes of the present study and an online corpus, consisting primarily of Google-based search queries run across selected domains and websites, particularly Indian quality newspapers. Drawing on such authentic spoken and written data, the author is able to test the validity and accuracy of claims made in a number of previous descriptions of IndE. Sedlatschek is thus in a position to criticize earlier feature-list descriptions of IndE, because 'many of the acclaimed Indianisms from the feature lists were too rare to be attested in the IndE databases' (p. 311). Other so-called 'Indianisms' were in fact not independent innovations, so that, according to results presented in this study, IndE differs structurally from other varieties of English, especially BrE, far less than some of its descriptions may suggest. However, the author also points out that speakers of IndE have nevertheless developed independent innovative strategies to make English meet their needs and to impress a kind of 'Indianness' on the English language at all levels of linguistic description. The study shows that speakers of IndE 'draw freely on the possibilities of English and make their own choices and this in a context-sensitive fashion' (p. 315), while adhering to the codified standard of BrE, which strongly limits the nativization process of this variety of English.

Indian English by Pingali Sailaja is a more accessible introduction to this variety of English in a textbook format. It follows the structure common to all volumes published in that series in that the introductory chapter provides the reader with background information on India, including information on the geography, demography, and sociolinguistics of the region. The second chapter describes the phonetics and phonology of IndE, and chapter 3 deals with morpho-syntactic characteristics. These include issues such as verb complementation, particle verbs, the progressive, tense concord in complex sentences, and auxiliary verbs, but also the use of articles and prepositions, topicalization, the formation of questions, and even some idioms, code-switching, and inflectional patterns, for example the pluralization of non-count nouns. Chapter 4 describes lexical and discourse features, but also other strategies of communication, such as aspects of politeness and style. In the next chapter, the author gives an account of the language history of India, starting with the first European, i.e. Portuguese, contacts and closing with the three-language formula of the post-independence period. This chapter also briefly mentions IndE pidgins and ongoing changes, most notably concerning the spelling of Indian words in English. Chapter 6 is an overview of previous publications and an annotated bibliography. The book closes with chapter 7, a collection of sample texts, including transcripts of two audio samples. The audio files to these transcripts can be accessed via the internet, where one can find four additional sound files with transcripts. To summarize, the book certainly resembles what Andreas Sedlatschek in his monograph criticizes as 'a feature-list descriptions of IndE' and remarks such as 'Despite serious attention to idioms and metaphors in school, comfortable use of idioms is rare' (p. 61) possibly suggest a slightly Anglocentric approach to the topic. However, as is made clear in the blurb on the back cover, the volume is intended to 'provide a starting point for anyone wishing to know more about [this] particular dialect', and this is what it does. It is a well-written introduction to IndE and can be recommended, and not only for students.

Among individual papers on IndE, there is Claudia Lange's '"Where Is the Party *Yaar*!": Discourse Particles in Indian English' (in Hoffmann and Siebers, eds., pp. 207–25), which is a systematic and thorough treatment of the Hindi-derived discourse particle *yaar* on the basis of the spoken part of ICE-India. In his paper 'The Lexicogrammar of Present-Day Indian English: Corpus-Based Perspectives on Structural Nativisation' (in Römer and Schulze, eds., *Exploring the Lexis-Grammar Interface*, pp. 117–35), Joybrato Mukherjee analyses four areas of IndE lexicogrammar, i.e. collocations, new prepositional verbs, new ditransitive verbs, and verb-complementation patterns, on the basis of ICE-India and ICE-GB, as well as web-derived corpora. He clearly shows that these four lexico-grammatical phenomena exhibit processes of structural nativization. In a similar vein, Chandrika Balasubramanian presents a corpus-based study of 'Circumstance Adverbials in Registers of Indian English' (*WEn* 28[2009] 485–508), comparing the uses of *also* and *too* in IndE to those in BrE and AmE. His results suggest that in terms of Edgar Schneider's Dynamic Model, IndE has in fact 'gone beyond nativization towards endonormative stabilization' (p. 507). Olga Maxwell and Janet Fletcher investigate in detail 'Acoustic and Durational Properties of Indian Vowels' (*WEn* 28[2009] 52–69) in the speech of speakers of IndE from northern India, who have Punjabi or Hindi as their L1, thus taking into account the linguistic diversity in India. Although their results to a large extent confirm those of earlier studies, they are able to draw a much more detailed picture of the inventory of monophthongal vowels in IndE. In '[V]at Is Going On? Local and Global Ideologies about Indian English' (*LSoc* 38[2009] 393–419), Vineeta Chand examines the v/w-merger in IndE and how this feature of Indian pronunciation is depicted and ideologized, for instance in American cartoons, and targeted, in Indian call centres, concluding that global standard language ideologies have an effect on Indians' self-evaluation of their English competence. Finally, in a column in *English Today* David Graddol shares with us some 'Thoughts from Kolkata on English in India' (*EnT* 100, 25:iv[2009] 21–3), on the question of English versus vernacular schooling.

Another South Asian variety of English is discussed in Ahmar Mahboob's paper 'English as an Islamic Language: A Case Study of Pakistani English' (*WEn* 28[2009] 175–89), which addresses questions such as whether English can carry the weight of Islamic experiences, cultures, and ideologies. Looking primarily at English-language newspapers and English-language textbooks used in Pakistan, the author concludes that English has ceased to be a colonizing language and is capable of representing South Asian Islamic values and identities. Two articles deal with Sri Lankan English: Michael Meyler identifies and describes 'Sri Lankan English: A Distinct Asian Variety' (*EnT* 100, 25:iv[2009] 55–60), and argues that Sri Lankan English is not a sub-variety of IndE, although the two varieties have much in common, most notably a partly shared history, shared religious and cultural practices, and common flora and fauna. Nevertheless, many Sri Lankans are themselves generally reluctant to accept Sri Lankan English as a variety in its own right.

The author hopes that with the publication of *A Dictionary of Sri Lankan English*, which is also discussed in this paper, attitudes will change. Attitudes are also the topic of a paper by Viktoria Künstler, Dushyanthi Mendis, and Joybrato Mukherjee, 'English in Sri Lanka: Language Functions and Speaker Attitudes' (*Anglistik* 20[2009] 57–74), which they have investigated with the help of a questionnaire. Albeit based on a limited sample, the survey suggests that Sri Lankan English has developed into 'an institutionalised second-language variety in its own right' (p. 72), serving a wide variety of functions and expanding even into personal domains. Finally, Suresh Canagarajah discusses 'The Plurilingual Tradition and the English Language in South Asia' (*AILA* 22[2009] 5–22), in more general terms, including a historical perspective.

Coming to Southeast Asia, Richard Powell discusses 'The Roles of English in Southeast Asian Legal Systems' (in Hoffmann and Siebers, eds., pp. 155–77). He notices an increasing importance of legal English in the region, coinciding with an expanding English/local language bilingualism. Despite this, there seems to be little evidence for the development of a distinct South Asian legal English variety. Singapore is the focus of a number of individual papers: Wendy D. Bokhorst-Heng and Imelda Santos Caleon present the results of a language attitude survey conducted among primary school students in their article on 'The Language Attitudes of Bilingual Youth in Multilingual Singapore' (*JMMD* 30[2009] 235–51). Similarly, 'Between Status and Solidarity in Singapore' by Francesco Cavallaro and Ng Bee Chin (*WEn* 28[2009] 143–59) is a report on their study of language attitudes towards SingE and Singlish; they suggest that governmental pressure and campaigns may explain the surprisingly low solidarity rating for Singlish. In her article 'Beyond Fear and Loathing in SG: The Real Mother Tongues and Language Policies in Multilingual Singapore' (*AILA* 22[2009] 52–71) Lisa Lim suggests that Singlish, plurilingual practices, and Chinese varieties should not be viewed as potential threats to the acquisition and intelligibility of English, but should instead be recognized as natural developments in a multilingual ecology. In another paper, 'Not Just an "Outer Circle", "Asian" English: Singapore English and the Significance of Ecology' (in Hoffmann and Siebers, eds., pp. 179–206), Lisa Lim argues again that the structural characteristics of a particular variety should be explained by taking ecological factors into consideration. Her argument for ecology is illustrated by an in-depth analysis of discourse particles in SingE. In their analysis of 'Colloquial Singapore English *Got*: Functions and Substratal Influences' (*WEn* 28[2009] 293–318), Nala Huiying Lee, Ling Ai Ping, and Hiroki Nomoto identify seven distinct uses of *got* in SingE. On the basis of a detailed cross-linguistic comparison of substrate languages, they come to the conclusion that Hokkien can be established as the primary source for the characteristics of this feature in SingE. Anne Pakir addresses the issue of language description versus language prescription in her article on 'Lexical Variations in "Singapore English": Linguistic Description and Language Education' (in Kawaguchi et al., eds., *Corpus Analysis and Variation in Linguistics* [2009] pp. 83–102). Taking examples from the lexicon of SingE, she claims that in Outer Circle countries, such as Singapore, the tension between traditional and emergent norms is more acute than in Expanding Circle countries, as the latter can easily adopt well-established Inner Circle standard varieties for pedagogical purposes, while the former need to define an acceptable standard model variety. Ulrike Gut presents results from her study of 'Past Tense Marking in Singapore English Verbs' (*EWW* 30[2009] 263–77), based on a corpus of spoken SingE. Her results suggest that phonological factors rather than morphological factors form the basis for the lack of many past tense markings in this variety of English. In addition, her study confirms observations, made in previous studies for written SingE, that present tense forms may have expanded in function so that they can be used to refer to habitual actions in the past, or to past events still relevant to the moment of speaking and can thus occur in contexts for which a past setting has already been established. Chonghyuck Kim and Lionel Wee aim at 'Resolving the Paradox of Singapore English *Hor*' (*EWW* 30[2009] 241–61), showing that this discourse particle is not only used as an attenuator but may also function in some discourse contexts as a booster of illocutionary force. Debra Ziegeler and Sarah Lee compare SingE to Malaysian English in their article 'A Metonymic Analysis of Singaporean and Malaysian English Causative Constructions' (in Panther et al., eds., *Metonymy and Metaphor in Grammar*, pp. 291–322). On the basis of an elicitation test, they show that the selection of a single-clause, conventionalized scenario structure over a causative-resultative in SingE, and to a lesser extent in Malaysian English, is due to a metonymic shift and possibly triggered by substratum influence. This brings us to three further publications on Malaysian English: Tan Siew Imm investigates eighty-five items of 'Lexical Borrowings from Chinese Languages in Malaysian English' (*WEn* 28[2009] 451–84) on the basis of the Malaysian English Newspaper Corpus, and shows that the preservation of Chinese culture and practices is reflected in the vocabulary of Malaysian English. Norizah Hassan and Azirah Hashim give an account of 'Electronic English in Malaysia: Features and Language in Use' (*EnT* 100, 25:iv[2009] 39–46), highlighting the creativity of this variety by examining a corpus of 2 million words collected from blogs, chat and instant messages, e-mails, and text messages. In addition to documenting the use of English as a lingua franca in electronic discourse, the authors also provide ample evidence for its distinctiveness. Azirah Hashim's paper 'Not Plain Sailing: Malaysia's Language Choice in Policy and Education' (*AILA* 22[2009] 36–51) discusses various aspects of language and education in Malaysia, including accounts of past and present language policies, conflicts between different ethnic groups relating to language choice in the country and nation-building, the emergence of a Malaysian variety of English, and the role of English as a regional lingua franca. Language policy and education is also the topic of T. Ruanni and F. Tupas's article 'Language as a Problem of Development: Ideological Debates and Comprehensive Education in the Philippines' (*AILA* 22[2009] 23–35), shifting the focus, however, to the Philippines. The authors' main point is that in discussions of educational and language policies attention should be shifted away from language issues to developmental issues.

Among East Asian varieties of English, eight publications deal with Hong Kong English (HKE). Taking up the issues of typology, ecology, feature pool, and substrate influence mentioned in several publications this year (especially in the relevant volume of *EWW*), Nikolas Gisborne discusses 'Aspects of the Morphosyntactic Typology of Hong Kong English' (*EWW* 30[2009] 149–69). Like many authors he also comes to the conclusion that the morphosyntax of HKE relating to tense and finiteness is heavily influenced by the substrate and that these should be viewed as systemic transfers and not as reflexes of imperfect second language acquisition. However Tony T.N. Hung, in his article on 'Innovation in Second Language Phonology: Evidence from Hong Kong English' (in Hoffmann and Siebers, eds., pp. 227–37), claims that some phonological features of HKE are neither transferred from the substrate languages nor attributable to the superstrate language. He believes that these phonological characteristics are genuine innovations, which may shed light on similar developments in other New Englishes. Andrew Sewell discusses an intelligibility-oriented approach for HKE pronunciation models in his article entitled 'World English, English as a Lingua Franca, and the Case of Hong Kong English' (*EnT* 97, 25:i[2009] 37–43). Winnie Cheng and Amy B.M. Tsui present results from a study of pragmatic aspects of HKE in their paper ' "Ahh (laugh) well there is no comparison between the two I think": How Do Hong Kong Chinese and Native Speakers of English Disagree with Each Other?' (*JPrag* 41[2009] 2365–80). They submitted data from naturally occurring English conversations, between Hong Kong Chinese non-native speakers of English and native speakers from Great Britain, the US, and Australia, to both qualitative and quantitative analysis. Their analyses confirm that some of the stereotypes relating to conversational behaviour and management of disagreement among Hong Kong Chinese, such as avoidance of confrontation and accommodation of the interlocutor's face wants, have a factual basis. However, their results also contradict some assumptions, for instance that Hong Kong Chinese disagree less often than their non-Chinese interlocutors. The authors point out that the specific context of a situation in which a disagreement occurs is an important key to understanding the social and cultural variables which determine the discourse behaviour of Hong Kong Chinese. In his article 'The Evolution of the English-Language Speech Community in Hong Kong' (*EWW* 30[2009] 278–301) Stephan Evans reconstructs the history of HKE in terms of Edgar Schneider's 'Dynamic Model' as proposed in the latter's 2007 publication *Postcolonial English* (*YWES* 88[2009] 95). Evans uses hitherto under-explored textual and statistical material to complete Schneider's account of this variety of English. Jonathan J. Webster portrays a change of perception of English in Hong Kong in his survey in 'Language in Hong Kong: Ten Years On (1997–2007)' (in Hoffmann and Siebers, eds., pp. 143–53); he claims that English has lost the negative connotation of a colonial language, being increasingly perceived positively, as a language of progress and upward mobility. He further claims that Hong Kong's language policy promotes and will continue to promote the development of biliteracy and trilingualism, a language policy 'which acknowledges the different roles played by Cantonese, Putonghua and English in Hong Kong society' (p. 152). This view is discussed in more detail by David C.S. Li in his article 'Towards "Biliteracy and Trilingualism" in Hong Kong (SAR): Problems, Dilemmas and Stakeholders'

Views' (*AILA* 22[2009] 72–84). As the author explains, the success of the language policy of English–Cantonese biliteracy and Cantonese–English–Putonghua trilingualism is hampered by the typological distance of the languages involved and by the absence of a language environment outside the classroom which allows the practice of English and Putonghua in authentic situations. Finally, Brian Hok-Shing Chan looks at 'English in Hong-Kong Cantopop: Language Choice, Code-Switching and Genre' (*WEn* 28[2009] 107–29), presenting a preliminary analysis of a corpus of Cantonese popular songs collected randomly from website archives. As he shows, the functions and poetic uses of code-switching in this music genre seem to resemble the pop music of other regions.

Emily Tsz Yan Fong presents results from a pilot study of the attitudes of the Chinese government and of Chinese overseas students in Australia in her article 'English in China: Some Thoughts after the Beijing Olympics' (*EnT* 97, 25:ii[2009] 44–9). Her results show that, especially in the context of the Beijing Olympics, English has received strong government support and is widely held by the public to be a universal modern skill. However, the variety of English generally accepted is AmE, not China English. This corresponds to the findings from Tian Bo Li and Gillian Moreira's survey, reported on in their article 'Learning English in Corporate China' (*EnT* 99, 25:iii[2009] 41–8). They administered a questionnaire in fifty-nine companies in five provinces of the People's Republic of China, and their analysis of the 296 responses shows that AmE is the variety of English that is mostly used by the informants. In addition, their results show that English is primarily a language of business and trade. Guiling Hu and Stephanie Lindemann also investigate the positive evaluation of AmE vis-à-vis negative stereotypes of Chinese English. In their article 'Stereotypes of Cantonese English, Apparent Native/Non-Native Status, and their Effect on Non-Native English Speakers' Perception' (*JMMD* 30[2009] 253–69) they present results from a matched guise experiment administered to Chinese learners of English. As their study shows, with regard to the perception of unreleased word-final stops, a stigmatized feature of Cantonese English but not of AmE, listeners who believed they were listening to a Cantonese speaker of English perceived the typical native speaker pronunciation, which is similar to the Cantonese English stereotype, as a feature of Cantonese English. Listeners who thought they were hearing a native speaker of AmE tended to not hear the unreleased stops. Similarly, Deyuan He and David C.S. Li investigate 'Language Attitudes and Linguistic Features in the "China English" Debate' (*WEn* 28[2009] 70–89), and their results largely confirm previous studies, in that native AmE is clearly preferred as a teaching model. However, their informants seem to accept many features of China English as a 'legitimate part of the local English curriculum' (p. 86). Anwei Feng's paper 'English in China: Convergence and Divergence in Policy and Practice' (*AILA* 22[2009] 85–102) describes policies and practices with respect to English language education at various governmental levels, pointing out that China's rapid development has caused a number of changes and transformations in the educational system, which may lead to inequalities and social and ethnic divisions in society.

I would like to close this section by drawing attention to the publication of a very interesting collection of articles presenting various aspects of life experienced by different groups of Asian Pacific Americans in the US and Canada. With *Beyond Yellow English: Toward a Linguistic Anthropology of Asian Pacific America*, Angela Reyes and Adrienne Lo have edited a volume which explores questions of language and culture, alongside identity negotiation and educational issues, and which makes a valuable contribution to the understanding of the experiences of Asians in North America and of diaspora communities in general. The first part of the book deals with identity formation and stereotypes at the individual level, while Part II takes this issue to the community level. Languages in contact and bilingualism are dealt with in Part III, while language use in the media and media representations are discussed in Part IV. The last part concerns itself with educational issues and questions of language acquisition. The book is rich in information and combines a broad variety of approaches to the topic.

Moving on to the African continent, a number of this year's publications deal with West African varieties of English. Paul N. Mbangwana and Bonaventure M. Sala present a book-length treatment of *Cameroon English Morphology and Syntax: Current Trends in Action*. The authors aim to establish CamE as a standard variety in its own right and describe its features as adaptations to Cameroonian ecological conditions and as the results of internal restructuring processes. They base their description on three novels by the Cameroonian author Linus Asong and on examples from recordings, as well as from 'general observation' of the spoken language and from texts produced by university students in the written language. After a foreword, a preface, and a prologue with a note on the data and methods of analysis, the book starts with a chapter on the general historical background of English in Africa. This chapter also deals with the question of language use in African literature, the problem of defining CamE and some aspects of New Englishes in general. Chapter 2 presents a wide array of theoretical issues, whose relevance to the overall theme of the book is not always evident, and a survey of some varieties of English, which contains some surprising mistakes, such as classifying 'West Indian English' as a variety of 'Indian English'. Chapter 3 lists some morphological characteristics of CamE, while the next two chapters deal with syntactic features of this variety of English. The final chapter summarizes and categorizes the findings of the earlier chapters and gives a brief outlook. The book is valuable for anyone interested in CamE, as it provides the reader with a number of genuine and interesting examples from this variety of English, particularly in the field of syntax. One of its biggest flaws, however, is the source and unsystematic analysis of the study's data. Furthermore, the bibliography is somewhat outdated and the authors seem to have disregarded a number of recent and relevant publications from the field.

With *The Sociolinguistics of English and Nigerian Languages* Dele Adeyanju has edited a collection of papers which treat all the well-known issues relevant to this topic in the era of globalization, from the development, maintenance, or endangerment of indigenous languages, and the indigenization of the English language, via language planning, policy formation, and pedagogical implications, all the way to the exploitation of sociolinguistic realities in literary works. The tenor of the contributions is summarized by the editor in the introduction to the volume: 'The papers generally opine that the prestige status and dominant role enjoyed by English over the indigenous languages in official contexts and the overwhelming positive attitude of the people to English at the expense of the indigenous languages pose a serious threat to the development and even the survival of such indigenous languages' (n.p.). Consequently this collection does not add very much new to the debate on linguistic imperialism, and one is even surprised by the obvious neglect of Nigerian Pidgin in this context. But it makes the writings of Nigerian researchers available to a wider public and is therefore certainly a useful source for anyone interested in the sociolinguistic situation of Nigeria and the interrelation between Nigerian indigenous languages and English.

More innovative is Diri I. Teilanyo's treatment of 'Literary Usage in English as a Second Language in Nigeria: A Study of "Icheoku" and "Masquerade"' (*Africa Today* 55:iv[2009] 73–121), which studies the use of English in two Nigerian television series, showing that the deviant use of idioms, proverbs, and aphorisms by the Igbo English bilingual characters, on the one hand, constitutes 'a realistic parody of a true-life challenge' and on the other has a 'significant impact on real-life use of English' (p. 93) in Nigeria. The ethnic variety of NigE referred to as Igbo English is also at the centre of another article. Emmanuel Ezejideaku and Esther Nkiri Ugwu examine 'Igbo English in the Nigerian Video Film' (*EWW* 30[2009] 52–67). They describe various forms of Igbo influence, mainly at the syntactical level and with regard to idiomatic expressions, but interestingly they also mention a mixed code, which they refer to as 'Engligbo' and which reminds one of similar phenomena described for other urban settings such as 'Sheng' in Kenya and 'Camfranglais' in Cameroon. 'The Functions of English in Nigeria from the Earliest Times to the Present Day' are surveyed by Rotimi Taiwo (*EnT* 98, 25:ii[2009] 3–10), giving a detailed account of the use of English in pre-colonial and colonial times, of the different functions English has assumed since independence, and the relation between English and indigenous languages today. Pragmatics aspects of CamE are examined in Yves Oufeu and Talla Sanda's 'Thanking Responders in Cameroon English' (*WEn* 28:4[2009] 544–51). Finally, Jemima Asabea Anderson discusses 'Codifying Ghanaian English: Problems and Prospects' (in Hoffmann and Siebers, eds., pp. 19–36). She reviews existing descriptions of the characteristics of Ghanaian English (GhE), which suggest the existence of a distinct Ghanaian variety. However, the standardization and codification of GhE are challenged by the negative attitudes expressed in publications, most notably by Ghanaian scholars, who usually refer to this variety as 'English in Ghana', while outsiders more readily describe the language as 'Ghanaian'.

East African varieties of English, or rather the mixing of English with indigenous languages, have also attracted the attention of a number of scholars. Christina Higgins, for instance, investigates *English as a Local Language: Post-Colonial Identities and Multilingual Practices* in Kenya and Tanzania. The author gives an historical overview of the sociolinguistics of multilingualism in the region, from pre-colonial times with Swahili trade via the colonial beginnings with German and later British colonization to the 'multivocality' in Kenya and Tanzania today. 'Multivocality' is described as 'the different "voices" or *polyphony* that single utterances can yield due to their syncretic nature. Creative language forms are frequently produced when speakers intermingle the languages and language varieties circulating in their lives' (p. 7). This can be described in the framework of a continuum between code-switching at one end and mixed or fused languages, such as Sheng, at the other. Higgins then explores the linguistic behaviour of multilingual East Africans in four different domains: the workplaces of office workers and journalists, beauty contests, hip hop culture and lyrics, and advertising. She demonstrates how this multilingual behaviour and the hybridity of their discourse is a response to the tensions felt between local African identities and the pressure of English as a global means of communication. Her book is therefore a very good demonstration of the creative linguistic and local forms of English that frequently develop in multilingual urban settings around the globe.

Charles Bwenge's *The Tongue Between: Swahili and English in Tanzanian Parliamentary Discourse* also deals with code-switching and code-mixing in East Africa. Taking the Tanzanian national parliament as his primary site of investigation, the author illustrates how the mixing of English and Swahili has led to an emerging new variety of Swahili, which he refers to as 'elite Swahili' (ES) and which he claims is a variety in its own right. The book contains six chapters, in the first of which he outlines the theoretical concepts and descriptions of code-switching in the literature. The second chapter gives an overview of the history of Swahili–English bilingualism and patterns of contact. Chapter 3 explores the language policies and patterns of language use of the Tanzanian parliament at a general level, while chapter 4 analyses linguistic behaviour during a typical day in parliament. In chapter 5 the author shows how the linguistic behaviour of politicians in parliament transfers to the language of electoral campaigns. By way of a conclusion, chapter 6 summarizes the author's main claims and aims to illustrate the vitality and high symbolic value of ES. In fact, this book is almost complementary to Christina Higgins's book, as it illustrates the concept of 'multivocality' for yet another domain, namely parliamentary discourse and the language of politicians. In addition, although it contains very little that is unexpected to readers familiar with studies in similar settings, this book definitely provides very interesting details and examples from Tanzania, a region which is frequently under-represented in accounts of English in Africa, more often than not being lumped together with Kenya and subsumed under the general heading of 'East Africa'. However, the book would have profited from better proofreading as the large number of books mentioned in the text but missing from the bibliography is very annoying and could easily have been avoided.

In her article ' "It's kuloo tu": Recent Developments in Kenya's Englishes' (*EnT* 97, 25:i[2009] 3–11), Christiane Meierkord also investigates the linguistic repertoire which East Africans, in this case Kenyans, can and do draw on for their communicative needs and identity construction in a multilingual society. In more detail, she describes 'Engsh', a Kenyan mixed code whose syntax is basically English and which incorporates lexical items from indigenous Kenyan languages and, most notably, from AmE. Meierkord analyses its use in various Kenyan newspapers and, as do Higgins and Bwenge discussed above, comes to the conclusion that 'language mixing has established itself as an accepted strategy for expressing one's identity linguistically . . . to indicate a "glocal" identity, which combines local modern Kenyan and global belonging' (p. 10). Finally, in her article 'Expanding Circles within the Outer Circle: The Rural Kisii in Kenya' (*WEn* 28[2009] 352–64) Martha M. Michieka questions the appropriateness of classifying Kenya as an Outer Circle country in the Kachruvian Circle model when it comes to describing the language situation in rural south-western Kenya. As she demonstrates, political, educational, economic, and historical factors mean that, in this part of the country, English functions as a foreign language and it would more accurately be classified as an Expanding Circle area.

Among work on South African varieties of English we find Ingrid Fandrych's article on 'The Importance of English Communication Skills in Multilingual Settings in Southern Africa' (*EnT* 99, 25:iii[2009] 49–55), which surveys the situation in Southern African states such as Lesotho, South Africa, and Namibia, stressing the importance of language teaching and the acquisition of English-language skills in these countries, for both intra-national and international communication and participation. With 'Deracialising the GOOSE Vowel in South African English: Accelerated Linguistic Change Amongst Young, Middle Class Females in Post-Apartheid South Africa' (in Hoffmann and Siebers, eds., pp. 3–18) Rajend Mesthrie presents a very interesting account of ongoing phonological changes among middle-class female students in South Africa. Preliminary results from a larger study suggest that middle-class female informants tend to realize the GOOSE vowel with a more fronted quality, once primarily associated with white speakers, and that black females seem to be leading this change, followed by 'coloured', while Indian South Africans seem to be most resistant to this development.

I will close this section by mentioning two publications on the language situation in Zimbabwe. Finex Ndhlovu explores *The Politics of Language and Nation Building in Zimbabwe*, drawing on a variety of material, using semi-structured open interviews with a total of fifty informants as the main source, combined with archival material, radio and television programmes, etc. After an introduction, the author gives a historical overview of the development of language policy from the colonial to the postcolonial period, with a focus on missionary activities in chapter 2. Chapter 3 gives a detailed description of the sociolinguistic ecology of the country, presenting among other topics the distribution of national and official languages and discussing the status of English. Most notably, the author makes clear that Shona and Ndebele, and not English, have been imposed as the languages of widest communication, and this imposition 'has significantly constricted the use of minority languages in the domains of education, media, law and administration' (pp. 76–7). In chapter 4, the author explores the relationship between ethnic, linguistic, and political loyalties from the early 1980s to the present, showing a tight connection between political party and linguistic affiliation. Chapter 5 describes how nation-building programmes promoting Shona, and to a lesser extent also Ndebele, have marginalized other minority languages and language communities. This issue is further elaborated in the following chapter, highlighting the hierarchical structure of the model of triglossia and introducing the notion of 'internal colonization'. The book closes with chapter 7, which sets into a wider perspective the discussion of the imposition of linguistic norms by a dominant ethnic group on minority groups and thus the issues of internal colonization. As the author stresses: 'the politics of linguistic imposition is not only or always associated with the spread of English as an international language. Rather, linguistic imperialism is something that is endemic and firmly resident in the seemingly stable relations among the speakers of different African languages in Zimbabwe' (p. 181). With this, as opposed to the collection by Dele Adeyanju mentioned above, the author develops a new perspective on the debate of linguistic imperialism, one that had already been suggested by Janine Brutt-Griffler in 2006 in her 'Language Endangerment, the Construction of Indigenous Languages and World English' (in Martin Pütz, Joshua A. Fishman, JoAnne Heff-van Aertselaer, eds., *'Along the Routes to Power': Explorations of Empowerment through Language*, pp. 35–53).

In 'A Survey of the Language Situation in Zimbabwe' (*EnT* 98, 25:ii[2009] 18–24), Muzi Mlambo reflects on the relationship between Shona and English in Zimbabwe and on the question of whether English in Zimbabwe could actually be referred to as 'Zimbabwean English'. The author believes in the existence of a localized variety of English that deserves the latter designation, but unfortunately he fails to give evidence for this view. The few rather impressionistic examples provided, such as *return back* for 'return' or *cousin brother* for 'cousin' can hardly be considered sufficient and are, in fact, also found in many other varieties of African English.

Turning our attention to varieties of English in the Caribbean, Christian Mair's contribution 'Corpus Linguistics Meets Sociolinguistics: Studying Educated Spoken Usage in Jamaica on the Basis of the International Corpus of English' (in Hoffmann and Siebers, eds., pp. 39–60) is an impressive account of a study undertaken on the basis of the spoken component of ICE-Jamaica. On the basis of five variables contrastively investigated in several ICE sub-corpora, Mair conclusively shows that the emerging Jamaican English (JamE) standard seems to be more influenced by AmE and Jamaican Creole than by BrE or shared L2 features and should therefore perhaps not be included among the British-influenced postcolonial standards anymore. Ingrid Rosenfelder analyses 'Rhoticity in Educated Jamaican English: An Analysis of the Spoken Component of ICE-Jamaica' (in Hoffmann and Siebers, eds., pp. 61–82), and her findings do not confirm traditional accounts, which classify this variety as generally rhotic. However, the results of her thorough analysis confirm impressionistic descriptions in earlier accounts of the factors influencing rhoticity, adding interesting new details; her study clearly demonstrates that 'rhoticity in educated Jamaican English can be considered to remain a complex phenomenon at the interplay of British, American and local norms of pronunciation' (p. 81). In her article 'Standard English in the Secondary School in Trinidad: Problems—Properties—Prospects' (in Hoffmann and Siebers, eds., pp. 83–104), Dagmar Deuber presents results of a study of language use in Trinidadian educational institutions. Using linguistic analyses based on transcripts of lessons from different secondary schools, coupled with semi-formal conversations for an assessment of language attitudes, Deuber concludes that a localized variety of StE is the major language of instruction in Trinidad, while creole is only used for complementary purposes. Glenda Alicia Leung investigates the 'Negotiations of Trinidadian Identity in Ragga Soca Music' (*WEn* 28[2009] 509–31) using the theoretical framework of Robert Le Page and Andrée Tabouret-Keller's 'acts of identity' model, and showing that the borrowing and appropriation of phonological Jamaican Creole features by raga soca artists is used to convey and represent their particular Trinidadian identity. In 'Caribbean ICE Corpora: Some Issues for Fieldwork and Analysis' (in Andreas Jucker et al., eds., pp. 425–50), Dagmar Deuber highlights some problems arising in the compilation of the spoken components of ICE sub-corpora in the Caribbean, where English is spoken alongside English-based creoles; she shows that strategies similar to those applied in the compilation of ICE-East Africa can be successfully applied. As she demonstrates, creole features 'are not necessarily excluded from a text whose language would overall be classified as English or Creolized English' (p. 427). Similarly, in her paper '"The English We Speaking": Morphological and Syntactic Variation in Educated Jamaican Speech' (*JPCL* 24[2009] 1–52), Deuber questions the accuracy of the creole continuum model for the description of the spoken language of educated Jamaicans, since her data from ICE-Jamaica fall in between the high acrolect and the upper mesolect. She concludes that syntactic and morphological variation in speech needs to be correlated with stylistic variation.

These last three articles bring us to the section on Creolistics. With *Gradual Creolization: Studies Celebrating Jacques Arends*, Rachel Selbach, Hugo C. Cardoso, and Margot van den Berg have edited an impressive volume dedicated to and celebrating the life and work of the late Jacques Arends. As the title suggests, the central theme of this book is the question of gradual creolization, and the editors have managed to bring together nineteen different papers, which deal with the pros and cons of this theoretical concept from different theoretical and empirical perspectives. In Part I of the book, Selbach et al. have grouped together articles which take a primarily linguistic perspective, examining the phonological, lexical, or morpho-syntactic structures of pidgin and creole (P/C) languages. For example, Philip Baker discusses 'Productive Bimorphemic Structures and the Concepts of Gradual Creolization' and tries to identify the length of time required for a P/C to develop consistency in the structure of interrogatives. Bettina Migge and Donald Winford investigate 'The Origin and Development of Possibility in the Creoles of Suriname' by drawing on data from early Sranan and Saamaka texts. Their findings show that the expression of possibility and thus 'the grammars of the Surinamese creoles continued to evolve over time, in accordance with Arends's gradualist hypothesis' (p. 152). Three more contributions in this section of the book deal with the creoles of Surinam. The origin of Saramaccan verbs and the frequency of Portuguese and English in this creole, investigated by Peter Bakker in his contribution 'The Saramaccan Lexicon: Verbs', provide evidence for the assumption that

English is the most important source for the lexicon of this language. George L. Huttar looks at 'The Development of a Creole Lexicon' in Ndyuka, which supports Arends's gradualist hypothesis. The same can be said of Marvin Kramer's contribution, which explores 'Gradualism in the Transfer of Tone Spread Rules in Saramaccan'. The papers in Part II of the collection are primarily concerned with the language-external and thus the sociohistorical and demographic issues of creolization. Of particular interest in our context are: Christine Jourdan's contribution on 'Bilingualism and Creolization in the Solomon Islands', an in-depth historical analysis of the multilingual ecology of the region, which links creolization to social change; Magnus Huber's paper entitled 'Lingua Franca in West Africa? An Evaluation of the Sociohistorical and Metalinguistic Evidence', which explores the nature and conditions of Afro-European linguistic contacts on the West African coast from the fifteenth to the eighteenth centuries; Norval Smith's reassessment of sociohistorical data gathered by Jacques Arends and the conclusions he drew concerning 'English-Speaking in Early Surinam?'; Silvia Kouwenberg's investigation of 'The Demographic Context of Creolization in Early English Jamaica, 1655–1700'; and finally Don E. Walicek's discussion of 'The Founder Principle and Anguilla's Homestead Society'. Given the high quality of the individual contributions, this volume is indispensable for anyone interested in particular P/C languages but also in the theory of creolization more generally.

Ingo Plag's two columns, 'Creoles as Interlanguages: Phonology' (*JPCL* 24[2009] 119–38) and 'Creoles as Interlanguages: Word-Formation' (*JPCL* 24[2009] 339–62), also deal with general theoretical aspects of creole genesis, giving further evidence for his 'interlanguage hypothesis'. This hypothesis was also the topic of his two last year's columns in the journal (see *YWES* 89[2010] 131), and Plag's detailed comparison of creoles and SLA data in two additional structural sub-systems (inflection and syntax being dealt with in last year's contributions) highlights yet again many striking similarities between these two sets of data, which can be taken as a proof that inter-language processes are the basis of many creole genesis features. 'Grammaticalization in Creoles: Ordinary and Not-So-Ordinary Cases' is discussed by Adrienne Bruyn (*SLang* 33[2009] 312–37). Focusing on definite and indefinite article use and locative items, as well as instances of sentence complementation and tense-marking in Sranan, the author shows that a grammaticalization approach can only be helpful in the context of creole studies, if different types of development are neatly distinguished and if substrate and adstrate languages are also taken into consideration. Marta Viada Bellido de Luna's account of 'The Use of English Lexified Creole in Anglophone Caribbean Literary' (in Smith et al., eds., *Caribbean without Borders: Literature, Language and Culture*, pp. 42–57) is a survey of well-known aspects of the literary use of creole languages, giving, however, a few interesting and genuine examples from Caribbean authors of different nationalities.

Among works on the description of individual P/C languages, Jeff Good analyses 'A Twice-Mixed Creole? Tracing the History of a Prosodic Split in the Saramaccan Lexicon' (*SLang* 33[2009] 459–98), giving further evidence that this language is a highly mixed lexifier creole with significant parts of the lexicon coming from Portuguese (cf. Bakker's paper mentioned above), and from African languages, in addition to English, the latter providing the language with lexical items marked for tone. Jacqueline Bunting investigates the early uses of *taki* and its variants, using a corpus of Sranan text from the eighteenth and nineteenth centuries, and presenting her findings in '"Give" and Take: How Dative *gi* Contributed to the Decline of Ditransitive *taki*' (*JPCL* 24[2009] 199–217). Miriam Meyerhoff also investigates substrate influences in 'Animacy in Bislama? Using Quantitative Methods to Evaluate Transfer of a Substrate Feature' (in Stanford and Preston, eds., *Variation in Indigenous Minority Languages*, pp. 369–96); her work is based on quantitative analyses of conversational Bislama and Tamambo. In his article 'Chinese Pidgin English in Southeastern Australia: The Notebook of Jong Ah Siug' (*JPCL* 24[2009] 306–37), Jeff Siegel provides us with interesting information about the linguistic features and the scarcely documented use of Chinese Pidgin English in Australia in the second half of the nineteenth century. His source of data is the recently discovered notebook of a Chinese immigrant, which also provides evidence that in Australia Chinese Pidgin English was used alongside and mixed with Australian and Pacific pidgins. 'Writing in Cameroon Pidgin English: Begging the Question' (*EnT* 98, 25:ii[2009] 11–7), by Bonaventure M. Sala, illustrates some of the (foreseeable) difficulties the author encountered when compiling a dictionary of contemporary Cameroon Pidgin. This article is thus an overview of issues pertaining to the writing of P/C languages, i.e. the decision for or against a spelling convention that closely reflects the orthography of the lexifier. This problem is more acute in the Cameroon case, where competing French- and English-oriented orthographies can be found.

11. Pragmatics and Discourse Analysis

In 2009 several new reference works for pragmatics were published. To begin with, the ten-volume series *Handbook of Pragmatics Highlights*, published by John Benjamins of Amsterdam and edited by Jef Verschueren and Jan-Ola Östman, is a topically organized series of paperbacks that aims to focus on the most salient topics in the field of pragmatics, dividing its wide interdisciplinary spectrum in a transparent and manageable way. Hence, each volume starts with an up-to-date overview of its field of interest and then presents a selection of some twelve to twenty of the most relevant entries from its more comprehensive sister publication *Handbook of Pragmatics* [1995–2009], intending to cover the major concepts, traditions, methods, and scholars in the respective field of research. The first five volumes appeared in 2009, the others are due in 2010 and 2011 respectively. Volume 1, *Key Notions for Pragmatics*, edited by Jef Verschueren and Jan-Ola Östman, introduces some fundamental concepts that pervade the pragmatic literature, such as deixis, implicitness, speech acts, and context, thereby situating the field of pragmatics in relation to a general concept of communication and the discipline of semiotics, also touching upon non-verbal aspects of language use and a comparison with non-human forms of communication. Volume 2, *Culture and Language Use*, edited by Gunter Senft, Jan-Ola Östman, and Jef Verschueren, reviews basic topics and traditions that place language use in its cultural context. Moreover, a number of contributions to this volume are devoted to aspects of methodology (e.g. ethnography and fieldwork), while others highlight the role of eminent scholars who have significantly shaped the study of cultural dimensions of language use (e.g. Franz Boas, Edward Sapir, William von Humboldt, and Benjamin Lee Whorf). The third volume, *Cognition and Pragmatics*, edited by Dominiek Sandra, Jan-Ola Östman, and Jef Verschueren, focuses on the interface between language and cognition, thus testifying to the success of cognitive approaches to language in the last decades. Volume 4, *The Pragmatics of Interaction*, edited by Sigurd D'hondt, Jan-Ola Östman, and Jef Verschueren, is dedicated to the empirical investigation of the way human beings organize their interaction in natural environments and how they use talk for accomplishing actions. It contains a selection of entries documenting the various levels of interactional organization and some topical articles on phenomena like reported speech and listener response. Moreover, the volume features overviews of specific traditions (e.g. conversation analysis, ethno-methodology) and articles on eminent researchers (Erving Goffman and Harvey Sacks) who had a formative influence on the field. Finally, the fifth volume *Grammar, Meaning and Pragmatics*, edited by Frank Brisard, Jan-Ola Östman and Jef Verschueren, looks at the field of linguistic pragmatics from the point of view of grammar, asking in which particular sense a variety of older and more recent functional (rather than generative) models of grammar relates to the study of language in use.

In addition to this handbook series, two encyclopaedias of pragmatics have been published. The *Routledge Pragmatics Encyclopedia*, edited by Louise Cummings, intends to capture the diversity of pragmatics, which has grown into a multi-disciplinary field that encompasses a range of theoretical and empirical concerns, in a comprehensive, single-volume edition. In over 200 entries, it covers concepts and theories that have traditionally been associated with pragmatics, but also recent areas of development within the field, scholars who have had a significant influence on pragmatics, interdisciplinary exchanges between pragmatics and other areas of enquiry, and major research trends. In a similar fashion, the second edition of the *Concise Encyclopedia of Pragmatics*, edited by Jacob L. Mey and Keith Brown, is a single-volume reference resource describing the discipline of pragmatics in more than 200 contributions from eminent scholars of pragmatics. Like its sister publications in the same series of Concise Encyclopedias of Language and Linguistics, it is a spin-off from the second edition of the *Encyclopedia of Language and Linguistics* (*ELL* 2) also published with Elsevier.

Some book-length publications address the wider scope of pragmatics and its application to other disciplines. To begin with, *Corpora: Pragmatics and Discourse*, edited by Andreas H. Jucker, Daniel Schreier, and Marianne Hundt, explores the relationship between pragmatics, discourse, and corpus linguistics. The book on the whole features current state-of-the-art discussions in corpus-based linguistic research of the English language presented at the 2008 International Conference on English Language Research on Computerized Corpora (ICAME 29) in Ascona, Switzerland (see also section 12). In its first of three thematic sections, entitled 'Pragmatics and Discourse', the book covers the field of corpus pragmatics and corpus-based discourse analysis, including studies of speech acts, conversational routines, referential expressions, and thought styles in the history of English, PDE, learner English, and political discourse. The ten papers are: 'Historical Corpus Pragmatics: Focus on Speech Acts and Texts' by Thomas Kohnen; 'The Pragmatics of Knowledge and Meaning: Corpus Linguistic Approaches to Changing Thought-Styles in Early Modern Medical Discourse' by Irma Taavitsainen; 'A Diachronic Perspective on Changing Routines in Texts' by Tanja Rütten; '*Friends* Will Be "Friends"? The Sociopragmatics of Referential Terms in Early English Letters' by Minna Nevela; 'Self-Reference and Mental Processes in Early English Personal Correspondence: A Corpus Approach to Changing Patterns of Interaction' by Minna Palander-Collin; '*Sort of* and *Kind of* in Political Discourse: Hedge, Head of NP or Contextualization Cue?' by Anita Fetzer; '"So er I just sort I dunno I think it's just because...": A Corpus Study of *I don't know* and *dunno* in Learners' Spoken English' by Karin Aijmer; '*On the face of it:* How Recurrent Phrases Organize Text' by Magnus Levin and Hans Lindquist; 'Research on Fiction Dialogue: Problems and Possible Solutions' by Karin Axelsson (see also section 12 below); and finally 'Establishing the EU: The Representation of Europe in the Press in 1993 and 2005' by Anna Marchi and Charlotte Taylor.

Gila Schauer's monograph *Interlanguage Pragmatic Development. The Study Abroad Context* deals with pragmatics in the field of SLA. Her study of interlanguage pragmatic development in English examines German learners of English at a British university over the course of a year. The focus is not only on the learners' productive pragmatic development but also on their pragmatic awareness, which is compared with their grammatical awareness.

Like 2008, this year yet again bears witness to the growing interest in the study of historical pragmatics. *Early Modern English News Discourse: Newspapers, Pamphlets and Scientific News Discourse*, edited by Andreas H. Jucker, is a collection of papers that examine the emergence of new textual genres and new publication channels in early modern Britain. In a period where news discourse became increasingly more important and reached wider audiences, newspapers appeared first on a weekly and then on a daily basis, while pamphlets became established as the first real mass media, and scientific news discourse in the form of letters exchanged between fellow scholars turned into academic journals. The papers are organized into three thematic sections preceded by the editor's introduction, 'Newspapers, Pamphlets and Scientific News Discourse in Early Modern Britain'. The first part contains studies of early newspapers that range from reports of crime and punishment to want ads, and from traces of religious language in early newspapers to the use of imperatives: 'Crime and Punishment' by Udo Fries; 'Reading Late Eighteenth-Century Want Ads' by Laura Wright; '"Alwayes in te Orbe of honest Mirth, and next to Truth": Proto-Infotainment in the Welch Mercury' by Nicholas Brownlees; 'Religious Language in Early English Newspapers?' by Thomas Kohnen; '"As silly as an Irish Teague": Comparisons in Early English News Discourse' by Claudia Claridge; and '"Place yer bets" and "Let us hope": Imperatives and their Pragmatic Functions in News Reports' by Birte Bös. The second part focuses on pamphlets and provides detailed analyses of news reporting and of impoliteness strategies: 'Comparing Seventeenth-Century News Broadsides and Occasional News Pamphlets: Interrelatedness in News Reporting' by Elisabetta Cecconi, and '"From you, my Lord, professions are but words—they are so much bait for fools to catch at": Impoliteness Strategies in the 1797–1800 Act of Union Pamphlet Debate' by Alessandra Levorato. The last section deals with scientific news discourse and traces the early publication formats in their various manifestations: '"Joyful News out of the Newfound World": Medical and Scientific News Reports in Early Modern England' by Irma Taavitsainen and 'News Filtering Processes in the *Philosophical Transactions*' by Lilo Moessner.

The Language of Daily Life in England (1400–1800), edited by Arja Nurmi, Minna Nevala and Minna Palander-Collin, is a state-of-the-art account of historical sociolinguistic and socio-pragmatic research mainly based on the *Corpus of Early English Correspondence*. The volume contains nine studies, presented in three thematic sections, and an introductory essay by the editors entitled 'The Language of Daily Life in the History of English: Studying How Macro Meets Micro'. The contributions discuss linguistic and social variation and change over four centuries. Each study tackles a linguistic or social phenomenon, and approaches it with a combination of quantitative and qualitative methods, always embedded in the sociohistorical context. The volume presents new information on linguistic variation and change, while evaluating and developing the relevant theoretical and methodological tools. Section I, 'Variation and Social Relations', contains the three papers that are most relevant for the present context: 'Negotiating Interpersonal Identities in Writing: Code-Switching Practices in Charles Burney's Correspondence' by Päivi Pahta and Arja Nurmi, 'Patterns of Interaction: Self-Mention and Addressee Inclusion in Letters of Nathaniel Bacon and his Correspondents' by Minna Palander-Collin, and 'Referential Terms and Expressions in Eighteenth-Century Letters: A Case Study on the Lunar Men of Birmingham' by Minna Nevala. The papers that appear in the other two sections of the book, i.e. 'Methodological Considerations in the Study of Change' and 'Sociohistorical Context' are discussed in sections 2 and 9 of the present chapter.

In addition to these two edited collections, several papers on the historical pragmatics of English have appeared in the *Journal of Historical Pragmatics*. In 'Empowerment and Disempowerment in the Glencairn Uprising: A Corpus-Based Critical Analysis of Early Modern English News Discourse' (*JHPrag* 10[2009] 23–55), Sheryl Prentice and Andrew Hardie offer a corpus-based, partly quantitative critical discourse analysis of the presentation of actors and groups on both sides of the Glencairn Uprising (1653–4), a military rebellion by Scottish Highlanders under the leadership of William, earl of Glencairn, against the English government of Oliver Cromwell. In 'Re-Visiting Salem: Self-Face and Self-Politeness in the Salem Witchcraft Trials' (*JHPrag* 10[2009] 56–83), Krisda Chaemsaithong investigates the accused individuals' response strategies in the Salem witchcraft trials from the perspective of pragmatic politeness in the sense of politeness to self, for the sake of one's face, arguing that the accused's responses were in part driven by 'what they thought others thought of them', which is part of their 'face'.

Alessandra Levorato studies the linguistic resources adopted by pamphlet writers to express their stance and engage their readers during the so-called Irish paper war that preceded the 1800 Union between Great Britain and Ireland in '"Be steady then, my countrymen, be firm, united and determined": Expressions of Stance in the 1798–1800 Irish Paper War' (*JHPrag* 10[2009] 132–57). Raymond F. Person, Jr., in '"Oh" in Shakespeare: A Conversation Analytic Approach' (*JHPrag* 10[2009] 84–107) compares the observations concerning *oh* in spoken ModE with *oh*/*O* in the First Folio and early quartos of William Shakespeare. The language of Shakespeare is also the topic of Evelyn Tribble's 'Languaging in Shakespeare's Theatre' (*P&C* 17[2009] 596–610), which discusses performance practices in the eModE period which were marked by a tension between improvisational here-and-now languaging practices, including the use of gesture in playing, and a new set of expectations based upon an emergent conception of plays as written documents.

The *Journal of Historical Pragmatics* also published a special issue in 2009. 'Historical Sociopragmatics' (*JHPrag* 10:ii[2009]), edited by Jonathan Culpeper, features the editor's introduction 'Historical Sociopragmatics: An Introduction' (*JHPrag* 10[2009] 179–86) and five full papers. 'Structures and Expectations: A Systematic Analysis of Margaret Paston's Formulaic and Expressive Language' by Johanna L. Wood (*JHPrag* 10[2009] 187–214) shows how a model based on a CDA approach, in conjunction with frame analysis, offers a systematic way to analyse fifteenth-century letters. In 'The Sociopragmatics of a Lovers' Spat: The Case of the Eighteenth-Century Courtship Letters of Mary Pierrepont and Edward Wortley' (*JHPrag* 10[2009] 215–37) Susan M. Fitzmaurice draws on relevance theory in a pilot analysis preliminary to the pragmatic coding of implicature and inference in a rich body of epistolary prose in the letters sub-corpus of the *Network of Eighteenth-Century English Texts* (*NEET*). Minna Nevala, in 'Altering Distance and Defining Authority: Person Reference in Late Modern English' (*JHPrag* 10[2009] 238–59), studies the use of nominal terms and pronouns as a means to refer to a third party, as well as to the writer him/herself and the addressee in written interaction on the basis of lModE letters and journals. Minna Palander-Collin, in 'Variation and Change in Patterns of Self-Reference in Early English Correspondence' (*JHPrag* 10[2009] 260–85), examines what gentlemen in early and late modern England could say about themselves in the first person, and whether there were any register or diachronic differences in typical self-reference, drawing on integrationist social theory and employing a set of quantitative and qualitative methods in the analysis of recurrent word clusters extracted from the *Corpus of Early English Correspondence* and its *Extension*. Finally, in 'Identifying Key Sociophilological Usage in Plays and Trial Proceedings (1640–1760): An Empirical Approach Via Corpus Annotation' (*JHPrag* 10[2009] 286–309), Dawn Archer and Jonathan Culpeper argue for another approach to the study of historical pragmatics they label 'sociophilology', demonstrating it can effectively be pursued by combining corpus annotation and 'keyness' analysis.

Turning to discourse studies, three new textbooks appeared in 2009. *Discourse, of Course: An Overview of Research in Discourse Studies*, edited by Jan Renkema, is designed as a textbook for graduate students. It comprises twenty short papers organized into seven sections that cover approaches from very different schools in discourse studies (from argumentation theory to genre theory, from the study of multi-modal metaphors to cognitive approaches to coherence analysis). The volume aims at presenting material for advanced courses in discourse studies, unfolding a display of research projects for future Ph.D. students, and providing an overview of new developments since 2004, when Renkema's introductory textbook for undergraduates *Introduction to Discourse Studies* was published. Next, *Confusing Discourse* by Karol Janicki is intended primarily for graduate students of linguistics, language, and communication. It identifies and addresses some of the sources of confusion in discourse (understood as part of the phenomenon of discourse in general) and offers ways of diminishing it. The last textbook to be mentioned here is one of a number of publications this year that present discourse-analytic studies of language used on the internet and the emergence of new genres on the web. *The Discourse of Blogs and Wikis* by Greg Myers is a textbook for upper-level undergraduates in linguistics and language studies that informs and offers insights into two major new types of discourse, weblogs (or blogs) and wikis, which have made a huge impact on electronic communication and provide a basis for the analysis of discourse and genres on the internet. The book addresses the questions of what makes these forms distinctive as genres, and what ramifications the technology has for the language.

Genres in the Internet: Issues in the Theory of Genre, edited by Janet Giltrow and Dieter Stein, is a collection that brings together for the first time papers taking diverse perspectives on genre, all addressing internet communication, an arena challenging to traditional ideas of genre which assume a conventional stability that is at odds with the unceasing innovations of online discourse. The papers show that genre study is a powerful means of testing commonplaces about the internet world and, in turn, that the web is a fertile field for theorizing genre. The book consists of an introduction by the editors, 'Genres in the Internet: Innovation, Evolution, and Genre Theory', and ten full papers: 'Re-Fusing Form in Genre Study' by Amy J. Devitt; 'Lies at Wal-Mart: Style and the Subversion of Genre in the *Life at Wal-Mart* Blog' by Cornelius Puschmann; 'Situating the Public Social Actions of Blog Posts' by Kathryn Grafton;, ' "Working Consensus" and the Rhetorical Situation: The Homeless Blog's Negotiation of Public Meta-Genre' by Elizabeth G. Maurer; 'Brave New Genre, or Generic Colonialism? Debates over Ancestry in Internet Diaries' by Laurie McNeill; 'Online, Multimedia Case Studies for Professional Education: Revisioning Concepts of Genre Recognition' by David Russell and David Fisher; 'Nation, Book, Medium: New Technologies and their Genres' by Miranda Burgess; 'Critical Genres: Generic Changes of Literary Criticism in Computer-Mediated Communication' by Sebastian Domsch; 'A Model for Describing "New" and "Old" Properties of CMC Genres: The Case of Digital Folklore' by Theresa Heyd; and finally 'Questions for Genre Theory from the Blogosphere' by Carolyn R. Miller and Dawn Shepherd.

Two journal articles provide further critical discourse/genre analyses of internet language. 'Give Me Liberty and Give Me Surveillance: A Case Study of the US Government's Discourse of Surveillance' (*CDS* 6[2009] 1–14) by Maria A. Simone reports a CDA analysis of www.lifeandliberty.gov, a website constructed by the US Department of Justice, with the express intention of explaining provisions of the USA PATRIOT Act, while in '"I am a very happy, lucky lady, and I am full of Vitality!": Analysis of Promotional Strategies on the Websites of Probiotic Yoghurt Producers' (*CDS* 6[2009] 111–25), Nelya Koteyko examines internet advertising of food and drinks containing probiotics using the framework of critical genre analysis. The discourse of food promotion is also the topic of '"But it's all true!": Commercialism and Commitment in the Discourse of Organic Food Promotion' by Guy Cook, Matt Reed, and Alison Twiner (*T&T* 29[2009] 151–73), who report on a research project which combined corpus analysis, interviews, and focus group discussions to investigate the discourse of organic food promotion in Britain, the thinking behind it, and how people react to it. 'Electronic Bumper Stickers: The Content and Interpersonal Functions of Messages Attached to E-Mail Signatures' (*DisS* 11[2009] 105–20), by Stephen A. Rains, Geoffrey R. Tumlin, and Mark L. Knapp, examines the content and communication function served by electronic bumper stickers, i.e. the sayings that are included in an e-mail signature file following personal identifiers such as one's name, phone number, and postal address.

Further studies of specialized genres outside electronic communication have also appeared. In 'Toward a Genre-Based Characterization of the Problem–Solution Textual Pattern in English Newspaper Editorials and Op-Eds' (*T&T* 29[2009] 393–414), Isabel Alonso Belmonte presents the results of discourse-analytic research on the problem–solution (PS) pattern of textual organization in a sample of English written newspaper editorials and op-eds, characterizing the linguistic realization of the PS-pattern in written opinion journalism and describing its textual variations. '"Just wondering if you could comment on that": Indirect Requests for Information in Corporate Earnings Calls' by Belinda Crawford Camiciottoli (*T&T* 29[2009] 661–81) is based on a corpus of thirty authentic question-and-answer sessions from earnings calls, i.e. multi-party telephone calls arranged through a tele-conferencing service during which executives present financial results to investment analysts. She investigates the language used by investment analysts to request information, with particular attention to indirect requests. Carita Paradis's '"This beauty should drink well for 10–12 years": A Note on Recommendations as Semantic Middles' (*T&T* 29[2009] 53–73) examines middle constructions in wine-tasting notes, arguing that the weakly deontic nature of recommendation fosters semantic middles and that the middle quality is directly derived from the discourse function of recommendation.

Academic discourse is the object of study of Ken Hyland's *Academic Discourse: English in a Global Context*, a genre-based introduction to academic discourse designed for undergraduate and postgraduate students of applied linguistics, TESOL, and English for Academic Purposes (EAP). It outlines the nature and importance of academic discourse in the modern world, describing the conventions of spoken and written academic discourse and the ways in which these construct both knowledge and disciplinary communities. On the same topic, Suomela-Salmi and Fred Dervin have edited *Cross-Linguistic and Cross-Cultural Perspectives on Academic Discourse*, a fine volume that examines spoken and written academic discourse from a cross-linguistic, cross-cultural, and cross-disciplinary perspective: as many as twelve scientific fields and eight different languages are considered. Concluding this overview of publications on academic discourse is Maicol Formentelli's 'Address Strategies in British Academic Setting' (*Pragmatics* 19[2009] 179–96), which sheds light on address strategies used by students and members of the teaching staff in academic interactions, using data from semi-structured interviews and video-recordings to outline an unmarked pattern of asymmetry between the parties, in which students mainly employ formal vocatives towards lecturers (title + surname, honorifics), while lecturers frequently use first names and other informal expressions.

The remainder of this section briefly highlights a number of special issues of journals that have appeared this year. To begin with, *Intercultural Pragmatics* has published a special issue on 'The Pragmatics of English as a Lingua Franca' (*IPrag* 6:ii[2009]), edited by Juliane House, that aims to contribute to current conceptualizations and descriptions of the nature of ELF as a phenomenon *sui generis*. Hence the papers do not look upon English as an L2 to be measured against an ideal native speaker norm, but as a special form of language use operating under different conditions than both native/native and native/non-native interactions, suggesting a need for a new kind of interactive pragmatics approach that involves the revision of key concepts and tenets of English-language research practices in the past. Following House's 'Introduction: The Pragmatics of English as a Lingua Franca' (*IPrag* 6:ii[2009] 141–5), Alan Firth's contribution, 'The Lingua Franca Factor' (*IPrag* 6:ii[2009] 147–70), addresses the central question of ELF research, namely whether there is in fact something that is special about ELF—whether there exists a 'lingua franca factor' at all. Firth argues that variability as a major characteristic of ELF is not to be equated with failure to fulfil native norms, but, rather, is something that lies at the core of ELF discourse, in which forms can be changed, adapted, and communicatively aligned whenever necessary. In 'Subjectivity in English as Lingua Franca Discourse: The Case of *You Know*' (*IPrag* 6:ii[2009] 171–93) Juliane House reanalyses the use of *you know* in ELF, arguing that it is predominantly used as a self-serving, non-other-oriented strategy which speakers employ in order to create coherence in their turns at talk and/or gain time for planning further talk. As such, it frequently co-occurs with *and*, *but*, and *because*, functioning as an expression of procedural meaning following a process of pragmaticalization. 'Accommodation and the Idiom Principle in English as a Lingua Franca' by Barbara Seidlhofer (*IPrag* 6:ii[2009] 195–215) provides empirical corpus-based evidence of the special nature of ELF discourse on the basis of the use of idioms. Seidlhofer shows that ELF users make use of idiomatic phrases, constructing and co-constructing them online for their own locally emerging needs and purposes. She argues that the co-construction of idiomatic phrases in ELF talk goes even further: over and above signalling co-operation it also serves to create shared affective spaces. In 'Chunking in ELF: Expressions for Managing Interaction' (*IPrag* 6:ii[2009] 217–33), Anna Mauranen focuses on phraseological patterns used in ELF discourse, providing further empirical evidence for the existence of unique features in ELF talk by highlighting ELF speakers' real-time innovative modifications of the pool of conventional forms. Lastly, 'Intonation as a Pragmatic Resource in ELF Interaction' by Lucy Pickering (*IPrag* 6:ii[2009] 235–55) deals with intonation and explores its role in linguistic, discursive, and pragmatic features of ELF. She argues that the use of intonation as a pragmatic resource in ELF interactions is unique in that speakers make tone and key choices predominantly in order to signal trouble spots and indicate their resolution, rather than making such choices for socially integrative and face-saving reasons as native speakers often do.

The second special issue of *Intercultural Pragmatics* is edited by Klaus P. Schneider and Anne Barron and deals with 'Variational Pragmatics' (*IPrag* 6:iv[2009]), a subdiscipline of intercultural pragmatics, investigating intra-lingual differences, i.e. pragmatic variation between and across L1 varieties of the same language, an emergent area of research which has been much neglected to date. Variational pragmatics can be conceptualized as the intersection of pragmatics with sociolinguistics, or, more specifically, with dialectology as the study of language variation. It is assumed that the social factors analysed in sociolinguistics also have a systematic impact on language use in interaction. The introductory chapter, 'Variational Pragmatics: Studying the Impact of Social Factors on Language Use in Interaction' (*IPrag* 6:iv[2009] 425–42), by the editors, outlines the framework that includes two components: one in which social factors are specified, and one in which levels of pragmatic analysis are distinguished. Of the six papers, four focus on English. In 'The Pragmatics of the *be* + *after* + V-*ing* Construction in Irish English' (*IPrag* 6:iv[2009] 517–34), Anne O'Keeffe and Carolina Amador Moreno discuss this construction from a pragmatic perspective, identifying its discourse functions and showing that it is widely used by both genders and also among younger speakers of Irish English today. They predict that it will remain an exclusive feature of this national variety. Fiona Farr and Bróna Murphy study the macro-social factors of gender and age, and the role played by genre in the study of language in use in 'Religious References in Contemporary Irish English: "For the love of God almighty... I'm a holy terror for turf"' (*IPrag* 6:iv[2009] 535–59). They establish that religious references used to signal emotions are primarily found in spoken language of an informal nature and that the use, and also the preferred pragmalinguistic means to signal emotions using religious references, differ by gender and age. In 'The Functional and Social Reality of Discourse Variants in a Northern English Dialect: I DON'T KNOW and I DON'T THINK Compared' (*IPrag* 6:iv[2009] 561–96), Heike Pichler investigates the use of localized and non-localized full and reduced variants of these discourse markers among working-class speakers from Berwick-upon-Tweed. Finally, in 'Adolescents and Identity' (*IPrag* 6:iv[2009] 597–612), Ronald K.S. Macaulay identifies a number of innovative forms of intensifiers and quotatives that have developed locally in the speech of working-class adolescents in Glasgow, also establishing age and gender differences.

Languages in Contrast published a special issue on 'Contrastive Pragmatics' (*LinC* 9:i [2009]), edited by Karin Aijmer, containing seven studies that address various topics and contrast English with other European languages: 'Modality and ENGAGEMENT in British and German political interviews' by Annette Becker (*LinC* 9:i [2009] 5–22); 'The Intersubjective Function of Modal

Adverbs: A Contrastive English-French Study of Adverbs in Journalistic Discourse' by Agnès Celle (*LinC* 9:i [2009] 23–36); 'Intersubjective Positioning in French and English: A Contrastive Analysis of *ça dépend* and *it depends*' by Bart Defrancq and Bernard De Clerck (*LinC* 9:i [2009] 37–72); 'Challenges in Contrast: A Function-to-Form Approach' by Anita Fetzer (*LinC* 9:i [2009] 73–97); 'Interruption in Advanced Learner French: Issues of Pragmatic Discrimination' by Marie-Noëlle Guillot (*LinC* 9:i [2009] 98–123); 'Closeness and Distance: The Changing Relationship to the Audience in the American TV News Show *CBS Evening News* and the Swiss *Tagesschau*' by Martin Luginbühl (*LinC* 9:i [2009] 124–43); and 'The Nominative and Infinitive in English and Dutch: An Exercise in Contrastive Diachronic Construction Grammar' by Dirk Noël and Timothy Colleman (*LinC* 9:i [2009] 144–81).

The *Journal of Pragmatics* published a thematic issue on 'Pragmatic Markers' (*JPrag* 41:v[2009]), edited by Neal Norrick. The papers that deal with pragmatic markers in English are 'Interjections as Pragmatic Markers' by Neal R. Norrick (*JPrag* 41:v[2009] 866–91), 'Topic Orientation Markers' by Bruce Fraser (*JPrag* 41:v[2009] 892–8), and 'Mind You' by David M. Bell (*JPrag* 41:v[2009] 915–20). Pragmatic markers are also examined by Phoenix W.Y. Lam in 'The Effect of Text Type on the Use of *So* as a Discourse Particle' (*DiSt* 11[2009] 353–72), Galina B. Bolden in 'Implementing Incipient Actions: The Discourse Marker "So" in English Conversation' (*JPrag* 41[2009] 974–98), and Bruce Fraser in 'An Account of Discourse Markers' (*IRPrag* 1[2009] 293–320).

Finally, *Pragmatics* published a special issue on 'Youth Language at the Intersection: From Migration to Globalization' (*Pragmatics* 19:i[2009]), edited by Mary Bucholtz and Elena Skapoulli, in which two papers are relevant for the present overview. 'Speaking Like Asian Immigrants: Intersections of Accommodation and Mocking at a U.S. High School' by Elaine Chun (*Pragmatics* 19:i[2009] 17–38) explores the relationship between immigrant and non-immigrant Asian American youth identities and the use of language to manage this relationship, focusing on everyday interactions at a high school in Texas. The second paper, ' "She's hungarious so she's Mexican but she's most likely Indian": Negotiating Ethnic Labels in a California Junior High School' by Jung-Eun Janie Lee (*Pragmatics* 19:i[2009] 39–63) examines how California youth employ a variety of concepts associated with ethnicity to classify themselves and others, suggesting that ethnicity is not a simple category, but rather a concept that youth in a multi-ethnic context actively construct and co-construct with the help of associated notions. Youth language is also the topic of ' "And then I'm really like...": "Preliminary" Self-Quotations in Adolescent Talk' (*DiSt* 11[2009] 401–19) by Joyce Lamerichs and Hedwig F.M. Te Molder, who demonstrate how the preface leading up to the self-quotation is designed as hard to counter, and instructs the hearer how to understand what comes next, while the self-quotation constitutes the assessment as a mere characterization that provides the speaker with a number of opportunities for testing the proposed view.

12. Stylistics

At a time when scholars all over the world find themselves more and more compelled to 'justify' their positions in academic departments, it is not surprising to find a wealth of academic publications every year. Stylistics is not free from this overwhelming need to 'publish or perish', but fortunately this pressing need has not compromised the quality of papers, monographs, and edited collections in the year 2009.

One term seems to have caught the imagination and scholarly interest of academics this year, that of 'texture', as demonstrated, for instance, by Gail Forey and Geoff Thompson's *Text Type and Texture*, Jan Renkema's *The Texture of Discourse: Towards an Outline of Connectivity Theory*, and Peter Stockwell's *Texture—A Cognitive Aesthetics of Reading*. These publications, however, do not coincide in the way the authors conceive the term. Forey and Thompson's *Text Type and Texture*, emerges out of the Systemic Functional Linguistics (SFL) tradition, whereby texture refers to the 'key quality which distinguishes a text' (M.A.K. Halliday and R. Hasan, *Cohesion in English* [1976] 2) as texts are not made out of sentences randomly put together. As the authors point out, SFL has traditionally identified various means for creating texture such as 'grammatical signals of cohesion (Halliday and Hasan 1976), lexical repetitions of various kinds (Hoey 1991), devices for encapsulation and prospection (Sinclair 1992/2004) and for participant tracking (Martin 1992), and... patterns of thematic choice' (p. 1). This volume collects work that focuses primarily on how texture manifests in the textual meta-function, especially in relation to theme, such as in Geoff Thompson and Susan Thompson's 'Theme, Subject and the Unfolding of Text' (pp. 45–69). Secondly, thematic aspects are considered in relation to text types and genre as in Hugh Gosden's 'Thematic Content in Peer Reviews of Scientific Papers' (pp. 94–107), or David Hyatt's '"To elicit an honest answer—which may occasionally be the same as the truth": Texture, Coherence and the Antagonistic Political Interview' (pp. 125–50). A third way in which texture is assessed is in relation to interpersonal patterns, as illustrated by Gail Forey's 'Projecting Clauses: Interpersonal Realisation of Control and Power in Workplace Texts' (pp. 151–74). Finally, the collection is brought to a close by J.R. Martin's 'Boomer Dreaming: The Texture of Re-Colonisation in a Lifestyle Magazine' (pp. 252–84), which looks at a magazine article by using some of the ideas previously developed by the rest of the contributors to the volume.

The second monograph dealing with texture is Jan Renkema's *The Texture of Discourse*. Renkema's concerns are relatively close to those in the previous collection, although he states that he is mainly interested in looking at texture from the perspective of what he calls 'connectivity': 'The aim of this study is... understanding the links between sentences, by exploring in depth what makes a sequence of utterances a discourse. The cover term chosen to refer to linking phenomena is *connectivity*' (p. 2). It appears that the issues identified in this book as 'texture of discourse' (p. 2) are roughly equivalent to what other scholars describe as discourse grammar. Hence, the author is interested in looking at topics such as 'elaboration', 'extension', and 'enhancement', on the one hand, and 'interjunction' (the way in which an addresser communicates with an addressee) on the other.

Finally, in Peter Stockwell's *Texture*, the emphasis on texture shifts to cognitive stylistics. The author states that this monograph can be viewed as an enriched and much more refined version of some of the principles initially outlined in his *Cognitive Poetics: An Introduction* [2002]. Following the stylistic tradition of implementing close textual analysis, Stockwell defines texture as 'the experiential quality of textuality' (p. 14), which he endeavours to account for by borrowing, primarily, from the cognitive grammar framework developed by Ronald Langacker in his *Foundations of Cognitive Grammar*, volumes 1 and 2 [1987, 1991], and *Cognitive Grammar: A Basic Introduction* [2008]. The present monograph is particularly successful at highlighting the complementary, non-discriminatory role that cognitive linguistic and cognitive psychological models can have for the more traditional textual approaches to texts. As the author states, 'texture . . . can be accounted for precisely neither by purely textual description nor by purely psychological modelling, but by a properly holistic blending of both aspects into a unitary analysis' (p. 15). The challenge, therefore, lies in achieving a balance concerning how writerly and readerly aspects contribute to meaning creation in texts. In general, though, and as stated in the title itself, this volume focuses on the investigation of the latter components. For instance, in his discussion of 'mind style', Stockwell argues that it can be defined as 'being the presentation of a highly deviant or at least very unusual worldview, judged of course by a reader against his own set of cultural norms' (p. 125). This definition is based both on the original characterization of the notion by Roger Fowler in *Linguistic Criticism* [1986] and the subsequent reworkings by other scholars. Whereas I concur with Stockwell concerning the need to consider readers' experiential side of those (usually unorthodox) world-views, I think this can only be achieved by equally bearing in mind the textual aspects of mind style; that is, the fact that readers are able to judge such a world-view 'against their own set of cultural norms' (p. 125) is only possible by first considering the linguistic (verbal or otherwise) forms that mark such a particular cognitive make-up, an aspect not so thoroughly developed in the monograph. In this connection, Stockwell's treatment of mind style appears to slightly overlook the way mind style has been generally defined as the linguistic (verbal, non-verbal, multimodal) representation of a particular mind.

There are a number of other introductory textbooks to different aspects of English that merit mentioning. There is, first of all, Christiana Gregoriou's *English Literary Stylistics*, which applies prototypically stylistic theoretical notions and frameworks such as deviation, parallelism, or speech and thought presentation to the analysis of poetry, narrative, and drama. In the field of narratology, two excellent volumes stand out, David Herman's *Basic Elements of Narrative* and Monica Fludernik's *An Introduction to Narratology*. Despite the fact that these volumes are marketed as non-specialist works, they do not merely contain basic information about narratology and its scope of analysis. They are written in a reader-friendly manner but they do not lose any of the sophistication or scholarly engagement that would be expected in works targeted at more advanced students or scholars new to the discipline.

Herman's study encompasses topics which range from a basic definition of narrative, both literary and non-literary, to notions such as world-creation, as also developed in cognitive stylistics. In contrast, Fludernik's work (translated from the original German) focuses primarily on aspects of fictional narratives but also includes detailed analyses besides general tips for future practitioners of narratology. Wendy Anderson and John Corbett's *Exploring English with Online Corpora: An Introduction* is also addressed to a non-specialist audience and focuses on corpus studies; this is a worthy introductory companion to other more sophisticated works such as some of those discussed later on. A far more comprehensive volume is *English Language: Description, Variation and Context*, edited by Jonathan Culpeper, Paul Kerswill, Ruth Wodak, Francis Katamba, and Tony McEnery. The contributors to this volume are all, or have previously been, based at Lancaster University. Their desire was to put together an introductory volume which was, nonetheless, research-led and to do so in the most holistic way possible. Thus, the collection is divided into six parts ranging from topics such as the structure of language, discussed among others by Geoffrey Leech in 'Words (and Phrases)' (pp. 111–29) (followed by two more chapters by the same author on clauses and sentences), to aspects of historical linguistics, such as Sebastian Hoffman's 'Lexical Change' (pp. 286–300), issues concerning style, such as Mick Short's 'Language in Literature: Stylistics' (pp. 464–76), and English learning and teaching, illustrated by Andrew Hardie's 'Language Acquisition' (pp. 609–25) (for more details see section 5(a) above). A final introductory work, part of the Routledge English Language Introductions series, is Alan Durant and Marina Lambrou's *Language and Media: A Resource Book for Students*. The aspect that undoubtedly stands out here, as is indeed the norm for the whole series, is the imminently practical nature of the book. Some of the issues discussed are typically linguistic, such as register and style, but these are then contextualized in their connection with media topics such as media storytelling, the relationship of words and images or blogs' speech.

The interface of language and media (in all its manifestations) is an issue that stylisticians are always keen to investigate, so work done in these areas subsequently finds its way into stylisticians' research, especially in the area of multimodal stylistics. Televisual adaptations of classical novels, for instance, illustrate this language/media interface, as argued by Chris Louttit in 'Cranford, Popular Culture, and the Politics of Adapting the Victorian Novel for Television' (*Adaptation* 2[2009] 34–8). Chris Louttit suggests that television adaptations of novels respond to a particular socio-economic and political period, clear and distinct from that in which the originals were created, for which purpose this author looks at Charles Dickens's *Bleak House* [1853] and Elizabeth Gaskell's *Cranford* [1853] in the 2005 version by Andrew Davies and the 2007 adaptation by Heidi Thomas, respectively. Christine Geraghty's 'Foregrounding the Media: *Atonement* (2007) as an Adaptation' (*Adaptation* 2[2009] 91–109) focuses instead on what is considered a cinematic sub-genre in its own right: the adaptation of literary works.

Further examples of the interconnections between language and media can be found in some of the chapters of Sandra Heinen and Rory Sommer's *Narratology in the Age of Cross-Disciplinary Research*. Published in the

Narratologia series, this edited collection aims at showing that narratologists are finding cross-fertilization to be not simply profitable but actually necessary. Wolfgang Hallet's 'The Multimodal Novel: The Integration of Modes and Media in Novelistic Narration' (pp. 129–53), Peter Verstraten's 'Between Attraction and Story: Rethinking Narrativity in Cinema' (pp. 154–69), and Silke Horstkotte's 'Seeing or Speaking: Visual Narratology and Focalization, Literature to Film' (pp. 170–92) seem to prove such a need. Hallet highlights that what he calls the 'multimodal novel' is a sub-genre still in need of much more adequate attention; in addition, he rightly points out that considering the multimodal novel has repercussions for narratology as a discipline, which, put simply, can no longer afford to focus on textual aspects exclusively. Verstraten, on the other hand, focuses on cinematic forms, and questions whether the 'traditional' notion of narrativity in film is still applicable to all cinematic forms, especially to those more experimental exercises characterized by what he calls 'filmic excess', where 'excess' refers to those cinematic characteristics capable of bringing the non-narrative components of film to the fore while relegating the narrative content to the background. Finally, Horstkotte, rather thought-provokingly, investigates what she considers to be an under-researched aspect of filmic narratives, that of the cinematic focalizer. She considers the notion of cinematic narrator (originally defined by Seymour Chatman in *Coming to Terms: The Rhetoric of Narrative in Fiction and Film* [1990]) to be, at best, contentious, arguing convincingly that the figure of the filmic focalizer is, still, more of an idealized abstraction, because even in the case of 'point of view' shots in which the audience uses the perspective of a filter other than the cinematic narrator, that is the focalizer, it is simply too problematic to actually, and effectively, separate the two figures as clear and distinct entities.

Multimodal stylistics also considers aspects of non-verbal communication irrespective of the medium or mode. This is illustrated by Victoria Carrington's 'I Write, Therefore I Am: Texts in the City' (*VC* 8[2009] 409–25). Carrington investigates the impact of graffiti work both as a form of textual expression and as a multimodal manifestation of the narrative construction of the self. In a similar fashion, Roi Tartakovsky, in 'e.e. cummings's Parentheses: Punctuation as Poetic Device' (*Style* 43[2009] 215–47) analyses traditional punctuation signs in poetry and argues that they are as much indicative of poetic tasks as traditional linguistic markers, especially those underscoring rhythm and rhyme: punctuation signs work 'for the eye as well as for the ear' (p. 241).

We now turn to a number of monographs and papers that deal with (the analysis of) poetry. Rhian Williams's *The Poetry Toolkit: The Essential Guide to Studying Poetry* defines traditional tropes and terms associated with poetic forms such as epic, ballad, elegy, or sonnet and subsequently illustrates those definitions with examples. Despite its ambitious scope and undeniable richness, it is nonetheless slightly disheartening to see that there are no references to stylisticians' work here; nor, indeed, is there any attempt at recognizing the usefulness of the linguistic frameworks that have investigated poetry from a variety of perspectives (iconicity and sound-symbolism, for instance, or lexico-semantic models in relation to 'word play', one of the headings in the book). Also dealing with poetry is Jean Boase-Beier's 'Translation and Timelessness' (*JLS* 38[2009] 101–14), with the author focusing on how to transpose expressions of time and uncertainty as used by poets, from German into English. Marta Dahlgren's 'Connoting, Associating and Inferring in Literary Translation' (*JLS* 38[2009] 53–70) combines elements from pragmatics, literature, and translation studies in order to assess notions that she considers need clearer definitions when applied to the field of translation studies: denotation, connotation, and association. Whereas Dahlgren's understanding of denotation very much coincides with the general view of the term in linguistics and stylistics, the latter two terms are explained in relation to the pragmatic concept of inference, whereby connotation is defined as the stereotypical meaning of any lexical item, and association emanates from the way individual speakers'/readers' experience influences their understanding of the item concerned. This crucial difference has considerable bearing on the way lexical items are to be translated.

In the *Journal of Literary Theory* two articles voice particularly well the way some literary critics position themselves in relation to developments in the cognitive sciences, and reflect on how this can affect literary studies in general. First, Gerhard Lauer's 'Going Empirical: Why We Need Cognitive Literary Studies' (*JLT* 3[2009] 145–54) presents an interesting case when viewed from the perspective of stylistics. Lauer highlights that whereas linguistics seems to be taking full advantage of the outcomes of the cognitive sciences, literary studies have not embraced these advances so fully. In his opinion, encompassing the methods and techniques of cognitivism could be 'the opportunity to release literary studies from its bourgeois conventions and to open it up for fascinating and innovative issues' (p. 152). Virginia Richter's 'I Cannot Endure to Read a Line of Poetry: The Text and the Empirical in Literary Studies' (*JLT* 3[2009] 375–88) is a response to the above. She argues that the kind of antagonistic view (cognitive vs. non-cognitive) purported by Gerhard Lauer is unnecessary or, simply, based on an erroneous assessment regarding where the boundaries of conventional literary studies actually lie. Richter claims that the hermeneutic practice of traditional literary studies does not necessarily entail the exclusion of a more empirical slant as would be illustrated by incorporating cognitive approaches to the study of literature. The influence of cognitive sciences on literature is also felt in many other articles. Timothy C. Baker's 'The (Neuro)-Aesthetics of Caricature: Representations of Reality in Bret Easton Ellis's *Lunar Park*' (*PoT* 30[2009] 471–515) echoes scholars' interest in cognitive methods to account for the nature of aesthetic response, in his case, as far as *Lunar Park* is concerned. Interestingly, this article like the two above, and somewhat confusingly for stylisticians, also seems to equal cognitive approaches and general empiricism; this approach stands out as slightly unusual when viewed from a stylistics angle. In stylistics, there has been a tendency to see these two approaches as clearly distinct—for some, even as antagonistic—perspectives. Whereas empirical studies would primarily involve the use of techniques that can 'demonstrate' by providing some kind of quantifiable results, cognitive approaches are normally associated with accounting for the readerly aspects of texts. Corpus stylistics and cognitive poetics would, quintessentially, illustrate the two most extreme takes on empirical versus non-empirical perspectives respectively. Stylisticians such as Willie van Peer and Elena Semino have clearly established how these two approaches are not mutually exclusive but in fact complementary and necessary if a fully comprehensive perspective is to be implemented.

Willie van Peer and Elena Semino are, in fact, two of the contributors to *Cognitive Poetics: Goals, Gains and Gaps*, edited by Geert Brône and Jeroen Vandaele. This is an impressive collection, in which established practitioners of cognitive poetics, narratology, and/or stylistics put forward arguments for and against this sub-discipline and discuss the numerous 'gaps' that are still to be filled. The editors, in fact, argue that the label itself, cognitive poetics, is still being brandished as a kind of umbrella term but its aims, objectives, and general scope are not necessarily always made explicit. Geert Brône and Jeroen Vandaele start by introducing the issue of whether a true cognitive poetics is feasible at all: 'Can we think of a field that combines cognitive insights in cognition and language structure with poetics' insights in literary meaning production?' (p. 6). They believe the answer to be positive if principles of cognitive linguistics are incorporated into the study of literary texts since, according to them, 'Cognitive linguistics, as a special branch of cognitive science, stands out as a paradigm mainly because it pays due attention to the rich phenomenology of thought and language, and is therefore compatible with the traditional project of poetics' (p. 6). They propose to refer to this principled way of dealing with issues of thought and language as 'indirect empiricism'. Whereas not all the contributors to the volume abide by such a definition (for instance, Rachel Giora, Ofer Fein, Ronie Kaufman, Dana Eisenberg, and Shani Erez's 'Does an "Ironic Situation" Favor an Ironic Interpretation?' (pp. 383–400) and Max Louwerse and Willie van Peer's 'How Cognitive is Cognitive Poetics? Adding a Symbolic Approach to the Embodied one' (pp. 423–45) argue for a more rigorous approach to empiricism), the editors claim that by incorporating indirect empiricism, a kind of middle ground can be actually reached. It is rather striking that such an impressive collection appears rather sloppy as far as its general editing is concerned because the bibliographical section of the introduction is unusually full of missing references.

One very exciting field into which more and more stylisticians seem to be moving is concerned with issues of emotion. Emotion is a broadly understood notion which relates not only to the way in which it is embodied in the language of characters in literary works, but also to the way readers perceive characters' emotions or to how readers experience emotions themselves. Hidetsugu Komeda, Miho Kawasaki, Kohei Tsunemi, and Takashi Kusumi's 'Differences between Estimating Protagonists' Emotions and Evaluating Readers' Emotions in Narrative Comprehension' (*Cog&Em* 23[2009] 135–51) evaluate two of these aspects in particular: they consider the way readers assess the various emotions felt by characters in narratives, before moving on to assess the emotions of the readers themselves. More interestingly, they investigate how these two appraisal exercises affect general comprehension in narrative reading. In 'Are You Joking? The Moderating Role of Smiles in the Perception of Verbal Statements' (*Cog&Em* 23[2009] 1504–15), Eva Krumhuber and Antony S.R. Manstead look further into how emotion is combined with non-verbal gestures and how the latter affect the assessment of the verbal component of the message. They conclude that one particular aspect, smiles, positively affects the way messages are perceived.

The field of corpus studies is, undoubtedly, one in which more and more papers, monographs, and edited collections are being written. This growth is not simply quantitative but also qualitative, as the range of scholars using corpora as a basis for their subsequent research in a variety of fields is also increasing. A clear illustration of the ever-expanding intent to combine corpus techniques and other disciplines is *Corpora: Pragmatics and Discourse* edited by Andreas H. Jucker, Daniel Schreier, and Marianne Hundt, which specifically wants to redress the lack of attention paid to the interface between corpus analysis and discourse analysis/pragmatics (see also sections 9 and 11 above). Of special relevance for stylistics is Karin Axelsson's 'Research on Fiction Dialogue: Problems and Possible Solutions' (pp. 189–202), which highlights not simply how under-researched fictional dialogue is in relation to naturally occurring speech, but also the inadequacy of some of the existing corpora to investigate this aspect. Axelsson points out that the way corpora tend to be annotated fails to account for the stylistic nuances of 'direct speech', understood as the verbatim presentation of a character's words. This author concludes that corpora require a more balanced illustration of various literary genres, different parts of novels, and 'different levels of literary quality' (p. 199). Although Axelsson's suggestions seem sound, it is not totally obvious, and, indeed, slightly controversial, to judge literary merit objectively, an issue which is not completely resolved in this paper.

Michael Toolan's *Narrative Progression in the Short Story: A Corpus Stylistic Approach* more specifically tackles stylistic issues related to the structure of short stories by means of a corpus analysis. The study explores how narrative texts guide the reader and claims that corpus tools can help us view the lexico-phrasal patterns that actually shape narrative progression. The author acknowledges that he has used a relatively small number of authors belonging to a very specific literary movement and temporal setting, that of the modern short-story genre (James Joyce, Katherine Mansfield, Raymond Carver, and Alice Munro among others), which might have skewed the results in favour of that specific genre and temporal setting. Nevertheless, the results indicate that narrative elements, explicitly or implicitly manifested, direct readers' assessment of progression in short stories. Some of the particular aspects investigated here are collocation, lexical diversity, top keyword analysis, repetition, and para-repetition.

The collection edited by Dawn Archer, *What's in a Word-List? Investigating Word Frequency and Keyword Extraction*, also addresses the hermeneutic possibilities of using computerized methods for the analysis of texts. The adjective hermeneutic is purposefully used here to indicate the authors' acknowledgement of the role of computerized methods as supplementary to, not substitutive for, the human researcher. Thus, Dawn Archer's 'Does Frequency Really Matter?' (pp. 1–15) emphasizes that keyword analysis helps the researcher to know more about those aspects which provide a key for the 'aboutness' of the text or can complement other aspects to study. David Hoover's 'Word Frequency, Statistical Analysis and Authorship Attribution' (pp. 35–54), on the other hand, suggests increasing the number of keywords selected to account for authorship attribution, whereas Dawn Archer, Jonathan Culpeper, and Paul Rayson's rather illuminating 'An Exploration of Key Domains in Shakespeare's Comedies and Tragedies' (pp. 137–58) proposes to study key semantic domains in Shakespeare's oeuvre which will provide empirical support for some of the conclusions drawn from implementing cognitive analyses of the plays. Jonathan Culpeper has extended the findings of the latter paper in his 'Keyness: Words, Parts-of-Speech and Semantic Categories in the Character-Talk of Shakespeare's *Romeo and Juliet*' (*IJCL* 14[2009] 29–59). Here he specifically argues that the analysis of literary texts can benefit from incorporating the study of key parts of speech and key semantic categories into key-word analysis. Most importantly, Culpeper highlights that exploring statistical data has occasionally been deprived of the appropriate contextualization and that the investigation of 'keyness' from three different perspectives might overcome such lack. In 'Keywords and Frequent Phrases of Jane Austen's *Pride and Prejudice*: A Corpus-Stylistic Analysis' (*IJCL* 14[2009] 492–523), Bettina Fischer-Starcke also argues for the applicability of principles and techniques of corpus linguistics to the language of literature, and suggests that such a profitable application has only recently begun to bear fruit for stylistics. Although her definition of stylistics seems to refer to approaches which have been reworked, reconsidered, and reassessed considerably since they were formulated—i.e. the structuralist tradition of Roman Jakobson's poetic function and M.A.K. Halliday's transitivity analysis of Golding's *The Inheritors*—she uses these two approaches to underscore the principles of replicability and rigour that can be achieved by undertaking a corpus-linguistic analysis of literary texts.

A really fascinating approach to corpus studies is presented in 'HeadTalk, HandTalk and the Corpus: Towards a Framework for Multi-Modal, Multi-Media Corpus Development' (*Corpora* 4[2009] 1–32) by Dawn Knight, David Evans, Ronald Carter, and Svenja Adolphs. When so many scholars are veering towards multi- and interdisciplinary work to combine aspects which were previously analysed and studied in isolation, a project based at the University of Nottingham has joined efforts by scholars from different departments to try and produce a truly comprehensive multi-modal and multi-medial corpus. They argue that, so far, academics have assessed multi-modal and corpus-linguistic issues from two different angles: multi-modal and multi-media studies of discourse on the one hand, and speech engineering and corpus annotation on the other. The authors of this article propose to combine these two perspectives so that the corpora of the future move away from the strictly textual and into the multi-modal. More examples of how scholars are finding the need to combine the tools, techniques, and expertise from different but cognate disciplines can be found in Sandra Mollin's 'Combining Corpus Linguistic and Psychological Data on Word Co-occurrences: Corpus Collocates versus Word Associations' (*CLLT* 5[2009] 175–200). Mollin argues that looking at the same phenomenon from the perspective of different disciplines might not just illustrate but perhaps even contravene tenets previously held, established, and accepted. For this reason she looks at a linguistic aspect traditionally analysed in corpus linguistics, that of collocation or the co-occurrence of words in proximity and in the same linguistic context. Next, she considers the phenomenon of word-association as understood in psychology, that is, the combination of words which are semantically affiliated. Mollin clarifies that in psychology, word-association is used as a common test. If corpus linguistics is to make claims in relation to language use, the suggestion is that it should also pay heed to psychology's account concerning the way language is produced.

The journal *Language and Literature* has devoted a special issue to the notion of the 'reader'. Daniel Allington and Joan Swann's 'Researching Literary Reading as Social Practice' (*L&L* 18[2009] 218–30) introduces the volume, provides an overview of the various ways in which this concept has been conceptualized in this same journal from 2004 to 2008, and finally summarizes findings from empirical investigations into this topic. A historical perspective is adopted in Katie Halsey's '"Folk Stylistics" and the History of Reading: A Discussion of Method' (*L&L* 18[2009] 231–46). Halsey uses the term 'folk stylistics' to refer to the way readers have historically voiced their concerns about style, which most of the time differ from professional assessments of the same concept by scholars. Her data have been gathered from the Research Project *The Reading Experience Database* (www.open.ac.uk/Arts/RED and www.open.ac.uk/Arts/reading), which collects information about the reading habits of British readers and overseas visitors to the UK in a period spanning five centuries, from 1450 to 1945. Joan Swann and Daniel Allington's 'Reading Groups and the Language of Literary Texts: A Case Study in Social Reading' (*L&L* 18[2009] 247–64), on the other hand, provides an assessment of how contemporary readers share their experience in reading groups as they analyse the discourse arising out of their discussions. The authors perform a qualitative analysis of those discussions but also emphasize that they have paid heed to empirical concerns by having used data which they consider to be 'naturalistic' in contrast with data obtained in other reading experiments generally taking place under more controlled, and hence inevitably more 'artificial', conditions. A different perspective on how to analyse the role of readers is presented by Katarina Eriksson Barajas and Karin Aronsson in 'Avid versus Struggling Readers: Co-Construed Pupil Identities in School Booktalk' (*L&L* 18[2009] 281–99). They focus primarily on the younger book-consumer (10 to 14 years of age) as their data emerge out of experiments conducted in the classroom; they conclude that a combination of discursive psychological methods and reception research can be profitable and can also benefit pedagogical concerns about literacy in schools. Bethan Benwell's '"A Pathetic and Racist and Awful Character": Ethnomethodological Approaches to the Reception of Diasporic Fiction' (*L&L* 18[2009] 300–15) stands out in so far as it reports on results obtained by looking at transnational book group meetings. Her findings rely on ethno-methodological techniques which, once again, imply a degree of artificiality despite the fact that this scholar is keen to point out, as did Swann and Allington above, that any mediation was kept to a minimum. This issue is brought to a close with two review articles by Greg Myers and Geoff Hall. Greg Myers's 'Stylistics and "Reading-in-Talk"' (*L&L* 18[2009] 338–44) highlights that investigating reader response can be viewed as much as a problem as an opportunity to broaden stylistic horizons. As he points out, 'readers do not necessarily address the concerns of literary stylistics, even when they are talking about language, literature, and style' (p. 338) as very often reader responses deal with all sorts of other issues not necessarily pertinent to stylistic investigation. Geoff Hall's 'Texts, Readers—and Real Readers' (*L&L* 18[2009] 331–7) underscores that stylistics might be in need of developing frameworks that redress the current imbalance in favour of textual analyses to incorporate research which focuses on the readerly components.

The same journal has explored many other aspects of the interface between language and literature, such as, for instance, the function of parentheticals in Free Indirect Style (FIS). In 'Parentheticals and Point of View in Free Indirect Style' (*L&L* 18[2009] 129–53), Diane Blakemore expertly traces the various perspectives that linguists interested in language as social interaction, syntacticians, and pragmaticians have viewed parentheticals from. The former, for instance, would consider parentheticals to be markers of unplanned discourse; syntacticians would view them as syntactically anchored structures of the non-restrictive relative clause type; and finally pragmaticians would define these forms as ways in which speakers form their utterances to retrieve particular information. The main focus of the article is on the way parentheticals are exploited in FIS in fictional discourse, and it underscores that these forms can create a 'multi-personal representation of consciousness' (p. 134) encompassing that of the author and that of the character. *Language and Literature* is also the forum for work which incorporates pragmatic principles for the study of fictional texts such as Billy Clark's 'Salient Inferences: Pragmatics and *The Inheritors*' (*L&L* 18[2009] 173–212) or Lisa Nahajec's 'Negation and the Creation of Implicit Meaning in Poetry' (*L&L* 18[2009] 109–27). Billy Clark provides an innovative pragmatic view on a text which has famously, and virtually canonically, been considered from the perspective of Systemic Functional Linguistics: Golding's *The Inheritors*. Lisa Nahajec initially focuses on negation as a pragmatic phenomenon but subsequently implements a cognitive stylistic analysis by looking at a small corpus of poems. Further perspectives employed in the analysis of fictional texts are those of Philip Seargeant's 'Ideologies of English in Shakespeare's *Henry V*' (*L&L* 18[2009] 25–44), which prioritizes an ideological analysis of a historical text, and Vera Tobin's 'Cognitive Bias and the Poetics of Surprise' (*L&L* 18[2009] 155–72) and Chantelle Warner's 'Speaking from Experience: Narrative Schemas, Deixis, and Authenticity Effects in Verena Stefan's Feminist Confession *Shedding*' (*L&L* 18[2009] 7–23), the latter two of which are both characterized by their cognitive slant.

Analyses of fictional and non-fictional narratives viewed from an array of different perspectives are dealt with in a considerable number of publications which either directly or indirectly influence work in stylistics. In 'Measuring Narrative Engagement' (*MPsych* 12[2009] 321–47), for instance, Rick Busselle and Helena Bilandzic attempt to measure a story's ability to engage audiences. To this end, they monitor readers' sensations alongside four dimensions of engagement: narrative understanding, attentional focus, emotional engagement, and narrative presence. On narratological aspects, Dan Shen's 'Non-Ironic Turning Ironic Contextually: Multiple Context-Determined

Irony in "The Story of an Hour"' (*JLS* 38 [2009] 115–30) investigates a type of ironic meaning which, according to the author, has so far been neglected. She calls it 'context-determined irony': unlike verbal or situational types, it emerges out of the context itself and gives rise to semantically rich interpretations because it allows a non-marked use of the textual components to co-occur alongside the marked ironic meaning. Paul Dawson's 'The Return of Omniscience in Contemporary Fiction' (*Narrative* 17[2009] 143–61), on the other hand, provides a really informative and stimulating take on the traditional notion of omniscience. He highlights a shift in the way the narrative voice of contemporary American and British fiction is marked, namely by means of an omniscient narrator reminiscent of the voices most commonly found in nineteenth-century novels. Having stated this, though, Dawson is keen to report on the distinct nature of this omniscient teller which, unlike its nineteenth-century counterpart, avoids the moral authority that characterized historical omniscience in favour of 'extraliterary claims to knowledge or expertise in postmodern culture' (p. 149). In the same journal, Brian McHale's 'Beginning to Think about Narrative in Poetry' (*Narrative* 17[2009] 11–27) proposes that the boundaries of what constitutes a narrative are in need of reassessment because the narrative aspects of poetry have been blatantly neglected for far too long.

Further prototypical aspects dealt with in narratology, and indeed stylistics, are those of point of view and focalization, discussed in *Point of View, Perspective and Focalization: Modeling Mediation in Narrative*, edited by Peter Huhn, Wolf Schmid, and Jorg Schonert. This collection is structured around the notion of 'mediation' used as an umbrella term to cover aspects of point of view, perspective, and focalization as they occur in literary and non-literary narratives. Most of the chapters in the collection propose some kind of reworking of the notion originally proposed by Genette, for instance, Uri Margolin's 'Focalization: Where Do We Go From Here?' (pp. 41–57), or Tatjana Jesch and Malte Stein's 'Perspectivization and Focalization: Two Concepts—One Meaning? An Attempt at Conceptual Differentiation' (pp. 59–78).

The concept of narrative, however, is also appraised in light of positions other than the literary-narratological, as demonstrated by Blake Stephen Howald's 'A Quantitative Perspective on the Minimal Definition of Narrative' (*T&T* 29[2009] 705–27). In his analysis of naturally occurring narratives detailing ten counts of murder by Dennis Rader, Howald encompasses recent developments in the search for a definition of minimal narratives; these new developments show that spatial linguistic markers alongside spatio-temporal narrative domains need to be considered in definitions of minimal narratives despite the fact that 'space', *per se*, is not functionally constitutive of narratives. Likewise, another volume encompassing concerns with narrative aspects viewed from perspectives other than the literary is *Narrative and Folk Psychology* edited by Daniel D. Hutto. The editor defines folk psychology as 'a specific sub-section of our everyday talk of, and thought about, the mental' (p. 10). The collection includes practitioners of disciplines as diverse as philosophy, computer science, psychology, and anthropology. Of special relevance for stylistics is David Herman's 'Storied Minds: Narrative

Scaffolding for Folk Psychology' (pp. 40–68) since he analyses the language of Ian McEwan's novel *On Chesil Beach* [2007]. Finally, Alan Palmer's 'Attributions of Madness in Ian McEwan's *Enduring Love*' (*Style* 43[2009] 291–308) and James Phelan's 'Cognitive Narratology, Rhetorical Narratology, and Interpretive Disagreement: A Response to Alan Palmer's Analysis of *Enduring Love*' (*Style* 43[2009] 309–21) further take on responses from well-established narratologists to new developments in the field of cognitive sciences. Palmer uses narrative thinking, attribution theory, and intermental thought to explicate the concept of madness in McEwan's novel, but he is keen to highlight that 'cognitive' in his analysis is not to be understood as the opposite of, but rather as complementary to 'psychoanalytical, historical/cultural, feminist, rhetorical and ethical criticism and so on' (p. 292). Phelan's paper responds to Palmer's definition of cognitivism by denying that such an approach necessarily underlies all other approaches, and opts instead for a rhetorical positioning which does not need to always 'start with cognitive analysis' (p. 310).

The treatment of the concept of mind style, as also discussed in relation to Peter Stockwell's *Texture* above, always finds a way into some publication on stylistic matters; Mari-Ann Berg's 'The Monologic Self as First-Person Narrator: Nadine Gordimer's "Good Climate, Friendly Inhabitants"' (*JLS* 38[2009] 39–52) is one such piece. Mari-Ann Berg argues that mind style can be regarded vis-à-vis the notion of monologism initially discussed by Bakhtin.

Discourse studies are also often relevant to students of stylistics. Jan Renkema's *Discourse, of Course* gathers a broad group of papers aimed at advanced students (see also section 11 above). One of the parts in the volume pertinent to this section is 'Stylistics and Rhetorics', which contains three chapters on 'the study of the varieties in wording and composition in discourse and the effects on its audience' (p. 5). In this volume, therefore, stylistic and rhetorical concerns seem to coincide, which results in a limited identification regarding the scope of modern stylistics. The chapters included in this section appear to confirm that the view on style presented here is indeed based on tenets which do not conform to those currently followed in stylistics. For instance, Martin Kaltenbacher's 'Style and Culture in Quantitative Discourse Analysis' (pp. 143–56) focuses on stylistic patterns and cultural identity by analysing American and Austrian tourist websites. Xinzhang Yang's 'Devices of Probability and Obligation in Text Types' (pp. 157–69), on the other hand, argues that different text types are characterized by different uses of probability and obligation markers. However, as interesting as these analyses are, it is regretful that literature is not viewed as an equally valid discourse type (cf. Paul Chilton's paper discussed below), and thus it has not found a way into this section misleadingly labelled 'Stylistics and Rhetorics'.

Douglas Biber and Susan Conrad's *Register, Genre, and Style* draws attention primarily to the notion of register, understood as those linguistic characteristics that singularize a particular text type without ignoring the context of situation in which that text is produced. The authors subsequently deal with a variety of texts ranging from newspaper writing and academic prose to fiction, e-mails, internet forums, and text messages, but, as they state, it is the framework itself that becomes the main asset of this publication. For instance, concerning the situational characteristics of registers, their framework takes into account who the participants are, what their relationship is, what channel is being used, what circumstances define the production of this text type, what setting is chosen, what the communicative purposes are, and what the topic is. These situational characteristics are followed, first, by an analysis of the typical linguistic characteristics of any particular register and, secondly, by looking at the functional reasons that explain why any set of linguistic features comes to be associated with any situational characteristic. The volume is also complemented by further exercises to provide practice with the framework and put it to the test. Kelly Benneworth's 'Police Interviews with Suspected Paedophiles: A Discourse Analysis' (*D&S* 20[2009] 555–69) brings to the fore a topic which, unfortunately, seems to be constantly on TV screens world-wide. Benneworth considers investigative techniques used by the police in the UK, with particular reference to the questioning of suspected paedophiles. The author is very keen to point out that her analysis is not to be seen as simply a criticism of the way the police conduct interviews; instead, she suggests that were interviewers to adopt a more co-operative stance by letting the suspects elaborate on their accounts as opposed to following a more institutionalized way of information-exchange, the interviewees might produce versions which could become self-incriminatory, and thus much more useful for a possible conviction.

The ever-expanding field of metaphor analysis has also been well researched in 2009. Three edited collections need mentioning as they provide a multifarious perspective on a variety of topics ranging from political discourse to multimodal representations of metaphors. *Politics, Gender and Conceptual Metaphors*, edited by Kathleen Ahrens, is specifically concerned with the linguistic realization of conceptual metaphors in the political arena as employed by both male and female politicians. The various chapters combine quantitative and qualitative approaches in order to investigate whether any possible differences in the actual use of metaphors emanate from gender differences. The results are inconclusive but yet illustrative of the inadequacy of explaining metaphor use exclusively as a result of a male–female dichotomy. For instance, Veronika Koller and Elena Semino, and Elena Semino and Veronika Koller, have conducted two studies on metaphor use in Germany and Italy in 'Metaphor, Politics and Gender: A Case Study from Germany' (pp. 9–35) and 'Metaphor, Politics and Gender: A Case Study from Italy' (pp. 36–61) respectively. Their methodology is primarily quantitative, but there is also some qualitative analysis. They conclude that metaphor use is defined by a combination of factors, including political and personal gain. In contrast, two other studies argue that metaphorical exploitation in politics is determined by gender. Encarnación Hidalgo Tenorio ('The Metaphorical Construction of Ireland', pp. 112–35) and Jonathan Charteris-Black ('Metaphor and Gender in British Parliamentary Debates', pp. 139–65) investigate the political sphere in Ireland and Britain respectively, and both conclude that some marked differences are directly determined by gender. Thus, Charteris-Black shows that male MPs use more metaphors than female MPs, whereas Hidalgo Tenorio demonstrates that the Irish president Mary McAleese included twice as many metaphor instances as the Irish prime minister Bertie Aherne. Finally, this volume also investigates the linguistic and multi-modal representation of females as depicted by politicians and advertisers. Interestingly, females seem to be stereotypically portrayed via gendered use of metaphors, as argued by Michelle M. Lazar in 'Gender, War and Body Politics: A Critical Multimodal Analysis of Metaphor in Advertising' (pp. 209–34).

The aim of the second collection, *Metaphor and Discourse*, edited by Andreas Mussolff and Jörg Zinken, is to try and formulate theoretical tenets about metaphors out of the empirical investigation of a variety of discourse types. This is, to say the least, an ambitious and challenging objective. Paul Chilton's 'Reading Sonnet 30: Discourse, Metaphor and Blending' (pp. 40–58) looks at a prototypical literary instance (Shakespeare's Sonnet 30) as an example of discourse event. Chilton employs cognitive frameworks, namely blending theory and conceptual metaphor theory, but also highlights the importance of viewing this discourse event as a sociohistorically situated product, for which CDA tools are particularly suitable. Paul Chilton successfully considers the discoursal aspects of the sonnet as 'microdiscourse', that is, as the linguistic aspects that project conceptual coherence, and as 'macrodiscourse', namely, as those practices that position the discourse event in relation to a society and culture. Jonathan Charteris-Black's 'Metaphor and Political Communication' (pp. 97–115), on the other hand, tentatively theorizes on the general role of metaphors in the political arena as imbued with mythical and ideological meanings. After looking at the metaphorical components of speeches by Fidel Castro and Tony Blair, the author concludes that the success of political leaders is, in part, due to the way in which audiences project their own meanings onto the political discourse event, thus finding 'a degree of socio-psychological and emotional gratification' (p. 97). The final part of the collection is devoted to presenting a historical perspective, and comprises Roslyn M. Frank's 'Shifting Identities: Metaphors of Discourse Evolution' (pp. 173–89) and Andreas Musolff's 'Metaphor in the History of Ideas and Discourses: How Can We Interpret a Medieval Version of the Body–State Analogy?' (pp. 233–47).

The third collection is *Multimodal Metaphor* edited by Charles J. Forceville and Eduardo Urios-Aparisi. Multi-modality is a term widely brandished and diversely understood by scholars. Charles Forceville, however, has for a while been working on a very specific definition of how to conceptualize multi-modality in relation to metaphorical meanings. His definition underscores that for any metaphor to be viewed as truly multi-modal it must present its source domain in one mode or modality, whereas the target domain must appear in a different one. In practice, though, Forceville admits that pure multi-modal metaphors are identified for 'analytical purposes only' (p. 430). The thoroughness with which this volume has been put together is also equalled by its richness. For instance, Gunnar Theodór Eggertsson and Charles Forceville review the use of the metaphor HUMAN VICTIM IS ANIMAL (in 'Multimodal Expressions of the HUMAN VICTIM IS ANIMAL Metaphor in Horror Films', pp. 429–47) in the films *Wolf Creek* [2005], *Calvaire* [2004], and *The Texas Chainsaw Massacre* [1974], and suggest that, far from being a localized metaphor, the HUMAN VICTIM IN

HORROR FILM IS ANIMAL USED AS RESOURCE metaphor actually pervades the whole of the horror film genre. Veronika Koller's 'Brand Images: Multimodal Metaphor in Corporate Branding Messages' (pp. 45–71), on the other hand, analyses how companies are represented by the metaphors BRANDS ARE LIVING ORGANISMS and BRANDS ARE PEOPLE, which allow these companies to be endowed with human personality traits, manifestly realized by verbal and visual features.

Finally, Norman MacLeod's 'Stylistics and the Analysis of Poetry—A Credo and an Example' (*JLS* 38[2009] 131–49) summarizes a debate which, despite the by now well-established tradition of this discipline, still regularly crops up among mainly, although not exclusively, literary critics (this debate is also echoed in Karina Williamson's '"A Proper Synthesis of Literary and Linguistic Study": C.S. Lewis and a Forgotten War' (*JLS* 38[2009] 151–69)). MacLeod finds himself defending the role of stylistics by reacting to Ben Yagoda's comments in 'Style: A Pleasure for the Reader, or the Writer?' (*Chronicle of Higher Education. The Chronicle Review* 50(49) [13 August 2004] B 16; http://chronicle.com/free/v50/i49/49b01601.htm), where the latter states that: 'Today in English departments in the United States and Britain, stylisticians are few and far between and tend to be graybeards approaching retirement.' Since the proof of the pudding is in the eating, MacLeod demonstrates how stylistics works by implementing a stylistic analysis of Keats's sonnet 'On First Looking into Chapman's Homer' [1816] and concludes that stylistics can account for how syntactic and grammetric patterns contribute to the success of such poem.

This review of the publications of 2009 seems to highlight the dynamism and healthy status of this discipline. Unlike what Ben Yagoda suggests in his assessment of stylistics, this is a discipline happily undertaken by many stylisticians who, like myself, are indeed neither 'graybeards approaching retirement' nor have any intention of stopping practising what we consider to be a vigorous, energetic, lively, and exciting enterprise.

Books Reviewed

Aarstad, Rich, Ellie Arguimbau, Ellen Baumler, Charlene Porsild, and Brian Shovers. *Montana Place Names from Alzada to Zortman*. Montana Historical Society. [2009] pp. xxix+347. pb $24.95 ISBN 9 7809 7591 9613.

Adams, Michael. *Slang: The People's Poetry*. OUP. [2009] pp. xv + 238. £12.99 ISBN 9 7801 9531 4632.

Adeyanju, Dele. *The Sociolinguistics of English and Nigerian Languages*. LINCOM. [2009] pp. 306. €73.20 ISBN 9 7838 9586 5794.

Ahrens, Kathleen, ed. *Politics, Gender and Conceptual Metaphors*. Palgrave Macmillan. [2009] pp. 288. £50 ISBN 9 7802 3020 3457.

Allan, Kathryn. *Metaphor and Metonymy: A Diachronic Approach*. Publications of the Philological Society 42. Wiley-Blackwell. [2009] pp. x+255. pb £22.99 ISBN 9 7814 0519 0855.

Anderson, Wendy, and John Corbett. *Exploring English with Online Corpora: An Introduction*. Palgrave. [2009] pp. xiii + 205. hb £49.50 ISBN 9 7802 3055 1398, pb £16.99 ISBN 9 7802 3055 1404.

Anderwald, Lieselotte. *The Morphology of English Dialects: Verb-Formation in Non-Standard English*. Studies in English Language. CUP. [2009] £60 ISBN 9 7805 2188 4976.

Ansaldo, Umberto. *Contact Languages: Ecology and Evolution in Asia*. CUP. [2009] pp. 276. $102 ISBN 9 7805 2186 3971.

Archer, Dawn, ed. *What's in a Word-List? Investigating Word Frequency and Keyword Extraction*. Ashgate. [2009] pp. 200. £55 ISBN 9 7807 5467 2401.

Auer, Anita. *The Subjunctive in the Age of Prescriptivism: English and German Developments during the Eighteenth Century*. Studies in Language History and Language Change. Palgrave. [2009] pp. xiv+221. £50 ISBN 9 7802 3057 4410.

Baker, Paul, ed. *Contemporary Corpus Linguistics*. Contemporary Studies in Linguistics. Continuum. [2009] pp. ix+357. hb £85 ISBN 9 7808 2649 6102.

Barber, Charles, Joan C. Beal, and Philip A. Shaw. *The English Language: A Historical Introduction*, 2nd edn. CUP. [2009] pp. ix + 306. hb £45 ISBN 9 7805 2185 4047, pb £17.99 ISBN 9 7805 2167 0012.

Beal, Joan C., Karen P. Corrigan, and Hermann L. Moisl, eds. *Creating and Digitizing Language Corpora*. Palgrave. [2007] vol. 1: *Synchronic Databases*. pp. xix+245. £60 ISBN 9 7814 0394 3668, vol. 2: *Diachronic Databases*. pp. xix+250. £55 ISBN 9 7814 0394 3675.

Berezowski, Leszek. *The Myth of the Zero Article*. Continuum. [2009] pp. 149. £45 ISBN 9 7814 4118 5136.

Berg, Lawrence D., and Jani Vuolteenaho, eds. *Critical Toponymies: The Contested Politics of Place Naming*. Ashgate. [2009] pp. 291. $115 ISBN 9 7807 5467 4535.

Berg, Thomas. *Structure in Language: A Dynamic Perspective*. Studies in Linguistics. Routledge. [2009] pp. xii+396. £95 ISBN 9 7804 1599 1353.

Biber, Douglas, and Susan Conrad. *Register, Genre and Style*. CUP. [2009] pp. 354. £65 ISBN 9 7805 2186 0604.

Blevins, James P., and Juliette Blevins, eds. *Analogy in Grammar: Form and Acquisition*. OUP. [2009] pp. xiv + 278. £60 ISBN 9 7801 9954 7548.

Boeckx, Cedric. *Bare Syntax*. OUP. [2008] pp. xiii + 295. hb £70 ISBN 9 7801 9953 4234, pb £22.99 ISBN 9 7801 9953 4241.

Boeckx, Cedric. *Language in Cognition: Uncovering Mental Structures and the Rules Behind Them*. Wiley-Blackwell. [2009] pp. 264. £55.00 ISBN 9 7814 0515 8817.

Bosch, Peter, David Gabelaia, and Jérôme Lang, eds. *Logic, Language, and Computation. 7th International Tbilisi Symposium on Logic, Language, and Computation*. Springer. [2009] pp. xii + 286. pb €45.95 ISBN 9 7836 4200 6647.

Botha, Rudolf, and Chris Knight, eds. *The Cradle of Language*. OUP. [2009] pp. xviii+386. hb $135 ISBN 9 7801 9954 5858, pb $45 ISBN 9 7801 9954 5865.

Brisard, Frank, Jan-Ola Östman, and Jef Verschueren, eds. *Grammar, Meaning and Pragmatics*. HopH 5. Benjamins. [2009] pp. xiii+308. pb €39 ($59) ISBN 9 7890 2720 7821.

Brône, Geert, and Jeroen Vandaele, eds. *Cognitive Poetics: Goals, Gains and Gaps*. MGruyter. [2009] pp. vii + 560. €118 ISBN 9 7831 1020 5602.

Bunt, Harry C. *Mass Terms and Model-Theoretic Semantics*. CUP. [2009] pp. xiii + 325. pb £35 ISBN 9 7805 2110 5910.

Bwenge, Charles. *The Tongue Between: Swahili and English in Tanzanian Parliamentary Discourse*. LINCOM. [2009] pp. 110. €53.60 ISBN 9 7838 9586 2366.

Chambers, J.K. *Sociolinguistic Theory*, Rev. edn edn. Wiley-Blackwell. [2009] pp. xxiv + 308. pb £22.99 ISBN 9 7814 0515 2464.

Clark, Patricia Roberts. *Tribal Names of the Americas: Spelling Variants and Alternative Forms, Cross-Referenced*. McFarland. [2009] pp. 313. pb $49.95 ISBN 9 7807 8643 8334.

Coffin, Caroline, Jim Donohue, and Sarah North. *Exploring English Grammar: From Formal to Functional*. Routledge. [2009] pp. xii + 449. hb $115 ISBN 9 7804 1547 8151, pb $39.95 ISBN 9 7804 1547 8168.

Collins, Peter. *Modals and Quasi-Modals in English*. Language and Computers: Studies in Practical Linguistics 67. Rodopi. [2009] pp. ix+193. €41 ISBN.

Copley, Bridget. *The Semantics of the Future*. Routledge. [2009] pp. xiv + 157. £75 ISBN 9 7804 1597 1164.

Coupland, Nikolas, and Adam Jaworski, eds. *The New Sociolinguistics Reader*. Palgrave Macmillan. [2009] pp. xii + 735. hb £85 ISBN 9 7814 0394 4146, pb £24.99 ISBN 9 7814 0394 4153.

Coventry, Kenny R., Thora Tenbrink, and John Bateman, eds. *Spatial Language and Dialogue*. OUP. [2009] pp. x + 216. $135.00 ISBN 9 7801 9955 4201.

Cowie, A. P, ed. *The Oxford History of English Lexicography*, vol. 1: *General-Purpose Dictionaries*, vol. 2: *Specialized Dictionaries*. *Clarendon*. [2009] vol. 1: pp. xviii+467 ISBN 9 7801 9928 5600, vol. 2: pp. xix+551 ISBN 9 7801 9928 5617, 2-vol. set £175 ISBN 9 7801 9928 5624.

Cox, Barrie. *The Place-Names of Leicestershire*. part 4: *Gartree Hundred*. English Place-Name Society. [2009] pp. xxviii+392. £40 ISBN 9 7809 0488 9826.

Crisma, Paola, and Giuseppe Longobardi, eds. *Historical Syntax and Linguistic Theory*. OUP. [2009] pp. xiii + 417. £70 ISBN 9 7801 9956 0547.

Culicover, Peter W. *Natural Language Syntax*. Oxford Textbooks in Linguistics. OUP. [2009] pp. xvii+490. hb £75 ISBN 9 7801 9923 0174, pb £29.99 ISBN 9 7801 9923 0181.

Culpeper, Jonathan, Francis Katamba, Paul Kerswill, Ruth Wodak, and Tony McEnery, eds. *English Language: Description, Variation and Context*. Palgrave. [2009] pp. x + 718. hb £55 ISBN 9 7814 0394 5891, pb £19.99 ISBN 9 7814 0394 5907.

Cummings, Louise, ed. *The Routledge Pragmatics Encyclopedia*. Routledge (Taylor & Francis). [2009] pp. 656. £130 ($225) ISBN 9 7804 1543 0968.

D'hondt, Sigurd, Jan-Ola Östman, and Jef Verschueren, eds. *The Pragmatics of Interaction*. HopH 4. Benjamins. [2009] pp. xiii+262. pb €39 ($59) ISBN 9 7890 2720 7814.

Dossena, Marina, and Roger Lass, eds. *Studies in English and European Historical Dialectology*. Lang. [2009] pp. 257. pb £46.40 ISBN 9 7830 3430 0247.

Dufter, Andreas, Jürg Fleischer, and Guido Seiler, eds. *Describing and Modeling Variation in Grammar*. MGruyter. [2009] pp. viii + 410. €98 ISBN 9 7831 1020 5909.

Durant, Alan, and Marina Lambrou. *Language and Media: A Resource Book for Students*. Routledge. [2009] pp. 288. hb £65 ISBN 9 7804 1547 5730, pb £17.99 ISBN 9 7804 1547 5730.

Duranti, Alessandro, ed. *Linguistic Anthropology: A Reader*. Blackwell. [2009] pp. xi + 522. hb £65 ISBN 9 7814 0512 6335, pb £24.99 ISBN 9 7814 0512 6328.

Durkin, Philip. *The Oxford Guide to Etymology*. OUP. [2009] pp. x + 347. £25 ISBN 9 7801 9923 6510.

Edwards, John. *Language and Identity*. CUP. [2009] pp. viii + 314. £60 ISBN 9 7805 2187 3819.

Endriss, Cornelia. *Quantificational Topics: A Scopal Treatment of Exceptional Wide Scope Phenomena*. Springer. [2009] pp. xi + 306. €139.95 ISBN 9 7890 4812 3025.

Enfield, Nick J. *The Anatomy of Meaning: Speech, Gesture, and Composite Utterances*. CUP. [2009] pp. xii + 264. £64.00 ISBN 9 7805 2188 0640.

Evans, Martha Walton, ed. *Relational Models of the Lexicon. Representing Knowledge in Semantic Networks*. Studies in Natural Language Processing. CUP. [1988, reissued 2009] pp. ix+390. pb £20.99 ISBN 9 7805 2110 4760.

Fernández-Domínguez, Jesús. *Productivity in English Word-Formation: An Approach to N+N Compounding*. Lang. [2009] pp. 204. pb £38 ISBN 9 7830 3911 8083.

Filppula, Markku, Juhani Klemola, and Heli Paulasto. *English and Celtic in Contact*. Routledge Studies in Germanic Linguistics. Routledge. [2008] pp. xix+312. £90 ISBN 9 7804 1526 6024.

Filppula, Markku, Juhani Klemola, and Heli Paulasto, eds. *Vernacular Universals and Language Contact: Evidence from Varieties of English and Beyond*. Routledge. [2009] pp. vi + 386. £90 ISBN 9 7804 1599 2398.

Fludernik, Monika. *An Introduction to Narratology*. Routledge. [2009] pp. 200. pb £16.99 ISBN 9 7804 1545 0300.

Forceville, Charles J., and Eduardo Urios-Aparisi, eds. *Multimodal Metaphor*. MGruyter. [2009] pp. xiv + 470. €118 ($183) ISBN 9 7831 1020 5152.

Ford, Cecilia E. *Women Speaking Up: Getting and Using Turns in Workplace Meetings*. Palgrave Macmillan. [2008] pp. xi + 202. £55 ISBN 9 7814 0398 7228.

Forey, Gail, and Geoff Thompson, eds. *Text Type and Texture*. Equinox. [2009] pp. 308. hb £55 ISBN 9 7818 4553 2147, pb £18.99 ISBN 9 7818 4553 9122.

Fowler, H.W. *A Dictionary of Modern English Usage: The Classic First Edition*, ed. David Crystal. OUP. [2009] pp. 832. hb £14.99 ISBN 9 7801 9953 5347, pb £9.99 ISBN 9 7801 9958 5892.

Ghim-Lian Chew, Phyllis. *Emergent Lingua Francas and World Orders: The Politics and Place of English as a World Language*. Routledge. [2009] pp. 288. $128 ISBN 9 7804 1587 2270.

Giltrow, Janet, and Dieter Stein, eds. *Genres in the Internet: Issues in the Theory of Genre*. P&BNS 188. Benjamins. [2009] pp. ix+294. €99 ($149) ISBN 9 7890 2725 4337.

Górecka-Smolińska, M., G.A. Kleparski, and A. Włodarczyk-Stachurska, eds. *Historical Semantics Brought to the Fore*. Galicia Studies in Language. WUS. [2009] pp. 118. pb [price not available] ISBN 9 7883 6037 1978.

Gregoriou, Christiana. *English Literary Stylistics*. Palgrave Macmillan. [2009] pp. 216. hb £52.50 ISBN 9 7802 3052 5436, pb £17.99 ISBN 9 7802 3052 5412.

Guo, Jiansheng, Elena Lieven, Nancy Budwig, Susan Ervin-Tripp, Keiko Nakamura, and Seyda Ozcaliskan, eds. *Crosslinguistic Approaches to the Psychology of Language: Research in the Tradition of Dan Isaac Slobin*. Psychology Press. [2009] pp. xx + 584. hb £117.00 ISBN 9 7808 0585 9980. pb £54.00 ISBN 9 7808 0585 9997.

Hayes, Bruce. *Introductory Phonology*. Wiley-Blackwell. [2009] pp. ix + 323. hb £55 ISBN 9 7814 0518 4120, pb £20.99 ISBN 9 7814 0518 4113.

Heinen, Sandra, and Roy Sommer, eds. *Narratology in the Age of Cross-Disciplinary Narrative Research*. MGruyter. [2009] £99.95 ISBN 9 7831 1022 2425.

Herman, David. *Basic Elements of Narrative*. Wiley-Blackwell. [2009] pp. 272. hb £50 ISBN 9 7814 0514 1536, pb £18.99 ISBN 9 7814 0514 1543.

Hicks, Wynford. *The Basics of English Usage*. Routledge. [2009] pp. vi + 184. pb $19.95 ISBN 9 7804 1547 0230.

Higgins, Christina. *English as a Local Language: Post-Colonial Identities and Multilingual Practices*. Multilingual Matters. [2009] pp. 176. $34.95 ISBN 9 7818 4769 1811.

Higman, B.W., and B.J. Hudson *Jamaican Place Names*. UWIndiesP. [2009] pp. xii + 319. $27 ISBN 9 7897 6640 2174.

Hilton, Mary, and Jill Shefrin, eds. *Educating the Child in Enlightenment Britain: Beliefs, Cultures, Practices*. Ashgate. [2009] pp. 254. hb £60 ISBN 9 7807 5466 4604.

Hinrichs, Erhard, and John Nerbonne, eds. *Theory and Evidence in Semantics*. CSLI. [2009] pp. xxvii + 261. hb $70 ISBN 9 7815 7586 5775, pb $32.50 (€22.50) ISBN 9 7815 7586 5768.

Höche, Silke. *Cognate Object Constructions in English: A Cognitive-Linguistic Account*. Language in Performance 41. Gunter Narr. [2009] pp. xii+312. €58 ISBN 9 7838 2336 4894.

Hoffmann, Thomas, and Lucia Siebers, eds. *World Englishes: Problems, Properties and Prospects:* Selected Papers from the 13th IAWE Conference. Benjamins. [2009] pp. 436. €99 ISBN 9 7890 2724 9005.

Hotta, Ryuichi. *The Development of the Nominal Plural Forms in Early Middle English*. Hituzi Linguistics in English 10. Hituzi Syobo. [2009] pp. xix+291. ISBN 9 7848 9476 4033.

Huhn, Peter, Wolf Schmid, and Jorg Schonert, eds. *Point of View, Perspective and Focalization: Modeling Mediation in Narrative*. MGruyter. [2009] pp. vi + 305. €99.95 ($155) ISBN 9 7831 1021 8909.

Hüllen, Werner. *Networks and Knowledge in Roget's Thesaurus from Ancient to Medieval*. OUP. [2009] pp. vii + 217. £49 ISBN 9 7801 9955 3235.

Hutto, Daniel D., ed. *Narrative and Folk Psychology*. IA. [2009] pp. 406. pb. £17.95 ISBN 9 7818 4540 1658.

Hyland, Ken. *Academic Discourse: English in a Global Context*. Continuum. [2009] pp. 256. hb £75 ($150) ISBN 9 7808 2649 8038. pb £24.99 ($39.95) ISBN 9 7808 2649 8045.

Jaffe, Alexandra, ed. *Stance: Sociolinguistic Perspectives*. OUP. [2009] pp. vii + 261. £48 ISBN 9 7801 9533 1646.

Janicki, Karol. *Confusing Discourse*. Palgrave Macmillan. [2009] pp. 248. £52 ISBN 9 7802 3023 2600.

Jaszczolt, K.M. *Representing Time: An Essay on Temporality as Modality*. OUP. [2009] pp. xiii + 192. hb £63 ISBN 9 7801 9921 4433, pb £26 ISBN 9 7801 9921 4440.

Jenkins, Jennifer. *World Englishes: A Resource Book for Students*, 2nd edn. Routledge. [2009] pp. 256. £17.99 ISBN 9 7804 1546 6127.

Jucker, Andreas H., ed. *Early Modern English News Discourse: Newspapers, Pamphlets and Scientific News Discourse*. P&BNS 187. Benjamins. [2009] pp. vii+227. €95 ($143) ISBN 9 7890 2725 4320.

Jucker, Andreas, Daniel Schreier, and Marianne Hundt, eds. *Corpora: Pragmatics and Discourse*. Papers from the 29th International Conference on English Research on Computerized Corpora (ICAME 29), Ascona, Switzerland, 14–18 May 2008. Rodopi. [2009] pp. 516. €105 ISBN 9 7890 4202 5929.

Kachru, Braj B., Yamuna Kachru, and Cecil L. Nelson, eds. *The Handbook of World Englishes*. Wiley-Blackwell. [2009] pp. 832. pb €36 ISBN 9 7814 0518 8319.

Kawaguchi, Yuji, Makoto Minegishi, and Jacques Durand, eds. *Corpus Analysis and Variation in Linguistics*. Benjamins. [2009] pp. 399. €95 ISBN 9 7890 2720 7685.

Kemenade, Ans van, and Bettelou Los. *The Handbook of the History of English*. Wiley- Blackwell. [2009] pp. xvi + 655. hb £110 ISBN 9 7806 3123 3442, pb £29.99 ISBN 9 7814 0518 7862.

Klein, Wolfgang, and Ping Li, eds. *The Expression of Time*. MGruyter. [2009] pp. 278. hb €98 ($137) ISBN 9 7831 1019 5811, pb €29.95 ($42) ISBN 9 7831 1019 5828.

Kleparski, G.A., Elżbieta Rokosz-Piejko, and Agnieska Uberman, eds. *Old Pitfalls, Changing Attitudes and New Vistas*. Galicia English Teachings. WUS. [2009] pp. 250. Pb [price not available] ISBN 9 7883 7338 4897.

Kretzschmar, William A., Jr. *The Linguistics of Speech*. CUP. [2009] pp. £55 ISBN 9760 5218 8703 8.

Leech, Geoffrey, Marianne Hundt, Christian Mair, and Nicholas Smith. *Change in Contemporary English: A Grammatical Study*. CUP. [2009] pp. xxviii + 370. £69 ISBN 9 7805 2186 7121.

Lieber, Rochelle, and Pavol Štekauer, eds. *The Oxford Handbook of Compounding*. Oxford Handbooks in Linguistics. OUP. [2009] pp. xx+691. £85 ISBN 9 7801 9921 9872.

Lim, Lisa, and Ee-Ling Low, eds. *Multilingual, Globalizing Asia: Implications for Policy and Education. AILA Review 22*. Benjamins. [2009] pp. 130. €93 ISBN 9 7890 2723 9945.

Lodge, Ken. *A Critical Introduction to Phonetics*. Continuum. [2009] pp. ix + 244. hb £75 ISBN 9 7808 2648 8732, pb £24.99 ISBN 9 7808 2648 8749.

Loureiro-Porto, Lucía. *The Semantic Predecessors of* Need *in the History of English (*c.*750–1710)*. Publications of the Philological Society 43. Wiley-Blackwell. [2009] pp. xvii+273. pb £22.99. ISBN 9 7814 0519 2705.

Macaulay, Ronald. *Quantitative Methods in Sociolinguistics*. Palgrave Macmillan. [2009] pp. xii + 138. hb £40 ISBN 9 7802 3057 9170, pb £14.99 ISBN 9 7802 3057 9187.

Machan, Tim William. *Language Anxiety: Conflict and Change in the History of English*. OUP. [2009] pp. x + 302. £30 ISBN 9 7801 9923 2123.

Maddieson, Ian. *Patterns of Sounds*. CUP. [Reissued 2009] pp. 436. pb £33 ISBN 9 7805 2111 3267.

Mbangwana, Paul N., and Bonaventure M. Sala. *Cameroon English Morphology and Syntax: Current Trends in Action*. LINCOM. [2009] pp. 200. €70.50 ISBN 9 7838 9586 5220.

McCully, Chris. *The Sound Structure of English: An Introduction*. CUP. [2009] pp. viii + 233. hb £50 ISBN 9 7805 2185 0360, pb £16.99 ISBN 9 7805 2161 5495.

McGregor, William B, ed. *The Expression of Possession*. MGruyter. [2009] pp. 435. hb €98 ($137) ISBN 9 7831 1018 4372, pb €29.95 ($29.95) ISBN 9 7831 1018 4389.

McIntyre, Dan. *History of English: A Resource Book for Students*. English Language Introductions. Routledge. [2009] pp. xiv+209. hb $125 ISBN 9 7804 1544 4309, pb $34.95 ISBN 9 7804 1544 4293.

Meier, Richard P., Helen Aristar-Dry, and Emilie Destruel, eds. *Text, Time, and Context. Selected Papers of Carlota S. Smith*. Springer. [2009] pp. lxiv + 404. €139.95 ISBN 9 7890 4812 6163.

Mesthrie, Raj, Joan Swann, Ana Deumert, and William L. Leap *Introducing Sociolinguistics*. EdinUP. [2009] pp. xxvi + 500. hb £80 ISBN 9 7807 4863 8437, pb £19.99 ISBN 9 7807 4863 8444.

Mey, Jacob L., and Keith Brown, eds. *Concise Encyclopedia of Pragmatics*, 2nd edn. Elsevier. [2009] pp. 1,180. $210 ISBN 9 7800 8096 2979.

Minkova, Donka, ed. *Phonological Weakness in English: From Old to Present-Day English*. Palgrave Macmillan. [2009] pp. xii + 357. £60 ISBN 9 7802 3052 4750.

Minkova, Donka, and Robert Stockwell. *English Words: History and Structure*, 2nd edn. CUP. [2009] pp. xiv + 219. hb £55 ISBN 9 7805 2188 2583, pb £19.99 ISBN 9 7805 2170 9170.

Mondorf, Britta. *More Support for More-Support: The Role of Processing Constraints on the Choice between Synthetic and Analytic Comparative Forms*. Studies in Language Variation 4. Benjamins. [2009] pp. xi+222. €95 ($143) ISBN 9 7890 2723 4841.

Mussolff, Andreas, and Jörg Zinken, eds. *Metaphor and Discourse*. Palgrave Macmillan. [2009] pp. 280. £50 ISBN 9 7802 3053 7309.

Myers, Greg. *The Discourse of Blogs and Wikis*. Continuum. [2009] pp. 192. hb £75 ($150) ISBN 9 7818 4706 4134, pb £24.99 ($44.99) ISBN 9 7818 4706 4141.

Nasukawa, Kuniya, and Phillip Backley, eds. *Strength Relations in Phonology*. MGruyter. [2009] pp. xviii + 400. £99.95 ISBN 9 7831 1021 8589.

Ndhlovu, Finex. *The Politics of Language and Nation Building in Zimbabwe*. Lang. [2009] pp. 227. €34.20 ISBN 9 7830 3911 9424.

Nevalainen, Terttu, Irma Taavitsainen, Päivi Pahta, and Minna Korhonen, eds. *The Dynamics of Linguistic Variation: Corpus Evidence on English Past and Present*. Studies in Language Variation 2. Benjamins. [2009] pp. viii+339. €105 ($158) ISBN 9 7890 2723 4827.

Nurmi, Arja, Minna Nevala, and Minna Palander-Collin, eds. *The Language of Daily Life in England (1400–1800)*. Benjamins. [2009] pp. vii + 312. €105 ISBN 9 7890 2725 4583.

Ogden, Richard. *An Introduction to English Phonetics*. EdinUP. [2009] pp. 208. hb £55 ISBN 9 7807 4862 5406, pb £15.99 ISBN 9 7807 4862 5406.

Panther, Klaus-Uwe, Linda L. Thornburg, and Antonia Barcelona, eds. *Metonymy and Metaphor in Grammar*. Benjamins. [2009] pp. 423. €99 ISBN 9 7890 2722 3791.

Peters, Pam, Peter Collins, and Adam Smith, eds. *Comparative Studies in Australian and New Zealand English: Grammar and Beyond*. Benjamins. [2009] pp. 406. €105 ISBN 9 7890 2724 8992.

Piattelli-Palmarini, Massimo, Juan Uriagereka, and Pello Salaburu, eds. *Of Minds and Language: A Dialogue with Noam Chomsky in the Basque Country*. OUP. [2009] pp. xii + 459. hb £30 ISBN 9 7801 9954 4660, pb £16.99 ISBN 9 7801 9954 4677.

Pichler, Pia. *Talking Young Femininities*. Palgrave Macmillan. [2009] pp. xi + 269. £52 ISBN 9 7802 3001 3285.

Pichler, Pia, and Eva Eppler, eds. *Gender and Spoken Interaction*. Palgrave Macmillan. [2009] pp. xxii + 241. £52 ISBN 9 7805 2057 4021.Portner, Paul. Modality. OUP. [2009] pp. xi+288. hb £68 ISBN 9 7801 9929 2424, pb £26 ISBN 9 7801 9929 2431.

Preece, Siân. *Posh Talk: Language and Identity in Higher Education*. Palgrave Macmillan. [2009] pp. xi + 214. £50 ISBN 9 7802 3057 3987.

Renkema, Jan, ed. *Discourse, of Course: An Overview of Research in Discourse Studies*. Benjamins. [2009] pp. vii + 393. hb €110 ($165) ISBN 9 7890 272 3258, pb €36 ($54) ISBN 9 7890 2723 2595.

Renkema, Jan. *The Texture of Discourse: Towards an Outline of Connectivity Theory*. Benjamins. [2009] pp. 213. £90 ISBN 9 7890 2723 2663.

Renouf, Antoinette, and Andrew Kehoe, eds. *Corpus Linguistics: Refinements and Reassessments*. Rodopi. [2009] pp. 462. £75 ISBN 9 7890 4202 5971.

Repp, Sophie. *Negation in Gapping*. OUP. [2009] pp. xi + 266. hb £68 ISBN 9 7801 9954 3601, pb £27 ISBN 9 7801 9954 3618.

Reyes, Angela, and Adrienne Lo, eds. *Beyond Yellow English: Toward a Linguistic Anthropology of Asian Pacific America*. OUP. [2009] pp. 424. $99 ISBN 9 7801 9532 7366.

Rohdenburg, Günter, and Julia Schlüter, eds. *One Language, Two Grammars? Differences between British and American English*. CUP. [2009] pp. xxiv + 461. £60 ISBN 9 7805 2187 2195.

Römer, Ute, and Rainer Schulze, eds. *Exploring the Lexis-Grammar Interface*. Benjamins. [2009] pp. 321. €99 ISBN 9 7890 2722 3098.

Room, Adrian. *Alternate Names of Places*. McFarland. [2009] pp. 257. pb $49.95 ISBN 9 7807 8643 7122.

Sailaja, Pingali. *Indian English*. EdinUP. [2009] pp. 184. £19.99 ISBN 9 7807 4862 5956.

Sairio, Anni. *Language and Letters of the Bluestocking Network: Sociolinguistic Issues in Eighteenth-Century Epistolary English*. Société Néophilologique. [2009] pp. 365. pb €45 ISBN 9 7095 1904 0318.

Sampson, Geoffrey, David Gil, and Peter Trudgill, eds. *Language Complexity as an Evolving Variable*. Studies in the Evolution of Language 13. OUP. [2009] pp. xiv+309. hb £65 ISBN 9 7801 9954 5216, pb £22.99 ISBN 9 7801 9954 5223.

Sandra, Dominiek, Jan-Ola Östman, and Jef Verschueren, eds. *Cognition and Pragmatics*. HopH 3. Benjamins. [2009] pp. xvii + 399. pb €39 ($59) ISBN 9 7890 2720 7807.

Sato, Kiriko. *The Development from Case-Forms to Prepositional Constructions in Old English Prose*. Linguistic Insights: Studies in Language and Communication 88. Lang. [2009] pp. 231. pb £37.80 ISBN 9 7830 3911 7635.

Schauer, Gila. *Interlanguage Pragmatic Development: The Study Abroad Context*. Continuum. [2009] pp. 280. £75 ($150) ISBN 9 7818 4706 5209.

Sedlatschek, Andreas. *Contemporary Indian English: Variation and Change*. Benjamins. [2009] pp. 363. €105 ISBN 9 7890 2724 8985.

Selbach, Rachel, Hugo C. Cardoso, and Margot van den Berg, eds. *Gradual Creolization: Studies Celebrating Jacques Arends*. Benjamins. [2009] pp. 392. €105 ISBN 9 7890 2725 2562.

Senft, Gunter, Jan-Ola Östman, and Jef Verschueren, eds. *Culture and Language Use*. HopH 2. Benjamins. [2009] pp. xiii+280. pb €39 ($59) ISBN 9 7890 2720 7791.

Shaer, Benjamin, Philippa Cook, Werner Frey, and Claudia Maienborn, eds. *Dislocated Elements in Discourse: Syntactic, Semantic, and Pragmatic Perspectives*. Routledge Studies in Germanic Linguistics. Routledge. [2009] pp. vii+478. £100 ISBN 9 7804 1539 5984.

Sharifian, Farzad, ed. *English as an International Language: Perspectives and Pedagogical Issues*. Multilingual Matters. [2009] pp. 304. $54.95 ISBN 9 7818 4769 1224.

Smith, Dorsia, Raquel Puig, and Ileana Cortes Santiago, eds. *Caribbean without Borders: Literature, Language and Culture*. CambridgeSP. [2009] £34.99 ISBN 9 7814 4380 0336.

Smith, Jeremy J. *Old English: A Linguistic Introduction*. Cambridge Introductions to the English Language. CUP. [2009] hb £45 ISBN 9 7805 2186 6774, pb £15.99 ISBN 9 7805 2168 5696.

Stanford, James N., and Dennis R. Preston, eds. *Variation in Indigenous Minority Languages*. Benjamins. [2009] pp. 519. €105 ISBN 9 7890 2721 8643.

Stockwell, Peter. *Texture: A Cognitive Aesthetics of Reading*. EdinUP. [2009] pp. 224. £57 ISBN 9 7807 4862 5819.

Styles, Moraq, and Evelyn Arizpe, eds. *Acts of Reading: Teachers, Texts and Childhood*. Trentham Books. [2009] pp. 256. pb £20.99 ISBN 9 7818 5856 4388.

Suomela-Salmi, Eija, and Fred Dervin, eds. *Cross-Linguistic and Cross-Cultural Perspectives on Academic Discourse*. P&BNS 193. Benjamins. [2009] pp. vi+299. €95 ($143) ISBN 9 7890 2725 4375.

Thrane, Torben. *Referential-Semantic Analysis: Aspects of a Theory of Linguistic Reference*. CUP. [2009] pp. xii + 256. pb £20.99 ISBN 9 7805 2110 5712.

Tieken-Boon van Ostade, Ingrid. *An Introduction to Late Modern English*. EdinUP. [2009] pp. x + 166. hb £55 ISBN 9 7807 4862 5970, pb £15.99, ISBN 9 7807 4862 5987.

Tieken-Boon van Ostade, Ingrid, and Wim van der Wurff, eds. *Current Issues in Late Modern English*. Linguistic Insights. Lang. [2009] pp. 436. pb €63 (£63, $97.95) ISBN 9 7830 3911 6607.

Toolan, Michael. *Narrative Progression in the Short Story: A Corpus Stylistic Approach*. Benjamins. [2009] pp. xi + 212. hb £84 ISBN 9 7890 2723 3387, pb £33 ISBN 9 7890 2723 3431.

Traugott, Elizabeth Closs, Alice ter Meulen, Judy Snitzer Reilly, and Charles A. Ferguson, eds. *On Conditionals*. CUP. [2009] pp. xi + 384. pb £26.99 ISBN 9 7805 2111 3274.

Trinklein, Michael J. *Lost States*. Quirk. [2009] pp. 157. $24.95 ISBN 9 7815 9474 4105.

Trips, Carola. *Lexical Semantics and Diachronic Morphology: The Development of* –hood, –dom *and* –ship *in the History of English*. Linguistische Arbeiten 527. Niemeyer. [2009] pp. x+267. pb €89.95 ($139) ISBN 9 7834 8430 5274.

Vanderveken, Daniel. *Meaning and Speech Acts*, vol. 1: *Principles of Language Use*. CUP. [2009] pp. x + 244. pb £20.99 ISBN 9 7805 2110 4906.

Vanderveken, Daniel. *Meaning and Speech Acts*, vol. 2: *Formal Semantics of Success and Satisfaction*. CUP. [2009] pp. x + 244. pb £17.99 ISBN 9 7805 2110 4913.

Verschueren, Jef, and Jan-Ola Östman, eds. *Key Notions for Pragmatics*. HopH 1. Benjamins. [2009] pp. xiii+253. pb €39 ($59) ISBN 9 7890 2720 7784.

Williams, Rhian. *The Poetry Toolkit: The Essential Guide to Studying Poetry*. Continuum. [2009] pp. 270. hb £60 ISBN 9 7818 4706 0488, pb £15.99 ISBN 9 7818 4706 0495.

Wolf, Hans-Georg, and Frank Polzenhagen. *World Englishes: A Cognitive Sociolinguistic Approach*. MGruyter. [2009] pp. 278. €98 ISBN 9 7831 1019 6337.

II

Early Medieval

PHILIP SHAW AND MARY SWAN

This chapter has the following sections: 1. Bibliography; 2. Manuscript Studies, Palaeography, and Facsimiles; 3. Social, Cultural, and Intellectual Contexts; 4. Literature: General; 5. The Exeter Book; 6. The Poems of the Vercelli Book; 7. The Junius Manuscript; 8. The *Beowulf* Manuscript; 9. Other Poems; 10. Prose. Sections 1 and 2 are by Mary Swan; section 3 is by Mary Swan with contributions by Philip Shaw; section 4 is by Philip Shaw with contributions by Mary Swan; sections 5, 6, 7, and 9 are by Philip Shaw; section 8 is by Philip Shaw with a contribution by Mary Swan; section 10 is by Mary Swan with a contribution by Philip Shaw.

1. Bibliography

Beginning with vol. 42[2009], *Old English Newsletter* returns to its original publishing schedule of two issues a year. From now onwards, it will print only the *Bibliography* (Spring) and *Year's Work in Old English Studies* (Fall); all other content will be published on the *OENews* website (www.oenewsletter.org/OEN/). *OENews* 42:i and 42:ii[2009] contains the year's work in Old English studies 2007. *OENews* 42:i online also includes an essay on 'Lexomics for Anglo-Saxon Literature' by Michael D.C. Drout, Michael Kahn, Mark D. LeBlanc, Amos Jones, Neil Kathok, and Christina Nelson, and reports on 'Two Articles from Roskilde Museum, October 2009' by John C. Niles, the 'Dictionary of Old English: 2009 Progress Report' by Joan Holland, and 'Anglo-Saxon Plant Name Survey (ASPNS): Eleventh Annual Report, 2009' by C.P. Biggam. *OENews* 42:iii online contains an essay by Ben Reinhard on 'The Opening Image of Junius 11' and the following reports and notices: 'Old English Core Vocabulary' by Christine Rauer, 'Inside the Evellum Scriptorium Series' by Bernard J. Muir, 'ISAS 2009: St John's Newfoundland' by Stacy Klein, and 'Anglo-Saxon Plant Name Survey (ASPNS): Twelfth Annual Report, 2010' by C.P. Biggam.

The Year's Work in English Studies, Volume 90 (2011)
doi:10.1093/ywes/mar007

2. Manuscript Studies, Palaeography, and Facsimiles

Rebecca Rushforth describes a new discovery of 'Two Fragmentary Manuscripts at St John's College, Cambridge' (*Scriptorium* 63[2009] 73–8). Both survive as flyleaves in later medieval manuscripts: Cambridge, St John's College F.10, which contains six flyleaves, five of which are from a tenth-century English copy of Alcuin's *In evangelium Iohannis*; and Cambridge, St John's College F.27, which contains a flyleaf bifolium from an eleventh-century English manuscript of a commentary on Donatus's *Ars grammatica* which provides the first indication that this text was known in Anglo-Saxon England.

George Hardin Brown offers a new examination of 'The St. Petersburg Bede: Sankt-Peterburg, Publichnaja Biblioteka, MS. Lat. Q.v.I.18' (in Kilpiö, Kahlas-Tarkka, Roberts, and Timofeeva, eds., *Anglo-Saxons and the North*, pp. 212–19), rejecting the theory that Scribe 4 is Bede himself and categorizing the St Petersburg manuscript as 'a copy of an exemplar close to Bede's original, perhaps an ideograph' (p. 129).

Daniel Anlezark's 'Understanding Numbers in London, British Library, Harley 3271' (*ASE* 38[2009] 137–55) examines this composite manuscript, rich in items with links to computus and prognostics, with particular reference to items written by its Scribe C. Anlezark argues that Scribe C played a role in compiling the collection and that it might have been intended for use in Latin teaching at a major centre, perhaps Winchester.

Matthew T. Hussey investigates the connections between 'Dunstan, Æthelwold, and Isidorean Exegesis in Old English Glosses: Oxford, Bodleian Library Bodley 319' (*RES* 60[2009] 682–704). Bodley 319 is written by the same scribe as the Exeter Book, and Hussey's analysis draws on lexical and stylistic data to propose links with Æthelwold, and concludes with the tantalizing suggestion that 'Bodley 319—and perhaps its sister volumes, Lambeth 149 and the Exeter Book—moved in the vernacular literary circles of Dunstan and Æthelwold in the dynamic decades following their study together' (p. 702). An appendix to the article provides a diplomatic edition of the Latin text of Isidore of Seville, *De fide catholica* and its Old English gloss in Bodley 319, fos. 74^r–75^r.

Two of the essays in *Texts and Traditions of Medieval Pastoral Care*, the Festschrift for Bella Millett edited by Cate Gunn and Catherine Innes-Parker, deal with Anglo-Saxon texts and their post-Conquest manuscript transmission. Elaine Treharne calls for a remapping of 'Scribal Connections in Late Anglo-Saxon England' (in Gunn and Innes-Parker, eds., pp. 29–46), which would involve us thinking 'of known centres of production as something more like the hubs of interconnecting networks of operation' (p. 29). With particular reference to Cambridge, Corpus Christi College MS 322, Treharne shows the circularity of arguments about localization, and she sketches out the wide range of circumstances under which books are known to have travelled within Anglo-Saxon England, considers post-Conquest Old English textual copying, with Oxford, Bodleian Library Bodley 343, London, Lambeth Palace 487, and Cambridge, Trinity College B.14.52 as examples of books which might not be the products of the major earlier centres, and then examines book production in Exeter in the decades around the Conquest.

Ralph Hanna's contribution is 'Lambeth Palace Library, MS 487: Some Problems of Early Thirteenth-Century Textual Transmission' (in Gunn and Innes-Parker, eds., pp. 78–88). He offers a new description of the manuscript and its contents, and then turns to consider the implications of its varied writing area and *mise-en-page* to 'construct a narrative of the book's production' (p. 83), with the scribe initially planning quite a small book of Old English texts, then expanding this as further source materials became available. Hanna argues persuasively that neither of the two bodies of source materials was continuously available to the scribe, and draws parallels, via their inclusion of Wohunge Group texts, with British Library, Cotton Nero A.xiv and Cotton Titus D.xviii to propose a scenario where source texts are 'available only fitfully and sporadically to book producers and the readers they served' (p. 88).

Jeremy Smith also offers a new study of Lambeth 487, this time from the point of view of spelling as an indicator of linguistic development, in 'The Spellings ⟨e⟩, ⟨ea⟩ and ⟨a⟩ in Two Wooing Group Texts (MSS London, Cotton Nero A.xiv and London, Lambeth Palace 487)' (in Chewning, ed., *The Milieu and Context of the Wooing Group*, pp. 84–95). Betty Hill includes some observations on the codicology and construction of Lambeth 487 in 'Notes on *The Conduct of Life*' (*N&Q* 56[2009] 9–12).

Aidan Conti continues to produce important studies of post-Conquest Old English manuscripts. This year he offers 'The Taunton Fragment and the Homiliary of Angers: Context for New Old English' (*RES* 60[2009] 1–33), in which he identifies the Latin source of this recently discovered Old English and Latin text and presents an overview of the Homiliary of Angers, its audience, sources, and manuscript transmission. Hussey then situates the Taunton Fragment text relative to the versions of the Homiliary of Angers to show that it represents one of the earliest known manuscripts and provides a reconstruction of the Fragment which highlights the Latin text it now lacks. Conti counters the idea that the author of the Taunton Fragment text is not fluent in Old English, and makes a case for the Taunton Fragment text being 'the consummation of stages in a process' of copying (p. 30) and reflecting the language of its scribe as the scribe works with the language of their exemplar, sometimes making copying errors. The Taunton Fragment, Conti suggests, might have been part of a book which was used outside a major intellectual centre, and perhaps outside of the Benedictine Reform.

Elaine Treharne also published a paper in 2008 on 'The Architextual Editing of Early English' (in Edwards and Kato, eds., *New Directions in Medieval English Editing*, pp. 1–13). Treharne proposes 'a different model for thinking about text, its representation and interpretation' (p. 1) with attention to the materiality of text in manuscript and the impossibility of representing it fully in any surrogate or edition. The manuscripts of the Eadwine Psalter and the Old English Hexateuch—Cambridge, Trinity College R.17.1 and London, British Library, Cotton Claudius B.iv—and Cambridge, University Library Ii.1.33 provide central examples for Treharne's discussion of textual textures and layers and the challenges they pose to scholars.

Working with Anglo-Saxon Manuscripts, edited by Gale R. Owen Crocker, provides a set of beautifully illustrated discussions of key topics which will be of immense use to those starting out in the field. Owen-Crocker writes the introduction, and then, with Maria Cesario, 'Handling Anglo-Saxon Manuscripts'. Alexander Rumble describes 'The Construction and Writing of Anglo-Saxon Manuscripts'; Donald Scragg gives an overview of 'Manuscript Sources of Old English Prose', and Elaine Treharne of 'Manuscript Sources of Old English Poetry'. Gernot R. Wieland adds 'A Survey of Latin Manuscripts', and Timothy Graham discusses 'Glosses and Notes in Anglo-Saxon Manuscripts'. Catherine Karkov surveys 'Manuscript Art' and Stuart D. Lee and Daniel Paul O'Donnell track new developments 'From Manuscript to Computer'. Guidance on further reading underpins the volume's usefulness.

Richard Pfaff's *The Liturgy in Medieval England*, reviewed in section 3 below, includes a most useful overview of the manuscript sources for Anglo-Saxon liturgical study.

3. Social, Cultural, and Intellectual Contexts

Handbooks and Companions continue to be genres popular with publishers and readers. This year, two wide-ranging new Companions contain much of interest to Anglo-Saxonists. Carol Lansing and Edward D. Heath edit *A Companion to the Medieval World*, in which many of the topic-based essays—in particular those in the 'Early Medieval Foundations' section—provide useful contexts and examples for the study of pre-Conquest England. *A Companion to the Early Middle Ages: Britain and Ireland c.500–c.1100*, edited by Pauline Stafford, provides a wealth of new studies of aspects of social organization and regionality, with a focus on 'areas of recent historiographical development and advance' (p. 3). The volume opens with a set of 'Introductory Matter', in which Stafford discusses the historiography and the sources, and is then structured chronologically into three further sections, each of which contains a range of specialist studies on places and topics, from 'Economy' (by Howard B. Clarke, pp. 57–75) to 'Queens and Queenship' (by Stafford, pp. 459–76). The volume will provide an excellent, nuanced, and thought-provoking overview for students new to early medieval studies, and will offer early medieval literary scholars informed insight into key current topics and approaches for political and religious historians.

More new work on Anglo-Saxon political and secular culture provides valuable context for textual scholars. A fitting reflection of its dedicatee's scholarly range, and a treasure-trove of new work, is offered in *Early Medieval Studies in Memory of Patrick Wormald*, edited by Stephen Baxter, Catherine Karkov, Janet L. Nelson, and David Pelteret. The collection is divided into six sections. The first, 'Patrick Wormald', contains 'The Writings of Patrick Wormald' and 'Patrick Wormald as Historian' by Sarah Foot; 'Patrick Wormald the Teacher' by Stuart Airlie; and 'Living with Patrick Wormald' by Jenny Wormald. 'Studies: Celtic and Anglo-Saxon Foundations' contains 'Archipelagic Thoughts: Comparing Early Medieval Polities in Britain and

Ireland' by James Campbell; 'Celtic Kings: "Priestly Vegetables"?' by T.M. Charles-Edwards; 'The *Bretwaldas* and the Origins of Overlordship in Anglo-Saxon England' by Barbara Yorke; and 'Royal and Ecclesiastical Law in Seventh-Century Kent' by Lisi Oliver. 'Gregory and Bede' contains 'Divine Justice in Gregory the Great's *Dialogues*' by David F. Johnson; 'Bede, the Britons and the Book of Samuel' by Alan Thacker; 'Bede and Benedict of Nursia' by Scott DeGregorio; 'After Bede: Continuing the *Ecclesiastical History*' by Joanna Story; and 'Chosen Arrows, First Hidden Then Revealed: The Visitation-Archer Sequence as a Key to the Unity of the Ruthwell Cross' by Éamonn Ó Carragáin.

'Carolingian Authority and Learning' contains 'Alcuin, Charlemagne and the Problem of Sanctions' by Henry Mayr-Harting; '"For it is Written in the Law": Ansegis and the Writing of Carolingian Royal Authority' by Stuart Airlie; 'Kings, Clergy and Dogma: The Settlement of Doctrinal Disputes in the Carolingian World' by Thomas F.X. Noble; 'Charlemagne's *Missi* and their Books' by Rosamond McKitterick; 'Charlemagne's Daughters' by Anton Scharer; and 'Hrabanus Maurus in Anglo-Saxon England: *In honorem sanctae crucis*' by William Schipper. 'English Politics and Law (Ninth–Twelfth Centuries)' contains 'The Fonthill Letter, Ealdorman Ordlaf and Anglo-Saxon Law in Practice' by Nicholas P. Brooks; 'An Anonymous Historian of Edward the Elder's Reign' by David A.E. Pelteret; 'Reform and Retribution: The "Anti-Monastic Reaction" in the Reign of Edward the Martyr' by Shashi Jayakumar; '*Đonne se cirlisca man ordales weddigeð*: The Anglo-Saxon Lay Ordeal' by Sarah Larratt Keefer; 'Trial by Ordeal in Anglo-Saxon England: What's the Problem with Barley?' by John D. Niles; 'Lordship and Justice in Late Anglo-Saxon England: The Judicial Functions of Soke and Commendation Revisited' by Stephen Baxter; '*The Making of English Law* and the Varieties of Legal History' by John Hudson; and 'Liturgy or Law: Misconceived Alternatives?' by Janet L. Nelson. 'Church, Cult and Memory in England' contains 'King Æthelred's Charter for Eynsham Abbey (1005)' by Simon Keynes; '*Si litterali memorię commendaretur*: Memory and Cartularies in Eleventh-Century Worcester' by Francesca Tinti; 'Emma's Greek *Scrine*' by Lynn Jones; 'Emma: Image and Ideology' by Catherine Karkov; 'The Bishop's Book: Leofric's Homiliary and Eleventh-Century Exeter' by Elaine Treharne; and 'The Dangerous Dead in Early Medieval England' by John Blair. The general index to the whole volume is supplemented by indices of Anglo-Saxon charters and of manuscripts.

'King Edgar and the Dee: The Ceremony of 973 in Popular History Writing', by Stephen Matthews (*NH* 46[2009] 61–74), surveys attitudes to and understanding of this event from the Anglo-Saxon period to the twelfth century and then focuses on nineteenth- and early twentieth-century representations to show a shared desire to exploit its symbolic potential.

Three of the essays in *St Edmund King and Martyr: Changing Images of a Medieval Saint*, edited by Anthony Bale, concern Anglo-Saxon topics: Bale surveys 'St Edmund's Medieval Lives' (pp. 1–25). Carl Phelpstead's 'King, Martyr and Virgin: *Imitatio Christi* in Ælfric's *Life of St Edmund*' (pp. 27–44) investigates the tensions in Ælfric's *Life* from the point of view of 'what it might mean for a king of Anglo-Saxons to follow the example of the King of the Jews' (p. 44). Alison Finlay's 'Chronology, Genealogy and Conversion: The Afterlife of St Edmund in the North' (pp. 45–62) compares the development of English representations of the death of Edmund with references in thirteenth- and fourteenth-century Icelandic texts.

Richard Mortimer edits a collection of new work on *Edward the Confessor: The Man and the Legend*. Mortimer's own contribution is an introductory essay with the same title as the volume, and this is followed by 'Edward the Ætheling (c.1005–16)' by Simon Keynes; 'Edward and Normandy' by Elisabeth van Houts; 'Edward the Confessor and the Succession Question' by Stephen Baxter; 'Edith, Edward's Wife and Queen' by Pauline Stafford;, 'Edward the Confessor's Westminster Abbey' by Eric Fernie; 'New Glimpses of Edward the Confessor's Abbey at Westminster' by Warwick Rodwell; 'Craftsmen and Administrators in the Building of the Confessor's Abbey' by Richard Gem; and 'The Sanctity and Canonization of Edward the Confessor' by Edina Bozoky. Timothy Bolton's *The Empire of Cnut the Great: Conquest and the Consolidation of Power in Northern Europe in the Early Eleventh Century* offers a comparative overview of Cnut's career in Scandinavia and England and its political contexts and ramifications.

Ad F.J. Van Kempen examines 'The Mercian Connection, Harold Godwineson's Ambitions, Diplomacy and Channel-Crossing, 1056–1066' (*History* 94[2009] 1–19) for indications of Harold's motives in travelling to northern France. He draws on the *Vita Ædwardi* and William of Poitier's *Gesta Guillelmi* to argue that Harold was gathering support for his claim to the English throne.

Andrew Rabin explores 'Female Advocacy and Royal Protection in Tenth-Century England: The Legal Career of Queen Ælfthryth' (*Speculum* 84[2009] 261–88), tracking examples of Ælfthryth acting as a legal advocate for female litigants in property disputes, and arguing that, 'for Ælfthryth, acting as an advocate offered a way of articulating both a space and a rhetoric of female authority in the otherwise masculine world of Anglo-Saxon law' (p. 262), and that Æthelthryth's actions add a dimension to the Benedictine Reform model of queenly patronage. Legal culture is also the subject of Nicole Marafioti's 'Punishing Bodies and Saving Souls: Capital and Corporal Punishment in Late Anglo-Saxon England' (*Haskins Soc Jnl* 20[2008] 38–57). Marafioti explores clerical attitudes to secular legal processes, and in particular to capital punishment, drawing on Ælfric's First Pastoral Letter for Wulfstan and *Life of St Edmund*, *De Penitentia*, and Wulfstan's legal writings.

'Hospitality in Pre-Viking Anglo-Saxon England', by Alban Gautier (*EMedE* 17[2009] 23–44), draws on examples from charters, laws, letters, heroic poetry, and hagiography to argue that hospitality was always framed as a binding exchange.

This year saw the publication of the first volume—hopefully the first of many—of lectures in honour of J.M. Kemble, *The Kemble Lectures on Anglo-Saxon Studies 2005–8*, edited by Alice Jorgensen, Helen Conrad-O'Briain, and John Scattergood. The volume includes an introductory biography of Kemble by John Scattergood, 'Introduction: John Mitchell Kemble (1807–1857)' (pp. 1–11), followed by the texts of the first four lectures: 'On the Disappearance of Old English', by Jane Roberts (pp. 12–44);

'Fear, Mainly in Old English', by Eric Stanley (pp. 45–63); 'Kemble, *Beowulf*, and the Schleswig-Holstein Question', by Tom Shippey (pp. 64–80); and 'On Reading Anglo-Saxon Graves', by Martin Carver (pp. 81–103). Roberts discusses the development of writing practices through the Old English period, but focuses in particular on the copying of Old English texts towards the end of the Anglo-Saxon period and across the Conquest, as well as touching on the practices associated with new composition in early Middle English. Stanley surveys the Old English lexis of fear, particularly as represented in poetic texts, but also touching on homiletic materials. Shippey's lecture is reviewed in the section on the *Beowulf* manuscript below. Carver discusses the interpretation of Anglo-Saxon burials, demonstrating the pitfalls of grand, essentializing narratives and the possibilities of work that recognizes the individual and the performative aspects of burials. [PS]

Ecclesiastical and intellectual culture continues to generate plentiful new work. *Anglo-Saxons in a Frankish World 690–900*, by James T. Palmer, offers an important overview of missionary activity in Germany and the Netherlands. Palmer draws on a range of textual sources, including letters, charters, and hagiography, to reassess the impact of Anglo-Saxon missionaries and key figures such as Boniface, Willibrord, and Willehad on the development of East Frankish culture.

Richard Pfaff's *The Liturgy in Medieval England: A History* includes two chapters with an Anglo-Saxon focus: 'Early Anglo-Saxon England: A Partly Traceable Story' (pp. 30–61) and 'Later Anglo-Saxon England: Liturgy for England' (pp. 62–100). The historiography of the subject is usefully traced; the dominance of Bede for our understanding of the early period is evaluated; and key topics are analysed: the Northumbrian tradition, liturgy for minster churches and secular clergy, and the role of Æthelstan, Leofric, Æthelwold, and Æthelnoth in the production of liturgical texts. A third chapter, 'The Norman Conquest: Cross Fertilizations' (pp. 101–56), tracks post-Conquest continuities and innovations in liturgical practice. Karmen Lenz analyses 'Liturgical Readings of the Cathedral Office for Saint Cuthbert' (*HeroicA* 12[2009], 27 paras) to show the influence of Bede's *Life of Cuthbert* on this tenth-century rhymed text, and to emphasize Æthelstan's donation of MS Cambridge, Corpus Christi College 183, one of the earliest witnesses to the Office, as a move to link the Wessex royal house with the cult of Cuthbert. Yitzhak Hen's 'Review Article: Liturgy and Religious Culture in Late Anglo-Saxon England' (*EMedE* 17[2009] 329–42) offers the perspective of a scholar of early medieval mainland Europe on some significant recent studies of late Anglo-Saxon ecclesiastical culture.

Steven Bassett's study of 'The Landed Endowment of the Anglo-Saxon Minster at Hanbury (Worcs.)' (*ASE* 38[2009] 77–100) examines this well-documented example of the transfer of a minster's land administration to a cathedral community with appeal to the authority of the royal family whose ancestors were associated with its foundation. The Fursey Pilgrims publish a further study this year: Jane Roberts's *Guthlac of Crowland: A Saint for Middle England*, which gives an overview of the pre-Viking context for Guthlac's life and then discusses Felix's *Life* in comparison with the *Transitus beati Fursei*, *Guthlac A* and *B* and Vercelli Homily XXIII to suggest that behind the Exeter and Vercelli Book texts lie 'lost Guthlac poems' (p. 30).

Austin Mason, Alecia Arceo, and Robin Fleming, 'Buckets, Monasteries, and Crannógs: Material Culture and the Rewriting of Early Medieval British History' (*Haskins Soc Jnl* 20[2008] 1–38), is made up of three studies, one by each of its authors, with an introduction and a conclusion. Aspects of religious custom and ritual and the use of material culture to address historical questions are at the core of all three essays: Mason's 'Buried Buckets: Rethinking Ritual Behavior Before England's Conversion' (pp. 3–18), Arceo's 'Rethinking the Synod of Whitby and Northumbrian Monastic Sites' (pp. 14–30), and Fleming's 'Political Innovation in a Forgotten Welsh Kingdom: Rethinking the Grand Narrative of Viking-Age Britain' (pp. 31–6).

New work on artistic and material culture includes *Form and Order in the Anglo-Saxon World, AD 600–1100*, edited by Sally Crawford and Helena Hamerow with Leslie Webster, which focuses particularly on iconographic form and order in a range of Anglo-Saxon art forms. Tania M. Dickinson, 'Medium and Message in Early Anglo-Saxon Animal Art: Some Observations on the Contexts of Salin's Style I in England' (pp. 1–12), assesses the frequency of Salin's Style I in nineteen published Anglo-Saxon cemeteries, noting the prevalence of the style in female graves, as well as some regional variations in the frequency of artefacts with Style I decoration. '"... And Pretty Coins All in a Row"', by Anna Gannon (pp. 13–17) elaborates seven 'principles of textuality' (p. 14) that can contribute to a reading of the iconography of Anglo-Saxon *sceattas* in terms of the response of their Anglo-Saxon users and producers to the coins' iconography. Richard N. Bailey considers 'Anglo-Saxon Art: Some Forms, Orderings and their Meanings' (pp. 18–30), discussing a range of Anglo-Saxon artwork, with a particular focus on stone sculpture, and arguing for the importance of form to such artwork, as exemplified by riddling and skeuomorphic forms. Jane Hawkes, 'The Church Triumphant: The Figural Columns of Early Ninth-Century Anglo-Saxon England' (pp. 31–44), examines the iconographic scheme of the figural column from Masham in relation to other columns from Dewsbury and Reculver, arguing that these columns reflect an early Christian model with associations with Constantine and the notion of a Christian *imperium*. 'From Metalwork to Manuscript: Some Observations of the Use of Celtic Art in Insular Manuscripts', by Susan Youngs (pp. 45–64), considers the influence of artistic motifs developed originally in metalwork in early insular manuscript art, particularly in the Book of Durrow and the Lindisfarne Gospels. The Book of Durrow also provides the focus for Nancy Netzer, who writes on 'Framing the Book of Durrow Inside/Outside the Anglo-Saxon World' (pp. 65–78). This is a stimulating discussion of the history of scholarship seeking to localize the Book of Durrow and its artistic style, arguing that many of the premises employed in such arguments are flawed, and that we might usefully reconsider an Irish origin for the Book of Durrow, and an abandonment of the idea of replacement of an Irish artistic style by Roman models in early Northumbria. Such styles may well, in fact, coexist, in Metzer's view. [PS]

Two studies focus on the representation of the chi-rho in manuscript art. Carol A. Farr discusses 'The Sign at the Cross-roads: The Matthean *Nomen*

Sacrum in Anglo-Saxon Gospel Books before Alfred the Great' (pp. 79–88), considering the varying uses of the chi-rho symbol in eighth- and ninth-century gospel books. 'The Last Chi-Rho in the West? From Insular to Anglo-Saxon in the Boulogne 10 Gospels', by Richard Gameson (pp. 89–107), provides a detailed discussion of Boulogne, Bibliothèque municipale, MS 10, an Anglo-Saxon gospel book of the early to mid-tenth century. Finally, Geoffrey Russom writes 'On the Distribution of Verse Types in Old English Poetry' (pp. 108–18). Russom examines verse types in *Beowulf*, *The Battle of Maldon*, and Cynewulf's poems in the light of the 'word-foot theory', which posits a normative two-foot verse pattern from which verse deviates in order to create tension and resolution across full lines of verse. The importance of the word-foot theory, according to Russom, is that it offers an interpretative model for the choices poets make in composing Old English verse, rather than simply providing a taxonomy of verse types: verse types may deviate to a greater or lesser extent from the normative pattern, and we can thus use this deviation in interpreting poets' compositional choices. [PS]

For a review of Richard Abels's 'What Has Weland To Do with Christ? The Franks Casket and the Acculturation of Christianity in Early Anglo-Saxon England', see section 4 below.

Admirably prompt and extraordinarily beautifully illustrated, a short British Museum guide to *The Staffordshire Hoard* by Kevin Leahy and Roger Bland is published this year. Setting out the circumstances of the discovery, key aspects of early Anglo-Saxon cultural and political contexts, and describing many of the finds which had been identified at the point of publication, this publication exemplifies the work of those involved in recovering and conserving the hoard to make information publicly available at the earliest opportunity, and thus to open out interpretations. This publication paves the way for years of detailed analysis of the finds, their context, and their implications for our understanding of Mercia in the early Anglo-Saxon period.

Three new publications in the British Archaeological Reports British Series examine aspects of Anglo-Saxon archaeology and architecture. Mary Chester-Kadwell surveys *Early Anglo-Saxon Communities in the Landscape of Norfolk* with particular reference to mortuary and settlement practices from the early fifth to early seventh centuries. She considers how to integrate the study of these two kinds of practices into a narrative of landscape use and symbolic significance. Chapters 1 and 2 of John F. Potter, *Patterns in Stonework: The Early Church in Britain and Ireland. An Introduction to Ecclesiastical Geography*, focus on Anglo-Saxon choice of stone, quarrying, and changes in architectural style. *Approaching Interdisciplinarity: Archaeology, History and the Study of Early Medieval Britain, c.400–1100*, edited by Zoë L. Devlin and Caroline N.J. Holas-Clark, addresses and exemplifies the intersections of key, and traditionally separate, disciplines via the following studies: 'A Dialogue of the Deaf and Dumb: Archaeology, History and Philology' by Alex Woolf; 'The Practical Implications of Interdisciplinary Approaches: Research In Anglo-Saxon East Anglia' by Morn Capper; 'Archaeology, History and Economics: Exploring Everyday Life in Anglian Deira' by Caroline Holas-Clark; 'The End of Anglo-Saxon Furnished Burial: An Interdisciplinary Perspective' by Zoë L. Devlin;

'Sculpture and Lordship in Late Saxon Suffolk: The Evidence of Ixworth' by Mike F. Reed; 'Reassessing Remoteness: Ireland's Western Off-Shore Islands in the Early Medieval Period' by Sharon A. Greene; 'Romans Go Home? An Archaeological And Historical Exploration of the Cult of Saints in Late Antique Britain' by Michael Garcia; 'Alcuin of York on Wisdom and Mary: Texts and Buildings' by Sarah Boss; and 'Approaching Interdisciplinarity' by Zoë L. Devlin.

A thorough case-study of *Wasperton: A Roman, British and Anglo-Saxon Community in Central England*, by Martin Carver, Catherine Hills and Jonathan Scheschkewitz, draws on the excavation and analysis, from the early 1980s onwards, of a complete cemetery to present an example of the transition from late Roman Britain to Anglo-Saxon England. Important contributions to this wider picture include the suggestion that 'territorial identity in central England up to the 7th century may actually be largely Iron Age, rather than Anglian or Saxon' (p. 139), emphasis on changing perspectives and self-presentation over time and on both 'British continuity and Germanic intrusion', and the fact that 'the style of burial shows not continuous immigration, but who is winning the argument' (p. 140).

Six of the essays in *Mortuary Practices and Social Identities in the Middle Ages*, a Festschrift for Heinrich Härke edited by Duncan Sayer and Howard Williams, concern Anglo-Saxon topics: '*Beowulf* and British Prehistory' by Richard Bradley (pp. 38–45), 'Anglo-Saxon DNA?' by Catherine Hills (pp. 123–40); 'Laws, Funerals and Cemetery Organisation: The Seventh-Century Kentish Family' by Duncan Sayer (pp. 141–69); 'On Display: Envisioning the Early Anglo-Saxon Dead' by Howard Williams (pp. 170–206); 'Variation in the British Burial Rite: AD 400–700' by David Petts (pp. 207–21); and 'Anglo-Saxon Attitudes: How Should Post-AD 700 Burials Be Interpreted?' by Grenville Astill (pp. 222–35).

Richard Holt surveys 'The Urban Transformation in England, 900–1100' (*ANStu* 32[2009] 57–78), with reference to a number of towns, and particular attention to Worcester, in order to map a 'complex series of changes within the English boroughs' (p. 58).

Waterways and Canal-Building in Medieval England, edited by John Blair, includes several studies of these features of the Anglo-Saxon landscape: 'Barrier or Unifying Feature? Defining the Nature of Early Medieval Water Transport in the North-West' by Fiona Edmonds (pp. 21–36); 'Uses of Waterways in Anglo-Saxon England' by Della Hooke (pp. 37–54); 'The Place-Name Evidence for Water Transport in Early Medieval England' by Ann Cole (pp. 55–84); 'Canal Construction in the Early Middle Ages: An Introductory Review' by James Bond (pp. 153–206); 'The Water Roads of Somerset' by Charles and Nancy Hollinrake (pp. 228–43); 'Glastonbury's Anglo-Saxon Canal and Dunstan's Dyke' by Charles and Nancy Hollinrake (pp. 235–43); 'Early Water Management on the Lower River Itchen in Hampshire' by Christopher K. Currie (pp. 244–53); and 'Transport and Canal-Building on the Upper Thames, 1000–1300' by John Blair (pp. 254–94).

The cultural implications of language study are brought to our attention in a number of new publications. Immo Warntjes examines 'The Earliest

Occurrence of Old English *Gerīm* and its Anglo-Irish Computistical Context' (*Anglia* 127[2009] 91–105), arguing that *gerīm*, in its technical sense of '(a period of) a certain number of (Julian calendar) days' (p. 105), is first attested in an early eighth-century Latin-language Irish computistical text, reflecting intellectual engagement between Irish and Anglo-Saxon scholars on computus. [PS]

Katrin Thier compares Old Norse and Old English vocabulary in 'Ships and their Terminology between England and the North' (in Kilpiö et al., eds., pp. 151–64) to show continuing contacts throughout the early Anglo-Saxon period. In the same volume, Debbie Banham explores 'Race and Tillage: Scandinavian Influence on Anglo-Saxon Agriculture?' (in Kilpiö et al., eds., pp. 165–91), and does not find great signs of it. Banham emphasizes that the influence of Scandinavian settlers on agricultural practices in England varied greatly from place to place; that Viking armies were not entirely made up of people of Scandinavian origin, and that influences from outside Scandinavia as well as inside could have been introduced via Scandinavian settlers.

A very early example of post-Conquest Anglo-Saxonism is explored by Tom Licence in 'History and Historiography in the Late Eleventh Century: The Life and Work of Herman the Archdeacon, Monk of Bury St Edmunds' (*EHR* 124[2009] 516–44). In the 1090s Herman wrote an account of the miracles of St Edmund, and Licence examines his career, the sources on which he drew for his text and his agenda in producing it.

Post-medieval interest in pre-Conquest England continues to generate interesting new work. Henry Summerson examines 'Tudor Antiquaries and the *Vita Ædwardi Regis*' (*ASE* 38[2009] 157–84), argues that the late sixteenth-century antiquaries responsible for the compilation of Holinshed's *Chronicles* used a now lost manuscript of the *Vita* once owned by John Stow, and offers a reconstruction of some passages missing from the surviving manuscript of the *Vita*, including the complete version of a poem describing a ship which Earl Godwine gave to Edward. An appendix to the article provides the text, and a modern English translation of the reconstructed ship poem and of the relevant extracts from the *Vita* in the work of Tudor antiquaries. Simon Keynes and Rosalind Love build on Summerson's work in 'Earl Godwine's Ship' (*ASE* 38[2009] 185–223) to examine its implications for the relationship between the *Vita Ædwardi* and the *Encomium Emmae* and the source used by John of Worcester and William of Malmesbury, and to support the argument that the *Encomium Emmae* is influenced by the *Vita Ædwardi*.

The Victorian (re)invention of the early Middle Ages continues to prompt new studies. Barbara Yorke views 'The "Old North" from the South Saxon in Nineteenth-Century Britain' (in Kilpiö et al., eds., *Anglo-Saxons and the North*, pp. 131–49), and finds Vikings portrayed as archetypal enemies reminiscent of threats to the nineteenth-century British empire. *The Vikings and Victorian Lakeland: The Norse Medievalism of W.G. Collingwood and his Contemporaries*, by Matthew Townend, provides an interesting insight into the career and context of one of the founders of the study of Anglo-Saxon stone sculpture and into key stages of work on English place names.

4. Literature: General

A range of new work on Old English verse is published this year. Thomas A. Bredehoft's monograph, *Authors, Audiences, and Old English Verse*, considers the nature of the production and consumption of Old English verse, arguing that literate-formulaic composition became increasingly important, and perhaps dominant, at least from the later ninth century onwards. This development, Bredehoft argues, challenges views of poetic production centred around oral-formulaic models. Consideration of groups of poems within this context suggests that Old English poetry (particularly anonymous poetry) may have circulated among 'small, well defined, and local audiences' (p. 202). A particularly intriguing example of this is discussed in chapter 2, 'The Audience for Saxon Songs in the Late Ninth Century', which argues on the grounds of shared formulas for the influence of Old Saxon verse on Alfredian composition, and suggests that Alfred's own library may have included texts such as *Genesis A*, *Genesis B*, *Solomon and Saturn*, *The Finnsburh Fragment*, and *The Dream of the Rood*. In chapter 3, 'Literate Poetic Composition in Tenth-Century Classical Poems', Bredehoft examines metrically conservative poems that he assigns to the tenth century, including Exeter Book Riddle 40, *The Menologium*, *The Battle of Maldon*, and the Chronicle poems. The evidence of the different metrical practices in these poems suggests, he claims, that Riddle 40 may be associated with Glastonbury (perhaps with Dunstan), while *The Menologium* and the Chronicle poems are metrically distinct, related to one another, and reflect the concerns of Æthelwold.

Three of the essays in Jefferson and Putter, eds., *Approaches to the Metres of Alliterative Verse*, touch on Old English metrical practices. Elizabeth Solopova discusses 'Alliteration and Prosody in Old and Middle English' (pp. 25–39), analysing developments in the linguistic conditions affecting alliterative metre from the Old English through into the Middle English period. Brief discussions of the Old English background to Middle English alliterative metre also appear in two other essays in the volume: Jeremy Smith, '"The metre which does not measure": The Function of Alliteration in Middle English Alliterative Poetry' (pp. 11–23), and Geoffrey Russom, 'Some Unnoticed Constraints on the A-Verse in *Sir Gawain and the Green Knight*' (pp. 41–57).

Kilpiö et al., eds., *Anglo-Saxons and the North*, also provides two essays on metrical issues. Geoffrey Russom discusses 'Why There Are Three Eddic Metres' (pp. 69–88), arguing that the three Eddic metres should be understood not as imperfect imitation of models from outside Scandinavia, but as effective native developments that reflect and work with changes in the structure of the Old Norse language. Russom makes frequent comparison with Old English metre, especially as represented in *Beowulf*, and his article may therefore be of some interest to Old English metrists. 'On Finnic and English Alliterative Metres', by Jonathan Roper (pp. 89–108), discusses the parallels between Old English alliterative metre and Finnish, Estonian, and Vadjan alliterative metres, arguing that comparisons between these traditions may help to illuminate issues such as the performance characteristics of Old English verse and the reasons for the eventual extinction of English alliterative verse.

Two essays in *Oral Tradition* this year deal with Old English verse in general. In 'The Word Made Flesh: Christianity and Oral Culture in Anglo-Saxon Verse' (*OralT* 24[2009] 293–318), Andy Orchard undertakes a wide-ranging survey of the evidence for traditional oral material in Old English verse, arguing that it is possible to discern some evidence for widespread orality in Anglo-Saxon culture, encompassing both newer compositions and re-compositions, and much older verse. Alice Jorgensen discusses 'The Trumpet and the Wolf: Noises of Battle in Old English Poetry' (*OralT* 24[2009] 319–36), examining descriptions of noise in battles and approaches to battle in Old English verse. Such descriptions, Jorgensen argues, serve to highlight the psychological impact of battle and its capacity for carrying spiritual meaning.

A new study of the ways in which Old English poetry engages with the past is offerred in Renée Trilling's *The Aesthetics of Nostalgia: Historical Representation in Old English Verse*. Trilling surveys Old English heroic and biblical poems, as well as Chronicle verse, drawing on the interpretative model of the 'constellation', elaborated in her article, also published this year, 'Ruins in the Realm of Thoughts: Reading as Constellation in Anglo-Saxon Poetry' (*JEGP* 108[2009] 141–67), on which the first chapter of this monograph is based. Trilling considers both the representation of different pasts—Germanic, Roman, and biblical—and the representation of the present through the lens of an imagined past, insisting on the importance of poetic form and its aesthetics in interpreting Old English uses and conceptions of the past. The discussion of Chronicle verse in chapter 4 ('Poetic Memory: The Canonical Verse of the *Anglo-Saxon Chronicle*', pp. 175–213) and chapter 5 ('Transitional Verse in the *Anglo-Saxon Chronicle*: Changing the Shape of History', pp. 214–52) provides an interesting appraisal of the changing formal characteristics of verse within the *Anglo-Saxon Chronicle*, seeking to align this with changing socio-political and literary concerns across the Norman Conquest.

Corinne Saunders, ed., *A Companion to Medieval Poetry*, provides an invaluable survey of the field, but also deliberately sets out to address the constraints of periodization of Old and Middle English poetry, and to demonstrate continuities as well as disjunctions. Essays dealing with Old English verse are: 'The World of Anglo-Saxon England', by Andy Orchard; 'The Old English Language and the Alliterative Tradition', by Richard Dance; 'Old English Manuscripts and Readers', by Rohini Jayatilaka; 'Old English and Latin Poetic Traditions', by Andy Orchard; 'Germanic Legend and Old English Heroic Poetry', by Hugh Magennis; 'Old English Biblical and Devotional Poetry', by Daniel Anlezark; 'Old English Wisdom Poetry', by David Ashurst; and 'Old English Epic Poetry: *Beowulf*', by Daniel Anlezark.

Jonathan Wilcox evaluates the relevance for Anglo-Saxon literary studies of the work of a Russian scholar of Icelandic literature in 'The Ghost of M.I. Steblin-Kamenskij: Interpreting Old English Literature through Saga Theory' (in Kilpiö et al., eds., pp. 109–20), with particular relevance to questions of narrative tone, historicity, time, authorship, and gesture.

Two of the essays in *The Blackwell Companion to the Bible in English Literature*, edited by Rebecca Lemon, Emma Mason, Jonathan Roberts, and Christopher Rowland, discuss Old English literature. Daniel Anlezark provides an introduction surveying Old and Middle English literary uses of biblical material (pp. 41–60), while Catherine A.M. Clarke addresses 'Old English Poetry' that draws on scriptural narrative (pp. 61–75).

This year also saw the publication of a volume of essays in honour of Helen Damico, *Poetry, Place, and Gender*, edited by Catherine Karkov. The volume's contents include: 'Introduction', by Patrick W. Conner (pp. 1–12); 'The Wearmouth Icon of the Virgin (A.D. 679): Christological, Liturgical, and Iconographic Contexts', by Éamonn Ó Carragáin (pp. 13–37); '*The Dream of the Rood* at Nones on Good Friday', by Sarah Larratt Keefer (pp. 38–59); 'Prophetic Vision in *The Dream of the Rood*', by Thomas N. Hall (pp. 60–74); '*þyle* as Fool: Revisiting *Beowulf*'s Hunferth', by Leslie A. Donovan (pp. 75–97); 'The *nathwylc* Scribe and the *nathwylc* Text of *Beowulf*', by Kevin Kiernan (pp. 98–131); 'Æðeldreda in the *Old English Bede*', by Paul E. Szarmach (pp. 132–50); 'Goscelin, the *Liber confortatorius*, and the Library of Peterborough', by Katherine O'Brien O'Keeffe (pp. 151–70); 'The Lady and the Vine: Putting the Horsewoman on the Hilton of Cadboll Cross-Slab into Context', by Kellie S. Meyer (pp. 171–96); 'Petitionary Poetry in Old English and Early Welsh: *Deor*, *Widsið*, *Dadolwch Urien*', by David N. Klausner (pp. 197–210); 'Revisiting Anglo-Scandinavian Settlement and Sculpture', by Christopher D. Morris (pp. 211–33); 'The *Málsháttakvæði* or "Proverb Poem" Englished', by Roberta Frank (pp. 234–51); 'From the Wound in Christ's Side to the Wound in his Heart: Progression from Male Exegesis to Female Mysticism', by George Hardin Brown (pp. 252–74); 'Translating Images: Image and Poetic Reception in French, English, and Latin Versions of Guillaume de Deguileville's *Trois Pèlerinages*', by Richard K. Emmerson (pp. 275–301); and 'Dante's Views on Judaism, Christianity, and Islam: Perspectives from the New (Fourteenth) Century', by Christopher Kleinhenz (pp. 302–18). The essays by Keefer and Hall are dealt with below in section 6, and Klausner's essay is discussed in section 5. Likewise, Donovan's essay and Kiernan's appear in section 8.

Ó Carragáin discusses the icons of the Virgin and apostles brought from Rome by Benedict Biscop and placed in the altar area of St Peter's at Wearmouth. These icons, he argues, do not reflect merely a desire to imitate Rome, but a specific concern with doctrinal concerns over the virgin birth, and an attention to maintaining up-to-date liturgical and theological norms at St Peter's. Szarmach compares the *Old English Bede* with Bede's *Historia Ecclesiastica Gentis Anglorum*, arguing that the Old English translation deserves renewed attention for the light it sheds on Anglo-Saxon attitudes to Bede's text and the concerns of a translator in reworking the narrative in Old English. Bede also features in Brown's wide-ranging exploration of devotion to the wounds and instruments of the Passion. O'Brien O'Keeffe compares the booklist in Oxford, Bodleian Library, MS Bodley 163, fos. 250–1 with the sources employed by Goscelin in composing his *Liber confortatorius*, finding some evidence that Goscelin used a book collection similar to that in the Bodley manuscript, and suggesting that the booklist and Goscelin's composition may both be traceable to Peterborough. Meyer examines the iconography of the Hilton of Cadboll cross-slab, noting the possibilities for interpretation in the light of Christian exegesis, and exploring the possible connections with the Columban church or with Northumbria. Morris considers Anglo-Scandinavian sculpture from Sockburn in County Durham, arguing that, while the site was probably an important ecclesiastical site in the eighth century, in the ninth and/or tenth centuries it came under secular control by individuals of Scandinavian or Anglo-Scandinavian extraction, whose patronage influenced the production of the sculpture visible today.

Welcome new light on both the prose and verse of the Vercelli Book comes from *New Readings in the Vercelli Book*, edited by Samantha Zacher and Andy Orchard. Its contents are: 'Introduction', by Samantha Zacher and Andy Orchard (pp. 3–11); 'The Vercelli Prose and Anglo-Saxon Literary History', by Paul E. Szarmach (pp. 12–40); 'Studies in the Language of Copyists of the Vercelli Homilies', by Donald G. Scragg (pp. 41–61); 'The Portents at Christ's Birth in Vercelli Homilies V and VI: Some Analogues from Medieval Sermons and Biblical Commentaries', by Thomas N. Hall (pp. 62–97); 'The Source of Vercelli VII: An Address to Women', by Samantha Zacher (pp. 98–149); 'Vercelli Homily XV and *The Apocalypse of Thomas*', by Charles D. Wright (pp. 150–84); 'The 'Homiletics' of the Vercelli Book Poems: The Case of *Homiletic Fragment I*', by Jonathan T. Randle (pp. 185–224); '*The Dream of the Rood*: Cross-References', by Andy Orchard (pp. 225–53); 'Vercelli Homilies XIX–XXI, the Ascension Day Homily in Cambridge, Corpus Christi College 162, and the Catechetical Tradition from Augustine to Wulfstan', by Michael Fox (pp. 254–79); 'The Reburial of the Cross in the Old English *Elene*', by Manish Sharma (pp. 280–97); 'The Journey Motif in the Poems of the Vercelli Book', by Patrick McBrine (pp. 298–317); 'The Vercelli Book and its Texts: A Guide to Scholarship', by Paul G. Remley (pp. 318–415). The essays are discussed in sections 6 and 10 below.

This year also saw the publication of the third edition of Joyce Hill's *Old English Minor Heroic Poems* (comprising *Widsið*, *Deor*, *Waldere*, and *The Finnsburh Fragment*). The new edition provides an updated introduction and notes, and improves on the already valuable glossary of proper names with references to primary sources for the figures listed. The result is a very useful tool for scholars of Old English verse and Germanic heroic tradition, while also fulfilling the editor's hope that 'it continues to be as student-friendly as it was originally designed to be in 1983' (p. vii).

In 'What Has Weland To Do with Christ? The Franks Casket and the Acculturation of Christianity in Early Anglo-Saxon England' (*Speculum* 84[2009] 549–81) Richard Abels discusses the iconographic programme of the Franks Casket—in particular the juxtaposition of Weland and the Magi—in the light of a number of Old English poems including *Deor*, *Beowulf*, and *The Battle of Maldon*. The casket, he concludes, 'may be read as a *speculum principum* for late-seventh- and early-eighth-century kings and lords' (p. 580) in which a symmetrical moral obligation to both gift-giving and feud is encoded.

In 'Monsters and the Exotic in Early Medieval England' (*LitComp* 6[2009] 332–48), Asa Simon Mittman and Susan M. Kim discuss a range of classical and early medieval English textual sources to show how depictions of the monstrous in early medieval England serve to define the normative and function as part of an English Christian world-view. Johanna Kramer reviews the last fifteen years of 'The Study of Proverbs in Anglo-Saxon Literature: Recent Scholarship, Resources for Research, and the Future of the Field' (*LitComp* 60[2009] 71–96), makes a case for studying proverbs in isolation as well as in context, and points up directions for future research.

Joseph P. McGowan, 'Giants and Snake-Charmers: OE *þyrs*' (*N&Q* 56[2009] 487–90), surveys the use of the word *þyrs* in Old English verse and glossaries, suggesting that the association of this term with sorcery as well as gigantism may derive from Aldhelm.

Michael D.C. Drout and Scott Kleinman, 'Philological Inquiries 1: Method and Merovingians' (*HeroicA* 12[2009] 23 paras.) promises to be 'the first of a series of columns on philology'. This piece is in part a plea for the central importance of philology to literary scholarship, illustrated by a case study of Tom Shippey's article, 'The Merov(ich)ingian Again: *Damnatio memoriae* and the *Usus scholarum*' (on which, see *YWES* 86[2007] 188), and a discussion of a project to produce a *Handbook of Philological Methods*.

David Clark's *Between Medieval Men: Male Friendship and Desire in Early Medieval English Literature* is an important study of male same-sex acts, identities, and bonds in a range of Anglo-Saxon texts, including penitentials, heroic, elegiac, and biblical poetry, hagiography, and schoolroom texts. By ranging across texts often boxed off into separate categories—Latin and vernacular; poetry and prose—Clarke is able to pose questions about how texts make identities in their production and reflection of cultural and linguistic meanings, and to make important points about the coexistence of competing ideologies and the need to make our readings of sexuality, love, and affection as subtle and complex as the textual records upon which we draw. Clark also publishes 'Old English Literature and Same-Sex Desire: An Overview' (*LitComp* 6[2009] 573–84), a survey of relevant work on gender studies, sexuality, and queer theory and its impact on Old English literary studies, and an indication of areas for new work. [MS]

5. The Exeter Book

A valuable addition to the literature on the Exeter Book riddles this year is Dieter Bitterli's monograph *Say What I Am Called: The Old English Riddles of the Exeter Book and the Anglo-Latin Riddle Tradition*. Bitterli addresses the multiplicity of riddling techniques employed in the riddles, with an emphasis on the ways in which the techniques of Latin sources are creatively reimagined and re-created in the Old English riddles. Discussion focuses around issues such as the use of runic cyphers and numerical patterning, etymology as an approach to understanding the nature of riddlic objects, and the ways in which the riddles engage with and examine the process of riddling itself. Bitterli also identifies an analogue for Riddle 9 in the eighth-century insular Latin pseudo-Bedan *Collectanea* in 'The "Cuckoo" in the *Collectanea* of Pseudo-Bede—An Unnoticed Latin Analogue to Exeter Book *Riddle 9*' (*N&Q* 56[2009] 481–2).

The challenge of solving some of the Exeter Book riddles continues to generate new work. Shannon Ferri Cochran, in 'The Plough's the Thing: A

New Solution to Old English Riddle 4 of the Exeter Book' (*JEGP* 108[2009] 301–9), argues that the riddle creature in this case is an ox in a plough team, explaining the numerous rings that occur in the riddle partly in terms of the wheels of a wheeled plough of the sort illustrated in London, British Library, Cotton Julius A.vi, folio 3. The linguistic difficulties presented by the riddles also attracted fresh attention this year from Elena Afros, who discusses 'Exeter Book *Riddle 49*: Linguistic Ambiguities Revisited' (*N&Q* 56[2009] 171–5). Bredehoft's monograph, reviewed in section 4, touches on the issue of the originary milieu of Riddle 40.

The other poems of the Exeter Book are less well represented this year. Klausner in Karkov, ed., *Poetry, Place, and Gender*, argues that *Deor* and *Widsith* can be read as 'petitionary poems' in which the poets provide an indication of the range and variety of their knowledge of narratives, and invoke the generosity of rulers and their provision of patronage to poets, implicitly requesting patronage for themselves. In Kilpiö et al., eds., *Anglo-Saxons and the North*, Joseph Harris examines 'The Rök Stone through Anglo-Saxon Eyes' (pp. 11–45). In a wide-ranging discussion, Harris argues for the influence of West Germanic legendary narrative material on the Rök inscription, paying attention to the parallels between the reference to Theoderic in the inscription and in *Deor* lines 18–19, and discussing the **Hrædgotan* in Old English verse, in particular in *Widsith*.

Brian O'Camb discusses 'Bishop Æthelwold and the Shaping of the Old English *Exeter Maxims*' (*ES* 90[2009] 253–73) and argues, mainly on the basis of lexical parallels, that lines 45–50a of *Maxims I* echo discussions of the treatment and training of oblates in Æthelwold's translation of the Benedictine Rule. The poem, O'Camb contends, reflects the concerns of reformed monasticism in the period around the mid- to late tenth century, and should not be treated simply as a storehouse of quotidian secular lore. Alfred Bammesberger locates 'A Reference to Martyrdom in Cynewulf's Ascension Poem (*Christ II*, 679a)' (*ANQ* 22:ii[2009] 5–7), interpreting the apparent tree-climbing in *Christ II*, lines 678b–679a, as a reference to martyrdom, presumably by crucifixion.

6. The Poems of the Vercelli Book

Four of the essays in Zacher and Orchard, eds., *New Readings in the Vercelli Book*, discuss the verse of the Vercelli Book. Patrick McBrine considers 'The Journey Motif in the Poems of the Vercelli Book' (pp. 298–317), arguing that this motif serves particularly as a way of dealing with the sufferings of life on earth and the need to prepare for the world beyond. In '*The Dream of the Rood*: Cross-References' (pp. 225–53), Andy Orchard discusses the poetic technique of the *Dream of the Rood* and its relationship with Old English literary traditions at large as well as specific connections that can be drawn with *Elene* and *Andreas*, arguing both for the skill of the *Dream*-poet's work, and the vitality of the poem's continued transmission and interaction with later verse. Jonathan T. Randle, 'The "Homiletics" of the Vercelli Book Poems: The Case of *Homiletic Fragment I*' (pp. 185–224), examines the structure, style, metre, and contents of *Homiletic Fragment I*, with a view to establishing the ways in which a homiletic style in Old English verse might operate, arguing that this text deploys a range of homiletic techniques in a skilful fashion. Manish Sharma examines 'The Reburial of the Cross in the Old English *Elene*' (pp. 280–97), arguing that *Elene* operates in two directions, containing not only a progressive movement towards conversion, but also a retrograde one reflected in the reburial of the cross.

Elene also receives attention from Christina M. Heckman, who examines 'Things in Doubt: *Inventio*, Dialectic, and Jewish Secrets in Cynewulf's *Elene*' (*JEGP* 108[2009] 449–80). Heckman reads the invention of the Cross in *Elene* in terms of a dialectical process in which Jewish wisdom plays a foundational role in Christianity. The poem, Heckman suggests, can be understood as allegorizing epistemological methods and presenting the Cross as a focal point for the establishment of Christian wisdom.

Two of the essays in Karkov, ed., *Poetry, Place, and Gender*, focus on *The Dream of the Rood*. Sarah Larratt Keefer compares the poem with the ritual of the Veneration of the Cross, suggesting that it particularly resembles the presentation of the Veneration of the Cross in eleventh-century *Regularis Concordia* witnesses, and may thus suggest situating the composition of the extant manuscript version of *The Dream of the Rood* in the context of the Benedictine Reform. In the same volume, Hall explores the visual description of the Cross in the opening lines of *The Dream of the Rood*, deploying interpretative models that draw on Gregory the Great's *Homilies on Ezechiel* and the idea of the hypostatic union of Christ's human and divine natures.

The question of the sources of *The Dream of the Rood* is the subject of Thomas D. Hill, 'The *Passio Andreae* and *The Dream of the Rood*' (*ASE* 38[2010] 1–10). Hill assesses the relationship between *The Dream of the Rood* and the *Passio Andreae*, arguing that the latter is an important source for numerous narrative details within the former.

The Mermedonians of *Andreas* are the subject of two articles this year. Alexandra Bolintineanu discusses 'The Land of Mermedonia in the Old English *Andreas*' (*Neophil* 93[2009] 149–64), considering the presentation of the Mermedonians and the landscape of Mermedonia in *Andreas* in comparison to its Latin and Greek analogues. Close analysis of the text reveals parallels with *Beowulf* in its treatment of the monstrous and of the landscapes in which monsters are to be found, while the transformation of the landscape within the poem can be situated within the discourses of exile and homeland with which Old English poets approach salvation. Shannon N. Godlove examines 'Bodies as Borders: Cannibalism and Conversion in the Old English *Andreas*' (*SP* 106[2009] 137–60), arguing that the Mermedonians of *Andreas* can be linked both with the Jews and with Vikings, seeking to situate the poem within the context of Viking incursions while also reading it as drawing on an Anglo-Saxon consciousness of a history of missionary activity on the Continent.

Fates of the Apostles is the subject of a brief discussion of a textual crux. Alfred Bammesberger examines 'Old English *Ende Gesealdon* (*Fates of the Apostles*, Line 85b)' (*N&Q* 56[2009] 170–1), interpreting *ende* in this verse as a mistaken replacement of *andan* (perhaps via an Anglian form *ande*) with a sense 'zeal', yielding a translation '[they] gave up their zeal' (p. 171).

7. The Junius Manuscript

While 2008 saw several publications on the poems of the Junius manuscript, 2009 has been relatively quiet. Douglas Simms examined 'Heavy Hypermetrical Foregrounding in the Old Saxon *Heliand* and *Genesis* Poems' (*HeroicA* 12[2009] 29 paras), analysing the small number of irregular or 'heavy' hypermetric verses containing four rather than three lifts in the Old Saxon *Heliand* and *Vatican Genesis*, and in the Old English *Genesis B*. These verses are employed, in Simms's view, to emphasize significant points in these narratives. The metrical characteristics of some of the Junius manuscript poems are also discussed in depth in Bredehoft's monograph, *Authors, Audiences, and Old English Verse*, reviewed in section 4 above. Clarke's piece in Lemon et al., eds., *The Blackwell Companion to the Bible in English Literature*, and Anlezark's piece in Saunders, ed., *A Companion to Medieval Poetry*, both discussed in section 4, also touch on verse from the Junius manuscript. For Reinhard's essay on 'The Opening Image of Junius 11', see section 1 above.

8. The *Beowulf* Manuscript

As always, *Beowulf* attracted considerable attention, but we begin with Dick Ringler's *Beowulf: A New Translation for Oral Delivery*, which was not noted here on its publication in 2007. It deserves a mention, however, as it may be of considerable interest to those who have to teach *Beowulf*, particularly if they lack the time and space in their syllabi to cover the whole text in the original. Ringler provides a substantial introduction, tackling basics such as 'The Story' and 'The Hero', but also addressing more problematic areas such as 'Oral and Written *Beowulfs*' and 'Christianity and the Problem of Violence'. Alongside *Beowulf*, Ringler also translates *The Fight at Finnsburh*, *Deor*, and *The Wanderer* (to which he applies the title *A Meditation*, arguing that the poem is too miscellaneous to support the traditional title). Ringler attempts a metre closely modelled on that of the original poem, and provides an appendix (pp. cx–cxiii) classifying his verse-types according to the system proposed by Bliss in *The Metre of Beowulf*. Interestingly, he observes the old-fashioned practice of setting out each half-line as a new line.

An important new book on *Beowulf* is John F. Vickrey's *Beowulf and the Illusion of History*. Vickrey discusses the Finnsburh episode and Beowulf's killing of Dæghrefn in detail, arguing for interpretations of these episodes in the light of folktale motifs. The problematic forms *eotena* and *eotenum* in the Finnsburh episode, often taken as anomalous forms of the ethnonym 'Jute', should, in Vickrey's view, be interpreted as regular forms of the word *eoten* 'giant'. The attack on the Danes in the episode can be seen in the light of such an interpretation as a description of an attack by giants, with the Frisians representing a secondary addition to the folkloric material. The recounting of the Finnsburh episode as part of the celebrations of Beowulf's defeat of Grendel, Vickrey argues, can be better understood in terms of a monster-fight narrative which parallels that of Beowulf himself. The champion of the Hugas, Dæghrefn, should be understood, according to Vickrey, as a humanized version of a monster in an earlier version of the narrative, whose name 'day-raven' reflects the association of other monsters in the text with particular times of day (e.g. *uhtsceaða* at line 2271 and *uhtfloga* at line 2760 for the dragon). The Finnsburh episode is also the subject of Keri Wolf's essay on 'Enacting Ties that Bind: Oath-Making vs. Oath-Taking in the Finnsburg "Episode"' (*Comitatus* 40[2009] 1–24).

The problems of interpretation presented by Unferth's apparently impolite behaviour attracted renewed attention this year. In 'Cei, Unferth, and Access to the Throne' (*ES* 90[2009] 127–41), William Sayers re-examines the character of Unferth in the light of early Welsh depictions of Kay (Cei), particularly in *Culhwch and Olwen*. Sayers identifies in *Beowulf* a series of three challengers to newcomers approaching a royal hall, of which the last is a senior royal official such as Kay or Unferth who seeks to test or reject (in these cases, unsuccessfully) the newcomer. Kay's contumacious characteristics in the later romance tradition are, Sayers argues, an echo of his earlier role—a role that can also help us to understand the apparently problematic depiction of Unferth. Unferth is also the subject of Donovan's essay in Karkov, ed., *Poetry, Place, and Gender*, which argues for interpreting him as belonging to a tradition of wise fools in court settings, who may be warriors and counsellors, and not simply entertainers. The negative aspects of Unferth's character, Donovan argues, have been exaggerated, and his behaviour can in fact be interpreted in terms of prudent testing of an untried newcomer.

The question of politeness in Beowulf's dealings with Hrothgar is the focus of Michael R. Kightley, 'Reinterpreting Threats to Face: The Use of Politeness in *Beowulf*, ll. 407–472' (*Neophil* 93[2009] 511–20). Kightley argues that Beowulf's request to Hrothgar for permission to fight Grendel constitutes a face-threatening act that Hrothgar handles by reinterpreting the request in terms of his relationship with Beowulf's father and the repayment of a debt incurred by Ecgtheow.

Textual cruces in *Beowulf* remain a live area of debate. J.R. Hall, 'Beowulf 3179a: Hlafordes (Hry)re' (*N&Q* 56[2009] 166–9) presents a reading of these two words that supports [*hry*]*re* and suggests that we are dependent on the Thorkelin transcript for the final *-s* of *hlafordes*. The author also briefly discusses the history of modern readings of this phrase. Alfred Bammesberger also addresses a problematic reading in 'Hrothgar's Plight (Beowulf, Line 936)' (*N&Q* 56[2009] 330–2). He defends the manuscript reading of this line as 'wea widscofen witena gehwylcne', arguing that it can be understood as an absolute participle construction yielding the sense 'woe having scattered widely every one of the councillors' (p. 332).

The manuscript text of *Beowulf* more broadly also attracts attention. The reverberations of Michael Lapidge's discussion of 'The Archetype of *Beowulf*' (*ASE* 29[2000] 5–41; reviewed in *YWES* 81[2002] 153) continue to be felt. George Clark, 'The Date of *Beowulf* and the Arundel Psalter Gloss'

(*MP* 106[2009] 677–85), seeks to rebut E.G. Stanley's rebuttal, in 'Paleographical and Textual Deep Waters: [a] for [u] and [u] for [a], [d] for [ð] and [ð] for [d] in Old English' (*ANQ* 15:ii[2002] 64–72; reviewed in *YWES* 83[2004] 3), of Lapidge's piece. Kiernan (in Karkov, ed., *Poetry, Place, and Gender*) discusses folio 179 of the *Beowulf* manuscript, which he believes to be a palimpsest produced by deliberate erasure and rewriting of the folio by a third scribe contemporary with the two main scribes of *Beowulf*. This episode of rewriting, Kiernan contends, may have served to bring together an account of Beowulf as a young man ending on folio 178 and the narrative of Beowulf's dragon fight, and he goes on to address in detail the palaeographical problems presented by the imperfect text of folio 179. A broader perspective on the context of the manuscript and its texts is provided by Matthew T. Hussey's work on 'The Possible Relationship of the *Beowulf* and the Blicking Homilies Manuscripts' (*N&Q* 56[2009] 1–4). Examining the similarities between these two manuscripts, he suggests that, while conclusive evidence for a relationship between the two is lacking, their shared features could indicate that they were both produced in 'the same literarily odd and codicologically unconventional cultural centre' (p. 4).

This year has also seen new work on orality and its representations in *Beowulf*. Patrizia Aziz Hanna Noel, 'Layers of Versification in *Beowulf*' (*Anglia* 127[2009] 238–60), re-examines the versification of *Beowulf*, arguing that its complexity arises from the preservation of older Germanic patterns of versification that are impacted by subsequent phonological change. The discussion also seeks to relate these findings to performance patterns, suggesting ways in which verse-forms could be mapped to musical realizations. In 'Where Now the Harp? Listening for the Sounds of Old English Verse, from *Beowulf* to the Twentieth Century' (*OralT* 24[2009] 485–502), Chris Jones discusses the problematic representations of oral delivery within *Beowulf*, arguing for a disquiet about the continuance of such traditions, and setting this against the imitation of Old English patterns of versification in the work of twentieth-century poets including W.S. Graham and Edwin Morgan. Marie Nelson, 'Prefacing and Praising: Two Functions of "Hearing" Formulas in the *Beowulf* Story' (*NM* 110[2009] 487–95), discusses the phrases 'we gefrunon', 'ic gefrægn' and 'ic gehyrde' in *Beowulf*, and their negated counterparts, arguing that the negated versions serve to introduce evaluative statements of a superlative nature, while the non-negated forms preface material of whose credibility the poet wishes to persuade the audience. Dana M. Oswald, '"Wigge under Wætere": Beowulf's Revision of the Fight with Grendel's Mother' (*Exemplaria* 21[2009] 63–82), argues that Beowulf's fight with Grendel's mother is presented as a sexualized confrontation, and that this motivates Beowulf to conceal or elide its details in recounting the battle to Hrothgar and to Hygelac.

This year also sees fresh work on the role of the hall in *Beowulf*. Frank Battaglia's essay, 'Not Christianity versus Paganism, but Hall versus Bog: The Great Shift in Early Scandinavian Religion and its Implications for *Beowulf*' (in Kilpiö et al., eds., pp. 47–67), argues that the conflict between humans and monsters associated with watery places in *Beowulf* in fact reflects the tensions between an older, gynocentric cultic practice in Scandinavia centred around wetlands, and a new religious model focused on the hall and on masculine deities. A contrasting approach is Helen T. Bennett's discussion of 'The Postmodern Hall in *Beowulf*: Endings Embedded in Beginnings' (*HeroicA* 12[2009] 23 paras.). Bennett seeks to argue that the image of the hall in *Beowulf* can be understood as thematizing the indeterminacy of 'meaning making' in Anglo-Saxon society.

Heike Sahm, 'Unversöhnte Motivierungen. Der Schatz als Hindernis kohärenten Erzählens im "Beowulf"' (*BGDSL* 131[2009] 442–60), reads the presentation of the dragon's hoard in *Beowulf* as inconsistent, undermining Beowulf after his death. Before the dragon fight, Sahm argues, Beowulf's actions are presented as a justified response to aggression, but after his death they are refigured as an attempt at plunder. Francis Leneghan considers 'The Poetic Purpose of the Offa-Digression in *Beowulf*' (*RES* 60[2009] 538–60), arguing that the digression (*Beowulf* vv. 1931b–1962) is not an insertion in praise of Offa of Mercia, but rather an integral allusion to a well-known character of the heroic past, emphasizing the importance of royal marriage to secure dynastic succession, and foreshadowing Beowulf's failure to marry.

In '*Beowulf* Off the Map' (*ASE* 38[2010] 11–40), Alfred Hiatt casts doubt on the notion that *Beowulf* provides a representation of an imagined homeland for its Anglo-Saxon audiences, and suggests that the treatment of place in the poem can best be understood in terms of the interrelations between peoples, rather than a geographical sense of the areas involved. Tom Shippey's lecture, 'Kemble, *Beowulf*, and the Schleswig-Holstein Question' (in Jorgensen et al., eds., pp. 64–80), considers the political backdrop to Thorkelin's and Kemble's editions of *Beowulf*, and examines the ways in which Kemble's edition interacts with political concerns over the status of Schleswig-Holstein in relation to Denmark and Germany.

Nathan A. Breen writes on '*Beowulf*'s Wealhtheow and the *Đeowwealh*: A Legal Source for the Queen's Name' (*ANQ* 22:ii[2009] 2–4), suggesting that the term *ðeowwealh*, used in the laws of Ine to refer to a non-free non-English individual, may have prompted the *Beowulf*-poet's creation of the name Wealhtheow. Yvette Kisor's essay, 'Numerical Composition and *Beowulf*: A Reconsideration' (*ASE* 38[2010] 41–76), provides a critique of previous arguments for numerical composition in *Beowulf*, arguing that broad agreement in results between different scholars suggests the genuineness of some of the larger patterns identified. The significance of such patterning, however, has not, in Kisor's view, been adequately addressed.

Two articles this year address the artistry of *Judith*. Mark Sundaram considers 'Anterior Future Constructions and the Structure of Old English Narratives' (*NM* 110[2009] 267–81), examining the use of modal constructions using preterite forms of modal verbs to express the future in the past in Old English poetry. Focusing on *Beowulf* and *Judith*, he argues that such forms are used in structuring narratives through the use of foreshadowing. In 'Poetic Exuberance in the Old English *Judith*' (*SP* 106[2009] 119–36), Howell Chickering seeks to counteract what he perceives as a tendency in recent scholarship on *Judith* to treat the text within wider contexts—literary, historical, exegetical—by analysing the poem in terms of its poetic style, arguing for an exuberance of stylistic effect that supports the poem's 'central themes of Judith's wisdom and faith and God's mercy and grace toward His faithful' (p. 136).

In '*Beowulf* and Poststructuralist Theory' (*LitComp* 6[2009] 56–70) Mannish Sharma reviews the responses of Anglo-Saxonists to poststructuralist theory, then surveys studies of the poem which use this theoretical framework and proposes new directions. Walter Goffart's 'Hetware and Hugas: Datable Anachronisms in *Beowulf*' is republished this year in his *Barbarians, Maps and Historiography: Studies on the Early Medieval West* (pp. 245–62). [MS]

9. Other Poems

This year saw the publication of two important new editions of Old English verse from outside the four main poetic codices. Jonathan B. Himes edits *The Old English Epic of Waldere* with a facing-page translation, and provides a substantial introduction that considers the Walter legend and seeks to place the fragmentary Old English poem within it, as well as discussing the manuscript and the narrative that it represents. The treatment of the manuscript is illustrated with a number of useful ultraviolet photographs of the text (figs. 2-1 to 2-7) and includes a detailed discussion of scribal error (pp. 27–35). Appendices consider 'Weapons and Wargear' (p. 97) and 'Heroic Vocabulary and Versification' (p. 119). Chapter 4, 'The Epic Voices', makes a very helpful attempt at sorting out who is speaking when in the surviving fragments of the poem.

Daniel Anlezark's new edition of *The Old English Dialogues of Solomon and Saturn* is particularly welcome. Anlezark provides a thorough and careful edition of the texts, and argues that they were originally composed in early West Saxon, probably within a close circle of individuals: although they seem to represent original Old English compositions they reflect, as Anlezark demonstrates, considerable learning and some familiarity with Irish scholarship, and he suggests that they can plausibly be associated with Glastonbury, and perhaps with Dunstan at a relatively early stage in his career.

Worthwhile advice for would-be editors comes from Kazutomo Karasawa, who discusses 'Some Problems in the Editions of the *Menologium* with Special Reference to Lines 81a, 184b and 206a' (*N&Q* 56[2009] 485–7). Karasawa argues that the poet of the *Menologium* tended to use irregular forms of words deliberately for metrical purposes, and that we should therefore bear in mind this tendency in the poet when considering emending the manuscript text.

Writing on 'The Oldest English Proverb in Verse' (*N&Q* 56[2009] 4–7), Alfred Bammesberger reappraises the supposed compound *daedlata* in *A Proverb from Winfrid's Time*, arguing that it should instead be read as two words *daed lata* constituting the direct object and subject respectively of the first clause. This leads to a reading of the first line of the proverb as meaning 'often a sluggard delays the deed for the sake of glory' (p. 7). Bammesberger also tackles '*Fusæ* in the Runic Inscription on the *Ruthwell Cross*' (*N&Q* 56[2009] 7–9), proposing a reading of this word as an adverb, rather than an adjective used substantively (as it appears to be used in the parallel passage in *The Dream of the Rood*). 'Altenglisch *Scepen* in *Cædmons Hymnus* (M)' attracts Bammesberger's attention as well (*Anglia* 127[2009] 106–14). Bammesberger examines the form *scepen* in the Moore manuscript text of *Cædmon's Hymn*, arguing that it can be satisfactorily etymologized without recourse to emendation to *sceppend*.

Two Old English charms containing metrical material are the foci of discussions this year. László Sándor Chardonnens writes on 'An Arithmetical Crux in the Woden Passage in the Old English *Nine Herbs Charm*' (*Neophil* 93[2009] 691–702), arguing that Woden's use of nine *wuldortanas* to strike a snake into nine parts can best be explained as the use of nine instances of some sort of weapon to strike a snake that bites its own tail (i.e. a circular snake) into nine parts, since nine divisions of a linear snake would produce ten parts rather than nine. The other discussion of a charm containing metrical material involves the identification of a hitherto unnoticed piece of Old English verse by Andrew Rabin in 'Hypermetric Verse in an Old English Charm against Theft' (*N&Q* 56[2009] 482–5). The charm is preserved in Cambridge, Corpus Christi College, MSS 190 and 383, in the *Textus Roffensis* and in London, British Library, Cotton Tiberius A.iii, and is not one of those identified as metrical by the *Anglo-Saxon Poetic Records*. As Rabin demonstrates, however, the charm does contain a pair of regular hypermetric lines.

In 'An Anglo-Norman Nun: An Old English *Gnome*' (*N&Q* 56[2009] 16–18), Jane Bliss notes the parallel between a snippet of the *Vie d'Edouard le Confesseur* and Byrhtwold's speech in *The Battle of Maldon*, and raises the possibility of the Old English poem being known to the twelfth-century Barking nuns.

10. Prose

This year is notable for a particularly rich crop of new work on Bede. George Hardin Brown draws on many years of specialist study to offer *A Companion to Bede*. The volume opens with discussion of aspects of 'Bede's Life and Times', and then turns to consider his writings, which are discussed in categories: 'Educational Works', 'Biblical Commentaries', 'Homilies, Hagiography, Martyrology, Poems, Letters', and 'Histories'. There follows an overview of the transmission and influence of Bede's works, from the Carolingian to the early modern period, with a brief summary of recent scholarly approaches. The thorough coverage of Bede's writings, and the indices of works cited and of Bede's works, in addition to the general index, make this a most useful volume both for those already familiar with aspects of Bede's output and for those approaching its study for the first time. Brown also identifies a 'Quotation from Isidore in Bede's Commentary on Genesis 4:25–26' (*N&Q* 56[2009] 163) and suggests that the same source is quoted by Bede in *On the Reckoning of Time*.

Vicky Gunn's focus is *Bede's 'Historiae': Genre, Rhetoric and the Construction of Anglo-Saxon Church History*, and she approaches this via comparative studies of Bede's works and other compositions, organized into chapters on Bede's audience, contemporary Northumbrian hagiography and history-writing, monastic superiority in the *Ecclesiastical History*,

Bede's approach to the genre of *Historia*, his *History of the Abbots*, *Martyrology*, and compositional techniques.

W. Trent Foley and Nicholas J. Higham examine 'Bede on the Britons' (*EMedE* 17[2009] 154–85) with reference to indications in the *Historia Ecclesiastica* of Bede's attitude to Britons in his own time, highlight a greater degree of internal inconsistency and nuance than has often been assumed, and stress the shifting narrative imperatives of different chapters of the work. Sarah Foote examines textual reflections of 'Anglo-Saxon "Purgatory"' (*StCH* 45[2009] 87–96), with reference to Bede's account of Fursa's and Dryhthelm's visions and Boniface's reporting of the vision of the monk from Wenlock.

George Molyneux's 'The *Old English Bede*: English Ideology or Christian Instruction' (*EHR* 124[2009] 1289–1323) revisits Patrick Wormald's work in various publications on the political impact of the *Historia Ecclesiastica* in eighth- and ninth-century England. Molyneux examines the choices made by the translator of the Old English *Historia*, in particular omissions and abbreviations, and then turns to a detailed comparison of the preface of the Latin and Old English versions. His overall conclusions are that the Old English translator is less concerned to present a divinely privileged English people and more interested in providing examples of good Christian conduct. 'Bede and the Papacy' by John Moorhead (*JEH* 60[2009] 217–32) notes that Bede's references to the papacy in the *Historia Ecclesiastica* and elsewhere do not seem to imply any great understanding of papal procedures and authority, and contrasts this with the apparently sharper understanding of Boniface and Stephanus to argue that Bede had a relatively unsophisticated knowledge of the papacy. In 'Bede's Castella and the Journeys of St Chad' (*NH* 56[2009] 137–9), Andrew Breeze proposes a new translation of the phrase from the *Historia Ecclesiastica* 'oppida rura casas vicos castella' as 'cities, country areas, towns, villages, and homesteads'. 'Locating Ingetlingum and Suthgedling: Gilling West and Gilling East' by Thomas Pickles (*NH* 46[2009] 314–25) argues that these are the locations of the founding of a religious house in the aftermath of a battle between Oswiu and Oswine described in the *Historia Ecclesiastica*, and of a vill granted to Cuthbert as described in the *Historia de Sancto Cuthberto*. Paul Szarmach's and George Hardin Brown's essays on Bede, in Karkov, ed., *Poetry, Place, and Gender*, are reviewed in section 4 above.

Supplementing this new work on Bede is the republication of some key articles by Walter Goffart, in his *Barbarians, Maps and Historiography*. In addition to some important articles on migration-period population movements, reprinted here are 'Bede's *uera lex historiae* Explained' (pp. 121–6), 'The *Historia Ecclesiastica*: Bede's Agenda and Ours' (pp. 127–44), and 'Bede's *History* in a Harsher Climate' (pp. 145–68).

Reading the Anglo-Saxon Chronicle: Language, Literature, History, edited by Alice Jorgensen, offers studies of a wide range of topics. Jorgensen's introduction surveys the versions of the *Chronicle* and scholarly understanding of their development, and gives an overview of the essays which follow. '*Malcolm and Margaret*: The Poem in Annal 1067D', by Thomas A. Bredehoft, argues for the poem extending further than editors of the

Anglo-Saxon Poetic Records recognized, explores the implications of this for the relationship between the D and E versions, and proposes that the poet of *Malcolm and Margaret* was influenced by Ælfric. An appendix to the article presents a preliminary edition and translation of the poem, with textual notes. 'The Production of the Peterborough Chronicle' is reconstructed by Susan Irvine with reference to the manuscript context and the relationship of the Peterborough text to Latin chronicles. Irvine argues for some of the compiler's source-materials being in English, supports the case for transmission of historical texts between Canterbury, Malmesbury, and Worcester in the third and fourth decades of the twelfth century, and adds Peterborough to this network. 'Double-Edged Déjà Vu: The Complexity of the Peterborough Chronicle', by Malasree Home, investigates the reconstruction of the E-text of the *Chronicle* at Peterborough, in particular in the First Continuation, and argues for the first two phases of the Peterborough Chronicle being the work of a single compiler who may also have had overall responsibility for the production of the text. In 'Sentence to Story: Reading the Anglo-Saxon Chronicle as Formulary', Jacqueline Stodnick reviews scholarly attitudes to the *Chronicle* as history or literature and argues that its repetitive style is 'part of a coherent historiographic technique that mediates difference and disorder in the historical record itself by means of a deliberately restricted idiom' (p. 95). Alice Jorgensen's 'Rewriting the Æthelredian Chronicle: Narrative Style and Identity in Anglo-Saxon Chronicle MS F' also focuses on style and voice; this time in the Æthelredian Chronicle and its adaptation in the F-version. 'The Representation of Early West Saxon History in the Anglo-Saxon Chronicle', by Barbara Yorke, examines the annals for the seventh and eighth centuries for indications of the circumstances of the *Chronicle*'s compilation and makes a case for 'considerable intervention by the team who produced the version put into circulation around 890×92' (p. 158). Anton Scharer's 'The Anglo-Saxon Chronicle and Continental Annal-Writing' also focuses on the ninth-century compilation, and makes comparison with mainland European annals to show how the *Chronicle* is at once drawing on Carolingian examples and making innovative use of the vernacular for the writing of history.

In the same volume, 'Marking Boundaries: Charters and the Anglo-Saxon Chronicle', by Scott Thompson Smith, takes as its starting point the annals for 910–46 and their accounts of territorial expansion, and compares them with charters to show the *Chronicle* 'using the writing of territorial bounds as a means of articulating and maintaining the legitimate possession of land' (p. 168). Ryan Lavelle maps 'Geographies of Power in the Anglo-Saxon Chronicle: The Royal Estates of Anglo-Saxon Wessex' through references to significant places and their royal associations. 'Reporting Scotland in the Anglo-Saxon Chronicle', by Alex Woolf, uses the A-version as its main source to track Wessex's transformation into a kingdom of England. In 'Coins and the Chronicle: Mint-Signatures, History, and Language', Jayne Carroll presents an alternative body of evidence for language use and development which, when compared with the *Chronicle*, reveals the latter to be linguistically conservative in some respects. Sara M. Pons-Sanz identifies and analyses 'Norse-Derived Vocabulary in the Anglo-Saxon Chronicle' to track the development of terms from specific association with new Scandinavian settlers to wider use, the relationship of them with court-sanctioned language, and the evidence they offer for language use in Scandinavianized areas of England. The volume closes with a select bibliography of *Chronicle* scholarship, an index of annals, and a subject index. Further new work on the poetry in the *Chronicle* is reviewed in section 9 above.

The Old English Boethius, edited by Malcolm Godden and Susan Irvine, is a most welcome resource for scholars working on poetry and prose, Old English translation, and the place of these complex texts in the textual culture of the ninth and tenth centuries. In the first of two substantial volumes, Godden and Irvine present an introduction which gives a succinct overview of the composition, dissemination, and glossing of Boethius' *De Consolatione Philosophiae* and of the Old English versions; describes each of the Old English manuscripts, their relationship to each other, and their place in the transmission of the text; explores the Old English prose version and metres and their composition; maps the relationship of the Old English Boethius to other texts associated with the Alfredian translation programme; and discusses authorship, date, language, and influence on later texts. Full editions of the B and C texts and the Napier Fragment are provided, along with editions of passages from the works of Ælfric which make use of the Old English Boethius. The second volume contains modern English translations of the B and C texts, textual notes, a commentary, and a glossary and list of proper names.

In 'The Transmission of Boethius' *De Consolatione Philosophiae* in the Carolingian Age' (*MÆ* 78[2009] 1–15) Adrian Papahagi reassesses whether the text was known in Britain before the ninth or early tenth century, and suggests that it is more likely that the text reached England from a Carolingian centre like Fleury, where he argues that it was rediscovered in the late eighth or early ninth century, than via Alcuin. Papahagi supports Malcolm Godden's case (reviewed in *YWES* 88[2009] 186) for the Old English translation of the text being made in the first half of the tenth century rather than in the late ninth. Michael Treschow, Paramjit Gill, and Tim B. Schwartz re-examine 'King Alfred's Scholarly Writings and the Authorship of the First Fifty Prose Psalms' (*HeroicA* 12[2009] 81 paras), using statistical analysis to argue that Alfred is not the translator of the psalms, and to confirm that he did not translate *Orosius* or the *Ecclesiastical History*. Questions of authorship are also addressed by Janet Bately, who reframes Godden's question in 'Did King Alfred Actually Translate Anything? The Integrity of the Alfredian Canon Revisited' (*MÆ* 78[2009] 189–215). Bately assesses the integrity of the Alfredian canon in the light of linguistic evidence, drawing on Treschow, Gill, and Schwartz's work, amongst others, and noting that statistical analysis tends to overlook the influence of the source-text on a translator's choice of one word over another. She concludes that there is no reason not to assume that 'there was one mind at work' on the Old English *Pastoral Care*, *Consolation of Philosophy*, *Soliloquies* and Psalms, and that 'it is reasonable to conclude that that mind was King Alfred's' (p. 209).

Rebecca Stephenson continues to open up our understanding of the textual-political dynamics of the Anglo-Saxon Benedictine Reform.

In 'Scapegoating the Secular Clergy: The Hermeneutic Style as a Form of Monastic Self-Definition' (*ASE* 38[2009] 101–35), she argues that the negative depiction of secular clerics in Byrhtferth of Ramsey's *Enchiridion* aims less to criticize its apparent targets than to shore up a Benedictine Reform monastic self-image by negative example. Latinity, and in particular exclusive hermeneutic Latin, in this instance, is key to monastic identity.

An essential new assessment of Ælfric is provided by the specially commissioned essays in *A Companion to Ælfric*, edited by Hugh Magennis and Mary Swan. Hugh Magennis surveys past and present 'Ælfric Scholarship' (pp. 5–34), pointing to a renewed vigour in studies of Ælfric and his writings, in particular in areas such as his theological thought, his sources, his Latin writings and the transmission and reception of his works. Joyce Hill's piece 'Ælfric: His Life and Works' (pp. 35–65) traces Ælfric's career in detail, and considers his authorial output within this context. 'Ælfric and the Limits of "Benedictine Reform"' (pp. 67–108), by Christopher A. Jones, questions the notion that Ælfric's concern with monasticism should be conceptualized in terms of reform, and argues that his works in fact reveal a number of ways in which his thinking differed from that of those of his contemporaries commonly identified as reformers. Mechthild Gretsch, in 'Ælfric, Language and Winchester' (pp. 109–37), discusses Ælfric's use of the vernacular, situating it within 'Standard Old English' and discussing his use of Winchester vocabulary, as well as providing a stimulating discussion of his approach to Latin and the processes involved in translating it. Malcolm R. Godden discusses 'Ælfric and the Alfredian Precedents' (pp. 139–63), examining Ælfric's attitude to Alfredian texts and the ways in which he used—and avoided using—such texts. 'Ælfric's Lay Patrons' (pp. 165–92), by Catherine Cubitt, discusses the lives of Æthelweard and Æthelmær and their activities as Ælfric's patrons, and considers the nature of Ælfric's patronage from lesser gentry figures such as Sigeweard, Wulfgeat, and Sigefyrth.

Thomas N. Hall considers 'Ælfric as Pedagogue' (pp. 193–216), addressing the evidence for pedagogical approaches in the *Grammar*, *Glossary*, *Colloquy*, and *De Temporibus Anni*. In 'Catechetic Homiletics: Ælfric's Preaching and Teaching During Lent' (pp. 217–46), Robert K. Upchurch provides an account of Ælfric's homilies for Lent, focusing on their use of exegesis in elaborating moral teaching. Mary Swan discusses 'Identity and Ideology in Ælfric's Prefaces' (pp. 247–69), considering the ways in which Ælfric constructs authorial voices and positions in order to support his ideological concerns and to negotiate the dynamics of the relationship between author and addressee. 'In Ælfric's Words: Conversion, Vigilance and the Nation in Ælfric's *Life of Gregory the Great*' (pp. 271–96), by Clare A. Lees, examines the ways in which Ælfric's *Life of Gregory* presents the conversion of the English both in terms of its significance for English identity and in relation to its wider theological implications.

Gabriella Corona discusses 'Ælfric's Schemes and Tropes: *Amplificatio* and the Portrayal of Persecutors' (pp. 297–320), tracing the influence of classical and late antique rhetorical practices, and considering the relationship between Ælfric's practice and that of Aldhelm. 'Boredom, Brevity and Last Things: Ælfric's Style and the Politics of Time' (pp. 321–44), by Kathleen Davis, considers the ways in which Ælfric constructs an unlearned audience, and seeks to relate this to concepts of salvation history. Jonathan Wilcox dissects the manuscript evidence for practical use of Ælfric's homilies in preaching in non-elite contexts in 'The Use of Ælfric's Homilies: MSS Oxford, Bodleian Library, Junius 85 and 86 in the Field' (pp. 345–68), arguing that the homilies may have enjoyed a substantial circulation in booklet form, and in portable, lower-status manuscripts that rarely survive. 'Assembling Ælfric: Reconstructing the Rationale behind Eleventh- and Twelfth-Century Compilations' (pp. 369–98), by Aaron J. Kleist, considers the manuscript relationships between Ælfric's *De duodecim abusivis*, *De falsis diis*, and the *Interrogationes Sigeuulfi in Genesin*, three texts that frequently travel together: the manuscript contexts of these texts and others in the Ælfrician canon reflect various and complex processes of compilation and transmission in the centuries after Ælfric. Elaine Treharne discusses the evidence in post-Conquest manuscripts for active engagement with Ælfric's writings in 'Making their Presence Felt: Readers of Ælfric, *c.*1050–1350' (pp. 399–422). [PS]

A new edition of *Ælfric's 'De Temporibus Anni'* is published by Martin Blake this year. In an introduction, Blake discusses Ælfric's career and the place of this work in his output, previous editions, the manuscripts, sources, and the wider topics of medieval cosmology, calendar, and computus. The edited text is presented without any on-page notes or collation, but with facing-page modern English translation; appendices compare Ælfric's biblical quotations with the Vulgate, and list biblical references in the text, parallels between the text and other works by Ælfric, and manuscript variants. An index to astronomical and calendrical terms, glossary, bibliography, and general index make the volume of use to scholars experienced and new.

In '*þam gecyrredum mannum* in Ælfric's Homily "Natale Sancti Pauli" (ÆCHom 1.27)' (*N&Q* 56[2009] 14–16), Petra Hofmann argues that 'gecyrredum' here means 'monastic'. 'A Demilitarized Saint: Ælfric's *Life of St. Sebastian*', by Damian Fleming (*Anglia* 127[2009] 1–21), compares Ælfric's text with its Latin source to show that his rendering of this saint's life differs from his treatment of other male secular military martyrs and argues that this might be the result of Ælfric's desire for narrative and moral clarity. Carl Phelpstead's essay on Ælfric's *Life of Edmund* is reviewed in section 3 above.

Mary Clayton ponders 'Suicide in the Works of Ælfric' (*RES* 60[2009] 339–70), via a survey of early medieval attitudes to suicide and with a focus on Ælfric's treatment of suicides in biblical narrative and in his *Catholic Homilies* for the feasts of Stephen, Matthew, and Martin. Clayton examines Ælfric's sources for narrative details and ideas on suicide and examines his linking of excessive fasting and suicide in his introduction to *De octo uitiis et de duodecim abuisiuis gradus* in order to emphasize his hard line on the guilt of a person who attempts suicide.

In 'Strange Hybrids: Ælfric, Vergil and the Lynx in Anglo-Saxon England' (*N&Q* 56[2009] 163–6), Emily V. Thornbury suggests that an alphabetical glossary such as the Corpus Glossary might lie behind Ælfric's conflation of the lycisca with the lynx in his own *Glossary*. Kiriko Sato offers a study of the influence of Latin on Ælfric's Old English writings in 'The Absolute Participle Construction in Old English: Ælfric's Exploitation of the Latinate Syntax in his Vernacular Prose' (*ES* 90[2009] 2–16), tracking his distinctive and changing use of the construction and linking it to his fluent and creative translation style.

Samantha Zacher publishes important new work on the Vercelli Homilies this year, in the form of a coedited collection of essays and a monograph. In *Preaching the Converted: The Style and Rhetoric of the Vercelli Book Homilies*, she offers the first sustained stylistic analysis of these texts, via chapters exploring questions of originality, themes, adaptation and compilation, body and soul, figurative language, generic ambiguity, rhetorical models, and modes of style. The variety of styles and techniques used across the Vercelli Homilies is emphasized, as is the influence of Latin and vernacular traditions. Appendices set out the contents of the Vercelli Homilies and selected variant texts and divisions in the manuscript, and the general index is supplemented by an index of passages cited.

In their introduction to *New Readings in the Vercelli Book* (pp. 3–11), Samantha Zacher and Andy Orchard emphasize the richness of the connections of the manuscript's contents with other texts and with wider Anglo-Saxon textual traditions, and summarize the collection's essays. 'The Vercelli Prose and Anglo-Saxon Literary History', by Paul E. Szarmach (pp. 12–40), contributes an invigorating argument that 'the Vercelli homilies offer the literary historian a book of styles that for later literary history has a double effect: the twenty-three prose pieces offer a baseline for what the later period will produce in direct development and for what the later period will develop on its own. The Vercelli prose is the *fons et origo* not precisely in a source relation but rather as a set of potential directions and paths for later prose writers' (pp. 12–13), and flags up the ways in which the work of Ælfric and Wulfstan can be seen as the development of different aspects of Vercelli homiletic style. 'Studies in the Language of Copyists of the Vercelli Homilies', by Donald G. Scragg (pp. 41–61), draws on the Manchester Centre for Anglo-Saxon Studies 'Inventory of Script and Spellings in Eleventh-Century English' database (http://www.arts.manchester.ac.uk/mancass/C11database/) to examine each manuscript which contains a Vercelli homily for indications of the language underlying the surviving version(s). He concludes that late Old English is less uniform than is often supposed, and calls for further study of the important, but often ignored, variations across texts.

'The Portents at Christ's Birth in Vercelli Homilies V and VI: Some Analogues from Medieval Sermons and Biblical Commentaries', by Thomas N. Hall (pp. 62–97), plots the relationship between a surprisingly wide range of texts which describe the portents of Christ's birth in ways which suggest connections with Vercelli V and VI, and analyses them to propose that both Vercelli homilies draw on traditions 'current in Hiberno-Latin exegetical literature by the late seventh or early eighth century' (p. 97), that Vercelli V is most likely drawing on a version of a text in the Homiliary of Saint Père de Chartres, and that Vercelli VI probably has access to the tradition at a later point of its development. Samantha Zacher reveals 'The Source of Vercelli VII: An Address to Women' (pp. 98–149) to be half of a Latin translation of John Chrysostomon's Homily XXIX on the epistle to the Hebrews. Zacher provides a tabulated comparison of Vercelli VII and its source, and notes that

Vercelli VII's interest in 'the behaviour and spirituality of women' (p. 127) is paralleled by two other texts in the Vercelli Book: *Elene* and Homily XVII.

In 'Vercelli Homily XV and *The Apocalypse of Thomas*' (pp. 150–84) Charles D. Wright focuses on Vercelli XV's alterations of its source to show that the Vercelli version emphasizes corruption amongst kings, popes, bishops, and ealdormen, and to propose that this might indicate a secular clerical response to the Benedictine Reform. An appendix to Wright's article discusses the authenticity of the letter of John XII to King Edgar, and argues that it is likely to be, or to be based on, a genuine original. 'Vercelli Homilies XIX–XXI, the Ascension Day Homily in Cambridge, Corpus Christi College 162, and the Catechetical Tradition from Augustine to Wulfstan', by Michael Fox (pp. 254–79), examines these homilies, the work of the same anonymous author, to argue that they follow Augustine's guidelines for educating catechumenates and foreshadow Ælfric's and Wulfstan's later preaching texts with the same aim. The volume closes with 'The Vercelli Book and its Texts: A Guide to Scholarship', by Paul G. Remley (pp. 318–415), a substantial bibliography of work on the Vercelli Book organized into sections for each of the poems and for the Vercelli Homilies.

Stephen Pelle investigates 'The *Revelationes* of Pseudo-Methodius and "Concerning the Coming of Antichrist" in British Library MS Cotton Vespasian D. XIV' (*N&Q* 56[2009] 324–30) to show that this text was definitely known to at least one Old English author, and to identify which recension was most likely available to them.

Peter J. Dendle offers 'The Old English "Life of Malchus" and Two Vernacular Tales from the *Vitas Patrum* in MS Cotton Otho C.i: A Translation' (*ES* 90[2009]: part 1, *ES* 90:v[2009] 505–15; part 2, *ES* 90:vi[2009] 631–52). The translations are preceded, in part 1 of the article, by a discussion of the texts, their histories, and the context of their copying into Otho C.i in mid-eleventh-century Worcester; a description of the manuscript; and textual sources. Part 2 of the article contains the edition and translation of the texts. In '*þoðer* and *top* in the Old English Apollonius of Tyre' (*N&Q* 56[2009] 12–14), William Sayers examines the translation choices behind the use of these two words.

Catherine Cubitt offers new insight into late Anglo-Saxon lay literacy in '"As the Lawbook Teaches": Reeves, Lawbooks and Urban Life in the Anonymous Old English Legend of the Seven Sleepers' (*EHR* 124[2009] 1021–49). Noting the unique example in this text of a reference to the use of a *domboc* by a reeve in sentencing a criminal, Cubitt sets this in the context of other late Anglo-Saxon references to laypeople using texts to demonstrate the likelihood of an environment of 'pragmatic literacy, administrative vitality and urban and economic sophistication' (p. 1048), and to argue that 'everyday justice was informed by the lawbooks' (p. 1049).

Katherine O'Brien O'Keeffe, *Stealing Obedience: Narratives of Agency in Later Anglo-Saxon England*, discusses the nature of agency in Wulfstan of Winchester's life of St Æthelwold, Ælfric's homily on St Benedict in the second series of the *Catholic Homilies* and in B's life of St Dunstan. Looking at narratives of monastic obedience, O'Brien O'Keeffe argues that obedience requires an act of interpretation on the part of someone who obeys an order. [PS]

Christopher M. Cain ponders 'Sacred Words, Anglo-Saxon Piety, and the Origins of the *Epistola Salvatoris* in London, British Library, Royal 2.A.xx' (*JEGP* 108[2009] 168–89). The manuscript in question was written in Mercia in the late eighth or early ninth century and contains a mixture of biblical and liturgical texts, apocrypha, and prayers. Cain's focus is on one of the apocryphal texts: the letter of Joseph to Abgar; he outlines the history of this legend, argues that it was probably known in the early Anglo-Saxon period, and examines the version in Royal 2.A.xx, which is the only direct Anglo-Saxon textual witness to the text. Cain proposes Theodore's Canterbury school as a context for the copying of the legend, and Bishop Oftfor of Worcester as the person who transmitted it from Canterbury to Worcester.

Books Reviewed

Anlezark, Daniel, ed. and trans. *The Old English Dialogues of Solomon and Saturn*. Brewer. [2009] pp. xii + 167 £50 ISBN 9 7818 4384 2033.

Bale, Anthony, ed. *St Edmund King and Martyr: Changing Images of a Medieval Saint*. York Medieval Press. [2009] pp. xi + 198. £50 ISBN 9 7819 0315 3260.

Baxter, Stephen, Catherine E. Karkov, Janet L. Nelson, and David Pelteret, eds. *Early Medieval Studies in Memory of Patrick Wormald*. Ashgate. [2009] pp. xix + 582. £85 ISBN 9 7807 5466 3317.

Bitterli, Dieter. *Say What I Am Called: The Old English Riddles of the Exeter Book and the Anglo-Latin Riddle Tradition*. UTorP. [2009] pp. xii + 218. $75 ISBN 9 7808 0209 3523.

Blair, John, ed. *Waterways and Canal-Building in Medieval England*. OUP. [2007] pp. xiii + 315. £67 ISBN 9 7801 9921 7151.

Blake, Martin, ed. and trans. Ælfric's '*De Temporibus Anni*'. Anglo-Saxon Texts 6. Brewer. [2009] pp. xii + 177. £50 ISBN 9 7818 4384 1937.

Bolton, Timothy. *The Empire of Cnut the Great: Conquest and the Consolidation of Power in Northern Europe in the Early Eleventh Century*. Brill. [2009] pp. xvi + 351 + 22. plates. €119 ($176) ISBN 9 7890 0416 6707.

Bredehoft, Thomas A. *Authors, Audiences, and Old English Verse*. UTorP. [2009] pp. xviii + 237. $65 ISBN 9 7808 0209 9457.

Brown, George Hardin. *A Companion to Bede*. Boydell. [2009] pp. ix + 167. £45 ISBN 9 7818 4383 4762.

Carver, Martin, Catherine Hills, and Jonathan Scheschkewitz. *Wasperton: A Roman, British and Anglo-Saxon Community in Central England*. Boydell. [2009] pp. x + 372. £60 ISBN 9 7818 4383 4274.

Chester-Kadwell, Mary. *Early Anglo-Saxon Communities in the Landscape of Norfolk*. BAR British Series 481. Archaeopress. [2009] pp. xi + 235. £50 ISBN 9 7814 0730 4168.

Chewning, Susannah M., ed. *The Milieu and Context of the Wooing Group*. UWalesP. [2009] pp. xiii + 236. £75 ISBN 9 7807 0832 0334.
Clark, David. *Between Medieval Men: Male Friendship and Desire in Early Medieval English Literature*. OUP. [2009] pp. xii + 229. £56 ISBN 9 7801 9955 8155.
Crawford, Sally, and Helena Hamerow, eds. (with Leslie Webster). *Form and Order in the Anglo-Saxon World, AD 600–1100*. ASSAH 16. Oxford University School of Archaeology. [2009] pp. 128. pb £35 ISBN 9 7819 0590 5133.
Devlin, Zoë L., and Caroline N.J. Holas-Clark, eds. *Approaching Interdisciplinarity: Archaeology, History and the Study of Early Medieval Britain, c.400–1100*. BAR British Series 486. Archaeopress. [2009] pp. 75. £26 ISBN 9 7814 0730 4410.
Edwards, A.G., and Takako Kato, eds. *New Directions in Medieval English Editing*. Poetica 71. Yushodo Press. [2008] pp. 104. ¥4500 ISBN 9 7848 4190 5175.
Godden, Malcolm, and Susan Irvine, eds. *The Old English Boethius: An Edition of the Old English Versions of Boethius's 'De Consolatione Philosophiae'*, 2 vols. OUP. [2009] pp. xlvi + 547. (vol. 1), pp. 631 (vol. 2). £215 ISBN 9 7801 9925 9663.
Goffart, Walter. *Barbarians, Maps, and Historiography: Studies on the Early Medieval West*. Ashgate Variorum. [2009] pp. xi + 331. £85 ISBN 9 7807 5465 9846.
Gunn, Cate, and Catherine Innes-Parker, eds. *Texts and Traditions of Medieval Pastoral Care: Essays in Honour of Bella Millett*. YMP. [2009] pp. xx + 217. £50 ISBN 9 7819 0315 3291.
Gunn, Vicky. *Bede's 'Historiae': Genre, Rhetoric and the Construction of Anglo-Saxon Church History*. Boydell. [2009] pp. 256. £50 ISBN 9 7818 4383 4656.
Hill, Joyce, ed. *Old English Minor Heroic Poems*, 3rd edn. Durham Medieval and Renaissance Texts 2. Centre for Medieval and Renaissance Studies, Durham University. PIMS. [2009] pp. viii + 131. pb $21.95 ISBN 9 7808 8844 5629.
Himes, Jonathan B., ed. and trans. *The Old English Epic of Waldere*. CSP. [2009] pp. xv + 142. £34.99 ISBN 9 7814 4380 5582.
Jefferson, Judith, and Ad Putter, eds. *Approaches to the Metres of Alliterative Verse*. LTM NS 17. School of English, University of Leeds. [2009] pp. 311. pb £40 ISBN 9 7808 5316 2766.
Jorgensen, Alice, ed. *Reading the Anglo-Saxon Chronicle: Language, Literature, History*. Brepols. [2009] pp. xvi + 344. €60 ISBN 9 7825 0352 3941.
Jorgensen, Alice, Helen Conrad-O'Briain, and John Scattergood, eds. *The Kemble Lectures on Anglo-Saxon Studies 2005–8*. School of English, Trinity College, Dublin. [2009] pp. vi + 103. pb £10 ISBN 9 7809 5550 2569.
Karkov, Catherine E., ed. *Poetry, Place, and Gender: Studies in Medieval Culture in Honor of Helen Damico*. MIP. [2009] pp. viii + 380. $70 ISBN 9 7815 8044 1278.

Kilpiö, Matti, Leena Kahlas-Tarkka, Jane Roberts, and Olga Timofeeva, eds. *Anglo-Saxons and the North: Essays Reflecting the Theme of the 10th Meeting of the International Society of Anglo-Saxonists in Helsinki, August 2001*. Medieval and Renaissance Texts and Studies 364. Essays in Anglo-Saxon Studies 1. ACMRS. [2009] pp. viii + 191. £32 ISBN 9 7808 6698 4126.

Lansing, Carol, and Edward D. English, eds. *A Companion to the Medieval World*. Wiley-Blackwell. [2009] pp. xii + 584. £110 ($132) ISBN 9 7814 0510 9222.

Leahy, Kevin, and Roger Bland. *The Staffordshire Hoard*. BMP. [2009] pp. 48. £4.99 ISBN 9 7807 1412 3288.

Lemon, Rebecca, Emma Mason, Jonathan Roberts, and Christopher Rowland, eds. *The Blackwell Companion to the Bible in English Literature*. Wiley-Blackwell. [2009] pp. x + 703. £110 ISBN 9 7814 0513 1605.

Magennis, Hugh, and Mary Swan, eds. *A Companion to Ælfric*. Brill. [2009] pp. xvi + 466. €146 ISBN 9 7890 0417 6812.

Mortimer, Richard, ed. *Edward the Confessor: The Man and the Legend*. Boydell. [2009] pp. xii + 203. £45 ISBN 9 7818 4383 4366.

O'Brien O'Keeffe, Katherine. *Stealing Obedience: Narratives of Agency in Later Anglo-Saxon England*. H.M. Chadwick Memorial Lectures 19. Department of Anglo-Saxon, Norse and Celtic, University of Cambridge. [2009] pp. 22. pb £5 ISBN 9 7809 5545 6893.

Owen-Crocker, Gale, ed. *Working with Anglo-Saxon Manuscripts*. UExeP. [2009] pp. xvi + 320. hb £65 ($115) ISBN 9 7808 5989 8409, pb £25 ($50) ISBN 9 7808 5989 8416.

Palmer, James. *Anglo-Saxons in a Frankish World, 690–900*. Brepols. [2009] pp. xii + 324. €70 ISBN 9 7825 0351 9111.

Pfaff, Richard W. *The Liturgy in Medieval England: A History*. CUP. [2009] pp. xxviii + 593. £80; $96 ISBN 9 7805 2180 8477.

Potter, John F. *Patterns in Stonework: The Early Church in Britain and Ireland. An Introduction to Ecclesiastical Geography*. BAR British Series 496. Archaeopress. [2009] pp. xxv + 191. £53 ISBN 9 7814 0730 6001.

Ringler, Dick, trans. *Beowulf: A New Translation for Oral Delivery*. Hackett. [2007] pp. cxiv + 188. pb £6.95 ISBN 9 7808 7220 8933.

Roberts, Jane. *Guthlac of Crowland. A Saint for Middle England*. Fursey Occasional Paper 3. Fursey Pilgrims. [2009] pp. 36. £3 ISBN 0 9544 7733 2.

Saunders, Corinne, ed. *A Companion to Medieval Poetry*. Wiley-Blackwell. [2010] pp. xviii + 683. £110 ISBN 9 7814 0515 9630.

Sayer, Duncan, and Howard Williams, eds. *Mortuary Practices and Social Identities in the Middle Ages: Essays in Burial Archaeology in Honour of Heinrich Härke*. UExeP. [2009] pp. xiii + 306. £60 ($110) ISBN 9 7808 5989 8317.

Stafford, Pauline, ed. *A Companion to the Early Middle Ages: Britain and Ireland c.500–c.1100*. Wiley-Blackwell. [2009] pp. xx + 554. £110 ($132) ISBN 9 7814 0510 6283.

Townend, Matthew. *The Vikings and Victorian Lakeland: The Norse Medievalism of W.G. Collingwood and his Contemporaries*. Cumberland

and Westmorland Antiquarian and Archaeological Society Extra Series 34. [2009] pp. xv + 328. £35 ISBN 9 7818 7312 4499.

Trilling, Renée R. *The Aesthetics of Nostalgia: Historical Representation in Old English Verse*. UTorP. [2009] pp. xiv + 296. $75 ISBN 9 7808 0209 9716.

Vickrey, John F. *Beowulf and the Illusion of History*. LehighUP. [2009] pp. 254. $57.50 ISBN 9 7809 8014 9661.

Zacher, Samantha. *Preaching the Converted: The Style and Rhetoric of the Vercelli Book Homilies*. UTorP. [2009] pp. xxviii + 348. CAN$75 ISBN 9 7808 0209 1581.

Zacher, Samantha, and Andy Orchard, eds. *New Readings in the Vercelli Book*. UTorP. [2009] pp. x + 426. £55 ISBN 9 7808 0209 8696.

III

Later Medieval: Excluding Chaucer

JENNIFER N. BROWN, CARRIE GRIFFIN,
JURIS G. LIDAKA, RALUCA RADULESCU,
MICHELLE M. SAUER AND GREG WALKER

This chapter has the following sections: 1.General and Miscellaneous; 2. Women's Writing; 3. Alliterative Verse and Lyrics; 4. The *Gawain*-Poet; 5. *Piers Plowman*; 6. Romance; 7. Gower, Lydgate, Hoccleve; 8. Malory and Caxton; 9. Middle Scots Poetry; 10. Drama. Sections 1 and 7 are by Juris Lidaka; sections 2 and 9 are by Jennifer N. Brown; section 3 is by Carrie Griffin; sections 4 and 5 are by Michelle M. Sauer; sections 6 and 8 are by Raluca Radulescu; section 10 is by Greg Walker.

1. General and Miscellaneous

This is a good year for reference tools. Margaret Connolly presents *The Index of Middle English Prose Handlist XIX: Manuscripts in the University Library, Cambridge (Dd–Oo)*, making available in a single large but handy volume the prose works scattered throughout the multi-volume catalogue by Charles Hardwick and Henry R. Luard roughly a century and a half ago. The collection has been well mined for quite some time, and the date of Hardwick and Luard's manuscript catalogue brings to the fore how necessary Connolly's welcome modern updates are: articles from the nineteenth through to the twenty-first century, EETS editions from early in the last century on, a host of key dissertations, and reference tools even from the last decade. A short history of the collection is followed by a more detailed description of the prose contents, most of which are religious and frequently anonymous; many are yet to be edited, such as some works by Richard Rolle, Eleanor Hull, and Lollards. Secular works include many by well-known names such as Chaucer and Trevisa, but extend to scientific materials, arboriculture, animal husbandry, physiognomy, alchemy, heraldry, and language. Not all the manuscripts in the two-letter classes were checked, of course, and over 800 that were checked proved to have no Middle English materials (a list of their shelfmarks is provided). Nor are incunabula and manuscripts in the Additional collection

The Year's Work in English Studies, Volume 90 (2011)
doi:10.1093/ywes/mar008

included. After a necessarily lengthy summary table of contents, the index itself follows in shelfmark order with the prose items individually detailed, including references to other manuscript copies of the texts, not simply printed references.

More than 300 manuscripts are catalogued in Jayne Ringrose's *Summary Catalogue of the Additional Medieval Manuscripts in Cambridge University Library Acquired before 1940*, including fragments that received Additional numbers but otherwise excluding collections of fragments, so some pieces of the *South English Legendary* are described here, as are some poems by Charles d'Orleans, miscellaneous English verse, and Thomas's *Roman de Horn*. Ringrose ascribes a good portion of this collection to the four scholar-librarians—Henry Bradshaw, William Robertson Smith, Francis John Henry Jenkinson, and Alwyn Faber Scholfield. The contents have been known, for the most part, but having a published summary catalogue greatly eases research for those without ready access to the university library itself. Additional 43, a fragmentary *Three Kings of Cologne*, is the only manuscript to have been described before, in 1867, as item 43 among the Patrick Papers in the fifth volume of *A Catalogue of the Manuscripts Preserved in the Library of the University of Cambridge* (p. 185). Complete or at least extensive works include Langland's *Piers Plowman*, Lydgate's *Siege of Thebes* (one the copy written by Stephen Dodesham), Gower's *Mirour de l'Omme*, a *Brut Chronicle*, the *South English Legendary* and other saints' lives in English and Latin, the *Prick of Conscience*, the *Speculum Vitae* possibly by William of Nassington, Nicholas Love's *Mirror of the Blessed Life of Jesus Christ* and more (one copy from his own priory), Hilton's *Scale of Perfection*, Gaytryge's *Lay Folks' Catechism*, several Wycliffite Bibles, Ranulph Higden's *Polychronicon*, Richard of Bury's *Philobiblon*, a chronicle roll in book form, and various histories, chronicles, devotional works, and sermons. As a summary catalogue, the volume aims to keep descriptive matters to a minimum, and both the works' entries and the notes on provenance are often highly detailed yet concise.

Equally thick but a much more imposing folio-sized volume is R.M. Thomson's *A Descriptive Catalogue of the Medieval Manuscripts of Merton College, Oxford, with a Description of the Greek Manuscripts by N.G. Wilson*. This catalogue's entries are different from the minimalist Latin entries in Henry Coxe's 1852 catalogue; for example, Coxe devoted nearly four full quarto columns to describing MS 248, a composite volume with many contents ranging across sermons, sermon aids, canon law, and John Beleth's *Summa de officiis ecclesiasticis*, and he added eight snippets of English verse in the sermons; however, Thomson presents about five folio columns and lists thirty-nine numbers from the *New Index of Middle English Verse*, along with much more information. Coxe's rare omissions are noted, but more importantly Thomson's introduction opens with manuscripts or parts of them that have moved elsewhere since Coxe. Merton was founded in 1264 and most of its manuscripts were in the library (a late fourteenth-century building) before the Reformation; naturally, the holdings represent the courses of study in Merton and Oxford more broadly: the arts, theology, philosophy, law, and medicine, which Merton's founder forbade. Accordingly, we find Gilbertus Anglicus'

Lilium medicinae, Anselm, Roger Bacon, Bede, Bracton, Robert Grosseteste, Walter of Henley, Albertus Magnus, Walter Map, Alexander Nequam, Ockham, *La terre des Sarazins* (not in Dean and Boulton no. 332), John of Salisbury, John Duns Scotus, *Spiritus Guidonis* (the widespread Latin prose behind various English versions known by titles such as the *Gast of Gy*), Philippe de Thaon's *Bestiary*, Nicholas Trevet, and William Woodford, but not Wyclif. Texts we might consider more literary include several works by Richard Rolle, the *Stimulus conscientiae* ascribed to him, Walter Hilton in Latin, William of Newburgh's *Historia rerum Anglicarum*, Richard de Castre's 'Prayer to Jesus', brief verses in margins, some prose selections, and French and English prose and verse in sermons, with additional matters in English. Very welcome and useful are the 100 plates illustrating, for example, the library itself, bindings, ownership, chaining, script, scribal names or script (including William of Malmesbury), and decoration.

Peter Kidd adds a 'Supplement to the Guide to Medieval and Renaissance Manuscripts in the Huntington Library' (*HLQ* 72[2009] 1–101) to Consuelo Dutschke's *Guide* of 1987, with twenty-seven manuscripts or fragments; in addition to service books, there is a copy of William Lyndwood's *Constitutiones provinciales* and some astrological treatises in English. Several minor prayers and legal materials in English appear, and one manuscript was owned by Bregett Jernegan, whose name is on the flyleaves of the Ellesmere Chaucer, while another refers to her father.

More editions also are made available to researchers. For EETS, Fiona Somerset has edited *Four Wycliffite Dialogues: Dialogue between Jon and Richard, Dialogue between a Friar and a Secular, Dialogue between Reson and Gabbyng, Dialogue between a Clerk and a Knight*. Each dialogue appears in a separate manuscript, all were composed apparently within two decades either side of 1400, and none have been published before (except in a thesis), although some were clearly consulted and studied as late as the early seventeenth century. Somerset finds some other reasons for placing these four together and notes that their argumentative form aids readers in learning about some of the basic ideas in 'lollardy' (uncapitalized throughout), here moving from antifraternal criticism through the correct mode of living to the relationship between church and state in England and that between the church in England and the church at large.

Although it is clear that authorship varies between them, a Midlandization of language and selected expressions and topics of concern helps confirm Lollard authorship, whether individual or committee. The first dialogue evidently alludes to Richard FitzRalph through the speakers' names and may refer to the end of *Piers Plowman*. The second addresses itself to the duke of Gloucester (probably Thomas of Humphrey) and is curiously tinged with Latinate academic disputation, while the third is a free rendering of Wyclif's *Dialogus* (or *Speculum ecclesie militantis*) and shares with the first dialogue the 'al if' conjunction common among Wycliffite sermons and a few other works. The fourth continues a tradition of dialogues concerning papal authority, such as one by Ockham and another translated by Trevisa, and it shows the typical Lollard belief that royal power is obligated to rein in clerical abuses. The linguistic analysis is keyed to LALME references, and the discussion of editorial method distinguishes between general procedures and those peculiar to the individual dialogues. The editions themselves are in usual EETS style, followed by explanatory notes that often focus on theological points, a glossary, and two short indexes. One novelty is the use of electronic sources: the texts of Ockham's *Dialogus* and Grosseteste's *Dicta* are only online, but online versions of some published texts (for example, the *Corpus iuris canonici*) were also used, no doubt because they are searchable.

John Mirk's *Festial* is being re-edited by Susan Powell, with the first of two volumes out this year and the second expected next year. Austin canon and later prior of the abbey of Lilleshall near the Welsh Marches, Mirk probably wrote the *Festial* in the late 1380s, placing sermons in order of the church year, from Advent onwards; not long after, it was revised nearby and organized into service-book order of *temporale* and *sanctorale*; after 1434, the sermons were rewritten and added to, and it was printed multiple times in the fourteenth and fifteenth centuries. His three works—the *Festial*, the *Instructions for Parish Priests* in couplets, and the Latin, more advanced *Manuale Sacerdotis*—were all envisaged as pastoral instruction and assistance for the under-educated parish priest. As often happens, the plan for the *Festial* was somewhat superseded during its execution, so to the original sixty-four sermons are added four more scattered within the original ones and six more added after them in selected manuscripts. This volume includes the opening prayer, prologue, and first forty-nine sermons, with the rest to come in the second volume, along with the explanatory notes and glossary.

Powell's introduction discusses Mirk, the sermons (with some emphasis on literary features) and their transmission, manuscript relationships, scribal production, and her choice of the base manuscript, and is followed by a bibliography. Linguistic comments on the base manuscript's several hands are included in the descriptions of those hands, each illustrated by a plate (reduced to nearly half-size), but there is no linguistic analysis of the work, although it is noted that Mirk was probably from the north of England, despite being in Shropshire when writing. Rather extensive codicological discussion is used to pose how the base manuscript was written and constructed, and the introduction ends with a summary of textual relationships among the witness manuscripts, reasons for choosing the base manuscript (date, contents, location, and indications of authorship), and editorial policy and procedures. The text is the usual EETS text, with page-bottom apparatus restricted to limited observations on the status of the text in the base manuscript and its readings when corrected.

Susanna Fein's TEAMS edition of John the Blind Audelay's *Poems and Carols* (Oxford Bodleian Library MS Douce 302) announces that it is the first to offer all works by Audelay († after 1426). Although technically that is correct, it overlooks some aspects of Ella Keats Whiting's 1931 EETS edition (OS 184): entitled *The Poems of John Audelay*, it did not intend to edit the prose (included here pp. 211–15) and thus omitted an embedded verse, it focused on the English verse and therefore excluded the long Latin poem (here pp. 222–3) but not some shorter Latin passages connected to larger English works, and—rather than wholly omitting 'Instructions for Reading 1' as implied on p. 31—it actually moved the quatrain to the introduction (p. vii);

unfortunately, it failed to record or even mention the 'Drawing of the Holy Face on the Vernicle' so handy for understanding the following poem (p. 173). Douce 302 is missing the opening leaves, perhaps nineteen of them, so the first surviving work begins (and ends) imperfect and the next is numbered XI; thus, probably nine prior works are lost in addition to portions on other leaves now missing. The scribe numbered thirty-eight items, but other numberings are possible; for example, there are twenty-five carols although the scribe numbered the whole sequence as one item. Fein and Whiting disagree in their editorial divisions, but the total number of poems is quite impressive, particularly in the organization, for overall the works are grouped by 'genre' and then arranged within each 'genre' according to a sequence determined for devotional effect. Most of the introduction is devoted to reading these 'genres' and their sequences, but special attention is paid to Audelay's consciousness of his authorship, unusual for its time but not ours. Pointedly mentioned but not detailed is Audelay's experimentation with verse form: 'to judge from the range of verse styles in his book, Audelay was an aficionado of metrical variety and musical form' (p. 3), including a favourite thirteen-line stanza $ababbcbc_4d_3eee_4d_3$ and occasional alliterative verse. The edition attempts to reproduce even the *ordinatio* of the manuscript, including underlining and marginal indicators, but not colour; however, while the manuscript places the carols' burdens at their beginnings and does not repeat them, the edition repeats them at stanza ends as they would be sung. As usual in TEAMS editions, difficult words and phrases are glossed to the side, or at the bottom if longer; Latin verses are translated alongside. Generous explanatory notes follow, with brief textual notes after, then an index of biblical references, a line index, a bibliography, and a brief glossary.

To accompany this edition, Susanna Fein edits a collection of essays, *'My Wyl and My Wrytyng': Essays on John the Blind Audelay*, resulting from sessions at the 2004 International Congress on Medieval Studies (Western Michigan University, Kalamazoo). Susanna Fein herself opens with 'John Audelay and his Book: Critical Overview and Major Issues' (pp. 3–29), ranging broadly among his life, the manuscript, poetic environment, and the essays to follow. In 'John Audelay: Life Records and Heaven's Ladder' (pp. 30–53), Michael J. Bennett reviews Audelay's patrons' assault on Sir John Trussell in St Dunstan's on Easter Sunday 1417, and supposes that Audelay's guilt for that may well be reflected in his poems. In 'The Vatic Penitent: John Audelay's Self-Representation' (pp. 54–85), Robert J. Meyer-Lee peers into the psychological effects of this self-representation and into how the works may have been intended to reach out to any readers. Comparing 'John Audelay and John Mirk: Comparisons and Contrasts' (pp. 86–111), Susan Powell sees both taking orthodox views, but Audelay as more private and subjective. To Oliver Pickering, 'The Make-Up of John Audelay's *Counsel of Conscience*' (pp. 112–37), the portion thus titled was probably not conceived as a single book though it seems Audelay grouped the works as if they were, and some may have been borrowed.

In 'Audelay's *Marcolf and Solomon* and the Langlandian Tradition' (pp. 138–52), Derek Pearsall finds Audelay more conventional, accepting of the friars, and probably referring to the popular tradition of Piers Plowman, not to Langland's poem. However, Richard Firth Green's 'Langland and Audelay' (pp. 153–69) finds a number of similarities, notably Lady Mede and selected alliterative formulae, and surmises that Audelay had read *Piers Plowman* but, especially with the events he lived through after Langland's time, was literarily and spiritually sympathetic but not deeply influenced by it. Robert Easting, in '"Choose yourselves whither to go": John Audelay's *Vision of Saint Paul*' (pp. 170–90), compares Audelay's poem and his Latin source. In 'John Audelay and the Bridgettines' (pp. 191–217), Martha W. Driver elicits some tantalizing clues for a closer connection than previously suspected, and suggests that Audelay's intent may have been for his work to be an indulgence and prayer. 'Audelay's Carol Collection' (pp. 218–29), Julia Boffey notes, is interesting in its contrasts with other carol collections and in its own internal order of carols. In '"Wo and werres . . . rest and pese": John Audelay's Politics of Peace' (pp. 230–48), John C. Hirsh finds similarities between Audelay's carol in praise of Henry VI and similar lyrics, such as 'The Agincourt Carol' and Lydgate's 'Praise of Peace'. Eric Gerald Stanley's 'The Alliterative *Three Dead Kings* in John Audelay's MS Douce 302' (pp. 249–93) uses lexicography to argue both for the quality of *Three Dead Kings* and against doubting Audelay's authorship. Finally, in 'Death and the Colophon in the Audelay Manuscript' (pp. 294–306), Susanna Fein returns to argue that there are three subsequent endings to his collection of works, all designed to help him end well.

Tony Hunt has edited *Three Anglo-Norman Treatises on Falconry* found in manuscripts from as early as the late thirteenth century; the third is also clearly an adapted translation of a Latin *Physica avium*, an edition of which (based on only one manuscript) is added in an appendix, for comparison with the three. The third text should be of special interest, for it survives in the well-known MS Digby 86 and in the miscellany of Friar William Herbert of Hereford, as well as another Anglo-Norman copy and a continental one. A short introduction provides a modicum of information about the manuscripts and texts, and then it summarizes the rearing, training, types, and care of birds of prey. The treatises follow, with generous use of white space, occasional textual or commentary footnotes, and a glossary (where sometimes abbreviations used in the notes may be found) at the end of each. The second treatise receives its own brief introduction, immediately before the text, while the first and third simply have their source manuscripts identified. Readers should note that the layout concerning textual variants changes in the third treatise, *Le medicinal des ioseus*, to asterisked groups of readings following each paragraph, except for rubrics. The appended *Physica avium* edition has abbreviated references to its sources or analogues placed within brackets in the text, not in commentary footnotes. A selected bibliography ends the volume.

Michael Van Dussen presents 'Three Verse Eulogies of Anne of Bohemia' (*MÆ* 78[2009] 231–60), Richard II's queen, in Latin by English authors and accompanied by an unstudied copy of Richard Rolle's *Super threnos Jeremiae* and other texts with English origins, written in Bohemia; he describes the two manuscripts briefly, offers an interesting account of them, one possibly by Richard Maidstone, and adds translations. Richard J. Moll edits and discusses '"O Lady Fortune": An Unknown Lyric in British Library MS Harley 2169'

(*N&Q* 56[2009] 192–4), a heraldic roll including some stanzas from Lydgate's 'Kings of England'; the new lyric was copied three times on the same page, perhaps as a 'poetic moment'. Not a literary text itself, but of interest to readers, is 'Relics at Glastonbury Abbey in the Thirteenth Century: The Relic List in Cambridge, Trinity College R.5.33 (724), fols. 104r–105v' (*MS* 71[2009] 197–234), in which Martin Howley edits the text and discusses its contents, particularly as related to the three other Glastonbury relic lists. Jack R. Baker finds a connection between 'Christ's Crucifixion and *Robin Hood and the Monk*: A Latin Charm against Thieves in Cambridge, University Library, MS Ff.5.48' (*TCBS* 14[2008] 71–85), not only due to their both being in the same manuscript, but in several motifs, which extend to a picture, below the charm, of a lion frightened by a cock.

Studies of manuscripts lead to interesting findings. For example, Betty Hill presents a number of largely palaeographical and codicological 'Notes on *The Conduct of Life*' (*N&Q* 56[2009] 9–12)—that is, the *Poema Morale*—making various observations on some of the manuscripts, their script, and marginalia, but also having to do with provenance. In 'British Library MS Harley 2253: A New Reading of the Passion Lyrics in their Manuscript Context' (*Viator* 40:i[2009] 271–307), Nancy Vine Durling argues that the Passion lyrics (items 49–69 on fos. 75–83) are designed with a page layout that turns five holes in the parchment into the five wounds of Christ. Carol M. Meale revisits 'London, British Library, Harley MS 2252, John Colyns' "Boke": Structure and Content' (*EMS* 15[2009] 65–122) to discuss the interrelatedness of that structure and the contents, which include a number of anonymous and Lydgate lyrics as well as Ipomydon B and the stanzaic *Le Morte Arthur*, not to mention numerous sixteenth-century materials, literary and practical. Timothy L. Stinson's 'Knowledge of the Flesh: Using DNA Analysis to Unlock Bibliographical Secrets of Medieval Parchment' (*PBSA* 103[2009] 435–53) provides a grounding for further study and suggests how DNA analysis can be used in localizing herds, studying the parchment trade, establishing construction of manuscripts, and other matters.

Catherine Eagleton's 'John Wethamstede, Abbot of Saint Albans, on the Discovery of the Liberal Arts and their Tools; or, Why Were Astronomical Instruments in Late-Medieval Libraries?' (*Mediævalia* 29:i[2009] 109–36) takes the 'Inuenire' section of Wethamstede's *Granarium* as indicative of broader contemporary attitudes about such instruments, giving information about the work, its survival, and sources, before noting that Merton College and the Austin friars of York are recorded as having instruments. Michael Thompson presents a short biography of 'John Hurte (d. 1476): A Nottingham Priest and his Books' (*NMS* 53[2009] 109–19), twenty-one of which are listed in his will, leaving a copy of Ranulf Higden's *Polychronicon* (2° folio 'ad ipsum') to his own church, St Mary's, Nottingham, and an Albertus Magnus *De homine* (2° folio 'animam esse') to Cambridge University.

Christopher Clarkson and Marina Stiglitz review 'The Gough Map: Its Nature, Conservation History and Display' (*BLR* 22[2009] 212–24): MS Gough Gen. Top. 16 is carefully described (but not dated here) to record its ownership and trace alterations which are the result of conservation efforts at various times, even now continuing. Rod Thomson briefly notices 'A New

Manuscript Belonging to Humfrey, Duke of Gloucester' (*BLR* 22[2009] 234–7), a small-format Bible *c.*1250–60 now Oxford, Corpus Christi College MS 1, with decorations in the styles of the William of Devon painter and the Glazier Bible, several marginalia, an inscription of college ownership which is peculiarly plain and in French, and one of the duke's ownership.

Let us turn, now, to more literary studies. Ronald E. Pepin's translation of *Anselm & Becket: Two Canterbury Saints' Lives by John of Salisbury* makes available in modern English the last untranslated works by the author best known for the *Metalogicon* and *Policraticus*. Both are quite short, which is perhaps why scholars have largely paid them little if any attention, but they can be illuminating. The life of Anselm, based on—but not limited to—Eadmer's *Vita Anselmi*, was written for Becket as part of a presentation to Pope Alexander III in 1163 in hopes of canonization for Anselm; the pope referred it to committee, and canonization occurred in 1494. Why Becket chose John is unclear, but John was a member of his household and must have impressed him. The life of Becket is based on a letter John wrote shortly after the murder, to which he is claimed to have been an eyewitness (neither text claims that, and other evidence indicates it to be doubtful). This letter—written years later but still the earliest account—is well within the usual mode of medieval historiography, idealizing and inventing for the sake of moral truth. Apparently he wrote the same letter to various friends, but the narrative of the martyrdom is used heavily for this *Life* with the latter portions much abbreviated. In both versions, John stresses Becket's independence and he is quick to refer to many miracles, though these are largely devoid of the details that typify many saints' lives. Because the volume is in the series Medieval Sources in Translation, the translation aims for faithful representation of the Latin, and it reads smoothly. Footnotes identify biblical sources, explain some references, and provide background; a selected bibliography is at the end.

Karen Bollerman and Cary J. Nederman's 'John of Salisbury's Second Letter Collection in Later Medieval England: Unexamined Fragments from Huntington Library HM 128' (*Viator* 40:i[2009] 71–91) argues that the fourteenth-century letter texts illustrated and transcribed here represent an early, independent tradition for John's second collection. Jan M. Ziolkowski's 'Cultures of Authority in the Long Twelfth Century' (*JEGP* 108[2009] 421–48) traces the uses of *auctor* and *auctoritas* in broadly philological contexts (grammar, rhetoric, exegetics) in the broad European tradition, but also glances at the likes of Walter Map, Geoffrey of Monmouth, Roger of Melun, Anselm of Canterbury, and Adelard of Bath. In 'Two Prophecies and a Talking Head—An Anglo-Norman Text in the Lanercost Chronicle' (*NMS* 53[2009] 38–52), Diana B. Tyson presents the text with its two tales of pride leading to great falls and places them in their historical situation, musing on what we might surmise about the text's history.

'Reconsidering Emending the Capital at Line 1711 of *The Owl and the Nightingale*' (*ANQ* 22:ii[2009] 13–18), Michael David Elam finds previous reasons for emending insufficient and argues that the division is correct; the poet shifts to the nightingale and makes her the subject of the present-tense verb two lines below (and, we should note, she need not be the indirect object in the prior clause). In 'Adam of Barking: Work in Progress' (*Journal of

Medieval Latin 19[2009] 219–49), George Rigg writes up his own progress and findings about Adam's **O**riginal **P**oem (as Rigg puts it), a long poem of the Six Ages of history, very much in process of revision with careful indications of where additions should go, probably in Adam's own hand, in Cambridge, Corpus Christi College MS 227.

Four of the eleven essays in C.P. Lewis's *Anglo-Norman Studies XXXI: Proceedings of the Battle Conference 2008* should interest readers. Catherine A.M. Clarke muses upon 'Writing Civil War in Henry of Huntingdon's *Historia Anglorum*' (pp. 31–48), specifically on how form and content match in style, voice, and structure in prose and verse in Book X on Stephen's reign. Ad Putter surveys 'Gerald of Wales and the Prophet Merlin' (pp. 90–103) in politics from Henry II through John, picking at the various references—including two Merlins—in Gerald's many works, with some emphasis on *The Prophetic History*. Björn Weiler's 'William of Malmesbury, King Henry I, and the *Gesta Regum Anglorum*' (pp. 157–76) probes into how William portrayed Henry I, why he did so for his audience, and how the *Gesta* fits into a wider historical context. And in 'Twelfth-Century Receptions of a Text: Anglo-Norman Historians and Hegesippus' (pp. 177–95), Neil Wright looks over how the Latin translation of Josephus' *Jewish War* was read and used by Alfred of Beverley, Geoffrey of Monmouth, Henry of Huntingdon, and William of Malmesbury.

Matthew Paris attracts quite a bit of attention this year. First, Björn Weiler studies 'Matthew Paris on the Writing of History' (*JMH* 35[2009] 254–78), teasing out Matthew's basic understanding of history out from the *Chronica majora*, the *Historia Anglorum*, *La Estoire de Seint Aedward*, and other works: since history is a compendium of information about past dangers to help present and future readers, writing history is therefore both a pious and an ethical duty. Second, Judith Collard's 'King John and the Symbol of the Falling Crown in the Chronicles of Matthew Paris' (*SMRH* 6[2009] 34–52) notes that *signa* (visual emblems or symbols) were 'designed to link prefatory or marginal imagery with the contents of the main text' and to emphasize 'its significant elements' (p. 42); the slipping crown mirrors the text's negative description, and it is echoed in the falling crowns of Offa and William the Lion, king of Scotland.

Third, Daniel K. Connolly ponders *The Maps of Matthew Paris: Medieval Journeys through Space, Time and Liturgy*, that is, travel, history, and devotion. He opens with some background necessary to understand Matthew, his milieu, and how meditation and reading maps and accounts of pilgrimages were deeply important to readers, who could then imagine themselves performing the pilgrimages as a meditative exercise. Then the itineraries—which look like trip planners or travel routes from modern online maps, with some tourist information about the destination—are examined in their manuscript format (including how moving the maps' flaps changes the route), devotional practices, and visual contexts. Thus, beholding and contemplating the map allows one to visit its locations vicariously. The placement of the itineraries at the start of the *Chronica maiora* and their formal similarity to genealogical and historical rolls is found to match the teleological *translatio imperii* wherein space and time meet purposively, culminating in

London long after Brutus came from Troy. Nevertheless, Jerusalem is the goal of his itineraries and indicates a sacral culmination: Matthew's apocalypticism (he believed the world would end in 1250) leads to a kind of liturgical dramatism that sits easily with monastic liturgical relations with history, geography, and travel. Finally, Connolly looks over the maps not readily associated with monastic environments, but with regal views concerning English power and destiny, and he argues that the map and the *Historia Anglorum* in BL MS Royal 14 C VII were made for Henry III or perhaps more probably Edward I after Matthew died. Both colour and monochrome illustrations are provided.

Medieval writers must have learned to read and write in school, so several essays in the latest *New Medieval Literatures* are particularly relevant for our readers, though most are far enough afield not to warrant coverage here. Christopher Cannon brings together what is known about 'The Middle English Writer's Schoolroom: Fourteenth-Century English Schoolbooks and their Contents' (*NML* 11[2009] 19–38), noting the contents of twenty-four probable schoolbooks, discussing a number of *latinitates*, and observing how translation exercises were mistaken for poetic creations. Manfred Kraus continues, describing 'Grammatical and Rhetorical Exercises in the Medieval Classroom' (*NML* 11[2009] 63–89) for earlier times and with a more broadly European scope, while maintaining an English emphasis. And Martin Camargo presents two case studies of fifteenth-century teachers in 'Grammar School Rhetoric: The Compendia of John Longe and John Miller' (*NML* 11[2009] 91–112), featuring—as Chaucer does—Geoffrey of Vinsauf's *Poetria nova*.

Politics and literature have long been interrelated, as have economics and law. Andrea Ruddick's 'National Sentiment and Religious Vocabulary in Fourteenth-Century England' (*JEH* 60[2009] 1–18) traces how political interests appropriated conventional literary rhetoric, particularly identifying England with Old Testament Israel in its sufferings. In 'The Economy of Need in Late Medieval English Literature' (*Viator* 40:i[2009] 309–31), Andrew Galloway lays out a 'legibility of need' from Jerome, Gratian, and Aquinas, and reads it in Wimbledon's sermon *Dives and Pauper*, the alliterative *William of Palerne*, Gower, Chaucer, and Langland. In 'Bromyard's Other Handbook: Canon and Civil Law for Preachers' (*SMRH* 6[2009] 93–123), Siegfried Wenzel studies the *Tractatus iuris ciuilis et canonici ad moralem materiam applicati* (or *Opus trivium*), which has 262 alphabetical keyword chapters, each in three conceptual divisions, providing grist for preachers, prelates, and teachers, much like his *Summa praedicantium*, but which seems less used, though evidently it was more popular.

'New Biographical Notes on Robert Mannyng of Brunne' (*N&Q* 56[2009] 197–201), by Andrew W. Taubman, poses some evidence and reasons for thinking that Robert was born in Nunburnholme near York, joined the Augustinians at Warter, and later joined the Arrouasians at Bourne, Lincolnshire, only to join the Gilbertines and move to Sixhills. Don C. Skemer has found a second version of 'The Story of Engle and Scardyng: Fragment of an Anglo-Norman Chronicle Roll' (*Viator* 40:ii[2009] 255–75) from the mid-fourteenth century, the first being in Robert Mannyng of

Brunne's *Story of Inglande*. He transcribes the text and adds the medallion portrait of Engle, with extensive discussion of the text, fragment, and their backgrounds.

In 'The Virtues of Balm in Late Medieval Literature' (*Early Science and Medicine* 14[2009] 711–36), Elly R. Truitt traces the development of ideas that balsam was a panacea and could even prevent putrefaction, which filtered from ancient natural history through the encyclopedias to works such as Lydgate's *Troy Book* and Mandeville's *Travels*. Karma Lochrie's 'Provincializing Medieval Europe: Mandeville's Cosmopolitan Europe' (*PMLA* 124[2009] 592–9) begins by asserting that Mandeville structures the *Travels* in accordance with both Jerusalem-centred maps and climatic zonal maps, which centre the equator and thus northern Africa, thereby provincializing Christian Europe; by marvelling at the knowledge and wisdom of the sultan, for example, and the amazing skill of the great khan's craftsmen, Mandeville reveals the limited, naive views of Europeans.

Maija Birenbaum's 'Affective Vengeance in *Titus and Vespasian*' (*ChauR* 43[2009] 330–44) traces some thematic similarities with the *Siege of Jerusalem*, in that this poem also seeks unity on God's behalf against the enemies of Christendom. In 'Antifraternalism and the *Upland Series*: Evidence from a Fifteenth-Century Ballad' (*N&Q* 56[2009] 24–6), J. Patrick Hornbeck II finds several elements in the ballad *Friar and Boy* that look back to the *Upland Series*: opposition between Jack and Tobias, and friars' litigiousness, adultery, and attachment to their habits. In 'Lord Fitzwarren and a Carol of 1470' (*N&Q* 56[2009] 23–4), Andrew Breeze identifies William Bourchier as the previously unidentified 'Lord Fueryn' in the unique 'Willikin's Return' carol.

Mary Raschko finds 'Common Ground for Contrasting Ideologies: The Texts and Contexts of *A Schort Reule of Lif*' (*Viator* 40:i[2009] 387–410), in that the Lollard *Schort Reule* is sufficiently orthodox to cast doubt on the effectiveness of Arundel's *Constitutions*; an appended edition of the *Schort Reule* shows variants adapting it for various audiences. Elizabeth Schirmer's 'William Thorpe's Narrative Theology' (*SAC* 31[2009] 267–99) finds that Thorpe turned to narrative for his *Testimony* in order to help his theology survive political and ecclesiastical repressions, at both diegetic or intradiegetic and metadiegetic levels (narrating the story and telling a story within this story); comparisons are made with sermons (including Wycliffite ones), the *Lanterne of Liȝt*, John Mirk's *Festial*, and even Robert Mannyng of Brunne's *Handlyng Synne*. In 'Textual Borrowings, Theological Mobility, and the Lollard Pater Noster Commentary' (*PQ* 88[2009] 1–23), Anna Lewis discusses the indebtedness and resemblance of three commentaries to orthodox materials.

In 'The Visibility of the Translator: The *Speculum Ecclesie* and *The Mirror of Holy Church*' (*Neophil* 93[2009] 537–52) Atsushi Iguchi provides some background materials on Edmund of Abingdon's Latin text and Middle English translations before turning to Bodleian Library MS Douce 25, which differs from other Middle English versions in anglicizing more of its vocabulary, often in doublets such as 'meditacioun eiþer þenkynge' for *meditacionem*.

Historical chronicling is not neglected this year, as evidenced first by Julian M. Luxford's 'An English Chronicle Entry on Robin Hood' (*JMH* 35[2009] 70–6), this being a note added perhaps in the 1460s to Higden's *Polychronicon*, observing that, according to popular opinion, in the late 1290s an outlaw called Robin Hood infested Sherwood Forest and other areas with continual robberies. David Green's 'Masculinity and Medicine: Thomas Walsingham and the Death of the Black Prince' (*JMH* 35[2009] 34–51) delves into the *Chronica maiora* for Edward's symptoms before Walsingham deleted them in his revised version and inspects several potential interpretations Walsingham might have had in mind. Alison Hanham's 'C.L. Kingsford: the Stonor Letters, and Two Chronicles' (*RES* 60[2009] 382–405) amasses a number of misreadings and several misinterpretations made by Kingsford in the Stonor documents, the second continuation of the Croyland chronicle, and John Hardyng's rhymed chronicles for Henry VI and Richard, duke of York. In 'A Source for the Anonymous "Kings of England"' (*N&Q* 56[2009] 194–7), E.A. Jones observes that Latin prose notes preceding the verses and the verses themselves greatly resemble a Latin chronicle once belonging to Bury St Edmunds.

Let us turn to works with a broader chronological span. *Poverty in Late Middle English Literature: The Meene and the Riche*, by Dinah Hazell, looks into how poverty appears in a broad range of works, mainly from the late fourteenth and early fifteenth centuries, organized by broad social environment. The first three chapters begin with socio-economic overviews, to which the fourth adds some historical background, and each is subdivided by the works surveyed. 'Aristocratic poverty' actually concerns romance knights who become impoverished (even for good reasons, such as charity or largesse) and how other themes may relate to their status before and after, with reference to *Ywain and Gawain*, *Sir Amadace*, *Sir Cleges*, *Sir Launfal*, and *Sir Orfeo*. 'Urban poverty' expands the genres and questions where boundaries occur between city and country in *Havelok the Dane*, *London Lickpenny*, Hoccleve's *The Regiment of Princes*, Chaucer's *Prioress's Tale*, and, especially, *The Simonie*. 'Rural poverty' explores the varying attitudes towards patient Griselda in Boccaccio, Petrarch, and Chaucer, and then moves on to Chaucer's *Nun's Priest's Tale* and the Corpus Christi *Shepherds' Plays*, taking the main characters as representations of actual peasants. 'Apostolic poverty' presents the oppositions between spiritual and worldly wealth, first through critical views as in Gower's *Vox Clamantis*, *The Land of Cokaygne*, *Why I Can't Be a Nun*, *Pierce the Ploughman's Crede*, the *Song against the Friars*, and Richard FitzRalph's *Defensio curatorum* (in John Trevisa's translation), and second through positive models, shown by selections from the *South English Legendary*, Capgrave's *Life of Gilbert*, *Godric of Finchale*, and *Sir Gowther*. At the end, 'Solutions and Attitudes' aggregates a number of views and activities concerning charity, true versus false poverty, redirections of responsibility, institutional responses by church and state, civic and individual reactions, and varying presentations of the ploughman as a figure, in *Piers Plowman* and other works.

Cate Gunn and Catherine Innes-Parker's *Texts and Traditions of Medieval Pastoral Care: Essays in Honour of Bella Millett* commends the well-known student of the *Ancrene Wisse*, prefaced by a scholarly biographical sketch by Derek Pearsall (pp. xiii–xiv) and a bibliography of her writings (pp. xv–xvii). E.A. Jones's '"Vae Soli": Solitaries and Pastoral Care' (pp. 11–28) ranges across a number of texts in Latin and Middle English—*Ancrene Wisse*, a *Cambridge Rule*, the *Rule of Celestine* and its translations—and some biographical materials to survey what guidelines spiritual advisers laid down for their solitaries and how some solitaries gave advice and guidance. Elaine Treharne proffers networks of 'Scribal Connections in Late Anglo-Saxon England' (pp. 29–46), with Worcester as a natural focus of discussion. Brian Golding's 'Gerald of Wales, the *Gemma Ecclesiastica* and Pastoral Care' (pp. 47–61) describes Gerald and his rambling, self-confident *Gemma* and comments on various aspects, such as its curious lack of Welshness and its status as a forerunner of the Fourth Lateran Council's products. Jocelyn Wogan-Browne's 'Time to Read: Pastoral Care, Vernacular Access and the Case of Angier of St Frideswide' (pp. 62–77) deals with *Dialogues de saint Grégoire*, a translation by Angier just after and quite opposite to Gerald, for it is more carefully and explicitly structured and audience-aware. Ralph Hanna's 'Lambeth Palace Library MS 487: Some Problems of Early Thirteenth-Century Textual Transmission' (pp. 78–88) uses codicological and linguistic evidence to argue that the manuscript (and the *Ancrene Wisse* manuscript British Library MS Cotton Titus D.xviii) developed as a series of accretions from Old and Middle English sources only intermittently available. Joe Goering's 'Pastoral Texts and Traditions: the Anonymous *Speculum Iuniorum* (c.1250)' (pp. 89–99) describes and summarizes the incomplete work, adding observations on what little can be known about the uncompleted portions.

Cate Gunn is interested in 'Reading Edmund of Abingdon's *Speculum* as Pastoral Literature' (pp. 100–14), that being the *Speculum religiosorum*, but cannot resist the *Speculum ecclesie* in addition. Nicholas Watson carries on beyond Gunn's work in 'Middle English Versions and Audiences of Edmund of Abingdon's *Speculum Religiosorum*' (pp. 115–31), the Middle English being late fourteenth-century and later, contrasting Edmund's perceived intention and audience with those of the vernacular versions, with comparative comments on the *Ancrene Wisse*. Bob Hasenfratz wishes to play on modern concerns in 'Terror and Pastoral Care in *Handlyng Synne*' (pp. 132–48) but in fact places Robert Mannyng of Brunne's amassed exempla within a broader, roughly contemporary theoretical 'theology of fear'. Mishtooni Bose's 'Prophecy, Complaint and Pastoral Care in the Fifteenth Century: Thomas Gascoigne's *Liber Veritatum*' (pp. 149–62) looks at *prophetia comminationis* ('prophecy of denunciation' here, or of threat or menace) in Gascoigne's work. Catherine Innes-Parker's 'Pastoral Concerns in the Middle English Adaptation of Bonaventure's *Lignum Vitae*' (pp. 163–77) turns to another thirteenth-century work vernacularized in the fifteenth century, wherein structure is changed to metaphor and contemplation is revised into instruction. Taking those at Syon Abbey as a touchstone, C. Annette Grise considers 'Prayer, Meditation and Women Readers in Late Medieval England: Teaching and Sharing through Books' (pp. 178–92), notes that pious women read as a devotional activity, offers as examples two manuscripts connected with Syon, and touches on Lady Margaret Beaufort and her translating activities as part of her broad devotion. Finally, in '"Take a book and read": Advice for Religious Women' (pp. 193–208), Alexandra Barratt surveys works addressed to women to discover that they clearly advocate reading suitable works but are rather vague about what those works are, except for the Vulgate, the works themselves, saints' lives, the *Meditationes vitae Christi*, and the *Stimulus amoris*.

The title of *Against All England: Regional Identity and Cheshire Writing, 1195–1656*, by Robert W. Barrett, Jr., comes from the early modern ballad *Bosworth Field*, wherein Richard III is preparing to fight Henry Tudor with Cheshire and Lancashire support. Barrett makes a case for Cheshire having long seen itself as neither English nor Welsh, but other. The volume treats Cestrian writing in two parts: the city Chester and the county Cheshire. City writing begins with the *Liber de Luciani laude Cestrie* of *c*.1195 (surviving in one manuscript) from the Benedictine abbey of St Werburgh, jumps to the 1506–13 *Life of St Werburge* by the monk Henry Bradshaw, and then looks at some early modern plays. Lucian's *De laude Cestrie* turns the geographical city into an allegorical one that can tropologically prefigure New Testament events and concepts; it even replaces Jerusalem as the *omphalos* of the world. Bradshaw's *encomium* is similar in its praise of Chester but enters politics by urging the maintenance of his monastery's ancient extensive rights; Henry VIII deemed otherwise, however, and Pynson's printed edition of 1521 put Bradshaw's *Life* into an anti-Lutheran context. The allegorizing and political refiguring return in the Chester Whitsun mystery plays, best understood when the changes of stations are considered in light of regulations concerning movement as well as contemporary social topography. In 1610, St George's Day celebrations printed as *Chester's Triumph in Honor of Her Prince* were highly successful, despite the absence of the soon-to-be Prince of Wales and earl of Chester; the producer, Robert Amerie, used the event and publication for personal political aggrandizement. County interests begin with the Wirral location in *Sir Gawain and the Green Knight* and continue into the Scrope–Grosvenor trial over duplicate arms in a topography of honour between a courtly (i.e. national) and a regional knight, whose armorial contest can be read back into a heraldic reading of *Sir Gawain and the Green Knight*. Barrett moves on to works devoted to the Stanley family and its interests, recorded after Bosworth field: *Bosworth Field*, *Lady Bessy*, *The Rose of England*, *Flodden Field*, *Scottish Field*, and *The Stanley Poem*; these are supplemented by accounts of the siege of Lathom House by parliamentarians, accounts of which are informed by various tropes and conventions of romance.

Danielle Westerhof's *Death and the Noble Body in Medieval England* is a historical study largely focused on the Anglo-Norman aristocracy from the late twelfth to the early fourteenth centuries, but provides much information for the literary researcher because the historical background necessarily underlies literary treatments and thereby interpretations. 'Death and the Cadaver: Visions of Corruption' surveys ideas about dying, death, and the dead body in the twelfth and thirteenth centuries, noting how dying in sin was a real concern, as literature and chronicles reveal. 'Embodying Nobility: Aristocratic Men and the Ideal Body' surveys ideas about what it meant to be a noble male, including aristocratic status and concepts of knighthood, where especially in literature the quality of the body implied the quality of the soul. 'Here Lies Nobility: Aristocratic Bodies in Death' begins to apply the concepts of the first two chapters to religious patronage and funerary practices; in the thirteenth century, the aristocracy asserted its moral and social superiority by these means, and the visible nature of their tombs and effigies perpetuated the family's status. 'Shrouded in Ambiguity: Decay and Incorruptibility of the Body' continues the work of the preceding chapter, including heart and visceral burials, whose dispersal did not reflect a division of personhood, although some attention was paid to a distinction between skeletal and visceral separation in burial. 'Corruption of Nobility: Treason and the Aristocratic Traitor' switches attention to when the noble is considered a threat to society, as seems increasingly common in the troubles of the late thirteenth and early fourteenth centuries; legal theory, chivalric manuals, and romances offered excision from society as the treatment for offenders against the king's peace, which came to be identified with the king himself. Finally, 'Dying in Shame: Destroying Aristocratic Identities' looks at how traitors were removed from society and their corruption exposed in practice—circumstances dictated whether specific cases were treated more lightly or more rigorously, but the sense was still one of excision from society.

In *St Edmund, King and Martyr: Changing Images of a Medieval Saint*, Anthony Bale collects essays distributed among various disciplines and ranging from early medieval into early modern times, the products of a seminar at Birkbeck College, University of London, in 2004. Bale's 'Introduction: St Edmund's Medieval Lives' (pp. 1–25) swiftly covers Edmund's life, the abbey at Bury St Edmunds and how the cult of Edmund was served there and elsewhere, and some modern scholarly approaches to hagiography. Then, Carl Phelpstead's 'King, Martyr and Virgin: *Imitatio Christi* in Ælfric's *Life of St Edmund*' (pp. 27–44) inspects Ælfric's life in its historical and hagiographical contexts. Alison Finlay's 'Chronology, Genealogy and Conversion: The Afterlife of St Edmund in the North' (pp. 45–62) looks backwards through Icelandic eyes at what the Danes might have seen. Paul Antony Hayward's 'Geoffrey of Wells's *Liber de infantia sancti Edmundi* and the "Anarchy" of King Stephen's Reign' (pp. 63–86) considers how Geoffrey altered Abbo's *Passio S. Eadmundi* (and others' accounts) to contrast Edmund with Stephen. Lisa Colton explores the relationship between 'Music and Identity in Medieval Bury St Edmunds' (pp. 87–110) based on surviving materials. Rebecca Pinner's 'Medieval Images of St Edmund in Norfolk Churches' (pp. 111–32) also uses surviving materials—this time visual—to look at Edmund's popularity in Norfolk. In 'John Lydgate's *Lives of SS Edmund and Fremund*: Politics, Hagiography and Literature' (pp. 133–44), A.S.G. Edwards turns to the origins and development of the paired lives, wondering about how they got into their sequence, one after the other. Anthony Bale himself provides 'St Edmund in Fifteenth-Century London: The Lydgatian *Miracles of St Edmund*' (pp. 145–61), a search for the 'environment' of the text, with its Bury St Edmunds connections. The first of its three miracles is interpreted as Lydgate's creation for the earl of Suffolk or his family. And, at the end, Alexandra Gillespie's 'The Later Lives of

St Edmund: John Lydgate to John Stow' (pp. 163–85) finds Lydgate's text not crystallized or superseded after the Dissolution but revalued according to changed values and interests.

Jonathan Good's *The Cult of Saint George in Medieval England* traces how St George developed into the patron saint of England from ancient through to modern times, beginning with an introductory chapter on saints' cults and nationalism in the Middle Ages—with an eye on St George and on England, with the growth in English literature 1290–1340 as an indicator of that nationalism—and another on the origins of St George in embarrassingly grotesque passion tales, through Bede, Leofric, Ælfric, and later tales during the Crusades of George as a warrior, on with the development of the dragon story after the *Legenda aurea*, until George could be associated with agricultural productivity, the military, and chivalry. England's special veneration was begun by Edward I, who had a special regard for St George and fought Wales and Scotland using the crusaders' patron; Edward III institutionalized St George through the Order of the Garter, and he and Henry V used banners with St George while fighting the Hundred Years War. By the time of Henry VII, the notion that George was the patron saint of England was well established, especially since use of him against unpopular kings supported belief in his protection of the realm, not the ruler. Hundreds of English churches, chapels, hospitals, and even guilds were dedicated to St George; lives of the saint are found in the *South English Legendary*, Mirk's *Festial*, Lydgate, the *Speculum sacerdotale*, Caxton's *Golden Legend*, and Alexander Barclay. The Protestant Reformation was not kind to any saint, but Elizabethan neo-medievalism allowed a rehabilitated return that became more political as the centuries passed, as Good traces swiftly up to the present. An appendix lists a number of pre-Reformation dedications of churches and the like, the top twenty dedications for comparison (George is nineteenth), stained glass images, murals, and guilds.

Levinas and Medieval Literature: The 'Difficult Reading' of English and Rabbinic Texts, edited by Ann W. Astell and J.A. Jackson, applies the ethical philosophy of Emmanuel Levinas to selected literary texts, some of which are not to our purpose. Valerie Allen briefly surveys the relevant aspects of Levinas's thought in 'Difficult Reading' (pp. 15–33). Susan Yager's 'Levinas, Allegory, and Chaucer's Clerk's Tale' (pp. 35–56) continues with a broader theoretical background applied to many late Middle English works to point out that allegory resists limitation to any single interpretation, with a closer look at Walter and Grisilde within this framework. In '"In his eyes stood a light, not beautiful": Levinas, Hospitality, *Beowulf* (pp. 57–84), Eileen A. Joy explores the inside versus the outside of the meadhall, and thus the political and ethical views about hospitality towards those from without, beginning with legal codes but moving on to Beowulf, Grendel, and his dam. Alexander L. Kaufman's 'There Is Horror: *The Awntyrs off Arthure*, the Face of the Dead, and the Maternal Other' (pp. 85–106) tweaks the relationship between Gaynour and her mother's ghost, effectively requiring that she mother her mother, a different obligation towards an Other. Turning to the male side of family relationships, in 'Doing Justice to Isaac: Levinas, the *Akedah*, and the Brome Play of *Abraham and Isaac*' (pp. 107–36), Daniel T. Kline views how

Isaac gets a voice and reveals how the sacrifice plays against the ethics of father–son relationships.

Two essays in the same volume turn to the face: first, James J. Paxson's 'The Personificational Face: *Piers Plowman* Rethought through Levinas and Bronowski' (pp. 137–56) considers the prosopopoeia of Anima in the B-version's Passus XV through various eyes, and, second, J.A. Jackson's 'The Infinite Desire of *Pearl*' (pp. 157–84) begins with seeing the face of the Pearl Maiden and moves on to how she works to resituate the Dreamer's desire. Love and the erotic are the heart of J. Allan Mitchell's 'Criseyde's Chances: Courtly Love and Ethics About to Come' (pp. 185–206), which explores her passivity in a gendered context against Troilus's passivity, when uncertainties contrive to affect the ethics. Cynthia Kraman follows with 'The Wound of the Infinite: Rereading Levinas through Rashi's Commentary on the Song of Songs' (pp. 207–26), and Sandor Goodhart on '"A land that devours its inhabitants": Midrashic Reading, Levinas, and Medieval Literary Exegesis' (pp. 227–53). In 'When Pardon Is Impossible: Two Talmudic Tales, Chaucer's *Pardoner's Tale*, and Levinas' (pp. 255–79), Ann W. Astell plays the three stories against each other to investigate forgiveness and, when it cannot be given, 'rubbing' it also against the *Parson's Tale* and Chaucer's Retraction. Moshe Gold closes with 'Those Evil Goslings, Those Evil Stories: Letting the Boys Out of their Cave' (pp. 281–303) comparing a talmudic story to one from the fourth day of Boccaccio's *Decameron*.

Jocelyn Wogan-Browne and others have assembled over thirty essays in *Language and Culture in Medieval Britain: The French of England c.1100–c.1500*, grouped broadly into four parts: 'Language and Socio-Linguistics', 'Crossing the Conquest: New Linguistic and Literary Histories', 'After Lateran IV: Francophone Devotions and Histories', and 'England and French in the Late Fourteenth and Fifteenth Centuries'. We will restrict our attention to the essays most relevant to literary points and authors. In '"'Fi a debles', quath the king": Language-Mixing in England's Vernacular Historical Narratives, *c*.1290–1340' (pp. 68–80), Thea Summerfield studies code-switching in six *Brut* chronicles equally split between Middle English and Anglo-Norman. In addition to the *Anglo-Norman Prose Brut to 1322*, 'John Barton, John Gower and Others: Variation in Late Anglo-French' (pp. 118–34) are studied by Brian Merrilees and Heather Pagan to show that some deliberately lean towards continental forms and vocabulary, perhaps in order to expand the anticipated audience. R.F. Yeager concurs in 'John Gower's French and his Readers' (pp. 135–45) and notes that Gower's linguistic acumen is matched by his political astuteness in dedications to targeted noble readers, adding that a Yorkshire translation of Gower's *Traité pour essampler les amantz marietz* may reveal unintended readers.

In 'From Old English to Old French' (pp. 164–78), Elizabeth M. Tyler uses the English tradition of vernacular writing to link Gaimar and the *Anglo-Saxon Chronicle* to a larger European pattern of writing history and poetry that reflected back into writing in French. Henry Bainton continues this with 'Translating the "English" Past: Cultural Identity in the *Estoire des Engleis*' (pp. 179–87), noting Gaimar's use of the *Anglo-Saxon Chronicle*'s aims to different ends. Turning elsewhere, Françoise H.M. Le Saux's

'The Languages of England: Multilingualism in the Work of Wace' (pp. 188–97) concludes that Wace felt allied with England, even if English was his second or, more likely, third language. Geoff Rector shows how French was 'An Illustrious Vernacular: The Psalter *en romanz* in Twelfth-Century England' (pp. 198–206), concerning Psalter translations and commentaries that flourished before the romances. In 'Serpent's Head/Jew's Hand: *Le Jeu d'Adam* and Christian–Jewish Debate in Norman England' (pp. 207–19), Ruth Nisse argues that the *Jeu*'s concerns about language extend beyond Latin and French to Hebrew. Monica H. Green explores the mystery of 'Salerno on the Thames: The Genesis of Anglo-Norman Medical Literature' (pp. 220–31), for more texts were available than were translated.

Broadening the scope, Jocelyn Wogan-Browne's '"Cest livre liseez . . . chescun jour": Women and Reading *c.*1230–*c.*1430' (pp. 239–53) begins work on penitential, devotional, and doctrinal materials with women audiences, taking as starting points specific images in the *Lambeth Apocalypse* and *La Reule*, a close French translation of *Ancrene Wisse*. Continuing this thread, Helen Deeming describes some 'French Devotional Texts in Thirteenth-Century Preachers' Anthologies' (pp. 254–65) in MS Harley 524, while Jean-Pascal Pouzet surveys some potential sources for vernacular devotion in 'Augustinian Canons and their Insular French Books in Medieval England: Towards an Assessment' (pp. 266–77). Laurie Postlewate dips into how Bozon manipulated his audience's values in '*Eschuer peché, embracer bountee*: Social Thought and Pastoral Instruction in Nicole Bozon' (pp. 278–89). Delbert W. Russell delves into 'The Cultural Context of the French Prose *remaniement* of the Life of Edward the Confessor by a Nun of Barking Abbey' (pp. 290–302). Through a variety of examples, Julia Marvin demonstrates 'The Vitality of Anglo-Norman in Late Medieval England: The Case of the Prose *Brut* Chronicle' (pp. 303–19), and Michael Bennett surveys various cultural displays of 'France in England: Anglo-French Culture in the Reign of Edward III' (pp. 320–33). Nicholas Watson wonders about making a case for 'Lollardy: The Anglo-Norman Heresy?' (pp. 334–46) because of earlier vernacular devotion in that language and modern academic separation of studies by language.

Rebecca June's 'The Languages of Memory: The Crabhouse Nunnery Manuscript' (pp. 347–58) is a literary discussion viewing the manuscript's jumbled contents in a different light. Tim William Machan undertakes a sociolinguistic study of 'French, English, and the Late Medieval Linguistic Repertoire' (pp. 363–72), and Carolyn Collette surveys 'Aristotle, Translation and the Mean: Shaping the Vernacular in Late Medieval Anglo-French Culture' (pp. 373–85) with an interest in mediation or moderation in texts in social bounds, not geographical. In 'Writing English in a French Penumbra: The Middle English "Tree of Love" in MS Longleat 253' (pp. 386–96), Julia Boffey introduces an unedited fifteenth-century poem and places it in the context of readers of French texts and English ones translated from French. Similarly, Ad Putter discusses 'The French of English Letters: Two Trilingual Verse Epistles in Context' (pp. 397–408), founding the love letters in a tradition of French epistolography in England. Godfried Croenen's 'The Reception of Froissart's Writings in England: The Evidence of the

Manuscripts' (pp. 409–19) concludes that French readers saw Froissart biased towards England, where his work gained popularity only with Lord Berners's translation of the *Chronicles*. Martha W. Driver's '"Me fault faire": French Makers of Manuscripts for English Patrons' (pp. 420–43) describes, illustrates, and lists a number of manuscripts made by Ricardus Franciscus and the Fastolf Master. In 'The French Self-Presentation of an English Mastiff: John Talbot's Book of Chivalry' (pp. 444–56), Andrew Taylor makes a case for seeing Talbot's self-promotion in the anthology he gave Margaret of Anjoy upon her wedding Henry VI: BL MS Royal 15 E VI. And Stephanie Downes's 'A "Frenche booke called the Pistill of Othea": Christine de Pizan's French in England' (pp. 457–68) looks into two of the many English manuscripts of the French text to show continuing engagement with French works late into the fifteenth century.

Medieval Grammar and Rhetoric: Language Arts and Literary Theory, AD 300–1475, edited by Rita Copeland and Ineke Sluiter, presents another corrective to the many volumes that skip from Aristotle to the Renaissance while surveying grammar, rhetoric, and their role in poetics and literary theory, combining both topics in one volume and offering most of its texts in their first English translations. England owes much to the continental tradition—especially Latin—and it is unwise for researchers and students to ignore that tradition; the anthology of translations, accordingly, works from late antiquity towards the twelfth and thirteenth centuries, finishing with later materials in Latin and English. The first part covers the first few centuries until just before the first millennium, with the expected Donatus, Martianus Capella, and Isidore of Seville but also with Bede and Alcuin. The second turns to discussions of the ablative absolute and etymology, including relevant passages from the prologue to the Wycliffite Bible about translating ablative absolutes and Osbern of Gloucester on etymology. The third to fifth parts cover new developments in the twelfth and thirteenth centuries, with the fourth targeting pedagogical works; English authors included are John of Salisbury, Alexander Neckam, Thomas of Chobham, and the peripatetic Geoffrey of Vinsauf and John of Garland. The sixth part turns to the late fourteenth and fifteenth centuries, with the first selection being a central European treatise on rhetorical colours. Then it turns to Gower's *Confessio Amantis* on rhetorical eloquence, giving some narrative examples; the prologue to the Wycliffite Bible on figurative language and how to deal with it; Lydgate's *Fall of Princes* on rhetoric, which adds to its source; and a late fifteenth-century Middle English text on the Seven Liberal Arts, based on and partly translating Robert Grosseteste's *De artibus liberalibus*. Each chapter employs footnotes for quick reference, and the volume ends with select bibliographies of primary and secondary sources, an index of Latin terms, one of ancient and medieval names, and a general index.

Ben Parsons's '"A Riotous Spray of Words": Rethinking the Medieval Theory of Satire' (*Exemplaria* 21[2009] 105–28) begins as a review article covering the last few decades' work and then considers 'more marginal, even eccentric' comments (p. 105), highlighting past ethical goals: Alexander Neckam, Nigel of Canterbury, and Henry Watson on Brant's *Stultifera navis*, with parodic bite showing in works like *Wynnere and Wastoure* and *Mum and the Sothsegger*. J. Patrick Hornbeck (this time without the 'II') takes a look at 'Theologies of Sexuality in English "Lollardy"' (*JEH* 60[2009] 19–44), *c*.1381–1521, concluding that the sexual status quo remained the norm except for swelling support for a married clergy, with some wobbling on church weddings; notions of libertinism are no doubt part of any charges of sexual vice made against perceived dissenters and heretics.

When we consider language this year, we should look to Richard Ingham's 'Mixing Languages on the Manor' (*MÆ* 78[2009] 80–97), for he reviews the status of French, English, and Latin through nested code-switching, keyed to English nouns and non-English articles or pronouns preceding them: English nouns were easily inserted into French and even Latin documents, despite how the spoken versions may have been rendered. The act of translating is the heart of Anne Mouron's '*The Manere of Good Lyvyng*: The Manner of a Good Translator?' (*MÆ* 78[2009] 300–22), a fifteenth-century translation perhaps for the Bridgettine sisters of Syon; it is a 'primary' translation, faithful while being free, and compares well to similar contemporary translations.

Companions or guides continue to appear. Larry Scanlon's *The Cambridge Companion to Medieval English Literature 1100–1500* opens with abbreviations, a list of contributors and their positions, a chronology, and the editor's introduction (teeing off from the *Cursor mundi*, elsewhere untouched) before the first part, on 'Contexts, Genres, and Traditions', where Wendy Scase begins with 'Re-inventing the Vernacular: Middle English Language and its Literature' (pp. 11–23), pointing out dialectal diversity in English and then multilingual literature before turning to varieties of versification and the early impetus towards regularization. Richard Firth Green's 'Textual Production and Textual Communities' (pp. 25–36) describes such communities through understanding how they share like-minded attitudes about a coherent set of texts: Lollard conventicles, Bokenham's women readers, a Thomas Lord Berkeley group, and John Shirley's circles. Richard Newhauser introduces 'Religious Writing: Hagiography, *Pastoralia*, Devotional and Contemplative Works' (pp. 37–55), not just delineating those broad genres but depicting their ubiquity, audience, and importance. Christine Chism performs a similar service for 'Romance' (pp. 57–69), touching on topical preoccupations, style, audiences, authors, and variety. Steven F. Kruger's 'Dialogue, Debate, and Dream Vision' (pp. 71–82) briefly looks at modern criticism about these popular works, but spends more time on the intellectual tradition and the uses of debates and visions.

Sarah Beckwith takes on 'Drama' (pp. 83–94) with comments on the various town cycle mystery plays and the morality, miracle, and saints' plays. Ardis Butterfield's chapter on the 'Lyric' (pp. 95–109, and using P/p for Þ/þ) emphasizes how messy lyrics are in the vernacular literary landscape but finds paths to understanding them through preachers' uses and sundry collections, adding brief comments on music. Rita Copeland brings this part to a close with a survey of 'Lollard Writings' (pp. 111–22) from a historical overview to reasons for vernacular scripture and the Wycliffite Bible to additional writings, such as polemics and even verse satire. The second part introduces a variety of popular late fourteenth- and fifteenth-century authors, beginning with Ralph

Hanna on 'William Langland' (pp. 125–38), with a brief biography and observations on versions, episodic development, and themes. Sarah Stanbury's 'The *Gawain*-Poet' (pp. 139–51) introduces all four poems with a predilection for descriptive focus. Diane Watt's 'John Gower' (pp. 153–64) follows an overview of Gower's major works with closer consideration of the *Confessio Amantis* and how it influenced Hoccleve and Lydgate.

Larry Scanlon reserves for himself the chapter on 'Geoffrey Chaucer' (pp. 165–78), taking a chronological stroll through the works with his eye on the ideas of poetic authority, tradition, and 'translation', or Chaucer's European sources or analogues, followed by a literature review. Lynn Staley's 'Julian of Norwich' (pp. 179–89) swiftly gives the known facts and embarks on a discussion designed to show Julian's learning and thought from the short to the long version, with careful negotiation of certain topics sensitive to orthodoxy. Ethan Knapp studies 'Thomas Hoccleve' (pp. 191–203) across early, mid-, and late career to show a wily poet working the angles as best he can. 'John Lydgate' (pp. 205–16), according to James Simpson, should be very important for six reasons, but compared to Chaucer was doomed to fail, and Simpson lacks room to redress this; instead, he turns to how Lydgate reacted to civil war and to Lollardy. Rebecca Krug asks if 'Margery Kempe' (pp. 217–28) wrote a treatise, not an autobiography, and finds that it teaches how to deal with insecurity in life. David Wallace gallops across 'Sir Thomas Malory' (pp. 229–41) in search of soft places. And Sally Mapstone's 'Robert Henryson' (pp. 243–55) offers background material in addition to overviews of the fables, *Orpheus and Eurydice*, and *The Testament of Cresseid*. Each chapter has its own notes, and at the end there is a 'Guide to Further Reading' (pp. 257–78), in general and for each chapter.

Marilyn Corrie's *A Concise Companion to Middle English Literature* also provides a number of topical considerations, eschewing discussions of selected authors, in four main parts. The first, 'Key Contexts', begins with Barry Windeatt's 'Signs and Symbols' (pp. 9–31), noting how a common culture allowed for symbolic readings which authors and readers both grasped, as we can see in Margery Kempe, Thomas Malory, Julian of Norwich, and the Scots Chaucerians. Marilyn Corrie herself follows up with 'Religious Belief' (pp. 32–53), explaining traditional education and engagement through plays, *Cursor mundi*, *Cleanness*, vision literature, and Langland's *Piers Plowman*, and the situation in the fifteenth century as seen through Nicholas Love's *Mirror*, *Everyman*, and Malory. Catherine Sanok discusses 'Women and Literature' (pp. 54–76), beginning with the usual notices about misogyny and interest in female sexuality and moving on to observations about analogies with social order, patience and protest, virginity, woman/women, identity, and women readers and writers; Chaucer is mined the most, with glances into Malory, Langland, the Katherine Group, Bokenham, Gower, Marie de France, and Lydgate. And Andrew Galloway reviews 'The Past' (pp. 77–96), or rather a literary 'obsession' with it from Geoffrey of Monmouth and Laȝamon onwards in biblical, classical, and medieval retellings of heroes and women that shift to new focuses, as in *Sir Gawain and the Green Knight*, Chaucer, and Lydgate.

Part II, 'The Production of Middle English Literature', starts with Alexandra Gillespie on 'Production and Dissemination' (pp. 99–119), meaning that literary texts were made and distributed under historical circumstances that changed with time, and so did their reception as audiences differed. It closes with Jane Griffiths contemplating 'The Author' (pp. 120–41), not only through theoretical *auctoritas* and Chaucer's musings in the *House of Fame* and *Troilus and Criseyde* but also through the instances where authors name themselves (Audelay, Langland, possibly Nicholas of Guildford) and Lydgate, Hoccleve, and Gower. Part III is 'Writing in Middle English; Writing in England', where Jeremy J. Smith summarizes 'Language' (pp. 145–65) with overviews of history, lexicon, grammar, graphemics, and dialects. Helen Cooper follows with the related matters of 'Translation and Adaptation' (pp. 166–87) from Latin or French predecessors, whether devotional, didactic, or secular—for example, the Wycliffite Bible, Nicholas Love's *Mirour*, various romances, and, of course, Chaucer. Helen Barr surveys 'Contemporary Events' (pp. 188–208), looking first at Gower and Chaucer on the 1381 Peasants' Revolt, then at Laurence Minot and Hoccleve on the Hundred Years War, several works on Richard II and on the Lollards, and Malory during the Wars of the Roses. Part IV turns to the modern times with 'Middle English Literature in the Post-Medieval World', wherein first Daniel Wakelin's 'Manuscripts and Modern Editions' (pp. 211–31) sets out how manuscript texts and edited texts differ, with many examples of variant readings in multiple manuscripts, and an excursus on original and reader-added marginalia. Finally, David Matthews muses upon 'The Afterlife of Middle English Literature' (pp. 232–52), following it through survival in the sixteenth century, decline in the seventeenth, and revival in the eighteenth and nineteenth, to academic study after about 1870, with some emergence of popular interest.

Daniel T. Kline's *The Medieval British Literature Handbook* is a very different volume, being in a series aimed at 'students in the twenty-first century' (p. xxii). Accordingly, Kline's introduction (pp. 1–22) describes the appeal the Middle Ages have for those who play 'Roll Playing Games' (*sic*, p. 1) or read *The Da Vinci Code* before defining parameters, surveying modern scholarly issues, and questioning ethical concerns for modern readers, all the while noting differences from popular misconceptions. Like the other chapters, it ends with a group of study questions and a 'web quest' for students to hunt for materials variously relevant. The next two chapters offer historical contexts for studying Middle English literature: first, Brian Gastle's 'Historical Context for Middle English Literature' (pp. 23–48) briefly describes about a dozen topics such as changes after 1066, the church, the Great Schism, the plague, the Hundred Years War, and the Wars of the Roses, and he adds a timeline from 1066 to 1492. Second, Julia Bolton Holloway, with Daniel T. Kline, give the dictionary-like 'Literary and Cultural Contexts: Major Figures, Institutions, Topics, Events, Movements' (pp. 49–81), with a paragraph or so for many entries such as anchoress, Arthurian literature, courtly love, the Ellesmere manuscript, Nicholas Love, Richard II, and virginity. The fourth and fifth chapters give case studies. Mathew Boyd Goldie's 'Case Studies in Reading I: Key Primary Literary Texts' (pp. 82–108) looks at several texts dealing with what some might consider issues contemporary with them, if not us: Marie de France's *Lanval*, representations of the Peasants' Revolt in 1381, Margery Kempe's *Book*, and *Mankind* in view of *The Treatise of Miraclis Pleyinge*. Gail Ashton's 'Case Studies in Reading II: Key Literary and Theoretical Texts' (pp. 109–32) selects issues highlighted in recent publications (and those works themselves) to survey some theoretical drives, for example Carolyn Dinshaw's *Chaucer's Sexual Poetics*, queer readings, secrecy, gender, Jeffrey Jerome Cohen's *Of Giants*, the body, and postcolonialism. In 'Key Critics, Concepts and Topics' (pp. 133–51), however, Bonnie Millar surveys some topics and critics separately, such as alterity, gender, marginal voices, the marvellous, orality, transmission, David Aers, Stephen Knight, Miri Rubin, and Paul Strohm.

John M. Ganim gives a historical overview of the last three decades in 'Changes in Critical Responses and Approaches' (pp. 152–83), ranging widely in topics such as the centrality of Chaucer, deconstruction, feminism, gender, queer studies, Marxism, new historicism, postcolonialism, psychoanalysis, ecocriticism, Lollardy and literacy, and reception theory. Nancy Bradley Warren offers a number of points and persons as 'Changes in the Canon' (pp. 184–98): for example, feminism and Julian of Norwich and Margery Kempe; new historicism and Lollardy; Osbern Bokenham and Thomas Hoccleve; and multilingualism, continental relationships, and postcolonialism. In 'Issues of Sexuality, Gender and Ethnicity' (pp. 199–225), Diane Cady expands upon some previous points and touches on several texts as relevant, as in feminism and the *Querelle de la Rose* and Chaucer's Wife of Bath, mysticism, gender, bodies, race and cultural differences, and crusades and conversion. 'Mapping the Current Critical Landscape' (pp. 226–46), by Sol J. Neely, takes a different view, passing through structuralism, poststructuralism, materialism, Marxism, deconstruction, Derrida, gender, and more to consider ethical readings as more responsible ways to approach literature. This is followed by a general glossary with nineteen entries, an appendix pointing to an online chapter, 'Teaching Medieval British Literature into the Twenty-First Century' by Susan Oldrieve with Joanna Wright Smith, and a general, annotated bibliography of references from the whole volume.

2. Women's Writing

As usual, Margery Kempe and Julian of Norwich were the most discussed English medieval women writers of 2009, although the work on Julian eclipses that on Margery. Lisa J. Kiser has written an article that brings Margery Kempe into the field of animal studies with her 'Margery Kempe and the Animalization of Christ: Animal Cruelty in Late Medieval England' (*SIP* 106[2009] 299–315), in which she discusses the implications of an analogy that Margery makes between the beaten Christ and seeing an animal so abused.

Margery's engagement with Mary Magdalene is the focus of Audrey Walton's 'The Mendicant Margery: Margery Kempe, Mary Magdalene and the *Noli Me Tangere*' (*MysticsQ* 35[2009] 1–29). Following Caroline Dinshaw's work, Walton looks at the 'queerness' of Margery's relationship to the *Noli me tangere* story, and in particular how Margery would have heard and processed the story as told by medieval preachers. Tara Williams examines how Margery navigates women's social roles in '"As thu were a wedow": Margery Kempe's Wifehood and Widowhood' (*Exemplaria* 21[2009] 345–62). She suggests that Margery constructs a kind of in-between identity that uses cultural measures of both the chaste virgin and the widow in order to forge her own, independent social role.

Karen Cherewatuk's '*Becoming Male, Medieval Mothering*, and Incarnational Theology in *Sir Gawain and the Green Knight* and the *Book of Margery Kempe*' (*Arth* 19:iii[2009] 15–24) discusses how these two different texts use references to Christ's nativity and Passion as commentary on gendered behaviour. She argues that ultimately Gawain is hindered in his attempt to reconcile his masculinity with Christ's humanity, while Margery is able fully to embrace it due to her social and personal experience as a mother.

Missed in 2008 was Brad Peters's article on Julian entitled 'Julian of Norwich's *Showings* and the *Ancrene Riwle*: Two Rhetorical Configurations of Mysticism' (*RhetR* 27[2008] 361–78), where he offers a close reading of rhetorical strategies in the anchoritic rule book and in Julian's *Showings*. He argues that she was familiar with the *Ancrene Riwle*, and that her book is in part meant to answer the dogma presented in the earlier text.

One of the most interesting books in recent years about Julian of Norwich was published in 2009: *Julian of Norwich's Legacy: Medieval Mysticism and Post-Medieval Reception*, edited by Sarah Salih and Denise N. Baker. In the introduction (pp. 1–12), the editors discuss Julian's 'many publics', academic and otherwise, who have embraced the mystic, her writing, and her symbolism. The collection examines Julian's post-medieval life, ranging from just after the Reformation to present day, but the editors give a short and comprehensive overview of Julian's known medieval readers and manuscript tradition. Because Julian's text had such little contemporary circulation and readership, it is especially interesting that she has such a rich and extensive afterlife. There are ten contributions to the volume, covering areas ranging from early manuscript and print history through to visual representations of Julian in present-day Norwich.

Alexandra Barratt's 'Julian of Norwich and her Children Today: Editions, Translations, and Versions of her Revelations' (pp. 13–27) opens the collection. Barratt, in an update to her 1995 study, surveys the editions of Julian's work from the surviving manuscripts through to the most recent print editions, examining the editorial policies and agendas of each text. Jennifer Summit's 'From Anchorhold to Closet: Julian of Norwich in 1670 and the Immanence of the Past' (pp. 29–47) follows, looking at aspects of Julian's 'early modernity' and how her subsequent readers are influenced by the seventeenth-century reading tradition of contemplative texts. After these two essays, the following ones in the collection deal with decidedly more modern material.

Anthony Cuda's 'W.B. Yeats and a Certain Mystic of the Middle Ages' (pp. 49–68) argues that Yeats used Julian's work as a touchstone for his own, using some references Yeats himself had made to the influences of medieval mystics and to Julian's work. Cuda focuses particularly on Yeats's idea of the 'mask and antiself', which he argues comes directly from his reading of Julian and other medieval mystics. Jewel Spears Brooker likewise looks at Julian's poetic influences in 'The Fire and the Rose: Theodicy in Eliot and Julian of Norwich' (pp. 69–86), using Eliot's direct quotation of Julian in his poem 'Little Gidding' as her starting point. Brooker suggests that Eliot found a way to write about evil through Julian's own confrontation with the concept.

The collection continues in the twentieth century with Denise N. Baker's 'Julie Norwich and Julian of Norwich: Annie Dillard's Theodicy in *Holy the Firm*' (pp. 87–100). Baker looks at how Dillard reconceptualizes Julian through the lens of American Transcendentalism in her character Julie Norwich. Susannah Chewning discusses how twentieth- and twenty-first-century popular fiction uses the figure of Julian in 'Julian of Norwich in Popular Fiction' (pp. 101–12), suggesting that most authors ignore Julian's faith and differences from modern-day women in favour of her likeness and ability to reflect them. In 'Playing Julian: The Cell as Theater in Contemporary Culture' (pp. 113–29), Jacqueline Jenkins examines three twentieth-century plays based on the life of Julian: James Janda's *Julian: A Play Based on the Life of Julian of Norwich*, Dana Bagshaw's *Cell Talk: A Duology between Julian of Norwich and Margery Kempe*, and Sheila Upjohn's *Mind Out of Time: A Play on Julian of Norwich*. Jenkins focuses specifically on the idea of the cell and how it is portrayed on stage.

Christiania Whitehead turns to how Julian was incorporated into later spiritual practices in '"A great woman in our future": Julian of Norwich's Functions in Late Twentieth-Century Spirituality' (pp. 131–51). Whitehead examines Julian's impact on Anglican, American Episcopalian, and Roman Catholic devotional practice and thought. Sarah Salih turns to visual culture in 'Julian in Norwich: Heritage and Iconography' (pp. 153–72), where she writes about the ways in which Julian has been translated into Norwich's material culture through artistic representations and a reconstruction of her cell. In 'In the Centre: Spiritual and Cultural Representations of Julian of Norwich in the Julian Centre' (pp. 173–89), Sarah Law closes the collection by also looking at present-day interest in Julian, especially through the work and audience of the Julian Centre and the reconstruction of her cell. Law argues, as does much of the collection as a whole, that Julian is appropriated by her audience for various purposes.

Ambram Van Engen argues that Julian's parable of the Lord and Servant does not reconcile the problem that Holy Church and God's teaching may be contradictory, but rather repositions the argument in such a way that God supersedes the church, in his article 'Shifting Perspectives: Sin and Salvation in Julian's *A Revelation of Love*' (*L&T* 23[2009] 1–17). Another parable, that of the hazelnut, is the point of examination in Jeanette S. Zissell's 'Universal Salvation in the Earthly City: *De Civitate Dei* and the Significance of the Hazelnut in Julian of Norwich's *Showings*' (in Classen, ed., *Urban Space in the Middle Ages and the Early Modern Age*, pp. 331–51). Zissell argues that Julian, both following in and disputing with the Augustinian tradition, adapts a conception of urban space in order to explain devotional and theological space, exemplified in her discussion of all creation as a hazelnut. Julian's theology is also central to Anna Lewis's 'Directing Reader Response: Julian's Revelation as Guided Meditation' (*MysticsQ* 35[2009] 1–27). Lewis examines the ways in which Julian both adheres to and departs from a kind of 'visionary script' (using Barbara Newman's term) that comes out of medieval meditative literature.

Nicola Masciandaro takes a different approach to Julian's writing and contemporary meditative literature in 'Eros as Cosmic Sorrow: Locating the Limits of Difference in Julian of Norwich's *Revelation of Love* and *The Cloud of Unknowing*' (*MysticsQ* 35[2009] 59–103), where he looks at the use of 'extreme sorrow' in Julian's text as well as the contemporary mystical treatise *The Cloud of Unknowing* and ponders how this intersects with the idea of eros and place.

Several of the essays in *Women and Experience in Later Medieval Writing: Reading the Book of Life*, edited by Anneke B. Mulder-Bakker and Liz Herbert McAvoy, will be useful to scholars of medieval women's writing. The essays focus on both insular and continental texts, including those by Heloise and Abelard, Hadewijch of Brabant, and other lesser-known women writers and readers. In their introduction to the collection, '*Experientia* and the Construction of Experience in Medieval Writing: An Introduction' (pp. 1–23), the editors suggest that medieval women have been portrayed as excised from the literate world of men and its implications, instead learning from the 'book of experience' and the ways of knowledge it implies. The collection, they argue, is meant to disrupt this comfortable and persistent dichotomy, focusing on the discourse women did and could use throughout the Middle Ages, producing texts that documented their *experientia*, going beyond simply lived experience and, rather, representing complex forms of knowledge and learning. Liz Herbert McAvoy's own contribution to the volume is most relevant to scholars of English medieval women as she focuses on the *Book of Margery Kempe*, examining Margery's use of secular, social language in order to express the mystical and theological concepts with which she wrestles. The result, McAvoy argues, is that the book Margery produces is her lived experience, her own actual *Book of Life*.

Many essays in *Women and the Divine in Literature before 1700: Essays in Memory of Margot Louis*, edited by Kathryn Kerby-Fulton, are of particular interest to those studying medieval English women writers, subjects, and readers. First, Kerby-Fulton's introduction, 'Skepticism, Agnosticism and Belief: The Spectrum of Attitudes Toward Women's Vision in Medieval England' (pp. 1–17), examines through a close reading the transmission and dissemination of the visions of St Perpetua and Christina of Markyate, suggesting that what has been passed down is an 'abridged' version of 'under-recorded' lives (p. 1). Linda Olson discusses St Augustine's mother Monica, and how she is interpreted in his writings—particularly later Middle English redactions—in 'Mother and More for the Middle Ages: Monica as Teacher, Visionary Philosopher and Mystic' (pp. 19–47). Thea Todd discusses Christina of Markyate in 'Revisiting Christina's Vow of Virginity: The Influence of Developing Marriage Law on Christina of Markyate's *Life*' (pp. 49–63), where she argues that, significantly, the hagiographic text is written after her life, when ecclesiastical marriage laws had changed and affected the view of the hagiographer.

Adrienne Williams Boyarin's 'Sealed Flesh, Book-Skin: How to Read the Female Body in the Early Middle English *Seinte Margarete*' (pp. 87–106) regards the early usage of the medieval motif of body as text, especially in the Katherine Group's *Seinte Margarete*. She argues that ultimately the text offers female self-authorization through its depiction of the feminized body, drawing on diverse contemporary images of contemporary seals, parchment, and jewels. Heather Reid looks at a much less studied Middle English text in 'Female Initiation Rites and Women Visionaries: Mystical Marriage in the Middle English Translation of *The Storie of Asneth*' (pp. 137–52). She compares the Hellenic Jewish *Asneth* story to the experiences of medieval female religious visionaries, suggesting that the 'initiation' rites of the former can be seen in the latter, for example in the funeral rites of the anchoress or the language of marriage used to join the visionary to the bridegroom Jesus.

Both Margery Kempe and Julian of Norwich have essays devoted to them in the collection. Johanne Paquette's 'Male Approbation in the Extant Glosses to the *Book of Margery Kempe*' (pp. 153–69) reviews the history of Kempe criticism following Sanford B. Meech and Hope Emily Allen's first edition of the *Book* through to current critics' reactions to the woman and her narrative, but then turns to Kempe's earlier readers evidenced by the red-ink annotator of British Library MS Additional 61823, the manuscript which contains the whole text. She looks at the annotator's symbols, surmising what they mean and noting where they are placed. The article concludes with a useful appendix laying these out. Jonathan Juilf's '"The boke is begonne . . . but is nott yett performyd": Compilations of Julian of Norwich's *A Revelation of Love*, 1413–1670' (pp. 171–84), similarly, is interested in the afterlife of Julian's text, beginning with the recent trend to anthologize both Margery Kempe and Julian of Norwich as part of the canon of medieval writers, and then turning to the early textual history of *A Revelation of Love*. Juilf is most interested in the 1670 edition of Julian's work by Hugh Cressy, and what the publication, 'packaging', and readership of the Cressy edition have done to influence Julian scholarship and reception afterwards.

The first full collection on the Wooing Group was published this year: *The Milieu and Context of the Wooing Group*, edited by Susannah M. Chewning, with eleven contributions focusing on the important anchoritic poems. In her introduction (pp. 1–25), Chewning surveys both the history of the Wooing Group manuscripts as well as its critical history, most of it beginning with W. Meredith Thompson's 1958 edition of *þe Wohunge of ure Lauerd*. She also gives attention to the language of the Wooing Group, discussed consistently since Tolkien first took it up in 1929, its generic and literary influences, and the anchoritic experience generally.

Bella Millett's essay 'The "Conditions of Eligibility" in *þe Wohunge of ure Lauerd*' (pp. 26–47) opens the collection, and situates the *Wohunge* in relation to contemporary continental devotional practices. Through close comparative readings, Millett demonstrates the influence and adaptation of many different texts associated with the Paris schools on the *Wohunge* author. Following Millett's is Chewning's own essay, 'Speaking of Flesh and Soul: Linguistic and Spiritual Translation in the Wooing Group' (pp. 48–65), where she looks at the sensual imagery inherent in the *Wohunge* texts and how the physical is translated into the verbal for anchoritic consumption. This essay is followed by Jennifer N. Brown's 'Subject, Object and Mantra in *þe Wohunge of ure Lauerd*' (pp. 66–83), where she discusses the poetic devices of the *Wohunge* author and how the poem creates a spoken dialogue out of a prayer meant to be read by a cell's solitary occupant.

Jeremy Smith's contribution to the volume, 'The spellings ⟨e⟩, ⟨ea⟩ and ⟨a⟩ in two Wooing Group texts (MSS London, Cotton Nero A.xiv and London, Lambeth Palace 487)' (pp. 84–95), offers a linguistic analysis, and the complications of, the so-called 'AB' language—originally classified as such by J.R.R. Tolkien—of the texts. Catherine Innes-Parker's '*þe Wohunge of ure Lauerd* and the Tradition of Affective Devotion: Rethinking Text and Audience' (pp. 96–122) examines not only the content of the *Wohunge*, which she suggests anticipates the devotional movements of the fourteenth and fifteenth centuries, but also the knowledge and expectations of its anchoritic audience, which she argues have been vastly underestimated in recent critical scholarship. In Michelle Sauer's '"þe blod þ[at] bohte": The Wooing Group Christ as Pierced, Pricked, and Penetrated Body' (pp. 123–47), she argues that the bleeding Christ figure is central to anchoritic devotion representing three things: 'eternal salvation, carnal reparation, and bodily purification' (p. 123).

Sarah Salih's essay, 'Transvestism in the Anchorhold' (pp. 148–64), looks at the idea of heteronomativity in the use of bridegroom/bride imagery and gendered personae in four of the *Wohunge*'s meditations: *On wel swuðe God Ureisum of God Almihti*, *On Lofsong of Ure Louerde*, *On Lofsong of Ure Lefdi*, and *þe Wohunge of ure Lauerd*. Anne Savage follows with 'The Wooing Group: Pain, Pleasure and the Anchoritic Body' (pp. 165–77), where she examines the emotional life of the anchoress and how this engages with the language of the passion inherent in the language of the *Wohunge*. Michael Sargent's 'What Kind of Writing is *A Talkyng of þe Love of God*' (pp. 178–94) engages with the language of taxonomy and categorization used to describe the *Talkyng* and its associated texts, in particular the meaning and use of the word 'mystical'. Finally, Nicholas Watson closes the volume with his 'Afterword: "On *Eise*"' (pp. 195–210), where he deftly pulls out the commonalities and conflicts among the essays and puts them in dialogue with one another.

Masha Raskolnikov also looks at anchoritic texts, in particular *Sawles Warde*, in her book *Body Against Soul: Gender and Sowlehele in Middle English Allegory*. The chapter entitled 'Defending the Female Self: "Sawles Warde" and *Sowlehele*' looks at the Katherine Group narrative in relation to the idea of 'sowlehele' that Raskolnikov defines as medieval texts that personify different aspects of the self, such as the body and soul. She separates 'Sawles Warde' from other body/soul debates of the time, particularly in its use of gendered language and because of its clearly female audience.

In '"Ryght worchepfull mastres": Letters of Request and Servants' Scripting of Margaret Paston's Social Self' (*Parergon* 26[2009] 91–114) Valerie Creelman writes about Margaret Paston's role in managing her estate by looking not only at Paston's letters, but also at her servants' written petitions to her and the kind of dialogue that ensues as a result of this back and forth. Margaret's own letters are the focus of Jennifer Douglas's '"Kepe wysly youre wrytyngys": Margaret Paston's Fifteenth-Century Letters' (*Libraries & the Cultural Record* 44[2009] 29–49), where she uses Margaret Paston's letter as a kind of case study in order to make some observations about women's literacy and writing practices, particularly when it comes to letter-writing, in the late Middle Ages. The Paston letters also come into the argument Shannon McSheffrey and Julia Pope make about 'Ravishment, Legal Narratives, and Chivalric Culture in Fifteenth-Century England' (*JBS* 48[2009] 818–36); while they focus on a narrative of ravishment of a local Norwich woman recounted by John Paston, it would be useful for scholars interested in the female Pastons or the idea of 'ravishment' in late medieval England.

Although the Pastons are generally the most studied letter-writers of medieval England, that other epistolary family, the Stonors, get their due this year in Elizabeth Noble's *The World of the Stonors: A Gentry Society*. Noble sketches out the critical history of the Stonor letters and other records in her introduction, outlining how much less attention their corpus has received than that of the Pastons. The chapters are somewhat oddly divided—neither clearly chronologically nor thematically—and would be hard to navigate if a reader wanted to look at only parts of the book and not the book as a whole. The first is logically devoted to 'The Stonors: A Gentry Family Biography', but it is then followed by 'Lineage', 'Landed Estate', 'The Stonors' Lords', 'Early Social Networks: Judge John to Thomas I', 'Later Social Networks and Gentry Values: Thomas II and William', and finally 'Conclusion: Gentry Networks, Culture, Mentality and Society'. The letters written by and about the Stonor women are interspersed throughout, and for someone who works on their writings or on the Paston women's writings this would be a most helpful introduction. Noble draws on the Paston letters as points of comparison, not so much in style as in content. While the Stonor letters are not as rich in women's writing as the Paston letters, they do provide an invaluable insight into the workings of a gentry family in late medieval England, and show women's roles in both the household and the wider society.

Anglo-Norman writers generally, and women writers in particular, have a banner year with the publication of *Language and Culture in Medieval Britain: The French of England c.1100–c1500*, edited by Jocelyn Wogan-Browne. This expansive volume has several articles of peripheral interest to scholars working in medieval women's writing and reading, and many that are specifically focused on the topic. In her 'General Introduction: What's in a Name: The "French" of "England"' (pp. 1–13), Jocelyn Wogan-Browne sets out the parameters of the significant volume, explaining the preference for the term the 'French of England' over 'Anglo-Norman' or 'Anglo-French' as intended to encompass divisions that have arisen by using one of the latter terms exclusively. She discusses the various uses and integrations of French in medieval English culture, suggesting that one of the purposes of the volume is to 're-position what has been often treated as a monoglot English culture within its multilingual actualities, and use more open and less prescriptive models of language and language-contact for thinking about the French of England' (p. 10). I will discuss only the articles most pertinent to women's writing and reading in medieval England (other articles are reviewed in the relevant sections of this chapter) but recommend the volume in its entirety.

Marilyn Oliva discusses 'The French of England in Female Convents: The French Kitcheners' Accounts of Campsey Ash Priory' (in Wogan-Browne, ed., pp. 90–102). The survival and subsequent study of convent records is fairly rare, so Oliva's discussion of the records from Campsey Ash Priory, a house of Augustinian nuns, is welcome. In discussing the accounts, she gleans implications about the wealth, health, diet, and lifestyle of the women who lived at the priory. Monica H. Green's 'Salerno on the Thames: The Genesis of Anglo-Norman Medical Literature' (pp. 220–31) looks at six Anglo-Norman medical texts that are both about women's health and, more significantly, addressed to women readers (although this address is not as simple as it seems, as Green teases out of the text). Green suggests that female patrons are behind the works as well.

Jocelyn Wogan-Browne's own contribution to the volume, '"Cest livre liseez...chescun jour": Women and Reading *c.*1230–*c.*1430' (pp. 239–53) extends her already remarkable contribution to the study of women's literacy practices in medieval England. Wogan-Browne turns her criticism towards penitential reading and its intersection with and relationship to francophone women's patronage and literary culture of the later Middle Ages. Among other texts, the article pays close attention to a diagram from the Lambeth Apocalypse (Lambeth Palace Library, MS 209), representing an allegory of penance featuring a noblewoman, which Wogan-Browne deftly parses and whose implications she explains. Ultimately, she argues that women's francophone literary culture is inextricable from the larger English literary culture within which it operates and which it influences. Delbert W. Russell also discusses women's literacy, as well as authorship, in 'The Cultural Context of the French Prose *remainement* of the Life of Edward the Confessor by a Nun of Barking Abbey' (pp. 290–302). Russell's subject is a reworking from poetry into prose of the Nun of Barking's life of Edward into a French manuscript, London BL Egerton 745; he looks at both the meaning of the text and its images, as well as the probably female patronage and ownership of the manuscript itself.

Rebecca June's 'The Languages of Memory: The Crabhouse Nunnery Manuscript' (pp. 347–58) discusses a conventual manuscript which, in addition to convent records, contains a miscellany of narratives written in both poetry and prose, in English, Latin, and French. June is interested in how the manuscript was read and used as a way of establishing the nuns' identity and the 'story of themselves' (p. 348). Finally, Stephanie Downes discusses Christine de Pizan's work in England in 'A "Frenche booke called the Pistill of Othea": Christine de Pizan's French in England' (pp. 457–68). Downes is interested in Christine's *Epistre d'Othea*, which, while translated into English in the Middle Ages, circulated in French in greater numbers in England. She focuses especially on the narrative's presence in MS Harley 219, situating the *Othea* in relation to its textual neighbours in the manuscript.

A few articles outside this volume look at some of the same works. Jane Bliss discusses some word and phrase usage in the Nun of Barking's *Vie d'Edouard le Confesseur* in 'An Anglo-Norman Nun: An Old English *Gnome*'

(*N&Q* 56[2009] 16–18). Jennifer N. Brown's '"Cut from its stump": Translating Edward the Confessor and the Dream of the Green Tree' (in Renevey and Whitehead, eds., *The Medieval Translator 12: Lost in Translation?*, pp. 57–70) also discusses the Nun of Barking's work, putting it in dialogue with other redactions of Edward's legend and the political climate at the time of their writing.

The French of Marie de France was another fruitful area of scholarship this year. First, however, a few articles were missed last year. Brian Sutton's '"A different kind of the same thing": Marie de France's *Laüstic* and Glaspell's *Trifles*' (*Explicator* 66[2008] 170–4) discusses how the medieval *lai* and the twentieth-century play both use the symbolism of a dead songbird to represent the death of the joy and dreams of its female characters. Matthieu Boyd looks at Marie's *Yonec* in 'The Ring, the Sword, the Fancy Dress, and the Posthumous Child: Background to the Element of Heroic Biography in Marie de France's *Yonec*' (*RomQ* 55[2008] 205–30). He is most interested in how the Celtic tradition is co-opted and used in order to bring together the themes of courtly love and Christianity in Marie's work. Monica Brzezinski Potkay explores the general prologue to Marie's collected *lais* in 'The Parable of the Sower and Obscurity in the Prologue to Marie de France's *Lais*' (*C&L* 57[2008] 355–78), focusing on a passage with a misattribution to the Latin grammarian Priscian and its implications for the writer and the reader. Potkay suggests that Marie is alluding to the biblical parable of the sower in her prologue, and that reading the troubling passage through that lens adds some clarity and comprehension to the work as a whole.

In 2009 Ashley Lee discussed two prologues in Marie de France's work—that to the collection of her *lais* and the specific prologue to the *lai Guigemar*—in her 'The Hind Episode in Marie de France's *Guigemar* and Medieval Vernacular Poetics' (*Neophil* 93[2009] 191–200). She suggests that these prologues reveal Marie's defence of her art and set up her authorial voice. Marie de France's *lais* are likewise the subject of Norris J. Lacy's 'Observations on Authority' (*Arth* 19[2009] 72–9), where Marie's *Chevrefoil* is used an example of how symbols and objects are used to relate the events of the text.

Animals were a big topic this year in medieval studies generally, but have always been a focus of those who look at Marie de France's fables and *lais*. Jill Mann's *From Aesop to Reynard: Beast Literature in Medieval Britain* devotes a chapter to 'Marie de France: The Courtly Fable' (pp. 53–97). Mann points out that Marie's fables survive in many more manuscripts than do her *lais*, and that they, like the *lais,* evoke a courtly world in their description and vocabulary. Mann looks at specific fables and parses the messages, morals, and ethos, both overt and implicit, that Marie incorporates.

Peggy McCracken also writes about animals in 'Translation and Animals in Marie de France's *Lais*' (*Australian Journal of French Studies* 46[2009] 206–18), arguing that Marie's project of translation does not merely include linguistic and cultural translations, but also the idea of animals' translation into men (and vice versa). She suggests that forms of animal–human translation inform Marie's other kinds of translation projects. Werewolves are the central animal in Amanda Hopkins's 'Why Arthur At All?: The

Dubious Arthuricity of *Arthur and Gorlagon*' (*ArthL* 26[2009] 77–95), where she looks at three textual cognates—*Bisclarel*, *Melion*, and *Arthur and Gorlagon*—in relation to Marie's *lai Bisclavret*, and particularly at how Arthur is or is not used in the narratives. Surprisingly, Marie's *lais* only figure peripherally in the hefty volume *A Companion to Arthurian Literature*, edited by Helen Fulton, despite the Arthurian overtones and content of many of them.

Jane Chance takes a pedagogical approach to Marie's *Lanval* in her essay 'Tough Love: Teaching the New Medievalism' (in Fugelso, ed., *Studies in Medievalism XVIII: Defining Medievalism(s) II*, pp. 76–98). She situates *Lanval*, in particular Guinevere's accusation of homosexuality directed at the eponymous character, in relationship to *Gawain and the Green Knight* and Tolkien's criticism of the poem in order to open up the text to a queer reading.

A Concise Companion to Middle English Literature, edited by Marilyn Corrie, contains Barry Windeatt's essay 'Signs and Symbols' (pp. 9–31), which looks at Margery Kempe's and Julian of Norwich's texts, among others, and these writers' use of symbols in comparison to the Middle Scots poet Robert Henryson. Corrie's own contribution to the volume, 'Religious Belief' (pp. 32–53), demonstrates how Julian of Norwich engages with scripture and the teachings of the church, particularly in their descriptions of their visions. Catherine Sanok's overview 'Women and Literature' (pp. 54–76) examines representations of women in medieval literature, for example, in Chaucer's *Legend of Good Women* or Hoccleve's *Letter of Cupid*, and the paradigms that are set up by these depictions. She then turns to texts written by women, such as Marie de France's *Guigemar*, or those directed at women, such as the *Ancrene Wisse*, and examines how the stereotypes of the anti-feminist tradition are used. She ends by briefly turning to Julian of Norwich and Margery Kempe and how their literary products respond to the masculine tradition.

As usual, there are several books and articles that may not address women's writing directly but are of interest to those who study women's writing and reading. The most significant of these is *Syon Abbey and its Books: Reading, Writing and Religion c.1400–1700*, edited by E.A. Jones and Alexandra Walsham. While all of the essays will be of interest to those who study convent culture in late medieval England, a few are particularly of note here. Virginia R. Bainbridge's 'Syon Abbey: Women and Learning c.1415–1600' (pp. 82–103) addresses the issue of women's education, literacy, and relationship to their books, looking at evidence from the Rule, the library, and certain individual manuscripts. Bainbridge also discusses the networks of patronage surrounding Syon and to what extent the nuns were integrated in and crucial to the functions of those networks. C. Annette Grisé examines printed books owned and read by the sisters of Syon in '"Moche profitable unto religious persones, gathered by a brother of Syon": Syon Abbey and English Books' (pp. 129–54). The essay serves as a survey of the most important books associated with the nuns, such as the Wynkyn de Worde 1519 edition of the *Orcharde of Syon*, but also situates the books in relation to each other and to the world outside Syon's walls. Several of the essays also serve to showcase the importance of Syon at the time of the Reformation and after, such as Claire Walker's 'Continuity and Isolation: The Bridgettines of Syon in the Sixteenth and Seventeenth Centuries' (pp. 155–76), Caroline Bowden's 'Books and Reading at Syon Abbey, Lisbon, in the Seventeenth Century' (pp. 177–202), and Ann M. Hutchinson's 'Syon Abbey Preserved: Some Historians of Syon' (pp. 228–51).

Peter Kidd's 'Codicological Clues to the Patronage of Stowe MS. 39: A Fifteenth-Century Illustrated Nun's Book in Middle English' (*Electronic BLJ* [2009] article 5, 1–12) is a study of the interplay between text and image in British Library, MS Stowe 39, which contains the texts *The Abbey of the Holy Ghost* and *The Desert of Religion*. Kidd suggests a provenance for the manuscript through his close study of both the manuscript itself and the symbolism of the images therein. One article that will certainly be of interest to scholars of medieval women and gender is Dyan Elliot's 'The Three Ages of Joan Scott' (*AHR* 113[2008] 1390–1403), which looks at how gender has been conceptualized and used in the past four decades of medievalist work through the lens and influential work of Joan Scott. Monica Green continues to publish fascinating work on medieval women's medical issues this year with her 'The Sources of Eucharius Rösslin's "Rosegarden for Pregnant Women and Midwives"' (*Medical History* 53[2009] 167–92), where she argues that there is an earlier source than previously believed for the popular medieval medical text for women, 'Rosegarden', and examines the effect of print culture on the dissemination and translation of the treatise.

Two essays in the collection *Texts and Traditions of Medieval Pastoral Care*, edited by Cate Gunn and Catherine Innes-Parker, address women as readers. C. Annette Grisé's 'Prayer, Meditation and Women Readers in Late Medieval England: Teaching and Sharing Through Books' (pp. 178–92) argues that there was a kind of lateral pastoral care between pious women (as opposed to the official hierarchical pastoral care provided by monks and priests) that was facilitated through the practice of sharing books. She takes as her case study a group of manuscripts from the Bridgettine Syon Abbey and the circulation of those texts. In the same volume, Alexandra Barratt's '"Take a book and read": Advice for Religious Women' (pp. 193–208) discusses to what extent religious women had prescribed reading, examining devotional texts directed at women and what they suggest about women's reading generally and specifically. Barratt looks at some obvious texts, such as the *Ancrene Wisse*, but also at less well known devotional treatises, especially those in Middle English.

The Medieval British Literature Handbook, edited by Daniel Kline, provides a user-friendly guide that would be useful to students entering into the field of British medieval studies, as it lists major authors, texts, critics, and critical approaches in an accessible format. A few of the essays touch on the subjects and women discussed in this chapter and are worth mentioning here. Julia Bolton Holloway and Daniel T. Kline's 'Literary and Cultural Contexts: Major Figures, Institutions, Topics, Events, Movements' (pp. 49–81) has brief entries on Julian of Norwich, Margery Kempe, Marie de France and the Paston Letters. Matthew Boyd Goldie's 'Case Studies in Reading I: Key Primary Literary Texts' (pp. 82–108) looks at both Marie de France's *Lanval* and *The Book of Margery Kempe*, discussing the cultural and critical issues surrounding the texts. Four of the essays discuss gender criticism and its use and history in medieval studies: Gail Ashton's 'Case Studies in

Reading II: Key Literary and Theoretical Texts' (pp. 109–32), Bonnie Millar's 'Key Critics, Concepts and Topics' (pp. 133–51), John M. Ganim's 'Changes in Critical Responses and Approaches' (pp. 152–83), and Diane Cady's 'Issues of Sexuality, Gender and Ethnicity' (pp. 199–225). Nancy Bradley Warren's 'Changes in the Canon' (pp. 184–98) discusses Julian of Norwich and Margery Kempe and how they are studied by feminist critics.

While Sarah McNamer's *Affective Meditation and the Invention of Medieval Compassion* only peripherally addresses women's writing, specifically Julian of Norwich's, her chapters 'Feeling Like a Woman' (pp. 119–49) and 'Marian Lament and the Rise of Vernacular Ethics' (pp. 150–73) are both particularly useful reading for scholars who work on devotional literature and gender (as is the book as a whole). In the former chapter, McNamer discusses Richard Rolle's effect on late medieval piety and devotion, arguing that he sets up a generic paradigm where 'feeling compassion like a woman' is part of the practice of devotion inherent in his writings. She demonstrates how this is transmitted to Rolle's readers, especially his dedicatee Margaret Kirby, as well as subsequent texts by other devotional writers. In the latter chapter, McNamer looks at how compassion for Christ is encouraged in its transference to ordinary Christians, opening her argument with quotes from both Julian of Norwich and Margery Kempe to demonstrate how this functions in practice. She argues that the use of the Passion and compassion through the popularity of Marian lyrics allows for a vocabulary and practice of ethical dissent against warfare in late medieval England.

Mary Dockray-Miller's edition *Saints Edith and Æthelthryth: Princesses, Miracle Workers, and their Late Medieval Audience. The Wilton Chronicle and the Wilton Life of St Æthelthryth* is a welcome addition for scholars of medieval women. Dockray-Miller lays out the important history of the Wilton texts, in relation to English history generally and medieval women's history specifically. Directed towards the nuns at Wilton Abbey, these narratives are essential reading for the understanding of women's conventual identities and literacy. The handsome volume contains facing-page translations of the *Wilton Chronicle* and *The Wilton Life of St. Æthelthryth*, and contains two helpful appendices as well: Stephen J. Harris's 'Founders and Sources Listed in the Wilton Manuscript' (pp. 407–21), and a transcription of additional lines listed at the end of the manuscript. There is also a useful glossary and an index of proper names.

3. Alliterative Verse and Lyrics

The past year has seen some important contributions to the field of study of short verse, in particular. Of these one the most significant must be Helen Barr's *The Digby Poems: A New Edition of the Lyrics*, which is the first complete edition of the lyrics since Joseph Kail's volume of 1904. Barr's work is comprehensive, supplying a lengthy introduction that begins with a description of Oxford, Bodleian Library, MS Digby 102, the work of a lone scribe, which contains, as well as twenty-four lyric poems, an incomplete C-text of *Piers*, the metrical paraphrase of the *Seven Penitential Psalms* by

Richard of Maidstone, and *The Debate between the Body and the Soul*, and the collection is unified by what Barr calls a 'demonstrable orthodoxy' comparable to that of the Vernon manuscript. The critical reception has been as fragmented as the editing of the poems, and Barr corrects this with a close reading of the texts that ought to facilitate new approaches and work on them. She pays particular attention to the issues and cruxes in dating, which allows her to provide a detailed historical analysis of each short verse. Poem 12, for instance, celebrates a new king at Easter, which correlates to Henry V's coronation in 1413 but, like Poem 14, which is comparable in part, it can also be dated to 1418. Barr also examines the sequence's concerns with 'bolstering devotional orthodoxy' (p. 19), its focus on penance and devotion, on the defence of the sacraments and, compellingly, on reform, the advocacy of which is so bold and unafraid as to be akin to some Lollard writings. Poem 18 is a plain-speaking and monitory appeal for the proper observance of monastic rule ('Gret hors, ne iewel, ne browded hood / Nes no cause of holynesse'). Barr is to be commended for her production of a fine edition of a fascinating, layered, and subtle verse collection, and this new volume will greatly aid teaching and encourage new research.

Equally welcome is Susanna Fein's admirable new edition of *John the Blind Audelay: Poems and Carols*. Scholars are treated to an entire book, expertly edited and introduced by Fein, which was completed by the chaplain John Audelay (assisted by two scribes) in 1426 and frequently inscribed with his name (sixteen times on thirty-five vellum leaves) as if, the editor suggests, 'to preserve his worldly memory and ensure for his soul's salvation' and in order to 'make the book identifiable as an anthology of the collected works of an early fifteenth century poet' (p. 1). Fein writes extremely well on the complexity of authorship in the fifteenth century generally, and specifically regarding Audelay in relation to his ancestors and contemporaries, and indeed to his book. For our purposes, however, the carols and poems preserved therein—some unique—represent one of the most dynamic personal compilations to survive from the period. One such text is Audelay's own—the alliterative *Marcolf and Solomon*, a text indebted to *Piers Plowman*; others may have been composed by Audelay—the alliterative *Paternoster* and *Three Dead Kings*. *Marcolf and Solomon* is an early work, probably before 1414, since it apparently reflects the political mood leading up to the Oldcastle rebellion. The carols, twenty-five in number, are 'convivial', some 'directed to women and seem meant for singing in a hall' (p. 7), are arranged in groups of five 'by topic' (p. 15), and are intended, as the headnote directs, to be sung at Christmas, though Fein notes that some of the longer ones—like the ceremonial ones dedicated to Henry VI and St Francis—are probably intended for reading. Taken together, the carols create what Fein calls 'a narrative of faith' (p. 19), but discovering for what occasion Audelay actually composed these carols is complicated by the existence of other, similar, versions, and the possibility that he borrows from other sources. However, it is also likely that other composers borrowed from Audelay's own compositions. Whatever his contemporary influence, the writings of Audelay provide a unique window onto the spiritual life, and the iteration of aspects of that life, of a fifteenth-century poet, lyricist, and reader. Fein's edition, complete with excellent textual notes and useful indexes, manages to provide readers with a useable textbook while simultaneously retaining a sense of the author-compiler's own book.

Fein is also responsible for the substantial and important volume of critical essays that acts as a companion to her edition. *'My Wyl and My Wrytyng': Essays on John the Blind Audelay*. It is rare to have an edition appear in tandem with criticism, since one usually follows the other; the benefit of publishing both is that this volume works in synergy in every way with the edition to provide a set of perspectives on the history of the book and the selection and the nature of texts. One of Fein's' contribution here—aside of course from her editorial input—is an overview of studies on Audelay who, she argues, has been neglected by the scholarly community despite his comparability to other writers of his time in his 'self-proclaimed displays of idiosyncratic autobiography, orthodox yet troubled allegiances, authorial proclivities and preoccupations, earnest refashioning of traditions, and dependency on scribal fidelity—all made more interesting when set against the social, political, and ecclesiastical forces of his day' (p. 3). Fein's second essay, 'Death and the Colophon in the Audelay Manuscript' (pp. 294–302), questions how much we can look to the book of Audelay to reconcile the public and the private man. As the chaplain to Lord Richard Lestrange, Audelay was no doubt affected by the crime committed by his patron and the very public penance meted out to him and his wife, and Fein offers the suggestion that the book 'serves... as part of an ongoing atonement before God and man' (p. 295). Here the endings in the book are most significant; Audelay is careful in one not just to warn readers not to deface his volume, but also to drive home the point that everything copied or written there (including endings) is done intentionally. The two alliterative poems that close the book's first ending, *Paternoster* and *Three Dead Kings*, are, Fein argues, afforded a position of honour, and written in a suitable medium for serious matter. The latter is 'the most accomplished literary piece in the book, an admonitory narrative of three kings who encounter the animated corpses of their fathers, receive warnings from them, and use these mirrors of what they will become to reform their ways in the world' (p. 300).

Audelay's endings are also ways into new beginnings. In 'John Audelay: Life Records and Heaven's Ladder' (pp. 30–53), Michael J. Bennett deftly pieces together what is known about the chaplain; the codex provides the only record of his activities after 1417. In 'The Vatic Penitent: John Audelay's Self-Representation' (pp. 54–85), Robert J. Meyer-Lee addresses one of the puzzles identified by Fein's edition: how a man responsible for so much 'ordinary' verse was capable of compiling Douce 302, an 'unprecedented', sophisticated collection compared to contemporary books like those of Hoccleve, for example. Meyer-Lee examines how a period with a fairly loose sense of authorship and book production spawned a volume with 'an extraordinary sense of book-consciousness' (p. 55). Susan Powell's contribution (pp. 86–111) concerns the commonality between John Audelay and John Mirk, who led very different lives but who 'lived within a generation of each other in time and wrote their extant works within fifteen miles of each other in space' (p. 86). Oliver Pickering, in 'The Make-Up of John Audelay's *Counsel of Conscience*' (pp. 112–37), takes Audelay's *Counsel of Conscience* as his topic, arguing for the compiler as a 'poet in his own right' (p. 113). The *Counsel* refers to the first of four groups of material identifiable in the manuscript; Pickering deals with the 'homogeneity' of this part, and asks if we can be sure whether Audelay composed the material. Included in this section, among seventeen other poems, is the alliterative *Marcolf and Solomon* (1,013 lines). The latter is also the subject of Derek Pearsall's contribution, 'Audelay's *Marcolf and Solomon*' (pp. 138–52), which is probably the most germane to this review. Locating it in the Langlandian tradition, Pearsall calls it a 'long and sprawling anthology of reproof and exhortation to the clergy, written in a complex thirteen-line stanza consisting of an octave of four-stress alliterative and semi-alliterative lines' (p. 139). In previous work, Pearsall has referred to *Marcolf* as being 'profoundly influenced by *Piers*'; here, he re-examines the nature of that influence. Richard Firth Green also takes Langland and Audelay as his subject in 'Langland and Audelay' (pp. 153–69); where Pearsall now questions whether Audelay knew *Piers*, he finds compelling evidence that he both read and used Langland. In an essay on Audelay's *Vision of Saint Paul*, '"Choose yourselves whither to go": John Audelay's *Vision of St Paul*' (pp. 170–90), Robert Easting examines the narrative poem, derived from a Latin source, to which Audelay adds about 155 lines. Coupled with *Our Lord's Epistle on Sunday* in the manuscript, Easting notes that the pairing is quite deliberate, and that the *Vision* is 'a priestly production in tones of voice and style, which Stanley has dubbed "sermonic"' (p. 171).

In the same volume, 'John Audelay and the Bridgettines' (pp. 191–217), Martha Driver writes on the *Salutation to Saint Bridget*, written by him in the Augustinian house of Haughmond Abbey, as providing insight into the daily habits of the Bridgettines, who were also governed by Augustinian rule. Julia Boffey's contribution, 'Audelay's Carol Collection' (pp. 218–29), centres on Audelay's fascinating and 'numerically significant' collection of carols. This collection is unusually large and relatively early; more important, however, and as Boffey states, '[I]n the context of other late Middle English manuscripts, it stands out as an especially unusual instance of the amassing of a selection of short poems, texts much more often relegated to positions as fillers or flyleaf jottings' (p. 218). Audelay exhorts that the carols be used at Christmas; however many—like those concerned with Henry VI, the four estates, and matters like childhood—seem not to respond to this specific instruction. John C. Hirsh, in '"Wo and werres . . . rest and pese": Audelay's Politics of Peace' (pp. 230–48), takes that carol written in honour of Henry, using it to examine Audelay's social and political context and his responses to the times in which he lived. Finally, in 'The Alliterative *Three Dead Kings* in John Audelay's MS Douce 302' (pp. 249–93), Stanley reasserts the literary value of one of the alliterative pieces in the manuscript. Angus McIntosh praised the poem, Stanley notes, but 'that it is not thought to be an item of Audelay's oeuvre is in large measure attributable to philological localization, insufficiently informed with the literary likelihood . . . that when a poet turns to heavily alliterative versified narration . . . he may look westwards' (p. 250). This is a heavily technical but rewarding essay, its main focus being the analysis of some of the important linguistic features of the alliterative *Three Dead Kings*.

This volume sheds new light on understudied alliterative verse and carols, as well as providing an excellent template for work on similar, and similarly neglected, personal compilations.

Ardis Butterfield contributes the section on lyric to the newest *Cambridge Companion to Medieval English Literature, 1100–1500*, edited by Larry Scanlon (pp. 95–122). Using the famous short lyric 'Westron winde' as her point of departure, and challenging its apparent simplicity, Butterfield skilfully posits ways and levels of reading and comprehending this most prolific of medieval textual genres. Butterfield's statement—that 'Westron winde' is 'more medieval than it looks'—is not quite as startling as it may read here when couched in Butterfield's concise but nicely tuned argument. The lyric is representative of a type of short verse, and thus typically medieval, but it also reads well as a modern poem: short, secular, erotic and intensely personal, slightly ironic. However its sole context, in a Tudor song book, and evidence of subsequent use in Masses throughout the sixteenth century, challenge its postmodern mocking tone. And this is the crux of Butterfield's article: that medieval verse continually interrupts our (well-founded) historical readings. There is a call here for a renewed appreciation of the lyric. Editions of lyric tend to be thematic in focus, thus frequently disregarding context and chronology; conversely, manuscript studies, compilation, circulation, and related issues have dominated research over the last two decades, a situation which is, Butterfield quite rightly states, no longer tenable. Some 2,000 verses have been recorded from 450 manuscripts; the majority of those are anonymously circulated, with little sense of self-image or fashioning. This anonymity may be evidence of the status of English as a literary vernacular, but—and again we see this duality in terms of the lyric—we still find performances of high art which, along with lyrical features such as repetition, ask us to consider relationships between text and sound, fragment and whole, individual and collective, political and personal, and, broadly, to accept anonymity as a gateway into an entire network of textual creation and public expression. Butterfield does a great service to lyric here, even in this short article. The same volume's treatment of alliterative verse is not as concentrated; however, where it does occur, it proceeds in line with the year's work in the field that sees the alliterative impulse not just as a poor imitation of older verse types, metre, and tradition, but as another tendency to the improvement of vernacular verse. In 'Re-inventing the Vernacular: Middle English Literature and its Language' (pp. 11–23) Wendy Scase notes that '[E]nrichment of versification and vocabulary was sought and displayed by alliterative poets' (p. 19), and offers a useful, concise description of the metre and language of alliterative verse.

As we might expect, a fair amount of work on alliterative verse is to be found in Dinah Hazell's *Poverty in Late Middle English Literature*. Hazell acknowledges the work that has been undertaken in this area, but she argues for a 'comprehensive focus on poverty: its existential reality, its place in medieval culture, its perception and treatment by the populace at all levels, and its literary function as reflector of ideals and ideologies of both audience and author in fourteenth-century England' (p. 11). *Pierce the Ploughman's Crede* is presented as an example of a text dealing with apostolic poverty, each of the four orders attacking the other on various points. The Austin friar accuses the Franciscan of wearing rich, elaborate clothes under his cope; the Dominican friar condemns the Austins as 'simoniacs who practice a "pur pardoners craft"' (p. 146). None of the friars can teach the narrator his creed and, Hazell notes, all are grouped together as 'fals freres' by Peres, who in turn answers the narrator's suspicion that he may have a grudge against the orders by reaffirming the validity of the poem's anti-fraternal charges as objective and well-intended.

The dating of the alliterative *Morte* is the subject of P.J.C. Field's paper (*MÆ* 78[2009] 80–97). In '*Morte Arthure*, The Montagus, and Milan', Field notes the general agreement amongst scholars that, of all of the Arthurian texts of the Middle Ages, the *Morte* reflects more of the affairs of the time. This premise, however, is complicated and affected by the problems in dating the poem. The two main scholars of the topic, Benson and Hamel, agree on *c*.1400, but this fairly close and definite dating is further complicated by the fact that the *Morte* almost certainly underwent revisions, and that the poem, as it stands, demonstrates at least three different dialects. Hamel's final assertion that the *Morte* was completed between 1396 and 1400–2 presents problems which are evaluated here; Field posits an 'outer limit' which relates to the copying of the manuscript (1420–50), and notes that echoes of the *Morte* in the *Awntyrs off Arthure* push the composition of the former back to the mid-1420s. Field's paper is a close and complex argument, concluding that, based on the (convincing) evidence, an earlier date of composition is likely.

Randy P. Schiff also contributes to work on alliterative verse in 'The Loneness of the Stalker: Poaching and Subjectivity in *The Parlement of the Thre Ages*' (*TSLL* 51[2009] 263–93). Taking on the space of the forest as the locus for political battles, and the symbolic potential of the successful poaching of deer to 'strike at the heart of royal power and prestige' (p. 263), Schiff examines the anonymous poacher-narrator of the text who, he reckons, emerges as a more threatening, individual, and troubling figure than many traditional outlaws like Robin Hood or poachers such as Ralph the Collier. The careful balance of class and landownership in relation to forest and hunting rights, instituted by a Ricardian statute of 1390, is challenged but hidden in the 'unassuming person of the poacher-narrator of *The Parlement*' (p. 265), and the framing narrative of the hunt constitutes a critique of forest laws. Schiff uses Bourdieu's work on assumptions about how much social behaviour is informed by abstract concepts to tease out this theory. In part the paper focuses on the aesthetic disjunction between frame and narrative, manifest in the poem in the figure of the lone poacher as fluid, moving between two worlds, 'immersed in the social circulation of an overdetermined symbolic good that brings pressure to bear on aristocratic self-understanding through privileged hunting and consumption' (p. 266). This is an informed paper, nicely combining theory, literature, and historical analysis.

Eric Nebeker's 'Broadside Ballads, Miscellanies and the Lyric in Print' (*ELH* 76[2009] 989–1013) challenges the received construction, via Puttenham and others, of the development of poetry in English. Nebeker notes that traditional accounts see improvements and refinements, inspired by the Renaissance and by humanism, as having passed from author to author, while new work in book history and print culture takes account of social contexts and the systems of literary production and dissemination in order to understand literary history more broadly. Using 'methods of reading' and 'quantitative analysis', Nebeker examines the development of the lyric, attitudes towards the lyric, and the relationship between it and other literary forms (the broadside ballad, chiefly) by charting the evolution of the lyric from manuscript contexts into the more commercial world of print. Nebeker argues, primarily, that the ballads helped to establish the reputation of the lyric in print and, following an overview of the paratextual features of broadsides in miscellanies (such as *Tottel's*, and those of Richard Jones and Henry Disle), finds that they tacitly comment on the quality of the verse that they disseminate by fostering a culture of exclusivity. Both Tottel and Disle appeal to the noble reader, while retaining the possibility of a wider audience; Jones, however, appeals with his later miscellany *The Gorgeous Gallery* [1577] to 'All Young Gentlemen'. Jones, as Nebeker states, does not just see gentlemen as part of his audience for miscellanies of lyric verse: they make up his audience in its entirety, and the paper briefly discusses Jones's career as a self-styled printer for young aristocrats. The focus shifts somewhat in the second half of this long article to examine metre, in particular the crossover between fourteeners and poulters in broadside ballads and miscellanies. Nebeker also comments on the deeper crossovers in image and metaphor, language and theme. Finally, the paper looks at the print culture associated with both formats, focusing on Jones, as mentioned.

A very solid introduction to the scansion of fourteenth- and fifteenth-century verse is published in the new volume of Wiley-Blackwell's *Companion* series: *A Companion to Medieval Literature and Culture, c.1350–c.1500*, edited by Peter Brown. Donka Minkova's chapter, 'The Forms of Speech' (pp. 159–75), is a clear and accessible tool for first-time students of alliterative verse (and, indeed, for those entrusted with the instruction of first-timers). Minkova discusses the phonology of verse, with the caveat that there can be no one, single overview of a political, literary and dialectical landscape that was in constant flux in the centuries following the Norman Conquest. Particularly relevant to this review are pages 162–3, where examples the practices of alliterative poets are used to illustrate the dialectical differences in the pronunciation of consonants, and the standard pronunciation of clusters such as 'kn' and 'gn'. Minkova also discusses the use of prefixes in alliterative verse; English prefixes were not stressed as were borrowings from French, despite the link in such verbs with prefixes on the etymological root. The same author, in the next chapter, 'The Forms of Verse' (pp. 176–95), writes about the demise of alliterative practice, the form favoured by the poets of the west Midlands and north-west, and the oldest form of poetic composition in English, which was indebted to the corpus of Old English writings. Minkova notes that the latest two outstanding pieces of alliterative verse that can be scanned strictly according to the rules of Old English versification are two short poems: *Durham* [*c.*1100] and *The Grave* [*c.*1150]. The rest of the early Middle English corpus, it is argued, is not comprised of alliterative verse, strictly speaking, but rather of 'hybrids' that combine rhyme, alliteration, and syllable-counting. It is not clear whether the imperfect fragments that remain from the later period are testament to the end of composition in this form, but Minkova argues that the continued interest in alliteration—including the fourteenth-century revival which, as a fashion, was relatively short-lived but which produced some fine literature—is evidence that the sonic appeal of alliteration, and its link to the past, contributed to its persistence. Minkova's work here—again with practical examples (of half-line distribution, the metrical components, and structure)—is most useful for the newcomer to alliterative verse, blending technical explanation and theoretical perspectives.

More on alliterative literature naturally finds its way into this *Companion* at various stages, too numerous to mention here in full. In particular, Thomas Hahn and Dana M. Symons, in 'Middle English Romance' (pp. 341–57), suggest that Thomas Malory's *Morte Darthur*, rather than giving us a snapshot of the nature of romance in England, in fact distorts the reader's sense of native performance of, attitudes to, and trends in the transmission of romances and versions of romances that extends across centuries. Indeed, as the authors note, most anthologies of Middle English writing contain excerpts from Malory and *Sir Gawain*, at the expense of other verse romance. The alliterative *Morte* usually suffers in such a manner, despite being one of the chief sources used by Malory in the compilation of his text; the authors cite its challenges to the (modern and contemporary) reader, both linguistic/structural and moral/political, as contributing to the *Morte*'s status as one of the greatest pieces of literature surviving in Middle English. Moreover, the duality of pieces like the *Morte*—straddling the native, oral tradition of popular verse, and the learned, bookish Latinate tradition—renders them fascinating from the perspective of audience and contemporary appeal.

Lyric is dealt with more directly in its own chapter by Rosemary Greentree, 'Lyric' (in Brown, ed., pp. 387–405). Beginning with a statement on the limitations of the genre, this chapter wisely advises the reader that the catch-all term operates as something into which almost any short poem in Middle English is gathered. Greentree also notes the constraints of the genre, including those of metre, rhyme, and theme and, sometimes, plot; the speaker-receiver model; and the directness and brevity of communication. Her survey responds to the variety and variability by treating of lyric in a broadly thematic fashion. Religious and secular lyrics are taken together, with the insistence that secular verse does not preclude spirituality. Political verses are numerous, offering advice, complaint, and voice to the downtrodden in general terms, and allegiance in specific conflicts (the Wars of the Roses). Language is an issue, too, for the student of the lyric in English, as the sections on macaronic verse and lyrics in other languages show. It is, perhaps, the courtly love lyric that is most familiar and most beloved, and Greentree does a good job here in a short space; she finds time to mention the lyrics of women, many of which are found in the Findern manuscript. Carols are by far the most numerous of this genre, unconfined by season or church calendar, defined by the round dance or *carole*, and expressive equally of politics, satirical comment, and joy.

Lyric also finds its way *passim* into this nicely structured and dialogic volume: in 'Manuscripts and Readers' (in Brown, ed., pp. 93–106), A.S.G. Edwards writes that neither the audience for lyrics in manuscript nor the contexts for their composition can be described with clarity, citing the example of 'An Anchoress' Hymn to the Virgin' which, in one of its two versions, is attributed to Lydgate. Edwards shows that lyric, perhaps more than any other medieval poetic genre, is suited to emendation, appropriation, and transformation: the variations on Richard de Caistre's Hymn is a case in point, as are the reworkings of parts of Chaucer's *Troilus* as courtly lyrics. Somewhat paradoxically, the textual instability of the lyric is arguably both a cause and an effect of these mercenary tendencies.

A number of short papers of interest appeared in *Notes and Queries* throughout 2009. Andrew Breeze contributes a note entitled 'Lord Fitzwarren and a Carol of 1470' (*N&Q* 56[2009] 23–4) relating to a four-stanza carol found in British Library MS Add. 19046, with the given title 'Willkin's Return'. The carol celebrates the return of Warwick and praises the Prince of Wales and the Lord Chamberlain, John Neville, marquess of Montagu. In the same issue J. Patrick Hornbeck II writes on 'Antifraternalism and the *Upland Series*: Evidence from a Fifteenth-Century Ballad' (*N&Q* 56[2009] 24–6). Hornbeck's focus is *Friar and Boy*, a ballad extant in five manuscripts (including the Percy Folio) and once printed by de Worde; he offers a summary of the ballad, argues for it as a 'potentially Wycliffite text' (p. 25), and points out its similarities to the *Upland* tradition, chief among them the use of the names Jack and Tobias. Finally, Richard J. Moll's note, '"O Lady Fortune": An Unknown Lyric in British Library MS Harley 2169' (*N&Q* 56[2009] 192–4) concerns an unrecorded Middle English lyric found in the famous heraldic roll. The lyric, on Fortune, is found copied three times, in three different hands, on the manuscript's final folio. The poem, reproduced here and nicely analysed by Moll, is a traditional complaint against Fortune, in the form of a dialogue between Lady Fortune and the plaintiff.

Alliterative verse, both generally and in relation to specific texts, receives some attention in the important essay collection *A Companion to Medieval Popular Romance*, edited by Raluca Radulescu and Cory James Rushton. Alliteration generally is treated by Karl Reichl in 'Orality and Performance' (pp. 132–48), where he discusses the issues surrounding the possibilities of the oral composition of alliterative verse, relating this to the notion that there is frequently a discernible formulaic structure. Ad Putter, in a paper entitled 'The Metres and Stanza Forms of Popular Romance' (pp. 111–31), calls on us to examine the formal options open to poets of the period. Putter points out that the alliterative long line, inherited from Old English poetry, was continued and refined by Laȝamon, who added end-rhyme to link the half-lines. Importantly, Putter points out that this innovation had begun to appear in Old English verse of the later period, where it is usually attributed by scholars to outside influences.

Also relevant here, and in the same volume, is Maldwyn Mills and Gillian Rogers's 'The Manuscripts of Popular Romance' (pp. 49–66); the manuscripts—both contemporary and post-medieval, it is pointed out, present a varied transmission history that has affected the subsequent reception history of romance. Mills draws parallels between the contexts in which romances survive and the modes in which they are written, stating that, frequently, the books preserving them and the romances themselves have multiple themes.

Thus *The Awntyrs off Arthure*, seen in two halves, is a 'stark warning against sin' and a 'combat between two knights'. Mills finds the same variety even in manuscripts which preserve only romances. He usefully surveys the manuscript contexts, noting that *The Awntyrs*, now Douce 324, once formed a book along with Rawlinson D 82 (*Seege of Thebes* and *Sege of Troy*) and Rawlinson Poet. 168 (Hoccleve's *The Boke of Governaunce*). Mills argues that, in the major romance manuscripts which survive, the texts can be variously grouped (he gives a handy summary account); so that, for example, in the London Thornton manuscript the *Segge of Melayne* has connections with the *Segge of Jerusalem* (which precedes it) but also with *Rowlande and Ottuell* following it.

The extremely impressive and valuable *Language and Culture in Medieval Britain: The French of England c.1100–c.1500*, edited by Jocelyn Wogan-Browne et al., contains much of interest, not least Julia Boffey's expert treatment of the (incomplete) Middle English *Tree of Love* contained in MS Longleat 253, 'Writing English in a French Penumbra: The Middle English "Tree of Love" in MS Longleat 253' (pp. 386–96). The *Tree of Love*, surviving alongside Scrope's translation of de Pizan's *Epistle d'Othea*, is also said to have been translated from French, though Boffey points out that nothing in the surviving part makes this explicit. The poem centres on the figuration of the tree as love and, thus, as something which needs to be nurtured, tended, and cared for. It also features a debate between Love and Reason. The manuscript evidence suggests that the intended marriage of text and image in the *Tree* was never realized, but Boffey argues that the elaborate scheme of decorations present in the French texts of the *Epistle*, and in the other two surviving English copies, and their survival co-located in Longleat, may indeed point to a French source. Boffey also suggests the *Somme le roi*, which operates at a similar allegorical level, as a close analogue.

4. The *Gawain*-Poet

This year saw the preliminary launch of a new journal, *Gawain-Poet Studies*, edited by Ross G. Arthur. The inaugural issue has not yet been published, but the mechanism for production, including an editorial board and an institutional home, is in place.

One full-length study of the *Gawain*-poet was published this year: *Looking Westward: Poetry, Landscape, and Politics in Sir Gawain and the Green Knight* by Ordelle G. Hill. Hill's central claim is that scholars have overlooked the west when considering the identity of the author, and by west, Hill means Wales and the Welsh Marches in particular. He undertakes a study of Welsh poetry in order to demonstrate the inherently Celtic nature of the *Gawain*-poet's works. Hill's claim that Celtic sources have been under-studied is a valid one, and could have provoked some interesting re-evaluations. The book fails to live up to its full potential, however, and is riddled with numerous, albeit mostly small, errors that prove distracting. Moreover, the 'evidence' Hill compiles is thin at best (for example, 'correspondences' and constructed scenarios). Nevertheless, the project is an intriguing one that deserves praise for its undertaking, and which may spur on future studies in this area.

Robert W. Barrett, Jr.'s *Against All England: Regional Identity and Cheshire Writing, 1195–1656* contains a complete chapter on the *Gawain*-poet. Addressing *Gawain* as a regional poem, Barrett connects the heraldic devices on Gawain's shield to his identity. Barrett situated this discussion with an overview of the local Scrope–Grosvenor controversy, in which heraldic devices were falsified and reputations were damaged through lies and insecurities. Similarly, Gawain's identity is destabilized throughout the poem. His body is subject to division, as are his honour and his loyalty. He travels through a space of uncertainty, only to find redemption coupled with more uncertainty at the end.

Myra Stokes, in 'Bilive and Blive: Distribution and Metrical Function' (*JEGP* 108[2009] 190–221), examines the adverbial distribution of variants of what is, essentially, 'believe'. The forms vary based on regional differences, and are most commonly found in poetry, not prose. Stokes goes on to claim that 'the behavior and distribution of this word make it potentially relevant to all kinds of linguistic, metrical, and literary investigations' (p. 220). She works through a number of poems pointing out instances of use, noting that *Piers Plowman*, for example, does not contain any instances. The *Gawain*-poet's works, however, contain it in numerous places, where it was chosen, she suggests, for metrical purposes rather than semantic ones. Stokes primarily concentrates on provenance and scribal contamination alongside metrical considerations, and this article is an interesting and engaging discussion of instances of adverbial overlap.

In 'The Alliterative *Three Dead Kings* in John Audelay's MS Douce 302' (in Fein, ed., pp. 249–93), Eric Gerald Stanley notes in passing that *Three Dead Kings* has much in common, poetically and metrically, with the works of the *Gawain*-poet. In the notes on specific words, however, Stanley reaffirms the standard scholarly belief that the lexicon demonstrates it is not by the *Gawain*-poet.

J.A. Jackson, in 'The Infinite Desire of *Pearl*' (in Astell and Jackson, eds., pp. 157–84), uses Levinas's ideas about the relationship between literature and ethics to produce a newly layered reading of *Pearl* in which he concentrates on the 'structural excessiveness' of the poem and its interplay with ethics. Infinite substitution mirrors the constant connection and reconnection of the divine and the human, and the constant excessiveness results in infinite beauty.

Pearl and *St Erkenwald* both figure in '"A reuer... brighter þen boþe the sunne and mone": The Use of Water in the Medieval Consideration of Urban Space' (in Classen, ed., pp. 245–72) by Britt C.L. Rothauser. Water was an urban space's most precious resource; thus medieval writers often prioritized descriptions of water in their portrayal of cities. One of the primary roles of water in poetry is definition. In *Pearl*, water both metaphorically and literally defines the New Jerusalem by revealing the city and hinting at its divine origin. Rothauser explores the reverberations of these dual levels of understanding as a way of defining not only the city itself, but also its functions. She goes on to elaborate the role that water and rivers play in protecting space in both *Pearl* and *St Erkenwald*. Rivers are barriers in both the positive and negative sense. Throughout her discussion, Rothauser also addresses other scholarship regarding water, especially sexual metaphors. Ultimately, however, she determines that water is a cleansing, protective agent.

Andrew Breeze, in 'Rheged and the *Gawain* Poet' (*N&Q* 56[2009] 190–1), notes that the Tolkien and Gordon edition of *Sir Gawain* incorrectly locates the kingdom of Rheged, with the correct location being in Cumbria. Lingering assertions that Rheged was in Wales are due to the eighteenth-century forger Iolo Morganwg, whose ideas influence the Tolkien edition.

In 'The Theatrical Lesson of the *Pearl*-Poet's *Patience*' (in Ciuk and Molek-Kozakowska, eds., *Exploring Space: Spatial Notions in Cultural, Literary and Language Studies*, volume 1: *Space in Cultural and Literary Studies*, pp. 270–9), Piotr Spyra reconfigures the 'negative exemplum' *Patience* into a space for performance, where Jonah participates in the 'unveiling of divine Providence' (p. 270). Thus, instead of being a penitential journey focused on the Ninevites, *Patience* becomes a study in how to interact with God. Jonah repeatedly fails to exhibit the title characteristic, patience, and must come to understand that God guides everything and has the patience to save.

Two different articles focused specifically on courtly ethics. Carl Grey Martin's 'The Cipher of Chivalry: Violence as Courtly Play in the World of *Sir Gawain and the Green Knight*' (*ChauR* 43:iii[2009] 311–29) considers what he calls 'the grotesque physical breaking and disfigurement of one knight by another' (p. 311) against the backdrop of various courtly gestures and rituals. Eventually, warriors enveloped by the chivalric code are able to rationalize their relation to violence and physical suffering, as a knight's test of military prowess and as a spiritual test of enlightenment.

Jill Mann, in 'Courtly Aesthetics and Courtly Ethics in *Sir Gawain and the Green Knight*' (*SAC* 31[2009] 231–65), discusses the notion of late medieval chivalry as a culture of 'display' and excess, provides a reading of *Gawain* in terms of 'this conscious cultivation of royal and courtly display', and argues that the poet identifies the reasons behind courtly excess (p. 235). First locating *Gawain* within the landscape, Mann connects the luxury in the poem to the luxury found in north-west England. She also addresses the deliberate distancing of homosexual implications, especially in light of accusations surrounding Richard II, but notes that Gawain could be connected to Richard's 'dear friend' Robert de Vere, and that assigning luxury to him could have been a way of connecting grace and chivalry with Richard's favourite. The *Gawain*-poet, then, does not rely on courtly display to impress the lower classes; rather, it becomes a way of subtly celebrating true courtly ethics and values that may or may not be directly connected with warriorship.

Karen Cherewatuk's '*Becoming Male, Medieval Mothering*, and Incarnational Theology in *Sir Gawain and the Green Knight* and the *Book of Margery Kempe*' (*Arth* 19:iii[2009] 15–24) situates her article as a nod to *Arthuriana* editor Bonnie Wheeler. Recognizing that she is addressing two disparate texts, Cherewatuk links them through incarnational theology, though she covers no really new ground. *Gawain* shows its dependence upon incarnational theology through its Christmas setting and Gawain's shield, thus proclaiming his personal connection to the 'fleshly Christ'. Despite this, he still reacts to the final outcome in a gendered way, debasing women in an effort to more fully align himself with God as man.

The only essay to address *Cleanness* was Amity Reading's '"The ende of alle kynez flesch": Ritual Sacrifice and Feasting in *Cleanness*' (*Exemplaria* 21[2009] 274–95). Here Reading argues that *Cleanness* relies on metaphors of sacrifice in order to represent purity as social custom. In this way, personal actions are governed by rules. This idea holds true throughout the poem, as all make ready for the feast. In this way, the poet is able to send a more complicated message than simple sexual purity; he is also able to address the idea that purity can be achieved through ritual sacrifice and submission to the divine.

Works by the *Gawain*-poet cropped up in modern-day readings of texts in several places. In 'Tough Love: Teaching the New Medievalisms' (in Fugelso, ed., pp. 76–98), Jane Chance uses *Sir Gawain and the Green Knight* as one of her examples of opening up the 'queer medieval' in her classroom. She acknowledges that Tolkien did not consider the possibility of a homosexual encounter in the poem, yet suggests that does not matter in creating a teaching moment. It is particularly useful, she suggests, to contrast the situation in *Gawain* with the events in *Lanval*.

Stefan Ekman's 'Echoes of *Pearl* in Arda's Landscape' (*TStud* 6[2009] 59–70) connects Tolkien's poem 'The Nameless Land' with *Pearl* through metre and descriptors. Ekman painstakingly points out the similarities between *Pearl*'s dreamscape and Arda's landscape, connecting both through visual imagery as well as visions. Finally, Ekman includes a discussion of temporal connections, focusing on how time 'runs differently' in these worlds.

Finally, 'A Murdochian Reading of *Sir Gawain and the Green Knight*' (*InteractionsAJ* 18:ii[2009] 149–59) by Zeynep Yılmaz Kurt examines the reinvention of *Gawain* by Iris Murdoch in her novel *The Green Knight* [1993]. Rather than providing a reading of *Gawain*, this article instead of focuses on reading Murdoch's novel through the lens of medievalism and allusions to the fourteenth-century poem, while changing the religious aspects into metaphysical twentieth-century concepts, or morals for a modern age.

5. *Piers Plowman*

A flurry of activity continues in *Piers Plowman* studies. A number of books devote chapters or parts of chapters to studies of the poem or texts related directly to it, such as the works of John Audelay. Articles and essays continue to be strong also, with a surprising variety of journals publishing such pieces. Katherine Zieman, in *Singing the New Song: Literacy and Liturgy in Late Medieval England* [2008], devotes a chapter and several other passages to the study of *Piers Plowman* from a liturgical performance perspective. At times, she suggests, Langland seems to deliberately incorporate liturgical discourse in order to make his poem more accessible to a wider audience. Elsewhere, however, he struggles with the 'inevitable forms of self-interest' that liturgical performance carries with it, and at least somewhat consciously revises the third vision with this in mind. In addition to this, Will's incorporation of reading and singing into his tools of labour suggest a prayer performance.

Elena Levy-Navarro's *The Culture of Obesity in Early and Late Modernity: Body Image in Shakespeare, Jonson, Middleton, and Skelton* [2008] contains a chapter that provides a careful investigation of Gluttony in Passus V. Although Langland's portrayal does include a grotesque body, ultimately Levy-Navarro suggests that the gluttonous form is not repulsive because of the obesity; rather, it becomes bestial and repulsive because of its commitment to the body instead of to the spirit. This reading is contextualized within contemporary views of the poor, suggesting that Langland is further sending a message about food and almsgiving.

Masha Raskolnikov's *Body against Soul* also incorporates a chapter about *Piers Plowman*. Here she considers the poem from a gendered perspective, paying particular attention to human dependence on company alongside the various female personifications which eventually collapse into a monolithic view. Women then become excluded from functional human society, seen as extraneous and useless, which challenges a traditional heterosexual model of society, although, as Raskolnikov points out, 'the alternative offered to active heterosexuality throughout *Piers Plowman* is, of course, celibacy, that state is envisioned by the poem as a relationship between a man and his (male) double' (p. 196). *Piers*, she argues, demonstrates the necessity of silence for men to communicate with a masculine self.

Susanna Fein has edited a new edition, the first complete one, of John the Blind Audelay's *Poems and Carols from Oxford*. Of important note here is the preservation of Audelay's alliterative poem *Marcolf and Solomon*, which most scholars hold to be directly descended from *Piers Plowman*. Fein provides an annotated and glossed transcription. Derek Pearsall takes up this very subject in 'Audelay's *Marcolf and Solomon* and the Langlandian Tradition' (in Fein, ed., pp. 138–52). Pearsall begins by re-examining his own earlier thoughts about the 'profound' influence *Piers Plowman* had on Audelay. After an outline of the poem meant to foreground the theme of 'concord' between friars and priests, Pearsall compares thematic links and topics, concluding that both Langland and Audelay 'draw upon a common body of popular complaint, satire, and prophecy' (p. 147), mostly an oral tradition, and that this is why modern readers see the overlap. In 'Langland and Audelay' (in Fein, ed., pp. 153–69), Richard Firth Green tackles this same topic, concluding that Langland had a profound influence on Audelay's work with regard to theme, metrics, and alliteration, but does not seem to influence Audelay's political views. He considers his evidence from the point of view that Audelay and Langland had personal attributes in common, particularly being in minor orders and holding a preacher's perspective. Green includes a table of alliterative phrases in Audelay and Langland for comparison's sake. Finally, in 'The Vatic Penitent: John Audelay's Self-Representation' (in Fein, ed., pp. 54–85), Robert J. Meyer-Lee assumes the direct connection between Langland and Audelay, dubbing him a 'Langlandian Poet', but suggests the influence is primarily on the idea of authorial biography. Although Audelay reveals few direct details about himself, Meyer-Lee posits the work's self-referentiality as an expression of penitential labour. Audelay tells his audience how to 'die well' in order to achieve salvation, making his text a work of prayer.

James J. Paxson, in 'The Personificational Face: *Piers Plowman* Rethought through Levinas and Bronowski' (in Astell and Jackson, eds., pp. 137–56), suggest that the concept of the soul (*anima*) in the B-text can be reconsidered through the use of postmodern theories, and combining the works of Emmanuel Levinas and the mathematician Jacob Bronowski. The questioning of Newtonian optics and the rise of studies in faciality allow for a particular hermetic discourse to arise, one that concerns itself with the 'personificational face' or the 'face which is not a face' or the 'face of the Other' (p. 156). The result is a new view of traditional allegory, one that is 'refreshing' and illustrates Langland's visual poetics.

The *Yearbook of Langland Studies* continues to provide a treasure trove of insightful scholarship on *Piers Plowman* and related works. Barbara Newman kicks off the volume with 'Redeeming the Time: Langland, Julian, and the Art of Lifelong Revision' (*YLS* 23[2009] 1–32). Here she looks at both *Piers Plowman* and *Revelation of Love* as products of revision, in light of authorial process and temporality. She suggests that the rough structures of each are deliberate authorial recollections of the writing process which allow for temporal collapse, thus providing a mechanism by which the authors can compare different times as well as 'earthly' time and 'spiritual' time. Thus they deliberately emulate the notion that revision is a lifelong process and cannot be 'finished'. Most significantly, Newman suggests that Julian wrote a 'B-text' of her own work between *A Vision of Love* (the short text) and *A Revelation of Love* (the long text), a suggestion she bases primarily on comparisons of the changes made between Langland's B-text and C-text to the final effects found in *A Revelation*.

Next, D. Vance Smith takes up the cause of 'Negative Langland' (*YLS* 23[2009] 33–59). He suggests that scholarship has overlooked the deliberately inconclusive nature of the poem. Instead of seeing it in conventional terms, particularly with regard to narrative, Smith proposes that we examine *Piers* in terms of its 'deep interest' in negation as a philosophical concept, with the negativities providing 'essential properties' of the poem (p. 39). He connects this proposition to apophatic texts and their anxiety over naming—a struggle traditional medieval linguistic theory finds problematic. The case study is situated within the poem's attention to the 'kynde name' and the resultant discussion of love.

Simon Horobin argues, in 'Adam Pynkhurst and the Copying of British Library, MS Additional 35287 of the B Version of *Piers Plowman*' (*YLS* 23[2009] 61–83), that the prominent scribe who copied the Hengwrt and Ellesmere manuscripts was responsible for the numerous emendations made to the manuscript in question. This is established through meticulous examination of the handwriting and semantics. Once identity is established, Horobin then argues that this has a profound effect on our understanding of the early London book trade. Most importantly, Horobin suggests that scribes operated individually, yet shared resources. Thus previous ideas about 'scribal schools' may not be as valid as once thought.

J.A. Burrow re-evaluates the standard arguments regarding Conscience's account of Christ's life in 'Conscience on Knights, Kings, and Conquerors: *Piers Plowman* B.19.26–198' (*YLS* 23[2009] 85–95). Problematically, previous readings have glossed over the deliberate three-part structure emphasized by Conscience: Christ begins as knight, rises up as king, and continues as conqueror (*Christus*). Burrow worries that by minimalizing Christ's role as conqueror, as other readings are wont to do, we miss the point of the Harrowing. Christ must become conqueror if he is to judge his subjects, and it is this particular power that he passed on to Peter.

In 'Failed Signification: *Corpus Christi* and *Corpus Mysticum* in *Piers Plowman*' (*YLS* 23[2009] 97–123) Jennifer Garrison looks at the failed Communion in Passus XIX of the B-text. She suggests that Langland considers the Eucharist as an allegorical sign—as the material bread unites with Christ's flesh, the physical reception of the host connects with the community of believers as they unite through its consumption. Garrison argues that, 'according to Langland, proper eucharistic reception requires that Christians recognize their own role as the signified corporate body of Christ, a body in which all members are equally important' (p. 121). Thus, the failed communion demonstrates the failed understanding of Will and the others to recognize that the Eucharist can assist them in connecting their divided social selves by forming a reflection of the divine unified body.

Macklin Smith's 'Langland's Alliterative Line(s)' (*YLS* 23[2009] 163–216) is published as part of the *YLS* editors bid to re-establish *Piers* as part of the alliterative tradition. Smith suggests that alliteration in *Piers* goes beyond the standards required by metrics. Langland's versatility with alliteration was deliberate, he argues, and compounding alliterative structures serve to link the poem both linguistically and thematically. Generally, Smith looks at alliteration within, between, and among lines and line groups, ultimately suggesting a new classification of interlinear alliterative forms, expanded to include 'anticipation', 'echo', and 'repetition'.

Stephen Barney contributes a review essay on Derek Pearsall's recently updated edition, 'A Revised Edition of the C Text' (*YLS* 23[2009] 265–88). Barney praises the revised edition, calling it 'trustworthy' and commendable. He addresses issues of presentation and editing as well as content before turning to the focus of his considerations, the overhauled critical apparatus. Barney praises the thoroughly revised introduction and overview of scholarship, but holds his highest praise for the wealth of annotation provided by Pearsall. Barney then discusses various editions, including Pearsall's previous one. Barney's major criticism of Pearsall's edition relates to the lack of attention paid to verse form. Barney believes Pearsall's attempts to address this topic are 'inadequate' and 'fail to exploit the opportunity' (p. 277). He reviews Langland's stress patterns as well as alliterative patterns in brief, and closes by thanking Pearsall for his continued dedication to the field.

Another contribution by Derek Pearsall, 'The Idea of Universal Salvation in *Piers Plowman* B and C' (*JMEMS* 39[2009] 257–81), addresses the primary question underlying the entire poem: 'How do I save my soul?'. Pearsall suggests the tempting answer is one concerning universal salvation—that is, the idea of Judgement Day as a merciful mission, rather than a vengeful proposition. This is not an orthodox view, and Pearsall goes on to examine Langland's supposed 'universal salvation' principle as a carefully thought out strategy, tracing Langland's developing thoughts throughout both the B-text and the C-text. One such idea is 'salvation witness' or a deathbed conversion based on a vision from God, a theory advanced by Uthred of Boldon, but condemned in 1368. Pearsall finally turns to Christ's speech in Passus XX during which he 'permits himself' the luxury of universal salvation.

Isabel Davis also contributed two pieces of scholarship to the body of work on *Piers Plowman*. In '*Piers Plowman* and the *Querelle* of the *Rose*: Marriage, *Caritas*, and the Peacock's "Pennes"' (*NML* 10[2008] 49–86), she suggests that *Piers Plowman* enters into the critical debates surrounding the *Roman de la Rose*. In particular, Davis concentrates on the issue of sexual ethics, suggesting that *Piers* engages with both the *Rose* and its sources in order to investigate sexuality. One glaring difference is the support for marriage found in *Piers* that is absent from *Rose*, although all texts exhibit concerns about potential same-sex desire and other challenges to ethical living.

Similarly, in 'On the Sadness of Not Being a Bird: Late-Medieval Marriage Ideologies and the Figure of Abraham in William Langland's *Piers Plowman*' (in Goldberg and Kowaleski, eds., *Medieval Domesticity: Home, Housing, and Household in Medieval England*, pp. 209–31), Davis examines the figure of Abraham as a representation of Langland's support of marriage. In particular, she argues that there is a thematic relationship between Passus XVI in the B-text and Abraham's discussion of the Trinity—both hark back to *De nuptiis et concupiscentia* by Augustine.

Lawrence Warner contributes two pieces of scholarship to the *Pier Plowman* ranks this year as well. His article 'New Light on *Piers Plowman*'s Ownership, ca. 1450–1600' (*JEBS* 12[2009] 183–94) suggests a new identity for a *Piers* manuscript owner, basing his conclusions on absence of evidence as well as materials not previously considered. Warner reviews the documented ownership of MS BL Additional 35287 by Thomas Danet, the gift inscription of a Crowley edition by a prioress, and the links between Archbishop Matthew Parker and *Piers* manuscripts in order to examine what is left out of these exchanges. The most important conclusion he reaches is that scholarship has relied to heavily upon the indications of readership that survive, rather than on explaining the absence of ownership, especially considering how popular the poem was.

Warner's second article, 'The Gentleman's *Piers Plowman*: John Mitford and his Annotated Copy of the 1550 Edition of William Langland's Great Poem' (*LaTrobe* 84[2009] 104–12, 130–1), examines the continuing impact *Piers Plowman* had on literary studies in the nineteenth century through the example of the Revd John Mitford (1781–1859), who owned an annotated copy of Crowley's edition. Mitford's annotations included a 'compendium' of *Piers* criticism dating back to the sixteenth century. Warner explores this side note in *Piers* ownership as a look into literary responses of the past and a representation of what past generations found significant.

In 'Will's Imagination in *Piers Plowman*' (*JEGP* 108[2009] 27–58), Michelle Karnes addresses scholastic theories of imagination as concerned with joining natural and spiritual knowledge, proposing that Will's spiritual development improves as does his reconciliation of nature and revelation. Furthermore, she emphasizes the role that experience plays in biblical and spiritual understanding as displayed by Will, and examines the idea that Will moves from present to past in a manner that aligns them more closely.

In 'Giving Each His Due: Langland, Gower, and the Question of Equality' (*JEGP* 108[2009] 310–35), Conrad van Dijk explores the differences between Gower's notion of justice and Langland's ideas of equity, concluding that, despite more overt differences, there is a surprising underlying similarity in position. Van Dijk first carefully defines equity, differentiating it from justice, and concluding that both authors use a Roman definition of justice. Next he considers each poet's attitude towards upholding the law. Finally, he considers the idea of justice tempered by mercy, and how that affects the practice of the law.

Gerald Morgan challenges the idea that Lady Meed is a fallen woman in 'The Dignity of Langland's Meed' (*MLR* 104[2009] 623–39). Detailed examination of the words Langland chooses to describe Meed indicates a level of respect other scholars have overlooked. Nevertheless, overall she is excessive and false, and cannot be trusted in any way. Lady Holy Church surpasses Meed in every sense of dignity and respect. Thus Morgan concludes that we should leave the poem wanting to suppress all dignity accorded to Meed.

Another multiple contributor, Simon Horobin, expands his ideas about scribal resource-sharing in 'The Criteria for Scribal Attribution: Dublin, Trinity College MS 244 Reconsidered' (*RES* 60[2009] 371–81), where he questions the findings of Alan J. Fletcher (*RES* 58[2007] 597–632; reviewed in *YWES* 88[2009] 249–50) who suggested that the London scribe Adam Pynkhurst copied the above-mentioned manuscript. Horobin believes that many significant features of Pynkhurst's hand are missing, while the ones that are present are inconclusive. Horobin also takes on Fletcher's idea of a 'Pynkhurst school', claiming that many of the supposed idiosyncrasies pointed out are really common scribal practice. In short, Horobin debunks Fletcher but advances no solid theory of his own.

Eugenie Freed's '"In that folie I raigned . . .": Reason, Justice, and the King in *Piers Plowman* and *King Lear*' (*SAJMRS* 13[2003] 15–41) focuses on Robert Crowley's 1550 edition of *Piers* in order to compare the kings in each text, concluding that *Lear* was influenced by *Piers*. Chih-hsin Lin's 'Salvation through a Literary Education: Biblical Interpretation and the Trivium in *Piers Plowman*' (*SiCS* 7[2009] 67–110) examines Langland's attitude towards Christian education as found in the B-text, especially in Passus VII–XII. This is particularly accomplished through Ymaginatif, who shows Will, rather than simply telling him, that education should be supplemented by spiritual interpretations of the Bible. In this manner, a preacher can assist students in taking up their responsibilities to study the word of God and discover a personal answer. *Piers Plowman* is briefly mentioned in 'Defining the Medieval City through Death' (in Classen, ed., pp. 182–204) by Kisha G. Tracy as one of a number of texts reflecting the important role of death in shaping migrations to the city. In particular, she cites city deaths as affecting rural religious practices.

Unavailable for review were Gillian Rudd, *Greenery: Ecocritical Readings of Late Medieval English Literature* (ManUP [2008]) and David Aers, *Salvation and Sin: Augustine, Langland, and Fourteenth-Century Theology* (UNDP [2009]).

6. Romance

This year's critical work on medieval romance is shaped, as noted with increased frequency in recent years, by questions of genre and audience (rather than theme or theory) which are receiving renewed attention in a number of book-length studies and shorter articles and chapters. Two book-length studies stand out in this year's output on this topic: Melissa Furrow's monograph *Expectations of Romance* and the collection of essays edited by Raluca L. Radulescu and Cory James Rushton, *A Companion to Medieval Popular Romance*.

Melissa Furrow's *Expectations of Romance: The Reception of a Genre in Medieval England* is the major contribution to this year's work on medieval romance. The monograph is divided into six chapters and an appendix; these tackle a range of topics, authors, and periods chronologically arranged, from the eleventh to the fifteenth centuries, and from Robert Manning of Brunne to Chaucer and Malory. Unsurprisingly, the monograph starts with an examination of 'The Problem with Romance' (chapter 1), in a similar vein to the *Companion* discussed below; Furrow tackles medieval reception from the earliest evidence, that is from the medieval tiles portraying Tristram and Isolde at the Benedictine Abbey at Chertsey, as well as tiles with links to these, such as those at Hailes Abbey in Gloucestershire, and Robert Manning of Brunne's positive reception of romance, evident in his prologue to *Handlyng Synne*, where he 'voices strong views . . . on the functionality of literature' (p. 20), and where he seems to indicate that he appreciates a good story, be it romance or religious. Alongside Robert Manning, other known (Denis Priamus) or anonymous authors of comments on romance (*Cursor Mundi*) point to the pleasures of reading afforded by the genre or indeed sometimes to the way an author, 'disgusted' by the 'compulsory moralizing' of romance, can still produce one, albeit differently. The latter is exemplified by Walter Map, whose *De societate Sadii et Galonis, Of the Friendship of Sadius and Galo*, Furrow argues, 'is not simply a romance, it is *about* romance, and the roles of author and audience in its telling' (p. 36).

In chapter 2, 'The Name and the Genre', Furrow engages, as her title indicates, in a thorough and bold scrutiny of definitions and labels attached to 'romance' through decades of scholarship, and points out the shortcomings of several important recent cases made by Helen Cooper, Rosalind Field, Paul Strohm, and others. Furrow sets out to show that even inclusive definitions, like Cooper's and Ad Putter's, based on the Wittgensteinian theory of family resemblance (according to which romances can be grouped by features even if not all of them are present in any one text), are subject to further debate as they cannot acknowledge the inclusion, for example, of blunt comments of a sexual nature, which would bring a text like Hue de Rotelande's *Ipomedon* closer to fabliau (at least in this respect). Furthermore Furrow makes her own case for using the theory of 'radial categories', put forward by the linguist George Lakoff, and which introduces more versatility into the 'family resemblance' theory. In other words, Furrow focuses on creating a 'central' set of variables that are core to romance, and proceeds to examine some exemplary romances (*Guy of Warwick*) and central characters (Guenevere).

Chapter 3, 'Genres, Languages, and Literary History', contains Furrow's careful analysis of insular romances' 'neighbouring genres', such as chronicle, fabliau, saints' lives, and so on. In particular, Furrow makes a persuasive case for the inclusion of *chansons de geste* with insular romances, and places emphasis on illuminating examples from fabliaux and romances, and the connections between them (beyond the usual critical consensus that fabliaux mock romance and courtly love conventions, for example). Ultimately, Furrow argues, 'English romance occupies a larger and more capacious territory for a while [after the ties with French romance are severed] before a new reconfiguration at the end of the fourteenth century' (p. 141).

In chapter 4, 'The Example of Tristram and Isolde' and chapter 5, 'Making Free with the Truth', respectively, Furrow takes two case studies (the latter being moralizing romance in the fifteenth century) and investigates the trajectory of one theme (the famous lovers) and one ethical principle (authority/truth). The 'Tristram and Isolde' chapter is fascinating in its attention to context (including the fourteenth-century Chester Cathedral misericord depicting the lovers' tryst under the tree, and the ramifications and connections of the Middle English *Sir Tristrem* in terms of sources and analogues. Chapter 5, on the fifteenth-century use of romance in service of 'truth' is particularly oriented towards integrating Chaucer's romances into the culture of the century that received them and highlighting the author's own concern with how his audiences would approach his work. In the conclusion to the book, 'Coda: The Reception of a Genre' and the appendix, 'Romances and the Male Regular Clergy by Order', Furrow draws together her argument that 'a wide range of medieval readings of romances all rely on the premise that the ethical is the main point' (p. 236).

A Companion to Medieval Popular Romance brings together ten chapters by leading scholars and emerging ones on a range of topics pertinent to the study of romance in medieval Britain. Unlike other companion volumes, which sometimes contain mainly surveys of the field, the essays in this one chart the current state of criticism in the field as well as pointing to future directions for research. As the editors, Raluca L. Radulescu and Cory James Rushton, state in their introduction, the *Companion* aims to go beyond previous pioneering essay collections such as Nicola McDonald's *Pulp Fictions* (*YWES* 85[2006] 210) and Ad Putter and Jane Gilbert's *The Spirit of Medieval Popular Romance* (*YWES* 81[2002] 194–5), which placed emphasis on the extraordinary, taboo, or sensational aspects of medieval romance, in an effort to draw modern attention to the valuable contribution of medieval romance to our understanding of medieval culture and society, against previous negative critical views. This year's *Companion* highlights the difficulties of categorizing romance by challenging previous labels and tackling head-on the drawback of the label 'popular', widely misused due to its modern connotations

(Rosalind Field, 'Popular Romance: The Material and the Problems'), and the modern critical tendency to look for classification as an essential dimension of understanding literary texts in the medieval romance category (Raluca L. Radulescu, 'Genre and Classification'). A more profitable avenue for investigation, Radulescu argues, is to take the versatility of this genre as a starting point and then look for intersections between it and other traditionally defined genres such as hagiography, chronicle, and even prophecy. The collection is thus organized in several parts, focusing on the material (classification, genre, manuscript, and print), themes (nationhood and gender), characteristics (metre and orality), and reception (young readers, and modern and academic reception).

Manuscript culture and the collocation of medieval romances with other genres, including the all-important question of what medieval scribes used for titles, are dealt with by Maldwyn Mills and, for the well-known post-medieval Percy Folio, Gillian Rogers ('The Manuscripts of Popular Romance') in a chapter that challenges, in part, previous assumptions about the nature of romance which were reached via discussions of individual texts rather than the context of the manuscript to which they belonged. Jennifer Fellows covers the transition from manuscript to print in her chapter on 'Printed Romance in the Sixteenth Century', focusing primarily on several romances, *Sir Eglamour of Artois*, *Syr Tryamowre*, and *Sir Bevis of Hampton*, *Guy of Warwick*, and *Sir Degaré*, all of which survive together or in groupings, ranging from the well-known early fourteenth-century Auchinleck manuscript (Edinburgh, National Library of Scotland, Advocates 19.2.1) to the late fifteenth- or early sixteenth-century Cambridge University Library Ff.2.38, followed by early print, thus attesting to the popularity of the romances contained therein. Thomas H. Crofts and Robert Allen Rouse ('Middle English Popular Romance and National Identity') inject new energy into the topic of nationhood, tackled in some medieval romances, by examining afresh a number of texts, including a close reading of *The Sege off Melayne* into their analysis, while Joanne Charbonneau and Désirée Cromwell ('Gender and Identity in the Popular Romance') extend previous critical discussion of gender by including issues of social and cultural identity, alongside the more established critical foci, masculinities and female domesticity.

Ad Putter ('The Metres and Stanza Forms of Popular Romance') presents a thorough review of the evolution of form in popular romance, which complements, albeit in the limited space afforded to a chapter, last year's monograph on tail-rhyme romance by Rhiannon Purdie (*YWES* 89[2010] 263), while Karl Reichl ('Orality and Performance') tackles the often debated questions related to 'popular' romance such as performance and transmission, a perennial critical crux both in the analysis of the genre and in the period in which it circulated. Last, but not least, Philippa Hardman ('Popular Romances and Young Readers') draws critical attention to the very fact that all of the earliest Middle English romances (before 1300) focus on children, and hence are shaped in ways which respond to questions of nurture and shaping identity in the household and in society. Cory James Rushton ('Modern and Academic Reception of the Popular Romance') concludes the volume with a summary of research and new critical directions in the study of the afterlives of medieval romance, taking as one of his main examples the 'Green Knights' of the genre.

Welcome attention is also paid this year to a number of less-studied romances. Ilan Mitchell-Smith, in 'Defining Violence in Middle English Romances: *Sir Gowther* and *Libeaus Desconus*' (*FCS* 34[2009]148–61), revisits acts of violence in these romances, which, he argues, are informed by the 'fair unknown' theme, and take place 'only within narrowly defined spaces and at appropriate moments . . . where this excessive violence is sanctioned and legitimized by the politico/Christian power structure' (p. 149). From this perspective Gowther's journey to salvation is charted from his wild, excessive behaviour while still thought to be the Devil's son, to the point where he is reformed, and becomes God's champion, under the rule of the pope and fighting the Saracens.

Arthur and Gorlagon, a romance relatively rarely discussed in recent criticism, receives attention this year in Amanda Hopkins's 'Why Arthur At All? The Dubious Arthuricity of *Arthur and Gorlagon*' (*ArthL* 26[2009] 77–95), where the author focuses on the werewolf's wife and cubs from the viewpoint of theological literature on bestiality, and echoes in the Welsh *Mabinogi*; read against this rich background Arthur's appearance in the text seems to alleviate the weight of sin.

The first chapter in Dinah Hazell's *Poverty in Late Middle English Literature* surveys the theme in the context of a number of romances, among which are *Ywain and Gawain*, *Sir Launfal*, *Sir Cleges*, *Sir Amadace*, and *Sir Orfeo*. Hazell argues that the presentation of the theme of noble or aristocratic poverty acts as evidence of the anonymous romance poets' socio-political and 'ethical concerns' (p. 56), using some of the evident concerns presented by romance as a genre in relation to class and politics, though no time- or period-specific associations are made. *Sir Launfal* forms the centre of Tory Vandeventer Pearman's investigation of disability. In his 'Refiguring Disability: Deviance, Blinding, and the Supernatural in Thomas Chestre's *Sir Launfal*' (*Journal of Literary & Cultural Disability Studies* 3:ii[2009] 131–46), Pearman argues that Guenevere's blinding by the fairy Tryamour exposes the queen as sinful (through the medieval association between blindness and sin), while she is also a representative of the corruption at King Arthur's court. The presentation of the fairy's intervention, as well as her obvious hypersexuality, help problematize the oppositional roles of the two female characters and their power in the story, showing Tryamour as a 'critique of the human system of justice and a proposal of an alternative to that system' (p. 145).

A number of contributions to *The Cambridge Companion to the Arthurian Literature* tackle medieval English Arthurian romance either by period or by theme, in chapters that include both broad surveys and directions for further research. In 'Part I: Evolution', Ad Putter, 'The Twelfth-Century Arthur', looks at the development of Arthurian romance and chronicle from Geoffrey of Monmouth's *Historia Regum Britanniae* to Wace's and Layamon's retellings, while J.A. Burrow, 'The Fourteenth-Century Arthur', charts the flourishing of the genre in *Sir Gawain and the Green Knight* alongside the Middle English *Ywain and Gawain*, *Syr Percyvell of Gales*, *Sir Landevale*, *Sir Launfal*, and *Lybeaus Desconus*. In 'Part II: Themes', a series of interconnected chapters deal briefly with some Middle English romances and their later adaptations through topics as varied as 'Questioning Arthurian Ideals' (Elizabeth Archibald), 'Arthurian Ethics' (Jane Gilbert), 'Imperial Arthur: Home and Away' (Andrew Lynch), 'Love and Adultery: Arthur's Affairs' (Peggy McCracken), and 'Religion and Magic' (Corinne Saunders) (see section 8(a) below for a discussion of the relevant material).

In the *Companion to Arthurian Literature*, edited by Helen Fulton, three chapters survey the development of the English romance tradition: Ad Putter provides new insights into three medieval romances in his 'Arthurian Romance in English Popular Tradition: *Sir Percyvell of Gales*, *Sir Cleges* and *Sir Launfal*' (pp. 235–51). He notes the 'impressive' narrative continuity in *Percyvell*, now transformed from Chrétien de Troyes's ambiguous tale *Conte du Graal* into a typical Middle English 'family romance' (p. 237); Putter also argues in favour of considering *Sir Cleges* an Arthurian romance (contrary to W.R.J. Barron's omission of the text from his major 1987 survey) and for a 'violently *anti*-bourgeois' attitude on Thomas Chestre's part in his *Sir Launfal*. Roger Dalrymple, 'Sir Gawain in Middle English Romance' (pp. 265–77), surveys the impressive bulk of extant Gawain romances by usefully splitting his analysis into three sections, focusing on 'The Heroic Gawain of the Chronicle Tradition', followed by 'The Fallible Gawain of Chivalric Romance' and 'The Exemplary Gawain of Popular Romance', while Tony Davenport looks at 'The Medieval English Tristan' (pp. 278–93; see section 8(a) below for a discussion of the relevant material) by comparing the unique, but poorly received, *Sir Tristrem* with Thomas Malory's own take on the Tristan story (for a discussion of the Malory part, see below).

Heidi Breuer, in her monograph *Crafting the Witch: Gendering Magic in Medieval and Early Modern England*, dedicates three chapters (one of which focuses on Malory, Shakespeare, and Spenser, for which see section 8 below) to the study of medieval romance. In chapter 2, 'Gender-Blending: Transformative Power in Twelfth- and Thirteenth-Century Arthurian Literature', Breuer uses early Arthurian romance and chronicle writing, including Geoffrey of Monmouth's and Layamon's, to explore the power of magic and love in enabling 'gender mutability', but 'only in male characters' (p. 21), and the prophet as androgyne (for example, Merlin displaying feminine attributes, such as extreme emotion, before prophesying). In chapter 3, 'From Rags to Riches, or the Step-Mother's Revenge: Transformative Power in Late Medieval Arthurian Romances', Breuer turns to the motifs of the loathly lady and the churlish knight in the Gawain romances, Chaucer's *Wife of Bath's Tale*, and Gower's 'Tale of Florent'.

Two other studies deal with the Gawain romances this year. In the first, Ralph Norris, 'Sir Thomas Malory and *The Wedding of Sir Gawain and Dame Ragnell* Reconsidered' (*Arth* 19:ii[2009] 82–102), revisits P.J.C. Field's argument that Thomas Malory was the author of the shorter romance. Norris examines the versions of the tale, in particular the similarity between Chaucer's and Gower's, as well as the relationship between the *Wedding* and the much earlier poem *The Awntyrs of Arthur at the Terne Wathelyn*, with respect to the mysterious name Gromer Somer Joure, found nowhere else apart from the French verse romance *L'âtre périlleux* and Malory. Despite the usual humorous appreciation of the romance, Norris finds 'dignified moments' which contribute to the uneven quality of the poem, a feature that, in Norris's view, may justify the association with Malory (p. 96).

The other Gawain romance which receives attention this year is *The Carl of Carlisle*, revisited by Sean Pollack in 'Border States: Parody, Sovereignty, and Hybrid Identity in *The Carl of Carlisle*' (*Arth* 19:ii[2009] 10–26). Pollack examines evidence about the self-consciousness of border literature and its readers, manifested not only in the issue of the Carl's identity (and the debate over courtesy), but also in sovereignty and power, especially in relation to the centre, represented by King Arthur and his court. Pollack notes that the romance's presentation of the killing of 500 deer appears 'tantamount to a hostile incursion not only on the rights of the local landowners, but also against the population in general' (p. 16); he further considers the place of this romance among the other Gawain romances, and the emphasis placed on courtesy and its display in these, as an exploration of class and aspirations.

A return to some of the Gawain romances is also in evidence in K.S. Whetter's 'Love and Death in Arthurian Romance' (in Cherewatuk and Whetter, eds., *The Arthurian Way of Death: The English Tradition*, pp. 94–114). Here Whetter explores the longstanding association between these two themes in romance in the Middle English texts *Ywain and Gawain*, the *Awntyrs off Arthure at the Terne Wathelyne*, the stanzaic *Morte Arthur*, and Sir Thomas Malory's *Le Morte Darthur* (the latter is discussed below in section 8(a)).

Karen Cherewatuk's own contribution to the same essay collection, 'Dying in Uncle Arthur's Arms and at his Hands' (pp. 50–70), contains an examination of the relationships between Arthur and Mordred, traced back to Geoffrey of Monmouth's *Historia Regum Britanniae*, Wace's *Roman de Brut*, Layamon's *Brut*, and the *Alliterative Morte Arthure*, while Siân Echard, '"But here Geoffrey falls silent": Death, Arthur and the *Historia Regum Britannie*' (pp. 17–32) deals with early modern responses to Geoffrey's text and Arthur's historicity, and Edward Donald Kennedy, 'Mordred's Sons' (pp. 33–49), discusses the differences between the death of Mordred's sons in Geoffrey and in the *Alliterative Morte Arthure*, respectively.

Stephen Knight's *Merlin: Knowledge and Power through the Ages* contains substantial discussions of the eponymous character in Geoffrey, Wace, Layamon and Malory, organized under different chapter headings, which correspond to the widening appeal of the wizard to later medieval writers, from the Welsh/southern Scottish wise man (chapter 1, 'Wisdom'), through to the royal counsellor at King Arthur's court (chapter 2, 'Advice') (see the discussion in section 8(a) below). Knight concludes that Geoffrey's Merlin is 'actually a condensation of the key roles of knowledge, both outside and inside the domain of power' (p. 30), while Wace reduced Merlin's role, transferring his power to that of 'an instrumental assistant to the extraordinary Western monarch' (p. 46), and thus preparing the ground for Layamon's Merlin, who becomes the hero of a national English epic. Knight also discusses the early fourteenth-century *Arthour and Merlin* (only rarely tackled in any depth in recent years, with the exception of Siobhan Bly Calkin's monograph, *Saracens and the Making of English Identity: The Auchinleck Manuscript* [2005], not reviewed in *YWES*) in which he identifies closer affinities to Layamon than to the French sources; here, although Merlin is not Layamon's national prophet, the anonymous author-translator still emphasizes the centrality of Merlin's character to a narrative of unity; in Knight's words, 'the hero of knowledge validates the hero of unified English power' (p. 88).

The *Alliterative Morte Arthure* features in yet another study this year: P.J.C. Field's '*Morte Arthure*, the Montagus, and Milan' (*MÆ* 78[2009] 98–117). Here Field argues for a much more precise dating of the poem in the light of internal evidence, based on a detailed analysis of the lines concerning Mordred's support from the 'Mownttagus and oþer gret lordys' (lines 3772–3). These lines reflect the disobedience of Earl John and the earls of Huntingdon, Kent, and Rutland in January 1400 against Henry IV and represent an anomaly from the point of view of versification; according to Field, line 3772 is a 'uniquely incompetent line in a very well-written poem' (p. 101), which indicates a scribal interpolation. In addition, through further examination of the 'Viscownte of valewnce' (line 2047) for the Viscount of Romae in the poem, Field identifies Giangaleazzo, viscount of Valenza, and son of Galeazzo II—also through his heraldic device, 'a dragon engowllede dredefull to shewe, / Deuorande a dolphin with dolefull lates' (lines 2053–4) contrary to previous critical opinion, that these are Edward III's arms depicted in the poem. An in-depth analysis of the intricate political power struggles in late fourteenth-century Italy, and the role played by *condottieri* such as Sir Richard Hawkwood, an English mercenary, in both Italian faction strife and in the wedding of Giangaleazzo's sister Violante to Lionel, duke of Clarence, son of Edward III, in 1368, further supports Field's thesis that the *Alliterative Morte Arthure* was written between 1375 and 1378, and not around 1400 as previously posited by Mary Hamel.

7. Gower, Lydgate, Hoccleve

(a) Gower

In 'Giving Each His Due: Langland, Gower, and the Question of Equity' (*JEGP* 108[2009] 310–35), Conrad van Dijk finds both authors believing equitable justice to be consistent, uniform, and reciprocal, less tinged with mercy than we may expect, but not wholly resolving its complications. In 'Gower's Beast Allegories in the 1381 *Visio Anglie*' (*PQ* 87[2008] 257–75), which we have as the first book of the *Vox clamantis*, David R. Carlson shows how the verse takes the revolting peasants to be animals but the prose mitigates that—it was their sins that made them less than human—and the ways in which Gower drew on Boethius and Ovid for models. Kathryn McKinley's 'The View from the Tower: Revisiting Gower, 1381, and *Vox Clamantis* Book 1' (*Mediævalia* 29:ii[2009] 31–52) works through how Gower encompasses the narrator/king seeking refuge in the Tower from the chaos and anarchy he has caused and is endangered by; particularly when compared to his source in Guillaume de Deguileville, Gower moves from blaming the mobs to royal guilt, finishing with a return to traditional attitudes.

Several articles focus on the *Confessio Amantis*. Given the propagandistic nature of many texts in the early years of Henry IV, Wim Lindeboom finds good cause for 'Rethinking the Recensions of the *Confessio Amantis*' (*Viator* 40:ii[2009] 319–48) and examines Macaulay's scheme of the recensions, the dating glosses, the political climate, Book VII, Chaucer's 'testament of love', and several other points, to find numerous faults with Macaulay's portrayals. Aidan Conti's 'The Gem-Bearing Serpents of the Trinity Homilies: An Analogue for Gower's *Confessio Amantis*' (*MP* 106[2008–9] 109–16) finds the analogue to the snake with a jewel in its head resisting its hunters' beguiling melodies by placing one ear against a rock or on the ground and its tail in the other (I.463–80), in the twelfth-century Trinity Homilies and in Bodley 343, in all cases as an exemplum on resisting temptation through the senses. In 'Composing the King, 1390–1391: Gower's Ricardian Rhetoric' (*SAC* 31[2009] 141–73), Kurt Olsson revisits the barge episode and the two epilogues in the *Confessio Amantis* to explore 'trouthe' and Gower's schemes for advising the touchy king without chastising him.

(b) Lydgate

Karen Elaine Smyth turns to 'The Astrological Subtext and Other Temporal Patternings in Lydgate's Theban History' (*Medievalia* 29:i[2009] 137–56), arguing that the opening's picture of judicial astrology prefigures the following story in structure, theme (temporal matters in particular), and rhetoric, especially when the astrological significances are observed. A.S.G. Edwards has found a connection between 'Gaskell's *North and South* and John Lydgate' (*N&Q* 56[2009] 399), in that the novel's closing verses come from *The Churl and the Bird*. With reference to Lydgate's 'Epistle to Sibille' and 'A tretise for lauandres', Anthony Bale reconstructs 'A Norfolk Gentlewoman and Lydgatian Patronage: Lady Sibylle Boys and her Cultural Environment' (*MÆ* 78[2009] 261–80), the former more certainly written for her than the latter, which is easily placed alongside other poems of domestic advice and illustrative of the kind of poem written for someone like her—a *Fürstenspiegel* for the higher gentry.

(c) Hoccleve

In '"What world is this? How vndirstande am I?": A Reappraisal of Poetic Authority in Thomas Hoccleve's *Series*' (*MÆ* 78[2009] 281–99), Sebastian James Langdell indicates that—after the Council of Constance and under Duke Humphrey's Protectorate—Hoccleve fears political polarization is divesting poetry of gradations of meaning. *Lerne to Die* is the focus of '"Your ensaumple and your mirour": Hoccleve's Amplification of the Imagery and Intimacy of Henry Suso's *Ars Moriendi*' (*Parergon* 25:ii[2009] 1–16) by Steven Rozenski, Jr., who spots the personification in both and discusses how Hoccleve selects his vocabulary carefully to help readers identify with the dying man.

8. Malory and Caxton

(a) Malory

This year's contributions to Malory studies have seen a surge of interest through indirect approaches to his work, either thematic, as the bulk of essays in *The Arthurian Way of Death* show, or character studies, as in Stephen Knight's *Merlin: Knowledge and Power through the Ages*.

Unsurprisingly, five essays in *The Arthurian Way of Death: The English Tradition*, edited by Karen Cherewatuk and K.S. Whetter, focus on Malory's treatment of the theme, while some of the remaining essays refer, mostly in passing, to his *Morte Darthur*, primarily due to his influence on later writers, from Tennyson to modern movies. The five essays on Malory form the middle part of the book (Part II: 'Middle English Romance and Malory'), but some of the topics tackled here are to some extent anticipated by, and linked to, Karen Cherewatuk's own contribution, 'Dying in Uncle Arthur's Arms and at his Hands' (discussed in section 6 above). In 'Love and Death in Arthurian Romance' (pp. 94–114) K.S. Whetter explores the link between these two themes in romance in the Middle English texts *Ywain and Gawain*, the *Awntyrs off Arthure at the Terne Wathelyne*, the stanzaic *Morte Arthur* (see section 6 above), and Sir Thomas Malory's *Le Morte Darthur*. Whetter's analysis of love and death focuses more specifically on Arthur's incest with his sister Morgawse, Elaine of Ascolat's love of Lancelot, and Lancelot and Guenevere's adulterous love; each of these love relationships is overshadowed by catastrophic consequences, ranging from personal harm (Elaine's suicide) to the destruction of the Round Table. Whetter's interesting argument finally centres on an exploration of the 'relationship between morality and mortality' (p. 113) in Malory's *Morte*.

Thomas H. Crofts's chapter, 'Death in the Margins: Dying and Scribal Performance in the Winchester Manuscript' (pp. 115–23), scrutinizes the marginalia in the only existing manuscript of the *Morte Darthur*. Crofts attends to, in particular, the murders of two minor characters, Harleus le Berbeus and Peryne de Mounte Belyarde, by the invisible knight Garlonde, which are accompanied by marginal notes (encased in shield-shaped obits) which draw attention to these knights' deaths while under Balin's 'conduyt' (p. 119), pointing to Balin's own uneasy progress in his own fate. Michael Wenthe, in 'The Legible Corpses of *Le Morte Darthur*' (pp. 124–35), focuses primarily on the 'Tale of Sir Gareth' and the gruesome presentation of the hanging bodies of forty knights killed by the Red Knight of the Red Lands, and explores the challenges to chivalric behaviour represented both by such unchivalric acts and by other examples of ambiguous death, be it of women or men, whose demise 'speaks for itself' or not, as the case might be.

Lisa Robeson, in her chapter 'Malory and the Death of Kings: The Politics of Regicide at Salisbury Plain' (pp. 136–50), revisits the political consequences for Arthur's heeding (or not) advice at the end of the *Morte* and the specific fifteenth-century conditions under which his behaviour would be judged. Robeson emphasizes both Arthur's position as a weak-willed king when he allows Gawain to take the lead in the vengeful war against Lancelot, and

Arthur's reasonable use of advice in other cases. Robeson also looks at Mordred's brief kingship and his own inability to rule, but Arthur's final act of killing Mordred demonstrates, according to Robeson, that 'Arthur seems to regain his royal will, but not his ability to receive and judge good counsel' (p. 147). The last chapter in this cluster is by Cory James Rushton, who writes persuasively in '"Layde to the colde erthe": Death, Arthur's Knights, and Narrative Closure' (pp. 151–68) about Malory's transformations of several crucial characters' deaths from his source, the *Alliterative Morte Arthure* to the end of his own *Morte*: Bedevere, Gawain, Kay, and finally Arthur take centre stage, in an essay that bridges the gap between Malory's sources and his own intended use of them, and also notes the potential in his writing to inspire generations to come, up to modern movie productions.

In his long article, 'Wounded Masculinity: Injury and Gender in Sir Thomas Malory's *Le Morte Darthur*' (*SP* 106:i[2009] 14–31), Kenneth Hodges challenges some previous critical views that injuries feminize men, and makes a case (following Andrew Lynch's *Malory's Book of Arms*, not reviewed in *YWES*) for reading wounds in Malory's work not as a sign of weakness or a violation of masculinity, but rather as essential in creating 'meaning out of conflict' (p. 16), in particular showing good knights a path to learning and close fellowship. Through perceptive, brief analyses of a variety of examples of male wounding as well as female agency in wounding or healing knights, Hodges argues for a deeper critical engagement with injury in the *Morte*, and a differentiated approach to male and female vulnerability.

Several survey chapters in the Wiley-Blackwell *Companion to Arthurian Literature*, edited by Helen Fulton, focus on Malory. Andrew Lynch, 'Malory's *Morte Darthur* and History' (pp. 297–311), charts critical opinion on reflections of Malory's identity and fifteenth-century politics in his Arthuriad; in particular, emphasis is placed on several topics of relevance: Malory's view of the institution of knighthood, much in tune with the aspirations of his contemporary gentry readers, the linguistic similarity (as well as the pragmatic understanding of social and political realities) in extant gentry letters from the period and the *Morte*, the 'historicity' of Arthur as a character, and the nostalgic view of the past. In the same volume, Elizabeth Archibald eloquently writes on 'Malory's Lancelot and Guenevere' (pp. 312–25), tracing the relationship of these famous characters back through layers of source material, and then back again in the *Morte*. Malory's much-debated choice to call Guenevere a 'trew lover', as well as his portrayal of her 'good ende' as a nun, point, in Archibald's view, to Ector's final eulogy for Lancelot, in which the latter is celebrated as both the 'hede of al Crysten knyghtes' and as a good lover—therefore upholding Guenevere's love (p. 324).

Raluca L. Radulescu, in 'Malory and the Quest for the Holy Grail' (pp. 326–39), reviews critical opinion of the 'Tale of the Sankgreal' in the *Morte* and reveals the layers of biblical interpretation stripped away by Malory in his translation and adaptation of the story. She presents the two sides of the critical debate, one of which states that Malory diminished the negative impact of the knights' failure to achieve the Grail adventure by exalting Lancelot's partial success, and the other that the heightened sense of religious feeling remains in the 'Sankgreal', even if partially, as a reminder of the fallen state of earthly chivalry (as in the French *Queste*).

Heidi Breuer, in her monograph *Crafting the Witch*, dedicates three chapters to the study of medieval romance (the first two are reviewed in section 6 above). Chapter 4, 'The Lady is a Hag: Three Writers and the Transformation of Magic in Sixteenth-Century England', focuses, as its title indicates, on the medieval (Malorian) roots of magic and its use by Shakespeare and Spenser. Breuer argues that negative uses of magic by female characters are more prominent in the works of these three authors and that the transition to scepticism about the benefits of using magic is in evidence here, resulting in a portrayal of almost all magic as demonic. Breuer's analysis of Malory's *Morte* prioritizes female practitioners in the context of increased anxiety over the effects of magic or intentions to use magic in fifteenth-century England.

Stephen Knight's *Merlin: Knowledge and Power through the Ages* contains, as expected, numerous points where the wise man, Arthur's adviser, appears in Malory's *Morte*. Knight's book is a persuasive tour de force through centuries of literature and a variety of languages, genres, and geographical locations, and the structure of the book (four chapters organized around the themes of Wisdom, Advice, Cleverness, and Education) means that Malory's Merlin features, to some extent, in all of them, either in the chronological sequence or as a major influence on later writing. In Malory's *Morte Darthur* Merlin reaches the apogee of his political position as the king's adviser, and the myth of national unity is reinforced through his agency in shaping at least part of Arthur's policies in his early reign.

Merlin also features in Rachel Kapelle's 'Merlin's Prophecies, Malory's Lacunae' (*Arth* 19:ii[2009] 58–81). In this article Kapelle focuses on Merlin's ambiguous predictions and their misunderstood or simply missed meanings (or 'gaps') in Malory's 'Tale of King Arthur'. Kapelle argues that the lack of response to prophecies in this tale, or, alternatively, various characters' refusal to engage with the content of the prophecies (a contrast to Malory's French source for this tale, the *Suite de Merlin*), explains Malory's well-known tendency to favour action over words—translated as a feature of the beginning of Arthur's reign and world. On the same topic of Malory's 'Tale of King Arthur', Jonathan Passaro makes a new case for 'Malory's Text of the *Suite du Merlin*' in this year's *Arthurian Literature* (*ArthL* 26[2009] 39–75). By using a comparative approach, he analyses passages in the tale with parallel ones in two *Suite de Merlin* manuscripts—Cambridge University Library Additional 7071 and London, British Library Additional 38117—and makes a case for the Cambridge manuscript as Malory's closest source, both on linguistic grounds and on Malory's life-records, which place him in the vicinity of the presumed medieval location of this manuscript in the period. The Cambridge manuscript also contains marginalia which attest to its early readers' awareness of the links between the story contained therein and Malory's *Morte*. Overall, Passaro's detailed comparative analysis seeks to prove that Malory's changes to the source enhance Arthur's stature in 'Tale I', so as to portray 'the ideal monarch and his courtiers' (p. 72).

As expected, several other articles in *Arthuriana* include new work on Malory and his *Morte Darthur*, though no general critical or new trend is noticeable either here or elsewhere in Malorian criticism this year. In the special issue dedicated to *Arthuriana*'s retiring chief editor Bonnie Wheeler (also its founder, and a well-known medievalist), K.S. Whetter, 'Characterization in Malory and Bonnie' (*Arth* 19:iii[2009] 123–35), re-examines Gawain's character while arguing that many Malorian characters remain misunderstood due to the disproportionate amount of attention paid by critics to Malory's Lancelot. In the earlier issues of this year's *Arthuriana* three other critics explore Malory's text. Michael W. Anderson, '"The honour of bothe courtes be nat lyke": Cornish Resistance to Arthurian Dominance in Malory' (*Arth* 19:ii[2009] 42–57), revisits 'The Book of Sir Tristram' from the point of view of chivalric prowess, both as a form of resistance and difference to Camelot and as an 'avenue by which the Arthurian court might recognize its troubles' (p. 54). Here the Welsh knight Lamerok sides with the Arthurian court in the test of the drinking horn (which is supposed to expose cuckolded husbands) by sending it to King Mark, and Arthur, as a *rex inutilis*, fails to recognize in Tristram and Isolde's relationship the mirroring of Lancelot and Guenevere's.

Jennifer Boulanger offers 'Righting History: Redemptive Potential and the Written Word in Malory' (*Arth* 19:ii[2009] 27–41), in which she argues for a new reading of tombs and inscriptions in the *Morte Darthur* as redemptive places, both inside the narrative and outside it. Through analyses of Balin and Balan's tomb, the inscription on Excalibur, and Arthur's own tomb, alongside the Fair Maid of Ascolat and Gawain's letters, Boulanger explores how Malory attempts 'to right history by writing history' (p. 37). Janet Jesmok, 'Guiding Lights: Feminine Judgment and Wisdom in Malory's *Morte Darthur*' (*Arth* 19:iii[2009] 34–42), returns critical attention to the feminine in Malory, in particular female agency in the transmission of knowledge and display of wisdom, associated not only with the many unnamed female helpers during chivalric adventures, but also with Igraine and Guenevere. In the same issue of *Arthuriana* Felicia Nimue Ackerman writes '"Your charge is to me a pleasure": Manipulation, Gareth, Lynet, and Malory' (*Arth* 19:iii[2009] 8–14). Ackerman uses an interdisciplinary approach to scrutinize, by means of contemporary analytic philosophy, Gareth's intentional manipulation of Lynet, and concludes that he exceeds the usual Malorian 'means justify the end' attitude (according to which Gareth is simply trying to improve Lynet's opinion of himself) by humiliating her.

Cory James Rushton contributes 'Malory's Idea of the City' (in Dietl and Lauer, eds., *Studies in the Role of Cities in Arthurian Literature and in the Value of Arthurian Literature for a Civic Identity: When Arthuriana Meets Civic Spheres*, pp. 95–116). Rushton explores Malory's important cities, such as London, Winchester, and Cardiff, but more specifically the episode involving King Harmaunce of the Red City, to highlight the 'rather utopian vision of a city united in the desire for strong, effective royal leadership—a vision of an aristocracy which is both respected and needed' (p. 106). By using other texts outside the *Morte* as well as offering close readings of the tournament at the

Red City, Rushton points to the mirroring between Arthur's own story and the tragic end of King Harmaunce.

One of the chapters in Allan J. Mitchell's new monograph, *Ethics and Eventfulness in Middle English Literature*, focuses primarily on the events surrounding Malory's treatment of Balin, the unfortunate knight. By comparing the *Morte* with the equivalent source for this tale, the French *Suite du Merlin*, Mitchell uncovers Malory's originality in cutting out the clear connection, announced by Merlin, between Balin and Eve, both seen as evildoers, but whose actions lead ultimately to the greater good; according to Mitchell, 'events in the *Morte* are deprived of obvious providential significance, and moral judgements are correspondingly moderated' (p. 126).

(b) Caxton

Jenny Adams edits William Caxton's own edition of Jacobus de Cessolis's *The Game and Playe of the Chesse* for the TEAMS Middle English Texts Series. She has chosen to use the 1483 edition rather than Caxton's first, dated 1474. Neither a manual for playing chess nor an entertaining piece of writing, Cessolis's thirteenth-century work is a serious political treatise or *speculum regis* which is informed by the earlier work of John of Salisbury, whose *Policraticus* established the allegorical image of the state as a human body where the members serve the command of the head, or the king. Cessolis, Adams reminds the reader, placed more emphasis on the contractual obligations of individuals as 'each piece corresponds to a specific professional identity, with all pieces being interdependent' (p. 3). The two editions differ in terms of prologue: Caxton's first prologue to the 1474 edition was dedicated to George, duke of Clarence; after the latter's execution, Caxton reissued his edition with a new prologue which emphasizes the nature of his translation of Cessolis as a 'mirror of a political body' instead of the previous thrust of the mirror for princes/kings text. The second difference between the editions is the presence of numerous woodcuts, well reproduced in Adams's edition, in Caxton's 1483 print of the work. Adams's edition contains a very helpful introduction, glosses placed at the bottom of each page, and generous explanatory notes, which will assist scholars in their exploration of this rich text and its appeal to Caxton's contemporaries.

Joseph A. Dane's new monograph, *Abstractions of Evidence in the Study of Manuscripts and Early Printed Books*, contains one chapter dedicated to Caxton's work. In chapter 8: 'What Is [a] Caxton? From Book to Text' (pp. 121–37), Dane scrutinizes the criteria by which the make-up and degree of authenticity and completeness (which makes appeal to the notion of a 'perfect and complete' Caxton) of Caxton's editions were established by generations of scholars following William Blades, Henry Bradshaw, and W.J.B. Crotch. Through careful analyses of the parameters of these scholars' work Dane singles out the drawbacks as well as scholarly advantages of creating certain editorial procedures, although he also shows the wide gap between the experience of the real early Caxton editions and those a modern reader is faced with; in other words, the latter are not 'a "textual" Caxton, but a vulgate one as well' in so far as the errors introduced by Caxton are 'an essential part of his craft, perhaps more essential to the art of printing than they are, say, to the art of literary production' (p. 137).

Kiyokazu Mizobata, ed., *A Concordance to Caxton's Morte Darthur (1485)* [Osaka Books [2009]), was not available for review.

9. Middle Scots Poetry

Overall this was a sparse year for studies in Middle Scots Poetry. A few articles missed last year, however, are worth mentioning before discussing the work produced in 2009. Joanna Kramer's '"Falsett no feit hes": A Proverb in William Dunbar's "In Vice Most Vicius He Excellis"' (*ES* 89[2008] 263–72) attempts to uncover some of the folkloric influences of Dunbar's poetry by searching for analogous proverbial phrases in other languages, since these are mostly lost from the Older Scots corpus. Kramer's project is as interesting as her process, and both are well described in the article. Andrew Breeze also offers etymological studies in 'Some Gaelic Etymologies for Scots Words: *Drubly, Blad, Gilravage* and *Gaberlunzie*' (*ScotLang* 27[2009] 43–50); these words are used by Henryson, Dunbar, and Douglas.

Nicola Royan contributed 'Some Conspicuous Women in the *Original Chronicle, Scotichronicon* and *Scotorum Historia*' (*The Innes Review* 59[2008] 131–44), where she looks at important medieval Scottish historiography and the roles that women play within the narratives. She argues that they sometimes hold symbolic representative positions within the texts, or otherwise fulfil important central functions in the stories, and notes that women are most often excised from works of historiography, and that, as a result, they demand more attention when they are left in.

Moving to 2009, in Corrie, ed., *A Concise Companion to Middle English Literature*, Barry Windeatt's essay 'Signs and Symbols' (pp. 9–31), which opens the volume, looks at Robert Henryson's work, specifically *Garmont of Gud Ladeis, Testament of Cresseid, Orpheus and Eurydice*, and his fable 'The Paddock and the Mouse'. Windeatt argues that Henryson's use of symbols demonstrates 'the sheer range of uses of signs and symbols in medieval writings' (p. 9). He places Henryson's work in dialogue with other texts of the late Middle Ages (such as Margery Kempe's *Book* or *Piers Plowman*), illustrating how symbols are manipulated throughout.

Henryson is also the subject of a chapter of Jill Mann's *From Aesop to Reynard: Beast Literature in Medieval Britain*, entitled 'Henryson: The Epicized Fable' (pp. 262–305). Mann closes her erudite book with this chapter, arguing that Henryson, in his *Morall Fabillis*, combines two separate strands of medieval beast literature: the Aesopic and the Renardian traditions. She suggests that this combination creates a new kind of fable under Henryson's hand, one that collapses the voice of Henryson and his animals in such a way that the reader is required to decide the effectiveness of a tale or appropriateness of its attending moral, and that this gestures towards what will come in later forms of fable (such as Orwell's *Animal Farm*). Henryson's *Testament* is the primary topic of Anna Czarnowus's 'Feminine Acedia in Robert Henryson's *The Testament of Cresseid*' (in Krygier and Sikorska, eds., *þe Laurer of Oure Englische Tonge*, pp. 115–25). She suggests that Henryson, more than Chaucer, invites the audience to 'read like a woman' and to see the disintegration of Criseyde's body as analogous to a loss in her soul after Diomede's rejection.

Joanna Martin's article 'Responses to the Frame Narrative of John Gower's *Confessio Amantis* in Fifteenth- and Sixteenth-Century Scottish Literature' (*RES* 60[2009] 561–77) discusses the influence of Gower, in particular his moral and ethical ideas, in three Scottish texts: the anonymously authored *The Spectacle of Luf*, Gavin Douglas's *The Palice of Honour*, and John Rolland's *The Court of Venus*. Anne Andrews Caughey writes about Gavin Douglas's work in '"The wild fury of Turnus now lies slain": Love, War and the Medieval Other in Gavin Douglas' *Eneados*' (in Ellis and Meyer, eds., *Masculinity and the Other: Historical Perspectives*, pp. 261–80). She argues that, in Douglas's translation of Virgil's *Aeneid*, he rejects the chivalric and courtly values that are imposed by his contemporaries (such as Chaucer) in their own translations of the work, and instead highlights and embraces the Roman values inherent in the original.

In 'Dunbar's Perfection: The Still Movement of Aureate Poetics in *The Thistle and the Rose*' (*AteneaPR* 29[2009] 69–90), Nickolas Haydock suggests that, while Dunbar is heavily influenced by Chaucer's *Parliament of Fowls* in the poem, he uses it as a starting point in order to explore a divergent vision of nature in his famous poem commemorating the marriage of James IV and Margaret Tudor. A.A. MacDonald also discusses Dunbar's *The Testament of Maister Andro Kennedy* in 'William Dunbar and Andro Kennedy: A Dental Challenge' in a note (*MÆ* 78[2009] 118–22), where he looks closely at the troubling Latin lines in the poem and their meaning, particularly the phrase 'sine de'.

In the inaugural issue of the *Scottish Literary Review*, Emily Lyle's 'Three Notes on *King Orphius*' (*ScotLR* 1[2009] 51–68) looks closely at a redaction of the Orpheus legend, *King Orphius*, preserved in a sixteenth-century Scottish manuscript. Juliette Wood discusses 'The Arthurian Legend in Scotland and Cornwall' (in Fulton, ed., pp. 102–16). Wood looks closely at the Scottish chronicles, suggesting that Arthur is portrayed ambivalently throughout, with some chroniclers naming Mordred (the son of the Scottish Loth) as the legitimate heir to Arthur's throne. She also surveys the surviving Scots Arthurian romances *Gologros and Gawaine* and *Lancelot of the Laik* and their relation to the Arthurian corpus at large.

10. Drama

Two book-length studies of early drama have been published this year, one a brief introduction to the field as a whole, the other a more detailed study of a particular and notably problematic text. Katie Normington's *Medieval English Drama* provides a brisk introduction to the diversity of genres and performance traditions that thrived in the period. Arranged around discussions of the principal auspices and locations for performance (ecclesiastical buildings, city streets, open spaces, and halls), this short and accessible book summarizes the state of play in current scholarship on the various dramatic genres discussed and offers students valuable orientation in the field.

More tightly focused in its scrutiny and exposition is Penny Granger's admirable analysis of the N-Town play, the first detailed monographic study of what remains in many ways the Cinderella of the religious cycle plays—if a cycle play is indeed what it is, rather than a collection of somewhat disparate materials. *The N-Town Play: Drama and Liturgy in Medieval East Anglia* is a detailed and impressive analysis of the separate dramatic materials that make up the N-Town manuscript, which draws out the overriding importance of the liturgy (and especially the Eucharist and the Magnificat) to its conception and effects. In this way Granger's book is a valuable companion piece to Pam King's recent study of drama and the liturgy in York, *The York Mystery Cycle and the Worship of the City* (Brewer [2006]; reviewed in *YWES* 87[2008] 50–1), adding richly to our sense of the interactions between performance, ritual, devotion, and lay religious practice in this period. In addition Granger looks more broadly across the dramatic and literary landscape, comparing and contrasting N-Town with the other extant English cycles, and also with Middle Dutch analogues to the Mary Play, *Die Eerste Bliscap van Maria* and *Die Sevenste Bliscap van Onser Vrouwen*. Her conclusion is that N-Town displays a distinctly East Anglian approach to its engagement with and deployment of liturgical materials, closer to surviving non-dramatic literature from the region than to religious drama produced elsewhere. A brief discussion of the possible history of the manuscript's compilation and ownership completes the study and argues tentatively that the work might helpfully be thought of as both a practical record of plays for performance and a text designed for devotional reading, perhaps in the context of influential female patronage or that of a female religious community. A detailed glossary, a bibliography, and a list of liturgical sources for the play complete this impressive monograph.

A number of the essays in the excellent collection *Shakespeare and the Middle Ages*, edited by Curtis Perry and John Watkins, discuss early drama in some depth. Most notably, perhaps, Michael O'Connell's '*King Lear* and the Summons of Death' (pp. 199–216) brilliantly explores Shakespeare's debt to both the religious cycle plays and the Moralities, before focusing on *King Lear* and its numerous echoes of earlier plays and dramatic motifs. Karen Sawyer Marsalek also looks to the cycle plays in her essay 'Marvels and Counterfeits: False Resurrections in the Chester *Antichrist* and *I Henry IV*' (pp. 217–40), suggesting how echoes of the Chester play of Antichrist inform the figure of Falstaff, 'a character unrepentantly, charmingly, and sometimes treacherously theatrical' (p. 231), who similarly conjures his own mock-resurrection on the battlefield of Shrewsbury.

Scholars interested in the political work performed by early drama will benefit from Scott C. Lucas's radical rereading of one of the 'great texts' of the mid-sixteenth century, *A Mirror for Magistrates*, not only because the *Mirror* is a source for many Elizabethan plays, but for the substantial reinterpretation of the text that Lucas offers. His study, '*A Mirror for Magistrates* and the Politics of the English Reformation', persuasively sets out the case that the tragic narratives in William Baldwin and his co-authors' work were not simply exercises in scholarly or populist historiography or *de cassibus* narrative, but active reflections upon, and interventions in, mid-Tudor politics, designed to address contemporary policies and attitudes.

Stephen Hamrick's stimulating study, *The Catholic Imaginary and the Cults of Elizabeth, 1558–1582*, focuses largely on the poetic literature of Elizabeth's first two and a half decades on the throne, but his discussion of the English poets' negotiation of the state's reappropriation of conventional Catholic forms and imagery to bolster Protestant rule provides valuable contextual material for the similar work done in the drama of the period. The conservative religious culture of the north in the sixteenth century is also explored in Michael Bush's detailed investigation of the textual and cultural aspects of the Pilgrimage of Grace of 1536–7: *The Pilgrims' Complaint: A study of Popular Thought in the Early Tudor North*.

The TEAMS edition of *Two Moral Interludes: 'The Pride of Life' and 'Wisdom'*, edited by David N. Klausner, offers two excellent working texts of these significant plays, the one fragmentary and somewhat less well known, the other substantial and rather more canonical, in a single handy volume. Alongside the clearly reproduced texts, with useful marginal glosses, Klausner offers a short, informative introductory essay, detailed interpretative notes, and, in appendices, extracts from suggested sources for the plays: *The Gesta Romanorum* and 'The Abuses of the Age' (from BL MS Harley 2251) for *The Pride of Life*; Heinrich Suso's *Orologium sapientiae*, Walter Hilton's *The Scale of Perfection*, and *Epistle on the Mixed Life* and other shorter extracts from contemporary religious texts for *Wisdom*. There is also a bibliography, glossary, and suggested songs (with their music) that might be used when performing the plays.

Two of the essays in *Literature and the Scottish Reformation*, a thought-provoking collection edited by Crawford Gribben and David George Mullan, focus on drama, and more specifically on Sir David Lyndsay's seminal work, *Ane Satire of the Thrie Estaitis*. Amanda J. Piesse's 'Allegory and Reformation in David Lindsay's *Ane Satire of the Thrie Estaitis* (1552–54)' (pp. 81–94) looks at both the theatrical and the political and social dynamics of the play. Building on the still vital work of Joanne Spencer Kantrowicz, Piesse teases out the problematics of allegory as a mode in the reformist mindset, and offers the intriguing suggestion that Lyndsay's play is in part an object lesson for godly audiences in how to resist drama's rhetorical and affective seductions. In 'Political Theatre or Heritage Culture? *Ane Satire of the Thrie Estaitis* in Production' (pp. 213–32), Adrienne Scullion looks closely at the play's modern revivals and offers a rather pessimistic account of its position in the contemporary performance repertoire, even in Scotland. More optimistically, however, she ends with a persuasive call for its resurrection, shorn of its 'heritage' trappings, as a potentially powerful political statement in an early twenty-first-century context. Further background to the religious and political contexts of both Lyndsay's work and the English drama can be found in Alec Ryrie's adept and engaging survey, *The*

Age of Reformation: The Tudor and Stuart Realms, 1485–1603. The book is especially useful for its willingness to compare and contrast the distinct experiences of religious and cultural change in Scotland and England through the long sixteenth century.

The latest issue of *Jewish Culture and History* (*JCH* 11:i–ii[2009]), a special issue on *Jewish Journeys: From Philo to Hip Hop*, edited by James Jordan, Tony Kushner, and Sarah Pearce, contains one essay on the early drama. Greg Walker's '"And here's your host . . .": Jews and Others in the Croxton *Play of the Sacrament*' (*JCH* 11:i–ii[2009] 41–56) looks at that play's more subtly subversive theatrical and cultural effects as well as surveying the existing scholarship on the nature and roles of the Jews in this intriguing East Anglian drama.

Among the specialist journals, the bulk of the articles in *Early Theatre* (*EarT* 12[2009]) this year are, as is frequently the case, focused on the later Elizabethan and Stuart drama, but there are some notable discussions of earlier material too. David Kathman's 'The Rise of Commercial Playing in 1540s London' (*EarT* 12:i[2009] 15–38) documents the existence of commercial stages (in halls, yards, inns, and houses) in the English capital well before the conventional dates for the advent of professional theatres in 1576 or 1567. Issue 12:ii is dedicated to the memory of the late Barbara D. Palmer, whose own work was focused on the earlier period, and especially on the religious drama and the Towneley plays, so fittingly there is rather more medieval and early Tudor material in its pages than is the norm. In 'Miraculous Rhetoric: The Relationship Between Rhetoric and Miracles in the York "Entry into Jerusalem"' (*EarT* 12:ii[2009] 15–31) Frank Napolitano looks at the rhetorical dimensions to humankind's attempts to engage with the divine and with the tenets of the Christian faith in this pivotal pageant in the York cycle. John Geck's article, '"On yestern day in Feverere, the yere passeth fully": On the Dating and Prosopography of *Mankind*' (*EarT* 12:ii[2009] 33–56), reads that early Morality in the light of local and national politics in the late 1460s, focusing on the list of East Anglian notables named in the play. Finally, in 'The Singing "Vice": Music and Mischief in Early English Drama' (*EarT* 12:ii[2009] 57–90), Maura Giles-Watson briskly catalogues the associations of the Vice figure in early drama with secular music and misrule, dwelling more substantially on Merry Report in John Heywood's *The Play of the Weather* and Sedition in John Bale's *King Johan*, and suggesting connections with the Vice-like figures on the Shakespearian stage, such as Falstaff and Iago.

A sense of the wider context of John Heywood's later career in the service of Princess Mary Tudor can be gained from J.L. McIntosh's innovative study, *From Heads of Household to Heads of State: The Preaccession Households of Mary and Elizabeth Tudor, 1516–1558*. While Heywood himself is not discussed, the princess's household culture through the years of her vicissitudes in the 1530s and 1540s is well sketched out in a book that is published in association with a clutch of additional web-based illustrations and other materials available at www.gutenberg-e.org. Given the sophistication of this multi-media format, however, the lack of an index in the book itself is disappointing, and makes navigating its riches somewhat more frustrating than necessary.

The role of drama in grammar-school education in the sixteenth century is discussed briefly at a number of points in Ian Green's excellent study of the diverse influences on the Tudor English schools and colleges, *Humanism and Protestantism in Early Modern English Education*. Green points usefully to the role of teachers who had been exposed to classical performances at university in the spread of Latinate drama into provincial schools, as when Thomas Ashton, a student at St John's Cambridge, developed a performing tradition at Shrewsbury School following his appointment there as headmaster in 1561 (p. 215).

The rhetorical dimensions to early modern learning and education are also the subject of a number of the essays collected in Nancy S. Struever's Variorum volume, *The History of Rhetoric and the Rhetoric of History*. Of particular interest to scholars of the drama will be the material scattered through the volume on the work of Vives, Valla, Petrarch, and Shakespeare. The essay 'Shakespeare and Rhetoric' (pp. 137–44), first published in *Rhetorica* 6[1988], is especially suggestive in its implications for the playwright's rhetorical technique. Proverbs and epigrams, the subject of a number of Struever's essays, are also the subject of Gerard Kilroy's valuable new edition of *The Epigrams of Sir John Harrington*. Presented with a detailed critical introduction and scholarly apparatus including a discussion of manuscript provenance, textual variants, and print history, the epigrams will now hopefully find a wider readership for their shrewd and often acerbic wisdom.

Books Reviewed

Adams, Jenny, ed. *William Caxton: The Game and Playe of Chesse*. TEAMS Middle English Texts. MIP. [2009] pp. viii + 156. $13 ISBN 9 7815 8044 1308.

Archibald, Elizabeth, and Ad Putter, eds. *The Cambridge Companion to Arthurian Literature*. CUP. [2009] pp. xx + 261. £18.99 pb ISBN 9 7805 2167 7882.

Astell, Ann W., and J.A. Jackson, eds. *Levinas and Medieval Literature: The 'Difficult Reading' of English and Rabbinic Texts*. Duquesne. [2009] pp. x + 374. hb $58 ISBN 9 7808 2070 4203, pb $24.95 ISBN 9 7808 2070 4210.

Bale, Anthony, ed. *St Edmund, King and Martyr: Changing Images of a Medieval Saint*. YMP. [2009] pp. xii + 202. £50 ($95) ISBN 9 7819 0315 3260.

Barr, Helen, ed. *The Digby Poems: A New Edition of the Lyrics*. UExeP. [2009] pp. 368. pb £18.99 ISBN 9 7808 5989 8171.

Barrett, Jr., Robert W. *Against All England: Regional Identity and Cheshire Writing, 1195–1656*. UNDP. [2009] pp. xvii + 306. £31.50 ($35) ISBN 9 7802 6802 2099.

Breuer, Heidi. *Crafting the Witch: Gendering Magic in Medieval and Early Modern England*. Routledge. [2009] pp. xii + 190. £65 ISBN 9 7804 1597 7616.

Brown, Peter, ed. *A Companion to Medieval Literature and Culture, c.1350–c.1500*. Wiley-Blackwell. [2009] pp. 688. £24.99 ISBN 9 7814 0519 5522.

Bush, Michael. *The Pilgrims' Complaint: A Study of Popular Thought in the Early Tudor North*. Ashgate. [2009] pp. xiv + 307. £65 ISBN 9 7807 5466 7858.

Cherewatuk, Karen, and K.S. Whetter, eds. *The Arthurian Way of Death: The English Tradition*. CUP. [2009] pp. xiv + 259. £50 ISBN 9 7818 4384 2088.

Chewning, Susannah M., ed. *The Milieu and Context of the Wooing Group*. UWalesP. [2009] pp. xiii + 236. £75 ($85) ISBN 9 7807 0832 0334.

Ciuk, Andrzej, and Katarzyna Molek-Kozakowska, eds. *Exploring Space: Spatial Notions in Cultural, Literary and Language Studies*, vol. 1: *Space in Cultural and Literary Studies*. CambridgeSP. [2009] pp. 475. $79.99 (£49.99) ISBN 9 7814 4382 1438.

Classen, Albrecht, ed. *Urban Space in the Middle Ages and the Early Modern Age*. De Gruyter. [2009] pp. vii + 757. $119.95 ISBN 9 7831 1022 3897.

Connolly, Daniel K. *The Maps of Matthew Paris: Medieval Journeys through Space, Time and Liturgy*. Boydell. [2009] pp. xiv + 224. £50 ($95) ISBN 9 7818 4383 4786.

Connolly, Margaret. *The Index of Middle English Prose Handlist XIX: Manuscripts in the University Library, Cambridge (Dd-Oo)*. Brewer. [2009] pp. lx + 470. £60 ($115) ISBN 9 7818 4384 0541.

Copeland, Rita, and Ineke Sluiter, eds. *Medieval Grammar and Rhetoric: Language Arts and Literary Theory, AD 300–1475*. OUP. [2009] pp. xii + 972. £95 ($192.50) ISBN 9 7801 9818 3419.

Corrie, Marilyn, ed. *A Concise Companion to Middle English Literature*. Wiley. [2009] pp. xii + 268. £60 ($104.95) ISBN 9 7814 0512 0043.

Dane, Joseph A. *Abstractions of Evidence in the Study of Manuscripts and Early Printed Books*. Ashgate. [2009] pp. viii + 176. £55 ISBN 9 7807 5466 5014.

Dietl, Cora, and Claudia Lauer, eds. *Studies in the Role of Cities in Arthurian Literature and in the Value of Arthurian Literature for a Civic Identity: When Arthuriana Meets Civic Spheres*. Mellen. [2009] pp. vii + 167. £64.95 ($100) ISBN 9 7807 7343 8927.

Dockray-Miller, Mary. *Saints Edith and Æthelthryth: Princesses, Miracle Workers, and their Late Medieval Audience. The Wilton Chronicle and the Wilton Life of St. Æthelthryth*. Brepols. [2009] pp. ix + 475. £73.17 ($116) ISBN 9 7825 0352 8366.

Ellis, Heather, and Jessica Meyer, eds. *Masculinity and the Other: Historical Perspectives*. CambridgeSP. [2009] pp. xii + 337. £39.99 ($67.99) ISBN 9 7814 4380 1515.

Fein, Susanna, ed. *John the Blind Audelay: Poems and Carols, from Oxford, Bodleian Library MS Douce 303*. TEAMS Middle English Texts. MIP. [2009] pp. 389. pb $23 ISBN 9 7815 8044 1315.

Fein, Susanna, ed. *'My Wyl and My Wrytyng': Essays on John the Blind Audelay*. MIP. [2009] pp. xx + 356. hb $50 ISBN 9 7815 8044 1353, pb $25 ISBN 9 7815 8044 1360.

Fugelso, Karl, ed. *Studies in Medievalism XVIII: Defining Medievalism(s) II*. Brewer. [2009] pp. xii + 292. £50 ($95) ISBN 9 7818 4384 2101.

Fulton, Helen, ed. *A Companion to Arthurian Literature*. Wiley-Blackwell. [2009] pp. xiv + 571. £105 ($209.95) ISBN 9 7814 0515 7896.

Furrow, Melissa. *Expectations of Romance: The Reception of a Genre in Medieval England*. CUP. [2009] pp. viii + 264. £50 ISBN 9 7818 4384 2071.

Goldberg, P.J.P., and Maryanne Kowaleski, eds. *Medieval Domesticity: Home, Housing, and Household in Medieval England*. CUP. [2009] pp. 332. $102 ISBN 9 7805 2189 9208.

Good, Jonathan. *The Cult of Saint George in Medieval England*. Boydell. [2009] pp. xvi + 200. £50 ($95) ISBN 9 7818 4383 4694.

Granger, Penny. *The N-Town Play: Drama and Liturgy in Medieval East Anglia*. Brewer. [2009] pp. x + 257. £50 ISBN 9 7818 4384 1890.

Green, Ian. *Humanism and Protestantism in Early Modern English Education*. Ashgate. [2009] pp. xvii + 373. £65 ISBN 9 7807 5466 3683.

Gribben, Crawford, and David George Mullan, eds. *Literature and the Scottish Reformation*. Ashgate. [2009] pp. ix + 260. £55 ISBN 9 7807 5466 7155.

Gunn, Cate, and Catherine Innes-Parker, eds. *Texts and Traditions of Medieval Pastoral Care: Essays in Honour of Bella Millett*. YMP. [2009] pp. xx + 228. £50 ($95) ISBN 9 7819 0315 3291.

Hamrick, Stephen. *The Catholic Imaginary and the Cults of Elizabeth, 1558–1582*. Ashgate. [2009] pp. 232. £55 ISBN 9 7807 5466 5885.

Hazell, Dinah. *Poverty in Late Middle English Literature: The Meene and the Riche*. Dublin Studies in Medieval and Renaissance Literature. FCP. [2009] pp. 238. £50 (€55, $70) ISBN 9 7818 4682 1554.

Hill, Ordelle G. *Looking Westward: Poetry, Landscape, and Politics in Sir Gawain and the Green Knight*. UDelP. [2009] pp. 203. $51.50 ISBN 9 7808 7413 0492.

Hunt, Tony, ed. *Three Anglo-Norman Treatises on Falconry*. Medium Ævum Monographs NS 26. Society for the Study of Medieval Languages and Literature. [2009] pp. iv + 184. £30 ($45) ISBN 9 7809 0757 0196.

Jones, E.A., and Alexandra Walsham, eds. *Syon Abbey and its Books: Reading, Writing and Religion c.1400–1700*. Boydell. [2009] pp. xvi + 267. £50 ($95) ISBN 9 7818 4383 5479.

Kerby-Fulton, Kathryn, ed. *Women and the Divine in Literature before 1700: Essays in Memory of Margot Louis*. ELS. [2009] pp. xi + 279. $30 ISBN 9 7815 5058 3830.

Kilroy, Gerard, ed. *The Epigrams of Sir John Harrington*. Ashgate. [2009] pp. xiii + 348. £60 ISBN 9 7807 5466 0026.

Klausner, David N., ed. *Two Moral Interludes: 'The Pride of Life' and 'Wisdom'*. TEAMS Middle English Texts. MIP. [2009] pp. 113. $13 ISBN 9 7815 8044 1346.

Kline, Daniel T., ed. *The Medieval British Literature Handbook*. Continuum. [2009] pp. xxii + 300. hb £57 ($120) ISBN 9 7808 2649 4085, pb 17.99 ($29.95) ISBN 9 7808 2649 4092.

Knight, Stephen. *Merlin: Knowledge and Power through the Ages*. CornUP. [2009] pp. xvii + 275 + 25 illustrations. $27.95 ISBN 9 7808 0144 3657.

Krygier, Marcin, and Liliana Sikorska, eds. *þe Laurer of Oure Englische Tonge*. Lang. [2009] pp. 149. £28.60 ($49.95) ISBN 9 7836 3159 0973.

Levy-Navarro, Elena. *The Culture of Obesity in Early and Late Modernity: Body Image in Shakespeare, Jonson, Middleton, and Skelton*. Palgrave. [2008] pp. 252. $80 ISBN 9 7802 3060 1239.

Lewis, C.P., ed. *Anglo-Norman Studies XXXI: Proceedings of the Battle Conference 2008*. Boydell. [2009] pp. xii + 210. £45 ($90) ISBN 9 7818 4383 4731.

Lucas, Scott C. *'A Mirror For Magistrate's' and the Politics of the English Reformation*. UMassP. [2009] pp. x + 275. £34.50 ISBN 9 7815 5849 7061.

Mann, Jill. *From Aesop to Reynard: Beast Literature in Medieval Britain*. OUP. [2009] pp. xii + 380. £63 ($110) ISBN 9 7801 9921 7687.

McIntosh, J.L. *From Heads of Household to Heads of State: The Preaccession Households of Mary and Elizabeth Tudor, 1516–1558*. ColUP. [2009] pp. xii + 251. £41.50 ISBN 9 7802 3113 5504.

McNamer, Sarah. *Affective Meditation and the Invention of Medieval Compassion*. UPennP. [2009] pp. viii + 309. £39; $59.95 ISBN 9 7808 1224 2119.

Mitchell, J. Allan. *Ethics and Eventfulness in Middle English Literature*. Palgrave. [2009] pp. 204. £50 ISBN 9 7814 0397 4426.

Mulder-Bakker, Anneke B., and Liz Herbert McAvoy. *Women and Experience in Later Medieval Writing: Reading the Book of Life*. Palgrave. [2009] pp. x + 194. £50 ($85) ISBN 9 7802 3060 2878.

Noble, Elizabeth. *The World of the Stonors: A Gentry Society*. Boydell. [2009] pp. xii + 224. £50 ($95) ISBN 9 7818 4383 4298.

Normington, Katie. *Medieval English Drama*. Polity. [2009] pp. xii + 177. £16.99 ISBN 9 7807 4563 6047.

Pepin, Ronald E. trans. *Anselm & Becket: Two Canterbury Saints' Lives by John of Salisbury*. Medieval Sources in Translation 46. PIMS. [2009] pp. viii + 108. $19 ISBN 9 7808 8844 2987.

Perry, Curtis, and John Watkins, eds. *Shakespeare and the Middle Ages*. OUP. [2009] pp. xiv + 295. £56 ISBN 9 7801 9955 8179.

Powell, Susan, ed. *John Mirk's 'Festial': Edited from British Library MS Cotton Claudius A.II*, vol. 1. EETS OS 334. OUP. [2009] pp. cxlvi + 190. £70 ($130) ISBN 9 7801 9957 8498.

Radulescu, Raluca, and Cory James Rushton, eds. *A Companion to Medieval Popular Romance*. Brewer. [2009] pp. 222. £50 ($90) ISBN 9 7818 4384 1924.

Raskolnikov, Masha. *Body against Soul: Gender and Sowlehele in Middle English Allegory*. OSUP. [2009] pp. 288. £31.47 ($44.95) ISBN 9 7808 1421 1021.

Renevey, Denis, and Christiania Whitehead, eds. *The Medieval Translator 12: Lost in Translation?*. Brepols. [2009] pp. xviii + 382. £70.16 ($109) ISBN 9 7825 0353 1397.

Ringrose, Jayne. *Summary Catalogue of the Additional Medieval Manuscripts in Cambridge University Library Acquired before 1940*. Boydell. [2009] pp. xxxvi + 340. £90 ($170) ISBN 9 7818 4383 4878.

Ryrie, Alec. *The Age of Reformation: The Tudor and Stuart Realms, 1485–1603*. Pearson/Longman. [2009] pp. xx + 333. £19.99 ISBN 9 7814 0583 5572.

Salih, Sarah, and Denise N. Baker, eds. *Julian of Norwich's Legacy: Medieval Mysticism and Post-Medieval Reception*. Palgrave. [2009] pp. viii + 217. £65 ($90) ISBN 9 7802 3060 6678.

Scanlon, Larry, ed. *The Cambridge Companion to Medieval English Literature 1100–1500*. CUP. [2009] pp. xx + 300. hb £45 ($80) ISBN 9 7805 2184 1672, pb £17.99 ($29.99) ISBN 9 7805 2160 2587.

Somerset, Fiona, ed. *Four Wycliffite Dialogues: Dialogue between Jon and Richard, Dialogue between a Friar and a Secular, Dialogue between Reson and Gabbyng, Dialogue between a Clerk and a Knight*. EETS OS 333. OUP. [2009] pp. lxxii + 152. £60 ($110) ISBN 9 7801 9957 8481.

Struever, Nancy S. *The History of Rhetoric and the Rhetoric of History*. Ashgate Variorum. [2009] pp. xx + 336. £70 ISBN 9 7807 5465 9990.

Thomson, R.M. *A Descriptive Catalogue of the Medieval Manuscripts of Merton College, Oxford, with a Description of the Greek Manuscripts by N.G. Wilson*. Brewer. [2009] pp. xlvi + 330. £95 ($180) ISBN 9 7818 4384 1883.

Westerhof, Danielle. *Death and the Noble Body in Medieval England*. Boydell. [2008] pp. xii + 190. £50 ($95) ISBN 9 7818 4383 4168.

Wogan-Browne, Jocelyn, et al., eds. *Language and Culture in Medieval Britain: The French of England c.1100–c.1500*. YMP. [2009] pp. xxii + 538. £50 ($95) ISBN 9 7819 0315 3277.

Zieman, Katherine. *Singing the New Song: Literacy and Liturgy in Late Medieval England*. UPennP. [2008] pp. 312. $59.95. £39 ISBN 9 7808 1224 0511.

IV

Later Medieval: Chaucer

KATHARINE W. JAGER AND JESSICA BARR

This chapter is divided into four sections: 1. General; 2. *The Canterbury Tales*; 3. *Troilus and Criseyde*; 4. Other Works. The ordering of individual tales and poems within the sections follows that of the Riverside Chaucer edition.

1. General

Via a series of far-ranging, often bilingual, close readings, Ardis Butterfield argues for a newly historicized multilingual context of medieval England in her *The Familiar Enemy: Chaucer, Language and Nation in the Hundred Years War*. Butterfield charts the relationship between French, English, and Anglo-Norman, ranging from Hengist and Horsa to Shakespeare. She notes that only 'a narrow sleeve of sea' separates England and France (p. xix), and that neither nation had a single vernacular literature. Using Derridean notions of translation to govern her analyses, as well as those of postcolonial theorists Spivak and Chakrabarty, she argues that Chaucer's London English 'was far more than English: it was English in a richly mobile and alien setting' (p. 210). In her readings of Chaucer she posits that 'Chaucer's writings do not display a single relationship between two languages, English and French, but a set of relationships between several language boundaries that are played out within England as much as they are across the Channel' (p. 275).

Building upon this research is the text of the biennial Chaucer lecture, addressed to the New Chaucer Society 2008 conference in Swansea. Ardis Butterfield's 'Chaucerian Vernaculars' (*SAC* 31[2009] 25–51) argues for a more capacious understanding of the term 'vernacular', noting that in the late medieval period 'vernacular in England does not mean only English' (p. 36). She explores the triangular relationship between French, Middle English, and Anglo-Norman and posits that 'the relationship between English and French, far from being a topic that has lost its way, is poised to transform our approach to both areas', and urges a reconsideration of Chaucer as a fully bilingual writer (pp. 31–4).

Carol Falvo Heffernan, in *Comedy in Chaucer and Boccaccio*, argues that Chaucer's comedy is best understood in relation to Boccaccio's writings.

The Year's Work in English Studies, Volume 90 (2011)
doi:10.1093/ywes/mar009

Asserting the possibility that Chaucer came into direct contact with more of Boccaccio's writings than has previously been assumed, Heffernan situates his comedic poems within an Italian tradition as well as within the French tradition that has most often been seen as his source. Heffernan approaches the relationship between Chaucer and Boccaccio from several different directions. Following a discussion of the possibility of Chaucer's having read the *Decameron*, she compares several of the comic episodes from the *Canterbury Tales*—the Miller's, Merchant's, Shipman's, and Reeve's tales—to similar episodes in the *Decameron*. In a consideration of anti-fraternal satire in Chaucer and Boccaccio, Heffernan argues that both Chaucer's Friar and his Pardoner, though the latter is not actually a friar himself, resemble in significant ways the Italian poet's satirical friars. Finally, she turns to *Troilus and Criseyde*, whose relationship to *Il Filostrato* has been well established, to consider the significance of Chaucer's comic additions to Boccaccio's poem. Chaucer's development of comedic threads in the *Troilus*, she concludes, is what gave rise to the extended comedy of Fragment I of the *Canterbury Tales*.

Daniel J. Ransom's 'Imprecise Chaucer' (*ChauR* 43:iv[2009] 376–99) surveys Chaucer's ambiguous use of words designating time to 'caution against assuming that Chaucer uses [them]...with reliable precision' (p. 376). Worrying about the precise meanings of his measurements is a distraction, Ransom contends, as Chaucer is unlikely to have concerned himself much with the accuracy of his measurements.

Julia Ruth Briggs, in '"Chaucer...the Story Gives": *Troilus and Cressida* and *The Two Noble Kinsmen*' (in Driver and Ray, eds., *Shakespeare and the Middle Ages: Essays on the Performance and Adaptation of the Plays with Medieval Sources or Settings*, pp. 161–77), discusses the performance history of Shakespeare's two most 'Chaucerian' plays, which are based on *Troilus and Criseyde* and the *Knight's Tale*, respectively. This article examines the 'medieval' elements that are present (or, especially in the case of *Troilus and Cressida*, typically lacking) in such performances.

Peter Holbrook's 'Vulgar, Sentimental, and Liberal Criticism: F.J. Furnivall and T.S. Eliot on Shakespeare and Chaucer' (*MP* 107:i[2009] 96–125) finds modern relevance in Furnival's and Eliot's approaches to criticism. Focusing on their treatments of Chaucer and Shakespeare, Holbrook favourably compares Furnival's 'sentimental' form of criticism to Eliot's more 'elitist' style to make an argument for literary criticism as an engaged practice and one that can contribute to individual and collective liberation.

Laura Kendrick, in 'Games Medievalists Play: How to Make Earnest of Game and Still Enjoy It' (*NLH* 40:i[2009] 43–61), examines the concept of 'play' in the Middle Ages and as a way of understanding medievalists' work. She argues that medievalists engage in a kind of play—a 'game' with 'rules'—when they seek to understand the Middle Ages from a 'medieval' perspective. Chaucer appears in this article as one of several sources employed in uncovering the development of the concepts of 'play' and 'game'.

John Ganim argues, in his 'Cosmopolitan Chaucer, or the Uses of Local Culture' (*SAC* 31[2009] 3–21), that Chaucer's deft use of other languages and poetic traditions establishes him as 'the most cosmopolitan' of late medieval writers (p. 9). Ganim notes that the shift between the local and the cosmopolitan in the *Canterbury Tales* is 'mandated by history' (p. 14), and calls for the New Chaucer Society to itself become an advocate for cosmopolitan technologies. In his 'Toward a Description of Chaucer's Verse Forms' (*SN* 81:i[2009] 45–52), Joseph A. Dane charts Chaucer's prosody, noting that he 'regularly accents syllable four' in his decasyllabic lines (p. 49). He observes that accent dominance appears as 'a distinct feature of English varieties of [Chaucer's] verse, rather that as its foundational principle' (p. 51).

James Wimsatt's revised edition of *Chaucer and the Poems of 'Ch.'* presents an expanded analysis of Chaucer's likely contribution to Pennsylvania MS French 15. He posits that 'while the mature Chaucer busily adapted Continental genres and subjects to the English language, the youthful Chaucer's first essays at court were no doubt composed in French' (p. 1). The largest grouping of a variety of anonymous French lyric *formes fixes*—*balade*, *rondeau*, *virelay*, *lay*, and five-stanza *chanson*—manuscript Penn French 15 contains fifteen lyrics headed by the initials 'Ch.' from approximately 1360, contemporaneous with Chaucer's service to the court as a young man. The manuscript, likely owned by Isabel of Bavaria, also contains copies of poems by Machaut, Granson, and Deschamps; those labelled 'Ch.' are 'among the best' therein (pp. 2–3). Wimsatt notes that the 'Ch.' poems seem allied with the style of Jean de le Mote, the poet deeply involved in mid-fourteenth-century English courtly poetic production who may have been the first 'prominent court poet that young Geoffrey Chaucer met' (pp. 5–6). Ten 'Ch.' poems are *balades*, and four use *royaux employ* stanzas and rhyme schemes much like le Mote's own work (p. 8). Most are love poems that strive for 'grace and sonorousness rather than striking originality' (p. 9). Likely presented orally, the 'Ch.' poems are 'particularly flexible in assuming dramatic personas' (p. 10). This edition does not include facsimile images of the manuscript, as the 1982 version does.

Simon Horobin, in 'The Criteria for Scribal Attribution: Dublin, Trinity College MS 244 Reconsidered' (*RES* 60[2009] 371–81), contests Fletcher's attribution of MS 244 to Adam Pynkhurst, arguing that such an attribution cannot be defended on palaeographic or linguistic grounds. Rather, Horobin proposes that MS 244 was copied by a scribe who, like Pynkhurst, was trained in *anglicana formata*, but who was otherwise unconnected with him. Horobin also offers the argument that Bodleian Library MS Bodley 619 might be the product of the prolific fifteenth-century Carthusian scribe Stephen Dodesham, in 'The Scribe of Bodleian Library MS Bodley 619 and the Circulation of Chaucer's Treatise on the Astrolabe' (*SAC* 31[2009]109–24).

Geoffrey Cooper and Peter Goodall's edition *Chaucer's Monk's Tale and Nun's Priest's Tale: An Annotated Bibliography, 1900 to 2000* offers an invaluable compendium of research. Noting that the *Monk's Tale* and the *Nun's Priest's Tale* are in many ways the 'odd couple' of the *Canterbury Tales*, their book charts a rich century of criticism on the two tales (p. xix).

Angela Florschuetz's essay '"A mooder he hath, but fader hath he noon": Constructions of Genealogy in the Clerk's Tale and the Man of Law's Tale' (*ChauR* 44:i[2009] 25–60) reads both the *Clerk's Tale* and the *Man of Law's Tale* as being 'fantas[ies] of autonomous patrilineal reproduction' (p. 27) in which the masculine characters are able to effectively erase the generative powers of the women under their control.

Of particular interest to Chaucer studies is Gerald Morgan's careful explication of the *Canterbury Tales* in his *The Shaping of English Poetry: Essays on Sir Gawain and the Green Knight, Langland, Chaucer and Spenser*, and specifically his chapters on the *General Prologue*, the *Man of Law's Tale*, and the *Pardoner's Tale*. In 'The Universality of the Portraits in the *General Prologue*', Morgan, following Jill Mann, posits that the portraits are collectively and individually 'organized in terms of a general conception of social class defined by means of function' (p. 111). He distinguishes between the 'intrinsic importance' of the detail given over to the physical and ethical aspects of the portraits and the 'structural significance' of their social aspects (p. 116), arguing that, ultimately, medieval people thought in generic rather than individual terms about the construction of character. Morgan builds upon this argument in 'Rhetorical Perspectives in the *General Prologue* to the *Canterbury Tales*', to argue for the 'specifically medieval dimensions of Chaucer's art' (p. 130). He notes that in medieval rhetoric 'the unity of perspective is aimed at in portraiture' (p. 137). His eighth chapter, 'A Defence of Dorigen's Complaint', situates the genre of the complaint within the larger medieval rhetorical tradition and argues that 'medieval poetry is distinguished by its moral and not its psychological subtlety' (p. 170). He similarly interrogates psychological studies of the *Pardoner's Tale* in 'The Self-Revealing Tendencies of Chaucer's Pardoner', parsing the literary sources of Chaucer's character in the *Roman de la Rose* among other texts.

The *Cambridge Companion to Medieval English Literature 1100–1500*, edited by Larry Scanlon, offers Chaucer studies several useful essays. In his introduction (pp. 1–10) Scanlon notes that the compilation aims 'to give the reader new to Middle English studies a map of what one might call the discursive economy of later Middle English literature' (p. 6) as well as consideration of individual authors. Wendy Scase considers the vernacular context in which Chaucer wrote, in her 'Re-inventing the Vernacular: Middle English Language and its Literature' (pp. 11–24), specifically his own claim regarding the 'gret diversite / In Englissh' (p. 11). She notes that it is difficult to pin down any medieval text to one vernacular, because 'real texts elude systematic dialectal categorization' (p. 12). Scanlon also contributes the chapter on 'Chaucer' (pp. 165–78), discussing Chaucer's biography and literary contributions. Scanlon notes that, in the *Canterbury Tales*, 'by mapping the tale-telling contest onto pilgrimage's therapy of distance, Chaucer makes tale-telling (and by extension, poetry itself) a worldly, non-sacral enterprise, or even a profane one—as we might expect of a tavern game' (p. 174).

Elizabeth Scala and Sylvia Federico, in their compilation *The Post-Historical Middle Ages*, offer a valuable series of essays, situating Chaucer studies within a new theoretical landscape, when they note in their introduction (pp. 1–12) that 'historicist practice has shifted neither the generalist scholarly audience nor the undergraduate curriculum. Despite their continued importance to popular culture, including film and fiction and new technological media, the Middle Ages are as academically marginal as ever'

(p. 4). They observe that the book 'signifies as a significant misnomer: think of it as a wish, an impossibility, a threat—but most of all as a provocation' (p. 10).

Patricia Clare Ingham, in her psychoanalytic analysis of Chaucer, Petrarch, and history, 'Amorous Dispossessions: Knowledge, Desire and the Poet's Dead Body' (pp. 13–36), argues that 'far from being a state that prohibits or constrains knowledge about literature . . . dispossession constitutes the occasion for the production of such knowledge' (pp. 15–16). She notes that 'something other than truth is at stake' in the 'intractable' questions of 'temporality, of literary history, of "medieval" and "early modern" that exist in the exclusion of Chaucer from Petrarch's "legacy"' (p. 16). Also taking a Lacan-influenced approach, George Edmondson's 'Naked Chaucer' (pp. 139–60) examines Helgeland's film depiction of Geoff Chaucer in *The Knight's Tale*. He resists the notion of 'historicism as the moral obligation to understand those who preceded us, and their worlds, exclusively in terms with which they themselves would have been familiar' (p. 140), arguing that 'historical time is not continuous, that there are breaks and ruptures, upheavals and overturnings' (p. 141), and wonders if the film offers us in a naked depiction 'a Chaucer that is more real than the empirical Chaucer, the one who lived and worked and wrote in the late fourteenth century' (p. 142). Thomas Prendergast and Stephanie Trigg likewise analyse the film *The Knight's Tale* in their 'The Negative Erotics of Medievalism' (pp. 117–38), arguing for a renewed interest in medievalism. They note that 'medievalism has the capacity to function as a challenge to many of our most complex debates about historicism', and that 'manifestations of medievalism allow us to get closer to the expression of human desire about the past, expressions that are often disarmingly unselfconscious' (p. 118).

In his beautifully constructed *Telling Images: Chaucer and the Imagery of Narrative*, volume 2, V.A. Kolve presents nuanced readings of both Chaucer's poetry and many corollary images. His first chapter, 'Looking at the Sun', argues that images of eagles, the sun, and Christ form the textual backdrop of Boccaccio. His second chapter, 'From Cleopatra to Alceste', looks at the characters of Cleopatra and Alceste in the *Legend of Good Women* and persuasively argues that Chaucer's death scene for Cleopatra, which imagines her entering a pit of vipers, must be understood alongside *transi* tombs and images of dead bodies eaten by worms. Chapter 3, 'Man in the Middle', explores the image of the carter in the *Friar's Tale*, seeing the carter as both an exemplum and as the 'imaginative center' of the tale (p. 68). The carter is poised between good and evil; Kolve argues that Chaucer presents in this positioning the idea that 'art is at liberty to evade . . . definitive closure [and] unqualified truth' (p. 92). Kolve's fourth and fifth chapters read the *Merchant's Tale* and the calendrical images of January and May. He argues that the figure of January is routinely figured as the god of gates and keys, while the month of May is often decorated with the twins of Gemini. These twins are frequently depicted naked, and occasionally as a heterosexual couple in the midst of trees. In his sixth chapter, 'Rocky Shores and Pleasure Gardens', Kolve discusses the 'poetics of illusion' (p. 198) in the *Franklin's Tale*, specifically analysing images of automata and pleasure gardens.

His seventh chapter reads the *Second Nun's Tale* and images surrounding St Cecilia and her bath of fire, and his final chapter, 'God-Denying Fools', argues for a reassessment of the contemporary atheism of critics by offering analyses of images of the god-denying fool.

Kathy Cawsey, in 'Disorienting Orientalism: Finding Saracens in Strange Places in Late Medieval English Manuscripts' (*Exemplaria* 21[2009] 380–97), examines manuscript images in BL Harley 2278 of figures that appear to be Saracens but are labelled Danes in Lydgate's *Lives of Saints Edmund and Fremund*, and then interrogates two 'orientalist' tales, Chaucer's *Man of Law's Tale* and Gower's *Tale of Constance*. She argues that the images of turbaned Danes 'speak to the fundamental affinity medieval people perceived between the Eastern Muslims and the Northern pagans', and that such a move is problematic for writers like Chaucer because it situates him alongside earlier pagan ancestors (p. 393).

Tison Pugh offers a queer reading of instances of troth-pledging between men in the *Friar's Tale*, *Pardoner's Tale*, and *Shipman's Tale*, in '"For to be sworne bretheren til they deye": Satirizing Queer Brotherhood in the Chaucerian Corpus' (*ChauR* 43:iii[2009] 282–310). He argues that through these satirical, homosocial representations of brotherhood oaths Chaucer 'causes narrative constructions of fraternal masculinity to founder' (p. 283).

Kathleen Kennedy thoughtfully discusses the trope of maintenance (that is, 'supportive behavior', p. 4) in late medieval literature, in her *Maintenance, Meed, and Marriage in Medieval English Literature*. She 'explores the culture of relationships between different kinds of masters and men in late medieval England', blending literary criticism with historiography (p. 2). Of particular interest to Chaucer studies are chapter 3, 'Attaining Women', and chapter 4, 'Retaining Men'. Chapter 3 analyses the inequalities of marriage, as seen through *Troilus and Criseyde*, the *Wife of Bath's Tale*, and the *Franklin's Tale* (p. 31), looking specifically at the trope of *raptus* and what she calls 'the sliding agency' of married women (p. 42). Chapter 4 looks at *Melibee* as depicting the fraught 'culture of service' to which men were subject (p. 62). Kennedy notes that *Melibee* 'points to how service's dual basis, loyalty and finance, could further social trouble as easily as ameliorate it' (p. 65).

In his *Constructing Chaucer: Author and Autofiction in the Critical Tradition*, Geoffrey Gust explores Chaucer's inconsistent, ironic narratorial personae, positing that Chaucer constructs an 'autofiction' or an autobiographical story that is fundamentally representational (p. 2). In his first chapter, Gust catalogues the theoretical history of persona theory and tries to rehabilitate the new-critical trope of 'persona'; he also offers what he calls a 'queer' view of Chaucer's personae in an attempt to disrupt 'the interpretive status quo' in a more capacious study of who these personae might be and to whom they are speaking (pp. 47–8). This queer study examines Chaucer the author 'as a poetic agent and manipulator, who thrived by both producing and responding to diverse implications of his material, whether social or textual, satirical or sexual' (p. 49). Further chapters look at the critical constructions of Chaucer's biography; his shorter works and the voice of memoir; the critical reception of the *Wife of Bath's Tale* and the *Pardoner's Tale* in light of Chaucer's persona as pilgrim; and Chaucer's self-representation in the *Tale of Sir Thopas*.

2. *The Canterbury Tales*

Following a discussion of Chaucer's military and diplomatic career, Gerald Morgan, in 'The Worthiness of Chaucer's Worthy Knight' (*ChauR* 44:ii[2009] 115–58), uses evidence of contemporary standards of knightly conduct to argue that Chaucer's description of the Knight is not ironic. Both the description and Chaucer's diplomatic experience suggest that the Knight has religious conviction, virtue, and a high seriousness of purpose. In '"Tu es pélérin en la sainte cité": Chaucer's Knight and Philippe de Mézières' (*SP* 106:iv[2009] 379–401), Stefan Vander Elst similarly rejects the idea that the description of the Knight is ironic, arguing that the fourteenth-century French soldier Philippe de Mézières may have served as Chaucer's model for the Knight. One implication of this claim is that the Knight is intended neither ironically nor as an unattainable chivalric ideal, but as a 'truthful description of human achievement' (p. 398). Like Morgan and Vander Elst, S.H. Rigby, in *Wisdom and Chivalry: Chaucer's Knight's Tale and Medieval Political Theory*, sets out to reclaim the Knight—or, rather, his tale—from modern critical scepticism. Rigby argues against the idea that Chaucer intends Theseus to be seen as a tyrant or unjust king; instead, by reading the tale in light of Giles of Rome's *De Regimine Principum*, he demonstrates that, on every level, the Duke of Athens adheres to the standards of conduct proper for a ruler. Beginning with the concept self-governance, Rigby argues that Theseus follows the standards of personal conduct and ethics laid out by Giles. For instance, he is sufficiently prudent, just, and temperate, and his construction of the stadium for Palamon and Arcite's combat demonstrates his magnificence, rather than being a symptom of his vainglory, as some critics have asserted. But Theseus's virtue does not end with his self-governance. Rigby argues further that his relationships with his wife, his sister-in-law, and the other members of his entourage indicate his proper governance of his household (the medieval definition of 'economics'). Moving outward to the political realm, Rigby compares Theseus's kingship favourably with the model of monarchical rule spelled out in Giles's *De Regimine*. Finally, Rigby reads the Duke's 'Prime Mover' speech, concluding that, despite modern critics' difficulty in accepting its message, it is not ironic but rather very much in accord with the Boethian and Aristotelian cosmography that was current in Chaucer's day. By reading the *Knight's Tale* in conjunction with contemporary political theory, then, Rigby claims that the story can be read as a sort of mirror for princes in the guise of a romance. According to this reading, the critically problematic Duke of Athens embodies the virtues required of a king.

Other scholars, by contrast, examine the tale's inconsistencies. Robert Emmett Finnegan, in 'A Curious Condition of Being: The City and the Grove in Chaucer's *Knight's Tale*' (*SP* 106:iii[2009] 285–98), discusses several contradictory moments in the *Knight's Tale*: Thebes is razed and then exists, and the grove is razed twice (p. 285). These moments, along with Theseus's 'Prime Mover' speech, reflect the instability of the tale's universe, despite its characters' ongoing quest for 'order and permanence' (p. 298). Their lack of surprise at the spontaneous regeneration of city and grove demonstrates their recognition of a universe that does not follow the principle of non-contradiction. Edward Wheatley, in 'Murderous Sows in Chaucer's *Knight's Tale* and Late Fourteenth-Century France' (*ChauR* 44:ii[2009] 224–6), speculates that the scene of a sow gnawing on a child referred to in the *Knight's Tale* may have been based on an incident at Falaise in which a sow ate the face of a child, and considers the implications of this connection for the dating of the tale.

Discussing the possible sources and analogues for the *Miller's Tale* laid out in Revard's 2005 article (reviewed in *YWES* 86[2007] 299), Frederick M. Biggs, in 'A Bared Bottom and a Basket: A New Analogue and a New Source for the *Miller's Tale*' (*N&Q* 56[2009] 340–1), argues that reading 'Le Chevalier et la Corbeille' and 'La Gageure' as analogues for the Chaucer's narrative underscores the abruptness of the ending of the *Miller's Tale*. In '*The Miller's Tale* and *Decameron* 3.4' (*JEGP* (108:i[2009] 59–80), Biggs also examines Chaucer's 'narrative borrowings' of religion, apology, and judgement from Boccaccio's *Decameron* (p. 60), and argues that Chaucer deepened the 'moral complexity' of Boccaccio's comic narrative (p. 80).

Karl P. Wentersdorf, in 'The "Viritoot" Crux in Chaucer's *Miller's Tale*' (*ChauR* 44:i[2009] 110–13), considers a feature of the tale that does not derive from any known source. Wentersdorf suggests that the hapax legomenon 'viritoot', whose meaning has not been established, derives from 'cum virtute', and means something along the lines of 'with manly ardour' or (as Donaldson has suggested) 'on the prowl'. Obscure words and their meanings take on additional significance in 'Ineloquent Ends: *Simplicitas*, Proctolalia, and the Profane Vernacular in the *Miller's Tale*' (*Speculum* 84[2009] 956–83). In this article, Gregory Heyworth explores the meanings of inarticulate expression and material objects in the *Miller's Tale* in order to theorize profanity as a linguistic category. Concluding that profanity 'is not irreligion but a category used by the literate to describe a non-textual mode of meaning they do not understand' (p. 983), Heyworth argues for the multivalence of the tale's scatology as well as of metanarrative moments such as the warning to readers at the end of the Miller's *Prologue*. Dawn Simmons Walts tackles the subject of time in her 'Tricks of Time in the *Miller's Tale*' (*ChauR* 43:iv[2009] 400–13). She argues that the *Miller's Tale* depicts the ways in which time and time management are linked to social prowess. As she notes, 'actions are quick and events are timely in the *Miller's Tale*' (p. 407), and Nicholas manipulates time in order to achieve multiple goals. To manage and control time, in the tale, 'is nothing less than the ability to control the narrative of one's life' (p. 412).

Nicole Nolan Sidhu, in '"To late for to crie": Female Desire, Fabliau Politics, and Classical Legend in Chaucer's *Reeve's Tale*' (*Exemplaria* 21[2009] 3–23), proposes that the *Reeve's Tale* foregrounds the clash between women's desire and assumptions of male authority over women's bodies, specifically fathers' power over their daughters' sexual choices. Sidhu argues that Chaucer's use of themes from classical legend, particularly those concerning rape and daughters using their sexuality to escape paternal control, distinguish the *Reeve's Tale* from most fabliaux and point to the tale's critique of the ideology of male martial domination evident in both the *Knight's Tale* and the *Miller's Tale*. In 'Chaucer's Strother and Berwickshire' (*N&Q* 56[2009] 21–3), Andrew Breeze argues that there are both linguistic and political reasons for believing that the 'Strother' referred to in the *Reeve's Tale* is most likely Westruther, in Scotland. If his hypothesis is correct, then the *Reeve's Tale* is probably English literature's first imitation of Scots dialect.

Jay Ruud and Stacy M. Jones take a novel approach to the *Canterbury Tales* in 'The Practice of PR and the Canterbury Pilgrims' (*CLCWeb: Comparative Literature and Culture* 11:ii[2009] article 11). Applying the public-relations concept of relationship management to the *Canterbury Tales*, they argue that the Wife of Bath's focus on communal, 'win–win' relationships makes her more appealing than the Pardoner, who is intent upon winning and thus confined to quid pro quo exchange relationships. Elizabeth Scala also compares pilgrims in 'Desire in the *Canterbury Tales*: Sovereignty and Mastery between the Wife and Clerk' (*SAC* 31[2009] 81–108). Scala argues that the Wife and the Clerk express desires seemingly contrary to their tales: the Wife yearns to be subject to masculine dominance, and the Clerk to be the dominating male. These desires are made manifest in the narrative and structural similarities between the tales: both narrators back away from their own lessons and end their narratives with discordant vituperation. In 'Interpreting the *Wife of Bath's Prologue* and *Tale* in a Contemporary Note to Thynne's 1532 Edition' (*ANQ* 22:iii[2009] 3–11), Antonina Harbus explores the meaning of a comment that appears at the end of a copy of Thynne's edition of Chaucer's *Works*. Ostensibly about the Wife of Bath's views of men and marriage, the comment does not accurately reflect her discourse but rather seems to articulate—and dismiss—popular anti-male sentiments.

Glending Olson, in his 'Measuring the Immeasurable: Farting, Geometry, and Theology in the *Summoner's Tale*' (*ChauR* 43:iv[2009] 414–27), argues that the final moment of the *Summoner's Tale* might be read as both satire and an invitation to consider 'efforts to measure or quantify abstract theological terms' (p. 414). The parodic ending of the tale is 'a comic triumph of geometric intelligence' (p. 420).

David Raybin, in 'Muslim Griselda: The Politics of Gender and Religion in Geoffrey Chaucer's *Clerk's Tale* and Pramoedya Ananta Toer's *The Girl from the Coast*' (*Exemplaria* 21[2009] 179–200), compares the gender politics of the *Clerk's Tale* and Pramoedya's novel, which, though set in 1960 s Indonesia, follows a parallel narrative line. Both texts articulate similarly the possibility of female agency in a patriarchal world and hint at the ways in which spiritual institutions can support oppressive political forces. Also considering gender roles, Lynn Shutters, in 'Griselda's Pagan Virtue' (*ChauR* 44:i[2009] 61–83), argues that Griselda can best be understood within the context of late medieval treatments of pagan female virtue. Griselda's devotion to Walter is consonant with other of Chaucer's (and other writers') works, suggesting that the question of virtuous pagan women's relationship to Christian women was a concern in the later Middle Ages.

Gerald Morgan, in. 'The Logic of *The Clerk's Tale*' (*MLR* 104:i[2009] 1–25), defends the Clerk from critical hostility, pointing out that his tale is consistent with the emphasis on his 'seriousness'. Walter's persecution of his wife follows a clear logic, and Griselda's response indicates that she personifies humility, patience, and obedience. What the tale points out, Morgan argues, is how uncomfortable the virtue of obedience really is, and the importance of victims shaping a 'moral response' (p. 15) to oppression. Susan Yager also reflects on the moral implications of the *Clerk's Tale* in 'Levinas, Allegory, and Chaucer's *Clerk's Tale*' (in Astell and Jackson, eds., *Levinas and Medieval Literature: The 'Difficult Reading' of English and Rabbinic Texts*, pp. 35–56). Beginning with the premise that elements of Levinas's writing parallel medieval allegory, Yager uses his ethical insights to read Walter and Griselda as an allegory of the transformative confrontation of the self with the ethical other. Nonetheless, one cannot simply 'apply' Levinas, as allegory requires openness to multiple interpretations. Laura F. Hodges, in 'Reading Griselda's Smocks in the *Clerk's Tale*' (*ChauR* 44:i[2009] 84–109), discusses the multivalence of Griselda's smocks within the context of medieval material and literary culture. The smocks are noteworthy because they are not elaborately described, despite the fact that clothing is an important signifier in the tale. Hodges also describes the likely style and appearance of Griselda's various costumes.

In her essay 'When Pardon Is Impossible: Two Talmudic Tales, Chaucer's Pardoner's Tale, and Levinas' (in Astell and Jackson, eds., pp. 255–79), Ann Astell argues that the *Pardoner's Tale*, like Levinas's reflections on talmudic tales, engages the concept of forgiveness. She proposes that the Old Man is a figure of the Pardoner himself, who suffers from the sin of despair, and concludes by reading the *Parson's Tale* and the retraction in light of Levinasian ethics, arguing that we must seriously evaluate Chaucer's plea for forgiveness—regardless of how we interpret his intent.

In his *Translations of Authority in Medieval English Literature: Valuing the Vernacular*, A.J. Minnis primarily examines the relationship between English and Latin, identifying the ways in which vernacularity was associated with late medieval heresy, and noting that the vernacular 'is far too potent to be strait-jacketed within the narrow sphere of language transfer' (p. 16). His sixth chapter, 'Chaucer and the Relics of Vernacular Religion', is of particular value to Chaucer studies. The chapter explores the ways in which Chaucer considers the Pardoner's relics and Harry Bailly's anger at being asked to kiss them, focusing on historical evidence suggesting that relics were believed to have power to cure urogenital illness (p. 131). He argues that the veneration of bodily relics might be understood as a 'vernacular' or lay practice (p. 136). Towards that end, he discusses the medieval tradition of kissing bodily relics and of dipping such relics in holy water that was then thought to be curative, and notes that excrement-stained saints' garments were regularly kissed.

Maidie Hilmo's 'Iconic Representations of Chaucer's Two Nuns and their Tales from Manuscript to Print' (in Kerby-Fulton, ed., *Women and the Divine in Literature before 1700: Essays in Memory of Margot Louis*, pp. 107–35) examines the Ellesmere and Caxton illustrations of the *Prioress's Tale* and *Second Nun's Tale* to argue that the depiction of their speakers suggests a growing interest in authorship. She contextualizes the speaker-portraits within contemporary illuminations and images, such as the iconography of St Cecilia in the early fourteenth-century Uffizi altarpiece.

Roger Dahood, in his 'English Historical Narratives of Jewish Child-Murder, Chaucer's Prioress's Tale, and the Date of Chaucer's Unknown Source' (*SAC* 31[2009] 125–40), argues that the *Prioress's Tale* combines themes of similar 'chorister' tales in which little boys are crucified by Jews

(p. 126), and posits that, by alluding to Hugh of Lincoln, Chaucer is referencing 'non-Marian, historical English narratives' related to the 1290 expulsion of the Jews from Britain (p. 140).

Patricia Clare Ingham uses a Lacanian psychoanalytic approach to read the *Squire's Tale* as a romance obsessed with drolleries and with courtly love, in her 'Little Nothings: *The Squire's Tale* and the Ambition of Gadgets' (*SAC* 31[2009] 53–80). She argues that the tale 'crosscuts rationalism with the kind of enchanted absorption in the new and unusual, a wonder to familiar to readers of romance but here considered in contradictory and complex terms' (p. 58). Newfangled objects are fascinating, she observes, but there is terrible pain when the beloved pursues new love (p. 59).

Cara Michelle Hersh's article, '"Knowledge of the Files": Subverting Bureaucratic Legibility in the Franklin's Tale' (*ChauR* 43:iv[2009] 428–54), explores the concepts of privacy, bureaucracy, and secrecy in the *Franklin's Tale* and notes that the tale's interplay between legibility and concealment reflects the tension between a householder's making his accounts legible to himself but illegible to the king and his agents. Roy J. Pearcy, in 'Épreuves d'amour and Chaucer's *Franklin's Tale*' (*ChauR* 44:ii[2009] 159–85), analyses the differences between the *Franklin's Tale* and several other romances to argue that the task that Dorigen sets for Aurelius and her reaction to its completion are incompatible with courtly love. The conflict between the demands of courtly love and the love that Dorigen and Arveragus feel for one another indicates the tensions between romantic love and Christian marriage. William Sayers, in 'Tregetours in the *Franklin's Tale*: Stage Magic and Siege Machines' (*N&Q* 56:iii[2009] 341–6), defends the possibility of a link between the word 'tregetour' in the *Franklin's Tale* and 'trebuchet', or siege machine, on the grounds of etymological and, especially, conceptual similarities. While we cannot assume that Chaucer was aware of a connection between the words, Sayers argues for their 'associational' relationship (p. 346).

In Martha Driver's 'Reading *A Midsummer Night's Dream* through Middle English Romance' (in Driver and Ray, eds., pp. 140–60), a discussion of the elements of medieval romance found in *A Midsummer Night's Dream*, Driver reviews the similarities between *The Tale of Sir Thopas* and the story of Piramus and Thisbe, focusing in particular on how the latter section of the play has been interpreted in twentieth-century performances.

Two essays discuss *The Tale of Melibee*, each situating the narrative in a distinctive context. One of these is Louise M. Bishop's 'A Touch of Chaucer in *The Winter's Tale*' (in Driver and Ray, eds., pp. 232–44). Contending that Shakespeare's *Winter's Tale* is in part an adaptation of Chaucer's *Melibee*, Bishop considers both texts' emphasis upon female utterance as an effective response to patriarchal violence. By situating Shakespeare with regard to his sources, she argues for the play's concern with authorial reputation and legacy. Jamie Taylor, in 'Chaucer's *Tale of Melibee* and the Failure of Allegory' (*Exemplaria* 21[2009] 83–101), reads *Melibee* through the discussion of ownership and sovereignty in Bracton's *De legibus et consuetudinis Angliae* to argue that the tale is concerned with the 'use' and 'ownership' of allegory. Finally, exploring Sophie's naming and subsequent dismissal from the tale,

Taylor suggests that Chaucer's text 'gesture[s] towards the referential absence at the heart of sovereignty' (p. 98).

Peter W. Travis's *Disseminal Chaucer: Rereading the Nun's Priest's Tale* is a 443-page reconsideration of the *Nun's Priest's Tale* that explores in depth a cluster of seemingly minor, but notoriously baffling, narrative and poetic details: for example, Chauntecleer's and the Priest's time-telling; Harry Bailly's description of the Priest's virility; and the startling comparison of the hens' clamour to the noise of the 1381 Peasants' Revolt. Arguing that the tale can be seen as Chaucer's *ars poetica*, Travis proposes that it forces readers—both medieval and modern—to examine their own interpretative and readerly practices by presenting insoluble ambiguities and calling parodic attention to the medieval liberal arts curriculum. Through theoretically informed close readings (Travis draws in varying degrees upon Ricoeur, Derrida, and de Man, among others), this book contends that the tale is best described as a Menippean parody, rather than a satire. Specifically, Chaucer is parodying the educational practices with which he would have expected his readers to be familiar: training in logic and rhetoric, new and old methods of time-telling, and the literary imitations that schoolboys were required to compose. The length of Travis's volume—and he admits that it is a rather long book about a rather short poem—is the result of his in-depth exploration of the various intellectual contexts for each parodic element of the tale. Finally, his close readings, theoretical reflections, and historical contextualization lead Travis to conclude that the *Nun's Priest's Tale* ultimately challenges readers to become aware of how they read and of the ambiguities inherent in literary interpretation at every level.

Nancy Mason Bradbury and Carolyn Collete read themes of time, timeliness, and clocks in the *Nun's Priest's Tale*, in their 'Changing Times: The Mechanical Clock in Late Medieval Literature' (*ChauR* 43:iv[2009] 351–75). They note that the tale contains an early reference to the word 'clokke' (p. 366). They argue that the tale's representation of time and timepieces requires 'readers to test the sententious pronouncements of received authority against newer allegiances to experience, quantification and proof' (p. 352). The rooster Chauntecleer is himself a 'natural clock' who lives not in historical time but in the time of the narrative fable, they note, and bears a resemblance to actual late medieval clocks adorned with roosters (pp. 367–8).

3. *Troilus and Criseyde*

In *The Cycle of Troy in Geoffrey Chaucer: Tradition and 'Moralitee'* José María Gutiérrez Arranz examines the Troy cycle in Chaucer's poetry, and posits that Chaucer had access to many classical texts. In his third chapter Arranz catalogues many of the medieval mythographies in a reading of *Troilus and Criseyde* as well as the *House of Fame*, providing a lengthy compilation of classical characters (pp. 31–126).

In 'Chaucer's "litel bok", Plotinus, and the Ending of Troilus and Criseyde' (*Neophil* 93:ii[2009] 357–68), Clíodhna Carney reads the ending of *Troilus and*

Criseyde in the light of Plotinus' Neoplatonic concept of emanation and return, through which she explores the triple movement of transcendence in the final stanzas of the poem. She concludes that these stanzas signify a recuperation of Troilus's tragic story.

Equally concerned with medieval philosophy, Noel Harold Kaylor, Jr.'s 'The Shape of Chaucerian Tragedy' (in Krygier and Sikorska, eds., *Þe Laurer of Oure Englische Tonge*, pp. 93–105) considers Chaucer's use of two different epistemological systems in *Troilus and Criseyde*: Boethius's hierarchical ascent from sensory to intellectual knowing, and a Dantean structure that reflects the cyclical movement of Fortune's wheel. The combination of these two systems, Kaylor argues, accounts for the poem's ambiguity as a tragedy.

Gary Lim, in '"Thus gan he make a mirour of his mynde": Fragmented Memories and Anxious Desire in *Troilus and Criseyde*' (*Neophil* 93:ii[2009] 339–56), uses medieval cognitive psychological theory and the principles of Kleinian analysis to argue that Troilus's anxiety shapes his desire for Criseyde, which in turn shapes his sense of self. These theories illuminate the obsessive quality of Troilus's despair over the loss of Criseyde and the persecutory anxieties that pursue him in Book V. Where Lim borrows from psychoanalysis to explore *Troilus and Criseyde*, J. Allan Mitchell, in 'Criseyde's Chances: Courtly Love and Ethics about to Come' (in Astell and Jackson, eds., pp. 185–206), employs ethics. Focusing on Criseyde, Mitchell uses Levinas to evaluate the moral dimensions of love and fortune in the text. Remarking that courtly love confers upon women only 'the privilege of subjection to an other' (p. 203), he suggests that it is too contingent and vulnerable to create 'the ethical relation' in a Levinasian sense (p. 206).

4. Other Works

Nancy Ciccone, in 'The Chamber, the Man in Black, and the Structure of Chaucer's *Book of the Duchess*' (*ChauR* 44:ii[2009] 205–23), traces the parallels between the images that fill the narrator's chamber as he falls asleep and the autobiography of the man in black. This reading of *The Book of the Duchess* suggests that the artefacts in the chamber can serve different purposes; their cultural value differs depending on one's subjective experience, reflecting the difficulties of expressing emotional realities.

Alasdair A. MacDonald, in 'Allegorical (Dream-)Vision Poetry in Medieval and Early Modern Scotland' (in Suntrop and Veenstra, eds., *Himmel auf Erden/Heaven on Earth*, pp. 167–76), explores the relationship between Chaucer's dream visions and the dream-vision poetry of late medieval and early modern Scottish writers. MacDonald argues that the latter demonstrate affinities with, while differing significantly from, Chaucer. The Scottish poems differ from Chaucer's in their use of personal experience and their movement away from the English poet's 'delicacy and ambiguity' (p. 173).

In *Visual Power and Fame in René d'Anjou, Geoffrey Chaucer, and the Black Prince*, Sunhee Kim Gertz examines the concept of 'visual power' (how authors—and stories—articulate complex concepts using iconic imagery and conventional narratives) through representations of fame in the writings of

René d'Anjou, Chaucer, and Edward III. Gertz grounds her investigation in the *Fürstenspiegel* genre, which instructs both princes and non-royal readers in the behaviour proper to a leader through the use of exempla and stock narratives. One of her major arguments is that the *Fürstenspiegel*, like other exempla, flatten individuals' lives in order to render them comprehensible and also to fit them into conventional interpretations—so Dido, in *The House of Fame*, could be an exemplum of the spurned lover, an interpretation that omits the details and singularity of her life. Thus, an important question becomes whether fame it/herself similarly 'flattens' and renders static the lives that it memorializes. In her chapter on Chaucer, Gertz focuses on *The House of Fame* (with brief incursions into the *Monk's Tale*). She argues that this text conflates the roles of readers and writers: just as Geffrey exists both as a reader of his dream and the events that occur to him and as an interpreting writer, so is the audience invited to interpret and 'write' the text's own fame. Ultimately, Gertz sees Chaucer as differing starkly from René d'Anjou in that the former recognizes the reader's power over the 'code' (in the Jakobsonian terms that Gertz employs throughout the study) of the text itself. The book concludes with the thought that fame is not, itself, conclusive; rather, the complexities of tales and their renegotiations by both writers and readers interfere with fame's flattening tendencies.

Simon Meecham-Jones sheds light on a detail of the *House of Fame* in '"Englyssh Gaufride" and British Chaucer? Chaucerian Allusions to the Condition of Wales in the House of Fame' (*ChauR* 44:i[2009] 1–24). Noting how few medieval English texts refer to Wales, Meecham-Jones analyses three possible references to Wales in the *House of Fame*. By calling Geoffrey of Monmouth 'Englyssh Gaufride', he argues, Chaucer obliquely refers to the pro-colonial uses to which his *Historia* was put, emphasizing the ways in which texts are beyond their authors' control.

Patrick Cheney, in 'The Voice of the Author in "The Phoenix and Turtle": Chaucer, Shakespeare, Spenser' (in Perry and Watkins, eds., *Shakespeare and the Middle Ages*, pp. 103–25), sees Shakespeare's poem *The Phoenix and the Turtle* as a commentary on authorship, exploring its relationship to Chaucer and Spenser. Discussing *The Parliament of Fowls* as a possible source and the poem's elements of Chaucerian self-effacement, Cheney also argues that Shakespeare reads Chaucer through Spenser's earlier appropriation of him.

Laura J. Campbell's 'Reinterpretation and Resignification: A Study of the English Translation of *Le Roman de la Rose*' (*Neophil* 93:ii[2009] 325–38) offers insight into medieval practices of translation. Using Holmes's 'mapping method', Campbell analyses the interpretative moves involved in Fragment A of the Middle English translation of *Le Roman de la Rose*. The translation, she argues, concretizes ambiguous imagery from the original and increases the narrator's presence, imposing Christian morality upon the original's courtly aesthetic.

In her essay 'The European Lending Library: Borrowing, Translating, and Returning Texts' (in Chantler and Dente, eds., *Translation Practices: Through Language to Culture*, pp. 17–29) Lynne Long notices that, in contradistinction to traditional polysystem theories of translation, for medieval writers literate in Latin as well as other vernacular languages 'translation was happening even when it was not strictly necessary to translate' (p. 20). She catalogues multiple translations of Boethius's *De Consolatione Philosophiae*, beginning with Jean de Meun and Chaucer and ending with Elizabeth I, and argues that 'translation was central to the literary polysystem' of the Middle Ages (p. 29).

Also examining Chaucer's translations of Boethius is Eleanor Johnson in her 'Chaucer and the Consolation of Prosimetrum' (*ChauR* 43:iv[2009] 455–72). Johnson analyses Chaucer's aesthetics and rhythmic prose in his translation of Boethius's *De Consolatione Philosophiae* in terms of the usage of time. She is then able to posit that Chaucer's manipulation of rhythmic time might be applied to a reading of the *Canon Yeoman's Tale*, and persuasively argues that 'the Yeoman is not so much a stand-in for Chaucer as he is a counterpoint to Boethius' (p. 463).

The following items were unavailable for review this year:

Laurel Amtower and Jacqueline Vanhoutte, *A Companion to Chaucer and his Contemporaries: Texts and Contexts* (Broadview); Albrecht Classen, ed., *Urban Space in the Middle Ages and the Early Modern Age* (De Gruyter); Robert M. Correale and Mary Hamel, eds., *Sources and Analogues of the Canterbury Tales*, vol. 2. (B&B); Joseph Dane, *Abstractions of Evidence in the Study of Manuscripts and Early Printed Books* (Ashgate); S. Dorsch, *Reader's Guide to Geoffrey Chaucer* (Centrum); Susanna Greer Fein and David Raybin, *Chaucer: Contemporary Approaches* (PSU); Andrew Hass and David Jasper, *The Oxford Handbook of English Literature and Theology*. (OUP); Maik Goth, *From Chaucer's Pardoner to Shakespeare's Iago: Aspects of Intermediality in the History of the Vice* (Lang); J. Allan Mitchell, *Ethics and Eventfulness in Middle English Literature* (Palgrave); A.R. Myers, *Chaucer's London: Everyday Life in London 1342–1400* (Amberley); Nicole R. Rice, *Lay Piety and Religious Discipline in Middle English Literature* (CUP); Nila Vazquez, *The Tale of Gamelyn of the Canterbury Tales: An Annotated Edition with Introduction, Translation, Commentary and Glossary* (Mellen).

Books Reviewed

Astell, Ann W., and J.A. Jackson, eds. *Levinas and Medieval Literature: The 'Difficult Reading' of English and Rabbinic Texts*. Duquesne. [2009] pp. x + 374. $58 ISBN 9 7808 2070 4210.

Butterfield, Ardis. *The Familiar Enemy: Chaucer, Language, and Nation in the Hundred Years War*. OUP. [2009] pp. 432. $95 ISBN 9 7801 9957 4865.

Chantler, Ashley, and Carla Dente, eds. *Translation Practices: Through Language to Culture*. Rodopi. [2009] pp. 279. $76 ISBN 9 7890 4202 5332.

Cooper, Geoffrey, and Peter Goodall, eds. Chaucer's Monk's Tale and Nun's Priest's Tale: An Annotated Bibliography, 1900 to 2000. UTP [2009] pp. xlviii + 338. $110. 9780802093202.

Driver, Martha W., and Sid Ray, eds. *Shakespeare and the Middle Ages: Essays on the Performance and Adaptation of the Plays with Medieval*

Sources or Settings. McFarland. [2009] pp. 276. $39.95 ISBN 978-0786434053.

Heffernan, Carol Falvo. *Comedy in Chaucer and Boccaccio*. Brewer. [2009] pp. 166. $90 ISBN 9 7818 4384 2019.

Gertz, Sunhee Kim. *Visual Power and Fame in René d'Anjou, Geoffrey Chaucer, and the Black Prince*. Palgrave. [2009] pp. 248. $85 ISBN 9 7814 0397 0534.

Gust, Geoffrey W. *Constructing Chaucer: Author and Autofiction in the Critical Tradition*. Palgrave. [2009] pp. 300. $95. ISBN 9 7814 0397 6437.

Gutierrez Arranz, Jose Maria. *The Cycle of Troy in Geoffrey Chaucer: Tradition and 'Moralitee'*. Cambridge Scholars. [2009] pp. 150. $53 ISBN 1443813079.

Kennedy, Kathleen E. *Maintenance, Meed, and Marriage in Medieval English Literature*. Palgrave. [2009] pp. 200. $85 ISBN 9 7802 3060 6661.

Kerby-Fulton, Kathryn, ed. *Women and the Divine in Literature before 1700: Essays in Memory of Margot Louis*. ELS. [2009] pp. 220. $30 ISBN 9 7815 5058 3830.

Kolve, V.A. *Telling Images: Chaucer and the Imagery of Narrative*, vol. 2. StanfordUP. [2009] pp. xxxvi + 368. $65 ISBN 9780804755832.

Krygier, Marcin, and Liliana Sikorska, eds. *Þe Laurer of Oure Englische Tonge*. Lang. [2009] pp. 149. $49.95 ISBN 9 7836 3159 0973.

Minnis, A.J. *Translations of Authority in Medieval English Literature: Valuing the Vernacular*. CUP. [2009] pp. 288. $98 ISBN 9 7805 2151 5948.

Morgan, Gerald. *The Shaping of English Poetry: Essays on Sir Gawain and the Green Knight, Langland, Chaucer, and Spenser*. Lang. [2009] pp. xiv + 299. $74.95 ISBN 9 7830 3911 9561.

Perry, Curtis, and John Watkins, eds. *Shakespeare and the Middle Ages*. OUP. [2009] pp. xiv + 295. £56 ISBN 9 7801 9955 8179.

Rigby, S.H. *Wisdom and Chivalry: Chaucer's Knight's Tale and Medieval Political Theory*. Brill. [2009] pp. 329. €119 ($169) ISBN 978 90 04 17624 9.

Scala, Elizabeth, and Sylvia Federico, eds. *The Post-Historical Middle Ages*. Palgrave. [2009] pp. 252. $90 ISBN 9 7802 3060 7873.

Scanlon, Larry, ed. *The Cambridge Companion to Medieval English Literature, 1100–1500*. CUP. [2009] pp. 314. pb £17.99 ($29.99) ISBN 9 7805 2160 2587.

Suntrop, Rudolf, and Jan R. Veenstra, eds. *Himmel auf Erden/Heaven on Earth*. Lang. [2009] pp. xx + 201. $57.95 ISBN 9 7836 3156 4202.

Travis, Peter W. *Disseminal Chaucer: Rereading the Nun's Priest's Tale*. UNDP. [2009] pp. 456. $40 ISBN 9 7802 6804 2356.

Wimsatt, James I. *Chaucer and the Poems of 'Ch.'*. TEAMS. MIP. [2009] pp. viii + 166. $13.95 ISBN 9 7815 8044 1322.

V

The Sixteenth Century: Excluding Drama after 1550

JOAN FITZPATRICK

This chapter has two sections: 1. Sidney; 2. Spenser. Sections 1 and 2 are by Joan Fitzpatrick.

1. Sidney

William E. Engel's 2009 monograph, *Chiastic Designs in English Literature: From Sidney to Shakespeare*, has a chapter on Sidney and one on Spenser (discussed in section 2 below). In the introduction to his study Engel explains that he will explore 'patterns that are part and parcel of early modern mnemonic culture', specifically those that make mortality 'momentarily intelligible' such as *memento mori* objects and 'emblematic conceits (such as echo poems)' (p. 1). Chapter 3, 'Echo in Arcadia: Sidney's Legacy', concentrates on Sidney's use of what Engel perceives to be echo-like sets of songs in the *Arcadia*, songs which 'are contextualized as being based on memory, especially the memory of loss' (p. 41). Allegory and death are the focus here, and the close reading by Engel of Book I of Sidney's poem uncovers chiastic patterns begun by Sidney and completed after his death by his sister Mary, countess of Pembroke. The chapter concludes with an appendix that prints the chiastic design of the 'barley-break eclogue' beside the chiastic design of Book I of *Arcadia*, revealing the patterns suggested by Engels.

In a collection of essays focusing on early modern romance in prose fiction and drama, Cyrus Mulready considers dramatic romance in the context of Sidney's *Defence of Poetry*, specifically his complaint that these plays disregard the classical unities of time, place, and action: '"Asia of the One Side, and Afric of the Other": Sidney's Unities and the Staging of Romance' (in Lamb and Wayne, eds., *Staging Early Modern Romance: Prose Fiction, Dramatic Romance, and Shakespeare*, pp. 47–71). Mulready provides a survey of plays conforming to the romance genre and what it was specifically that

The Year's Work in English Studies, Volume 90 (2011)
doi:10.1093/ywes/mar010

Sidney objected to, before focusing on one play that is representative of the genre, Thomas Dekker's *Old Fortunatus*. Dramatic romance was especially attractive to those wishing to tell stories 'that take place in many places and over many times' (p. 62), something acceptable in prose, and reflecting the early modern interest in new lands, but not the dramatic practice laid down by Aristotle in his *Poetics*. Mulready includes a useful appendix listing the works of dramatic romance between 1572 and 1662 and stating the romantic sources to which they are indebted.

In this year's first issue of the *Sidney Journal* Michael Brennan considers an unjustly neglected portrait of Philip Sidney by Renold Elstrack, an engraver working in London during the reign of James I, in 'The Sidney Family and Jacobean Portrait Engravings' (*SidJ* 27:xxii[2009] 9–30). As Brennan points out, it is surprising the portrait has not been given more attention since, in reverse, it formed the model for the folio engraved portrait of Sidney that is usually included facing the title pages of the 1655 and 1674 editions of *The Countess of Pembroke's Arcadia*. Brennan asks a number of important questions regarding the portrait's origins and what it might tell us about the Sidney family's reputation at the time. After outlining Elstrack's biography, he concludes that the engraving is possibly based on an original oil painting of Sidney, which would suggest that Elstrack had access to important private collections. Brennan thinks that Robert Sidney might well have personally commissioned the portrait, which would have acted as a powerful reminder of the family's military heritage and public service.

Matthew Zarnowiecki is concerned with the evidence for what he terms 'lyric surrogacy' in Sidney's poetry, specifically lyric poems in the *Arcadia*, in 'Lyric Surrogacy: Reproducing the "I" in Sidney's *Arcadia*' (*SidJ* 27:i[2009] 31–53). In the *Defence of Poetry* Sidney presents the common conceit of the author as parent and his work as offspring, as well as the poet's ability to move the reader; in the *Arcadia* he goes even further, by imagining readers as 'co-creators or surrogate creators of the work' (p. 33). It has been acknowledged that Sidney's poetry inspired many spin-offs, as well as efforts to complete his own unfinished work, and Zarnowiecki argues that this is mirrored by the manner in which Sidney 'repeatedly dramatizes, in the poetry of the *Arcadia*, a process in which poetry is reproduced in successive generations' (p. 34). The essay traces Sidneian poetic surrogacy in the dedication of the *Arcadia*, in several poems from the *Arcadia*, and in epitaphs written by readers of Sidney's work.

The second issue of this year's *Sidney Journal* opens with an essay that will be of particular interest to Sidney's biographers: Roger Kuin's 'The Bogus Baron, his Elusive Earldom, and the Aborted Assassination: A Newly Discovered Letter to Sir Philip Sidney' (*SidJ* 27:ii[2009] 1–11). Kuin reports the discovery of a letter to Sidney by Edmond Neville, an English Catholic nobleman who had fought alongside the Spanish and later was accused and acquitted of treason. Usefully, Kuin transcribes the letter in full in original and modern spelling, and provides an interesting history of its author in the context of Neville's eventful life and his ill-fated attempts to consolidate his position in England.

Robert E. Stillman considers Sidney's debt to the Continental reformer Philip Melanchthon in *The Arcadia*, specifically the revised *Arcadia*'s third and final book, in 'Fictionalizing Philippism in Sidney's *Arcadia*: Economy, Virtuous Pagans, and Early Modern Poetics' (*SidJ* 27:ii[2009] 13–37). Stillman argues that it is through the character of the pagan Pamela that Sidney presents Philippist ideas, specifically 'reason's power to complement revelation in its testimony to God's existence as a maker and preserver' (p. 27), as presented in Melanchthon's nine 'proofs' that comprise an important source for Pamela's refutation of Cecropia.

While scholars of Sidney are usually concerned with the views of one specific female reader of Sidney, his sister the countess of Pembroke, Clare Kinney considers another female reader, the less well-known 'Mrs. Stanley', who published her *Sir Philip Sidney's Arcadia Moderniz'd* in 1725, in 'The Gentlewoman Reader Writes Back: Mrs. Stanley's *Sir Philip Sidney's Arcadia Moderniz'd*' (*SidJ* 27:ii[2009] 39–70). In this work Stanley, whose first name remains unknown, reworked Sidney's prose; as Kinney puts it, she 'characteristically flattens out Sidney's conceits... and turns compressed oxymoron into spelled-out paradox' (p. 42). Stanley also made additions and indulged in some bowdlerizing of Sidney's more risqué passages. Previous critics have tended to ridicule Stanley's efforts as simplistic and sentimental, but Kinney, while acknowledging Stanley's limitations, argues that her interjections were rather more thoughtful than they are usually considered, specifically her decision to highlight the moral agency of Sidney's heroines and cut those moments focusing on the abused female body. Also, unlike Sidney, Stanley provides the poem with closure and a firm moral, even if it is one that, as Kinney points out, seems rather at odds with Sidney's poem.

In other journals published in 2009, a number of essays emerged on Sidney's epic romance, *The Arcadia*. V.L. Forsyth is concerned with Sidney's pastoral landscape, specifically the contradictory nature of the location presented in the *Arcadia*, in 'The Two Arcadias of Sidney's Two Arcadias' (*SEL* 49:i[2009] 1–15). He argues that, although critics have recognized Sidney's debt to Sannazaro's pastoral romance *Arcadia*, they have tended to overlook his use of Polybius's description of the land of Arcadia in the fourth book of his *Histories*. These sources present two very different versions of the pastoral: Polybius presents an Arcadia that 'is realistic, complex, and definitely not a pastoral idyll' (p. 2), a marked contrast to Sannazaro's beautiful and unrealistic world. Polybius was a historian, not a poet, and he described 'a realistic and complex Greek state' (p. 5), one that, for Sidney, represented a model for the perfect Protestant state, the discipline of which is missing from Sannazaro's Arcadia, where leisure dominates. Forsyth traces Sidney's use of these two Arcadias in both the *Old Arcadia* and the *New Arcadia*, what he takes from each, and, specifically, the tensions and reconciliations that emerge between the two.

Tom McFaul traces Sidney's depiction of friendship as a humanist ideal in the two versions of the *Arcadia* in 'Friendship in Sidney's Arcadias' (*SEL* 49:i[2009] 17–33). Tracing Sidney's debt to Cicero's *De Amicitia*, which argues that friends should be brought up together, McFaul explores the relationship between Pyrocles and Musidorus in the *Old Arcadia*, a friendship that demonstrates the ideal of 'mutually improving emulation' (p. 18). McFaul argues that in the *New Arcadia* the friendship between the princes is given more depth by their separation, where each experiences different yet related events. Comparing this friendship to other relationships in the *New Arcadia*, including Amphialus's exclusion from friendship, McFaul concludes that in much sixteenth-century literature there is a link between friendship, which is 'in the realm of grace' (p. 31), and freedom since, as with divine grace, friendship facilitates escape from the severe rule of law.

Jenny C. Mann's essay, 'Sidney's "Insertour": Arcadia, Parenthesis and the Formation of English Eloquence' (*ELR* 39:iii[2009] 460–98), continues the focus on Sidney's *Arcadia*, specifically its structure and its impact upon early modern literary culture. Using as her starting point Anne Bradstreet's criticism of Sidney's poem, a criticism within parenthesis, Mann proceeds to demonstrate the rhetorical significance of parenthesis in Sidney's poem, and its pertinence to plot, something critics have hitherto regarded merely as punctuation. After tracing early modern attitudes to parenthesis, especially the notion that 'the figure constitutes belated and thus expendable textual matter' (p. 467), Mann shows that it shapes Sidney's text in a very specific way: repeated interruptions and qualifications often reinforce the mental state of the speaker and provide the reader with psychological realism. Mann concludes by considering the parenthetical nature of the revisions, supplementations, and alterations that produced the *New Arcadia* and subsequent early modern responses to Sidney such as that by Bradstreet.

Essays also emerged this year on Sidney's sonnet sequence *Astrophil and Stella*. Jennifer Bess questions Tom Parker's criticism of Sidney's Sonnet 49, in which Stella is dehumanized as a horse, as 'contrived and bestial', in 'Schooling to Virtue in Sidney's *Astrophil and Stella*, Sonnet 49' (*Expl* 67:iii[2009] 186–91), a criticism made in his 1998 monograph *Proportional Form in the Sonnets of the Sidney Circle: Loving in Truth*. Bess argues, rather, that the sonnet, in which Astrophil compares himself to a horse, situates the speaker as horse and rider, master and student. Providing a detailed analysis of the sonnet and how it fits Sidney's thesis in his *Defence of Poetry*, Bess shows that Sidney interrogates the complex process of poetry-writing, whereby the poet is not master in any simplistic fashion but, rather, achieves his objective via 'invention, co-creation, and nurturing' (p. 189), a synergy that mirrors the ideal relationship between horse and rider.

Sidney's sonnet sequence is also the focus of Hong Won Suh's essay 'Philip Sidney's Poetical Rhetoric in *Astrophil and Stella*' (*MES* 17[2009] 243–58). With specific reference to the first sonnet in the sequence, the essay explores the tension between Sidney's use of rhetoric, specifically invention, and the extent to which he 'writes without invention, looking directly into his heart and writing what he sees there' (p. 247). The point is that Sidney gets to have his cake and eat it since he 'depends upon the hiding of art within the fore-conceit, the rhetoric behind the poetic' (p. 253), that is, his claim to naturalness is, in fact, artificial.

Focusing on Sidney's prose work, James A. Williams reads Sidney's *Defence of Poetry* in the light of Stephen Gosson's *The Schoole of Abuse* in 'Erected Wit and Effeminate Repose: Philip Sidney's Postures of Reader-Response' (*MLR* 104:iii[2009] 640–58). Gosson famously denounced romance fiction and stage plays as effeminizing, and called upon readers to devote themselves to books that could develop a properly masculine mind, specifically the work of classical philosophers, historians, and rhetoricians. In his *Defence* Sidney argued that poetry was superior to other kinds of literature because it inspired the male reader's virtuous and martial sensibilities in ways that instruction from either the philosophical tract or historical example could not. Yet Williams suggests that Sidney's work 'also traffics in a notion of poetry as an agent of consciousness-altering pleasure, a means by which the reader suffuses his mind with phantasmal images of impossible beauty and allure' (p. 647). As Williams puts it, 'Sidney suggests that what is most commendable about poetry is not its ability to fashion masculine minds by providing templates of virtuous disposition and behaviour but to facilitate experiences of psychological ecstasy.' Sidney's belief that poetry should instil pleasure in the reader is also evident in the dedicatory epistle to the countess of Pembroke that prefaces the original version of Sidney's *Arcadia*, a text which ostensibly presents the poem specifically for the female reader but that Williams argues is intended also for the male.

This year's *Notes and Queries* saw three pieces relevant to Sidney, with particular focus on what other writers and readers made of his work. Andrew Hadfield identifies a reference to Philip Sidney in the opening lines of Ben Jonson's poem 'To Penshurst' in 'Ben Jonson and Philip Sidney' (*N&Q* 56[2009] 85–6). As Hadfield points out, critics have noted that Jonson comments on the relative poverty of the Sidneys compared with other aristocratic families and that their house was made to look more ancient than it was in order to suggest they were part of the old nobility. Hadfield asserts that Jonson also alludes to Philip Sidney's sonnet from the sequence *Astrophil and Stella*, 'Queen *Vertue's* Court', since the first three lines of Jonson's poem echo the precious materials mentioned by Sidney, thus suggesting that the Sidney wealth resides in literature rather than property.

Scholars of Sidney ought to be interested in Paul Salzman's account of Anne Clifford's consumption of the *Arcadia* in 'Anne Clifford's Annotated Copy of Sidney's *Arcadia*' (*N&Q* 56[2009] 554–5). Sidney's poem was read to her by her waiting women at Knole in 1617, and annotations can be found in her copy of the work recently deposited in the Bodleian Library. As Salzman points out, it is disappointing that there are no annotations in the margins, but the underlining of the work, perhaps indicating two separate encounters with it, suggests 'an intense and concentrated reading'.

Hannah Leah Crumme considers a less well-known reader of Sidney, William Scott, who wrote his own work in response to Sidney's *Apology for Poetry* while still a student in 'William Scott's Copy of Sidney' (*N&Q* 56[2009] 553–5). A copy of this work, *The Model of Poesy*, is located in the British Library, and was first drawn to our attention by the Shakespearian, Stanley Wells; Scott's own copy of *The Model of Poesy* can be found in Cambridge University Library. Also in Cambridge is an edition of *The Countess of*

Pembroke's Arcadia that also belonged to Scott and which contains Sidney's *Apology for Poetry*; the passages in Sidney that Scott commented upon in his own work are underlined and, as Crumme rightly points out, the relationship between the two demands closer analysis by scholars.

2. Spenser

A number of monographs devoted exclusively to Spenser, or including Spenser amongst studies of other authors, appeared in 2009. Two relevant monographs were published by Ashgate: Jane Grogan's study *Exemplary Spenser: Visual and Poetic Pedagogy in The Faerie Queene*, and that by William E. Engel, *Chiastic Designs in English Literature: From Sidney to Shakespeare*. Grogan is concerned with the didactic nature of Spenser's epic poem and the relationship he forges with the reader through the visual dynamics at work in his poetry. She begins her impressive study by tracing the views of some important readers who have 'misread' Spenser, amongst them W.B. Yeats, whose view of Spenser she characterizes as 'rosy', with Yeats praising Spenser for a pictorialism that 'frees him from the smear of politics' (p. 2); yet Yeats did not get it all wrong since he recognized the importance of images in Spenser's poetry, even if he did misread the pictures. Grogan contends that Spenser has also been misread by some modern critics as a mouthpiece for the Elizabethan state, a view that she argues 'ignores the inquiring nature of Spenser's poetry, its empowering of readers', 'the ambiguous view of the queen that it affords them' and 'the radicalism and brinkmanship of Spenser's visual strategies' (p. 12). Influenced by Plato's banishment of poets from his ideal republic, Spenser was living amongst those who denounced poetry as harmful and so, like Sidney before him, he set about 'to redeem the good nature of poetry by emphasizing its didactic potential' (p. 15), an emphasis that Grogan contends is apparent not just in the *Letter to Raleigh* but throughout *The Faerie Queene*.

Grogan's study is divided into four chapters, the first of which, 'To Fashion a Gentleman or Noble Person: Xenophon and English Protestant Poetics', considers the *Letter to Raleigh* via its slippery genre and considers the significance of Spenser's preference for Xenophon over Plato as a model for his 'doctrine by ensample'. Chapter 2, 'Spenser's "Gallery of Pictures"', investigates Spenser's engagement with Renaissance theories of vision where he reveals the limitations and vulnerability of vision in his epic poem; idolatry is one danger of not seeing properly (as with the False Florimell in Book III) and spiritual ignorance is another (as with Corceca in Book I). Chapter 3 concentrates on ekphrasis (the visual represented by the verbal), especially in Books II and III of Spenser's poem, and here Grogan traces the paradoxes evident in 'the invitation to look and know' (p. 104) when the poem being presented is an allegory mediated through a narrator. The book's final chapter considers the difficulties of representing courtesy, a virtue with predominantly verbal values, through visual means; at Mount Acidale Calidore fails to see the vision before him, which Grogan interprets as a moment of crisis for Spenser.

William E. Engel's chapter on Sidney is discussed in section 2 above, and his book also considers Spenser's *Faerie Queene* in chapter 4, 'Mirror and

Allegory: Spenser's Calling'. Here Engel discusses what he terms 'the double movement' of Spenser's work on epic poetry and allegory. Lodowyck Bryskett characterized Spenser's *Faerie Queene* as a 'goodly cabinet', and Engel traces the chiastic implications of Spenser's poem as a type of container, one that holds treasure. In Book II of his epic poem, specifically in the two books that appear within it, *Briton moniments* and *Antiquities of Faerie lond*, Spenser evokes 'two aspects of a larger thematic pattern', a pattern that reveals both the achievements of the past and the significance of memory in recalling them.

Another monograph on Spenser that emerged in 2009 was by M.L. Stapleton, *Spenser's Ovidian Poetics*. Stapleton begins his book by tracing the critical history of Spenser's debt to Ovid, attending to important commentaries emerging in the eighteenth century, specifically the philological work of John Jortin; early twentieth-century critics who focus on Spenser's use of Golding's translation of Ovid; and later critics who have 'a more theoretical and much less unified approach to Spenser's use of Ovid' (p. 20). Also considered are those commentators of the last thirty years who have analysed the tension between Ovid and Virgil in Spenser. Chapter 1, 'Colin Clout and Old Palemon Read the *Tristia*', concentrates on Spenser's reading of *Tristia* (Ovid's ruminations on exile), as well as Thomas Churchyard's *The Three First Bookes of Ouid de Trisbus Translated into English*. Stapleton argues that Spenser may have learnt from both authors, and these works account for the images of exile and alienation that dominate his writings. In chapter 2, '"So swelles myne inward minde": The *Heroides* and Spenser', Stapleton considers Spenser's debt to Ovid's work of 'literary transvestism' when the classical poet 'adopts the personae of mythic women who lament the amatory crimes of the men they love' (p. 74). Stapleton detects a debt to Ovid via the translations of Churchyard's contemporary, George Turberville, when he argues that his *Heroycall Epistles of the Learned Poet Publius Ouidius Naso, in Englishe Verse* influenced Spenser's presentation of female voices in *The Shepheardes Calender* and *The Faerie Queene*; in this chapter he also detects a debt to Isabella's Whitney's *The Copie of a letter, lately written in meeter, by a yonge gentilwoman: to her vnconstant louer*. Chapter 3, 'Spenser's Golding', sees Stapleton trace Spenser's reading of Arthur Golding's well-known translation of Ovid's *Metamorphoses*, showing that although Spenser would have read Ovid in the original Latin he learnt much from Golding; indeed, 'they read the same Ovidian material similarly' (p. 122). Chapter 4, 'Anamorphic and Metamorphic Patterning in Spenser', traces the influence of the *Metamorphoses* upon *The Faerie Queene*, specifically Golding's translation, while chapter 5, '"Loue my lewd Pilott": Spenser's *Ars Amatoria*', provides evidence for the assertion that Spenser 'raids' Ovid's poem for the various depictions of love and lechery in his epic poem and elsewhere. The focus of the final chapter, 'Devoid of Guilty Shame: Ovidian Tendencies in Spenser's Erotic Poetry', is Ovid's *Amores* and its impact upon Spenser's shorter poems, the *Amoretti*, *Epithalamion*, and *Fowre Hymnes*. This well-researched and thoughtful study should be of interest to all Spenserians since it adds considerably to our knowledge of Spenser and Ovid and complements the 2005 monograph *Spenser and Ovid* by Syrithe Pugh, which was published by Ashgate.

We have seen that memory interested Engle in his monograph on chiastic designs (reviewed above); also on memory is an essay by Chris Ivic from a collection of essays on the topic 'Spenser and Interpellative Memory' (in Beecher and Williams, eds., *Ars Reminiscendi: Mind and Memory in Renaissance Culture*, pp. 289–310). The collection, published by the Centre for Reformation and Renaissance Studies and introduced by Donald Beecher, is broad in scope, with essays on Erasmus and *Paradise Lost*, amongst other subjects. Like Engel, Chris Ivic focuses on Book II of Spenser's *Faerie Queene*, but his context is Ireland, specifically Spenser's *A View of the Present State of Ireland*. Ivic argues that Spenser's prose work and *The Faerie Queene* both 'reveal a commitment to memory's role in the preservation of identity as well as a fear of the erosive, degenerative effects of forgetting' (p. 290). In *The Faerie Queene* memory is integral to nation-building, and characters such as Verdant or Grill stand for the dangers of failing to remember. In the *View* it is the Old English who, like Verdant, are guilty of having forgotten their allegiance to England; the Irish too have forgotten since their bodies that were once tamed have become bestial (Spenser describes them as shaking off their bridals and beginning to 'colt anew'). Ivic argues that Spenser does not simply condemn those who have forgotten but, rather, highlights the power of the memory 'to discipline, rescue, and recuperate those who have forgotten themselves' (p. 293), what Ivic refers to as 'interpellative memory'.

Abigail Shinn's essay on the influence of the almanac on Spenser's *Shepheardes Calender* appears in a collection of essays on highbrow literature and less esteemed culture in early modern England in '"Extraordinary discourses of vnnecessarie matter": Spenser's *Shepheardes Calender* and the Almanac Tradition' (in Dimmock and Hadfield, eds., *Literature and Popular Culture in Early Modern England*, pp. 137–49). Having traced the history of the almanac form, Shinn argues that Spenser takes the almanac as his model in *The Shepheardes Calender* in an attempt to transform this low and popular genre into one that is more sophisticated. Shinn provides comparisons between some well-known almanacs and Spenser's poem in order to demonstrate influence, and suggests that Spenser's utilization of the form reflects his new English pastoral, something that is indebted to classical and popular genres and that can effectively compete with its European literary rivals.

This year's *Spenser Studies* is a special issue on 'Spenser and Platonism', guest-edited by Kenneth Borris, Jon Quitslund, and Carol Kaske, who open the volume with an introductory essay explaining the rationale for their choice of topic and how their contributors have approached it (*SSt* 24[2009] 1–14). The first contribution to the volume is by Carol Kaske, one of the volume's editors, who is concerned with definitions and their application, identifying Platonic terms and concepts that appear in Spenser in 'Hallmarks of Platonism and the Sons of Agape (*Faerie Queene* IV.ii–iv)' (*SSt* 24[2009] 15–71). The terms and concepts considered are the Ideas or forms, the four beneficent frenzies, the concomitance of physical and spiritual beauty, ladders of love, the pre-existence of the soul, and emanation. Kaske considers Spenser's use of these in a number of his works, including *The Faerie Queene*, and specifically the episodes in Book IV featuring the sons of Agape. She compares Spenser's engagement with Platonic terms and concepts with that of the Italian

Platonist, Flaminio Nobili, arguing that Spenser is the more indebted of the two to Platonic ideas. Following Kaske's essay, Valery Rees also compares Spenser's take on Platonism with that of another Platonist, Marsilio Ficino, in 'Ficinian Ideas in the Poetry of Edmund Spenser' (*SSt* 24[2009] 73–134). Tracing Ficino's treatment of a range of topics such as stability and change, beauty, love, and the soul, Rees demonstrates that Spenser's debt to Ficino, across a number of texts, was significant. Usefully, the essay contains an appendix tracing the availability of Ficino's works and Plato's works to Spenser at Cambridge and to other English readers beyond the university.

Following an essay by Eugene D. Hill, the focus of which is Everard Digby, a contemporary of Spenser at Cambridge, rather than Spenser himself, Anne Lake Prescott compares Spenser with another contemporary, the French poet, Guy Le Fèvre de la Boderie, in 'Hills of Contemplation and Signifying Circles: Spenser and Guy Le Fèvre de La Boderie' (*SSt* 24[2009] 155–83). Prescott notes how Le Fèvre's long poem *La Galliade* contains a prefatory sonnet sequence with lines on the 'mount of contemplation' from which the ecstatic soul can see the New Jerusalem, and which she compares to a similar passage in *The Faerie Queene*, Book I, when Redcross, guided by Contemplation, sees the same city. She concludes that each poet is indebted to a combination of Platonic and Christian ideas, despite coming from distinctly Catholic and Protestant traditions; other texts also combine the Christian and Platonic in the context of contemplation, specifically via images of ascent.

Andrew Escobedo's focus is on Spenser's engagement with erotic rapture, a concept evident in medieval love poetry and the Petrarchan lyric but most significantly in Plato's *Symposium* and *Phaedrus*, in 'The Sincerity of Rapture' (*SSt* 24[2009] 185–208). For Plato, succumbing to erotic rapture meant relinquishing reason and decision-making faculties, and it is in this context that Escobedo explores the motives of Scudamour in *The Faerie Queene* Book IV. Scudamour's behaviour suggests he is a lover who has not wholly given himself to love and so is able, indeed compelled, to decide whether or not he will pursue Amoret. Unfortunately, this lack of rapture, which enables reason, also makes Scudamour insincere; without suggesting that Scudamour does not love Amoret, a convincing argument emerges that his lack of abandonment to love presents a lover who remains rather too self-involved. Kenneth Borris attempts to resolve the tension between Spenser's poetic depictions of Platonic ideals that promote virtue and truth and the fact that Plato denounced poetry in *The Republic* in 'Platonism and Spenser's Poetic: Idealized Imitation, Merlin's Mirror, and the Florimells' (*SSt* 24[2009] 209–68). In episodes from Books III and IV of *The Faerie Queene*, specifically those featuring Merlin's mirror and the creation of the False Florimell, Spenser explores the distinction between true and false art, suggesting that it is the use to which art is put and the role of the poet as philosopher that lie at the heart of his poetic project.

Drawing upon the work of Frances Yates, Catherine Gimelli Martin considers Spenser's *Faerie Queene* in the context of geography and place, specifically the mapping of psychology and virtue, in 'Spenser's Neoplatonic Geography of the Passions: Mapping Allegory in the "Legend of Temperance", *Faerie Queene*, Book II' (*SSt* 24[2009] 269–307). Martin concentrates on Book II of *The Faerie Queene*, reading Guyon's adventures in the context of Plato's four elements of earth, water, air, and fire. As Martin points out, these elements 'simultaneously chart the physical and spiritual ascent of the hero and his passions' (p. 272); along the way our hero must negotiate myriad paths where he will either pass unscathed or become trapped. Book II is also the focus of Jon Quitslund's essay, specifically Guyon's descent into Mammon's cave, which he reads via Marsilio Ficino's description of melancholia in his *Three Books of Life* and his suggestion that magic provides a cure, in 'Melancholia, Mammon, and Magic' (*SSt* 24[2009] 309–54). In tracing Spenser's debt to Ficino, Quitslund also makes comparisons between the episode featuring Mammon and a number of other episodes in Spenser's poem, including the Garden of Adonis canto in Book III, which he thinks Spenser conceived with the Mammon episode in mind. The Garden of Adonis is the main subject of an essay by Kenneth Gross, which argues that Spenser's garden is an allegory of the mind or thought: 'Green Thoughts in a Green Shade' (*SSt* 24[2009] 355–71). Gross traces Spenser's debt to Plato and a number of Neoplatonists, and finds analogy for an allegory of the mind in a passage from Nicholas of Cusa's *De Mente Idiota*.

Spenser's *Fowre Hymnes*, a text often overlooked by critics, makes a welcome appearance in Ayesha Ramachandran's essay, 'Edmund Spenser, Lucretian Neoplatonist: Cosmology in the *Fowre Hymnes*' (*SSt* 24[2009] 373–411), a piece that considers Spenser's interest in cosmology and natural philosophy, specifically the syncretic relationship between Christian Neoplatonism and the celebration of Epicurean philosophy by the Roman poet Lucretius in his *De rerum natura*. The *Hymnes* are also the subject of the 'Forum' section that provides a kind of coda to this year's volume of *Spenser Studies*, with essays by Richard McCabe, Kenneth Borris, Gordon Teskey, and Jon Quitslund. McCabe's fine essay, 'Spenser, Plato, and the Poetics of State' (*SSt* 24[2009] 433–52), considers the influence of Plato's *Republic* on Spenser's poetry, contextualizing Plato's denunciation of poets in the light of Burghley's criticism of Spenser. Spenser's defence of himself as poet while, as a colonist, attacking the Irish bards, reveals not only the inherent contradictions of his position but also that 'both the defenders and the detractors of poetry were fully agreed on its efficacy, moral or immoral as the case might be' (p. 437). McCabe argues that Spenser's defence of epic and amatory verse in the second instalment of *The Faerie Queene* was strengthened by the publication of the *Fowre Hymnes* in the same year (1596) since the hymn was one genre that Plato found acceptable.

Questioning Robert Ellrodt's view that all four hymns were composed after the second instalment of Spenser's *Faerie Queene*, Kenneth Borris argues that at least the first two came earlier, in 'Reassessing Ellrodt: Critias and the *Fowre Hymnes* in *The Faerie Queene*' (*SSt* 24[2009] 453–80). Borris reads the *Hymnes* as a sort of guide-book to the epic poem, 'indicating potential philosophical and theological subjects and illuminating doctrinal resonances of his diction, tropes, and imagery' (p. 454). Gordon Teskey focuses on the *Hymnes* themselves and, in an original take on them, proposes reading them out of sequence, specifically backwards, in 'A Retrograde Reading of Spenser's *Fowre Hymnes*' (*SSt* 24[2009] 481–97). The trajectory of the poems as presented by Spenser, argues Teskey, suggests that philosophical and religious wisdom are privileged over human wisdom and human love, but upon reversing the order a more complex picture emerges, one that highlights continuity between the heavens and this world. Closing the forum on the *Hymnes*, and this year's volume, is Jon Quitslund's essay comparing the *Hymnes* to other poetic writings by Spenser and highlighting specifically their consideration of the heavenly origins of physical beauty, a theme that recurs in his early poetry, a number of key episodes from Book I of *The Faerie Queene*, and that poem's unfinished *Cantos of Mutabilitie*, in 'Thinking about Thinking in the *Fowre Hymnes*' (*SSt* 24[2009] 499–517). Before leaving the essays in this year's *Spenser Studies* it is worth mentioning Paul Suttie's piece since it provides an important challenge to the notion that Spenser was a Platonist: 'The Lost Cause of Platonism in *The Faerie Queene*' (*SSt* 24[2009] 413–30). Suttie argues that, although Platonic ideas influenced Spenser's writing, his main aim was rhetorical and political rather than philosophical, and *The Faerie Queene* offers 'praise of a particular regime', that of Queen Elizabeth I, rather than some higher 'luminous truth' (p. 145).

A final point on this year's *Spenser Studies*: it is rather odd that Borris and Quitslund, who are both editors of this special issue of the journal, should each have two bites of the cherry (three if we count their contribution to the introductory essay as well as the lengthy essay by each that appears in the main section of the journal); Carol Kaske, the other guest editor, does not appear in the forum on the *Fowre Hymnes* but, like her fellow-editors, has an essay in this volume. While including contributions by editors is acceptable in a book of essays, arguably guest editors of a journal ought not to have such a high profile in their own volume (aside from introducing it) since this raises concerns about impartiality, concerns that would not be so prominent were it not for the fact that *Spenser Studies* does not operate a policy of blind peer review.

In other journals published in 2009 there was a distinct focus on Spenser's *Faerie Queene* and amongst the topics discussed was the poet's engagement with gender, colonialism, and oratory, as well as Spenser's biography. Building upon an argument first presented in her 2005 study *Translating Investments: Metaphor and the Dynamic of Cultural Change in Tudor-Stuart England* Judith H. Anderson's essay is concerned with Britomart in Books III, IV, and V of *The Faerie Queene*, specifically her armour, in 'Britomart's Armor in Spenser's *Faerie Queene*: Reopening Cultural Matters of Gender and Figuration' (*ELR* 39:i[2009] 74–96). As Anderson puts it, her aim is 'to highlight the *Venus armata* composite as Venus-Mars and to explore how a doubled perception of Britomart's gender develops' (p. 75); Britomart evolves as her narrative unfolds 'and her armour conspicuously participates in—indeed, figures—both the development of her integrity and its loss' (p.75). Although Britomart wears the armour of a Saxon queen, it marks her as male, and she is interpreted as such by those who meet her. The armour has a dynastic function, and while it serves to protect her it also renders her duplicitous, for example in her dealings with Amoret, even if this duplicity is necessary for self-protection. Anderson fully explores the multivalence of Britomart's armour, something she detects in Britomart's combat with Artegall but that she considers lost by the time Britomart's confrontation with Radigund is over.

Chih-hsin Lin also interrogates Amoret's suffering in the episodes in which she appears in *The Faerie Queene* in 'Amoret's Sacred Suffering: The Protestant Modification of Courtly Love in Spenser's *The Faerie Queene*' (*SP* 106:iii[2009] 354–77). Amoret has been characterized, most famously by C.S. Lewis, as a victim of courtly love, but the essay asks a number of questions that complicate any straightforward reading of her experiences: is it necessary for the chaste married woman in to suffer in courtly culture? is she innocent or implicated in her own suffering? and why does she feel such pain in courtly culture? Having considered the critical views that Amoret is entirely innocent and entirely to blame for the situations in which she finds herself, the essay analyses the similarities and differences between her relationships with Busyrane and with Scudamour. Via Protestant conceptions of suffering and married love, together with treatises on courtly love and writings on the theme of love and suffering, the essay concludes that Amoret represents the ideal Protestant wife: she accepts a modified version of the codes of courtly love, one that privileges chastity and the good Christian who will build a sexual relationship with her husband, not a lover.

David Scott Wilson-Okamura is concerned with Spenser's depiction of virginity and celibacy in *The Faerie Queene*, specifically via Belphoebe and Gloriana, in 'Belphoebe and Gloriana' (*ELR* 39:i[2009] 47–73). He traces various critical approaches to the topic, exploring why Spenser decided to omit description of Belphoebe's 'bikini area' (p. 50), something that bothered Louis Montrose, and he also explores Belpheobe's origins, considering how she compares to other women warriors in the Renaissance epic. Notably, Gloriana is immune to the criticism of Elizabeth's surrogates elsewhere in the poem, and he suggests that this is due to the fact that Spenser perceived Gloriana not as the queen but as queenship, the very monarchy itself. He argues that Spenser's decision to make Gloriana absent from his poem is partly due to its unfinished nature, and that a completed poem 'would have been Gloriana's book' and would have included 'a critique, not just of personalities, but of institutions' (p. 73).

Joseph Campana's original essay explores what he terms 'the pleasurable liquidity' (p. 466) that pervades Book II of *The Faerie Queene* in 'Boy Toys and Liquid Joys: Pleasure and Power in the Bower of Bliss' (*MP* 106:iii[2009] 465–96). Campana questions the usual moral readings of the destruction of the Bower of Bliss at the climax of Book II, arguing that those critics who side with Guyon and the Palmer miss the point. According to Campana, Spenser explores physical pleasure in his poem, thus suggesting that poetry itself is pleasurable, not to condemn pleasure as inherently corrupt and corrupting but in order to present it as a form of resistance. As Campana points out, 'Spenser deploys Guyon and the Palmer to dramatize the disastrous consequences of the attempt to moderate pleasure and deploy bodily energy as violence in the service of heroic, moral agendas' (p. 478). Vulnerability to pleasure allows masculinity to disarm, something Spenser specifically calls for in the proem to Book I of his epic poem.

Spenser and sport are the focus of John Wesley's fascinating article that investigates the presence of wrestling in Book II of *The Faerie Queene*, in 'The Well-Schooled Wrestler: Athletics and Rhetoric in *The Faerie Queene* Book II'

(*RES* 60[2009] 34–60). Wrestling was a serious exploit for educated young men in the early modern period, as well as for their classical predecessors, and advice on how to wrestle like an educated courtier can be found in Castiglione's *The Courtier* and Elyot's *The Boke Named the Governour*. Wesley suggests another source for Spenser's conception of wrestling in *The Faerie Queene*, one that, unlike Castiglione's and Elyot's texts, emphasizes virtue, specifically temperance. This was by Richard Mulcaster, Spenser's schoolmaster; his *Positions*, a theory of education, considers the art of wrestling in the context of what it takes to be a good orator, and he specifically recommended upright rather than pancratic wrestling (a form that used 'a combination of holding and boxing' p. 45), upright wrestling being associated with the order, controlled strength, and courage necessary for a skilled orator. Wesley finds parallels between the advice offered by Mulcaster and the actions of Spenser's Guyon, and traces several other examples of gestures in *The Faerie Queene* that he argues are consistent with Mulcaster's conception of the gentlemanly wrestler.

Kasey Evans argues that in Book II of *The Faerie Queene*, and especially in the Cave of Mammon episode, Spenser presents a critique of humanist resistance to the march of time, in 'How Temperance Becomes "Blood Guiltie" in *The Faerie Queene*' (*SEL* 49:i[2009] 35–66). Evans suggests that, for the early moderns, the virtue of temperance became a kind of proto-capitalistic ethos of time management (one based on thrift, industry, frugality) and, moreover, 'a secular virtue adduced to justify the ethically insupportable conditions of European colonialism' (p. 36). In the Cave of Mammon she argues that Spenser engages specifically with the issue of slave labour in the New World, and condemns the enslavement and 'violent theft' (p. 37) necessary for the enrichment of an emerging capitalist society, an enslavement and violence in which Guyon is implicated. The argument is a convincing one, but Evans might have more fully engaged with Spenser's personal involvement in the violent theft that also took place in colonial Ireland.

Justin Kolb's '"In th'armor of a pagan knight": Romance and Anachronism East of England in Book V of *The Faerie Queene* and *Tamburlaine*' (*EarT* 12[2009] 194–207) is part of an 'Issues in Review' section of the journal *Early Theatre*. The essays included in this section were originally written for a research seminar organized by Linda McJannet and Bernadette Andrea at the Shakespeare Association of America annual meeting in 2009. The theme of the papers presented, and introduced by Linda McJannet, is 'Early Modern English Drama and the Islamic World' and, as McJannet points out, the papers are from 'emerging scholars' (p. 189, notes). Kolb's essay is concerned with moments of cross-over between the pagan and Christian knights that populate Book V of Spenser's *Faerie Queene* and Marlowe's *Tamburlaine*. Both authors, claims Kolb, engage in a process whereby anachronism and mimesis are evident; as Kolb puts it, 'making the Muslim other a figure in a transhistorical drama and appropriating aspects of his identity for one's own self-fashioning were central to the construction of both the Turk and the Englishman in Elizabethan literature' (p. 195). Kolb considers Spenser influenced by the historical figure known as Scanderbeg, a 'Christian-turned-Muslim-turned-Christian hero' (p. 197), who he argues 'parallels the syncretic identity adopted by Arthur and Artegall in their fight with the Souldan' (p. 198), specifically Artegall's disguise as a Turk and Arthur's mirror-like shield that reflects his pagan enemy. Kolb mentions the Protestant tradition of conflating Catholic and Muslim enemies, but (like Evans, above) perhaps ought to have engaged with Ireland, especially given Richard McCabe's important point, in the context of Ireland, that 'the "pagans" of romance fiction are the Catholics of reformed politics' (see the 1989 essay by Richard A. McCabe 'The Fate of Irena: Spenser and Political Violence', in Coughlan, ed., *Spenser and Ireland: An Interdisciplinary Perspective*, Cork University Press, pp. 109–25).

Benjamin P. Myers argues that the Irish context of Spenser's *Faerie Queene* can no longer be considered a 'special subtopic' of Spenser studies since it effectively dominates *The Faerie Queene*, in 'The Green and Golden World: Spenser's Rewriting of the Munster Plantation' (*ELH* 76:ii[2009] 473–90). Myers reads Book VI of Spenser's poem as a continuation of Book V, the Book of Justice, and relates the efforts of English colonists 'to bring English pastoralism to Ireland' (via enclosure and other methods) to Calidore's experiences in Book VI. When Calidore befriends the shepherds who represent the New English colonists, Spenser depicts an ideal pastoral world that omits the fractious nature of the relationship between the New English colonists, each eager to grab land for himself. That Spenser's shepherds live in the 'open fields', that is common land, rather than 'private farms' (*FQ* VI.ix.3, VI.ix.4) also belies the reality of colonial Ireland and is part of the idealizing thrust of the pastoral; Spenser's shepherds work on common land but, unlike their Irish counterparts, retire to their private quarters and their private lives, thus indicating an ancient English edenic world rather than a contemporary Irish one. Myers considers Meliboe a key figure in Spenser's desire to make a pastoral idyll of Ireland, with the New English as ideal shepherds; like Colin in *Colin Clouts Come Home Again*, Meliboe stands for the New English who have found life at court difficult and made a home for themselves in this pastoral land, one that must keep the indigenous Irish peripheral.

In a welcome focus on Spenser's shorter poems, and his sources, Katherine Little traces Spenser's debt to medieval pastoral, specifically William Langland's *Piers Plowman*, in *The Shepheardes Calender*, in 'The "Other" Past of Pastoral: Langland's *Piers Plowman* and Spenser's *Shepheardes Calender*' (*Exemplaria* 21[2009] 160–78). Critics have hitherto emphasized the continuity between medieval pastoral and its early modern successor, but Little suggests, rather, that a distinct break with the Catholic past is evident in Spenser's poem. After exploring in detail the significance of Langland's poem, Little considers Spenser's figure of Piers, who appears in the May and October eclogues of his pastoral poem. Far from asserting a kinship with Langland, Spenser signals his distance from the medieval tradition. Crucially, whereas Langland's Piers is a labourer, Spenser's Piers does not work. For Little, this carries religious significance for it underlines the Protestant attitude towards Catholic good works as a means of gaining spiritual reward. When rural labour is detached from its medieval Christian significance, it is no longer imbued with reformist possibilities (individual and social reform). For Piers, Spenser's shepherd-poet, poetry is a gift that cannot be earned through labour, just as, for Protestants, grace is a gift that cannot be earned through good works.

Andrew Hadfield builds upon his earlier consideration, in *The Times Literary Supplement*, of Spenser's use of the girl's name Rosalind in *The Shepheardes Calender* in 'Spenser's Rosalind' (*MLR* 104:iv[2009] 935–46). Critics have identified Rosalind as a young woman from the north of England Spenser actually knew, as Spenser's wife, and as Queen Elizabeth herself. Hadfield claims that, if we read *The Shepheardes Calender* and letters to Spenser from Gabriel Harvey, it becomes clear that Rosalind is Maccabaeus Chylde, Spenser's first wife, but that Rosalind later takes on a new identity, that of his second wife, Elizabeth Boyle. Hadfield also suggests Shakespeare's debt to Spenser in his use of the name Rosaline in *Romeo and Juliet*, suggesting a link between Spenser's first and second wives, just as Romeo's former love is the woman who 'remains as a trace, the supplanted love whose impact disappears when a real woman appears' (p. 945). Most interestingly, Hadfield claims another supplanting, this time of one poet by another since he argues that Shakespeare is here asserting his literary dominance over Spenser.

This year's *Notes and Queries* saw several pieces on Spenser, and it was a busy year for Andrew Hadfield. In the first of three notes by him in 2009, 'Edmund Spenser and Samuel Brandon' (*N&Q* 56[2009] 536–8), he adds to our knowledge of the connection between Edmund Spenser and Samuel Brandon, who made allusion to the Mutabilitie Cantos from Spenser's *Faerie Queene* in his play *The Virtuous Octavia*. Back in 1923 Frederick Ives wondered if Brandon may have read the cantos in manuscript, a suggestion rejected by Evelyn May Albright five years later. Albright's dismissal of Ives's suggestion has not hitherto been challenged, but Hadfield provides convincing evidence that Brandon did indeed have access to the cantos prior to their publication.

Another of Spenser's famous readers occupies Arthur Sherbo in 'Gleanings from Thomas Warton's *Observations on the 'Faerie Queene' of Spenser*' (*N&Q* 56[2009] 252–3). In his *Observations* the eighteenth-century critic Thomas Warton perceived the debt owed to Spenser by a number of authors including Milton, observations carefully traced and commented on here by Sherbo. In another note, '"Range" in the *OED*' (*N&Q* 56[2009] 63–4), Sherbo remarks upon the perceived influence of Spenser in Shakespeare's *Antony and Cleopatra*. The Shakespearian Edmund Malone tentatively suggested that Antony's exclamation 'Let Rome in Tyber melt! and the wide arch / Of the rang'd empire fall' (I.i.33–4) was indebted to Spenser's use of the term 'ranged' in *The Faerie Queene*, which he thought a reference to mason-work; another Shakespearian, George Steevens, was less tentative, and this definition of Spenser's word is the one currently in use in the *OED*.

A collection of manuscripts containing three poems dedicated to Spenser by 'J.S.' is the subject of another note by Hadfield, 'Spenser and John Stow' (*N&Q* 56[2009] 538–40). It has been assumed that the initials 'J.S.' refer to the poet Joshua Sylvester or the satirist Joseph Hall, but Hadfield argues that the initials in this only example of a printed work dedicated to Spenser refer to John Stow. He further suggests that Stow probably knew Spenser personally, and since the poems in the collection are medieval a dedication to Spenser, who shared an interest in the past, would seem fitting.

The last of this year's pieces on Spenser by Hadfield in this year's *Notes and Queries*, 'Spenser's Reference to Censorship' (*N&Q* 56[2009] 532–3), detects allusion in Spenser's dedicatory letter to the *Fowre Hymnes* to the suppression of his previous *Complaints*. Hadfield suggests that Spenser's use of the phrase 'call in' is an in-joke that refers to the seizure of his previous work due to the sensitivities surrounding *Mother Hubberds Tale*, which was contained in the volume.

Kate McClune suggests that the process whereby an identical rhyme scheme was developed by Spenser and Scottish sonneteers at the court of James VI is owed to more than mere coincidence in 'The "Spenserian Sonnet" in Sixteenth-Century Scotland' (*N&Q* 56[2009] 533–6). She traces the possible means by which Spenser may have accessed the Scots forms and rightly observes that more work on the literary relationship between England and Scotland in this period would be productive.

Kathryn Walls questions the usual critical conclusions reached regarding Una's words of advice to Redcross when he battles with Errour in Book I of *The Faerie Queene* in '"Add faith vnto your force": The Meaning of Una's Advice in *The Faerie Queene* I.i.19.322' (*N&Q* 56[2009] 530–2). As Walls points out, her advice that he 'Add faith' to his 'force' is inconsistent with Protestant teaching that we ought to be justified by faith only. Via reference to the *OED* and a seventeenth-century poem by Charles Cotton, she concludes that Una may not be invoking faith in God but, rather, that Redcross ought to have faith in his own strength.

John Wesley suggests real-life inspiration for Spenser's choice of the name 'Wrenock' in the December eclogue of the *Shepheardes Calender* in 'Spenser's "Wrenock" and an Anglo-Welsh Latimer' (*N&Q* 56[2009] 526–30). Drawing upon historical and literary sources, Wesley makes interesting connections between Spenser's figure and the Powys family who owned Whittington Castle in Shropshire, revealing important implications for Spenser's relationship with his schoolmaster Richard Mulcaster, often considered the source for Wrenock.

Matthew Woodcock examines the hitherto overlooked pamphlets that emerged commemorating the death of Elizabeth I in 1603 in 'Edmund Spenser and Commemorations of the Death of Elizabeth I' (*N&Q* 56[2009] 43–6). As Woodcock shows, these reveal important information about Spenser's posthumous reputation, specifically the sense in which he was regarded as 'dominant mythographer of Elizabeth and her reign' (p. 43). There is a perception amongst some that if Spenser were still alive he would be the best person to commemorate the nation's loss, an interesting point since this puts Spenser and Elizabeth in a similar position: both celebrated figures associated with myth-making who are no more.

Jean Brink asserts that Spenser was born not in 1552, as critics usually suggest, but 1554, the same year as Philip Sidney, in 'Revising Edmund Spenser's Birth Date to 1554' (*N&Q* 56[2009] 523–7). Brink provides persuasive evidence for this opinion: Spenser's likely age when he first entered Cambridge, given his strong academic ability; evidence regarding his relationship with Gabriel Harvey; and Spenser's reference to his own age in the *Amoretti*.

In a piece that ought perhaps to be read alongside Campana's fine essay (reviewed above), John Considine, 'Lascivious Boys in the Bower of Bliss: A Note on *Faerie Queene* II V 28 and II XII 72' (*N&Q* 56[2009] 42), questions critical interpretations of the 'lascivious boys' who appear in Acrasia's Bower of Bliss in Book II of *The Faerie Queene*. In a gloss to his second edition of the poem A.C. Hamilton thought the boys clearly signalled pederasty, whereas elsewhere Catherine Belsey reads them, more innocently, as cupids. Considine concludes that since the word 'boy' could refer to men as well as children in the early modern period and 'lascivious' might merely mean amorous, Hamilton's interpretation is not convincing. This is reinforced by other references to 'lascivious boys' in a number of texts before 1640 where it is clear that men are intended.

Books Reviewed

Beecher, Donald, and Grant Williams, eds. *Ars Reminiscendi: Mind and Memory in Renaissance Culture*. Centre for Reformation and Renaissance Studies. [2009] pp. 440. $37 ISBN 9 7807 7272 0481.

Dimmock, Matthew, and Andrew Hadfield, eds. *Literature and Popular Culture in Early Modern England*. Ashgate. [2009] pp. 219. £65 ISBN 9 7807 5466 5809.

Engel, William E. *Chiastic Designs in English Literature: From Sidney to Shakespeare*. Ashgate. [2009] pp. 165. £50 ISBN 9 7807 5466 6363.

Grogan, Jane. *Exemplary Spenser: Visual and Poetic Pedagogy in The Faerie Queene*. Ashgate. [2009] pp. 226. £55 ISBN 9 7807 5466 6981.

Lamb, Mary Ellen, and Valerie Wayne, eds. *Staging Early Modern Romance: Prose Fiction, Dramatic Romance, and Shakespeare*. Routledge. [2009] pp. 261. £75 ISBN 9 7804 1596 2810.

Stapleton, M.L. *Spenser's Ovidian Poetics*. UDelP. [2009] pp. 271. £53.50 ISBN 9 7808 7413 0805.

VI

Shakespeare

GABRIEL EGAN, PETER J. SMITH, ELINOR PARSONS, CHRIS BUTLER, CHLOE PORTER, DANIEL CADMAN, RICHARD WOOD, STEVE LONGSTAFFE, KATE WILKINSON AND NAOMI McAREAVEY

This chapter has four sections: 1. Editions and Textual Matters; 2. Shakespeare in the Theatre; 3. Shakespeare on Screen; 4. Criticism. Section 1 is by Gabriel Egan; section 2 is by Peter J. Smith; section 3 is by Elinor Parsons; section 4(a) is by Chris Butler; section 4(b) is by Chloe Porter; section 4(c) is by Daniel Cadman; section 4(d) is by Richard Wood; section 4(e) is by Steve Longstaffe; section 4(f) is by Kate Wilkinson; section 4(g) is by Naomi McAreavey.

1. Editions and Textual Matters

One major critical edition of Shakespeare appeared in 2009: James R. Siemon edited *Richard III* for the third series of the Arden Shakespeare. An abortive Arden edition of *Romeo and Juliet* also appeared in the form of an appendix to a monograph, but it was so poorly executed that it needs little notice. There were also four major monographs directly on our topic and a further two with important contributions, the usual number of essays in book-format collections and more than the usual number of relevant journal articles.

Siemon's 123-page introduction has nothing to say on the complex textual situation of *Richard III*, because an extended appendix deals with the matter. At times Siemon's tone is rather too colloquial—'cue victim number one' (p. 6), 'goofy' (p. 7), and 'Sound familiar?' (p. 8)—and is unhelpfully aimed at readers who already know the play. He makes the valuable point that Richard's character, and his stichomythic wooing, are somewhat dependent upon the character of Dissimulation in Robert Wilson's play *Three Ladies of London*, before exploring more familiar analogues in Thomas Kyd's *The Spanish Tragedy* and Christopher Marlowe's *The Jew of Malta*. Siemon points out that the character of Richard in this play is rather different from the one seen in the preceding history plays, where he was vengeful but not a loner, not

The Year's Work in English Studies, Volume 90 (2011)
doi:10.1093/ywes/mar018

anti-family. Not until his soliloquy in Act III of *3 Henry VI* does he become the 'theatrical, scheming, wicked, ironic' (p. 40) figure we see in *Richard III*.

Composition of the play could not have preceded the publication in 1587 of the second edition of Raphael Holinshed's *Chronicles*, a major source, and must have been complete before the play's entry in the Stationers' Register on 20 October 1597. Siemon considers it highly likely that *Richard III* postdates *3 Henry VI*, on which it builds, so that makes it after the spring of 1592 once allusions by Robert Greene and Thomas Nashe are factored in, and Siemon goes for the summer of 1592. He adopts John Jowett's nomenclature for the lost manuscripts underlying early editions, but calls them QMS and FMS rather than Jowett's MSQ and MSF. If *Richard III* was in performance before the closure in June 1592—which lasted until December 1593 except for five weeks in December 1592 and January 1593—then it ought to be mentioned in Philip Henslowe's records, but it is not, and we would expect Nashe to mention it when praising the depiction of Talbot in *1 Henry VI* and when lauding Lord Strange (whose ancestors the play depicts positively), and he does not. So, *Richard III* was probably first performed by the new Chamberlain's men company when they began in June 1594 at the Theatre, with Richard Burbage in the lead. Siemon offers a useful summary of the sources (pp. 51–67), indicating the crucial importance of Thomas More's biography as well as how Holinshed, Edward Hall, and *The Mirror for Magistrates* tell the play's stories.

A digression (pp. 69–74) on a family-tree pageant for Elizabeth I on the way to her coronation in 1559 contains an odd mix of colloquialism ('Sound familiar?' again) and obscure words such as *scapular* (twice) for 'pertaining to shoulders' and *nuntius* for 'messenger'. A play on the same topic, Thomas Legge's *Richardus Tertius*, introduced the wooing scenes absent in other sources, and as Siemon notes, the anonymous Queen's men's play *The True Tragedy of Richard III* contains the line 'A horse, a horse, a fresh horse'. Siemon's introduction ends, conventionally, with a brief stage history (pp. 79–123), which contains the familiar story common to Shakespeare's plays of an adaptation (here, Colly Cibber's) holding the stage from 1700 to the early nineteenth century. Quoting Henry James's account of Henry Irving as Richard from the essential compilation *Eyewitnesses to Shakespeare*, Siemon fails to give its author Gāmini Salgādo the accents in his name (p. 101, n.1). This section (and hence the introduction) ends abruptly with a description of Jonathan Slinger's remarkable performance as Richard for the Royal Shakespeare Company in 2007–8.

Before turning to the text, it will be useful to survey Siemon's Appendix I on the early editions (pp. 417–60). He gives the hypothetical stemma, and necessarily it is complicated; in compensation Siemon quotes Barbara Mowat and Paul Werstine's excellent summation that 'the first printed version, almost all scholars agree, provides a second state of the play, and later printings of this second state, in turn, influenced the printing of the play in the first state' (p. 418). For III.i.1–III.i.166 and V.iii.49–end, about one-sixth of the play, the Folio simply reprints Q3 (a reprint of Q2, which reprinted Q1) and hence Q1 of 1597 is Siemon's copy text for these parts. F is his copy text for the rest of the play. Siemon charts the general twentieth-century preference for F, with

Q1 rising in editorial popularity towards the end of the century, culminating in Jowett's edition for the Oxford Shakespeare, which preferred Q1 as more theatricalized. (This edition was reviewed in *YWES* 81[2002], covering work published in 2000.) Siemon makes the case that the inextricable linking of Q1 and F means that an editor has to use both—that is, conflate them—but his policy is to prefer F overall and bring in from Q1 what he needs, using the symbols $^{Q}\dots^{Q}$ to mark it off, except where F merely reprints Q3, for which parts Q1 is basic, and $^{F}\dots^{F}$ is used to mark what is taken from there. These symbols have not been seen in the Arden3 series since R.A. Foakes introduced them for his *King Lear*. Because of F's dependence on Q6, Siemon has to collate all six pre-Folio quartos.

In a subsection on Q1 (pp. 422–31), Siemon repeats Peter W.M. Blayney's claim that plays were not particularly attractive to publishers, without acknowledging Alan B. Farmer and Zachary Lesser's counter-claim (reviewed in *YWES* 86[2007], covering work published in 2005), which did not appear too late to be noticed. At 3,480 lines, Q1 is much longer than other plays and Siemon awkwardly describes how the play must have been cut for performance: 'Sometime between some version of what Shakespeare wrote and what found its way into print as Ql, someone—perhaps Shakespeare, the acting company, a theatrical scribe, the printers or their employees—shortened the text' (pp. 424–5). Here there is slippage between the terms 'time' and 'text': Siemon ought to have written 'Some time between the writing of some version... and the writing of what found its way...'. The words 'Some time' are required because 'Sometime' means formerly or occasionally.

Valentine Simmes printed sheets A–G and Peter Short printed sheets H–M of Q1, both for Andrew Wise. The copy was cast off and, to judge from the results, fairly accurately, although there is in places severe cramping that may well have necessitated shortening of stage directions in a way that altered the action. Siemon traces the dispute between MacDonald P. Jackson and Susan Zimmerman about the number of compositors who set Short's sheets H–M, but he omits the final blow in the exchange, an article by Jackson published in 2001. (This reviewer missed it at the time too, because it appeared in the fairly obscure *Bibliographical Society of Australia and New Zealand Bulletin*; it ought to have been reviewed in *YWES* 82[2003].) Siemon also uses only two of Alan E. Craven's four relevant articles on Simmes's compositor A, whose habits Craven rather over-confidently detected across a number of jobs over the years. The over-confidence resided in Craven's assumptions that one man's habits would be relatively stable over time, that compositors did not share typecases, and that from the variants in an edition the extent of its proof-reading can be inferred; all three assumptions are unreliable. Siemon mentions challenges to Craven's work on Simmes's compositor A (p. 429, n. 1), without going into the details.

Having acknowledged, albeit under-represented, the extent of, the Jackson/Zimmerman dispute about Short's sheets of Q1, Siemon writes that 'less has been asserted about personnel' (p. 429) in Short's shop than has been asserted about Simmes's compositor A; in fact the debates are about equally extensive. Then comes a howler '... printing by formes requires setting all pages for one side of a sheet and printing them before setting the pages for the other side of the sheet' (p. 429). In fact, the setting of the second side can be done simultaneously with the setting of the first, or during the printing of the first. Indeed, being able to set both sides simultaneously is one of the reasons for bothering with casting off and setting by formes, as the procedure allows more flexible and rapid reallocation of labour in the printshop.

A single variant introduced during stop-press correction of Q1 is of considerable importance. Where the uncorrected state of L2r reads 'greatest number' the corrected state reads 'vtmost number', and at this point F reads 'vtmost power'. Siemon reckons that F's agreement with Q1c in having *vtmost* (a reading not found in Q2–6) shows an F/Q1 relationship independent of F's derivation from Q2–6, since it is most unlikely that F got this reading, and nothing else, from Q1c. If so, QMS and FMS were closely related. However, as Siemon points out, the next word shows the opposite, since it is hardly likely that Q1's compositor would make the correction of *greatest* > *vtmost* (which is so unmotivated that it must have followed from consultation of copy) without also fixing *number* if his copy showed that *power* was the correct word. Thus it cannot be the case that QMS and FMS agreed on the second word, so we have evidence for and against these manuscripts being closely related. Siemon reckons that Q1/F's exclusive agreements (that is, against Q2–6) show the closeness of QMS/FMS but their differences show that QMS derived from FMS. To prove this, he turns to Q2–8.

Siemon's subsection (pp. 431–41) on these derivative quartos characterizes the Q2–8 line as essentially monogenous, although Q5 drew on Q3 as well as Q4. Q3 supplied one-sixth of the copy for F, and for the other five-sixths Q3 and/or Q6 was printed copy for F that was first marked up by reference to FMS. F frequently agrees with one or more of Q2–6 against Q1, which could be coincidence but could also happen because F got those readings from Q2–6. Thus the need to collate Q1–6 and F. Q2 supplies two lines absent from Q1 and an important question is how they got there. One possibility is that these lines were in a corrected exemplar of Q1, now lost, which was copy for Q2. The alternative, supported by Jowett, is that for these two lines the copy for Q1 was consulted in the making of Q2; Andrew Wise would still possess that copy, being the publisher of both. Siemon finds evidence for this alternative in the crowding of the preceding page of Q2: the compositors would not need to crowd if they were just reprinting an exemplar of Q1 that had these lines, but would need to crowd if they discovered during setting that the Q1 they were reprinting had two lines missing. (Actually, this is not quite true, since the corrected exemplar of Q1 they were reprinting might itself have the crowding, created during press correction when it was realized that two omitted lines had to be squeezed in, and since Q2 is a page-for-page reprint of Q1 it would reproduce this crowding.) As Siemon points out, the signs of crowding (a turn-up and a catch-word sharing a line with dialogue) appear elsewhere in Q1 and Q2 so they do not tell us much. Weighing it all up, Siemon plumps for the idea that Q2 was reprinted for an exemplar of Q1 (now lost) that contains these two lines, added during press correction. Thus nowhere in Q2–6 was QMS consulted: they are pure reprints. Jowett argued that Q3's small improvements over its copy Q2 betray consultation of QMS, but Siemon thinks that a clever printshop worker could have made them and he itemizes the evidence (pp. 436–7).

Q1 gets right ('ix' months), Q2 gets wrong ('xi' months), and Q3 gets right ('ix' months) the age of Henry VI at his coronation, but this did not require consultation of QMS since the fact was well known. A crucial case is Q3's reordering of the speaking of the ghosts, which Jowett thinks Q1 and Q2 get right—in the sense of showing what got performed, since its order is more efficient in casting—and Q3 gets wrong by putting the ghosts in the order in which they died. Jowett came up with possible explanations for Q3's ordering of the ghosts' appearance, such as unclear transposition marked in QMS, a change in the staging that Wise knew about, or Shakespeare's insistence that the ghosts appear in the book in the order they died rather than in the order they appeared on stage for purely practical reasons; Siemon finds them all unconvincing. He adds his own possibility: whereas Q2 reprints Q1 page for page, Q3 reprints Q2 without preserving its pagination, and Siemon reckons that 'It could not have been easy to mark up so many repaginations' (p. 438). But in fact there would have been no need to mark them up if Q3 was set seriatim, and Siemon offers no evidence that Q3 was instead cast off to be set by formes. Siemon notices that Q3 corrects a speech-prefix error in Q1 and Q2 regarding one of the ghosts: Rivers' ghost's condemnation is attributed to '*King*' in Q1 and Q2 (both on L4r) and correctly to '*Riu*[*ers*]' in Q3 (L3r). Thus someone in the printshop making Q3 was paying close attention to Q2, and such a person might easily read Buckingham's 'The last was I that felt thy tyrannie' (Q2, L4r) and decide that all the ghosts' speeches ought to appear in order of death, and altered the text to make them do so. On this supposition, Siemon rejects Q3's ordering of the speeches (which is F's, but then F just reprints Q3 at this point) and goes back to Q1's.

Siemon then turns to the evidence for the other five-sixths of F not printed from Q3 being printed from Q6. There are a dozen F/Q6 agreements against Q1–5. Importantly, where Q1–5 have 'Is colder tidings, yet they must be told', Q6 has 'Is colder news, yet they must be told', and F has 'Is colder Newes, but yet they must be told'. For F to be independent of Q6 requires either that FMS had *news* and that Q6 got its *news* by accidentally picking it up from two lines earlier, or that F and Q6 both independently picked it up from there. However, F has *but* which would not metrically fit with *tidings*, and this *but* is most easily explained as an attempt in the making of F to bring the erroneous reading in Q6 back to good metre. Since F is at this point simply reprinting Q6, Siemon returns to Q1's reading.

Siemon discusses the creation of F by compositors A and B, noting that no press variants implying consultation of copy have been found. Unfortunately, he takes over from Antony Hammond's Arden2 edition of the play the quite meaningless claim that page q6r is 'the last of the inner forme of gathering q' (p. 443, n. 2). Gathering q, made of three sheets, has three inner formes and three outer formes, and Siemon means that pages q6r and q1v make up the last inner forme of gathering q to be set and printed. There are signs of stretching of copy on this page, towards the end of gathering q, and Siemon (following Hammond) sees in this compositor B attempting to meet an agreed end-of-gathering break predetermined by casting off. This makes no sense unless the next gathering had already been cast off too, and neither Siemon nor Hammond gives a reason for thinking that happened here. The standard work they follow is Charlton Hinman's *The Printing and the Proof-Reading of the First Folio of Shakespeare*, which describes the normal method as setting seriatim in the second half of the quire and letting the next gathering start where it will. (Hinman gives exceptions to this—occasions where multi-gathering casting off was done—but gatherings q and r are not among them.) Werstine has shown that the second half of a gathering might be cast off if its setting was to be shared by compositors, but that is not the case here.

Over 200 lines in F do not come from a quarto, so there was a manuscript involved too. Conversely, Q1 has nearly forty lines not in F, so we need to consider the QMS/FMS relationship. There are Q1/F agreements against Q2–5 that seem to come from QMS/FMS agreement rather than consultation of Q1 when printing F. Siemon does not go into the detail of how we know that these are not cases of Q1 itself influencing F, which is that around these Q1/F agreements against Q2–5 the copy for F is clearly Q3 or Q6, so unless the compositors were flitting furiously between different forms of copy—that is, if they were doing the sensible thing and just alternating between exemplars of Q3 and Q6 marked up from an authoritative manuscript—the Q1/F agreements must come from that manuscript. The line 'Harpe not on that string Madam, that is past' is in Q1, missing in Q2–5 (making nonsense of a dialogue exchange), and present in F, but in the wrong place. The obvious inference is that it was written in the margin of F's quarto copy (when it was noticed that this line in FMS was absent from that quarto copy) with an indication of where it should be inserted, but the indication was badly made or badly followed when setting F. The fact that QMS was derived from FMS (and not the other way around) is shown by Q1's garbling of things correct in F. For example, in F Richard is sarcastically advised to woo princess Elizabeth by sending her, to wipe her eyes, a handkerchief dipped in her brother's blood, whereas in Q1 the advice is to send a handkerchief dipped in Rutland's blood; the latter would mean nothing to her.

Siemon surveys claims that QMS was made by collective, legitimate memorial reconstruction by the company, ending with Jowett's proof (from variation in speech prefixes) that QMS and FMS are related by transcription, not memory. (Jowett's article was reviewed in *YWES* 81[2002], covering work published in 2000.) Siemon accepts that QMS must derive from FMS since Q1 is more theatricalized than F, although he notices that the theatricalization sometimes hurt the meaning of dialogue, as when streamlined casting gives Lovell and Ratcliffe's tasks to Catesby alone, but the references to those actions retain plural pronouns. Likewise, in Q1 Ratcliffe takes over the Folio Sheriff's role as Buckingham's executioner, yet in Q1 Buckingham treats his executioner as someone he does not know rather than as a former ally. In Q1 Catesby takes over from Lovell and Ratcliffe (in F) as Hastings's executioner, yet in Q1 Hastings fails to reproach Catesby, his former friend and confidant. (Hastings has no such close relationship with Ratcliffe and Lovell, so it is plausible that he would not reproach them.). There is a similar wrinkle with the streamlining that makes Dorset, in Q1, rather than a messenger (as in F) bring to his mother in II.iv the news of the imprisonment of members of their family: she and he express no concern for one another, and she talks as if he was not there, as indeed he was not in F.

How should an editor respond to this textual situation (pp. 456–60)? If we accept FMS > QMS revision, then mostly it was a matter of cutting lines, although Q1 has the jack-of-the-clock episode absent from F. Was it added in? Was it censored when F was printed? Siemon does not know. In some verbal variants Q1 is closer to the sources than F is, but in others it is further. F has certain geographical errors that Q1 fixes, such as getting from Stony Stratford to London via Northampton (II.iv.1–2), but Siemon thinks this a miscorrection in the sense that F reflects the sources. That is, F's route, which indicates turning back and heading away from London, is indeed what the party historically did after Richard intervened at Stony Stratford to arrest Rivers, Grey, and Vaughan. The trouble with this argument is that it leaves the Archbishop trying to reassure the others on stage that the royal party is on its way to London, yet naming a sequence of places that indicates, to the geographically knowledgeable at least, that they are heading in the opposite direction.

Siemon is not convinced that authorial correction explains the difference between F's treatment of Woodville, Rivers, and Scales as three men (apparently arising from ambiguous phrasing in the source Hall) and Q1's historically correct reduction of these names to one man. It could, he thinks, just be theatrical economy. He decides to let the route-to-London geographical error stand (that is, he follows F) since an unauthorized change by a geographically knowledgeable printshop worker might account for Q1's correction. On balance he decides that the reduction of Woodville/Rivers/Scales to one man is not something that could have happened in the printshop, so it was a fix authorized by someone in the know and Siemon's retains this fix (that is, he follows Q1). The famous error of Richard saying that Richmond was raised at 'our mother's cost' (V.iii.324) instead of 'our brother's cost' is not fixed by Siemon because it seems to be what Shakespeare really thought happened, having been misled by a misprint in Holinshed. Overall and in general this edition 'sides with F' (p. 460).

Let us see how these ideas affect the words chosen for the text of the play. Siemon uses one collation band for everything, and where there is a choice of Q1 or F wording, he goes for one or other, usually favouring F. Where one edition has something the other lacks he imports it inside $^{Q}\ldots^{Q}$ and $^{F}\ldots^{F}$ symbols. Modern editions are collated very occasionally, and although he refers to the corrected and uncorrected states of formes of Q1 Siemon does not indicate where the exemplars containing them are located nor give a list of all their press variants. Siemon uses F for 'Plots have I laid, inductions dangerous' (I.i.1.32), rejecting Q1's reading (defended and adopted by Jowett for the Oxford Shakespeare series) of *inductious* as an adjective. F is also followed for Clarence's 'but I protest | As yet I do not. But, as I can learn' (I.i.52–3), although Q1 makes the first *but* into *for* (which makes smoother sense), and one might argue that the F compositor picked up *but* from the next line; Siemon thinks the *but*... *but* phrasing might be intended to show Clarence's inarticulate excitement. Siemon has Richard say that the queen 'tempers him [the king] to this extremity' (I.i.65) using *tempers* from Q1 because it fits the sense of women moulding men, whereas F's *tempts* does not. The limitation of the edition's typographical conventions is clear in the first of Siemon's importations for Q1: 'Heard you not what an humble suppliant | Lord Hastings was ^{Q}to her^{Q} for his delivery?' (I.i.74–5). Aside from *to her* there is another Q1/F variant in this line—*her/his* as the penultimate word—but it is buried in the collation. This mixture of conventions makes it hard for the reader to appreciate that Q1 reads 'Lord Hastings was to her for his deliuery' and F reads 'Lord Hastings was, for her deliuery?' Siemon has Richard swear by 'Saint John' (I.i.138), the Folio reading, rejecting the quartos' variant *Saint Paul* although the sources attest to his use of it and he says it elsewhere in the play.

Siemon offers a textual note on the three-way press variant in Q1 'set downe your honourable l' versus '... honourable lo' versus '... honourable lo:' (I.ii.0), pointing out that the last word might mean *lord* instead the familiar *load*, but he does not adopt Q1 for his edition, and he does not go into the two-stage correction that this press variant is witness to. Indeed nowhere does he make systematic comments on press variants and their significance for the editor. For the complex set of Q1/F variants in Anne's speech 'Stabbed by the same hand ... cursed ... Cursed ... Cursed ... blood from hence' (I.ii.11–16) Siemon just follows F, noting but not being persuaded by the arguments in favour of emendation, such as the first *hand* being contradictory of *3 Henry VI* where all three York brothers stabbed her son, nor by the argument for reordering the lines to make better poetic sense. Although following Q1 for 'Unmannered dog, stand thou when I command!' (I.ii.39) where F has '... stand'st thou ...', Siemon tries in a note to make sense of F's reading which 'could be a demand in the form of a question: i.e. are you going to stand still or not when I issue the order?'. There are twelve lines at I.ii.158–69 that appear in F and are absent from Qq, forming a speech about how he, Richard, has forborne weeping until now. Siemon surveys the arguments about these lines—an addition to FMS? a deletion from QMS?—and decides that 'Speed [of theatrical performance] seems the most likely motivation for omission', so clearly his edition is not trying to present the play as performed else he would remove these lines.

Despite the colloquialisms noted above, certain aspects of Siemon's edition are rather old-fashioned. There is a recurrent pattern of cross-referencing to other literary works without comment, as when the note for lines I.ii.177–81, where Richard offers his naked breast to the sword, begins 'Cf. Seneca, *Hercules Oetaeus*, 1000–1, 1015'. It is hard for a reader to know if she should take the trouble to find these lines in Seneca without first being given a hint about why it is worth doing. Likewise for 'Cf. Berowne's surprise and consternation at the absurdity of his falling in love (*Love's Labour's Lost* III.i.169–200)' (I.ii.230–40n.), which seems to betray an educator's concern for comparing the plays more than an editor's concern for explaining this one. Siemon follows F to give '[your hatred] Makes him [the king] to send, that he may learn the ground' (I.iii.68) where Q1 has 'Makes him to send that thereby he may gather | The ground of your ill will and to remoue it'. The thought is rather more completed in Q1, but Siemon is right that F makes sense on its own and needs no improvement.

Siemon combines F and Q1 to produce 'What? Threat you me with telling of the King? | ^{Q}Tell him and spare not. Look what I have said^{Q} | I will avouch't in presence of the King' (I.iii.12–14). The trouble here is that *avouch't*, from F, seems necessary because F lacks the Q-only words. That is, the *it* of *avouch't* refers back to an earlier speech Richard made, while in Q1 the corresponding word is *avouch* because the antecedent 'what I have said' is present in the sentence. To conflate Q/F here is to change the meaning of 'Look what I have said', which appears only in Q1, where it is the subject of *avouch*. The conflation makes it into a separate thought roughly equivalent to 'think on what I'm saying', and that is rewriting Shakespeare. At I.iii.322 Siemon gives '*Exeunt all but* ^{Q}*Richard*^{Q} [, *Duke of*] *Gloucester*', and it is not clear why Siemon bothers to mark that this first name comes from Q1 since ordinary regularization of character names would in any case warrant the intervention. Another odd use of the superscripted ^{Q}...^{Q} markers occurs at the end of I.iii, the suborning of the two murderers. It is clearly the end of a scene as the location is about to change, and F has '*Scena Quarta*' as the next line, yet Siemon prints '^{Q}*Exeunt*^{Q}'. Using superscripted markers instead of confining variants to the collation band is usually justified as a way of highlighting plausible alternative readings, but here there is no alternative: the scene must end with a clearing of the stage.

The next scene, including Clarence's murder (I.iv.84–282), is where the quartos differ from F most extensively. Siemon follows F for almost all readings except where he thinks it reflects censorship of swearing or profane religious matter, for which he reverts to Q1. Just how he represents these interventions is not immediately clear. At I.iv.125 Q1 reads 'Zounds he dies, I had forgot the reward' while F has 'Come, he dies: I had forgot the Reward', and Siemon follows Q1 (with some minor repunctuation). There is no indication in the body text that he has done this: the information is buried in the collation. Yet at I.iv.143–4 Q1 reads 'Zounds it is euen now at my elbowe perswading me | Not to kill the Duke' and F has 'Tis euen now at my elbow, perswading me not to kill the Duke', and Siemon again departs from his usual authority, F, to here follow Q1. But this time he puts *Zounds* inside ^{Q}...^{Q} and omits to mention it in the collation. The rule seems to be that where Siemon rejects a copy-text word and adopts a non-copy-text word, he need not draw attention to this in his body text—just mentioning it in the collation will do—but where he adopts a non-copy-text word for which his copy text has no word he draws attention to it with ^{Q}...^{Q}. It is not clear why his copy text having no word at the point of Siemon's departure from it should cause him to mark the departure more heavily than he does when his copy text has a word he rejects: is not the rejection of an erroneous blank essentially the same editorial action as the rejection of an erroneous word?

There are several such moments of apparent inconsistency in this scene. At I.iv.188–9 Q1 reads 'I charge you as you hope to haue redemption, | By Christs deare bloud shed for our grieuous sinnes' and F has, in place of these, just the single line 'I charge you, as you hope for any goodnesse'. Siemon follows Q1 to print 'I charge you, as you hope to have redemption, | ^{Q}By Christ's dear blood, shed for our grievous sins,^{Q}'. The logic of Siemon's intervention in adopting Q1's reading is that the alteration of *to haue redemption* to *for any goodnesse* was part of the same act of censorship that struck out the entire second line present in Q1, and indeed he considers the whole matter in one textual note covering both lines' censorable religious content. But his rules about use of ^{Q}...^{Q} markers means that he has to treat this single act of censorship in different ways in the two lines: *to haue redemption > for any goodnesse* is noted only in the collation, while the inclusion of Q1's 'By Christs deare bloud shed for our grieuous sinnes' gets the full ^{Q}...^{Q} treatment and is not recorded in the collation. Siemon believes that a single intervention for a single reason produced this variant—and he rightly wants to undo it—so it is hard to see why he thinks different signals for parts of essentially one variant are the best way to make the modern reader aware of what happened and what has been done to reverse it.

A surprising choice is that Siemon sticks with F for 'I hope this passionate humour of mine will change' (I.iv.117–18) where Q1 calls it a *holy humor*. Since Siemon thinks that religious censorship has affected the whole of the murderers' scene and that the play's 'generally ironic treatment of religion ... may have occasioned particularly close scrutiny' so that a hope for *redemption* was revised to a hope for *goodness* (I.iv.188–9n.), it is odd that he does not think *holy > passionate* part of that process. I mentioned that for almost all readings Siemon follows F, but at I.iv.236 F omits the quarto line 'And chargd vs from his souls, to loue each other'. Because Siemon thinks this necessary to the meaning of the speech it appears in, he concludes that it was most likely accidentally omitted by F's compositors and he reinstates it. In fact the passage makes just as good sense without the line, although it is less moving, so one could argue for F and Q1 offering equally viable alternatives. In a passage absent in Q1, F has Clarence ask 'Which of you ... If two such murtherers ... came to you, | Would not intreat for life, as you would begge | Were you in my distresse' (I.iv.256–60). The problem is 'as you would begge', which seems ungrammatical. *The Oxford Complete Works* fixed it by putting a dash after *distress* to show that Clarence is cut off, unable to complete his thought, but Siemon goes for the solution used by his Arden2 predecessor Hammond and emends *as* to *Ay*.

At II.i.5, F has the king reconcile his relatives so that 'more to peace my soule shall part to heauen', while the corrected state of Q1 has the more meaningful 'now in peace my soule shall part to heauen'; the uncorrected state of Q1 has the impossible reading '... depart from heauen'. Siemon thinks F wrong, but rather than adopt Q1c he goes for Nicholas Rowe's conflation of 'more in ...', noting that 'editors often follow it' but without making a case for it. He does a similar thing at I.iv.236n., writing that 'Most editors include this Qq line [that F omits] as essential ...' before specifying why he thinks they are right to do so. Likewise at II.ii.145 he writes that 'Most recent editors include this Qq line [that F omits]' and again at II.iv.21 ('Most editors assign ...'). Siemon seems a tad too concerned with the editorial tradition, and although he generally gives the reasons for his decisions he repeatedly prefixes them with an observation that he is doing as others have done. Siemon adopts from Qq the king's requirement that Hastings and Rivers reconcile themselves, over F's line that has Dorset and Rivers do it (II.i.7), on the perfectly reasonable grounds that Dorset says nothing and there is no reason to suppose he is at enmity with his uncle Rivers. Siemon adopts another Q1 reading of *God* over F's *heauen* (II.i.39) on the grounds of likely religious censorship. At II.i.57 Richard apologizes if he has offended anyone *unwillingly* (F) or *unwittingly* (Q1) and Siemon thinks the former possible but he nonetheless departs from his copy text F to follow Q1. At certain times it does not take much to make Siemon depart from his copy text.

Occasionally Siemon offers a speculation that appears not to have been entirely thought through. At II.ii.145 the quartos contain a line absent from F—'*Ans.* | With all our hearts'—which Siemon includes in his edition. Siemon speculates that its coincidence with a column break in F might have caused it to be overlooked. This could be the case only if the compositors stopped setting when they had completed exactly one column, and there is no reason to suppose that they did. From the reuse of rules Hinman concluded that ordinarily the centre rule was added as soon as the first column was in type, but since adjustments for balance would have to be made for every page this implies no more than pausing somewhere near (not exactly at) the column end. Where the columns were set by different men, a marker approximately dividing the copy might be useful, but this page was not shared.

At III.i.86 Siemon retains the spelling *valure* for 'His wit set down to make his valure live' despite noting that 'it has the same triple meaning as "valour"'. He appears to prefer the word's obsolete spelling because it 'reminds one of its polysemousness', but if the meanings are the same as the modern *valour* this decision seems to contradict his general principle on modernization. Siemon follows F in having a priest enter to Hastings and exchange a few words with him before Buckingham enters and comments on this conference (III.ii.105–10). Q1 has the same action except that the priest says nothing: Hastings simply acknowledges the priest and speaks in his ear. Thus Q1 saves a speaking part. Strangely, Siemon imports from Q1 the stage direction '*He whispers in his ear*' (putting it inside $^{Q}\ldots^{Q}$ markers), which surely is an action arising from the saving of a speaking part and ought not to be conflated with F's alternative version. That is, either talking openly with the priest (as in F) or whispering with him (as in Q) will do to motivate Buckingham's question 'talking with a priest?' and his comment on shriving, so there's no need to import Q1's stage direction.

Siemon follows F in having Ratcliffe enter at the start of Act III, scene iv, set in London despite the fact that he was in the previous scene set in Pomfret, West Yorkshire. Not only does this create a temporal/geographical problem for the reader and audience—when did he make the long journey down to London?—but it also violates the Law of Re-entry. Siemon decides that these inconsistencies are 'probably preferable to Qq's awkward and inconsistent substitutions of Catesby for Ratcliffe and Lovell' (III.iv.77n.). Siemon sticks to F's highly unmetrical 'Well, well, he was the covert'st sheltered traitor | That ever lived. | Would you imagine, or almost believe' (III.iii.33–5), where the problem is the short line in the middle, rather than patch it from Q1 where there is a clearly displaced half-line obtruding in the previous speech ('Looke ye my Lo: Maior'), which half-line fits perfectly the gap here. The logic of those who patch F from Q1 here is that 'Looke... Maior' was written in a manuscript in such a way that it got displaced in Q1 and omitted altogether in F. Siemon, following recent editors, prefers F's unmetrical short line and plausibly suggests that Buckingham is here displaying his talent for histrionic pauses and breakings-off. Also based on Buckingham's character is the attribution to him of the lines 'I never looked for better at his hands | After he once fell in with Mistress Shore' (III.v.50–1), as in F, rather than the mayor who gets them in Q1. This attribution requires Buckingham to switch between *I* and *we* pronouns in one speech, which Siemon explains is not the intermittent intrusion of a royal plural but Buckingham distinguishing between his own opinions and those he shares with Richard (III.v.56n.).

Siemon is convinced that Shakespeare used *mine* before words beginning with a vowel when he did not want to emphasize the possessive and *my* when he did, so that in place of F's 'And when my Oratorie drew toward end' he has Buckingham say 'And when mine oratory drew toward end' (III.vii.20), using *mine* from Q1. As Siemon acknowledges when treating the same problem elsewhere in his edition, compositors appear to have imposed their own preferences regarding *my/mine* before a vowel and deciding whether the possessive is to be emphasized is subjective. Given these causes for doubt, it is surprising that the otherwise conservative Siemon should here depart from his F copy without giving a compelling reason for thinking it wrong. Q1 has Buckingham say 'Come Citizens, zounds ile intreat no more' to which Richard replies 'O do not sweare my Lord of Buckingham', whereas F has Buckingham say the much less objectionable and less forceful 'Come Citizens, we will entreat no more' and omits Richard's response (III.vii.218–19). As Siemon points out, censorship that removed Buckingham's swearing (*zounds ile* > *we will*) obviously entailed cutting of Richard's objection to it, so Siemon restores Q1's readings here. Having accepted the crown, Q1 has Richard pretend to return to his devotions with 'Farewel good coosine, farwel gentle friends' where F has the plural 'Farewell my Cousins ...' (III.vii.246). Siemon adopts F's wording but with the singular *cousin* from Q1, on the grounds that 'It seems improbable that he would be so familiar with mere citizens, since he has expressly distinguished his own *degree* from their *condition* (p. 142)'. But Richard wants to appear to have relented over the course of this scene—no longer aloof and accepting the honour thrust on him—so an overly familiar term might be just what he thinks he should use at this point. Again, a departure from his copy when it makes reasonable sense is inconsistent with Siemon's conservatism elsewhere.

F has the Duchess of York notice the entrance of 'My Neece Plantagenet, | Led in the hand of her kind Aunt of Gloster?' whereas Q1 cuts the second line (IV.i.1–2). This affects the casting, as in F's reading the niece must be Clarence's daughter—to whom Anne, Richard's wife, is aunt—while Q1's reading allows the niece (a relationship used loosely) to be Anne herself. In accepting F's reading Siemon is obliged to follow Lewis Theobald's lead and emend the scene's opening stage direction to include Clarence's daughter, who is mentioned in neither Q1 nor F's direction. Following F, Siemon is obliged at IV.ii.81 to omit the Q-only exchange in which Richard asks about the murder of the princes in the Tower: 'Shal we heare from thee Tirrel ere we sleep?', and the murderer's reply 'Ye shall my lord', which is almost exactly the same as an exchange between Richard and Catesby at III.i.188–9. The editors of the *Oxford Complete Works* argued that this exchange is connected to the 'clock-passage' near the end of the scene, where Richard is anxious about time in a way quite unnoticed and unappreciated by Buckingham, and they import it from Q1 for that reason. Editing the single-volume Oxford Shakespeare edition, Jowett decided that the echo was deliberate—a possibility that Gary Taylor did not consider for the *Oxford Complete Works*—and included the exchange in both scenes. By following F, Siemon has included the exchange in III.i where it does not make a lot of sense—Catesby does not go to sound out Hastings until the next morning—and omitted it in IV.ii where it makes a great deal of sense in relation to Richard's insomnia and impatience, and where it connects with Richard's appalling desire to enjoy hearing the full story of the princes' murder as an 'after-supper' treat (IV.iii.31).

Siemon includes the whole 'clock-passage' exchange, present in Qq and absent in F, surveying the various explanations for its absence in F and noting that 'most commentators agree that it is Shakespearean' (IV.ii.97–114n.). Apart from this consensus, Siemon gives no reasons for his including it—against F's authority—and this is all the more surprising since on F's authority he omitted the Richmond/Tyrrel exchange (IV.ii.81) about hurrying back with news of the princes' murder, which plausibly can be connected to this passage. Siemon chooses not to adopt Q1's version of Buckingham's response to Richard's jack-of-the-clock insult, which is a clearly petulant 'Whie then resolue me whether you wil or no?', preferring instead F's simple repetition of the polite question Buckingham has been pursuing all along: 'May it please you to resolve me in my suit?' (IV.ii.115). There is an argument to be made that Q1's petulant question goes with Q1's inclusion of the 'clock-passage', while F's polite question goes with F's omission of the 'clock-passage', in which case Siemon's conflation of Q1 and F has produced a contradiction. That is, Siemon makes Richard deeply insulting in calling Buckingham a jack, but Buckingham appears not to notice. However, Siemon rightly comments that the seemingly polite line for Buckingham that he has adopted 'could be inflected many different ways, expressing frustration, despair, incredulity or any combination of these emotions mixed with a desire not to offend' (IV.ii.115n.).

At IV.iv.37–9 Q1 reads 'And let my woes frowne on the vpper hand, | If sorrow can admitte societie, | Tell ouer your woes againe by vewing mine', where F has almost the same (except *woes* > *greefes*) but omits the last line, which Siemon restores using his $^{Q}\ldots^{Q}$ notation. In fact, F makes good sense on its own because the 'If...' can just as well, or even better, refer back to its preceding line—to mean 'if we can share these pains then mine is foremost'—as it can refer forward to the missing line to mean 'if we can share these pains then count your sorrows again in hearing mine'. Oddly, Siemon gives no defence for importing F's missing line from Q1. F has 'That reignes in gauled eyes of weeping soules: | That excellent grand Tyrant of the earth' (IV.iv.51–2) which, as Siemon says, makes better sense if one puts the second line first. But he also moves the preceding line of F, 'That foule defacer of Gods handy worke', to after this pair, admitting that it may stay where it is in F 'without spoiling the sense'. So why move it? At IV.iv.64 Siemon uses Q1's 'Thy other Edward dead...' in place of F's 'The other Edward dead...', but admits that F might be right because although it introduces added ambiguity into an already notoriously confusing exchange that might be intentional: 'might interchangeability have been the playwright's point?'.

Siemon has Queen Elizabeth call words of complaint 'Airy succeeders of intestate joys' (IV.iv.128), which draws on Q1's *intestate* rather than F's *intestine*. As he admits, this choice of metaphor—words as empty-handed inheritors of joy that died leaving nothing behind—suppresses a much ruder possibility of words as farts. I would have thought F's reading particularly attractive since Queen Elizabeth goes on to say of them 'yet do they ease' (IV.iii.131). Of the means to woo Queen Elizabeth's daughter, Folio Richard says to her 'That I would learne of you' (IV.iv.268), but Siemon follows Q1 to read 'That would I...', giving no more reason than 'Most recent editors prefer' it. Siemon follows Q1 to have Queen Elizabeth refer to the children left fatherless by Richard who will wail it 'in their age' (IV.iv.392) rather than F's 'with their age', but he sounds scarcely convinced, pointing out that F's reading provides a parallel with the next line but one in which Q1 and F agree that the parents left childless by Richard will also wail it 'with their age'. However, Siemon might have defended his choice by saying that 'in their age' means when the children grow up while the parents wailing 'with their age' means now, in their old age.

As this long scene moves to its final phase, Siemon notes that in F Queen Elizabeth exits before Richard has told her to bear his kiss to her daughter, and he thinks this is due to there being not enough room for the stage direction to take its correct place near the bottom of page s5v, so it got displaced upwards. This may be, but the reader is left wondering why matter could not be carried over from the bottom of s5v to the top of s6r, where there is room. Siemon's explanation would make sense if the compositors were particularly lazy or in a hurry, or if s6r were already printed or about to be and they did not want to disturb it. But the usual practice was for the pages in the second half of a Folio quire, here s4r to s6v, to be set in reading order by one compositor (for this quire, compositor B) while the pages in the first half of the quire were set in reverse reading order by the other compositor (here, A). It so happens that this order was slightly departed from in that compositor A jumped in and set page s6r in the second half of the quire (compositor B's half). It could be argued that compositor A did this because compositor B was falling behind and that in response they agreed the s5v/s6r page boundary to enable compositor A to start on s6r while compositor B completed s5v. But unless forme s1v:6r actually went to press before what would normally be its predecessor, s2r:5v—and we have no evidence that it did—the simplest expedient to solve crowding at the bottom of page s5v would be to move a line or two to the top of s6r.

It might be argued that moving a line to the top of the next page—which is all that would be needed to make room for Queen Elizabeth's exit direction to appear in its correct place—would create an unattractive page because s5v's column b would end on the centred words *Exit Queene*. However, several columns in this quire and elsewhere end with such a lonely stage direction, for example r6vb, s1ra, s3rb, and s4ra. The truth is we do not know why at the bottom of s5v compositor B squeezed a stage direction in at the end of a line and seemingly too early, and we cannot say that he was forced to by the exigencies of printing. For all of Siemon's edition from V.iii.49 to the end, Q1 is his copy text because F is clearly a simple reprint of Q3. Yet, within this, Siemon departs from Q1's perfectly meaningful line 'Richard loues Richard, that is I and I' (V.iii.186) to favour F's '... I am I', on purely poetical grounds. After the text there are three appendices. The first, on textual matters, is discussed above. The second is a doubling chart showing that thirteen men and seven boys are needed for the play as it appears in this edition; that is a rather a lot of boys for a playing company of the period. The third appendix gives genealogical tables for the aristocratic families depicted in the play.

Had things gone according to previous planning, there would be another Arden Shakespeare edition to review this year: Lynette Hunter and Peter Lichtenfels's *Romeo and Juliet*. For reasons not disclosed in the book, it has instead appeared as part of a monograph called *Negotiating Shakespeare's Language in Romeo and Juliet: Reading Strategies from Criticism, Editing and the Theatre*. The edition itself appears as an electronic text included with a DVD tucked into the back cover of the monograph, which latter will be reviewed first. A blurb page before the title page says that this book includes 'on CD-Rom the first modern edition of the text of *Romeo & Juliet*', and it is hard to know what is meant by this; presumably it depends on what one understands by 'modern'. The oddness of the entire project is apparent from the introduction (pp. 1–5), which includes personal material that normally is found in an acknowledgements section, such as the recollection that its authors, who are married, spent Christmas holidays walking in Yorkshire. The first two chapters, 'The Reader and the Text' (pp. 9–31) and 'The Actor and the Stage' (pp. 33–58), are not relevant to this review. The third chapter is called 'The Editor and the Book' (pp. 61–82), and much of it is repetition of work already published.

Because John Danter printed sheets A–D of Q1 *Romeo and Juliet* and Edward Allde printed sheets E–K, Hunter and Lichtenfels think in terms of 'Danter beginning the project and Allde finishing it' (p. 65), but of course we do not know that: they could have worked simultaneously. Unfortunately their consideration of the padding in Allde's section is ignorant of Jowett's argument that Henry Chettle extended the stage directions, perhaps from memory of performance. They refer to the 'current consensus' on the matter (p. 65), but support their account of it with references to R.B. McKerrow writing in 1933 and Harry R. Hoppe writing in 1948. Not knowing the argument that the padded stage directions probably come from Chettle, Hunter and Lichtenfels incorporate them into their edition under the misapprehension that they provide 'a wealth of information about stage props and stage actions, as well as some indication of what theatre practitioners thought about the movement of the play, pace and timing' (p. 66). Far from exemplifying the explanatory power of what they call the 'transdisciplinarity' of their approach—that is, theatrical and editorial knowledge coming together—Hunter and Lichtenfels unintentionally exemplify the danger that a lack of knowledge in one field may create a vacuum that is filled by irrelevant knowledge from the other.

Hunter and Lichtenfels's knowledge of key works in the bibliographical tradition is scant to the point where it would, if presented in a Ph.D. dissertation, imperil the awarding of the degree. They think that in his classic *The Stability of Shakespeare's Text* [1965] E.A.J. Honigmann argued that 'there could be no "definitive" text for Shakespeare's plays partly because the full detail of their historical production is lost' (p. 69). They have no idea that he was primarily concerned with authorial tweaking when copying out fairly. Hunter and Lichtenfels think that Taylor's essay 'Swounds Revisited' explains that *zounds* was 'a word apparently so strong that the Folio editors 20-odd years later would not set it' (p. 73). They appear to believe that the Folio's 'editors' (John Heminges and Henry Condell?) set type. In two paragraphs Hunter and Lichtenfels gallop through McKerrow's best-text principle of editing, W.W. Greg's response to it in his essay 'The Rationale of Copy-Text', and recent work by David C. Greetham, Peter L. Shillingsburg, and G. Thomas Tanselle. All this careful scholarship is thoroughly garbled in their accounts of it. A taste of this can be had from a sentence that follows a confusion of McKerrow's emphasis on recension with Greg's on emendation: 'We have to have better reasons for using Q2 than copy text theory, to provide more appropriate guidelines for reading the text today' (p. 79). Hunter and Lichtenfels do not use English words the way the rest of us do, objecting that 'traditional editorial practices can be evasive and implicitly authoritative' (p. 80) when they surely mean by that last word authoritarian. Or perhaps they think editions ought not to be authoritative, which would help account for theirs.

Chapter 4 (pp. 85–131) is called 'The Family: Behaviour, Convention, Social Agreement and their Breakdown', so it was a surprise that here Hunter and Lichtenfels place their summary of how early books were made. They call the spaces between words 'slugs' (p. 103), which is in fact the name for a line of type created as a single piece of metal by a Linotype machine. They seem to think that wooden printing presses of Shakespeare's time were fundamentally different from the 'compact steel printing presses of the nineteenth and twentieth centuries' (p. 103), but in fact little changed over this period, and of course the metal used to make presses was iron, not steel. They date the replacement of the compositor by the computer to exactly '1987' (p. 103), whereas in fact stereotyping and mechanized compositing (cold- and hot-metal) had been putting compositors out of work since the nineteenth century, and mid-twentieth-century phototypesetting and offset lithographic printing were the bridge to the nearly complete abandonment of setting type by hand in the 1980s. Hunter and Lichtenfels imagine a compositor at work 'setting the line from right to left' (p. 104), which a moment's reflection should have told them would be impossible for prose—unless the copy were written to be read from right to left, as in Hebrew and Arabic—since each line ends when there is no room for another word, and one cannot know in advance when that will be. Right-to-left setting is not impossible for verse, where the line endings are set by the poet, but it is awkward and quite unnecessary. Hunter and Lichtenfels make bizarre references to compositors 'measuring out' (p. 104) type when setting seriatim, where I think they must mean 'set type continuously without regard for line breaks'. They think that casting off manuscript copy means 'mentally estimating' (p. 105) how much of it will occupy each printed page, but of course Joseph Moxon's seventeenth-century manual of printing gives detailed descriptions of how it is worked out on paper. All this garbled stuff about printing is included only so that Hunter and Lichtenfels can explain (poorly) G. Blakemore Evans's speculation about why the Queen Mab speech is mislined as prose in Q2.

To explain a transition from setting speeches as prose to setting speeches as verse in Q1—and without mentioning which they think the speeches should be—Hunter and Lichtenfels suggest that perhaps a second compositor began setting the first page of sheet D before his colleague had finished setting the last page of sheet C, and hence this second compositor forced the first to compress his speeches, to set them as prose, on the last page of sheet C (pp. 120–1). It is clear that Hunter and Lichtenfels assume that page C4v was the last page of sheet C set in type and that page D1r was the first page of sheet D set in type. Even if this were the case, the compression at the bottom of C4v could be relieved by one compositor simply passing a few lines to the other. But in fact C4v was not the last page set on sheet C. Type-recurrence evidence uncovered by Frank E. Haggard in 1977 shows that C(outer), comprising C1r, C2v, C3r, and C4v, was set before C(inner), comprising C1v, C2r, C3v, and C4r. Thus pressure on C4v, noticed when it was set to a predetermined sheet-break, could have been relieved by transferring lines to its predecessors C4r and C3v that were not yet set. Also, there is no reason to think that sheet D was begun before sheet C was complete, so lines could also have been transferred forward from a tight ending of C to the beginning of D. All this does not make it impossible that C4v is crowded because the casting off was misjudged, but it takes away from the power of the mechanical explanation that Hunter and Lichtenfels offer for the setting of prose and verse on C4v and on D1r.

The remainder of the book—chapters 5 ('The Humours: Anarchy and Doubleness', pp. 133–78) and 6 ('Governance: The Law, Medicine and the Recuperation of the Social' pp. 179–212)—is outside the scope of this review. The electronic edition of the play, provided as an e-text on a disk, has a copyright date of 2007 while the printed book's is 2009. The first line of the play text is its title '*Romeo and Juliet*', for which Hunter and Lichtenfels provide the startling collation note 'TITLE] *this edn;*'. A check of their list of abbreviations confirms that they mean by '*this edn*' what we would expect: 'a reading adopted for the first time in this edition'. But of course they are not the first editors to call the play *Romeo and Juliet* and it is not clear why they think they are. The opening stage direction is '*Enter* SAMPSON *and* GREGORY, *of the house of Capulet, with swords and bucklers*' and at the back of the edition this is glossed with a Longer Note beginning 'Heavy swords and shields were the ordinary weapons of servants; gentlemen wore rapier and dagger'. These words are a direct quotation from G.L. Kittredge's 1946 edition (in the collection *Sixteen Plays*), but Hunter and Lichtenfels do not put it in quotation marks nor attribute it to him. An undergraduate who did this in an essay could escape a charge of plagiarism only by pleading guilty to the lesser charge of incompetent referencing. Hunter and Lichtenfels miss the interesting point that Charles Edelman drew attention to: wearing a sword was fairly unremarkable but nobody normally went around the streets of early modern London carrying a shield, so the stage direction indicates that the characters are either anticipating trouble or are heading for Smithfield (or rather Verona's equivalent) where fencing was practised on Sunday mornings. At I.i.74 Hunter and Lichtenfels offer the collation note 'crutch, a crutch] *F*; crowch, a crowch *Q2–4*'. Since *OED* attests that *crowch* was an ordinary sixteenth-century spelling of *crutch* there is no need for a collation note. Hunter and Lichtenfels appear to be unaware of the basics of modernization and their edition falls below the threshold for further consideration here.

Four monographs wholly relevant to this review were published in 2009, but only two will be noticed. It is regrettable that University of Delaware Press was unable to provide review copies of Adele Davidson's *Shakespeare in Shorthand: The Textual Mystery of King Lear* and Paul Menzer's *The Hamlets: Cues, Qs, and Remembered Texts*; they will be noticed next year. The third monograph is Hugh Craig and Arthur Kinney's *Shakespeare, Computers, and the Mystery of Authorship*, which offers compelling arguments for the attributions of certain works. The book's only significant flaw is that it misses an opportunity to explain to a Shakespearian audience the mathematics used in stylometry, such as Principal Component Analysis, and instead points readers to existing textbooks that few of them will understand. In the Preface and Acknowledgements (pp. xv-xix), Craig and Kinney assert that there are Shakespearian things we can measure that underlie the variations in the speeches of 'Hal, Falstaff, and Hotspur' and that can distinguish them from the characters of other dramatists (p. xvi). Brian Vickers having done the groundwork for five of Shakespeare's collaborations—presumably *Titus Andronicus*, *Timon of Athens*, *Pericles*, *Henry VIII*, and *The Two Noble Kinsmen*—this book will concentrate on *Edward III*, *Arden of Faversham*, additions to *The Spanish Tragedy*, Hand D of *Sir Thomas More*, *Edmond Ironside*, Folio *King Lear*, *1 Henry VI*, and *2 Henry VI*. The electronic texts used are transcriptions of early editions and software did the work of bundling the various spellings (such *folly/follie/folie*) under one headword (*folly*). The book is based on a corpus of 165 play e-texts created by the authors rather than on texts drawn from Literature Online. The book is here described as having 'four authors' (p. xix) and it is noticeable that the title page does not report that it is 'edited by' anyone, so although it looks like a collection of essays it is really a collaboratively authored monograph for which two of the authors are simply not mentioned on the title page.

The introduction (pp. 1–14) makes a weak start by giving a rather imprecise summary of where neuroscience stands on the individuality of language, which marvels at the combinatorial potential of millions of neurons' connections but does not indicate how they produce idiosyncratic language or personality. There is rather a lot of irrelevant writing about DNA, RNA, and protein biosynthesis. Things pick up when Craig and Kinney describe the phenomenon of the characteristic collocations of two-, three-, and four-word groups and observe that even when they are deliberately impersonating another's style, writers betray their authorship to 'tests of common words, rare words, and word pairings' (p. 9). One test alone is seldom reliable so investigators need a battery of them. Function words, that is those having a syntactical function rather than a semantic one, are most commonly counted, but they tend to fluctuate simply according to genre. Collocations—what Craig and Kinney call word-combinations—are particularly good for working up an authorial signature. Stylometrics, they observe, does not have to confine itself to authorship attribution: we can also date texts and group them according to various kinds of likeness.

In chapter 2 (pp. 15–39) Craig and Kinney describe the methods that will be used in the book's case studies. Shakespeare uses the word *gentle* nearly twice as frequently as do other dramatists of his time, in all the genres. To turn this knowledge into a test, one must divide Shakespeare's work and others' into segments of a fixed length (say 2,000 words) and compare how often a Shakespeare segment contains *gentle* with how often a non-Shakespearian segment contains *gentle*. (This technique tends to discount clusters of *gentle* since a segment is counted as a container of *gentle* whether it has one or ten uses of the word.) Likewise, Shakespeare's avoidance of *yes*, *brave*, *sure*, and *hopes*, and his liking for *answer* and *beseech* make him stand out from his fellow dramatists. Add a few hundred more marker words to this batch—some he used a lot, some he avoided—and one has a reasonable test: does the unknown passage lack the words he avoids and feature the words he likes? If so, it is by Shakespeare. If it features the words he avoids and lacks the words he likes, it is non-Shakespearian. Craig and Kinney admit that in doing their work with this kind of test they used strings rather than linguistic words, so that for example *hope* and *hopes* are counted as different things not as variant forms of one word. They explain that this is done to avoid introducing arbitrariness and inconsistency, and neglect to mention that it is also a lot of work to lemmatize a text. In any case, it is wrong to imply that lemmatizing is arbitrary or inconsistent. Fortunately, unlemmatized texts are perfectly valid for their tests so long as all the dramatists are treated equally.

An important test of a stylometrician's method is to ask whether it properly distinguishes all of Shakespeare's work from everyone else's. Craig and Kinney use 2,000-word segments from twenty-seven of his core sole-authored plays, and the question to be asked is whether the Shakespearian segment with the least number of words he favoured nonetheless has more of those words than has the non-Shakespearian segment with the greatest number of them. The question also should be asked of the words he avoided, with a view to determining the overlap between Shakespeare's usage and everyone else's. Craig and Kinney give a detailed account of how they validated their test. They took *Coriolanus* out of their core set of twenty-seven Shakespeare plays and found 500 words that appear in many of the segments from the remaining twenty-six plays and appear infrequently in the segments from the non-Shakespearian plays. Specifically, for each word they counted how many segments by Shakespeare it appeared in and divided that by how many Shakespeare segments there are, thus producing a score between 0, for words that appear in no segments, and 1 for words that appear in all segments. To this they added a score derived by counting how many non-Shakespearian segments lack the word and dividing that by how many non-Shakespearian segments there are. Thus a word with an ideal score of 2 is in every Shakespeare segment and no non-Shakespearian segment. In the event, the highest score (for *gentle*) was 1.24 and the lowest was 1.03, and Craig and Kinney simply took the words with the top 500 scores. The whole procedure was repeated in reverse to find non-Shakespearian markers.

At this point Craig and Kinney mention that they excluded function words from the segments before they started; for these they have a different procedure. For each segment of play text, Craig and Kinney counted how many Shakespeare marker words it has and divided that by total number of different words in that segment—or rather the number of strings, since they did not lemmatize—in order to show how frequently that segment uses his favourite words. They did the same for the words he avoids, and, plotting for each segment its place on a graph whose axes are 'words Shakespeare uses more than others do' and 'words others use more than Shakespeare does', the segments visibly cluster into two populations. The Shakespeare segments are all high on the 'Shakespeare likes' axis and low on the 'Shakespeare avoids' axis, and the non-Shakespearian segments are all low on the 'Shakespeare likes' axis and high on the 'Shakespeare avoids' axis. The graph shows two variables at once, and if only one had been used—either the x-axis, frequency of appearance of words Shakespeare likes, or the y-axis, frequency of appearance of words Shakespeare dislikes—the overlap would be considerable: it is the two-at-once procedure that makes the populations largely non-overlapping. Putting into the graph the *Coriolanus* segments, which played no part in setting up the test, they all appear comfortably in the Shakespeare zone so we could have assigned them to him with confidence using just this test. Doing the whole thing again for a non-Shakespearian play abstracted from the non-Shakespearian set—Thomas Middleton's *Hengist, King of Kent*—showed that all but one of its segments comfortably sit in the non-Shakespeare zone of the graph.

For a new test to combine with the existing one, Craig and Kinney take the very common function words and count their frequencies, using *Titus Andronicus*, *Timon of Athens*, *Henry VIII*, and *The Two Noble Kinsmen* as their texts because the boundaries of collaboration in them (with George Peele, Middleton, John Fletcher, and John Fletcher respectively) are well established, as are the collaborators' other plays, whereas for *Pericles* we have only one other George Wilkins play. If successful, this ought to be a rigorous test because in collaboration writers generally try to produce something self-consistent using the same materials and genre, so the ability to tell their shares apart is impressive. Craig and Kinney work with whole scenes of at least 1,500 words, of which *Titus Andronicus* has five: I.i (Peele) and II.iii, III.i, V.ii, and V.iii (all Shakespeare). Rather than use all the function words, Craig and Kinney set out to discover the ones that most distinguish Peele from Shakespeare in *Titus Andronicus* using what is known as Student's t-test. This procedure governs all the function-word tests in the book: only those words for which the authors being tested have a significant preference or dislike are used, and this set of words will obviously be different for each test; Craig and Kinney ought to have spelt that out at this point. They define the statistical concepts of mean, variance, and standard deviation, and point out that for a normal distribution (a concept they do not gloss) around two-thirds of the values will be above or below the mean by no more than the standard deviation value; that is, they will be within the first standard deviation.

Here the mathematics gets tricky. The t-value is the difference between the means for Shakespeare counts and Peele counts—how often they use a particular word in each of their segments—divided by the standard deviations for all the counts. So, a high t-value happens when the two means are far apart and the standard deviation is low, which happens when the means—the rates of usage of a particular word—for Shakespeare and Peele are markedly different but the readings for both men considered together are not terribly widely spread. If the readings were widely spread, of course, then the differences in the two men's means could be generated by chance alone. Craig and Kinney calculate the t-values for 200 function words in twenty-seven Shakespeare plays and four Peele ones, and fifty-five of them turned out to be good discriminators of the authors. In particular, *and* and *thy* are words that Peele uses a lot more than Shakespeare, and *it* and *very* ones that Shakespeare uses a lot more than Peele. At this point Craig and Kinney introduce Principal Component Analysis (PCA), but rather than explain it they point the reader to standard textbooks. However, they offer a useful analogy borrowed from a textbook: if one had a set of data that showed the height of several people and another set that showed their weight, one could derive from them a Principal Component called 'size' that combines these data for each person. This value would not capture all the detail, since some people are tall but light, others short but heavy, but it would account for most of the correlation between height and weight.

Craig and Kinney use as their PCA variables the frequencies within each play segment—the 2,000-word segments from twenty-seven Shakespeare plays, the 2,000-word segments from four Peele plays, and the five 1,500-word or more scenes from *Titus Andronicus*—of the words known to be the best discriminators of Shakespeare and Peele. On a graph where each segment's position along the x-axis is its first Principal Component score and its position on the y-axis is its second Principal Component score, the Peele and Shakespeare writings occupy fairly distinct zones, and scene I.i belongs with the other Peele writing. Craig and Kinney repeat the process—finding the most discriminating function words, then graphing the PCA results—for the bits of *Timon of Athens* by Shakespeare and Middleton. Interestingly, among the markers from Middleton is '*that* as a demonstrative' (p. 34), but Craig and Kinney do not tell the reader how the demonstrative use is distinguished from other uses, having earlier indicated that words are treated as merely strings of characters without lemmatization. Again there appear distinct zones for each author on the graph and the investigators find that the bits of *Timon of Athens* attributed to each author by other means mostly sit in their respective zones. Likewise for *Henry VIII* and *The Two Noble Kinsmen* with Fletcher. So, thus validated, Craig and Kinney have at their disposal two tests—one excluding function words and one using them—that give good but not perfect results when used with bits of plays where we know the authors. In the rest of the book the authors and their co-investigators apply these two tests to segments of plays of unknown authorship.

Chapter 3 (pp. 40–78) is by Craig alone, and concerns 'The Three Parts of *Henry VI*'. Craig acknowledges the problem that if collaborators worked together on a small unit such as a scene, or revised one another's work, the chances are they would erase the evidence of individual authorship. Craig divides the three plays into 2,000-word segments, which—because not following natural boundaries such as scene division—are likely each to contain mixed authorship. Since he does not yet know the boundaries of the collaboration, that is all he can do. Using the lexical and function-word tests described above, these segments were compared with the known Shakespeare plays, providing for each segment two measures of likeness-to-Shakespeare. Taking first just some early Shakespeare plays—*Richard III*, *Richard II*, *King John*, *The Two Gentlemen of Verona*, *The Comedy of Errors*, and *Love's Labour's Lost*—Craig plots their likeness to the rest of the securely attributed Shakespeare set, that is the twenty-seven known Shakespeare plays minus, for each test, the play being tested. This produces a graph showing where each segment from each of these six plays sits in its likeness to Shakespeare, with the score from the function-word test along the x-axis and the score from the lexical-word test along the y-axis. This graph shows that most 2,000-word segments from these plays are more like than unlike Shakespeare. The worst outlier is one segment from *Richard II*, that fails both tests (function-word and lexical-word) and there are thirteen other segments (out of fifty-eight segments in all for the six plays) that fail one or other of the tests and are falsely declared non-Shakespearian. Craig concludes that since only one segment in fifty-eight is misclassified by both tests, 'the methods are more reliably used together than separately' (p. 47).

With the tests now calibrated, Craig repeats the operation for the 2,000-word segments from *1 Henry VI*, and they turn out to be mostly—in eight of out the ten segments—to be unlike other Shakespeare writing of his early period. This suggests mixed authorship. Likewise for *2 Henry VI*, but not quite so much unlike Shakespeare; this also suggests mixed authorship. But most of *3 Henry VI* turns out to be much like Shakespeare. The part of *1 Henry VI* most like Shakespeare on these tests is IV.ii.56–IV.vii.40, including Talbot and his son dying at the siege of Bordeaux, which Edmond Malone subjectively judged to be the only Shakespearian part of the play. John Dover Wilson and Taylor also gave this part to Shakespeare, and it is the part that Nashe celebrates in *Pierce Penniless*. Other parts that score highly on these 'like Shakespeare' tests are ones that many critics have thought distinctly Shakespearian, including the Temple Garden rose-picking scene.

Instead of arbitrary 2,000-word segments, Craig decides to use the division of the play proposed by Taylor but expressed in 4,000-word segments. The outcome confirms Taylor's claim: II.iv and IV.ii–IV.vii.31 are like Shakespeare, the rest, especially the first act, are not. Taylor, like others, thought that Nashe wrote the first act of *1 Henry VI*, but unfortunately the only certain Nashe works we have to compare it with are in prose. Craig uses 4,000-word segments from Nashe's *Pierce Penniless*, *Strange News*, and *The Unfortunate Traveller* and equally sized segments from forty-nine single-authored pre-1600 plays, and applies the lexical-word test described above using the top 500 Nashe marker words and the top 500 not-Nashe marker words. The resultant graph shows two zones, and the first act of *1 Henry VI* falls in with the plays by others and far from Nashe's prose works. But it is closer to the Nashe prose works than any other bit of the play is, and tweaking the test so that the comparison is just with Shakespeare (rather than forty-nine plays by others) also shows that it is a bit nearer to Nashe than anything else Shakespeare did. 'The Nashe hypothesis survives, then' (p. 55). Contrary to Vickers's 2008 article (reviewed in *YWES* 89[2010]), Craig's test shows 'no affinities between Kyd and *1 Henry VI*' (p. 56) since there is clear separation on both dimensions of Craig's graph, although he admits that the sample of known Kyd drama is so small that the results may not be reliable. Tweaking the test to bring in *Soliman and Perseda*—accepting for the nonce the claim that it is his—and limiting the others' drama to pre-1600 work does not help: *1 Henry VI* stays firmly with the non-Kyd material.

As Craig explains, Vickers's tests worked by finding collocations that appear in the suspect text and author X's work, but not in the works by other authors, yet Vickers is not scrupulous on this last step. Craig points out that Thomas Merriam has found phrases common to *1 Henry VI* and plays in the Marlowe canon and nowhere else, but this does not necessarily prove anything: we need to know how often, in general, a phrase appears in writer X's work and in writer Y's work and in no one else's work. If that is fairly common—say there are phrases that only Shakespeare and Marlowe use—then Vickers's methodology is invalid. (The same point about Vickers's methodology is made in an article by Jackson considered below.) Merriam has shown that rates of function-word usage and collocations-in-common give reasons to suppose that Marlowe wrote the Joan of Arc parts of *1 Henry VI*. To test this, Craig pulls out the 1,803 words of *1 Henry VI* in which she appears and uses his lexical-word analysis to see where they fall in a test that separates the six reliably Marlovian plays from 130 plays by other writers. Comparing the word usage in the early, middle, and late Joan passages, Craig finds the early to be non-Marlovian and the middle and late to be Marlovian. Craig surveys the various objections that have in the past been raised against Marlowe's contributing to *1 Henry VI*, and finds them all weak. Imitation of Marlowe's style, a popular explanation, would not give false positives on the function-word tests used in this book because words used by a writer imitating Marlowe would drop out of the calculations here, since the method is to find words that Marlowe uses that others do not and vice versa. Craig does not admit it, but his method would be fooled by a writer able to imitate perfectly Marlowe's word preferences (for and against) across hundreds of words, but that is a tall order.

Craig returns to the analysis of *2 Henry VI* in 2,000-word segments using lexical words and function words in order to explore the possibility that Act III is Shakespearian but the rest of the play is not. Two of the 2,000-word segments—numbers 10 and 11 covering lines IV.iii.160 to V.i.13—turn out to be markedly Marlovian, and Craig notes that these contain Jack Cade's rebellion, which is notably detachable and out of keeping with York's description of Cade when revealing in III.i the plan to incite him. Running a battery of tests, Craig repeatedly finds that segments 10 and 11 look like Marlowe. Thus Cade and the devil-dealing Joan of Arc are Marlovian characters, both characteristically claiming high birth and dying defiantly. *2 Henry VI* also has recurrent decapitation, a characteristically Marlovian device. Comparing the Cade rebellion with the popular uprisings in *Julius Caesar*, *Coriolanus*, and *Sir Thomas More*, it is notable that the last three all are nearer to Shakespeare's norm than Marlowe's in lexical and function-word tests, whereas the Cade rebellion comes out nearer to Marlowe than Shakespeare by the same tests. It does not seem that subject matter is displacing the results. The conclusion of this chapter, then, is that *1 Henry VI* and *2 Henry VI* are collaborations.

Chapter 4 (pp. 78–99), by Kinney alone, is about *Arden of Faversham*, and after an extended discussion of past attributions, including to Shakespeare, he begins his analysis using scene boundaries to generate segments. Each he subjects to a variant of the lexical-word test of 500 words common in Shakespeare and rare outside Shakespeare in plays from 1580 to 1619, and vice versa for words others use and Shakespeare avoids. (No reason for the date limits is given.). The Shakespearian and non-Shakespearian segments form clear zones on a graph of Shakespeare-uses (x-axis) against Shakespeare-avoids (y-axis). This puts scenes 4, 5, 6, 7, 9, and 16 on the Shakespeare side and scenes 1, 2, 3, 8, 10, 11, 12, 13, 14, 15, 17, 18, and Epilogue on the non-Shakespearian side. Kinney is rightly cautious about this result as the scenes concerned are rather short. From this hint about possible division of labour, he constructs larger segments to test: 1–3 (putatively non-Shakespearian), 4–7 (putatively Shakespearian), 8–9 (a bit of both), and 10–18 (putatively non-Shakespearian). The ones that he seems to assign to the wrong side are 8 and 9, which were in any case borderline, and 16, which is short. Repeating his lexical-word test for these larger segments, 1–3 are confirmed as non-Shakespearian, 4–7 are confirmed as Shakespearian, and 8–9 and 10–18 are confirmed as non-Shakespearian. The function-word test produces the same discrimination in that scenes 4–7 look like Shakespeare, but scenes 8–9 now also look like Shakespeare.

Instead of creating a test of Shakespearian versus a non-Shakespearian group of plays to compare bits of *Arden of Faversham* with, Kinney reruns the lexical-word tests using Shakespeare-versus-Kyd—first just *The Spanish Tragedy* and *Cornelia*, then *The Spanish Tragedy*, *Cornelia*, and *Soliman and Perseda*—and then Shakespeare-versus-Marlowe. These tests put all four *Arden of Faversham* segments on the Shakespeare side of the graph, which shows not that Shakespeare wrote them but that neither Marlowe nor Kyd wrote them. Kinney repeats this procedure using function-word frequencies, which for Marlowe-versus-Shakespeare gives rather a lot of overlap because their function-word habits are similar, and into this area of overlap most of the play falls. The bit that does not, scenes 10–18, falls closer to Shakespeare than Marlowe. On function words, Kyd versus Shakespeare also has a lot of overlap, but here the segments of *Arden of Faversham* are even more distinctly not Kydian. That is, they fall into the Shakespearian zone, not because he wrote them but because they are unlike the rival candidate Kyd. Kinney does not explain why he tests each segment of *Arden of Faversham* on a

Marlowe-versus-Shakespeare spectrum and then a Kyd-versus-Shakespeare spectrum rather than testing them on a Marlowe-versus-everyone-else spectrum and then a Kyd-versus-everyone-else-spectrum. There are quite a few such questions that this book raises in the mind of the reader and does not answer. Kinney's conclusion is that, in collaboration with someone who was not Kyd or Marlowe, Shakespeare co-wrote *Arden of Faversham,* concentrating on the middle, around scenes 4–7 and maybe as far as scenes 8–9.

In chapter 5, about *Edmond Ironside* (pp. 110–15), Philip Palmer begins with a history of the play's reception, including E.B. Everitt's 1950s and Eric Sams's 1980s attributions of it to Shakespeare. Palmer tests *Edmond Ironside* against Shakespeare's plays and eighty-five other single-authored plays, using two new procedures described in chapter 7, reviewed below. (It would have been better if the tests and the methods of processing the results had all been laid out in advance, since to bring in new techniques halfway through the book, and without fully explaining them, enhances the non-specialist's sense that this work is incomprehensible computer 'magic' and raises the suspicion that the procedures were changed in the light of the intermediate outcomes.) The first new procedure is Discriminant Analysis of the frequencies of 200 function words in each 2,000-word segment under test. Palmer validates his test by taking out of the sample a play of known authorship and seeing whether the test assigns each of its 2,000-word segments to the correct author. His test was right 84 per cent of the time, which Palmer considers rather good, although it means that one time in six this test will be wrong. All seven 2,000-word segments of *Edmond Ironside* were deemed non-Shakespearian by this test. Turning to the lexical-word test that the book has already made much use of—in which the distinct Shakespearian and non-Shakespearian zones on graphs are by now familiar—all the *Edmond Ironside* segments fall on the non-Shakespearian side. So, by both tests Shakespeare is not a likely candidate.

Palmer takes the candidates Greene, John Lyly, Marlowe, and Peele, for whom substantial sole-authored play canons are already known, and for each he makes a candidate-versus-others graph—so, starting with words Greene favours more than others and words Greene neglects more than others—and plots where the *Edmond Ironside* segments fall on it. For each, *Edmond Ironside* is either firmly in the 'others' zone or in the overlap area where the zones are not distinct, so none of these four men is the author. To look beyond these four, into the authors whose known canons are small, Palmer switches methods and simply counts how many words in *Edmond Ironside* occur in other dramatists' plays, common words and proper nouns excluded. The dramatists are Lyly, Peele, Marlowe, Greene, Anthony Munday, Chettle, Thomas Lodge, Kyd, George Chapman, Nashe, and Shakespeare. Shakespeare's word usage comes out as particularly unlike that of the author of *Edmond Ironside*, but by Palmer's admission this test is not particularly convincing since Lyly comes out on top here even though the lexical-word test showed *Edmond Ironside* to be most unlike his writing. Palmer reports but does not graph his attempt at lexical-word tests for, in turn, Chapman, Thomas Heywood, Ben Jonson, and Kyd being the author of *Edmond Ironside* and in each case the play's segments fell into the 'others' category. Thus all the candidates put forward by Sams, plus some more, are eliminated as possible authors of *Edmond Ironside*. Shakespeare did not write it and we do not know who did.

Chapter 6 (pp. 116–33) is by Thomas Irish Watt and is concerned with *Edward III*. Its opening remarks are somewhat confused, beginning correctly with the Stationers' Register entry of the play on 1 December 1595 but then going on 'In 1599, Burby entered a second quarto in the Register' (p 116). Of course manuscripts, not printed books, were entered in the Stationers' Register and in any case there is no such entry in 1599. (It is bad form to give only a year for a Stationers' Register entry as the reader has to trawl the register to find it, or, as here, not find it.). This error is not a simple slip but a thorough confusion since Watt goes on to discuss these 'two entries in the Register' being 'the only evidence of performance on record' (p. 116). The Stationers' Register entry makes no reference to performance: it is the play's title page that tells us about performance 'about the Citie of London'. Further inaccuracy creeps into Watt's history of the play's reception, such as the claim that Shakespeare's fellow actors 'Heminge and Condell published the 1623 Folio' (p. 117). Something goes wrong with the referencing on page 120 as a quotation from Edmund King is supported by footnote 13 that reads '*Ibid.*, p. 9', pointing the reader back to a book by Edward Armstrong from 1946 cited in footnote 12, when in fact Watt means to point the reader back to footnote 5 where King's Master's degree dissertation is cited. Watt usefully points out that Eliot Slater's stylometric analysis of the play published in 1988 (and reissued by Cambridge University Press in 2009) uses a hopelessly flawed methodology.

Sections of the play that stand out as fairly unconnected to the rest are I.ii–II.ii, which shows Edward's failed attempt to woo the Countess of Salisbury, and III.i–IV.iii, which shows his campaign against the French; each contains around 6,500 words. Watt divides the twenty-seven single-authored Shakespeare plays into 6,000-word segments (why not 6,500?) and does the same for the eighty-five single-authored non-Shakespearian plays from 1580 to 1619. First he tries the function-word test, which does not produce highly distinguished zones on the Principal Component Analysis graph but nonetheless the I.ii–II.ii segment falls close to the Shakespearian zone and the III.i–IV.iii segment falls within the non-Shakespearian zone. Then comes this book's usual lexical-word test based on 500 words commoner in Shakespeare's segments than in the others' segments and vice versa, which for these 6,000-word segments produces a clear separation of the zones on the graph. Pleasingly, the I.ii–II.ii segment falls (just) inside the Shakespearian zone and the III.i–IV.iii segment falls (just) inside the non-Shakespearian zone. To validate this last test, Watt reruns it several times with one play removed from first the Shakespearian set and then the non-Shakespearian set, producing the new zones based on this slightly smaller dataset, and then tests the extracted play to see where the procedure would place it. Graphs show that the test consistently puts Shakespeare's *King John*, *1 Henry IV*, and *Henry V* in the Shakespearian zone and the non-Shakespearian plays *James IV*, *Edward I*, and *Edward II* in the non-Shakespearian zone.

So far Watt's tests have used plays from across several decades, and since there is evidence that dramatic language changed around 1600 he reruns all the tests with his dataset confined to pre-1600 plays. This produces zones that are a little more clearly defined for the function-word test and puts the two *Edward III* segments nearer the centre of their respective zones: I.ii–II.ii is more clearly Shakespearian, III.i–IV.iii more clearly non-Shakespearian. Under this new date restriction the lexical-word test still provides a clear separation of the zones for Shakespeare's plays and the non-Shakespearian plays, but although III.i–IV.iii falls within the non-Shakespearian zone, I.ii–II.i falls between the two zones. Replicating what Palmer did for *Edmond Ironside*, Watt tries one more test and simply counts how often the words in the *Edward III* segments appear in the segments by Shakespeare and the segments by each of fifteen other dramatists for whom we have two or more plays, but excluding common words, meaning those that appear in more than 40 per cent of the segments. This test shows that the unusual words in *Edward III* I.ii–II.i are words that appear more often in Shakespeare's plays than in anybody else's—as we would expect if he wrote this segment—and that the unusual words in *Edward III*, III.i–IV.iii are ones not favoured by Shakespeare but favoured by Marlowe (most strongly of all), then Peele, then Kyd. This gives Watt three new candidates for authorship of *Edward III* III.i–IV.iii, so he reruns his lexical-word tests, but rather than sorting the segments into two heaps of Shakespeare-versus-the-rest he uses Marlowe-versus-the-rest, Peele-versus-the-rest, and then Kyd-versus-the-rest. In all the tests, I.ii–II.i and III.i–IV.iii of *Edward III* fall into the zones of 'the rest' rather than Marlowe, or Peele, or Kyd. Watt's conclusion, then, is that Shakespeare wrote section I.ii-II.i of *Edward III* and not section III.i–IV.iii, whose author is unknown but is not Marlowe, Peele, or Kyd. (Actually, Watt does not make that last point explicitly but it must be the reasonable conclusion from his work since if he trusts his lexical-word tests in one part of his argument he must trust them throughout.)

Watt also wrote chapter 7, on *Sir Thomas More* (pp. 134–61), of which the Hand D section plus Addition III—More's soliloquy beginning 'It is in heaven that I am thus and thus'—add up to 1,214 words. Watt performs the book's standard lexical-word test by dividing twenty-seven Shakespeare plays and eighty-five non-Shakespeare plays into 1,200-word segments and finding the top 500 words used more by Shakespeare than by the others and the 500 words used less by Shakespeare than by the others. For each segment he plots the frequency with which it uses each of the words Shakespeare favoured and those he disliked, and the graph shows two fairly clear zones formed by the Shakespeare segments and the non-Shakespeare segments, with a little overlap. 'Hand D + Addition III' sits centrally within the Shakespeare zone. To validate the test, Watt takes one play at a time out of the procedure—in turn, Thomas Dekker's *The Shoemaker's Holiday*, Heywood's *If You Know Not Me*, Jonson's *Volpone*, Middleton's *The Phoenix*, Shakespeare's *Hamlet*, and John Webster's *The Duchess of Malfi*—recalculates the zones, and then checks where the removed play's segments fall on the graph: 90 per cent of the segments are correctly identified as Shakespearian or non-Shakespearian.

Watt then reruns the lexical-word test using not 1,200-word segments but the whole of each play, and this gives much better separation of the zones because in bigger samples the local variations cancel one another out. Here 'Hand D + Addition III' is much nearer the centre of the Shakespeare zone than the centre of the non-Shakespeare zone. Watt changes the comparison so that rather than Shakespeare-versus-others it is Dekker-versus-others, and this time 'Hand D + Addition III' is much closer to the others than to Dekker, so he did not write it. Repeating this procedure for each of them in turn, Watt establishes that it was not written by Heywood, Jonson, Middleton, or Webster. In function-word tests the 1,200-word segments are just too small for meaningful Principal Component Analysis, so Watt switches to Linear Discriminant Analysis, for the classificatory power of which he gives a short and not terribly helpful explanation in discursive prose. His explanation uses no analogies and the description is highly abstract, as for example when he explains the danger of over-training the test so that 'it struggles with new instances from the same class' (p. 153). The reader is left wondering what it can mean for a test to struggle.

Using the validation method he previously used for the lexical-word test, Watt counts the frequencies of the top 100 most author-specific function words in the set of 1,200-word segments from Shakespeare's *Hamlet* (called Group One) and, in turn, the sets of 1,200-word segments from each of Dekker's *The Shoemaker's Holiday*, Heywood's *If You Know Not Me*, Jonson's *Volpone*, Middleton's *The Phoenix*, Shakespeare's *Hamlet*, and Webster's *The Duchess of Malfi* (each called, in turn, Group Two) and uses Linear Discriminant Analysis to say whether the 1,200-word segment from 'Hand D + Addition III' belongs in Group One or Group Two. In every case the test shows that 'Hand D + Addition III' belongs in Group One, meaning it is Shakespearian. However, this test also wrongly indicates that two-thirds of *A Shoemaker's Holiday* were not written by Dekker. Rather than abandon the test, Watt decides that the validation 'underestimates the power of the method' (p. 153), which seems an odd way to describe a failure.

As a final test, Watt discards proper nouns, function words, numbers, and 'imprecations' from 'Hand D + Addition III', and then searches among the remaining words for those that appear in no more than 40 percent of the project's collection of 136 single-authored plays. There is an ambiguity here: did Watt look for words that appear in no more than fifty-four of the plays (40 per cent of 136) or in no more than 40 per cent of the 1,200-word segments from all the plays? Watt looks for these relatively rare words in plays from 1580 to 1619, and finds the highest set of matches with *Othello*, even after adjusting for the differing lengths of different dramatists' plays, since a long play has a better chance of matching with the rare-word set than a short one. Moreover of the top ten plays when listed in order of how many times they use these rare words, seven are by Shakespeare. Watt rather long-windedly (and confusingly) explains how he adjusted for the different sizes of the canons: how he 'correlated' (an ambiguous word in this context) the scores with the number of plays by each dramatist. After this adjustment, Shakespeare was still the front-runner for rare-word links with 'Hand D + Addition III'. Watt then runs the test in reverse, looking for the relatively rare words absent from

'Hand D + Addition III'. Here we would expect Shakespeare to be the lowest scorer if he were the author of 'Hand D + Addition III', and in the event he is the second lowest, with Jonson as the lowest, which shows that Jonson generally avoids the words that 'Hand D + Addition III' avoids.

Thus we can be reasonably sure that 'Hand D + Addition III' is by Shakespeare. To date the writing, Watt divides the 1,200-word Shakespeare play segments into two classes: up to 1599, and 1600 onwards, and repeats his tests but treating these two sets as though they were the work of different dramatists. In the lexical-word tests the two classes form fairly distinct zones on the graph, and 'Hand D + Addition III' sits on the edge of the 1600 onwards zone. How come, Watt then asks, 'Hand D + Addition III' fails two of Ward E.Y. Elliott and Robert J. Valenza's tests for Shakespearian authorship? As Jackson pointed out, Elliott and Valenza's test using word and sentence length can be thrown off by a manuscript source, and their function-word test used samples of writing that were just too small: they compared only the words common in *Macbeth* and uncommon in Middleton's *The Witch*, and vice versa, to create their list of Shakespeare-favours and Shakespeare-neglects markers. Watt reruns Elliott and Valenza's function-word test with certain modifications whose effects are hard to predict, such as including prose as well as verse, and finds that 'Hand D + Addition III' no longer fails it. Watt's conclusion is that, as other studies have shown, Shakespeare composed the 'Hand D + Addition III' material after 1600, and since it seems not to be scribal he presumably did the handwriting of Hand D too.

Chapter 8 (pp. 162–80), by Craig, is about the additions to Kyd's *The Spanish Tragedy* that first appeared in the 1602 edition. Addition One is fifty-four lines, Addition Two is ten lines (replacing two lines), Addition Three is forty-eight lines, Addition Four is 169 lines, and Addition Five is forty-eight lines incorporating some existing lines. We do not know who wrote them, but Philip Henslowe's Diary records two payments to Jonson for making additions to the play, on 25 September 1601 and 22 June 1602. However, Addition Four is parodied in John Marston's *Antonio and Mellida*, written in 1599, so presumably it was already in performance then and hence cannot be what Jonson was paid for in 1601–2. Jonson's own *Cynthia's Revels* (first performed 1600) also implicitly alludes to revision in *The Spanish Tragedy* by referring to 'the old Hieronymo (as it was first acted)', again before Jonson was paid by Henslowe. *The Spanish Tragedy* is recorded by Henslowe as 'ne[w]' in 1597, so maybe the additions that appeared in the 1602 edition were already written by 1597 and Jonson's additions were something else now lost.

Craig decides to use Jackson's method of looking for collocations in Literature Online (LION), but for an unexplained reason he uses Chadwyck-Healey's Verse Drama CD-ROM, part of the original basis for LION, rather than LION itself. This is bound to skew the results by disregarding all prose drama. At page 170, n. 41, Craig admits to missing the word *unsquared* in Marston's *What You Will* because it is not in the Verse Drama CD-ROM, but he caught it because *OED* mentions it. How many others did he miss because *OED* does not mention them? This is poor methodology. Craig starts with the additions' phrases that Warren Stevenson decided were rare when arguing for Shakespeare's authorship. Some of the phrases turn out to be so common as to be useless, but the collocation *things/called/whips* occurs only in *2 Henry VI* and Addition Three, *pry/crevice/wall* only in *Titus Andronicus* and Addition Four, *hand/lean/head* only in *The Rape of Lucrece* and Addition Four, and *brow/jutty* only in *Henry V* and Addition Four. Other collocations might, however, be conscious reworkings of famous lines from other plays (as with Pistol's speeches in *2 Henry IV*), and Craig mentions other of the additions' links with Shakespeare that are not unique but rather rare. Having dealt with the rare words/phrases that Stevenson found, Craig finds his own: 'as massy as' occurs only in *Much Ado About Nothing* and Addition Four, [*un*]*delve/mine* only in *Hamlet* and Addition Four, and there is one further rare but not unique link.

Then comes a fresh approach. Craig takes 136 confidently sole-authored plays from 1576 to 1642 by thirty-five dramatists, and to match the 2,663 words in the additions he divides these plays into 2,500-word segments. The first test is of frequencies of function words and Discriminant Analysis is able to assign segments to their correct authors for 98.9 per cent of the segments. The procedure is not clearly described here, and at one point it is implied that the classification into author groups was made by hand for the software to work on: 'Each author's segments were assigned to a group . . .' (p. 172). But this would render meaningless the claim that nearly all the segments 'were assigned to the correct author' by the software (p. 172). The Discriminant Analysis is then asked to assign the additions to an author group, and it chooses Shakespeare. To validate the test Craig takes all the segments for one play at a time out of the dataset, reruns the test, and then asks the Discriminant Analysis to assign these (known-author) play segments to one of the thirty-five authors: 93 per cent of the Shakespeare segments are correctly identified as being by Shakespeare (so 7 per cent of them are wrongly ascribed to someone else) and 86 per cent of the non-Shakespearian segments are correctly identified as not being by Shakespeare (so 14 per cent of them are wrongly ascribed to Shakespeare). Craig seems to think that these are good results, but it means that about one time in seven the test will say something is by Shakespeare when it is not.

Next comes the by now familiar turn to the lexical-word tests. Since critics have settled on four frontrunner candidates for the author of the additions—Jonson, Shakespeare, Dekker, and Webster—Craig puts them head to head, starting with Shakespeare-versus-Jonson and using 2,500-word segments. On a graph whose x-axis shows the segment's use of words Shakespeare favours and Jonson neglects and whose y-axis shows the segment's use of words Jonson favours and Shakespeare neglects, the segments fall into two distinct zones, one for each author. The additions are well within the Shakespeare zone. Doing the same test for Shakespeare-versus-Dekker also produces well-defined zones, and although this time the additions are not within the Shakespeare zone they are a lot nearer to its centre than they are to Dekker's zone's centre. Shakespeare-versus-Webster has well-defined zones, and the additions fall on the edge of the Shakespeare zone, a long way from the Webster zone. And so on for Lyly, Marlowe, Greene, Peele, Heywood, Fletcher, and Middleton: on this test (that is, each man versus Shakespeare) the additions always come out nearer the Shakespeare centre than the rival's centre. Craig tries just testing Addition Four, comprising nearly 1,500 words, but when the test is validated—by taking away a segment, recalculating the zones, and then seeing where this isolated segment falls on the new graph—a lot of the segments are wrongly attributed, so he has little faith in this test. Craig admits that when he ran the kind of test used in previous chapters, a lexical-word test of Shakespeare-versus-all-the-others-at-once, the additions came out as being not by Shakespeare, but mentions that when he confined this test to plays first performed up to 1602 they came out as Shakespeare again. His conclusion is that the additions to *The Spanish Tragedy* are most probably by Shakespeare, and if not by him then Jonson is a particularly unlikely alternative.

The final chapter, by Kinney, is concerned with the revision of Shakespeare's *King Lear* (pp. 181–201). Without explanation, Kinney gives the date of publication of Q1 *King Lear* as 1607–8. Blayney reckons printing started in the middle of December 1607 and was finished in the middle of January 1608, and all surviving exemplars are dated 1608, so it is not clear what Kinney means by his date of 1607–8. Kinney gives an extended account of the textual condition of Q1 and Folio *King Lear*, the former lacking 100 lines that are in the latter and the latter lacking 300 lines that are in the former, with 1,000 words variant, and he gives a history of the explanations for these differences. Kinney wrongly credits the collaboratively written *Textual Companion* to the *Oxford Complete Works* for explaining how F came to have press-variant errors from Q1 despite being set from Q2 in which those errors do not appear. The credit rightly belongs to Taylor alone, appearing in his contribution to the collection called *The Division of the Kingdoms* [1983]. Another curiosity is a garbled sentence about 'leaves written in the margins of pages of the original manuscript' (p. 185), which I can make no sense of. Kinney also makes the common error of referring to a 'heath' (p. 189) in *King Lear* although the word appears nowhere in the play.

Q and F show small differences that seem to reflect a consistent set of changes: *which* becomes *that*, *doth* becomes *does*, *these* becomes *this/those*, and *thine* becomes *thy*. While Kinney is right that random corruption cannot do this, he is wrong to imply that the only alternative is artistic revision since scribes also imposed their preferences to this extent. Kinney offers bar charts about uses of *which*, *doth*, *these*, and *thine*, but it is not at all clear how they relate to his claim of substitution of one word in Q with another in F, since the charts show only proportions and ratios of these words in each act. There are passages amounting to 902 words present in F and absent from Q, so using this book's function-word test Kinney pitches Shakespeare against Fletcher using 900-word segments from their reliably sole-authored works. The resulting graph shows reasonably distinct zones, with the F-only passages of *King Lear* falling squarely in the Shakespeare zone. Using the same segments, Kinney performs the lexical-word test and again produces distinct zones, but this time the F-only passages of *King Lear* fall on the border of the Shakespeare zone, just where it meets the Fletcher zone. According to Kinney these two tests rule out Fletcher as a candidate for composition of the F-only passages of *King Lear*.

Kinney repeats the test by pitching Shakespeare against, in turn, Chapman, Jonson, Philip Massinger, Middleton, and Webster. Rather than give the graphs, Kinney uses a table that summarizes the 'distance' that the F-only passages lie from the centres of the two zones. (There is a linguistic slip here: the final column of the table is supposed to show the 'difference between' numbers in two preceding columns, but this final column's numbers are themselves all negative; by definition a difference cannot be negative.) It is clear from this table that the author zones for these comparisons are not so clearly defined as in previous tests, yet in every case the F-only *King Lear* passages are nearer the centre of the Shakespeare zone than the centre of the other author's zone. The chapter's conclusion is that Shakespeare was the reviser of *King Lear*. The book ends with a general conclusion by Kinney: Shakespeare collaborated more than we used to think and we must add *2 Henry VI*, *Arden of Faversham*, and *The Spanish Tragedy* to the previously known list of *1 Henry VI*, *Edward III*, *Sir Thomas More*, *Titus Andronicus*, *Timon of Athens*, *Henry VIII*, *The Two Noble Kinsmen*, *Pericles*, and (posthumously) *Macbeth* and *Measure for Measure*. One of his collaborators, on *1 Henry VI*, was Marlowe. Notwithstanding this reviewer's objections in passing, this book is a most impressive achievement of scrupulous scholarship whose conclusions represent the current state of knowledge.

The fourth and last of this year's monographs is Lukas Erne's *Shakespeare's Modern Collaborators*, which argues that the editing of Shakespeare is necessary and enabling. In his introduction (pp. 1–11), Erne explains why unediting is impossible and why we need to improve on previous editing, not abandon it. The uneditors' argument that we should return to the early editions overlooks the fact that we cannot apprehend them as their first readers did since 'What was modern spelling for Shakespeare's contemporaries seems unfamiliar to us' (p. 6). Erne does not mention it, but this is essentially the problem faced by investigators of original staging: we cannot become the early modern audience who saw doublet and hose as modern dress. The problems have the same solution: we can somewhat train ourselves to think like them. Chapter 1, on 'Establishing the Text' (pp. 13–42), is concerned with the necessity of modernizing spelling and punctuation, and the dangers of emendation, including of lineation. Margreta de Grazia and Peter Stallybrass pointed out that returning to the early texts' fruitfully ambiguous spellings does not really restore the ambiguities that early moderns enjoyed because modern readers have internalized the distinctions: we cannot hear both *human* and *humane* in the early modern spelling *humane*. (I am not sure this is true: surely Erne would be unable to make this point, would be incomprehensible, if we had entirely lost the capacity to hear both senses.) Erne makes the surprising assertion that 'none of Shakespeare's playbooks published during his lifetime contained any act or scene divisions' (p. 35). In his edition of *Romeo and Juliet* for the New Cambridge Shakespeare Early Quartos series, Erne pointed out that the 1597 quarto has decorative bars 'inserted between scenes or scenic movements' (p. 39), and it is not clear what has changed his mind about this.

Chapter 2, on 'Framing the Text' (pp. 42–58), discusses editorial provision of collations and introductions, but largely neglects the problems of providing explanatory notes. Erne offers an interesting discussion of the rethinking of the plays' order of composition that must have occurred between publication of the *Oxford Complete Works*' first edition in 1986 and the second edition of 2005, the latter shuffling a handful of plays to new positions. In fact, the years of composition assigned by the *Oxford Complete Works* editors did not change much, but rather where a single year contained more than one play they rethought the order within that year. Discussion of chronology in the edition's *Textual Companion* indicates that they were seldom confident about precedence within a single year. Only once did they shift a play by more than one year, with *All's Well that Ends Well* moving from 1604–5 (in the 1986 first edition) to 1606–7 (in the 2005 second edition). In Chapter 3, on 'Editing Stage Action' (pp. 59–85), Erne gives examples of indeterminate and absent, yet necessary, stage directions in the early editions, and surveys the arguments—by, amongst others, Stanley Wells, M.J. Kidnie, A.R. Braunmuller, and John D. Cox—over the extent to which an editor should intervene to resolve ambiguities. He finds Wells mistaken in asserting that editors should undoubtedly help readers to imagine the original performances. Why not, Erne asks, help readers to imagine the action in its fictional locations, and so respect the differences between a book and a performance? He acknowledges that early editions' stage directions refer explicitly to doors even where there should be none (as in a forest) and to things happening on 'the stage'; that is, they refer to the theatre fabric rather than the fictional locations. But they also refer, he points out, to fictional places such as 'the walls' of a city, 'a window', 'the grave', 'the cave', and so on. It would be reasonable, he decides, for an editor expanding the stage directions of her play to include fictional rather than theatrical ones.

Almost all of the first half of Erne's final chapter, on 'Editing the Real *Lear*' (pp. 87–102), is about how the play ends differently in Q1 and F, and the second half is concerned with the ways in which editions have chosen to respond to the Q/F differences. He makes the valid point that the editors of the *Oxford Complete Works* of 1986 claimed, shortly after its publication, that they regretted not splitting *Hamlet* as they had split *King Lear*, and yet they did not do so when they had the chance in the second edition of 2005, which added *Edward III* to the canon and represented all of *Sir Thomas More* where formerly they gave only Shakespeare's contributions. In fairness, we should remember that their hands might have been tied, since the publisher could likely countenance the extra expense of adding two new plays to the edition because it enhanced the book's attractiveness to readers, while splitting *Hamlet* would likely be perceived as harming its appeal. In his conclusion (pp. 103–4) Erne looks forward to more editions produced along fresh editorial lines, and in particular the splitting of not only *King Lear* and *Hamlet* but also *Othello*, *Troilus and Cressida*, *2 Henry IV*, *Henry V*, and *Romeo and Juliet*.

Two monographs published in 2009 had individual chapters that fall within this review's purview. The first 140 pages of Margaret Jane Kidnie's *Shakespeare and the Problem of Adaptation* are about various theatre and screen adaptations of Shakespeare. Kidnie describes the invitation of the BBC (the United Kingdom's state-run television broadcaster) that viewers 'press the red button' on their handsets in order to enter into an interactive relationship with broadcasts such as adaptations of Shakespeare. As Kidnie rightly points out, 'For those with analogue television, the invitation to press a non-existent red button on their remote controls seemed to summon up the promise of another world as inaccessible to their eyes as the fairy world of *Dream* is to the eyes of the young lovers' (p. 128). In fact this was not the only disappointment the invitation generated. Thousands of complaints were received from viewers who reported that pressing the red button made their television sets stop working altogether: on older television handsets the power button is red.

The last of Kidnie's chapters is on 'Textual Origins' (pp. 140–64) and begins with a sketch of the present textual situation of Shakespeare, with some editors constructing elaborate hypotheses about what happened to a play before it got printed—Taylor and Jowett on *Measure for Measure* is her archetype—and others trying to avoid doing that. She describes the New Folger Library Shakespeare editions edited by Barbara Mowat and Paul Werstine as ones that chose 'not to write or otherwise rely on textual histories that seek to recover from early printed texts, manuscript authorities' (p. 155), and approves of 'Mowat's and Werstine's refusal to make editorial choices on the basis of what one believes can be said about the manuscript(s) that provided copy for an extant printed text' (p. 156). Yet, as Kidnie acknowledges, the choice to base a New Folger Library Shakespeare on a substantive early edition (rather than a derivative one) indicates that Mowat and Werstine must have some sense of the *work* as distinct from its manifestation in particular *documents*, since they treat the early documents as not all equal. What else could they be measuring them against except some notion of the disembodied *work*? Actually, Mowat and Werstine's position is even more incoherent than that, since by their definition a substantive edition is one printed from a manuscript rather than an existing book. Contrary to their protestations of having nothing to do with the editorial divination of underlying manuscript copy, they engage in it at least as far as the determination that the copy *was* manuscript rather than print.

Kidnie concludes with the presentist observation that all editions serve the market for which they are created and are products of their times. Editions 'are not authoritative in and of themselves, but have authority conferred on them through reference to certain culturally accepted criteria' (p. 162), and hence we are free to do what we like in editing. We can, if we choose, 'release editorial practice from imperatives to represent in new editions of the works reconstructions of the past' (p. 164) and instead promote 'culturally engaged editorial practices'. Let us not, Kidnie argues, be driven just by a historicist impulse to be faithful to the past. Her closing sentence sums up what she sees as the new possibilities. 'In short, to resist the dominant inclination to regard past histories as foundational to editorial labour would be to insist on the realization that textual, no less than theatrical, efforts to recover "what happened" can only be pursued alongside efforts to shape "what is happening" in terms of work recognition and the ever-shifting boundaries that separate work from adaptation' (p. 164). What has dropped out of the equation here is the editorial duty to represent the author's intentions, and

Kidnie's whole book is an argument that we should not worry too much about that. Such an argument cuts both ways, since any writer who feels free to ignore another writer's intentions can hardly complain if her own receive the same treatment. If I have misrepresented Kidnie's thinking, her own logic would deny her grounds to object.

The first 130 pages of Paul Eggert's *Securing the Past: Conservation in Art, Architecture and Literature* are about historic buildings and paintings and so not relevant here. Chapter 7 (pp. 131–53) is called 'Materialist, Performance or Literary Shakespeare?' and considers Erne's recent arguments (reviewed in *YWES* 83[2004] and 84[2005], covering work published in 2002 and 2003) that Shakespeare wrote for a market of readers as well as for the stage. We already knew from reader-response theory that reading is a kind of performance in the head—novels are not quite so unlike plays—so why, asks Eggert, should Erne's ideas so greatly surprise us? Eggert thinks that the *Oxford Complete Works*' two *King Lear*s came about partly through the success of post-structuralist thinking. (I would have said they came out of a purely empiricist approach and happened to arrive by a circuitous route at a destination to which post-structuralism took a short cut.) Eggert conflates the move to stage-centredness with the post-structuralist turn, and critiques the materialist Shakespeare movement. In it he perceives evasive uses of the word *text* to sometimes mean the mental object, sometimes the physical object, and sometimes both, and he decries the movement's futile attempts to magic away agency. 'Objects *point* [at someone]' (p. 146), he writes. Eggert's own solution to the quandaries arising from Erne's work is that we should edit separately for the performer and the reader. For the former, the editor's model of agency would include all those involved in the original performances, and all that they acted would be included and what they cut would be excluded. In editions for readers, on the other hand, all that got written by Shakespeare (but no one else) would be included.

At least two, and possibly three, essays from book-format collections were relevant this year, but only two will be noticed. The University of Virginia Press was unable to supply a review copy of Stephen Burt and Nick Halpern's collection *Something Understood: Essays and Poetry for Helen Vendler*, which contains William Flesch's essay 'The Bounds of the Incidental: Shakespeare's View of Accuracy'; it will be noticed next year if it turns out to be relevant. In the first of the two essays that could be examined, Richard Dutton's '*The Famous Victories* and the 1600 Quarto of *Henry V*' (in Ostovich et al., eds., *Locating the Queen's Men, 1583–1603: Material Practices and Conditions of Playing* (pp. 133–144)), the author argues that the 1600 quarto of *Henry V* is not a cut-down version of the play better seen in the Folio, but rather is a version first performed in the late 1590s. Dutton first made this argument, from different evidence, in an article reviewed in *YWES* 86[2007], covering work published in 2005. Here he explores the play's debt to *The Famous Victories of Henry the Fifth* (published 1598), which is extensive in the quarto. None of the Folio *Henry V* material that is absent from the quarto draws on *Famous Victories*, and hence, unless the process that cut down the manuscript underlying the Folio text to make the manuscript underlying the quarto managed somehow to cut only material not in *Famous Victories*, we have to conclude that, as Dutton maintains, the situation was reversed. That is, the manuscript underlying the quarto (indebted to *Famous Victories*) must have been enlarged to make the manuscript underlying the Folio, and by addition of material not indebted to *Famous Victories*. Dutton addresses James Bednarz's argument (reviewed in *YWES* 87[2008], covering work published in 2006) that the *Henry V* Chorus's reference to conveying the audience across the English Channel is mocked in Jonson's *Every Man Out of His Humour* (first performed 1599) and hence was in the original performances of *Henry V*. Dutton considers the verbal and conceptual link between *Henry V* and *Every Man Out of His Humour* to be tenuous in the latter's quartos of 1600, becoming real mockery only in the 1616 Folio version, which reflects extensive authorial revision.

The authorial revision of the quarto version of *Henry V* to make the Folio version Dutton dates to 1602. Q makes no mention of Ireland, F makes several, and in 1602 Ireland was safely back under English control. Dutton details just how closely the quarto follows, action by action, the events in scenes 9–20 of *Famous Victories*, and there are a number of close verbal parallels. A particularly telling point is that, compared to the quarto, 'F loses Clarence and Warwick, replacing them with the earls of Westmorland, Salisbury and Shrewsbury (Talbot), seemingly concentrating on warriors already made famous in *1 Henry VI*—possibly anticipating the Epilogue's reminder of what would follow from all this' (p. 140, n. 16). Dutton accepts Scott McMillin and Sally-Beth MacLean's theory that the text for *Famous Victories* came from a good, non-piratical, memorial reconstruction by the actors dictating their lines to a rather inaccurate scribe. This they did to produce a script of a revised version of the play, cut for fewer actors, and of course Andrew Gurr also claims aural transmission for quarto *Henry V*. There are some tangles in *Henry V* that might be explained by the existence of a now lost even earlier version of the play in which Falstaff is alive, since in the play that we have Pistol seems married to Doll Tearsheet (Falstaff's whore) and describes himself as old, a word more suitable in Falstaff's mouth. Revision to remove Falstaff from such a lost early version of *Henry V*, in order to make the play we have in Q, might have occasioned collective dictation to a scribe.

Famous Victories was published in 1598, having been entered in the Stationers' Register on 14 May 1594, presumably because the international situation near the end of the century was much like the situation just before the Armada of 1588, when *Famous Victories* was first performed as a patriotic confidence booster. An uncomplicatedly patriotic *Henry V*, as we find in the 1600 quarto, would be an appropriate response by Shakespeare to such a situation a decade later. That *Famous Victories* and *Henry V* were felt to be competitive texts would explain why Thomas Creede, who had the rights to the former, printed the latter: he compelled *Henry V*'s owners, Thomas Millington and John Busby, to pay him to print *Henry V* because he had the rights to all stories about Prince Hal making good and conquering France. This might also explain why *Henry V* was printed in 1600 (and indeed twice reprinted, 1602 and 1619) without Shakespeare's name on the title page: Creede was marking that Shakespeare did not really deserve credit for the story. Dutton does not directly address the problem of the Bishop's speech being mangled in the 1600 quarto so that he refers to 'King *Pippins* title' and 'King *Charles* his satisfaction' (A2v) having not spoken the Folio-only lines that ought to precede these allusions in order for them to make sense. Part of the traditional argument for Q representing a cut-down version of the play underlying F is that no one intentionally writes meaningless snippets of an allusion, so MSQ > MSF makes no sense while MSF > MSQ is perfectly plausible as botched reduction. However, this evidence could also be accommodated within the aural theory of transmission that Dutton accepts: the antecedents were dropped by the actor forgetting his lines or the scribe failing to capture them.

The other book chapter of certain relevance this year is Margreta de Grazia's argument that John Benson's 1640 edition of Shakespeare's *Poems* is not as bad as is frequently claimed: 'The First Reader of *Shake-speares Sonnets*' (in Barkan et al., eds., *The Forms of Renaissance Thought: New Essays in Literature and Culture*, pp. 86–106). De Grazia sees it as not so much a pirating of the 1609 *Sonnets* as a reading of it, and modelled on the Folio albeit in octavo format. Putting into his collection the non-Shakespearian matter that appeared under Shakespeare's name in the 1612 edition of *The Passionate Pilgrim*, Benson was simply misled by its title page rather than wilfully dishonest. De Grazia insists that the 1640 book is not an edition of *Sonnets* because 'In order to have an edition, an editor is needed' (p. 89). She seems aware that this is not the usual meaning of the word edition but she does not retract the claim. The reason Benson's edition was not a piracy is that the rights to *Sonnets* seem to have been worthless: no one had reprinted it in thirty years, and by 1640 the sonnet form was well out of date. Benson's bundling of *Sonnets* with poems from *The Passionate Pilgrim* and his giving them titles were attempts to demystify and organize the miscellany. Stanley Wells and Paul Edmondson have a low opinion of Benson, but their grouping of the sonnets in a monograph published in 2004 matches Benson's in a number of ways. Giving the sonnets descriptive titles was nothing new: manuscript copyists, and owners, did that all the time, and like Benson they assumed a heterosexual norm. Also, Benson's titles are, according to De Grazia, pretty good. Readers in any case knew such titles to be provisional, and sometimes crossed them out and wrote in their own. The reproduction sonnets are heavily indebted to Erasmus's epistle on marriage, and there is a kind of self-conscious invitation to textual reproduction in Shakespeare making his verse so easy to quote in a commonplace book, as indeed happened. Contrary to the impression created by the Variorum editor Hyder Edward Rollins, Benson was a responsible man who published other poetry and was perhaps the first to introduce the innovation of numbering lines in vernacular works, as if they were classics. He also introduced emendations to the sonnets that we still use. We used to think that Thomas Thorpe himself, publisher of the 1609 *Sonnets*, was a rogue. But whether or not he had Shakespeare's permission to print the book, he presumably was responsible for its structure, which we now admire.

Of the journal articles this year, much the most surprising title was Paul Werstine's 'The Continuing Importance of New Bibliographical Method' (*ShS* 62[2009] 30–45). Werstine argues that Greg's characterization of dramatists' authorial foul papers as necessarily messy came largely from his misinterpretation of the evidence of scribe Edward Knight's transcript of Fletcher's play *Bonduca*. Greg thought that this transcript differs from the text of the play printed in the 1647 Beaumont and Fletcher Folio wherever Knight could not read the foul papers (because they were messy), but in fact, Werstine proves, Knight was inclined to capricious departures from his source, exacerbated in this case by a desire to avoid making corrections in what was to be a presentation copy. Greg somehow failed to follow his own New Bibliographical procedures in studying *Bonduca*.

In his undated transcript, Knight uses the term 'fowle papers' to describe what he was copying and explains why some scenes in the fifth act were 'wanting'; presumably he recalled seeing them performed, else how would he know they were missing? In an essay not published until 1990, Greg explored what Knight meant by foul papers by studying the variants between the manuscript and the Folio, which latter has the missing scenes. Greg found twenty-two gaps in the manuscript where Knight left a space and F has meaningful words or phrases, and he diagnosed Knight's inability to read the foul paper and his scrupulous avoidance of misreading. Thus according to Greg, Knight's transcript was the best copy that could be made of the foul papers. Greg had already decided that the missing scenes were contained on two folded sheets (eight pages) of the foul papers that became detached from the rest before Knight made his transcript, and noticed that in the transcript some lines or part-lines were displaced from the F location, frequently to the damage of metre. This Greg attributed to the lines being additions to the foul papers that were awkwardly placed and so misled Knight about where they belonged, which led Greg to his idea that foul papers were the dramatist's final draft, too untidy to be used to run a play. Greg thought that in copying out his own foul papers to make the basis for the promptbook, Fletcher introduced a final layer of revision detectable in the transcript/F variants, and so Greg anticipated Honigmann's *The Stability of Shakespeare's Text*.

For his Malone Society reprint of *Bonduca* Greg changed his mind and reattributed a number of transcript/F variants—differences of wording and of placing of lines—to failures by Knight to read the foul papers correctly rather than authorial revision. What Greg should have noticed, Werstine argues, is that the Knight transcript is not obviously 'wanting' anything at all and indeed is more coherent than the version of the play in F. The additional two-and-a-half scenes in F that come before the ending—as it appears in the transcript and in F—make that ending nonsensical because two characters who are supposed to be pinned down in a cave are, in the first of these additions, seen to leave it. Thus the additions are not by Fletcher, who would hardly butcher his own play's logic. Someone other than Fletcher was able to copy the author's foul papers, add the additional material, and so make the book that Knight calls the one 'where by it was first Acted from', which supplied copy for the Folio. Greg must have been wrong to think that the author's foul papers were illegible to anyone but the author, and Werstine proposes that in fact 'foul papers' meant simply any document from which a fair copy was made.

His transcript of Nathan Field, Massinger, and Fletcher's *The Honest Man's Fortune* (for which we also have the Folio text) shows that Knight was prone to eye-skip that made him miss out whole lines. When he realized what he had done he corrected his writing with crossings out and insertions, but because his *Bonduca* transcript was to be a presentation copy to an important person Knight was much less keen to make visible corrections. When he realized that eye-skip had made him miss out whole lines, he crossed nothing out but simply inserted the omitted lines further down the same page, at the point where he realized his error. This, and not the difficulty of his copy as Greg maintained, is the reason for transposed lines in the *Bonduca* transcript. Also, we know from his work on *The Honest Man's Fortune* that Knight was capable of dropping whole lines even where there is no reason for eye-skip. Perhaps, reasons Werstine, Knight's gaps in the transcript do show that where he could not read Fletcher's foul papers he left a space to be filled later, but in some cases it is clear that he later filled such spaces with words of his own invention. At this point something goes wrong in the typesetting of Werstine's article, where it reads 'It is clear that the last word "troopes" has been written in later—first, because it angles up toward the right, while the other words in the line tend to angle down, and, second, because the initial t of "troopes" is italic, unlike the secretary 's found earlier in the line in "the" and "through"' (p. 40). There is no secretary 's in the words *the* and *through*, and Werstine confirms in private communication that a symbol in his typescript representing the secretary *t* was garbled in typesetting.

One of the written-in-later words is *troopes*, and the Folio reading is *Carts*, which is the better word in this context. Werstine reports from LION that Fletcher's phrase *armed carts* is 'not recorded as appearing before *Bonduca*' (p. 41) and hence Knight would not have known it; thus the *troops/carts* variant shows Knight substituting a commonplace phrase for an unusual one. Here Werstine is mistaken, as LION shows that George Puttenham in *The Art of English Poesy* [1589] referred to the Nubians' use of *armed cartes*, and EEBO-TCP shows that Richard Knowles in *The General History of the Turks* [1603] also used the phrase in a description of machines of war; it was not so unusual a phrase and did not originate with Fletcher's account of the ancient Britons' chariots. Another substitution is *trac't* interlined over a boxed *trasht*, where in fact *trasht* (meaning encumbered) is right and is in F, again showing Knight overruling his copy where it has a word he does not know. Werstine shows that quite a few of the gaps and written-in-later words in the transcript appear where the Folio reading is an unusual word, so Knight's not knowing, or not liking, the new word is the best explanation for the transcript/Folio variant at that point.

Indeed, Knight seems to have interfered even when Fletcher's word was not unusual. He was just an interfering scribe, so Greg was wrong to see the transcript/F differences as essentially a matter of the foul papers (copied to make the transcript) being hard to read. According to Werstine, Fredson Bowers's characterization of these matters was more accurate and he was right to assert that authors submitted fair copy to the players. The only Shakespeare play in which Knight's hand is detectable is the 1634 quarto of *The Two Noble Kinsmen* with his production notes in it. But if a scribe like Knight could interfere as much as he did in *Bonduca*, producing variant readings that fooled Greg into thinking they were signs of authorial revision, then we should not assume that the three *Hamlet*s, two *Othello*s, and two *King Lear*s are the result of authorial alteration. The scenes added to the fifth act of *Bonduca*—absent from the transcript based on foul papers and present in F—ruin the play artistically, but were essential because Fletcher wrote only 167 lines for this final act. Theatrical adaptation, then, might not be a polishing for the stage. Werstine finds that *Bonduca* challenges Gurr's maximal/minimal text theory since the shorter version of it is authorial and the longer is theatrical. Knight shows concern that his transcript should reflect what got acted and the 1647 Folio shows that concern too (since it is the acted version), so Gurr's idea that printed playtexts do not reflect performed versions is probably wrong. The term foul papers is certainly pejorative, but is essentially relational: when papers were used as the basis of a transcript they were called foul papers no matter how clean they were. Thus Greg's own New Bibliographical methods—the means for finding the agents of textual alteration—reveal his error about the foul papers of *Bonduca* and about foul papers generally.

Werstine's article appeared in the same volume of *Shakespeare Survey* as two others of relevance here. In the first, 'The Popularity of Shakespeare in Print' (*ShS* 62[2009] 12–29), Lukas Erne undertakes a series of counts that show that in his lifetime Shakespeare's books were much more popular than other playwrights' books. To start considering how big a deal Shakespeare was in the publishing world of his day, Erne approximates that 300 titles were published in the year 1600, one-third of them on religion. About another third, around 100, are on what we would call literature, and these include the first editions of Shakespeare's *Henry V*, *Much Ado About Nothing*, *2 Henry IV*, *A Midsummer Night's Dream*, and *The Merchant of Venice* and the second editions of *The Contention of York and Lancaster* and *Richard Duke of York*, and the fourth and fifth editions of *The Rape of Lucrece*. Moreover, Shakespeare's words were excerpted in three collections, making twelve books in all, or 4 per cent of the entire book market. The highly popular *Venus and Adonis* (ten editions in his lifetime) might make us think, as Roger Chartier and Peter Stallybrass did (in an essay reviewed in *YWES* 88[2009], covering work published in 2007), that in the book world Shakespeare was known as a poet not a playwright, but it is worth remembering that *Sonnets* [1609] did not get a second edition until 1640. Also, because more of his plays were published than his poems, there were more editions: forty-five play editions in his lifetime (twenty-six of them naming him on the title page), and only twenty poetry editions.

What, then, was Shakespeare's reputation in his time, compared to other dramatists? Erne starts counting editions as an index of popularity, treating co-authored plays as one hit for each of the dramatists involved and counting each collection as one investment by a publisher, not as one-hit-per-play. From the beginnings of play printing to the closure of 1642 Shakespeare had seventy-three editions, way out in front of the next most published writer, Heywood, with forty-nine, and more than three times as many as Jonson with twenty-two. The picture is the same if we take the endpoint of 1660 instead of 1642: Shakespeare out in front, Heywood next, Jonson way behind. A switch to counting each play in a collection separately (so the 1623 Folio counts thirty-six times) makes Shakespeare's lead over his rivals increase still further: up to 1642 he had three times as many, up to 1660 twice as many, as anyone else.

Turning to reprints—so, capturing not what publishers predicted would sell but what actually did sell out and had to be reprinted—Blayney's figure of around 50 per cent of plays published 1583–1622 getting reprinted inside twenty-five years is pertinent, because within these limits the reprint rate for Shakespeare was 85 per cent. (The utility of the endpoint being 1622 is that it excludes an unexplained drop in reprints in the Caroline period identified by Alan B. Farmer and Zachary Lesser.) Erne compares that reprint rate to each of a number of Shakespeare's contemporary and successor dramatists, none of whom, he discovers, was anything like as popular in print. The closest to Shakespeare in reprint rates are Marlowe, Webster, Beaumont, and Fletcher. Slicing the data another way, Erne looks at the average number of reprints per play (as opposed to just asking if any reprinting happened) and tabulates them by author. The table is headed by Beaumont at two reprints per play, then Shakespeare (1.6), then Fletcher (1.45), Marlowe (1.4), then a big drop to the next writer Heywood (0.9). But Erne worries that writers with small oeuvres are distorting this table, so he recalculates it for writers with at least ten plays to their name. This puts Shakespeare back on top and with a reprint rate three or four times that of Middleton, Jonson, and Dekker. If we now require that the reprints being measured had to happen within ten years of the first edition, Shakespeare streaks ahead even further.

So Shakespeare was wildly more popular with readers than Jonson was, although Erne concedes that perhaps Jonson was more popular with other writers, as their frequent allusions to him and his work suggest. Erne now turns his attention back to Shakespeare's lifetime by counting sheer numbers of editions up to 1616. Shakespeare is way out on top at forty-five, then Heywood at twenty-three, and Jonson at fifteen. In his own lifetime Shakespeare was a play publishing giant, and in fact he achieved this by 1600, when he had twice as many editions out as his nearest rival, Lyly. What about Shakespeare's name being absent from early title pages: does this invalidate Erne's reckoning of his popularity in print? No, because even counting just title-page ascriptions, rather than all editions, Shakespeare rockets into the lead from 1598 when his name starts to appear on his books. Shakespeare could hardly have been unaware of his pre-eminence in the field of printed plays; he not only wanted to be a successful literary author—he was one. Whether or not he was the most popular of the pre-Commonwealth dramatists as far as Restoration audiences and readers were concerned—and Erne is willing to accept that he might not have been—in the first half of the seventeenth century Shakespeare stood head and shoulders above everyone else.

The last article of relevance from this year's *Shakespeare Survey* is by Sonia Massai, 'Shakespeare, Text and Paratext' (*ShS* 62[2009] 1–11), and argues that Shakespearian paratexts should be given the same status as texts. Defending the non-peripherality of books' preliminaries, Massai claims that they were generally the last part of a book to be printed only because of 'the practical challenge of casting-off the printer's copy before the presswork started' and not because of 'any perceived difference' in their status compared to the main text (p. 2). This cannot be true because (i) they were printed last even in books for which the copy was not cast off, and (ii) their status was manifestly different since the copy for the preliminaries came on separate pieces of paper and, as she freely acknowledges in her own footnote (p. 2, n. 4), they might not be attached to all exemplars in the print run. Massai gives some examples of prologues and choruses being half-in and half-out the play and includes in the things we must treat as being part of Shakespeare's text such print entities as act and scene divisions and even running-titles. This is quite a mix of disparate materials, since running-titles have no dramatic equivalent and are seldom found in manuscript playbooks. Such things have only a mechanical or even an accidental explanation, and to overstress the paratextual can be to mistake the mechanical/accidental for the meaningful.

Massai reproduces the epilogue to *Locrine* that was printed in 1595 as 'Newly set foorth, ouerseene and corrected by W.S.' and writes that she is not interested in whether Shakespeare wrote it but in the fact that the epilogue refers to the monarch in the 'here and now' (p. 7). In fact the line 'That eight and thirtie yeares the scepter swayd' refers to Elizabeth I in the past tense and is numerically inaccurate: not until November 1596 had she reigned for thirty-eight years. Massai thinks the epilogue's here-and-nowness betrays a 'company man' concerned with serving his patron, but even if Shakespeare had once been a Queen's man he was in 1595 under a different patron as a Chamberlain's man. Massai makes a convoluted argument that perhaps the act intervals in Folio *As You Like It* do not reflect theatrical practice, since they do not mark temporal breaks, as though this were the only way of using intervals. The events of *The Tempest* happen more or less in real time, but Massai nonetheless agrees that its intervals reflect theatrical practice. More importantly, it is not obvious why act intervals count as paratext at all rather than just being the structure of the text. The intervals themselves are, to be literal about it, not texts but gaps between pieces of text.

In a surprising volte-face in the middle of her article, Massai objects that modern editions of *As You Like It* retain its merely scribal/editorial act divisions when they should in fact jettison them as nothing to do with Shakespeare. Yet she had earlier complained that because of New Bibliography's legacy—especially the lingering 'tendency to identify the printer's copy rather than the printed text as the ultimate source of textual authority'—we find in modern editions that 'all those features that were added to the printer's copy as the dramatic manuscript was transmitted into print and transformed into a reading text tend to be overlooked' (p. 1). It seems that now she wants to revert to the authority of the underlying copy too, and remove the Folio's editorial layer. Bravo, but why criticize others for doing the same? Massai wants the paratext to be edited in the same way as the text, and hence is surprised that the act intervals she has identified as non-theatrical have not been edited away in modern editions. The difficulty, of course, is that it is not clear that these intervals are entirely mechanical and can be got rid of: perhaps those in *As You Like It* and Folio *The Merry Wives of Windsor* (her other example) reflect what happened when a play that was written for continuous performance was revived after the use of intervals became normal. That is, the breaks we find unsatisfactory might nonetheless have been used in performances. Even if we were certain that the intervals were imposed by a scribe or a printshop worker for the purpose of making the Folio, it would still be no easy matter to remove them, since we would have to speculate about—and try to restore for the modern reader—the scribe or the printshop worker's underlying copy. That is the very New Bibliographical project that Massai complains about at the start of this argument.

The second issue of this year's volume of the journal *Critical Survey* is devoted to the topic of 'Questioning Shakespeare', which turns out to mean asking the silliest question of all: did he write the plays? The first of the issue's four articles is Roger Stritmatter and Lynne Kositsky's repetition of their groundless claim that *The Tempest* is not dependent on the Strachey Letter report of the shipwreck of the *Sea Venture* off Bermuda '"O Brave New World": *The Tempest* and Peter Martyr's *De Orbe Novo*' (*CS* 21:ii[2009] 7–42). (Their previous attempt to establish this point is comprehensively invalidated in an expert study reviewed below.) Stritmatter and Kositsky argue that Richard Eden's *Decades of the New World* of 1555—a translation of Peter Martyr's *De Orbe Novo*—is the prime source for *The Tempest*, listing (and at certain points tabulating) what they think are striking parallels. Of course no one denies that Eden is a minor source—for example, providing the name of Sycorax's god Setebos—so the whole argument depends on the reader sharing the authors' conviction that long-acknowledged tenuous links are actually strong ones.

The second article, '*Cymbeline*: "The First Essay of a New Brytish Poet"?' (*CS* 21:ii[2009] 43–59), is Penny McCarthy's claim that *Cymbeline* was begun in the early 1590s and continually revised by Shakespeare until, but not after, the death of Elizabeth. McCarthy argues that thematically *Cymbeline* does not quite so tightly form a group with *The Winter's Tale* and *The Tempest* as has been supposed: other, earlier plays have elements present in what has been called the Romances group and *Cymbeline* could have been written much earlier than 1609. (The main things to be overcome here are the copious stylometric evidence and the dependence upon Beaumont and Fletcher's *Philaster* that both put *Cymbeline* around 1609; McCarthy has nothing to say about them.) The connection with *The Tempest* as a late play McCarthy tries to weaken by pointing to the anti-Stratfordians' claim that the play is not indebted to the Strachey Letter, and she focuses on loose parallels between aspects of *Cymbeline* and things happening, and works published, in the 1590s and early 1600s. She finds great significance in coincidences, such as Innogen having a 'cinque-spotted' mole and the fact that 'the personal emblem of Robert Dudley was a cinque-foil' (p. 53). This kind of 'evidence' leads McCarthy to the clairvoyant conclusion that 'Shakespeare long nursed a secret but rather vain desire, as did all the Dudley faction, that an alien Scot should not succeed to the "British" throne—leaving the way clear for the true British, the Dudleys' (p. 56).

The third article is by Roger Stritmatter alone, 'The Tortured Signifier: Satire, Censorship, and the Textual History of *Troilus and Cressida*' (*CS* 21:ii[2009] 60–82), and needs no close examination. It is a literary-critical argument about personal satire, censorship, and topicality in *Troilus and Cressida*, built on slender evidence and attempting to co-opt to its own ends the bibliographical facts of the play's publication. The attempt is frustrated by the author's ignorance of most recent discussions of the topic, evident in his treatment of Alice Walker's 1950s scholarship as if it were the latest thing. The last article, 'Shakespeare Authorship Doubt in 1593' (*CS* 21:ii[2009] 83–110), is by Rosalind Barber and aims to show that doubting Shakespeare's authorship was not a nineteenth-century innovation but first arose in the 1590s. Her logic is bizarre. Because scholars suspect that the verdict of the inquest into Marlowe's death was inaccurate—recording it as self-defence where we think it was murder—the evidence of the death itself should be disregarded as unreliable. This is like arguing that those who believe that the 1972 Widgery Report into the Bloody Sunday killings by the British army in Derry came to the wrong conclusion—determining that the soldiers acted in self-defence—are obliged to remain open to the possibility that, although thirteen bodies were buried, no one was killed that day. We should not believe that the body buried was Marlowe's, argues Barber, because the witnesses were known liars.

The remainder of Barber's article relies upon the reader accepting her absurd premise that Marlowe did not die in 1593. In the line of duty, however, this reviewer read to the end and can report that the full panoply of anti-Stratfordian irrationality is present, including the idea that Shakespeare was not known as a writer in 1593, which requires that the allusion in *Greene's Groatsworth of Wit* (published 1592) to a 'Shakes-scene' and the line about a 'tiger's heart wrapped in a woman's hide' from *3 Henry VI* have nothing to do with Shakespeare. Barber repeatedly mentions that certain works were entered into the Stationers' Register 'anonymously'—in the sense of their authors not being named, although the stationers' names are present—as if this should raise our suspicion of something untoward. In truth, of course, it did not matter to the stationer at this point who the author was, since it was his own exclusive right to publish on a particular topic, as expressed in the work's title, that entry in the register helped to establish. It does the reputation of the journal *Critical Survey* harm to publish articles as ill informed and prejudiced as the four that are supposed to be 'Questioning Shakespeare'.

A much better quartet of articles appeared in *Shakespeare Quarterly*. In the first, 'The Anachronistic *Shrews*' (*SQ* 60[2009] 25–46), James J. Marino argues that editors have come up with unwieldy narratives to avoid acknowledging that perhaps Fletcher revised *The Taming of the Shrew* around 1619–23. In the Folio text, the Lord praises one of the visiting players for his previous performance of a character whose name the Lord has forgotten, and the reply is '*Sincklo*. I thinke 'twas *Soto* that your honor meanes' (sig. S3r). *Sincklo* is clearly the actor of that name, who seems to have been a hired man. *Soto* is presumably the character of that name in Fletcher's *Women Pleased*, who does what the Lord says he saw performed: dresses up in his master's clothes to woo a gentlewoman. The action of Fletcher's play is like the class cross-dressing of *The Taming of the Shrew*, but it is dated much later, at 1619–23. So, the speech prefix ties *The Taming of the Shrew* to the 1590s and early 1600s—because Sincklo is in the plot of *2 Seven Deadly Sins* and is last heard of in 1604, while the Soto reference ties it to the late 1610s or early 1620s. The standard editorial explanation, from the Cambridge New Shakespeare of 1928, is to say that either this line in *The Taming of the Shrew* (and those around it) are later interpolations, or there was once an earlier play with another Soto in it. The New Shakespeare editors were writing just after Peter Alexander made the claim that the manuscript underlying Folio *The Taming of the Shrew* preceded the one underlying the 1594 quarto of *The Taming of a Shrew*, which claim they accepted, so they found Soto an embarrassment to be got around.

We cannot, Marino insists, simply invent lost plays to solve our puzzles, and we cannot assume that just this small segment of Folio *The Taming of the Shrew* is late: why might not the whole play have been revised after Shakespeare's death? Marino rather unfairly mocks Wells for considering the possibility that Soto was a late authorial insertion into *The Taming of the Shrew*, which Marino thinks silly because *Women Pleased* was first performed around 1620, when Shakespeare was four years dead (p. 31, n. 15). This is unfair because Wells makes his suggestion in the context of considering the possibility that *Women Pleased* might have been first performed rather earlier than this, since the cast list that gives us the 1620 date—which appeared in the 1679 Beaumont and Fletcher Folio—need not be the cast list of the first performances. When complaining of the *Oxford Complete Works* editors' treatment of the problem, Marino gives no credence to the stylometric tests that unequivocally indicate an early date for *The Taming of the Shrew*. There are significant errors in Marino's handling of the detail of this problem. He is under the misapprehension that the term 'foul papers' is used in 'a letter from Edward Knight' (p. 34, n. 25), the King's men's scribe, but of course it is in Knight's transcript of Fletcher's *Bonduca*, and he misidentifies the 1595 octavo edition of *Richard Duke of York* as a quarto from 1594 (p. 41). Marino writes that 'In fact, John Sinckler or Sincklo's first name is only known to us because it appears in a playhouse manuscript that mixes actors' and characters' names indiscriminately' (p. 37). Presumably, he is here thinking of *2 Seven Deadly Sins*, and that is not an accurate description: every fictional character is named and many are glossed with actors' names; no mixing happens.

Regarding Sincklo's career, Marino rightly observes that we need not assume it ended with his appearance the print edition of *The Malcontent* in 1604. Indeed, oddly enough his name repeatedly turns up in connection with Chamberlain's/King's men's plays that came to them from other companies: *The Taming of the Shrew*, *3 Henry VI* (both Pembroke's), *2 Henry IV* (which has some connection with the Queen's men's *Famous Victories*), and the Induction to *The Malcontent*, which is about how the play jumped from one company to another. Aside from the desire to locate the manuscript underlying Folio *The Taming of the Shrew* before, and as the origin of, *The Taming of A Shrew*, 'all of the other available evidence places *Women Pleased* between 1619 and 1623' (p. 43). This is rather overstating the matter, since the only evidence for that date is the cast list in the 1679 Beaumont and Fletcher Folio. Marino finds it hard to believe that Shakespeare's foul papers would have been kept for thirty years and then allowed to be destroyed to print F, but in fact it is not necessary to suppose that F *The Taming of the Shrew* was based on foul papers to believe all the things that Marino says we should not believe. Moreover, the Folio project was big enough that Heminges and

Condell might well have done some rummaging and found the neglected—because no longer needed—foul papers in the theatre library. Referring to its plot inconsistencies, Marino also finds it hard to believe that Shakespeare would have left the play uncorrected for twenty years. But again, the obvious retort is that Shakespeare could have corrected any inconsistencies without altering the foul papers. It is easier to believe, according to Marino, that Fletcher revised Shakespeare's play and introduced those tangles. Marino's characterization of the preciousness of Shakespeare scholarship seems dated when he supposes a prejudice against the 'implicitly forbidden hypothesis that Shakespeare's works might have been substantially improved by his collaborators' (p. 44). I should have thought that such hypotheses are rather popular. Marino concludes by admitting that he has not got his own explanation of the Sincklo/Soto problem, which is rather a disappointment.

Michael Hattaway's article, 'Dating *As You Like It*, Epilogues and Prayers, and the Problems of "As the Dial Hand Tells O'er"' (*SQ* 60[2009] 154–67), shows that, contrary to recent arguments by Juliet Dusinberre, we do not have a new epilogue to *As You Like It*, nor can we date the play's first performance to Shrovetide 1599. *As You Like It* is not mentioned in Francis Meres's *Palladis Tamia*, entered in the Stationers' Register on 7 September 1598, but must have been written by the time its own 'staying entry' was made in the Register on 4 August 1600. The internal evidence for dating *As You Like It* is weak, as is the performance evidence such as the play's Robin Hood theme being perhaps an answer to the Admiral's men's Robin Hood plays at court during Christmas 1598 or Shrovetide 1599. We have a record of the Chamberlain's men being paid for a court performance on 20 February (Shrove Tuesday, Pancake Day) 1599 at Richmond Park, where Elizabeth liked to hunt and where there was a recently refurbished sundial. All three—the pancakes, the hunting, the sundial—are links with *As You Like It*, hence Dusinberre's suggestion that this was the first performance. Hattaway objects that the play's pancake jest would work just as well some time after this day, and that the play contains an allusion to the June 1599 Bishops' Ban burning of satiric books, which allusion could also work some time later. The allusion itself is 'for since the little wit that fools have was silenced, the little foolery that wise men have makes a great show' (I.ii.84–6). Moreover, the Chamberlain's men played at court during Christmas 1599 and on Shrove Sunday 1600, so if *As You Like It* were first performed at court it could have been during either of these visits.

The poem 'As the Dial Hand Tells O'er', dated 1598 in Henry Stanford's commonplace book, was clearly written for the queen at Shrovetide, but as Hattaway points out the Admiral's men also played at court on Shrove Sunday 1599 so it could as likely be theirs as the Chamberlain's men's, who played there on Shrove Tuesday 1599. The style of the poem—trochaic, with use of uninflected genitives—is more Jonsonian than Shakespearian. Also, it seems to wish the queen several dozen more years of life, which in 1598 would be ridiculous, and uses a phrase close to Mary Queen of Scots' motto, which would be unwise after her execution in 1587. In fact, Hattaway argues, there is no reason to suppose that it is an epilogue at all. It does not do the usual epilogue work of asking people to think well of the play, and is more like a prayer, which might itself form part of an epilogue. Hattaway ends by surveying what we know about *As You Like It*'s earliest performances, including the transition from William Kempe to Robert Armin as company clown, and the sign and alleged motto of the Globe. Much of this is speculation, he points out.

The last article from *Shakespeare Quarterly* in 2009 to be noticed here is only tangentially relevant. Jeffrey Todd Knight, in 'Making Shakespeare's Books: Assembly and Intertextuality in the Archives' (*SQ* 60[2009] 304–40), tells the history of the binding, rebinding, putting together, and taking apart of early editions by Shakespeare and others. Knight subscribes to the contentious idea popularized by D.F. McKenzie that 'forms effect meaning' (p. 306), which appears to be driving a fresh interest in the ways that purchasers chose to have their books bound together as collections. (Erne's article reviewed above also touches upon this.) It is easy to overstate the importance of these choices, since an element of happenstance must enter into them. Binding decisions may be driven by purely practical needs, and the fact that even modern libraries shelve books by size should warn us against over-reading physical juxtaposition. Knight makes the interesting point that when bound together the Thomas Pavier quartos of Shakespeare did not always preserve the continuity of signatures across plays that is usually taken to indicate that he was attempting to make a collected works. Some volumes even bound non-Shakespearian plays with the Shakespeare ones (pp. 324–6). Knight makes an unfortunate slip in claiming that *Pericles* depicts 'a Governor of Tarsus whose starving people rise up to kill their leader' (p. 332). In fact the people rise up against Cleon and his family, in anger at the attempt on the life of Marina, many years after the city's hunger is relieved by her father Pericles; during these years Marina is born and grows to adolescence.

In an article from *Shakespeare Quarterly* overlooked last year, 'William Strachey's "True Reportory" and Shakespeare: A Closer Look at the Evidence' (*SQ* 59[2008] 245–73), Alden T. Vaughan shows that William Strachey's Letter, or 'True Reportory', is indeed a source for *The Tempest* despite the contrary claim by Stritmatter and Kositsky in their article 'Shakespeare and the Voyagers Revisited' (reviewed in *YWES* 88[2009], covering work published in 2007). Richard Hakluyt was clearly preparing a third edition of *Principal Navigations* after the second edition of 1600, although it never appeared. Equally clearly, the Reverend Samuel Purchas acquired the material that Hakluyt was accumulating, with a view to putting together a posthumous third edition of Hakluyt. Purchas's 1625 volume *Purchas's Pilgrims*, where 'True Reportory' was first published, used the letter H (for Hakluyt) or P (for Purchas) before each item in the table of contents to show who was responsible for it, and Strachey's 'True Reportory' is marked with an H. After Strachey's Letter Purchas prints extracts from the Virginia Company's publications and it is likely that Hakluyt himself did the editing necessary to include 'True Reportory' in this larger narrative of exploration. Essentially, Purchas printed 'True Reportory' as he got it from Hakluyt.

'True Reportory' would not have pleased the Virginia Company in 1610, as it revealed bad behaviour by the colonials and it made Bermuda sound so attractive that Spain would be encouraged to try to take it. But by 1625 it would be innocuous: Bermuda was secure and the Virginia Company had ceased to exist. There would be no reason for Purchas to meddle with 'True Reportory' when publishing it, other than adding a few notes, nor to give it a false date. Vaughan gives an account of the discovery in 1983 of a nineteenth-century transcript of Strachey's Letter that seems to derive from a version different from the one published. He thinks it likely to be based on Strachey's draft, written while still in Bermuda, whereas the published one was a more polished account later completed in Jamestown. Stritmatter and Kositsky claimed that 'True Reportory' cannot have been written in Jamestown because it describes the voyage back to England of Sir Thomas Gates, which voyage carried 'True Reportory' to London. Vaughan points out that this is a misreading of 'True Reportory', which says only that Gates is 'now bound for England', meaning that he is waiting for embarkation at Point Comfort, 40 miles from the Jamestown colony. Jamestown did not have the resources for a transatlantic voyage and fleets rendezvoused at Point Comfort; while the ships preparing to sail to England were gathering there, they took on board Strachey's letter.

Stritmatter and Kositsky's claim that 'True Reportory' is Strachey's answer to a request for information from Richard Martin, secretary of the Virginia Company, is implausible, Vaughan points out, since it is addressed to an anonymous 'lady' and reports many things Martin did not ask about. Having asserted rather than shown that 'True Reportory' was written in 1612 or later, Stritmatter and Kositsky accuse it of plagiarizing other works that, if anything, plagiarized it. However, Vaughan thinks in fact there was no real plagiarism: the ideas they have in common are simply ones shared by people in this circle. The survival of the shipwrecked passengers of the *Sea Venture* was extraordinary news in London in September 1610, and was made much of in pamphlets. Strachey's manuscript account, 'True Reportory', would have been very popular and widely repeated. The parallels with *The Tempest* are ample and well documented, and while Shakespeare certainly could have got them from a whole set of other sources, Strachey's account 'bundled them conveniently . . . at just the right moment for dramatic adaptation' (p. 272).

The volume of *Studies in Bibliography* published in 2009 was 'for 2007–8', which raises hope that it will soon return to currency. Three articles are of relevance to this review. The first, 'Mind and Textual Matter' (*SB* 58[2009 (for 2007–8)] 1–47), is by Richard Bucci and argues that the Greg–Bowers editorial techniques provide much the best way to present old texts to modern readers and that their detractors are ill informed and confused. Bucci provides a fine critique of the illogicality of postmodern positions on editorial theory such as Stephen Orgel's, and of inaccurate characterizations of Greg by Werstine. The postmodern textualist movement entirely misunderstood Greg's ideas about accidentals, and Bucci insists that editors who are author-centred—instead of concerning themselves with the socialized text—are not necessarily Platonists, nor blind to the instability of texts or their social contexts. Bucci describes how the Greg–Bowers approach affected the editing of American literature, for which it is more suitable than it was for early modern drama because the evidence of authorial revision, indeed the documentary evidence in general, is more plentiful. This is an interesting line of argument, since it is more commonly held that the Greg–Bowers approach ought not to have been applied beyond early modern drama. Bucci continues his history of this line of thinking to embrace its extension by G. Thomas Tanselle and brings in a useful discussion of the tension between the editorial principles of *usus scribendi* (look for the author's usual practice) and *lectio difficilior potior* (the more difficult reading is preferable). To apply this to a concrete case we may observe that the recent Arden3 edition of *Hamlet* (reviewed in *YWES* 87[2008], covering work published in 2006) has Osric say that he speaks *sellingly* of Laertes (V.ii.93), from the uncorrected state of Q2, rather than *feelingly* as most editions do, using the corrected state. The Arden editors applied the principle of *lectio difficilior potior* (*sellingly* being unique to this text) while others apply *usus scribendi*, noticing that *feelingly* is used by Shakespeare in a number of plays. Bucci ends with examples of modern editions made along author-centred lines that he thinks particularly fine.

S.W. Reid, 'Compositor B's Speech-Prefixes in the First Folio of Shakespeare and the Question of Copy for *2 Henry IV*' (*SB* 58[2009 (for 2007–8)] 73–108), shows that Folio *2 Henry IV* was most likely set from annotated quarto copy, since it preserves features of the 1600 quarto's speech prefixes that are unlikely to have survived in an intervening manuscript. The forms of Folio compositor B's speech prefixes can tell us what kind of copy he had, since he was conservative, tended to repeat the form of a name he had just set in a stage direction, and preferred short to long names. Looking at his work in *Much Ado About Nothing*, *Love's Labour's Lost*, *A Midsummer Night's Dream*, *The Merchant of Venice*, *1 Henry IV*, *Titus Andronicus*, and *Romeo and Juliet* it is clear that he frequently set two-, three-, or four-letter speech prefix forms even when there was room on the line to set longer ones. He strongly preferred three-letter forms and imposed them even when his quarto copy had longer forms, although this preference is more strongly marked in the comedies than the histories and tragedies, where he let his copy influence him into tolerating more four-letter ones. Compositor B seems to have wanted to avoid ending a speech prefix with a vowel, which accounts for a number of four-letter forms instead of three such as *Leon* and *Brag*. However, contrary to Bowers's description, he did not go for maximally abbreviated forms: he demonstrably set more letters than were needed for disambiguation of characters in a number of cases. Compositor B frequently first encountered a name in the middle of a scene—because of the order of page setting in a folio-in-sixes—and did not know the character's full name. For this reason it sometimes took him a while to settle on a preferred form of the speech prefix, and of course he could not expand a short form in his copy if he had not yet encountered the full name.

Reid traces compositor B trying to settle on a standard speech prefix for Poins in *1 Henry IV*, given his quarto copy's use of *Poy* and *Po*. The important thing to figure out is when compositor B discovered a character's full name; once that happened he used a three- or four-letter form right away in almost all cases. Compositor B's preference for his speech-prefix forms seems to have persisted even in long lines that show abbreviation elsewhere in the line, including extreme abbreviation such as setting an ampersand for *And*, and

Emp in place of *Emperour* in a line of dialogue. Occasionally he would lengthen a speech prefix just to help justify a line. In general, the evidence shows that where compositor B departed from his adopted form of a name—changing to a different name for the same character, or using a form longer than he was wont to do—it is because his copy showed this variation. Thus, with compositor B's general habits defined, we can use them to speak of the characteristics of other Folio plays for which we do not know the copy, such as *2 Henry IV*. Reid summarizes the arguments over the past 150 years about whether Folio *2 Henry IV* was set from an authoritative manuscript or a quarto annotated by reference to an authoritative manuscript, or something else. Evidence from compositor B's speech prefixes in *2 Henry IV* should help, although the matter is complicated by a casting-off error that made the compositors first try to compress the play to fit into a standard quire g and then to expand the play when it was decided to add an eight-leaf quire $^{\chi}$gg.

In quire g compositor B departed from his usual practice by setting full-length speech prefixes (such as *Hostesse* and *Snare*) that are identical to the quarto speech prefixes at the corresponding points, so presumably his copy had the quarto speech prefixes and they influenced him to break his abbreviating habit. Some of these long settings might have been done for the sake of justification, but not all. Moreover, this happens even where we have reason to suppose he was trying to save rather than waste space because of casting-off error. The same use of full-length names as speech prefixes happens on quire $^{\chi}$gg, although of course this is harder to evaluate since compositor B here needed to expand his copy to fill the quire. But there are several full-length speech prefixes here in lines that are short, so there was no hope of making a new line by using the long name. The obvious conclusion is that, since the longer forms are in Q, he was following copy that had Q's longer forms. There is some counter-evidence—compositor B setting long forms where Q has abbreviated ones—but Reid disposes of them as special cases induced by local matters, such as the need to expand copy or the influence upon compositor B of the appearance of a full name in a stage direction just before the speech prefix. Reid's conclusion is that either compositor B was setting Folio *2 Henry IV* from quarto copy or, much less likely, he was setting from manuscript copy that slavishly followed the forms of Q's speech prefixes.

Reviving an explanation of textual origin that has until recently been neglected, Gerald E. Downs, in 'Memorial Transmission, Shorthand, and John of Bordeaux' (*SB* 58[2009 (for 2007–8)] 109–34), argues that the manuscript of the play *John of Bordeaux* was created by stenographic recording of performance, and perhaps other surviving play texts have this origin too. G.I. Duthie's rejection of stenography as not the cause of the errors in Q1 *King Lear* is, as Adele Davidson has argued, not a logically strong one: all that Duthie achieved was to show that stenography does not have to be the cause of those errors, not that it cannot be. In any case, Duthie was not sufficiently expert in stenography and found problems in it that do not exist. Moreover, if we think Folio *King Lear* is an adaptation of Q1—the dominant view since the 1980s—then the F/Q differences cannot easily be used as evidence for Q's copy. The evidence from reprints, with authorial corrections, of sermons first printed from stenographic recording indicates that the preachers considered those accounts to be good enough versions of what they had preached. *John of Bordeaux* is a manuscript written out by a scribe who, to judge from certain errors, cannot be its author, and it is lightly annotated by theatrical hands; it has the name of the actor John Holland in three marginal notes, and there is an added speech in the hand of Henry Chettle. It is a sequel to Greene's *Friar Bacon and Friar Bungay*, so presumably he is its author. Verse is lined as prose but with punctuation falling where the lines should end, as if the scribe recognized that it was verse, and there are plenty of unmetrical lines mixed with metrical ones.

Downs finds evidence of eye-skip in the manuscript, and points out that this can occur when a stenographer expands his shorthand symbols to make a longhand version. Downs spots a couple of repetitions best explained by an actor coming in with the wrong speech, ad-libbing to get himself out of trouble, and then repeating those lines later in the correct place. In the manuscript the first of these two speakings is deleted, but the ad-libbing remains, and Downs reckons this could not have happened in dictation, only in notes taken during performance. Downs quotes a garbling in Q1 *Hamlet*, first noted by B.A.P. van Dam, that is hard to explain other than as an actor coming in with the wrong one of his speeches and another actor noticing the mistake and adjusting his speech to make up for it. Claudius says to Laertes 'content your selfe, be rulde by me, | And you shall haue no let for your reuenge' to which Laertes replies (meaninglessly) 'My will, not all the world', which is in fact the correct response to 'Who shall stay you?', a question present in Q2 and F but not in Q1. Spotting the error, the actor of Claudius comes back with 'Nay but Leartes, marke the plot I haue layde' (H3r) to restore the exchange to sense. Downs finds in this a parallel for his claims about actors recovering from error in *John of Bordeaux*. There are also misnamed characters that are best explained by a stenographer not knowing who is who in an early entrance of several people—because stage directions are not spoken but witnessed—and getting ascriptions wrong in a way much more difficult to do in the transcription of writing.

There are strange, phonetic spellings in *John of Bordeaux* such as *grattewlat* for *gratulate* and *anenstrewment* for *an instrument*, and while it is true that spelling in this period was variable, a scribe who was this idiosyncratic would not get much work. More likely is that these are the effects of stenography, especially where the manuscript has gibberish Latin, for which the stenographer presumably could do no more than represent the sound he heard because he did not know the language. As Downs points out, Greg argued the same kind of aural corruption as the source for the gibberish Latin in the memorially reconstructed quarto of *Orlando Furioso*, where Edward Alleyn's actor's part has it basically right. In stenography the *p*/*b* distinction would not be recorded but rather left to be recovered later, from context, when writing out longhand, and there are a number of *p*/*b* errors in *John of Bordeaux*, some corrected by subsequent overwriting. Similarly, stenographic use of the same symbol for *k*/*c*/*q* would explain a number of odd spellings and subsequent corrections. In a number of places the manuscript makes the *u*/*v* distinction based on sound (as we now do) rather than on place in the word (as was more normal at the time), so this too points to notes taken by ear. Downs draws attention to other manuscript oddities, such as *in cappable* for *incapable*, that he thinks are best explained from stenography. Since the attempt to correct *John of Bordeaux* to remove the errors arising from stenography could have gone much further, it is distinctly possible that many other plays we have were copied this way and then tidied up so well that we cannot see how they were made.

The Review of English Studies contained one article of relevance this year, 'Did Shakespeare Own His Own Playbooks?' (*RES* 60[2009] 206–29), in which Andrew Gurr argues that perhaps a playing company did not always own its own playbooks but rather the players owned them personally, as did impresarios and authors. With one exception, playbooks containing performance licences never went to the printer, and there are only two extant licensed playbook manuscripts: Middleton's *The Second Maiden's Tragedy* (Lansdowne 807) and Massinger's *Believe as You List* (Egerton 2828). The exception is the printing of *The Walks of Islington and Hogsdon* in 1657 from the allowed book and including its licence. Who owned the allowed book? We assume the company did, but our model for this is Shakespeare's relationship with the Chamberlain's/King's men. The Admiral's men and other companies seem to have operated differently. Shakespeare is the obvious candidate for being the agent by whom his pre-1594 plays entered the repertory of the newly formed Chamberlain's men, but who brought Marlowe's plays to the newly formed Admiral's men in 1594? The inventory of playbooks owned by the Admiral's men in 1598 contains only twenty-nine plays, yet since 1594 they had performed ninety-four plays at the Rose, so who owned the other sixty-five? Perhaps it was Alleyn personally. How did *Titus Andronicus* get from Derby's to Pembroke's to Sussex's to Chamberlain's men by 1594? If by Shakespeare's personal ownership of it, this would violate our idea of the obligations of a sharer in a joint-stock company. Perhaps these obligations emerged only after 1594. Gurr thinks that there was a variety of different forms of each play, so there can be no editorial singularity to represent them all.

An entire issue of the journal *Textual Cultures* (formerly *TEXT*) was devoted to W.W. Greg because 2009 contained the fiftieth anniversary of his death. A.C. Green's article, 'The Difference between McKerrow and Greg' (*TC* 4:ii[2009] 31–53), is irritatingly written, with half its words as discursive footnotes, as if attempting to tell two stories at once. After some rather inconsequential discussion of terminology—just who meant what by (New) Bibliography and when—the article ends up using personal correspondence plus manuscripts and typescripts of Greg's lectures, articles, and books (conserved at the Beinecke Library of Yale University) to throw light on the genesis of McKerrow's *Prolegomena for the Oxford Shakespeare* [1939] and Greg's *The Editorial Problem in Shakespeare* [1942]. Apparently the former felt put out by the latter stealing his thunder, and Greg's responses to McKerrow's book—plus his interactions with Paul Maas—led to his celebrated essay 'The Rationale of Copy-Text' [1950–1]. A useful tidbit is that in manuscript correspondence just before his death McKerrow qualified his view on the drying of sheets between printing and perfecting, having wrongly described in his *An Introduction to Bibliography* [1927] their being hung up for this purpose.

A.S.G. Edwards's article, 'W.W. Greg and Medieval English Literature' (*TC* 4:ii[2009] 54–62), is unfortunately outside the scope of this review, being concerned with Greg's (largely dropped) interest in Old English and medieval literature. Likewise T.H. Howard-Hill's 'W.W. Greg as Bibliographer' (*TC* 4:ii[2009] 63–75), a description of neglected early work by Greg (before 1902) that was preparatory to his *Bibliography of the English Printed Drama*, which reveals how his ideas were emerging, and Laurie Maguire's 'W.W. Greg as Literary Critic' (*TC* 4:ii[2009] 76–87), a brilliant analysis of Greg's 1917 essay 'Hamlet's Hallucination' and the ways in which his literal editorial mind responded to the duplications and contradictions of the play by trying (and failing) to reduce them to coherent singularities. Gary Taylor, 'In Medias Res: From Jerome through Greg to Jerome (McGann)' (*TC* 4:ii[2009] 88–101), concerns himself with a comparison of St Jerome as a translator of the Hebrew Bible into Latin and Greg as a transcriber who refused to translate and for whom modernization was a form of translation. Taylor finds that the transcription/translation binary is not terribly secure and that all such activities—which he sees as existing along a spectrum—necessarily 'remediate' the text to a greater or lesser extent, according to the needs of the target audience. Unmediated transmission is, of course, impossible. Implicitly opposing Maguire's argument, Sukanta Chaudhuri, in 'W.W. Greg, Postmodernist' (*TC* 4:ii[2009] 102–10), sees Greg as a proto-postmodernist in that he accepted and embraced textual multiplicity and resistance to closure. Or at least Greg became a proto-postmodernist between writing *The Calculus of Variants* [1927] and 'The Rationale of Copy-Text' [1950–1]. Annoyingly, Chaudhuri repeatedly references a work by Jerome J. McGann given as '(McGann 2001)' for which there is no corresponding entry in the list of works cited.

In the journal *Shakespeare* co-edited by this reviewer, B.J. Sokol, 'A Warwickshire Scandal: Sir Thomas Lucy and the Date of *The Merry Wives of Windsor*' (*Shakespeare* 5:iii[2009] 55–71), finds a historical allusion indicating that *The Merry Wives of Windsor* was written in or after 1600. Leslie Hotson came up with and popularized the dating of the first performance of *The Merry Wives of Windsor* to an Order of the Garter feast at Westminster on 23 April 1597, although there is little evidence for it. Shakespeare undoubtedly knew of Sir Thomas Lucy (<1532–1600), who was tutored by John Foxe and who had Shakespeare's mother's second cousin arrested as a Catholic conspirator in 1583 and subsequently executed. Sokol lists other less horrific connections between Lucy—and his son and grandson, both also called Thomas—and Shakespeare's cultural and social world in London. Lucy's granddaughter Elizabeth Aston was orphaned, and Lucy looked after her and her siblings at Charlecote, hiring for them a tutor called Bartholomew Griffin. In 1600 Elizabeth Aston ran away to marry, against her family's wishes, a former servant from Charlecote called John Sambach of Broadway. Lucy engaged the Attorney General Sir Edward Coke to fight the marriage in court, alleging that Griffin helped the couple in the hope of financial gain. Elizabeth Aston, then, was like Anne Page in the play: old enough to marry of her free will, in possession of a small inheritance, and likely to do a lot better financially if she married according to her family's wishes. But whereas Lucy fought the marriage, and kept Elizabeth Aston from part of her inheritance, the Pages accept their daughter's choice.

In the play, Shallow says that his family coat contains 'a dozen white luces' (I.i.14), meaning a type of fresh water fish, and the Lucy coat also contains luces, but only three. Sokol shows that we can find twelve luces in a picture of an early Lucy in the first edition of William Dugdale's *The Antiquities of Warwickshire Illustrated* [1656]. The charges Shallow wants to bring against Falstaff in the play—riot, park breaking, and deer stealing—are the ones that the historical Lucy brought in complaint against the abduction of his granddaughter Elizabeth Aston, if we allow one 'cherished creature' (p. 365) to stand for another. The allusion to Elizabeth Aston's marriage would date composition of *The Merry Wives of Windsor* to 1600 or later, and hence after the completion, with *Henry V*, of the second tetralogy. This would make sense of *The Merry Wives of Windsor* bringing on Shallow, Bardolph, Nym, and Pistol at its beginning and then not using them very much, since if they were already known and loved—from *1 Henry IV*, *2 Henry IV*, and *Henry V*—then such exploitation would 'attract spectators who were already familiar with them' (p. 368), as G.R. Hibbard put it. Conversely, if *The Merry Wives of Windsor* were written in 1597 it makes little sense for the tetralogy to expand on these minor figures from it, especially as Nym is not used again until *Henry V* in 1599.

Alan Galey, 'Signal to Noise: Designing a Digital Edition of *The Taming of a Shrew* (1594)' (*CollL* 36:i[2009] 40–66), gives an account of the editorial attempts, especially in the eighteenth century, to patch *The Taming of the Shrew* with bits of the metatheatrical framing material from *The Taming of A Shrew*, and shows how he will present these plays' relationship in his new digital edition. Gefen Bar-On Santor, 'The Culture of Newtonianism and Shakespeare's Editors: From Pope to Johnson' (*ECF* 21[2009] 593–614), argues that eighteenth-century editors used the language of Newtonianism and the new sciences to describe Shakespeare's contributions to knowledge, which were especially concerned with human motivations. Anthony James West, 'Ownership of Shakespeare First Folios over Four Centuries' (*The Library* 10[2009] 405–8), tabulates according to social class (or 'institution' such as a library) the known owners of First Folios since 1623, and finds that the institutional ownership took off in the nineteenth century and now dominates the field.

The journal *Research Opportunities in Renaissance Drama* changed its name to *Research Opportunities in Medieval and Renaissance Drama* in 2006, and this seems to have made it almost invisible to the Modern Language Association's International Bibliography (MLA-IB), which lists just three articles under this title although many more have appeared. Because MLA-IB omits them, a couple of articles relevant to this review were missed in 2007 and 2008 and will be examined now. In the first, 'The Date and Authorship of *Thomas of Woodstock*: Evidence and its Interpretation' (*ROMRD* 46 [2007] 67–100), MacDonald P. Jackson shows that Samuel Rowley wrote the play *Thomas of Woodstock* in 1598–1609, comprehensively refuting Michael Egan's claim (reviewed in *YWES* 87[2008], covering work published in 2006) that the play is early Shakespeare and should be called *Richard II Part One*. It is unfortunate that at one point (p. 96, n. 2) Jackson attributes Egan's claim to this reviewer, but hopefully use of the correct first name (Michael, not Gabriel) in his body text will prevent this misattribution spreading. Around 1599–1600 a lot of colloquial contractions that had not been used before became popular in drama, as David J. Lake showed. *Thomas of Woodstock* has these in abundance and in lines where they perfectly fit the metre, so those lines were probably composed after 1600 as opposed to being revised then. Other features such as rates of feminine endings and distributions of pauses within lines also point to post-1600 composition for the play, as Jackson has previously shown. The play also has a collection of linguistic features that are fairly rare but occur abundantly in Rowley's play *When You See Me You Know Me*, so he is probably the author of *Thomas of Woodstock*.

Jackson works through some of the thirty-seven words that he previously showed are in *Thomas of Woodstock* but were not common before 1598, refuting in each case Egan's claim that they were available in the early 1590s. (In fact, Jackson mainly shows that they were still in use in the early 1600s, not that they were unavailable before then.) Jackson concedes that *Thomas of Woodstock*'s phrase describing the king of England as 'Superior Lord of Scotland' would likely infuriate James I, but would have been innocuous before 1603. However, Jackson thinks it could have been written, incautiously, after 1603 but then excised by the censor or the self-censoring company before first performance, and indeed it is marked for deletion in the *Thomas of Woodstock* manuscript. From a hint given by Egan, Jackson has realized that the appearance together of unapostrophized *bith*, *oth*, *ith*, and *tother* (for *by the*, *of the*, *in the*, and *the other*) is unique to Rowley's *When You See Me You Know Me* and the *Thomas of Woodstock* manuscript and *Wily Beguiled*, which last has, on other grounds, been tentatively attributed to Rowley. Jackson adds five contractions/colloquialisms—*ant* for *an it*, *ont* for *on it*, *ist* for *is it*, *thart* for *thou art*, and *tush*—that are never seen together outside these three plays. *Thomas of Woodstock* also shares more expletives with *When You See Me* than it does with any Shakespeare play, and they are listed by Jackson.

Feminine endings and run-on lines became increasingly common in drama over the period 1580–1642, and the caesura shifted from after the fourth to after the sixth syllable. *Thomas of Woodstock*'s rate of 21 per cent of lines having feminine endings is way above what Shakespeare was averaging in early 1590s history plays, and likewise its rate of rhyming couplets, and especially the scene-ending rhyming couplet, which was a Jacobean practice. The proportion of caesuras falling after the sixth syllable in Shakespeare's 1590s plays varies from 16.9 per cent of lines (*3 Henry VI*) to 23.1 per cent (*Julius Caesar*), whereas *Thomas of Woodstock*'s proportion is 32.2 per cent, far outside of Shakespearian practice; not until well into the 1600s does Shakespeare's caesura practice start to resemble that of *Thomas of Woodstock*. These figures derive from use of punctuation, but more reliable is measurement taken from the splitting of a verse line between characters, for that phenomenon is more certainly authorial. Using just these more reliable data, the results point the same way: the pause patterns in *Thomas of Woodstock* are unlike Shakespeare's 1590s practices, and indeed unlike anyone else's 1590s practices. (In fairness, caesuras falling in the breaks where verse lines are split between speakers are still not entirely reliable evidence, since the early editions have no consistent way of marking such shared verse and it has to be inferred by modern editors.)

There is yet more evidence on Jackson's side and against Egan's. *Thomas of Woodstock* and Rowley's *When You See Me You Know Me* have strikingly high frequencies of polysyllabic rhyming, such as *tyranny/eternally*, which frequencies are considerably higher than those found in Shakespeare's 1590s plays, even the ones that are full of other kinds of rhyme. Mid-speech rhyming couplets are frequent in *Thomas of Woodstock* at 112 (out of 492 rhyming lines), while Shakespeare used only 116 in his entire career. *When You See Me You Know Me* has ninety-eight such mid-speech rhyming couplets out of 454 rhymed lines and so is much like *Thomas of Woodstock*. Other features such as two rhyming couplets separated only by a line of blank verse connect *Thomas of Woodstock* and *When You See Me You Know Me*, their having eighteen and seven respectively, and are extremely rare in Shakespeare. Likewise, assonantal rhymes are rare in Shakespeare and common in *Thomas of Woodstock* and *When You See Me You Know Me*. The Rowley rhyming features are also prominent in the additions that he and William Birde contributed to *Doctor Faustus*. Early Shakespeare is fond of *-eth* endings (as opposed to *-es*) for verbs in the third person singular, but *Thomas of Woodstock* almost entirely uses the more modern *-es* endings. These linguistic features cannot be accounted for by saying that *Thomas of Woodstock* was an early 1590s play revised in the early 1600s, as they are too deeply embedded: the whole thing would have to be rewritten to put them in. The fact that they are also found in Rowley's *When You See Me* makes him the likely author and 1598–1609 the likely date.

The second overlooked article from *Research Opportunities in Medieval and Renaissance Drama*, 'New Research on the Dramatic Canon of Thomas Kyd' (*ROMRD* 47[2008] 107–27), is also by Jackson, and in it he argues that Brian Vickers's methodology for adding *Arden of Faversham*, *King Leir*, *Fair Em*, and bits of *1 Henry VI* to the canon of Thomas Kyd is fatally flawed and the attributions are false. Vickers's attribution appeared in the *Times Literary Supplement* and was reviewed in *YWES* 89[2010], covering work published in 2008, where its methodological weakness was overlooked by this reviewer. Vickers first set out to find the three-word collocations, 'triples' he called them, in the unattributed plays and in the known Kyd canon of *The Spanish Tragedy*, *Soliman and Perseda*, and *Cornelia*; having found them he sought to discover how common these triples are in the rest of the pre-1596 drama. (Or rather, not all the pre-1596 drama but the seventy-five plays that he has electronic texts of.) A substantial number of the triples that link *Arden of Faversham* to the Kyd canon are found in no other play. As Jackson points out, the mistake is in first finding the shared triples and only then looking to see how often they occur elsewhere, since a certain number of them are bound to be common only to *Arden of Faversham* and one other playwright's canon. Had Vickers look for triples shared by the *Arden of Faversham* and the Marlowe canon and then excluded all those that also appear in other men's plays, he would have been bound to likewise get a residue of triples unique to

Arden of Faversham and Marlowe, but this does not mean that Marlowe wrote the play.

Vickers used plagiarism detection software to pick up the triples within the Kyd canon, which is smart as such software is intended to find approximate (sometimes called fuzzy) matches as well as perfect ones, and hence does not require the matches to have identical spelling. But when hunting these triples in the rest of the canon Vickers used simple string-searching software that demands perfect identity, so he probably missed a few matches because of spelling differences. Jackson repeated Vickers's methodology, but first searched for triples common to *Arden of Faversham* and the known Shakespeare play *2 Henry VI*, using modernized, regularized texts and a different plagiarism package, and then hunted in LION for the same triples occurring in plays from 1580 to 1596. (LION's 'variant spelling' feature is not perfect, he points out, since it misses the common spelling of *hart* for *heart*.) In any case LION found all the matches identified by Vickers, and 437 triples shared by *Arden of Faversham* and *2 Henry VI*. Of these 437, fifty are unique to these two plays and a further six are found only in *Arden of Faversham*, *2 Henry VI*, and another Shakespeare play. Thus *Arden of Faversham* has fifty-six unique matches with *2 Henry VI*, more than the number of unique matches with any one of Kyd's plays. Jackson interrogates Vickers's list of triples unique to *Arden of Faversham* and the Kyd canon, which list is supposed to be on the website of the London Forum for Authorship Studies, but was not there when this review was written in November 2010. Jackson works through Vickers's list, whittling away entries that in fact appear outside *Arden of Faversham* and the Kyd canon but were overlooked, for example because Vickers was searching for exact strings, not for words in their variant spellings. This whittling leaves twenty-one collocations unique to *Arden of Faversham* and *The Spanish Tragedy*, twenty-nine unique to *Arden of Faversham* and *Soliman and Perseda*, and four unique to *Arden of Faversham* and *Cornelia*. None comes close to the fifty-six collocations that Jackson found to be unique to *Arden of Faversham* and *2 Henry VI*.

Jackson repeats the process for *Arden of Faversham* and *The Taming of the Shrew* and finds forty-four unique matches, and four more that appear only in these two plays plus another Shakespeare play. Thus Vickers's methodology is useless for proving that *Arden of Faversham* was written by Kyd, since it can also—with greater strength of evidence—be used to show that Shakespeare wrote *Arden of Faversham*. Because Vickers's own tables (publicly available when Jackson was writing) show the numbers of triples shared by plays in his new expanded Kyd canon (that is, *The Spanish Tragedy*, *Soliman and Perseda*, *Cornelia*, *Arden*, *King Leir*, *Fair Em*, and bits of *1 Henry VI*) and the numbers of these triples that do not occur elsewhere in the drama of 1580–96, Jackson is able to calculate the proportion of unique matches—those not appearing outside Kyd—as a percentage of the total matches shared amongst the Kyd canon. Topping the list are the uncontroversial Kyd plays, *The Spanish Tragedy*, *Cornelia*, and *Soliman and Perseda*. Why should they have more unique shared links than the other plays? The obvious answer is that they really are Kyd plays and the ones further down the list are not. A statistical procedure called Wilcoxon's signed-rank test shows that it is most unlikely that coincidence would put these three plays at the top of the list if all seven plays were by the same person. Jackson dices the data several ways and the outcome is always the same: the three plays definitely by Kyd—*The Spanish Tragedy*, *Soliman and Perseda*, and *Cornelia*—have stronger links with one another than with the four Vickers claimants for Kydness. Jackson dices the data yet another way, looking at unique matches per 1,000 lines, and the results are the same: the accepted Kyd plays are like one another and the ones Vickers wants to add to the Kyd canon are unlike them.

Yet a third Jackson article was overlooked in previous *YWES* reviews: 'Is "Hand D" of *Sir Thomas More* Shakespeare's? Thomas Bayes and the Elliott-Valenza Authorship Tests' (*EMLS* 12:iii[2007] n.p.). In it he argues that there are flaws in the tests by Ward E.Y. Elliott and Robert J. Valenza that deny Shakespeare's composition of 'Hand D + Addition III' of *Sir Thomas More* and the bits of *Edward III* normally attributed to him. (Elliott and Valenza's tests were also critiqued by Thomas Irish Watt in his essay reviewed above.) Jackson thinks Elliott and Valenza did not apply the correct procedure for working out how likely it is that something is the case when the test for that something is known to be less than perfect. Jackson explains the statistics of Bayes' Theorem, which is appropriate to such cases yet produces decidedly counter-intuitive results. Suppose that in cancer screening a test is 79 per cent reliable, meaning that when the patient has a cancer the test will indicate this 79 per cent of the time, and hence will falsely indicate no cancer (despite there being one) 21 per cent of the time. Suppose also that for cancer-free patients the test indicates this freedom 90 per cent of the time, and (falsely) comes back positive for cancer 10 per cent of the time. Finally, suppose that the actual rate of cancer in the population is 1 per cent. If I take the test and it comes back positive, what is the likelihood that I really have cancer? Most people guess that it is highly likely I have cancer, but in fact it is most unlikely. The formula relies on two statistics. The first is the rate-of-true-positives times by the real-cancer-rate, so here $0.79 \times 0.01 = 0.0079$. The second is the rate-of-false-positives times the real-no-cancer-rate, so here $0.1 \times 0.99 = 0.099$. (The real-no-cancer-rate is 1 minus the rate of cancer in the population, in other words the proportion of the human population not suffering cancer.) The Bayes formula divides the first of the above statistics (0.0079) by the sum of the two statistics (0.1069), which gives 0.074. So in fact if this test indicates that I have cancer, there is only about a 1 in 13 chance I really have it.

Elliott and Valenza give figures for how often their tests declare something to be by Shakespeare when it is by Shakespeare and when it is not by Shakespeare, the true positives and false positives, and how often they declare something to be not by Shakespeare when it is by Shakespeare and when it is not by Shakespeare, the false negatives and true negatives. But we lack one number, equivalent to the real-cancer-rate: what is the actual probability—independent of the test—that Hand D is by Shakespeare? It seems odd, of course, that in order to establish how likely it is that Hand D is by Shakespeare we must first put a figure on how likely it is that Hand D is by Shakespeare. Jackson's idea, though, is to plug into the formula various estimates of this likelihood—reflecting the range of scholarly opinion—in order to determine how likely it is that Elliott and Valenza's tests give a false verdict. Jackson summarizes the purely palaeographical evidence that Hand D is Shakespeare's composition, and mentions that LION confirms that the unusual spellings in Hand D of *scilens*, *iarman*, *elamentes*, *a levenpence*, *deule*, and *argo* are extremely rare outside of Shakespeare. A lot of the highly odd spellings in Hand D are absent from all printed works in LION but present in a few manuscripts, and they seem to have been considered old-fashioned in the 1590s. Thus, the reason that they do not occur in other Shakespeare works is probably that those works are printed and these spellings were routinely modernized by compositors. It is well known (and apparent to the casual reader) that there are thematic and imagery links between Hand D and Shakespeare's works.

Overall, and in the light of all this independent evidence pointing the same way, Jackson reckons the likelihood of Hand D being by Shakespeare is 99.9 per cent. Putting this number into Bayes' Theorem shows that, on this assumption, it is 97.8 per cent likely that Hand D is by Shakespeare despite the fact that it fails Elliott and Valenza's tests. It is hard not to respond to this by saying that of course if one starts with a near-certainty of Shakespearian authorship as one's premise, one is bound to conclude that Elliott and Valenza's demurral is wrong. Jackson tries lowering the initial likelihood to 99 per cent and finds that this makes the chance that Elliott and Valenza are wrong fall to around 80 per cent, and with 95 per cent as the initial likelihood it drops to about even money, 50:50. Starting with what Jackson thinks is the highly sceptical view that the likelihood of Hand D being by Shakespeare is only 80 per cent, the chance that the tests are wrong and it really is by Shakespeare drops to 15 per cent.

Jackson examines closely one of Elliott and Valenza's tests that Hand D fails, which is called 'grade level', meaning the complexity of the writing as measured by determining what grade (year) a person would have to reach in (presumably American) school in order to be able to understand it. He shows that the software used to calculate this might well count numbers of words wrongly and points out that because Hand D is unlike all other Shakespeare in being a foul papers manuscript, where quite a few things seem not to be fully worked out, the test for complexity might be thrown off. The other of Elliott and Valenza's tests that Hand D fails is based on two lists of high-frequency words that are (list *a*) more frequent in *Macbeth* than in Middleton's *The Witch* and (list *b*) less frequent in *Macbeth* than in *The Witch*. Elliott and Valenza established upper and lower frequency limits—within which a sample must fall to be declared Shakespearian by this test—by running all the Shakespeare plays through the test. That is, they counted the total of list *a* words in the play, subtracted the total of list *b* words, then divided this by the total number of occurrences for both lists, and they finally scaled up the answer to avoid dealing with small decimal fractions. Jackson notices that this test is highly sensitive to genre, with tragedies and histories rating highly, so a tragical history such as *Sir Thomas More* would rate highly in any case. Jackson also objects to Elliott and Valenza's tests being created from analysis of just seven plays, which arose because some of their procedures depend on linguistic data that are available only for these plays. Finally, he objects to the tests being developed and refined alongside their application. The better procedure is to perform a blind process of developing sets of Shakespearian and non-Shakespearian writing by randomized sampling and then calibrating the tests once it has been determined how well they attribute authorship under conditions that prevent the investigator unconsciously tipping the scales.

So, finally, to *Notes and Queries*. Christopher Mead Armitage argues that Dr Caius in *The Merry Wives of Windsor* is indeed a mockery of the historical figure Dr John Caius (1510–73) of Gonville and Caius College in 'Dr Caius: Cambridge Scholar, Shakespearean Buffoon' (*N&Q* 56[2009] 46–8). Todd Pettigrew made an argument (reviewed in *YWES* 81[2002], covering work published in 2000) that the play's Caius was supposed to be someone impersonating the historical figure. The play alludes to the real Caius's reputation as a stickler for pronunciation—hence the fictional one is a terrible mispronouncer of English—and to his views on the Latin and Greek pronunciation to be taught to boys, hence William's Latin lesson in the play. The historical figure also published a book on English dogs, the classifications of which match those in Macbeth's speech to the two murderers (III.i.93–102).

Thomas Merriam has three notes this year. In the first, 'Six-Word Collocations in Shakespeare and *Sir Thomas More*' (*N&Q* 56[2009] 48–51), he argues that Shakespeare contributed not merely the Hand D and Addition III parts of the play *Sir Thomas More*, but was also one of the authors of the original text that is in Munday's hand in the manuscript. Merriam has found seven of what he calls six-word collocations in *King Lear* that first occurred in previous Shakespeare plays, and five of these seven are unique to Shakespeare's canon while the other two are very rare (up to five other occurrences) outside Shakespeare. (The notion of collocation is usually indifferent to word order—so *blue skies* and *skies blue* would count as a match—but Merriam's matches comprise six words in a particular order.) Merriam has found two seven-word collocations and two six-word collocations that are common to *1 Tamburlaine* and *2 Tamburlaine* but are not found in Shakespeare. He has also found six six-word collocations that *The Comedy of Errors* shares with other Shakespeare plays, and of these two are unique to Shakespeare while the other four are very rare (up to three other occurrences) outside Shakespeare. The point he is making (none too clearly) is that such long collocations are a good test of authorship as they are fairly frequently shared by works in one writer's canon—because he self-plagiarizes—but are rarely shared across canons.

The Munday section of *Sir Thomas More* shares one six-word collocation with Munday's *John a Kent and John a Cumber*, and shares it also with *1 Henry IV* and *The Two Gentlemen of Verona* and more than five other works (he lists only five), so it is not very rare. Munday's *John a Kent and John a Cumber* shares two six-word collocations with the thirty-six plays in the Shakespeare Folio. But, and this is the important point, the Munday section of *Sir Thomas More* shares seven six- to eight-word collocations with Shakespeare's plays, of which four are not found anywhere else and of which three are very rare (each having only one occurrence) outside Shakespeare. One of these seven is tricky as it is 'God save the King! God save the King' being used twice (twenty-three lines apart) within one scene of the Munday section of *Sir Thomas More*, and being used twice (seventy-four lines apart) in two successive scenes in *2 Henry VI*, which repetition happens in only one other work Merriam has found. Merriam does not make clear that it is the double exclamation being repeated that constitutes the collocation, and he muddies the waters by also indicating which other works use 'God save the King! God save the King' without repeating it. This example is rather unlike his other six collocations. Of Merriam's seven collocations, two have a further connection: the two lines containing them are adjacent in the Munday section of *Sir Thomas More* and their corresponding lines in Shakespeare are not only in the same play, *2 Henry VI*, but are just ten lines apart in it. In a sense, then, these collocations themselves collocate, which is most rare. Merriam concludes that either this is all extraordinary coincidence, or the writers of the Munday section of *Sir Thomas More*, supposedly Munday and Chettle, borrowed from Shakespeare or vice versa, and perhaps by ear since the plays were unpublished. (The uncertainty about the direction of borrowing arises from uncertainty in dating *Sir Thomas More*.) Or, more likely still, Shakespeare was one of the writers of the whole of *Sir Thomas More*.

Merriam's second note, 'Feminine Endings in *King John*' (*N&Q* 56[2009] 576–8), argues that Shakespeare co-wrote *King John* with a person or persons unknown. Rates of usage of feminine endings in blank verse are an important statistic for stylometricians, but unfortunately there is no agreed way to count them. For example, does a weak ending caused by the last syllable of a proper noun count? Merriam tabulates the counts for the first sixteen Shakespeare plays (in chronological order), as counted by six scholars, and although there are discrepancies there emerges enough correlation to say that feminine ending counts are sufficiently agreed upon for meaningful analysis to use them. Merriam presents a diagram containing curiously shaped polygons that he says show 'the two central quartiles of the Shakespeare feminine ending counts for the sixteen plays' (p. 577) in the preceding table. The vertical axis shows the rate of feminine-ending use (from 0 to 15 per cent of all lines) and the horizontal axis represents the different scholars' counts, so the polygon for E.K. Chambers's counts stands horizontally adjacent to the one for Elliott and Valenza's counts. Thus the widths of the polygons have in fact no meaning: these quartiles should be lines running vertically to represent minima and maxima, not overlapping polygons. The diagram shows that everyone puts Shakespeare's feminine-ending use above 5 per cent and Merriam adds in P.W. Timberlake's counts that show that across forty-nine non-Shakespearian plays of the same period the rate of feminine-ending use is below 5 per cent. Thus feminine endings are a good discriminator of Shakespearian from non-Shakespearian drama. In his book *Co-Authorship in King John* (reviewed in *YWES* 88[2009], covering work published in 2007) Merriam used different criteria to divide the Shakespearian and non-Shakespearian parts of the play. Merriam now shows that feminine-ending use in what he ascribed the non-Shakespearian parts falls below the 5 per cent threshold and in the Shakespeare parts falls above it, so this is an independent confirmation of his conclusion in that book.

In his third note, 'Marlowe Versus Kyd as Author of *Edward III* I.i, III, and V' (*N&Q* 56[2009] 549–51), Merriam tries to show that the non-Shakespearian parts of *Edward III* were not written by Kyd. The word *the* occurs more often in Marlowe's work than in Kyd's, and the words *but*, *for*, *I*, *me*, and *not* occur less often in Marlowe's work than in Kyd's. By counting occurrences of these function words in the non-Shakespearian parts of *Edward III* Merriam hopes to work out if Marlowe or Kyd wrote them. In other words, assuming that one of these two men wrote the non-Shakespearian parts of *Edward III*, which is it? He is not aiming to establish that either of them is the actual author, and, as we saw above, Timothy Irish Watt offers evidence to reject both. Counting the frequencies of these words in the non-Shakespearian parts of *Edward III*, the values are typical of Marlowe not Kyd. Principal Component Analysis enables the plays to occupy positions on a graph if we represent the first component along one axis and the second along the other. On such a graph, the proximity of the non-Shakespearian parts of *Edward III* to Marlowe's works is clear, as is their distance from Kyd's works. Merriam claims that the same result is obtained if other function words are used in place of his six. Thus the non-Shakespearian parts of *Edward III* are not by Kyd, as Brian Vickers claims. Merriam stops short of claiming that these parts of *Edward III* were written by Marlowe, since obviously any number of writers (except Kyd) might have word-usage habits that are closer to those of Marlowe than those of Kyd.

Brett D. Hirsch, in 'Rousing the Night Owl: Malvolio, *Twelfth Night*, and Anti-Puritan Satire' (*N&Q* 56[2009] 53–5), discerns in Sir Toby's singing to 'rouse the night-owl' and draw three souls out of one weaver (*Twelfth Night* II.iii.57–8) a reference to Malvolio, since *owl* (a roundhead) and *weaver* (a Flemish Calvinist refugee of that profession) were slang terms for Puritans. Dennis McCarthy, in 'A "Sea of Troubles" and a "Pilgrimage Uncertain": *Dial of Princes* as the Source for Hamlet's Soliloquy' (*N&Q* 56[2009] 57–60), finds in Thomas North's translation of Antonio de Guevara's *Dial of Princes* [1557] a source for Hamlet's 'To be . . .' speech. We know that Shakespeare used whole phrases, as well as the stories, from North's translation of Plutarch, and McCarthy thinks that in *Dial of Princes* Shakespeare found the ideas of death as sleep, as a pilgrimage, as a place from where no one returns, and as an escape from suffering. (These ideas seem rather too commonplace to count as sources.) More specifically, North uses the phrases 'sea of troubles' and 'of so long life' that appear in Hamlet's speech, and also collocates the words *sleep*, *perchance*, and *dream*. McCarthy goes looking for these words and phrases in others' writing using EEBO (he means EEBO-TCP) and discovers that 'sea of troubles' is not rare: fifteen other works of the period use it. But 'of so long life' is fairly rare: only three other works use it. The collocation of *sleep*, *perchance*, and *dream* is, according to McCarthy, unique to *Hamlet* and *Dial of Princes*, and the order of ideas in Hamlet's speech also follows that of *Dial of Princes*. McCarthy is mistaken about the collocation. He reports that his EEBO-TCP search term was 'sleep near perchance near dream', and applied to EEBO-TCP at the time of writing of this review this search term also hits John Florio's *First Fruits* [1578], which contains 'if perchaunce thou aske me, because thou hast dreamed it, sleping'. Perhaps the

Florio book was added to EEBO-TCP after McCarthy looked. Scholars should be aware, and make clear in their work, that the searchable texts of EEBO-TCP currently represent only about 20 per cent of EEBO, but the percentage is rising all the time as more works are keyboarded.

Brian Vickers, 'Shakespeare or Davies? A Clue to the Authorship of "A Lover's Complaint"' (*N&Q* 56[2009] 62–3), thinks that 'A Lover's Complaint' is by John Davies of Hereford, not Shakespeare, despite being published in the same volume as *Sonnets* [1609], but MacDonald P. Jackson has evidence that Vickers is wrong. In 'A Lover's Complaint' there are three uses of the article *a* instead of *an* before a word beginning with *h*: *a hill*, *a hell*, *a heart*. Shakespeare always put *a* not *an* before these words whereas in his known works Davies prefers *a* over *an* half the time for *a*/*an hell*, one time in six for *a*/*an hill*, and one time in ten for *a*/*an heart*. Thus the chance that Davies would write *a hill*, *a hell*, *a heart* together in one work is half a sixth of a tenth, or 1 in 120. Jackson reports that he used an online concordance, but the printed URL has been truncated and does not work (p. 63, n. 3); the correct URL is http://www.it.usyd.edu.au/~matty/Shakespeare/test.html. Jackson does not report which edition of Shakespeare this concordance is based upon. I repeated Jackson's searches using an electronic text of the 1863–6 Cambridge–Macmillan edition, which produced a few more hits for *a hill*, *a hell*, *a heart* than Jackson counts, and none for *an hill*, *an hell*, *an heart*, so his case is not weakened. In a second note, 'Arcite's Horsemanship: A Reading in *The Two Noble Kinsmen*, II.v.13' (*N&Q* 56[2009] 605–7), Jackson considers Arcite's boast of his 'feat in horsemanship' (II.v) in the 1634 quarto of *The Two Noble Kinsmen*. It is an odd phrase and editors would be tempted to emend to *feats* were not the singularity emphasized in the next line ('it was'). Yet *feat* cannot easily mean *ability*. No one seems to have noticed that when the play appeared in the second Beaumont and Fletcher Folio [1679] the line was 'seat in horsemanship', which makes much better sense and a simple long s/f confusion would explain Q's reading.

Roger Stritmatter, in 'Shakespeare's *Ecclesiasticus* 28.2–5: A Biblical Source for Ariel's Doctrine of Mercy' (*N&Q* 56[2009] 67–70), reckons that one passage from Ecclesiasticus on the subject of mercy is a Shakespearian source. Unfortunately, Stritmatter's sense is harmed by what seems to be a printing error on page 68, for a paragraph ends 'To these must be added, although previously undetected in the secondary literature, a line from *Romeo & Juliet*:' and the reader does not find out what the line is. Lord Say's attempt to dissuade the rebels in *2 Henry VI* by saying that to receive mercy from God they must show mercy to their fellow men (IV.vii), Henry V's similar reproach to the conspirators Cambridge, Scroop, and Grey (*Henry V* II.ii), Ariel's reproach to Prospero for lacking mercy (*The Tempest* V.i), and Prospero's epilogue about the audience's hopes to be pardoned, are based on Ecclesiasticus 28:2–5, according to Stritmatter. He admits, though, that the necessity for reciprocal forgiveness appears throughout Shakespeare's work and need not have just one source. Stritmatter shares the common misapprehension that Jack Cade says 'kill all the lawyers' in *2 Henry VI*, but this is Dick the Butcher's line (p. 69, n. 21). Howard Jacobson, in '*King Lear* I.i.271–2' (*N&Q* 56[2009] 63), reckons that Cordelia's 'the jewels of our father' (said of her sisters when parting from them in the first scene) comes from the story of Cornelia, the mother of the Gracchi, as told by Valerius Maximus, who called her sons her jewels. Jacobson neglects to name the Roman source, giving only the cryptic reference 'Val. Max.4.4 praefatio', but it is Maximus's *Factorum Dictorumque Memorabilium* (*Memorable Words and Deeds*). As well as being a famous anecdote, the story of Cornelia saying this is in Robert Burton's *Anatomy of Melancholy*.

Katherine Duncan-Jones, in 'Shakespeare, Guy of Warwick, and Chines of Beef' (*N&Q* 56[2009] 70–2), finds that Shakespeare's knowledge of the legend of Guy of Warwick is apparent in his plays. In *King John* I.i the Bastard responds to being called 'good Philip' with, in the Folio's styling, '*Philip*, sparrow'; editors vary their styling and punctuation according to their sense of what this means. Duncan-Jones thinks this an allusion to the play *Guy of Warwick*, since Colbrand the Giant, who was killed by Guy, is mentioned by the Bastard six lines earlier, and Sparrow is the name of Guy's attendant clown in the play. Shakespeare's *Henry VIII* V.iii also alludes to Guy of Warwick in the lines 'I am not Samson, nor Sir Guy, nor Colbrand . . . Let me ne'er hope to see a chine again— | And that I would not for a cow, God save her!' In the legend and the play of it, Guy slew the enormous Dun Cow of Dunsmore Heath and its huge rib was hung up in Warwick Castle. We know there was such a huge bone on display in Warwick Castle in the middle of the sixteenth century, and Duncan-Jones thinks this bone prompted the chine mentioned in *Henry VIII* in the context of an imagined contest between adversaries of unequal size. Another unequal fight featuring the word chine is between hungry Jack Cade and Alexander Iden in the latter's garden in *2 Henry VI*. Duncan-Jones reckons Shakespeare may have seen the Dun Cow bone at Warwick Castle and that he would also have been familiar with such sights from the slaughterhouses of Stratford-upon-Avon.

Boris Borukhov, in 'Was the Author of *Love's Martyr* Chester of Royston?' (*N&Q* 56[2009] 77–81), shows that the Robert Chester who wrote *Love's Martyr* was not Robert Chester of Royston, as is often claimed. *Love's Martyr* was published as 'by Robert Chester' in 1601 with Shakespeare's poem 'The Phoenix and the Turtle' alongside it, and there are two candidates for its authorship: Robert Chester of Royston in Hertfordshire and Robert Chester of Denbighshire. The latter is not known to have existed, but is inferred from the name in *Love's Martyr* and the book's dedicatee, John Salusbury, being from there. The recent Arden3 edition of Shakespeare's poems, edited by Katherine Duncan-Jones and H.R. Woudhuysen (reviewed in *YWES* 88[2009], covering work published in 2007) favoured Robert Chester of Royston, but Borukhov lists a number of reasons why he is not likely to be the man. He was not closely associated with John Salusbury, he was not Welsh (there is evidence of Welsh pronunciation in *Love's Martyr*), his signature does not match the one of the Robert Chester who we know was connected to Salusbury, he was an esquire (whereas the author of *Love's Martyr* would have boasted of that if he were), and he was Salusbury's equal (whereas the author of *Love's Martyr* makes clear his dependence on Salusbury).

Continuing his work on the 1821 Boswell–Malone edition of Shakespeare, Arthur Sherbo published three notes this year. In the first, 'More on the Bible in Shakespeare' (*N&Q* 56[2009] 270–4), he lists a collection of Shakespeare's uses of biblical terms and ideas that do not appear in Naseeb Shaheen's standard works on the topic but are recorded by editors cited in the Boswell–Malone edition. Most are really quite tenuous and we need not think that Shakespeare was consciously echoing Scripture. The second note, 'Pope and Gray: Gleanings from the 1821 Boswell–Malone *Shakespeare*' (*N&Q* 56[2009] 274–6), lists echoes of Shakespeare found in poems by Alexander Pope and Thomas Gray, as noted in the Boswell–Malone edition, and the third, 'Military Language in Shakespeare' (*N&Q* 56[2009] 607–10), lists some military language that Sherbo considers well glossed in Boswell–Malone but not in modern editions nor in Charles Edelman's dictionary on the subject. William Sayers, 'Two Etymologies: *Inkle* and *Natty*' (*N&Q* 56[2009] 350–4), traces the etymologies, unknown to *OED*, of the words *inkle*, a linen tape mentioned in a few Shakespeare plays, and *natty*, which has no Shakespearian uses.

Daniel Pollack-Pelzner, in '"Another Key" to Act Five of *A Midsummer Night's Dream*' (*N&Q* 56[2009] 579–83), decides that, as in the Folio, Egeus should be the manager of mirth in the last act of *A Midsummer Night's Dream*, rather than Philostrate as the 1600 quarto has it. Both versions have Philostrate be the man ordered to manage the merriment in the first act, but according to Pollack-Pelzner Egeus performs a kind of prologue function in saying 'Stand forth Demetrius . . . Stand forth Lysander' in the first scene and saying 'this is my daughter . . . this Lysander; this Demetrius . . . This Helena' when he finds the lovers sleeping in IV.i. Egeus keeps bringing in a tragic tone to disrupt Theseus's desire for a comic atmosphere—in the first scene, and when the hunt comes across the lovers—so it has to be him whom Theseus overrules regarding the lovers and regarding the choice of play-within-the-play. The titles of possible entertainments that he lists embody the genre confusion the play is concerned with. In *Hamlet* III.ii Hamlet calls Polonius 'so capitol a calf' when he refers to acting the role of Caesar in a play where he was killed by Brutus. As well as alluding to the play *Julius Caesar* (in which the actor of Polonius may well have played Caesar), Steven Doloff, in 'Killed Behind the Curtain: More on Hamlet's Calf Allusion' (*N&Q* 56[2009] 583), thinks the joke alludes to the itinerant shadow-play entertainment of killing a calf behind a curtain, because Polonius himself will soon die that way. When Sir Toby says 'they have been grand-jurymen since before Noah was a sailor' (*Twelfth Night* III.ii), Horst Breuer thinks he is referring to Fabian's family background as a local magistrate with a long and distinguished pedigree, rather like Shallow and Silence in *2 Henry IV*; such a man would plausibly organize a bear-baiting and resent the new, upstart servant ('"They have been grand-jurymen since before Noah was a sailor": A Note on Shakespeare's *Twelfth Night*, III.ii.12–13' (*N&Q* 56[2009] 584–5)).

Cheering up Cordelia as they are being taken off to prison, Lear says in F 'The good yeares shall deuoure them' and it is not clear who 'them' are, nor what he means by 'good yeares'. Editors have suggested a number of emendations for 'good yeares', but Stephen Rollins, in 'The Good Years in *King Lear* V.iii.24' (*N&Q* 56[2009] 585–8), thinks F's reading is fine: Lear is reversing the events of Pharoah's dream from Genesis 41 in which the seven lean cows (seven bad years) eat the seven fat cows (the seven good years); in reversal the good shall eat the bad. Confused after his capture by Cordelia's men, Lear asks if he is in France. This means not only that he remembers that Cordelia married the king of France, but also that he remembers the play's sources, for as Heather Hirschfeld points out in '"Am I in France?": *King Lear* and Source' (*N&Q* 56[2009] 588–91), in all the sources Lear goes to France to meet Cordelia. Hirschfield finds it a metatheatrical comment, reminding the audience of the sources precisely because Shakespeare is going to depart from them in order to create a tragic ending.

Oliver R. Baker's note, 'Duncan's Thanes and Malcolm's Earls: Name Dropping in *Macbeth*' (*N&Q* 56[2009] 591–5), cannot properly be summarized because this reviewer does not understand it. Holinshed's *Chronicles* names eight thanedoms turned into earldoms by King Malcolm of Scotland: Fife, Menteth, Atholl, Leuenox, Murrey, Cathnes, Rosse, and Angus. Six of these thanes appear in *Macbeth*, and if we exclude Fife (Macduff) then Shakespeare chose five from seven, leaving out Moray (Murrey) and Atholl. Baker looks for meaning in this choice, but there is a typo in his formula for calculating how many ways there are of picking a five-person committee from a list of seven candidates. The factorial symbol ('!') has been omitted after the first *n*, and the formula should read $n!/(r!(n-r)!)$. More seriously, Baker's grasp of probability is faulty. Because there are twenty-one ways to pick five men from seven, he thinks that 'the chances of Shakespeare's selections from Holinshed being random are 1 in 21, or less than 5 per cent' (p. 592, n. 6). This is like saying that the draw for the National Lottery is unlikely to be random because there was only a 1 in 10 million chance that the numbers selected would come up. Random means unguided or haphazard, not unlikely. The remainder of the note (pp. 592–5) is almost incomprehensibly written, mainly because the argument is unevenly split between the footnotes (amounting to 2,230 words) and the body text (just 1,200 words). The thrust might be that a study of Scottish and English history shows that Shakespeare was pandering to contemporary aristocratic sensibilities in leaving out Moray and Atholl.

Richard M. Waugaman, in 'The Sternhold and Hopkins *Whole Book of the Psalms* is a Major Source for the Works of Shakespeare' (*N&Q* 56[2009] 595–604), thinks that there are echoes of Thomas Sternhold and John Hopkins's *The Whole Book of Psalms Collected into English Metre* [1565] in Shakespeare's *Sonnets*. The echoes he lists are faint, including common words such as *save*, or even just common prefixes such as *mis-*. In certain cases, the meaning differs in the two uses: *save* means *rescue* in the psalm and *except* in the sonnet. There are ideas in common too, but again the connections are loose, and when Waugaman finds links between the psalms and *Macbeth* and *The Rape of Lucrece* the result is equally unconvincing. Claire R. Waters, in '*The Tempest*'s Sycorax as "Blew Eye'd Hag": A Note Toward a Reassessment' (*N&Q* 56[2009] 604–5), thinks that the handwriting of the scribe Ralph Crane, who provided the Folio copy for *The Tempest*, can help solve an old crux. Prospero calls Sycorax a 'blew ey'd hag'—Waters misquotes this as 'eye'd'—and the problem is whether to modernize to *blue* or something like *blear*. Bleared eyes certainly were associated with witchcraft, but looking at Crane's handwriting in surviving manuscripts Waters decides that a confusion of *-ar* for *-w* is distinctly possible, and so she supports the *blear* emendation. Azar Hussain, in 'The Reckoning and the Three Deaths of Christopher Marlowe' (*N&Q* 56[2009] 547–8), thinks that the Jailer's lines in *Cymbeline*, 'A heavy reckoning for you . . . fear no more tavern bills' (V.v), are an allusion to Marlowe's death, as are Falstaff's 'A trim reckoning! . . . He that died o' Wednesday' (*1 Henry IV*,V.i), since Marlowe was indeed killed on a Wednesday. This last claim seems improbable. For members of one generation President Kennedy's assassination is supposed to be highly memorable, and for another 11 September 2001 is indelible. Who remembers that these were a Friday and a Tuesday respectively?

2. Shakespeare in the Theatre

Erica Sheen's *Shakespeare and the Institution of Theatre: 'The Best in this Kind'* (what is the point of that subtitle?) considers the emergence of the professional theatre during the Elizabethan period and its eventual arrival at a position of cultural invulnerability: by 1601, Shakespearian theatre 'was above political accountability' (p. 109). Jacobean patronage puts this establishment beyond contention: 'Shakespearean theatre had achieved generic institutional status in the London theatrical scene' (p. 112). This is a brave book in as much as it challenges the last thirty-odd years of new historicist and cultural materialist scholarship which, in spite of their differences, share (broadly) the contention that early modern theatre was occasionally, potentially, incipiently subversive. As we know, the Elizabethans were a litigious lot and Sheen charts the formation of the institution of professional theatre in the light of complicated debates to do with family law, property law, monopolies, and contract. This is a complicated and (it must be said) not always interesting technique. At the end of a particularly murky summary of property and right, title and possession, phrased in terms of a series of questions, Sheen offers the lacklustre 'And so on' (p. 114). Occasionally the book is just plain hard going. As she discusses the connections between property law and the actor–audience relationship in *The Merchant of Venice*, she asserts that it is 'not simply that Shakespeare did not observe strict principles of continuity. It is, rather, that these complex spatio-temporal articulations create a continuum of dramatic duration within which Antonio's stipulation of Bassanio's witness of the embodied display of his ruin maps the term of Shylock's "merry bond" and the conditions for its satisfaction onto the organisation of the text and the audience's experience of the play' (pp. 86–7). It is not a user-friendly sentence, and indeed much of the book occludes the already foggy world of early modern law with a critical discourse that is neither concise nor lucid. Her assertion is that 'in Shakespeare's plays, legal thinking opens an intellectual threshold for the creation of a special property in theatre' (p. 48). For instance, *The Taming of the Shrew* dramatizes 'the contrast between love as industry and marriage as conveyance' (p. 50), while in the case of *Richard III* 'the principle of beneficial ownership provided the basis of a fully fledged principle of dramatic action' (p. 71). But in places such suggestive propositions are undermined by reliance upon 'legal allusion[s] so oblique' (p. 77) that one wonders whether early modern playwrights or their audiences could have had the first idea of their significance. That the emergence of theatre as a wholly new and professionalized institution occurred during the period Shakespeare was writing is both undeniable and wholly fortunate. That this accomplishment can be (or indeed need be) demonstrated with reference to contemporary legislative complexities is less certain.

In 'Feasting and Starving: Staging Food in Shakespeare' (*ShJE* 145[2009] 11–28), Peter Holland argues that 'Shakespeare's central interest is in the process of food as analogy, as social system, as symbolic discourse' (p. 13). He notes the paradox that while they are 'Packed . . . with references to food by the thousand, the plays largely resist showing us food, restricting the visibility of eating, the sight of the materials of consumption' (p. 11). While this is a consequence of the practical difficulties of preserving foodstuffs in a pre-refrigeration age as well as a rapidly changing repertory which required new props (edible or not) from night to night, it is also, argues Holland, to do with Shakespeare's characteristic capacity to transform an object into 'a complex social and cultural metaphor' (p. 28). As Holland elegantly puts it, 'The differing availability of food, the gap between conspicuous consumption and famine, serves as a central social and political definition of the ways in which, for example, states govern themselves, in which power is located in marriage or in which patterns of social behaviour operated both in Shakespeare and in the realities that lie outside the drama' (p. 28). Holland offers, in support of this fascinating assertion, several pertinent examples. Of *The Comedy of Errors*, he shows how mealtimes offer 'a diurnal rhythm' (p. 19) to the play which is ruptured in *Macbeth* with its association between the witches and food, in particular in their ghoulish goulash—'by far the most detailed construction of a concoction Shakespeare creates' (p. 18). He also deals with Banquo's banquet apparition and the ways in which political disorder is figured in the breaking down of commensality. Holland deals with the importance of starvation and hunger in plays as various as *The Taming of the Shrew*, *Timon of Athens*, and, of course, *Coriolanus*, the play that begins with a famine that is man-made. Holland concludes this powerful essay with the suggestion that 'Shakespeare explores the extremes of food, in *Coriolanus* and elsewhere, precisely as signals, staged to our view, of the collaborations and failures of sympathy in human interaction' (p. 28).

Edward L. Rocklin is interested in torture rather than hunger. In 'The Smell of Mortality: Performing Torture in *King Lear* III.vii' (in Kahan, ed., *King Lear: New Critical Essays*, pp. 297–325), he examines the blinding of Gloucester in the context of early modern politics and treatment of traitors. This is not always convincing. For instance, he suggests that the blinding is exceptional since it 'was never used as a punishment for treason by Tudor and Stuart monarchs' (p. 304), to which one might retort that the legality is less important than the dramatic effect of such a moment (as is suggested too by the threatened blinding of Arthur in *King John*). Again of the First Servant's attempt to prevent the brutality, Rocklin writes, 'There is no direct parallel for such an intervention in the records of the Tudor and Stuart regimes' (p. 305) as though surprised that Shakespeare's fiction does not reflect Elizabethan or

Jacobean penal codes with perfect fidelity. The onstage blinding of Gloucester is both spectacular and hideous—why need it enact the legal processes of the day? Occasionally the essay illustrates the awkwardness of some writing about performance: 'at a recent production of *The Winter's Tale* at my university's studio theatre, where I was inches away from the action, I was surprised to feel . . . an impulse to join the courtiers' (p. 315). So what? Is Rocklin really suggesting that proximity to the actors concentrates audience empathy as though there were a mathematical formula relating vicinity to the stage and the intensity of audience emotion? Might it not just be that Rocklin is a sensitive soul? This is impressionistic stuff. However, when Rocklin discusses the language of the scene from *King Lear* he is on firmer ground. Of 'flies to wanton boys', for instance, he writes, 'One reason why this speech has become famous is because it offers an epigrammatic expression of a primal image, but it also resonates so intensely because in performance it is incarnated before it is articulated' (p. 311)—just so. (There is a howler when Rocklin quotes Goneril's determination to do 'something, and *that* i' th' heat' (p. 300) where the 'that' is an unfortunate authorial interpolation.)

Coen Heijes analyses, in forensic detail, a 'largely unexplored subfield within Shakespeare studies' (p. 242). His '"Strike up the drum": The Use of Music in the Boyd History Cycle' (*ShakB* 27[2009] 223–48) leaves no stone unturned—multiple viewings of the productions both separately and in their cycle incarnations, interviews with actors, composers, musicians, and directors as well as reference to reviews and other secondary literature. The result is a credible, assiduous, but occasionally mechanical piece. Heijes distinguishes carefully between music within the story of the plays (which he calls diegetic), such as a song embedded in the text, and that with which he is more concerned here (exegetic), which refers 'to a world external to the filmed or staged scenes, particularly when a specific mood is called for' (p. 224). Heijes is concerned to demonstrate how this kind of music adds further interpretative layers to the production. Methodically, he divides the music into various kinds and illustrates each type. For instance, he talks of 'character music' and demonstrates how various motifs appear around the Cade rebels, the French, or the internecine English. 'Event' music is repeatedly associated with coronations, funerals, or episodes of civil strife. Most indeterminate is what he calls 'mood' music, designed to connect 'parts of the history cycle which were not logically connected by similar events' (p. 236) such as the unrelated deaths of young Talbot and Suffolk. There is much detailed analysis of various sequences and particular moments within this epic production, and Heijes has an acute eye for detail. However, in conclusion he ponders the sixty-four thousand dollar question: 'No matter how intricate the idea behind the musical motifs was, and no matter how consistently music was employed throughout the cycle, the question remains whether the audience really picked it up' (p. 241). Such loose talk could put all performance scholars out of a job!

Robert Shimko considers John Crowne's rewrites of 2 *and* 3 *Henry VI* during the 1680s to be contemporary political commentaries. 'The Miseries of History: Shakespearian Extremity as Cautionary Tale on the Restoration Stage' (*THStud* 29[2009] 81–94) is a persuasive and intriguing account which offers yet another illustration of the ease with which Shakespeare's plays can be appropriated to address immediate cultural or political crises. Unsurprisingly, following the Restoration, republican ideas became taboo. 'But as the political situation circa 1678–9 came more and more to resemble 1641–2, memories of open rebellion as well as the persecution of the theatre seemed more likely to repeat themselves in the present' (p. 81). Shimko notes how social tensions surrounding the Popish Plot as well as frictions between Charles II and parliament over the Exclusion Crisis encouraged 'royalist playwrights to thrust visceral memories of the Civil War back into the popular imagination as a warning' (pp. 81–2). Issues to do with stagecraft were no less important to Crowne than those of statecraft, argues Shimko, as theatre professionals regarded censorship as a rejuvenation of Puritan objections to the theatre which characterized the period running up to and during the Interregnum. Shimko shows how Crowne intensified the violence of *Henry VI* and superimposed the Wars of the Roses, the English Civil War, and the imminent threat of political collapse: Crowne's 'revision of Shakespearian dramaturgy and his amplification of Shakespeare's violent imagery reflect the royalist program of selective historiography and scare tactics meant to deter the Whigs from renewing their challenge to royal authority' (p. 85).

Farah Karim-Cooper (head of Courses and Research in Globe Education at Shakespeare's Globe) and Kate Rumbold (co-ordinator of the Shakespeare Institute's research project entitled 'Interrogating Cultural Value in the Twenty-First Century: The Case of Shakespeare') swap notes in the lively 'Literary Heritage: Stratford and the Globe' (*E&S* [2009] 147–54). They identify two prevalent contrasting myths of Shakespeare—the rural, solitary genius of Stratford and the 'edgy, urban playwright working in London' (p. 147). Such idea(l)s generate differing audience expectations, albeit that in both settings, Shakespeare is 'a brand that sells!' (p. 149). Karim-Cooper suggests that the increase in participatory Shakespeare (in the tourist experience as well as in the vogue for thrust stages and promenade productions) is the result of the digital age. Rumbold responds, 'Partly in response to new digital technologies, theorists are locating authenticity not in the place which you visit but in the experience of the tourist. You can have an authentic experience anywhere' (p. 149). But she also notes, perhaps disconcertingly, that there has been 'a big move in cultural funding policy towards the idea that the public should decide which institutions deserve public money' (p. 149). The increased political clout of Tommy Taxpayer may yet see the demise of expensive cultural institutions in these straitened times. The Globe, exempt from the responsibilities of justifying demands on the public purse, is forced to choose a greater evil, corporate sponsorship which generates programme titles like 'Playing Shakespeare with Deutsche Bank' (p. 151). Unsurprisingly, this is a malign pressure Karim-Cooper is keen to play down: 'It may look like the Globe is quite corporate' (p. 151), to which we might respond, much virtue in that 'may look like'. In spite of their contrasting funding structures, the two companies share educational and creative imperatives. One example mentioned here is the funding of new writing. Karim-Cooper cites the instance of Che Walker's 'brilliant new play' (p. 153) *Frontline*, and Rumbold mentions Adriano Shapiro's *The Tragedy of Thomas*

Hobbes. I left the first play at the interval and fell asleep during the second—proof either of my obtuseness or of the companies' misplaced aspirations.

Karim-Cooper has co-edited the most thorough and diverse collection of essays on the Globe to date. *Shakespeare's Globe: A Theatrical Experiment* [2008], co-edited with Christie Carson collects sixteen essays by actors, directors, education practitioners, academics, costume designers, and composers, all of whom have some degree of intimacy with the building, its productions, its architecture, or its theatrical or educational practices. The volume, write its editors, aims 'to re-establish a dialogue between the scholar and the practitioner' (p. 6), but it also admits that 'The Globe Theatre has been a disappointment to many scholars' (p. 9). In spite of the editors' desire for a rapprochement between the actor and the academic, occasionally the resentments get the better of the contributors. Director Tim Carroll muses venomously about the assumptions critics make 'in their shallow way' (p. 39) and later bitterly opines that an audience 'can cope with anything—a lot more, at any rate, than most critics' (p. 42), though one wonders whether audience or critic could make sense of Carroll's admiration of 'the divine *flatus* of imagination' (p. 44)—good job it's an open-air theatre, I suppose.

Carson introduces a section of the volume dedicated to 'Original Practices' and bravely declares that OP raised as many problems as it solved: 'The very real demands of the audiences and the building as a tourist centre at times were at odds with the serious approach taken to recreating the period' (p. 33). Of course authenticity is more of a Holy Grail than an achievable outcome (and has since been abandoned by the current artistic director, Dominic Dromgoole). Alan C. Dessen's '"Original Practices" at the Globe: A Theatre Historian's View' emphasizes, in the teeth of the editors' aspirations about bringing practitioners and scholars together, the distinctiveness of the communities: 'the findings of theatre historians have had little impact on today's productions'. One reason for this, he suggests, is the deeply conservative nature of theatrical thinking, where concepts such as character, human nature, and 'psychological or narrative realism' (p. 46) remain in the ascendant. Perhaps most intriguingly, Dessen suggests that in spite of—or perhaps because of—our scholarly and technical advances, we have lost touch with the world of these plays: 'are we today with our superior know-how and technology missing images or linkages that would have been obvious, even italicised to original playgoers?' (p. 52.) In 'Exploring Early Modern Stage and Costume Design' Jenny Tiramani is wisely sceptical about OP, noting that 'every OP production we did in the first ten years at the Globe proposed a particular interpretation of the evidence we have' (p. 57). She is also rightly dismissive of the tendency of designers to augment the Globe stage in a way that clutters the production rather than expressing the story. Often, she writes, it has 'resulted in a confused, jumbled stage picture that was not helpful to the unfolding narrative of the play' (p. 60). Claire van Kampen's 'Music and Aural Texture at Shakespeare's Globe' and David Lindley's 'Music, Authenticity and Audience' both argue, like Dessen above, for the Elizabethan currency of particular connotations which have since vanished. Each discusses the tantalizing possibility that certain tunes (such as military music) or instruments (such as the lute and the viol, 'which signified a royal or noble character', p. 81) carried particular associations which are now lost on a modern audience. Scholarship, argues Lindley, ought to try to recover these associations. Van Kampen is rather less persuasive when she offers as justification for its inclusion the audience expectation for there to be a jig at the end of each production: they 'would consider the play "unfinished" if it were not there' (p. 87). This is neither artistically nor historically justified but submits to the worst populist tendencies of the Globe. In 'Research, Materials, Craft: Principles of Performance at Shakespeare's Globe' Mark Rylance—probably the Globe's best performer and its most confused artistic director—is typically mysterious, talking about 'the Globe's spirit [and] the sacred geometry of the architecture' (p. 109). He endorses Carroll's disdain for the critics: 'He [Carroll] certainly learned that reading theatre critics was a waste of time' (p. 110). In 'Democratising the Audience?' Carson is much more astute and circumspect when she asserts that 'The work of the Globe Theatre has destabilised what had been seen as accepted truths about Shakespearean performance' (p. 125).

Karim-Cooper introduces the volume's second section, 'Globe Education and Research', and underlines the Globe's stress on placing 'the learner at its centre' (p. 131). Contributions follow from the director of Globe Education, Patrick Spottiswoode, whose 'Contextualising Globe Education' details the history of its foundation and its centrality to the Globe project as a whole. He recounts how in 1974 Sam Wanamaker asked Warren Mitchell to give the Shakespeare sermon in Southwark Cathedral 'in the persona of his infamous comic TV character, Alf Garnett. The Bishop and clergy walked out in high dudgeon and refused to speak to Sam again' (p. 135). In ' "That scull [*sic*] had a tongue in it and could sing once": Staging Shakespeare's Contemporaries' James Wallace offers an account of the Globe's aspiration to give rehearsed readings of the 500 or so extant plays of the period (160 and counting) in the 'Read not Dead' series. Interestingly (and revealingly) these hastily mounted productions—rehearsed and performed in a single day—depend on an ensemble rather than a director as 'a single pole of authority' (p. 153). Fiona Banks, in 'Learning with the Globe', describes the similarities between playing a role on the stage of the Globe and being in front of a class. In places though, she is distinctly mawkish: 'The universality of Shakespeare's stories and the dilemmas faced by his characters have great resonance with twenty-first-century students' (p. 157). In 'Research and the Globe' Martin White notes that the discussions about the building continue: 'there is a high level of speculation about the physical nature of the building itself' (p. 166). Like many of the other contributors to the volume, White is prepared to admit that the Globe is a best guess, and his scepticism extends to the idea of OP: 'Just as building a physical reconstruction might convince us that its solutions are therefore more solid, so we must beware of believing that Globe performances provide a similarly reliable window into past practices' (p. 172).

The final section, 'Research in Practice, Practice in Research', adds little to the above. Carson and Karim-Cooper, in their introduction to this section, call for a 'more rigorous approach to criticism of the "original practices" aesthetic, which takes into account its full developmental process' (p. 179). In 'Performing Early Modern Music at Shakespeare's Globe' Claire van

Kampen, Keith McGowan, and William Lyons reiterate the points made by van Kampen and Lindley above—that certain specific kinds of music may well have carried particular associations that are lost on a modern audience. At one point, Lyons deftly torpedoes the entire OP project: 'The trouble with being a purist is that you do not actually know what happened in the theatre' (p. 192). Mark Rylance, Yolanda Vazquez, and Paul Chahidi describe the experience of acting on the Globe stage in 'Discoveries from the Globe Stage', during which Vazquez comes up with the delightfully nonsensical pronouncement that 'Women walk with parallel feet and men walk with one foot in front of another' (p. 202). 'Directing at the Globe and the Blackfriars: Six Big Rules for Contemporary Directors' does exactly what it says on the tin, although there is nothing essentially Globish or Blackfriarish about these rules. Indeed any theatre company would do well to follow exhortations to 'have actors attend strictly to the words' (p. 213) or 'challenge your audience and do not be afraid to make them work' (p. 222). Cohen's wholly admirable fear of litigation is noteworthy—'Actors should be careful never to touch an audience member' (p. 221)—especially in the light of Vazquez's earlier delight in doing precisely that: 'You can push audience members around and play with them and see what their reactions are going to be, which can be fun' (p. 201). 'Conclusions' manifests Carson's and Karim-Cooper's misplaced optimism in the Arts and Humanities Research Council, which has funded Globe research in the past and whose generosity is as much a distant memory as the original Globe itself. Gordon McMullan's 'Afterword' describes the working relationship between the theatre and King's College London's Department of English, which is not particularly useful in terms of drawing the volume's diverse contributions (both in topic and in quality) together. Historians of the Globe will need to be cognizant of this book, though in no way will it be the last word on the subject.

It sounds as though David Tennant is hostile towards the idea of OP: 'I think that the whole doublet and hose thing is, not insurmountable, but it is a barrier to connecting with a modern-day audience' (p. 301). 'Interview: David Tennant on *Hamlet*' (*Shakespeare* 5[2009] 291–301) is a frank and intelligent exchange with Abigail Rokison about the casting, rehearsal processes, and some of the particular production decisions made during Greg Doran's RSC version of the play, which opened in the Courtyard Theatre in July 2008 before transferring to the Novello during December 2008/January 2009. Tennant is incisive on the differences between the two theatre spaces: 'I thought that I would hate moving to a pros. arch in the West End, but the Novello is such a beautifully designed theatre, that nobody feels very far away' (p. 300). He is also disarmingly frank on the play's Oedipal readings: 'I don't really see where he wants to fuck her [Gertrude]' (p. 299), as well as on the character's possible madness: 'Whether or not he is mad is for an audience or a doctor to decide, it's certainly not for Hamlet to decide' (p. 299). The production will be remembered for the shifting of scenes and the brilliant touch of placing the interval after Hamlet's 'Now might I do it pat' (III.iii.73), plunging the audience into darkness as Hamlet stood behind and upstage of a kneeling Claudius (Patrick Stewart): 'If you have never seen *Hamlet* before you should believe that he is going to plunge the knife into his back. Or even if you have seen it before, you might just for a second go, "Is he . . . ?"' (p. 297). But for all the production's innovations, Tennant is complacently aware that this is still the most canonical play for the most canonical company: 'it's *Hamlet* at the Royal Shakespeare Company, which is where you would want to play Hamlet if you're going to do it' (p. 292).

3. Shakespeare on Screen

In 2009 just two books focused exclusively upon screen adaptations. Both texts chart the chronological extremities of the scholarly area. Judith Buchanan's monograph, *Shakespeare on Silent Film: An Excellent Dumb Discourse* offers a rewardingly close study of films released between 1899 and 1922. *Apocalyptic Shakespeare: Essays on Visions of Chaos and Revelation in Recent Film Adaptations*, edited by Melissa Croteau and Carolyn Jess-Cooke, collects the work of twelve scholars on a range of films released between 1976 and the present day.

Judith Buchanan gives sustained and detailed attention to the earliest Shakespeare films, and her nuanced examination attests to the intriguing interpretations offered by these films. It is a significant study—the only previous book-length study of 'silent' Shakespeare was published in the late 1960s. Buchanan acknowledges her debt to Robert Hamilton Ball's scholarship, and her book builds on the research published in his *Shakespeare on Silent Film: An Eventful History* [1968], while also drawing extensively on his archive (held at the Folger Shakespeare Library). Although 250 to 300 Shakespearian silent films were evidently made, Buchanan suggests only forty have survived. Twenty-three are analysed in some detail here, combining a number of the extant films (several of which have been released on DVD) and some 'lost' adaptations (such as J.M. Barrie's 1916 *The Real Thing at Last*), which are interpreted through archival research. The rationale behind the choice is straightforwardly subjective: 'All case-study films . . . are chosen for their capacity to illustrate with particular clarity, grace or piquancy some of the symptomatic issues raised by silent Shakespeare films as a more extensive body' (p. 5). Buchanan's movement between a personal response (as in her engagement with her variety of viewing contexts) and a collective 'we' testifies to a current tension about the positioning of the viewer which it might perhaps have been rewarding to examine.

Buchanan's interest in what might be learnt about early film-making drives the study. Although the case-studies provide material for the consideration of perspectives and attitudes towards the plays at the time, attention is most clearly directed towards what can be gleaned about 'the film industry' (p. 17). That singular phrase suggests a unity in the behaviour and style of the American and European film-makers which is consistent with the first chapter's interest in the extent to which a nineteenth-century preoccupation with Shakespeare manifested itself on both sides of the Atlantic. The first chapter suggests fluid connections, and it establishes a range of antecedents to filmed Shakespeare. Buchanan focuses upon five areas: 'the magic lantern, the pantomimic and spectacular stage traditions, the quest for theatrical realism, the desire to frame performance and the taste for narrative' (p. 24).

Exploration of the prevalence of Shakespearian images in the magic lantern shows provides especially fascinating original research.

The second chapter examines the 'production, character, exhibition and reception' (p. 58) of the oft-cited 1899 *King John* film. Buchanan concludes by making explicit her wish to maintain a chronological progression through the material. Tree's starring role in *Macbeth* [1916] is discussed in the sixth chapter in recognition that 'films of 1916 belong to a different world—a world of commercially ambitious, technically proficient, interpretively attentive, market-canny, star-driven, multi-reel production' (p. 73). In chapters 3, 4, and 5, Buchanan considers 'the transitional period' between 1907 and 1913. The third chapter focuses on the English 1908 *The Tempest* and the Italian 1909 *Otello*, both of which have, until now, received limited scholarly attention, and Buchanan draws attention to the 'stylistic divisions' (p. 88) in both films. Chapter 4 concentrates on the Vitagraph Company in America and suggests that the twelve films from that studio can 'sit more lightly to the notion of heritage and so dare to embrace cinematic inventive possibility, and indeed self-parody' (p. 104). The breadth of that chapter's analysis shifts when the study focuses on two *Hamlet* versions, the English 1913 version with Forbes-Robertson as Hamlet and the Italian 1917 *Amleto* with Ruggeri in the title role. By tracing connections between the earlier film and the later, Buchanan directs attention towards shifts in the physical performances of the respective protagonists, reflecting upon 'the differing cultural registers of the variant styles of acting for the camera' (p. 187).

The sixth chapter functions in a climactic way by including films from 1916, the tercentenary of Shakespeare's death. The British–American axis dominates the discussion of the *Macbeth*, *Romeo and Juliet* (both English), and an American *Romeo and Juliet*. Attention is drawn to how the styles from different sides of the Atlantic are parodied in another 1916 film, J.M. Barrie's *The Real Thing at Last: The 'Macbeth' Murder Mystery*. Chapter 7 proceeds to locate Svend Gade and Heinz Schall's 1920 *Hamlet* and Dimitri Buchowetzki's 1922 *Othello* firmly within the 'artistically ambitious German film industry' (p. 192). Buchanan's decision to complete her analysis by engaging briefly with the work of Synetic Theater provokes valuable questions about the relationship between the early films and contemporary Shakespearian interpretations. Synetic Theater is a company based in Washington, DC, and Buchanan grants space to an interview with the director and lead actor, Paata Tsikurishvili. The generalized focus upon 'what cultural prejudices wordless performances of Shakespeare have to combat' (p. 21) seems to work against much of the more context-specific analysis earlier in the book. In chapter 1 balletic interpretations were confined to a footnote, and that neglect is perhaps more glaring in the absence of any reference to dance versions in the final chapter's engagement with non-verbal Shakespeare in the twenty-first century. Buchanan's brief consideration of how 'silent' can be a misnomer offers a signal to areas which might be fruitfully developed by others. Buchanan's text is provocative and stimulating and, set against her enthusiasm, rigorous research, and thought-provoking analysis, the majority of the year's output is frankly dull.

Apocalyptic Shakespeare struggles to maintain the dynamic promise of its title. The eleven essays all engage with films realized over the past two decades. Melissa Croteau's introduction, 'Beginning at the Ends', celebrates the ways in which the 'apocalyptic is such a multivalent and versatile phenomenon' (p. 9). Her emphatic tone strikes an overly defensive note at the beginning of the text and the range of approaches taken in the essays means that the book's argument fails to cohere. As a collection the essays struggle to combat the perspective of film scholar Jon Stone, who Croteau cites in her introduction, suggesting that his worries that apocalypse is a 'catch-all metaphorical category' merely demonstrate his 'more orthodox or conservative' credentials (p. 8). Too often throughout this collection of essays repeated attempts to define apocalyptic, post-apocalyptic, post-cataclysmic, and postmodern frames of reference obscure a more direct engagement with the film texts. Perhaps part of the problem is that the 'Shakespeare on screen' scholarly field has come close to saturation point with the pre- and post-millennial film work, such as Luhrmann's *Romeo + Juliet* [1996], Almereyda's *Hamlet* [2000], Taymor's *Titus* [2000], Levring's *The King is Alive* [2000], and Radford's *The Merchant of Venice* [2004].

The customary 'Shakespeare on Film' issue of *Literature/Film Quarterly* similarly struggles to group its articles in a rewarding way. They are loosely combined by the theme of '"Rewriting" Shakespeare, Rewriting Films'. Elsie Walker, the editor, seeks to suggest that the title accentuates the articles' adoption of methods which resist the 'deadening power of fidelity-led adaptation studies' (p. 82). However, the disparate mix of approaches within the volume labour to inject life when revisiting films such as Olivier's *Richard III* [1955], Kozintsev's *Hamlet* [1964] and *Korol Lir* [1970], Pacino's *Looking for Richard* [1996], and Rogerson's *Shakespeare Behind Bars* [2005]. Amanda Kane Rooks offers what is perhaps the most stimulating article on the 2006 Australian *Macbeth*: 'Macbeth's Wicked Women: Sexualised Evil in Geoffrey Wright's *Macbeth*' (*LFQ* 37:ii[2009] 151–60). Her piece engages with the play's critical context and the film's cultural moment in order to engage in a sensitively complex way with the film's relationship with current 'oppressive ideologies' (p. 159).

Shakespeare Bulletin includes a similar mixture of essays. John Blakeley's discussion of the ending of *Shakespeare in Love* [1997]—'Shakespearean Relocations: The Final Scene of John Madden's *Shakespeare in Love*' (*ShB* 27:ii[2009] 249–59)—makes peculiarly generalized assumptions about Hollywood's attitude towards Shakespeare, about Gwyneth Paltrow's centrality in *Shakespeare in Love*, and about critical attitudes towards *The Tempest*. Ayanna Thompson edited the autumn issue of the journal, entitled 'Shakespeare, Race and Performance' (*ShB* 27:iii[2009]), and she provides the sole film-orientated contribution. The form of 'Two Actors on Shakespeare, Race and Performance: A Conversation between Harry J. Lennix and Laurence Fishburne' (*ShB* 27:ii[2009] 399–414) can be related to the practitioner interview which completes Buchanan's monograph. The actors' reflections situate their own acting experiences in a wider context—Lennix played Aaron in Julie Taymor's 2000 *Titus* and Fishburne was Othello in Kenneth Branagh's 1995 film. Thompson provides a short preface to the interview suggesting that 'performance historians and theorists will find a wealth of material in this conversation' (p. 399). The absence of any analysis following the transcription in combination with the meandering structure of the conversation makes it hard to discern the value of such general reflections.

It is perhaps useful to set the discursive conversation alongside the written materials cited in Cary M. Mazer's analysis when he considers more structured actor accounts and memoirs. These written materials form the concluding part of Mazer's article, which examines 'Sense/Memory/Sense-Memory: Reading Narrative of Shakespearian Rehearsals' (*ShS* 62[2009] 328–48). The essay explores actor training and focuses on the implications of 'the Stanislavskian paradigm—the reciprocal discovery of the self in the role and the role in the self' (p. 342). Mazer takes Branagh's *In the Bleak Midwinter* [1995] as a point of departure for his consideration of 'the persistence of the Stanislavskian, emotional-realist paradigm in contemporary English-language Shakespeare performance' (p. 332). Mazer points to an anxiety in audience responses to the close identification between actor and their role: 'such identification, and such presence, [is] oddly terrifying' (p. 332). He then casts back to George Cukor's *A Double Life* [1947] which, he notes, yokes psychoanalysis and Stanislavskian acting. The Coleman/Tony/Othello role in the film 'becomes a dramatized lesson in Method-acting' (p. 334). The argument progresses to draw thoughtfully precise connections between Richard Eyre's *Stage Beauty* [2004], the Canadian television mini-series *Slings and Arrows* [2003–6], and Hank Rogerson's *Shakespeare Behind Bars* [2005]. The final section of the article engages with a written account of rehearsal process in the form of Antony Sher's *Woza Shakespeare!* Mazer strengthens the connection between this kind of material (he notes that there are more than a dozen book-length eyewitness reports on theatre productions) by recognizing an element of crafting, shaping, and fictionalizing in these written narratives. He sees this as similar to the creation of those films which are more openly fictions. Mazer's conclusion suggests that collectively they amplify the idea that 'theatre—and Shakespeare in particular—is transformative' (p. 347). They celebrate the 'redemptiveness of Shakespeare' (p. 341). Mazer resists the kind of distant, dismissive scholarly positioning which has become all too common. He grants authority to the engaging energy and popularity of his materials. His article provides a refreshing corrective to esoteric rejections of whatever meets mainstream approbation.

The winter issue of *Shakespeare Bulletin* includes two screen-related articles. Rob Conkie, in 'Shakespeare Aftershocks: Shylock' (*ShB* 27:iv[2009] 549–66), suggests that there are aftershocks from *The Merchant of Venice* present in *Star Wars: Episode 1—The Phantom Menace* [1999], *Borat* [2006], and *Tropic Thunder* [2008]. The focus on the intention behind the three films, 'why these kinds of aftershock effects should (re)surface within the last decade' (p. 550), perhaps provides Conkie with an unanswerable question. The abrupt movement between mainstream contemporary film and British stage production signals an unresolved tension in the links the article attempts to forge: 'Borat, of course, screams anti-Semitic controversy not less vehemently than

Laurence Olivier's vanquished and exiting Shylock in Jonathan Miller's Victoria-era production of 1970' (p. 550).

The most incisive and stimulating journal article this year comes from Michael D. Friedman: 'Horror, Homosexuality, and Homiciphilia' (*ShB* 27:iv[2009] 567–88). He provides a detailed, invigorating, and tightly woven argument. The piece responds to Peter S. Donaldson's work on Loncraine's *Richard III* [1995], and seeks to reframe Donaldson's suggestion of necrophilia as '"homiciphilia" ... the sexual pleasure that McKellen's Richard appears to derive from homicide' (p. 568). Friedman makes rewarding connections with classic Hollywood horror films of the 1930s which work convincingly to display Richard III's 'conservative sexual politics' (p. 572) in contrast to Jarman's *Edward II* [1991], which 'concedes nothing to the straight establishment' (p. 569). The use of precise detail from both films adds considerable authority to the argument. Friedman justifies his decision to consider Richard III and Edward II alongside each other on a textual and extra-textual level. There are strong parallels drawn between the attitudes of both men to their respective screenplays, and also thoughtful connections with contemporary events, such as Jarman's public reaction to McKellen accepting a knighthood in 1991. The essay usefully complicates the relationship between on- and off-screen personae.

One aspect of Friedman's argument chimes with the sole screen-specific essay in Paul Yachnin and Jessica Slights's edited collection, *Shakespeare and Character: Theory, History, Performance and Theatrical Persons*. Trevor Ponech's 'The Reality of Fictive Cinematic Characters' (pp. 41–61) promises an engagement which might usefully complement the more genre-inflected and time-period-driven perspectives offered elsewhere in the field this year. It is a shame, therefore, that critical rhetoric clouds and obscures Ponech's broadly conceived discussion of 'cinema's ontology' (p. 45). The preoccupation with the 'Stroboluminescent display (SLD)' dominates a limitingly literal approach to questions of realism in Kurosawa's *Throne of Blood* [1957].

There are several references to Shakespeare on screen in the essays in Martha W. Driver and Sid Ray's collection, *Shakespeare and the Middle Ages: Essays on the Performance and Adaptation of the Plays with Medieval Sources or Settings*. The editors introduce the volume by establishing a cinematic context. Al Pacino's decision to set his version of *Richard III* (in *Looking for Richard* [1996]) in New York City's Cloisters museum is, Driver and Ray suggest, symptomatic of the way that the film offered a 'pastiche of old and new' (p. 7). As the syntax of the introductory statement attests, screen versions predominate. The volume examines 'films, television productions, and staged productions of Shakespeare's plays, specifically those that derive from medieval sources or are set in the Middle Ages' (p. 7). All too often the connections are briefly sketched (as the Pacino reference demonstrates). The piece is prefaced by a transcript of a conversation between the film director Michael Almereyda and theatre practitioner Dakin Matthews (pp. 1–6). The interview provides a third example from this year's body of work of a desire to give space to contemporary voices. The interview, it is suggested, offers evidence of the ways in which 'Shakespeare's medieval narratives continue to be reshaped and replayed' (p. 7). The legacy of scholarly studies published in

2009 would seem to be an emerging impulse to craft polyvocal accounts and to redirect attention towards early Shakespearian cinema. It will be interesting to see what kind of response 2010 brings.

4. Criticism

(a) General

Postcolonialism and interculturalism continue to be useful lenses through which to consider Shakespeare and his works. The general section this year begins by looking at three books which amply demonstrate the insights to be gained from research conducted in these two areas. Themed collections of new essays, monographs, miscellaneous volumes, and journal articles will then be reviewed in turn.

Chinese Shakespeares: Two Centuries of Cultural Exchange is a fascinating and important study by Alexander C.Y. Huang. The prologue and chapters 1–3 tell the history of Chinese Shakespeare, starting with the arrival of Jesuit missionaries in 1582 and proceeding to the rise of imperial Western culture in the nineteenth century, when Chinese intellectuals first began seriously to question traditional (Confucian) cultural norms. In the early twentieth century, Shakespeare's history plays in particular were enlisted to support the interests of 'the male elite class' (p. 7). On the other hand, urban centres such as Hong Kong and Shanghai placed different emphases. Silent film versions of Shakespeare comedies (*The Woman Lawyer*, based on *The Merchant of Venice* [1927] and *A Spray of Plum Blossom*, a version of *The Two Gentlemen of Verona* [1931]) promoted the 'new woman's movement', especially with regard to the entry of women into the legal profession (p. 8). Shakespeare's stories first appeared in Chinese in a 1904 adaptation of the Lambs' *Tales from Shakespeare* [1807]. Two competing strains of Chinese Shakespeare emerged: traditional/Confucian and westward-looking/historical. Reflecting this split, Lao She's novel *New Hamlet* [1936] was 'based on the premise that modern China in a time of transition displays a Hamlet complex' (p. 87).

Chapter 4 discusses silent film and early theatrical versions of Chinese Shakespeare. Huang Zuolin's 'highly political' Shanghai production *The Hero of a Tumultuous Time* [1945] was based on Li Jianwu's play *Wang Deming* [1944], itself an adaptation of *Macbeth*. Huang stresses the importance of location. Li Jianwu and his fellow dramatists declined to write plays for the occupying Japanese army in Shanghai. However, Li changed his mind in 1942, possibly because he thought the theatre's commercial nature left it relatively free from Japanese control. Nonetheless, Li 'was faced with the moral and practical question of how to turn theatre into a force of resistance' (p. 108). Commercial imperatives did not always serve such a benign function, however. In Chinese films, the 'new woman' motif became 'a channel through which the spectators' voyeuristic curiosity about the life of educated, professional woman is satisfied' (p. 113). Chapter 5 provides 'site-specific' readings of versions of *Hamlet* staged in a Confucian temple and a labour camp respectively. Huang also describes how, in 1957, *Much Ado About Nothing* was employed as a safe non-political vehicle by the Soviet drama expert Yevgeniya Lipkovskaya, with the connivance of the state. Given this, Huang's assertion that '[t]he actors and director were not at all interested in making the play relevant' does not seem plausible. As Huang notes, several members of the cast suffered persecution. Huang says this was not linked to *Much Ado* but occurred because the actors in question 'had committed antirevolutionary "crimes" in the past' (p. 151). Apparently, Huang seems to doubt the presence of social commentary because of the production's emphasis on psychological realism. Elizabethan authors, it might be argued, created a notion of a performative subjectivity (just as the Stanislavsky quotation supplied by Huang seems to recommend) in order to ward off the intrusive attentions of a regime which demanded shows of loyalty.

Chapter 6 treats the 1980s and the tendency 'to essentialise *xiqu* ['Chinese opera'] and Shakespeare' as a consequence of interculturalism (p. 168). The relationship between actor-disciple and master-instructor is explored in chapter 7. Huang notes that the twenty-first century has seen Chinese actors bring their 'personal stories' to their interpretations of Shakespeare (p. 197). This trend is especially noticeable in 'marginal' localities such as Taiwan, Hong Kong, and Singapore (p. 200). In the Taiwan-based actor Wu Hsing-kuo's *Lear is Here*, '[t]he tension between father and child in *King Lear* is turned into an allegory about Wu's uneasy relationship with his *jingju* master', which relates in turn to the dialogue between conflicting theatrical traditions and political ideologies (p. 220). Finally, in the Epilogue, Huang diagnoses 'asymmetrical cultural flows', whereby Asian visuality is consumed as global fad while, at the same time, 'ethnic authenticity' is rejected by members of the culture being appropriated (p. 20).

Also focusing on intercultural Shakespeare is the special section ('South African Shakespeare in the 20th Century') of *Shakespeare International Yearbook* 9, guest-edited by Laurence Wright. In his introduction, 'South African Shakespeare in the 20th Century' (*ShIntY* 9[2009] 3–28), Wright summarizes twentieth-century South African Shakespeare scholarship. In the first of the special section's essays, 'Loyal Memory: The Tercentenary in Colonial Cape Town' (*ShIntY* 9[2009] 29–45), Peter Merrington uses the Cape Town celebrations of the tercentenary of Shakespeare's death as a springboard for consideration of Shakespeare in relation to colonialists' claims to moral authority. In the context of the First World War's demonstration that Germany and Britain did not share the same values and goals, it became clear that high culture was no guarantee of civilization or colonialists' right to govern. How, in that case, to celebrate the Bard's tercentenary? In Cape Town, Merrington observes, the answer was either to rely on pageantry and nostalgia (p. 37) or to insist on Shakespeare's patriotism. Staying with the 300th anniversary of the Stratfordian's demise, Victor Houliston, in '*The Merchant of Venice* in the City of Gold: The Tercentenary in Johannesberg' (*ShIntY* 9[2009] 46–65), ponders the choice of staging *The Merchant of Venice* as the main event of Johannesberg's celebrations given the fact that '[s]ome of the richest men in the city were Jews' (p. 46). Houliston points out that Shakespeare's Elizabethan works (not his Jacobean ones) were 'the product on sale in the colonies' (p. 55) because 'Elizabethan' stood for English courage, chivalry, expansion, and so forth. The essay brings out points of contrast between the capital city and Merrington's Cape Town. Johannesberg was still finding its identity in 1916; there was much new money, and the rich were young and less 'establishment' in their attitudes. Interest in Shakespeare, therefore, had to be whipped up, not always with success (as Houliston shows).

In 'The Colonial Encounter and *The Comedy of Errors*: Solomon Plaatje's *Diphoso-phosho*' (*ShIntY* 9[2009] 66–86), Deborah Seddon focuses on Plaatje's translation of Shakespeare's early comedy. Plaatje, whose *Mhudi* is considered 'the first novel in English by a black South African' (p. 66), saw the translation of Shakespeare's texts as a means of preserving aspects of his native language, Setswana, especially proverbial material. This view was based on an apprehension of Shakespeare's own relationship to an endangered oral culture. Plaatje chose to translate *The Comedy of Errors* because the play's representation of 'repeated errors of perception match[es] the colonial alien's misapprehension of the indigenous South Africans' (p. 70). However, where Shakespeare's Antipholus of Syracuse 'reiterates the sense of being overwhelmed by sorcery', Plaatje's translation stresses 'the fundamental concept of sociality among [Tswana] people' (p. 76).

Rohan Quince, in 'Shakespeare on the Apartheid Stage: The Subversive Strain' (*ShIntY* 9[2009] 87–104), describes subversive Shakespeare productions in South Africa between the Second World War and the first democratic elections in 1994. The first production with a black cast was a staging of *The Tempest* in 1946. Quince objects to the chief aim of the white liberals behind the production, however—this apparently being to show that blacks were capable of 'doing' high culture. In 1947 came the first Shakespeare production with Afrikan actors: *Hamlet*, in an Afrikaans translation. 'Parallels between Hamlet's claim to the throne and Afrikaners' claim to political control of their land were articulated among the cast' (p. 89). The production was well received. Indeed, the moment was evidently ripe: a year later Jan Smuts's United Party lost power to D.F. Malan's National Party, 'and the apartheid era began in earnest' (p. 90). The first Indian Shakespeare production in South Africa (*The Comedy of Errors* [1968]) was more muted. 'The much later date, relative to other groups, suggests the Indian community's resistance to the idea of Shakespeare as a litmus test of civilisation' (p. 90). The 1970s saw the development of 'consciously subversive Shakespeare' organized by university drama departments, independent theatres, and state-sponsored arts councils (pp. 87–8). A preview of a 1970 production of *Titus Andronicus* performed before black stagehands and their families had an explosive effect: 'When Aaron made his speech pledging to train his son to become a warrior, the audience rose screaming to their feet, with women running down the aisles holding up their babies—presumably as potential warriors in the anti-apartheid struggle' (p. 92). In the 1980s multiracial casts were at last allowed (in *Othello Slegs Blankes*, a 1972 version of *Othello*, the title character never appeared on stage). Quince also discusses a 1985 production of *Julius Caesar* which 'avoided the ultimately pessimistic outcome', seeming thereby to intimate that assassinations might be justified and effective (p. 97). Finally, Quince considers possible reasons why the government tolerated subversive

Shakespeare productions: perhaps it was concerned for the state's international reputation, or the ideological content was not obvious enough to represent a threat, or theatre audiences were considered too small to worry about, or allowing such performances was an easy way to keep middle-class intellectuals happy.

Guest-editor Wright contributes '*Umabatha*: Zulu play or Shakespeare Translation?' (*ShIntY* 9[2009] 105–30), describing the genesis of *Umabatha*, a 'Zulu drama on the theme of *Macbeth*', first performed in 1972 in Durban (p. 121). The play went on to international success, attracting criticism as a product of apartheid ideology. Nonetheless, as Wright notes, the apartheid regime opposed the play's performance in London. The work's Zulu author, Welcome Msomi, turned *Macbeth* into a black comedy. 'In Zulu culture', Msomi remarked, 'we celebrate the death of a king.' Wright contends that this attitude is 'far removed from Shakespeare' (p. 116). But is it? One thinks of the jigs witnessed by contemporary audience members at the ends of plays such as *Julius Caesar*.

Robert Gordon, in 'Iago and the *Swart Gevaar*: The Problems and Pleasure of a (Post)colonial *Othello*' (*ShIntY* 9[2009] 131–51), assesses the 1987 Market Theatre production of *Othello*, whose director, Janet Suzman, was returning to South Africa after success with the RSC. Despite its having the first black Othello to play before mixed-race audiences in South Africa, Gordon finds Suzman's production guilty of liberal white implicit racism. Likewise, Natasha Distiller, in 'Tony's Will: *Titus Andronicus* in South Africa 1995' (*ShIntY* 9[2009] 152–70), detects narcissism in the expatriate South African actor Anthony Sher's published diary response to South African indifference to, and criticism of, the production of *Titus* he staged in his native country (with director Gregory Doran).

Finally, in 'Giving Place to Shakespeare in Africa: Geoffrey Haresnape's *African Tales from Shakespeare*' (*ShIntY* 9[2009] 171–91), Rebecca Fensome discusses three stories from South African poet and academic Geoffrey Haresnape's collection of narratives, considering 'the role of Shakespeare's plays in colonial and post-colonial conceptions of Africa' (p. 172). 'Sooth to Say', for example, tells the story of *Antony and Cleopatra* through the eyes of the Soothsayer, who 'in his sweeping condemnation of all things Roman, makes the reader question the dichotomy drawn between Egyptian and Roman, or Europe and Africa' (p. 181).

Roshni Mooneeram's study *From Creole to Standard: Shakespeare, Language, and Literature in a Postcolonial Context* comes with a preface in which Jonathan Hope observes how the birth of languages may be studied during 'the process of creolisation'. In particular, the conflicting demands imposed by language standardization (i.e. 'a reduction in variation' and 'an increase in the possible registers of a language') may be registered in the literary productions of a given creole language. (p. ix). Chapters 1–3 of Mooneeram's text provide sociolinguistic, literary, historical, and theoretical background, while chapters 4 and 5 concentrate on the Mauritian Creole (MC) writer Dev Virahsawmy's Shakespeare translations. However, after noting that, in the 'literary history of young languages', poetry and theatre are the forms which develop first, chapter 2 also discusses Virahsawmy's early 'protest play', *Zeneral Makbef* [1981] (p. 71). The author initially intended to write a translation of *Macbeth* but, finding the task too difficult, used Shakespeare's text as a launchpad for his own political satire. Nonetheless, the plot of *Macbeth* was seen to reflect the postcolonial history of several African countries close to Mauritius. Accordingly, Virahsawmy's play 'warns against two types of oppression facing post-colonial countries, the risk of becoming puppets in the hands of superpowers and of becoming victims of their own leaders' (p. 75). In this context, it is intriguing that Virahsawmy found himself obliged to collaborate with the Catholic Church in Mauritius in order to secure a 'national consensus' with regard to MC orthography (p. 43). It is also noteworthy that Virahsawmy's version of *Macbeth* 'takes its cue from the overthrow of tyranny by collective action which concludes Shakespeare's play' (p. 75).

In chapter 4, Mooneeram analyses *Toufann*, Virahsawmy's 'iconoclastic' rendering of *The Tempest*, to show how Shakespeare's texts were consciously employed as a means of enhancing the translator's language (p. 142). In particular, Mooneeram discusses the methods by which Virahsawmy compensated for his inability to render Shakespeare's diction, metalanguage, metrical effects, word-doubling, puns, and allusions precisely. These strategies led to a massive extension of MC's expressive and stylistic range. Other alterations were more ideological in intent. For example, in *Toufann* Caliban is 'a brilliant technician' who 'will eventually reign as king and partner to Kordelia, Prospero's daughter' (p. 144). Furthermore, Mooneeram ponders Virahsawmy's use of 'code-switching', previously discussed in relation to *Zeneral Makbef*. Code-switching occurs when characters 'switch from one dialect or language to another as a means of register variation, since the dialects and languages which are in contact fulfil the same stylistic function as the different varieties of a language in a monolingual community' (p. 81). By treating MC as the higher register and having characters express their immorality by occasional switches to French or English, Virahsawmy 'alleviates some of the anxiety surrounding the [use of Shakespeare] in a postcolonial context' (p. 149).

Chapter 5 covers Virahsawmy's *Prins Hamlet* and *Enn ta Senn dan Vid* (*Much Ado About Nothing*). With reference to the translator's response to the hyper-neological *Hamlet*, Mooneeram notes that 'Virahsawmy's coining of hybrid terms' recalls the practice of his source (pp. 170–1). 'Whereas other Elizabethan writers often created innovations from homogeneous morphemes, Shakespeare created hybrid forms from Latinate and English morpheme combinations' (p. 171). As may be inferred, Virahsawmy selected examples from different genres to maximize the developmental effect on MC. Comedy, however, presented particular problems. Whereas in the case of *Hamlet* Virahsawmy retained classical allusions, in *Enn ta Senn dan Vid* he used popular culture references and anachronistic idioms to convey humour. Thus, 'she would have made Hercules have turned spit' became 'Sa, li kapav fer Rambo souiside' ('She would cause Rambo to commit suicide') (p. 179), and 'a skirmish of wit' is turned into 'fer satini laservel' ('make brain chutney') (p. 182). In the conclusion, Mooneeram suggests that chapters 4 and 5 confirm Itamar Even-Zohar's theory that 'the part played by translation in a literature is inherently connected with the historical evolution of that literature' (p. 226). However, unlike Even-Zohar, Mooneram (in line with the work of André Lefevere) stresses 'extra-literary factors', attending to the 'rationale behind the choice of a particular text for translation' (p. 134).

A concern with intertextual relations between nominal cultural/political centre and periphery also informs the essays in *Identity, Otherness and Empire in Shakespeare's Rome*, edited by Maria Del Sapio Garbero. In the collection's introduction Del Sapio Garbero explains that the essays will focus on Rome not so much as an ideal to be emulated but as one pole in a 'combative two-directional fashioning process' (p. 10). The book's first half asks 'What is it to be a Roman?' In the opening essay, 'Shakespeare's Romulus and Remus: Who Does the Wolf Love?', Janet Adelman argues that though Shakespeare often draws metaphorically on the Romulus and Remus legend in his Jacobean Roman plays, those plays do not feature actual brothers. Perhaps, in returning to Rome, the playwright re-encounters the 'psychic mechanism' that impelled the murderous brothers of earlier works (p. 20). The association of the rival twins motif with hunger, moreover, seems to signify an inherited wolfishness that instils tyrannical urges. Discussing *Cymbeline*, Adelman claims that Shakespeare undoes the *Lucrece* rape (Imogen is not violated). This may indicate the playwright's disillusionment with republican values. The Romulus and Remus legend is also revised in that play: Cymbeline's two sons are raised not by a female wolf, but in a male pastoral retreat. In this way, the romance purifies Roman origins prior to the translation of Rome's imperial authority to Britain.

In 'Acting the Roman: *Coriolanus*', Manfred Pfister observes that, 'far from being author of himself' as he claims, Shakespeare's Coriolanus is ' "authored" by his mother and kin, and by Rome' (p. 40). Especially interesting in this context of culturally fashioned identity is the revelation that the historical Coriolanus never existed. Rather, he was 'a fiction concocted from legendary materials to glorify a plebeian family who had made it into nobility' (p. 46). Pfister also suggests that, in contrast to Montaigne and Spenser, who attributed ancient Rome's fall to moral decadence, for Shakespeare what made Rome great were the same qualities that occasioned its collapse. The following essay, 'Antony's Ring: Remediating Ancient Rhetoric on the Elizabethan Stage', by Maddalena Pennacchia, argues that *Julius Caesar* represents Rome's alteration from republic to empire 'as a shift in communication practice'. Once a speaker is no longer required to persuade a learned council in the Senate, but, instead, must sway illiterate masses, the orator who best adapts to the new circumstances will thrive. Thus Brutus's style of ancient oratory is remediated as demagogic theatre by Antony.

A different type of style is explored by Paola Colaiacomo in 'Other from the Body: Sartorial Metatheatre in Shakespeare's *Cymbeline*'. Colaiacomo notes that, in the century after Caesar's conquest of Britain, 'Roman fashions began to be adopted by the island's chieftains and their sons' (p. 65). In Elizabethan and Jacobean England, however, '[n]otwithstanding the worship of antiquity professed by Renaissance artists, the prevailing look was one of bodily constriction, more Gothic than Latin' (p. 65). Drew Daniel, in ' "I am more an antique Roman than a Dane": Suicide, Masculinity and National Identity in

Hamlet', examines Roman attitudes to suicide, as filtered through early modern representations (here, specifically, the final scene of *Hamlet*), and how these relate to classical and Renaissance concepts of masculinity. Daniel invokes Elizabeth Freeman's term 'temporal drag', which denotes 'a salutary yet disorienting "tug backwards" at play in certain specifically queer performances of trans-historical identification'. Thus Daniel ponders the extent to which Horatio, in vowing to be 'Roman' in committing suicide in order to achieve 'communion-in-death with Hamlet', when he is not, in fact, in Rome, represents an example of temporal drag (p. 83). Next comes Del Sapio Garbero's 'interchapter', 'Fostering the Question: "Who Plays the Host?"'. The piece marshals Derrida's understanding of hospitality, according to which, when a guest is instructed to feel at home, a host is asserting his or her ability to impose laws. Del Sapio Garbero sees Shakespeare as aggressively 'hosting' Rome in *Titus Andronicus* by assembling fragments of classical culture. In addition, banquet imagery in *Antony and Cleopatra* figures a 'struggle for mastery' (p. 101). Cleopatra insists on hosting Antony but also envisages future comedians in another culture hosting *her* by restaging her parties. Likewise, *Julius Caesar* is read as an exercise in chewing over the significance of Caesar's sacrifice.

The book's second half addresses 'The Theatre of the Empire'. Gilberto Sacerdoti opens proceedings with a recondite essay: '*Antony and Cleopatra* and the Overflowing of the Roman Measure'. Early modern radical thinkers, maintains Sacerdoti, cherished 'the idea of a new, "natural" religion, superseding a Christian, "supernatural" religion', whereby peace might be procured instead of war (p. 108). Traces of this commitment may lurk in *Antony and Cleopatra*, in the form of, for example, the 'holy priests' in Act II, scene iii, who '"bless" Cleopatra not in spite of, but *because* of her very unchaste and lustful voluptuousness' (p. 109). Sacerdoti then discusses a possible allusion to Bruno's theory of an infinite universe in the play's opening scene, when Antony claims that 'new heaven, new earth' must be found if his love for Cleopatra is to be measured. Infinite space logically deprives the deity of any transcendental habitat. Thus, 'hierarchical distinctions of "low" and "high"... are completely abolished' (p. 111). Bruno, moreover, tended to personify this 'new divine and infinite nature... as a female magician or goddess'. Worship (i.e. love) of her could occasion 'the rebirth of the ancient Egyptian wisdom' (p. 116). Hence the opposition of Rome and Egypt in Shakespeare's play is appropriate to a representation of the tragic failure, under hostile political conditions, of a loving relationship between a heroic product of a masculine, supernatural religion and the female avatar of a natural religion. In 'Romans versus Barbarians: Speaking the Language of the Empire in *Titus Andronicus*', Barbara Antonucci wonders who, exactly, is producing imperial discourse in Shakespeare's early revenge tragedy. Antonucci suggests that the greatest violence in this violent work is arguably textual/linguistic. Cultural interchange between Rome and Shakespearian text is also assessed in Nancy Isenberg's 'Shakespeare's Rome in Rome's Wooden "O"'. The essay reports that a replica Globe theatre was built in Rome in 2003 in the Villa Borghese park. The venue lacked a specific cultural agenda until 2004, when it hosted 'Notes from William Shakespeare's Roman Tragedies'.

The project's director, Walter Pagliaro, coming from a classical background, combined *Julius Caesar* and *Antony and Cleopatra* with *Titus Andronicus* (in that sequence) to trace the rise and fall of republican and imperial Rome. Finally, in a coda to the book's essays, '"They that have power": The Ethics of the Roman Plays', Giorgio Melchiori analyses single scenes from *Julius Caesar*, *Coriolanus*, and *Antony and Cleopatra* from an ethical standpoint. Melchiori finds that scenes which might be considered dramatically unnecessary in these plays, such as the one depicting Cinna's lynching by the Roman mob, are 'important because they contain the ideological message of a play' (p. 196). Thus, though Shakespeare's Roman plays reflect the exemplary approach of Plutarch, where the actions of great men are considered pivotal, the dramatist adds seemingly inconsequential details which indicate that the actions of supposedly great men are themselves regulated by the combined influence of a multitude of minor events. For instance, where Plutarch's Coriolanus remembers to free his Volscian benefactor, Shakespeare's hero forgets the latter man's name. Melchiori claims that the playwright thus removes 'any possible ambiguity about his hero's character' (p. 199): the Jacobean Coriolanus is 'fundamentally indifferent towards other people' (p. 198). Attention is also paid to the relevance of Sonnet 94 ('They that haue powre to hurt...') and the Shakespeare-attributed scenes in *Edward III* to the Plutarchan concern with morality which informs the Roman plays (p. 194).

Two collections of new essays entitled *Shakespeare and the Middle Ages* appeared in 2009; one, edited by Martha W. Driver and Sid Ray, maps out its territory with a subtitle: *Essays on the Performance and Adaptation of the Plays with Medieval Sources or Settings*. Both medieval and early modern scholars contribute essays to the volume, which is superbly illustrated in a larger-than-usual format (a few millimetres taller and wider than the Blackwell Shakespeare companions). The book is divided along generic lines into four parts (covering histories, tragedies, comedies, and romances). The histories section opens with '"Richard's himself again": The Body of *Richard III* on Stage and Screen' by Jim Casey. The essay focuses on performances of Richard's wooing of Anne, pondering the foregrounding of Richard's bodily presence. Casey discusses Olivier's 1955 film version in detail before turning to various other Richards of stage and screen. In 'Falstaff in America', Catherine Loomis argues that Falstaff embodies individualism for American audiences, mocking as he does the feudal values rejected by America's European settlers. Meanwhile, 'Scoring the Fields of the Dead: Musical Styles and Approaches to Postbattle Scenes from *Henry V* (1944, 1989)', by Linda K. Schubert, discusses medieval elements in two film versions of *Henry V* from a musicologist's perspective, paying particular attention to the scoring of the post-battle scenes.

Martha W. Driver's introduction to Part II includes discussion of Kurosawa's application of Noh dramatic conventions to Shakespearian tragedies. Then, in '"We're everyone you depend on": Filming Shakespeare's Peasants', Carl James Grindley considers the role of the medieval peasant in *Romeo and Juliet* and three films related to the play. Patrick J. Cook's 'Medieval *Hamlet* in Performance' examines representations of *Hamlet*'s medievalism in stage and screen versions of the tragedy. Sid Ray analyses representations of Lady Macbeth in four film treatments of the

Scottish play in the light of references to her equivalent, Gruoch, in Shakespeare's chronicle sources (such as Boece's *Scotorum Historiae* [1527]). Though lacunae in the play-text offer opportunities to be filled in performance and commentary, Ray observes that scholars often research Macbeth's historical claims to the throne but neglect Gruoch's status as princess. Polanski's and Welles's diminution of Lady Macbeth's role in their respective film versions offers a contrast to the feminist reading in Chris Terrio's film *Heights* [2005], which occludes Macbeth and puts Glenn Close, playing an actress rehearsing the part of Lady Macbeth, in the foreground.

Ray also contributes the introduction to Part III, which discusses medieval aspects of *As You Like It*. Ray suggests that the play, 'with its five songs, may have been a very early prototype for musical theatre'. This speaks to the play's relationship with the *Chanson de Roland*, which, of course, is itself musical (p. 137). In 'Reading *A Midsummer Night's Dream* through Middle English Romance', Driver concentrates on the influence of Middle English romance on Shakespeare's play, especially *Huon of Burdeux* and Chaucer's 'Sir Thopas'. Also concerned with Chaucerian sources is '"Chaucer . . . the story gives": *Troilus and Cressida* and *The Two Noble Kinsmen*' by Julia Ruth Briggs.

Part IV opens with '"The Quick and the Dead": Performing the Poet Gower in *Pericles*', in which Kelly Jones explores Gower's liminal function as the Prologue figure in *Pericles*. R.F. Yeager addresses the same play in 'Shakespeare as Medievalist: What It Means for Performing *Pericles*'. Yeager contends that Shakespeare used one of Thomas Berthelette's two editions of the *Confessio Amantis* [1532 and 1554] in writing the romance. Yeager summarizes Howard Felperin's reading of *Pericles* as Shakespeare's resuscitation of the medieval Catholic miracle play, but wonders how relevant such arguments are to modern performance. Accordingly, he discusses various productions: the 1854 revival deleted Gower, references to incest, and the brothel scenes; the RSC version of 1947 also left out Gower but reinstated the brothel. When Gower finally returned in the 1957 RSC production he was 'a Trinidadian calypso singer'; then, in 1969 (again RSC), Gower was a Welsh bard. In recent versions at Washington in 2004 and 2005, Gower was absent once more (p. 223). Thus, Yeager concludes, modern productions tend to take out the medievalism that Shakespeare carefully included. Louise M. Bishop, meanwhile, finds 'A Touch of Chaucer in *The Winter's Tale*'. Shakespeare, argues Bishop, uses elements from the *Tale of Melibee* to 'place himself in England's literary history' (p. 232). Endorsing Lukas Erne's arguments, Bishop describes a Shakespeare who cared about establishing his *literary* reputation. In the book's final essay, 'Caliban's God: The Medieval and Renaissance Man in the Moon', Kim Zarins pays detailed attention to the reference to the Man in the Moon in *The Tempest*, suggesting that Caliban is aligned with this figure. 'The English folkloric tradition', Zarins explains, 'is largely the story of a man sent to the Moon as a punishment for stealing either thorns or brushwood, which he must now carry forever' (p. 247). The moon's dark spots are the signs of this outcome. Zarins discusses medieval and early modern representations of the Man in the Moon in splendid detail before considering Caliban's shifting allegiances to Setebos, Prospero, Miranda, and Stephano in the light of his relationship to the lunar figure.

The second collection of essays entitled *Shakespeare and the Middle Ages*, edited by Curtis Perry and John Watkins, is also multidisciplinary but more committed to questioning the customary binary model opposing the early modern to the medieval. Christopher Warley, in 'Shakespeare's Fickle Fee-Simple: *A Lover's Complaint*, Nostalgia, and the Transition from Feudalism to Capitalism', challenges the Marxist habit of seeing economics as the key to everything that happens in a culture. Accordingly, in his reading of *A Lover's Complaint*, Warley seeks to retain Richard Brenner's 'accidental' model while avoiding Marxist determinism. Thus he finds that the *Complaint* 'helps to create new social positions out of the logic of older social relations' (p. 24). Rather than simply bemoaning 'the loss of a former wholeness', as the speaker in a conventional love complaint might do, the 'I' in Shakespeare's text (whose identity is unstable) becomes abstract, commodifying social power. The 'fickle maid', moreover, is not merely in a subject relation to 'the transition from feudalism to capitalism'; she is the (inadvertent) cause and location of that transition (p. 38). As may be inferred, such a summary does not do justice to Warley's subtle and thought-provoking essay.

The volume's high standard is maintained by Sarah Beckwith's contribution, 'Shakespeare's Resurrections'. Beckwith investigates the apparent resurrections of Shakespearian characters presumed dead at some point in their respective narratives. These returnings offer opportunities for redemptive transformation to the characters (re)visited. A quasi-religious note is also sounded in Elizabeth Fowler's contribution, 'Towards a History of Performativity: Sacrament, Social Contract, and *The Merchant of Venice*'. Fowler asks: 'If the sacraments perform and thus produce community . . . then what happens when they are radically altered in the Reformation . . . How is society achieved?' (pp. 68–9). Social contract theory, therefore, informs Fowler's analysis of *The Merchant of Venice*, in which play Shakespeare 'revives romance topoi', with their emphasis on consent, but also interrogates them via jurisprudential concerns (p. 70).

William Kushkin, in 'Recursive Origins: Print History and Shakespeare's *2 Henry VI*', approaches *2 Henry VI* on the assumption that it was Shakespeare's first play to be printed (anonymously in 1594). Kushkin's thesis is that 'texts do not emerge simply by linear means, and so a literary history premised on linearity . . . fails to capture the essentially self-referential nature of literary reproduction' (pp. 129–30). Brian Walsh, meanwhile, in 'Chantry, Chronicle, Cockpit: *Henry V* and the Forms of History', argues that Shakespeare was not primarily concerned with conveying 'a general sense of worldly mutability'. Rather, in plays such as *Henry V*, the dramatist 'historicises practices of historiography, and in so doing, demonstrates a rupture in English historical culture between what we now call the Middle Ages and his own late-sixteenth-century moment' (p. 153). The Reformation is relevant here, of course. Since the intercessory rituals Shakespeare's Henry arranges for Richard II are not in the usual sources (Holinshed, Hall, Grafton, and Stow), William Caxton's late-fifteenth-century continuation of the *Brut* may be an additional source. Regardless of whether the representation of 'popish' practice in *Henry V* is positive or negative, Walsh prudently concludes, it places Henry conspicuously in a '*past* era' (p. 157). This is only one example of the way in which 'the form and language of *Henry V* work to assert *discontinuity* between time periods' (p. 171).

In '"For they are Englishmen": National Identities and the Early Modern Drama of Medieval Conquest', Curtis Perry finds the construction of national identity in early modern culture to be grounded in 'Elizabethan and early Stuart medievalism' (p. 173). Following Richard Helgerson, Perry sees Shakespeare's histories as achieving a 'consolidated, royalist sense of the nation only by systematically excluding alternative perspectives' (p. 175). These perspectives, however, were included in other history plays, especially Henslowe-sponsored works such as *Fair Em* and *Edmund Ironside*. Such plays celebrate the English 'ability to resist conquest by absorbing external threats'. Perry, therefore, regards these works as medievalist in their opposition to exclusionary nationalism and association of 'monarchical tyranny with the Norman yoke' (p. 177). The discussion of the Henslowe plays here is welcome and enlightening, but the 'jingoistic' Shakespeare required by Perry's thesis seems one-dimensional (p. 182).

In '*King Lear* and the Summons of Death', Michael O'Connell argues that medieval drama, especially the mystery plays, affected Shakespeare more than other playwrights of his time because of his 'generational and geographic positioning' (p. 199). For O'Connell, *King Lear* is the play by Shakespeare which demonstrates this influence most clearly. Moreover, Shakespeare's evident assumption that his audiences would 'share something of his own early knowledge of these traditions' challenges the modern tendency to impose labels such as '"early modern" and "late medieval" on theatres that were in fact adjacent' (p. 216).

Karen Sawyer Marsalek's contribution, 'Marvels and Counterfeits: False Resurrections in the Chester *Antichrist* and *1 Henry IV*', points out that scenes of resurrection in early English drama were sometimes parodic distortions of Christ's resurrection and, accordingly, reads Falstaff's fake death and apparent recovery in *1 Henry IV* as mockery of the eucharistic sacrament.

Finally, in 'Shakespeare's Medieval Morality: *The Merchant of Venice* and the *Gesta Romanorum*', Rebecca Krug traces 'the way the *Merchant* takes up four moral tales drawn from or related to the *Gesta Romanorum*', a collection gathered by medieval preachers, probably in the late thirteenth century (p. 242). Noting how, in adapting these tales, Shakespeare 'pushes aside the allegorised morals that medieval preachers found so useful', Krug points out that this does not necessarily confirm 'the divide between the medieval and early modern' (p. 260). More probably, medieval readers appreciated the same aspects of the stories Shakespeare retained; that is, moral terminals do not necessarily indicate allegorical habits of reception.

Shakespeare and Religious Change is edited by Kenneth J.E. Graham and Philip D. Collington. In the opening piece, 'Sanctifying the Bourgeoisie: The Cultural Work of *The Comedy of Errors*', Richard Strier reads *Errors* as a 'celebration of ordinary bourgeois life' which reveals 'holiness in everyday activities' (p. 4). Hence, Strier concludes, the play 'must be seen as consciously Protestant' (p. 27). Similarly, Glenn Clark, in 'Speaking Daggers: Shakespeare's Troubled Ministers', finds the Erasmian stance of scholars such as Jeffrey Knapp 'hard to accept as something wholeheartedly Protestant' (which indicates the latter quality is something he seeks in Shakespeare's texts). Clark argues that Shakespeare's drama is 'recognisably Reformed in the thematic significance it gives to the internal struggles and professional failures of pastors' (p. 178). Clark uses Prince Hamlet and *Measure for Measure*'s Duke Vincentio as examples in support of this view.

Jeffrey Knapp's own contribution, 'Author, King, and Christ in Shakespeare's Histories', also arrives at a quasi-sectarian conclusion. As in his important study, *Shakespeare's Tribe* [2002], Knapp persuasively counters the standard view that Shakespeare offered 'a secular religion of the nation' (p. 218). More specifically, here, Knapp argues that Shakespeare made good the loss of authorial sovereignty and respectability inherent in writing for the early modern stage by elaborating a sacrificial model of drama authorship according to which the playwright, like God, makes fictional worlds and characters and gifts them to the audience, just as God sacrificed his own Son for the world's benefit. The poet John Weever's rivalry with Shakespeare as literary and dramatic author is discussed in this context, and aspects of *Henry V* are pondered. For example, Henry's responsibility for the deaths of his soldiers, maintains Knapp, renders *his* imitation of Christ inferior to the playwright's, which entails only bloodless fictional deaths as sacrificial offering. Thus, for Knapp, 'Shakespeare's distinction between actual and theatrical bleeding better accords with [Protestant] sacramental theory than the Catholic view' (p. 233).

Deborah Shuger's essay, '"In a Christian Climate": Religion and Honour in *Richard II*', recalls how Xenophon's Cyrus won the loyalty of not only his own people but also those he conquered, thereby converting the zero-sum logic of conventional conquest (I win, you lose) into the win-win logic of mutual gain. In *Richard II*, Shakespeare shows Richard wrestling with related issues, including the cardinal problem of reconciling Christian values with the chivalric honour ethic. Shakespeare's play, claims Shuger, is more ambivalent on this score than Holinshed's history, Samuel Daniel's *Civil Wars* [1595], or John Hayward's *Henrie IIII* [1599]. Hayward, for example, implies Richard's deposition was justified, while Daniel and Holinshed criticize Richard from the honour-ethic standpoint. Unlike Shakespeare's play, '[n]one of these works attributes religious propensities to Richard' (p. 41). Read in this light, the last-minute cancellation by Shakespeare's Richard of the duel between Mowbray and Bolingbroke represents an imitation of Christ's work of atonement. However, Richard fails where Cyrus conquered because Richard enacts not 'Xenophon's win-win solution' but 'the Christian transvaluation of failure' (p. 44). For Shuger, moreover, Robert Devereux, second earl of Essex, resembles Shakespeare's Richard: both are tragic figures oscillating chaotically from Christian resignation to chivalric defiance. Finally, Shuger counters the view that *Richard II* enacts the movement from 'sacral kingship' to 'demystified realpolitik' (p. 54), pointing out that such a reading makes little sense historically, since sacral kingship was largely a Tudor invention. Rather, the split from Rome occasioned the intensification of monarchical mystique.

In 'Staging Allegiance, Re-membering Trials: *King Henry VIII* and the Blackfriars Theatre', Karen Sawyer Marsalek recalls that Henry VIII's 1529 divorce hearing was conducted in the very space that became the Blackfriars theatre, where Shakespeare's collaboration with John Fletcher was possibly staged. Discussing the play (*Henry VIII*), Marsalek suggests that the context of the Jacobean Oath of Allegiance informs the playwrights' representations of 'Katherine as an admirable Catholic and Wolsey as a despicable one' (p. 134). Thus the play's first audiences 'saw different perspectives on this issue worked out on stage' (p. 146).

Elizabeth Williamson's contribution, 'Things Newly Performed: The Resurrection Tradition in Shakespeare's Plays', traces the influence of 'performance traditions that developed around the use of tomb properties' in plays such as *Much Ado About Nothing* and *The Winter's Tale* (p. 110). In medieval drama, the problem of representing Christ's resurrection was handled 'by emphasising the separation between the actors and the persons depicted in the narrative'. Thus the three 'Maries' in the tenth-century *Regularis Concordia* 'are referred to using the masculine pronoun to indicate the monks' status as actors' (p. 115). In Williamson's view, early modern plays, when figuring the Resurrection, work to overcome equivalent 'representational challenges' (p. 118).

Tom Bishop's 'Othello in the Wilderness: How Did Shakespeare Use his Bible?' demonstrates that Shakespeare probably drew upon glosses to the Geneva Bible in writing *Othello*. Bishop discusses biblical allusions in the tragedy, arguing for Shakespeare's particular interest in Exodus and related texts. Iago's representation of Othello, in Act I, scene iii, as currently an eater of locusts, recalls John the Baptist's diet. Thus, though now happily married, Othello's time in the desert (Iago implies) is not over. Finally, in 'The Secular Theatre', Anthony B. Dawson pursues his commitment to regarding early modern theatre as a secularizing institution.

Two contributions to *Locating the Queen's Men, 1583–1602: Material Practices and Conditions of Playing*, edited by Helen Ostovich, Holger Schott Syme and Andrew Griffin, have notable Shakespeare content. In '"The Curtain is Yours"', Tiffany Stern discusses the Chamberlain's men's relationship with the Curtain theatre, where the company performed between 1597 and 1599. The theatre had a reputation, circa 1598–9, for being a place where people could go to acquire language and behavioural tips for erotic encounters. Thus, when *Romeo and Juliet* was (arguably) revived there, the play may have been performed in a 'hammily sexual' manner displeasing to its author (p. 84). Turning to *Henry V*, Stern suggests the play's extant prologue and choruses may have been written for performance at the Curtain. Arguing this view, Stern notes that Jonson apparently parodies *Henry V*'s prologue and/or choruses in *Every Man Out of His Humor* [1600]; secondly, *Henry V*'s prologue and choruses' 'doing-down of their stage' does not seem appropriate to performance at the Globe (p. 88); finally, Exeter's claim that 'the king will come to France 'in fierce Tempest…In Thunder and in Earth-quake' may allude to the earthquake which shook the newly built Curtain in 1580 (p. 89). Stern also suggests that Will Kempe, unlike his fellow company members, was 'delighted to find himself at the Curtain', since jigs were popular there (p. 93). This may have influenced the clown's subsequent decision to leave the Chamberlain's men.

The dating of the choruses in *Henry V* is also relevant to Richard Dutton's contribution, '*The Famous Victories* and the 1600 Quarto of *Henry V*'. The piece is a sequel to Dutton's 2005 essay '"Methinks the truth should live from age to age": The Dating and Contexts of *Henry V*' (*HLQ* 68 [2005]), which argued that the Folio *Henry V* dated from 1602 not 1599. In the present article, Dutton maintains that the 1600 quarto *Henry V* (Q) is not 'an inadequate redaction' of the Folio text but 'a (version of a) play that was almost certainly performed in its own right', being 'highly indebted' to the *Famous Victories of Henry V* (*FV*; first published 1598) (p. 135). Supporting this contention, Dutton observes that the celebratory tone of the Chorus in Q2 is inappropriate to England's political isolation in 1599. The choruses may have been added in 1602 following English victory at the battle of Kinsale; in that case, the Chorus to Act V would celebrate Mountjoy as 'Generall' not Essex. Secondly, Dutton notes the absence of references to Ireland in Q and *FV*, though censorship may have been responsible for this silence. In addition, *FV* 'provided Shakespeare with the essential *shape* of Q', though there are 'relatively few *verbal* links' between the two plays (p. 138). Dutton then considers the rising stock of Q among editors following the waning of the 'bad quarto' orthodoxy. However, under current orthodoxy, editors see Q as Shakespeare's work in progress, with F being the consummate article. Perhaps, though, Q was a finished article in its own right; possibly it featured a living Falstaff—but why was such a play staged in 1599? A clue may reside in Thomas Creede's decision to publish *FV* in 1598, four years after entering it in the Stationers' Register. All the other plays Creede acquired from the Queen's men in 1594 were published within a year. Since *FV* was probably first written before mid-1587, i.e. 'in a moment of looming crisis to stir up patriotic fervour', then its republication in 1598 makes sense (p. 143). Likewise, Shakespeare delivered Q, the text the nation needed at such a moment (Dutton evidently supposes that the rival companies and playwrights had similar political agendas/constituencies). Finally, Dutton notes that in 1600, when *A Midsummer Night's Dream*, *The Merchant of Venice*, *2 Henry IV*, and *Much Ado About Nothing* appeared in print with Shakespeare's name prominently displayed, Q *Henry V* came out anonymously. Dutton suggests that, since Creede was the printer of Q, leaving off Shakespeare's name was his way of saying Q was really a version of his property, *FV*. In closing, Dutton soundly observes that the conflated versions readers encounter in modern editions of *Henry V* are texts that 'Shakespeare never wrote, and no one ever saw or read' (p. 144).

Presentism, Gender, and Sexuality in Shakespeare is edited by Evelyn Gajowski. In her polemical introduction, 'The Presence of the Past', Gajowski avers that the recent dominance of historicism in literary studies has led to the present going untheorized. Also protesting is the book's opening essay, 'Resexing Lady Macbeth's Gender—and Ours', where Bruce R. Smith argues that presentism, unlike historicism, is able to 'entertain models of gender and sexuality that existed before Shakespeare's time as well as after and not be particularly worried about the currency of those models in 1606' (p. 27). Presumably, therefore, where new historicists have been accused of selecting contemporary anecdotes to suit their arguments, presentists may select anecdotes from any moment to suit theirs. The editor contributes '"Mirror[s] of all Christian kings": Hank Cinq and George Deux', which finds analogies in *Henry V* to George W. Bush's career as president and invader of Iraq.

Kathryn Schwarz, in 'Ventriloquised Sentimentality, or, the Theory and Practice of Women in War', meanwhile, examines war as a homosocial activity, comparable to sport. Noting the greater consequentiality of war, Schwarz maintains that militaristic discourse tends to be grounded in a culture's key values, as represented via female tropes. Schwarz registers tension within the concept of the 'figure', which denotes the body but also the linguistic trope and thus 'informs the practices of signifying femininity' (p. 91). The essay proceeds to probe 'the intersection of maternal rhetoric and violent acts' (p. 95) by looking, for example, at Constance's response to the announcement of the truce in *King John*. Schwartz shows how 'instrumental femininity', i.e. the act of fighting in the name of one's 'mother country' or 'mother church', turns into 'volitional femininity', whereby 'feminine abstractions become not motives for masculine efficacy, but disciplinary instruments against masculine inadequacy' (p. 98).

In 'A Presentist Analysis of Joan, la Pucelle: "What's past and what's to come she can descry"', Kay Stanton reads the Joan of *1 Henry VI* as 'a champion of the anti-historical voice', noting how women are progressively marginalized in Shakespeare's history plays until, after Henry V's death, one is (in terms of chronology) 'thrown back into the woman-dominated world of Henry VI' (p. 105). Thus, *Henry V* represents not the end of Shakespeare's history cycle but the centre of its recursive structure. This speaks to Joan's use of circle imagery: 'Glory is like a circle in the water...'. For Stanton, moreover, Shakespeare 'ultimately aligns himself with... the oppositional voice of Joan' (p. 106).

Michael Mangan, in '"My hand is ready, may it do him much ease": Shakespeare and the Theatre of Display', pursues Marjorie Garber's notion that 'fetishism is fundamental to the theatre itself' (p. 145). Mangan focuses on the Freudian understanding of 'fetish' as a substitute for the mother's missing penis. Hence, the fetishistic theatrical experience is erotically 'encoded' (p. 149). Having covered this ground, Mangan offers a 'presentist' reading of *The Taming of the Shrew* as an exercise in sado-masochistic role-play.

In 'Uncivil Unions', Linda Charnes dwells upon the paradoxical situation in America, where a perceived need for legislation against same-sex marriage is synchronous with greater tolerance of public exhibitions of homosexuality. As Charnes points out, currently there is no capitalist imperative for heterosexual marriage to be policed. Therefore, anxiety over same-sex marriage wears a ritualistic aspect. Turning to *Twelfth Night*, Charnes suggests that the play does not emphasize 'family values' *because of* the reliance of late sixteenth-century and seventeenth-century culture on the institution of heterosexual marriage; i.e. given the perceived pragmatic need, idealized ratification was not necessary. 'By contrast, today's discourse... floats a raft of sentimentalist fictions.' Thus Charnes describes modern attitudes as 'cynically idealist' (p. 202). *Twelfth Night*, by contrast, engages with genuine cynicism. That cynicism is even more apparent in *Measure for Measure*, which demonstrates that the authority of law is proven only when *senseless* edicts are obeyed. In *The Merchant of Venice*, meanwhile, the demonstration of the continued need for '"same sex" partnership within the institution of marriage' interrogates the Aristophanic fetish of wholeness (p. 205).

Likewise concerned with marriage is Arthur L. Little, Jr.'s '"A local habitation and a name": Presence, Witnessing and Queer Marriage in Shakespeare's Romantic Comedies'. For Little, plays such as *Twelfth Night* '*act* out heterosexual desire' and marriage, but 'they *play* with queer desire' (p. 210). Attention is also paid to the setting of *A Midsummer Night's Dream*, Athens being the birthplace of Western law. The play may be read as concerned with regulatory practices relating to human relationships, showing awareness of the need to police the seeming randomness of heterosexual attraction.

The year 2009 was a strong one for monographs on Shakespeare-related matters, with a number of important volumes published. *Shakespeare and the Institution of Theatre: 'The Best in this Kind'*, by Erica Sheen, for example, is a path-forging study which indicates that literary criticism has neglected the concept of the institution. Studying institutions, Sheen contends, offers a more nuanced understanding of intentionality, treating the latter not as relating to isolated mental events but as activity enmeshed within contingent social systems. Such an approach is valuable for the study of 1590s drama because the precarious nature of aristocratic patronage meant that the Elizabethan theatre companies had to prioritize popular performance. Since patrons consequently had to accommodate their political projects to the commercial repertoire, they were obliged to interact with the theatre as institution, not as servant. Sheen acknowledges that Elizabethan theatre was a capitalist institution but stresses the capacity of individuals to transform the institutions to which they belong, without, however, transforming the structural conditions enabling the existence of those institutions. Thus, behaviour which new historicism might seek to label 'subversive' is, on the contrary, 'creative of institutional *durée*' (p. 15). After all, subversion aimed at social superstructures would threaten the continued existence of the theatrical institution itself (a piece of logic which the company of child actors referred to in *Hamlet* seems not to appreciate). One reason why Sheen's argument is especially pertinent to Shakespeare is the unique status of the Chamberlain's men, arising from the ownership of their own theatre.

Close attention is first paid to a Shakespearian text in chapter 3, which argues that, from the very beginning of his career, Shakespeare regarded his relationship with commercial theatre in institutional terms. Thus, the performance of *The Taming of the Shrew* by a company of players visiting a lord 'presents a dialectical image of theatre looking back at its origins in service and forward to its status as a profession' (p. 49). Here, as in chapter 2, Sheen makes excellent use of contemporary legal cases to demonstrate the subtler sociocultural implications of her argument. For example, *Fyllol v. Assheleygh* (1520) decided that pleasure was not 'purely personal' but 'a form of profit' (p. 44). Thus, Kate's willingness, in *Shrew*, to obey Petruchio might not represent female submission so much as 'the profitable transformation of a wild thing into a thing of pleasure' for all parties (p. 51). Chapter 4 continues the focus on the motif of plays-within-plays as institutional meta-discourse, noting that, during the inset performance in *Sir Thomas More*, More acquires a positive understanding of the institutional viability of theatre. *Richard III* takes this process a step further, for Richard makes the spectator a participant with him in the institutional process. The arrival of the 'star performer', therefore, is synchronous with a more direct address to 'skilful, active spectators' (p. 69). However, after Act IV, scene v, 'the spectator's grasp of the plot exceeds Richard's'. Sheen equates the 'decisive interest' of a third party (i.e. a spectator) with an emergent notion of passive (nominally female) agency. Thus, when Richard attempts to woo Elizabeth in Act IV, scene iv, he thinks he is repeating his successful wooing of Anne in Act I, scene ii, but actually, and unwittingly (in accordance with the law of unforeseen consequences), he is acting on behalf of a third party (the 'nation' or the 'people') (p. 72). Chapter 5 focuses on other Elizabethan comedies, examining the notion of clashing duty-circles in *The Two Gentlemen of Verona*, and the treatment of 'conflicting durations of indebtedness' in *The Merchant of Venice* as a reflection of the troubles facing Shakespeare's company in 1596–7 (p. 94). *As You Like It* is assessed in the light of 'its contemporary role in the play-by-play renegotiation of the bond between the Shakespeare company and what the plays themselves quite clearly see as an increasingly identifiable audience' (p. 90). Accordingly, Rosalind and Celia form a new type of partnership (like the company who are performing their host-play at the new Globe, as Sheen assumes). Unlike previous comedy heroines, that is, the two women become owners of property. Chapter 6 considers the issue of monopoly in the period 1580–1600, arguing that Robert Greene saw Shakespeare 'not just as a competitor, but as the very embodiment of monopoly' (p. 98). Elsewhere in the chapter, Seneca's *Troades*, by way of Jasper Heywood's *Troas* [1581], is identified as a more significant source for the Dido play seen by Prince Hamlet than Marlowe and Nashe's text. Chapter 7 turns to *King Lear* by way of answering the question: what happened to the theatrical institution under James I? Sheen perceives a move from 'the mutuality of the Elizabethan commonwealth' to 'the culture of praise and profligacy that attended the rise of Jacobean absolutism' (p. 113). Cordelia's silence, therefore, represents a powerful example of Shakespeare's ongoing exploration of passive agency. Sheen does at times seem troubled by textual issues, testing as they do the interface between the theatrical institution and other cultural agencies such as censors, printers, and authors. Nonetheless, in the context of the various *Lear* texts, Sheen notes that 'there is perhaps something within an agency of writing that keeps a play open to structural transformation'. That something may be akin to fraudulent editorial practice, but 'fraudulent' in the sense of 'the Elizabethan law of fraudulent conveyance: the transfer of one's property to another owner in order to avoid its loss to contractual obligations'; that is, textual confusion may be a deliberate self-protective strategy on the part of the theatrical institution (p. 127). This is an avenue that invites further exploration. Chapter 8 asks another question: did Shakespeare find the post-1608 two-theatre arrangement less satisfactory than the previous state of affairs? Considered in this light, the need to cater to the Blackfriars audience bears an intriguing relation to Ben Jonson's promotion of the rival institution of literature. Sheen views *The Tempest* as Shakespeare's retort to Jonson's classicism. Thus, 'Shakespeare presents a Jonsonian sovereign–master [Prospero] whose . . . "art" may be "power" but is demonstrably not agency' (p. 136). At the same time, Shakespeare again privileges passive agency via Miranda's role as third party.

Narrating the Visual in Shakespeare, by Richard Meek, recalls Roland Barthes's observation (in *S/Z*) that a sense of realism is created not by imitating the supposed 'real' but 'by representing *other* modes of representation'. Consequently, for Meek, ekphrasis may figure 'what all representation tries to achieve' (p. 6). This suggestion is brought to bear upon Shakespeare's habit of including long narrative descriptions in his plays. As Meek cogently observes: 'There are various events throughout Shakespeare's plays that he chooses to represent in narrative form, moments that he could have staged' (p. 11). Given Shakespeare's commitment to ekphrasis, Meek suggests that Shakespeare doubted drama's superiority over language. However, he is not arguing that Shakespeare was anti-theatrical (that might be a tall order), 'but rather that the plays themselves debate the question of text versus performance' (p. 25). Meek's first two chapters discuss *Venus and Adonis* and *The Rape of Lucrece* respectively. A problem faced by Lucrece, Meek observes, is how to convey her grief adequately in writing. When her glance alights upon a painting of the fall of Troy, 'Lucrece appears to believe that this piece of visual art will provide a more reliable or authentic means of depicting the world than language can offer' (p. 72). Meek stresses that Lucrece is deceived by the painting, attacking it with her nails. 'The creation of a visual 'reality' in the poem can thus be seen as a complex confidence-trick'; that is, Shakespeare is implying that 'both visual and verbal works of art are incomplete' (p. 80). Chapter 3, on *Hamlet*, quotes James Calderwood's description of Horatio as 'an ideal teller who . . . can recapture to everyone's satisfaction all that has taken place'. Meek counters with a quotation from Walter Benjamin's 'The Storyteller': 'the perfect narrative is revealed through the layers of a variety of retellings' (p. 114). Not Horatio alone, nor any one performance of the play can adequately embody its 'message'. For Meek this is because the ideal that is being imitated is, in fact, elusive. Chapter 4 applies the argument to *King Lear*, while the importance of the theme of 'con-trickery' comes to the fore in chapter 5, concerning *The Winter's Tale*. For Leontes, Meek points out, the spider in one's drink is only poisonous 'if one *sees* it' (p. 152). If vision makes things real, then the resemblance of a con-man such as Autolycus to the dramatist becomes more pertinent: the skill of both lies in making their audiences believe their fictions have real existence. This notion informs the possible resurrection of Hermione. Meek does not consider the role of Paulina in the 'deception' but does provide welcome discussion of the relevance of the *trompe l'œil* artist Giulio Romano. Meek's 'Coda' points out that fourteen of Shakespeare's plays conclude with a request for explication. This device appears to have been originated by Shakespeare, though Lyly uses it in *Gallathea* [1595]. In a Lacanian vein, Meek suggests that the device seem to imply that desire is incapable of satisfaction, at least within the confines of art.

Scott F. Crider's *With What Persuasion: An Essay on Shakespeare and the Ethics of Rhetoric* addresses many issues raised by Meek's study. Crider maintains that the historicist approach to Shakespeare's rhetoric has focused too much on Latin and early modern English models (Quintilian, Cicero, Thomas Wilson, etc.). Shakespeare's evident concern with 'the ethics of rhetoric' needs to be considered in the light of Aristotle's defence of same in response to 'the Platonic critique' (p. 4). Chapter 1, on *Hamlet*, echoes points made by Meek. Prince Hamlet's 'first tragic error' is that he does not understand that fictions can 'help us understand ourselves, but they are much less helpful in understanding others' (p. 10); his second error is that 'he begins to fashion representations that have no purpose other than decadent sport' (a conclusion, says Crider, with resonance for modern academic practice) (p. 11). The importance of fiction, therefore, is not that it enables the understanding of others, but that it provides 'the concreteness and flexibility' lacking in 'general formulations' (p. 21, quoting Martha Nussbaum). Consequently, the purpose of a mimetic relation is not to achieve maximum verisimilitude. The calibre of such a relation will depend 'on who we desire to be'. The receptor's disposition to receiving the text is presupposed; hence, '[t]he ethical effect of representation is its cause' (p. 22). In passing, it may be noted that Crider's treatment covers non-aesthetic aspects of the rhetorical exchange unexplored by Meek, with his privileging of ekphrastic set-speeches as sites of rhetorical activity (valuable though that focus certainly is). '[M]any Renaissance writers', Wayne Rebhorn has argued, 'do not limit rhetoric to formal speeches; they conceive of it instead in the widest terms as being present practically wherever communication and persuasion are occurring' (quoted by Crider, p. 36). In any case, Shakespeare acknowledges the arguments of Plato and the anti-theatricalists of his own day to the extent that he includes examples of rhetorical skill and mimesis having negative effects in his works. However, he also includes positive examples so 'we can discern the difference in our own perceptions' (p. 24). Accordingly, if Prince Hamlet is seen as admirable then the play itself may be regarded as decadent. Crider laconically notes that 'Hamlet's actions are seldom criticised in the secondary literature' (p. 33). Hence, for Crider, it is important to consider the extent to which Shakespeare's later plays function as criticisms of Hamlet's activity.

Before going on to consider some of those plays, Crider argues, in chapter 2, that Shakespeare, like Plato and Aristotle but unlike Quintilian and Quintilian-influenced contemporaries such as Wilson, did worry about the purpose rhetoric was made to serve. Thus *Julius Caesar* shows that when unethical rhetoric 'becomes the norm, the future of one's rhetorical culture will be brief' (p. 47). The character of Caesar himself is left ambiguous in the play because that is not the important thing. What *is* important is the ethical stances of such as Cassius and Brutus in seeking to depose Caesar. Moreover, while Brutus's ends are shown to be ethically sound (the general good of the state), his means are ineffective because he assumes his audience loves liberty and hates monarchy. The same chapter discusses *Henry V*. Crider infers, from the dramatist's adaptation of his sources, that Shakespeare did not hold to the same 'good' as Henry and his soldiers; hence, Holinshed's insistence upon the justice of the war is omitted in the play. Rather, 'Shakespeare emphasises Henry's democratic appeal' (p. 74). As evidenced earlier, Crider chooses to represent Shakespeare's use of rhetoric as an aspect of his development as a dramatist. Thus, as Shakespeare matures he comes to perceive 'a universal ethics of rhetoric' (p. 6). The problem is, of course, that a 'universal ethics' will tend to coincide with the values of the scholar describing them. Hence Crider finds democratic values being promulgated in *Henry V*. Against Crider, it might be argued that Shakespeare adapted his rhetorical practice to suit contingent events.

Crider's third chapter analyses *All's Well That Ends Well*, arguing that rhetoric can be distinguished from force. Chapter 4 assesses Iago's unethical rhetoric in *Othello*. Chapter 5 examines 'the erotic nature of rhetoric' in relation to *Measure for Measure* and also considers how 'weaknesses in the audience' (i.e. Angelo) can imperil an ethical rhetorical project (p. 6). Like Meek, Crider finds *The Winter's Tale* especially relevant to a study of Shakespeare's use of rhetoric. Unlike Meek, Crider focuses on Paulina as 'ideal rhetor' (p. 6). The materials Paulina is obliged to work with as orator, moreover, include suffering and time. Crider points out that the Pygmalion story in *Metamorphoses*, often regarded as a source for the play's statue scene, is told by Orpheus, who, having lost Eurydice, 'forsakes the love of women' and sings five songs (p. 164). Of these five songs, only the third, telling the Pygmalion story, is inconsistent with Orpheus's misogynous project. Thus, the tale of a miraculous vivification of a statue of a woman is centrally accented in Ovid's text. After noting Pygmalion's credit-winning faith in Venus, Crider observes that Orpheus's own attempt to transform the real through mimesis had failed through doubt. Arguably, therefore, Leontes is both Pygmalion and Orpheus, combining the error of Orpheus's doubt with the faith of Pygmalion to merit a miraculous outcome. Nonetheless, Crider maintains that Shakespeare deliberately left ambiguous the question of whether Hermione actually dies. The scene is designed so that it can be performed either way because Shakespeare is seeking to rise above 'religious factionalism' (p. 177). Accordingly, Crider's Epilogue suggests that the pressures of censorship actually provided Shakespeare with the means to 'enact' a religion which can 'inhabit multiple forms' (p. 180).

Chiastic Designs in English Literature from Sidney to Shakespeare is a monograph by William E. Engel which examines the role of chiastic patterns in early modern mnemonic culture. Engel argues that Spenser and Shakespeare, in particular, explored 'symmetrically arranged plot structure, themes, and sentences'. Major precedents for these practices may be found in Virgil and in Scripture, especially (with regard to the latter example) in 'the alpha-numeric design and ring structure of Daniel's Lamentations' (p. 2). 'Ring structure' occurs when chiastic patterning 'appears in structures longer than a single sentence' (p. 3). The 'medial element' in such structures (especially as used by Sidney and Shakespeare) 'takes on special significance because it is not echoed directly' (p. 4). Engel devotes two chapters to discussion of Shakespearian texts: chapter 5 includes discussion of triadic Diana imagery, reading the hunt as a metaphor for the pursuit of truth, in *Cymbeline*, *Pericles*, *The Two Noble Kinsmen*, and *Love's Labour's Lost*; chapter 6 analyses Shakespeare's use of music in Pericles to heighten chiasmic effect.

In *Early Modern Drama and the Eastern European Elsewhere: Representations of Liminal Locality in Shakespeare and his Contemporaries*, Monica Matei-Chesnoiu notes a tendency towards romance in many early modern texts when 'the geographical limits of cognition' are reached (p. 12). Marginal venues (especially those on the fringes of the Roman empire) offer space for innovation because they are scarcely documented; when it comes to describing what occurs in such zones, the historian Sallust admits his account lacks authority: 'Let euery man give credite, as he pleaseth to fancie it.' Such gaps act as 'generators of fictions', which, in turn, are embodied in theatrical representations (pp. 39–40). Thus, 'space becomes discourse and layers of fictionalised assumptions gradually efface real places and people's features' (p. 12). Nonetheless, though participating in this process, early modern theatre also complicates it 'through the ambivalence of dramatic personation' (p. 15). What is avowedly fantastic in a written fiction is physically present to an extent in the act of dramatic representation.

Matei-Chesnoiu's first chapter looks at ancient representations of the Black Sea area. Plutarch, for example, rejects using such exotic locations to generate 'wonder', restricting himself to a sober comparative method in his *Parallel Lives*. However, Matei-Chesnoiu suggests, this only made his readers more curious about the blank geographical spaces he was obliged to mention. This, in turn, encouraged a perception of the rhetorical function of the exotic in historical discourse. 'Readers are confronted with an ontological order that lies at the border between the symbolic and the actual.' Thus, exotic 'beings and nations are conceived to exist only for the [rhetorical] uses to which others can put them' (p. 49). As mentioned, however, there is a difference between narrative and dramatic modes in this regard. By way of securing rhetorical effect, narrative stimulates curiosity about alien people and places. Shakespeare's 'references to alien places such as Colchis, Thracia, Scythia' and so on, however, 'are used to reinforce, subvert, diminish, or anticipate the expressiveness of the representation on stage' (p. 49). Thus in *Titus Andronicus*, the dramatist could invoke the Goths, known to 'carve their children to pieces and eat them for supper' (p. 36). However, this 'barbaric' behaviour is shown to be characteristic of Shakespeare's supposedly civilized Romans. Likewise, Hippolyta in *A Midsummer Night's Dream* is a conspicuously non-savage Amazon wedded to the sceptical and poetry-deaf Theseus. Matei-Chesnoiu, moreover, argues that such passing allusions to classical exotica in Shakespeare's plays invariably signal treatment of contemporary English mores.

Discussing *Julius Caesar* and *Antony and Cleopatra*, chapter 2 demonstrates Shakespeare's combination of the Plutarchan comparative and anti-Plutarchan 'wonder'-evoking rhetorical methods. However, while the evaluation of rhetorical modes in *Julius Caesar* interrogates Rome's cultural centrality, the competing locations of *Antony and Cleopatra* offer scope for complex explorations of space as rhetorical dimension. Chapters 4 and 5 extend the discussion to plays by other authors. Throughout the book, Matei-Chesnoiu implies that Shakespeare in particular employed the strategies described by her thesis. From these chapters, however, it is clear that she considers other dramatists to have done the same kind of thing. The only exceptions discussed are Ben Jonson's vociferously anti-romance plays. Chapter 6, focusing on romance plays, includes discussion of *Pericles* (concentrating on the brothel scenes, where the horizontal plane of Renaissance Europe promiscuously interacts with the vertical plane created by the narrative's antiquity), *The Winter's Tale* (with comments on the link between Hermione's Russian origins and her failed attempt at legal self-defence), *Cymbeline*, and *The Tempest*.

What Matei-Chesnoiu does for *topos*, David Houston Wood does for *chronos* in *Time, Narrative and Emotion in Early Modern England.* Modern scholars, in Wood's view, often treat time transhistorically in a post-Cartesian manner, disregarding the more unified, porous humoral model available to early moderns. Given the vital role of 'dynamism and flux' in humoral theory, moreover, time is a crucial factor in the early modern humoral experience of emotion (p. 17). Wood therefore enlists psychoanalytic theory, citing Freud, Klein, and Lacan. Indeed, Lacan is central to chapter 3's discussion of Iago's 'manipulation of narrative time' in *Othello* (p. 43). Wood argues that Shakespeare puts volatility, rousing, and rupture 'at the core of his characters' subjective experiences' (p. 83). Here may be noted a tendency towards essentialism in the book's argument (a tendency the author acknowledges), for Wood relates to Shakespeare's characters as 'real' people, possessed of 'cores' and (shades of Bradley) 'subjective *experiences*'. That said, Wood's analysis of Iago is complex and groundbreaking: Iago keeps 'rousing' other characters, making them hurry, become emotional, passionate, and jealous—a one-man cultural overload. Thus Iago works upon the black bile in his patients. This particular humour, by virtue of its susceptibility to alteration, was understood in the period 'as the material cause not only for a range of depressive psycho-physiological illnesses, but also for the series of outstanding qualities that comprise the heroic identity' (p. 86). Hence by means of a humanist-style manipulation of empathy Iago is able to infiltrate his victims' psyches in the manner of a demonic analyst. Chapter 4 focuses on *The Winter's Tale*. In contrast to previous psychoanalytical readings, Wood suggests that Leontes does not project self-hatred upon Hermione so much as misrecognize Hermione as a result of a mistaken belief in his unified selfhood (as Cartesian subject). Failing to know his 'self' as a porous humoral system, seeking perhaps to make himself as self-contained as a Bohemia without coastal inlets, Leontes succumbs to humoral melancholy, 'a synecdoche for the postlapsarian melancholy of formalised Christianity' (p. 115). Wood also employs Hilary P. Dannenberg's suggestion that the force of recognition found in stories such as *The Winter's Tale* amounts to a shift across alternative worlds, its power deriving from a 'competition for actuality' between those worlds (p. 133). Wood implies that such insights offer a virtual wormhole by means of which one may cross the historical distance separating the post-Cartesian from the humoral cognitive apparatus. Dannenberg, in quotation, associates trauma with the recognition scene, not the confused or wrongful actions which precede the redemptive recognition. Accordingly, Wood dwells on Leontes' apparent failure to mature even by the end of the play. Thus, Wood suggests the romance ending offers not closure but 'an unsettled status quo' (p. 135). Such indeterminacy is characteristic of the melancholy humour, 'a fundamentally dangerous and irrational force within early modern English culture', which is also 'at the root of all patriarchal systems' (pp. 136–7).

Michael J. Redmond's *Shakespeare, Politics, and Italy: Intertextuality on the Jacobean Stage* scrutinizes the relationship between Renaissance Italy and early modern English culture. Chapter 4 is concerned with the genre of the Italianate 'disguised ruler' play. As Redmond notes, Machiavelli's *Principe* 'refers to the exact Italian states featured in *The Tempest* [i.e. Naples and Milan] as part of its denunciation of the complacency of the hereditary rulers of the peninsula' (p. 121). The relevant passage in John Wolfe's 1584 Italian-language edition of the *Principe*, moreover, concludes with the word *tempesta.* Thus the ships in both Machiavelli's tract and Shakespeare's play figure the ship of state. 'The great leaders are powerless against the tempest', Redmond comments, 'because their titular authority does not coincide with any practical ability to govern the vessel' (p. 123). According to Machiavelli, princes must cultivate cynicism and acquire political skills to retain power. Hence '[t]he story of Prospero's newfound ability to dominate his enemies conforms with the narrative line of the Italianate disguised ruler play, a theatrical plot structure that emerged around the time of the succession of James I to the English throne' (p. 124). *Measure for Measure* is an earlier example of the genre. In the *Hecatommithi* and *Epitia*, 'Cinthio provided *Measure for Measure* with a model for representing the virtuous prince defined by post-Tridentine theology', according to which reason of state should not be allowed to dictate a realm's religion, for the sovereign is responsible for the souls of his subjects (p. 146). This religious context informs 'the unique choice of disguise that Shakespeare assigns his ruler' (p. 147). Conversely, Shakespeare also ironizes Vincentio, for the outcome of the rather sordid bed trick gratifies the Duke's own desire. Furthermore, Shakespeare complicates the generic schema. Redmond persuasively argues that the Tridentine rejection of Machiavellianism informed Cinthio's adoption and championing of the mixed genre of tragicomedy: once Providence replaces reason of state as the regulator of politics in dramatic fiction, tragic outcomes are jettisoned. Moreover, events may go unexplained: *Epitia* 'envisages a spectator left unaware of key events in the plot'. God's workings thus remain, to an extent, enigmatic. But in Act III of *Measure for Measure* Shakespeare's Duke provides an accurate summary of how matters will end. Thus, the work is not a 'problem play' for its spectators, only for certain of its characters. However, Shakespeare thus creates an absolutist drama: Vincentio controls all; the audience's role is only to watch the situation unfold. At the same time, Shakespeare foregrounds the Duke's desire to be loved. Redmond then considers whether Shakespeare's play contains a satirical portrait of James I and/or an interrogation of the king's reliance upon dynastic marriage with regard to foreign policy.

The following chapter challenges the critical consensus that reads *Cymbeline* as Shakespeare's conscious attempt to link ancient Roman virtues with the concept of Britain in line with Jacobean policy. The standard reading views the Jachimo plot as deliberately anachronistic, working to distinguish corrupt Renaissance Italy from the imperial Roman ideal. Against this, Redmond points out that, departing from his sources, Shakespeare names the villain in the wager plot Jachimo, 'a variant of the Italian word for James' (p. 171). English classical scholars in the early modern period were indeed inclined to represent classical Rome in ideal terms—the aim being, in Redmond's view, 'to represent England as the true heir of classical Rome'. However, 'the crucial distinction between ancient and modern is lost when Jachimo, the over-determined representative of every English discourse of Italianate vice, takes his place among the commanders of the Augustan legions' (p. 175). Indeed, by the end of the play all forms of emulative identity have been thrown into question (the mole on Guiderius's neck is 'the only unequivocal sign of identity in *Cymbeline*', p. 202). Redmond thus concludes that the play implies that 'the only way to retain your identity is to stay at home' (p. 204). This does not, however, commit one to 'exclusive nationalism' as spouted by the Queen and Cloten, but it does require acknowledgement of difference and the environmental contingency of values. Consequently Redmond finds equivocation in Shakespeare's apparent endorsement of British unification.

Aware that 'popular' can be taken to mean conformist, Stephen Purcell, in *Popular Shakespeare: Simulation and Subversion on the Modern Stage*, argues that the adjective implies 'a theatre of the people, speaking to them in their own idioms, voicing their own concerns' (p. 10). The study looks mainly at post-1990 British-based live performances of Shakespeare texts but also refers, at times, to older examples, films and non-British-based performances. For Purcell, popular theatre embraces 'roughness', i.e. a 'non-elaborateness of presentation', which constantly switches between 'modes of reception'. In performance, this quality makes for a collective experience shared by actors and audience. This can appear politically problematic if conservative norms are being affirmed; thus, there is a simultaneous requirement 'to instil a 'critical' attitude' in the community being fashioned (pp. 15–16). Robert Weimann's *locus/platea* model is cited as relevant here. Chapter 2 identifies two types of anachronism: 'assimilative' (i.e. unselfconscious) and 'disjunctive' (p. 32). Rather dubiously, Purcell celebrates *Shakespeare in Love* for its positive application of the latter type (where is the film's *platea* to its normative heterosexual *locus*?). In any case, Purcell suggests the *Shakespeare in Love* approach (the creation of a new vehicle) might be more intellectually 'honest' than rewriting a Shakespeare text according to modern notions of political correctness (p. 48). This latter option might be considered something of a straw person, however: politically correct is not the same as politically aware. Purcell expresses understandable impatience at the self-consciousness of 'irreverent' productions which seek to justify their departures and interpolations by claiming they are being true to Shakespeare's disjunctive intentions. However, given that such productions avowedly explore disjunctivity, *Shakespeare in Love*, in offering a contrast to that approach, is presumably univocal and, therefore, not critically popular according to Purcell's terms.

Chapter 3 deplores the equation of Hamlet's views on improvisation with Shakespeare's own attitude to same. Regardless of Shakespeare's position, Purcell champions improvisation. Ad-libbing, it turns out, 'tends to be found more often at the Globe than any other mainstream Shakespearean theatre today' (p. 88). This is probably due to the space itself, with its highly visible audience and the regular intrusion of noises from the outside world. When actors ad-lib with seeming spontaneity in response to, say, passing helicopters, audience response is usually appreciative, but longer obviously considered departures seem to be resisted by not only reviewers but also portions of the audience. Chapter 4 maintains that the tendency of vehicles of popular culture to engage in parody fosters 'double consciousness' (p. 96). On the other hand, parody can be elitist, requiring knowledge of parodied texts. Moreover, parody seems to falter when employed over long stretches. More successful examples of parody tend to explore, in a carnivalesque vein, possible continuities between parody and parodied, not distinctions, as in Rick Miller's *MacHomer* [1996]. Chapter 5 considers the construction of group identity. This is especially relevant to theatre as the relationship between actors and audience is what sets the medium apart from film. Patrick Tucker's Original Shakespeare Company performs unrehearsed just as (Tucker believes) Elizabethan actors did, having been given only their own lines and cues. Thus, the actors 'experience the play at one with the audience' (pp. 145–6). Purcell, however, worries about the implicit appeal to a universal set of (communal) values in such approaches. An equivalent occurs in the genre of the Shakespeare-play-in-rehearsal film: *Shakespeare in Love*, *Dead Poets' Society* [1989], Branagh's *In the Bleak Midwinter* [1995], and Tommy O'Haver's *Get Over It* [2001] all end with triumphant performances, actors and audience united by joy. For Purcell, popular communality might better be regarded as 'a *simulacrum* of *communitas*: an idealized *copy* of a phenomenon which never really existed in the first place' (p. 157). Chapter 6 explores the political nature of space and includes a concise history of Shakespearian staging. Purcell also discusses the use of 'found' or 'appropriated' spaces in Shakespearian performances. The book's argument culminates in chapter 7 by suggesting that meaningful distinctions between (Shakespearian) text and metatext can no longer be upheld.

Kiernan Ryan's *Shakespeare's Comedies* covers the Elizabethan comedies, being examples of 'a kind of comedy which Shakespeare quite consciously brought to an end with *Twelfth Night*' (p. xi). Though a general study aimed at students and teachers, the book has a strident edge. 'If one is disinclined to immure Shakespeare's drama in its early modern milieu', the preface declares, 'by shackling it to extraneous archival material . . . then most of what currently passes for Shakespeare criticism is of little value.' I suppose it depends on what one considers 'extraneous'. The positive side of Ryan's truculence in this regard is that he draws instead on 'the great Shakespeare critics of the distant past' (such as Chesterton, Hazlitt, Johnson, Murry, and Shaw)—oft-neglected resources (p. xii). Positing *The Comedy of Errors* as Shakespeare's earliest comedy, chapter 1 describes Ephesus as 'the first in a long series of licensed realms . . . which allow the characters to inhabit a parallel universe of alternative possibilities' (pp. 1–2). *Errors* is thus an early salvo in Shakespeare's war 'on conceptions of time that clamp people into the predictable scripts of their culture'. Hence, the 'autonomous vitality' of Dr Pinch comes in for special attention (p. 4). One danger arising from Ryan's refusal to engage with new historicism emerges as the discussion proceeds.

'Commodified, linear time with a price-tag is the product of early modern capitalism', he avers (p. 8). By refusing to historicize 'capitalism', Ryan runs the risk of idealizing non-historical time, i.e. of positing an ideal realm free of capitalism's evils and projecting that idealism onto the plays. Refusal to historicize, in other words, can 'immure Shakespeare's drama' as much as card-carrying new historicism. Chapter 2 defends *The Taming of the Shrew* as a 'scandalous affront to the norms of patriarchal class society' (p. 29); Chapter 3 argues that *The Two Gentlemen of Verona* is 'unjustly neglected' (p. 55); and chapter 4 champions *Love's Labour's Lost*, maintaining that in this play 'Shakespeare reverses the patriarchal poles of the form he is creating and defies its demand for a conjugal resolution' (p. 56). Students struggling with any one of these three plays, therefore, might benefit from reading the appropriate chapter here.

In chapter 5, Ryan argues that the double frame of *A Midsummer Night's Dream*—formed by the Athenian and acting troupe scenes—makes 'Bottom's dalliance with Titania' the play's centrepiece (p. 86). Thus the reduction of a queen to a tradesman's concubine is foregrounded. Chapter 6 contains profound analysis of *The Merchant of Venice*. 'The true root cause of Antonio's sadness', Ryan suggests, 'is his grief for the death of himself' (p. 123). Having the title role, Antonio might be mistaken for the play's hero. This mismatch between title and character, Ryan suggests, is Shakespeare's way of registering 'the play's disenchantment with the early modern capitalist culture Antonio personifies' (p. 124). Belmont, meanwhile, is an ideal realm, comparable with Illyria or Arden, but also 'a cosmetically enhanced version of Venice, to whose values it tacitly subscribes' (p. 126). Here Ryan seems to counter the charge of idealism I made earlier. On the other hand, this conclusion does not lead Ryan to suspect that all of the 'ideal' realms in Shakespeare's comedies might be likewise compromised.

One strength of Ryan's book, however, is its commitment to regarding plays that are often slighted as the equals of their genre companions. Thus *The Merry Wives of Windsor* receives welcome attention here. Ryan points out that the play seems to be Shakespeare's version of a 'citizen' comedy (p. 139) but set in a 'Berkshire market town' instead of London (p. 151). Since 'Windsor is also best known as the seat of majesty', ironic tension is created by the fact the heroines are 'middle-aged, bourgeois housewives' (pp. 151–2). The play's 'democratic inclusiveness' is confirmed, moreover, by the pointed absence of royalty, given the Windsor setting and the presence of Falstaff (p. 153). Consequently, the play's action seems contemporary with the world of Shakespeare's popular audience. Perhaps, then, the play is an imagining of a non-monarchical England, which might explain its appeal to Friedrich Engels (p. 155).

Much Ado About Nothing, meanwhile, presents '*modes* of manhood that deserve to be discarded as the postures of a bygone era' (p. 168; emphasis added). Fashion is, therefore, a key term. Accordingly, the spurious character 'Deformed' (invented by Dogberry) is discussed in detail. 'The Watchman's aside harbours an encrypted understanding of the power of fashion to disguise and distort the reality of human beings.' Nonetheless, 'the terms "fashion" and "Deformed" remain abstractions, which preserves the recognition that their operation is impersonal and endemic, and cannot be attributed to the conscious agency of individuals' (p. 167). Ryan astutely notes that 'the accidental invention of Deformed creates an individual culprit', on whom the law may 'pin the rap ... for the crime of stealing people from themselves and leaving perfect duplicates in their place to walk and talk as if they were the real thing' (p. 170). Indeed, but it might be argued that Ryan has been doing something similar throughout this study with 'early modern capitalism'. Not that he is wrong to vilify an abstraction for the purpose of analysis, but the importance of historical specificity (as conceivably enabled by new historicism) becomes more evident as a result of his superb observations here. As he says, everyone is the victim of the crime attributed to 'Deformed', but likewise 'everyone is unwittingly complicit in its perpetration'. Thus Don John emerges as a 'fall guy' rather than the 'real criminal mastermind in *Much Ado*' (p. 170). Ryan tightens the knot even further by pointing out that Don John has 'a strange bedfellow ... in Beatrice', who 'behaves in a way that is eccentrically at odds with the approved conventions of courtship' (p. 173). In addition, Ryan rightly objects to directors' habit of staging 'the hoax at Hero's chamber window', as, for example, Kenneth Branagh does in his film version of the play. Doing this, such directors 'miss the point completely ... By not dramatising what Claudio is said to have seen, Shakespeare refuses to mitigate his subsequent conduct' (p. 181).

In chapter 9, on *As You Like It*, Ryan again polarizes the actual and the ideal, opposing the court to 'the uncorrupted country' (p.199). In what sense, though, is Arden uncorrupted, given the shepherdess Phoebe's pride? Unlike other chapters in the book, Ryan's discussion of *As You Like It* perpetuates received wisdom instead of challenging it. Much better, in my view, is the book's final chapter, on *Twelfth Night*, which Ryan holds to be 'a virtuoso reprise' of elements from the previous comedies (p. 236). Ryan distinguishes *As You Like It* and *Twelfth Night* from other Shakespeare plays featuring females disguised as males on the grounds that in those two comedies 'the pretext of protective male disguise is soon rendered redundant and sexual impersonation becomes a structural device integral to the vision of the play' (p. 239). It thus becomes all the more intriguing that after circa 1601 (the presumed year of *Twelfth Night*'s composition) Shakespeare set this strategy aside (the only later cross-dressed Shakespearian heroine, *Cymbeline*'s Imogen, adopts a male guise, says Ryan, as 'a purely practical ploy', p. 240). The sad mood of *Twelfth Night*, despite its being a comedy, is, therefore, suited to its title, denoting 'the last evening of the holiday season, after which the routine burdens of the workaday world had to be shouldered once again' (p. 245). Surely it is worth wondering whether the impending regime change is relevant here. Be that as it may, Ryan makes a convincing case for *Twelfth Night* being the ultimate expression of Shakespeare's assault on 'the concept of a core identity' (p. 264). In particular, Feste, for Ryan, is 'a revenant from a future purged of the conflicts that warped the minds and cramped the lives of men and women in Shakespeare's time'. The clown thus emerges as the spokesman for Ryan's ideal 'futurity'. Worth stressing, then, is Feste's inhuman lack of sincere relation to others ('[h]e is disinterested and attached to nobody in the play', Ryan notes).

In *The Tainted Muse: Prejudice and Presumption in Shakespeare and his Time*, Robert Brustein maintains that Shakespeare's personal prejudices may be diagnosed by paying close attention to 'extreme statements [in the works] supported neither by the plot nor by the character' (p. 5). The book's six chapters discuss six prejudices: misogyny, 'effemiphobia' (dislike of effeminate courtiers), 'machismo' (admiration for the plain-speaking courtier or soldier), elitism, 'racialism', and religious prejudice. Each chapter provides an overview of the cultural context for its respective prejudice. In chapter 1, for instance, Brustein looks at examples of misogyny in Shakespeare's works (such as Hamlet's verbal assaults upon Gertrude and Ophelia) but also discusses texts by John Knox, Middleton, Dekker, Marston, Beaumont and Fletcher, Chapman, Donne, Jonson, William Burton, and Barnabe Barnes. Referencing of sources is haphazard. Nonetheless, there is useful historical analysis. For instance, Brustein notes that, aside from criticism of shrews, 'one does not find attacks on women . . . to any noticeable extent in the drama until 1599, though the expression of male misogyny is common enough in other forms of literature' (p. 26). This date is significant, of course, because literary satire was banned in London that year. Hence, Brustein plausibly concludes, misogyny migrated to the stage. Ranging genially over the entire canon, Brustein's text does contain inaccuracies and over-generalization. For example, in chapter 2 *As You Like It*'s Jaques is said to have previously been a courtier. Elsewhere, Brustein considers it 'a fact that Essex had commissioned Shakespeare's [*Richard II*] on the day of the rebellion', when, of course, certain followers of Essex commissioned a single performance, and it is by no means a 'fact', as Paul Hammer has recently stressed (*SQ* 59[2008]), that it was meant to coincide with a 'rebellion' (p. 136). Nonetheless, anyone studying Elizabethan literary texts in relation to any of the prejudices Brustein covers would profit from consulting the relevant chapter of this highly readable book.

Dorothea Kehler's *Shakespeare's Widows* is the first critical study to be devoted to its titular topic. Shakespeare, Kehler observes, seems both to reproduce and to contest fixed categorizations, employing stereotypes (lusty widows, chaste widows, etc.) but also showing widows negotiating their circumstances by performatively exploiting those stereotypes. (*Titus*'s Tamora and *The Comedy of Errors*' Aemilia are strong examples, discussed at length in chapters 2 and 6 respectively). Kehler uses an emphatically materialist approach, insisting that '[r]eal-life widows were largely an economic category, their actions more apt to be determined by materialist than theological considerations' (p. 10). Thus, Kehler sees literary representations as idealistic and ethically prescriptive, but also effectively impotent. Similarly, for all the complexity Shakespeare brings to the characterization of his widows, his plays 'urge a male point of view' (p. 11). These conclusions derive from Kehler's reliance on Marxist theory. 'As Marx realized', she avers, '"it is not the consciousness of men that determines their existence, but their social existence that determines their consciousness"' (p. 83). Consequently, Kehler circumscribes the agency of 'working-class' women thus: 'Lacking class-consciousness and power, they are not political rebels . . . Rather, they trespass to ease the friction between themselves and the social order' (p. 137).

Kehler also tends to read history in schematic, linear terms. Catholicism prioritized celibacy, one is reminded, while Protestantism championed marriage. However, many Protestant authors chastised widows who remarried and praised ones who remained chaste. Kehler accounts for this by suggesting that such authors have failed to shake off Catholic values. Hence, she concludes, 'Protestant John Webster writes like a Catholic when he opposes "An ordinarie Widdow" to "A Vertuous Widdow"' (p. 23). In lieu of this schematicism, it might be observed that misogynist discourse operates across confessional boundaries. Within its materialist parameters, however, the study offers a thorough account of social, economic, and political conditions which, Kehler argues, provide greater understanding of Shakespeare's widows.

Chapter 1 summarizes classical and Christian prescriptions for widows, including excellent discussion of relevant early modern legal and social customs. Chapter 2 focuses on four female characters from comedies and romance plays who are uncertain or mistaken as to whether they are wives or widows. The cases of Aemilia (*Errors*), Thaisa (*Pericles*), Paulina (*The Winter's Tale*), and Imogen (*Cymbeline*) are analysed at length. Kehler's choice of topic leads her to discuss some neglected characters, such as Widow Capilet from *All's Well That Ends Well* in chapter 3, which spotlights 'problematic widowed mothers'. This chapter also contains a convincing apology for *Coriolanus*' Volumnia, associating her case with the celebration of motherhood in modern fascist regimes. The following two chapters treat of war widows and working widows respectively, while chapter 6 looks at the stereotype of the lusty and demonic remarried widow, key examples being Tamora and Queen Gertrude. Finally, chapter 7 ponders widows who die for love, such as (most famously) Juliet, exploring this category in relation to recent debates on the custom of sati. Also, Kehler considers the role played by contrasting pagan and Christian attitudes to self-slaughter in Shakespeare's representation of the dichotomous pressures bearing upon young widows.

Sean Benson's monograph, *Shakespearean Resurrection: The Art of Almost Raising the Dead*, reads recognition scenes in Shakespeare's plays as 'quasi resurrections' (p. 1). Such scenes enable Shakespeare not only to produce powerful aesthetic effects, but also to gesture to 'something beyond' the material world (p. 15). Accordingly, for Benson, materialist criticism of all stripes (Marxist, new historicist, cultural materialist, and so forth) is not equipped to discuss this aspect of Shakespeare's texts adequately. However, the 'beyond' Benson's Shakespeare points to is not specifically Christian. The poet-playwright seized the opportunity provided by his humanist inheritance 'to conflate pagan and Christian understandings' (p. 19). Benson's first chapter discusses 'resurrections' in five comedies (*The Comedy of Errors*, *Much Ado About Nothing*, *Twelfth Night*, *All's Well That Ends Well*, and *Measure for Measure*); chapters 2 and 3 attend to 'frustrated recognition scenes' in *Romeo and Juliet*, *Othello*, and *King Lear*; Chapters 4 and 5 discuss the romances; finally, an appendix looks at mock-resurrections in *1 Henry IV* and *Antony and Cleopatra*.

Narcissism and Suicide in Shakespeare and his Contemporaries, by Eric Langley, is an important intervention in debates concerning the early modern focus on subjectivity. Langley discusses early modern 'suicentric figures' (characters who either love or kill themselves) to show the period's 'intellectual commitment to reflexive models of self-knowledge and consciousness' (p. 2). Though narcissists and suicides believe they escape reflexive relations, they merely internalize reflexivity, intensifying it to crisis point. Refreshingly, Langley also aims 'to identify an earlier grammar of self-reflection', obviating the need to employ Freudian or Lacanian terminology (p. 4). Chapter 1 examines English Renaissance versions of the Narcissus myth. Uniquely among Tudor translators of Ovid's phrase *adstupet ipse sibi* (describing the effect of Narcissus seeing himself reflected in the pool), Shakespeare, in *Venus and Adonis*, employs two reflexive pronouns: 'Narcissus so himself himself forsook' (p. 33). The words 'himself himself' not only signal an 'impossible distinction between subject and object (so we feel the incongruity of a single subject so divided), but the visual mirroring of word against itself, pronoun against pronoun—*impossible in the inflections of the Latin source*—simultaneously insists on that single state' (p. 35; emphasis added). English, with its lack of inflection, cannot render the Latin original adequately. Shakespeare, however, turns that into a means for demonstrating what a lack of inflection enables. As Langley notes, 'this is a divided self, but defiantly an insistent agent, inescapably passive in its self-defeat, but actively assertive, resounding the subject' (p. 35).

Chapter 2 investigates the competing Galenic and empirical models of conceptualizing vision. Again, *Venus and Adonis* is relevant as the poem pits the two visual regimes against each other. Venus seeks to participate extramissively with Adonis as object, while Adonis wishes to remain isolated. The poem, therefore, figures the scholastic/scientific divide, by way of Ficino's Plato versus Lucretius. Aware that the critical consensus is against Shakespeare having direct knowledge of Lucretius's text, Langley argues for 'the refracted influence of Lucretius' upon the Stratfordian's work (p. 77). Narcissism is not, however, restricted to the specular. Also pertinent is the function of echo. 'We are deluded by the echo', Langley contends, 'tricked by a mere auditory event into believing in a communicative world' (p. 92). Thus Shakespeare's Venus is unable to tell from the 'dismal cry' of Adonis's hounds whether or not the youth has been killed.

In chapter 3 Langley discusses *Romeo and Juliet* as a dramatization of the relationship between self-love and suicide. Chapter 4 observes how Stoicism threatens Christian social order by condoning suicide, reading *Julius Caesar* in this context. Also discussed here is Aristotle's celebration of friendship as a facilitator of self-knowledge. Langley notes that it would seem straightforward to suppose that the early modern introspective model would relocate the 'friend' within the self. Langley finds a precedent for this development, however, in the case of Seneca, who, given his 'precarious position as a tyrant's confidant', was obliged to fashion a discreet inner self (p. 149). Similarly, Seneca could view his suicide as 'assertive self-slaughter' (p. 161). *Julius Caesar* is ultimately ambiguous on this score: Brutus, in committing suicide, rediscovers his 'will'; however, Antony then 'repackages' Brutus's death as being 'for the "common good"' (p. 164). Chapter 5 continues the investigation of suicide, analysing *The Rape of Lucrece* and *Antony and Cleopatra*. Langley suggests that, in the latter work, 'Enobarbus displays a Roman perspective while acknowledging his propensity for Egyptian excess' (p. 177) and succumbs to self-loss. Antony, on the other hand, taught by Cleopatra's example, learns to anticipate not noble (Roman) isolation in death-by-suicide but reciprocation. Chapter 6 looks at the representation of self-murder in other Renaissance texts, including *Hamlet*. Finally, in the conclusion, Langley notes the positive valence awarded to Desdemona's claim to be responsible for her own death, thus reclaiming the field for reciprocity from the 'aggressively introspective' Iago (p. 260). Indeed, Iago's 'I', however split, is extremely strong, being 'an *I* that will not look beyond itself, that knows no other referent but itself, self-divided only in order to be self-referential' (p. 273). Thus, Iago achieves 'absolute controlled indeterminacy' but also commits 'murder on the level of the pronoun' (pp. 273–4). Indeed, this self-annihilation is what allows Iago to insert himself so ably into the minds of his victims. The only way to avoid such a threat, Langley suggests, is to 'let your owne conscience be your own praiser' (p. 279, quoting Grey Bridges's *A Discourse Against Flatterie* [1611]). Langley claims this remedy 'cannot be condemned as narcissism' as it involves only 'an introspective retreat', as sought by Adonis, not an aggressive desire to invade the being of another. Not only self-reliance but marriage is perhaps promoted here: 'Shakespeare's nostalgic vision sees Iago and his egotistic solipsism as a threat to the kind couple' (p. 279).

Helen Hackett's *Shakespeare and Elizabeth: The Meeting of Two Myths* explores the extent to which the unconscious of culture has been reflected in its confection of and response to the idea of a relationship between Shakespeare and Elizabeth I. Chapter 1 discusses the presence of Elizabeth in eighteenth-century Shakespearian secondary texts, such as Rowe's 1709 biography and the Samuel Ireland forgeries, which included a letter purportedly from Elizabeth to the poet-playwright. Chapter 2 investigates representations of Elizabeth in nineteenth-century Shakespeare biography, paying particular attention to the moment when Shakespeare supposedly paused in mid-performance to pick up a glove dropped by the queen. In addition to tracing the development of historical fiction following the success of Walter Scott's *Waverley* [1814] (Scott's *Kenilworth* [1821] is analysed in some detail), the chapter considers the relevance of representations of the relationship between Shakespeare and Elizabeth to the Victorian era and its imperial project. Various novels, plays, and paintings imagining meetings between the Stratfordian author and Elizabeth I are then examined.

Chapter 3 turns to relevant American material. Hackett argues that while Americans sought to distance themselves from British monarchical tyranny, they also claimed Shakespeare as an advocate of their founding fathers' ideals. Chapter 4 examines supposed references to Elizabeth in Shakespeare's works. Oberon's vision in *A Midsummer Night's Dream* II.i receives close attention. As Hackett notes, Rowe's identification of Oberon's 'fair vestal' as Elizabeth has become a standard reading. However, Hackett records dissenting voices, such as Louis Montrose's. Hackett also argues that *Dream* was written for the 1596 wedding of Elizabeth Carey, the Lord Chamberlain's granddaughter, and Thomas Berkeley, noting that the bride 'had a known interest in dreams' (p. 124). Additionally, the chapter traces links between *Richard II* and the 'Essex Rebellion' and possible allusions to Elizabeth I in Shakespeare's poetry

('The Phoenix and the Turtle' and the sonnets). Female characters in the plays who have been interpreted as figures for the queen are then assessed, especially Joan la Pucelle and Gertrude. Also discussed is the manuscript poem 'As the diall hand tells ore', arguments for Shakespeare's authorship of which have recently been lodged (p. 147).

Chapter 5 covers anti-Stratfordian texts that represent Queen Elizabeth as either Shakespeare's mother, lover, or true identity. In chapter 6, twentieth-century fictional representations of Shakespeare and Elizabeth are discussed, including the inevitable *Shakespeare in Love* and other well-known works such as Virginia Woolf's *Between the Acts* and Caryl Brahms and S.J. Simon's comic novel *No Bed for Bacon* [both 1941]. Also covered are lesser-known texts such as Frank Harris's play *Shakespeare and His Love* [1910], Alfred E. Carey's novel *The Dark Lady* [1919], the 1924 British film *Old Bill 'Through the Ages'*, Sara Hawks Sterling's novel *Shake-speare's Sweetheart* [1905], George Bernard Shaw's playlet *The Dark Lady of the Sonnets* [1910], Cunliffe Owen's novel *The Phoenix and the Dove* [1933], Dario Fo's play *Elizabeth Almost by Chance a Woman* [1984], and Robert Nye's novel *The Late Mr Shakespeare* [1998]. Finally, in the epilogue, Hackett scans the twenty-first-century mediascape for associations of Elizabeth and Shakespeare, discussing Timothy Findley's play *Elizabeth Rex* [2000], recent arguments for a Catholic Shakespeare in Richard Wilson's *Secret Shakespeare* [2004] and Clare Asquith's *Shadowplay* [2005], and the 2007 *Doctor Who* episode, 'The Shakespeare Code'.

Stuart Sillars's *The Illustrated Shakespeare, 1709–1875* analyses illustrated editions of Shakespeare from Rowe's 1709 volume to late nineteenth-century publications. The work functions, to an extent, as a history of ways of reading, as refracted through the interrelationship of text and image in Shakespeare editions. Since the latter corpus in itself maintains a complex relationship between the visual and the conceptual, the significance of illustrated Shakespeare for a study of cognition as enacted in reading practices is readily apparent. Sillars stresses that 'from the very earliest printed versions of theatrical texts, illustrations have sought not to represent stage action' but rather to re-enact the plays conceptually (p. 6). In any case, readers process static visualizations differently to the way in which audience members register stage action. Sillars usefully distinguishes between the function and effects of frontispieces and the role of illustrations included within the play-text itself. In addition, changes in illustration technology and other aspects of book production are discussed in detail.

Chapter 2 arguably constitutes the book's greatest contribution to Shakespeare scholarship in general, rectifying the dismissal of the illustrations in Rowe's edition arising from the misapplication of naturalist criteria. Rowe's publisher Jacob Tonson did not regard Shakespeare's works as being of comparable cultural worth to Dryden's *Virgil* or Milton's *Paradise Lost*. Thus, he recruited a pair of unknown artists: François Boitard and engraver Elisha Kirkall. Boitard's images drew heavily on the European Baroque. Hence, 'a kind of modified naturalism' is combined with 'elements founded on earlier techniques of visualizing space and narrative' (p. 37). Consequently, in order to read these images one should dispose of certain modern assumptions.

The simultaneous presentation of multiple narrative moments, as in medieval or Renaissance religious painting, conveys particular significance; emblems and allusive details 'must be given as much importance as any larger, descriptive whole'. This entails 'a degree of decryption that immediately separates the reader from the empathic experience produced in the novel'. Moreover, where the pictures do allude to performance, the reference is invariably to the earlier staging theories of Serlio, Sabbatini, and Inigo Jones. In addition, the images use 'devices common in Catholic painting, but rigorously suppressed by Protestant reformers in England' (p. 38). This lineage indicates that there is an 'element of meditative reading involved' (p. 39). Also noteworthy is the use of perspective in these images. The perspective lines created by Inigo Jones's staging meant that, among the audience, only the king would have the 'perfect view' of all the action (p. 45). Boitard follows this technique, thus allowing the reader to occupy the monarch's position. In Rowe's second edition of 1714, the illustrations by Louis du Guernier are more naturalistic. 'The gain in reader involvement . . . is considerable; yet the losses in terms of visual embodiment of concepts should not be underestimated' (p. 67). However, typological aspects do remain: Isabella's pose in the 1714 *Measure for Measure* plate replicates that of Mary Magdalene greeting the resurrected Christ, as depicted in sixteenth-century religious paintings.

The book's other chapters offer similarly rich accounts of later trends in the production and reception of Shakespearian illustrations. Chapter 3 is concerned with the work of rococo illustrators, including Hubert Gravelot (Theobald's second edition of 1740) and Francis Hayman (Sir Thomas Hanmer's edition of 1743–4). Chapter 4 considers late eighteenth-century editions, which began the practice of including illustrations of renowned actors in character. Images, moreover, began to be sited opposite the textual elements they represented. This diminution of the role of the frontispiece indicates a 'shift from an imposed concern for the structure as a whole to a greatly enhanced involvement with one local incident' (p. 124). Chapter 5 discusses illustrating trends in popularizing editions published from 1780 to 1840, including the 1805 A.C. Chalmers edition with frontispieces by Henry Fuseli. Also covered is James Woodmason's *Irish Shakespeare Gallery*, a rival project to the Boydell scheme (analysed in chapter 6). Woodmason's series was published in Ireland with a view to reviving Irish painting, and perhaps also promoting Irish independence, by laying claim to the perceived celebration of nationalism in Shakespeare's works. Accordingly, M.W. Peters's *Tempest* image broke with custom in portraying Caliban as no less human than Prospero and Miranda. Chapter 7 examines 'extra-illustrated' editions, which, by including multiple representations of the same textual moment, break up the continuous dialogue between text and illustrated interpretation and invite a comparative style of reading; chapters 8 and 9 assess Victorian populism. Chapter 10 observes that illustrated editions of Shakespeare became victims of their own success, with all available markets saturated. Illustrations ceased to function as a reliable indicator of contemporary reception. A manner of renewal came in the production of editions for collectors.

Minako Nakayasu's *The Pragmatics of Modals in Shakespeare* is a study in linguistics, the aim of which is 'to make a reappraisal of the modals in

Shakespeare's language from the pragmatic viewpoint', paying particular attention to SHALL/WOULD and WILL/WOULD (p. 10). The book's first chapter provides theoretical background; chapter 2 covers the literature on modals, especially with reference to early modern English (with early modern defined as 1500–1700, p. 51). Historical background is provided in chapter 3, while the following two chapters provide detailed analysis of Shakespeare's usage of the targeted modals, using *Antony and Cleopatra*, *Julius Caesar*, and *Love's Labour's Lost* as corpora. The final chapter looks at contracted forms, 'focusing on "LL"' (p. 11).

In *Shakespeare's Foreign Worlds: National and Transnational Identities in the Elizabethan Age*, historian Carole Levin and literary scholar John Watkins write a chapter apiece about three plays from the 1590s (*1 Henry VI*, *The Merchant of Venice*, and *The Taming of the Shrew*) with relation to the multifarious social and cultural consequences of emergent nation-state conditions. The two authors commendably oppose all demarcation of territory (academic and otherwise) and read 'foreign' as internal to the nation as well as external. Notwithstanding this emphasis on overthrowing demarcations, Levin and Watkins's unwillingness to engage with the collaboration issue in relation to *1 Henry VI* enervates the arguments of the first two chapters. They insist they are 'less interested in Shakespeare as an individual author' than in the cultural message of the plays attributed to him. That is a valid stance, but it is inconsistent with the book's recurrent insistence upon Shakespeare's intentional role in 'writing' the English nation. Levin and Watkins state that 'stylistic analysis is insufficient to prove or disprove the authorship [of *1 Henry VI*]'. The saving word here, of course, is 'prove', but it is noticeable that Levin and Watkins repeat Cartelli's argument that the play 'may have been written at such an early period in Shakespeare's career that he was still experimenting with a range of stylistic possibilities' (p. 16). This is circular logic: only by assuming Shakespeare wrote the bulk of the play can one maintain it is his early work.

In chapter 3, discussing *The Merchant of Venice*, Levin examines documentary evidence for the presence of Jewish women in Shakespeare's England. In Watkins's chapter on the same play, Elizabethan worries that England was turning into another Venice are diagnosed. Watkins ponders Shakespeare's adaptation of his main source, a tale from Ser Giovanni's *Il Pecorone*, especially with regard to the latter's counterpoising of Venice and Florence. Shakespeare, of course, excised Florence from his version, thus replacing Giovanni's historical context with something more inward-looking. Jewish issues are pertinent here also. 'Venice was one of the first major Italian cities to allow Christian residents to borrow money from Jews; Florence was one of the last'. Florence experienced a pattern of events typical of such city-states: the arrival of Jewish moneylending 'tended to coincide with the decline of the republican communes and the rise of despots' (p. 124). Venice, however, was an exception, apparently because the republic was more accommodating to the Jewish presence, allowing Jewish moneylenders to operate within the mainland suburb of Mestre. The cultural and doctrinal mutability of England, therefore, may function as an index of the successes and failures of its hybrid polity.

The book's final two chapters approach *The Taming of the Shrew* as Shakespeare's exploration of the impact of humanism and the Reformation on the English household. Levin finds 'an analogue for Katherine's struggles in Foxe's account of Katherine Parr's struggles with Henry VIII' (pp. 142–3). Thus, Shakespeare's Kate represents 'a new kind of Englishwoman empowered by Reformation teaching to play a leading role in the country's evangelisation' (p. 143). Watkins, meanwhile, reads *Shrew* by way of Ariosto's *I suppositi*, which would have informed Shakespeare that Renaissance Italian women (unlike their English equivalents) retained a title to their dowries. Watkins finds, however, that Shakespeare's play does not accurately represent either country's legal practices in this regard. Rather, the dramatist creates 'a powerful fantasy', envisioning circumstances where 'women might control the kind of wealth that would underwrite significant free agency' (p. 191). In line with the play's emphasis on the relative liberty consequent upon effective education, Watkins argues that the London theatres were the main channels by which empowering humanist culture reached a wider public.

Four books find themselves categorized as miscellaneous volumes this year. One of these, *Essaying Shakespeare*, collects eleven essays by Karen Newman (dating from 1983, with three previously unpublished) on matters related to the poet-playwright. As Newman says in her introduction, a collection such as this can provide 'a useful overview of recent Shakespeare studies' (p. xii). Thus, in 'Myrrha's Revenge: Ovid and Shakespeare's Reluctant Adonis' [1985], Newman finds biographical and historical explanations for Adonis's coyness in Shakespeare's epyllion unsatisfactory. Instead, Newman enlists Lacan's emphasis on the importance of the 'not-said' for acts of interpretation. Newman also makes good use of her experience in the field of Latin literature. Thus, she suggests that the lack of direct reference to the crime of Adonis's mother Myrrha in Shakespeare's poem would have prompted educated contemporary readers to recall the Ovidian tale of Myrrha's incest. That story occupied the central strand of *Metamorphoses* X, which book is concluded by the Venus and Adonis section. Newman's comparative analysis holds up well, but her feminist re-evaluation of psychoanalytical interpretations of the myth and poem seems more dated, or at least appears convoluted to the apprehension of this reader. Revisionist history (the influence of which upon literary studies postdates the first appearance of Newman's essay) might encourage one to consider Lacan's 'not-said' in political-theological terms, rather than Oedipal ones. Interesting to note, therefore, that a recipe for this development is implicit in the last section of Newman's essay, where she considers 'the nature of myth itself' (p. 10). Lévi-Strauss and the structuralists, she observes, regard myth as being 'preoccupied with mediation . . . between the opposing terms and contradictions of a given social system' (p. 11).

Though Newman modestly describes the following piece, 'Hayman's Missing *Hamlet*' [1983], as 'a note', it may be fruitfully read in conjunction with the relevant chapter of Stuart Sillars's study of Shakespeare illustrations (reviewed above). The following two essays, 'Renaissance Family Politics and Shakespeare's *The Taming of the Shrew*' [1986] and '"And wash the Ethiop white": Femininity and the Monstrous in *Othello*' [1987], Newman describes as 'the anchors of this volume' (p. xiii). They offer a now familiar combination of feminism, poststructuralism, race-related issues, and psychoanalysis. In a less well-worn vein, 'Cultural Capital's Gold Standard: Shakespeare and the Critical Apostrophe in Renaissance Studies' [1998] considers *Timon of Athens* in the context of canon formation. To avoid economic determinism, Newman invokes Bourdieu's post-Marxist insistence upon the importance of 'symbolic capital', but also observes that 'economics has always been implicated in the processes of symbolisation' and vice versa (p. 98). Thus *Timon*, allowed in the canon but often neglected or depreciated, provides a liminal test case for a discussion of the symbolic economies of canonization. For example, Newman notes that influential scholars of the 1960s and 1970s tended to minimize Shakespeare's use of Plutarch as a source for this play. Apparent Plutarchian source-material for *Timon* foregrounds Alcibiades' homoeroticism. Perhaps, therefore, *Timon*'s 'gold standard' rating is low as it is not heteronormative (no doubt significantly, it seems to have been admitted to the 1623 Folio when copyright issues regarding *Troilus and Cressida* created a gap that needed to be filled).

'Charactery' is the first of the volume's three previously unpublished essays. As part of a vigorous assault upon Harold Bloom's *Shakespeare: The Invention of the Human* [1998], the essay points out that Bloom's reliance upon a non-Shakespearian sense of the term 'character' is no less theoretical as a critical paradigm than an insistence upon gender, class, or race. In 'Sartorial Economies and Suitable Style: The Anonymous *Woodstock* and Shakespeare's *Richard II*', Newman notes that, unlike the author of *Woodstock*, 'Shakespeare seems deliberately to avoid description of Richard's sartorial excess' (p. 130). That is, Shakespeare does not contrast 'Plain Thomas' with 'gaudy Richard' but opposes two Richards: the one in the play's first half who wears 'gay apparel', and the 'unaccommodated man' of the second half (p. 131). Newman closes the essay by pondering whether modern academic preoccupation with courtly fashions and expenditure (and concomitant neglect of poorer classes' attire) may derive from an unacknowledged desire to 'collaborate fully with commodity fetishism' (p. 135). Finally, 'French Shakespeare: Dryden, Vigny's *Othello*, and British Cultural Expansion' 'offers a prospectus for [Newman's] new project on Shakespeare and cultural translation' (p. xvii). Newman's larger argument will be that cultural globalization did not begin in the twentieth century. The current essay discusses the 'long cultural rivalry between England and France' by way of Dryden's *Of Dramatic Poesy* and Alfred de Vigny's 1829 translation of *Othello* (p. xviii).

Jonathan Bate describes his *Soul of the Age: The Life, Mind and World of William Shakespeare* as an 'intellectual biography' of Shakespeare (p. 4). Since the materials for such an artefact are arguably lacking, Bate's book could also be viewed as a collection of entertaining essays, mini-essays, and notes aimed at the general reader, loosely held together by a 'seven ages of man' framing device. Many quotations and allusions are unreferenced, and there is no list of works cited. That said, scholarly insights and interventions of worth are scattered throughout the volume. For example, Bate makes a good case for the view that Henry Chettle was apologizing to George Peele not William Shakespeare in *Kind-Harts Dream*. He suggests Shakespeare may have played William the Conqueror in *Fair Em* and tentatively implies the Stratfordian may have died of syphilis (witness the playwright's premature baldness and the mention of the 'seething bath' in Sonnet 153 (p. 188)). The pursuit of one-to-one identifications for the Dark Lady or fair youth of the sonnets is worthily admonished. However, Bate then paradoxically asserts that John Davies of Hereford may have been the 'rival poet' of that sequence. The accompanying argument does not strike me as persuasive, but Bate makes excellent use of recent computer-generated stylometric analysis which suggests Sonnets 78–86 and 104–26 have Jacobean dates of composition. Bate thus associates these mini-sequences with the 'cynical and harder-edged' ambience of James I's court (p. 225).

The book's fourth section, 'Soldier', offers a crystal-clear account of the textual complications surrounding Essex's downfall, demonstrating that the 1601 performance of *Richard II* was not commissioned to incite rebellion. Bate notes that he had not seen Paul Hammer's essay (in *SQ* 59), which reaches similar conclusions. The present book, however, puts this reading of events into the mainstream and will, one hopes, influence future accounts. The book's 'Sixth Age', 'Pantaloon', complicates the usual retirement-to-Stratford narrative of Shakespeare biography, arguing that Shakespeare returned to Stratford for extended periods prior to 1611 and, conversely, spent considerable time in London after that year. Bate is also good on the Poets' War, using Occam's Razor to make a convincing case that Shakespeare's acting in Dekker's *Satiromastix* represented the purge administered to Ben Jonson. (In a note, Bate resurrects a nineteenth-century argument by W. Bernhardi that Shakespeare himself wrote the relevant scene in Dekker's play.) Section 7, 'Oblivion', argues for an Epicurean Shakespeare who imbibed Lucretian notions by reading Montaigne. Also noteworthy is the detailed coverage given to annotations by William Johnstoune in the latter's personal copy of the First Folio.

The Shakespeare Encyclopedia: The Complete Guide to the Man and his Works (chief consultant A.D. Cousins) is not an equivalent of *The Spenser Encyclopedia* but a generously illustrated guide aimed at general readers. The opening section, 'The World Before Shakespeare', provides historical context, with subheadings such as 'The European Renaissance' and 'The Virgin Queen'. The influence of revisionist history may be traced in the brief but sympathetic account of the Jesuit poet Robert Southwell and the observation that '[r]eligious toleration had not been achieved in the culture Shakespeare inhabited' (p. 17). (One sometimes sees respectable scholars aver otherwise.) The next section is entitled 'Shakespeare the Man'. The text is understandably noncommittal on the religious question. More daringly, the Cobbe portrait, which appears here (p. 21), is the only putative image of Shakespeare on the volume's cover. Chapters on the 'Canonical Works', disputed works (*Sir Thomas More*, *Edward III*, and *Cardenio*, mentioned here, do not have entries in the 'Plays' section), and on Shakespeare's language are likewise up to date and uncontroversial. The latter section has some novel features, however: the short entry on 'Punctuation Marks' contains an enlightening summary of the functions of the colon in Shakespeare's time, while under 'Silence' it is argued that 'incomplete lines of verse in the Folio may . . . indicate intended silences' (p. 33).

After two somewhat less focused sections on Shakespeare as 'Universal Phenomenon' and 'Shakespeare's Enduring Appeal' comes the section which makes up the bulk of the volume: 'The Plays'. Each play has a separate entry, ranging from two pages in length for works such as *1 Henry VI* and *The Two Noble Kinsmen* to ten pages for the likes of *Hamlet* and *King Lear*. Each section has a plot summary, followed by a brief account of the action's historical context (in the case of the histories), sources apparently used by Shakespeare, discussion of thematic, stylistic, and structural issues, and a summary of performance history. Boxed insets list 'Dramatis Personae' and frame choice quotations. A third box contains facts: date of composition, setting and period, number of characters, acts, scenes, and lines. Some of these statistics might prove useful for compiling Shakespeare quizzes for the winter evenings. For example: 'Which Shakespeare play has the fewest characters?' Plays with longer entries also include 'Family Tree' diagrams showing the relationships between all the characters. One can imagine this feature being valued by students of the history plays. Missing from these sections is any account of critical reception. Readers have to turn to the back of the volume for short lists of further reading. Speculative content, therefore, tends to be presented as fact. For instance, it is stated that 'Essex was plotting to overthrow the queen' (p. 59). As noted, the volume is lavishly illustrated with many stills from productions and films (mainly recent, but many older ones, too) and large, clear reproductions of contemporary images, including expected items such as the de Witt sketch (p. 22) and contextual ones such as the Wilton diptych (*c.*1395–9) showing Richard II kneeling beside John the Baptist (pp. 58–9); there are also many reproductions of imaginary visualizations such as a cover of *Illustrazione Italiana* featuring a painting of Falstaff as he appeared in Verdi's eponymous 1893 opera (p. 119). The section on 'The Poems' has entries on *Venus and Adonis* and *The Rape of Lucrece* (four pages each), *The Passionate Pilgrim*, *The Phoenix and the Turtle*, and *A Lover's Complaint* (two pages apiece), and the sonnets (twelve pages). Because the poems lack performance histories, cursory accounts of critical trends are supplied. Nonetheless, the relevant section for *Venus and Adonis* focuses instead on a staging of Shakespeare's text using puppets.

The Shakespeare Handbook is a resource for new students of Shakespeare. Chapter 1, by the book's editors Andrew Hiscock and Stephen Longstaffe, provides a summary of critical reception of Shakespeare's works, starting with contemporary examples. After a timeline in table form comes a chapter on Shakespeare's historical context, in which religious change features prominently. 'Commercial and Military Exchanges' are discussed in a subsection, offering basic but useful purchase to students encountering cultural materialist discourse. Chapter 3 (literary and cultural context) and chapter 4 are aimed at new students. In particular, undergraduates may value chapter 4's exposition of early modern verse conventions.

In chapter 5, Mark Robson discusses Shakespeare and critical theory. Stephen Greenblatt's 'Invisible Bullets' essay is considered with reference to its debt to Foucault and its use of Thomas Hariot's *Brief and True Report*. Other sections cover '"Race" and Ethnicity' (with a focus on *The Tempest*), 'Gender and Sexuality' (discussion of the sonnets) and 'Psychoanalysis and

Deconstruction'. Stuart Hampton-Reeves's chapter on Shakespeare in performance and film uses *Macbeth* as a case-study divided in three parts: first, Simon Forman's experience of seeing *Macbeth* at the Globe is discussed; then, a performance workshop-based approach to reading Shakespeare scenes in seminar is outlined; finally, Hampton-Reeves provides insightful analysis of two *Macbeth* productions: the BBC *Complete Works* 1982 version and the 'Patrick Stewart' 2007 run. In sum, Hampton-Reeves brings out the importance of performance as text. In chapter 7, Adrian Streete discusses influential critical interventions in relation to a series of key critical concepts and topics. For example, with reference to 'Authority', Robert Weimann's *Authority and Representation in Early Modern Discourse* and Andrew Hadfield's *Shakespeare and Republicanism* are usefully counterpoised. As with the book as a whole, this chapter could be used to organize a series of seminars: prompts for further discussion on each topic are included, with specific scenes suggested as cues for closer reading. Lisa Hopkins (chapter 8) provides a summary of recent critical responses and approaches. New historicism's fatalistic preoccupation with power is diagnosed, and the differences between new historicism and cultural materialism are explained. There are also illuminating sections on recent movements such as presentism, performance studies, ecocriticism, and 'British studies'.

Gabriel Egan's chapter discusses new biographical contexts for studying Shakespeare (working habits, texts, and the archaeology of relevant buildings). With reference to the 'religious question', Egan maintains that 'if Shakespeare were secretly Catholic . . . it would put an end to the long-cherished idea that Shakespeare saw both sides of every argument, and indeed was capable of articulating both sides' (p. 175). This seems discriminatory. The Shakespeare long thought to be so fair-minded was also held to be Protestant without anyone making the same objection. On other topics, Egan is more enlightening. He provides a useful résumé of recent discussion of the nature of Shakespeare's collaborative contributions, suggesting (with reference to *Titus Andronicus*, *1 Henry VI*, and *Henry VIII*) that scholars should 'work to a finer reticulation, investigating collaboration *within* scenes' (p. 181, emphasis added). Especially informative and thought-provoking is Egan's concluding discussion of the reconstructed Globe in relation to issues of authenticity. Chapter 10 houses Willy Maley's spirited discussion of recent 'issues' in Shakespeare studies, while, in chapter 11, Ros King argues for Shakespeare's plays as *theatrical* texts, averring that existing evidence does not support Lukas Erne's claim that Shakespeare wrote 'specifically for publication in print' (p. 211). In an appendix, a website address offers access to an additional chapter of teaching materials. Finally, there is an annotated bibliography by Robert C. Evans, which, unfortunately, omits articles.

Journal articles of general relevance to Shakespeare scholarship are reviewed in the following subsection. In 'Body Politics between Sublimation and Subversion: Critical Perspectives on 20th Century All-Male Performances of Shakespeare's *As You Like It*' (*ShIntY* 9[2009] 248–69) Stephan Baumgärtel discusses four twentieth-century productions of *As You Like It* in order 'to understand what kind of subject position they offer to their audiences' (p. 249). Clifford Williams's 1967 production with the National Theatre at the

Old Vic used minimalist geometric staging. The visual style was intended to 'conjure up a time of magical release from material dominion' (p. 250). Baumgärtel is dubious about this metaphysical utopianism. Petrica Ionescu's 1976 German production of *As You Like It* was an 'anti-bourgeois' version which appeared unconcerned with any 'tension between different layers of identity' (p. 254). Rather, '[t]he concept was . . . to lie down, jump on, and shag' (p. 258). As with Katharina Thalbach's 1993 Berlin production, which also showed 'a lack of interest in psychological characterisation' (p. 258), over-reliance on irony can fail to produce audience empathy, thus rendering the play 'politically less effective' (p. 260). Finally, Declan Donnellan's 1991 Cheek by Jowl production is considered. Donnellan's book, *The Actor and the Target*, notes Baumgärtel, stresses the 'narcissist function of everyday frames' (p. 263). Plays such as *As You Like It* allow us to relativize those frames, but also reveal that all frames are related to a governing norm.' Thus, 'instead of investing in a kind of camp aesthetics that makes fun of its own game of make-believe, [Donnellan's] production counterbalanced the theatrically stylized identity with a behaviour full of signs taken from the tradition of emotional realism' (p. 264).

In 'Understanding Shakespeare's Perfect Prince: Henry V, the Ethics of Office and the French Prisoners' (*ShIntY* 9[2009] 195–213), Conal Condren objects to the anachronistic application of modern notions of selfhood to Shakespeare's plays, as this fails to register that, in early modern culture, moral behaviour was judged in relation to a person's role or office. Condren refers to this tendency as 'an ethics of office', which may be characterized as 'contextual and casuistic' (p. 197). Hence, it may be argued that 'reason of state' was not coeval with 'Tacitean "new humanism"' but had a long tradition, acknowledged by Aquinas (p. 198). Condren then persuasively defends the actions of Shakespeare's Henry V at Agincourt, on the basis of an 'ethics of office'.

Natasha Distiller, in 'Shakespeare and the Coconuts: Close-Encounters in Post-Apartheid South Africa' (*ShS* 62[2009] 211–21), wonders if black South African appreciation of Shakespeare can ever not be taken as evidence that one is a 'coconut' (the latter word being a derogatory term for one who is black on the outside but white on the inside). Distiller contrasts the Shakespeare-quoting South African president Thabo Mbeki with his successor, the plain-speaking Jacob Zuma. Distiller does not note, however, that the South African cartoon strip she reproduces, which ridicules Mbeki, is itself clearly modelled on American political-satirical cartooning styles. High culture is understandably associated with imperialism and colonialism, yet pervasive cultural influence in a modern capitalistic context can go unassessed.

Katharine Duncan-Jones argues for greater attention to be paid to Shakespeare's career as an actor in 'Shakespeare, the Motley Player' (*RES* 60[2009] 727–43). The reference in *Greene's Groatsworth of Wit*, for example, may target Shakespeare's acting skills. The article also suggests that Henry Chettle may have found out how 'gentle' Shakespeare was as an actor by witnessing the latter playing the role of Summer in Nashe's *Summer's Last Will and Testament* in a private performance at Archbishop Whitgift's country residence, Croydon Palace.

Lukas Erne, in 'The Popularity of Shakespeare in Print' (*ShS* 62[2009] 12–29), wonders how popular Shakespeare was, and whether he was more popular as poet or dramatist. Erne tabulates and discusses the numbers of editions of playbooks published up to 1660, including reprints, demonstrating that Shakespeare was published, bought, and read 'on a scale unrivalled by any other early modern dramatist' (p. 28).

Paul Franssen examines representations of ghosts of Shakespeare in literary texts (especially plays) in 'Shakespeare's Afterlives: Raising and Laying the Ghost of Authority' (*CS* 21:iii[2009] 6–21). Diagnosing trends in these portrayals across time and location, Franssen shows Shakespeare is invoked as a moral and/or cultural authority but also as an object of ridicule. Particularly interesting is the use Thomas Betterton's company at the Lincoln's Inn Fields theatre made of Shakespeare's ghost, in the early eighteenth century, in their rivalry with the Drury Lane theatre.

Lorna Hutson's article, 'Imagining Justice: Kantorowicz and Shakespeare' (*Rep* 106[2009] 118–42), finds that the 'participatory legal culture' described by Kantorowicz 'bears a very close relation to the development of a new naturalism in dramatic fiction' (p. 123). Hutson, moreover, contests (mis)readings of Kantorowicz which align the king's body with the commonwealth. Rather, more abstract conceptions were entertained by both medieval and early modern legal thinkers. Relevant here is the concept of equity, according to which the particular circumstances of a given case are allotted a crucial role in the formulation of a just verdict. In sixteenth-century England this concept 'fostered a more . . . fictively dense and "realistic" mode of dramatic narrative'. Correspondingly, a decision which goes against precedent should not be regarded as the arbitrary intervention of an absolute monarch, but 'an interpretative enlargement of law by fiction' (p. 132). In *Richard II*, therefore, Shakespeare subjects Richard's claim to divine authority to the audience's judgement. Similarly, at the start of the play Shakespeare creates an expectation that the contest between Mowbray and Bolingbroke will go ahead, so that when Richard intervenes he is shown to be 'aborting . . . the judicial process' (p. 138).

The associations of gardens for early modern receptors are discussed by Mariko Ichikawa in '*Enter Brutus in his Orchard*: Garden Scenes in Early Modern English Plays' (*ShIntY* 9[2009] 214–47). Early modern gardens were usually enclosed, Ichikawa explains, were regarded as a suitable meeting-place for lovers, and 'also frequently associated with beneficial solitude and the love of God' (p. 216). Ichikawa appraises the balcony scene in *Romeo and Juliet* and 'the less clearly romantic garden' in *The Two Noble Kinsmen* (p. 218). The different uses to which garden scenes are put in extant early modern plays are then categorized: garden as 'site for intimate talks and secret meetings' (*Twelfth Night*, *Cymbeline*, *Troilus and Cressida*, and *2 Henry VI*); garden as setting for melancholy speeches (*Twelfth Night* and *Edward III*); garden as site for eavesdropping (*Twelfth Night* and *Much Ado About Nothing*). Ichikawa also discusses the use of garden properties in early modern plays (*1 Henry VI* II.iv needs 'two rose bushes', p. 232). Particular attention is paid to *Julius Caesar* II.i, set in Brutus's orchard. Ichikawa comments: 'No other place would have been more appropriate than [Brutus's] orchard for the setting of the scene where he makes up his mind to sacrifice his private self for the public good' (p. 240).

'Making Shakespeare's Books: Assembly and Intertextuality in the Archives' (*SQ* 60[2009] 304–40), by Jeffrey Todd Knight, examines 'the processes of assembly and reassembly through which Shakespearean texts . . . are made available and read' (pp. 305–6). Such an examination is especially pertinent to the consideration of Shakespeare's texts because of the high stakes involved in the editing and dissemination of his works. Knight notes that, prior to the nineteenth century, 'printed books were . . . customisable objects' (p. 309). A copy of *The Passionate Pilgrim* offers a case in point, having been discovered in 1920 bound with other texts including Shakespeare's *Venus and Adonis* and *Lucrece*, and Middleton's *The Ghost of Lucrece*. In such a context, the opening lines of *Pilgrim* resonate with the theme of role reversal explored in *Venus and Adonis*, drawing attention to possible relationships between Venus and the Dark Lady and Adonis and the fair youth respectively. Similarly, Middleton's Lucrece returns as a ghost demanding vengeance and, therefore, seems 'closer' to Shakespeare's Venus or Dark Lady than the Stratfordian's own version of the Roman heroine (p. 330). Such connections can be obscured by hermetic modern editions. In any case, consulting these 'composite volumes . . . can help us read Shakespeare historically' (p. 338).

In 'A Play of Modals: Grammar and Potential Action in Early Shakespeare' (*ShS* 62[2009] 69–80), Lynne Magnusson maintains that, by the 1590s, modal auxiliary verbs 'had a significant role to play . . . in the playwright's invention of possible worlds' (p. 70). Thomas Linacre appears to have introduced the category 'potential' to the list of acknowledged verb-moods in the early sixteenth century, noting that it was similar to the Latin subjunctive. Editions of William Lily's *A Shorte Introduction of Grammar*, which ubiquitous school text Shakespeare's earliest plays in particular refer to repeatedly, incorporated Linacre's innovation from mid-century. Thus, the emergence of English modal forms enabled the perception of a distinction between the way the English and Latin languages formulated potentiality. Magnusson discusses passages from *Titus Andronicus* and *Richard III*, showing Shakespeare's collaboration with 'the ever-evolving collective resources of the language' (p. 72).

In 'William Shakespeare, "Our Roscius"' (*SQ* 60[2009] 460–9), Alan H. Nelson and Paul H. Alrocchi record the discovery of a handwritten reference to Shakespeare as 'Our Roscius' in a copy of the 1590 third edition of Camden's *Britannia*.

In '"Talk to him": Wilde, his Friends, and Shakespeare's Sonnets' (*CS* 21:iii[2009] 22–40) Reiko Oya investigates the interconnections between Oscar Wilde, Alfred Douglas, George Bernard Shaw, and Frank Harris in relation to each man's reading of various of Shakespeare's sonnets.

Chloe Porter, in 'Idolatry, Iconoclasm and Agency: Visual Experience in Works by Lyly and Shakespeare' (*L&H* 18:i[2009] 1–15), argues that English visual culture did not perish with the reformation but underwent 're-formation' (p. 21). Accordingly, in the Prologue to *Henry V* and the statue scene in *The Winter's Tale*, Porter finds not nostalgia for Catholic practice but restructuring of visual experience.

Building on his study *The Vanishing* [2000], Christopher Pye's "To throw out our eyes for brave Othello': Shakespeare and Aesthetic Ideology' (*SQ* 60[2009] 425–47) offers a reading of *Othello*. However, the article makes the larger claim that the play 'exemplifies the emergence of the aesthetic as such' in English literature (p. 425). Two responses included in the same journal—'Shakespeare's Citizen-Subject: Distracting the Gaze, Contracting the City—A Response to Christopher Pye' by Julia Lupton (*SQ* 60[2009] 448–53) and 'Theory "After Theory": Christopher Pye's Reading of *Othello*' by Hugh Grady (*SQ* 60[2009] 453–9)—extend the debate further.

In 'Merry, Marry, Mary: Shakespearean Wordplay and *Twelfth Night*' (*ShS* 62[2009] 81–91), Thomas Rist suggests that the word 'marry' had a second meaning in the early modern period, referring to the Virgin Mary. The oath 'marry', meaning 'by the Virgin Mary', is especially frequent in Shakespeare's works compared to other dramatists' usage. Rist discusses *Twelfth Night* in this context, claiming that, by the end of the play, 'to "marry" and "Mary" are "one and the same"' (p. 91).

Hanna Scolnicov finds Marc Chagall's own experience as a Jewish 'exile' very much present in the artist's little-known series of black and white lithograph illustrations of *The Tempest*, in 'Chagall's *Tempest*: An Autobiographical Reading' (*ShS* 62[2009] 151–61).

Wolfgang Weiss provides a useful résumé of nineteenth-century German scholarly attitudes to Shakespeare in 'The Debate about Shakespeare's Character, Morals, and Religion in Nineteenth-Century Germany' (*CS* 21:iii[2009] 87–102).

In 'Boys Should be Girls: Shakespeare's Female Roles and the Boy Players' (*NTQ* 25:ii[2009] 172–7), Stanley Wells argues that all female roles were played by boy actors on the Shakespearian stage. Therefore it is mistaken to regard the performance of older female parts by adult men in current Globe productions as indicative of original practice.

(b) Comedies

Kiernan Ryan's *Shakespeare's Comedies* is the only study published in 2008–9 that, as the directness of the title suggests, focuses entirely on the comedies on their 'own terms' (p. xii). Ryan discusses the first ten comedies, starting with *The Comedy of Errors* and concluding with *Twelfth Night*, in a study which is unencumbered by footnotes or a bibliography, and which adopts a unique critical stance. Having decided to 'steer clear of current Shakespeare criticism as far as possible', Ryan avoids concerns with historical contexts and textual matters in favour of a turn to 'the great Shakespeare critics of the distant past' (p. xii). The invocation of the 'greatness' of past critics may not appeal to readers concerned with the politics of critical canonicity, but Ryan's references to figures such as William Hazlitt, Nicholas Rowe, Samuel Johnson, and George Eliot do complement some very incisive readings of the comedies. A fascinating discussion of *The Comedy of Errors* as a play which displays 'capacity for disenchantment with its own powers of enchantment' (p. 17), for example, unravels from Ryan's agreement with Hazlitt that the minor character of Dr Pinch is 'a very formidable anachronism' (p. 3). An Elizabethan character in the 'archaic fantasy land of Ephesus', for Ryan, Pinch 'encapsulates' the dislocation of time and deviation from the plot central to Shakespeare's first ten comedies (p. 4). Particularly enjoyable in this discussion is Ryan's emphasis on the extent to which Shakespeare's early comedies depend on characters blithely wasting time, while the audience is urgently aware of fast-approaching deadlines such as the impending execution of Egeon.

Although Ryan's avoidance of current critical trends frees up space for some fascinating interpretations of the comedies, the stripping back of critical frameworks and footnotes can be frustrating (a criticism which Ryan anticipates in his preface, p. xii). The intended audience for this study seems to be balanced precariously between undergraduate and scholarly readers; for the former, *Shakespeare's Comedies* provides very sophisticated yet highly accessible analyses of the plays. It is exactly this sophistication, however, that may prompt specialist readers to wish for some detailed footnotes and further elaboration of the historical and cultural contexts which do inform Ryan's discussions. For example, considering Shakespeare's interest in 'insubstantiality' (p. 167) in *Much Ado about Nothing*, Ryan focuses on the significance of 'fashion' as a 'process' through which 'individuals are unconsciously "deformed"...to fit the current cultural mould', and also as something which 'is immaterial and intangible' (p. 167). I felt prompted here to think more about the links between early modern concepts of 'deformity', immateriality, and fashion, particularly given Ryan's allusion to the anxieties of post-Reformation visual culture, 'a world where nothing is what it appears to be and people are not what they think they are' (p. 184). The absence of conventional academic apparatus in Ryan's study, however, discourages the intellectual inquisitiveness that is simultaneously stimulated by his lively readings of the comedies.

Most works on Shakespeare's comedies continue to pursue more conventional critical approaches (although two methodologically 'new' works on the comedies are discussed at the end of this section). Concerns with historical contexts and/or questions of genre, for example, inform a number of publications on *The Merchant of Venice* from 2008–9, as this play's disturbing mix of hostile religious interactions and comic conventions continues to make it an appealing site for critical enquiry. Aaron Kitch's 'Shylock's Sacred Nation' (*SQ* 59[2008] 131–55) is an earlier version of a chapter entitled 'Shylock's "Sacred Nation": Commerce, Statehood, and the Figure of the Jew in Marlowe's *Jew of Malta* and Shakespeare's *Merchant of Venice*', in Kitch's monograph *Political Economy and the States of Literature in Early Modern England*. In both publications, Kitch explores *The Merchant of Venice* in relation to the formation of 'a Jewish nation based on trade' (p. 133). Also focused on *The Merchant of Venice*, though with less attention to early modern religious, economic, and political contexts, is Gene Fendt's 'Sweet Use: Genre and Performance of *The Merchant of Venice*' (*P&L* 33[2009] 280–95). Fendt discusses the troubling question of genre in the play, deploying a critical style that unfortunately interferes with an otherwise sound engagement with the status of the play as tragedy or 'romantic comedy' (p. 285). As a critical framework for the play, this latter opposition between tragedy and comedy is, for example, dismissed as 'unhelpful and untrue' (p. 285). The 'unhelpful' is convincing here, but we might ask whether invocations of 'truth' are helpful for literary analysis. Perhaps most unhelpful, however, is the informally derogatory tone of a discussion of the instance in III.ii in which Bassanio attempts the casket test. Fendt refers to Portia in this scene as 'the girl who cannot sing' who 'croaks a tune' for Bassanio as he makes his selection; in the next paragraph, Portia is a 'crow' who 'squawks out fearful hints about the correct choice' (p. 284). Finally, Fendt rounds on Portia as 'the woman whose picture is in a casket of lead' and 'has herself a heart of just that value, though her hair be gold' (p. 284). Such oddly personalized descriptions of Portia make for uncomfortable reading, and potentially alienate the reader from an argument which depends in part on an assumed common sense of confusion as to the choices made by 'our comic poet' (p. 287).

A more sophisticated reading of Portia can be found in Natasha Korda's 'Dame Usury: Gender, Credit, and (Ac)counting in the Sonnets and *The Merchant of Venice*' (*SQ* 60[2009] 130–53). Korda here explores the language of accounting and the 'the gendered bonds of credit' (p. 130) in *The Merchant of Venice* and early modern theatre more broadly. The author points to the intriguing significance of early modern female money-lenders for the establishment and everyday business of the commercial playhouses, highlighting examples such as Elizabeth Burbage, 'mentioned as a creditor in the will of actor Nicholas Tooley (also known as Wilkinson)' (p. 137). The author speculates that 'gendered bonds of credit' in operation in early modern London 'may have influenced the depiction of credit relations onstage' (p. 138), and thus mounts a very convincing reading of Portia as a skilled money-lender, rather than 'the bountiful heiress who willingly hands over her portion to pay her husband's debts' (p. 144). Further to this, Korda suggests that this figuring of Portia as creditor 'points to a broader cultural shift that destabilized the ideal of marriage as a reciprocal debt' (p. 153). This suggestion is introduced briefly at a late stage in Korda's argument; I hope that this is therefore a starting point for further work on links between women's accounting and early modern marriage.

Shakespeare Quarterly provided a rich source for essays on the comedies in 2009. Also included in the summer edition that presents Korda's essay is Michael Hattaway's 'Dating *As You Like It*, Epilogues and Prayers, and the Problems of "As the Dial Hand Tells O'er"' (*SQ* 60[2009] 154–67). Hattaway is sceptical about the suggestion that the dial poem might be an epilogue for *As You Like It* (or for any play), and sensibly concludes that 'the debates over both dates and venues for the earliest performances of *As You Like It* along with the authorship of the dial poem must... remain open' (p. 167). Equally sensible in approach to textual matters in Shakespeare's comedies is James J. Marino's 'The Anachronistic *Shrews*' (*SQ* 60[2009] 24–56). Here, Marino attacks scholarly attempts to fix the date of *The Taming of the Shrew* so that this play remains the predecessor to the 1594 quarto *The Taming of a Shrew*. In such attempts, Marino identifies an investment in 'preserving Shakespeare's individual authority' that can lead to the tacit 'altering of protocols when it seems that William Shakespeare's honour is at stake', as textual criticism remains focused on the pursuit of 'a definitive text' (pp. 25–6). Also published in *Shakespeare Quarterly* in 2009 was Martine Van Elk's ' "This sympathizèd one day's error": Genre, Representation and Subjectivity in *The Comedy of Errors*' (*SQ* 60[2009] 47–72). Van Elk argues that the mixing of romance and farce in *The Comedy of Errors* creates 'a space' between both modes 'in which the audience is momentarily transported from one mode to the other and back' (p. 52). The author explores the implications for subjectivity that arise from this intermingling of genres, emphasizing that the construction of identity in the farcical scenes is connected to the 'exchange of goods', and that romance and farce espouse contrasting Christian and 'worldly' world-views (p. 57).

How we might progress critically from the perspectives offered by new historicism and cultural materialism is the concern of my final selection of publications. I refer here to two exciting studies of *A Midsummer Night's Dream*; Henry S. Turner's 'Life Science: Rude Mechanicals, Human Mortals, Posthuman Shakespeares' (*SCRev* 26[2009] 197–217), and Hugh Grady's pioneering revisiting of aesthetics in his monograph *Shakespeare and Impure Aesthetics*. Where Kiernan Ryan seeks to stand outside critical discourse by avoiding it as far as possible, Turner and Grady attempt new approaches to Shakespeare which build more overtly on new historicist and postmodern foundations.

Turner's essay appears in a special edition of the *South Central Review* which, as editor Carla Mazzio writes in her introduction 'Shakespeare and Science, c.1600' (*SCRev* 26[2009] 1–23), recommends a 're-assessment of Shakespearean drama in terms of the arts and science and sciences of art in, as well as beyond, the early modern period' (p. 11). Turner's is the only article in this collection which is fully focused on a comedy, although William N. West's 'What's the Matter with Shakespeare? Physics, Identity, Playing' (*SCRev* 26[2009] 103–26) refers to *A Midsummer Night's Dream* and *Twelfth Night* as part of a fascinating discussion of the significance of physics in early modern conceptualizations of transformation.

Turner is very much concerned with newness. Drawing on 'the history and the philosophy of science', the author seeks 'new concepts and new techniques for making sense of Shakespeare, new ways for asking questions about his work and for proposing answers to the questions that his own work asks of us' (p. 198). Turner's pursuit of newness is largely a response to a perceived critical stagnation within the boundaries of new historicism; the article identifies in the concepts of 'bare life' expounded by Giorgio Agamben a 'model for what we might call a "new new historicism" if not quite... posthistoricism', that is 'motivated as much by argument as archive, or by concept rather than object' (pp. 198–9). Turner's argument is theoretically dense, turning to *A Midsummer Night's Dream* for evidence of what happens when the ' "concept-in-life" ' as described by Foucault, Foucault's mentor Canguilhem, and Agamben, 'gets *theatricalized*' (p. 201). It is the metatheatrical pull of *A Midsummer Night's Dream* that underlies this argument however, as Turner looks at dramatic characters as a form of 'life', asking 'in what *way* is a dramatic character alive?' (p. 204). Turner points out that in the early modern imagination, the distinction between 'fictive' and 'real' is encapsulated within the broader question of the relationship between art and nature, which, in turn 'formed the discursive domain for many arguments that we would today describe as "scientific" or "technological"' (p. 204). From this view, Turner moves to a thrilling discussion of the early modern theatre as a 'machine' (p. 204), 'a device with which to experiment with different forms of life according to a variety of codes and "scripts"' (p. 209). Noting that for Shakespeare and his contemporaries the word 'character' would mean something close to 'code' (p. 210), for example, the author understands Peter Quince, assigning characters amongst the mechanicals, as 'a "compiler", a program written to match patches of code to the other simple programs, objects, and functions they are supposed to perform' (p. 211). At times, Turner's argument can seem to be doing little more than deploying a technological frame of reference within a discussion of a metatheatrical complexity in *A Midsummer Night's Dream* of which we are already well aware. Turner's exploration of the mechanicals as parts of an assembly within the machine of the theatre, for example, leads to the relatively familiar observation that in the performance of the play-within-the-play, 'the "character" is empirically identical to the actor and yet is not the actor; the character treads at the threshold of the person and opens it up to a double form' (p. 213). Furthermore, statements such as that *A Midsummer Night's Dream* reveals that 'unaccommodated man really is no more than such a poor, bare forked animal' (p. 213) raise the spectre of postmodernist attacks on the 'human', a subject which Turner does not fully address in this otherwise ambitious article. Turner's 'new new historicist' analysis, then, suggests some exciting possibilities for criticism of Shakespeare's comedies, but does not fully convince here.

A Midsummer Night's Dream was particularly popular with critics interested in developing new approaches to the study of Shakespeare in 2008–9. Hugh Grady's 'Shakespeare and Impure Aesthetics: The Case of *A Midsummer Night's Dream*' (*SQ* 59[2008] 274–302) is an earlier version of a chapter on *A Midsummer Night's Dream* in Grady's monograph, *Shakespeare and Impure Aesthetics*. As the title of the article indicates, *A Midsummer Night's Dream* is used as a case study for Grady's own response to our current post-postmodern critical position. In his monograph, Grady proposes a return to a focus on aesthetics, embracing postmodernist attacks on notions of unity to formulate an 'impure aesthetics' which rejects a Romantic 'aesthetics of unity' (p. 3). Again, the metatheatricality of *A Midsummer Night's Dream* underpins the application of a 'new' critical approach, as Grady considers the 'meta-aesthetics' of the play as 'a sign of modernity and a prerequisite for consciousness of the modern concept of the aesthetic' (p. 55). Grady considers the complex, 'multi-level' world presented in the play as 'utopian', in that 'it defines an ideal space, clearly designated as such, in which it is possible to represent and contemplate determinate human needs, wants and desires in various stages of their satisfaction' (p. 61).

Grady's argument is more refined and effective than that of Turner, with the insistence that it is possible to discuss ideology alongside aesthetics a particularly compelling suggestion (p. 54). Grady points out that current understanding of the sexual politics of *A Midsummer Night's Dream* is linked to 'old' understandings of aesthetics in terms of unity, as the submission of the female characters leads to a 'comedic knitting together of the plots' in which 'aesthetic harmony ... is tinged with the ideology of male supremacy' (pp. 67–8). We need to update our aesthetic frame of reference, Grady suggests, demonstrating the way forward with an intricate, politicized analysis of the 'impure aesthetics' of the play. The author argues that in the distinction between the fairy and human worlds, the play demonstrates 'one of the fundamental possibilities of aesthetic representation', as the fairy world, representative of 'a utopian or aesthetic sexuality unrestrained by the institution of marriage', invites us to imagine 'other modes of loving and living' than those offered by the patriarchal ideology of marriage (p. 69). Like Turner, Grady finds an endpoint in the play's highly metatheatrical fifth act. The author observes that the activities of the mechanicals in the production and performance of *Pyramus and Thisbe* reveal the 'constructedness' of the play's 'magic'; thus the 'meta-aesthetics' of *A Midsummer Night's Dream* are understood as shaped by a very postmodern materiality (pp. 88–9). It may be mere coincidence that critics interested in fresh approaches to Shakespeare in 2008–9 were so attracted to Shakespeare's most famously metatheatrical comedy; it will interesting to see how these 'new' critical approaches might be exploited in future discussions of the comedies.

(c) Problem Plays

This year has seen a number of varied critical approaches focusing on all three of the problem plays. *Measure for Measure* gained the most critical attention with the articles largely focusing on the moral, legal, and ethical issues provoked by the play. Such is the case with Andrew Majeske's 'Equity's Absence: The Extremity of Claudio's Prosecution and Barnardine's Pardon in Shakespeare's *Measure for Measure*' (*L&L* 21:ii[2009] 169–84), which argues that the concept of equity, the necessary mediation of certain laws in order to avoid extremities of rigour or clemency, which has been identified as an important feature in *Measure for Measure* by numerous critics, is in fact an elusive element in the play. Majeske suggests that Angelo's single-minded interpretation of the law and Vincentio's seemingly excessive pardons at the end ultimately negate the concept of equity in the play, which takes second place to some shrewd political manoeuvring on the Duke's part. Appropriating the recognized parallels between Machiavelli's account of the premiership of Cesare Borgia and the behaviour of Duke Vincentio, it is suggested that Vincentio actually wishes to achieve the refounding of his state. He does so by allowing Angelo to make an exemplary prosecution before distancing himself from him, not by executing him (as was the fate of Remirro de Orco, the deputy of Cesare Borgia) but by pardoning the unrepentant Barnardine. Majeske argues that this pardon 'precisely counteracts Angelo's confoundingly strict application of the law in Claudio's case' and emerges as 'a breathtaking display of the Duke's power over his subjects on a scale designed to surpass their comprehension' (p. 178). The article concludes by raising the possibility of a connection between the pardon of Barnardine and the imprisonment of Sir Walter Raleigh, proposing that 'the play might be suggesting that James should pardon Raleigh just as the Duke pardons Barnardine' (p. 179). However, this is the only mention that this context receives, resulting in its emergence as a rather underdeveloped argument. Unfortunately, this signals a rather abrupt ending to what is an otherwise engaging article.

The legal issues provoked by the play are also considered in Jeremy Tambling's elegant article 'Law and Will in *Measure for Measure*' (*EIC* 59[2009] 189–210). Appropriating biblical outlooks on law and justice, as well as those from figures such as Jacques Derrida, Tambling analyses a number of key passages and incidents in Shakespeare's play, especially those involving the interaction of Isabella with Claudio and Angelo, and the instances of self-examination by Angelo. He sets out to argue that 'the supremacy of the "will" of "Authority"' is at the core of the play, and does so by illustrating that this is the case 'in terms hardly flattering to the law, so giving an emphasis differing from much criticism of the play, which, however tacitly, usually agrees on seeing it as the necessary centre' (p. 191). The enactment of the law thus depends, above all, upon the will of the sovereign. In the case of Angelo, his unexpected attraction to Isabella emphasizes the fact that his will is 'sexual' and 'self-dividing' (p. 193), a premise which is read alongside St Paul's views of inner sinfulness and the Puritan practice of self-examination, as well as considering the ways in which it motivates him to abuse the divinely sanctioned power of the law. The article also considers the way in which the law's preoccupation with bawdiness—a vice whose 'quality as sin is contingent on the law calling it so' (p. 203)—exemplifies the fact that 'the law is not self-evidently the eternal law of God, but actually more like a comic structure which presents itself as one thing, when personified in Angelo's straightness of character, but which is actually, hypocritically, another' (pp. 203–4). Tambling also goes on to consider Isabella's forgiveness of Angelo which, he argues, goes against the teachings of the Gospels on adultery, as well as giving up 'the idea of measure being followed by measure, which also means surrendering any idea that justice is what Derrida calls "calculable"' (p. 206). He also suggests that if 'the Duke is to be thought of as like God, then that shows that theocracy depends on the assertion of the will, which includes the power of forgiveness' (p. 207) and considers the possibility that Isabella's famous silence after the Duke's proposal may be motivated by the fact that 'the power of saying "I will", and the power of the will, have been so questioned by the play' (p. 207). This is a lucid article which represents a significant contribution to the already robust range of material focusing on the legal issues raised in *Measure for Measure*.

Robert B. Pierce's 'Being a Moral Agent in Shakespeare's Vienna' (*P&L* 33:ii[2009] 267–79) explores the ways in which the characters of Vincentio, Isabella, and Angelo can be viewed in relation to the concept of moral agency and focuses on the ways in which their separate brands of idealism, and the challenges they face, are portrayed in the play. Pierce explains his choice of play for this subject by suggesting that *Measure for Measure* is 'perhaps the most systematic exploration of idealists trying to live by their ideas' and that each of the three principal characters 'set out on that project in a world that the play analytically divides into four environments for their moral testing: the court, the convent, the tavern-brothel, and the prison' (p. 268). According to Pierce's reading, both Angelo and Isabella face obstacles or challenges which serve to test their personal codes of morality. For Angelo, it is the discovery of a repressed sexual passion, while Isabella's plea for mercy on Angelo's behalf is a test case for her allegiance to a personal moral code informed by her chastity as well as her preoccupation with family honour. For the Duke, however, Pierce argues that no such test case occurs; he can be viewed as 'a man who honestly seeks to bring intellectual probity to politics' (p. 276) and who 'confronts the sustained task of imposing his vision of a just and nurturing order on Vienna, shaping his society as Isabella seeks to shape her life' (p. 277). *Measure for Measure* is also considered in 'On the "Prenzie" Crux in *Measure for Measure*', a short note by Karl P. Wentersdorf (*SN* 81:i[2009] 33–5). This note proposes that the repeated use of the word 'prenzie' in Act III, scene i, can be emended to 'frenzy' (or 'phrenzie') in the first instance relating to Angelo, and 'friezy' in the second, which refers to the guards. Both emendations are based on the grounds that the *f*/*ph* substitution was not uncommon in contemporary texts.

An elegant reading of *All's Well that Ends Well* is provided by Gary Waller in 'Shakespeare's Reformed Virgin' (in Eisenbichler, ed., *Renaissance Medievalisms*, pp. 107–19). Waller's essay considers the final scene of *All's Well That Ends Well* against the context of representations of the Virgin Mary in medieval art, particularly Piero della Francesca's fresco *Madonna del Parto*. Waller is careful to clarify that he is not arguing that Shakespeare had seen the fresco first-hand in Italy, but rather that 'he would have been aware of the artistic representations of the pregnancy of the Virgin Mary, which was, even in Protestant theology, part of the verification of the genuine humanity of Christ and had scriptural basis' (p. 110). Works like Piero's fresco represent a conscious attempt to consolidate the paradox of Mary as both virgin and mother, an issue which, as Waller observes, was the source of some considerable tension between Catholics and the Reformers: her 'independence of sexuality was a subject of centuries of discussion and dogma' (p. 112). This emerges in *All's Well That Ends Well* through the representation of Helena in the play's final scene in which she appears to an awe-struck gathering of characters who are forced to come to terms not only with the prospect of her apparent resurrection, but also with the premise that this apparently virginal woman is pregnant as a result of the play's bed-trick, effectively making the scene a Marian moment.

The infamous 'bed-trick', and its implications, are also at the heart of Maurice Hunt's 'Bertram, the Third Earl of Southampton, and Shakespeare's *All's Well That Ends Well*: A Speculative Psychosexual Biography' (*Exemplaria* 21:iii[2009] 319–42). Hunt's article proposes two contexts relating to *All's Well*: first, a re-examination of the long-established affinities between Bertram and Henry Wriothesley, the third earl of Southampton, and some possible explanations for the representation of a number of Bertram's negative characteristics unwarranted by Shakespeare's source; second, the suggestion that Shakespeare was examining his own conscience about the adulterous relationship he records in the sonnets and that the bed-trick, which is adultery only in a spiritual rather than a literal sense, emerges as a form of 'wish fulfillment' (p. 336), providing as it does 'a way of indulging adulterous desire without incurring moral blame' (p. 337). The negative portrayal of the earl leads Hunt to suggest that the play can be dated during Southampton's brief period of incarceration between February 1601 and April 1603, on the basis that such a portrayal would only have been possible during a period when the earl had fallen out of favour. Hunt reads *All's Well* alongside the sonnets and argues that the possible premise that Southampton, often identified with the young man of the sonnets, betrayed Shakespeare by having an affair with his mistress, the Dark Lady, thus provoking a grudge between the two which is at the root of the negative portrayal of Bertram. Hunt also argues that the play can be read alongside some of Shakespeare's later plays dealing with the issue of adultery, such as *King Lear* and *The Winter's Tale*; the latter in particular, with the death of Mamillius emerging as a punishment for the father's vices. Hunt suggests that the characterization of Bertram provides an explanation which 'may involve Southampton's involvement in Shakespeare's guilty feelings about the death of his son and the Earl's involvement in not only the playwright's adultery but also his homosexual desire' (p. 332). One of the key weaknesses of Hunt's article is his adoption of an overly cautious tone. At some points he describes his argument as 'pronouncedly speculative' (p. 320), 'one that never transcends speculation' (p. 323), and on one occasion he qualifies a statement by labelling it 'an assumption I ask my reader provisionally to grant' (p. 326). Such statements serve ultimately to undermine the force of some of his arguments, highlighting the fact that much of the content of this essay remains, as the title suggests, speculative.

Troilus and Cressida is considered briefly in Peter Scheckner's 'Renegades in the Literature of War: From Homer to Heller' (*WLA* 21[2009] 197–206). This article considers the figure of Thersites as a precedent for the stock figure of the renegade in war literature, responding to that which Hegel labelled 'Thersitism'. As well as the realization of this character in Homer and Shakespeare, Scheckner argues that he can be compared to such figures as Falstaff, Brecht's Mother Courage, Josef Švejk in Jaroslav Hašek's *The Good Soldier Švejk*, and Yossarian in Joseph Heller's *Catch-22*. Scheckner emphasizes the satirical elements of Shakespeare's play, arguing that in 'no other play does Shakespeare more openly expose the incompatibility of war and honor' and in this context, 'Thersites, by conventional social standards the most scurrilous of characters, rises above the real depravity of those war lovers for whom life is trivial' (p. 201). Although *Troilus and Cressida* is only scrutinized fleetingly in this article, it could be a good starting point for those whose interests in Shakespeare extend to the affinities of his characters with those in other, non-contemporary, works of literature.

A more detailed analysis of *Troilus and Cressida* is provided in Christopher Paris's 'Poetic Drama as Civic Discourse: *Troilus and Cressida*, an Allegory of Elizabeth I's Common Weal' (*RR* 28:ii[2009] 128–47). This article reads Shakespeare's play as an allegory of the declining years of the reign of Elizabeth I which engages with a number of the social and political issues which marked this era, as represented through several of the play's key characters from a number of different perspectives. In this way, Paris suggests that the problems with the generic classification of this play can be addressed by considering it as an 'allegorical artifact' (p. 129) and 'a dramatized *mythopoesis* that illuminates, interprets, and argues England's recent journey of history and politics to a dramatic self-realization, a moment of grace for Queen and Realm that affirms—at least for that historical moment—her "Common Weal"' (pp. 129–30). According to Paris's reading, the play contains numerous clues which suggest its potential for contemporary application; like Troy, London's city walls had six gates, and the play's reference to the number 'sixty and nine' in the prologue could allude to the sixty ships sent in pursuit of the remains of the Armada fleet which were commanded by nine ministers, thus suggesting that 1588 is a point of departure for the allegory. Paris's reading also focuses on individual characters who, he argues, can be identified with key individuals or groups of people. He suggests that the play provides a 'dichotomous allegorical model for Elizabeth' (p. 135) through Cressida and Helen who both represent two facets of Elizabeth I; Helen, Paris argues, represents the queen's public persona, while Cressida emerges as an analogue for the more intimate personality known to her advisers and confidantes. Paris also reads the reference to 'wards' (I.ii.254) as a means for Pandarus to act as an allegorical representation of Sir William Cecil, Lord Burghley, particularly in his role of Master of the Court of Wards, which involved acting as an intermediary between Elizabeth and her suitors. Paris also argues that other characters are metonymic of certain groups: he proposes, for example, that Ajax is representative of the emergent class of gentry who were viewed as 'highly ambitious and self-serving' and as 'objects of derision by their noble kin' (p. 139), while Thersites is the 'voice of a threatening subjugated social class' (p. 141). Paris concludes that the action of the play ultimately reaches an optimistic conclusion by stating that 'Shakespeare's allegorized mythopoetic message participating in a civic arena of diverse and conflicting voices offers a positive reality for a nation's understanding of itself' (p. 145). This article provides some interesting conclusions, albeit of an occasionally tenuous and ultimately somewhat conservative nature, and makes a spirited case for the role of rhetorical criticism as an approach to literary texts.

(d) Poetry

As in other years, the publications on Shakespeare's poems that appeared in 2009 were mostly on the sonnets. To mark the 400th anniversary of their publication, this year's *Shakespeare* devoted a special issue to them. In the introductory article, subtitled 'Tradition and the *Sonnets*' (*Shakespeare* 5:iii[2009] 215–18), Raphael Lyne testifies to the complexity of the relationship between Shakespeare's sonnets and the sonnet tradition, in terms of both inheritance and legacy. Briefly, Lyne contrasts the interaction between Shakespeare's poems and the tradition, which is 'not easily traced', and the corresponding position of Petrarch's *Canzoniere* relative to the history of the form, which is characterized as 'more systematically present, active, and profound'. As such, in Lyne's assessment, the essays that follow 'display Shakespeare's perpetually shifting and thoughtful demeanour towards tradition' (p. 216). The first essay, 'Will in the *Sonnets*' (*Shakespeare* 5:iii[2009] 219–34), by Elizabeth Heale, identifies within Shakespeare's sonnets the influence of an 'anti-idealizing' discourse more in line with the sonnets of an earlier period of English sonneteering (that of Thomas Wyatt, *Tottel's Miscellany*, and Philip Sidney) than with the practice of Shakespeare's time. Wyatt's 'cynicism about love', added to the idealism of Petrarch (p. 219), is present in Sidney's *Astrophil and Stella*, and it is to Sidney's Astrophil that, in Heale's reading, Shakespeare's poet/lover is so indebted. Sidney creates a sympathetic speaker with strong authorial associations whose 'mistakes and the final tragedy of his entrapment in a self-destructive passion' may, nevertheless, be judged unsympathetically and as a negative exemplum (pp. 221–2). Here, the poet/lover illustrates the tension in Sidney's own poetic manifesto between the 'infected will' and the 'erected wit'; the latter being a wit, as Heale notes, 'inspired by the human (not beastly) gift "to discern beauty"' (p. 224). Shakespeare's sonnet sequence reflects this tension in its themes of timeless beauty (Sonnet 116) and a beloved who is both fair and true (Sonnet 105), which are also 'questioned both within the sonnets in which they are expressed, and by their juxtaposition with other sonnets adjacent, or elsewhere in the sequence, that predictably depict the idealized beloved, as well as the idealizing lover/poet, as subject to time and infections of the will' (p. 226). Broadly speaking, Heale's schema identifies the Dark Lady with such 'infections', the 'poet/lover... positioned as a social outsider, an embodiment of the infected will, yearning for, yet sceptical of, the idealized perfection of the aristocratic young man' (p. 219).

Sean Keilen's essay from the same issue, 'The Tradition of Shakespeare's *Sonnets*' (*Shakespeare* 5:iii[2009] 235–52), explores what the sonnet sequence meant in a time when 'tradition [scientific, philosophical, and religious]... fell into disrepute' (p. 235). Ultimately, rather than positing new truths, the sequence, in Keilen's view, functions as a mechanism for dealing with the instability that such fundamental change and concomitant doubt entail. Keilen situates Shakespeare's poems among other creations of 'a doubting age', including Francis Bacon's *New Organon* and René Descartes's *Discourse on Method*. Focusing on sonnets 1–129, Keilen highlights the poems' preoccupation with their own validity as expressions of 'true plain words' and 'true-telling' friendship (Sonnet 82), in the context (applicable to most of the chosen poems) of an older poet, arguably identified with the authority of tradition, addressing a younger man (p. 237). Bacon's 'well-known doubt about the validity of Aristotelian science', characterized as over-reliant 'upon the consensus of textual authorities', and Descartes's abandonment of the study of 'ancient Greek and Latin textual traditions' for the pursuit of 'doubt itself as an infallible method' provide a broad scientific and philosophical backdrop to a reading of the sonnets in which Shakespeare's poet-lover 'travels from loving certainty about the younger man and his poems to doubts about their virtues, and from those doubts to new/renewed belief that he ought to love the youth and keep writing anyway'. As such, Shakespeare is portrayed as differing from Bacon and Descartes: they equate reason with truth and tradition with falsehood, while the poet, like Montaigne, portrays 'doubt... as frail as other aspects of human judgement' (pp. 239–40). Keilen also offers a meditation on the consequences of his reading for the relationship between the poet, truth, tradition, and the divine, in a Reformation and a contemporary context. Shakespeare's sonnets, in particular, are a dramatization of the poet's effort 'to change his lover's perishable flesh into the undying, indubitable word of secular scripture' (p. 245), and, although he makes no claims about Shakespeare's faith, Keilen concludes that 'the *Sonnets* imply that for better and for worse, the meaning of experience lies *within*' (p. 249, emphasis in the original).

In a reading that aligns Shakespeare with the Aristotelian philosophical tradition, Bradin Cormack's essay, 'On Will: Time and Voluntary Action in *Coriolanus* and the *Sonnets*' (*Shakespeare* 5:iii[2009] 253–70), identifies three registers in the poet's use of time. In Book 3 of his *Nicomachean Ethics*, Aristotle maintains that sequential time—the time within which a human action occurs—affects the conclusion as to whether the action is voluntary or involuntary, and therefore, in Aristotle's system, virtuous or not. Put more simply, 'narrative matters for judgement' (p. 256). This distinction is made evident in *Coriolanus* when, in Act IV, the Citizens who 'willingly consented to [Coriolanus's] banishment' seem, without self-contradiction, to have done so against their will (*Coriolanus*, IV.vi.151–3). Adopting Aristotle's analysis, it is quite possible, in the case of 'a political engagement that unfolds, necessarily, in time', that what was 'voluntary in relation to the time of its doing' may be later regarded as involuntary (pp. 255–6). The significance of this for the sonnets is first illustrated with reference to Sonnet 129, where Cormack unpicks the knot of kinds of knowledge (specifically related to sexual desire and fulfilment) evident in the poem: common knowledge, which is 'the inefficacious knowledge that cannot *do* anything', and experiential knowledge, which is 'the knowledge that cannot "shun" the doing'. The former kind attends to the contemplation of the act, and the latter is 'sealed off in the present . . . is nothing except the doing itself'. This leaves knowledge 'full in relation to its content . . . and empty in relation to its time', and presents 'the act of lust, voluntary in itself, oddly involuntary in relation to its time [of doing]'; this is a classic instance of Aristotle's 'mixed action' (p. 257, emphasis in the original). Cormack finds two further registers of time and action in Shakespeare's sonnets. Sonnets 133 and 134 represent occasions of Aristotle's 'problem of mixed action' in juridical contexts: bail and mortgage. Here the triangular relationship between the poet, the youth, and the mistress, from whose bonds the poet wishes to free the youth, provides Shakespeare, in Cormack's reading, with the opportunity to suspend, metaphorically, 'strict legal time into a legal- and lyric-conditional mode that allows a subordinate will . . . to operate' temporarily as if with full agency; such freedom is, however, only momentarily apparent (pp. 257–65). Sonnets 135 and 136 'recast' the 'temporal waver between freedom and boundedness' of the previous poems 'as a semantic waver', punning on 'Will' (the speaker), 'will' (the 'capacity for choice'), 'will' (the sexual appetite), and 'will' (the sexual object). The wordplay results in a compression of 'the temporality of action into a dazzling all-at-onceness' that renders 'the elements of action . . . visible for lyric analysis, but only so as to end by becoming invisible, too, once subject and object are conflated' (pp. 265–8). Cormack's lyric analysis might be judged similarly dazzling.

Cathy Shrank's essay, 'Reading Shakespeare's *Sonnets*: John Benson and the 1640 *Poems*' (*Shakespeare* 5:iii[2009] 271–91), reconsiders the 'lyric analysis' of a much older critic: John Benson, whose edition of Shakespeare's *Poems* has often been denigrated for its reordering and grouping of the sonnets. Placing the publication firmly in its historical time, Shrank rehabilitates Benson's practice as a significant milestone in the transmission and reception of Shakespeare's poems. Benson stresses the gentlemanly status of the author, and the use of the title 'Poems', as opposed to 'Sonnets', is apparently another reflection of Benson's desire to elevate Master Shakespeare's work above what was, in 1640, regarded as the rather 'demotic vein of sonneteering' (p. 276). Shrank also discerns 'some underlying plan to Benson's rearrangement of the 1609 *Sonnets*', and a readily explicable design in his use of titles, which, as Shrank stresses, 'offer a record of how someone has read—and how contemporary readers were being invited to read—the verses beneath'; it stands as 'one of the earliest critical and imaginative responses that we have to a work which otherwise has left scant imprint on the literature of seventeenth-century England' (pp. 278–9, 273).

Beyond the special issue of *Shakespeare*, Vin Nardizzi's article, 'Shakespeare's Penknife: Grafting and Seedless Generation in the Procreation Sonnets' (*Ren&R* 32:i[2009] 83–106), argues that an appreciation of the sixteenth- and early seventeenth-century practice of plant grafting, which 'was regarded . . . as *both* an analogue to procreation *and* a form of writing', is the key to understanding the organization of 'the discourses of generation and genealogy' in Shakespeare's procreation sonnets (p. 83, emphasis in the original). Significantly, Nardizzi insists on 'the fusion of that which [Bruce R.] Smith's reading of Sonnet 15 separates out rhetorically (procreation and poetic creation)' (p. 84; see Bruce R. Smith, *Homosexual Desire in Shakespeare's England: A Cultural Poetics* [1991]). Making extensive and fruitful use of Renaissance gardening books, Nardizzi observes the relationship between the sexualization of plant grafting in such books and the offer made by the speaker of Sonnet 15 to the young man: to use grafting for procreation, the youth having eschewed the biblical call to 'increase and multiply'; tellingly, 'seeded' means of botanical generation are not sexualized in the same horticultural publications. Grafting, a distinctly seedless means of reproduction, provides the means for the 'gardener-poet' to tend the 'plant-like body' of the young man in a 'queerer' manner than would be the case in 'the "seeded" generational act of human procreation' (p. 85).

Fred Blick, in his article, ' "Duble Vantage": Tennis and Sonnet 88' (*UCrow* 28[2009] 82–93), explores a hitherto unrecognized example of Shakespeare's use of a tennis metaphor in, as it turns out, an appropriately numbered poem. Blick reassesses the metaphorical significance of words such as 'set', 'faults', 'fight', 'loosing', 'win', 'gainer', and 'vantage', 'which could arise in a legally fought case of slander, but they are also tennis terms' (p. 83). Such a reconsideration alters the psychological force of the poem, providing the speaker with, in tennis terms, a 'duble vantage', what Blick terms 'a covert, ego-preserving, psychological victory in the feeling of being "one up" ' (p. 85).

Indeed, in the French Rules of tennis of 1592, 'duble vantage' may mean 'winning two games in succession to win a set at a score of, say, 8–8' (p. 83). The small victory for the speaker in the contest of Sonnet 88 is, in Blick's reading, a presage for 'more violent, physical imagery' in the sonnets that follow, and fits in with the author's interpretation of the progress of the sonnets' broader narrative. A discussion of the possibility of a connection to Henry Wriothesley's taste for tennis rounds off the article (p. 87).

Another unusual approach to Shakespeare's poems is delineated in Bruce R. Smith's article, 'How Should One Read a Shakespeare Sonnet?' (*EMLS* special issue 19[2009] 2.1–39). Smith uses film and photographic stills of Crescenciano (Chris) Garcia's American Sign Language (ASL) interpretation of Sonnet 29, embedded in the text of his article for the online journal *Early Modern Literary Studies* to illustrate his case that, contrary to what might be thought, in all languages (including ASL and early modern English) gesture precedes speech. In an example of theoretically adept literary criticism, Smith's discussion ranges across the fields of modern psychology, linguistics, quantum mechanics, early modern acting technique, theology, and, naturally, the sign language that he places at the heart of his thesis. Smith makes particularly effective use of John Bulwer's treatises, *Chirologia: or the Natural Language of the Hand* and *Chironomia: or the Art of Manual Rhetoric*, published together in 1644. Usefully for Smith's thesis, Bulwer, in his *Chirologia*, 'regards hand gestures not as ornaments that occur *after* verbal signifiers... but as meaning-formations that occur *before* verbal signifiers—and that often outpace them' (paragraph 20, emphasis in the original). In the light of Smith's embodied mode of meaning, the rules of grammar and syntax in languages such as Latin, Flemish, and English, as articulated by authors such as Cicero, Erasmus, and Jonson, are reassessed. Returning to Shakespeare's poetry, Chris Garcia's ASL version of the passage from Sonnet 29—'and then my state, | Like to the lark at break of day arising, | From sullen earth sings hymns at heaven's gate' (ll. 10–12), interpreted as 'bird/wake/inspire/chirp/sing/offer up/towards heaven'—merges the 'three possible actors' ('I', 'lark', and 'my state') into the one gesture: 'bird' (para. 37). This allows Smith to assert that the subject positions of Shakespeare's sonnets ('I', 'he', and 'thou') are merged into the 'useful but now rarely heard pronoun "one"', which 'implies mutual understanding'. As such, in Smith's terms, when *one* reads a Shakespeare sonnet in this way, 'difference-marking might not be the beginning of meaning-making' (para. 39).

Isabelle Schwartz-Gastine's article, 'Les Sonnets de Shakespeare revus et corrigés par le XIXe siècle français' (*La Revue LISA* 7:iii[2009] 368–93), commemorates the quatercentenary of the publication of the sonnets by examining the history of their translation into French. The article reveals a relatively recent story (beginning as late as the nineteenth century) of translation, mostly into prose, with numerous occasions on which the translator thought it necessary to 'improve' the originals. Where verse was employed, Shakespeare's pattern of metre and rhyme was abandoned for a preferred scheme of alexandrines arranged in two quatrains and two tercets. François-Victor Hugo's translation was a prose version of the whole sequence, though he placed the poems in his own preferred order. Moreover, as

Schwartz-Gastine observes, his reading of the sonnets favoured the typically Romantic autobiographical approach: 'Après avoir souffert des caprices de l'amour avec une maîtresse perfide, Shakespeare, selon Hugo, aurait, à la suite de Montaigne pour La Boétie, trouvé une belle amitié en la personne de son aristocrate mécène, véritable Adonis personnifié. Et Hugo de citer le sonnet 65 (qu'il place en 53ème position) pour corroborer sa théorie' (p. 379).

Amanda Rudd's 'A Fair Youth in the Forest of Arden: Reading Gender and Desire in *As You Like It* and Shakespeare's Sonnets' (*Journal of the Wooden O Symposium* 9[2009] 106–17), was the top undergraduate paper selected from those given at the annual Wooden O Symposium hosted by Southern Utah University. This symposium often includes a panel of undergraduate papers within its programme, from which the best gains peer-reviewed publication. Rudd gives overdue, serious consideration to the similarity between the personae in *As You Like It* and the sonnets, particularly with respect to 'the poet's constructions of gender and desire' (p. 106). Likening the fair youth of the sonnets to the role of Ganymede played by Rosalind in the play, the author explores the several parallels between their characters: the 'master-mistress' of Sonnet 20 'is a lurking presence in the relationship between Ganymede and Orlando'; and 'just as Shakespeare's sonnets . . . urge the fair youth toward . . . heterosexual relationships, the tensions between Orlando and Ganymede finally resolve in Orlando's marriage to Rosalind' (pp. 107–9). The characters of Phoebe and Audrey combine to represent the play's version of the Dark Lady of the sonnets, and Audrey's love triangle with Touchstone and William echoes the three-sided relationship seen in the later poems of Shakespeare's sonnet sequence. The suggestiveness of the name 'William' in both texts does not go unnoticed either. Rudd observes numerous other analogous details between the two works, in terms of how they relate to early modern society, classical precedent, and generic orthodoxy, resulting in a meticulous and comprehensive account.

William Nelles, in his article for *English Literary Renaissance*, 'Sexing Shakespeare's Sonnets: Reading Beyond Sonnet 20' (*ELR* 39:i[2009] 128–40), attempts to unify the two main points of view that have dominated the discussion about the coherence (or otherwise) of the sonnets as a sequence. Amanda Rudd's paper, discussed above, is a pertinent example of a contribution to this debate; Rudd slides down Nelles's 'slippery slope' into a discussion of the sonnets' dramatis personae. As Nelles notes, approaches to this subject fall into two broad kinds: 'either the Young Man and Dark Lady sonnets are read as belonging to sustained and usually interlaced narrative sequences, or the sonnets are seen as a series of *n* number of contiguous mini-sequences connected by themes and images; we might call these the strong and weak sequence theories'. Nelles endeavours to clear the field of unsubstantiated claims and provide 'new lines of analysis' with a greater basis in logic (p. 130). Beginning with a graphical representation of the gender of each sonnet's addressee, Nelles demonstrates the proliferation and increasing size of the 'gaps to be filled' where the gender of the addressee is not readily determined. The willingness of adherents to the 'strong sequence theory' to infer the gender of the addressee of a particular sonnet from the gender of the addressee of its neighbouring sonnets proves to be somewhat alarming (pp. 130–5). A further experiment, targeting the 'weak sequence' theorists, based on the critical judgements of thirty of his students, who were presented with random sequences of five of Shakespeare's sonnets, shows that, in Nelles's terms, critics are 'reciting' a kind of sonnet 'playlist' for their own literary iPods. The sequences of sonnets, whether chosen by random or by sequence theorists, are intelligible and coherent on the basis of several literary-critical conventions, but this is demonstrably not evidence for the validity of any particular arrangement that can be attributed to Shakespeare's own intricate design (pp. 135–40).

Natasha Korda, in her article, 'Dame Usury: Gender, Credit, and (Ac)counting in the Sonnets and *The Merchant of Venice*' (*SQ* 60[2009] 129–53), analyses the gendered language of credit, bonds and accounting in Sonnets 134, 135, and 136, and, at greater length, in *The Merchant of Venice*. The rise of the female money-lender and the advent of married female creditors in early modern England are thoroughly explored and provide the context for reading Portia as a skilful agent in a world of metaphorical bonds of credit. Korda reads the play as associating 'Portia's will and skill with surety, contrasting it with the risks of male (ad)venture', and, against the grain of early modern misogyny, 'aligns it with an emergent ethos of virtuous, Christian exactitude' (p. 143). Portia is likened to the figure of the female usurer that appears in Sonnets 134–6. The female addressee of these sonnets is, however, more readily associated with inexactitude than any other virtue, as is Shylock. In the end, Portia's 'rhetoric of just measure' may be to her credit, but it does not bode well for marital harmony in Korda's balanced account (pp. 152–3).

Dan Decker and Stephen Denning provide an altogether different kind of scholarly publication from Korda's *Shakespeare Quarterly* article in their joint exposition, 'The Two Roses: A Suggested Interpretation of Shakespeare's Sonnets' (*New England Theatre Journal* 20[2009] 15–47). In attempting to explain the sonnet sequence in a 'single-theory account of the entire story' they no doubt fall into the category of 'strong sequence' theorists devised by William Nelles in his article discussed above. Nevertheless, this is an extensive, if often fanciful, examination of the relationship between Shakespeare's life, times, theatrical works, and the sonnets that leaves very few stones unturned; they deliberately 'exclude the lunatic fringes of criticism', which, in their account, appears to mean the suggestion of an author other than Shakespeare as the poems' creator (p. 16). The article quickly displays its credentials as following a biographical method of discovery. The authors' attempt to discount a particular theory about the sonnets addressed to a young man, on the basis of Henry Wriothesley's personality as evident 'from the historical record', is just one of several similar examples of this approach: 'how could the world's greatest writer, with such a deep understanding of human nature, have loved such a man in such a way?' (p. 18). Whether reliable or not, Decker and Denning's method leads them to make much of the 'rose' metaphors present in a number of sonnets. Taking the possibility that Wriothesley was pronounced 'Rosely' together with the unlikelihood, as they see it, of a significant relationship between Shakespeare and Southampton himself (who is nevertheless accepted as the 'Fair Youth'), they posit a close relationship between the author and the earl's mother, who is, in this account, thought likely to have commissioned the poems in order to persuade Southampton to marry Lady Elizabeth Vere. It is the earl's mother, Lady Mary, countess of Southampton, then, who arranged the sonnets in the order in which they were published, primarily out of a desire to promote those poems which addressed her son. The first 'rose' of the article's title is, therefore, Henry Wriothesley, and the second is his mother, who, in Decker and Denning's increasingly speculative account, is also a hidden lover in the sonnets, one who gives the poet syphilis, as is evident in Sonnets 34–6. The two 'roses' are presented as the key to the sonnets and other works in Shakespeare's canon by marshalling a great deal of material that is already familiar to students of Shakespeare biography. Nevertheless, the particular synthesis presented by Decker and Denning is decidedly less familiar.

R.H. Winnick, in an article for *Literary Imagination*, '"Loe, here in one line is his name twice writ": Anagrams, Shakespeare's Sonnets, and the Identity of the Fair Friend' (*LitI* 11:iii[2009] 254–77), also attempts to identify one of the personae represented in the sonnets. Winnick, like Decker and Denning, presents a case for Henry Wriothesley being the 'Fair Friend' of the sonnets, though his method relies on a detailed description of 'a previously unrecognized, significant nexus binding Q's [the quarto publication of the sonnets of 1609] onomastic and anagrammatic wit' rather than the narrative-based means employed by these authors (p. 255). Winnick notes the phonetic echo of Wriothesley in the repeated use of 'rose', utilized both simply and anagrammatically, but it is his delineation of numerous examples of hidden onomastic anagrams based on the third earl of Southampton's name that justifies his conclusion that 'the dismissal of the Fair Friend's identity as a topic worthy of serious inquiry . . . predicated on its presumed irrelevance' is not as tenable as it once was (p. 277).

Clinton Heylin's book-length study, *So Long as Men Can Breathe: The Untold Story of Shakespeare's Sonnets*, in providing a 'biography' of the 400-year-old quarto, rows back on recent scholarship that sees the publication of the sonnets in 1609 as approved by their author. For Heylin, the sonnets remain a 'bookleg': 'an unauthorized collection of previously unavailable material that has been published, usually surreptitiously, without the author's permission' (p. xi). Following the fate of the 154-sonnet collection, Heylin divides his book into chapters that correspond to particular eras in which the reception of Shakespeare's poems was coloured by the learned (or not so learned) fashion of the time, the divisions also providing opportunities to examine the classic debates that surrounded the poems from that particular period onwards. Section I, on 1590–1640, includes five chapters: one on the conditions surrounding the first publication (1609); two chapters on parts of the back story (1590–1603 and 1593–1603), including the pre-existence of many of the poems and the social context in which the poems were written; another on the question of the status—authorized or unauthorized—of Q and its immediate afterlife (1609–39); and a fifth on John Benson's 1640 edition. Section II, on 1709–2009, brings the story up to date and includes detailed discussions of many modern scholarly debates: chapter 6 (1709–1821) begins with the publication of Nicholas Rowe's edition of the *Dramatic Works* and his scepticism as to the authenticity of the sonnets; chapter 7 (1821–1973) is inaugurated by the Boswell–Malone edition of the *Plays & Poems*, and covers the conjecture about the identities of the various personae presented in the sonnets; chapter 8 (1841–2007) considers the 'disintegrationist' tendency begun by Charles Knight in 1841; chapter 9 (2007–8) tackles the authorship question surrounding *A Lover's Complaint*; and the final chapter (2009) invokes the spirit of the 'booklegger' in its discussion of the secret circulation and collecting of the poems, not unlike the modern-day fan of Bob Dylan in search of the singer's 'little red notebook' (pp. 224–5). Heylin usefully includes all of Shakespeare's sonnets at the end of his stimulating account of their 400-year journey.

Robert Arbour's short article for *Explicator*, 'Shakespeare's Sonnet 60' (*Expl* 67:iii[2009] 157–60), elucidates the said poem's concern not with love but 'the relentless and destructive march of time'. Most significantly, Arbour discusses the metre, rhyme, and acoustic devices of the sonnet as 'creators of meaning' (p. 157). The interplay of each of these elements, the measured use of trochees and spondees, the clever punning that is suggestive of the military theme, and the rhyming of 'light' and 'fight' to imply the battle against the advance of time, all combine 'to demonstrate the futility of attempting to resist the passage of time without seeking immortality through literature' (p. 159).

MacDonald P. Jackson adds to the continuing debate over the authorship of *A Lover's Complaint* in a short entry in *Notes and Queries*: 'Shakespeare or Davies? A Clue to the Authorship of "A Lover's Complaint" ' (*N&Q* 56[2009] 62–3). Here, Jackson provides 'a further scrap of evidence against [Brian] Vickers's theory' that John Davies of Hereford wrote the poem (p. 63). Essentially, the evidence from the works of both Shakespeare and Davies suggests that the use of the indefinite article 'a' (as opposed to 'an') preceding words beginning with 'h' in *A Lover's Complaint* is more in line with Shakespeare's practice than that of Davies.

Jürgen Kamm's essay, ' "She murders with a kiss": The Mentality of Passion in Shakespeare's *Venus and Adonis*' (in Kamm and Lenz, eds., *Shakespearean Culture—Cultural Shakespeare*, pp. 65–85), returns to the relationship between Shakespeare and Henry Wriothesley, earl of Southampton. Here, the context is that of Lord Burghley's desire, as the man entrusted with Southampton's wardship, for the young earl to marry Lady Elizabeth Vere, Burghley's granddaughter, and Southampton's apparent opposition to the match. In his essay, Kamm wishes 'to study the text in precisely this context and to identify Shakespeare's cautious approach both to Burghley's intention and to Southampton's inclination' (p. 67). In order to achieve this, Kamm's reading is structured according to a proposed order for Venus's 'strategies of seduction', which, the author argues, 'push the hapless Adonis through the four ages of Man [youth, adolescence, manhood, and death] and . . . every rite of passage is accompanied by a transformation of genre and mood, reflected in the change of the respective humours [phlegmatic, choleric, sanguine, and melancholic]'. The sudden changes in mood are, in this reading, indicative of the poem's debt to the sensibilities of contemporary stage performance (p. 70). Southampton, clearly identified with Adonis, is encouraged 'in his resistance to accept a female who was thrust upon him as well as supporting him in his wish "to know himself" ". There is, however, a clear sense of anxiety in the poem about Adonis's taste for adventure, which would have found its parallel in the earl's 'hopes of martial glory', later manifested in his active support for the earl of Essex, Lord Burghley's arch political rival (p. 81).

Following his 2005 article for *Critical Survey* 'Rome's Disgrace: The Politics of Rape in Shakespeare's *Lucrece*' (*CS* 17:iii[2005] 15–26), Peter J. Smith returns to the narrative poem for an article in *Shakespeare*: 'Exonerating Rape: Pornography as Exculpation in Shakespeare's *The Rape of Lucrece*' (*Shakespeare* 5:iv[2009] 407–22). On this occasion, Smith aims to justify what he acknowledges may be an unpopular claim: 'that Shakespeare's narrative poem attempts to exculpate Tarquin's offence'. In the process, and including Sonnet 129, *Hamlet*, and Philip Larkin's 'Deceptions' in the scope of his analysis, Smith devises 'a theory of pornography as that which allows the titillation of a masculine reader while clearing him of any moral culpability' (p. 407). Contrary to the view of Ian Frederick Moulton (*Before Pornography: Erotic Writing in Early Modern England* [2000]), Smith argues that early modern texts can be termed pornographic, not least because 'the absence of affection, the loathing of the sexual object, the objectification of the female and the power of the male gaze' are characteristics of early modern examples just as much as they are of any other, properly designated, instance of pornography (p. 409). In a context where 'masculine sociality' enables the circulation of poems like *The Rape of Lucrece*, Smith contends that 'we must be forthright enough to assert the *possibility*' that Shakespeare's readers 'would not automatically be anti-pathetic to a poem of sexual assault which demonstrates compassion with and indeed, further, attempts to exculpate a male aggressor' (p. 412). For Smith, the 'process of exoneration' is an essential feature of pornography, and he persuasively demonstrates the participation of Shakespeare's poem, from its very beginning, in this process (pp. 413–8). Moreover, Tarquin's exoneration, as emblematic of 'patriarchal constructions of gender and power', explains what Smith terms the 'anxious incapacity' of feminist literary criticism to confront the poem's issues head-on (pp. 407, 418).

(e) Histories

Meredith Evans, in 'Rumor, the Breath of Kings and the Body of Law in *2 Henry IV*' (*SQ* 60:i[2009] 1–24), begins from the position that, *contra* King Henry's words at the opening of *2 Henry IV*, there is no such thing as 'good' news in that play, because news 'proves a labile compound of speculation and misrepresentation, endowed with a disturbing power to transform established ideas and forms of political organization' (p. 1). Rumour is 'disruptive of authority per se' 'reconstitutes sovereignty', and 'institutes a new and demotic form of authority' (pp. 3, 4). These are large claims indeed, and are followed by larger ones: 'In Shakespeare, rumor disastrously fails to constitute or confirm sovereign power and can actively undermine that power. Of course, it can also have the opposite effect' (p. 8). The problem I have with this discussion of rumour is its abstract nature: the relation between rumour, sovereignty, legitimacy and other hypostasized concepts are probed as if this weren't a play about a civil war, when by definition a polity is in flux. Evans thinks that through Rumour 'the play draws attention to the contingent, labile, and fundamentally contestable nature of *any* given political configuration' (p. 5). Rumour is also, in Evans's hands, a word with a lability Humpy Dumpty might have envied. 'Like civic discourse' 'she' 'contrasts sharply with... sovereign decision-making' (p. 4), to whom it 'acts as the unreliable deputy' (p. 8). 'She' is 'co-constitutive with paternity' (p. 18) but her 'boasts about her virility echo... in the space vacated by stable biological succession' (p. 20). Hal is a polyglot, like Rumour (p. 21), who 'actively works to elude both embodiment and scapegoating; in this respect she is similar to Falstaff' (p. 23).

Keith Botelho takes a very different tack in his *Renaissance Earwitnesses: Rumor and Early Modern Masculinity*, pointing to the multiplicity of the 'many tongues of counsel' (including, implicitly, rumour) to which the monarch gives ear. Rumour is particularly dangerous on the battlefield, but it is what the monarch does with the rumours he hears—or starts—that is important, not rumour's ontological status per se. The Henriad presents not a mirror for princes but an 'auditory training ground' (p. 61), in which Hal develops a 'discerning ear' when dealing with Falstaff's lies and exaggerations, and indeed ends up confronting rumours about his own transgressions. Rumour's power, such as it is, is licensed, part of Hal's decision to put himself in the way of potentially effective intelligence and counsel at all times.

Nina Taunton, in 'Food, Time and Age: Falstaff's Dietaries and the Tropes of Nourishment in *The Comedy of Errors*' (*ShJE* 145[2009] 91–105), contrasts Falstaff's fatness with Henry IV's leanness, literally and metaphorically, setting up a contrast between the former's 'disorderly eating' and the latter's 'eating disorder' (which she calls 'anorexia' at one point). The fat knight outlasts the king, whose 'self-starving' is an equally poor example to his son. Though Falstaff's relationship to food and drink is plentifully exemplified, and placed in relation to a range of early modern writings on diet, the comparison with the king is hobbled through lack of comparable emphasis in the text: indeed, Taunton's vision of him as having an eating disorder seems to depend more upon the need to produce a satisfactory binary for Falstaff's whole-hearted approach to food and drink than on what we are told about him in the play. Christian Billing takes a refreshingly sceptical line with 'humoral' criticism, identifying Falstaff as increasingly cold, earthy, and feminine. This overly textual approach takes verbal references to humours at face value, and does not help to account for the immediate and continuing theatrical vitality and energy of the character. Billing proposes, rather, that Falstaff's corporeality constitutes a 'satirical critique' of his Galenic self-descriptions, so that 'Falstaff's linguistic descent into femininity and earthiness is frequently ironic, always metaphorical' (p.71). Falstaff does not fit with all the robustly masculine characters he shares the duration of the play with—but this means that he offers a different kind of masculinity, inviting the audience 'to read Falstaff as a site of resistance whose words and deeds are used to critique dominant assumptions about what it is to be and to behave like a man' (p. 73). The homosocial and homoerotic world of these plays defines the benefits for masculinity of a 'number of playful performative shifts that allow men to choose between a number of alternative social, erotic and sexual identities' (p. 79); these shifts are not into femininity, but between masculinities, and Billing provides some interesting expositions of homoerotic gags to point the moral.

The Norton edition of *Richard III* commissioned a new essay from Harry Berger Jr. on the play, 'Conscience and Complicity in *Richard III*' (in Cartelli, ed., pp. 400–17). Building on the work of Rossiter, Brooke, Parker, and Charnes, Berger finds a complex dynamic to Richard's duplicity: 'the speaker tells himself one thing and tells everyone else onstage another, and among the things he tells himself is that he tells himself one thing and tells everyone else onstage another' (p. 402). Yet, Berger proposes, Anne deprives herself of agency, exercising the 'power of self-disempowerment', in a game which takes two to play. Richard's later stringing out of his acceptance of the throne is, in part, a demonstration of how much everyone lets him get away with it. And, given their own varying guilts and complicities, when the ghosts confront Richard towards the end of the play he appears 'to be the target of a conspiracy of bad faith' (p. 415). As usual with Berger's work, a summary doesn't do justice to his sparkling close readings of the play's rhetoric. Jessica Walker compares *Richard III* to Walpole's *The Castle of Otranto* as Gothic texts in '"We are not safe": History, Fear and the Gothic in *Richard III*' (in Desmet and Williams, eds., *Shakespearean Gothic*, pp. 181–97). Though she spends some time on the easily identified Gothic conventions—ghosts, nightmare, curses, prisons, and the like—Walker focuses on the play's relationship with its medieval past, with the house of York being, as it were, the 'haunted house', and the Wars of the Roses 'reassembled like Frankenstein's creature, pieced together from bits of dead memories and revived as a monster that stalks the stage' (p. 182).

Carole Levin and John Watkins include two chapters on Joan of Arc in their *Shakespeare's Foreign Worlds*. Levin's chapter draws on sixteenth-century cases of women pleading pregnancy in an attempt to defer execution, including the story of Perotine Massey, a Guernsey Protestant during the reign of Mary, who, according to Foxe, gave birth while being burnt for heresy. The wide range of cases examined, and of attitudes towards them, testifies to the indeterminacy of Joan's status as perhaps-pregnant malefactor. Sometimes women survived by pleading pregnancy, sometimes they did not. Watkins suggests that the misogyny of the play is related to women's centrality to an increasingly outmoded mode of diplomacy, based upon traditional dynasty-merging marriage. English national foreign policy by the time of Elizabeth had become uncoupled from the fate of the house of Tudor. In *1 Henry VI*, 'Shakespeare attributes England's disgrace to the apparatus through which medieval dynastic diplomacy had been conducted: the relaxation and reassertion of feudal obligations, marriage alliances between former belligerents, and submission to the international authority of the Roman Church' (p. 60). Chivalry, too, as a pan-European code, is clearly inadequate as a means of conducting the conflict. Philippa Shepherd reaches back into alternative treatments of Joan of Arc in 'The Puzzle of Pucelle or Pussel: Shakespeare's Joan of Arc compared with Two Antecedents' (in Eisenbichler, ed., pp. 191–209). The antecedents are in Christine de Pisan's poem *Ditié de Jehanne d'Arc*, written shortly after Joan had defeated the English at Orléans and Fronton du Duc's 1580 play *The Tragic History of La Pucelle of Domrémy*, and Shepherd provides a predominantly descriptive account of the differences between the three texts. Wolfram Keller, Astrid Lohöfer, and Christian Pauls offer a more substantial reading of Shakespeare and de Pisan in 'What's at Stake: Jeanne d'Arc between Historiography and Propaganda' (in Fielitz, ed. *Literature as History/History as Literature: Fact and Fiction in Medieval to Eighteenth-Century British Literature*, pp. 43–60). They conclude that Joan's pursuit of Burgundy after Rouen 'shows the integrative potential of Joan's self-created sanctity and doubleness for unifying France' (p. 55). Moreover, this changeableness is part of the theatrical vitality making her the dominant character in the play. Dominique Goy-Blanquet writes very readably on the *Henry VI* plays in 'Shakespeare, Burgundy, and the Design in the Arras' (in Mayer, ed., *Representing France and the French in Early Modern English Drama*, pp. 49–67). In particular, she rehabilitates the French chronicler Robert Gaguin, whose work fed, via Fabyan, into Hall and thus into Shakespeare. Goy-Blanquet compares the English chronicle treatments with what Shakespeare made of them, concluding that he 'knew more about things French than the Tudor chroniclers' (p. 58).

Deborah Shuger, in '"In a Christian climate": Religion and Honor in *Richard II*' (in Graham and Collington, eds., *Shakespeare and Religious Change*, pp. 37–59), suggests that Shakespeare's play wrestles with the 'problem of how to transcend the honor politics of zero-sum' (p. 40) (or the 'you win, I lose' scenario imagined in Richard's metaphor of the buckets). Shuger points out that Shakespeare's play is not particularly concerned with whether Richard deserved his deposition; rather, its focus is on Richard's attempt to see himself as something other than a loser once Bolingbroke 'wins' the crown. Indeed, Richard's early cancellation of the combat can be read as an attempt to find an alternative to the honour community's values. Tudor–Stuart Christianity can be read as a 'system for hallowing loss' (p. 44), and Richard reaches into various kinds of Christian selfhood—hermit, penitent, sacral king, even suffering Christ—in his unsuccessful attempts to fashion himself anew. However, he fails to keep at bay his bitter sense of loss, and does not die well. In this he resembles the earl of Essex, in whose later years and fall Shuger traces the same tension between the self as constituted by honour or religion. The piece ends by challenging the often identified modern realpolitik of the play; for Shuger, the play centres (via Richard) on the relationship between Christianity and political power.

Richard Wilson's '"A stringless instrument": *Richard II* and the Defeat of Poetry' (in Meek et al., eds., *Shakespeare's Book: Essays in Reading, Writing and Reception*, pp. 102–19) finds in the play an allegory of Shakespeare's own shift, following the death of his patron Stanley, from the putative poet to the quality of the narrative poems to provider of plays for the theatrical marketplace. Bolingbroke's player-king charisma trumps Richard's poetry. Indeed Richard's sabotaging of his own princely power-on-display moment at the play's opening 'enacts the attention drift the plot confirms, from princely to public stage, and patronage to playhouse' (p. 110). Jennifer Vaught devotes a chapter to *Richard II* in her monograph *Masculinity and Emotion in Early Modern English Literature*. She delineates the ways in which Richard's 'emotionally expressive, masculine identity' includes affective use of rhetoric, a tendency towards privacy and interiority, and retreat from honour-code self-definition. Richard himself seeks pity through 'woeful rhetoric', passivity, and lament; via the play the potency of such 'feminized means of resistance' is reaffirmed, at a time when violent and militaristic versions of masculinity were 'crumbling' at the Elizabethan court.

Karen Sawyer Marsalek considers the site-specific nature of early performances of *Henry VIII* in 'Staging Allegiance, Re-membering Trials: *King Henry VIII* and the Blackfriars Theater' (in Graham and Collington, eds., pp. 133–50). The Blackfriars was the location of Katherine of Aragon's divorce trial; but Marsalek points out that it had also housed Wolsey's parliamentary trial, as well as a range of heresy trials of Wycliffites in the fourteenth century. The heresy link further strengthens *Henry VIII*'s implication in the issue of papal authority, as well as to some extent further 'Englishing' Katherine as a martyr with Protestant overtones (something visible, for example, in her attitudes towards Latin and English). It also inflects Cranmer's trial late in the play for heresy. In the context of James's Oath of Allegiance, the relationship between political and confessional identities had renewed topicality—a topicality whose complexities were clearly revealed in bodying forth (or 're-membering') on the Blackfriars stage. Jennifer Richards's essay on 'Shakespeare and the Politics of Co-Authorship: *Henry VIII*' (in Armitage et al., eds., *Shakespeare and Early Modern Political Thought*, pp. 176–94) begins from the position that the play poses in a particularly acute form the question of Shakespeare's own politics, particularly because the reflection on Wolsey's fall at IV.ii, for Richards the 'moral centre' of the play, however 'Shakespearian', is by Fletcher. However, Richards discerns a coherent political and moral core to the play: that 'honesty' (in its early modern or Ciceronian sense of moderation, decency, and decorum) is more trustworthy than 'truth', and, as a means of managing different viewpoints, is a way to avoid 'sectarian tragedy'. Richards then rereads several uses of 'honest' or 'honesty' to shift the centre of gravity of the play's politics away from the question of 'truth'. Truth, or claims to truth, and temperance are not always bedfellows, and both dramatists' representations of Wolsey cohere in this respect.

Jeffrey Knapp's *Shakespeare Only* investigates the concentration of references to Christ, the Mass, and the word 'sacrament' in the Lancastrian histories (the chapter also appears as 'Author, King, and Christ in Shakespeare's Histories' in Graham and Collington, eds., pp. 217–37). One cluster is around hypocrisy, a person trading 'on the spiritual power of Christ's death and resurrection in particular' (p. 110); but two of the main pretenders, Richard II and Falstaff, cannot be easily boxed into that category, not to mention a third, Hal/Henry V. The epilogue to *Henry V* characterizes the author as generating 'unbloody versions of sacrifice'—a new communion, as it were, but out of the hands of untrustworthy clerics—and in doing so generating a new conception of authorship where the author's pen yields to the power of the actor's body.

Dorothea Kehler's *Shakespeare's Widows* is largely descriptive, and devoted to demonstrating, in a commonsensical way, the uncontroversial thesis that Shakespeare's widows are not all stereotypical. It offers a series of rather old-fashioned character studies, including some fairly speculative excursions into motivation ('Mistress Quickly remarries, perhaps to console herself for a lost mate—or the lost title she had dreamt of—perhaps for companionship, even desire, but surely for a helpmate to help keep her business solvent', p. 129). Anne in *Richard III* is dismissed as constructed 'out of derogatory topoi'; Margaret of Anjou is a 'pastiche of misogynistic commonplaces and canards laced with xenophobia and English jingoism' (pp. 101, 102). Carole Levin's *Dreaming the English Renaissance* has a chapter on dreams in the histories; however, it is primarily descriptive and does not offer a thesis about dreams other than that dramatists 'used dreams to emphasise the issues of sexuality and power in the founding of the Tudor dynasty and in the political and religious challenges to that dynasty' (p. 126).

Eric Heinze's 'Power Politics and the Rule of Law: Shakespeare's First Historical Tetralogy and Law's Foundations' (*Oxford Journal of Legal Studies* 29:i[2009] 139–68) explores the way in which the first tetralogy 'explores . . . the conditions for the possibility of a legal order' (p. 142), and in particular the necessity for such an order to not merely work, but to be just. Henry VI, though he is constantly undermined by the aristocracy (and indeed the corruption of lawyers themselves, as suggested in the Temple Garden scene of *1 Henry VI*) offers a model of due process. Heinze defends Henry against his detractors, suggesting that though any attempt to impose the rule of law without a corresponding civil society will fail, this does not mean that Henry could have succeeded had he been temperamentally more able to dictate. The tensions between violence and the rule of law revealed in this play are not simply a function of the individual characters within it; rather, Heinze suggests, they are embedded in the foundations of law itself. Heinze returns to Henry VI, in a study of four different kinds of legitimacy embodied by Richard II, Henry IV, Henry VI, and Richard III, in 'Heir, Celebrity, Martyr, Monster: Legal and Political Legitimacy in Shakespeare and Beyond' (*Law Critique* 20[2009] 79–103). Heinze suggests four kinds of legitimating discourse, those of 'transcendent right', 'secular duty', 'secular right', and 'transcendent duty'. Richard III's 'might is right' translates into 'secular right'; Bolingbroke's more principled version into 'secular duty'; Henry VI grounds his legitimacy in 'transcendent duty', and Richard II, unsurprisingly, relies on 'transcendent right'. Such a schema opens up interesting points of comparison which have the potential to challenge current schematic understandings—for example, the emphasis on Bolingbroke's concern for 'duty' frees him from the equally schematic characterization of him as a Machiavellian pragmatist.

Rachana Sachdev considers the 'gratuitous' references to breastfeeding in *Richard II* (V.iii.90) and *Richard III* (II.ii.30) in 'Of Paps and Dugs: Nursing Breasts in Shakespeare's England' (*ELN* 47:ii[2009] 49–57) to confirm the role of the two duchesses of York in disrupting the patriarchal order, in the one case by splitting son from father and in the other by engendering the monstrous Richard.

David Schalwyk writes on 'Proto-Nationalist Performatives and Trans-Theatrical Displacement in *Henry V*' (in Henke and Nicholson, *Transnational Exchange in the Early Modern Theater*, pp. 197–213). For him, Henry's project differs from that of the Elizabethans in Ireland in that, while the Irish were constructed as 'Other', both Henry's war and the eventual settlement are predicated on his kinship with the French. It is not '*really* about Ireland or even English nationalism' (p. 198). Rather, the play embodies a tension between performance and the performative: all those speech acts represented are not really happening. The Chorus's 'histrionic sleight of hand' is duplicated by the king himself, especially in his deployment of the rhetoric of nationalism: Schalwyk notes that 'the Chorus promises Mars, but delivers a mercurial wordsmith' (p. 204). Henry is closer to Pistol than he seems, and 'vacuous speech acts' pervade the play. Rhetoric of all kinds is exposed by its performance in the theatre. Robin Bates, in *Shakespeare and the Cultural Colonization of Ireland* focuses instead on the dynamics of the play whereby Henry is transformed from personal character into a national figure. In the course of this, Henry 'sheds personal companions and replaces them with an abstract—an assortment of embodiments of Britain's holdings' (p. 41) in a kind of 'cultural impressment'. This move seems to me to be more partial than Bates supposes, however—there is some continuity in Henry's companions, who are not *all* 'replaced'.

Bradin Cormack starts from the position that 'English military nationalism was unimaginable except as a version of the Conquest in 1066' in his *A Power to Do Justice: Jurisdiction, English Literature, and the Rise of Common Law, 1509–1625* (p. 181). Conquest of France in *Henry V* reverses 'the' Conquest 'by acknowledging that, far from being a simple other, France is a pressure internal to and generative of English national identity' (p. 200). Cormack reads the plays through the discourse of 'legal nationalism', the early modern attempts to account for the presence of French language within English legal discourse, disrupting the attempt to ground it respectably in and on Latin, and through it the classical past. The ironies increase as Henry is figured as Julius Caesar, who conquered both England and France. Cormack also points out the iterative irony of casting Richmond in *Richard III* as a conqueror—but of the English, rather than the French—'re-enacting the foundational moment of Englishness' (p. 204). There is a linguistic turn to this politics also—embodied in Pistol's mishearings and mistranslations of French—and visible in the final article in *Henry V*, which institutes Henry's new title in French and Latin, a sign that English law already inhabits this macaronic territory. Jean-Christophe Mayer takes a broader perspective on the 'plurivocality' of the play in 'The Ironies of Babel in Shakespeare's *Henry V*' (in Mayer, ed., pp. 127–41). Not only do Pistol and Nym mangle French and Latin (with a bit of Irish thrown in), but Katherine's 'English lesson' pushes the audience's linguistic competence. Indeed, spectators are given a 'kind of lesson in French', as the French (for once) speaking their own language (or at least Shakespeare's version of it), suggesting that 'foreignness is only a construction, and indeed a question of perspective' (p. 131). In the truce scene, Katherine speaks broken English and French while other French nobles speak perfect English; Henry seizes the chance to propose a new hybrid Anglo-French cultural identity for their child 'half French, half English, that shall go to Constantinople and take the Turk by the beard'. But the play's epilogue ironizes this epic reversal of the Babel curse.

Malcolm Pittock reconsiders 'The Problem of *Henry V*' (*Neophil* 93:i[2009] 175–90), proposing that the play's oft-remarked ambiguity is difficult to ground in Elizabethan attitudes towards the king. Pittock's alternative explanation is that the text we have is the product of a tension between 'Shakespeare the man' (a simple patriot) and 'Shakespeare the universal artist' (with an eye on universal appeal, including to the French). He then provides plentiful evidence, from the play and from contemporary attitudes to war and politics, to support the idea of Shakespeare the artist at work. Shakespeare the simple and non-artistic patriot is rather less evident, however, which undermines the duality with which the article begins and ends. Aysha Pollnitz considers a history alongside a tragedy in 'Educating Hamlet and Prince Hal' (in Armitage et al., eds., pp. 119–38), concluding that Hal's education is distinctly 'un-Erasmian'. Despite this, his success as king means suggests that the prince educated to best sixteenth-century standard may not make the best ruler.

David Coleman writes on the 1599 text of *Henry V* in 'Ireland and Islam: *Henry V* and the "War on Terror"' (*Shakespeare* 4:ii[2008] 169–80). He sums up critical arguments that, notwithstanding the reduced 'Irish' presence in the quarto, it 'remains a text deeply implicated in the strategies of colonial violence undertaken by Elizabethans in Ireland' (p. 172). He then notes a variety of deployments of *Henry V* in (particularly) journalism dealing with the invasion of Iraq, and the parallels between representation of Irish republicanism and Islamic terrorism. However, the relationship between the play and the journalism, and the events of which it treats, is not fully spelt out, and the conclusion leaves the links unclear: the 'surprising conflation of Irish and Islamic alterity' is 'perhaps as a result of the tendency to read current politics through the lens of *Henry V*' (p. 178). Diana E. Henderson also considers the play in relation to contemporary wars in 'Meditations in a Time of (Displaced) War: *Henry V*, Money, and the Ethics of Performing History' (in King and Franssen, eds., *Shakespeare and War*, pp. 226–42). In the only scripted battle scene in the play—between Pistol and Le Fer—Henderson finds 'a farcical epitome of systematic corruption, foregrounding the economic motive that repeatedly jars with the rhetoric of warrior glory' (p. 232). Indeed, Henderson advises us to 'follow the money' in the play—not merely the traitors' or clerics' fiduciary motives, but Henry's own use of the language of 'mercantile enterprise' in his musings before battle. Such readings, she suggests—in critical and theatrical work—might help to challenge the co-optation of the play as pro-war ongoing in the US since the invasion of Iraq. R. Scott Fraser reads the play as embodying a tension between what the audience sees and what it is told (by the Chorus and Henry) in '*Henry V* and the Performance of War' (in King and Franssen, eds., pp. 71–82). Historically, the siege of Harfleur was successful because the Dauphin could not relieve the town; in the play, it is Henry's violent rhetoric which wins the day. As Henry's words have no direct counterpart in the material he worked from, Shakespeare can here be seen to be interrogating the Henry 'myth', a technique which reaches its high spot in the representation of the killing of the French prisoners. This is the only part of the play beyond Henry's 'stage-managing', and starkly poses 'implied questions about the war: its justification, its performance, and its mythology' (p. 82).

Finally, Laurence Lerner's *Henry IV* in the British Council's Writers and their Work series offers a sensible introduction to the play aimed at the undergraduate or non-specialist reader. The book begins with the historical events recounted before taking the reader through the play and subsequent criticism. In this last chapter the main currents are well covered, and it would function well to introduce undergraduates to a range of critical approaches.

(f) Tragedies

Shakespeare's tragedies continued to generate a lot of interest in 2009 and a number of critical enquiries covering the full spectrum of titles were published. While the more popular plays continue to offer scholars subject for debate, the perhaps less popular titles also saw a number of essays. This survey offers first a discussion of the contributions on the tragedies in more general book collections before going on to cover articles on specific plays.

Maria Del Sapia Garbero edited a collection of essays, entitled *Identity, Otherness and Empire in Shakespeare's Rome*, which study how Shakespeare used the idea of Rome not only to discuss the political sphere but also to discuss the culture of ancient Rome in Elizabethan England.

In the chapter 'Acting the Roman: *Coriolanus*', Manfred Pfister notes the omnipresent importance of refashioning to England in the early modern period and the interest of drama in republican rather than imperial Rome as a part of this. Pfister highlights the Romanness of *Coriolanus* in terms of the use of the word Rome, the accuracy of topography, and the fact that 'it is *about* Rome and about *romanitas*, about what constitutes Rome as a social and political space' (p. 37, emphasis in original). Pfister discusses Shakespeare's anatomization of the body politic extended to Coriolanus 'in his deeply disturbed attitude towards his own body' (p. 38), and goes on to address Coriolanus as acting a role of masculinity. Pfister relates the idea of the self to the idea of *romanitas*, stating that 'there is something demonstrative about *romanitas* which puts the true Roman always on stage: as a *man*... as a *politician*... as a *warrior*... as an *orator*... as a philosopher' (pp. 42–3, emphasis in original), and concludes that Coriolanus is 'forever the performer, acting the Roman in order to suppress the un-Roman "boy of tears" (V.vi.103) within him' (p. 44).

In his essay '"I am more an antique Roman than a Dane": Suicide, Masculinity and National Identity in *Hamlet*' Drew Daniel studies Horatio's refusal to perform Hamlet's dying request and asks what is meant by being 'more an antique Roman than a Dane' and what idea of Romanness is assumed by Shakespeare to be understood by his English audience. Daniel explores the patrician idea of the nobility of self-killing and what it means in terms of the individual agency of free men and slaves, and contrasts this with the Christian teaching on the sanctity of life and ideas related to suicide. He asserts that self-killing is central to *Hamlet* and discusses it in the light of the Senecan celebration of suicide as 'the ultimate expression of self-possession' (p. 81). He reads Seneca as 'the linchpin connecting a Stoic philosophy that celebrated suicide for intellectual reasons with a dramatic context in which suicide was subjected to aesthetic apotheosis as the defining act of tragic grandeur' (p. 81). Daniel discusses the idea of national identity which is inherent in Horatio's words and suggests that his 'cross-identification is not only national but historical' (p. 83) and relates this to notions of masculinity. He concludes that *Hamlet* ultimately shows that 'the greater suffering, the greater masculinity, the greater witnessing, the greater obedience, lie not in suicide but in mandatory survival' (p. 87).

In her chapter on 'Romans versus Barbarians: Speaking the Language of the Empire in *Titus Andronicus*', Barbara Antonucci argues that although binary differences between the civilized and the barbarous appear to be established at the beginning of the play, in fact 'the racial boundaries . . . progressively crumble: the cultural differences/boundaries between the Romans, Goths and Aaron collapse on the grounds of their common literary heritage and . . . ability to "speak" the language of the Empire which confounds cultural distinction' (p. 121). She refers to the language of Act I, scene i, to explore notions of barbarity and who occupies the barbarous space in the play, noting that each group equates the other with barbarity. Antonucci looks at the classical allusions in *Titus Andronicus* and addresses which characters speak this language, its power, and the role of Lavinia as 'a loud "silent" presence onstage' (p. 121). Antonucci discusses how Lavinia's rape and her family's attempts to decipher her signs is the point at which 'the connections of episodes to legendary narratives becomes crucial' by 'channelling the episode into an epic frame' (p. 125) both in the rape and in the punishment of Chiron and Demetrius. Antonucci suggests that setting the play on the eve of the empire's collapse shows Shakespeare mocking Rome and its classical authors.

Paul Yachnin and Jessica Slights's collection, *Shakespeare and Character: Theory, History, Performance, and Theatrical Persons* boldly asserts that 'character has made a comeback' (p.1) and that consequently a 'new character criticism' (p.1) is emerging. The volume of essays is split into four sections: the 'first three . . . group essays according to the primary critical approaches of their authors . . . the fourth . . . offers three essays that demonstrate what a theoretically sophisticated and historically informed new character criticism can accomplish when it is alert to the nuances of theatrical performance and intellectual history' (p. 12). Of the three essays in the collection on the tragedies, two fall into this final section, while the first, James Berg's 'The Properties of Character in *King Lear*' (in Yachnin and Slights, eds., pp. 97–116) is in the second section entitled 'History'. Berg's essay addresses how all elements constituting a character should be considered as '*reading material*'. In this context, 'all character *is* property, where property represents not just what persons seem to own, but things that properly belong *with* them' (p. 98).

Anthony Dawson's contribution to the collection seems to challenge the idea of character, its title asking 'Is Timon a Character?' Dawson suggests that a character as a person must possess a level of complex self-awareness which Timon, although an attractive creation, does not. Through looking at Timon's presence and his command of 'elegiac language' (p. 201), and the notion that *Timon of Athens* was written during 'one of Shakespeare's most productive periods... and one in which he was exploring the extremities of character' (p. 203), Dawson concludes that Timon 'is a sort of extremity, an experiment in character making... a distilled element—pure and unmixed' (p. 207).

Sarah Werner's essay on 'Arming Cordelia' takes a stage direction in the Folio version of *King Lear* which suggests that Cordelia is figured as the head of the French army in Act IV, and that as such it can be assumed that she wears armour. Werner addresses what it might mean for a woman to wear armour, invoking Margaret from the *Henry VI* plays and Philippa from *Edward III* along the way, to challenge notions of appropriate feminine behaviour.

In '*Macbeth* and Old Wives' Tales: Gendering Conflicts in Burke's Amphibious Subject' (in Dimmock and Hadfield, eds., *Literature and Popular Culture in Early Modern England*, pp. 179–91), Mary Ellen Lamb establishes how interest in women since the 1980s has changed 'the landscape of popular culture' and sets out to explore 'the effect of women's agency by gendering the implications of Peter Burke's brilliant insight that early modern educated males are "amphibious"' (p. 180). Lamb discusses the role of women in raising men and the power of old wives' tales through the different cultures experienced by growing men, Lamb offers *Macbeth* as 'a decisive test case' for this discussion as laying 'bare the gendered conflicts of its day' (p. 181). Lamb discusses old wives' tales as a denigrating term which also suggests their frightening power, both in terms of real fear and also pleasure. Lamb perceives a threat in the relationship between 'female narrators and children' (p. 181) to later masculinity, and reads this fear as evident in *Macbeth* citing the example of III.iv.61–7. Lamb highlights the power of tales by arguing that, although read by Lady Macbeth as figments of his imagination, the dagger and the ghost are very real to Macbeth and also, potentially, to the audience. In relation to Lady Macbeth, Lamb argues that 'Early moderns would have understood [Macbeth's] regression [to dependence on a woman] in terms of a persistent and widespread anxiety that a man might relapse to the unfixed gender identity of a childhood dominated by women' (p. 183). Lamb suggests that the role of the witches 'enacts a humiliating awareness... of the dependence of early modern males... on the lower-class women who also nursed them' (p. 185).

Early Modern Literary Studies published a special issue in 2009 entitled 'Embodying Shakespeare', a number of contributions to which focused on the tragedies. In '"Enamoured of thy parts": Dismemberment and Domesticity in *Romeo and Juliet*' (*EMLS* 19[2009] 31 paras.), Arian M. Balizet reads *Romeo and Juliet* in relation to early modern domestic guides in the play's deep investment 'in the anatomization of masculine qualities' (para. 1). Balizet states that 'Juliet is looking to make Romeo into her husband' (para. 1) and that the play's engagement with ideas of domesticity as seen in the guides shows its 'rejection of contemporary domestic ideology' and 'the extent to which early modern models of domestic order depend upon fantasies of corporeal violence' (paras. 1–2). For example, Balizet demonstrates how Capulet presents Paris to Juliet 'as a collection of parts fashioned into a suitable husband' (para. 4) in Act III, scene v. However, Balizet notes that in presenting a whole made up of parts, Paris is 'anatomized for Juliet's scrutiny' (para. 4). Balizet explores two models through the article—embodiment in medical treatises and domesticity in marriage manuals—and explores a range of medical and political treatises which illustrate the Elizabethan conception of the body as a microcosm of the state, before going on to discuss domestic treatises. Balizet then relates these discussions to the play: the penetration of Juliet's body figured in Romeo's trespasses into Capulet's house; the headless Capulet family; Juliet's disobedience as against Elizabethan ideals of family management. Balizet concludes by stating that '*Romeo and Juliet* dramatizes the dismemberment of patriarchal domestic authority at each opportunity' (para. 31).

In her short article, 'Hamlet, the Pirate's Son' (*EMLS* 19[2009] 11 paras.), Mary Floyd-Wilson discusses Hamlet's rescue by the sea pirates in terms of Dutch heritage and identity. Floyd-Wilson sets out to address the previously unexplored notion of 'how Hamlet's sea-voyage succeeds in locating a seemingly crucial moment of character development beyond the reaches of psychological inwardness' and points towards 'Shakespeare's investment in the barbarism of his source material' (para. 1). Floyd-Wilson spells out previous critical approaches to the pirates, briefly looking at historical accounts which link the Danish with a history of piracy which then leads to a new reading of *Hamlet*'s sources in Saxo Grammaticus and François de Belleforest stressing the 'significant references to piracy' (para. 6) in their works. Floyd-Wilson thus reads this as gesturing towards Hamlet's own heritage. Floyd-Wilson argues that 'Hamlet's disparagement of his low origins and his proud assertion ... "This is I, / Hamlet the Dane" ... mirrors ... tension at work in the early modern literary and historiographical turn towards northern sources' (para. 9). Floyd-Wilson also argues that it is the change in air as a consequence of the sea-voyage that leads to Hamlet's change in behaviour, and concludes, in contrast to other critics who suggest Hamlet's voyage and rescue bring out internal qualities, that it is external forces that change his exterior temperament.

By way of introduction to his essay '"A nature but infected": Plague and Embodied Transformation in *Timon of Athens*' (*EMLS* 19[2009] 18 paras.), Darryl Chalk invokes Artaud's *The Theatre and its Double* to illustrate the notion of theatre as a plague 'capable of infecting and transforming both body and mind' (para. 1). Chalk links this idea to the rhetoric of Renaissance anti-theatricalists and theatre closures during the Renaissance which were caused by outbreaks of plague. Chalk cites John Rainolds (1599) and his concerns for actors who might be infected by the characters they played. In so doing, Chalk historicizes the play to argue that the links between the theatre and plague were present not just in anti-theatrical tracts but in early modern plays themselves. He reads Timon's 'extreme transformation from philanthropy to misanthropy' (para. 3) in this context. Chalk argues for a more gradual transformation which is foreshadowed and signalled through 'the conscious organization of onstage and offstage space' (para. 3) than critics have previously suggested. Chalk gives a brief historical context of plague in the period and the causes which were perceived by early modern pamphleteers.

Chalk explores the idea of the link between plague and social disorder, leading to a reading of *Timon of Athens* as a 'despairing and vehement evocation of plague as chaotic undifferentiation' (para. 7), while highlighting instances in the text where plague, illness, and medicine are either spoken of, discussed, or invoked in the language used. Chalk particularly notes Timon's tirade in Act IV, scene i, which calls for pestilence bringing 'catastrophic inversions and behavioural transformations identified by Dekker and Girard' (para. 7). In so doing, Chalk argues that speech 'demonstrates Shakespeare's appropriation of the understanding of plague in medical discourse as communicable contagion' and that 'Timon's speech harnesses fear of undifferentiation and fear of plague' (para. 7). Chalk goes on to discuss early modern accounts of theatre as a contagion, a drug, and a poison with 'a powerful capability to infect others' and 'spread the disease of theatricality with an efficiency as dangerous as any plague epidemic' (para. 8). A thorough discussion of anti-theatrical attitudes in this regard, focusing on the writing of John Rainolds, follows. Chalk then goes on to discuss the transformation of Timon and reads the drama as a bubonic plague-play. He discusses how Timon is established as 'king of his own court' (para. 18) in the first part of the play, and illustrates where the change is foreshadowed before discussing the actual transformation in mind and body. Chalk highlights how Timon's 'vitriolic rhetoric mimics the repetitive style of anti-theatrical polemic' (para. 23) and argues that 'Timon's apparently affected role is... also a kind of infection, a contagious entity he caught from his overtly theatrical lifestyle' (para. 26). Chalk concludes that 'Unlike the early modern actor... the anti-theatricalists lack that self-conscious doubleness, the awareness of the "seam" between actor and character' which is revealed in Shakespeare's work. In *Timon of Athens*, Shakespeare 'reinscribes the anti-theatrical identification of acting as a plague, responding to anti-theatrical sentiment with parodic effect' (para. 28).

In a short article, 'Is There Life After Sex? *Macbeth* and Post-Sexuality' (*EMLS* 19[2009] 13 paras.), Helen Ostovich argues that new performances build on and play with texts, performances, images, and ideas that have come before. Ostovich argues that 'the Jonson/Middleton creation of blackly comic covens of mothers and grandmothers may be closer to Shakespeare's conception of the Weird Sisters than other critics have allowed' (para. 2), and that 'By playing with the play' readers create a 'compilation of impressions... [which] adds to our understanding of the play by generating new possible meanings' (para. 2). Ostovich uses 'the postmodern theatrical choice of stirring tangentially related versions of stories together in a cauldron to create a deliberately dispersed presentist vision with layers of possible meaning' (para. 3) and discusses the witches in terms of different stories—such as the Grey Women in the Perseus myth—which create understanding of Shakespeare's witches. In historicizing the witches, Ostovich discusses the role of James VI of Scotland in creating the 'singing and dancing witches as performance prelude' (para. 6) to the *Macbeth* play after commanding Gillis Duncan to dance when he interrogated the North Berwick witches. This discussion leads on to the exploration of the sociability and warmth of witches. Ostovich goes on to discuss the sexuality of witches as 'a routine part of their exuberant undifferentiating embrace of the chaos in which they live', but reads it as 'unmoralized and unpunished' impotence (para. 7). Ostovich talks about the Jonson/Middleton witches as 'figments of comedy' (para. 10) but observes that 'the real harm is Macbeth's belief in the witches' power to control him' (para. 10). Ostovich brings the idea of the witches up to date in a discussion of *The Triplets of Belleville*, reading the triplets in the light of Shakespeare, Middleton, and Jonson before concluding that 'there is more to the Weird Sisters... and performance experiments are key' (para. 13).

Carla Mazzio's philosophical essay 'The History of Air: *Hamlet* and the Trouble with Instruments' (*SCRev* 26:i–ii[2009] 153–96) discusses early modern approaches to air from Francis Bacon and John Donne, and sets out to argue that 'an aesthetics of affect' grew out of 'the otherwise threatening power of an element that could not be directly seen, understood, controlled, or subjected to "capture"' (p. 154). Mazzio examines how 'innovations in the representation of affect... evince powerful traces of a "history of air"' (p. 154), Shakespeare's *Hamlet* being one such innovation. In the first section of the article, Mazzio discusses various meanings of air in Shakespeare's England—for example, ghost or breath—which have significance in relation to *Hamlet*, and addresses a number of contemporary philosophical enquiries into the idea of air. Mazzio asserts the importance of air in Shakespeare's England, not least because of the common knowledge about the threat of air which carried plague and pestilence. Mazzio goes on to discuss how air cannot be easily manipulated and the repeated failings in *Hamlet* to manipulate it. For example, Mazzio refers to the recorder exchange between Hamlet, Rosencrantz, and Guildenstern in Act III, scene ii, drawing the conclusion that 'Such an emphasis on air at the limits of governance, knowledge and manipulability might well be understood as a metaphoric subset of larger problems of illegitimate governance and vexed theology that dominate *Hamlet*' (p. 159). Mazzio also explores the atmospheric air of the play and how the element is reflected within speech as well as action within the play. Mazzio also discusses Dürer's illustration *Melencolia I* in relation to *Hamlet* since both texts deal with air as being at the limits of the philosophical. In the first part of the essay, Mazzio discusses the philosophical background to the issue of air. In the second part, she goes on to discuss how these discourses relate to *Hamlet*. Mazzio reads a 1563 meteorological text by William Fulke as informing *Hamlet* in terms of 'how such *meteorological* debates of the period can help us to understand the ghost within Hamlet as something other than a haunt of Catholicism or a phantasmatic product of a son unable to mourn his father' (p. 171). Mazzio finds moments in *Hamlet* that echo the ideas within Fulke's text. Mazzio also discusses the 'fumes and vapours' (p. 177) that fill the play and signal corruption, linked again to the fear of the spread of illness through the air. Mazzio concludes with reference to J.M. Barrie's *My Lady Nicotine* [1915] and the idea of air as inspiring—in this context, smoke inspiring Shakespeare with the idea of *Hamlet*.

Elizabeth Williamson's article 'The Uses and Abuses of Prayer Book Properties in *Hamlet*, *Richard III*, and *Arden of Faversham*' (*ELR* 39:ii[2009] 371–95) highlights the importance of prayer-books to post-Reformation Protestantism in spite of the move to remove material objects from the object of mediation. Williamson notes that dramatists of the period were drawing attention to 'the inescapable corporeality of early modern worship' (p. 374). The essay thus examines scenes in *Hamlet*, *Richard III*, and *Arden* in which prayer books are used, in order to demonstrate how the physical materiality of worship was highlighted through the analogy of prayer-book as simultaneously stage prop and tool for meditation. Williamson also asserts that 'the Protestant reformers' attempts to deploy representations of women readers as emblems of true piety were often undercut by misogynist stereotypes' (p. 374) on the stage. Williamson discusses *Hamlet* in terms of the falsification of worship and meditation that is evident in Polonius's instructions to Ophelia to use her prayer-book as a prop in a trap with which to catch Hamlet out. That Hamlet does not recognize this immediately as a ploy underlines the appearance of sincerity and the threat of the false meditation. Williamson goes on to read prayer in *Richard III* as linking Richard's Machiavellianism with 'the errors of medieval religion, presenting an apparently straightforward endorsement of anti-Catholic stereotypes' (p. 381). Williamson focuses this discussion on Act III, scene vii—a 'classic example of political propaganda, but it is also a quintessentially hypocritical use of the prayer book as prop' (p. 382). Williamson highlights how, in both *Hamlet* and *Richard III*, the characters using prayer-books are directed to do so by others, underlining the dual falsity of the scene and use of the book. She also highlights the negative presentation of devout women in these instances: in the use of Ophelia as actor in the set-up, and in Buckingham's instruction to Richard to 'play the Maid's part' (III.vii.51). Williamson concludes that 'the surprising likeness between theatrical props and religious ones elegantly exposes the investment in material things that Protestants, whether they admitted it or not, shared with Catholics, and with the commercial theatre' (p. 395).

In a similar vein, Joseph Sterrett begins his article 'Confessing Claudius: Sovereignty, Fraternity and Isolation at the Heart of *Hamlet*' (*TPr* 23:v[2009] 729–62) by noting the isolation in which Claudius speaks his confession: unheard on an empty stage. Noting the significance of confession as a theme of *Hamlet* and the important triangulation of three confession scenes in Act III, Sterrett asserts the notion that one of the 'principal concerns of the play is articulated in these scenes—the failure of confession'. The article is built on two strands: in the first, Sterrett historicizes the play, looking at 'the culture of confession that surrounded the play's moment of production' (p. 740), focusing on the earl of Essex's confession as a powerful example of failure, before going on to discuss *Hamlet* by way of Derrida's exploration of *The Confessions* of St Augustine, 'which offers a valuable theoretical framework for confession in the ideal' (p. 740). Sterrett discusses the background of confessing both in the Catholic and post-Reformation Anglican churches. In so doing, he references the iconography of confession, especially in the confession box. However, Sterrett pays particularly close attention to published confessions and their implications in terms of readership and purpose linked to the notion of the attractiveness of the 'idea that the truth of oneself could be expressed in words' (p. 744). Sterrett concludes this section of discussion by suggesting the intention and expectation of an audience for all published and public confessions. Sterrett then reads the earl of Essex's confession in light of this conclusion as embodying two aspects of the 'confessional genre its outward appeal and the indeterminate nature of the truth' (p. 747). He discusses contemporary questioning of Essex's sincerity, in part related to the uniformity of scaffold confessions, stating that 'The lingering and captivating undecidability of the Earl's confession stimulated a debate for decades to come' (p. 748). A significant alignment between this and *Hamlet* is then drawn, suggesting that 'If in the end, these confessions either fail to give expression to a "real" interiority, or fail even to be heard, it can only point to an underlying anxiety that the story . . . can never be told "aright"' (p. 749). The Mousetrap is discussed in terms of the ambiguity of Claudius's response, observing that Horatio does not clearly state what he has witnessed. Sterrett discusses the bedroom scene in the same vein, observing that Gertrude also fails to give a clear confession. Sterrett reads Claudius's confession scene as 'the key to the play's programme of failed confessions' (p. 752), asking why Claudius confesses at all. In so doing, Sterrett links his discussion of *Hamlet* to Derrida's of St Augustine. Sterrett concludes that there is a problem associated with the Protestant emphasis on praying directly and inwardly: no confessor means no certainty of absolution. This is the theme that Sterrett argues is at the heart of *Hamlet*.

Derek Cohen's article 'The Malignant Scapegoats of *King Lear*' (*SEL* 49:ii[2009] 371–89) begins with a thorough illustration of the deaths that take place in *King Lear*: who dies and where their death takes place, on- or off-stage. Cohen points out that 'the context of each of the deaths is unique . . . in terms of the emotional and dramatic energies that are released by the fact of death' (p. 371). The analysis of these energies is what makes up the article: Cohen first discusses Lear's own death, which is striking in that 'alone among those who die onstage, Lear in his last moments shows no awareness that he is dying' (pp. 371–2). Cohen then goes on to emphasize the significance of final words and dying statements and then focuses on the dying moments of Cornwall, Oswald, and Edmund, observing 'an almost visible progression of intensity in the order of these three deaths' (p. 378). Of particular interest is Cohen's account of Oswald, who dies proclaiming his patriotism: Cohen discusses how Oswald, who is usually '[lumped] in with the evil forces . . . because he participates in evil actions' (p. 381), is problematical because of his patriotism. Cohen states that 'when the nation is threatened, even if it is governed by the likes of Goneril, Regan, Edmund, and Albany, most people will choose to defend their country' (p. 380), and this 'profoundly complicates questions about [Oswald's] moral locus in the play' (p. 381). What Cohen focuses on is the confusion Shakespeare creates in the moment of death: even the presence of the Captain as Lear dies 'as an evil witness to the spectacle, is profoundly confusing' (p. 383). Cohen concludes that the 'existential despair' these confusions create 'brings into being a powerful dramatic image of nihilism and thus, a viable alternative to the clean and monologic conclusion that many have argued for'. Cohen writes that despite committing acts of violence and evil, 'the question remains whether any of these characters [Cornwall, Oswald, or Edmund] commits the crime of endangering the safety of the community . . . in greater degree than any other characters . . . And in this sense they are innocent and thus, in their deaths, fulfil the function of scapegoats in their plays' (p. 386).

Edward Wheatley, in his article 'Voices of Violence: Medieval French Farce and the Dover Cliff Scene in *King Lear*' (*CompD* 43:iv[2009] 455–71), sees clear alignments between 'the humiliation of the recently blinded Gloucester at the hands of his supposedly loving son' (p. 455) and the farce drama of medieval France. Wheatley draws attention to four such plays and gives a synopsis of each, highlighting the role that servants play in humiliating, stealing from, and beating the blind man, frequently disguising their voices in order to present different characters to their master. Wheatley briefly rehearses previous criticism which has linked French farce to sixteenth-century English drama, before more thoroughly exploring the similarities between the genre and *King Lear*. Wheatley marks the differences too within these parallels, for example noting that 'Gloucester cannot be robbed, because he almost instantly hands Poor Tom his purse as payment' (p. 464). However, Wheatley also notes that 'the structure of the Dover Cliff scene has parallels with the plot device of a guide abusing a blind character in early French farce' (p. 467), before concluding that the scene 'might actually have been intended or received as comic light relief' and that 'it is remarkable that Shakespeare could have a putatively comic plot device that demeans and humiliates . . . and turns it into what, at least for a while, affirms both life and the love of a son for his father' (p. 469).

Laurie Shannon's '"Poor, bare, forked": Animal Sovereignty, Human Negative Exceptionalism, and the Natural History of *King Lear*' (*SQ* 60[2009] 168–96) takes Lear's words (III.iv.105–7) as a starting point from which to offer a zoographic reading of *King Lear*, offering a challenge to 'the historical and intellectual adequacy of what commentators have repeatedly posited as "*the* question of *the* animal"' (emphasis in original) and stating that reading *King Lear* in this way 'suggests evolving historiographic ways to see humankind within a larger cross-species milieu' (p. 169). Shannon discusses Pico della Mirandola's *On the Dignity of Man* as showing 'something less binary than a sheer human-animal divide' indeed suggesting a '*menagerie* of man' (emphasis in original), and goes on to highlight how usage of the term 'animal' was uncommon in the early modern period. Shannon highlights this in Shakespeare's plays, and argues that there is, rather, a sense of a range of animal types rather than a binary opposition. Shannon reads *King Lear* as seeing man as exceptional but in negative terms. She goes on to consider 'by what logic . . . this "human negative exceptionalism" [can] be articulated' (p. 175). In answering this, Shannon gives 'an archaeology of the terms of what may be [King Lear's] most singular statement' (p. 175). Shannon does this by addressing the vulnerability of immortal souls to sin before discussing Renaissance natural history and the idea of sovereignty. Shannon discusses 'the ways that . . . animal sovereignty . . . comes to define human conditions' (p. 185) and how 'the human estate also comes down to a matter of dress, or . . . a state of undress' (p. 185). The article concludes by reading 'a natural-historical circle' (p. 195) in *King Lear*; Shannon states that 'Lear thus not only anatomizes man philosophically, and finds him wanting: it taxonomizes man, literally, and finds him naked' (p. 196).

In his short article on 'Hybridity, Othello and the Postcolonial Critics' (*ShSA* 21[2009] 23–9), Daniel Roux challenges the way in which postcolonial critics have read *Othello* and Othello as 'an Othello that lives beyond the text even as he inhabits it' (p. 23): the character as existing in a real sense beyond the play. Roux uses Christopher Marlowe's *Dido, Queen of Carthage* to highlight the distance between the signifier of the character and the character's sense of his own identity. In so doing, Roux argues that the plays engage with early modern humanism. Othello, then, is concerned with the notion of the '*unformed*', 'an alien in an alien world, precariously holding on to an identity that is incessantly undercut' (p. 26). Roux concludes that '*Othello* works so well as a postcolonial text because post-colonialism draws so many of its terms and preoccupations from a dialectical understanding of humanist subjectivity' but that '*Othello*... offers the reading of post-colonialism' and not vice versa (p. 28).

Sam Wood's 'Where Iago Lies: Home, Honesty and the Turk in *Othello*' (*EMLS* 14:iii[2009] 27 paras.) reads Iago's motivations as related to issues of home and identity, and, further, as related to Shakespeare's audience's fears and concerns regarding religious and national identity and conversion. Wood begins by detailing arguments from Stephen Greenblatt, Marvin Rosenberg, and Daniel Viktus that suggest Iago is merely satanic, before challenging them by suggesting that such views '[risk] stripping Iago of his humanity' and that the character is 'in fact, profoundly discomforted by his ability to manipulate his victims, and that we are able to find a motivation in this discomfort' (para. 1). Wood finds this motivation through the play's focus on home and truth, which Wood relates to contemporary shifts in foreign policy, stating that 'the play is set in and is the product of a culture increasingly uncertain of where and how it belonged' (para. 13). In relation to Iago, Wood reads Othello's desire for a home and Cassio's 'daily beauty' in his sense of belonging 'in his context' (para. 20) as factors in Iago's motivations because of his own sense of homelessness.

In 'Iago's Art of War: The "Machiavellian Moment" in *Othello*' (*MP* 106:iii[2009] 497–529), Ken Jacobsen explores the influence of Machiavelli on Iago's rhetorical performance, focusing on Machiavelli's 1521 treatise *The Art of War*, which Jacobsen observes 'critics have generally ignored' (p. 498) in relation to Shakespeare. The article discusses the ways in which rhetoric and warfare are linked, and the article is divided in a way which reflects this. Jacobsen argues that Iago 'represents an authentic application of the inner logic of Machiavellism to a particular set of contingent circumstances' and as such *Othello* represents J.G.A. Pocock's idea of the 'Machiavellian Moment' (p. 500). Jacobsen does this by analysing the rhetoric of the play, noting the significance of rhetoric to military leadership and noting the clash in the play between old and new styles of speaking as well as old and new concepts of warfare. This is 'most pointedly' (p. 503) evident in the contrast between the characters of Iago and Othello. In this context, 'According to the standards of *The Art of War*, Othello... lacks the acumen for calculation and strategy required of a modern general' (p. 504). After illustrating how Othello fails in Machiavellian terms, Jacobsen discusses Iago in two sections 'under the headings of traditional rhetoric: the *pisteis*... and the canons' (p. 507). In the first of the two sections, Jacobsen discusses what ethos and pathos mean and, using examples, demonstrates how Iago uses and 'exploits' (p. 508) them to fashion himself as a Machiavellian general, before going on to illustrate how Iago 'demonstrates his mastery of the canons of rhetoric' (p. 512). In a thorough character study, Jacobsen persuasively shows how rhetoric is embodied in Iago and how the language of warfare relates to Iago's manipulations of Othello. In concluding, Jacobsen brings the reader back to the idea of the 'Machiavellian Moment', arguing that '*Othello* is, among other things, a reflection on the subversive, anti-social implications of Machiavellian thought' (p.523).

In 'Music and the Crisis of Meaning in *Othello*' (*SEL* 49:ii[2009] 355–70), Erin Minear discusses how *Othello* 'repeatedly questions and blurs the distinctions that separate different kinds of music' (p. 355). These different kinds of music may be the music of poetry or of the ordered cosmos, or of the tavern fiddler. Minear suggests that 'the two poles of empty noise and transcendent poetry . . . occupy the same space' (p. 356). In the article, Minear explores how Othello's speech disintegrates through the play—from poetry to prose, music to noise. She goes on to discuss how this motif is reiterated throughout the play and how the relationship between the two 'illustrates and informs the play's treatment of language in general' (p. 359), but Minear also points out the apparent paradox: 'for Othello, warlike noises are musical in the sheer sonic pleasure they arouse' (p. 361). Minear also highlights how Desdemona's actions follow a similar path to Othello's language. Questions are raised throughout the article about the relationship between music and noise: for example, 'are the musical moments of the moments of violent noise actually different moments?' (p. 358), 'is war musical to Othello because it is orderly?' (p. 361). The Willow Song is discussed, and Minear states that 'Emilia offers the best commentary on [the song] and the efficacy of dying words' (p. 365) before concluding that 'the sonic aspects of *Othello* work against a neat encapsulation of the play's meaning' (p.367).

Christopher Pye's essay '"To throw out our eyes for brave Othello": Shakespeare and Aesthetic Ideology' (*SQ* 60[2009] 425–47) explores *Othello*'s 'political entailments and its aesthetic status' (p. 425), arguing that the aesthetic emerges in the play and that the play 'suggests how intimately this modern transformation entails a set of political correlates' (p. 425). Pye argues that 'Any account of the play . . . needs to attend to a supervening shift in the meaning of the literary-aesthetic, especially in that aesthetic dimensions relation to the law' (p. 425). In relation to this, Pye suggests that 'race functions in the play as the means through which universalism reinscribes itself as a signifying form' (p. 425). In exploring Act II, scene i, Pye discusses the different responses found in Desdemona's and Montano's accounts of waiting for Othello. Pye argues that Montano's words at II.i.36–40 suggest that in focusing fixedly on something, one loses oneself, but that Desdemona's reserve and 'dallying' with Casio show 'a certain capacity to beguile oneself' which 'can be saving' (p. 427). Pye goes on to discuss such moments of 'distraction' (p. 427) elsewhere in the play and relates it to the aesthetic arguing that the vanishing point which is focused on without distraction signals the limits of Shakespearian tragedy and the 'illimitability' of the aesthetic 'as representational form' (p. 428). Pye also invokes *Hamlet* and *King Lear* to make this argument. Pye builds on the arguments of Joel Fineman that *Othello* exemplifies the 'coming into being of a modern literary subjectivity' found in Shakespeare's work (p. 429). However, Pye also acknowledges that Shakespeare was a part of a wider 'set of political and historical transformations' (p. 429). Pye argues that *Othello* asks 'what holds our attention in a play when we know too much' (p. 430) and suggests that 'all know and all are captivated because everything functions within a fictive or aesthetic field, an autochthonic, self-begotten domain, which inscribes audience and characters alike' (p. 431). Pye studies Act I, scene iii, in order to 'consider the play's reflection on its own grounds' (p. 433), a scene which Pye considers to be the '*Ur*-scene' of the play (p. 433). Pye describes Othello's stories as 'a cannibal narrative' in their power to consume both the teller and the listener (p. 435). Pye argues that with Othello's death 'it is difficult to avoid the sense... he has somehow narrated his own end' (p. 437) and that 'such an effect, recalling the cannibalizing narrative of the opening, is intimately bound up with the problem of aesthetic autochthony and the interpretive ethic it implies' (p. 437). In the final part of the essay, Pye discusses the 'fragile' distinction between fiction and law (p. 440). To explore 'the level at which the autochthonic work engages the question of symbolic foundations most radically', Pye looks at the numerous references in the play to hands and the functions that they fulfil. Pye goes on to conclude that 'it is the rise of the aesthetic that problematizes anything like an outright developmental account, whether historical or textual' (p. 446) and that 'the negative, universal subjectivity that *Othello* articulates emerges expressly as an effect of the illimitability of its own figurative grounds' (p. 447).

In 'Physics Divined: The Science of Calvin, Hooker and *Macbeth*' (*SCRev* 26:i–ii[2009] 127–52) Kristen Poole offers a thorough discussion of Calvin's God and man's place in the cosmos and how this relates to *Macbeth*. Poole discusses Calvin, theology, and science and Calvin's 'theological mission... to re-orient his readers in their perception of their place in the universe' (p. 129). Poole explores this in order to create a basis for an argument 'about the Calvinist physics operative in Shakespeare's *Macbeth*' (p. 129). Poole notes the importance of Calvin during the late sixteenth century and how widely read he was, although she also acknowledges the increasing distortion of his theology. Poole goes on to discuss Hooker as a contributor to the cloudiness of 'Understandings of God and cosmos at the turn of the seventeenth century' (p. 137) and aligns Hooker with Calvin in his basing 'his text on a discussion of the relationship between God and creation that fundamentally constructs his theology' (p. 138). Poole reads *Macbeth* in the light of this theology, stating that 'the play [explores] how an understanding of the operations of the cosmos and an individual's relationship to the time, space and matter of the environment influence their sense of themselves and of the divine' (p. 141). Poole then discusses the unpredictable environment of the play and especially the difficulty of fixing time; Poole notes that 'within the world of *Macbeth* we encounter early modern formulations of space-time' (p. 143) which 'opens questions of human and divine agency' (p. 144). Poole argues that, in contrast to Calvin, 'For the inhabitants of *Macbeth*, an environmental self-consciousness could only result in a recognition that there is no stability' (p. 145). Poole thus addresses the conflict between *Macbeth* and Calvin, reading

Macbeth's 'recognition of cosmic instability' as leading him 'to play God' (p. 146).

Vernon Guy Dickson opens his article, '"A pattern, a precedent, and lively warrant": Emulation, Rhetoric, and Cruel Propriety in *Titus Andronicus*' (*RenQ* 62[2009] 376–409), by discussing the death of Livinia at Titus's hands. Dickson highlights the disparity between Saturninus's two responses to Titus's hypothetical predicament and to his action. Dickson states that the 'characters are continually presented as modelling themselves on their history and historical fictions' and this 'reflects the play's involvement in examining emulation and related rhetorical and educational practices and beliefs' (p. 377). Dickson sets out to 'explore the significance of emulative practices' in *Titus Andronicus*, which ultimately offers a critique of those practices through the destruction of Titus and his family. Dickson argues that the 'excessive repetition of emulative strategies' (p. 380) in the play is a challenge to 'straightforward humanist models of character, judgement, self, and decorum' (p. 380) evident in the presentation of education in the play. In so doing, Dickson builds on the practices of new historicism. Dickson discusses emulation in the Renaissance, using contemporary examples from works by Roger Ascham, Quintilian, Thomas Wilson, and George Abbot. Dickson argues that *Titus*, in the emphasis on contrast between theory and action, '[questions] humanist reliance on imitative learning practices' (p. 388). The article moves on to discuss the teaching of boys in the play, highlighting the parallels in the play's structure of Marcus and Titus teaching the Boy and Aaron and Tamora teaching Chiron and Demetrius.

John Feerick, in 'Botanical Shakespeares: The Racial Logic of Plant Life in *Titus Andronicus*' (*SCRev* 26:i–ii[2009] 82–102), bases his article on the shifts of epistemology in the seventeenth century as set out by Foucault to ask 'how scientific knowledge informed literature and how literature may have enabled the movement towards differentiation, classification, and compartmentalization'. In contrast to previous studies which have read literature in the light of medical texts, Feerick explores how botanical discourse may inform readings of literature, suggesting that drama uses such discourses to make sense of human difference. In relation to *Titus Andronicus*, Feerick argues that, in contrast to criticism that suggests the play is forward-looking in terms of racial logic, the play 'understands difference in relation to quality of blood' (p. 83). Feerick acknowledges other criticism which views the image in the play of the state as a body, but goes beyond this to read the state as a vegetative body, stating that 'for Shakespeare and his earliest auditors and readers, laws of kind were similar among people as among plants' (p. 86). As an example of this, Feerick draws on 'The Rape of Lucrece' and demonstrates how, in both *Titus* and 'Lucrece' 'Shakespeare draws on the distinctions underpinning well developed botanical hierarchies to work through notions of human difference' (p. 87). Indeed, Feerick goes further, arguing that in *Titus Andronicus* botanical images and discourses 'are made to carry complex social valences' (p. 87). Feerick discusses the etymology of the word 'kind' and its various meanings in the period—both in terms of blood relation and race—and links this to Titus through the notion in the play of the Roman family. Feerick draws attention to how differences emphasized between Titus and Saturninus embody these different meanings of 'kind'. This is then related back to botanical discourse as 'one of the play's preferred discursive registers for sorting through these distinctions' (p. 89). Feerick persuasively gives evidence for the different aspects of the botanic state in reference to Tamora in the forest in Act II, scene ii, and the different ends to which she uses botanical imagery, first with Aaron and then with Lavinia and Bassianus. Feerick also reads botanical discourse as significant to Titus's presentation of himself and his family, and suggests that consequently it is this that Tamora attacks: 'the buds and branches that line this tree' (p. 92). Titus's downfall, then, is the result of Tamora not allowing Titus to construct his notion of race. Feerick conducts an interesting discussion of Aaron as a constructed outsider who separates different 'kinds' of blood: 'He is a master of courtly discourses and the serpentine paths to power' (p. 95). The article concludes that 'Aaron's blackness emerges as the crucial axis of difference which enables the resolution to the epistemological crisis regarding notions of kind' (p. 99), but points out the ambiguity of the ending, which shows blood lines continuing through both Titus's and Aaron's lines.

(g) Late Plays

The Cambridge Companion to Shakespeare's Last Plays, edited by Catherine M.S. Alexander, represents one of the most significant contributions to work on Shakespeare's late plays this year. Adopting the term 'last' rather than 'late' to describe the plays written towards the end of Shakespeare's theatrical career, the collection considers all of Shakespeare's last plays—*The Winter's Tale*, *Cymbeline*, *The Tempest*, *Pericles*, *The Two Noble Kinsmen*, *Henry VIII*, even the lost *Cardenio*—and its attention to the collaborative as well as the single-authored plays is a key strength of the collection. The decision to abandon the term 'late' in favour of 'last' sidesteps the problematic assumptions attached to the term, which have been exposed and undermined in recent years by Gordon McMullan (who also contributes a chapter to the volume), and the collection as a whole goes some way in challenging attitudes to 'late Shakespeare' that have dominated critical approaches to Shakespeare's last plays. *The Cambridge Companion to Shakespeare's Last Plays* represents a timely and important contribution to our understanding of the late plays, and it will undoubtedly become essential reading for anyone interested in Shakespeare's theatrical career.

In the first chapter of the book, McMullan addresses the crucial question: 'What is a "late play"?' He vigorously contests the critical assumption that Shakespeare's last plays constitute 'a small subset of plays that post-date the major tragedies, forming a chronologically, generically and stylistically distinct group characterized by the sensibility of an old man reaching the end of an extraordinary career and ready to drown his art' (p. 6). In a genuinely groundbreaking argument (although one that has admittedly been doing the rounds for a couple of years now), he disputes each of these assumptions in turn with the ambition of debunking the myth of 'late Shakespeare'. Pointing out that criticism generally groups *Cymbeline*, *The Winter's Tale*, and

The Tempest as Shakespeare's 'late plays', he explores what happens when the other plays written around the same time—the co-authored *Pericles*, *Cardenio*, *Henry VIII*, and *The Two Noble Kinsmen*—are added to this group. Aiming 'to clear the air of some of the presumptions and myths' (p. 14) that surround 'late Shakespeare' in order to come to a fuller understanding of the last plays, McMullan offers some alternative ways of reading all of the plays as a group. While his proposed thematic topics (such as the issue of return) have only limited appeal, the issue of collaboration and repertory has, I think, exciting potential. McMullan argues that, in the context of repertory production, the late plays, especially the Shakespeare–Fletcher collaborations, become pivotal, 'not supplementary or fragmentary but the locus of institutional transition' (p. 24) as Fletcher takes over from Shakespeare as principal house playwright for the King's men. With further work in this area having the potential to transform our understanding of the joint- and single-authored plays alike, the future of scholarship on Shakespeare's late plays looks very bright indeed.

In his contribution to *Shakespeare's Late Plays*, David Lindley takes up McMullan's challenge to relocate Shakespeare's plays in the repertory of the King's men, although his essay focuses on other changes experienced by the company late in Shakespeare's career. 'Blackfriars, Music and Masque: Theatrical Contexts of the Last Plays' tackles the question of how the acquisition of the Blackfriars shaped Shakespeare's last plays, arguing that 'exactly how and to what extent is far from self-evident' (p. 29). Two features of Shakespeare's last plays that have typically been associated with the acquisition of the Blackfriars—music and masque—are discussed by Lindley, but their debt to the new theatre is questioned. In a subtle and carefully argued essay, Lindley proves that while changing theatrical conditions undoubtedly influenced the dramatist, 'They are not, of course, sufficient explanations of the exploratory and experimental nature of Shakespeare's late plays' (p. 43). Lindley's essay thus reopens the debate about the impact of the Blackfriars on Shakespeare's plays, a topic that is taken up in a very different way by Erica Sheen, whose book is discussed below.

A more traditional approach to the influences on Shakespeare's last plays is taken by Charles Moseley in his contribution to Alexander's volume. 'Elizabethan and Jacobean drama is an untidy thing' (p. 47), he writes at the beginning of 'The Literary and Dramatic Contexts of the Last Plays', and this point is reflected in his essay, which traces the elaborate weave of influences upon the themes of Shakespeare's plays, exploring classical and medieval, Continental and English, contexts for his late writing. Significant in its inclusion of all the last plays, the essay is nevertheless reluctant to engage with some of the issues raised by other contributors; Moseley begins his discussion of *The Two Noble Kinsmen*, for example, by remarking that 'there is no reason why a collaboration should not be successful' (p. 64), which seems to assume the inferiority of collaborative authorship. This essay thus sits a little uneasily with the volume's revisionary aim, which suggests that its efforts to debunk the myth of 'late Shakespeare' still has some way to go, even if *Pericles*, *Cardenio*, *Henry VIII*, and *The Two Noble Kinsmen* are included in the category.

One of the primary objectives of *Shakespeare's Last Plays* is to relocate the plays in the Jacobean period, which Alexander suggests has received less critical attention than the Elizabethan. With this in mind, the book provides a useful historical timeline, prepared by Clare Smout, which summarizes the early print and performance history of Shakespeare's last plays and also charts key political events, events in the lives of Shakespeare and the King's men, other theatrical events, and the cultural context of Shakespeare's last plays. Some of the essays also aim to resituate the plays in their Jacobean context. In 'Politics, Religion, Geography and Travel: Historical Contexts of the Last Plays', Karen Britland investigates 'the political, geographical and religious issues prevalent in England during James's reign, examining how they were reflected in Shakespeare's late plays' (p. 72). Charting a complex web of allusions, the essay traverses questions of James's absolutism, his desire for the unification of England and Scotland, royal marriages, relationships between Ireland, Scotland, and England, exploration and conquest, Protestantism, and many other topics. One of the essay's more interesting discussions connects the representation of incest in *Pericles* and *Cymbeline* (and perhaps similar suggestions in *The Winter's Tale*, although Britland does not mention these) to James's unification project. The essay uses a wide variety of contemporary sources to illuminate the plays' contemporary resonances, and it helpfully synthesizes the work of a range of critics (Gossett, Lindley, McMullan, and many others) who have shown how Shakespeare's last plays reflect the key debates of Jacobean England. Although Britland's essay certainly fulfils its modest claim to show in the plays 'allusions to contemporary anxieties and events' (p. 87), the allusive—and elusive—nature of the discussion is a little unsatisfying. Nevertheless, it is important work, which proposes several topics for further research.

Russ McDonald's groundbreaking research on Shakespeare's late style is sampled in his wonderful essay for *Shakespeare's Last Plays*, '"You speak a language that I understand not": Listening to the Last Plays'. He argues that towards the end of his career Shakespeare developed 'a poetic style like nothing he (or anybody else) had composed before: it is audacious, irregular, ostentatious, playful, and difficult' (p. 91). McDonald offers a clearly illustrated descriptive account of Shakespeare's late verse under the categories of elision, syntax, repetition, and metrics, and he makes a powerful case for the distinctiveness of the language of *Pericles*, *Cymbeline*, *The Winter's Tale*, and *The Tempest*. I would have liked him to address the difficulty of discussing *Shakespeare*'s late style in the co-authored *Pericles*, however, and I would also have liked him to explore whether this late style can be detected in the other collaborative works that constitute Shakespeare's last plays. Despite these limitations, however, McDonald offers significant insight on the technical features of Shakespeare's language, which he links back to 'the larger topics of meaning and purpose' (p. 104). His work also points to the fact that attention to the style of the last plays has the potential to enrich our understanding of Shakespeare's collaborative authorship, even though this is not something McDonald examines in this essay.

While McDonald discusses Shakespeare's 'late style' to the exclusion of the collaborative plays, the volume as a whole prefers the term 'last' to include the entire group of plays written between 1607/8 and 1613. The editor also justifies the choice of 'last', 'in part, by the connotations in the word of survival and endurance' (p. 3). Indeed, what is striking about Alexander's collection is its attention to the rich and varied afterlives of Shakespeare's last plays. Illuminating the changing fortunes of the play from its earliest stagings to late twentieth-century productions, Patricia Tatspaugh's '*The Winter's Tale*: Shifts in Staging and Status' offers a beautifully drawn performance history of one of Shakespeare's best-loved plays (Alexander does something similar in '*Cymbeline*: The Afterlife'). Tatspaugh's essay focuses productively on two of the most troubling aspects of the play—the staging of Leontes' jealousy and the statue scene—to showcase how directors of the twentieth century defied earlier critics to prove that *The Winter's Tale* is 'one of Shakespeare's most compelling, powerful and ingenious plays' (p. 113).

While Tatspaugh charts *The Winter's Tale*'s growth in popularity, Eugene Giddens shows that *Pericles* was highly esteemed in the early seventeenth century before falling out of favour. In '*Pericles*: The Afterlife', Giddens shows how consideration of the play's afterlife (in performance and criticism) can raise interesting questions and generate new analytical approaches to the play. In my favourite of the chapters on Shakespeare's 'lasting' last plays, Giddens also attends more to *Pericles*' reception through the seventeenth century, and other issues of contextual interest, such as its problematic textual status (it only exists in a 'bad' quarto). Making a good case for the play's timeliness, Giddens's hope for a resurgence of critical interest in *Pericles* following its recent stage success seems well founded.

Giddens's and Tatspaugh's essays show the ways in which ideas of worth in Shakespeare are historically contingent, and their arguments have important implications for the volume's revisionary purpose. I would have liked more attention to this topic in the introduction, however, which would have helped to bind the two strands of its subject—Shakespeare's last and lasting plays—a little more closely. One essay that does engage fully with this question is Suzanne Gossett's '*The Two Noble Kinsmen* and *King Henry VIII*: The Last Last Plays', which concludes the collection. This essay explores the Shakespeare–Fletcher collaboration, showing how the collaborative origin of the plays has contributed to their marginalization in the Shakespeare canon, and indeed their lack of critical attention generally, maintaining that 'the more the plays were viewed as Shakespearean, the more they were appreciated and produced' (p. 186). Gossett charts the complex production and publication history of the 'last last plays' (including the lost *Cardenio*), and discusses their critical reception through the centuries. Arguing that the authorship debate has always been at the heart of their reception, Gossett contextualizes the collaboration and treats seriously the plays that were created through this process. With one of the many strengths of this essay its use of modern productions as a springboard for detailed textual analysis, Gossett's essay indicates the rich potential for further study of these two plays.

It is therefore gratifying that this year's work on Shakespeare's late plays sees a growth in publications on Shakespeare and Fletcher's jointly authored *Henry VIII*. Jennifer Richards interrogates the play's collaborative authorship in the course of looking for evidence of Shakespeare's political thought in her essay, 'Shakespeare and the Politics of Co-Authorship: *Henry VIII*' (in Armitage et al., eds., *Shakespeare and Early Modern Political Thought*). In a highly nuanced exploration of the nature of their collaboration, she speculates about 'the extent to which Shakespeare and Fletcher really did collaborate, working across the play together, discussing their work and sharing ideas about it' (p. 177). In response to previous critiques of the play, she poses the question: 'is the play really such a fractured text, or does it evidence a consistent thematic as well as political concern that unites its different elements?' (p. 177). Arguing that through its complex depiction of Wolsey the play advocates moderation in judging him and other fallen characters, Richards attributes this to 'Shakespeare *and* Fletcher's contrasting representation of Wolsey, as well as by the compromised moral stance assumed by Wolsey's accusers in scenes by both authors' (p. 194). Richards is highly attuned to the complexities of the play's collaborative authorship, and her essay exhibits both the challenges and rewards of attending to the nuances of the collaborative process.

In an essay that evades the collaboration issue altogether, Karen Sawyer Marsalek's essay for Kenneth J.E. Graham and Philip D. Collington's *Shakespeare and Religious Change* relocates the play to its Jacobean context and connects it in interesting ways to the Blackfriars theatre. 'Staging Allegiance, Re-membering Trials: *King Henry VIII* and the Blackfriars Theater' reads the play in the context of King James's Oath of Allegiance and the conflict that it provoked among English Catholics when asked to distinguish their spiritual from their temporal loyalties. Making a solid case that the play was performed at the indoor playhouse, Marsalek suggests that the King's men took advantage of the meta-dramatic potential of the Blackfriars space—alive as it was with memories of Catherine of Aragon's divorce trial, the parliamentary trial of Cardinal Wolsey, and the heresy trials of Wycliffite martyrs, all of which took place there—to enhance the play's multifaceted exploration of allegiance. The essay focuses on the complex characterization of Katherine, Wolsey, and Cranmer, arguing that each offers different perspectives on the thorny issue of English Catholic loyalties. In doing so, it offers some intelligent analyses of the text; the attention to the queen's control of the spectacle of her trial (p. 137), the discussion of the cardinal's 'mere performance of allegiance' (p. 142) and the foreshadowing of Cranmer's martyrdom (p. 144) are particular highlights. Ultimately Marsalek asserts that 'the play's palimpsest of trials insists that the interactions between confessional identity and spiritual and temporal loyalties are much more complex that King James's legislation and rhetoric would acknowledge' (p. 146), and her essay illuminates the play's exploration of Catholicism in the Jacobean era.

Thomas Cogswell and Peter Lake consider another highly charged performance of *Henry VIII*, but this time at the Globe theatre nearly twenty years after its notorious first performance there. In their genuinely pioneering essay, 'Buckingham Does the Globe: *Henry VIII* and the Politics of Popularity in the 1620s' (*SQ* 60[2009] 253–78), Cogswell and Lake analyse a performance of *Henry VIII*, specially commissioned and attended by the soon-to-be-murdered duke of Buckingham, which took place in August 1628. In the midst of a theatrical event that they liken to the more famous staging of *Richard II* on the eve of the Essex rising, they describe how, at a significant juncture in the play, the duke and his entourage spectacularly left the theatre. Situating this dramatic moment in the context of the political crisis in which Buckingham had found himself in 1628, which it describes in helpful detail, and seeing it as a climax in his use of theatre as a political tool, this excellent article persuasively argues that Buckingham appropriates *Henry VIII* in an attempt to turn the tide of public opinion in his favour. He does so, they argue, by adopting a strategy also evident in a masque that he patronized and in which he performed, Jonson's *The Gypsies Metamorphosed* [1621], as well as Middleton's *Game at Chess* [1624], the run of which he seems to have supported. As in those performances, Buckingham evokes the negative stereotype of the evil counsellor and corrupt favourite to which he was popularly likened—represented in Shakespeare's play by Wolsey—in order to define himself as its opposite—in *Henry VIII* his namesake, and Wolsey's most vocal critic, Buckingham; the duke and his entourage dramatically left the play immediately after the staging of Buckingham's execution in Act II, scene i, providing credence to this analysis. In a richly drawn argument, Cogswell and Lake not only illustrate 'the role of theater as a means of staging the most controversial political issues of the day' (p. 277), but they also offer further evidence of how Shakespeare's plays were received and appropriated immediately after his death. In doing so, their researches shed new light on the play itself, highlighting the importance of Buckingham, and especially his gallows speech, in its interrogation of monarchical authority.

As with *Henry VIII*, this year's work on *Cymbeline* is primarily concerned with locating the play in its historical context. This work connects in different ways to the play's representation of ancient Rome. Rereading as a Roman play a play that has been variously categorized as romance, tragedy and history, two essays on *Cymbeline* are included in Maria Del Sapio Garbero's *Identity, Otherness and Empire in Shakespeare's Rome*. The first of these, Paola Colaiacomo's 'Other from the Body: Sartorial Metatheatre in Shakespeare's *Cymbeline*', focuses on the representation of clothing in the play, arguing that '*Cymbeline* offers an interesting example of sartorial metatheatre: no longer a stage property, and not yet a full round character, but a hybrid between the two, the "garment" is there given a role to perform which takes it very close to being a character on its own, though one whose words have to receive a voice from the "regular" actors' (p. 67). Colaiacomo's essay emphasizes the centrality of Posthumous–Cloten's garments in the play. However, its attempt to link the hybridity of clothing to the play's setting at the crossroads of Rome and Britain, and thus to its representation of national hybridity, is quite strained.

More convincing in its exploration of identity and location is Laura Di Michele's 'Shakespeare's Writing of Rome in *Cymbeline*'. Reading the play in the light of the changing relationship between England and 'Britain' under James's composite monarchy, the essay argues that Shakespeare's play reveals 'the instability and porousness of the opposed categories adopted to design the spaces of "Rome" and "not Rome"' (p. 158). This essay benefits from reading *Cymbeline* in the context of Shakespeare's other Roman plays, including

Titus Andronicus, which allows Di Michele to compare the representation of Rome and otherness; the link perceived in Marcus's response to the mutilated Lavinia and Imogen's response to what she understands to be the dead body of Posthumous is particularly illuminating in its unpacking of the relationship between gender and nation in the two plays.

'"No more a Britain": James I, Jachimo, and the Politics of Xenophobia in *Cymbeline*', the concluding chapter of Michael J. Redmond's *Shakespeare, Politics, and Italy*, also reads the play in the context of contemporary debates about Anglo-Scottish union. But rather than focusing on its depiction of ancient Rome, as Di Michele has done, Redmond, by examining the character of Jachimo, 'a stock Italianate stage villain' (p. 169), highlights what he sees as the play's anachronistic references to early modern Italy. Emphasizing Jachimo's participation in the Roman conquest of Britain, Redmond argues that *Cymbeline*'s inability to resolve the tensions between its story of British resistance and its ultimate submission to Rome is linked to English unease about obedience to a foreign, Scottish, king. While his thesis is not unique, Redmond's attention to the play's allusions to early modern Italy adds a new dimension to understandings of the play's engagement with the question of 'Britain'.

Defying this year's other interpretations of *Cymbeline*, and even risking the play's exclusion from this section of the review, Penny McCarthy has launched a provocative challenge to the identification of *Cymbeline* as one of Shakespeare's late plays with her article, '*Cymbeline*: "The First Essay of a New Brytish Poet"?' (*CS* 21:ii[2009] 43–59). Placing it not in 1609–10 as generally accepted but early in Shakespeare's career, McCarthy disputes point by point the work of scholars from Emrys Jones to Ros King who have emphasized the play's Jacobean topicality. Asserting that *Cymbeline* was, rather, conceived and written in Shakespeare's early career and then revised before James succeeded to the throne in 1603, she reads the play as being both anti-Tudor and anti-Stuart, suggesting that its sympathies lie instead with the Sidneys. She thus concludes that Shakespeare 'was the Pembroke family's laureate. *Cymbeline* was one of his most worked-over and deeply felt pieces of propaganda for them—a history of "their" Britain, a Britain in which phoenixes are not only reborn, but also crowned' (p. 57). McCarthy's article is thought-provoking, and although her arguments fail to compel absolutely, she offers an intriguing alternative to the identification of *Cymbeline* as a 'late' or even a Jacobean play. And as she exposes the lack of certainty in the dating of Shakespeare's plays, she also contests our understanding of 'late Shakespeare'.

One of the most interesting pieces on *The Tempest* this year responds to McMullan's challenge to rethink Shakespeare's late plays in the context of the repertory of the King's men. Rather than focusing on Shakespeare's collaborations with Fletcher, however, the concluding chapter of Erica Sheen's *Shakespeare and the Institution of Theatre* considers how changes experienced by the King's men towards the end of Shakespeare's career impacted upon his relationships with the writers with whom he did not collaborate, and she explores how these relationships were reflected in his writing. Maintaining that the purchase of the Blackfriars theatre impacted upon the institutional identity of the King's men (thus taking a very different approach to Lindley), Sheen suggests that it fed the rivalry of two of its most famous writers, its shareholder Shakespeare and the freelancer Jonson. This perspective helps Sheen generate an original and inventive analysis of *The Tempest*, proposing that it engaged in a 'face-off' (p. 130) with Jonson's *The Alchemist* over their different roles in the company. In doing so, Sheen offers an interesting new take on the play's exploration of 'sovereignty and collective labour' (p. 135). Although the connections drawn between the experiences of the King's men and the themes of *The Tempest* can only be speculative, Sheen's invigorating discussion of the play's institutional context offers a credible account of the fraught and endlessly fascinating relationship between the two rival playwrights.

'"Backward and abysm of time": Negotiating with the Dead in *The Tempest*', Brinda Charry's contribution to *Emissaries in Early Modern Literature and Culture: Mediation, Transmission, Traffic, 1550–1700*, which she edits with Gitanjali Shahani, thinks further about Prospero's role in the play. Focusing on its representation of otherness, Charry reads Shakespeare's play in terms of 'the changing attitudes to "foreign" knowledges in the early modern period and the emerging ideology of Eurocentrism that arose in the context of early modern England's encounter with the Muslim world' (p. 208). Although the Europeans could not deny the learning of the Muslim world (as they did that of the New World), Charry points out that they did disavow the exchange of knowledge that characterized their shared history. She studies *The Tempest* allusively in this context, reading Prospero 'as an emissary who negotiates between European self and foreign Other, as well as past and present time' (p. 207). Comparing Prospero with the gone-but-not-forgotten Sycorax, Charry argues that Sycorax, like the Muslim world, is 'relegated to the past' and 'characterized by degeneration and decay' (p. 219). Prospero's continuity with Sycorax is thus downplayed in *The Tempest*, just as the European debt to Muslim learning is denied, and Prospero's difference from Sycorax and her son is reinscribed. As she offers new insight into the play's complex exploration of otherness, Charry's work also makes an important contribution to our understanding of European responses to the Muslim world in the early modern period.

Moving from a Muslim-centred approach to a Jewish perspective on the play, Hanna Scolnicov's 'Chagall's *Tempest*: An Autobiographical Reading' (*ShS* 62[2009] 151–61) demonstrates how the Jewish artist Marc Chagall's experiences during the revolution in Russia and the Second World War in France caused him to respond to Prospero's deposition and exile from Milan. In a beautifully illustrated essay, Scolnicov brings Chagall's black and white lithographs illustrating *The Tempest* to critical attention for the first time, and shows how autobiography can shape one's understanding of Shakespeare's plays, and how attention to modern Shakespearian adaptation can make valuable contributions to our understanding of the plays. (Virginia Mason Vaughan, in 'Literary Invocations of *The Tempest*', which she contributes to *The Cambridge Companion to Shakespeare's Last Plays*, takes a similar approach).

Another discussion of *The Tempest* this year also attends to contemporary adaptations of the play that prioritize the theme of exile. As part of her book-length study on women's cross-gender casting in Shakespeare, Elizabeth Klett provides a stimulating analysis of Vanessa Redgrave's turn as Prospero in Lenka Udovicki's 2000 production of *The Tempest* at the Globe theatre. While showing how Redgrave's 'androgynous' performance illuminates Prospero's depiction as both mother and father, Klett's suggestion that in doing so she also 'questioned the construction of masculine and feminine' (p. 104) is perhaps a little overstated. Moreover, her proposal that 'exile'—a theme privileged in Udovicki's production of the play—'necessitated him becoming androgynous, incorporating both parenting roles' (p. 107) is also a bit strained. The strength of the analysis, I think, is Klett's attention to critical responses to Redgrave's performance. Provocatively arguing that women's cross-gender performances are 'deemed acceptable only if they are seen as potentially bolstering Shakespearean authority and English national identity' (p. 110), Klett highlights the pre-season buzz that surrounded the casting of the acclaimed British actress and international star, which was quite different from the more hostile reactions to the casting of the Irish actress Fiona Shaw as Richard II. However, Klett suggests that the poor reception of Redgrave's performance ultimately betrays the underlying assumption that 'women's cross-gender performances of Shakespeare will always be inadequate or "illegitimate"' (p. 111)—as Shakespeare, as male, and as English. This thesis is convincingly argued through detailed citation from the reviewers, and although Klett's analysis of the gender and national dynamics of Redgrave's Prospero does not entirely satisfy, her reference to one reviewer for the *New York Times* who noted that this was 'the first Prospero I have seen who might have nurtured a daughter from babyhood to adolescence' (p. 113) indicates the interpretative potential of cross-gender casting. Beyond her specific focus, Klett's attention to the staging conditions of the Globe theatre—specifically her focus on its lack of realism—once again reminds us of the exciting possibilities offered by this wonderful performance space.

Performance issues seem to dominate analyses of *The Winter's Tale* this year. The most unusual of these, Paul Yachnin and Myrna Wyatt Selkirk's contribution to *Shakespeare and Character: Theory, History, Performance, and Theatrical Persons*, edited by Yachnin with Jessica Slights, is based on a theatrical experiment at McGill University in 2003 in which a group of student actors was asked to explore the interconnections between metatheatre and character in a performance of *The Winter's Tale*. Seeking 'to understand just how metatheater helps to produce the particular phenomenon of Shakespearean character, especially in performance and in the presence of an audience' (p. 141), Yachnin and Selkirk staged a production of *The Winter's Tale* that emphasized its metatheatrical elements, and they encouraged the actors to build a relationship with the audience and to reflect on its effects. Using *The Winter's Tale* as a case study for thinking about Shakespearian metatheatre in general, Yachnin and Selkirk's essay draws on the students' experiences of performing in the play, and offers significant insight into the play itself (exploring the metatheatrical elements in the performances of Leontes and the Clown, for instance, illuminated both characters in interesting ways), as well as into the performance of character more broadly in Shakespeare. Ultimately Yachnin and Selkirk argue that, although 'Shakespeare has set certain verbal, behavioral, social, generic, and relational parameters', he has also 'created very many opportunities for constitutive interactions among the actors, and between the actors and the audience' (p. 152), which accentuates 'the dynamic and collaborative nature of character creation' (p. 153). Shakespeare, of course, was an actor, and his plays are undoubtedly shaped by his professional experiences. By focusing attention on the vital relationship between actor and audience, Yachnin and Selkirk's work brings new life to *The Winter's Tale* and to Shakespeare's plays overall.

'"Here's a sight for thee": The Claims of Narrative in *The Winter's Tale*' is the concluding chapter of Richard Meek's *Narrating the Visual in Shakespeare*, and it represents an important contribution to our understanding of spectacle in the play. Like the other texts in his study, Meek argues that *The Winter's Tale* 'explores the rival claims of visual and verbal modes of representation, and, implicitly, the relationship between narrative and drama' (p. 147). He proposes that while Shakespeare 'might *appear* to privilege the visual immediacy of dramatic performance', his decision to narrativize so many events in the play—along with the power of those acts of narration—suggests that the playwright ultimately 'remains undecided about the status of both theatrical and narrative representations' (p. 148). By reading the play's verbal modes of representation (Antigonus's dream-narrative, the Clown's account of Antigonus's death, and the gentlemen's description of the reunion of Leontes and Perdita) against the more renowned visual elements of the play, Meek offers a highly nuanced analysis of the play's complex representation of the relationship between narrative and drama, and the unreliability of both. He claims the centrality of Autolycus in his argument, proposing that the con artist signifies the unreliability of both visual and verbal representations. Focusing on critical responses to the play's staging of the so-called 'miracle' of Hermione's statue, he also intriguingly suggests that Autolycus's inclusion in the play 'is itself an Autolycus-like confidence trick, inasmuch as the very presence of a confidence trickster reflects, but may also distract us from, the extent to which we are "taken in" by Shakespeare's artistry' (p. 162). Meek's excellent essay beautifully shows that there is much more to the spectacular effects of *The Winter's Tale* than meets the eye.

Writing for Pascale Drouet's *The Spectacular in and around Shakespeare*, Josée Nuyts-Giornal's 'Shakespearean Virtuosity in *The Winter's Tale* and the Mannerist *Tour de Force*' takes Shakespeare's reference to 'the rare Italian master, Giulio Romano' as a prompt to situate the play 'within the spectacular scene of Mannerist artists, whose graphic works, engravings, drawings, paintings and statues emphasized theatricality and extravagant, mobile gestures and postures' (p. 63). In an essay that brings an interesting new (non-literary) context to bear on the play, she argues: 'The spectacular character of Giulio Romano's breath-taking statue serves as a foil to what drama is capable of—namely, giving breath or life to its characters. The intricate but commonplace concept of nature conferring eternity upon art is staged in the enigmatic form of Mannerist aesthetics prizing emulation and invention in order to create amazement amongst spectators' (p. 75). Privileging Shakespeare's play above its prose source (something that is strongly opposed by Mary Ellen Lamb and Valerie Wayne's excellent *Staging Early Modern Romance: Prose Fiction, Dramatic Romance, and Shakespeare*, which will be reviewed next year), Nuyts-Giornal argues that Shakespeare transforms Greene's *Pandosto* in the spectacular style of the Mannerists.

While simultaneously engaging in a wider debate on the role of text and performance in Renaissance literary studies, Donavan Sherman's curious essay 'The Absent Elegy: Performing Trauma in *The Winter's Tale*' (*ShakB* 27:ii[2009] 197–221) offers a fresh analysis of Mamillius's function in the play. Reading Mamillius as the embodiment of a traumatic mode of theatricality, Sherman sees his absent presence in the ending of the play, which he argues represents the not entirely successful attempt 'to rewrite total textuality onto Mamillius's total performativity' (p. 199). Identifying Leontes as 'a surrogate scholar-audience', he suggests that we too 'are called upon to decide between text and performance, between seeing either a fixed statue or an actor trying not to tremble' (p. 200). Heavily influenced by trauma theory, Sherman's article is highly theoretical but a little strained at times and occasionally unwieldy. Nevertheless, its attention to Mamillius is welcome, and its identification of the 'textual' Perdita as the surrogate of the 'theatrical' Mamillius is inspired. I particularly enjoyed Sherman's exploration of the possibility of casting the same actor in both roles. Suggesting that double casting 'makes vivid the fissures between the traumatic event and the recovery; the body, as performative residue, persists while the text seemingly forgets' (p. 214), Sherman showcases the importance of attending to the intermingling of performance and text.

A more successful exploration of 'surrogation' in *The Winter's Tale* is offered by Joseph Roach in '"Unpath'd waters, undream'd shores": Herbert Blau, Performing Doubles, and the Makeup of Memory in *The Winter's Tale*' (*MLQ* 70:i[2009] 117–31), who defines it as a process through which 'memory both reproduces and interrogates itself' (p. 122). Using Herbert Blau's writing on the death of his mother (to whom Roach owes the concept of 'makeup of memory'), Roach focuses on the 'three-sided relationship among memory, performance and substitution' (p. 122) in *The Winter's Tale*. As he explores the many doublings in the play (Leontes and Mamillius, Leontes and Perdita, Polixenes and Florizel, Leontes and Polixenes, Florizel and Mamillius, Mamillius and Perdita), Roach interrogates what he dubs the 'perverse' theatrical tradition of doubling Hermione and Perdita, arguing that such a manoeuvre downplays the play's attention to the ravages of time. He speaks instead about the effect of Shakespeare's likely doubling of the same boy actor as Mamillius and Perdita, which he argues evokes the memory of the lost son while emphasizing his absence: 'the final tableau can effect a partial surrogation only, whose suture marks appear in the aging face of the wronged queen and bereaved mother and, most tellingly, in the eloquent redress of her unremarked silence to Leontes' (p. 131).

Sarah Dewar-Watson also attends to the play's ending in 'The *Alcestis* and the Statue Scene in *The Winter's Tale*' (*SQ* 60[2009] 73–80). Revisiting the long-recognized connection between Shakespeare's statue scene and Euripides' *Alcestis*, she substantiates the link with Euripides by pointing out some previously overlooked verbal correspondences between Shakespeare's play and George Buchanan's Latin translation of the *Alcestis* [1539]. Persuasively suggesting that the statue motif, along with Perdita's name, have their origins in Buchanan's *Alcestis*, Dewar-Watson rightly calls for greater critical attention to the influence of neo-Latin writers on Shakespeare.

Phebe Jensen similarly situates *The Winter's Tale* in its literary contexts, but in the concluding chapter of her monograph *Religion and Revelry in Shakespeare's Festive World* she focuses on contemporary Protestant recuperations of festivity. In 'Singing Psalms to Hornpipes: Festivity, Iconoclasm and Catholicism in *The Winter's Tale*', she returns to a topic that animated so much of last year's scholarship on the play—its Catholic subtexts. Reading the play's exploration of festivity against contemporary anti-Catholicism, Jensen identifies Leontes and Perdita with iconoclasm, but suggests that an 'antidote' is provided by the festive celebrations in Act IV and the statue scene in Act V. She thus argues that the play explores 'the dangers of Protestant iconoclasm' and endorses 'exactly those aspects of traditional pastimes—their link to a Catholic past, and affinity with Catholic forms of ritual behavior—that had been mostly purged from customary pastimes' (p. 212). In refocusing attention on the festivities in Act IV, and offering an illuminating analysis of that scene and its importance in the play, Jensen uncovers in *The Winter's Tale* and Shakespeare's other festive plays a subtle sympathy for Catholicism.

In bringing my review of the year's work on Shakespeare's late plays to a close, I would like to mention Nicholas Tredell's *Shakespeare's Late Plays: Pericles, Cymbeline, The Winter's Tale, The Tempest*, which is part of Palgrave's Readers' Guides to Essential Criticism series. In line with other books in the series, Tredell aims to provide easy access to criticism on Shakespeare's late plays, and he charts critical responses to the plays from the eighteenth, nineteenth, twentieth, and into the twenty-first centuries, concluding with some speculations on future directions of research. Although Tredell mentions *Cardenio*, *Henry VIII*, and *The Two Noble Kinsmen* in his introduction, they are excluded from detailed discussion, apparently on the basis that they have 'never excited much critical interest' (p. 3). Tredell seems to connect this to the fact that they were co-written with John Fletcher, although at the same time he acknowledges the collaborative authorship of *Pericles*, which he suggests may be the reason for its exclusion from the First Folio. *Shakespeare's Late Plays* ably guides the student through criticism on some of the late plays, although its decision to exclude *Henry VIII* and *The Two Noble Kinsmen* continues to propagate the myth of 'late Shakespeare', the dismantling of which has undoubtedly represented the most exciting development in criticism on the late plays in this and recent years.

Books Reviewed

Alexander, Catherine M.S. *The Cambridge Companion to Shakespeare's Last Plays*. CUP. [2009] pp. 244. pb £18.99 ISBN 9 7805 2170 8197.

Armitage, David, Conal Condren, and Andrew Fitzmaurice, eds. *Shakespeare and Early Modern Political Thought*. CUP. [2009] pp. 302. £59 ISBN 9 7805 2176 8085.

Barkan, Leonard, Bradin Cormack, and Sean Keilen. *The Forms of Renaissance Thought: New essays in Literature and Culture*. Palgrave Macmillan. [2009] pp. xii + 284. hb £50 ISBN 978-0230008984.

Bate, Jonathan. *Soul of the Age: The Life, Mind and World of William Shakespeare*. Penguin. [2008] pp. xii + 500. £10.99 ISBN 9 7801 4101 5866.

Bates, Robin. *Shakespeare and the Cultural Colonization of Ireland*. Routledge. [2008] pp. viii + 170. £71.25 ISBN 9780 4159 5816 4.

Benson, Sean. *Shakespearean Resurrection: The Art of Almost Raising the Dead*. Duquesne. [2009] pp. x + 219. $56 ISBN 9 7808 2070 4166.

Billing, Christian. *Masculinity, Corporality and the English Stage 1580–1635*. Ashgate. [2008] pp. 248. £55. ISBN 9780754656517.

Botelho, Keith M. *Renaissance Earwitnesses: Rumor and Early Modern Masculinity*. Palgrave. [2009] pp. xvi + 199. £52 ISBN 9 7802 3061 9418.

Brustein, Robert. *The Tainted Muse: Prejudice and Presumption in Shakespeare and his Time*. YaleUP. [2009] pp. 280. £18.99 ISBN 9 7803 0011 5765.

Buchanan, Judith. *Shakespeare on Silent Film: An Excellent Dumb Discourse*. CUP. [2009] pp. 340. £59 ISBN 9 7805 2187 1990.

Carson, Christie, and Farah Karim-Cooper, eds. *Shakespeare's Globe: A Theatrical Experiment*. CUP. [2008] pp. xxii + 268. £15.99 ISBN 9 7805 2170 1662.

Cartelli, Thomas, ed. *Richard III*. Norton. [2009] pp. xiv + 423. £6.99 ISBN 9 7803 9392 9591.

Charry, Brinda, and Gitanjali Shahani, eds. *Emissaries in Early Modern Literature and Culture: Mediation, Transmission, Traffic, 1550–1700*. Ashgate. [2009] pp. 278. £55 ISBN 9 7807 5466 2075.

Cormack, Bradin. *A Power To Do Justice: Jurisdiction, English Literature, and the Rise of Common Law, 1509–1625*. UChicP. [2007] pp. xv + 406. £24 ISBN 9780 2261 1624 2.

Cousins, A.D., ed. *The Shakespeare Encyclopedia: The Complete Guide to the Man and his Works*. Apple. [2009] pp. 304. £20 ISBN 9 7818 4543 3390.

Craig, Hugh, and Arthur F. Kinney, eds. *Shakespeare, Computers and the Mystery of Authorship*. CUP. [2009] pp. xix + 234. £59 ISBN 9 7805 2151 6235.

Crider, Scott F. *With What Persuasion: An Essay on Shakespeare and the Ethics of Rhetoric*. Lang. [2009] pp. xii + 210. £52.50 ISBN 9 7814 3310 3124.

Croteau, Melissa, and Carolyn Jess-Cooke, eds. *Apocalyptic Shakespeare: Essays on Visions of Chaos and Revelation in Recent Film Adaptations*. McFarland. [2009] pp. viii + 230. £32.50 ISBN 9 7807 8643 3926.

Del Sapio Garbero, Maria, ed. *Identity, Otherness and Empire in Shakespeare's Rome*. Ashgate. [2009] pp. xiii + 231. £55 ISBN 9 7807 5466 6486.

Desmet, Christy, and Anne Williams, eds. *Shakespearean Gothic*. UWalesP. [2009] pp. xii + 286. hb £75 9 7807 0832 0938, pb £19.99 ISBN 9 7807 0832 0921.

Dimmock, Matthew, and Andrew Hadfield, eds. *Literature and Popular Culture in Early Modern England*. Ashgate. [2009] pp. xiii + 234. $124.95 (£65) ISBN 9 7807 5466 5809.

Driver, Martha W., and Sid Ray, eds. *Shakespeare and the Middle Ages: Essays on the Performance and Adaptation of the Plays with Medieval Sources or Settings*. McFarland. [2009] pp. viii + 276. £32.50 ISBN 9 7807 8643 4053.

Drouet, Pascale, ed. *The Spectacular in and around Shakespeare*. CambridgeSP. [2009] pp. 180. £34.99 ISBN 9 7814 4381 1057.

Eggert, Paul. *Securing the Past: Conservation in Art, Architecture and Literature*. CUP. [2009] pp. 302. £19.99. ISBN 9 7805 2172 5910.

Eisenbichler, Konrad, ed. *Renaissance Medievalisms*. Centre for Reformation and Renaissance Studies, Toronto. [2008] pp. 360. C$36 ISBN 9 7807 7272 0450.

Engel, William E. *Chiastic Designs in English Literature from Sidney to Shakespeare*. Ashgate. [2009] pp. viii + 158. £50 ISBN 9 7875 4666 363.

Erne, Lukas. *Shakespeare's Modern Collaborators*. Shakespeare Now! Continuum. [2008] pp. 144. £13.99 ISBN 9 7808 2648 9968.

Fielitz, Sonja, ed. *Literature as History/History as Literature: Fact and Fiction in Medieval to Eighteenth-Century British Literature*. Lang. [2007] pp. 214. £36.40 ISBN 9 7836 3156 8798.

Gajowski, Evelyn, ed. *Presentism, Gender, and Sexuality in Shakespeare*. Palgrave. [2009] pp. 308. £50 ISBN 9 7802 3022 3837.

Grady, Hugh. *Shakespeare and Impure Aesthetics*. CUP. [2009] pp. 272. £59 ISBN 9 7805 2151 4750.

Graham, Kenneth J.E., and Philip D. Collington, eds. *Shakespeare and Religious Change*. Palgrave. [2009] pp. 296. £52 ISBN 9 7802 3021 3098.

Hackett, Helen. *Shakespeare and Elizabeth: The Meeting of Two Myths*. PrincetonUP. [2009] pp. xiii + 295. £24.95 ISBN 9 7806 9112 8061.

Henke, Robert, and Eric Nicholson. *Transnational Exchange in the Early Modern Theater*. Ashgate. [2008] pp. xv + 264. £60 ISBN 9 7807 5466 2815.

Heylin, Clinton. *So Long as Men Can Breathe: The Untold Story of Shakespeare's Sonnets*. Da Capo. [2009] pp. 288. £7.99 ISBN 9 7803 0681 8707.

Hiscock, Andrew, and Stephen Longstaffe, eds. *The Shakespeare Handbook*. Continuum. [2009] pp. xviii + 261. £17.99 ISBN 9 7808 2649 5785.

Houston Wood, David. *Time, Narrative, and Emotion in Early Modern England*. Ashgate. [2009] pp. x + 199. £50 ISBN 9 7807 5466 6752.

Huang, Alexander C.Y. *Chinese Shakespeares: Two Centuries of Cultural Exchange*. ColUP. [2009] pp. xiii + 350. £58.50 ISBN 9 7802 3114 8481.

Hugh, Craig, and Arthur F. Kinney *Shakespeare, Computers, and the Mystery of Authorship*. CUP. [2009] pp. 254. £59 ISBN 9 7805 2151 6235.

Hunter, Lynette, and Peter Lichtenfels. *Negotiating Shakespeare's Language in Romeo and Juliet: Reading Strategies from Criticism, Editing and the Theatre*. Ashgate. [2009] pp. 252. £50 ISBN 9 7807 5465 8443.

Jensen, Phebe. *Religion and Revelry in Shakespeare's Festive World*. CUP. [2009] pp. 280. £53 ISBN 9 7805 2150 6397.

Kahan, Jeffrey, ed. *King Lear: New Critical Essays*. Routledge. [2008] pp. x + 374. £60 ISBN 9 7804 1577 5267.

Kamm, Jürgen, and Bernd Lenz, eds. *Shakespearean Culture—Cultural Shakespeare*. Stutz Verlag. [2009] pp. 267. €38 ISBN 9 7838 8849 2587.

Kehler, Dorothea. *Shakespeare's Widows*. Palgrave. [2009] pp. x + 245. £52.50 ISBN 9 7802 3061 7032.

Kidnie, Margaret Jane. *Shakespeare and the Problem of Adaptation*. Routledge. [2009] pp. 232. £20.99 ISBN 9 7804 1530 8687.

King, Ros, and Paul J.C.M. Franssen, eds. *Shakespeare and War*. Palgrave. [2008] pp. xii + 250. £50 ISBN 9780 2302 0508 9.

Kitch, Aaron. *Political Economy and the States of Literature in Early Modern England*. Ashgate. [2009] pp. 228. £99.95 ISBN 9 7807 5466 7568.

Klett, Elizabeth. *Cross-Gender Shakespeare and English National Identity: Wearing the Codpiece*. Palgrave. [2009] pp. 220. £50 ISBN 9 7802 3061 6325.

Knapp, Jeffrey. *Shakespeare Only*. UChicP. [2009] pp. xvi + 238. £24 ISBN 9 7802 2644 5717.

Langley, Eric. *Narcissism and Suicide in Shakespeare and his Contemporaries*. OUP. [2009] pp. xi + 312. £50 ISBN 9 7801 9954 1232.

Lerner, Laurence. *William Shakespeare: Henry IV*. Northcote. [2008] pp. viii + 78. hb £40 ISBN 9 7807 4631 1912, pb £12.99 ISBN 9 7807 4630 8516.

Levin, Carole. *Dreaming the English Renaissance*. Palgrave. [2008] pp. xiv + 210. hb £45 ISBN 9 781 4039 60894, pb £17.99 ISBN 9 7802 3060 2618.

Levin, Carole, and John Watkins. *Shakespeare's Foreign Worlds: National and Transnational Identities in the Elizabethan Age*. CornUP. [2009] pp. xiv + 217. £36.95 ISBN 9 7808 0144 7419.

Matei-Chesnoiu, Monica. *Early Modern Drama and the Eastern European Elsewhere: Representations of Liminal Locality in Shakespeare and his Contemporaries*. FDUP. [2009] pp. 246. £48.95 ISBN 9 7808 3864 1958.

Mayer, Jean-Christophe, ed. *Representing France and the French in Early Modern English Drama*. UDelP. [2008] pp. 247. £51.50 ISBN 9 7808 7413 0003.

Meek, Richard. *Narrating the Visual in Shakespeare*. Ashgate. [2009] pp. viii + 222. £55 ISBN 9 7807 5465 7750.

Meek, Richard, Jane Rickards, and Richard Wilson, eds. *Shakespeare's Book: Essays in Reading, Writing and Reception*. ManUP. [2008] pp. x + 273. £55 ISBN 9 7807 1907 9054.

Mooneeram, Roshni. *From Creole to Standard: Shakespeare, Language, and Literature in a Postcolonial Context*. Rodopi. [2009] pp. xi + 239. £50 ISBN 9 7890 4202 6230.

Nakayasu, Minako. *The Pragmatics of Modals in Shakespeare*. Lang. [2009] pp. viii + 281. £49.30 ISBN 9 7836 3159 4001.

Newman, Karen. *Essaying Shakespeare*. UMinnP. [2009] pp. xix + 199. £22.50 ISBN 9 7808 1665 5908.

Ostovich, Helen, Holger Schott Syme, and Andrew Griffin, eds. *Locating the Queen's Men, 1583–1603: Material Practices and Conditions of Playing*. Ashgate. [2009] pp. xiii + 269. £55 ISBN 9 7807 5466 6615.

Perry, Curtis, and John Watkins, eds. *Shakespeare and the Middle Ages*. OUP. [2009] pp. xiv + 295. £56 ISBN 9 7801 9955 8179.

Purcell, Stephen. *Popular Shakespeare: Simulation and Subversion on the Modern Stage*. Palgrave. [2009] pp. ix + 262. £50 ISBN 9 7802 3057 7039.

Redmond, Michael J. *Shakespeare, Politics, and Italy: Intertextuality on the Jacobean Stage*. Ashgate. [2009] pp. x + 242. £55 ISBN 9 7807 5466 2518.

Ryan, Kiernan. *Shakespeare's Comedies*. Palgrave. [2009] pp. xiii + 284. £14.99 ISBN 9 7803 3359 9327.

Sheen, Erica. *Shakespeare and the Institution of Theatre: 'The Best in this Kind'*. Palgrave. [2009] pp. viii + 172. £50 ISBN 9 7802 3052 4804.

Siemon, James R. *Richard III*. Arden, Methuen. [2009] pp. Methuen456. £9.99 ISBN 9 7819 0343 6899.

Sillars, Stuart. *The Illustrated Shakespeare, 1709–1875*. CUP. [2008] pp. xxii + 394. £60 ISBN 9 7805 2187 8371.

Tredell, Nicolas. *Shakespeare's Late Plays: Pericles, Cymbeline, The Winter's Tale, The Tempest*. Palgrave. [2009] pp. 184. hb £40 ISBN 9 7802 3020 0494, pb £12.99 ISBN 9 7802 3020 0500.

Vaught, Jennifer. *Masculinity and Emotion in Early Modern English Literature*. Ashgate. [2008] pp. xii + 244. £60 ISBN 9 7807 5466 2945.

Yachnin, Paul Edward, and Jessica Slights, eds. *Shakespeare and Character: Theory, History, Performance, and Theatrical Persons*. Palgrave. [2008] pp. 278. £50 ISBN 9 7802 3057 2621.

VII

Renaissance Drama: Excluding Shakespeare

SARAH POYNTING, ELEANOR COLLINS, JESSICA DYSON, ANDREW DUXFIELD AND SAM THOMPSON

This chapter has three sections: 1. Editions and Textual Scholarship; 2. Theatre History; 3. Criticism. Section 1 is by Sarah Poynting; section 2 is by Eleanor Collins; section 3(a) is by Jessica Dyson; section 3(b) is by Andrew Duxfield; section 3(c) is by Sam Thompson.

1. Editions and Textual Scholarship

There were two interesting volumes of early modern drama this year: Henry Burkhead's *A Tragedy of Cola's Furie, or, Lirenda's Miserie*, edited by Angelina Lynch with an introduction by Patricia Coughlan, and a collection of *Three Renaissance Usury Plays* edited by Lloyd Edward Kermode, containing Robert Wilson's *The Three Ladies of London*, William Haughton's *Englishmen for my Money*, and Robert Tailor's *The Hog Hath Lost his Pearl*.

The play by Burkhead (not to be confused with Henry Birkhead, founder of the Professorship of Poetry at Oxford, and also an amateur playwright) comes as part of a very welcome new venture from Four Courts Press of English-language literary texts from seventeenth- and eighteenth-century Ireland. The play, which was, according to the title page, written in 1645 and published in Kilkenny in 1646, focuses on the wars in Ireland in 1642–3 following the rebellion of 1641, and on the foundation of the confederation of Kilkenny. Historical figures and places are depicted under pseudonyms, to which Coughlan provides a guide in an appendix (though some remain unidentified—'Lirenda' proves to be misleadingly simple in this respect). Her excellent and detailed introduction sets out clearly the play's context, explaining the complex interrelationships between the groups and individuals involved, and how Burkhead uses contemporary events to create a drama of incident and sensation, bearing strong resemblances to the shorter English pamphlet plays of the later 1640s. It is, as she convincingly demonstrates, 'a good deal more... than a versified chronicle' (p. 11), whose stage directions

The Year's Work in English Studies, Volume 90 (2011)
doi:10.1093/ywes/mar011

appear to indicate that it may well have been intended for performance, whether or not it ever received one. The theatrical possibilities open to Burkhead in 1640s Dublin and Kilkenny are outlined without ever coming to any conclusion; here the connections between play and context seem a little tenuous. Coughlan investigates who Burkhead—probably a merchant originally from Bristol—may have been, and what his connection with Ireland was that impelled him to write the play. Short sections are devoted to its language, which bears possible signs of Anglo-Irish dialect idioms (without ever descending into cod-Irish), and to the three commendatory verses that precede the text of the play. I cannot help feeling that Daniel Breede's encomium to the effect that Burkhead combines the dramatic talents of Jonson, Shakespeare, and Fletcher ('and all'), as well as displaying the descriptive powers of Rubens and Van Dyck, manifests greater friendship than judgement.

Coughlan also analyses the play as drama, and not merely as a piece of political-literary history, with stimulating discussions of its dramaturgy, emblematic characterization, Burkhead's use of the supernatural in the onstage appearances of Mars, Bellona, Pallas, Mercury, and the figure of Revenge, and the deployment of low comedy. If some of the parallels with other early modern plays seem a little far-fetched at times, these never reach Breede-like proportions, and encourage readers to examine the play from a theatrical as well as a historical perspective.

The text is a transcription of the single surviving quarto copy of *Cola's Furie* in the British Library; while this new edition is mostly very clear and readable, it is not without some minor problems. Lynch makes slight emendations to certain words ('than' for 'then'; 'too' for 'to') and rather more substantial alterations to punctuation, modernizes 'u/v' and 'i/j', and regularizes the spelling of names. It seems a slightly odd decision to make substantive changes in an otherwise near-diplomatic transcription, and the emendations are not applied with total consistency. This line-by-line version has, though, a major advantage for an editor in that no judgement needs to be made as to what Coughlan describes as 'uncertain, often rather approximate blank verse' (p. 10), which often appears to be intended as—and certainly reads as—prose, despite the layout in the quarto of the text in consistently short lines which, however, lack initial capitals. From the reader's point of view, it might have been useful had Lynch attempted to disentangle likely verse from prose, particularly given the play's generic and tonal variety.

Footnotes are signalled by degree symbols, rather unnecessarily since the commentary is (usually) on the same page as the line to which it refers. While it is generally helpful, it's relatively light, and again there's rather a lack of consistency as to choice of words or classical references explicated: Pluto and Medea are annotated, but not 'the furies' or 'stix'; 'celeritie' is defined, but not the use in the stage directions of 'preter' (i.e. 'praeter', 'except'). The explanation of 'sinquapace' ignores the reasonably common 'cinquepace' dance, which, combined as it is with 'frisk about', is surely meant; while the information that Agamemnon was murdered by his wife Clytemnestra and her lover Achilles should not have got past the editors. In view of the contentious nature of the activities of Lord Herbert (later earl of Glamorgan) in Ireland in 1645 under the secret directions of Charles I, I would also have appreciated rather more on the implications of the dedication of the play to him. The few lines on him in the introduction are decidedly bland.

Lloyd Edward Kermode's edition of Wilson, Haughton, and Tailor adds to the enormously useful and enterprising list brought out in the Revels Plays Companion Library, which continues to publish lesser known (and much less available) early modern plays in full scholarly versions. As the joint title of *Three Renaissance Usury Plays* suggests, these all focus, in quite different ways, on the issue of money-lending and commerce, and Kermode's very interesting introduction provides us with the developing legal, political, and conceptual contexts within which they were performed (though there are times throughout it when I felt it could be more clearly structured and written). He demonstrates the degree of doublethink concerning lending money at interest as it became an economic necessity in a mercantile society that still saw it as problematic in moral and religious terms, and as potentially dangerous, both individually and socially. Kermode describes the statutes controlling usury in England, and the ways in which these are reflected in the literature of the period (including *The Jew of Malta* and *The Merchant of Venice*), seeing the 1581 proclamation on usury, for example, as possibly generating, at least in part, Robert Wilson's *The Three Ladies of London* of the following year. Different systems of money-lending are examined, along with the distinction drawn between illicit usury and legitimate interest (a distinction on which, as he shows, writers failed to agree as to where it should lie). The relationship between money-lending, trade, and foreigners in London, both actual and literary, is explored at some length, before Kermode discusses the history of Jews in England and their stereotypical representations as usurers on the stage.

This general—and very thorough—introduction is followed by individual sections on each play, which provide a biographical outline of the playwrights (in so far as they can be certainly identified), the performance possibilities in terms of playing company, space, and actors, and a critical piece on the place and function of usury. The influence of the morality play on *Three Ladies* (characters include Lady Lucre, Usury, Simony, and Fraud) is touched on, but Kermode is understandably more interested in examining the surprisingly sympathetic figure of the Turkish Jewish moneylender Gerontus, whose remarks on Christian hypocrisy he sees reflected in speeches by Barabas and Shylock. However, the idea of Jews as inherently driven by money still functions within the play, in which Gerontus is seen as an exception in his generosity, and his very activity as moneylender as corrupting of the social and religious fabric of the nation.

Haughton's *Englishmen for My Money* of 1598 of course postdates both *Jew* and *Merchant*, and Kermode views Haughton as drawing on the former, as well as on other Marlowe plays, for its protagonist, the Portuguese Jew Pisaro, a widower resident in London whose wife was English. With his three rebellious daughters trying to elope with their English lovers, this is more city comedy, Kermode suggests, than morality play. He argues that the '"foreignness" and "strangeness" of the usurer ... is shifted towards a familiarity and domesticity in the endenizened Pisaro' (p. 44), complicating the way that the issue of usury is dealt with, though Pisaro is still shown as obsessed with gold. Critical reactions to the ambiguities—indeed, contradictions—that

Haughton has built into *Englishmen* are assessed, together with critics' recent interest in gender in the play. A sketch map in an appendix shows the London places mentioned in it to illustrate the density of local detail, though I cannot help feeling you have to know London quite well to make sense of it—simply labelling the Thames and London Bridge would have helped.

Tailor's *The Hog Hath Lost his Pearl* of 1613 (published 1614) has a particularly interesting performance history, its amateur actors at the Whitefriars—apprentices according to Sir Henry Wotton—being arrested at an unlicensed performance; City gossip claimed that the lord mayor Sir John Swinnerton was attacked as the 'Hog'. Kermode looks at Dekker's *Troia-Nova Triumphans*, performed for the mayor in 1612, as a way of judging Swinnerton's reputation and attitudes to his financial dealings, and hence the likelihood of this identification, despite a perhaps disingenuous claim in the Prologue to the *Hog* that no such personal invective was intended. The text appears to have suffered on its way to publication, Kermode being of the opinion that 'overt political material' may have been excised, leaving a play with an episodic structure that shifts uneasily between melodrama and more subtle passages of dialogue (p. 53). Once again one thread of the plot concerns the conflict of a daughter with her usurer father, Hog, but more important in much of the play are themes of heterosexual sex versus male friendship, and the possibility of redemption following penitence for misdeeds, played out through a mix of comedy and sermonizing whose religious message is regularly undercut, Kermode suggests, through jokes about good works and salvation. Hog's conversion in Act V, when issues surrounding usury, and its effect on both the individual and urban society take centre stage, is seen by him as necessarily equivocal.

Textual apparatus collates the small number of later editions with early versions of all the plays, Haughton's and Tailor's each surviving in only one quarto edition. Q1 of *Three Ladies* [1584] is used as copy text in preference to Q2 [1592], whose revisions may reflect performance practices occurring in the interim: Kermode expresses a strong preference for presenting an early 1580s version in his own edition. The commentary is helpful and informative, and Kermode is to be congratulated for taking on all three plays.

A new series of critical editions, Arden Early Modern Drama, was launched this year, beginning with Webster's *The Duchess of Malfi* edited by Leah Marcus, and Beaumont and Fletcher's *Philaster* edited by Suzanne Gossett; unfortunately, I have been unable to see either of these, so can do no more than note their arrival and hope that I may be able to give them more attention next year.

The most substantial article was published in *Studies in Bibliography*, reappearing after something of a hiatus and bearing a volume date that suggests a long gestation period. In 'Memorial Transmission, Shorthand, and *John of Bordeaux*' (*SB* 58[2007–8] 109–34) Gerald E. Downs re-examines the vexed question of 'bad quartos' in general and the manuscript playtext of *John of Bordeaux* in particular, coming to the conclusion that stenographic recording of a stage performance is the likeliest mode of transmission for the text. He summarizes critical arguments on 'memorial reconstruction' before exploring early modern systems of shorthand, references to its use in the period (especially by Heywood, whom he regards as a more reliable witness than has been sometimes supposed), and the likely results of using shorthand to record a text, as well as the reasons that it has been rejected, apparently decisively, by previous scholars. This is argued in relation to the first quarto of *Lear*, as well as the use of shorthand for the transmission of sermons, where, through a comparison of editions, Downs finds the standard of reporting to be surprisingly high without being absolutely accurate. He applies his findings to a consideration of *John of Bordeaux*, one of the plays analysed by Laurie Maguire in *Suspect Texts*, supporting her dismissal of memorial reconstruction, but taking issue with her conclusions on lineation of verse and prose and on verbal repetition. Following a minutely detailed argument, Downs finds that the text's anomalies can best be ascribed to shorthand recording, which accommodates evidence that other theories fail to explain, and suggests that this has major implications not only for other 'bad quartos', but for our study of published playtexts that retain signs of being 'good performances well reported'.

There was a wide variety of shorter articles on issues of editorial interest, with Marlowe attracting most interest. Thomas Merriam's 'Marlowe versus Kyd as Author of *Edward III* I.i., III and V' (*N&Q* 56[2009] 549–51) looks at theories about the play's authorship following Brian Vickers's argument in 2008 that it is mostly by Kyd. Through detailed analysis of 'function words' Merriam finds possible Marlovian responsibility in some scenes, conflicting with the evidence presented by Vickers, which he suggests bears further investigation. The question of authorship is also the focus of Donna M. Murphy's '*Locrine*, *Selimus*, Robert Greene, and Thomas Lodge' (*N&Q* 56[2009] 559–63), in which she supports, on the basis of a search of key words and phrases in *EEBO*, Alexander Grosart's attribution of *The Lamentable Tragedy of Locrine* [1595] to Greene, rejecting Nashe—a frequent candidate—whose vocabulary does not match the play's. She further argues that its sister play, *Selimus*, was by Greene and Lodge.

Source-hunting is found in two articles this year. Anna Fahraeus, in 'A Source for William Rowley's *All Lost for Love*' (*N&Q* 56[2009] 84–5), discusses early Spanish and Arabic tales of the fall of Iberia to the Moors published in an anthology *Christians and the Moors in Spain*, edited by Colin Smith, Charles Melville, and Ahmad Ubaydli [1988–92], which show that the story was 'either common knowledge in the early seventeenth century or Rowley had access to it', although it is impossible to pinpoint the precise source. Rather less tentatively, Adrian Streete's 'Samuel Rowland's "Fawnguest" and Marston's *The Dutch Courtesan*' (*N&Q* 56[2009] 615–16) identifies a source for the opening scene, the gulling of Mulligrub by Cocledemoy, in Rowland's *Greenes ghost haunting conie-catchers* of 1602.

Marston turns up again in 'Lampatho's "Delicious sweet" in Marston's *What You Will*' (*N&Q* 56 [2009] 610–12) by Charles Cathcart, in which he considers who is being satirized in the figure of Lampatho Doria. Exploring Marston's poem 'Adored excellence, delicious sweet', as well as *Antonio and Mellida*, he finds Marston recycling his own phrases, and suggests that, though it cannot be proved, there may be an element of self-parody in the character, lending support to other critics who have argued this. Cathcart moves on to (probably) Heywood in '*How a Man May Choose a Good Wife from a Bad* and *The Taming of the Shrew*' (*N&Q* 56[2009] 612–15), looking at what he sees as 'concentrated echoes' from Shakespeare's play (published in 1623) in the anonymous *How a Man* of 1602. He suggests that there is an 'inverted relationship' between the plays, with the echoes reversing the meanings they hold in *Shrew*; he also finds 'memories' of both *A Midsummer Night's Dream* and *Romeo and Juliet*. He agrees with the attribution of the play to Heywood, and draws attention to its significance in the repertoire of Worcester's Men, which seems to reflect a wider interest in the drama of marital relations, given their commission of *A Woman Killed with Kindness* and performance of the lost *A Medicine for a Curst Wife*.

In 'A Compositorial Error in Lodowick Carlell's *Osmond the Great Turk*' (*N&Q* 58[2011] 207-9), Friederike Hahn examines textual corruption at the end of Act II of the 1657 quarto, suggesting on the basis of a detailed bibliographical analysis that it is more likely to be the result of a mistake by the compositor than, more excitingly, the outcome of censorship, as proposed by G.E. Bentley (*N&Q* 56[2009] 207-9). By contrast Mark Hutchings rejects the existence of textual corruption where it has normally been perceived, in Middleton's single appearance for the year in 'A Textual Crux in *The Changeling*' (*N&Q* 56[2009] 625–9). This closely argued piece concerns a line by De Flores which comes in the dialogue with Beatrice-Joanna after De Flores presents her with Alonzo's ring, complete with finger, and her offer of money to him. The line which in the 1653 quarto reads 'And mine own conscience might have' was extended by 'slept at ease' by Dilke in 1815, and all editors since (including *The Complete Middleton*) have interpolated similar phrases, which Hutchings usefully compares. He points out that there is no metrical need for this, given the looseness of Middleton's metre, and the fact that the lines are also unnecessarily relineated by Dilke. He further argues that emendation is redundant in terms of both grammar and meaning, since the unfinished clause can be read parenthetically, with 'conscience' the object rather than the subject of 'might have', to mean 'I might still have my conscience'. He shows that the consequence of emendation is to alter the subtleties of the significance of the preceding line on 'hir[ing] a journey-man in murder'. It seems rather convincing to me; N[igel] W. Bawcutt might justifiably be puzzled at being turned into a woman, though.

2. Theatre History

The year 2009 was a strong one in repertory studies with the publication of Andrew Gurr's *Shakespeare's Opposites: The Admiral's Company 1594–1625* and the multi-authored *Locating the Queen's Men, 1583–1603: Material Practices and Conditions of Playing*, edited by Helen Ostovich, Holger Schott Syme, and Andrew Griffin. The first of these—a monograph that refocuses Gurr's dedication to company 'biography'—provides a comprehensive and judicious critical history of the Admiral's Men and their repertory; the other half of the government-sponsored duopoly that dominated theatrical London from 1594 to 1603—or, as Gurr puts it, 'the mirror to the other great theatrical success story of those fertile years', the Chamberlain's Men (p. 7). Gurr's rationale for this study of the Admiral's Men stems in part from the company's status as 'opposites' to Shakespeare's company; and so while the project seeks to reposition the Admiral's Men as a successful and innovative commercial rival to Shakespeare, its premise remains dependent in part on the continued (co-)centrality of the King's Men in the telling of theatre history—more so, perhaps, than those of other repertory studies. Yet this reading provides the opportunity to establish new, positive oppositions between the Admiral's and the Chamberlain's Men, which emphasize for the first time the Admiral's Men's divergent theatrical strategies as advantages rather than disadvantages. These alternative strategies included playing in outdoor venues throughout the winter, favouring the collaborative strategies of playwrighting that are evidenced so abundantly by the advances, loans, and instalments recorded in Henslowe's diary, and the innovative exploitation of the 'metatheatrical trick' of disguise in the composition and performance of the plays themselves.

Gurr's central and original argument here is that the use of disguise in the repertory arose as a direct consequence of having to entertain audiences on a daily basis within a theatrical duopoly. Under these circumstances—which entailed limited theatrical competition and choice for London playgoers—the company's audiences grew to recognize the actors they came to see perform, and became intimately familiar with the theatrical necessity of doubling. The dramatic strategy of disguise thus offered the Admiral's Men the opportunity to experiment with theatrical expectations, and present their audiences with inventive and fresh twists on dramatic formulae that might otherwise have become worn and predictable. For Gurr, it also offers the opportunity to engage in detail with the content of the repertory and its unique dramatic features. This is crucial to the success of the repertory study, combining an intimate knowledge of the distinctiveness of the troupe's drama with the scholarly rigour demanded by interpretation of Henslowe's diary and attention to the architecture of the Rose theatre. Gurr's study is of importance not only with respect to furthering knowledge of the Admiral's Men therefore, but also in terms of its methodological reach across theatre history. He presents a company analysis that comprises conclusions rendered by archaeological digs, performance criticism, and a renewed engagement with the recurrent underlying concerns of theatre history, including questions of playbook ownership, the theatrical roles played by company personnel, the economics of theatre, and the extent of company involvement in dramatic publication. The book plays an important role in bringing the extant evidence relating to the Admiral's Men into a coherent narrative line, and is the rewarding result of decades of committed research in theatre history.

Locating the Queen's Men is a collaborative repertory project on the first Queen's Men, formed in 1583. This volume of collected essays features work by nineteen researchers in the field, and sets out to develop and test the research that Scott McMillin and Sally Beth Maclean conducted on the troupe in *The Queen's Men and their Plays* by combining theatre history with literary criticism. At the same time, the research findings of the book have grown as much out of performance projects and conferences as from the archive, and as such the book is deeply invested in working through the premises and methodologies of repertory study. A range of approaches are drawn together here to provide evidence for the commercial importance of the Queen's Men, and revise the critical consensus of the troupe as in decline: overly reliant on an older, increasingly outdated, and 'more ostentatiously theatrical form of drama' (p. i). The book is divided into quarters, and treats in turn the playing spaces and touring conditions of the company; the repertory on page and stage; repertory content; and the distinctive performance style of the company. With particular focus on the troupe's morality and history plays, contributions engage with the evidence now available through the REED project, editorial questions of the textual provenance of the plays, the position of the company in a trajectory of early modern drama and dramatic tradition, and the performance potential of the plays.

Part I—'In and Out of London'—features essays on performance conditions while the company was on tour, alongside David Kathman's exploration of the London Inns that the company performed in and an analysis by Tiffany Stern of the social and historical 'situation', the 'branding and advertising', site and reputation of the Curtain theatre (at which the Queen's Men performed). Roslyn L. Knutson and Richard Dutton both contribute stand-out essays to Part II—Knutson's on the problems inherent in determining repertory content and identifying the characteristics of the drama, and Dutton's on the relationship between the Queen's Men's *Famous Victories of Henry V* and the 1600 quarto of Shakespeare's *Henry V*. Dutton argues here that *Famous Victories* provided the 'shape' of Shakespeare's 1600 quarto text, adding more weight to the argument that the quarto is '(a version of a) play that was almost certainly performed in its own right in 1599' rather than 'an inadequate redaction of the much larger folio text' (p. 135). Part III focuses on character analysis and the dramatic traditions present in the Queen's Men's repertory, and includes detailed and subtle essays by Alan C. Dessen and Karen Oberer on the appropriation of allegorical devices and the application of 'popular tradition to historical event' respectively. Finally, Part IV includes an engaging discussion of the jig and its changing theatrical role, by William N. West. West argues that the noise, chaotic exuberance, and physical exhaustion caused by the performance of the jig 'returned the order of the play to the noisiness of everyday life in a spectacular whirl of increasing disorder' (p. 214), in which the actor upon the newly institutionalized stage of Elizabethan England becomes, rather than a collaborator with the audience, a 'spectacle' for the paying patrons, 'gamely staging his own subordination to their pleasures' (p. 215). Finally, Peter Cockett recounts the experiences and conclusions offered by the rehearsal and performance of some of the Queen's Men's repertory during the project. Cockett discusses the questions of company make-up and issues of doubling in performance, alongside 'the effect of the rehearsal and performance process on the ideology of the plays' (p. 230). The findings that he presents here centre on the observation that '[t]he experience of producing these . . . plays encourages us to see the Queen's Men as a process, changing, evolving, and adapting to meet the pragmatic challenges of theatrical production' (p. 235). At the same time, he suggests that the time limitations on rehearsal and the variable availability of actors required simple character choices, blocking, and other forms of 'theatrical shorthand', with the aesthetic and ideological effect that 'the world of each play became remarkably consistent and relatively conservative in outlook' (p. 238). The editors' accomplished introduction brings the themes of these essays together and draws out wider conclusions and implications, rescuing the volume from the potential danger of presenting a collection of related, but ultimately freestanding, essays. *Locating the Queen's Men* puts the Queen's Men back on the map, revises current narratives of late Elizabethan theatre, and contributes to the ongoing debate on the direction that theatre history should take, how it should be researched, and what its priorities should be.

Roberta Barker also puts the possibilities afforded by performance to academic use in her article in *Early Theatre*: '"An honest dog yet": Performing *The Witch of Edmonton*' (*EarT* 12:ii[2009] 163–82). Barker's critical approach hinges around the extent to which the reality of Dekker, Ford, and Rowley's play is 'at once prosaic and suffused with the workings of the numinous' (p. 164); she works to establish its painstaking representation of a rural English community while taking account of the historical and cultural context of the play—particularly the 'firm belief in the devil's real spiritual and physical presence in the world' (p. 167). Barker's discussion of the incongruous and, to modern sensibilities, faintly ridiculous physical presence of the play's devil dog addresses the implied tension between '"realist" mimesis and . . . a more presentational and symbolic mode'—between 'the everyday social world and the demonic realm' (p. 169)—by arguing that within the context of original performance, the devil's canine visage should be interpreted as 'as much a costume for [the devil] as it is for the human actor who plays the role' (p. 169). This 'clinches' the play's moral message, by underscoring the characters' 'inability to perceive the concrete presence of the devil in their own lives' (p. 169). Barker recounts the performance choices and rationale behind a production of *The Witch of Edmonton* in which she was involved at Dalhousie University in order to evoke the play's original social and cultural resonance and demonstrate the means by which the 'disturbing image of evil's presence in [an audience's] own everyday lives' (p. 164) can be revealed to modern spectators. This essay blends historical, literary, and dramatic approaches to present an original reading of a canonical early modern text and provide a convincing interpretation of the problematic devil dog, attributing to it a specific theatrical and cultural function that is dependent upon, not marred by, its overt sensationalism.

Also accounting for spectacle is Holly Crawford Pickett's article 'Dramatic Nostalgia and Spectacular Conversion in Dekker and Massinger's *The Virgin Martyr*' (*SEL* 49:ii[2009] 437–62), which explores the theatrical and ideological use of spectacle on the early modern stage. Crawford Pickett argues that the play performs a radical interrogation of conversion by 'testing the sincerity' of converts throughout the plot, and by examining the corruptible nature of reason and the potential emptiness of rhetoric—a central 'converting agent' in 'contemporary conversion culture' (p. 445). This strategy is combined with the play's emphasis on the 'instantaneous, spectacular, and miraculous' conversions, which represent 'an older, miraculous brand of transformation more at home in a medieval saint's play than on the 1620s London stage' (p. 451).

Crawford-Pickett suggests here that 'spectacle—not rhetoric—is the play's most effective conversion tool' (p. 455)—and that this metadramatic dimension of the play draws attention to theatre as a 'vehicle of spiritual transformation', in which conversion 'in the play is finally and importantly inseparable from its theatrical representation' (p. 455). This carefully crafted argument makes a compelling case for the extent to which the aesthetic and doctrinal choices of Dekker and Massinger are here interwoven, and provides a new reading independent of any analysis of the play's strict allegiances to either Catholic or Protestant ideologies.

Moving the question of religious dedication forwards into the study of 1630s drama, Rebecca A. Bailey's *Staging the Old Faith: Queen Henrietta Maria and the Theatre of Caroline England, 1625–1642* provides an attentive and elegantly composed study of Caroline theatre and its relationship to Roman Catholicism and Roman Catholic audiences, which ranged from powerful royal patrons to the clergy and the laity. This is one of the strengths of the work; while the book is ostensibly concerned with Queen Henrietta Maria's impact on Caroline drama, Bailey takes care to assess the extent to which the Roman Catholic concerns of whole communities and identifiable individuals influenced the drama of the commercial stage. She argues that Caroline theatre should be viewed as 'a space where the concerns of the English Catholic community are staged and as a shaping force in the survival of the tenaciously adaptable old faith' (p. 2), and provides examples from the drama performed by Queen Henrietta Maria herself, as well as from plays written by her 'servant' playwrights, James Shirley and William Davenant. At the same time, and alongside these dramatic interpretations, Bailey offers an overview of the more broadly political and religious climate of the years of Charles I's reign, a backdrop that she establishes as central to the preoccupations, and subsequent interpretation, of the dramatic endeavours of this period. This study reveals a 'dialogue' between the elite and the commercial stage—one that it is only possible to trace in the subtle blend of early modern theatre history and religious history that Bailey offers here. The book is noteworthy for its sustained attention to the relationship between canonical Caroline playwrights, the commercial theatre, and the influence of court patronage and private performance—an intersection rarely studied in such depth and detail. In striking this balance so well, Bailey makes an eloquent and substantiated case for the importance of 1630s drama and its theatrical and political vitality, and reinforces the extent and complexity of Queen Henrietta Maria's impact upon 1630s drama, culture, and politics.

The influence of women on theatre more broadly is the subject of a selection of essays introduced by Marion Wynne-Davies in *Medieval and Renaissance Drama in England*, which examines the dynamics between the representation of women on stage and their presence as audience members. Her paper, 'Orange-Women, Female Spectators, and Roaring Girls: Women and Theater in Early Modern England' (*MRDE* 21 [2009]), begins by posing the bold questions of 'how and why women went to the theatre, what they expected of it, who they were, and how they were represented' (p. 19). Answering these questions proves to be far from straightforward, but Wynne-Davies argues that the vocal presence of orange-women, the 'amorous female spectators', and audience members like Mary Frith 'suggest[s] that a more complex analysis of the way in which women negotiated their roles as mute viewers within a space dominated by men is necessary' (p. 19). She identifies a 'gender-specific discourse' inherent to the behaviour and identity of such women 'which ran parallel with the authorized entertainment being acted out on stage' (p. 22)—a discourse based on class, sexual transgression, and vocalization. The distinction drawn here between theatrical representations of fictional female characters and an independent discourse employed to describe female audience members is not as convincing as it could be, given that much evidence relating to women playgoers is itself often theatrical, satirical, or performative in some important sense. (The question of theatrical or social 'authorization' is also more complex than is acknowledged here.) But this selection of papers raises interesting questions about the ways in which women 'engaged with the experience of early modern theatre . . . ways that, in turn, complicate how criticism interprets the roles of female characters on stage', given that 'the early modern theaters would have been alive with women's actions and voices' (p. 23). Nora L. Corrigan extends and opens up the discussion with an essay on 'The Merry Tanner, the Mayor's Feast, and the King's Mistress: Thomas Heywood's *1 Edward IV* and the Ballad Tradition', which analyses the role of the play's original audience and works to establish a connection between female audience members—spectators and women selling their wares—and the character of Jane in the play. Elizabeth Hodgson's '"A fine and private place": Chapman's Theatrical Widow' examines the materials and evidence provided by the ballad tradition and surviving conduct books in order to present a new reading of Chapman's play—and particularly his representation of the widow. Finally, Yvonne Bruce's essay, '"That which marreth all": Constancy and Gender in *The Virtuous Octavia*', examines the role of closet drama—and closet drama written by women—in the construction of women on stage and in society, exploring 'the complex negotiation between how women were represented on stage and how they presented themselves as playgoers' (p. 24).

Kelly J. Stage's article, 'The Roaring Girl's London Spaces' (*SEL* 49:ii[2009] 417–36), also engages with questions of gender and female power in an analysis of the representation of Moll Cutpurse. In her detailed reading of Dekker and Middleton's play, Stage analyses the ways in which Moll 'achieves success by maneuvering through London's spaces and by taking advantage of normative social practices', drawing a direct correlation between her 'ability to navigate' London and her distinctive brand of 'urban competency' (p. 417). In doing so, Stage reconceptualizes the character of Moll herself, refiguring her in any one of her accepted roles as 'a heroine, a protofeminist, a roarer, a criminal, or a rebel' into an independent and unique dramatic figure who is able to 'restage . . . social structures', and 'bend . . . theatrical London's social space to fit her' (p. 418). Stage scrutinizes the use of dialogue, asides, and the choreography of space in the play to make a powerful argument both for Moll's ability to arrange and construct space around her and for the extent to which Moll stands apart from the other communities and characters of the play, outside and beyond any of its socially designated and gendered spaces. On the one hand Stage argues that 'she must move because she has nowhere to stand' (p. 424); on the other, she makes convincing the claim that 'Moll is always at home and she is always her own mistress' (p. 429). This subtle tension is brought to an imaginative, poised, and (crucially) tentative reconciliation in Stage's construction of Moll's identity as dependent on her ability to judge and create distance: we are shown that Moll 'has no plot of her own, per se, but she has a path' (p. 431). Here, Stage reveals the attempts of other critics to fix Moll's position and 'insist' on resolution as reductive, an unnecessary fiction that is in any case unhelpful; like Moll, she is able to maintain 'a metropolis of possibilities' (p. 433). This thoughtful reading exemplifies the benefits of detailed and sustained attention to the text, and introduces a new, and newly liberated, configuration of the roaring girl.

The *Oxford Handbook of Early Modern Drama*, edited by Richard Dutton, promises to have the most lasting impact on the field of this year's publications, if only for its tremendous scope and ambition. Drawing together thirty-six essays by a distinguished host of scholars, the collection presents the most recent research across a wide range of approaches to theatre history, and features a body of challenging and innovative new work. Richard Dutton's intention as editor is to encourage contributors 'to engage with the research frontiers' rather than offer overviews or generalizations, and to take account of the multiplicity of early modern stages (there is also, in the preface, a note of regret that more repertory-based studies on individual companies could not have been included). The result is a collection that goes far beyond the remit of a student handbook, but which should be read and studied by professional scholars for years to come. In testament to this, William Ingram begins the discussion in his introduction: 'Theatre History: Where We Are Now, How We Got Here, Where We Go Next'. Ingram's analysis is structured around two questions: 'Is theater history a form of social or cultural history, and if so, do those disciplines have theoretical underpinnings (however untested) that should be of interest to theater historians?' and ('impertinently', as he admits) 'Where is the boundary between theater history and fiction?' (p. 2). Ingram offers a sharp, if not stern, reminder of the duty of theatre historians to engage reflectively with questions of historical method and theory; to remember that giving extant documents the benefit of the doubt is 'an act of faith' or 'a choice we make, not a requirement of our discourse' (p. 6). The question of historical training in the discipline surfaces more than once, and recognition of the danger that theatre history might be 'the uncritical sum of what practicing theater historians happen to be doing at any given time'—rather than a justified, premise-based discipline—reveals an anxiety that is ultimately necessary, Ingram argues, to 'the health in our discipline' (p. 15). This is a fascinating—slightly daunting—but rousing opening; one that raises expectations and also takes care to emphasize that such fundamental methodological concerns are not indicative of 'inadequacy' in the ensuing work.

The essays thereafter range from an analysis of the theatre companies in Part I—which treats each decade from 1583 in individual chapters and includes separate entries on pre-1583 theatre and the boy companies—to analysis of theatrical and social space and practices. Part II, on the London playhouses, provides accounts of the inn-yards (David Kathman), the Theatre (Gabriel Egan), the Globe (Andrew Gurr), the second Blackfriars (Ralph Alan

Cohen), the Red Bull (Mark Bayer), and a comprehensive investigation and comparison of the architectural structure, history, and management of the Phoenix and the Cockpit-in-Court, by Frances Teague. The next part—on 'Other Playing Spaces'—presents essays on more marginal performance spaces, both culturally, as is the case with London street theatre (accounted for by Anne Lancashire) and touring practices (see Peter Greenfield's essay), and also in terms of the critical attention they have received. Suzanne Westfall investigates household entertainments, followed by an exploration by Alan H. Nelson of theatrical culture at the universities and the Inns of Court. The court itself counts as an 'other' place of performance here; John Astington provides a summary account. It is refreshing to see the court represented here as one of many alternative performance spaces, rather than as a dominant cultural and theatrical presence.

The comparative emphasis on social practices (the subject of Part IV), before the analysis of theatrical practices, is also noticeable; eight essays present fresh insight into various aspects of the economic and cultural factors brought to bear on theatre. In each, the specialist knowledge of the contributors is newly cited—Alan Somerset's work on the patronage of early modern theatre; the relationship between the master of the revels and the theatre companies by Richard Dutton, and between the City of London and the theatre by Ian W. Archer; and the economics of theatre and the role of its entrepreneurs by S.P. Cerasano. David Kathman also considers the players' relation to the livery companies and the apprenticeship model, and Kathleen E. McLuskie writes on the Lady Elizabeth's Men here, with respect to 'the means of production, consumption, distribution, and exchange in the early modern theatrical market' (p. 432). Finally, Heather Hirschfield represents recent interest in literary authorship in her essay, and Natasha Korda re-evaluates the place and role of women in the theatre, with reference to their place within the economy and a 'gendered division of labor' (p. 458).

In the last section of this far-reaching volume—'Evidence of Theatrical Practices'—subjects under discussion include naturalistic acting on the Globe stage (Jacalyn Royce), actors' parts (Tiffany Stern), stage directions and the difficulties of their interpretation (Alan C. Dessen), and an analysis of lighting effects in a variety of early modern theatres (R.B. Graves). Lucy Munro provides a considered account of musical traditions within the playhouses and the use of other sound effects, and Andrew Sofer attempts to 'set early modern properties imaginatively in motion once more' (p. 560), considering 'the property demands' made on the King's Men during the staging of Jonson's *Alchemist* and Shakespeare's *Tempest* (p. 563); the article includes an inventory of required properties at its end. Thomas Postlewait presents a new methodology in theatre history by analysing 'visual evidence for theater in early modern England', investigating the methods, problems, and offerings of visual sources including drawings, paintings, maps, sculptures, and tapestries. Closing the collection, Eva Griffith presents a detailed analysis of the theatrical entrepreneur Christopher Beeston, and his control of his assets—including the theatrical properties of his company. Griffith offers a new reading of Beeston's theatrical role, and a new interpretation of historical biography and its relevance to theatre history. The success of this volume as a whole is due to the extent to which it covers all of the essential questions asked by the theatre historian, but in doing so breaks new ground and incorporates all of the recent work and trends of the discipline. Each essay pushes beyond offering a mere synopsis and develops that recent work in new directions, theorizes its position, and poses new questions about the evidence. This book will surely be a mainstay for the foreseeable future; a valuable resource for student and scholar alike.

Finally, and reaching back into the past, 2009 saw the republication of Charles Jasper Sisson's *Lost Plays of Shakespeare's Age*, originally published in 1936. While the volume's contents are now outdated in many ways and the essays can feel almost like relics or curiosities of theatre history, their new availability in paperback is enriching and curiously timely. The attempt to study lost plays and in doing so prioritize unexplored, elusive, and neglected drama speaks directly to the current direction of early modern theatre history and its recent attempts to push towards and beyond the margins of an accepted canon; Sisson's focus on lost plays and jigs, for instance, picks up on some of the themes that emerge from *Locating the Queen's Men* (discussed above). His reluctance 'to accept with confidence the belief that all the best of this abundant drama survived, and that the worst only is buried in the oblivion that fell upon almost all plays neglected by the printer' (p. 1) is particularly salient in the context of the last decade's focus on dramatic publication, literary authorship, and the role of the book trade in the shaping of early modern drama. His attention to the 'obscure dramatists' that might have 'stood forth . . . with the great ones' had their works been preserved in print, and the book's attentive scrutiny of the works of Chapman, Dekker, Ford, Webster, and a host of anonymous writers of verse, places him as a (retrospective) forerunner of the kind of critical focus that is now brought to the early modern dramatists that have suffered in Shakespeare's shadow. While the collection's fascination with 'the never-ending drama of human life . . . the intimacies of Elizabethan England' (p. 11), and the frank conjecture that constitutes some of the reconstructed plot and content of the lost plays may be doubtful now as a scholarly methodology, Sisson's work remains both important and relevant.

Sisson's way into these plays and their subject matter is through the records of the Star Chamber Court, Court of Requests, Delegates' Court, and a range of other circumstantial historical documents. This has the potentially misleading effect of treating each lost play with respect to its once libellous content, but also leads to fascinating discussion of the means by which Chapman's *The Old Joiner of Aldgate* and Dekker, Rowley, Ford, and Webster's *Keep the Widow Waking* came about—both in the historical development of the events upon which the plays were based and in the dramatic composition. His exploration of the Elizabethan jig, short verse-plays, provincial plays, and the May Game also centres on their potentially scandalous and libellous content, providing context to the ban on jigs that the Middlesex justices introduced in 1612 and the 'tumults' they might result in (p. 126), and speaking directly to William N. West's interpretation, discussed above. The new availability of Sisson's work offers insight into the historical development of theatre history—analysed so pertinently by Ingram in the *Handbook* introduction—and reanimates old debates and interpretations. Rather than being replaced by new work, this example shows how past scholarship—which could be described as lost in some important sense itself—can augment and fortify our understanding of the practice of theatre history.

3. Criticism

(a) General

Beginning with monographs, Kim Solga's *Violence Against Women in Early Modern Performance: Invisible Acts* provides an interesting and extremely valuable feminist intervention in reading both early modern drama and its modern production. Devoting one chapter to each of her four plays—*Titus Andronicus*, *A Woman Killed with Kindness*, *The Duchess of Malfi*, and *The Changeling*—Solga provides a critical reading of each text, followed by a critical engagement with modern performances of these plays. Chapter 1, 'Encounters with the Missing: From the Invisible Act to In/visible Acts', addresses the nature of the acts of 'percepticide' which lead to the making invisible of the acts of violence perpetrated against women. Thus, the 'in/visible act…argues for performance's power to bear witness to its own complicity in the disappearing act, as well as history's indebtedness to such acts for the authority of its representations' (p. 17). In chapter 2, 'Rape's Metatheatrical Return: Rehearsing Sexual Violence in *Titus Andronicus*', Solga explores the legal processes surrounding rape in the period as a cultural rehearsal, a theatrical re-representation, that 'divorc[es] rape from the body of the victim' (p. 26) and shifts attention to the honour of her male relatives. Solga's reading of the play emphasizes the ways in which Lavinia is a role to be performed, and a role in which Lavinia has to perform. Chapter 3, 'The Punitive Scene and the Performance of Salvation: Violence, the Flesh, and the Word', reads Thomas Heywood's *A Woman Killed with Kindness* in relation to domestic violence and contemporary conduct manuals which required women to offer a 'self-abnegating performance of salvation' (p. 66) in order to prevent the patriarchal order of 'reasonable correction' becoming disorderly. Building on the idea of such performances of salvation, Chapter 4, 'Witness to Despair: The Martyr of Malfi's Ghost', argues that, unlike Heywood's Anne, Webster's Duchess of Malfi refuses to disavow the 'rage, pain and loss with which she struggles'; rather 'she will be…the witness who questions, who pulls at the threads linking sacrifice, subjectivity, statehood, and sexed and gendered embodiment' (p. 99). Solga's excellent analysis goes on to show how, through her return as 'echo', 'the Duchess, martyrdom's conscientious objector, becomes fully domesticated, literally transformed into the ghostly remnant of Duchess-as-Martyr' (p. 101). Chapter 5, 'The Architecture of the Act: Renovating Beatrice Joanna's Closet', examines the 'in/visible act as a function of theatrical architecture' (p. 141). Solga argues that in Middleton and Rowley's *The Changeling*, 'spaces-off repeatedly mangle the distinction between sexual violence and obsessive passion, lust and trauma' (p. 143), limiting our acts of witness to violence. She argues that modern tendencies to read Beatrice-Joanna as vixen rather than victim, however the play is performed, is down to the influence of critical tradition which colludes with the men who betray her. This particular refusal to witness the elision of violence against women in drama, making it 'invisible in plain sight' (p. 177), Solga concludes, is representative of all such readings. She ends her book with a plea for a more active witness to in/visible acts, and a wider recognition of feminist intervention on stage in modern performance. This is an important book which provides a vital and engaging reassessment of the plays it discusses, on the page and on the stage.

Solga's is not the only monograph on Renaissance drama to be produced in 2009, but it was the only one available in time for review. Others will, therefore, be included in next year's review. Moving on to shorter studies in scholarly journals, then, we have two items which also engage with the representation of women and (theatrical) space. First, Michelle M. Dowd's article, 'Delinquent Pedigrees: Revision, Lineage, and Spatial Rhetoric in *The Duchess of Malfi*' (*ELR* 39[2009] 499–526). In this interesting essay, Dowd argues that the inscrutable off-stage world of the Duchess's family and sexuality provides an alternative to the seemingly incontrovertible ideology of patrilineal inheritance espoused in Webster's source. However, she also asserts that such a questioning takes place in the margins, arguing that the Duchess's power in such matters is only presentable off-stage. In '"You were an actor with your handkerchief": Women, Windows, and Moral Agency' (*CompD* 43[2009] 473–96), Cynthia Lewis provides an insightful analysis of Shakespeare's *The Merchant of Venice* and *Much Ado About Nothing*, Jonson's *Volpone*, and Middleton's *Women Beware Women* in regard to the positioning of women at 'real' or imagined windows. She describes the complicated implications of agency and sexuality created for Jessica, Margaret, Celia, and Bianca, developing a detailed reading of how 'women framed by windows involve their audience in moral dilemmas, moral questions, or moral concerns' (p. 473).

There are two items this year concerning Dekker, Rowley, and Ford's play *The Witch of Edmonton*. In her carefully argued 'Female Bodies, Speech, and Silence in *The Witch of Edmonton*' (*EarT* 12:i[2009] 69–91), Sarah Johnson discusses the way in which the early modern association of women's silence with chastity, and loose speech with loose bodies, informs and is challenged by the representation of women in the play. If Mother Sawyer's loose tongue brings the devil to her, she argues, the devil is also paralleled with the men who abuse her body because of her speech. Johnson suggests that *The Witch of Edmonton* presents women's silence too as a challenge to patriarchal authority, commenting that, with speech or with silence, Sawyer and Susan Carter 'cannot "win"' (p. 86). Rather, in the fates of Mother Sawyer and Susan, and in Winnifride's self-preservation through an ability to speak or be silent as necessary, 'the play demonstrates ... that for women such a preoccupation is necessary' (p. 88). In contrast with Johnson's essay, which provides a sympathetic response to Dekker, Rowley, and Ford's Elizabeth Sawyer, Katherine O'Mahoney's 'The Witch Figure: *The Witch of Edmonton*' (*SC* 24[2009] 238–59) reassesses the play in light of its source material in Goodcole's pamphlet and now non-extant ballads, and emphasizes the wickedness of the witch. Reading the play with regard to contemporary religious and legal understandings of suicide, O'Mahoney convincingly argues that Anne Ratcliffe's suicide serves 'as a dramatic instrument to stigmatize the witch-figure' (p. 248). This is further emphasized, she suggests, by the forgiveness given to the murderer, Frank Thorney, but not afforded to Mother Sawyer, since the 'dramatised witch becomes not merely responsible for Ratcliffe's death, but also for the damnation of her soul' (p. 254).

Staying with Dekker, Katrine K. Wong's interesting article offers 'A Dramaturgical Study of Merrythought's Songs in *The Knight of the Burning Pestle*' (*EarT* 12:ii[2009] 91–116). Wong summarizes the classical and contemporary understanding of the purpose and nature of music, particularly its divarication as potentially divine and damning, and the use of music in contemporary plays to indicate seduction, masculinity, or femininity, or as a potential cure. In this context, she provides a detailed discussion of Merrythought's songs and singing as 'an indispensable component of the metatheatrics' of the play, connecting the play and its on stage (play) audience (p. 110), and as a defining part of his character, both to Merrythought himself and the audience. She argues that 'his singing establishes him as a representation of everything non-mercenary in this city comedy, which aims to satirize the mercantile values of the society', while also 'accommodating an expression of the contemporary belief in music's duality' (p. 110).

In 'Fletcher, Massinger, and Roman Imperial Character' (*CompD* 43[2009] 317–54), John E. Curran Jr. examines the Roman rulers featured in Massinger and Fletcher's collaborative and individually authored Roman plays. He suggests that each ruler is individualized, despite the use of such tyrant tropes as lust/lechery and theatricality, because 'histrionics and desire can both work to personalize and particularize the emperors, especially for the dramatist imagining them through the lens of the historical—including the biographical—tradition' (p. 319). Thus, he argues, Massinger and Fletcher engage not only with the generic imperial character but with the characters of individual emperors in *The False One*, *The Prophetess*, *Rollo, Duke of Normandy*, *The Roman Actor*, *Valentinian*, and *The Emperor of the East*. Curran offers insightful readings of each play, along with instructive parallel readings, in order to demonstrate that 'a tyrant's particular point along the axes of desire and histrionics makes him highly idiosyncratic' (p. 341), and his article constitutes an attempt to reconstruct the real, historic character of each ruler.

Bradley J. Irish's 'Vengeance, Variously: Revenge before Kyd in Early Elizabethan Drama' (*EarT* 12:ii[2990] 117–34) provides an overview of the extent and prominence of the revenge theme in drama of a variety of genres. Irish argues that 'Before revenge came to inhabit its own generic space, it functioned as a widely versatile thematic and dramaturgical element in countless plays, ranging from raucous comedies to stately classical histories' (p. 118), and he traces the idea through examples of comedy, history, hero plays, and classical or biblical histories. He concludes that 'revenge was a narrative and thematic element of the utmost importance to early Elizabethan theatre, much earlier than is usually recognized' (p. 129). This survey provides an important beginning to further developments in this area. Sheetal Lodhia also engages with revenge tragedy in '"The house is hers, the soul is but a tenant": Material Self-Fashioning and Revenge Tragedy' (*EarT* 12:ii[2009] 135–61). In this essay Lodhia discusses ideas of the relationship between the body and soul in *The Maiden's Tragedy*, *The Revenger's Tragedy*, and *The Duchess of Malfi*, arguing that these plays anticipate the Cartesian *cogito* while simultaneously investing the body with an agency divorced entirely from the spirit or soul. She is particularly concerned with the ways in which 'acts of bodily modification divest the body of spiritual immanence' (p. 142) in the eyes of those who fashion them. Despite this, she argues, there remains a deep concern in all three plays with the Catholic investment in the wholeness of bodies and their spiritual being.

Staying with revenge tragedy, but moving on to ideas of nationalism and national identity, we have Eric Griffin's 'Nationalism, the Black Legend, and the Revised *Spanish Tragedy*' (*ELR* 39[2009] 336–70). This article discusses the three texts related to *The Spanish Tragedy*: that is, *The Spanish Tragedy* [1592], *The Spanish Tragedy* [1602], and *The First Part of Hieronimo* [1605], in relation to national and racial discourses regarding Spain, arguing, that in its 'successive emendations we may audit important shifts in the way "the Spaniard" was constructed for the stage' (p. 339). Particularly, Griffin explores the way in which these plays trace and perhaps contribute to the development of the Black Legend of Spanish colonial activity, arguing that 'In taking up the arguments for ethnicity, the later versions of *The Spanish Tragedy* are very much of their day' (p. 366). Continuing with dramatic constructions of national identity, Jesús López-Peláez Casellas discusses early modern English national identity through the concept of the semiosphere and its boundaries in '"Race" and the Construction of English National Identity: Spaniards and North Africans in English Seventeenth-Century Drama' (*SP* 106[2009] 32–51). He argues that while the Africans constituted the absolute Other, the Spanish were on the periphery of the semiosphere, with Spain functioning as a place of cultural translation. This position, he suggests, presents Spain as more threatening to English identity than Africa, since it is the enemy within the European semiosphere, and thus, potentially duplicitous. Casellas explores this 'proto-racist thinking' (p. 34) through the representation of Moors and Spaniards in Rowley's *All's Lost by Lust* and Dekker's *Lust's Dominion*, asserting that 'these plays embody fears and anxieties of a world that tried to offer rigid classifications of a fluid reality, and they attempt to provide imaginary resolutions to these fears by safely signalling the Other . . . with the simultaneously gradable, comfortable, and disquieting brand "non white"' (p. 51). Andrea Stevens's essay 'Mastering Masques of Blackness: Jonson's *Masque of Blackness*, the Windsor Text of *The Gypsies Metamorphosed,* and Brome's *The English Moor*' (*ELR* 39 [2009] 396–426) is also concerned with race, but through the lens of the practicalities of performance and the use of blackface paint. Taking subtle and intelligent note of the emphasis on the theatrical property of paint in these texts and performances, Stevens argues that Jonson and Brome are concerned with the relationship between inner and outer selves, complicated by the use of make-up. In this interesting and clearly argued piece, Stevens comments that Jonson's engagement with anti-cosmetic and climate geo-environmental discourses destabilizes the idea of blackness in order to privilege whiteness in *The Masque of Blackness*, but emphasizes the temporary properties of blackface paint to assert the essential gentlemanly nature of the Duke of Buckingham through the Windsor additions to *Gypsies Metamorphosed*. Finally, she highlights Jonson's anxieties over his mastery of this theatrical property through a discussion of Brome's mastery and excessive onstage use of blackface paint in *The English Moor*.

Staying with Caroline drama, Christopher Marlow's essay 'A Crisis of Friendship? Representation and Experience in Two Late University Plays' (*ShakS* 37[2009] 54–66) highlights the distinction between real friendships amongst university students who require broad social alliances for a secure future and the classical ideal of perfect friendship in Peter Hausted's *The Rivall Friends* (staged at Cambridge in 1631–2). Marlow goes on to argue that in Robert Mead's *The Combat of Love and Friendship* (staged at Oxford, 1634–8?), 'the seriousness with which [the conventions of classical friendship] are traditionally taken is exploited to such an extent that it is not just the friendship . . . that reaches crisis point but the discourse of friendship itself' (p. 61). Marlow places both plays in dialogue with the revived Platonic tradition at the Caroline court. Also engaging with the Caroline context, in '"You see the times are dangerous": The Political and Theatrical Situation of *The Humorous Magistrate*' (*EarT* 12:i[2009] 93–118), Mary Polito and Jean Sébastien Windle discuss the untitled and undated manuscript play usually referred to as *The Humorous Magistrate* in relation to legal reforms in the Caroline period. They argue that its detailed engagement with such documents as the Book of Orders in the character of Justice Thrifty dates the play's composition to 1632–40, and its revised version to *c*.1642. In addition to useful contextual information, the essay also provides an interesting analysis of issues kingship and government in the play.

Regarding monarchy, the final two items discuss performances at royal progresses and processions. First, Elizabeth Zeman Kolkovich's 'Lady Russell, Elizabeth I, and Female Political Alliances through Performance' (*ELR* 39:ii[2009] 290–314) gives a detailed analysis of the 1592 entertainment at Bisham performed for Queen Elizabeth I by the ladies of the Russell household. Kolkovich's analysis traces the ways in which the entertainment subtly positions the advice of men as unworthy, and potentially critical of the queen, emphasizing the loyalty and capabilities of Lady Russell and her daughters. Anne Lancashire's article, 'Dekker's Accession Pageant for James I' (*EarT* 12:i[2009] 39–50) asserts that the probable purpose of Thomas Dekker's unperformed Genius Pageant found in his *The Magnificent Entertainment* was to be performed during James I's accession entry to London in 1603, but was not performed because the king entered London by a different route. She suggests that Jonson's Genius Pageant for the coronation entry in 1604 may have used Dekker's original as a source.

(b) Marlowe

The only monograph of 2009 dedicated to Marlowe is Patrick Cheney's *Marlowe's Republican Authorship: Lucan, Liberty, and the Sublime*. Cheney's book, which builds on the work of his well-received *Marlowe's Counterfeit Profession*, examines the Marlowe canon through the lens of its most critically neglected component: his translation of the first book of Lucan's *Pharsalia*, the civil war epic which depicts and laments the fall of Roman republicanism. Through this process Cheney identifies a republican strain to Marlowe's work, reading it in the context of both classical republican ideas and the writing of late sixteenth-century European political theorists such as Niccolò Machiavelli and Philippe du Plessis Mornay. In Cheney's own words, the book attempts to 'situate Marlowe's poems and plays within a long history of republican thought, stretching from Polybius and Tacitus, to Machiavelli and Thomas Smith, to Algernon Charles Swinburne and David Norbrook' (p. 188). In the introduction, entitled 'Was Marlowe a Republican?', Cheney offers clarification of his use of the term 'republican', stating that in relation to Marlowe it constitutes more a mode of literary representation or construction of authorial identity than a programmatical political outlook; the author draws a distinction between Marlowe's own politics, which he acknowledges we have no access to, and his 'republican authorship', which is brought into being through the literary texts. Having highlighted Marlowe's interest in liberty as a literary theme, Cheney introduces the idea, central to the book's argument, that both Lucan's and Marlowe's work are infused with the notion of the sublime as characterized by the Greek writer Longinus, and that this notion of the sublime is bound up with ideas of democracy, freedom, and republicanism. Cheney suggests that, while many critics have identified the grandiloquent overreaching tendencies of Marlowe's protagonists, few have associated this with a formalized notion of the sublime, and none with a full consideration of republican authorship. It is this gap that his book aims to fill. The first chapter, 'Republican Representation: Marlowe, the Age of Elizabeth, and Lucan's First Book', establishes the context for discussion of republicanism in Marlowe's work. It first concentrates on biographical intimations of Marlowe's association with republicanism, focusing in particular on the poet's connections with France, the Netherlands, and Scotland, all of which were active centres of republican thought. The discussion then moves on to the cultural context in which Marlowe emerged as a writer, citing the influence of republican thinkers such as Machiavelli and Bodin, and drawing attention to Thomas Kyd's under-examined closet drama *Cornelia* as an early Elizabethan republican text, before suggesting that 'Elizabethan tragedy, with Marlowe its pioneer, emerges in its own period on the brink of breakdown, in a clash between monarchism and republicanism' (p. 41). The chapter ends with a brief discussion of Marlowe's *Lucan's First Book*, arguing that the Elizabethan poet harnesses the spirit of Lucan's text, and in the process 'invents a poetry of sublime dissolution' (p. 46). The rest of the book is devoted to a closer analysis of the Marlowe canon in the light of the contexts established in the introduction and first chapter. In chapter 2, Cheney turns his attention to what he classes as 'Marlowe's Ovidian Poems' (*The Passionate Shepherd*, *Hero and Leander*, and the translation of the *Elegies*). Identifying a sublime notion of liberty in these erotic poems, Cheney draws out of them a Lucanian republican ethic, before going on to demonstrate how later seventeenth-century authors, including Milton, accentuated these elements of the poems in their own appropriations of Marlowe's Ovidian lyric. Chapter 3 groups together the three plays which most clearly demonstrate an interest in empire, *Dido* and the two parts of *Tamburlaine*, examining them in terms of the tension in contemporary political discourse between the need for a state to expand its boundaries and the need for it to maintain a policy of liberty. Through this lens, as well as through identifying Lucan as a source and theorizing Marlowe's persistent self-quotation of the rhetoric of *The Passionate Shepherd*, Cheney delineates a republican dynamic at play in each of these three plays. Civil war is the primary context of the fourth chapter, which offers discussion of *The Jew of Malta*, *The Massacre at Paris*, and *Edward II*. Foregrounded in each of these plays are intertextual links with the *Pharsalia*, and hence with a civil Roman conflict between republicanism and tyranny. Cheney also complicates the standard readings of Marlowe's engagement with Machiavelli in these plays by offering detailed consideration of the *Discourses* as a context as well as the more frequently cited *The Prince*. The final chapter focuses its sole attention on *Doctor Faustus*, and, as with the readings of the other works, brings under scrutiny the influence of Lucan on the play. Tracing a link between scepticism and the Lucanian sublime, Cheney explores the treatment of these themes in the play, and suggests that it represents the apex of Marlowe's sublime authorship. The book's afterword (which is a brief version of an article entitled 'Milton, Marlowe, and Lucan: The English Authorship of Republican Liberty' (*MiltonS* 49[2009] 1–19), as well as offering concluding thoughts on the argument of the book, also takes a look forward, sketching Marlowe's influence on later republican authors such as Milton, who, Cheney argues, models his Satan on 'the tragic Marlovian superhero', and in the process 'locates Marlowe within a distinct literary genealogy in the formation of Christian republican authorship' (p. 192). It is Marlowe's place in this genealogy that Cheney's book argues we should acknowledge.

Cheney's focus on Lucan and Marlovian authorship is nicely complemented by José-María Perez Fernandez, whose 'From Virtue to Compulsion: Epic, Translation and the Significance of Early Modern Blank Verse' (*CahiersE* 75[2009] 1–16) places the emergence and success of early modern blank verse into a literary-philosophical context. Perez Fernandez argues that blank verse, with its eschewal of rhyme and its 'natural'-sounding rhythm, disguises its status as poetry, and thus makes less obtrusive the 'veil of words' that Neoplatonic thought conceived of as the mediator between the sense perception of the reader and transcendental essence of the text. The article focuses on instances of verse translation, namely Surrey's *Aeneid* and Marlowe's rendition of the first book of the *Pharsalia*, suggesting that these two very different examples—'Surrey's experimental hands and Marlowe's radical workshop' (p. 1)—demonstrate the versatility of blank verse which would allow it to shoulder the burden of the development of modern subjectivity and secularization.

While Cheney's was the only sustained full-length study of Marlowe published in 2009, *Shakespeare Bulletin* made a significant contribution to the year's output by dedicating a special issue, guest-edited by Pierre Hecker and Roslyn L. Knutson, to discussion of Marlowe's plays in performance and adaptation (*ShakB* 27:i[2009]). It's opening essay, Evelyn Tribble's 'Marlowe's

Boy Actors' (*ShakB* 27:i[2009] 5–17), examines the interaction between roles performed by boys—either female or juvenile characters—and those performed by adult male actors, in the process underlining the early modern theatre company's approach to training young boy actors. Discussed in particular detail is 'scaffolding', a technique by which characters played by boys (whether female adults or young boys) are led onto and around the stage by characters played by adult males, and addressed in a way that provides clear cues for their speaking parts. Tribble shows, with particular reference to *Tamburlaine* and *Edward II*, how scaffolding enables the introduction of boy actors into fairly complex roles with the help of more experienced actors, and also demonstrates how patterns of scaffolding often reflect the thematic content of the play itself; when the young Edward III takes the stage unguided for the first time (previously having been led, physically and morally, by Isabella and Mortimer) it is as the new king—he becomes independent as an actor and as a character simultaneously. In 'Marlowe's Knifework: Threat, Caution, and Reaction in the Theatre' (*ShakB* 27:i[2009] 19–26), Rick Bowers delineates a visceral element to Marlowe's dramaturgy that elicits a response from the audience that occurs prior to intellectual or moral perception. Bowers engages with Janet Clare's application of Artaud's theatre of cruelty to Marlowe, but suggests that while this account discusses the rhetorical effects of Marlowe's stage violence, in fact 'the critical vocabulary and the governing aesthetics of violence inhere in the physicality of theatre itself' (p. 20). Focusing on *Tamburlaine* and *Edward II*, and in particular on their preoccupation with stabbing weapons, this essay emphasizes the immediacy of Marlowe's kinaesthetic dramaturgy, and its instantaneous neuro-sensory impact upon its audience. Tom Rutter's contribution to the issue, 'Marlovian Echoes in the Admiral's Men Repertory: *Alcazar*, *Stukeley*, *Patient Grissil*' (*ShakB* 27:i[2009] 27–38), aims to unpack the relationship between the Marlovian texts, particularly *Tamburlaine*, and other plays being performed shortly afterwards by the Admiral's Men. Rutter draws a distinction between allusion and imitation (the former being a practice which makes incidental reference to old material and presents it in a new light, and the latter being a common-sense commercial tactic), and offers numerous examples of both in *The Battle of Alcazar* and *Thomas Stukeley*. While the imitation highlighted can be characterized as an uncritical regurgitation of identifiably Marlovian linguistic features, the allusions can be demonstrated to be more sophisticated; *Stukeley* employs Tamburlainean rhetoric in order to present its protagonist's sense of himself as a warrior hero, yet goes on to undercut this sense through allusion to other dramatic styles. Finishing with an allusion in Dekker, Chettle, and Haughton's *Patient Grissil*, in which the would-be poet Laureo inveighs in a Marlovian tone alien to the rest of the play, Rutter asserts the influence of Marlowe on writers both real and imagined. Lucy Munro's 'Marlowe on the Caroline Stage' (*ShakB* 27:i[2009] 39–50) focuses on the ambivalence of the Caroline reception and reproduction of older Elizabethan and Jacobean plays, paying particular attention to Marlowe's work. Munro discusses the paratexts accompanying *The Jew of Malta* in its 1633 publication (its first), and particularly their focus on aspects of performance—it is the memory of Edward Alleyn's performances, rather than the work of the author, that figures most forcefully in the play's dedicatory epistle—before going on to examine allusions to Tamburlaine (allusions that are clearly informed by an impression of the role in performance) in Randolph's *Hey for Honesty, Down with Knavery* and Cowley's *The Guardian*. Marlowe's work in the Caroline period, Munro suggests, had not yet become a nostalgic curiosity, but had maintained a steady performance history and continued to exert influence on writers and performers of the age. Stacy Pendergraft's essay, 'Marlowe Mee: Constructing the Marlowe Project' (*ShakB* 27:i[2009] 51–62), describes the rationale behind and implication of a student drama project at the University of Arkansas at Little Rock which culminated in a performance before delegates of the Marlowe Society of America conference, held in Canterbury in 2008. 'The Marlowe Project' resulted in an ensemble piece that offered a medley of radically reconceived scenes from *Tamburlaine*, *The Jew of Malta*, *Doctor Faustus*, and *Edward II*, devised in the spirit of Charles Mee's 're-making' approach to theatre. Pendergraft here details both the pedagogical and performance value of such an approach. This flexibility of verse and meaning is precisely the topic of Lois Potter's 'What Happened to the Mighty Line? Recent Marlowe Productions' (*ShakB* 27:i[2009] 63–8), which looks at the privileging of cultural currency over poetry in recent (early/mid-twentieth century onwards) productions of Marlowe plays. Potter looks at how modern directors tend to see Marlowe's text as freely interchangeable, asking why the mighty line is 'being replaced by the moving line' (p. 66). In '"There is nothin' like a dame": Christopher Marlowe's Helen of Troy at the Royal Shakespeare Company' (*ShakB* 27:i[2009] 69–79), Laura Grace Godwin provides a survey of the representation of Helen of Troy in four RSC productions of *Doctor Faustus*. Godwin details how the portrayals, from Maggie Wright's 1968 performance—the first nude appearance on an English stage—to Vincent Regan's overtly homoerotic turn in 1989, offer a register of sexual taboos at the time of each production, but concludes that the company's consistent figuring of the character in a politically and sexually transgressive manner, and the resultant focus of the press on this aspect of the drama, has obscured the content of Marlowe's play and helped to reinscribe the playwright's position as 'other'. The issue is brought to a close by David Fuller's 'Love or Politics: The Man or the King? *Edward II* in Modern Performance' (*ShakB* 27:i[2009] 81–115). Fuller, like Godwin, offers a survey of productions of one of Marlowe's plays, this time focusing on *Edward II*. Fuller analyses the treatment of the play's themes in three productions: the Prospect Theatre Company in 1969–70, the Globe in 2003, and David Bintley's ballet, choreographed for the Stuttgart Ballet in 1995 and revised for the Birmingham Royal Ballet two years later. Fuller argues that the more successful productions were those which maintained the indeterminacy which runs through Marlowe's text rather than presenting a more unilateral treatment of sexuality or politics, and judges firmly in favour of the Prospect and ballet productions in this respect. This wealth of material on Marlowe in performance and adaptation is complemented elsewhere by Bert Cardullo, whose '"Outing" Edward, Outfitting Marlowe: Derek Jarman's Film of *Edward II*' (*LFQ* 37:ii[2009] 86–96) offers an analysis of Jarman's film adaptation of *Edward II* which refutes contemporary critical responses that accused it of being a vehicle for a heterophobic agenda. Cardullo suggests rather that the film adroitly employs the ambiguity inherent in Marlowe's dramaturgy to enable a bleak but balanced discussion of the politics of sexuality, arguing that, in true Marlovian style, the 'film's vision of *all* sexuality, all human relationships, is equally dark and deadly' (p. 91).

This entry covers four pieces which focus on issues relating to Marlowe's life, and to his relationship, professional or otherwise, with contemporary writers, particularly with Shakespeare. Robert Sawyer's 'Shakespeare and Marlowe: Re-Writing the Relationship' (*CS* 21:iii[2009] 41–58) surveys the development of the critical and popular account of the relationship between Shakespeare and Marlowe over the course of the twentieth and early twenty-first centuries. Sawyer examines the redrawing of the relationship against particular historical contexts: after looking at early accounts by Swinburne and Eliot, he goes on to place the adversarial characterization by Irving Ribner in a Cold War frame, before suggesting that the more congenial representations of the relationship in popular appropriations by Anthony Burgess and in the movie *Shakespeare in Love* reflect the 'political climate of peace and prosperity' (p. 52) post-Berlin Wall and pre-9/11. Azar Hussain's note, 'The Reckoning and the Three Deaths of Christopher Marlowe' (*N&Q* 56[2009] 547–8), offers further consideration of this relationship. The three deaths in question are in fact three putative Shakespearian references to Marlowe's death, the first of which is Touchstone's well-known quip about the danger of great reckonings in little rooms in *As You Like It*. The other two, in *Cymbeline* and *1 Henry IV*, are allusions newly proposed by Hussain, and both revolve around the use of the word 'reckoning', which of course also featured prominently on the coroner's report pertaining to Marlowe's demise. Hussain argues that Shakespeare's apparent preoccupation with the circumstances of his peer's death might indicate both that he knew 'what really happened at Deptford on that fateful Wednesday in 1593' (p. 548) and that he harboured a degree of indignation about it. A further link between the two playwrights is suggested by Thomas Merriam, whose 'Marlowe versus Kyd as Author of *Edward III* I.i, III, and V' (*N&Q* 56[2009] 549–51) tests a suggestion made by Sir Brian Vickers in late 2008 that Thomas Kyd may have been the author of the 'non-Shakespeare' (p. 549) parts of *Edward III*. Suggesting that an *Edward III* co-authored by Shakespeare and Marlowe would complete a neat authorial and historical transition from *Edward II* to *Richard II*, Merriam tests Marlowe's claim to the sections in question against Kyd's, using his own computerized analysis of relative frequencies of key function words (Vickers had reached his conclusion using plagiarism detection software). The results of Merriam's analysis, which examines the relevant sections of *Edward III* along with works attributable to Marlowe and Kyd, draw a clear distinction between work by Kyd and that by Marlowe, and place the non-Shakespearian sections of *Edward III* clearly among the latter. Merriam ends by asserting the need to for further work in order to reconcile his and Vickers's results. Andrew Power's 'Marlowe's Chamber Fellow and a Dramatic Disturbance at Cambridge in 1582' (*N&Q* 56[2009] 39–40) highlights the involvement of Marlowe's Corpus Christi roommate and fellow Parker scholar Robert Thexton in an incident involving the two things with which Marlowe tends to be most associated—drama and violence. Thexton had his head 'broken' in a disturbance that followed a theatrical performance at Pembroke Hall which had already upset the college authorities with its representation of the mayor of Cambridge. Two days later, in what Power suggests may have been a related incident, a Pembroke scholar was beaten for interrupting a performance hosted by Corpus Christi. It is not unlikely, Power suggests, that Marlowe may have been involved in this edgy atmosphere of controversial theatrical performance and inter-college rivalry in his days at Cambridge.

Doctor Faustus and *Tamburlaine* were the recipients of the overwhelming majority of critical attention in what was a quiet year for Marlowe's other works. On *Faustus*, Andrew Sofer's 'How To Do Things with Demons: Conjuring Performatives in *Doctor Faustus*' (*TJ* 61:i[2009] 1–21) offers a revealing critique of the play's employment of stage magic in terms of speech-act theory. Sofer refers to J.L. Austin's account of the performative speech act (hinted at in the title of the essay), which discounted speech acts in theatrical performance or a literary context as 'hollow' or 'inefficacious' (saying 'I do' in a wedding ceremony on stage, for instance, doesn't bring into being an *actual* marriage), before examining applications of speech-act theory to literature by Jacques Derrida and Judith Butler which complicate this distinction. Concentrating on the ambiguity inherent in the Elizabethan use of the word 'perform' (meaning both to bring into being and to enact in a theatrical sense), Sofer examines the performative language of the play, particularly in its scenes of conjuration (another word whose ambiguity is explored), and argues that it allows the play to maintain an ambiguously liminal position between representing black magic and damnation and bringing them into being—an actor reciting a conjuration on stage, for example, may not be trying to conjure a devil himself, but, as far as the Elizabethan audience was concerned (and this is what matters), his uttering of the words may have had the power to do so in spite of his intentions. Similarly, Edward Alleyn's performance of blasphemy might be seen to edge dangerously close to a performative rejection of God. Elsewhere, drawing upon an anecdotal account of Cornelis Drebbel's early seventeenth-century exhibition of his newly invented submarine, Mickael Popelard's 'Spectacular Science: A Comparison of Shakespeare's *The Tempest*, Marlowe's *Doctor Faustus* and Bacon's *New Atlantis*' (in Drouet, ed., *The Spectacular in and around Shakespeare*, pp. 17–40) examines the relationship between 'science', or what that term can be said to represent in the Renaissance, and spectacle, and argues that the distinction between theatre and magic is a hazy one. Popelard draws similar conclusions on *The Tempest* and *Doctor Faustus*, namely that both plays exhibit science as a practice that is so bound up in the illusory as to be practically useless. The chapter finishes by contrasting these representations of science/magic with that in Bacon's *New Atlantis*, which marks a change in attitude, and encourages the separation of science from the kind of strangeness and ostentatious associations that are evident in the two plays.

In '"Falling to a diuelish exercise": The Copernican Universe in Marlowe's *Doctor Faustus*' (*EarT* 12:i[2009] 141–9) Gabrielle Sugar expands on the work of Leah Marcus, who identified an ideological shift between the two texts of *Doctor Faustus* that correlated with the differing brands of Reformation theology associated with their respective settings, Wertenberg (almost always, prior to Marcus's work, dismissed as a textual corruption) and Wittenberg. Sugar notes a similar correlation with respect to Copernican astronomy. Wittenberg, Faustus's university in the 1616 B-text, accepted Copernicus's idea as a mathematical model but not as a physical reality. Wertenberg (a common contemporary anglicization of Würtemburg) was home to the Doctor Faustus of the 1604 A-text, and also to the University of Tübingen, where Johannes Kepler espoused a more radical adoption of the Copernican cosmos as both a theoretical and physical reality. Having established that the Copernican model is something of a dangerous idea (even Mephistopheles will not discuss it with Faustus), Sugar identifies a key difference between the texts that occurs when the Chorus describes Faustus's journey around the universe; the Wertenberg text describes only a mythological cosmos, leaving open the possibility of a Copernican one existing in actuality, whereas the Wittenberg text expands on the journey in such a way that it establishes the universe as unmistakably Ptolemaic. This more conservative astronomical outlook, Sugar suggests, reflects the location of the 1616 version, and is reflected in the more severe punishment that is ultimately meted out to Faustus in this text.

One of three shorter pieces on *Faustus*, Joseph Candido's 'Marking Time in *Doctor Faustus* 5.2' (*EarT* 12:i[2009] 137–9), examines Marlowe's playful use of, and commentary on, time in Act V, scene ii, of *Doctor Faustus*. Candido considers the generally unremarked fact that the striking of the clock during this scene (the clock strikes eleven, once for half-past, and then twelve, giving a total number of strikes—twenty four—that fittingly matches the number of Faustus's fleeting years of earthly pleasure) would be experienced by an audience as a slow, uncomfortable passage of time. In contrast, the time between them flies by at an increasing pace (the thirty minutes between eleven and half past are gone in thirty lines, the following half-hour in just twenty). Candido suggests that this various speeding up and slowing down of theatrical experience reflects the fluidity of our perception of time, and offers an ironic comment on the painfully finite terms on which Faustus surrenders his soul. Matthew Steggle's '*Doctor Faustus* and the Devils of Empedocles' (*N&Q* 56[2009] 544–7) identifies an echo in the final soliloquy of *Doctor Faustus* of fragment 107 of the pre-Socratic philosopher-poet Empedocles. Fragment 107, which exists only as a quotation in Plutarch, offers an account of the journey through the elements undergone by the spirit, or devil, that has fallen from Heaven, a journey whose structure is replicated, Steggle argues, in Faustus's famous final invocations to the elements to absorb him (the sequence, in both cases, is air–sea–earth–evaporation–air). Steggle closes by suggesting that this reference opens a new line of enquiry into the play, especially given its references to the old philosophers, and its use of good and bad angels (also a feature of Empedoclean philosophy). Wrapping up the work on *Doctor Faustus*, Donna Murphy's note 'The Date and Co-Authorship of *Doctor Faustus*' (*CahiersE* 75[2009] 43–4) lends support to the case for an early *Doctor Faustus*, arguing that it was in performance by March 1588, when *Perimedes the Blacksmith* was registered with the stationers. Robert Greene's preface to *Perimedes*, Murphy argues, makes reference to *Faustus*, in addition to its well-known nod to 'that atheist Tamburlan'. Positing Robin as a mocking reference to Greene, Murphy goes on to suggest that this early date bolsters the case for Thomas Nashe as the author of the comic prose scenes in Faustus—with the undeveloped style and mocking of Greene providing a good match for Nashe's early pre-Marprelate career.

Moving on to Tamburlaine, Matthew R. Martin's '"This tragic glass": Tragedy and Trauma in *Tamburlaine Part One*' (in Allard and Martin, eds., *Staging Pain, 1580–1800: Violence and Trauma in British Theater*, pp. 15–29) examines, through a Lacanian reading of the play, the place of *1 Tamburlaine* in the developmental process of early modern tragedy. Martin argues that the play stands not as a crucial part of a linear progression from the earlier Elizabethan moralizing tragedy (of the *Mirror for Magistrates* mould) to the later and more complex Shakespearian tragedy, but rather as an obstacle in that progression, differing from the drama at both ends of that simplified continuum in its treatment of trauma. In the moralizing tragedy, Martin contends, trauma exists only as part of an overarching scheme in which moral balance is always restored, while Shakespearian tragedy 'works through' trauma until the final cathartic closure allows it to be contained 'safely in coherently representable past' (p. 17). While these models of tragedy present trauma as something external that happens to an already realized being, Martin argues that the generically ambiguous *Tamburlaine* enacts trauma in a more Lacanian sense, as prior to and constitutive of subjectivity. The play firmly resists closure as Tamburlaine compulsively enacts traumatic repetition, in an attempt to assert a unified identity—in order to assert 'his own ontological significance' (p. 23). Javad Ghatta, in '"By Mortus Ali and our Persian gods": Multiple Persian Identities in *Tamburlaine* and *The Travels of the Three English Brothers*' (*EarT* 12:ii[2009] 235–49), seeks to complicate the notion that the early modern English perception of Islam reductively conflated Muslims of North Africa, Persia, India, Asia Minor, and South-East Asia into the concept 'Turk'. Rather, Ghatta argues, the early seventeenth-century stage, with a particular example being Middleton's *The Travels of Three English Brothers*, registers a keen awareness of separate Islamic identities—Safavid Persia as distinct from the Ottoman empire, Shi'a Islam as opposed to Sunni. Ghatta here suggests that the development of this recognition is anticipated and inspired by Marlowe's *Tamburlaine*. Marlowe invests Persia with a curiously classical, non-Islamic identity in the plays, but Tamburlaine himself harbours associations with Shi'a Islam (the historical Timur claimed to be descended from Mortus Ali, the cousin of Mohammed revered by Shi'a Muslims), and his audacious challenge to Mohammed-as-godhead could be seen as a rejection of a particularly Sunnite understanding of the prophet. Marlowe's tacit acknowledgement of the complexity of various eastern and Islamic identities, Ghatta argues, prepares the ground for later writers, like Middleton, to explore this complexity more fully. Occupying similar territory is Justin Kolb's '"In th'armor of a Pagan knight": Romance and Anachronism East of England in Book V of *The Faerie Queene* and *Tamburlaine*' (*EarT* 12:ii[2009] 194–207), which examines instances of Elizabethan literary encounters with Islam, focusing on Book V of *The Faerie Queene*, in which Arthur and Artegall face the Souldan, and Marlowe's *Tamburlaine*, whose eponymous protagonist engulfs the east and wages terrible war on the Ottoman Turks. Both instances, Kolb suggests, ostensibly contain the contemporary Islamic threat within framework of national romance, disarming the alien by swallowing him into familiar myth. Yet, in both cases, the distinction between self and other is destabilized in such a way that it makes alien the self—Artegall must temporarily 'turn turk' to defeat the Souldan (which he does using a mirror), and Tamburlaine effectively takes the place of the Islamic tyrants he deposes; to contain the Muslim threat is to risk a bidirectional assimilation. 'Tamburlaine in Two Broadside Ballads: "A Brave Warlike Song" and "Saint George's Commendation to all Souldiers"' (*N&Q* 56[2009] 551–3), another contribution to the year's work on Marlowe by Rick Bowers, discusses references to *Tamburlaine* in two early seventeenth-century patriotic and militaristic ballads. Bowers notes that the ballads assimilate Tamburlaine into English and Christian tradition, placing his deeds alongside those of St George and of biblical warrior heroes, and suggests that these allusions provide evidence of Tamburlaine being used as a call to arms, in this case in the face of the pacifist foreign policy being employed by James I.

Of the remaining commentary, Lucy Potter provides the lone work on *Dido, Queen of Carthage* with her note 'Marlowe's *Dido*: Virgilian or Ovidian?' (*N&Q* 56[2009] 540–4). Potter re-examines the critical near-consensus that the play, with its frolicking gods and fallible male lead, represents a departure from the Virgilian gravity of *The Aeneid*, its primary source, and an inclination towards the more ironic tone of Ovid, whose *Heroides* retold the myth from the perspective of the jilted Dido. This view, Potter argues, is predicated upon a reductive reading of Virgil's epic as presenting an unproblematic portrayal of its hero, and fails to take into account critical output on *The Aeneid* since the 1970s, particularly that of the Harvard school, which emphasizes its darker, more cynical characteristics. A more complicated understanding of Virgil, the note argues, would lead to a more fruitful understanding of the uses to which he was put in the Renaissance. Finally, Andrew Hadfield's 'Marlowe's Representation of the Death of Edward II' (*N&Q* 56[2009] 40–1) questions the editorial tradition that introduces the hot poker to the death scene of *Edward II*, thus bringing the climactic event into line with Holinshed's account of Edward's demise. Hadfield instead argues that we might consider Edward's crushing under a table (the only murder implement mentioned in the stage directions of the playtext) as an instance of *peine fort et dure*, a method of execution by crushing referred to in a number of Shakespeare plays and which was reserved for defendants who refused to appear before a jury. The advantage for the victim would be that by dying unconvicted they could avoid the forfeiture of their estate or dynasty. As this 'favour' was not extended to those who committed treason, Hadfield suggests that the nature of Edward's death may represent a tacit acknowledgement that his crimes did not extend to that level.

(c) Jonson

One monograph this year is devoted to Jonson. Lynn S. Meskill's *Ben Jonson and Envy* argues that, although biographers often represent Jonson as an envious person, critics have not analysed the 'persistent thematic issues derived from envy' in the works themselves (p. 2). Jonson's thematics of envy are linked with his obsessive concern with the reception of his work: readers and audiences are 'dominated by invidiousness' (p. 7), and 'necessarily distort, pervert and deform the meaning of the text' (p. 5). This is a threat, but also a stimulus: in *Poetaster*, for instance, 'literary creation is produced in confrontation with envy or "bad" readers' (p. 94), and Jonsonian authorship in general involves 'meeting, anticipating and diverting envious curiosity by confounding and baffling it or camouflaging the object of its gaze' (p. 24). For Jonson, the reader's envious gaze possesses 'the power attributed to the eye to harm' (p. 29) by early modern physiology, and the effort to evade this harm generates a pervasive self-consciousness in the work, 'a split in the writer, who turns his gaze upon his own text in anticipation of the gaze of the reader and proceeds to defend the text against his own envy' (pp. 73–4). In turn, this drives Jonson's project of monumentalizing himself in print, and the 1616 Folio represents 'Jonson's Gorgon gaze upon his own work' (p. 40), figuratively turning it to the stone of a classic, impregnable by envy. For example, in the Folio text of *The Masque of Queenes*, with its supporting marginalia, 'we can literally see Jonson's negotiation with posterity and fame', and 'the anti-masque and masque narrate a battle between the poet and the forces of envy against which he must build an everlasting monument to protect his name' (p. 153). Because in 1616 'Jonson enfolioed himself . . . as a dead classical author' (p. 188), the later plays, from *The Staple of News*, are written in the shadow of that earlier self. Envy is also the theme of Marlin E. Blaine, 'Envy, Eunoia, and Ethos in Jonson's Poems on Shakespeare and Drayton' (*SIP* 106[2009] 441–5), which examines how Jonson 'explicitly reckons with his reputation as a scornful egotist when he sets out to laud a fellow author' (p. 441): as well as praising his subjects, he is concerned with developing his own *ethos* by confronting his reputation for 'peevishness and egocentrism' (p. 455).

V.A. Moul, 'The Poet's Voice: Allusive Dialogue in Ben Jonson's Horatian Poetry' (in Houghton and Wyke, eds., *Perceptions of Horace: A Roman Poet and his Readers*), considers Jonson's 'intertextual conversation' with Horace, seeing this as 'a primary source of the texture and tone' (p. 220) of his verse. Moul uses manuscript evidence to argue that 'To Sir Robert Wroth' is shaped intertextually by Horace's second epode, and traces how Jonson's work 'tracks its model' (p. 225) in a range of poems and masques, producing 'an allusive dialogue of great flexibility and nuance, at once rigorously competitive and minutely textual' (p. 238). Another aspect of the Horatian tradition is considered in Paul Baines and Pat Rogers, 'Pope's First Horatian Imitation: Ben Jonson's Crispinus and the Poisoning of Edmund Curll' (*RES* 60[2009] 78–95), which relates the vomiting purge in *Poetaster* to the 'notorious incident in which Pope spiked the rogue bookseller Edmund Curll's drink with an emetic' (p. 78), and suggests that Pope eventually came closer than Jonson to turning *Poetaster*'s fantasies of poetic justice into reality: 'In time, Pope was able to co-opt actual court decisions' to his satiric project (p. 95).

Ben Jonson and the Politics of Genre, edited by A.D. Cousins and Alison V. Scott, is a volume of essays by eight scholars on Jonson's use of the 'resources of kind' to 'offer representations of the political' and 'refigure . . . the political actualities of early Stuart society' (p. 1). A.D. Cousins, 'Feigning the Commonwealth: Jonson's Epigrams', reads the *Epigrams* as 'feigning' a Jacobean utopia: the poems represent idealized communities of national worthies and judicious understanders, both subordinate to the mythologized figure of the king. Through this community of national heroes (which 'expresses difference as well as sameness' (p. 20), in a modification of Stanley Fish's concept of the 'community of the same'), the poems imagine 'a level of existence—an ideal political economy—beyond the economy of the market-place' (p. 32). Robert C. Evans, 'The Politics (and Pairing) of Jonson's Country House Poems', proposes that the adjacent placement in the 1616 Folio of 'To Penshurst' and 'To Sir Robert Wroth' 'practically forces us to read them together, as commentaries on each other' (p. 80): the former poem is utopian and the latter dystopian, but by pairing them Jonson reminds us 'that his own political vision is not escapist, naive, or sycophantic, let alone mendacious' (p. 84), and finally conveys scepticism of 'utopian dreams and schemes' (p. 87). John Roe, 'Style, Versatility, and the Politics of the Epistles', interrogates the critical commonplace of Jonson as a poet 'caught in a contradiction', an idealist who is nevertheless 'a shrewd exploiter of patronage' (p. 91). In the verse epistles he emerges as a humanist counsellor, negotiating the politics of patronage but also furthering a larger 'concern for peace' (p. 97): 'While he writes invariably with an eye to the main chance, he can with justice claim to strike an ideal note, and often in the midst of the most material and personal of circumstances' (p. 112). Marea Mitchell, 'Jonson's Politics of Gender and Genre: Mary Wroth and "Charis"', follows critics like W. David Kay and Helen Ostovich in suggesting a specific connection between 'A Celebration of Charis in Ten Lyric Pieces' and Jonson's patron and fellow poet, Mary Wroth. Both Wroth and Jonson 'experiment with models of feminine behaviour that escape conventional models', and 'Charis' 'constructs a dialogue that allows not one but two women to speak, and also gives them the last word' (p. 117), redefining female desire 'as an active rather than a negative virtue' (p. 118).

Moving to drama, in the same volume Richard Dutton, 'Jonson's Metempsychosis Revisited: Patronage and Religious Controversy' emphasizes the influence of Donne's poem 'Metempsychosis' on 'Jonson's own "metempsychosis" entertainment' (p. 147) in *Volpone*, arguing that Robert Cecil is 'the key topical link between the two works' (p. 150). *Volpone* 'reflects on a spiritual malaise that grips the whole society', and 'lays the blame for it squarely at Cecil's door' (p. 146). Dutton proposes that 'the play as a whole is about patron/client relations': 'there is a sense in which Volpone represents Cecil', and the struggle between Mosca and Volpone can be read as 'Jonson's imaginary turning on the patron he undoubtedly resented, even as he recognized the need he had of him' (pp. 153–4). Another form of topical meaning, Jonson's humanist 'use of history to illuminate contemporary events' (p. 172) is the topic in Tom Cain, 'Jonson's Humanist Tragedies'. Rather than attempting psychological complexity, the tragedies raise questions about 'the business of government and the dynamics of power' (p. 165): Jonson 'saw *Sejanus* as a play about freedom of speech and the responsibilities of the historian to the state' (p. 178), while *Catiline* 'is a treatment of classical republicanism which must at least qualify the characterization of Jonson as an ardent monarchist, an authoritarian in politics as in his attitude to his literary output' (p. 184). Alison V. Scott, 'The Jonsonian Masque and the Politics of Decorum', discusses 'the paradoxical nature of the [masque] genre's political work'; Jonson's masques 'keep multiple truths in play at once' (p. 43), reconciling political contingencies with universalized values. Through readings of the *Masque of Oberon*, *Pleasure Reconciled to Virtue*, *Neptune's Triumph*, and others, Scott argues that the masques are 'always at once engaged with Platonism and Sophism, the affirmation of immutable truth and the adaptation to contingent truth' (p. 64). Last in this collection, Eugene D. Hill, 'A Generic Prompt in Jonson's *Timber, or Discoveries*', suggests that the quotation from Persius's fourth satire which Jonson used as the epigraph for *Discoveries* may direct us to 'an uncanvassed function' of the text: 'like Persius, Ben had in mind an assemblage of applicable commonplaces for political writing', so that 'the book stands as a perpetual invitation to topical appropriation' (p. 195).

The concerns of several of these essays are taken up, too, in the periodical literature. On the country house poems, Lisa Celovsky, 'Ben Jonson and Sidneian Legacies of Hospitality' (*SIP* 106[2009] 178–206), reads Jonson's praise of the Sidney family in 'To Penshurst', and the rest of *The Forest*, as informed by the idea that 'the Sidneys of the seventeenth century were as much "new capitalists" as they were..."feudal aristocrats"' (p. 179). *The Forest* registers how, 'in the face of earthly transience and frustrated fertility', the Sidneys maintain traditions of hospitality but also 'work within emerging economies to find viable ways to transmit their heritage' (pp. 203–5). Andrew Hadfield, 'Ben Jonson and Philip Sidney' (*N&Q* 56[2009] 85–6), finds in the opening lines of 'To Penshurst' an echo of Philip Sidney's sonnet 'Queene *Vertue*'s court', implying that the Sidneys' 'heritage is probably in the family's literary endeavours as much as its social attainments' (p. 86). Elizabeth Moran, '"Devils Liquore" and "Virgins Milke": Fashion, Fetishism and Jonson's Line' (*Parergon* 26:i[2009] 141–73), again raises the issue of family lines, arguing that Jonson sees 'fashionable consumption' in 'the nascent consumer culture of early modern London' (p. 141) as corroding 'the feudal virtues of hierarchy, stasis, and above all, lineage' (p. 147). 'To Penshurst' resists 'fashion's challenge to the hierarchy of rank' (p. 154), while *Epicoene* and *The Devil is an Ass* 'crystallize Jonson's preoccupations with attire, line and nobility' (p. 160).

Adrian Curtin, 'Dumb Reading: The Noise of the Mute in Jonson's *Epicene*' (*CompD* 43:i[2009] 45–62), addresses another aspect of *Epicoene*, focusing on Jonson's 'dramaturgically complex, if not contradictory' (p. 45) treatment of noise in the acoustic environment of the Blackfriars theatre, and on the figure of Morose's servant Mute, who may be overlooked on the page, but brings on stage 'the gestures of the dumb show, and the frivolous antics of the clown': a 'performative "noise of signs"' (p. 58) that partially eludes the control of the dramatist. Contemporary performance conditions are also the focus of Andrea Stevens, 'Mastering Masques of Blackness: Jonson's *Masque of Blackness*, the Windsor text of *The Gypsies Metamorphosed*, and Brome's *The English Moor*'

(*ELR* 39:ii[2009] 396–426). Reading the two masques in which Jonson uses 'race-altering paint as a stage device' (p. 397) alongside Brome's 'comedy about a miscarried masque of blackness' (p. 400), Stevens explores the relation between the evolution of make-up technology and the masques' signification: Jonson's narratives of racial transformation are constrained by the technical difficulties of removing black paint, which also has a 'provocative and paradoxical status as a figure for antitheatricality' (p. 426). Last on the masques, John Mulryan, ' "The primrose way to the everlasting bonfire": The Choice of Hercules in Shakespeare, Jonson, and Milton' (*BJJ* 16[2009] 148–67), compares Jonson's treatment of the Choice of Hercules in *The Masque of Pleasure Reconciled to Virtue* with Milton's and Shakespeare's handling of the trope: Jonson's masque resolves the choice between the easy path of pleasure and the rocky road to virtue by seeking 'both pleasure and virtue in the arduous pursuit of truth, a lifelong journey up the mount of contemplation' (p. 158).

Jeffrey Kahan, ' "Shakespear wanted arte": Questioning the Historical Value of Ben Jonson's Conversations with Drummond' (*BJJ* 16[2009] 132–47), challenges the literary and historical value of Jonson's *Conversations* with Drummond, noting that the underlying manuscript 'is neither in Jonson's nor Drummond's holograph, nor is the extant manuscript even remotely contemporaneous to Jonson's visit' (p. 133). He traces the transmission of Drummond's manuscript, arguing that we should see its transcriptions 'not as relatively faithful copies of a Renaissance document but as unique, eighteenth-century literary objects' (p. 139). However, in spite of its questionable status as historical evidence, '*Conversations* is a portrait of Jonson that has become vital to *our* portrait of Jonson, or at least to our ever-evolving literary construction of Jonson' (pp. 144–5). On other textual matters, Grace Ioppolo, 'The Monckton-Milnes Manuscript and the "Truest" Version of Ben Jonson's "A Satyricall Shrubb" ' (*BJJ* 16[2009] 117–31), compares the version of Jonson's satire 'A Satyricall Shrubb' printed in *Underwoods* in the 1640 Folio with the version found in the Monckton-Milnes manuscript, a verse miscellany dating from the early seventeenth century, and assesses the claims of scribal and printed texts to represent the 'truest' version of the poem. The 1640 text is an abbreviation of the 'more sexually explicit and more personal' (p. 125) manuscript text, and Ioppolo argues that Jonson revised the poem because the earlier version was too revealing of his 'unconstructed self, not the formally constructed and artificial self that was institutionalized in print' (p. 129).

Adam McKeown's *English Mercuries: Soldier-Poets in the Age of Shakespeare*, a study of the writings of early modern military veterans, argues that 'Jonson had little sympathy for wars and soldiers' (p. 145), in spite (or because) of his personal experiences: his Elizabethan and early Jacobean representations of soldiers are 'vitriolic', and he is keen to 'slip the grim reality of war into his audience's mind' (pp. 151–2). Finally, Boris Borukhov, 'Ben Jonson's "Widowed Wife": A New Candidate' (*N&Q* 56[2009] 86–91), suggests that the 'widowed wife' addressed in the epigram in *Underwoods* beginning 'The wisdom, Madam, of your private life', often identified as Elizabeth, countess of Rutland, is instead Frances Howard, countess of Essex.

Books Reviewed

Allard, James Robert, and Matthew R. Martin, eds. *Staging Pain, 1580–1800: Violence and Trauma in British Theater*. Ashgate. [2009] pp. 232. £55 ISBN 9780 7546 6758 8.

Bailey, Rebecca A. *Staging the Old Faith: Queen Henrietta Maria and the Theatre of Caroline England, 1625–1642*. ManUP. [2009] pp. 320. £50 ISBN 9 7807 1907 6732.

Cheney, Patrick. *Marlowe's Republican Authorship: Lucan, Liberty, and the Sublime*. Palgrave. [2009] pp. xiii + 248. £50 ISBN 9 7814 0393 3416.

Cousins, A.D., and Alison V. Scott, eds. *Ben Jonson and the Politics of Genre*. CUP. [2009] pp. 230. £53 ISBN 9 7805 2151 3784.

Drouet, Pascale, ed. *The Spectacular in and around Shakespeare*. CambridgeSP. [2009] £34.99 ISBN 9781 4438 1105 X.

Dutton, Richard, ed. *Oxford Handbook of Early Modern Drama*. OUP. [2009] pp. 752. £85 ISBN 9 7801 9928 7246.

Gurr, Andrew. *Shakespeare's Opposites: The Admiral's Company 1594–1625*. CUP. [2009] pp. 328. £53 ISBN 9 7805 2186 9034.

Houghton, L.B.T., and Maria Wyke, eds. *Perceptions of Horace: A Roman Poet and his Readers*. CUP. [2009] pp. 378. £60 ISBN 9 7805 2176 5084.

Kermode, Lloyd Edward, ed. *Three Renaissance Usury Plays*. Revels. ManUP. [2009] pp. 380. £60 ISBN 9 7807 1907 2628.

Lynch, Angelina, and Patricia Coughlan, eds. A Tragedie of Cola's Furie, or Lirenda's Miserie *by Henry Burkhead*. FCP. [2009] pp. 118. £24.95 ISBN 9 7818 4682 1080.

McKeown, Adam. *English Mercuries: Soldier Poets in the Age of Shakespeare*. VanderbiltUP. [2009] pp. 208. £53.50 (£22.50) ISBN 9 7808 2651 6633.

Meskill, Lynn S. *Ben Jonson and Envy*. CUP. [2009] pp. 242. £53 ISBN 9 7805 2151 7430.

Ostovich, Helen, Holger Schott Syme, and Andrew Griffin, eds. *Locating the Queen's Men, 1583–1603: Material Practices and Conditions of Playing*. Ashgate. [2009] pp. 284. £55 ISBN 9 7807 5466 6615.

Sisson, Charles Jasper. *Lost Plays of Shakespeare's Age*. CUP. [2009] pp. 252. £14.99 ISBN 9 7811 0800 2431.

Solga, Kim. *Violence Against Women in Early Modern Performance: Invisible Acts*. Palgrave. [2009] pp. 224. £50 ISBN 9 7802 3021 9540.

VIII

The Earlier Seventeenth Century: General and Prose

JOHN R. BURTON AND AMRITESH SINGH

This chapter has two sections: 1. General; 2. Women's Writing. Section 1 is by John R. Burton; section 2 is by Amritesh Singh.

1. General

This year sees for the first time the complete collected works of Gerrard Winstanley published together in two annotated volumes which include, aside from his published works, manuscript prose attributed to him and writings by him which appeared in other publications. The substantial introduction not only establishes Winstanley's significant contributions to the political discourse of the period, but also signals the exhaustive scholarship underpinning this modern edition: Thomas Corns, Ann Hughes, and David Loewenstein have given each individual work an introduction with bibliographical details, and each is followed by endnotes illustrating Winstanley's extensive biblical allusions. In all, the volumes form the first edition to collect Winstanley's entire known works, and with earlier attempts missing significant earlier writings, readers can now appreciate the rightful place Winstanley enjoys as a prose stylist as well as a political idealist.

The impact of Cervantes on English literature is considered by Dale Randall and Jackson Boswell in *Cervantes in Seventeenth-Century England: The Tapestry Turned*, a volume which gathers for the first time more than a thousand references to Cervantes and his works in English literature in the period up to 1700. The significant introductory passage traces the early English reception of Cervantes in general terms and the main body of the work is arranged by year, offering a unique survey of references found in both literary and non-literary printed material. Indeed, aside from the obvious translations of Cervantes' works and the many references to him in English drama and prose, the volume includes references made in diaries and letters, and thus forms a fascinating broad cultural survey. Each reference is

The Year's Work in English Studies, Volume 90 (2011) © *The Author 2011. Published by Oxford University Press on behalf of the English Association.*
doi:10.1093/ywes/mar012

annotated and contextualized, and a full bibliography permits scholars to locate each reference with ease.

In the entry Robert Burton wrote for himself in his expansive work *The Anatomy of Melancholy*, the reader is instructed that on this subject they may also see the entry 'Libraries'. So Emily Anglin informs us in her article '"The glass, the school, the book": *The Anatomy of Melancholy* and the Early Stuart University of Oxford' (*ESC* 35[2009] 55–76). Aside from the significant impact Burton's personal contribution made to the Bodleian with the gift of his collection, Anglin evaluates the impact of Oxford and its library on Burton's work as he responds to his experience of confinement with books and collections during his sequestration. Burton is also shown to respond to the burgeoning numbers of well-born students whose ambitions were aimed at advancement rather than learning (p. 72), who stood accused by Burton of eroding the humanistic basis upon which the new library had been founded. Anglin's reading of *Melancholy* is informed by Burton's sequestration to Oxford's libraries, in which he considers himself simultaneously free and imprisoned, a sentiment echoed by King James during his visit to Oxford and repeated by Burton; 'If it so that I were a prisoner, if I might have my wish, I would desire to have no other Prison than a library' (p. 63).

Colonial book ownership is evaluated in Jennifer Mylander, 'Early Modern "How-To" Books: Impractical Manuals and the Construction of Englishness in the Atlantic World' (*JEMCS* 9:i[2009] 123–46). The value and place of distinctively English early seventeenth-century texts in the New World is given prominence by Mylander, who considers them pivotal to determining identity in responding to the degeneration threatened by the new land and its indigenous people. Aside from manuals by Gervase Markham and Nicholas Culpeper, the article also references tobacco pamphlets, and in all Mylander's study explores transatlantic book circulation and the how early colonists evaluated and used texts in the formation of a new national identity.

2. Women's Writing

The initial euphoria surrounding the recovery of works by Judith Shakespeare was matched, rightly so, by a cluster of critical studies that focused on them in an exclusive manner. However, the time is ripe to study texts by women writers in conjunction with or parallel to works by their canonical male counterparts. This juxtaposition not only illuminates the manner in which female authors contributed to contemporary socio-political and cultural discourse but also rescues them from being banished into the scarcely traversed ghettoes of literary criticism by making them integral rather than ancillary to a discussion of texts from the period.

Early Modern Women and Transnational Communities of Letters is a remarkable study that highlights a steady traffic of texts and ideas that trespassed over national boundaries. This collection of essays edited by Julie Campbell and Anne Larsen foregrounds intellectual networks across Europe that facilitated female scholarship and authorship. Although the editors are sensitive to the prohibitive cultural precepts that conditioned the works of most female writers, they urge critics to recognize the literary communities that blossomed in the period that 'enabled [women writers] to step outside traditional female roles' (p. 3). This recognition, they emphasize, empowers us to read texts written by women writers as more than the material tokens of a heroic triumph over unsympathetic social norms. Crucially, Campbell and Larsen recognize both male and female literary figures as participants in and beneficiaries of these intellectual communities. Although the collection boasts several finely written essays, those of particular interest to this section are ones by Carol Pal, Sarah Ross, Sharon Arnoult, and Meredith Ray.

In her essay entitled 'Forming *Familles d'Alliance*: Intellectual Kinship in the Republic of Letters', Carol Pal challenges the 'vision of a collaborative intellectual landscape populated by learned men alone' (p. 251). Through its focus on the correspondence of the Dutch scholar Anna Maria van Schurman, Pal's meticulous study highlights the discursive strategies adopted by female scholars that allowed them to participate in the Republic of Letters. Schurman's letters to figures as notable as André Rivet, Marie de Gournay, and René Descartes, among others, reveal an eager appetite for learning characterized by daring enterprise and quiet, but unmistakable, independence. Pal highlights how women in the Republic of Letters constructed 'a layer of female mentorship to supplement the mentoring relationships they shared with their male colleagues' (p. 259). A close examination of the intellectual consanguinity that the Republic of Letters promoted demonstrates not only the conflicting attitudes towards female learning but also the strategies that female scholars adopted to confront them and the extent to which their networks with other erudite women enabled them do so.

Sarah Ross's essay, 'Esther Inglis: Linguist, Calligrapher, Miniaturist, and Christian Humanist', emphasizes the extent to which Esther Inglis's intellectual bonds with her father, Nicholas Langlois, and her husband, Bartholomew Kello, advanced her learning and its public recognition. Concurrently, Ross also establishes how this '"domestic" self-fashioning performed crucial cultural work for ambitious women in early modern Europe' (p. 168). Ross details how Inglis deployed the appreciation and admiration she received from her male peers 'to prove that she was no mere calligrapher, but a divinely inspired artist and author' (p. 175). In her attempt to chart the manner in which Inglis 'participated in a strong tradition of continental and English women intellectuals, and engaged with a European community of Christian humanists' (p. 181), Ross signals a new approach towards female scribal publication.

Sharon Arnoult studies the relationship between female authorship and devotional literature in her essay '"Some improvement to their spiritual and eternal state": Women's Prayers in the Seventeenth-Century Church of England'. Arnoult recognizes key points in 'the personal writings of women in this period' that dramatically fuse the public and private nature of prayer. In borrowing phrases and expressions from the Book of Common Prayer to author their personal prayers, women infused them with credibility and irrefutable moral strength. Further, Arnoult carefully details how 'the writing down of a prayer was understood to be the crucial first step in turning it into a common prayer, and while not every prayer that was written down might take on this aspect, every written prayer was, implicitly, extending, at least potentially, beyond its individual author, to be shared, whether between two persons, or among a familial group, or even in a worship service, whether the formal and public one of the community, or the semi-formal, quasi-public one of the household' (p. 132). Lady Pakington's prayers, Arnoult argues, simultaneously display their public and private nature and are 'surprisingly direct' in their ability to 'comment on the political through the religious' (p. 134).

The relationship between public engagement and religious devotion is also examined in Meredith Ray's essay in the collection, 'Letters and Lace: Arcangela Tarabotti and Convent Culture in Seicento Venice'. Ray questions the neat understanding of convents as a space characterized by retirement and confinement by focusing on Arcangela Tarabotti's 'incisive polemical works investigating the social and political underpinnings of enforced monachization' (p. 49). Through her study of Tarabotti's letters, Ray shows how the nun was 'a kind of cultural broker who initiated and facilitated the exchange of books (often her own), the production of lacework, and the fostering of social connections' (p. 50). Further, Ray convincingly argues that the nature of Tarabotti's participation in the contemporary intellectual milieu through published works and debates with male authors tested and transgressed the boundaries that the institution of the convent sought to set. Ray's work thus presents itself as a template to rewrite existing understanding of life within the convent.

In *Desire and Dramatic Form in Early Modern England*, Judith Haber studies the relationship between aestheticism and sexuality/sexual difference, discovering nuances that transcend the historical specificity of textual production while cautiously refraining from making claims that are essentialist in nature. Drawing inspiration from Judith Roof, Haber argues that '[c]onventional "unified" dramatic structure is regularly associated with orthodox male sexuality and disrupted by deviations from the norm' (p. 5). When studied alongside her male peers and predecessors, especially Marlowe, Cavendish's diegetic devices reveal, Haber posits, a deep scepticism of and ambivalence towards the nature and function of narrative closure. For Haber, Cavendish is evidently invested in revising her male narrative legacy by attempting to create 'something new—something that she images as the tales of young virgins' (p. 8). In displaying Cavendish as both in opposition to and the beneficiary of experimentations in narrative by her male coevals, Haber's critical stance is both shrewd and delicate. Haber argues that 'Cavendish does not entirely escape the tradition she criticizes—nor does she entirely desire to do so; but she repeatedly opposes it with evocations of the performative, the static, the singular, the unrelated' (p. 118). In her discussion of Cavendish's prefatory materials, Haber teases out the dual tones in their self-reflexive confessions of ignorance which are simultaneously disarming and defiant, inviting and belligerent. Haber sees Cavendish's plays as consistently challenging the alliance between narrative coherence and patrilinear discourse through implosive devices of cross-dressed characters, lyric arias and orations that impede dramatic pace, and abrupt and unexpected denouements. Haber highlights how in the figure of the young virgin, frequently central to her drama, Cavendish creates 'the formal equivalent of . . . non-procreative sexuality' and signals the 'possibility of telling new tales' (p. 130).

Cavendish's authorial self-representation also comes under close scrutiny from Amy Greenstadt. In her book *Rape and the Rise of the Author: Gendering Intention in Early Modern England*, Greenstadt draws a compelling analogy between the private landscape of a woman's will and authorial intention. Greenstadt posits how 'many literary writers began to compare their authorial position with that of the chaste woman threatened with rape' (p. ix). Further, she focuses on how the Augustinian notion of chastity and sexual purity as a state of mind, independent of the sexual violence that the body may have experienced, lent itself as a credible metaphor for early modern writers 'to assert the virtue and autonomy of their intentions despite the sinful misreading to which their textual bodies might be subject' (p. 20). In the chapter entitled 'Cavendish's Willing Subjects' Greenstadt parses the discursive techniques employed by Cavendish to negotiate and bargain for a position distinct and apart from her male peers. Yet even as Greenstadt details how Cavendish identified herself as an 'interloper' (p. 133) in a literary scene populated by male authors, she emphasizes how Cavendish's position in current criticism could scarcely be less so by juxtaposing her works with those of Milton, Shakespeare, and Sidney. Particularly illuminating is Greenstadt's account of how Cavendish unsettled contemporary notions of chastity by plaiting it with the anarchic impulses of creativity and authorship: 'Rather than defining chastity as the absence or suppression of desire, Cavendish describes a mental wantonness that is "*honest*, *Innocent*, and *harmlesse*" because it substitutes for and prevents the acting out of fantasies in the external world'. Furthermore, 'by designating literature as the space of "Fancies" . . . chastity [emerges as] the product of a kind of masturbatory activity women can enjoy without male participation' (p. 139). Greenstadt's study of Cavendish's *Assaulted and Pursued Chastity* leads her to conclude how the unexpected narrative treatment of the threat of rape showcases the author's virtuosity.

Bernadette Andrea laments 'the effacement of women's agency in recent studies on Anglo-Ottoman relations, most of which focus on gendered representations in male-authored travel narratives and dramas to the exclusion of sustained attention to women's cultural productions' (p. 2) and seeks to redress the balance in her book *Women and Islam in Early Modern English Literature*. Her chapter 'The Imaginary Geographies of Mary Wroth's *Urania*' approaches the text with a refreshing critical insight. Situating Mary Wroth's prose romance against the competing imperial ambitions of Christian and Islamic powers, Andrea's incisive interpretation reveals how the mass conversion to Christianity decreed by the king of Cyprus at the end of the first part of the epic romance (Cyprus, Andrea pithily observes, was under Ottoman rule at the time of *Urania*'s creation) dramatizes 'the suppression, not of a subdued colonial other, but of an immensely powerful imperial alternative' (p. 38). Andrea's careful consideration of contemporary texts in relation to Urania leads her to conclude how '[w]ith her aggressive emphasis on Christian proselytizing and her increasing fetish on whiteness, Wroth . . . positions herself on the side of western European imperialism' (p. 52). While such a representation may not be appealing to current political and cultural sensibilities, it nonetheless underscores Wroth's participation in and allegiance to contemporary perspectives and helps us achieve an understanding of her as a cultural agent rather than an outsider.

The year's publications continued to expand the canon of early modern women's writings. Rebecca Laroche's book *Medical Authority and Englishwomen's Herbal Texts 1550–1650* aims to 'advance our understanding of early modern Englishwomen's engagement with herbal signifiers and thus medical authority' (p. 2). In one of her chapters, Laroche studies the recently discovered autobiography of Elizabeth Isham in conjunction with Margaret Hoby's diary and Grace Mildmay's written legacy to her daughter and grandson. In the process Laroche urges us to be alert to 'the variety of meanings available through the representation of one kind of text, even when that text is not literary' (p. 134).

The year also saw the publication of Katherine Chidley's works as part of Ashgate's series, The Early Modern Englishwoman: A Facsimile Library of Essential Works. In her brief introduction to the book, Katharine Gillespie emphasizes how 'Chidley contributed to the 'Puritan' thinking about religious and political liberty that characterizes such seventeenth-century figures as John Milton and in some ways anticipates such theorists as John Locke with the claim that the principle of spiritual equality implies certain political rights' (p. ix). By establishing Chidley as part of a larger tradition of political activism and spiritual ideology, frequently expressed through polemical writing, Gillespie provides a contextual and critical apparatus with which to approach Chidley's writings. The edition reproduces three of Chidley's texts, all of which argue for a separation of the church and the state and put forward a persuasive case for individual freedom of conscience: *The Ivstification of the Independant Chvrches of Christ* [1641], *A New-Yeares-Gift, or A Brief Exhortation to Mr Thomas Edwards* [1645], and *Good Counsell, to the Petitioners for Presbyterian Government* [1645].

Finally, it is heartening to see that the commendable forays into researching early modern women's writings are being matched by similar advances in pedagogy. *The Cambridge Companion to Early Modern Women's Writing*, edited by Laura Knoppers, is an extremely desirable addition to the growing corpus of critical writings on the subject. Knoppers notes how the *Companion* offers 'basic historical, methodological and textual information [to] upper-level undergraduates, graduate students and scholars'. The edition has essays by the leading critics in the field, including Danielle Clarke, Wendy Wall, James Daybell, Marta Straznicky, and Susanne Wood. It is thus likely to be a vital resource for teaching and to prove itself indispensable to fledgling scholars in the field.

Books Reviewed

Andrea, Bernadette. *Women and Islam in Early Modern English Literature*. CUP. [2009] pp. 196. pb £17 ISBN 9780 5211 2176 7.

Campbell, Julie D., and Anne Larsen, eds. *Early Modern Women and Transnational Communities of Letters*. Ashgate. [2009] pp. 352. £65 ISBN 9780 7546 6738 4.

Corns, Thomas N., Ann Hughes, and David Loewenstein, eds. *The Complete Works of Gerrard Winstanley*, 2 vols. [2009] pp. 600. (vol. 1), pp. 465 (vol. 2). £180 ISBN 9 7801 9957 6067.

Gillespie, Katharine. *Katharine Chidley*. The Early Modern Englishwoman: A Facsimile Library of Essential Works—Printed Writings, 1641–1700, series 2, pt. 4. Ashgate. [2009] pp. 142. £50 ISBN 9780 7546 6231 0.

Greenstadt, Amy. *Rape and the Rise of the Author: Gendering Intention in Early Modern England*. Ashgate. [2009] pp. 204. £55 ISBN 9780 7546 6274 7.

Haber, Judith. *Desire and Dramatic Form in Early Modern England*. CUP. [2009] pp. 224. £53 ISBN 9780 5215 1867 3.

Knoppers, Laura Lunger, ed. *The Cambridge Companion to Early Modern Women's Writing*. Cambridge Companions to Literature. CUP. [2009] pp. 344. pb £19 ISBN 9780 5217 1242 2.

Laroche, Rebecca. *Medical Authority and Englishwomen's Herbal Texts 1550–1650*. Ashgate. [2009] pp. 208. £55 ISBN 9780 7546 6678 3.

Randall, Dale B.J., and Jackson C. Boswell. *Cervantes in Seventeenth-Century England: The Tapestry Turned*. OUP. [2009] pp. xlii + 719. £98 ISBN 9 7801 9953 9529.

IX

Milton and Poetry, 1603–1660

DAVID AINSWORTH, JAMES DOELMAN,
GREGORY KNEIDEL AND ALVIN SNIDER

This chapter has four sections: 1. General; 2. Herbert; 3. Donne; 4. Milton. Section 1 is by David Ainsworth; section 2 is by James Doelman; section 3 is by Gregory Kneidel; section 4 is by Alvin Snider.

1. General

In '"Pulchrum Spargitur Hic Chaos": Crashaw's Meta-Commentary' (*JEMCS* 9:i[2009] 147–59), Stephen Guy-Bray writes about one of Crashaw's Latin poems, 'Bulla' ('bubble'). 'Bulla', published at the end of Daniel Heinsius's *Crepundia Siliana*, a commentary on the Latin poem *Punica*, sets out to describe a bubble through poetry. Guy-Bray argues that Crashaw deliberately sets himself an impossible task in order make a comment upon writing generally and scholarly writing specifically. If a bubble is beautiful because of its disorganization, its chaos, then perhaps a poetic text can be called beautiful for the same reasons. Guy-Bray suggests that Crashaw plays off of other meanings of 'Bulla', contrasting the association with childhood ('bulla' as a young boy's clothing) to a more modern meaning of 'bulla' as 'bull', an important document associated with authority. Crashaw emphasizes the former meaning while noting the latter, suggesting that he wants to explore the idea of writing (and poetry) as a childish or insubstantial thing, a mere bubble. Guy-Bray relates 'Bulla' to Crashaw's epigrammatic poetry and to 'The Flaming Heart', which also represents the inadequacy of representation while offering a textual description of a visual illustration which clearly cannot capture its subject as well as a poem. The poem itself, however, is ultimately no more than a bubble, a chaotic and unstable object easily carried out of sight. Guy-Bray concludes by suggesting that his own commentary lacks substance, offering Elliott Carter's 'Symphonia' as a musical response to the poem which better captures the mingling of artistic forms addressed in and embodied by Crashaw's poem.

In 'Richard Crashaw's Indigestible Poetics' (*MP* 107:i[2009] 32–51), Kimberly Johnson examines Crashaw's epigram on Luke 11, arguing that

The Year's Work in English Studies, Volume 90 (2011) © *The Author 2011. Published by Oxford University Press on behalf of the English Association.*
doi:10.1093/ywes/mar014

his poem both engages with the problematic overtones of the Eucharist—sexual, incestuous, cannibalistic—and with the hermeneutic challenge it presents. Crashaw, Johnson argues, does not refute transubstantiation but engages with the difficulty in perceiving eucharistic transformation, figuring the challenge of faith through a challenge of language. In translating his own poem from Latin into English, Crashaw moves from the ritualistic reiteration of 'bibet' to the ambiguous and troubling 'suck', easily associated with erotic or physical contexts outside the bounds of eucharistic ritual. Crashaw, Johnson argues, problematizes Christ's body by manifesting it physically and materially. She also considers Crashaw's poems on the circumcision and Passion, where he again challenges the orthodox and sacramental elements of the stories with corporeal terms which stress indigestibility, an inability to fully reconcile symbol with physical reality. Johnson cautions that the hermeneutic challenge Crashaw investigates cannot be simply resolved along orthodox lines, but warns against seeing Crashaw as embracing blissful profligacy. Rather, she emphasizes the ambivalence Crashaw feels towards the Eucharist, his discomfort with the very ambiguity he brings out in his poems. Crashaw is not, Johnson suggests, embracing the material body so much as he is caught up in it.

William M. Russell concentrates upon the role of reason in Crashaw's poetry in '"Spell it wrong to read it right": Crashaw's Assessment of Human Language' (*JDJ* 28[2009] 119–45). He argues that Crashaw writes, not to settle doctrinal questions, but to engage with them, to interrogate and not to answer. Across a range of Crashaw's poems, Russell examines a series of inversions between hope and despair, suggesting that Crashaw finds the most hope where he finds fallen language to be redeemable or redeemed. Language mediates between humanity and the divine, but the inherent instability of human language forces Crashaw to vacillate, knowing as he does that language must often work against itself to act as mediator. Russell coins the phrase 'doubtful hope' to describe the resulting emotional response, tracing moments in Crashaw's poetry where he perceives this dynamic between hope and despair to operate. Russell also examines paradoxical language in Crashaw's poetry, suggesting that such paradoxes may communicate something of the divine mystery, pointing towards the ineffable by speaking something which cannot be spoken literally. The breakdown of language in one of Crashaw's poems, then, represents not a failure or an erasure but a generative incapacity, where what cannot be said nevertheless registers itself through the paradoxical attempt to articulate it.

In '"Times trans-shifting": Chronology and the Misshaping of Herrick' (*ELR* 39:i[2009] 163–96), John Creaser argues for chronological caution in dating and historically interpreting Herrick's *Hesperides*. Taking a wide range of historicist critics to task for assuming composition dates for poems which don't match the chronological evidence, Creaser suggests that the resultant misreadings also misconstrue *Hesperides* as a coherent response to its historical moment of publication (1648). Creaser presents Herrick's collection as diverse and contradictory, with Herrick himself concentrating on the level of the poem, not the book. He also expresses severe reservations about political or religious interpretations of Herrick's poetry which do not acknowledge that, for Herrick, poetry itself is the end and not a means to some other end. Creaser offers a schedule of Herrick's poetic production, placing many poems in a range of a few years within which they were written and providing approximate dates for 190 poems in total. He concludes that *Hesperides* is indeed a life's work, covering poetry spread across a forty-year period, and that Herrick's greatest poetic accomplishments come earlier in his career, the product of high ambition not yet dashed by the English Civil War. For Creaser, the late Herrick is content with limitation and at times merely goes through the motions of poetic production. And Herrick's poetic exhaustion does not reflect unity in his poetic collection, but rather continuity, an association between poems which relies on no larger narrative or framework to make sense out of it. Creaser concludes with a sample of his method for dating Herrick's poems and then provides the schedule itself.

In 'Embracing Lucia: Reading Robert Herrick's "The Vine"' (*JDJ* 28[2009] 147–58), Abigail Scherer argues against a purely phallocentric reading of that poem, suggesting that the vine may permit the speaker of the poem to still his gaze's object and thus evoke the imagined ideal of woman through poetry. Scherer turns towards criticism of 'The Vine' as focused on language, on the delights and limits of aesthetic discourse, as an extension of her interpretation of the poem's erotic content. The fantasy of the poem, Scherer writes, involves not simply an erotic fantasy, but a poet's fantasy that he might entwine and preserve a feminine ideal within the lines of language. The sinuous motion of the vine throughout the poem, then, becomes a metaphor for the ways in which the poetic lines sketch out and define Lucia. 'The Vine', Scherer argues, represents not a simple bondage fantasy, but an attempt to bind Lucia aesthetically, both containing and preserving her within the poem. When the speaker awakes, then, the promise of eternity bound within the vine and the poem is thwarted by mortality and inadequacy.

In '"Devils Liquore" and "Virgins Milke": Fashion, Fetishism and Jonson's Line' (*Parergon* 26:i[2009] 141–73), Elizabeth Moran discusses Jonson's satires of fashion, concentrating on *Epicoene* and *The Devil is an Ass* but also examining many of Jonson's poems. In particular, Moran considers Jonson's concern that fashion, as part of a growing consumer culture, might endanger or destroy the family line and displace a generative appetite for bodies to a fetishistic appetite for objects. In particular, she considers the shift from clothing as a means of identifying one's family to fashion as a mode of self-expression, and she demonstrates how Jonson satirizes the latter trend and sets it in direct conflict with the former. She suggests that Jonson links fashion and abandonment of the family line with self-consumption, the wasting of resources meant to be passed on to future generations of the family in the name of immediate consumption. Jonson links modish women to sexual licentiousness which is either barren or produces bastards, while he links women of chaste privacy to the generative capacity vital to sustain and propagate the family line. Moran also considers the complexities inherent in Jonson's criticism of fashion while he works in a trade exempted from sumptuary laws and driven in part by fashion. Jonson, she suggests, tries to resolve these complexities through appeal to a patrilineal tradition of *imitatio*, situating his own works within a long line of poetry and drama stretching back to ancient Rome. Moran argues that Jonson ultimately places blame on men who fetishize women and thus transfer their desire from an actual woman who can reproduce to an object (or a woman treated as an object), which endangers the family line by threatening its propagation.

In 'Envy, Eunoia, and Ethos in Jonson's Poems on Shakespeare and Drayton' (*SIP* 106:iv[2009] 441–55), Marlin E. Blaine discusses the strategies Jonson uses when writing encomiums of other authors to compensate for his own reputation as an egotist. Jonson structures his poems in praise of Shakespeare and Drayton to disavow envy and stress his good will (or *eunoia*) towards the writers he praises. Approaching his task from a rhetorical viewpoint, Jonson heeds his own warnings in *Discoveries* and constitutes his poetic *ethos* with care to acknowledge and refute his own reputation for envy. Regarding his poem on Shakespeare, Blaine argues that Jonson opens with a potentially egocentric examination of poetry and praise in order to conjure the spectre of his own envy and exorcise it from the poem. Through a concentration on the rhetorical processes of encomium, Jonson underlines the appropriateness of his own expression of praise in an attempt to assert its genuine character. In addressing Drayton, Jonson presents himself as a generous judge to make an ethical appeal to his readers that his praise of Drayton represents good will and good judgement. Blaine concludes his essay with a brief acknowledgement that Jonson's rhetorical efforts failed, with his two poems considered both now and in the period as evidence of his envy.

Lisa Celovsky examines Jonson's 'To Penshurst' in 'Ben Jonson and Sidneian Legacies of Hospitality' (*SIP* 106:ii[2009] 178–206), placing emphasis on Jonson's association between masculine behaviour and hospitality in *The Forest*. Celovsky suggests that *The Forest* uses the lives of the Sidneys to imply a partnership between a rising capitalist movement and the restorative powers of hospitality. Jonson can also critique elements of a new capitalism through reminders of old standards of civic obligation. He sets past traditions of hospitality within a context of order, relating masculine practices of householding to order in the state. Hospitality becomes a link between the modern Sidneys and their ancestors, a legacy which the current Sidney family lives up to magnificently. Celovsky provides an overview of the period's understanding of hospitality as a masculine virtue, turning to letters between Barbara and Robert Sidney as evidence of their own division of labour. Celovsky also considers the tensions between a poem which sets Sidney's hospitality as an example to be emulated and a poem which attempts to write Sidney as an exemplary host in order to praise him, in effect comparing 'To Penshurst' to itself and questioning the dynamic between constructing hospitality and constructing Robert Sidney as hospitable. This article acknowledges and examines a range of tensions associated with masculinity and hospitality in *The Forest*, in particular reading 'To Sir Robert Wroth' as an example of a man who falls short. It concludes with an examination of inheritance and legacy, considering how *The Forest* holds out the future potential of the Sidney family in direct relation to the legacy of its past generations.

In '"Owning" in Aemilia Lanyer's *Salve Deus Rex Judæorum* ("Hail God King of the Jews")' (*SIP* 106:i[2009] 52–75), Audrey E. Tinkham suggests that

Lanyer reinterprets classical civic virtue by questioning whether a notion of virtuous citizenship can properly exclude women. By conjoining intellectual property and real property, Lanyer authorizes herself as a citizen and transforms recognition of her as an author into recognition of women's right to speak and thus shape the commonwealth. Lanyer draws upon the disjunction between the language of patronage in civil or religious contexts and the ends of that patronage: in civil contexts, individual advancement; in religious contexts, union with God. By stressing the meaning of the word 'virtue', Lanyer argues that women ought to speak and act publicly. Tinkham places Lanyer's poem within the context of classical humanism, noting that she draws upon Christian notions of virtue to refute the Aristotelian claim that women's inferiority prevents them from being citizens. If humility and lowliness are not impediments to virtue or honour, as they are not in a Christian context, then a woman's inferior status need not bar her from civic virtue. Tinkham approaches the tensions in the text between gender differences and class differences from a perspective of female public agency which implicates both kinds of difference. A woman of higher class may be empowered to speak but may also be muzzled by her status, while Lanyer herself is empowered through her ownership of her own speech. As an author, Lanyer possesses ownership in a form distinct from the often contested right to a title or an estate. Lanyer bolsters her own ownership rights by likening herself to Christ, appropriating an authority rooted in virtue and humble or lowly origins. She strengthens this association by feminizing Christ, emphasizing his speech in particular as feminine. Christ's authority thus justifies Lanyer's position that women deserve to be, and indeed should act as, virtuous citizens.

2. Herbert

The year saw no book-length studies of Herbert, but there was a rich supply of articles (some based on conference proceedings), particularly from the two issues of the *George Herbert Journal*. While the poems of *The Temple* continued to elicit finely focused close readings—more than is common in our time with other poets—Herbert's writings and activities beyond these poems also came in for significant treatment.

In '"Generous Ambiguity" Revisited: A Herbert for All Seasons' (*GHJ* 30[2006–7] 19–41), published in 2009, Daniel Doerksen offers a more historically grounded understanding of the 'generous ambiguity' that Louis Martz first identified in Herbert. His fine overview presents both a Church of England and a Herbert that were more Calvinist than is often supposed. His description of the early Stuart church owes much to Anthony Milton and persuasively suggests that our notions of 'Calvinism' have been too often shaped by looking at its most extreme expressions. Thus, he identifies Herbert as a moderate, Calvinist, conforming figure, whose theology encouraged a pastoral rather than combative approach. This, along with his wide reading in both Roman Catholic and Protestant writings, equipped Herbert to reach out in *The Temple* to different Christians at different points, thus producing the 'generous ambiguity' celebrated by Martz. The portrait of Herbert may not be new, perhaps, but the article's emphasis on a more nuanced, less caricatured Calvinism than is often encountered is an important corrective.

Herbert's 'generous ambiguity' is also manifest in the breadth of readers he attracted in the decades following his death. Helen Wilcox's 'In the *Temple* Precincts: George Herbert and Seventeenth-Century Community-Making' (in Sell and Johnson, eds., *Writing and Religion in England, 1558–1689: Studies in Community-Making and Cultural Memory*) explores the 'textual communities' of Herbert readers that crossed denominational bounds. She argues that many readers were conscious of the broad popularity and influence of *The Temple*, and that this was a community gathered largely by religious rather than literary interest. The term 'community' here might be stretched to fit the volume of papers in which this article appears, but Wilcox's discussion is a rich example of reception history, showing the breadth of Herbert's readers and the variety of purposes to which Herbert's poems were put. Her idea of 'sub-groups' comprised of 'family, location, epistolary network and religious groups' is the strongest part of the article. The title of *The Temple* itself offered fruitful ambiguity: to ceremonialists it was a reminder of the significance of formal worship; for non-conformists it could be read as a reference to the individual heart as Temple of the Holy Spirit.

Anne-Marie Miller Blaise, 'George Herbert's Distemper: An Honest Shepherd's Remedy for Melancholy' (*GHJ* 30[2006–7] 59–82), suggests that Herbert's crisis of the mid-1620s might be understood as melancholy, and that this might reconcile some of the debate over whether his move towards the church was pragmatically driven by frustrated ambition or piously motivated. While 'melancholy' is not mentioned in *The Temple* or *The Country Parson*, in Herbert's condition she finds causes and symptoms described in Burton's *Anatomy of Melancholy*. While Blaise begins with this biographical supposition, the bulk of the article explores the melancholic aspects of Herbert's *Memoriae Matris Sacrum* and *The Temple*. The grief-based pastoral melancholy of the former is eventually turned away from as the poet seeks 'pastoral employment'. Most significant is her suggestion that in *The Temple* melancholy (including or especially religious melancholy) is tempered by the sacrament of Communion, and that in turning to song and 'employment' Herbert is drawing on traditional antidotes to the condition.

Joyce Ransome's 'George Herbert, Nicholas Ferrar, and the "Pious Works" of Little Gidding' (*GHJ* 31[2007–8] 1–19), published in 2009, provides an excellent overview of Herbert and Nicholas Ferrar's work with Juan de Valdes's *One Hundred and Ten Considerations*. Working from a thorough understanding of Little Gidding, Ransome sees the translation and Herbert's notes as part of the larger project there, and suggests that Ferrar and others found in Valdes's writings an emphasis upon experience led by the Holy Spirit that fitted with their developing practices at Little Gidding, which included vigils and mortification. This heterodox Roman Catholic of the previous century offered views on justification that appealed to the conciliatory approach of Herbert and Ferrar. She finds their work on Valdes consistent with the broader project at Little Gidding in cultivating communal and personal piety, and with their desire for Christian unity.

This same work is the subject of 'Holiness as a Psychological State in Herbert's *Briefe Notes on Valdesso's Considerations*' (*GHJ* 30[2006–7] 109–24) by Sean McDowell, who argues that, in these responses to the Spanish Catholic, Herbert shows his typical concern with the cultivation of personal holiness. Repeatedly Herbert notes the effect of the Holy Spirit on the psychological state of the believer; as part of this McDowell suggests that earlier scholars have neglected that 'motions' in the period might refer to merely human 'passions' or affections as well as those prompted by the Holy Spirit.

In '"Resorting to Sermons": The Place of Preaching in William Baspoole's *The Pilgrime* and George Herbert's *The Country Parson*' (*GHJ* 30[2006–7] 42–58) Kathryn Walls compares William Baspoole's *The Pilgrime* (*c*.1630–3) with the original French medieval manuscript work upon which it was based, and finds that the text and illustrations augment the significance of preaching. She goes on to suggest that Herbert in a similar way indirectly affirms the balanced combination of preaching and sacraments in his *Country Parson*.

In '"Shepherds are honest people": Herbert and Pastoral' (*GHJ* 30[2006–7] 83–95), Margaret Turnbull identifies Herbert as an anti-pastoral poet, one who rejects the distorting fictions of that tradition as represented particularly in 'pastoral love-lyrics' (in contrast to, say, Spenser). Such poems as 'Jordan (I)' engage in resistance to the humanist tendency to syncretic absorption of classical traditions into Christian verse. She argues that Herbert places God (rather than himself as poet) against the aspirations of pastoral poets. Ultimately, she suggests that Herbert offers a 'true pastoral', one which takes seriously his responsibilities as pastor, and hails the 'true shepherd and king' in such poems as 'The 23d Psalme'.

In 'Typology and the Self in George Herbert's "Affliction" Poems' (*GHJ* 31[2007–8] 63–82), A.E. Watkins extends Daniel Rubey's earlier (1980) argument that the 'Affliction' poems show a development from self-absorption to devotion by stressing the significance of Renaissance concepts of the body–self relationship. Watkins finds typology at work in the series as a whole, not just at its end. The article is compelling in arguing that Herbert's poems find self-identity not in the body, but in relation to others as known through the Scriptures: 'Their storie pennes and sets us down'. It first provides an overview of recent studies on corporeality in the period, and then turns to the relationship of typology to corporeality. Watkins finds in 'Affliction (I)' a 'typological pairing of the speaker's body with Eden' (p. 64) as he mistakenly thinks in the early stanzas that his life is an unfallen Paradise. In the final poem of the sequence the speaker finds a new role as a 'Christological type': his body is now recognized as a member of Christ's body (which is also the Church) rather than as the enclosed Garden.

In her study of the literary uses of Mary Magdalene in early modern poetry, *The Maudlin Impression: English Literary Images of Mary Magdalene, 1550–1700*, Patricia Badir considers Herbert's 'Marie Magdalene' within the context of emblematic illustrations of her washing of Christ's feet. She finds in the poem's epigrammatic conciseness a parallel to visual depictions of an already well-known scene. She argues that the poem is like many other treatments of Mary Magdalene in that it does not present a close affinity of the central figure with the poet's voice (and thus rejects Schoenfeldt's perception of sexual unease in the poem). The image of Mary is placed in the background by the poem, as 'it nimbly illustrates the grace that lies at the center of reformed piety' (p. 144). Finally, Badir suggests that the relationship of visual moment and textual commentary in Herbert's poem has affinities to the juxtaposition of image and biblical text in the Little Gidding *Harmonies*.

Warren M. Liew also revisits the topic of Herbert's use of erotic language and tropes in 'Reading the Erotic in George Herbert's Sacramental Poetics' (*GHJ* 31[2007–8] 33–62), and convincingly places these in the context of Augustinian understandings of the Incarnation. Like poetic wit, bodily desire is both worthy and suspect, and as language is fallen, its capacity to articulate a prelapsarian sexuality is limited, apart from a revelation of transcendent divine grace. Thus, like Badir, Liew probes the anxieties about erotic language identified by Michael Schoenfeldt.

Focusing on 'Jordan (I)', 'Easter Wings', and 'Prayer (I)', Jean-Louis Breteau (*Revue LISA/LISA e-journal* 7:iii[2009] 120–40) compares Herbert's use of biblical imagery and typology with that of John Donne.

Among articles providing interpretations of individual poems the most ground-breaking is Roberta Albrecht's '"The Pulley": Rundles, Ropes, and Ladders in John Wilkins, Ramon Lull, and George Herbert' (*GHJ* 30[2006–7] 1–18). Through an explanation of the wide variety of complex pulleys in use at the time, Albrecht shows how the compound pulley is that which is consistent with the details of the poem, particularly the 'tossing' up of a man to God. The second half of the article explores the pervasive influence of the medieval philosopher Ramon Lull's 'Ladder of Ascent and Descent' in the Renaissance, and how this is also part of the context of 'The Pulley'. Thus, 'Herbert invents a machine that combines Lullian logic with Archimedes's concept of mechanical advantage in order to lift an otherwise too heavy object to God' (p. 15).

In 'Herbert's "Peace"' (*Explicator* 67[2009] 105–8), Philip Harlan Christensen offers a clear and succinct close reading of the poem that says little that is new about it, but persuasively argues that the 'reverent good old man's' words at the end render it an invitation to readers to 'Take of this grain'. Also noteworthy is the article's emphasis on the numerical structuring of the poem.

To the scholarship on George Herbert and music, Jonathan Nauman, 'Herbert and Monteverdi: Sacred Echo and the Italian Baroque' (*GHJ* 30[2006–7] 96–108), adds the suggestion that Herbert's poem 'Heaven' responds to sacred Italian echo songs (such as Monteverdi's 'Vespers of the Blessed Virgin'), and that his brother Edward Herbert served as a conduit for such influence. He argues that Herbert's poem acts as a cautious Protestant response to the Counter-Reformation echo poem, as it questions the echo until certain of its consistency with Holy Scripture. While he does not use the term 'generous ambiguity', Arthur F. Kinney's 'George Herbert's Early Readers' (*BJJ* 16[2009] 77–98) shows something like that to be achieved in 'Love (III)'. He argues that in spite of its basis in the Holy Communion service of the Book of Common Prayer, it is open and ambiguous enough to draw in Roman Catholic and Puritan readers as well.

In a second article, 'Herbert, Coleridge, Hopkins: Usefulness' (*GHJ* 31[2007–8] 83–111), Margaret Turnbull explores the long-noted dependence of Coleridge's 'Work without Hope' and Hopkins's 'Thou art indeed just' on Herbert's 'Employment (I)'. Overall, she shows how the religious thought of the three poets led to distinct representations of the meaning of work. For Herbert, the ultimate work is the praise of God, from whom also flows the ability to perform that work. The poet aspires to do so in words, where the flower and bees offer a mute work of praise. While 'Employment (I)' and other Herbert poems articulate the dismay and frustration of one who feels that he falls short, the poems stand both as works of praise in themselves and as that which might prompt praise (of God) in others. Coleridge 'uses Herbert's words but refuses his theology' (p. 97); his difference from Nature at work is a manifestation of a separation from Nature, rather than from God. His desire to work as poet/priest/prophet of Nature, as expressed in the poems of his early career, has been stymied. The focus remains upon his own situation, rather than what his work might offer to others or God. Thus, the indebtedness of the poem to Herbert's is on the level of imagery and situation only, not the significance of that situation. While the influence of 'Employment (I)' on 'Thou art indeed just' is less certain, Hopkins's poem shares the earlier poem's theology and understanding of poetic purpose, even while it pushes beyond that poem in its probing of God's justice. Like Herbert, Hopkins aspires to work for God, not for the wreath of poetic accomplishment sought by Coleridge.

The reception of Herbert's works today goes far beyond the academy, and his place as part of our living culture is manifest in two projects. Published with volume 31 of the *George Herbert Journal* was Paulette S. Goll's DVD, 'Setting George Herbert's Lyrics', a collection of musical settings of the poetry from Herbert's time up to our own. Also appearing in this issue (*GHJ* 31[2007–8] 20–32) are the results of the George Herbert Poetry Competition, 2008, which recognized poems 'written in the style of George Herbert', along with commentary in a Judges' Report by David Jaspar and Helen Wilcox.

3. Donne

In the unusual absence of a full monograph devoted to Donne, two studies of attempts to recontextualize his love poetry stand out as the most sustained and original contributions to Donne studies in 2009. The first study is actually a clutch of essays published in the *John Donne Journal* on lithographs made by the American artist June Wayne in the 1950s to accompany various Donne poems. With her Parisian collaborator Marcel Durassier, Wayne produced some fifty of these lithographs; the most important are the fifteen prints collected (along with three 'rejected' prints) in her 1958 *John Donne Songs & Sonets*, a *livre d'artiste* that, while never technically lost, had hitherto escaped the notice of Donne scholars. 'A Gallery of Words and Images' (*JDJ* 28[2009] 173–96) reproduces eleven of Wayne's plates with their accompanying poems. Four interpretative essays follow. Paul A. Parrish's '"Forming new wholes": John Donne and June Wayne' (*JDJ* 28[2009] 217–26), provides a cogent history of Wayne's engagement with Donne and stresses her strongly romantic visual interpretations of his poems. In 'Donne's "Breake of Day" and the Female Perspective in June Wayne's Timeless Lithograph' (*JDJ* 28[2009] 197–206), Helen B. Brooks shows that Wayne's image for this poem, an unusual dramatic monologue with a female speaker, creates for the lovers a 'womb-like space' around an ominously eclipsed sun in such a way that the 'subjective inner reality—or sanctuary—of the female single speaker' becomes 'the cognitive locus of the poem' (p. 203). In his superb essay, '1590/1950: John Donne, June Wayne, and Concrete Expressionism' (*JDJ* 28[2009] 207–16), Jonathan F.S. Post situates the Wayne Donne in the context of earlier print and text collaborations, from Dürer's *Apocalypse* [1496] to the Matisse-illustrated New York edition of Joyce's *Ulysses* [1935]. Noting that Donne in the 1950s was at the pinnacle of his New Critical prestige, Post further positions Wayne's folio-sized edition of Donne as a pointed rejoinder to the abstract expressionism of the 1950s that was associated 'with the post-war empire, with New York City, not Paris, as the new economic and cultural capital of the world, and . . . with the work of male painters like de Kooning and Pollock with their huge canvasses' (p. 213). And lastly, Ann Hurley, author of *John Donne's Poetry and Early Modern Visual Culture* [2005], and Jebah Baum, a New York City visual artist, collaborate on the longer article, 'June Wayne and John Donne: Reverse *Ekphrasis* Exemplified and Explored' (*JDJ* 28[2009] 227–50). Baum describes in detail the process of lithographic print-making and he explains that it was a dying art that Wayne helped to revive thanks to a Ford Foundation grant that she was awarded soon after her Donne book (she used the grant funding to establish the celebrated Tamarind Lithography Workshop). Hurley offers exemplary readings of several Wayne prints, especially those of 'Twicknam Garden' (pp. 238–41), 'A Valediction: Forbidding Mourning' (pp. 241–5), and 'The Exstasie' (pp. 245–8). Hurley and Baum conclude that the strongest connection between Donne and Wayne is that they both typically 'depict thinking about [an] image rather than the image itself' (pp. 248–9). Wayne 'responded visually to [Donne's] verbal skills' and gave 'visual embodiment to [his poetry's] intensification of her own effort to produce the "seeable"' (p. 249).

The second study that recontextualizes Donne's love poetry is Joshua Eckhardt's monograph *Manuscript Verse Collectors and the Politics of Anti-Courtly Love Poetry*. Donne is central to Eckhardt's broader study because he 'played a major role' in forming the genre of the anti-courtly (or anti-Petrarchan) love poem and because verse 'collectors made Donne the most popular poet in early modern literary manuscripts by preserving some 5,000 extant copies of his individual works' (p. 6). Both confirming and complicating recent political readings of Donne's love poetry—especially the often copied elegies 'The Anagram', 'The Autumnall', and the ubiquitous 'To His Mistress Going To Bed'—Eckhardt identifies manuscript verse collections that seem to position Donne's anti-courtly love poetry purposefully with or against explicitly political libels. Eckhardt discusses (and, in several instances, reproduces in an appendix) political libels on the major scandals of Donne's adult life. There are chapters on Sir Walter Ralegh and his colonialist ambitions; on the sordid Overbury affair (1613–16); on the 1623 controversy over the Spanish Match, the possible marriage between Prince Charles and the Infanta, Donna Maria Anna of Spain, orchestrated by James I's favourite George Villiers, soon to be duke of Buckingham; and on the assassination of Buckingham in August 1628 at the hands of the army officer John Felton. Eckhardt's epilogue examines the print history of three of Donne's most copied and bawdiest anti-courtly poems, 'To His Mistress Going To Bed', 'Loves Progress', and 'Loves War', which very early on ran afoul of the censors and which were not published in a single-author volume until the seventh, 1669, edition of Donne's *Poems*. Eckhardt takes earlier, mid-century printings of these poems in multi-author anthologies as examples of Donne's anti-courtly poetry being 'redeployed' against a puritanical Protectorate government that was 'determined to advance moral reform' (p. 162). Of all these chapters, the most complex is Eckhardt's investigation of the Overbury affair, in which Donne's patron Robert Carr, the future earl of Somerset, and his wife Frances Howard, whose marriage to Robert Devereux, third earl of Essex, had only recently been nullified, were convicted of conspiring to murder Carr's mentor, Sir Robert Overbury, whose vacated position as secretary to Carr Donne briefly filled. Donne wrote an epithalamion celebrating the 1613 Somerset wedding, and he attempted to gather together his disparate poems in order to produce a volume dedicated to Somerset (this volume, of course, never materialized). Eckhardt speculates that it was Donne's attempt to gather in his poems that led directly to a burst of scribal copying of them, often in the context of Somerset libels, so that the 'verse collectors established an association between the sexualized and disgraced women who are the subjects of the two genres' (pp. 84–5). In doing so, these 'verse collectors effectively turned Donne's writings against his own patron' (p. 85).

Of the other three dozen or so essays and articles on Donne from 2009, several split Eckhardt's dual focus on Donne's love poetry and political satire and treat these topics more or less separately. In 'Reading 'More Wit' in Donne and Catullus' (*BJJ* 16[2009] 33–56), M. Thomas Hester argues that Donne took from Catullus a 'paradoxical amatory and poetic *problem*' (p. 34), specifically a novel desire, one 'without name in [Catullus's] culture', for a love that 'transcend[s] the social, the political, and the sexual' (p. 37). According to Hester, several of Donne's profane and sacred poems reiterate 'Catullus's vexed portraits of sexual love's limitations as well as [its] overwhelming promise of transcendence' and employ 'the language of an incarnate "impossible love" to portray... just what Catullus's powerful plaints of desire strove to name' (p. 38). In 'Eying the Thought Awry: The Anamorphosis of John Donne's Poetry' (*ELR* 39:i[2009] 141–62) Anna Riehl links the logic and rhetoric of 'The Exstasie' and 'To M.M.H.' to the Renaissance vogue for anamorphic or perspectival painting. As in anamorphic paintings, 'The Exstasie' attempts 'to imagine the viewpoint that in a flash will turn 'nothingness' into a shape, make the souls visible and audible, and thus exchange confusion for profound understanding' (p. 148). Likewise imitating the experience of viewing anamorphic art, the verse epistle 'To M.M.H.' graphically recounts the confused and voyeuristic adventures of Donne's 'mad paper' in a way that leads the reader 'from nonsensical obscurity to muteness to brilliantly sensible speech to silence that is no longer troublesome but instead advantageous' (p. 157). Both poems proceed according to the 'three act' 'drama of anamorphosis': 'puzzlement, recognition, and mediation' (pp. 161–2).

A.W. Barnes includes two chapters on Donne in *Post-Closet Masculinities in Early Modern England*. In 'Juggling John Donne's Manliness' (pp. 31–55), Barnes argues that Donne defines masculinity in *The First Anniversary* 'by employing the rhetoric of science and in particular the advances in anatomy in which the flesh of a woman was meant to construct a new world in which masculinity could be firmly grounded' (p. 33). Likewise, many of Donne's *Songs and Sonets* use Copernican cosmographic theory in order to 'construct his masculine subjectivity somewhere in between the threatening body of Woman and the impossibility of leaving her body behind' (p. 55). A subsequent chapter, entitled 'Dissecting John Donne's Masculinity', traces the critical tradition of labelling Donne's verse 'masculine' or 'manly' and finds in Renaissance alchemical treatises analogues to Donne's treatment of 'distilled' masculinity in his love poetry (p. 73). Barnes concludes that Donne's 'masculinity is queer' because it is a 'de-essentialized identity' positioned between 'the body of Woman' and 'the figure of the sodomite', neither of whom is 'given a voice' and neither of whom 'is able to respond to Donne's positioning' (pp. 77–8). And in 'Sighs and Tears: Biological Signals and John Donne's "Whining Poetry"' (*P&L* 33:ii[2009] 329–44), Michael A. Winkelman evaluates from the perspective of evolutionary biology Donne's conventionally weepy lovers. Casting the lover's tears as a form of 'costly signaling' (p. 329), Winkelman argues that Donne recognized 'the potential duplicity of female weeping' and that his innovative adaptation of this tired Petrarchan conceit can be thought of as itself as kind of costly signal designed to 'evince an intellect correlating to high mating fitness' (p. 331).

In his chapter on Donne in *English Mercuries: Soldier Poets in the Age of Shakespeare* ('John Donne's Emblem of War', pp. 63–82), Adam N. McKeown reviews Donne's military adventures during the 1590s and surveys the martial imagery in his sermons and especially in his youthful verse epistles and elegies. Linking Donne's writings on war to an emblem tradition that depicts it in 'complicated and internally conflicted' terms (p. 105), McKeown argues that for Donne war is both 'a consummate terror that must be avoided' and 'a focal point for a country and its citizens, a testing ground for personal valor, and a means of learning true humility not easily replaced in peacetime or even understood outside the context of war' (p. 102). In 'Jonson's Metempsychosis Revisited: Patronage and Religious Controversy' (in Cousins and Scott, eds., *Ben Johnson and the Politics of Genre*, pp. 134–61), Richard Dutton triangulates Donne's *Metempsychosis* [1601], Jonson's *Volpone* [1606], and Donne's Latin commendatory poem to that play ('Amicissimo et meritissimo BEN. JONSON') and proceeds to argue that Donne and Jonson were united in their animus against Robert Cecil, the powerful state councillor who engineered the fall of the earl of Essex in 1599, the 'government-sponsored paranoia' (p. 149) surrounding the Gunpowder Plot in 1605, and the exploitation of English Catholics at the end of Elizabeth's reign and beginning of James I's. Paul J. Stapleton's 'A Priest and a "Queen": Donne's Epigram "Martial"' (*JDJ* 28[2009] 93–118) contends that the epigram's two halves pit Jesuit religious hypocrisy against Calvinist religious hypocrisy and cloak both 'as sexual license' (p. 112). The queenly allusions of the final line—'As Katherine, for the Courts sake, put down Stewes'—offers a further 'veiled' rebuke of the English monarchy. And David Ian Hopp, in 'John Donne's "The Curse" as Themes and Variations' (*N&Q* 56[2009] 72–5), suggests that the proverbial phrase 'confess, and die' in 'The Curse' echoes the opening lines of Act II, scene iii, of Shakespeare's *The Merchant of Venice*, and that both works protest against 'the state's use of judicial torture' against English Catholics (p. 73).

In a stimulating essay entitled 'Satire III and the Satires: John Donne on True Religion, Memory and Community' (in Sell and Johnson, eds., pp. 127–49), A.D. Cousins argues that the enigmatic Satyre III is best understood: (1) in the context of the treatment of religion in Donne's other four formal verse satires, in which 'unexplained and inexplicable aberration' seems to be the 'archetypical predicament of the Christian consciousness' (p. 134); and (2) as an example of a *suasoria*, as that form was described by the Roman rhetorician Quintilian (p. 140). Cousins concludes that 'Donne's speaker advocates, as regards the pursuit of religious truth, inquiry into the authority of the Church and State . . . yet in doing so he at once affirms and denies the power of cultural memory, through which such an investigation would . . . need chiefly be conducted' (p. 129).

On a more technical (and metrical) note: In a long and enriching chapter in *Wit's Voice: Intonation in Seventeenth-Century English Poetry* ('John Donne', pp. 59–112), John R. Cooper catalogues the great number of intonational effects that Donne achieves in his verse, the innovative techniques that differentiate his iambic pentameter from earlier practitioners, and the influence of generic norms on his metrical practices (in the *Holy Sonnets*, for example, Cooper detects 'a falling off in stylistic variety and dramatic power' (p.103)). In Cooper's estimation, 'Donne's reputation for metrical irregularity is in excess of the facts, and the harshness or difficulty of his verse is most often a result not of irregularity but rather of the strain of maintaining meter against considerable syntactic and semantic resistance' (p. 71). From her even more technical application of the principles of generative metrics to Donne's poetry in 'Nonlexical Word Stress in the English Iambic Pentameter: A Study of John Donne' (in Hanson and Inkelas, eds., *The Nature of the Word*, pp. 21–61), Kristin Hanson concludes that Donne's metrical practice was more systematic than is often thought, and that with regard to stresses in lexical words in specific his 'practice may be extreme within the English tradition, but . . . not outside it' (pp. 47–8).

Donne's religious writings, especially those we know or, in the case of the *Holy Sonnets*, think were written in the period between his marriage (1601) and his ordination (1615), continue to garner considerable scholarly interest. In an essay especially focused specifically on this period, 'Donne the Layman Essaying Divinity' (*JDJ* 28[2009] 1–30), Kate Narveson argues that Donne's *Essayes in Divinity* (published 1651) should not be read as 'an apprentice work anticipating the master craftsman's sermons, or as evidence of Donne's theological development' but rather as one of several instances of a lay gentleman 'venturing into exegesis'. Properly situated between the pulpit and the prayer closet, Donne's *Essayes* reflect a 'mix of pragmatism and religious commitment that was not unusual among gentlemen... in early Stuart London' (p. 4). The *Essayes*, however, do 'not exhibit the confidence of a right or even duty to promote public piety' (p. 21) that is typically found in writings by early Stuart judges and lawyers, but instead present Donne as a Paul-like authority who 'transcends the lay/clerical distinction' while still exemplifying the experience of the 'ordinary Christian who knows the futility of knowledge in the face of possession by sin' (pp. 29–30).

In 'Donne's Catholic Conscience and the Wit of Religious Anxiety' (*BJJ* 16[2009] 57–76), R.V. Young ranges widely over Donne's poetic corpus in order to argue forcefully that

> Donne is important to us now... not as a 'player' in the power politics of the English Church in the early seventeenth century, but as an artist who helps us come to terms with the conflicts that beset us by framing them in an imaginative vision. In fact, we may learn more about what it was like to be a Catholic recusant from Donne's poems *because* he abandoned the Church and thereby reveals more than the solid faithful about the emotional pressure of the persecution they faced. What is more, we can learn as much about this from his profane love poetry as from his devotional poetry, because Donne envisages both religion and sexual love in unconventional, highly personal terms, intimating a private intensity that is part of the legacy of the Reformation in the modern world. (p. 59)

Robert C. Evans's '"Despaire behind, and death before"' (*BJJ* 16[2009] 99–116) offers a detailed comparison of Donne's *Holy Sonnets* and the twenty-six religious sonnets published by Anne Vaughan Lock in *A Meditation of a Penitent Sinner* [1560]. Evans concludes that in some respects, especially vocabulary, 'Lock seems to have much more in common with Donne' than with other early modern religious poets (p. 107); still, partly because of his penchant for personal scrutiny, Donne is 'the more adventurous, inventive, and talented writer of the two' (p. 112).

Kathleen Quiring's '"Mourne with some fruit": John Donne and the Redemptive Power of Religious Melancholy' (*JDJ* 28[2009] 31–51) counters modern critics who diagnose religious melancholy as either a sin or a form of mental illness. She argues instead that melancholy is a more varied state in Donne's religious writing and that ultimately 'Donne's propensity for grief and fear is conducive to his religious devotion, and is thereby redemptive' (p. 50). Tina Skouen's lengthy and broad-ranging essay 'The Rhetoric of Passion in Donne's *Holy Sonnets*' (*Rhetorica* 27:ii[2009] 159–88) highlights the numerous passions at play in Donne's religious poetry and situates them within ancient, patristic, and especially early modern discussions (in, for example, Thomas Wright's *The Passions of the Minde in General* [1604] and Edward Reynolds's *A Treatise of the Passions and Faculties of the Soule of Man* [1640]) of how to stir and steer violent passions 'in a virtuous direction' (p. 171). She concludes that the *Holy Sonnets* 'offer some instruction on how to handle the passions. But they also provide examples [such as 'Since she whom I lov'd hath payd her last debt'] that are not worthy of imitation' because they give 'vent to uncontrolled emotion' (p. 180).

In 'Division in Communion: Symbols of Transubstantiation in Donne, Milton, and Dryden' (in Duncan, ed., *Religion in the Age of Reason*, pp. 1–17), Anne Barbeau Gardiner argues that 'Good Friday, 1613. Riding Westward' 'tells of a private journey that leads to an encounter with the real presence' of Christ, an encounter that is then 'followed by a substantial interior conversion' (p. 5). The poem's narrative, then, enacts Donne's abridging, interiorizing, and repurposing of the Catholic doctrine of transubstantiation. In 'Squaring the Circle: Neoplatonic Versions of the Self in Early Modern Poetry' (*Symbolism* 9[2009] 13–39) Verena O. Lobsien argues that the iambic pentameter lines of Donne's poem on the Sidney Psalter 'practice what they praise in . . . contemporary attempts to supersede the Sternhold–Hopkins psalter, for they strive to form part of the ancient circulation of the inspired word they describe—above all by their central conceit, which casts the transmission and tradition of the psalmic praise of God into the mould of a circle' (p. 30). Norman Vance, 'Donne's "Death Be Not Proud" and the *Book of Homilies*' (*N&Q* 56[2009] 75–6), finds key themes and phrases from Donne's most famous holy sonnet anticipated in 'An Exhortation against the Death', originally published in the *Book of Homilies* [1547]. And In 'Tears in the Desert: Baroque Adaptations of the Book of Lamentations by John Donne and Francisco de Quevedo' (*JMEMS* 39:i[2009] 31–42), Hilaire Kallendorf draws out biographical contrasts and stylistic parallels between the English and Spanish poets, noting especially their 'shared spiritual formation involving Jesuit meditational techniques' (p. 34). Kallendorf concludes that Donne, despite leaving Roman Catholicism, 'produced a more beautiful, more successful (but only because . . . more "Catholic") rendition of the biblical text of Lamentations' (p. 39).

A chapter on Donne in Molly Murray's *The Poetics of Conversion in Early Modern English Literature* ('John Donne and the Language of De-Nomination', pp. 69–104) convincingly demonstrates that Donne's most studied writings about his and others' conversions—for example the preface to *Pseudo-Martyr*, Satire III, the *Holy Sonnets*—are not as idiosyncratic as critics sometimes suppose. Instead, these writings belong to the early modern genres of the conversion narrative and what Murray calls 'texts of resolution' (p. 86). Of *Pseudo-Martyr* in particular she observes that what is 'unusual' about Donne's argument is his 'failure to describe in clear terms what he came to believe *after* [a] period of 'irresolution'—his failure, in short, to write the end of his own story' (p. 79). Like many others, Donne 'insists on conversion as the source of individual spiritual authenticity', but he also asserts that 'the truth, once found, must remain hidden for each of us, and from all of us' (p. 104). Piers Brown's curiously like-minded essay 'Donne's Hawkings' (*SEL* 49:i[2009] 67–86) tracks Donne's analogy between hawking and composing poetry. This analogy 'presents composition as not one, but two imbricated movements: the spiraling flight of the hawk-like mind, which ranges upwards and outwards, hunting material, and its center, the riding falconer whose forward motion orders and disciplines the ranging imagination' (p. 68). Brown shows further that 'the interlinked motions of hawking' become 'an organizing metaphor' for 'Donne's images of presence and abstraction' and a template 'for the mental trajectories of both writer and reader', specifically in Satyre I, 'Good Friday, 1613. Riding Westward', and 'A Valediction: Forbidding Mourning' (p. 69).

Turning to Donne's sermons and his career as a churchman, one focal point of political readings of Donne over the last decade has been the sermon he delivered to the Virginia Company on 13 November 1622, shortly after a deadly attack on English colonists by the Powhatan confederacy and shortly before the dissolution of the fractious company in 1624. In 'The Metaphysics of Labor in John Donne's Sermon to the Virginia Company' (*SP* 106:i[2008] 76–99), Thomas Festa argues that Donne's sermon, by articulating 'an idea of the *vocation* of empire as a civilizing mission that would result from sacrifices made through enforced and sustained labor', becomes 'emblematic of the first step in a peculiarly English transformation of the [religious] cleric into an imperial clerk' (p. 82). Though he argues for charity towards the Indians and denounces the ruthlessness of Spanish colonialism, Donne commodifies the souls of the natives in such a way that he 'comes dangerously close to switching merely from one form of inhumane exploitation to another' (p. 94), especially when he advocates transporting London's poor to the colonies to do the work that the Indians resist. According to Festa, by intervening on 'behalf of a humanitarian cause—the effort to prevent retributive violence against indigenous peoples—Donne indirectly voiced the theoretical basis for future forms of enslavement in the New World' (p. 99).

John T. Shawcross, in 'Penance and Passion Week: John Donne's Sermon on Psalm 6:6–7, and Charles I' (*JDJ* 28[2009] 53–65), dates the sermon to April 1628 and speculates that Donne may have intended to provoke the 'autocratic' Charles I to imitate David and exhibit humiliation, deprecation, and repentance as he confesses his sins to God 'at this most special of religious times' (p. 62). Marie-Christine Munoz's '"*Bellum Symbolum Mali*": War and Peace in John Donne's Sermons or the Study of a Contest' (in Teulié and Lux-Sterritt, eds., *War Sermons*, pp. 53–68) portrays Donne as steadfastly loyal to James I and Charles I, who as monarchs were in Donne's view responsible for establishing and maintaining peace. Munoz explains further that although Donne never preached a war sermon, his sermons consistently and creatively invoke 'the theme of war as the embodiment of divine punishment against sin' (p. 55). Maria Salenius's chapter, '"...those marks are upon me": John Donne's Sermons for a Community in Transition' (in Sell and Johnson, eds., pp. 151–68), focuses on four sermons from the 1620s and illustrates how, 'as a preacher, Donne unites the parishioner...with the preacher of the new [Protestant] religion' and how Donne 'compares notes about God with a congregation which is still to some extent moving from the context of the "old" religion (that is, Catholicism) to the "new" Protestant faith' (p. 152).

Two essays by Chanita Goodblatt appraise the life and scholarship of Evelyn Simpson, who is best known as co-editor with George Potter of the standard twentieth-century edition of Donne's sermons. In '"The University is a Paradise, Rivers of Knowledge are There": Evelyn Mary Spearing Simpson' (in Hurley and Goodblatt, eds., *Women Editing/Editing Women*, pp. 257–83),

Goodblatt offers a compelling account of Simpson's eventful life—her Victorian upbringing; her early education at Cambridge; her service as a VAD nurse in the First World War; her time at Oxford, where she became the first woman to be awarded the D.Phil.; and her relationships with her husband Percy Simpson, with Potter (who died suddenly one year into what would become the ten-year project of publishing the *Sermons*), and with her friend (and sometime rival) Helen Gardner. Goodblatt also provides a bibliography of Simpson's works, including a 1917 war memoir, *From Cambridge to Camiers under the Red Cross*, that Virginia Woolf reviewed for the *TLS*. Goodblatt's 'An Unpublished Manuscript on John Donne: Retrospect and Prospect' (*JDJ* 28[2009] 67–91) supplements this account of Simpson's academic career and prints for the first time her essay, 'Donne and the Elizabethan Stage' (pp. 73–91), which tracks references to plays and the theatre in Donne's writing and argues for the indelible imprint left by 'the masterpieces of Marlowe, Shakespeare and Ben Jonson' on both 'Donne the poet and Donne the preacher' (p. 91). In a third, shorter, note, 'The Presence of Abraham Ibn Ezra in Seventeenth-Century England' (*ANQ* 22:ii[2009] 18–24), Goodblatt tracks references to and citations from the twelfth-century Jewish scientist, exegete, and poet in Donne's sermons (a Latin translation of Ibn Ezra's medical-astrological work *Sefer Ha-Me'orot* was published in 1507) and observes similarities between the two poets' styles.

In 'Experiencing Pain in John Donne's *Devotions upon Emergent Occasions* (1624)' (in Dijhuizen and Enenkel, eds., *The Sense of Suffering: Constructions of Physical Pain in Early Modern Culture*, pp. 323–45), Mary Ann Lund argues that 'Donne's treatment of pain reveals important aspects of his attitude to medicine and sickness, as well as his [Calvinist] theological outlook' (p. 324). Likewise, the metaphors he uses to represent personal suffering—metaphors of torture by pressing, of flooding water, and of the action of vapours—'resist the idea that another's pain is unimaginable' while also hinting at 'a specific and authentic experience of physical suffering' (p. 343). In a chapter on Donne in his *Plague Writing in Early Modern England* (pp. 189–213), Ernest B. Gilman concentrates on three of Donne's works published in the years around London's horrific 1625 plague: *Devotions upon Emergent Occasions* [1624], which recounts Donne's recovery from relapsing fever late in 1623; a rushed 1625 edition (probably not authorized by Donne) of his long elegy for Elizabeth Drury, *The First Anniversary or An Anatomie of the World* [1611]; and a 1626 sermon on Exodus 12:30 ('For there was not a house where there was not one dead'), Donne's only contribution to the genre of the plague sermon. Gilman highlights Donne's repetitive, typological reasoning—by which the plagues afflicting London are prefigured by the plagues in the Exodus narrative—and he concludes that Donne's three works 'represent . . . the last "successful" accommodation of the plague to theology in the seventeenth century. . . . In Donne's view, any one outbreak [of plague] forms one more link in a legible sequence of epidemics, each representing and represented in the others, and all of them under the supervision of a divine Physician pledged to restore his patients to health' (p. 312).

The final two essays surveyed here explore the influence of Donne on twentieth-century religious poetry and theology. Kalyan Chatterjee,

'Cross-Cultural Transactions: Rabindranath Tagore, John Donne, and Peter Damian' (*ANQ* 22:iv[2009]: 33–42), traces the erotic spirituality of the Nobel Prize-winning Bengali poet Rabindranath Tagore (1861–1941) to Donne and through him to the eleventh-century Benedictine monk Peter Damian and ultimately to the biblical Song of Solomon. And in 'Why I Still Read John Donne: An Appraisal of Grace Jantzen's *Becoming Divine*' (in Graham, ed., *Grace Jantzen: Redeeming the Present*, pp. 55–68), Frances Ward contrasts the obsession with death, with sex, and with the afterlife in the writings of Donne with competing concepts in the writings of Jantzen, a twentieth-century feminist theologian. Ward contends that Donne's dangerously masculinist form of Christianity is redeemable partly because he 'stimulates greater understanding of the nature of desire, with a breadth and depth that has seldom been surpassed, with his eyes fixed, ultimately, on death and dying' (p. 68).

4. Milton

Written in studious retirement, Annabel Patterson's *Milton's Words* belongs with earlier studies of Miltonic style by Christopher Ricks, Thomas Corns and John K. Hale. Patterson sets out to study 'Milton's brilliant way with words' (p. 146), in particular, how his words become laden with the burden of political and personal meaning. Databases and other computational resources no doubt contributed something to Patterson's project, but her command of the details of the Miltonic oeuvre, her insight into Milton's life and the political life of the period, are such that the assistance of such tools might seem superfluous.'A proper stylistician would count all the instances [of double negatives] in *Paradise Lost,* and draw statistical conclusions about Milton's negativity, here and elsewhere' (p. 190), she concedes at one point. Patterson's analysis of Milton's characteristic lexical choices, however, needs no quantitative crutch. Nor does she make much reference to Milton scholarship, preferring to sail freely between Milton's poetry and prose with minimal scholarly citation to supply the wind at her back. Raymond Williams's *Keywords: A Vocabulary of Culture and Society* (rev. ed., 1983) has shaped aspects of her methodology, but Patterson does not limit herself to looking at contested political terms, terms freighted with political associations and capable of mobilising people to action (for example, *liberty, heresy*). Some of the words she chooses are Latinate polysyllables (*indefatigable*), some of them odd (*by-ends*), some periphrases ('to grind in the mill of an undelighted and servile copulation'), and some basic English vocabulary (*perhaps, book, death*). Psychologically astute and always readable, the book places a heavy burden of interpretation on word frequency. That 'the word "liberty" appears a mere 12 times' in *Paradise Lost,* and that 'nine of these are demonic', while three seem parodic of the sort of liberationist rhetoric Milton uses in *A Readie & Easie Way to Establish a Free Commonwealth* (p. 88), admits no contradiction. Not everyone will agree that the avoidance of a particular lexical item is in itself sufficient to close off a line of interpretation, or that attempts to bend the major poems 'to our Whiggish will' (p. 89) will inevitably founder on data gleaned from a concordance or database searching. Patterson's conclusion about the relation of the poetry to the prose pamphleteering, however, seems impossible to quarrel with: what Milton decided 'was to prune and pare the vocabulary of the great poems to make sure that the revolutionary keywords had been bracketed, restricted, or ironized. Consequently, he died in his bed' (p. 93). *Death* itself is a common but difficult (and sometimes taboo) word in Milton, one that recent criticism has moved closer to the centre of *Paradise Lost* and that Patterson comments on with anything but solemnity. Patterson reserves another chapter for 'Rude Words', polemical fighting words that we might find disturbing, 'billingsgate', 'trash talk', and the like. The Milton who appears to posterity as a writer who 'could wield scurrility with as much flair as he could raise his reader's aspirations' (p. 147) has received less attention than he deserves. Although the work of reconstructing this side of Milton might seem an unpleasant task, Patterson does not hesitate to muck in. Such abusive tactics reach backwards in England to the Marprelate tracts and forward to Marvell's *Rehearsal Transpros'd,* but something distinctly Miltonic remains in the gallimaufry of insults he concocts, many of them focused on lower-body functions. About Milton's propensity for using negative forms to express core convictions ('Worthy to have not remained so long unsung'), Patterson observes that his 'syntactical negativity is the sign of vocational doubt, the negative mirror image of his remarkable confidence' (p. 175). In *Paradise Regained* and *Samson Agonistes*, however, Paterson finds that negative constructions decrease in frequency and become semantically simpler. Overall, what impresses most about this book is its success in engaging multiple audiences, its having something to offer both the neophyte and the polyglot professional Miltonist.

The last several years have witnessed the publication of several encyclopaedic consolidations of Milton scholarship presumably intended for a wide audience, and Nicholas McDowell and Nigel Smith's *Oxford Handbook of Milton* serves the author well in this respect. Like Patterson's brief guide to the life and works, it does double duty as a primer and resource for advanced study. Readers who have lived through the seismic shifts in the field of literary study since the 1980s will note certain emphases and lacunae in this volume, especially when compared to collections assembled during the period when the excitement of deconstruction, feminism, new historicism and the theory boom still coursed through the profession's bloodstream. *The Oxford Handbook* 'seeks to incorporate developments in what can broadly be termed historical criticism over the last twenty years' (p. v), and arranges its material under rubrics keyed to Milton's biography, the shorter poems, prose, major poems, his influence and so forth. Many of the thirty-five scholars gathered here write on aspects of Milton developed in their earlier, often very influential work: thus, among the thirty-eight essays we find Joseph Wittrech on 'Miltonic Romanticism', Martin Dzelzainis on 'The Politics of *Paradise Lost*', Paul Stevens on 'Milton and National Identity', Gordon Campbell and Thomas N. Corns on *De Doctrina Christiana,* for example. A couple of the pieces have appeared before (Gordon Teskey on 'Milton's Early English Poems: The Nativity Ode, "L'Allegro", "Il Penseroso,"' and Stephen B. Dobranski's excellent 'Editing Milton: The Case against Modernization'). Most of the articles are impressively fresh and their overall achievement is to provide readers with a crash course in historically oriented approaches to Milton, with particular emphasis on politics and, to a lesser extent, religion. On balance, Milton's prose seems to elicit deeper engagement than the poetry, where the rehearsal of critical concerns can sometimes seem dutiful and pro forma. What follows are thumbnail sketches of most of these essays.

Edward Jones's careful review of the life of the young Milton ('"Ere half my days": Milton's Life, 1606–1640') and Nicholas von Maltzahn on 'John Milton: The Later Life (1641–1674)' effectively raise the question of consistency across his Milton's career, especially important to critics who seek to understand Milton's political and religious development. Estelle Haan, 'The "adorning of my native tongue": Latin Poetry and Linguistic Metamorphosis' examines 'the linguistic versatility exhibited by Milton's 'bilingualism', in light of 'Renaissance pedagogical theory and practice' (p. 55). Ann Baynes Coiro finds *Comus* full of contradictions in '"A thousand fantasies": The Lady and *The Maske*', describing the work as an unstable 'amalgam of court masque and English drama, of theatrical performance and dramatic poem, of idealistic beliefs and the realities of human life, and of feminism and paternalism' (p. 91). Nicholas McDowell's '"Lycidas" and the Influence of Anxiety' (pp. 112–35) looks at Ovidian and Marlovian strains in early poetry. With a finely tuned ear, John Leonard attends to 'The Troubled, Quiet Endings of Milton's English Sonnets', 'the tensions they create (in themselves and us) by their opposed impulses towards opacity and tranquility' (p. 137).

One of the volume's editors, Nigel Smith, takes on 'The Anti-Episcopal Tracts: Republican Puritanism and the Truth in Poetry', which he treats as Milton's 'chance to make poetics do the work of theological argument' while declaring an allegiance to the 'Puritan cause' (p. 172). In '"A Law in this matter to himself": Contextualizing Milton's Divorce Tracts', Sharon Achinstein situates the tracts somewhere between domestic turmoil and political conflict, somewhere near the faultline where marital vows and political obligation both break down (pp. 174–85). A second essay on these texts, by Diane Purkiss, 'Whose Liberty? The Rhetoric of Milton's Divorce Tracts' (pp. 186–99), fills in an issue that she claims has received comparatively little attention, Milton's ideology of gender and marriage. *Areopagitica* also receives the honour of having two essays devoted to it. The first, by Ann Hughes on 'Milton, *Areopagitica,* and the Parliamentary Cause' (pp. 200–17), looks at parallels between Milton's text and parliamentary debate and his associating the regulation of printing with a hard-line Presbyterian faction in the Westminster Assembly that feared heresy. Blair Hoxby's '*Areopagitica* and Liberty' includes some illuminating remarks on monopoly power and the Licensing Order as an attempt to monopolize truth and make of it what Milton called 'a staple commodity of all the Knowledge in the Land', handling books in a manner better suited to 'our broad cloath, and our wooll packs' (p. 227).

Stephen M. Fallon's contribution on '"The strangest piece of reason": Milton's *Tenure of Kings and Magistrates*'(pp. 241–51) detects a strain between lofty ideals and pragmatic concerns, pointing to the unstable political ground of the 1640s as well as to Milton's internal contradictions. Nicholas

McDowell's 'Milton's Regicide Tracts and the Uses of Shakespeare' turns to submerged Shakespearean allusions in the prose, most productively in *Macbeth,* arguing that, despite Milton's association of the dramatist with the culture of the Stuart court, he found in the Scottish play materials useful 'in offering him an affective language for his argument and animus against the Presbyterians and the Scots' (p. 267). Joad Raymond's 'John Milton, European: The Rhetoric of Milton's Defences' ushers forward a portrait of the author as both a busy civil servant and, in a more flattering self-portrait,'as a champion of liberty in a Europe-wide context...an orator and an Englishman among wider non-national networks' (p. 290). Elizabeth Sauer writes on the subject of 'Disestablishment, Toleration, the New Testament Nation: Milton's Late Religious Tracts', showing how, 'at a time when the majority supported establishment and the reinstatement of a national religion, Milton upheld a minority, oppositional position, that severed Christianity and national election from Jewish antecedents' (p. 341).

Part V of this 700-page compilation deals concisely with 'Writings on Education, History, Theology,' beginning with a fine essay by William Poole on 'The Genres of Milton's Commonplace Book'. Poole includes sections on the document's provenance, the practice of commonplacing, the sorts of materials gathered, and Milton's techniques for note-taking, studying the artefact' as an object in its own right, structured not just by Milton's own polemical concerns, but by his educational background and the priorities it continued to exert" (p. 380). Poole notes, in one useful example, that Milton gathered texts on marriage 'before his first, initially disastrous marriage' (p. 381), making his defence of conjugal liberty far more than an exercise in autobiography. We see in Milton's commonplacing basic assumptions about the organization of knowledge and the division of subjects. Timothy Raylor's essay on 'Milton, the Hartlib Circle, and the Education of the Aristocracy' (pp. 382-406) detects outlines of the French noble academy behind the reformed institution that Milton sketches in *Of Education,* and Martin Dzelzainis takes up the 'Conquest and Slavery in Milton's *History of Britain*' (pp. 407–23), slavery now having become an inescapable issue in assessments of Milton as a theorist of human liberty.

The classicist Charles Martindale takes on the assignment of discussing 'Writing Epic: *Paradise Lost*' (pp. 439-61), re-focusing attention on the reception of ancient literature in early modern England, for which Milton traditionally has served as a focal point. The editors allow us a small taste of formal analysis with John Creasar's essay '"A mind of most exceptional energy": Verse Rhythm in *Paradise Lost*', a nod to the inexhaustible subject of Milton's innovative use of meter and prosody (pp. 462–79). Nigel Smith writes on '*Paradise Lost* and Heresy', without the benefit of much earlier criticism (or the assistance of Stephen B. Dobranski and John P. Rumrich's collection of essays, *Milton and Heresy* [Cambridge UP, 1998]), and another unavoidable topic gets dispatched by Stuart Curran in an essay bracingly titled 'God' (pp. 525–33). Gender studies make a cameo appearance in the volume with Susan Wiseman's 'Eve, *Paradise Lost*, and Female Interpretation', which surveys seventeenth-century writing on the nature of women, and situates Milton's Eve 'in the specific context of writing on obedience by seventeenth-century women' (p. 535), in particular, by Aemelia Lanyer, Rachel Speght, Anna Trapnel and Margaret Fell.

Laura Lunger Knoppers's '"England's Case": Contexts of the 1671 Poems', reprises and expands her editorial work on the 1671 *Poems* in the Oxford *Complete Works* (vol. 2., 2008), paying special attention to readers of Milton's own time, whose indexes and markings provide a lens into how they understood these texts (pp. 571–88). John Rogers's "*Paradise Regained* and the Memory of *Paradise Lost*' sets out to explain, building on Barbara Lewalski's influential argument in *Milton's Brief Epic* (1966) about the Son's recognition of his divinity, 'a way in which the poet crafted his sequel to serve not just as the culmination, but, in a remarkable way, the actual *revelation*, of the story of Christian history' (p. 590) begun in the earlier poem. Regina M. Schwartz's '*Samson Agonistes*: The Force of Justice and the Violence of Idolatry' turns to the question of divinely sanctioned violence and whether we should 'understand Samson as a saviour or destroyer, a success or failure' (p. 635), together with a series of broader questions (with obvious contemporary resonances) involving violence between groups and religious toleration.Many readers will agree with Schwartz's conclusion, that despite his endorsement of free inquiry, 'Milton is not living in a multicultural, pluralistic space where all religions are equally valid. In his writing, we encounter, again and again, and with much discomfort, the limits of toleration. And those limits are always idolatry' (p. 647). In the volume's final section, on 'Aspects on Influence', an essay by Anne-Julia Zwierlein titled 'Milton Epic and Bucolic: Empire and Readings of *Paradise Lost*, 1667–1837' shows how eighteenth-century adaptations construct Milton 'to appear simultaneously imperial *and* domestic' (p. 671) and how in later georgic and pastoral the poet becomes a source for a colonialist discourse of landscape appreciation.

The scant attention paid to Milton's angelology since Robert H. West's standard (but now dated) *Milton and the Angels* (1955) represents one of the more surprising gaps in Milton scholarship, a hiatus that Feisal G. Mohamed admirably fills in his 2008 *In the Anteroom of Divinity: The Reformation of the Angels from Colet to Milton*. Angelology's scholarly decline, at least relative to demonology, might seem especially surprising to readers in the United States, where 87 percent of members of Evangelical churches agree 'completely' or 'mostly' in a recent survey that angels and demons are active in the world (figures remain comparably high for mainline churches). Three of Mohamed's chapters read Milton's views of angels against the theological and political controversies of the mid-seventeenth century, especially the revival of Dionysius the Pseudo-Areopagite and his theory of nine angelic orders, which Milton and his protestant contemporaries rejected in favour of other angelologies. Despite Milton's scepticism concerning Dionysian orders of angels and his inversion of the Dionysian model (with archangels at the top of the chain and cherubim and seraphim at the bottom), Milton positions his angelic characters in a fixed celestial order. Mohamed turns to Henry Lawrence and Sir Henry Vane—both subjects of Milton sonnets and writers of texts steeped equally in republicanism and spiritualism—and argues that 'Milton's employment of angels in *Paradise Lost* shares the emphasis on election and illumination evident in both of these men' (p. 104), and that

Raphael and Michael play roles consistent with an illuminationist understanding of angels. Mohamed treats Raphael in light of his association with medicine and moral philosophy, which arises from the Book of Tobit where Raphael removes the curse that makes marriage to Sarah a perilous undertaking and also restores Tobit's eyesight. Milton casts Raphael in a manner 'consistent with Renaissance perception of this "celestial physician,"' and the dialectical and curative method associated with him (p. 140). The final chapter in the sequence uses the figure of Michael to put pressure on the question of Milton's apocalypticism, how Michael's portrayal in *Paradise Lost* puts the poet at a distance from the nationalist eschatology of the anti-prelactical tracts of 1641–42. In Michael we see the same impulse that animates the tracts of 1659: while the earlier prose 'emphasizes the rise of an elect nation', Milton grows 'sceptical of national progress' and Michael's history recalls that 'God's election of Israel is a fleeting moment in biblical history' and that the promise of salvation extends to 'the faithful few of all nations' (p. 162).

Angelology also assumes a central position in N. K. Sugimura's *'Matter of Glorious Trial': Spiritual and Material Substance in Paradise Lost,* offering additional evidence that angels have returned in force to Milton studies. (Joad Raymond's book on *Milton's Angels: The Early-Modern Imagination* appeared in 2010, further confirmation that angels, who long have figured in film and popular culture, have reassumed a place in the academic world.) Where Mohamed's orientation is political and theological, Sugimura adopts a philosophical and linguistic approach that aims to refute 'the prevailing scholarly consensus that Milton's poetry supports monist materialism' (p. ix). Stephen Fallon's view of Milton's monism as distinct both from Hobbesian materialism and the dualism of the Cambridge Platonists, as neither mechanistic nor committed to a notion of 'incorporeal substance', continues to provoke debate but remains the account with which Miltonists must reckon. The 'Matter of glorious trial' (*PL* 9.1176) referred to in Sugimura's title draws attention not to the test in the garden but to an inquiry on substance that Milton conducted from his early years at Cambridge to the end of his poetic career. A key chapter, on 'Milton's Angelology: Intelligential Substance in *Paradise Lost*', finds Milton tirelessly grappling with conflicting traditions regarding angels. In this segment alone Sugimura invokes intellectual movements and writers as disparate and difficult as Averroism, Pietro Pomponazzi, Aquinas, Bonaventure and Scholastic commentators on Aristotle to buttress her reading.Wandering through a maze of sources, elementary Hebrew etymologies, and passages in the epic where Milton would seem to puzzle over the intricacies of materialism, the chapter argues against conceiving of angels as material, as Fallon and Raymond do, and positions the poem in relation to late sixteenth- and early seventeenth-century scholastic views on angelic cognition. Already thorny theological and philosophical problems have undergone further complication earlier in the book as Sugimura moves back and forth among Milton, Aristotle and Neoplatonism, while trying not to lose sight of the poetry, and arguing the plausible case that 'against the bleached backdrop of the story of Milton's monist materialism, there are brilliant moments of opposition, such as when the intellect shimmers with immateriality like the 'radiant forms' of Milton's angels' (p. xxiv).

The sixth chapter, 'From Angels to the Almighty: Accommodation and the Problem of Narrative Intelligibility', modulates decisively from the key of metaphysics to literary expression, with the diapason closing full in Milton's poetics. How Milton materializes abstruse ideas, or accommodates the understanding of his readers to matters beyond human reason, has engaged the attention of Miltonists for some time, and few will doubt that *Paradise Lost* attempts to make the divine intelligible as something narrativized and embodied. Milton's alleged materialism, Sugimura argues, does not account for the complexities of his thinking or literary practice. Her comments on analogy, the War in Heaven and depictions of the divine in general are all worth having, even if they reduce to the truism 'Milton closed his eyes to see' (p. 230). Inevitably, the argument of this wide-ranging book defies abridgement or paraphrase. Readers will come away from it convinced that Milton embraces a shifting and sophisticated notion of substance, one that operates within and outside the boundaries of Aristotelian metaphysics, and that the poetry of *Paradise Lost* provides a vehicle for Milton's 'complex and confused' (p. 281) thinking about matter. Whether the study can succeed in dislodging the current view of Milton's monist materialism might depend on the success of the study's own critical method, which casts a large net into the sea of intellectual history and gathers texts of every kind, without throwing much away.

Noam Reisner's *Milton and the Ineffable* speaks to some of the same concerns, while engaging, in his exploration of inexpressibility, 'to define the exact terms I am concerned with as precisely as possible, as well as the intellectual-historical forces which shaped those terms' (p. 2). Milton's struggle to articulate the inarticulable has provoked commentary before, yet Reisner's approach opens up the question in an unusually productive way. Well versed in biblical and classical scholarship, he surveys the problem of ineffability in the Western tradition, from Moses in Exodus, through Greek reflections on the logos, to medieval theology, Reformation philology, down to English Protestant humanism. Milton, he contends, 'wants to be *seen* to say the unsayable without *actually* saying it, and without once sacrificing either intelligibility *or* the sense of mystery which authorizes such intelligibility' (p. 7). When Milton invokes the presence of the ineffable he inevitably engages with a tradition of apophatic theology, and the problem of talking around and about God provides the framework for understanding his entire poetic career. Reisner's close readings of Milton's early paraphrase of Psalm 114 and of pieces from the 1645 *Poems* lay the groundwork for his analysis of *Paradise Lost*, which achieves some of its most powerful effects by positioning itself against intimations of the ineffable while incorporating, as critics often note, a biblical theory of accommodation. Reisner works across the entire poetic oeuvre and complicates critical thinking about the problem of representation in language by showing how Milton only pretends to say what cannot be said, and does not (indeed, cannot) aspire to exceed the bounds of the effable. Reisner inserts Milton into a framework where, as a reader of biblical texts, the poet assumes the position of 'author' of these texts, so that the already-accommodated text becomes his own and no longer requires accommodation. In keeping with a Protestant emphasis on interiority, Milton centres the ineffability of *Paradise Lost* on the mystery of poetic inspiration, the power to bring the spectacle of heaven, hell and Eden before our eye and ears. *Paradise Lost* achieves far more than a translation of abstractions into metaphors and allegories.What Milton aspires to elicit from his readers is both a reverent silence and also the sort of logocentric response recorded in the endless commentary provoked by the poem. In a final chapter, on *Paradise Regained* and *Samson*, Reisner anticipates resistance from readers who understandably might find in these poems few signs of the ineffable divinity that surfaces in the earlier poetry.Yet there too he successfully excavates Milton's poetry for a discourse of apophasis at the centre of Protestant theology that motivated Milton's lifelong struggle to say (and not say) the unsayable.

Alluding to Sigmund Freud's very different book of a similar title, Abraham Stoll's *Milton and Monotheism* argues that *Paradise Lost* 'relies extensively on the seventeenth century study of polytheism' (p. 7), making heavy use of John Selden's *De diis Syris syntagmata* (1617), an important source of the mythography for Book One of the poem. The significance of *monotheism* to the seventeenth century emerges with the word's first recorded use, in 1660 by the Cambridge Platonist Henry More in *An Explanation of the Grand Mystery of Godliness*. Moving towards a consideration of some of the same issues that concern Sugimura and Reisner, Stoll finds the significance of monotheism to reside in its implicit opposition to a specific logic of representation: 'Monotheism has a structural tendency toward silence and erasure—an endpoint that is sometimes called aniconism for the total absence of representability in the divine economy' (p. 9). Stoll comes at the old question of the representation of God in book 3 of *Paradise Lost* through the theophany of Genesis 18, where God appears to Abraham ('The Lord appeared to him by the terebinths of Mamre; he was sitting at the entrance of the tent as the day grew hot'). He considers the theological difficulties of this extraordinary text crucial to the key exchanges between Adam and Raphael in Books Three through Eight and elsewhere in the poem. In chapter three Stoll connects Milton's understanding of this theophany to Henry More's 'personal, revealed God' (p. 107), while in the first two chapters treats the incorporation of Selden's book into *Paradise Lost* as plunging Milton into debates surrounding the unitary concept of God found in the Abrahamic religions, although Islam plays no part in Stoll's account. Jeffrey Einboden's 'A Qur'ānic Milton: From *Paradise* to *al-Firdaws*' (*MiltonQ* 43[2009] 183–94, fills some part of this gap by looking at Muhammad 'Inānī's 1982 translation into Arabic and describing how this text renders *Paradise Lost* intelligible within the language and traditions of Islam. Stoll constructs Milton's views as eclectic and heterodox, while making *Paradise Lost* into something of a relativist critique of religious first principles. Much of this depends on what one means by 'monotheism', a central theologoumenon that need not entail a passionate embrace of heresy. Stoll positions his subject somewhere between Selden and More, arguing that while Selden detects a type of monotheism hidden within polytheism and thus denies any single religion a monopoly on religious truth,

More considers monotheism the exclusive preserve of Christians. According to Stoll, the foundational but nevertheless mysterious concept of monotheism ('Who am alone / From all eternity', *PL* 8.405–6) flies in a straight line to eighteenth-century deism: 'the assertion of a single God leads to the absolute abstraction of the deist godhead . . . and deism views itself as expressing a purer form of monotheism' (p. 183).This argument lays the groundwork for the second half of his book, which installs Socinianism and deism as the theological contexts most meaningful to *Paradise Regained* and *Samson Agonistes* and thus augments a substantial body of criticism that affixes heretical labels such as 'mortalism' and 'Arianism' to Milton's thinking on religion. Stoll prefers the descriptors 'anti-trinitarian' and 'monotheistic' when speaking of Milton's positions, but distinctions tend to get blurred in the course of folding radical heresies into a theology of monotheism.

Stoll allows Milton to maintain the theological version of plausible deniability in *Paradise Regained,* a text that he reads in chapter 6 as 'at once a radical statement of Antitrinitarianism, and an irenic intervention in the debates over the Trinity' (p. 263), in other words, as a serious experiment in and response to Socinianism. The poem registers a descent from the divine and narrates 'a Son who is almost entirely human' (p. 233), bringing Milton close to an embrace of a Socinian Christology—this despite some rather clear contrary indications of the Son's pre-incarnate existence. For Stoll, the paradox at the core of Milton's theology, his ambivalent aniconism, drives the major poetry, especially *Samson*, in which we find Milton 'on the threshold of the radical theology of the deists and the relativistic perspectives of nascent comparative religion' (p. 308)—all, apparently, the outgrowth of an ontological monotheism. John T. Shawcross's approach to *The Development of Milton's Thought: Law, Government, and Religion* stresses changes in his thinking over time, and pricks holes in any implication that his anti-trinitarianism opens the floodgates to a cascading series of heresies: 'His subordinationist position, as it has been called, is seen as a heresy, although it is *not* Arian or Socinian, despite similarity as to the relationship of the Son to the Father . . . It is similar to the problem of calling him an Arminian and even a Calvinist; acceptance of certain ideas does not make such labelling cogent' (p. 118). The product of a lifetime's reflection and writing, Shawcross's book both refutes any residual notion of 'Milton's unchanging mind' and demonstrates the difficulty of branding contentious categories onto Milton's writings.

A collective, as opposed to a personal, consolidation of Milton scholarship that stretches over generations, the new volume of *A Variorum Commentary on the Poems of John Milton* on *Samson Agonistes* stands on a foundation of notes compiled by William Riley Parker before 1968, and takes 1970 as its cut-off date. Although the balance of critical attention has shifted over time, the political and religious questions we ask of *Samson* have a long and illustrious lineage. Anyone interested in Milton scholarship as a historical institution will find Stephen B. Dobranski's annotations and Archie Burnett's introduction useful for their judicious filtering of materials. One of a projected six volumes, the book appears under the imprint of Duquesne University Press, which has shouldered the task of publishing the *Variorum Commentary* that Columbia

University Press set down in the 1970s, and the complete set will include updated commentaries with coverage of scholarship produced between 1970 and 2000.

If literary studies continue to provide new (and some old) answers to questions about Milton's thought, Louis Schwartz's *Milton and Maternal Mortality* takes up an issue hidden in plain view in the poetry, the gendered consequences of the Fall and Milton's 'pained feeling that women bore a greater burden of suffering for original sin than men' (p. 2). In this lucidly written and tightly focused project, Schwartz pays relatively little attention to a Christian theology of suffering but does devote some pages to examining 'the role religious discourses played in the management of obstetric anxieties' (p. 9). He argues that in labour and delivery women experienced a form of suffering exclusively their own, a fact Milton confronted at important junctures of his career in the deaths in childbirth of three women: Lady Jane Paulet, Mary Powell and Katherine Woodcock. In 'An Epitaph on the Marchioness of Winchester', 'On Shakespear', *A Mask,* and Sonnet 23, and Schwartz finds the poet struggling with his own sense of a vocation, and the deaths of these women count among the causes that eventually motivated Milton to write *Paradise Lost*. In preparation for these readings, the study outlines a social history of childbirth, of 'churching' and other rituals, while taking special note of maternal mortality and the childbed prayers and meditations meant to help expectant mothers overcome fear and strengthen their faith. These conditions give rise, he argues, to Milton's construction of childbirth as a means of figuring literary ambition and 'the perplexity of the will in the face of severe suffering' (p. 73).

In a detailed and astute excursus on Milton's sonnet 'Mee thought I saw my late espoused saint', Schwartz detects a newly discovered sense of poetic vocation behind the bereavement as Milton stages a foray into the problem of Christian consolation in the face of terrible suffering.The analysis, then, weaves together biography and literary history with a fair amount of psychological penetration and novelistic attention to detail, painting, for example, this slightly speculative portrait of Milton after Mary Powell's death in 1652: 'The image of that veiled woman, who did not return from her last lying-in to unveil herself and help him care for the children, who had, in fact, barely begun her month of lying-in when she died, and who had left him with not only a fourth child, but a third child vulnerable to the neglect of a woman not his mother, must have tapped deep currents of ambivalence, loss, and helplessness for Milton, whether or not he gave expression to those emotions in verse at the time' (p. 188). In chapter eight Schwartz looks at *Paradise Lost* in eschatological terms, moving from the allegory of Sin and Death to Milton's understanding of birth as both the carrier of sin from one generation to another and the vehicle whereby sin gets overthrown. To treat Book Two as reflecting the reality of contemporary obstetric practice requires reading the allegory much more literally than usual, but Schwartz balances medical discourses with passages from Phineas Fletcher, Spenser and Ovid. It might not seem an overreach to say that the final two books of the epic bring the theological significance of difficult birth into conjunction with the Nativity, 'the master figure of a birth that will make possible the redemption of all human suffering' (p. 233). But the book seems perhaps too much in the grip of its powerful thesis when it proceeds to argue, in the closing chapter, that reproductive imagery also provides a key for understanding Milton's cosmology. The fifteen pages allotted to the subject cannot do it justice. Still, most readers will come away from the book convinced that 'allusions to contemporary obstetric conditions and to Milton's own biographical experience of them are of central importance to *Paradise Lost*' (p. 245), and that a good deal of anxiety attached to reproductive trauma among Milton and his contemporaries.

Mandy Green's *Milton's Ovidian Eve* studies the interplay between the *Metamorphoses* and *Paradise Lost*, not only delving into strategies of allusion and mythological structures in the poem but re-opening critical debates involving gender relations and Milton's attitude towards women. Following the same line of thought pursued by Schwartz, she observes that 'Ovid and Milton are unusual among epic poets for the attention both give to the uniquely female experience of birth and motherhood' (p. 91). Green describes her study as offering 'a fresh account of poetic influence' (p. viii), a goal that recedes into the rear-view mirror as she settles into arguing her main thesis, that 'Milton's manipulation of Ovidian motifs enables his handling of the relationship between the sexes before the Fall to be more complex and fluid than the rigidly hierarchical conception of gender designation offered by our first introduction to the human couple' (p. 13).Thoroughly documented and well aware of the Miltonist's anxiety of influence in handling such familiar materials, Green's first three chapters go far beyond a reading of the poolside creation scene and its recapitulation of the Narcissus myth to examine other uses of Ovidian figurations: Milton's allusion in book 4 to Daphne's flight from Apollo, the pursuit of Chloris-Flora by Zephyr, parallels between Sin and the monstrous Scylla, and Eve's alignment with Proserpina all receive scrupulous treatment. Chapter four chases the argument down different alleys, showing how Eve, associated with springtime and flowers through her identification with Flora and Proserpina, ascends several notches in the poem as 'she assumes the role of graceful goddess of beauty and love, Venus herself' (p. 99). Green contends that proper valuation of Eve's superior beauty presents'a genuine conundrum experienced at times by Satan, Adam, Eve and the narrator himself, and proves a dilemma for the reader too' (p. 115). Chapter five describes Eve's association with the vine as located at the intersection of classical texts and scripture: the 'fruitful vine' migrates from Psalm 128 to the marriage service and also recalls Pomona's wedding of the vine to her elm. (Not entirely literary in origin, the practice of training vines to grow around elms dates back to the Romans and continued for centuries as a standard agricultural technique). Eve plays multiple roles throughout the epic, making her anything but the static figure subject to patriarchal containment imagined by some critics, her identity constantly shifting and suffused with myth. Green conveniently summarises her thesis—had we lost sight of it amongst all the interwoven close readings, echoes and cross-references—in the final chapter: 'She is both one and many: first the solitary Narcissus, then the reluctant Daphne, hotly pursued; now the softly sensuous *mater florum* or even Venus herself, queen of the graces. She is both the all-powerful mother goddess

Ceres and the frail, vulnerable Proserpina or the doomed Eurydice. As she leaves Adam to garden alone, Eve has the "Virgin Majestie" of Diana, yet she more nearly resembles the independent-spirited but unwary gardener Pomona, armed only with her gardening tools' (181). In her final metamorphosis (and in the closing chapter) we see Eve step forward as Deucalion's virtuous wife, 'chaste Pyrrha' (*PL* 11.12), here the prototype of the redemptive agency and Christian heroic patience fulfilled by the Son.

Readers would have a hard time identifying particular trends or emphases from what appeared on Milton in the journals during 2009, some portion of which I consider below. We might think of Milton studies as analogous to the engineering of a fail-safe design, the building of systems to a standard where they continue to work even if one component should become less than fully operational. Milton's reputation does not rise or fall together with any one methodology. Among the wide array of approaches deployed by Miltonists, studies that attend to allusion and gender, to scriptural sources and theology, show no sign of fading from the scene. Katherine R. Kellett, 'The Lady's Voice: Poetic Collaboration in Milton's *Mask*' (*MiltonS* 50[2009] 1–19) builds her argument on our current sense of the workings of early modern textuality to reveal how the Lady's verbal authority depends on exchange, how the solitary author inevitably gives way to collaboration and multiple voices, and how dialogue renders Milton's text multivocal and networked. According to David Quint, 'Ulysses and the Devils: The Unity of Book Two of *Paradise Lost*' (*MiltonS* 49[2009] 20–48), Milton constructs Book 2 around the figure of Ulysses, appropriating a series of scenarios from various classical sources, and reproducing versions of the Greek hero in Belial and Beelzebub, as well as in Satan. Taken together, the allusions form a web that binds together parts of the book whenever readers encounter versions of Ulysses. Book Two thus repeats itself again and again, and the repetition forms part of its meaning. Richard J. Du Rocher, '"Tears such as Angels weep": Passion and Allusion in *Paradise Lost*'(*MiltonS* 49[2009] 124–45), argues that far from soft-pedalling epic's traditional reliance on the passions, Milton devises his epic to raise the volume on affect, that 'through a series of allusions to the *Aeneid*, Milton emphasizes the analogy between his God and Virgil's impassioned gods, particularly Juno, thus forcing readers to observe the similarities and isolate the differences between them' (p. 124), and that Milton's God is a God of feeling, although with emotions much finer than our own. Daniel Shore's 'Things Unattempted . . . Yet Once More' (*MiltonQ* 43[2009] 195–200) yet once more glosses the line 'Things unattempted yet in Prose or Rhime' (*PL* 1.16), reminding us, for example, of a neglected source in Matteo Maria Boiardo's *Orlando Innamorato*, and of the multi-layered tissue of irony underlying the novelty *topos*.

In 'The Horseless Epic' (*MiltonQ* 43[2009] 1–16), Bruce Boehrer takes his cue from animal studies to argue a tripartite thesis, striking in its obvious rightness and stated with commendable clarity from the outset: first, that *Paradise Lost* 'is distinguished by an almost complete absence of the equestrian imagery and references to be found in its most important classical antecedents; second, that this virtual absence provides insight into the thematic and formal qualities that differentiate Miltonic epic from its

Homeric and Virgilian forebears; and third, that in the very few cases, when equestrian references do appear in Milton's late poetry, they function consistently as invidious discriminators, associated with fallen experience, corrupt notions of sociopolitical order, and debased language and literature' (p. 1). Anthony Welch in 'Milton's Forsaken Proserpine' (*ELR* 39[2009] 527–56), studies allusions to Pluto's rape of Proserpina, which extend across Milton's entire poetic career. In *Paradise Lost* the scene of Pluto's crime undergoes erasure since with this myth of abduction and sexual violence Milton must 'confront a range of anxieties' surrounding death, together with 'deep misgivings about his investment in a pagan literary heritage' (p. 529). In the final two books of the epic, Welch concludes, Milton orchestrates the effacement of the Proserpina myth and 'of the erotic *locus amoenus* that has by now been stained by mortality' (p. 555).

Victoria Kahn's 'Job's Complaint in *Paradise Regained*' (*ELH* 76[2009] 625–60) re-visits the poem's allusions to the book of Job and discerns in its dialogue and structure traces of Job's ironic rhetoric: 'The Son's Jobean rhetoric is thus crucial for understanding the Son's nature, including the political, hermeneutical, and literary exemplarity of the Son as "perfect man"' (p. 626), she writes. As he toys with the literal-minded Satan, the Son deploys such techniques as parody, wordplay, quotation and mimicry in a manner that signals an affinity with Job, whose impatience with his comforters some commentators (including Milton) thought of as exemplifying a higher patience. According to Kahn, Milton adopts the dialogue of Job as a pattern for his own complaining and legitimate questioning of God, and the convergence 'insinuates a Job-like complaint, a subliminal counterplot questioning the God who permitted the crucifixion' (p. 643). Rather than staging *Paradise Regained* as theodicy, Milton models Jesus as a figure of ironic critique and human resistance to temptation, basing his portrait on a literary reading of Job.

Kent R. Lehnhof's 'Performing Masculinity in *Paradise Lost*' (*MiltonS* 50[2009] 50–64) denies that Milton's outlook on gender is essentialist. Rather, riding in the slipstream of 1990s queer theory, he sees the treatment of gender in *Paradise Lost* as primarily a question of performance: masculinity appears most stable, Lehnhof contends, when it does not appear coextensive with sexual identity, a principle supposedly exemplified by Milton's angels.

Let me end this year's review by mentioning that William Poole, in the *Oxford Handbook* entry discussed above, quotes Milton from *Of Prelatical Episcopacy* on the mind-numbing task of studying patristics and the Church Fathers' 'immeasurable, innumerable, and therefore unnecessary and unmerciful volumes' (p. 379). Milton offers a characteristically acerbic take on the exasperation early modern readers experienced, their sense of being overwhelmed and exhausted by the ceaseless production of books and writing. Ann Blair's *Too Much to Know: Managing Scholarly Information before the Modern Age* (Yale UP, 2010), demonstrates how complaints similar to Milton's became a constant refrain in humanist culture. Early modern readers availed themselves of dictionaries, commentaries, books of quotations, indexes, omnibus reviews and other tools useful for managing vast bodies of knowledge. Of making many books there is no end, and readers have worried over mental fatigue and eyestrain from antiquity down to the present. Twenty-first century consumers of print in its various forms, however, have good reason to feel optimistic about the production of so many books and articles on Milton, living (as I think we do) in a golden age of Milton criticism.

Books Reviewed

Badir, Patricia. *The Maudlin Impression: English Literary Images of Mary Magdalene, 1550–1700*. Notre Dame. [2009] pp. 300. $38 ISBN 9 7802 6802 2150.

Barnes, A.W. *Post-Closet Masculinities in Early Modern England*. BuckUP. [2009] pp. 211. $49 ISBN 9 7808 3875 7185.

Cooper, John R. *Wit's Voice: Intonation in Seventeenth-Century English Poetry*. UDelP. [2009] pp. 254. $55 ISBN 9 7808 7413 0591.

Cousins, A.D., and Alison V. Scott, eds. *Ben Jonson and the Politics of Genre*. Cambridge. [2009] pp. xi + 218. $93 ISBN 9 7805 2151 3784.

Dijkhuizen, Jan Frans van, and K.A.E. Enenkel, eds. *The Sense of Suffering: Constructions of Physical Pain in Early Modern Culture*. Brill. [2009] pp. xxiii + 501. $148 ISBN 9 7890 0417 2470.

Dobranski, Stephen. B. *A Variorum Commentary on the Poems of John Milton*, vol. 3: *Samson Agonistes*. Duquesne. [2009] pp. xviii + 501. $85 ISBN 9 7808 2070 4159.

Duncan, Kathryn, ed. *Religion in the Age of Reason*. AMS. [2009] pp. xx + 233. $84.50 ISBN 9 7804 0464 8534.

Eckhardt, Joshua. *Manuscript Verse Collectors and the Politics of Anti-Courtly Love Poetry*. OUP. [2009] pp. viii + 306. $99 ISBN 9 7801 9955 9503.

Gilman, Ernest B. *Plague Writing in Early Modern England*. UChicP. [2009] pp. xi + 295. $35 ISBN 9 7802 2629 4094.

Graham, Elaine L., ed. *Grace Jantzen: Redeeming the Present*. Ashgate. [2009] pp. x + 269. $34.95 ISBN 9 7807 5466 8237.

Green, Mandy. *Milton's Ovidian Eve*. Ashgate. [2009] pp. xi + 235. $99.95 ISBN 9 7807 5466 6660.

Hansen, Kristin, and Sharon Inkelas. *The Nature of the Word: Studies in Honor of Paul Kiparsky*. MIT. [2009] pp. xvi + 750. $90. ISBN 9 7802 6208 3799.

Hurley, Ann, and Chanita Goodblatt. *Women Editing/Editing Women: Early Modern Women Writers and the New Textualism*. MIT. [2009] pp. xviii + 295. $67.99 ISBN 9 7814 4380 1782.

McDowell, Nicholas, and Nigel Smith, eds. *The Oxford Handbook of Milton*. OUP. [2009] pp. xxii + 715. $150 ISBN 9 7801 9921 0886.

McKeown, Adam N. *English Mercuries: Soldier Poets in the Age of Shakespeare*. VanderbiltUP. [2009] pp. xi + 208. $59.95 ISBN 9 7808 2651 6626.

Mohamed, Feisal G. *In the Anteroom of Divinity: The Reformation of the Angels from Colet to Milton*. UTorP. [2008] pp. xiv + 242. $57 ISBN 9 7808 0209 7927.

Murray, Molly. *The Poetics of Conversion in Early Modern English Literature*. CUP. [2009] pp. xi + 205. $80. ISBN 9 7805 2111 3878.

Patterson, Annabel. *Milton's Words*. OUP. [2009] pp. viii + 212. $34.95 ISBN 9 7801 9957 3462.

Reisner, Noam. *Milton and the Ineffable*. OUP. [2009] pp. xii+321. $95 ISBN 9 7801 9957 2625.

Schwartz, Louis. *Milton and Maternal Mortality*. CUP. [2009] pp. xi + 269. £53.00 ISBN 9 7805 2189 6382.

Sell, Roger D., and Anthony W. Johnson, eds. *Writing and Religion in England, 1558–1689: Studies in Community-Making and Cultural Memory*. Ashgate. [2009] pp. xvi + 498. £65 ISBN 9 7807 5466 2785.

Shawcross, John T. *The Development of Milton's Thought: Law, Government, and Religion*. Duquesne. [2008] pp. x + 283. $60 ISBN 9 7808 2070 4111.

Stoll, Abraham. *Milton and Monotheism*. Duquesne. [2009] pp. xi + 377. $60 ISBN 9 7808 2070 4104.

Sugimura, N. K. *"Matter of Glorious Trial": Spiritual and Material Substance in Paradise Lost*. YaleUP. [2009] pp. xxix + 402. $55 ISBN 9 7803 0013 5596.

Teulié, Gilles, and Laurence Lux-Sterritt, eds. *War Sermons*. CambridgeSP. [2009] pp. xviii + 265. $59.99 ISBN 9 7814 4380 5469.

X

The Later Seventeenth Century

HELEN BROOKS AND JAMES OGDEN

This chapter has one section: 1. Drama. Section 1(a) is by Helen Brooks; section 1(b) is by James Ogden.

1. Drama

(a) General

'Does Performance Studies Speak to Restoration Theatre?' (*LitComp* 6:iii[2009] 668–79), Deborah Payne Fisk asks provocatively this year. In this challenging essay Fisk identifies a connection between declining interest in Restoration theatre and drama, and the resistance to a performance studies (PS) approach to the field, making a compelling argument for the need to revitalize scholarly approaches. She draws attention to Restoration drama's distinctive resistance to a PS approach by highlighting the incorporation of PS into neighbouring fields and historic periods (such as Shakespeare, early modern, and nineteenth-century theatre studies), and she explains this resistance as being a consequence of the textuality of Restoration theatre, of the institutional privileging of the literary, and of the perception of work on stagecraft and performance as being anti-intellectual. The oddity she notes is that while PS has impacted only loosely on the field, 'the Restoration reveled in those very attributes—textuality, sophistication, pleasure, and aesthetic form—disdained by performance theorists' (pp. 668–9). While arguing that the resistance to a PS approach has limited consideration of such important subjects as theatrical reception and the large-scale material context of performance, Fisk also recognizes the difficulties of applying PS to the Restoration. She identifies PS's elusive nature, its focus on non-scripted events, its celebration of hybridity, its location on the margins, and its commitment to social action, as being at odds with the thrust of the largely elite, white, male, and privileged Restoration theatre. Yet despite its problems, Fisk concludes, it is only by engaging with the varied methodological approaches offered by PS that the field will be opened up to new, important foci such as neighbourhood geographies, audience sociologies, strategies of scenic representation, the material history of scripts or modes of commercial

The Year's Work in English Studies, Volume 90 (2011)
doi:10.1093/ywes/mar013

and theatrical exchange (p. 676). Performance studies, Fisk suggests, is central to the future of studies in Restoration theatre and drama.

Two essays which speak to Fisk's call for a performance studies approach do so through their consideration of sexual identity and queerness. In '"The Queen was not shav'd yet": Edward Kynaston and the Regendering of the Restoration Stage' (*ECent* 50:iv[2009] 309–26) George E. Haggerty turns his attention to the largely unresearched area of transvestite theatre. Contextualizing his essay with the argument that the male actor was as subject to the theatrical male gaze as the female actress, Haggerty offers an engaging analysis of Kynaston's presentation of both male and female roles and uses this to explore the codification of gender difference in performance. He charts Kynaston's development from playing female to male roles between 1660 and 1700, focusing in particular on Kynaston's performance of a man who masquerades as a woman in the titular role in *Epicoene* [1661] as a transitional moment in this development. In this play, Haggerty argues, the audience's knowledge of Kynaston's female performances and Epicoene's gender performance worked together to undermine constructions of gender both on stage and in society. Positioning this performance as marking Kynaston's shift from playing female to playing male roles, the second part of the essay then turns to Kynaston's performance of male characters, focusing on his performance of Harcourt in *The Country Wife*. In this role, Haggerty argues, Kynaston articulated a new, abject, sensitive, and slightly feminized model of theatrical masculinity which was distinct from either the libertine or the fop. Recognizing that models of gender were shifting in similar ways outside the theatre, it was through presenting himself as a model of abject masculinity, Haggerty concludes, that Kynaston was able to promote himself as a central figure on the Restoration stage.

Haggerty's previous work on queerness and the Restoration stage is the starting point for Kristin Hunt's essay 'I Greedily Resign: *Lucius Junius Brutus* as Queer Transcultural Object' (*RECTR* 24:ii[2009] 63–79). Hunt argues for the use of queer theoretical approaches in studying the period's theatre, demonstrating their potential in a queer analysis of a play which she argues has been the subject of a scholarly 'straightening impulse' (p. 69), Nathaniel Lee's *Lucius Junius Brutus* [1680]. Hunt argues that the multiple narratives and ideologies on offer in the play are best understood through an analysis of it as a queer transcultural object, where transcultural is understood as working across time periods, rather than geographical space. Hunt identifies potential sites for a queer reading in both the content and in its structure, and concludes that, with the more sympathetic characters being the more queer, such an approach relocates the play's slippery resistance to definition as a celebration of the queer. A secondary but related thread throughout Hunt's essay is a concern with Restoration theatre as heritage and the need for a refocus on past theatre's potential to broaden our understanding of, and intervention in, the present (p. 78), an argument which segues to the second strand in this year's work.

The number of studies examining drama at points of political uncertainty and crisis presents an interesting comment upon the contemporary context from which these studies emerge as well as speaking to Hunt's argument for past theatre to speak to the present moment. Elaine McGirr's book *Heroic Mode and Political Crisis* takes up the theme, with a comprehensive examination of the heroic's association with Stuart rule over the years 1660–1745. McGirr presents the heroic mode as a fulcrum linking the Restoration to the mid-eighteenth century (p. 26), analysing the ways in which the changing connotations of the heroic provide a lens through which to look at cultural and ideological change. Demonstrating the heroic's shift from being a dramatic form to being a mood or cultural experience, McGirr argues for its continuance after 1671 in a variety of cultural forms including poetry, cultural events, and drama, and her analysis of plays at moments of cultural crisis demonstrates the use of the heroic as a shorthand for ideological debates over authority, masculinity, and British national identity. Beginning at the Restoration with Orrey's *The Generall* and Davenant's *Siege of Rhodes* [both 1663], McGirr presents the heroic as the dominant cultural aesthetic, highlighting both its affiliation with the court and its celebration of post-war unity and peace. Moving on to consider responses to the heroic, McGirr identifies attacks on the mode as the consequence of the ambiguity of the heroic's form, its association with James, and an increasing gap between reality and the heroic ideal. Concluding chapter 1 with a detailed analysis of the most prominent attack, Buckingham's *The Rehearsal* [1672], chapter 2 shifts forwards to consider the development of these attacks during the Exclusion Crisis, arguing that by 1680 the Whigs' use of the heroic to represent popery, tyranny, and the cultural embodiment of fears of James's reign had transformed its meaning. With an interwoven analysis of plays, poetry, cultural artefacts, and critical works, McGirr makes a convincing case for the heroic's independent life during this period. She considers the ways in which plays like Otway's *Venice Preserv'd* [1682] cultivated an ambiguity which spoke both to a Whig public and a Tory theatrical institution, but concludes that by the time of James's accession the combined impact of the Whigs' control of the meaning of the heroic and James's lack of interest in the political potential of theatre resulted in a neglect of the heroic. As well as seeing in James's reign the reasons for the dramatic drought experienced by the United Company, McGirr presents the Tories' failure to reclaim the heroic as an effective counter-model as being a factor in James's loss of the crown. Moving forward to the final years of the seventeenth century in chapter 3, McGirr argues that the meaning of the heroic mode had now shifted fundamentally. No longer celebrating the present, but instead looking back to 1660 in the hope of a second restoration, post-Glorious Revolution heroic productions served to allow Jacobites to both escape their present and also, through a shared cultural language, recognize each other. Turning from here to the eighteenth century, McGirr's subsequent two chapters consider the heroic during the Whig ascendancy and finally during the 1745 Jacobite rebellion. In its sophisticated analysis of dramatic, cultural, and literary texts, McGirr's book provides an excellent frame for a number of further essays this year.

The theme of the heroic is a central feature of Laura Linker's essay, '"Decencies of behavior": Dryden and the Libertines in *Marriage-à-la-Mode*' (*RECTR* 24:i[2009] 47–60). Considering this play as an evaluation of the meaning of pleasure (p. 49), Linker suggests that Dryden uses the concurrent heroic and comic plots to comment on the political dangers of the court's hedonist impulses and to call for a return to classical notions of self-control. Seeing in this play the influence of Dryden's reading of Lucretius, Linker argues that, while it is not didactic, the play certainly offers a disapproving stance towards libertine behaviour. David Bywaters's challenge to the standard narrative that immediately post-Restoration plays in London reflect an unqualified royalism also speaks to McGirr's argument. In 'Representations of the Interregnum and Restoration in English Drama of the Early 1660s' (*RES* 60[2009] 255–70) Bywaters offers an analysis of post-Restoration plays informed by an understanding of the heterogeneous audiences to which they were performed, arguing that playwrights 'were careful in various degrees, while wooing the royalists, to provide also some reassurance to those who had collaborated with the interregnum regimes, or cherished some reservations about the new one' (p. 255). In an extensive and detailed analysis of the twenty-six original plays produced between 1660 and 1665, Bywaters compares the approaches taken by comedies and tragedies to the subject of the interregnum and Restoration. He identifies seven tragedies or tragicomedies as representing the Restoration or usurpation in an elevated style, and in doing so questions these plays—including Orrery's *The Generall* and Robert Howard's *Indian Queen*—as allegories for the Restoration. Edward Howard's *The Usurper*, Bywaters argues, is the one tragicomedy to represent usurpation and Restoration in the period, although he recognizes that it does so by distancing itself from the specificity of Charles II's restoration. The five comedies or tragicomedies which represent the interregnum do so, Bywaters concludes, in a plainer style. He considers the approach to the political subject in John Tathams's *The Rump*, Abraham Cowley's *Cutter of Coleman-Street*, Robert Howard's *The Committee*, Etherege's *Comical Revenge*, and John Lacy's *The Old Troop, or Monsieur Raggou*. In both Howard and Tatham he identifies a strategy of translating the ambiguities of politics into the certainties of anti-feminist mockery, and concludes that these plays' rhetorical subtleties can help us to understand the complex and ambivalent attitudes of the theatrical audiences. Leticia Álvarez-Recio's analysis of the representation of legitimate succession in 'Nahum Tate's *The History of King Richard the Second* (1681): Politics and Censorship during the Exclusion Crisis' (*RECTR* 24:i[2009] 17–30) proves a useful companion-piece to Bywaters's study. In this essay Álvarez-Recio focuses on the only one of Tate's plays to consider the theme of legitimate succession, arguing through a detailed analysis of the alterations made to characters from the Shakespearian source-text that Tate was moving towards an affective drama which combined political engagement and sentimentalism, but that the sentimental was a response to concurrent dramatic trends rather than to the political subject. Álvarez-Recio challenges the idea that the play was censored for presenting a feeble, credulous monarch, suggesting instead that this transformation of Richard into a weaker and more tolerant king was a move to create an affective and compassionate response, while the play's censorship was a result of its intertextual relationship to contemporary polemical writings. It is the implications of the Catholic question which preoccupy Judy A. Hayden in her essay 'Harlequin, the Whigs, and William

Mountfort's *Doctor Faustus*' (*SEL* 49:iii[2009] 573–93). Examining the ways in which Mountfort adapted the play, Hayden focuses on the introduction of elements of *commedia dell'arte*, arguing that these functioned as a destabilizing force. Hayden frames her analysis through an understanding of the play as performed in the spring of 1688, and argues that it specifically draws on the hysteria of the Popish Plot in order to suggest the destructive long-term effects of the current frenzy. Lora Geriguis's essay, 'Monarchs, Morality, and English Nationalism in the Comedies of Etherege, Steele and Sheridan' (*RECTR* 24:i[2009] 31–46), also engages with the Popish Plot, considering Etherege's *The Man of Mode* in the light of the preceding paranoia. Geriguis prompts us to rethink the presentation of national identity in a play often seen as contrasting French and English identities. Drawing attention to the comparisons made between the French and English, Geriguis presents the play as an expression of conciliation between the two nations before continuing to develop her argument into the eighteenth century.

The shifting quality and understanding of embodiment in seventeenth-century London is the subject of Kate Cregan's *The Theatre of the Body: Staging Death and Embodying Life in Early-Modern London*. Arguing that the seventeenth century was a period when the body was being medically abstracted, Cregan considers the ways in which legal, anatomical, and theatrical practice worked concurrently to codify and rewrite the body, identifying a shift in the perception of subjectivity across both anatomy manuals and later seventeenth-century plays. The first two parts of the book consider the spectacle of anatomy in the spaces of law, theatre, and medicine, focusing on the years leading up to 1660. In Part III Cregan turns to the Restoration, drawing connections between the changing presentation of the body in anatomical drawings and the types of characters populating the Restoration stage. Chapter 7 develops this point in more detail through a detailed analysis of two of Edward Ravenscroft's adaptations of earlier plays: *Titus Andronicus, or the Rape of Lavinia* [1679] and *The Anatomist, or The Sham Doctor* [1696]. Examining these dramas in light of the overlaps between audiences for dramatic and anatomical theatre, Cregan demonstrates the ways in which anatomical practices mirrored the construction of embodiment offered on the Restoration stage. The theme of scientific work as public spectacle is continued in a second work this year. In 'Theatrical Space and Scientific Space in Thomas Shadwell's *Virtuoso*' (*SEL* 49:iii[2009] 549–71) John Shanahan combines a history of science and the theatre in order to show how the Royal Society attempted to distinguish its work from models of theatricality in response to its concern about the theatricality of experimentation. Shadwell's 1676 play, Shanahan argues, was an attempt to counter this effort. By representing experimental laboratory work on-stage, rather than off-stage as had been done in previous plays, Shanahan argues that Shadwell transformed these private spaces into public spaces and erased their mysticism. In drawing a direct parallel between natural philosophy and theatrical discourse Shadwell attacked not only the self-aggrandizement of the virtuoso but also the new spaces of scientific modernity they had created for themselves. Shadwell makes a second appearance this year in Peter Craft's essay, 'The Contemporary Popular Reception of Shadwell's *A True Widow*'

(*RECTR* 24:i[2009] 5–16). Examining the reasons for the play's failure, Craft reconsiders both Shadwell's own explanation and twentieth-century critics' responses before identifying two primary reasons for the critical contemporary response. The specificity and attack on the audience during the 'play within a play' in Act IV, Craft concludes, was a significant factor, failing to distance the audience from the play's ridicule of them, but equally significant, he argues, was Dryden's prologue, which conflated the play with his own play, *The Kind Keeper*, which had failed ten days earlier. Overall Craft makes an important argument for the need to consider contemporary reception in the light of preceding productions, and for understanding the full range of factors which might inform audience responses.

The final two volumes this year offer detailed historical analyses of specific texts and themes. *Music and Musicians on the London Stage, 1695–1705*, by Kathryn Lowerre, is the first book to consider music's place in the staging of dramatic representations in the period following the lapse of the Licensing Act, and as such it offers a valuable insight into an area often ignored by textual analysis while attesting to Fisk's perception of an increased attention to baroque music and dance in the Restoration (p. 675). The first half of the book takes a topical approach, introducing and explaining the characteristics of different forms of music and their use. Revealing that only three texts out of ninety failed to indicate performed music (p. 17), Lowerre demonstrates the centrality of musical events to comedy, continuing by contrasting this to the lack of music's dramatic integration in tragedy. In the early chapters Lowerre highlights the ways in which music interacted with both the text and the non-textual performance conventions, placing a particular emphasis on examining the repertoire, the creators, and the performers. The second half of the book builds on this grounding, offering a chronological theatre history from a musical perspective. Lowerre highlights the ways in which musical conventions were imitated and extended through a season-by-season analysis of change and adaptation. Drawing on a comprehensive understanding of the wider political context, Lowerre analyses the competition between houses, the comparative musical resources of each house, and audience responses in order to explain performance choices and the changing pattern of music's place in theatre. She concludes with a demonstration of the ways in which musical-theatrical practices continued after 1705. Offering a detailed analysis of both canonical and non-canonical plays and the music within them, Lowerre presents a comprehensive picture of the diversity of, and specific differences between genres and theatres. The structural organization and the extensive notes, explanations, and glossary make this volume accessible to the music specialist and non-specialist alike.

Jorge Braga Riera's, *Classical Spanish Drama in Restoration English (1660–1700)*, also focuses on theatrical practice and reception. Through the lens of translation studies, Riera undertakes a detailed analysis of the relationships between source and target texts, examining a corpus of Spanish golden age comedies translated into English over the period. Informed by an understanding of the social and political contexts and theatrical conventions, and through detailed comparative analysis of themes, plots, characters, titles, structure, stage directions, extralinguistic factors, and theatrical spaces, Riera sheds light on the decisions made by adapters and translators, and demonstrates a shift over the period from a respect for original texts to a more dynamic relationship in which the target culture dominates. With each chapter divided into small, focused sections each concentrating on a specific theatrical convention, this study provides a wealth of easily accessible information on the practices of translation in the plays.

(b) Dryden

I noted two articles on the heroic plays. In 'Unrecorded Allusions to Dryden in Thomas Southerne's *The Wives' Excuse*' (*N&Q* 56[2009] 230–1) Joseph Pappa notes that Lovemore's flattery of Mrs Friendall in this play echoes Almahide's praise of Almanzor in *The Conquest of Granada*: the sexes are reversed, but generally Lovemore's bravado resembles Almanzor's. It is not surprising that these fleeting allusions had not been recorded. In 'Dryden's Transformation of Bernier's *Travels*' (*Restoration* 33:ii[2009] 47–55) Peter Craft takes up a point made in the dedication of *Aureng-Zebe* to the earl of Mulgrave, that Charles II himself suggested changes to the source. Bernier had made it clear that Aureng-Zebe was ambitious and ruthless, but he could not be so portrayed for fear of injuring the East India Company's trade with the Mughal empire, over which Aureng-Zebe still ruled; Dryden did his best to make him appear virtuous and heroic.

At present critics find the adaptations especially interesting, above all those of Shakespeare's *The Tempest* and Milton's *Paradise Lost*. In 'Spaces of Patronage: *The Enchanted Island* and *Prospero's Books*' (*Folio* 15:ii[2008] 5–19) Juan-Francisco Cerdá compares Shakespeare's play, the Dryden–Davenant version, and the Peter Greenaway film of 1991. In 'Adapting the Adaptors: Staging Davenant and Dryden's Restoration *Tempest*' (*Journal of Adaptation in Film and Performance* 2:i[2009] 65–77) Tim Keenan discusses a performance at Hull University. In '*Paradise Lost* and the Stage Directions of Dryden's *The State of Innocence*' (*Restoration* 33:ii[2009] 1–24) Lara Dodds focuses on the theatrical elements of this adaptation to argue that the form of semi-opera enabled Dryden to transform Milton's sublime images into dramatic spectacle, and to challenge his theodicy. This is an elegant and persuasive defence of Dryden's work against adverse criticism. In 'Milton's Ideal of Innocence' (*CritQ* 24:ii[1982] 17–23) I considered implications of a stage-direction not mentioned by Dodds, which shows that Dryden's Adam and Eve were to wear clothes, even before their fall. In '*Paradise Lost* and the Contest over the Modern Heroic Poem' (*MiltonQ* 43:iii[2009] 153–65) Barbara K. Lewalski briefly compares Milton with Davenant, Cowley, Dryden, and others, and maintains that where Milton emphasized that 'freedom (however difficult and dangerous) is the prime good', Dryden rewrote his politics in royalist terms, and expressed 'a desire for authoritative control to avoid evil'. Milton, of course, won the contest.

To conclude: in 'The Cost of Dryden's Catholicism' (*Logos* 12:ii[2009] 144–77) Bryan Berry is primarily concerned with *The Hind and the Panther* in relation to the poet's career and reputation. But a full cost-benefit analysis would remark on his loss of royal patronage and return to the commercial theatre.

Books Reviewed

Cregan, Kate. *The Theatre of the Body: Staging Death and Embodying Life in Early-Modern London*. Brepols. [2009] pp. 349. €70 ISBN 9 7825 0352 0582.

Lowerre, Kathryn. *Music and Musicians on the London Stage, 1695–1705*. Ashgate. [2009] pp. 412. £60 ISBN 9 7807 5466 6141.

McGirr, Elaine. *Heroic Mode and Political Crisis, 1660–1745*. UDelP. [2009] pp. 245. $56 ISBN 9 7808 7413 0430.

Riera, Jorge Braga. *Classical Spanish Drama in Restoration English (1660–1700)*. Benjamins. [2009] pp. 330. $149 ISBN 9 7890 2722 4293.

XI

The Eighteenth Century

ELIZA O'BRIEN, SANDRO JUNG, DAVID SHUTTLETON AND CHRISY DENNIS

This chapter has four sections: 1. General and Prose, 2. The Novel, 3. Poetry and 4. Drama. Section 1 is by Eliza O'Brien; section 2 is by Sandro Jung; section 3 is by David Shuttleton; and section 4 is by Chrisy Dennis.

1. General and Prose

The year 2009 belongs to Samuel Johnson. *The Age of Johnson* returned in Johnson's tercentenary year with a range of essays offering its usual detailed readings of Johnson's writings, those of his circle, and from the period more widely: biblical satire, poetry, jokes, biography, linguistics, sentimental novels, and immigration in late eighteenth-century novels. Of relevance to this section are the following essays. Earl A. Reitan's 'Samuel Johnson, the *Gentleman's Magazine*, and the War of Jenkins' Ear' (*AgeJ* 19[2009] 1–8) examines Johnson's contributions to the *Gentleman's Magazine* regarding the 'Lilliputian Debates' from 1738 onwards. H.J. Jackson, in 'A General Theory of Fame in the *Lives of the Poets*' (*AgeJ* 19[2009] 9–20), considers Johnson's differentiation between 'present praise and posthumous recognition' (p. 11) and the elements which compose Johnson's conception of fame. Anthony W. Lee's 'An Intertextual Node: Johnson's *Life of Dryden*, *Rambler* 31, and *A Letter from a Gentleman to the Honourable Ed. Howard, Esq.*' (*AgeJ* 19[2009] 21–8) examines Peter Cunningham's 1850 article in *Gentleman's Magazine* which attributes authorship of the letter in question to Richard Flecknoe, and examines Johnson's use of this letter in his section on Dryden in his *Life*. Julie Crane, in 'Johnson and the Art of Interruption' (*AgeJ* 19[2009] 29–45), tracks the importance of casual encounters, or 'diversions' (p. 30) in Johnson's life, and the effect these had on his writings. Robin Dix locates three previously unknown references to Johnson in manuscript form in 'Fugitive References to Johnson in Eighteenth-Century Manuscripts' (*AgeJ* 19[2009] 47–52), uncovering a letter from Charles Adams to John Gilbert Cooper, an anonymous review in *The Museum; or, Literary and Historical Register 3* [1747] of Johnson's *Dictionary*, and a poem written in defence of Mark

The Year's Work in English Studies, Volume 90 (2011)
doi:10.1093/ywes/mar002

Akenside in response to Johnson's *Lives* in or shortly after 1781, possibly by Jeremiah Dyson who was the son of Akenside's patron. Robert G. Walker, in 'Boswell's Use of "Ogden on Prayer" in *Journal of a Tour to the Hebrides*' (*AgeJ* 19[2009] 53–68), explores the text of Samuel Ogden's sermons and Boswell's references to and use of them, arguing that Ogden is not Johnson's favourite preacher (as has been suggested, where Ogden has been considered at all) but Boswell's.

In a substantial and detailed consideration of the satirical 'lesson' or 'chronicles' based on biblical scripture, Michael F. Suarez, S.J. examines the popularity of this type of satire and the manipulation of the Bible to produce such writings, in 'Secular Lessons: Biblical Satire, Parody, Imitation, and Emulation in Eighteenth-Century Chronicles of British Politics' (*AgeJ* 19[2009] 69–128). David Fairer's ' "Fishes in his Water": Shenstone, Sensibility, and the Ethics of Looking' (*AgeJ* 19[2009] 129–47) argues for a new way of figuring the gaze, at once subjective and objective rather than in an oppositional or binary mode, in relation to the cultivation of William Shenstone's estate. William Gibson, in 'Smollett, Goldsmith, Nash, and Tobit's Dog: The Biography of a Joke' (*AgeJ* 19[2009] 149–66), investigates the genesis and afterlife of a joke through the connections between biography, fiction, jestbooks, and cultural myths. In 'Perfect Patterns of Conjugal Love and Duty: George Ballard's Domestic Ideologies in his Lives of Elizabeth Egerton and Margaret Cavendish' (*AgeJ* 19[2009] 167–85), Emily Bowles-Smith interrogates the 'posture of objectivity' (p. 168) in Ballard's *Memoirs of Several Ladies of Great Britain* [1752] and explores how the subjects of Ballard's work have been reshaped according to the didactic purpose of the biographer. Brijraj Singh's 'Revisiting *Purley*: John Horne Tooke's Logocentrism' (*AgeJ* 19[2009] 187–212) turns to *Epea Pteroenta* and persuasively argues that Horne Tooke's writings as a linguist and etymologist, rather than as a political radical, anticipate twentieth-century theories of language, and that his linguistic theories were as radical as his politics, or indeed, were the site of his radicalism. In the review essays, Robert Folkenflik, in ' "Little Lives and Little Prefaces"? Lonsdale's Edition of Johnson's *Lives of the Poets* (*AgeJ* 19[2009] 273–83), evaluates Roger Lonsdale's valuable work, and Nora Nachumi's 'Living Large: The Women in *Women's Theatrical Memoirs* (*AgeJ* 19[2009] 285–99) considers the real lives behind the self-representations offered in Pickering & Chatto's collection of that name, edited by Sharon Setzer, Sue McPherson, and Julia Swindells [2007].

Chief among the reconsiderations of Johnson's work this year is Greg Clingham and Philip Smallwood's edited collection of essays, entitled *Samuel Johnson After Three Hundred Years*. This volume seeks to establish the nature of Johnson's impact upon past critics and writers as well as upon possible future ones. It aims to find 'legitimate and responsible ways of bringing [Johnson] into conversation with issues—political, cultural, theoretical, and philosophical as well as literary—that engage modern readers, and that can contribute profoundly to the way in which modern readers think' (p. 4). The fourteen essays focus on moral philosophy, philosophical theory, jurisprudence, biography, non-literary arts, individual literary works, his literary influence, and literary heirs, in ways which emphasize Johnson's work within his historical context, but also, importantly, within the development and progression of thought and literary theory more broadly. Compelling arguments within a very strong collection are found in the following: '"We are perpetually moralists": Johnson and Moral Philosophy' (pp. 15–32) by Fred Parker, which examines Johnson's resistance to easy classification, and 'Samuel Johnson's Politics of Contingency' (pp. 73–94) by Clement Hawes, which investigates critical misunderstandings of Johnson's ethics and politics, arguing that they are not separate spheres and cannot be compartmentalized. In 'The Life of Johnson, *The Life of Johnson*, the *Lives* of Johnson' (pp. 131–44) Jack Lynch explores the connections between Johnson's theory of lives and works, and his influence upon the genre of life writing, arguing successfully that we are so much Johnson's inheritors in this genre that we fail to notice his development of it from previous models. David Fairer's 'The Awkward Johnson' (pp. 145–63) looks at the challenges posed to politeness, the mind, and art by Johnson's understanding of and engagement with the playful side of awkwardness and resistance. 'Johnson's Criticism, the Arts, and the Idea of Art' (pp. 164–85) by Philip Smallwood considers Johnson's criticism of non-literary art forms and his particular critical terminology, and O.M. Brack Jr. offers a fascinating account of the editor's reasoning and rationale in producing the Yale Edition of the Works of Johnson (1958–), and poses questions about Johnson's place in literary history, in 'The Works of Samuel Johnson and the Canon' (pp. 246–61).

The subject of fraud and deception in eighteenth-century writing continues to provide a rich vein of scholarship. This year sees the arrival of Thomas Curley's long-awaited monograph on Johnson and the Ossian controversy, after a series of influential articles, with *Samuel Johnson, the Ossian Fraud, and the Celtic Revival in Great Britain and Ireland*. Curley's main focus is upon Johnson's belief in the importance of literary truth, and how Macpherson's fabrication is involved in both the construction of national cultural myths and the disruption of authentic historical (as well as literary) narrative. Beginning with a broad discussion and evaluation of the history of criticism of Macpherson and then turning to the deception itself, Curley investigates Johnson's tireless enquiry into the nature of truth throughout his career, with a special focus on *A Journey to the Western Isles of Scotland*. The second half of the book turns to the Celtic revival and the exploration and construction of national identity, illuminating Johnson's connections with Scottish and Irish scholars and patriots. The book also includes the pamphlet *A Reply to Mr Clark's Answer* in an appendix, a contribution to the Ossian controversy written by the linguist William Shaw and edited for publication by Johnson in 1782. Curley brings us to a greater understanding of the moral and literary significance of fraud and deception for Johnson and his contemporaries. The breadth of his discussion of Macpherson criticism makes this a useful introduction to the controversy; the depth of analysis and steady, careful argument makes this a significant contribution to Johnson studies.

There is a special section devoted to Johnson in *Dictionaries: Journal of the Dictionary Society of North America*, edited by William Frawley: 'Lexicography and Samuel Johnson' (*Dictionaries* 30[2009] 95–135). Lisa Berglund explores the background to Hester Lynch Piozzi's *British Synonymy* and her attempts to distinguish her work from that of Johnson in 'Fossil Fish: Preserving Samuel Johnson within Hester Lynch Piozzi's *British Synonymy*' (*Dictionaries* 30[2009] 96–107). Kate Wild considers Johnson's use of prescriptive language in the *Dictionary* and argues that it is not as widespread as is commonly described, in 'Johnson's Prescriptive Labels—a Reassessment' (*Dictionaries* 30[2009] 108–18). Chris P. Pearce examines Johnson's definitions of science and the often already outmoded sources he used for information, in 'Samuel Johnson's Use of Scientific Sources in the *Dictionary*' (*Dictionaries* 30[2009] 119–29). Finally, Richard W. Bailey compares Johnson's explanations of American sayings in his *Dictionary* with definitions presented in similar publications both prior to the *Dictionary* and subsequent to it, in 'Dr. Johnson and the American Vocabulary' (*Dictionaries* 30[2009] 130–5). Elsewhere, in 'Reference Point: Samuel Johnson and the Encyclopedias' (*ECLife* 33:iii[2009] 37–64), Paul Tankard traces references to Johnson and critiques of his work in eighteenth-century encyclopaedias, examining the construction of his reputation and the contemporary responses to his many writings. Christopher Vilmar explores critical perceptions of Johnson's writings (or lack of them) on satire in 'Johnson's Criticism of Satire and the Problem of the Scriblerians' (*CQ* 38[2009] 1–23).

Ruth Mack's *Literary Historicity: Literature and Historical Experience in Eighteenth-Century Britain*, a rewarding and challenging read, sets about analysing the following questions: what does the past mean for eighteenth-century writers? And what relation does fiction or literature bear to truth? Mack interrogates ideas of fiction and history, as well as both fictional and historical writings, and argues that the lack of division in the eighteenth century between history and fiction means that current criticism needs to radically rethink its approach to these subjects as separate disciplines. She suggests that rather than looking for investigations into historical knowledge within historical or at least non-fiction discourse we can see these debates playing out 'most strikingly in prefaces, novels, and literary criticism' (p. 3). For Mack, such writings do not emphasize the apparent opposition between fact and fiction but are concerned instead with organization, hence the validity of comparing history with poetry, or biographical narrative with fictional narrative. Writers under consideration here include Lord Bolingbroke, Samuel Johnson, Henry Fielding, Charlotte Lennox, Horace Walpole, Laurence Sterne, and William Warburton. Her analysis of Johnson and history in chapter 1, 'Johnson and Historical Authorship' (pp. 33–58), is especially compelling. It discusses the connections between the individual subject, history, and experience as presented by Johnson in his Preface to *The Dictionary of the English Language*, and looks at how the Preface investigates the idea of the historical subject: how can the individual's experience be considered as history? Mack suggests that Johnson answers this by making experience the basis for a historical relation to the individual self, rather than a basis of fact. This in turn is linked to Johnson's *Lives of the Poets*, which Mack argues is a demonstration of Johnson's method of the historicization of the individual's authorship and the individual's experience through narrative form.

A welcome reissue this year is Robert DeMaria's *Samuel Johnson and the Life of Reading*, originally published in 1997. DeMaria's erudite, perceptive, and absorbing study of readers and the act of reading, with Johnson as the exemplar, brims with a steady enthusiasm amidst its effortless theorization of and investigation into this most fundamental of activities. Presumably reissued for the tercentenary, DeMaria's work will be of interest to all English scholars in eighteenth-century studies and beyond. Another classic reissued for Johnson's tercentenary was Hibbert's lively account of Johnson's life, *Samuel Johnson: A Personal History* [1971], with a new introduction by Henry Hitchings. It provides an entertaining introduction to Johnson and the wider culture of the eighteenth century. Hibbert supplies plenty of interesting and amusing detail, and the chatty tone of his biography is enhanced by its structure, which is divided chronologically into four sections but with much commentary and description in each chapter reaching across the decades, rather than a year-by-year account, which adds to the lively pace of the narrative.

A significant event in Johnson biography is the publication of the first critical edition of Sir John Hawkins's work from 1787, *The Life of Samuel Johnson, LLD*, taken from the second edition published the same year and edited by O.M. Brack. This is an exceedingly valuable addition to Johnson biography, given that it is based on first-hand observation, shared interests, particularly pertaining to religion, deep friendship, and respect, and benefits from Hawkins's access to Johnson's legal documents as his executor. Hawkins's work was first greeted by hostile reviews and later superseded by Boswell's biography, so its recovery is of great value. Brack has corrected the typographical errors (listed in the emendations) but has reproduced the actual text of the second edition unadorned, with substantial and learned annotations kept to the notes. Though Brack writes '[t]he focus of the annotations is to illuminate the text, not to provide elaborate discussions of related literary, cultural, and political matters' (p. xi), the notes contain a wealth of scholarly information and the work as a whole is a testament to Brack's patient, thorough, and intelligent editorial work that is exemplified by his Yale Johnson work. The introduction recovers the value of Hawkins's first-hand account of Johnson's life against the more familiar version by Boswell, and unpicks some of the contradictory political and religious opinions held by Johnson and Hawkins. It also discusses the contributions made to the manuscript by Hawkins's daughter, Laetitia-Matilda. The edition is complete with notes, a textual commentary, a list of emendations, a list of cancellations in the 1787 edition, and the preliminaries to volume 1 of *The Works of Samuel Johnson, LLD* from 1797.

Amongst so many biographies of Johnson, David Nokes's *Samuel Johnson: A Life* stands out. In his scholarly discussions of Johnson's work and life Nokes frames his own work with Johnson's belief that 'an individual's works [should be] seen in the context of the turmoils of his life' (p. 357). His ability as a writer enables him to retell the many well-known anecdotes and significant encounters in Johnson's life in a way that makes them appear fresh and absorbing after more than 200 years of repetition. The biography, broadly chronological in order, begins in the weeks leading up to the publication of the first edition of Johnson's *Dictionary*, when Johnson, after some anxious written appeals and visits, waited for his degree from Pembroke College, Oxford, to be awarded so that he could print it after his name on the title page of his new work. Out of this mixture of hard-earned triumph, reputation, effort, and anxiety Nokes draws Johnson's character and intellectual activities into a fully realized, coherent, engaging, and astute account.

In *Anna Seward: A Constructed Life. A Critical Biography* by Teresa Barnard the representation that Seward made of herself in her public and private letters, which she then rewrote with a view to publication, is recovered from the interventions of Seward's editors, chiefly Walter Scott, who cut and censored and contravened Seward's clear instructions. Barnard argues that correspondence was the main means by which Seward carefully constructed her own literary image, so to consider Seward as a writer means that we must return to her own extant letters, both the original forms and the rewritten versions for publication, before the editors set to work. Seward emerges from these original letters as a very different character: political, independent, supportive of other writers, intellectually rigorous, and adventurous. The chapters on Seward's juvenile letters illuminate these early writings, and are especially informative as to how Seward used these early letters as a form of diary within which she could test out her literary ambitions. The final chapter reads Seward's legal will as another form of autobiography, a substantial public document that allows its author one final, posthumous way of presenting and controlling her self-image.

J.A. Downie's *A Political Biography of Henry Fielding* begins with a useful author's note: 'I think a political biography of Fielding should attempt two interrelated tasks; first, to offer an account of his life which concentrates on the political aspects of his career in all its twists and turns, including his various and varying political allegiances; second, to trace the development of his political ideas—his political ideology, if you will' (p. ix). This clarity of purpose is followed unwaveringly through Downie's text, and the result is a much-needed exploration and analysis of the developments and changes to Fielding's political thought (namely, that he wrote for money and seemed easily bought) which has often puzzled or wrong-footed critics. Downie argues convincingly that Fielding's political allegiances are entirely coherent when considered against exactly which type of Whig policies he supported, rather than viewing him as moving awkwardly between certainty and uncertainty, and that while writing for money may be unsavoury, 'it is imperative to recognize that this involved no sacrifice of political principle on Fielding's part' (p. 207). A particularly rewarding chapter in this excellent book is its ninth, ' "A Hearty Well-Wisher to the Glorious Cause of Liberty": *Tom Jones* and the Forty-Five' (pp. 173–84), which offers a persuasive argument accounting for Fielding's inclusion of the Jacobite uprising of 1745 among the scenes of Tom's adventures, and how this may be viewed as adhering to Fielding's politics overall in relation to the Protestant succession, rather than as a contradiction of them.

Following on from Fielding, a further addition to Pickering & Chatto's extremely useful series is *A Political Biography of Richard Steele*, by Charles A. Knight. It is a thorough, precise, and painstaking work (though unfortunately not entirely free from typographical errors), clarifying and contextualizing the often obscure and restlessly changing political situation and allegiances of the early eighteenth century. Knight structures his chronological investigation into Steele's political principles and allegiances around his work for his most famous periodicals: *Gazette* and *Tatler* in chapter 2, *Spectator* in chapter 3, *Guardian* and *Crisis* in chapters 4 and 5 respectively, before a discussion of his theatrical writings. This thematic arrangement is especially rewarding in that it allows for a sustained and nuanced investigation into Steele's political activities and his differing literary strategies and motivations in each case. Steele's many varied roles—soldier, writer, propagandist, dramatist, member of parliament—become newly coherent as engagements with the public world which, when mapped upon his political views, pose interesting questions about principle, necessity, and contingency in Steele's overall career.

Biography of a different kind is the subject of Rebecca Bullard's steady and thorough investigation into the form of the secret history. In *The Politics of Disclosure, 1674–1725: Secret History Narratives* Bullard sets out 'to provide the first integrated account of early modern secret history, in which both its literary and its partisan characteristics are considered, in detail, together' (p. 5). This ambitious project illuminates not only this form of history writing in all its political complexity, but also its influence upon the emerging form of the novel as well as satirical and polemical writing, playing with questions of fact and fiction and making claims to truthfulness that, given the integral role of secrecy within the form, can be impossible to prove. Bullard argues that 'secret history is, at its heart, a self-conscious form with Whig origins, which was nonetheless appropriated by eighteenth-century writers of different political opinions' (p. 22), and she structures her study accordingly, moving from Whig historical and political writings in the late seventeenth century in Section I, to a nuanced analysis of the various appropriations of the form by Tory writers. In Section II, 'Secret History in the Eighteenth Century: Variations and Adaptations' Bullard turns her attention to works that engage with the rhetorical conventions of the anti-absolutist Whig secret history but which yet do not strictly belong to that tradition, discussing in turn Delarivier Manley's *romans-à-clef The New Atalantis* and *Memoirs of Europe*, Addison and Steele's *The Spectator*, Defoe's *The Secret History of the White Staff*, and Eliza Haywood's *roman-à-clef Memoirs of a Certain Island Adjacent to the Kingdom of Utopia*.

Our Coquettes: Capacious Desire in the Eighteenth Century, by Theresa Braunschneider, is a nuanced and incisive study of the figure of the coquette and how from her appearance in society and literature in the early eighteenth century she is defined through choice, consumption, and resistance against constraint. Before coquetry became almost exclusively (and erroneously) synonymous with flirtation, it signified the emergence of a type of young woman newly mobile in society, possessed of a certain amount of money and therefore a certain degree of independence from dominant codes of society regarding travel, sexual conduct, and consumption. The various activities of the coquette, as Braunschneider shows, were the result of the historical moment, with her array of choices produced by the market. By examining the apparently stock character of the frivolous coquette in eighteenth-century satire, drama, and novels, Braunschneider argues, we may see how representations of this new female type can be used as a means for writers to reflect upon their own society's progress into modernity, in terms not only of women's public participation in society but of virtuous, or feminine, or fashionable behaviour, and what these changes say about the society that represents and interrogates them. 'By taking seriously this ostensibly trivial figure' Braunschneider suggests, 'we can analyze the cultural and ideological work performed by the *attribution* of triviality to women who unapologetically embrace the world of consumer goods, who insist on determining their own sexual destiny, who (at least temporarily) want many instead of one' (p. 8). This numerical opposition, of many choices versus one, is something that defines the discourse surrounding coquetry, and it is the coquette's refusal of restriction that eventually results in the representation of the coquettish mode changing from one of amusement and entertainment, at the start of the century, to one of punishment and disaster (with her refusal viewed as a threat to marriage and domesticity) at the end. Braunschneider's erudition, matched to a lively and expressive writing style, makes this a thoroughly engaging work.

An ambitious study by Karen O'Brien, *Women and Enlightenment in Eighteenth-Century Britain*, opens new ground on the debate about women as writers of history and as individuals subject to the historical process during the Enlightenment. It examines the re-evaluation of history during the long eighteenth century, and in turn causes us to reconsider current thoughts about eighteenth-century history and the role women played in the development of Enlightenment society. O'Brien draws upon a vast range of sources for this work of intellectual history, with educational, economic, and theological works among the literary and historical writings discussed. Part of the reconsideration results from O'Brien's focus upon the Whiggish view of history and writing, rather than the Tory one, and explores the continuities between philosophical Whigs and radical Dissenters. Beginning with the engagement of women writers such as Mary Astell, Catherine Cockburn and Damaris Masham with Locke's ideas about morality and society, this study covers Scottish moral philosophy and its implications for women, especially Hume's idea of artificial virtues, and also examines how Gothic, Roman, and medieval history, and chivalry, were used to shape the debate on women's place in society. Catherine Macaulay and Mary Wollstonecraft are given a chapter each, with O'Brien's discussion on Macaulay's place in the development of the theory of historical progress particularly fruitful, positioning her between Cockburn and Wollstonecraft in the train of influence. The study ends with female historians and the aftermath of Malthus's *Essay on the Principle of Population*, with Austen, Elizabeth Hamilton, and Hannah More among the range of writers discussed. O'Brien's range is impressive, and she never falters in her dedicated examination of writing by and about women for its ability to unlock the meaning of history.

A different investigation into gender and society is offered in *Domestic Affairs: Intimacy, Eroticism, and Violence between Servants and Masters in Eighteenth-Century Britain*, by Kristina Straub. This fascinating and richly detailed study sheds much-needed light upon a central subject of eighteenth-century life: the role of the servant in both public and private spheres. Straub analyses a wide array of literary sources, from novels (*Roxana*, *Pamela*, *Joseph Andrews*, *Humphry Clinker*, and *Caleb Williams* among them) to dramas, conduct books, pamphlets, periodicals, and polemical writings. She explores the sexual and social forces that lend the servant's role its peculiar charge, at once familiar/familial and threatening or sexually available, as well as the developing economic forces and labour market that affect the servant's personal agency. The different responses to and exploitation of male and female servants, physically, morally, or sexually, are examined in detail. Straub argues convincingly that paying attention to representations of the eighteenth-century servant provides us with new ways of understanding the later formation of theories of gender and sexuality especially in relation to the notion of deviance, which Straub discusses here regarding the writings on the notorious cases of Elizabeth Canning and Elizabeth Brownrigg. Particularly intriguing is chapter 5, 'Performing the Manservant, 1730–1760' (pp. 110–40), which analyses the roles of masculinity, authority, and violence in the interplay between representations of male servants on the stage and the forgotten controversy regarding the behaviour of servants in the Footmen's Gallery at London's Drury Lane Theatre.

A special edition of *Eighteenth Century: Theory and Interpretation* this year is devoted to 'The Future of Feminist Theory in Eighteenth-Century Studies'. In her introduction the volume's editor Laura J. Rosenthal discusses canon formation and the significance of feminist theory in the ongoing recovery of women writers in Restoration and eighteenth-century studies (*ECent* 50[2009] 1–11). Ellen Pollak explores the changes and developments in feminist theory and its involvement with Enlightenment thought and the articulation of an emerging modernity (*ECent* 50[2009] 13–20). Alison Conway, in 'Future Conditional: Feminist Theory, New Historicism, and Eighteenth-Century Studies' (*ECent* 50[2009] 25–31), argues for the importance of feminist theory's place within eighteenth-century studies as a corrective against new historicism's tendency to lean towards realism. Melissa Mowry explores the difficulties facing feminist theory as it continues to argue for its own relevance in the field of historical studies, in 'Feminism and Eighteenth-Century Studies: Working in the Bordello of History' (*ECent* 50[2009] 33–41). Judith P. Zinsser considers the challenges of biographical writing, criticism, and history and explores some solutions in 'Feminist Biography: A Contradiction in Terms?' (*ECent* 50[2009] 43–50).

Felicity Nussbaum, in '"More Than a Woman": Early Memoirs of British Actresses' (*RCEI* 58[2009] 89–103), considers the representation of female virtue in the lives of Anne Oldfield, Nell Gwyn, and Lavinia Fenton. In 'Hospitable Harem? A European Woman and Oriental Spaces in the Enlightenment' (*Paragraph* 32[2009] 87–104) Judith Still questions Lady Mary Wortley Montagu's *Turkish Embassy Letters* in the context of hospitality, both in a critical approach to Montagu's writings and in Montagu's representation of Turkish society. In 'Talking to the Margins: Lady Mary Wortley Montagu at the Nadir of Communications' (*Lumen* 28[2009] 111–25), by Isobel Grundy, Montagu's resistance to patriarchy, authority, and monarchy is explored in an investigation of her annotations to an heraldic tome. In 'Unsexed Souls: Natural Philosophy as Transformation in Eliza Haywood's *Female Spectator*' (*ECS* 43[2009] 55–74) Kristin M. Girtin focuses upon Haywood's engagement with philosophy as part of her wider project within her periodical writing to explore and modify the public sphere for women. Rebecca M. Mills, in '"To be both Patroness and Friend": Patronage, Friendship, and Protofeminism in the Life of Elizabeth Thomas (1675–1731)' (*SECC* 38[2009] 69–89), examines the tensions between authority and affection in Thomas's letters, poetry, and prose writings.

Tensions of a different sort are the focus of Laura Mandell's 'Prayer, Feeling, Action: Anna Barbauld and the Public Worship Controversy' (*SECC* 38[2009] 117–42), which looks at the role Barbauld played in the religious pamphlet wars in the late eighteenth century, in her response to Wakefield's *Enquiry into the Expediency and Propriety of Public or Social Worship*. Issue iii of *Journal for Eighteenth-Century Studies* has a special focus on religion in the eighteenth century, the result of the 2008 conference of the British Society for Eighteenth-Century Studies. In his introduction, 'Transforming "the Age of Reason" into "an Age of Faith"; or, Putting Religions and Beliefs (Back) into the Eighteenth Century' (*JECS* 32[2009] 287–305) Jeremy Gregory emphasizes the plurality of religious belief and also the importance of lay religious activity in the eighteenth century; we must reconsider how reason and belief are interrelated, rather than straightforwardly opposed to each other, in Enlightenment literature. The journal's articles range widely across the genres, as well as across forms of belief. Jane Shaw, for instance, explores strange happenings, ghostly apparitions, and superstitions across the century in 'Mary Toft, Religion and National Memory in Eighteenth-Century England' (*JSECS* 32[2009] 321–38), while Joanna Cruickshank examines the representation of female friendships and the influence of shared religious belief in '"Friend of my Soul": Constructing Spiritual Friendship in the Autobiography of Mary Fletcher' (*JECS* 32[2009] 373–87).

In '"Matchless Sufferings": Intimate Violence in the Early Modern Apparition Narratives of Daniel Defoe and Elizabeth Boyd' (*WW* 16[2009] 425–44) Heather Harper explores issues surrounding justice, class, and representations of sexual violence in the short-lived literary form of the apparition narrative. Sheldon Rogers argues for the recognition of 30 September 1659 as Defoe's official birthday, evaluating the evidence in 'Daniel Defoe's Birth Date' (*N&Q* 56[2009] 226–8). In 'Defoe, Dissent, and Early Whig Ideology' (*HistJ* 52[2009] 595–614) K.R.P. Clark argues for the de-attribution of several anonymous pamphlets relating to the 1688 Revolution which have been credited to Defoe, and explores the political and religious significance for Defoe via this de-attribution. Stephen H. Gregg's *Defoe's Writings and Manliness: Contrary Men* addresses the 'failure of manliness' across Defoe's writing (p. 1). Gregg examines the contemporary language and terms which are used to construct, represent, and discuss masculinity in Defoe's novels as well as in his non-fiction writing, and structures his analysis around the central themes of trade, manners, myth, and friendship. The way in which Defoe's particular type of manliness is constructed upon the notion of contrariness is a unifying thread in the study, relating to both Defoe's attitudes as a writer and to the construction of gender itself. To be contrary, Gregg writes, 'is to be aware of the parameters of both sides, of heterodoxy and orthodoxy, to willingly ply between the hegemonic and the transgressive, the ideal and the corrupt' (p. 166). The exploration of this trope allows Gregg to present a coherent study that is successfully balanced between investigating Defoe's representations of failing types of masculine behaviour and developing a theory of the functioning of such failure in Defoe's writings.

Volume 7 of Defoe's *A Review of the State of the Nation* is now in print, covering the period 1710–11 and edited by John McVeagh. The publishing history of the *Review* in these years is complicated by the fact that Defoe published it as separate editions in London and Edinburgh, but suspended the Edinburgh reprints of the London edition in June 1720, after thirty-five editions. The editions, with their slight variances, are clearly headed and footnoted. The introduction contextualizes Defoe's writings with his activities at this period, and the political animosity that surrounded him, with brevity and clarity. In the *Review* numbers in this volume Defoe positions himself somewhere between the failing Whig ministry and that of the Tory administration led by Robert Harley after the October election. Defoe controversially balances and mediates opposing political views throughout, promoting non-party politics and eventually losing his Whig supporters. His vivid writings on the Sacheverell crisis in March and April are matched by the creativity of his allegorical accounts of Credit in August, and followed in turn by the intense satire of his descriptions in September and October of the election preparations. War in France, commerce, and credit end the 1711 editions.

Defoe's Footprints: Essays in Honour of Maximillian E. Novak, a Festschrift for Novak edited by Robert M. Maniquis and Carl Fisher, is a provocative and inspiring collection of essays. The provocation comes from the contributors' determination to overturn critical commonplaces and to push eighteenth-century scholarship further with a combination of lively prose and rigorous scholarship. The inspiration comes from Novak's influential and erudite work; the contributors position themselves in relation to his scholarship, wide-ranging literary interests, and precise theorization of eighteenth-century studies, resulting in this compelling collection that interrogates accepted perspectives on forms of representation and knowledge, the novel, literary influence and inheritance, and the figure of the writer. The majority of the essays discuss Defoe's fiction and some poetry, but Stuart Sherman, in 'Defoe's Silences' (pp. 12–31) examines representations of sound and silence, narration and absence, in Defoe's prose writings—*A Journal of the Plague Year*, *Continuation of Letters Written by a Turkish Spy at Paris*, and Robinson Crusoe's essay 'On Solitude' among others—delving into the consciousness of the print form. Carl Fisher's '"The Project and the People": Defoe on the South Sea Bubble and the Public Good' (pp. 170–88) provides a thorough discussion of Defoe's pamphlets and his economic theories. He analyses Defoe's optimism and faith in speculation and credit, with his concerns for its abuses and lack of regulation; transparency, regulation, and principled dealing are necessary to ensure stability. Manuel Schonhorn, in 'The Writer as Hero from Jonson to Fielding' (pp. 189–205), examines the construction of the writer's public self in the changing print market.

The Postcolonial Enlightenment: Eighteenth-Century Colonialism and Postcolonial Theory, edited by Daniel Carey and Lynn Festa, is a significant publication. The eight essays, substantial introduction, and coda that make up this collection mark an important development in both Enlightenment studies and postcolonial criticism: each is considered in relation to the other, addressing the previous critical neglect of the role which Enlightenment thought played in the construction and critique of European colonial ideology. As the editors write in the introduction: '[i]t is our hope that an engagement between postcolonial theory and Enlightenment colonialisms may allow us to qualify theoretical concepts—even to elaborate new categories—so as to move beyond the impasse created by the polarization of the two fields' (p. 24), but they are alert too to the 'paradoxical if not anachronistic status' of the collection's title (p. 33). The collection addresses canonical and non-canonical writers and texts, with fiction, poetry, philosophy, law, natural sciences, religion, and political economy among the areas discussed. The essays are divided into three sections. Part I, 'Subjects and Sovereignty', consists of 'Hobbes and America' (pp. 37–70) by Srinivas Aravamudan, which addresses the colonization of Virginia and Bermuda and the presence of imperialism in Hobbes's writings on sovereignty and David Lloyd's 'The Pathological Sublime: Pleasure and Pain in the Colonial Context' (pp. 71–102) on the aesthetic representation of the suffering body, which completes the first section. In Part II, 'Enlightenment Categories and Postcolonial Classifications', Daniel Carey's 'Reading Contrapuntally: *Robinson Crusoe*, Slavery, and Postcolonial Theory' (pp. 105–36) investigates Defoe's novel in the light of Edward Said's theory of contrapuntal reading; 'Between "Oriental" and Blacks So Called, 1688–1788' (pp. 137–66) by Felicity A. Nussbaum examines the space between the discourses of different subjects of colonialism where such discourses overlap and develop in relation to each other, particularly regarding slavery; and Siraj Ahmed's 'Orientalism and the Permanent Fix of War' (pp. 167–203) turns to the role played by the East India Company in rewriting Indian property law in the eighteenth century, using Enlightenment economic and colonial theory to position itself within the emerging global financial network. Part III, 'Nation, Colony, and Enlightenment Universality', contains three essays: 'Of Speaking Natives and Hybrid Philosophers: Lahontan, Diderot, and the French Enlightenment Critique of Colonialism' (pp. 207–39) by Doris L. Garraway, on the roles of speech, mimicry, and writing in dialogue form as critique or attempted recovery of the voice of the colonized other; 'Universalism, Diversity, and the Postcolonial Enlightenment' (pp. 240–80) by Daniel Carey and Sven Trakulhun, which considers religious tolerance in British, French, and German philosophical writings, particularly those of Kant; and '"These Nations Newton Made his Own": Poetry, Knowledge, and British Imperial Globalization' (pp. 281–303), in which Karen O'Brien interrogates theories of universality and cosmopolitanism and the ways in which poets like Cowper, Thompson, and Akenside engaged with them. The collection concludes with an urgent coda by Suvir Kaul, 'How to Write Postcolonial Histories of

Empire?' (pp. 305–27), about the dangers of recent justifications of eighteenth- and nineteenth-century British imperialism, which are being used to support current American political and economic expansion.

The latest book in the series Postcolonial Literary Studies from Edinburgh University Press is Suvir Kaul's *Eighteenth-Century British Literature and Postcolonial Studies*. It offers a fuller exploration of the concerns raised in his coda in Carey and Festa's *The Postcolonial Enlightenment*. The return of empire via Anglo-American contemporary politics, which argues for expansion on the basis of political and economic security, has given itself a moral justification for its actions. The activity of postcolonial scholars who examine and re-examine the arguments for empire, interrogating accepted reasoning and overturning assumptions, is more relevant than ever. As part of this clear, informative series Kaul's book contains a broad critical survey of existing scholarship with suggestions for further reading, explanations of key terms and debates, a survey of literary texts and case studies for closer readings of such texts, and a timeline. Kaul contextualizes a broad range of canonical texts by Behn, Defoe, Addison and Steele, Johnson, and Smollett, as well as less-discussed writers like Phillis Wheatley and Ukawsaw Gronniosaw, and addresses poetry, drama, prose, fiction, and periodicals. As an introduction to postcolonial studies and the eighteenth century it would make an invaluable student textbook, but it is Kaul's important reappraisal of primary texts and his engagement with the problematic concept of empire that make this work indispensable. Another work which at once provides an introduction to the subject of empire and heralds new critical directions for it is Lynn Festa's 'Sentimental Visions of Empire in Eighteenth-Century Studies' (*LitComp* 6:i[2009] 23–55), which combines a substantial survey of recent publications and critical trends relating to sentimentality and empire with an identification of gaps in current scholarship and suggestions for further research, particularly interdisciplinary studies which will investigate the broad impact sentimentality had on all areas of eighteenth-century imperial discourse and representation.

A comprehensive analysis of the emergence of civil society in the late eighteenth century is presented by James Livesey in *Civil Society and Empire: Ireland and Scotland in the Eighteenth-Century Atlantic World*, which explores the differences between the idea of civil society and the practice of association in England, Ireland, and Scotland from the late seventeenth century up to 1799. As Livesey writes, 'the goal [of this book] is to identify the innovations that renamed association as civil society' (p. 2). Among these social and institutional innovations examined here are the popular coffee-house, empire, Scottish moral philosophy, and the development of discourses of improvement and morality by political, religious, and intellectual societies. Livesey pays close attention throughout to what is meant by, and understood by, 'civil society'. His sustained interrogation of this idea and its use is matched by his painstaking analysis of the particularities of eighteenth-century discourse and his commitment to examining association on its own terms. He investigates the debates and conflicting ideologies of civil society, noting in particular its failure and collapse in Ireland in the 1790s. This monograph is sure to be of interest to all scholars of sociability, improvement, and empire, as well as being of particular use to those working in Irish and Scottish studies.

A new collection of essays, *Liberating Medicine, 1720–1835*, edited by Tristanne Connolly and Steve Clark, aims to bridge the gap between the disciplines of science and literature by exploring the similarities between the two in relation to the concept of freedom: freedom from pain, from ignorance, from mortality. This study examines the emergence of medicine in the eighteenth century as a recognizably modern form, and one which can be explored in tandem with developments in literature rather than in opposition to them. The editors describe in their introduction how the essays 'are as interested in how Enlightenment medicine might underpin, as much as undermine, Enlightenment ideals of liberty. Both medicine and liberty are tied to rationality and improvement, and to sensibility's delicate balance of health, virtue, and physical-emotional response' (p. 8). This sets a broad horizon for enquiry into the professionalization of the figures of the doctor or surgeon and the writer, for investigation into the causes of human suffering, for spiritual, social, physical, and mental illness or disturbance, and, crucially, how illness itself is represented and a medical discourse is developed in eighteenth- and early nineteenth-century literature. The sixteen essays in the collection are divided into five sections. Part I, 'Spiritual Sickness and Hypochondria', examines consumption, religious conversion, and slavery in the work of Hemans, Ignatius Sancho, Carlyle, and Stowe. In Part II, 'Health and Emancipation', the writings of Defoe, Wollstonecraft, and Blake are discussed in relation to social and political freedom. The development of discourses of suffering in Wordsworth, Hogg, and writings on King George's illness, are the focus of Part III, 'Madness'. Part IV, 'Anatomized and Aestheticized Bodies', turns to animal magnetism in Godwin and the use of anatomy in the work of George Stubbs, as well as Frances Burney's suffering body, and John Armstrong's writing on sex. Finally, Part V, 'Birth', contains an investigation into Barbauld's poetic representation of motherhood, and concludes with maternal elegy in Barbauld and Gray.

The idea of adventure is an intriguing basis for an essay collection. *Adventure: An Eighteenth-Century Idiom. Essays on the Daring and the Bold as a Pre-Modern Medium*, edited by Serge Soupel, Kevin L. Cope, and Alexander Pettit, presents a variety of ways in which the either the activity of adventuring (exploration, travel, conflict) or the concept (risk, contingency, imagination) functions in fiction, biography, travel writing, poetry, and history. There are four sections: Part I, 'Adventures of the Mind', Part II, 'Adventures in Genre', Part III, 'The Places of Adventure', and Part IV, 'Adventure as Social Process'. This is a rather uneven collection, perhaps because of its breadth, but it poses some interesting questions and invites consideration of what it means to be adventurous in eighteenth-century thought, activity, and genre. Of relevance here are, in Part I, Allan Ingram's 'Boswell's Big Adventures: London, Scotland, London' (pp. 3–22), addressing life-writing, expectation, and imagination, and Elisabeth Soubrenie's 'Chance, Providence, and Fate: The Spiritual Adventures of John Bunyan and William Cowper' (pp. 23–39), which discusses episode-writing and poetry, but also examines the activity of reading as an adventure in relation to chance and predestinarian theology.

Part II is concerned with novels (*Roxana* and *Gulliver's Travels*) and poetry (William Falconer's *The Shipwreck*), but Guyonne Leduc presents an interesting exploration of two anonymous narratives which describe female soldiery, in 'The Adventure of Cross-Dressing: Hannah Snell (1723–92), a Woman Soldier' (pp. 145–67). Part III provides accounts of Defoe's activities in Scotland and Thomas Grey's travel writings, and in Andrew Varney's 'Fielding's Last Adventure: *The Journal of a Voyage to Lisbon*' (pp. 221–32) the interplay of travel writing, personality, and narrative fiction is considered. Pierre Carboni provides a thoughtful exploration of historical narrative and myth, examining an episode of romantic myth-making in a travelogue in 'Boswell and the Extraordinary Adventures of Prince Charles Edward Stuart in the Hebrides' (pp. 211–20), which he links to the subsequent development of the historical novel. Part IV turns again to the novels of Defoe and Swift, but there are also two essays on the historical process, H.J.K. Jenkins, 'A Looking-Glass Adventure: Lord Orfords's Fenland Cruise in 1771' (pp. 251–73), and James P. Carson's 'Interracial Adventures: The Black Caribs of St Vincent' (pp. 305–24).

An excellent discussion of print culture is presented in Anthony Pollock's *Gender and the Fictions of the Public Sphere, 1690–1755*, which analyses public discourse, periodicals, and the construction of gender in representations of publicness, or spectatorial reading. Informed by Mandeville's identification of the troubling position of the female reader, his scepticism about Whig authority, and Pollock's interpretation of Mandeville's view of the public sphere as one of 'regressive antagonism and competitive emulation in which readers vie to establish who among them can most convincingly reproduce the culture's ideology of propriety' (p. 2), this study poses a challenge to the Habermasian construction of the public sphere and to existing theories of gendered models of reading and subjectivity. It is divided into two parts, 'Models and Countermodels of English Public Discourse, 1690–1714' and 'Tory Feminism and the Gendered Reader, Astell to Haywood'. The focus in Part I is upon the print market in the final years of censorship and the development of Addison and Steele's periodicals from existing forms of public discourse: a borrowing, rather than an invention, but one which produces an important new model for a spectatorial public sphere, which is critiqued in turn by the *Female Tatler*. Part II moves from general concerns about readership to a more particularized analysis of female readers and writers, engaging primarily with the work of Astell and Haywood in relation to Whig and Tory discourse.

In 'After Design: Joseph Addison Discovers Beauties' (*SEL* 49[2009] 615–35) Michelle Syba argues that Addison develops a distinctive theory of reading in his critical writings on eighteenth-century neoclassical aesthetics which explores the tension between authorial intention and reader empowerment. 'An Unknown Author' (*JECS* 32[2009] 173–96) by Thomas Mautner examines the evidence which attributes various anonymous publications in early eighteenth-century periodicals such as *The Spectator* and *Tatler* to the obscure writer John Morrice. David Chandler examines the public sphere, print culture, and emerging literary tradition in a provincial case study in

'"The Athens of England": Norwich as a Literary Center in the Late Eighteenth Century' (*ECS* 43[2009] 171–92).

Amanda Vickery's *Behind Closed Doors: At Home in Georgian England* investigates the very fabric of the private home. This richly illustrated and detailed account of the domestic world of the long eighteenth century examines the home as the central location for theories of society, politeness, economics, authority, and gender. Households of different class and rank are explored, and the differing roles and responsibilities of men and women are discussed, as well as the importance of architecture, furniture, and the decorative arts. The varying degrees of significance attributed to home ownership, the labour and implements required for domestic cleanliness, and the objects, inhabitants (familial or otherwise), and occupations that constituted a household are brought to life by imaginative engagement with and thoughtful interpretation of a wide array of manuscript sources: diaries, account books, household inventories, letters, commonplace books, business ledgers, sale catalogues, bills, and more. The voices of Vickery's Georgian characters are skilfully woven through the text, continually reminding us of the psychological importance of the household and the home to individuals from all backgrounds, as well as the symbolic and practical purpose of the house within society.

A very different conception of the domestic space is explored and represented in *Horace Walpole's Strawberry Hill*, edited by Michael Snodin. This vast tome functions as the catalogue for the Victoria and Albert and Yale touring exhibition of engravings, sketches, paintings, curiosities, and objects from Walpole's collection, but also aims to become the standard critical work on Walpole and his collection, on the art of collection, and on display. It is richly illustrated with full-colour (where applicable) photographs of the collection, but also of the house itself in 2008, striking even in its empty desolation. The contributors of the sixteen essays are art historians and consultants, curators, and English literature scholars, and the essays explore the interplay of historical interest, space, works of art, and the written word within Walpole's house. Single artefacts are the focus of some essays, while others discuss the politics of collecting and display, sourcing art, antiquarianism, printing, and Walpole's writings. It is an astonishing record of a fabled house and contents, as well as an absorbing representation of Walpole's life's work in all its highly detailed facets. Sean R. Silver, in 'Horace Walpole's Gothic Historiography' (*ECF* 21[2009] 235–64), offers an account of Walpole's collection of antiquities that argues for its significance in providing a form of history that is material rather than textual.

The use, value, and significance of gift-giving across a variety of genres is examined in *The Culture of the Gift in Eighteenth-Century England*, a substantial collection of essays edited by Linda Zionkowski and Cynthia Klekar. The editors state that their aim is 'to demonstrate how gift transactions both produced and responded to changes in traditional concepts of class, gender, national and personal identity, social authority, and property' (p. 2), and the nuanced, scholarly investigations in the essays that follow perfectly achieve this aim. The collection is divided into four sections—'Theories of Benevolence', 'Conduct and the Gift', 'The Erotics of the Gift', and 'The Gift and Commerce'—and the following essays are of particular interest to this section: 'Rights and Reciprocity in the Political Discourse of Eighteenth-Century England' by Anna Moltchanova and Susannah Ottaway (pp. 15–35), which examines natural rights and exchange following on from Locke's writings; 'Charity Education and the Spectacle of "Christian Entertainment"' by Jad Smith (pp. 37–54), which addresses children's education and the spectacle of reform; and 'Debt without Redemption in a World of "Impossible Exchange": Samuel Richardson and Philanthropy' by John A. Dussinger (pp. 55–75), which explores Richardson's status as donor and debtor, and his involvement in the Charitable Corporation. Correct forms of behaviour and gratitude are explored in Marilyn Francus's 'Tis Better to Give: The Conduct Manual as Gift' (pp. 79–106). Dorice Williams Elliott, in 'The Gift of an Education: Sarah Trimmer's *Oeconomy of Charity* and the Sunday School Movement' (pp. 107–22), discusses Trimmer's anxiety about gift-giving and the undermining of social relations that may result. Obligation is also the focus of 'Josiah Wedgewood's Goodwill Marketing' (pp. 197–213) by Susan B. Egenolf, and in 'Anson at Canton, 1743: Obligation, Exchange, and Ritual in Edward Page's "Secret History"' (pp. 215–33) Robert Markley examines narrative structure (history writing, travel writing and poetry) and the language of gifting and deference.

Two books in Ashgate's series Studies in Childhood were published this year, and they form a complementary pairing. *Educating the Child in Enlightenment Britain: Beliefs, Cultures, Practices*, edited by Mary Hilton and Jill Shefrin, is a substantial collection of essays, which developed from a 2005 conference on children and education. The editors declare the aim of the book is the redefinition of education 'as a cultural, rather than a political, social or purely instructive practice' (p. 1) and wish to position it as part of 'an ongoing silent revolution in the history of education' (p. 3). The interdisciplinarity of the resulting work offers rewarding and satisfying accounts of the varieties of eighteenth-century theories and practices of education, with a strong emphasis on the role played by religion, including Methodism and Catholicism, and developments in the print market. The substantial introduction offers a very helpful contextualization of current critical debates in this interesting and rapidly expanding area of research, the range of which is perhaps best illustrated by essay titles themselves: '"Oh miserable and most ruinous measure": The Debate between Private and Public Education in Britain, 1760–1800' (pp. 21–39) by Sophia Woodley; 'Evangelicalism and Enlightenment: The Educational Agenda of Hannah More' (pp. 41–55) by Anne Stott; '"Familiar Conversation": The Role of the "Familiar Format" in Education in Eighteenth- and Nineteenth-Century England' (pp. 99–116) by Michèle Cohen; 'Marketing Religious Identity: Female Educators, Methodist Culture, and Eighteenth-Century Childhood' (pp. 57–75) by Mary Clare Martin; 'Learning and Virtue: English Grammar and the Eighteenth-Century Girls' School' (pp. 77–98) by Carol Percy; 'Hosting the Grand Tour: Civility, Enlightenment and Culture, c.1740–1790' (pp. 117–30) by Jennifer Mori; '"Superior to the rudest shocks of adversity": English Jesuit Education and Culture in the Long Eighteenth Century, 1688–1832' (pp. 131–46) by Maurice Whitehead; 'Colonizing the Mind: The Use of English Writers in the

Education of the Irish Poor, c.1750–1850' (pp. 147–61) by Deirdre Raftery; '"Adapted for and Used in Infants' Schools, Nurseries, &c.": Booksellers and the Infant School Market' (pp. 163–80) by Jill Shefrin; and 'Delightful Instruction? Assessing Children's Use of Educational Books in the Long Eighteenth Century' (pp. 181–98) by M.O. Grenby. Such variety nonetheless produces a coherent sense of this relatively new subject of study. The literary texts surveyed in this collection are enriched by Anja Müller's exploration of visual print culture in *Framing Childhood in Eighteenth-Century English Periodicals and Prints, 1689–1789*. The many reproductions are clear, and her focus upon early eighteenth-century periodicals bridges a particular gap in critical discussions of childhood, which often tend to focus on the post-Rousseauvian response rather than what precedes Rousseau. Müller's concern is with the construction of childhood, and how this construct was in turn enabled by developments in print and visual media in the long eighteenth century. The representation and education of children's bodies and minds, breastfeeding, the duration of childhood, the family, and the position of the child in the public world are among the areas of analysis in Müller's lucid study.

Will Pritchard, in 'New Light on Crumb's Boswell' (*ECS* 42[2009] 289–307) considers the visual and non-visual elements in Boswell's *London Journal* through Robert Crumb's rendition of the narrative as a comic book. In 'Condorcet, Social Mathematics, and Women's Rights' (*ECS* 42[2009] 347–62) Guillaume Ansart discusses the connections between Condorcet's mathematical writings and his theories on individual rights, particularly relating to women's intellectual ability and education. Chad Wellmon explores embodied reason and ideas of emotional adjustment and social engagement in 'Kant and the Feelings of Reason' (*ECS* 42[2009] 557–80). In a thoughtful and thought-provoking monograph, *The Evolution of Sympathy in the Long Eighteenth Century*, Jonathan Lamb presents a significant analysis of an integral part of eighteenth-century literary and philosophical discourse, addressing the work of Spinoza, Hume, Smith, Descartes, Mandeville, Burke, and many more. Beginning with the use and function of sympathy within power relations, Lamb investigates the value of sympathetic engagement, its role in testimony and the experience of reality, how the term is understood as part of eighteenth-century discourse, and the ways in which it can be experienced and manipulated. Lamb categorizes sympathy in five ways: 'mechanical, moral, theatrical and (after Hume) "compleat"' (p. 46), as well as horrid sympathy, and explores the different values of each of these in turn while investigating the connections between each form and the rest. His framework for investigation continues into the twenty-first century, and produces an illuminating and persuasive account of the ways in which sympathy and passion rival reason and will in determining what it means to be human, to be engaged, to be real.

The Eighteenth-Century Literature Handbook, edited by Gary Day and Bridget Keegan, offers an excellent introduction to students. It contains a detailed timeline, an extensive and annotated bibliography, and a glossary, but it is the organization of the contents that makes this book so useful. The ten sections include discussions of key topics in eighteenth-century writing, genre, context, canonicity, case studies, and the current critical field, offering a fully rounded perspective on the subject. The chapters in full are as follows: 'Contexts, Identities and Consumption: Britain 1688–1815' (pp. 32–47) by Ruth M. Larsen; 'Literary and Cultural Figures, Genres and Contexts' (pp. 47–69) by Gavin Budge, Michael Caines, Daniel Cook, and Bonnie Latimer; 'Case Studies in Reading 1: Key Primary Texts' (pp. 70–96) by Anne Chandler; 'Case Studies in Reading 2: Key Theoretical and Critical Texts' (pp. 96–118) by Steven Newman; 'Key Critical Concepts and Topics' (pp. 119–33) by Richard Terry; '"Dead Keen on Reason?" Changes in Critical Response and Approaches to the Eighteenth Century' (pp. 134–54) by Philip Smallwood; 'Questioning Canonicity' (pp. 155–67) by Bridget Keegan and Amber Haschenburger; 'Gender, Sexuality and Ethnicity' (pp. 168–86) by Chris Mounsey; and 'Mapping the Current Critical Landscape' (pp. 187–200) by Donna Landry. The contents of each chapter are clearly set out, firstly in the detailed contents page and then again in the overview at the beginning of each chapter, making the book extremely easy to navigate. Of particular practical use to students here are the chapters providing case studies and 'Key Critical Concepts and Topics'. Overall, the immense body of information is expressed in a lucid and lively manner, and the seemingly effortless synthesis of so many different aspects of eighteenth-century writing and culture presented here makes it an exciting, stimulating, and welcoming text for newcomers, as well as a very handy source for teachers and scholars.

Published in 2008 but not reviewed last year was volume 8 of the *Cambridge Edition of the Works of Jonathan Swift*, edited by Bertrand A. Goldgar and Ian Gadd. *English Political Writings 1711–1714: The Conduct of the Allies and Other Works* is well illustrated throughout with title pages and prints, and there is a substantial chronology as well as a detailed introduction which offers a full contextualization of Swift's activities and political opinions during these years. As well as Swift's acknowledged writings there are attributions to Swift included here: 'The New Way of Selling Places at Court' (pp. 155–62), 'It's Out at Last: Or, French Correspondence Clear as the Sun' (pp. 181–6), 'A Dialogue upon Dunkirk, between a Whig and a Tory' (pp. 187–92), 'A Hue and Cry after Dismal' (pp. 193–9), 'A Letter from the Pretender, to a Whig-Lord' (pp. 199–203), 'The Importance of the Guardian Considered' (pp. 217–41), and 'Contributions to the Post Boy and the Evening Post' (pp. 317–24). The texts used for this volume are the first editions, not the final revised ones, in line with editorial practice, as there is no guarantee that Swift was involved with or approved subsequent editions of his writings. The exception to this is 'The Conduct of the Allies', the fourth edition of which has been taken as the copy-text as Swift was involved in its production and so it is an authoritative text.

Also published in 2009 but not available for review are the following: Stephen Bygrave, *Uses of Education: Readings in Enlightenment England* (BuckUP), Nicola Parsons, *Reading Gossip in Early Eighteenth-Century England* (Palgrave), and Betty Schellenberg, *The Professionalization of Women Writers in Eighteenth-Century Britain* (CUP). These will be covered with material from 2010.

2. The Novel

With two major Cambridge University Press editorial projects—*The Cambridge Edition of the Works of Samuel Richardson* and *The Cambridge Edition of the Correspondence of Samuel Richardson*—under way, a reinvigorated interest in Richardson's writings can be identified. Richardson's fiction inspired the greatest number of scholarly articles in the period under review. Apart from two substantial book-length studies of Richardson's *Clarissa*, E. Derek Taylor's *Reason and Religion in Clarissa* and Lynn Shepherd's *Clarissa's Painter*, *Eighteenth-Century Fiction* alone published six articles on subjects as varied as discourses of prostitution and moral reformation, architectural symbolism, and the empowering qualities of pity. Taylor's book traces and examines the presence in *Clarissa* of a nowadays little-known clergyman, poet, and philosopher, the 'famous' John Norris, of Bemerton, and interrogates the extent to which Richardson endorsed a Lockean approach to perception (and especially the senses). Offering a sensitive matrix of Richardson's philosophical indebtedness to Norris's anti-Lockean ideas, steeped in the theosophy of Nicolas Malbranche, Taylor argues for readers' widespread familiarity, in the first half of the century, with Norris and his ideas; at the same time, he sets out to redress previous critics' 'shortsighted, misplaced, or self-defeating' (p. 37) insistence on identifying Locke as the basis of the novelist's engagement with perception and truth. While the first chapter offers a painstaking account and a detailed consideration of the semantic ambiguities of the term 'sense' that Richardson underpins philosophically by adopting the paradigms that distinguish Norris's works from Locke's, the second chapter introduces some of Richardson's female contemporaries (including Mary Astell and Elizabeth Carter) and traces their uses of Norris. Taylor succeeds in presenting an effective comparative analysis of the Lockean and anti-Lockean features of Lovelace and Clarissa, which interprets Richardson's 'hero and heroine on opposite sides of the mind-body divide' (p. 41). In fact, while Clarissa's 'sense' is related to Richardsonian synonyms such as 'intellect' or 'soul', Lovelace's is related to bodily sensuality as well as 'his inability to eschew the physical senses that led him to rape Clarissa' (p. 42). It is shown that Lovelace manipulates Clarissa's senses by turning them against the heroine, thereby 'providing sensory evidence in support of a ruse that will draw the heroine from her putative safe haven' (p. 45). In Taylor's view, Richardson's third, redacted edition of *Clarissa*, especially in its addition of footnotes, represents the author's attempt at clarifying his intention as to how the text should be read in terms that Norris has popularized in his writings. Consulting both Norris and the writings of Astell, Richardson is portrayed as a writer who skilfully managed to combine his conservative religious vision with the more progressive, proto-feminist agenda of Astell, ultimately creating a theological experiment that utilizes Norris's influence as an enabling element in Clarissa's sense-driven resistance against Lovelace. Taylor's book offers a fresh and timely contextual approach to Richardson's complex religious vision and successfully manoeuvres the philosophical territory informing Richardson's writing process that earlier critics have largely traced to Locke.

The second major contribution to Richardson studies, Lynn Shepherd's book offers a detailed investigation of the painterly responses to *Pamela* (and *Pamela II*), *Clarissa*, and *Sir Charles Grandison*. Approaching Richardson's works via the cultural materialism that Thomas Keymer and Peter Sabor explored in *Pamela in the Marketplace* [2005], Shepherd argues for the overarching significance of portraiture in the visual renderings—in the forms of book illustrations and paintings—of iconographic moments from the works illustrated. She contends that, while previous critics have focused on the dramatic action of Richardson's novels, specifically in *Pamela* and *Clarissa*, eighteenth-century readers largely highlighted their pictorial evocativeness; in fact, Richardson deliberately 'borrowed techniques and terminology from the visual' (p. 3) and utilized the conventions of mid-century portraiture—as 'a particularly rich nexus of contemporary notions of public and private, heroic and domestic, and masculine and feminine' (p. 12)—to generate what Shepherd terms 'modern moral romance' (p. 86). She creates an analytic narrative engaging with a range of different images whose composition and representational gender-specific ideologies as well as power relations she examines by offering a consideration that takes into account the social factors that influenced the cross-fertilization of two analogously developing genres, the one literal, the other painterly. Wide-ranging and detailed in its sophisticated art-historical approach to the paintings of the Richardson family and his works, the print culture of the period, more popular visualizations of the novels, and insightful accounts of the rise of the mid-century genre piece, *Clarissa's Painter* offers an important contribution to the social and material cultural history of reading and consumption. It effectively sheds light on the interpretative and artistic processes by which painters and illustrators appropriated Richardson's texts and centralizes the importance of portraiture for the cultural commodification of literary bestsellers at mid-century. Above all, Shepherd persuasively charts the ways in which Richardson's exposure to new practices in painting facilitated his adopting a new vocabulary for the articulation of interpersonal relationships. Also, the pictorial and compositional techniques that Richardson derived from the visual arts had an extended literary life and were adopted by, among others, Jane Austen, who deployed not only Richardson's compositional frameworks of portraiture, but also 'his narrative technique and scenic form' (p. 232).

The issue of cultural adaptation, ideational translation, and appropriation, this time for an audience of children, is also centrally explored in Bonnie Latimer's 'Leaving Little to the Imagination: The Mechanics of Didacticism in Two Children's Adaptations of Samuel Richardson's Novels' (*L&U* 33[2009] 167–88). Latimer's '"Apprehensions of Controul": The Familial Politics of Marriage, Choice and Consent in *Sir Charles Grandison*' (*JECS* 32[2009] 1–19), focusing on the marriage of the novel's minor character, Miss Mansfield, explores the issue of coerced marriage and to what extent the female's consent was necessary to enter into a marriage contract. By the same author, 'Pious Frauds: "Honest Tricks" and the Patterns of Anglican Devotional Thought in Richardson' (*JECS* 32[2009] 331–51) interrogates Clarissa's honesty on the occasion of writing a letter to Lovelace, which deceives him by using ambiguity as a means to escape his persecution. Deliberately constructing a spiritual meaning which she expects Lovelace will understand literally, she enters a realm of 'ethical dubiousness' (p. 340). Latimer persuasively argues that 'certain species of fraud and secrecy are not regarded as incommensurate with "piety"' (p. 340). Consulting Richard Hooker's 'ends-oriented morality' (p. 344), Latimer shows that the 'honest trick' that Clarissa plays on Lovelace can be justified, especially in the light of tenets current in popular devotional literature.

While E. Derek Taylor explained Clarissa's empowerment via Norris and Astell, Chad Loewen-Schmidt, in 'Pity, or the Providence of the Body in Richardson's *Clarissa*' (*ECF* 22[2009] 1–28), examines the history and literary uses of the concept of pity with which Richardson engages both intra- and extra-textually. Clarissa's inability to evoke a kind of proactive pity that could save her intra-textually is remedied by her readers, with whom she 'develop[s] an abstract zone of intimacy apart from the law that is capable of being both outside and inside herself' (p. 15). It is the 'jurisdiction' (p. 14) of this extra-textual pity that, ultimately, will culminate in poetic justice for the heroine. Whereas Taylor and Loewen-Schmidt focus on the religious and moral fabric of the novel, Karen Lipsedge's '"I was also absent at my dairy-house": The Representation and Symbolic Function of the Dairy House in Samuel Richardson's *Clarissa*' (*ECF* 22[2009] 29–48) concerns itself with a promising new area of interest. She explores the cultural-historical phenomenon of a dairy house, placed in a landscaped garden, and inscribed in Richardson's novel with narratives of ownership, morality, and self-definition. Linked with the pastoral realm in which it is set, the dairy serves as an architecturally symbolic locus of 'Clarissa's labour, good deeds, and virtue' (p. 36).

Examining Richardson's conservative morality and his views on reintegrating penitent prostitutes into society, Martha J. Koehler's 'Redemptive Spaces: Magdalen House and Prostitution in the Novels and Letters of Richardson' (*ECF* 22[2009] 249–78) traces the ways in which the discourses of reform and prostitution are centrally reworked and articulated in, among others, *Clarissa*. By contrast, Jessica L. Leiman's '"Booby's Fruitless Operations": The Crisis of Male Authority in Richardson's *Pamela*' (*ECF* 22[2009] 223–48) considers the central problems of Mr B.'s desire for Pamela and his supposed inability to rape her. She reads Mr B.'s crisis of masculinity not so much in terms of his predatory intention to possess Pamela physically but rather as his attempt at silencing the voice of the epistolary narrator whose female voice would otherwise dominate the novel. His vacillating behaviour, especially what previous critics have interpreted as a failed attempt on Pamela's honour, represents his shift from action to verbal assertiveness, a process reflecting 'the readiness with which his amorous impulses yield to his narrative ambitions' (p. 228). Carol Stewart's '*Pamela* and the Anglican Crisis of the 1730s' (*JECS* 32[2009] 37–51) interprets Richardson's novel as advocating an Anglican ethos of rewarding virtue 'to promote the worldly Christianity of the Latitudinarians' (p. 38) at a time when the authority of the Anglican clergy was widely contested. Parson Williams is read as failing in his duty 'to exhort his patron to reform' and thereby as facilitating (and condoning)

Mr B.'s 'licentious conduct' (p. 37). Stewart argues 'that a significant context for Richardson's composition of *Pamela*...is a perception of the clergy as inadequate advocates of the Anglican position, and of the Church itself as weak, corrupt or remote' (p. 39), a more topical, historically grounded interpretation than has hitherto been attempted.

Although not principally concerned with Richardson's novel, Laura E. Thomason's stimulating 'Hester Chapone as a Living Clarissa in *Letters on Filial Obedience* and *A Matrimonial Creed*' (*ECF* 21[2009] 323–44) explores the resonance of the character that Richardson established with his paragon of virtue. Equally, Emily C. Friedman, in 'Remarks on Richardson: Sarah Fielding and the Rational Reader' (*ECF* 22[2009] 309–26), offers an account of Richardson's reader that complements Loewen-Schmidt's on the pitying reader. Nicholas D. Nace has examined the intertextuality of *Clarissa*, and in 'More Aaron Hill in *Clarissa*' (*N&Q* 56[2009] 247–8) has identified two quotations from Hill's 'Picture of Love', cited by Lovelace in the fourth and sixth volumes of the first edition. The former quotation was excised for the second edition of the novel. While Richardson criticism has largely focused on *Pamela* and *Clarissa*, Tita Chico, in 'Details and Frankness: Affective Relations in *Sir Charles Grandison*' (*SECC* 38[2009] 45), discusses Richardson's adoption of 'a nostalgic model' of kinship, one that safeguards her against the economic pressures of the marriage market. In her view, Sir Charles 'meditates upon the mechanisms through which affective communities are constructed' (p. 45) but also actively influences affective exchanges, as when he encourages the public ('narrative') reading of letters from correspondents known to the general audience.

As in previous years, the range of subjects published in *Eighteenth-Century Fiction* is indicative of trends in the study of the eighteenth-century novel. The fiction of Eliza Haywood has generated significant scholarly engagement this year. Sharon Harrow, in 'Having Text: Desire and Language in Haywood's *Love in Excess* and *The Distressed Orphan*' (*ECF* 22[2009] 279–308), discusses two of Haywood's amatory novels, examining the ways in which she rescripts the conventions of narratives of seduction and patriarchy's regulatory mechanisms. By contrast, Elizabeth Gargano offers a different approach to the gendered language of desire and, in 'Utopian Voyeurism: Androgyny and the Language of the Eyes in Haywood's *Love in Excess*' (*ECF* 21[2009] 513–34), explores 'the erotically charged language of the eyes' (p. 513)—inflected, as it is in Haywood, by 'the texture of an extended discourse, replete with nuanced meaning' (p. 514)—in the light of its ability (through voyeurism, for instance) to empower the female and emphasize the woman's agency. In 'Haywood's Thinking Machines' (*ECF* 21[2009] 201–28), Joseph Drury grounds his discussion of morality in the materialist philosophy of the early eighteenth century, arguing that morality and 'the automatism of Haywood's characters in her signature erotic scenes' (p. 202) are compatible; he contends that her 'mechanical fiction...privileges the intensity and complexity of female consciousness produced in the material experience of subjection over the straight arrow of masculine desire, thereby claiming the emergent psyche as a compensatory sphere of female dominance' (p. 204). Concerned with the novelist's didactic agenda, Kristin M. Girten's

'Unsexed Souls: Natural Philosophy as Transformation in Eliza Haywood's *Female Spectator*' (*ECS* 43[2009] 55–74) offers Haywood's argument in favour of a sensible female education via the study of natural philosophy. In her work, 'natural philosophy equalizes the masculine and the feminine, the male and the female, and thereby helps to promote women's self-assertion' (p. 63). In his reception studies account Peter Damrau's 'Eliza Haywoods *Geschichte des Fräuleins Elisabeth Thoughtless* (1756): Frühe Selbsterkenntnis und Ehekritik in der englischen Übersetzungsliteratur' (*GQ* 82[2009] 425–46) examines the German translations of Haywood's *Betsy Thoughtless* and embeds the author's critique of the institution of marriage within the cultural contexts of German debates of the subject. Also concerned with the role of women in eighteenth-century society and the negotiation of a proper educational process, Johanna Devereaux's 'A Paradise Within? Mary Astell, Sarah Scott and the Limits of Utopia' (*JECS* 32[2009] 53–67) examines Astell's *A Serious Proposal* and Sarah Scott's *Millenium Hall* as responses to contemporary male philosophers and argues that these texts are not straightforwardly utopian but rather identify how the correct kind of philosophical education can provide benefits for women's social and spiritual worth.

The Festschrift for a doyen of eighteenth-century studies, John Richetti, published as a special double number of *Eighteenth-Century Novel*, edited by George Justice and Albert J. Rivero, introduces the work of a number of eminent scholars in the field. One contribution, by J. Paul Hunter, needs singling out, since it indicates a new direction in the study of form and the novel. His 'Rethinking Form in *Tom Jones*' (*ECN* 6–7[2009] 309–34) offers a reading that moves away from those interpretations of the novel that highlight its formal perfection, symmetry, and Palladian design. Hunter suggests popularized versions of the biblical wisdom writings as significant intertexts which help Fielding to structure his text. He argues that 'Fielding draws . . . not on learned technicalities and abstract theory but simple popular manifestations that any amateur Protestant reader or hearer of Bible stories would readily understand' (p. 321). His essay is followed by Adam Potkay's 'Liberty and Necessity in Fielding's *Amelia*' (*ECN* 6–7[2009] 335–58) and Jack Lynch's '*Tristram Shandy* and the Rise of the Novel; or, Unpopular Fiction after Richardson' (*ECN* 6–7[2009] 359–77). Potkay argues that *Amelia* 'is less a Christian than a philosopher's book, and Fielding the novelist a cannier moral philosopher than is often remarked' (p. 339). Lynch, considering the difficult-to-classify, eccentric generic hybridity of *Tristram Shandy*, contends that 'there is no better way to discover what is at stake in different conceptions of the history of the novel than to examine how Sterne fits into them' (p. 361). He states that the insistence of Anglo-American literary historians of Sterne on utilizing the term 'novel' (and its traditional binary opposite 'romance') is unhelpful in that it cannot accommodate the uniqueness of Sterne's text. Rather, he suggests, 'international criticism, without the habit of distinguishing romance from novel' (p. 374), has found ways of comprehending *Tristram Shandy* within its contextual frameworks of imaginative prose fiction.

In the Festschrift the history and theory of the novel are explored in a range of essays on 'The Paradigms of Popular Culture' (Paula R. Backscheider),

'The Novel as Modern Myth' (John Bender), and '*Memoirs of a Woman of Pleasure* and the Culture of Pornography' (Robert Folkenflik). These historical and theoretical essays are followed by essays on the 'new' eighteenth-century novel, especially two stimulating pieces on Frances Burney, by Laura Brown and Susan C. Greenfield. Brown's 'Shock Effect: *Evelina*'s Monkey and the Marriage Plot' (*ECN* 6–7[2009] 379–408) presents an in-depth discussion of the monkey as a humanoid symbol of the monstrous, inviting simultaneously proximity/intimacy and revulsion, at the same time favouring extended comparisons between man and ape. Tracing the figure of the monkey in Restoration and eighteenth-century drama, Brown contextualizes it as a commodity within the growing early eighteenth-century market for pets. Mr Lovel, the fop, is rendered in those terms of effeminacy and humanity that are otherwise used for the monstrous monkey whom he encounters in *Evelina*. Greenfield's 'Monkeying Around in *Evelina*: Identity and Resemblance Again' (*ECN* 6–7[2009] 409–28) engages with the issue of physical similarity (Evelina–her mother; Mr Lovel–the monkey) and notes that 'the heroine and the monkey are twinned in their joint roles *as* twins' (p. 411). Extending her discussion of resemblance by considering the complex issue of 'identity boundaries' in *Evelina*, Greenfield addresses 'problems of nation, race, gender, and class' (p. 415) engendered in the characters of the novel. Megan Woodworth, in '"If a man dared act for himself": Family Romance and Independence in Frances Burney's *Celia*' (*ECF* 22[2009] 355–70), reading the novel in the context of contemporary debates on the politics of independence, reveals the origins of the political stakes for the public and private actions of men in the novel and interprets the subdued ending as Burney's dissatisfaction with the status quo.

Chapters 4 and 5 of Kirsten T. Saxton's *Narratives of Women and Murder in England, 1680–1760* centrally discuss the representation of murderesses in Defoe's *Roxana* and Fielding's *Amelia*, especially Fielding's 'fictional foray into Mary Blandy's case' (p. 6) in *Amelia*, and in the latter chapter the competing narratives of Fielding's novel and Blandy's amatory fiction. Saxton's wide-ranging study is not only useful for its mining of a multi-generic and experimental realm of fiction featuring the murderess; also, it explains convincingly the mechanisms by which a literate (and literary) murderess produces an imaginative apology that skilfully avoids or resists her inscription as 'a monstrous anomaly' (p. 4).

Stephen H. Gregg's *Defoe's Writings and Manliness* is the major critical intervention in Defoe studies this year and concerns itself with 'Defoe's abiding interest . . . in *failures* of manliness' (p. 1). It addresses questions regarding the ways in which manliness can accommodate both 'a gentlemanly honour transformed via middle-sorts values' and the idea of 'the born gentleman whose virtue had a civic function to perform' (p. 7). Gregg's book covers the whole range of Defoe's major fiction and offers stimulating analyses of masculinity, male friendship, the position of man in varying social contexts, and Defoe's implicit questioning of patriarchal sexual hierarchies. In his chapter on *Robinson Crusoe*, he interprets the protagonist's choice to leave his native country and his repeated expressions of despair as unmanly and effeminate. He embeds his reading within the discursive frameworks of idleness and luxury and relates these dangers to manliness to the encounter with the exotic. Crusoe's 'language of a hypochondriac malaise' (p. 60) is indicative of the ways in which he gives in to temptation, even to the extent that he indulges in self-pity rather than in action to reject or overcome temptation. Chapter 5, 'Singleton, Friendship and Secrecy', especially reveals the author's ability to unravel the gender-conceptual nuances of Defoe's fashioning of male–male friendship. Gregg consolidates his considerations of the issues of manliness by including extensive exploration of the notion of contrariness in Defoe's fiction, since 'manliness is shaped by the intermittent tensions and fitful syntheses between a variety of contrary forces in Defoe's writings: between, for example, commerce and civic humanism; Christian and Classical virtue; patriarchy and companionate marriage; gentility and gentlemanliness; or between private friendship and public spirit' (p. 14). Given the extensive body of work on gender and Defoe's fiction, Gregg has identified a critical issue that is largely unexplored and succeeded in original ways in producing a fresh account of the conceptual complexities of manliness that also comprises interesting discussions of the contrariness of Defoe's characters and his writing generally.

Focused studies of tropes, the supernatural, and publishing contexts complement Gregg's study. In 'The Early Novel and Catastrophe' (*Novel* 42[2009] 443–50), Scott J. Juengel engages with Defoe's conceptualization of catastrophe by considering *Robinson Crusoe* as well as four further texts, also by Defoe, which range from satirical essay to more substantial accounts of natural disasters. In his more extended uses of the catastrophe trope, Defoe is shown to develop in the framework of his fictions 'a discursive network . . . that at once takes measure of the tragedy while disaggregating any omniscient, or even adequate, point of view' (p. 447). Heather Harper investigates the genre of the apparition narrative, popular at the beginning of the century, in '"Matchless Sufferings": Intimate Violence in the Early Modern Apparition Narratives of Daniel Defoe and Elizabeth Boyd' (*WW* 16[2009] 425–44). Pat Rogers's 'Nathaniel Mist, Daniel Defoe, and the Perils of Publishing' (*Library* 10[2009] 298–313) contributes to our understanding of the publishing contexts of Defoe's fiction, specifically the pirated editions of *Captain Singleton*, whereas Nicholas Seager's 'Prudence and Plagiarism in the 1740 Continuation of Defoe's *Roxana*' (*Library* 10[2009] 357–71) investigates the publishing history and critical fortunes of Defoe's novel. Seager revisits *Roxana* in a contextualization of the mid-century novel in 'The 1740 *Roxana*: Defoe, Haywood, Richardson, and Domestic Fiction' (*PQ* 88[2009] 103–26). Christina L. Healey's '"A perfect Retreat indeed": Speculation, Surveillance, and Space in Defoe's *Roxana*' (*ECF* 21[2009] 493–512) examines economically inscribed spaces and the importance of surveillance practices for the success of an individual in a competitive, market-driven world. In her analysis of the ways that women of business negotiate space through speculation and surveillance, Healey considers 'how their entrepreneurial activities affect the social spaces of the novel' (p. 494) and indicates that *Roxana* instructs readers in good business practices.

Thomas Keymer's *The Cambridge Companion to Laurence Sterne* follows in the tradition of Cambridge University Press's excellent 'companions' to eighteenth-century novelists such as Defoe and Fielding and will prove a useful resource for students and scholars alike. It features twelve contributions by some of the most distinguished Sterne scholars, four of whom centrally engage with the study of his imaginative prose: 'Scriblerian Satire, *A Political Romance*, the "Rabelaisian Fragment", and the Origins of *Tristram Shandy*' (Marcus Walsh, pp. 21–33); 'Tristram Shandy, Learned Wit, and Enlightenment Knowledge' (Judith Hawley, pp. 34–48); '*Tristram Shandy* and Eighteenth-Century Narrative' (Robert Folkenflik, pp. 49–63); and '*A Sentimental Journey* and the Failure of Feeling' (Thomas Keymer, pp. 79–95). Other chapters of particular interest reflecting modern approaches to Sterne include 'Words, Sex, and Gender in Sterne's Novels' (Elizabeth W. Harries), 'Sterne and Print Culture' (Christopher Fanning), and 'Sterne and Visual Culture'. Investigating the origins of *Tristram Shandy*, Walsh studies two early works of Sterne's, *A Political Romance* and 'Rabelaisian Fragment', identifying Swiftian methods and models for Sterne's satires and focusing on the fragmentary—especially in its intertextual anthologizing of earlier authors. What Walsh terms Sterne's 'ironic method' centrally draws on 'overt allusion, covert allusion, and occasional local verbal theft' (p. 25), still a fruitful area for exploration. Starting with the eighteenth-century conception of long fictional works, Folkenflik defines Laurence Sterne's *Tristram Shandy* in the literary tradition of the comic romance running from Cervantes to Fielding, and explores some of the work's generic characteristics. The presence and influence of Cervantes is also explored in *The Cervantean Heritage: Reception and Influence of Cervantes in Britain*, edited by J.A.G. Ardila, especially in Brean Hammond's contribution to the volume, 'The Cervantic Legacy in the Eighteenth-Century Novel' (pp. 96–103). Hawley traces the Sternian agenda of instructing his readers in the variety of 'possible sexual connotations that he and his characters use': 'Readers should be alert to the many registers of language, rhetorical to bawdy to metaphorical; they must read asterisks, dashes, blank spaces, as well as the many connotations of the words themselves' (p. 112). Hawley's useful chapter investigates Sterne's sexual(ized) language by reading it as an effective (and entertaining) way of access 'to the half-suppressed . . . world of sexuality in its most physical form' (p. 113). Keymer reads Sterne's *A Sentimental Journey* in the context of eighteenth-century sensibility and discusses a fundamental ambiguity in the work, suggesting that 'sentiment and satire coexist and compete in shifting proportions, allowing readers to read the text according to their rubric' (p. 90). The various contributions to Keymer's volume introduce a range of approaches to Sterne's work that will surely stimulate further research and consolidate research areas such as the study of print culture.

Independently published essays on Sterne include Andreas Mahler's '"Doing" Things with Words: Laurence Sterne's *Tristram Shandy* und die Praxis des narrativen Sprechaktes' (*Anglia* 127[2009] 41–64), which, in the author's own words, 'shows how Tristram-the-narrator, in reporting speech and thereby surreptitiously including the very act of his creation, textually . . . self-begets a Tristram-as-character, which serves Sterne as a source of (potentially endless) textual play' (p. 41). In 'The Literary History of the Sash Window' (*ECF* 22[2009] 171–94), Rachel Ramsay introduces a capsule history of the sash window and then reads it in cultural terms, especially in terms of its literary significance. She traces the occurrence of the sash window in early modern works ranging from *Gulliver's Travels* and *Tristram Shandy* to Johnson's *Journey to the Western Islands* and Austen's *Northanger Abbey*. Sterne is put into comparative perspective in Scott Nowka's 'Talking Coins and Thinking Smoke-Jacks: Satirizing Materialism in Gildon and Sterne' (*ECF* 22[2009] 195–222). Nowka highlights the ways in which Charles Gildon's *The Golden Spy* and Sterne's *Tristram Shandy* reveal the dangers of materialistic ideas as well as the cultural pervasiveness of materialist thinking in eighteenth-century Britain.

Few scholars have engaged with Smollett's fiction. Lee F. Kahan, in 'Fathoming Intelligence: The "Imperial" Novelist and the Passion for News in Tobias Smollett's *Ferdinand Count Fathom*' (*ECF* 21[2009] 229–58), argues that Smollett develops a dialectic between the periodic and the novelistic mode and their competing economies of information in the central characters Fathom and Renaldo. This dialectic results in the emergence of the objective novelist as the work's real principal personage, who is 'necessary [not only] to preserve... the integrity of information but also to prevent the reader from becoming too involved in the intelligence he consumes' (p. 231). Pierre Dubois's 'Perception, Appearance and Fiction in *The Adventures of Roderick Random* by Tobias Smollett' (*EA* 62[2009] 387–400) charts Roderick's development to see beyond the veil of superficial appearances and underpins his discussion with reference to Locke's stress on visual perception in the acquisition of knowledge and the epistemological crisis caused by the issue of appearance and reality. Dubois argues that the 'dialectics of appearance and reality is thus at the heart of Smollett's literary endeavor and is used to articulate an implicit theory of fiction' (p. 387). Alex Wetmore's 'Sympathy Machines: Men of Feeling and the Automaton' (*ECS* 43[2009] 37–54) relates the eighteenth-century automaton to notions of masculinity and offers comparative considerations of the linked subjects of automata and men in the works of Sterne, Smollett, and Henry Mackenzie. Wetmore argues that the man of feeling's spontaneous (i.e. automatic) responsiveness in terms of sensibility destabilizes the clearly defined boundary between the inanimate machine and human beings, thereby renegotiating this boundary in novel ways.

Horace Walpole's *Castle of Otranto*, as in previous years, has been explored in a range of different contexts. *1650–1850: Ideas, Aesthetics, and Inquiries in the Early Modern Era* published a special feature section, edited by Peter Sabor, in which three articles address Walpole's fiction. Stephen Clarke's 'Horace Walpole's Architectural Taste' (*1650–1850* 16[2009] 223–44), Marcie Frank's 'Horace Walpole's Theatricality' (*1650–1850* 16[2009] 309–27), and 'Laura Baudot's 'A Voyage of Un-Discovery: Deciphering Horace Walpole's *Hieroglyphic Tales*' (*1650–1850* 16[2009] 329–61) complement scholars' continued efforts to historicize *The Castle of Otranto* in literary and architectural terms, as in Robert B. Hamm's 'Hamlet and Horace Walpole's *The Castle of Otranto*' (*SEL* 49[2009] 667–92) and Sean R. Silver's 'Visiting Strawberry Hill: Horace Walpole's Gothic Historiography' (*ECF* 21[2009] 535–64). Clarke's architectural focus, demonstrating Walpole's critical attitude towards the work of some of the foremost architects of his day, offers a useful background for further studies of an architectural vocabulary which characterized the literary Gothic that Walpole had helped to popularize. Frank's essay aligns Walpole's generic innovation with Shakespeare's, and Walpole's preoccupation with dramatic theory is central to his 'style of authorship and his concept of fiction' (p. 311). Silver offers 'an experiment in reassembling the villa [Strawberry Hill] and its collection' (p. 537), in the process producing a useful account of Walpole's conception of Gothic historicity.

Not having arrived on time to be included in this review, two books—*Defoe's Footprints: Essays in Honour of Maximillian E. Novak*, edited by Robert M. Maniquis and Carl Fisher, and *Adventure: An Eighteenth-Century Idiom: Essays on the Daring and the Bold as a Pre-Modern Medium*, edited by Serge Soupel, Kevin L. Cope, Alexander Pettit, and Laura Thomason Wood—will be reviewed next year in this section. Both are covered elsewhere in this chapter: the former in section 1 and the latter in sections 1 and 3.

3. Poetry

This year saw no full-length studies of eighteenth-century poetry, but a number of substantial essays and articles appeared covering a wide range of poets and themes. These studies do not suggest any significant new critical trends but rather a continuing commitment to an expanded canon and broadly historicist and ideological approaches. This said, these predominantly cultural concerns frequently combine with a continuing commitment to the modes of close reading and attention to matters of poetic language, form, and genre. The potential strengths of such a critical marriage are exemplified in '"Nature to Advantage Drest": Chinoiserie, Aesthetic Form, and the Poetry of Subjectivity in Pope and Swift' (*ECS* 43:i[2009] 75–94) by Eugenia Zuroski Jenkins, an engaging example of what can be achieved when fresh cultural insights are brought to bear upon two such familiar poems as Pope's *The Rape of the Lock* and Swift's *The Lady's Dressing Room*. Following pointers in earlier studies of women, consumerism, and domestic taste by Maxine Berg, Laura Brown, Robert Jones, Elizabeth Kowaleski-Wallace, Marcia Pointon, and David Porter, Jenkins draws attention to the consequences for women of the establishment in the early eighteenth century of 'a new set of aesthetic skills and practices associated with the "Chinese taste" in personal ornament and decoration' (p. 76). In doing so she seeks to address 'some of the particular syntactical relationships that bound the eighteenth-century British woman to the Chinese object in cultural sites such as the dressing room and the tea-table, as well as in the textual space of poetry' (p. 75). What this reveals is a collusion between material culture and poetry to generate and then dismantle a particular form of female subject who is being defined by her relationship to decorative objects either imported from the Orient or, as in the example of Chippendale 'Chinese' furniture, being produced in Britain in an oriental style (as Jenkins makes clear, 'Chinese' in this context might cover objects and styles originating in Japan and other parts of Asia). Jenkins illustrates how women, as 'consuming subjects', were encouraged to become conversant in how to acquire, use, and display these decorative objects and how the resulting 'material practices of beautification followed a poetic logic' by examining a range of contemporary instructive manuals which sought to encourage a particular principle of aesthetic ordering that accorded with Pope's sense of 'Order in Variety' (pp. 76–7). This analysis of a neglected sub-genre provides the social and aesthetic context for Jenkins's consideration of the related yet contrasting negotiations of this cultural territory in *The Rape of the Lock* and *The Lady's Dressing Room*. She argues that although Pope and Swift both 'look to women's aesthetic work in the home to illustrate the consequences of certain boundary violations' this also 'entails a change in the social life of china'; but while, for Pope, 'dressing room china is a foreign object that can be assimilated by women into British culture' since it 'stands for and sublimates the mercantile ambitions of a cosmopolitan early modernity, in which the interior qualities of taste and judgment can be displayed on the surface, whether in a room or on a woman's body'; for Swift, in contrast, surface and depth were placed 'in decisive opposition' (p. 91). This is a conceptually sophisticated comparative reading which avoids simply treating the poems as mere source material to be ransacked by the cultural historian. In so doing it offers an informative, genuinely interdisciplinary exercise in feminist cultural and literary analysis (for two further essays on Pope, arriving too late for detailed discussion, see the close of this section).

Last year I neglected to mention a couple of recent accounts of Swift's poetry in the established journal *Swift Studies: The Annual of the Ehrenpreis Center*. J.A. Downie's bibliographical article 'Swift's "Corinna" Reconsidered' (*SStud* 22[2007] 161–8) offers a convincing argument for dating the composition of this poem (first published on 7 March 1728 in the third, so-called 'Last Volume' of the Pope–Swift *Miscellanies in Prose and Verse*) to 1726 rather than 1712 as has often been the case since Faulkner's 1735 edition of *Swift*. Downie's argument, based on detailed analysis of all the available circumstantial evidence, begins with his recognition that all claims for the earlier dating derive from an often repeated, but now wholly disputable, identification of 'Corinna', with Delarivier Manley that can be traced back to a footnote in John Hawksworth's 1755 edition of Swift's *Works* in which two crucial lines of the original poem are silently excised. Downie presents a convincing case for dating the time of composition of the poem to shortly before Swift visited England to oversee the publication of *Gulliver's Travels* in 1726 and for identifying, in the use of the name Corinna a deliberate slight against the poetess Elizabeth Thomas.

In her short but engaging article 'Viewing "the diamond midst the dunghill shine": Anna Young Smith's Poetic Response Upon Reading Swift's Poems' (*SStud* 23[2008] 147–55), Kirsten Juhas draws attention to a neglected response to *The Lady's Dressing Room* and the other voyeuristic satires. As Juhas notes, ever since it reputedly caused Laetitia Pilkington's mother to throw up her dinner, *The Lady's Dressing Room* has prompted some violent responses, not least from women readers. Two early poetical ripostes have become familiar since their recovery in Roger Lonsdale's ground-breaking 1989 Oxford anthology of *Eighteenth-Century Women Poets*: the rather simplistic *The Gentleman's Study; In Answer to* [*Swift's*] The Lady's Dressing

Room, by a 'Miss W—' (untraced), and *The Dean's Provocation for Writing the Lady's Dressing Room*, attributed to Lady Mary Wortley Montagu, which presents a more sophisticated debunking of Swift as impotent misogynist while taking a derisive side-sweep at Pope. Juhas provides the biographical and critical context for the first known response by an American woman poet, the verses 'On Reading Swift's Works' by Anna Young Smith (1756–80), who, having been partly educated in the household of 'the most learned woman in America', her aunt, Elizabeth Graeme Fergusson (1737–1801), became a member of a small circle of well-educated women poets based in and around Philadelphia. Young's poetic response, in which she combines condemnation of Swift for indulging in such disgusting and 'vengeful satire' against 'helpless woman' with admiration for his 'wit almost divine', was composed in 1774 and first published posthumously in 1790. No holographs of Young's poetry survive, but Juhas provides a transcription of a variant manuscript copy Fergusson made for fellow-poet Annis Boudinot Stockton in 1787, and compares this with the published version.

In his essay 'Salomon Gessner and Collins's *Oriental Eclogues*' (*Neophil* 93[2009] 369–76), Sandro Jung addresses the early reception of the poetry of William Collins on the continent by drawing attention to a neglected German translation of his *Oriental Eclogues* [1757] (first published as *Persian Eclogues* in 1742). Entitled *Orientalische Eclogen von Wilhelm Collins. Nebst einigen anderen Gedichten. Aus dem Englischen*, and published at Zurich in 1770, this translation was the work of the Swiss poet, bookseller, and engraver, Salomon Gessner (1730–88) who was well known throughout Europe for his own collections of pastorals including *Idyllen* [1756]. As Jung explains, although in Britain Collins was best known for his *Odes on Several Descriptive and Allegoric Subjects* [1746], their use of abstractions hindered the work of translation whereas the more concrete *Eclogues* proved more amenable. Gessner's translation of the *Eclogues*, the second to appear in German, is of particular interest for bearing a theoretical preface in which Gessner, seeking to illustrate his own theory of pastoral, also translates and discusses John Langhorne's 'Observations on the Oriental Eclogues' [1765]. We are reminded that Collins, who has limited modern appeal, was popular amongst late eighteenth-century readers, and Jung concludes his brief account of the translated poems by noting the interest that Gessner's own theory and practice of the idyll held for British Romantics, notably Samuel Taylor Coleridge. Jung's relatively short but practical essay not only advances our knowledge of the transmission of Collin's poetry in Europe but also touches on the wider development of his reputation as a writer of pastoral.

Another poet who tends to baffle modern tastes is the Edward Young of *Night Thoughts*. In 'Venture and Adventure in Edward Young's Night Thoughts (1742–1746)' (in Soupel et al., eds., pp. 63–87), John A. Baker observes that although Young's poem was widely admired until the mid-nineteenth century, it is now 'probably one of the least read important poems in the English language' (p. 67). *Night Thoughts*, Baker suggests, has never really recovered from George Eliot's *ad hominem* yet 'talented and insightful demolition job' in her article 'Worldliness and Other-Worldliness', published in 1857 three years after James Nichols's edition of Young's

Complete Works (p. 77). Baker does not flinch from admitting the challenge posed by *Night Thoughts*—for example, he refers to 'the sometimes rarefied and unbreathable atmosphere of the poem'—but working within the overall theme of the volume in which his essay appears, he teases out Young's largely metaphorical engagement with adventure and venturing (p. 76). Ironically, in an age of travel and adventure, Young largely stayed put, yet one undoubted facet of *Night Thoughts* is 'the poetry and adventure of travel, and the adventure of the imagination, reined in intermittently by the poem's evident and self-avowed didactic leanings' (p. 68). For Baker it is 'a work that ranges, roams, wanders, roves (all Young's words) straining at every turn to leave this world and reach out to the heavens' (p. 69). Baker draws attention to the likely biographical prompt for Young's obsessive concern with mortality and the night-time of the soul when he suffered a triple bereavement between 1736 and 1740, but bucking the trend towards contextual, cultural approaches, this stylish essay is primarily a meditation on language, metaphor, and rhetoric. Without wholly defending Young against the implications of Eliot's charge that he 'is equally impressed by the momentousness of death and of burial fees' (or, as Baker deftly puts it, the hypocrisy of 'a sort of spiritual insider trading'), this essay is partly devoted to a consideration of 'the extent to which economic and religious terms overlap' in *Night Thoughts* and the theological discourses within which it participates (p. 80). The very opening of Baker's sustained close reading seeks to forge some contrasting analogies with Philip Larkin's poem 'Days' from *Whitsun Weddings*. This exercise is a little hampered by a copyright restriction on direct quotation, but this framing comparison does allow Baker to conclude that Young is, above all, 'a poet of negativity, in which the moral and nocturnal poetic adventure is the negative, in photographic terms, of the diurnal and the worldly (p. 87). Overall this lively essay offers a rewarding exploration of *Night Thoughts* which we are invited to read as not so much insincere, but rather 'Young's faithful reflection on and of an inner state of emotional turmoil, self-questioning, worldly disappointment, and the expression of the need for hope' (p. 87).

Victoria Bridges Moussaron's contribution to the same volume is entitled 'The Adventure of a "Sublime Subject": *The Shipwreck* (1762) by William Falconer' (pp. 125–43). *The Shipwreck*, which was published in three variant editions during Falconer's lifetime (in 1762, 1764, and 1769), is another example of a once popular but now neglected poem. Loosely modelled on classical and neoclassical epics, it tells the tale of a return voyage to 'Albion' of a sailor-poet who is one of only three people to survive a shipwreck. As Moussaron explains, the poem has unique resonances as both autobiography and prophetic warning since Falconer, who based the story on his own experience of being one of only thee survivors of a shipwreck, was to die in another shipwreck in 1769. In his 1764 preface Falconer tells his readers that he had composed the poem for 'the gentlemen of the sea, for whose entertainment it was chiefly calculated' and to whom, it is implied, he had originally recited the poem on board ship. By drawing attention to the twofold Latin etymology of adventure '*ad* plus *venire*' which 'includes an element of the unknown which belongs to the future' and how this is in potential tension with the notion of a tale of *past* adventure, Moussaron explores how Falconer's poem negotiates the twin poles of 'time' and 'truth'. To begin, she draws attention to questions of performance and address. Falconer, who terms himself 'A *Sailor*' on the poem's title page, claims to be addressing his tale to fellow seafarers, but by the time he presents his set-piece account of the storm there are several implied listeners: 'The final verse includes the audience, the spectators, and the victims turning the tale into a *mise en abîme* of referentiality' (p. 128). Falconer was commended by contemporaries for his command of accurate nautical language but, as Mousarron observes, he was faced with the problem of satisfying two audiences, 'demanding, on the one hand, a verisimilitude of unfailing nautical accuracy for the seafarers and, on the other hand, for his literary readers, mastery of the art of storytelling equal to that of the classical authors' (p. 129). Mousarron goes on to examine how Falconer adapts various classical topoi, notably that of the witness, presenting himself as 'the cantor of those who died in the shipwreck' (p. 131). Seeing *The Shipwreck* as, in part, an attempt to apply Burke's theories of the sublime to a storm at sea (what the poet himself terms 'a sublime subject'), and drawing a comparison between Falconer's declaration that he is a singer of 'a *Native* Song' (p. 139) and similar claims in the Preface to the *Lyrical Ballads*, Moussaron concludes that *The Shipwreck* 'illustrates a poetics which anticipates that of Coleridge and Wordsworth' (p. 141). This is an engaging close reading that certainly drew my attention back to this neglected but not negligible poem (*The Shipwreck* is also one of several poems discussed in an essay on empiricism by Kevin L. Cope to be addressed below).

It should be noted that William Roberts's essay 'Thomas Gray's Adventures in Scotland and the English Lake District', to be found in the same volume (Soupel et al., eds., pp. 171–88), makes passing reference to the poetry, but is largely concerned with encouraging us to read Gray's travel journals, including his account of his visit to the Highlands of Scotland in 1765 when he visited Ben More, from where, as an admirer of Macpherson's *Ossian* fragments, he looked down 'on the tomb of Fingal' (p. 174). The essays in *Crossing the Highland Line: Cross-Currents in Eighteenth-Century Scottish Writing*, edited by Christopher MacLachlan and derived from the Association of Scottish Literary Studies annual conference in 2005, are largely concerned with Gaelic prose and poetry but three contributions, all to some extent engaged with questions of nationalism and genre, warrant notice here. Kenneth Simpson's contribution addresses 'the Place of Macpherson's Ossian in Scottish Literature' (pp. 113–22). This is a panoramic attempt to locate Macpherson's work 'poetically and politically' in relation to its immediate context of production and lasting influence. In a wide-ranging account that embraces David Hume and Irvine Welsh while taking in Lord Shaftesbury, Alexander Pope, Tobias Smollett, Henry Mackenzie, Robert Burns, and Walter Scott along the way, Simpson argues for seeing *The Poems of Ossian* as a typically inventive Scottish performance embracing a commendably 'creative conflation of a range of sources' (p. 117). Drawing upon Macpherson's often overlooked pre-Ossian poetry, Simpson pays particular regard to the role of more immediate literary influences, notably the patriotic identification of Scotland with 'purity of feeling and action' in John Home's tragedy *Douglas* [1754]. Looking beyond the role of Rousseau in providing the conditions within which Macpherson's 'romantic melancholy' was conceived and received, Simpson ties the Ossianic emphasis upon noble sensibility down to a more distinctly Scottish philosophical ethos derived from Francis Hutcheson and Adam Smith in which potentially elitist inflections of sensibility sometimes tip over into crude sentimentalism (pp. 114–16). Simpson concludes by remarking on the inherent irony in the fact that 'while Macpherson may have been unwittingly responsible for mapping out a constraining course for Scottish literature, he is undeniably, in company with Burns, one of the most influential of Scottish writers internationally' (p. 121).

Gerard Carruthers opens his contribution to the same volume, '"Poured out extensive, and of watery wealth": Scotland in Thomson's *The Seasons*' (in MacLachlan, ed., pp. 21–30), by drawing attention to the irony in how Thomson, a poet of 'empirical landscape observation' who not only pays 'close attention to the natural environment but also to the human geography of Great Britain', has become a writer 'of rather uncertain territory' (p. 21). As Carruthers observes, this is partly a consequence of his marginalized standing in his native Scotland where Thomson is largely ignored by critics despite being, second only to Scott, its most successful international writer. Reassessing Thomson's Scottishness, Carruthers challenges a traditional polarization of Ramsay as the poet of the 'vernacular' and Thomson of the 'non-vernacular' by drawing attention to the latter's role as a poetic revivalist (the Spenserian stanza in *The Castle of Indolence*) and also to the combined influence of both poets upon Fergusson and Burns later in the century. Addressing how Thomson's more rational, less spiritually inspired mode of natural description was indebted to William Derham and other Newtonian physico-theologians, Carruthers talks of Thomson's 'Presbyterian devotional eye' while urging that the poet's 'response to recent British history informed by moderate Presbyterianism, where divine providence and purpose are to be read in the world, is the context in which his attention to nature is crucial' (p. 23). Countering the 'distracting tendency' in Thomsonian criticism to place the impulses behind *The Seasons* within a long native tradition stretching back to the Middle Ages (Gavin Douglas and Robert Henryson), Carruthers is concerned with Thomson's remaking of tradition in the light of more contemporary history and politics. Here he describes an emerging Presbyterian Whig context, as exemplified in the *Edinburgh Miscellany* [1720], to which Thomson contributed, and traces Thomson's appropriation of William Wallace as a patriot in 'Autumn'. He also discusses the invocations, throughout *The Seasons*, of a 'water pastoralism' in which, in contrast to England's green pastures, Scotland's rivers, lochs, and seas are identified as unique and underused resources. Carruthers thus illustrates how Thomson was 'seeking to draw continuity between the ancient Scottish patriotic past' and what he 'took to be the best of Hanoverian Britain' (p. 26). Warning against readings that too readily view Thomson's invocations of 'Briton' in the debased light of later nineteenth-century imperialism, Carruthers reminds us that for his immediate contemporaries, and also for 1790s radicals, Thomson represented an oppositional 'Presbyterian Real Whig' for whom 'Briton' signified 'the aspiration of industrious, non-luxurious living founded on reasonable thinking and conscientious political involvement' (p. 27).

This informed essay admirably fulfils its own call for a serious reassessment of Thomson as 'yes, a complex Scottish writer, but not as someone to be effectively excluded from discussions of Scottish literature for being not Scottish enough or for being too British' (p. 29).

Murray Pittock's 'The Jacobite Song: Was There a Scottish *Aisling*?' (in MacLachlan, ed. pp. 85–95) is a version of an essay appearing under the same title in *The Review of Scottish Culture* (19[2007] 45–53). In this self-declaredly provisional, but very well informed analysis, Pittock examines the various points of intersection between the Jacobite song tradition and the traditional aisling. Alongside a running critique of the essentialist and delimiting nationalist terms within which the aisling has been traditionally claimed as a uniquely Irish sub-genre, Pittock examines a number of common concerns and motifs. These include some intriguing observations on the symbolic use of the blackbird in both Irish and Scottish song where, as he quips, these 'avian connections of birdic nationalism are almost entirely unexplored' (p. 92). 'Was there a Scottish *aisling*?' Pittock asks in rhetorical conclusion: 'Nearly; and for those who think that is not enough, one may also ask whether Aristotle would think *Macbeth* a tragedy or Pindar recognize himself in Cowley's verse' (p. 93).

William J. Christmas's essay, '"From threshing corn, he turns to thresh his brains": Stephen Duck as Laboring-Class Intellectual' (in Krishnamurthy, ed., *The Working-Class Intellectual in Eighteenth- and Nineteenth-Century Britain*, pp. 25–48), usefully revisits what has often been Duck's somewhat uncomfortable positioning within this tradition. The descriptive epithet 'thresher-poet' has stuck to Duck since he first read his poem *The Thresher's Labour* at court in 1730 and became, albeit briefly, a Hanoverian literary celebrity. As Christmas observes, this reductive identification continues with the recent resurgence of critical interest, although somewhat ironically this probably owes much to the championing of Mary Collier's proto-feminist response, *The Woman's Labour* [1739]. Tracing the tendency to identify Duck with *The Thresher's Labour* as his 'best' poem down through the Robert Southey of *The Lives and Works of the Uneducated Poets* [1831] to Duck's first modern biographer Rose Mary David writing in the 1920s, Christmas observes how political or ideological readings have more recently 'given way to a return to formalism' in a proliferation of essays concerned with the aesthetic and generic innovations of this one poem (p. 25). Inclined to accept that on both ideological and aesthetic grounds *The Thresher's Labour* is Duck's best poem, Christmas's concern is rather to address the consequences of approaches that claim that Duck only achieved 'authenticity' 'when he wrote about his class-specific labor experiences, and that such authenticity should be valued above all other concerns' (p. 26). The usual consequence of such privileging has been the production of a standard downhill narrative of Duck's career, starting with his 'discovery' by a clergyman and his being brought to court, where he gained Queen Caroline's patronage, to a Latin education which meant that he resorted to writing 'blasé neo-classical verse and fawning panegyric' that eventually crushed his 'natural' poetic potential and led to depression and suicide (p. 26). Aiming to 'challenge this narrative of deracination and corrupted authenticity' by considering Duck within a more 'transhistorical context of working-class intellectualism', Christmas draws attention to what is truly extraordinary in Duck's development from 'natural' genius to 'a man of remarkable learning' whose primary goal was quite evidently assimilation into the dominant culture (p. 26). This has presented a particular problem to left-field historians, who tend to derive their models of labouring-class intellectualism from the radicals of the 1790s. By drawing upon Gramsci's contrasting model of 'traditional' and 'organic' intellectuals and taking Duck's educational achievements seriously, Christmas offers a new approach to this problem. In the process he pays close attention to Duck's later attempt to assert poetic authority through a series of Horatian imitations and in his late patriotic prospect poem *Caesar's Camp; or, St George's Hill* [1755]. Without making any radical argument for aesthetic reassessments, this thoughtful essay invites us to reconsider the broader trajectory of Duck's literary career from a different, notably less judgemental perspective. (This essay was provided in proof-copy by the author but the volume reached my desk too late for me to address Monica Smith Hart's contribution, 'Protest and Performance: Ann Yearsley's *Poems on Several Occasions*', this year.)

Sandro Jung's substantial, closely argued essay 'Shenstone, Woodhouse, and Mid-Eighteenth-Century Poetics: Genre and the Elegiac-Pastoral Landscape' (*PQ* 88[2009] 127–49) addresses very similar questions over the matter of deracination to those considered in Christmas's review of Stephen Duck's career, but here in relation to 'the shoemaker poet' James Woodhouse. Engaging with debates over the relative value of ideological and formalist approaches to labouring-class poetry as articulated in the earlier work of H. Gustav Klaus, Steve van Hagen, Bridget Keegan, Donna Landry, and Christmas himself, Jung confronts an established assumption that Woodhouse had two mutually exclusive poetic personae: on the one hand, a poet who conforms to neoclassical aesthetic norms as represented by a polite canon, and on the other 'the alternative, different, and plebeian poet, engaging with political issues of self-representation and class struggle on whom critics of labouring-class poetry have concentrated' (p. 127). Addressing this bias against poems that do not address socio-economic themes, Jung observes how, as a consequence Woodhouse's early poems have received cursory attention 'as the productions of a sycophantic imitator', but for Jung this has meant a 'failure to recognize Woodhouse's considerable skill in the use of forms and the lyric mode that few of his more expansive works demonstrate' (p. 128). Jung also alerts us to the fact that class distinctions become blurred once we take on board that Woodhouse's patron, the poet and garden designer William Shenstone, was well placed to act as a mentor because he was himself from a relatively humble background; Shenstone was never entirely comfortable in polite society and, although he attended Pembroke College, Oxford, he was largely self-taught. Jung presents a detailed assessment of Shenstone's influence on Woodhouse's early lyric and pastoral poetry and, in particular the representation of landscape inspired by Woodhouse being granted access to his patron's gardens and *ferme ornée* at Leasowes. Noting that 'imitation—integral to eighteenth-century poetics—entailed a process of experimentation, interpretation and invention', Jung devotes the core of this detailed essay to formal readings of Woodhouse's early lyric verse, which enables him to be 'restored to being a man of his time engaging with the literary culture of the mid-century' rather than a declassed, sycophantic copyist of the models Shenstone offered (p. 129). This detailed study reassesses Shenstone as pastoralist and elegist as well as providing an important account of Woodhouse's neglected early poetry.

We return to the poetic representation of rural labour in 'Labor and Commerce in Locke and Early Eighteenth-Century English Georgic' (*ELH* 76[2009] 963–88), where Robert P. Irvine addresses the relevance of John Locke's analysis of the relationship between labour, commerce, and the state in chapter 5 of the *Second Treatise of Government* [1669; revised 1698] when reading early eighteenth-century georgic. The first half of this essay outlines how Locke, in seeking to establish the priority of property rights over those of political institutions, accords labour 'the rhetorical role of legitimating the money economy in the face of the traditional (Aristotelian) objections', such that labour functions to both signify and naturalize 'a commercial system in which it is fully integrated, and which is historically and morally prior to the state' (p. 963). Taken on its own this offers a valuable account of Locke on labour that is fully cognizant of the range of available interpretations. In particular Irvine draws attention to Locke's 'rhetorical strategy ... to use "labor" as a synecdoche for commerce, so that the moral meaning of plowing and reaping can be extended to trading and banking as well' (p. 971). The rest of the essay considers the 'georgic moment' of John Philips's *Cyder* [1708] and Alexander Pope's *Windsor-Forest* [1713] which, as Irvine analyses in some detail, are to be read as being in a subtle dialectical relationship with, on the one hand, a classical Virgilian georgic ethos within which values invested in the land are deemed to be at risk of erosion by a commercial, money economy and, on the other, Locke's more recent assimilation of labour to commerce. In both analyses agricultural labour serves, as it does in Virgil's georgics, as a 'political symbol', but with Locke having 'inscribed labour as an element within the money economy', Irvine argues that Philips and Pope can only reassert the political difference of land from other types of property by asserting the autonomy of agriculture from the circulation of commodities that the money economy makes possible' (p. 973). Irvine concludes that 'Locke's *Second Treatise* provides a crucial context for early English georgic, because the priority of the commercial over the political for which he argues is just what these poems set out to reverse' (p. 973). He presents these readings by way of supplement to the earlier work of Pat Rogers, who has identified the encoding of specific party-political commitments in the two poems (see Pat Rogers, 'John Philips, Pope and Political Georgic', *MLQ* 66[2005] 411–42). While acknowledging that the last twenty years have seen much excellent work on the genre, Irvine is keen to counter a tendency to read 'each poem as an example of a genre performing essentially the same ideological function throughout the period, and developing only in response to its own internal logic' (pp. 963–4). His essay does indeed mount a convincing case for recognizing the quite distinctive ideological work being undertaken in *Cyder* and *Windsor-Forest* and for not simply subsuming these quite specific, early georgic deployments into a tradition that includes James Thomson's *The Seasons* [1730–46] or John Dyer's *The Fleece* [1757] which, as Irvine observes, 'make no bones about the participation of rural labour in international commerce' (p. 984).

Eighteenth-century Britain witnessed dramatic developments in travel and communications that are registered in a flowering of epistolary literature but, despite increasing attention being paid to travel writing as an important literary genre, relatively little attention has been given to poetry concerned with travelling. It is in this context that Bill Overton presents his essay 'Journeying in the Eighteenth-Century British Verse Epistle' (*StTW* 13[2009] 3–25), in which he surveys twenty-five examples of verse epistles concerned with travelling (all usefully listed at the close). Writing for a journal concerned with travel studies rather than poetics, Overton is careful not to imply that the one can straightforwardly 'read off' socio-historical information from this literary material. He draws on established studies of epistolary writing to preface his accounts of the actual poems with a useful discussion of the importance of paying attention to verse forms, modes of address, literary voice and biographical contexts (written en route or in retrospect for public or private circulation). He then details his examples of verse epistles according to mode of transport: on foot, on horseback, by carriage, by water, and 'by various means' (p. 16). The writers include only two familiar names—John Gay and Stephen Duck—but as Overton notes, they cover a wide social range indicative of a society on the move; three labouring-class poets, members of the Anglican clergy and the professional and commercial bourgeoisie as well as an aide-de-camp in the American Revolutionary Army and several gentry. Their journeys stretch from a day's ride to a nine-month sea journey and embrace an extraordinary variety of destinations both at home and abroad. There is a wealth of engaging detail concerning the lived experience of travelling in this period: everything from the state of the roads to fellow-travellers, from food to sea-sickness and the particular impressions of a stagecoach trip taken by Priscilla Pickering, who was blind. Overton makes no special aesthetic claims here—we are warned that some examples are rather dull—but he does unearth an occasional gem like William Cocklin's 'A Familiar Epistle from the Country to Mr. G[eorge] R[omne]y Painter in London' of 1776, which includes some lively verses on the many inconveniences of travelling by stagecoach: 'To bed, to board, to stool, now out, now in, / Jog, jog, a-jog (ye Gods!) through thick and thin...' (p. 11). In other examples humour is mixed with serious reflection, as in Thomas Pearson's remarkable verse epistle recording a nine-month voyage to Calcutta via Rio de Janeiro—some of it probably written en route—which includes Shandean quips, descriptions of everyday shipboard life, meditations on the meaning of movement, and concerns over the progress of the Seven Years War (p. 16). In this informed essay Overton mines a rich seam; a neglected poetic sub-genre of interest to social historians and literary scholars and one to which future compilers of anthologies should be alert.

Daffyd Moore's cultural study 'Patriotism, Politeness, and National Identity in the South West of England in the late Eighteenth Century' (*ELH* 76[2009] 739–62) is primarily concerned with what *Poems Chiefly by Gentlemen of Devonshire and Cornwall* [1792] and a related 1796 essay collection compiled by 'a Society of Gentleman at Exeter' can reveal to the social historian concerning the assertion of a conservative, patriotic regional identity in the 1790s, but it is worth a brief notice here since most of the surprisingly numerous local contributors to these anthologies, notably Hugh Downman, Richard Polwhele, Richard Hole, and William Jackson, had poetic careers beginning earlier in the century.

Disruptions to the British postal service caused by an unusually early fall of snow were partly to blame for Kathryn Duncan's edited volume *Religion in the Age of Reason: A Transatlantic Study of the Long Eighteenth Century* not reaching my desk in time for me to do justice to the two contributions concerned with poetry. In the first of these, 'Fading Fast but Still in Print: The Brink of Visibility and the Form of Religious Experience, Spinoza to Cowper' (pp. 19–42), Kevin L. Cope is concerned with the degree to which many notions of 'empiricism' and 'experience' in the long eighteenth century are in fact non-empirical. Having summarized the largely sidelined ontological models available in Spinoza and Leibniz, Cope surveys 'an array of British poets who have received less than their fair share of modern attention precisely because their writings epitomize the broader notion of "experience" that was at play during the "empirical century"' (p. 20). These include Edmund Waller, Abraham Cowley, George Berkeley (as poet), and William Falconer (*The Shipwreck*). Cope detects a 'symphony of invisibility' as Falconer, 'by concentrating attention on non-visible phenomena... summons a surplus of information from a minimum of experience' (p. 37). His account clearly meshes with some of Mousarron's concerns with motifs of 'venturing' in the poem (as discussed earlier). In a short coda, Cope concludes with a brief reading of William Cowper's *The Castaway*. The same volume also includes Katherine M. Quinsey's 'Dualities of the Divine in Pope's *Essay of Man* and *The Dunciad*' (pp. 135–57). This substantial discussion of how *The Dunciad* represents the 'unholy relative' of the *Essay on Man* is supported by a number of black and white illustrations depicting headpieces from Pope's *Works* [1717–35] (p. 135). The two poems are read in relation to Milton and as 'expressing two sides of Pope's religious imagination; one, rationalizing, optimistic, attempting to make sense of suffering through a "balance of Opposites": the other, visionary, irrational, and subversive of balance and order' (p. 153).

In conclusion, I wish to thank Professor Hermann J. Real for clarifying the matter of the title of Kirsten Juhas's book *'I'll to my Self, and to My Muse Be True': Strategies of Self-Authorization in Eighteenth-Century Women Poetry* to which I referred last year (*YWES* 89[2010] 592). As he has kindly explained, 'women poetry' is a direct translation of a well-recognized German term for a distinct poetic tradition. I must also thank him for alerting me to a typographical error that it was too late to amend in proof; please note that the reference on the same page to where Kirsten Juhas gained her doctorate should have read Westfälische Wilhelms Universität, Münster. Finally, I regret being unable to access Hye-Soo Lee's article 'Mock-Epic and "Novelization": Alexander Pope's the *Rape of the Lock*' (*JELL* 55[2009] 865–83) in time for inclusion in this entry.

4. Drama

[Chapter XI in *YWES* 89[2009] did not cover eighteenth-century drama, so this section reviews publications from both 2008 and 2009, plus one monograph missed from 2007. The author is grateful to Marjean Purinton for contributing substantial notes on works from 2008.]

Interest in the eighteenth-century actress continues to enrich drama and theatre scholarship but it is also invaluable to the ongoing debates about eighteenth-century gender construction and the changing status of women. Moira Goff's fascinating work, *The Incomparable Hester Santlow: A Dancer-Actress on the Georgian Stage* adds to this body of knowledge with the first full-length study of Hester Santlow (later Booth). Santlow is not an easy subject for a biographical study as she left no letters or personal memoirs and therefore the research has been drawn from family papers, advertisements of Santlow's performances, texts of the plays, and contemporary and newspaper reports. Goff charts Santlow's life from dancer to actress and mistress to wife whose story ends with a 'long and exemplary Life of Widowhood' (p. 161) showing that women could transcend the actress/whore paradigm and be seen as living a life of independent respectability. Alongside her meticulously researched biography, Goff delivers a cogent study of early eighteenth-century theatre as she charts Santlow's rise from her apprenticeship with René Cherrier to Drury Lane's lead dancer and one of the company's leading actresses until her retirement in 1733. Santlow worked with actors, writers, managers, and actresses such as Colley Cibber, Barton Booth (whom she married), Richard Steele, Susanna Mountfort, Margaret Bicknell, and many others. Discussion of these figures adds depth to the narrative and provides Goff with the opportunity to examine the rivalries and jealousies between competing companies or individual actors as well as battles with the Lord Chamberlain over theatre licences. Particularly interesting is Goff's chapter on 'Mimes and Pantomimes 1723–1728' and her discussion of John Thurmond's *Harlequin Doctor Faustus* and John Rich's *The Necromancer or, Harlequin Doctor Faustus*, which examines the 'pantomime rivalry between Drury Lane and Lincoln's Inn Fields' (p. 115). Goff argues that despite criticisms in the press of this illegitimate and low-cultured art form, pantomimes drew large audiences and were enjoyed by the educated as well as the masses. Also of interest to dance scholars are Goff's 'Glossary of Early Eighteenth-Century Dance Terms' and the plates describing Santlow's dance compositions.

Marc Martinez also examines the rivalry between the two patent theatres of Lincoln Inn Fields and Drury Lane. In his article 'The Tricks of Lun: Mimesis, Mimicry in John Rich's Performance and Conception of Pantomimes' (*THStud* 29[2009] 148–70) Martinez asserts that most theatre scholars have concentrated on Rich's commercial reasons for promoting his pantomimes but have not discussed them in terms of artistic merit. He argues that Rich can be viewed as having had a 'dual identity': Rich the theatre manager and his performing alter ego, 'Harlequin under the pseudonym of Lun' (p. 149). It is through this duality, Martinez suggests, that Rich can 'straddle the roles of entrepreneur and performer' (p. 149). There is no denying that Rich was an excellent showman and entrepreneur, although one who transgressed the theatrical codes of the day in his afterpieces. However, with Martinez's analysis of Rich's dumbshows it is clear to see these were not just dependent on magic, tricks, and tumbling; rather, these afterpieces 'fused elements of elite and popular culture' (pp. 158–9) that could be seen as part of Rich's destabilizing practice, but which ensured his box-office success.

We return to the eighteenth-century actress in Felicity Nussbaum's '"Real Beautiful Women": Actresses and *The Rival Queens*' (*ECLife* 2[2008] 138–58). In her article Nussbaum examines the new phenomenon of the star actress, arguing that actresses such as Elizabeth Barry, Anne Bracegirdle, Anne Oldfield, Kitty Clive, Peg Woffington, George Anne Bellamy, and Frances Abington crafted a public identity that demonstrated 'another kind of exchange value in the culture' (p. 140). Through her analysis of Charlotte Lennox's *The Female Quixote* [1752], and in particular Nathaniel Lee's *The Rival Queens* [1677], Nussbaum argues that, despite the negative images that surrounded the celebrated actresses, their professional achievements and significant economic power in a market where women's roles were a scarce commodity allowed the actress to transcend the actress/whore delineation that tainted so many. It was well known that these actresses were often their own agents and managed their contracts, benefits, and costumes as well as negotiating their roles. Therefore, as Nussbaum suggests, they invented 'a new kind of labor and identity for women' (p. 140). In her conclusion Nussbaum argues that these actresses provided a form of 'real' woman that the women spectators could emulate, and were more central to the eighteenth-century stage than has been previously recognized.

Bridging the gap between drama and the novel, Emily Hodgson Anderson's excellent *Eighteenth-Century Authorship and the Play of Fiction: Novels and the Theatre, Haywood to Austen* explores how the novel was influenced by eighteenth-century drama. Anderson focuses on women writers who 'through their own authorial choice [chose] to work between two specific eighteenth-century genres, novels and plays' (p. 2) She also discusses the divisions between scholars of the novel and those who work on drama and argues that this generic divide should be bridged, given that the sales of playbooks and manuscripts were often greater than the sales of novels and play-going was an integral part of the lived experience of readers, writers, and of their fictional characters. She also argues that the constraints on types of authorship and restrictions of the modes of expression open to eighteenth-century women writers turned them towards theatrical frameworks, such as drama and the masquerade, to help articulate ideas, truths, and passions that could not be otherwise expressed. Through her analysis of the work of five women novelists and playwrights—Eliza Haywood, Frances Burney, Elizabeth Inchbald, Maria Edgeworth and Jane Austen—Anderson suggests that the fictional text 'could function as an act of disguise; and authorship could become an act of performance' (p. 2). Of particular importance for this section is Anderson's chapter 'Rehearsing Desire: Eliza Haywood's Self-Conscious Performance'. In this chapter she suggests that, as an actress, playwright, bookseller, translator, editor, and novelist who wrote more than eighty works, Haywood is an 'ideal initial test case to search for the continuities of early to mid-eighteenth-century literature' (p. 17). Haywood began her career at a time of negative public opinion about both the actress and the female playwright. This, and the long duration and range of her canon, offers scholars the opportunity to examine developments in women's writing across the century. The link between the reception of the woman and her writing has long been made. In her early career Haywood teased her audience and her readers with suggested connections between herself and her subject matter. This may well have led to the attack by Pope in *The Dunciad* [1728], with his assertion that only lascivious women could write lascivious tales. However, as fashions changed Haywood moved away from her early amorous novellas and seductive fictions and wrote more didactic work such as *The History of Miss Betsy Thoughtless* [1751]. This shift, Anderson suggests, prepared the way for Burney's *Evelina* and the didactic and sentimental literature that was to follow.

Hsin-yun Ou's essay 'Gender, Consumption and Ideological Ambiguity in David Garrick's Production of *The Orphan of China* (1759)' (*TJ* 60[2008] 383–407), examines how the production of *The Orphan of China* 'represented a variant of English national identity shaped by cultural representations of gender, colonial expansion and the Orient' (p. 383). Working within the assumption that eighteenth-century English society associated women with consumerism, Ou suggests that the play achieves its negotiations of national identity through a series of analogies: (1) the conflicts between the Mandarins and Tartars as representative of the tensions between England and France; (2) that the character Mandane, who opposed both her husband's patriotism and patriarchal authority, is the author's spokesperson against Chinese and French oppression; (3) that the ideologically charged figure of Mary Anne Yates as a woman of fashion and rank may have undercut Mandane's potency as an authorial voice; and (4) that the audience and the makers of the play collaborated and worked together to construct layers of social meaning through the dramatization, staging, and costumes. In her analysis Ou further suggests that the presence of a defiant oriental woman in the play provides a female body upon which English debates about the role of women in society and emerging views about female sexuality could be examined.

Interest in David Garrick, actor–manager–dramatist, continues, and he has long been written about as Shakespeare's champion or high priest with his adaptations, or rather as Vanessa Cunningham suggests, in *Shakespeare and Garrick*, 'alterations' of Shakespeare's plays for the eighteenth-century audience. Cunningham asserts that it would be difficult to overstate 'the contribution made by Shakespeare to the growth of Garrick's reputation' (p. 4). However, Cunningham's aim is not to add to the already large number of biographical works, but to examine Garrick as a literary figure, arguing for his centrality in all matters Shakespearian while he lived. Cunningham argues that Garrick was, first and foremost, a Shakespearian editor, and he made alterations to Shakespeare's drama in the context of his associations with the eighteenth-century literary club and his profound sense of eighteenth-century audience tastes. Cunningham convincingly demonstrates this point in the analysis of Garrick's 1744 alteration of *Macbeth* and his 1748 alteration of *Romeo and Juliet*. Garrick played the role of Romeo sixty times between 1748 and 1760, and so his alterations also favoured particular performers and their relationships with the audience. Second, Cunningham asserts that Garrick 're-bottled' Shakespeare into performable texts for staging at Drury Lane. Garrick's 1754 alteration of *The Taming of the Shrew* and his 1756 reworking of *The Winter's Tale* demonstrate the kind of performance refashioning that appealed to eighteenth-century theatre-goers. Garrick scripted the Jubilee celebrations at Stratford in the fall of 1769 that are often cited as the catalyst for the age's bardolatry and the association of Shakespeare with nationalism, patriotism, and genius. According to Cunningham, Garrick's textual modifications and performances of *King Lear* and *Hamlet* reveal his knowledge of the Shakespearian editions from the Renaissance to the mid-eighteenth century as well as the tragedies' inherent familial tensions. The study concludes with the admonition that Garrick left a powerful legacy to Shakespeare studies that deserves serious scrutiny and credit.

Taking a different approach, John Pruitt's 'David Garrick's Invisible Nemeses' (*RECTR* 23[2008] 2–15) discusses the 'unrestrained contentions [that] arose between Garrick, theatre enthusiasts, and the population of unemployed performers he rejected for roles on the stage' (p. 2) during his management of Drury Lane from 1747 to 1776. Pruitt suggests that Garrick was criticized for rejecting his own sensibility, which was vital for an actor, and for rejecting the spirit of the theatre and its need for novelty. Garrick was further criticized as thinking only as a manager and concerned merely with attracting and keeping his audiences, which resulted in him offering re-adaptations of established plays. Garrick was the subject of many satires such as *The Theatrical Manager* [1751], *A Dialogue in the Green-Room upon a Disturbance in the Pit* [1763], and *The Stratford Jubilee* [1769]. Each satire accused Garrick of the commercialization of both the theatre and his craft, which his detractors felt degraded all actors. However, Pruitt concludes that it was Garrick's acting sensibility that ensured his success as a manager.

There are two texts that discuss nationalism and Britishness. Louise H. Marshall's *National Myth and Imperial Fantasy: Representations of Britishness on the Early Eighteenth-Century Stage* examines the influence of drama, especially history plays written and performed between 1719 and 1745, on early eighteenth-century political discourse. For Marshall, the early eighteenth-century London stage dramatized Britain as a 'paragon state' with prologues and epilogues dedicated to its glorious past (p. 1). Although plays remained primarily a commercial venture, the theatre could be seen as a powerful commentator on, and respondent to, public debates or, as Marshall argues, as 'the nation's mirror, a microcosmic version of the state' (p. 1). The book is organized around the examination of groups of plays with discussions of their key themes, beginning with the introduction 'Dramatising Britain: Nation, Fantasy and the London Stage, 1719–1745', and followed by 'Ancient Britons and Liberty', 'Kings, Ministers and Favourites: The National Myth in Peril', 'Shakespeare, the National Scaffold', 'Britain, Empire and Julius Caesar', 'Turks, Christians and Imperial Fantasy', and her conclusion, 'History, Fantasy and the Staging of Britishness'. Marshall's study demonstrates the relationship between history, theatre, and nationhood as portrayed in stage spectacle. Her chapters discuss a range of ideas, from favouritism and patriotism as building blocks in the national myth; the role of Shakespeare and adaptations of Shakespeare's history plays in the building of the national fantasy and a 'gendered interpretation of Britishness'; and Romans and the Roman empire as favourite foreign histories for early eighteenth-century playwrights and a gauge by which Britain could judge its own imperial fantasy and activity, to the ways in which British playwrights appropriated foreign history to comment upon contemporary British politics so as to accommodate the nation's sense of itself as an emerging colonial power. *National Myth and Imperial Fantasy* concludes with a brief discussion about how London theatres promoted and 'sustained notions of Britishness and a sense of communal identity' (p. 183). Marshall points out that although all the plays examined in this study featured ideas of British liberty and patriotism, they varied in their definitions of the British national character, an identity that may on the surface seem shared but was, in fact, evasive and exclusionary.

Lora Geriguis's essay 'Monarchs, Morality and English Nationalism in the Comedies of Etheredge, Steele and Sheridan' (*RECTR* 24[2009] 2–15) also examines theatre and nationalism. In it, she argues that the portrayal of English identity on stage reflected the rise of the country as a 'political, military and economic presence in the world' (p. 31). Geriguis suggests that George Etherege, Richard Steele, and Richard Brinsley Sheridan defined Englishness 'in ways that were relevant to their differently challenged monarchs' (p. 32). Through her analysis of Etherege's *The Man of Mode* [1676], Steele's *The Conscious Lovers* [1722], and Sheridan's *School for Scandal* [1777] Geriguis asserts that although their views of Englishness varied the cultural influences in their nationalistic commentaries can be explicitly linked to the individual sovereign and his, and therefore the country's, preoccupations. Geriguis concludes that despite the playwrights' differences and although their sentiments were based on hopeful thinking rather than reality, English comedy was 'the potter's wheel upon which national identity was shaped, smoothed and stiffened' (p. 45).

Elizabeth J. Heard suggests that changes in eighteenth-century staged comedy were the result of intense experimentation, by writers and dramatists such as William Congreve, Colley Cibber, John Vanbrugh, Richard Steele, Susanna Centlivre, and George Farquhar. In her monograph, *Experimentation on the English Stage, 1695–1708*: *The Career of George Farquhar*, Heard asserts that each of the above adapted the traditional comedic elements of late seventeenth-century drama and infused their work with innovations that significantly changed stage comedy by the early eighteenth century. *Experimentation on the English Stage* is organized chronologically, with textual readings of the standard plays as evidence for the changes in popular theatre that the study seeks to explore. Through an in-depth analysis of Farquhar's *The Recruiting Officer* and *The Beaux' Stratagem*, Heard outlines the differences between his early and later plays to demonstrate how Farquhar experimented with characterization in his humane comedies. Heard asserts that Farquhar's 'A Discourse on Comedy' discloses the playwright's creative process and his concerns about the definitions, rules, and models of British comedy. Farquhar's theory emphasized the importance of instruction in comedy, and especially how these new elements enabled an actor to connect with English theatre-going audiences. In assessing the importance of Farquhar's contributions to the development of British comedy, Heard maintains that his work was influential to the extent that it was capable of stimulating paradigmatic changes in British comedy. Heard also considers the contributions Farquhar made to Anglo-Irish comedy, his struggles to resist the 'stage Irishman' stereotype, and his efforts to render more complex, intelligent Irish characters in his dramas.

In her essay '"Adieu Buttock": Censoring Restoration Comedies for the Early Eighteenth-Century Stage' (in Swenson and Lauterbach, eds., *Imagining Selves: Essays in Honor of Patricia Meyer Spacks*, pp. 132–54), Deborah Kaplan suggests that theatre companies were only intermittently cowed and censored by political and religious polemicists in the first decade of the eighteenth century, for it was more likely that theatre personnel, rather than the state's representative, were responsible for censorship following the Restoration. Kaplan's essay examines this first wave of self-censorship on a moral and religious basis by London theatres with the intent of enriching understanding about the complex relationship between the theatre and society that made the self-censorship a temporary practice. Often the censored segments of staged drama can be traced to extant promptbooks, as Kaplan demonstrates with a Drury Lane promptbook for Durfey's *Love for Money; or, the Boarding School* and a Drury Lane promptbook for Congreve's *Old Batchelor*.

Marjean Purinton's essay 'Teaching Orientalism through British Romantic Drama: Representations of Arabia' (in Cass and Peer, eds., *Romantic Border Crossings*, pp. 135–46) examines theoretical and practical avenues of late eighteenth-century orientalism depicted in two eighteenth-century plays among several representing Romantic drama: Richard Cumberland's *The Arab: A Tragedy in Five Acts* [1785] and Elizabeth Inchbald's *The Egyptian Boy* [1790]. Because Arabia was important to Britain's imperial project, these plays provide spaces for the interrogation of effective colonial leadership and a masculinized British presence not tempered by feminine sensibility.

The final text in this section is *Staging Pain, 1580–1800: Violence and Trauma in British Theatre*. This study, edited by James Robert Allard and Mathew R. Martin, concentrates primarily on the early modern in its exploration of the theories and histories of the staging of pain and trauma in the British theatre. The essays are collected into four parts. Part I looks at 'Traumatic Effects', Part II examines the 'Pedagogies of Pain', and Part III examines 'Bodies (Im)politic'. However, it is Part IV, 'Spectacular Failures', that is most relevant for this section, as it includes Cecilia A. Feilla's essay 'Sympathy Pains: Filicide and the Spectacle of Male Heroic Suffering on the Eighteenth-century Stage' (pp. 151–67). Feilla examines the trope of a father who kills his offspring in the 'heroic and bourgeois tragedies' of the eighteenth century (p. 151) such as John Dennis's *Appius and Virginia* [1709], George Lillo's *The Fatal Curiosity* [1736], and Charles Kemble's *The Point of Honour* [1800]. Feilla suggests that an examination of these plays across the century shows a shift in the presentation and reception of filicide on stage from 'painful and horrific to beautiful and profound' as the pain these characters felt became proof of their virtue (p. 153).

Romanticism and Celebrity Culture 1750–1850 edited by Tom Mole arrived too late to be included in this review but will be included next year.

Books Reviewed

Allard, James Robert, and Mathew R. Martin, eds. *Staging Pain, 1580–1800: Violence and Trauma in British Theatre*. Ashgate. [2009] pp. xii + 220. £49.50 ISBN 9 7807 5466 7582.

Anderson, Emily Hodgson. *Eighteenth-Century Authorship and the Play of Fiction: Novels and the Theatre, Haywood to Austen*. Routledge. [2009] pp. 181. £70 ISBN 0 4159 9905 7.

Ardila, J.A.C., ed. *The Cervantean Heritage: Reception and Influence of Cervantes in Britain*. MHRA. [2009] pp. xiii + 273. £45 ISBN 9 7819 0654 0036.

Barnard, Teresa. *Anna Seward: A Constructed Life. A Critical Biography*. Ashgate. [2009] pp. viii + 200. £55 ISBN 9 7807 5466 6165.

Braunschneider, Theresa. *Our Coquettes: Capacious Desire in the Eighteenth Century*. UPVirginia. [2009] pp. ix + 189. $39.50 ISBN 9 7808 1392 8098.

Bullard, Rebecca. *The Politics of Disclosure, 1674–1725: Secret History Narratives*. Political and Popular Culture in the Early Modern Period. P&C. [2009] pp. viii+250. £60 ISBN 9 7818 5196 9692.

Carey, Daniel, and Lynn Festa, eds. *The Postcolonial Enlightenment: Eighteenth-Century Colonialism and Postcolonial Theory*. OUP. [2009] pp. xiii + 378. £55 ISBN 9 7801 9911 9147.

Cass, Jeffrey, and Larry Peer, eds. *Romantic Border Crossings*. Ashgate. [2008] pp. 225. $99.95 ISBN 9 7807 5466 0514.

Clingham, Greg, and Philip Smallwood, eds. *Samuel Johnson After Three Hundred Years*. CUP. [2009] pp. xiv + 291. £59 ISBN 9 7805 2188 8219.

Connolly, Tristanne, and Steve Clark. *Liberating Medicine, 1720–1835*. P&C. [2009] pp. 317. £60 ISBN 9 7818 5196 6325.

Cunningham, Vanessa. *Shakespeare and Garrick*. CUP. [2008] pp. 231. £58 ISBN 9 7805 2188 9773.

Curley, Thomas M. *Samuel Johnson, the Ossian Fraud, and the Celtic Revival in Great Britain and Ireland*. CUP. [2009] pp. x + 338. £59 ISBN 9 7805 2140 7472.

Day, Gary, and Bridget Keegan, eds. *The Eighteenth-Century Literature Handbook*. Literature and Culture Handbooks. Continuum. [2009] pp. xvi+256. hb $49.95 ISBN 9 7808 2649 5228, pb $29.95 ISBN 9 7808 2649 5235.

DeMaria Jr., Robert. *Samuel Johnson and the Life of Reading*. JHUP. [2009] pp. xviii + 270. pb $30 ISBN 9 7808 0189 2424.

Downie, J.A. *A Political Biography of Henry Fielding*. Eighteenth Century Political Biographies. P&C. [2009] pp. x+267. £60 ISBN 9 7818 5196 9159.

Duncan, Kathryn, ed. *Religion in the Age of Reason: A Transatlantic Study of the Long Eighteenth Century*. AMS. [2009] pp. xx + 225. £71.20 ISBN 9 7804 0464 8534.

Goff, Moira. *The Incomparable Hester Santlow: A Dancer-Actress on the Georgian Stage*. Ashgate. [2007] pp. 189. £55 ISBN 9 7807 5465 8054.

Goldgar, Bertrand A., and Ian Gadd, eds. *The Cambridge Edition of the Works of Jonathan Swift, vol. 8: English Political Writings 1711–1714: The Conduct of the Allies and Other Works*. CUP. [2008] pp. xxx + 546. £87 ISBN 9 7805 2182 9298.

Gregg, Stephen H. *Defoe's Writings and Manliness: Contrary Men*. Ashgate. [2009] pp. ix + 197. £55 ISBN 9 7807 5465 6050.

Hawkins, Sir John. *The Life of Samuel Johnson, LLD*, ed. O.M. Brack Jr. UGeoP. [2009] pp. xxxvi+554. $59.95 ISBN 9 7808 2032 9965.

Heard, Elisabeth J. *Experimentation on the English Stage, 1695–1708: The Career of George Farquhar*. P&C. [2008] pp. 170. £60 ISBN 9 7818 5196 9715.

Hibbert, Christopher. *Samuel Johnson: A Personal History*. Palgrave. [2009] pp. xii + 364. pb $19.95 ISBN 9 7802 3061 4277.

Hilton, Mary, and Jill Shefrin, eds. *Educating the Child in Enlightenment Britain: Beliefs, Cultures, Practices*. Studies in Childhood, 1700 to the Present. Ashgate. [2009] pp. ix+243. £55 ISBN 9 7807 5466 4604.

Kaul, Suvir. *Eighteenth-Century British Literature and Postcolonial Studies*. EdinUP. [2009] pp. xviii + 188. hb £70 ISBN 9 7807 4863 4545, pb £19.99 ISBN 9 7807 4863 4552.

Keymer, Thomas, ed. *The Cambridge Companion to Laurence Sterne*. CUP. [2009] pp. 224. £18.99 ISBN 9 7805 2161 4948.

Knight, Charles A. *A Political Biography of Richard Steele*. Eighteenth Century Political Biographies. P&C. [2009] pp. viii+288. £60 ISBN 9 7818 5196 9135.

Krishnamurthy, Aruna, ed. *The Working-Class Intellectual in Eighteenth- and Nineteenth-Century Britain*. Ashgate. [2009] pp. 268. £49.50 ISBN 9 7807 5466 5045.

Lamb, Jonathan. *The Evolution of Sympathy in the Long Eighteenth Century*. P&C. [2009] pp. 181. £60 ISBN 9 7818 5196 8541.

Livesey, James. *Civil Society and Empire: Ireland and Scotland in the Eighteenth-Century Atlantic World*. YaleUP. [2009] pp. x + 294. $45 ISBN 9 7803 0013 9020.

Mack, Ruth. *Literary Historicity: Literature and Historical Experience in Eighteenth-Century Britain*. StanfordUP. [2009] pp. viii + 230. $50 ISBN 9 7808 0475 9113.

MacLachlan, Christopher, ed. *Crossing the Highland Line: Cross-Currents in Eighteenth-Century Scottish Writing*. ASLS. [2009] pp. £9.95 pp. vii+215 ISBN 9 7809 4887 7889.

Maniquis, Robert M., and Carl Fisher, eds. *Defoe's Footprints: Essays in Honour of Maximillian E. Novak*. UTorP. [2009] pp. 273. $65 ISBN 9 7808 0209 9211.

Marshall, Louise H. *National Myth and Imperial Fantasy: Representations of Britishness on the Early Eighteenth-Century Stage*. Palgrave Macmillan. [2008] pp. 223. £50 ISBN 9 7802 3057 3376.

McVeagh, John, ed. *Defoe's Review of the State of the British Nation*, vol. 7: *1710–11*. 2 vols. P&C. [2009] pp. xxxii+752. £195 ISBN 9 7818 5196 9098.

Müller, Anja. *Framing Childhood in Eighteenth-Century English Periodicals and Prints, 1689–1789*. Studies in Childhood, 1700 to the Present. Ashgate. [2009] pp. x+263. £55 ISBN 9 7807 5466 5038.

Nokes, David. *Samuel Johnson: A Life*. Faber. [2009] pp. xx + 415. £25 ISBN 9 7805 7122 6351.

O' Brien, Karen. *Women and Enlightenment in Eighteenth-Century Britain*. CUP. [2009] pp. viii + 310. £53 ISBN 9 7805 2177 3492.

Pollock, Anthony. *Gender and the Fictions of the Public Sphere, 1690–1755*. Routledge. [2009] pp. viii + 232. £75 ISBN 9 7894 1599 0042.

Saxton, Kirsten. *Narratives of Women and Murder in England, 1680–1760*. Ashgate. [2009] pp. 162. £45 ISBN 9 7807 5466 3645.

Shepherd, Lynn. *Clarissa's Painter: Portraiture, Illustration, and Representation in the Novels of Samuel Richardson*. OUP. [2009] pp. 288. £68 ISBN 9 7801 9956 6693.

Snodin, Michael. *Horace Walpole's Strawberry Hill*. YaleUP. [2009] pp. xvi + 368. $85 ISBN 9 7803 0012 5740.

Soupel, Serge, Kevin L. Cope, and Alexander Pettit, eds. *Adventure: An Eighteenth-Century Idiom: Essays on the Daring and the Bold as a Pre-Modern Medium*. AMS. [2009] pp. xx + 327. £128.95 ISBN 9 7804 0464 8589.

Straub, Kristina. *Domestic Affairs: Intimacy, Eroticism, and Violence between Servants and Masters in Eighteenth-Century Britain*. JHUP. [2009] pp. ix + 223. $55 ISBN 9 7808 0189 0499.

Swenson, Rivka, and Elise Lauterbach, eds. *Imagining Selves: Essays in Honor of Patricia Meyer Spacks*. UDelP. [2008] pp. 325. $64.50 ISBN 9 7808 7413 0126.

Taylor, E. Derek. *Reason and Religion in Clarissa: Samuel Richardson and 'The Famous Mr. Norris, of Bemerton'*. Ashgate. [2009] pp. 178. £55 ISBN 9 7807 5466 5311.

Vickery, Amanda. *Behind Closed Doors: At Home in Georgian England*. YaleUP. [2009] pp. xviii + 382. pb $28 ISBN 9 7803 0016 8969.

Zionkowski, Linda, and Cynthia Klekar, eds. *The Culture of the Gift in Eighteenth-Century England*. Palgrave. [2009] pp. xi + 263. £50 ISBN 9 7802 3060 8290.

XII

Literature 1780–1830: The Romantic Period

ORIANNE SMITH, LUKE WRIGHT, FELICITY JAMES, DAVID STEWART, JASON WHITTAKER, CHRISTOPHER MACHELL AND JEREMY DAVIES

This chapter has five sections: 1. General; 2. Prose; 3. Prose Fiction; 4. Poetry; 5. Drama. Section 1 is by Orianne Smith; section 2 is by Luke Wright; section 3 is by Felicity James; section 4 is by David Stewart, Jason Whittaker, and Christopher Machell; section 5 is by Jeremy Davies.

1. General

The most important and original book published this year in the category of general Romanticism is Andrew Elfenbein's *Romanticism and the Rise of English*. This book explores the disappearance of philology or the history of the English language as a valid area of study for literary criticism. As Elfenbein notes, English professors today study everything but English. One reason for this is that philology does not lend itself well to historicist or formalist interpretations of literature; it can in fact be remarkably resistant to attempts to tell a cohesive story about language, language use, and history. Yet the relevance of philology to literary studies, particularly Romantic-era studies, is too great to ignore. As Elfenbein reminds us, the eighteenth century witnessed the standardization of English, and Romantic writers were the first generation of writers who self-consciously negotiated this new rule-laden literary landscape. They and their contemporary audiences were deeply aware of, and attuned to, the subtle ways in which their language choice, style, and diction measured up to or resisted the newly minted standards of correct English, as dictated by what Elfenbein describes as the 'English experts' (p. 14). These English experts included Samuel Johnson, but also other names less familiar to us today such as George Campbell, Lindley Murray, and John Walker. The first chapter explores the prescriptive efforts of these writers as an answer to the accessibility of print culture to more and more diverse audiences. The advent of pure English provided a reassuring road map for writers and readers to follow, but the 'purification' of the English language also forced

The Year's Work in English Studies, Volume 90 (2011)
doi:10.1093/ywes/mar003

aspiring poets and novelists to strike a balance between individual style and the increasingly complex linguistic expectations of their chosen genre. The next chapter takes up two examples of eighteenth-century prescriptivism—the condemnation of double negatives and the will/shall distinction—and their effect on Romantic-era literary production, including the most canonical of poets and poems, such as Wordsworth's 'Tintern Abbey'.

As chapter 3, 'Bad Englishes', demonstrates, the standardization of English had its dark side. English experts fretted about the possibility that their efforts at purifying the English language would drain it of its vitality, and the negative examples of bad English usage that they employed often corroborated their fears by representing an enviable primitivism. The next chapter explores the relationship between Romantic-era poetry and novels and the development of two very distinct educational schools for the dissemination of pure English: elocution and expository prose. Whereas novels tended to replicate elocutionary markers and exposition in their descriptions of dialogue and the use of the third-person omniscient narrator, late eighteenth-century poetry rebelled against the normative elements of both schools, and evolved into what Elfenbein describes as 'percussive Romanticism' (p. 16), a form of poetry in which the force of the metre overrides or subverts elocutionary expectations. The well-formed sentence posed a greater problem for novelists throughout the eighteenth century. Even early on, novelists tended to be less confident in the ability of the sentence to adequately describe human experience. As different as they may be in other respects, Johnson's *Rasselas* and Sterne's *Tristram Shandy* register doubt about the myopic purview of the sentence and its inadequacy as a descriptor of the rich and varied scope of human existence. Romantic-era novelists like Austen and Scott addressed this problem in different ways: Austen's novels focused more on the ability of sentences to flow together to intensify a particular mood, and Scott introduced a new novelistic sentence that placed the burden of clarity on the narrative rather than on the typographical sentence. The issues surrounding the well-formed sentence in novels were transferred to the demands placed on Romantic poetry by the popular practice of excerpting. As Elfenbein demonstrates, Romantic-era poets were by and large as resistant as their novel-writing counterparts to the idea of a discrete part representing the whole, and wrote stanzas that stubbornly refused extraction from the larger narratives of the poems themselves. *Romanticism and the Rise of English* represents a significant contribution to our understanding of the pressures of philology on Romantic-era poetry and prose as well as the fundamental transformation of the English language during this period.

Another excellent book published this year in the category of general Romanticism is Denise Gigante's *Life: Organic Form and Romanticism*. The one question that comes up repeatedly in the poetry of this era is 'What is life?' As Gigante reveals in this well-written and consistently insightful book, Romantic poets drew upon contemporary biological theories to think through the ways in which literary works were themselves living or organic forms. During the period 1760–1830, the Aristotelian theory of epigenesis was revisited by European scientists who were interested in exploring embryogenesis as a process of self-generation compelled by an internal, vital power.

Epigenesis conflicted with another prevalent theory, 'preformation', which argued that organic form was static and that each species was designed by God. The search for the source of vital power converted natural researchers into natural philosophers and transformed poets like Christopher Smart, William Blake, Percy Shelley, and John Keats into life scientists who used their art to trace the mysterious power embedded in the structures of nature.

Gigante's *Life* argues that the poetry written by these poets was informed by an epigenesist poetics, and tackles four of their most difficult poems to illustrate this point. Comparing the seemingly open-ended poetic organization of Smart's *Jubilate Agno* to the epigenetic progression from unorganized fluid matter to organic form, Gigante argues that this poem's defiance of typical generic patterns was similar to the revolutionary scientific theory proposed by Smart's contemporary, Caspar Friedrich Wolff. As Gigante persuasively notes, Wolff's radical departure from the disciplines of anatomy and physiology in his assertion that organic form did not depend on structure is strikingly similar to Smart's rejection of identifiable form in *Jubilate Agno*. Gigante suggests that Blake's final prophecy, *Jerusalem*, was similarly engaged with contemporary life science in its emphasis on the regenerative process of living form and its resistance to readings that focus on the parts rather than the whole. The second half of Gigante's book focuses on the monstrous capabilities of the organic process as exemplified by Shelley's 'The Witch of Atlas' and Keats's *Lamia*. Shelley's Witch and Keats's Lamia embody organic form in all of its dangerous beauty and its potential excesses. As Gigante reveals, the Romantic fascination with monstrosity was an offshoot of the fears associated with the anarchic and potentially monstrous energies of organic form reproducing itself ad infinitum. *Life: Organic Form and Romanticism* reveals an important and overlooked connection between some of the more difficult and abstruse poems in the Romantic canon and the principles of Romantic-era vitalism.

Students of Romanticism who enjoyed Julie A. Carlson's *England's First Family of Writers: Mary Wollstonecraft, William Godwin, Mary Shelley* [2007] will welcome another book published this year on the subject of the pressure of familial relations on literary Romanticism: Scott Krawczyk's *Romantic Literary Families*. Like Carlson before him, Krawczyk argues that it is impossible to interpret the works of members of Romantic-era literary families without taking into consideration their familial networks. Where this study differs from Carlson's book is in its treatment of the family itself as an author, exploring each family member's works as part of a larger collaborative effort. This familial collaboration is exemplified by the relationship between Anna Barbauld and her brother, John Aikin. According to Krawczyk, the collaboration between these two prolific siblings can be divided into three distinct stages: the Warrington stage (1758–74), when the two were living under the same roof at the Warrington Academy; the reformist and education stage (1774–1802), which enabled them to put the Warrington ethos into practice in their explicitly activist and politically engaged works; and the canon-formation stage (1802–20), when they drew upon their collective wisdom and experience over the years in compiling two significant new collections of British literary works: Barbauld's *The British Novelists* [1810] and Aikin's *Select Works of the British Poets* [1820].

The first chapter of *Romantic Literary Families* examines the simultaneous publication, in March 1790, of their two political tracts—Barbauld's *Address to the Opposers of the Repeal of the Corporation and Test Acts* and Aikin's *Address to the Dissidents of England on their Late Defeat*—as an example of shared labour amongst family members. Although written on the same topic—the controversial series of acts upheld in England that discriminated against Dissenters—their tracts deliberately and strategically targeted two very different audiences: 'the Opposers' and 'the Dissidents'. Another significant pair of works from Barbauld and Aikin that Krawczyk discusses are the two essays in *Miscellaneous Pieces in Prose* [1773] that concern themselves specifically with aesthetics: Aikin's 'On the Pleasure Derived from Objects of Terror' (with *Sir Bertrand*) and Barbauld's 'An Enquiry into those Kinds of Distress which Excite Agreeable Sensations' (with *A Tale*). Once again, this is a concerted effort, with Aikin leaving the discussion of the sentimental entirely to Barbauld. Reading the two essays back to back reveals their overall 'collaborative consciousness' (p. xiv), a term that Krawczyk uses to describe a collective will to reform that points to the Jungian notion of the collaborative animus as well as the Lockean idea that working towards a shared goal will result in the growth of a shared consciousness. Throughout their lives and works, as Krawczyk demonstrates, this brother-and-sister pair worked in tandem on educating and reforming their middle-class readers by pooling their respective talents.

The next brother-and-sister pairing examined in *Romantic Literary Families* is the collaborative relationship between William and Dorothy Wordsworth. In contrast to Aikin and Barbauld, who spent much of their childhood and young adult years under the same roof and under the tutelage of a kind and loving father, the early years for Dorothy and William were characterized by a sense of profound loss: the loss of their parents at a young age, and the subsequent separation of the two until they reunited in 1795. The time they lived together (from 1795 to 1802, the year of William's marriage) was, therefore, a time in which they mutually sought to recapture a shared childhood that they never had. Krawczyk argues that the intensity of their literary collaboration as well as Dorothy's commitment to sacrificing her own writing career for that of her brother stemmed from those childhood years they spent apart.

The chapters that follow widen the scope from real-life sisters and brothers to the desire amongst other Romantic-era writers to replicate familial structures outside the family. One example was Coleridge, whose longing for a literary family, Krawczyk argues, informed his early efforts to establish the unrealized Pantisocracy, and also underwrote his intensely collaborative and intensively competitive relationship with Wordsworth. The final chapter probes the collaborative consciousness of Mary and Percy Shelley in their intergenerational explorations of their familial connections to Godwin and Wollstonecraft in works such as *Frankenstein*, 'Ode to the West Wind', *Valperga*, and the prefatory poem to *Laon and Cynthia* (*The Revolt of Islam*).

The tensions between nationalism and cosmopolitanism at the end of the eighteenth century and the beginning of the nineteenth century have generated a great deal of interest amongst Romantic-era scholars over the past few years. What sets *Romantic Cosmopolitanism*, by Esther Wohlgemut, apart from other recent studies on this subject is its nuanced understanding of cosmopolitanism not in opposition but as an alternative approach to nationalism during this period. Wohlgemut's study probes the connections between Enlightenment philosophy and the emergent sense of nationhood in Great Britain by contextualizing cosmopolitanism within British political thought and then revealing how the notion of cosmopolitanism is refracted in the literature of second-generation Romantics. *Romantic Cosmopolitanism* takes as its point of departure two influential essays by Kant: 'Idea for a Universal History with a Cosmopolitan Purpose' [1784] and 'On Perpetual Peace' [1795]. These essays provide a helpful summary of the eighteenth-century debate on cosmopolitanism, and gesture to cosmopolitanism as a non-unified model of nationhood. Wohlgemut revisits the famous debate between Richard Price and Edmund Burke as the paradigmatic instance of the increasing divide between radicals such as Price who, like Kant, endorsed a cosmopolitan understanding of the social contract, and conservatives such as Burke, who perceived cosmopolitanism as a threat to the idea and ideals of the British nation. Cosmopolitanism continued to be a fraught subject in the early decades of the nineteenth century, as Wohlgemut demonstrates in her investigation of how the *Edinburgh Review* under Francis Jeffrey utilized the political economy of Adam Smith to endorse a cosmopolitan model of commerce based on the interdependence of nations. As *Romantic Cosmopolitanism* reveals, the *Edinburgh Review*'s advocacy of cosmopolitanism was also reflected in the unapologetically international scope of the literary reviews by Jeffrey, James Mackintosh, and Thomas Carlyle, which drew upon Germaine de Staël's understanding of the politics of literature in a European context.

The second half of *Romantic Cosmopolitanism* turns to four case studies of literary figures in the early nineteenth century whose work reflected a continued belief in cosmopolitanism: Maria Edgeworth, George Gordon Byron, Madame de Staël, and Charles Robert Maturin. Edgeworth's domestication of cosmopolitanism is evident in her Irish tales such as *Castle Rackrent* [1800], *Ennui* [1802], *The Absentee* [1812], and *Ormond* [1817], all of which reconcile Burke's local conception of nationhood with an Enlightenment world-view. Whereas Edgeworth incorporates the narrative structure of the eighteenth-century 'philosophical tale' in her novels, Byron similarly imports the figure of the 'philosophical traveller' or 'cosmopolitan' in his representation of the cosmopolitan Childe Harold. Undeterred or perhaps encouraged by negative reviews that cast his cosmopolitanism as a threat to the emergent sense of nationhood in Britain, Byron went on to create one of the most thoroughgoing cosmopolitan figures of the nineteenth century: Don Juan. *Romantic Cosmopolitanism* concludes with an investigation of how the cosmopolitan heroines of Stael's *Corinne; or Italy* [1807] and Maturin's *Milesian Chief* [1812] sounded a dissonant note in Great Britain's emergent sense of national identity. As the epilogue reminds us, cosmopolitanism is not always progressive in its aims: Robert Southey's *The Colloquies* [1829] and Mary Shelley's *The Last Man* [1826] are two examples of reactionary cosmopolitanism that take up in different ways the moral repercussions of ignoring the Enlightenment idea of a universal history.

Toby Benis's *Romantic Diasporas: French Émigrés, British Convicts, and Jews* approaches the issues of local and global community from an entirely different perspective. Although the tens of thousands of French émigrés who flocked to England between 1789 and 1794 benefited from the cosmopolitan perspective of many members of their host country, their profound sense of displacement—and the ambivalent and often hostile reactions to these exiles—is not captured by the figure of the cosmopolitan. *Romantic Diasporas* explores how Romantic national identity was shored up by literary representations of exiled or marginalized groups. The first chapter explores the émigré experience from the perspective of two novels from the 1790s: Charlotte Smith's *The Banished Man* [1794] and Mary Robinson's *Hubert de Sevrac* [1796]. Smith's novel depicts a French aristocrat travelling throughout Europe, pondering his purpose and duty in life before attaching himself to a English family with a female head of the household (who is a writer not unlike Smith herself). Another aristocrat émigré is the subject of Robinson's novel as well: *Hubert de Sevrac* traces the journey of Hubert and his family, who flee to Italy during the Terror, and reveals how this displacement enables him to realize his complicity in the victimization of the French people. These two novels by two of the most celebrated female novelists of the late eighteenth century underscore similarities between the ambiguous position of women and the French émigrés in the polity. In *The Wanderer* and in the representation of the De Lacey family in *Frankenstein*, Frances Burney and Mary Shelley use the figure of the émigré to critique abuses of tyrannical male authority and to call into question issues of citizenship in a post-revolutionary age.

At the same time as record numbers of foreigners were flocking to England, England was doing everything in its power to rid itself of its undesirables by transporting them to Australia. The next two chapters turn from the émigré experience to the experiences of these transported convicts. In his popular published account of his transportation to Botany Bay, George Barrington, the so-called prince of pickpockets, suggested that rehabilitated criminals like himself were the ideal representatives of Britain abroad, affirming and protecting the cultural and moral imperatives of the British nation. The political dimension of transportation is revealed in Benis's analysis of the trial defences and first-hand accounts of the Scottish Martyrs, five reformers who were tried for sedition in Edinburgh in 1793 and 1794, and sentenced to transportation. The final chapter explores the ambiguous position in British society of another marginalized group: the Jews. Taking Maria Edgeworth's novel *Harrington* [1817] as a point of departure, Benis argues that the persecution of the Jews between the 'Jew Bill' controversy of 1750s and the Gordon riots reveals how vulnerable marginalized groups are in times of political and social instability.

Two other popular subjects in the area of general Romanticism—transatlantic studies and ecocriticism—are explored in another very good book published this year: Kevin Hutchings's *Romantic Ecologies and Colonial*

Cultures in the British Atlantic World, 1770–1850. Building upon the insights of James McKusick's ground-breaking *Green Writing: Romanticism and Ecology* [2000], this study investigates a transatlantic effort amongst American and British authors during the Romantic period to explore and critique the pernicious effects of human 'progress' on the natural world. One of the merits of *Romantic Ecologies and Colonial Cultures* is the attention it pays to lesser-known authors and works. The first two chapters investigate how local ecosystems and the people who were sustained by them were undermined by colonial governments which invoked contemporary ideologies of racial and cultural hierarchy that naturalized the subordination of the indigenous races. As Hutchings notes, one strategy was to characterize Africans and North Americans as less noble than savage—the progeny of barbaric landscapes who could only benefit from the civilizing practices of the West. This discussion of contemporary discourses of animality and environmental determinism provides a foundation for the close readings that follow. Chapter 3 probes the relationship between natural philosophy, colonialism, and gender in William Blake's *Visions of the Daughters of Albion* [1793]. The subject of chapter 4 is a poem by Coleridge that has hitherto not received much critical attention, 'To a Young Ass, its Mother Being Tethered Near It' [1794]. Coleridge's argument that animals deserve humane treatment is discussed from the perspective of contemporary British animal-rights activists such as John Oswald, Humphry Primatt, and John Lamb. Chapters 5 and 6 examine the representation of Native American people and the North American landscape in the work of two Romantic-era Scottish poets, William Richardson and Thomas Campbell. The final chapter explores how the Romantic concepts of nature and culture informed the naturalism and ethnography of the nineteenth-century Anishinaabe or Ojibwa author George Copway (also known by his traditional name Kahgegagahbowh, or Standing Firm), whose writings reveal the influence of British writers such as Robert Burns, Walter Scott, Southey, and Byron.

Two excellent collections of essays published this year fall into the category of general Romanticism: *Romanticism, History, Historicism: Essays on an Orthodoxy*, edited by Damian Walford Davies, and *Romanticism and the Object*, edited by Larry H. Peer. *Romanticism and History* is a continuation of a spirited conversation amongst Romantic-era scholars on the past, present, and future of new historicism that began at the 2004 'Romanticism, History, Historicism' conference organized by Davies along with Richard Marggraf Turley. In the first chapter, 'The Incommensurable Value of Historicism' (in Davies, ed., pp. 14–31), Tim Milnes argues that the source of the problems confronting postmodern historicism today is its tendency to fetishize the idea of criticism as repetition with difference without recognizing or reconciling the interdependence of truth, value, and communication. Erik Gray's 'The Hair of Milton: Historicism and Literary History' (pp. 32–42) explores the tensions and parallels between the synchronic model of history in new historicism and the diachronic approach to literary history as modelled in a poem by Keats on the relic of Milton's hair. Keats is also the subject of Kelly Grovier's essay, '"In Embalmèd Darkness": Keats, the Picturesque, and the Limits of Historicization' (pp. 43–59), which asserts that the aesthetic of the picturesque enables scholars to synthesize the two most influential yet apparently contradictory conceptions of Keats's imagination: his ambivalence towards his subjects and the pressure of the political on his poetics. In ' "Telling Lives to Children": Young Versus New Historicism in *Little Arthur's History of England*' (pp. 60–78), Michael Simpson argues that the romance of history that attracts Romantic scholars to new historicism can be traced back to a Romantic source—children's histories like Lady Maria Callcott's *Little Arthur's History of England* [1835]—that deploy a series of complex strategies to simultaneously engage and estrange its young readers from their nation's historical narrative.

The first four chapters of *Romanticism, History, Historicism* emphasize the limits or problems confronting new historicism today. The next three chapters trace a series of lost 'histories' of the 1790s. Kenneth R. Johnston's essay, 'Whose History? My Place or Yours? Republican Assumptions and Romantic Traditions' (pp. 79–102) catalogues the tremendous personal, political, and literary losses experienced as a consequence of Pitt's efforts to suppress British radicalism during this period. Judith Thompson's 'Overlooking History: The Case of John Thelwall' (pp. 103–25) points to the critically overlooked work of Thelwall to argue that Romantic ideology is alive and well, despite the best efforts of McGann et al. In 'Byron's *Cain* and the "History" of Cradle Songs' (pp. 126–42), Damian Walford Davies asserts that the form and content of the cradle song are particularly susceptible to a historical reading because it 'ponders the location of the human subject in history, generational difference, heredity and the historical and psychological condition of parenthood' (p. 126).

The following three chapters examine the negotiation of history by Romantic women writers as well as the relatively recent phenomenon of feminist historiographies of this era. Anne K Mellor and Susan J. Wolfson are the joint authors of 'Romanticism, Feminism, History, Historicism: A Conversation' (in Davies, ed., pp. 143–62), which summarizes the roles played by women in the formation of literary print culture in the 1790s, discusses the influence of feminist literary theory on Romanticism, and gestures to the future of gender and Romantic-era studies. Gary Kelly's 'Romanticism and the Feminist Uses of History' (pp. 163–81) investigates recent feminist interventions in historical studies as well as the rich dialogue between Romanticism and feminist historiography that was already taking place during the Romantic era in the works of women writers as diverse as Mary Wollstonecraft, Hester Thrale Piozzi, Jane Austen, and Joanna Southcott. In 'New Historicism, New Austen, New Romanticism' (pp. 182–202), Robert Miles reveals how the recent attempts to historicize Austen have positioned her 'not on the fringes, but in the center of a reimagined Romanticism' (p. 199). *Romanticism, History, Historicism* concludes with Nicholas Roe's 'Leigh Hunt and Romantic Biography' (pp. 203–20), in which Roe points to the recent revaluation of Hunt as a key point of departure in an area that has not received the critical attention it deserves—Romantic biography.

Romanticism and the Object, expertly edited by Larry H. Peer, offers a collection of essays that explore Romanticism's aesthetic use of objects.

Marilyn Gaull's '"Things Forever Speaking" and "Objects of All Thought"' (pp. 9–16) explores the difference between 'things' and 'objects' in Wordsworth's poetry and amongst Wordsworth's contemporaries in the Romantic period. As Gaull notes, the word and the concept of 'things' originated in Scandinavia and survived in the oral tradition of the north country as a flexible word signifying something that tends to be living or organic. The word and concept of 'objects', in contrast, is Latinate and was transmitted in the written tradition through Old French to English. An object is a subset of things that is made, manufactured, acquired, or inanimate. As Gaul notes, the difference between the genesis and Romantic-era usage of these two words/concepts is crucial to our understanding of the process in Wordsworth's poetry, in which memory transforms things into objects. In '"Perfectly Compatible Objects": Mr. Pitt Contemplates Britain and South America' (pp. 17–36), Jocelyn M. Almeida explores the importance of the negotiations between Francisco de Miranda and William Pitt in the creation of Latin America as an object for Britain. Lisbeth Chapin's 'Children as Subject and Object: Shelley v. Westbrook' (pp. 37–49) takes up Percy Shelley's custody trial following the death of his wife, Harriet, and reads his letters about the trial within the context of Shelley's ethics of victimhood. These letters, Chapin argues, are Romantic objects pointing to the necessity of resisting tyrannical authority, and the child at the centre of this trial becomes the chief object of tragic innocence. In '"I'll Contrive a Sylvan Room": Certainty and Indeterminacy in Charlotte Smith's *Beachy Head, The Fables, and Other Poems* (1807)' (pp. 51–69), Mark Fulk situates Smith's fables in relation to the genre of the fable in the Enlightenment, and argues that Smith's appropriation of this form enabled her to deal with and contain the epistemic collapse described in *Beachy Head*. Rodney Farnsworth's '"A Better Guide in Ourselves": Objects, Romantic-Protestant Ethics, and Fanny Price's Individualism' (pp. 71–94) argues that Austen's representation of Fanny's individualism was rooted in the radical Protestant belief in the soul's unmediated connection to Providence. In 'The Literal and Literary Circulation of Amelia Curran's Portrait of Percy Shelley' (pp. 95–107), Diane Long Hoeveler explores the way in which this portrait functioned as the inspiration for the ghostly portrait of Jeffrey Aspern in the novella *The Aspern Papers* as a homosocial fetishized exchange object signifying masculine creativity.

The afterlife of Percy Shelley as object is the subject of Michael Gamer's essay as well. In 'Shelley Incinerated' (pp. 109–16), Gamer argues that the 'Shelley Myth' that sprang up after his death was a collaborative effort amongst his executors, who deliberately manipulated his poetic remains in order to create Shelley as an intellectual and cultural 'object'—a project that satisfied the tendency amongst many Romantic writers to form themselves into coteries. Magdalena M. Ostas's 'Keats and the Impersonal Craft of Writing' (pp. 117–35) argues that Keats's poetics draw upon a visual idiom through his deployment of a unique grammar of enunciation and representation in his verse. In '"Tun'd to Hymns of Perfect Love": The Anglican Liturgy as Romantic Object in John Keble's *The Christian Year*' (pp. 137–57), Chene Heady argues that Keble's bestselling book of poetry reconfigured

Romanticism in terms of orthodox Anglicanism and served as an object of reference for Romantic ideas of time and nature.

The final two chapters of *Romanticism and the Object* address this topic from a transnational perspective. William S. Davis's 'Journeys to the East: Shelley and Novalis' (pp. 159–75) compares the mysterious 'Singer' in Novalis's *Hymns to the Night* [1800] to the nameless 'Poet' in Shelley's *Alastor* [1816], arguing that these two poems share the fantasy of a pilgrimage to a romanticized East 'that functions as the site for the fulfillment of a very Western dream of overcoming distance, alienation, misunderstanding, and loss through a form of communion that exceeds the limitations of linguistic signs—paradoxically employing Otherness as a vehicle for sameness' (p. 159). In 'Weighing It Again' (pp. 177–99), Charles J. Rzepka points to the need articulated in different ways throughout this collection for a more reflexive and flexible understanding of Romantic facts and objects, suggesting that it is time to throw away our preconceived expectations and our desire to fit Romanticism into a neat package—to, in effect, 'weigh it again'.

Two essays that fall into the category of general Romanticism conclude this section. The first essay, Esther Schor's 'Universal Romanticism' (*ERR* 20[2009] 271–87), investigates three Romantic-era 'universalisms': universal language, universal rights, and universal egotism. Schor argues that Romantic evocations of music as a 'universal language' offered an alternative to reading the universe as the 'Book of God'. As Schor demonstrates, for poets like Shelley and Wordsworth, what she describes as the 'sonic sublime' (p. 276) followed the pattern of the Kantian sublime, which enabled the poet to articulate the immensity of the universe as a mysterious and wild harmony. The second essay, Dawn M. Vernooy-Epp's 'Teaching Mary Darby Robinson's Reading List' (*Pedagogy* 9[2009] 13–34) discusses her use of Mary Robinson's *Letter to the Women of England* [1799] in the classroom as a tool to help students think about canon formation. As Vernooy-Epp notes, Robinson's list of eighteenth-century women writers functions as an alternative canon to the one drawn up by Samuel Johnson in his *Lives of the Poets* [1779–81]. Robinson's *Letter* is a Romantic-period text that models the decision-making process that goes into the creation of a canon, and invites students to consider the sociopolitical, historical, and gendered implications of anthologies then and now.

2. Prose

I am going to begin with a general review of an important collection of essays on various aspects of the Romantic period, *Spheres of Action: Speech and Performance in Romantic Culture*, edited by Alexander Dick and Angela Esterhammer. I will provide general comments first and then discuss three specific essays in some detail; other essays are reviewed elsewhere within this volume.

Spheres of Action seems almost an attempt to take stock of what the authors argue is a reconstructed view of Romanticism which has arisen over the first decade of the twenty-first century, and then to articulate this view. The title itself is descriptive of this project:

> Theory and practice, discourse and agency, behaviour and identity, performance and audience response are the terms addressed by the contributors to this collection. Some of their essays explicitly seek to recover the Romantic Speaking voice; some explore the function of gesture, dress and other forms of embodiment; and some address the journalism, and the novel. (p. 4)

The collection is divided into two parts. Part I is entitled 'Public Speaking', and Part II 'Body Language'. Within the scope of the project the authors desire to

> capture these shared concerns of Romanticism and postmodernity in the concept of 'spheres of action', a resonant phrase that occupied different places on the scientific-philosophical continuum between the sixteenth and nineteenth centuries. The 'public spheres' and 'separate spheres' that figure prominently in recent criticism deriving from Habermas and gender studies respectively, have a long (if largely unacknowledged) pre-history that begins in the early modern period and takes on new meaning during the late eighteenth century. (p. 8)

They argue its change of definition in the eighteenth century is relevant to the Romantic enterprise itself. In 'Public Speaking' they argue for a return to an aurality of interpretation which seems fundamentally right-headed—especially where verse is interpreted, as verse is written to be heard, whether aloud or in the mind's ear. 'Body Language' moves the sphere of influence to what I might call the practical: the House of Commons, the stage, sport, and the salon (p. 16). Each part contains five essays. 'Public Speaking' has a discussion of Thelwall and the practice of elocution by Judith Thompson (pp. 21–45); Sarah Zimmerman on Coleridge as lecturer (pp. 46–72); Alexander Dick on 'Wordsworth's Lament' (pp. 73–99); Victoria Myers on parody as a weapon in blasphemy trials (pp. 100–23); and Richard Van Oort discussing '*Frankenstein*, Romanticism, and the Tragedy of Human Origin' (pp. 124–48). 'Body Language' has Frederick Burwick on 'Telling Lies with Body Language' (pp. 149–77); Marjean D. Purinton on cross-dressing in comic plays by women (pp. 178–93); Daniel O'Quinn on drama influencing the political sphere (pp. 194–221); Joshua Lambier on the 'foreignizing' (*sic*) effect of cultural translation, in which he argues that Romanticism strove against Enlightenment cosmopolitanism by focusing on local issues (pp. 222–47); and Thomas C. Crochunis on the subject of sport—pedestrian races specifically (pp. 248–72). The collection is carefully planned, and the coalition of the essays does not seem forced. The essays are all of a high calibre and they are all fascinatingly creative. The volume is paradigmatic, however, and there is a general tendency within it to stray too far towards imposing critical theory on history for my taste. Be that as it may, even with that substantive reservation, I find great value in this work. Its attempt to be a book which takes stock of a decade of work on Romanticism is successful in my opinion. Its attempt to turn Romantic studies onto a slightly different vector using the hinge of aurality and the dramatic will, in my opinion, be successful in time if it is widely read.

I will treat, in reverse order of their appearance in the volume, O'Quinn's 'Fox's Tears: The Staging of Liquid Politics' (from 'Body Language') first and then discuss Zimmerman and Myers essay (from 'Public Speaking'). O'Quinn's central point is that during the 1790s the theatre began to influence real life rather than be a mimesis of it. He takes as his proof-text Fox and Burke's exchange during the Quebec debate of 6 May 1791, during which Fox wept openly while delivering his riposte. O'Quinn does significantly good detective work in his line-by-line attribution of the sources upon which Burke drew to compose the invective (Shakespeare's *Macbeth* was one) and gives a very thorough treatment of how the newspapers and satirical cartoonists documented and embellished the incident. His argument is that Fox used theatrical tears to underscore his own rhetoric and to attempt to gain the favour of the House back from Burke; what he does not allow for is even the possibility that Fox's tears were emotionally real and stemmed from an honest wounding through the public humiliation by a lifelong friend; this is odd considering how much time he spends discussing the exceptionalism of Burke's rant when compared to concurrent invectives against Fox. He demonstrates conclusively that theatre affected the debate in the House (perhaps to be more fair to him I should argue that he says that the participants in the debate affected the theatre) and he gives an elegant description of how the debate was subsequently reported. All this is first-rate. O'Quinn then goes on to argue that Fox employed the use of the bodily fluid of tears to bring to the mind of other members of the House the bodily fluid of blood spilled by British troops across the empire. This proposed link between bodily fluids seems implausible in the historical context, and O'Quinn does not fully take into account the medicinal aspects of blood-letting in this period. The essay is essentially written in three sections, and two-thirds of it is tremendous; one-third is unconvincing.

Sarah M. Zimmerman's 'Coleridge as Lecturer: A Disappearing Act' argues that because Coleridge's lectures were often delivered extemporaneously without a full script, and because no accurate transcript has survived, his great series of lectures on literature need to be analysed employing the tools fashioned by historians of drama. In other words the rooms in which they were delivered, the manner of their performance, the reception by the audience, and the transmission of that reception through the interpretation and press reports all should be brought into consideration when constructing an understanding of the lectures. The essay dovetails nicely with Judith Thompson's 'Re-sounding Romanticism: John Thelwall and the Science and Practice of Elocution' (the seminal essay in 'Public Speaking') and Zimmerman outlines Coleridge's debt to Thelwall in a precise way. Within this treatment we receive what might almost be called a short biography of the Royal Institution (the only room in which Coleridge lectured that still survives). This is not misplaced, as part of her argument is that the 'theatre' itself is important to comprehending the 'drama' that Coleridge performed, and delineating the work of other 'performers' in the venue gives insight into what the *audiences* would provide in their own interpretations (in other words identifying the cultural presuppositions of those audiences); indeed, this consideration of the nature of the audience helps to define the very genre she argues for the existence of. Zimmerman points out that Coleridge himself argued that this genre contributed to a 'nascent culture of celebrity' (p. 57). She carefully points out that both Southey and Wordsworth derided the genre of public lecturing and attempted to dissuade Coleridge from the enterprise but succeeded only in delaying his delivery of his various series of lectures.

As a lecturer Coleridge sought not to impart information so much as to tease the audience with intellectual questions; Zimmerman cites an 1819 letter to John Britton in which he describes his own lecturing style as 'a theatre of meditative spontaneity' in response to Britton's invitation to lecture at the Russell Institution (p. 65). The final section of the article argues that in his lectures on Shakespeare Coleridge found much to identify with in Hamlet, and that this self-identification shaped his larger views on Shakespeare; there is merit in this view and it is substantiated with sufficient quotations to make the argument persuasive. The lectures are undoubtedly an important section of Coleridge's collected works, and Zimmerman's paradigm for viewing them as performance rather then set texts may well provide an avenue of understanding which will make our greater view of the way they fit within the corpus or system created by his published works more cogent. She is certainly correct in her assertion that taking into account the elements involved in their delivery will give greater insight into early nineteenth-century public lectures, and this is a compelling argument which reaches far beyond Coleridge.

Whereas O'Quinn demonstrates conclusively that drama influenced action and diction in the political realm in 'Body Language', Victoria Myers demonstrates that the legal system was a fertile ground for art to imitate life in the final essay of 'Public Speaking': 'Blasphemy Trials and *The Cenci*: Parody as Performative'. Her starting point is a deep analysis of four trials for blasphemy (Daniel Isaac Eaton's 1812 trial for publishing Part III of Thomas Paine's *Age of Reason* and William Hone's three trials for publishing deliberate satires of the Catechism, the Litany, and the Creed.) Her overarching point is that the use of satire by the two defendants was an influence on Shelley when he composed *The Cenci*, and she has the epistolary evidence from Shelley to back this up. This essay is extremely dense, and its arguments very technical indeed (as are all legal interpretations); they are logically progressive, however, and in no way does Myers seek to obfuscate her point through using technical legal jargon. Though dense and technical, each one of her arguments is clear. She notes that both Eaton and Hone used satire in different ways during their trials in such a way as to diminish the credibility of the legal system: both, to differing extents, pointed out that conducting the trial required them to cite their works in evidence, which effectively put the state in the position of partaking in the blasphemy by forcing them to be read out again. Both of the defences mounted were compelling to radical sensibilities, including Shelley's; both defendants succeeded in emasculating the apparatus of state on its own ground to a not inconsiderable extent. The final third of the essay is a close reading of *The Cenci* in which Myers argues that Cenci himself is parodied by Shelley to represent both the fabric of the Established Church (in this case Roman Catholicism) and the desire of the Enlightenment mind to move away from it. 'My interpretation . . . emphasizes Cenci's conflict with constituted authority, but without relinquishing the ways in which he repeats that authority—especially his claiming the religious ground to sanction his violent (speech) acts' (p. 114). Likewise she sees Beatrice as portraying the Enlightenment rebellion against religious authority following the murder when she presents her 'defence' at her 'trial' in which the guests represent a symbolic hand-picked jury (similar to the hand-picked jury which Eaton faced). This is a paradigmatic reading no doubt, but Myers has the quotations, the contemporary commentary by Shelley, and the rhetorical skill to draw elegant parallels between the trials and the text of *The Cenci*. Myers certainly appears to have demonstrated a source text for *The Cenci* in the form of the two blasphemy trials; anyone with any interest whatsoever in *The Cenci* or in Shelley generally would benefit from reading this article, which—to pardon the pun—cannot be given full justice in a brief review.

The second major essay collection concerned with Romantic prose published in 2009, *The Oxford Handbook of Samuel Taylor Coleridge*, edited by Frederick Burwick, is nothing short of stunning. This is bar none the best resource for teaching the thought of Coleridge in existence. It might almost have been better titled an encyclopedia, because like an encyclopedia it has thirty-seven discrete articles on general topics written by experts in each particular field, and many of these are divided into even more discrete sub-sections, but the choice to opt for concision and to aim the articles at a general audience was a very wise one. When the authors of *YWES* 2009 divided up their reviews, I agreed to make general comments about both this book, and *Spheres of Action*, and so though I will discuss only a limited selection of essays, I will stitch general comments throughout the paragraphs. Though what general comment one can make other than to praise the project eludes me. Every aspect of Coleridge's thought, writings, and influences is addressed somewhere in this volume; though sometimes the placement of a particular subject is counterintuitive: I suspect that this was unavoidable considering the breadth of scope of the volume. All of the chapters seek to be polemical, and because of this every one of them could serve as an introduction to a section of Coleridge studies. This makes Coleridge's works and thought accessible even to senior undergraduates in a way that they were not before. This volume will open a pathway to Coleridge for a much wider academic audience. Each chapter also provides a genuine 'encyclopedic' bibliography on the particular aspect under discussion, which will allow the generalist to become (at the very least) a person of far more than competence on that aspect of Coleridge's works. The handbook contains eleven essays specifically on Coleridge's prose works by Peter Kitson, Michael John Kooy, Angela Esterhammer, Matthew Scott, Raimonda Modiano, Pamela Edwards, Jeffrey Hipolito, H.J. Jackson, Paul Cheshire, David Vallins, and Murray Edwards, but many more essays are broadly relevant to Coleridge's prose writings. While I discuss three significant essays here, readers are advised to explore all the contributions to this collection.

Douglas Hedley's essay 'Coleridge as Theologian' is an excellent example of how the material is often broken down into small, digestible, discrete, and complete units: fifteen in all. Each one of them has a beginning and an end of argument. Each one of them teaches the novice the basics of theology. Hedley demonstrates why Coleridge wrote what he wrote, why what he wrote is important, how it fits with Coleridge's greater project, why it is theologically important, and often what influences contributed to its conceit. This article successfully navigates a beautiful 'white-water rapid' between historical theology and Coleridge's constructive contribution to an attempt at systematic theology that will both provide the opinions of *the* undisputed authority on Coleridge's theology and an education for the Romanticist who requires a reference point from which to consult on a particular interpretation. Anyone who knows Coleridge's poetry but not his theology will emerge from having read this article with not only an understanding of Coleridge's theology but, far more importantly, of the basic theological doctrines and issues in Coleridge as a whole. Likewise, in 'Coleridge and Philosophy', Christopher Bode divides his essay into five sections. The title of this essay gives the author absolute claim to discuss everything he does, presenting a largely Germanic interpretation of Coleridge. The same ground is covered elsewhere in the volume, but with less acumen. Speaking personally, I found a more complete picture of Coleridge's philosophical influences in Hedley's essay, because despite his German training he is intent on bringing out the constructive influences on Coleridge from ancient Greek theology, but I would not dream of disagreeing with what Bode points out. Again, it is a good particular introduction to the influence of German philosophy for a student. Staying on similar themes in Coleridge's prose, Pamela Edwards's 'Coleridge on Politics and Religion: *The Statesman's Manual, Aids to Reflection*, and *On The Constitution of The Church and State*' has no discrete divisions. This is disappointing. Having said that, she takes a largely chronological approach. There is nothing in any way controversial in this essay, though there is arguably nothing novel either. The chapter is shorter than most in the volume, but it is a fine précis of a consistent theme within multiple works. It is a useful introduction to the subject, which takes a broad-ranging approach, presenting the 'received wisdom' on its topic straightforwardly. This essay does not reach for the stars, but it accomplishes what it set out to do.

The Oxford Handbook of Samuel Taylor Coleridge is truly a wonderful volume. Burwick has created exactly what he intended to: a volume which will enable Coleridge's thinking on various topics to become accessible to anyone who desires to put the time into reading it. This volume will live in the reference rooms of libraries (rather than languish in the stacks) for the foreseeable future. We are all lucky to have it: linguist, scholar, translator, philosopher.

James Vigus wrote his monograph *Platonic Coleridge* while a Ph.D. student at Clare College, Cambridge, so Douglas Hedley figures large in its creation; it is therefore no surprise that we are met with an exceedingly well crafted piece of philosophical interpretation. Earlier parts of the book are discussed elsewhere in this chapter; it is my task to discuss his chapter 5: 'Restoring Plato's "System": The *Friend* and the *Opus Maximum*'. Vigus's central point within the volume is that Plato provided a central constructive influence upon Coleridge which has been underestimated by previous critics. Whether or not it has been underestimated it has probably been under-reported, or openly remarked upon less than it should. Some will argue that Vigus overplays his hand, but I shall not be one of them. Granted, Coleridge's mind was a sponge which absorbed so many influences that concentrating only on one substantive influence would leave other influences unilluminated and give an incomplete picture. The title of this book is not 'Coleridge the Platonist', however, it is *Platonic Coleridge*, and Vigus is careful to select particular parts of particular works to delineate as Platonic. He furthermore protects himself from the accusation of being too one-sided by keeping Kant as a bridge figure firmly in the interpretation throughout, devoting an entire chapter to him. In his discussion of the *Friend* of 1816, for instance, Vigus chooses specific essays to demonstrate Plato's influence—arguing that Coleridge saw himself as a modern Plato (which is heavy-handed but probably entirely consistent with Coleridge's ego) and that he was trying to resurrect Plato's own project. Throughout chapter 5 Vigus carefully discriminates between works intended for different audiences, and particularly published and therefore public works versus those intended for smaller audiences: hence he treats the *Friend* as a work for a published audience and the *Opus Maximum* as a work for a private audience. This delineation is seen as Platonic at its root; as Vigus makes clear at the outset of his discussion of the *Essays on Method*: 'By his painstaking analysis of how truth should be communicated to a particular audience, and disavowal of financial motives for writing, Coleridge distances himself vehemently from what he labels "sophistry": the using of language in the service of Truth. Coleridge looks to the authority of Plato for his anti-sophistic Project' (p. 129). I find it odd that this quotation is met with no comment on its irony by Vigus, since the *Friend* of 1809 was a subscription journal designed to provide Coleridge with a living (his second attempt at such a project, *The Watchman*, being the first) and the *Friend* of 1816 was a rejig of the journal into a longer form designed to provide Coleridge with a livelihood from royalties. But this is a minor issue.

What I do disagree with is Vigus's heavy emphasis on the difference between exoteric and esoteric writing. He views the *Friend* as the former and the *Opus Maximum* as the latter. His argument is that because the *Opus Maximum* was intended for an esoteric audience Coleridge was able to develop his ideas on the Will and the Divine Idea more completely because he had no need to explain them to a general audience. I have a fundamental problem with the logic of this argument: Vigus admits that Coleridge intended to publish the *Opus Maximum* eventually. I cannot see the *Opus Maximum* as intended only for a small circle of illuminati who hovered around Highgate (though such a society certainly existed); it is simply yet another work that Coleridge never managed to get into print. Vigus proposes that the ideas that are inchoate in the *Friend* were more fully developed in the *Opus Maximum* because of the audience; I propose they were more fully developed because Coleridge had been cerebrating on them for another decade. Vigus's interpretation as a whole, though, unquestionably stands. There are simply too many similarities between Plato's system and Coleridge's system presented in the *Opus*

Maximum for it to be coincidence. This is a wonderfully strong book which anyone interested in Coleridge's philosophical writings will find fascinating.

Julian Knox's essay 'Coleridge's Transnational Concept of Translation' (in Class and Robinson, eds., *Transnational England: Home and Abroad, 1780–1860*, pp. 249–70) argues that Coleridge's approach to translation can be best understood by an image he hinted at to Southey in a letter of 1799 and which he was still fascinated with in a notebook entry of 1825. That image is two self-conscious mirrors facing one another so that the contents of the one become an equal part of the contents of the other. Knox argues that the image of mimesis is more apt for Coleridge as a translator than the image of the lamp that is usually given to Romanticism. In other words, Knox is arguing that Coleridge viewed translation as the translator putting both of the two poets or philosophers into the product in a mutual, self-conscious exchange. Knox concludes that, for Coleridge, the enterprise of translation was to give the two mirrors a common focus. There is more discussion of the theory of translation than examples of the proposed paradigm in Knox's essay, though in the final section he does quote extensively from Coleridge's *Wallenstein*, and there is a fine post-twentieth-century discussion of how this concept of translation feeds into the *Biographia Literaria* debate on 'plagiarism'. Other essays in this volume will doubtless be of interest to readers of this article, especially David Fallon's piece on Blake.

David P. Haney's essay 'Coleridge's "Historic Race": Ethical and Political Otherness' (in Wehrs and Haney, eds., *Levinas and Nineteenth-Century Literature: Ethics and Otherness from Romanticism through Realism*, pp. 61–88) draws parallels between the ethical and political writings of Levinas and Coleridge. Haney knows a tremendous amount about the political and ethical writings of both philosophers, and this article will be of great interest to those who are familiar with their works. For those who are coming to Levinas for the first time this essay will be difficult, though Haney must be given credit for a very fine introduction to his essay which sets the philosophical scene (and, after all, the essay collection is about Levinas and not Romanticism). There are indeed striking parallels between Levinas and Coleridge, both of whom chose to give primacy to ethical relationships. For Levinas, one does not have to encounter the Other; there is no empiricism in his philosophy. He started to talk of 'the face' but changed to 'proximity' to counter this possibility of misunderstanding him. We are as obligated to someone we will never meet in Africa as we are to our neighbour; Coleridge would hold that we are equally obliged to all persons because all are equal creatures: created by the Trinitarian God. None of the parallels Haney draws is forced, and his premise that Coleridge's distinction between 'the subjective freedom of "juridical law" and the absolute command of the moral law bears some resemblance to Levinas's distinction between justice and ethics' (p. 71) is basically indisputable. Haney's decision to concentrate on comments concerning race (which was not in any way a subject central, prevalent, or even uncommon in Coleridge's thought) when he could so easily have chosen other subjects relating to personal responsibility to others on which Coleridge wrote much more extensively, is more problematic, and I would have liked to see more discussion of the *Opus Maximum*—very fertile ground for the kind of parallels Haney draws—in this essay.

Jeffery W. Barbeau's *Coleridge, the Bible, and Religion* [2008] should have been reviewed last year, and the fault is entirely mine for not doing so. Barbeau takes the view that Coleridge's religious thought was integral to all his thought throughout the entire course of his life, arguing that anyone writing about Coleridge must make a decision about Coleridge's faith. What he hopes to convey by this is the interpretation that Coleridge's faith and interpretation of the Bible simmered over time and matured. Barbeau wishes to point out that, though conflicted at different points in his life about how the Bible should be properly read by the individual and by the community, Coleridge was on a 'journey' of faith. The language may be overly dramatic, but I am in substantial agreement with this opinion. Coleridge changed his mind often, and at times nearly capriciously, on matters of religion in precisely the same way that he changed his mind often about nearly everything else. What Barbeau is in fact arguing against is the possibility of a secularist approach to reading any part of Coleridge's works: an entirely valid perspective. The majority of the book seeks to discuss Coleridge's hermeneutical approach during his mature years, and the three texts Barbeau focuses on are (unsurprisingly) *Aids to Reflection*, the *Opus Maximum*, and *Confessions of an Inquiring Spirit*. He also has gone to substantial lengths to tease a unified vision of Coleridge's biblical commentaries out of the hodge-podge that are the *Notebooks*. I may disagree with him in his assertion that the *Confessions* are the most focused or comprehensive (again his terms) treatment of the Christian religion, but I find his interpretation that Coleridge was a defender of Reformation theology accurate, and though he has received criticism which argues that this emphasis diminishes his portrayal of Coleridge's thought on practical hermeneutics, I do not think this criticism entirely fair. Barbeau started his journey through the thought of Coleridge with *Confessions* and has broadened his scope over time. This book presents a fine introductory treatment of Coleridge on the Bible, and pushes outward to attempt to come to grips with the question of what, precisely, was his faith.

Ronald Wendling's position in 'Presence and Distance: Samuel Taylor Coleridge and the Meaning of Modernity' (*CStA* 25[2009] 101–22) is that philosophically Coleridge struggled not with empirical understanding itself but with the tendency of the early nineteenth-century mind to idolize it and separate it from imagination and a Platonic understanding of reason. Wendling is certainly correct to present Coleridge as interested in empiricism, *and* idealism *and* Platonism, and to be frustrated that the wider society wished to prioritize empiricism over other methods of philosophy. He correctly ties this to Coleridge's fixation on discriminating between the reason and the understanding, and again correctly identifies Coleridge's frustration with the faculty of understanding being given a primary role over the faculty of reason by empiricists. This is a good, broad-ranging discussion of Coleridge's philosophical commitments which takes into account some of the poetry as well as prose works and treats its subject comprehensively while remaining concise.

Monika Class in her article ‘Coleridge and the Radical Roots of Critical Philosophy’ (*WC* 40[2009] 51–5) argues that Coleridge became infatuated with Kant through the ‘translation’ (as she points out, largely a condensation and interpretation) in English which was produced by Friedrich August Nitsch under the title *A General and Introductory View,* and which circulated through the Radical circles in which Coleridge moved during the early 1790s. Members of those circles also attended lectures given by Nitsch. Coleridge later lied in the *Biographia Literaria* about how he came to be aware of Kant’s philosophy. Class has compelling evidence to demonstrate that Coleridge must have been captivated by Nitsch’s work *before* his trip to Germany and that this influence had political ramifications because Nitsch’s work was inexorably tied to Jacobinism. This link between Nitsch and Jacobinism was one which Coleridge sought aggressively to distance himself from in his later life—which is likely why he embellished and lied in the *Biographia*. When Coleridge ventured to Germany and learned the real system of Kant it became a pervasive constructive influence on his thought. Class is right in pointing out that Coleridge must have been introduced to Kant previous to the voyage, and right in tracing the likely source; though her comments on the veracity or otherwise of the *Biographia* are less novel.

Andrew Elfenbein writes what is essentially a ‘review’ of *On the Constitution of the Church and State* as a part of a larger project inviting scholars to suggest primary sources to students of Victorian literature, and in a rather wonderful piece of irony it precedes an article by Len Findlay on *Manifest der Kommunistischen Partei* (*VR* 35[2009] 19–23). Elfenbein clearly did not know the ordering of the articles else he would have remarked upon the irony that where Marx and Engels saw the church as the destroying cancer of society (conveniently ignoring the fact that its theology had produced the philosophical principles of equality and beneficence on which they based their work), Coleridge saw it as the guardian of all that was good in society. What Elfenbein chooses to concentrate on in this short (and excellent) piece is the clerisy, not in its administrative form, but rather in its form as the guardian of education in England. He focuses particularly on the figure of the village schoolmaster. Elfenbein points out that there was no figure more commonly the source of satirical derision than the village schoolmaster within Victorian and eighteenth-century literature. Coleridge, he argued, constructively elevated (rehabilitated perhaps) the image of the marginally literate sadist or hopelessly incompetent intellectual which was so often the standard representation. Elfenbein sees *On the Constitution of the Church and State* as posing a challenge to literary authors: did their work provide anything of equal value to the education provided by the schoolmaster? Were Coleridge to have been posed that challenge, he would unquestionably have answered that of course literary authors produce equal, and far higher, value, but that the schoolmasters, as guardians of their product (which Coleridge specifically called ‘national treasures’), were necessary for the preservation of that treasure in the community of readership. Elfenbein finishes the piece by ‘sketching the effects of Coleridge’s work on one Victorian text, Charles Dickens’s *The Old Curiosity Shop*’ (p. 22). He argues that with this text Dickens fundamentally changes his portrayal of schoolmasters ‘for reasons that previous critics have never explained but that make sense in light of Coleridge's book' (p. 22). I am certainly in Elfbein's camp that students of Victorian literature should read *On the Constitution of the Church and State:* especially as Gladstone cited it as his bedrock influence in *The State in its Relations with the Church*.

Kazuyoshi Oishi's article 'The "Scions of Charity": Cowper, the Evangelical Revival, and Coleridge in the 1790s' (*SEL* 50[2009] 45–64) posits that the poetry of Cowper (which he thoroughly demonstrates to be invocative for both Methodism and wider Evangelicalism alike) 'provided a model for Coleridge to solve [his] politico-religious dilemma and drove him away from the pale of Unitarian radicalism in late 1797' (p. 58). The argument is that Cowper's philosophy of philanthropy as presented through the medium of his poetry became a substantive influence on Coleridge's own philosophy and poetry. Kazuyoshi argues that it was a constructive influence on *The Ancient Mariner*, seeing that poem as an attempt to 'transplant Cowper's evangelical language of Charity in a supernatural, and yet, in essence, evangelical context' (p. 60). Kazuyoshi has done excellent work in bringing Cowper to the foreground of the Evangelical movement, and I can easily see Cowper being influential to some degree on the young Coleridge (Kazuyoshi has a couple of quotations from the letters to substantiate this interpretation, but the evidence can only be called persuasive and not compelling).

Helen Boyles's 'Hazlitt's Gendered Distinction between Gusto and Enthusiasm and its Application to Coleridge's Pulpit Rhetoric' (*ColB* 33[2009] 34–41) seeks to examine and reflect upon Hazlitt's use of the word 'gusto' throughout his writings—particularly discriminating it from 'enthusiasm'. She also seeks to explore the masculine and feminine attributes of the way he used the words. A principal hermeneutic she employs is Hazlitt's reaction to Coleridge's preaching and religious writings. A good example of her exegesis can be found in the following passage: 'The traditionally feminine, atmospheric metaphors which Hazlitt applies to the oracular style, structure and content of Coleridge's *Lay Sermons* contrast with the vigorous and muscular metaphor applied in the earlier tributes. The changing language seems to reflect the way in which the original gusto of a rationally focused conviction has progressively dissolved into fluid and elusive speculation, or been inflated into balloons of visionary abstraction' (p. 38). In other words Hazlitt wrote about Coleridge's early preaching (in the pulpit that his own father was vacating no less) with 'gusto' while he wrote about the *Lay Sermons* with enthusiasm—'gusto' has more masculine qualities. Her conclusion is that 'Hazlitt's very different estimations of Coleridge's enthusiasm reflect the extreme and contrasting responses which the enthusiastic style typically provokes, while the degree of gusto which he detects in Coleridge's discourse will to some degree reflect the extent to which he identifies with its political and moral perspective' (p. 40). The tracing of the use of a particular word through Hazlitt's writings is an interesting project, and Coleridge provides a consistent subject to conduct the trace on.

Kerri Andrews's '"More's polish'd muse, or Yearsley's muse of fire": Bitter Enemies Write the Abolition Movement' (*ERR* 20[2009] 21–36) makes no pretence to have discovered the rivalry between More and Yearsley; instead Andrews posits a genesis for the rivalry in More's original patronage of

Yearsley, and desires to make a case for both of the women being taken more seriously as poets. I find the idea that More thought Yearsley was getting too big for her bonnet entirely plausible (More particularly mentions with derision Yearsley wearing gauze bonnets in a letter written in August 1785); More could be an entirely distasteful, self-centred, conceited, and downright nasty woman when it suited her politically. She was also fundamentally classist in her view of society, and so having a female rival from a lower social class, whom she had originally provided patronage to, become an equally popular poetic voice must have galled her to the core. The fact that Yearsley wrote from the perspective of the lower classes and addressed 'A Poem on the Inhumanity of the Slave Trade' to a wider audience than the power elite, and that it spoke from a working-class voice more able to understand the horrors of slavery because it understood the horrors of near-poverty and hunger at home in Britain also irritated More's sensibilities on class consciousness. Much of what Andrews wants to accomplish within this article is to get us to read the poems on their own merits. I sense an implicit, and at times explicit, argument within the article that when they are taken side by side Yearsley emerges as a better poet than More, though Andrews' object in the article is to encourage the reading of both poems, and I must confess that I find Yearsley's imagery of righteous indignation more haunting and gripping than More's highly stylized poem. In a sense Andrews has already succeeded in her objective of getting scholars to treat both women as serious poets, because anyone who reads this article will be thinking more of the poetry than the rivalry by the end of the piece.

'"As Long-Winded as Possible": Southey, Coleridge, and *The Doctor &c.*' by David Chandler (*RES* 60[2009] 605–19) could serve as a polemical introduction to a new edition of the work (there isn't one, but perhaps in light of Chandler's findings there ought to be). Not only does he trace the tortuous history of its composition in a crisp précis of the appearance of each volume (much of it was published posthumously, and its attribution to Southey was only made public after his death, though those in his circle certainly knew who was writing it), he has gone to exacting lengths to demonstrate source material that Southey incorporated into his version. It is well known that Southey got the idea of the story from Coleridge, who was performing it as a set piece of after-dinner entertainment from very early in the 1790s, but Coleridge had no proprietary claim on the threads of the story. In fact those threads appear to lead all the way back to Smart. For instance Chandler notes that 'The central story of Daniel Dove and Nobs had, then, been printed at least six times before Southey started writing *The Doctor &c.* around 1813. All but one of the later printings are clearly derivative from *The Midwife*, but the story had entered popular culture and any association with Smart was lost early on. As noted earlier, Southey appears to have known none of these published versions of his story, despite being exceptionally widely read' (p. 610). Chandler goes to some length to detail the interaction of Southey and Coleridge concerning the story of Daniel Dove of Doncaster and his horse Nobs, and argues that it was clearly a long-running inside joke between them. There is a long—perhaps over-long—discussion of Coleridge's claims on the story, and of how the two men saw the story differently: Coleridge as a story to be enacted verbally over several nights and never told the same way twice, and Southey (of course) as a rich vein to mine for constructive satirical humour in print.

Chandler uses a very good metaphor in 'long-winded' because Coleridge's long-windedness in voice suited his performative model, while Southey's long-windedness in print served as an obstacle to the release of the work overall. An important point that Chandler makes subsequent to this discussion is that Southey was 'temperamentally adverse to writing about himself in the direct autobiographical manner employed on occasion by Wordsworth and Coleridge, but *The Doctor &c.* indirectly presents at least a full portrait of its author as any of the more avowedly confessional 'Romantic' texts. The irony here, one that says a good deal about Southey, is that he was intent on disguising his authorship' (p. 617). This article really is a comprehensive treatment of *The Doctor &c.* and if there is any justice in the world of letters it may spark renewed interest in it.

J. Mark Smith performs good old-fashioned philology (lexicography more precisely) in 'The Rippling of *Verschiedenheit*: Wilhelm von Humboldt on Philology, Usage and Intra-Linguistic Diversity' (*EER* 20[2009] 237–45). He begins with a discussion of the English word 'desynonymization' (invented by Coleridge) and James McKusick's argument that it gave justification to the editors of *A New Dictionary of the English Language* (misidentified as *The Oxford English Dictionary* which its second edition would become) to include historical examples and variant forms under their own entries. Smith describes Von Humboldt as an 'alternative' (his term) to Coleridge's linguistic philosophy of desynonymization, and summarizes Von Humboldt's stance as arguing that 'everything diverse in language forms or structures springs from the 'inner freedom 'of individual thought, which is intimately related to its activity'(p. 238). He has a constructive argument and I should let him speak for himself:

> Coleridge's concept of desynonymization cannot explain the comedy-of-errors dimension of public shiftings of usage. It tells us nothing about the force of the normative, or about how the energy of language must necessarily, much of the time, *fail* to bind its speakers together. But nor perhaps does Humboldt emphasize enough how the action of speaking or writing falls short, or rings hollow, or makes a poor trial, how the modified utterance comes never to be 'echoed from a stranger's mouth' (*On Language* 56) . . . any consideration of verbal action must take into account not just instances of the felicitous or infelicitous, exemplary or erroneous, but also of usage that is merely ordinary. (pp. 242–3)

Smith has probably caused more questions to crop up in this article than he has answered, and it seems pretty clear that this was his intention. It is a discussion of the philosophy on innovation in language and I am not entirely sure that it sought to have a meta-conclusion, but rather be concluded with a meta-question.

Finally, all scholars of Romantic prose should note that the letters of Leigh Hunt, an invaluable resource to both Hunt scholars and others, were placed online by the University of Iowa in 2009 (this project is discussed elsewhere in this volume). Letters usually are covered under the prose section in *YWES* but there was not a natural place for such a discussion to fit in this article, and furthermore there is little general commentary I could make other than effusively praising Iowa for funding this project and thanking the editors for their work. Thomas Fuller once wrote that 'the best History is Letter-History', and I am a firm believer in that position today.

3. The Novel

Should there be a section on Romantic prose fiction? Why rule it out from our discussion of Enlightenment literature—or then again, from the nineteenth century? Which authors should we consider here, and why? Questions which have long vexed the field—not to mention *YWES* editors—come to the fore in Miriam L. Wallace's edited collection, *Enlightening Romanticism: Romancing the Enlightenment, British Novels from 1750–1832*. This is an important volume. It builds on the growing body of work on Romantic fiction and sets it in extended dialogue with criticism of the long eighteenth century: not, it transpires, to do away with periodicity, but to reveal 'the elucidating power of cross-period scholarship' (p. 19). Margaret Case Croskery's essay, 'Novel Romanticism in 1751: Eliza Haywood's *Betsy Thoughtless*', sets a good opening challenge. Haywood as Romantic novelist? Yes, this essay argues, outlining the ways in which Betsy learns to value passion and experience sympathy, and suggesting that Haywood's novel 'thematizes an essentially Romantic stance to the absorptive pleasures of fiction at both the level of form and content' (p. 23). Haywood makes, as Case Croskery admits, 'an unlikely herald of Wordsworth', but this is a powerful argument for an alternative narrative of sympathetic identification across the eighteenth and early nineteenth centuries. Peter Walmsley, in 'The Melancholy Briton: Enlightenment Sources of the Gothic', goes on to suggest that the flowering of post-revolutionary Gothic should be seen in the light of earlier eighteenth-century graveyard literature, gloomy musings which may be traced back to Locke, and then to Addison's *Spectator* essays, before emerging in Young's *Night Thoughts* and Sterne's *Tristram Shandy*. Moreover, this Enlightenment Gothic offers a 'dark obverse' of British pragmatism and commercialism: a portrait of 'the Briton as pathologically melancholy, incapacitated and obsessed about the past' (p. 40–1). Walmsley's long history of Gothic, then, gives a different narrative of national identity. As well as these large panoramas of period and nation, essayists try to question more local categories, such as 'Jacobin' and 'anti-Jacobin'. Scott C. Campbell analyses the epistolary experiments of Charlotte Smith's *Desmond*, and Daniel Schierenbeck looks at Jane West's *The Advantages of Education*, both arguing for a temporary removal of, in Schierenbeck's words, 'the blinding binaries of Jacobin and anti-Jacobin' (p. 84). Shawn Lisa Maurer reads the relationships between men in the radical fiction of William Godwin and Thomas Holcroft against the backdrop both of their own friendship and of changing attitudes to male friendship in the 1790s. Social debates of the period also inform Shelley

King's essay on *Adeline Mowbray*. Just as Maurer shows how Holcroft and Godwin look back to and test earlier concepts of friendship, King discusses the ways in which Opie reuses staples of eighteenth-century fiction—in particular, the duel—to negotiate contemporary ideologies. Christopher Flynn's 'Frances Trollope's America: From Enlightenment Aesthetics to Victorian Class', later in the volume, also shows the long after-history of eighteenth-century readings, arguing that Trollope 'uses her eighteenth-century aesthetics as they were taught by Gilpin to the traveller to create an aristocratic sensibility in a world that is moving towards a less clear structure' (p. 178).

As Shelley King concludes in her essay, we can only appreciate the writers of the period through unravelling 'the sophisticated web of textual affinities that mark their works' (p. 130). In the case of the rare novel *The Woman of Genius* [1821–2], by Elizabeth B. Lester, these are complex indeed, as Julie Shaffer explains. Few copies of Lester's novel exist, but Shaffer's chapter makes a good case for tracking them down, showing how it might be read alongside *Corinne* as an exploration of female genius and border-crossing. Like this collection of essays itself, Lester's novel questions categories of genre, periodization, and gender; it 'addresses the question of which genres of literature produced in the period merit attention', and 'asks whether there is a feminine and a masculine Romanticism' (p. 143). Shaffer closes by emphasizing the importance of the 'mixed heritage' of both protagonist and protégée in Lester's novel, which open up the genre to larger perspectives. The global reach of the Romantic novel is also tackled in Tara Ghoshal Wallace's 'Reading the Metropole: Elizabeth Hamilton's *Translations of the Letters of a Hindoo Rajah*', which analyses Hamilton's mixed feelings about the British empire. In part, the novel does justify British rule in India, as Felicity Nussbaum and Isobel Grundy have suggested. But Wallace argues that 'this text is deeply troubled by the consequences of the imperial mission'; Hamilton uses Hindu spokesmen to 'articulate her critique of the metropole' (p. 131), and her narrative ventriloquism and double-voicing complicate and unsettle views of the empire (Wallace's comments on Hamilton's narrative complexity are paralleled, incidentally, by Susan Egenolf and Fiona Price in monographs which will be discussed later).

So does *Enlightening Romanticism* offer any solutions to the problems of periodization and categorization? Two response essays at the end of the volume give a thoughtful summary of some of the issues involved in reading the Enlightenment/Romantic/Victorian novel. Patricia Spacks, in 'How We See: The 1790s', admits the usefulness of classification, but suggests that our constructions of literary history should perhaps 'focus, at least in part, not on artificially designed periods but on arbitrary, limited stretches of time' (p. 187). Stephen C. Behrendt closes the collection on an optimistic note, inspired by 'more and increasingly sophisticated critical and theoretical equipment for assessing the novels that were produced and read during this protean period' (p. 205). We have access to unprecedented amounts of this fiction, too, and will begin to find new ways of evaluating and contextualizing it, as this collection has already begun to do; in Behrendt's words, scholarship of the Romantic-era novel at present 'offers so much promise, so many opportunities' (p. 205).

This is an exciting moment, then, for Romantic fiction criticism—and Behrendt's confidence in the future is borne out by several very strong monographs this year. In *Revolutionary Imaginings in the 1790s*, Amy Garnai takes up Spacks's challenge of a close focus on a specific period, and 'attempts to recover a particular historical moment and a scene of cultural production within it' (p. 1), looking at the revolutionary writing of three authors: Charlotte Smith, Mary Robinson, and Elizabeth Inchbald. Moving with ease between poetry, plays, and fiction, Garnai's book is an excellent account of women's political and literary participation in the public sphere, inflected by recent work on radical networks and sociability, in particular the Godwin circle. Garnai quotes Charlotte Smith's rhetorical question, 'women, it is said have no business with politics.—Why not?' (p. 12), and provides a nuanced and specific answer. Her focus on particular authors—and, especially, her close reading of novels including Smith's *Desmond* and *The Banished Man*, Robinson's *Walsingham*, and Inchbald's *Nature and Art*—allows an insight into the different radical trajectories of writers in the period and the interplay of politics and creativity. A detailed reading of the changes in Smith's narrative style across the decade, for example, not only helps towards an understanding of the novelist herself but also demonstrates how 'literary form itself becomes a marker of cultural crisis' (p. 15). Unfortunately, Arnold A. Markley's *Conversion and Reform in the British Novel in the 1790s: A Revolution of Opinions*, which promises to be a most interesting study of the same period—from an author who has a track record as editor of Smith, Holcroft, and Godwin—did not arrive in time to be considered in this year's survey, and will instead be explored with work from 2010.

Smith's question about women and politics might also be taken as a useful starting point for Susan B. Egenolf's *The Art of Political Fiction in Hamilton, Edgeworth and Owenson*, which takes an unusual approach to women's narrative strategies. Garnai concentrates on a specific period; Egenolf focuses on a particular device. Informed by theories of book history, including H.J. Jackson's work on Romantic marginalia, and Gérard Genette's concepts of 'paratext' and 'intertitle', Egenolf carefully studies the self-conscious glosses used by these three writers. Hamilton's 'Preliminary Dissertation' in *Letters of a Hindoo Rajah* and her glossary of 'Oriental' terms should be seen, Egenolf argues, as a subversive act, allowing an insight into 'the creative generic negotiations of a woman writer taking on a political topic' (p. 17). Egenolf sets Hamilton's use of paratexts alongside Edgeworth's preface, notes, and glossary to *Castle Rackrent*, suggesting that the tension between these and Thady's central narrative constructs a 'highly complex and negotiable history', and reflects on the uneasy relationship between colonizer and colonized. Tracing these glosses—often ironic, always questioning—through *Belinda*, *The Wild Irish Girl*, *Cottagers of Glenburnie*, and *The O'Briens and the O'Flahertys*, and also considering other modes of interdisciplinary commentary on the texts, Hamilton's engaging and original book builds up a layered picture of women's political and literary engagement in the period. Nora Nachumi, *Acting Like a Lady: British Women Novelists and the Eighteenth-Century Theater*, also looks at three women writers—Elizabeth Inchbald, Frances Burney, and Jane Austen—in detail, placing them in a broader context of attitudes towards playwriting, performance, and theatre. All these novelists themselves also had (very different) relationships with the stage, whether through playwriting, family theatricals, acting, or play-going. All, as Nachumi analyses, used images and tropes 'which helped them to dramatize the performative nature of female experience' (p. xvii). To 'act like a lady' was itself a role, and Nachumi suggests that the use of theatrical images and tropes by these writers 'called into question the ideals of femininity that their novels seem to support' (p. 175). Nachumi's argument is strongest in the case of Inchbald—her career as an actress and playwright fed directly into her novel-writing, and Nachumi reads *A Simple Story* and *Nature and Art* in the light of Inchbald's thoughts on the relationship between actor and audience, and the potential dangers of performance. A large appendix details almost 400 female novelists from 1660 to 1818, a good proportion of whom were also playwrights or performers—a spur, perhaps, to further work on the interplay between women's novels and theatre in the period.

Fiona Price's *Revolutions in Taste, 1773–1818: Women Writers and the Aesthetics of Romanticism* offers perhaps the most comprehensive and striking reading of a range of Romantic novels this year, putting forward a reassessment of female commentary on taste in the period. Price begins with a thoughtful, critically nuanced analysis of why, and how, we might approach women writers of the Romantic period separately from their male counterparts; not to underline any essential, gender-based similarities, but because 'the complication of gender discourse in the late eighteenth century gave women writers a common and particular point of entry into discussions on taste' (p. 7). Female writers might approach the issue in different ways: in her opening chapter, for example, Price sets Clara Reeve alongside Anna Letitia Barbauld, discussing their differences but showing how both are highly aware of the cultural power of the discourse of taste. Both embark on canon-forming, tradition-building enterprises—Reeve's 1785 *Progress of Romance* and Barbauld's edition of *British Novelists*—but both also 'show an awareness of the malleability of tradition' too (p. 16). If Reeve and Barbauld were promoting the mental independence of female readers, women such as Wollstonecraft were simultaneously proclaiming their independence as writers. Price's next chapter shows the difficulties in Wollstonecraft's self-positioning, and argues for a reassessment of women's attitudes to originality and genius in the period. This opens into a larger discussion of ways in which women writers might try to direct aesthetic experience and to imagine a 'revolution in taste'. As Price points out in her introduction, 'disputes over taste frequently took place in marginalized forms themselves regarded as being in bad taste: the Gothic, the sentimental novel, the romance, and the tale' (p. 2), and she therefore examines a wide range of marginalized—but popular—novels. Alongside major authors such as Wollstonecraft, Austen, and Edgeworth, it is particularly welcome to have Price's discussion of Eliza Fenwick, Priscilla Wakefield, Elizabeth Hamilton, and Mary Brunton, among others, and to see, for example, Elizabeth Gooch's *Wanderings of Imagination* placed alongside Owenson's *Florence Macarthy: An Irish Tale* to form a detailed account of the national tale. Angela Esterhammer also made a striking case for the ways in which a 'minor' author and a forgotten work might help us trace the elusive nature of the Romantic novel, in 'London Periodicals, Scottish Novels, and Italian Fabrications: *Andrew of Padua, the Improvisatore* Re-membered' (*SiR* 48[2009] 469–90). Esterhammer exposes a remarkably successful Romantic forgery: the novel *Andrew of Padua* which presents itself as an eighteenth-century Italian text, an anonymous translation of a novel by Abbate Francisco Furbo. Indeed, the novel is still catalogued in libraries as the work of Furbo. But Esterhammer finally reveals Furbo as a fictional author, a pseudo-scholarly hoax complete with biography, bibliography, and reception history. It seems a slight plot-spoiler to reveal Esterhammer's attribution to John Galt, an identification which she supports with compelling evidence, and which she then opens out into a discussion of literary imposture and improvisation. This is, Esterhammer shows, an 'exemplary' Romantic novel—a typical example of an ephemeral literary commodity which is also 'exceptional in the way it thematizes the conditions' of the Romantic literary marketplace.

Attention to form and style marked some good work on Charlotte Smith this year. Melissa Sodeman, in 'Charlotte Smith's Literary Exile' (*ELH* 76[2009] 131–52), considers novels such as *The Old Manor House* in light of Smith's art of imitation—or, as more hostile readers such as Anna Seward termed it, 'plagiarism'. Sodeman sites Smith's 'imitative aesthetic' firstly in eighteenth-century debate around imitation and originality and then in the context of Smith's interest in exile and wandering, drawn both from autobiography and from literary cliché. The very use of cliché, repetition, and familiar tropes, argues Sodeman, means that the novels 'figure their derivative nature as a formal effect of exile, styling their repetitive narratives and entrenched form as an aesthetic of estrangement and alienation'. Suzie Park's 'Compulsory Narration, Sentimental Interface: Going through the Motions of Emotion' (*ECent* 50[2009] 165–83) looks at the complex, and sometimes frustratingly limited, portrayals of feeling in the sentimental novel, from Smith's *Emmeline* to Austen's *Sense and Sensibility*: 'Often doing the reverse of what it seems designed to do, the sentimental novel strips its dialogues—both inner and outer—of efficiency in communication and reliable markers of emotion'.

A special issue of *Women's Writing*, introduced by Antje Blank, gave some welcome reinterpretations of Smith's novels. '"Empire without End": Charlotte Smith at the Limits of Cosmopolitanism', by Adriana Craciun (*WW* 16[2009] 39–59), builds on Craciun's 2005 study *Citizens of the World* to discuss the reach, and (importantly) the limitations, of Smith's 'feminist and revolutionary cosmopolitanism'. Focusing on two later works, *Montalbert* and 'The Story of Henrietta', Craciun dissects Smith's ambivalent colonial attitude, considering her own financial entanglement in the family plantations in Barbados: in Smith's colonial romance, perhaps, we see 'a marker of the limits of one vision of Romantic cosmopolitanism'. Kari Lokke's 'Charlotte Smith's *Desmond*: The Historical Novel as Social Protest' (*WW* 16[2009] 60–77) places *Desmond* as the original historical novel, with a strong activist purpose, conceived 'in explicit opposition to the romance and courtship novel'. Smith's portrayal of extramarital love, and her challenging depiction of the shortcomings of marriage, Lokke argues, also have a powerful impact on the development of the British novel, and *Desmond* may be seen 'as the progenitor of a tradition of strong feminist novels', including Wollstonecraft's *The Wrongs of Woman* and Anne Brontë's *The Tenant of Wildfell Hall*. Antje Blank's 'Things as They Were: The Gothic of Real Life in Charlotte Smith's *The Emigrants* and *The Banished Man*' (*WW* 16[2009] 78–93) discusses Smith's changing attitude both to the situation in France and to Gothic literature. She sees *The Banished Man* and *Avis au Lecteur* as 'a departure from the sentimental Gothic of Smith's earlier romances', and discusses the possible reasons for this, chief among them the lesson, driven home by *The Banished Man*, 'that valid causes for human fear originate in the material world'. James Holt McGavran, Jr., in 'Smuggling, Poaching and the Revulsion against Kinship in *The Old Manor House*' (*WW* 16[2009] 20–38), reads the novel in the context of Smith's knowledge of the contraband trade and poaching in Sussex: local criminality which had a continental reach, and which was mirrored by, and connected to, government corruption. This 'nightmare vision of British criminality and vice' shapes *The Old Manor House*, argues McGavran, and seeps into its portrayal of family. Mark K. Fulk looks at Smith's innovative, and sometimes difficult, narrative strategies in 'Mismanaging Mothers: Matriarchy and Romantic Education in Charlotte Smith's *The Young Philosopher*' (*WW* 16[2009] 94–108). Far from being a flaw in the novel, he argues that the interpolated story and interrupted conclusion of *The Young Philosopher* should be seen as 'deliberate ideological choices made by Smith to explore the social problem of disempowered mothers who suffer at the hands of matriarchal women'. An interesting perspective on Smith's literary versatility is offered by Elizabeth A. Dolan in 'Collaborative Motherhood: Maternal Teachers and Dying Mothers in Charlotte Smith's Children's Books' (*WW* 16[2009] 109–25). This argues for a proper consideration of Smith's writing for children—including *Rural Walks, Rambles Farther* and *Minor Morals*—as experimental and innovative in form and content. In particular, Dolan suggests that we look closely at Smith's portrayal of motherhood, which she imagines as 'a collaborative, recursive, and mutual endeavour'.

Other work worth noting on children's fiction in the Romantic period is contained in the special issue of the *Charles Lamb Bulletin* celebrating the bicentenary of *Mrs Leicester's School* and *The Adventures of Ulysses* (*ChLB* 147[2009] 90–132). Pamela Clemit, in 'William Godwin's Juvenile Library' (*ChLB* 147[2009] 90–99), investigates the political and literary significance of the Godwins' bookshop, reminding us that this is an important context for an understanding of the Lambs' children's writing. This is echoed by Susan Manley's '*Mrs Leicester's School* and Schools for Treason' (*ChLB* 147[2009] 116–121), which shows the potentially transgressive power of the Lambs' stories, with their emphasis on a 'sympathetic, non-judgemental and non-authoritarian approach'. Malini Roy discusses the different approaches adopted by Godwin and Lamb, while emphasizing their 'imaginative contribution to children's books' (*ChLB* 147[2009] 122–130). Mary Wedd comments on the 'artistic skill and human understanding' of *Mrs. Leicester's School* (*ChLB* 147[2009] 100–106), and Felicity James on the allusions and potential influence of *The Adventures of Ulysses* (*ChLB* 147[2009] 107–115).

Maria Edgeworth's narrative art—and its political and national implications—is considered in several pieces this year. Like Susan Egenolf in *The Art of Political Fiction*, Jean Fernandez analyses the subversive nature of Maria Edgeworth's editorial strategies in 'Thady's Grey Goose Quill: Historiography and Literacy in Maria Edgeworth's *Castle Rackrent*' (*NewHibR* 13[2009] 133–46). Fernandez reads Thady's 'illiteracy' alongside the 'deranging effects' of English literacy: Sir Murtagh, with 'a lawsuit for every letter in the alphabet', is hedged about by papers, endlessly rewriting and ligitating, a 'prisoner and victim', Fernandez suggests, 'of his own powers of literacy'. Such images are echoed and furthered by Edgeworth's own 'double-edged editorial ironies' which, concludes Fernandez, 'disturb "literate" English reading responses'. 'Castle Stopgap: Historical Reality, Literary Realism, and Oral Culture', by Katherine O'Donnell (*ECF* 22[2009] 115–30), also looks at the interplay of the oral and the literary in *Castle Rackrent*, taking as its starting point George III's supposed comment on the book, 'what what—I know something now of my Irish subjects'. What what, indeed: O'Donnell asks what *can* be known in the novel, and its ways of 'knowing the Irish subject'. O'Donnell also tackles the topic of editorial glosses, but reads them here as a demonstration of authorial anxiety, reminding us of the ways in which Thady's oral narrative is presented as having 'a superior claim to veracity'. O'Donnell is particularly interested in the ways in which the Edgeworths' own family troubles feed into the story, which comes to function as 'a theatrical stopgap in the midst of fluctuation, uncertainty, and dramatic change, where all signifiers of allies and enemies were open to change'. Similarly, Emily Hodgson Anderson's 'Autobiographical Interpolations in Maria Edgeworth's *Harrington*' (*ELH* 76[2009] 1–18) shows how the autobiographical might be a useful tool in our understanding of this novel—yet emphasizes the importance of recognizing that it is not, therefore, an autobiography.

Mary Wollstonecraft's voice and discourse were the focus of much scholarly enquiry this year. Naomi Jayne Garner, in '"Seeing through a glass darkly": Wollstonecraft and the confinements of eighteenth-century femininity' (*JIWS* 11[2009] 82–95), offers a well-argued interpretation of Wollstonecraft's use of 'male discourse'. Garner suggests that Wollstonecraft's stance foreshadows Luce Irigaray's theories of the speculum, before moving on to discuss the use of 'subversive mimesis' in *Vindication of the Rights of Woman*, and arguing that this text becomes 'a mirror that reflects a distorted and hence revelatory vision of men back at themselves'. Dustin Friedman's '"Parents of the Mind": Mary Wollstonecraft and the Aesthetics of Productive Masculinity', (*SiR* 48[2009] 423–46) revisits debates about Wollstonecraft's treatment of desire and sexuality and instead chooses to examine her 'representation of men's sexuality', and her role as 'theorist of masculinity'. Exploring the complex portrayal of benevolent men in *Vindication of the Rights of Woman* and *The Wrongs of Woman*—Maria's kindly uncle being one example—Friedman argues for a form of 'avuncular non-normative masculinity' which we might trace through Wollstonecraft, Inchbald, and Dickens. Their portrayal of men who remain outside marital, heterosexual, reproductive relationships allows us to construct 'a literary genealogy that attempts to recognize, represent, and theorize the political and ethical importance of non-heterosexual identities'.

Meanwhile, Wollstonecraft's treatment of femininity was re-examined in 'Vindicating Paradoxes: Mary Wollstonecraft's "Woman"', by Kirstin R. Wilcox (*SiR* 48[2009] 447–67). Wilcox suggests that Wollstonecraft still has much to offer modern feminism: in particular, the ways in which she recognizes 'the conceptual limitations of the category of "woman" that is available to her'. From these limitations, argues Wilcox, she 'invokes an unprecedentedly fluid notion of female identity' which still has resonance.

Two interesting pieces examined Godwin's portrayal of his wife in his *Memoirs of the Author of a Vindication of the Rights of Woman.* Cynthia Richards, in 'The Body of Her Work, the Work of Her Body: Accounting for the Life and Death of Mary Wollstonecraft' (*ECF* 21[2009] 565–92), analyses a particularly disturbing moment in the biography, as he describes 'procur[ing] puppies to draw off the milk'. Modern biographers shrink from this detail, labelling it 'grotesque', 'bizarre', 'odd'; in Richards's words, 'careful to be more discreet than the grief-stricken Godwin'. What makes the episode so unsettling? Richards suggests that the answer may lie in its 'profound violation of what is deemed proper to human representation', and uses this as her starting point for a thoughtful exploration of the problems of such representation. Ildiko Csengei's 'Godwin's Case: Melancholy Mourning in the "Empire of Feeling"' (*SiR* 48[2009] 491–519) carefully considers not Godwin's portrayal of Wollstonecraft so much as his mourning, seeing in the *Memoirs* a 'complex and emotionally ambivalent psychological process'. They are read as a case study which 'probes the meeting points of mourning and melancholia as they take place in writing'. Meanwhile, William Godwin's novels were explored in '"The Business of War": William Godwin, Enmity, and Historical Representation' (*ELH* 76[2009] 343–69), by Thomas Campbell, which looks at the ways in which Godwin writes 'English history as war'. Campbell analyses approaches to enmity in *Political Justice* and 'On History and Romance', before tracing these ideas into *Caleb Williams* and *Mandeville*. He sets Godwin's concern with 'the so-called end of history' alongside the historical romance of *Waverley*, both of which display particular problems with the fictionalization of war; however, as Campbell concludes, '*Mandeville* contests Scott's efforts to consign enmity to the past'. Emily R. Anderson, in '"I will unfold a tale—!": Narrative, Epistemology, and *Caleb Williams*' (*ECF* 22[2009] 99–114), shows how *Caleb Williams* interrogates the construction of narrative, getting to the heart 'of the empirical problem: are the stories we tell about the world true?'

As ever, there was a good deal of strong work on Jane Austen. While a full discussion of scholarship on adaptation of her writing is beyond the scope of this essay, I will just mention *The Cinematic Jane Austen: Essays on the Filmic Sensibility of the Novels*, by David Monaghan, Ariane Hudelet, and John Wiltshire. The essays in this collection ask whether film criticism and the study of cinema might allow us a new awareness of the 'distinctive qualities of Austen's art'. The 'cinematic qualities' of her writing are discussed, from the visuality of her novels, to the questions about perception and interpretation raised by her writing, and the 'broad mythological structures that underpin Austen's socially specific plots' (p. 15). These essays offer a good way of understanding 'the interplay between the novels and their film adaptations' as a mutually rewarding relationship. Two books shed light on the ways in which Austen might be read alongside other writers: Peter W. Graham's *Jane Austen & Charles Darwin, Naturalists and Novelists* [2008] and Eric C. Walker's *Marriage, Writing, and Romanticism: Wordsworth and Austen after War*. Graham's study connects with *The Cinematic Jane Austen* in its willingness to consider new, interdisciplinary perspectives on Austen's work: 'the ampersand in this book's title is meant to signal that I am "shipping" (as fan fiction would put it) Jane Austen and Charles Darwin . . . through juxtaposition I'm creating a relationship that did not actually exist' (p. xi). Through four interconnected essays, however, Graham makes an involving case for a reading of Austen and Darwin alongside one another. Those later terms in the title are also well chosen—both authors function as 'naturalists' and 'novelists', both skilled in microscopic, particular observation, and at drawing out larger conclusions from tiny detail. This is a pleasingly personal study, drawn from close reading and careful thought, which prompts larger questions about the relationship of two authors who might at first seem opposed. Walker's more traditional, but no less provocative, reading of Wordsworth and Austen traces unexpected connections, showing how their writing about marriage 'confesses itself in a variety of forms perplexed, stymied, or otherwise balked by the nuptial, for better or for worse' (p. 6). Why put these authors together? Austen 'ducks marriage in her own life and appears to write about nothing else'; Wordsworth 'seems to have disappeared into marriage but appears never to write about it' (p. 3). Walker shows how we might productively read the complex and ambivalent portraits of marriage in their writing alongside other forms of relationship, with siblings and friends, and in the broader context of nineteenth-century marriage theories—Hegel, Kierkegaard, and Schelling—and modern philosophical approaches, where Walker finds the work of Stanley Cavell particularly useful. In a range of readings which set novels and poetry alongside one another—*Emma* and *Persuasion* discussed in light of Wordsworth's Waterloo poems as texts published 'in the wake of war'—Walker shows, first, the (contested) importance of marriage as a theme in the Romantic era and, second, how we might further understand the deep connections between Austen and the Romantic poets.

The 2009 AGM of JASNA was held in Philadelphia, and to celebrate the city of brotherly love, the theme was 'brothers and sisters', which has given rise to some good articles in *Persuasions* (31[2009]). Austen's relationship with her own brothers and sister is explored in articles by Maggie Lane, who looks at the literary aspirations of James and Henry (*Persuasions* 31[2009] 13–32), Peter Sabor, who traces the thought and care which shaped Austen's dedications to her siblings in her *Juvenilia* (*Persuasions* 31[2009] 33–46), and the appropriately named Sheila Johnson Kindred, who has previously made a strong case for the prize-winning abilities of naval captain Charles, and here argues for the potential influence of Charles' experiences on *Persuasion* and *Mansfield Park* (*Persuasions* 31[2009] 115–129). More generally, the nature of sibling relationships in the period is analysed. Essays probe the usefulness for Austen's novels of concepts such as Lawrence Stone's 'affective individualism' and Ruth Perry's recent work on family transformation in the period. Jan Fergus, in '"Rivalry, treachery between sisters!": Tensions between Brothers and Sisters in Austen's Novels' (*Persuasions* 31[2009] 69–88), takes as her starting point the assertion that 'the eighteenth century in general took deep sibling rivalry for granted in ways that might surprise or disturb us'. Fergus contextualizes her readings of the Watson and Bennet siblings through a close study of contemporary attitudes to family—in, for example, Chapone, Gregory, and Gisborne—and shows how rivalries can coexist with intimacies in Austen's novels. Sisterly intimacy was also the subject of John Mullan's contribution (*Persuasions* 31[2009] 59–68), which revisits the 'surely mischievous' *LRB* debate over the shared bed with Cassandra—'Was Jane Austen Gay?', ran the 1995 headline. As Mullan notes, the whole idea was an 'imaginist' controversy, since Cassandra and Jane had separate beds in any case; he rewardingly speculates, however, on the special place of shared bed*room* conversation in Austen's life and fiction, and also on the more 'disturbing sisterly confidences' of rival siblings, such as half-sisters Mrs Grant and Mary Crawford, the treacherous Steeles, or the 'baleful sisterly confederates' Caroline Bingley and Louisa Hurst. As in Fergus's essay, Mullan shows how Austen's images of siblings are defined as much by rivalry as by love. Rivalries also haunted Susan Allen Ford's essay, '"Exactly what a brother should be"? The Failures of Brotherly Love' (*Persuasions* 31[2009] 102–114), and Juliet McMaster's exploration of sibling 'matchmakers and matchbreakers' (*Persuasions* 31[2009] 89–101). William Galperin, in 'Lady Susan, Individualism, and the (Dys)functional Family' (*Persuasions* 31[2009] 47–58), discusses the connections between changing ideas of family and narrative practice, looking closely at the epistolary origins of Austen's fiction. Using the epistolary form in *Lady Susan*, argues Galperin, Austen turns back time, 'to the extent at least that she can stand outside, or apart from, the individualism with which her narrative practice is otherwise aligned'. Jocelyn Harris, meanwhile, looks at the close of Austen's career. In 'Frances Burney's *The Wanderer*, Jane Austen's *Persuasion*, and the Cancelled Chapters' (*Persuasions* 31[2009] 130–144), Harris gives a thorough and convincing account of the parallels between the two novels, until the close of *Persuasion* which, she argues, 'swerves' away from the prior model: this is an insightful account of narrative influence and difference, and Austen's 'patterns of inspiration, resistance, and creativity'.

Several of the essays in *Persuasions* make reference to the great Austen event of 2010, the launch of the *Jane Austen's Fiction Manuscripts Digital Edition*, <www.janeausten.ac.uk>, which presents images and searchable transcripts of Austen's manuscripts from libraries in New York, Cambridge, Oxford, and London. This will be covered in more detail in *YWES* [2010], but it is worth noting how work on Austen in 2009 looks forward to this opening up of original material, an invaluable piece of scholarship which will allow wider access to and more thorough appreciation of Austen's development as a writer. Peter Sabor, in his discussion of Austen's juvenilia (mentioned above), comments that 'Jane Austen's private dedications have thus become public at last', and an essay by Jenny McAuley, research assistant to Kathryn Sutherland on the digitization project, '"A long letter upon a jacket and petticoat": Reading Beneath Some Deletions in the Manuscript of *Catharine*, or *The Bower*' (*Persuasions* 31[2009] 191–8), explores new readings of Austen's manuscript changes to her early fiction.

There is growing recent interest in language-based studies of Austen's novels. One outstanding contribution to (and furthering of) the field is Massimiliano Morini's *Jane Austen's Narrative Techniques: A Stylistic and Pragmatic Analysis*. This attempts to bridge the gap between literary-critical readings of the novels and linguistically minded analysis, and succeeds in offering an accessible account of the usefulness of post-war linguistics and pragmatics to a study of Austen's work. While it might appear at first uncomfortable to accept a critical assessment which views Austen's works as 'dialogic machines', Morini engagingly shows how we might advance our technical understanding of Austen's 'indeterminacy' and 'narrative unreliability' (pp. 7, 23). He looks closely at the narrators of each major novel, and gives a particularly interesting account of 'evaluative opacity' in *Mansfield Park* which concludes that 'the initial orientation of [the novel] resembles a report written by a very careful double-dealing spy for his superiors: the text leads its readers to evaluate a situation in a certain manner; yet no single word is traceable that commits the writer to the evaluation which the text unmistakably proposes' (p. 76). Morini takes issue with certain historicist readings of Austen's work, showing—and *proving*—the difficulty of securely advancing any single-mindedly ideological reading of the novels, and providing 'a (technical) framework which accounts for the existence of a plethora of interpretations' (p. 146). Three articles of note which also adopt a language-based approach are Candace Nolan-Grant's 'Jane Austen's Speech Acts and Language-Based Societies' (*SEL* 49[2009] 863–78), Laura Buchholz's 'The Morphing Metaphor and the Question of Narrative Voice' (*Narrative* 17[2009] 200–19), and 'Verbal Conflicts in Austen's *Pride and Prejudice* and Burney's *The Wanderer*' (*English Text Construction* 2[2009] 111–20) by Laure Blanchemain. Nolan-Grant shows the potential importance of speech-act theory to an analysis of Austen's fictional societies, and the character dynamics of her novels. Marie-Laure Ryan's work on what computers might teach us about narrative theory lends Buchholz the metaphor of 'morphing' to 'help define the changing nature of a narrator's voice throughout a text'. She uses this to probe the use of voice, and specifically the use of free indirect discourse, in *Emma* and in Salman Rushdie's *Shame*. Blanchemain looks at moments of argument and verbal warfare between women in order to analyse conversational patterns and the questions they raise about gender. Austen's narrative was explored from a slightly different angle by Kelly A. Marsh, 'The Mother's Unnarratable Pleasure and the Submerged Plot of *Persuasion*' (*Narrative* 17[2009] 76–94). This offers a theoretical account of the concept of the 'submerged plot', informed by feminist narrative theory as well as work on plot and progression, before turning to the 'unnarratable story' in *Persuasion*—that of Anne Elliot's mother, constantly present, Marsh argues, in Anne's own marriage plot. Rachel Provenzano Oberman, in 'Fused Voices: Narrated Monologue in Jane Austen's *Emma*' (*NCL* 64[2009] 1–15), focuses on Austen's manipulation of voice, and, in particular, the 'double-voicedness of narrated monologue'.

Some new perspectives on the contextualization of Austen's novels were offered this year. 'Managing Propriety for the Regency: Jane Austen Reads the Book', by Kristin Flieger Samuelian (*SiR* 48[2009] 279–97), is a gripping account of several seduction stories: Lydia's elopement and Georgiana Darcy's near-ruin set in a larger context of the Princess Caroline affair. 'The Book' is the Commission Report into accusations of Caroline's adultery, published in the same year as *Pride and Prejudice*, and Samuelian suggests how both exhibit similar concerns with feminine behaviour: Lydia's 'boisterous sexuality has its contemporary counterpart in the reports of and ongoing fascination with the Princess of Wales', which we might read alongside Georgiana's more conventional narrative of near-seduction. Both, of course, shape the narrative of Elizabeth's 'authorized romance', and Samuelian suggests that Austen's plot thus reflects wider interest in the Caroline affair, its reception, and what she terms 'a cultural management strategy, in which the illicit energies residing in the royal family could be consumed, appropriated and eventually retracked into culturally normative modes'. Hidden stories of sexual excess also inform a surprising article by Janine Barchas, 'Hell-Fire Jane: Austen and the Dashwoods of West Wycombe' (*ECLife* 33[2009] 1–36). Just who are the Dashwoods? While 'Austen's fictional Dashwoods have now thoroughly displaced their namesakes in the cultural zeitgeist', Barchas suggests that we have forgotten the notoriety of the name in 1811, when it 'remained synonymous with diabolism, sexual lewdness, and the dubious privileges of wealth' thanks to the bad behaviour of Sir Francis Dashwood and the Hell-Fire Club. She offers evidence—an extensive accumulation of small, telling links and allusions—for Austen's enduring interest in this context. Reading *Sense and Sensibility* in a larger eighteenth-century context illuminates this backstory of libertinism and scandal, allowing us a new understanding both of Austen's reading and of the origins of her dangerous rakes. Barchas turns an attentive eye on landscape, discussing the ribald gardens of West Wycombe in detail; in another article this year, 'Mapping *Northanger Abbey*: Or, Why Austen's Bath of 1803 Resembles Joyce's Dublin of 1904' (*RES* 60[2009] 431–59), she explores an outwardly more respectable context for Austen's writing. Just as Barchas uncovers the hidden history of the Dashwood name, so here she investigates the Allens, suggesting the importance of Ralph Allen—and his shaping influence on Bath's turn-of-the-century landscape—to the novel. Using contemporary maps and evidence, Barchas re-creates Austen's minute attention to the detail of Bath's geographical and social scene, which, she suggests, looks forward to the specificity of Joyce's *Ulysses*, and must be taken as seriously.

Understanding the detail of Austen's fiction is also the driving aim of Rachel Ramsey's 'The Literary History of the Sash Window' (*ECF* 22[2009] 171–94, also discussed in Chapter XI of this volume). Plenty of contexts are deemed 'neglected', but this is a truly unusual angle on Austen's work. Ramsey reminds us of the long fictional history of sashes: Richardson's sequel to *Pamela* opens with a debate about casements versus sashes; Gulliver, initially pleased with the sash windows in his box, must contend with Brobdingnagian wasps making their entrance through them; Tristram Shandy, of course, has the unluckiest encounter with a sash in eighteenth-century fiction. By the time we get to *Northanger Abbey*, suggests Ramsey, the two sashes in Mrs Tilney's bedroom play a pivotal role in banishing Catherine's fears about the General—yet his role in the novel is hardly transparent, and the mention of the windows helps to register 'the ambivalent attitudes of the eighteenth century towards progress, social display and nationalistic pride'. Kathleen Anderson, meanwhile, looks closely at Austen's approach to gender in 'Lounging Ladies and Galloping Girls: Physical Strength and Femininity in *Mansfield Park*' (*WS* 38[2009] 342–58), and suggests how difficult it is to understand all the implications of female strength and weakness in the novels. Elsewhere, Hazel Jones's *Jane Austen and Marriage*, while not seeking to break new critical ground, is a readable overview of the biographical and historical context of marriage in the late eighteenth and early nineteenth centuries, illustrated with affectionate close readings of the novels. She makes good use of Austen's letters and juvenilia, conduct books, and periodicals. James Fordyce and Thomas Gisborne make their appearance, the latter condemning the 'rage of rambling', and brandishing the Bible 'as a big stick to beat wandering females back indoors' (p. 121).

Several articles employed different approaches to examine Austen's use of Gothic in *Northanger Abbey*. Barbara MacMahon, 'Metarepresentation and Decoupling in *Northanger Abbey*', an article in two parts (*ES* 90[2009] 518–44, 673–94), hardly offers a conventional literary-critical approach: MacMahon uses Austen's novel as a case study to show how 'certain cognitive and evolutionary psychological approaches can help us to understand the nature of literary fiction and relate it to other cognitive and communicative processes'. This is a complex undertaking, since MacMahon uses several approaches: relevance theory, a modular theory of mind-reading, and a general theory of 'decoupled mental processes'. In the first part of the article, she explains each concept in detail in an accessible way, outlining key models, before moving on to her own analysis of literature as 'richly metarepresentational' and explaining the relevance of these cognitive/evolutionary approaches to readings of fiction. *Northanger Abbey*, with its evasive narrative and moments of parody, offers a good case study. Towards the close of the first article, and in the second, MacMahon gives a thorough analysis of 'Gothic syntactic structures' in passages from Austen and from *The Mysteries of Udolpho*, to suggest a deeper, interdisciplinary understanding both of Austen's irony, and of 'the nature and complexity of the literary reading process'. From a more traditional perspective, Susan Zlotnick's 'From Involuntary Object to Voluntary Spy: Female Agency, Novels, and the Marketplace in *Northanger Abbey*' (*SNNTS* 41[2009] 277–92) is an enjoyable exploration of 'the intimate connection between the literary and the economic' in the novel, beginning with the bathetic washing-bill Catherine discovers in the black cabinet. Catherine has arrived at the washing-bill moment through her reading of the Gothic: her 'participation in the literary marketplace', as Zlotnick puts it. But Zlotnick shows that this participation is by no means straightforward in the novel, and suggests some ways in which we might assess 'Austen's complicated exploration of women's "value" in the marriage market'—and as novel-readers. Sheila Graham-Smith suggests a different source for *Northanger Abbey* in 'The Awful Memorials of an Injured and Ill-Fated Nun: The Source of Catherine

Morland's Gothic Fantasy' (*Persuasions* 31[2009] 199–208). Arguing for the importance of T.J. Horsley Curtis's *Ancient Records; or The Abbey of St. Oswythe*, Graham-Smith concludes that Austen's novel 'contains a series of in-jokes and references that, like Catherine's cabinet, may have been "at first unlocked", till we ourselves, through our ignorance of their sources, succeeded in re-locking them'.

So how might we 'unlock' eighteenth-century approaches to the Gothic? Partly this involves looking again at our categorizations and key critical terms, and two major studies this year offer different ways of doing this: *The Female Gothic: New Directions*, edited by Diana Wallace and Andrew Smith, and *The Gothic and Catholicism: Religion, Cultural Exchange and the Popular Novel, 1785–1829*, by Maria Purves. *The Female Gothic* is a timely and interesting collection. It begins, in its introduction and first essay by Lauren Fitzgerald, with a shrewd assessment of the rise of the 'Female Gothic' in twentieth-century criticism, from Ellen Moers onwards. The term was first popularized by Moers's *Literary Women* [1976]—with its origins in a Warwick lecture heckled by Germaine Greer—and the collection sees this 1970s moment as crucial for our understanding of the entanglement of Gothic and feminism. Indeed, Fitzgerald makes a powerful case for understanding Moers as a sort of Ann Radcliffe herself: 'neither is quite the "originator" of Female Gothic, as tradition or critical category', she writes, 'but their importance as "pioneers" in both is indisputable'. However, both essay and book go on to outline some of the problems caused by 'hitching the Gothic's wagon to feminism's star', in Fitzgerald's words, discussing debates of the 1990s in detail, and asking whether there is still a place for 'Female Gothic'. All the essays critically examine the use of this term. Diana Wallace's essay, for example, analyses the persistent interest in Gothic metaphors associated with women—hauntings, imprisonments, graves—not only within late eighteenth-century culture but also in modern critical theories of the Gothic. Robert Miles similarly revisits Moers and examines the centrality of 'Mother Radcliff' in conceptualizing female Gothic; Angela Wright argues for a slightly different, non-Radcliffean, vision, based on Isabella's voracious and uncritical reading of the Gothic in *Northanger Abbey*. Key tropes and recurrent themes are critically examined—Alison Milbank looks at the figure of 'the bleeding nun' as a way of understanding the female grotesque; Marie Mulvey Roberts examines Bluebeard from Austen to Carter; Avril Horner and Sue Zlotnik read Daphne du Maurier and Iris Murdoch in light of a female Gothic fascination with incest, and Andrew Smith places the work of Shirley Jackson in a larger context both of women's Gothic writing and of female Gothic criticism. Essays trace different traditions and adaptations of female Gothic: both Meredith Miller and Anya Heise-von der Lippe emphasize the ways in which female Gothic might be used to question racial and national identity, Miller in the context of Southern Gothic, and Heise-von der Lippe through a rereading of Toni Morrison. Kirsti Bohata explores new perspectives on nationhood offered by anglophone Welsh female Gothic writing, and Carol Margaret Davison's closing essay chooses Iain Banks's *The Wasp Factory* and Alisdair Gray's *Poor Things* as explorations—vexed, comic, and dark—of Scottish nationality and independence. Early in the collection, Fitzgerald begins her essay with the provocation, 'does Female Gothic have anything left to offer?' This volume, informed by issues of historicism, national identity, sexuality, and race, moving across periods and cultures, proves that it still does have its uses: the book is a valuable contribution to our understanding of a key critical tradition. In a related article, JoEllen DeLucia, 'From the Female Gothic to a Feminist Theory of History: Ann Radcliffe and the Scottish Enlightenment' (*ECent* 50[2009] 101–15), offers a very useful progression of the debate around female Gothic: her work, like earlier feminist criticism, analyses 'the uneven and repetitious qualities' of Radcliffe's work, reading this not in psychological terms but 'as attempts to theorize gaps in eighteenth-century narratives of historical progress'. She strives to historicize and contextualize such moments against Scottish Enlightenment thought, and, in particular, stadial theory. Like much of the best scholarship on Romantic novels this year, DeLucia attempts to place work of the 1790s in a longer eighteenth-century context, and suggests that Radcliffe's fiction might be read not simply as registering historical shifts, but as a 'meta-commentary on the problems involved in producing history'. A different angle on female Gothic is taken by Sandro Jung in 'Sarah Pearson's Gothic Verse Tales' (*WW* 16[2009] 392–407). Jung explores the little-known work of Pearson, a domestic servant from Sheffield, who wrote essays, a novel, and several verse tales: Jung's essay focuses on the verse tale, and Pearson's poetic experimentation, but is useful for a deeper understanding of women's writing in different Gothic genres.

The anti-Catholic and anti-clerical sentiment expressed by Gothic novels has become a critical commonplace of Gothic studies: the description of the 'despotic sway' of superstition in Madrid which opens *The Monk*, for example, is very often cited as a key to understanding the anti-Catholicism of the Gothic, along with corrupt monks, sensual nuns, and the horrors of the Inquisition. But in an important book which encourages a new approach to scholarship and teaching of the Gothic, Maria Purves argues that we should reread attitudes to Catholicism, both literary and social, in the Romantic period. *The Gothic and Catholicism* begins by taking apart some key critical views on literary Gothic's anti-Catholic sensibilities; most importantly, perhaps, Victor Sage's assertion that the whole rise of Gothic might be linked to the 'growth of the campaign for Catholic Emancipation from the 1770s onwards' (p. 8). Purves takes this argument seriously, and convincingly refutes it. In her first chapter she examines attitudes to Catholicism in the late eighteenth century, looking closely at the Gordon Riots but showing that this should not preclude our awareness of sympathy towards Catholics in the period, helped along by Burkean Church and King factions who painted Dissent as the real danger. When Burke spoke in Parliament in sympathy for the suffering of Roman Catholic clergy in France in May 1791, 'the House cheered in support' (p. 31), and Purves shows how this sympathy manifested itself towards French émigré clergy in the 1790s. She cites the establishment of monastic communities in England—Ushaw College, Ampleforth, and Downside Abbey, for instance—and local interest in and kindness towards émigré monks and nuns. How might this fit, then, with the 'anti-Catholic sensibilities' of Gothic novels? Having begun with a firm historical grounding, Purves then moves to examine a large range of Gothic literature, extending back into the early eighteenth century (the treatment of the Abelard and Heloise story; Yorick's exchange with the Franciscan monk) before focusing on turn-of-the-century authors and themes. Major authors, including Horace Walpole, Matthew Lewis, and Ann Radcliffe, are examined in detail, alongside novels we now know less well, such as Regina Maria Roche's *The Children of the Abbey*. In Roche's work Sister Mary is hardly a 'delicate Eloisan maiden... but a robust middle-aged Irishwoman', rosy and healthy, and her abbey is a happy and bustling place which turns our Gothic expectations upside down: the contemporary popularity of Roche's novel shows us how positive representations of the Catholic were circulated and well received. Roche, argues Purves, 'was writing for an audience which she knew would be receptive to pro-Catholic sentiment' (p. 123). This is a small example of the ways in which Purves attempts to recontextualize and reassess our understanding of Gothic Catholicism: the cumulative effect of her book is deeply persuasive. It has implications beyond Gothic scholarship, too: using recent work by scholars such as Robert Ryan, Purves argues for a more detailed reading of religion in contemporary scholarship, 'a more extensive treatment of religious topics in eighteenth-century texts is key to an enhanced and nuanced understanding of those texts, their genres and the cultural and historical moments they describe' (p. 209). Her book shows the rich possibilities of such an approach.

There were several other articles and teaching resources relating to the Gothic which should be noted this year. 'Is Nothing Sacred? Christ's Harrowing through Lewis's Gothic Lens' by Melanie Griffin (*OrbisLit* 64[2009] 167–74) makes a good case for reading the rescue of Agnes alongside Christ's Harrowing of Hell, and offers an interesting interpretation of Lewis's *The Monk*. Some of the larger ideas about 'the anti-Catholic sentiment so prevalent in Protestant Reformation dialogue' might, however, be usefully questioned by *The Gothic and Catholicism*, and it will be interesting to see how Gothic scholarship reacts to Purves's findings. Elsewhere, Marilyn Brock, in 'Desire and Fear: Feminine Abjection in the Gothic Fiction of Mary Wollstonecraft' (in Brock, ed., *From Wollstonecraft to Stoker: Essays on Gothic and Victorian Sensation Fiction*, pp. 17–29), uses Kristeva to explore Wollstonecraft's use of Gothic, focusing on the 'subjugated female body' in works such as *Wrongs of Woman*. Tom J. Hillard, in '"Deep into that darkness peering": An Essay on Gothic Nature' (*Isle* 16[2009] 685–95), asks 'what might a Gothic lens bring to ecocriticism?': looking at the darker side of Gothic nature writing might, he suggests, highlight our own fears, doubts, and phobias. Meanwhile, of particular interest for those teaching the Gothic, a revised edition of *The Handbook of the Gothic*, edited by Marie Mulvey-Roberts, was issued this year; previously *The Handbook to Gothic Literature*, the new title reflects the increasing interdisciplinarity of the subject, and the considerable expansion of the field since its original publication in 1998. The *Handbook* now includes additional entries on Wilkie Collins and Charlotte Dacre, as well as twentieth-century authors such as Susan Hill, Shirley Jackson, and Stephen King, with a new filmography and list of 'Gothicized websites', and still boasts an enviable list of international contributors.

James Hogg was very well served in 2009 by a collection of essays edited by Sharon Alker and Holly Faith Nelson, *James Hogg and the Literary Marketplace: Scottish Romanticism and the Working-Class Author* (also discussed in section 4 of this chapter). This begins with an overview of Hogg's shifting critical fortunes, and of the ways in which he has become recognized as vital to an expanded understanding of Romanticism, which encompasses Scottish culture, labouring-class aesthetics, and periodical writing. The essays in this volume, on his songs, verse, novels, and *Blackwood's* writing, 'establish that these works deserve a central place in Romantic studies', and also, as Alker and Nelson note, 'demonstrate that they anticipate and address many of the recent concerns voiced in contemporary discussions of literature' (p. 12), concerns which might include our readings of oral culture, nationalism and colonialism, class, history, and historicism. The essays on Hogg's poetry and songs are addressed elsewhere in this section, but I will just comment on some new readings of Hogg's novels, and identity as a novelist, which emerge in this collection. Peter Garside, in 'Hogg and Scott's "First Meeting" and the Politics of Literary Friendship' (pp. 21–42), examines narratives and images of the encounter between the two novelists, tracing changing critical appraisals of their work and the dynamics of their relationship. The relationship between Hogg and Scott, and their differing attitudes towards oral culture, are also discussed in Suzanne Gilbert's 'James Hogg and the Authority of Tradition' (pp. 93–110). Meiko O'Halloran, in 'National Discourse or Discord? Transformations of *The Family Legend* by Baillie, Scott, and Hogg' (pp. 43–56), gives an absorbing account of the motif of the 'family legend', 'a piece of primitive Highland history', and its different incarnations from Joanna Baillie's stage production of Hogg's *Blackwood's* story, 'A Horrible Instance of the Effects of Clanship' and his *Tales of the Wars of Montrose*. Hogg's renderings of the story, informed by oral storytelling and folklore culture, intensify the violent energies which Baillie and Scott had struggled to keep under control: his ominous prose asserts 'the continuing potency of primitive native traditions' (p. 55). O'Halloran's attention to Hogg's sources fits well alongside H.B. de Groot's 'The Labourer and Literary Tradition: James Hogg's Early Reading and its Impact on him as a Writer' (pp. 81–92). This traces the literary lineage of Hogg's novels back to *Don Quixote* and *Tristram Shandy*, and argues for 'an alternative tradition' of the novel which might include Rabelais, Sterne, Flann O'Brien—and Hogg. Hogg's place in the literary marketplace is analysed by Thomas C. Richardson in 'James Hogg and *Blackwood's Edinburgh Magazine*: Buying and Selling the Ettrick Shepherd' (pp. 185–200), and Janette Currie explores his American reputation. There are also new readings of Hogg's novels. Ian Duncan sets *Confessions of a Justified Sinner* in the context of 'the discourses of the so-called Scottish Enlightenment', showing how it criticizes Adam Smith's concept of sympathy. Instead, its portrayal of fanaticism and dangerous religious enthusiasm might reflect Dugald Stewart's fears about the 'contagious', 'infectious' nature of 'sympathetic imitation', and the novel might thus be seen as a critique of modernity itself. Gillian Hughes, in 'Robert Wringhim's Solitude' (pp. 71–80), offers a more psychological reading, considering Hogg's ownership of Zimmermann's *On Solitude*, and suggesting that the treatise might feed into the novel's examination of 'the breakdown of personality under conditions of extreme social isolation'. Essays by Graham Tulloch (pp. 157–174) and Caroline McCracken Flesher (pp. 175–184) discuss the complex work *The Three Perils of Man*: as McCracken Flesher suggests, this is a narrative of excess, 'overfull of plots and of people', but opening up pathways to a broader understanding of nation and history (p. 184).

A special issue of *Modern Language Quarterly* (*MLQ* 70[2009]) was a rich collection of recent approaches to Walter Scott and his wider context. Janet Sorensen, in 'Alternative Antiquarianisms of Scotland and the North' (*MLQ* 70[2009] 415–41), explored the ways in which collections of ballads and songs by Scottish and northern song collectors might be presented and viewed. Samuel Baker, in 'Scott's Stoic Characters: Ethics, Sentiment, and Irony in *The Antiquary*, *Guy Mannering*, and "the Author of *Waverley*"' (*MLQ* 70[2009] 443–71), suggests that not only are Scott's characters, Guy Mannering and Jonathan Oldbuck, Stoics, so too is Scott himself, albeit a compromised one. Ina Ferris's '"On the Borders of Oblivion": Scott's Historical Novel and the Modern Time of the Remnant' (*MLQ* 70[2009] 473–94) reads the 'figure of the remnant' in Scott's historical novels as a way of understanding disconnections in the present. Michael Gamer's '*Waverley* and the Object of (Literary) History' (*MLQ* 70[2009] 495–525) questions the claim that *Waverley* might be 'the first historical novel', suggesting that this status is largely self-created by Scott, and reading the work as not simply historical, but also literary-historical. Another good insight into a range of current approaches to Scott was the collection of essays edited by Evan Gottlieb and Ian Duncan, *Approaches to Teaching Scott's Waverley Novels*. The book is divided into two parts, with the first, 'Materials', giving an overview of critical backgrounds and editions, and the second, 'Approaches', containing essays on the history and language of Scott's novels as well as questions of Romantic authorship and intertextuality. There are also some useful case studies on the particular challenges of teaching Scott in diverse ways—alongside Austen, for example, or in the context of queer theory, or to open up questions of gender and multiculturalism.

Roderick S. Speer's *Byron and Scott: The Waverley Novels and Historical Engagement* charts Byron's 'extraordinary enthusiasm' for Scott's work. Often seen as opposites in the nineteenth century, Speer shows why and how we should read the two authors together, discussing their meeting in 1815, and their subsequent relationship, literary and affectionate. This is not simply a biographical account, although the study does shed light on an enduring friendship—it is a subtle reading of the ways in which Byron's life and work might have been shaped by Scottian ideals. Scott, Speer argues, 'put Byron in touch with the positive ideals of his boyhood, ideals essential for Byron's turn to action' (p. x); in turn, Byron's historical dramas, *Don Juan*, and *The Island* may owe surprising debts to Scott's heroes. Claire Lamont offers an insightful reading of Wordsworth's literary relationship with Scott in 'Wordsworth, *The White Doe of Rylstone*: A Reading with Reference to Scott' (*ChLB* 145[2009] 24–33). This sets Wordsworth's long poem—seldom, as Lamont admits, 'a favourite'—alongside both *The Lay of the Last Minstrel* and *Waverley*, showing how comparison with Scott might bring out some of the qualities of Wordsworth's narrative verse.

Erik Simpson's '"A good one though rather for the foreign market": Mercenary Writing and Scott's *Quentin Durward*' (*SiR* 48[2009] 667–85) suggests that Scott's treatment of mercenary fighting might shed light on his attitude to mercenary writing. Scott resists writing simply with profit in mind, shows Simpson, and instead, in an attempt to negotiate with and 'justify' economic ambition, constructs an image of the writer as 'latter-day minstrel'. Simon J. White, in '*Ivanhoe*, Robin Hood and the Pentridge Rising' (*NCC* 31[2009] 209–24), reads Scott's twelfth-century England against the turmoil of the 1810s. White notes that Scott deliberately associates *Ivanhoe* with 1817, and therefore draws out telling parallels, both explicit and implicit, with the Pentridge Rising of that year. The links in some ways 'represent the power of the people as a threat', but, argues White, this threat 'strangely brings with it the seeds of political and social transformation'. Opening up this historical parallel might show us new ways of understanding the ambiguities of Scott's novel.

There was stimulating research on the afterlives of Scott: Victorian, American, and cinematic. Rosemary Mitchell's 'Charlotte M. Yonge: Reading, Writing, and Recycling Historical Fiction in the Nineteenth Century' (*NCC* 31[2009] 31–43) is a particularly interesting case study of one of Yonge's lesser-known novels, *Chantry House* [1886], and its connections with Scott's *Talisman*: her exploration of allusion and intertextuality succeeds in reconstructing 'something of the early Victorian upper and middleclass reader's reading experience of, interaction with, and utilisation of historical fiction'. 'Scott's Victorian Readers' (*NCC* 31[2009] 19–29), by Annika Bautz, explores the widespread and persistent popularity of Scott's novels across the century, and Emily B. Todd's 'Establishing Routes for Fiction in the United States: Walter Scott's Novels and the Early Nineteenth-Century American Publishing Industry' (*BoH* 12[2009] 100–28) traces the immense success of the Waverley novels in America. This, Todd argues, challenges 'not only the models we have for studying American literary history but also the models we have for studying the history of the book'. She outlines what we might gain from a global perspective on book history, and uncovers a new narrative of publishing history through examining the transatlantic reception and consumption of Scott's novels. Juliet Shields, in 'Savage and Scott-ish Masculinity in *The Last of the Mohicans* and *The Prairie*: James Fenimore Cooper and the Diasporic Origins of American Identity' (*NCL* 64[2009] 137–62), begins her comparison by citing the *North American Review* of 1822, dubbing James Fenimore Cooper 'the Scott of America'. While Cooper may have resented this, Shields, through close reading of the depiction of Scots in two Cooper novels, shows that he was nevertheless indebted to Scott. Taking his model from Scott, Shields suggests, Cooper uses the historical romance to help form national identity, and gradually constructs 'a genealogy of American identity determined by cultural appropriation rather than by blood inheritance'. Jonathan Stubbs, meanwhile, in 'Hollywood's Middle Ages: The Development of *Knights of the Round Table* and *Ivanhoe*, 1935–53' (*Exemplaria* 21[2009] 398–417), uses different versions of screenplays to examine Hollywood's reinterpretation of Scott's vision of medieval Britain to suit changing political contexts.

Julia V. Douthwaite and Daniel Richter examine a strange precursor to Mary Shelley's novel in 'The Frankenstein of the French Revolution: Nogaret's Automaton Tale of 1790' (*ERR* 20[2009] 381–411): François-Félix Nogaret's *Le Miroir des événemens actuels, ou la belle au plus offrant: Histoire à deux visages* (The Looking Glass of Actuality, or Beauty to the Highest Bidder: A Two-Faced Tale [1790]). The story features a contest in which six inventors compete to win a woman's love—the fifth of these inventors, 'a Gaul named Wak-wik-vauk-on-son-frankénsteïn (shortly thereafter nicknamed "Frankénsteïn")' creates a wonderful automaton flautist; the sixth presents a female automaton 'demonstrating powers of speech and locomotion and bearing precious gifts'. Douthwaite and Richter point out that their purpose is not to prove 'Shelley's debt to Nogaret, but rather to share with readers a constellation of themes and ideas relating to artificial creation and the French Revolution'. Nogaret's automatons are kindly and docile, used for benevolent social (and political) purposes: the optimism of 1790 has dwindled by the time we reach Shelley's lonely creature. Jeanne M. Britton's 'Novelistic Sympathy in Mary Shelley's *Frankenstein*' (*SiR* 48[2009] 3–22) looks at the ways in which Shelley might extend Adam Smith's account of sympathy through her narrative techniques in the novel. Although sympathy may not always survive in face-to-face exchanges, the written word—and specifically 'the transcribed narrative'—compensates for such failures. In 'Time and the Sibyl in Mary Shelley's *The Last Man*' (*SNNTS* 41[2009] 141–56), Timothy Ruppert casts the novel as 'a capstone achievement in British visionary literature'. Ruppert revisits recent critical perspectives on *The Last Man* which see it as an imperial critique and a register of contemporary anxieties. He argues, rather, for a positive reading of the novel as a prophecy of hope, an act of faith in the transformative power of imagination.

Two intriguing articles took *Valperga* and *Matilda* as a starting point for wider investigations of Romantic attitudes. Sonia Hofkosh's 'Euthanasia's Handkerchief; or, The Object at the End of History' (*ERR* 20[2009] 689–97) starts with a focus on the white handkerchief washed up at the close of *Valperga*, which tells us, indirectly, of Euthanasia's fate. Hofkosh looks closely at the handkerchief—'in its knot were a few golden hairs' and also knotted up within it is an allusion to *Othello*—to emphasize the power of the mundane, ordinary object in Romanticism. Here, the object offers 'a way to think about the representation of history in Shelley's novel', and the history of representation itself, since it is at once palpable, yet unknowable. Joel Faflak, in 'The Inoperative Community of Romantic Psychiatry' (*ERR* 20[2009] 721–31), reads *Matilda* in terms of the rise of psychiatry. This is examined firstly through a reading of Wordsworth's depressed figure Margaret in *The Ruined Cottage* in the 1790s, alongside the first emergence of psychiatry, and then through a reading of *Matilda* itself, product of the Regency, and a resistance, Faflak argues, to 'the post-1790s paradigm of morally useful man'.

Perhaps the last word on the Romantic novel this year should go to a pair of articles which suggest (and contest) further critical approaches. What to do with our new wealth of statistical and bibliographical knowledge about the

Romantic novel? Franco Moretti's 'Style, Inc.: Reflections on Seven Thousand Titles (British Novels, 1740–1850)' (*CritI* 36[2009], 134–58) draws on the work of James Raven and Peter Garside to argue for the explanatory power of 'abstract models' in dealing with such huge sets of data. Looking at the metamorphosis of eighteenth-century titles, as they shrink across the century, Moretti shows that 'the market expands, and titles contract'; important, argues Moretti, because 'readers, faced with this type of title, have to change their expectations: the first thing they are told about the novel asks them to imagine, not so much a story, but *the point* of the story: the point of the story as a single, unifying concept'. Quantitative stylistics might allow us to understand such units of language across the whole field of the British novel 1740–1850, and how 'powerfully they contribute to the construction of meaning'. But Katie Trumpener's perceptive response in the same issue raises some productive difficulties with such a statistical approach. She makes the case for an equally important approach to the novel, arguing 'rather for the continued usefulness of older comparative methods, particularly those associated with the discipline of comparative literature'. Trumpener's essay begins with an image of herself as teenage bookshop browser, thinking about the difference between German and American titles, and outlines the continuing need for the 'distinctly informal, unsystematic' and cross-cultural response of the individual reader. She calls for 'Browsing in addition to quantification; incessant rather than distant reading', and concludes that 'the unsystematic nature of our discipline is actually its salvation'. Her conclusion is borne out by the variety, excitement, and range of current scholarly approaches to the deeply unsystematic genre of the Romantic novel.

4. Poetry

[In this section David Stewart covers poets from A to J; Christopher Machell covers poets from K to Z. Blake is covered by Jason Whittaker.]

It was once rare that studies of Romantic poetry discussed either form or organicism except to debunk the terms, but two studies this year took both very seriously. The first, Denise Gigante's *Life: Organic Form and Romanticism* (also discussed in section 1 above), begins with a discussion of them in scientific discourse in the late seventeenth and early eighteenth centuries. Theories of the 'Epigenetic', or 'self-shaping' (p. 26), force had important political and aesthetic ramifications. Discussions like these, in which questions of organicism structured an approach to scholarship which connected spheres of influence to each other, ended, for Gigante, with the development of cell theory in the 1830s. Her book is a call for a return to the enthusiasms of a model of thinking that conceives of Romanticism as 'a genuinely cross-disciplinary, transnational approach to living form' (p. 35), going against 'decades of historical challenge to the rubric of Romanticism as a shared intellectual project' (p. 3). She discovers that unity in a shared commitment to vitality. Accordingly, this is a rather brave attempt to reshape thinking about poetry in the period, and an important reorientation of the growing return to formalism in studies of Romantic poetry. The 'era of vitalism' begins at the earliest reaches of the period, with Christopher Smart's highly idiosyncratic *Jubilate Agno* [1759–63]. A chapter on this poem is paired with one on Blake's *Jerusalem*, both of which, straining at the limits of the 'form' of poetry, nonetheless represent a form of epigenesis that persists because of their 'disjointed textual and visual elements' (p. 108). The final two chapters focus on Shelley's 'The Witch of Atlas' and Keats's *Lamia*. These poems are far more stable formally (using ottava rima and couplets respectively), but, as Gigante demonstrates, they can be read as part of an aesthetic education that sought to rework 'power in all its relations' (p. 159). Both poems contain monstrous female characters at their centre, but that monstrosity is not an emanation of fear but an embrace of 'uncontainable vitality' (p. 207) that, as this significant study suggests, was at the centre of political, aesthetic, and scientific thinking in the period.

The second book, David Fairer's *Organising Poetry: The Coleridge Circle, 1790–1798*, is tighter in its historical and literary focus but offers a more detailed and cogent thesis. The notion of the organic has been a problematic part of a definition of Romanticism. The power of the imagination to draw contradictions into a transcendent unity has been characterized as a typically Romantic evasion. Fairer opposes this notion in three ways. First, he does not attempt to offer an account of 'Romanticism', but of the poetry produced by a particular group of poets (principally Coleridge, Southey, Wordsworth, Thelwall, Lamb, and Lloyd) in the 1790s. He also disputes the conclusions of those critics who would blame these poets for their political 'evasions'. But his biggest claim is a redefinition of the term 'organic'. Rather than seeing these poets as embodying a radical (or Romantic) break with the past, Fairer uncovers a poetics which values continuity and growth both in its relationship with other contemporary poets but also with the poetic past. Thomas Warton, the author of the first narrative history of English poetry, is a hero of the book, becoming a 'channel of communication between young poets and their literary past' (p. 106). These poets, rather than breaking with the past, might be considered as being 'rooted in the *genial*, the creatively sustaining climate' (p. 12) of the eighteenth century. This is very much a book of the 'long eighteenth century'. Fairer's formidable knowledge of eighteenth-century poetry allows him to discover the threads of allusion between his circle and writers as diverse as Sterne, Locke, Burke, Cowper, Warton, Chatterton, and Bowles. The major achievement of the book lies in the cogency with which Fairer argues for the subtle interweaving of the poetic past into the poetry of his key writers. This requires not just a very wide knowledge, but also a deft touch, which Fairer employs superbly. There is a brilliant reading of *The Ruined Cottage* as a georgic rather than pastoral poem that allows Wordsworth to 'combine a language of alienation and loss with one of growth and continuity' (p. 275). The difficulties and complexities of shared projects are wonderfully unravelled by focusing on the difference between Lamb's method of 'unresolved wondering—the thread that holds his fragile text together' (p. 215) and Coleridge's mistrust of it. There are also excellent chapters on Southey's Wartonian sense of literary history and Coleridge's relationship with Chatterton. The final chapter reconsiders the apparently evasive politics of 'Fears in Solitude', contextualizing the poem thoroughly with reference to Sheridan's speech in Parliament which made 'strategic retreat' an 'urgent topic' (p. 298). Fairer describes the conventional critique of Coleridge's patriotism at this moment as 'extraordinary' (p. 307). It is perhaps this strain of the book that will make it most controversial. Fairer's organic tradition is consciously Burkean, and deliberately resists a Paineite sense of the revolutionary 'moment'. This, he argues, is a rather more 'dynamic and committed' (p. 60) position than has been granted. But it nonetheless rejects a dominant strand of Romantic criticism. It is all the more powerful for that. This is a deft, rigorous, scholarly study. It is the most significant book published on Romantic poetry this year, and it is likely to have a substantial influence.

Much work this year focused on issues of celebrity and the afterlives of the poets. Julian North's *The Domestication of Genius: Biography and the Romantic Poet* brought these two concerns together in a consideration of the biographies of the Romantic poets published between the 1820s and the early 1840s. These biographies have often provoked hostility in both poets and critics, and North's book is an eloquent call for their reappraisal. The dominant model provided by Boswell's *Life of Johnson* is placed alongside eighteenth-century collective biographies of women to establish the association with a middle-class marketplace that '[alarmed] the Romantic poets' (p. 11). Biography thus comes to represent a peculiarly vexed form for male poets. As North points out, biographies 'underwrote and perpetuated the Romantic identification of the author with his work' (p. 31) while also threatening the autonomy of that creation by writing the poet's life for him. Moreover, by insisting on the domestic nature of that life, biography feminized the poet, and brought him down to earth. Byron, of course, did much himself to draw attention to his domestic entanglements, and in a subtle reading of his work alongside that of his biographers (particularly Thomas Moore), North suggests how 'Byronism produced and was produced by' biography (p. 100). Victorian biographies of Shelley have often been blamed for doing mischief to the poet's reputation. But they were not, for North, simply idealizing mystifications but critical engagements with a sentimental Shelley already present in popular culture. De Quincey's notorious accounts of the Lakers in *Tait's Magazine* are read in the context of that magazine's appeal to a female audience. The final chapter considers Lives of Hemans and Landon. If the poets were wary of biography because 'to domesticate was to democratize' (p. 6), such concerns took a twist with female poets. These biographies drew on the techniques adopted by biographers of their male compeers, but suggested the superiority of the poetesses in their ability to actively engage with readers.

Eric Eisner's *Nineteenth-Century Poetry and Literary Celebrity* discusses the culture of literary celebrity that arises after Byron's sensational arrival into the literary market. Eisner argues that the common assumption that the period's poets were actuated by a desire to escape the enervating effects of celebrity is mistaken. In studies of Byron, Keats, Shelley, Landon, and Barrett Browning, Eisner shows how these poets exploited a system which allowed readers to encounter poets through 'seductive forms of literary presence' (p. 13). The celebrity industry, with its reviews, its fan letters, and its celebrity biographies, is discussed in ample detail. But Eisner does not let this historical scaffolding obscure the poetry itself. Instead, he offers a series of subtly argued case studies of individual poems which suggest the way that poets encountered, manipulated, and engaged with the system of celebrity. Byron provides a model for all subsequent poets, but even in his 'Fare Thee Well' he offers 'an effect of immediacy' (p. 29) which self-consciously reflects on the conflation of public and private the occasion of the poem produces. *Don Juan* takes this a step further, engaging with readers not by ignoring the culture of celebrity, but in placing reader and writer in 'a shared location within print culture' (p. 39). The *Adonais* myth of Keats, dying to live in posterity, has, for Eisner, obscured Keats's 'sophisticated negotiation' in poems like *Sleep and Poetry* and *The Fall of Hyperion* with 'mass-market structures' (p. 52). A pair of chapters on Shelley consider *The Cenci* as a model for Shelley's thinking about the relationship between 'authorial charisma' and 'readerly fascination' (p. 69) before discussing how that very fascination structured thinking about Shelley's authorial presence in the Victorian period. A brilliant chapter on Landon suggests the ways in which she swerves from a Byronic model of sympathetic feeling, profoundly questioning its implications and considering its effects on the professional female author. This is a subtle, intelligent book that revitalizes the poetry under discussion. It is also an important reflection on the continuing significance of the figure of the author, and the relationship between critics and fans.

Maria Schoina's *Romantic 'Anglo-Italians': Configurations of Identity in Byron, the Shelleys, and the Pisan Circle* offers a timely and subtly argued consideration of the later Romantic poets' engagement with questions of place and identity. The author develops a sophisticated theoretical apparatus in order to do so. Italy played a crucial imaginative role in British cultural thought. Schoina cogently suggests that 'imaginative geography affects real geography' (p. 24), and she demonstrates the unusual interpenetration of the real and the imaginative in the period. The post-Waterloo opening up of the Continent to British travellers provoked anxiety and excitement in equal measure. On the one hand, superficial travellers were seen to have failed to appreciate the true charms of Italy; but this may not have been as bad as 'going native'. The hyphenated status, 'Anglo-Italian', that Mary Shelley proposes moves between these two poles, retaining an 'Anglo' superiority while also fully immersing oneself in the other culture. The literary products of this 'betweenness' (p. 62) bore the marks of this instability. A brilliant reading of a *Capriccio* by William Marlow focuses on the sense of flux that water introduces into many similar poetic juxtapositions of the English and the Italian, such as Percy Shelley's *Lines Written Among the Euganean Hills* and the conclusion to Byron's *Childe Harold*, canto IV. Byron seemed to contemporaries the most 'authentic' Anglo-Italian, and he exemplifies the dynamic that Schoina identifies. For him, the presence of the masquerade typifies his experience of identity in Italy, involving 'inclusion and exclusion, identification and detachment' (p. 91). In discussion of Percy Shelley and Leigh Hunt's attempt to construct a Pisan circle, Schoina notes how significant it is that very few Pisans were involved. Shelley, like Hunt, addressed an Anglo-Italian, not an Italian, audience. There are some important readings of individual poems, but the real strength of this study lies in the range of Schoina's erudition and her problematization and historicization of theories of place and identity. Paul Stock also considered this circle in 'Liberty and Independence: The Shelley–Byron Circle and the State(s) of Europe' (*Romanticism* 15[2009] 121–30). Their commitment to concepts like freedom and liberty were complicated by their understanding of patriotism. The circle, Stock shows, was divided between an understanding of Europe connected by liberty, and one in which individual states expressed their freedom through their separation from each other.

In the rapidly growing field of Romantic women writers, Stephen C. Behrendt, in *British Women Poets and the Romantic Writing Community*, presents a bold and compelling study of British female poets between 1770 and 1835. Justifying his broad demarcation of the Romantic period, Behrendt points out that he has deliberately selected the start date 'to include the early works of poets (like Mary Robinson, Anna Seward, and Eliza Ryves) who were already active before the more familiar starting dates in 1780s' (p. 29). Behrendt's aim in this volume is not simply to disrupt the traditionally male-dominated canon of the Romantic period, but also to weaken the rigid and homogenous stability of what has, until recently, constituted the Romantic genre. This position is summarized in Behrendt's introduction, where he states that 'The plain fact is that it [the Romantic period] was a poetry-mad era . . . One result was an extraordinary range of aesthetic quality in poetry that ranged from the splendid to the truly wretched' (p. 13). Here, Behrendt suggests a heterogeneity to Romantic-era writing that has not yet been adequately explored, resulting in an unbalanced, male-dominated canon. He points to this as he describes the process of writing his volume: 'it became clear to me that the road lay through a literary and cultural landscape that is still being remapped in a number of important ways' (p. 28). Over the course of six chapters, then, Behrendt begins to redress the balance, although he rightly acknowledges that the adequate remapping of the Romantic canon is a project not likely to be completed in the near future. His methodological approach, interestingly, is three-tiered, examining various poets and their works from the perspectives of British radicalism, questions of genre and poetic form, and the discussion of Irish and Scottish poets as specifically Irish and Scottish, as opposed to the blanket term 'British'.

This intriguing approach means that Behrendt is able to tailor his analyses to the needs of the poets, thereby avoiding the pitfalls of rigid generic constraints that he sets himself against in his introduction. Chapter 1, for example examines radical female writers such as Wollstonecraft and Mary Robinson. Behrendt argues that despite scholars' reluctance 'to acknowledge either the nature or the extent of Romantic-era women writers' involvement in radical politics . . . many women laboured against' the growing climate of reactionary politics and policy (p. 37). Crucially, he positions the poetry of these and other radical writers at the centre of a public discourse on contemporary politics, and he argues convincingly and clearly that 'the Romantic period may mark the last time in British literary and cultural history in which poetry stood in this fashion at the crossroads of cultural discourse' (pp. 41–2). In contrast to the context-centric approach of chapter 1, chapters 3 and 4 of this volume concentrate on the ways that female Romantic poets worked and experimented with poetic form, and the contrast between privately written and publicly published poems, within a social and political framework. Behrendt's varied yet coherent approach results in not only a bold and important study of women writers in the Romantic era, but also an extremely enjoyable and compelling discussion.

In a new and groundbreaking study, *Rhyming Reason*, Michelle Faubert examines the poetry of Romantic-era psychologists—a body of work that Faubert posits is virtually unknown, let alone sufficiently understood. In her preface, Faubert sets to 'show how psychologists used literary methods to develop their professional identities and psychological theories', an investigation which ultimately 'leads us to far-ranging new insights about Romantic-era subjectivity and the relation of disciplinary power to literature' (p. xi). In this section, Faubert justifies her Foucauldian theoretical approach convincingly, and she is successful both in establishing a sense of canon-expansion, which she argues is 'unavoidably influenced by Foucauldian theory', and in moving scholarly discussion forward from recent, related studies such as Philip W. Martin's *Mad Women in Romantic Writing*, or Allan Ingram's *Patterns of Madness in the Eighteenth Century*.

Faubert introduces her study proper with a brief, but welcome, overview of the early history of psychology in England, stating that the field began there during the period 1790–1850 (p. 2). She argues that early psychologists 'regarded their roles as public, in a way that necessitated the use of an appealing form of writing, specifically poetry', and suggests that 'the field of psychology required, to some extent, the poetic medium for communicating ideas, just as statisticians need graphs' (p. 4). 'For the psychologist-poets', Faubert posits, 'medicine is not framed by poetry . . . Rather, poetry is framed by medicine' (p. 4). Chapter 1 yields further intriguing analysis, with Faubert's investigation of Erasmus Darwin, James Beattie, and Nathaniel Cotton, positioned as psychologist-poets. She argues in this chapter that Romanticism was 'synchronous with the reification of the discipline of psychology' (p. 29). Part of her aim in this chapter is to establish a 'pre-Romantic scene' in which the tradition of the psychologist-poet was developed. She begins by examining Darwin, because, as she states, 'Darwin's verse serves as a good introduction because he represents the Scottish Enlightenment idea; of the scientist as polymath . . . his verse shows[s] the broad range of scientific interests for which students of the Scottish Enlightenment are celebrated' (p. 29). Furthermore, she argues in this chapter that the liberal atmosphere of the Scottish Enlightenment was essential in fostering the psychologist-poet, pointing out that 'Darwin, like so many of his fellow students in Scotland and psychologist-poets of the Romantic period, was radical in his politics'.

Further on in her study, Faubert turns to the psychologists Thomas Trotter, William Perfect, and Thomas Beddoes by arguing that they 'expand our notions of the role of the psychologist in Romantic-era culture'. Here, she posits that 'Perfect, Beddoes and Trotter show their indebtedness to the distinctly democratic culture of the Scottish Enlightenment . . . by addressing in poetry and prose the concerns of the wider population and less wealthy members of British society' (p. 117). Faubert concludes *Rhyming Reason* with the statement that the project's aim was to 'illustrate one aspect of the development of psychology that has been overlooked hitherto, an absence in intellectual history about the connections between literature and psychology' (p. 198). Undoubtedly, given the breadth of her analysis and success at breaking new scholarly ground, she has achieved this aim.

A new volume edited by Beth Lau, entitled *Fellow Romantics, Male and Female British Writers, 1790–1835*, brings together several fascinating essays that investigate the common ground male and female British writers shared in the Romantic period. Lau introduces the volume's major theme by suggesting that 'men and women of the late eighteenth and early nineteenth centuries participated in many of the same literary traditions ... they influenced and interacted with one another in dynamic and fruitful ways' (p. 1). This is a period where female writers of the Romantic period are rightly receiving increased critical attention, but Lau's volume brings value to recent studies in examining male and female authors as writing in a common marketplace of literary ideas and traditions.

The first chapter, for example, by Jacqueline M. Labbe and entitled 'Revisiting the Egotistical Sublime: Smith, Wordsworth, and the Romantic Dramatic Monologue' (pp. 17–38), suggests that 'the egoistic personae developed by William Wordsworth and Charlotte Smith function as [the] Romantic version' of the dramatic monologue (p. 17). Labbe notes that critics have not yet properly explored the importance of dramatic monologues in the autobiographical poems of the Romantic period, but that it is vital to realize that Wordsworth's 'persona is not nearly as coherent as it pretends to be' (p. 21). It is crucial, Labbe argues, to read the autobiographical as 'meta-autobiographical' in both the poetry of Wordsworth and Smith, as it 'means that we can interpret some of the "I"s of the *Elegiac Sonnets* and the *Lyrical Ballads* as a characterization of selfhood' (p. 23). Lau contributes her own essay in chapter 3, 'Romantic Ambivalence in *Frankenstein* and *The Rime of the Ancient Mariner*' (pp. 71–98). Here, Lau points out that despite Mary Shelley's 'conspicuous references' to Coleridge's poem in *Frankenstein*, few critics have examined or even observed 'Coleridge's importance for Mary Shelley' (p. 72). Pointedly, Lau suggests that the intertextual relationship between Coleridge and Shelley has been missed because critics have traditionally been more interested in Shelley's textual relationships with her family. Moreover, she argues that, in contrast to previous scholars' positions, 'Coleridge was a profoundly sympathetic and congenial figure to Mary Shelley whose beliefs, themes, and literary techniques resonated with and helped shape her own' (p. 74). Lau's intriguing discussion is followed by Susan J. Wolfson's chapter '"Something must be done": Shelley, Hemans, and the Flash of Revolutionary Female Violence' (pp. 99–122), which argues that 'Reading Hemans in relation to the male poets who long dominated the scholar's Romantic canon represents a new phase in criticism, not only of Hemans, but of Romantic-era women's poetry generally' (p. 123). In chapter 6, Julie Melnyk discusses the meeting of Wordsworth and Hemans as the meeting of the first and second generations of Romanticism, speaking to the major theme of the volume, not only of the shared poetic traditions across male and female writers, but also of shared generational traditions. Michael O' Neill contributes the penultimate chapter, in which he discusses the intertextual relations between Percy Shelley and Letitia Elizabeth Landon. O'Neill suggests that Landon's poetic imagination is 'profoundly intertextual . . . one saturated in the dominant tropes of the Romantic poets', focusing on 'Landon's intricate relationship with Shelley, a poet to whom she responds in a fluid and complex manner' (p. 211). Overall, *Fellow Romantics* presents a varied and consistently excellent collection of essays. In their variety, however, they are united by an important and fascinating discussion of the techniques, ideas, and literary traditions that male and female writers shared in the Romantic period in Britain.

Two strong essays on Romantic poetry appeared in Monika Class and Terry F. Robinson, eds., *Transnational England: Home and Abroad, 1780–1860*. Dana Van Kooy delivers a fascinating study, entitled 'Improvising on the Borders: Hellenism, History and Tragedy in Shelley's *Hellas*' (pp. 41–57). Van Kooy speaks to the growing interest in Romantic studies in genre, suggesting that 'improvisation provided a new model for mixing genres' (p. 42). In the same volume, Shelley Meagher discusses Thomas Moore's sense of a dual-national identity in her essay, 'Thomas Moore, Ireland and Islam' (pp. 233–48). Meagher suggests that Moore's dual identity 'plays a fundamental role in his *Irish Melodies*', and is particularly convincing in her argument that Moore's references to Islam 'evince a surprisingly deep and informed engagement with Islamic history' (p. 233).

There were three articles of general interest on Romantic poetry. Norbert Lennartz's 'Icarian Romanticism—The Motif of Soaring and Falling in British Romantic Poetry' (*Romanticism* 15[2009] 213–24) considers the forgotten figure of Icarus in Romantic poetry, focusing particularly on poems by Southey, Shelley, Wordsworth, and Byron. Mark J. Bruhn addresses an increasingly central aspect of Romantic studies in 'Romanticism and the Cognitive Science of Imagination' (*SiR* 48[2009] 543–64). Bruhn remarks on the unlikely similarity between Romantic theories of the imagination and contemporary cognitive science. Both, he notes, must depend on introspection as an empirical method. This makes Romantic cognitive experiments, notably poems by Wordsworth, Coleridge, and others, potentially relevant as 'prototypical examples and revealing limit cases' (p. 549) of contemporary theories of imagination. Laura Stocker's 'Sea, Self and Sustainability' (*LW* 6:i[2009] 133–41) offers an impressionistic appreciation of her own relationship with the sea as seen through the eyes of Coleridge, Shelley, and Byron. Her understanding of the poems is unfortunately rather naive.

In 'Fighting Words: Representing the Napoleonic Wars in the Poetry of Hemans and Barbauld' (*ERR* 20[2009] 327–43), Evan Gottlieb considers Anna Barbauld's *Eighteen Hundred and Eleven* in tandem with Felicia Hemans's rather more triumphalist *England and Spain*. Importantly, Gottlieb draws attention to the fact that they helped 'readers conceptualize Britain's place in the world at large' (p. 340) and so might be taken as a contribution to Romanticism's global perspective. Laura Mandell's 'Prayer, Feeling, Action: Anna Barbauld and the Public Worship Controversy' (*SECC* 38[2009] 117–42; also discussed briefly in Chapter XI) considers Barbauld's intervention in a debate in the early 1790s on the propriety of public prayer, most particularly her pamphlet addressed to Gilbert Wakefield. Mandell's article subtly explores Barbauld's public prose, and is particularly helpful in insisting on the diverse nature of Dissenting thought in this period. In 'Talking Animals and Reading Children: Teaching (Dis)obedience in John Aikin and Anna Barbauld's *Evenings at Home*' (*SiR* 48[2009] 641–66), Darren Howard offers an important consideration of the political efficacy of literature for children in the 1790s. He discovers, persuasively if surprisingly, that the 'politics of children's literature is inextricable from the way the genre depicts animals' (p. 644). Barbauld and Aikin train their young readers as social critics by encouraging them to consider sympathetically the animals they depict.

Robert Bloomfield's relationship with Romanticism was considered in a fine article by Tim Fulford, 'To "crown with glory the romantick scene": Robert Bloomfield's "To Immagination" and the Discourse of Romanticism' (*Romanticism* 15[2009] 181–200). Fulford presents the full text of Bloomfield's 1800 ode, newly edited from the manuscript. He then uses Bloomfield's decidedly 'Romantic' topic to question the assumptions both of those who excluded poets like Bloomfield from a conception of the Romantic and those who seek to reclaim him as an 'oppositional' labouring-class voice.

The year 2009 saw a flurry of book publications on Blake, one of the most erudite being *William Blake and the Art of Engraving* by Mei-Ying Sung. Sung begins with a simple observation that while Blake's technique of relief etching has attracted considerable academic interest in recent decades, his engraving processes—including, remarkably, the archive of surviving copper plates—have been much neglected. Sung suggests that the main reason for this is that engraving as a technology of reproduction is obsolete and consequently downgraded, but a (slightly) more positive reason may be that Blake's technique of relief etching was so innovative, particularly with regard to the illuminated books produced using this method, that it has been a much more obvious source of academic enquiry. Related to this is the much more ambivalent and frustrating factor that Blake as an artist is frequently treated as secondary to Blake as poet.

Sung's opening technical argument provides a deft and scholarly summary of a controversy that dogged Blake studies for several years (and which often appears opaque and esoteric to general appreciators of Blake's art) between Robert Essick, Joseph Viscomi, and Michael Phillips. She provides a usefully concise version of that controversy, with a conclusion that is rather damning towards Phillips while also observing that all experts involved confined themselves to the prints while ignoring—more or less completely—the thirty-eight copper plates that survive. It is by considering these artefacts in detail that Sung's work provides her most rigorous innovations in Blake studies, most notably how Blake had to work and rework his plates using a technique known as *repoussage*, as well as providing fascinating detours through subsequent experiments to renovate Blake's techniques by artists such as Ruthven Todd, Joan Miró, and William Stanley Hayter. In particular, she shows how the emphasis on relief etching as well as the experiments of the Surrealists has skewed our understanding of Blake's actual practice. Sung notes that differences in etching and engraving techniques could have a significant difference on the amount of correction required to complete a work, and this provides important context for her subsequent observations. Sung's careful examination indicates that 'the evidence of the plates and Blake's alterations to them shows not only the development of ideas but also modifications of errors', and that this leads us 'to reconsider the limits of [Joseph] Viscomi's concept about Blake's technique being original creation rather than secondary reproduction', the *Job* engravings being a 'mixture of experiments and trial and error' (pp. 85, 118). *William Blake and the Art of Engraving* is an incredibly detailed, highly technical and scholarly work, one that contributes greatly to our understanding of Blake's techniques of production in a tradition that includes figures such as Bentley, Viscomi, Essick, and Phillips. Her most important addition is to refocus specifically on Blake's work as an *engraver*, and throughout the book Sung demonstrates remarkable and comprehensive attention to the minute particulars of his craft that allows her to challenge easy assumptions about the theory of his creative practice.

In *Blake's Margins: An Interpretative Study of the Annotations*, Hazard Adams turns his attention to the marginalia which, perhaps appropriately, have largely been a peripheral subject in Blake studies. What critical commentary there is has previously been provided by R.J. Shroyer, and G. Ingli James in introductions to their facsimiles of Lavater's *Aphorisms on Man* and Bishop Watson's *An Apology for the Bible*, as well as essays by Morton Paley, Thomas McFarland, and H.J. Jackson and a smattering of others, as well as one book, Jason Allen Snart's *The Torn Book: UnReading William Blake's Marginalia*. As Adams observes, his own approach—dealing directly with Blake's words with a special emphasis on providing a descriptive context for each text that Blake annotates—is very different to the postmodernist and deconstructionist line taken by Snart. Eleven volumes bearing Blake's comments have survived, along with sheets of notes to Wordsworth's *The Excursion* and a transcript of the annotations to Spurzheim's *Observations on the Deranged Manifestations of the Mind*. Adams deals with the annotations more or less in chronological order, although it is also clear that what has survived tends to fall into three areas: psychology and philosophy, the arts, and religion. Of chapters dealing with the former, Blake is of course considerably more benevolent towards Lavater, which is very clear when turning to Bacon. As Adams points out (following other commentators before him), Blake's damning verdict on Bacon is expressed less by his words and more by a marginal illustration of a devil's arse dropping excrement on the words 'A King' (p. 84). Blake is a little more sympathetic when annotating George Berkeley's *Siris*, although the fact that he does not mark at all the first two-thirds of the book which discuss the beneficial properties of tar-water do not provide us with knowledge of whether Blake agreed or disagreed with Berkeley's foolish opinions.

Turning to the arts, Blake's antipathy to Sir Joshua Reynolds is notorious, and Adams notes that the annotations to the *Discourses* 'range from angry accusations and denunciations to the occasional agreement' (p. 109). It is uncertain whether Blake read all of Reynold's *Discourses*, but throughout it is clear that the two artists held fundamentally different opinions as to the purpose of imagination. The annotations to Henry Boyd's translation of

Dante's *Inferno*, by contrast, are less angry, though still motivated by disagreement with regard to what he saw as Boyd's deism and the role of morality in religion. More interesting for later readers are the comments on William Wordsworth's *Poems*, published in 1815 and lent to Blake by Henry Crabb Robinson. On religion, a substantial chapter is devoted to Bishop Richard Watson's *An Apology for the Bible*, published in 1796 and annotated by Blake in 1798. Blake's interest, suggests Adams, flagged after the first three letters, after he had made clear his political sympathy with Paine and irritation with 'Watson's barely concealed snobbishness' (p. 79). At the end of the artist's life, comments in Robert John Thornton's *The Lord's Prayer, Newly Translated* [1827] provide an entertaining, pithy, and radical blast against the often eccentric doctor, introduced to Blake via John Linnell, who had commissioned Blake for a series of woodcuts to Virgil's *Eclogues*. Although Snart's deconstructivist approach is more sophisticated, Adams's book is a much clearer introduction to several works which, obscure now, provide considerable insight into Blake's ideas and philosophies on a range of subjects.

Published to accompany the exhibition at Tate Britain in 2009 that recreated Blake's private show of 1809, Martin Myrone, *Seen in My Visions*, provides Blake's one-man show with a cultural significance that would have astonished the Romantic artist's contemporaries. Divided into four sections, the book includes the *Descriptive Catalogue* itself along with a bibliographical essay, catalogue of the paintings that were included in the Tate exhibition, and a glossary of art terms. Myrone's essay, 'The Grand Style of Art Restored', is concise but extremely informative, providing within its few pages a comprehensive (and comprehensible) account of the contexts of the fine art scene as it existed in the late eighteenth and early nineteenth centuries. Myrone's main concern is the institutional practice of the Royal Academy, designed as a showcase to promote contemporary British artists and one that very quickly prompted opposition that resulted in alternative one-man shows, beginning with Nathaniel Hone's exhibition in 1775. Leading artists such as Gainsborough, Barry, and Fuseli sought alternatives to the hegemony of the Academy; Blake's decision to exhibit was thus by no means as eccentric as (in the eyes of those few contemporaries who saw them) were the works of art on display. As Myrone concludes, Blake was not that unusual, and many artists 'had tried to acquire a public reputation, and avoid the pitfalls of the big annual exhibitions, by setting up their own shows' (p. 18).

The plates of surviving works (eleven out of sixteen included in the 1809 show) include some of Blake's most famous images, such as *The Spiritual Form of Nelson Guiding Leviathan* and *Christ in the Sepulchre, guarded by Angels*, as well as early, more conventional examples of Blake's art such as *The Penance of Jane Shore*, which he had painted in 1793 for exhibition in the Royal Academy. Some of these paintings, notably the rich temperas of which *Satan Calling up his Legions* is a good example, have suffered considerably over time, the canvas having cracked and darkened. By displaying mainly biblical subjects or those drawn from contemporary poetry (for example Gray's *The Bard*), rather than those figures that comprised his own mythology, Blake attempted to present himself in a relatively conventional light, yet the non-mimetic, gradiose figures elevated from flat, pre-Renaissance backgrounds could not have appeared as anything other than impossibly bizarre to most viewers at the time. The book as a whole has been designed as a catalogue for general readers (and visitors to the 2009 show) rather than academics, and the strength of Myrone's style is his ability to convey the complexities of art history with an assured, light touch. Blake's painting, in contrast to his poetry and printmaking, tends to be a neglected subject, but recent exhibitions and the continuing interest of twenty-first-century artists in Blake indicate that *Seen in My Visions* probably marks the start of a new trend in Blake studies that will pay more attention to that art.

Magnus Ankarsjö's *William Blake and Religion* shares some themes with his earlier title, *William Blake and Gender* [2006] in that one of the aims of this book is to take recent discoveries about the religious background of Blake's family and explore these in relation to his views on sexuality. Most important for Ankarsjö's thought is the work undertaken by Marsha Keith Schuchard in *Why Mrs Blake Cried* [2006], and by Keri Davies in various essays, that has uncovered links between Blake's mother and the Moravian Church. In addition to the research of Schuchard and Davies (to which may be added Robert Rix's re-evaluation of Blake's relations to the various religious sects of his day in *William Blake and the Cultures of Radical Christianity* [2007]), the most important critical figures for *William Blake and Religion* are David Worrall, who cast fresh light into the activities undertaken by Swedenborgians at the end of the eighteenth century, and Helen Bruder because of her re-evaluation of Blake and gender studies in her extremely influential and important book, *William Blake and the Daughters of Albion* [1997]. Ankarsjö sets out his relation to these foundational critics in his introduction, explaining that his task is to focus on the effect that newly discovered materials relating to Moravianism will have on our understanding of Blake. As such, with particular emphasis on both religion and sexuality, *William Blake and Religion* is probably one of the first of what is likely to be a growing number of texts that will explore the intersection between Blake and the Moravian Church. In addition, in his first and best chapter Ankarsjö also pays attention to the continuing influence of Swedenborgianism, the teachings and church established by the Swedish mystic Emanuel Swedenborg, who claimed constant and visionary experiences of the spiritual world, throughout the 1790s, as well as a more prickly relationship with Unitarianism, which influenced a number of his contemporaries, that Blake would have encountered via the circle gathered around the publisher Joseph Johnson. Ankarsjö is clear and convincing when outlining these religious contexts, and makes some extremely interesting and relevant observations, for example in his repetition of Keri Davies's comment at the Blake 250 conference in 2007 that the position of Moravianism as neither dissenting from, nor wholly within, the mainstream Anglican Church means that we shall probably have to revise many oft-repeated (and dearly held) assumptions about the dissenting radicalism of Blake's background.

The following chapter on 'Blake's Religion' is somewhat more confusing. First of all, Ankarsjö tends to cherry-pick texts, looking for ones that may reinforce his approach to Moravianism in particular but also that suggest Blake continued to look towards Swedenborgianism. This leads to a more general point: few other English writers (or, indeed, artists) spent more time than Blake in dealing with the topic of religion and the divine, but any attempt to pin down Blake in terms of a particular sect appears to me doomed to failure because of the idiosyncrasies of his spiritual vision, his fairly consistent refusal to participate in a church (unless, perhaps, this is because as Keri Davies has suggested the Anglican Church was, in the end, broad enough to encompass his vision). My problem with this part of *William Blake and Religion* results from a degree of confusion as to whether Ankarsjö is proposing what we may call a 'strong' theory of Blake and Moravianism, where that religion helps to explain more or less completely the framework of Blake's belief—the evidence for which I find rather hard to accept; or whether he is working towards a 'weak' theory, in which Blake's Moravian background predisposes him towards a number of tenets and attitudes, for example with regard to ecumenicism and sexual love, which, by contrast, does appear extremely enlightening.

Although I found myself somewhat confused as to Ankarsjö's aims in the chapter on Blake's religion, a more serious flaw is to be encountered in his chapter on Blake's sexuality. Before turning to this flaw, it is right to remark on where Ankarsjö's comments are illuminating, for example in reinforcing the attitudes towards 'free love' that were developing both among Blake's radical associates of the eighteenth century and 'conjugal love' that existed in the Moravian Church and Swedenborgianism. *William Blake and Religion* has much to say that is useful in this regard, although again the tendency to jump between different Blakean texts can be confusing. However, the flaw is that Ankarsjö's apparent desire to claim Blake as a proto-feminist can be rather unsophisticated and extremely problematic. The repeated assertion by Anne Mellor as to Blake's intrinsic sexism is a coarse and unhelpful position, one which Helen Bruder in particular has treated to appropriate criticism (and which has also been aided by more work by scholars such as Davies into Blake's early female collectors). However, Bruder maintains a healthily caustic attitude to Blake's sexual politics which seems largely to vanish in *William Blake and Religion*. Ankarsjös desire to read white where others read 'Blake' leads him, in my opinion, into occasionally bizarre interpretations.

Laura Quinney begins *William Blake on Self and Soul* with the observation that Blake was 'both a political radical and a radical psychologist' (p. xi). That Blake was deeply concerned with the experience of consciousness and of the self and addressed such experience in profound ways is an instantly recognizable assertion for anyone who has read his prophetic works in any detail. As Quinney observes, such readings stem at least from the interpretations from Northrop Frye and Harold Bloom to those of critics such as Mary Lynn Johnson and Peter Otto, and her own desire to understand Blake's reformulations of self and selfhood exists against a wider contemporary critical background in which Charles Taylor and Jerrold Siegel, among others, have been mapping the construction of the modern self. Blake was living and writing at a time when the investigations of the Enlightenment were replacing the concept of the 'soul' with that of the 'self', which was, in turn, to be replaced by the 'subject'—and all three to be undermined by post-structuralist and postmodern philosophy. Quinney, however, returns attention to the problematic experience of the self and the 'intuition of selfhood' that does not disappear for all that the self (and, with it, the soul and the subject) is threatened with disintegration. Indeed, for Blake 'essential topic is the unhappiness of the subject within its own subjectivity, or to use a more plangent idiom, the loneliness of the soul' (p. 11). Blake's original solution to the problem of the self—and of the soul—stems from the recognition that the isolated, atomistic self must always be fearful in its isolation, must always be anxious and threatened and so, to strengthen itself, becomes an iron-willed selfhood that is actually even more troubled. At the same time, Blake attacks the old conception of a personal immortal soul as just another version of selfhood; he does not call for the recovery of the 'true self'—itself another form of egotism—but rather a discovery of the transcendence of the soul now, in a multiplicity of experience, what Quinney calls 'immanent transcendence' that 'reconciles the self to actuality' (p. 22).

In her readings of Blake's works, she explores how a false notion of self as a passive *tabula rasa* on which the external world is written leaves no way of exercising the intuited self on the interface between subject and stimuli. It is against this limited materialism—as well as the egotistical selfhood of traditional conceptions of the soul—that *The Marriage of Heaven and Hell* and Lambeth Prophecies direct their invective. Because Locke had reduced all operations of the mind, even reflection, to a mechanical status, the actions of the self are debased and thus despair. In her chapter on Blake, Plato, and Wordsworth, she sees Wordsworth's self as literally 'haunted' by the impressions it receives from the outside world, alienated by its inability to cross the gulf it has itself created between subject and object: the outside is never quite assimilated to the inner self and so 'Wordsworth spelled out and bequeathed to psychoanalysis the notion of self-estrangement that is inherent in Locke's picture' (p. 77). By contrast, Blake's immortality of the soul is not the promise of the survival of the ego in the face of the apparent indifference of nature, but the ability of imagination to recognize the eternal now of all aspects of existence, including that of the self. That such awareness proves elusive is clear from her reading of *The Four Zoas*, which, as with the interpretations of *Milton* and *Jerusalem*, is particularly supple and effective. If there is one criticism, it is that her final reading of the revision of self-annihilation that takes place between *Milton* and *Jerusalem* is slightly less satisfactory. It seems to me that she is on the correct track—and an added subtlety is added in her recognition that even the prophet Los is subject to self-deceit, so that we should not simply take his word on trust. Unfortunately, such emphases are rather glossed over at the end of the book, though the work as a whole remains a valuable contribution on the dangers of our rush to reconsider the role of self, subjectivity, and even that tarnished notion, the soul.

Of journal articles for 2009, one of the most fascinating is Céline Mansanti's 'William Blake in *Transition* Magazine (Paris 1927–38): The Modalities of a Blake Revival in France during the 1920s and 1930s' (*Blake* 43[2009] 52–60). This is a marvellously detailed look at the ways in which Blake's work could be revived in a particular context and period, providing a finely nuanced exploration of an invocation of the poet and artist in the context of avant-garde modernism. Thus the 'Manifesto for "The Revolution of the

Word'' [1929] invokes Blake's Proverbs of Hell to illustrate and demonstrate that such a revolution has already been accomplished in awakening language from the banality of modernity, and indicating some of the ways in which a radical revisioning of Blake could operate in the twentieth century. As well as Bentley's survey of publications for 2008 in 'William Blake and his Circle: A Checklist of Publications and Discoveries in 2008' (*Blake* 43[2009] 4–48) and Robert Essick's summary of Blake sales, 'Blake in the Marketplace' (*Blake* 42[2009] 116–46), other substantial publications in *Blake: An Illustrated Quarterly* included Mark Crosby's charming exposition on 'William Blake's Miniature Portraits of the Butts Family' (*Blake* 42[2009] 147–52).

The significance of Blake's reception by subsequent artists and writers continues to be a growing theme in Blake studies, and in 'Dreams of Freedom: Magical Realism and Visionary Materialism in Okri and Blake' (*Romanticism* 15[2009] 18–32) Matthew Green explores what he identifies as a 'strand of messianic hope' in Ben Okri's essays *A Way of Being Free* that derive ultimately from Blake's prophetic vision. What is particularly important for Okri and which, argues Green, he takes from Blake, is the notion that spiritual renewal will be effected through the corporeal effects of artistic practice—that art itself, through its imaginative engagement with transforming the world around us, is precisely what enables such prophetic acts without recourse to metaphysics. While the contexts for Green's essay are fresh and vivid, this also draws quite profoundly on the line of argument expounded in his 2005 book, *Visionary Materialism in the Early Works of William Blake*, in which he offered a provocative and extremely well-considered opinion of what materialism could actually mean to Blake, in contrast to the rather tired and obvious stock denunciations that had once been a commonplace in Blake studies for a considerable period.

Two papers from 2009 can be taken together here in that they deal with vitalism and living form. Denise Gigante's 'Blake's Living Form' (*NCLE* 63[2009] 461–85; see also her full-length book on the topic, reviewed above) explores the epic poem *Jerusalem* in the light of theories of Romantic vitalism in their historical context, in particular how Aristotelian theories surrounding epigenesis had been revived and modified to understand embryonic growth as motivated by a vital force. Until this point, Gigante argues, theories of development had remained largely creationist, but theories of a vital power provided the basis for evolutionary change, hence this paper's suggestion that this particular form of organicism allowed Blake to develop what Gigante calls an 'epigenecist poetics', one in which the aesthetic organization of *Jerusalem* itself becomes vital and open. In the same issue, Nicholas M. Williams's 'Blake Dead or Alive' (*NCLE* 63[2009] 486–98) offers a reformulation of Blake's interest in the living body after phenomenological theories, particularly those of Merleau-Ponty, especially as it points to the problems of perceiving (and explaining) motion in life as conceived in Aristotelian or Newtonian forms. Motifs of life as movement, Williams observes, are scattered throughout Blake's works, though he concentrates in greater detail on the climactic rise and fall of Albion in *Milton*. Williams also approaches a similar topic from a different perspective in ' "The Sciences of Life": Living Form in William Blake and Aldous Huxley' (*Romanticism* 15[2009] 41–53), in this instance exploring

Huxley's association of Blake with vitalism in essays such as 'Literature and Science' [1963], in which Huxley, seeking a more complex and fuller relation between the two cultures, figures Blake as 'a singular hinge in intellectual history' (p. 44), one able to anticipate the twentieth-century sciences of life. Finally, in *Nineteenth-Century Literature*, Steven Goldsmith's 'William Blake and the Future of Enthusiasm' (*NCLE* 63[2009] 439–60) returns to a subject that, for the past twenty years, has been something of a minor staple and manages to present it in a new light. While considerable work has been undertaken on Blake's relations to religious enthusiasm in the context of the 1790s in particular, Goldsmith's innovation is to view scholars' interest in the subject in the light of their own modern ambitions to energize 'a future beyond modernity'. As such, Blake's apocalyptic visions of a machine world serve a very different function when taken out of immediate historicist concerns, looking ahead to critiques of postmodern philosophers concerned with ideological systems, which Goldsmith relates particularly to ideas from Sartre. While the connections between the particular theorists discussed in this paper and Blake occasionally appear a little opportunistic, what Goldsmith does achieve is to indicate the relevance that enthusiasm can have outside a purely historicist setting.

From other journals, 'William Blake's Golgonooza and *Jerusalem*: A Conversation in Visionary Forms Dramatic' (*ERR* 20[2009] 289–307) by Clint Stevens offers a dialogic interpretation of Blake's epic that focuses on the ways in which epistemology is figured through conversational approaches. Such an approach has begun to figure significantly in some aspects of Blake research (for example in the work of Jon Mee, although his exploration of conversation and meaning is by no means restricted to Blake), and Stevens offers a fair exposition of what some of the consequences of this approach could mean, although the somewhat abstract philosophical approach of this particular essays does make some of its assertions somewhat harder to follow than they would otherwise be. Somewhat more fruitful for this reader, at least, was Andrew M. Cooper's 'Freedom from Blake's *Book of Urizen*' (*SiR* 48[2009] 187–218), which begins with a formal problem faced by Blake in the 1790s: how to present his social critique of the conservative religious and political ideologies gaining currency in England in reaction to the French Revolution. Cooper also indicates just how radical Blake's narrative solution to this dilemma was in *The Book of Urizen*, in that it not only criticized notions such as original sin as the root of man's current state but also refuted Whiggish notions of an ideal progression to a preferred civilization in its final 'decrescendo', a self-contradictory fall that renders *Urizen* one of those 'self-consuming artifacts' designed to liberate the agency of the reader from the text itself.

A number of articles from 2009 present close historicist readings of Blake in the context of the Romantic period. In '"That I may awaken Albion from his long & cold repose": William Blake Addresses the Nation' (in Class and Robinson, eds., pp. XX–XX), David Fallon examines how Blake's self-appointed role as a prophet ostensibly allowed him to adopt a universal subject position but also exposed anxieties in relation to his other concern with avoiding this kind of generalization. An interesting consequence of this, suggests Fallon rather persuasively, is that it was precisely that apparently objective, universalist discourse that had dominated eighteenth-century patriotism that hindered its adoption of democratic and progressivist ends, so that Blake's negotiations between patriot and prophet enabled him to explore a much more radical attack on the corruptions of his own country. An excellent example of the micro-biographical technique being pursued by a new generation of scholars following in the steps of figures such as G.E. Bentley, Jr., is provided in Mark Crosby's '"A Fabricated Perjury": The [Mis]Trial of William Blake' (*HLQ* 72[2009] 29–47), exploring in some detail the legal and historical contexts of Blake's trial in January 1804 to test Blake's claim that the charges against him were fabricated. Crosby's findings indicate considerable sympathy towards Blake's claims, in that the Sussex magistrates appeared willing to misinterpret the laws against sedition in order to try Blake as an example to the local population.

Two contributions by great Blake scholars, G.E. Bentley, Jr., and Morton Paley, also appeared in the same issue of the *Huntington Library Quarterly*. In 'Blake's Murderesses: Visionary Heads of Wickedness' (*HLQ* 72[2009] 69–105), Bentley provides an entertaining and vivid description of the artistic curiosity of Blake's later years, stories of which attracted more attention after his death than the illuminated works for which he has since become more famous. Bentley concentrates on four of these visionary heads, those depicting murderesses, information on which must have come from contemporary pamphlets or the 'Newgate Calendar'. While most critical writings have concentrated on the exemplary mythical or historical characters from this series of sketches, conducted between 1819 and 1825, the focus here on minute particulars from Blake's own time offers an insight into some of the artist's everyday engagement with early nineteenth-century culture, as well, argues Bentley, as acting as a refutation that the physiognomy of these women revealed some monstrous moral character. Paley's '"A Virgin of Twelve Years": Ololon in Blake's *Milton*' (*HLQ* 72[2009] 106–12) deals not only with the female sexuality of this character from Blake's epic poem, but also considers some of the influences on Blake's poetry, particularly with regard to Christian apocrypha. As Ololon appears to Blake in his garden at Felpham in a spirit of prophecy, Paley ponders quite rightly why her age is defined so precisely, locating the suggested association with the Virgin Mary in the Protoevangelium Jacobi (Infancy Gospel of James) that was published in English 1798. Working (quite convincingly and carefully) from this clue, Paley observes other ways in which the Protoevangelium contributes to Blake's apocalyptic imagery in *Milton*, offering some fruitful contexts for the poet's wide-ranging appropriation of Christian symbolism.

Substantial work was undertaken on the William Blake Archive (http://www.blakearchive.org) during 2009. New copies of *Milton a Poem* (copy B), *The Song of Los* (copies C and E), and *Europe a Prophecy* (copy G) were published, along with the engraved illustrations to William Hayley's *Designs to a Series of Ballads* and *Ballads... Relating to Animals*, and Mary Wollstonecraft's *Original Stories from Real Life*. In addition, the Book of Job water colours and sketchbooks were republished with ImageSearch and iNote functions.

As might be expected there was a great deal of attention paid to Robert Burns in 2009, the 250th anniversary of his birth; some popular, some scholarly, most of it somewhere in between. There were two major new biographies, and one, issued initially to mark the 200th anniversary of his death in 1996, revised and reissued. The latter is Ian McIntyre's *Robert Burns: A Life*, formerly *Dirt and Deity: A Life of Robert Burns*. He has added a pleasant, rather wry, round-up of the development of the Burns industry (worth, he tells us, £157 million annually to the Scottish economy) in the intervening years. It remains a thoughtful, balanced popular biography, though it is unlikely to prompt much scholarly response. The same cannot be said, for better or for worse, of the two new biographies published in 2009, Robert Crawford's *The Bard: Robert Burns, A Biography* and Patrick Scott Hogg's *Robert Burns: The Patriot Bard*. Scott Hogg was co-editor of the controversial *Canongate Burns* [2001], and his work has been at the forefront of attempts to radicalize Burns's image. His biography is an explicit attempt to place this 'visionary democrat' (p. 16) firmly in context. That the biography is weighted heavily towards the 1790s, with much new information about regional political activity in that period, will make it of great interest to Romanticists. Scott Hogg employs a punchy and often rather funny prose style: wondering if Burns visited Edinburgh brothels, he regrets that 'we do not have CCTV footage' (p. 138). Scott Hogg takes aim at a perception that Burns was less than fully committed to the radical cause. Inevitably, this is often speculative (we don't have the footage), and some of the scholarship is likely to prove contentious. The air of polemic in the book is perhaps understandable in a popular biography, but it is certainly to be hoped that the debate will be constructive. Scott Hogg also offers two radical essays published in 1794 and 1795 as essays by Burns. Almost in spite of his efforts, Scott Hogg cannot help suggesting a decidedly protean poet. He wishes to 'strip away the layers of myth to find the real flesh and blood man' (p. 16), but also recognizes the part Burns played in fashioning these myths, 'playing the part of the inspired rustic with panache' (p. 139) in Edinburgh. The 'political Burns' was a necessary corrective to the twee Burns of immortal memory, but one wonders whether it might be time to move beyond the polemic.

Crawford's biography is less concerned to offer a particular version of the poet. Instead, he seeks to build a nuanced sense of the cultural world which Burns inhabited and in which he was formed. It is a remarkably fair-minded book. Old enemies like the Kirk are evaluated rather than denounced, and Crawford's subtle understanding of the contexts of debates over Presbyterianism allows him to explain that if Burns critiques the church he does so from a position firmly within it. Burns's relationship with the Scottish Enlightenment is subtly explained rather than treated as an embarrassment. But the biography's real strength is its literary focus. It is certainly pleasing that Burns has found a biographer so readily attuned to the poet's craft. There are a number of excellent close readings of individual poems which use the life to explain the context of key works. The book will prove particularly useful in reminding scholars of the range of Burns's reading. Alongside the traditional key influences (Allan Ramsey and Robert Fergusson), Crawford claims of Pope that 'no other poet was then more important to his intellectual development' (p. 102), while Shenstone emerges as a kind of touchstone that Burns returned to repeatedly throughout his life, a model for the bardic vocation. The deftness with which Crawford combines a claim for Burns's distinctive Scottishness while placing him in a web of international influences is particularly heartening, as is the way in which he powerfully states Burns's radicalism without seeming partisan. *The Bard* is sure to become the standard life of the poet. Crawford's emphasis on nuance and a recognition of the importance of registering Burns's links to a wide variety of cultural and literary contexts may just signal a new start for Burns scholarship.

Gerard Carruthers might agree. Having recounted the many ways that Burns has been co-opted by all sides, he argues that 'we are now on the verge of a new and exciting phase of Burns criticism and scholarship' (p. 3). The appearance of his *Edinburgh Companion to Robert Burns* justifies the claim. The essays, by leading critics of Scottish literature, Romanticism, and the eighteenth century, are particularly notable for the diversity of the connections they draw between Burns and political, scientific, philosophical, and literary traditions. Carruthers's carefully argued piece 'Burns and Publishing' suggests how cannily Burns positioned his own texts in a burgeoning print market. Sarah Dunnigan, Colin Kidd, and Nigel Leask are similarly cautious and scholarly in approaching the touchy subjects of women, politics, and slavery respectively; like Carruthers, they promote a sense of the complexity of the contemporary culture to which Burns responded. Burns's literary influences are thoroughly covered. Rhona Brown sheds new light on Burns's appreciation of Robert Fergusson, and Kirsteen McCue expertly analyses Burns's brilliant songwriting. Chapters by Kenneth Simpson and Steven R. McKenna draw welcome attention to Burns's classical inheritance. An excellent chapter by Corey E. Andrews discusses Burns's use of eighteenth-century critical ideas to argue for a perception of the poet as one 'deeply invested in his craft' (p. 112). Fine chapters by Fiona Stafford and Alison Lumsden look afresh at Burns's Romantic inheritors, a topic that is finally receiving the attention it deserves. These two sensitive readings ought to prompt further research. The book, broad in reference and ambitious in scope, is fittingly concluded by Leith Davis's discussion of 'Burns and Transnational Culture'. This fine collection suggests a real flourishing in Burns scholarship.

Burns studies has long had difficulty negotiating the divide between the popular and the academic, symbolized perhaps most effectively by the apparent inability of the Enlightenment figures Burns met in Edinburgh to appreciate fully the poet of the people. An important new collection of essays on Burns, *Fickle Man: Robert Burns in the 21st Century*, edited by Johnny Rodger and Gerard Carruthers, situates itself between those two poles, and suggests the extent to which conflicts like this are integral to any understanding of Burns. A subtle piece by Ralph Richard McLean reconsiders that relationship, concluding that Burns was 'both of, and not of, the enlightenment' (p. 25). Similarly, Ken Simpson's 'The Vernacular Enlightenment' attempts to suggest the common ground between these two terms; by foregrounding the 'humanism' (p. 96) of the Enlightenment one might see the vernacular poetry of the likes of Ramsay, Fergusson and Burns as part of that movement. These attempts to have it both ways characterize the collection as a whole. The Burns that emerges is 'fickle' in the sense that he made himself, as Byron realized, 'antithetical'. In this collection he is as interested in bawdry as Adam Smith, as Jacobite as Jacobin. His own self-figuration explains a constantly mutating posthumous legacy that has made him curiously open to appropriation by anyone of any persuasion, 'not so much an everyman as a delivery man peculiarly proffering back to many commentators' (p. 9). Essays consider his appropriation by satirists, biographers, painters, architects, filmmakers, and even Sinn Fein. There are important considerations of the vexed issues of Burns's political attachments and his relationship with Ireland in general and Ulster in particular. The book will do much to stimulate debate about the way Burns continues to be appropriated.

Burns's relationship with Ulster was considered in greater depth in *Revising Robert Burns and Ulster: Literature, Religion and Politics, c.1770–1920*, edited by Frank Ferguson and Andrew R. Holmes. This is a rather more weighty literary-historical project, concerned to probe and question easy assumptions made about an influence that, when the 'national, cultural, linguistic and spiritual' (p. 11) factors are taken into account, becomes intriguingly anxious. The most obvious connection is that between Burns and Ulster Scots Presbyterians. But, as Holmes shows in his chapter, that group was far from homogeneous. Beyond the expected interest in Burns amongst radically inclined weaver poets, Holmes shows that Burns was appropriated in different ways by Presbyterians of many political hues, and indeed by poets of Catholic, Anglican, and Methodist faith. Ferguson's chapter also seeks to question the simplistic political assumptions of earlier critics. Burns, he argues, 'provided as much inspiration to conservative poets and literary networks' (p. 83) as he did to radicals, focusing in particular on Anglican-led literary coteries. Carol Baranuik, indeed, suggests that Burns did not have as much influence as has been assumed on weaver-poets like James Orr, shifting the focus away from a 'Scoto-centric' model in which Ulster is accorded 'subaltern' status (p. 64). Jennifer Orr's consideration of Samuel Thomson's politics continues this thesis, emphasizing his interest in a wider tradition, including Allan Ramsay and Robert Fergusson. Other chapters look at Burns's appearances in Ulster newspapers and his commemoration as a kind of 'people's poet' in Belfast, and two chapters focus on Burns's influence on Ulster fiction. This ground-breaking collection challenges lazy stereotypes and provides fascinating new perspectives on Burns's legacy and the politics of poetry in the north of Ireland; it ought to prompt much new research.

John Burnett's *Robert Burns and the Hellish Legion* is an entertaining, well-illustrated discussion of eighteenth-century Lowland Scots folk-beliefs and their importance to Burns, particularly in 'Tam o' Shanter'. The book celebrates rather than patronizes folk-belief and is a thoroughly and accurately researched account of its subject. It is an important reminder of the vitality of the traditions of which Burns made such brilliant use. James Currie's *Life* of Burns is beginning to take its place as the central document in the poet's Romantic reputation, and Jane Darcy's important article, 'The Medical Background to Currie's *Account* of the Life of Burns' (*ERR* 20[2009] 513–27), builds on Nigel Leask's contributions to the field. Rather than Burns's taste for drink, Currie's central interest in the *Life* is to understand him in the eighteenth-century medical tradition of melancholy. This, for Darcy, places Currie in the vanguard of radical medicine in the 1790s. J. Derrick McClure considers Burns's European reputation in 'August Corrodi's Translations of Burns' (*SLR* 1[2009] 45–61). Corrodi saw parallels between Scots and Swiss German at the level of particular words and also in its seeming 'sturdiness' in comparison with a more dominant tongue. McClure suggests both the strengths and the limitations of his attempts. Luke R.J. Maynard, in 'Hoddin' Grey an' A' That: Robert Burns's Head, Class Hybridity, and the Value of the Ploughman's Mantle' (in Krishnamurthy, ed., *The Working-Class Intellectual in Eighteenth- and Nineteenth-Century Britain*, pp. 67–84) provides a balanced reading of the problematic attempts of Burns critics, particularly in the nineteenth century, to read Burns as a 'working-class intellectual', a status that, Maynard points out, did not really exist in Burns's lifetime. This subtly historicized piece mobilizes Cixous's notion of a 'hybridized viewpoint' to reshape the debate.

Martin Garrett's *The Palgrave Literary Dictionary of Byron* will prove an invaluable source for scholars. It is part of a new series intended to provide the reader with 'immediate access to reliable information' (p. xi) on major authors. With any author this is a difficult task, and Byron's incessantly varied interests and Europe-wide influence make Garrett's achievement all the more impressive. The volume begins with an excellent and thorough chronology, and concludes with a concise bibliography. In between are short entries on almost anything one could imagine, from the poet's early lovers to his attitudes on classical literature to the opinions on him held by the likes of Browning and Ibsen. Garrett offers longish treatments of major works and central thematic areas and short discussions of people and things Byron knew or referred to, or who refer to him. Inevitably, some things will be missed, but given the challenges involved in producing such a volume, Garrett is to be commended. One of the real strengths of the collection is its sense of balance. The entry on 'Politics' exemplifies this. Garrett stresses Byron's continual interest in politics, but notes the counter-arguments by the likes of Malcolm Kelsall, who see his political positions as empty bluster. Rather than offering one side or the other, Garrett allows the reader to follow up both. The entry on Pope notes Byron's celebration of him while also remarking on the intriguing fact that 'Byron does not often write like Pope' (p. 227). The book never seeks to close off argument, but always to prompt readers to make connections, and to find out more. Its primary readership will be amongst those students and scholars relatively new to Byron, but such is Garrett's erudition that even seasoned experts will be inspired by it.

Ghislaine McDayter's *Byromania and the Birth of Celebrity Culture* complements and extends the substantial recent interest in the growth of celebrity culture, particularly in relation to Byron, notably Tom Mole's *Byron's Romantic Celebrity* [2007] and Julian North and Eric Eisner's work, discussed above. That this is a relatively new field is germane to McDayter's argument. The critical desire to disconnect Byron's poetry from his fans is a product, she argues, of a period which sought to separate high culture from a popular culture associated with the hysterical and diseased passions of a newly democratized public sphere. Most particularly, Byron attracted, and his critics wish to distance him from, women. For McDayter, rather than a distraction, this connection with 'feminine hysteria, with popular culture . . . marked him as one of the most dangerous political forces of the period' (p. 7). Fears of the kind of sympathetic, enthusiastic response that Byron's poetry aroused were part of a long-running set of anxieties connected to the expansion of the print market and the French Revolution. McDayter focuses in particular on the Turkish Tales that are often presented as Byron's aesthetic low, the point at which he pandered to the tastes of the market. These tales are placed in a context of radical enthusiasm and popular representation of revolutionary sentiment. *The Giaour* is read as 'a scathing critique of the moderate republican stance endorsed by so many of Byron's contemporaries' (p. 72). If Byron gets angry with the Byromaniacs, that is because of his 'perception of their capricious betrayal of democracy' (p. 104). Although one might question the way McDayter conflates anxieties about the feminization of literature and anxieties about political radicalism, her readings are incisive and provocative. There is a fine chapter on Byron's relationship with the periodicals, and an excellent consideration of the role of desire in the act of reading and interpretation. This is a thoughtful, lively, and theoretically astute reading of an issue of central importance.

Ian Dennis's *Lord Byron and the History of Desire* builds an impressive theoretical framework in a substantial new reading of Byron's relationship with the market and his readers. It shares much with recent work on Byron's celebrity discussed above, but his use of a framework that derives largely from Eric Gans's theory of 'generative anthropology' pushes the debate in intriguing new directions. Gans's work takes its impetus from René Girard's idea of imitative, or 'triangular', desire, a notion that has some immediate application in Byron's courting of his readers through a pose of aristocratic indifference. Gans develops this, positing a complex web of triangulated desires focused on a relationship between a common centre and competing peripheries. It is a remarkably broad basis for a study of the poetry, but it produces illuminating results. The first two cantos of *Childe Harold*, for Dennis, represent a movement towards an increasingly complex understanding of the relationship between speaker and persona, interacting with and partially thwarting a desiring readership. The Eastern Tales are, in this view, less expressions of political despair than a celebration of the energies that produced that situation. As Byron's career progresses, his understanding of these dynamics strengthens and deepens. *Cain* and *Manfred* 'demystify' (p. 29) this earlier relationship with his audience, toying with concepts of sincerity in a way that Dennis sees as complementary to Byron's interests in an anthropological understanding of 'the basic principles of human life and culture' (p. 138). *Don Juan* receives the greatest share of attention. The poem is, for Dennis, a full-scale analysis of market-driven desire. But the reader is not simply ironized out of existence. Instead, Dennis finds a 'new sort of comforting and helpful alliance' (p. 30) that provides a suitably hopeful conclusion to a stimulating contribution to Byron studies.

Peter Cochran's *'Romanticism'—and Byron* offers thirteen chapters which discuss Byron's relationship with his contemporaries. It begins with an introduction which takes vigorous swipes at the term 'Romanticism' but will perhaps prove less controversial than Cochran hopes. Southey (about whom Cochran is amusingly if unfairly rude) is a key presence in the chapters which follow. An excellent chapter on Byron's odd relationship with William Gifford discovers Byron panicking: 'the more he asserts distance from Southey, the more he acknowledges that they're the same' (p. 33). Byron's allusions to Sheridan's *The Critic* reveal a similar anxiety, and the relationship between the two hangs over Byron's uneasy engagement with Wordsworth and Shelley. Cochran suggests that 'In his enemies, he sees himself' (p. 364). Southey is the most spectacular example of such a relationship, and the book presents compelling evidence for Byron as a poet who is obsessed by his enemies. The relationship with Coleridge is represented in more positive terms, but things bubble below the surface: 'imitation by inversion was an instinctive method with the antithetically-minded Byron' (p. 65). Similarly, it is not during the Shelley-influenced period that Byron engages most significantly with Wordsworth, but when he was insulting him in *Don Juan*. There are other relationships discussed. Cochran's knowledge of the papers of Byron's less famous peers such as Gifford, Lord Holland, Isaac Nathan, and Teresa Guiccioli provides some important new information and fresh insights regarding Byron's work. Alongside the more generous readings of Byron's 'antithetical' relationship with his peers, Cochran reveals an unfortunate tendency to stick the boot into writers he dislikes, particularly Southey, Wordsworth, Keats, and Hunt. Putting such moments aside, however, there are many intriguing insights in the book that help one think about Byron's distinctive relationship with the full range of his period's culture.

Byron's relationship with the Gothic was amply discussed in a collection of essays edited by Cochran, *The Gothic Byron*. Nearly half of the volume consists of a long introductory essay by Cochran entitled 'Byron Reads and Rewrites Gothic'. Cochran suggests that any opposition between Romanticism and the Gothic is false before considering Byron's use and abuse of a wide variety of Gothic writers, including Ann Radcliffe, William Beckford, and Joanna Baillie. Like *'Romanticism'—and Byron*, discussed above, Cochran uses a Harold Bloom-esque antithetical method, proposing that the slighter Byron's attention to a text the greater his debt. Byron rarely mentions either *Frankenstein* or *Caleb Williams*, but Cochran persuasively suggests their influence on *The Giaour*, *Manfred*, and *The Deformed Transformed*. Particular attention is devoted to excellent readings of Byron's relationship with Charlotte Dacre and Friedrich Schiller's *Der Geisterseher*. Byron is attracted to the Gothic for its capacity to '[allow] contraries to float about free' (p. 77). There are then ten short essays examining that relationship from a range of angles. Mirka Horová picks up on Cochran's lead and talks eloquently about *Don Juan*'s 'serious laughter' (p. 118) about the Gothic. Bernard Beatty discusses Byron's 'complex, daring, and thoughtful' (p. 89) engagement with Catholicism in the Gothic. Malcolm Kelsall offers a timely discussion of the political repressions of the Gothic spectre, while Cochran, in a separate piece, argues that Byron returns social satire to the Gothic form. Monika Coghen discusses Byron's Gothic drama, David Herbert talks about ghosts at Newstead Abbey, and Cristina Ceron examines the relationship between *Manfred* and the Brontës' *The Professor* and *Wuthering Heights*. Richard

Cardwell and Shona Allen look at Byron's ghostly afterlives in, respectively, Spain and Germany.

Joshua Lambier's 'Citational Cosmopolitics: Staël, Byron, and the Foreignizing Effect of Cultural Translation' (in Dick and Esterhammer, eds., pp. 222–47) seeks to recalibrate the relationship between nationalism and localism and Enlightenment cosmopolitan aspiration in an excellent study of Byron and Staël's border crossing. Both the 'English Cantos' of *Don Juan* and *Corinne* refuse to recognize cultures' claims to self-containment, instead seeing identity as something performed in a cross-cultural context. Byron's relationship with place was further considered by Juan L. Sánchez in 'Byron, Spain, and the Romance of *Childe Harold's Pilgrimage*' (*ERR* 20[2009] 443–64). Spain has not had as much attention as other Byronic locales, such as Italy, Greece, and Scotland. Sánchez focuses on canto I of *Childe Harold* to propose that Byron remains committed to a poetics of ambivalence that figures Spain as an idealized location tied to a romance tradition from which Byron cannot free himself. Byron's Scottish connections have been the subject of increasing critical attention lately, and Murray Pittock's 'Byron's Networks and Scottish Romanticism' (*ByronJ* 37[2009] 5–14) will do much to further the dialogue. Pittock uses his own concept of the 'fratriot' identity to challenge perceptions of Byron's personal Scottish networks. Byron's links with Scottish figures were not simply literary; rather, they pervaded his life.

Jim Cocola's 'Renunciations of Rhyme in Byron's *Don Juan*' (*SEL* 49[2009] 841–62) offers a sparkling reading of Byron's brilliantly inconsistent rhyming habits in *Don Juan*. It is always a pleasure to be reminded of rhymes like 'martyrs hairy / Virgin Mary', and Cocola lists many more, including revised rhymes and polyglot rhymes. The article does not come to any particular conclusions, but makes some intriguing suggestions about Byron's oppositional politics. Susan J. Wolfson's 'Byron's Ghosting Authority' (*ELH* 76[2009] 763–92) looks, with her customary subtlety, at Byron's ability to joke about the dead. Focusing on *Don Juan*, Wolfson shows how Byron's rhymes 'collate comedy and anxiety' (p. 779), undermining without dispelling the notion of ghostliness. Irony allows him to become a ghostly author, there and not there. In 'Byron and Montaigne' (*ByronJ* 37[2009] 33–41), Anne Fleming looks for reasons as to why Byron should compare *Don Juan* with Montaigne's *Essays*. Both were purposefully contradictory, and while they shared a contempt for war, they both felt war could be used to relieve oppression. Gavin Hopps's '"Eden's Door": The Porous Worlds of *Don Juan* and *Childe Harold's Pilgrimage*' (*ByronJ* 37[2009] 109–20) challenges the perception of the poet as sceptical and earthly. Hopps's subtle study of entrances and exits in his two major works suggests that Byron might be seen in theological terms as a seeker of ecstasy precisely in his focus on the quotidian. Trevor Hart's '*Cain*'s Byron: A Mystery—On the Inscrutability of Poetic Providence' (*ByronJ* 37[2009] 15–20) suggests that the difficulties of ascribing a theological position to the play are unsurprising. Byron was addressing theological issues for which finding a clear answer is beside the point.

In 'Byron's Orphic Poetics and the Foundations of Literary Modernism' (*TSLL* 51:iii[2009] 361–82), Christopher A. Strathman offers an important reorientation of Byron studies. Recent critical opinion has found him valuable precisely in so far as his poetry reveals its historically situated status. Strathman seeks to reverse this by emphasizing, first, Byron's position in an Ovidian tradition of fragmentary poetic expression of deep loss and, second, his influence on modernists like Joyce, Pound, and Eliot through the way he makes sincerity a theatrical gesture. Alex Watson's important 'Byron's Marginalia to *English Bards and Scotch Reviewers*' (*ByronJ* 37[2009] 131–9) presents and discusses Byron's annotations to the poem. These comments prompt Watson to conclude that scholars ought to reconsider the position of such texts. They are neither text nor paratext; they take their cue from the 'master' text, but they also offer judgement upon it. Maurizio Ascari, in '"Not in a Christian Church": Westminster Abbey and the Memorialisation of Byron' (*ByronJ* 37[2009] 141–50), looks at the complex of cultural issues raised by attempts to memorialize Byron in a space that served both religious and national functions. In 'Lord Byron's "The Dream" and *Wuthering Heights*' (*BS* 34:i[2009] 31–46) Meridel Holland argues that the parallel between Heathcliff and the protagonist of 'The Dream' is far greater than has previously been recognized. The narratives of the two are structurally parallel, and Holland shows that there are also numerous verbal echoes. Adam Gyngell's 'Romance and Romanticism: Byron, Keats, and the Quest' (*KSR* 23[2009] 28–33) discusses the trope of quest in poems such as *Childe Harold's Pilgrimage* and *Endymion*. The worryingly adolescent nature of such quests shapes *Don Juan* in turn, which drives forward, reflecting and critiquing the notion of 'romantic art as a journey without a destination' (p. 32). Jane Stabler's '"True Impossibility": Editing Byron' (*WC* 40[2009] 73–7) offers a pleasant discussion of the difficulties of editing that she and her co-editors (Andrew Nicholson, Gavin Hopps, and Peter Cochran) of the Longman seven-volume Byron have begun to face. Kasahara Yorimichi's 'Byron's Dying Gladiator in Context' (*WC* 40[2009] 44–51) traces the many sources of Byron's depiction of the statue in *Childe Harold's Pilgrimage* IV to a hitherto unrecognized source in William Hayley's 1800 poem *An Essay on Sculpture*, and records for particular note Robert Chinnery's strong influence on Byron's version. In 'Byron's Voice' (*ByronJ* 37[2009] 121–30), Christine Kenyon Jones considers the fascinating, if challenging, possibility of reconstructing the sound of Byron's speech. Byron's Aberdonian upbringing and subsequent London life would have made him acutely aware of the importance of accents; Jones provides some fascinating analysis to probe the issues.

John Williams considers Thomas Chatterton's ongoing reputation in 'Peter Ackroyd's *Chatterton*, Thomas Chatterton, and Postmodern Romantic Identities and Attitudes' (*Romanticism* 15[2009] 33–40). Despite his apparent rejection of a 'Romantic attitude' represented by Chatterton, the figure of Chatterton, for Williams, continues to shape and structure the thinking of Ackroyd and others in a way that suggests the redundancy of their apparent postmodernism. Daniel Cook's 'The Critical and the Curious: Thomas Chatterton's First Reviewers' (*Romanticism* 15[2009] 109–20) considers Chatterton's treatment at the hands of the *Gentleman's Magazine* and the *Monthly* and *Critical Reviews*. That debate has usually centred on questions of authenticity, but, Cook shows, they were as much about the definition of literature and the reliability of claims of scholarly authority. Chatterton's reputation was considered further by Nick Groom in '"With certain grand Cottleisms": Joseph Cottle, Robert Southey and the 1803 *Works of Thomas Chatterton*' (*Romanticism* 15[2009] 225–38). The edition is particularly significant because of Cottle's 'tampering', which took the opportunity to emphasize the mystical Rowley poems over the political satire. Southey, as Groom shows, was rather more attracted to, and influenced by, the strange mixture of politics and medievalism. In 'Five Poems Wrongly Attributed to Thomas Chatterton' (*N&Q* 56[2009] 357–9), Groom presents evidence that poems attributed by Donald Taylor to Chatterton should not have been, and in 'Who Plagiarized Thomas Chatterton's "Elegy"?' (*N&Q* 56[2009] 359–60) he discusses the plagiarism in *The Ipswich Magazine* [1799] of 'Why blooms the radiance of the morning sky', most likely by the editor's son, James Hews Bransby.

Sarah Houghton-Walker's *John Clare's Religion* offers an important and compelling argument to support her original claim that 'we cannot read John Clare's verse adequately if we ignore that his own vision is informed by a religious awareness that is both intellectual and experiential' (p. 1). The book begins with a subtle and attentive reading of the neglected satire *The Parish*. Houghton-Walker's reading of the poem is informed by the contemporary historical context (Clare is, she points out, rather more abrasive than the reality merited) but also attuned to the way that Clare modulates his verse to reflect an attitude to communality that suggests, despite the poem's tone, his commitment to what religion offers. *John Clare's Religion* provides much-needed contextualization (Clare's interests in Methodism and folk superstition were alternative to Anglican faith, but were nonetheless 'a phenomenon within them' (p. 59)), but the book's principal aim is to explore fully the operation of forms of faith in the poetry. The sublime is explored as a key concept in his poetry, a 'rapture' that is inspired by nature but whose terminology is 'reinforced by religious doctrine' (p. 139). The experience of ecstasy is itself, for Clare, a kind of 'poetry' he tries to recreate in his poems as a mode of accessing God. Clare's thorough knowledge of the Bible and Milton structure his ideas of Eden, evil, and Heaven as they are described both in the early poems and in the asylum poems. Houghton-Walker examines a wide variety of Clare's poetry in a series of subtle, intelligent readings. She studies 'what he did believe, when he did believe' (p. 223), without being blind either to the doubts that he had, or to the fact that 'he changes his mind frequently, and is able to entertain apparently mutually exclusive possibilities simultaneously' (p. 4). But these contradictions and uncertainties, as she shows, can best be considered as an aspect of the poet's continuous relationship with aspects of faith.

In 'Listening with John Clare' (*SiR* 48[2009] 371–90), Stephanie Kuduk Weiner offers a subtle and sensitive close reading of Clare's 'middle period poetry' that suggests the significance of Clare's attempts to find a poetic form that reflected the sounds of nature. For Clare, language is a crucial mediating force, not a simple reflection of nature. His understanding of sound is part of a 'productively vexed relationship with the written word' (p. 373). In 'John Clare: "The Man of Taste"' (*JCSJ* 28[2009] 38–54), Adam White offers the challenging and rather refreshing proposal that Clare was energized by eighteenth-century aesthetic notions of the picturesque and taste. In doing so, White argues, Clare consciously adopted 'culturally sophisticated positions' (p. 45) that distanced him from the labouring class. 'Clare's Gypsies and Literary Influence', by Sarah Houghton-Walker (*JCSJ* 28[2009] 71–93), considers the gypsy in Clare's work. Rather than, as the figure is usually taken, a symbol of a desire for the liminal or an expression of alienation, Houghton-Walker argues that Clare's gypsies are part of a history of literary representation, notably in the work of Samuel Rogers. Simon J. White's 'John Clare's Sonnets and the Northborough Fens' (*JCSJ* 28[2009] 55–70) focuses on sonnet sequences written around the time of his move from Helpstone to Northborough. Rather than a simple revulsion from the flat fenland, Clare produced a careful response to a quite new environment, based on 'unsettling formal innovation' producing a 'new kind of sonnet for a new kind of place' (p. 68). In 'John Clare, the Popular Wood-Cut and the Bible: A Venture into the History of Popular Culture' (*WC* 40[2009] 121–5), Eric Robinson begins by noting Clare's devotion to the Bible. He was particularly attached to a Scottish Bible which included wood-cuts by Thomas Bewick. Wood-cuts were Clare's first artistic love, and Robinson suggests that he continued to enjoy such work in art by the likes of Hogarth, Cruikshank, and Rowlandson. Ian Waites's '"The prospect far and wide": An Eighteenth-Century Drawing of Langley Bush and Helpston's Unenclosed Countryside' (*JCSJ* 28[2009] 5–22) reproduces a drawing of Clare country by the Flemish artist Peter Tillemans. Waites's thorough understanding of both Clare and artistic representations of landscape help bring out the subtleties of both. The *John Clare Society Journal* also published 'An Unpublished Letter and Poems by John Clare', provided by Eric Robinson and Robert Hayes (*JCSJ* 28[2009] 94–8). The letter is to James Hessey; the poems are a romantic lyric, a sonnet celebrating nature, and a poem written on seeing a copy of the Venus de Medici.

Two articles considered Hartley Coleridge's poetry. Nicola Healey's important '"A living spectre of my Father dead": Hartley Coleridge, Samuel Taylor Coleridge, and Literary Reputation' (*ColB* 33[2009] 96–105) may do much to correct views of Hartley which see him simply in the shadow of his father. Hartley's poems to STC, Healey argues, must be considered public rather than private documents, and an attack on readers who fail to differentiate between a private and a public poetic identity. Andrew Keanie continues his fine work on the poet in 'Hartley Coleridge and his Art of Dovetailing Miscellaneous Particulars' (*ColB* 33[2009] 106–13). Much of the reason for the neglect Hartley has faced stems from his own poetic practice, which privileged immediate impulses over considered expression; yet this, as Keanie suggests, is precisely what makes his poetry so compelling.

The most important contribution to studies of Samuel Taylor Coleridge this year is *The Oxford Handbook of Samuel Taylor Coleridge*, edited by Frederick Burwick. Given that Coleridge's all-encompassing erudition seemed to defeat Coleridge himself, it is not unreasonable that the student faced with the complete works of Coleridge, concluded in 2002 following forty years of meticulous editing, should feel daunted. As Robert M. Maniquis puts it in his contribution, 'critical writing about Coleridge is labyrinthine, not unlike Coleridge's own prose, but no serious reader of Coleridge disdains a labyrinth'

(p. 713). This volume will provide an excellent guide, not only for students, but also for specialists in a particular aspect of Coleridge's work who wish to gain a foothold in an unfamiliar area. There are thirty-seven essays, arranged under five headings: 'Biography', 'The Prose Works', 'The Poetic Works' (which also includes drama), 'Sources and Influences', and 'Reception'. The chapters cover the established ground, explaining key positions, while also attempting, in most cases, to push the discussion forward. Richard Gravil's fine chapter on Wordsworth and Coleridge efficiently summarizes recent critical debate (broadly drawn into either 'symbiosis' or 'radical difference' camps) before offering a delicate, winding path between those extremes. Anya Taylor's discussion of 'Coleridge's Self-Representations' takes a less common topic, but, similarly, suggests new directions for scholars, not least in the notion that he 'lived his identity as a physical being at the centre of texts' (p. 107). Much of the important work that this volume does is to explicate and provide a guide to the complexities of Coleridge's thinking on topics like allegory and symbol (Nicholas Halmi), politics and religion (Peter J. Kitson and Pamela Edwards) and philosophy (Murray J. Evans, Elinor Shaffer, and Christoph Bode, amongst others). These chapters are uniformly excellent; lively and informative while also providing clear accounts of Coleridge's thought, even in the *Opus Maximum*. The volume is also notable for pointing readers down less-trodden paths. Angela Esterhammer's splendid discussion of Coleridge's work for newspapers, periodicals, and annuals asks us to reimagine Coleridge's relationship with his public; H.J. Jackson's essay on Coleridge's reading habits and his marginalia brilliantly demonstrates that he was 'a remarkable reader but not beyond compare' (p. 272). Of particular relevance to this section are essays by David Fairer on 'Coleridge's Early Poetry', which elegantly draws out the 'disparate strands' of his early verse that would contribute to his 'maturity'; Michael O'Neill, who discusses 'Coleridge's Genres'; and Christopher R. Miller, who suggests Coleridge's indebtedness to and difference from poets like Gray, Cowper, and Collins. Those sections focusing on Coleridge's prose are discussed in section 2 above.

There has been much important recent work which attempts to reframe the relationship between poetry and philosophy in Coleridge's thought, and James Vigus's *Platonic Coleridge* (also discussed above) will do much to further that discussion. While Coleridge's engagement with Kant has always been clear, Plato represents a far more shadowy presence in his thought. Yet that very shadowiness is an aspect, for Vigus, of the way in which Coleridge adopted Platonic ideas. The first key phase of his argument is to set Coleridge's relationship with Plato in a historical context that explores the politicization of his reception. Vigus also shows how Coleridge used Plato to test the boundaries of Kant's thought. Coleridge's apparent esotericism is connected to his anxieties about his status as the sage explaining metaphysics to the nation, but it is also, for Vigus, an aspect of the Platonic way in which Coleridge investigates language and truth. Esoteric philosophy, spoken to an inner circle, offers the opportunity to develop a 'poetic philosophy that appears to leave things unsaid, and so offers a tantalizing sense of esoteric doctrines lying beyond the text' (p. 6). The apparent division between poetry and philosophy lies at the heart of the book. Kant rejects poetry which aspires to the philosophical, as poets were banished from *The Republic*. Coleridge, following Plato in this respect, is fundamentally ambivalent about this issue, agreeing with Kant yet placing faith in the poetic cognition embodied by the Imagination. Vigus shows this ambivalence at work in a brilliant reading of 'Kubla Khan' and its preface, suggesting how the two texts move between two Platonic models of poetic inspiration as part of a '"critical scrutiny" of his imagination' (p. 86). Even in the *Opus Maximum*, thinking in poetry remains a structuring influence, as witnessed by a series of key allusions to Milton. This intelligent, enjoyable book is original and stimulating, and ought to help and challenge those scholars who see the poetic and the philosophical as mutually supportive aspects of Coleridge's thought.

Christopher R. Stokes's impressive 'Radical Sympathy and Retributive Violence: The Sublime of Terror in "The Destiny of Nations"' (*ERR* 20[2009] 57–75) considers the importance of Coleridge's Unitarianism to his political poetry. Coleridge resists Burke's sense that the sublime is solitary, imbuing it with a Unitarian social function. Yet the poem also suggests a turn away from the optimism of his youthful religious creed. Manu Samriti Chander's 'Romantic Controversialism and Universalist Vision of "Fears in Solitude"' (*ColB* 34[2009] 9–16) argues that the Romantic period was witness to the rise of a culture of controversy so pervasive that it became an 'ism'. Coleridge's 'Fears in Solitude' responds to this by offering a universalism that accommodates rather than denies dissent. Coleridge's rather daring 1794–5 political poetry was ably discussed by Katy Beavers in 'Public Expression and Political Repression—Coleridge on William Pitt the Younger' (*ColB* 34[2009] 25–33). Beavers examines Coleridge's changing position on radical politics between the sonnet to Pitt and 'Fears in Solitude'. In what is itself a rather daring move, Beavers suggests he '[outgrew] his radical adolescence' (p. 33).

The issue of Walter Scott's apparent plagiarism from *Christabel* in *The Lay of the Last Minstrel* is readdressed by Phillip B. Anderson in 'Scott's *The Eve of St John* and the "Influence" of *Christabel* on *The Lay of the Last Minstrel*' (*PhilRev* 35[2009] 1–10). Scott does indeed use the accentual metre that Coleridge had employed, but Scott had already used the metre in 1799's *Eve of St John* which draws on the ballad tradition. Tom Clucas defends Coleridge from the charge (made by De Quincey) of plagiarism in 'Allusion to *Samson Agonistes* in Coleridge's "France: An Ode"' (*N&Q* 56[2009] 365–7); he was creatively alluding, not stealing. In 'Shadowy Nobodies and other Minutiae: Coleridge's Originality' (*ColB* 33[2009] 1–12), R.A. Foakes traces Coleridge's development as both poet and critic. In 1798 he wrote much indifferent verse; the reason, for Foakes, was that he was only beginning to realize that his true originality lay in his conversation poems rather than his public, political poetry. The continuing debate over the attribution of an edition of *Faust* to Coleridge was surveyed by Chris Murray in '"Give it up in Despair": Coleridge and Goethe's *Faust*' (*Romanticism* 15[2009] 1–15). The evidence presented, Murray argues, is not sufficient to warrant the attribution.

The remarkable afterlife of *The Rime of the Ancient Mariner* received further attention from John Tallmadge in 'Shackleton in the Antarctic: Tragedy, Initiation, and the Epic of Endurance' (*ILStud* 10:ii[2009] 43–55). Shackleton's disastrous 1915–18 expedition is narrated in terms which suggest 'the hidden meaning of events' (p. 43) despite their apparent arbitrariness revealing his dependence on the plot structure of Coleridge's *Rime*. In 'Coleridge's Uncertain Agony' (*SEL* 49[2009] 807–39), Harry White provides a very funny, and rather thoughtful, treatment of *The Ancient Mariner*. The poem dramatizes Coleridge's own sense of guilt, which he worried was either a product of original sin or a symptom of his melancholy. White provides a great deal of historical and literary material to explore the issue. In 'Crossed Lines: The Vernacular Metaphysics of the *Ancient Mariner*' (*C&L* 59:i[2009] 51–83), Graham Pechey suggests that the *Ancient Mariner* might be considered a 'staging-post' (p. 52) on the poet's journey from Unitarian to Trinitarian belief. With intensive attention to the detail of words and phrases, Pechey reconsiders the significance of figures of the line and the cross. Somewhat differently, 'Coleridge's Dilemma and the Method of "Sacred Sympathy": Atonement as Problem and Solution in *The Rime of the Ancient Mariner*' by Russell M. Hillier (*PLL* 45:i[2009] 8–36) attempts to undo the apparently contradictory nature of the *Rime* by understanding the poem with reference to a 'rigorously Unitarian or subordinationist perspective in regard to Christology' (p. 10). Similarly, the redemption that the Mariner achieves is used by Hillier, ingeniously, to suggest the continuities of Coleridge's philosophy over the full span of his career. In 'Coleridge, the Rime, and the Image of God: Humanness as Communion with Creator' (*ColB* 34[2009] 42–8), Christopher Dinkel examines the *Opus Maximum*'s outline of what Dinkel sees as an issue 'foundational to his entire system of theology and philosophy' (p. 42): the person. *The Rime of the Ancient Mariner*, Dinkel argues, is an expression of Coleridge's view that the capacity to love is what makes us human.

Onita Vaz-Hooper's '"If dead we cease to be": The Logic of Immortality in Coleridge's "Human Life"' (*ERR* 20[2009] 529–44) considers a late, neglected poem. 'Human Life' seems a typical example of Coleridge having it both ways. Vaz-Hooper shows how he enters the vitalist debate by proposing that materialists mistake the case: because God made humans, humans have a rational compulsion to believe in their own immortality. Shelley Trower's 'Nerves, Vibration, and the Aeolian Harp' (*RoN* 54[2009] 31 paras.) offers a materialist take on the medical context to Coleridge's 'Eolian Harp' and 'Dejection: An Ode'. Rather than an ability to transcend the mind, Coleridge displays an interest in Hartleyan associationalism and contemporary medical theories that means he, like Shelley and Robert Bloomfield, retains an interest in the harp as metaphor for the creative mind despite the growing doubt about nervous sensibility. Nishi Pulugurtha's 'Community, Domestic Space and the Self in Coleridge's Conversation Poems' (*ColB* 34[2009] 49–55) examines a wide range of these poems, suggesting that Coleridge achieved perfection of the work, but not the man. His life was fragmented, but his poems offered hope of an ultimate communal wholeness. William Ulmer's 'Radical Similarity: Wordsworth, Coleridge and the Dejection Dialogue' (*ELH* 76[2009] 189–213) begins with the apparently antithetical dialogue between the poets in the 'Immortality Ode' and the version of the 'Dejection Ode' addressed to Wordsworth. These poems, he suggests, have far less of a philosophical difference than has been suggested. Ulmer uses this basis to propose an important reorientation of the whole Wordsworth/Coleridge opposition that may have a significant scholarly impact. In 'The Paradoxes of Nature in Wordsworth and Coleridge' (*WC* 40[2009] 4–9), John Beer ponders what the content of Wordsworth and Coleridge's 1790s conversations may have been, considering the evolving role of nature in both poets' work. Coleridge found at times the 'treachery of nature' (p. 8); Wordsworth began to devote himself to those aspects of nature 'friendly to human beings' (p. 9).

Mary Wedd's excellent 'Hell and Resurrection' (*ColB* 33[2009] 24–34) considers Coleridge's lifelong engagement with ideas of the afterlife. John Powell Ward, in '"Weave a circle round him thrice": Three Takes on "Kubla Khan"' (*ColB* 33[2009] 35–44), merrily considers the 'divine dictation', Christian, and 'Person from Porlock' conceptions of the poem. A.D. Harvey's 'Elinor Shaffer and the Genesis of Coleridge's Non-Existent *The Fall of Jerusalem*' (*N&Q* 56[2009] 367–70) makes a rather elegant claim for the importance of attentive scholarship, convincingly contradicting Elinor Shaffer's assumptions about the sources for 'Kubla Khan' as conveyed in her *'Kubla Khan' and The Fall of Jerusalem* [1975]. Morton D. Paley's 'Coleridge's Captain Derkheim' (*WC* 40[2009] 82–7) provides a full biographical survey of a man who took him from Livorno to Britain and 'saved his life three times over' (p. 86).

Five articles in the *Coleridge Bulletin* discussed Sara Coleridge's poetry. Peter Swaab's 'Sara Coleridge: Poems and their Addressees' (*ColB* 33[2009] 45–64) offers an elegant reading of her verse, taking as its starting point the fact that so few of her poems were published in her lifetime. This, as Swaab demonstrates, was something Sara put to 'creative use' (p. 46), and Swaab provides a fine call for Sara's skill as a poet and for the importance of attending to the relationship between a poem and its readers. In '"Amaranths" and "Poppies": Sara Coleridge, Poet's Daughter and Poet' (*ColB* 33[2009] 65–73), Robin Schofield is similarly attentive to the texture of her poetry, mounting an argument for considering Sara as 'enabled by, yet distinct from, the paternal legacy' (p. 65). The article, like Swaab's, encourages a reinterpretation of the relationship between 'Romantic' and 'Victorian' poetics through a study of her poetry of the 1830s. Katie Waldegrave, in 'Sara Coleridge: A Poet Hidden' (*ColB* 33[2009] 74–9), is tempted to see Sara as a victim of a series of patriarchs, but her research at the Harry Ransom Centre on Sara's manuscripts has caused a reinterpretation of 'Sara-as-Victim' (p. 76). Rather, her decision to hide herself might be styled a positive, if historically determined, decision. In 'Suffering Servant: Grief and Consolation in Sara Coleridge's Poems' (*ColB* 33[2009] 81–8), Jeffrey W. Barbeau argues that Sara's reading in her father's theology, allied with time spent in her Uncle Southey's extensive library, imbued her poetry with an unusually powerful religious sense. Her poems' depictions of the mother–child relationship are, for Barbeau, not simply personal, but an aspect of a theology that had departed from her father's position. Sara D. Nyffenegger's 'The Mirror, Friend or Foe? Sara Coleridge and the Ill Effects of Society's Judgment on Female Appearance' (*ColB* 33[2009] 89–95) focuses on Sara's essay 'On the Disadvantages Resulting from the Possession of Beauty' [1826], gathering together an interesting array of historical evidence to suggest why she felt that her period was witness to a new tyranny directed against the beauteous.

Noel Jackson's 'Rhyme and Reason: Erasmus Darwin's Romanticism' (*MLQ* 70[2009] 171–94) provides a remarkably perceptive take on a poet who has been revived in the past quite consciously in spite of his aesthetics. Instead, Jackson suggests, Darwin is interesting and politically challenging because of his formal innovations which expressed their political and philosophical positions *as* poetry, rather than offering two separate aims. Alan Bewell's 'Erasmus Darwin's Cosmopolitan Nature' (*ELH* 76[2009] 19–48) also offers an important claim for reading Darwin on his own terms. Bewell's elegant and scholarly piece places Darwin's poem *The Botanic Garden* [1796] alongside Henry Jones's 'Kew Garden' to suggest at once the historicity and the contemporary relevance of Darwin's approach. Darwin, he argues, presented 'a natural world that was undergoing ceaseless change and transformation and was inescapably bound up with global commerce, industry and consumption' (p. 20).

Michael O'Neill places Felicia Hemans in mutually sustaining dialogue with her fellow Romantics in '"A Deeper and Richer Music": Felicia Hemans in Dialogue with Wordsworth, Byron and Shelley' (*ChLB* 145[2009] 3–12). Hemans's poetry, for O'Neill, is densely allusive but also deft in its ability to open itself to alternative possibilities. Nikki Hessell describes a remarkable story of Hemans's influence in 'Romantic Literature and Indigenous Languages: Reading Felicia Hemans in Te Reo Māori' (*ERR* 20[2009] 261–70). Hemans's 'The Hour of Prayer' was translated into the Māori language as a teaching tool in schools, which, as Hessell shows, subtly engage with the linguistic possibilities inherent in te reo Māori. Rather than simply an imposition of the colonizer's culture on the colonized, the translations suggest 'a conversation between two cultural standpoints' (p. 269). Jason R. Rudy's *Electric Meters: Victorian Physiological Poetics* (discussed in Chapter XIII) contains an important chapter on Hemans and Mary Robinson's response to physiology ('The Electric Poetess', pp. 17–43). These poets, unlike Wordsworth, require little distance between experience and communication, producing a poetics that is vitally conscious of the politics of sensibility. In 'Translating the Elgin Marbles: Byron, Hemans, Keats' (*WC* 40[2009] 29–36), Angela Esterhammer subtly unravels three poets' ambivalent responses to the Elgin Marbles based on their sense of the commercial nature of the imperial translation of ancient Greece to modern Britain. Byron condemns such activity by insisting on his capacity (as one who has been to Greece) to embody history. But, Esterhammer shows, this depends on an all too similar 'commodification of antiquity' (p. 32). Noah Comet provides an important reconsideration of Hemans's Hellenism in 'Felicia Hemans and the "Exquisite Remains" of *Modern Greece*' (*KSJ* 58[2009] 96–113). Paying due attention to form and history, Comet suggests how Hemans 'fragments the monumentalizing poetics and tropes of traditional Hellenism' (p. 98); despite her approval of Elgin's pillaging, she suggests that Britain's monuments, too, are 'ephemeral' (p. 113). Rodney Stenning Edgecombe argues for the influence of Hemans on Keats in 'Felicia Hemans's "Modern Greece" and the "Ode to Psyche"' (*KSR* 23[2009] 51–2).

James Hogg's songs received welcome attention this year. Kirsteen McCue's excellent 'From the Songs of Albyn to German Hebrew Melodies: The Musical Adventures of James Hogg' (*SHW* 20[2009] 67–83) focuses on the years between 1815 and 1819 in which Hogg was engaged in a remarkable range of projects, and, centrally, an investigation of Scottish and biblical song traditions. McCue argues that the Scottish elements prevail, but equally her readings of the songs suggest the interpenetration of these cultural spheres. McCue's 'Singing "more old songs than ever ploughman could": The Songs of James Hogg and Robert Burns in the Musical Marketplace' (in Alker and Faith, eds., pp. 123–37) emphasizes that if Hogg would be Burns's successor, he saw that role largely as 'protector and evangelist of the Scottish song tradition' (p. 124). Yet despite his remarkable skill in this field, Hogg remained, in the eyes of the nineteenth-century musical marketplace, firmly in second place. Murray Pittock's 'James Hogg: Scottish Romanticism, Song, and the Public Sphere' (in Alker and Faith, eds., pp. 111–22) examines Hogg's role as one who recognized but also resisted the effects the market was having on the local song tradition; as song began to lose its Dissenting heritage and local roots in search of politeness, Hogg reflected the 'paradox of cultural and social bifurcation' (p. 122). In 'Hogg's Bardic Epic: *Queen Hynde* and Macpherson's *Ossian*' (in Alker and Faith, eds., pp. 139–55), Douglas S. Mack argues that in placing his poem as a Scottish epic, Hogg offers it, not as an imitator of *Ossian*, but an 'alternative' to it (p. 140). Hogg resists Macpherson's elegiac national dirge and celebrates 'new beginnings' and the 'energies of youth and spring' (p. 154). Other essays in this collection are discussed in section 3. Work on Leigh Hunt is discussed in section 2.

The year 2009 was a relatively lean one for Keats studies in terms of individual articles, though his poetry does feature in several general studies and collections discussed above. Besides those discussed above, *Romanticism and Popular Culture in Britain and Ireland*, edited by Philip Connell and Nigel Leask, includes an essay on Keats. Gillian Russell discusses how Keats 'offers a test case of how the categories of popular culture, theatre, and Romanticism might be conjoined' (p. 196) in 'Keats, Popular Culture, and the Sociability of Theatre' (pp. 194–213). Keats's relationship with Leigh Hunt was considered by Arnd Bohm in 'Hunt's *The Descent of Liberty* and the Seasonal Politics of Keats's "To Autumn"' (*Romanticism* 15[2009] 131–43). Hunt's strange and rather brilliant masque offered an explicitly political reading of autumn that, as Bohm suggests, would surely have influenced Keats. Bohm adds his voice to those who see Keats's 'perfect' ode as principally political in its aims. Speaking to recent discussions on the Romantic fascination with disease, particularly consumption, Brendan Corcoran observes that 'death as an actuality and an enigma thoroughly permeates Keats's thought' (p. 321), in 'Keats's Death: Towards a Posthumous Poetics' (*SiR* 48[2009] 321–48). Corcoran's essay provides an interesting and valuable contribution to the growing discourse on Romantic disease and mortality. Lastly on Keats, two pieces by Deborah Forbes and Christopher R. Miller featured in *Something Understood: Essays and Poetry for Helen Vendler*, edited by Stephen Burt and Nick Halpern. This collection was not available in time for review this year but will be covered with material from 2010.

Ian Haywood's superb essay, 'Shelley's *Mask of Anarchy* and the Visual Iconography of Female Distress' (in Connell and Leask, eds., pp. 148–73), suggests that Shelley's *Mask* 'has the most impeccably "popular" credentials of all canonical Romantic poems' (p. 148). Haywood focuses on Shelley's use of 'allegorized female agency' in his poem, which, he argues, 'plays a key role in Shelley's mission' towards reform (p. 149). Joel Faflak offers a new interpretation of Shelley's 'Triumph of Life', in his article 'The Difficult Education of Shelley's "Triumph of Life"' (*KSJ* 58[2009] 53–78). Drawing on previous readings of Shelley by Paul de Man and Tilottama Rajan, Faflak suggests that 'our critical purchase on history is as much about the desire for and trauma of knowledge through a scene of psychoanalysis' (p. 54). Following his excellent 2008 volume *The Reception of P.B. Shelley in Europe*, coedited with Susanne Schmid, Michael Rossington delivers a fascinating discussion of Shelley's view of the role of poetry in creating freedom, in his article, 'Theorizing a Republican Poetics: P.B. Shelley and Alfieri' (*ERR* 20[2009] 619–28). Rossington posits that 'From his Italian vantage-point' Shelley wishes to show that poetry can actively promote and 'effect' political freedom (p. 620). Also published in Shelley studies was *The Unfamiliar Shelley*, edited by Alan M. Weinberg and Timothy Webb. The volume was covered in last year's *YWES*, but Jeremy Davies covers the chapters on Shelley and drama this year in section 5 below.

Elizabeth Heckendorn Cook directs her attention to the natural-historical allusions in Charlotte Smith's 'The Swallow', in her article 'Charlotte Smith and "The Swallow": Migration and Romantic Authorship' (*HLQ* 72[2009] 48–67). Cook asserts that Smith's poem 'is a remarkable conflation of pastoral, erotic, religious and natural-historical allusions' (p. 48), setting the scene for both a fascinating analysis of Smith's work, and a worthy contribution to the growing critical interest in animal imagery in Romantic literature. Lily Gurton-Wachter's article, '"An Enemy, I suppose, that Nature has made": Charlotte Smith and the Natural Enemy' (*ERR* 20[2009] 197–205), traces the fascinating history of the term 'natural enemy', and specifically offers an analysis of Charlotte Smith's use of the phrase in her 1807 poem *Beachy Head*. Gurton-Wachter's thorough investigation offers a unique and refreshing analysis of Smith's poem. In 'The hybrid poems of Smith and Wordsworth: Questions and Disputes' (*ERR* 20[2009] 219–26), Jacqueline Labbe argues that the hybridized titles of Wordsworth's *Lyrical Ballads* and Smith's *Elegiac Sonnets* actively engage with contemporary debates over what constitutes poetry. Labbe posits that Smith and Wordsworth force their works to ask 'What is a poem?', and combine 'forms to produce something else altogether' (p. 225). Melissa Sodeman argues in her essay, 'Charlotte Smith's Literary Exile' (*ELH* 76[2009] 130–52) that Smith's fascination with exile was inextricably linked to concerns over poetic form, and that a full understanding of Smith's life is the key to her work.

In a monumental achievement, editor Linda Pratt and assistant editors Carol Bolton, Tim Fulford, and Ian Packer have collected the complete letters of Robert Southey in eight parts. Primarily funded by the AHRC and supplemented by grants from several other bodies such as the Leverhulme Trust, the British Academy, and the Humanities Research Centre at the

University of Nottingham, the collection is a significant contribution to a new understanding of Southey as 'a consummate, even an "entire" man of letters, intimately involved in the culture of his time' (General Introduction). The collection itself is undeniably the best edition of Southey's letters available, edited with precision and care, providing a new and invaluable resource for Southey scholars. Moreover, because it has been published electronically, the collection is not only as widely available as possible, but also its clear layout, and the inclusion of an engine to search for specific letters, make this resource supremely accessible for newer readers and researchers. In addition to the letters, the collection includes a general introduction and specific introductions to each of the eight parts, a selective chronology of Southey's life, a list of his correspondents, biographies of those connected with Southey, and a summary of significant places in his time. The last three of these provide extremely valuable contextual information, helping to build a concise but clear picture of the environment Southey wrote his letters in. Aside from the impressive scholarly rigour and attention to detail on display here, the collection's strongest aspect is that it has been published in electronic format. *The Collected Letters of Robert Southey* is the supreme example of electronic resources being used effectively to further scholarly research: not only is it the definitive collection of Southey's letters, it is highly accessible while remaining rigorous and effective, and undoubtedly points the way for future electronic research projects of this kind. Southey was also the subject of one scholarly article, 'Formal Relocations: The Method of Southey's *Thalaba the Destroyer* (1801)' (*ERR* 20[2009] 671–9), in which Dahlia Porter reads Southey's *Thalaba the Destroyer* against the backdrop of the 'Enlightenment Science of Man and its analogical framework' (p. 671). In a concise but thorough investigation, Porter argues that 'The uncomfortable collusions definitive of *Thalaba* arise out of the methodological paradigms Southey was working within' (p. 676).

Judith Thompson provides one of this year's only discussions of the radical poet and satirist John Thelwall. In 'Why Kendal? John Thelwall, Laker Poet?' (*WC* 40[2009] 16–22), Thompson claims that a thrilling discovery in 2004 of Thelwall's complete poems 'prove[s] that Thelwall's poetry is more ambitious and original than he has been given credit for' (p. 17).

Scholars of Wordsworth will be pleased to see that the poet received much critical attention this year. In the final chapter of Connell and Leask, eds., *Romanticism and Popular Culture*, 'How to Popularize Wordsworth' (pp. 262–82), Philip Connell considers the difficulty with which critics have wrestled with the issue of Wordsworth's popularity. Intriguingly, he suggests that Wordsworth's supplementary 'Essay' to the first collected edition of his poems 'offers a fascinating demonstration of the way in which discourse on literary popularity in this period could shift' (p. 265). In his article 'Communicable Dis-Ease: Wordsworth's Discharged Soldier' (*Selected Proceedings from the Canadian Society for Eighteenth-Century Studies* 28[2009] 139–50), James Allard discusses Wordsworth's poem 'The Discharged Soldier' to investigate 'popular representations of the medical profession in Britain in the late eighteenth and early nineteenth centuries' (p. 141). Allard provides an interesting and useful foray into the growing body of work on literature and medicine. David Bromwich supplies a fascinating investigation into the origins of Wordsworth's concept of community in 'The "Ode to Duty" and the Idea of Human Solidarity' (*WC* 40[2009] 9–16). Bromwich concentrates on the division between the poet's early concerns with imagination and his later sense of 'duty' (p. 9). In 'The Making of Meaning in Wordsworth's *Home at Grasmere* (Speech Acts, Microanalysis and "Freudian Slips")' (*SiR* 48[2009] 391–421), Sally Bushell analyses Wordsworth's *Home at Grasmere* in relation to the nature of speech acts, and the 'exploration of the making of meaning through "micro-analysis" of acts on the page and the interpretation of unintended meaning' (p. 391). Bushell links this to Wordsworth's poem by noting that the fact that the work 'never achieved a lifetime published state' makes it perfect for this kind of analysis (p. 391). In 'Some Youngian Echoes in Wordsworth' (*N&Q* 56[2009] 364–5), Rodney Stenning Edgecombe compares passages from Young's *Night Thoughts* to Wordsworth's Immortality Ode, arguing that Wordsworth seems to have taken over the bleak rocky landscape of Young's visionary image' (p. 365). In '"Another race hath been": Vaughan, Milton, and the "Immortality Ode"' (*ChLB* 148[2009] 134–40), Ian M. Emberson examines the influence of Milton's *Paradise Lost* and Henry Vaughan's *The Retreat* on Wordsworth's 'Immortality Ode'. Emberson suggests that rather than simply highlighting Wordsworth's 'echoes' of Milton and Vaughan, the consideration 'of these influences can throw light on the full meaning of the "Ode" itself' (p. 134). Aaron Fogel introduces his essay on Wordsworth's 'We Are Seven' by stating that, 'By unusually silent implication, [the poem] makes poetry, not prose, the first, most dangerously concise medium through which to record conflicts over "population" in the larger scene' (p. 23). Fogel thus posits 'We Are Seven' as acting out 'a deliberately lowest variant of the eighteenth century's English population debates' (p. 24). In '"Long Meg" and the Later Wordsworth' (*EIC* 59[2009] 37–58), Tim Fulford suggests that Wordsworth's sequence of poems entitled 'Composed or Suggested During a Tour in the Summer of 1833' has received little critical attention not because of its lack of poetic merit, but because of the 'typical biases' of Romanticists (p. 37).

A.C. Goodson brings us his essay, 'The Voices of Others: Wordsworth's Poetics of Recognition' (in Wehrs and Haney, eds., pp. 45–60), in which he argues that 'Wordsworth's hospitality to the voices of others became a signature of his new kind of verse' (p. 46). In 'Wordsworth and Touch' (*English* 58[2009] 4–23), Francis O'Gorman provides a fascinating discussion of Wordsworth's reluctance to engage with the concept of physical human touch in his poetry. O'Gorman opens his essay by asking simply 'Why is touch between human beings so unusual in Wordsworth's poetry?' (p. 4). The analysis that follows proves both enlightening and compelling. Richard Gravil discusses, in 'Helen Maria Williams: Wordsworth's Revolutionary *Anima*' (*WC* 40[2009] 55–64), Wordsworth's infatuation with Helen Maria Williams, suggesting that 'if there ever were a conclusive instance of the male writer absorbing the female, it is this strangely unsung instance of the use he clearly made of the work of this "scribbling trollop"' (p. 56). Felicity James, in her article 'Neighbours: Wordsworth and Harriet Martineau' (*ChLB* 58[2009] 13–23), discusses the relationship between Wordsworth and Martineau. James's focus is on the latter, offering 'a broad biographical introduction'

(p. 15) to Martineau. Sandro Jung examines Wordsworth's interest in the works of the poet William Collins, in 'Wordsworth and Collins' (*ANQ* 22[2009] 19–24). Jung posits that Collins's appeal to the Romantics was threefold, but for Wordsworth, Collins was 'a direct literary forebear from whom he derived his own unique brand of Romanticism' (p. 24). In her article 'Wordsworth, *The White Doe of Rylstone*: A Reading with Reference to Scott' (*ChLB* 58[2009] 24–33), Claire Lamont examines the poem that Francis Jeffrey described as having 'the merit of being the very worst poem we ever saw imprinted in a quarto volume' (p. 24). Lamont's article analyses this divisive poem in relation to the works of Walter Scott, in order to 'shed light on its particular qualities' (p. 24). In a brief but enlightening discussion, Daniel Lewis investigates 'regimentation' and 'officialdom' (p. 80) in 'Pedestrian Politics: William Wordsworth's "The Old Cumberland Beggar"' (*Expl* 67[2009] 80–3). Lewis argues convincingly that these themes are 'the poem's keynote' and that 'Wordsworth's poem actually celebrates order, predictability, and certainty' (p. 83). Emma Mason and Rhian Williams's article 'Reciprocal Scansion in Wordsworth's "There Was a Boy"' (*LitComp* 6[2009] 515–23) forms part of a cluster that has its origins in the recent 'Metre Matters' conference. Mason and Williams argue that 'The current resurgence of interest in prosody is . . . beneficial . . . because it offers us a way of finding . . . routes into the past' (p. 522).

Brian McGrath opens his discussion of the 'desire for sensational tales' (p. 572) in 'Wordsworth, "Simon Lee," and the Craving for Incidents' (*SiR* 48[2009] 565–82) by summarizing two kinds of readers of Wordsworth: those who favour 'the spontaneous overflow of powerful feelings', contrasted with those 'who privilege the importance of "recollection" . . . that subordinates immediate sensation to reflective judgement' (p. 565). In 'Behind the Dream of the Arab: The Non-Publication of Wordsworth's *The Prelude*' (*OrbisLit* 64[2009] 127–40), Peter Simonsen investigates why Wordsworth did not publish *The Prelude* in 1805. Simonsen suggests that it is not necessary not to 'think of *The Prelude* as a "book" just because Wordsworth did not push it to print' (p. 127), but that he did not publish it dramatically alters the way that readers must read the work.

5. Drama

The product of a very deep engagement with the theatre of the Romantic period, Frederick Burwick's *Romantic Drama: Acting and Reacting* was the year's most significant contribution to the field. Burwick offers a treasure-house of interpretation and appreciation of stage plays that have fallen into neglect. His priority is the recovery of individual texts—much room is given over to summaries of their plots—rather than the drawing of general conclusions, but there emerges a strong sense of how theatrical culture developed through processes of adaptation, borrowing, and pastiche, often across national and linguistic boundaries. The desire to respond to controversies and anxieties of the moment, and to keep up with rapid shifts in fashion, led playwrights and theatre managers to produce patchworked and recycled dramas that sometimes inverted comprehensively the ideological bearings of their originals. Burwick's first chapter introduces the Scottish gentleman of leisure John Waldie, whose lifelong theatre journal is mined throughout the book for its insights into contemporary actors and audience responses. Burwick traces Waldie's development from a rather gauche teenage lover of the theatre into an indefatigable play-goer who travelled widely across Europe, and finds in his homosexuality a partial explanation for his fascination with 'the otherness of the stage' (p. 32). The second chapter deals with French stereotypes in plays adapted from French originals, set in France, starring French characters, or just satirizing the adopters of French affectations. The French are typically presented as procuresses, smugglers, schemers, and boasters, but what is striking, for Burwick, is how rarely they are truly vilified. Instead, there is a consistent awareness of the extent of French influence on English manners and society. The next chapter describes how the extremes of realism and fantasy could merge into one another. Topical documentary dramas like *The Gamblers* (staged by William Thomas Moncrieff) provided a dizzyingly rapid theatricalization of sensational crimes; supernatural thrillers, like Edward Fitzball's *The Flying Dutchman*, made much use of phantasmagoric stage effects. Both were self-consciously illusionistic and sought to dazzle their audiences with spectacle.

Chapter 4 is concerned with the theories of stage gesture and expression developed by Henry Siddons and others, and especially with the problem of playing characters—such as Iago and Richard III—who themselves dissimulate or feign their emotions. The fifth explores texts that hint at the representation of homosexual desire. Cross-dressing is the obvious way in which same-sex attraction could be implied on stage, but Burwick's most compelling discussion is of Elizabeth Inchbald's *The Widow's Vow*, in which the comedy arises instead from the mistaken belief that a male suitor is a cross-dressed woman. The device allows Inchbald to approach 'much closer to the forbidden boundaries of homosexual touch than most plays of the period' (p. 123). The next chapter—an extensively altered version of an essay described here last year—discusses sets and settings: both the work of the landscape painters commissioned to produce ever more elaborate backdrops, and the interpretative consequences of setting plays in either remote or familiar locations. Adaptations often involved a change of location: later chapters discuss George Colman's 1798 version of *Blue-Beard*, which was the first to turn this western European tale into a fable of Turkish despotism, and Charles Nodier, who made possible the splendid title of the final chapter, 'Vampires in Kilts', by first transposing the vampire legend to Scotland. The last three chapters are all concerned, in one way or another, with the 'presence of the comic in plays of dark melodrama' (p. 200). A chapter on the Gothic precedes those on Bluebeard and vampires, and includes a memorable discussion of how the child actor Master Betty was able to play depraved middle-aged villains to great acclaim. The many versions of *Blue-Beard* were used predominantly as vehicles for misogynistic sexual fantasy rather than as opportunities to pursue a critique of the oppression of women. 'The vampire melodrama', however, 'provided an apt post-Revolutionary commentary on an aristocracy feeding upon the lower classes' (p. 257). John Polidori's

The Vampyre served in England, France, and Germany as a thrilling—albeit easily parodied—source for dramas representing the dangers of unrestrained sexual appetite.

Christine A. Colón's *Joanna Baillie and the Art of Moral Influence* is a methodically argued study that commends Baillie as a Christian and didactic writer—for Colón, the two qualities that caused her to be disregarded for so long. Her didacticism gave rise to the tension that drives her theatre theory and practice. On the one hand, the playhouse is the perfect venue for making the most of the universal propensity for sympathetic curiosity, which means that playwrights have a special power to shape moral responses. On the other, Baillie is above all concerned with individual responsibility and freedom of choice, a principle that Colón traces to her theological standpoint (Presbyterianism spiced with an interest in Unitarianism). Her fear was that the dramatist's 'influence may ultimately become manipulation and impinge upon the freedom of the audience' (p. 82). *Rayner* is a rare play in which the protagonist is able fully to live up to his responsibilities and master his passions; more often, dramatizing freedom of interpretation means presenting characters who collapse into destructive misinterpretation. Baillie's preoccupation with ethical autonomy is also the reason for her persistent critique of the gendered division between public and private spheres of influence: to make feminine mildness responsible for taming masculine aggression is to damage the moral standing of both sexes. Colón reflects on many of Baillie's plays, and on her *View of the General Tenour of the New Testament*, but *De Monfort* seems once more to justify its status at the heart of the Baillie canon, eliciting the lengthiest and most stimulating discussion. Jane de Monfort is seen as a source rather than a healer of strife. She embodies the domestic sphere too completely, as sister, mother, and lover in one, and De Monfort must be sacrificed 'so that no threat of incest taints her pristine character' (p. 144). It is likewise through *De Monfort* that James Robert Allard examines Baillie's dramatic theory in 'Joanna Baillie and the Theater of Consequence' (in Allard and Martin, eds., *Staging Pain, 1580–1800: Violence and Trauma in British Theater*, pp. 169–83). Allard is concerned with the relative failure of the play's 1800 production, and with what that failure tells us about the priorities of its audiences. *De Monfort*, he argues, interrogates sympathetic curiosity as well as inciting it: 'Baillie feeds the "natural desire we have to look" precisely to [draw our] attention to that desire' (p. 182).

A group of four essays in Class and Robinson, eds., *Transnational England: Home and Abroad, 1780–1860* (also covered in *YWES* 89[2010] under 'The Novel') explores ethnic and national hybridity in the period's drama. In 'Women's Cosmopolitanism and the Romantic Stage: Cowley's *A Day in Turkey, or the Russian Slaves*' (pp. 22–40), Greg Kucich finds in Hannah Cowley's topical comedy of 1791 a 'politically charged kind of embodied female cosmopolitanism' (p. 34). Kucich reads the play in the light of the new genre of female-authored 'global histories of women's experience' (p. 29) and their enthusiasm for the pacifying effects of love-affairs that cross racial boundaries—a creative mixing that is reflected in the generic mishmash of what one reviewer called Cowley's 'tragic-comedy-operatical-pantomimical farce' (p. 29). Dana Van Kooy's 'Improvising on the Borders: Hellenism,

History, and Tragedy in Shelley's *Hellas*' (pp. 41–57) associates *Hellas* with popular stage melodrama and pantomime, and with the tradition of reflections on empire and slavery in topical theatre. The text represents history as a dialectical process of struggle: '[t]he dramatic action of *Hellas* concludes with Mahmud achieving a lyric consciousness of history' (p. 54). The essay by Frederick Burwick that follows (pp. 58–91) is a version of the second chapter of his *Romantic Drama*, discussed above. Lastly, Michael Eberle-Sinatra's 'Performing Leigh Hunt's 1840 Play *A Legend of Florence*' (pp. 92–110) tells the story of Hunt's negotiation of the difficult transition from theatre critic to playwright. That transition was complicated by some aspects of his dramatic theory—which celebrated readerly imagination over the contemporary star system—but his winningly ingenuous approach to the writing and staging of his tale of escape from domestic abuse helped to make the production a success.

Heather McPherson's 'Siddons Rediviva: Death, Memory and Theatrical Afterlife' (in Mole, ed., *Romanticism and Celebrity Culture, 1750–1850*, pp. 120–40) argues that the caricatures of Sarah Siddons produced at the time of the Old Price riots marked the beginning of a loss of control over her public image in the later years of her life. Henry Perronet Briggs's double portrait of Siddons and her niece Fanny Kemble suggests disjunction rather than continuity within the Kemble acting dynasty. Yet since her death stage and film artists have found many different ways to commemorate and celebrate her career. Cheryl Wanko's contribution to the same collection deals mainly with a slightly earlier period. 'Patron or Patronised? "Fans" and the Eighteenth-Century English Stage' (in Mole, ed., pp. 209–26) describes the shifting power-relations between actors and their audiences. Aristocratic patrons of the theatre increasingly had to compete with the 'patron-function' exercised by the rest of the house, while the performers themselves acquired ever more cultural capital. In the absence of a fully developed commodity market for dramatic performance, however, the Romantic period saw only developments in the patronage system, rather than the emergence of a modern fan culture. Another exploration of Romantic celebrity, Michael Gamer and Terry F. Robinson's 'Mary Robinson and the Dramatic Art of the Comeback' (*SiR* 48[2009] 219–56), is concerned with Mary Robinson's theatrical career from 1782 onwards—that is, *after* her retirement from the stage. Robinson's appearances as a spectator rather than a performer at the opera and the playhouse were covered breathlessly in the press, and Gamer and Robinson narrate an enjoyably colourful history of the way in which she performed her sexual and fashionable identity, a topic that leads, via a reading of Cowley's *A Bold Stroke for a Husband*, to her flirtatious *entrée* into the Della Cruscan circle in 1788.

Diego Saglia's 'Introduction: The Survival of Tragedy in European Romanticisms' (*ERR* 20[2009] 567–79) serves as a preface to a group of essays on tragedy in continental European literatures, but it draws the British experience into its purview through a discussion of William Hazlitt. Hazlitt's vacillation as to whether tragedy was undergoing a disintegration or a reinvention on the contemporary stage was, Saglia shows, just one version of debates taking place across Europe. The two essays on Shelley's dramas in *The*

Unfamiliar Shelley, edited by Alan M. Weinberg and Timothy Webb (discussed in *YWES* 89[2010] under 'Poetry') both touch on their relationship to the stage tradition: *Swellfoot the Tyrant* is a 'pantomimic satyr play', writes Timothy Morton in 'Porcine Poetics: Shelley's *Swellfoot the Tyrant*' (pp. 279–95), while Nora Crook, in 'Shelley's Late Fragmentary Plays: "Charles the First" and the "Unfinished Drama"' (pp. 297–311), locates those texts within the busy theatrical activities of the Shelley circle in early 1822. Morton describes a grotesque carnival in which pigs are reduced to the status of walking food even as they are anthropomorphized, mobilizing tropes of consumption, vomiting, and disgust. Crook reconstructs the skeins of imagery buried within Shelley's disorderly late manuscripts; worries about faithlessness and corruption seem to have been much on his mind.

Monika Coghen argues for the influence on Byron of contemporary Gothic stage plays—works by M.G. Lewis and Charles Maturin, and the pantomime tradition—in 'The Gothic in Byron's Dramas' (in Cochran, ed., pp. 97–110). *Werner* is the most obvious example, but even his overtly neoclassical plays adopt Gothic tropes and the theme of a bloody past's stranglehold upon the present. In 'National Discourse or Discord? Transformations of *The Family Legend* by Baillie, Scott, and Hogg' (in Alker and Nelson, eds., pp. 43–55), Meiko O'Halloran discusses Walter Scott's ambitious 1810 production of Baillie's *The Family Legend*. Staged as a grand expression of pro-Union Edinburgh high culture, Baillie's play envisaged the harnessing of inter-communal Highland aggression to imperial military ends. James Hogg was among the audience, but his reworking of the drama in two prose tales played up the anxieties about the destructiveness of primitive clan culture that even Baillie and Scott had not managed completely to contain.

Two excellent essays in *The Byron Journal* showed how modern performances can illuminate Romantic texts. Both of the productions described were rehearsed readings rather than full stagings, and in Michael Simpson's 'Byron's *Manfred* and the King's Head: Having Words with Bodies' (*ByronJ* 37[2009] 43–54), this mode of performance that involves actors 'not merely dramatising a text but also dramatising the act of reading a text' (p. 44) is seen as an adroit way of offering up a drama that belongs somewhere between the closet and the stage. Simpson's subtle, associative meditation on da Vinci's *The Last Supper*, death and resurrection, Orpheus, and Frankenstein's Creature finds that *Manfred* is troubled by the political resonances of its own charismatic appeal. Bernard Beatty's '*Sardanapalus* at the Globe: 3 April 2009' (*ByronJ* 37[2009] 55–6) is a brief, penetrating description of how performance can change our sense of the tone and qualities even of a very familiar text. In 'Wordsworth at the Theater: Illegitimate Spectacle in Book 7 of *The Prelude*' (*ERR* 20[2009] 77–93), David Francis Taylor examines the Sadler's Wells episode in Book VII of *The Prelude* in the light of recent scholarship on London's illegitimate theatres. Wordsworth's description of a performance of *Jack the Giant Killer* expresses his enthusiasm for a marginal theatrical culture, while the legal suppression of speech on the non-patent stage illustrates for him the way in which vocalization is overwhelmed by the metropolis. Yet his enthusiasm sits uneasily with a Burkean fear of disorderly mass spectatorship; Burkean, too, is the sentimental portrayal of the Maid of Buttermere through which those anxieties are held in check.

Books Reviewed

Adams, Hazard. *Blake's Margins: An Interpretative Study of the Annotations*. McFarland. [2009] pp. 204. £32.50 ISBN 9 7807 8644 5363.

Alker, Sharon, and Holly Faith Nelson, eds. *James Hogg and the Literary Marketplace: Scottish Romanticism and the Working-Class Author*. Ashgate. [2009] pp. xvi + 261. £49.50 ISBN 9 7807 5466 5694.

Allard, James Robert, and Mathew R. Martin, eds. *Staging Pain, 1580–1800: Violence and Trauma in British Theater*. Ashgate. [2009] pp. xii + 220. £49.50 ISBN 9 7807 5466 7582.

Ankarsjö, Magnus. *William Blake and Religion: A New Critical View*. McFarland. [2009] pp. 163. $39.95 ISBN 9 7807 8644 5592.

Barbeau, Jeffrey W. *Coleridge, the Bible and Religion*. Palgrave. [2008] pp. 234. £42.50. ISBN 9 7802 3060 1345.

Behrendt, Stephen C. *British Women Poets and the Romantic Writing Community*. JHUP. [2009] pp. xii + 368. £67 ISBN 9 7808 0189 0543.

Benis, Toby R. *Romantic Diasporas: French Émigrés, British Convicts and Jews*. Palgrave Macmillan. [2009] pp. ix + 194. £50 ISBN 9 7802 3061 0651.

Brock, Marilyn, ed. *From Wollstonecraft to Stoker: Essays on Gothic and Victorian Sensation Fiction*. McFarland. [2009] pp. 220. £31.50 ISBN 9 7807 8644 0214.

Burnett, John. *Robert Burns and the Hellish Legion*. National Museums Scotland. [2009] pp. x + 132. pb £9.99 ISBN 9 7819 0526 7316.

Burwick, Frederick, ed. *The Oxford Handbook of Samuel Taylor Coleridge*. OUP. [2009] pp. xx + 758. £85 ISBN 9 7801 9922 9536.

Burwick, Frederick. *Romantic Drama: Acting and Reacting*. CUP. [2009] pp. viii + 345. £53 ISBN 9 7805 2188 9674.

Carruthers, Gerard. *The Edinburgh Companion to Robert Burns*. EdinUP. [2009] pp. ix + 198. £18.99 ISBN 9 7807 4863 6488.

Class, Monika, and Terry F. Robinson, eds. *Transnational England: Home and Abroad, 1780–1860*. CambridgeSP. [2009] pp. xiv + 283. £40 ISBN 9 7814 4380 1966.

Cochran, Peter, ed. *The Gothic Byron*. CambridgeSP. [2009] pp. viii + 201. £40 ISBN 9 7814 4380 2444.

Cochran, Peter. *'Romanticism'—and Byron*. CambridgeSP. [2009] pp. lv + 395. £44.99 ISBN 9 7814 4380 1133.

Colón, Christine A. *Joanna Baillie and the Art of Moral Influence*. Lang. [2009] pp. vii + 214. £48 ISBN 9 7814 3310 5364.

Connell, Philip, and Nigel Leask, eds. *Romanticism and Popular Culture in Britain and Ireland*. CUP. [2009] pp. 332. £53 ISBN 9 7805 2188 0121.

Crawford, Robert. *The Bard: Robert Burns, A Biography*. Cape. [2009] pp. xiii + 466. £20 ISBN 9 7802 2407 7682.

Davies, Damian Walford, ed. *Romanticism, History, Historicism: Essays on an Orthodoxy*. Routledge. [2009] pp. xx + 234. £85 ISBN 9 7804 1596 1127.

Dennis, Ian. *Lord Byron and the History of Desire*. UDelP. [2009] pp. 266. £48.95 ISBN 9 7808 7413 0669.

Dick, Alexander, and Angela Esterhammer, eds. *Spheres of Action: Speech and Performance in Romantic Culture*. UTorP. [2009] pp. viii + 306. £42 ISBN 9 7808 0209 8030.

Egenolf, Susan B. *The Art of Political Fiction in Hamilton, Edgeworth and Owenson*. Ashgate. [2009] pp. x + 210. £55 ISBN 9 7807 5466 2037.

Eisner, Eric. *Nineteenth-Century Poetry and Literary Celebrity*. Palgrave Macmillan. [2009] pp. vii + 204. £50 ISBN 9 7802 3022 8153.

Elfenbein, Andrew. *Romanticism and the Rise of English*. StanfordUP. [2009] pp. viii + 278. £49 ISBN 9 7808 0477 3621.

Fairer, David. *Organising Poetry: The Coleridge Circle, 1790–1798*. OUP. [2009] pp. xiv + 345. £50 ISBN 9 7801 9929 6163.

Faubert, Michelle. *Rhyming Reason: The Poetry of Romantic-Era Psychologists*. P&C. [2009] pp. 304. £60 ISBN 9 7818 5196 9555.

Ferguson, Frank, and Andrew R. Holmes, eds. *Revising Robert Burns and Ulster: Literature, Religion and Politics, c.1770–1920*. FCP. [2009] pp. 198. £45 ISBN 9 7818 4682 1974.

Garnai, Amy. *Revolutionary Imaginings in the 1790s*. Palgrave. [2009] pp. 256. £50 ISBN 9 7802 3057 5165.

Garrett, Martin, ed. *The Palgrave Literary Dictionary of Byron*. Palgrave Macmillan. [2009] pp. xx + 332. £65 ISBN 9 7802 3000 8977.

Gigante, Denise. *Life: Organic Form and Romanticism*. Yale. [2009] pp. xiii + 302. £27 ISBN 9 7803 0013 6852.

Gottlieb, Evan, and Ian Duncan, eds. *Approaches to Teaching Scott's Waverley Novels*. MLA. [2009] pp. vi + 202. pb $19.75 ISBN 9 7816 0329 0364.

Graham, Peter W. *Jane Austen & Charles Darwin, Naturalists and Novelists*. Ashgate. [2008] pp. 214. £55 ISBN 9 7807 5465 8511.

Houghton-Walker, Sarah. *John Clare's Religion*. Ashgate. [2009] pp. x + 254. £55 ISBN 9 7807 5466 5144.

Hutchings, Kevin. *Romantic Ecologies and Colonial Cultures in the British Atlantic World, 1770–1850*. McG-QUP. [2009] pp. xi + 226. £55 ISBN 9 7807 7353 5794.

Jones, Hazel. *Jane Austen and Marriage*. Continuum. [2009] pp. 256. $34.95 ISBN 9 7818 4725 2180.

Krawczyk, Scott. *Romantic Literary Families*. Palgrave Macmillan. [2009] pp. xvi + 224. £52 ISBN 9 7802 3060 4759.

Krishnamurthy, Aruna, ed. *The Working-Class Intellectual in Eighteenth- and Nineteenth-Century Britain*. Ashgate. [2009] pp. x + 257. £60 ISBN 9 7807 5466 5045.

Lau, Beth, ed. *Fellow Romantics, Male and Female British Writers, 1790–1835*. Ashgate. [2009] pp. 278. £55 ISBN 9 7807 5466 3539.

McDayter, Ghislaine. *Byromania and the Birth of Celebrity Culture*. SUNYP. [2009] pp. xiii + 242. pb £24.95 ISBN 9 7814 3842 5269.

McIntyre, Ian. *Robert Burns: A Life*. Constable. [2009] pp. xvi + 480. pb £9.99 ISBN 9 7818 4529 4694.

Mole, Tom, ed. *Romanticism and Celebrity Culture, 1750–1850*. CUP. [2009] pp. xi + 296. £53 ISBN 9 7805 2188 4778.

Monaghan, David, Ariane Hudelet, and John Wiltshire, eds. *The Cinematic Jane Austen: Essays on the Filmic Sensibility of the Novels*. McFarland. [2009] pp. vi + 197. £31.50 ISBN 9 7807 8643 5067.

Morini, Massimiliano. *Jane Austen's Narrative Techniques: A Stylistic and Pragmatic Analysis*. Ashgate. [2009] pp. 172. £55 ISBN 9 7807 5466 6073.

Mulvey-Roberts, Marie, ed. *The Handbook of the Gothic*. Palgrave. [2009] pp. 384. pb £16.99 ISBN 9 7802 3000 8540.

Myrone, Martin. *Seen in My Visions: A Descriptive Catalogue of Pictures*. Tate. [2009] pp. 128. £12.99 ISBN 9 7818 5437 8637.

Nachumi, Nora. *Acting Like a Lady: British Women Novelists and the Eighteenth-Century Theater*. AMS. [2008] pp. xxvi + 347. $94.50 ISBN 9 7804 0464 8503.

North, Julian. *The Domestication of Genius: Biography and the Romantic Poet*. OUP. [2009] pp. xii + 253. £55 ISBN 9 7801 9957 1987.

Peer, Larry H., ed. *Romanticism and the Object*. Palgrave Macmillan. [2009] pp. xii + 223. £50 ISBN 9 7802 3061 7384.

Pratt, Linda, ed., with Carol Bolton, Tim Fulford, and Ian Packer. *The Collected Letters of Robert Southey*. Romantic Circles. [2009]. Available online: http://www.rc.umd.edu/editions/southey_letters/Part_One/index_part1.html.

Price, Fiona. *Revolutions in Taste, 1773–1818: Women Writers and the Aesthetics of Romanticism*. Ashgate. [2009] pp. 204. £55 ISBN 9 7807 5466 0262.

Purves, Maria. *The Gothic and Catholicism: Religion, Cultural Exchange and the Popular Novel, 1785–1829*. UWalesP. [2009] pp. 192. £75 ISBN 9 7807 0832 0914.

Quinney, Laura. *William Blake on Self and Soul*. HarvardUP. [2009] pp. 195. $39.95 ISBN 9 7806 7403 5249.

Rodger, Johnny, and Gerard Carruthers, eds. *Fickle Man: Robert Burns in the 21st Century*. Sandstone. [2009] pp. xi + 319. £23.99 ISBN 9 7819 0520 7275.

Rudy, Jason R. *Electric Meters: Victorian Physiological Poetics*. OhioUP. [2009] pp. xiii + 222. £39.95 ISBN 9 7808 2141 8826.

Schoina, Maria. *Romantic 'Anglo-Italians': Configurations of Identity in Byron, the Shelleys, and the Pisan Circle*. Ashgate. [2009] pp. ix + 192. £55 ISBN 9 7807 5466 2921.

Scott Hogg, Patrick. *Robert Burns: The Patriot Bard*. Mainstream. [2009] pp. 368. pb £7.99 ISBN 9 7818 4596 4856.

Speer, Roderick S. *Byron and Scott: The Waverley Novels and Historical Engagement*. CambridgeSP. [2009] pp. xiv + 116. $34.99 ISBN 9 7814 4380 5872.

Sung, Mei-Ying. *William Blake and the Art of Engraving*. P&C. [2009] pp. 220. £60 ISBN 9 7818 5196 9586.

Vigus, James. *Platonic Coleridge*. DavidB. [2009] pp. xii + 188. £45 ISBN 9 7819 0654 0067.

Walker, Eric C. *Marriage, Writing, and Romanticism: Wordsworth and Austen after War*. StanfordUP. [2009] pp. 304. pb $23.95 ISBN 9 7808 0477 3652.
Wallace, Diana, and Andrew Smith, eds. *The Female Gothic: New Directions*. Palgrave. [2009] pp. 240. £50 ISBN 9 7802 3022 2717.
Wallace, Miriam L., ed. *Enlightening Romanticism: Romancing the Enlightenment, British Novels from 1750–1832*. Ashgate. [2009] pp. x + 229. £55 ISBN 9 7807 5466 2433.
Wehrs, Donald R., and David P. Haney, eds. *Levinas and Nineteenth-Century Literature, Ethics and Otherness from Romanticism through Realism*. UDelP. [2009] pp. 298. £56.50 ISBN 9 7808 7413 0577.
Weinberg, Alan M., and Timothy Webb, eds. *The Unfamiliar Shelley*. Ashgate. [2009] pp. xix + 369. £54 ISBN 9 7807 5466 3904.
Wohlgemut, Esther. *Romantic Cosmopolitanism*. Palgrave. [2009] pp. viii + 203. £50 ISBN 9 7802 3023 2044.

XIII

The Nineteenth Century: The Victorian Period

WILLIAM BAKER, GREGORY TATE, MARTIN DUBOIS, ALEXIS EASLEY AND DAVID FINKELSTEIN

This chapter has five sections. 1. Cultural Studies and Prose; 2. The Novel; 3. Poetry; 4. Drama; 5. Periodicals and Publishing History. Sections 1 and 2 are by William Baker; section 3 is by Gregory Tate and Martin Dubois; section 4 is by Alexis Easley; section 5 is by David Finkelstein.

1. Cultural Studies and Prose

(a) General

A truly illuminating study for 2009 takes an innovative turn. In *The Transatlantic Indian, 1776–1930*, Kate Flint examines how imaginary boundaries connect American and British cultures—specifically how Native American figures informed British cultural narratives. This study broadens the field of Victorian studies. Chapters include 'Figuring America' (pp. 1–25); 'The Romantic Indian' (pp. 26–52); ' "Brought to the Zenith of Civilization": Indians in England in the 1840s' (pp. 53–85); 'Sentiment and Anger: British Women Writers and Native Americans' (pp. 86–111); 'Is the Indian an American?' (pp. 112–35); 'Savagery and Nationalism: Native Americans and Popular Fiction' (pp. 136–66); 'Indians and the Politics of Gender' (pp. 167–91); 'Indians and Missionaries' (pp. 192–225); 'Buffalo Bill's Wild West and English Identity' (pp. 226–55); 'Indian Frontiers' (pp. 256–87); and 'Conclusion: Indians, Modernity, and History' (pp. 288–96). Margaret Linley's 'The Early Victorian Annual (1822–1857)' (*VR* 53[2009] 13–19) explores the once flourishing hybrid book as a source for continuing study. Anne Anderson's ' "Fearful consequences . . . of living up to one's teapot": Men, Women, and "Cultchah" in the English Aesthetic Movement *c.*1870–1900' (*VLC* 37[2009] 219–54) is a work in progress article on the significance of the teapot that helpfully draws upon late nineteenth-century prose writing and illustrations of teapots. Kate Flint's special issue on 'Materiality and Memory' in (*RaVoN* http://www.ravon.umontreal.ca/) includes her essay 'Photographic

The Year's Work in English Studies, Volume 90 (2011)
doi:10.1093/ywes/mar004

Memory'. James Eli Adams, *A History of Victorian Literature* promises much as its author is well known in Victorian studies. In his preface Adams boldly announces that 'this is a narrative history addressing to students and readers wishing to learn more about the world of Victorian literature' (p. ix). Following 'Introduction: Locating Victorian Literature' (pp. 1–26), Adams's work is divided into three sections: '"The times are unexampled": Literature in the Age of Machinery, 1830–1850' (pp. 27–142); 'Crystal Palace and *Bleak House*: Expansion and Anomie, 1851–1873' (pp. 143–292); and 'The Rise of Mass Culture and the Specter of Decline, 1873–1901' (pp. 293–428). There is a brief 'Epilogue' (pp. 429–34), a listing of works cited (pp. 435–50) and a detailed index (pp. 451–62). Each section has subdivisions: for instance, the third section begins with 'Science, Materialism, and Value' (pp. 296–305) and then moves on to 'Twilight of the Poetic Titans' (pp. 305–14). Two sections later, we are on to 'The Aesthetic Movement' (pp. 325–9) followed by a section on 'Aesthetic Poetry' (pp. 329–33). Divided into neat capsules, the volume, with its 'strong chronological thrust . . . aim[s] . . . to sketch a complex, changing field of literary production and reception without surrendering the rich particularity of individual works and authors' (p. ix).

A fascinating study, Anthony Bateman's *Cricket, Literature, and Culture: Symbolising the Nation, Destabilising Empire* is well illustrated with black and white pictures, amongst others of W.G. Grace taken from C.B. Fry's *The Great Batsman: Their Methods at a Glance* [1905]. Bateman's book 'seeks to explore the ways in which Cricket literature produced and reproduced ideas of the national and imperial cultures between the publication of the Reverend James Pycroft's *The Cricket Field* in 1851 and the mid-1980s'. Bateman writes that 'in the four decades following the first publication of *The Cricket Field*, cricket became the most popular, written-about and symbolically significant sport in England and the British Empire' (p. 2). Of particular pertinence to Victorianists are the introduction (pp. 1–13), the first chapter '"More mighty than the bat, the pen [. . .]": Culture, Hegemony, and the Literaturisation of Cricket' (pp. 16–54), and the fourth chapter, 'Cricket Literature and Empire 1850–1939' (pp. 121–56). There is an enumerative bibliography (pp. 205–27) and an index (pp. 229–36).

Writing the Pre-Raphaelites: Text, Context, Subtext, edited by Tim Barringer and Michaela Giebelhausen, 'addresses some key issues raised by the Pre-Raphaelite archive' (p. 11). The editors in their introduction, 'Pre-Raphaelite Mythologies' (pp. 1–16), present a clear account of the purpose of their collection. Deborah Cherry writes on 'In a Word: Pre-Raphaelite, Pre-Raphaelites, Pre-Raphaelitism' (pp. 17–51); her essay has 141 footnotes which fortunately are placed at the end of the essay and not at the foot of the individual page. Julie F. Codell writes on 'Pre-Raphaelites from Rebels to Representatives: Masculinity, Modernity, and National Identity in British and Continental Art Histories, *c.*1880–1908' (pp. 53–79). David Peters Corbett writes on '"A Soul of the Age": Rossetti's Words and Images, 1848–73' (pp. 81–99). Julie L'Enfant's subject is 'Reconstruction Pre-Raphaelitism: The Evolution of William Michael Rossetti's Critical Position' (pp. 101–16), and Michaela Giebelhausen writes on 'The Quest for Christ: William Holman Hunt and the Writing of Artistic Motivation' (pp. 117–37). William Vaughan writes on 'Written Out? The Case of Ford Maddox Brown' (pp. 139–50). Jason Rosenfeld's subject is 'Absent of Reference: New Languages of Nature in the Critical Responses to Pre-Raphaelite Landscapes' (pp. 151–70). Colin Cruise writes on 'Poetic, Eccentric, Pre-Raphaelite: The Critical Reception of Simeon Solomon's Work at the Dudley Gallery' (pp. 171–91). Matthew Plampin's preoccupation is 'Exhibiting the Avant-Garde: The Development of the Pre-Raphaelite "Brand"' (pp. 193–214), and Malcolm Warner writes on 'Millais in Reproduction' (pp. 215–36). There is a useful enumerative bibliography (pp. 237–53) and an index (pp. 255–62) to this excellent collection, which also contains a number of black and white illustrations.

Galia Ofek's fascinating and richly illustrated *Representations of Hair in Victorian Literature and Culture* is a study 'of the socio-cultural, and literary history of mid-to-late Victorian representations of women's hair'. Her aim is 'to examine how pervasively [such representations] were constructed, disseminated and eventually accepted as a common, almost self-evident framework of signification which played a major role in the negotiations and production of gender identity' (p. x). Writers and artists discussed range from Elizabeth Gaskell, George Eliot, and Margaret Oliphant to Charles Darwin, Anthony Trollope, Elizabeth Barrett Browning, Eliza Lynn Linton, Mary Elizabeth Braddon, Herbert Spencer, Dante Gabriel Rossetti, Edward Burne-Jones, Charles Dickens, Thomas Hardy, and Aubrey Beardsley. This is a very well produced study; the only caveat in this uncovering of the 'unread text in the margins of Victorian culture and literature' (p. 31) is a certain degree of opaqueness which creeps into the text. In the realm of politics in Victorian culture studies, a special issue of *Nineteenth-Century Contexts* features 'Politics and Public Display in Britain, America, and France', and includes 'Festival: Event, Representation, Context' by Peter J. Manning (*NCC* 31[2009] 99–112); 'Can the Mummy Speak? Manifest Destiny, Ventriloquism, and the Silence of the Ancient Egyptian Body' by Charles D. Martin (*NCC* 31[2009] 113–28); 'The 1889 World Exhibition in Paris: The French, the Age of Machines, and the Wild West' by Susanne Berthier-Foglar (*NCC* 31[2009] 129–42); and 'Dickens and the Female Terrorist: the Long Shadow of Madame Defarge' by Teresa Mangum (*NCC* 31[2009] 143–60). Kathryn Miehle, in 'Horse-Sense: Understanding the Working Horse in Victorian London' (*VIJ* 37[2009] 129–40), draws upon Victorian prose writing in order to 'consider the ways in which humans have identified with animals as animals'. For Miehle 'the introduction of the animal as animal into the discussion of human culture reveals a level of complexity in life and history that is all too easily overlooked' (p. 129). In addition to Darwin, Miehle utilizes writing by Conway Lloyd Morgan, George John Romanes, W.J. Gordon, Henry Curling, C. Forbes, and others, including *Times* correspondence from August 1874 by Edward F. Flower on the 'cruel' 'use of the bearing rein' on carriage horses (p. 135), and George Fleming's response to it. Miehle concludes that 'Victorians took seriously the attempt to express the inexpressible as a means of encouraging others to consider what steps might be taken to ameliorate suffering' (p. 138).

An important contribution to cultural studies is Monica Flegel's *Conceptualizing Cruelty to Children in Nineteenth-Century England: Literature, Representation, and the NSPCC*, part of the Ashgate Studies in Childhood, 1700 to the Present series. Chapters include 'Creating Cruelty to Children: Genre, Authority, and the Endangered Child' (pp. 9–38); '"Animals and Children": Savages, Innocents, and Cruelty' (pp. 39–72); '"What Eyes Should See": Childhood Performance and Peeping Behind the Scenes' (pp. 73–108); '"Cannibalism in England": Commerce, Consumption, and Endangered Childhood' (pp. 109–46); 'The Dangerous Child: Juvenile Delinquents, Criminality, and the NSPCC' (pp. 147–80); and 'Conclusion: Inspector Stories: The Inspector's Directory and the Cruelty Man' (pp. 181–94). *'The Jew' in Late-Victorian and Edwardian Culture: Between the East End and East Africa*, edited by Eitan Bar-Yosef and Nadia Valman, contains eleven essays. The editors in their introduction write on 'Between the East End and East Africa: Rethinking Images of "the Jew" in Late-Victorian and Edwardian Culture' (pp. 1–27). Following this, Adrienne Munich writes on 'Jews and Jewels: A Symbolic Economy on the South African Diamond Fields' (pp. 28–44); Nadia Valman contributes 'Little Jew Boys Made Good: Immigration, the South African War, and Anglo-Jewish Fiction' (pp. 45–64); Lara Trubowitz writes on 'Acting like an Alien: "Civil" Antisemitism, the Rhetoricized Jew, and Early Twentieth-Century British Immigration Law' (pp. 65–79); Nicholas J. Evans writes on 'Commerce, State, and Anti-Alienism: Balancing Britain's Interests in the Late-Victorian Period' (pp. 80–97); Ben Gidley writes on 'The Ghosts of Kishinev in the East End: Responses to a Pogrom in the Jewish London of 1903' (pp. 98–112); Simon Rabinovitch writes on 'Jews, Englishmen, and Folklorists: The Scholarship of Joseph Jacobs and Moses Gaster' (pp. 113–30); David Glover writes on 'Imperial Zion: Israel Zangwill and the English Origins of Territorialism' (pp. 131–43); Meri-Jane Rochelson writes on 'Zionism, Territorialism, Race, and Nation in the Thought and Politics of Israel Zangwill' (pp. 144–60); Jasmine Donahaye writes '"By whom shall she arise? For she is small": The Wales–Israel Tradition in the Edwardian Period' (pp. 161–82); Eitan Bar-Yosef writes on 'Spying Out the Land: The Zionist Expedition to East Africa, 1905' (pp. 183–200); and finally, Mark Levene writes on 'Herzl, the Scramble, and a Meeting that Never Happened: Revisiting the Notion of an African Zion' (pp. 201–20). Obviously some of the essays are more interesting than others, depending on the reader's perspective, and some are written with greater clarity than others.

Joy Dixon argues for continued study of Ellis's and Symonds's work in 'Havelock Ellis and John Addington Symonds, *Sexual Inversion* (1897)' (*VR* 35[2009] 72–7). Janet Lyon, in 'Sociability in the Metropole: Modernism's Bohemian Salons' (*ELH* 76[2009] 687–711), 'sketches the confluent histories of Bohemia, modernist sociability, and Roman culture' in late nineteenth-century and Edwardian Britain. Lyon argues 'that the dissident salons associated with modernism staged a formal . . . sociability', based on the ideas of George Simmel 'that became a vehicle for the circulation of experimental aesthetics' (p. 687). Inevitably, such an article is prone to generalizations: Lyon's account is largely restricted to very limited culture milieus in metropolitan capital cities that are in no way representative of what went on elsewhere. *Nineteenth-Century Gender Studies*, available at www.ncgsjournal.com, features 'The Serious Mrs. Stopes: Gender, Writing and Scholarship in Late-Victorian Britain' by Stephanie Green (*NCGSJ* 5[2009]), '"A New Servitude": Pedagogy and Feminist Practice in Brontë's *Jane Eyre*' by Kirstin Hanley; 'Female Prescriptions: Medical Advice and Victorian Women's Travel' by Narin Hassan; 'Amelia Edwards's Picturesque Views of Cairo: Touring the Land, Framing the Foreign' by Julia Kuehn; and '"I saw him looking at me": Male Bodies and the Corrective Medical Gaze in Sheridan le Fanu's "Green Tea"' by Daniel Lewis. Gail Marshall's *Shakespeare and Victorian Women* is another valuable volume in the Cambridge Studies in Nineteenth Century Literature and Culture series, discussed in more detail elsewhere. In 'Journal-istic Propaganda and Queen Victoria's Construction of Scotland in *Leaves from the Journal of a Life in the Highlands*' (*VIJ* 37[2009] 47–65), Carla E. Coleman asserts that the queen invites her readership, as well as all of England, to experience her version of Scottish culture and history, thereby recapturing the British spirit that England's more advanced society seemed to have lost. Bennett Zon's 'C. Hubert H. Parry, *The Evolution of the Art of Music* (1893/96)' nicely sketches an outline of Victorian theories of music, then celebrates Parry's work as a key text for continued study (*VR* 53[2009] 68–72).

A Cultural Citizen of the World: Sigmund Freud's Knowledge and Use of British and American Writings, by S.S. Prawer, is based on an intensive study of the original German text of Freud's writings, letters, and journals. This is the first book to make a full and systematic map of Freud's use of English literature. Freud was fascinated by writings from many nations and languages, and his use of English shows the great range of his reading: from Shakespeare to Bernard Shaw, Henry Fielding to George Eliot, Mark Twain to Thornton Wilder; from scientific works by Maxwell and Darwin to the economics of Adam Smith, Malthus, and Keynes, and from psychology and anthropology to the origins of religion. Though he was a reader *par excellence*, he was also a case study in how world literature can be used by men and women who are not professional literary scholars or critics—and of how much it can come to mean to them, and to their sense of who they are. Chapters include 'Shakespearean Autobiography' (pp. 5–20); 'Demolished Idols and Satanic Spokesmen' (pp. 21–34); 'Enlightenment' (pp. 35–44); 'Imperfect Sympathies' (pp. 45–52); 'Cultural Community' (pp. 53–60); 'Adventures of Body and Mind' (pp. 61–8); 'Our Highly Interesting Family Novel' (pp. 69–80); 'Just So Stories' (pp. 81–90); 'Ideological Interlude' (pp. 91–100); 'Old Wine in New Bottles' (pp. 101–4); and 'Bloomsbury and Beyond' (pp. 105–26). Leslie Howsam's *Past into Print: The Publishing of History in Britain 1850–1950* 'is about the publishing history of history; it tells a story of how knowledge of the past was captured in books and periodicals in Britain between 1850 and 1950'. Further, 'its human protagonists are historians and publishers and its theoretical concerns lie with historiography and bibliography' (p. 10). In addition to a clearly written preface, 'Narrative and Discipline' (pp. x–xv), Howsam has chapters on 'Every Schoolboy Knows: Publishing the Narrative of England's Liberty, 1850–1863' (pp. 1–23); 'Quality and Profit: New Histories of England, 1863–1880' (pp. 24–48); 'Breaking the Drowsy Spell of Narrative, 1880–1914' (pp. 49–75); 'Historians and Publishers in an Age of War and Revolution, 1914–1929' (pp. 76–96); and 'Knowledge in the Marketplace, 1930–1950' (pp. 100–21). There is a succinct 'Epilogue: History out of Print' (pp. 122–8) followed by notes (pp. 129–54), a chronology (pp. 155–61), a bibliography (pp. 162–77), and a rather brief index (pp. 178–81).

Isaac Yue's 'Missionaries Representing China: Orientalism, Religion, and the Conceptualization of Victorian Cultural Identities' (*VLC* 37[2009] 1–10) closely examines Victorian perceptions of 'Orientalism' focusing upon missionaries and their reactions to experiences in China, and in particular the writings of the Reverend Samuel Kidd. Kidd, following years in the Far East, became the first professor of Chinese at University College London. Yue cites from Kidd's *China, or Illustrations of the Symbols, Philosophy, Antiquities, Customs, Superstitions, Laws, Government, Education, and Literature of the Chinese* [1841] and his earlier *Lecture on the Nature and Structure of the Chinese Language* [1838]. Curiously, Kidd's dates of birth and death are absent, none of his other works are drawn upon, nor is his academic career discussed. Shanyn Fiske's 'Asian Awakenings: Alicia Little and the Limits of Orientalism' (*VLC* 37[2009] 11–26) draws primarily upon Alicia Little's *Intimate China* [1899] and her other writings, including her *A Marriage in China* [1896]. Fiske shows that Little's perceptions display 'variable subjectivities that Europeans can adopt in their interactions with the Far East' and posits 'an attentive basis for understanding nineteenth-century Sino-British relations and for constructing critical views of the orient in our own time' (p. 23). Bennett Zon's '"Loathsome London": Ruskin, Morris and Henry Davey's *History of English Music* (1895)' (*VLC* 37[2009] 359–75), is mis-titled as its focus is not primarily Ruskin and Morris but the neglected musicologist Henry Davey (1853–1929) with special attention to his 'principal work, his *History of English Music*' first published in 1895 and revised in 1921. This work is 'significant for three reasons'. First, 'it *is* the first monograph published in England to have covered the full expanse of English music history in any scholarly detail'. Second, it seems 'to have been widely read and discussed' by Davey's contemporaries 'and continues to be read to this day with great critical interest'. Third, it provides 'a parameter of the way in which contemporary ideological currents and trends not usually associated with music histories influence music historical thinking of the time'. Zon isolates Davey's mentions of Ruskin and Morris with particular reference to London, their 'unabated aesthetic repugnance' for the metropolis (pp. 361–3), and Davey's attitude towards London. Zon concludes his fascinating article: 'For Davey, like Ruskin and Morris, it is ultimately the past which represents the future, and only through overturning the city can society progress' (p. 372). Valerie Sanders's clearly written *The Tragic Comedy of Victorian Fatherhood* draws upon Dickens, Darwin, Huxley, and Gladstone in a perceptive exploration of the complex relationship between the public and the private lives of four Victorian fathers. J. Martin Stafford draws parallels between two important but today neglected Victorian writers in his 'Herbert Spencer and William Henry Hudson' (*N&Q* 56[2009] 404–6). Two Victorian writers who seem to have been totally ignored are the subject of the seventh chapter, 'Romanticism, Colonialism, and the "Natural Man" in the Writings of

Sir Francis Bond Head and George Copway', in Kevin Hutchings, *Romantic Ecologies and Colonial Cultures in the British Atlantic World 1770–1850* (pp. 154–75).

(b) Prose

Carol Hanbery Mackay has edited an extremely useful edition of Annie Besant's autobiographical sketches. The spring 2009 issue of the *George Borrow Bulletin* opens with George Hyde's 'Armenian Lessons with George Borrow' (*GBB* 38[2009] 9–19). Hyde explores 'the peculiar (not very extensive, but strangely significant) attention Borrow accords, via his *alter ego*, to the Armenian language' (p. 9). Peter Missler's 'Lost in Lugo' (*GBB* 38[2009] 20–36) is an illustrated account of a visit to modern-day Lugo, where Borrow stayed in July 1837. Borrow, as the editor Ann M. Ridler indicates, in a headnote to Philip Ivory's 'George Borrow and Pushkin: Borrow's Translation of Pushkin's "The Talisman"' (*GBB* 38[2009] 36–41), was 'only the second Englishman to publish any translation of Pushkin during the poet's lifetime' (p. 36). This is followed by 'Presentation Copies of Borrow's Books, an Unfinished Paper by the Late Sir Angus Fraser' (*GBB* 38[2009] 41–9). Additionally the issue contains Peter Missler's 'Presentation Copies of the *Gypsy Luke*' (*GBB* 38[2009] 50–1) and Ann M. Ridler's 'Presentation Copy of *The Sleeping Bard*' (*GBB* 38[2009] 51). A regular informative feature of the journal is its 'Notes and Queries' and the spring 2009 issue is no exception. There are nine: 'Eve Deceived by a Baboon, a Query Arising from Correspondence between Ann Ridley and Kathleen Cann'; the late Sir Angus Fraser's 'Frederick Ganning'; Ann M. Ridler's 'Italian or English? A Query on Borrow's Reading'; John Hentges, 'The Re-building of London Bridge'; Kedrun Laurie's 'Lady Eleanor Smith and *Lavengro*', and 'Information Please: Who Is the Author of "In Borrow's Country"?'; Simon R. Keeon's 'Spanish Shadows'; Ann M. Ridler's 'The Sad Fate of Lady Bowring' and 'A Note on Borrow's Grave, by Ann M. Ridler, from Information in Correspondence from the Late Sir Angus Fraser' (*GBB* 38[2009] 51–69). There is a detailed review by David Chandler of Philip Davis's discussion of Borrow in his *Oxford English Literary History*, vol. 8 [2002] (*GBB* 38[2009] 70–3). Chandler writes: 'it is frankly embarrassing to find so much concentrated error in a prestigious Oxford publication' although 'Davis' impressive interpretative and critical efforts' are excluded from such adverse observations (p. 73). The issue concludes with David Price's 'Borrow-on-line', a Note on Borrow 'on Facebook', and 'George Borrow as a Portraitist' (*GBB* 38[2009] 75–9).

The autumn 2009 issue of the *George Borrow Bulletin* contains David Chandler's '"Incidents on my journey": The Influence of Sir Richard Phillips on Borrow' (*GBB* 39[2009] 6–22) and Richard Shepheard's 'The Unresolved: Borrow's Gypsies' (*GBB* 39[2009] 22–37). There are nine 'Notes and Queries': 'Lavengro and the Evil Chance, a Note by Simon R. Keeton, Illustrated by the Author'; 'Borrow Downgraded at the Bodleian, a Note from David Chandler'; 'Borrow and Pushkin, a Response from Alan Todd to the Note in *Bulletin 38*';

'Frederick Charles Ganning, a Response from Ron Fiske to the Note in *Bulletin* 38'; 'Mutiny on the Bounty, a Response to Angus Fraser's Query in *Bulletin* 38, Compiled by the Editor [Ann Ridler] from Her Own Notes and Contributions from Ron Fiske, Peter Missler, and Phyllis Stanley'; 'New Light on George Burrow's Brother John, Compiled from Information Received from Peter Henderson'; 'Two Borrovian Mysteries: (i) Up and Down Manxland; (ii) Stone Heads at Icolmkill, by Ann M. Ridler'; 'Spanish Shadows—a Response to Simon Keeton's Note in *Bulletin* 38, from Laurence Shand' (*GBB* 39[2009] 37–59). Leslie Howsam reviews Peter Missler's *A Daring Game: George Borrow's Sales of the Scio New Testament* (Madrid [1837]): 'Missler has produced a narrow and scrupulous work of scholarship, devoted to understanding the circumstances of Borrow's activities in Spain from 1836 to 1840.' He 'does not aim to contribute to a broader scholarship on the Bible as a book, or on the history of the book in Spain, but students of those subjects may well find valuable material embedded in this meticulous work of scholarship' (*GBB* 39[2009] 60–2). In addition to other book reviews there is a section on 'Borrow On-line' (*GBB* 39[2009] 62–78), and an account of the George Borrow Society Meeting in London Held on 25–6 July 2009, by Ann M. Ridler, including photographs of Borrovian's site today (*GBB* 29[2009] 79–89). Other items of interest in this issue include John Hentges, 'Borrow and Dickens at Greenwich Fair' (*GBB* 29[2009] 89–109), and Ivan Bunn, 'New Light on George Borrow's Grave' (*GBB* 29[2009] 109–12). This issue, in common with others, is accompanied by excellently reproduced and illuminating black and white photographs.

Carlyle Studies Annual for 2009 opens with Janet Ray Edwards's 'The Coterie Speech of Jane Welsh Carlyle' (*CStA* 25[2009] 5–25), which 'throws fresh light on the intricacies of 'coterie speech', the private language of Thomas and Jane Welsh Carlyle' (p. 1). Owen Dudley Edwards, in his 'Christopher Harvie's *A Floating Commonwealth* a Carlylean Commentary' (*CStA* 25[2009] 27–47), supplies an extensive review essay of Harvie's 2008 book. Edwards regards Harvie's book as 'great' (p. 28): 'what Harvie has done is epoch-making for the student of Carlyle' (p. 46). Jude V. Nixon's 'Thomas Carlyle's Igdrasil' (*CStA* 25[2009] 49–58) is dedicated '(In memory of G.B. Tennyson)' (p. 49), and includes an appendix: 'Igdrasil: From the Norse' (*CStA* 25[2009] 59–60), first published in *Igdrasil: Journal of the Ruskin Reading Guild* (1:ii[February 1890] 41–2). Nixon writes that, 'although the title infers it to be a translation, the language and ideas it contains appear to [him] sufficient to stamp it as Carlyle's original work' (p. 60). He also observes: 'the sacred tree known as the Yggdrasil was an essential metaphor for Thomas Carlyle' (p. 49). David R. Sorensen's '"Symbolic Mutation": Thomas Carlyle and the Legacy of Charles Darwin in England' (*CStA* 25[2009] 61–81) examines John Tyndall's efforts to include Carlyle as the advocate of the legacy of Charles Darwin in the last quarter of the nineteenth century. Carlyle's use of memory is the subject of Ian Campbell's' '"True to the life": Thomas Carlyle's *Reminiscences*' (*CStA* 25[2009] 83–100). Ronald C. Wendling's 'Presence and Distance: Samuel Taylor Coleridge and the Meaning of Modernity' (*CStA* 25[2009] 101–27) re-examines Carlyle's reading of Coleridge's work. Rodger L. Tarr's '*The Passion:* Some Personal

Reminiscences of collecting Thomas Carlyle' (*CStA* 25[2009] 123–7) is followed by a listing of 'The Carlyle Collection of Rodger L. Tarr, Armstrong Browning Library, Baylor University' (*CStA* 25[2009] 130–49). David Southern describes 'Carlyle's Photograph Albums Butler Library, Columbia University' (*CStA* 25[2009] 151–73) with accompanying photographs. Brent E. Kinser gives an account of 'The Letters Relating to John Linnell's Portrait of Thomas Carlyle' (*CStA* 25[2009] 177–83). This is followed by an unattributed note 'Viewing Ford Madox Brown's *Work*, 1865' (*CStA* 25[2009] 183–4) and Terry E. Meyers, 'Two Letters from Thomas Carlyle and Beverley Tucker' (*CStA* 25[2009] 184–90). David Taylor provides the background and notes in ' "I must write": Vernon Lushington, the Brownings, John Ruskin, and Thomas Carlyle' (*CStA* 25[2009] 190–6).

David A Sorensen, one of the indefatigable editors of *CStA*, describes the context for the 'Letters from John A. Carlyle and Charles Butler' (*CStA* 25[2009] 147–213) and 'An Afterword . . . "A Great Moral Tonic": Lecky on Carlyle and *The French Revolution*' (*CStA* 25[2009] 213–17). This is followed by two Lecky texts revealing his 'appreciation of Carlyle's achievement and enduring significance both as a thinker and a historian' (p. 216): 'Carlyle's Message to his Age. A Sunday Afternoon Lecture to Working-Men', originally published in the *Contemporary Review* (60[October 1891] 520–8) (*CStA* 25[2009] 217–25), and Lecky's introduction to *The French Revolution*, published in New York by Appleton in 1904 (*CStA* 25[2009] 226–44). There are reviews of three important works. Beverly Taylor writes that the very expensively priced (at $145) *Florentine Friends: The Letters of Elizabeth Barrett Browning and Robert Browning to Isa Blagden, 1850–1861*, edited by Philip Kelley and Sandra Donaldson with Scott Lewis, Edward Hagan, and Rita S. Patteson, is 'fastidiously edited, richly annotated, and carefully documented' (*CStA* 25[2009] 247–55: p. 247). Marylu Hill's subject is *The Collected Letters of Thomas and Jane Welsh Carlyle*, covering the years November 1859 to September 1860 (*CSTA* 25[2009] 257–60). Omitted from *YWES* 89 covering work published in 2008, this great edition edited by Ian Campbell, Aileen Christianson, and David Sorensen, with Brent Kinser, Jane Roberts, Liz Sutherland, and Jonathan Wild, in the words of Marylu Hill, 'continue[s] the long process of bringing a complete picture of the Carlyles and their world to light'. Volume 36 of *The Collected Letters of Thomas and Jane Welsh Carlyle* 'offers more than just crankiness and petulance. There are also poignant and touching parts, especially the letters relating to the decline and death of Nero, [Jane Welsh Carlyle's] little dog of eleven years' (pp. 258–9). Mention should be made too of the latest addition to the ongoing series. Volume 37 covers the period October 1860 to October 1861, during which Carlyle was immersed in writing *Frederick the Great*, the third volume appearing in 1862. He involved himself in championing the writings of Ruskin and continued his onslaught on political economy. All the letters available to date are searchable at http://earlyletters.dukejournals.org/. The third review is by David Southern and focuses on Christopher Stray's edition of *An American in Victorian Cambridge: Charles Astor Bristed's 'Five Years in an English University'* (*CStA* 25[2009] 261–8): see *YWES* 89[2010] 686). Following details of contributors to this fascinating issue of *CStA*, there is Brent E. Kinser's succinct 'One Word More . . . The Cover of *Carlyle Studies Annual 25*' (*CStA* 25[2009] 273–4), explaining the background of Whistler's 1872 portrait of Thomas Carlyle, today in the Glasgow Museum and Art Gallery, and 'a masterpiece' (p. 273). Priced at $20 and £15 for individual subscribers and institutions, this 274-page issue of *CStA* is a remarkable value.

Thomas De Quincey (1785–1859) lived through the Romantic period into the mid-Victorian era. His dates are inconvenient for literary scholars, and he often gets overlooked. Robert Morrison's detailed *The English Opium Eater: A Biography of Thomas De Quincey* opens with a bold statement that he 'wrote some of the most eloquent and searching prose of the nineteenth century'. Morrison's 'is the first biography of De Quincey in nearly three decades, and it takes into account a vast array of new material that has come to light in recent years' (p. xiv). This biography considers 'the complete range of [De Quincey's] published and unpublished writings' and it demonstrates 'both the vital role he played in shaping his own age, and his enduring relevance to ours' (p. xvii). Anne Maxwell's '*Oceana* Revisited: J.A. Froude's 1884 Journey to New Zealand and the Pink and White Terraces' (*VLC* 37[2009] 377–90) is an insightful analysis of Froude's neglected *Oceana, or, England and her Colonies* [1886], the book Froude published in the twilight years of his literary career, after completing a six-month tour of South Africa, Australasia and the United States. Maxwell 'investigate[s] the effect that visiting New Zealand had on Froude's sanguine view of the British Empire and his idea that the center of that empire could be transferred from London to the South Seas' (p. 378). John Toman's *Kilvert's Diary and Landscape* is the first extensive analysis of Kilvert's prose and a detailed treatment of the rural writer's *Diary*. Toman delves into the diarist's background and influences to present new insights into the writer and the culture in which he wrote. First published between 1938 and 1940, edited by William Plummer, the diary contains the record of the writer's experiences in the Victorian countryside. Toman's focus is on 'the literary influences and religious that caused [Kilvert] to write in the way that he did' (p. 9).

Rodney Stenning Edgecombe's 'A Half-Concealed Allusion in an Essay by Macaulay' (*N&Q* 56[2009] 390–1) picks up an allusion in Macaulay which many others have missed. Unless the present writer has missed items, 2009 has seemed a particular thin year for discussion on William Morris's prose. Megan Ward's 'William Morris's Conditional Moment' (*RaVoN* http://www.ravon.umontreal.ca/) should not be ignored. Another great Victorian prose expositor who tends to be neglected in literary analysis is John Stuart Mill. His *On Liberty* [1859] is the subject of Mordecai Roshwold's 'Toleration, Pluralism, and Truth'' (*Diogenes* 53[2008] 25–34). A Broadview edition by Lou J. Matz and a note by Helen Taylor on *Three Essays on Religion* were also published in 2009.

The October issue of *Cahiers victoriens et édouardiens* is devoted to John Henry Newman. Jacqueline Clais-Girard, in 'Newman's Letters' (*CVE* 70[2009] 15–24), attempts to begin to assess the significance of the completion of the great edition of Newman's letters (see *YWES* 89[2010] 700). Keith Beaumont's 'Newman: Satirist and Polemicist' (*CVE* 70[2009] 25–62) focuses upon irony, satire, and Newman's 'typically English form of self-deprecating humour' (p. 9) in his *The Tamworth Reading Room* [1840], *Lectures on the Present Position of Catholics* [1851], *Discourses in University Education* [1852], and the *Apologia Pro Vita Sua* in its 1864 first edition and revisions of the following year. Michael Durand's 'Newman the Novelist' (*CVE* 70[2009] 63–78) argues that Newman's two novels *Loss and Gain* [1848] and *Callista* [1856] are 'not mere diversions but form an integral part of his overall vision'. Durand examines both Newman's strengths and his 'weaknesses as a novelist, the (relative) value of his historical tableaux and, most importantly, the autobiographical content and the religious dimension of each, in particular *Callista*' (p. 12). Bertrand Lentsch, in his '"One man's meat is another man's poison": The Rhetoric of Dissent in John Henry Cardinal Newman's *Apologia Pro Vita Sua* (1864)' (*CVE* 70[2009] 79–114), examines the motivation underlying *Apologia Pro Vita Sua*. For Lentsch the rhetoric of Newman's 'dissent is . . . but his will and his way to emphasize the artless beauty of antique simplicity' (p. 13). Paul Chavasse's 'Newman the Preacher' (*CVE* 70[2009] 115–28) argues that 'it is above all in his exploration of the intricate relationship existing between dogma, ethics, and spirituality, combined with his keen psychological penetration, that Newman's greatness as a preacher lies' (p. 10) Edward Ondrako also writes about Newman's preaching, as does C.J. Talar. Ondrako, in his 'The Intellectual and Developmental Character of Cardinal Newman's University Preaching Style' (*CVE* 70[2009] 129–70), looks at central components in Newman's university preaching starting with his last sermon given to the Oxford University faculty in 1843. Ondrako also discusses Newman's Dublin sermons and his cardinal's acceptance speech of 1879. Talar's 'Henri Bremond: Preaching Newman the Preacher' (*CVE* 70[2009] 171–86) is an examination of Henri Bremond's (1865–1933) psychological biography *Newman: La Vie chrétienne*, first published in 1906, which devoted a part of the work to Newman as a writer and preacher. For Bremond, Newman's sermons provided 'clues to deciphering the man who preached them'. Bremond's study reveals its subject 'as an existential thinker' (p. 16).

Terrence Merrigan's 'The Imagination in the Life and Thought of John Henry Newman' (*CVE* 70[2009] 187–218) argues that 'for Newman . . . the adequate appropriation of the object of Christian faith requires both an act of the imagination and a willingness to engage in critical, historical reflection' (p. 13). Robert C. Christie's '"Echoes from home": The Personalist Ground of Newman's Ecclesiology. Affection as the Key to Newman's Intellectual Discernment on the Issue of Church' (*CVE* 70[2009] 219–50), in spite of its wordy title, is a detailed discussion of Newman's *Essay on the Development of Christian Doctrine* [1845] and its genesis in Newman's earlier work. Christie usefully draws attention to neglected Newman work including for instance 'the little-studied Liturgy Sermon series of 1830'. Christie uses such works 'to substantiate the thesis that affectivity, or [personalism], was the ground of Newman's ecclesiology'. Christie adds 'Upon identifying the Roman community as the "home" for his spirit, [Newman] synthesized his ecclesiological search with his affectivity driven epistemology, concluding his voyage and 'coming into port after a rough sea (*Apologia*, ed. Ker, 214)' (p. 11). In the penultimate contribution to this very valuable issue of *Cahiers victoriens et édouardiens*, Pádraic Conway writes on 'Journal of a Frustrated Soul: John

Henry Newman's Dublin Diary (November 1853–March 1856) and the Perceived Failure of the Catholic University of Ireland' (*CVE* 70[2009] 251–64). Conway's analysis draws upon unpublished Newman journals he kept during the period from November 1853 to March 1856 and first published in volume 32 (supplement) of *The Letters and Diaries of John Henry Newman* (see *YWES* 89[2010] 700). The final contribution is by Keith Beaumont. His 'John Henry Newman (1801–1890): Chronology' (*CVE* 70[2009] 265–8) provides a useful but brief chronology of important landmarks in the life and work of its subject.

David Livingstone's *Missionary Travels and Researches in South Africa* [1857], an extensive account of his travels, is the central text for Adrian S. Wisnicki's opaquely titled work in progress 'Interstitial Cartographer: David Livingstone and the Invention of South Central Africa' (*VIJ* 37[2009] 255–71). His account 'garnered numerous favorable reviews, sold some 70,000 copies, and ultimately made the explorer a rich man' (p. 255). For Wisnicki, 'In *Missionary Travels*, the text that permanently secures his fame, David Livingstone reinvents south central Africa in a manner which invites British intervention and colonization.' Livingstone spent 'sixteen years in the interior'; as Wisnicki concludes, 'the future agents of empire and capitalist expansion would not have the luxury or the patience' to spend such a long period 'and would certainly not cultivate the cultural sensitivity that Livingstone prescribed for and envisioned in his successors' (p. 267). Geoffrey Johnston Sadock examines Walter Pater as master of the Gothic, focusing on Pater's short stories, *Marius the Epicurean*, and the unfinished novel *Gaston de Latour* [1889, revised text 1995] in 'Dark Aesthete' (*CVE* 69[April 2009] 77–96). In the same issue, Martine Lambert-Charbonnier writes, in 'Old Age in Walter Pater's Works: Humanity and Aesthetics of Culture', on how old age becomes an opportunity for starting again and on age's import through essential elements of the arts (*CVE* 69[April 2009] 115–30). Claire Masurel-Murray's '"A chalice empty of wine": L'Imaginaire sacramental dans la littérature fin de siècle en Angleterre' (*EA* 62[2009] 56–72) investigates Pater's vision of religion and of Christian rituals amidst the fascination in English literary circles with Catholicism. 'Walter Pater's "Strange Veil of Sight"' is a chapter in Catherine Maxwell's *Second Sight: The Visionary Imagination in Late Victorian Literature* (pp. 68–113). Peter Betjemann discusses late nineteenth- and early twentieth-century attitudes toward the crafts tradition in Britain and American, situated against Marian and general attitudes towards industrial labour, in 'Craft Telos, and the Representation of Labor: Nineteenth-Century Readings of Benvenuto Cellini' (*NCP* 36[2009] 1–30). Michael Helfand examines the differences in idealistic aesthetics between Ruskin and Wilde in relation to the scientific theories of Darwin and Spencer in 'Ruskin and Wilde on Realism: Evolutionary Change in Idealist Aesthetics' (*NCP* 36[2009] 185–94).

Florence Nightingale: The Nightingale School, volume 12, edited by Lynn McDonald, recounts the founding of her school at St Thomas Hospital and her leadership in its teaching for the rest of her life. Volume 13, *Extending Nursing*, also edited by McDonald, recounts the introduction of professional training and standards outside St Thomas, beginning with London hospitals and others in Britain, followed by hospitals in Europe, America, Australia, and Canada. Also presented is material on work in India, Japan, and China. The challenge of raising standards in the tough workhouse infirmaries is reported, as is Nightingale's fostering of district nursing. A chronology in this volume provides a convenient overview of Nightingale's work on nursing from 1860 to 1900. Both volumes give biographical sketches of key nursing leaders. Kate Flint advocates further study of the Albert Memorial in 'Gilbert Scott, The Albert Memorial (1872)' (*VR* 35[2009] 45–9). *The Collected Letters of A.W.N. Pugin*, volume 3: *1846–1848*, edited with notes and an introduction by Margaret Belcher, illuminates several high points in Pugin's professional career: the September 1846 dedication of the church of St Giles at Headle, Staffordshire; approximately six months later, the opening of the most magnificent portion of the new House of Lords in London; and on 4 July 1848, the consecration of what would become the cathedral of St George in Southwark, London. Yet Pugin's letters reveal a less than confident man. Editorial procedure in this volume is consistent with that of the initial two volumes. All transcripts of Pugin's letters have been made from the manuscripts except for the letter to the postmaster at Ramsgate and the letter to John Knill of August 1846; the printed letter to Pelham Maitland is also taken from a photocopy. Though dating on some letters is challenging, those included come from January 1846 to December 1848, presented in six segments.

In the realm of art, *The Correspondence of Dante Gabriel Rossetti: The Last Decade, 1873–1882: Kelmscott to Birchington II*, volume 7: *1878–1879*, edited by William E. Fredeman, and completed by Anthony H. Harrison, Joan Cowan, Roger C. Lewis, and Christopher Newall, is presented by years, including 'Major Works of the Year' (both literary and artistic) as a heading for each year, followed by a 'Summary of the Year's Letters'. *John Ruskin's Correspondence with Joan Severn: Sense and Nonsense Letters*, edited by Rachel Dickinson, contains letters chronicling an important epistolary relationship of Ruskin's later years, shared with his Scottish cousin Joan (Agnew Ruskin) Severn. These more than 3,000 letters are heretofore unpublished. Ruskin scholars have found these challenging, with their baby-talk, apparent nonsense, and unelaborated personal references, yet they contain important expressions of Ruskin's opinions on travel, fashion, the ideal arts and crafts home, effective education, and other questions, and Ruskin often used his letters to Severn as a substitute for his personal diary. Amy Woodson-Boulton's 'John Ruskin, Letters to James Allanson Picton: The Ruskin Society in Manchester (1880s)' (*VR* 35[2009] 60–4) promotes Ruskin's letters as fertile ground for study because of their multiplicity of interpretations. Isabelle Case's 'John Ruskin, prophète du désastre dans "Traffic"' (*EA* 62[2009] 3–15) details the 1864 conference at Bradford which prompted Ruskin to pen 'Traffic', in which he sternly warned the residents of impending dangers unless prompt action was taken. Anne-Florence Gillard-Estrada's '"Passing into the great romantic loves of rebellious flesh": Medieval Religion and the Body in Walter Pater's "Poems by William Morris" and "Two Early French Stories"' (*EA* 62[2009] 16–27) treats hitherto ignored Pater stories. Anne C. Colley's 'John Ruskin: Climbing and the

Vulnerable Eye' (*VLC* 37[2009] 43–66) demonstrates the significance of Ruskin's actual climbing experiences. Colley writes that she wishes 'to suggest that Ruskin's climbing—his physical and kinetic relationship to the mountains—is essential to his understanding of them' (p. 43). Colley draws upon his sketches as well as his prose writings in her fascinating and insightful account. Attention should be drawn to 'The Eighth Lamp: Ruskin Studies Today', edited by Anurandha Chatterjee. Electronically based, this useful research tool may be found at http://groups.yahoo.com/group/oscholarship/.

There are few items to record this year for Edward Lear studies. A notable exception is Jenny Gaschke's *Edward Lear Egyptian Sketches*. This includes excellent reproductions of Lear's watercolour sketches made while he travelled the Nile. Gaschke's succinct introduction is informative concerning Lear as an important artist recording his own life and his Egyptian travels, especially along the Nile. Suzy Anger's 'Thomas Huxley: "On the Hypothesis that Animals are Automata" (1874)' (*VR* 35[2009] 50–52) celebrates possibilities for future study in Huxley's notions of consciousness and its influence on the body. In 'Typography in the *Poor Man's Guardian*' (*VIJ* 37[2009] 225–43), Rob Breton analyses how *Poor Man's Guardian* [1831–5] expanded in content and politicized its audiences through typography. Excerpts from the periodical are included. The eighth volume of the *Letters of Benjamin Disraeli*, edited by M.G. Wiebe, contains 566 letters, of which more than 400 are hitherto unpublished. These letters were written during a tumultuous period in European history—years that witnessed the Italian revolution, the Polish revolt against Russia, anxiety about Napoleon III's intentions in Europe, and the American Civil War. They provide revealing insights into Disraeli's thoughts on political and social issues; they also illuminate the inner workings of the Conservative party and his style of leadership. This eighth volume of the *Letters of Benjamin Disraeli* also includes recently recovered letters from years covered by previous volumes, including four to Lionel de Rothschild that reveal a hitherto unknown collaboration between Rothschild, Disraeli, and Lord George Bentinck on an anonymous pamphlet that promoted Jewish political rights. Fully annotated, this volume is a welcome addition to the series.

In *Lionel Trilling and Irving Howe, and Other Stories of Literary Friendship*, Edward Alexander links history and personality by pairing intellectual friends: Lionel Trilling and Irving Howe, Thomas Carlyle and John Stuart Mill, D.H. Lawrence and Bertrand Russell, George Eliot and Emanuel Deutsch, Theodore Roethke and Robert Heilman. Chronologically the essays range from the early 1830s, when Carlyle and Mill discovered each other, to 1975, when Lionel Trilling died. The essay that gives this volume its title is also the most ambitious. Alexander examines Trilling and Howe in relation to one another and to Jewish quandaries, Henry James, politics and fiction, anti-Semitic writers, literary radicals, 1960s insurrectionists, the State of Israel, and the nature of friendship itself.

The year 2009 was Darwin's bicentenary, and not surprisingly a number of publications concentrated on his works. Grace Kehler's 'Charles Darwin *On the Origin of Species* (1859)' (*VR* 35[2009] 32–7) celebrates Darwin's seminal work as a key text for continued study. *Narrative* features 'Shapes of the Past and the Future: Darwin and the Narratology of Time Travel' by Elana Gomel (*Narrative* 17[2009] 334–52). A special issue of *Twentieth-Century Literature* is devoted to 'Darwin and Literary Studies', a topic introduced by Jonathan Greenberg (*TCL* 55[2009] 423–44). This is followed by Omri Moses' 'Gertrude Stein's Lively Habits' (*TCL* 55[2009] 445–84), Laura Otis's 'Monkey in the Mirror: The Science of Professor Higgins and Doctor Moreau' (*TCL* 55[2009] 485–509), Dana Carluccio's 'The Evolutionary Invention of Race: W.E.B. Du Bois's "Conversation" of Race and George Schuyler's *Black No More*' (*TCL* 55[2009] 510–46), Susan McCabe's 'Survival of the Queerly Fit: Darwin, Marianne Moore, and Elizabeth Bishop' (*TCL* 55[2009] 547–71), Keith Leslie Johnson's 'Darwin's Bulldog and Huxley's Ape' (*TCL* 55[2009] 572–97), and Deirdre Coleman's 'The "Dog-Man": Race, Sex, Species, and Lineage in Coetzee's *Disgrace*' (*TCL* 55[2009] 598–617). In '"England of the East": Metonymies of Absence in Charles Dilke's *Greater Britain*' (*VR* 35[2009] 64–8) Anna-Barbara-Graf analyses Dilke's travelogue *Greater Britain: A Record of Travel in English-Speaking Countries during 1866 and 1867* [1869], revealing Dilke's reading of Indian landscapes as copies of English originals and further revealing a privileging of an abstracted English ideal.

The Crimean War in the British Imagination, by Stefanie Markovits, is the first study of the impact of the Crimean War (1854–56) on British literary culture, investigating how mid-Victorian writers and artists reacted to the original 'media war'. The book is organized into four parts, precede by the introduction, which includes 'The Blossom of War' (pp. 1–5) and 'A Brief History of War' (pp. 6–11). Part I, 'Rushing into Print: Journalism and the Crimean War', includes '"The *Times* War"'; '"Mr. Russell's 'War'"'; and 'The People's War' (pp. 12–42); Part II, 'From Anyas Leigh to Aurora Keigh: Gender and Heroism in the Novels of the Crimean War', includes 'Eastward Ho? The Kingsleys and Heroic Manliness'; 'From East and West to *North and South*', and 'Heroic Womanhood' (pp. 63–122); Part III, '"The song that nerves a nation's heart": The Poetry of the Crimean War', includes 'The Poetic Battle-Field' and 'Giving Voice to the War: Tennyson's "Charge" and Maud's Battle-Song' (pp. 123–67); and Part IV, 'Painters of Modern Life: (Re)Mediating the Crimean War in the Art of John Leech and John Everett Millais', includes 'Nothing like Knowing the Country', 'Playing at War', and '*Peace Concluded?*' (pp. 168–209), as well as the afterword, 'Elizabeth Thompson, Lady Butler, *The Roll Call*, and the Afterlife of the Crimean War' (pp. 210–18).

Declan J. Foley edits a collection of essays devoted to *The Only Art of Jack B. Yeats: Letters and Essays*. Bruce Stewart's foreword (pp. xi–xvii) and Declan Foley's 'Men of Destiny: John Butler Years and his Son Jack B. Yeats' (pp. 1–11) are followed by previously unpublished letters which then receive commentary. 'Letters of Jack B. Yeats to Sarah Purser: 1888–9' is succeeded by Leslie Waddington's 'Mr. Yeats and Mr. Waddington (pp. 13–21); 'Letters of Jack B. Yeats to John Quinn: 1903–11' is followed by 'Eamonn Andrews Interviews Jack B. Yeats on Radio Éireann' and John Purser's 'Frisky Minds: Jack B. Yeats, Bishop Berkeley, and a Soupcon of Beckett' (pp. 22–39). 'Letters of John Butler Yeats to his Son Jack B. Yeats (1909–10)' is followed by 'John Sloan: The Artist in Modern Life' by John Loughery (pp. 40–51);

'Letters of John Butler Yeats to his Son Jack B. Yeats: 1912–13' is followed by Hilary Pyle's 'Jack B. Yeats and the Stencil' and Arnold Harvey's 'Sketches from the Letters of Jack B. Yeats' (pp. 52–75). 'Letters of John Butler Yeats to his Son Jack B. Yeats with a Letter of Jack B. Yeats to John Quinn: 1914' is followed by Betsy Fahlman's 'Irish Modern: Jack B. Yeats and the Armory Show' (pp. 76–98). 'Letters of John Butler Yeats to his son Jack B. Yeats: 1915' is followed by Giovanna Tallarico's 'A Part of or Apart? The Possible Influence of European Expressionism on Jack B. Yeats' (pp. 99–108). The 'Letters of John Butler Yeats to his Son Jack B. Yeats: 1916' is followed by Avis Berman's 'Yeats at Petitpas: The Path to a Picture' (pp. 109–27); 'Letters of John Butler Yeats to his Son Jack B. Yeats: 1917–18' is followed by Maureen M. Murphy's '"Of loyal nature and of noble mind": Jack B. Yeats and his Siblings' (pp. 128–43). 'Letters of John Butler Yeats to his Son Jack B. Yeats: 1919' is followed by Róisín Kennedy's 'Jack Yeats and Dublin' (pp. 144–58). The main body of the text concludes with 'Letters of John Butler Yeats to his Son Jack B. Yeats: 1920–22' (pp. 159–76). In addition to notes (pp. 177–85), there is a glossary of names (pp. 186–92) and four appendices: 'Jack B. Yeats: Chronology' (pp. 193–4); 'Commentary by Contemporaries' (pp. 195–6); 'Some Notes on References' (pp. 197–8); and 'A Miscellany' (p. 199). The bibliography (pp. 200–2) is followed by 'Notes on Contributors' (pp. 203–4). Unfortunately there is no index to this fascinating volume which is accompanied by many black and white and colour illustrations.

The Middle Eastern encounters between the biblical scholar William Robertson Smith (1846–94) and the explorer Richard Burton (1821–90) are the focal point for Gordon K. Booth's 'Comrades in Adversity: William Robertson Smith and Richard Burton' (*VLC* 37[2009] 275–84). Booth writes that 'at first sight these two eminent Victorians appear to be most incongruous traveling companions'. The former was a 'relatively austere young professor' and a member of 'the Free Church of Scotland'. Burton, on the other hand, was 'a mature, hard-swearing, short-tempered, thoroughly agnostic trouble maker with a concealed *penchant* for oriental erotica'. Both 'provoked widespread controversy' and were perceived by some as 'unusual' (p. 275). Burton's letters to Smith have survived and are utilized in Booth's account of the two, who 'had been drawn together by chance in Egypt, both comrades in adversity, but the attraction, it's fair to say, was primarily on Burton's side' (p. 282) Sigrid Anderson Cordell's '"A beautiful translation from a very imperfect original": Mabel Wotton, Aestheticism, and the Dilemma of Literary Borrowing' (*VLC* 37[2009] 427–45) discusses the life and importance of the relatively forgotten Mabel Wotton (1863–1927). Drawing upon recently discovered correspondence by Meri-Jane Rochelson between Wotton and Israel Zangwill, Cordell writes that 'far from a reclusive, starving artist, Wotton was deeply involved in the cultural and social life of turn of the century London' (p. 428). Her work 'seems to dramatize the vexed question of creating art that is not irrevocably bound up with its source material, as well as inextricably mired in the necessity of producing a marketable commodity' (p. 442).

2. The Novel

(a) General

A fresh look at the nineteenth-century novel is offered by Heidi Kaufman in *English Origins, Jewish Discourse, and the Nineteenth-Century British Novel: Reflections on a Nested Nation*, which explores ways in which the novel expanded ideas about more than England, additionally attempting to reconcile conflicts between racial and theological aspects of national identity. Chapters include 'Nested Nation' (pp. 1–26); 'England in Blood: Jewish Discourse in Edgeworth's *Harrington* and Dickens's *Barnaby Rudge*' (pp. 27–58); 'Right of Return: "Zionist" Crusades in Tonna's *Judah's Lion* and Disraeli's *Tancred*' (pp. 59–92); 'Becoming English: (Re)Covering "Jewish" Origins in Charlotte Brontë's *Jane Eyre*' (pp. 93–130); '"This inherited blot": Jewish Identity in *Middlemarch*'s English Part' (pp. 131–62); '*King Solomon's Mines*? African Jewry, British Imperialism, and H. Rider Haggard's Diamonds' (pp. 163–92); and the concluding chapter, 'The Connecting Thread' (pp. 193–6). A useful bibliography is included as well.

Utilitarianism and the Victorian novel is the focus of Kathleen Blake's *Pleasures of Benthamism: Victorian Literature, Utility, Political Economy*. Blake examines the frequently censured and misunderstood traditions of Utilitarianism and political economy and their bearing on Victorian literature and culture. Chapters include 'Victorian Literature, Utility, Political Economy: The Case of *Bleak House*' (pp. 1–41); 'Pleasures of Benthamism—Utility, or, "People mutht be amuthed": Bentham and *Hard Times*' (pp. 42–81); 'Pains—"Work while it is called Today": Utility, Political Economy, Carlyle, and Trollope' (pp. 82–110); 'Pains—Capital Versus the Gift in *The Mill on the Floss*' (pp. 111–37); '"On Liberty" and Laissez-Faire' (pp. 138–64); 'Time and the Textile Industry: Gaskell and Tagore' (pp. 165–94); and 'Utilitarian Political Economy and Empire: Mill as Liberal Imperialist' (pp. 195–231).

From Sketch to Novel: The Development of Victorian Fiction presents an innovative approach to the sketch as an important branch of Victorian fiction, showing the ways in which sketch-writing influenced the later work of Victorian novelists. Amanpal Garcha thoroughly reveals this process from sketch to novel through four parts: Part I 'Introduction: From Sketch to Novel', including 'Modern Change and Aestheticized Stasis in the Early Nineteenth Century' (pp. 3–24) and 'Plotless Styles in Novel History and Theory' (pp. 25–52); Part II, 'Journalism, Modernity, and Stasis in the Paris Sketch Book and the History of *Pendennis*', including 'Capitalist Excess, Gentlemanly Atavism: Thackeray's Devils in his Early Sketches' (pp. 60–83) and '*Pendennis*'s Stasis and Thackeray's Professional Sensibilities' (pp. 84–110); Part III, 'Styles of Stillness and Motion: Charles Dickens's Lower-Class Descriptions', including '*Sketches by Boz*: Narrative Form and Market Culture' (pp. 118–43) and 'Narrating Stasis, Describing Reform: *Nicholas Nickleby*' (pp. 144–68); Part IV, 'Elizabeth Gaskell's Individualism, from "Sketches among the Poor" to *Cranford*', including '"Leave me, leave me to repose": Gaskell's Descriptive Individualism' (pp. 174–200) and '*Cranford*'s

Individualistic Style' (pp. 201–18), as well as the conclusion, '"Nothing democratic": Intelligence, Abstraction, and Avant-Garde Plotlessness' (pp. 219–40).

Another source of pervasive influence on Victorian literature is analysed at length in *Milton and the Victorians*, by Erik Gray. Gray poses the paradox that Milton's influence was less visible yet more pervasive during the Victorian period. This situation arose from the 'classic' status of Milton's works, so familiar that they are constantly in the background. Gray supports this thesis with incisive analysis of examples from authors such as Elizabeth Barrett Browning, Christina Rossetti, Matthew Arnold, Alfred Tennyson, and George Eliot. Chapters include 'Dark with Excessive Bright: The Victorian Milton' (pp. 1–24); 'Milton as Classic, Milton as Bible' (pp. 25–59); 'Milton, Arnold, and the Might of Weakness' (pp. 60–91); 'Milton and Tennyson: Diffusive Power' (pp. 92–129); 'Middlemarch and Milton's Troubled Transmissions' (pp. 130–51); and 'The Heirs of Milton' (pp. 152–70).

Garrett Stewart's *Novel Violence: A Narratography of Victorian Fiction* is committed to an intensive reading of selected Victorian novels. These include *Little Dorrit*, *The Tenant of Wildfell Hall*, *The Mill on the Floss*, and *Tess of the D'Urbervilles*. For Stewart, violence is as structural as is the concept of form. Stewart's work is heavily influenced by the ideas of Georg Lukács. Indeed, each of Stewart's chapters begins with an epigraph from Lukács's work. It must be admitted that *Novel Violence* makes for hard reading and Stewart makes demands upon his readers. An amazing feat is encompassed in the second edition of John Sutherland's *The Longman Companion to Victorian Fiction*, which contains over 900 biographical entries, the synopses of over 600 novels, and extensive background material on publishers, reviewers, and readers, making this the fullest account of Victorian fiction ever published. The first edition was published in 1988; this edition is greatly enlarged in response to subsequent expansions of the *Oxford Dictionary of National Biography* in 2004, publication of the *Feminist Companion to Literature in English* in 1990, and publication of the *Oxford Companion to Edwardian Fiction* in 1997.

Karen Chase adds to the important contributions concerning the Victorian novel in 2009 with *The Victorians and Old Age*. Chase examines how old age was constructed in Victorian social and literary cultures, focusing on the centrality of institutions and the generational divide, tracking both power and powerlessness through character and individuals. Chapters include 'Faces and Spaces: Locating Age in the Dickens World' (pp. 11–61); 'Almshouse to Empire: What is "Enough" for Old Age?' (pp. 62–112), in which Anthony Trollope's *The Fixed Period* notably figures; 'Creases and Crevices, Heights and Depths: Narrative Extremities and Age' (pp. 113–52); and 'Victoria to Victorian: The Queen and her Age' (pp. 153–99), in which Lewis Carroll's *Alice* books, Margaret Oliphant, and Elizabeth Gaskell's works enter the discussion; 'Artistic Investigations and the Elderly Subject' (pp. 200–31), which considers *The Picture of Dorian Gray*; 'The Politics and Personality of Age at the Fin de Siècle' (pp. 232–53), which begins with examples from William Morris's *News from Nowhere*; and 'Gravestones, Obituaries, Epitaphs' (pp. 254–75). Also delving into particulars of Victorian life and a specific period of the life cycle is Kay Heath's *Aging by the Book: The Emergence of Midlife in Victorian Britain.* This book offers a unique look at the ways in which middle age, for centuries considered the prime of life, was transformed during the Victorian era into a period of decline. Looking at novels, advertisements, cartoons, and medical and advice manuals of the period, this study reveals how this ideology of decline spread throughout a changing culture. Chapters include 'The Rise of Midlife in Victorian Culture' (pp. 1–24); 'Age Anxiety in the Male Midlife Marriage Plot' (pp. 25–72); 'Female Desexualization at Midlife' (pp. 73–114); 'The Remarrying Widows of Frances Trollope and Anthony Trollope' (pp. 115–44); 'Victorian Age Construction and the Specular Self' (pp. 145–70); 'Advertising and Late Victorian Age Anxiety' (pp. 171–98); and 'Afterword: The Future of Midlife' (pp. 199–202).

An intriguing new study applied to a collection of Victorian authors' works is *Embodied: Victorian Literature and the Senses*, by William Cohen. The five chapters include 'Subject: Embodiment and the Senses' (pp. 1–26); 'Self: Material Interiority in Dickens and Brontë' (pp. 27–64); 'Skin: Surface and Sensation in Trollope's "The Banks of the Jordan"' (pp. 65–85); 'Senses: Face and Feelings in Hardy's *The Return of the Native*' (pp. 86–107); and 'Soul: Inside Hopkins' (pp. 108–30). *Making a Man: Gentlemanly Appetites in the Nineteenth-Century British Novel*, by Gwen Hyman, makes use of food history and theory, literary criticism, anthropology, gender theory, economics, and social criticism to read gentlemanly consumers such as the vampire and the men who hunt him in Bram Stoker's *Dracula*. Hyman argues that appetite is a crucial means of casting light on the elusive identity of the gentleman, a figure who is the embodiment of power and yet is hardly embodied in Victorian literature. Key chapters of interest to the Victorian scholar are '"An infernal fire in my veins". Drink and Be Merry: *The Tenant of Wildfell Hall*' (pp. 54–87); '"By Heaven I must eat at the cost of some other man!" Gluttons and Hunger Artists: *Little Dorrit*' (pp. 88–126); 'An "insatiable relish for horrors". Truffles and Womanflesh: *The Law and the Lady*' (pp. 127–68); '"Those appetites which I had long secretly indulged". Cocaine Supergents: *Strange Case of Dr. Jekyll and Mr. Hyde*' (pp. 169–201); and '"His special pabulum". Thirsting to Connect: *Dracula*' (pp. 202–41). Christine Bayle Kortsch's *Dress Culture in Late Victorian Women's Fiction: Literacy, Textiles and Activism* 'does not focus exclusively on "new women" authors but instead traces the currents of debate that engage writers that claim a variety of perspectives'. Kortsch's close readings of novels by Olive Schreiner, Ella Hepworth Dixon, Margaret Oliphant, Sarah Grand, and Gertrude Dix is accompanied by an exploration of 'the history of women's education, sewing and needlework, mainstream fashion, and alternative dress movements, working class labor in the textile industry, and forms of social activism' (p. 18).

Barbara Leikie, in her '"A preface is written to the public": Print Censorship, Novel Prefaces, and the Construction of a New Reading Public in Late Victorian England' (*VLC* 37[2009] 447–62), uses John Keats's words from an 1818 letter. These provide the foundation for a consideration of selected 'prefaces to novel editions published by Vizetelly and Co. between 1884, when the new publishing company was formed, and 1887, the year before the only nineteenth-century censorship trial in England to target a literary text' (p. 447). The prefaces are to the English translation of Zola's *The Assommoir* [1884], Flaubert's *Madame Bovary* [1886], George Moore's fascinating and neglected *A Mumma's Wife* [1886] and Moore 's preface to Zola's *Piping Hot!* [1887]. Lecky then discusses the 1888–9 censorship trials in which Vizetelly was successfully prosecuted and fined 'for the publication of Zola's *La Terre*' (p. 458). In 'Rich Woman, Poor Woman: Toward an Anthropology of the Nineteenth-Century Marriage Plot' (*PMLA* 124[2009] 421–36), Elsie B. Michie 'examines the implication of one of the most common marriage plots in the nineteenth-century English novel: the story of a hero positioned between a wealthy, materialistic, status-conscious woman who would enhance his social prestige' and the alternative, 'a poorer, more altruistic, and psychologically independent woman, who is the antipode of her rich rival' (p. 424). In order to illustrate her contention, Michie draws upon Jane Austen's *Pride and Prejudice*, Charlotte Brönte's *Jane Eyre*, and Dickens's *Great Expectations*, as well as other works. She concludes that 'the rich women who represent all that is psychologically and socially detrimental about the possession of wealth have been positioned as undesirable marital choices' (p. 433). Michie has interesting things to say in spite of her essay being sprinkled with unhelpful references to Lacan and other literary theorists. In another general essay, Tamara Silvia Wagner appropriates a metaphor for the approaching commuter railways from Anthony Trollope's *The Three Clerks* [1858] in her discussion of the versatile ways in which writers as different as Trollope, Charles Dickens, Wilkie Collins, and the little-known domestic novelist Emily Eden made the most of what became a rapidly evolving space, in 'London's Great Starfish: the Construction of Mid-Victorian Suburban Fiction' (*CVE* 69[2009] 151–70).

There is a contribution to record on the interesting but neglected Richard Marsh. In a review essay Christopher Pittard writes on ' "The Unknown—with a Capital U!" Richard Marsh and Victorian Popular Fiction' (*Clues* 27[2009] 94–103). The focus is on five reprintings of Marsh's *The Beetle* [1897], *Curious: Some Strange Adventures of Two Bachelors* [1898], *The Datchet Diamonds* [1898], *Philip Bennion's Death* [1897], and *The Seen and the Unseen* [1900]. Published in 2007 and 2008, these texts are reasonably priced, *Curious* is priced at $16.95 and the others at $2 more. They are issued on demand. Pittard's review account omits important primary Marsh research and criticism published during the 1990s. He correctly concludes that 'the value of these attractive editions lies in the opportunity they make available to modern readers of key popular texts of the fin de siècle—a literature of the curious and of the singular' (p. 103). Minna Vuohelaine, who introduces the edition of *The Beetle*, is the author of a well-argued and written item previously missed in *YWES*: 'Richard Marsh's *The Beetle* (1897): A Late-Victorian Popular Novel' (in *Working with English: Medieval and Modern Language, Literature and Drama*, 2.1: *Literary Fads and Fashions* [2006] 89–100). *Victorian Review* features 'Greater Britain and the Imperial Outpost: The Australasian Origins of *The Riddle of the Sands* (1903)' (*VR* 35[2009] 79–95), the 2008 Hamilton prize-winning essay by Philip Steer, in which Steer demonstrates that attending to Greater Britain markedly modifies the genealogy of the invasion novel.

Looking into the emergent sensationalism of the 1850s and its significance to the development of the novel genre, Tamara Wagner brings together two women writers usually dismissed as anti-feminist and therefore sold short for their subversive potential. In 'Stretching "The Sensational Sixties": Genre and Sensationalism in Domestic Fiction by Victorian Women Writers' (*VR* 35[2009] 211–28), Wagner asserts that Charlotte M. Yonge's *The Heir of Redclyffe* [1853] and Eliza Lynn Linton's *Patricia Kemball* [1875] offer versions of the domestic Gothic novel which illustrate both the ambiguities of domesticity's sensationalism and the development of the novel as a genre. Wagner's *Antifeminism and the Victorian Novel: Rereading Nineteenth-Century Women Writers*, in addition to the editor's 'Introduction: Narratives of Victorian Antifeminism' (pp. 1–18), contains Pamela K. Gilbert's 'Feminism and the Canon: Recovery and Reconsideration of Popular Novelists' (pp. 19–36); Susan Hamilton's 'Marketing Antifeminism: Eliza Lynn Linton's "Wild Women" Series and the Possibilities of Periodical Signature' (pp. 37–56); Kristine Moruzi's '"The Inferiority of Women": Complicating Charlotte Yonge's Perception of Girlhood in *The Monthly Packet*' (pp. 57–76); Lynn Shakinovsky's 'Domestic History and the Idea of the Nation in Charlotte Yonge's *The Heir of Redclyffe*' (pp. 77–96); Talia Schaffer's 'Maiden Pairs: The Sororal Romance in *The Clever Woman of the Family*' (pp. 97–116); Elizabeth Juckett's 'Cross-Gendering the Underwoods: Christian Subjection in Charlotte Yonge's *Pillars of the House*' (pp. 117–36); Tamara S. Wagner's 'Marriage Plots and "Matters of More Importance": Sensationalizing Self-Sacrifice in Victorian Domestic Fiction' (pp. 137–58); Amy Robinson's 'An "Original and Unlooked-for Ending?": Irony, the Marriage Plot, and the Antifeminism Debate in Oliphant's *Miss Marjoribanks*' (pp. 159–76); Leila Walker's 'Ghosts in the House: Margaret Oliphant's Uncanny Response to Feminist Success' (pp. 177–96); Heather Milton's 'The Female Confessor: Confession and Shifting Domains of Discourse in Margaret Oliphant's *Salem Chapel*' (pp. 197–216); Kate Mattack's 'Mary Elizabeth Braddon's Secret: An Antifeminist Amongst the New Women' (pp. 217–34); Heather L. Braun's 'Idle Vampires and Decadent Maidens: Sensation, the Supernatural, and Mary E. Braddon's Disappointing Femme Fatales' (pp. 235–54); Kiran Mascarenhas's '*John Halifax, Gentleman*: A Counter Story' (pp. 255–70); Ann-Barbara Graff's 'Annesley Kenealy and Sarah Grand: Biopower and the Limits of the New Woman' (pp. 271–96); and finally, Kate Macdonald's 'Ignoring the New Woman: Ten Years of a Victorian Weekly Fiction Magazine' (pp. 297–316).

In *Becoming a Woman of Letters: Myths of Authorship and Facts of the Victorian Market*, Linda H. Peterson selected six women of letters whose careers brought to light new possibilities for the professional woman author and whose remarks on their literary lives reveal the obstacles they faced as well as the strategies by which they succeeded. Chapters include 'The Nineteenth-Century Profession of Letters and the Woman Author' (pp. 13–60); 'Inventing the Woman of Letters: Harriet Martineau in the Literary Marketplace of the 1820s and 1830s' (pp. 61–95);

'Working Collaboratively: Mary Howitt and Anna Mary Howitt as Women of Letters' (pp. 96–130); 'Parallel Currents: *The Life of Charlotte Brontë* as Mid-Victorian Myth of Women's Authorship' (pp. 131–50); 'Challenging Brontëan Myths of Authorship: Charlotte Riddell and *A Struggle for Fame* 1883' (pp. 151–70); 'Transforming the Poet: Alice Meynell as *Fin-de-Siècle* Englishwoman of Letters' (pp. 171–206); and 'The Woman of Letters and the New Woman: Reinventing Mary Cholmondeley' (pp. 207–24). Twenty-eight halftones are also included. Bishnapriya Gush's comparative 'The Colonial Postcard: the Spectral/Telepathic Mode in Conan Doyle and Kipling' (*VLC* 37[2009] 335–57) explores their mutual 'fascination with... forbidden epistemologies multiplying at the edges of Empire' (p. 335). Gush's focus is upon these two writers, although he argues more generally that in 'colonial fiction on occult practices, written between 1880 and 1920, we see how writers preoccupied with telepathy move well beyond handling it thematically as an excursion into semi- or illegitimate scientific experiments'. Gush's observations on Conan Doyle's and Kipling's 'experiments, wagers, and failures can be generalized to include much occult fiction written in this period' (p. 337).

In *Masking the Text: Essays on Literature and Mediation in the 1890s*, Nicholas Frankel provides superb essays on British literature of the 1890s. Divided into two parts, 'Mediating the Text' and 'Literature and the Medium of the Book', the collection covers subjects ranging from Oscar Wilde, Michael Field, George Meredith, Aubrey Beardsley, and James McNeill Whistler to William Morris, the Rhymers' Club, collecting forgery, typography, and the literary ramifications of the typewriter. Frankel is preoccupied with the belief that readers 'have much to learn from a remarkable body of work from the early 1890s attesting to the truth of masks and the importance of dress for illusion'. He brilliantly interweaves critical and textual theory, the history of the book, literary criticism, study of print media, aesthetics, and history. Particularly noteworthy chapters include 'The Typewritten Self: Media Technology and Identity in Oscar Wilde's *De Profundis*', 'James McNeill Whistler and the Politics of the Page', and 'Poem, Book, Habitat: The World of George Meredith's Poetry'.

The Technology of the Novel: Writing and Narrative in British Fiction, by Tony E. Jackson, explores the connection between speech and writing, explaining how the technology of alphabetic writing has determined the nature of the modern novel. Through striking new readings of works by Austen, Mary Shelley, Dickens, Forster, Woolf, Lessing, and McEwan, Jackson reveals how the phenomena of speech and storytelling interact with the technological characteristics of writing. Jackson's claims are grounded in a contemporary understanding of human cognitive capacities and constraints. Of special interest to Victorian scholars will be the chapter entitled 'Letters and Spirits in *Bleak House*' (pp. 79–102). Helena Michie's 'Victorian(ist) "Whiles" and the Tenses of Historicism' appears in *Narrative* (17[2009] 274–90). An inventive commentary on literary criticism, *The Prodigal Sign: A Parable of Criticism*, by Kevin Mills, makes a case for a hybrid form that combines the critical with the creative. Mills's monograph includes interesting readings of Edmund Gosse's *Father and Son* [1907] and Stevenson's *The Strange Case of Dr. Jekyll and Mr. Hyde* [1886]. The March 2009 issue of

Victorian Literature and Culture concludes with three review essays. Herbert Sussman's 'Victorians Live' (*VLC* 37[2009] 287–310) assesses the Victorian's afterlife. Sally Mitchell's focus is 'Victorian Journalism in Plenty' (*VLC* 37[2009] 311–21) and Mark Knight's 'Figuring Out the Fascination: Recent Trends in Criticism on Victorian Sensation and Crime Fiction' (*VLC* 37[2009] 323–33) tackles the issue of the attraction of 'sensation novels'.

(b) Individual Authors

In 'Math for Math's Sake: Non-Euclidean Geometry, Aestheticism, and *Flatland*' (*PMLA* 124[2009] 455–71), Andrea Henderson explores how Edwin Abbott's 1884 *Flatland* speaks to the crisis in development of non-Euclidean geometry in its influence on aesthetics amidst the influences of Euclidean geometry. Lauren Gillingham's 'Ainsworth's Jack Sheppard and the Crimes of History' (*SEL* 49[2009] 879–906) discusses the literary environment in England during the 1830s. Gillingham's centre of attention is Ainsworth's *Jack Sheppard* [1839–40] and its criminal hero. The recent revived interest in Mary Elizabeth Braddon continues with the reissue by Valancourt Books of her novel *Thou Art The Man*, first published in 1894. This edition is edited by Laurence Talairach-Vielmas. Eva Badowska's 'On the Track of Things: Sensation and Modernity in Mary Elizabeth Braddon's *Lady Audley's Secret*' (*VIJ* 37[2009] 157–75) is another contribution to the recent revival of interest in Braddon, and in *Lady Audley's Secret* in particular. Badowska writes that 'the critical hostility directed against' the novel 'at the moment its greatest success in the 1860s also had the effect of exposing the seeds of transience that constitute the paradoxical essence of novelty' (p. 157). A detached discussion of the sensation novel and the ways in which it is expressed in Braddon's *The Doctor's Wife* [1864] is complemented by readings of contemporary reviews of the novel and subsequent writing on the sensation novel. Badowska's article demonstrates that *Lady Audley's Secret* is capable of sustaining multiple readings. *The Days of Bruce: A Scottish Romance* [1833], by Grace Aguilar, is the focus of Katherine Klein's 'Scottish Angels in the Reign of Victoria' (*VIJ* 37[2009] 7–29), in which Klein positions *Days of Bruce* in its broader political and cultural environment of mid-Victorian England to show that Aguilar makes Scottish women the model for what would become the Victorian domestic goddess.

A useful overview source for study is *A Reader's Guide: Charlotte Brontë, Jane Eyre*, by Sara Lodge. The guide includes feminist readings, Marxist and postcolonial criticism, topical analysis of recent developments, and information on adaptations performed on stage and screen, as well as other prose works. 'A Brief Guide to Further Reading' will be especially helpful (pp. 168–71). The initial issue of *Brontë Studies* for 2009 includes Christopher Heywood's 'The Column in Branwell's "Pillar" Portrait Group' (*BS* 34[2009] 1–19); Susan Lydon's 'The Gendering of Art and Science in Charlotte Brontë's *Villette*' (*BS* 34[2009] 20–30); Meridel Holland's 'Lord Byron's "The Dream" and *Wuthering Heights*' (*BS* 34[2009] 31–46); Alison Hoddinott's 'Perils of Biography: Charlotte Brontë and Tennyson' (*BS*

34[2009] 47–56); Graeme Tytler's 'Eating and Drinking in *Wuthering Heights*' (*BS* 34[2009] 57–66); Diana Parson's 'Charlotte Brontë and Henrietta Asseretti: Neighboring Governesses?' (*BS* 34[2009] 67–75); Stephen Whitehead's 'Remembering Sir James Roberts' (*BS* 34[2009] 76–80); and Judith Bland's 'Winifred Gérin's Papers at the Parsonage!' (*BS* 34[2009] 81). The special issue for July focuses on 'Staging the Inner Self: Charlotte and Emily Brontë and Jean Rhys', beginning with 'Auctorial (Im)postures in Emily Brontë's *Diary Papers*' (*BS* 34[2009] 93–106), in which Augustin Trapenard analyses the rhetoric which moulded Emily as speaker, woman, and writer in order to keep any intrusive reader from authorizing Emily Brontë, Charlotte Borrie writes on 'From Shrine to Stage: Inner Space and the Curtain in *Jane Eyre*' (*BS* 34[2009] 107–16), Catherine Lanone 'Arctic Spectacles in *Jane Eyre* and *Villette*' (*BS* 34[2009] 117–26). '"Portrait of a Governess, Disconnected, Poor and Plain": Staging the Spectral Self in Charlotte Brontë's *Jane Eyre*' (*BS* 34[2009] 127–37) is by Laurence Talairach-Vielmas; 'Charlotte's Transvestites' (*BS* 34[2009] 138–46), by Bernadette Bertrandias; 'Inside Out: *Jane Eyre* on the Victorian Stage' (*BS* 34[2009] 147–54), by Patsy Stoneman; 'The Other Stage: From *Jane Eyre* to the *Wide Sargasso Sea*' (*BS* 34[2009] 155–61); and a most moving tribute to Professor Ian Jack (*BS* 34[2009] 162), written by Margaret Smith. The final issue of *Brontë Studies* for 2009 features Bob Duckett's 'Mr Wise and Mr Wood: Two Brontë Bibliographers in Harmony. Part 1' (*BS* 34[2009] 185–208); Nicholas Armitage's 'Melting Miss Snowe: Charlotte's Message to the English Church' (*BS* 34[2009] 209–19); Leila S. May's 'How Lucy Snowe Became an Amnesiac' (*BS* 34[2009] 220–33); Jen Cadwallader's '"Formed for labour, not for love": Plain Jane and the Limits of Female Beauty' (*BS* 34[2009] 234–46); Ian M. Emberson's 'Three Quartets: The Rossettis, the Mendelssohns and the Brontës' (*BS* 34[2009] 247–54); James Ogden's 'A Brontë Reading List: Part 3' (*BS* 34[2009] 255–62); and Ann Dinsdale's 'Recent Acquisitions at the Brontë Parsonage Museum' (*BS* 34[2009] 263–6).

Patricia McKee's 'Racial Strategies in *Jane Eyre*' (*VLC* 37[2009] 67–83) argues that 'multiple discursive strategies' in the novel 'contend with the difficulty of determining racial identity'. McKee's intention is 'to clarify the usefulness of ambiguity to the narrative's racialism' (p. 67). It could be argued that, rather than clarifying it, she complicates it: her article contains rather a lot of generalization. For instance, she concludes: 'English freedom is constituted by circulation among the spaces of empire, in movements that prove that no place can contain the English spirit or resist the improvements made by white capitalist culture' (p. 82). Catherine Lanone's attention is to 'Secret Pastures in *Jane Eyre*' (*EA* 61[2008] 415–26). For Lanone, 'Jane shifts from being crushed by dark secrets to resilient, secretive empowerment' (p. 425). Priti Joshi, in 'Masculinity and Gossip in Anne Brontë's *Tenant*' (*SEL* 49[2009] 907–24), discusses the feminism of Anne Brontë's *The Tenant of Wildfell Hall* [1848]. Judith E. Pike '"My name was Isabella Linton": Coverture, Domestic Violence, and Mrs. Heathcliff's Narrative in *Wuthering Heights*' (*NCL* 64[2009] 347–83) is concerned with Emily Brontë's 'use of the framed narrative in *Wuthering Heights*' and the critical neglect of Isabella Heathcliff 'as the third narrator' (p. 382). Anne Longmuir's '"Reader, perhaps you were never In Belgium'': Negotiating British Identity in Charlotte Brontë's *The Professor* and *Villette*' (*NCL* 64[2009] 163–88) reconsiders the Belgium setting in Brontë's *The Professor* and *Villette*. These settings 'are not . . . merely a product of Brontë's own personal experience [rather] they reflect both Brontë's own concern with the clash of British and French values and in particular mid-Victorian understanding of the significance of Belgium to British national identity'. Longmuir's is an interesting article; however, insufficient consideration is given to the complicated notions of 'British national identity' or for that matter 'British and French values' (p. 187) whatever these may have been then or are now! Kate Lawson and Lynn Shakinovsky, in their 'Fantasies of National Identification in *Villette*' (*SEL* 39[2009] 925–44) pay particular attention to the heroine's professional role and transformed perceptions of the idea of national identity.

Mark M. Hennelly Jr.'s 'Alice's Adventures at the Carnival' (*VLC* 37[2009) 103–28) presents a carnival tradition reading of Lewis Carroll's Alice novels. His article is accompanied by twelve fascinating illustrations from Carroll's drawings and notes. Critical reactions to 'Lewis Carroll's *Alice* books' (p. 103) preoccupy Andrew R. Wheat in 'Dodgson's Dark Conceit: Evoking the Allegorical Lineage of *Alice*' (*Renascence* 61:ii[2009] 103–21). For Wheat, following a careful analysis of readings of Carroll's novels, 'Like Columbus, Carroll . . . may have been unaware of the real country he hit upon.' Further, 'Intentionally or by chance . . . he opened a passage to a new allegorical dark continent that writers have been exploring, colonizing, and in some cases, demonizing ever since' (p. 120). In *Wilkie Collins, Medicine and the Gothic*, Laurence Talairach-Vielmas examines how Collins's interest in medical matters evolved through investigation of his revisions of late eighteenth-century Gothic novels on through his last novels. The book explores these developments chronologically, recording how Collins utilized such devices as Gothic adaptations with archetypal castles replaced by modern medical institutions, with heroines fearing the scientist's knife instead of ghosts. Chapters include '"Sensation is [his] Frankenstein": Monomaniac Obsessions in Basil, "Mad Monkton" and *The Woman in White*' (pp. 18–52); 'The Substance and the Shadow: Invisibility and Immateriality in *Armadale*' (pp. 53–72); '"My grave is waiting for me there": Physiological Prisons in *The Moonstone*' (pp. 73–92); 'Transformation, Epilepsy and Late Victorian Anxieties in *Poor Miss Finch*' (pp. 93–118); 'The Shadows of the Past: Digging Out Hidden Memory in *The Haunted Hotel*' (pp. 119–36); 'Mad Scientists: *Jezebel's Daughter* and *Heart and Science*' (pp. 137–57); 'The Quest for Knowledge in "I Say No"' (pp. 158–80); and 'Born to Kill: the Haunting Taint in *The Legacy of Cain*' (pp. 181–202). In 'Wilkie Collins, *The Woman in White* (1859–60)' (*VR* 35[2009] 37–41), Dallas Liddle argues for the ongoing fertility of the novel's pertinence in the twenty-first century. In her essay, 'The Law and the Nation: Wilkie Collins and Scottish Identity' (*VIJ* 37[2009] 67–91), Teresa Huffman Traver illustrates how Collins's 1874 novel *The Law and the Lady* contrasts elements of English and Scottish national character to support a specific outlook of the 'marriage' between England and Scotland which symbolizes the British Union. Aviva Briefel, 'Cosmetic Tragedies: Failed Masquerade in Wilkie Collins' *The Law and the Lady*' (*VLC* 37[2009]

463–81) provides a moving reading of Collins's novel from the perspective of the 'profound anxiety about the far-reaching consequences of a woman's inability to embellish herself' (p. 464). Mark Mossman, 'Representation of the Abnormal Body in *The Moonstone*' (*VLC* 37[2009] 483–500), argues 'that the representation of [abnormality] in *The Moonstone* become the location of a disabled perspective on the workings of Victorian cultural practice' (p. 483). Collins's 'work is defined by the active translation of individual, unique experience into a larger social framework and set of meanings'. Consequently his narratives, like *The Moonstone*, reflect a particular kind of thinking or 'cultural' mentality that Mossman defines 'as the emergence of this disability being defined as a perspective on cultural practices' (p. 497). Mossman has interesting things to say about *The Moonstone* once the opaque quality of his prose, in which he is not alone, is deciphered. Some of the articles and monographs reviewed in this section really do need to be written in clear, concise English.

The most important contribution to a fertile year in Dickens studies is undoubtedly Michael Slater's long-awaited biography *Charles Dickens*. Slater writes clearly and his assessments are judicious and not without a tinge of scepticism. His unrivalled knowledge of his subject shines through every page. Slater has been 'primarily concerned to place [Dickens's] novels in the context of the truly prodigious amount of *other* writing that he was constantly producing' alongside his serial writing, 'and to explore the web of connections between them and it, as well as connections with his superlative letters and his personal life' (p. xiv). Another significant work, but this time devoted to a single Dickens novel, is Michael Cotsell's excellent *The Companion to Our Mutual Friend*. Natalie B. Cole's *Dickens and Gender: Recent Studies, 1992–2008* is a welcome and vital contribution to Dickens studies. The introduction itself is quite useful in its overview and logical explanations of chapter titles, which include the following: 'Review Essays and "Quick Takes" on Gender' (pp. 3–8); 'Families' (pp. 9–31), incorporating the following topics: 'Marriage, Spousal Abuse, and the Law' (pp. 13–18), 'Mothers and Surrogates' (pp. 18–22), 'Fathers and Surrogates' (pp. 23–6), 'Daughters' (pp. 26–8), and 'Children' (pp. 28–31); 'Sexualities' (pp. 32–82), which includes the following topics: 'Lesbian Erotics and Queer Theory' (pp. 32–6), 'Homoerotics and Queer Theory' (pp. 36–43), 'Bachelor Masculinities' (pp. 43–7), 'Odd Women' and 'Fallen Women' (pp. 47–55), 'Relational Femininities and Masculinities' (pp. 56–68), 'Incest' (pp. 68–72), and 'Victorian Bodies' (pp. 72–82); 'Work' (pp. 83–104), which includes the following topics: 'Masculinities and Work' (pp. 83–91), 'Femininities and Work' (pp. 91–9), and 'Redefinitions of Domesticity and Domestic Space' (pp. 99–104); 'Victorian and Other Cultural Contexts' (pp. 105–28), including the following topics: 'Intertextual Readings of Dickens' (pp. 105–9), 'Empire and Nationalism' (pp. 109–14), 'Cultural Authorities' (pp. 114–17), 'Industrialism and Urban Contagion' (pp. 117–22), and 'Archetypes, Icons, and Myths' (pp. 122–8); and 'Gender, Genre, and Narrative' (pp. 129–41), including 'Genre and Gender' (pp. 129–33), 'Gender and Narration in *Dombey and Son* and *David Copperfield*' (pp. 133–6), 'Dickens Symposium at Kingston University', and a useful appendix organized by novels and miscellaneous writings. An item of relevance to *David Copperfield* that should not be ignored is Clare Pettit's 'Peggotty's Work-Box: Victorian Souvenirs and Material Memory' (*RaVoN* http://www.erudit.org/revue/ravon/2009/v/n53). Also, in the same electronic accessible issue on 'Materiality and Memory', edited by Kate Flint, Adelene Buckland contributes '"Pictures in the Fire": The Dickensian Hearth and the Concept of History'.

Expanding upon Anne Lohrli's *Household Words: A Weekly Journal* [1973], Sabine Clemm, in *Dickens, Journalism, and Nationhood: Mapping the World in Household Words*, examines how Dickens's magazine *Household Words* dealt with nationhood and national identity. This recommended work includes the following chapters: '"Amidst the heterogeneous masses": *Household Words* and the Great Exhibition of 1851' (pp. 16–47); '(Un-)Englishness and National Character in *Household Words*' (pp. 48–79); '*Household Words*' Treatment in Ireland' (pp. 80–97); '"Continental ways and means": Europe in *Household Words*' (pp. 98–126); and '"Interlopers in the East": *Household Words* and India' (pp. 127–56). Work and character development across Dickens's career is at the centre of *Dickens's Secular Gospel: Work, Gender, and Personality*, by Chris Louttit. Following the introduction, 'Dickens, Work, and the Victorians' (pp. 1–8), are the chapters: 'Work and the Shaping of Personality' (pp. 9–35); 'Gendering the Laboring Body' (pp. 36–60); 'Dickens and the Professions' (pp. 61–88); 'Dickens and Domestic Management' (pp. 89–107); and 'Dickens's Idle Men' (pp. 108–30); along with the epilogue, 'Occupation, Disguise, and Personality in Dickens's Late Novels' (pp. 131–6).

A useful contribution to study of *A Tale of Two Cities* as well as the cultural history of events in France is *Charles Dickens, A Tale of Two Cities and the French Revolution*, edited by Colin Jones, Josephine McDonagh, and Jon Mee. Chapters include 'Introduction: *A Tale of Two Cities* in Context' by the editors (pp. 1–23); 'The New Philosophy: The Substance and the Shadow in *A Tale of Two Cities*' by Mark Philp (pp. 24–40); 'The Redemptive Powers of Violence? Carlyle, Marx and Dickens' by Gareth Stedman Jones (pp. 41–63); 'A Genealogy of Dr. Manette' by Keith Michael Baker (pp. 64–74); 'From the Old Bailey to Revolutionary France: The Trials of Charles Darney' by Sally Ledger (pp. 57–86); 'Face Value in *A Tale of Two Cities*' by Kamilla Elliot (pp. 87–103); 'Counting on: *A Tale of Two Cities*' by John Bowen (pp. 104–25); 'Mimi and the Matinee Idol: Martin-Harvey, Sydney Carton and the Staging of *A Tale of Two Cities*, 1860–1939' (pp. 126–45); 'Sanguine Mirages, Cinematic Dreams: Things Seen and Things Imagined in the 1917 Fox Feature Film *A Tale of Two Cities*' by Judith Buchanan with Alex Newhouse (pp. 146–65); 'Two Cities, Two Films' by Charles Barr (pp. 166–87); and 'Afterword' by Michael Wood (pp. 188–96). Teresa Mangum, 'Dickens and the Female Terrorist: The Long Shadow of Madame Defarge' (*NCC* 31[2009] 143–60), is concerned with the afterlife of Madame Defarge and her appearance in *A Tale of Two Cities*. Usefully drawing upon Hablot Browne's (Phiz's) illustrations to the novel and accounts of the terror of revolutionary France, Mangum considers Dickens's models for Defarge and perceptions of 'women terrorists' (p. 154). She sees 'Madame Defarge in a pool of blood, which in this novel signifies terrible thirst, hunger, lust, drunkenness, sustenance, bonds, and brutality all at once (p. 158). In '"A place for more than the healing of bodily sickness": Charles Dickens, the Social Mission of Nineteenth-Century Pediatrics, and the Great Ormond Street Hospital for Sick Children' (*VR* 35[2009] 153–73), Katharina Boehm traces influences from Dickens's *Oliver Twist* [1837–9] to his collaborative Christmas story *A House to Let* [1858]. Though both pieces involve an unfortunate marriage, an orphaned child, a secret will, and inheritances, Boehm examines Dickens's shift within a larger social framework of mid-nineteenth-century medicalization of children of the poor.

As usual, *The Dickensian* offers much of interest. The first issue for 2009 features Jeremy Clarke's 'Dickens's Dark Ride: "Traveling Abroad" to Meet the Heritage' (*Dickensian* 105[2009] 5–14). Jerome Meckier contributes '"A Wife in Two Volumes": the "Something Wanting" in *David Copperfield* and *The Woman in White*' (*Dickensian* 105[2009] 14–20), followed by Jan Lokin on 'Realism and Reality in Dickens's Characters: Dickens Seen Through the Eyes of Dutch Writers' (*Dickensian* 105[2009] 21–32); then Paul Schlicke writes on 'Macrone, Cruikshank and the Proposed Part-Issue of *Sketches by Boz*: A Note' (*Dickensian* 105[2009] 33–5). Angus Easson, Margaret Brown, Leon Litvack, and Joan Dicks contribute the very useful 'The Letters of Charles Dickens: Supplement XI' (*Dickensian* 105[2009] 36–53). The summer issue of *The Dickensian* opens with David McAllister's 'Artificial Respiration in *Our Mutual Friend*' (*Dickensian* 105[2009] 101–21). Irina Gredina and Philip V. Allingham contribute the most interesting 'The Countess Vera Sergeevna Tolstya's Russian Language Adaptation of *Great Expectations* (1895)' (*Dickensian* 105[2009] 122–34). Angus Easson, Margaret Brown, Leon Litvack, and Joan Dicks contribute 'The Letters of Charles Dickens: Supplement XII' (*Dickensian* 105[2009] 135–53). These include some fairly lengthy letters to Georgina Hogarth (see, for instance, pp. 138–41). The winter 2009 *Dickensian* opens with John Bowen's 'John Dickens's Birth Announcements and Charles Dickens's Sisters' (*Dickensian* 105[2009] 197–201). David Parker contributes 'The Topicality of *Pickwick Papers*' (*Dickensian* 105[2009] 202–12). This is followed by Robert D. Butterworth's 'The Significance of Fagin's Jewishness' (*Dickensian* 105[2009] 213–24): one would have thought that Butterworth was flogging a dead horse and that enough had been said on the subject. According to Butterworth, 'Dickens establishes Fagin's Jewish identity as such not so that he can indulge in meretricious anti-semitism. On the contrary, far from pandering to his readers' prejudices, Dickens plays on them to jolt his respectable Christian readers out of their complacency' (p. 223). Of course, one could reply that this is special pleading and Butterworth does not take into account the impact on young, sensitive Jewish children growing up in post-Second World War Britain of Dickens's portrayal of Fagin. Indeed, in some cases, it could be enough to put them off Dickens for life! Angus Easson, Margaret Brown, Leon Litvack, and Joan Dick again contribute 'The Letters of Charles Dickens: XII' (*Dickensian* 105[2009] 225–39). Each issue of *The Dickensian* is followed by excellent reviews and in some instances film reviews and notes and news related to the Dickens Fellowship.

In 'All in the Mind: The Psychological Realism of Dickensian Solitude' (*DQu* 26[2009] 15–123), Stella Pratt-Smith explores Dickens's portrayal of the contemporary relationship among interior spaces, individual identity and psychology. In 'Dickens, Niagara Falls and the Watery' (*DQu* 26[2009] 60–78), Natalie McKnight analyses Dickens's response to Niagara Falls in the context of other British travel narratives of the previous decade, and examines the ways in which Niagara speaks to Dickens of life after death, as well as the influences of the Niagara experience in shaping climactic and transcendent moments in his subsequent novels (after 1842). Sally Ledger's talk given at Genoa from the 2007 International Conference, 'Dickens, Victorian Culture, Italy' is printed in '"God be thanked: a ruin!" The Rejection of Nostalgia in *Pictures from Italy*' (*DQu* 26[2009] 79–85). Ledger explores Dickens's diverse reactions to Italy in its focus on the past, alongside his endorsement of popular culture and modernity. *The Chimes*, *Household Words, and Little Dorrit* are brought into the discussion as well. In 'Charles Dickens's and Apollo Korzeniowski's *Hard Times*' (*DQu* 26[2009] 86–107), Ewa Kujawska-Lis explores the relatively less popular Dickens title in Poland. As translated by Korzeniowski, father to Joseph Conrad, this earliest full translation of *Hard Times* is still the prevalent one today, Michael Hollington offers a moving tribute to Sally Ledger in 'Sally Ledger Remembered' (*DQu* 26[2009] 121–3). Margaret Flanders Darby's 'The Conservatory at Gad's Hill Place' (*DQu* 26[2009] 137–50) explores the paradoxes of Dickens maintaining his conservatory at Gad's Hill. A photo of Dickens and his daughters from about 1860 and photos of Gad's Hill, as well as a floor plan, are included. Darby traces Dickens's plans to build the conservatory, beginning with letters from September 1857, the influence of Joseph Paxton, and Dickens's expectations as a host at Gad's Hill, to the completion of the conservatory, including a subterranean route to the house, and Dickens's related actions within days of his own death.

Susan Shatto's 'Mr. Pickwick's First Brush with the Law: Civil Disobedience in *The Pickwick Papers*' (*DQu* 26[2009] 151–64) explores Miss Witherfield's dreamt duel between Pickwick and Magnum as a parody of contemporary social disturbances enumerated in extensive detail. In the essay 'Dick Swiveller's Bed' (*DQu* 26[2009] 165–74), Joel J. Brattin points out the multi-purpose aspects of Swiveller's bed as evidenced in *The Old Curiosity Shop*, as well other objects noted in Forster's *The Life of Charles Dickens*, 'Brokers and Marine-Store Shops', *The Pickwick Papers*, *Oliver Twist*, *Nicholas Nickleby*, *American Notes*, *Martin Chuzzlewit*, and *Little Dorrit*, among other Dickens works. Brattin further discusses the utility of these furniture pieces in highlighting various themes. In 'Terror Foreign or Familiar—Pleasure on the Edge, Translating *A Tale of Two Cities* into French' (*DQu* 26[2009] 175–86), Christine Raguet questions 'whether the translators of the novel stuck to the principle of "elegance" and brought something "more" to the text or attempted to respect Dickens's own principles and tried to reflect an outsider's observations in their work' (p. 175). She goes on to portray images French readers have perceived over the past 150 years, as well as how these images might correlate to the original text. Interestingly, Raguet answers these queries across three translations: Henriette Loreau's 1861 translation for its long life, Emmanuel Bove's for its political resonance, and Jeanne Métifeu-Béjeau's for its intellectual resonance. *Dickens Quarterly*

26:iv[2009] contains three main contributions: Gareth Cordery 'Quilp, Commerce, and Domesticity: Crossing Boundaries in *The Old Curiosity Shop*' (*DQu* 26[2009] 209–34); Paola Venturi, '*David Copperfield* Conscripted: Italian Translations of the Novel' (*DQu* 26[2009] 234–48); and Jerome Meckier's '*Great Expectations*, "A Good Name?"' (*DQu* 26[2009] 248–58).

The fortieth volume of *Dickens Studies Annual* features discussions of novels written across various stages of Dickens's career. Contributions include the following: 'In Pursuit of Pickwick's Hat: Dickens and the Epistemology of Utilitarianism' by Paul Schacht (*DSA* 40[2009] 1–21); 'The Erotics of *Barnaby Rudge*' by Natalie McKnight (*DSA* 40[2009] 23–36); 'Reading Laura Bridgeman: Literacy and Disability in Dickens's *American Notes*' by Karen Bourrier (*DSA* 40[2009] 37–60); '*Dombey and Son* and the "Parlour on Wheels" 'by Michael Klotz (*DSA* 40[2009] 61–79); 'Dickens, Collins, and the Influence of the Arctic' by John Kofron (*DSA* 40[2009] 81–93); 'Darkness, Light, and Various Shades of Gray: The Prison and the Outside World in Charles Dickens's *A Tale of Two Cities*' by Jan Alber (*DSA* 40[2009] 95–112); 'The Illustrations for *Great Expectations* in *Harper's Weekly* (1860–1) and in the Illustrated Library Edition (1862)—"Reading by the Light of Illustration"' by Philip V. Allingham (*DSA* 40[2009] 113–69); 'Dolls and Imaginative Agency in Bradford, Pardoe, and Dickens' by Victoria Ford Smith (*DSA* 40[2009] 171–97); '"Opium is the true hero of the tale": De Quincey, Dickens, and *The Mystery of Edwin Drood*' by Robert Tracy (*DSA* 40[2009] 199–214); 'Intoxication, Provocation, and Derangement: Interrogating the Nature of Criminal Responsibility in *The Mystery of Edwin Drood*' by Stephanie Peña-Sy (*DSA* 40[2009] 215–30); and 'Before Boz: The Juvenilia and Early Writings of Charles Dickens, 1820–1833' by Robert C. Hanna (*DSA* 40[2009] 231–364). Natalie McKnight's very useful narrative account of articles, book chapters, and books of literary criticism dealing with Dickens published during 2007, 'Recent Dickens Studies: 2007' (*DSN* 40[2009] 365–431) concludes this most useful issue of *Dickens Studies Annual*.

Dickens is the focal point of three recent articles in *PMLA*: Daniel Siegel's 'Griffith, Dickens, and the Politics of Composure' (*PMLA* 124[2009] 375–89), which brings together science, film, and Dickens; Sarah Gates's 'Intertextual Estella: *Great Expectations*, Gender, and Literary Tradition' (*PMLA* 124[2009] 390–405); and Robert E. Loughy's 'Dickens and the Wolf Man: Childhood Memory and Fantasy in *David Copperfield*' (*PMLA* 124[2009] 406–20). Brian Cheadle's well-written 'Improvising Character in *Our Mutual Friend*' (*EIC* 59[2009] 211–33) argues that 'characters are essential to discussions of Dickens, for they provide the fields of energy through which he conducts his improvisations' (p. 211). Cheadle examines the various characters in *Our Mutual Friend*, paying special attention to Eugene Wrayburn, his relationships within the novel, and critical reactions to *Our Mutual Friend* from 1865 (the date of its initial publication, not '1965' as a misprint in the notes states (p. 230)) to the present. For Cheadle, 'what makes the presentation of Eugene disconcerting . . . is the radical depth of his self-division' (p. 226). Perceptively Cheadle writes in his final sentence that 'In literary terms . . . Eugene's fragmentation of self is a century before its time, and his discontinuous intensities might well seem more true to what individuals are like than is the unity of personality taken for granted by all humanistic psychologies and indefatigably fictionalised' (p. 230).

Eileen Gillooly and Deirdre David, editors of *Contemporary Dickens*, have several aims: to present 'some of the most intriguing work being undertaken in Dickens studies; to review the Victorian genesis of many of the issues that critically concern us today; and to especially illuminate 'late Dickens—as a novelist, reformer, activist, ethicist, psychologist, anthropologist, and biographical subject' (pp. 2–3). There are three parts to *Contemporary Dickens*. The first, 'Ethics and Narrative', has five essays: George Levine on 'Dickens, Secularism, and Agency' (pp. 13–34), centred on *Little Dorrit* and its author's dramatization of 'the limits of secularity' (p. 31); Robert Newson on 'Dickens and the Goods' (pp. 35–52), which examines the complexity of its subject's 'ethical force' (p. 37); then *Bleak House* engages Nancy Yousef in her 'The Poverty of Charity: Dickensian Sympathy' (pp. 53–74); John Bowen writes on 'Uncanny Gifts, Strange Contagion: Allegory in *The Haunted Man*' (pp. 75–92); and *Hard Times* is the focus for Richard H. Moye's 'Storied Realities: Language, Narrative, and Historical Understanding' (pp. 93–109). The second part, on 'Material Culture', also contains five contributions: Joseph W. Childers writes on Dickens's perception of Christmas in 'So, this is Christmas' (pp. 113–30); ecology preoccupies Karen Chase and Michael Levenson in 'Green Dickens' (pp. 131–51); Elaine Freedgood's 'Commodity Criticism and Victorian Thing Culture: The Case of Dickens' (pp. 152–68) is partly reprinted from her *The Ideas in Things: Fugitive Meaning in the Victorian Novel* ([2006]; *YWES* 87[2008] 780); Tatiana M. Holway writes on 'Funny Money' (pp. 169–88); and James Buzard's subject is 'Enumeration and Exhaustion: Taking Inventory in *The Old Curiosity Shop*' (pp. 189–206). The third and final section of the collection is entitled 'Contextual Reading'. There are four contributions: Eileen Gillooly, 'Paterfamilias' (pp. 209–30); James Eli Adams, 'Reading with Buzfuz: Dickens, Sexuality, Interrogation' (pp. 231–44); Deirdre David, '*Little Dorrit*'s Theatre of Rage' (pp. 245–63); and Deborah Epstein Nord, 'The Making of Dickens Criticism' (pp. 264–87). Nord, in her account, curiously ignores Q.D. Leavis's important contribution to Dickens criticism. This challenging collection concludes with an alphabetically arranged enumerative bibliography (pp. 289–303), 'Notes on Contributors' (pp. 305–7), and a helpful index (pp. 309–15).

Rachel Teukolsky, 'Pictures in Bleak Houses: Slavery and the Aesthetics of Transatlantic Reform' (*ELH* 76[2009] 491–522), analyses *Bleak House* and American novels protesting against American slavery or, in the case of *Bleak House*, wage slavery in Dickens's Britain. Carolyn Vellenga Berman, in '"Awful unknown quantities": Addressing the Readers in *Hard Times*' (*VLC* 37[2009] 561–82), argues that *Hard Times* 'betrays a marked self-consciousness about the Victorian novel's divergent audiences'. The novel 'is deeply concerned about' what Berman refers to as 'two abstractions: Reader and People'. For Berman, *Hard Times* 'is deeply concerned about both [with] their shared tendency to make incommensurate subjects commingle' (p. 562). Lisa Rodensky, in 'Popular Dickens' (*VLC* 37[2009] 583–607), asks 'why was Charles Dickens so popular when he broke onto the scene in the late 1830s?' She also asks 'what did the terms "popular" and "popularity" mean when applied to [Dickens] at this signal moment in the development of the novel?' (p. 583). Rodensky primarily concerns herself with the early Dickens; however, she pays much attention to the criticism of George Henry Lewes, David Masson, and others in a clearly written account that fully acknowledges the work of others in the field and not just recent scholarship. Molly Clark Hillard, in her 'Dickens's Little Red Riding Hood and Other Waterside Characters' (*SEL* 49[2009] 945–73), draws upon the use by Dickens of the Red Riding Hood story with particular attention to his 1850 essay 'A Christmas Tree' and *Our Mutual Friend.* Melvin New contributes 'Taking Care: A Slightly Levinasian Reading of *Dombey and Son* (in Wehrs and Haney, eds., *Levinas and Nineteenth-Century Literature*: *Ethics and Otherness from Romanticism through Realism*, pp. 236–63). Following a discussion of selected illustrations to very early editions of the novel, New presents a reading of *Dombey and Son* with particular reference to chapter 59, 'Retribution'. Holly Furneaux's *Queer Dickens: Erotics, Families, Masculinities* 'endeavors to chart a two-directional literary genealogy, through which Dickens gained his understanding of, and access to, methods of representation of queer desire and adapted these, often compulsively and repeatedly, across his work to develop influential modes of queer expression' (p. 8). Furneaux has interesting things to say and illuminates many areas of Dickens work; however, it can only be wished that she expressed herself in a less convoluted manner.

Anna Neill, in her 'The Savage Genius of Sherlock Holmes' (*VLC* 37[2009] 611–26), suggests that the Sherlock Holmes stories 'resist the contamination of degeneracy, less via the sanitizing influence of the ordered, reasoning mind, than through the more obscure workings of genius, something which in turn anticipates the spiritualist focus of Doyle's later work'. In addition 'Holmes's genius . . . is atavistic rather than degenerative, intuitive rather than rational, and as worthy an object of psychical investigation as are the strangest phenomenon of the séance room' (p. 611). For Sherlock Holmes and Doyle aficionados this is interesting. Nathalie Saudo-Welby's 'The "over-aesthetic eye" and the "monstrous development of a phenomenal larynx": Du Maurier's Art of Excess in *Trilby*' examines how *Trilby* [1894], in its seductions and dangers of aesthetic transformation, sheds light on George Du Maurier's own practice in which he simultaneously brings the reader to see and finds a voice for himself (*EA* 62[2009] 28–41). Laura Vorachek's 'Mesmerists and Other Meddlers: Social Darwinism, Degeneration, and Eugenics in *Trilby*' (*VLC* 37[2009] 197–215) is a reading of the significance of a seventeen-page digression on *The Origin of Species.* This occurs roughly 'two thirds of the way through George Du Maurier's *Trilby* (1894)' (p. 197). Vorachek's well-written and clearly argued essay, accompanied by appropriate illustrative material, argues that 'in *Trilby* Du Maurier rejects any artificial interference with sexual selection, whether meddling mother's, society's preference for wealth and status, or . . . plans for preserving the middle classes'. In short 'For Du Maurier, the future of the human race may lie with individual free will and not the kind of mass phenomenon induced by mesmerists and eugenicists' (p. 211). An item on Du Maurier that should not be ignored is James Ogden's 'Henry James, James Russell Lowell, and George Du Maurier in Whitby' (*N&Q* 56[2009] 411–13). Athena Vrettos writes on '"Little Bags of

Remembrance": Du Maurier's *Peter Ibbetson* and Victorian Theories of Ancestral Memory' (*RaVoN* http://www.ravon.unmontreal.ca/).

The year 2009 brought a special issue of *The George Eliot Review*, celebrating the 150th anniversary of *Scenes of Clerical Life* in volume form. This issue includes 'How George Eliot Came to Write Fiction' (*GER* 40[2009] 7–14), by Rosemary Ashton; '*Scenes of Clerical Life*: George Eliot's Version of Conversion?' (*GER* 40[2009] 15–24), by Alain Jumeau; 'Idlers and Collaborators: Enter the Dog' (*GER* 40[2009] 25–36), by Beryl Gray; '"The stream of human thought and deed" in "Mr. Gilfil's Love-Story"' (*GER* 40[2009] 37–42), by Melissa Raines; 'Orphic Variations in *Scenes of Clerical Life*' (*GER* 40[2009] 43–7), by Renichi Kurata; '"Indications that I can touch the hearts of my fellow men": Reading *Scenes of Clerical Life* from a Kleinian Psychoanalytic Perspective' (*GER* 40[2009] 48–57), by Toni Griffiths; and 'Death and Recollection: The Elegiac Dimension of *Scenes of Clerical Life*' by John Rignall (*GER* 40[2009] 58–67). *Middlemarch* continues to inspire critical articles in Sybil Oldfield's 'Who Was Mrs. Nassau Senior? Was She the Inspiration for George Eliot's *Middlemarch*? (Thirty-Seventh George Eliot Memorial Lecture, 11 October 2008)' (*GER* 40[2009] 7–17) and Miriam Henson's 'George Eliot's *Middlemarch* as a Translation of Spinoza's *Ethics*' (*GER* 40[2009] 18–27). The issue also features Margaret Harris's 'J.W. Cross Defends G.H. Lewes' (*GER* 40[2009] 28–37); Lorna J. Clark's 'George Eliot and the Female Tradition: A Little-Known Source' (*GER* 40[2009] 38–48); Jennifer Jones's 'Orchestrating Society: The Merging of Language and Voice to Create Social Bonds in *Romola*' (*GER* 40[2009] 49–56); and Barbara Hardy's 'George Eliot to Martha Jackson: A New Holograph Letter with Unpublished Passages' (*GER* 40[2009] 57–61). There are also the usual book reviews and parochial notes.

George Eliot–George Henry Lewes Studies opens with June Skye Szirotny's detailed 'Some More Addenda and Corrigenda' (*GEGLHS* 56–7[2009] 11–48). This is a supplement to the nine-volume *George Eliot Letters*, edited by Gordon S. Haight [1954–5, 1978]. Peter Garratt writes illuminatingly on '"That old Glasgow suit": *Middlemarch*, Scotland and the Universities' (*GEGLHS* 56–7[2009] 49–61). David A. Reibel's 'Acts of Imagination: George Eliot, Charles Dickens, and Lindley Murray and his *English Grammar*: *A Divertissement* on Literature and Language' (*GEGLHS* 56–7[2009] 61–91) is replete with interesting information, some of it rather abstruse, on grammatical highways and byways. Glenda Sacks writes on 'George Eliot's Boudoir Experiment: Dorothea as Embodied Learner' (*GEGLHS* 56–7[2009] 92–119). Inna Volkova also has interesting things to say in her 'Public Spaces and the Political Underworld in George Eliot's *Felix Holt, The Radical*' (*GEGLHS* 56–7[2009] 119–32). Donald Hawes contributes his usual most helpful 'Articles on George Eliot in 2009: A Selective Survey' (*GEGLHS* 56–7[2009] 133–9), and also writes on '*Felix Holt, The Radical:* A Radio Dramatization' (*GEGLHS* 56–7[2009] 139–40). Patrick Streeter, a descendant of the eminent Victorian jeweller and mining entrepreneur Edwin Streeter, contributes an interesting short note on 'Florence Streeter and George Eliot' (*GEGLHS* 56–7[2009] 140–1). The usual reviews are followed by Barbara Hardy's 'Dante's Ghosts'. These consist of extracts from her 'poem-sequence freely based on the three cantice (books) of Dante's *Divina Commedia*' (*GEGLHS* 56–7[2009] 148–51).

In '"Exotic Eroticism": Gwendolen Harleth and Daniel Deronda' (*CVE* 69[April 2009] 97–114), Julia Kuehn examines the relationship between the two protagonists of *Daniel Deronda*, arguing that Gwendolen Harleth's interest in Daniel Deronda is better viewed through a concern for the ethnic otherness he represents rather than through the lens of class. Also focusing on *Deronda* is K. M. Newton's 'Winning, Losing, and Luck in the Ethics and Politics of *Daniel Deronda*' (*English* 58[2009] 297–317). Catherine Brown's well-argued '*Daniel Deronda* as Tragi-Comedy' (*EIC* 59[2009] 303–23) uses George Eliot's epigraph to chapter 6, which draws upon Bernard le Bouyer de Fontenelle's *Entretiens sur la Pluralité des Mondes* [1866], in order to usefully illuminate the relationships or non-relationships between the Gentile and Jewish characters of *Daniel Deronda*. Ilana M. Blumberg, in her '"Love yourself as your neighbor": The Limits of Altruism and the Ethics of Personal Benefit in *Adam Bede*' (*VLC* 37[2009] 543–60), observes that 'Eliot's unequal treatment of her protagonists was a moral cost which troubled the novelist herself'. Further, *Adam Bede*, 'keenly alive to the inseparability of the ethical and economic ... reflects not only the extraordinary demands of Victorian notions of altruism and the insufficient half-measures of such alternatives as utilitarianism, but also the intractable realities of a material world in which desire and need are felt by all but only attained by some' (p. 557). Blumberg has interesting things to say: perhaps she has been unduly influenced by the length of sentences in George Eliot's novels! Brief mention should be made of *The Jewish Odyssey of George Eliot*. This is not amongst Gertrude Himmelfarb's better works and is derivative, with its author adding very little to what is already known. Rachel Hollander's '*Daniel Deronda* and the Ethics of Alterity' (in Wehrs and Haney, eds., pp. 264–87), following a review of the 'many reasons for the recent surge of critical interest in George Eliot's final novel' (p. 264), concludes that the work's 'double ending' and 'profound ambivalence about the ability of the realist form to do for justice to an ethics of otherness ... establishes the truly radical nature of *Daniel Deronda*' (p. 284). Attention should be drawn to Susanna De Schepper's 'George Eliot on the Dutch Market, 1860–1896' (in Toremans and Verschueren, eds., *Crossing Cultures: Nineteenth-Century Anglophone Literature in the Low Countries*, pp. 83–97). John H. Mazaheri draws upon George Eliot's writing and previous critical studies in his evaluation of 'George Eliot and War' (in Glunz and Schneider, eds., *Krieg und Literatur Jahrbuch / War and Literature Yearbook XII*, pp. 64–74). June Skye Szirotny has useful information in her 'Seeing the Stars by Daylight in George Eliot's *Middlemarch*' (*N&Q* 56[2009] 383–6). Elizabeth Kraft writes on 'Pictures of the Prodigal Son in *Mill on the Floss* (*N&Q* 56[2009] 286–8). Jonathan Farina has some interesting insights in his '*Middlemarch* and "That Sort of Thing"' (*RaVoN* http://www.ravon.umontreal.ca/). Finally, *Narrative* features 'Sympathy Time: Adam Smith, George Eliot, and the Realist Novel' by Rae Greiner (*Narrative* 17[2009] 291–311).

In '"Mere Outward Appearances?": Household Taste and Social Perception in Elizabeth Gaskell's *North and South*' (*VR* 35[2009] 190–210), John Paul Kanwit illustrates how Gaskell employs household details in her novels to mobilize deep political statements. J.G. Voller published a short piece on 'Misstated Identity in Gaskell's "The Old Nurse's Story"' (*N&Q* 56[2009] 398–409). *Adaptation: The Journal of Literature on Screen Studies* features an insightful piece by Chris Louttit entitled 'Cranford, Popular Culture, and the Politics of Adapting the Victorian Novel for Television' (*Adaptation* 2[2009] 34–48). Sue Zemka, in her 'Brief Encounters: Street Scenes in Gaskell's Manchester' (*ELH* 76[2009] 793–819), applies Bakhtin's ideas to her reading of street scenes in Elizabeth Gaskell's *Mary Barton* and *North and South*. A.S.G. Edwards makes interesting parallels in his 'Gaskell's *North and South* and John Lydgate' (*N&Q* 56[2009] 399). Nancy S. Weyant's extremely useful 'A Bibliographical Supplement: Gaskell Scholarship 2002–2009' may be found on her website http://nancyweyant.com/. The *Gaskell Society Journal* contains many contributions of considerable interest, and the 2009 issue is no exception. It contains Shirley Foster's 'Space in Gaskell's Landscapes' (*GSJ* 23[2009] 1–15); Caroline M. Jackson-Houlston's '*Cranford*: Elizabeth Gaskell's Most Radical Novel?' (*GSJ* 23[2009] 16–31); Graham Handley's 'Elizabeth Gaskell, George Eliot, and Scenes of Clerical Life' (*GSJ* 23[2009] 32–9); Emily Jane Morris's '"Ready to hear and to help": Female Agency and the Reclamation of the Fallen Woman in Elizabeth Gaskell's "Lizzie Leigh"' (*GSJ* 23[2009] 40–53); Alan Shelston's 'Elizabeth Gaskell and the Crimean War' (*GSJ* 23[2009] 54–63); Mariko Tahira's 'The Translation of Elizabeth Gaskell's Short Stories and Non-Fiction Writing into Japanese' (*GSJ* 23[2009] 64–5); and Tomoko Kanda's 'Politics and Everyday Life: Translating "Morton Hall" into Japanese' (*GSJ* 23[2009] 66–7). Also of interest is Malcolm Pittock's '*Cranford* and Cruelty: An Interpretation' (*CQ* 38[2009] 95–119). Janine Barcas writes on 'Mrs. Gaskell's *North and South*: Austen's Early Legacy' (*Persuasions* 30[2008] 53–66). Lastly, Maria Granic-White explores a neglected Gaskell in her '*Ruth*: An Analysis of the Victorian Signifieds' (in Brock, ed., *From Wollstonecraft to Stoker: Essays on Gothic and Victorian Sensation Fiction*, pp. 147–63).

Paul Delany's edition of Gissing's *New Grub Street: The 1901 Revised Text* compares Gabrielle Fleury's 1899 French text of *New Grub Street* with Gissing's English version. This 'was of average length for a three-decker, about 187,000 words' (p. xvii). The French text reduces this by 26 per cent. Delany has an informative introduction and 'A Note on the Text'. With accompanying notes (pp. ix–xx), the English translation then follows (pp. 1–328). There are two 'Notes on the Text' (pp. 331–3) in this excellent addition to Gissing scholarship. The following 2009 issues of the *Gissing Journal* have come to our attention. *GissingJ* 45[2009] contains Roger Milbrandt's 'How Secure was George Gissing? A Study of Gissing's Income between 1889 and 1903' (*GissingJ* 45:i[2009] 1–24) and 'A Revision of George Gissing's "Account of Books"' (*GissingJ* 45:i[2009] 25–34). This fascinating research is followed by Andrew Harrison's 'Art and Money: George Gissing, D.H. Lawrence and the Literary Marketplace' (*GissingJ* 45:i[2009] 35–50). The subsequent issue includes Markus Neacey, 'Gissing's Scarcest Story: Redemption "At Nightfall" or Tribute to a Virtuous Woman' (*GissingJ* 45:ii[2009] 3–16); Bouwe Postmus, 'Gissing's Membership of the Association for the Improvement of Public Morals' (*GissingJ* 45:ii[2009] 16–21); Pierre

Coustillas, '"A Very Decent Fellow, Intelligent and Cordial": Gissing's Contact with the American Journalist Joseph Anderson' (*GissingJ* 45:ii[2009] 21–3); and Bouwe Postmus, 'A Collector's Lament' (*GissingJ* 45:ii[2009] 23–5). There is an unsigned obituary of Francesco Badolato (1926–2009) (*GissingJ* 45:ii[2009] 25–7), who was 'certainly the best known commentator on Gissing's work in Italy' (p. 25). The following issue includes Anthony Petyt 'The Sinden Bequest' (*GissingJ* 45:iii[2009] 1–5). This is a description of the 'collection of the Gissing family memorabilia' presented by John Sinden to the Gissing Trust. 'The gift was given in the name of his late wife Doris Georgina Marjorie Sinden (1914–2007) who was a distant relative of the Gissing family' (p. 1). Other contributors include Robert L. Selig, 'Depressive Gissing: Reconsidering Gillian Tindall's Diagnosis' (*GissingJ* 45:iii[2009] 5–15); Anthony Petyt, 'The Gissings' Wakefield Circle: VII—Samuel and Lucy Bruce' (*GissingJ* 45:iii[2009] 15–30); Vincenzo Pepe, 'Gissing Horace' (*GissingJ* 45:iii[2009] 31–7); Christine DeVine, 'Gissing in French Louisiana' (*GissingJ* 45:iii[2009] 37–42): this is a report of the session on Gissing presented at the 5–7 March 2009 'annual Louisiana Conference on Literature, Language, and Culture . . . at the University of Louisiana at Lafayette, in the heart of French Louisiana' (p. 37). Pierre Coustillas's 'Manchester 1911–1914: Gissing Slandered and Extolled: Homage to Percy Withers, C.H. Herford and A.N. Monkhouse' opens the fourth number (*GissingJ* 45:iv[2009] 1–24). This is followed by Markus Neacey's 'Arthur C. Clarke Looking Backward 1967–1898 and Morley Roberts Anticipating: A Literary Oddity' (*GissingJ* 45:iv[2009] 24–40). The title of this article is clever and there is no misprint! Some of the 2009 issues of the *Gissing Journal* contain 'Notes and News' of interest to Gissing scholars. The second issue contains useful book reviews by Bouwe, Postmus, and Coustillas (*GissingJ* 45:ii[2009] 28–38)

The year 2009 was a good one for Kenneth Grahame's *The Wind in the Willows* with two extensive useful complementary editions. Annie Gauger's *The Annotated Wind in the Willows* contains an introduction by Brian Jacques (pp. xi–xviii) and Annie Gauger's 'Preface and Notes to the Text' (pp. xix–lxxxiv). The text (pp. 1–301) is followed by letters from the author to his son from May 1907 to September of the same year (pp. 303–33) and then 'Fifty-Seven Letters from Naomi Stott, Alastair's Governess to Elspeth Grahame' (pp. 334–52). There are four appendices: 'Alastair Grahame's Bookshelf' (pp. 357–9); 'Critical Reception' (pp. 361–4); 'Kenneth Grahame on Abridgement by Eleanor Grahame' excerpted from her *Kenneth Grahame: A Walck Monograph* (New York: Henry Z. Walck [1963]) (pp. 365–6); and 'The Rural Pan, An April Essay', Grahame's 1891 essay and 1893 *Pagan Papers* (pp. 367–70). The acknowledgements (pp. 371–5) are extensive, and there is an enumerative bibliography (pp. 377–8) of works by Kenneth Grahame, followed by 'Other Sources' (pp. 378–84). Lavishly illustrated, printed in double columns, and nicely presented in quarto format with a decorative cover, this edition contains much of interest but is slightly let down by series of misprints, including some in the table of contents (pp. ix–x). Seth Lerer's *The Annotated Wind in the Willows* contains illustrations, an 'Afterword: Illustration and Illusion' (pp. 261–70), and a bibliography (pp. 271–3). The strength of Lerer's edition lies in his excellent annotation of Grahame's language, contexts, and allusions. Ideally, students of Grahame should purchase both volumes.

Naomi Lloyd's 'The Universal Divine Principle, The Spiritual Androgyny, and the New Age in Sarah Grand's *The Heavenly Twins*' (*VIJ* 37[2009] 177–96) discusses the possible connections between Sarah Grand's novel and articles by Mrs A. Phillips. These all appear in the feminist journal *Shafts*. The editor of the journal, Margaret Sibthorpe, 'added a note to Phillips's second article urging her readers to work towards the formulation of a gospel that would facilitate women's emancipation'. This February 1893 issue included a review of *The Heavenly Twins* also initially published in 1893. Lloyd interestingly reads Grand's novel within the context of Phillips's articles and Sibthorpe's note highlighting 'the possibility that the novel might constitute an attempt to reconfigure discourses of religion and gender, of the kind Sibthorpe had called for and Phillips undertaken' (p. 177). Further, Lloyd demonstrates that 'Helene Blavatsky's writings afforded Grand a modest reworking of dominant religious discourse which, while reinstating the spiritual basis of women's cultural authority, annexed the discourse of rationality to religion and aligned femininity with rationality' (p. 193). Though *The Diary of a Nobody* [1892] has been in print continually, it has failed to gain an edition which illuminates its lost social and literary contexts. Peter Morton's Broadview edition addresses this inadequacy. George and Weedon Grossmith's fictional diary of Charles Pooter is greatly enhanced by Peter Morton's treatment, beginning with the acknowledgements and introduction (pp. 7–43); 'Brief Chronology' (pp. 44–7); 'A Note on the Text', which includes material from the inception of the novel as a serial of twenty-five instalments to the book edition for Arrowsmith in 1892, and the addition of thirty-three witty pen and ink sketches by Weedon Grossmith (pp. 48–52); 'Appendix A: Contemporary Reviews', from such sources as the *Saturday Review*, the *Athenaeum*, and the *New York Times*, over a period of twenty-eight years (pp. 190–8); 'Appendix B: The Clerk's Lot in Life' (pp. 199–215); 'Appendix C: Domestic Economy at The Laurels' (pp. 216–23); 'Appendix D: Suburban Fictions in the Wake of the Day' (pp. 224–33); 'Appendix E: Séances in the Suburbs' (pp. 234–40); and 'Appendix F: Suburban Life and its Critics' (pp. 241–9), as well as recommended reading and works cited. H. Rider Haggard's *Eric Brighteyes* [1891] and *Narda the Lily* [1892] are the focus of the argument that Haggard was more nuanced and self-aware than is commonly supposed in 'Haggard's Questioning of the Heroic' by John Coates (*CVE* 69[2009] 17–40). Patricia Murphy's 'In "the sumptuous rank of the signifier": The Gendered Tattoo in [Haggard's] *Mr. Meeson's Will*' (*VR* 35[2009] 229–51) examines a trio of key paths which focus upon the novel's tattooing incident as a way to explore its gender implications.

Bringing together a wide array of eminent scholars in Hardy studies is *A Companion to Thomas Hardy*, edited by Keith Wilson. Chapters include the following. Part I, 'The Life': 'Hardy as Biographical Subject' by Michael Millgate (pp. 7–18); Part II, 'The Intellectual Context', including 'Hardy and Philosophy' by Phillip Mallett (pp. 21–35); 'Hardy and Darwin: An Enchanting Hardy?' by George Levine (pp. 36–53); 'Hardy and the Place of Culture' by Angelique Richardson (pp. 54–70); '"The hard case of the would-be-religious": Hardy and the Church from Early Life to Later Years' by Pamela Dalziel (pp. 71–85); 'Thomas Hardy's Notebooks' by William Greenslade (pp. 86–101); '"Genres are not to be mixed.... I will not mix them": Discourse, Ideology, and Generic Hybridity in Hardy's Fiction' by Richard Nemesvari (pp. 102–16); and 'Hardy and his Critics: Gender in the Interstices' by Margaret R. Higonnet (pp. 117–29); Part III, 'The Socio-Cultural Context', including '"His Country": Hardy in the Rural' by Ralph Pite (pp. 133–45); 'Thomas Hardy of London' by Keith Wilson (pp. 146–61); '"A thickness of wall": Hardy and Class' by Roger Ebbatson (pp. 162–77); 'Reading Hardy through Dress: The Case of *Far From the Madding Crowd*' by Simon Gatrell (pp. 178–93); 'Hardy and Romantic Love' by Michael Irwin (pp. 194–209); 'Hardy and the Visual Arts' by J.B. Bullen (pp. 210–22); and 'Hardy and Music: Uncanny Sounds' by Claire Seymour (pp. 223–37); Part IV, 'The Works', including 'The Darkening Pastoral: *Under the Greenwood Tree* and *Far From the Madding Crowd*' by Stephen Regan (pp. 241–53); '"Wild regions of obscurity": Narrative in *The Return of the Native*' by Penny Boumelha (pp. 254–66); 'Hardy's "Novels of Ingenuity" *Desperate Remedies*, *The Hand of Ethelberta*, and *A Laodicean*: Rare Hands at Contrivances' by Mary Rimmer (pp. 267–80); 'Hardy's "Romances and Fantasies", *A Pair of Blue Eyes, The Trumpet-Major, Two on a Tower,* and *The Well-Beloved*: Experiments in Metafiction' by Jane Thomas (pp. 281–98); 'The Haunted Structures of *The Mayor of Casterbridge*' by Julian Wolfreys (pp. 299–312); 'Dethroning the High Priest of Nature in *The Woodlanders*' by Andrew Radford (pp. 313–27); 'Melodrama, Vision, and Modernity: *Tess of the d'Urbervilles*' by Tim Dolin (328–44); '*Jude the Obscure* and English National Identity: The Religious Striations of Wessex' by Dennis Taylor (pp. 345–63); '"... into the hands of pure-minded English girls": Hardy's Short Stories and the Late Victorian Literary Marketplace' by Peter Widdowson (pp. 364–77); 'Sequence and Series in Hardy's Poetry' by Tim Armstrong (pp. 378–94); 'Hardy's Poems: The Scholarly Situation' by William W. Morgan (pp. 395–412); and 'That's Show Business: Spectacle, Narration, and Laughter in *The Dynasts*' by G. Glen Wickens (pp. 413–29); and Part V, 'Hardy the Modern', including 'Modernist Hardy: Hand-Writing in *The Mayor of Casterbridge*' by J. Hillis Miller (pp. 433–49); 'Inhibiting the Voice: Thomas Hardy and Modern Poetics' by Charles Lock (pp. 450–64); and 'Hardy's Heirs: D.H. Lawrence and John Cowper Powys' by Terry R. Wright (pp. 465–78).

The Hardy Review (2[2009]), in addition to extensive book reviews, contains 'Uncollected Items: Florence E. Dugdale, "Baby Brother" Introduced by Rosemarie Morgan' (*HR* 2[2009] 5–11). Dugdale was encouraged by Hardy, whom she initially met during the 'winter of 1905–06' (p. 5). Judith Mitchell provides a 'Reprint on the Thomas Hardy Association's Gender Page' (*HR* 2[2009] 12–13): 'this web page provides information on Hardy and gender-studies' and consists of a 'selected bibliography of secondary materials on Hardy and gender; a separate list of secondary materials on Hardy and masculinity'. In addition there is 'a selection of pertinent quotations from Hardy's fiction, poetry, essays, letters, and critics'. The webpage address is http://web.uvic.ca/-mitchell/ (p. 12) A regular feature of the journal is an online discussion of a Hardy poem, on this occasion the choice is 'By the Runic Stone'. The discussion with black and white illustrations may be found on pp. 15–25. Patrick Roper writes on 'Some Reflections on "Under the Waterfall"' (*HR* 2[2009] 26–30), and Laurence Estanove on 'A Lament and Sigh: Voicing Disillusionment in Thomas Hardy's Verse' (*HR* 2[2009] 31–40). Jane Bownas, in 'Exploration and Post-Darwinian Anxiety in Thomas Hardy's *Two on a Tower*' (*HR* 2[2009] 52–61), 'examine[s] Hardy's use of astronomical imagery' in the novel. *The Hardy Review* (2:ii[2009]) contains a report on Hardy studies in 2008–9 by Jeanie Smith in her 'Report on the Thomas Hardy Association's Checklist Page http://www.yale.edu/hardysoc/members/MRRHome.htm' (*HR* 2[2009] 82–6). A regular *Hardy Review* feature is introduced by Peter Lennon. 'Uncollected Items: Revisiting Young Thomas Hardy with Laurence Whistler' (*HR* 2[2009] 87–9), reprints Laurence Whistler's letter to the *TLS* (2 May 1975) in which 'he questions' Robert Gittings's contention in the first volume of his biography *Young Thomas Hardy* [1975] 'that Hardy may have been impotent' (p. 87). The regular 'The Poem of the Month' with 'Contributions: Completed and Edited by Rosemarie Morgan' is devoted to Hardy's 'Waiting Both' (*HR* 2[2009] 101–15). There is an obvious misprint to the heading where 'Poem Host' reads 'Potm Host' (p. 90)! Christina Cerom contributes 'Hardy's Poems: Writing Memory to Resist Annihilation' (*HR* 2[2009] 101–15). Suzannah Bowser's curiously entitled 'Aeneas Manston: Deadly Emasculation of a Fascinating Voluptuary' (*HR* 2[2009] 116–32) focuses on Hardy's depiction of Aeneas Manston in *Desperate Remedies*. Selected Hardy poems are the primary concern of Ilaria Mallozzi's 'Darwin, Hardy, and Bergson—A Glimpse of Continuity?' (*HR* 2[2009] 133–40). Her intention 'is to highlight how Hardy starts from Darwin's concept of inheritance, to come close to Bergson's statement about the innate "autonomy" of the past which is able constantly to preserve itself, without any special faculty' (p. 133). Ross Murfin contributes a detailed review essay on Herbert F. Tucker's *Epic: Britain's Heroic Muse 1790–1910*' (*HR* 2[2009] 144–50). Keith Wilson's extensive review of Martin Ray's *Thomas Hardy Remembered* [2007] is followed by Rosemarie Morgan's and Lynda Kiss's observations on its importance (*HR* 2[2009] 151–8). This excellent issue of *The Hardy Review* concludes with Arthur Efron's 'Reconsiderations on *Experiencing Tess of the d'Urbervilles*: A Deweyan Account' (*HR* 2[2009] 159–64), provoked by the author's reflection that 'after five years in print [his] book on experiencing Hardy's *Tess* is still not being read' (p. 159). Zena Meadowsong, 'Thomas Hardy and the Machine: The Mechanical Deformation of Narrative Realism in *Tess of the d'Urbervilles*' (*NCLE* 64[2009] 225–48) reviews critical responses to the novel. According to Meadowsong, these are primary readings of *Tess* 'as a novel concerned with the industrial demolition of agrarian England'. Meadowsong argues that the novel 'internalizes the problem of mechanization at the level of both story and narrative form' (p. 248).

Cahiers victoriens et édouardiens features a series of thought-provoking examinations in Stephanie Bernard's 'Moments of Vision: Thomas Hardy and the Act of Writing' (*CVE* 69[2009] 171–86); Annie Escuret's 'The Poetics of Stone in Thomas Hardy's Works: From the Book of Stone to The Book of

Life' (*CVE* 69[2009] 187–208); Laurence Estanove's '"The Church-Builder" and "The Chapel-Organist": Thomas Hardy's Poetry from Dramatic Monologue to "Theatre of the Voice"' (*CVE* 69[2009] 209–24); Isabelle Gadoin's '"Small Prose Poems": Poetic Form in Hardy's *Tess of the d'Urbervilles*' (*CVE* 69[2009] 225–40); Catherine Lanone's 'Syncopation as Symptom in Thomas Hardy's Poetry and Fiction' (*CVE* 69[2009] 241–54); Jean-Charles Perquin's 'Thomas Hardy Somewhere in between Fiction and Poetry' (*CVE* 69[2009] 255–66); and Annie Ramel's 'A Peculiar Poetical-Like Murmur: Repetition and Poeticality in *The Mayor of Casterbridge*' (*CVE* 69[2009] 267–82). Brigid Lowe's 'Thomas Hardy, *Tess of the D'Urbervilles* (1891)' (*VR* 35[2009] 56–60) celebrates the novel as a key text ripe for continued study through its exploration of Victorian myths. Michael J. Franklin's '"Market-Faces" and Market Forces: [Corn-]Factors in the Moral Economy of Casterbridge' (*RES* 59[2008] 46–8), missed last year, provides a most useful illumination of neglected factors from Hardy's novel. Franklin is proving to be a most promising Hardy critic and scholar and we eagerly await his further productivity. Ruth Bernard Yeazell's clearly written 'The Lighting Design of Hardy's Novels' (*NCL* 64[2009] 48–75) is a helpful illumination of Hardy and 'the phenomenology of light [that] affords a key to his representation of subjectivity' (p. 75). Yeazell draws upon the early *Desperate Remedies* [1871], *Jude the Obscure* [1895], and *The Well-Beloved* [1897]. Toru Sasaki writes on 'John Schlesinger's *Far from the Madding Crowd*: A Reassessment '(*FilmQ* 37[2009] 194–200). Elizabeth L. Knauer, in 'Unconscious Sue? Selfishness and Manipulation in *Jude the Obscure*' (*HR* 2[2009] 41–51), argues that 'a fresh and direct approach to the text, which considers important (but not central) social and political issues in their proper places, shatters the victimization myth that has long surrounded Sue and forces a reevaluation of reader's sympathies with that controversial heroine' (p. 41).

The spring newsletter of the Richard Jefferies Society contains a warm and touching obituary for honorary life member of the society Roger Frith, who played an active part in promotion of Jefferies's work (*RJSJ* 18[2009] 27–30). Included in the *Richard Jefferies Society Journal* is a Jefferies excerpt, 'The Peripatetic Philosopher and the Boy Preacher' (*RJSJ* 18[2009] 3–6); 'Who Read Richard Jefferies? The Evidence of the North Fund Subscription List' by Kedrun Laurie (*RJSJ* 18[2009] 6–30); 'The Healing Benefits of "Meadow Thoughts" by George Leslie Irons (*RJSJ* 18[2009] 31–3); 'Bevis's American Snap-Shooter' by Mark Daniel (*RJSJ* 18[2009] 33–4); and 'Poem "From some letters never sent"' by Neil Curry (*RJSJ* 18[2009] 35–6). Kimberly Snyder Manganelli, 'The Tragic Mulatta plays the Tragic Muse' (*VLC* 37[2009] 501–22), is a welcome exploration of a rarely discussed or read Charles Kingsley novel *Two Years Ago* [1857]. Manganelli's focus is upon 'Marie Lavington, the runaway slave [who] reenters the public marketplace by refashioning herself into the Italian diva, La Cordifiamma' (p. 501).

David Sergeant's 'Kipling's Descriptions' (*EIC* 59[2009] 324–46) effectively presents the case for an aesthetic as distinct from a 'historical, cultural, and biographical contextual' (p. 324) reading of Kipling. Sergeant's focus is Kipling's descriptive power. He observes 'the fascinating thing about Kipling's descriptions is their discrete multifariousness, their retention of the watermarking impression of their source even when manifesting across a variety of settings, genres, and contexts' (p. 325). Particular attention is paid to the early 'The Mark of the Beast' [1890], Kipling's journalism in *From Sea to Sea* [1889, 1900], *On the City Wall* [1889], the Mowgli stories in *The Jungle Books* [1894–5], and *Kim* [1901], among other works, including 'Then' [1904]. Sergeant's 'Whispering to the Converted: Narrative Communication in Rudyard Kipling's *Letters of Marque* and Indian Fiction' (*MLR* 104[2009] 26–40) presents a reading of Kipling's early *Letters of Marque*. This is 'a series of travel articles on the native states of Rajputana that Kipling wrote late in 1887, shortly after he left the Punjab-based *Civil and Military Gazette* to take up a position at its sister publication, the Allahabad *Pioneer*' (p. 26). Sergeant compares and contrasts *Letters of Marque* with two examples of Indian fiction to demonstrate that the *Letters* '[embodies] the moment when the diversion between . . . two kinds of story begin to emerge' in his work: 'its brilliantly controlled contradictions draped like veils over the granite certainties of its particular Anglo-Indian position' (p. 40). The March 2009 *Kipling Journal* features articles including Rodney Atwood '"Across our fathers' graves": Kipling and Field Marshall Earl Roberts' (*KJ* 83:330[2009] 9–28); David Sergeant's '"The Church that was at Antioch": A Reading' (*KJ* 83[2009] 29–42); and Muhammad Sufeer Awan's '"Transcending the Self"? Appropriation of Eastern Mystical thought in Kipling's Work, with the Focus on *Kim*' (*KJ* 83[2009] 43–57). The April issue is largely devoted to Margaret Muir's 'Kipling's Letters to Maitland Park' (*KJ* 83:331[2009] 5–67). This consists of eighteen letters Kipling wrote to Maitland Park (1862–1921), his friend and former colleague on the *Pioneer* of Allahabad, and to his son. Twelve of these were inherited by Park's granddaughter, who writes an introduction to the letters, transcribes them, annotates them, and places them in their new context. The letters range from 1889, when Kipling was preparing to leave India, to August 1926, when he wrote to Maitland's son, who survived active service in the First World War and the subsequent flu epidemic to serve on the home front in the Second World War and die in 1969.

The June 2009 *Kipling Journal* leads with John F. Bosher's 'Vancouver Island and the Kiplings' (*KJ* 83:332[2009] 9–22), followed by Charles Allen's 'Ruddy's Search for God: The Young Kipling and Religion' (*KJ* 83:332[2009] 23–37) and Jan Montefiore's 'Food and Cookery in Kipling: From the Cave-Woman's Magic to the Scout's Bacon and Eggs' (*KJ* 83:332[2009] 40–55). The September issue contains Amrit Joshi's 'The Problem of Identity in "The Gardener": An Impact of War' (*KJ* 83:333[2009] 8–16); Richard Holmes's 'Kipling's Soldiers' [*KJ* 83:333[2009] 22–9); Thorsten Sjölin's 'Rudyard Kipling and Selma Lagerlöf' (*KJ* 83:333[2009] 30–2); and Tim Connell's 'Rudyard Kipling and Saki Compared' (*KJ* 83:333[2009] 54–65). The December 2009 issue has considerable interest. It contains Toko Omomo's 'Technology and IT: The Transition of the Imperial Vision in *Traffics and Discoveries*' (*KJ* 83:334[2009] 7–21); Ray Beck's 'A Military Execution in India' (*KJ* 83[2009] 22–30); Alastair Wilson's 'So Where Exactly *Did* "Kipling", Kysh, Pyecroft, Hinchcliff, and the Unfortunate Policeman Go in "Steam Tactics"?' (*KJ* 83[2009] 31–42); and Naveen K. Mehta's 'Aspects of the Indian Notions of Spirituality in Kipling's *Kim* (Exploring Buddhism)' (*KJ* 83[2009] 43–7). This is followed by the texts of two stories by Kipling that initially appeared in the *St. James's Gazette*, on 21 and 30 November 1889, 'The Comet of a Season' and 'Gallihank's Pup' (*KJ* 83[2009] 48–58). David Page, the editor of the *Kipling Journal*, provides informative notes on them (*KJ* 83[2009] 59–61).

William Hurrell Mallock is today forgotten, so Anthony Kearney's 'Lady Ambrose's Querulous Historian in Mallock's *New Republic*: The Likely Original' (*N&Q* 56[2009] 406–8), and its examination of the author's historical sources, is most welcome. In '"Write a little bit every day": L.T. Meade, Self-Representation, and the Professional Woman Writer' (*VR* 35[2009] 132–52), Janis Dawson argues that girls' fiction author Meade was a knowledgeable professional writer who was guided by earlier models of Victorian authorship such as Anthony Trollope and Harriet Martineau, and framed her work on sensational incidents and contemporary debates in the periodical press. Dawson goes on to explain how *fin-de-siècle* women writers accessed debates and popular literary genres of the period in order to build their careers. The Spring 2009 issue of the *Victorian Newsletter* is devoted to the elusive William North (1824–54), who in 1852 left England for America, and two years later committed suicide in New York. Patrick Scott opens his 'Introducing a "Lost" Victorian Novel: The Elusive William North and *The City of the Jugglers* (1850)' (*VN* 115[2009] 7–15) by asking 'What is the least known but most relevant novel of the 19th century?' (p. 7). Scott's admirable introduction to the University of South Carolina Press reprint was noted in *YWES* (89[2010] 735). Scott in *VN* makes high claims for *The City of the Jugglers*: 'North's book is perhaps the only English novel fully to take up the challenge of 1848 and the revolutions elsewhere in Europe, and to imagine such a revolution is possible in the nation of shopkeepers' (p. 14). Lanya Lamouria's 'North's *The City of the Jugglers* (1850) and the European Revolutions of 1848' (*VN* 115[2009] 16–28) 'locates the novel in the broader context of Victorian writing about the 1848 revolutions'. For Lamouria, '*City* proposes that the British government is undermined not by the rise of politicized proletarians but by the crash of a speculative market' (p. 18). 'North's posthumous influence' (p. 4) is the subject of Edward Whitley and Robert Weidman's 'The (After) Life of William North among the New York Bohemians' (*VN* 115[2009] 29–45), 'positing that his theatrical suicide in the wake of thwarted romance and literary obscurity became an ideological inspiration to the transatlantic bohemian movement' (p. 4) centred in New York. Rebecca Stern's '*The City of the Jugglers* and the Limits of Victorian Fiction' (*VN* 115[2009] 46–51) 'highlight[s] the challenges this book poses for current literary criticism, and the problems and opportunities it presents' (p. 47). Stern concludes 'Given how productively *The City of the Jugglers* challenges its readers, it may well be that North's novel's time has come, and that the beginning and the audience he had sought in 1850 have arrived at last' (p. 51). Allan Life and Page Life, 'North versus North: William North (1825–1854) in Light of New Documentation' (*VN* 115[2009] 55–94), is a detailed examination of what we know and don't know about the life, work, and personality of William North. The essay concludes with the fact that his stepmother survived her stepson's suicide 'almost to the day, by 56 years, dying, aged 94, in London on 15 November 1910' (p. 90). The final contribution to this special issue consists of Page Life, Patrick Scott, and Allan Life, 'A Preliminary Checklist of Writings by and about William North (1835–1854)' (*VN* 115[2009] 95–114). Their research reveals 'a surprisingly substantial list for an author who has been largely unknown even to Victorian specialists', however 'a substantiated part of North's work is either unidentified or lost' (pp. 95–6). The partly annotated chronologically arranged checklist is divided into 'Manuscripts'—a poem in W.M. Rossetti's hand is now with the Angeli–Dennis Collection, University of British Columbia, Rare Books and Special Collections (p. 98)—'Books, Translations, Edited Periodicals, etc.' (pp. 98–103), 'Periodicals Contribution' (pp. 103–7), and 'Selected References about William North' (pp. 107–14).

Jamie Bartlett, 'Meredith and Ends' (*ELH* 76[2009] 547–76) provides a welcome reading of Meredith's *The Egoist*, applying Wittgenstein's 'theorization of intention as a "detail in the darkness"' (p. 547) to read the novel. Gisela Argyle's 'George Meredith's Fictional Transformations of Female Life-Writings' (*SEL* 49[2009] 975–95) focuses upon Meredith's fictional treatment of two controversial women, Caroline Norton and Helene von Racowitza. Both caused scandals in Victorian England as they had affairs with men in the public eye and wrote about their experience. Meredith transformed their accounts into ones in which emotions were perceived as feminine and the opposite seen as male traits. Bringing light to a seldom studied subject, William Baker and Jeanette Roberts Shumaker present a biography on the 'novelist's novelist', as J.M. Barrie referred to Merrick, author of a dozen novels, nine collections of short stories, and five plays. In *Leonard Merrick: A Forgotten Novelist's Novelist*, in addition to an introduction (pp. 11–16) outlining Merrick's life (1864–1934) and critical reception, there are chapters on his 'Early Novels' (pp. 17–45); 'The Middle Novels' (pp. 46–71); 'The Novels of the Early 1900s' (pp. 72–95); 'Later Novels' (pp. 96–127); 'Short Stories I' (pp. 128–47); 'Short Stories II' (pp. 148–64); 'Drama and Motion Pictures' (pp. 165–91); and a brief 'Conclusion' (pp. 192–3) reassessing Merrick's achievement. The bibliography is divided into primary materials (pp. 201–4) and alphabetically arranged writings about Merrick and other work used in the monograph (pp. 204–12), with a listing of films referenced (p. 213). There is a useful index (pp. 215–26). In 'Fact-Based Initiatives: Reform in Margaret Oliphant's *Some Passages in the Life of Margaret Maitland*' (*VIJ* 37[2009] 31–46) Mary M. Husemann focuses solely on the relationship between Mary and Mr Allan in the 1849 novel. Husemann argues that Oliphant infuses women with the power to make creative positive change and that progress made by men has to be tempered by female piety. Thomas Love Peacock (1785–1866), perhaps best known for his *Headlong Hall* [1816], *Melincourt* [1817], *Nightmare Abbey* [1818], and *Crotchet Castle* [1831], tends to fall between the cracks as he lived on well into the Victorian period. His late satirical novel *Gryll Grange* didn't appear until 1860–1. This late novel is the subject of 'Artful Womanhood: Thomas Love Peacock's Reinvention of St. Catherine of Alexandria as an English Bride' (*VIJ* 37[2009] 245–74), in which Kathy Nixon argues that the St Catherine passages are central to the novel. Andrew Nashe's 'William Clark Russell: An Unattributed Early Work by the Victorian Novelist of the Sea' (*N&Q* 56[2009] 396–8) draws attention to a totally forgotten but most interesting novelist.

David Wayne Thomas, in 'Liberal Legitimation and Communicative Action in British India: Reading Flora Annie Steel's *On the Face of the Waters*' (*ELH* 76[2009] 153–87) is a most welcome discussion of a neglected writer with especial attention to Flora Annie Steel's (1847–1929) single-volume *On the Face of the Waters* [1897]. This novel is set during the Indian Mutiny. Thomas applies the ideas of Jürgen Habermas to illuminate it. Harriet Hustis, in 'Hyding Nietzsche in Robert Louis Stevenson's Gothic of Philosophy (*SEL* 49[2009] 993–1007), considers ethical concerns in Stevenson's *Strange Case of Dr. Jekyll and Mr. Hyde* and focuses upon Jekyll, deploying Nietzsche's *Beyond Good and Evil* and his perception of morality. Loraine Fletcher's interesting 'Long John Silver, Karl Marx, and the Ship of State' (*CS* 19[2007] 34–48) was missed in the previous *YWES* and provides a worthwhile account of Stevenson as a political writer. *Victorian Review* features Sandy Feinstein's 'Dracula and Chloral: Chemistry Matters' (*VR* 35[2009] 96–115), in which it is argued that the tension between the potentiality and the limitations of science refers not only to Darwinian biology, but especially to chemistry. Dejan Kuzmanovic, in 'Vampiric Seduction and Vicissitudes of Masculine Identity in Bram Stoker's *Dracula*' (*VLC* 37[2009] 411–25), attempts to ring the changes on critical responses to *Dracula* by focusing attention upon a neglected character. Critics 'tend to overlook the unique position that the young Jonathan Harker occupies in the narrative: he is the only character that is an object of the vampire's seduction and an agent of his own destruction' (p. 411).

A better year to report for Thackeray studies. Micael Clark introduces *The Complete Works of William Makepeace Thackeray*, volumes 1–27. In 'Thackeray's Young Men: Bohemia and Manliness in the Novels of William Makepeace Thackeray' (*VIJ* 37[2009] 165–93), April Bullock investigates the novelist's later works for examples of Bohemia as the space in which young men developed or retained gentlemanly qualities of manners, honesty, and personal honour. Stanley Kubrick's cinematic adaptation of *Barry Lyndon* is the subject of Kim Newman's 'From Romance to Ritual' (*S&S* 19[2009] 22–3). Sarah Rose Cole, in her discussion of *Pendennis*, focuses attention on Thackeray's treatment of the 1848 revolution in 'National Histories, International Genre: Thackeray, Balzac, and the Franco-British *Bildungsroman*' (*RoN* 48[2007] 20). April Kendra's 'Silver-Forks and Double Standards: Gore, Thackeray, and the Problem of Parody' (*WW* 16[2009] 191–217) assesses the influence of Catherine Gore's work on Thackeray's *Vanity Fair*.

Ruth Colette Hoffman's excellent *Without Education or Encouragement: The Literary Legacy of Flora Thompson* is the first study of a neglected and significant author. Remembered largely for one book, the rural trilogy *Lark Rise to Candleford* [1945], Thompson's (1876–1947) career traverses the Edwardian period to include poetry, short fiction, and essays published in women's periodicals before the Second World War. Her rural upbringing has never been examined; nor have her freelance writing for women's periodicals or her posthumously published *Heatherly* [1974] or *Still Glides the Stream* [1947]. Hoffman's well-written account includes analysis of 'the nature essays... published in *The Catholic Fireside*' (p. 35), *The Peverel Papers* [1926]; 'The Major Works: *Lark Rise to Candleford, Heatherly, and Still Glide the Stream*' (pp. 72–101) and 'The Minor Works: Short Fiction, Poetry, and Literary Essays' (pp. 102–34). There is a perceptive chapter on 'Thompson and the Intellectual Life of the Working Classes' (pp. 135–58), followed by 'Flora Thompson Revealed' (pp. 59–163). There are four appendices: 'Sources of Literary Quotations in *The Peverel Papers*', revealing Thompson's readings, including 'Victorian Poetry' (pp. 165–8); 'Selected Poems from *Bog Myrtle and Peat*' (pp. 169–71); a listing of her 'Literary Essays in *The Fireside Reading Code*' (pp. 173–4); and a note on her unpublished novel '*Gates of Eden*' (pp. 175–6). There is an extensive primary and secondary bibliography (pp. 197–207).

The year 2009 seems to have been a fruitful one in Trollope studies. Leading the way as a major contribution is *The Politics of Gender in Anthony Trollope's Novels*, edited by Margaret Markwick, Deborah Denenholz Morse, and Regenia Gagnier. Offering original readings of Trollope in a multitude of areas for cultural and literary studies, this collection is organized around four parts, preceded by Margaret Markwick and Deborah Denenholz Morse's introduction. Part I, 'Sex, Power and Subversion', includes '(A)genda Trouble and the Lot Complex: Older Men–Younger Women Relationships in Trollope' by Robert M. Polhemus (pp. 11–29); '*He Knew He Was Right*: The Sensational Tyranny of the Sexual Contract and the Problem of Liberal Progress' by Kathy Alexis Psomiades (pp. 31–44); 'Bastards to the Time: Legitimacy as Legal Fiction in Trollope's Novels of the 1870s' by Jenny Bourne Taylor (pp. 45–59), and 'Out of the Closet: Monoerotics in Trollope's Novels' by Margaret Markwick (pp. 61–74). Part II, 'Imperial Gender', includes '"Some Girls who Come from the Tropics": Gender, Race, and Imperialism in Anthony Trollope's *He Knew He Was Right*' by Deborah Denenholz Morse (pp. 77–98); 'Anthony Trollope's *The Eustace Diamonds* and The Great Parliamentary Bore' by Lauren M.E. Goodlad (pp. 99–116); '"Two Identities": Gender, Ethnicity, and Phineas Finn' by Mary Jean Corbett (pp. 117–29); and 'The Rough and the Beautiful in "Catherine Carmichael": Class and Gender in Trollope's Colonial Aesthetic' by Helen Lucy Blythe (pp. 131–44). Part III, 'Genderized Economics', includes 'Mister Trollope, Lady Credit, and *The Way We Live Now*' by Nathan K. Hensley (pp. 147–60); 'A Woman of Money: Miss Dunstable, Thomas Holloway, and Victorian Commercial Wealth' by Elsie B. Michie (pp. 161–75), and 'Otherwise Occupied: Masculine Widows in Trollope's Novels' by Christopher S. Noble (pp. 177–90); and Part IV, 'The Gender of Narrative Construction', includes 'Trollope at Fuller Length: Lord Silverbridge and the Manuscript of *The Duke's Children*' by Steven Amarnick (pp. 193–206); '"Depth of Portraiture": What Should Distinguish a Victorian Man from a Victorian Woman?' by David Skilton (pp. 207–26); and 'The Weight of Religion and History: Women Dying of Virtue in Trollope's Short Fiction' by Anca Vlasopolos (pp. 221–33); as well as the conclusion, 'Gender, Liberalism, and Resentment' by Regenia Gagnier (pp. 235–68). Lauren M.E. Goodlad utilizes Trollope's Barsetshire novels, as well as his travel writings, in 'Trollopian "Foreign Policy": Rootedness and Cosmopolitanism in the Mid-Victorian Global Imaginary' (*PMLA* 124[2009] 437–54). John N. Hall, the eminent biographer of Trollope, writes on 'Glue and Daydreams: Trollope at Work' (in Sullivan and Harper, eds., *Authors at Work: The Creative Environment*, pp. 79–99). Deborah Morse's '"It went through and through me like an electric shock": Celebrating Vulgar Female Desire and the Realist Novel in Trollope's *Ayala's Angel*' (in Bernstein and Michie, eds., *Victorian Vulgarity: Taste in Verbal and Visual Culture*, pp. 153–68) discusses the treatment of women's desires in Trollope's neglected novel. *Phineas Finn* and its treatment of social progress preoccupy Geoffrey Baker in his *Realism's Empire: Empiricism and Enchantment in the Nineteenth-Century Novel*.

A 2008 contribution on Oscar Wilde, *Oscar Wilde and Modern Culture*, contains an impressive collection of essays, including the introduction by Joseph Bristow (pp. 1–45); 'Oscar Wilde, Lady Gregory, and Late-Victorian Table-Talk' by Lucy Diamond (pp. 46–62); 'Sexuality in the Age of Technological Reproductibility: Oscar Wilde, Photography, and Identity' by Daniel A. Novak (pp. 63–94); 'Salomé as Bombshell, or How Oscar Wilde Became an Anarchist' by Erin Williams Hyman (pp. 95–109); 'Oscar Wilde and the Politics of Posthumous Sainthood: Hofmannsthal, Mirabeau, Proust' by Richard A. Kaye (pp. 110–32); 'The Trouble with Oskar: Wilde's Legacy for the Early Homosexual Rights Movement in Germany' by Yvonne Ivory (pp. 133–53); 'Staking Salomé: The Literary Forefathers and Choreographic Daughters of Oscar Wilde's "Hysterical and Perverted Creature"' by Julie Townsend (pp. 154–79); '"Surely you are not claiming to be more homosexual than I?": Claude Cahun and Oscar Wilde' by Lizzie Thynne (pp. 180–208); 'Oscar Wilde's *An Ideal Husband* and Somerset Maugham's *The Constant Wife*: A Dialogue' by Laurel Brake (pp. 209–33); 'Transcripts and Truth: Writing the Trials of Oscar Wilde' by Leslie J. Moran (pp. 234–58); 'The Artist as Protagonist: Wilde on Stage' by Francesca Coppa (pp. 259–84); 'Wilde Lives: Derek Jarman and the Queer Eighties' by Matt Cook (pp. 285–304); and 'Oscar Goes to Hollywood: Wilde, Sexuality, and the Gaze of Contemporary Cinema' by Oliver S. Buckton (pp. 305–38). Christine Ferguson argues for renewed study of one of Wilde's essays as fodder for a re-evaluation of Wilde's aesthetic Darwinism and its uses of determinism in 'Oscar Wilde, "The Critic as Artist" (1891)' (*VR* 35[2009] 64–8). Lastly on Wilde, 'Illustrer *The Picture of Dorian Gray*: Les Paradoxes de la représentation' (*EA* 62[2009] 28–41), by Xavier Giudicelli, examines the modalities and the stakes of illustration through the analysis of images taken from three illustrated editions of the novel.

The online publication *Neo-Victorian Studies* features as its second issue a special edition entitled '"Swing Your Razor Wide ...."' The issue is available free at www.neovictorianstudies.com and contains 'Scarlet Carsons, Men in Masks: The Wildean Contexts for V. for Vendetta' by Ellen Crowell (*NVS* 2[2008/9] 17–45); 'The Angel' by Lee Jackson (*NVS* 2[2008/9] 46–51); 'The Victorian Criminal Underworld and the Musical Carnivalesque' by Scott Freer (*NVS* 2[2008/9] 52–77); 'Hyde and Seek in an Age of Surveillance: Stevenson's *The Last Strange Case of Dr. Jekyll and Mr. Hyde* and the BBC's

Jekyll' by Anna Lepine (*NVS* 2[2008/9] 78–102); 'Who Killed Cock Robin?' by Lucy Sussex (*NVS* 2[2008/9] 103–20); and 'Re-Viewing the Situation: Staging Neo-Victorian Criminality and Villainy after *Oliver!*' by Benjamin Poore (*NVS* 2[2008/9] 121–47).

3. Poetry

In this section, Martin Dubois reviews publications on Arnold, Edward FitzGerald, Hopkins, William Morris, the Rossettis, women poets, working-class poets, poetry from 1830 to 1880, and work by Gregory Tate. Gregory Tate reviews publications on the Brownings, Michael Field, Swinburne, and Tennyson, and poetry from 1880 to 1900. Thomas Hardy's poetry is currently covered in Chapter XIV, section 2.

The most wide-ranging study of Victorian poetry published in 2009 was Jason R. Rudy's *Electric Meters: Victorian Physiological Poetics*. Rudy's book manages to be both comprehensive and detailed in its analysis of Victorian poetry's engagement with two related areas of Victorian science: physiology and electricity. All Victorian poets, Rudy suggests, have a view on physiology, either celebrating or denying the role of the body in the composition and reading of poetry, and these writers consistently approach this issue through the trope of electricity. Chapter 1 of *Electric Meters* examines the work of Mary Robinson and Felicia Hemans, arguing that these Romantic poetesses remain aloof from embodied experience. Subsequent chapters consider what Rudy calls 'Victorian poetry's turn to the body' (p. 21). Chapter 2 looks at Tennyson's fascination with physical sensation in the first half of his career and suggests that electrical metaphors, and particularly that of the telegraph, were vital to his portrayal of sensation. Chapter 3 builds on recent critical interest in Spasmodic poetry to identify this short-lived movement of the 1850s as the epitome of Victorian physiological verse, while chapter 4 shows how poets such as Coventry Patmore and, to a lesser extent, Hopkins reacted against Spasmodism, developing prosodic systems that emphasized the disembodied nature of metre and poetry. Chapter 5 argues that theories of electromagnetism and evolution enabled a renewed focus on the body in the later nineteenth century, a trend evident in the work of Swinburne and Mathilde Blind. In his conclusion Rudy suggests that even Victorian spiritualism, and the poetry that it inspired, made use of physical and electrical conceits, thus affirming his contention that physiology was a central concern of all strands of Victorian poetry.

Monique R. Morgan's book *Narrative Means, Lyric Ends: Temporality in the Nineteenth-Century British Long Poem* considers nineteenth-century lyric and narrative poetry not as separate genres, but as distinct modes that coexist within individual poems. As is suggested by the title, this book differentiates lyric and narrative in terms of their relation to time, through their 'respective simultaneity and temporal progression' (p. 12). This idea threatens to make for a rather narrow definition, particularly of lyric, but Morgan's application of it to specific long poems is surprisingly fruitful. The introduction to the book provides a slightly rushed but nonetheless informative account of recent theoretical and critical perspectives on narrative and lyric. After this, Morgan moves on to case studies of nineteenth-century poetry, and in her first chapter she argues that the multiple narratives of Byron's *Don Juan* are presented through an essentially atemporal, static lyric voice. The second chapter of the book focuses on *The Prelude*, examining how Wordsworth attempts to sustain the simultaneity of lyric across a long poem by assimilating his succession of lyric passages into a narrative structure. Morgan's next two chapters move forward to consider Victorian poetry, specifically that of the Brownings. Chapter 3 argues that Elizabeth Barrett Browning juxtaposes lyric and narrative in *Aurora Leigh* in order to interrogate the gendered connotations of these poetic modes and to explore the limitations of narrative authority, while chapter 4 suggests that Robert Browning 'achieves a seamless blend' (p. 155) of narrative and lyric in his use of the dramatic monologue form in *The Ring and the Book*. In her postscript Morgan offers readings of two Victorian poems which she claims do not conform to her view of nineteenth-century poetry as a mixture of lyric and narrative: Tennyson's *Idylls of the King* and George Meredith's *Modern Love*.

In *The Age of Eclecticism: Literature and Culture in Britain, 1815–1885*, Christine Bolus-Reichert argues that historical, philosophical, and artistic eclecticism is a crucial but often neglected aspect of nineteenth-century culture. Bolus-Reichert's book has Victorian poetry, with its eclectic range of forms and concerns, at its heart. The first three chapters of *The Age of Eclecticism* map out three contexts for the eclecticism of Victorian Britain: chapter 1 deals with the presence of eclectic discourses in nineteenth-century art and architecture; chapter 2 with the eclectic and synthetic philosophical system of Victor Cousin; and chapter 3 with the celebrations and criticisms of eclecticism found in earlier nineteenth-century writers, including Coleridge, Carlyle, and Macaulay. The rest of the book attends to Victorian writers' responses to the perceived eclecticism of the age. In chapter 4 Bolus-Reichert considers Tennyson's *The Princess*, and the critical debates surrounding it, arguing that this poetic 'medley' embraces the heterogeneity of modern culture by amalgamating diverse poetic styles and intellectual viewpoints. This strategy was not uncontroversial, and chapter 5 focuses on Charles Kingsley's condemnation of unthinking 'naïve eclecticism' (p. 167) in his novel *Hypatia*. Chapter 6 returns to poetry, suggesting that the scholarly, speculative character of Arnold's verse prefigures the 'volitional eclecticism' (p. 191) of his criticism, his desire to find and synthesize the 'best' of different cultures and literatures. Chapter 7 examines two novels, Hardy's *A Laodicean* and Pater's *Marius the Epicurean*, arguing that both texts present cultural and intellectual eclecticism as a means of individual self-development. In the afterword that concludes the book, Bolus-Reichert brings her rehabilitation of eclecticism forward to the present day as she insists that the concept retains great significance in relation to debates about globalization and multiculturalism.

Another 2009 publication of interest to scholars of Victorian poetry is John Holmes's study of poetic responses to Darwinism, *Darwin's Bards: British and American Poetry in the Age of Evolution*. This is an ambitious and expansive book, covering poets from across the twentieth century as well as Victorian authors. Organized thematically rather than chronologically, *Darwin's Bards* contains few chapters solely dedicated to Victorian poetry, but Victorian poets' examinations of evolution often form the starting-point of Holmes's discussions. In his first chapter Holmes makes the case for a 'Darwinian tradition in modern English and American poetry', originating in the poetry of George Meredith and Thomas Hardy and representing 'an important and powerful counterweight to modernism' (p. 25). Meredith and Hardy are key figures for Holmes, but in chapter 2 he considers the work of other Victorian poets. Mathilde Blind, Swinburne, and Tennyson, he argues, participated in a 'non-Darwinian revolution' (p. 37) that pervaded late Victorian culture, responding to the troubling implications of Darwin's theories by writing poems that drew on older, teleological models of evolution. Chapter 3 of *Darwin's Bards* explores the impact of Darwinism on poets' views about God, and Holmes here gives an astute reading of Browning's 'Caliban upon Setebos'. Subsequent chapters consider the presence of Darwinian ideas about death, the natural world, animals, and sexuality in the work of a number of poets, including Meredith, Hardy, and Constance Naden, the author of the 1887 sequence 'Evolutional Erotics'. The final chapter of Holmes's book neatly brings together the strands of his argument through nuanced readings of two mid-Victorian responses to Darwin: Meredith's 'Ode to the Spirit of Earth in Autumn' and Tennyson's 'Lucretius'.

A different perspective on Victorian poetry is to be found in *The Blackwell Companion to the Bible in English Literature*, edited by Rebecca Lemon, Emma Mason, Jonathan Roberts and Christopher Rowland, which contains several essays on Victorian poets. Kevin Mills's piece on the Brownings (pp. 482–95) shows that Browning and EBB adopted very different viewpoints towards contemporary debates about the Bible, with the former being far more willing than the latter to engage with the conclusions of the Higher Criticism. Kirstie Blair's fine essay on Tennyson (pp. 496–511) notes that he too was interested in contemporary biblical scholarship, but the main thrust of Blair's argument is that Tennyson employs biblical quotations in his poetry primarily for their sentimental and affective force. A discriminating outline of Christina Rossetti's relationship to the Bible is provided by Elizabeth Ludlow in her contribution to the volume (pp. 551–62), which adduces the major influences on Rossetti's approach to biblical interpretation. And Paul S. Fiddes offers an engaging introduction to biblical inspirations for Hopkins's poetry in his essay (pp. 563–76), even if the decision to confine biblical reference to two Anglican translations is curious given Hopkins's linguistic range and confessional sensitivities.

There are several poetry-centred contributions in Mariaconcetta Constantini, Francesco Marroni, and Anna Enrichetta Soccio's collection *Letter(s): Functions and Forms of Letter-Writing in Victorian Art and Literature*, including John Woolford's essay on 'Textual Materiality in the Victorian Verse-Letter' (pp. 21–38). Alongside brief discussions of Patmore and Browning, Woolford gives consideration to the way in which epistolary convention in Clough's *Amours de Voyage* provides an index to its characters' varying attitudes to social communication. Biancamaria Rizzardi Perutelli's essay in the same volume, 'The Influence of Ovid's *Heroides* on Victorian Love

Poetry' (pp. 39–48), argues for classical influence on Victorian lyric portrayals of the abandoned woman. Joseph Feeney's contribution, 'The Playfulness of Gerard Manley Hopkins: A Touch of Theory, a Spate of Letters, Two Poems' (pp. 129–46), reproduces material which appears in Feeney's 2008 monograph, *The Playfulness of Gerard Manley Hopkins*.

Mike Sanders's *The Poetry of Chartism: Aesthetics, Politics, History* is a major achievement. Sanders mounts a vigorous case for the importance of poetry to the political destiny of the Chartist movement; he no less forcefully argues that Chartist poetry should not be thought marginal or alternative to more canonical verse, but rather alters our perception of the nature of Victorian poetry generally. As Sanders observes in a chapter summarizing previous scholarship on the subject, there has been something of a resurgence of interest in Chartist poetry in recent years. What distinguishes this study from most previous work, however, is its concern with the stylistic and formal aspects of the poems it examines. The aesthetic is not suspect in Sanders's account; on the contrary, he is interested in 'the political effect of poetic affect' (p. 13). Three absorbing chapters focus on the poetry column of the *Northern Star*, the leading Chartist newspaper, arguing for the importance of poetry in shaping contemporary appraisals of the 1839 Newport uprising; for its influence on developments in Chartist political and economic analysis during the mass strikes of 1842; and on Chartist perspectives on the European revolutions of 1848. A final chapter takes a different approach, focusing on a single poet, Gerald Massey, and enlisting Walter Benjamin's reflections on messianism to probe the relation between past, present, and future in Massey's work. There is an appendix giving a complete publication record of the *Northern Star*'s poetry column.

Sanders's concern with temporality and religious belief in Chartist poetry also finds reflection in Pamela K. Gilbert's 'History and its Ends in Chartist Epic' (*VLC* 37[2009] 27–42). Noting the traffic with eschatological discourse of long poems by Thomas Cooper and Ernest Jones, Gilbert considers how they attempt to correlate particular and universal temporal orders. Other publications on working-class poetry this year include Kirstie Blair's '"He Sings Alone": Hybrid Forms and the Victorian Working-Class Poet' (*VLC* 37[2009] 523–41). Blair adopts the concept of 'hybridity' to explore the relationship of working-class poets to the literary canon. She finds that borrowings and appropriations from high poetic culture, rather than diluting political and social radicalism, may constitute both an assertion of literary right and a highlighting of working-class poetry's exclusion from the established literary tradition. In 'From Langham Place to Lancashire: Poetry, Community, and the Victoria Press's *Offering to Lancashire*' (*VP* 47[2009] 517–32), Julie M. Wise traces the political and social implications of a gift book with unexpected ambitions, being an anthology of poems published in 1862 in support of cotton workers then suffering under the trade embargo caused by the American Civil War. Florence Boos offers a brief but compelling introduction to Janet Hamilton's 'A Plea for the Doric' in a forum on 'Key Victorian Texts' in *Victorian Review* (*VR* 35[2009] 41–5).

The bicentenary of the birth of Edward FitzGerald received early celebration in a *Victorian Poetry* special issue in 2008, but is marked in the year itself by the publication of Daniel Karlin's new edition of the *Rubáiyát of Omar Khayyám*. There are editorial dilemmas aplenty for any modern editor of the poem, for FitzGerald was an inveterate reviser of his texts: four versions of the *Rubáiyát* alone were published during his lifetime. Christopher Decker, in his 1997 critical edition, reprints all four; Karlin prefers the first 1859 text, although he includes a lengthy section detailing later revisions. Something of the fullness of Karlin's attention to FitzGerald's alterations can be known from the fact that although the poem occupies less than forty pages, the edition as a whole stretches to well over 200. As well as editorial notes, there is a brief account of the publication history of the *Rubáiyát*, a chronology of FitzGerald's life, and a selection of early critical responses to the poem. The edition also reprints Tennyson's 'To E. FitzGerald'. Karlin's superb introduction steers a careful course through the tangle of attribution this work of compound authorship represents, combining attention to Persian contexts and the circumstances of FitzGerald's own life with close attention to the formal and stylistic properties of the poem itself. The edition will surely be the standard reading text for many years to come.

Perhaps the most important of the year's publications, in terms of its effect on the future direction of Victorian poetry studies, was *Michael Field, the Poet: Published and Manuscript Materials*, edited by Ana Parejo Vadillo and Marion Thain. Bringing together a wide range of writings by the two women who worked under the name 'Michael Field', this single-volume edition is a product of the growing scholarly interest in this important *fin-de-siècle* writer, and it will surely be a spur to further work on the poet. The volume opens with an economical introduction that positions the work of Katherine Bradley and Edith Cooper within the contexts of late nineteenth-century feminism and aestheticism. There follows a generous selection from their poetry across their career, which reveals the brilliant sensuousness of Michael Field's verse, as well as its rich engagement with classical literature and with painting and sculpture. The volume also includes extracts from the journal *Works and Days*, which Bradley and Cooper kept for twenty-six years between 1888 and 1914, and from their correspondence. These prose writings display a rich vein of humour; they also shed light on Bradley and Cooper's relations with figures as diverse as Ruskin, Browning, and the artists Charles Ricketts and Charles Shannon. The volume concludes with a brief but nonetheless revealing selection of contemporary reviews of Field's work. This book is a work of great editorial skill, bringing together a wide range of material in one accessible volume, and it will make a major contribution to future work on Michael Field and on late Victorian poetry more broadly.

Patricia Rigg's *Julia Augusta Webster: Victorian Aestheticism and the Woman Writer* is a notable contribution to the study of Webster's life and poetry. The biographical insights culled from Rigg's extensive archival research would by themselves have significance, but the particular merit of her book lies in the sensitivity with which she brings such insights to bear upon the poems. Rigg's approach is chronological, beginning with lesser-known early work, in which she sees the seed of Webster's later aestheticism, and ending with the sonnet sequence written in the period before Webster's death, and published posthumously. On the way, there are apt considerations of the relation of Webster's labours on behalf of the suffrage movement to her poetic commitments as well as of her work on the London School Board. There is extensive discussion of Webster's journalism, especially her articles and reviews for the *Examiner*. The thoroughness with which Rigg documents Webster's diverse literary activities cannot be faulted, even if—perhaps as a consequence of her biographical slant—the book's local arguments are never fully combined into an overarching thesis. If there is a thesis underlying Rigg's study, it might be that the aestheticist thread to Webster's thought is present from the beginning, but this is a line of reasoning which comes and goes depending on the chapter. Given the comprehensiveness of her treatment, Rigg might have allowed herself to stake out a rather larger claim for Webster's importance than the muted, page-long outline of Webster's legacy with which her study ends. The book's value for comprehending Webster's achievement is, however, undoubted.

In *Women Writers and the Dark Side of Late-Victorian Aestheticism*, T.D. Olverson argues for the distinctiveness of literary renderings of ancient Greek myth and culture by a number of Victorian women writers. This is one of a number of recent studies—Yopie Prins's *Victorian Sappho* [1999] is another—to have paid attention to the engagement of Victorian women with Hellenism. Webster's sustained engagement with ancient Greek literature began with her 1866 translation of Aeschylus's *Prometheus Bound.* The first chapter of Olverson's book considers the translation alongside Webster's later poetry, in which the women of Greek mythology, especially Medea and Circe, are strong presences. Chapter 2 finds that Amy Levy enlists the Medea myth, and the story of Xantippe, the wife of Socrates, to offer poetic opposition to the marginalization of women in Victorian society. Emily Pfeiffer, a subsequent chapter argues, concerned with some of the same myths and stories in her poetry, has a similar ambition in mind: the subversion of male power. In chapter 4 Olverson turns to Michael Field, contending that Hellenism is a crucial means to exploring homoerotic desire in Bradley and Cooper's poetry. The maenads and Dionysiac religion have a particular importance in their reimagining of sexual and gender identity. Finally, chapter 5 discusses the importance of Medea for a range of *fin-de-siècle* writers, chiefly Mona Caird and Vernon Lee. In each of these chapters, Olverson reveals the way in which adaptations and appropriations of Greek literature and myth serve as a commentary on Victorian social and political life. The attention to Pfeiffer—as Olverson notes, a poet still too little studied—is particularly welcome.

In terms of other work on women poets, Kathryn Ledbetter's *British Victorian Women's Periodicals: Beauty, Civilization, and Poetry*, which considers a raft of lesser-known women poets alongside more familiar names, is covered in section 4. Clare Broome Saunders's wide-ranging *Women Writers and Nineteenth-Century Medievalism* has a large concern with Victorian poetry, discussing, amongst others, EBB and Augusta Webster. A notable aspect of Broome Saunders's book is the claim it seeks to make for lesser-known writers, especially Louisa Stuart Costello, who, among other things, published a poetic version of the Lady of Shallott legend. Kate Flint's 'The "Hour of Pink Twilight": Lesbian Poetics and Queer Encounters on the Fin-de-Siècle Street' (*VS* 51[2009] 687–712), is mostly concerned with short fiction, but has some astute commentary on urban encounter in Amy Levy's poetry. Amy Levy is also the subject of Linda K. Hughes's 'Discoursing of Xantippe: Amy Levy, Classical Scholarship, and Print Culture' (*PQ* 88[2009] 259–81). Hughes discusses Levy's classical turn in 'Xantippe', finding that it allowed her to navigate between a variety of discourses, including classical scholarship, higher criticism and print culture. Rob Breton attempts to broaden critical debate around George Eliot's poetic writing in 'The Thrill of the Trill: Political and Aesthetic Discourse in George Eliot's *Armgart*' (*VR* 35[2009] 116–31), finding that *Armgart* reflects not only a concern with gender, but can also be read in light of anxieties about sensationalist popular theatre, revealing the ambivalences in Eliot's attitude to social reform.

Other 2009 articles cover a broad range of subjects within Victorian poetry. Discussing a number of writers, including Tennyson, EBB, and Michael Field, Anna Barton's article 'Boz, Ba and Derry Down Derry: Names and Pseudonyms in Victorian Literature' (*LitComp* 6[2009] 799–809) gives a fascinating account of these authors' interest in the complex signification of names, a preoccupation which 'corresponds directly with concerns about authorial identity' in Victorian culture (p. 806). Sue Edney's excellent article on William Barnes, ' "Times be badish vor the poor": William Barnes and his Dialect of Disturbance in the Dorset "Eclogues" ' (*English* 58[2009] 206–29), makes a striking claim for the social alertness of Barnes's poetry, even while acknowledging his wariness of political radicalism. Barnes's personal encounters with agricultural upheaval are sensitively brought alongside the poetry. T.L. Burton and K.K. Ruthen discuss the potential for broadening critical interest in Barnes and dialect poetry in 'Dialect Poetry, William Barnes, and the Literary Canon' (*ELH* 76[2009] 309–42), giving particular scrutiny to the possibilities offered by sound recording. Their call for the recognition of the importance of dialectology in Victorian culture is well made. Francis O'Gorman's 'Poetry in the Age of New Sound Technology: Mallarmé to Tennyson' (*CVE* 69[2009] 41–58) considers poetic responses to the invention of the electric telegraph and advances in sound technology in the work of Barnes, Tennyson, Swinburne, and others. O'Gorman relates this to a concern with preserving the voices of the dead.

William Morris's poem *Sigurd the Volsung* provides the focus for Simon Dentith's adroit reflections on epic and the pre-modern in 'Morris, "The Great Story of the North", and the Barbaric Past' (*JVC* 14[2009] 238–54). Dentith explores the poem's complex relation to Morris's desire for modern social transformation by considering its archaizing manner and portrayal of violence. Megan Ward defends Morris's 'The Defence of Guenevere' from the charge of escapism in 'William Morris's Conditional Moment' (*RaVoN* 53[2009]), suggesting that because moments in time are primarily experienced through the senses in the poem, they have an immediacy which disturbs the expectation of progressive historical narrative. Lewis Carroll's nonsense poem *The Hunting of the Snark* is the subject of Jed Mayer's 'The Vivisection of the Snark' (*VP* 47[2009] 429–48). Mayer sets Carroll's poem in the context of opposition to vivisection in the 1870s, observing how it troubles the division between human and non-human subjects and poses a satirical challenge to claims of scientific authority.

A monograph entirely devoted to Matthew Arnold's poetry is something of a rarity these days. Antony H. Harrison's *The Cultural Production of Matthew Arnold* makes an appeal for a renewal of interest in Arnold's poetic oeuvre by focusing attention on its social and cultural contexts. Harrison finds the political engagements of Arnold's poetry underwhelming, and contends that in this lies their importance. The opening chapter expresses frustration with the obscurity of the contact had by several poems with civil disturbance and political radicalism in the 1840s, but finds that the medievalism of *Tristram and Iseult* turns this obscurity into an ideological stratagem, distracting attention from the tumult of contemporary events. In his second chapter, Harrison attempts to read broad cultural significance into Arnold's encounters with Keats and the Spasmodics. Chapter 3 considers the way Arnold draws on the tradition of sensibility as found in Hemans and Landon even as the values propagated in his prose writings contributed to its decline. Arnold's ambivalent representation of the gypsy figure in 'The Scholar-Gipsy' and other poems at once reflects broader social pressures and displaces them, a final chapter argues. It is refreshing to see that Harrison has cast a wide net over Arnold's poetic corpus, considering poems such as 'Revolutions' alongside better-known works. His conclusion that the seeming political and social detachment of Arnold's poems is itself ideological does not break new ground, but the argument is forcefully put, and given that Arnold's poetic star has undergone so steep a decline in recent decades, efforts at restoration are very much to be welcomed. That only one article on Arnold's poetry was published in 2009 indicates the scale of the challenge. Bringing to prominence a traditionally marginal figure, the third part of Arnold's reworking of the Tristram and Iseult legend, focusing on the 'second' Iseult (of Brittany rather than Ireland), is cognizant of the potential for domestic life to turn sour, suggests Ingrid Ranum in 'A Woman's Castle is her Home: Matthew Arnold's *Tristram and Iseult* as Domestic Fairy Tale' (*VP* 47[2009] 403–28).

Scholars of the Brownings were well served with new editions this year. *Florentine Friends*, edited by Philip Kelley and Sandra Donaldson, comprises letters written by Browning and EBB to their close friend Isabella Blagden between 1850 and 1861. Although some of these letters have already been published by the same editors and publisher in The Brownings' Correspondence series, and although the remainder will appear in that series in the future, it is hard to disagree with the editors' opinion that collecting the Brownings' letters to 'dearest Isa' in a single place enables readers to gain a greater sense of 'the immediacy of their friendship' (p. xii). Given the intimacy and duration of that friendship, this volume is also welcome for the wealth of biographical information it provides about Isa Blagden, especially the editors' exhaustive (and apparently conclusive) research into her paternity. And while the letters themselves contain little of the Brownings' views on their own work or on poetry in general, they do shed significant light on other topics, such as the depth of EBB's engagement with Italian politics in the two years before her death. There is also a fascinating appendix reproducing the photographs of the major players in Italian affairs that EBB collected in 1860–1.

It is also important to note the appearance, over recent years, of new volumes of *The Brownings' Correspondence*. Volume 15, edited by Edward

Hagan, Philip Kelley, and Scott Lewis and published in 2005, spans the eventful years 1848 and 1849. The letters feature numerous analyses (mostly by EBB) of the 1848 revolution in France as well as first-hand accounts of political developments in Florence, the poets' new home. On a more personal level, the volume also takes in the events of March 1849, which saw both the birth of Pen Browning and the death of Robert Browning's mother. Volume 16, produced by the same editorial team and published in 2007, covers September 1849 to January 1851, a period in which professional matters once again became more prominent in the Brownings' lives. There are references here to the publications of *Christmas-Eve and Easter-Day* and *Sonnets from the Portuguese*, and to the question of who should replace Wordsworth as Poet Laureate after his death in 1850. EBB was seen as a likely candidate by many commentators, but she welcomes the appointment of Tennyson in a letter from December 1850. The letters in these volumes will be of inherent interest to scholars of Victorian poetry, and their appeal is heightened by the usual high production standards of this series. Volumes 17 and 18 of the series, published in 2010, will be discussed next year.

Jane Stabler, in 'Romantic and Victorian Conversations: Elizabeth Barrett and Robert Browning in Dialogue with Byron and Shelley' (in Lau, ed., *Fellow Romantics: Male and Female British Writers, 1790–1835*, pp. 231–53), offers a rare comparative reading of the Brownings' work, arguing that their responses to Byron and Shelley in their early writings enable them to fashion 'an imaginative androgyny that questions rigid gender identities' (p. 232). Turning to publications specifically on EBB, Heather Shippen Cianciola, in '"Mine earthly heart should dare": Elizabeth Barrett's Devotional Poetry' (*C&L* 58[2009] 367–400), claims that the 1838 volume *The Seraphim and Other Poems* presents a radical critique of contemporary religious writing and of women writers' place in the devotional tradition. Some of Cianciola's argumentative leaps are a little forced, but this remains an impressively thorough analysis of EBB's devotional concerns. In a rich and complex essay—'"Our deep, dear silence": Marriage and Lyricism in the *Sonnets from the Portuguese*' (*VLC* 37[2009] 85–102)—Rhian Williams argues that EBB's courtship sonnet sequence uses the trope of silence to deconstruct the unified lyrical subject and to fashion a lyricism that is 'neither male or female, but vigorously conjugal' (p. 89). There are also chapters on EBB in Eric Eisner's *Nineteenth-Century Poetry and Literary Celebrity* and in Claire Knowles's *Sensibility and Female Poetic Tradition, 1780–1860*, both discussed in the Romantic poetry section (Chapter XII).

This year saw the publication of volume 15 of Oxford University Press's *The Poetical Works of Robert Browning*, edited by Stefan Hawlin and Michael Meredith. Bringing together Browning's last two collections of poetry, *Parleyings with Certain People of Importance in their Day* [1887] and *Asolando* [1889], this impressive edition will hopefully stimulate new interest in these under-appreciated late works. Both texts represented a return to the past for Browning: *Parleyings* comprises seven addresses to figures whose work had interested the poet in his youth, while *Asolando* contains many short poems that recall Browning's lyrical verses of the 1840s and 1850s. Hawlin and Meredith's introductions to the two collections and to each individual poem are excellent, combining detailed accounts of the immediate (often biographical) impulse that lay behind composition with insightful discussions of Browning's views on art, politics, and theology in his final years. However, it is a pity that the editors do not always draw attention to the numerous moments in which these works reaffirm or rework ideas or images from Browning's earlier poems. Overall, though, this edition attains the impressive standard set by previous volumes in this series. The text of *Parleyings* and *Asolando* is both rigorously edited and very readable, and the poems themselves, complex and varied, deserve to be read and studied more widely. Evgenia Sifaki studies another late Browning work in her article 'Masculinity, Heroism, and the Empire: Robert Browning's "Clive" and Other Victorian Re-constructions of the Story of Robert Clive' (*VLC* 37[2009] 141–56). Sifaki positions Browning's 'dramatic idyll' in the context of other nineteenth-century narratives about Clive, claiming that the poem challenges received Victorian notions about ostensibly heroic concepts of masculinity and imperialism.

Paul Mariani's new biography of Hopkins, *Gerard Manley Hopkins: A Life*, arrived too late for inclusion in last year's *YWES*. Mariani is already the author of a noted commentary on Hopkins, and his immersion in Hopkins's poetry is evinced on every page of this biography, to the extent that his own prose is laced with words or phrases taken (mostly unattributed) from his subject's work. These borrowings, part of an attempt to cultivate a lyrical prose style, provide one of several of Mariani's innovations in biographical method. Another is the decision to write most of his book in the present tense. The result is curious, a narrative which is certainly fast-paced, but which rarely moves to interpret the details it has accumulated. If there is a central thread running through the book, it is Mariani's sympathy with Jesuit life and spirituality. Given that a marked suspicion of the Jesuits is sometimes thought to be the chief fault of the standard biography of Hopkins, Norman White's *Hopkins: A Literary Biography* [1992], this might have stood Mariani in good stead. As it is, the perspective is skewed too far the other way: that only fifty pages are devoted to the period before Hopkins's conversion, compared to nearly 400 pages on his life as a Roman Catholic, is a major imbalance, obscuring the fact that almost half the poet's years were spent as an Anglican. The lack of discussion of Hopkins's homoeroticism, sceptical or otherwise, also has to be counted a serious flaw.

Brian Willems's monograph *Hopkins and Heidegger* proposes that poet and philosopher might be brought into productive contact, even if there is no possibility of direct influence (Heidegger was born in the year Hopkins died and had no discernible interest in Victorian poetry). At the core of Willems's book is his attempt to relate Hopkins's notion of 'inscape' to the enigmatic concept Heidegger termed *Ereignis*, in which cause he enlists a myriad assortment of modern philosophers and cultural theorists. The argument is difficult to summarize, especially given the absence of a conclusion, but a persistent theme is that for both Hopkins and Heidegger the particular quality of the poetic resides in its potential for revealing the true nature of being, something which other kinds of linguistic exchange tend to conceal. Each of the four chapters takes a single poem as a basis for forays into philosophical debate, returning to analyse the poem in their light. What value the book holds for interpreting Heideggerian philosophy is hard to judge, but, for all that it shows a wide familiarity with criticism of the poet's work, Willems's study does not add significantly to the terrain already mapped out in Roger Ebbatson's *Heidegger's Bicycle: Interfering with Victorian Texts* [2006], which offers more cogent reflections on Hopkins in relation to modern German cultural theory and philosophy.

Articles in this year's *Hopkins Quarterly* are almost all biographical in nature. Nicolas Hawkes's 'The Other Hopkinses' (*HQ* 36[2009] 3–24) presents the fruit of the author's researches into Hopkins's extended family, most notably into the life of his second cousin, Sir Frederick Gowland Hopkins, a Nobel prize-winning biochemist. James Pribek, SJ's 'Fr. Darlington's Memories of Hopkins: A More Favorable Appraisal' (*HQ* 36[2009] 25–55) attempts to rehabilitate the reputation of one of Hopkins's Dublin colleagues from under the censure of several previous commentators. Darlington may be discredited as a source for information about Hopkins's life, Pribek contends, but he held no personal malice towards his fellow Jesuit. Considering Hopkins's best-known sermon, on the beauty of Christ, Michael P. Kuczynski's 'Gerard Manley Hopkins and the Apocryphal *Epistola Lentuli*' (*HQ* 36[2009] 73–97) discusses Hopkins's likely source for his assertions about the physical attractiveness of Christ. The detailed research undertaken is impressive, but the article is short on interpretation of this passage, especially given how often it has been cited in recent studies of Hopkins's homoeroticism. Blaise Cirelli finds parallels between Hopkins's conception of nature and that of Teilhard de Chardin, an idiosyncratic Jesuit thinker known for his work in palaeontology, biology, and philosophy, in 'Gerard Manley Hopkins and Teilhard de Chardin: The Poetic and Scientific Reconciliation of Spirit and Matter' (*HQ* 36[2009] 98–114). Mary Hewitt's 'Felix Randal's "Battering Sandal": What Did It Look Like?' (*HQ* 36[2009] 115–18) describes the horse 'pattens' Hopkins may have been describing at the end of his sonnet on the death of a Liverpool blacksmith. Joseph Feeney considers recent dramatizations of Hopkins's poetry in 'Hopkins On Stage, Sumptuously, in Sante Fe' (*HQ* 36[2009] 119–22).

One 2009 number of the bilingual *Revue LISA/LISA e-journal* is a Festschrift in honour of French scholar René Gallet, who has published extensively on Hopkins, and includes a number of new articles on the poet, as well as reprinting one of Gallet's own pieces. Joseph Feeney's 'Is Hopkins' "The Windhover" about Christ? A Negative Response, with a Whimsical Postscript' (*La Revue LISA* 7:iii[2009] 94–9) makes a provocative case for the absence of reference to Christ in Hopkins's best-known sonnet, observing that Hopkins only added his dedication of the poem to Christ several years after it had been written. Gildas Lemardelé's 'La Mer et l'insistance paradoxale dans quelques poèmes de G.M. Hopkins' (*La Revue LISA* 7:iii[2009] 101–8) surveys the various significances with which Hopkins imbues the sea, finding analogies between it and God's nature in the poems. Catherine Phillips's '"Nothing is so beautiful": Hopkins's Spring' (*La Revue LISA* 7:iii[2009] 109–19) explores Marian contexts for Hopkins's passion for the season of spring, giving consideration to how this traditional association functions in a number of his poems, and its convergence with his artistic and scientific interests. Cary H.

Plotkin's 'Hopkins the Darwinian: a Contextual Unriddling' (*La Revue LISA* 7:iii[2009] 476–89) finds a puzzle in the equanimity of Hopkins's brief responses to Darwin's theories in his letters, concluding that the absence of a doctrinal pronouncement from Rome on evolution in Hopkins's lifetime allowed for considerable variation in the attitudes of individual Catholics to evolutionary theory. Maureen Moran's 'Hopkins and Victorian Responses to Suffering' (*La Revue LISA* 7:iii[2009] 570–81) contends that Hopkins's response to physical torment, especially that leading to martyrdom, mixes Catholic and Protestant influences. The manner in which martyrdom is tied to the cause of the English nation in *The Wreck of the Deutschland*, she finds, is an attempt to appropriate a familiar trope of Protestant martyrological discourse.

Of the other articles published on Hopkins this year, perhaps the most important is Pamela Coren's 'Gerard Manley Hopkins, Plainsong and the Performance of Poetry' (*RES* 60[2009] 271–94). Coren relates Hopkins's interest in plainsong, a rhythmically fluid form of liturgical music, to his approach to prosody. Her view of sprung rhythm as essentially a pure stress rhythm is contentious, but the approach to this oldest of debates through Hopkins's musical interests is innovative and insightful. Also notable is Simon Humphries's critique of editorial conventions in respect of the poem he prefers to call 'Hark, Hearer, Hear What I Do', but which is usually (and erroneously, Humphries argues) titled 'Epithalamion' (*ANQ* 22:i[2009] 27–33). Elsewhere, Alan C. Christensen offers a Lacanian interpretation of nautical journeys in Hopkins and Tennyson in 'Navigating in Perilous Seas of Language: *In Memoriam* and "The Wreck of the Deutschland"' (*VP* 47[2009] 379–402), suggesting a metaphorical relation to the linguistic practice of the poets. Particular attention is given to moments when language appears in both poems to be forced beyond its capacities, as in the vision of Christ experienced by the tall nun in Hopkins's poem. Francis O'Gorman's note, 'Gerard Manley Hopkins and George MacDonald on Immortality' (*N&Q* 56[2009] 399–400), raises the possibility of an echo in one of Hopkins's late poems of MacDonald's novel *At the Back of the North Wind*.

Several of this year's articles on the Rossettis are concerned with sound. Angela Leighton is finely attuned to the verbal music in the poetry of Christina and Dante Gabriel in 'On "the Hearing Ear": Some Sonnets of the Rossettis' (*VP* 47[2009]: 505–16). Listening with the ear rather than the mind, she suggests, might allow for new kinds of thinking in poetry to take place. Ernest Fontana considers the potential a number of Dante Gabriel's poems offer for dramatic vocalization in 'Exercitive Speech Acts in the Poetry of Dante Gabriel Rossetti' (*VP* 47[2009] 449–58), proposing that this interest in questions of voice is especially prominent when Rossetti writes in a sceptical or transgressive mode. In 'Listening: Dante Gabriel Rossetti and the Persistence of Song' (*VS* 51[2009] 409–21), Elizabeth Helsinger traces the ways in which Rossetti's thinking about musical song shapes his approach to sound in poetry, giving close and sensitive attention to the song poems he included in an 1870 collection.

Of the other articles on Dante Gabriel Rossetti, Andrea Henderson's 'The "Gold Bar of Heaven": Framing and Objectivity in D.G. Rossetti's Poetry and Painting' (*ELH* 76[2009] 911–30) contends that Rossetti's aspiration to represent ideal female beauty in both art and poetry is coupled with an awareness of the inescapable subjectivity of his own imaginings. Brian Donnelly considers the commodification of female desire in Dante Gabriel's poetry and painting in 'The Consuming Aesthetic of Dante Rossetti's "The Orchard-pit" and *Bocca Baciata*' (*JPRS* 18[2009] 4–26), sensitively tracing his multifaceted responses to Christina's 'Goblin Market'. Lawrence J. Starzyk pursues a comparison between D.G. Rossetti and Robert Browning in '"My soul another echo there": Rossetti's "The Portrait" and Ekphrastic Disavowal' (*JPRS* 18[2009] 27–40), discussing the relation of word and image in a number of their 'portrait poems'. Two little-discussed sonnets Rossetti wrote to accompany an 1875 drawing are the focus for D.M.R. Bentley's '"Impenetrable Dooms": Dante Gabriel Rossetti's *The Question* and Explanatory Sonnets' (*VN* 116[2009] 53–65). Bentley remarks interestingly on the way Rossetti's concern with the fate of the soul after death is framed by the interplay between the sonnets and the drawing. Difficulties with elucidating one of Rossetti's most languorous lyrics are explored by Matthew Paul Carlson in 'A Secret Kept: Interpreting Rossetti's "The Stream's Secret"' (*Expl* 67[2009] 135–9). A number of engaging articles on Christina Rossetti appeared in 2009. William Baker and Emily Kingery provide details of a recently discovered letter and fragment of devotional prose by Christina Rossetti in their note, 'Some New Christina Rossetti Materials' (*N&Q* 56[2009] 394–6). John Woolford ponders Rossetti's response to William Blake in 'Christina Rossetti and the "Rossetti Manuscript" of William Blake' (*JPRS* 18[2009] 72–84), observing that Blakean moments in her poetry are moderated by a resistance to misogyny and by the pursuit of religious orthodoxy. Bertrand Lentsch's '"Thou whole burnt offering!": The Mystical Ecstasy in Christina Rossetti's Poems' (*CVE* 69[2009] 131–49) is obscurely written and ranges eclectically over Rossetti's poetic corpus, but is most of all concerned with the paradoxes in Rossetti's ascetical aesthetic.

As one might expect, the Rossettis feature prominently in Julia Straub's monograph *A Victorian Muse: The Afterlife of Dante's Beatrice in Nineteenth-Century Literature*. Their father Gabriele's allegorical theorization of Beatrice provides the point of departure for a chapter considering Dante's importance for the Rossetti family. The encounters with the *Commedia* had by the Rossetti children, Straub finds, variously acknowledge and resist their father's interpretation. A subsequent chapter is focused more narrowly on Christina's sonnet sequence *Monna Innominata* and Dante Gabriel's poetry and painting, especially his 1861 anthology of translations, *Early Italian Poets*. As well as chapters on George Eliot and Walter Pater, Straub also devotes a chapter to discussing the possibility that Arthur Henry Hallam is consciously attributed with some of Beatrice's qualities in Tennyson's *In Memoriam*.

The year 2009 saw the centenary of the death of Swinburne, an anniversary that was marked by relatively few publications. Jonathan Bate's essay in the *Times Literary Supplement*, 'Libidinous Laureate of Satyrs' (*TLS* [10 July 2009] 14–15), focuses (unsurprisingly, given its title) on the salacious aspects of Swinburne's work and life, but is also a serious and forcefully argued vindication of Swinburne's poetry, celebrating both its radical exploration of sexual feeling and its metrical brilliance. Another article discussed the editing of Swinburne's poetry, drawing attention in the process to the continuing need for an authoritative critical edition of his work. Lakshmi Krishnan's 'Editing Swinburne's Border Ballads' (*MLR* 104[2009] 333–52) delves deep into the British Library's Swinburne manuscripts, using the ballad 'Burd Margaret' to illustrate the numerous editorial questions that surround Swinburne's verse. Swinburne was also represented by a special issue of *Victorian Poetry* in 2009. After an introduction by Rikky Rooksby and Terry L. Meyers (*VP* 47[2009] 611–18) which offers a survey of developments in Swinburne criticism over the last forty years, the volume opens with Jerome McGann's article on 'Wagner, Baudelaire, Swinburne: Poetry in the Condition of Music' (*VP* 47[2009] 619–32), a stimulating account of the influence of Wagner's theories of music, as mediated by Baudelaire, on the sound and the prosody of Swinburne's poetry. Baudelaire also features in Tony W. Garland's contribution, 'Brothers in Paradox: Swinburne, Baudelaire, and the Paradox of Sin' (*VP* 47[2009] 633–45). Garland makes some thought-provoking points about Baudelaire and Swinburne's simultaneous attraction to and repulsion from the concept of sin, but his article gives no really new insight into the artistic connection between the two poets.

In 'A Theory of Poetry: Swinburne's "A Dark Month"' (*VP* 47[2009] 661–73), Yisrael Levin claims that the often maligned 'A Dark Month' can shed important light on Swinburne's conception of poetry in his later career. Employing detailed close readings, Levin traces Swinburne's development, over the course of the poem, of a non-representational and subjective poetics encapsulated in the figure of the child. In 'Intimations and Imitations of Immortality: Swinburne's "By the North Sea" and "Poeta Loquitur"' (*VP* 47[2009] 675–90), Andrew Fippinger gives a new perspective on Swinburne's fascination with the sea through a sensitive study of these two poems, reading the latter as a self-parody of the former. Julia F. Saville's article on 'Cosmopolitan Republican Swinburne, the Immersive Poet as Public Moralist' (*VP* 47[2009] 691–713) posits that the sensual means of Swinburne's verse often serve political or moral ends. The examples that Saville takes from Swinburne's poetry do not always add a great deal to her argument, but this remains an intriguing and suggestive piece. Katie Paterson's contribution, '"Much regrafted pain": Schopenhauerian Love and the Fecundity of Pain in *Atalanta in Calydon*' (*VP* 47[2009] 715–31), studies *Atalanta* through the lens of Schopenhauer, interpreting the destructive effects of love in Swinburne's drama as evidence of a pessimistic world-view that pervades the text. Catherine Maxwell's piece on 'Swinburne and Thackeray's *The Newcomes*' (*VP* 47[2009] 733–46) details the ways in which Thackeray's novel was important to Swinburne. Maxwell traces the similarities between Ethel Newcome and Swinburne's beloved cousin Mary Gordon, as well as examining how the relationships depicted in Thackeray's book influenced some of Swinburne's writing about love and sexuality.

Two of the contributions explore the links between classicism and sex in Swinburne's verse. Jason Boulet's essay '"Will he rise and recover[?]": Catullus, Castration, and Censorship in Swinburne's "Dolores"' (*VP* 47[2009] 747–58) gives a formidably detailed and well-researched account of the ways in which Swinburne borrows from Catullus in order to challenge Victorian conventions of literary and sexual propriety. T.D. Olverson, in 'Libidinous Laureates and Lyrical Maenads: Michael Field, Swinburne and Erotic Hellenism' (*VP* 47[2009] 759–76), concentrates on female sexuality. Olverson studies Swinburne's dramatic poems *Atalanta in Calydon* and *Erechtheus* together with Michael Field's play *Callirrhoë*, arguing that Field builds on Swinburne's example to fashion a more active and more radically feminist conception of women's sexuality. The issue ends with two pieces that focus on the textual dimensions of Swinburne's work. T.A.J. Burnett offers 'Some Reflections on the Text of Swinburne's Unfinished Novel, the so-called "Lesbia Brandon"' (*VP* 47[2009] 777–86), undertaking a careful assessment of the manuscripts of the novel and making a case for a new edition of this important text. Benjamin F. Fisher, in 'Swinburne's "A Nympholept" in the Making' (*VP* 47[2009] 787–800), studies the manuscripts of 'A Nympholept' in order to reconstruct the development of Swinburne's ideas as he composed and revised the poem. Although Fisher is at times too assertive in his interpretations, this article is an illuminating analysis of Swinburne's method of composition. Another contribution to the issue is the late Margot K. Louis's 'Erotic Figuration in Swinburne's Tristram of Lyonesse, Canto 2: The Vanishing Knight and the Drift of Butterflies' (*VP* 47[2009] 647–59). This article presents a nuanced analysis of a single passage of Swinburne's poetry, beautifully explicating the ways in which he questions phallocentric models of sexuality through his evocation of female sexual pleasure.

Louis is also the author of the posthumously published *Persephone Rises, 1860–1927: Mythography, Gender, and the Creation of a New Spirituality*. This wide-ranging and illuminating book adopts a historicist approach to mythography, exploring the various ways in which British and American writers have appropriated the figure of Persephone or Proserpine in response to changing historical circumstances. Swinburne, unsurprisingly, is at the heart of the book; for Louis, Swinburne's focus on Proserpine's role as the queen of the dead is evidence of the growing influence of philosophical pessimism on nineteenth-century culture. At the same time, Louis also considers how Victorian women poets foregrounded the gender issues, inherent in the Persephone myth, which were largely ignored by male poets. Discussing the work of Jean Ingelow, Dora Greenwell, Mathilde Blind, and Katherine Bradley (one half of 'Michael Field'), Louis studies these writers' representation of Persephone in poems that explore questions of female agency, sexual experience, and the mother–daughter relationship. After an introduction which examines nineteenth-century theorizations of myth, the first chapter of Louis's book traces the development of the Persephone story from ancient Greece to the Romantic period. The second chapter focuses on the work of Ingelow and Greenwell, while the third concentrates on Swinburne and on those writers, including Tennyson, George Meredith, Robert Bridges, and Edith Wharton, who responded to the issues raised in his Proserpine poems. Chapter 4 considers Persephone's role as a symbol of fertility in the novels of Willa Cather and Thomas Hardy, and chapter 5 looks at the presence of the goddess, and the enduring influence of Swinburne, in modernist writing, particularly that of H.D., William Carlos Williams, and D.H. Lawrence.

This year also brought the bicentenary of Tennyson's birth, and as a result Tennysonians were treated to a vast range of publications. Perhaps the most significant of these was *Tennyson Among the Poets: Bicentenary Essays*, edited by Robert Douglas-Fairhurst and Seamus Perry, a substantial collection that examines the relations of influence and exchange between Tennyson and other writers. After a short 'Prefatory Note' by Christopher Ricks, the volume opens with Douglas-Fairhurst's incisive introduction, which sets the scene for the following essays by examining Tennyson's own mixed feelings about living 'among the poets', surrounded by the writings of his more or less distinguished forebears and contemporaries. The first essay in the volume, 'Tennyson's Dying Fall' by Peter McDonald, undertakes detailed close readings of a number of poems, arguing that the 'dying fall' of Tennyson's metrical cadences, and indeed the presence of the word 'fall' itself, is crucial to understanding the emotional nuances of his verse. Dinah Birch, in 'Tennyson's Retrospective View', offers a new take on the question of Tennyson's interest in the past, examining his engagements with history, myth, and legend and arguing that those engagements influenced and anticipated the work of writers as diverse as A.E. Housman and T.S. Eliot. In 'Tennyson's Limitations', one of the most original essays in the volume, Christopher Decker considers those Tennyson poems, such as 'Morte d'Arthur' and 'Ulysses', that retell or build on the narratives of other writers, arguing that the 'intertextual manoeuvres' of these poems reveal Tennyson's writing to be 'imaginatively open to other texts' (p. 58).

Another impressive piece in the same volume, Aidan Day's 'Tennyson's Grotesque', makes a perhaps counter-intuitive but thoroughly convincing case for Tennyson as a writer of chaos and grotesque. According to Day, 'Tennyson's exquisitely finished poetic manner' both hides and exposes 'a dissonance, an incoherence which contradicts and is unassimilated to the finish of the style' (p. 78). In 'Tennyson, Browning, Virgil', Daniel Karlin succeeds in shedding light on Tennyson's relations both with classical and with contemporary poets. Karlin presents a detailed analysis of the different ways in which Tennyson and Browning, in 'To Virgil' and 'Pan and Luna' respectively, respond to the writing and the figure of Virgil. A.A. Markley, in 'Tennyson and the Voice of Ovid's Heroines', gives another perspective on Tennyson's engagement with the Latin poets, arguing that Ovid's *Heroides* should be viewed as 'an influence on the development of the dramatic monologue in the nineteenth century' (p. 117) and on Tennyson's monologues in particular. Subsequent essays focus on Tennyson's responses to the English poetic tradition. Eric Griffiths's piece 'On Lines and Grooves from Shakespeare to Tennyson' studies Tennyson's view of Shakespeare, and his understanding of metre, through an examination of the typographical practices of various nineteenth-century editions of Shakespeare's works. N.K. Sugimura's nuanced and well-argued essay 'Epic Sensibilities: "Old Man" Milton and the Making of Tennyson's *Idylls of the King*' examines the ways in which Milton's writing, particularly *Paradise Lost*, influenced Tennyson's conception of epic and the composition of his Arthurian poem. In another excellent piece, 'The Wheels of Being: Tennyson and Shelley', Michael O'Neill presents the book's most sustained discussion of Tennyson's engagement with Romanticism, arguing that 'the paths travelled by much of his greatest work take their point of departure from Shelley' (p. 198).

The next two essays in *Tennyson Among the Poets* focus on Tennyson's relations with his contemporaries. In '"Brother-Poets": Tennyson and Browning', Donald S. Hair provides a neat summary of Tennyson and Browning's personal relationship, their respective conceptions of poetry, and their often divergent opinions on a range of subjects. Marion Shaw's piece 'Friendship, Poetry, and Insurrection: The Kemble Letters' draws on an unpublished archive of letters to Tennyson's university friend John Mitchell Kemble to examine the Cambridge Apostles' involvement in the 1830 insurrection in Spain, and its influence on Tennyson. Matthew Bevis, in 'Tennyson's Humour', studies an often ignored aspect of Tennyson's work, exploring Tennyson's sense of humour and concluding, for example, that the numerous parodists of Tennyson take their cue from the poet himself, 'teasing out the smile that lay buried yet implicit in his printed page' (p. 238). Richard Cronin touches on similar issues in 'Edward Lear and Tennyson's Nonsense'. Cronin draws some illuminating comparisons between the preoccupations of Tennyson and Lear, and argues that Lear, in his rewritings of Tennyson, 'does not so much make a nonsense of' Tennyson's verse 'as release a nonsensicality already implicit in it' (p. 263). In '"Men my brothers, men the workers": Tennyson and the Victorian Working-Class Poet', Kirstie Blair offers a reciprocal account of Tennyson's relationship to working-class writers, examining such writers' engagements with Tennyson's work as well as Tennyson's own (very mixed) opinions about their poetry. Linda K. Hughes's piece '"Frater Ave"? Tennyson and Swinburne' looks at Tennyson's complicated personal and poetic links to the poet many Victorians saw as his natural successor. Hughes argues, convincingly, that the 'oppositional gestures' found in the two poets' writings are more than counterbalanced by the 'kindred practices' which unite them (p. 299).

The rest of the volume concentrates on Tennyson's influence, positive or negative, on subsequent writers. In 'After Tennyson: The Presence of the Poet, 1892–1918', Samantha Matthews maps out a range of responses to Tennyson and his work in the quarter-century after his death, taking in forms such as tribute verses, biographies, and critical commentaries. Angela Leighton's piece 'Tennyson, by Ear' begins and ends with Virginia Woolf, exploring the novelist's ambivalent reactions to the sounds and rhythms of Tennyson. In between, Leighton digresses to consider the links between Tennyson's poetry and that of Christina Rossetti, suggesting that the unique acoustics of Tennyson's verse can be heard throughout Victorian and modernist writing. In 'Hardy's Tennyson', Helen Small convincingly makes the case that Hardy's response to Tennyson's poetry was one of 'respect', rather than the 'resistance' identified by many critics (p. 363). Small demonstrates her argument through a consideration of the annotations in Hardy's copy of Tennyson, and through a nuanced close reading of Hardy's elegy 'The Going'. John Morton's piece on 'T.S. Eliot and Tennyson' does a fine job of assessing Eliot's views on Tennyson. Morton takes in both Eliot's early criticisms and his later appreciations of his predecessor, as well as examining the substantial allusions to Tennyson in *Murder in the Cathedral* and the drafts of *The Waste Land*.

After this, John Fuller's essay on 'Tennyson and Auden' provides another example of a twentieth-century poet whose stated ambivalence about the Victorian laureate was accompanied by a persistent engagement with Tennyson's language and rhythms. Fuller's essay is impressive in its close attention to the intricacies of the Tennysonian echoes found in Auden's verse. The volume is rounded off in fine fashion by Seamus Perry: 'Betjeman's Tennyson' is a suitably exuberant piece which demonstrates how Betjeman's intense regard for Tennyson's writing worked itself into his own poetry. All in all, it would be difficult to imagine a more comprehensive assessment of Tennyson's position in the poetic canon than this book.

Tennyson's significance for other cultural forms was also considered this year. Jim Cheshire's edited volume *Tennyson Transformed: Alfred Lord Tennyson and Visual Culture* explores the ways in which the poet's image and work pervaded Victorian visual art. The book accompanies the exhibition, also called 'Tennyson Transformed', that Cheshire curated at The Collection, Lincoln, and, without wanting to be unjust to the informative essays that form the first half of the book, it is fair to say that the main attraction of the volume is the beautifully presented catalogue of the exhibition. Cheshire's introduction to the book provides fascinating contextual information about the world of Victorian art and illustration. The book's first chapter, by Julia Thomas, presents a survey of Victorian illustrations of Tennyson's work, while chapter 2, by Colin Ford, focuses on the poet's association with photographer Julia Margaret Cameron. In the third chapter, Leonee Ormond looks at responses to Tennyson's verse by Victorian painters, particularly the Pre-Raphaelites. Chapters 4 and 5 turn to portraits of Tennyson, with Ben Stoker discussing the various informal sketches that were made by the poets' acquaintances, and John Lord focusing on the sculptures of Tennyson that were produced when his fame was at its height, both before and after his death. The exhibition catalogue that closes the book is a treasure-trove: it includes illustrations of Tennyson's poems and drawings, as well as portraits and sculptures of the poet himself, neatly demonstrating his centrality to the development of Victorian ideas of visual culture.

There was also, of course, the 2009 edition of the *Tennyson Research Bulletin*. Observing the unevenness in the poem's early critical reputation, Gregory Tate's '"A fit person to be Poet Laureate": Tennyson, *In Memoriam*, and the Laureateship' (*TRB* 9[2009] 233–47) questions whether the success of *In Memoriam* was as significant a factor in Tennyson's appointment as Poet Laureate as has been claimed. A detailed look at the chronology, Tate finds, suggests otherwise. Erik Gray's informative note, 'The Title of *In Memoriam*' (*TRB* 9[2009] 248–51), discusses the occasional tendency of editors and, to a lesser extent, critics, to mis-title the elegy as *In Memoriam A.H.H.*, and elucidates the textual history that has led to such confusion. James Williams, in 'Tennyson's Once and Future King' (*TRB* 9[2009] 252–69), offers a sensitive analysis of ideas of the apocalypse in *Idylls of the King*. Tennyson's deployment of apocalyptic thinking and imagery, Williams argues, sheds new light on his conception of time, both past and future, in the *Idylls*; an apt subject for the poet's bicentenary year. In an article that neatly complements Williams's, 'Tennyson, Morris and the Guinevere Complex' (*TRB* 9[2009]

270–9), Eleonora Sasso compares early poems about Guinevere by Tennyson and William Morris in order to argue that, early in their careers, both poets used the queen as a powerful multivalent symbol of sensual desire, natural beauty, and the irretrievable past.

The 'Tennyson at Two Hundred' special issue of *Victorian Poetry* was the other main publication marking Tennyson's bicentenary. The issue was edited by Herbert F. Tucker, who introduces the essays with a short but erudite piece that studies Tennyson's own writing about dates and anniversaries (*VP* 47[2009] 1–6). After this, the first article in the issue is Richard Maxwell's 'Unnumbered Polypi' (*VP* 47[2009] 7–23), an informative and enjoyable exploration of the literary and biological contexts that float around the fifteen lines of 'The Kraken'. This is followed by an intriguing essay by Linda H. Peterson, 'Tennyson and the Ladies' (*VP* 47[2009] 25–43), which seeks to rehabilitate the oft-maligned 'lady poems' of 1830 and 1832 by arguing for their 'participation in a contemporary debate over the "characteristics of women"' (p. 25). Next comes Erik Gray's 'Getting It Wrong in "The Lady of Shalott"' (*VP* 47[2009] 45–59), which subtly analyses the function of error, and particularly of deliberate or 'conscious error' (p. 48), as an aspect of artistic creativity in the 1832 and 1842 versions of 'The Lady of Shalott', and also in 'Lancelot and Elaine'. Gregory Tate's 'Tennyson and the Embodied Mind' (*VP* 47[2009] 61–80) explores Tennyson's concern with the physical nature of mental processes against the background of Victorian psychological theory. There is an insightful reading of 'Ulysses', with Tate finding ambivalence in Tennyson's presentation of the human will's capacity to escape material conditions. In 'Tennyson and Zeno: Three Infinities' (*VP* 47[2009] 81–99), W. David Shaw offers readings of a range of poems, particularly 'Ulysses' and *In Memoriam*, in order to demonstrate that Tennyson gestures towards three types of infinity in his verse: 'physical infinities of space and time', 'recursive images of a mindscape', and 'an Absolute that is unlimited or boundless' (p. 89). James Nohrnberg's 'Eight Reflections of Tennyson's "Ulysses"' (*VP* 47[2009] 101–50) is a suitably epic consideration of the various explorers, literary and historical, that may have influenced Tennyson's poem of anticipated and deferred adventure, particularly James Cook, Columbus, and Dante's Ulysses.

In D.B. Ruderman's impressive essay 'The Breathing Space of Ballad: Tennyson's Stillborn Poetics' (*VP* 47[2009] 151–71), the author begins by giving a sensitive reading of the brief elegy that Tennyson wrote for his stillborn son in 1851, before proceeding to consider the ways in which stillbirth operates as a metaphor for literary production and reception in Tennyson's writing. Irene Hsiao, in her article 'Calculating Loss in Tennyson's *In Memoriam*' (*VP* 47[2009] 173–96), succeeds impressively in giving a fresh interpretation of Tennyson's elegy, as she examines the significance of tropes of counting, calculation, and measurement to the psychological and metaphysical concerns of the poem. Timothy Peltason's 'What the Laureate Did Next: *Maud*' (*VP* 47[2009] 197–219) challenges readings that see *Maud* as a sort of anti-laureate piece, arguing instead that Tennyson uses this poem to negotiate between the private and public aspects of poetry, linking 'the voiced reflections of an isolated and idiosyncratic sensibility' to communal and national concerns (p. 208). Another essay on *Maud*, Anne C. McCarthy's '"Who knows if he be dead?": *Maud*, Signification, and the Madhouse Canto' (*VP* 47[2009] 221–39), draws on theoretical and historical perspectives to argue that this pivotal section of the poem can be read as 'a speculative fiction concerning the unknowability of death' (p. 223).

As the issue goes on, the focus shifts to *Idylls of the King*. Ingrid Ranum, in 'An Adventure in Modern Marriage: Domestic Development in Tennyson's *Geraint and Enid* and *The Marriage of Geraint*' (*VP* 47[2009] 241–57), argues that these two idylls are deeply concerned with the question of how contemporary gender roles should fit into the institution of marriage. Similarly, Robert L. Patten's 'The Contemporaneity of *The Last Tournament*' (*VP* 47[2009] 259–83) suggests that this Arthurian idyll is heavily invested in nineteenth-century preoccupations. Patten adduces a number of contemporary contexts for the poem, ranging from debates about evolution and religion to the Franco-Prussian war. Other articles shed light on often neglected contexts for Tennyson's work. Dennis Taylor, in 'Tennyson's Catholic Years: A Point of Contact' (*VP* 47[2009] 285–312), argues for the importance of Catholic theology to Tennyson's poetry, particularly 'The Holy Grail', and explores the poet's links to Catholicism through friends such as Aubrey de Vere, Sir John Simeon, and Wilfrid Ward. Anna Barton, in 'Delirious Bulldogs and Nasty Crockery: Tennyson as Nonsense Poet' (*VP* 47[2009] 313–30), considers Tennyson's friendship with Edward Lear. In a similar manner to Richard Cronin's essay, discussed above, Barton's piece argues for an inherent nonsensicality in Tennyson's writing, traceable in the sonic exuberance of his verse and in his love of exotic place names. The final essay in the issue, William H. Pritchard's 'Epistolary Tennyson: The Art of Suspension' (*VP* 47[2009] 331–47), studies a specific subset of Tennyson's oeuvre, his 'verse epistles', in order to argue for the existence of 'a more "social" Tennyson, conveyed in a poetic voice from whose register urbanity and humor were not excluded' (p. 331).

Tennyson continued to be represented in *Victorian Poetry* throughout the year. In '"Of happy men that have the power to die": Tennyson's "Tithonus"' (*VP* 47[2009] 355–78), Henry Weinfeld uses this particular dramatic monologue as a means of exploring a range of contexts and approaches that help to illuminate Tennyson's views on mortality and immortality. Allison Adler Kroll's 'Tennyson and the Metaphysics of Material Culture: The Early Poems' (*VP* 47[2009] 461–80) offers an original take on Tennyson's 'passion for the past', arguing that his early writing participates in concerns about the preservation of the material objects of cultural history, concerns which led to the birth of the heritage industry. Stefanie Markovits's essay 'Giving Voice to the Crimean War: Tennyson's "Charge" and Maud's Battle-Song' (*VP* 47[2009] 481–503) presents a detailed account of the ways in which the form and language of *Maud* and "The Charge of the Light Brigade" reflect Tennyson's 'ambivalence' and 'bewilderment' (p. 487) about the Crimean War, a bewilderment that was felt throughout Victorian Britain.

Elsewhere, Molly Clark Hillard's article '"A perfect form in perfect rest": Spellbinding Narratives and Tennyson's "Day Dream"' (*Narrative* 17[2009] 312–33) studies a poem which, the author argues, has been 'virtually absent from criticism' (p. 313). Hillard argues persuasively that Tennyson's sleeping beauty poem is an important example of the consideration of temporality that informs so much of his poetry. In 'Hengist's Brood: Tennyson and the Anglo-Saxons' (*RES* 60[2009] 460–74), Damian Love offers an indirect and rather narrow reading of Tennyson's interest in Old English, and of the role of the Saxons in *Idylls of the King*, through a study of the poet's Old English vocabulary, particularly his use of the word 'mere' to refer to the sea. M. Wynn Thomas examines Tennyson's transatlantic reach in 'Whitman, Tennyson, and the Poetry of Old Age' (in Burt and Halpern, eds., *Something Understood: Essays and Poetry for Helen Vendler*, pp. 161–82). Through an analysis of the two poets' differing but complementary representations of old age, Thomas concludes that Tennyson was as important to Whitman at the end of his career as he was at its start. There is also a chapter on Tennyson in Sally Bushell's *Text as Process: Creative Composition in Wordsworth, Tennyson, and Dickinson*. This book is an exercise in genetic criticism, and the Tennyson chapter concentrates on the manuscripts and composition history of *Idylls of the King*. Bushell argues, fairly uncontroversially, that Tennyson was a '"reproductive" writer' (p. 120), a poet whose method of composition involved recording and reorganizing preformed phrases and ideas.

4. Drama

One of the highlights of 2009 was the publication of *Ruskin, the Theatre and Victorian Visual Culture*, a collection of essays edited by Anselm Heinrich, Katherine Newey, and Jeffrey Richards. The first part of the volume focuses on intersections between Victorian drama and Ruskin's cultural and aesthetic theories. J.A. Hilton's chapter, for example, examines Gilbert and Sullivan's adaptations of Ruskin's ideas in *Patience,* the *Mikado*, and other operettas performed at the Savoy Theatre (pp. 42–57). The second part of the volume focuses more broadly on intersections between visual culture and the theatre. For example, Shearer West examines photographic portraiture of Ellen Terry and Henry Irving (pp. 187–215), and Jim Davis investigates cartoons and caricature of Victorian drama in the popular press (pp. 216–38). The volume also includes chapters by Jeffrey Richards, Rachel Dickinson, Andrew Leng, Anselm Heinrich, Andrew Tate, Janice Norwood, David Mayer, and Richard Foulkes. Taken together, these essays illuminate 'intersections of Ruskin, the word, and the image with the locus of the theatre and real or imagined dramatic space which vivifies late Victorian modes of expression' (p. 9).

In her introduction to *Ruskin, the Theatre and Victorian Visual Culture*, Katherine Newey points out that Victorian drama had the 'capacity to absorb and incorporate all other art forms' (p. 5). This view is certainly supported by Gail Marshall's *Shakespeare and Victorian Women*, which highlights the myriad ways women engaged with Shakespeare's plays, both on and off the stage. Marshall emphasizes the importance of Shakespeare in women's education, not only in terms of formal instruction but also the more indirect influence of the visual arts. She examines the significance of Shakespeare in the careers of women writers and activists, including Elizabeth Barrett Browning, George Eliot, Marie Corelli, Mathilde Blind, and Eleanor Marx. She also investigates the role of Shakespearian performance in the acting careers of Ellen Terry, Sarah Bernhardt, Fanny Kemble, and Helen Faucit. Marshall highlights how women 'translated' Shakespeare through their reading, writing, and performances, reinventing his work as a means of countering prevailing gender stereotypes and facilitating their own careers. 'For these women', she notes, 'the only possibility was to produce readings which ran counter to conservative gender ideologies, and which not only articulated their freedom from the thrall of a prescriptive and limiting Victorian femininity but also freed Shakespeare from the trammels of institutionalised relevance' (p. 44).

Like Gail Marshall, other recent feminist scholars have examined the role of theatre and performance in Victorian women's everyday lives. Amy Lehman, in *Victorian Women and the Theatre of Trance: Mediums, Spiritualists and Mesmerists in Performance*, explores domestic and popular entertainments associated with the spiritualist movement. Female trance performers were able to transgress the boundaries of conventional behaviour by assuming the identities of spirits from the great beyond. Lehman offers a variety of short case studies from England and America to support her argument about the theatricality of trance performances. This includes investigation of the career of British medium Florence Cook, who invoked a fully materialized spirit named Katie King in popular séances during the 1870s. Lehman also includes a short chapter linking spiritualist performance to trends in Victorian theatre, including theories of acting.

On the stage, women's issues were addressed in plays attuned to sexual politics in the popular press. In 'Medea in the Courtroom and on the Stage in Nineteenth-Century London', Nicola Goc examines plays, operas, and burlesques based on Euripides' play performed in London,1834 to 1870 (*AuVSJ* 14[2009] 29–44). At the same time that *Medea* was gaining popularity on the London stage there was an increase in the number of actual infanticides in London. Drawing upon news reports, theatre reviews, and letters to the editor published in the *Times*, Groc demonstrates how the public expressed sympathy for Medea, partly in response to the master performances of actress Madame Adelaide Ristori during the 1850s. Meanwhile, real-life Medeas were treated harshly in the press and the juridical system. Goc speculates that Victorians responded so enthusiastically to *Medea* on the stage because they saw a relationship between 'Medea's plight and that of the destitute, unmarried mothers who, through the introduction of a harsh new law, the 1834 New Poor Law with its iniquitous Bastardy Clause, were driven to kill their babies' (p. 32). It was not until the 1834 Poor Law was amended, forcing men to assume joint responsibility for illegitimate children, that the rate of infanticide dropped and *Medea* finally failed to seize the imagination of London audiences.

In *The Ancient World on the Victorian and Edwardian Stage*, Jeffrey Richards also focuses on the revival of classic drama during the Victorian era. In addition, he focuses on the immense popularity of 'toga plays' set in ancient Rome and Greece, as well as plays set in Egypt, Babylon, and the Holy Land. He begins by examining the popular mania associated with the literature, painting, sculpture, and archaeology of the ancient world. He then analyses the careers of major actor-managers, such as Henry Irving, Wilson Barrett, and Herbert Beerbohm Tree, illuminating their instrumental role in the popularization of ancient texts and motifs on the Victorian stage. Richards also draws attention to how the production of plays set in the ancient world provided an opportunity for actors and managers to address issues of gender, faith, politics, and national identity. 'Interestingly', Richards notes, 'each area of the Ancient World could serve as an arena to discuss contemporary problems that Victorian audiences understood and with which they could engage' (p. 24). In his analysis of the reception history of these plays, Richards draws extensively upon contemporary theatre reviews. He also analyses several plays, including highly popular adaptations of Edward Bulwer-Lytton's novel *The Last Days of Pompeii* and Lew Wallace's novel *Ben-Hur: A Tale of the Christ*. In addition, he examines productions of Shakespeare's plays set in the ancient world, including *Julius Caesar*, *Coriolanus*, and *The Winter's Tale*.

The central role of Shakespeare in the formation of mid- to late Victorian notions of national identity and stagecraft is also addressed in Lynne Walhout Hinojosa's *The Renaissance, English Cultural Nationalism, and Modernism, 1860–1920*. Hinojosa briefly addresses the role of Shakespeare in the *fin-de-siècle* debate over the establishment of a national theatre. The Elizabethan age, she argues, was viewed as the 'model period of national culture to which the present should typologically and allegorically return' (p. 150). She then explores how the elevation of Shakespeare and Renaissance nationalism during the 1890s was reinforced in the years leading up to the First World War.

At the *fin de siècle* the stage became a central locus for addressing the Woman Question. Two recent essays highlight issues of gender and sexuality in the early plays of Bernard Shaw. Bernard Dukore, in his essay 'Boy Gets Girl' (*ShawR* 29[2009] 28–40), recounts stages in the 'duel of sex' between Valentine and Gloria in Shaw's 1897 romantic comedy, *You Never Can Tell*. Charles Carpenter, in '*Homo Philanderus* as Created and Embodied by Bernard Shaw' (*ShawR* 29[2009] 4–16), focuses on *The Philanderer* [1893]. Carpenter acknowledges that the play is to some degree autobiographical, given Shaw's philandering ways during the 1890s. However, he argues that there are a number of key differences between Shaw and Leonard Charteris, the play's protagonist. Unlike Shaw, Charteris was 'rationalist' and 'heartless' in his treatment of women (p. 13).

Heather Anne Wozniak, in her essay 'The Play with a Past: Arthur Wing Pinero's New Drama' (*VLC* 37(2009) 391–409), examines the intersection between the discourse on the New Drama and controversies over the New Woman at the *fin de siècle*. Through her analysis of *The Second Mrs. Tanqueray* [1893] and *The Notorious Mrs. Ebbsmith* [1895], Wozniak argues that modern playwrights, like New Women, faced censorship and narrow-minded conventionalism. Some contemporary critics, such as William Archer, insisted on the masculine vigour of the New Drama, while authors such as Pinero emphasized the compromised status of the playwright. Just as social restrictions prevented fallen women from escaping the past and assuming roles as New Women, so did modern British playwrights face social judgements and literary conventions that impeded the progress of their art. Consequently, Pinero's work suggests that the 'transgressive woman must be killed or maimed, just as the fledgling New Drama finds itself dead and restricted' (p. 404). Although Pinero 'manages to provoke an intellectual engagement with the systems that regulate gender and genre', he is not able to achieve the same degree of autonomy and self-definition as Ibsen, who, in *A Doll's House*, was able to imagine a truly modern New Woman and a truly ground-breaking New Drama (p. 399).

Of all *fin-de-siècle* dramatists, Oscar Wilde continues to receive the most critical attention. Emmanuel Vernadakis focuses on *Salomé* and *La Sainte Courtisane* in his essay, 'Oscar Wilde, Tennessee Williams and the Palimpsest of the Courtesan' (in Letissier, ed., *Rewriting/Reprising: Plural Intertextualities*, pp. 229–40). Vernadakis argues that the courtesan-heroines of these early plays, Salomé and Myrrhina, are complex figures incorporating a variety of literary references and allusions. Just as Wilde 'reprises' a variety of 'historical, philosophical, mystic and literary hypotexts' in his adaptation of the courtesan figure, so, too, does Tennessee Williams evoke Salomé and Myrrhina in his creation of Alma, the courtesan heroine of 'The Yellow Bird' [1947], *Summer and Smoke* [1947], and *The Eccentricities of a Nightingale* [1964] (p. 230).

To what extent do the characters in Wilde's plays express the playwright's own viewpoints? In her essay 'Wilde's "Puritanism": Hester Worsley and the American Dream' (*Wildean* 35[2009] 52–61), Margaret Wright situates *A Woman of No Importance* [1893] within Wilde's broader reflections on America, particularly his idealism about American industriousness and youthful purity. Wright argues that Wilde uses American Hester Worsley as a device for questioning British decadence and arguing for an 'open-minded, tolerant morality rooted in love and compassion' (p. 60). Colleen Denney, in her chapter on Wilde's *A Woman of No Importance* in *Women, Portraiture, and the Crisis of Identity in Victorian England: My Lady Scandalous Reconsidered*, acknowledges that 'Wilde keeps us guessing as to his own views about politics and women's issues in his plays' (p. 213). Yet she also points out that there are a number of topical references in *A Woman of No Importance* that suggest Wilde's awareness of the complex roles and identities women often assumed in *fin-de-siècle* culture. Denney argues that Wilde, through his depiction of Gertrude and Mabel Chiltern in the play, was alluding to real-life controversies surrounding Lady Dilke, Millicent Garrett Fawcett, and Sarah Grand. The play thus serves as commentary on the 'true nature of the characters' self-identities, but also how London society shaped those identities through its somewhat hypocritical expectations' (p. 212).

Gregory Mackie, in his essay 'The Function of Decorum at the Present Time: Manners, Moral Language, and Modernity in "an Oscar Wilde Play"' (*MD* 52[2009] 145–67), focuses on the competing discourses of etiquette and conventional moralism in Wilde's comedies. Mackie situates these works within the broader discourse on etiquette at the *fin de siècle*, which demonstrated how adherence to the rules of decorum might be divorced from moral goodness. Through his use of epigrams and other devices adapted from conduct literature, Wilde exposes the hollowness of conventional morality and proposes an alternative ethical code. Mackie contends that the 'sophistication of good manners' serves to 'interrogate, and to subvert, the generally *un*sophisticated assumptions informing good morals' (p. 150). His comedies thus have much in common with the New Drama of Ibsen and Shaw. However, *The Importance of Being Earnest* differs from Wilde's earlier comedies, Mackie asserts, because it 'offers a less discernible positive alternative to the social norms it critiques' (p. 146).

In *Acting Wilde: Victorian Sexuality, Theatre, and Oscar Wilde*, Kerry Powell examines the variety of Wilde's public performances during his career as well as his exploration of the theatricality of selfhood. 'To appreciate and understand Wilde's performative achievement', Powell argues, 'it is necessary above all to situate him in the controversies of his historical moment regarding gender and subjectivity, while at the same time attending to the archival record of his hesitations and second guesses as a playwright for the late-Victorian stage' (p. 2). As a way of investigating these 'hesitations and second guesses', Powell analyses all existing manuscripts of Wilde's plays as well as a recently discovered transcript of the first Wilde trial. These texts reveal a 'contingent and conflicted' Wilde, who was enmeshed in controversies over gender and sexuality at the *fin de siècle* (p. 3). Powell includes chapters on Wilde's American tour, trials, major plays, and imprisonment. Taken together, these investigations reveal how Wilde's work spoke to the concerns of its time period and 'set the agenda for modern drama' (p. 174).

Recent scholarship on theatre at the *fin de siècle* not only highlights the work of major dramatists such as Wilde, Shaw, and Pinero but also examines important developments in stagecraft. Beth Hannant makes a significant contribution to this field of enquiry in her essay, 'From Gas to Electric Lighting in London Theatres of the Late Nineteenth Century' (in Frayling, King, and Atkinson, eds., *Design and Popular Entertainment*, pp. 15–35). In Great Britain, she notes, theatres were the first buildings to be fitted with electric lighting technology in the 1880s. Hannant acknowledges that it is difficult to theorize the actual use of lighting technology given the situational nature of performance. However, through close analysis of contemporary cultural materials, she is able to make several insightful observations about changes in lighting technology and their likely effect on Victorian audiences. She uses three theatres as case studies: the Gaiety, which was the first London venue to introduce electric light in 1878; the Savoy, which became the first theatre to light an entire building with electric light in 1881; and Henry Irving's Lyceum, which experimented with electric stage lighting in innovative ways. The use of artistic, on-stage lighting effects, she argues, was associated with the emergence of modernist theatre at the *fin de siècle*.

The adaptation of prose works for the Victorian stage remains an area of keen interest within the scholarly community. In *Bluebeard: A Reader's Guide to the English Tradition*, Casie Hermansson traces the history of the Bluebeard fairy tale from Charles Perrault's original 1697 text through three centuries of Bluebeard variants, including a chapter focused on comic adaptations of the fairy tale during the Victorian era. In her investigation of Bluebeard on the Victorian stage, she focuses on popular pantomimes and burlesques, including *Blue Beard: An Extravaganza* [1839] and *Blue Beard Re-Paired* [1866].

Hermansson also focuses on amateur performances based on the Bluebeard tale, including *Blue Beard, or Female Curiosity, a Sensation Drama in Two Acts and Two Scenes* [1871]. The study concludes with an extensive bibliography that includes the titles of several adaptations of Bluebeard for the Victorian stage.

The practice of theatrical adaptation during the Victorian era is also addressed in Patsy Stoneman's 'Inside Out: *Jane Eyre* on the Victorian Stage' (*BS* 34[2009] 147–54). Stoneman builds upon her 2007 anthology of plays, *Jane Eyre on Stage*, by providing analysis of selected adaptations of the novel performed in England and America, from 1848 to 1882. Working within melodramatic conventions, playwrights brought the novel's subtext into the foreground, creating characters who vocalized contemporary concerns about the politics of class and sex. Stoneman focuses on two early adaptations performed in working-class theatres, John Courtney's *Jane Eyre, or the Secrets of Thornfield Manor* [1848] and John Brougham's *Jane Eyre* [1849]. She then briefly addresses later versions, including James Willing's *Jane Eyre, or Poor Relations* [1879] and W.G. Willis's *Jane Eyre* [1882].

Joss Marsh explores the adaptation of Dickens's *A Tale of Two Cities* for the stage in his essay, 'Mimi and the Matinée Idol: Martin-Harvey, Sydney Carton, and the Staging of *A Tale of Two Cities*, 1860–1939' (in Jones, McDonagh, and Mee, eds., *Charles Dickens, A Tale of Two Cities and the French Revolution*, pp. 126–45). Marsh focuses primarily on *The Only Way*, a wildly popular adaptation of *A Tale of Two Cities* that appeared at the Lyceum from 1899 to 1939. Marsh explains the success of the play by suggesting that it resonated with *fin-de-siècle* expressions of nationalist pride while at the same time exploring notions of doubleness and 'masked homosexual desire' (p. 139). Marsh briefly alludes to earlier adaptations of *A Tale of Two Cities*, including *All for Her!*, which was first staged in London in 1875, with revivals in 1884 and 1897.

Dickens's engagement with the Victorian theatre world was perhaps best expressed through his collaborative relationship with Wilkie Collins. In 'Dickens, Collins, and the Influence of the Arctic' (*DSA* 40[2009] 81–93), John Kofron explains the popularity of Collins's *The Frozen Deep* by situating it within popular discourse on Arctic exploration during the mid-Victorian period. A major source of inspiration for *The Frozen Deep* was the failed Franklin expedition of 1845, which Dickens highlighted in an 1854 series of articles in *Household Words*, entitled 'The Lost Arctic Voyagers'. Dickens and Collins adapted motifs from *The Frozen Deep* in their subsequent novels, *A Tale of Two Cities* [1859] and *No Name* [1862]. However, they interpreted the narrative of Arctic adventure in different ways. Kofron notes that 'while Dickens was attracted to Arctic exploration as a moral struggle (resulting in moral victory), it appealed to Collins as an image of quest and defeat' (p. 83).

The subject of theatrical collaboration was the focus of a variety of scholarly studies this year. Michael Holroyd, in his biography, *A Strange Eventful History: The Dramatic Lives of Ellen Terry, Henry Irving, and their Remarkable Families*, tells the stories of Terry's and Irving's intersecting lives and theatrical projects, including their joint rise to fame and their North American tours. Holroyd entwines the biographies of Terry and Irving with the experiences and achievements of their children. Irving's sons followed him into the theatre but never achieved lasting fame. Even more fascinating are Ellen Terry's children, feminist Edy Craig and modernist stage designer Gordon Craig. Holroyd tells these interlocking stories in an engaging way and creates a fully realized portrait of the theatre world during the late Victorian and modernist eras.

It is conventional to refer to 'Gilbert and Sullivan' as an inclusive term denoting one of the most productive collaborations in Victorian theatre history. However, as Regina Oost points out in her book, *Gilbert and Sullivan: Class and the Savoy Tradition, 1875–1896*, the success of Gilbert and Sullivan's comic operas depended not only on synergy between the two artists but also on the shrewd business and marketing practices of their collaborators. Richard D'Oyly Carte, manager of the Savoy, played a crucial role in the success of the operettas, helping to attract affluent audiences and establish the theatre as a national cultural phenomenon. Through her reading of diverse cultural materials, including advertisements, playbills, and account books, Oost situates the success of Gilbert and Sullivan within the broader context of the West End theatrical marketplace, which constituted a 'small, competitive band of entrepreneurs' (p. 4). Like other theatres of the era, the Savoy attempted to establish its own brand, thus distinguishing itself from other theatres while attempting to ensure 'repeat patronage' and a 'family countenance' (p. 12).

The trend towards situating the Gilbert and Sullivan operettas within a broader network of cultural meanings and materials is also apparent in Monica Cohen's 'Noblemen Who Have Gone Wrong: Novel-Reading Pirates and the Victorian Stage in Gilbert and Sullivan's *The Pirates of Penzance*' (*TSLL* 51[2009] 341–60). Cohen explores the meanings of 'piracy' in the play, focusing specifically on the ways in which it highlighted controversies over copyright infringement while at the same time engaging in 'creative borrowing' from the novels of Dickens and other sources (p. 342). *The Pirates of Penzance* was created as a direct response to the explosion in the number of pirated versions of *H.M.S. Pinafore* on the British and American stage. By the end of the operetta, she argues, 'what substitutes for any securing of intellectual property is a representation of Englishness that is self-consciously and exuberantly ironic, anticipatory even of twentieth-century camp' (p. 342).

The role of children on the Victorian stage has been an area of keen scholarly interest in recent years. In *Artful Dodgers: Reconceiving the Golden Age of Children's Literature*, Marah Gubar challenges scholarly understanding of the Victorian cult of childhood by arguing that juvenile literature of the period both asserted and questioned the ideal of childhood innocence. While there were undeniably efforts to preserve childhood as a state of purity separate from adulthood, Victorians nonetheless questioned whether such a separation was natural or realistic. Gubar includes two chapters on children's theatre that explore the development of children's drama and associated controversies over the appropriateness of children's roles as actors and audiences in the Victorian theatre world. The popularity of child actors and children's theatre, she argues, not only reflects a cultural fascination with childhood innocence but also an obsession with childhood precocity. In this way, children's literature for the stage tended to 'ignore, deny, or unsettle the adult–child binary that activists were struggling to establish' (p. 180). She includes extended analysis of J.M. Barrie's *Peter Pan* and Frances Hodgson Burnett's *Little Lord Fauntleroy*. These works are often viewed as key texts in the establishment of the children's play as a distinct theatrical genre. Yet, as Gubar points out, both authors seemed intent on 'keeping the line between childhood and adulthood blurry' (p. 175).

New reference works in the field of Victorian drama include Angela Courtney's *Nineteenth-Century British Dramatists*, vol. 344 in the Dictionary of Literary Biography series. Contributors include useful biographical overviews and bibliographies for each of the thirty-five playwrights featured in the volume. Also noteworthy is the republication of Allardyce Nicoll's classic reference, *A History of English Drama, 1660–1900*. Volumes 4 and 5 of the series, now available in paperback, cover the early and late nineteenth century. Nicoll provides a wealth of information about theatrical genres, venues, actors, audiences, and managers on the Victorian stage. Volume 6 provides an eminently useful catalogue of plays performed or produced in England between 1660 and 1900.

5. Periodicals and Publishing History

Work this year has covered a great deal of ground across a range of literary genres and subjects. Weighty tomes of fine academic quality covering Victorian publishing history, periodicals studies, and print culture were also in abundance. One fine example was Dallas Liddle's *The Dynamics of Genre: Journalism and the Practice of Literature in Mid-Victorian Britain*. Liddle makes a persuasive argument for re-examining the role of Victorian journalism in the 1850s and 1860s in the formation of key literary works and genres from that period. Significant figures of the period, Charles Dickens, George Eliot, Anthony Trollope, and Harriet Martineau among others, engaged directly with journalistic forms and material, adapting or rejecting its techniques in their literary fiction. However, Liddle argues, under-appreciated has been the manner in which periodical genres competed ideologically and economically with literary genres, and the way in which mid-century literary production responded to the challenges of the cascade of text created as literary journal production expanded exponentially.

The same theme is taken up by Matthew Rubery in *The Novelty of Newspapers: Victorian Fiction after the Invention of the News*. Rubery uses case studies of Dickens, Trollope, Conrad, and Henry James, among others, to follow through on the place of journalistic conventions in contemporary fiction. Rubery also draws attention to the significant role of peripheral periodical and newspaper material—advertisements, correspondence columns, obituaries and personal notices—in the plotlines of popular fiction of the later nineteenth century. The insertion of journalistic text and items into fiction would find clear expression in such popular texts as Conan Doyle's *Sherlock Holmes* stories, or Mary Elizabeth Braddon's sensation novel *Lady Audley's Secret*. Rubery also offers useful insight into the 'interview' genre that would dominate news pages in the last quarter of the century, and the filtration of its stylistic conventions into the fiction of Henry James, whose disapproval of contemporary journalistic practices and invasion of personal privacy manifested itself in the many negative characterizations of news reporters present throughout his work.

Print as a site of intellectual contestation is not new in academic studies of publishing and the periodical press. Adrian Johns, in *Piracy: The Intellectual Property Wars from Gutenberg to Gates*, however, has garnered much praise for his sweep through space and time and his wide-ranging study of 500 years of piracy in the scientific, cultural, and commodified spheres. Print features large in his debates, which draw our attention to the parallels that exist between past attempts to curb the pirating of literary texts and current efforts to contain piracy of digital media. Some superb case studies uncover forgotten examples of intellectual property battles, particularly during the nineteenth-century period of commercial and technological expansion.

A significant addition to our knowledge of small magazine and periodical studies is Peter Brooker and Andrew Thacker's magnificently edited compendium, *The Oxford Critical and Cultural History of Modernist Magazines*, vol. 1: *Britain and Ireland 1880–1955*. The contributors to this work provide much-needed context for evaluating the cultural history and production background from which modernist and postmodernist periodicals emerged. Though much of the volume is focused on twentieth-century entrants to the little magazine market, there are significant sections on Victorian and *fin-de-siècle* precursors that offer valuable material on both known and less recognized examples of literary periodical production. Contributions in these sections include the following from well-known experts in the field of periodical studies: Kyriaki Hadjiafxendi and John Plunkett, 'The Pre-History of the "Little Magazines", (pp. 33–50); Marysa Demoor, 'In the Beginning, There Was *The Germ*: The Pre-Raphaelites and "Little Magazines"' (pp. 51–68); Laurel Brake, 'Aestheticism and Decadence: *The Yellow Book* (1894–7), *The Chameleon* (1894), and *The Savoy* (1896)' (pp. 76–100); David Peters Corbett, 'Symbolism in British "Little Magazines": *The Dial* (1889–97), *The Pageant* (1896–7), and *The Dome* (1897–1900)' (pp. 101–19); and Imogen Hart, '"The Arts and Crafts Movement": *The Century Guild Hobby Horse* (1884–94), *The Evergreen* (1895–7), and *The Acorn* (1905–6)' (pp. 120–44).

Some of the same contributors also appear in *The Lure of Illustration in the Nineteenth Century: Picture and Press*, a multifaceted collection of essays focused, as the editors Laurel Brake and Marysa Demoor suggest in their valuable introduction, on text and image, text alongside image, and text *as* image. The focus of the fourteen essays featured in this wide-ranging volume is on the shifts in illustrations featured in nineteenth-century magazines, whether of the weekly, monthly, or quarterly format. From wood engravings and steel plates of the earlier nineteenth century, to photography and decorative art featured at the century's end, the contributions commingle technological detail with the form, function, and editorial constructions evident in the pages of key examples of the periodical press. As the volume clearly demonstrates, research into the porous and interlocking links between textual and visual representations, whether of fiction, news, or non-fictional prose, has progressed remarkably since studies of the form and function of the periodical press began in earnest in the 1960s. A listing of the contributions is as follows: Brian Maidment, 'The *Illuminated Magazine* and the Triumph of Wood Engraving' (pp. 17–39); Sarah Dewis, 'Accurate Dreams or Illustrations of Desire: Image and Text in the *Gardener's Magazine* (1826–44), Edited by John Claudius Loudon' (pp. 40–59); David E. Latané, Jr., 'Alaric "Attila" Watts, the *Fraser's* Portrait Gallery, and William Maginn' (pp. 60–75); Malcolm Chase, '"The Original to the Life": Portraiture and the *Northern Star*' (pp. 76–96); Beryl Gray, 'Man and Dog: Text and Illustration in Dickens's *The Old Curiosity Shop*' (pp. 97–118); Joanne Shattock, 'Elizabeth Gaskell: Journalism and Letters' (pp. 119–27); Lorna Huett, 'Among the Unknown Public: *Household Words*, *All the Year Round* and the Mass-Market Weekly Periodical in the Mid-Nineteenth Century' (pp. 128–48); Frank Murray, 'Often Taken where a Tract is Refused: T.B. Smithies, the *British Workman*, and the Popularisation of the Religious and Temperance Message' (pp. 149–67); Laurie Garrison, 'Seductive Visual Studies: Scientific Focus and Editorial Control in *The Woman in White* and *All the Year Round*' (pp. 168–83); Christopher Kent, 'Depicting Gentlemen's Fashions in the *Tailor and Cutter*, 1866–1900' (pp. 184–202); James Mussell, 'Science and the Timeliness of Reproduced Photographs in the Late Nineteenth-Century Periodical Press' (pp. 203–19); Linda K. Hughes, 'Aestheticism on the Cheap: Decorative Art, Art Criticism, and Cheap Paper in the 1890s' (pp. 220–33); Anne Humpherys, 'Putting Women in the Boat in the *Idler* (1892–1898)' (pp. 234–50); and Edward H. Cohen, 'Images of Englishness: The *Daily Chronicle* and "Proposed Laureates" to Succeed Tennyson' (pp. 251–63).

Science in periodicals is the subject of two useful journal articles produced this year by James Mussell, who featured in the collection just noted. In 'Arthur Cowper Ranyard, "Knowledge" and the Reproduction of Astronomical Photographs in the Late Nineteenth-Century Periodical Press' (*BJHS* 42[2009] 345–80), he examines the reproduction of astronomical photographs in support of scientific pieces in the popular monthly *Knowledge*. Founded in 1889 by Richard Anthony Proctor, under the editorship of Arthur Cowper Ranyard the journal increasingly featured high-quality collotype images to illustrate its scientific arguments. The form in which he manipulated such material to support contentions about the formation of the Milky Way, however, created great dispute amongst the scientific community about the validity of such supposedly objective material in support of contentious scientific claims.

Similarly, disputes over how to represent material that scientists imagined but did not know in concrete form thread their way through Mussell's piece, 'Cohering Knowledge in the Nineteenth Century: Form, Genre and Periodical Studies' (*VPR* 42[2009] 93–103). Mussell argues that particular attention should be paid to forms through which journals framed the scientific events that they reported. The article uses as case study John Tyndall's 'Discourse on the Scientific Use of the Imagination' to argue that imaginative recreations of scientific unknowns involved substituting system and structure for natural disorder. Scientific journalism filtered complexity to fit into allocated spaces in newspaper columns, in the process imposing order and familiar structures on previously unknowable types of information. In this way, as Mussell concludes, the forms of the press operated in a similar fashion to the scientific imagination, displacing the new with the familiar, the unknown with the yet-to-be-known, and chaos with system.

Technology and print culture come together in Mike Esbester's interesting piece on railway timetables, 'Designing Time: The Design and Use of Nineteenth-Century Transport Timetables' (*Journal of Design History* 22[2009] 91–113). Esbester tackles reader reception, analysing how the complexity of designing printed timetable information for railway users was shaped by both functionality and reader interaction. Here, societal notions of time and space met in printed form. The result was digests and publications that shaped the 'functional literacy' and 'functional reading' of their users, and provided tools for individuals to navigate daily lives increasingly dominated by schedules and an industrialized, time-bound society.

Another example of note of a scientifically focused study of Victorian 'new media' and periodicals is Paul Fyfe's award-winning graduate essay, 'The Random Selection of Victorian New Media' (*VPR* 42[2009] 1–23). Fyfe's study of Victorian appraisals of popular literature suggests that several commentators adopted a process of random selection to generalize about its contents. Faced with an unrelenting flood of what was variously called 'cheap literature', 'popular literature', and 'reading for the million', critics sought to make sense of it by dipping into this cornucopia in arbitrary fashion, much in the manner of current scientific random sampling. Equally the panicked mode of response among such appraisals echoes contemporary concerns about the profusion and access of electronic materials, a salutary lesson in the way one can find resonances of past debates in modern settings.

Mathematics features in two strong contributions this year. First there is Joe Albree and S.H. Brown, '"A valuable monument of mathematical genius": *The Ladies' Diary* (1704–1840)' (*Historia Mathematica* 36[2009] 10–47). Their piece looks at mathematics work featured throughout the long publishing history of *The Ladies' Diary*. From a position of strength and leadership in the early development of British mathematics, *The Ladies' Diary* would slowly move towards the sidelines of scientific journals as the evolution of mathematical theory, and the competition from professionalized journals in the field, overtook it. Maths also features in Timothy David Harding, 'Kings and Queens at Home: A Short History of the Chess Column in Nineteenth-Century English Periodicals' (*VPR* 42[2009] 359–91). Columns catering to chess in English periodicals grew from a feature seen in a few titles at mid-century into one that was almost required reading in a weekly paper by the 1880s. Widely circulated journals such as the *Illustrated London News* included popular chess columns, with several targeting new audiences such as young readers and women. As Harding notes, the interest in chess was partly driven by the way the columns approached the game, showing examples of good play, offering advice of various kinds, running competitions, and providing interactive puzzles for readers to solve.

Punch gets its share of analysis in several pieces this year. Among them, two works by Henry Miller, including 'The Problem with *Punch*' (*HistR* 82:ccxvi[2009] 285–302). Here, Miller contextualizes *Punch*'s visual imagery in relation to that of other British periodicals from the 1860s through to the

1900s. His argument is that *Punch*, as opposed to some of its rival contemporaries, maintained a clearly metropolitan outlook, ignoring provincial life in favour of material aimed at a middle-class audience steeped in London-centred culture. Miller also explores the place of *Punch* artist John Leech in creating its metropolitan imagery in 'John Leech and the Shaping of the Victorian Cartoon: The Context of Respectability' (*VPR* 42[2009] 267–91). Leech's influential work for *Punch* set standards and greatly shaped what Victorian readers expected comic cartoons to look like. Miller solidly contextualizes Leech's work within the publishing contexts of the period, noting how the development of wood engraving and the demand for visual imagery in such journals worked to enhance the financial, social, and artistic position of artists such as Leech.

Women and periodical work remain at the forefront of research this year. Among notable examples are both generalist and specialist case studies covering well-known and forgotten voices of Victorian literary culture. A key text that revitalizes debate about the development of nineteenth-century literary careers for women is Linda H. Peterson's *Becoming a Woman of Letters: Myths of Authorship and Facts of the Victorian Market*. The bulk of the work is taken up with case studies of six female literary figures or their works at key points between 1830 and 1900: Harriet Martineau, Mary and Anna Mary Howitt, Elizabeth Gaskell's biographical treatment of Charlotte Brontë, Charlotte Riddell, Alice Meynell, and Mary Cholmondeley. Each section is lucidly presented and underpinned by in-depth scholarly archival work. Most valuable is the way in which such authorial activity is contextualized within current scholarly work on the literary marketplace, in which literary work is seen as a consequence of a variety of social, cultural, and economic factors. The work is a valuable addition to Victorian periodical studies, as well as a welcome insight into the varied fortunes of women positioning themselves within evolving professional structures.

Cheryl Wilson, in 'Placing the Margins: Literary Reviews, Pedagogical Practices, and the Canon of Victorian Women's Writing' (*TSWL* 28[2009] 57–74), takes a strongly literary critical approach in her analysis of sample literary reviews and critical essays by Victorian women literary stalwarts such as George Eliot, Margaret Oliphant, and Anne Thackeray Ritchie. Her argument rehearses by now standard themes that periodical press work should be situated within the contexts of canon studies and reception theory to inform contemporary pedagogical practices. In contrast, Sally Mitchell's 'Ephemeral Journalism and its Uses: Lucie Cobbe Heaton Armstrong (1851–1907)' (*VPR* 42[2009] 81–92), explores the challenges of unearthing information about freelance contributors to general publications of the period. Some of the detective work needed to recuperate the work of jobbing women journalists is now made easier through online access to scanned pages of nineteenth-century journals and periodicals.

Author–editor relationships are fruitfully explored in Deborah Logan's '"I am, my dear slanderer, your faithful malignant demon": Harriet Martineau and the *Westminster Review*'s Comtist Coterie' (*VPR* 42[2009] 171–91). Between 1852 and 1858, Harriet Martineau contributed to the *Westminster Review* under John Chapman's editorship. Her literary connection with the *Westminster Review* interwove itself with her role as member of Chapman's socio-literary circle, and her financial role as a key investor who, for a time, held its mortgage. Logan fruitfully explains the repercussions of Martineau's financial and professional involvement with the Chapman coterie and journal, which ultimately proved ill-advised. The results make for a dramatic story intermingling the public and private, familial and professional, the morally high-handed and the scandalous.

The *Westminster Review* also featured large in George Eliot's early working life, as Fionnuala Dillane discusses in 'Re-reading George Eliot's "Natural History": Marian Evans, "the People", and the Periodical' (*VPR* 42[2009] 244–66). In this case, Dillane offers a case study of George Eliot's 'The Natural History of German Life', which appeared in the *Westminster Review* in July 1856. The piece plays a significant part in George Eliot studies for its famous articulation of her 'doctrine of sympathy', which underpinned the author's efforts at literary realism in her novels. Dillane argues that in fact the piece reveals more about Eliot's discomfort with reviewing and with her place in the pages of the *Westminster*: a fractured piece, ironic, evasive, and subversive, it compares quite strongly with George Henry Lewes's contribution in the same issue of the *Review*, written more in line with standard nineteenth-century reviewing traditions.

The editorial mission of women is drawn to our attention in Beth Palmer's '"Chieftaness," "Great Duchess," "Editress! Mysterious Being!": Performing Editorial Identities in Florence Marryat's *London Society* Magazine' (*VPR* 42[2009] 136–54). In this case, archival correspondence is mined for insight into how mostly male contributors constructed their relationship with Florence Marryat in her capacity as editor of the shilling monthly *London Society* between 1872 and 1876. The results interestingly demonstrate a negotiation of gendered roles, played out in the type of articles and illustrations subsequently featured by Marryat in the journal. Carol Hanberry Mackay turns our attention to the editorial work of Annie Besant in 'A Journal of Her Own: The Rise and Fall of Annie Besant's *Our Corner*' (*VPR* 42[2009] 359–91). Besant founded and edited the monthly journal *Our Corner* from 1883 to 1888. Her struggle to issue a journal that reflected her socialist convictions yet provided accessible combinations of material on politics, science, literature, and the arts did not fare as well as could be hoped. As her hopes and beliefs in social reform began to diminish, and with finances too tenuous to support journal production, Besant terminated its publication, leaving editorial work behind to concentrate on promoting theosophy in print and in person.

In Romantic-period studies, discussions of publishing history and the periodical press are integral to the field, and this year was no exception. Several publications from 2009 are also relevant to Victorian studies. A useful entry this year is a collection of essays focused on the early history of the *Encyclopedia Britannica*, Frank A. Kafker and Jeff Loveland's edited *The Early Britannica: The Growth of an Outstanding Encyclopedia*. Though focused primarily on the late eighteenth-century development of this crucial reconfiguration of historical compendia, the contributors do move into the early nineteenth century to offer archivally based insights into how the early editors of the *Encyclopedia* shaped its contents, and how such material shaped later British culture. Other decent examples of new work on Romanticism and print include William Christie, 'Francis Jeffrey in Recent Whig Interpretations of Romantic Literary History' (*ELH* 76[2009] 577–97). Christie looks at the *Edinburgh Review* and its chief architect through political and trenchant literary lenses. Theoretically dense but informed, the piece suggests that there are key binary oppositions we cannot avoid when studying the material in its pages, between Whig and Tory politics, Scotland and England, critic and poet, revolutionary and romantic. David Stewart points our attention to the conservative-tinged material of a successor journal, *Blackwood's Magazine*, in 'Filling the Newspaper Gap: Leigh Hunt, *Blackwood's*, and the Development of the Miscellany' (*VPR* 42[2009] 155–70). From its 'relaunch' in October 1817, *Blackwood's Magazine* strove to situate its material as a staunch, conservative yet reactionary bulwark against the reformist Leigh Hunt and the 'Cockney' school of writers grouped around his *Examiner* newspaper. Stewart convincingly argues that, despite the obvious antagonism, the model of 'miscellaneity' evident in Hunt's innovatory journalism for *The Examiner* would directly influence *Blackwood's* content and organization. The influence would remain unacknowledged.

Two monographs produced this year on topics of Romanticism and print culture are also worthy of note. First, in *Scottish Men of Letters and the New Public Sphere, 1802–1834*, Barton Swaim makes a coherent argument for re-evaluating the significance of Scots in the shaping of British periodical and intellectual culture in the first third of the nineteenth century. Whether as editors, contributors, or supporters of both London- and Scottish-based periodical reviews and magazines, Scots were significantly involved in shaping material read by cultural elites of the time. Swaim takes us through some of the key examples and texts in which Scots writers and editors were engaged, and posits that through such means a British 'public sphere' was shaped through which Scots were able to participate in a manner not available to them politically. Mark Schoenfield draws on similar territory in *British Periodicals and Romantic Identity: The 'Literary Lower Empire'*. However, rather than focusing on individuals and national identifiers, Schoenfield approaches similar questions through examining in the first section of his work the key periodicals emanating from or in response to Scottish input, namely the *Edinburgh Review*, *Blackwood's Magazine*, and the Scots-founded but London-based *Quarterly Review*. The latter half of the volume concentrates on individual critics and figures who loom large in the history of periodical production during this period, namely, Hazlitt, Byron, and James Hogg. The work is theoretically dense but important in its conclusions about the place of periodical culture in consolidating literary reputations and shaping cultural understanding of Romanticism as a literary movement and force in intellectual terms.

Several works and articles from this year tackle what is becoming a major focus in Victorian studies: the interface between journalism, culture, and the periodical press. E.M. Palmegiano offers a mini-survey in 'The First Common Market: The British Press on Nineteenth-Century European Journalism' (*Media History Monographs* 11[2009] 1–44). Her piece draws on material from forty-four British periodicals to offer general insights into the themes prevailing in reportage of European journalism. Most articles draw attention to the state of journalism in France, with Germany, Italy, and Russia close behind in popularity. Among the general themes emerging from this survey is the concentration on the tension between governments and journalists, the character of the press and its personnel, and the professionalization of journalism from a sideline to a paying career.

European journalism marked the start of the career of George Augustus Sala, a key mid-Victorian journalist and critic. Sala's career is partly studied in Catherine Waters, '"Much of Sala, and but little of Russia": "A Journey Due North", *Household Words*, and the Birth of a Special Correspondent' (*VPR* 42[2009] 305–23). Sala's journalistic career had its start through assignment by Charles Dickens as a special correspondent for *Household Words* covering Russia post-Crimean War. His twenty-two contributions to the journal, which appeared in weekly instalments from 4 October 1856 to 14 March 1857, are interesting for their vibrant, ethnographically informed style, setting a tone to be found in other travel writing of the period.

War and its ephemeral traces in popular culture are the fascinating subject of Richard Fulton's 'The Sudan Sensation of 1898' (*VPR* 42[2009] 37–63). After a two-year campaign culminating in September 1898, an Anglo-Egyptian force under Lord Herbert H. Kitchener defeated the army of the Khalifa at his capital of Omdurman in the Sudan. Fulton deftly explores how public fascination with the event, which had been widely reported in the British press, found further expression in an insatiable demand for merchandise associated with it, an opportunistic movement of geopolitical events from war zones into popular-culture settings.

Victorian seaside and holiday reading are pleasurably explored in Margaret Beetham, '"Oh! I do like to be beside the seaside!": Lancashire Seaside Publications' (*VPR* 42[2009] 24–36). In the late nineteenth century Manchester's vigorous periodical press included publications which offered appropriate reading for the seaside holiday. Working-class families that began going on holiday to British beaches could be found bringing with them annuals and reprints of stories from such publications as *Ben Brierley's Journal*. These offered themselves both as representations of the time/space of the seaside holiday and as part of its pleasures.

On the topic of readership, how the concept of the 'teenage market' could be located in mid-Victorian periodical production is Louis James's intriguing premise in '"Now inhale the gas": Interactive Readership in Two Victorian Boys' Periodicals, 1855–1870' (*VPR* 42[2009] 64–80). James draws out examples from the pioneering *Boy's Own Magazine* [1855–74], edited by Samuel Beeton, and contrasts them with the *Boys' Journal* [1863–71], to demonstrate how both set out to cater to perceived needs of a teenage male readership, using a mixture of tales of adventure, popular science, targeted competitions, and sympathetic correspondence columns.

Reading of a different sort is explored in Sharon Murphy's empirically informed and detailed piece, 'Imperial Reading? The East India Company's Lending Libraries for Soldiers, *c.*1819–1834' (*BH* 12[2009] 74–99). Murphy draws on lending-library records of military stations overseas to illustrate that readership for popular British fiction was not only aimed at a 'reading public' confined to the British Isles. The correspondence between the novel and empire-building is most interestingly seen in such reading outposts, which have been little explored for their records of reader interaction.

A more unusual subject is that of Michael Heller's 'British Company Magazines, 1878–1939: The Origins and Functions of House Journals in Large-Scale Organisations' (*MedHis* 15[2009] 143–66). Heller draws valuable attention to the early history of corporate journals and internal newsletters, which emerged in the 1880s partly as a consequence of the burgeoning contemporary growth in weekly, monthly, and quarterly magazines catering to both popular and professional interests. The area is under-researched and deserving of more study.

In the area of publishing history, Walter Scott featured in several strong pieces this year. Among them were Emily B. Todd, 'Establishing Routes for Fiction in the United States: Walter Scott's Novels and the Early Nineteenth-Century American Publishing Industry' (*BH* 12[2009] 100–28). Todd provides valuable details of how Walter Scott's work was marketed in the US, and how, via such methods as cheap pirate editions produced for example by the Boston-based firm Wells and Lilly, they were incorporated into the American cultural imagination. In 'Sir Walter Scott, *The Vision of Don Roderick*, 1811' (*JEBS* 4[2009] 69–72), Brian McMullin offers a short bibliographical comparison between the 1811 first Edinburgh and London printings of Walter Scott's dramatic poem, noting differences between the two that have been previously unchronicled by Scott scholars.

Andrew Nash offers some interesting observations about Kailyard literature and publishing contexts in 'Ian Maclaren: Some Notes on the Publication of his Work from the Files of A.P. Watt, Literary Agent' (*JEBS* 4[2009] 49–59). Drawing on unpublished letters and documents from the A.P. Watt archives in the University of North Carolina, Chapel Hill, Nash traces the publishing history, popularity, and significant income derived from the Scottish Kailyard works of Ian Maclaren from 1896 through to the interwar years, showing how strong sales attested to a public enthusiasm for the type of material produced in this genre by Maclaren.

History and print feature very strongly in work produced this year. A fine example is Leslie Howsam's *Past into Print: The Publishing of History in Britain, 1850–1950*. Howsam takes as her subject the publishing of history books in Britain (or more accurately England, as she excludes Welsh and Scottish examples) during the nineteenth and early twentieth centuries. Though acknowledging at the start that this is more a work in progress than a final statement on the matter (the linked chapters evolved from a series of lectures delivered in Oxford in 2006), this work is challenging and insightful. It aims to draw together history, book history, and bibliography by reminding us that the study of the material production and shifting themes of past historical texts is a neglected area of historical enquiry in contemporary historical circles. Howsam concentrates her efforts on case studies gleaned from the archives of Macmillan, Cambridge University Press, and Oxford University Press. Covering a sweep of late nineteenth- and early twentieth-century publishing history, she pinpoints an interesting shift in the production of such textbooks, from anecdote-led accounts to scientifically aimed, objective, and rigorous presentations of historical material. She concludes very persuasively that formulas that are enshrined in current history textbook production have their roots in actions taken in the past. The general point is significant: history textbooks, much like any other work subject to commercial concerns, were actively shaped by mediating agencies and factors we would do well to interrogate more closely.

Similar interrogations are evident in contributions to John Hinks, Catherine Armstrong and Matthew Day's edited volume, *Periodicals and Publishers: The Newspaper and Journal Trade, 1740–1914*. The latest in the Print Network series, the volume offers a mixture of fine-grained, localized case studies ranging across the eighteenth and nineteenth centuries, with one exception focused on the early twentieth century, Stephen Colclough's telling example of 1914 print disruption, '"The Retail Newsagents of Lancashire ARE ON STRIKE": The Dispute between the Lancashire Retail Newsagents and the "Northern Wholesalers", February–September 1914' (pp. 203–22). The tone and focus of the volume are set by Iain Beavan's general piece, 'Forever Provincial? A North British Lament' (pp. 1–20), which wrestles with what the term 'provincial book trade' actually stands for in current book history terms. As Beavan persuasively argues, it is a misnomer to label as provincial all non-London book-trade activity in the eighteenth and nineteenth centuries. The term, suggesting a passive role for booksellers as mere conduits of London-produced material, ignores the many examples (some documented in this volume of essays) of regional printers whose influence and trade sales extended beyond the provinces. The volume is divided equally between studies of book-trade personnel in Scotland, Ireland, and the north of England and historical accounts of small but telling moments of conflict in periodical trade circles. In the former cluster, studies of particular interest to the nineteenth-century scholar include Elizabeth Tilley's solidly researched 'National Enterprise and Domestic Periodicals in Nineteenth-Century Ireland' (pp. 185–202), a case study of staunchly nationalist businessman James Duffy, responsible for launching key domestic periodicals in Dublin between 1830 and 1870. An intriguing piece is Ria Snowdon's 'Sarah Hodgson and the Business of Print, 1800–1822' (pp. 119–38), an astute appraisal of a Newcastle-based female printer and proprietor who between 1800 and 1822 ran one of the most significant weekly newspapers of the region, the *Newcastle Chronicle*. Less successful in this respect was George Miller of Dunbar, the subject of Graham Hogg's 'Latter Struggles in the Life of a Provincial Bookseller and Printer: George Miller of Dunbar, Scotland' (pp. 139–60), which begins as a summary of extant manuscript material and concludes more usefully as a study of the print trade career of a little-known early nineteenth-century Scottish provincial town bookseller and printer. Michael Powell and Terry Wyke shift the focus in 'Manchester Men and Manchester Magazines: Publishing Periodicals in the Provinces in the Nineteenth Century' (pp. 161–84). Their piece makes a convincing case for the argument that during the nineteenth century Manchester, despite its regional status and distance from the declared centre of journalism (London), could lay claim to being an influential and vibrant participant in British periodical culture.

Their comparative survey of the number of journals founded and produced in Manchester in the 1830s, 1850s, and 1880s demonstrates a substantive rise in titles and influence, culminating in the serial publication and family journal title boom of the 1880s, of which George Newnes's *Tit-Bits*, founded in 1881, was the best known. Where such material might have been distributed and how is the focus of Lisa Peters and Kath Skinners' detailed quantitative survey of newspaper distribution networks across the Wrexham region in the second half of the nineteenth century, 'Selling the News: Distributing Wrexham's Newspapers, 1850–1900' (pp. 203–23). This playful piece uncovers startling examples of unconventional newsagents, including coachmen, a Baptist minister, a ship chandler and nail maker, and a coroner. Regrettably, little information is provided as to how these balanced news distribution with their regular positions.

Other titles worth noting in the area of publishing history include Richard Abel and Gordon Graham's edited volume *Immigrant Publishers: The Impact of Expatriate Publishers in Britain and America in the 20th Century*. Drawn from at times anecdotal features published in the journal *Logos*, and focused mainly on mid- to late twentieth-century publishers such as Robert Maxwell, Paul Hamlyn, George Weidenfeld, and Jacques Schiffrin, there is some context provided linking contemporary practitioners with Victorian exponents. Weightier and more valuable is the *Cambridge History of the Book in Britain*, volume 6: *1830–1914*, edited by David McKitterick. This multi-authored compendium digs out valuable information contextualizing print culture activity during one of the most significant technological periods of British book production. A plethora of detail on the technology and production of books during the Victorian period is accompanied by valuable contributions on authorship, readership, distribution, literary and non-literary textual production, serials, and illustrations. The volume takes its place as another landmark example of national book history work that both explicates current knowledge on the subject and points towards areas for further expansion.

More focused but nevertheless an important addition to our understanding of author–publisher interaction in the nineteenth century is Leila Koivunen's study of the production of images for African exploration narratives, *Visualizing Africa in Nineteenth-Century British Travel Accounts*. The work ably links cultural history, visual culture, and book history concerns through consideration of the publishing, editorial, and production processes and factors that shaped the visual content of key texts of British encounters with Africa by the likes of David Livingstone, John Hanning Speke, Samuel Baker, and Henry Stanley, among many. It deserves attention for the careful and valuable way in which Koivunen contextualizes the development and publication of such material within contemporary anthropological, social, political, and cultural arenas.

Before concluding it is worth pointing out Palgrave Macmillan's continuing commitment to issuing useful studies on the nineteenth-century print culture and the periodical press. Four good examples under their imprint demonstrate this continuing support. Alberto Gabriele's *Reading Popular Culture in Victorian Print: Belgravia and Sensationalism* provides a great deal of new material and insight into Mary Elizabeth Braddon's editorial management of the journal *Belgravia* and her approach to producing, advertising and promoting its sensational fiction contents. Kathryn Ledbetter's insightful *British Victorian Women's Periodicals: Beauty, Civilization and Poetry* devotes attention to how advice on style, taste, and approach to social respectability, dispensed in the pages of periodicals, was also refracted in the poetry appearing alongside such didactic material, making periodicals a significant space for assessing the reading practices of women and their assimilation of literary and non-literary texts into their everyday lives. Tara Moore's thoughtful *Victorian Christmas in Print* delves into the variety of ways in which constructions of Christmas were shaped by both texts and genres, whether in the periodical whimsies in *Punch*, or the use of poetry to add a contemplative and reflective tone to periodical spaces, or Dickens's fashioning of the public appetite for Christmas ghost stories in *Household Words* and *All the Year Round*. Finally, there is *Literary Tourism and Nineteenth-Century Culture*, ably edited by Nicola J. Watson. The volume includes some interesting pieces of book history and periodical studies interest, notably Julian North, 'Literary Biography and the House of the Poet' (pp. 49–62); Barbara Schaff, 'John Murray's *Handbooks to Italy*: Making Tourism Literary' (pp. 106–18); and Margaret D. Stetz, 'Selling Literary Tourism in *The Bookman*' (pp. 119–27).

Finally, journal articles with relevance to periodical and publishing history studies that have appeared this year and not yet mentioned include the following: Peter Blake, 'George Augustus Sala and the English Middle-Class View of America' (*19* 9[2009] www.19.bbk.ac.uk); Anthony Cummins, 'Emile Zola's Cheap English Dress: The Vizetelly Translations, Late-Victorian Print Culture, and the Crisis of Literary Value' (*RES* 60[2009] 108–32); Jonathan V Farina, '"A Certain Shadow": Personified Abstractions and the Form of *Household Words*' (*VPR* 42[2009] 392–415); Isobel Hurst, 'Ancient and Modern Women in the *Woman's World*' (*VS* 52[2009] 42–51); Barbara Leckie, '"A Preface is Written to the Public": Print Censorship, Novel Prefaces, and the Construction of a New Reading Public in Late-Victorian England' (*VLC* 37[2009] 447–62); Mary Elizabeth Leighton and Lisa Surridge, 'The Transatlantic *Moonstone*: A Study of the Illustrated Serial in *Harper's Weekly*' (*VPR* 42[2009] 207–43); Leah Price, 'From the History of a Book to a "History of the Book"' (*Rep* 108[2009] 120–38); Sharon Ragaz, 'The Spurious *Tales of My Landlord*' (*Library* 10[2009] 41–56); and Virginia Zimmerman, '"The Weird Message from the Past": Material Epistemologies of Past, Present, and Future in the *Nineteenth Century*' (*VPR* 42[2009] 114–35).

Books Reviewed

Abel, Richard, and Gordon Graham, eds. *Immigrant Publishers: The Impact of Expatriate Publishers in Britain and America in the 20th Century*. Transaction. [2009] pp. 222. £35 ISBN 9 7814 1280 8712.

Adams, James Eli. *A History of Victorian Literature*. Wiley. [2009] pp. 480. $131.53 ISBN 978 0 6312 2082 8.

Alexander, Edward. *Lionel Trilling and Irving Howe, and Other Stories of Literary Friendship*. Transaction. [2009] pp. 124. £29.93 ISBN 1 4128 1014 0.

Baker, Geoffrey. *Realism's Empire: Empiricism and Enchantment in the Nineteenth-Century Novel*. OhioUP. [2009] pp. ix + 246. $40 ISBN 9 7808 1421 0987.

Baker, William, and Jeanette Roberts Shumaker. *Leonard Merrick: A Forgotten Novelist's Novelist*. FDUP. [2009] pp. 226. £52.25 ISBN 978 0 7546 6456 2.

Barringer, Tim, and Michaela Giebelhausen, eds. *Writing the Pre-Raphaelites: Text, Context, Subtext*. Ashgate. [2009] pp. xiv + 262. $99.95 ISBN 9 7807 5465 7170.

Bar-Yosef, Eitan, and Nadia Valman, eds. *'The Jew' in Late-Victorian and Edwardian Culture: Between the East End and East Africa*. Palgrave Macmillan. [2009] pp. xii + 241. £50 ISBN 9 7814 0399 7029.

Bateman, Anthony. *Cricket, Literature, and Culture: Symbolising the Nation, Destabilising Empire*. Ashgate. [2009] pp. xii + 236. €55 ISBN 9 7807 5466 5373.

Belcher, Margaret, ed. *The Collected Letters of A.W.N. Pugin*, vol. 3: *1846–1848*. OUP. [2009] pp. xviii + 712. $102.25 ISBN 978 0 1992 2916 3.

Bernstein, Susan David, and Elsie B. Michie, eds. *Victorian Vulgarity: Taste in Verbal and Visual Culture*. Ashgate. [2009] pp. xi + 259. No price given. ISBN 9 7807 5466 4055.

Blake, Kathleen. *Pleasures of Benthamism: Victorian Literature, Utility, Political Economy*. OUP. [2009] pp. 267. £47.50 ISBN 978 0 7801 9956 3265.

Bolus-Reichert, Christine. *The Age of Eclecticism: Literature and Culture in Britain, 1815–1885*. OSUP. [2009] pp. vii + 296. $44.95. ISBN 9 7808 1421 1038.

Brake, Laurel, and Marysa Demoor, eds. *The Lure of Illustration in the Nineteenth Century: Picture and Press*. Palgrave. [2009] pp. 279. £50 ISBN 9 7802 3021 7317.

Bristow, Joseph, ed. *Oscar Wilde and Modern Culture*. OhioUP. [2009] pp. 448. $28.95 ISBN 978 0 8214 1838 6.

Brock, Marilyn, ed. *From Wollstonecraft to Stoker: Essays on Gothic and Victorian Sensation Fiction*. McFarland. [2009] pp. viii + 212. $35 ISBN 9 7807 8644 0214.

Brooker, Peter, and Andrew Thacker, eds. *The Oxford Critical and Cultural History of Modernist Magazines*, vol. 1: *Britain and Ireland 1880–1955*. OUP. [2009] pp. 955. £100 ISBN 9 7801 9921 1159.

Broome Saunders, Clare. *Women Writers and Nineteenth-Century Medievalism*. Palgrave. [2009] pp. 244. $90 ISBN 9 7802 3060 7934.

Burt, Stephen, and Nick Halpern, eds. *Something Understood: Essays and Poetry for Helen Vendler*. UPVirginia. [2009] pp. ix + 335. $59.50 ISBN 9 7808 1392 7848.

Bushell, Sally. *Text as Process: Creative Composition in Wordsworth, Tennyson, and Dickinson*. UPVirginia. [2009] pp. 320. $55 ISBN 9 7808 1392 7749.

Campbell, Ian, Aileen Christianson, and David R. Sorensen (senior editors); Brent E. Kinser, Jane Roberts, Liz Sutherland, and Jonathan Wild (editors). *The Collected Letters of Thomas and Jane Welsh Carlyle*, vol. 36: *November 1859–September 1860*. DukeUP. [2008] pp. xxxvii+301. $30 (institution) $60 (individual). ISBN not supplied.

Campbell, Ian, Aileen Christianson, and David R. Sorensen (senior editors); Brent E. Kinser, Jane Roberts, Liz Sutherland, and Jonathan Wild (editors). *The Collected Letters of Thomas and Jane Welsh Carlyle*, vol. 36: *October 1860–October 1861*. DukeUP. [2009] pp. xxxvii + 301. $60 (institution), $30 (individual). ISBN 9 7808 2236 7178.

Chase, Karen. *The Victorians and Old Age*. OUP. [2009] pp. 284. £55.10 ISBN 978 0 1995 6436 1.

Cheshire, Jim, ed. *Tennyson Transformed: Alfred Lord Tennyson and Visual Culture*. LH. [2009] pp. 160. £40 ISBN 9 7818 4822 0034.

Clemm, Sabine. *Dickens, Journalism, and Nationhood: Mapping the World in Household Words*. Routledge. [2009] pp. 247. $92.80 ISBN 9 7804 1595 8462.

Cohen, William H. *Embodied: Victorian Literature and the Senses*. UMinnP. [2009] pp. 182. £14 ISBN 978 0 8166 5013 6.

Cole, Natalie B. *Dickens and Gender: Recent Studies, 1992–2008*. AMS. [2010] pp. 214. $94.50 ISBN 0 4046 4474 0.

Constantini, Mariaconcetta, Francesco Marroni, and Anna Enrichetta Soccio, eds. *Letter(s): Functions and Forms of Letter-Writing in Victorian Art and Literature*. Aracne. [2009] pp. 238. €16 ISBN 9 7888 5482 6243.

Cotsell, Michael. *The Companion to Our Mutual Friend*. Routledge. [2009] pp. 316. £80 ISBN 9 7804 1548 2400.

Courtney, Angela, ed. *Nineteenth-Century British Dramatists*. Gale. [2009] pp. 485. £55 ISBN 9 7807 8768 1628.

Delany, Paul, ed. *New Grub Street: The 1901 Revised Text*, by George Gissing. UVict. [2009] pp. 333. $20 ISBN 978 1 5505 8384 0.

Denney, Colleen. *Women, Portraiture, and the Crisis of Identity in Victorian England: My Lady Scandalous Reconsidered*. Ashgate. [2009] pp. 260. £55 ISBN 9 7807 5466 8794.

Dickinson, Rachel, ed. *John Ruskin's Correspondence with Joan Severn: Sense and Nonsense Letters*. Legenda. [2009] pp. 300. $89.50 ISBN 1 9059 8190 2.

Douglas-Fairhurst, Robert, and Seamus Perry, eds. *Tennyson Among the Poets: Bicentenary Essays*. OUP. [2009] pp. xvi + 436. £50 ISBN 9 7801 9955 7134.

Flegel, Monica. *Conceptualizing Cruelty to Children in Nineteenth-Century England: Literature, Representation, and the NSPCC*. Ashgate. [2009] pp. 208. £52.25 ISBN 978 0 7546 6456 2.

Flint, Kate. *The Transatlantic Indian, 1776–1930*. PrincetonUP. [2009] pp. 376. $39.50 ISBN 978 0 6911 3120 1.

Foley, Declan J., ed. *The Only Art of Jack B. Yeats: Letters and Essays*. Lilliput Press. [2009] pp. xvii + 204. €30 ISBN 9 7818 4351 1557.

Frankel, Nicholas. *Masking the Text:: Essays on Literature and Mediation in the 1890s*. Rivendale. [2009] pp. 279. £40 ISBN 978 1 9042 0114 8.

Frayling, Christopher, Emily King, and Harriet Atkinson, eds. *Design and Popular Entertainment*. ManUP. [2009] pp. 208. £45 ISBN 9 7807 1908 0166.

Fredeman, William E., ed. *The Correspondence of Dante Gabriel Rossetti: The Last Decade, 1873–1882: Kelmscott to Birchington,* vol. 7: *1878–1879*. Brewer. [2009] pp. 428. $250 ISBN 978 1 8438 4131 2.

Furneaux, Holly. *Queer Dickens: Erotics, Families, Masculinities*. OUP. [2009] pp. 282. $84.68 ISBN 0 1995 6609 7.

Gabriele, Alberto. *Reading Popular Culture in Victorian Print: Belgravia and Sensationalism*. Palgrave. [2009] pp. 275. £55 ISBN 9 7802 3061 5212.

Garcha, Amanpal. *From Sketch to Novel: The Development of Victorian Fiction*. CUP. [2009] pp. 278. $100 ISBN 978 0 5215 1358 8.

Gaschke, Jenny. *Edward Lear Egyptian Sketches*. National Maritime Museum. [2009] pp. 61. £9.99 ISBN 9 7819 0636 7206.

Gauger, Annie, ed. *The Annotated Wind in the Willows*. by Kenneth Grahame; introd. Brian Jacque. Norton. [2009] pp. xi + 377. $39.95 ISBN 9 7803 9305 7744.

Giebelhausen, Michaela, and Tim Barringer, eds. *Writing the Pre-Raphaelites: Text, Context, Subtext*. Ashgate. [2009] pp. 276. $99.95 ISBN 978 0 7546 5717 5.

Gillooly, Eileen, and Deirdre David, eds. *Contemporary Dickens*. OSUP. [2009] pp. xii + 316. $49.95 ISBN 9 7808 1420 2852.

Glunz, Claudia, and Thomas F. Schneider, eds. *Krieg und Literatur / War and Literature XII*. Universitätsverlag Osnabrür. [2009] pp. 160. €41 ISBN 9 7838 9971 5019.

Gray, Erik. *Milton and the Victorians*. CornUP. [2009] pp. 183. $32.54 ISBN 978 0 8014 4680 5.

Gubar, Marah. *Artful Dodgers: Reconceiving the Golden Age of Children's Literature*. OUP. [2009] pp. 264. £40 ISBN 9 7801 9533 6252.

Hagan, Edward, Philip Kelley, and Scott Lewis, eds. *The Brownings' Correspondence*, vol. 15. Wedgestone. [2005] pp. xvi + 432. $110 ISBN 9 7809 1145 9302.

Hagan, Edward, Philip Kelley, and Scott Lewis, eds. *The Brownings' Correspondence*, vol. 16. Wedgestone. [2007] pp. xvi + 432. $110 ISBN 9 7809 1145 9326.

Harrison, Antony H. *The Cultural Production of Matthew Arnold*. OhioUP. [2009] pp. 160. $49.95 ISBN 9 7808 2141 8994.

Hawlin, Stefan, and Michael Meredith, eds. *Parleyings with Certain People of Importance in their Day and Asolando*, by Robert Browning. OUP. [2009] pp. xix + 514. £116 ISBN 9 7801 9812 3514.

Heath, Kay. *Aging by the Book: The Emergence of Midlife in Victorian Britain*. SUNYP. [2009] pp. 247. $75 ISBN 978 0 7914 7657 X.

Heinrich, Anselm, Katherine Newey, and Jeffrey Richards, eds. *Ruskin, the Theatre and Victorian Visual Culture*. Palgrave. [2009] pp. 242. £50 ISBN 9 7802 3020 0593.

Hermansson, Casie. *Bluebeard: A Reader's Guide to the English Tradition*. UMP. [2009] pp. 289. £22 ISBN 9 7816 0473 2313.

Himmelfarb, Gertrude. *The Jewish Odyssey of George Eliot*. Encounter. [2009] pp. 180. £14.39 ISBN 1 5940 3251 3.

Hinks, John, Catherine Armstrong, and Matthew Day, eds. *Periodicals and Publishers: The Newspaper and Journal Trade 1740–1914*. BL/OakK. [2009] pp. 251. £25 ISBN 9 7807 1235 0747.

Hinojosa, Lynne Walhout. *The Renaissance, English Cultural Nationalism, and Modernism, 1860–1920*. Palgrave. [2009] pp. 247. £48 ISBN 9 7802 3060 8313.

Hoffman, Ruth Colette. *Without Education or Encouragement: The Literary Legacy of Flora Thompson*. Rosemont. [2009] pp. 213. $45 ISBN 978 0 8386 4206 3.

Holmes, John. *Darwin's Bards: British and American Poetry in the Age of Evolution*. EdinUP. [2009] pp. xiv + 288. £65 ISBN 9 7807 4863 9403.

Holroyd, Michael. *A Strange Eventful History: The Dramatic Lives of Ellen Terry, Henry Irving, and their Remarkable Families*. FS&G. [2008] pp. 620. £25 ISBN 9 7803 7427 0803.

Howsam, Leslie. *Past and Present: The Publishing History in Britain 1850–1950*. UTorP. [2009] pp. 192. $50 ISBN 1 4426 4057 X.

Howsam, Leslie. *Past into Print: The Publishing of History in Britain, 1850–1950*. BL/UTorP. [2009] pp. 181. £50 ISBN 9 7807 1235 0273.

Hutchings, Kevin. *Romantic Ecologies and Colonial Cultures in the British Atlantic World 1770–1850*. McG-QUP. [2009] pp. xiii + 226. $80 ISBN 978 0 7735 3579 9.

Hyman, Gwen. *Making a Man: Gentlemanly Appetites in the Nineteenth-Century British Novel*. OhioUP. [2009] pp. 309. £21.38 ISBN 978 0 8214 1854 8.

Jackson, Tony E. *The Technology of the Novel: Writing and Narrative in British Fiction*. JHUP. [2009] pp. 234. £27.08 ISBN 0 8018 9244 9.

Johns, Adrian. *Piracy: The Intellectual Property Wars from Gutenberg to Gates*. UChicP. [2009] pp. 626. £24 ISBN 9 7802 2640 1188.

Jones, Colin, Josephine McDonagh, and Jon Mee, eds. *Charles Dickens, A Tale of Two Cities and the French Revolution*. Palgrave. [2009] pp. 240. £55 ISBN 9 7802 3053 7781.

Kafker, Frank A., and Jeff Loveland, eds. *The Early Britannica: The Growth of an Outstanding Encyclopedia*. Voltaire Foundation. [2009] pp. 349. £65 ISBN 9 7807 2940 9810.

Karlin, Daniel, ed. *Rubáiyát of Omar Khayyám*. by Edward FitzGerald. OUP. [2009] pp. 224. $19.95 ISBN 9 7801 9954 2970.

Kaufman, Heidi. *Jewish Discourse, and the Nineteenth-Century British Novel: Reflections on a Nested Nation*. PSUP. [2009] pp. 272. $85 ISBN 978 0 2710 3526 9.

Kelley, Philip, and Sandra Donaldson, eds. with Scott Lewis, Edward Hagan, and Rita S. Patteson. *Florentine Friends: The Letters of Elizabeth Barrett Browning and Robert Browning to Isa Blagden*, 1850–1861. Wedgestone and ABL. [2009] pp. ii + 538. $145 ISBN 9 7809 1145 9333.

Koivunen, Leila. *Visualizing Africa in Nineteenth-Century British Travel Accounts*. Routledge. [2009] pp. 351. £60 ISBN 9 7804 1599 0011.

Kortsch, Christine Bayles. *Dress Culture in Late Victorian's Women's Fiction: Literacy, Textiles, and Activism*. Ashgate. [2009] pp. x + 201. €55 ISBN 9 7807 5466 5106.

Lau, Beth, ed. *Fellow Romantics: Male and Female British Writers, 1790–1835*. Ashgate. [2009] pp. xi + 266. £55 ISBN 9 7807 5466 3539.

Ledbetter, Kathryn. *British Victorian Women's Periodicals: Beauty, Civilization, and Poetry*. Palgrave. [2009] pp. 236. £45 ISBN 9 7802 3060 1260.

Lehman, Amy. *Victorian Women and the Theatre of Trance: Mediums, Spiritualists and Mesmerists in Performance*. McFarland. [2009] pp. 202. £40 ISBN 9 7807 8643 4794.

Lemon, Rebecca, Emma Mason, Jonathan Roberts, and Christopher Rowland, eds. *The Blackwell Companion to the Bible in English Literature*. Wiley-Blackwell. [2009] pp. 703. £110 ISBN 9 7814 0513 1605.

Lerer, Seth, ed. *The Annotated Wind in the Willows*, by Kenneth Grahame. HarvardUP. [2009] pp. xiv + 274. $35 ISBN 9 7806 7403 4471.

Letissier, Georges, ed. *Rewriting/Reprising: Plural Intertextualities*. CambridgeSP. [2009] pp. 250. £40 ISBN 9 7814 4381 3884.

Liddle, Dallas. *The Dynamics of Genre: Journalism and the Practice of Literature in Mid-Victorian Britain*. UPVirginia. [2009] pp. 234. £36.95 ISBN 9 7808 1392 7831.

Lodge, Sara. *A Reader's Guide: Charlotte Brontë: Jane Eyre*. Palgrave. [2009] pp. 181. $24 ISBN 978 0 2305 1815 X.

Louis, Margot K. *Persephone Rises, 1860–1927: Mythography, Gender, and the Creation of a New Spirituality*. Ashgate. [2009] pp. xvi + 171. £55 ISBN 9 7807 5466 4550.

Louttit, Chris. *Dickens's Secular Gospel: Work, Gender and Personality*. Routledge. [2010] pp. 182. $111 ISBN 978 0 4159 9136 6.

Mackay, Carol, ed. *Hanbery: Autobiographical Sketches*. by Carol Hanbery Mackay. Broadview. [2009] pp. 376. $ 24.95 ISBN 978 1 5511 1448 8.

Mariani, Paul. *Gerard Manley Hopkins: A Life*. Viking. [2008] pp. 496. $34.95 ISBN 9 7806 7002 0317.

Markovits, Stefanie. *The Crimean War in the British Imagination*. CUP. [2009] pp. 304. $87.95 ISBN 0 5211 1237 0.

Markwick, Margaret, Deborah Denenholz Morse, and Regenia Gagnier, eds. *The Politics of Gender in Anthony Trollope's Novels*. Ashgate. [2009] pp. 260. $99.95 ISBN 978 0 7546 6389 2.

Marshall, Gail. *Shakespeare and Victorian Women*. CUP. [2009] pp. 207. £53 ISBN 9 7805 2151 5238.

Matz, Lou J., and Helen Taylor, eds. *Three Essays on Religion*. by John Stuart Mill. Broadview. [2009] pp. 300. $24.95 ISBN 9 7815 5111 7683.

Maxwell, Catherine. *Second Sight: The Visionary Imagination in Late Victorian Literature*. ManUP. [2008] pp. 260. £52.25 ISBN 978 0 7190 7144 5.

McDonald, Lynn, ed. *Collected Works of Florence Nightingale*, vol. 12: *The Nightingale School*. WLUP. [2009] pp. 935. $15 ISBN 9 7808 8920 4676.

McDonald, Lynn, ed. *Collected Works of Florence Nightingale*, vol. 13: *Extending Nursing*. WLUP. [2009] pp. 946. $150 ISBN 9 7808 8920 5208.

McKitterick, David, ed. *The Cambridge History of the Book in Britain*, vol. 6: *1830–1914*. CUP. [2009] pp. 808. £110 ISBN 9 7805 2186 6248.

Mills, Kevin. *The Prodigal Sign: A Parable of Criticism*. SussexAP. [2009] pp. 167. $52.50 ISBN 978 1 8451 9154 4.

Missler, Peter. *A Daring Game: George Borrow's Sales of the Scio New Testament*. Madrid 1837. Dunwich Publishing. [2009] pp. 189. No price given. ISBN 9 7819 0594 6044.

Moore, Tara. *Victorian Christmas in Print*. Palgrave. [2009] pp. 194. £52.50 ISBN 9 7802 3061 6547.

Morgan, Monique R. *Narrative Means, Lyric Ends: Temporality in the Nineteenth-Century British Long Poem*. OSUP. [2009] pp. x + 233. $47.95 ISBN 9 7808 1421 1113.

Morrison, Robert. *The English Opium Eater: A Biography of Thomas De Quincey*. W&N. [2009] pp. 462. £17.29 ISBN 978 0 2978 5279 5.

Morton, Peter, ed. *The Diary of a Nobody*. by George and Weedon Grossmith. Broadview. [2009] pp. 259. $19.95 ISBN 978 1 5511 1704 5.

Nicoll, Allardyce. *A History of English Drama, 1660–1900*, 7 vols. CUP. [1930, 1955, repr. 2009]. £265 ISBN 9 7805 2112 5482.

Ofek, Galia. *Representations of Hair in Victorian Literature and Culture*. Ashgate. [2009] pp. xii + 271. £55 ISBN 9 7807 5466 1610.

Olverson, T.D. *Women Writers and the Dark Side of Late-Victorian Aestheticism*. Palgrave. [2009] pp. 248. £50 ISBN 9 7802 3021 5597.

Oost, Regina. *Gilbert and Sullivan: Class and the Savoy Tradition, 1875–1896*. Ashgate. [2009] pp. 168. £50 ISBN 9 7807 5466 4123.

Parejo Vadillo, Ana, and Marion Thain, eds. *Michael Field, the Poet: Published and Manuscript Materials*. Broadview. [2009] pp. 384. $26.95 ISBN 9 7815 5111 6754.

Peterson, Linda H. *Becoming a Woman of Letters: Myths of Authorship and Facts of the Victorian Market*. PrincetonUP. [2009] pp. 289. £19.95 ISBN 9 7806 9114 0179.

Powell, Kerry. *Acting Wilde: Victorian Sexuality, Theatre, and Oscar Wilde*. CUP. [2009] pp. 204. £59 ISBN 9 7805 2151 6921.

Prawer, S.S. *A Cultural Citizen of the World: Sigmund Freud's Knowledge and Use of British and American Writings*. Legenda. [2009] pp. 200. $89.50 ISBN 978 1 9065 4042 X.

Richards, Jeffrey. *The Ancient World on the Victorian and Edwardian Stage*. Palgrave. [2009] pp. 267. £52 ISBN 9 7802 3022 9365.

Rigg, Patricia. *Julia Augusta Webster: Victorian Aestheticism and the Woman Writer*. FDUP. [2009] pp. 312. $62.50 ISBN 9 7808 3864 2207.

Rubery, Matthew. *The Novelty of Newspapers: Victorian Fiction after the Invention of the News*. OUP. [2009] pp. 233. £40 ISBN 9 7801 9536 9267.

Rudy, Jason R. *Electric Meters: Victorian Physiological Poetics*. OhioUP. [2009] pp. xiii + 222. $44.95 ISBN 9 7808 2141 8826.

Sanders, Mike. *The Poetry of Chartism: Aesthetics, Politics, History*. CUP. [2009] pp. 314. £50 ISBN 9 7805 2189 9185.

Sanders, Valerie. *The Tragic Comedy of Victorian Fatherhood*. CUP. [2009] pp. xii +246. $95 ISBN 9 7805 2188 4785.

Schoenfield, Mark. *British Periodicals and Romantic Identity: The 'Literary Lower Empire'*. Palgrave. [2009] pp. 296. £40 ISBN 9 7802 3060 9471.

Slater, Michael. *Charles Dickens*. YaleUP. [2009] pp. 696. $23.10 ISBN 978 0 3001 1207 6.

Stewart, Garrett. *Novel Violence: A Narratography of Victorian Britain*. UChicP. [2009] pp. 280. $36 ISBN 978 0 2267 7458 9.

Straub, Julia. *A Victorian Muse: The Afterlife of Dante's Beatrice in Nineteenth-Century Literature*. Continuum. [2009] pp. 178. $120 ISBN 9 7808 2644 5896.

Sullivan, Ceri, and Graeme Harper, eds. *Authors at Work: The Creative Environment*. English Association Essays and Studies. Brewer. [2009] pp. xii + 180. £30 ISBN 9 7818 4384 1951.

Sutherland, John. *The Longman Companion to Victorian Fiction*, 2nd edn. Pearson Education. [2009] pp. 736. $ 33.36 ISBN 978 1 4082 0390 1.

Swaim, Barton. *Scottish Men of Letters and the New Public Sphere, 1802–1834*. BuckUP. [2009] pp. 219. £45.50 ISBN 9 7808 3875 7161.

Talairach-Vielmas, Laurence, ed. *Thou Art the Man*. by Mary Elizabeth Braddon. Valancourt. [2008] pp. 372. $16.95 ISBN 9 7819 3455 5378.

Talairach-Vielmas, Laurence. *Wilkie Collins, Medicine and the Gothic*. UWalesP. [2009] pp. 224. $85 ISBN 978 0 7083 2223 9.

Thackeray, William Makepeace. *The Complete Works of William Makepeace Thackeray*. vols. 1–27. Introd. Micael Clarke. CambridgeSP. [2009] £259.99 ISBN 9 7814 4380 3526.

Toman, John. *Kilvert's Diary and Landscape*. Lutterworth. [2008] pp. 402. $57.50 ISBN 978 0 7188 3095 4.

Toremans, Tom, and Walter Verschueren, eds. *Crossing Culture: Nineteenth-Century Anglophone Literature in the Low Countries*. LeuvenUP. [2009] pp. 218. $52.25 ISBN 9 7890 5867 7334.

Vuohelaine, Minna, ed. *Curious: Some Strange Adventures of Two Bachelors*. by Richard Marsh. Valancourt. [2007] pp. 156. $16.95 ISBN 9 7819 3455 5255.

Vuohelaine, Minna, ed. *Philip Bennion's Death*. by Richard Marsh. Valancourt. [2007] pp. 168. $18.95 ISBN 9 7819 3455 5304.

Vuohelaine, Minna, ed. *The Beetle*. by Richard Marsh. Valancourt. [2008] pp. 416. $18.95 ISBN 9 7819 3455 5491.

Vuohelaine, Minna, ed. *The Devil's Diamonds*. by Richard Marsh. Valancourt. [2007] pp. 148. $16.95 ISBN 9 7819 3455 5019.

Vuohelaine, Minna, ed. *The Seen and the Unseen*. by Richard Marsh. Valancourt. [2007] pp. 244. $18.95 ISBN 9 7819 3455 5002.

Wagner, Tamara, ed. *Antifeminism and the Victorian Novel: Rereading Nineteenth-Century Women Writers*. Cambria. [2009] pp. 350. $119.99 ISBN 9 7816 0497 6076.

Watson, Nicola J., ed. *Literary Tourism and Nineteenth-Century Culture*. Palgrave. [2009] pp. 230. £50 ISBN 9 7802 3022 2816.

Wehrs, Donald R., and David P. Haney, eds. *Levinas and Nineteenth-Century Literature: Ethics and Otherness from Romanticism through Realism*. UDelP. [2009] pp. 298. $23.90 ISBN 978 0 8741 3057 3.

Wiebe, M.G. et al. *Benjamin Disraeli: Letters: 1860–1864*. UTorP. [2009] pp. 656. $130.46 ISBN 978 0 8020 9949 1.
Willems, Brian. *Hopkins and Heidegger*. Continuum. [2009] pp. 144. £45 ISBN 9 7814 4116 9563.
Wilson, Keith, ed. *A Companion to Thomas Hardy*. Wiley-Blackwell. [2009] pp. 488. £99.75 ISBN 9 7814 0515 6684.

XIV

Modern Literature

ANDREW RADFORD, SAM SLOTE, ANDREW HARRISON, ERIC SANDBERG, NICK BENTLEY, REBECCA D'MONTÉ, GRAHAM SAUNDERS, MATTHEW CREASY AND MARIA JOHNSTON

This chapter has six sections 1. Pre-1945 Fiction; 2. Post-1945 Fiction; 3. Pre-1950 Drama; 4. Post-1950 Drama; 5. Pre-1950 Poetry. 6. Irish Poetry. Section 1(a) is by Andrew Radford; section 1(b) is by Sam Slote; section 1(c) is by Andrew Harrison; section 1(d) is by Eric Sandberg; section 2 is by Nick Bentley; section 3 is by Rebecca D'Monté; section 4 is by Graham Saunders; section 5 is by Matthew Creasy; section 6 is by Maria Johnston.

1. Pre-1945 Fiction

(a) British Fiction 1900–1930

The most salient feature of 2009 concerning research into early twentieth-century British fiction has been the increasingly probing analysis of lesser-known women writers who merit little close scrutiny—or indeed any mention at all—in Peter Nicholls's second edition of *Modernisms: A Literary Guide*. Nicholls acknowledges in his preface that the thirteen years since the publication of this groundbreaking guide have witnessed an extraordinary burgeoning of interest in the charged and complex aesthetic and political terrain of modernism. He does well to include an incisive new chapter on African American authors, but his otherwise scrupulously structured account keeps the story of 'the formation and evolution' of a plurality of modernisms (p. viii) rather too tightly focused. This reviewer would have liked him to finesse Robert Scholes's more inclusive, revisionary enterprise in *Paradoxy of Modernism* [2006], which canvasses figures who do not fit easily into a 'high' modernist paradigm. Scholes energetically casts 'a wider net for useful texts' (p. xi) and interprets the conservative middlebrow fiction of Dornford Yates (who also features in Clive Bloom's second edition of *Bestsellers* [2008]) as sedulously as he does Joyce's *Ulysses*.

The Year's Work in English Studies, Volume 90 (2011)
doi:10.1093/ywes/mar017

In marked contrast to Ann Ardis's *Modernism and Cultural Conflict, 1880–1922* [2002], Chris Baldick's *The Modern Movement* [2004], Tim Armstrong's *Modernism* [2005], and Pericles Lewis's *Cambridge Introduction to Modernism* [2007], which all stimulated lively interest in the period bracketed by the two world wars by removing simplifications produced through measuring 'vernacular' against 'elite' literary expression, Nicholls sidelines the revenants of a forgotten modernism. Chief casualties of his approach are Mary Butts, Sylvia Townsend Warner, and Olive Moore, who all tirelessly mapped the bohemian borders of interwar culture. As Jane Garrity argues in her review article 'Found and Lost: The Politics of Modernist Recovery' (*Mo/Mo* 15[2008] 803–12), such authors who have suffered what Roger Boylan wittily terms the 'dead-writer rollercoaster of obloquy and oblivion, rediscovery and restitution', were maverick practitioners of a literary art that warrants—and richly rewards—the most punctilious attention. Garrity urges literary historians to pinpoint and overturn those trends by which these provocatively transgressive figures, once feted and ebulliently reviewed, come to be belittled and excluded from the canon. Rod Rosenquist's *Modernism, the Market and the Institution of the New* and Langford, ed., *Textual Intersections: Literature, History and the Arts in Nineteenth-Century Europe* variously elaborate Garrity's thesis by evoking a period dominated by anxieties about cultural worth, urgent dialogues between avant-garde and middlebrow art forms, and the relationship of history to iconoclastic verve.

The year 2009 saw the welcome reissue in paperback of Patrick Wright's *On Living in an Old Country: The National Past in Contemporary Britain*. First published in 1985, this analytically sophisticated book boasts a compelling chapter on the turbulent life and literary career of interwar novelist Mary Butts (pp. 84–120). Wright is admirably alert to the cultural context which lends her novelistic voice its dissident difference. He was one of the first British scholars to confront and process the vexed racial and class politics underpinning Butts's preservationist pamphlets and fiction, especially *Ashe of Rings* [1925] and *Armed with Madness* [1928]. Rochelle Rives's '"No Real Men": Mary Butts's Socio-Sexual Politics' (*Connotations* 18[2009] 246–58) canvasses with eloquent energy this wilfully obscure writer's 'frequently hostile' attitude 'to modernist sets, groups, and imperatives' (p. 246). Rives consolidates and deepens this project in 'A Straight Eye for the Queer Guy: Mary Butts's "Fag-Hag" and the Modernist Group' (in Durao and Williams, eds., *Modernist Group Dynamics: The Politics and Poetics of Friendship*, pp. 95–118). Through a stringent reading of *Armed with Madness* that focuses confidently on interlinked issues of violent disorder, storytelling brio, and unchecked desire, Rives charts Butts's insistent debunking of 'heterosexual romantic trajectories' and 'individual narratives of development' (p. 112).

Renée Dickinson's *Female Embodiment and Subjectivity in the Modernist Novel: The Corporeum of Virginia Woolf and Olive Moore* brings a bracing new focus to the unjustly neglected and oracular fiction of Olive Moore, whose 1930 novel *Spleen* gauges what Beatrice Monaco calls in *Machinic Modernism* [2008] the 'simultaneously creative and political impulses that characterize modernism as a cultural movement' (p. 5). In Dickinson's account *Spleen* is positioned as a productive forum for assessing the inscription of gendered identities and sexed bodies in literary media. Like Kristyn Gorton's *Theorising Desire: From Freud to Feminism to Film* [2008], which measures gendered differences as they are encrypted within various media, moving between the textual and the visual, Dickinson addresses the carefully rehearsed artifice which offers itself as a survival strategy to an embattled yet questing femininity. Little is known about Moore's social and intellectual upbringing, and, after publishing four novels during the interwar period, she slipped beneath the radar of literary history. It was not until the 1990s that her novels were republished posthumously by the Dalkey Archive Press. Her slyly sardonic and densely layered narrative of female pilgrimage deserves the same keen analysis that has been accorded to Mary Butts, thanks largely to the sedulous biographical scholarship of Nathalie Blondel and Jane Garrity's exceptionally detailed *Step-daughters of England* [2003].

Olive Moore's corpus epitomizes a strand of 'intermodernism', a new critical and historical category which provides the title to Kristin Bluemel's essay collection. *Intermodernism: Literary Culture in Mid-Twentieth-Century Britain* is particularly strong on those underestimated women writers such as Sylvia Townsend Warner (pp. 38–55), Rebecca West (pp. 150–70), and Storm Jameson (pp. 21–37) whose work emerged from the Great War and its aftermath. Like David James's trenchant essay 'Localizing Late Modernism: Interwar Regionalism and the Genesis of the "Micro Novel"' (*JML* 32[2009] 43–64) Bluemel's book concentrates well on three types of 'intermodern' features in texts that are undervalued by rival accounts of the modern movement: working-class culture; political theory; and the middlebrow as a stylistic repertoire as well as a 'mass' genre. Glib assumptions about the retrogressive or timorous nature of fiction from the 1930s and 1940s have been subverted by recent reappraisals of this era. What is less widely canvassed, Bluemel contends in her shrewdly angled introduction, is the extent to which such different writers as Warner, Jameson, and Rosamond Lehmann exploited the advancements of their modernist-Impressionist precursors to refine challenging modes for engagement with provincial and liminal geographies.

Bluemel's volume weighs competing ideologies of 'Englishness' by searching and subtle forms of rhetorical analysis. So national belonging becomes, in the words of Simon Featherstone in *Englishness: Twentieth-Century Popular Culture and the Forming of English Identity*, 'a diverse and surprisingly heterogeneous field for study and argument' (p. 4). This is also manifest in Ashton and Kean, eds., *People and their Pasts: Public History Today* and especially in Watson ed., *Literary Tourism and Nineteenth-Century Culture*, whose cross-disciplinary research on figures such as Rudyard Kipling, H. Rider Haggard, and J.B. Priestley emphasizes the degree to which regional affiliation and canon formation are intertwined with 'pilgrimages to literary destinations' (p. 3).

Wendy Gan's elegantly written and erudite book *Women, Privacy and Modernity in Early Twentieth-Century British Writing* postulates that privacy is a complex marker of modernity in selected novels by Rose Macauley, Sylvia Townsend Warner, and Dorothy Richardson. Like Andrea Adolph's *Food and Femininity in Twentieth-Century British Women's Fiction*, Darling and Whitworth, eds., *Women and the Making of Built Space in England,*

1870–1950 [2007], Heather Love's *Feeling Backward* [2007], and Scott and Keates, eds., *Going Public: Feminism and the Shifting Boundaries of the Private Sphere* [2004], Gan debunks with psychological acuity the well-entrenched assumptions about separate spheres in the field of literary enquiry. As Maya Higashi Wakana also demonstrates in *Performing the Everyday in Henry James's Late Novels*, the 'hinterland' of private life is a generative and seminal site for our grasp of 'literary modernism' (p. 5). Gan shows that an obsession with domestic interiors reverberates through Dorothy Richardson's *Pilgrimage*, a text which draws its conceptual repertoire from the lexicons of domestic architecture and interior design. Gan finesses a concept of psychic interiority that is anchored in tropes, debates, and ideas about architectural nooks and crannies. Maria Diaz's 'An Analysis of Poetic and Cinematic Features in Dorothy M. Richardson's *Pilgrimage*' (*ES* 90[2009] 57–77) is not only responsive to these concepts but also ponders poetic language and cinematic technique by building on Laura Marcus's meticulous research in *The Tenth Muse* [2007].

Like Jane Garrity in *Step-daughters of England* and Garrity and Doan, eds., *Sapphic Modernities* [2006], Gan suggests that ostensibly humble domestic recesses and the design of living spaces variously adumbrate potent formal and thematic potentialities. Saikat Majumdar's 'Katherine Mansfield and the Fragility of Pakeha Boredom' (*MFS* 55[2009] 119–141) is also attuned to issues of privacy and how 'the calm texture of quotidian domesticity' (p. 120) reveals psychic fault-lines and fractures synonymous with the colonial predicament. Majumbar posits that as a colonial writer who had so assiduously pursued 'entry into Bloomsbury, and one who was both granted entry and derided for her colonial origins', Mansfield constructs vivid tales of existential ennui in a milieu where 'desires are teased but never satisfactorily fulfilled' (pp. 120–1).

Tatiana Kontou's *Spiritualism and Women's Writing: From the Fin de Siècle to the Neo-Victorian* asks a crucial question with regard to the 'modernist experiments' of Dorothy Richardson's *Pilgrimage* and May Sinclair's *Mary Olivier: A Life* respectively: can core components of literary modernism be relocated in 'the textual and performative practices of the Edwardian séance' (p. 43)? By tracing out such 'a spectral chain of connection' Kontou invites us to reconfigure hidebound notions about the 'history of literary innovation' (pp. 43–80). Kontou does well to privilege the work of two women writers who do not feature prominently in Helen Sword's *Ghostwriting Modernism* [2002], which also explicates the complex 'implications of popular spiritualist tropes' (p. 46) for the modernist canon.

The recent scholarly work on the polyphonic textual strategies of Djuna Barnes (see for example Diane Warren, *Djuna Barnes' Consuming Fictions* [2008], which usefully compares *Ryder* [1928] with Sylvia Townsend Warner's *Lolly Willowes*) has also illuminated Radclyffe Hall's 1928 novel of lesbian life *The Well of Loneliness* and how it figures the gay subject's emergence out of the specifically modern, capitalist contradiction between the public domain of industrial production and the private domain of pleasure and consumption. Building on the achievements of Jeffrey Weeks's *Making Sexual History* [2000] and Laura Doan's *Fashioning Sapphism* [2001], which variously unpick the equation of gender variance and same-sex desire, Elisa Glick focuses on Hall as 'the monocled lesbian dandy' who represented in the 1920s 'the newest face of homosexual aestheticism' (p. 64) in *Materializing Queer Desire: Oscar Wilde to Andy Warhol* (pp. 63–81). Julie Abraham considers Radclyffe Hall and the Chicago school in *Metropolitan Lovers: The Homosexuality of Cities* (pp. 141–68). Abraham methodically traces 'culturally resonant accounts' of the modern city not only as a site of over-stimulation, perceptual shock, and decentring of self, but more importantly as mirroring the complex 'convergence of homosexuality and urbanity' (p. 143). Mary A. Armstrong's 'Stable Identity: Horses, Inversion Theory, and *The Well of Loneliness*' (*LIT* 19[2008] 47–78) and Micki Nyman's 'Displaced Deviance in Radclyffe Hall's *The Well of Loneliness*' (*FemSEL* 16[2008] 79–101) interrogate rival definitions of aberrant passion in Hall's definitive lesbian novel.

Laura Heffernan's 'Reading Modernism's Cultural Field: Rebecca West's *The Strange Necessity* and the Aesthetic "System of Relations"' (*TSWL* 27[2009] 309–25) addresses West's extraordinarily variegated body of work that includes reportage, memoir, and critical and lyrical essays. Heffernan's eloquent essay builds on the signal achievements of Schweizer, ed., *Rebecca West Today: Contemporary Critical Approaches* [2006], especially Debra Rae Cohen's chapter on West's 'playful generic iconoclasm' (pp. 143–56) in the 1920s. Heffernan considers West's overlooked 1928 volume of essays *The Strange Necessity* and its treatment of the aesthetic values that would eventually be consecrated as literary 'modernism' to be due in no small part to T.S. Eliot's critical precepts and imperious judgements, especially his championing of 'impersonality'—the key notion around which an initial modernist canon of formally ambitious, typically male-authored works was fashioned. Heffernan asks what it would mean to privilege West as 'a forgotten critic of modernism', and how we might assess the 'institutional formation of modernism as eclipsing not just literary styles, but alternative modes of interpretation and critical practice' (p. 310).

Alissa G. Karl's *Modernism and the Marketplace: Literary Culture and Consumer Capitalism in Rhys, Woolf, Stein, and Nella Larsen* effectively positions Jean Rhys as a writer whose early novels—especially *Quartet* [1928] and *After Leaving Mr. Mackenzie* [1930]—both enact and interrogate the contradictions of consumer choice. Karl construes Rhys not only as an architect of a deracinated modern subjectivity but also as a writer obsessed by 'the internal points of friction within the marketplace's circuit of seemingly endless desire' (p. 34). The fraught trajectory of Rhys's protagonists—also canvassed by Patricia Moran in *Virginia Woolf, Jean Rhys, and the Aesthetics of Trauma* [2007]—demonstrates the extent to which commodity logic dominates female sexuality. Indeed their reliance upon men for economic survival 'inheres with their status as sexualised commodities' (p. 34). Karl persuasively concludes that consumerism is not simply the trope which augurs the fate of these female protagonists; rather, it is the remorseless 'logic' by which these novels become comprehensible (pp. 34–42).

Cathleen Maslen's *Ferocious Things: Jean Rhys and the Politics of Women's Melancholia* amplifies Karl's shrewd insights. Maslen focuses on the articulation and inscription of feminine anguish in the early fiction, resisting glib generalizations with regard to Rhys's portrayal of women's psychic pain. Like Karl, Maslen is responsive to the subtle and significant inflections of sexual, cultural, and ethnic displacement imbuing the trials of Rhys's heroines. Rhys's corpus, according to Maslen, simultaneously certifies and complicates basically Eurocentric and anti-feminist paradigms of melancholia and elegiac yearning. In short, the existential ennui of Jean Rhys's female voices poses constructive paradoxes and points of departure for feminist and postcolonial debates in the twenty-first century.

Lilian Pizzichini's *The Blue Hour: A Portrait of Jean Rhys* owes a signal debt to Carole Angier's 1991 biography, *Jean Rhys: Life and Work*, though this succinct new account adopts a more measured stance towards her subject's traumatic childhood sexual experiences. While Angier's sprawling project presents Rhys as a 'borderline personality' (p. 126), Pizzichini develops a less judgemental approach by showing Rhys as an author of remarkable gifts whose fiction returns repeatedly to the turmoil of not being able to follow the strictures of her own family, as well as the hidebound and humourless bourgeois society in which she struggled to locate a secure, fulfilling niche. Read against Angier's exhaustive biography, Pizzichini's short book is not always convincingly sourced, plus she falls into the trap of making a few reductive links between the angry energy of Rhys's felt experience and her encrypted literary responses. Pizzichini is at her best when investigating the ruptured mother–daughter relationship and how the acute fear of abandonment infuses Rhys's spare, tautly structured *Quartet* and *After Leaving Mr Mackenzie*.

Claire G. Jones's *Femininity, Mathematics and Science, 1880–1914* supplies a thorough contextual account for the reappraisal of under-studied women writers such as Edith Ayrton Zangwill, whose 1924 novel *The Call* has recently garnered judicious scrutiny: see Meri-Jane Rochelson, 'Edith Ayrton Zangwill and the Anti-Domestic Novel' (*WS* 36[2007] 161–83). Bray, Gavin, and Merchant eds., *Re-embroidering the Robe: Faith, Myth and Literary Creation since 1850* [2008] offers myriad critical tools by which to assess how women writers from this literary period 're-minted' mythic archetypes into 'fashions' or 'skins' more 'wearable in the modern world' (p. 1). Paul March-Russell's *The Short Story: An Introduction* sets out in twenty crisply written chapters an incisive and well-informed portrait of this literary mode, its history, culture, aesthetics, and economics. March-Russell's key strength is his ability to compare European innovators such as Chekhov and Flaubert with British and New Zealand practitioners such as Katherine Mansfield and Rebecca West.

In 2009 an array of scrupulously researched contextual studies appeared which set out misconstrued facets of Anglo-American modernism's shell-shocked history. Admirers of Great War novels such as Richard Aldington's *Death of a Soldier* [1929], Frederic Manning's *The Middle Part of Fortune* [1929], and Ford Madox Ford's *No Enemy* [1929] will find valuable material in Herzog, ed., *Brutality and Desire: War and Sexuality in Europe's Twentieth Century*, which affirms 'the transformation of European military history from a marginal enclave into a major growth area' (p. 1). Erika Kuhlman's *Reconstructing Patriarchy after the Great War: Women, Gender, and Postwar Reconciliation between Nations* [2008] should be scrutinized by scholars of

Rebecca West, Mary Butts, and May Sinclair, especially the fourth chapter, on women's historical involvement in post-war reconciliation (pp. 105–37). Like Smith, ed., *Gender and Warfare in the Twentieth Century: Textual Representations* [2004] Kuhlman's enterprise raises vital sociocultural questions regarding women's ability to 'participate politically in the nation-state' (p. 108).

Ana Carden Coyne's *Reconstructing the Body: Classicism, Modernism and the First World War* is impressive both in scope and depth as it inspects the cultures of 'resilience' and the institutions of post Great War reconstruction in Britain, Australia, and the United States. Coyne's thesis is that bodies damaged by global conflict were not locked away as tortured or blighted memories. Like Leo van Bergen in *Before My Helpless Sight: Suffering, Dying and Military Medicine on the Western Front, 1914–1918*, Coyne shows that wounded bodies became a focus for rigorous cultural commentary, fierce debate, the objects of radical rehabilitation and 'commodities of desire' in global industries (p. 34). Coyne is particularly skilful in showing that government agencies, physicians, beauty and body therapists, and visual artists variously referred to classical figurations as devices by which to heal a ravaged home culture and its desensitized citizens.

These deeply pondered arguments are extended in Lamberti and Fortunati, eds., *Memories and Representations of War: The Case of World War I and World War II*; Knights, ed., *Masculinities in Text and Teaching* [2008]; Jessica Meyer's *Men of War: Masculinity and the First World War in Britain*; and Trudi Tate's 'The First World War: British Writing' (in McLoughlin, ed., *The Cambridge Companion to War Writing*, pp. 160–74). Sean Brady's essay, 'Masculinity and the Construction of Male Homosexuality in Modern Britain before the First World War' (in Ellis and Meyer, eds., *Masculinity and the Other: Historical Perspectives*, pp. 115–37), canvasses the 'cultural abhorrence of sexuality between men' (p. 116) through developments in masculinity as a social status, especially in relation to parliamentary legislation and Home Office directives, the medical profession, and middlebrow journalism. Brady's searching analysis is greatly amplified in his *Masculinity and Male Homosexuality in Britain, 1861–1913* which Palgrave has now published in paperback.

In the ongoing stock exchange of literary evaluations, Ford Madox Ford's critical worth has soared over the past fifteen years. Paul McCormick's 'Claims of Stable Identity and (Un)reliability in Dissonant Narration' (*PoT* 30[2009] 317–52) addresses the fractured narrative of *The Good Soldier* while Jeffrey Mathes McCarthy's '"The Foul System": The Great War and Instrumental Rationality in *Parade's End*' (*SNNTS* 41[2009] 178–200) explores how Ford's most acclaimed novel constructs the 'enemy' as those who actively remodel human beings according to the unforgiving 'logic of production' (p. 178). McCarthy is particularly adept at showing the myriad ways in which Ford targets the industrial, bureaucratic society behind the conflict. *Parade's End*, in McCarthy's trenchant account, documents 'a massive shift in lived experience, otherwise obscured by the dust and sorrow of conflict' (p. 179).

Patrick Deer's *Culture in Camouflage: War, Empire, and Modern British Literature* addresses writers such as Ford Madox Ford, Elizabeth Bowen,

Siegfried Sassoon, and Wilfred Owen, who all challenged the dominant narratives of war disseminated by a powerful mass media and culture industry. Deer's definition of 'war literature' is productively open to popular cultural forms and mass communications, as well as the pamphlets of war strategists and the 'projections of new technologies of violence' (p. 56). Deer is convincing when detailing Ford Madox Ford's formulation of selfhood in terms of its tortured relationship with intensive bureaucratization and state technologies veiled by such civic institutions as matrimony. Ford also ruthlessly debunks the modern war culture's drive to police the entire wartime cultural field, and thereby to monopolize the documentation of the conflict and its causes. Deer also provides an incisive chapter on Ford Madox Ford's propaganda pieces concerning the psychology of active service (p. 15). Ford's imagination, according to Deer, 'specifically his ability to visualize, refuses to cooperate' (p. 15). Ford's 1916 essay entitled 'A Day of Battle' offers a panorama of the war-ravaged landscape that seems both palpably present yet stubbornly 'unreadable' (p. 16). Deer's enterprising account of the 'map' of Great War literature also throws into sharper focus debates about cartographic theory and praxis summarized in Dodge, Kitchin, and Perkins, eds., *Rethinking Maps: New Frontiers in Cartographic Theory*.

Sarah Henstra's *The Counter-Memorial Impulse in Twentieth-Century English Fiction* contains a percipient chapter on Ford's 1915 novel *The Good Soldier* (pp. 40–79). Henstra focuses on the notions of 'grieving Englishness' and melancholic loss triggered by the 'lapse of the British empire and its attendant ideologies' (p. 4). Through a discerning close reading, Henstra fashions a compelling case for viewing *The Good Soldier* as a 'counter-memorial hybrid of elegy and satire' in which honouring a failed national identity becomes rather 'the opportunity' for a slyly sardonic 'critique of that identity's investment in colonial exploitation and self-delusion' (p. 5). Henstra's nuanced argument should be read alongside Gabriel Koureas's *Memory, Masculinity and National Identity in British Visual Culture, 1914–1930: A Study of 'Unconquerable Manhood'* [2008], which appraises the complexities emerging from issues of traumatic bereavement, cultural expressions of sexuality, and the ways in which these are encoded in commemorative objects.

Aulich and Hewitt, eds., *Seduction or Instruction? First World War Posters in Britain and Europe* [2008], with its pointed stress on the Great War as a socio-political as well as martial event, nicely complements these titles given that the war poster from this period acquired a new respectability in terms of its ideological repackaging of the active serviceman as an epitome of extrovert virility. Scholars intrigued by Ford Madox Ford's overt propaganda efforts such as *When Blood is their Argument* [1911] will find much to ponder in this invigorating and richly textured account which salvages the 'wider discursive context' in which posters were designed and disseminated, anchoring them in a milieu in which government campaigns exploited 'the agencies, methods and sites of the new advertising profession' (p. 96), especially what Stephen Donovan calls the 'textual' prestige of 'newsprint' (in Donovan et al., eds., *Authority Matters: Rethinking the Theory and Practice of Authorship* [2008], p. 168).

Colombino, ed., *Ford Madox Ford and Visual Culture* is the eighth volume in the International Ford Madox Ford Studies series and reveals a diverse array of exegetical and theoretical methodologies which position this author in the 'forefront' of the 'philosophical, social and political developments of his age', and as a writer who anticipated many of 'the polemical and theoretical' concerns of the present day (pp. 3–4). As Laura Colombino posits in her crisply written introduction, 'vision' pervades this writer's corpus just as his life was 'thoroughly permeated with the presence of painters and artists in various media' (p. 17). Vita Fortunati's essay on Ford's art criticism (pp. 39–50) demonstrates that theories and themes delineated in *Rossetti* [1902] and *The Pre-Raphaelite Brotherhood* [1907] were crucial to Ford's poetics, such as the 'seeing eye' and the 'cross-cultural approach to literature' (p. 20). Sarah Haslam's lively essay (pp. 85–96) starts from Ford's preoccupation with the Pre-Raphaelites to show that Ford's conception of colour as material, tangible substance becomes a formidable means of expressing and triggering affect in *The Portrait* [1910], *Ladies Whose Bright Eyes* [1911], and *The Panel* [1912], and also in the later *Parade's End* [1924–8].

Petra Rau's *English Modernism, National Identity and the Germans, 1890–1950* focuses brilliantly on the metamorphosis of the Anglo-German Hermann Hueffer into Ford Madox Ford, who offers, like E.M. Forster, 'largely positive representations of Germans' (p. 13). This is in striking contrast to Joseph Conrad, whose *Lord Jim* shows 'modernity' as 'a traumatic loss for which the Germans became a melancholic catalyst' (p. 13). Rau contends that for Ford 'hybridity' and the 'power to assimilate' were 'the strongest qualities of the English people' and the English had to rediscover how they transmuted, 'incorporated and appropriated these influences into their national character' (p. 14). Rau offers a perspicacious assessment of *The Good Soldier*, most of which is set in a German spa town, and of how the trope of the spa vouchsafes 'one way of dealing with the sexual allure of foreign bodies, or with desires most foreign to the English novel' (p. 14). Rau's effectively structured thesis extends the methodologies of cultural and literary research that scrutinizes colonial, sexual, and ethnic others such as Brian Cheyette's *Modernity, Culture and 'the Jew'* [1998], Garrity and Doan, eds., *Sapphic Modernities: Sexuality, Women and National Culture* [2006], and Jennifer Cooke's *Legacies of Plague in Literature, Theory and Film* (pp. 115–40).

Max Saunders's essay on 'Burgess, Joyce and Ford: Modernity, Sexuality and Confession' (in Roughley, ed., *Anthony Burgess and Modernity* [2008], pp. 190–206) demonstrates with intellectual verve that Burgess's admiration for Ford is rooted in shared views about 'literary form' and the delineation of 'sexuality and desire in realistic terms' (p. 9). Saunders's careful reading of Ford's techniques, especially impressionism, underscores the 'view of art incarnated in Burgess's own novels' (p. 195). Ford's child characters and concerns in works such as *Christina's Fairy Book* [1905] are touched upon in Gavin and Humphries, eds., *Childhood in Edwardian Fiction: Worlds Enough and Time*. This volume also boasts a wide-ranging essay by Elizabeth Hale on Saki's 'beastly children and childlike beasts' (pp. 191–207). Brian Gibson's essay, 'Murdering Adulthood: From Child Killers to Boy Soldiers in Saki's

Fiction' (pp. 208–23), also notes the 'sardonic maliciousness' (p. 191) imbuing 'Sredni Vashtar' [1910], 'The Penance' [1910], and 'The Lumber-Room' [1913]. With an elegant sureness of touch Gibson contends that children in these stories 'battle their indoctrinating guardians' by finessing 'an inner story frame, becoming authors of their own re-ordering fictions' (p. 209). Paul March-Russell's essay (pp. 23–36) argues that E.M. Forster's fictional preoccupation with various mystical traditions and codes 'supplied a set of ideas with which to oppose the hegemonic values of efficiency, routine and hierarchy' (p. 30).

March-Russell's essay provides an intriguing companion piece to Ambreen Hai's 'Forster and the Fantastic: The Covert Politics of *The Celestial Omnibus*' (*TCL* 54[2008] 217–46). Hai postulates that the six short stories written between 1902 and 1910 and collected as *The Celestial Omnibus*, so often denigrated as mannered whimsy, encrypt a radical politics that engages with homosexual yearning as well as 'interlocking forms' of social 'oppression' (p. 217). Kim Shirkani's 'The Economy of Recognition in *Howards End*' (*TCL* 54[2008] 193–216) offers a timely reassessment of Leonard Bast, a character so often used to demonstrate Forster's 'most embarrassing blind spot' in the novel (p. 193). Praseeda Gopinath's 'An Orphaned Manliness: The Pukka Sahib and the End of Empire in *A Passage to India* and *Burmese Days*' (*SNNTS* 41[2009] 201–23) convincingly details 'the gradual progression of the devolution of imperial manliness in the long twilight of empire' (pp. 202–3). Gopinath broadens and buttresses the examination of embattled imperial masculinities during the *fin de siècle* by Anjali Arondekar, Tim Middleton, and Sarah Cole. Gopinath focuses specifically on 'gentlemanliness', especially 'its articulated constituent traits', with a vigorous discussion of the 'contrapuntal production' of English national culture and selfhood in 'the interwar years' (p. 202).

Don Adams's *Alternative Paradigms of Literary Realism* offers a spirited analysis of the undervalued modernist writer Ronald Firbank (pp. 75–94) and how his narrative fabric, with its often puckish deployment of allegory, elegiac pastoral, and existential parable, subverts the conventions of naturalistic mimetic fiction. Adams's chapter is perceptive on Firbank's dogged refusal to 'adopt a self-conscious and subjective manner, avoiding nearly all commentary on the material he is presenting' (p. 75). Adams is also adept in detailing how Firbank's stylistic innovations energized the next generation of British novelists, especially Ivy Compton-Burnett and Henry Green.

Ronald Firbank was a key influence on Forster, who has been extremely well served recently by two fine editions of his miscellaneous writings, especially popular criticism for established print-media venues such as the BBC. Heath, ed., *The Creator as Critic and Other Writings by E.M. Forster* [2008], and Lago, ed., *The BBC Talks of E.M. Forster* [2008] both illuminate an enigmatic ambivalence which marks this author's formidable corpus of non-fiction prose; between the stance of chilly elitism synonymous with the modernist author and the rapidly evolving scope and impact of the popular media to which Forster eagerly contributed. Ardel Thomas's essay, 'Gothic Landscapes, Imperial Collapse and the Queering of Adela Quested in E.M. Forster's *A Passage to India*' (in Hughes and Smith, eds., *Queering the Gothic*, pp. 89–104), addresses the emotional and physical cartography of the novel and how it raises questions about fractured identities and existential emptiness.

Ambreen Hai's *Making Words Matter: The Agency of Colonial and Postcolonial Literature* also weighs these issues in two vigorously argued chapters entitled 'Forster's Crisis' and 'At the Mouth of the Caves'. Alison Sainsbury's essay, '"Not yet not there": Breaking the Bonds of Marriage in E.M. Forster's *A Passage to India*' (*CS* 21[2009] 59–73), ties Forster's urgent discussion of male friendships to the presentation of gendered desire and imperial expansion. Tony E. Jackson's chapter on 'The De-Composition of Writing in *A Passage to India*' (in Jackson, ed., *The Technology of the Novel: Writing and Narrative in British Fiction*, pp. 103–22) proposes that theories of writing considered as an invented technology permit us to appreciate hitherto neglected facets of Forster's most acclaimed novel. Nicholas Royle's chapter, 'Impossible Uncanniness: Deconstruction and Queer Theory' (pp. 113–133), from *In Memory of Jacques Derrida*, canvasses Forster's *The Longest Journey*. While not a 'queer novel', Royle asserts, 'we are still in need of inventing a critical language to respond to it' (p. 122). Royle's thoughtful response is especially alert to the 'switching and multiplying of sexual identities' in arguably Forster's most maligned work of fiction (p. 122).

Of the other notable essays on Forster's oeuvre it is worth mentioning Tess Cosslett's 'Revisiting Fictional Italy, 1887–1908: Vernon Lee, Mary Ward, and E.M. Forster' (*ELT* 52[2009] 312–28), which shows that *Where Angels Fear to Tread* [1905] and *A Room with a View* [1908] are informed by earlier literary examples of 'mapping' the Mediterranean. Cosslett's thesis reflects how resourcefully Forster's early fiction has been construed with reference to the politics of place, cultural geography, and especially environmental history, a rapidly expanding area of historical enquiry which exploits a dizzying array of disciplines for its insights, as evidenced by Sörlin and Warde, eds., *Nature's End: History and the Environment*, and Becket and Gifford, *Culture, Creativity and Environment* [2007].

Evelyn Cobley's *Modernism and the Culture of Efficiency: Ideology and Fiction* seeks to merge the 'excavating insights' of 'social scrutiny' with the nuanced exactitude of literary analysis in her chapter on 'Criminal Efficiency' in Conrad's *Heart of Darkness* (pp. 185–202). Cobley calibrates the terms in which protagonists both challenge modern civilization and buttress its fierce investment in efficiency (p. 13). Core preoccupations with sexual relations, family structures, identity crises, social ambitions, and moral dilemmas camouflage from the reader 'how much space is often devoted to the efficiency calculus surfacing' in delineations of 'instrumental reason' and 'capitalism' (p. 13). This thesis resonates powerfully with the efficient Wilcoxes in *Howards End* (pp. 246–81), the scrupulous Leonora in Ford's *The Good Soldier* (pp. 224–45), and the exceptionally driven Kurtz in *Heart of Darkness*. However, Cobley throws into sharper focus the 'ambiguous, slippery, and often contradictory ideological work performed by efficiency' (p. 13). Her argument demonstrates that the ideology of efficiency 'has seeped unannounced into' the entire 'social fabric' of *The Good Soldier* (p. 229).

Ross, ed., *Modernism and Theory: A Critical Debate* seeks 'to recapture the continuities among modernism and theory', and addresses specific concerns about the relationship between historical and theoretical approaches to modernism (in its various definitions), local and transnational locations, canonical and marginalized thinkers, and political and philosophical readings (pp. 3–4). Ross's elegantly structured introduction rightly affirms the degree to which 'the new modernist studies' have been 'a boon' for scholars of this literary period (p. 1). Such an energizing turn has 'reopened modernism to a more comprehensive gaze' (pp. 1–2), embracing the full gamut of culture from approximately 1890 to 1950: little magazines, manifestoes, realist writing, scientific treatises, women's writing, advertising, toys, even cookbooks. Ross indicates that behind all this is a 'renewed vision of modernism as a variegated response to a manifold modernity' (p. 1). Melba Cuddy-Keane's incisive essay on 'Ethics' (pp. 208–18) employs Forster's *Howards End* and Conrad's *Lord Jim* to foreground 'the problematics of instinctual response versus duty, mercy versus responsibility, and love versus loyalty to a code' (p. 212).

Stephen Ross also contributes a perceptive essay on 'Uncanny Modernism, or Analysis Interminable' to Caughie, ed., *Disciplining Modernism* (pp. 33–52). Ross's research is not only a dexterous appraisal of 'modernism's brand name' (p. 36) but also amplifies some of the key findings in Collins and Jervis, eds., *Uncanny Modernity: Cultural Theories, Modern Anxieties* [2008].

Dryden, Arata, and Massie, eds., *Robert Louis Stevenson and Joseph Conrad: Writers of Transition*, contains a particularly fine essay on 'Cross-Cultural Encounters in *In the South Seas* and *Heart of Darkness*' (pp. 92–108) by Monica Bungaro. The key strength of this essay, as of the volume as a whole, is how thoroughly it details points of intersection between Stevenson's richly varied writing and the modernist themes of imperial assertion and biting anxiety (p. 93). For Conrad, as for Stevenson, Bungaro contends, the 'story of progress is not one of colonial mastery but of degeneration and atavism' (p. 95). In Stevenson's tales of human duality, chaotic instinctual appetite, and deep colonial scepticism there is a signal 'crossover' between high Victorian literature and the birth of the modern movement (p. 1). The chronicle of degeneration which Bungaro's essay relates is greatly complicated by Peter Melville Logan's *Victorian Fetishism*, whose astute chapter on E.B. Tylor's anthropological science (pp. 89–114) raises questions about the cross-fertilization between ethnographic investigation and the imperial romance mode variously epitomized and critiqued by Conrad, Stevenson, and H. Rider Haggard.

Baxter and Hand, eds., *Joseph Conrad and the Performing Arts*, showcases a diverse array of theoretical perspectives to gauge major and overlooked works within the context of the performing arts: the improvisation of ethnic identity in the Malay fiction; Conrad's sardonic and parodic procedures; his adroit manipulation of melodramatic and Gothic tropes; his interest in operatic convention and the visual culture of early cinema; plus his complex relationship with Shakespeare. Moreover, since the first screening of *Victory* in 1919, Conrad remained a notable 'source for screen adaptation', a task 'facilitated when one recognizes how remarkably and consistently cinematic many of Conrad's works are' (p. 4). As Katherine Baxter eloquently contends in her lucid opening gambit, Conrad is a novelist who is energized by the performing arts as a fund of complex intertextual reference and allusion. Indeed, the collection's key strength is its flexible and provocative interpretation of 'performative modes' (p. 9) so as to canvass how political power is 'staged'. This approach can be measured against Judith Brown's project in *Glamour in Six Dimensions: Modernism and the Radiance of Form*, which indicates that Kurtz's ability to seize and consolidate power is inextricably related to his 'aura' as a charismatic figurehead whose fascinating rhetoric cannily re-brands the pernicious excesses of 'the colonial system' (p. 12).

Tabish Khair's *The Gothic, Postcolonialism and Otherness: Ghosts from Elsewhere* reassesses Conrad's *Heart of Darkness* in terms of the challenge of narrating the 'subaltern' in a postcolonial context (pp. 72–85). Khair's account places a shrewd emphasis on this much-discussed text's 'subterranean anxiety and awareness' of a vengeful revenant that was 'already stalking England, but which mainstream novelists' elected to view predominantly in the most remote recesses of the British empire (p. 9). Vilashini Cooppan's *Worlds Within: National Narratives and Global Connections in Postcolonial Writing* also prioritizes *Heart of Darkness* (pp. 55–97) as 'haunted ground' to which postcolonial literature and criticism return 'as if to the scene of a crime or prophecy' (p. 55). Cooppan deploys psychoanalytical paradigms with adroit skill to expose how the text shares with the Freudian fetish a 'compulsion' to articulate an underlying misgiving about 'the very existence of difference'. Indeed, *Heart of Darkness* becomes in this thesis the 'traumatic kernel for a whole series of fetishistic displacements' (pp. 70–1).

Daniel Darvay's 'The Politics of Gothic in Conrad's *Under Western Eyes*' (*MFS* 55[2009] 693–715) construes Conrad's 1911 novel through the interpretative lens of Gothic figurations as well as the treatment of Slavic identity, especially Polish–Russian relations. Vilashini Cooppan's *Worlds Within: National Narratives and Global Connections in Postcolonial Writing* offers a bold reappraisal of *Heart of Darkness* by adding a complex psychoanalytical dimension to its consideration of nationalism and racial identity.

Paul Kirschner's *Comparing Conrad* is a self-published work by a seminal Conrad scholar whose research spans nearly half a century, from the volume's opening essay, 'Conrad and Maupassant' [1965], to the carefully pondered coda, 'Conrad, James and the "Other Self"' [2007]. Kirschner's patient textual analysis teases out a plethora of striking correspondences and apparent contradictions in this most paradoxical of authors. Kirschner is especially attuned to Conrad's multifaceted relationship with other writers from the period. One of the recent developments in the study of Conrad and intertextuality has been the informed discussion of his riddling attitude towards the mainstream marketplace, visual technology, and advertising practices (see for instance Stephen Donovan's sedulously researched *Joseph Conrad and Popular Culture* [2005]). *Comparing Conrad* is more preoccupied with measuring Conrad's formidable achievements against those of Dostoevsky and Henry James rather than H. Rider Haggard and Robert Louis Stevenson.

Michael John DiSanto's *Under Conrad's Eyes: The Novel as Criticism* discusses Conrad's borrowings from and often radical revaluations of some of his nineteenth-century precursors—especially Thomas Carlyle, Charles Dickens, George Eliot, Dostoevsky, and Nietzsche. DiSanto's interpretation of *Heart of Darkness* and *Victory* prioritizes questions concerning 'the will to know' and the 'avoidance of knowledge' (pp. 3–32). His detailed examination of how Conrad transmutes facets of *Bleak House* into *The Secret Agent* and *Middlemarch* into *Nostromo* demonstrates that Conrad's fictions are not just 'highly complex' works, but also vehicles of stringent 'literary criticism' (p. 24).

Like DiSanto, Ludwig Schnauder's *Free Will and Determinism in Joseph Conrad's Major Novels* is fascinated by the competing instincts for self-preservation and self-annihilation; especially the 'forces' which conspire to derail the fortunes of his major fictional protagonists. Schnauder canvasses the core philosophical dilemma the protagonists' predicament raises: that of the 'freedom-of-the-will' (p. 3). Schnauder's resourceful readings of *Heart of Darkness*, *Nostromo*, and *The Secret Agent* uncover a beguiling paradox: how Conrad stresses the need for moral responsibility, presupposing 'the existence of free will' (p. 55), in a materialist universe which seems to gainsay it at every turn. Tanya Agathocleous's percipient introduction to her new Broadview edition of *The Secret Agent* also raises important questions about this nagging paradox.

Carey, ed., *Empires of Religion* [2008], broaches the 'currently contested status of missionary history' (p. 2) and is only indirectly concerned with issues of textual interpretation. However, this compelling essay collection, with its astute examination of the logic of imperial expansion, should be of considerable interest to Conrad specialists who admired Robert Hampson's thesis in *Writing Malaysia: Cross-Cultural Encounters in Conrad's Malay Fiction* [2000], as well as to postcolonial theorists and scholars of gender studies and race relations. Like Ulrike Hillemann in *Asian Empire and British Knowledge: China and the Networks of Imperial British Expansion*, the contributors to Carey's volume set out in telling detail the history of foreign missions in an age of acquisitive imperialism, especially in West Africa and the Malay archipelago. Carey irradiates misunderstood facets of what Leila Koivunen calls, in *Visualizing Africa in Nineteenth-Century British Travel Accounts*, Conrad's portrayal of a 'threatening' continental interior which also operates as a cipher for a philosophical 'darkness' within European culture (p. 2). The exhaustive work of both Carey, ed., and Koivunen, which says much about the modernist transmutation of novelistic and pictorial space, should be surveyed alongside the equally impressive Kuehn and Smethurst, eds., *Travel Writing, Form, and Empire: The Poetics and Politics of Mobility*, and Ben Grant's *Postcolonialism, Psychoanalysis and Burton: Power Play of Empire*.

Amar Acheraïou's *Joseph Conrad and the Reader: Questioning Modern Theories of Narrative and Readership* adopts an innovative, theoretically informed approach to the fiction by construing Conrad's 'slippery, nomadic aura' (p. 19) through the lens of urgent debates about visual strategies, audience expectation, and the ethics of authorship. Acheraïou is at his most persuasive when gauging Conrad's imaginative debt to nineteenth-century

French novelists such as Flaubert, whose 'theory of authorship' Conrad 'elaborates' in surprising ways (p. 17). The discerning textual analysis of *Under Western Eyes* operates to show that for Conrad 'the modern writer is not dead, nor exiled, nor epistemologically irrelevant', as deconstructionist pundits propose. Rather, Acheraïou demonstrates that 'the modern author haunts the interstices of his/her indeterminate, multilayered narratives' (p. 186). Such an authorial revenant underscores that 'the writer in modern texts' rarely 'ceases to be a potential epistemic and signifying site of power' (p. 186). Yet this power, as the closing chapters indicate, is 'always chameleon-like, functioning stealthily, by means of veiling and subtle manipulation' (p. 185). That Conrad's treatment of reader-response theory and narrative form exemplifies the presence of a 'constant dialogue' (p. 185) with ancient as well as modern concepts is admirably borne out by some ingenious analysis of *Lord Jim* and *A Personal Record*.

Pearson and Singer, eds., *Detective Fiction in a Postcolonial and Transnational World*, situates Conrad's *Heart of Darkness* and *The Secret Agent* in relation to classic detective fiction and its 'close cousin the spy story' in which mystery tropes and figurations are aligned with deep misgivings over 'contamination, irrationality, and the threat posed to imperial modernity by unassimilated racial and cultural difference' (p. 4). This argument builds on the recent research of Upamanyu Pablo Mukherjee (*Crime and Empire* [2003]) and Caroline Reitz (*Detecting the Nation* [2004]), who have variously shown that early twentieth-century crime fiction developed in tandem with the formation of imperial sway and prestige.

Salisbury and Shail, eds., *Neurology and Modernity: A Cultural History of Nervous Systems, 1800–1950*, effectively construes texts as diverse as John Galsworthy's *Man of Property* [1906], Arnold Bennett's *The Old Wives' Tale* [1908], William Le Queux's *The Count's Chauffeur* [1907], and John Buchan's *Prester John* [1910], using 'a broad range of cultural discourses' that both emerged from and delineated modernity as a 'singularly neurological, determinedly nervous' condition (p. 2). Neurology vouchsafed 'several major components of modernity's particular conception of somatic and psychological experience' (p. 23), and it is one of this volume's signal strengths that it permits us to view how Ford Madox Ford and Joseph Conrad variously sought to render 'nervous strain' (p. 187) in the imaginative patterns of their fiction. Roger Luckhurst's *The Trauma Question* [2008] persuasively anchors many of these insights in a discussion of shell-shock and its place in the 'war ecology' (pp. 49–59).

Sean Gaston's *Derrida, Literature and War: Absence and the Chance of Meeting* boasts a rigorously theorized chapter on Conrad's 'The Duel' (pp. 117–39), which was published in 1908 in a collection of shorter fiction, *A Set of Six*. Gaston's account ponders what it means to 'fight a duel', to pursue a 'private contest' as 'insane artists' in a time of bitter internecine strife (p. 121). Conrad's elliptical perspective in this story seems to oscillate between 'half sceptical yearning' for the ostensibly more structured milieu of the early nineteenth century, and a debunking of two hopelessly 'outdated' figures who struggle against 'the imperial *realpolitik* of the day' (pp. 121–2).

Andrew Bennett's discriminating assessment of 'Conrad's Blindness' in *Ignorance: Literature and Agnoiology* (pp. 132–53) weighs the condition of not being 'able' to 'see' as a core thematic concern of Conrad's short fiction and its 'relation to his life' (p. 133). Bennett's argument is delivered with emphatic assurance, and he concludes that it is through a profound perceptual 'disturbance'—the loss of sight or ebbing of light—that Conrad's stories 'get written' (p. 133). Indeed, the peculiar intensity of these texts, such as 'The Secret Sharer', Bennett avers, is rooted in a radical ambivalence about their 'ultimate literary merit' (p. 137).

Deborah McLeod's 'Disturbing the Silence: Sound Imagery in Conrad's *The Secret Agent*' (*JML* 33[2009] 117–31) contends that while myriad pundits have delineated the impressionist aspects of *The Secret Agent*, few have canvassed the equally complex and extensive evocations of sound. As McLeod rightly asserts, both painters and musical composers influenced literary impressionism, and Conrad deploys aural imagery in the novel both thematically and descriptively. Allen MacDuffie's 'Joseph Conrad's Geographies of Energy' (*ELH* 76[2009] 75–98) ponders Conrad's multilayered use of the rhetoric of energy and entropy in his scathing critique of imperial dependency and inefficiency. MacDuffie punctiliously contextualizes *Heart of Darkness* and *The Mirror of the Sea* not simply in terms of their fierce engagement with Victorian thermodynamic discourse, but by reference to the specific ways in which concerns about energy use and depletion were inextricably intermingled with expressions of the imperial project at the start of the twentieth century.

Matthew Olivier's essay, 'Conrad's Grotesque Public: Pornography and the Politics of Reading in *The Secret Agent*' (*TCL* 55[2009] 209–32), asks a question that has preoccupied myriad scholars of this espionage novel over the last decade: why is *The Secret Agent* located in a pornography shop? Rather than amplifying the thesis of John Lutz—that the culture of insurgency in the novel shares with the consumption of pornography an abject retreat from the crowding urgencies of the modern moment—Olivier suggests that pornography epitomizes 'a more politically subversive element' (p. 209) Indeed, the essay makes a compelling and eloquent case for how the pornographic underscores the novel's 'larger practice' of employing 'the grotesque' to undercut any concept of 'secure, homogeneous reading publics' (pp. 209–10).

Cannon Schmitt's 'Rumour, Shares and Novelistic Form: Joseph Conrad's *Nostromo*' (in Henry and Schmitt eds., *Victorian Investments: New Perspectives on Finance and Culture*, pp. 182–201) underscores Britain's ominous 'extension of its financial sector into ever more remote parts of the no –European world' (p. 6); becoming a mode of imperialism that 'however different from classic imperialist expansion in its workings, is similar in its results' (p. 188). For Schmitt, *Nostromo* not only indicts informal imperialism but also dissects the pernicious repercussions of 'the culture of investment' (p. 189) in which 'value' is often shaped by the impact of scurrilous rumour, malign innuendo, and misinformation campaigns.

David M. Earle's *Re-Covering Modernism: Pulps, Paperbacks and the Prejudice of Form* explains that between 1900 and 1930 modernist works appeared not only in obscure little magazines and books published by small-scale exclusive presses but also in literary reprint magazines of the 1920s and pulp magazines of the 1930s. This discussion of the publishing and marketing of modernist works is especially helpful in relation to Joseph Conrad, whose use of 'the imperial adventure form' operates, in Earle's estimation, as an 'overture' to the modernist exploitation of the pulp genre (p. 176). Earle's argument resonates with some of the key findings of Andrea White's [2008] *Joseph Conrad and the Adventure Tradition* as well as Linda Dryden's [1999] *Joseph Conrad and the Imperial Romance* by returning Conrad's early narratives to the mainstream milieu of 'their initial appearance' (pp. 177–8).

Anne Veronica Witchard's *Thomas Burke's Dark 'Chinoiserie': 'Limehouse Nights' and the Queer Spell of Chinatown* focuses on Burke's bestselling collection of short stories, *Limehouse Nights* [1916], and assiduously contextualizes the burgeoning cult of 'Chinatown' in turn-of-the-century London. Witchard's vibrant interdisciplinary perspective allows her to overturn the rigid partitions that have characterized Chinese studies, textual analysis, gender studies, critiques of orientalism, and diasporic research. Witchard rethinks Burke's influence and how his fictional tactics both mirrored and subverted the cultural concerns of Western art and literature.

Lawrence Rainey's 'From the Fallen Woman to the Fallen Typist' (*ELT* 52[2009] 273–97) examines four British novels from 1908 to 1922, most notably Arnold Bennett's *Lillian* [1922] and its presentation of a new occupational category that only sprang into existence after 1880: the female secretary. Rainey's essay is acute in its depiction of the secretary's visibility as a distinctively modish and metropolitan phenomenon. Like Price and Thurschwell, eds., *Literary Secretaries/Secretarial Culture* [2005], Rainey gauges the newly working and independent woman of the present in Bennett's text who engages in premarital consensual sex, thus situating her within the older Victorian category of the 'fallen woman', which entailed social ostracism.

Justin E.A. Busch, in *The Utopian Vision of H.G. Wells*, Steven McLean in *The Early Fiction of H.G. Wells: Fantasies of Science* (pp. 151–88), and Richard Nate's essay 'Discoveries of the Future: Herbert G. Wells and the Eugenic Utopia' (in Pordzik, ed., *Futurescapes: Space in Utopian and Science Fiction Discourse*, pp. 79–109) all throw into sharper relief Wells's abiding interest in questions of social engineering and racial cleansing in such prose works as *A Modern Utopia* [1904] and *Men Like Gods* [1922–3]. Christoph Ehland's 'The Watchdogs of Eden: Chesterton and Buchan Look at the Present and Future' (in Pordzik, ed., pp. 171–98) appraises the trope of the Garden City in G.K. Chesterton's *The Man Who Was Thursday* [1908] and John Buchan's 1919 spy novel *Mr Standfast*. Ehland calibrates the elaborate strategies by which these writers of a 'pointedly conservative stance' (p. 171) not only denigrate the supposedly idyllic space of the garden suburb but also fashion reactionary counter-utopias.

Slavoj Žižek's 'From Job to Christ: A Paulinian Reading of Chesterton' (in Caputo and Alcoff, eds., *St. Paul among the Philosophers*, pp. 39–58) canvasses the treatment of anarchism in *The Man Who Was Thursday* as well as its coding of Christian theology. Žižek's bracing and witty essay, along with Alison Milbank's *Chesterton and Tolkien as Theologians* [2007] reflects an encouraging revival of scholarly interest in Chesterton's status as a public intellectual and the more problematic components of his fictional repertoire, such as his relationship with liberal 'Little Englanders', his hectoring populist patriotism, and his idiosyncratic reworking of late Victorian anti-imperialist tropes.

(b) James Joyce

It is hardly common for a work of Joyce criticism to find itself on the bestseller lists, but for a short time in Dublin in 2009 Declan Kiberd's *'Ulysses' and Us* accomplished such a feat. In part, its popular success could be attributed to Kiberd's sure-footed explication of each of *Ulysses*' eighteen episodes, which makes this one of the better introductory volumes available. However, the main reason for the media attention was the polemic Kiberd signals in the title and develops in his opening chapters: his is a populist *Ulysses*, a book which he argues works better when untainted by the 'scholastic stink'. He makes a cogent, although not completely original, argument that even though Joyce's works were appreciated by an avant-garde audience, he never saw himself as an avant-garde author. For Kiberd, Joyce is fundamentally an ethical writer, and this point has been missed by the assimilation of Joyce into university curricula. Kiberd reads *Ulysses* as an example of 'wisdom literature' in which Joyce 'sought a new style which would show the dignity of everyday living' (p. 29), and, in so doing, he 'would explore modes of teaching and learning which answer the emotional and intellectual needs of ordinary people in search of a wiser way of life' (p. 63). Such a thesis leads Kiberd to organize his readings of the individual episodes under rubrics such as 'Walking', 'Thinking', 'Dying', 'Eating', and (inevitably) 'Drinking'. In effect, Kiberd reads Joyce's encyclopedism as a commodious self-help manual. In Kiberd's reading, *Ulysses* is an ethical book in spite of its stylistic complexity—he even endorses Roddy Doyle's claim from 2004 that 'many passages stood in dire need of an editor' (p. 30). Furthermore, he castigates the 'Joyce industry' for denaturing Joyce with all sorts of jargon-laden technical studies that alienate it from its valorization of the quotidian, thereby scaring readers away from Joyce. Kiberd unambiguously blames the professoriate for erecting obstacles for the lay reader to finding wisdom in *Ulysses*. To be sure, most deconstructive readings of Joyce, to take just one example, hardly help his popular appeal, but I'm not so sure that they would hurt it either, at least not to the extent that Kiberd claims. Perhaps the specialization of academic study has not been cause of the decline of the popular appreciation of difficult books and instead both are symptoms of other cultural forces. While the anti-academy polemic is somewhat simplistic, overall Kiberd's book offers an energetic and sympathetic reading of *Ulysses* and does deserve to be taken seriously. Indeed, a number of other critical works from 2009 pick up on some of the themes Kiberd discusses: his critique of the 'bloodless, technocratic explication of texts' (p. 15) is not uniquely his and one can find it made even by bloodless technocrats themselves.

David Earle's book *Re-Covering Modernism* offers an alternative trajectory of the popular and academic reception of Joyce to the one that Kiberd proposes, and indeed, his study is one that has been sorely missing from modernist studies in general. While his book covers a range of modernist authors, Earle does devote considerable attention to Joyce, and reading his book in parallel with Kiberd's is instructive. Earle, in effect, proposes a redefinition of modernism as an elitist, avant-garde movement by looking at the varied publishing histories modernist authors had beyond the small magazines and limited editions. By turning away from the privileging of first publications Earle teases out the history of what he calls 'pulp modernism'. The journals and publications Earle covers enjoyed circulations that were considerably larger and more diverse than the forms of publications traditionally associated with modernist writers. The larger argument of his book is that modernism had a greater and more democratic appeal than has been assumed and, indeed, counter to Kiberd's claims the academy's hold on modernism and modernist writers was perhaps never quite so hegemonic. While some of the magazines that Earle discusses published Joyce because of his reputation as a writer of obscene books, he cogently argues that the pulp interest in Joyce and other modernists went beyond simple matters of prurience. Indeed, my favourite example of his is that *American Girl,* the official magazine of the Girl Scouts of America, published some of Joyce's poems in 1927, a time when *Ulysses* was still a prohibited commodity in the US. While Earle focuses on the US, he does bring up some examples of British pulp modernism. His study is enlivened by pictures of the various publications he discusses. Earle's book thus has the potential to inaugurate a redefinition of modernism and its reception by problematizing the high-versus-low dichotomy entrenched in much academic study.

Cambridge University Press has introduced a new series to complement its stalwart Companions and, as with that series, Joyce is the first author to be covered with *James Joyce in Context*, edited by John McCourt. Perhaps a better title would be 'in contexts' since the scope and range of the essays in this volume are anything but monolithic. As opposed to the lengthy essays in the Companion, McCourt's volume consists of thirty-two short and targeted essays that are arranged under three broad rubrics, 'Life and Works', 'Theory and Critical Reception', and 'Historical and Cultural Contexts'. Some of the essay topics are expected and even necessary for such a volume (and overlap a bit with the Companion), but others—such as Vike Martina Plock's essay on medicine and Jolanta Wawrzycka's on translation—are fresh and innovative. The sheer range of different contexts in both genre (theoretical, historical, biographical, bibliographical, etc.) and type testifies to the vitality of Joyce criticism and also works to encourage more work and new approaches. The various studies of Joyce's critical reception—especially Sean Latham's study of 'Twenty-First Century Critical Contexts'—in some ways counter but in some ways also reinforce Kiberd's argument about how 'bloodless' academics have estranged Joyce from a popular readership. Each essay offers a cogent survey of its specific topic and, when taken together, they form an invaluable volume for postgraduate students and seasoned Joyceans in their survey of the contexts of Joyce's works and their critics.

Lee Spinks's *James Joyce: A Critical Guide* is a more compact and traditional version of McCourt's volume in that he offers a survey of the various contexts that have informed Joyce's works and their reception. Spinks divides his study into three main sections: 'Life and Contexts', 'Work', and 'Criticism'. As an introduction to Joyce and his works, Spinks's book is certainly capable, but not more so than any number of other recent volumes. Like Kiberd's book, Spinks's uses as its cover image the photograph of Marilyn Monroe reading from Arthur Miller's copy of *Ulysses*; hopefully this is not the start of a new trend in Joyce criticism.

A more successful introductory volume is Peter Mahon's *Joyce: A Guide for the Perplexed*, which primarily focuses on just the major works. Beyond simply explicating themes and passages, Mahon provides his readers with strategies on how to approach Joyce through analysing the evolution of styles across his works. Mahon does an elegant job of applying what could be called theoretical readings in an accessible manner.

Joining the recent surge of books on *Finnegans Wake* is Edmund Lloyd Epstein's *A Guide through 'Finnegans Wake'*. Epstein's is a prescriptive guide rather than a descriptive one. That is, avoiding issues of *Wakean* equivocation, he tells his reader what the *Wake* is about (or, less charitably, what he claims it is about) rather than illustrating a protocol with which one may approach reading it on one's own. Aside from the introduction, Epstein devotes his book to a through, but reductive, summary of a narrative line that is presented as if it were the essence of the *Wake* distilled and unencumbered by linguistic tomfoolery. True, he admits that individual passages can denote multiple meanings, but, within his argument, such multiple denotation is always narratologically delimited. Despite these criticisms, there is much to recommend Epstein's book. While his summaries and paraphrases are arguably reductive, they nonetheless result from a highly informed and engaged critical perspective. He avoids Campbell and Robinson's grand mythopoesis and, instead, posits the *Wake* as the story of the sexual awakening of the young generation and the concomitant decline of their parents, a story that is told simultaneously through various registers of characters. In some ways this is a reductive view harking back to readings from before the 1980s; on the other hand, Epstein presents this particular narratological disposition with such clarity and perspicacity that it has great force. As much as I objected to some of his readings, I found myself agreeing, at least in general, with the broad outlines of the argument he propounds. In particular, I very much appreciated that he emphasizes that the *Wake* is a human book and is thus concerned with human foibles and imperfections, a thesis that in its broad strokes parallels Kiberd's reading of *Ulysses*.

Unlike recent years, 2009 was not a strong year for monographs on Joyce. However, in addition to McCourt's volume, two edited volumes appeared, both of which collect conference papers. The 2004 Bloomsday Centennial Symposium in Dublin is marked by a volume edited by Morris Beja and Anne Fogarty, *Bloomsday 100: Essays on 'Ulysses'*. Although the symposium itself was unusually large in scale—with over 500 papers presented—this volume maintains a focus on *Ulysses*, perhaps as a symptom of the current trend in publishing that avoids conference collections as such unless they are themed.

Of particular note are Katherine O'Callaghan's paper on 'Sirens' and Margot Norris's on 'Calypso'. Michael Gillespie's essay, 'When to Stop Reading Joyce Criticism', is compatible with Kiberd's invective against 'bloodless' critics, although Gillespie's argument is not fully formed.

The 2007 Austin Joyce Conference is represented by a volume in the European Joyce Studies series, *De-Familiarizing Readings*, edited by Alan Friedman and Charles Rossman. There is less thematic consistency among these essays than can be found in the Bloomsday Centennial volume. Margot Norris's paper on the 'Ballad of Little Harry Hughes', as sung by Stephen in 'Ithaca', is an important contribution to the analysis of this important crux in the text. She begins by going through the range of possible critical responses as to why Stephen sings this blatantly anti-Semitic song to Bloom in order to conclude that this remains a fundamentally insoluble problem but that this insolubility is essential to Joyce's narrative technique and to the overall human dimension of *Ulysses*.

Along with the 2009 Buffalo Joyce Conference, the Poetry Collection at the University of Buffalo produced an exhibition of their substantial Joyce holdings. Accompanying this exhibition is the volume *Discovering James Joyce*, edited by James Maynard. Along with an exhibition checklist (although not a full catalogue) are essays by Michael Groden, Luca Crispi, and Sam Slote, and a reprint of Oscar Silverman's account of how Buffalo came to acquire such a significant collection of Joyce's manuscripts and personal effects. The volume is well illustrated, but, sadly, issues of copyright precluded the printing of any images of manuscripts.

Daniel Ferrer has an important essay, '*Ulysses* de James Joyce: Un homérisme secondaire', in Most et al., eds., *Révolutions homériques*, which collects papers from a 2006 colloquium devoted to Homer at the École Normale Supérieure in Paris. Looking across the drafts of *Ulysses* as the text evolved over its seven years of composition, Ferrer shows how the Homeric references—a critical chestnut ever since *Ulysses* was first published—were initially slight but became reinforced during Joyce's extensive revisions, in a process he calls 'retrospective Homerisation' (p. 141). Ferrer's essay is an important contribution to the continuing discussion about Homer's impact on Joyce, and he offers a brilliant case study in applied genetic criticism.

Philip Kitcher has an excellent essay in the 2009 *Joyce Studies Annual,* which continues to publish first-rate work (*JoyceSA* [2009] 188–211). Kitcher's essay, 'Collideorscape: *Finnegans Wake* in the Large and in the Small', complements his 2007 book *Joyce's Kaleidoscope* and, in his attention to *Wakean* polysemy, offers an advance over that work. He presents a painstakingly close reading of the ninth question in chapter I.6—the famous 'collideorscape' passage—to demonstrate how the *Wake* suggests 'the philosophical struggle to vindicate a human life' (p. 206). This essay, along with Kiberd's book, points towards a concern with ethical questions emerging within Joyce studies.

The second issue of the *Dublin Joyce Journal* contains a range of impressive articles, ranging from papers on historical contexts—for example on Garryowen and Eugene Stratton—to more theoretical concerns. Dirk Van Hulle's analysis of how Joyce incorporated references to Darwin in the *Wake* and how these references evolved and mutated over the course of revisions is a detailed and instructive application of genetic criticism.

Articles of note include Joseph Valente and Margot Backus's '"An iridescence difficult to account for": Sexual Initiation in Joyce's Fiction of Development' (*ELH* 76[2009] 523–45). Following from Lacan's reading of Joyce, through close readings of passages from *Dubliners* and *A Portrait*, they argue that Joyce plays with the erotic potentialities of language and signification. This essay is an important contribution to Lacanian readings of Joyce.

Another essay of note is Adrienne Janus's 'From "Ha he hi ho hu. Mummum" to "Haw! Hell! Haw!": Listening to Laughter in Joyce and Beckett' (*JML* 32:iii[2009] 144–66). Janus traces out how both Beckett and Joyce, working from the linguistic theories of Fritz Mauthner, deploy tropes of laughter as an index of the unreliability of language as a representational medium. While the influence of Mauthner on Joyce and Beckett has been well explored, Janus's focus and analysis are original and insightful.

(c) D.H. Lawrence

D.H. Lawrence criticism and scholarship were well served by the items published during 2009. In addition to two challenging collections of essays on the author and a monograph on sexual desire in the prose works, there were three journal articles, new numbers of the *Journal of D.H. Lawrence Studies* and *Études Lawrenciennes*, two new volumes in the Cambridge edition of Lawrence's works, plus a fresh selection of his critical writings.

New D.H. Lawrence, edited by Howard J. Booth, contains nine essays by a new generation of Lawrence scholars in Britain, the USA, and Italy, showcasing a range of recent critical approaches to the author in the academy. The contributors, in addition to the editor, are Andrew Harrison, Holly A. Laird, Hugh Stevens, Jeff Wallace, Stefania Michelucci, Bethan Jones, Fiona Becket, and Sean Matthews, and their approaches range from book history to postcolonialism, ecocriticism, psychoanalysis, philosophy, gender studies, and war writing. In an essay entitled 'D.H. Lawrence, Language and Green Cultural Critique', Fiona Becket draws on the writings of Freya Mathews, Val Plumwood, and Mary Midgley to argue that Lawrence 're-imagined our relationship to the material world in ways which have been ignored by the critical establishment' (p. 157); Lawrence goes well beyond a dualistic attitude to the urban/rural or the city/country, and even questions the 'human/non-human dualism' (p. 156), imputing consciousness to rocks and thus joining Plumwood in refusing to privilege the human or the human-like in the order of creation. Becket suggests that Lawrence's poetry, and especially the poems of *Birds, Beasts and Flowers*, 'goes beyond the human to redeem nature's others from the margins' (p. 166). In '51/49: Democracy, Abstraction and the Machine in Lawrence, Deleuze and their Readings of Whitman', Jeff Wallace concentrates on a 'strange' moment in Lawrence's essay 'Democracy' when he implies a mathematical ratio of spontaneity and mechanism in humans corresponding to '51% spontaneity, 49% mechanism'. The moment is uncharacteristic, 'even unfortunate' (p. 99), because it occurs in an essay that pointedly critiques the abstract thinking that underpins ideas of democracy. Wallace asks whether the anomaly might reveal, in contrast to Lawrence's own privileging of spontaneity over mechanism, that abstraction 'in fact characterizes Lawrence when he is *most* himself, though least aware of it' (p. 102). Wallace is not merely concerned to 'play the game of turning Lawrence's rhetorical and conceptual weapons against himself'; instead, he finds something 'sad' in 'Lawrence's fundamentalising of subjectivity' (p. 111), comparing it to the '*good* abstraction' implicit in Deleuze and Guattari's notion of Nature as 'an immense Abstract Machine' (p. 113). Wallace's essay embodies one of the strengths of this collection in the way it reads Lawrence's work as adopting a conflicted, troubling, potentially paradoxical, but also fascinating and revealing position in relation to debates central to his time and our own.

Windows to the Sun: D.H. Lawrence's 'Thought-Adventures', edited by Earl Ingersoll and Virginia Hyde, brings together revised versions of several papers first delivered at the tenth international D.H. Lawrence conference in Santa Fe, New Mexico, in 2005. The conference theme that year was 'Lawrence and the Frontiers', and the majority of the contributors to this volume foreground the transgressive aspects of Lawrence's 'thought-adventures', identifying his readiness to traverse various sexual, cultural, and ideological faultlines. The editors stress Lawrence's unflinching confrontation with a range of contemporary issues, including 'wartime and postwar malaise, fascism, eugenic marriage patterns, racism, sexism, ecological crisis, and the prospect of censorship' (p. 8). As this list suggests, the issues at stake here are very broad indeed, and the treatment of them is variable as regards the depth and quality of analysis. There are nine essays, covering a range of texts and issues, including Lawrence's engagement with Herman Melville (Earl Ingersoll), his subversive recourse to eugenic discourses in *The Lost Girl* (Theresa Mae Thompson), and his use of a kind of magical realist technique in *The Plumed Serpent* (Jamie Jung Min Woo). The two best contributions come from John Worthen and Christopher Pollnitz. In '"Over Some Frontiers" at Monte Cassino: Lawrence and Maurice Magnus', Worthen revisits his recent biography, *D.H. Lawrence: The Life of an Outsider* [2005], suggesting that it underplayed the significance of the interactions between Lawrence and Magnus, the down-at-heel American ex-pat whose financial recklessness, openly homosexual lifestyle, and eventual suicide fascinated, moved, and appalled Lawrence in equal measure. Worthen feels that his biography mistakenly 'normalized' (p. 50) the author's short stay with Magnus in Monte Cassino in February 1920; where it dismissed as spiteful gossip Magnus's statement to Norman Douglas that Lawrence expressed a personal interest in seeking out bisexual types for himself, Worthen now gives some credence to the account. He does not believe that Lawrence was a practising bisexual at that time, but he does feel that, through Lawrence's willingness to entertain the idea of bisexual attraction in himself, he sought to draw Magnus out, asking him to describe sexual experiences beyond the range of Lawrence's own understanding. He suggests that Lawrence may have persuaded Magnus to make explicit mention of his homosexual experiences in *Dregs*, the memoir of the time he spent in the Foreign Legion; in turn, Worthen speculates that their frank discussions informed the kinds of relationship Lawrence explored in *Aaron's Rod*, in (for instance) Aaron Sisson's tortured affair with the Marchesa. This account of 'their frontier-crossing exploration of sexual experience normally beyond Lawrence's reach' (p. 56) is psychologically compelling and richly suggestive. In 'Keeping his Flag Flying: Censorship and Lawrence's Poetry', Christopher Pollnitz redresses two common misconceptions about the censorship of Lawrence's texts. First, he shows that Lawrence's texts were censored not purely on sexual grounds, but also for religious and political reasons; second, he shows that it was not only his novels that fell foul of the censors, but also 'his short fiction, his nonfiction, and (just as relentlessly) his poetry' (p. 166). He pays close attention to the censorship of the poetry collections *Love Poems and Others*, *Look! We Have Come Through!*, *New Poems*, *Birds, Beasts and Flowers*, *Pansies*, and *Nettles*.

The year's single monograph, *Destinies of Splendor: Sexual Attraction in D.H. Lawrence*, by Douglas Wuchina, is 'principally concerned with the clear positive examples of sexual attraction' in Lawrence's novels (p. 18), focusing on *Sons and Lovers*, *The Trespasser*, *The Rainbow*, *Women in Love*, *Mr Noon*, *The Lost Girl*, and *Lady Chatterley's Lover*. The interesting decision to consider *The Trespasser* after *Sons and Lovers*, thus reversing the chronology of their completion, is justified by Wuchina on the grounds that *The Trespasser* 'tells us a good deal about the sensibility that accompanies love, and [has] a sustained romantic focus that *Sons and Lovers* lacks' (p. 71). Unfortunately, the book fails to engage in any systematic way with recent Lawrence criticism or biography. Wuchina's opening claim that the amount of critical attention devoted to Lawrence and sexuality 'remains essentially the same as it was over fifty years ago' (p. 1) strikes a very hollow note indeed. He cites just two articles on Lawrence and sex, from 1962 and 2003 respectively, but he makes only superficial use of the three-volume Cambridge biography, and he fails to mention (for example) James C. Cowan's *D.H. Lawrence: Self and Sexuality* [2002] or David Ellis's article on 'D.H. Lawrence and the Female Body' (*CQ* 46:ii[1996] 136–52). There are only two entries on homosexuality in the index, and there is no mention of Howard J. Booth's essay on 'D.H. Lawrence and Male Homosexual Desire' (*RES* 53[2002] 86–107). Without the kind of critical dialogue that an attention to such texts might have fostered, Wuchina's analyses frequently give way to a largely unfocused and monotonous attempt simply to describe instances of sexual attraction in the texts. One soon tires of reading platitudes like the following: 'There is no doubt that Paul's perception of Miriam is skewed as a result of his sexual struggles' (p. 59); '[Anton Skrebensky's] secret is his emotional impotence' (p. 121); 'Gudrun can't be blamed for being who she is' (p. 130); 'The main fact about Clifford is his impotence' (p. 189). Few readers will share Wuchina's appreciation of *The Trespasser* as 'Lawrence's most enjoyable novel', nor recognize his description of its 'freshly romantic holiday atmosphere' (p. 71).

Turning to this year's journal articles, in 'D.H. Lawrence, "An Opportunity and a Test": The Leavis–Eliot Controversy Revisited' (*CQ* 38:ii[2009] 130–46), Brian Crick and Michael DiSanto offer a critical reappraisal of the complex background to Leavis's longstanding quarrel with Eliot over Lawrence's posthumous reputation. They suggest that some of Eliot's more pointed and dismissive published references to Lawrence may have been occasioned by his professional contacts with John Middleton Murry, whose memoir of Lawrence, *Son of Woman* [1931], sought to dismiss the author as a case study in sexual failure. The intensity of Leavis's dismissal of Eliot, in turn, is said to have been conditioned by his early sense of indebtedness to Eliot as critic, and by certain of his early writings on Lawrence, which show that he shared some similar reservations about, for instance, *Women in Love*. Faced by Eliot's silence in the 'debate', Leavis increasingly implied that Lawrence himself was opposed to Eliot and his journal, *The Criterion*, whereas in fact he contributed several pieces to it and initially described it in glowing terms. The opposition which Leavis insisted on in his critical writings (Lawrence *or* Eliot) was an artificial one. Eliot can be seen to have been profoundly ambivalent about Lawrence's art throughout his life. Crick and DiSanto suggest that the situation demonstrates 'how extraordinarily difficult it is to do justice to an opponent's argument when it attacks a position to which one is deeply committed' (p. 130); they counsel us to reconnect the judgements of the two critics with the context of their arguments.

In '"His Father's Dirty Digging": Recuperating the Masculine in D.H. Lawrence's *Sons and Lovers*' (*MFS* 55:ii[2009] 242–64), Ronald Granofsky seeks to augment and extend a range of modern psychoanalytic approaches to *Sons and Lovers* by demonstrating how its symbolism reveals Paul Morel's unconscious wish to counter his mother's influence through an identification with his reviled and abjected father, Walter. Granofsky focuses on the dirt symbolism in the novel, suggesting that the miner's synecdochic oneness with the dirt of the pit is firmly established by his wife, Gertrude, to whom it represents disorder, low social status, and filthy manners. Paul and his brothers adopt their mother's prejudice, but Paul can be said to unconsciously seek out the dirt which stands in for his father: 'Paul yearns for the dirt his mother has taught him is disgusting' (p. 249). The approach produces a fascinating reappraisal of the famous and resonant scenes in which the young Paul burns his sister's broken doll, and later burns the loaves which he is tending on behalf of his mother; in both cases, Paul's actions register 'the oblique presence of the neglected figure of the father' (p. 253) through the blackened arms and legs of the doll, and the burnt coke on the surface of the loaf. Granofsky is acute in his observation that the 'wisdom of the writing is in its subtle reaching out to Walter even as he is shunned by his family' (p. 255): he tellingly directs us to an easily overlooked scene shortly after Mrs Morel's death in which the father acts as the nourisher, giving Paul the hot milk which stands in for the gift of the vanquished mother. Unfortunately, the sharpness and sensitivity of such insights is offset by an absurdly opaque and strained interpretation of 'the famous lily scene' (p. 251), and by severely abbreviated and largely unconvincing readings of the later poems 'Man and Bat' and 'Snake' as staging a 'recuperation of the masculine' (p. 255) comparable to *Sons and Lovers*.

Finally, in 'Art and Money: George Gissing, D.H. Lawrence and the Literary Marketplace' (*GissingJ* 45:i[2009] 35–50), Andrew Harrison assesses the anxieties of the young Gissing and Lawrence when confronted by the literary marketplace at the start of their careers. He compares the depiction of struggling artist-figures in Gissing's short story 'The Artist's Child' and Lawrence's *Sons and Lovers*, suggesting that they reveal their authors' fears of a failure to adapt to the literary marketplace (Gissing) and an inability to 'wrest back some sense of art's value from the commercial arena where it is sold and appreciated' (Lawrence) (p. 47).

There was no new number of the *D.H. Lawrence Review* published in 2009. However, there *were* new numbers of the annual *Journal of D.H. Lawrence Studies* and of the biannual *Études Lawrenciennes*.

This year's issue of the *Journal of D.H. Lawrence Studies* contains the 'Further Letters of D.H. Lawrence', plus essays or review-essays by Colm Kerrigan, Keith Sagar, Judith Ruderman, Keith Cushman, Jim Phelps, Lynn K. Talbot, Howard J. Booth, Paul Eggert, Christopher Pollnitz, and Jonathan Long. In 'Lawrence at *Bay*: "Hand-Printed and Beautiful, 7/6 a Copy"' (*JDHLS* 2:i[2009] 103–21), Keith Cushman documents the troubled negotiations between Lawrence and the publisher Cyril Beaumont over the limited edition publication of Lawrence's poetry collection *Bay*, which finally appeared in November 1919. He also discusses Anne Estelle Rice's ten watercolour illustrations for the expensive volume, seven of which are reproduced at the end of the essay. Judith Ruderman's 'Louisa Victrix: Female Initiative in "Daughters of the Vicar"' (*JDHLS* 2:i[2009] 81–100) makes a refreshing feminist reappraisal of one of Lawrence's most accomplished early stories, arguing that it 'marks a step in the direction of the more complex exploration of female emancipation that Lawrence undertook [in *The Rainbow*]' (p. 97).

Volumes 39 and 40 of *Études Lawrenciennes* were devoted to 'A Plurality of Selves and Voices' and 'Power and Authority in D.H. Lawrence's Work' respectively, containing essays by, among others, Earl Ingersoll, Gerald Doherty, Elizabeth Fox, and Neil Roberts (volume 39), and Juliette Feyel, Jacqueline Gouirand-Rousellon, and Helen Baron (volume 40). In the former volume, Keith Cushman's 'Middleton Murry, Catherine Carswell, and the Boundaries of Memoir' (*EL* 39[2009] 9–30) looks at the spate of memoirs written about Lawrence in the 1930s, focusing on the controversy surrounding the publication of Carswell's *Savage Pilgrimage* [1932], which provoked legal action over its treatment of Middleton Murry. Carswell had been angered by Murry's earlier study of Lawrence, *Son of Woman*, which Cushman describes as 'poisonous' in its combination of 'animosity' and 'smarmy *faux* sympathy' (p. 15). The publishers of Carswell's book, Chatto & Windus, were forced to withdraw it, but it was reissued in a revised edition by Martin Secker. Cushman notes that Murry and Carswell present contrasting versions of Lawrence: 'the tortured, self-divided misogynist and latent homosexual' and 'the priest of love, the man of rich spirit and immense passion and vitality' (p. 28). In volume 40, Peter Preston takes a broadly postcolonial approach to one of Lawrence's least well known books in 'Roman Power: Politics in *Sketches of Etruscan Places*' (*EL* 40[2009] 9–28). He identifies two narratives in the book: the 'transhistorical, cross-cultural encounter with the Etruscan people, achieved through visits to their tombs and other remains' (p. 9) and the more mundane and contingent narrative of 'the fortunes of Lawrence and [Earl] Brewster as travellers' (p. 10). He discusses Lawrence's critical treatment of the colonizing power of the Romans, who effectively erased traces of the Etruscan civilization, and his allusions to Mussolini, who appropriated Roman models 'in order to increase the prestige and effectiveness of his own regime' (p. 12).

Two new volumes in the Cambridge edition of Lawrence's works appeared this year. *The Vicar's Garden and Other Stories*, edited by N.H. Reeve, collects together early versions of the short stories 'The Shadow in the Rose Garden', 'A Fragment of Stained Glass', 'The White Stocking', 'Odour of Chrysanthemums', 'The Witch à la Mode', 'The Shades of Spring', 'The Thorn in the Flesh', 'The Blind Man', and 'Wintry Peacock'. The texts date from 1907 to 1919, but they are particularly revealing for the insights they offer into Lawrence's crucial development as a writer of fiction between 1907 and 1914. *Mornings in Mexico and Other Essays*, edited by Virginia Hyde, contains the *Mornings in Mexico* essays; ten other short pieces by Lawrence on New Mexico and Mexico written between 1922 and 1928; plus 'Just Back from the Snake Dance', and early versions or fragments of 'Indians and an Englishman' and 'Certain Americans and an Englishman', 'Pan in America', and 'See Mexico After, by Luis Q.'. It also reproduces two Lawrence pencil sketches, 'The Corn Dance' (p. 69) and 'A Koshare' (p. 72), both of which are in the possession of the Charles Deering McCormick Library, Northwestern University.

Selected Criticism: D.H. Lawrence, edited by Brian Crick and Michael DiSanto, offers a judicious selection of Lawrence's critical writings. It prints parts of the 'Study of Thomas Hardy', celebrated essays from *Studies in Classic American Literature* on 'Fenimore Cooper's Leatherstocking Novels', 'Nathaniel Hawthorne and *The Scarlet Letter*' and 'Herman Melville's *Moby Dick*', plus the renowned essays on the novel from 1923 and 1925, including 'Surgery for the Novel—Or a Bomb' (published in the Cambridge edition of *Study of Thomas Hardy and Other Essays* as 'The Future of the Novel'). Among the less familiar pieces it reproduces are the preface to Lawrence's translation of Giovanni Verga's *Cavalleria Rusticana*, 'The Theatre' (section III of *Twilight in Italy*), and the third part of the long 1919 essay 'Democracy' (a section entitled 'Personality'). The editors present Lawrence as a writer whose discriminating critical insights offer a vital alternative to 'literary criticism at the present time' (p. viii). Whether or not we agree with their negative assessment of 'academic theory' (p. xxii), we can feel their enthusiasm for the liveliness, originality, and integrity of Lawrence's insights. Crick and DiSanto justifiably assert Lawrence's right to be placed alongside Henry James and Virginia Woolf as one of those 'rare' things: 'a major critic and a major novelist' (p. viii). However, for all its admirable qualities I do have some lingering reservations about the volume. The editors note that the texts of the essays are taken from '*Phoenix* (1936), *Studies in Classic American Literature* (1923) and *Twilight in Italy* (1916)' (p. 307). This clearly implies that they have used the American Seltzer edition of *Studies*, since the British Secker edition was not published until 1924, but we are left wondering whether they used the Duckworth or the Huebsch edition of *Twilight in Italy* (as both were published in 1916). Their vagueness here seems to reflect a lack of interest in, or even outright disdain for, textual scholarship. This is also felt in the brevity of the explanatory notes, which is defended on the extraordinary grounds that Matthew Arnold was against them, preferring 'a literary book which schools can and will use', rather than 'a school-book' (p. 307). The scholarly underpinnings of the collection will not withstand too much scrutiny, but—for all its flaws and eccentricities—this new volume offers a fresh and engaging alternative introduction to Lawrence's critical writings.

(d) Woolf

R.S. Koppen's *Virginia Woolf, Fashion and Literary Modernity* adopts an unusual but rewarding approach, offering a 'comprehensive reading' of Woolf 'in the context of the modern interest in fashion' (p. ix). Koppen begins by tracing Woolf's personal engagement with fashion, including her ambivalence towards clothing, the Omega Workshop's 'sartorial venture', and her participation in the famous Dreadnought hoax, 'a signal moment of anti-establishment satire performed through costume' (p. 23). She then moves on to look at 'Woolf's writing through its clothes', describing a movement in *Freshwater*, *Orlando*, and *A Room of One's Own* from satirical attacks on Victorian sartorial conventions of 'claustrophobic concealment and totalitarian gender segregation' to the emergence of the androgynous woman as a figure of modernity and modern writing (p. 50). These readings are grounded in contemporary intellectual history such as Havelock Ellis's study of transvestism and J.C. Flügel's *The Psychology of Clothes*, published by the Hogarth Press in 1930. In a reading of *Mrs Dalloway* influenced by Walter Benjamin's vision of fashion as connected to both a pre-modern allegory of 'transcendence' and a modern allegory of 'rupture and lack', Koppen argues that clothing in the novel interweaves 'the quotidian and the profound', a tendency she also identifies in the sartorial historiography of *Between the Acts* (pp. 66, 74). She then employs Wyndham Lewis's 'anti-fashion critique' as a departure point for an examination of Woolf's 'analysis of the commodity culture and its structures of experience' (p. 102). This is carried out through fascinating readings of some of Woolf's less well-known work including the 'The Docks of London' and 'Moments of Being: "Slater's Pins Have No Points"'. *Virginia Woolf, Fashion and Literary Modernity* goes on to offer a study of the interwar progressive counter-culture's association of 'modernity, democracy and pacifism with the liberate (nude) body' (p. 121). While nudity and Woolf do not necessarily sit comfortably together in the mind, Koppen's discussion of *Three Guineas* and its examination of clothing as participant in 'the language of commodities, of exchange value, of advertisement' and of 'mystification and veiling', situates Woolf's polemic within its historical context of resistance to fascism (p. 130). Particularly illuminating is the contrast between *Three Guineas* and Leonard Woolf's *Quack, Quack*. However, perhaps the most interesting part of the book is its use of clothing to reread the mystical and impassioned elements of *The Waves*, which have, as Koppen points out, generally been treated as either parodic and satirical or contextualized within contemporary developments in theoretical physics. For Koppen, the employment of sartorial motifs and garments in the novel acts to mediate between 'the mundane and the sublime' and thus to reconcile opposed readings of Woolf's novel as satire and elegy (p. 160).

In *Virginia Woolf's Ethics of the Short Story*, Christine Reynier describes Woolf's ambivalent attitude towards her short stories, arguing that 'she took short story writing more seriously than she chose to say' (p. 4). This is the departure point for an exploration of a range of issues surrounding Woolf's short stories, including an interesting account of their posthumous publication history that raises the question of generic instability: much of Woof's work crosses boundaries between, for example, essay and story. Reynier goes on to describe the Woolfian short story as 'belonging to a space characterized by circulation, incompletion and inconclusion' and sets out to provide a 'synthetic reading' of this important body of work (pp. 15, 17). In her first chapter she reads Woolf's essays to uncover her critical vision (influenced by Anton Chekhov) of the short story as a location for 'a new reading process' based on a 'shift from intellect to affects and from morality to ethics' (p. 34). In the second chapter, Reynier sets out the heart of her argument: the Woolfian short story is 'based on contradictory impulses', and simultaneously registers 'completion and lack of completion, framing and an absence of framing, fragmentation and unity' (p. 56). She then applies this principle to the ethical implications of the short story as 'a space of encounter between . . . the self and the other' (p. 60). This takes the form of a 'conversation' or 'a space of exchange' both between characters within the text and between the 'story-teller' and the reader (p. 88, 90). This conversational or 'dynamic space', Reynier argues, is 'an aesthetic space with an ethical turn that opens . . . onto the political' (p. 111). This convincing argument establishes clear links between a large number of seemingly disparate stories. While *Virginia Woolf's Ethics of the Short Story* offers little in the way of close readings of individual stories, it successfully situates them as a whole in a theoretical and interpretative framework.

Roberta Rubenstein's *Virginia Woolf and the Russian Point of View* opens by drawing an analogy between Orlando's first encounter with Sasha, the beautiful and elusive Russian princess, and England's encounter—and Woolf's—with Russian literature in the early twentieth century. The comparison is an apt one, and Rubenstein's book helps to trace the contours of Woolf's encounters with Dostoevsky, Chekhov, Tolstoy, and Turgenev, dedicating a chapter to her responses to each of these 'giants of Russian literature' (p. 16). Rubenstein acknowledges previous work done in this area, including her own substantial contributions, and sets out to bring together in one place 'all the strands of this important dimension of her critical and creative oeuvre' (p. 16). The chapter on Dostoevsky covers familiar but important ground, exploring Woolf's responses to the portrayal of thought in Dostoevsky in relation to both the development of her own prose and to her disputes with the Edwardian writers Arnold Bennett, John Galsworthy, and H.G. Wells. In her chapter on Chekhov, Rubenstein highlights 'the radical modernity of his method', and links this, like Christine Reynier in her *Virginia Woolf's Ethics of the Short Story*, to developments in Woolf's short stories (p. 61). The chapter on Tolstoy, a 'fixed star in Virginia Woolf's literary imagination', is particularly interesting (p. 129). As Rubenstein points out,

Tolstoy's name appears more frequently than that of any other Russian author in Woolf's writing, yet the critical community has paid far more attention to her responses to Dostoevsky and Chekhov. Finally, in the fifth chapter Rubenstein makes fascinating connections between Woolf's responses to Turgenev and her novel *The Years*. Also included in the text are useful transcriptions of Woolf's reading notes for *The Possessed*, *Anna Karenina*, *War and Peace*, and several works by Turgenev, as well as an unpublished review in which Woolf uses Chekhov to read Pope's *The Rape of the Lock*.

Virginia Woolf's Mrs. Dalloway: Invisible Presences by Molly Hoff attempts both to explain the seductiveness of Woolf's prose and to prove that *Mrs Dalloway* is an 'essentially metafictional' text (p. 1). While some of Hoff's claims, for instance that 'Woolf's stated object of criticising . . . the social system . . . is often lost in the study of this novel', seem to ignore much contemporary Woolf criticism, other elements are more innovative (p. 2). The bulk of Hoff's book takes the form of meditative annotations on *Mrs Dalloway*, generally linking specific passages in the text with classical intertexts, tracing what she calls the 'prevailing poetics of intertextuality', but also departing into wider interpretative spaces (p. 4). This form is rewarding, both operating as a textual gloss allowing quick identification of readings of particular passages, and building up an argument concerning the classical metafictionality of the novel without losing a tactile connection with text. Problems arise, however, with some of Hoff's readings: is it sufficient to assert that the famous line 'Mrs. Dalloway said she would buy the flowers herself' refers to the myth of the abduction of Persephone who 'is carried away when she had been gathering flowers' (p. 10)? Hoff herself points out that Europa was abducted by Zeus while she was picking flowers, which surely muddies the mythical waters, and in neither case is it clear that the mythical parallel holds true for Woolf's novel: Clarissa is neither carried off to the underworld nor abducted for carnal purposes. Other annotations are perceptive but potentially tendentious: Sir William Bradshaw's 'curious exercise with the arms' is indeed 'reminiscent of a fascist salute' to a modern reader, but Hoff provides no historical context for this observation. Would a contemporary reader have been likely to make this association, or would Woolf herself have made it, given that the novel was published in 1925 when the so-called roman salute was in the early days of its association with fascism? Similarly, does the cliché 'come a cropper' as applied to Peter Walsh clearly suggest 'a sexual relationship gone sour' (p. 159)? Does the line 'a small girl sucked her thumb' really relate to the unreferenced fact that 'a part of Isis-worship includes sucking her thumb, according to Plutarch', and can it really be said that 'the referent is ambiguous as to whose thumb is being sucked by whom' (p. 191)? Surely Hoff does not think that the girl is sucking Rezia's thumb, or even more bizarrely that Rezia is sucking the girl's thumb? If she is proposing this unusual reading, it should be supported by more than scholarly innuendo. Hoff is no doubt correct in pointing out that 'the complexity of such a text as *Mrs. Dalloway* . . . fosters a multiplicity of interpretations' (p. 244), and has done a valuable service in offering a novel approach to identifying, discussing, and clarifying them. However, too many of the interpretations she proposes are tendentious or insufficiently argued.

The greatness of Woolf's novel does not depend on esoteric interpretations or recondite allusions.

Madelyn Detloff includes a chapter on Woolf in *The Persistence of Modernism: Loss and Mourning in the Twentieth Century*, a book which looks to 'modernist strategies of resilience' to provide 'conceptual resources' for dealing with the twenty-first century's 'war, terror, and trauma' (p. 3). For Detloff, Woolf's attentiveness to both visible and invisible structures of power and her lifelong resistance to the early twentieth century's 'ideology of death' make her an appropriate departure point for a study of modernism's responses to loss (p. 23). The chapter approaches Woolf from two angles. Detloff first contrasts Woolf's own attempts to articulate a response to personal trauma such as abuse, grief, and mental illness with reifying readings that identify Woolf either as 'primarily a trauma survivor' or 'primarily mentally ill' (p. 25). Woolf developed, Detloff argues, a literary equivalent of 'negative space' which allowed her to communicate 'the psychic pain of loss *as loss*' (p. 27). She goes on to argue that for Woolf pain, illness, and loss were not limitations but opportunities, not indictments 'of the limitations of language' but indications 'of its future possibilities' (p. 29). In the second half of the chapter Detloff examines Woolf's responses to the threat of fascism and war in *Between the Acts*, tracing the ways in which 'thinking was Woolf's fighting' particularly in terms of the linkages Woolf establishes between 'violent exclusion' of the sexual other and the formation of an apparently unifying national bond (p. 35). Woolf's non-linear and associative prose is an attempt, then, to destabilize 'cultural constructs' such as national identity and history, a process Detloff traces in a close and perceptive reading of Woolf's last novel (p. 39). Much of the material in this chapter builds on familiar readings of *Between the Acts*, but Detloff assembles her argument carefully and persuasively, making this a useful orientation to the text.

In *Mourning, Modernism, Postmodernism*, another exploration of the connections between modernist fiction and 'the need to mourn a range of cataclysmic social events', Tammy Clewell similarly argues, in a chapter on the First World War and Woolf, that her response to grief and loss 'constitutes a positive achievement' (p. 26). Woolf's vision of mourning as 'anti-consolatory' and 'perpetual' is placed in relation to the trauma of the First World War through readings of *Jacob's Room* and *To the Lighthouse* (p. 26). Clewell is well aware of the scholarly tradition underlying her work, pointing out that Winifred Holtby's 1936 study of Woolf identified the 'elegiac dimension' of her work (p. 25). Her discussion of *Jacob's Room* is thus grounded in critical tradition, but contributes revealing and insightful readings to bolster the argument that 'the traditions of consolation' are represented in the novel as 'complicitous in the production of wartime loss' (p. 30). In a similarly well-grounded argument, Clewell links the narrator of *Jacob's Room*'s refusal of interpretative authority with the 'ethical imperative of mourning' (p. 38). She then traces this imperative further in her reading of *To the Lighthouse*, which she situates in opposition to the Victorian practices of consolation and redemption represented by Leslie Stephen's *Mausoleum Book*. Through close readings of the second and third sections of the novel, Clewell examines Woolf's attempt to 'strip the pathetic fallacy of all consolatory effects' and her figuring of the need to 'resist . . . art's consolatory powers', culminating in a powerful reading of the famous final brushstroke as both a 'thematic and structural' division (p. 49).

In a third book dealing with the theme of trauma, *Trauma, Postmodernism, and the Aftermath of World War II*, Paul Crosthwaite has included Woolf in odd company: it is unusual and refreshing to see Woolf discussed next to Thomas Pynchon, J.G. Ballard, and Michael Moorcock. Crosthwaite argues that *Mrs Dalloway* displays a 'fine balance between public and private aspects of everyday life' through its use of indirect interior monologue (p. 124). However, as in postmodern fictional responses to the Second World War, this balance breaks down in *Between the Acts* into a 'dissolution of subjective boundaries' represented through a 'radical use of the indirect interior monologue technique' in which characters are allowed occasional direct access to one another's thoughts (p. 116). While this is a feature of Woolf's narrative technique that has been widely noted—and one which is present in other works, such as *The Waves*—Crosthwaite contends that it is 'best understood . . . as a metaphor for Woolf's vision of community in war' (p. 126).

Renée Dickinson's *Female Embodiment and Subjectivity in the Modernist Novel: The Corporeum of Virginia Woolf and Olive Moore* gives a chapter each to *Mrs Dalloway* and *The Waves* within a comparative study of the ways in which Woolf and Moore 'examine four crucial incarnations of female embodiment and subjectivity', or physical, national, textual, and geographical bodies, these being what Dickinson refers to as 'the *Corporeum*, an interconnected . . . network of representations of physical and ideological embodiments' (p. 1). In her discussion of *Mrs Dalloway*, Dickenson connects Clarissa Dalloway's identity, an idealized pastoral vision of England and a constructed version of national and imperial identity. She argues that Woolf is able to challenge 'female embodiment in physical, geographical and national bodies' through her 'textual experimentation' (p. 26). Problematically, however, Dickinson identifies Woolf's textual innovation in *Mrs Dalloway* with 'the boundless form of stream-of-consciousness explored by other modernists such as James Joyce and Dorothy Richardson' (p. 49). Nomenclature aside, this seems to represent both a misreading of Woolf's narrative technique, minimizing the significance of the differing levels of narrative intimacy achieved by free indirect discourse, and a simplification of her complex relationship to Joyce and Richardson. In her chapter on *The Waves*, Dickinson offers a postcolonial reading of the novel's interludes, focusing on their concern 'with the politics of empire' (p. 52). In contrast to Jane Marcus, she emphasizes the endlessness of the imperial drive, which shares in the cyclical nature of the sun and waves, continually employing women and the female body as 'figureheads of patriarchy and imperialism' (p. 57). Dickinson's discussion is situated within feminist and postcolonial readings of *The Waves*, and traces a movement in the interludes from the feminine to androgyny, savagery and darkness, a movement linked to an attack on 'the feminized, domestic spaces of the homeland' (p. 60). Ultimately, Dickinson argues, the interludes offer 'new possibilities for women and the text to develop away from the light of empire' (p. 73). While this is in many ways a convincing reading, it may ignore the polysemous nature of Woolf's text: surely, for instance, Bernard's 'final cry of defiance' is, as Koppen argues in *Virginia Woolf, Fashion and Literary Modernity*, more than a demonstration of the 'the anxiety about the return of the empire to the homeland' (p. 70).

Alice Staveley situates her 'Marketing Virginia Woolf: Women, War, and Public Relations in *Three Guineas*' (*BH* 12[2009] 295–339) as part of an emerging body of work on the historical-material contexts of modernist cultural production. Her claim that 'women novelists—even the distinctly canonical Woolf—remain underrepresented' in this field is perhaps debatable: Staveley herself lists several such studies (p. 300). Nonetheless, this essay offers a substantial and extremely detailed reading of the networks of mainstream and feminist periodicals instrumental in the launching of *Three Guineas*. Staveley analyses the role played by Norah Nicholls, briefly manager of the Hogarth Press, in the extension of these networks to minor feminist publications not generally associated with literary criticism such as *The Woman Engineer* and *The Catholic Citizen*.

Rebecca Wisor's 'Versioning Virginia Woolf: Notes toward a Post-Eclectic Edition of *Three Guineas*' (*Mo/Mo* 16[2009] 497–535) similarly locates itself within a scholarly tendency, in this case the 'surge of interest' in textual editing (p. 497). She sets out to establish post-eclectic editorial principles which both accommodate an expansive notion of textual boundaries and reveal 'something of the social and cultural context' within which Woolf's polemic 'was conceived, composed, published, and transmitted', a project that has clear affinities with Stavely's (p. 499). Wisor explores the theoretical and practical issues involved in parallel-text and genetic editions of *Three Guineas*, but ultimately argues that an edition based on John Bryant's fluid-text principles is 'especially promising . . . in its ability to accommodate and narrate both the extensive pre-publication and post-publication documents that are known to be in existence' (p. 529).

Paul Tolliver Brown's 'Relativity, Quantum Physics, and Consciousness in Virginia Woolf's *To the Lighthouse*' (*JML* 32:iii[2009] 39–62) is another example of historical contextualization, although with an emphasis on intellectual rather than material factors. He builds on the work of critics such as Michael Whitworth and Ann Banfield who have identified points of contact between Woolf's fiction and early twentieth-century developments in theoretical physics, relativity, and quantum mechanics, attempting to 'establish the specific ways in which the ideas she shared with the preeminent subatomic scientists of her time work into the characters and themes of some of her most important novels' (p. 40). Brown's argument is in addition located in the context of nineteenth-century debates over the relationship between objective reality and perception, disputes in which Leslie Stephen was deeply involved. Brown's close readings of *To the Lighthouse* cover generally familiar ground—identifying Mr Ramsay with separation and Mrs Ramsay with unification, for instance—but are linked metaphorically to the concepts of modern physics: Mrs Ramsay's creation of unity at her famous dinner party is 'relativistic' insofar as 'she orders her environment like a large body of mass influencing the curvature of spacetime', while her sense of identification with the lighthouse beam is a form of 'quantum interconnectedness' (p. 44, 51). Moving beyond these scientific metaphors, Brown argues that 'in contrast to the fields of physics, Woolf's characters are bound to one another and to the world via their consciousness' (p. 53).

In her 'Developing an Ear for the Modernist Novel: Virginia Woolf, Dorothy Richardson and James Joyce', Angela Frattarola (*JML* 33:i[2009] 132–53) argues that while vision was 'the dominant sense for exploring the world in the Victorian period', it was during the modernist period that the novel became 'saturated with sound' (p. 134). Building on Steven Connor's work on the relationship between aural perception and challenges to 'Cartesian concepts of subjectivity', Frattarola reads Woolf, alongside Richardson and Joyce, as a writer for whom 'audition draws characters together while vision separates them' (pp. 137, 138).

Studies of Woolf's exploration of private and public spheres, in the tradition of Anna Snaith's 2000 *Virginia Woolf: Public and Private Negotiations* and Snaith and Michael Whitworth's 2007 collection *Locating Woolf: The Politics of Space and Place* continue. Stephen M. Barber's 'States of Emergency, States of Freedom: Woolf, History, and the Novel' (*Novel* 42:ii[2009] 196–206) describes how Woolf's late attempts to 'devise by means of her art a critique' of power involve the interrelated shaping of both a new aesthetic form for the novel and a trenchant critique of contemporary forms of power, both tending towards the attainment of a 'unique form of freedom' as exemplified in *Three Guineas* and *The Years* (p. 196). Barber focuses interestingly on what he describes as the second phase of Woolf's 'apprenticeship' in her 'turn to freedom', during which she attempted to integrate ethics into 'political analysis and practice' (p. 197). Both texts are, Barber argues, 'thought experiments' and 'spiritual exercises', simultaneously explorations of politics and aesthetics respectively and 'spiritual' articulations of subjectivity (p. 197). This is a term which Barber carefully and valuably situates through comparison with Foucault's late work as part of the ancient Greek philosophy of self-mastery and self-care, an 'art of life that is at once and also a critique of who we are . . . *and* an experimental work on freedom that brings into existence new subjective possibilities' (p. 199). This is played out, according to Barber, in the ways in which *The Years* 'attains to the disclosure of multiple ontologically heterogeneous strata', allowing the novel to connect the personal and the political in its diagnosis of, and struggle against, fascism (p. 201). *Three Guineas* continues this project, explicitly answering the question of how to live a non-fascist life, particularly for the emerging class of professional women, who must not 'repeat conventional passive and subordinate relations to the state' (p. 204). While Barber's readings of the connections between these two texts are familiar, his linkage of the two with the notion of a 'philosophical non-philosophy' of care of self is valuable.

Wendy Gan's 'Solitude and Community: Virginia Woolf, Spatial Privacy and *A Room of One's Own*' (*L&H* 18:i[2009] 68–80) situates Woolf's call for women to have a room of their own as part of a transition from a traditional location of female privacy 'within the inner and inviolable space of the mind' to a twentieth-century demand for 'for physical space to accompany the inner space of refuge' (p. 68). She complicates this transition, however, by locating it within early twentieth-century transformations in spatial awareness and by focusing on Woolf's insistence on the gender-neutral space of a room rather than the traditionally male study. In the first stage of this argument, Gan compares Florence Nightingale's *Cassandra*, which emphasizes women's lack of private time and solitude and was included in Ray Strachey's 1928 *The Cause*, with Woolf's focus on a material and spatial solution to this problem in *A Room of One's Own*. Gan then moves on to contrast the 'insularity' of the male study with the 'flexible and multi-tasking room of one's own', a contrast which reveals that the 'female author is involved in a series of negotiations between private and public' (pp. 73, 78).

The spring issue of *The Virginia Woolf Miscellany* focused on Virginia Woolf and the city, the same theme as the 2009 New York Woolf Conference, but with essays in this issue also considering Woolf's interactions with rural environments (*VWM* 75[2009]). The fall issue offered an interesting selection of essays on Woolf's involvement with periodicals. Some of the essays approach traditional issues in Woolf scholarship with the help of periodical evidence, while others place Woolf's writing in detailed publication contexts (*VWM* 76[2009]).

2. Post-1945 Fiction

The year 2009 was a reasonably productive one in post-1945 British fiction, with monographs and edited collections, and books that balance new research with an introductory approach aimed at the student market.

Lena Steveker's monograph *Identity and Cultural Memory in the Fiction of A.S. Byatt: Knitting the Net of Culture* offers a range of sophisticated and thought-provoking analyses of Byatt's fiction. She concentrates on six novels in particular *Possession: A Romance*, *The Biographer's Tale*, and Byatt's tetralogy of novels from *The Virgin in the Garden* [1978] to *A Whistling Woman* [2002]. Her approach is to focus on three aspects of Byatt's fiction: identity, literature, and cultural meaning. She sets out this scope in a short but useful introduction. The book is then divided into two sections each containing six chapters. The first section focuses specifically on Byatt's exploration of the cultural notion of identity drawing on relevant theoretical perspectives from Jürgen Straub, who discusses the idea of identity as a kind of aspiration against which people attain an awareness of self, and Paul Ricoeur's hermeneutics of the self. Both these theoretical areas are discussed with erudition and sensitivity in terms of their intersection with Byatt's fiction. The first two chapters in this section concentrate on *Possession* and *The Biographer's Tale*, and detail, as Steveker puts it, 'the hermeneutic impulse of Byatt's novels and the underlying possibilities and limitations of understanding another's life' (p. 3). This approach is particularly useful in the discussion of the dual historical narratives in *Possession*. Steveker points out the way in which that novel 'highlight[s] the problems and limitations of accessing and presenting an individual's past, and consequently, of writing about a person's life' (p. 23). The next four chapters in this section discuss Byatt's tetralogy. Chapter 3 looks at the way in which identity is developed in each of the novels, while chapters 4, 5, and 6 focus on issues of gender, in terms of both feminine and masculine identity, against the historical contexts in which the range of novels in this sequence develops (from the 1950s to the late 1960s). The second part of the book extends the discussion of identity to engage with ideas of cultural memory, and the place of literature in this context. Chapter 7 establishes the way in which Byatt's novels combine individual and collective memories, an idea that is taken forward in chapters 8 and 9 to the place of two historical figure-tropes in her fiction: Elizabeth I and Shakespeare. In the last three main chapters Steveker thoughtfully explores the way in which literature generally, and Byatt's fiction in particular, works to both reflect and articulate cultural memory. As she persuasively argues, 'Byatt's tetralogy and her novel *Possession* exemplify the eminent role pertaining to literature within cultural memory, since they negotiate their protagonists' processes of identity formation within the context of British memory, which the texts both activate and contribute to through their rich intertextual depositories' (p. 5). Overall, Steveker's book offers original and rich analyses of Byatt's fiction while also succeeding in producing thoughtful discussion of the nature of literature generally in relation to identity formation and cultural memory.

One of the main edited collections to come out this year is *Doris Lessing: Border Crossings*, edited by Alice Ridout and Susan Watkins, conveniently published to coincide with Lessing being awarded the Nobel Prize in literature. The collection is based on selected papers given at the Second International Doris Lessing Conference at Leeds Metropolitan University in July 2007. The book aims to take a broad view of Lessing's fiction over the past sixty years or so with an emphasis on the diversity of works she has produced that have complicated geographical, ideological, and generic categories. The 'border crossing' in the title of the book relates to four main areas: feminism and anti-feminism; Marxist and reactionary politics; British and postcolonial writing; and realism and science or (speculative) fiction. After an interesting introduction from the editors, the nine essays collected in the book are arranged chronologically with respect to their treatment of Lessing's fiction. Edith Frampton offers the first essay, in which she produces a fascinating Kristevan reading of the place of the abject in *The Grass is Singing*. Frampton argues convincingly that the novel represents a return from the symbolic order to the semiotic for the main character Mary Turner. This process is a result of her physical affair with the African 'houseboy' Moses, with regard to whom she has previously experienced a simultaneous repulsion and attraction analogous to the ambivalences of the Kristevan abject. The contact with the African body carries with it broader social and political contexts: 'Moses's first physical touch, so shocking to Mary, can thus be seen as skin-to-skin contact that breaches a fundamental social boundary, calling Mary's autonomous fortified identity, as a member of the white ruling class, into question' (p. 20). She also shows how this repulsion/attraction is focused on her observation of African women suckling their children, which itself signals a form of border crossing that recalls the semiotic state before the Law of the Father imposes its bar between mother and child. As Frampton argues, breastfeeding thus 'violates the conceptual boundaries between inside and outside, at the same time that it threatens those between self and other' (p. 21). In chapter 2, Pat Louw discusses Lessing's examination of the inside and outside spaces of the

African landscape in some of her African stories, emphasizing their focus on the crossing of those borders. As Louw argues, this concentration on physical space allows Lessing to 'illustrate... the crossing of boundaries in colonial space to construct complex subjectivities' (p. 27). This argument is pursued thoughtfully in careful readings of several of Lessing's African stories, including 'Home', 'The De Wets come to Kloof Grange', and 'the Old Chief Mshlanga'. In the latter of these, Louw argues, the meeting between an old African chief and the young daughter of a white colonial farmer repositions the latter 'in relation to the black people of the country and leads her to reflect critically on her identity as a colonizer' (p. 37). This is followed by an essay by Nick Bentley (the present reviewer) that traces the influences on the formal experiment that is *The Golden Notebook*. This essay identifies this experiment as a form of 'critical fiction' that produces a novel which simultaneously critiques the limits of the novel form itself. The chapter argues that the book represents a transition point between two politically engaged forms of fiction, one based on Lukács's critical realism, the other on Bertolt Brecht's call for an engaged, experimental literature that Lessing transfers to the novel by experimenting with dramatic form in her 1958 *Play with a Tiger*. Roberta Rubenstein, in 'Doris Lessing's Fantastic Children', takes up the theme of border-crossing with respect to the novelist's experimentation with literary genre, and in particular with respect to her juxtaposition of realistic and fantastic modes in the novels *The Four-Gated City*, *The Memoirs of a Survivor*, and *The Fifth Child*. Drawing on theories of the fantastic in the work of Tzvetan Todorov and Rosemary Jackson, Rubenstein concentrates on the representations of child figures in each of these novels that extend beyond realistic description, and their presentation as liminal figures between realism and fantasy. The representation of the feral children in *Memoirs* and the evolutionary 'throwback' of Ben in *The Fifth Child* show how Lessing's interest in the crossing of generic borders opens up philosophical questions concerning identity. As Rubenstein concludes, 'The fantastic children in Lessing's narratives... challenge the boundaries of narrative mimesis... Thematically, they function subversively and even trangressively, obliging the reader to ponder the significance of their exceptionality' (p. 72). Susan Watkins's chapter focuses on the Jane Somers hoax, where Lessing invented a pseudo-novelist to test out the institutional parameters of the publishing industry. Watkins extends the extant criticism on the novels to argue convincingly on the 'integral relationship' of the 'issues raised by the hoax and the subject matter of the novels' (p. 76). In terms of the issues raised, Watkins shows how the hoax, as Lessing realized, did not '*escape* the commercial constraints of modern literary production so much as exchange one set of constraints (those of a well-established literary celebrity) for another (a woman journalist who has made a first attempt at breaking into the world or "literary" fiction publishing)' (pp. 79–80). Watkins's reading of the *Diaries of Jane Somers* shows how this exploration into the nature of literary production is in part the subject matter of the text, emphasized in Lessing's adoption of the first-person narration of Janna, herself a writer working in a number of genres. As Watkins concludes, 'The Jane Somers hoax allowed Lessing to cross the borders of the authorial persona; in doing so she was at the forefront of an increasing body of work . . . that examines the relationship between gender, authorship and commercial literary culture' (p. 89). In chapter 6, Ruth Robins looks at the way in which Lessing's *The Fifth Child* and Lionel Shriver's *We Need to Talk About Kevin* open up questions about received literary representations of motherhood. They do this, argues Robins, in their destabilization of generic conventions. Robins begins by challenging powerful 'male gaze' representations of childbirth in William Wordsworth's 'Intimations' ode and W.B. Yeats's 'The Second Coming', which she contrasts with a reading of the maternal drawn from Julia Kristeva's work on the abject. In thoughtful close readings of the novels by Lessing and Shriver, Robins shows the way in which each writer uses 'narrative structures that unsettle the reader' to the end that 'their texts imply that neither version of the maternal institution of ideologically constructed ideal nor the real experience of motherhood . . . are adequate representations' (p. 95). The genre instability in both Lessing's and Shriver's texts raises the question of whether these are realistic depictions of 'abnormal' children or fantastic monster narratives. As Robins cogently argues, it is in the ambiguity between the two generic modes in which the power of both narratives lies. In the next chapter, Alice Ridout explores Lessing in the context of 'Third Culture Kids' (TCK), drawing on theories of cosmopolitanism by Vertovec and Cohen, Pollock and Van Reken, and Bruce Robbins. She interrogates the concept of the TCK and adapts it to Lessing's particular background arguing that while many theories of cosmopolitanism tend to identify individuals with a non-political outlook, 'Lessing's life-long political commitments demonstrate that detachment is not a necessary consequence of a cosmopolitan or TCK upbringing' (p. 111). She goes on to discuss fiction and non-fiction by Lessing in this context, including *Under My Skin*, *In Pursuit of the English*, and *The Grass is Singing* showing how the concept of the TCK and comparison with other writers offer an intriguing a new focus on Lessing's work. Fiona Becket's chapter examines Lessing's 'Ifrik' novels in the context of ecocriticism. She begins by critically surveying some important concepts and works in ecocriticism, ranging from Jean-François Lyotard's posthuman notion to Rachel Carson's 'object' invocation of scientific investigation as a support for ecocriticism. This forms the basis of her erudite analysis of a number of Lessing's novels, most notably her 1999 futuristic novel *Mara and Dann*. Becket emphasizes the way that this novel as a 'postmodern (posthuman) fable decentres, therefore, displaces the human subject from the narrative of the familiar' (p. 135). The last main chapter in the book, by Phyllis Sternberg Perrakis, looks at Lessing's 2007 novel *The Cleft*, focusing on the way in which Lessing 'portrays the porous nature of . . . three borders, genre, gender and species' (p. 143). Drawing heavily on Dominick LaCapra's notion of 'empathetic unsettlement', the chapter argues that *The Cleft*, through its central narrative voice (the Roman historian Transit), establishes a detachment from the prehistoric context for the development of humanity in the novel. Perrakis also argues that Lessing has been misrepresented by critical reviews of the novel, suggesting that she is 'both more sophisticated and more even-handed in her creation of a gendered myth of origins than some of her detractors have realized' (p. 150). She concludes that 'Lessing's prophetic voice [demands] that we cast a speculative and detached eye on the gender assumptions governing our own civilization' (p. 156). The book ends with an afterword by Judith Kegan Gardiner that places the preceding chapters in the context of a long view on Lessing's career. Taken together, the essays provide a fresh critical engagement with one of the most important international writers of the past sixty years.

There have been two monographs this year concentrating on the work of Jeanette Winterson. Sonia Front's *Transgressing Boundaries in Jeanette Winterson's Fiction* is part of Peter Lang's Literary and Cultural Theory series, and offers an in-depth analysis of a range of aspects of Winterson's fiction including the writer's focus on issues of gender, sexuality, and identity and her use of a number of postmodern narrative techniques. Front identifies Winterson's quest in her fiction as an exploration through her characters of the 'process of finding a new identity' (p. 11). This focus is pursued in particular in relation to Winterson's engagement with a sexual politics foregrounded through lesbianism, and Front draws on theories related to French feminism in teasing out these themes. The book has five main chapters, the first of which explores the 'divergence between the sexes in patriarchal sociosymbolic order of Winterson's books' drawing on relevant theory from Judith Butler, Elisabeth Grosz, and Michel Foucault. This theoretical triptych is brought into play in interesting readings of a number of Winterson's texts, including *Oranges Are Not the Only Fruit*, *Sexing the Cherry*, *Gut Symmetries*, and *Art & Lies*. The following chapters follow this pattern of looking at a range of Winterson's work from one particular thematic and theoretically informed focus. Chapter 2 identifies Winterson's treatment and deconstruction of the notion of love, drawing heavily on Roland Barthes's *A Lover's Discourse*, while chapter 3 succeeds in exploring 'Winterson's hybrid identities and sexualities by means of lesbian/queer mythology' (p. 17). The fourth chapter shifts the focus to identifying the 'quest' as a paradigmatic form in many of Winterson's novels, in relation to the themes identified in the previous two chapters, and to the theme of war. This analysis is pursued against theories from Erich Fromm and, again, Barthes. The last chapter turns our attention to the representation of time, memory, and history in Winterson's work, identifying a particularly psychoanalytical aspect of her exploration of these themes. Front concludes that Winterson's 'subversion of phallologocentric narrative and scenarios entails a re-envisaging of relations between the sexes/genders and reconceptualization of female desire' (p. 193). The book as a whole is an important contribution to Winterson studies.

The second book on Winterson this year is Sonya Andermahr's *Jeanette Winterson*, in Palgrave's New British Fiction, an important series in the field that is aimed at both literary scholars and students. Like the previous volumes in this series, Andermahr's book succeeds in achieving this balance. Her prose style is both accessible and erudite, and she is able to engage critically with the difficult aspects of Winterson's work with lucidity. In line with the conventions of the series, Andermahr's book begins with a timeline that identifies significant political, cultural, and economic events in world history alongside Winterson's biography and publishing history. This is followed by a brief introduction that sets out the parameters of the book's analysis of Winterson in terms of her status as a contemporary writer; a postmodern writer; and a feminist/lesbian writer. The introduction also serves to establish what Andermahr sees as the three main themes in Winterson's work: 'love as a transcendent value'; 'art as an absolute value through time . . . and storytelling as a constant means of expression of human life'; and, thirdly, Winterson's emphasis on how reality and identity are 'radically unstable contexts' (p. 25). There is a second main chapter in this introductory section that details aspects of Winterson's biography read against her fiction. As Andermahr argues, this biographical-critical approach is appropriate to a writer such as Winterson because as her 'unique biographical intertextuality attests, many of the major tropes in her work have their echo if not their origins in Winterson's life' (p. 46). In particular, Andermahr identifies the author's focus on metaphors of flight, escape, and liberation in this context. The middle section of the book consists of detailed and engaged readings of Winterson's major works, arranged in broadly chronological order. Chapter 3 looks at *Oranges Are Not the Only Fruit*, *The Passion*, and *Sexing the Cherry*, and there's an interesting reading of the first of these novels as an engagement and partial deconstruction of the traditional *Bildungsroman*. Chapter 4 looks at *Written on the Body*, *Art & Lies*, and *Gut Symmetries*, and the last chapter in this section looks at Winterson's twenty-first-century novels *The PowerBook*, *Lighthousekeeping*, and *Weight*. Part III, 'Criticisms and Contexts', includes an interview with Winterson in which she discusses issues ranging from identifying dominant narrative forms in her fiction to her engagement with the intersection of literature and science; her writing other than fiction; and an indication of the thinking behind her move to science fiction in her most recent novel (at the time of writing) *The Stone Gods*. This leads nicely into a section where Andermahr looks at Winterson's writing beyond the main novels: short stories; essays; children's fiction; original work for TV, radio and film; adaptations for stage and screen; journalism; and her 'virtual' presence/writing. This section in particular covers areas that have often been overlooked in Winterson criticism. The last chapter traces the critical reception of Winterson's fiction. Overall, the book is a valuable addition to the growing critical body of work on this central figure in contemporary British fiction.

There were two books published in Continuum's Contemporary Critical Perspectives series this year: *Ian McEwan*, edited by Sebastian Groes; and *Kazuo Ishiguro*, edited by Sean Matthews and Sebastian Groes. Each volume follows a series format, with eight chapters written by established and emerging critics of contemporary fiction, a timeline detailing the main events in the author's life, and an interview with the author. The series editors are Jeanette Baxter, Sebastian Groes, and Sean Matthews. The book on Ian McEwan begins with a foreword from Matt Ridley that identifies McEwan's interest in the workings of the mind both in the neurological and the psychological senses. This is followed by an introduction by Groes that details McEwan's centrality in contemporary fiction, his courting of controversial subjects, including his use of disturbing moral scenarios in his fiction, his pronouncements on the relationship between science and art, and his support of the war in Iraq. Groes emphasizes McEwan's engagement with a wide variety of contemporary subjects and the way in which his fiction intersects with his role as a cultural commentator. In the first main chapter, Jeanette Baxter explores McEwan's early fiction: the short story collections *First Love, Last Rites* [1975] and *In Between the Sheets* [1978], and his first novel *The Cement Garden* [1978]. She focuses on the 'unsettling aspect of reading' this early work because of its engagement with stories of 'incest, paedophilia, erotic violence, sex and death' (p. 13). Baxter frames the discussion of the fiction with respect to Georges Bataille's dissident Surrealist philosophy of desublimation, with a focus on McEwan's examination of the pornographic imagination in *First Love, Last Rites*; the desublimating drives of materialism in *In Between the Sheets*; and the troubling eroticism of transgression and taboo in *The Cement Garden*. In the second chapter, M. Hunter Hayes and Sebastian Groes discuss an often overlooked area of McEwan's work, his writing for the screen. They provide an interesting analysis of the way in which McEwan's TV film *The Imitation Game* intersects with his fiction. They also celebrate what they call McEwan's 'Anti-Thatcherite Triptych' of works, *The Ploughman's Lunch*, *The Good Son*, and *Sour Sweet*. Following this chapter, Claire Colebrook explores the representation of childhood in McEwan's *The Innocent*, arguing that the focus on innocence in the novel produces an anti-Freudian stance that challenges the importance of childhood in adult psychology. Drawing on Deleuze and Guattari's *Anti-Oedipus*, Colebrook argues that McEwan is a 'profoundly anti-Oedipal writer, because his work, at the level of form and narration, displays a libidinal economy that goes beyond the imaginary and the familial' (p. 45). She goes on to show that this tendency in McEwan's work has a political context in terms of a rejection of the fixation on childhood innocence becoming a way of evading the desire for adults to project a master-narrative of authority onto political figures. This is achieved by disrupting the oppositions between knowing and not-knowing and between adult and child. She produces a convincing argument: '*The Innocent* shows that such political modes of care and solicitation are also the moments of extreme paternalism and violence, for it is precisely through monitoring, documenting and educating that one is creating the other as nothing more than an image of the self' (p. 53). The three following chapters all discuss *Atonement*, emphasizing the importance of that novel in McEwan's corpus. Natasha Alden offers an interesting reading by focusing on how the idea of plagiarism intersects with postmodern ideas of the relationship between history and fiction. She tackles this question through recourse to Linda Hutcheon's oft-cited concept of 'historiographic metafiction', but argues that McEwan's novel problematizes postmodernism's focus on the fluidity of all narratives. As she argues, '*Atonement* is still a metafictional novel, but McEwan is reasserting the history/fiction divide, broken down by postmodern historiography, in order to interrogate it, while retaining the freedom fiction gives the author to explore the past—to go *beyond* the factual record' (p. 61). This ethical nature of the relationship between fiction and fact (or history) is also the focus on Alastair Cormack's chapter on the novel. Cormack begins by identifying the range of intertextual references McEwan uses in *Atonement* which serve to self-reflexively place the novel within a canon of a certain kind of English realist fiction. He argues, however, that this recourse to tradition establishes the novel's central metafictional lie, which is disrupted by the jarring effect of its postmodern ending. He explores the novel's metafictional forms through a reading of its reflection of modes: realist, modernist, and postmodernist, and attempts to argue that *Atonement*, despite its postmodern elements, ultimately accepts a grounding notion of a real set of events behind the main character Briony's romanticization of the world of the novel. This leads him to register connections between McEwan and the empirical humanism found in F.R. Leavis's literary criticism. There is an element of reduction in Cormack's argument here, as McEwan's metafictional twist does more than suggest a fault with Briony's perception, it also recognizes the power of fictionalizing the world to do good as seen in the Luc Cornet episode of the novel. However, Cormack raises interesting issues in his analysis of McEwan's engagement with literary form. Laura Marcus concentrates on the treatment of time in *Atonement* and McEwan's 2005 novel *Saturday* as well as looking back to his earlier *The Child in Time*. Marcus argues that McEwan adopts a 'modernist time' model in each of these novels for differing ends. In *The Child in Time* an 'ideological time-lapse' is employed to focus on the discrete outlooks and politics of differing generations achieved by McEwan's disruption of linear time. This is grounded in his interest in physics, especially around the notion of the fluidity of time with respect to space, and through his focus on the bringing together of 'the languages of science and literature' (p. 87). This focus on modernist time is explored in Marcus's reading of *Atonement*, whereby the disjunction between real and imaginative (or fictional) time is emphasized. Marcus identifies McEwan's interest in Virginia Woolf's modernist treatment of time as a model for both *Atonement* and *Saturday*. In terms of the latter she draws on Paul Ricoeur's notion of 'monumental time' as opposed to subjective time, and on Mark Currie's reading of the novel in his book *About Time* [2007]. In chapter 7, Sebastian Groes also focuses on the modernist elements of *Saturday*, and in particular the representation of the city in the novel. Groes argues cogently that McEwan's view of twenty-first-century London as a place of darkness, crime, and poverty represents earlier modernistic visions of London. Groes identifies this kind of representation of the urban landscape in some of McEwan's earlier fiction, including many of the short stories in *First Love, Last Rites* and *The Child in Time*. Drawing on Raymond Williams's *The Country and the City* and references to T.S. Eliot's *The Waste Land*, Groes shows how McEwan is influenced by a 'literary mythology of London as a monstrous and unjust place where young innocents are corrupted' (p. 99). He goes on to show the modernist trait of multiple intertextual references in *Saturday*, and in particular (as with Marcus) the centrality of Virginia Woolf in McEwan's reference to modernist writing. The last section, however, makes a valid case that McEwan in *Saturday* is perhaps rejecting earlier misrepresentations of London as a 'dark place' through his evocation of Matthew Arnold's cultural politics, dramatically represented in the main character Perowne's attempt to reconnect public and private by way of countering media representations of news events. This attempt is not fully realized and, as Groes argues, leaves the novel with an uncertain representation of the contemporary urban environment: 'McEwan's representation in *Saturday* thus corrects his earlier "darkest

London" by supplementing it with the traditional vision of the city as a place of light and learning, but new uncertainties, a new darkness, are brought to the fore in the post-9/11 metropolis' (p. 111). Dominic Head's chapter on *On Chesil Beach* closes the critical analysis part of the book with a reading of McEwan's use of the novella form in this work and his earlier *Amsterdam*, arguing that he achieves a greater depth of social commentary than is normally associated with the form. Head counters some of the critical readings of *On Chesil Beach* as being simply about the period before the Swinging Sixties, and makes the case that it expands debate beyond culturally specific mores of sexuality and their impact on individual lives. Head argues convincingly that the two main characters are more than emblems of the period before the "sexual revolution", registered in their atypical backgrounds. This, coupled with 'a sexually knowing narrator manipulating his innocent creations', opens the novel to wider ethical and cultural debates around contemporary attitudes to sexuality (p. 122). The book closes with an interview with Ian McEwan carried out by Jon Cook, Sebastian Groes, and Victor Sage, in which the author discusses a number of issues including the representation of children in the media, his creative method, and his increasing interest in neuroscience as revealed in his fiction. Overall this edited collection provides a valuable contribution to the growing corpus of literary criticism on Ian McEwan and Groes has done a good job in collecting together interesting and new readings of his fiction.

The second book in the Contemporary Critical Perspectives series this year is *Kazuo Ishiguro* edited by Sean Matthews and Sebastian Groes. Ishiguro is currently attracting a lot of critical attention, and this book adds significantly to that corpus. After a short foreword by Haruki Murakami, there is an introduction by Matthews and Groes in which they argue for Ishiguro's place in the canon of international contemporary fiction, and identify the focus in his work on the complexities of aesthetic practice. Brian W. Shaffer offers the first main chapter on Ishiguro's short fiction, arguing that many of the themes set out in the early 'Japanese' stories are returned to in his later fiction, especially his attempt to 'understand psychological trauma' (p. 19). In particular, Shaffer discusses 'A Family Supper', 'Waiting for J', and 'Getting Poisoned' in relation to Ishiguro's first novel *A Pale View of Hills*. Ishiguro has stressed his aim to be an international writer, and Motoyuki Shibata and Motoko Sugano produce a fascinating account of how this aim can be both enhanced and frustrated by the concept of translation. They discuss Ishiguro's use of universal and timeless themes as a way of identifying across cultures, but also the way in which the crossing of national languages inevitably produces nuances of meeting distinct to each translation. They offer interesting readings in this context of Japanese translations of *A Pale View of Hills* (translated by Takeshi Onodera) and *An Artist of the Floating World* (translated by Shiego Tobita and published in Japan as *Ukiyo no gaka*). In chapter 3, Sebastian Gores and Paul-Daniel Veyret consider Ishiguro's writing for television and film, arguing that this work visits similar themes to his fiction but often with a more overtly political approach. They identify Ishiguro's 1993 comic-Gothic screenplay *The Gourmet*, in which a famous gastronome travels to Britain in order to eat a ghost, as a critique of

Thatcherite policies in the 1980s. Groes and Veyret show how the screenplay draws on other magic realist writers, especially Angela Carter, Salman Rushdie, and Peter Ackroyd. They go on to discuss two further screenplays, *The Saddest Music* and *The White Countess*, both set in the inter-war years, arguing that the absurd logic and experimental form of *The Saddest Music* is reminiscent of German Expressionist film of the 1920s and 1930s, and that *The White Countess* is 'a film that simultaneously celebrates but also warns against the artistic imagination' (p. 44). The fourth chapter in the book, by Justine Baillie and Sean Matthews, concentrates on *A Pale View of Hills*. The chapter argues that Ishiguro's focus on the memory of traumatic experience in the novel connects with recent feminist criticism, and especially gender theories related to postmodernism. They begin by referring to Jean-François Lyotard's idea that the Holocaust disrupted the grand narrative of human progress through its irrationality and connect this to Ishiguro's representation of the Nagasaki atomic bomb in *A Pale View of Hills*. They go on to offer a reading of the central character Etsuko's experiences in Japan post-Nagasaki. They identify the contradictions in Etsuko's narrative and her ambivalence to motherhood read against Julia Kristeva's theories of the maternal, and Judith Butler's critique of Kristeva. They make the point that 'the Bomb, ironically, exposes Etsuko to new opportunities, to the ambiguous challenge of new forms of individualism and fulfilment, and this guilty fact may be at the heart of her ambivalence to maternity' (p. 53). The next four chapters concentrate individually on what are probably Ishiguro's best-known novels. David James begins by identifying the distinctiveness of Ishiguro's style as both reserved and at the same time idiosyncratic, and goes on to show how this control of style is achieved, especially in *The Remains of the Day*. As he argues. 'to become absorbed in what happens within the world of this novel is also to be made aware of *how* our absorption can coalesce with . . . a heightened awareness of Ishiguro's craft' (p. 55). Richard Robinson explores Ishiguro's use of naming in *The Unconsoled*, where he uses famous footballers and characters from Josef von Sternberg's *Der blaue Engel* as intercultural and intertextual references. This naming is discussed with respect to the varying conventions in realist and postmodernist fiction, showing that *The Unconsoled* 'seems to share some sense of postmodernist arbitrariness but without the characteristic postmodern relish for the poststructuralist omni-directionality of the signifier' (p. 74). Hélène Machinal looks at the detective narrative form in *When We Were Orphans*. She argues that Ishiguro goes to great pains to set up what appears to be a conventional detective framework, but gradually disrupts this epistemological form as the novel moves forwards, especially in the central Shanghai sections of the novel, in which the move into Surrealist and psychological modes as the reader's suspicions of the central character Banks's narrative reliability are increasingly heightened. She argues convincingly that the detective persona Banks has initially projected is seen to be performative and itself drawn from literary conventions. In a neat turn, Machinal then goes on to show how the novel can be read as a critique of the political and imperial contexts of the turn-of-the-nineteenth-century British detective mode. In the last main chapter in the book, Mark Currie offers an examination of the formal technique and structure of Ishiguro's dystopian novel *Never Let Me Go*. He begins by identifying the juxtaposition of the popular and serious contexts of the novel's title and (following Kafka) Ishiguro's defamiliarization of metaphors. This is followed by a close analysis of the rhetorical style of the novel's narrator, Kathy H., arguing that it uses the 'proleptic past perfect' tense as a way of both remembering the past and simultaneously misremembering potentially traumatic or worrying aspects of the situation in which Kathy and her peers find themselves. This unsettling narrative style is what Currie sees as the power of the narrative to disturb. As he concludes, it is in the 'chasm between two realities, one a closed institution, the other a brutal domain of inequality and social injustice, that the temporal structures of remembered forgetting and recollected anticipation are deployed' (p. 103). John Mullan takes up the unsettling nature of the narrative voice of *Never Let Me Go* in an afterword that details his experience of first reading the novel. The book ends with an interview with Ishiguro carried out by Sean Matthews, in which the author talks about the dangers of biocritical readings of his fiction; his relation to literary traditions (British and Japanese); the variety of narrative techniques he has used in his fiction; and his feelings towards film adaptations of his novels. Taken together, the chapters in this book are a valuable contribution to the increasing body of work on Ishiguro.

There have been works on Angela Carter that are worthy of mention. A second edition of Linden Peach's 1998 groundbreaking study *Angela Carter* has been published this year. The new edition contains the original chapters (although some with additions and reworked titles), as well as new chapters on post-feminism and Gothic form in *Shadow Dance*; the influence of Federico Fellini on *Nights at the Circus*; and an erudite discussion of the representation of the body and ageing in Carter's work generally. In addition, Sarah Gamble's study of the author, *Angela Carter: A Literary Life*, first published in 2006, has come out in a paperback edition this year.

3. Pre-1950 Drama

Several useful theatrical biographies have appeared recently, including Michael Holroyd's work on Ellen Terry and Henry Irving, together with their respective families. Jeffrey Richards's book on the depiction of the ancient world in the nineteenth and early twentieth centuries is a useful accompaniment to this. Further biographies are Selina Hastings's *The Secret Lives of Somerset Maugham*, David Slattery-Christie's *In Search of Ruritania: The Life and Times of Ivor Novello* [2008], and Nicolas Ridley's memoir of his father, *Godfrey's Ghost*. Andy Merriman's *Margaret Rutherford* pays tribute to the stalwart character actress who appeared in Daphne du Maurier's stage version of *Rebecca*, which Rebecca D'Monté also writes on in Rachel Carroll's volume on *Adaptation in Contemporary Culture*, and in David James and Philip Tew's *New Versions of Pastoral*. Barry Day continues to publish on Noel Coward, with his *Essential Noel Coward Compendium*. Two very different types of theatre have been the focus of a couple of books: Graeme Smith writes on Glasgow's Theatre Royal, while Don Chapman provides a history of the Oxford Playhouse. The early part of Olivia Turnbull's *Bringing down the*

House: The Crisis in Britain's Regional Theatres [2008] provides an illuminating insight into the rise (and possible fall) of regional theatre, and along the way explores how the seeds of the Arts Council were sown during the Second World War. *The Cambridge Companion to War Writing*, edited by Kate McLoughlin, misses an opportunity to address the numerous theatrical outputs on this subject, but nonetheless provides some useful contextual issues.

After writing on various figures of the early twentieth century (Lytton Strachey, Augustus John, Bernard Shaw), Michael Holroyd has now turned his attention to the two theatrical giants of the Victorian and Edwardian period, Ellen Terry and Henry Irving. However, in the well-presented *A Strange Eventful History: The Dramatic Lives of Ellen Terry, Henry Irving and their Remarkable Families* [2008], it is Terry's son and daughter that are of interest. Edith ('Edy') Craig was born illegitimately in 1869, Gordon Craig following in 1872; their father was the architect Edward William Godwin. Edy Craig's role in developing suffrage and community theatre has until comparatively recently been neglected. Julie Holledge's *Innocent Flowers* [1981] did much to give her the prominence she justly deserves, followed by other writers such as Joy Melville, Christine Dymkowski, and, most notably, Katharine Cockin. Cockin's research has helped not only to show Edy Craig's role as theatrical innovator, but also to test the parameters of the theatrical canon. Being split between several figures, Holroyd's biography is unable to fully tease out the intricacies of the lives of Terry's children. This is particularly true of Gordon Craig. Although it is pointed out that, ironically, it was Craig's immersion in Irving's intricate staging which led to his obsession with minimalism, the innovative nature of his stage design is glossed over. Nevertheless, Holroyd is the consummate biographer, and this is an engrossing read for anyone interested in the theatre.

As its title suggests, *The Ancient World on the Victorian and Edwardian Stage* by Jeffrey Richards outlines various ways in which plays of this time depicted ancient Rome, Greece, Egypt, Babylon, and the Holy Land. This theatrical codification became a way to contrast contemporary urbanization and industrialization with an imagined golden age, to comment on national identity through the figure of the intrepid explorer/educator, and to titillate an audience with images of the exotic other. Sir Herbert Beerbohm Tree followed in the footsteps of Sir Henry Irving, both of whom were 'masters of the pictorial stage' (p. 152). Tree had already scored successes with plays like *Julius Caesar* [1898], which was the opening show for his new theatre, Her Majesty's in the Haymarket. He went on to produce a string of classically inspired plays: *Herod* [1900], *Ulysses* [1902], and *Nero* [1906], all written by Stephen Phillips, the rising star of the Edwardian theatre, who drank himself to death by 1915. The literary 'worthiness' of the plays was emphasized through the *mise-en-scène*, which revelled in vivid colour, sumptuous settings, and triumphal music. In this way, directors presented the ancient world in much the same way as artists of the time, such as Alma-Tadema: as a spectacle, which had little to do with historical accuracy.

Like Holroyd, Selina Hastings is a skilled biographer, having written on the likes of Evelyn Waugh, Rosamond Lehmann, and Nancy Mitford. Her new work on W. Somerset Maugham is welcomed, after Jeffrey Meyers's poorly received attempt in 2005. Hastings's title hints at Maugham's creation of a public persona, designed to hide his promiscuous homosexual liaisons, and the guilt and shame they caused him. While known mainly as a writer of novels, such as *Of Human Bondage*, *The Moon and Sixpence*, and *The Painted Veil*, as well as a prolific short-story writer, Maugham's exposure to theatre during his time at university in Germany fired his passion, and ended with him becoming one of the most important playwrights of the interwar period. In fact, as Hastings points out, he only wrote novels as a means of attracting the attention of theatre managers. His first piece, a one-act play, *Marriages are Made in Heaven* [1898], was rejected by London managers, but produced by Max Reinhardt's company in Germany four years later. J.T. Grein, who produced his plays at the Stage Society, a private theatre devoted to experimental work, eventually saw his promise. Hastings does much to display Maugham's enthusiasm for the theatre and the influence of Ibsen and Wilde on his drama. Although Maugham has fallen out of critical favour since his death in 1965, his plays deserve a wider audience, and Hastings has firmly put him back on the map.

At first glance, David Slattery-Christie's *In Search of Ruritania: The Life and Times of Ivor Novello* also attempts to draw attention to a man who was once one of England's most popular entertainers, and whose contribution to theatre, like Maugham, has seldom been recognized. Novello was a remarkable figure whose highly successful career ran from the First World War to the 1950s. He was equally adept at stage and film acting, composing, and directing. His musicals have been lampooned as 'Ruritania' for their overuse of the royalty of imaginary foreign countries, although Novello himself was not above parodying his own work, as with his last musical, *Gay's the Word*, whose title may well have been a reference to his own homosexuality. Unlike Selina Hastings, though, Slattery-Christie presents a hagiographical account of a man who is obviously his idol. Much more could have been said of Novello's ability to judge the mood of the moment, and to present work that carries, beneath all its froth, some topical commentary. For example, *The Dancing Years*, produced on the eve of war, carries a message about fascism's threat to art, and his 1945 musical *Perchance to Dream* is steeped in nationalistic pride. This would certainly suggest that a serious critical study of Novello's work is long overdue.

In a similar vein, Nicolas Ridley gives an affectionate portrait of his father in *Godfrey's Ghost: From Father to Son*. Arnold Ridley is best known nowadays as Private Godfrey in the long-running television series *Dad's Army*. However, during the interwar years, he wrote over thirty plays, including his one smash hit, *The Ghost Train* [1923], *Keepers of Youth* [1929], and *Recipe for Murder* [1936]. However, dogged by bad luck, wrong decisions, and poor health (exacerbated by two world wars), Ridley never considered himself a success, even after he had become a household name on television. The book provides extracts from Ridley's personal papers that give a flavour of what it must have been like to tour around the provinces or work in repertory, but his son's concern is to create a tribute rather than give any analysis of the period.

One of Britain's best-loved character actresses is under discussion in Andy Merriman's *Margaret Rutherford: Dreadnought with Good Manners*. Rutherford was brought up in a difficult household, where her mother committed suicide when she was only 2, and her father's mental illness led him to kill his own father: for the actress, fear of her own fragile mental health continued to haunt her. Merriman's workmanlike style moves the narrative along at a good pace, and provides plenty of information about Rutherford's stage and film career. While there is always the feeling that the author never fully gets to grips with his subject, nevertheless there is much here to appreciate. Coming late to acting, Rutherford made her stage debut at the Old Vic in 1925, aged 33, and through persistence rose to prominence in plays such as *Spring Meeting*, written by M.J. Farrell and John Perry in 1938. With this Rutherford found her niche as the blustery spinster that she played with comic insouciance for much of her career. While on a tour of wartime Britain, as Mrs Danvers in *Rebecca*, Daphne du Maurier's adaptation of her popular novel, she was sent the script of Noel Coward's *Blithe Spirit* [1941]. The role of Madame Arcati, the idiosyncratic spiritualist, ended up being one of her best stage roles, and the play went on to hold the record for the longest run on the English stage—until it was broken by Agatha Christie's *The Mousetrap*—with 1,997 performances at the Piccadilly Theatre. By an ironic twist of fate, Rutherford became well-known for another doughty spinster, Miss Marple, in a series of 1960s films.

Rebecca D'Monté's chapter, 'Origin and Ownership: Stage, Film and Television Adaptations of Daphne du Maurier's *Rebecca*', appears in *Adaptation in Contemporary Culture: Textual Infidelities*, edited by Rachel Carroll. D'Monté's work focuses on the stage, film, and television adaptations of du Maurier's 1939 novel to consider the ways in which notions of origin and authorial ownership can be problematized, as a means of exploring the effect of context and form upon subjectivity and meaning. Du Maurier's own stage adaptation of her novel came in 1940, the same year that Alfred Hitchcock's celebrated film appeared. D'Monté considers the radically different ending in the stage version, which leaves the aristocratic Manderley unravaged at the end, and argues that this gave wartime audiences a potent symbol of Englishness at a time of renewed energy in nationalistic pride.

D'Monté also looks at *Rebecca* in her chapter 'Feminizing the Nation and the Country House: Women Dramatists, 1938–1941' (in James and Tew, eds., *New Versions of Pastoral: Post-Romantic, Modern, and Contemporary Responses to the Tradition*). Here she explores how three women playwrights during the 1930s and 1940s—du Maurier, Dodie Smith, and Esther McCracken—drew on literary traditions such as the retirement, georgic, and pastoral genres in order to emphasize the Englishness of England at a time of national crisis. Ultimately, she suggests, a shift was taking place in the representation of the country house, from the aristocratic Manderley in *Rebecca* to the more middle-class versions represented in *Dear Octopus* and *Quiet Weekend*.

After publishing Noel Coward's lyrics, letters and quotations, Barry Day continues his almost solo efforts to return Coward from critical oblivion with *The Essential Noel Coward Compendium*. That this brings together selections drawn from all aspects of his career—plays, songs, novels, short stories, poetry, and film—makes one aware of Coward's extraordinarily wide-ranging talent. However, there is also the sense that Day is mining his previous work in order to keep the Coward treadmill going. The chapter on his stage work includes extracts from three of his best-known plays, *The Vortex*, *Private Lives*, and *Hay Fever*, together with scattered quotes on theatre ('The theatre ... is a house of strange enchantment, a temple of dreams', p. 45) and acting ('acting is not a state of being ... It's giving an *impression* of feeling', p. 85).

If J.T. Grein was seen by Hastings to help along the theatrical career of Somerset Maugham, Olivia Turnbull shows how he was also instrumental in establishing the repertory system in England, along with such figures as Harley Granville Barker, George Bernard Shaw, and William Archer. This is mentioned at the beginning of her meticulously researched *Bringing Down the House: The Crisis in Britain's Regional Theatres*. Turnbull goes on to explain how the First World War had nearly brought about the closure of the repertory movement, due to loss of staff and support, and the fear was that this would also happen during the next war. In fact, the Second World War actually strengthened its position. This was partly because of the strange dichotomy imposed by wartime conditions: on the one hand, travel was restricted and so audiences were encouraged to make the best of their local theatres; on the other hand, the population was increasingly mobile so new audiences continued to flow into different areas. Again, Turnbull charts the way in which the present-day Arts Council sprang from the Council for the Encouragement of Music and the Arts (CEMA), set up in 1940. The Theatre Royal, Bristol (better known as the Bristol Old Vic) became the first theatre to receive state funding via CEMA, and 'it was done in such a way as to emphasize "good drama" as a right of the nation, not just the metropolis' (p. 23). Perhaps the most fascinating part of the book is the information it gives on John Maynard Keynes. He was one of CEMA's first directors, before helping to set up the Arts Council. The decisions he made in these early days, Turnbull convincingly argues in her richly referenced work, continue to influence arts policy in England. One example she gives is of Keynes's privileging of London over the regions, and of professional theatre over amateur, beliefs that ran counter to the original CEMA constitution.

Graeme Smith turns his attention to Scottish theatre with his book *The Theatre Royal: Entertaining a Nation*. This charts the history of the Glasgow theatre from its inception as the Royal Colesseum (*sic*) and Opera House by James Baylis. At the turn of the twentieth century, there was a wide range of entertainment on offer at the theatre, from hosting a Japanese company from Tokyo, 'possibly linking with the Japanese Pavilion at a nearby International Exhibition', to 'the American La Loie Fuller in her "sensational dances" involving red, blue and white lights being projected onto her white silk costume—marrying light and dance' (p. 102). The Theatre Royal was firmly rooted in the community and celebrated Scottish culture: Sir Harry Lauder, for example, topped the bill for a number of years with his song 'Ma Scotch Bluebell', character actor Will Fyffe sang about 'Sailing Up the Clyde' and

'I Belong to Glasgow', and local playwright Graham Moffat's work was staged at the theatre, before he campaigned after the First World War for Glasgow to have its own municipal theatre. Again, in 1932, the Sir Walter Scott's centenary saw a month at the Theatre Royal dedicated to his greatest works. Smith's book sometimes lacks clarity, as there can be several different narrative threads in one chapter, and even on the same page. Nevertheless, it is handsomely illustrated, and gives a fascinating account of how a major regional theatre came into being, and survived. Pantomimes, variety, and even cinematic showings all helped to keep the theatre going, as well as straight drama. It also staged the early work of the Glasgow Unity Theatre, which started in 1941. The rise of television led to a farewell performance being given in 1957 when, ironically, it became STV's television studios. It was restored in 1975, becoming the home of the Scottish Theatre Company, Scottish Opera, and the Scottish Ballet.

Don Chapman explores the history of another theatre in his *Oxford Playhouse: High and Low Drama in a University City* [2008], looking at its two manifestations, starting with the Woodstock Road building in 1923 (originally a big-game museum), and then the purpose-built theatre in Beaumont Street fifteen years later. Throughout Chapman chronicles the tensions between 'town and gown', and even between Oxford University and its own drama society, OUDS. He posits, correctly, that 'commentators have persisted in regarding Oxford's role as crucial to Britain's dramatic well-being' (p. 1). In 1947 J.B. Priestley asserted that, to preserve the future of theatre in Britain at least four universities needed to become involved, naming Oxford, Cambridge, London, and either Glasgow or Edinburgh as suitable choices. An absorbing account is given of the response to this challenge, as a fight began to set up England's first university drama department. Oxford finally lost out to Bristol. This was due to the difficulty Oxford University had with seeing drama as a subject worthy of academic study, as well as the long-held objection that theatre was a corrupting influence on the young. The Oxford Playhouse would only be deemed a wholly university theatre from 1961, when student work was finally able to be staged alongside a resident professional company. Chapman's scholarly but readable book goes beyond a straightforward history, delving into some of the key issues at stake: the balance often required between commercialism and experimentation, the shifting boundaries between amateur and professional theatre, and the educative links that can be forged between the practical and the theoretical.

Finally, Kate McLoughlin's edited volume *The Cambridge Companion to War Writing* will be of little help to those interested in theatre. While situating war within a wider theoretical framework about the concept of war, and difficulties of finding a language to convey this experience, the book also covers a range of historical events around the world: from classical times to the Cold War, taking in Britain, America, and Spain along the way. This makes it all the more frustrating that barely any plays are mentioned. Apart from a fleeting mention of R.C. Sherriff's *Journey's End* and Terence Rattigan's *Flare Path*, there is nothing of the wealth of plays written about the First and Second World Wars: this is an area ripe for further research.

4. Post-1950 Drama

While this year marked a slowing down of output in this particular field, 2009 has been notable for several significant monograph studies and journal articles on individual playwrights together with related work on theatre censorship and documentary/verbatim drama.

Work on Samuel Beckett, however, still continues apace. Questions over Beckett's Irish heritage occupied two monographs this year. Emile Morin's *Samuel Beckett and the Problem of Irishness* puts forward a case that Beckett's drama (together with the prose and poetry) turned towards European modernism in a bid to avoid incorporation within an Irish literary tradition. Morin concludes that, at least in terms of his drama, Beckett was less successful. In the chapter 'Beckett and the Irish Literary Revival' (pp. 21–54), Morin looks at his early play-going between 1923 and 1927 as a university student at the Abbey Theatre, and argues that the influence of W.B. Yeats's verse drama and, later, Sean O'Casey's Dublin realism had a lasting influence on Beckett's stagecraft. Later chapters, such as 'Representing Scarcity' (pp. 96–126), detail how motifs from the literary revival find their way into Beckett's writing, particularly the dramatic representation of poverty. Here Morin draws some interesting comparisons between Lady Gregory's short comic play, *The Workhouse Ward* [1908], whose bare set with two old men trapped in beds make for obvious comparisons with *Waiting for Godot* [1952] and *Endgame* [1957]. The allusions to poverty in these two plays are discussed in some detail, as well as the Irish language that betrays itself in the English exchanges between Vladimir and Estragon. In a closely observed comparison between Beckett's own French and English versions Morin points out the differences between small but telling moments such as the different names for Pozzo's pipe: in *En attendant Godot* it is an Abdullah, 'linking Pozzo's position of authority and French colonial rule in north Africa', while the 'Kapp and Peterson' in the English version has associations with a type of pipe smoked in Ireland by women (p. 113).

Rina Kim's *Women and Ireland as Beckett's Lost Others: Beyond Mourning and Melancholia* argues that Beckett (who in his early life underwent psychoanalysis), displays an awareness in his prose and drama of concepts of Freudian and Kleinian analysis and the 'lost others' of the title. Kim argues that, after 1937 with Beckett's self-imposed French exile, this becomes significant for the representation of both geographical place and ideas of Irish nationhood and womanhood. In chapter 3, 'The Gender of Mourning and Melancholia in Beckett's Early Drama' (pp. 76–106), Kim identifies the sense of women speaking as nation through the figure of Mrs Rooney in the wireless play *All That Fall* [1956]. This is then developed in work that follows such *Krapp's Last Tape* [1958] whereby male protagonists begin to associate loss with Ireland but are able to address this sense of mourning through language. In the chapter 'Beyond Mourning and Melancholia: Kleinian Approaches' (pp. 115–30), Kim sees earlier Freudian echoes in the drama and prose of the 1950s giving way to Kleinian analysis. Drawing on essays such as 'A Contribution to the Psychogenesis of Manic Depressive States' [1935] useful readings are opened up for exploring Winnie's growing manic highs and lows in *Happy Days* [1961], and the growing sense of paranoia that afflicts the protagonist of *Film* [1964]. Kim argues that it also explains the growing importance of the role that the mother occupies in Beckett's drama from the 1970s onwards. Plays such as *Footfalls* [1975] and *Rockaby* [1980] are termed 'project[s] of revision' which aim to restore the 'damaged and abjected [female subject] in [Beckett's] early fiction' (p. 18) in order for Beckett to understand his own sense of alienation from Ireland and clinging maternal bonds.

Beckett's relationship with the country of his birth is just one of the fifteen short chapters in Mark Nixon and Matthew Feldman's highly readable edited collection, *The International Reception of Samuel Beckett*. It is surprising that a volume charting the responses to Beckett's work in different countries has not been attempted before. While restrictions of space (which the co-editors openly acknowledge in their introduction, p. 3) prevent an exhaustive global survey, the countries considered range widely, from more familiar Anglo-American accounts to little-known reception histories in countries such as Spain, Portugal, Poland, and New Zealand. Chapters generally concentrate on the area of each contributor's expertise: hence Shane Weller's account of Beckett's reception in France, 'Beckett among the *Philosophes*' (pp. 24–39) concentrates on the prose work (and particularly its reception by critical and philosophical theory) over drama: clearly this is inevitable when considering a writer such as Beckett. Many of the chapters also consider the contested place of national boundaries when appropriating Beckett's work, and also the problematic relationship with Ireland, his practice of writing first in French then English, and his Anglo-German work for television. Several chapters also consider the premieres of plays such as *Ohio Impromptu* [1980] in America. Other contributions look at the dissemination of the work through a multilingual series of publishing houses alongside Beckett's own translations in French, English, and German. Despite the disparate histories of reception that make up the volume there are many points of cohesion, such as the impact that *En Attendant Godot* made throughout Europe in several fascinating accounts, such as its profound impact on the subsequent development of theatre in the Netherlands during the 1950s.

Jonathan Bignell's *Beckett on Screen: The Television Plays* despite a substantial discussion of Beckett's *Film* [1964] and the ambitious *Beckett on Film* [2001] project, is mainly devoted to Beckett's place in broadcasting. Bignell's monograph provides a welcome contribution to this relatively neglected area of Beckett scholarship. Previous work, including Clas Zilliacaus's influential study *Beckett and Broadcasting* [1976], Grayley Herren's *Samuel Beckett's Plays on Film and Television* [2007], and, more recently, Ulrika Maude and David Pattie's edited collection for the *Journal of Beckett Studies*, *Beckett on TV* [2009], has concentrated on Beckett's response to television as an experimental medium in itself. Bignell's approach is somewhat different, with its emphasis on Beckett's place within the television industry. Starting with the BBC and its wider history of television drama, Bignell traces how Beckett gradually became seen as canonical writer who represented the experimental values of high modernism against competing duties to broadcast popular drama and light entertainment programmes.

This new approach to Beckett's work on television is aided by extensive use of the BBC Written Archives. These sources do much to clarify several of the chief arguments put forward. For instance Bignell's access to audience surveys reveals interesting material that says much about the BBC's high regard for Beckett as a serious dramatist, whose audiences would almost by definition be small and select. Moreover, small but telling details about Beckett's standing at the BBC are revealed, such as the fact that he was paid one-sixth more than was usually allocated for the commission of a new television play (p. 149).

In a very different approach to Beckett, Paul Kintzele's article 'Sacrifice, Inhibition, and Oedipal Fantasy in *Krapp's Last Tape* (*MD* 52:ii[2009] 207–19) gives an alternative reading to the popular interpretation of the play being about Krapp's sacrifice to literature through his 39-year-old self on tape bidding 'farewell to love'. Kintzele points out that nowhere in the play do the younger or older Krapp equate the speech with sacrifice, and argues that the decision can better be understood by looking closer at the unresolved Oedipal conflicts that are present throughout the play in Krapp's references to his mother's death. It is through seeing *Krapp's Last Tape* in terms of what Kintzele calls a 'drama of inhibition' (p. 207) that we are allowed to interpret fully its protagonist's dealings with a whole succession of women, including his mother.

Caryl Churchill is the subject of Siân Adieshiah's monograph *Churchill's Socialism: Political Resistance in the Plays of Caryl Churchill.* As its title suggests this is a detailed study of the author's perceived transition from socialist-feminist in the 1970s and 1980s to the quasi-absurdist and postmodern experiments of the last twenty years. Adieshiah attempts to refute this view. The study makes a case for more recent works such as *A Number* [2002] still containing a discernible socialist impulse; chapters look at the politics of utopianism, such as the period of the mid-1970s when Churchill produced Marxist-feminist historiographic plays such as *Light Shining in Buckinghamshire* [1976] and *Vinegar Tom* [1976]. Class and gender identities are also discussed in the chapter 'The Politics of Utopia' (pp. 37–92), on two of Churchill's most significant plays of the early 1980s, *Fen* [1983] and *Top Girls* [1982]. These are later revisited in the chapter 'The Triumph of Capitalism' (pp. 165–94), which analyses Churchill's response to the high days of Thatcherism in the City of London, the collapse of the Soviet bloc, and the advent of postmodern slogans, such as the 'end of history', 'globalization', and 'the hyperreal', that held sway. Adieshiah's penultimate chapter, 'Still a Socialist? *The Skriker* and *Far Away*' (pp. 195–218) uses the two plays as case studies to question the extent to which these seemingly postmodern plays can still recall previous socialist models. As well as close readings of a number of plays by Churchill, chapter 1, 'Socialist Contexts' (pp. 7–30), provides a highly detailed overview of the history and principal positions taken by the British left after 1945. A notable feature of the book is its presentation of factually based material, such as the history and features of utopianism, and of Marxist historians such as Christopher Hill, who influenced writers such as Churchill in the mid-1970s.

Chapter 5, 'The Triumph of Capitalism? *Serious Money* and *Mad Forest* (pp. 165–93) also forms the basis of Adieshiah's article 'Revolution and the

End of History: Caryl Churchill's *Mad Forest*' (*MD* 52:iii [2009] 283–99). Here, post- Ceauşescu Romania is used as a case-study to explore the failure of the left to take account of the speed with which the capitalism of liberal democracies colonized former communist states in eastern Europe. Adieshiah argues that the play does not so easily yield to this reading, and through considering the different historical perspectives (looking at events both pre- and post-revolution as well as the different styles of performance employed)—from domestic scenes showing family life to the use of documentary-style testimony—refutes Francis Fukuyama's 'end of history' and the triumph of liberal democracies over alternative forms of political or economic ideology.

Caryl Churchill's *Top Girls* [1982] also forms a major part of Rebecca Cameron's thoughtful article, 'From Great Women to *Top Girls*: Pageants' of Sisterhood in British Feminist Theater' (*CompD* 43:ii [2009] 143–66). Celebratory stagings of heroic women from the past featured in a number of British suffragette dramas, but in Churchill's play this gives way to a more problematic sisterhood. Cameron sees Churchill's use of the all-female cast of historical characters who gather in the first scene of *Top Girls* as representative of the debates and divisions in the women's movement of the early 1980s. Yet while it is now a familiar argument that the first scene's gradual collapse into anarchy represents the failure of feminism to connect with a wider political movement, Cameron argues that 'Churchill does not deny the possibility beyond the social conditions represented in the play' (p. 144).

Matters of gender and the representation of sexuality also occupy Andrew Wyllie's *Sex on Stage: Gender and Sexuality in Post-War British Theatre*. The monograph sets itself a difficult task in attempting to assess the impact of feminism, masculinities, *and* gay/lesbian identities in post-war British playwriting from the 1950s to the mid-1990s in fewer than 160 pages. The book also re-rehearses some already familiar arguments over a number of equally familiar plays such as Shelagh Delaney's *A Taste of Honey* [1960] and Caryl Churchill's *Cloud Nine* [1979]. However, there are perceptive readings of lesser-known dramatists such as Olwyn Wymark, some clear-sighted analysis of Arnold Wesker's *Trilogy*, and a welcome discussion of Timberlake Wertenbaker's much-underrated *Break of Day* [1995]. There are also interesting readings presented on proto-feminist men (whom Wyllie terms 'boy feminist writers', pp. 65–72) and the misogynistic anxieties in the late plays of John Osborne and the work of Patrick Marber. A strong case is also put forward for the early work of Howard Barker expressing clear feminist impulses from *Claw* [1975] to *Ursula: Fear of the Estuary* [1998]. However, his breathless attempt to cover so many contentious area of gender identity over such an extensive period means that all too often there is not sufficient space for Wyllie to sufficiently develop his arguments.

David Ian Rabey's *Howard Barker: Ecstasy and Death. An Expository Study of his Drama Theory and Production Work, 1998–2008* is a welcome companion to his earlier monograph *Howard Barker: Politics and Desire*, published in 1989 (reissued by Palgrave with a new introduction and updated chronology), which has been the foundation for much scholarship that has followed. A great virtue of this book is its scope—both published and unpublished plays are included and attention is also paid to Barker's long relationship with writing for BBC wireless. The chapters are logically set out and broadly follow a chronological mapping of Barker's work since 1988. After outlining the distinctive features of Barker's drama in the introduction, the second chapter, '"The Ecstasy of Vanishing Meaning": Arguments for a Theatre; Death, the One and the Art of Theatre' (pp. 18–30), looks at Barker's own theoretical writings. This then allows the philosophical and aesthetic ideas about theatre to inform the remainder of the book. Insightful analyses of the plays are followed by discussion of the work in its performance contexts, often based around a major British production. Detailed consideration is also given to Barker as a director and designer of his own work in plays such as *Ursula* [1998], *The Twelfth Battle of Isonzo* [2001], and *Gertrude—The Cry* [2002]. Groups of plays are also brought together in terms of shared themes or developments in style. Unusually in the work of a living dramatist attention is also given to work that so far has been neither produced nor published.

Alison Forsyth and Chris Megson's *Get Real: Documentary Theatre Past and Present* is a timely study that considers, in part, the recent popularity of documentary forms in theatre since the late 1990s. The collection looks across a range of work since the 1930s, but chapters on British theatre since 1950 include Colin Chambers's exploration of Unity Theatre, where documentary sources were used to further a socialist/communist agenda. Derek Paget concludes the volume by expanding upon his pioneering work in this field to outline the didactic purpose of documentary-based drama in the 1960s and its increasing use as a yardstick and a bulwark against the forces of postmodernism and a partisan mass media.

David Hare's mixture of documentary sources and fictional episodes in the build-up to the second Iraq war in *Stuff Happens* [2004] is the subject of J. Chris Westgate's article, '*Stuff Happens* in Seattle: Taking a Sober Account' (*ConTR* 25:iv[2009] 402–18). Westgate provides a thoughtful account of a 2007 production of the play in Seattle. Here despite the best efforts of the theatre's marketing department to highlight its controversial London opening, Westgate argues that Seattle audiences were not sufficiently challenged by Hare's play because the very drama itself 'encourages liberal audiences to defer accountability for the war in Iraq onto the Bush administration' (p. 410). Westgate also observes that the three-year interlude between the London and Seattle productions 'demonstrated the short shelf-life of *Stuff Happens*' (p. 412), which carries with it implications for the genre of documentary theatre.

Stuart Young's article, 'Playing with Documentary Theatre: *Aalst* and *Taking Care of Baby*' (*ConTR* 25:i[2009] 72–87), also looks at two recent examples of documentary theatre. Here he argues that Dennis Kelly's play *Taking Care of Baby* [2007] and its masquerade as a creditable piece documentary theatre undermines important claims made by verbatim and testimony forms owing to their claims for veracity. Young argues that Kelly's play shows clearly how documentary theatre can construct its own version of events, to which audiences all too willingly surrender themselves because 'audiences recognize verbatim testimony as being of a different mimetic order from fictional drama' (p. 75). Consequently, when it is revealed that they have been duped Young notes that both critics and audiences could not help but betray their disappointment (p. 85). While plays such *Taking Care of Baby* are useful in providing a critique of a type of drama that has been one of the dominant theatrical forms of the millennial decade, Young concludes that its manipulation 'may implicate ... and even collude with the mechanisms of injustice which they seek to oppose' (p. 86).

Richard Eyre's *Talking Theatre: Interviews with Theatre People* is an entertaining as well as informative collection of transcripts taken from the interviews conducted during Eyre's BBC television series *Changing Stages* [2000]. Although the format of the interviews is hampered by a series of set questions, the responses given are of interest by virtue of the range of views which his interviewees have about a particular subject, such as Brecht's *Galileo* [*c.*1947]. Many of the best insights come from younger writers and practitioners such as Patrick Marber, Deborah Warner, and Simon McBurney, rather than the more established figures such as Peter Hall, Harold Pinter, and Peter Brook, who have a tendency to recycle familiar stories and anecdotes.

Aleks Sierz's interview with the playwright Philip Ridley, '"Putting a new lens on the world": The Art of Theatrical Alchemy' (*ConTR* 25:iv[2009] 109–17), allows his subject no such indulgence. As a consequence this becomes a wide-ranging and informative interview. Sierz's youthful insouciance, as a tactical approach, seems to make the normally reticent playwright open up more fully than he has done in the past when discussing such topics as the early reception of *The Pitchfork Disney* [1991] and the importance of ritual and London's East End (p. 112). Ridley also discusses the problems in getting his controversial play *Mercury Fur* [2005] published (p. 114), and the destructive family relationships in *Vincent River* [2000] and *Leaves of Glass* [2007].

Harold Pinter's death in December 2008 is the subject of personal tributes (*NTQ* 25:i[2009] 3–5) by the theatre director Charles Marowitz and critic Simon Trussler. *Contemporary Theatre Review* also includes contributions from academics Mark Taylor-Batty and Carlota Benet (*ConTR* 19:ii[2009] 204–13). Pinter's friend and fellow playwright Simon Gray, who died earlier, in August 2008, is also the subject of a tribute from the actor Simon Callow in 'Simon Gray: A True Original in Life and Art' (*ConTR* 19:ii[2009] 107–8).

Pinter's short early play *The Dumb Waiter* [1959] is the subject of an edited collection by Mary F. Brewer, *Harold Pinter's The Dumb Waiter*, which aims to bring together emerging scholars and more seasoned voices. The volume also produces some fruitful reappraisals of a play that has already attracted a great deal of critical attention. For instance, Basil Chiasson's '(Re)Thinking Harold Pinter's Comedy of Menace' (pp. 31–54) and Marc E. Shaw's 'Unpacking the Pinteresque in *The Dumb Waiter* and Beyond' (pp. 211–30) retrospectively examine the terms 'Pinteresque' and 'Comedies of Menace' not only in regard to *The Dumb Waiter*, but also with respect to how useful these terms are today. Catherine Rees's 'High Art or Popular Culture: Traumatic Conflicts of Representation and Postmodernism in Pinter's *The Dumb Waiter*' (pp. 111–26) and Michael Patterson's 'Pinter's *The Dumb Waiter*: Negotiating the Boundary between "High" and "Low" Culture' (pp. 127–42) are also two intelligent 'dialogues' over the play being representative of high modernism set against its more obvious borrowings from popular forms of entertainment. David Pattie's 'Feeding Power: Pinter, Bakhtin, and Inverted Carnival' (pp. 55–70) is also a notable contribution, drawing as it does upon inverted notions of the alimentary process where Gus and Ben return the food back to its mysterious source via the device of the dumb waiter. Pattie also makes comparisons to later plays such as *Party Time* [1991] and *The New World Order* [1991], where food is associated with privilege and abuse (p. 63). Whereas increasingly exotic culinary dishes such as bamboo shoots and char siu are delivered to Gus and Ben during the play, some of the contributions in the volume are less digestible: here less obfuscation and recourse to arcane theory in place of original ideas would have been welcome.

Another short play by Pinter, written later in his career is the subject of Stephen Watt's 'Things, Voices, Events: Harold Pinter's *Mountain Language* as a Testamental Text' (*MD* 52:ii[2009] 38–56). Taking Alain Badiou's comment about Beckett's prose work *Worstward Ho* [1983] as a testamental text in the respect that it encapsulated Beckett's intellectual perspective, Watt makes the same case for Pinter's *Mountain Language* [1988] being illustrative of the repressive power structures that have operated in Pinter's work since *The Room* [1957]—namely the human voice and the significance of domestic objects taking on sinister power onstage.

One of the major themes of *Mountain Language* is censorship of thought through repression of language. Helen Freshwater's monograph *Theatre Censorship in Britain: Silencing, Censure and Suppression* follows on from recent work including David Thomas, David Carlton, and Anne Etienne's *Theatre Censorship: From Walpole to Wilson* [2007] and several recent high-profile articles on contemporary issues in censorship. However, whereas existing work to date on the subject mainly concentrates on the history of British censorship via the system upheld by the Lord Chamberlain until its abolition in 1968, the case-studies in Freshwater's book look at issues of censorship beyond Britain and 1968. This is particularly so where other forms of censorship—manifested for example through the activities of special interest groups—have attempted other interventions. The first half of the book looks at a number of events that took place up to the abolition of censorship in Britain, while the second part looks in detail at a number of case-studies. Even when familiar events are covered, such as the furore over Howard Brenton's *The Romans in Britain* [1980], Freshwater is able (through comparing the original production to its 2006 revival) to provide some fascinating new perspectives. Freshwater's eclectic approach also provides a stimulating contribution on the National Theatre's attempts to stage Rolf Hochuth's *Soldiers* [1968] and the role of historian (and later infamous Holocaust denier) David Irving, who at the time acted as Kenneth Tynan's adviser on the play. There is also a chapter that considers the ways in which economic pressures can produce other insidious forms of censorship, with a number of examples, including Diane Dubois's *Myra and Me* [1998] and the Jerwood Foundation's sponsorship of the Royal Court. There are also absorbing chapter-length discussions of cases where the issue of religion and theatre censorship has become a major national event, such as Gurpreet Kaur Bhatti's *Bezhti* (*Dishonour*) [2004] and *Jerry Springer: The Opera* [2003].

Kate Dorney's *The Changing Language of Modern English Drama 1945–2005* is a rare example where a critical approach, borrowed from linguistic stylistics, is used to analyse the long-standing tensions within post-war British theatre and its attitudes towards language. Dorney is less interested in overtly theatrical forms such as the soliloquy, and more in the way ordinary speech is produced and received in a live environment. Early chapters reveal that the question of language for writers, audiences, and critics has been a continual site of conflict, which Dorney terms 'language minding' (p. 4). The opening chapter outlines the main forms this takes—ranging from the use of slang to sexual or violent language (used most infamously by the so-called 'in yer face' dramatists of the 1990s). Yet the book does not insist on some prelapsarian moment followed by deterioration; language minding is also taken to mean the concerns both of those dramatists who attempted to maintain an artificial lingua franca (the exemplar being Noel Coward) and of those who sought to produce a more realistic theatre language which could attempt to match the ways syntax and grammar existed beyond the theatre foyer—most famously with Osborne's *Look Back in Anger*. In chapters 1 and 2 Dorney looks at, amongst others, Beckett's and Pinter's use of language as a counterpoint between the demotic and the poetic in order to illustrate the problems inherent in the reception of 'life-like' (Dorney's preferred term) to that of 'authentic' (p. 4). Far from subscribing to Martin Esslin's widely upheld interpretation that the language of Beckett and Pinter is in a state of entropic decay, Dorney locates the pair far nearer to the realism of the kitchen sink dramatists. Yet even here Dorney is circumspect and points out that 'a great deal of post-war British drama continues to prefer articulacy over realism' (p. 12); this perhaps explains why Jimmy Porter's and Bill Maitland's epic set-piece speeches are still held in high regard by audiences and theatre scholars alike.

Yael Zahry-Levo's 'The Making of Artistic Reputation: Dennis Potter, Television Dramatist' (*TRI* 34:i[2009] 37–49) locates a rare phenomenon—namely Potter's dual status, both as a high-profile television dramatist and as a long-standing television newspaper critic. Zahry-Levo identifies this as being achieved by other critics 'extensive reliance on, and endorsement of [Potter's] commentaries as both a dramatist and critic' (p. 37). The importance of the dramatist as a television critic is emphasized as the principal means by which Potter could 'establish the grounds for the evaluation of his own innovative work' (p. 37).

Tom Stoppard's *Indian Ink* [1995] is the subject of Nandi Bhatia's 'Reinventing India through "A quite witty pastiche": Reading Tom Stoppard's *Indian Ink*' (*MD* 52:ii[2009] 220–36). Despite a recognition of Stoppard's research into colonial India and part of his own childhood spent there, Bhatia sees the play as highly problematic: while recognizing that Stoppard sets out 'to destabilize colonialist myths... and interrogate "impartial" claims of a historian's history' (p. 221), she argues that Stoppard's familiar trademarks of linguistic playfulness and the shift between past and present also dismantle 'boundaries between empire and colony and engage [the] audience in a rethinking of the cross-cultural fluidity between the two' (p. 222). While Bhatia acknowledges that Stoppard attempts to disengage from the clichés of the Raj that dominated English film and television during the 1980s, she concludes that 'the playwright reveals a version of India that is consistent with the kind of orientalism that framed earlier writings of the Raj' (p. 224).

The 2007 West End revival of Peter Shaffer's *Equus* [1973] is the subject of Ryan M. Claycomb's substantial article 'Middlebrowing the Avant-Garde: *Equus* on the West End' (*MD* 52:i[2009] 99–123). In a detailed comparison between the two productions Claycomb compares the revival with its original première at the National Theatre and traces its avant-garde leanings against the middle-class anxieties that it also reveals—namely its reliance on psychiatry as a tool in explaining aberrant behaviour and the casting of Harry Potter actor Daniel Radcliffe in the new production.

In 'New Writing: Scanning the Horizon' (*ConTR* 19:i[2009] 131–3) Aleks Sierz provides another of his fiery ongoing reports about the state of British theatre through several of its new writing venues. Sierz observes that a number of productions at the Royal Court, including Anthony Neilson's *Relocated* [2008], Mike Bartlett's *My Child* [2007], and debbie tucker green's *Random* [2008], have all experimented with space, while other productions, such as Levi David Addai's *Oxford Street* [2008], were staged some distance from Sloane Square in an empty shop in London's Elephant and Castle shopping centre. Sierz also notes the rather less successful attempts by the National Theatre and Shakespeare's Globe to revive the fortunes of verse drama; here Sierz's customary youthful scorn is poured on Tony Harrison's *Fram* [2008] and Glyn Maxwell's *Liberty* [2008], which he describes as 'among the best ways of driving audiences to narcolepsy' (p. 132).

New writing is just one of the targets of Gregory Motton's equally polemical *Helping Themselves: The Left-Wing Middle Classes in Theatre and the Arts*. The main agenda of Motton's book is that since the 1950s the British leftish-leaning middle classes have hijacked major cultural and theatrical institutions, with a corresponding disempowerment of working-class aspirations. In setting out to make his case Motton divides his book into a series case-studies including chapters on the Arts Council, the 1960s satire boom, and the Oz trial. Motton also has much to say about landmark plays and defining genres of British post-war theatre. For instance, notwithstanding *Look Back in Anger*'s many qualities, Motton feels it to be hamstrung by Osborne's 'disinclination to think outside his own ego' (p. 90), and an alternative case is made for *Luther* [1961] being Osborne's true masterpiece. Motton also holds Osborne responsible (together with the film *Rebel Without a Cause*) for the promotion of youthful disaffection and rebelliousness without a clear target: for Motton this has produced disastrous consequences, ranging from Edward Bond's *Saved* [1965] to Sarah Kane's *Blasted* [1995], which dislocate disaffection from violence, but ignore the real social consequences whereby 'rebellion has turned into oppression . . . in the housing estates [and] streets of our cities' (pp. 94–5). Much of the responsibility for this situation is laid at the door of the Royal Court, which Motton views as an institution largely cocooned from the wider society it has always purported to reflect. Moreover, he challenges the myth that the theatre was ever truly the home of working-class playwrights. To hammer this point home Motton even produces a chart that, while certainly not comprehensive, clearly shows that the Royal Court's major writers and directors throughout its history have all followed a gilded route through public school and Oxford/Cambridge (with Oxford overwhelmingly favoured) (pp. 102–3). Genuine working-class playwrights and directors such as Arnold Wesker, Edward Bond, and John Dexter are distinct aberrations. Motton in particular takes John Arden and Anne Jellicoe to task—both from privileged backgrounds and both key to the Royal Court myth—for what he sees as their irresponsible and dangerous romanticizing of what would now be termed 'the underclass 'in *Live Like Pigs* [1958] and *The Sport of My Mad Mother* [1958]. Motton describes the former as 'the middle class writer's contempt of any feeble working class pretensions of bourgeois comfort or sophistication [which] makes a big noise for supporting the neighbours from hell' (p. 108). Such splenetic assessments of landmark plays is as good a way as any to end this review of work in post-1950 drama criticism for 2009.

5. Pre-1950 Poetry

The year 2009 was a rich one for T.S Eliot studies: it saw a revised first volume and a long-awaited second volume of his letters, with Hugh Haughton supplementing the editorial efforts of Eliot's second wife Valerie. The first volume is now approximately 250 pages longer, partly because of new material (including twenty letters from Eliot's first wife, Vivien). There are also noticeable changes in annotation which now firmly emphasize scholarly interconnections and background material over biography. The majority of newly published letters from Eliot himself are short and functional, so there are few revelations. There is, however, considerable new material from the early 1920s and a fuller picture of arrangements for publishing *The Waste Land* and Eliot's activities in preparing the first issues of the *Criterion* emerges.

Although it only covers 1923 to1925, the second volume of Eliot's letters is also nearly 900 pages. Presumably this reflects an editorial aspiration towards absolute inclusivity—otherwise, letters and notes confirming the addresses of *Criterion* contributors might seem redundant. Most of this volume concerns workaday matters: these are the years in which Eliot wrote and published *The Hollow Men* and his collection of essays *Homage to John Dryden*, and the volume concludes with Eliot resigning from Lloyds Bank in order to take up a position at the publishers Faber & Gwyer. However, amidst the professional correspondence is a startling picture of the deepening misery of his marriage, his wife's illnesses, and the toll upon Eliot of coping with the demands of his professional and personal life. In 1925 he confesses to John Middleton Murry that 'I have deliberately died—in order to go on with the outward form of living' and asks 'Does it happen that two persons' lives are absolutely hostile? Is it true that sometimes one can only live by another's dying?' (p. 627). These outbursts seem all the more extraordinary given Eliot's previous hostility towards Murry. It's clear that, with some qualifications, these volumes are an important achievement and will become a standard point of reference for scholars.

Another major publication during 2009 is the *Companion to T.S. Eliot*, edited by David Chinitz. As with other volumes in Wiley-Blackwell's *Companion* series (including that on Thomas Hardy, discussed below), this is a significant resource for students of all levels. The majority of essays address their chosen facet of Eliot's writing career or life in general terms. So Anthony Cuda provides a clear and straightforward account of Eliot's life, listing the personal and marital crises which prompted him to write poetry as a form of psychological release or escape; Gareth Reeve probes the coherence and political context of Eliot's *Coriolan* sequence; Tony Sharpe considers the Ariel poems and scrutinizes *Ash Wednesday*; Lee Oser examines the links between literature and spirituality in *Four Quartets*; Sarah Bay-Cheng outlines Eliot's metrical games in *Old Possum's Book of Practical Cats*; Richard Badenhausen tackles Eliot's prose after 1927, from his views on individual writers to the connections between his public proclamations about poetic drama and his own practice; John Timberman Newcomb describes Eliot's career as a publisher and his role in shaping the 'High Modernist canon' while working at Faber; Nancy Gish surveys critical responses to Eliot's work from the 1930s to the early 1960s; and Gail McDonald looks to the afterlife of Eliot's criticism, examining the influence of *The Sacred Wood* in shaping the New Criticism. Such survey essays have virtues of their own and obviously play an important role within a work of this kind, but they are not always the most compelling contributions.

Other essays adopt a thematic approach: Patrick Query considers Eliot's career in terms of 'sexuality' and 'improper desire', charting a movement from 'intense fascination with human sexuality' (p. 351) in the early poems towards an emphasis upon 'communion' (p. 357) in his later work. Cyrena Pondrom reviews Eliot's career in relation to 'Women and Gender', starting with the frustrations of J. Alfred Prufrock, who hesitates, she suggests, to 'disturb' the social 'universe' of constricting, constructed gender roles (p. 326). Kevin J.H. Detmar explores 'Eliot as a Religious Thinker', considering the value of epiphanic moments of revelation or mystical experience in his poetry, the influence of Hulmean classicism, and Eliot's relationship to the church. He concludes with an appeal to recent appreciations of 'the depth, influence, complexity and contradictions of Eliot's religious faith' (p. 374).

Lawrence Rainey lifts his summary of key Eliotan concepts 'tradition', 'objective correlative', and 'impersonality' from tedium by analysing the poet's syntax and use of metaphor. Eliot's classicism, Rainey argues, coexists uneasily with 'the histrionic' (p. 308)—a fascination with the grisly side of popular culture. In 'Not One, Not Two: Eliot and Buddhism', Christina Hauck outlines the Buddhist concept of *shunyata*, commonly translated as 'emptiness', but more properly connoting a lack of self-nature or fully individuated perspective separate from other things and places. She provides thoughtful readings of *The Waste Land* and *The Cocktail Party* that contrast the attitudes of Buddhism and Christianity towards selfhood and ponder Eliot's appreciation of the differences. Michael Coyle's essay on *The Waste Land* attempts to recover a sense for the poem's difficulty from its professional explicators. Distinctively, Coyle indicates that the irregular patterns of rhyme echo Eliot's general intentions—promising conclusions which never come and surprising readers with unexpected repetitions. He also suggests that, despite their shared interest in comparative anthropology, the modernism of *The Waste Land* lies in tensions between J.G. Frazer's rationalism and Jessie Weston's primitivism.

Collectively many essays supply a useful picture of trends in Eliot criticism. Several contributors dwell on Eliot's interest in French Symbolism: Francis Dickey reveals significant verbal connections between Arthur Symons's account of Jules Laforgue in *The Symbolist Movement in Literature* and Eliot's construction of J. Alfred Prufrock. Barry Faulk takes a 'larger view' of French Symbolism and its influence on Eliot, arguing that Symbolism was inextricably linked to the metropolis. Faulk connects Symons's interest in music halls and dancing girls to Eliot's fascination with popular culture, as well as the savage anthropology of his 'unreal City'. And Jayme Stayer points to Laforgue's influence on Eliot's achievement of an 'edgy' voice (p. 109) in his early poems (published posthumously as *Inventions of the March Hare*).

Several essays dwell on the formative importance of Eliot's graduate work on F.H. Bradley. Michael Levenson connects Eliot's concern with politics to the questions of authority addressed in his early philosophical study of Bradley, but also gives space to his increasing disillusion with the social order after the First World War and the influence of Christopher Dawson's political thought upon Eliot in the 1930s. Amongst the best contributions to the volume, Leonard Diepeveen's account of Eliot's essays up to 1927 emphasizes the importance of the theory of knowledge espoused in Eliot's doctoral thesis on F.H. Bradley to understanding his criticism, rather than localized concepts such as 'the dissociation of sensibility' or 'objective correlative'. Diepeveen tackles Eliot's 'seriousness' as a critic and identifies Eliot's characteristically discerning approach, which demands contrast and comparison in order, as Eliot puts it, 'to treat a book austerely by criteria of art and art alone' (p. 267).

Two contributors touch in detail upon previous accusations of anti-Semitism against Eliot. Edward Brunner's essay on 'Gerontion' examines that tricky monologue's place in relation to the satirical quatrains elsewhere in *Poems (1920)* and considers its status as 'serious' poetry. Placing the anti-Semitism in 'Gerontion' within a complex dramatic context, Brunner suggests that we should hear the poem as a monologue channelling the experiences of Henry Adams through a layer of Jamesian dramatic irony. Bryan Cheyette brings together Eliot's treatment of 'Jews, Irish and Black' under the heading of 'race'. As forms or echoes of 'Semitic discourse', he argues that Eliot seems to imagine transgressive others, from Bleistein to King Bolo, in terms which evoke Jewishness.

Many contributors recapitulate their most important previously published work. Chinitz explains in his preface that the volume aims to take account of 'the "new" T.S. Eliot' (p. xiv) emerging from recent criticism: his own essay reprises ground covered in *T.S. Eliot and the Great Divide* [2004]. Exploring Eliot's interest in popular culture produces, Chinitz argues, a 'more involved, more ambivalent and . . . more interesting' (p. 67) picture of Eliot's career than accounts which align him exclusively with high art. Ann Ardis offers a broad account of Eliot in relation to 'something called modernism', focusing on the material historical culture of modernism and the relation between Eliot's career and reception and the 'professionalization of literary studies' (p. 315). Marc Manganaro pursues Eliot's interest in anthropology, from his declared debt to the comparative studies of Jessie Weston and J.G. Frazer in *The Waste Land* and his particular interest in the work of Lucien Lévy-Bruhl on primitive mentalities. Manganaro traces connections between Lévy-Bruhl and Eliot's 'Sweeney' poems and 'The Hollow Men', before concluding with an examination of his later thought on 'culture'.

Jason Harding's essay on 'Eliot's Editorship of the *Criterion*' focuses upon critical controversies within the review pages. Eliot's stance towards John Middleton Murry serves as a barometer here, from fierce disagreements regarding the claims of Romanticism against classicism in the late 1920s to a 'softening' of stance (p. 397) identified by Harding in the 1930s.

Jewel Spears Brooker concentrates on Eliot's philosophical studies at Harvard, Paris, and Oxford from 1906 to 1916. She emphasizes Eliot's shift towards scepticism; the influence of anthropology and social studies upon his thinking; and his rejection of the dualism of Descartes in favour of Bradley and (unusually) of Aristotle's view of facts and objects. Aaron Jaffe begins his examination of Eliot as a big name and 'pre-sold property' by citing the description of a public reading by Eliot as 'socko' (p. 423). The main body of the essay considers a variety of responses to Eliot's death by other poets and critics. Where I.A. Richards notes 'we are all products of his work' (p. 431), Jaffe perceives traces of a Bloomian anxiety of influence amidst the 'worn coins' of obituary (p. 428).

The best essays, however, manage to give a new or interesting twist to material that is otherwise familiar. Sanford Schwarz offers an imaginative reading of 'Tradition and the Individual Talent' which understands Eliot's 'tradition' as an alternative to 'pedantic' historical criticism, reads his impersonal poetics as self-transformation instead of 'self-suppression' and places the whole essay in context with the epistemological scepticism of Eliot's graduate work on Bradley. He manages to couple this with able readings of Eliot's allusive practice within his poetry.

Vincent Sherry explores Eliot's 'imaginative apprehension of living in a late historical age ... of Decay as a condition of general existence' (p. 91), arguing that the First World War gave Eliot direct experience of 'the unreason of history' (p. 95). The Great War, claims Sherry, provided Eliot with 'a ground and warrant' for the Decadent sensibilities he had been cultivating in his immature verse under the influence of nineteenth-century French writing. Sherry is particularly sensitive to Eliot's rhyming practice and suggests that the 1916 Easter Rising (and the decline of the British empire in Ireland) may have inspired the figure of Sweeney.

Jeffrey M. Perl's essay on *Poems (1920)* starts with another compellingly clear reading of Eliot's work on Bradley. Having identified Eliot's characteristic philosophical perspective as ambivalence, Perl claims that Eliot used his quatrain poems to take on the contesting forces he perceived as vying for epistemological superiority. As a consequence, this phase of his poetic career is, unusually, not ambivalent, but 'disambivalent (rather than confident) and, thus, insecure' (p. 143). John Xiros Cooper provides a thoughtful and complex account of Eliot's social criticism. After exploring Eliot's debt to French thinkers from Joseph De Maistre to Charles Maurras and examining his interest in Coleridge and Arnold, Cooper summarizes astutely the later writings on Christian society and culture, emphasizing Eliot's 'interdisciplinary temper' and urging his appreciation of 'the complex unity of social and cultural life' (p. 288). Cooper's decision, however, to exclude *After Strange Gods* from his account as 'intemperate' (p. 289) and unrepresentative may be seen by some as controversial.

It is unlikely that anyone other than a reviewer would plough through a volume of such length. Although not always rewarding, there are definite highlights and it certainly provides a thorough picture of the field.

In theory Steve Ellis's *T.S. Eliot: A Guide for the Perplexed* offers a fresh approach to writing an introductory guide. Instead of a sequential account of Eliot's life and work, he reads the poetry through Eliot's prose, placing the early poems, for example, in relation to Eliot's critical speculations about the 'mind of Europe'. This approach means that Ellis reads *The Waste Land* against Eliot's notes and reviews critical opinion regarding their use as an interpretative source. The results can, however, be a little perplexing when poems and essays are read out of sequence and context. Nevertheless, Ellis strives to sustain his overall argument that there is an 'underlying consistency of outlook in Eliot's writing' (p. 4) and that Eliot's later Christian conservatism can be reconciled with an early commitment to classicism.

Observing recent biographical speculation about Eliot's sexuality and accusations of anti-Semitism, John Worthen offers *T.S. Eliot: A Short Biography* as an attempt to trace Eliot's 'intense inner existence' (p. 3) across his life and poetic output. Worthen gives short shrift to claims that Eliot was a frustrated homosexual, and deals with Eliot's attitude towards Jews by conceding that he made anti-Semitic remarks but denying that he was an 'anti-Semitic *writer*' (p. 77). Instead, his readings of Eliot's poetry (particularly the account of *Ash Wednesday*) dwell upon whether Eliot was having sex with Vivien. Worthen offers a bluff and fast-paced overview of Eliot's life, informed by recent scholarship.

Joseph Maddrey's *The Making of T.S. Eliot: A Study of Literary Influences* is an ambitious survey, covering Eliot's career from 1905 to 1930 (the publication of *Ash Wednesday*) and itemizing influences in short sub-sections. It is striking for the sheer number of authors Maddrey cites and, as such, functions as a snappy intellectual biography. But, necessarily, it is unable to devote a great deal of space to individual authors (even with sub-sections on each chapter of *The Waste Land*), so that what it offers in terms of scope sometimes means a loss in terms of depth.

The essays in G. Douglas Atkins's *Literary Paths to Religious Understanding: Essays on Dryden, Pope, Keats, George Eliot, Joyce, T.S. Eliot, and E.B. White* all start from Eliot's intimation of the Incarnation as 'The hint half guessed, the gift half understood' in *The Dry Salvages*. Atkins focuses upon the lay function performed by literature and poetry and upon the concept of understanding as a process. The essay on *Four Quartets* starts by examining Eliot's response to Pascal and his conception of the link between passion and reason in religious thought, then presents the encounter with the 'familiar compound ghost' in *Little Gidding* as a narrative of progressive religious understanding. Atkins concludes by emphasizing the redemptive power of writing and the connections between writing and reading.

Barry Spurr's *'Anglo-Catholic in Religion': T.S. Eliot and Christianity* derives from Eliot's famous description of himself in 1928 as 'classicist in literature, royalist in politics and anglo-catholic in religion'. Critics have failed, Spurr asserts, to understand the specific implications of the latter term, classifying it generally with Anglicanism. His study traces religious influences, from the Unitarian background of Eliot's family in Missouri, through his unhappy marriage and his public Christian commitments as a poet and social critic. Spurr is combative, scolding critics for failing to notice the specifically Anglo-Catholic nuances within Eliot's attitude towards confession, prayer, and the Blessed Virgin Mary. This intellectual biography is larded with historical contextual material relating to a revival of the popularity of Anglo-Catholicism in the 1920s.

In 'Sweeney Among the Marionettes' (*EIC* 59[2009] 116–41), Ann Stillman investigates Eliot's interest in marionettes from his earliest poetry under the influence of Arthur Symons's reading of Jules Laforgue to the presentation of mechanical human behaviour in 'Sweeney Among the Nightingales'. Stillman deftly places this in the context of a late nineteenth- and early twentieth-century vogue for puppetry from Alfred Jarry to Stravinsky's *Petrushka*—even J.M. Keynes was drawn to this figure. As something artificial in construction but human in appearance, the marionette, Stillman suggests, represents tensions between the experience of individuals and broader historical developments, but can also stand for the complex interrelation between levity and seriousness in Eliot's poetry.

Noting Eliot's appeal for the 'coming of a Satirist', in 'Eliot's Last Laugh: the Dissolution of Satire in *The Waste Land*' (*JML* 32:ii [2009] 65–79), Robert S. Lehman investigates the erasure of a satirical passage couched in couplets from an early draft of 'The Fire Sermon'. As his conception of 'tradition' bound the creative to the critical, Lehman argues, so Eliot saw satire as an 'immanent means of managing literary history' (p. 66). He concludes, however, that satire eluded Eliot's control, so that he turned to the 'mythical method' as a means of mediating literary past and present instead.

Having established the lack of material connections between 'The Lovesong of J. Alfred Prufrock' and Jean-Paul Sartre's *Nausea*, William Irwin compares the two in 'Prufrock's Question and Roquentin's Answer' (*P&L* 33:i[2009] 184–92), on the basis that Prufrock's 'overwhelming question' must 'essentially' be Roquentin's 'question to himself "Can you justify your existence then? Just a little?"' (p. 185). Irwin's synopses bring out shared concerns with the roles foisted upon modern man by society and the fundamental inauthenticities imposed upon Prufrock and Roquentin by modern life.

In addition to Christina Hauck's contribution to the *Companion*, discussed above, two further essays in 2009 proposed connections between *The Waste Land* and Buddhism: 'T.S. Eliot, Dharma Bum: Buddhist Lessons in *The Waste Land*' by Thomas Michael LeCarner (*P&L* 33:ii[2009] 402–16) and 'Theravada Buddhist Influence in *The Waste Land*' by Lheisa Dustin (*N&Q* 56[2009] 417–20). LeCarner outlines *samsāra* or the 'wheel of life', whereby the cycle of birth and death brings pain and suffering to the unenlightened and compares this with mythical cycles of futility in *The Waste Land*. Eliot aimed, LeCarner concludes, to direct his readers towards a Buddhist emptying out of the desires that protract such suffering. Dustin's essay adopts a more empirical approach, tracing links between 'The Fire Sermon' and Henry Clarke Warren's translation and commentary upon Buddhist scriptures. LeCarner's identification of Buddhist affinities within Eliot's work requires him to pass over the specifically biblical and Christian nuances of phrases such as 'son of man' and 'the peace which passeth understanding' (not to mention other, Hindu, sources), but Dustin argues that 'an asymmetry between Christian and Buddhist modes of salvation emerges as one of the poem's main concerns' (p. 417).

Reinaldo Silva's interests are largely biographical in 'T.S. Eliot and the Premio Camões: A Brief Honeymoon and Anointment of Portuguese Fascist Politics' (*YER* 26:ii[2009] 16–23). Silva attempts to connect Eliot's decision to sit on the jury for the Camões prize in April 1838 to affinities towards the right-wing Catholic politics of Antonia de Oliveira Salazar. Lacking other materials, the essay is more informative about Portuguese writers and politics than about Eliot's own views.

Modernism/Modernity published Susan Matthias's translation of Greek poet George Sefaris's 'Introduction to T.S. Eliot' (*Mo/Mo* 16:i[2009] 143–60). Writing in 1936, Sefaris saw Eliot as a poet responding to a 'world in dissolution, a sick and benumbed world' (p. 154); he acutely identifies the general influence of nineteenth-century French literature and the particular influence of Laforgue upon Eliot, and writes about the resonance of allusion in Eliot's poetry as a means of achieving community through shared mythic resources. As Matthias points out, it is clear from his account of Eliot's difficulty as a poet (although Sefaris denies that Eliot is obscure) and the way that he examines the tensions between the formal demands of personal and impersonal expression that much of the essay also meditates upon Sefaris's own development as a poet and negotiations with Eliot's influence.

Angelo Arciero's essay, ' "Politics has become too serious a matter to be left to the politicians": T.S. Eliot and George Orwell' (translated by Gianna Fusco, in Ricci, ed., *Morality and the Literary Imagination*, pp. 85–108), discovers surprising grounds for comparison between Eliot (self-declared 'monarchist') and Orwell: both writers perceived the 1930s as a time of social crisis and disdained the moral and political effects of industrialization—a convergence typified for Arciero in similarities between Eliot's Prufrock and George Bowling in Orwell's *Coming Up for Air*. Although Orwell disdained the right-wing editorial politics of the *Criterion*, the two writers shared a distrust of political dogmatism and, Arciero suggests, they 'tend to converge' (p. 99) in their understanding of the problematic relationship between individuals and power.

As ever, *Notes and Queries* provides continuing speculation about Eliot's sources and influences. In 'Another Possible Source for T.S. Eliot's "Handful of Dust" ' (*N&Q* 56[2009] 420), Andrew Souter suggests that *The Waste Land* contains more echoes of Nathanial Hawthorne's *The Marble Faun* than hitherto realized. In 'A Figure Behind T.S. Eliot: W.H. Schofield' (*N&Q* 56[2009] 420–4), John Morgenstern explores connections between Eliot and the Professor of Comparative Literature who taught him at Harvard. Morgenstern suggests that Schofield may have had a significant influence upon Eliot's theories of tradition and poetic impersonality, as well as shaping the presentation of J. Alfred Prufrock and Professor Channing Cheetah in his poems. Similarly, in 'Sully Prudhomme's "Juin" in T.S. Eliot's *The Waste Land*' (*N&Q* 56[2009] 416–17), James Womack traces 'concrete parallels' between a sonnet by Sully Prudhomme and 'The Burial of the Dead'. It is to be regretted that a copy of Nancy Hargrove's biographical and contextual study *T.S. Eliot's Parisian Year* was not made available for consultation.

Hardy studies are richer for Keith Wilson's *A Companion to Thomas Hardy* from the same series as the Eliot *Companion* discussed above. Wilson's introduction notes admiringly his contributors' capacity to 'range confidently' between Hardy's novels and poetry, as if to break down 'Hardy's bifurcated literary position' (p. 1): while this is true of some, many contributions still adhere to old divisions. Essays which do manage it include Ralph Pite's account of 'Hardy in the Rural' (pp. 133–45), which moves thoughtfully between *Tess*, Hardy's essays, and a close reading of 'Geographical Knowledge' from *Time's Laughingstocks*. Hardy's rural characters and communities are, Pite observes, typically troubled by division and disharmony, and 'the rural' cannot be insulated from the modern. Wilson's own essay on Hardy's relationship with London (pp. 146–61) draws mostly upon letters and the *Life* Hardy connived to write with his second wife, but concludes by quoting the rendition of London in his poetry. Hardy absorbed from London, Wilson argues, various 'strategies of observation' (p. 151), including a restless feeling for rootless movement through a cityscape, akin to Eliot's Prufrock.

Roger Ebbatson's account of Hardy and issues of class (pp. 162–77) moves fluently between the novels, an essay on 'The Dorsetshire Labourer', and key poems such as 'The Self-Unseeing' and 'The Little Old Table'. These are employed as illustrations of key stages in a broader argument about the fluctuation of Hardy's sensitivity to class issues and his conflicted tendency to find himself seduced away from his roots by the social mobility conferred by his status as a successful writer.

Michael Irwin shifts swiftly between Hardy's novels and poems in his account of 'romantic love' (pp. 194–209), which he identifies as 'Hardy's central theme' (p. 194). The essay itself is more discriminating than this sounds, examining the various impulses that draw characters together in the novels and considering the passage of time in Hardy's poems and the capacity of romantic attraction to weather the ageing of physical bodies.

Claire Seymour suggests that music was Hardy's 'consuming, even controlling passion' (p. 226), functioning as a trigger for memory and experience; as a transforming influence, Seymour compares its effects to Freud's theory of the Uncanny (pp. 223–38). William Greenslade's account of 'Hardy's Notebooks' (pp. 86–101) devotes some pages to a description of the 'Poetical Matter' notebook and its relationship to Hardy's very last years of poetic composition.

Other essays focus more exclusively upon different forms. Tim Armstrong's essay adopts an unusual and innovative approach by using mathematical theory to explore 'Sequence and Series in Hardy's Poetry' (pp. 378–94).

He cites Hardy's interest in Henri Bergson and Josiah Royce, among others, as an 'oblique' connection to broad questions about the experience and representation of order and sequence. A concluding section on birds and birdsong identifies them as 'an emblem of the seriality of life' (p. 392) for Hardy. It is a thought-provoking essay, rife with close attention to the concept of 'seriality' at the level of poem sequences and at the level of sound and rhyme patterns within individual poems.

William W. Morgan provides an informative overview of editions of the poetry, of Hardy's letters and notebooks, and biographies, along with short summaries of the available electronic resources and some of the critical work on Hardy from the last sixty years, although these are not extensive or exhaustive (pp. 395–412). Charles Lock begins by considering Hardy's reception by modernist contemporaries in the first half of the twentieth century and pointing out that those readers who favour Hardy's poetry tend to do so at the cost of the novels (pp. 450–64). For Lock, however, 'Hardy's poetics are those of a novelist' (p. 543). He draws heavily on the work of Dennis Taylor to argue that, in place of the shifting narrative perspectives in his novels, Hardy's poems use language, rhythm, and register to unsettle the voice. It is in such startling shifts of diction and word choice, he concludes, that Hardy is a true contemporary of Pound and Eliot.

There were two significant publications on the poetry of D.H. Lawrence in 2009. *D.H. Lawrence: Poet* [2008] brings together several essays by Keith Sagar into an invigoratingly opinionated overview of Lawrence's poetic career from the influence of Walt Whitman to the genesis of 'Snake'. Sagar is not afraid to criticize Lawrence's early poetry, describing his rhythmical choices in one instance as 'a dog's breakfast' (p. 31). He does not, however, stint in praise and admiration for Lawrence's achieved verse (particularly the poems written in the last decade of his life), hailing his decision to abandon rhyme in favour of free verse and commending Lawrence's capacity to generate 'analogues' for emotions and experiences from natural phenomena without reducing the strange, alien, and diverse forms of nature to mere tokens or symbols of feeling. His admiration for Lawrence's capacity to give voice to 'the living poem' (p. 11) is so warm that Sagar sounds like his subject at times. The volume concludes with a useful checklist of critical work on Lawrence's poetry.

In *The Poet as Botanist* [2008], M.M. Mahood identifies 'the floweriness of Lawrence's fictional worlds' and argues that his 'lifelong interest in plants' (p. 183) was central to all of his writings. These observations belong to a larger study of 'the ways in which poets see plants' (p. 1) and although Mahood emphasizes 'the richness and intricacy and life-giving importance of the plant-world' she is cautious about 'ecology' and distances herself from 'ecopoetics' (p. 6). The chapter on Lawrence (pp. 183–225) traces his enthusiasm for plants from his adolescence and formal training in botany at Nottingham's University College through to encounters with foreign forms of plant life in New Mexico and Australia. Fascinated by cell life under the microscope, Mahood reveals the figurative and symbolic power of plant life for Lawrence as a means to express his understanding of women, the possibility of renewal, and abiding natural forces. Her account of his poetic career maps Lawrence's understanding of the Persephone myth and concludes with a reading of his final poems, in which a 'painterly delight' (p. 224) in flowers becomes connected to his appreciation of 'the living dark which is the source of all life' (p. 225).

In the absence of a copy of Victoria Arana's *W.H. Auden's Poetry: Mythos, Theory and Practice*, criticism of Auden is limited in 2009 to several articles. In 'For the Love of Nothing: Auden, Keats and Deconstruction' (*P&L* 33:ii[2009] 345–57), Jo-Anne Cappeluti compares Auden's 'Caliban to the Audience' with Keats's *Endymion*. Both poets, she claims, 'write in the Romantic mode' and 'dramatize the self-thwarting attempts of the intellect to dissect and dismiss what it claims is nothing' (p. 346). She reads both poems as meditations upon a self-reflexive criticism which exposes a significant 'Nothing' within the power of language.

John Farrell offers a closely attentive reading of 'Spain, 1937' in 'Auden's Call to Arms: "Spain" and Psychoanalysis' (*CQ* 38[2009] 225–42). Scrutinizing Auden's engagement with the tensions between poetry and politics step by step, Farrell concludes that the poem is a kind of brilliant failure in which Auden uses psychoanalytic thinking to confront ambiguities in his own sense of political commitment. In 'Auden's Sacred World' (*EIC* 59[2009] 234–54), Jonathan Hufstader outlines the imaginative appeal to Auden of abandoned lead mines on the Yorkshire moors as the source of a 'private secondary sacred world' (p. 234). His reading of *New Year Letter* identifies this landscape as figure for humanity's potential, one which integrates 'the savage and the cultivated' (p. 239), whereas Hufstader's reading of 'In Praise of Limestone' draws out contradictions and a sense of perplexed self-scrutiny. The essay shows thoughtfully how, in his imagination, this landscape helped Auden to figure his attempts to reconcile his Christian faith and his hedonistic impulses; and balance his conception of a 'faultless' Christian love with his experience of suffering in love and life.

Edward Quipp's essay 'Versions of an "Intimate Relation": Difficulty and Lightness in the Thirties Auden' (*OL* 64:iv[2009] 300–23) is ambitious in its scope and aims. Quipp identifies a severance between the internal grammar and syntax of Auden's poetry from the 1930s and the fluidity of these poems when read aloud. He assesses 'the readerly experience' (p. 302) of Auden's poems, paying particular attention to his 'light' verse and using the relationship between poetry upon the page and poetry spoken aloud to explore Auden's political commitments.

'Literature', asserts David Garrett Izzo in *The Influence of Mysticism on 20th Century British and American Literature*, 'is the means to an end and that end *is* mysticism' (p. 5). Relevant to this section are chapter 2, 'Aldous Huxley and W.H. Auden: Mysticism as a Literary Theory' (pp. 23–61), and a subsection on T.S. Eliot within a general chapter about mystical theory and twentieth-century British literature (pp. 104–6). Izzo reads Auden through a mystic understanding derived in part from Huxley, and links him to four key tenets: conveying the thoughts of the 'wise man' in ordinary speech, bringing fresh insight, telling the truth, and intimating an experience of 'awe' (p. 32). Similarly, the pages on Eliot cite his studies as a graduate student, then point out Eliot's use of Brahmanic texts in *The Waste Land*. They are part of a broader argument connecting Eliot to other writers on the grounds that 'chance is the residue of design' (p. 107).

Reading the poems and radio broadcasts of John Betjeman against the fiction and non-fiction of George Orwell, Peter Lowe discovers surprising similarities between these two writers from seemingly opposite political poles in 'Englishness in a Time of Crisis: George Orwell, John Betjeman and the Second World War' (*CQ* 38[2009] 243–63). For different reasons, Lowe suggests, both writers disdained the stifling effect of suburban life and architecture prior to the Second World War, but adopted defensive postures towards suburbia once its physical structures came under threat from bombardment. Fretting over the cultural legacy of war, Betjeman and Orwell expressed similar fears at losing hold of an abiding Englishness.

David Williams's *Media, Memory and the First World War* constitutes a significant and new approach to the literature of the First World War, and two chapters are relevant to this section: 'Cinematic Memory in Owen, Remarque, and Harrison' (pp. 103–37) and '"Spectral Images": The Double Vision of Siegfried Sassoon' (pp. 138–57). Williams's overall thesis emphasizes the value of memory as a medium which conditions and channels retrospective understanding of events. Literature of and about the First World War, he argues, is suffused with the 'strangely invasive power of cinema' (p. 109), which determines the manner in which it is recalled. 'In Owen's poetry', he writes, 'much as in Sassoon's fiction, the speakers tend to be haunted by "spectral images" from the past that invade the present with cinematic immediacy' (p. 8). The chapter on Owen begins by recounting the general effects of cinema upon perceptions of events. Its presentation of events as moving images constituted a particular form of encounter with their *actualité*. Williams then describes Owen's ambivalent attitude towards cinematography, expressed in his letters, but a reading of the poetry culminates in an account of 'Dulce et Decorum Est' as 'cinematic' in its presentation of soldiers suffering the effects of gas. The chapter on Sassoon is predominantly concerned with 'the cinematic epistemology' of his fiction, such as *The Memoirs of George Sherston*. But Williams gives prominence to *Picture-Show* [1919]—a privately printed collection of poems which uses the cinematic screen as a metaphor to express distance between suffering of soldiers and onlookers and a sense for the hopelessness of their situation. The concept of cinema allowed Sassoon, Williams argues, a form of imaginative doubling or distance from the sufferings he sought to depict and his own experience of trauma in the war. Whatever its local discoveries, *Media, Memory and the First World War* should clearly be seen in the broader context of other recent work on the influence of early cinema upon twentieth-century literature, such as Laura Marcus's *The Tenth Muse* [2007] and David Trotter's *Cinema and Modernism* [2007]. It is an important contribution to the critical literature of both cinema and the First World War.

Joanna Scutts offers a wide-ranging examination of the public commemoration of the war dead in 'Battlefield Cemeteries, Pilgrimage, and Literature after the First World War: The Burial of the Dead' (*ELT* 52:iv[2009] 387–416). Starting with Rupert Brooke's 'The Soldier' and the involvement of Rudyard Kipling with the War Graves Commission and the design of war cemeteries, the essay broadens to examine literary responses to the post-war culture of pilgrimage to these sites. Scutts also manages to trace further connections to work by T.S. Eliot and Katherine Mansfield, examining their attempts to commune with the dead.

Kaley Joyes's essay 'Regenerating Wilfred Owen: Pat Barker's Revisions' (*Mosaic* 42:iii[2009] 169–83), strictly concerns the *Regenerations* trilogy of novels by Pat Barker. Joyes, however, explores the ways in which Barker reworks key poems by Owen into a 'subtle intertexuality' (p. 171). Scholars of his poetry might therefore be interested to read Joyes's account of how the minutiae of Owen's revisions to his own poems in manuscript are translated into the novels' dramatic texture.

This year also saw publication of a new selection of Wilfred Owen's letters and poems, edited by Helen Cross. Clearly and simply presented and prefaced by an essay putting 'Wilfred Owen in Context', this is solidly aimed at a high school audience, with activities and discussion points at the end of the book for both students and teachers.

In 'Gurney and Fritz' (*EIC* 59[2009] 142–56), Tim Kendall explores the sudden emergence of references to the opposing side ('Fritz') in a sequence of poems by Ivor Gurney written in 1925 that revisit his experiences during the First World War. Kendall emphasizes Gurney's oxymoronic formulations and 'tonal performances' (p. 149) in order to bring out the humour and moral complexities of Gurney's response to his wartime experiences.

William Empson received limited attention in 2009. David Reid's essay 'William Empson: Two New Tropes?' (*UTQ* 78:iii[2009] 851–80) vaunts the discovery of two new figures of speech ('Mutual Comparison' and 'Mutual Metaphor') in *The Structure of Complex Words*, ably unpicking Empson's thinking and his appreciation of attempts to express the ineffable. Empson's critical thought also naturally recurs as a point of reference in David James and Philip Tew's collection, *New Versions of Pastoral*, but receives particular attention in Nick Hubble's contribution, 'Intermodern Pastoral: William Empson and George Orwell' (pp. 123–35). Starting from the apparent dismissal of 'Proletarian Literature' in *Some Versions of Pastoral*, Hubble compares Empson's views on the possibility of literature for and about the proletariat with those of George Orwell. He calls for Orwell and Empson and their writings from the 1930s to be seen in the light of the recent critical concept 'intermodernism' (p. 130). Hubble proposes their merits in contrast with T.S. Eliot and Virginia Woolf as 'radical eccentrics' (p. 130).

Raymond-Jean Frontain, 'Kipling's "Follow Me 'Ome" and 2 Samuel 1' (*ANQ* 22:ii[2009] 37–48) explores the bonds between soldiers within 'the homosociality of the military world' (p. 39) as it is represented in Kipling's poetry. Frontain thoughtfully ponders various readings for the voices in the poem 'Follow Me' Ome' and considers an allusion to the relationship between the Old Testament's King David and Jonathan in relation to the broader resonance of this ambiguously erotic male friendship within late Victorian culture.

This year produced a number of interesting contributions relative to familiar writers who tend to suffer critical neglect. Angela Leighton places two poems by Walter de la Mare ('The Listeners' and 'Some One') at the centre of her

F.W. Bateson Memorial Lecture, 'Poetry and the Imagining Ear' (*EIC* 59[2009] 99–115). She situates them alongside poems by Robert Frost and prose by Edward Thomas and James Joyce, as part of her argument that 'the literariness of the text' lies in its 'capacity to make us listen, not necessarily *to* anything, just to listen' (p. 107). This is deft and poised writing, attuned to the aural summonings of syntax, rhythm, and acoustic effect. In 'Charlotte Mew's Aftereffects' (*Mo/Mo* 16:ii[2009] 255–80), Joseph Bristow attempts to explain Mew's poor literary reception and the slow appreciation of her work until recent years. He describes her literary career, from the publication of her story 'Passed' in the *Yellow Book* of July 1894 to the appearance of a volume of her poems, *The Farmer's Bride*, in 1915 and her suicide in 1928. Considering biographical criticism of her work and the failure of her contemporaries to decide whether she was a throwback to the *fin de siècle* or an intimation of the modern, Bristow judges that the world was not ready for her abstracted, deathly monologists, the 'disconnectedness' of her narratives (p. 263), and her aesthetics of misgiving. Modern audiences may be better prepared, he muses, to appreciate the hint of trauma that persists in relation to her work.

Bruce King's *Robert Graves: A Biography* [2008] is a vigorous and necessarily lively account of Graves's unorthodox life, loves, and writing. King outlines Graves's poetic career against his shambolic personal life, from his origins as a soldier poet in the First World War to his eventual transformation into the hierophantic poet, pursuing incarnations of his Muse in a succession of different women. This isn't a particularly scholarly life of Graves, but it is refreshingly brusque in parts and prepared to confront how unpleasant (and misguided) he could be.

Dylan Thomas occasionally inspires obsessive devotees: David Thomas's *Fatal Neglect: Who Killed Dylan Thomas?* [2008] scrutinizes his final days in meticulous detail (it includes the poet's post-mortem) in an attempt to discover whether there were sinister circumstances behind an initial failure to ascribe Thomas's death to prolonged pneumonia. It doesn't contain much to detain anyone interested in the poetry for long, but it tries very hard to make a gripping murder story. Thomas is also the subject of a chapter in Harri Garrod Roberts's Kristevan study of Welsh verse, *Embodying Identity: Representations of the Body in Welsh Literature*, which attempts to rescue his early poetry from accusations of immaturity (pp. 90–113). Roberts argues that the acoustic properties of his verse enact a 'childlike relationship to language' (p. 92) that also constitutes an active resistance to social pressures to conform.

The essays and reviews in William Pritchard's *On Poets and Poetry* span over twenty years. Of particular interest to this section are his essays on Hardy's poetry of old age (pp. 95–115), on A.E. Housman's letters (pp. 116–25), and on Eliot's 'mischievous prose' (pp. 273–91). The essay on Hardy explores relations between voice and perspective in the very late poems, considering their moral and ethical implications. An 'undercurrent of sensual cruelty' (p. 100) is juxtaposed with Hardy's quiet but isolated sense of achievement and retrospect. The essay on Housman weighs up the virtues of Archie Burnett's edition of Housman's correspondence in order to explore Housman's virtues as a letter-writer, and the essay on Eliot identifies unexpected turns of wit and sly humour in his critical prose. As might be expected in a volume that alludes to Eliot in its title and is dedicated to Christopher Ricks, Pritchard offers close readings largely innocent of theoretical concerns, and dedicated to quotation, nuance, and the occasional larger critical judgement.

6. Irish Poetry

The year 2009 was a great one for the distinguished over-sixties in Irish contemporary poetry. Ciaran Carson entered his sixth decade while Michael Longley and Seamus Heaney celebrated their seventieth birthdays, with the 'Heaney at 70' weekend in the Irish media (the voice of Heaney reciting his poems over the airwaves could be heard all weekend long on national radio) replacing what was formerly known as the Easter weekend. As a further mark of respect to Famous Seamus, Cambridge University Press dedicated one of its coveted *Companions* to his work, with the *Cambridge Companion to Seamus Heaney*, edited by Bernard O'Donaghue, becoming another of the very few titles in this series on the work of a living writer. The *Companion* kicks off with Rand Brandes's reflection on Heaney's working titles; working titles in literary history more broadly have proven to be a subject of some interest as scholars brood on how, for example, *The Great Gatsby* might have been a very different book had it been published as *Trimalchio* or *The High-Bouncing Lover*. The degree to which editorial intervention and marketing strategies have shaped Irish poetry is an overlooked subject in critical narratives, and Brandes's essay misses its chance to investigate it. Moreover, Brandes also overlooks the extent to which Heaney's relationship with other poets must also have influenced his choice of titles. Thus, although Brandes briefly notes that Heaney's 'Rite of Spring' was initially entitled 'Persephone', he does not think to link this to Michael Longley's 'Persephone' even though both poems must have been written around the same time in the 1960s under Philip Hobsbaum's auspices. Almost entirely disowned by Heaney later as 'a crude piece of work', the poem might well speak of Heaney's struggle to forge his own poetics away from Longley's influence. Instead of considering these potentially productive lines of influence and exchange, Brandes simply attributes the change of title to Heaney modestly 'diminishing the mythic magnitude of the poem'. Too often throughout the essay Brandes deems the discarded titles as 'too literary' or 'too self-conscious', thus beatifying Heaney as a benign, humble, and thoroughly unselfconscious poet; all of which ties in with a tendency throughout the *Companion* as a whole to downplay Heaney's own ingenuity. Indeed, in an oft-related anecdote, Heaney has revealed how his dropping of the title 'Alder' from *District and Circle* was in fact occasioned by a wisecrack made by Paul Muldoon about Heaney as the 'Alder Statesman'. Here again it is the conversations between Heaney and other poets and not some worthy self-deprecating impulse that in fact shapes the work.

Edited as it is by Bernard O'Donaghue, who is both a Heaney scholar and a poet heavily influenced by Heaney, there is a real sense throughout that it might have been better entitled *The Cambridge Celebration of Seamus Heaney* as the weight of Heaney's compelling influence on his own critics is strongly felt. The image of Heaney sending faxes to Rand Brandes in the opening essay imprints itself on much of what follows as Heaney's own statements on his poetry, poetics, and politics are given voice and rarely questioned or unpicked. Dennis O'Driscoll, though very much in the role of chief celebrant, does offer a very fine, assiduously researched essay on Heaney as a public figure, and one which raises essential questions regarding Heaney's reflex reactions to criticism of his work. This brand of investigative analysis ranges throughout the collection, even if answers are rarely pursued, and it is hoped that these lines of enquiry will be picked up by future scholars. After much lingering over Heaney's reception and his title as 'Ireland's unofficial poet laureate', Fran Brearton's critically engaged essay on representations of the feminine in Heaney comes as a breath of fresh air. Developing previous work by Patricia Coughlan, Brearton reads Heaney in terms of gender theory and, more intriguingly still, in terms of the image of the female in nationalist and Catholic discourses. A later essay by Guinn Batten which also takes on the subject of the feminine and displacement in Heaney's work is not as convincing in its argument and ends inconclusively. Justin Quinn provides a much-needed examination of the nature of Heaney's engagement with east European poets, many of whom, as Quinn outlines, Heaney looks to as models of the poet under political pressure at particular moments in his career. Quinn sets out by rightly observing how Heaney is 'hermetically sealed from the original texts of the Slavic poetry' which he so often invokes, but the implications of this are left unexplored, even as David Wheatley in a later essay observes how Heaney's use of these poets is 'misjudged'. Many of the other essays look at various influences on Heaney's work; Neil Corcoran writes on Yeats in Heaney with characteristic acuity and scholarly flair. Heather O'Donoghue presents a fascinating consideration of Heaney's use of Old Norse myth (with the focus mainly on *Njál's Saga*) to illuminate Heaney's handling of the integral themes of tribal violence and the continuity of the past. Even if the basic material will be familiar to those who have read Conor McCarthy's *Seamus Heaney and Medieval Poetry* [2008], her reading of *North* and 'Funeral Rites' in the light of her own expertise as a scholar of Old Norse myth is expertly done and with clean attention to detail. Interestingly, for those unacquainted with developments in the field, she reveals how recent scholarship on bog bodies is sceptical of the theory of death by ritual killing. O'Donoghue's specialist knowledge makes for a convincing and exhilarating argument as she proves how Heaney's adroit use of this literature may be regarded as 'intertextuality of the highest order'. The collection is rounded off with a lengthy, suggestive essay by John Wilson Foster which deals mainly with Heaney's work from *Seeing Things* onwards and thus gestures to the future, appropriately for a poet whose work is still in progress. Overall, this is a valuable companion to Heaney, for undergraduate students primarily, and one which lays out ample ground for further investigations into a body of work that seems bottomless in its interpretative possibilities.

David Wheatley's assured essay, 'Professing Poetry: Heaney as Critic', in *The Cambridge Companion* begins by considering that slippery, hyphenated term 'poet-critic' and variants thereof. As Wheatley's essay bears out, Heaney falls into the category of 'critic-poet' (other examples being T.S. Eliot and

Dr Johnson, 'whose prose dwarfs their poetry in volume and surrounds it like a protective cocoon'). Although Wheatley's offering is vital—particularly in the way that he covers so much critical ground in such a short space—the reader comes away feeling somewhat disappointed by his unwillingness to attribute Heaney's critical manoeuvres to anything other than 'magnanimity'. 'Heaney is simply not an authoritarian critic, and not concerned to police the canon or impose himself on his material', Wheatley avows by way of a rejoinder to Peter McDonald (incidentally, the absence of this authoritative Heaney scholar from the *Companion* is grievous). The case is surely more complicated than Wheatley cares to admit here; one thinks of how critic-poet Eliot was dubbed 'the literary dictator' by Delmore Schwartz.

One turns then to Michael Cavanagh's monograph *Professing Poetry: Seamus Heaney's Poetics* expecting to find a more penetrating approach to the subject of Heaney as critic. Sadly, such hope soon evaporates. Cavanagh's suitability is called into question on the opening page when he attributes Heaney's trademark critical term 'exemplary' to the Heaney scholar Neil Corcoran. Corcoran himself, unlike Cavanagh, has shrewdly picked up on the ethical as well as aesthetic implications of the term, and Cavanagh's unfortunate slip also points attention to just how indebted so many of the essays in the *Cambridge Companion* are to Corcoran's scholarship (his 1998 study *Seamus Heaney: A Critical Study* remains indispensable). Here again, as with Wheatley, it is to Corcoran's seminal work on Heaney's literary criticism that Cavanagh turns. Further problems arise in the introductory pages as Cavanagh relates how his own study of Heaney was 'written in emulation of Heaney's own prose', thus setting his own critical study up as an act of hero-worship. Added to this, Cavanagh, in his acknowledgements, unctuously thanks the poet for his 'encouraging words about the two chapters I sent him' as he unabashedly advertises Heaney's endorsement of his scholarship. From this it would appear that there will be little prospect of anything less than respectful in Cavanagh's probings of Heaney's critical oeuvre. So much for a 'critical' examination of the critical prose then, one might think, and this is largely the case. Far from being Philip Larkin's 'Gombeen man', Heaney is a poet and critic of sharp intelligence and artfulness—to overlook this fact and concentrate only on the charm and sanguinity of his persona is to deny him the true force of his critical savvy—and his prose deserves a much more rigorous reading than the awe-filled Cavanagh can provide. One review of *The Government of the Tongue* which Cavanagh has not read is by the scholar-poet Eiléan Ní Chuilleanáin, in which she rightly points out some of the 'tenuous connections' that Heaney as a critic makes between writers (as he fits them to his own needs, one might add). Cavanagh refuses to allow critical voices that do not toe the Heaney line into his study and it is all the more impoverished for that. There is not room here to go through every chapter in Cavanagh's prolix study, but by far the oddest chapter concerns Robert Lowell's influence on Heaney. Of all of the literary influences on Heaney discussed here—Cavanagh, after two chapters that provide general summaries of Heaney's critical engagements, considers his relationship with Lowell, Dante, (fleetingly) Wordsworth, and then finishes with Larkin and Yeats—that of Lowell has perhaps received the least amount of critical interest. Bizarrely, in order to argue for Heaney's *Field Work* as a 'repudiation' of Lowell's *Life Studies* Cavanagh has to persuade the reader of Lowell's 'hostility to the past', of his 'confessionalism and obsession with family and friends', his 'swagger and selfishness' in *Life Studies*; Lowell, in short, as a poet who 'fights against his dreadful past' is a 'self-serving, false poetic father' to Heaney. The problem here is that Cavanagh does not understand Lowell's poetics and, as a result, delivers the most extraordinarily inaccurate comments on *Life Studies*, such as those above. Had Cavanagh read Heaney's 1981 comments on *Life Studies* he would have learnt that it has the poet taking 'intense elements of his own experience and rendering them symptomatic' (exemplified most powerfully in Lowell's 'Skunk Hour'). For Heaney, *Life Studies* is a 'public book. It profiles its figures against public reality', and not a self-indulgent work of confessionalism (a highly contentious critical term) as Cavanagh has it. Cavanagh's limited understanding reaches its nadir in his reading of 'Skunk Hour', by now a canonical poem, which he (predictably) pitches against Heaney's 'The Skunk'. As the high point of *Life Studies*, 'Skunk Hour' has to be downgraded in order for Cavanagh's argument to hold, and so is dismissed as a mere satire of New England's hypocrisies. Instead, Cavanagh looks to 'For the Union Dead' as the truly exemplary poem for its '"drifting", loosely organized structure'. Here, Cavanagh loses the plot entirely as his praise of 'For the Union Dead' as a poem in which Lowell 'raises a personal drama to a cultural one' is more accurately a description of 'Skunk Hour'. Moreover, as any undergraduate reader of mid-twentieth-century American poetry will know, 'Skunk Hour', Lowell's breakthrough poem into a 'new style', is dedicated to Elizabeth Bishop precisely because of its use of the 'drifting description' that he learned from her. Unsophisticated, poorly informed readings such as these speak of confusion and a slipshod approach that cannot inspire confidence. This is not to say that Cavanagh does not make some salient points, but had he properly done his research and assembled all of the basic material for his purposes he would have encountered Heaney's other writings on Lowell in both prose (Heaney's valuable essay for *Critical Inquiry*) and poems such as 'Pit Stop Near Castletown'.

Another of the book's failings concerns its conspicuous lack of engagement with Heaney's *District and Circle* [2006], a collection that must be key to Heaney's developing poetics of return, that obviously signals Heaney as a profoundly Wordsworthian and Dantean poet, that contains elegies to Miłosz and others, and that is key, too, in exploring Heaney's complex connection to the United States and its poetry and politics. Moreover, other works of Heaney scholarship such as Conor McCarthy's brilliant recent study (mentioned above) are never consulted. Indeed, much of the scholarship that is referred to is quite dated. The chapter on Larkin and Heaney repeats much of what has already been said about this relationship (by Larkin scholars such as James Booth for instance), but Cavanagh might have deepened his consideration by reflecting on the fact that Larkin did not simply renounce Yeats and his 'Celtic fever' for Thomas Hardy. As Andrew Motion and others have shown, Larkin merges both of these predecessors in his later work. The final chapter on Yeats and Heaney provides relatively nothing new on this relationship either, and readers would do better to consult Corcoran's scholarship on the topic. Cavanagh's study is ambitious in its scope, and its efforts must be applauded. In many ways, though, it falls short of its aims and ultimately becomes merely a study of influence (although Cavanagh crucially never defines what he means by 'influence') which quotes often from Heaney's prose writings and interviews in order to plot his changing relationship to his most pervasive poetic predecessors. Remarkably, neither of Heaney's most prominent contemporaries and fellow high-ranking members of the 'Ulster Renaissance', Michael Longley and Derek Mahon, is mentioned even once. It is strange too that, given Cavanagh's focus on Heaney's problems with Larkin's 'Aubade', he never looks at Heaney's similarly conflicted view of Sylvia Plath and Heaney's oft-quoted, high-minded castigation of her 'Daddy' as a poem that 'rampages so permissively in the history of other people's sorrows'. An investigation into this would have yielded much-needed insights into the heavily moralistic tone of some of Heaney's assessments as well as showing how this criticism of Plath might well be read as a veiled self-criticism which echoes the similar accusations levelled at his own procedures in *North*.

Michael Longley's seventieth birthday revels were decidedly more low-key than Heaney's, but the poet was the subject of a very handsomely produced Festschrift edited by Robin Robertson (Longley's publisher at Cape) and which included a variety of tributes from his contemporaries—poets, publishers, critics—in Ireland, the UK, and beyond; these include Fleur Adcock, Andrew Motion, Sharon Olds, Donald Hall, Douglas Dunn, Ciaran Carson, Paul Muldoon, and Derek Mahon. Comprised of poems and essays, *Love Poet, Carpenter* stands as a true mark of the deep respect in which Longley is held by his peers, and in this way it testifies to his centrality as one of the pre-eminent Irish poets of his generation. Although for a time not as critically acclaimed as his contemporaries Mahon and the inescapable Heaney, Longley's poetry has by now been well served by critics. Fran Brearton's accessible companion to the poetry (*Reading Michael Longley* [2006]) went a long way towards extending his readership and confirming his achievement, and her contribution here is a sensitive reading of Longley's 'The Pattern' which cements Longley's importance as a major love poet. In other contributions, the American Donald Hall pays tribute to 'The Ice-cream Man' as a significant poem of the Troubles while Patricia Craig resituates Longley in Belfast as not only a poet of the city (as well as, more obviously, of the west of Ireland), but also a key player in its cultural life.

Not only has Longley had a defining role as a poet and educator over the past few decades, but, as *Love Poet, Carpenter* confirms, his enabling presence as Writer in Residence at Trinity College Dublin in the 1990s was key in bringing together what would become the next generation of Irish poets (and critics), many of whom were involved with the renowned journal of international poetry *Metre*, co-founded by David Wheatley and Justin Quinn. In an evocative and deeply appreciative portrait of Longley's writing workshops during this time, O'Reilly credits him with having 'opened windows of possibility' for her as she began to write. As Heather Clark's 2006 study proved, Longley's long relationship with Trinity College Dublin complicates neat ideas of a Belfast-centred, Northern Ireland renaissance—it was in

Dublin that he became a poet as an undergraduate and part of a unique community of poets, only to return some decades later as an inspiring, Buddha-like mentor to a rising generation of poets—and this side of Longley is captured in Quinn's 'Front Square' and in Brendan Kennelly's 'I Hear Young Longley Laughing' as 'the Homer of Botany Bay' and 'a special Homer of modern Irish poetry'. Throughout, it is the poetic conversations that are of most value. Heaney's poem to Longley unites both poets through their shared aesthetics of shedding 'Homeric light'. Though necessarily approaching through their own 'different gates', both are in their poetry 'more pastoral/ lyrical than epical' as Heaney frames his own achievement with Longley's in mythic terms. Interestingly, a stray remark in Kevin Crossley-Holland's contribution asserts that it was Heaney who convinced Crossley-Holland, then poetry editor at Macmillan, to publish Longley's first collection of poetry but this is surely an instance of misremembering as it contradicts previous accounts that credit Philip Hobsbaum with this crucial intervention. Ciaran Carson singles out Longley's 'Galapagos' for its importance to his own writing, reading it as both a 'jazz riff' and 'two parts of a traditional Irish reel'. In so doing he both signals Longley as an influence while also redirecting attention to the jazzy side of a poetics that is too often thought of as 'tight-arsed'. The dominant themes and techniques of Longley's poetry are affirmed and reiterated throughout, as the continuing contribution of this poet, scholar, and teacher to artistic and cultural life in Ireland and beyond is validated. This is a timely and engaging work of record and one which will be of use for further readings in Longley's copious oeuvre.

Ciaran Carson's work to date was also the subject of a collection of critical essays, the majority of which started life as conference papers at a 2002 symposium. The essays are prefaced with a 'conversation' between Carson and the editor Elmer Kennedy-Andrews that sets up the obvious thematic and technical aspects of Carson's work while also making the reader aware of Carson's living presence. Interestingly, one of the 'formative influences' that Carson lists is Alan Gillis, who also contributes one of the book's keenest essays. Kicking the essays off, Peter Denman's scrupulous syllable-counting makes for an erudite study of Carson's prosody, if a somewhat dry analysis of how sound and structure combined create sense. The long digression into examples of long lines in modern poetry seems somewhat unnecessary for the educated reader but overall Denman's attention to technical detail is exemplary. In the essay that follows, David Wheatley provides a defter illumination of Carson's line manoeuvres by presenting, for the purposes of explication, an example of what the poem 'Breath' would have looked like had Carson cast it in alexandrines. This is indeed instructive as Wheatley performs a nimble exegesis of Carson's *Breaking News*.

After two essays that are models in their attentiveness to Carson's formal dynamics at the level of the line, it comes as a surprise to learn, in John Goodby's contribution, that 'generally, in Carson's poems, the line-break is arbitrary'. Goodby, in an essay on 'Walking in the City', never quite makes the connection between walking and form, almost totally ignoring the ambulatory procedures of the poems, and prefers to offer a few points for discussion rather than a sustained exploration. This is surely one of the dangers that attend the project of turning a short, suggestive conference paper into a synthesized essay. Likewise, Eamonn Hughes's essay fails to attend to the poetry in a close way and remains at a general level. A most glaring inaccuracy sullies Hughes's reading of Carson's famous poem 'Belfast Confetti', where he incorrectly inserts line-breaks—thus completely ruining the effect of the long line—only to then omit the all-important line-break in the sentence 'What is / My name?'. All of which makes one all the more grateful for Denman and Wheatley's meticulous readings. Stan Smith's lucid essay on the space of hyphenation that Carson inhabits as a poet shows how valuable such contributions can be when they aim to meaningfully interpret the poetry rather than impose theoretical frameworks on it. Yet in saying this, it must be acknowledged that one of the best essays in the book—Michael McAteer's on Carson and commodification—puts a variety of critical theories to very good use, as it does so in a bid to educate rather than impose a monothematic reading and shows no signs of theory anxiety.

The longest essay in the book—by Kennedy-Andrews—rehearses a good deal of what has gone before and at greater length. It is most interesting in its final pages where what should perhaps have been a full-length essay on Heaney and Carson is mooted only briefly. Had this been extended it would have added more dimensions to a collection which features a good deal of repetition in terms of both the poems and themes covered. As mentioned, Gillis rounds off the book by reading Carson as a poet of essences and, by so doing, reveals his own deep-rooted affinities with his precursor and Belfast cohort. As the lost opportunity in Kennedy-Andrews's own essay highlights, some important aspects of Carson's work are overlooked; in place of a rather dutiful and uninspiring essay that looks at Carson's obvious use of tradition—the influence of Keats, Borges, and others—space should have been given over to Carson's complex dialogues with his poetic contemporaries, both in Ireland and elsewhere (John Ashbery's influence is perhaps most apparent). Also, although Carson has repeatedly signalled Italo Calvino's influence, none of the essays refers to Calvino, and his powerful presence warrants serious scrutiny. Indeed, how exactly the collection of essays asserts (as the blurb advertises) Carson's 'major role in the internationalization of contemporary Irish poetry' is never clear. However, these quibbles merely confirm the need for further scholarship on the work of this most challenging postmodern poet. There are a number of infelicities throughout—stylistic inconsistencies, unfinished sentences, incorrect spellings, incorrect references given—but most glaring of all is the attribution of Marvell's 'Horatian Ode Upon Cromwell's Return from Ireland' to John Milton (in Frank Sewell's otherwise competent essay on Irish and the oral tradition in Carson). The editor should have spotted this, and the general carelessness may be in part due to the fact that so many of these essays started life as papers for oral delivery (indeed, Sewell gives himself away in his opening paragraph with his reference to 'this paper', and a number of essays end in tell-tale fashion by presenting long quotations that were no doubt left undigested because of the twenty-minute time limit). Nonetheless, egregious elements aside, this is a welcome addition to Carson studies which does very well in its privileging of expert close readings.

Kennedy-Andrews' own study of home, place and identity in Northern Irish poetry failed to make it to this reviewer when it was published last year but it deserves mention here as a comprehensive work of poetry scholarship and a detailed survey of issues that go to the heart of the poetry and poetics of Northern Ireland. In 'Writing Home: Poetry and Place in Northern Ireland 1968–2008', Kennedy-Andrews charts the representation of place and 'home' and the key concepts of rootedness and exile in the work of an extensive range of poets. In his introduction the author begins by defining the concepts of 'space' and 'place' and asserting the importance of 'place' to Irish poets historically; Yeats' 'Prayer for My Daughter' is presented first off as a 'celebration of rootedness'. The author notes how in Northern Ireland place is a contested site of division and opposition and it is this fact that justifies his selective criteria. Thus, the study begins with a chapter on Patrick Kavanagh (not obviously Northern Irish but a poet of Ulster as Kennedy-Andrews explains), John Hewitt and MacNeice as precursors and then devotes chapters to John Montague (as 'global regionalist'), Heaney and Muldoon, Padraic Fiacc and James Simmons, Longley, Mahon, Tom Paulin, Carson, Medbh McGuckian and finishes up with a short discussion of the evolving work of the younger postnational poets Peter McDonald, Sinéad Morrissey, Alan Gillis and Leontia Flynn. The trajectory may thus simply be viewed as one that moves from the national level to the postnational but this neat view is surely complicated by the nomadic MacNeice most of all, and his significant influence in this regard on this newest generation of postnationalists should have been mentioned at the very least. What is more, the degree to which these younger poets are indebted to their elder contemporaries—Muldoon and Carson in particular—in their ability to move easily across boundaries should have been discussed. The idea of place and displacement is by now an overly-familiar one in the context of Northern Irish poetry but what remains of most value throughout this study is Kennedy-Andrews' ability to bring together the existing lines of critical scholarship on Northern Irish poetry and read the poems in the light of these. 'What is the significance of the prevalence of classical Latin and Greek influences in Northern Irish place writing? What is the importance of translation as an aspect of cultural adaptation and transfer?' Kennedy-Andrews asks in his introduction but neither of these important questions are revisited. Throughout, Kennedy-Andrews keeps a steady eye on American-Irish interconnections rather than broadening his scope to include European ones and does not consider translations from other languages; this continues to be an area of study that, although routinely held up as an essential one, has yet to be adequately examined in an expert way. The chapter on Longley's relationship to the landscape of the west of Ireland is one of the most engaging while that on McGuckian's gendered spaces is somewhat tedious as Kennedy-Andrews summons Kristeva and other heavy-weight theorists to bolster his reading of this notoriously challenging poetry. The chapter that reads Muldoon and Heaney through Robert Frost is clearly informed by the author's reading of Rachel Buxton's 2004 study. As an unquestionably committed reader of Irish poetry Kennedy-Andrews is at his best when he is relaxing on familiar ground; elucidating the poems with close, well-researched readings and consolidating recent critical accounts of

Northern Irish poetry that present its poets as boundary crossers who are ever in transit and who are all, in their different ways, at home in the world; a world that MacNeice set out as being 'various', 'crazy', 'incorrigibly plural'. All of this in one compact volume makes for an eminently student-friendly affair.

Despite the fact that it would be difficult to think of a prominent Irish poet whose output does not include some translation from non-anglophone languages, poetry in Ireland is not often read under the rubric of translation studies. With his study *Poetry and Translation in Northern Ireland: Dislocations in Contemporary Writing* Rui Carvalho Homem provides a useful basis for examining the vast subject of inter- and intra-linguistic translation in Northern Irish poetry and Irish poetry more broadly—individual chapters are devoted to the work of Paul Muldoon, Michael Longley, Derek Mahon, Ciaran Carson, and Seamus Heaney—which takes as its own obvious starting-points Michael Cronin's seminal *Translating Ireland: Translations, Languages, Cultures* [1996] and Brian Friel's *Translations*. Homem cites Friel's line on how the Irish 'feel closer to the warm Mediterranean' to support his critical view that Irish poetic engagements with non-anglophone European cultures are rooted in a desire to 'counter the gravitational pull of English culture'. This ideologically charged assertion is dropped as soon as it is aired, however. Homem also overlooks the crucial fact that all of the above poets have also, albeit to varying degrees, translated from the Irish language, and the study routinely fails to examine this important fact—perhaps because Homem's professional linguistic competence does not extend to the Irish language—thus making for an incomplete view. Homem lays his groundwork by quoting a plethora of other theorists on the nature of 'place' and the relational connection between text, space, and time, to conclude, via the oft-quoted dictum of James S. Duncan and Trevor J. Barnes, that 'places are intertextual sites'. One fears throughout this opening gambit that this theory-heavy approach will not be conducive to readings of the literary work of poets who actively resist such narrow, prescriptive perspectives, and the reader must wonder if any fresh approaches to the poetry itself can come out of this. However, still in the lengthy introduction, Homem's theoretical acuity makes for an interesting and helpful critique of the term 'translation studies' itself as he teases out the implications of spreading it too far. Yet despite its own warning against extending the term 'translation' into vague abstraction his study goes on to do just that.

The main problem lies in its attempt to do too much within the available space. Accordingly, the author is restricted in his ability to develop points; there are few new insights into the work of any of the poets—the most that can be provided is an encapsulation of existing critical narratives and how these relate to the themes of dislocation and translation. One comes away feeling that the study has far more to do with ideas of 'dislocation' than linguistic translation. The chapter on Heaney is too diffuse, and readers interested in Heaney's translations would be better off with Conor McCarthy's superbly detailed 2008 study which gives a truer sense of the reach of Heaney's art as a translator. The chapter on Mahon seems to be more concerned with place and 'desolation' (a word that is repeated so often it ceases to have any meaning) than with his work in translation. There are moments of real interest in the chapter on Mahon when Homem engages with the original texts in French and notes Mahon's swerves, but there should have been more of this. Each of the chapters begins with a lengthy preamble that merely consolidates existing criticism on each of the writers. It is difficult to know what market this study is aimed at. The academic specialist will find nothing new here while the undergraduate student will find the lack of close readings and the densely compacted style frustrating, if not difficult, to disentangle. The most lucid chapter is on Paul Muldoon as it begins by asserting the fundamental importance of linguistic translation to Muldoon's poetics. However, even here, in a startling oversight, Muldoon's high-profile translations of Nuala Ní Dhomhnaill's work—his 'The Language Issue' and the acclaimed *The Fifty Minute Mermaid*—are never as much as referred to. Indeed, Homem's view is blinkered throughout as he writes as though there is no poetry being written in Ireland outside of these Northern male poets. This translational poetics is hardly a Northern Irish male phenomenon—to take one example from elsewhere in Irish poetry, the multilingual scholar, poet, and translator Eiléan Ní Chuilleanáin has written of how, for her, writing poetry in English is itself an act of translation. Homem's frame of reference is disappointingly narrow. Only a very general engagement with translations of poetry from other languages is in evidence; perhaps the book might better have been entitled *Poetry and Dislocation in Northern Irish Poetry* as it seems to be far more concerned with place, language, and identity than with the exact and complex art of translation itself, and Homem is far more comfortable when writing about these themes than about the technique, as his oversight regarding Muldoon's best-known translations shows. Nonetheless, this thoughtful and well-researched study does provide a good, basic overview to which many students will be indebted and will no doubt inspire further investigations and readings of contemporary poetry under this rubric.

Thomas Kinsella's *Prose Occasions: 1951–2006* comes with a number of disclaimers regarding the flaws of some of the pieces selected for inclusion. It repays forbearance however, once the stuffy, self-regarding tone of the early work develops and matures into some of the more engaging pieces, the stand-outs in this regard being the reminiscences and appreciation of Sean Ó Riada—full of wonderful vignettes—as well as Kinsella's pronouncements on the rich tradition of poetry in Irish, a subject that he came to late in his career (as he puts it) but to which he has contributed much service since his conversion. The editorial decision to separate the reviews from the other prose pieces is highly questionable. Surely a chronological sequence would have made more sense; it also would have made the tedious repetition of material in the first section less obvious. Instead, the reviews are relegated to the back and so we have to go back in time as we begin reading them after finishing the first section; the reader finds himself having to place the reviews in time and in their correct order. Curiously, although the book has been 'edited' by Andrew Fitzsimons one finds no editorial statement, no critical reflection from a Kinsella scholar on the material and its value and relevance to our understanding of the poet's oeuvre. As a result, a lot of the work is left to the reader. Kinsella's reviews are for the most part dutiful pieces written under obligation, and the reader feels similarly dutiful in having to read every one of them. However, when Kinsella's passions are truly stirred the writing becomes far livelier, even stimulating, and it is in these moments that the worth of the book emerges. Here we find Kinsella in the 1950s absorbing poets such as Ezra Pound (his 'spray of sparkling free verse'), Stevens (his 'poems are of the school of the oriole, an American bird of brilliant plumage and pure song'), and others. It is clearly the American poets—as 'pioneers' of a new language—that truly excite him, and his prose is charged accordingly: 'Where is Richard Eberhart's "Groundhog"?', he laments in an all-too-rare outburst of passion. Of the Irish poets, Clarke and Kavanagh are both commended (unsurprisingly Kinsella keeps coming back to Clarke's 'Martha Blake at Fifty-One') and, importantly, Kinsella's review of the long-overlooked Patrick MacDonogh ('sensitive, intelligent' with 'the gift of creating the memorable phrase, the precise and singing cadence') places fresh emphasis on why this poet deserves proper critical attention. There is the odd moment—again, all too rare—when Kinsella's critical tongue sharpens, as when he describes Kathleen Raine's voice as that of the 'well-groomed Pythoness'. This chortle-inducing style is not typical, however, and Kinsella studiously takes pains to pull his punches, a tendency which very often makes for a uniformity of response. 'Eccentric' seems to be a favourite adjective; when applied to Marianne Moore it must be a term of praise, and Kinsella captures with remarkable understanding the 'eccentric' style of Moore's own prose occasions, her *Predilections*. 'Interesting enough to wring forgiveness from the laziest reader', Kinsella concludes of Moore's literary criticism; his own *Prose Occasions* beg the same forgiveness, but the book as a whole will be useful as a convenient and eminently portable, all-in-one resource for students of Kinsella to dip in and out of (even if the absence of an index will make this more of a chore than it should be).

In his editor's introduction to *Flowing Still: Irish Poets on Irish Poetry*, Pat Boran flogs the increasingly tired horse of the term 'Irish poetry', offering up the present collection of essays, in appropriately militaristic parlance, as a continuing 'interrogation' of that term. One will recognize in this a rehashing of Justin Quinn's argument in his provocative *Cambridge Introduction to Modern Irish Poetry*, and Boran takes issue with Quinn's theory of the 'Disappearing Ireland' (and woefully misinterprets it in the process) to no intelligible end. In the twenty-first century the nationalist paradigm of Irish poetry simply does not hold up, as Boran must know. Boran's objections to Quinn's study seem to lie most of all with Quinn's failure to take account of, in Boran's fighting words, 'so many of the most active presences on the contemporary scene', many of whom are published by his own Dedalus Press. (Boran delivers his sales pitch some sentences on as he directs the reader—for 'reader' read 'potential Dedalus customer'—to the Dedalus website.) Possible agendas aside, the value of this collection is highly debatable. Of the book's two sections, all of the essays in the first were previously published in the 1999 anthology *Watching the River Flow*. Surely, many of the poets here, who would have made their selections in 1999, would, in the intervening years have found reason to revise their judgements? Time has not stood 'still'. Moreover, to reprint these essays without including the poems that they introduce seems illogical. But it is not only the first section of the book that is recycled; the second half will also be familiar to any reader of Irish poetry criticism. David

Wheatley's is the only proper, scholarly essay here and it is already eight years old. The services of a good proof-reader should also have been enlisted as the lack of scholarly precision in matters of style (Boran's essay lacks footnote references and all of his quotations sound as though they have come straight from blurb endorsements) only augments the lack of substance. Overall, the essays in the first section, though still of great value as comments by poets on the previous century's poetry, hardly required to be repackaged in this way. A distinct sense of déjà vu dogs the whole, and one has to wonder what purpose the book was intended to serve.

One of the surprising verdicts on Irish poetry delivered in Kinsella's *Prose Occasions* concerns Louis MacNeice's *Autumn Sequel*, a poem that has not enjoyed critical approbation, but which Kinsella declares 'a considerable poem' and 'the work of an old master who has achieved great ease and style, and who has taken the world personally'. In his introduction to *Louis MacNeice and the Poetry of the 1930s*—the first study of MacNeice's poetry since the major publication in 2007 of Peter McDonald's new edition of the *Collected Poems*—Richard Danson Brown pays tribute to McDonald's scholarship for the way that it allows readers 'to read MacNeice's poetry as it was originally published'. McDonald's scholarship on MacNeice is a constant touchstone for Brown throughout, as he rarely makes a point without citing either him or his other eminent predecessor Edna Longley for support. It should be noted that the title of Brown's study is somewhat misleading as the book does not focus exclusively on MacNeice's poetry of the 1930s but moves chronologically across the entire oeuvre. More curiously still, Alan Gillis's study *Irish Poetry of the 1930s* is never mentioned and is not listed in the bibliography; an unfortunate oversight given that Gillis treats MacNeice in his study along with other notable Irish poets of this decade. Moreover, Gillis's sharp, considered reading of *Autumn Journal* and other Thirties poems would surely have added to Brown's understanding. An early chapter that discusses the work of the other members of MacSpaunday seems to have little bearing on the rest of the proceedings, as these poets are peremptorily dropped once the 1930s is out of sight, and Brown's reading does nothing to assert their importance either to MacNeice or to modern poetry more broadly. This makes for a strangely diffuse argument that lacks direction. Moreover, Brown makes little in the way of helpful comment on the connections between Spender, Day-Lewis, and MacNeice, for example, on the possible intertextual connection between MacNeice's famous 'The Sunlight on the Garden' (the title of which Brown repeatedly gives incorrectly as 'Sunlight in the Garden') with its line 'We shall have no time for dances' and the title poem of Day-Lewis's 1935 collection *A Time to Dance and Other Poems*. Because the study provides an overview of MacNeice's entire career, and not just his poetry of the 1930s, perhaps a better title would have foregrounded MacNeice as a poet of conflict or dialectical struggle.

Although Brown is an enlightened reader, little of original insight is offered throughout; he has clearly learned much from his predecessors and as he relies heavily on established readings of MacNeice's work many of the major points in his thesis will already be familiar. As a major conference event at Queen's University Belfast in 2007 testified, MacNeice is not a poet for whom posterity is in doubt; his legacy is profound and his reputation assured. One of the aspects of MacNeice's oeuvre that McDonald's *Collected Poems* redirected focus onto was the important sequence *The Last Ditch* [1940]. This and *Plant and Phantom* [1941] were shaped by MacNeice's experience of being between Ireland and the US at the start of the Second World War. Instead of benefiting from the possibilities for critical enquiry opened up by McDonald's work, Brown is content to merely revisit the critical heritage. Indeed, Brown's knowledge of the American poetic landscape seems sketchy as, later in the study, he devotes much attention to MacNeice's 'The Snow Man', a title that immediately calls to mind the American modernist poet Wallace Stevens's poem of the same title—it is extremely interesting that MacNeice follows Stevens by opting for 'Snow Man' rather than the usual 'Snowman'—and with which it shares many of the same wintry philosophical concerns. The potential links between these two poems would have been fascinating to explore, and a consideration of MacNeice's engagement with the US, its poetry and culture at this crucial moment would have opened up MacNeice's work in new ways. The lack of critical focus on MacNeice's elsewheres is compounded in the book's final pages when Brown briefly points to Muldoon's '7, Middagh Street' as a tribute to MacNeice the 'internationalist'; the true international force of MacNeice's poetry has not been examined in any meaningful way. Had Brown made this a central aspect of his own study, then it would have at least contributed something new to MacNeice scholarship and built on the revelations that McDonald's *Collected Poems* made available. But, although earnestly researched and presented, the study remains at the level of suggestion. It is difficult to know whom the study is aimed at. Given the already strong body of criticism on MacNeice by ground-breaking scholars such as Longley, McDonald, and Gillis, it will be hardly be required reading for undergraduates. What seems to be more urgent is a well-researched critical biography of the poet to replace Jon Stallworthy's.

'Coffey and Devlin have remained obdurately hard to revive', Bernard O'Donoghue writes in his contribution to *Flowing Still: Irish Poets on Irish Poetry*, an observation that, though by now over ten years old, still holds true, of Coffey in particular. A major attempt to correct the incontestable fact of Coffey's critical neglect is undertaken in *Other Edens: The Life and Work of Brian Coffey*, a sizeable collection of essays edited by Benjamin Keatinge and Aengus Woods. Mounting their defence in their opening sentence, the editors acknowledge that, 'there are perhaps few Irish poets on whom critical opinion is so divided as Brian Coffey', before launching into an account of the appraisals that Coffey's work has received (most negatively in recent evaluations of his work by Quinn and Gillis) and what they see as the various reasons for his low visibility in modern poetry and in critical narratives of poetic modernism. Here, as one would expect, the battle between 'mainstream' and avant-garde, between local or 'insular' and European and modernist, is momentarily replayed, but the editors are clear-sighted enough to admit that these too-easy binaries are no longer useful in mapping Irish poetry. This, then, is a work of careful re-evaluation which the editors clearly believe is long overdue; their focus on the discrepancy between the low-key affair that was the 2005 centenary symposium on Coffey's work (at which event many of the essays here were first aired) and the main event that was the Beckett centenary the following year is telling, and Coffey's links with other figures in modernism, particularly with Beckett, are reiterated throughout the volume (one of the book's fine illustrations reprints a postcard sent to Coffey from Beckett). Yet Keatinge and Woods are careful not to sugar-coat the issue of Coffey's obscurity. As they concede: 'if Coffey's poetry still demands to be read, it can also be puzzling, difficult, elliptical as well as liberating'.

(As the current reviewer is a contributor to the volume the remarks that follow will be in no way evaluative and will attempt only to describe the content.) All of the scholarly essays here build on the pioneering scholarship of both the veteran Coffey admirer J.C.C. Mays and Dónal Moriarty, whose *The Art of Brian Coffey* [2000] is still the only monograph on Coffey's poetry. Throughout the collection the reader is granted a sense of the whole of Coffey's career and not just the 1930s contexts. Following an introductory personal reminiscence by Augustus Young, Gerald Dawe starts the scholarly proceedings with an essay on Coffey's critical reception. Coffey's poems receive close attention throughout the book; Thomas Dillon Redshaw considers Coffey's *Third Person* as a *livre d'artiste*; Woods teases out Coffey's love poems in the light of Emmanuel Levinas; 'Missouri Sequence' is the focus of essays by Keatinge and James Matthew Wilson (who reads the sequence through Coffey's profound interest in the philosophy of Jacques Maritain), while *Advent* and *Death of Hektor* are treated by Andrew Goodspeed, Harry Gilonis, and Wacław Grzybowski. Geoffrey Squires, in his essay on Coffey's prosody, shows a particular debt to Moriarty's study. Many of the contributors focus on Coffey's relationship with other writers, artists, and cultural figures: the George Reavey scholar Sandra O'Connell examines the friendship between Coffey and Reavey, while Thomas Dillon Redshaw adds Mallarmé to the mix, Kit Fryatt reads Coffey through the work of the contemporary Irish poet Maurice Scully, and Mays investigates links between Coffey's work and Beckett's *Murphy*. Other contributions include more personal reminiscences of Coffey, by his son John and by contemporary poets who are indebted to Coffey such as Young, Billy Mills, and Michael Smith as well as a startling reminiscence by Coffey himself on his friendship with Beckett. The range of contributors alone suggests Coffey's lasting relevance, and this collection will no doubt inspire further scholarship on Coffey's poetry, not least because of its inclusion of a descriptive checklist of books and pamphlets by Coffey and a bibliography of works by and on Coffey.

The poet Gerald Dawe has been a prominent critical voice in Ireland for decades. As director of the Oscar Wilde Centre for Creative Writing at Trinity College Dublin, where he is also a senior lecturer in English, he has worked tirelessly as an educator, and his *The World as Province: Selected Prose 1980–2008* has him in precisely this mode as it gathers his essays and lectures from across the past three decades on matters to do with Irish literature and culture. (I should here disclose that the current reviewer was taught by Dawe at Trinity College Dublin and proof-read part of the book under review.) The main shortcoming concerns matters of scholarly reference. Dawe, widely seen as a highly respected commentator and well-known advocate of poetry in Ireland, is no doubt trying to reach beyond a specialist academic readership, but the lack of footnote referencing throughout makes for an unsatisfying read and detracts from the scholarly merit of the whole. This aside, the book itself is full of Dawe's characteristically unbiased insights and careful readings of Irish poetry. Rarely routine in his perceptions, Dawe is an involved, informed reader of Irish poetry and its contexts, and the ease with which he discusses the breadth of literature in Ireland is impressive as he travels from the nineteenth-century poet Raftery to the present via William Carleton, Yeats, Beckett, Devlin, Mahon, Thomas Kilroy, and Van Morrison (the essay 'The First Time I Heard' is an engaging musical autobiography).

Over the years Dawe has often foregrounded poets deemed critically unfashionable, asserting their literary and cultural worth through sensitive readings of poems that knowingly move beyond the restrictive, generic term 'Irish Poetry'. Thus, he holds up iconoclasts such as Brian Coffey (whose *Death of Hektor* 'flies in the face of current poetic practices') and Denis Devlin (who 'creates his own terms of reference'), as well as contemporary poets such as Harry Clifton, Paul Durcan ('a liberating force'), and Frank Ormsby, who are seen to be shifting the imaginative focus of Irish poetry away from the rural landscape and onto the city. Dawe champions poets who defy expectation, who challenge orthodoxy and complacency, and is a forthright critic of sectarianism and small-mindedness. In a substantial essay on Kinsella's 'strange, uncommon poetic vision' he rails against how Irish poetry is 'read in the strict and increasingly constrictive terms of national categories'. As Terence Brown remarks in his preface: 'Dawe's own complex Irish migrations...have enforced on the author an awareness of Irish heterogeneity at a time of marked social and political change'. Northern Ireland is a complex phenomenon, as Dawe is all too aware. Like Heaney in his critical prose, Dawe presents autobiographical material so as to underpin his critical views with personal experience, particularly that of growing up in Belfast and the effects of the Troubles in Northern Ireland. However one might argue with some of his assessments of the merits of individual poets, no one could argue that Dawe writes with anything other than conviction. It comes as no surprise to learn that he worked as a postman during his student years; he knows his territory in its entirety and gets on with the business of decoding, opening lines of travel and communication, even if this means that the line between journalism and literary criticism is constantly blurred throughout. Lastly, it must be acknowledged that this is a much slighter affair than Dawe's *The Proper Word: Ireland, Poetry Politics*, edited by Nicholas Allen (Creighton University Press [2007]), and it perhaps confirms that a substantial, properly edited volume of Dawe's collected prose writings is now required.

Finally, Irish poetry criticism must at certain points concern itself with taking stock and reflecting on its own discourse and value systems. 'Poems that Matter' is the suggestive title of a special issue of the *Irish University Review* edited by that most dexterous close reader, Peter Denman. But 'matter' in what way? What matters in poetry? In 'Irish' poetry more pertinently? Does a poem have to make ethical or political points in order to have value? Must it refer to the Irish context? Does it have to be engaged with society and culture? Does the poem matter more if it is an 'original' rather than a translation from another source? Can a poem matter simply because it gives pleasure? These are some of the issues raised by the appearance of this intriguing volume of essays. (As I myself was a contributor to this issue I will again limit myself to general comments rather than evaluative statement.) What is most revealing here is not simply the poems that are chosen but the poets. One can only speculate on how the judges set out to make their choice; did they first think of a poet who 'matters' and then settle on a poem, or was the identity of the poet of no matter? As Denman writes in his careful introduction: 'the underlying idea was not so much the identification of "important" poems, but rather to see why poems might be identified as significant by selected, informed readers of Irish poetry'. Be this as it may, it is the omissions (never 'accidents', as Marianne Moore observed) that are most revealing. No one will be surprised to see Mahon's 'A Disused Shed in Co. Wexford', Eavan Boland's 'Mise Eire', or Longley's 'Wounds', but where are Louis MacNeice, John Montague, Carson, Vona Groarke, or Nuala Ní Dhomhnaill? Poetry in the Irish language is well represented by Seán Ó Ríordáin's 'Adhlachadh mo Mháthar', Gabriel Rosenstock's 'Mussolini ag dul ar Neamh', and Biddy Jenkinson's 'Gleann Maoiliúra', so that issue at least will not stoke controversy. That the youngest poet selected was born in 1951 (Paul Muldoon) raises questions. Is this because the contributors lacked the bravery to stray from the safety of established reputations or is this a negative critical indicator of the achievement of Irish poets born after 1951? The critical output on Irish poetry in this year might suggest that the latter is the case and that the old-timers still hold sway in critical evaluations of Irish poetry.

Books Reviewed

Abraham, Julie. *Metropolitan Lovers: The Homosexuality of Cities*. UMinnP. [2009] pp. xxii + 357. £55 ISBN 9 7808 1663 8185.

Acheraïou, Amar. *Joseph Conrad and the Reader: Questioning Modern Theories of Narrative and Readership*. Palgrave. [2009] pp. x + 233. £50 ISBN 9 7802 3022 8115.

Adams, Don. *Alternative Paradigms of Literary Realism*. Palgrave. [2009] pp. ix + 200. £52 ISBN 9 7802 3062 1862.

Adieshiah, Siân. *Churchill's Socialism: Political Resistance in the Plays of Caryl Churchill*. CambridgeSP. [2009] pp. 261. £39.99 ISBN 1 4438 1318 4.

Adolph, Andrea. *Food and Femininity in Twentieth-Century British Women's Fiction*. Ashgate. [2009] pp. viii + 183. £60 ISBN 9 7807 5466 7346.

Agathocleous, Tanya, ed. *Joseph Conrad's 'The Secret Agent'*. Broadview. [2009] pp. 320. £9.99 ISBN 9 7815 5111 7843.

Andermahr, Sonya. *Jeanette Winterson*. New British Fiction. Palgrave. [2009] pp. ix + 194. hb £42.50 ISBN 9 7802 3050 7609, pb £9.99 ISBN 9 7802 3050 7616.

Arana, Victoria R. *W.H. Auden's Poetry: Mythos, Theory and Practice*. Cambria. [2009] pp. 364. $119 ISBN 9 7816 0497 5956.
Ashton, Paul, and Hilda Kean, eds. *People and their Pasts: Public History Today*. Palgrave. [2009] pp. xiv + 304. £50 ISBN 9 7802 3054 6691.
Atkins, G. Douglas. *Literary Paths to Religious Understanding: Essays on Dryden, Pope, Keats, George Eliot, Joyce, T.S. Eliot, and E.B. White*. Palgrave. [2009] pp. xxii + 173. $80 ISBN 9 7802 3062 1473.
Aulich, James, and John Hewitt. *Seduction or Instruction? First World War Posters in Britain and Europe*. ManUP. [2008] pp. xx + 218. $49.95 ISBN 9 7807 1907 5902.
Baxter, Katherine Isobel, and Richard J. Hand, eds. *Joseph Conrad and the Performing Arts*. Ashgate. [2009] pp. 165. £55 ISBN 9 7807 5466 4901.
Beja, Morris, and Anne Fogarty, eds. *Bloomsday 100: Essays on 'Ulysses'*. UPFlorida. [2009] pp. 254. $70 ISBN 978-0 8130 3402 7.
Bennett, Andrew. *Ignorance: Literature and Agnoiology*. ManUP. [2009] pp. iv + 260. £50 ISBN 9 7807 1907 4875.
Bignell, Jonathan. *Beckett on Screen: The Television Plays*. ManUP. [2009] pp. 230. £50 ISBN 9 7807 1906 4203.
Bloom, Clive. *Bestsellers: Popular Fiction since 1900*. Palgrave. [2008] pp. xx + 425. £14.99 ISBN 9 7802 3053 6890.
Bluemel, Kristin, ed. *Intermodernism: Literary Culture in Mid-Twentieth-Century Britain*. EdinUP. [2009] pp. viii + 254. £50 ISBN 9 7807 4863 5092.
Booth, Howard J., ed. *New D.H. Lawrence*. ManUP. [2009] pp. xvi + 200. £55 ISBN 9 7807 1907 8361.
Boran, Pat, ed. *Flowing, Still: Irish Poets on Irish Poetry*. Dedalus Press. [2009] pp. 194. €25 ISBN 9 7819 0661 4058.
Brady, Sean. *Masculinity and Male Homosexuality in Britain, 1861–1913*. Palgrave. [2009] pp. viii + 265. £18.99 ISBN 9 7802 3023 8565.
Bray, Suzanne, Adrienne E. Gavin, and Peter Merchant, eds. *Re-embroidering the Robe: Faith, Myth and Literary Creation since 1850*. CambridgSP. [2008] pp. 278. £34.99 ISBN 9 7818 4718 6089.
Brewer, Mary F., ed. *Harold Pinter's The Dumb Waiter*. Dialogue 6. Rodopi. [2009] pp. 269. pb £54 ISBN 9 7890 4202 5561.
Brown, Judith. *Glamour in Six Dimensions: Modernism and the Radiance of Form*. CornUP. [2009] pp. xiv + 200. £50 ISBN 9 7808 0144 7792.
Brown, Richard Danson. *Louis MacNeice and the Poetry of the 1930s*. Northcote. [2009] pp. 158. pb £12.99 ISBN 9 7807 4631 1851.
Busch, Justin E.A. *The Utopian Vision of H.G. Wells*. McFarlane. [2009] pp. vii + 204. £50 ISBN 9 7807 8644 6056.
Caputo, John D., and Linda Martin Alcoff, eds. *St. Paul among the Philosophers*. IndUP. [2009] pp. 195. £25 ISBN 9 7802 5322 0837.
Carey, Hilary M., ed. *Empires of Religion*. Palgrave. [2008] pp. xii + 350. £50 ISBN 9 7802 3020 8803.
Carroll, Rachel, ed. *Adaptation in Contemporary Culture: Textual Infidelities*. Continuum. [2009] pp. xi + 212. pb £19.99 ISBN 9 7808 2642 4628.
Caughie, Pamela, ed. *Disciplining Modernism*. Palgrave. [2009] pp. xi + 296. £55 ISBN 9 7802 3023 5084.

Cavanagh, Michael. *Professing Poetry: Seamus Heaney's Poetics*. CUAP. [2009] pp. 254. $59.95 ISBN 9 7808 1321 6713.
Chapman, Dan. *Oxford Playhouse: High and Low Drama in a University City*. UHertP. [2008] pp. xx + 343. pb 9.99 ISBN 9 7819 0280 6877.
Chinitz, David, ed. *Companion to T.S. Eliot*. Wiley. [2009] pp. xviii + 483. £105 ISBN 9 7814 0516 2371.
Clewell, Tammy. *Mourning, Modernism, Postmodernism*. Palgrave. [2009] pp. viii + 185. £50 ISBN 9 7802 3023 1948.
Cobley, Evelyn. *Modernism and the Culture of Efficiency: Ideology and Fiction*. UTorP. [2009] pp. x + 344. £60 ISBN 9 7808 0209 9570.
Colombino, Laura, ed. *Ford Madox Ford and Visual Culture*. Rodopi. [2009] pp. 269. £55 ISBN 9 7890 4202 6353.
Cooke, Jennifer. *Legacies of Plague in Literature, Theory and Film*. Palgrave. [2009] pp. x + 226. £50 ISBN 9 7802 3021 9342.
Cooppan, Vilashini. *Worlds Within: National Narratives and Global Connections in Postcolonial Writing*. StanfordUP. [2009] pp. xxiii + 354. £60 ISBN 9 7808 0475 4903.
Coyne, Ana Carden. *Reconstructing the Body: Classicism, Modernism and the First World War*. OUP. [2009] pp. xiii + 344. £60 ISBN 9 7801 9954 6466.
Crick, Brian, and Michael DiSanto, eds. *Selected Criticism: D.H. Lawrence*. Brynmill. [2009] pp. xxiii + 316. £14.40 ISBN 9 7809 5599 9611.
Cross, Helen, ed. *Wilfred Owen: Selected Poems and Letters*. Oxford Student Texts. OUP. [2009] pp. ix + 163. pb £9.99 ISBN 9 7801 9832 8780.
Crosswhite Hyde, Virginia, ed. *Mornings in Mexico and Other Essays*, by D.H. Lawrence. CUP. [2009] pp. lxxxi + 370. £83 ISBN 9 7805 2165 2926.
Crosthwaite, Paul. *Trauma, Postmodernism, and the Aftermath of World War II*. Palgrave. [2009] pp. vii + 222. £50 ISBN 9 7802 3020 2955.
Dawe, Gerald. *The World as Province: Selected Prose 1980–2008*. Lagan Press. [2009] pp. 222. £12.99 ISBN 9 7819 0465 2687.
Day, Barry, ed. *The Essential Noel Coward Compendium: The Very Best of his Work Life and Times*. Methuen. [2009] pp. 374. pb £16.99 ISBN 9 7814 0810 8697.
Deer, Patrick. *Culture in Camouflage: War, Empire, and Modern British Literature*. OUP. [2009] pp. xi + 329. £50 ISBN 9 7801 9923 9887.
Detloff, Madelyn. *The Persistence of Modernism: Loss and Mourning in the Twentieth Century*. CUP. [2009] pp. xii + 213. £53 ISBN 9 7805 2189 6429.
Dickinson, Renée. *Female Embodiment and Subjectivity in the Modernist Novel: The Corporeum of Virginia Woolf and Olive Moore*. Routledge. [2009] pp. xii + 180. $121 ISBN 9 7804 1599 3838.
DiSanto, Michael John. *Under Conrad's Eyes: The Novel as Criticism*. McG-QUP. [2009] pp. xv + 253. £55 ISBN 9 7807 7353 5107.
Dodge, Martin, Rob Kitchin, and Chris Perkins, eds. *Rethinking Maps: New Frontiers in Cartographic Theory*. Routledge. [2009] pp. xviii + 246. £85 ISBN 9 7804 1546 1528.
Donovan, Stephen, Danuta Fjellestad, and Rolf Lunden, eds. *Authority Matters: Rethinking the Theory and Practice of Authorship*. Rodopi. [2008] pp. 302. £50 ISBN 9 7890 4202 4830.

Dorney, Kate. *The Changing Language of Modern English Drama 1945–2005*. Palgrave. [2009] pp. 259. £50 ISBN 9 7802 3001 3292.
Dryden, Linda, Stephen Arata, and Eric Massie, eds. *Robert Louis Stevenson and Joseph Conrad: Writers of Transition*. TTUP. [2009] pp. xii + 273. £60 ISBN 9 7808 9672 6536.
Durao, Fabio A., and Dominic Williams, eds. *Modernist Group Dynamics: The Politics and Poetics of Friendship*. CambridgeSP. [2009] pp. 275. £39.99 ISBN 9 7818 4718 5082.
Earle, David M. *Re-Covering Modernism: Pulps, Paperbacks and the Prejudice of Form*. Ashgate. [2009] pp. viii + 246. £55 ISBN 9 7807 5466 1542.
Eliot, Valerie, and Hugh Haughton, eds. *The Letters of T.S. Eliot*, vol. 1: *1898–1922*. rev. edn. Faber. [2009] pp. xl + 871. £35 ISBN 9 7805 7123 5094.
Eliot, Valerie, and Hugh Haughton, eds. *The Letters of T.S. Eliot*, vol. 2: *1923–1925*. Faber. [2009] pp. xxxiv + 878. £35 ISBN 9 7805 7114 0817.
Ellis, Heather, and Jessica Meyer, eds. *Masculinity and the Other: Historical Perspectives*. CambridgeSP. [2009] pp. xii + 337. £45 ISBN 9 7814 4380 1515.
Ellis, Steve. *T.S. Eliot: A Guide for the Perplexed*. Continuum. [2009] pp. ix + 169. pb $19.99 ISBN 9 7818 4706 0174.
Epstein, Edmund Lloyd. *A Guide through 'Finnegans Wake'*. UPFlorida. [2009] pp. 314. $60 ISBN 978-0 8130 3356 3.
Eyre, Richard. *Talking Theatre: Interviews with Theatre People*. Nick Hern Books. [2009] pp. 331. £20 ISBN 9 7818 4842 0465.
Featherstone, Simon. *Englishness: Twentieth-Century Popular Culture and the Forming of English Identity*. EdinUP. [2009] pp. vi + 202. £60 ISBN 9 7807 4862 3655.
Forsyth, Alison, and Chris Megson. *Get Real: Documentary Theatre Past and Present*. Palgrave. [2009] pp. 256. £50 ISBN 9 7802 3022 1154.
Freshwater, Helen. *Theatre Censorship in Britain: Silencing, Censure and Suppression*. Palgrave. [2009] pp. 212. £45 ISBN 9 7802 3022 3783.
Friedman, Alan W., and Charles Rossman, eds. *De-Familiarizing Readings: Essays from the Austin Joyce Conference*. Rodopi. [2009] pp. 114. pb €28 ISBN 978-9 0420 2570 7.
Front, Sonia. *Transgressing Boundaries in Jeanette Winterson's Fiction*. Literary and Cultural Theory. Lang. [2009] pp. 211. £33.50 ISBN 9 7836 3158 9533.
Gamble, Sarah. *Angela Carter: A Literary Life*. Palgrave. [2009] pp. viii + 239. pb £19.99 ISBN 9 7802 3058 0985.
Gan, Wendy. *Women, Privacy and Modernity in Early Twentieth-Century British Writing*. Palgrave. [2009] pp. ix + 182. £55 ISBN 9 7802 3053 5855.
Gaston, Sean. *Derrida, Literature and War: Absence and the Chance of Meeting*. Continuum. [2009] pp. xxi + 220. £24.99 ISBN 9 7818 4706 5537.
Gavin, Adrienne E., and Andrew F. Humphries, eds. *Childhood in Edwardian Fiction: Worlds Enough and Time*. Palgrave. [2009] pp. viii + 236. £50 ISBN 9 7802 3022 1611.
Glick, Elisa. *Materializing Queer Desire: Oscar Wilde to Andy Warhol*. SUNYP. [2009] pp. xiv + 220. £55 ISBN 9 7814 3842 7263.

Gorton, Kristyn. *Theorising Desire: From Freud to Feminism to Film*. Palgrave. [2008] pp. x + 182. £50 ISBN 9 7814 0398 9604.

Grant, Ben. *Postcolonialism, Psychoanalysis and Burton: Power Play of Empire*. Routledge. [2009] pp. xi + 209. £60 ISBN 9 7804 1545 0867.

Groes, Sebastian, ed. *Ian McEwan*. Contemporary Critical Perspectives. Continuum. [2009] pp. xiv + 176. hb £40 ISBN 9 7808 2649 7215, pb £14.99 ISBN 9 7808 2649 7222.

Hai, Ambreen. *Making Words Matter: The Agency of Colonial and Postcolonial Literature*. OhioUP. [2009] pp. xi + 377. £60 ISBN 9 7808 2141 8819.

Hargrove, Nancy. *T.S. Eliot's Parisian Year*. UFlorP. [2009] pp. 336. hb $69.95 ISBN 9 7808 1303 4010, pb $29.95 ISBN 9 7808 1303 5536.

Hastings, Selina. *The Secret Lives of Somerset Maugham*. Murray. [2009] pp. 614. pb £10.99 ISBN 9 7807 1956 5557.

Heath, Jeffrey M., ed. *The Creator as Critic and Other Writings by E.M. Forster*. UTorP. [2008] pp. 814. $90 ISBN 9 7815 5002 5224.

Henry, Nancy, and Cannon Schmitt, eds. *Victorian Investments: New Perspectives on Finance and Culture*. IndUP. [2009] pp. viii + 250. £35 ISBN 9 7802 5322 0271.

Henstra, Sarah. *The Counter-Memorial Impulse in Twentieth-Century English Fiction*. Palgrave. [2009] pp. x + 182. £50 ISBN 9 7802 3057 7145.

Herzog, Dagmar, ed. *Brutality and Desire: War and Sexuality in Europe's Twentieth Century*. Palgrave. [2009] pp. xi + 290. £50 ISBN 9 7802 3054 2532.

Hillemann, Ulrike. *Asian Empire and British Knowledge: China and the Networks of British Imperial Expansion*. Palgrave. [2009] pp. x + 262. £50 ISBN 9 7802 3020 0463.

Hoff, Molly. *Virginia Woolf's Mrs. Dalloway: Invisible Presences*. ClemsonUDP. [2009] pp. x + 286. pb $29.95 ISBN 9 7809 7960 6670.

Holroyd, Michael. *A Strange Eventful History: The Dramatic Lives of Ellen Terry, Henry Irving and their Remarkable Families*. C&W. [2008] pp. xviii + 620. £25 ISBN 9 7807 0117 9878.

Homem, Rui Carvalho. *Poetry and Translation in Northern Ireland: Dislocations in Contemporary Writing*. Palgrave Macmillan. [2009] pp. 254. £50 ISBN 9 7802 3022 1161.

Hughes, William, and Andrew Smith, eds. *Queering the Gothic*. ManUP. [2009] pp. xii + 195. £55 ISBN 9 7807 1907 8156.

Ingersoll, Earl, and Virginia Hyde, eds. *Windows to the Sun: D.H. Lawrence's 'Thought Adventures'*. FDUP. [2009] pp. 249. £49.50 ISBN 9 7808 3864 1972.

Izzo, David Garrett. *The Influence of Mysticism on 20th Century British and American Literature*. McFarland. [2009] pp. 185. pb $39.95 ISBN 9 7807 8644 1068.

Jackson, Tony E. *The Technology of the Novel: Writing and Narrative in British Fiction*. JHUP. [2009] pp. ix + 234. £60 ISBN 9 7808 0189 2448.

James, David, and Philip Tew, eds. *New Versions of Pastoral: Post-Romantic, Modern, and Contemporary Responses to the Tradition*. FDUP. [2009] pp. 285. $62.50 ISBN 9 7808 3864 1897.

Jones, Claire G. *Femininity, Mathematics and Science, 1880–1914*. Palgrave. [2009] pp. x + 264. £55 ISBN 9 7802 3055 5211.

Karl, Alissa G. *Modernism and the Marketplace: Literary Culture and Consumer Capitalism in Rhys, Woolf, Stein, and Nella Larsen*. Routledge. [2009] pp. xiii + 183. £50 ISBN 9 7804 1598 1415.

Keatinge, Benjamin, and Aengus Woods, eds. *Other Edens: The Life and Work of Brian Coffey*. IAP. [2009] pp. 304. €39.95 ISBN 9 7807 1652 9101.

Kennedy-Andrews, Elmer. *Ciaran Carson: Critical Essays*. FCP. [2009] pp. 288. €45 ISBN 9 7818 4682 1561.

Khair, Tabish. *The Gothic, Postcolonialism and Otherness: Ghosts from Elsewhere*. Palgrave. [2009] pp. vi + 198. £50 ISBN 9 7802 3023 4062.

Kiberd, Declan. *'Ulysses' and Us*. Faber. [2009] pp. 399. pb £15 ISBN 978-0 5712 4254 2.

Kim, Rina. *Women and Ireland as Beckett's Lost Others: Beyond Mourning and Melancholia*. Palgrave. [2009] pp. 210. £50 ISBN 9 7802 3023 0477.

King, Bruce. *Robert Graves: A Biography*. Haus. [2008] pp. 266. £16.99 ISBN 9 7819 0579 1941.

Kinsella, Thomas. *Prose Occasions: 1951–2006*, ed. Andrew Fitzsimons. Carcanet. [2009] pp. 227. pb £18.95 ISBN 9 7818 4777 0080.

Kirschner, Paul. *Comparing Conrad: Essays on Joseph Conrad and his Implied Dialogues with Other Writers*. [2010] Paul Kirschner, Geneva (self published).

Koivunen, Leila. *Visualizing Africa in Nineteenth-Century British Travel Accounts*. Routledge. [2009] pp. xvi + 351. £60 ISBN 9 7804 1599 0011.

Kontou, Tatiana. *Spiritualism and Women's Writing: From the Fin de Siècle to the Neo-Victorian*. Palgrave. [2009] pp. x + 245. £55 ISBN 9 7802 3020 0050.

Koppen, R.S. *Virginia Woolf, Fashion and Literary Modernity*. EdinUP. [2009] pp. x + 182. £60 ISBN 9 7807 4863 8727.

Koureas, Gabriel. *Memory, Masculinity and National Identity in British Visual Culture, 1914–1930: A Study of 'Unconquerable Manhood'*. Ashgate. [2008] pp. xiv + 217. £55 ISBN 9 7807 5466 0170.

Kuehn, Julia, and Paul Smethurst, eds. *Travel Writing, Form, and Empire: The Poetics and Politics of Mobility*. Routledge. [2009] pp. ix + 255. £60 ISBN 9 7804 1596 2940.

Kuhlman, Erika. *Reconstructing Patriarchy after the Great War: Women, Gender, and Postwar Reconciliation between Nations*. Palgrave. [2008] pp. xiii + 246. £50 ISBN 9 7802 3060 2816.

Lago, Mary, Linda K. Hughes, and Elizabeth Macleod Wells. *The BBC Talks of E.M. Forster, 1929–1960: A Selected Edition*. UMinnP. [2008] pp. 512. £53.50 ISBN 9 7808 2621 8001.

Lamberti, Elena, and Vita Fortunati, eds. *Memories and Representations of War: The Case of World War I and World War II*. Rodopi. [2009] pp. 343. £55 ISBN 9 7890 4202 5219.

Langford, Rachael, ed. *Textual Intersections: Literature, History and the Arts in Nineteenth-Century Europe*. Rodopi. [2009] pp. 231. £45 ISBN 9 7890 4202 7312.

Logan, Peter Melville. *Victorian Fetishism*. SUNYP. [2009] pp. 206. £16.99 ISBN 9 7807 9147 6628.

Luckhurst, Roger. *The Trauma Question*. Routledge. [2008] pp. x + 240. £25 ISBN 9 7804 1540 2712.

Maddrey, Joseph. *The Making of T.S. Eliot: A Study of Literary Influences*. McFarland. [2009] pp. x + 179. pb £39.95 ISBN 9 7807 8644 2713.

Mahon, Peter. *Joyce: A Guide for the Perplexed*. Continuum. [2009] pp. 197. pb £13 ISBN 978-0 8264 8792 6.

Mahood, M.M. *The Poet as Botanist*. CUP. [2008] pp. xii + 269. £58 ISBN 9 7805 2186 2363.

March-Russell, Paul. *The Short Story: An Introduction*. EdinUP. [2009] pp. x + 291. £17.99 ISBN 9 7807 4862 7745.

Maslen, Cathleen. *Ferocious Things: Jean Rhys and the Politics of Women's Melancholia*. CambridgeSP. [2009] pp. xi + 267. £34.99 ISBN 9 7818 4718 6614.

Matthews, Sean, and Sebastian Groes, eds. *Kazuo Ishiguro*. Contemporary Critical Perspectives. Continuum. [2009] pp. xvi + 151. hb £40 ISBN 9 7808 2649 7239, pb £14.99 9 7808 2649 7246.

Maynard, James, ed. *Discovering James Joyce: The University at Buffalo Collection*. SUNYP. [2009] pp. 112. $30. pb ISBN 978-0 9226 6823 6.

McCourt, John, ed. *James Joyce in Context*. CUP. [2009] pp. 414. £60 ISBN 978-0 5218 8662 8.

McLean, Steven. *The Early Fiction of H.G. Wells: Fantasies of Science*. Palgrave. [2009] pp. ix + 242. £55 ISBN 9 7802 3053 5626.

McLoughlin, Kate, ed. *The Cambridge Companion to War Writing*. CUP. [2009] pp. xxiv + 266. hb £25 ISBN 9 7805 2172 0045, pb £18.99 ISBN 9 7805 2172 0045.

Merriman, Andy. *Margaret Rutherford: Dreadnought with Good Manners*. Aurum. [2009] pp. 296. 18.99 ISBN 9 7818 4513 4457.

Meyer, Jessica. *Men of War: Masculinity and the First World War in Britain*. Palgrave. [2009] pp. x + 216. ISBN 9 7802 3022 2014.

Monaco, Beatrice. *Machinic Modernism: The Deleuzian Literary Machines of Woolf, Lawrence and Joyce*. Palgrave. [2008] pp. viii + 213. £55 ISBN 9 7802 3021 9366.

Morin, Emile. *Samuel Beckett and the Problem of Irishness*. Palgrave. [2009] pp. 234. £50 ISBN 9 7802 3021 9861.

Most, Glenn W, Larry F. Norman, and Sophie Rabau, eds. *Révolutions homériques*. Edizioni della Normale. [2009] pp. 162. pb €25 ISBN 8 8876 4236 2.

Motton, Gregory. *Helping Themselves: The Left-Wing Middle Classes in Theatre and the Arts*. Levellers Press. [2009] pp. 207. pb £10 ISBN 9 7809 5643 6405.

Nicholls, Peter. *Modernisms: A Literary Guide*. Palgrave. [2009] pp. xiii + 406. £25 ISBN 9 7802 3050 6763.

Nixon, Mark, and Matthew Feldman, eds. *The International Reception of Samuel Beckett*. Continuum. [2009] pp. 309. £80 ISBN 9 7808 2649 5815.

O'Donoghue, Bernard, ed. *The Cambridge Companion to Seamus Heaney*. CUP. [2009] pp. 260. pb £18.99 ISBN 9 7805 2154 7550.

Peach, Linden. *Angela Carter*, 2nd edn edn. Palgrave. [2009] pp. viii + 206. hb £47.50 ISBN 9 7802 3020 2825, pb £15.99 ISBN 9 7802 3020 2832.

Pearson, Nels, and Marc Singer, eds. *Detective Fiction in a Postcolonial and Transnational World*. Ashgate. [2009] pp. ix + 214. £60 ISBN 9 7807 5466 8480.

Pizzichini, Lillian. *The Blue Hour: A Life of Jean Rhys*. Norton. [2009] pp. 322. £30 ISBN 9 7803 9305 8031.

Pordzik, Ralph, ed. *Futurescapes: Space in Utopian and Science Fiction Discourses*. Rodopi. [2009] pp. 366. £60 ISBN 9 7890 4202 6025.

Pritchard, William H. *On Poets and Poetry*. OhioUP. [2009] pp. xvi + 361. hb $48.96 ISBN 9 7808 0401 1143, pb $24.95 ISBN 9 7808 0401 1150.

Rabey, David Ian. *Howard Barker: Ecstasy and Death: An Expository Study of his Drama Theory and Production Work, 1998–2008*. Palgrave. [2009] pp. 289. £50 ISBN 9 7814 0399 4738.

Rau, Petra. *English Modernism, National Identity and the Germans, 1890–1950*. Ashgate. [2009] pp. x + 233. £55 ISBN 9 7807 5465 6722.

Reeve, N.H., ed. *The Vicar's Garden and Other Stories*. by D.H. Lawrence. CUP. [2009] pp. xxxvii + 265. £83 ISBN 9 7805 2186 7108.

Reynier, Christine. *Virginia Woolf and the Ethics of the Short Story*. Palgrave. [2009] pp. ix + 179. £50 ISBN 9 7802 3022 7187.

Ricci, Gabriel R., ed. *Morality and the Literary Imagination*. Religion and Public Life 36. Transaction. [2009] pp. xiv + 187. pb £29.95 ISBN 9 7814 1280 8392.

Richards, Jeffrey. *The Ancient World on the Victorian and Edwardian Stage*. Palgrave Macmillan. [2009] pp. xi + 267. £50 ISBN 9 7802 3022 9365.

Ridley, Nicolas. *Godfrey's Ghost: From Father to Son*. Mogzilla Life. [2009] pp. 258. pb £9.99 ISBN 9 7819 0613 2989.

Ridout, Alice, and Susan Watkins, eds. *Doris Lessing: Border Crossings*. Continuum. [2009] pp. x + 172. £60 ISBN 9 7808 2642 4662.

Roberts, Harri Garrod. *Embodying Identity: Representations of the Body in Welsh Literature*. Writing Wales in English. UWalesP. [2009] pp. xii + 195. pb £18.99 ISBN 9 7807 0832 1690.

Robertson, Robin, ed. *Love Poet, Carpenter: Michael Longley at Seventy*. Enitharmon. [2009] pp. 125. £15 ISBN 9 7819 0463 4904.

Rosenquist, Rod. *Modernism, the Market, and the Institution of the New*. CUP. [2009] pp. ix + 210. £60 ISBN 9 7805 2151 6198.

Ross, Stephen. *Modernism and Theory: A Critical Debate*. Routledge. [2009] pp. xi + 264. £30 ISBN 9 7804 1546 1573.

Roughley, Alan R., ed. *Anthony Burgess and Modernity*. ManUP. [2008] pp. xx + 297. £55 ISBN 9 7807 1907 8866.

Royle, Nicholas. *In Memory of Jacques Derrida*. EdinUP. [2009] pp. xv + 192. £19.99 ISBN 9 7807 4863 2961.

Rubenstein, Roberta. *Virginia Woolf and the Russian Point of View*. Palgrave. [2009] pp. viii + 265. £55 ISBN 9 7802 3061 8732.

Sagar, Keith. *D.H. Lawrence: Poet*. Troubador. [2008] pp. 188. pb £15 ISBN 9 7818 4760 0684.

Salisbury, Laura, and Andrew Shail, eds. *Neurology and Modernity: A Cultural History of Nervous Systems, 1800–1950*. Palgrave. [2009] pp. xiv + 298. £50 ISBN 9 7802 3023 3133.

Schnauder, Ludwig. *Free Will and Determinism in Joseph Conrad's Major Novels*. Rodopi. [2009] pp. 268. £55 ISBN 9 7890 4202 6162.

Slattery-Christie, David. *In Search of Ruritania: The Life and Times of Ivor Novello*. AuthorHouse. [2008] pp. xvi + 267. pb 15.99 ISBN 9 7814 2594 9440.

Smith, Graeme. *The Theatre Royal Entertaining a Nation*. Glasgow Publications. [2008] pp. 310. pb £19.95 ISBN 9 7809 5594 2006.

Sörlin, Sverker, and Paul Warde, eds. *Nature's End: History and the Environment*. Palgrave. [2009] pp. xii + 368. £60 ISBN 9 7802 3020 3464.

Spinks, Lee. *James Joyce: A Critical Guide*. EdinUP. [2009] pp. 233. pb £17 ISBN 978-0 7486 3836 9.

Spurr, Barry. *'Anglo-Catholic in Religion': T.S. Eliot and Christianity*. Lutterworth. [2009] pp. xiv + 325. £25 ISBN 9 7807 1883 0731.

Steveker, Lena. *Identity and Cultural Memory in the Fiction of A.S. Byatt: Knitting the Net of Culture*. Palgrave. [2009] pp. xix + 200. £50 ISBN 9 7802 3057 5332.

Thomas, David N. *Fatal Neglect: Who Killed Dylan Thomas?* Seren Books. [2008] pp. 232. pb £9.99 ISBN 9 7818 5411 4808.

Turnbull, Olivia. *Bringing Down the House: The Crisis in Britain's Regional Theatres*. Intellect. [2008] pp. 237. pb £27.50 ISBN 9 7818 4150 2083.

van Bergen, Leo. *Before My Helpless Sight: Suffering, Dying and Military Medicine on the Western Front, 1914–1918*. Ashgate. [2009] pp. x + 528. £35 ISBN 9 7807 5465 8535.

Wakana, Maya Higashi. *Performing the Everyday in Henry James's Late Novels*. Ashgate. [2009] pp. ix + 193. £60 ISBN 9 7807 5466 7445.

Warren, Diane. *Djuna Barnes' Consuming Fictions*. Ashgate. [2008] pp. xviii + 188. £50 ISBN 9 7807 5463 9206.

Watson, Nicola J., ed. *Literary Tourism and Nineteenth-Century Culture*. Palgrave. [2009] pp. xi + 230. £50 ISBN 9 7802 3022 2816.

Williams, David. *Media, Memory and the First World War*. Studies in the History of Ideas. McG-QUP. [2009] pp. xii + 321. $59.95 ISBN 9 7807 7353 5077.

Wilson, Keith, ed. *A Companion to Thomas Hardy*. Wiley. [2009] pp. xiv + 488. £105 ISBN 9 7814 0515 6684.

Witchard, Anne Veronica. *Thomas Burke's Dark 'Chinoiserie': 'Limehouse Nights' and the Queer Spell of Chinatown*. Ashgate. [2009] pp. x + 292. £55 ISBN 9 7807 5465 8641.

Worthen, John. *T.S. Eliot: A Short Biography*. Haus. [2009] pp. 330. £16.99 ISBN 9 7819 0659 8358.

Wright, Patrick. *On Living in an Old Country: The National Past in Contemporary Britain*. OUP. [2009] pp. xxviii + 290. £8.99 ISBN 9 7801 9954 1959.

Wuchina, Douglas. *Destinies of Splendor: Sexual Attraction in D.H. Lawrence*. Lang. [2009] pp. vii + 241. £43.50 ISBN 9 7814 3310 6651.

Wyllie, Andrew. *Sex on Stage: Gender and Sexuality in Post-War British Theatre*. Intellect. [2009] pp. 160. pb £20.50 ISBN 9 7818 4150 2038.

XV

American Literature to 1900

MICHAEL COLLINS, CLARE ELLIOTT, ANNE-MARIE FORD AND THERESA SAXON

This chapter has two sections: 1. General; 2. American Literature to 1900. Section 1 is by Theresa Saxon; section 2 is by Michael Collins, Clare Elliott and Anne-Marie Ford.

1. General

American Literature has contributed significantly to studies of nineteenth-century American literature in 2009. In a special edition on literature and law for the first issue of 2009, the journal published a series of articles, collected by special editors Britt Rusert and Priscilla Wald, relating to nineteenth century writing. In '"Freedom with a Vengeance": Choosing Kin in Antislavery Literature and Law' (*AL* 81:i[2009] 7–34), Edlie Wong examines the controversy over the enactment of fugitive slave legislation, particularly the largely overlooked role of abolitionists in bringing cases against slave-owners who had brought their slaves with them in their travels to New England, through a study of literary output of the time, as well as news accounts and legal pamphlets. Jeannine Marie DeLombard's 'Salvaging Legal Personhood: Melville's *Benito Cereno*' (*AL* 81:i[2009] 35–64) locates Melville's short tale within a wider exploration of legal documentation that demonstrates the law to be contingent and temporary. Andrea Stone, in 'Interracial Sexual Abuse and Legal Subjectivity in Antebellum Law and Literature' (*AL* 81:i[2009] 65–9), examines the literary evocation of sexual abuse of enslaved women in the context of legal property/possession and power relations, particularly through Harriet Jacobs's *Incidents in the Life of a Slave Girl* [1865]. In 'Fugitive Obscura: Runaway Slave Portraiture and Early Photographic Technology' (*AL* 81:i[2009] 93–120), Sarah Blackwood explores how the developing literacy of slaves in slave narratives (notably Frederick Douglass's *Narrative* [1845] and Jacobs's *Incidents* [1861], both of which commented on the development of photographic technologies) and the African American press, argued for a visual literacy that would combat the whiteness of the word and bring injustice into sharp relief. The work of

The Year's Work in English Studies, Volume 90 (2011)
doi:10.1093/ywes/mar005

Frederick Douglass also features in Lance Newman's 'Free Soil and the Abolitionist Forests of Frederick Douglass's "The Heroic Slave"' (*AL* 81:i[2009] 127–52), comparing the novella of 1853 to *My Bondage, My Freedom* [1855], which are situated as shaped by a republican pastoralism, in distinction to his earlier works, in which 'nature' appears as a sinister wilderness. Andy Doolen, in '"Be cautious of the word 'rebel'": Race, Revolution, and Transnational History in Martin Delany's *Blake; or, The Huts of America*' (*AL* 81:i[2009] 153–79), examines Delany's novel as a challenge to white histories of slavery, widening the context of the debate to a transnational arena that eroded the historical narrative of reliance for black Americans on the ideologies of a specifically white American revolutionary fervour.

Later issues of *American Literature* also feature essays by nineteenth-century literary scholars. In the second issue of 2009, Maurice S. Lee's 'Probably Poe' (*AL* 81:ii[2009] 225–52), explores 'The Murders in the Rue Morgue' [1841], 'The Mystery of Marie Roget' [1842–3], and 'The Purloined Letter' [1844] as registers of rationality through their engagement with probability theory, in contradistinction to general criticism, which has located Poe as the Gothically framed imp of the perverse. In the same issue, Mark Noble, in 'Whitman's Atom and the Crisis of Materiality in the Early *Leaves of Grass*' (*AL* 81:ii[2009] 253–79), examines Whitman's enthusiasm for popular science in an account of his poetic engagement with the compatibility of the spiritual and the material. Nick Bromell's 'Reading Democratically: Pedagogies of Difference and Practices of Listening in *The House of Mirth* and *Passing*' (*AL* 81:ii[2009] 281–303) asserts a specific connection between Edith Wharton's *The House of Mirth* and Nella Larsen's *Passing* in their relative, albeit distinctive, assessments of the value of difference within and between citizens.

In the third issue of 2009, Jake Mattox's 'The Mayor of San Juan del Norte? Nicaragua, Martin Delany, and the "Cotton" Americans' (*AL* 81:iii[2009] 527–54) takes Delany's claim to have been made mayor of San Juan del Norte as a point of departure for his discussion of *The Condition, Elevation, Emigration, and Destiny of the Colored People of the United States* [1852] and *Blake* [1859, 1861–2], in an assessment of the racialized politics of the actual Nicaraguan election that was contextualized by a rising interest in travelling and emigration for African Americans and a conflict in definitions of nationhood and citizenship. In the same issue, Stephanie LeMenager's '"Geographical Morality": Place and the Problem of Patriotism in John W. De Forest's Civil War Realism' (*AL* 81:iii[2009] 555–82) also explores location in an assessment of De Forest's *Miss Ravenel's Conversion from Secession to Loyalty* (written between 1864 and 1867) alongside Whitman's *Specimen Days*, arguing that this novel of realism offers insights into current debates over liberalism and cultural nationalism, rights and constitution, and a moral attachment to place that resonates with Whitman's 'erotics of patriotism'.

In the fourth 2009 issue of *American Literature*, Jeffrey Insko, in 'The Logic of Left Alone: *The Pioneers* and the Conditions of U.S. Privacy' (*AL* 81:iv[2009] 659–85), examines Cooper's 1823 novel as participating in an uneven discourse of rights to privacy that have perpetuated in the

United States. Hsuan L. Hsu's 'Vagrancy and Comparative Racialization in *Huckleberry Finn* and "Three Vagabonds of Trinidad"' (*AL* 81:iv[2009] 687–717) also looks to mobility as a key topic, in this instance examining the distinctions between experience of mobility in racialized America, through the legal impediment of the vagrancy laws. Nicholas Gaskill, in 'Red Cars with Red Lights and Red Drivers: Colour, Crane, and Qualia' (*AL* 81:iv[2009] 719–45), locates Crane's absorption in 'colour' as informed technological developments of synthetic dyes, developing a literary style that translates colour to human senses, in a technique that, argues Gaskill in his discussion of Goethe's *Theory of Colours* [1810], matches the remit of qualia. Michael Lundblad, in 'Epistemology of the Jungle: Progressive-Era Sexuality and the Nature of the Beast' (*AL* 81:iv[2009] 747–73), revisits Eve Kosofsky Sedgwick's assessment of homosocial operations outlined in the *Epistemology of the Closet* [1990], which, Lundblad argues, overlooks the significance of what he terms the 'discourse of the jungle', drawing on animality studies, as an alternative to Freud and Darwin, in an assessment of Henry James's 'The Beast in the Jungle' [1903] as one of a series of socially relevant but critically ignored 'sexual histories of the beast'. *American Literature* also continues to provides important scholarly resources, as well as articles of interest to the general reader, in the 'Book Reviews' and 'Brief Mentions' sections of the quarterly publication.

The *Modern Language Association International Bibliography* (*MLAIB*), proves a useful resource for scholars, with full and detailed bibliographic listings of books, articles, review essays, notes and dissertations of the annual publication. *American Literary Scholarship: An Annual* (*AmLS*) constitutes an exhaustive bibliographical survey of the year's critical writing. This year's edition (2009) covers critical material published in 2007. The edition is sectioned: Part I deals with American literary greats and Part II provides a chronological view of the year's output. Editor David J. Nordloh, and the team of contributing scholars, as ever cover extensive ground in this valuable resource, which includes sections on Emerson, Thoreau, Fuller, and Transcendentalism; Hawthorne; Melville; Whitman and Dickinson; Mark Twain; Henry James; Wharton and Cather, as well as providing a general guide to scholarship on nineteenth-century literature. *American Literary History* continues to offer a substantial scope of resources for students and specialists in American literature. Issue *AmLH* 21:iv[2009] features a special forum on Abraham Lincoln, which will be of significant interest to scholars of American literature and history. Notable articles for literary specialists are Robert Milder's 'Hawthorne and the Problem of New England' (*AmLH* 21:iii[2009] 464–91), which examines Hawthorne's preoccupation with writing about and from a specific place; Michael T. Gilmore's '"Speak, man!": Billy Budd in the Crucible of Reconstruction' (*AmLH* 21:iii[2009] 492–51), which examines the concepts of language and silence in the context of Reconstruction's racial voices and voicelessness; and Wendy Graham's 'Notes on a Native Son: Henry James' New York' (*AmLH* 21:ii[2009] 239–26), which builds on current studies of James's connectivity with concept of modernism/postmodernism. *American Literary History* also features a range of essays throughout the year which continue to address a range of studies that will be of use to scholars of nineteenth-century literature.

2. American Literature to 1900

Since Walter Benn Michaels first suggested a new path for literary criticism with his influential work, *The Gold Standard and the Logic of Naturalism* [1987], critics have been slow to follow his lead in relating federal economic policy to historical theories of identity. As the power of fiscal policy to shape lives has become such a crucial issue in contemporary culture, perhaps it is unsurprising that 2009 saw the release of a number of works directly reflecting upon how the modern triumvirate of concerns in Americanist scholarship, 'race, class, and gender', are related in complex and often subtle ways to how we spend, accumulate, and think about money. In *Paper Money Men: Commerce, Manhood, and the Sensational Public Sphere in Antebellum America*, David Anthony avoids the problem of making general claims about the connection between identity and money by providing a more materialist critique, based around careful archival research, and rooted in a particular time and place: the print culture of the 1840s and 1850s. Adding to a recent boom in texts that have paid close attention to the institutional logic of the publishing industry in the antebellum era, Anthony does not privilege racial identity as separate from other identitarian concerns. Where race does become a key factor, especially in chapter 2 ('Shylock on Wall Street') and chapter 5 ('Success and Race in *The House of the Seven Gables*'), it is connected with gender, sexuality, religion, and class through the author's exploration of the antebellum 'sensational public sphere'. It is Anthony's sophisticated understanding and deployment of this term that makes the work groundbreaking and essential for scholars of the American Renaissance. By showing how the construction of masculine authorial identity was bound up in ideas of indebtedness, across numerous cultural genres (theatre, the short story, the novel, journalism, and illustration), Anthony establishes an important beachhead into the muddled and carnivalesque world of the antebellum literary marketplace. Subverting older readings that have related antebellum sensationalism to the feminine-gendered sphere of social relations, Anthony explores a masculine 'sensational public sphere', comprising texts dealing with 'all states of affect stemming from the residual question: what was the originary relationship between men and money, and how did it go so horribly wrong?'. In an impressive piece of counterintuitive logic, the author effectively shows how the definition of a productive, urban manhood in the mid-nineteenth century relied more upon 'the possession of a highly emotional, feeling body' that represented the new market economy than upon the inviolate, patriarchal forms of masculine self-possession that had characterized revolutionary manhood. Indeed, in an ingenious reading of the journalism of 'enterprising newspaperman' James Gordon Bennett, Jr., the author demonstrates how, through the deployment of authorial postures of submission in the *New York Herald*, Bennett was able to fashion the penny press as the voice of the disenfranchised working-class male. This creative reimagining of the public sphere serves the author brilliantly in his readings of stories such as 'Bartleby, The Scrivener; A Story of Wall Street' [1853] and *The House of the Seven Gables* [1851], which are frequently groundbreaking. By elegantly fusing readings of lesser-known figures with more canonical concerns, Anthony has produced a work that is essential for scholars of mid-nineteenth-century literature.

Jaime Osterman Alves's *Fictions of Female Education in the Nineteenth Century* examines American infancy and socialization in gendered terms. Covering writing by Elizabeth Stoddard, Oliver Wendell Holmes, S. Alice Callahan, and Frances E.W. Harper, as well as a variety of non-fiction texts, this study argues for seeing nineteenth-century schools as 'crucial components in a network of social and cultural institutions' that worked together to build ideal American female citizens. Alves claims that girls' schools in the nineteenth century were at the centre of a gathering of institutions all interested in shaping female domestic roles, sexuality, reproduction, and education. In the fiction she examines, public and private realms blur for the female characters, largely as they would in life beyond the pages of novels. Alves fruitfully examines the narratives of 'real' schoolgirls alongside these fictional constructions of girlhood. Chapter 1 looks at the relationship between the family and the girls' school in New England of the 1810s, 1820s, and 1830s in Elizabeth Stoddard's *The Morgesons*. Chapter 2 argues that debates over education, and in particular education for females, took place in the 1830s through the 1850s as the family became a less stable social force. Alves's argument moves to discourses of science, medicine, and education and how those discourses worked in the 1830s to 1850s to produce an educational programme aimed at normalizing female sexuality. Girls were no longer being schooled in behaving as dutiful daughters (as a precursor to becoming dutiful wives) but in preparation to become 'ideal mates' for young American males. Alves makes an important point about Oliver Wendell Holmes as a major scientific thinker of his time. Mostly remembered in nineteenth-century studies as the man who pronounced Emerson's 'American Scholar' as 'our intellectual declaration of independence', Holmes was also a medical doctor and man of letters. Dr Holmes is being rediscovered in nineteenth-century studies as an important figure in mid-century literary circles, and Alves rightly identifies the convergence of medicine and literature as shaping his life-long interest in the female intellect, and the pathologizing of adolescent female sexual and intellectual development at school. In a dramatic shift, the third chapter turns to the study of two Native American tribes over a period of more than six decades and the published writings of actual schoolgirls. Elias Boudinot, a Cherokee editor, worked with white missionaries in the 1820s and 1830s to raise funds for the establishment of a tribal school and a newspaper. As such, young Cherokee schoolgirls began publishing in the newspaper, expressing their dual identities by writing in English using American pen-names and in Cherokee under their birth names. Alves goes on to trace fictional accounts of similar phenomena in S. Alice Callahan's novel *Wynema: A Child of the Forest*, in which a young Creek schoolgirl uses newspaper reading to negotiate the two worlds she straddles—coming to terms with her role as an educated female living among whites and Natives, to mediate and translate events (the career of Buffalo Bill, in one case) as they are portrayed in the press. The last chapter explores another fictional account of a female adolescent, one depicted in Frances E.W. Harper's *Trial and Triumph* [1888–9]. Harper's neglected serial novel addresses questions about her vision of African American female education through the schooling of the heroine Annette Harcourt. In this work, Annette is prepared by educated black adults in the community for her role as a female race leader. Alves argues that its serialization in *Christian Recorder*, a small but influential black Christian newspaper, ensured the impact of the tale on a predominantly black audience. Alves essentially asks questions about what it meant to be female in the American 1800s and plausibly stresses the emergence of schoolgirl culture in fiction as a mainstream social force in the nineteenth century.

The Civil War is the subject of Janet Kemper Beck's *Creating the John Brown Legend: Emerson, Thoreau, Douglass, Child and Higginson in Defense of the Raid on Harpers Ferry*. Its excellent achievement is to draw together the threads of support for John Brown within literary circles in the nineteenth century. John Brown's reputation, even into the twenty-first century, has been uneven to say the least. Celebrated by W.E.B. Du Bois as the hero of black struggle in his biography *John Brown* [1909], the martyr of Harpers Ferry was initially mythologized as the saviour of slaves. After Du Bois's work, much historiography constructed Brown in quite different terms, more as a madman or fanatic, and recently (post-9/11) as a terrorist. Despite these two extreme perceptions of John Brown, the raid on Harpers Ferry was a vital event triggering the beginnings of the Civil War, and one to which nineteenth-century writers and thinkers devoted extensive reflection. Until now it has been a surprise to read of Emerson's interest in and support for Brown, and not much has been known about the influential but often neglected Lydia Maria Child's comments on the raid. Beck's work offers a coherent and full account of the literary reactions to Harpers Ferry by illustrating not only the support that Brown received within literary circles, but how literature began to rewrite history and indeed fictionalize Brown. Devoting chapters to each writer in turn, Beck presents the writings on Brown by Emerson, Thoreau, Frederick Douglass, Lydia Maria Child, and Thomas Wentworth Higginson. Two fascinating chapters, respectively entitled 'History's Version' and 'Literature's Version', address the layered complexities of Brown's mythology. With photographs, maps, and a timeline of the events surrounding the raid, this volume will serve American studies students and scholars well, not least by reminding us of the stubborn entanglement of historiographical and literary meanings in the nineteenth century.

Diane N. Capitani's *Truthful Pictures: Slavery Ordained by God in the Domestic Sentimental Novel of the Nineteenth-Century South* examines antebellum sermons and writings and their influence on the sentimental fiction of the period. Capitani begins by contemplating the function of women writers and the cult of domesticity. Women, as the moral centre of the home, must exert their influence for good; yet the dilemma was the perception of what was right. In tension with the anti-slavery text *Uncle Tom's Cabin* by the Northern writer Harriet Beech Stowe, were the Southern women writers Caroline Hentz and Mary H. Eastman. Hentz was horrified by what she believed to be Stowe's total ignorance of conditions on the Southern plantations. *The Planter's Northern Bride* [1854] was her response and it was immediately popular, establishing the pattern of the Southern, domestic, pro-slavery novel. Hentz insists that planters felt a great responsibility towards their slaves and that the planter's wives were angels of goodness, who had frequent recourse to the scriptures, which, it was argued, defended slavery. Another defender of slavery using Christian scripture was Eastwick, whose 1852 novel *Aunt Phillis's Cabin* (published the same year as Stowe's *Uncle Tom*) teemed with biblical references, and claimed abolition to be fanatical. In her story the slaves are actually referred to as servants throughout, and enjoy their lives on the plantation. The character of Aunt Phillis is employed to reflect on the lack of superiority of the black races, arguing that they had been placed in their lowly estate by God himself; a particular reference being to Simon of Cyrene, who was black, and who helped Jesus carry his cross to Calvary. Another such novelist who wrote of the Southern world of domesticity was Maria McIntosh, who was infuriated by Stowe's attack on the institution of slavery. She argued, in *The Lofty and the Lowly* [1852], that the movement from Africa into bondage had been a positive one; slaves had learnt about Christianity from the white man, and in coming to know God had embraced a better life. What is most telling about these texts is the compulsion the authors felt to write back to Stowe, to refute her abolitionist theme, and to argue for the positive values of slavery. They were not the only ones, and the divisions between North and South grew into a political storm. This study offers a thoughtful discussion of the way in which scripture was perverted to defend racism and slavery, although a deeper and more detailed exploration of both novels and sermons would have been illuminating. *Truthful Pictures* allows the reader the opportunity of tracing increasing racial tensions in the years preceding the Civil War and some interesting line drawings are included. A bibliography of primary and secondary sources is useful as the basis for further exploration of the subject.

It is a truism that to understand American literature one must first understand the Gothic, the imaginative expression of fears and forbidden desires. Charles L. Crow, in *History of the American Gothic*, begins by exploring the influence of America's wild landscape, and perhaps the most popular writer of wilderness adventures in the pre-Civil War period, James Fenimore Cooper. The study describes *The Last of the Mohicans* [1826] as a Gothic romance, pondering whether Gothic tales are genuinely subversive, or whether they reinforce the values of the dominant culture; he develops the idea of dark Romantics through the writings of Edgar Allan Poe, Nathaniel Hawthorne, and Herman Melville. Hawthorne's 'Young Goodman Brown' [1835] and his most celebrated novel, *The Scarlet Letter* [1850], both employ the wilderness of the dark wood as an arena where the ambiguities of human psychology and those of nature interact. *The House of the Seven Gables* [1851] is often referred to as Hawthorne's most Gothic text, with its haunted house, ancient crimes, ancestral curse, and sinister villain; its conclusion describes an attempt to escape from a corrupt world. Hawthorne was a profound influence upon another New England author, Melville, and the symbolism of Hawthorne's writing can be traced, especially, in Melville's *Moby-Dick*

[1851]. Masked and veiled images, a common Gothic trope, are also favourite themes with both writers, and appear most memorably in Hawthorne's *The Blithedale Romance* [1852] and Melville's *The Piazza Tales* [1856]. The borders of Poe's Gothic, meanwhile, are dreamscapes between madness and death. Images of disease, death, and decay held powerful sway in Poe's imagination. Emily Dickinson, arguably America's foremost poet, shared a Gothic sensibility with these writers, exploring a sense of alienation, reflecting, in poem 670, 'One need not be a Chamber—to be Haunted'. And haunted she certainly was, by death, by separation, by desire and longing. Although it was not until the following century that Dickinson's genius would be recognized, her work demonstrates the power of the Gothic and its hold on the imaginative processes of literary artists during her lifetime. Meanwhile, regionalism, generally the province of women writers, continued to explore Gothicism. The stories of Alice Cary, *Clovernook* [1852] and *Clovernook, Second Series* [1853], fall into this category, and the genre was to reach its zenith in the fiction of Sarah Orne Jewett, Mary E. Wilkins Freeman, and Kate Chopin. Crow also cites Henry James as a Gothic 'master' who drew upon the traditions of his American predecessors, especially Washington Irving and Hawthorne, and discusses in some detail James's tale of the haunted governess, *The Turn of the Screw* [1898]. The writings of Mark Twain (Samuel Clemens) are also investigated, especially his fascination with such Gothic symbols as twins, doubles, and alter egos. His most powerful Gothic writing is based on the enduring American tragedy of race, *Pudd'nhead Wilson* [1894], a story about racial identity which employs the motif of twins and doubles as a key to the novel itself. Perhaps the most celebrated Gothic story of the closing years of the century is Charlotte Perkins Gilman's 'The Yellow Wallpaper' [1892], which anticipates twentieth-century narratives of mental illness, such as Sylvia Plath's compelling *The Bell Jar* [1963]. Gilman's character tells a story of a haunted house, male oppression, and female disintegration into madness. Crow's *American Gothic* includes detailed notes and a comprehensive bibliography that encourages a wider examination of the significance and pervasiveness of the Gothic in American literature and culture.

Thoreau is quoted by Monika Elbert and Marie Drews as noting that 'some berries which I have eaten on a hill-side had fed my genius'. Thoreau's doubleness of body and mind is examined in a broader context by Elbert and Drews's edited collection, *Culinary Aesthetics and Practices in Nineteenth-Century American Literature*. Published in Palgrave's Nineteenth-Century Major Lives and Letters series, the collection uses the trope of food (feast, famine, consumption, and cannibalism) to reread familiar texts and authors, including Dickinson, Chopin, and Henry James. Among its many striking insights is the revelation that 'abstemious attitude and predilection for a vegetable diet [was] shared by many in the mid-nineteenth-century United States', while going on to develop the human palate as a methodological focal point for analysing literary culture. The editors' thesis claims that, just as the American republic of the nineteenth century saw aesthetic movements which aimed to cut the political and literary apron strings with Europe, those apron strings were being cut in American kitchens as a 'culinary declaration of independence' took place. They notice that Whitman, the national poet, celebrates the land of milk and honey in 'Starting from Paumanok' in a poem which becomes a long list of American produce which includes 'sugar, rice!... wheat, beef, pork!' Connecting these essays is a tension between abundance and scarcity; Thoreau and Harriet Beecher Stowe preach about the dangers of excess while Whitman celebrates the bounty of the American landscape. Maura D'Amore, Mark McWilliams, Andrew Dix, and Lorna Piatti examine the influence of capitalism and class structure on culinary practice, with the focus on excessive eating within larger social tensions of the Gilded Age. Robert T. Tally, Marie Drews, and Kim Cohen present arguments around the social dynamics of food, but this time with a focus on marginalized characters in Melville's *Moby-Dick*, Harriet E. Wilson's *Our Nig*, and Catherine Owen's cookbook novels. Lorinda B. Cohoon, Cree LeFavour, and Monika Elbert discuss how nineteenth-century writers in their representation of food and etiquette comment on the Americanness or foreignness of their characters and as such have the play to assert their allegiance to one nationality over another. For example, Monika Elbert focuses on Nathaniel Hawthorne's critique of American and British diets, recovering Hawthorne's telling ambivalence towards both nations' cultural identities. Finally, Hildegard Hoeller, Yvonne Elizabeth Pelletier, Elizabeth Andrews, and Lance Rubin examine representations of hunger in nineteenth-century literature, noticing an abstinence from American excess countered with an alluring side of food repression. These essays form a vivid cultural history, as well as a literary argument, about an essential everyday mode of consumption that links landscape and labour with cultural practices (social rituals, bodily regimes, prohibitions) and in turn with food's more abstract meanings (appetite's relation to aesthetics, pleasure, and replenishment).

The field of transatlantic literary studies will welcome Tim Fulford and Kevin Hutchings's edited collection, *Native Americans and Anglo-American Culture 1750–1850*. The essays in this collection explore the Atlantic world between 1750 and 1850, examining the lives of Britons, Native Americans, and Anglo-Americans in that period. As a whole the collection argues that the interconnections between these nationalities shaped the canonical and non-canonical literature of the nineteenth century. Genuinely interdisciplinary in approach, its chapters scrutinize literary texts, travel accounts, traders' memoirs, historical documents, captivity narratives, autobiographies, newspaper articles, and visual arts. The divergent essays share a common objective: to explore the transatlantic literary culture that thrived against a backdrop of colonial unrest in North America. The collection focuses on the period from 1750 to 1850 because Britain's war with France in America reshaped the social and cultural landscape on both sides of the Atlantic, which augmented the relationships between Native Americans, Britons, and Anglo-Americans. Fulford and Hutchings point out that by the 1840s, after the war of 1812 had heightened white power in North America, most Indian nations east of the Mississippi had been forced into exile. This collection raises interesting questions about cultural hybridity and its impact on identity and agency, and acknowledges the controversy of hybridity as a concept: Mohawk scholar Taiaiake Alfred is quick to point out that this can often mask the negation of difference, 'cultural pollution' leading to 'cultural blanks'. Given this shrewd qualification, questions of cultural purity as well as hybridity are critically engaged. Fulford and Hutchings argue that distinct academic categories cannot do justice to the complexities of this undertaking, and their volume transcends institutional boundaries. A helpful summary of developments in Romantic studies, American and Canadian literary studies and Native American studies is offered, yet the editors do not locate their volume in the interdisciplinary home of transatlantic literary studies which aims to explore hybridity and postcolonial theory and transcend national and genre boundaries. The collection sits most obviously in this emergent zone of scholarly enquiry, but difficulty placing it attests only to merits of scope, rigour, and originality.

Eric Gardner's *Unexpected Places: Nineteenth-Century African American Literature*, is a welcome and timely addition to the exploration of the writings of early African Americans, and recovers the work of unknown writers and editors, as well as revisiting the writings of William Wells Brown, Hannah Crafts, and Maria Stewart. *Unexpected Places* offers critical considerations of those it argues are significant literary figures, including William Jay Greenly, Jennie Carter, Lizzie Hunt, and Polly Wash. The books examines them through their physical locations, leading to an investigation of the way region is linked to genre, publication circumstances, ideologies, authorship, and mobility. Chapter 1, 'Gateways and Borders', bases itself in St Louis during the 1840s and 1850s. One of Garner's sources, the records of the St Louis Circuit Court, is where over 300 cases brought by enslaved African Americans fighting for their freedom are documented. One such case file is that of Polly Wash. While the story is shaped by her experiences, and the depositions of those involved in the case, not one word is, of course, authored by Polly Wash herself, and the mark she made in place of a signature appears to confirm that she was illiterate. Nevertheless, it was her story and the recognition of her freedom that became part of the story of St Louis itself. The subsequent chapter is located in Indiana, in the years between 1857 and 1862. It considers the writings of the Reverend Elisha Weaver, a black man, in the local periodical, the *Repository of Religion and Literature and of Science and Art*, as well as Greenly's collection of plays, *The Three Drunkards* [1858], which may well be the first such collection by a black author. The third chapter looks to northern California and beyond, during the postbellum era, and writers such as William H. Newby, who penned a column for *Frederick Douglass's Paper* under the playful pseudonym of 'Nubia'. Another major figure in California's black literary world was Jennie Carter, who wrote extensively for the *Elevator*, her earliest columns focusing on advancing domestic principles. 'Beyond Philadelphia' is the title of the fourth chapter in this study, referencing one of the northern black women who travelled south to teach newly freed African Americans, Sarah Louise Daffin, and her contributions to the black press, principally the *Christian Recorder*. A contemporary, Jane Elizabeth Hart, also published letters and poems in this journal. Gardner argues that Hart's rhetorical skill, awareness of current events, and her gender make her especially interesting for scholars of nineteenth-century African American writings, mainly because her sense that the national was the local, and vice versa, shaped all her contributions. Gardner's epilogue centres on Hannah Crafts. Assumed to be writing under a pseudonym, Crafts recounts a rich first-person story of a young woman's experience of slavery, *The Bondwoman's Narrative* [2002]. Poignantly, the main character's developing sense of personal autonomy is represented through her increasing mobility, and her eventual escape places her in a particularly unexpected location, rural New Jersey. Ultimately, the excellent notes and bibliography are just the beginning of an exploration of under-studied, but significant, African American writers and texts.

Michael Germana's *Standards of Value: Money, Race and Literature in America*, like David Anthony's *Paper Money Men*, while distinct in terms of their outward concerns, suggest key ways in which engagement with coinage and monetary debates is fertile ground for contemporary discussions of nineteenth-century literature. Michael Germana's work begins with the intriguing proposition that rather than attempting to negate race as a category, nineteenth-century authors such as Harriet Beecher Stowe, Charles Chesnutt, Mark Twain, George Washington Cable, and Frank L. Baum reflected upon how race operated within 'a cultural economy in which signs are exchanged' and in which the subject is 'always already racialised'. This leads to the supposition that socially progressive authors from the Jacksonian era onwards sought to 'change the *value* of racial difference within that economy' through racial passing or play. In effect, Germana follows Michaels in positing that competing economic theories concerning the necessity, or otherwise, of a hard currency based on specie created a valence in society's parallel conceptions of the value of racial purity. In what is the strongest chapter of the book, 'Jacksonian Abolitionism: Money, Minstrelsy and *Uncle Tom's Cabin*', the author offers a brilliant example of the ways in which debates in national policy can be brought to bear on the reading of texts. Taking as a background Andrew Jackson's 'war' against the Second Bank of the United States, Germana provides a fascinating account of the strategic engagements of blackface minstrelsy with white working-class fears over wage slavery and the move from a 'hard currency' to a paper-based, market-oriented, speculative economy. Germana then provides a reading of *Uncle Tom's Cabin* [1852] that focuses upon the metaphorical connections drawn between Tom and the 'silver dollar' he carries around his neck, showing how Stowe inverts white racism by transforming Tom into 'the minstrel guise to self-reflexively reveal his role as both blackface Christ and Jacksonian hard money martyr'. His outward blackness thereby becomes a sign of his essential worth, connecting ideas of the importance of value in coinage to the changing value of race. In so doing, Germana suggests, Stowe generates a connection between an anti-slavery position and fears over wage slavery that were increasingly seen as connected to capitalist paper-money policy, in order to appeal to a potential white, working-class readership more often drawn to the Democratic Party's slavery advocacy. Towards the end of the book Germana begins to question the limits of the strategic essentialism he finds useful in reading Stowe's, Cable's, and Chesnutt's work. Indeed, the post-structuralist interest in performativity that motivates his early readings serves a discussion of race in the mid- to late nineteenth century extremely well. Where Germana extends beyond the nineteenth century he seems to be on less certain ground, as he is often unable to successfully account for writers of the Harlem Renaissance who seemed to favour genuinely essentialist conceptions of racial difference. It is interesting that while the author is fascinated by the interconnected ideologies of money and race, he finds little space for a discussion of class. At times, the desire to produce a generalized critique of race and money overwhelms the subject. Indeed, Germana privileges racial identity to the point of neglecting intersectionalist debates that would connect religion, class, and gender more holistically. Even as he critiques it, racial identity is premiumized. It inadvertently becomes the gold standard of his text.

A. Robert Lee's collection of essays, *Gothic to Multicultural: Idioms of Imagining in American Literary Fiction*, is a similar undertaking in that it begins with the Gothic in nineteenth-century American literature and opens up an expansive study across twentieth-century texts in multiple literary genres. Indeed, its breadth feels almost intimidating, gathering as it does twenty-three of Lee's essays from four decades in which he robustly evokes 'a coalescing thread' of an imagined American geography. Early essays in the collection deal with Charles Brockden Brown, James Fenimore Cooper, and Edgar Allan Poe. As with Michaud's book, reviewed below, the revolutionary era becomes the informing context of Gothic fiction: Brown's work is set in Independence-era Pennsylvania and in Cooper's first American novel *The Spy* [1821] 'War and Peace vie ambiguously'. In sum, this is nothing less than a tour de force of American literature, broad yet detailed, rich and incisive, establishing intellectual maps across the Gothic-national imaginary while continuously making close readings that encompass the might of Fitzgerald, Faulkner, and Hemmingway as well as less canonical zones of literary culture such as Native American fiction and the contemporary African American novel.

Alan Marshall's *American Experimental Poetry and Democratic Thought* stretches from nineteenth-century poetry through the twentieth century, and scholars and students of nineteenth-century American literature will be interested in the chapters on Whitman and Emily Dickinson in particular. The book argues that the persistent traditions of American experimental poetry, beginning with Walt Whitman, are politically motivated. Marshall claims that twenty-five years of literary criticism have been interested in the formal achievements of experimental poetry and its history, and that now it is time to turn to the democratic principle behind it. However, the political, for Marshall, has to be distinguished from the merely ideological, and the book draws on the work of political philosopher Hannah Arendt. Poetry is studied in parallel to the political philosophy of a series of 'thinkers' in a study of 'visionary history'. Marshall adopts the term 'experimental' with more than a nod to Emerson, Dickinson, and Thoreau, who all used the label to identify their own poetic undertakings, signalling the freeing of verse and the liberation of poetic meaning in a spirit of democratic enactment—rather than an elusive formalism as so often assumed of Dickinson and later modernists.

The striking resurgence of the Gothic continued in 2009 with Marilyn Michaud's *Republicanism and the American Gothic*, a comparative transatlantic study that sees the American Gothic as emerging directly from the republican tradition of the British Enlightenment. For Michaud, the revolutionary fears of deterioration and depravity translate fluently onto the American landscape. The usual psychological readings of the Gothic are replaced in this study by an exploration of republicanism in the late eighteenth century, setting up the terms for a reading of these continued fears in Cold War America in the mid-twentieth century. The juxtaposition of the late eighteenth century with the early postwar decades of the twentieth century, suggestively grouping the years 1780–1800 and 1950–70, produces a plausible recontextualization of Gothic literature. Tracing the historical development of what is termed the republican paradigm, Michaud presents both postwar moments in American history as periods when questions of national identity and social stability were most pressing. The threat to liberty by 'external treachery and internal decay' characteristic of both eras reflected the persistence of a discourse of classical republicanism and its important role in the articulation of cultural anxieties. Moreover, these parallel moments were at once decisively progressive historical openings and also marked by crisis and reactionary zeal. Michaud's book is a refreshing and valuable contribution to a field of intensifying scholarly interest, particularly in relation to the political contours of vampirism, and the chapters on the eighteenth century's violent encounter with democracy will be of interest to students and scholars of early America as well as those interested in the emergence of Gothic literature.

Boys at Home: Discipline, Masculinity, and 'The Boy-Problem' in Nineteenth-Century American Literature by Ken Parille examines work by male and female authors during the period 1830–1885. Whereas most studies of nineteenth-century boyhood have been concerned with postbellum male novelists, Parille's work broadens the scope to include a reading of Louisa May Alcott's *Little Women* in this study of boys, boyhood, and masculinity. *Boys at Home* is structured around five pedagogical modes: play-adventure, corporal punishment, sympathy, shame, and reading. Chapter 1 argues that scenes of play in boys' novels mimic domestic values. Chapter 2 discusses debates about corporeal punishment as a cultural source of ideas around gender difference. The third chapter is concerned with mother–daughter and mother–son bonds in fiction, with chapter 4 turning to *Little Women* to explore cultural narratives about what it means to 'be a man'. The last chapter explores the effect that narratives (fictional, historical, and biographical) had on the young man's sense of himself and his masculinity. The book contributes valuably to our knowledge of masculinity in the period, and therefore to the growing body of critical work being done on masculinity in general, while also reorienting interpretation of a central literary text of the period.

Finn Pollard's *The Literary Quest for an American National Character* concerns the desire for pre- and post-revolutionary writers to construct a national character in literature that reflected the conditions of the new American experience. The notion that the American Revolution conferred upon the American people a distinct national character has been so much out of vogue in recent years that the presence of Pollard's book is either a timely reinvigoration of an under-represented concern or a rather conservative restatement of first principles. The author navigates this territory by relying less on the idiom of literary studies to illuminate the works of Franklin,

Crevecoeur, Brackenridge, Irving, and Cooper than on the techniques of documentary history. Indeed, Pollard 'hopes to persuade the reader that a quest for and different definitions of national character existed, but offers documentary evidence, rather than imposing a theoretic framework'. However, the lack of this theoretical framework produces a weakness in the work. In Pollard's reading, what seems to connect these writers is how their texts question the political establishment, especially the Jeffersonian and Monrovian sense of 'rising glory', and are concerned with debates over American identity. Often the texts are used as 'evidence' that conflicts existed over national character, without sufficient acknowledgement of how they function as literature. This is most apparent in the manner in which Franklin's memoirs are treated as possessing equivalent value as historical documents as fictional works such as Irving's satires of New York democracy. Considerable time is given here to the biographical details of the authors' lives, much of which is illuminating. It is in tracing the strategic political engagements of these various writers (Franklin with the British empire, Brackenridge with the bloodthirsty world of western Pennsylvania campaigning, and Cooper with Indian land claims) that the author makes the most valuable contribution to scholarship. In terms of literary analysis of style and theme, Pollard is on his surest footing with the fiction authors whose critical lineage is the most established. The chapters on Washington Irving's *A History of New York* and Fenimore Cooper's early work provide a valuable complement to the more overtly literary and theoretic work of other critics.

Susan Zieger's *Inventing the Addict* does not contemplate the lives of writers who are addicted, but is, rather, a compelling and wide-ranging investigation into drugs, race, and sexuality as they are represented in nineteenth-century American writings. An important book for Americanists, the theme of addiction throughout the century examines a number of literary and cultural materials, including canonical novels, such as Harriet Beecher Stowe's *Uncle Tom's Cabin* [1852], and the writings of former slave Frederick Douglass. This reference to slavery is key to the manner in which the first section of this book, 'Travel, Exile, and Self-Enslavement', explores and compares the theme of addiction to that of chattel slavery. The intemperance of slave owners in Douglass's writings is steeped in the irony that the master cannot master himself. Douglass extends his references to addiction to include that of tobacco; he speaks of the way in which tobacco and rage combine to deform the body and mind of a slave-owner. This, however, is unusual, and a sign of a slaver's vicious and coarsened sensibility was more generally linked to alcohol. Stowe's slave-master, Simon Legree, who symbolizes habitual drinking, is especially cruel and also attempts to use brandy to manage his sexual coercion of Cassy and Emmeline. Here, temperance is positioned, principally, as a condition of white masculinity. The insidiousness of drunkenness and chattel slavery emerges in Legree's frenzied bouts of drinking and violence, the dysfunctional plantation, and his eventual death, in delirium tremens. Both Douglass and Stowe also contemplate the power of alcohol to subdue, and further enslave, the slaves themselves, by giving them occasional access to rum, believed to make them more agreeable to their state. Certainly, temperance ideals surrounded and helped define the abolitionist theme and Stowe was to return to the subject of temperance in two of her later novels, *My Wife and I* [1871] and *We and Our Neighbours* [1875]. However, in the postbellum era the links with slavery and plantations were no longer foregrounded; rather, addiction came to be seen as a disease. This allowed for the creation of more sympathetic characters and opened new fictional possibilities for its portrayal. Zieger expands these ideas to investigate the growing addiction, during the 1870s and 1880s, to morphine and the use of the hypodermic needle. She follows this, in Part II, 'Disease, Desire, and Defect', with a chapter entitled 'Needling Desires', in which Maria Weed's *A Voice in the Wilderness* [1895], published in the United States, depicts a woman, Helen Matthews, who becomes addicted to morphine. This text moves from the stereotypical addict as male, and investigates female addiction, albeit still representative of male abuse of power. Helen's addiction is, after all, the result of a male doctor's treatment of her, following her experience of a train wreck. Moreover, the addiction is conceived here as erotic, symbolizing female longing and desire. In *Inventing the Addict* the author therefore demonstrates how the addict became a figure of both disease and desire, developing from earlier images of vicious slave-masters and drunkards. The merging of ideas and themes in both literary and non-literary works offers powerful representations of the social and cultural experiences of the period, and excellent notes supplement this fascinating study.

In *On The Cusp: Stephen Crane, George Bellows, and Modernism*, John Fagg shows how these two master practitioners of different art forms (the literary sketch and genre painting respectively) can be linked through their use of a similar set of technical devices, specifically cliché, aphorism, frame, and ellipsis. Through intricate close reading of Crane's language and Bellow's composition, Fagg suggests that these artists sought to consciously position their work between older codes of nineteenth-century realism and an emergent aesthetic modernism. The interdisciplinary nature of the book works particularly well in highlighting 'the complex social practices of "urban visuality"' that were developing in the late nineteenth and early twentieth centuries in response to a period of rapid change and development in the material landscape. For example, by suggesting in chapter 6 that both Crane and Bellows used cliché drawn from older folk stories and forms of genre painting within their depictions of the modern city to explore 'the language of mass culture', Fagg avoids the pitfall of assuming that modernism developed a unique and utterly original aesthetic vocabulary in isolation from the experience of mass culture in urban space. Instead, Fagg suggests that modernist abstraction was one of a range of possible means for the representation of urban experience. Fagg's reading of Bellows's work alongside the Ashcan School of John Sloan and others provides an interesting account of the painters' 'move away from the Ashcan emphasis on social observation and evidence of local knowledge' seen in their interest in slum life, and towards 'compositions made up of more solid, heavily worked planes'. This logic of more 'detached and withdrawn' painting has parallels with Crane's work, which, in later years, moved away from the formal conventions of the city sketch and urban anecdote towards the 'scientific and pseudo-scientific discourse of sociology and anthropology' in works such as

The Open Boat [1897]. In chapter 5, Fagg's reading of Crane's use of aphorism, recalling Emerson, while looking forward to modernists like Pound and Eliot, is excellent and provides an especially valuable addition to Crane scholarship that locates him at the important, and seldom explored, bridge between realism and modernism. Overall *On the Cusp* is an enlightening work that manages to balance equally work across two disparate disciplines with grace. Fagg manages to use the language of painting to enhance readings of Crane, while also suggesting a way in which devices normally associated with literature, such as aphorism, might usefully be brought to bear on art criticism. In addition, the author's knowledge of the culture of late nineteenth- and early twentieth-century New York is rich and detailed, suggesting this work would be of interest to specialists and general readers alike.

Domhnall Mitchell and Maria Stuart, editors of *The International Reception of Emily Dickinson*, offer a response to Dickinson's 'This is my letter to the World' (441) by exploring the responses her writings evoked outside North America. The collection begins with Sabine Sielke's '"The Mind Alone?": Reading Emily Dickinson in Germany, Austria and Switzerland'. She ponders what Dickinson's vision offers to a German reader, exploring a number of critical theories, and identifying her unique voice as one that speaks to a German-reading public of what they most appreciate, single-mindedness and disregard of traditions of writing, as well as of wisdom. Chapter 2, David Palmieri's '*La Hurleuse discrète*: Emily Dickinson in Francophone Europe and North America', discusses the manner in which Dickinson's artistic presence grew in France and Quebec over the last decades of the twentieth century, in which her poetry speaks disturbing truths, while the following chapter, 'Emily Dickinson in the Low Countries', by Marian de Vooght, observes a much earlier interest in the poet, dating from an essay on the art of Emily Dickinson by Simon Vestdijk, published in 1933 in the journal *Forum*. The impact of this essay, and Vestdijk's subsequent translations of some of her poems, was impressive, and a lively interest in her work as a source of wisdom grew apace. Chapter 4, 'Emily Dickinson in Norway', by Mitchell, offers amusing comments by Dickinson of her view of Norway; she speaks of it, in a letter to a friend, as comparable to the month of November, and of a snowy January as 'Norwegian Weather'" Clearly, Norway was, for Dickinson, a metaphor for cold and winter. So how did Norway see Dickinson? Throughout the process of her Norwegian reception there was a fascination with her biography; the poetry, as Mitchell asserts, was a more difficult journey, which has only just begun. The subsequent essay, Lennart Nyberg's '"I Dwell in Possibility": The Reception of Emily Dickinson in Sweden', records the initial site of her emergence in the writings of the critic and essayist Klara Johanson, published in 1916. Nyberg argues that the trajectory of her reception in Sweden has developed over the century into a role of what is possible, especially for female recipients of her work. The sixth chapter, by Ana Luisa Amaral and Marinela Freitas, 'Meteors, Prodigies, Sorcerers: Emily Dickinson in Portugal', cites the poet and novelist Jorge de Sena as the means by which Dickinson was to meet her Portuguese public. His important volume of translations, *80 Poemas de Emily Dickinson*, was published posthumously as late as 1979. The following chapter, 'Emily Dickinson in

Brazil', by Carlos Daghlian, records a growing engagement with Dickinson's poetry, and the various translations, over the decades, concluding that the development of Dickinson scholarship predicts a promising future. In chapter 8, 'Called Back: Emily Dickinson in Hebrew', Lilach Lachman points out that, since her first book-length translation into Hebrew in 1965, Dickinson has been encountered by three generations, each with a distinct perception of the poet and her work. Different images emerge, from a Romantic, to a reclusive lover, to a revolutionary sceptic. As the struggle to translate her original and iconoclastic voice into an authentically Hebrew one continues, so does a profound growth in academic and artistic interest. Chapter 9, Masako Takeda's 'Dickinson in Japan', strikes me as a particularly complex task, yet its roots may be traced to the visit of the astronomer and Amherst college professor David Todd to Japan, to observe the solar eclipse of 1896. He was accompanied by his wife Mabel, an early editor of Dickinson's poetry. After such an early introduction to Dickinson's poems, interest slowly developed until, in 1941, Takeshi Saito, a respected Japanese scholar, acknowledged Dickinson as the greatest American woman poet, in his influential history of American literature. As a result, Dickinson's reception in Japan has progressed, and continues to do so, with increasing energy. The subsequent chapter contemplates 'Dickinson in the Ukraine: Slavic Traditions and New Perspectives', by Anna Chesnokova, who records that it was as late as the 1990s that Dickinson's poems began to appear in libraries and bookshops; prior to that Dickinson scholars struggled to obtain her writings and literary critiques of her work. Modern technology has changed all this, and young Ukrainian readers explore Dickinson's work through internet forums. Although the poet's position within the culture may seem relatively modest, a growing body of translation and an active interest amongst students point forward to an optimistic future. Maria Stuart's 'Dickinson in England and Ireland' reminds us that cultural transplantation is itself a form of translation. The sheer scale of the critical reception of Dickinson's poetry in England has been amazing, and her position as a superior American poet has been consolidated over the years. Meanwhile, the earliest examples of the poet's presence in Ireland can be found in the library of Trinity College, dating from 1891 onwards. Yet there seems little evidence of her influence upon Irish writers and critics. Although some interest can be traced in the years following the Second World War, it was not until the closing decades of the century that her work achieved the popular recognition she so richly deserved. The final essay, '"Into Van Diemen's Land": Emily Dickinson in Australia', by Joan Kirkby, also records early copies of Dickinson's work in libraries and educational establishments, and her work achieved inclusion in examination papers from the 1970s. Critical reception was somewhat sporadic, although a number of poets have made explicit references to Dickinson in their work since the 1960s. The contributors to this body of work explore the variety of impacts the New England poet and her work have had outside her native country and, in doing so, chart her influence, appropriation, and appreciation over more than a century, offering new insights and fresh perspectives.

First We Read, Then We Write: Emerson on the Creative Process is Robert D. Richardson's new book. Richardson is the pre-eminent Emerson biographer, and as such offers a distinctly insightful view of Emerson's approach to writing and specifically its imaginative genesis. Crucially, Richardson knows Emerson—the man and the life—not just Emerson's work. Thus Emerson's insistence that he was above all a *poet* (a fact regularly overlooked in Emerson scholarship) is taken seriously here. To read Emerson as a poet and not merely an inconsistent essayist is to glean much more from his oeuvre than is typically permitted. For scholars of Emerson, the extensive work Richardson has undertaken with his journals and marginalia will be of great interest, recovering a treasury of Emersonian insight into other writers (particularly the British Romantic poets), tumultuous feelings about the Church, and magnified grief at the loss of his first wife. Above all, Richardson highlights what others seem to miss when consulting the journals: the great detail and unconventional advice on how to write—on compositional practice and the beginnings of creative expression. Emerson's highly developed aphoristic habit ('the way to write is to throw your body at the mark when your arrows are spent') may perhaps offer little practical guidance to students of creative writing, but the book's original triumph is to cast Emerson as a theorist of literary aesthetics and poetic judgement. Richardson returns Emerson's notes on writing to their historical and biographical context while opening up his own writing to fresh readings. Students and scholars of Emerson will also learn more about the writer's habits of literary consumption, as details of Emerson's library provide an ongoing narrative of their own. Moving interestingly between literary-critical territory and the realm of creative practice, the book seeks to advise readers who are themselves writers, while describing Emerson's reading and giving new attention to the well-known essays.

Charles Crow's suggestion (in *History of the American Gothic*, reviewed above) that a daguerreotype of Poe came to represent the image of the *poète maudit*, is echoed in what might be seen as a complementary study of Poe as a writer of the Gothic, Kevin J. Hayes's *Edgar Allan Poe*. Several black and white photographs and line drawings illustrate this exploration of Poe's life and work, and Hayes notes the influence Poe was to have on Continental writers, including Daniel Baudelaire, Guy de Maupassant, and Jules Verne. Hayes begins his study by focusing on Poe's competitive and argumentative spirit, before exploring the roots of his temperament in his troubled and desolate childhood. This is followed by an examination of Poe's obsession with the terrifying beauty of the dying woman. References to letters help to flesh out Poe's responses to other writers and editors, including those to James R. Lowell and Sarah J. Hale. The author also explores a number of Poe's most famous short stories, including 'The Masque of the Red Death' [1842], a narrative powerful in its visual imagery and symbolic resonance. This study also contemplates the poverty in which Poe lived for most of his life; in spite of the fact that 1844 was one of his most productive years, during which 'The Raven' was written, Poe's labour could never guarantee sufficient income. His fascination with death, which runs through his work, seems especially acute in his writings during this year, perhaps reflecting the failing health of his wife Virginia. Poe's subsequent relationship with Frances Osgood is discussed, as well as the ensuing gossip, prior to his wife's finally succumbing to tuberculosis in January 1847. Poe wrote little during this year, save for one masterful poem, 'Ulalume'. Another woman, the poet Sarah Helen Whitman, was to enter Poe's life at this time, and he proposed marriage. Whitman was indecisive and Poe equally confused by strong feelings he had for a married woman, Annie Richmond. Richmond was wise enough to maintain the relationship on a platonic basis and advised him to marry Whitman. In a delusional state, Poe took a near-fatal dose of opium; Whitman now made up her mind to refuse Poe, and he began drinking heavily. When he returned to Whitman's house, drunk and despairing, she was induced to change her mind, and agreed to marry him, so long as he gave up drinking. This made Poe turn to the bottle even more desperately, and they eventually parted. Such destructive behaviour by Poe was to be repeated in 1849 with his childhood sweetheart, Elmira Royster Shelton. Ultimately, Poe went on a drinking binge from which he would never recover, dying on 7 October 1849. Extensive references to magazine and journal articles of the period, as well as to contemporary literary criticism, complete this study, which may perhaps best be seen as a potted version of his life rather than a detailed exploration of his literary output, but which nonetheless offers some interesting connections between the work and the life.

William B. Allen's *Rethinking Uncle Tom: The Political Philosophy of Harriet Beecher Stowe* provides an enriching experience in the field of Stowe scholarship. He divides his study into two distinct parts, Book I, 'The Ghostly Cry: *Uncle Tom's Cabin*', and Book II, 'Non-Utopian Optimism: Harriet Stowe's Evangelical Liberalism'. The first section focuses not only on her seminal text, but also on the world she wrote out of and, especially, her husband's influence upon her intellectual responses to the social, cultural, and religious anxieties of her time. Allen explores, in great detail, the characters of the novel, and discusses the subtext in a scholarly search for the meaning of equality and humanity, as it is represented in the book. A close reading of the text is often revelatory and engages thoughtfully with the many Stowe scholars whose readings inform Allen's view, as well as those with whom his perceptions are at odds. Careful notes at the close of each chapter of this great work elaborate on a range of ideas, giving opportunities for the reader to focus their research anew. Allen's many references to modern criticism are powerfully illuminating in his consideration of Stowe's text, and he celebrates the manner in which she succeeds in adapting a didactic novel into a tale of moral persuasion. Stowe, he points out, was a preacher, like her husband Calvin, and *Uncle Tom's Cabin* is a passionate, beautifully structured sermon in which events are juxtaposed so as to create a silent commentary which aims to prompt the reader to question their own beliefs. The second section commences with Stowe's 'American Campaign Abroad', which led to the publication of *Sunny Memories of Foreign Lands* [1854]. Here, the author points to Stowe's use of artifice. She begins her journey, she informs the reader, on the ship *Niagara*, and concludes her account with the image of Niagara Falls as a symbolic expression of the sublime truths concerning things American, which her book celebrates. The truth, Allen comments, is that Stowe sailed on the royal mail steamer *Canada*, a fact that would not allow Stowe to form the artistic and literary circle she wished. This foregrounds the close examination of Stowe's private letters, which make up her journal, and the way in which they are rewritten for public consumption in *Sunny Memories*. Allen also elaborates on Stowe's silences, in terms of public speaking, during the trip, and on the way in which her husband spoke for her. Although this was not unusual at the time, what was a little strange, perhaps, was the enthusiasm with which Calvin took up this role. Often contentious, and frequently repetitive, her husband's speeches are investigated through a range of newspapers and journals, some of which describe these public performances as 'tedious'. Finally, Allen embraces the Utopian dreaming of Stowe's late books, focusing particularly on *Oldtown Folks* [1869], frequently perceived as an example of New England regionalism; he argues that it is instead a richly allegorical tale. Stowe tells the reader, in her preface, that she will remain passive 'as a looking glass', an affectation which emphasized the reader's need to seek their own reflection in her reversed images. If her works were explicitly didactic, they were not merely so. The ultimate expression of her writing is a vision of an ideal. *Rethinking Uncle Tom* allows a closer engagement with the moral discourse of abolition and reform and a vision of America as capable of producing a nobility of soul, represented in Uncle Tom, who was a model for the human condition expressed in the possibility of the sublime. Such exhaustive notes as are offered, together with a detailed bibliography, help to create a tour de force that elaborates on the political and philosophical debates of the mid-nineteenth century, in its sparkling and innovative approach to the moral questions of the time.

Jack Turner's edited collection *A Political Companion to Henry David Thoreau* sheds new light on Thoreau's literary repertoire. Given that *Civil Disobedience* sits proudly at the centre of nineteenth-century political essays, it is surprising that this is the first volume devoted exclusively to Thoreau's political thought. There are sixteen essays in the collection and the opening pieces engage with classical and modern elements of democratic theory and Thoreau's democratic ideals of equality and individual liberty. The collection also serves Thoreau well by setting him apart from his literary contemporaries and in particular their political and social attitudes. Where Emerson shied away from the subject of slavery for much of his career and Whitman famously denounced abolition as a threat to the union, Thoreau's political thought is unveiled here as being staunchly anti-slavery, extending to his protest at the subjugation of Native Americans. The essay on 'Thoreau and John Brown' adds importantly to our understanding of Thoreau's thought on race and slavery. A second area where he parts company with Emerson, his common literary partner, is the adumbration of transcendental metaphysics. Susan McWilliams argues for Thoreau's distinctive concern with doubleness, or 'double(ness) trouble', in so far as Thoreau's preoccupation with the embodied mind and mindful body caused him deep unrest since he intuited that 'the outward and the inward life correspond'. McWilliams animates this philosophical concern with reference to Thoreau's journals to show us his troubled assertions that 'If I have got false teeth, I trust that I have got a false conscience.' Thoreau is thus made to stand apart from Emerson's religiosity, that radical disembodiment by means of which the self becomes 'part or parcel of God'. Later essays in the collection make philosophical comparisons between Thoreau and Rousseau, Adorno and Gandhi, which lift Thoreau out of the American literary canon and recontextualize his work within the traditions of political theory. As such, researchers working beyond the confines of nineteenth-century literature will benefit greatly from this collection.

Ted Genoways has devoted his new work on Walt Whitman to the two years when America slid into Civil War—1860–2. *Walt Whitman and the Civil War: America's Poet During the Lost Years of 1860–1862* has many strengths: scholarly precision, narrative drama, and historical documentation. Most interestingly it serves as a long-missing preface to those later, dark years, when postbellum Whitman went off the boil and sank into a personal depression mirroring the national postwar gloom. In the two 'missing' years, Genoways depicts Whitman as the poet finding his voice and morphing into the 'kosmos' with which critics would later wholly identify him. By rediscovering a concealed Whitman, one who had all but disappeared from the literary scene, Genoways fleshes out his forming attitudes to the Civil War. His silence, as it has been understood up until now, shows not a disregard for the war itself, but a troubled participation in it through unpublished letters and never-before-seen manuscripts.

Books Reviewed

Allen, William B. *Rethinking Uncle Tom: The Political Philosophy of Harriet Beecher Stowe*, Lexington. [2009] pp. xx + 462. hb £59.95 ISBN 9 7807 3912 7988, pb £24.95 ISBN 9 7807 3912 7995.

Alves, Jaime Osterman. *Fictions of Female Education in the Nineteenth Century*, Routledge. [2009] pp. xv + 187. £75 ISBN 9 7804 1599 6761.

Anthony, David. *Paper Money Men: Commerce, Manhood, and the Sensational Public Sphere in Antebellum America*. OSUP. [2009] pp. 225. $43.95 ISBN 9 7808 1421 1106.

Beck, Janet Kemper. *Creating the John Brown Legend: Emerson, Thoreau, Douglass, Child and Higginson in Defense of the Raid on Harpers Ferry*. McFarland. [2009] pp. vii + 206. pb £31.50 ISBN 9 7807 8643 3452.

Capitani, Diana N. *Truthful Pictures: Slavery Ordained by God in the Domestic Sentimental Novel of the Nineteenth-Century South*. Lexington. [2009] pp. 146. £34.95 ISBN 9 7807 3911 2328.

Crow, Charles L. *History of the American Gothic*. UWalesP. [2009] pp. 236. pb £19.99 ISBN 9 7807 0832 0440.

Elbert, Monika, and Marie Drews, eds. *Culinary Aesthetics and Practices in Nineteenth-Century American Literature*. Palgrave Macmillan. [2009] pp. viii + 267. £50 ISBN 9 7802 3061 6288.

Fagg, John. *On The Cusp: Stephen Crane, George Bellows, and Modernism*. UAlaP. [2009] pp. 280. £44.50 ISBN 9 7808 1731 6518.

Fulford, Tim, and Kevin Hutchings, eds. *Native Americans and Anglo-American Culture, 1750–1850*. CUP. [2009] pp. xi + 263. £53 ISBN 9 7805 2188 8486.

Gardner, Eric. *Unexpected Places: Nineteenth-Century African American Literature*. UPMissip. [2009] pp. 258. $50 ISBN 9 7816 0473 2832.

Genoways, Ted. *Walt Whitman and the Civil War: America's Poet During the Lost Years of 1860–1862*. UCalP. [2009] pp. vii + 210. £16.95 ISBN 9 7805 2025 9065.

Germana, Michael. *Standards of Value: Money, Race and Literature in America*. UIowaP. [2009] pp. 220. £35.50 ($39.95) ISBN 9 7815 8729 8189.

Hayes, Kevin J. *Edgar Allan Poe*. Reaktion Books. [2009] pp. 184. pb $16.95 (£10.95) ISBN 9 7818 6189 5158.

Lee, A. Robert. *Gothic to Multicultural: Idioms of Imagining in American Literary Fiction*. Rodopi. [2009] pp. 543. £87 ISBN 9 7890 4202 4991.

Marshall, Alan. *American Experimental Poetry and Democratic Thought*. OUP. [2009] pp. viii + 315. £53 ISBN 9 7801 9956 1926.

Michaud, Marilyn. *Republicanism and the American Gothic*. UWalesP. [2009] pp. 197. £75 ISBN 9 7807 0832 1461.

Mitchell, Domhnall, and Maria Stuart, eds. *The International Reception of Emily Dickinson*. Continuum. [2009] pp. x + 320. £75 ISBN 9 7808 2649 7154.

Parille, Ken. *Boys at Home: Discipline, Masculinity, and 'The Boy-Problem' in Nineteenth-Century American Literature*. UTennP. [2009] pp. x + 153. £25 ISBN 9 7815 7233 6773.

Pollard, Finn. *The Literary Quest for an American National Character*, Routledge. [2009] pp. 258. £75. ISBN 9 7804 1596 3732.

Richardson, Robert D. *First We Read, Then We Write: Emerson on the Creative Process*. UIowaP. [2009] pp. vii + 101. £17.95 ISBN 9 7815 8729 7939.

Turner, Jack. *A Political Companion to Henry David Thoreau*. UPKen. [2009] pp. ix + 483. £35.50 ISBN 9 7808 1312 4780.

Zieger, Susan. *Inventing the Addict*. UMassP. [2009] pp. 304. pb £32.96 ISBN 9 7815 5849 6804.

XVI

American Literature: The Twentieth Century

JAMES GIFFORD

This year's chapter has one section, Poetry, by James Gifford. The other sections—Fiction 1900–1945; Fiction since 1945; Drama; African American Writing; Native, Asian American, Latino/a, and General Ethnic Writing—will recommence in *YWES* 91[2012].

1. Poetry

The year 2009 continued many trends in critical study already noted in 2007 and 2008, including both reissued critical works and important critical editions, as well as a continued emphasis on the new modernist studies. ELS Editions, which has published strong monographs on Susan Howe by Stephen Collis and Gertrude Stein by Karin Cope, has added to the recent spike in critical works on Sylvia Plath. Lisa Narbeshuber's *Confessing Cultures: Politics and the Self in the Poetry of Sylvia Plath* is a well-timed critical intervention in to the continued growth of Plath scholarship in the wake of the publication of *Ariel: The Restored Edition* in its near-original form in 2004 by Frieda Hughes (HarperCollins [2004]). Narbeshuber focuses on Plath's post-1961 poetry, *Ariel* in particular, in order to argue against the received sense of Plath's poetry as confessional in contrast to W.H. Auden and the impersonality of T.S. Eliot. Narbeshuber instead contends that Plath's later works shun egocentric confessional tropes in order to develop a critique of capitalist, patriarchal culture, which is the real confession of her various facades and personas in the poems of *Ariel.* It is doubtless the case that several scholars will disagree with Narbeshuber's revision to the established confessional readings of Plath's works. The previous year saw several publications on Plath, and of those concerned with her poetry rather than her prose, archival and editorial matters dominated; however, implicit in these works is a sense of immediacy between the author and the narrative voice in Plath's poetry. Bethany Hicok's *Degrees of Freedom: American Women Poets and the Women's College, 1905–1955* (reviewed in *YWES* 89[2010]), contains a

The Year's Work in English Studies, Volume 90 (2011)
doi:10.1093/ywes/mar019

strong chapter on Plath that retains the established focus on biographical alignment of the poetic works and the restoration of her own vision for *Ariel* prior to Hughes's editorship. Hicok's focus on the educational background that led to Plath's works is her major innovation. Unfortunately, Narbeshuber's work is too close in time to respond to Hicok or to Anita Helle's edited collection, *The Unraveling Archive: Essays on Sylvia Plath* (reviewed in *YWES* 89[2010]), from the same year. Both would have given Narbeshuber more to contrast her reading against, which would have been productive. A telling revision to preceding scholarship appears in Narbeshuber's reading of Plath's bee poems: 'The bee poems, like most of Plath's later poetry, display her subjects' terrible condition... to map out a torturous social machinery... Plath's later work traces and challenges the reifying social conditions under which people lose their humanity, flatten into a single dimension' (p. 3). Narbeshuber's contribution is sure to arouse responses in Plath scholarship as well as fresh ways of teaching Plath in the classroom, in particular for such standard works as 'Daddy' and 'Lady Lazarus'. Scott Knickerbocker adopts a similar rejection of the 'confessional' reading paradigm for Plath and instead proposes ecopoetics as a polemical correction (*CollL* 36[2009] 1–27). Although Knickerbocker's polemic differs significantly from Narbeshuber's, their synchronous revision is poignant, as can be seen in Knickerbocker's assertions that 'As both cause and consequence of Plath's categorization as a confessional poet, the dramatic and famously tragic events of her life have also contributed to the abundance of biographically driven criticism' (p. 1), and 'Another significant result of emphasizing Plath's interiority and confessional mode is that many critics overlook and even flatly deny her connection to the outside world' (p. 2). Both comments from Knickerbocker would be as at home in Narbeshuber's book as they are in his article, and Plath scholarship will certainly respond.

A new collection of works by Audre Lorde is a timely release from Oxford University Press in its series Transgressing Boundaries: Studies in Black Politics and Black Communities. Rudolph P. Byrd, Johnnetta Betsch Cole, and Beverly Guy-Sheftall edited *I Am Your Sister: Collected and Unpublished Writings of Audre Lorde*, which also includes critical chapters on Lorde by each of the three editors (with Byrd's functioning as the introduction) as well as Alice Walker, bell hooks, and Gloria I. Joseph. Byrd's chapter, which opens the volume, does the most to contextualize Lorde critically and to develop a critical vision based on archival study of her works, from which several of the book's chapters were selected. The volume also includes Lorde's critical comments in her journal, in which she reflects on her poetic production while fighting cancer. There is also a strong chapter on Pat Parker's poetic works, as well as several short chapters, such as 'Poetry Makes Something Happen', in which she reflects on the function and social relevance of poetic practices and teaching. A critical discussion of the role of the archive, akin to what appeared the previous year in Helle's *The Unraveling Archive*, would have been very welcome. The different purposes of the two collections is clear, yet a broader discussion of the state of the Lorde archives, editorial practices in her works, and the recuperative potential of the archive for silenced or marginalized voices would have given this collection on Lorde a greater appeal to those following the current rush in archival interests in twentieth-century American poetry in general. The collection also follows on the biography of Lorde by Alexis DeVeaux, *Warrior Poet: A Biography of Audre Lorde*, which has garnered significant critical praise (Norton [2004]). A number of unseen book chapters concerned Lorde also appeared in 2009, primarily from smaller publishing houses, including Kirsten Ortega's 'Claiming the "House of Difference": New York as Home Space in the Life Narratives of Audre Lorde and Diane di Prima' (in Sabrina Fuchs-Abrams, ed., *Literature of New York*, CambridgeSP [2009] pp. 113–31); Stephanie Li's 'Becoming her Mother's Mother: Recreating Home and the Self in Audre Lorde's *Zami: A New Spelling of My Name*' (in Verena Theile and Marie Drews, eds., *Reclaiming Home, Remembering Motherhood, Rewriting History: African American and Afro-Caribbean Women's Literature in the Twentieth Century*, CambridgeSP [2009] pp. 139–63); and Jennifer Browdy de Hernandez's '"Mother" as a Verb: The Erotic, Audre Lorde, and Female Genital Mutilation' (in Tobe Levin and Augustine H. Asaah, eds., *Empathy and Rage: Female Genital Mutilation in African Literature*, Ayebia Clarke [2009] pp. 64–74). To see this increase in scholarship following on DeVeaux's 2004 biography is surely no coincidence and indicates further work to come, which already appears to be true for 2010, even at this early date.

Critical work on George Oppen has also continued to develop significantly in 2009. I first noted this continuing development of critical works in the opening page of 2007's reviews, and this trend has continued through 2008 and 2009. Previous years have included reviews of Lyn Graham Barzilai's *George Oppen: A Critical Study* (McFarland [2006]), which was followed by Peter Nicholls's major work *George Oppen and the Fate of Modernism* (OUP [2007]) and Stephen Cope's critical edition of Oppen's *Selected Prose, Daybooks, and Papers* (UCalP [2007]). John Lowney's *History, Memory, and the Literary Left: Modern American Poetry, 1935–1968* (UIowaP [2006]) also included a chapter on Oppen to conclude the volume, perhaps the most engaging chapter of the book. In 2008 two other works kept Oppen scholarship in prominence: G. Matthew Jenkins's *Poetic Obligation: Ethics in Experimental American Poetry after 1945* (UIowaP) included a chapter dedicated to Oppen, as did Bonnie Costello in *Planets on Tables: Poetry, Still Life, and the Turning World* (CornUP). This stunning critical output in a three-year period is extended by Steve Shoemaker's 2009 edited collection from the University of Alabama Press, *Thinking Poetics: Essays on George Oppen*, which combines new materials and excerpts from previous publications. The included authors come as no surprise given the previous productions. Peter Nicholls contributes a chapter on 'Oppen's Heidegger' extracted from his previous book, which explored Oppen's engagement with Heidegger and Hegel extensively, in particular with regard to ontology, as most reviewers have noted. Michael Davidson's excerpt from his 1988 *Postmodern Genres* is also effective. Since nearly all chapters are taken from previously published materials, the effect is to create a lineage or genealogy of Oppen criticism, which Shoemaker does effectively as an editor. In this regard, the book will be most useful for students and for the classroom as well as a convenient reference for scholars, through most would prefer to use the full text of the original publications rather than their excerpted form here. Of the five newly written chapters, including the preface and introduction, Kristin Prevallet's 'One Among Rubble: George Oppen and World War II' is useful for tying Oppen to the critical scholarship on war poetry in the 1940s, such as Paul Fussell (one almost expects to find Bernard Bergonzi here). Shoemaker's preface to the volume is also helpful for giving a biographical precis; however, it is impossible not to note that fully three of the five newly composed contributions to the book are penned by the collection's editor, Steve Shoemaker, including a divided preface and introduction. Tom Fisher's article in *Arizona Quarterly*, 'A Political Poetics: George Oppen and the Essential Life of the Poem', would have made a natural political extension of the works in Shoemaker's collection. Fisher turns to Oppen's cessation of poetry-writing after joining the Communist Party. The article benefits from comparison to the political and ethical exegeses undertaken by Jenkins's and Lowney's chapters in 2008, and Fisher makes extended use of Nicholls's article that preceded his monograph, 'George Oppen: The New or the Avant-Garde?' (*JML* 28:iv[2005] 1–12). Fisher's political reading of Oppen's later works aligns clearly with these earlier pieces of research. Apart from this volume of Oppen scholarship, perhaps the most striking feature of the recent burst of research is its unity and interlaced references. As a critical mass for Oppen scholarship, these few years have charted a clear direction for future work and have provided the basis necessary for major pedagogical incorporations of Oppen into national and historical survey courses.

Oppen is also the main subject of Susan Bernstein's chapter 'Conference Call: Ronell, Heidegger, Oppen' in Diane Davis's collection *Reading Ronell* (pp. 49–59). Ronell's philosophical production is daunting in its complexity and scope, but Bernstein draws from Ronell's *The Telephone Book* and intriguing points of intersection between Heidegger, Oppen's 'Route', and Ronell's complex sense of reading and authorship (or 'operation'). Although the chapter is short and does not develop its discussion of Ronell as much as might be desired, the project it begins gives every impression of being extraordinarily fruitful, in particular in the context of recent Oppen scholarship and Nicholls's work.

Akin to Shoemaker's collection on Oppen, John Edgar Tidwell and Steven C. Tracy's *After Winter: The Art and Life of Sterling A. Brown*, from Oxford University Press, combines new chapters with previously published works. As a 'portable Sterling A. Brown', the book will be quite valuable, in particular for classroom use. It is also, in many respects, a companion volume to Tidwell and Mark Saunder's earlier critical edition through Oxford of Brown's works, *A Negro Looks at the South* [2007]. A very large portion of this new book is drawn from the journal *Callaloo*, which provides ten chapters, and another seven from *Black American Literature Forum* and *African American Review*. For scholars and students without ready access to these established journals, this collection is a significant resource. One hesitation arises from the dust-jacket promise of 'An updated version of the most comprehensive bibliography of Brown's published writings', which consists of Robert G. O'Meally's updates to his bibliography published in *Callaloo* (*Callaloo* 21[1998] 822–35). With this proviso noted, Steven C. Tracy's new discography does significantly extend the bibliographical scope of scholarship in his newly composed chapter for the book, '"Fear did not catch his tongue and throttle his breath": A Discography of Recordings by and Related to Sterling A. Brown' (pp. 445–8). The chronology and introduction to the book will also be of significant use to scholars of Brown's poetry and work. Tidwell and Tracy's opening suggestion in their 'Introduction: Sterling A. Brown's Odyssey into the Heart of Blackness' (pp. 3–18) that Brown's comparatively slight poetic production has limited his literary reputation and attainment of canonic status is reasoned. However, the second suggestion that 'Brown has been shunted aside by some white critics, who for racist reasons have not been exposed to his work or don't have the resources to understand his employment of the folk idiom' is not likely to garner sympathy, in particular given their immediately preceding comparison of Brown's production to such canonical figures as Ralph Ellison and Langston Hughes, as well as Brown's perennial discussion in relation to the Harlem Renaissance. Without doubt, racism is alive and well in academia and literary studies, but Tidwell and Tracy's own detailed demonstration of the difficulties of Brown's limited poetic output in comparison to many of his contemporaries is hardly a straw man to this argument. Their subsequent precis of Brown's biography and interracial position of liminality in American culture and society is cogent and helpful for the reader using the book as an introduction to Brown's works. Moreover, by continually shifting their own critical vision between academia and popular culture that derives from folk idioms, they offer proof of Brown's significant influence on American literary studies and their own critical paradigms. Deborah E. McDowell's lengthy review article on Tidwell's very fine previous work through Oxford, 'Turning Southward: Sons Journeying Home' (*AML* 21[2009] 902–22), shows what could have been accomplished in this new work had more new critical perspectives been integrated.

The trade reissue of Leigh Anne Duck's *The Nation's Region: Southern Modernism, Segregation, and U.S. Nationalism* largely pursues prose works by Zora Neale Hurston, Erskine Caldwell, and William Faulkner, yet integrates several useful linkages to the likes of Sterling Brown, Langston Hughes, and several of the New Critics. Although Duck's main critical perspective is shaped by theories of American exceptionalism and the attempt to present a new history from the perspective of the oppressed, in many ways akin to Howard Zinn's *A People's History of the United States*, her perspective implicitly argues for a rereading of American modernism through the perspective of Southern writers. Although Ezra Pound figures only in passing, as do T.S. Eliot, John Crowe Ransom, and Cleanth Brookes, an expansion of her polemic seems clear. The historical and social drive for her work is foregrounded, but it does encourage the reader to consider segregation and exceptionalism as aporetic presences in American modernism in general.

Anthony K. Webster's *Explorations in Navajo Poetry and Poetics* marks an intriguing foray into this often overlooked component of American poetic production. Webster's position as a linguistic anthropologist shapes his perspective in a manner that is likely to be unfamiliar to literary readers; however, his work here is engaging and demands critical attention. He emphasizes the social use of both Navajo and English in poetic practices in tandem with both the oral performance of written works and the poetics of linguistics' discourse analysis. As a study in ethnopoetics, Webster's book is continually drawing readers between anthropology, cultural studies, and poetics. Although the readership for his primary topic is relatively small, his method would apply well to a great number of areas, and the success he achieves in the book indicates its applicability elsewhere. His sensitivity to bilingualism or multilingualism in poetic works, especially the poetics of bilingualism, is particularly useful for those considering the use of quotation or allusion in modernist poetry or even the shifting languages in North American poetry to be found in recent Canadian works by Peter Midgley (*perhaps i should / miskien moet ek* [2010]) or Comfort Adesuwa Ero's 'Pieces of a Journey' (in Goyette, ed., *The Story That Brought Me Here: To Alberta from Everywhere*, [2008] pp. 103–11).

For this reviewer, the most prominent critical work of the year in American poetry is Julian Murphet's *Multimedia Modernism: Literature and the Anglo-American Avant-Garde*, from Cambridge. Murphet's work focuses on the fourteenth issue of *Camera Work*, the first issue of *Blast*, Gertrude Stein, Ezra Pound, Wyndham Lewis, and Louis Zukofsky, although T.S. Eliot, Pablo Picasso, and Sergei Eisenstein also figure prominently. As this list makes clear, Murphet's critical intervention bridges media studies and the new modernist studies, and it does so in several productive ways. The critical perspective develops from Frederic Jameson more than any other theorist, and the paradigm is overtly Marxist, yet Murphet ranges widely and offers resolutions to the theoretical disagreements between Raymond Williams's notion of a bidirectional influence between infrastructure and superstructure within the social formation and other media-oriented notions of technological determinism. This critical view is not new, but its development at the point of conflict between media studies and literary studies is highly productive and will appeal to a broad readership. The post-subjective and anti-humanist approach to technology during the modernist revolution in literary and artistic production leads to several critical perspectives that strongly indicate Murphet's base in media studies. The primarily Marxist interpretation of Slavoj Žižek and Murphet's emphasis on the conditions of production and technology in modernity for his examination of the new modernist studies. This leads Murphet to the compelling theses of 'a new materialism according to which not the utterly unknowable matrix of subjectivity but the perfectly objective historical destinies of the various media might serve as the primary referent of modern cultural phenomena' and 'Literature's desire to be a thing, the very story that this book tells, is a desire that leads the entire system of the arts, in the critical years 1910–14, to refashion itself as a "media system" proper, both in order to accommodate itself to the congeries of newer mechanical media, and to protect the gamut of its own practices' (pp. 4, 5). Much of Murphet's critical perspective here is derived from the notion of remediation put forward by Jay David Bolter and Richard Grusin in 2000 (*Remediation: Understanding New Media*, MITP), which entails the representation of one medium within another via hypermediacy, most often in a passive form and increasing the bound nature of the work to the culture industry. This leads to a number of highly provocative strong readings of established modernist tropes, such as 'a revision of Eliot's "Tradition" as a reflexive by-product of mechanical reproduction [that] permits us to see it as a technologically mediated, arbitrary system, every bit as rationalized and differentiated as the reviled products of the Culture Industry' (p. 29). The densely theoretical introduction from Murphet stands well on its own, as does each of the subsequent chapters, of which 'The Vorticist Membrane', on the first issue of *Blast*, is particularly fine. Scholars at work on Louis Zukofsky should also take note of the polemical reading of 'A', which is sure to lead to critical responses.

If Murphet's monograph stands out for 2009, the critical collection that cannot be overlooked is Stephen Ross's *Modernism and Theory: A Critical Debate*. Ranging across prose and verse works, and primarily focused on the relationship between modernism itself and the theoretical works that both shaped and subsequently interpreted it, the book proposes a convincing revision to the antagonism between the new modernist studies and the resistance to 'theory' often aligned with the new criticism. Charles Altieri's chapter, 'Aesthetics' (pp. 197–207), returns attention to William Carlos Williams's *Spring and All*, while C.D. Blanton's 'Invisible Times: Modernism as Ruptural Unity' (pp. 137–52) generates a fresh perspective on T.S. Eliot and Ezra Pound (and periodization) via Louis Althusser and Frederic Jameson. Bonnie Kime Scott's 'Green' (pp. 219–24) also turns attention to an ecopoetics reading of H.D. and Virginia Woolf in contrast to the Futurism and *techne* she aligns with Pound and Wyndham Lewis. Scott's contribution is certain to initiate further work, and elegantly demonstrates the rich reading opportunities available for ecopoetic examinations of the modernist canon. However, the scope of Ross's introduction, 'Theory's Modernism: Concrete Connections' (pp. 1–17), makes it the real reading treasure in the collection, even set next to the contributions from Jameson and Susan Stanford Friedman. Ross stitches together the broad grasp of the collection, from traditional figures such as Pound, Joseph Conrad, Woolf, and Eliot to Gilles Deleuze and Félix Guattari's sense of corporeality, Michel de Certeau's extension of the same in everydayness, Lacanian psychoanalysis, and a range of Marxisms from Antonio Gramsci to Jameson. Ross's chapter creates a conversation between the differing components of the book in a way that moves beyond the expected continuity constructed by an editor and forges a dialogue that would not otherwise have stood out for the reader. Once the book has been read through as a whole, it is difficult to disagree with Ross's opening contention that 'concepts today associated chiefly with Gilles Deleuze and Félix Guattari, Jacques Derrida, Henri Lefebvre, and Giorgio Agamben derive in many cases directly from encounters with D.H. Lawrence, Georges Bataille, André Breton, Virginia Woolf, and Walter Benjamin', or with 'how modernism had already begun to think about how art, philosophy, and science think; the postmodern sublime; the everyday; and messianic time well before their contemporary theoretical articulations' (p. 1). The collection is also unique for incorporating response chapters to each major contribution, such that debate and dialogue are genuinely both subject and form here.

Alan Marshall's *American Experimental Poetry and Democratic Thought* is aligned on its inside jacket with other recent Oxford books of major repute,

Giles's *American Republic*, Nicholls's *George Oppen and the Fate of Modernism*, and Rachel Potter's *Modernism and Democracy*, all of which have been reviewed in *YWES* (88[2009] and 89[2010]). This marker of status by the publisher is well founded and places Marshall in good company. Although his approach is more oriented to usability than to revising previous views, Marshall's work excels in both areas. He uses Hannah Arendt's sense of free connection and her distinction between thought and knowledge, such that 'Democratic thought then is any thought that thinks about the meaning of democracy' such that 'truth' is secondary to the consideration of 'meaning' (p. 3). This central theme allows *American Experimental Poetry and Democratic Thought* to range broadly from Walt Whitman to Ezra Pound and to link Emily Dickinson, Mina Loy, and Lorine Niedecker in a single chapter. Notably, all single-author chapters are dedicated to male writers. Marshall's discussion of George Oppen develops from Peter Nicholls's recent *George Oppen and the Fate of Modernism* (also mentioned above) and continues the development of Oppen criticism, in particular in relation to Heidegger, which has already been noted in this year's reviews. A short conclusion on Frank O'Hara leaves the reader wanting more, and it seems likely Marshall is preparing further work on this topic to develop from his previous articles in the same field. They are to be watched for.

Adam Piette's *The Literary Cold War: 1945 to Vietnam* opens with an extremely useful literature review for those working through the textual history of the Cold War and mid-century cultural studies. His writing is both clear and insightful even while moving through Derrida's sense of the impossibility of post-nuclear thinking or difficult histories. His poetic interests in the book focus on Allen Ginsberg's 'Kaddish' in contrast to Vladimir Nabokov's *Lolita* and the Distant Early Warning Line of radar stations in the Arctic, as well as images of mechanization in Sylvia Plath and Ted Hughes. The combination of Plath and Hughes, in which mechanized destruction and nuclear war lead Piette to a nuanced re-examination of the predilections of both poets, is the high point of the book. As with Narbeshuber's polemical revision of Plath scholarship to turn attention away from the confessional element, Piette's readings of her works are firmly political and contextually defined rather than relying on her personal relationships and capacity for self-expression.

Jed Rasula's *Modernism and Poetic Inspiration: The Shadow Mouth* takes up his daunting titular theme by opening with reference to Robert Graves's *The White Goddess*, a book known for its grand sweep perhaps more than for its specific content, and this bold range leads him to productive comparisons of poetics from the ancient and modern worlds, with particular attention to Pound, Oppen, Charles Olson, Rainer Maria Rilke, and Stéphane Mallarmé. Although Graves does not appear beyond this opening gesture, his subsequent notion of the Black Goddess from his lectures during his term as Professor of Poetry at Oxford would have worked very well with Rasula's subsequent explorations of the 'dark mouth' of poetic inspiration. Rasula's scope is kept manageable by his thematic unity and his close attention to the relations between form and content, as well as to the role of language and pre-discursive rhythm in poetic inspiration. Although his book focuses largely on modernism and the linkages between French and American modernist poetics in particular, Rasula's work also articulates perennial concerns for contemporary poetry and poetics, and hence serves a dual function. Balancing his insightful forays into the critical works of Walter Benjamin, Jacques Lacan, Michel Foucault, and Jacques Derrida, Rasula keeps his reader charmed by anecdotes and a narrative prose style that is remarkably clear, even in the midst of discussions of the problems of language and pre-linguistic thought via Continental philosophy after the linguistic turn. For this pleasure in reading Rasula's criticism, acknowledgement must be made of his important position as an editor and author in contemporary American poetry.

Liesl Olson has garnered significant praise for her *Modernism and the Ordinary*, in which she proposes a re-examination of the commonplace or everyday experiences in modernist literature as opposed to the transcendental, schismatic, or rupture-oriented perspectives that tend to dominate critical discourse. Her work would have benefited from a more extensive response to Bryony Randall's *Modernism, Daily Time and Everyday Life*, which was released by the University of Glasgow Press in 2008. Olson integrates acknowledging annotations, but the proximity in publication of the two books likely prevented any further responses. Olson's deft manoeuvres through the critical terrain, from Henri Lefebvre to Raymond Williams and Rita Felski, is impressive and aligns with the current pedigree of the new modernist studies. The book succeeds admirably in this regard, although its original incorporation of the term 'unselfconscious' everydayness in its dissertation form in 2004 would have allowed for a more significant discussion of Henri Bergson if revisions had been developed more. The only chapter concerned with poetry discusses Wallace Stevens's notion of 'commonplace'. Stevens scholars should take note, though the chapter is very much akin to her 'Wallace Stevens' Commonplace' (*WSJour* 29:i[2005] 106–16).

A comparison between two experimental mediums is articulated in Daniel Kane's *We Saw the Light: Conversations between the New American Cinema and Poetry*. Kane is convincing here, and develops his argument on the basis of unpublished manuscript and correspondence materials, mainly from the literary perspective, though he is adept in handling both poetry and film in his analyses. The opening of his project is a thesis that Donald Allen's 1960 anthology *The New American Poetry* was both informed by the practices of experimental film and served as the first major introduction of the poetic generation comprised of Robert Duncan, Allen Ginsberg, John Ashbery, and Frank O'Hara. This is a daunting range, but Kane manages it well, and his work on Duncan is the most engaging in the volume. While it is well known that Duncan dedicated *Bending the Bow* to the filmmaker Kenneth Anger, Duncan's further ties to Stan Brakhage and James Broughton do not necessarily garner as much attention. This leads Kane to useful reinterpretations of Duncan's 'The Torso, *Passages* 18' through Anger's *Fireworks*.

One of the most intriguing combinations of disciplines appears in Cathy Gere's *Knossos and the Prophets of Modernism* from the University of Chicago Press. Gere proposes that the archaeological excavations by Arthur Evans of the Palace of Knossos on Crete had a wide-reaching influence on critical thought and artistic production during the interbellum and post-Second

World War years. Of particular interest is her reconsideration of both H.D. and Robert Graves in relation to their interest in Evans. H.D. garners the greater share of Gere's attention, and her outline of H.D.'s relationship with Bryher is likely to spark significant response from H.D. researchers. Nonetheless, her central thesis that a cultural studies approach (likely deriving from her background primarily in science and technology studies and history of science) to the impact of Evans's excavations is startlingly effective and gives a rich new perspective on core critical concepts in both Graves's and H.D.'s literary production as well as the literary works of modernism, ranging from Joyce's *Ulysses* to H.D.'s *Trilogy*. Although a prose work, Gere's argument is perhaps best demonstrated through her brief reference to Henry Miller's *The Colossus of Maroussi*, which narrates his pre-Second World War travels in Greece, and its overlooked reliance on Evans's archaeological work on Crete: 'Miller displays a touching fidelity to Evans's political agenda With the Second World War already looming, pacifist Knossos lost its whiff of nihilistic decadence and began to look like an unambiguous paradise' (p. 153). Such a short note encapsulates the revision to charges of apolitical affiliation, decadence, and social reform that Gere undertakes with regard to each of the authors she discusses who responded to Evans. It is a striking realignment of our critical vision of each author. That Gere can manage such a dazzling project that recontextualizes H.D. and Graves while also integrating a nuanced reading of the archaeological materials and Aegean Bronze Age histories is impressive.

12 × 12: Conversations in 21st-Century Poetry and Poetics, edited by Christina Mengert and Joshua Marie Wilkinson, takes up the intriguing project of combining conversations between poets and their primary works. The titular '21st century' is provocative, but a good deal of the matter concerns works from the last decades of the twentieth century. The initial project was to invite twelve younger poets to interview twelve senior poets or influences of their choosing; however, as Wilkinson notes in the introduction, this modest aim was quickly outgrown by the scope of the interviews. Although the project was ostensibly about influence and mentorship, the conversations themselves chart a larger narrative arc of the history of influences in American poetry and poetics, with Christine Hume and Rosemarie Waldrop dwelling on Ezra Pound and William Carlos Williams (pp. 76–88), Mark Yakich and Mary Leader engaging in the archival turn to discuss the manuscript states of Emily Dickinson and T.S. Eliot's works (pp. 199–216), and Jennifer K. Dick and Laura Mullen repeatedly turning their conversation to Gertrude Stein (pp. 4–13). In each instance, the references are telling and create a genealogy. The innovative integration of poetry by each conversationalist demonstrates the direct relationship between the topics of discussion and their creative practices, which makes this volume useful to both writers and scholars.

Stephen Burt's collected essays on new poetry have been released as *Close Calls with Nonsense: Reading New Poetry*. Burt's collection unabashedly discusses pleasure and personal likes while aiming for a general readership outside academia. Nevertheless, he is an insightful reader, and the generally casual tone should not distract from his fine critical eye and capacity for prolixity on the subject of modern American verse. Each of the main chapters began as a review in the likes of *TLS* or the *London Review of Books*, and their collection here retains that original sense of audience. For scholars there are few new revelations, but the compression of the materials is useful, and each chapter is ideal for an undergraduate introduction to each poet. In many respects, the volume would be extremely useful for undergraduate lecture preparations when a model for convenient overviews and clear reading methods is needed. The chapter on Lorine Niedecker (pp. 317–28) is strong, and the sweep of the opening and closing sections of the book will appeal to critical readers, in particular given Burt's ability to range widely across a coterie of poets while constructing a cogent narrative that binds their works.

Oxford has released a trade edition of Paul Giles's *Atlantic Republic: The American Tradition in English Literature*, the third volume in his trilogy about the relations between British and American literary cultures. As many reviewers have noted, this third volume is exceptionally strong and has already significantly influenced critical work. Its appearance in an affordable edition is welcome. Yale has also produced Lawrence Rainey's latest edited collection, *Futurism: An Anthology*, co-edited with Christine Poggi and Laura Wittman, which follows on his very successful *Modernism: An Anthology* from Blackwell in 2005. The book is divided into three parts, each selected, translated, and introduced by its respective editor. Rainey's general introduction to the volume as a whole is particularly strong (pp. 1–39). The focus in each part is on the primary materials of Futurism, and hence references to American poets and Americans in general are rare, but allusions to Walt Whitman and American industry will prove useful to scholars at work on the Futurist elements of William Carlos Williams, Hart Crane, and Mina Loy.

Blackwell's new *Companion to T.S. Eliot*, edited by David Chinitz, lives up to the high expectations raised by previous volumes in the 'Companion' series. As a resource for both scholars and students the book is very strong, and stand-out contributions come from John Xiros Cooper, on Eliot's social critiques (pp. 287–97), and John Timberman Newcomb's reconsideration of Eliot's influence as an editor (pp. 399–410), in which he notes the sometimes overlooked role Eliot played not only in British modernism but also, with Pound, in shaping the public face of the likes of Oppen, Louis Zukofsky, and Marianne Moore. The collection as a whole, finely edited by Chinitz, will be a necessary reference for students.

John Worthen's *T.S. Eliot: A Short Biography* lives up to its subtitle and provides and excellent introduction to lay readers and students. However, he avoids much of the recent critical work on Eliot in an overly simplified manner. The discussions of anti-Semitism and homosexuality that have enlivened much recent critical discussion of Eliot, as evidenced in Chinitz's collection, are avoided rather than dealt with. Worthen rebukes the authors who discuss homosexual themes in Eliot's 'Columbo' verses by simply stating 'All three writers overstate their cases' and attributing the homosexual themes to a longstanding trend among male students (p. 30). Anti-Semitism receives the same quick dismissal. Nonetheless, the writing is very clear and Eliot's biography is drawn in close relation to his poetry, which has the virtue of being useful for the classroom and for studies of Eliot's milieu.

Late arrivals for 2008 include Stephen Cheeke's *Writing for Art: The Aesthetics of Ekphrasis*. Cheeke ranges from the Romantics and classical texts to several American modernist poets, W.H. Auden and Wallace Stevens in particular. His analysis of Auden's 'Musée des Beaux Arts' in relation to Pieter Brueghel's *Fall of Icarus* offers significant revisions to established interpretations of this perennially taught work, in particular by bringing it into dialogue with works by William Carlos Williams and Randall Jarrell. Given the frequency with which this poem is used in the classroom, this chapter is sure to have a very broad appeal and a great deal of use for instructors. Cheeke is also adept in his introduction at covering the range of debates concerning ekphrasis, which has enjoyed much critical attention over the past twenty years. His rereading of the critical approaches to Stevens's responses to Picasso is also deft and equally useful for scholarly and pedagogical purposes. Also from 2008 is Robert Faggen's *The Cambridge Introduction to Robert Frost*, which is both thorough and readable. Faggen's biographical precis of Frost is helpful, and his detailed close readings of specific works are sure to be an aid to both students and professors. The strength of the volume as an introduction, however, is its brief summary of critical responses to Frost, which establishes Frost's influence on his contemporary poets as well as the trends in criticism.

Books Reviewed

Burt, Stephen. *Close Calls With Nonsense: Reading New Poetry*. Graywolf. [2009] pp. 360. $19 ISBN 9 7815 5597 5210.

Byrd, Rudolph P., Johnnetta Betsch Cole, and Beverly Guy-Sheftall, eds. *I Am Your Sister: Collected and Unpublished Writings of Audre Lorde*. OUP. [2009] pp. 280. £17.99 ISBN 9 7801 9534 1485.

Cheeke, Stephen. *Writing for Art: The Aesthetics of Ekphrasis*. ManUP. [2008] pp. xii + 203. £50 ISBN 9 7807 1907 6503.

Chinitz, David, ed. *A Companion to T.S. Eliot*. Blackwell. [2009] pp. xvii + 483. £105 ISBN 9 7814 0516 2371.

Davis, Diane, ed. *Reading Ronell*. UIllP. [2009] pp. 264. $75 ISBN 9 7802 5203 4503.

Duck, Leigh Anne. *The Nation's Region: Southern Modernism, Segregation, and U.S. Nationalism* (reissue). UGeoP. [2009] pp. x + 340. $24.95 ISBN 9 7808 2033 4189.

Faggen, Robert, ed. *The Cambridge Introduction to Robert Frost*. CUP. [2008] pp. ix + 189. £39 ISBN 9 7805 2185 4115.

Gere, Cathy. *Knossos and the Prophets of Modernism*. UChicP. [2009] pp. 277. $27.50 ISBN 9 7802 2628 9533.

Giles, Paul. *Atlantic Republic: The American Tradition in English Literature* (reissue). OUP. [2009] pp. xii + 419. £27 ISBN 9 7801 9956 7034.

Goyette, Linda. *The Story That Brought Me Here: To Alberta from Everywhere*. Brindle and Glass. [2008] pp. 214. $24.95 ISBN 9 7818 9714 2349.

Kane, Daniel. *We Saw the Light: Conversations between the New American Cinema and Poetry*. UIowaP. [2009] pp. 270. $39.95 ISBN 9 7815 8729 7885.

Marshall, Alan. *American Experimental Poetry and Democratic Thought*. OUP. [2009] pp. xi + 315. £53 ISBN 9 7801 9956 1926.

Mengert, Christina, and Joshua Marie Wilkinson, eds. *12 × 12 Conversations in 21st-Century Poetry and Poetics*. UIowP. [2010] pp. 294. $29.95 ISBN 9 7815 8729 7915.

Midgley, Peter. *perhaps i should / miskien moet ek*. Kalamalka Press. [2010] pp. iv + 87. $15 ISBN 9 7809 7380 5796.

Murphet, Julian. *Multimedia Modernism: Literature and the Anglo-American Avant-Garde*. CUP. [2009] pp. 220. £53 ISBN 9 7805 2151 3456.

Narbeshuber, Lisa. *Confessing Cultures: Politics and the Self in the Poetry of Sylvia Plath*. ELS Editions. [2009] pp. 103. $18 ISBN 9 7815 5058 3854.

Olson, Liesl. *Modernism and the Ordinary*. OUP. [2009] pp. x + 200. £40 ISBN 9 7801 9536 8123.

Piette, Adam. *The Literary Cold War: 1945 to Vietnam*. EdinUP. [2009] pp. 246. £60 ISBN 9 7807 4863 5276.

Rainey, Lawrence, Christine Poggi, and Laura Wittman, eds. *Futurism: An Anthology*. YaleUP. [2009] pp. 604. $60 ISBN 9 7803 0008 8755.

Rasula, Jed. *Modernism and Poetic Inspiration: The Shadow Mouth*. Palgrave. [2009] pp. 251. £45 ISBN 9 7802 3061 0941.

Ross, Steven. *Modernism and Theory: A Critical Debate*. Routledge. [2009] pp. xi + 264. £19.99 ISBN 9 7804 1546 1573.

Shoemaker, Steve, ed. *Thinking Poetics: Essays on George Oppen*. UAlaP. [2009] pp. 283. $54.50 ISBN 9 7808 1735 5463.

Tidwell, John Edgar, and Steven C. Tracy, eds. *After Winter: The Art and Life of Sterling A. Brown*. OUP. [2009] pp. xxv + 470. £27.50 ISBN 9 7801 9536 5801.

Webster, Anthony K. *Explorations in Navajo Poetry and Poetics*. UNewMexicoP. [2009] pp. 278. $34.95 ISBN 9 7808 2634 8012.

Worthen, John. *T.S. Eliot: A Short Biography*. Haus. [2009] pp. 330. £16.99 ISBN 9 7819 0659 8358.

XVII

New Literatures

FEMI ABODUNRIN, TABEA BERGOLD,
SALLY CARPENTIER, MRIDULA NATH CHAKRABORTY,
LEIGH DALE, ELIZABETH HICKS, IRA RAJA,
PAUL SHARRAD, TONY SIMOES DA SILVA,
JANE STAFFORD, MARK STEIN, CHRIS TIFFIN,
IAN WHITEHOUSE AND MARK WILLIAMS

This chapter has six sections: 1. Africa; 2. Australia; 3. Canada; 4. The Caribbean; 5. The Indian Subcontinent and Sri Lanka; 6. New Zealand. Section 1 is by Femi Abodunrin and Tony Simoes da Silva; section 2 is by Leigh Dale and Chris Tiffin; section 3 is by Sally Carpentier and Ian Whitehouse; section 4 is by Tabea Bergold, Elizabeth Hicks, Paul Sharrad, and Mark Stein; section 5 is by Mridula Nath Chakraborty and Ira Raja; section 6 is by Jane Stafford and Mark Williams.

1. Africa

(a) West Africa

The maiden issue of *Nigerian Literature Today: A Journal of Contemporary Nigerian Writing* (*NLT*), edited by Allwell Abalogu Onukaogu and Ezechi Onyerionwu, appeared this year. Described as a 'a medium of projection for the developments on and about one of the most exciting national literatures in the world' (p. 6), this journal recalls *African Literature Today* (*ALT*), that midwife to the continent's literature from the early 1960s. *NLT*'s avowed desire to emphasize 'contemporary . . . developments in Nigerian literature' (p. 7) will be welcomed by many who have longed to see critical recognition of those who have taken over from the founding authors. Incorporation of visual material, according to the editors, will 'inject an aesthetic element into the literary journal tradition' (p. 7). This issue features four interviews, seven essays, six reviews of recent Nigerian creative and intellectual texts, and seven tribute articles on prominent writers and critics, living and dead. Section I, 'Conversations', comprises Ezechi Onyerionwu's '"Nigerian literature has

The Year's Work in English Studies, Volume 90 (2011)
doi:10.1093/ywes/mar016

always been a global phenomenon": Interview with Francis Abiola Irele' (*NLT* 1[2009] 17–25), Olu Obafemi's '"My snail-sense feminist theory accommodates the menfolk": Interview with Akachi Adimora-Ezeigbo' (*NLT* 1[2009] 27–33), Ismail Bala's '"Writing comes naturally to me": Interview with Razinat Mohammed' (*NLT* 1[2009] 35–44), and Ezechi Onyerionwu's 'Present Day Nigerian Literary Scholarship Should Be Involved in the Conversation of National Retrieval: Interview with James Tar Tsaaior' (*NLT* 1[2009] 45–9). According to Irele, literary criticism in Nigeria has evolved in three phases, beginning with documenting surveys of the early literature, after initial reviews of individual texts: 'One thinks here of the work of Margaret Amosu and later, Hans Zell' (pp. 18–19). This was followed by what Irele describes as early criticism of the literature in articles almost exclusively by westerners—figures such as John Povey and pioneering critic and editor of *Black Orpheus*, Ulli Beier. This phase also witnessed the appearance of a handful of books, such as G.D. Killam's monograph on Achebe and Gerald Moore's *Seven African Writers*. A third decisive phase, 'in which Africans became involved in the criticism of their literature', soon followed. This phase was marked by clarification of aspects that had to do with local culture and 'was inaugurated with the publication of Obiechina's path-breaking work on the African novel' (p. 19). Like the continent's literature, Nigerian literature today is on the verge of a fourth phase of 'being absorbed into the field of the postcolonial, with all the heavy theorizing that goes with the term', although Irele is not sure of the benefits of this. After a distinguished career editing influential journals such as *Présence Africaine*, *Black Orpheus*, *The Horn*, *Benin Review*, and *Research in African Literatures*, Irele still upholds the oral tradition and performance as central aspects of African literature (p. 22). In her conversation with Olu Obafemi, leading Nigerian female writer Akachi Adimora-Ezeigbo sympathizes with 'the shattering of closure made possible by postmodernism' and the ways in which this has empowered many women writers, but argues that because feminism is culture-based, African women must adopt the shade of feminism that reflects their culture positively: 'Various names have been given to this brand of feminism: Africana womanism (Clenra Hudson-Weems), Black feminism, womanism (Alice Walker), African womanism (Chikwenye Okonjo-Ogunyemi and Mary Kolawole), femalism (Chioma Opara), Nego-feminism (Obioma Nnaemeka), Motherism (Catherine Acholonu), Stiwanism (Molara Leslie-Ogundipe), Snail-sense womanism (Akachi-Ezeigbo)' (p. 29). However, given what Irele describes as 'our dysfunctional and crisis-ridden society, bearing all the signs of what I consider an ambiguous modernity' (p. 23) vis-à-vis Obafemi's perception of 'the deteriorating landscape of the Nigerian democratic culture' (p. 32), Adimora-Ezeigbo sees the writer as 'a sensitive point in his or her society [who] must guide the people back to what Ayi Kwei Armah called "The Way" in his novels, *The Healers* and *Two Thousand Seasons*' (p. 33). Ismail Bala's and Ezechi Onyerionwu's conversations with Razinat Mohammed and James Tar Tsaaior, respectively, focus on contemporary literature. While Mohammed talks about her work, the challenges of being a female anglophone writer from northern Nigeria, and the enterprise of criticism and Nigerian literature generally, Tsaaior articulates the burdens of newness as an 'up-and-coming young Nigerian literary critic and scholar' in ways reminiscent of Harold Bloom's famous notions of 'anxiety and influence'. Again, Tsaaior advocates a process through which the younger generation of Nigerian literary scholars can 'productively engage in national retrieval' (p. 48), while Mohammed sees the need to have 'recourse into the rich reservoir of oral tradition by recollecting or asking elders to explain phenomena that [they are] not able to reconcile with today's happenings' (p. 38).

Section III, 'Essays and Reflections on Nigerian Literature', includes G.G. Darah's 'Revolutionary Pressures in Niger Delta Literatures' (*NLT* 1[2009] 99–122); Hyginus Ekwuazi's 'Portrait of the Nigerian Poet' (*NLT* 1[2009] 123–8); Chibueze Prince Orie's 'The Short Fiction as an Elastic Genre: Multiple Ventures in Atta's *Lawless and Other Stories*' (*NLT* 1[2009] 129–41); Ismail Bala's 'The Broom Takes Flight: Odia Ofeimun and the New Nigerian Poet' (*NLT* 1[2009] 143–58); and Chibueze Prince Orie's 'Voicelessness, Post-Coloniality and Woman Beings: C.N. Adichie Joins the Conversation with *Purple Hibiscus*' (*NLT* 1[2009] 159–73). Darah's contribution explores the 'nexus between the arts and literature, on the one hand, and the politics of resistance and emancipation in the Niger Delta region, on the other' (p. 99). The avaricious grip of the Federal Government of Nigeria and its international allies has prompted 'a titanic struggle for human dignity and freedom from oppression [which] has been going on in the Niger Delta since the mid 1960s' (p. 101), and that delta is the 'locomotive of the Nigerian economy as well as the centre of gravity of the best traditions of the nation's literatures and letters' (p. 112). Orie examines short fiction by Sefi Atta, claiming 'Lawless' as the study that captures societal temperament and the short story as 'the zenith genre' of the twenty-first century (p. 131). Ismail Bala focuses on a member of the younger generation of Nigerian poets, Odia Ofeimun, whose controversial debut, *The Poet Lied* [1980], 'establishes a fresh departure in modern Nigerian poetry from a stylistic point of view, when it uses poetry to criticise poetry' (p. 144). Along with 'the poet of the market square', Niyi Osundare, Ofeimun occupies the last in Ekwuazi's six-part classification of Nigerian poets. Ofeimun is 'the poet as a troubadour' characterized by 'imploding anger' (p. 126) but influential socially through both his poetry and his political journalism' (pp. 143–4). In relation to Chimamanda Ngozi Adichie's acclaimed debut novel, *Purple Hibiscus* [2004], Orie argues that, while the debate for and against female violence and even murder as instruments of woman liberation, depicted in novels such as Nawal el Saadawi's *God Dies by the Nile* and *Woman at Point Zero*, rages, *Purple Hibiscus* shows there is little choice when confronted by patriarchs such as the anti-hero Eugene, whom society sees as a philanthropist but who in reality is a fanatic who bullies his household, and is poisoned by his wife, Beatrice. The book is a cry against 'silencing the woman being' (p. 171). Sunday Francis Okoh's 'The Impact of Oral Tradition on Contemporary Children's Fiction in Nigeria' (*NLT* 1[2009] 175–87) and Alexander Kure's 'The Use of Language in the Novels of Audee Tanimu Giwa' (*NLT* 1[2009] 189–210) complete the essays on contemporary Nigerian literature. Okoh explores the impact of oral tradition on contemporary children's fiction and the ways in which 'oral tradition can help in stimulating African children to read' (p. 175). Kure argues that the so-called minor writers, such as northerner Giwa, have made innovative shifts that 'include a conscious effort to stick to the use of standard but simple English that addresses a wider readership', while introducing 'very vibrant coinages' as embellishments that express discontent with the social status quo (p. 189).

Although not literary in focus, *Critical Perspectives on Dance in Nigeria* examines an art form central to much Nigerian writing. Edited by Ahmed Yerima, Bakare Ojo-Rasaki, and Arnold Udoka, it is a collection of essays on what theatre scholar Dapo Adelugba describes as 'the primordial art' and one that serves 'as an auxiliary to drama—drama, that is, as a performing art' (p. 213). Exploring dance as a global art and placing it within the cultural consciousness of society, 'in order to find historical studies of the development of the dancer, and the dance as a body of knowledge' (p. 11) are, according to the editors, some of the primary motivations for the volume. New terminologies in dance discourse and dance theory and written criticism are also canvassed. The volume opens with Ahmed Yerima's 'Nigerian Traditional Dancers: History and Practice' (pp. 17–44), which divides Nigerian traditional dances into two major categories—ritual and social dances. Yerima examines the various stages of the evolution of dance in Nigeria, from the pre-colonial era through the colonial period, culminating in the contemporary post-colonial milieu. When independent Nigeria was divided into three major regions 'each region developed its cultural identity, and celebrated its heritage also in the form of dance, music and drama' (p. 31), but 1977, according to Yerima, 'with Nigeria's hosting of the Second World Black and African Festival of Arts (FESTAC)... was the turning point for the Nigerian traditional dancer and indeed, the Nigerian arts' (p. 34). However, the National Troupe of Nigeria was established only in 1989 under the theatre director and foremost dramatist Hubert Ogunde. The 'New Traditional Dancer' that has emerged is a blend of western and local, and dance critics have been concerned that new works do not become so abstract in content and form, that they are 'lost to the owners of the dances and the traditional content—Nigerians' (p. 38). Chris Ugolo's 'Dance Documentation and Preservation in Nigeria' (pp. 45–54) continues on the same note and argues that 'the ephemeral and transitory nature of dance arts makes it imperative for strategies/methodologies of documentations to be established and properly outlined' (p. 45). While urging critics not to confuse reviewing with the art of criticism, Jeleel Ojuade's 'Dance Criticism in Nigeria' (pp. 55–63) underscores the importance of vibrant critical approaches to dance, noting that dance itself 'is an exercise in interpretation and such exercise has a set of principles underlying it' (p. 58). The playwright and choreographer Bakare Ojo-Rasaki's twin contributions, 'The Contemporary Choreographer in Nigeria: A Realistic Culture Preserver or a Harmful Distortionist?' (pp. 64–75) and 'Towards a Choreographic Theory of Indigenous West African Dance Movements' (pp. 76–91), also seek to balance contemporary choreography with preservation of traditional African dances: 'Perhaps, the issue the two groups have not seriously considered is that of context. Questions like: in what context and under what circumstance can a traditional dance be diffused or distorted? And what kind of traditional dances can be diffused or distorted should be answered' (p. 65). Choreography that is sensitive to 'details of the indigenous dance movements of these communities' is vital (p. 76). Gladys Ijeoma Akunna's 'Traditional Nigerian Dance Forms and Womanhood: Some Authentic Expressions' (pp. 92–109) and 'Expressions of Womanhood in Modern Nigerian Dance Forms' (pp. 110–23) examine the interwoven variety of cultures and ethnic groups to which Nigerian women belong, and the ways in which such variety is portrayed in the dances within their communities, in both traditional and modern settings. She considers how modernity and technology have modified or accentuated some unedifying expressions of womanhood, and asserts that 'women participated in varied dance forms to project positive self-images while contributing to the maintenance of well ordered peaceful co-existence and general well-being to their communities' (p. 110). Ahmed Yerima's 'Symbols and Images in Nigerian Dances' (pp. 124–34) uses semiology to show how the use of symbols and images in Nigerian dances 'becomes an expansion of the linguistic pattern of a group of people' (p. 124). Yeside Dosunmu's 'Masquerade Dancing in South-Western Nigeria' (pp. 135–50), S.O.O. Amali's 'Idoma Dances and their Continued Relevance to the Society: The Analysis of Idoma-Otukpo Icica and Aleku Dance of Benue' (pp. 151–65), Iyorwuese H. Hagher's 'The Dynamics of Dance in Tiv Culture' (pp. 166–91), Peter Badejo's 'Dance and Music: Essential Elements of Bori Survival' (pp. 192–211), and Samuel Ayemide Kafewo's 'Cult Dances in Northern Nigeria: An Appraisal' (pp. 258–75) map an even wider variety of Nigerian dance art. Other essays in the volume include Dapo Adelugba's 'The Interrelationships Between Dance and Other Arts' (pp. 212–31), B.I.C. Ijomah's 'The Uses of Dance with Respect to Religious Beliefs and Worships' (pp. 221–31), Agbo Folarin's 'Scenographic Art in Nigerian Dance and Some Suggestions Concerning its Revitalisation' (pp. 232–44), Meki Nzewi's 'Dance and Curriculum Development' (pp. 245–57), Arnold Udoka's 'Dance in Search of a Nation: Towards a Sociopolitical Redefinition of Dance in Nigeria' (pp. 276–92), Shaibu Husseini's 'From Natural Talent to Professionalism: The Challenges of the Nigerian Dancer' (pp. 293–304), and Arnold Udoka's 'Nigerian Traditional Dances at the Digital Archival Frontiers: Prospects of the Motion Capture Project with Ritsumeikan University, Kyoto, Japan' (pp. 305–13).

Iba: Essays on African Literature in Honour of Oyin Ogunba, edited by Wole Ogundele and Gbemisola Adeoti, is collection of twenty-two essays in honour of a pioneer critic of African literature who 'made his mark in two major fields, Literary and Dramatic Criticism and Oral African Literature' (p. vii). Ogunba's groundbreaking *The Movement of Transition: A Study of Wole Soyinka's Plays* [1975] has become part and parcel of Nigeria's literary history and epitomizes what the editors have described as 'the heady political and intellectual idealism that suffused the Nigerian academia of the mid-1970s and early 1980s' (p. vii). Dapo Adelugba's 'Foreword' (pp. v–vi) and Femi Osofisan's 'For Oyin Ogunba, an Incantation' (pp. 1–6) contextualize further the politics and poetics of this heady era. As active participants in the diatribes that characterized disagreements between the ill-defined left and right of Nigerian literature of the mid-1970s, Adelugba insists that the panel of leftist critics, himself included, that critiqued Ogunba's debut did nothing wrong, while Osofisan describes his contribution as 'tantamount to an intellectual recantation' (p. 1): '*The Movement of Transition* was sociological, whereas what we were seeking was ideology. Our judgement was therefore bound to be wrong, because we were assessing it for what it did not seek to do' (p. 4). Another influential member of that panel, Biodun Jeyifo, in his 'New Perspectives on the Postcolonial Literatures of the Developing World' (pp. 63–73), invokes Terry Eagleton in his discussion of unrhymed free verse and its critics. However, dismissing his relatively young intellectual assailants 'affably as rascals', Ogunba, as the next three tributes testify, simply moved on and, according to Osofisan, 'no other teacher has turned out as many students of literature, and particularly African literature, as Oyin Ogunba. He has earned himself in the process the reputation of being the most benign and the most compassionate teacher of literature in the Nigerian university system' (p. 6). Ahmed Yerima's 'Oyin Ogunba: A Great *Omo Alare*' (pp. 7–9), Mabel I.E. Evwierhoma's 'Oyin Ogunba: A Pioneer Critic of the Nigerian Theatre' (pp. 10–17), and Olalere Oladitan's 'Literature, Collective Administration of Rights, and the Development of a Systematic Cultural Economy in Africa' (pp. 17–39) are eloquent testimonies to Ogunba's lasting impact. Evwierhoma examines Ogunba's groundbreaking *The Movement of Transition* [1975] and *Theatre in Africa* [1978], which Ogunba co-edited with Abiola Irele, and concludes that 'The study of indigenous culture, which he attempted, was still "new". Ogunba can be said to be the critic who found a place for traditional African theatre at a time when postcolonial studies had not yet been heard of. The book emerged at the right time, when FESTAC '77 was fully planned, nearing execution. Through the book, more pride was accorded what is African and authentically so' (p. 10). Oladitan concludes his essay 'by drawing attention to the role of Oyin Ogunba in the ongoing projects of organising the professions in the literary academy and the establishment of a system of collective administration of rights as part of steps towards evolving organized cultural economy on the African continent' (p. 17). Akin Adesokan's 'The Return of *Ajantala* as Siamese Twins: Reflections on the "Grand Gestures" of African Literature' (pp. 40–62), Aderemi Raji-Ojelade's 'Myth and Ideology in Nigerian Drama: Reading the Early Plays of Femi Osofisan and Bode Sowande' (pp. 74–89), Gbemisola Remi Adeoti's 'Traditional Cleansing Rites and State Reconstruction in Contemporary Nigerian Drama' (pp. 89–99), Tejumola Olaniyan's 'Suicide and Ideology in Nigerian Drama: A Conceptual Investigation' (pp. 100–8), Dele Layiwola's 'African Drama and Dilemmas of Identity' (pp. 109–21), and Femi Fatoba's 'Language and Symbols of Time and Transition in Wole Soyinka's *Death and the King's Horseman*' (pp. 122–8) focus on Nigerian and African theatre and aesthetics vis-à-vis rituals of purification. Olaniyan's borrows 'the medical terms *prognostic* and *diagnostic*' (p. 100, original italics) to connect two dominant modes of suicide to the concept of honour, which 'in Nigerian drama [is] regrettably, largely aristocratic and idealistic, and consequently, conservative' (p. 105). Layiwola's rigorously theorized linking of drama to identity uses three plays which 'happen to be examples of poetic drama: Ebrahim Hussein's *At the Edge of Thim* (1988, transl. 1995), J.P. Clark's *Song of a Goat* (1966) and Ola Rotimi's *The God's Are Not to Blame* (1971)' (p. 110) to demonstrate the centrality of a dilemma of how to navigate transition in a history of competition for scarce resources. In this context 'constructing newfangled identities [entails] communalism . . . giving way to new forms of individualism' (p. 120). Again, in this context we can consent to Fatoba's primary conclusion that 'it is, therefore, not an accident that the play *Death and the King's Horseman* opens with a scene in a marketplace' (p. 122).

In the same volume, Lanrele Bamidele continues the ritual interest in 'Sango Myth and its Challenges in Science, Art and Religion' (pp. 178–86), but other contributions range more widely. Uko Atai's 'The Rhythm of Festive Comedy and the Spirit of Man in Oyono Mbia's *Three Suitors, One Husband*' (pp. 129–36) focuses on the Cameroonian playwright's 1960 classic drama, first written in French as *Trois Prétendants Un Mari*. The comic pattern of boy meets girl, parents object to their marriage, boy and girl struggle and triumph, play ends in celebration reflects the optimism of the independence era. Obododinma Oha's 'The Rhetoric of Cross-Cultural Engagement and the Typology of Memory in Remi Raji's America-Travel Poetry' (pp. 137–50), Toyin Jegede's 'Towards A Conceptual Definition of the Poetics of New Nigerian Poetry in English' (pp. 151–60), and Olusegun Adekoya's 'Towards a Classification of Yoruba Oral Poetry' (pp. 187–98) are accompanied by Ayo Kehinde's 'Intertextuality and the Contemporary African Novel' (pp. 161–77) and more work on dance: Sola Olorunyomi's 'What Is Contemporary African Dance?' (pp. 199–204) and Matthew M. Umukoro's 'The Dance Metaphor: Three Parables in the Nigerian Theatre' (pp. 205–17). The volume ends with Niyi Osundare's 'The Rhetoric of Lament: A Socio-Stylistic Study of Obituaries and *In Memoriams* in Nigerian Dailies' (pp. 219–36), Wale Adeniran's 'Towards the Decolonisation of Foreign Language Teaching in Nigerian Universities: The Case of French' (pp. 237–56), and Wole Ogundele's 'Early Yoruba Cultural Nationalism contra Nigeria Nationalist Historiography: A Reassessment (Or Where Angels Fear to Tread)' (pp. 257–72).

Introduction to African Oral Literature and Performance, by Bayo Ogunjimi and Abdul-Rasheed Na'Allah, puts together two earlier volumes by the authors first published in 1991 and 1994, respectively, under the title *Introduction to African Oral Literature*. The present volume has been revised by Abdul-Rasheed Na'Allah, who stresses the importance of performance to African oral traditions, noting that 'dramatic art alone, written or oral, does not constitute African performance even in the twenty-first century' (p. xiii). The present volume comprises a lucid introduction and conclusion and fifteen chapters, which are divided further into two sections: 'Oral Narrative Performance' and 'Oral Poetry Performance'. Chapter 1 tracks 'The Sources and Origins of African Oral Performance' (pp. 9–29) while chapter 2 considers 'Fieldwork Practice and Research Methodology in Oral Literature and Performance' (pp. 31–46). Chapters 3 to 8 are focused on the subgenres of African oral performance: archetypes, myths, legends, folktales, proverbs, riddles, and jokes. The section ends with a discussion of 'Stylistics and the Performance of Narratives' (pp. 101–20). Section II opens with a general introduction, and, from chapters 10 to 15 discusses topics 'from religious poetry, incantatory poetry, funeral poetry, occupational poetry, topical poetry to lullaby and occasional poetry' (p. xii). This highly readable single volume provides access to work across several cultures and will, without doubt, enhance the teaching of African oral performance.

Similarly, pioneer critic of African literature Charles Nnolim's *Approaches to the African Novel: Essays in Analysis* is the third edition of essays on major African novelists. The 1992 and 1999 editions have been expanded for gender and geographical balance. Two essays, 'Flora Nwapa: Writer as Woman' (pp. 175–83) and 'The Novelist as Historian: Craft in Peter Abraham's *Wild Conquest*' (pp. 185–94), have been added. Nnolim's 'approach is formalistic and exponential, in the manner of the New Critics: [aiming] to pin-point the principle that allows the work to reveal itself' (p. ix). Chapters 1, 2, and 3 are entitled 'The Form and Function of the Folk Tradition in Achebe's Novels' (pp. 1–9), 'Jungian Archetypes and the Main Characters in Oyono's *Une Vie de Boy*' (pp. 11–15), and 'From Nostalgia to Myth: An Archetypal Interpretation of Camara Laye's *The Dark Child*' (pp. 17–27). It is no surprise, then, that Nnolim expresses disdain for 'art that deals with trade disputes, economics and strikes . . . hardly interesting material for imaginative literature' (p. 30). However, in 'Craft in Marxist Garb: Bread, the Social Issue in Sembene's *God's Bits of Wood*' (pp. 29–42) he sees Sembene's book as saved by its recourse to a mode of storytelling technique and artistry that transcends materialist banality (p. 31). Chapters 5 and 6 consider background setting and structure and theme in Ngugi's *The River Between* and *A Grain of Wheat* to show that the inability of people 'to connect' 'lies at the core of Ngugi Wa Thiong'o's tragic vision' (p. 43). And while chapters 7 to 12 are focused on the works of 'the newer and less studied African writers'—Saro-Wiwa, Aniebo, Okri, Munonye, and Mazrui—chapter 13 returns to Achebe's *Things Fall Apart* as 'An Igbo National Epic' (pp. 145–9), reading the novel along the lines of the Anglo-Saxon epic, *Beowulf* and classical epics like Homer's *Odyssey* and Virgil's *Aeneid*. Apart from the two added chapters already mentioned, Nnolim analyses 'The Journey Motif: Vehicle of Form, Structure and Meaning in Mongo Beti's *Mission to Kala*' (pp. 151–8) and 'Technique and Meaning in Achebe's *Arrow of God*' (pp. 159–74). Finally, describing the Nigerian novel as dynamic rather than static, chapter 18 surveys 'Trends in the Nigerian Novel' (pp. 195–205).

Outside book publication, Andrea Powell also returns to Achebe in 'Problematizing Polygyny in the Historical Novels of Chinua Achebe: The Role of the Western Feminist Scholar' (*RAL* 39:i[2008] 166–84). Achebe's gender-determined blind spot raises, according to Powell, the larger issues of African polygyny and the place of the Western feminist critic in relation to it: 'how can we talk about polygyny in a productive way, in a way that advances the agenda of African feminism, without projecting a "West is best" ideology onto our discourse and without silencing the women who are actually involved in polygynous relationships?' (p. 168). Omar Sougou's 'Transformational Narratives: Hearing/Reading Selected Senegalese Folktales by Young Women' (*RAL* 39:iii[2008] 26–38), Devin Bryson's 'The Submitted Body: Discursive and Masochistic Transformation of Masculinity in Simon Njami's *African Gigolo*' (*RAL* 39:iv[2009] 83–104), Jane Bryce's '"Half and Half Children": Third-Generation Women Writers and the New Nigerian Novel'

(*RAL* 39:ii[2008] 49–67), and Unoma Azuah's 'Women Writers' Roundtable: Of Phases and Faces: Unoma Azuah Engages Sefi Atta and Chika Unigwe' (*RAL* 39:ii[2008] 108–16) examine different aspects of what Powell has described as 'important gender issues that continue to plague many postcolonial African countries' (p. 167). Sougou examines 'coding strategies used . . . to deal with power and marginality' (p. 28) in a collection of folktales from young housemaids originating from the rural region of Fatick, Senegal, as evidence of transformational trends in gender relations. Besides providing a space of enunciation, the stories' coded messages situate their tellers 'beyond the limits imposed on women in the social formation in which the stories are set' (p. 37). Bryson seeks to correct the lack of study of representations of masculinity and male sexuality in male writers in francophone Africa. He charts the odyssey of Njami's protagonist Moise Ndoungue, an immigrant from Cameroon, who came to Paris ten years prior in order to continue his studies; Bryson argues that 'in contemporary African novels immigration is a transformative experience for masculinity and, in turn, transgressive male sexuality creates a discursive space to contest normalizing discourse and redefines literary political engagement' (p. 85). Bryce's essay traces the new directions that fictional accounts of women's identities are taking in Nigeria through her examination of seven novels by third-generation Nigerian women writers that have been published since 2000: 'I suggest that the forms of feminine identity evident in earlier women's writing, constrained by nationalist priorities that privileged the masculine, have given way to a challenging reconfiguration of national realities in which the feminine is neither essentialized and mythologized nor marginalized, but unapologetically central to the realist representation of a recognizable social world' (pp. 49–50). Two of the seven writers studied in Bryce's essay feature in Azuah's 'Women Writer's Roundtable' and their problematization 'of Phases and Faces', Atta taking the pessimistic view that their prominence is merely a passing trend: 'It's a matter of time before the male establishment decides we're out' (pp. 109–10).

Lydie Moudileno's 'The Troubling Popularity of West African Romance Novels' (*RAL* 39:iv[2008] 120–32), Shirin Edwin's 'Subverting Social Customs: The Representation of Food in Three West African Francophone Novels' (*RAL* 39:iii[2008] 39–50), and David Murphy's 'Birth of a Nation? The Origins of Senegalese Literature in French' (*RAL* 39:i[2008] 38–60) address different trends in West African cultural production and literature. Moudileno's study focuses on what he has described as the phenomenally successful but troubling popularity of the new Adora series: love stories specifically tailored to an African public. The series is troubling in 'its capacity to let readers break away from the real and the "idea" of Africa, allowing them to forget, if just for a couple of hours, the frustration in their daily lives in the postcolony', but is appealing exactly because it offers escape from the ubiquitous images 'of a tragic, doomed, and distressed continent' that also permeate more canonical literature (p. 124). Reminding us that West African writing in English exists in dialogue with francophone Africa, Edwin's essay focuses on the symbolism of food in Ahmadou Kourouma's *The Suns of Independence* [1968], Mariama Ba's *So Long a Letter* [1979], and Aminata Sow Fall's *The Ghost* [1979]. The three novelists 'extend the symbolism embedded in food from social conviviality, bonding, and all positive symbols, to lay bare the social ills and excesses of the politics of their societies' (p. 49). David Murphy's study of the complex web in which African texts in French circulate raises the larger question of whether 'Senegalese literature in French [can] be deemed a "national" literature at all when the majority of the population neither reads nor writes in this language' (p. 49). Finally, John C. Hawley's 'Biafra as Heritage and Symbol: Adichie, Mbachu, and Iweala' (*RAL* 39:ii[2008] 15–26) examines the handling of the Biafran conflict by three contemporary Nigerian writers, almost forty years after Eddie Iroh had looked into the future and observed that writers of his generation who had lived through the conflict 'were too close to the suffering to write the definitive accounts of the war' (p. 15), and Kacke Gotrick, in 'Femi Osofisan's *Women of Owu*: Paraphrase in Performance' (*RAL* 39:iii[2008] 82–98), discusses the rewriting of *Women of Troy* as a Nigerian drama.

(b) North Africa

As usual, North Africa does not generate much by way of writing in English, but some figures do circulate in the wider anglophone discussions of the Black diaspora and postcolonial cultural politics. Anne Donadey's 'African American and Francophone Postcolonial Memory: Octavia Butler's *Kindred* and Assia Djebar's *La Femme sans sepulture*' (*RAL* 39:iii[2008] 65–81) compares African American and Algerian fictional rewriting of history. While *Kindred* uses the time-travel device to send its narrator, Dana Franklin, 'a modern day African American woman, back to the antebellum South' (p. 67), Djebar's narrative 'focuses on the ghostly presence-absence of disappeared freedom fighter Zoulikha, whose disembodied voice paradoxically highlights her own embodiment and the geography of her body' (p. 69) and breaks up under torture. *Kindred* and *La Femme* both 'demonstrate the impossibility of fully accounting for the horrors of the trauma with words and yet the necessity of trying to articulate the gruelling experience as part of a process of healing and surviving' (p. 70).

James Adam Redfield, in 'Cultural Identity from *Habitus* to *Au-delà*: Leïla Sebbar Encounters her Algerian Father' (*RAL* 39:iii[2008] 51–64), interviews Sebbar regarding her 2003 fictionalized memoir *Je ne parle pas la langue de mon père* (*I Don't Speak My Father's Language*), 'as Sebbar's response to the transition between colonial and postcolonial spaces of cultural identity' (p. 51). Redfield locates Sebbar's writing and critical gaze between Bourdieu's *habitus*-like 'hypersensitive sensibility' and Homi Bhabha's *au-delà*.

(c) Southern and East Africa

Michael Meyer introduces *Word and Image in Colonial and Postcolonial Literatures and Cultures* as a book 'that pays attention to the gaze and the voice in both visual and verbal representations of post/colonial spectacles' (p. xvii). In 'Word & Image—Gaze and Spectacle' he draws on a detailed discussion of French anthropologist Jean Rouch's 'ethnographic film

Les Maîtres fous about a Hauka ritual in the British colony Gold Coast' (p. xvii) to frame a collection of essays from the annual conference of the Association for the Study of New Literatures. Meyer quotes the Michael Taussig's *Mimesis and Alterity* [1993]: '[t]o become aware of the West in the eyes and handiwork of its Others, to wonder at the fascination with their fascination, is to abandon border logistics and enter into the "second contact" era of the borderland where "us" and "them" lose their polarity and swim in and out of focus' (p. xxxv). This the essays seek to do through a critical engagement with cultural artefacts from across much of the formerly colonized world. In 'A Black and White Nation? The "New" South Africa in Zapiro's Cartoons', Sonja Altnöder (spelt 'Altnoeder' on p. xxxvii), 'explore[s] some meanings of the rainbow metaphor—arguably the most acclaimed, but notably also the most debated national symbol of post-apartheid South Africa' (p. 107). The essay calls attention to Zapiro's 'creative despair in the face of an overwhelming flood of the latest frontpage news about racism, crime, and economic crisis in South Africa' (p. 108) and the cartoons' work as 'a critical subtext of South Africa's cultural narrative of self-proclamation' (p. 108). Altnöder endorses Natasha Distiller and Melissa Steyn's view in *Under Construction: 'Race' and Identity in South Africa Today* [2004] that the rainbow is little more than an empty slogan aimed at selling South Africa as a tourist destination. While conceptually interesting—Zapiro's work often is nothing short of political dynamite in its pushing at the limits of what can be said in South Africa—the essay falls back into rather simplistic analyses of the selected cartoons. What is missing here is a broader discussion of how racism remains in South Africa not as the political or familial baggage of Afrikaners such as the Olympic athlete Herstrie Cloete or her family (p. 116) but as that of every living (and dead) South African. Similarly, a rather misleading description of the South African flag 'being dragged down towards the ground' (p. 117) leaves a cartoon concerned with the enormous weight of what was expected of and for the New South Africa, *that* Rainbow Nation, appearing almost naively anti-ANC. Zapiro's work is much too complex to be understood as either pro- or anti-Rainbow Nation.

A second essay in this collection, Marita Wenzel's 'Zakes Mda's Representation of South African Reality: *Ways of Dying*, *The Madonna and the Excelsior* and *The Whale Caller*', argues that 'Zakes Mda perceives art as a form of self-expression that includes self-knowledge, acts as a survival technique or crutch, and enables insight and transcendence through the imagination' (p. 125). In an approach that veers between hagiography and a retelling of the novels, Wenzel shows the limitations of a tendency in contemporary South African studies, and in some quarters of postcolonial studies, to read fiction merely as sociological and autobiographical tracts. Mda's complex, contradictory, and provocative texts (not unlike Zapiro's in their overt irreverence) are reduced here to yet another account of the bleakness of the New South Africa. The discussion of magical realism, which is a key 'device' in Mda's work, is rushed and irrelevant. The repeated use of terms such as *irony*, *ironical*, and *ironically* does little to explain or explore the complex levels of meaning in Mda's writing.

In the same collection, Heilne Du Plooy's 'Looking Out and Looking In: The Dynamic Use of Words and Images in the Oeuvre of Breyten Breytenbach' examines 'identity and self-representation [as] prominent themes' by tracking 'resemblances between his poetic and painterly approach' (p. 147). Du Plooy proposes that Breytenbach is 'working for two muses [and] emerges from both [poetry and painting] as an enigma, as so many elusive figures, as the eternal chameleon' (p. 149). Although potentially an interesting study of a deeply complex artist, the essay resembles Wenzel's in its hagiographic tone. The author explains rather than analyses a number of poems and paintings, including the perplexing and poignant covers of *The True Confessions of an Albino Terrorist* [1984], but the essay is weakened by a fragmented structure. Despite the stated intention to juxtapose poetry and paintings, the section on poetry clearly is the winner length-wise.

In the last essay dedicated to South African texts, Susan Arndt draws on whiteness studies and Roland Barthes's work on myth to explore 'the disguised markers of the characters' "racial positions" as being interrelated with the negotiation of *whiteness* in general and the rhetorical figure of "race evasion" in particular' (p. 169). This allows her to undertake an original reading of Coetzee's *Disgrace* ('*Whiteness* as a Category of Literary Analysis: Racialising Markers and *Race*-Evasiveness in J.M. Coetzee's *Disgrace*'). It is expanded through references to the work of Toni Morrison and bell hooks on the cultural constructedness of race. Specifically, Arndt highlights the paradox at the heart of a discourse that posits whiteness as at once invisible and thus harmless while allowing its wearers what Richard Dyer (*White* [1997]) calls a 'passport to privilege' (p. 22). Central to Arndt's reading is George Yancy's view that whiteness is 'not an individual choice but a systemic position which is a form of inheritance that needs to be acknowledged and faced' (p. 175). She goes on to propose that in *Disgrace* Coetzee is aware of the complex processes of 'race-evasiveness' and 'toys provocatively with the asymmetry of marking. In the process he evokes the rhetoric of "race-evasiveness" in order to identify it as having contributed to a new crisis of *whiteness* in post-apartheid South Africa' (p. 178). Some attention to Paul Ricoeur's work on class as an 'evasive marker' in the sense Arndt ascribes to race would have been useful; it is very unlikely that a South African reader would ever find 'the whiteness of Coetzee's character, David Lurie [to be] masked' (p. 181), for the codes of his whiteness are spoken in his profession, in his cultural interests, in his visits to a discreet brothel in Cape Town's Greenpoint; even, indeed, in the transgressive inter-racial transactions that drew white men to break the law for sex with non-white women. Nonetheless, this is an insightful reading and the author does justice both to the novel and to the critical approach she adopts.

Neo-Imperialism in Children's Literature about Africa is co-authored by Yulisa Amadu Maddy and Donnarae MacCann. Conceptually and methodologically indebted to Edward Said's *Orientalism* [1978] and in the African context to the work of V.Y. Mudimbe [1988], the collection seeks to examine the persistence of certain myths and fantasies about Africa and their insidious effect on young readers (chapter 1 is entitled '"Darkest Africa": A Persistent Western Fantasy'). In their introduction to the work, they ask: 'Why does this mis-education persist? We critiqued books about Africa in 1996

(*African Images in Juvenile Literature*) and again in 2001 (*Apartheid and Racism in South African Children's Literature, 1985–1995*), but there has been no appreciable movement' (p. 3). This is a heartfelt but rather naive comment; Said's analysis of orientalist and colonialist discourses showed how ingrained and self-perpetuating ideological systems are, and that stereotypes of Africa persist despite the industry of postcolonial studies proves his point. Only one chapter is of relevance to a survey of scholarship on Southern Africa, namely Maddy and MacCann's analysis of Beverley Naidoo's short story collection, *Out of Bounds* [2001]. The stories are read against or with reference to the 1976 Soweto massacre, when schoolchildren protesting against the quality and intent of their 'Bantu education' were killed by the police in apartheid South Africa. Naidoo writes fiction, and much as one of the strengths of fiction is its ability to connect with the real world, the authors take to her work as if each story was a cooking recipe with set amounts of political commitment, anti-apartheid ideology, or good liberal thinking. Given the aims of the collection, a far more rewarding and ideologically apt approach would have been to identify ways of bringing alive writing such as Naidoo's in teaching it to young children, and to allow the fiction to counter the work of the persistent fantasies of the West and others.

It is tempting to see 2009 as 'The Year of J.M. Coetzee', such was the attention his work received. Yet it is likely that many other years may yet come to deserve the title far more. In addition to a number of critical essays concerned wholly or partly with his best-known novel, *Disgrace* [1999], five full-length books were published in 2009. Carrol Clarkson's *J.M. Coetzee: Countervoices* offers an erudite and very engaging discussion of J.M. Coetzee's writing, and of the ways in which he seeks (not) to explain his work. Rather than adopting a thematic or chronological approach, Clarkson pairs the fiction and Coetzee's own critical writings, especially as they 'speak to each other'. Clarkson's conversation with Coetzee's 'work of criticism' (p. 57) is strongly influenced by structural linguistics and structuralism. The discussion juxtaposes each body of evidence, as it were, to seek in the one echoes of the other. Coetzee the 'pure artist' is privileged as she traces both the author's and his fiction's debt to a profound commitment to and obsession with the world of language and linguistics. Occasionally there is a tendency to privilege 'Eureka' moments when Coetzee, his work, his influences, and Clarkson's own concerns all align, and we are led to believe that this was always so. This is particularly noticeable because Clarkson is less inclined to read such perfect alignments as she sees between Coetzee's criticism and his fiction when she considers other writers and their work. Besides, Clarkson relies a good deal on Coetzee's own scholarly work on structural linguistics in the 1970s, whereas much of the fiction was written well after this period. Indeed, Jane Poyner notes in another 2009 study of Coetzee's work, *J.M. Coetzee and the Paradox of Postcolonial Authority*, that the positions Coetzee adopted or defended earlier in his career are not always those he advocates in the present (p. 7). Moreover, she points out, in a cautionary note worth reiterating, that 'we should not feel obliged as readers to the whims or will of the author or the effects the author intends' (p. 34). Nevertheless, Clarkson's book rewards its readers with a close reading of fiction and criticism, and the rich intertextuality

(Clarkson herself prefers the Lacanian term 'countervoices') of Coetzee's writing is especially well handled.

It would be unfair to comment on the delicate way Clarkson's work handles Coetzee the writer and his work without noting that this is an attitude reflected in pretty much all the other texts surveyed here. *Secretary to the Invisible: The Idea of Hospitality in the Fiction of J.M. Coetzee* is the work of well-known Coetzee scholar Mike Marais, with David Attwell perhaps one of the most sympathetic readers of his work. The study engages with the whole of Coetzee, though chapters actually centre on six novels, and it is supported by a comprehensive knowledge of the veritable industry that surrounds Coetzee's oeuvre. Its key thesis is that Coetzee's writing is concerned with an ethics of writing (p. 36) and with an ethics of reading; as a writer, Coetzee reflects on his position while engendering ways to provoke his readers to do the same. Argued at times *contra* Derek Attridge, perhaps Coetzee's foremost 'ethical' critic, Marais's study nevertheless privileges well-travelled paths that detect in Coetzee's work a tension between the politics of art and the art of politics. As is the case in so much recent work on Coetzee, it is *Disgrace* that most starkly divides (and unites) readers, and Marais is no exception. Marais is correct to challenge the view that the novel *is* racist and/or reflects its author's own racism; *pace* Chinua Achebe in his response to *Heart of Darkness* [1903], such readings are ultimately reductive and sterile. Nevertheless, in Marais's case the desire to do battle on behalf of J.M. Coetzee risks weakening his argument. It may not make sense to say that the novel is racist but it does to describe it as a polemic, a (poisonous) comment on the enduring force of racial ideologies in post-apartheid South Africa. Discussing *Disgrace*, Marais proposes that we read an earlier essay by Georgina Horrell ('Postcolonial *Disgrace*: (White) Women and (White) Guilt in the "New" South Africa' [2008]) as a corrective response to Grant Farred's earlier attack on Coetzee ('Bulletproof Settlers: the Politics of Offense in the New South Africa' [2001]). He himself argues that Coetzee aligns 'the reader of the text with [the male white character] Lurie, the reader-figure in the text, through his management of point of view' (p. 183), as though this will prevent a non-white reader or a woman reader from resisting such an authorial conceit. If alignment there is, Coetzee arguably creates it precisely so that a certain kind of reader—*any* reader—is at liberty to consume the text as she or he wishes. How useful is it to make Coetzee a saint when the man and the writer have spent a lifetime foregrounding the subtlest flaws in the human condition? *Secretary to the Invisible* is the work of a hugely knowledgeable critic and makes a valuable intervention in Coetzee studies. That said, it tries perhaps a bit too hard to show the right way to read Coetzee.

Like Marais, Jane Poyner, in *J.M. Coetzee and the Paradox of Postcolonial Authority*, adopts a more conventional approach to Coetzee's writing in so far as she begins with *Dusklands* [1974] and concludes with his later writing—what she calls 'Coetzee's Acts of Genre' (pp. 167–85). As the title of the book suggests, Poyner is concerned with examining the power Coetzee exerts in South Africa and outside it, both through his work and as a literary figure. Opting to place him as 'a postcolonial late-modernist' (p. 10), Poyner investigates the tension inherent in a position that commands significant authority through the critical acclaim Coetzee's oeuvre has attracted and through the writer's own subjectivity while being at the centre of a concerted undoing of discourses of power and authority in South Africa. She writes: 'What is important to Coetzee is the staging of debate, challenging orthodoxy and nurturing an agential, critical readership but one that nevertheless is not expected to forgo the pleasure of the text' (p. 9). Indeed. Poyner is a sympathetic reader of Coetzee's writing but also a judicious one; the point is not no defend Coetzee from unfriendly fire, but rather to show how the writer himself sets the scene for such exchanges. As she states at the end of the introduction, '[t]his book, in its detailed analysis of the writer figure in Coetzee's work, hopes to elucidate Coetzee's ideas on authorial authority so that they [can] be applied more widely to colonial and postcolonial literatures' (p. 13). In work of meticulous analysis, Poyner brings into play Coetzee's own careful attention to detail, to intellectual pursuit and political commitment, and to his 'enduring belief in fiction', in words she quotes from Dominic Head (p. 73). Poyner negotiates her way through the work of some of the key figures in Coetzee studies, such as Head, David Attwell, Teresa Dovey, and Derek Attridge, to articulate a lucid and persuasive argument that is underpinned by rich and original readings of the novels. *J.M. Coetzee and the Paradox of Postcolonial Authority* constitutes a *tour de force* in its engagement with the unique weaving of ethics and politics, writing and reading positions in Coetzee.

In yet another full study of Coetzee's writing, though this time centred on *The Lives of Animals* [1999] and *Elizabeth Costello* [2003], Stephen Mulhall writes, in *The Wounded Animal: J.M. Coetzee & the Difficulty of Reality in Literature and Philosophy*, that Elizabeth Costello, the novelist character in both of the above works, allows Coetzee a surrogate philosopher position through which philosophers such as 'Aquinas, Plato and Descartes' are critiqued, their human-centred philosophies taken apart and mocked (p. 43). Mulhall's strategic use of Coetzee's writing underpins a series of complex disquisitions on the rivalry between literature (poetry) and philosophy, but also between warring philosophical traditions. Part of the appeal of this study is the way Mulhall seems to have no vested interest one way or another, drawing on the selected texts to test his own thinking. Although himself also a reader who aligns closely with Coetzee, Mulhall is interested in the characters the writer creates and how they stage the debates that Poyner refers to as a key intention of Coetzee the novelist.

James Graham opens *Land and Nationalism in Fictions from Southern Africa* by stating that '"Land" and "nation" are two very powerful ideas in the modern history of southern Africa' (p. 1). This he attributes to the long and contested 'history of human settlement in the region' (p. 1), notably its underlay of imperial, postcolonial, and neocolonial experiences. The book is framed by a series of questions that relate to land and its meaning as represented in contemporary Southern African literature. Although 'not the first comparative study of literature in southern Africa . . . it is, somewhat remarkably, the first to focus on common themes in fictions from two countries as intimately related as South Africa and Zimbabwe' (p. 3). In a series of close textual readings, Graham ponders the shifting signification of land in the region, oscillating between colonial and postcolonial temporal and political settings, seeking to attend to the fraught local histories of race and gender relations, but also of evolving neocolonial conditions. Focusing on an extensive body of writing published in the last thirty years or so, Graham brings side by side quasi-canonical postcolonial novels such as J.M. Coetzee's *Disgrace* [1999], Tsitsi Dangarembga's *Nervous Conditions* [1988], Yvonne Vera's *The Stone Virgins* [2002], and Nadine Gordimer's *The Conservationist* [1984], and lesser-known works by André Brink, Laureta Ngcobo, and Alex La Guma. Both in the strength, originality, and subtlety of its argument and in the breadth of texts it examines, Graham's study makes a significant contribution to an area of studies—literary representations of land—that remains absolutely central in Southern Africa. Initially intended to include writing from the former Portuguese colonies of Mozambique and Angola, the work is no less influential for focusing exclusively on anglophone writing. On occasion there is a programmatic tendency to fault some of the works for failing to represent and/or conceive of a collective resistant subjectivity, but overall this is only a minor quibble. Indeed, he writes of Bessie Head that '"the land" takes centre stage in an alternative narrative of rural but also transnational *development*, rather than simply *liberation* (African nationalism) or *consolidation* (white nationalism)' (p. 95). It is in this attention to the multiple levels of signification attributed to land, place, and self that Graham's work is especially good.

Edited by Toyin Falola and Fallou Ngom, *Oral and Written Expressions of African Cultures* brings together essays devoted to close examinations of politics, media, literature, and music. In their introduction, 'Orality, Literacy and Cultures', Falola and Ngom propose that Africa and Africans respond in diverse and knowing ways to foreign cultures and ideas. They write, for example, that '[t]he new linguistic innovations attested in African languages today triggered by the new forces of globalisation reflect the dynamism of African societies and cultures, and their ability to cope with new realities' (p. xxiii). Moreover, although largely concerned with an encounter between Africa and Europe, they also note that 'racism and prejudice toward Black Africans are by no means exclusive to Europeans. Racist views are also well document in the Arab literature' (p. xix). Similarly to Maddy and MacCann, Falola and Ngom are keen to present a picture of Africa that challenges colonial and neocolonial stereotypes. In its place they propose an Africa that is dynamic and progressive, both at home and in its web of diasporic communities. 'A New Grammar of Dialogue: The Media and the Cultural Restyling of Political Representation in Kenya', by George Ogola, undertakes a series of case studies of the way Kenyan politicians reinvent their old selves for the new, technology-savvy electorate. In a rather waffly but otherwise very engaging essay, Ogola draws on Achille Mbembe's work to argue that 'the public face of power is a performance' (pp. 5–6). Among those selected for close examination is a cast of usual suspects such as Mwai Kibaki, Uhuru Kenyatta, and Raila Odinga, but also lesser-known figures such as Charity Ngilu and Kalonzo Musyoka. Although not concerned with literature in any way, Ogola's essay addresses basic issues around textual selves. Far more relevant to the present survey is Colette Guldimann's reading of the South African magazine *Drum*, essentially aimed at black readers. Entitled

'"Imported from America" or Fugitive Forgeries: *Drum* Magazine and 1950s Apartheid South Africa', the essay explores a short story by William 'Bloke' Modisane, 'The Dignity of Begging', as 'inextricably linked to the transformation of a publication, a country, and the forging of a new form of black identity' (p. 47). These are big claims, but Guldimman does them justice, despite the occasional flaw (at one point the author cites Mphahlele's words spoken in 1962 to illustrate a point about 1958, and the references to Alan Paton's *Cry the Beloved Country* [1949] are somewhat tendentious). Her case that 'Modisane's story is forging *Drum*'s fugitive culture' (p. 64) is a persuasive attempt at making sense of an emerging body of writing by black South Africans, one that draws overtly and strategically on a wide range of cultural influences. In chapter 6 of the same collection, Francis Lukhele examines the work of a couple of South African poets whose writing is frequently engaging and certainly never dull. In fact, to engage with the work of oral poets Lesego Rampolokeng and Kgafela oa Magogodi requires a degree of analytical dexterity that few critics could muster, not least because both poets choose to write in the kind of 'mongrel' diction that urban South Africa nurtures so well. In 'Chisels that Cause Blisters in the Eardrums of Society: South African Word Poetry', Lukhele reads 'these poets' work as a severe indictment of the new South Africa' (p. 95), particularly of the Rainbow Nation kind. Sadly, the argument is pursued through a rather tedious retelling of each line and what each poet intends in its writing (and reading). There is a sense that the peculiarly insular tone of essays such as Lukhele's may reflect a desire to focus on an Africanness that much too often is undermined and overwhelmed by comparisons with work produced elsewhere. Yet in this case a comparison with dub poets from the Caribbean or Britain, or rappers in the USA, would have enriched the reading of two provocative voices in contemporary African poetry.

Zazel Tafadzwa Ngoshi writes, in 'Recovering the Tongue: Memorialising Grieved Women through Spirit Possession and Ritual in Zimbabwean Literature' (*AfI* 7:iv[2009] 451–61), that 'Zimbabwean national and cultural discourses' tend to reflect views that dominate at particular times—to put it simply, they are biased. Her essay aims to show how literature can undermine, or at least complicate, hegemonic portraits of the Zimbabwean past. She undertakes this task through a close reading of Chenjerai Hove's *Ancestors* [1996] and Alexandre Kanengoni's *Echoing Silences* [1997], highlighting 'spirit possession' (p. 460) as one of the ways in which the novels allow for transcendence of trauma and a reappraisal of the position of women in Zimbabwean literature and culture. For Ngoshi, working off research by K. Muchemwa (2005) and Maurice Vambe (2004), it is important to resist a simplistic desire often reflected in the postcolonial setting to foreground the narrative of celebration and acclaim of the postcolonial nation. Yet, as Ngoshi asserts, such 'dissident' insights take time to gain purchase, for '[i]t was [only]... after the waning of the euphoria with independence that we began to see texts that interrogate and problematise [nationalist] mega-narratives' (p. 458).

This concern with other voices is taken up by Liz Johanson Botha in '"Them and Us": Constructions of Identity in the Life History of a Trilingual

South African' (*AfI* 7:iv[2009] 463–76). Specifically, Botha examines how in apartheid South Africa 'there was no place for "in-between" people . . . Such as "white" people who speak a "black" language' (p. 463). She asks: 'How did they construct their identity in relation to the society around them, both during apartheid times and now, in the post-apartheid democracy?' (p. 463). The study is based on a series of interviews with a South African man, 'George', an 'English-speaking descendant of German and Portuguese settlers born in the Eastern Cape in 1968' (p. 464), and is inspired by her own condition as a trilingual white South African woman 'wrestling with issues of my own' (p. 464). While not concerned with the work of literature, the focus on story-telling and self-telling bears close resemblances to how literature is being deployed in settings such as South Africa to articulate new personal identities. Yet George's case highlights a crucial aspect of such discourses: without the right vocabulary, George can neither tell of his heroic opposition to apartheid, as an English-speaking white liberal would, nor fall back into the established space of white racism. Poorly educated, George's 'discourse does not seem adequate to the task' (p. 470). Ultimately Botha shows that under apartheid he had to deal with suspicion about his closeness to black South Africans (he spoke a 'black' language), but now he is insufficiently peculiar, as it were. In this new South Africa, for white people to speak a 'black language', even if just a smattering of one, no longer holds the frisson of old.

It is to be expected that a South African-based publication should be the surest place to stage debates about such issues as are raised in Botha's essay. In 2009 *Scrutiny2* published an issue under the heading 'History, Fiction, Autobiography'. The essays collected here vary widely in focus and methodology. In 'Watch this Woman' (*Scru2* 14:ii[2009] 9–24), Natasha Gordon-Chipembere discusses the biography she is writing about her mother-in-law, a Malawian gender activist and politician, also the 'widow of one of the nation's heroes, Henry Blasius Masauko Chipembere' (p. 9). Written in collaboration with Catherine Chipembere herself, the essay highlights aspects of that collaboration, historical record, and some of the ways in which gender impacts on political activism and the writing of a life. This is a persuasively argued essay, setting out in much detail the difficulties of writing the story of the woman activist in many African societies. Natasha Gordon-Chipembere is at pains to avoid overwhelming Catherine's story in the manner of so much auto/biography mediated by academics and journalists. Yet, in an odd irony, Catherine Chipembere herself never makes it onto the page; she emerges as a transcribed portrait that combines admiration, love, perhaps even pity, for a woman caught up in the ruthless post-Hastings Banda Malawian politics.

In 'Voice and Audience in African Auto-Biography' (*Scru2* 14:ii[2009] 25–7), Hlonipha Mokoena offers a succinct and provocative take on Gordon-Chipembere's essay. Using it as a catalyst for a broader discussion of voice in auto/biography that is traced to the work of Slovenian scholar Mladen Dolar (2006), Mokoena asks a series of pertinent questions, but then offers few answers. A return to Gordon-Chipembere's essay towards the end of the discussion suggests that '[w]hat is unique in Chipembere-Gordon's [*sic*] treatment of Catherine Chipembere is that she is doubly aware of the dangers of imposing her own voice, while also being unhappy with the impasse that results from merely observing the limits of her role as "author"' (p. 27). But postcolonial life-writing and indigenous life narratives in particular have long foregrounded this dilemma.

In 'Narrative Miscegenation in Zoë Wicomb's *David's Story*' (*Scru2* 14:ii[2009] 72–86) Minesh Dass borrows from the work of Mikhail Bakhtin 'to show that *David's Story* deconstructs the authority of hegemonic discourses (such as historical discourse and the discourse of "shame" associated with miscegenation) by exposing the so-called monologism of those discourses as false' (p. 72). *David's Story* fits Bakhtin's definition of a polyphonic novel because, Dass proposes, no voices 'can (or seem willing to) lay claim to this story, no voice can ultimately claim authority or superiority' (p. 75). In what is often a brilliantly insightful reading, Dass shows that to read the novel is to confront a difficult ethics of reading: 'the freedom to disagree with what we deem unethical in and about *David's Story* has already irrevocably implicated us *as subjects* of that unethical behaviour' (p. 79). It is in this way that the novel constitutes 'a historical document in the most literal sense' (p. 82), allowing readers access to moments and accounts in South African history while insisting that they make their judgement about ownership of and authority over personal narratives.

Ethical questions also mark Georgina Horrell's essay, 'White Lies, White Truth' (*Scru2* 14:ii[2009] 59–71), a discussion of selected life-writing narratives by white Southern African authors. She is especially interested in examining the role the child narrator plays in such works, and in how perspective and focalization inflect the multilayered negotiation of personal and historical truth. Ultimately, however, the essay casts its net far too widely, bringing together texts that hail from very specific social, historical, and political conditions. Despite an impressive bibliography of white life-writing, few of those texts make it into the essay, and perhaps that is just as well: like Mokoena's, Horrell's essay too might have benefited from a discussion a vocabulary of life-writing and its criticism with reference to the conditions in Southern Africa.

Claire Scott's 'Changing Nation, Changing Self' (*Scru2* 14:ii[2009] 40–7) falls within a growing body of critical work that focuses on the response of white South Africans to life in the Rainbow Nation (a metaphor perfectly suited to post-apartheid white South Africa's bland bleaching of the bleak dichotomies of the recent past). Antjie Krog's *A Change of Tongue* [2003] is one such response. Although not exclusively concerned with the place of white people in the new South Africa, It is essentially the product of a white consciousness. That in itself is not a weakness; in fact, attention to that aspect would elicit some interesting observations about the new in-between spaces opening up for whites willing to reflect on their own identity in the present and in the past. Krog writes as a liberal white intellectual *and* as an Afrikaner, a member of the ethnic group most commonly associated with apartheid and with its denial. Scott's essay sets out to understand the role that works such as Krog's perform in the acknowledgement of the difficulties of 'transition, displacement and transformation' and the way it 'suggests how the individual might claim a sense of national belonging within a changing society' (p. 40).

Scott makes some interesting observations in her treatment of *A Change of Tongue*, but the essay is weakened by some poor use of sources. Some of the critics invoked in the discussion, such as Homi Bhabha, have little to contribute to it, while the use of Carli Coetzee's work (pp. 44–5) is simply wrong, attributing to *A Change of Tongue* [2001] remarks Coetzee was making about *Country of My Skull* [1997].

Felicity Horne concludes her essay, 'What Does AIDS Mean? Dominant Metaphorical Models in a Selection of Southern African AIDS-Related Poetry' (*Scru2* 14:i[2009] 31–48), by stating that 'the metaphorical models considered in this article are not peculiar to southern Africa because they exist in the general AIDS discourse of many countries, but when analysed within the southern African situation they can take on a different significance' (p. 45). This willingness to think locally through a critical framework that draws on theoretical work on AIDS produced outside Africa allows Horne to make an original contribution to readings of Southern African literature that situate it as part of a global body of writing. Horne argues the obvious point that readers always respond to texts in culturally and politically inflected ways and that the meaning accorded AIDS varies depending on race, class, and education, but she underpins her point through careful, insightful, and sensitive examinations of the selected poems.

Lynda Spencer's 'Young, Black and Female in Post-Apartheid South Africa' (*Scru2* 14:i[2009] 66–78) shifts the attention from the usual engagement with canonical South African writers such as J.M. Coetzee and Nadine Gordimer, with occasional work on Zakes Mda and Zoë Wicomb, to examine Kopano Matlwa's novel, *Coconut* [2007]. *Coconut* explores what Spencer calls 'the essence of the black experience in post-apartheid South Africa' (p. 67). Despite the unhelpful use of such terminology—even before the end of apartheid black experience came in many shapes—Spencer offers a critically nuanced reading of *Coconut*, frequently making effective use of Frantz Fanon's work on race and identity in *Black Skin, White Mask* [1952]. In contrast to work focused on how white people are trying to make sense of the new South Africa, here attention turns to black South Africans, especially a younger group. Matlwa's characters, Fifi and Fiks, provide two contrasting portraits of the opportunities and subjectivities available to black people in the post-apartheid nation. Yet, as the title implies, the novel offers 'a biting critique' (p. 68) of how '[f]or both Fifi and Fiks, aspiration toward a new social position is enclosed in "whiteness"; their journeys ultimately end in entrapment because of the ways in which freedom has been encoded' (p. 68) in the new South Africa. In a thesis that resonates (unintendedly) with sociologist Melissa Steyn's work (2001), Spencer asserts that English now performs the ideological work once done by race qualifications.

Dobrota Pucherova's 'Re-Imagining the Other: The Politics of Friendship in Three Twenty-First Century South African Novels' (*JSAS* 35:iv[2009] 929–43) is, on the whole, an engaging and valuable reading of work by three lesser-known South African writers, Ahmat Dangor, Kabello Sello Duiker, and Ishtiyaq Shukri. However, occasional claims need more careful wording: 'the figure of the homosexual . . . once considered foreign to Africa . . . has been co-opted into the centre of the national project' (p. 930). But where, and to what effect? South Africa and Uganda alone would provide very different scenarios. That said, this study offers a counter-voice to work on more established South African writers and to a critical focus on race and skin colour. Pucherova argues that some new South African fiction figures an 'affective impulse…of hospitality and friendship directed towards the foreigner' that is reconfigured as 'instances of self-othering' (p. 929), but her selected texts imagine an exchange of love that goes beyond token gestures. She writes of Duiker's *The Quiet Violence of Dreams* [2001]: 'The yearning for far-away, exotic lands such as the Congo or Brazil, imagined as ideal, welcoming, utopian places where people "love to live" and are "into celebrating their different cultures", is ethical because it signifies a longing for liberation from racism and xenophobia that prefigures social change' (p. 939). Central to the essay is a discussion of masculine identities and behaviour that are framed by political conditions of particular periods. Pucherova notes of Duiker's work, for instance, that it owes much to the views of the Black Consciousness movement (p. 938). Framing her discussion through a reference to a politics of hospitality that has long had considerable attraction in southern African literary studies, Pucherova asserts that '[i]n the recent South African context of escalating violence against immigrants and the emergence of new nationalism based on "race" or "ethnicity", such moments of friendship for the other are decidedly radical' (p. 943).

Nicole Devarenne's essay, 'Nationalism and the Farm Novel in South Africa, 1883–2004' (*JSAS* 35:iii[2009] 627–42) traces the emergence of the genre through a detailed study of the key characteristics that distinguish it, of some foundational farm novels, and of more recent takes on the genre. She states: 'The genre is an important one not only because it investigates the relationship between white supremacy and land ownership, but also because it offers an insight into how certain constructions of race and gender come to be established as "natural" in a nationalist context' (p. 642). In the course of the essay she explores how the motif of the farm is used by English-speaking and Afrikaans-speaking Southern African writers, the latter working with the *plaasroman*. Content for the most part to demonstrate how each novel conforms to or deviates from the model she outlines, Devarenne offers a series of very powerful readings of the selected works. She is especially strong in her explication of Etienne van Heerden's writing, and concludes by noting that perhaps the greatest challenge the genre faces relates to 'its ability to make room for those stories about South African people and land that have not yet been told' (p. 642). In other words, what novels might the redistribution of land produce in South Africa? In Zimbabwe not only has this phenomenon begun to impact on literary production but it has generated a growing body of childhood memoirs by white people telling some of the stories left out of new, hegemonic, nationalist paradigms.

In '"Not Home but Here": Rewriting Englishness in Colonial Childhood Memoirs' (*ES* 90:iv[2009] 435–59) Rosalia Baena examines works written by children born in India and Africa but taken back to live in Britain. As Baena shows, '[o]ne of the immediate effects of their childhood time in the colonies is their ambiguous and problematic relationship with England' (p. 446), not least because it no longer feels like home, yet the new home is only too precarious and sometimes unfriendly. One of the most rewarding aspects of the essay is the focus on how such works both create and help to circulate a myth of Englishness while almost always struggling to contain their animosity towards it.

New writing and new voices are also the focus of Njeri Githire's essay, 'New Vision, New Voices: Emerging Perspectives in East African Fiction' (*Transition* 102[2009] 182–8). This is an energetic, informed, and provocative contribution to the historiography of contemporary East African writing, tracing both its genesis and its ongoing struggle to gain adequate support and recognition. In a discussion that ranges deftly across time periods, literary genres and influences, and political climates more or less unconcerned with writing and the arts, Githire argues that '[c]entering the debate around the region's [East Africa's] literary production and redefining its landscape will go a long way to enrich East Africa's literary historiography and to bolster the region's visibility' (p. 188). Elsewhere, she writes that '[t]he under-representation and invisibility of East African women within the African literary canon is disquieting' (p. 184) and challenges the continuing reliance of African writers on being '"discovered" through Western-instituted and supported initiatives' (p. 186).

Gail Fincham is another critic working on Zakes Mda. She assesses the impact and function in Mda's work of selected paintings by Belgian-born South African painter Frans Claerhout in 'Zakes Mda: Towards a New Ontology of Postcolonial Vision?' (*Kunapipi* 31[2009] 22–42), arguing that 'Claerhout's distorted, impassioned expressionist-symbolist paintings refuse voyeuristic hegemonic ways of knowing and seeing. This is why Zakes Mda appropriates them for *The Madonna for Excelsior*' (p. 40). The process works to 'destabilise conventional patriarchal perspectives' (p. 23). Altering our way of seeing 'begins to construct . . . a new ontology of postcolonial vision, one that transcends our contemporary sense that vision always implies surveillance or coercion' (p. 23). Claerhout's paintings are generously and beautifully reproduced in the essay, and its take on Mda's appropriation of other artists' work is noteworthy because this is an issue that has generated considerable debate amongst scholars and between Mda and some of his critics. (Fincham sketches the argument over Mda's alleged plagiarism in a long footnote (p. 41), although her attack on Offenberger seems to deny someone who happens not to be South African and not to feel obliged to think the South African way the interpretative freedom Mda's use of Claerhout supposedly promotes.)

In *The Grammar of Identity*, Stephen Clingman states that his 'book is premised on the idea that there is a phenomenon called transnational fiction which is of great importance as an "inner" map of the world we have inherited and currently inhabit' (p. 3). In seeking the meaning of transnational fiction, Clingman also wants to discover 'what kind of boundaries' (p. 5) remain in place in a world described by 'popular "sages" such as Thomas Friedman' (p. 4) as flat. Clingman undertakes a series of close readings of work by writers such as Salman Rushdie, W.G. Sebald, and Joseph Conrad. Chapter 6 addresses the work of two South African writers, J.M. Coetzee and Nadine Gordimer, reading, *inter alia*, *Waiting for the Barbarians* [1980], *July's People* [1981], and *The Pickup* [2001].

Stefan Helgesson also pursues the transnational, claiming that in his book it should be understood as 'a condition, a predicament of literature in southern Africa, not a programme or an ideology' (p. 1). However, in *Transnationalism in Southern African Literature* he is especially interested in unpicking the web of relations brought about 'by the cultural, economic, and political impact of late colonialism and by the migratory potential of the print medium' (p. 1) in the region. The book adopts a comparative approach to examine a body of writing produced in South Africa, Angola, and Mozambique between 1945 and 1975 to argue that it reflected a strong sense of cross-cultural engagement. Literary production, he argues, constituted one of the media through which anglophone and lusophone Southern Africa 'spoke' to each other, and looked outwards to the Caribbean, the US, and European cultural centres. Helgesson traces in the poetry and novels of writers such as South Africans Lewis Nkosi and Wopko Jensma, Mozambicans Rui Knopfli and José Craveirinha, and the journals *Drum* and *Itinerário* a common concern with language and representation in societies that shared despite the differences that separated them. This is an original work that sometimes understates the degree to which writers and intellectuals moved between Johannesburg and the then Lourenço Marques. Helgesson nonetheless clearly shows how for 'these disparate groups of intellectuals in southern Africa, literature allowed for a home in the modern world to be imagined, or for the homelessness of the colonial subject to find expression' (p. 3). Helgesson concludes his study with a plea for the power of the work of imagination over the limitations of material conditions in societies where intellectual pursuits remain an elite activity.

2. Australia

(a) General

The politics of literature is out, and spatiality is back: so we might say of 2009 studies of Australian literature, which continue to demonstrate considerable methodological and thematic diversity, and which dramatically increased in number this year. Paul Genoni's 'The Global Reception of Post-National Literary Fiction: The Case of Gerald Murnane' (*JASAL* special issue[2009]) sought to continue the debate about local undervaluing of literary fiction, but his defence of Murnane seemed like the alibi for an attack on the *enfant terrible* of this long-running quarrel, Ken Gelder. The other critic to come out punching was Graham Huggan. 'Globaloney and the Australian Writer' (*JASAL* special issue[2009]) is a bracing gallop, with swipes at that 'cultural nationalism' which yet 'provide[s] the ideological bedrock for debates about the future of Australian literature' (p. 2). The urgency of this struggle for control of the grand narrative of Australian literary studies is evident in *YWES* reports of interventions by the dirty half-dozen—David Carter, Mark Davis, Robert Dixon, Ken Gelder, Andrew McCann, and Huggan himself—over the last decade. However, since it is evident that this 'debate' is being ignored by most others, we declare our determination to give it prominence no longer.

The year saw the publication of two large compendia of criticism, *Reading Down Under: Australian Literary Studies Reader*, edited by Amit and Reema Sarwal, by far the most ambitious work on Australian literature ever to have been published in India, and *The Cambridge History of Australian Literature*, edited by Peter Pierce. *The Cambridge History* is the latest exemplum of that difficult genre that aims at authority and compendiousness without becoming monumental and unreadable. Pierce has succeeded pretty well. It is a large book—over 600 pages—which follows the familiar model of discrete chapters written by an extensive range of contributors. Its twenty-four chapters are arranged by genre (poetry, fiction, short story, drama) in up to three chronological tranches, usually divided at 1890 and 1950. There are, however, subtle variations as the literature evolves: 'Australian Drama 1850–1950' is matched by 'Theatre from 1950', 'Fiction in Australia to 1890' by 'Australian Fiction since 1950'. There are also more significant divergences and incorporations, no doubt to accommodate contributors' expertise or preference. Thus the reader moves from 'Australian Colonial Poetry 1788–1888' to 'Poetry, Popular Culture and Modernity 1890–1950'. Other genre-focused chapters include 'Autobiography' and 'Australian Children's Literature'. Genre-based chapters account for only half the book, the remainder being devoted to an imaginative range of thematic or contextual studies. There are two chapters on Australia's relationship to Britain ('Britain's Australia' and 'Australia's England 1880–1950'), as well as a chapter on nationalist models ('Australia's Australia') and one on spatial and regional conceptions of (or within) Australia ('Nation, Literature, Location'). There are several chapters on literary infrastructure: 'The Beginnings of Literature in Colonial Australia', 'Publishing, Patronage and Cultural Politics: Institutional Changes in the Field of Australian Literature from 1950', and 'The Novel, the Implicated Reader and Australian Literary Cultures, 1950–2008'. Identity-based essays ('Representations of Asia' and 'Early Writings by Indigenous Australians') accompany 'left-field' chapters: 'Romantic Aftermaths', 'Groups and Mavericks', and 'The Intersections of History and Fiction'.

Such imaginative flexibility is mirrored in the individual essays, which adjust or abandon the judicious chronological overview, once the stock in trade of literary histories. Stephen Torre's 'The Short Story since 1950' adopts a fairly traditional approach, giving a meticulous, largely chronological account of its material, dividing up each sub-period by focus (such as rural and provincial, international perspectives, experimental writers, ethnic writers) and still managing to comment neatly on key individual stories. Other chapters adopt a more distinctive approach, or commit to a strong reading of the material. Tanya Dalziell's 'No Place for a Book? Fiction in Australia to 1890', for example, thickens her own account of the nineteenth-century novel with the opinions of contemporary critics like William Walker and G.B. Barton, resulting in a richer sense of a self-conscious and dynamic literary culture. David McCooey, in 'Autobiography', traverses other issues such as gender politics and the writer's authenticity, but ultimately identifies 'the uncanny' as the (skeleton) key to unlock Australian autobiography. Dennis Haskell supplements his discussion of individual poets ('Scribbling on the Fringes: Post-1950 Australian Poetry') with an informative survey of the period's anthologies, arguing that they provide 'a sense of the level and range of activity' (p. 468).

The non-genre essays offer even more scope for individuality of approach. Ken Stewart opens his study of 'Britain's Australia' by comparing landscapes and demographies in the two countries, but then demonstrates the intellectual dependency of the colonies on England by documenting their exposure to the ideas of several Victorian sages—John Stuart Mill, Thomas Carlyle, and John Ruskin—and also to popular writers such as Shakespeare, Dickens, Gilbert and Sullivan, and Wilde. Stewart does not see this dependency as entirely passive, but rather as a negotiation towards cultural self-determination, framed as the 'contest between utilitarian materialism and aesthetic, spiritual and moral idealism' (p. 33). Peter Morton's answering chapter, 'Australia's England 1880–1950', does not continue the account of influence in either direction, concentrating on what England meant for the early twentieth-century Australian writer or artist in terms of inspiration, audience, and financial recompense. Morton charts the brain drain of 'several dozen, at least, of the brightest and most creative minds that Australia produced over 70 years' (p. 264) as they left for London. *The Cambridge History of Australian Literature* offers an impressive sample of the criticism of Australian literature early in the twenty-first century, although sadly, national optimism seems to have diminished in the past twenty years. In the index to *The Penguin New Literary History of Australia* [1988] there were twenty references to 'utopia' and its cognates and not a single one to 'dystopia'; in the *Cambridge History* index there are just two references to 'utopia' and four to 'dystopia'.

Reading Down Under: Australian Literary Studies Reader, which also tops the 600-page mark, is edited by Amit and Reema Sarwal, whose anthologizing credits already include *Fact and Fiction: Readings in Australian Literature* [2008] and *Creative Nation: Australian Cinema and Cultural Studies Reader* [2009]. This collection is partly a repackaging of earlier criticism, and even the new essays have the flavour of an overview for student use, but the compilation is extensive, sometimes quirky, and well produced, with extensive lists of 'Works Cited' in lieu of formal bibliographies. Its fifty-two chapters cover most of the topics critics currently worry about, and have particularly strong sections on 'Multicultural Realms', including an essay on 'Slovene Migrant Literature in Australia' by Igor Maver and a section, with nine essays, on 'Austral-Asia Dialogues'. Readers interested in the Austral-Indian connection should also consult Sissy Helff's 'Multicultural Australian and Transcultural Unreliable Narration in Indian-Australian Literature' (in Dolce and Natale, eds., *Bernard Hickey, a Roving Cultural Ambassador*, pp. 135–47), which pays particular attention to Suneeta Peres da Costa's novel *Homework* [1999].

Bill Ashcroft, Frances Devlin-Glass, and Lyn McCredden's *Intimate Horizons: The Postcolonial Sacred in Australian Literature* treats literary fiction and poetry in roughly equal measure. Its claims about the sacred come to seem strained and even defensive at times, not least because of the frequency with which they are made. But the more substantive weakness of this interesting book is that some chapters on major writers, such as Judith Wright and Patrick White, operate as though the work of critics like Veronica Brady did not exist. This sense of working in isolation is not helped by the tone of some remarks about critics critical of Christianity or notions of the sacred, most notably in the chapter 'The Moving Image of Place: Judith Wright'. While ignoring the work of Shirley Walker—essential when discussing Wright's understanding of language and the ineffable—the chapter seems to be overly concerned with establishing its opposition to comments by Paul Kane and, in particular, Andrew McCann. More successful are those chapters which engage with prior scholarship, offer complication and nuance rather than polemic, and which are long enough to allow a substantial engagement with the creative texts. Among these are the essays on 'the pastoral zone' (referring to the pastoral industry, but clearly punning on the poetic reference), which consider the work of Xavier Herbert, Alex Miller, and Kim Mahood in the light of contemporary feminist eco-philosophy, and compare Xavier Herbert's *Poor Fellow My Country* [1975], Kim Scott's *Benang* [1999], and Alexis Wright's *Carpentaria* [2006]. Overall, the impression is of a project which has not had quite enough time for its constituent parts to 'gell'. One wonders what insights might have developed had the brief discussion of Kevin Hart's 'The Great Explorers' been put into dialogue with the reading of James McAuley's *Captain Quiros*, or the observations about Les Murray's interest in deft presentations of the demotic epiphany been set against the longer discussion of the transcendent and the mundane in the novels of Alexis Wright.

The Intimate Archive: Journeys through Private Papers, edited by Maryanne Dever, Sally Newman, and Anne Vickery, is a discussion of three bio-textual problems concerned respectively with Marjorie Barnard, Lesbia Harford, and Aileen Palmer. It is also a meditation on the possibilities and limitations of biographical archival research. The first essay, Dever's 'Marjorie Barnard Falls in Love', poses the problem of understanding the significance of Barnard's eight-year affair with Frank Dalby Davison when so little correspondence (a scant half-dozen letters) between the two has been preserved. Dever squeezes what she can from these letters, but depends more on Barnard's correspondence with others such as Nettie Palmer, and on very cautiously drawn inferences from their respective fiction. Anne Vickery's essay, 'Lesbia Harford's Romantic Legacy', addresses the role of the private in Harford's public socialist and legal endeavours, exploring the ways in which her lyric poetry (much of it unpublished) contributes to a public ethical stance. This enquiry includes examination of Harford's early manuscript poetry and what it suggests about her personal relationships or, more accurately, her desire. Sally Newman's 'Aileen Palmer's Textual Lives' emphasizes the self-conscious nature of all personal writing, but argues that in Palmer's case it is necessary also to take account of the impact of the treatment she underwent for mental illness. The essay attempts to decode the cryptic diary and letter evidence concerning a group of homosocial women at Melbourne University around 1932 into which Palmer was inducted. None of the essays solves the problem it poses for itself: 'In the end there is no one story of Marjorie's involvement with Frank waiting to be uncovered' (p. 72); 'Yet the private world of Lesbia remains a mystery' (p. 126); 'I have had to resist the impulse toward narrative closure . . . [and allow] the story of her intimate life to remain unresolved and ambiguous' (p. 164), but the lack of definite conclusions hardly seems to matter.

The Intimate Archive was just one marker of a renewed interest in the Palmer family in 2009. Sylvia Martin's 'Aileen Palmer—Twentieth Century Pilgrim: War, Poetry, Madness and Modernism' (*Hecate* 35:i–ii[2009] 94–107) considers the younger Palmer's writing, her political commitments, and her sexuality, while Martin's own journey to Spain in 'Tracing Aileen Palmer: A Biographer's Journey' (*Heat* 20[2009] 67–82) reflects on Palmer's involvement in the Spanish Civil War. John Barnes's 'Remembering the Palmers' (*LaTrobe* 83[2009] 56–67) offers interesting reminiscences of Aileen's parents, Vance and Nettie, and shows how a critic's personal knowledge can be both a help and a hindrance to criticism. Barnes suggests that Vance's emotional reserve ultimately limited the achievement of his fiction, and accounted for some of the difference between his and Nettie's mapping of Australian literature. Nettie Palmer also receives praise in Robert Dixon's essay, 'Home or Away? The Trope of Place in Australian Literary Criticism and Literary History' (*Westerly* 54:i[2009] 12–17): her *Modern Australian Literature1900–1923* [1924] is heroic for being strategic in its praise of home *and* away. Dixon's villain is Miles Franklin's *Laughter, Not for a Cage* [1956] for being a defence of the local.

Deborah Jordan's '"Elusive as the fires that generate new forms and methods of expression in every age and country": Nettie Palmer and the Modernist Short Story' (in Dolce and Natale, eds., pp. 134–49), pays particular attention to the relationship between Palmer and Katharine Susannah Prichard, as well as to a 1928 anthology, edited by Palmer and featuring a story by Prichard, which in Jordan's view presents a far more 'experimental' account of Australian literature than was then commonly available. Readers of Jordan's essay will be wondering whether this anthology is the same one discussed by Victorian Kuttainen (it is), who accuses Palmer of 'strident nationalism' (p. 174) in assembling the collection. Kuttainen's 'A Lost Australian Story: "Man" in the 1930s' (*LiNQ* 36[2009] 161–80) offers a lively survey of book history and the place of periodicals before zeroing in on Depression culture and the launch of *Man* magazine. *Man*, which 'began as an ambitious local publishing enterprise that accurately perceived a yawning gap in the market for an aspirational gentleman's magazine that was modern, urbane, and cosmopolitan' (p. 164), was 'consciously modelled... on America's *Esquire*' (p. 163). Kuttainen argues that *Man*'s combination of the highbrow (to outwit the censors) and titillation (to draw in readers) has led it has to be overlooked by critics, thereby obscuring a cache of some 500 Australian short stories that appeared in a period usually regarded as unproductive.

Brigid Rooney's *Literary Activists: Australian Writer-Intellectuals and Public Life* analyses the participation of writers such as Patrick White, Judith Wright, Ooodgeroo, Tim Winton, and Helen Garner in the public sphere as activists and commentators. Rooney is less interested in measuring social prominence *per se* than in exploring how writers negotiate the problem of maintaining their reputation as 'serious' while engaging in messy public debate. Rooney's critique is both astute and relentlessly judicious in presenting the contradictions, troubling some reviewers. However, whereas this reader found the book opaque about the author's own opinions, that reviewer accused Rooney of cynicism towards her subjects. Something of the contradictions and volatility Rooney captures in individual careers and in public discussion of literature emerges from Wenche Ommundsen's 'Literary Festivals and Cultural Consumption' (*ALS* 24:i[2009] 19–33), a limpid and thoughtful analysis of the ambivalent attitudes to literary festivals, which have enthusiastic followers, but which are often criticized (or sneered at) for offering an experience more to do with celebrity-chasing than with serious reading and thinking about literature. The discussion is supported by the results of surveys of festival attendees, to conclude that festival-going is literary enactment in the public sphere and that while 'light', does not signal the death of a more profound literary engagement.

Creative Lives: Personal Papers of Australian Writers and Artists, by Penelope Hanley, offers brief but richly illustrated biographical essays on twenty writers and two artists, which the author admits 'cherry pick' from, rather than fully analysing, the manuscripts and related material at the National Library of Australia. The book could be a useful 'crib' for students looking for thesis topics, or serve as a general introduction to the kinds of objects held by the NLA. Other appealing essays with biographical impulses come from Wallace Kirsop and Graham Willett. Kirsop's '"Romancing the Stone": R.H. Horne, Daniel Deniehy and Lithography' (*S&P* 33:i–iv[2009] 217–21) is a 'modest footnote' on Deniehy as book owner and lithographer, and his bibliographical relations with R.H. Horne. Despite its subtitle, Willett's 'Moods of Love and Commitment: Laurence Collinson in Melbourne' (*LaTrobe* 83[2009] 77–90) is a gossipy and richly detailed account of literary circles in Brisbane in the 1940s and Melbourne in the 1950s. Collinson was a poet and dramatist of modest output who was so well connected that his name is linked with a surprisingly large range of literary endeavours, from the Ern Malley hoax (he had a poem in the issue of *Angry Penguins* that featured in the obscenity trial) to the then new world of ABC television drama. Virginia Blain, in '"Our Serious Frolic": Ern Malley's Postwar Trip to England' (in De Groen and Kirkpatrick, eds., *Serious Frolic: Essays on Australian Humour*, pp. 157–70), argues that perpetrators McAuley and Stewart hoped to entrap English critic Herbert Read with the Malley poems, but the premature revelation of the hoax in Australia prevented that. Nevertheless, some of the Malley poems were republished in an Oxford University undergraduate magazine, the editor of which had not heard of the hoax.

Cyril Hopkins' Marcus Clarke, edited by Laurie Hergenhan, Ken Stewart, and Michael Wilding, publishes for the first time the manuscript reminiscences of Clarke by his schoolfriend, the brother of Gerard Manley Hopkins. Although long known to Clarke scholars and used heavily in Brian Elliott's critical biography *Marcus Clarke* [1958], Hopkins's account of Clarke's schooldays and his redaction of Clarke's letters from Australia are virtually the only witnesses to parts of Clarke's life. Hopkins did not keep the original letters, however, and the editors carefully rehearse all the difficulties and ambiguities they faced in evaluating the evidence that his memoir presents.

Overseas connections are also the subject of Susannah Fullerton's *Brief Encounters: Literary Travellers in Australia 1836–1939*, a very readable account of a number of English and American writers who visited Australia. Some came to promote their books or give lecture tours (Mark Twain); some were there before, or early in, their literary career (Joseph Conrad, Rudyard Kipling); and some came for an entirely different purpose, but were treated as literary lions anyway (Arthur Conan Doyle). Fullerton is faced with vastly different amounts and types of source material but orders the chapters through constant reference points such as the writers' impressions of Australia, the use made of Australia in their subsequent work, and the plaque to each of the eleven writers (except H.G. Wells and Agatha Christie) in the Sydney Circular Quay literary walk.

Papers from the 'Resourceful Reading' conference held at the University of Sydney in 2007 have been collected as *Resourceful Reading: The New Empiricism, eResearch and Australian Literary Culture*, edited by Katherine Bode and Robert Dixon. The editors' introduction, 'Resourceful Reading: A New Empiricism in the Digital Age?', describes a post-theory critical movement in which some of the materialist concerns of the book historian combine with theoretical inflection and quantitative methodology from cultural studies. David Carter's 'Structures, Networks, Institutions: The New Empiricism, Book History and Literary History' is a proposal for a 'new paradigm' in Australian literary studies that neatly brings together a number of the intellectual patterns that have been developing over more than a decade. Identifying a post-theory moment, he sees twin paths forward. On the one hand there needs to be a 'dissolving or integrating [of] the literary into a more heterogeneous field of books', and on the other a reinspection of the literary 'bearing all the traces of its institutional history' (p. 48). Literary studies then will become aware of a broader range of frames and contexts, but will still retain a profound interest in what makes a text individual, effective, and persistently valuable. Paul Eggert's 'The Book, Scholarly Editing and the Electronic Edition' examines the ontological differences between print and electronic texts in order to establish that there is still a need for properly edited texts in the age when a version of a text can be summoned by a few keystrokes. He describes the processes involved in preparing a scholarly edition, using his recent edition of *Robbery under Arms* [1882; 2006] as a case study. Carol Hetherington's 'Old Tricks for New Dogs: Resurrecting Bibliography and Literary History' finds that after several decades' marginalization, bibliography is claiming a place at the centre of Australian literary studies, partly through the powerful example of the flagship AustLit database, and partly through renewed interest in empiricist book history. She argues that the greater accessibility and power of modern electronic bibliographical tools means that users' need for bibliographical training has increased rather than diminished. Robert Dixon's 'Australian Literature in the Translation Zone: Robert Dessaix and David Malouf' applies the ideas adumbrated in the introduction. Dixon characterizes the project as an attempt to supplement close reading of texts with 'distant reading' (the term is Franco Moretti's) derived from contextual analysis. He demonstrates by exploring the European translations of Dessaix and Malouf, examining first the settings and geographical allusions of Dessaix's *Night Letters* and then the pattern of translation of the two authors in relation to such promotional forces as tours, interviews, and prizes.

Roger Osborne's 'Australian Literature in a World of Books: A Transnational History of Kylie Tennant's *The Battlers*' comes from a project to investigate the literary relations between Australia and the US in times when the Australian market was dominated by the UK. Despite some successes, such as Eleanor Dark's *The Timeless Land* [1941] becoming a Book of the Month Club selection, Australian authors had difficulty in achieving American publication, and an attempt in the late 1940s to funnel Australian fiction to US readers by using an Australian agent failed. Osborne concludes with a revealing comparison of the reviews of Tennant's *The Battlers* in the US, the UK, and Australia. Robert Thomson and Leigh Dale's 'Books in Selected Australian Newspapers, December 1930' adopts a 'slice' approach to the data that Thomson generated for AustLit, concentrating on one month in 1930. The title refers to advertisements and reviews of books, not serializations of them. One of the strengths of the article is that it analyses newspapers from outside the state capitals, as well as the metropolitan dailies and weeklies, and speculates on the different nature of reading communities in provincial and metropolitan environments.

Ivor Indyk's 'Magical Numbers' recounts the failure of a publisher's attempt to devise a mathematical model for predicting a book's profitability, then takes three examples of literary fiction to show: that sales and critical esteem do not necessarily track each other (Gerald Murnane's *Tamarisk Row* [1974]); that initially unsuccessful books can become bestsellers if they are set on high school and university reading lists (Peter Skrzynecki's *Immigrant Chronicle* [1975]); and that some books eventually succeed because of protracted acts of faith by publishers and supporting institutions (Rosa Cappiello's *Oh Lucky Country* [1984]). Deborah Jordan's 'Emerging Black Writing and the University of Queensland Press' is a survey of two publishing programmes for indigenous writing run by UQP—the David Unaipon Award and the Black Writers series—and evaluates their importance for indigenous publishing and race politics. Mark Davis's 'Making Aboriginal History: The Cultural Mission in Australian Book Publishing and the Publication of Henry Reynolds' *The Other Side of the Frontier* [1981]' argues that Reynolds's book exemplifies the broad nationalist progressive 'cultural mission' manifest in Australia from the 1960s to the 1980s, before it succumbed to 1990s 'globalisation, marketisation and corporate publishing models' (p. 179). Making extensive use of the Penguin archives, Davis shows a balance between pragmatic economics and cultural responsibility in 'eighties publishing through impressive sales figures for radical books'.

Katherine Bode's 'From British Domination to Multinational Conglomeration? A Revised History of Australian Novel Publishing, 1950–2007' challenges an accepted model of Australian publishing moving from British domination in the 1950s and 1960s to independent local production in the 1970s and 1980s to global corporate control from the 1990s. She notes that in the 1950s Australian publishers, not British ones, filled the top three places in the list of fiction publishers. However, this was based on an enormous output of formula novelettes. The author writes a companion piece, 'Along Gender Lines: Reassessing Relationships between Australian Novels, Gender and Genre' (*ALS* 24:iii–iv[2009] 79–95), in which she interrogates the view that a hegemony of Anglo-Celtic male writers was overcome temporarily in the 1970s, but that this 'golden age' (p. 79) of gender and multicultural authorial diversity was undercut by the 1990s through global economic forces. The apparent success of women writers moving from authorship of 17 per cent of Australian novels in 1960–9 to 54 per cent in 2000–6 is modified by the old male genres of formula fiction being replaced in that period by romance with 91 per cent female authorship. This article exemplifies observations made by Jason Ensor: that the AustLit database is now so important for Australian literary research that its policies of inclusion and classification partly define research paradigms, and that there are friction points to be smoothed over between a quantitative approach in which a Marshall Grover 'western' is interchangeable with a Shirley Hazzard novel, and a literary approach which struggles to identify what is meaningful in the texts. (At this point we should note our indebtedness to AustLit for the initial bibliography supporting this essay.)

Julieanne Lamond and Mark Reid's 'Squinting at a Sea of Dots: Visualising Australian Readerships Using Statistical Machine Learning' (also in Bode and Dixon) presents some innovative research approaches using the Australian Common Reader Database. The article concentrates on visualization as a form of knowledge, and the relationships that can be mapped by the statistical algorithm gloriously named 't-distributed Stochastic Neighbour Embedding'. Analogous to words appearing in differential font sizes according to their frequency, a technique now familiar in cloud representations on Amazon, this software presents each borrowing of a book by a dot; size and proximity to other dots indicate frequency of borrowing and overlaps in readership. The article proposes readership patterns as an alternative to genre as a way of grouping books. Jason Ensor's 'Is a Picture worth 10,175 Australian Novels?', in a wide-ranging, even magisterial, argument, considers the methodologies and protocols of machine learning and data manipulation. He points out that the conclusions of 'distant reading' are vulnerable to inadequacies in the original data; that the mode of visual presentation of results is not innocent but itself hermeneutically tendentious; and that data from ongoing enumerative bibliographies can be thought of as having a half-life similar to unstable elements. Ensor's other paper, '"Still Waters Run Deep": Empirical Methods and the Migration Patterns of Regional Publishers' Authors and Titles within Australian Literature' (*Antipodes* 23:ii[2009] 197–208), argues that considering reprints of novels and changes in the place of publication from first to later novels greatly complicates the traditional view that Sydney and Melbourne have totally dominated Australian publication. The argument is supported by thirty-one graphs of data on publishing culled from the AustLit database. Ensor's work is self-conscious and nuanced and is already offering micro-explanations for the macro-patterns in publishing which it reveals. Finally, in Bode and Dixon, Gillian Whitlock's 'Voices from the Past: Gender, Politics, and the Anthology' compares a feminist anthology that Whitlock edited in 1989, also using data derived from the AustLit database, with other late twentieth-century Australian anthologies. Whitlock finds the anthologizing process 'was an important part of emerging feminist critique' (p. 285).

Humour has always seemed central to Australian literary consciousness but has proved difficult to discuss, so it is useful to have a new collection, *Serious Frolic*: *Essays on Australian Humour*, edited by Fran de Groen and Peter Kirkpatrick. The book republishes Ken Stewart's 1983 essay '"The Loaded Dog": A Celebration', which argues that this story epitomizes two essential emphases in Henry Lawson's vision of Australian bush life: 'human gregariousness' and 'the hardness of things', the dog in the story representing the acme of gregariousness. Jessica Milner Davis, in '"Aussie" Humour and Laughter: Joking as an Acculturating Ritual', points out that claims for examples of specifically Australian humour founder when the same joke occurs as an Irish or Scottish or Italian one. She considers it useful, therefore, to examine humour in its social context, and examines ethnic and multicultural humour in Australia, especially the self-mocking humour that disarms aggression and attack. Michael Wilding's 'Writing Humour' is a cultural and political contextualization of his own humorous work sprinkled with bons mots by other writers. The article is indispensable for anyone interested specifically in Wilding, but is also more generally rewarding for its racy sweep through several decades of Australian writing culture.

John McLaren, in '"This is Serious": From the Backblocks to the City' (to continue with De Groen and Kirkpatrick), takes a historical view of Australian humorous writing, arguing that it is a response to difficult and degrading circumstances depicted first in the bush and then in the poor suburbs of cities. He compares late nineteenth-century Australian humour with that found at the time in England, and considers twentieth-century Australian humour in the context of Labor politics. Elizabeth Webby's '"To Write or Not to Write": Australian Literary Parodies 1820–1850' is a brief survey of period Australian newspaper parodies such as the co-opting of the Witches from *Macbeth* to satirize the popular defence of the perpetrators of the Myall Creek massacre. Thomas Hood's 'Song of the Shirt' also proved popular as a satirical template. Fran de Groen, in 'Risus Sardonicus', charts numerous Second World War examples of Australian POWs responding to degrading, life-threatening experiences with a sardonic 'gallows humour'.

Peter Kirkpatrick's '"We are but dust, add water and we are mud": The Comic Language of *Here's Luck*' compares the linguistic surrealism of Lenny Lower's novel with that of his newspaper columns, arguing that the novel extends Lower's range by allowing 'a coherent organizing consciousness within a closely observed social milieu' (p. 109). Bruce Bennett's 'Seriously Funny: Happy Returns of Humour in Australian Short Fiction' notes Miles Franklin's emphasis on humour in her 1956 critical survey of Australian literature (*Laughter, Not for a Cage*) and declares his intention to 'spotlight some examples of seriously funny Australian stories and their authors with an eye to the traditions they represent and the literary friendships or partnerships they have developed across generations' (p. 125). This leads to an imaginative pairing of Steele Rudd with Frank Moorhouse, but the comparison of Rosa Praed with Elizabeth Jolley and Thea Astley, and the concluding discussion of Aboriginal humour via Herb Wharton, are less successful. Lillian Holt's

'Aboriginal Humour: A Conversational Corroboree' floats miscellaneous ideas about Aboriginal verbal humour that suggest it coheres in a response to situations of social oppression. The article is informed by a survey of a small number of Aboriginal correspondents.

Among the more substantial and interesting stand-alone essays of the year was Ian Henderson's '"Freud has a name for it": A.A. Phillip's "The Cultural Cringe"' (*Southerly* 69:ii[2009] 127–47). Henderson analyses the import of this now famous term from its first mention in passing to the two essays with that title published in 1950 and 1958, and argues that Phillips's concern shifted from being the problem of writers earning a living to being the psychic structures of aesthetic value (p. 128). Formulating an understanding of the colonial sense of inferiority as paralleling the function of the superego, which recalls and replays the child's subordination to the father, Henderson declares his belief 'that Phillips is arguing that Australians mistake the English accent for the sound of the superego's voice' (p. 135). Henderson concludes that what is needed is a kind of reading cure: 'a discerning Australian audience would be produced if more Australians read critics whose own cadences were Australian' (p. 141). Lydia Wevers's 'The View from Here: Readers and Australian Literature' (*JASAL* special issue[2009] 10), delivered as the 2008 Dorothy Green memorial lecture, likewise takes up the relationship between the act of reading and ways of conceptualizing readership but comes to the opposite conclusion on the value of nation to conceptualizations of reading position. Canvassing limitations of the idea of nation, referencing the example set by Dorothy Green and Wevers's own assertion that 'Being a reader is a primary form of self-fashioning' (p. 5), the essay moves into its stride when it describes Wevers's research based on the two libraries of a large New Zealand farm, one a collection of 'serious' books (or 'literature' in the more general nineteenth-century sense) and a collection of what can be termed 'light reading', a distinction Wevers uses to problematize notions of the literary. Wevers's essay makes intriguing reading when set against Henderson's claim that critics, consciously or unconsciously, assert the value of their own work in terms of performing 'exemplary' reading—although Wevers is not so immodest as to do this overtly. Her discussion of the work of skilled readers—Green, Janet Frame, and, in particular, of critic Chadwick Allen's readings of indigenous writers—is directed towards problematizing the idea of a national literature.

Dorothy Green's life and work are opened out much more fully in Willa McDonald's biography, *Warrior for Peace: Dorothy Auchterlonie Green*, which attends to the love of literature, the social activism, and the personal life of this renowned critic. Another scholar/activist, Veronica Brady, also earns the distinction of a full-length biography: Kath Jordan's *Larrikin Angel* will interest critics for the chapters on teaching Australian literature (pp. 76–95) and the writing of Brady's biography of poet and activist Judith Wright (pp. 216–44). Harry Heseltine's *In Due Season. Australian Literary Studies: A Personal Memoir* forestalls the biographers, interspersing Heseltine's account of his career teaching university English with essays published during that career, illustrative of trends in criticism of Australian literature.

Heseltine's experience was unusual for his direct encounter, as a graduate student at Louisiana, with American new criticism.

A 'worried' reading of Stephen Muecke, Krim Benterrak, and Paddy Roe's landmark collaboration of narratives about the Roebuck Plains in Australia's north-west, *Reading the Country* [1984], is presented by Tim Youngs in a fine essay, 'Making It Move: The Aboriginal in the Whitefella's Artifact' (in Kuehn and Smethurst, eds., *Travel Writing, Form and Empire: The Poetics and Politics of Mobility*, pp. 148–66). The question that concerns Youngs, as it concerned Muecke, is the cultural effect of deploying different kinds of textual forms—in *Reading the Country*, visual art and story-telling—in ways such that they honour and authenticate indigenous knowledge without appropriating it. The ambition of indigenous people is that a range of voices is heard (p. 151). This is slightly different from the 'ideas of fragmentation, contradiction and fluidity' (p. 155) that Muecke brings through his immersion in twentieth-century French philosophy, and which underpin the logic and the aspirations of *Reading the Country*. Robert Clarke's 'Reconciling Strangers: White Australian Travel Narratives and the Semiotics of Empathy' in the same volume (pp. 167–79) is a more wide-ranging survey which argues for a fundamental change in representations of relations between indigenous and non-indigenous peoples in the wake of the *Bringing Them Home* report [1997]. Marc Delrez's '"The Spirit of the Land": The Purposes of Mysticism in Recent Australian Literate Culture' (in Dolce and Natale, eds., pp. 101–8) attacks white Australian writers who claim (Les Murray) or depict (David Malouf) a relationship to the land that invokes the mystical relationship with country usually ascribed to Aborigines. Delrez sees this claim to comparable contiguity to land as a strategy to 'short-circuit the strenuous intellectual processes and the lucid analyses that the settler inheritance today requires' (p. 108). Delrez allows that some spiritual connection is possible and cites positively that developed in Andrew McGahan's *The White Earth* [2004].

Penny van Toorn's 'A Book By Any Other Name? Towards a Social History of the Book in Aboriginal Australia' (*ALS* 24:ii[2009] 5–20) canvasses a range of issues arising from the meeting of oral and literate cultures, including the purpose of written text, the respective values of written and oral evidence, and the social limitations on the circulation of knowledge. Van Toorn explores the implications of the differences for Aboriginal–white collaboration on printed books. Jennifer Jones's *Black Writers White Editors: Episodes of Collaboration and Compromise in Australian Publishing History* mixes forensic biographical detail with textual criticism in an investigation of the strong interventions by white editors in three early publications by Aboriginal women: Oodgeroo, Monica Clare, and Margaret Tucker. The final chapter, 'Questioning Collaboration' (pp. 206–36), provides a very useful analytical survey of collaborations between indigenous women writers and non-indigenous women editors, as well as the debate those collaborations have generated. Robin Freeman's '"We must become gatekeepers": Editing Indigenous Writing' (*NewW* 6:ii[2009] 133–49) is useful in offering a historical overview of indigenous contributions to this debate. A similar interest in memory, representation, and debates about indigenous identity is evident in Laura Basu's 'The Ned Kelly Memory Dispositif, 1930 to 1960: Identity Production'

(*Traffic* 10[2008–9] 59–74), a thoughtful essay that will be of particular use to anyone considering the rich collection of fiction about Kelly.

Studies in Australian Weird Fiction continues to be pitched mainly at fans, with writer interviews and brief essays on 'forgotten' writers or books. For example, James Doig's 'William Sylvester Walker ("Cooee"): A Neglected Colonial Writer of the Australian Outback' (*StudWF* 3[2009] 5–10) combines biographical and plot summaries to conclude that Walker 'wrote competently of the Australian bush' and, more audaciously, that as a writer he is 'the equal of Rosa Praed and Ernest Favenc' (pp. 9–10). The online journal *Peril* continues to carry interesting (if usually brief) commentaries and interviews with writers, one of the best being Alice Pung's 'The Original Introduction to *Growing up Asian in Australia*' (*Peril* 8[2009]). Pung offers an overview of the different forms of representations of Asian Australian experience in the 2008 anthology; *Peril* 9 is a special issue on 'creatures'. Nick Jose offers a breezily informative overview of cultural and literary relations between Australia and China in 'Australian Literature Inside and Out' (*JASAL* special issue[2009] 13). Jose considers the complex connections and diplomatic work done by creative writers and writing.

Although not, strictly speaking, criticism, we should also mention the appearance in 2009 of the *Macquarie PEN Anthology of Australian Literature*, edited by Jose and a strong cast of assistants, which is to appear in the United States under the Norton banner. As the first substantial historical anthology since Goodwin and Lawson's *Macmillan Anthology* [1990], the book is obviously directed at the education market, as well as the curious general reader. Pieces display literary merit and other cultural significance: outlaw Ned Kelly is represented, along with Australia's longest-serving prime minister, Robert Menzies; we hear the voice of Chinese Australian Taam Sze Pui (1853–1926) from his book *My Life and Work* [1925], and that of Mandawuy Yunupingu from his song 'Treaty'. Although there is some non-fiction and short fiction, the *Anthology* is dominated by poetry and by extracts from novels, with most writers (other than some fifty poets) represented by one piece of writing. Each writer—and there are more than 300—is introduced in a paragraph which also explains the significance of the selected work. There are interesting background stories on the *Anthology* in the November 2009 issue of the *Sydney PEN Magazine*, available online.

Three very useful review essays appeared in the mid-year issue of *Westerly*, although readers should note that the titles given here follow those printed with the essay, not those from the contents page. Tony Simoes da Silva's cumbersomely entitled 'We're One and Many: Remembering Autobiographically: The Year's Work in Non-Fiction 2008–2009' (*Westerly* 54:i[2009] 148–57) surveys general works as well as literary criticism, concurring with last year's *YWES* in naming Philip Mead's *Networked Language* 'head and shoulders above the rest' (p. 148). Susan Midalia's 'The Year's Work in Fiction 2008–2009' (*Westerly* 54:i[2009] 51–64) is more marketing department than critique, Christos Tsiolkas's *The Slap* the only work to miss out on laudatory phrases on the grounds of its being 'a deliberate assault on bourgeois sensibility and value' (p. 57). Julian Croft's essay is the only one of the three *Westerly* surveys which gives serious consideration to questions about publishing context and trends. 'At the Crossroads: Australian Poetry 2008–2009' (*Westerly* 54:i[2009] 115–27) suggests some emerging dialogue between criticism and creative writing.

(b) Fiction

Ken Gelder and Paul Salzman's *After the Celebration: Australian Fiction 1989–2007* is a major retrospective which follows a comparable 1989 survey by the same two authors, *The New Diversity: Australian Fiction 1970–1988*. The new book is divided into six chapters, only one of which is explicitly on 'literary fiction', although three of the other chapters are actually about fiction that would normally be seen in that category. However, one of the book's agendas is to cut literary fiction down to size by giving it no more space than is given to genre fiction in the 'hope that readers . . . are . . . less inclined to write contemporary Australian genre fiction off' (p. 178). The discussion of the fiction is as politically and socially aware as that in *The Cambridge History of Australian Literature* discussed above, but seems to be particularly haunted by former prime minister John Howard, who appears in the first line of the first chapter, 'Belonging'. This chapter is both an indirect satire on Howard's political goal of making Australians 'relaxed and comfortable', and a reprise of Gelder's earlier thesis that white Australian consciousness is haunted by its repressed memory of atrocities committed on Aborigines.

To make sense of almost twenty years of literary and genre fiction, the authors use new labels freely. Novels are grouped in sub-genres, such as 'rural apocalypse fiction', 'gothic settlement', and 'eco-genealogical fiction'. Other issues clustering around 'belonging' are treated under headings such as 'home', 'diasporic genealogies', 'authenticity', and 'indigenous genealogies'. Like the final chapter, the discussion sometimes focuses on controversy around fiction rather than the fiction itself. Salzman's chapter on historical fiction and the History Wars is particularly deft and economical in concentrating on the literary extensions of the dispute rather than rehearsing the original Reid and Reynolds versus Windschuttle contestation. Key texts are David Malouf's *Remembering Babylon* [1993] and Kate Grenville's *The Secret River* [2005], and the issues are less those of fact and forgetting than of speaking position and authority. That said, it is axiomatic to the book's position that any sympathetic depiction of a white settler is to be excoriated as a 'complacent, post-settler' (p. 88) position. Salzman believes that what the historical novelist should aim at is 'constructive alienation' (p. 89) which engages sympathy for Aborigines without allowing readers to think that they can comprehend the Aboriginal psyche in any satisfactory way.

Gelder and Salzman's other chapters also treat some prolific novelists individually: Peter Carey and Elizabeth Jolley, for example, who each published seven novels in the period surveyed, and Brian Castro, who produced six. One of the most substantial and engaging sub-sections is on novels that deal variously with the idea of Europe: they may rework the earlier idea of Europe (or England) as having superior culture and values; they may obliquely reprise that view; they may depict Europe as allowing Australians cultural mobility or hybridity; they may explore Europe as site of necessary knowledge for Australians; or they may reject Europe (or at least scrutinize it warily) as a locus of danger, corruption, or perverted self-destruction. The final chapter, on 'literary politics', covers some of the political interventions in literary sponsorship and administration during the Howard years, and controversies such as those around Helen Demidenko's *The Hand That Signed the Paper* [1994], Helen Garner's *The First Stone* [1995], and Elliot Perlman's *Three Dollars* [1998]. Gelder is disappointed by writers who remain 'disaffiliated' (p. 232), and he joyously flagellates right-leaning critics for their 'notion of the apolitical, timeless literary classic and the purity of the "literary experience"' (p. 248). This is a rewarding book not only for the chronicling of so much fiction over nearly two decades and its interpretation of the accompanying cultural climate, but also for the suggestive groupings, contrasts, and mini-genealogies that it both offers and provokes.

Catriona Elder's *Dreams and Nightmares of a White Australia: Representing Aboriginal Assimilation in the Mid-Twentieth Century* analyses popular representations of so-called 'mixed-race relations' in popular twentieth-century novels. Colonization is refigured here as a family drama in which white men are both *the* danger and *in* danger; white women are 'repositories for a displaced hatred of assimilation' (p. 236). Wildly popular works such as E.V. Timms's *The Scarlet Frontier* [1953], which was claimed by its publisher to have sold 850 000 copies, and Gwen Meredith's novel *Beyond Blue Hills* [1953], drawn from the iconic ABC radio serial *Blue Hills* which ran from 1949 to 1976, are implicitly contrasted with less well-known and less reassuring texts that dramatize the anxieties inhering in desire for indigenous sexual partners. Elder concludes that although the dominant ideology of assimilation generally underpins these texts, there was a commensurate wish among white Australians 'that assimilation should not work', as well as anxiety or hostility about the fact that Aboriginal people themselves did not actually seem to want to become like whites (p. 234). Although *Dreams and Nightmares* retains some signs of its origins as a thesis, with an overly long and respectful introductory account of key terms, these weaknesses are more than countered by the originality and persuasiveness of the readings.

The renewal of interest in place and in questions of gender and gender difference is marked in diverse essays on fiction. Anne Maxwell's 'Postcolonial Criticism, Ecocriticism and Climate Change: A Tale of Melbourne Under Water in 2035' (*JPW* 45:i[2009] 15–26) argues that postcolonial thinking offers ways of engaging with the current crisis of global warming, a case Maxwell makes through a reading of George Turner's short story 'The Fittest' [1985]. The first half of the essay includes a thoughtful appraisal of the state of postcolonial criticism considered in terms of the intersection of institutional politics, global intellectual currents (of writing in English), and the political imperatives created by the increasing gap between rich and poor. Interestingly, Maxwell offers praise for many whom Graham Huggan, in his perhaps too ambitiously entitled 'Postcolonial Ecocriticism and the Limits of Green Romanticism' in the same issue (*JPW* 45:i[2009] 3–14), finds reason to dismiss, including Judith Wright. Another useful contribution to this topic, Scott Brewer's '"A Peculiar Aesthetic": Julia Leigh's *The Hunter* and Sublime Loss'

(*JASAL* special issue[2009] 11), is a thought-provoking critique of attitudes to critical theory evident in ecocriticism—notably in essays collected in *The Littoral Zone* [2007], which was discussed in *YWES* 88[2009]. Brewer uses Leigh's 1999 novel as the basis for an incisive discussion of the place of literature and the literature of place in contemporary theorizing of environment and representation. The attention to philosophy never overwhelms the discussion, but informs a critique of the problems of representing extinction. It is hard to imagine this essay will make its author friends among the ecocriticism community, but like Maxwell's it deserves wide reading for its provocative insights.

Special issues of *Southerly* (on animals), *JAS* (on modernism, mainly in the visual arts), and *Hecate* and *ALS* (on feminism) appeared in 2009. The most substantial of the *Southerly* essays is Helen Tiffin's 'Animal Writes: Ethics, Experiments and Peter Goldsworthy's *Wish*' (*Southerly* 69:i[2009] 36–56), which in its first half ranges widely over issues germane to this burgeoning field. The starting point of Tiffin's argument is that repression of the contradictions of the representational forms and actual experiences of animals is essential to the logic which legitimates mass slaughter of animals for human consumption. This is, for Tiffin, a process in which animals are changed into 'meat and metaphor' (p. 41); such epigrammatic phrases are used throughout the richly literate essay, which in its second half moves into an enthusiastic reading of Goldsworthy's 1995 novel. In the same issue Andrew Game's 'Pecked, Naked and Stuffed: Paul Wenz on the Suffering of Animals' (*Southerly* 69:i[2009] 225–33) argues that Wenz 'champions the cause of the white man who explores the wild, claims it for himself and tames it' (p. 233) while Yvonne Smith's 'Hunter or Hunted? David Malouf's Poetic of the Human and Inhuman' (*Southerly* 69:i[2009] 167–81) is a swiftly moving but interesting account of Malouf's representation of animals and animal encounters with humans in his poetry and fiction. Smith finds that these are characterized by a desire for empathy that is tempered by an awareness of the obstacles to articulating such feelings.

Sneja Gunew opens with a sharp set of questions about the term 'diaspora' before moving into a consideration of the work of three writers, among them Yasmine Gooneratne, in a weighty essay, 'Resident Aliens: Diasporic Women's Writing' (*CWW* 3:i[2009] 28–46). As Gunew notes, neither the political and intellectual complexities of the concept of diaspora nor those of adjacent terms such as 'the transnational', 'the global', and 'migration' can be resolved in a single essay, but an awareness of complexities can animate the argument, the main line of which is to express (with reference to Althusser, Homi Bhabha, Rosi Braidotti, Ghassan Hage, and Vijay Mishra, among others, all inspired by psychoanalysis) a commitment to considering local specificities. The expanded frame of reference—thought through, rather than being the nod to authorities such citations sometimes become—makes this a rich contribution not only to critical studies of the writers considered—the other two are Anita Rau Badami and Shani Mootoo—but to the theorizing of diaspora studies.

The death of Elizabeth Jolley in 2007 occasioned a number of reconsiderations of her work, three of which were published in *ALS* (24:i) after being delivered as papers in a 'tribute' session at the annual ASAL conference. Barbara H. Milech's 'Friendship in a Time of Loneliness' (*ALS* 24:i[2009] 97–110) discusses Jolley's ideas on, and depiction of, love. Because she saw relationships as having a potential to degenerate into calculating and stultifying coupledom, Jolley preferred the idea of 'friendship'. Friendship, in Jolley's sense, combines the possibility of discovery, eroticism, and intimacy with the realization of the possibility of limitation or failure, and 'an ethic of restraint' (p. 102). The article exemplifies the various forms that this restraint takes in a number of the stories. Bronwen Levy's 'Jolley's Women' (*ALS* 24:i[2009] 111–20) finds that in Jolley's fiction 'the emphasis is on thought, movement, and activity rather than on identity and definition' (p. 112). Jolley's women desire each other in a 'gynocentric universe' (p. 112) in which narration is discontinuous and 'stylistically feminine' (p. 113); these women are often observed from the perspective of a half-outsider. The ambiguity of Jolley's depiction of female longing draws partly on an ambiguity or occlusion in the author's own position. Delys Bird's 'Elizabeth Jolley's Late Work' (*ALS* 24:i[2009] 121–33) uses Edward Said's *On Late Style* as a way of approaching the last four novels, finding *The Orchard Thieves* transitional, and the remaining three obscure, with increasing tendencies to farce. In canvassing them, Bird is able to point to many of the qualities identified by Said as characteristic of 'late work'. If Jolley was a disappointment to second-wave feminists, Larissa McLean Davies seeks to rehabilitate her for the third wave. In 'Reading Institutional Women: A Nexus Approach to Bourdieu, *Summer Heights High*, and the Fiction of Elizabeth Jolley' (*ALS* 24:iii–iv[2009] 66–78), Davies adopts Rachel Blau du Plessis's call for a less binary mindset in feminist critique by comparing the institutional women in Jolley's novels with those in a TV comedy written by a male. Her rather subtle conclusion is that 'although Jolley suggests that women's writing facilitates the appropriation of institutional space, she ultimately leaves this transformation to future texts to be created by her protagonist' (p. 76).

Maureen Lynch Pèrcopo's 'Generational Change: Women and Writing in the Novels of Thea Astley' (in Barthet, ed., *Shared Waters: Soundings in Postcolonial Literatures*, pp. 167–77) is an extremely useful discussion of Astley's novels and critical responses to them in the light of debates about her representation of women, largely generated by the author's own oft-quoted claim that she had had to 'neuter' her writing. In 'Questioning Belonging in Thea Astley's *Vanishing Points*' (in Dolce and Natale, eds., pp. 265–72) Serena Saba credits her approach to Gelder and Jacobs's *Uncanny Australia* [1998], but actually makes more effective use of Paul Genoni's edenic reading of Astley in her discussion of the novella 'The Genteel Poverty Bus Company'. Susan Sheridan, 'Some Versions of Coastal: Thea Astley, Captain Simpson and the North Queensland Coast' (in Hosking et al., eds., *Something Rich and Strange: Sea Changes, Beaches and the Littoral in the Antipodes*, pp. 114–26), contrasts Astley's depiction of the northern littoral with that of Beckford Simpson, a ship's captain sent north from Sydney to search for traces of Edmund Kennedy's expedition. The article also flirts with the idea of 'coastal' as a geographical alternative to 'pastoral'. Anne Collett's 'The Significance of the Littoral in Beverley Farmer's Novel *The Seal Woman*' (*ALS* 24:iii–iv[2009]

121–32) is a poetic argument about a poetic novel. Collett explores aspects of the narrative and its settings that are transitional, undefined, liminal, or littoral, relating them to the myths of the selkie's wife who crosses from sea to land and yearns to return, and also to Farmer's interest in the androgynous.

The turn to spatiality mentioned at the beginning of this review is also revealed in Susan Hosking's 'The Australian Midsummer Dream: From Beach Shack to Titania's Palace' (in Hosking et al., eds., pp. 35–46). It describes the 'shack' as egalitarian, ingenious, liberating, and a site for nostalgia, and discusses two stories that use shacks as a setting, Patrick White's 'Dead Roses' and Elizabeth Harrower's 'A Beautiful Climate'. While White's story plays with the idea that the liminal space of the beach house appears to offer a transcendence of class and conformity, ultimately the whole scenario is controlled by the possessors of 'property' and 'material wealth' (p. 40). Harrower's story explodes another myth: of the tolerant and genial family culture of the shack. Far from the shack offering a pleasurable family holiday space, it enables punitive, even sadistic, patriarchal control. Jonathan Bollen's essay in the same collection, 'White Men, Wet Dreams: Fishing Fatherhood and Finitude in Australian Theatre, 1955–2004' (pp. 62–74), argues that in Australia the beach has joined (perhaps displaced) the bush as a primary locale for testing masculinity.

Michael Sharkey's 'Why Men Leave Home: The Flight of the Suburban Male in Some Popular Australian Fiction 1900–1950' (in De Groen and Kirkpatrick, eds., pp. 110–23) is about the comic elements of gender politics in a series of novels that have long since disappeared from sight. Sharkey offers an illuminating mapping of the fictionalized fantasies of generations of Australian males, and provides a brief coda on what the marriage terrain looked like from the women's point of view. Xavier Pons's *Messengers of Eros: Representations of Sex in Australian Writing* offers a wider range of reference to literary texts—the book's strength and weakness. The more wide-ranging chapters are too reliant on essentialist generalization and flippancy; those selectively focused, in contrast, offer useful engagements with the texts (although not with the work of other critics, ignored in most cases). This determination to fly solo is especially evident in the chapters on *Coonardoo* [1928] (pp. 157–78), which refers also to Xavier Herbert's *Capricornia* [1938]; on Beverley Farmer (pp. 179–95); and on Carey's *The Tax Inspector* [1991] and Tsiolkas's *Dead Europe* [2005]. Pons is good on Carey, perhaps because he seems more comfortable discussing heterosexual relations (from a male point of view) than the representation of women or gay men.

'Delivering a Punch: Michael Williams Talks to Christos Tsiolkas' (*Meanjin* 68:ii[2009] 142–53), is one of the best of the interviews with writers that appear regularly in this journal. Tsiolkas reflects on the experiences and reading which inform *The Slap* [2008], as well as earlier works including *Dead Europe* [2005] and *Loaded* [1995]. The interview touches on questions about violence, family relationships, and the invisibility of poverty, as well as being emphatic on what *The Slap* is *not* about. Heather Smyth brings together the history of sexuality (via the work of Eve Sedgwick) and the history of Irish peasant revolutionaries (via writers such as Natalie Zemon Davis) to argue for the transgressive 'gendering of Australian nationalism' (p. 214) in Peter Carey's Ned Kelly novel. 'Mollies Down Under: Cross-Dressing and Australian Masculinity in Peter Carey's *True History of the Kelly Gang*' (*JHSex* 18:ii[2009] 185–214) shows an ambiguous representation of the outlaws as cross-dressing and, possibly, as desiring men. There is a sense here that the critic might have a richer set of ideas than the text. The same is true of Vivienne Muller and Penny Holliday's '"When everything old is new again": Class, Consumerism and Masculinity in Alasdair Duncan's *Metro*' (*JAS* 33:iv[2009] 431–43), a lively account which incorporates observations on the micro-geographies of the city of Brisbane.

Patrick White is back in the critical spotlight following the public release of his manuscripts in 2008 and several ensuing conferences. The most extensive work is Cynthia vanden Driesen's detailed study of *Voss* [1957], *Riders in the Chariot* [1961], and *A Fringe of Leaves* [1976]. *Writing the Nation: Patrick White and the Indigene* argues for the significance of White's portrayal of Aboriginal people (*contra* Simon During and Terry Goldie), particularly in *A Fringe of Leaves*, in part on the basis of an acceptance of White's own claim to want to write for or even to create 'a race possessed of understanding' (p. 174). The book concludes that White's Aboriginals are not simplistic stereotypes. An equally focused contribution to White criticism reads *Voss* as negotiating the shift from the geographical to the mystic. Deb Narayan Bandyopadhyay, in '"It overflows all maps": Culture, Nationalism, and Frontier in Patrick White's *Voss*' (*Antipodes* 23:ii[2009] 125–31), is less interested than vanden Driesen in the indigenous, arguing that White's novel proposes a remade form of cultural nationalism. Antonella Riem Natale, 'The Goddess Slid into the Australian Desert: *Voss* a Revisitation' (in Dolce and Natale, eds., pp. 251–63) rereads *Voss* as myth, plotting the novel's characters onto a twelve-stage Jungian model of persona development. The major stages proposed are Ego (Preparation), Soul (Journey), and Self (Return), the Return being a dissolution rather than a reaffirmation of the abrasive Ego. Although the discussion in places sounds like a tarot reading, the novel lends itself remarkably well to such chthonic mapping. Lorraine Burdett's 'Synthetics, Surveillance and Sarsaparilla: Patrick White and the New Gossip Economy' (*JASAL* special issue[2009] 11) presents a case for the importance of White's awareness of the development of a 'suburban surveillance culture' operating in parallel with 'gossiping intelligence networks' (p. 1) in the United States. Burdett, making passing comparisons between White and Philip Roth, contends that White's concern about the effect of this 'collective narrow-mindedness' on the heroic loner is particularly evident in his novels *Riders in the Chariot* [1961] and *The Solid Mandala* [1966]. More overtly historical and biographical, Peter Ferguson's 'Patrick White, Green Bans and the Rise of the Australian New Left' (*MHJ* 37[2009] 73–88) argues for the impact of the bans and the chief force behind them, Jack Mundey, on White's involvement in environmentalism and other political debates. This issue of *Melbourne Historical Journal* features several tributes to historian Greg Dening, whose work has been influential in literary and cultural studies in the Pacific region.

Giselle Bastin's 'The 1970s Gossip Girls: Gossip's Role in the Surveillance and Construction of Female Social Networks in Helen Garner's *Monkey Grip*' (*Antipodes* 23:ii[2009] 115–20) praises Garner's 1977 novel for its representation of talk between women. Bastin's conclusion—that gossip crosses borders rather than policing them—might seem optimistic, as well as being at odds with her earlier observation that the novel ultimately shows its key female characters as having 'very clear views about appropriate and inappropriate female behaviors' based on 'a vigilant adherence to the old rules of romantic love' (p. 118). The latter judgement about Garner's work accords with the arguments put by Larissa McLean Davies in 'Sensational Story: Rereading Female Heterotopias in Helen Garner's *Cosmo Cosmolino*' (in Uhlmann et al., eds., *Literature and Sensation*, pp. 61–72), which finds that this 1992 novel reinforces the limitations of Garner's imagination of domestic space. But Garner finds another friend in Denise Varney, whose 'Radical Disengagement and Liquid Lives: *Criminology* by Arena Theatre Company' (*ADS* 54[2009] 125–41) describes a performance piece which theatricalized the events described by Garner in *Joe Cinque's Consolation: A True Story of Death, Grief and the Law* [2004], an account of the death of a young man in Canberra and the subsequent trial of two students of the Australian National University.

We are used to arguments that argue that a particular city or region exerts a special (positive) inspiration on a writer. Russell Smith's 'The Literary Destruction of Canberra' (*ALS* 24:i[2009] 78–94) offers something quite different: a discussion of Australians' ambivalent, sometimes sardonic, attitude to the capital city. Smith argues that Canberra is seen variously as sterile and utopian (over-planned), dystopian (seedy with high drug consumption), or isolated and out of touch (self-obsessed and political). Consequently, a number of recent narratives conclude with its destruction in a displaced national wish-fulfilment. The most substantial examples discussed are Andrew McGahan's *Underground* [2006] and Marion Halligan's *The Point* [2003]. Much more respectful of its geographical subject is Susan Carson's 'Spun from Four Horizons: Re-Writing the Sydney Harbour Bridge' (*JAS* 33:iv[2009] 417–29). Carson contends that colonialism is just as influential a context as modernity in representations of the bridge, not least because among the first proponents of the project was convict architect Francis Greenaway, who argued to then governor Lachlan Macquarie that a bridge on this site would give 'an idea of strength and magnificence' that would be to the 'credit and glory' of New South Wales and England (p. 420). Carson has a nice eye for the monumental and the ridiculous, and thereby demonstrates the bridge's astonishing cultural plasticity.

Gay Breyley's 'Fearing the Protector, Fearing the Protected: Indigenous and "National" Fears in Twentieth-Century Australia' (*Antipodes* 23:i[2009] 43–8) is an especially valuable piece not so much for the framing material on policy in the early twentieth century as for its account of material from *Over My Tracks* [1993], Evelyn Crawford's memoir of growing up on a station, then at the Brewarrina Mission. Counterpointed with discussion of the re-enactment of the moment of invasion in the 1838 sesquicentenary celebrations in Sydney is Crawford's account of twenty-five men being taken from the mission to perform a 'corroboree'. The men were incarcerated and intimidated in Sydney during the 'celebration'. Some related political issues are canvassed in the journal *Life Writing*, as issues 6:i and 6:ii both contain essays on testimony to violence and trauma by refugees which bear either generally or specifically on Australian texts and contexts, while questions of history and place are the focus of four essays in *South Atlantic Quarterly* (108:i[2009] 1–84) by Larissa Behrendt, Ian Henderson, Katrina Schlunke, and Irene Watson. Although none is directly concerned with literary texts, these, along with the *Life Writing* essays, form a substantial contribution to ongoing debates about race, identity, and nation that inform literary studies in Australia.

Rich Pascal's 'The Telling of Marmel's Story' (*ALS* 24:ii[2009] 54–68) identifies Bill Harney's *Brimming Billabongs* [1947] as the first book to use an Australian Aboriginal voice to tell an Aborigine's story. He argues that Marmel lists the violent offences of whites against Aborigines and criticizes the destructive effects of the 'introduction of white values into the individual and communal thinking of the native peoples' (p. 59). Rachael Weaver in the well-documented 'Colonial Violence and Forgotten Fiction' (*ALS* 24:ii[2009] 33–53), surveys short fiction from late nineteenth-century story collections, magazines, and newspapers that depicts frontier conflict. She argues that violence was often played down or suppressed in real life at the time, but that its frank depiction in the fiction manifests a collective guilt revealed in motifs of nemesis undermining the colonizers' self-assumed superiority to the 'tragically self-annihilating' (p. 6) and anachronistic natives. Naomi Oreb's 'Mirroring, Depth and Inversion: Holding Gail Jones's "Black Mirror" against Contemporary Australia' (*SSEng* 35[2009] 112–27) argues that *Black Mirror* [2002], although so far mainly read in terms of postmodernity, in fact is a demonstration of its author's continuing concern with the lasting effects of colonization. Oreb's fluent essay will lead the reader back to the novel.

Paul Sharrad's 'Beyond Capricornia: Ambiguous Promise in Alexis Wright' (*ALS* 24:i[2009] 52–65) canvasses reviews of Wright's *Carpentaria* [2006] and the much less well-known *Plains of Promise* [1997] to estimate the novels' effectiveness in steering between a too rigorous depiction of Aboriginal society that might alienate readers who found it depressing, and a more hopeful depiction that might allow them to disengage from her call for amelioration with the excuse that problems are already being solved. However, the article is ultimately concerned with Wright's narrative and linguistic strategies that constitute an 'imaginative freedom in which social restrictions . . . are transcended in parables truer because they envisage a larger reality' (p. 64). Maria Renata Dolce, in 'Telling the "Truth" about Australia's Past: Reconciliation as Recognition in Society and Literature' (in Dolce and Natale, eds., pp. 109–25), revisits at length the history of white–Aboriginal relations, arriving at what seems to be a relativist position: Aboriginal and non-Aboriginal versions of history 'are multifarious [and] disclose positive and negative sides of a fraught relationship . . . which constantly needs negotiation' (p. 117). The essay praises Wright's *Carpentaria* as an example of a literature of '"understanding", caring and partnership' (p. 124). Laura Joseph's 'Opening the Gates of Hell: Regional Emergences in *Carpentaria* [2006] and *Dreamhunter* [2005]' (*Southerly* 69:ii[2009] 66–80) argues that the two novels present a sense of place that is both 'regional' and 'vertical'. In Joseph's view, these two works privilege 'ascent over descent' and in that sense are 'anabatic' narratives, as against 'katabatic' descents to the underworld.

Michela Vanon Alliata's 'A Land of Ghosts: Peter Carey's *Oscar and Lucinda*' (in Dolce and Natale, eds., pp. 301–12) concentrates on the themes of Aboriginal dispossession and of gambling in a brisk and lucid reading of one of Carey's best novels.

Caterina Colomba, 'Kate Grenville Explores the Murky Depths of Australia's Past in *The Secret River*' (in Dolce and Natale, eds., pp. 85–100), is a surprisingly free-wheeling discussion of colonization, Australian identity anxiety, the History Wars, and Grenville's antagonization of historians by her claims of fiction's greater imaginative insight. Grenville herself meditates on climate change as being, in part, 'a problem of the imagination' (p. 54), thence on the passions, possibilities, and responsibilities of literature in 'The Writer in a Time of Change: Learning from Experience' (*GriffithR* 26[2009] 53–64), an essay which offers an eclectic range of reference, from Keats to neuroscience. A different scientific problem, that of the passing of time, is a theme in Terence O'Neill's essay 'Joan Lindsay: A Time for Everything' (*LaTrobe* 83[2009] 41–55), which O'Neill follows in the next issue of the journal with 'A Bibliography of the Works of Joan Lindsay' (*LaTrobe* 83[2009] 113–18). Lindsay's relationship with time seems to have been idiosyncratic—she boasted that if she wore a watch it would stop—but her provision of an ending which 'explained' the mystery on which her novel *Picnic at Hanging Rock* [1967] turns suggests a disappointing confidence in the power of rationality to resolve artistic puzzles.

Peter Otto's 'Rereading David Malouf's *Fly Away Peter*: The Great War, Aboriginal Dispossession, and the Politics of Remembering' (*ALS* 24:i[2009] 35–51) takes Malouf to task for narrativizing white Australian loss of innocence in the First World War instead of writing about Aboriginal loss at the hands of whites. In a way that is not explained, for Otto the omissions simply evoke presences ('ghosts') (p. 44) which are so pervasive in the novel as to become 'annoying' (p. 46). He drives home this argument by discussing a painting from the Great Sandy Desert, the Ngurrara Canvas, which he says 'is closely related to stories of loss and return' (p. 47). Jo Jones considers a related question in her excellent 'Ambivalence, Absence and Loss in David Malouf's *Remembering Babylon*' (*ALS* 24:ii[2009] 69–82). Jones draws on the trauma theory of Dominick La Capra, especially the distinction between 'trauma', which is 'devastatingly individual' (p. 72) and 'absence', which is 'a general, and often ahistorical, foundational trauma for a culture or community in which a previous state of harmony or unity has been disrupted and is now missing' (p. 72). She sees Malouf's vision as typical of a 'liberal empathy that conflates loss and absence and denies historical specificity' (p. 79) without which any attempt at reconciliation will be futile.

There were several studies of Tim Winton published, including a beautifully presented book from Cambridge University Press. Hannah Rachel Bell's *Storymen* compares the understanding of place evident in Winton's fiction with that of indigenous intellectual David Mowaljarlai. The book is directed towards a general audience, but is significant for literary scholars in arguing a connection in Winton's fiction that has not so far been discerned. The most ostentatiously polemical contribution on Winton is Nathanael O'Reilly's '"No one gives a fuck about Australia": Aussies Abroad in *The Riders* and

Homesickness' (in Dolce and Natale, eds., pp. 207–15), which reads novels by Winton and Murray Bail to confirm O'Reilly's own observation that in Europe Australians are treated with hostility or indifference. Concise and clear explications of the novels to some extent make up for the theoretical paucity of the argument. Stephen Torre's 'Turning as Theme and Structure in Tim Winton's Short Stories' in the same collection (pp. 281–92) argues that Winton's theme in *The Turning* is the omnipresence of 'turn' or change. There are gestures to Iser and to narratology, but the essay remains rather plot-bound, and hence, because it is about Winton, interesting but depressing.

Susan Carson's 'Finding Hy-Brazil: Eugenics and Modernism in the Pacific' (*Hecate* 35:i–ii[2009] 124–33) argues that Eleanor Dark's novel *Prelude to Christopher* [1934] offers an insight into local debates about the agendas and consequences of science, medicine, and, in particular, the eugenics movement. This essay is part of the special issue of *Hecate*, edited by Carole Ferrier and Bonnie Kime Scott, which presents useful discussions of the intersection of feminism, modernism, and literary culture and a panoramic essay by the latter author, 'First Drafts for Transnational Women's Writing: A Revisiting of the Modernism of Woolf, West, Fauset and Dark'. Ann Vickery offers detailed analysis in 'An Uncanny Vernacular: Comparing the Radical Modernisms of Lorine Niedecker and Lesbia Harford', while Susan Sheridan's 'When Was Modernism? The Cold War Silence of Christina Stead' suggests that Stead's lack of literary output from the early 1950s until the end of the 1960s reflected the difficulties of categorizing her writing, which was 'neither high modernist nor social realist'. Brigid Rooney's 'Manifesto of the Senses' (*ALS* 24.iii–iv[2009] 53–65) discusses the paradox of 'blind sightedness' in Stead's *For Love Alone*. There is a double level of vision whereby neither Teresa nor the reader can resolve puzzles or anxieties of which they are aware until the conclusion of the novel, which clarifies Teresa's position in relation to both Crow and Quick. An indication of this resolution, but not a simple key to it, is the revelation of Crow's colour-blindness. Michael Ackland's 'Modelled on Blake? Christina Stead's Communist Affiliations and her Problematic Fellow-Travellers' (in Dolce and Natale, eds., pp. 17–31) argues that Stead was actually more strongly Marxist than current views (anchored by Hazel Rowley's biography) allow. Ackland claims that there is ample evidence by the mid-1930s of Stead's commitment to communist principles, although she rebelled against the conformity the Party sought to impose on its writers. She found support from the Marxist author Ralph Fox, which enabled her to write novels in which the politics seem 'tantalisingly... open-ended' (p. 25).

Ann Vickery was, with Margaret Henderson, co-editor of the special issue of *ALS* entitled 'Manifesting Feminisms', with contributions by Rachel Blau du Plessis and Susan Sheridan, among others. Sheridan's 'Generations Lost and Found: Reading Women Writers Together' (*ALS* 24:iii–iv[2009] 39–52) argues that because of the nature of the feminist project there is merit in considering a group of women artists together. Her subject is women writers who flourished (or should have) in the 1940s and 1950s, including Judith Wright, Dorothy Hewett, Dorothy Green, Thea Astley, Elizabeth Jolley, Ruth Park, and Kylie Tennant. Of these, only Wright and Astley achieved timely success. Sheridan canvasses reasons (personal circumstances, male control of the cultural and intellectual agenda) for the invisibility of these women writers. Anthea Taylor's 'Dear Daughter: Popular Feminism, the Epistolary Form and the Limits of Generational Rhetoric' (*ALS* 24:iii–iv[2009] 96–107) is a review of stringent criticisms of two senior second-wave feminists' advice to the next generation. Phyllis Chesler's *Letters to a Young Feminist* [1998] and Anne Summers's 'Letter to the Next Generation' (which was included in the 1994 edition of her influential feminist history of Australia, *Damned Whores and God's Police* [1975]) have been critiqued for their 'generational' (p. 101) rhetoric, with its tropes of handing on the torch and tone of needing to recall to duty unthinking offspring. Perhaps most notable of all, the essays were criticized for presenting their view of feminist history as secure, homogeneous, and unproblematic, thereby evincing the very patriarchal complacency they abjure.

Sharyn Pearce's 'Constructing a "New Girl": Gender and National Identity in *Anne of Green Gables* and *Seven Little Australians*' (in Blackford, ed., *100 Years of Anne with an 'e': The Centennial Study of Anne of Green Gables*, pp. 229–45) is concerned with the relationship between literary representation and national identity, arguing that there is a popular and powerful—if temporary—personification of nation via each 'cultural hero' protagonist of these children's classics. A similar but more wide-ranging comparative discussion is Janet Wilson's 'Constructing the Metropolitan Homeland: The Literatures of the White Settler Societies of New Zealand and Australia' (in Keown et al., eds., *Comparing Postcolonial Diasporas*, pp. 125–45). Wilson moves quickly across many texts, mainly novels, to show the different ways available to represent the connection to England. In a subtle and astute essay Elaine Minor challenges novelist Christopher Koch's self-described abhorrence of popular culture, arguing that ample evidence of his interest in comics is demonstrated in his fiction, particularly *Highways to a War* [2004] (see pp. 5–6). 'Christopher Koch: Drawn to Comics' (*JASAL* special issue[2009] 11) concludes that this novel reflects its author's capacity to bring popular and high culture together, albeit in ways that reflect a deep nostalgia for a lost Australian identity. A slightly different conclusion is reached in Chad Habel's comparative study of Koch and Thomas Keneally, 'Christopher Koch: Crossing Sea Walls' (in Hosking et al., eds., pp. 224–31), which proposes that the two writers differ in their deployment of 'ancestry'. While Keneally focuses on national identity and Koch on gender, 'Keneally promotes a positive sense of identification, whereas Koch focuses on absence and loss, underscoring missed opportunities' (p. 224). Habel claims that Koch's novels are unified by consistently showing protagonists attempting to cross borders or liminal spaces only to be frustrated and defeated.

Maggie Nolan's 'Who's a Weird Mob? Imagining Assimilation in Postwar Australia' (in Summo-O'Connell, ed., *Imagined Australia: Reflections around the Reciprocal Construction of Identity between Australia and Europe*, pp. 265–76) analyses reviews of John O'Grady's *They're a Weird Mob* [1957], purportedly the autobiography of an Italian journalist who quickly and happily assimilates to his new home in Australia. Nolan offers a perceptive view of the book's nonchalant approach to conflict and inequality in Italy and in Australia. Marilena Parlati's 'Looking for/at Australia: Roots and

Repulsion in Contemporary Australian Women's Writing' (in Summo-O'Connell, ed., pp. 257–60) offers a vigorous but sadly brief engagement with the translation and criticism of Rosa Cappiello's influential novel *Paese Fortunato* [1981]—in English, *Oh Lucky Country* [1984]—being distracted at first by a lengthy set of meditations on key terms. Contrastingly, Roberta Trape's 'Italy and the Transformation of the Traveller in Robert Dessaix's *Night Letters*' does much more than it promises, presenting a useful survey of representations of Italy in Australian writing before considering Dessaix's dialogue with Dante's *Inferno* in his 1996 novel. A different perspective from Parlati's is presented by the translator of *Paese Fortunato*, Gaetano Rando, in his tribute to Cappiello (who died in 2008). In 'The Cappiello Legacy' (*HEAT* 20[2009] 209–19), Rando discusses the translating of *Paese Fortunato* in some detail and thereby explains some of the issues raised by Parlati.

The year saw a peculiar convergence of interest in genre fiction and the Australia–France connection, manifested in an efflorescence of interest in mid-century detective novelist Arthur Upfield. Alistair Rolls's anchor essay in his edited collection *Mostly French: French (in) Detective Fiction*, 'An Uncertain Space: (Dis-)Locating the Frenchness of French and Australian Detective Fiction' (pp. 19–51) relates the spatial indeterminacy of earlier Australian detective novels (presumably to maximize an international readership) to more abstract indeterminacies in French detective fiction resulting from (1) its post-war commencement with translations of American texts, (2) its adoption of the spirit of modernism and the *flâneur*, (3) French loss of identity resulting from the German occupation, and (4) French detective fiction's recent evolution towards self-reflexive criticism. In 'Lost—and Found—in Translation: The Frenchification of Australian Crime' John West-Sooby discusses the translation of titles of Australian novels into French in the contexts of series conventions and paratextual social signals. He compares rhetorical effects such as alliteration in titles and their translations, and notes the predilection of the translations for more indirect or 'second-degree themes and devices' (p. 131). The article includes a select bibliography of Australian novels that have been translated into French, from Upfield to the present.

Susan Barrett's 'The Translation and Marketing of Australian Literature in France' (in Dolce and Natale, eds., pp. 17–31) shows how, despite the Australian government's programmes for subsidizing translation and bringing French publishers to Australian literary festivals, apart from travel guides, children's books on Aborigines and fauna, and Upfield novels, there has been less interest in commissioning French editions of Australian books than there has in commissioning South African or New Zealand ones. Judith Johnston's 'L'Amour aux Antipodes: Tasma, Australia and the French Connection' (*CVE* 69:viii[2009] 59–76) discusses Tasma's only known story in French to argue that the feebleness of the love plot was overlooked because the story otherwise connected with the intersection of anticlericism and feminism in France when the story was first published in 1880.

Jean Fornasiero, in 'Wakefield Queens of Crime Go to Paris: The Publishing Adventures of Patricia Carlon and Charlotte Gay' (in Rolls, ed., pp. 141–54), points to a dilemma that crime authors face: 'At what point does local identity or colour conflict with the suitability of a work for international publication, or conversely, enhance its chances?' (p. 144). This conundrum is explored in the careers of Carlon and Gay, whose detective fiction was published in the UK and the US in the 1950s and 1960s but then went out of print until it was republished in a 'classics' series by the independent Adelaide publisher Wakefield Press. This led to republication in the US and thence to French translations. A brief discussion of translation issues points out that sometimes even an exact verbal translation has to be nuanced by adjustments to punctuation. Sue Ryan-Fazilleau, in '*Murder in Montparnasse* and Kerry Greenwood's French Connection' (pp. 77–92), considers Greenwood's only Phryne Fisher novel set in France, which is explicated in terms of plot and stereotype, and more interestingly in relation to the real-life people attending the 1920s literary salon run by American expatriate Natalie Barney. Toni Johnson-Woods's 'Crime Fiction's Cultural Field: Carter Brown in France' (pp. 53–73) shows that more of the novels were translated and published in France than were republished in the US. After speculating on the reasons for this Gallic popularity, Johnson-Woods cites examples of arbitrariness in the translation and illustrations on the covers of the French editions.

In 'Re-Assessing Arthur W. Upfield's Napoleon Bonaparte Detective Fiction' (in Rolls, ed., pp. 93–120), John and Marie Ramsland argue that Upfield's appeal came from the realism of his nature depictions and the divided heritage of his protagonist. This essay is a broad introduction to Upfield's series without much emphasis on the French connection, although the authors do give examples of 'a fine thread of French referential language' (p. 16) in the novels, and mention some remarks by Upfield's French translator. Carol Hetherington, likewise considering the puzzle of Upfield's popularity, denies that Upfield's appeal relies on 'an exotic setting and sensational events'. In 'Bony at Home and Abroad: The Arthur Upfield Phenomenon' (*JASAL* special issue[2009] 12) she analyses Upfield's readership, his relations with overseas publishers, editors, and translators, and the contribution to Upfield studies made by fans. This is all part of a case for the seriousness of this writer; the point that the covers of English paperback editions of Upfield's novels were sometimes 'crudely and misleadingly suggestive' is conceded (or concealed) in footnote 5.

Huang Dan's 'Chinese Culture Cures: Ouyang Yu's Representation and Resolution of the Immigrant Syndrome in *The Eastern Slope Chronicle* [2002]' (*Antipodes* 23:ii[2009] 179–84) notes that Australian academics are represented as 'white businessmen': 'Chinese intellectuals are treated as suppliers of raw material about China' (p. 182), an ironic reversal of the trade in raw materials from Australia to China. More broadly, the essay considers the novel's complex treatment of migration and racism. Catriona Ross's survey of some thirty books in 'Paranoid Projections: Australian Novels of Asian Invasion' (*Antipodes* 23:i[2009] 11–16) is part of a special issue devoted to the topic of 'fear' in literature and film. Ross remarks that these books are notable for their astonishing sameness over a century or more (pp. 11–12), seeking to warn a city-dwelling and feminized Australian population of the horrifying threat posed by Asian peoples. Ross's thoughtful survey links nicely with Donna Coates's discussion of two accounts which are strongly critical of the political mendacity and military ineptitude in response to an actual military threat to Australia. Coates's '"Reality Bites": The Impact of the Second World War on the Australian Home Front in Maria Gardner's *Blood Stained Wattle* [1992] and Robin Sheiner's *Smile, the War Is Over* [1983]' (*Antipodes* 23:i[2009] 49–55), analyses responses to the bombing of northern Australian towns; Coates also contributes the chapter 'War Writing in Australia, Canada, and New Zealand' to Marina MacKay's *Cambridge Companion to the Literature of World War II* (pp. 149–62).

Roslyn Weaver's 'The Shield of Distance: Fearful Borders at the Edge of the World' (*Antipodes* 23:i[2009] 69–74) considers books which critique the 'complacency and optimism' that are the cultural effects of Australia's relative geographical isolation. Weaver concentrates on Neville Shute's apocalyptic novel *On the Beach* [1957], but offers a kind of 'lucky country' thesis, in referring to numerous texts which warn against an optimism that 'can prove unfounded and false' and thereby 'lead to catastrophe and disaster' (p. 69). The argument works interestingly (if not always congruently) with Richard Carr's account of five recent novels that implicitly contrast a new and dangerous world with 'an older, safer country' (p. 63), in '"A World of... Risk, Passion, Intensity and Tragedy": The Post-9/11 Australian Novel' (*Antipodes* 23:i[2009] 63–6). An older and more prevalent theme is considered in Elspeth Tilley's 'The Uses of Fear: Spatial Politics in the Australian White-Vanishing Trope' (*Antipodes* 23:i[2009] 33–41), which uses postcolonial precepts and psychoanalytical terms to consider a wide range of texts representing the trauma of being 'lost in the bush'. The failure of psychoanalysis to become popular in Australia is explained by Jean-François Vernay in 'Freudianism in Dire Straits: The Representation of Psychoanalysis in Contemporary Australia' (*AUMLA* 112[2009] 81–96). The essay is delightfully authoritative in its use of superlatives, and scolds Carmel Bird and Peter Goldsworthy for their insufficiently respectful portrayals of psychiatrists in *The White Garden* [1985] and *Three Dog Night* [2003] respectively.

Gavin De Lacy's 'Three Neglected Women Writers of the 1930s: Jean Campbell, "Capel Boake", and "Georgia Rivers"' (*LaTrobe* 83[2009] 26–40) notes that all three women have faded from the pages of literary history, but De Lacy argues that the fall of Marjorie Clark ('Rivers') has been greater than that of any other literary figure of the same period. Of the other two, both Campbell, *the* Melbourne literary celebrity of the 1930s, and Doris Boake Kerr, 'Boake', wrote of Jewish life in Melbourne, the latter in *Brass and Cymbals* [1933] and *The Babe is Wise* [1939]. Richard Freadman's 'Once Tortured, Forever Tortured: Testimony and Autobiography in Jacob Rosenberg's *East of Time* and *Sunrise West* (*PAns* 7:ii[2009] 279–98) begins with a broad-ranging introduction to the Jewish community in Melbourne and its literary production in the post-war period, dominated (in part for institutional reasons) by Holocaust memoirs. Freadman is alert to questions of definition as they pertain to relationships across autobiography, testimony, trauma, and torture, but is keen to argue the literary value of Rosenberg's oeuvre. John Scheckter's 'Morris Lurie: "Certainly There Is Irony"' (in Dolce and Natale, eds., pp. 273–80) is a stylish argument that Lurie exploits a secular

Jewishness that offers no rounded spiritual comfort, but rather sharpens the sense of awkwardness, aspiration, and disappointment. Scheckter proposes that Lurie's greatest achievement is in 'coming to an ironic truce with contemporary life' (p. 273).

(c) Poetry

Two biographies of major poets appeared in 2009, and as with other literary forms place and spatiality were prevalent themes in critical discussion. John McLaren offers a sympathetic portrait of his subject in *Journey without Arrival: The Life and Writing of Vincent Buckley*, a microscopically detailed examination of Buckley's personal life and institutional positions. Another scholar-poet is the subject of Stephany Steggall's *Bruce Dawe: Life Cycle*. Unlike McLaren's book (which is very strong on context and culture), this one foregrounds the poetry. Steggall's is the less convincing work, in part for being heavily dependent on its subject as informant. Lyn McCredden's 'The Locatedness of Poetry' (*JASAL* special issue[2009] 10) makes claims for a contingent but positive value of the local, illustrated through reference to the writing of Tony Birch, Lionel Fogarty, and Sam Wagan Watson. Jennifer Strauss's 'Building the Heart or Troubling the Mind?' (*Westerly* 54:i[2009] 18–24), which has the energy and speculative mode of a spoken piece, considers representations of place in the poetry of Gwen Harwood, Mary Gilmore, and Judith Wright. Christopher Lee presents a sensitive interview with poet Jean Kent, 'The Country of Unspoken Feeling' (*Antipodes* 23:i[2009] 88–92), in which Kent reflects on the influence of her country and small-town childhood, as well as her profession of counsellor and psychologist, on a poetry deeply concerned with memory, grief, and place. Kent resists, but casts interesting light on, Lee's attempts to consider her work in terms of a 'writing career' and the contemporary poetry scene.

Kevin Hart's '"Only This": Reading Robert Gray' (*Southerly* 69:ii[2009] 19–49) rehearses Hart's interest in 'thisness', read through Gray's own interests in Buddhism and his similarities to (and differences from) some key Western thinkers, notably Husserl. The essay ranges across philosophical questions, drawing the reader into agreement via co-opting plurals that might obscure the idiosyncrasy of some readings. A certain fastidiousness about the world emerges from Hart's own metaphors, which occasionally risk obfuscation: 'There is a sense in which we can say that Gray is a philosophical poet, perhaps even a religious poet, if we thoroughly rinse both adjectives and use them with care' (p. 33). A similarly dense and fertile essay, Ian Cooper's '"Equanimity": Les Murray, Levinas and the Breath of God' (*L&T* 23:ii[2009] 192–206), puts the case for Murray's poetry exemplifying 'a theology of grace' (p. 192). In a turn that might surprise Murray himself—and some of his critics even more—this 'grace' is paralleled with the ethics of Levinas's openness to the other.

Oral literature and forms of orality are imaginatively considered in Katherine Russo's substantial essay 'On Indigenous Post-Nostalgia: Transmedia Storytelling in the Work of Romaine Moreton' (*Anglistica*

13:i[2009] 73–87). Russo's intellectual starting point is her observation that 'academic criticism often reiterates the trope of media convergence as loss or as the replacement of a vanishing narrative tradition' (p. 75); her narrative starting point is an arresting account of the 'last man' trope used by anthropologist T.G. Strehlow to justify his publication of secret/sacred stories told to him by Arrente men in the 1930s. Russo argues that the denial of the capacity of indigenous peoples to access and to use creatively new technologies for cultural expression is a marker of the determination of colonizing cultures to lock indigenous people into a time/place of premodernity (pp. 77–8). Characterizing Romaine Moreton's poetry and poetry performance as 'transmedia storytelling', Russo offers an evocative analysis of the strategies by which Moreton's performances challenge non-indigenous accounts of temporality and white control over technologies of sound production.

Geoff Page's *Sixty Classic Australian Poems* offers brief critical essays on each of the selected poems, and shows a particular alertness to poetic form. The book will be especially useful to students for its models of reading, and seems designed to foster interest rather than close off discussion. In speaking of classics, Tracy Ryan's opening to 'Cold Greed and Rankling Guilt: A Re-reading of A.D. Hope's "The Cetaceans"' (*Southerly* 69:i[2009] 146–69) offers the seemingly bold claim that Hope's work is a form of cultural critique, particularly aimed at prompting 'self-examination' on the question of kindness to animals, a sentiment explicitly lampooned by Hope in another context. But Ryan's claims are well supported in a panoramic but closely argued exegesis that claims 'Cetaceans' is, in fact, noteworthy in being 'anti-speciesist' (p. 157). John McLaren's 'Kingdoms of Neptune: Seas, Bays, Estuaries and the Danger of Reading Skua Poetry (It May Embed in Your Skull)' (in Hosking et al., eds., pp. 161–71) offers a litany Australasian writers who have said something about the sea or the littoral (Kenneth Slessor, Allen Curnow, James Baxter, Vance Palmer, Thea Astley, Kate Grenville) before concentrating on Robert Adamson, who displays 'the symbolism of water as life, flight as freedom, and the fisherman as the participant observer who brings them into unity' (p. 166).

Anne Collett's 'Of Sages and Sybils: Alec Hope and Judith Wright' (*ALS* 24:i[2009] 66–77) is a detailed analysis of these two poets' criticism of each other's writing in light of their personal communications. Collett charges Hope with being made uneasy by Wright's poetry and rendered incapable of criticizing it insightfully because of his inability to surmount 'a patriarchal linguistic and aesthetic theory of creative process' (p. 74). John McLaren's 'Unsettling the Southland: Myths of Possibility and Origin' (in Dolce and Natale, eds., pp. 195–205) looks at three mid-twentieth-century monumentalizing poems about Australia by Hope, James McAuley, and Vincent Buckley that he finds essentially pessimistic or confused, and compares them with the more indirect poems of Wright and Dorothy Hewett, both associated with rural life rather than cities. McLaren finds a rejuvenation from land and a sense of history in Wright and Hewett, qualities which make their poems more effective 'national odes' (p. 204). Philip Butterss's '"Compounded of Incompatibles": *The Songs of a Sentimental Bloke* and *The Moods of Ginger Mick*' (in De Groen and Kirkpatrick, eds., pp. 16–27) reminds us that C.J. Dennis's argot is not authentic, but rather a mixture of street slang and educated (Australian) English. Much of the humour of these successful books depended on a series of oppositions, especially those between language register and situation. While it was a comparatively simple task to exploit such oppositions in the romance of the Bloke and Doreen, getting the tone of *Ginger Mick* right in the context of the war was a much more difficult task, especially given the impassioned debate over conscription.

Poets' use of the classical, the canonical, and the kitsch as inspiration caught the eye of critics. Luisa Pèrcopo, in 'Wizards and Witches of Oz: The Transformative Power of Words in Anna Walwicz's *Boat*' (in Dolce and Natale, eds., pp. 239–49) uses Salman Rushdie on the 1939 film *The Wizard of Oz* and David Malouf's *An Imaginary Life* [1978] on language to argue that Walwicz's poetry 'reshapes her sense of identity and re-signifies Australia' (p. 242). Amy Brown charts connections between James Joyce's *Ulysses* [1922] and 'ΠO's *24 Hours*: Ulysses in Fitzroy' (*Cordite* 31[2009]), emphasizing the implications of using epic, in keeping with the theme of the journal's special issue. Katrina Hansord analyses the use of the Lilith figure in 'C.J. Brennan's Femme Fatale: Representations of Female Sexuality in *Poems*' (*JASAL* 9 [2009]), paying particular attention to Christianity. Her argument is perhaps pressed too far where it aligns Brennan with early twentieth-century feminism. Toby Davidson's 'John Shaw Neilson: "Something of a Mystic"' (*JASAL* 9[2009] 13) characterizes Neilson as an Australian Christian Mystical Poet (we admit that the latter two capitalizations are misquotations, although they fairly characterize the tone). Davidson draws attention to 'distortions' in previous readings, which have underestimated Neilson's familiarity with symbolism, and misrepresented the nature of mysticism. Bernadette Brennan is rather less emphatic in 'Tracing the Spectre of Death in Francis Webb's Last Poems' (*JASAL* 9[2009] 12), which puts the case that Webb was increasingly prepared to contemplate and to represent death (or 'the void') in his very late poems. Walter Struve's 'In Search of "Herr O"' (*ZAus* 23[2009] 42–57) offers vignettes of a journalist and writer, later resident in Australia, whose novel *These Glorious Crusaders* [1934] Brennan translated from the German.

Oliver Haag's 'Indigenous Australian Literature in German. Some Considerations on Reception, Publication and Translation' (*JASAL* special issue[2009] 17) is a largely statistical study—nearly half of the seventeen pages are taken up by tables and documentation—which concludes that, while translation of their work into German is valuable for indigenous Australian writers, there are also examples of carelessness about property rights. Estelle Castro's 'Making Memory, Making Poetry: The Sovereignty of the Mind and Imagination in Contemporary Indigenous Australian Literature' (in Devy et al., eds., *Indigeneity: Culture and Interpretation*, pp. 269–78), offers an original, sympathetic, and erudite perspective on the poetry of Lisa Bellear, Romaine Moreton, and Kerry Reed-Gilbert, informed equally by French philosophy and indigenous perspectives on the personal and cultural uses of literature. Bonnie Cassidy's 'The Music of Fact: Sense, Place and a Network in Australian Poetry' (in Uhlmann et al., eds., pp. 228–43) is an ambitious attempt to consider the nature of bodily sensation and relationship to place as it is expressed in the work of some canonical Australian poets, with Cassidy acknowledging that 'connecting literary discourse with . . . the senses continues to feel a little intrepid' (p. 229). Adrian Curtin's study 'Alternative Vocalities: Listening Awry to Peter Maxwell Davies's Eight Songs for a Mad King' (*Mosaic* 42:ii[2009] 101–17) is far bolder in making such a coupling. This essay makes only passing reference to the work of librettist Randolph Stow, but offers a fascinating study of queer approaches to vocality.

(d) Drama

Two books on plays and theatre appeared in 2009, of which John McCallum's survey *Belonging: Australian Play Writing in the 20th Century* is the most likely to catch the interest of non-specialists. *Belonging* is centred firmly in the latter part of the century, with chapters on each of the last four decades as well as on Patrick White, David Williamson, Aboriginal theatre, and general themes. The book sacrifices depth for breadth, but will be useful to students and researchers new to the field in offering brief accounts of critical and cultural debates, key theatres and personnel, and, in particular, the plays (as opposed to performances). In keeping with this focus, there is a helpful list of published plays. The same chronological arrangement is evident in Christine Comans's *La Boite: The Story of an Australian Theatre Company* which, although it covers the Brisbane company's foundation in the 1920s (as the Brisbane Repertory Theatre Society), is interested mainly in the period since the late 1960s. The book highlights the contribution of two founders of the theatre: speech and drama teacher Barbara Sisley, and academic J.J. Stable. Gabriela Zabala complains that no history has been written of the Communist New Theatre in 'New Theatre—Unacknowledged and Out of the Mainstream: The Life of "A Theatre With a Purpose"' (*Southerly* 69:ii[2009] 187–200), the essay itself being a substantial attempt to fill this gap by paying particular attention to the encouragement of local writers, and the pursuit of political issues. Theatre historians are likewise well served by Mimi Colligan's 'Theatre in the Neild Scrapbooks' (*LaTrobe* 83[2009] 113–19), which details the contents of the Victorian state library's scrapbooks of James Edward Neild, prominent theatre critic in Melbourne in the second half of the nineteenth century.

Elizabeth Webby's 'Harlequin in Van Diemen's Land' (*S&P* 33:i–iv[2009] 176–84) traces the history of the pantomime in nineteenth-century Tasmania, scrounging what details she can from programmes and newspaper accounts where the play scripts have not survived. Webby argues that because the genre depends more on action than on words, performers were able to evade censorship and the 'panto' became a powerful satirical mode in the colony. Local businesses also paid for mentions in the panto—an early form of product placement. Robert Jordan's 'Australia's Worst Actor? The Life, Art and Business Practices of Mr. Henry Kemble of Drury Lane, Monopolylogist' (*S&P* 33:i–iv[2009] 185–216) is an exhaustively researched account of the career of a colonial actor notorious for his performances of Shakespeare plays in which he acted all the parts. The promises of cultural analysis in the arrestingly scatological opening of Russell Smith's contribution to 'Samuel Beckett's Reception in Australia and New Zealand' (in Nixon and Feldman, eds., *The International Reception of Samuel Beckett*, pp. 108–22) are not quite kept, as the argument is quickly overwhelmed by discussion of Beckett's plays and critical responses to performances. Two papers discuss an evolving theatre resource that Australian literature scholars need to know about, although it operates at the theatre-as-practice end of the drama spectrum. Jonathan Bollen et al., 'AusStage: e-Research in the Performing Arts' (*ADS* 54[2009] 178–94), describes the genesis of the database on theatre productions (accessible at www.ausstage.edu.au), and sketches the type of research that it has facilitated. Three specific functions discussed are its ability to show the geographical pattern of productions including the movement of touring productions; the 'sociogram' representation of networks of involvement by cast and crew in different productions; and the charting of (and participation in) blog discussions of Australian theatre. The article repeats Franco Moretti's warning that a quantitative research tool like this one 'provides data, not interpretation' (p. 178). Neal Harvey, Helena Grehan, and Joanne Tompkins, 'AusStage: From Database of Performing Arts to a Performing Database of the Arts' (in Bode and Dixon, eds., pp. 325–33) supplements Bollen et al. by providing more detail on the conception of the database and, crucially, its relation to AustLit. Whereas the basis of AustLit's records is 'the work', which has a new manifestation each time it is translated or adapted, AusStage's primary unit is the individual performance, called an 'event'. Thus it is not primarily a database of plays but of performances of plays. The article also discusses issues in the listing of theatrical ephemera and formal criticism.

Those concerned with modern theatre will also find interest in Brent Salter's *Copyright, Collaboration and the Future of Dramatic Authorship*. In the light of widely differing views among playwrights and theatre companies about who among writer, actor, director, and theatre company has the right and responsibility to control and profit from a play script, it is difficult to make a 'standard industry agreement' workable. Salter is impatient with 'the Romantic myth of the author', arguing that allocating sole copyright to the playwright does not reflect collaborative practices, nor the risks taken by production companies in developing the work of new writers, in particular. This question, of the fate of the author, is central to Susan Sheridan's 'Dorothy Hewett's Paths to the *Chapel Perilous*' (*Westerly* 54:i[2009] 170–88), which is less a study of the play than of the biographical contexts which saw Hewett famously transformed from communist writer of the late 1950s and 1960s to feminist of the 1970s. Sheridan gives considerable attention to the historical contexts of the relationship between, and Hewett's association with, these movements and boxes happily with most critics who have considered this period of Hewett's life and the 1971 play, called a founding document of women's liberation. Discussions of an author's juvenilia tend to overstate the way youthful productions prefigure mature works. Christine Alexander largely avoids this in '"In the hollow of the heart": Dorothy Hewett's Early Imaginative Life' (*ALS* 24:i[2009] 1–18). Drawing on Hewett's manuscripts at the Australian National Library and her autobiography *Wild Card* [1990], Alexander gives a charming picture of the child Hewett's intoxication with language, and the adaptations of fairytale imaginaries to her own strongly possessed locale.

Susan Lever's '"Lookatmoiye! Lookatmoiye!": Australian Situation Comedy and Beyond' (in De Groen and Kirkpatrick, eds., pp. 221–38) finds the accepted view that Australians write good soap operas for television but not situation comedy to be generally true, partly because Australian sitcom draws more on a vaudeville performance tradition than a script-based one. Geoffrey Atherden's *Mother and Son* remains an honourable exception. In the same collection John McCallum's 'Comedy and Constraint: Lenny Bruce, Bernard Manning, Pauline Pantsdown and Bill Hicks' (pp. 202–20) discusses comedy as licensed critique and explores three modern cases in which social and/or legal constraints were deployed against the comic. The parodic songs of Pauline Pantsdown were successfully injuncted during the 1998 Australian federal election campaign by their target, Pauline Hanson, and the defence that comedy does not operate in a real world was rejected in an appeal. McCallum argues that such a defence was misguided because it denies the very basis of comedy's relevance. Anne Pender's '"The Rudiments of Satire": Barry Humphries' Humour' (pp. 189–201) discusses Humphries' early career and decides that, fifty years later, he has not entirely abandoned 'his more perverse Dadaist antics' (p. 201).

3. Canada

(a) General

Image Technologies in Canadian Literature: Narrative, Film and Photography, edited by Carmen Concilio and Richard Lane, is an eight-essay exposition of the ongoing influence of film and photography on Canadian literary narratives. Covering modern, postmodern, and postcolonial authors and artists, the collection examines the role of image texts and technologies in relation to dialectic images, history, memory, performance, picture poetics, and translation. Applying key theorists of film and photography such as Roland Barthes, Walter Benjamin, and Susan Sontag to authors, artists, and poets such as Leonard Cohen, Joseph Dandurand, Stan Douglas, Robert Kroetsch, Ann-Marie MacDonald, Daphne Marlatt, and Michael Ondaatje, the book offers timely insights into the study of hybrid forms of Canadian literature and the theories that underwrite them. A good example is 'Dialectic Images in Canada: Joseph Dandurand, Stan Douglas, and the Conjectural Order' by Richard Lane. Lane explores how, within a theoretical framework provided by Walter Benjamin, Kwantlen First Nations poet and playwright Dandurand and photographer/film installation artist Douglas 'create powerful, revolutionary images that *cross* and at times *disrupt* theoretical domains, or, more accurately speaking, are complex constellations' (p. 137). To illustrate his point, Lane examines Dandurand's poem 'Fort Langley' and its accompanying image: a photograph by Frederick Dally entitled 'Indians, Fraser River circa 1868'. Dandurand found the photograph at his local library at Fort Langley, BC. Lane notes that Dandurand has cropped the image, removing Dally's handwritten caption: 'Indians shamming to be at prayer for the sake of photography. At the priest's request all the Indians kneel down and assume an attitude of devotion. Amen' (Davison, quoted in Lane, p. 140). By juxtaposing the photograph and the poetic text, Dandurand has taken the 'sham' and recoded it: 'instead of indigenous peoples performing a mode of belief imposed upon them by colonialism, the image is now seen as a "sham" imposed by Dally' (p. 140). For Lane, this creates a dialectical image with an explosive potential to deconstruct the discourse of authenticity while gesturing to its own presence in history.

'*Ladies and Gentlemen ... Mr. Leonard Cohen*: The Performance of Self, Forty Years On', by Keith Harrison, is another essay in *Image Technologies in Canadian Literature* that compels attention for its style and content. Harrison reviews the making and 1965 release of the National Film Board of Canada's documentary on Leonard Cohen. He begins his essay with a brief history: although the documentary began with the idea of filming Earle Birney, Phyllis Gotlieb, Irving Layton, and Leonard Cohen on their reading tour, the initial result was less than engaging and only survived re-edited and revised to feature just Cohen. Harrison then leads us through how this self-reflexive documentary was constructed, from voice-over to inserted footage of Cohen's childhood taken by his father, to a scene of a very young Cohen skiing. Harrison demonstrates how the film shows its own constructed nature and that of the celebrity, and is able 'to register the contradictions and ambivalences of both a poet and a nation at a time of shared emergence' (p. 80).

'Sunshine Cases of a Little Constitution' (*JCSR* 43:iii[2009] 146–68), by Ed Morgan, begins with the assumption that the ongoing development of Canadian law and literature has involved a process of continual national self-contemplation. He compares the leading constitutional cases of the Privy Council from the turn of the twentieth century with the writings of the leading literary figure of the time, Stephen Leacock, observing that 'Canada's constitutional jurisprudence has historically been characterized more by its fractured quality than its rational synthesis, while its literary output has been characterized more by incompleteness and diversity than by stylistic or thematic unity' (p. 147). Morgan also explores who and what serves the function, in Canada, of constitutional reviewer, as John Marshall did in the US, and who offers for Canada the literary enquiry and reflection that a Herman Melville or a Mark Twain did for the US. Morgan utilizes three short stories from Leacock's *Sunshine Sketches of a Little Town* for his comparison with Canadian historic case law. The essay, like the Canadian constitution itself, was created, 'with a unique, if fractured and partly accidental aesthetic' (p. 164), but one that rewards those with a reflective yet comedic temperament.

'Here the Country is Uncertain: Canadian Incarcerated Authors Transcribing Prison' (*Biography* 32:i[2009] 102–13), by Deena Rymhs, examines how life-writing by prisoners translates their experiences in the social and psychological spaces of internment to those outside the prison walls. Beginning with the little-known correspondence between Allen Ginsberg and Rik McWhinney, an inmate who at the time was serving a life sentence at the BC Penitentiary, Rymhs explores how the prison context not only influences the texts that are produced but also the subjectivity that produces them. Rymhs explores how this kind of writing might also allow prisoners to represent themselves differently to the way in which the law and prison construct them. She also considers the relationship between prisoner-writer and non-imprisoned reader. Aside from presenting prison as society in its most realized form and, alternatively, as a space of radical difference, Rymhs insists that 'these texts prompt a recognition of literature as social praxis at the same time as they urge us to question how we might read differently as we cross the threshold from one social space to another' (p. 103).

'The Return of Irony to Myth' *Revista de Filologia Hispánica* (*RILCE* 25:i[2009] 63–8), by Brian Graham, draws on Northrop Frye's *Anatomy of Criticism*. For Frye, there were five basic modes of literature: mythic, romantic, high mimetic, low mimetic, and ironic. Pertinent to Graham's argument is a particular passage in *Anatomy of Criticism*: 'Irony descends from the low mimetic: it begins in realism and dispassionate observation. But as it does so, it moves steadily towards myth, and dim outlines of sacrificial rituals and dying gods begin to reappear in it' (Frye, p. 42). For Graham, this return of irony to myth suggests a way of understanding postmodernism in general, and magic realism, specifically. Frye claims that ghosts are inadmissible in low mimetic and the better part of ironic fiction, but that in true myth there is no consistent distinction between ghosts and the living. Taking his lead from David Lodge, who argues in *The Art of Fiction* that in magic realism the marvellous and the impossible coalesce, Graham then argues that the return to myth, as it is incorporated in magic realism, is a return to a serious literature that can—indeed, often does—incorporate the supernatural without the loss of credibility. Frye thought that science fiction was a part of this return, blending a mode of romance with an intrinsic tendency to myth and closing the gap between serious and popular literature, and Graham sees this too as a characteristic of the postmodern. Using Frye's model, we find a literature moving beyond sign and symbol, away from plot structure into a poetic, thought-based work. The change is not simply stylistic but deeply epistemological, working with cyclical time and the eternal return of Nietzsche, Yeats, and Joyce. We also have the return of the reader as participant, as hero, in a creative process. 'The Return of Irony to Myth' is itself a return to one of Canada's great literary minds, and in this return there is even promise of more, for Brian Russell Graham's *The Necessary Unity of Opposites*: *The Dialectical Thinking of Northrop Frye*, published by University of Toronto Press, is due out at the end of December 2010. If his book on Frye is as articulate and informed as this short essay, it will be well worth the read.

(b) Fiction

In 'Trick of the Aesthetic Apocalypse: Ethics of Loss and Restoration in Thomas King's *Truth and Bright Water*' (*CJNS* 29:i–ii[2009] 237–55), Jesse Rae Archibald-Barber looks at theory and practice in King's novel. Symbolism and irony are elements often used in Native literatures, and Archibald-Barber argues that Western readers misread what looks familiar by assuming they carry the same epistemic system. She organizes the article as an introduction and five sub-sections that first address the novel's structure and its levels of meaning, then its symbolism and irony. In King's writing, the 'term "tribal" refers to stories accessible only to specific Indigenous communities, while "interfusional" describes works that combine oral traditions and contemporary written forms, and "polemical" indicates writing that represents conflicts between Native and non-Native cultures' (p. 238). What Archibald-Barber highlights, however, is King's use of Western literary conventions infused with 'tribal' customs to create a 'pan-Native' understanding. It is this cross-cultural context from which meaning derives: 'By working at this level, King, at least in theory, can situate his stories in the context of a Native community and also reach a more universal audience, while maintaining the integrity of an ethical Indigenous criticism' (p. 239). King's use of a fictionalized reserve setting allows him to 'associate the community with several Plains Indian cultures in general, as part of his pan-Native approach to writing' (p. 239) and also to infuse his characters and plotline with specific tribal histories showing the many conflicts felt through colonization. Archibald-Barber points out that King's pan-Native approach 'further set[s] up the critique of authenticity' (p. 240). As a consequence, in *Truth and Bright Water* 'the source of Native identity is elusive and paradoxical, because it has been both intentionally and unintentionally obscured' (p. 252).

For decades intentionally obscured, the effects of historic trauma transmission are conspicuously present in contemporary Aboriginal Canadian literatures. In line with this presence, Keavy Martin's 'Truth, Reconciliation, and Amnesia: *Porcupines and China Dolls* and the Canadian Conscience' (*ESC* 35:i[2009] 47–65) 'explores the desire for closure that governs not only novels like Alexie's but also national discourses around Aboriginal issues—in particular, the legacy of residential schools' (p. 49). Utilizing the lived realities of fictional characters in Arthur Alexie's 2002 novel *Porcupines and China Dolls*, Martin argues that 'rather than arriving at the expected denouement and hopeful, happy ending, we watch the characters continue to struggle, drink, and die' (p. 49). We are not able to turn the page—to begin anew—through a simple act of apology like that given by Canada's prime minister Stephen Harper on 11 June 2008. Martin suggests that, 'While healing and reconciliation are certainly desirable occurrences . . . these concepts can also entail a fixation upon *resolution* that is not only premature but problematic in its correlation with *forgetting*' (p. 49). She asserts that the apology was 'less about the well-being of Aboriginal peoples and communities than about freeing non-Native Canadians and their government from the guilt and continued responsibility of knowing their history' (p. 49). Alexie's novel, Martin believes, never allows the reader the cathartic moment of healing: 'the author does not allow his readers the comfort of watching his characters recover. The forward movement of their small personal victories and temporary relief from the memories of the past are always counteracted by renewed despair, further tragedy, and sometimes simply the inactivity or indifference of everyday life' (p. 60). As a result, she argues, characters and indigenous readers are 'forced to face the unpleasant, tedious, and exhausting continuation of a life . . . [along with] government rhetoricians and average Canadians alike' (p. 61).

Given the attention-demanding realities of the residential school experiment, what often becomes lost is that which is forever present within Aboriginal communities: humour. John Xiros Cooper explores this in 'Eva Gruber: *Humour in Contemporary Native North American Literature: Reimagining Nativeness*' (*ESC* 35:ii–iii[2009] pp. 214–18), arguing that literary humour 'opens a space for readers to re-imagine and renegotiate disempowering, predominantly colonial representations of Native identity' (p. 214). Cooper writes that 'Native literary humour is vital because the discourses so deployed subvert—often from within—Euroamerican stereotypes that justify the oppression of North America's original nations' (p. 214). Humour, Cooper argues, also allows 'Aboriginal people to reconfigure their own sense of themselves in the face of potentially overpowering institutional and media constructions' (p. 214) and literature can play a part in this.

The significance of humour within Aboriginal storytelling is also the focus of Kristina Fagan in 'Weesageechak Meets the Weetigo: Storytelling, Humour, and Trauma in the Fiction of Richard Van Camp, Tomson Highway, and Eden Robinson' (*SCL* 34.i[2009] 204–26). For Fagan, humour is a means of survival for a people who have suffered horribly at the hands of the government and church. She writes, 'laughter enables their people to bear the unbearable and thus to survive' (p. 204). Fagan observes that, regardless of the prevalent literature today that supports an awareness of humour within Aboriginal writing, 'humour and Aboriginal trauma [have] rarely been theorized in an academic context' (p. 204). Using *The Lesser Blessed* and *Kiss of the Fur Queen*, she investigates 'Aboriginal Trauma Theory' and advances a counter-argument to its validity by providing examples from 'Queen of the North' and *Monkey Beach* (p. 205). Against contemporary psychology explaining lived realities as a consequence of trauma, Fagan draws on anthropologist Michael Kenny to validate traditional storytelling as an alternative model: 'When we consider that Aboriginal societies have their own distinct traditions of storytelling, it makes sense to consider that Aboriginal people may express the connections between past and present pain in ways that differ from Western therapeutic models' (pp. 205–6). Fagan argues that it is important to critique Aboriginal theory but as an attempt to more fully understand it: 'seeking out "Native perspectives" on Aboriginal literature is a worthwhile act, and is essential within an academy that has generally not considered those perspectives... They have the potential to reveal aspects of Aboriginal literature that may not be considered, or may even be obscured, by Western theoretical approaches' (p. 223).

A new literary perspective is also now common in stories of pending global disaster. What is new is not the theme but the agent of destruction. It is not the Bible-inspired apocalyptic fiction of the past that William Deresiewicz in 'Honey and Salt' addresses but the dystopian variety in Margaret Atwood's *The Year of the Flood* (*Nation* 289:xiv[2009] 25–32). Deresiewicz points out that 'terrors of the modern apocalypse are not... to be dismissed, for they differ from the traditional kind in one crucial respect. It used to be that God would end the world, because only God could. Technology has made us capable of exterminating ourselves' (p. 25). He reminds readers of the literature produced during the twentieth century with its urban industrial setting—H.G. Wells's *The War of the Worlds*—and the Cold War—Nevil Shute's *On the Beach*—and notes that Atwood's second novel in her proposed trilogy continues to explore the plight of humankind as a direct result of science's genetic modifications. Deresiewicz asserts that *The Year of the Flood* 'is not, or not only, an extrapolation of current trends but something necessarily more radical: an investigation into what it means to be human. In the wake of universal disaster, amid extremes of scarcity and threat, the essential drives and qualities are laid bare' (p. 26). For Deresiewicz, it will not be for Atwood's lack of skill as a novelist that we don't understand the potential destruction of the earth because she removes the option of thinking that the problems only happen somewhere else.

Our compulsion to forget finds an artful antidote in Frances Sprout's 'Ghosts, Leaves, Photographs, and Memory: Seeing and Remembering Photographically in Daphne Marlatt's *Taken*' (in Concilio and Lane, eds.) Citing a significant body of writing—Joy Kogawa's *Obasan*, Thomas King's *Medicine River*, and Timothy Findley's *The Piano Man's Daughter*—Sprout makes the case that much 'Canadian writing [is] compulsively photographic' (p. 81). Sprout theorizes that Marlatt continues to pull on the 'photochemical play between light and dark, positive and negative—to suggest more inclusive ways of knowing and remembering' (p. 81). Photographic images give us access to memory, but Sprout argues that it is not what the photograph represents that is important but, on the contrary, what is not being represented. In the novels under examination, 'narrators also remember what the photographs fail to represent' (p. 81). What is critical for Sprout is that through this way of knowing, 'we see, remember, and memorialize the unseen' (p. 98).

Issues of Canadian national identity find expression in Michael Buma's 'Soccer and the City: The Unwieldy National in Dionne Brand's *What We All Long For*' (*SCL* 202[2009] 12–27). Buma shows how Brand represents sport as 'an important aspect of culture, a major site through which meanings and identities are produced, transmitted, and expressed' (p. 12). Brand's recollection of her attendance at a boxing match with many friends—'Latvian-Canadians... Russian-Canadians, African-Canadians... Anglo-Canadian, [and] even a Russian-Canadian promoter' (p. 12)—indicates the 'hyphenated-Canadianness... [which] reflects the urban realities of Toronto, Montreal, Vancouver, and other cities across the country' (p. 13). Because this hyphenism is a reality for many in Canada, Buma argues that the novel 'foreclose[s] entirely on the possibility of any homogenous national identity' (p. 13). She suggests that 'although soccer appears only briefly in *What We All Long For*, it offers significant insight into the tension between global and national categories' (p. 12), with Brand suggesting that 'Citizenship and belonging give way to becoming... [and] are constantly being reinvented' (p. 13). It is in the city, after the fictionalized retelling of the '2002 Federation Internationale de Football Association (FIFA) World Cup Round 16 match between Italy and Korea' (p. 15), that Torontonians identify with one or another country's nationalism—where the individual's cultural and ethnic backgrounds are realized not through characteristics thought of as essentially

Canadian but rather through the realization that Canada is a mosaic of difference.

Christian J. Krampe continues the exploration of the multifarious issues of Canadian identity in 'Inserting Trauma into the Canadian Collective Memory: Lawrence Hill's *The Book of Negroes* and Selected African-Canadian Poetry' (*ZGKS* 21:i[2009] 62–83). He claims that Canadian national memory is constructed largely on the basis of favourable recollections that 'strengthen a positive self-perception ... Victories are more easily memorized than defeats' (p. 63). However, Krampe points out that *national* memory suppresses many peoples' histories: 'Those memories deemed important for a group are kept "alive", while memories either unimportant or harmful to a group's identity are deleted' (p. 65). A nation's identity is dependent upon a 'coherent memory version and thus [on] an identity that is positive and devoid of major contradictions' (p. 65). For African Canadians, 'the historical denial of actual freedom and equality is closely followed by the denial of the existence of slavery and racism in the first place' (p. 75). Krampe suggests, then, that 'African-Canadian literature thus constitutes a counter-memory whose goal is a restructuring of the prevalent, "whitewashed" national memory of Canada' by undermining 'common stereotypes and notions of Canadian moral superiority and acknowledges memories that have been virtually purged from mainstream discourse for centuries' (p. 63). He demonstrates his thesis on three levels: *The Book of Negroes* supports the personal perspective through the protagonist Aminata and social perspectives through the other characters in the novel. He further employs other works of poetry and non-fictional writings to demonstrate the more theoretical components of his argument.

Significant contributions to understanding issues of identity are found in Ellen McWilliams's *Margaret Atwood and the Female Bildungsroman*. McWilliams argues that the *Bildungsroman*, traditionally associated with the male coming-of-age story, is turned on its heels and redirected by the female perspective in Margaret Atwood's novels: *The Nature Hut* [1966], *The Edible Woman* [1969], *Surfacing* [1972], and *Lady Oracle* [1976]. Moreover, McWilliams's book looks at the 'coming of age of a writer, a genre, and a national literature' (p. 1). The book is organized in three parts: 'Margaret Atwood and the Canadian Female Bildungsroman', 'Canadian Literary Apprenticeship: Atwood's Early Fiction', and 'Towards Maturity: Atwood's Later Novels', all of which provide a historical perspective and build a comprehensive case for McWilliams's thesis.

Another text that explores the female coming-of-age story is Kiley Kapuscinski's 'Exis-tensions: Surviving the *Red Shoes* Syndrome in Margaret Atwood's *Lady Oracle*' (UTQ 78:iii[2009] 902–23). The essay explores the paradox between the cultural limitation on female existence—a woman cannot be both female and artist without suffering dire consequences—and the same culture's belief in self-fashioning. Kapuscinski uses *Lady Oracle*'s protagonist Joan Delacourt, who is both female and artist, to analyse how her overeating is not so much an attestation of self-destructiveness as a coping strategy: 'while Joan's obesity signals her conflicted identity as a female artist and can thus be aligned with the self-harm anticipated by the *Red Shoes* syndrome, her projecting her creative talents onto various alternate identities can be read as a dissociative survival strategy that, for a time, permits her to maintain her divided identity as a woman artist' (p. 903). Kapuscinski observes that it is not until Joan is able to acknowledge her own internalized conflicts, born through her experience with other women in her early life, that she is able to find resolution: 'Joan ultimately refuses to allow her creativity to become the vehicle of her self-destruction, opting instead to use her capacity to imagine her world Other-wise' (p. 908). Kapuscinski concludes that Joan's 'resolution to maintain her identities as both woman and artist "but to keep the two roles separate"' (p. 909) is what Atwood herself has done in order to 'resist prescriptive cultural narratives' and to avoid the 'deadly designs of the *Red Shoes* syndrome' (p. 909).

(c) Poetry

An English Canadian Poetics, volume 1: *The Confederation Poets*, edited by Robert Hogg, with an introduction by D.M.R. Bentley, is the first of a series that seeks to present the most significant essays on poetic theory, written in English by Canadian poets, from the time of confederation to the early decades of the twentieth century. Volume 1 is a collection of thirty-one essays by Canada's 'Confederation Poets'. Blending a Romantic preoccupation with Beauty, Nature, and Truth with a Victorian sense of formal structure, these Canadian-born poets came to maturity in a post-1867 Canada, and being men—'members of the sex most qualified (according to the gender assumptions of the time) to celebrate in poetry the nation-building enterprise of the immense and young Dominion of Canada' (p. 38)—believed, like Sir Philip Sidney, that a great nation needs a great literature. As a consequence, they followed nineteenth-century European nationalism and endorsed the importance of poetry in the creation of a distinctive national identity. This initial volume offers a nuanced understanding of a poetic period and its genesis in the great movements of European art and literature. As a primer to current critical discussions involving identity, poetry, and national and transnational literature, *An English Canadian Poetics*, volume 1: *The Confederation Poets* is a valuable resource.

In the same literary-historical mode, Joel Baetz's *Canadian Poetry from World War I* is the first anthology solely devoted to Canadian poetry from one of the most dramatic and defining events of the twentieth century. Included in the collection are many of the nation's most important writers, from Helena Coleman to E.J. Pratt, from Charles G.D. Roberts to Robert Service. Biographical notes and historical references provide a context for understanding the salient images of Canada at war, and the enduring hope that found expression through the voices of early twentieth-century Canadian poets. Besides being a unique collection of poems, this anthology also deserves attention for including criticism and correspondence between poets and from poets to friends and kin.

Erica Kelly's 'Was Ever an Adventure without its Cost?' (*CanL* 200[2009] 37–54) is an exploration of the ambiguities of Canada's nation-building through the medium of E.J. Pratt's 1952 Governor General's Award-winning poem *Towards the Last Spike*. For Kelly, during the early phases of the Second World War, Canada began to imagine its post-war status as a nation free of the rule of the empire, while simultaneously fearing for its newly established freedom. Unlike many critics who read Pratt's poems as a simple celebration of Canadian history and *Towards the Last Spike* as a final spike in his own literary career, Kelly's close reading suggests that the poem is one rich in irony and in a complexity that questions both the cost of nation-building and the destructive legacy of the new powers in a post-war world made suddenly different by the splitting of the atom. Kelly also reads in the poem the problematic history of the Métis and the CPR's involvement in the silencing of their Red River Rebellion. The poem becomes a site of contesting forces in which Canada's history and its way to nationhood are critiqued: Macdonald has nightmares of Riel and the rebellion; he is also sickened by the demands of 'treaty-wise' Natives and the land claims that would need to be addressed. In the end, says Kelly, *Towards the Last Spike* is not so much about the 'then' of Canadian history but its problematic 'now'.

Part of that problematic now, or at least its expression from a literary perspective in *Transnational Canadas: Anglo-Canadian Literature and Globalization*, by Kit Dobson, is the institutionally sponsored literature around which the Canadian nationalism of the 1960s and 1970s sought to consolidate its identity itself coming into radical encounter with multiculturalism in the 1980s and 1990s, dismantling in the process its ethnocentrism. Adding to that transformation, it has now been conjoined with globalization. As a consequence, says Dobson, there is now a need to read Canadian literature in wider contexts and to carefully reconsider questions of belonging and the subjectivities that a world of global capitalism constructs. Dobson uses transnational theory to recontextualize Canadian literature written since the 1967 national centennial. One of his points of entry is the writing of Jeff Derksen, a BC poet and social critic, who first came to prominence through his work with the Kootenay School of Writing. Dobson analyses 'Jerk', a poem from Derksen's collection *Transnational Muscle Cars* [2003]. The speaker in the poem addresses the pervasive presence of capitalism and the way in which its strategy of branding has named, and claimed as commodity, the urban and rural landscapes. Derksen's poetry is an intervention, as personal as it is political, inviting consideration of the shifting sense of our subjectivity in a world of global capitalism.

Another writer of interest for Dobson is the Métis poet Gregory Scofield, whose effort to evade a state-imposed identity in favour of a fluid sense of indigenous selfhood based upon traditional and contemporary knowledges is particularly instructive. Scofield's poem 'Mix Breed Act', from *Native Canadiana* [1996], begins with the line 'How do I act without an Indian Act', artfully encapsulating the constraints and possibilities that moving beyond identity politics allows for 'other rezless Indians'. Dobson finds in Scofield and other writers similarly positioned a spirit of 'rezless/restless and resistant flexibility...in a complex relationship with the nation-state, its funding bodies, and its literary market place, all of which entail compromise and negotiation' (p. 206). Following Michel Foucault, Dobson believes that our ability to think about our subjectivity and the way in which we are governed and constituted as subjects is key to moving forward.

Shane Neilson's *Approaches to Poetry: The Pre-Poem Moment* moves from a focus on the future to an enquiry into origins. In fact, Neilsen's anthology asks of its poet contributors a simple question: how did the poem come to be? His motivation to collect the thoughts of other poets began with his own sense of reverence for those ringing lines that stop our flight of thought and startle us into the pure pleasure of reflecting on the life of a poem and its context. In answer to Seamus Heaney's question in *Stepping Stones*—'Who's to say where a poem begins?'—Neilsen provides an anthology of inspired responses, from Wayne Clifford's 'Beginning' to Claire Sharpe's 'On "Aperture"', that offer an understanding of the origins of poetic inspiration.

'Having a Conversation with the Place You're In: Discussing the Past, Present, and Future of Atlantic-Canadian Poetry with Brian Bartlett, Ross Leckie, Lindsay Marshall and Anne Simpson' (*DR* 89:i[2009] 25–37), by Alexander Macleod, is an interview with four of Atlantic Canada's leading authors that addresses the existence of a distinct Atlantic Canadian literature and the duality of regional/national culture. Relation to place, the role and importance of mentors, the responsibility of writers, the value of community, and advice for young poets are all topics in this engaging conversation.

Revisioning the genealogy of Canadian literary modernism, Di Brandt and Barbara Godard edit an impressive array of essays on the contributions of women critics, cultural activists, experimental prose writers, and poets Elizabeth Brewster, Dorothy Livesay, Jay Macpherson, Anne Marriott, P.K. Page, Elizabeth Smart, and Miriam Waddington in *Wider Boundaries of Daring: The Modernist Impulse in Canadian Women's Poetry*. While their role has been ignored in the making of a Canadian modernism, these women are the real founders, the contributors to this anthology argue, not only for their literary experiments but also for their wide-ranging cultural activism. Besides fulfilling the roles of wives, mothers, social workers, editors, teachers, and critics, they also established literary magazines, formed writers' groups, wrote newspaper columns, and engaged on public radio in intellectual and aesthetic debates. The editors divide the anthology into two parts. The first, 'The Making of Canadian Literary Modernism', includes Sandra Djwa's engaging semi-biographical essay, 'P.K. Page: Discovering a Modernist Sensibility'. Djwa traces Page's intellectual and aesthetic growth from its early beginnings in the international modernism of Virginia Woolf and Katherine Mansfield, through a middle period in which she immersed herself in modern art, literature, and psychology, to her close association with poets connected to Patrick Anderson's left-wing *Preview*. The second part of the anthology, 'Literary Modernism as Cultural Act', documents the range and diversity of these talented women. Pauline Butling's essay, 'Phyllis Webb as Public Intellectual', is a case in point. It details Webb's time as a founding director of CBC Radio's influential programme *Ideas*, how that work impeded her poetic production, and the way in which her position as director of a public forum on social, cultural, and political issues afforded her insight into the overwhelming male character of Canadian public institutions, insight which would later 'galvanize her to seek a more feminist-inflected community and writing practice' (p. 19). Candida Rifkind further demonstrates the anthology's thesis in 'A Collection of Solitary Fragments: Miriam Waddington as Critic', re-examining Waddington's critical writing from the 1950s to the 1970s and her exhortation for women writers to make more 'aggressive' feminist interventions in the public sphere.

While *Wider Boundaries of Daring* seeks to incorporate women into the Canadian modernist archive, Courtenay Richardson argues that poet David McGimpsey labours to expose the 'Can Lit' identity as a self-delusion that dismisses the enormous influence of American mass commodity culture. In 'Can Lit tm: National Branding and Canadian Literary Identity in David McGimpsey's Poetics' (*CanPo* 64[2009] 96–111), Richardson shows how brand names, fictional and factual, figure prominently in all of McGimpsey's collections. Richardson begins her analysis with his second collection, *Dogboy* [1998], in particular the poem 'Brands of Coffee/Literary Terms'. Juxtaposing 'Folgers' with 'Faustian' and 'Blue Mountain Blend' with 'Black Mountain Poets', McGimpsey effectively effaces the difference, argues Richardson, 'between the branding of tangible commodities like coffee and various cultural products, especially those that name or "brand" formal literary phenomena' (p. 97). Readers are invited to consider the financial realities of marketing a cultural product like literature and the complicity of academic institutions in the promotion of certain cultural concepts most beneficial to themselves.

Susan Gingell's 'Coming Home through Sound: See-Hear Aesthetics in the Poetry of Louise Bennett and Canadian Dub Poets' (*JWIL* 17:ii[2009] 32) moves away from the politics of commodity into the politics and poetics of community. In Gingell's case, it is the phonetics of the Jamaican oral tradition in the poetry of Louise Bennett and its relation to Canadian dub poets such as Jamaican-born Lillian Allen, Klyde Broox, and d'bi young, or the Canadian-born but of Jamaican ancestry amuna baraka-clarke. In analysing Bennett's textualization of Jamaican orality, Gingell argues that the great cultural activist, affectionately know as 'Miss Lou', creates a see-hear aesthetic that beckons her listeners home. Bennett's use of Jamaican English Creole, like that of the Canadian dub poets, also serves as a decolonizing act, giving voice and right of place to another dialect, reminding those who hear its resonance that a 'national language' is simply a dialect with an army.

In the process of creating their anthology *Prismatic Publics: Innovative Canadian Women's Poetry and Poetic*, editors Kate Eichhorn and Heather Milne were dogged by the question of why, when their stated concern is with innovative poetry and poetics, they would edit an anthology bound by the constraints of gender and nation. Their concern was heightened by the most significant debate on feminist poetics in a decade—an exchange between Jennifer Ashton ('Our Bodies, Our Poems') and Jennifer Scappettone. The debate became known as 'Numbers Trouble', and grew out of Ashton's claim that anthologies of innovative women's writing are inherently contradictory in that the writing itself seeks to destabilize notions of the gendered body while the very category of 'women's writing' maintains a logic of essentialism. The rebuttal to Ashton's position focused on the number of women writers actually represented in innovative writing communities. While the debate emerged in America, Eichhorn and Milne assessed Ashton's numbers in terms of Canada and responded with an important collection of women writers, few of whom have an uncomplicated relationship to nation and most of whom, 'maintain a complex relationship to gender and its implied identitary and political bonds' (p. 12). Beginning with the writings of Nicole Brossard and finishing with the works of Lisa Robertson, *Prismatic Publics* features women writers united in their effort 'to engage in the construction and interrogation of publics', with accompanying interviews that provide critical insight into their individual works (p. 12).

Malcolm Woodland's poetry review in *University of Toronto Quarterly* (*UTQ* 78:i[2009] 25–75) is as surprising and delightful an invitation to explore Canadian poetry and its criticism as one could hope to encounter. It is an honest, humorous, intelligent, and insightful review of a wide range of Canadian poets published in 2007. Woodland begins his essay with a refreshing response to 'Heart', from Margaret Atwood's *The Door*, and its equation of criticism with cannibalism. Posing as a respectful cannibal, Woodland assembles his critical menu along the lines of 'relatively conventional lyric works; then, some novel-like long poems and strongly unified collections; third, some more avant-garde or experimental collections; and, finally, some strong volumes from veteran poets whose work has begun to take on a retrospective and valedictory quality' (p. 26). Beginning with a lucid analysis of Monica Kidd's collection of poems entitled *Actualities* and ending with a final tip for the pleasures of Atwood's 'Heart', Woodland's review is a wonderful example of what creative sensibility appropriately applied can produce.

In a similar mode, Kit Dobson's review of poetry received in *The Dalhousie Review* entitled 'Experiments in Disaster: Recent Canadian Poetics' (*DR* 89:i[2009] 13–23) begins by charting a shift in the concerns of recent Canadian poetry from what it means to be a Canadian to what it means to live in today's world. Dobson finds in the poetry selection 'an abiding focus on ecology, upon the earth, and upon the imminence of environmental collapse' (p. 14). To support his thesis, Dobson first cites A.F. Moritz's *The Sentinel*, a book shortlisted for the Governor General's Award, and then *Jeremiah, Ohio*, by Adam Sol. In the latter, a wandering prophet-like figure, Jeremiah, 'decries the follies of the world to the locals' (p. 14), damning billboards, dumpsters, McDonald's customers, and fast food chains as symptoms of a world in crisis. Dobson's review is necessarily selective, but is an excellent introduction to a number of new poets unified in their concern about our environmental and psychological ecology.

'Discourses of Nations, National Ecopoetics, and Ecocriticism in the face of the US: Canada and Korea as Case Studies', by Simon Estok (*CompAS* 7:ii[2009] 85–97), begins with the assumption that the environmental crisis is global but that local systems, bearing different cultural valencies, will produce an ecocriticism differing significantly in its material application from an American ecocriticism which has tended to dominate this new field. To right this imbalance, Estok argues for a continued alliance between postcolonial and ecocritical studies in order to examine critically the interconnections between discourses of nations and national ecopoetics.

'*Eunoia*: Beauty or Truth (or What?)' (*AR* 67:i[2009] 138–52), by Jerome McGann, is a memorable piece with which to end our review of some of the more salient criticism of poetry published in 2009. It is staged as a take-home exam with a final question, for extra marks, that invites discussion of *Eunoia* [2001], a book of univocalic poetry by Christian Bök, as an example of 'beautiful thinking'. McGann's criticism emerges in the form of a dialogue between two students preparing for the exam. 'Eunoia', we learn, 'is the shortest word in English to contain all five vowels and the word quite literally means "beautifully thinking"' (*Eunoia*, p. 103). Bök found it in William Hayley's 1780 poem 'The Triumphs of Temper', and an etymological search reveals that its cognates are 'kindness' or 'good will'. Bök combines these ideas, dividing *Eunoia* into five chapters; each is a univocal lipogram—the first chapter has A as its only vowel, the second E, and so on. Each vowel takes on its own distinct personality: 'the I is egotistical and romantic, the O jocular and obscene, the E elegiac and epic (including a retelling of the Iliad!)', notes the publisher, Coach House Books, in its promotional script. While the pre-exam enquiry is an excellent prelude to readers unfamiliar with Bök's linguistic dexterity, McGann does not confine his review to *Eunoia* but ventures into another of Bök's books, *Pataphysics: The Poetics of an Imaginary Science* [2001], a ludic exploration of the potential for the combination of alphabetical signs. Bök's exploration, we learn through McGann's student researchers, redefines the realm of poetic truth, creating a science of speculative possibilities: 'The truth of the ludic abides no belief; instead, such truth is *entertained* as one of many hypothetical alternatives. It is merely a potentiality' (*Pataphysics*, p. 73).

(d) Drama

Potentiality, of course, is what interested Aristotle most about drama. Indeed, in response to Plato's attack on art and poetry in Book X of *The Republic*, Aristotle argues, in *Poetics*, that we learn by imitation and that drama, the art of imitation, presents the greatest stage for learning about what is possible. While traditional thought has imagined the direction of that learning as flowing from playwright, play, and stage through actors and actresses to audience, the Fall 2009 edition of *Canadian Theatre Review* 140 is dedicated to the changing nature of audiences, performances, and performance sites. The edition, appropriately entitled 'Audiences', begins with the acknowledgement that a shift in control has occurred from the producers to consumers of entertainment, art, popular culture, and news (*CTR* 140[2009] 5–7). As citizens of a 'digital democracy', we can vote, by remote, on our choice of drama, music, or cinema. If spectatorship is changing, the issue queries, 'how is (or should) theatre be keeping up?' (p. 5). The issue begins with 'The Peripatetic Audience' (*CTR* 140[2009] 8–13), an essay by Susan Bennett that studies how site-specific theatre increases our understanding of the relationship between performance and spectator. Bennett starts by gesturing to the now frequent audience-performance engagements such as the '"Shakespeare in-the-Park" companies; re-enactments ... designed to reproduce "authentic" history for the visitors of heritage parks, museums and other significant sites; entertainments in everyday settings like shopping malls; community-based dramas conceived with and for particular constituency groups' (pp. 8–9). These performances are part of her larger research interest in the mobilization of theatricality as a method of place branding for a world-wide tourist industry. In this essay she is concerned specifically with the ways in which the infrastructure of an area becomes a series of site-specific performances that create both pleasure and spending in an audience that simultaneously is being asked to view place as fundamentally theatrical. Utilizing Robert Lepage's *The Image Mill*, a spectacular multi-media celebration of Quebec City's 400th anniversary celebration in 2008, Bennett re-examines the performance–audience relationship from a reception theory perspective. As Bennett observes, 'For the tourist, a performance can be a way to learn about a place and, at the same time, can be instrumental in the production of memory: it is both an event experienced live and an archive-turned-souvenir' (p. 9). While Lepage's theatricality exists in the intersection of performance arts, digital media, and traditional theatre, Bennett argues that any site-specific performance requires a diverse, collaborative, and mobile activity, and one that rewrites for a peripatetic audience the contract between production and reception.

'*Uqquaq, the Shelter*: Building a Space for Intercultural Exchange' (*CTR* 140[2009] 45–50), another article in the same edition, is an interview between Lydia Wilkinson and the creators of the performance and video installation *Uqquaq, the Shelter*, Geneviève Pepin and Laurentio Q. Arnatsiag. Wilkinson begins with a memory of waiting for a friend outside a Toronto studio on a freezing night in February, before a performance of the collaborative work of Pepin, a dance interpreter, coach, performer, and dance teacher from Montreal, and Arnatsiag, an Inuit hunter, drum dancer, and artist, from Igoolik, Nunavut. She also recalls being asked to remove her shoes, put on slippers, and take a seat on the floor with other audience members who encircled the performance space, as the two performers set to work creating a shelter out of sealskin rope and wool. Two blank screens are suspended above the two performers, and Inuit singing is being transmitted from nearby speakers. In time, the singing and music stop and the screen displays images from both cultures: images of the Montreal comedy festival and the Arctic community and hunting scenes. The artists make no attempt to merge the two distinct cultures but, through performance, build a metaphorical shelter in which the difference between the two can be respected and celebrated. In one of her questions, Wilkinson remarks on the convivial nature of the setting, with its intimate enclosure and replications of the elements of an informal community. Arnatsiag replies that 'I wanted to create a piece that would be contemporary and that would be based on my life experience—hunting, fishing, clan life, solitude. I wanted to open a new point of view of my Inuit life. I didn't want to be traditional... For us, *Uqquaq, the Shelter* became a celebration of the birth of a new world, marked by harmonious cohabitation of dissimilar codes and legends' (p. 47). In a follow-up question, Wilkinson asks how the intimacy of the performance space affected the performance itself. Pepin responds that the impact was clearest in terms of space and movement. Because members of the audience were free to occupy the space in a variety of ways that they chose, 'sometimes, they took up space in which we had rehearsed certain parts a few hours before... Sometimes, someone's breathing or even certain movements would inspire me to create new gestures; similarly, Laurentio would be inspired to alter the intensity of his drum dance' (p. 47). The rest of the interview examines the depth of the intercultural exchange in the performance and its reception in Vienna as part of a project called North/South Lab, which incorporated participants from around the world. Wilkinson's interview, and her critical response to *Uqquaq, the Shelter*, builds a space for intercultural exchange and understanding, and for this alone she deserves applause.

'Inventing New Social Relations: Théâtre-Femmes and the Creation of the Feminist Self in Québécois Women's Plays', by Emine Fisek (*CTR* 140[2009] 91–3), is a review of editor Louise H. Forsyth's *Anthology of Quebec Women's Plays in English Translation*, volume 1 [1966–86]. The two decades between 1966 and 1986 were characterized by the rapid growth of the 'théâtre-femmes' movement in Quebec, and Forsyth identifies some of those plays written by 'québécois' women, translated into English, that subvert the patriarchal order and its theatrical space and are part of a larger théâtre-femmes movement. Fisek praises the selection of plays, Forsyth's comprehensive introduction, and the helpful notes on the plays themselves, which contribute to understanding the place each play assumes within the playwrights' respective works. Fisek also highlights Forysth's indexing of the feminist theatre's technique of *monstrance* (demonstration, or simply showing) as a critical element in women's innovations in theatrical writing. Fisek situates this technique within a lineage of confessional identity practices that surfaced in both Europe and North America in the last half of the twentieth century as a way of occupying civic space. Fisek also links the challenge of reading *monstrance* to the transformative capacity of language. Rather than adjudicate the plays by the scale of the transformation that they did create, Fisek suggests that performativity be rethought, not in terms of audience reception, but in relation to the plays that 'bring into being new understanding of the feminine self, understandings imagined, and, indeed experienced by the artists involved in the production' (p. 93).

If Fisek shifts the focus from the audience to the actors in the theatre, Floyd Favel, a theatre and dance director, playwright, essayist, and journalist from the Poundmaker First Nations in Saskatchewan, in 'Poetry, Remnants, and Ruins: Aboriginal Theatre in Canada' (*CTR* 139[2009] 31–5), laments the place of Aboriginal people in the current theatre system. Watching the Inuvialuit Drum Dancers perform at the Talking Stick Festival in Vancouver inspired Favel to write about what differentiates Aboriginal theatre from other theatres and the remnants and ruins upon which an indigenous Canadian theatre might be built. He begins by dismissing the differences as simply reducible to ethnicity and then insists that what is to be created must not be built on grants. Rather, for Aboriginal artists, 'Our words, gestures and feet originate in the ground in which our umbilical cords have been buried; this is where we should build our art... For there to be an Indigenous Canadian theatre, the theatre would have to be influenced and changed by the cultures and techniques that existed before colonialism relegated our cultures to folklore or the past' (p. 32). Favel believes that the rhythms of the land need to come on stage, not in their ritual form, but through a theatrical process that acts as a transformative bridge. He points to how Tadashai Suzuki has adapted Japanese performance principles from Noh theatre and combined them with Western performance structures and stories. For Favel, looking at these different cultures frees us to look at and perceive the world in a different way, in a way not defined by the limitations imposed by the English language. He conceives of theatre as a brother of ritual tradition: they share the same characteristics—action, narrative, and the use of a specialized or sacred space. Aboriginal theatres will not develop in the current Canadian theatre system but in the quiet interactions between the past and the present: 'This is the process from which a new theatre can be born, built on the whispered memories and tears of our elders' (p. 35).

4. The Caribbean

(a) General

For different reasons, both 'New Literatures' and 'The Caribbean' are not self-evident terms; the 'New Literatures' are neither as new and historyless as the name suggests, nor do they, as is implied, rely on an older body of (British) texts to achieve definition. Likewise, the regional approach taken in this section of *YWES* relies on a geographical logic that the Caribbean, in particular, does not sustain unproblematically. As Peter Hulme has suggested, the unstable signifier 'Caribbean' points to an 'Other America', the Glissantian term which Michael Niblett and Kerstin Oloff deploy in their collection *Perspectives on the 'Other America': Comparative Approaches to Caribbean and Latin American Culture*. In his essay contained therein, Hulme in fact does support a regional approach to Caribbean cultural production but argues for 'Expanding the Caribbean'; more specifically, he encourages comparative literary studies and area studies to engage with each other. He suggests we pay 'much *less* attention to propriety' (p. 43) and thus allow for consideration of early Caribbean texts, the voices of visitors born elsewhere, texts which are not easily categorized in terms of genre, and selected texts from bordering nation-states, such as Colombia and the USA. Advocating 'imaginative mass trespass over the established boundaries of literary history' (p. 45), Hulme is intent on expanding the Caribbean—not in an imperial sense, enlarging its territory at the expense of its neighbours, but by capitalizing on geographical, cultural, linguistic and historical overlaps.

Michael Niblett's reading of Eric Walrond's *Tropic Death* [1926], not in the context of Afro-American writing and the Harlem Renaissance but that of the Caribbean, might be one example of what Hulme has in mind. 'The Arc of the "Other America": Landscape, Nature and Region in Eric Walrond's *Tropic Death*' argues that Walrond maps out the violent character (in a Glissantian sense) of landscape, and by depicting the inhabitants as living on the land and controlling it, supersedes imperialist paradigms as they root themselves 'in the arc of the Other America as home' (p. 69). In the same volume, Theo D'haen's 'Exile, Caribbean Literature, and the World Republic of Letters' explores reasons for the international appeal of particular Caribbean texts. His thesis is that writers successfully separate themselves from their national literary tradition, thereby becoming part of a greater anglophone Caribbean one. He cites George Lamming's *The Pleasures of Exile* as an example of 'self-imposed geographical exile from [one's] native land' and claims that this gives Lamming, Maryse Condé, and others 'access to a world market of writing from which in their original native languages, and writing solely about their own native cultures, they would most probably have been banned' (p. 226). Kerstin D. Oloff is also interested in the conditions of international success. In 'Wilson Harris, Regionalism and Postcolonial Studies' she questions Harris's canonical position, attributing it to a correspondence between his work and the main concerns of postcolonial studies in the 1990s. She consequently calls for an expansion of the Caribbean canon to include texts that have 'been more resistant to being streamlined' in accordance with dominant theoretical predilections (p. 254).

In keeping with moves towards a more comparative approach to the field, Christopher Winks, 'A Great Bridge that Cannot be Seen: Caribbean Literature as Comparative Literature' (*CompL* 61:iii[2009] 244–55), sees the Caribbean as a transcultural site exemplifying Ngugi's and Spivak's calls for a decentralized postcolonial comparatism, mapping some of the commonalities (such as magic realism) as found in the region's theorists and writers. One example of how this might work, David Álvarez's, ' "Dis Poem is Vex bout Apartheid" ' (*JCL* 44:ii[2009] 107–22), includes a study of how three West Indian poems—'Soweto' by Kamau Brathwaite, 'Azania in Our Children's Names' by Lorna Goodison, and 'We Are Formed from Volcanoes' by Opal Palmer Adisa—represent South Africa in relation to its apartheid past. Brathwaite and Goodison draw a parallel between the South African struggle and anti-colonialist movements in the West Indies. The third poem takes a different approach, pointing out that South Africa functions as a 'static signifier for colonial and postcolonial wrongs' (p. 118). Allison Carruth provides another in reading Toni Morrison's *Tar Baby* against its Caribbean setting and a history of global hunger and First World consumption of sugar and chocolate in ' "The Chocolate Eater": Food Traffic and Environmental Justice in Toni Morrison's *Tar Baby*' (*MFS* 55:iii[2009] 596–619). Jeannine Murray-Roman, 'Writing Rehearsals: The Uses of Performance in Contemporary Caribbean Literature' (*DAI* 69:xi[2009] 4322–3), analyses French, Spanish, and English writing within a frame of performance studies, arguing that the unique/repeated nature of performance captures key aspects of creolization and that written texts draw on this. She charts different effects of textual, stage, cyberspace, and life sites of performance and political effects of work directing the performative towards the future or the past. Pedro Perez Osorio, 'Caribbean Worldliness' (*DAI* 70:vi[2009] 2040), brings poetry by Victor Hernández Cruz and Lorna Goodison together, analysing their common interests in travel, music, Sufi, and popular religion and magical realism to sketch a transnational poetic grounded in creolization.

By considering Barbadian and Nigerian poetry side by side, Curwen Best's *Kamau Brathwaite and Christopher Okigbo: Art, Politics, and the Music of Ritual* 'seeks to create a greater interest in the area of cross-cultural poetics' (p. 13). It draws a parallel between the two poets in respect of the colonial setting and the time of writing, their choice of similar themes, and the centrality of their work to Caribbean and West African poetry, respectively. This is also a study of colonialism, as selected poems are shown to have been shaped by the colonial experience. Other points of interest are the spiritual quest and the musicality of both poets' work. Music plays a pivotal role in Brathwaite's poetry, and is one means of including indigenous influences, as when he takes up the style of the tuk band, the indigenous Barbadian percussion ensemble. Brathwaite's approach here is described as being more pan-cultural than that of Okigbo, who focuses rather on understanding the individual and overcoming the contrast between art and politics.

Postcolonial Ghosts/Fantômes post-coloniaux expands and connects the Caribbean through intertextuality and intermediality. Edited by Mélanie Joseph-Vilain and Judith Misrahi-Barak, it addresses ghosts in their various historical, spatial, intertextual, and translational manifestations, linking them to poetic practice via Gerry Turcotte's poems, which run the length of the book. Anthony Carrigan's 'Haunted Places, Development, and Opposition in Kamau Brathwaite's "*The Namsetoura Papers*"' critiques the 'exploitative and often neocolonial practices' (p. 157) in the Caribbean tourism industry, reflecting on how cultural production can offer resistance and add to sustainability. Carrigan reads Brathwaite's encounter with the slave ghost Namsetoura of CowPastor as a celebration of the landscape's sacredness, showing 'how ghosts of the past have the potential to help augment more equitable social and environmental developments' (p. 171). Maurizio Calbi's 'Writing with Ghosts: Shakespearean Spectrality in Derek Walcott's *A Branch of the Blue Nile*' analyses Shakespearian influences in Walcott's play of a Trinidadian theatre company's staging of *Antony and Cleopatra*. Calbi concludes that Walcott moves 'from a "writing against or without" Shakespeare to a more complex sense of writing *with* Shakespeare' (p. 197). Prudence Layne's 'Reincarnating Legba: Caribbean Writers at the Crossroads' elaborates on works of Edgar Mittelholzer, Michelle Cliff, and Patricia Powell and their treatment of 'crossroad characters', arguing that these 'are the conduits between the spirit world, nature and the past and a shared vision for a peaceful and sustainable future' (p. 366). Timothy Weiss's 'The Living and the Dead: Translational Identities in Wilson Harris's *The Tree of the Sun*' reads Harris's novels as a revision of folklore and myth, situated at the interstice between life and death. Limbo dancing is just one metaphor of a process of transformation, which allows the readers 'to plunge, like limbo dancers, across the boundaries that fix us in narrow identities enclosed by time and place' (p. 385). Kerry-Jane Wallart's 'The Ghost in Wilson Harris's *The Guyana Quartet*: "Matter that Matters"' explores Harris's reconsideration of classical and postcolonial literary themes in his first four novels, claiming that its strength lies in its doing away with Eurocentric ideas of progress and its characteristic aesthetics of magic realism.

The region as a whole is theorized by Ulrick Charles Casimir as a circuit of local writers 'exporting' product to be validated by Britain and North America, which thus exerts a shaping influence on further Caribbean production. 'Conceptualizing the Caribbean: Reexportation and Anglophone Caribbean Cultural Products' (*DAI* Section A 69:x[2009] 3956) concentrates on Samuel Selvon and the films *The Harder They Come* by Perry Henzell and *Pressure* by Horace Ové.

The 'prehistory' of Caribbean literature is visited by Keith Standiford, who considers 'Space and Anxiety of Empire in Matthew Lewis's *Isle of Devils*' (*InteractionsAJ* 18:ii[2009] 123–40) and examines how time operates in the same text (*AteneaPR* 29:iv[2009] 35–54). Timothy Whelan assesses the anti-slavery press in 'William Fox, Martha Gurney and Radical Discourse in the 1790s' (*ECS* 42:iii[2009] 397–411). Slave-era writing also engages Christer Petley in '"Home" and "This Country": Britishness and Creole Identity in the Letters of a Transatlantic Slaveholder' (*AtS* 6:i[2009] 43–61) and Simon Lewis, in 'Slavery, Memory and the History of the "Atlantic Now": Charleston, South Carolina and Global Racial/Economic Hierarchy' (*JPW* 45:ii[2009] 125–35). Lewis draws on Toni Morrison's statement that '[f]reeing yourself was one thing; claiming ownership of that freed self was another' (p. 125) in an analysis of Charleston's black history. The article shows how the borderlands of the Caribbean might also be part of the region's story. Lewis criticizes the dominant narrative of Charleston as a prosperous port because this marginalizes the slavery that contributed to such prosperity. While acknowledging attempts in Charleston to commemorate past injustices, Lewis charges that 'current tourist practice... cannot be delinked from the racialized system of global capital made possible by the transatlantic slave trade' (p. 132).

Trans-Caribbean material is accompanied by work considering internal differences. These can be ethnic: Patricia Mohammed, 'The Asian Other in the Caribbean' (*Small Axe* 29[2009] 57–71) or sexual—queering the Caribbean continues to be a strong theme: Keguro Macharia's thesis, 'Queer Natives' (*DAI* Section A 69:xi[2009] 4322–3) discusses work by Nella Larsen, Claude McKay, Senghor, Kenyatta, and Fanon, arguing that the black diaspora challenges standard theories of sexuality. Kelly Baker Josephs, in 'Dissonant Desires: Staceyann Chin and the Queer Politics of a Jamaican Accent' (*Mosaic* 42:ii[2009] 153–70), considers how poetry slamming in the US by a lesbian Jamaican performs both community-building and communal blocking as accent, performance mode, and aspects of identity jar against each other. Comparisons are made to other Jamaican 'dialect' poets and Brathwaite's 'nation language' theory.

Complexities within the region can inspire new work across disciplinary boundaries too. Fiona Darroch's *Memory and Myth: Postcolonial Religion in Contemporary Guyanese Fiction and Poetry* is situated at the crossroads between religious and English studies. Its aim is to re-establish religion as an approach to Caribbean literature and postcolonial cultural production more generally. Analysing works of Harris, Agard, Nichols, and Dabydeen, among others, Darroch states that these add a religious dimension to both history and landscape, while also constantly renegotiating physical and psychological boundaries. Her approach focuses on landscape, memory, and trauma within a psychoanalytical frame. Darroch here uses the term 'religious imagination', a form of awareness linked to the world of dreams and fantasy, in which communal and historical memories interact. Psychoanalysis, when stripped of its individualist constraints, is seen to enable rereading of postcolonial literature. The monograph locates religion within postcolonial studies, showing how it has been shaped by colonialism. Darroch then reads selected texts against Guyanese history, presenting them as religious expressions that hold a healing power, and the act of writing itself as therapeutic. Harris's work is one example of how Guyanese literature can benefit historians, religious studies scholars, and postcolonial theorists alike due to its 'ability to recover painful memories' (p. 74), while at the same time transforming Western psychoanalysis into a postcolonial tool.

Diaspora remains a common framework for comparisons. Linda A. Winterbottom, for example, looks at 'Elsewhere Consciousness in the Fiction of Edwidge Danticat, Paule Marshall and Jamaica Kincaid' (*DAI* Section A 69:xi[2009] 4341–2), building on theorizing of 'elsewhereness' by Carole Boyce Davies and Michael Hanchard, while Keidra Morris shows how black American identity has shifted from 1960s homogenizing race solidarity to a mosaic of ethnicities in 'Troubled Migrations: An Analysis of Caribbean-American Women's (Im)migration Literature' (*DAI* Section A 69:x[2009] 3950–1). Matthew Mead revisits the *Empire Windrush* as 'The Cultural Memory of an Imaginary Arrival' (*JPW* 45:ii[2009] 137–49), and Nadia Ellis Russell considers 'Colonial Affections: Formulations of Intimacy between England and the Caribbean 1930–1963' (*DAI* Section A 69:x[2009] 3959). She focuses on the period 1930–62 and on works by Lamming, Salkey, and C.L.R. James. Her work is innovative in combining literary texts with essays, letters, policy documents, films, and interviews (including a discussion of homosexuality and cross-racial contacts centred on the Jamaican dancer Richie Riley).

Beyond the purely literary enclave, research into music and film remains a feature of Caribbean cultural analysis. Timothy Rommen, '"Come Back Home": Regional Travels, Global Encounters and Local Nostalgias in Bahamian Popular Musics' (*LAMR* 30:ii[2009] 159–83), situates the local 'rake and scrape' folk style in historical flows of labour, tourism, and inter-island musical forms. Juan Otero Garabís casts his eye over the corners and crossroads of the urban Caribbean in its music and literature ('Esquinas y/o encrucijadas: Una mirada al Caribe urbano en música y literatura' *RIa* 75:ccxxix[2009] 963–81). David Lizardi Sierra examines 'Jean, Dinah, Dorothy and the Rest: Representations of Women in Calypso and Literary Works of the Caribbean' (*DAI* Section A. 70:vi[2009] 2040). Folk traditions continue to attract scholarly attention. Robert W. Nicholls tracks the origins of the bull masquerade in the Lesser Antilles back to West Africa, tracking its modification to fit British traditions, in 'Running John Bull' (*Folklore* 120:i[2009] 133–56). Walter Rodney remains a point of interest as a political writer in Anthony Bogues, 'Black Power, Decolonization and Caribbean Politics: Walter Rodney and the Politics of *The Groundings with my Brothers*' (*Boundary* 36:i[2009] 127–47).

Cross-language work includes Nadège Veldwachter's 'Paratextes et pré-textes: Traduction de la littérature francophone antillaise en anglais' (*PALARA* 13[2009] 75–87) and Françoise Pfaff's 'Translating Maryse Condé's Caribbeanness into English' (*CLAJ* 53:ii[2009] 145–61). Veldwachter also deals with translations of Schwarz-Bart, Condé, and Confiant (*RAL* 40:ii[2009] 228–39). Aimé Césaire, in Martin Munro's 'Listening to Aimé Césaire' (*FPS* 7:i[2009] 44–60); Patrick Chamoiseau, in H. Adlai Murdoch's 'Autobiography and Departmentalization in Chamoiseau's *Chemin d'Ecole*' (*RAL* 40:ii[2009] 16–39); Edouard Glissant and Puerto Rican author Mayra Santos-Febres, in Juana María Rodríguez, ('Translating Queer Caribbean Identities in Sirena Selena vestida de pena' *MELUS* 34.iii[2009] 205–23); and Rosario Méndez Panedas, in ('El sujeto caribeño o la seducción de la alteridad en Nuestra Señora de la Noche de Mayra Santos Febres' *Espéculo* 43[2009] n.p.) all receive attention, many of them in the special number on the francophone Caribbean, *Small Axe* 30. Following the comparatist path, Peter Manuel, 'Transnational Chowtal' (*AM* 40:ii[2009] 1–32), examines Bhojpuri folk song as it moves from north India 'to the Caribbean, Fiji and beyond'. Ann Albuyeh tracks 'Reflections of African Language and Culture in Puerto Rico' (in Toyin Falola and Fallou Ngom, eds., pp. 143–62).

The African connection is reprised in Nereida Prado Rodríguez's thesis, 'African Caribbean Spirituality in West Indian Novels: From Realism to Spiritualism' (*DAI* Section A 70:ii[2009] 571), and Joseph McLaren, in 'African Diaspora Vernacular Traditions and the Dilemma of Identity' (*RAL* 40:i[2009] 97–111), highlights the discrepant valuings of Ebonics/creole in real life and in literature across Africa, the US, and the Caribbean.

(b) Journals

In *Literature & Theology* Rebecca Moore's 'Jonestown in Literature: Caribbean Reflections on a Tragedy' (*L&T* 23:i[2009] 69–83), applies Mikhail Bakhtin's concepts of centripetal and centrifugal forces and the carnivalesque to Caribbean narratives of the Jonestown catastrophe. The central narrative of Jonestown: 'all about crazy cultists who drank the Kool-Aid under the coercion of a lunatic' (p. 72) is challenged by four 'counter-narratives'. Shiva Naipaul reads the rise of the People's Temple as a consequence of decadent 1960s Californian culture. Guyana's own decay is reflected in the regime's corruption and the extremist opposition. Naipaul mourns a country 'mortally wounded by its colonial past' (p. 75). Secondly, Gordon K. Lewis ties Jonestown to the history of the Caribbean as El Dorado and stresses the multiple links between it and the government. Fred d'Aguiar's 'Jonestown' poem calls for a 'Bill of Rights' to combat the oppression and domination exhibited in the world by Jim Jones and colonialism alike. Lastly, Wilson Harris's novel *Jonestown* stands out for its non-linear narrative techniques and for placing Jonestown into the larger picture of imperial history, although this approach might be offensive to the victim's families.

David Winks's 'Forging Post-Colonial Identities through Acts of Translation?' (*JACS* 21:i[2009] 65–74) reflects on how translation can be repossessed by postcolonial subjects despite its long-standing history as means of oppression. Winks shares Rushdie's belief that 'something can be gained' (p. 65) from translation, and cites Achebe's *Things Fall Apart* as an example of overcoming binary oppositions and inscribing a marginalized culture into the dominant one. Erna Brodber's *Myal* entails subversive elements in its critical reading of colonialist education, as when the main character, Ella, reinterprets the colonial text 'Mr. Joe's Farm'. Winks does not neglect the difficulties that go with questions of representation, but calls on the 'post-colonial subject [to] continue to intervene and insert themselves into the dominant text' (p. 73).

Small Axe 28[2009] is entitled 'Reconstructing Womanhood: A Future Beyond Empire' and stems from a 2007 symposium honouring Hazel V. Carby and her work *Reconstructing Womanhood: The Emergence of the Afro-American Woman Novelist*. In 'Preface: The Paradox of Beginnings' (*Small Axe* 28[2009] vii–xiv), David Scott casts a backward glance at the roots of *Small Axe* in earlier journals (*New World Quarterly* and *Savacou*), while also outlining changes in the journal's methodology and philosophy up to the present issue, which represents a new relationship with Duke University Press. Scott notes a move to feature 'visual projects and art critical essays' (p. xiii) and signals a future literary competition for short fiction and poetry as well as an increased focus on history and the social sciences.

Saidiya Hartman and Tina Campt, in 'A Future Beyond Empire: An Introduction' (*Small Axe* 28[2009] 19–36) describe Carby's writing as depicting 'the constellation between our era and the earlier formative moment of black modernity in the Atlantic slave trade' and interrogating 'the ideology and conventions of womanhood that banished black women from the category of woman and the racialized exclusions constitutive of humanist discourse' (p. 20). Carby herself begins her 'Lost (and Found?) in Translation' (*Small Axe* 28[2009] 27–40): 'I am continually modifying my understanding of what it means to be a "child of empire"' (p. 27). Welsh Jamaican, Carby analyses the subject positions of her parents, her father's being partially formed by the British poetry he read in the *Royal Reader*. She also examines her own motives for further study, seeing members of her future college as 'allies in the fight against the increasingly authoritarian and conservative forces being mobilized against the poor, the working class, the black, and the immigrant' (p. 36).

In '"Oceans Apart"' (*Small Axe* 28[2009] 41–9), Ingrid Pollard presents a series of photographs in which images of 'state-sanctioned and educational authorities are placed alongside those preserved on family albums and the throwaway colloquialisms of letters' (p. 41). Via this archive she explores connections between the Caribbean, England, and Europe. Rinaldo Walcott also deploys visual material (filmic and artistic) in 'Reconstructing Manhood; or, The Drag of Black Masculinity' (*Small Axe* 28[2009] 75–89), and uses Hazel Carby's definition of representation as a stepping-off point to argue that black manhood is currently defined by 'neoliberalism's new managerial regime in which black masculinities are understood to be underperforming' (p. 79) and that cultural analysis should take neoliberalism into account.

Robert F. Reid-Pharr, in 'The Stranger's Work' (*Small Axe* 28[2009] 90–7), asserts that is would be easy to bemoan the lack of improvement in the lives of the subjects of Carby's *Reconstructing Womanhood* in the years since its publication. However, he celebrates two aspects of Carby's text, the first being that she discusses the work of black intellectuals as part of the mainstream. He compares her work to C.L.R. James's treatment of Herman Melville. Secondly, he believes that Carby 'turns to those many awkwardly fashioned characters that one finds in black women's literature' in order to provide 'fresh readings of how questions of similarity and difference were negotiated, with more or less success, in the variety of black Atlantic traditions' (p. 95). Another assessment of Carby's work comes from Lisa Lowe in 'Autobiography out of Empire' (*Small Axe* 28[2009] 98–111). For Lowe, Carby's 'insistence on the inseparable articulation of race, class, and gender structured in dominance opened up such possibilities for scholarship about black women and provided a critical paradigm for inventing and excavating materials others would have dismissed as lost to history' (p. 98). She discusses examples of autobiography, including Olaudah Equiano's and Carby's own autobiography-in-progress. She concludes that the latter is 'an incomparable and gracious reconstruction and a deconstruction of the genre' (p. 111).

Small Axe 29[2009], guest-edited by Glyne A. Griffith, presents essays from the 'Blackness Unbound' conference at the State University of New York, Albany, in 2007. Griffith states that the symposium title was 'meant to link the Prometheus myth to the traumatic recollection of the New World plantations harnessing and confining black bodies and black experiences' (p. 1) in the Caribbean and Latin America, in 'Blackness Unbound: Interrogating Transnational Blackness' (*Small Axe* 29[2009] 1–3). Silvio Torres-Saillant, in 'One and Divisible: Meditations on Global Blackness' (*Small Axe* 29[2009] 4–25), employs personal anecdotes, using the example of Dominican negrophobia as a starting point for his warning 'to exercise caution when we deploy blackness as a transnational category' (p. 17). He analyses the 1973 novel *The Friends* by Trinidadian Rosa Guy, which 'fictionalizes the ethnic antipathy that a West Indian girl encounters among African American classmates in a Harlem school' (p. 19).

In 'What Is This *Black* in Black Diaspora?' (*Small Axe* 29[2009] 26–38), Michelle Stephens points to Stuart Hall's 1991 question about black pop culture as marking the 'convergence of black British cultural studies and African American studies' (p. 26). Stephens analyses the terms 'colour consciousness' and 'race consciousness' in the writings of Frantz Fanon, arguing that 'Fanon's collective unconscious can usefully be read as one way of understanding the *black* in black diaspora' (p. 32). She then discusses ways of accommodating gender and sexuality within this framework, using examples from bell hooks, and concludes by advocating use of the insights of Fanon and W.E.B. Du Bois 'into the bodily aspects of our racial identities to expand our discussion of black genders and sexualities across the diaspora' (p. 38).

Evelyn O'Callaghan, in 'The Unholy Moment: Frieda Cassin's Nineteenth-Century Antiguan Novel and the Construction of the White Creole' (*Small Axe* 29[2009] 95–106), focuses on the question of 'how race signifies within and among *white* communities in the Caribbean and what "experiences of racialization" occur when members of such (putative?) communities move abroad' (p. 97). She uses Cassin's 1890 novel *With Silent Tread* to examine the different ways whiteness was constructed in the West

Indies and England. In the narratives of Mary Prince, Mary Seacole, and Jean Rhys, 'the bleakest account of migration "back to center" is that of the white creole' (p. 104), and for Cassin's heroine, too, her rejection by England and subsequent journey home is a negative experience. The complications of Caribbean colour are also examined in 'Deconstructing Jamaican Whiteness: A Diasporic Voice' (*Small Axe* 29[2009] 107–17). Kim Robinson-Walcott asks what it means to be a white Jamaican, focusing on the work of Anthony C. Winkler, whose writing addresses 'the floating-signifier of racial identity' (p. 108). In Jamaica, 'colour' refers to blood, behaviour, class, and economic power. While some signifiers of Africanness are seen as inappropriate by white Jamaicans, Winkler finds whiteness a mixed blessing, as he finds himself vilified by black Jamaicans. Winkler himself describes his experiences as a white Jamaican writing about black and brown characters who speak English and patois in 'What Do Jamaicans Mean by *Ole Negar*?' (*Small Axe* 29[2009] 118–27). Jamaicans, he says, 'openly describe people by their many and varied complexions' (p. 119), and the term 'ole negar' appears to refer to the poorest black people of Jamaican society, but is also a way of vilifying these people on the grounds of indiscipline, a concept imposed by the colonizer.

Writing in *Changing English* (*ChE* 15:ii[2009] 179–88), Velma Pollard, 'The Americas in Anglophone Caribbean Women Writers: Bridges of Sound', points out how migrants' sounds evoke a sense of longing and belonging in selected literary texts. The author recalls particular sounds from her childhood and observes that all of her literary examples establish a connection of sounds that enable moments of reconciliation with the characters' families, their native countries, or their long-forgotten histories. Olive Senior's 'Hurricane story, 1951' tells of a family torn apart by a hurricane. In the course of their lives their voices are silenced, until the day when the mother, while sweeping the floors, hears her son's voice in the bucket's swirling water. Although they are never to meet again, the son reconnects with his mother as he hears the echo of his calls. For Pollard, this marks 'the effectiveness of the bridge of sound over (troubled?) sea water' (p. 181). In Paule Marshall's *Praisesong for the Widow* an Afro-American widow finds 'the African self she has neglected' (p. 184) on her trip to the Caribbean and encounter with African sounds, while Erna Brodber's *Louisiana* links the history of two women from Jamaica and the US through shared songs.

Joseph Keith's 'At the Formal Limits. C.L.R. James, *Moby Dick* and the Politics of the Novel' (*Interventions* 11:iii[2009] 352–66) takes C.L.R. James's *Mariners, Renegades and Castaways: The Story of Herman Melville and the World We Live In* not only as a rereading of *Moby-Dick*, but, significantly, also 'as an effort to decentre the realist novel as the privileged form of postcolonial representation' (p. 353). While citing Pease and Scott, Hazel Carby and Belinda Edmonsen, Keith mainly draws on Alex Woloch's *The One vs. the Many* and its thesis that the realist novel fails to represent the many in favour of the few. For Keith this explains Melville's shift from the crew to Ahab, the collective story being 'as yet beyond the limits of the mid-nineteenth-century bourgeois political imagination' (p. 359). James extends both this imagination and the associated narrative form of the realist novel. The editing of James's conclusion to his book, where he addresses the issue of representation, once more attests to the marginalization of these stories.

(c) Books

We are used to depictions of the Caribbean as a group of small islands isolated but linked by sea. Christopher Winks begins his *Symbolic Cities in Caribbean Literature* with this 'thalassa' concept, relates it to Kamau Brathwaite's 'tidalectics', and extends the connections back to Greece and Rome and to Orisha and Olokun to posit a consistent Caribbean literary engagement with the idea of the city. His focus is on Hispanic writing, particularly that relating to Cuba (notably José Lezama Lima, Virgilio Piñeiro, Alejo Carpentier, Reinaldo Arenas, Calvert Casey, and Guillermo Cabrera Infante), but his impressively fluid prose and comparative reach wash around writers and theorists in both French (Césaire, Glissant, Dany Laferrière) and English (Brathwaite, Walcott, C.L.R. James, David Dabydeen, Wilson Harris, Martin Carter). The book challenges Angel Rama's thesis of the 'ciudad letrado' by pointing to the plantation as a city-machine and to the counter-city ideal behind maroon communities. Winks also explores the magical city tradition, one invoking memories of West African 'ancestral houses', whether real or mythical (as in the vanishing and reappearing Wagadu) and of utopian dream (El Dorado). The dystopic city figured in the plantation and the urban slum is set against the city as a site of transformation and renewal. Points of interest include reading Italo Calvino's *Invisible Cities* via links to the Caribbean through his Cuban birth and friendship with Calvert Casey, and attending to *Black Albino* [1961] by Jamaican Namba Roy. Winks also revisits Wilson Harris's *The Whole Armour* [1962] and *The Secret Ladder* [1963] and makes good use of a wide range of Brathwaite's work, his use of jazz as an aesthetic model providing one motif connecting to the Havana world at the heart of the study.

(d) Single-Author Studies

Paola Loreto's *The Crowning of a Poet's Quest* (Rodopi, Cross Cultures 108) is a study of Derek Walcott's *Tiepolo's Hound*. Loreto first reflects on Walcott's roots in an aesthetic tradition that can be traced back to Emerson. She then points out 'wanderer' parallels between Walcott and Nabokov on both a personal and a professional level (p. ix). In the third chapter, Loreto expands the idea expressed in the title of her work—that Walcott has been on a quest to develop a Caribbean aesthetic which has now culminated in *Tiepolo's Hound*. Its 'triple achievement' is in the writing of an 'autobiography in verse... the writing of his personal version of a *Künstlerroman*, and the development of a Caribbean or "mulatto" aesthetic, or aesthetic of the island artist' (p. 43). The concept of the *Künstlerroman* is explored in the ensuing chapter, and the final chapter praises Walcott's employment of the metaphor of light as an example of his poetic mastery and his reliance on both European and Caribbean literary cultures.

The *Journal of West Indian Literature* 17:ii is devoted to Jamaican-British poet Louise Bennett. Ifeoma Kiddoe Nwankwo introduces articles by Janet Neigh, 'The Lickle Space of the Tramcar' (*JWIL* 17:ii[2009] 5–19)—a feminist reading interested in transport and public space), Carol Baily's postcolonial reading (*JWIL* 17:ii[2009] 20–31), Susan Gingell's analysis of 'see-hear aesthetics' in relation to dub poetry and creole (*JWIL* 17:ii[2009] 32–48), and Jahan Ramazani's assessment of Bennett's transnational qualities (*JWIL* 17:ii[2009] 49–64).

Jean Rhys continues to attract scholarly attention. The suffering, alienation, and melancholic identification of her female protagonists have long been a dilemma for feminist critics, but Cathleen Maslen, in *Ferocious Things: Jean Rhys and the Politics of Women's Melancholia*, shows how both self-articulation and textual inscription of female psychic suffering can be read as transgressive strategies. The discourse of melancholia is not only celebrated but also undermined and resisted in Rhys's texts. Maslen acknowledges the difficulties arising from her understanding of 'Rhys's work as an appropriation of the melancholic identity on behalf of the marginalized and socially isolated woman' (p. 184), as it might be seen to perpetuate masculinist and Eurocentric discourses. But based on readings of *Quartet*, *After Leaving Mr Mackenzie*; *Good Morning, Midnight*, *Voyage in the Dark*, and *Wide Sargasso Sea* from postcolonial and feminist perspectives, Maslen accuses some of Rhys's critics of reducing a wider political agenda to a personal account of depression, and defends Rhys against accusations of her non-feminist portrayal of women's weaknesses and sufferings.

Sylvie Maurel, in 'The Other Stage: From *Jane Eyre* to *Wide Sargasso Sea*' (*BS* 34:ii[2009] 155–61), analyses Rhys's much-studied rewriting of Brontë's *Jane Eyre* from a 'wintry' into a 'tropical' romance. In allowing Bertha Mason, 'the unspeakable figure of otherness' (p. 155), to take centre stage, Rhys places the story of Rochester and his first wife into the 'Gothic delirium' of the Caribbean, thereby setting free the elements of Gothic romance already present in *Jane Eyre* and thus detaching 'Gothic fantasy from the strictures of the subtext in which it is confined' (p. 159). Likewise, she liberates the romance from its realistic limitations in the original.

Nicole Terrien looks at intertextual links to Rhys's most famous work: 'A Stitch in Time ... (How Travel Notes and a Short Story Written by Anthony Trollope Shape the Plot of Jean Rhys's *Wide Sargasso Sea*, as Rhys's Novel Will Shape the Fiction of Jenny Disky)' (in Letissier, ed., *Rewriting/Reprising: Plural Intertextualities*, pp. 138–51).

Another staple of Caribbean literary studies these days is Caryl Phillips (whose various locations illustrate the opening remarks about how the Caribbean is an unstable space). Rezzan Kocaoner Silku's 'Postcolonial Routes and Diasporic Identities: Belonging and Displacement in Caryl Phillip's *The Final Passage* and *A Distant Shore*' (*JPW* 45:ii[2009] 163–70) examines the concept of identity conveyed in both novels, thereby stressing the hybridity of the diasporic subject as experienced by the author himself. Space is central to identity formation, as the characters in both novels find themselves far from home and estranged in their host countries. Their responses differ: some (like Leila) feel disconnected from their ancestral history and dream of going home, while others are forced to stay and adapt. If Phillips makes black Britons visible on the 'map of Britishness' (Silku cites Lawson Welsh here), he is more concerned with the nature of individual identity, and with blackness as a facet of it (p. 167). Thus in *A Distant Shore* he 'discusses the othering process as a universal issue in terms of race and gender' (p. 167). Caryl Phillips locates himself as between spaces, and envisions 'a new world order in which there will soon be one global conversation with limited participation to all, and full participation available to none' (p. 166).

Anne Collett, 'Ritual Masking and Performed Intimacy: The Complex "I" of Edward Kamau Brathwaite's Life Poem' (*LW* 6:i[2009] 97–110), begins from a reading of Kamau Brathwaite's *Born to Slow Horses* [2005] to bring together the early 'public' voice and the post-'Time of Salt' personal poems under the rubric of life-writing and the poet's concern to confront trauma in order to create healing. The stuttering repetitions of the hesitant or traumatized poet-speaker are performed in intimate oral exchange with a compassionate audience to become drumbeat and Vodun transformation (pp. 99–100). Collett considers how Brathwaite's creole is a performed intimacy between poet and 'the people', and how (based on reading of *The Arrivants* [1973] and *The Zea Mexican Diary* [1993]) his public address masks private angst while the personal voice is also a mask for speaking about public concerns.

V.S. Naipaul remains part of Caribbean studies despite his progressive immersion in English society. Lucienne Loh's 'Rural Routes/Roots: India, Trinidad and England in V.S. Naipaul's *The Enigma of Arrival*' (*JPW* 45:ii[2009] 151–61) is another attempt to come to terms with the controversial author by engaging with his semi-autobiographical novel. She reinterprets Naipaul's apparently uncritical colonial nostalgia for the English countryside—criticized by Derek Walcott as an affirmation of 'the squirearchy of club and manor' (p. 152)—as a source of comfort and inspiration. Loh suggests that Naipaul has experienced a twofold alienation, given that he felt no connection with either India or Trinidad, a place where Indians 'sickened and died' (p. 155); for him, England became an escapist fantasy. Loh argues that Naipaul recognizes that England blossomed due to the exploitation of Trinidad's workforce and the destruction of the island's countryside.

Another transnational Caribbean writer is Jamaica Kincaid. 'In the Vicinity of the Almost: The Stylistics of Jamaica Kincaid's *Mr. Potter*' (*JCL* 44:i[2009] 81–99), by Nicole Matos, links the syntactic structure of the novel to the inner world of its protagonist. Matos rejects criticisms that the parataxis of the text is an expression of its nihilism or lacking coherence. On the contrary, she suggests that this forces the reader to ascribe meaning to the text; it allows the reader to sympathize with Mr Potter and leaves room for different interpretations. Matos claims that Kincaid uses 'a "land of the almost" to supplement the land of the real' (p. 82). She finds this is a characteristic of Kincaid's other works, citing Spivak's analysis of a 'subjunctive mode' in *Lucy* and drawing a comparison between *At the Bottom of the River* and *Mr. Potter*.

Maria Mårdberg has also written on *The Autobiography of My Mother* (see the following section).

(e) Essays in Edited Collections

In *Transcultural English Studies: Theories, Fictions, Realities*, editors Frank Schulze-Engler and Sissy Helff address transculturalism in a globalized world in four contexts: theory, material reality, cultural production, and mediation through didactics. According to Sabrina Brancato, transcultural issues are 'distinctly Caribbean' (p. 234). In 'Transcultural Perspectives in Caribbean Poetry' she differentiates four categories: transculturation, transculturality, transnational connections, and transculturalism/transnationalism, describing them as 'progressive stages of the transcultural process tending towards transnationalism as a worldview or an ideology' (p. 235). She understands transculturation as 'a process of assimilation, through selection and invention, of a dominant culture by a marginal group' and links this process to the 'counter-discursive practice of "writing back"' (p. 236). One of several examples is Grace Nichols's poem 'With Apologies to Hamlet', with its distinctive line 'To pee or not to pee'. Brancato criticizes the terms creolization and hybridity for their geographical limitation and their lack of a cultural dynamic, respectively, proposing transculturality instead. In the same volume, Sissy Helff's 'Shifting Perspectives: The Transcultural Novel' discusses the added value of transcultural approaches to postcolonial studies. She affirms John McLeod's criticism that postcolonial studies are obsessed with the notions of difference and subversion, while transcultural movements suggest connection (and are not necessarily subversive). However, Helff finds that the term transculturalism 'runs the danger of reducing the multiregional and multicultural reality of modern societies' (p. 79). Helff reads Onya Kampadoo's *Tide Running* as an example of a transcultural novel: its multiperspectival narrative structure by means of an unreliable narrator 'challenges essentialist modes of identity construction' (p. 82).

Mara de Gennaro's 'Césaire and Brathwaite: Negritude and Imagining across Cultures' (in Constant and Mabana, eds., *Negritude. Legacy and Present Relevance*, pp. 125–40) compares Césaire's and Brathwaite's depictions of women in their poetry. Césaire and Brathwaite differ in their approach to culture, or so the argument goes, with the former advocating the existent heterogeneous culture be 'lived internally as homogeneity' (p. 129), and the latter embracing different cultural influences as an enrichment of African culture. Still, both stress the importance of localized popular culture for Caribbean cultural expression. While Césaire's focus is on the denial of rights to particular groups in society, in his combat for recognition as a man of colour he seems to 'other' women. In the words of Susan Adrade, he 'repeats, albeit rhetorically, the same territorializing and sexualizing actions of the colonizers' (p. 131). It is Brathwaite who actually puts into practice Césaire's call for 'a poet free to be a comrade' in ridding himself of negritude's representation of women (p. 138).

M.B. Hackler's collection, *On and Off the Page: Mapping Place in Text and Culture*, produced with editorial assistance from Ari J. Adipurwawidjana, takes its title from the seventh annual Louisiana Conference on Literature, Language, and Culture. The book contains essays with traditional approaches to place in literature, and some that explore the political implications of place.

Paul A. Griffith's essay, 'Space, Time and Interval: Charting Roots and Routes through Myth and Mythos in Selected Works of Kamau Brathwaite and Derek Walcott' (pp. 105–40), singles out their understanding of history as a main point of difference between the two writers. While Brathwaite sees history as a source of inspiration and a crucial part of the colonized's identity, Walcott claims that 'amnesia is the history of the New World' and pictures the Caribbean artist as a 'second Adam' (p. 107). The essay goes on to analyse limbo, calypso, and the Trinidadian folk ritual of *mamagying* in both the artists' books as forms of resistance to colonialist oppression, concluding that '[w]hether dancer or musician, the artist is a parodist who enters imaginatively into colonial history to transform it' (p. 139).

In *Voices and Silence in the Contemporary Novel in English*, edited by Vanessa Guignery, Christina Mesa, 'Still Life and Performance Art: The Erotics of Silence and Excess in Jamaica Kincaid's *Lucy* and Zadie Smith's *On Beauty*' (pp. 231–48), compares the lives as black women of the two main characters. Both Lucy and Victoria question gender roles by actively seeking sexual encounters as a way of finding themselves (p. 248). Mesa's surprising suggestion is that, because of her reserved manners, Lucy is actually more independent than today's exuberant Victoria, though she also states that actually not much has changed for young black women: they are still felt to be 'out of place', their beauty is still considered an invitation for men, and they still try to attach to someone to attain a sense of belonging. Thus Victoria's freewheeling rootlessness might be a problem rather than a sign of liberation, and it is actually Lucy who, trying to reconnect with her history, achieves the self-fulfilment she seeks.

A Sea for Encounters: Essays Towards a Postcolonial Commonwealth, edited by Stella Borg Barthet, collects essays from the 2005 European Association for Commonwealth Language and Literature Studies' Malta conference 'Sharing Places', some of which focus on the Caribbean. Jogamaya Bayer's 'Crossing the Borders in Monica Ali's *Brick Lane* and V.S. Naipaul's *Half a Life*' successfully links these two novels to a broader discourse on motivations for migration and the global economic system. Both texts focus on the repercussions of migration on the individual and—*contra* Syed Manzurul Islam and Hardt and Negri—question the ideal of the 'postcolonial who continually crosses territorial and racial boundaries as the hero of our time' (p. 42). Lourdes López-Ropero's 'The Pleasures of Slave Food: The Politics of Creolization in Austin Clarke's *Pigtail'n Breadfruit*' outlines the anti-essentialist identity politics in Clarke's memoir, a text that links recipes, historical anecdotes, and socio-historical information on a range of dishes. While Clarke takes pride in the history of slave food, calling souse the 'sweetest thing handed down by our ancestors' (p. 85), he also stresses the diversity in the Caribbean, asserting an ongoing 'Creole continuum' from slave plantations to modern-day diaspora. Clarke avoids homogenising the Caribbean region, citing 'serving souse warm as evidence of the enormous cultural chasm that separates St. Kitts and the Bahamas from Barbados' (p. 86). Concepción Mengíbar Rico's 'The Carnivalesque into Theatre: Carnival and Drama in the Anglophone Caribbean' explores the history of carnival and its relevance to Caribbean theatre. Since the time of ancient

Rome, in which slaves dressed up as their masters and vice versa, it has had a tradition of reversing relations of power (p. 325), and its theatrical elements, such as masks and music, led Errol Hill to promote a national Caribbean theatre based on the ever popular celebration of carnival, comparing it to Greek theatre's imitation of Dionysian rituals. Carnivalesque elements can be found in plays by Derek Walcott as well as the calypso tradition. Carnival also has the potential of connecting diverse cultures, and as such has remained a vital cultural component of the Caribbean and its dramatic arts.

Reclaiming Home, Remembering Motherhood, Rewriting History: African American and Afro-Caribbean Women's Literature in the Twentieth Century, edited by Verena Theile and Marie Drews, contains Maria Mårdberg's essay, '"*A bleak, black wind*": Motherlessness and Emotional Exile in Jamaica Kincaid's *The Autobiography of My Mother*' (pp. 2–28). The study asserts that before colonial times motherhood was a capacity ascribed to all women, so that women as mothers were not confined to the home, but fully participated in the community. Xuela is, however, estranged from her 'othermothers', as these have suffered colonial alienation, 'the hostility and mistrust of Xuela's family relations [being] indicative of the level of hostility and mistrust in her society' (p. 13). When she finally meets a nurturing othermother, she is unable to accept the given love because of her negative experience, and in the end is unwilling to become a mother herself. Kincaid's novel shows how, under colonialism, 'family as such disintegrates as patriarchal and colonial significations determine and, ultimately, prevent bonding within the family' (p. 16). Magali Cornier Michael's 'Telling History Other-Wise: Grace Nichols' *i Is a Long Memoried Woman*' (pp. 210–32) analyses how Nichols's poem sequence questions the Western masculinist historiography of the slave trade. Nichols employs diverse narrative strategies by deviating from the historian's perspective, by outlining the creole background of suffering women, and by moving away from standardized forms of poetic form and language. While relying on empirical and geographical data to underscore the legitimacy of her narrative, Nichols questions written history by herself citing and perpetuating oral traditions. Nichols draws on the idea of linearity predominant in Western historical discourse while at the same time mocking it. Her 'supplement' simultaneously adds to and reshapes the historical record.

5. The Indian Subcontinent and Sri Lanka

(a) Books

A preoccupation with the diaspora emerges as the strongest theme in this year's list, and once again it is Salman Rushdie who garners the lion's share of the attention. At the same time, significant moves are also made towards expanding diaspora studies to include hitherto neglected non-Western contexts which, while influenced by literary developments beyond their borders, are also centres of literary activity in their own right.

Two single-author studies are reviewed in this year's essay. Rohini Mokashi-Punekar's book on Vikram Seth is a convenient introduction to the writer's work and includes several features aimed at an undergraduate readership. Aside from the introductory chapter with its somewhat programmatic interweaving of biographical detail and textual references, this volume offers close analysis of virtually all of Seth's work, reserving whole chapters for discussion of each of his five major books, a separate chapter for the discussion of his poetry, an overview of his chief thematic concerns, a bibliography, and an impressive list of topics for further discussion. A special strength of the study is the author's references to the work of other Indian critics who have commented on Seth's writings, giving the reader a vivid sense of his reception in India.

The focus of Nicole Weickgenannt Thiara's *Salman Rushdie and Indian Historiography: Writing the Nation into Being* is narrower, in that she examines only two of Rushdie's novels, *Midnight's Children* and *The Moor's Last Sigh*, although she does broaden to analyse Rushdie's concept of the nation against different ideological perspectives on India as presented in Indian historiography. Disputing the view of Rushdie's novels as offering 'a counternarrative' to established modern Indian history, Thiara observes that the field of Indian historiography is too complex and contested for any novelist simply to be able to produce an 'alternative' account (p. 4).

Feminism and subaltern theory are prominent strands in Thiara's study. In her discussion of *The Moor's Last Sigh* in chapter 4, perhaps the best chapter of the book, she situates Rushdie's interrogation of the concept of Mother India alongside three other versions of the Mother in Bankim Chandra Chatterjee, Katherine Mayo, and Mehboob Khan. *The Moor's Last Sigh*, she argues, stresses the dangers of blind passion which the image of Mother India is geared to arouse in (Hindu) nationalist discourse. By highlighting and magnifying the incestuous undertones of the relationship, the novel serves to 'denaturalise' nationalist fervour focused on the image of the mother (p. 156). Analysis of *Midnight's Children*, particularly Thiara's attempt to explore the case against the novel's misogyny as 'a shortcoming' on the part of its author, likewise leads to an interesting line of argument (p. 57). Rushdie's tendency to portray his powerful female characters as endowed with a monstrosity that is almost always directed against men (p. 70), she claims, is a deliberate and multi-layered strategy aimed at chastising the nationalist patriarchy for ostracizing women who transgress the nationalist ideal of good wives and mothers (p. 76). Thiara concedes that at the same time Rushdie's powerful condemnation of Indira Gandhi and her Emergency regime would not have the impact it does if it was not for its reliance on the strategy his work purportedly condemns (p. 85). The reading of 'ambivalence', so often helpful in rescuing Rushdie from various unsavoury political positions, thus would seem to be less useful in relation to his characterization of women in *Midnight's Children*, and while Thiara's argument goes some way towards nuancing existing critiques of Rushdie's misogyny, it is finally inadequate to the task of challenging that broad consensus.

A second chapter on *The Moor's Last Sigh* proceeds to read the novel against the subaltern perspective on Indian history, making special use of Thomas Blom Hansen's account of Hindu nationalism in his books *The Saffron Wave* [1999] and the *Wages of Violence* [2001]. Thiara argues that, although the novel's representation of the rise of Hindu nationalism in Bombay stresses the need to see it as not just a communalization of the city but also as an aspect of its increasing democratization (a shift of balance that may be mapped on to a transition from civil society to what Partha Chatterjee has called political society), this perception is precluded by Rushdie's foregrounding of a narrator who clings to the battered myths and ideals of the Nehruvian state until the very end (pp. 97, 120).

Naheem Jabbar approaches an apparently similar set of questions in *Historiography and Writing Postcolonial India*, but from a much more broad-based, philosophical perspective. Offered as a critical examination of postcolonial Indian history-writing, Jabbar's book makes only nominal references to the work of professional historians. Rather, it examines the writings of nationalist ideologues such as Gandhi, Savarkar, Nehru, and Ambedkar, and creative writers such as V.S. Naipaul and Salman Rushdie, to understand the ways in which India's millennial past was appropriated in the search for solutions to India's predicament as a postcolonial state. While all the writers discussed in the book set out to offer ostensibly objective and scientific accounts of India's past, Jabbar's analysis demonstrates that the boundaries between the emotional and the objective are not always easy to mark.

Irony as a literary strategy comes in for special attention in Jabbar's critique. Repeatedly in Rushdie's writing, he claims, 'the ironic mode returns from the complex arena of actual or material history to the consoling vagaries of individual temperament'. Hence it is that Rushdie urges the reader 'to forget the usual dichotomies of history, of left-right, capitalism-socialism, black-white' and recognize instead that the 'true dialectic of history' lies in 'epicure against the puritan . . . Virtue versus vice, ascetic versus bawd, God against the Devil' (p. 184). Rushdie's fiction, Jabbar argues, represents the desire of historical man to raise himself to the 'suprahistorical' perspective, from where he can recognize 'the essential condition of all happenings' (p. 185). Jabbar contends that Rushdie's writings may be called postmodernist only in the limited sense of deploying an ironic mode, which is by itself hardly adequate to the task of 'questioning the veracity of historical truth'. More typically, his writings are 'Romanticist in orientation, idiographic in their chief mode of argument and anarchist in the conclusions they draw about the relationship between human nature and the forces of history' (p. 181). Refreshing as this demystification of Rushdie's politics is, the book itself is leisurely paced and widely allusive, and can be frustrating as the reader finds herself lost in its ponderous prose and its many digressions.

Ambreen Hai's *Making Words Matter: The Agency of Colonial and Postcolonial Literature* works in an altogether different economy of words. This engaging, rigorous contribution to ongoing debates in postcolonial theory about agency and the body opens them up to newer questions of 'literary agency' (p. 10). Colonial as well as postcolonial literature, Hai observes, is haunted and shaped by a preoccupation with the autonomy and subjection of texts in the world. Questions of agency bear special resonance for writers such as Rudyard Kipling, E.M. Forster, and Salman Rushdie, the fraught political contexts of whose times had momentous implications for their personal lives (p. 312). In her fine, intensive readings of their fiction, essays, letters, and travel accounts, Hai finds the individual body to occupy a central place because it uniquely concretizes the complexities of human agency (p. 6). Being at once 'the site of autonomy, instrumentality and subjection', it is specially placed to help writers explore the function and status of art as both a manifestation and the working out of central links between human language, the body and the world (pp. 8–9).

Critical interest in Rushdie continues in Gaurav Majumdar's *Migrant Form: Anti-Colonial Aesthetics in Joyce, Rushdie, and Ray*, which begins with the claim that the relationship between anti-colonial arguments and formal modes and strategies of postcolonial texts has not received sustained attention (p. 1). Through a deft overview of the work of John Ruskin, Edmund Burke, Matthew Arnold, and Thomas Macaulay, Majumdar examines the centrality of unity in colonial aesthetics as a trope for control, co-operation, and harmony between the conqueror and the conquered (p. 2). The colonial ambitions of these writers stand on what he calls the aesthetics of expansion, valorizing largeness, continuity, restraint, subordination, and absorption. By contrast, anti-colonial aesthetics, as witnessed in the work of James Joyce, Salman Rushdie, and Satyajit Ray, dramatize 'combinative truncation, disjunction, and covert or subtle association, with an accompanying openness to ethical scrutiny' (p. 11). Majumdar gives these aesthetic practices the name of 'migrant form', where the term migrant signifies not so much the movement between places as a new sense of home which allows for multiple affinities at once, as the result of such movement (p. 14).

To show how the preferred political modes of migrant form—such as partiality, reconfiguration, instability, and multiplicity—are instantiated in fiction, Majumdar turns to the 'disorienting' effect of humour in *Midnight's Children* (p. 80). In contrast to Naheem Jabbar's scepticism about the usefulness of irony as a subversive mode, Majumdar grants ironic humour a special role in 'aiding indefinition' (p. 87). Humour in Rushdie, he argues, 'transgresses the limits of forms to activate a series of significative possibilities, mirroring and conflating stories, employing the pun for explicitly uncontrollable semiosis, and displacing the boundaries between the inside and the outside' (p. 80). This all generates a radical historiography that plays with notions of knowledge, culture, reality, and the stability of the text (p. 80).

In his second chapter on Rushdie, Majumdar resumes his argument with Ruskin, in particular with his rhetoric in *The Stones of Venice*, where the absence of familiarity, order, and the reassuring display of 'feeling consistent with itself' is the source of the grotesque. The status of the grotesque in Ruskin is decided by its lack of virtues attributed to 'noble' forms (p. 101). In *The Satanic Verses*, Rushdie mobilizes the grotesque to raise ethical questions about literary invention, authorship, and the migration of people and their stories (p. 99). The grotesque is a combinative form that problematizes the inside and the outside in much the same way that migration conflates the familiar and the unfamiliar. Majumdar argues for the figure of the migrant to be seen as a form of the grotesque and vice versa (p. 102). The two together produce 'an interpretive deficit', where the reader/viewer finds herself inadequate to the task of fully unpacking the formulations that the text's language, structure, and references might encode. Having to choose without an authoritative reading position involves an ethical curiosity characteristic of a cosmopolitan world-view, along with the concession that reading is necessarily incomplete, and open to reshaping.

Of the eight books published so far in the Postcolonial Studies series edited by Maria C. Zamora, Majumdar's book is probably the best. Well-written, insightful, and erudite, it has also been proof-read more carefully than other books from Peter Lang reviewed here, although the structure of the book—it is divided into four 'parts', each further carved into two 'sections'—warrants a firmer editorial hand.

If Majumdar uses the term migrant mainly as a metaphor for an anti-colonial aesthetics, Mariam Pirbhai's *Mythologies of Migration, Vocabularies of Indenture: Novels of the South Asian Diaspora in Africa, the Caribbean, and Asia-Pacific* works with the actual historical phenomenon of migration. Pirbhai's book examines the under-studied topic of South Asian migration, mostly undertaken by indentured labour across the greater part of the nineteenth and the early twentieth century. This migration spread a diverse array of languages, knowledge systems, religious beliefs, social mores, and cultural traditions from the Indian subcontinent to every part of the world (p. 3). Pirbhai's book is an important contribution to the field of diaspora studies not least because it opens new channels for intellectual traffic between non-Western societies and cultures as against the dominant paradigm which characteristically privileges the Western metropolis (p. 37). Analysing the writings of South Asians who trace their ancestors to the indentured labour diaspora, Pirbhai focuses mostly on first novels from regions that have only recently come to the attention of a wider international readership (p. 31). Writers studied include, from Mauritius, Deepchand Beeharry; from Uganda and South Africa, Peter Nazareth and Farida Karodia; from Guyana, Rooplall Monar and Narmala Shewcharan; from Trinidad, Lakshmi Persaud and Sharlow Mohammed; from Malaysia and Singapore, K.S. Maniam and Gopal Baratham; and from Fiji, Satendra Nandan.

The next two books discussed both deploy feminist frameworks. Hena Ahmad's *Postnational Feminism: Postcolonial Identities and Cosmopolitanism in the Works of Kamala Markandaya, Tsitsi Dangarembga, Ama Ata Aidoo, and Anita Desai* undertakes a comparison of feminist consciousness across novels by women from India, Ghana and Zimbabwe. Part of a broadly conceived series, American University Studies, this volume is aimed at undergraduates approaching these writers for the first time and presents a postcolonial Third World feminist perspective. Several interconnected factors characteristic of counter-narratives by women from the Third World, most notably the writers' cosmopolitanism, their diasporic connections, their sense of being simultaneously insider and outsider, bring these narratives together under the sign of what Ahmad calls 'postnational feminism' (p. 3). With reference to Kamala Markandaya's *Nectar in a Sieve*, she argues that while the author's colonial heritage and her diasporic consciousness were responsible for her ambivalence towards nationalism, her literary imagination was nonetheless inspired by a national culture and history (p. 36). In Anita Desai's *Clear Light of Day*, it was 'a position of rootedness in the nation, within national spaces, by taking women's issues, in a sense, beyond the nation' which lent force to Desai's opposition of both colonial legacy and indigenous tradition (p. 84). Both texts seem to call for a 'rooted cosmopolitanism' which simultaneously rejects and reinforces the national to create a new cosmopolitan space for Third World feminism (pp. 20, 80).

Literature in translation is increasingly part of anglophone postcolonial theorizing. In *Haram in the Harem: Domestic Narratives in India and Algeria* Mohanlakshmi Rajakumar brings a postcolonial feminist perspective to bear upon three Muslim women writers from the mid-twentieth century: one from Algeria, Assia Djebar, and two from the Indian subcontinent, Ismat Chughtai and Khadija Mastur. Through a close reading of two short stories by each, Rajakumar explores the lives of women in three distinct contexts: the Algerian revolution, middle-class Muslim reform, and the Partition of India. While in each case, it was the outside world which was seen to pose a threat to women's safety, Djebar, Chughtai, and Mastur show not only the negative mental, emotional, and physical consequences of confining women to domestic spaces but also how the challenge to the debilitating status quo often came from the women themselves, from inside the much-vaunted safety of the home, rather than externally. Stories discussed relevant to this chapter are Chughtai's 'The Quilt' and 'The Rock' and Mastur's 'They are Taking Me Away, Father, They are Taking Me Away' and 'The Miscreant'.

Talat Ahmed's *Literature and Politics in the Age of Nationalism: The Progressive Episode in South Asia, 1932–56* tracks the history of the All-India Progressive Writers Association (AIPWA) which flourished between 1936 and 1956, and had a formative influence on the ideas of both Ismat Chughtai and Khadija Mastur, mentioned above. Of special interest to readers will be the interaction of various national and international forces operating at the time, and their impact on the formation and eventual decline of the Progressive Writers' project. These include the national struggle for independence, the drive for social transformation within India, and the savage international polarization between fascism and democracy in the 1930s, as well as lines of influence, continuity, and rupture between the agenda set by Indian writers in English, often based in Europe, and their counterparts from various Indian languages, most of whom were in India. It was Mulk Raj Anand, for instance, an influential member of the AIPWA, who prepared the first draft of the manifesto formulating the aims and objectives of the AIPWA. A revised version of this manifesto appeared in the old *Left Review* in London and was subsequently published in *Hans*, the Hindi magazine edited by Premchand, as well as being translated into a number of other Indian languages (p. 19). Ahmed's useful, if somewhat uninspired, account of this turbulent and exciting period challenges popular perception that anglophone fiction in India lacks a literary genealogy within the nation. For a full account of the intertextual lines of influence in Indian writing in English which are confined neither to the literary nor to other anglophone writers alone, one must turn to Priyamvada Gopal's *Literary Radicalism in India* [2005].

Finally, in this section I discuss two books whose focus is the English language itself and its usage in literary texts and the print media. Sumana Bandyopadhyay's *Indianization of English: Analysis of Linguistic Features in*

Selected Post-1980 Indian English Fiction offers an overview of the key linguistic aspects of the English language as used in the literary register in the second-language setting and multilingual context of contemporary India. The author stresses how Indian English has adapted to homegrown realities while remaining a major variant of a world language. The phonological, lexical, functional, and structural aspects of Indian English discussed are illustrated with examples drawn from some of the best-known living practitioners of IWE. The time-span chosen starts with Salman Rushdie's epoch-making *Midnight's Children* [1981] and includes Vikram Chandra, Upamanyu Chatterjee, Amitav Ghosh, Manju Kapur, Rohinton Mistry, Arundhati Roy, and Vikram Seth. Bandyopadhyay concludes her study by stressing the vital and dynamic Indianness of today's English as handled by Indian writers who can be anywhere from Mexico—as in Anita Desai's *The Zigzag Way* [2004]—to Kashmir, France, and the USA (Rushdie's *Shalimar the Clown* [2005]).

Also worthy of attention alongside literature proper is the flourishing world of the English-language press in India. *The Times of India*, which dates from 1838 and has editions published from ten Indian cities, proclaimed a circulation of 1.4 million in 1997 and has since rebranded itself as the world's biggest-circulation English-language substantive newspaper. Print journalism in the big dailies is read all over the country and is quick to absorb and influence changes in spoken language. Asima Ranjan Parhi's *Indian English through Newspapers* conducts a lexical, syntactic, and semantic enquiry into the usage of English in Indian daily newspapers. An initial analysis of the socio-cultural factors behind the coinage of new words and expressions is followed by a meticulous list of new words and expressions collected by random sampling between 1996 and 2002. An analysis of the internal linguistic mechanism at work in the process of new-word formation is followed by a discussion of the syntactical changes that follow from the morphemic variation. Although we do not find a radical transformation of English structural patterns in the English dailies in India, Parhi concludes that there is a steady drive towards frequent code-mixing, proverbializing, and functional English.

(b) Chapters in Anthologies

Three chapters in Frank Schulze-Engler and Sissy Helff's edited collection *Transcultural English Studies* address issues of identity in diasporic literature from the subcontinent. Barbara Schaff's discussion of Hari Kunzru's *The Impressionist* in 'Trying to Escape, Longing to Belong' (pp. 281–92) shows how Kunzru's use of mimicry, while destabilizing fixed notions of self and its Other, produces a non-entity, a complete void. In the process it shears the concept of some of the glamour it has enjoyed since Bhabha's original formulation of it. Nadia Butt's analysis of Zulfikar Ghose's semi-autobiographical novel *The Triple Mirror of the Self* [1992] in 'Fictions of Transcultural Memory' (pp. 293–308) draws on Maurice Halbwach's notion of cultural memory to unpack the at once real and imaginary dimensions of the central character's self as it emerges in the context of diverse cultures and continents. Christine Vogt-William's 'Routes to the Root' (pp. 309–22) uses a film and a novel that both coincidentally bear the title 'Bombay Talkie' to argue that roots and transculturality are not mutually exclusive (roots can in themselves be transcultural), and that 'roots' alone are not the basis of an authentic cultural identity.

Stella Borg Barthet's edited collection *A Sea for Encounters* includes a couple of articles on the Indian novel in English. Evelyne Hanquart-Turner's essay, 'Amit Chaudhuri's *Afternoon Raag*: Interplay and the Translation of Chronotopes' (pp. 143–8), sees the novel as a significant illustration of the Bakhtinian chronotope: 'the place where the knots of narrative are tied and untied'. The novel moves through a succession of miniatures from the present into different pasts, from Bombay to Oxford and Calcutta. Each chapter contributes in multiple ways to the tying and untying of links between various times and spaces as they are filtered through memory and imagination. As such, each chapter shares in the whole utterance of the work, a chronotope mingling the experiences of the narrator in an implicit dialogue between East and West. The second essay, by Tuomas Huttunen, explores ethics and language in the novels of Amitav Ghosh (pp. 335–48). Huttunen argues that exploring ethics in literature frequently takes the form of probing how to represent otherness in the context of interpersonal relationships. In Ghosh's novels the encounter with the other often underscores the inadequacy of language to represent emotions. What emerges is a poststructuralist emphasis on difference, on the one hand, and a humanist transcending of discourse on the other. Huttunen aligns this with Levinasian ethics.

Included in *Shared Waters*, another collection of essays in the same series, also edited by Stella Borg Barthet, are at least six essays of potential interest to scholars of the subcontinent, each pushing for a dynamic understanding of space. Christine Vogt-William's 'Smells, Skins and Spices' (pp. 151–65) offers an analytical overview of Indian spice shops as gendered diasporic spaces in the novels of Chitra Banerjee, Radhika Jha, and Preethi Nair. Vogt-William shows how the spice shop serves as a backdrop as well as a spatial instigator of transcultural interrogation and strategies paving the way for greater autonomy on the part of their protagonists. Melanie A. Murray's 'The Sea and the Erosion of Cultural Identity in Romesh Gunesekera's *Reef*' (pp. 217–27) uses Homi Bhabha's concept of 'double relation' to show how the novel challenges notions of the island as timeless and insular, reflecting the author's transnational identity through an emphasis on movement and regeneration. T. Vijay Kumar's 'Sharing Nation Space: Representations of India' (pp. 323–33) considers the emergence in recent years of the 'local' Indian novel in English, signalling a shift in the balance of power from metropolitan India to provincial India. The recent surge in aggressive self-expression on the part of the small town is part of a larger, ongoing process of de-elitization and the assertion of the under-represented—or what Kumar calls 'provincialising postcolonialism' (p. 331). The problematization of space and identity is also the focus of Devon Campbell-Hall's essay, 'Writing Second-Generation Migrant Identity in Meera Syal's Fiction' (pp. 289–305), which argues that second-generation British Asian youth in Syal's novels are less concerned with their state of cultural marginalization than they are with the material realities of their everyday existence. These unwitting intermediaries between East and West offer an instantiation of Peter van der Veer's argument that non-Western cultures are no longer located outside the West, but form an increasingly important social element of the Western cultural scene itself.

Recovering the Asian (and black) literary heritage in Britain is the aim of Pallavi Rastogi and Jocelyn Fenton Stitt's edited collection *Before Windrush*. Julie F. Codell's 'Transposing Travel Narrative: Irony, Ethnography and the Guest Discourse in Indian Travel Writing' (pp. 88–116) focuses on writings by the increasing number of Indians who travelled overseas in the last quarter of the nineteenth century. This writing has been recently the subject of scholarship but little attempt has been made to analyse its literary quality. Pallavi Rastogi's 'An Easterner in the East End: Unsettling Metropolitan Discourses in Olive Christian Malvery's *The Soul Market*' (pp. 117–40) examines the Anglo-Indian, upper-class Malvery's experiences as an undercover journalist in her book of sketches of the London poor. Rastogi comments on Malvery's skilful use of metropolitan racial discourses—colonial rhetoric, the racialization of the working class, and anti-Semitism—in order to unsettle those modes of representation. She also shows how Malvery's writing highlights the rifts in a seemingly anglophile persona to foreground the contradictory affiliations of colonized identities in the metropolis. A third essay, 'The Noble Savage and the Savage Noble: Mulk Raj Anand's Deconstruction of Identity in *Conversations in Bloomsbury*' (pp. 179–97), by Margaret Lucille Trenta, shows how Anand's encounters with members of the Bloomsbury group, narrated nearly fifty years later, allowed him the freedom to re-present the history of Britain in the 1920s as his own. According to Trent, it is through both the content and the publication and creative history of *Conversations in Bloomsbury* that Anand decentres colonization in the structure of cultural identity to celebrate its multiplicity.

Seeking the Self—Encountering the Other: Diasporic Narrative and the Ethic Representation, edited by Tuomas Huttunen et al., is yet another volume of collected essays on diasporic literature which includes at least one article of relevance to Indian writing in English. Ene-Reet Soovik's 'Polyphony by a Polluted River' (pp. 168–80) discusses the presence of diaspora and hybridity in Arundhati Roy's *The God of Small Things*. The novel, Soovik argues, is not a tale of dispersal and exile so much as a return to familial roots. Yet the notion of the diasporic repeatedly surfaces in the text, occasionally also exposing the confluence of diaspora with globalization.

Writers of the Indian diaspora continue to exercise the imagination of literary scholars in an edited collection by Jaspal Singh and Rajendra Chetty, *Indian Writers: Transnationalisms and Diasporas*. The volume opens with an article by Aparajita De, 'Pariah or Messiah' (pp. 11–21), which studies the complications of diasporic identity formation and postmodern citizenship through the character of Gogol Ganguly in Jhumpa Lahiri's debut novel *The Namesake*. Ronit Frenkel's 'Writing South Africa in Diaspora' (pp. 23–43) theorizes place and identities in the South African and Indian diasporas in relation to place, gender and love in Imraan Coovadia's *The Wedding*. Jaspal Singh's 'The Indian Diaspora in Burma and the Politics of Globalisation in

Amitav Ghosh's *The Glass Palace* and Mira Kamdar's *Motiba's Tattoos*' (pp. 45–65) interweaves a personal narrative with textual analysis to probe the dialectics of dislocation. Ryan Paul Singh (pp. 69–86) challenges popular readings of Bharati Mukherjee's *Jasmine* as the story of a young immigrant woman's self-discovery and empowerment. The Americanized, commodified, consumerist, professional caregiver is not a subaltern and cannot speak the subaltern truth from her Iowan space. In 'Life-Writing: The Migrating Selves of Meena Alexander' (pp. 87–96), Sam Naidu engages with recent scholarly debates about life-writing and fiction, the reading of autobiographical texts as part of new ethnographic projects, and literary self-representations and their relationship to subjectivity with reference to Meena Alexander's memoir *Fault Lines* [1992]. We return to Bharati Mukherjee in Alison Graham-Bartolini's 'The Advantage of Estrangement in Mukherjee's *Jasmine*' (pp. 97–106) to see how the protagonist's 'nomadic, decentered, and contrapuntal' subjectivity provides her with a clear advantage over those who cannot adjust to cultural multiplicity, or those who, in an effort to stave off vulnerability, view themselves as fixed and uniform by nature. Rajendra Chetty's 'Mapping Durban in Aziz Hassim's *The Lotus People*' (pp. 109–20) takes us to the representations of Durban and the construction of the South African geographical space during apartheid, while Christopher Larkosh's 'Reading "South Asia" in Dangerous Times (and Other Lessons from the Future)' (pp. 121–31) argues for the need to challenge North–South models of transcultural communication in favour of a South–South exchange, illustrated through a discussion of two new writers in English from South Asia: Samrat Upadhayay from Nepal and Maniza Naqvi from Pakistan. Charles Wesley's 'The Function of "Good" and "Evil" in *The Satanic Verses*: A Query' (pp. 133–45) argues that while binary categories may play an important role in negotiating daily life, terms like good and evil need to be nuanced so as to indicate their complicity with power as tools of influence and persuasion within a range of contexts. The evolution of key metaphors in Indo-Fijian literature is the focus of Seri Inthava Luangphinith's article (pp. 147–57), which explores the linkage between Indian diasporic studies extraneous to Fiji with Indian heritage writing emanating from within Fiji, and the opportunity this linkage presents for deconstructing the universalizing tendency of the former while interrogating Fijian Indian ideas surrounding national identity and larger discussions of 'who' constitutes the 'nation' in the latter. The last two essays in the volume, by Peter Simatei and James Gifford, both look at the work of M.G. Vassanji. Simatei reads Vassanji's work against Ngugi wa Thiong'o's to show how the former claims historical time and space by disavowing the homogeneous history of the nation, while Gifford compares Vassanji with Lawrence Durrell to highlight the links and parallels between them.

This useful collection for undergraduate students could, however, have done with greater care and attention from its editors. The introductory essay appears to have been written before the collection was finalized and includes two references to pieces that were evidently dropped from the published volume. This carelessness is also evident in the introduction to Hena Ahmad's book discussed above, also from the same publisher, where virtually the same paragraph gets repeated in quick succession, in what is clearly an editorial oversight.

(c) Journal Articles

The year 2009 was a productive one for all the 'big guns' in subcontinental English writing, with numerous articles on Amitav Ghosh, Romesh Gunesekera, V.S. Naipaul, Michael Ondaatje, Salman Rushdie, Arundhati Roy, Shyam Selvadurai, and Vikram Seth. But it was also a significant one for some of the oft-forgotten stalwarts, such as Anita Desai, E.M. Forster, Rudyard Kipling, Sarojini Naidu, R.K. Narayan, Paul Scott, and Kamala Markandaya. In listing these names, I am not making nationality-based distinctions, but rather uniting them under their predominant literary locale. In doing so, I wish to emphasize the importance of geopolitical 'place' that inevitably shapes the imaginative in writers, especially at a time when the amorphous category of 'world literature' (read literature available in English, in the original as well as in translation) threatens to overtake all other affiliations of being and belonging.

Rosemary Marangoly George, in 'Where in the World Did Kamala Markandaya Go?' (*Novel* 42:iii[2009] 400–9), makes a timely intervention into the current debates concerning world literature in order to explore the limitations of contemporary postcolonial theory. This has rested on a rubric of the geopolitical entities that wrested self-governance from colonial powers. George suggests that Markandaya is an unusual example of a writer who refuses to board the nationalist ship at a time when Third World literatures were expected to be predominantly patriotic in character. Instead, Markandaya charts out a cosmopolitan career that uneasily straddles being 'Indian literary ambassador to the world' and 'European intellectual' (p. 401). However, apart from the urgent call to consider Markandaya more seriously as an example of world writing, George does not offer sustained analysis of the writer's work to support her case. Markanadaya is undoubtedly located as a subcontinental writer in her rich corpus of novellas bearing witness to catastrophic transformations of that region. Nevertheless, this is a timely appeal and may spark renewed interest in Markandaya's cultural brokering within and beyond postcolonial studies.

Anupama Arora shows how Sarojini Naidu's epistolary reflections and public lectures during her North American tour (1928–9) presented her as 'a self-confident cosmopolitan Indian woman, a poet and writer, and a female nationalist with her own mind' ('The Nightingale's Wanderings: Sarojini Naidu in North America' *JCL* 44:iii[2009] 87–105). Like Markandaya, Naidu's performance of modern Indian womanhood negotiated a mix of gendered nationalism and inter-imperial relations. It is still worth quoting from Naidu's Presidential Address at the All India Woman's Committee in Bombay on January 1930, given after she returned from her trip to North America: 'It was as a woman of this ancient race with its millennia of experience that in my travels last year, I looked at the lives of those child countries of Europe and those kindergarten countries of America. They expected me to fit into their notion of what an Indian woman should be, a timid woman, a modest woman, a jump-on-to-a-chair-at-mouse woman who had come to learn from them. But Sarojini had come to them as a free woman' (quoted in Arora, p. 87). While locating Naidu within the gendered politics of the Indian National Congress, where she had to constantly justify her poetic work as equally significant for the independence movement, Arora also makes explicit some of the problematic aspects of Naidu's speaking position. Travelling in North America as one of India's educated elite, Naidu views the African American struggle with some condescension, using tropes of the noble savage inherited from her European schooling. The article is a good illustration of the complexities of postcolonial feminisms.

Similar technologies of colonial gender lie at the heart of Alex Tickell's analysis of 'Cawnpore, Kipling and *Charivari*: 1857 and the Politics of Commemoration' (*L&H* 3rd series 18:ii[2009] 1–19). Tickell looks at narratives of assault, mourning, and rebellion focused on 'rape' as an apparatus of colonial distinction between grievable and non-grievable lives. At the zenith of Victorian funereal culture, 1857 provided a geography of remembrance to unite colonies and Britain as one imperial community. Tickell suggests that, in co-authoring the atrocity scripts of the Cawnpore and Lucknow revolts, and thereby justifying their retribution, British relief forces participated in *charivari*, a scapegoating carnivalesque ritual. The sites of supposed/constructed carnage mobilize mourning that then upholds violence as a state prerogative enshrined in the rule of law. Tickell goes on to explore how Kipling refused to write *the* historical novel of the 'Mutiny', preferring instead to invest in the meta-historical, even in his early journalism that anticipates *Kim*, although 'In the year '57' [1887] and 'The Little House at Arrah' [1888] suggest that public memorialization of the Mutiny was suspect. This is a rich essay, putting together material from the colonial archives and theoretical perspectives from Giorgio Agamben, Peter Stallybrass, and Allon White.

Jesse Oak Taylor's 'Kipling's Imperial Aestheticism: Epistemologies of Art and Empire in *Kim*' (*ELT* 52:i[2009] 49–69) suggests that imperial ideology actually leads to an aesthetic crisis in Kipling's depiction of masculinities in *Kim*. The tension between muscular masculinity and the more dissident masculinities of the dandy, the aesthete, and the *flâneur* reaches breaking point when Kipling's men of authority have to rely on Indian 'translators'. In this context, Kim offers the possibility of an epistemological 'third space' that Taylor contends is best understood as a form of aestheticism. Taylor suggests that the consumer culture heralded by the Great Exhibition of 1851 both spread the dandy's aesthetic and domesticated it, so that Kim's self-fashioning is as much a function of his 'Britishness' as a freedom of movement enabled by costumes and cross-dressing. Though the novel's denouement claims Kim's *flâneur* as imperial servant par excellence, Taylor concludes that it does so at the expense of an aesthetics that belied Kipling's belief in imperialism as moral imperative.

Sune Borkfelt, in 'Colonial Animals and Literary Analysis: The Examples of Kipling's Animal Stories' (*ES* 90:v[2009] 557–68), interrogates the imperial ruse of pitting heroic adventurers against aggressive savages, of both the human and the animal kind. Anthropomorphic animal tales such as *The Just*

So Stories and *The Jungle Book* served as cautionary examples to both children and adults and stood in for the exoticization and stereotyping of the human beings that inhabited colonized territories. These are valid suggestions, yet Borkfelt's somewhat simplistic listing of Kipling's various animals and their characteristics limits her argument. This shortcoming is addressed somewhat by David Sergeant in 'Kipling's Descriptions' (*EIC* 59:iv[2009] 324–46), where he argues that Kipling's descriptions are an essential unifying characteristic of his entire oeuvre. The sheer visuality of Kipling's work, embedded as it is in 'spatial situation', 'precise delineation', 'insubstantial mobility', and 'unfixed sensuality' (p. 332) bears the impression of its sources and carries it beyond the local.

Alison Sainsbury shifts focus to another colonial figure. '"Not Yet... Not There": Breaking the Bonds of Marriage in E.M. Forster's *A Passage to India*' (*CS* 21:i[2009] 59–73) opens with the novel's concluding question, 'Why can't be friends now?' and analyses the conventions of the Anglo-Indian domestic novel, wherein a young English girl arrives in India to marry and fulfil the heteronormative logic of empire. The impossibility of individual members of the empire having organic relationships becomes the theme of this essay. Sainsbury rehearses much that has been written about Forster's adjectival insistence on the unspeakability of encounter with a hostile land (reminiscent of Conrad's *Heart of Darkness*). The essay moves into a reading of the female body as a primary index for India, the Marabar Caves supplying the threat of rape that was a collective fantasy of the Anglo-Indian community. Sainsbury concludes that, rather than a political critique of British imperialism coded as the rules of marriage, the novel is an anguished albeit disguised lament at the utter impossibility of personal relationships between men.

Mahmoud Salami discusses how Forster's discursive technique is revealed in music in 'The Narratological Discourse of Music in E.M. Forster's Novels' (*ArielE* 40:ii–iii[2009] 135–51). Music is a means both to reveal authorial intentionality and to explore the plurality of ideological meanings and thus offer a powerful redemptive aesthetic to address the contestations of art and life. Salami uses the work of musicologists such as Simon Frith, Wendy Steiner, and John Blacking to excavate the musical underpinnings of several novels, including *A Passage to India*.

Echoing Jesse Oak Taylor's interest in colonial masculinity, Steph Cesaro and Patricia Connolly consider 'The Destabilization of Masculinity in *A House for Mr Biswas* and *The Mimic Men*' (*Mosaic* 42:iii[2009] 109–27). The essay considers the emasculating effects of colonial rule and postcolonial consciousness upon Indo-Caribbean men in Trinidad, who compensate by performing hyper-gender roles that are crossed with race, class, ethnicity, and nation. Creolization is the other fulcrum on which self-posturing and interpersonal relationships turn. (For more on Naipaul, see the Caribbean section above.)

The colonial house as a metaphor for the colonized island or bound colonial space is explored in Melanie A. Murray's 'Empire and the House in Postcolonial Fiction: Lawrence Scott's *Witchbroom*, Romesh Gunesekera's *The Sandglass* and Jean Arasanayagam's "Time the Destroyer"' (*JPW* 45:iv[2009] 438–48). Houses operate as spaces of confinement, where women replicate the insularity of empire. Murray sketches the three writers' biographies and turbulent postcolonial geopolitics. She goes on to question how far Bhabha's notion of hybridity offers a useful frame of reference for these contested territories. The passage recuperation of female silenced voices is effected through invested descendants, as memories of the house reveal both nostalgia and insecurity. Murray contends that the narrators try to reconcile their hybrid ancestry with present-day realities, but are unable to do so from their marginalized position within sites of unreconciled conflict.

Heather Smythe looks at 'Indigenizing Sexuality and National Citizenship: Shyam Selvadurai's *Cinnamon Gardens*' (*ArielE* 40:ii–iii[2009] 1–23). This important article links the surveillance of reproductive functions in 1927–8 Ceylon to the tensions between endogamy and exogamy, and understands constitutionalism and anti-colonial reform in terms not only of ethnic sameness/conflict, but also of same-sex/different-sex relationships. Selvadurai makes rich use of such political figures as Ceylonese nationalist Ponnambalam Arunachalam and radical British political thinker Edward Carpenter. The backdrop of the Donoughmore Commission's inquiry into the possibility of Ceylon's self-rule is intertwined with questions of kinship, which are troubled by ethnic and homophobic persecution, providing convenient regulative mechanisms for Sri Lanka's turbulent politics of ethno-nationalism.

Colonial nostalgia and gendered sunderings remain concerns in Jacqueline Banerjee's 'Women of Affairs: Contrasting Images of Empire in Paul Scott's *The Raj Quartet*' (*JCL* 44:iii[2009] 69–85). Banerjee traces the genesis of Scott's four novels and their television adaptation by Granada to two Victorian images, both concerning 'Women of Affairs' or women *in* affairs. The first is a coloured engraving of Queen Victoria receiving tribute from a native prince, and the second is of a running woman, evoking memories of rape and massacre at Cawnpore's Bibighar and the Jallianwallah Bagh. Banerjee exonerates Scott from the charge of being ambivalent about the loss of the Jewel in the Crown and instead sees *The Raj Quartet* as 'a final audit on the imperial account' (p. 82). What seemed impossible for Forster or Naipaul is a real hope in Scott: love and birth as the balm to atrocities on both sides, but, most of all, redemptive relationships between individuals, even though they might be cogs in the machinery of empire. I find somewhat problematic, however, Banerjee's suggestion that *The Raj Quartet* be read as a multicultural text.

Joel Baetz's 'Cricket Matters: The English Game and Rohinton Mistry's *Tales from Firozsha Bagh*' (*CanL* 202[Autumn 2009] 50–66) starts with the proposition that, contrary to the belief of enthusiasts, sport functions not as a unifier but rather as the arbiter of social distinctions and hierarchies. In the colonial context, the cricket bat is 'as much a weapon designed to enforce racial boundaries as it is a figurative phallus and a sign of hegemonic masculinity' (p. 50). The inhabitants of Firozsha Bagh understand all too well the sociological implications of the game, not as a gentleman's civil and civilizing pursuit, but as a polarizing pastime with investments in nationalism, ethnicity, and indigenous masculinity. Baetz is interested not so much in Mistry's realist portrayals of the activity, but in understanding how the writer recognizes cricket's colonial history in order to explore the limits of story-telling and representation. Mistry does not present cricket as a postcolonial opportunity for resistance but as the legacy of the British empire, which in turn becomes a vehicle for the maintenance of imperial fantasies about race and culture.

Ideas of cultural purity are enmeshed with religious orthodoxy in Jill Didur's '"An Unremembered Time": Secular Criticism in Pankaj Mishra's *The Romantics*' (*JCL* 44:ii[2009] 65–85). Didur begins with Mishra's ongoing concern with the failure of modernity to stem the rise of religious extremism and majoritarianism in India. Mishra links a tide of hyper-individualism to financial and social security of an elite Hindu class formation in his 2000 novel. Tracing a genealogy to Gita Mehta's *Karma Kola* [1979], Didur claims *The Romantics* is also a satirical look at selfhood as defined by the quest for religious/spiritual enlightenment, and thus falls into the tradition of Saidian 'secular critique' (p. 67). Using Said's notion of modernist affiliation, Didur makes a palimpsestic link between orientalist and Hindu nationalist attitudes in postcolonial India. She supplements her reading of Mishra's novel with two of his journalistic pieces, 'The Invention of the Hindu' and 'Edmund Wilson in Benaras', and concludes that *The Romantics* disrupts the idea of the nation as a unified concept, especially one supported by an unremembered time of a romantic, idealized, *religious* self. This conforms with the needs of exilic selves, who have a contrapuntal relationship to a remembered secular nation of origin.

Angelia Poon, too, explores the limits of a singular identity at a time when Islam is being portrayed as *the* Othered religion. 'To Know What's What: Forms of Migrant Knowing in Monica Ali's *Brick Lane*' (*JPW* 45:iv[2009] 426–37) starts with a timely distinction in the terms of migrancy with reference to the work of postcolonial scholars such as Benita Parry, Laura Chrisman, Neil Lazarus, and Susheila Nasta, as opposed to celebrators of hybridity such as Salman Rushdie and Homi Bhabha. The first four insist on recognizing the material conditions of migrants, while the latter two privilege an ideal of unfettered creative sensibility made possible by their liberation from territory and patriotism. *Brick Lane* restages the question of home by fixing on other, quotidian, ways of knowing the world, thus somewhat relinquishing its hold on origins, territory, or even memory, but still rejecting unboundedness. Nazneen makes sense of her narrow and constrained life, not untouched by history, but at an everyday remove from it, by 'making do' (Poon invokes Michel de Certeau, p. 430). Unlike the epistemic certainty of the hybrid Chanu harking back to his Bengali literary heritage, Nazneen's unlearning makes available to her an agency that is dependent on epistemological uncertainly as the only basis for an ethics of living. Poon's is a nuanced reading that champions functional know-how over abstract knowledge as a way of understanding the fraught lives of modern migrants.

Sarah Brouillette offers a more pointed analysis of inhabitation in 'Literature and Gentrification on Brick Lane' (*Criticism* 51:iii[2009] 425–49). Using theories of urban geography, Brouillette suggests that literary texts such as Monica Ali's *Brick Lane* [2003], Tarquin Hall's *Salaam Brick Lane: A Year in the New East End* [2005], and Rachel Lichtenstein's *On Brick Lane* [2007] actually partake of and contribute to the area's gentrification. Criticism of these works needs to consider the effect they have in capturing the 'intellectual property' behind the East End's remaking. The population of Brick Lane is fast getting polarized between a service class (of mostly immigrants) and a more bohemian avant-garde that 'revitalizes' it and moves on, allowing a moneyed group to move in. Brouillette excavates the story of *Brick Lane*'s genesis and reception, where Ali made *Granta*'s list of best young novelists even before she had published a word, and where long-time dwellers of Brick Lane felt more familiarized with their living environs after reading the novel but protested at the movie based on it. Working beyond the usual bounds of literary criticism, this essay offers valuable ways of grasping the nexus between global publishing regimes, capital development, creative circulation of ideas, and the transformation of lives.

Jesse Patrick Ferguson looks at place as an entry into knowledge in 'Violent Dis-Placements: Natural and Human Violence in Kiran Desai's *The Inheritance of Loss*' (*JCL* 44:ii[2009] 35–49). Using de Certeau's formulation of places as having '"fragmentary and inward-turning histories"' (p. 36), this essay understands place as space that is necessarily defined by violence. Desai's 2006 novel narrativizes the personal and private histories of landed occupiers in tension with 1980s agitations for a Nepali Gorkhaland in Darjeeling and Kalimpong. Ferguson suggests that nature's fecundity constantly replaces human edifices and thereby makes space for new existences and edifices, but that it offers little solace to the downtrodden, whether in the voluptuous greens of the mountains or in the scurry of cockroaches in the New York of Biju, the cook's son who emigrates to escape poverty and violence. Biju cannot lay claim to any place-ness either at home or abroad, hostage to either the constant vagaries of nature or the shifting of established hierarchies in contested social spaces.

Terri Tomsky also addresses environmental and human concerns in 'Amitav Ghosh's Anxious Witnessing and the Ethics of Action in *The Hungry Tide*' (*JCL* 44:i[2009] 53–65). Unlike the failure of cosmopolitanism in *Brick Lane* and *The Inheritance of Loss* (as understood by Poon and Ferguson above), Tomsky suggests that it is the civic possibilities created by the agency of the cosmopolitan individual that make justice and ethical action possible. She considers the extent to which the characters of Ghosh's 2004 novel implicate the reader into accounting for the subaltern in conceptually and geographically distant sites of the world. Ghosh's fundamentally humanist answer echoes Said's concept of 'anxious witnessing' where '"ethical intervention is only effective when accompanied by the economic agency of the transnational bourgeoisie"' (p. 54). *The Hungry Tide* is also a meditation on how affective relationships between individuals open them up to cultural-political and psychosocial change. In its depiction of the Morichjhãpi massacre the novel shows cosmopolitan subjectivity confounded by hunger and natural catastrophe, on the one hand, and governmental brutality and intellectual apathy on the other. Ghosh's idea of love not only questions conventional forms of humanitarianism but also radicalizes intervention in norms of community and the nation-state.

Four different essays on Ghosh's fourth novel identify the roots of his fiction, his continued engagement with alternative historiographies, and the importance of the 'witness' in recording them. Jenni G. Halpin's 'Gift Unpossessed: Community as "Gift" in *The Calcutta Chromosome*' (*ArielE*

40:ii–iii[2009] 23–40) looks at Ghosh's postcolonial interrogation of the Western scientific method in his reinterpretation of the story of Nobel Prize-winner Ronald Ross's research on the transmission of malaria. Ghosh rewrites both content and style of the history, creating a disjunctive non-sequential plot, and generating an invisible community able to interact only via technology. The transfer of personalities and a hyperspace created through such an imagined community of the creative non-material is, Halpin suggests, an attempt to delineate an anti-colonial nationalism. The 'counter-science' and vernacular Indian stories in the novel further disrupt space and time and break down borders through which identities can now move. Such a narrative inevitably evokes questions of justice and the possibility of community.

Claire Chambers continues the debate on knowledge and power in 'Network of Stories: Amitav Ghosh's *The Calcutta Chromosome*' (*ArielE* 40:ii–iii[2009] 41–63). Chambers, too, focuses on the shape-shifting subaltern figures operating within the cult of an Indian counter-science that demands the coexistence of conventional knowledge and its mysterious antithesis, 'not-knowledge' (p. 42). She explores the indeterminacy that challenges Western science's 'claim to know' and uses Gerard Genette's 'architextuality' and 'hypertextuality' to understand the multiple discourses and modes of enunciation in Ghosh's text. The essay uses Manuel Castell's notion of a network society to engage with the idea of disparate community that can only interact through textual references, international computer-mediated communication, and that harbinger of modernity, the railway. In each of these three essays so far, we see an attempt by critics to locate Ghosh's work within an ethics of community-making, but each time the readings are arrested by a highly involved textuality and reference to privileged modes of knowledge-making. However enamoured Ghosh may be of 'not-knowledge', and however desirous his commentators of recuperating the subaltern, their analyses remain rooted in an old-fashioned and ultimately committed textuality. I wonder if a larger point needs to be made here about the kind of function that literature performs and whether we are a bit misguided in imagining 'active' praxis through such modes of interpretation?

James H Thrall's 'Postcolonial Science Fiction? Science, Religion and the Transformation of Genre in Amitav Ghosh's *The Calcutta Chromosome*' (*L&T* 23:iii[2002] 289–302) also sees the novel as raising questions about the nature of knowledge in its negotiations between Western rationality and Eastern esotericism, the normativeness of the former being countered by the mysticism of the latter. Tracing the roots of science fiction to colonialism, and its fraught relationship with religion to an emergent secularism, Thrall sees Ghosh using the genre's interest in alternative histories/realities to explore tensions between religion and rationality via a cult of counter-science that includes biological transmigration of personalities and Hindu beliefs in reincarnation. The medical detective narrative becomes 'both commentary on and projection beyond the postcolonial world of contemporary India' (p. 292). Thrall compares Ghosh with Nalo Hopkinson as taking up the new field of postcolonial science fiction's offer of innovative methods to resolve old binaries.

All the themes outlined in these essays on Ghosh come together in Hilary Thompson's 'The Colonial City as Inverted Laboratory in *Baumgartner's Bombay* and *The Calcutta Chromosome*' (*JNT* 39:iii[2009] 347–68). Thompson proposes that these two novels go beyond a simple postcolonial critique to create emblematic and enabling environments in which indigenous knowledge and rooted consciousness come together in a conglomeration of the past, present, and future. The cities in these novels function as test-sites of invention and accident where colonial science needs to legitimize itself in order to make an 'obligatory passage point' of the vast experimental space of the colony (p. 362). But this space is not merely an object of detached study; the enquiry has to tunnel into the psychoanalytical realm of transference, in precisely the way that the transmigration of souls happens in Ghosh's counter-science cult. Paradoxically, Anita Desai's Bombay-based novel has to bring opposite hemispheres and domains into convergence in the black hole of Calcutta. This is an intriguing essay that links Desai's text of 'mourning and malaise' with Ghosh's novel of 'malaria and mutation' (p. 356).

From the city to the backwaters: three essays consider Ayemenem in terms of ecology, aesthetics, and cosmopolitanism. Elisha Cohn takes up 'Radical Aesthetics: Arundhati Roy's Ecology of Style' (*ArielE* 40:ii–iii[2009] 161–82), John Lutz looks at 'Commodity Fetishism, Patriarchal Repression and Psychic Deprivation in Arundhati Roy's *The God of Small Things*' (*Mosaic* 42:iii[2009] 57–75) and Aarthi Vadde considers 'The Backwaters Sphere: Ecological Collectivity, Cosmopolitanism and Arundhati Roy' (*MFS* 55:iii[2009] 522–44). Cohn prefaces her study with Roy's essay 'The End of Imagination' and rehearses the work of Isobel Armstrong, Brian Massumi, and Eve Kosofsky Sedgwick to cover postcolonial debate over the aesthetic autonomy of art, finding a politicized humanism to be the strength of Roy's novel. This involves an appreciation of beauty that does not succumb to either cultural compromise or unapproachable otherness. Instead, Roy offers an experiential and affective form of knowledge that marks the limit to a politics of anti-globalization bereft of beauty and fights to retain that beauty uncompromised and available to ideological debate.

Lutz reads the potential of *The God of Small Things* in the characters who seize upon the material and the imagistic and thus operate as a site of resistance. Baby Kochamma's obsession with American television, the Ayemenem house's dependence on a market economy, the airport's gift shop, Cochin Harbor Terminus's cheap plastic toy sale, all these suggest the awfulness of the present as an outcome of reductive history. The degradation of the landscape and subordination of life to market forces makes explicit the human need for aesthetic fulfilment, and herein lies the hope of the book.

Vadde locates Roy's literary work at the troubled intersection of ecocriticism and cosmopolitanism, two fields she thinks are antithetical to each other and to the project of epistemic revolution. Kerala is one centre of Indian debate on environmentalism versus development, and its backwaters represent for Vadde a social space in which to negotiate ecological collectivity. But it takes a convoluted detour through Kant to arrive at an idea of 'terrestrial cosmopolitanism' (p. 537), which Vadde declares to be a strategic tactic of Roy to 'foster solidarity among English language readers and India's rural and tribal populations who are, in the end, cultural and linguistic strangers' (p. 540)—a tall claim that underscores the limits of current discourses of cosmopolitanism.

Form was the preferred mode of analysis of Salman Rushdie, who continues to attract major scholarship. Chun-yen Chen, in 'Betrayal of Form: The 'Teeming' Narrative and the Allegorical Impulse in Rushdie's *Midnight's Children*' (*JCL* 44:iii[2009] 143–61), uses Walter Benjamin to argue the impossibility of the postcolonial subject's breaking free of the colonial legacy. Rushdie's life and writing have been yoked to an allegory of postcolonialism and yet the formal and material features of allegorical sign remain undecoded. Interrogating the overdetermined retrievalist demand of a nationalist narrative, Rushdie offers a redemptive historiography that is played out through repeated leitmotifs. Gaurav Majumdar, too, argues that Rushdie's form in all the novels since *Midnight's Children* performs a discordant and inappropriate dynamics of cultural transfer and transformation. In 'The Jolt of the Grotesque: Aesthetics as Ethics in *The Satanic Verses*' (*SubStance 120* 38:iii[2009] 31–50), Majumdar traces an itinerary of the grotesque from John Ruskin through Heinrich Schneegans to Erich Auerbach, and launches into a very interesting discussion of expressive and repressive grotesques. Rushdie's vision of violence, transgression, and the monstrous in his controversial novel sets up the fantastic as a symptom of politically resistant utopianism, and an opportunity for reconstruction.

The *Journal of Postcolonial Writing* carried four articles on Rushdie this year: Joy Wang's 'Othello Revisited: Metropolitan Romance in Fanon's *Black Skins, White Masks* and Rushdie's *The Satanic Verses*' (*JPW* 45:i[2009] 49–59), Florian Stadtler's 'Terror, Globalization and the Individual in Salman Rushdie's *Shalimar the Clown*' (*JPW* 45:ii[2009] 191–9), Vassilena Parashkevova's 'New Cities out of Old Ones: Catoptric Echoes and Reversals in Salman Rushdie's *The Ground Beneath Her Feet*' (*JPW* 45:iv[2009] 414–25), and Stuti Khanna's 'Postcolonial Politics of the Possible: City and Nation in the Fiction of Salman Rushdie' (*JPW* 45:iv[2009] 401–13). Without going into the individual merits of each of these articles, it can safely be said that scholarship on Rushdie is at least as prolific as his own output and that solid literary criticism is alive and kicking in the postcolonial journals.

'The Politics of Life after Death: Ondaatje's Ghost' (*JPW* 45:ii[2009] 201–12) relates Foucault's idea of biopolitics to Mbembe's notion of necropolitics in order to discuss Michael *Anil's Ghost* [2000]. Surveying the contradictory receptions of the novel as partisan and apolitical, Lesley Higgins and Marie-Christine Leps suggest that Ondaatje situates the Sri Lankan crisis within a broader geopolitical struggle where power–knowledge networks cut across national and ideological divides. Ondaatje's particular aesthetic method of textual assemblage and multiform epistemic space becomes an argument for heterotopia and archaeological liberation from the space of empire. Milena Marinkova, in '"Perceiving . . . in one's own body" the Violence of History, Politics and Writing: *Anil's Ghost* and Witness Writing' (*JCL* 44:iii[2009] 107–25)' finds that Ondaatje's representation of historical whitewashings and excisions generates anxiety. His witness writing is thereby not a redemptive counter to the realities of war, but offers micropolitical empowerment through an intimate and affective ethics of testimony. Reminiscent of haptic historiographies in *Running in the Family*, this trauma narrative offers an elemental and immanent tactility rather than a monumental or teleological unity. Art does not redeem history, but it does offer the possibility of intimacy and corporeality.

Cameron Fae Bushnell turns to the 'Art of Tuning: A Politics of Exile in Daniel Mason's *The Piano Tuner* and Vikram Seth's *An Equal Music*' (*ConL* 50:ii[2009] 332–62). Bushnell takes up Bruce King's provocative consideration of what the postcolonial 'industry' inclines us to expect and contends that the refusal to be native informants for their countries of origin is the reason Mason's and Seth's novels have received little attention. However, Bushnell argues that their representations of music pose a politics of exile that is staged as separation from standards operative in Western classical music. The protagonists assert their right to write differently from *within* the metropolis in order to interrogate its cultural politics while denying privilege to any teleological resolution. In this unsatisfactory inaudibility and irresolution, the novels become the very model for the politics of exile that they represent.

Last, a look at what was being said about world literature on the pages of *Wasafiri*, a magazine that almost single-handedly pioneered engagement with 'other' literatures in the heart of Britain's metropolis. Maya Jaggi's 'Opening the Universe a Little More' (*Wasafiri* 24:iii[2009]12–17) recounts her career as a cultural journalist and critic and maps out a terrain of world literature from a British perspective. Anita Desai narrates her journey from a time when Indian writers in English were accorded only 'loser' status to a time when there is prolific agreement that 'it's good to be an Indian English writer'. But the cultural-political work that Susheila Nasta, the editor, does is evident most in Ananya Vajpeyi's 'The Indo-Persian Sublime: From Amir Khusro to Shahzia Sikander' (*Wasafiri* 24:ii[2009] 36–46), where an English-language readership is opened up to a genuine sense of the breadth of world literature.

6. New Zealand

It is thirty years since C.K. Stead addressed the question of the literary value of James K. Baxter's 'Jerusalem Sonnets' [1970] and their place in a New Zealand poetry tradition learning to accommodate modernism ('From Wystan to Carlos: Modern and Modernism in New Zealand Poetry', *Islands* 7:v[1979] 467–86). Since then, Kai Jensen has explored the Jungian Baxter (*Whole Men: The Masculine Tradition in New Zealand Literature* [1996], pp. 127–48), while various writers have considered Baxter's 'tribal' affiliations, his relations to Maori, and the limitations of guru status. Yet what Leigh Davis in *Willy's Gazette* [1983] called Baxter's 'big ghost' still haunts the literary as well as the cultural landscape. If he cannot be exorcized, then he must be better understood.

An important step towards cultural-historical understanding is provided by a new study of the late Baxter and his community at Jerusalem. In *The Double Rainbow: James K Baxter, Ngati Hau and the Jerusalem Commune* John

Newton resists the familiar binary which sets Baxter the poet against Baxter the prophet, arguing instead that '"Jerusalem" was never an alternative to the poetry; it was part of it, its logical destination, even its most vivid accomplishment' (p. 171). This seems an ingenious way of recapturing the poet without expelling the prophet: the commune, in words Newton cites from Murray Edmonds in 'The Idea of the Poet' (*Cave* 4[1973] 36–7), was 'a poem which would speak to men' (p. 181). The placing of a socio-religious experiment at the heart of the literary legacy gives a novel context with which to reread Baxter's later works, which range from the scabrous to the contemplative, from social vilification to utopian optimism, from doubt to spiritual fervour, and from the holy to the silly.

Newton is right when he argues that the confrontation with the warmth of Maori culture produces in Pakeha an awareness 'of something apparently deficient in their own culture', but that sense of deficiency has steadily abated since the cross-cultural enthusiasm of the 1970s and 1980s (p. 88). If Pakeha are now to understand their own culture's strengths as well as its limits, its past as well as its present, its eccentricities as well as its conformity, they will need to return both to Baxter the poet who wrote great and wayward work and to the prophet who speculated that his final testament lay in a collection of idealists, outcasts, and voyeur-visitors on the damp banks of the Whanganui River.

Newton considers Baxter's various legacies: bicultural, counter-cultural, Maori, and Christian. He aspires, above all, to produce a 'work of *bi*cultural history' (p. 17), and has done the hard work in terms of learning Maori language and consulting with local Maori (as well as nuns, hippies, gang members, and counter-cultural Catholics). *The Double Rainbow* is singular and instructive in its methodology, a major work of cultural history that recognizes the exemplary role of Baxter's experiment in cross-cultural communalism at Jerusalem in the revolution in relations between Maori and Pakeha named biculturalism. The crucial work of literary revision, recuperation, sorting, and revaluation since Stead's essay remains to be done—and that will require some further disentangling of the social and the literary legacies. Someone, perhaps Newton, himself a fine poet as well as an alert close reader of poetry, needs now to give us that balanced estimation of Baxter that still eludes his critics by attending to both those legacies, but particularly the latter.

The alluring but confusing notion of 'culture' still dominates literary-critical and literary-historical practice twenty-five years after the defining texts of the Maori Renaissance appeared and the nation embraced biculturalism. But 2009 also saw some worrying at the bicultural idealism that Baxter encouraged Pakeha to adopt. In *The Dragon and the Taniwha: Maori and Chinese in New Zealand*, edited by Manying Ip, two essays consider the Chinese presence in New Zealand from a literary perspective, deprivileging the relation between colonizer and colonized in favour of that between two non-dominant cultures. This kind of multicultural perspective is common in post-settler societies, but has been largely absent in New Zealand because of the exclusive preoccupation with Maori–Pakeha relations. Kathy Ooi (pp. 319–37) examines the misunderstandings that occur when reading fiction is governed by 'inconsistent ascriptions of ethnicity' (p. 319). The problem she confronts is that we tend to read narrative in terms of the ethnic identities we attribute to authors, who are thus made to represent whole communities. Mark Williams (pp. 300–18) addresses the fundamental differences between bi- and multiculturalism, arguing that the Chinese presence has been occluded by the dominant pattern, and that the binary relationship serves to freeze both of the Treaty partner cultures at the point of colonial contact.

Melissa Kennedy, 'Are You for Real? Witi Ihimaera's Eidolon Camouflage', pushes past the limits of a bicultural/postcolonial approach to Maori writing in an essay on the reception of Witi Ihimaera in '"New" New Zealand Literature', in a special issue of the University of Leeds journal *Moving Worlds*, edited by Stuart Murray and Mark Williams (*Moving Worlds* 8:ii[2008] 107–19). Kennedy usefully observes that local literary critics have failed 'to attend to the playfulness in [Ihimaera's] fiction' (p. 107); she offers us a trickster novelist whose 'shiftiness allows him to change positions towards his Maori subject and Maori and Pakeha/Western readership' (p. 115). Kennedy directs critical attention away from the fixed concentration on Ihimaera as a Maori novelist, arguing that the dominant postcolonial and bicultural modes of reading his writing fail to respond to the range of styles and kinds it employs, or to the continually changing interests of the author.

Moving Worlds contains a number of critical essays which explore general and theoretical issues, such as Stephen Turner's 'Compulsory Nationalism', which contests 'the premise of criticism and culture for the nation's sake' (*Moving Worlds* 8:ii[2008] :18) or James Meffan's anatomy of 'Culturalism Gone Mad' (*Moving Worlds* 8:ii[2008] 27–43), which considers the way cultural rhetoric works within current discourses of national identity. Michelle Keown investigates New Zealand's 'increasing cultural diversity' by way of the popular television cartoon, 'bro-Town' in 'Can't We All Just Get Along? *Bro'Town* and New Zealand's Creative Multiculturalism' (*Moving Worlds* 8:ii[2008] 44–58). Jane Stafford, 'Irrevocably Mute, For Ever Mourned': George Grey and his Collaborators' (*Moving Worlds* 8:ii[2008] 65–81), examines the vexed issues of transmission, translation, and transliteration in colonial New Zealand, focusing on Sir George Grey and his Maori collaborator, Te Rangikaheke. Kirstine Moffat, 'The River and the Ocean: Indigeneity and Dispossession in Vincent Ward's *River Queen*' (*Moving Worlds* 8:ii[2008] 92–106), probes the even more vexed problems of representing indigenous culture and history in contemporary film, concluding in film's favour. Clare Barker applies the perspective of disability studies to Maori writing in '"Bionic Waewae" and "Iron Crutches": Turangawaewae, Disability, and Prosthesis in Patricia Grace's *Dogside Story*' (*Moving Worlds* 8:ii[2008] 120–33), while Julie Adams analyses an exhibition of Pacific art at the British Museum in 'Carving a Space: George Nuku and *Power and Taboo: Sacred Objects from the Pacific 1760–1860*, at the British Museum' (*Moving Worlds* 8:ii[2008] 134–50).

Meffan's '"New" New Zealand' essay is taken further in 'Culturalisms', which appears in an eponymous issue of *New Literatures Review*, which he edited with Diana Brydon and Williams (*NLitsR* 45–6[2009] 41–67). The issue offers a critical testing of the ideas informing biculturalism and multiculturalism: what does the term culture mean when expressed by agencies of the state, and how is this different from its uses by indigenous peoples? Are there limits to cultural 'politeness'? The introduction critically outlines culturalist discourse and state-cultural practice in Canada, Australia, and New Zealand (*NLitsR* 45–6[2009] 1–21). Closely argued essays by Simon During, 'The Limits of Culture' (*NLitsR* 45–6[2009] 23–40), Diana Brydon, 'Canadian Multiculturalism and Contemporary Citizenship Debates (*NLitsR* 45–6[2009] 113–32), Chris Prentice, 'Beyond Biculturalism: From Culturalist Discourse to Symbolic Exchange' (*NLitsR* 45–6[2009] 157–83), Marguerite Nolan, 'Mistaking Multiculturalism: Culotta, Demidenko and Khouri' (*NLitsR* 45–6[2009] 95–112), Winfried Siemerling, 'Bi-culturalism, Multiculturalism and Contemporary Citizenship Debates' (*NLitsR* 45–6[2009] 133–56), Morgan Thomas, 'Aboriginal Art and the "Ethnographic Turn"' (*NLitsR* 45–6[2009] 69–93), and Meffan test the unexamined assumptions that govern the ubiquitous use of the word 'culture'.

Another collection of essays on contemporary writing also registers changes in post-nationalist New Zealand literature: *Floating Worlds: Essays on Contemporary New Zealand Fiction*, edited by Anna Jackson and Jane Stafford. Published by the source of much of the best New Zealand literature over the last two decades, Victoria University Press, *Floating Worlds* seeks to redress the lack of serious yet accessible criticism of contemporary New Zealand fiction. The introduction surveys changes in literary culture, theory, and practice over the last twenty years, noting especially the increasing redundancy of cultural nationalism as an organizing trope, the influence of the university creative writing class, the increasing willingness to locate New Zealand fiction in non-New Zealand (in the case of Elizabeth Knox's *The Vintner's Luck*, non-terrestrial) settings, and the way a global context might alter critics' and readers' view of the idea of a national literature.

Floating Worlds is text-focused. In '"Poor Mr Yate": History, Sex and the Closet in Annamarie Jagose's *Slow Water*' (pp. 93–107), Lydia Wevers decodes the colonial and gay narratives entwined in that novel, which follows the colonial journey from Britain of William Yate, the missionary censured for sexual affairs with young Maori men. In 'Tenderness and Postmodernism: Damien Wilkins' *The Miserables*' (pp. 23–36), Nicholas Wright considers the work's complex play of conflicting elements—tenderness and the postmodern. Erin Mercer attends to the shifting and fragile experiences of cultural identity in 'Urban Spaces, Hybrid Faces: Rethinking Identity in Paula Morris' *Hibiscus Coast*' (pp. 124–41). Jane Stafford examines the theological systems, both the conventional and the fantastic, implicit in Elizabeth Knox's novel in 'Antipodean Theologies: Elizabeth Knox's *The Vintner's Luck*' (pp. 52–69). Kirstine Moffat looks at the recurring motifs and symbols—chiefly those of stones, water, and blood—in 'The Unifying Power of Imagery in Catherine Chidgey's *In a Fishbone Church*' (pp. 37–51). In 'What the Dickens: Storytelling and Intertextuality in Lloyd Jones' *Mr Pip*' (pp. 142–63), Jennifer Lawn deals with the novel's storytelling, its relationship with the literary canon, and its less than subversive postcolonial representation of tradition. The emergence of experimental and innovative forms is noted in Anna Jackson's discussion of Anne Kennedy's verse novel, 'Genealogy as Headland: Anne Kennedy's *The Time of the Giants*' (pp. 108–23), and in

'Smoke at Anchor: Dylan Horrocks' *Hicksville*' (pp. 70–92), Mark Williams and Hamish Clayton's examination of Horrocks's graphic novel, with its blend of high culture and low culture, comics and the art of Colin McCahon.

Christina Stachurski's *Reading Pakeha? Fiction and Identity in Aotearoa New Zealand* is the first sustained critical monograph on the field of New Zealand fiction in more than two decades. Stachurski is critically combative and applies a determinedly theoretical approach to reading New Zealand fiction. If the book is limited, it is by virtue of the texts it focuses on and by the familiarity of the arguments it rehearses. There might still be some purchase to be gained from considering the role of fictional representations of Maori and Pakeha in shaping notions of identity, but the terms of engagement have shifted significantly over the last decade, as Mercer demonstrates in her reading of *Hibiscus Coast* in *Floating Worlds*. The difficulty is that Stachurski's central stable of novelists—Mulgan, Hulme, Duff—speaks to arguments about nation and identity that have lost force and focus.

The critical method of *Reading Pakeha?* might also have benefited from turning away from the postcolonial politics of representation towards more nuanced historical interpretation and by granting the force of the literary. Stachurski's reads texts like *Man Alone* [1939] and *the bone people* [1983] in sociological terms, treating them as symptomatic of shifting cultural patterns. Social history and social science are cited alongside literary criticism, and are used *as* literary criticism. The literary complexity in the act of 'reading' referred to in the book's title is dissipated by the insistent recourse to 'social and cultural contexts' and to reviewers' responses. Stachurski quotes a reviewer's objection that Duff is '*reporting* (rather than creating fiction)'; a similar practice is implicit in her own stance: '*the bone people* can be read as reifying essentialism and masculinism, since it is the metaphoric erasure of Kerewin's femaleness that enables her to embody a revised masculine myth' (pp. 128, 63). *Once Were Warriors* [1990], we learn, signals the redundancy of a unitary notion of national meaning. Given that we thus live after that redundancy, it might have been useful to shift the balance of the book substantively towards fiction published since 1990 that makes more significant literary capital of the fact than Duff's novel.

Alistair Fox, in 'Inwardness, Insularity, and the Man Alone' (JPW 45:iii[2009] 263–73) also adopts a sociological approach, considering how familiar canonical texts, rehearse the operations of the 'Man Alone' theme, from Samuel Butler's *Erewhon* [1872], through John Mulgan's eponymous novel [1939], Maurice Gee's 1972 *In My Father's Den* to, once again, *the bone people*. The addition of Lloyd Jones's 2006 novel *Mr Pip* in this context offers an opportunity to refresh the discourse, though it is disappointing that Fox does so without reference to debates current at the time of *Mr Pip*'s publication. And John Newton's work on colonialism, homophobia, and the South Island myth is a surprising absence from the critical parameters of his discussion ('Colonialism above the Snowline: Baughan, Ruskin and the South Island Myth', *JCL* 34:ii [1999] 85–96). That Fox's essay is a digest of his 2008 book, *The Ship of Dreams: Masculinity in Contemporary New Zealand Fiction*, means that some of the concepts—coloniality, postcoloniality, masculinity, anxiety—are treated as if their meaning were self-evident rather than being argued for. Above all, the ground of the discussion suffers from what is common to many areas of recent New Zealand critical writing, a reluctance to venture outside the now somewhat tired parameters of local literary criticism and foundational postcolonial theory into related and potentially productive areas of social and cultural—not to mention literary—history. Fox's use of Matthew Arnold's troubled expression of his placement between the two worlds suggests that it wasn't only the colonial setting that produced such anxiety.

The last twenty-five years have seen a welcome extension and remodelling of critical discussion—a kind of technological updating, with 'technologies' supplied partly by imported theory, applied inventively to New Zealand literary texts, and partly by a broader attention to the meanings of culture than cultural nationalism had allowed. The main sources of this updating are to be found in new energies in the Auckland University English Department of the early 1980s. The 2009 number of the *Journal of New Zealand Literature* reminds us of that reformist period by marking the passing in 2009 of two major figures, associated with the department. The first of these, Terry Sturm, as Professor of English at Auckland from the early 1980s professionalized the study of New Zealand literature, editing both editions of the *Oxford History of New Zealand Literature in English* [1991, 1998] and directing scholarly attention to neglected areas such as popular fiction, while maintaining a steady critical eye on the major figures, notably Curnow, and supervising innumerable thesis students. The other was Leigh Davis, who died aged 54. Davis was perhaps the most striking and memorable of the avant-garde, theory-centred group that arrived in the department in the mid-1980s. A banker, poet, and dynamiter of ingrained cultural attitudes, Davis's legacy will certainly last, though in what sphere remains uncertain. Together these two enormously energetic and gifted intellectuals represent the active centrality of Auckland University English Department to shifts in literary and cultural attention over the last thirty years.

JNZL over the last decade has become the reliable journal not just of record but also of critical engagement and historically based literary scholarship, encompassing the colonial period, settler studies, modernism, and contemporary writing. The critical study of New Zealand literature here does not mean a narrowly inward gaze. Notable in the strong line-up of articles in *JNZL* 27 is Dougal McNeill's 'Japan in the Supermarket of the Kiwi Psyche' (*JNZL* 27[2009] 131–54). McNeill engages with the anti-globalization argument, articulated notoriously in Patrick Evans's critique of the internationally successful young writers from Bill Manhire's creative course, where he champions the postcolonial over the global ('Spectacular Babies: The Globalisation of New Zealand Fiction', *Kite* 22[July 2002] 4–14). McNeill pays welcome attention to current literary treatment of Japan (pp. 143–5). Surveying recent treatments, mainly poetic, McNeill finds a disappointingly thin range of stock images—haiku and blossom, tourists and Sanyo televisions—despite the steady level of contact, not least the JET scheme in which since 1987 over 2,000 New Zealanders have taught in Japan. Observing that Japanese imagery acts 'metonymically for that which is to be excluded from authentic New Zealand experience', McNeill argues that it has 'travelled from being a sign of perplexity and exclusion to being a marker for that which must be, linguistically and politically, excluded' (p. 145). For McNeill, the tormenting question of loyalty to the local referent or to what Allen Curnow called 'Overseasia' is answered, after cultural nationalism, by the binary-dissolving question: why either or?

Hulme's *the bone people* is the focus of Erin Mercer's article, '"Frae ghosties and ghoulies deliver us"' (*JNZL* 27[2009] 111–30), but her mode of approach is by way of genre rather than Stachurski's nebulous reading constituencies. Despite its rapturous reception by a New Zealand reading public—the title of Joy Cowley's review, 'We are the bone people', says it all—Mercer argues that it is more profitable to read the novel in terms of the literary Gothic rather than the more common frames of nation and ethnicity. *The bone people*'s 'secrets and traumas', Mercer explains, focus on the central preoccupations of classic Gothic fiction, identity and heritage (p. 115). Yet in this novel the Gothic mode is not 'redemptive', as has been argued for the New Zealand Gothic in general. The conflict and potentiality for violence are still present at the novel's conclusion, as are the disruptive elements inherent in the bicultural state.

Kristevan theories of the maternal are used by Isabel Michell in 'The Maternal as Site of Possibility in Janet Frame's "Fictional Exploration"' (*JNZL* 27[2009] 90–110). Kristeva posits, for the child, the omnipresence and all-embracing significance of the mother—perilously mimicked in Frame's assurance in 'Swans' that 'mother knew always'. Mitchell traces the disappearance of the actual mother in Frame's work and notes that the maternal figure there is not treated with Kristevan reverence (p. 106). And she follows the pattern of journey and quest, arrival and placelessness—central features of Frame's writing that disclose a permanent condition of migration, where subjectivity is a process rather than a mode of perception.

Two essays in this issue deal with museums' historical modes of presentation and their present practice. In 'Re-enactment and the Museum Case' (*JNZL* 27[2009] 48–69), Anna Boswell discusses what she calls the 'capacious construct' of re-enactment, defined as 'a form of historiography or a type of historical representation or engagement which involves the performative recreation of the past' (p. 49), in terms of the static setting of the museum. Using the example of the collections of the Peabody Essex Museum, Boswell shows how the juxtapositions and exclusions of the Oceanic and Native American displays can be read as a performance of the original values and perspectives of the donors rather than a way of honouring the makers. 'Who has the right to frame the past in this way?' asks Boswell, and 'How else might this history be understood?' (p. 62).

In '"Too perfectly historical for words": Reading Sociably at the Katherine Mansfield Birthplace/ Te Puakitanga' (*JNZL* 27[2009] 70–89), the journal's 2009 Prize Essay, Cameron McLachlan examines a different kind of museum, the literary birthplace, which delivers a more sharply focused form of re-enactment. Using the concept of 'sociable reading' (that is, reading centred not on a text but based around 'an assemblage of objects, persons and places surrounding a text'), the essay suggests that, far from encouraging the reading of Mansfield's work, the museum 'allows the avoidance of reading in the search for physically verifiable detail' (p. 70). Within this frame, Mansfield stories are used as source material for a past enacted in the furnishings of the museum—the piano gestures to that in 'A Birthday', the wallpaper to that in 'The Aloe'. Personal objects with a verifiable link to Mansfield, objects that correlate to the material details of the stories, and historical objects from the same period as Mansfield's habitation of the house are, McLaren suggests, brought uneasily together. This stands in contrast to the museum's more successful purposes. Detached from its function as a literary shrine, McLaren suggests, the house can be seen as 'enlighteningly generic and communicates specific points of late Victorian social history' (p. 76).

As a consequence of children's literature studies establishing itself in New Zealand English departments in the last decade, local literary critics and postgraduate students are paying increasing attention to canonical writers such as Frame, who dabbled in the genre, and Margaret Mahy, whose reputation as a children's author has long been established. Marc Delrez's 'The Legacy of Invention' (*JPW* 45:i[2009] 27–35) focuses on Janet Frame's sinister 1969 children's story, *Mona Minim*, which she ingenuously claimed was 'her favourite among all her books'. Arguing that, despite the intended audience, there are 'thematic continuities' between *Mona Minim* and the rest of Frame's work, Delrez suggests that the genre—in particular the licence to deploy animal characters—enables rather than constrains Frame's fascination with 'alternate ontologies' and her expression of 'concern with creativity' (p. 27). The essay notes Frame's reliance on and divergence from the traditional fairy-story forms with *Mona Minim*'s opening 'Once upon a time, not long ago, almost now . . .' and the story's sense of uncharacteristically grim quotidian wedded to the more conventional tropes of quest and test. That the animals in Frame's story are ants (in Frame's words, 'publishers prefer children's literature to be about rabbits') enables, as Delrez argues, 'a correlation between cultural stagnation and stasis of identity'. This is critically valuable but overlooks the sly humour that Frame directs at her adult as well as child readers (p. 33).

The postcolonial theories that energized critics in the 1990s as New Zealand texts were placed within an exciting global context now seem tired and broad-brush. Saikat Majumdar, 'Katherine Mansfield and the Fragility of Pakeha Boredom' (*MFS* 55:i[2009] 119–40) considers the boredom of settler existence, especially that of settler women undercut by a sense of the dark current of colonial violence. This is promising literary-historical terrain, but closer attention to local literary criticism and cultural history and theory of the last decade might have assisted in positioning the discussion in the rather more historicized, complex, and nuanced local discourses of the present. Factual accuracy is important here: the Treaty of Waitangi was signed in 1840, not 1848; the military engagements between Maori and settler began after, not before, the signing; Mansfield's husband was John Middleton Murry not Murray; and it is not usual to employ the terms 'massacre' and 'genocide' in the context of nineteenth-century New Zealand history. It is not enough that important international journals *notice* the postcolonial interest of, say, settler New Zealand to a historical discussion of the novel genre. The relations between local and international scholarship, and between the distinct history of a given settler colony and the larger frame of empire, need to be negotiated with care, precision, and awareness of divergences from the familiar pattern, both small and large.

Two essays dealing with contemporary Maori literature appearing in international journals display closer knowledge of those local and specific contexts, while taking the scholarly study of Maori writing in new directions. In 'Radiation Ecologies and the Wars of Light' (*MFS* 55:iii[2009] 468–98) Elizabeth DeLoughrey applies a heliographic perspective to James George's novel, *Ocean Roads*. The 'planetary' point of view here is rather arcane, but DeLoughrey directs serious critical attention at a Maori novelist who has not received such attention in New Zealand, and relates his work to the effects of nuclear weapons testing in the Pacific. Her cultural approach here recalls Anna Boswell's concluding remarks about western versus indigenous temporalities in 'Re-enactment and the Museum Case': 'a past that may lie in the future, or in the exchange of stories around a campfire, or in wind patterns or ocean currents, or in other places well beyond the conventional boundaries of western historical consciousness' (p. 66).

Bridget Orr uses the better-known Maori writer Robert Sullivan to re-enter the debate about Polynesian perceptions of Captain Cook and the meaning of his death, by bringing into new relation indigenous and anthropological explanations of Cook in Polynesia, Sullivan's epic poetry of Maori and Pacific contact, history, and myth. '"Maui and Orphic Blood": Cook's Death in Contemporary Maori Poetry' (*ECent* 49:xii[2008] 165–79) nicely refers back to J.G.A. Pocock's tribute to Allen Curnow's poetry, articulating 'the problematic of unsettled and mobile oceanic identities' (p. 166). Orr examines a complex act of revision in which Cook's death is seen to be 'both symbolically and literally absorbed by Moana Nui a Kiwa (the Pacific Ocean) and her people' (p. 167).

Jane Stafford and Mark Williams, in 'Indian Mysteries and Comic Stunts: the Royal Tour and the Theatre of Empire' (*JCL* 44:ii[2009]: 87–105), look at three royal tours—that of Queen Victoria's youngest son Prince Arthur in Canada in 1869, that of the duke and duchess of York (later King George and Queen Mary) in New Zealand in 1901, and that of the Prince of Wales (later and briefly King Edward VIII) to New Zealand and the Pacific in 1920. On all three occasions the indigenous subject performs in an appropriate and expected manner, but also has an active role in shaping the tone and import of their performance.

Anne Maxwell, in 'Oceana Revisited: J.A. Froude's 1884 Journey to New Zealand and the Pink and White Terraces' (*VLC* 37:ii[2009] 377–91), reads travel writing as cultural history. On his journey around New Zealand, Froude initially celebrated the potentialities of the colony and its ability to restore and regenerate the culture of the tired mother country. But, argues Maxwell, he became less certain when he encountered Maori at the Pink and White Terraces, a tourist attraction in the central North Island, and saw both the confident self-assertion of the local Maori and their perceived degeneracy. Maxwell sees parallels between the beauty of the terraces and the horror of the nearby volcanic and laval landscapes and this dual view of Maori as both noble and degenerate, a natural part of a landscape and a hindrance to European settlement.

At the other end of New Zealand's colonial/postcolonial history, Mark Houlahan, in '*Romeo and Tusi*: An Eclectically Musical Samoan/Māori *Romeo and Juliet* from Aotearoa/New Zealand' (*ConTR* 19:iii[2009] 279–88), considers the efforts of Oscar Kightley, co-author of the 1997 Polynesian *Romeo and Juliet*, to 'bring a big fat picnic' to its staging. Here Shakespeare finds his truly postcolonial embodiment in a production replete with contemporary hip-hop, jazz, and rap, where the Prologue is delivered by the *fa'afafine* (third gender) Ruby.

Katherine Mansfield's fiction continues to provide critics with unexpected critical approaches. Diane Blakemore, in 'Parentheticals and Point of View in Free Indirect Style' (*L&L* 18[2009] 129–53), offers a technical analysis of the familiar narrative technique, given new point by her comparison to its uses by Malcolm Lowry and Virginia Woolf. Analysing the role these asides play, Blakemore concludes that they allow the narrator 'to represent thoughts from a variety of perspectives—including his own' (p. 150). Mansfield is an author who repays such close attention to the precise workings of her design-governing strategies, and such attention is welcome alongside the vagaries that attend some of her postcolonial treatments

The image of the spiral as a structural motif in New Zealand fiction, counter to the Pakeha-centric linearity, has been much employed at least since *the bone people*'s association with the feminist publishing collective, Spiral. In 'Along "the many-stranded circle": Narrative Spiralling from Isolation to Homecoming in Patricia Grace's *Cousins*' (*JPW* 45:iv[2009] 459–71) Doreen D'Cruz gives it another tug. Building on an earlier essay of DeLoughrey on Grace's *Potiki* [1986] that explores the distinction between 'western "linear" time and "climatic" time', D'Cruz demonstrates that in *Cousins* [1992] the narrative journeys of the central characters away from isolation are founded again on 'spiral temporality' (p. 2).

Chris Prentice, in 'From Visibility to Visuality: Patricia *Grace's Baby No-Eyes* and the Cultural Politics of Decolonization' (*MFS* 55:ii[2009] 321–48), applies a much more densely written and argued case to Patricia Grace's *Baby-No-Eyes* [1998]. Grace has remained the most disciplined and lucid of fiction writers while developing an increasingly complex narrative method to directly involve her readers in the bicultural politics of language and culture. Here Prentice indicates a further turn in the complexity of those politics, arguing that she 'offers a rich depiction of contemporary cultural politics in Aotearoa/New Zealand as a complex contention between the conditions that have sustained a Maori politics of visibility and those that inform a more recently emergent culture of visuality' (p. 322). This might be seen as a (perhaps overly) sophisticated deployment of the postcolonial saw of representation politics. But Prentice carries Grace's fiction into unfamiliar territory. She argues that Grace moves beyond politics as asserting presence to an engagement with digital technologies. Thus in *Baby No-Eyes* the political impulse gives ground to 'changes in the structural order of representation' and this means that Grace's narrative method is situated where 'reality and truth emanate from signs' (p. 322).

New Zealand critics are disadvantaged in publishing in international forums that require a back story and explanatory context. This is seen in the stock rehearsals of colonial history, the Treaty of Waitangi, and Maori cultural revival that appear routinely in internationally published articles. This disadvantage is obvious in *Reading Pakeha*, where not just history but cultural history is rehearsed and one notices the effort of explaining and justifying, where New Zealand is a quaint little place of interest because it points to more important things outside itself. By contrast *JNZL* essays such as McNeill's are able to assume a high level of knowledge of their subject in their readers, and thus engage in a more complex and sophisticated discussion—but limited in that they are about New Zealand and addressed to a New Zealand audience.

A direct and original response to the difficulty is taken by Melissa Kennedy in 'Inside the Text: The Private Side of Maori writing' (*JPW* 45:i[2009] 61–9). Kennedy compares the situations of minority literatures in New Zealand and France, arguing that the differences in interpretative method in the two countries should be synthesized. Her own focus is on Witi Ihimaera's Maori operas, which allows her to avoid the usual postcolonial approaches to Maori writing and the habit of seeing indigenous writers as 'representative of and primarily concerned with promoting cultural and socio-political concerns (p. 61). As she observes: 'While the French approach may be criticized as denying the cultural distinctiveness of minority groups, the pervasiveness of New Zealand's discourse of difference tends to eclipse other interpretative frameworks for creative writing' (p. 61).

While theory still exerts its glamour and the postcolonial possesses the lure of political purpose, there has been a shift in the critical and scholarly attention directed at New Zealand literature towards the neglected but invigorating efforts of recovery and primary research. In the last several years a growing body of attention has been paid not just to settler society or colonial history but to the vast outpourings of literary writing—from novels to diaries—throughout the nineteenth century. Important vehicles in the recovery, editing, and dissemination of these texts have been the New Zealand Electronic Text Centre at Victoria University and the nineteenth-century website of newspapers, Papers Past.

New Zealand's journal of notes and queries, *Kotare*, has also been important in directing scholarly attention to this material and in giving critical shape to the industrious effort in archives and, increasingly, via digital primary material. Rebecca Burns's use of Phoebe Meikle's planned biography of the colonial novelist Edith Searle Grossmann demonstrates the value of this work. Meikle, a writer and editor who died in 1998, collected papers relevant to the project, which were deposited in the Alexander Turnbull Library in 2007. Burns has used them, as well as other family papers and newspaper reports, in 'Snapshot of a Life Reassessed: Edith Searle Grossmann', an essay published in *Kotare* ([2009]; http://www.nzetc.org/tm/scholarly/tei-corpus-kotare.html). While earlier writers had robustly defended Grossman from charges of mental incompetence, believing them to have been fabricated by her estranged husband, Burns finds enough contemporary evidence to suggest that Grossmann, at least in later life, 'was prone to psychiatric ill-health' and may have been a patient in Avondale Hospital. Nevertheless, Burns is able to demonstrate the wide range of Grossmann's activities as a journalist and as a promoter of New Zealand writing while she was in England and Europe.

Perhaps what is needed now after such prolonged assault on the canonical force of cultural nationalism is a new balance between the literary, the cultural, and the critical, instead of returning to the body of work that was sieved too finely by Curnow, Brasch, and Stead. Robin Hyde has been at the centre of an effort of revaluation, but another neglected figure deserving to be drawn into the light, O.E. Middleton, has languished. Lawrence Jones's edition of Middleton's short fiction, *Beyond the Breakwater, Short Stories 1948–1998*, is thus to be welcomed. Jones, as one would expect, comes to the task of revaluation with a thorough and argued introduction that makes the case for this author not fading from view. Jones's piece reminds us of the holes in our knowledge of the writing of the mid-twentieth century. The recent reissue of David Ballantyne's 1968 novel, *Sydney Bridge Upside Down*, by the Australian publisher Text is a hopeful sign here, and it is to be hoped that critical practice will catch up with an astute publisher's sense of what matters in the New Zealand literary legacy.

Books Reviewed

Ahmad, Hena. *Postnational Feminisms: Postcolonial Identities and Cosmopolitanism in the Works of Kamala Markandaya, Tsitsi Dangarembga, Ama Ata Aidoo, and Anita Desai*. Lang. [2010] pp. 148. $69.95 ISBN 9 7808 2045 2470.

Ahmed, Talat. *Literature and Politics in the Age of Nationalism: The Progressive Episode in South Asia, 1932–56*. Routledge. [2009] pp. 205. Rs595 ISBN 9 7804 1548 0642.

Ashcroft, Bill, Frances Devlin-Glass, and Lyn McCredden. *Intimate Horizons: The Post-Colonial Sacred in Australian Literature*. ATF. [2009] pp. vi + 364. pb A$36.95 ISBN 9 7819 2151 1790.

Baetz, Joel, ed. *Canadian Poetry from World War I*. OUPC. [2009] pp. 198. C$21.95 ISBN 9 7801 9543 1711.

Bandyopadhyay, Sumana. *Indianization of English: Analysis of Linguistic Features in Selected Post-1980 Indian English Fiction*. Concept. [2008] pp. xl + 184. Rs550 ISBN 9 7881 8069 7036.

Barthet, Stella Borg, ed. *A Sea for Encounters: Essays towards a Postcolonial Commonwealth*. Rodopi. [2009] pp. xiv + 412. €85 ISBN 9 7890 4202 7640.

Barthet, Stella Borg, ed. *Shared Waters: Soundings in Postcolonial Literatures*. Rodopi. [2009] pp. xiii + 412. €85 ISBN 9 7890 4202 7664.

Bell, Hannah Rachel. *Storymen*. CUP. [2009] pp. xiii + 264. A$39.95 ISBN 9 7805 2175 9960.

Best, Curwen. *Kamau Brathwaite and Christopher Okigbo: Art, Politics, and the Music of Ritual*. Lang. [2009] pp. 228. $112.99 ISBN 9 7830 3911 7161.

Blackford, Holly, ed. *100 Years of Anne with an 'e': The Centennial Study of Anne of Green Gables*. UCalgaryP. [2009] pp. 306. C$29.95 ISBN 9 7815 5238 2523.

Bode, Katherine, and Robert Dixon, eds. *Resourceful Reading: The New Empiricism, eResearch and Australian Literary Culture*. SUP. [2009] pp. x + 368. A$40 ISBN 9 7819 2089 9455.

Brandt, Di, and Barbara Godard, eds. *Wider Boundaries of Daring: The Modernist Impulse in Canadian Women's Poetry*. WLUP. [2009] pp. 417. C$42.95 ISBN 9 7815 5458 0323.

Clarkson, Carrol. *J.M. Coetzee: Countervoices*. Palgrave Macmillan. [2009] pp. 230. £50 ISBN 9 7802 3022 1567.

Clingman, Stephen. *The Grammar of Identity*. OUP. [2009] pp. 288. £59 ISBN 9 7801 9927 8497.

Comans, Christine. *La Boite: The Story of an Australian Theatre Company*. Playlab. [2009] pp. 352. A$55 ISBN 9 7809 0815 6719.

Concilio, Carmen, and Richard J. Lane, eds. *Image Technologies in Canadian Literature: Narrative, Film and Photography*. Lang. [2009] pp. 166. $42.95 ISBN 9 7890 5201 4746.

Constant, Isabelle, and Kahiudi C. Mabana, eds. *Negritude. Legacy and Present Relevance*. Foreword by Jane Bryce. CambridgeSP. [2009] pp. xii + 321. £39.99 ISBN 9 7814 4380 1126.

Darroch, Fiona. *Memory and Myth: Postcolonial Religion in Contemporary Guyanese Fiction and Poetry*. Rodopi. [2009] pp. xxxii + 202. €50 ISBN 9 7890 4202 5769.

De Groen, Fran, and Peter Kirkpatrick, eds. *Serious Frolic: Essays on Australian Humour*. UQP. [2009] pp. xxviii + 296. A$39.95 ISBN 9 7807 0223 6884.

Dever, Maryanne, Anne Vickery, and Sally Newman, eds. *'The Intimate Archive: Journeys in Private Papers'*. National Library of Australia (NLA). [2009] pp. v+ 198. A$34.95. pb. ISBN 9 7806 4227 6827.

Devy, G.N., Geoffrey V. Davis, and K.K. Chakravarty, eds. *Indigeneity: Culture and Interpretation. Proceedings of the 2008 Chotro Conference on Indigenous Languages, Culture and Society*. OBSwan. [2009] pp. xvi + 405. Rs795 ISBN 9 7881 2503 6647.

Dobson, Kit. *Transnational Canadas: Anglo-Canadian Literature and Globalization*. WLUP. [2009] pp. 223. C$44.30 ISBN 9 7815 5458 0637.

Dolce, Maria Renata, and Antonella Riem Natale, eds. *Bernard Hickey, a Roving Cultural Ambassador: Essays in his Memory*. ForEd. [2009] pp. 422. €28 ISBN 9 7888 8420 5445.

Eichhorn, Kate, and Heather Milne, eds. *Prismatic Publics: Innovative Canadian Women's Poetry and Poetics*. Coach House. [2009] pp. 407. C$29.95 ISBN 9 7815 5245 2219.

Elder, Catriona. *Dreams and Nightmares of a White Australia: Representing Aboriginal Assimilation in the Mid-Twentieth Century*. Lang. [2009] pp. 260. £40.10 ISBN 9 7830 3911 7222.

Forsyth, Louise H., ed. *Anthology of Quebec Women's Plays in English Translation,* vol. 1 *1996–1986*. PlaywCP. [2007] pp. 300. C$55 ISBN 9 7808 8754 8680.

Fullerton, Susannah. *Brief Encounters: Literary Travellers in Australia 1836–1939*. Pan Macmillan. [2009] pp. xx + 396. A$34.99 ISBN 9 7814 0503 9505.

Gelder, Ken, and Paul Salzman. *After the Celebration: Australian Fiction 1989–2007*. MelbourneUP. [2009] pp. xii + 292. A$29.99 ISBN 9 7805 2285 5975.

Graham, James. *Land and Nationalism in Fictions from Southern Africa*. Routledge. [2009] pp. 203. £85 ISBN 9 7804 1599 5818.

Guignery, Vanessa, ed. *Voices and Silence in the Contemporary Novel in English*. CambridgeSP. [2009] pp. ix + 292. £39.99 ISBN 9 7814 4381 2474.

Hackler, M.B., ed. eds. with Ari J. Adipurwawidjana. *On and Off the Page: Mapping Place in Text and Culture*. CambridgeSP. [2009] pp. vii + 347. £44.99 ISBN 9 7814 4380 5681.

Hai, Ambreen. *Making Words Matter: The Agency of Colonial and Postcolonial Literature*. OhioUP. [2009] pp. xi + 377. pb $26.95 ISBN 9 7808 2141 8819.

Hanley, Penelope. *Creative Lives: Personal Papers of Australian Writers and Artists*. NLA. [2009] pp. 204. A$39.95 ISBN 9 7806 4227 6568.

Helgesson, Stefan. *Transnationalism in Southern African Literature*. Routledge. [2009] pp. 164. £90 ISBN 9 7804 1546 2396.

Hergenhan, Laurie, Ken Stewart, and Michael Wilding, eds. *Cyril Hopkins' Marcus Clarke*. ASP. [2009] pp. xlvii + 339. A$44 ISBN 9 7819 2150 9124.

Heseltine, Harry. *In Due Season. Australian Literary Studies: A Personal Memoir*. ASP. [2009] pp. 337. A$39.95 ISBN 9 7819 2150 9285.

Hogg, Robert, ed. *An English Canadian Poetics*, vol. 1: *The Confederation Poets*. Talonbooks. [2009] pp. 73. C$29.95 ISBN 9 7808 8922 6135.

Hosking, Susan, Rick Hosking, Rebecca Pannell, and Nena Bierbaum, eds. *Something Rich and Strange: Sea Changes, Beaches and the Littoral in the Antipodes*. Wakefield. [2009] pp. xi + 320. A$29.95 ISBN 9 7818 6254 8701.

Huttunen, Tuomas, Kaisa Ilmonen, Janne Korkka, and Elina Valovirta, eds. *Seeking the Self-Encountering the Other: Diasporic Narrative and the Ethic of Representation*. CambridgeSP. [2008] pp. 364. $59.99 ISBN 9 7818 4718 6317.

Ip, Manying, ed. *The Dragon and the Taniwha: Maori Chinese Encounters in New Zealand*. AucklandUP. [2009] pp. 374. NZ$49.99 ISBN 9 7818 6940 4369.

Jabbar, Naheem. *Historiography and Writing Postcolonial India*. Routledge. [2009] pp. 244. £80 ISBN 9 7804 1548 8471.

Jackson, Anna, and Jane Stafford. *Floating Worlds: Essays on Contemporary New Zealand Fiction*. VictUP. [2009] pp. 193. NZ$40 ISBN 9 7808 6473 6017.

Jones, Jennifer. *Black Writers White Editors: Episodes of Collaboration and Compromise in Australian Publishing History*. ASP. [2009] pp. 273. A$44 ISBN 9 7819 2150 9063.

Jones, Lawrence, ed. *Beyond the Breakwater, Short Stories 1948–1998* by O.E. Middleton. OtagoUP. [2008] pp. 368. NZ$49.95 ISBN 9 7818 7372 2810.

Jordan, Kath. *Larrikin Angel: A Biography of Veronica Brady*. RHP. [2009] pp. 294. A$32.95 ISBN 9 7809 8061 0802.

Jose, Nicholas, and gen, eds. *Macquarie PEN Anthology of Australian Literature*. A&UA. [2009] pp. xxxviii + 1,464. hb $69.99 ISBN 9 7817 4175 4407, pb $49.99 ISBN 9 7817 4175 4391.

Joseph-Vilain, Mélanie, and Judith Misrahi-Barak, eds. *Postcolonial Ghosts/Fantômes post-coloniaux*. PULM. [2009] pp. 484. €32 ISBN 9 7828 4269 8850.

Keown, Michelle, David Murphy, and James Proctor, eds. *Comparing Postcolonial Diasporas*. Palgrave Macmillan. [2009] pp. xvi + 230. £50 ISBN 9 7802 3054 7087.

Kuehn, Julia, and Paul Smethurst, eds. *Travel Writing, Form, and Empire: The Poetics and Politics of Mobility*. Routledge. [2009] pp. x + 255. $110 ISBN 9 7804 1596 2940.

Letissier, Georges, ed. *Rewriting/Reprising: Plural Intertextualities*. CambridgeSP. [2009] pp. vii + 256. £39.99 ISBN 9 7814 4381 3884.

Loreto, Paola. *The Crowning of a Poet's Quest: Derek Walcott's 'Tiepolo's Hound'*. Rodopi. [2009] pp. xix + 225. €47 ISBN 9 7890 4202 6384.

MacKay, Marina, ed. *Cambridge Companion to the Literature of World War II*. CUP. [2009] pp. 258. pb £18.99 ISBN 9 7805 2171 5416.

McCallum, John. *Belonging: Australian Playwriting in the 20th Century*. Currency. [2009] pp. xi + 484. A$49.95 ISBN 9 7808 6819 6589.

McDonald, Willa. *Warrior for Peace: Dorothy Auchterlonie Green*. ASP. [2009] pp. 233. A$44 ISBN 9 7817 4097 1478.

McLaren, John. *Journey without Arrival: The Life and Writing of Vincent Buckley*. ASP. [2009] pp. 377. $39.95 ISBN 9 7819 2150 9292.

McWilliams, Ellen. *Margaret Atwood and the Female Bildungsroman*. Ashgate. [2009] pp. 170. $99.95 ISBN 9 7807 5466 0279.

Maddy, Yulisa Amadu, and Donnarae MacCann. *Neo-Imperialism in Children's Literature about Africa*. Routledge. [2009] pp. 175. £80 ISBN 9 7804 1599 3906.

Majumdar, Gaurav. *Migrant Form: Anti-Colonial Aesthetics in Joyce, Rushdie, and Ray*. Lang. [2010] pp. 169. $69.95 ISBN 9 7814 3310 5036.

Marais, Mike. *Secretary to the Invisible: The Idea of Hospitality in the Fiction of J.M. Coetzee*. Rodopi. [2009] pp. 249. €53 ISBN 9 7890 4202 7138.

Maslen, Cathleen. *Ferocious Things: Jean Rhys and the Politics of Women's Melancholia*. CambridgeSP. [2009] pp. xi + 267. £34.99 ISBN 9 7818 4718 6614.

Meyer, Michael, ed. *Word and Image in Colonial and Postcolonial Literatures and Cultures*. Rodopi. [2009] 379 €84 ISBN 9 7890 4202 7435.

Mokashi-Punekar, Rohini. *Vikram Seth: An Introduction*. CUPI. [2008] pp. 218. pb Rs195 ISBN 9 7881 7596 5898.

Mulhall, Stephen. *The Wounded Animal: J.M. Coetzee and the Difficulty of Reality in Literature and Philosophy*. PrincetonUP. [2008] pp. 272. $78.50 ISBN 9 7806 9113 7360.

Neilson, Shane. *Approaches to Poetry: The Pre-Poem Moment*. FroH. [2009] pp. 206. C$60 ISBN 9 7809 8103 5444.

Newton, John. *The Double Rainbow: James K. Baxter, Ngati Hau and the Jerusalem Commune*. VictUP. [2009] pp. 224. NZ$40 ISBN 9 7808 6473 6031.

Niblett, Michael, and Kerstin Oloff, eds. *Perspectives on the 'Other America': Comparative Approaches to Caribbean and Latin American Culture*. Rodopi. [2009] pp. 270. €54 ISBN 9 7890 4202 7046.

Nixon, Mark, and Matthew Feldman, eds. *The International Reception of Samuel Beckett*. Continuum. [2009] pp. xiv + 309. £80 ISBN 9 7808 2649 5815.

Nnolim, Charles. *Approaches to the African Novel: Essays in Analysis*. Malthouse. [2009] pp. 209. $26.99 ISBN 978 978 8244 19 8.

Ogundele, Wole, and Gbemisola Adeoti, eds. *Iba: Essays on African Literature in Honour of Oyin Ogunba*. OAUP. [2007] pp. 274. £12.95 ISBN 9789 7813 6136 4.

Ogunjimi, Bayo, and Abdul-Rasheed Na'Allah. *Introduction to African Oral Literature and Performance*. AWP. [2008] pp. 256. $26.99 ISBN 9781 5922 1151 8.

Page, Geoff. *Sixty Classic Australian Poems*. NSWUP. [2009] pp. 311. A$34.95 ISBN 9 7819 2141 9796.

Parhi, Asima Ranjan. *Indian English through Newspapers*. Concept. [2008] pp. 272. Rs700 ISBN 9 7881 8069 5070.

Pierce, Peter, ed. *The Cambridge History of Australian Literature*. CUP. [2009] pp. x + 612. A$140 ISBN 9 7805 2188 1654.

Pirbhai, Mariam. *Mythologies of Migration, Vocabularies of Indenture: Novels of the South Asian Diaspora in Africa, the Caribbean, and Asia-Pacific*. UTorP. [2009] pp. 262. $65 ISBN 9 7808 0209 9648.

Pons, Xavier. *Messengers of Eros: Representations of Sex in Australian Writing*. CambridgeSP. [2009] pp. x + 361. £29.99 ISBN 9 7814 4380 5230.

Poyner, Jane. *J.M. Coetzee and the Paradox of Postcolonial Authority*. Ashgate. [2009] pp. 204. £55 ISBN 9 7807 5465 4629.

Rajakumar, Mohanlakshmi. *Haram in the Harem: Domestic Narratives in India and Algeria*. Lang. [2009] pp. 120. $62.95 ISBN 9 7814 3310 7122.

Rastogi, Pallavi, and Jocelyn Fenton Stitt, eds. *Before Windrush: Recovering an Asian and Black Literary Heritage within Britain*. CambridgeSP. [2008] pp. 233. $52.99 ISBN 9 7818 4718 4139.

Rolls, Alistair, ed. *Mostly French: French (in) Detective Fiction*. Lang. [2009] pp. viii + 204. SF50 ISBN 9 7830 3911 9578.

Rooney, Brigid. *Literary Activists: Australian Writer-Intellectuals and Public Life*. UQP. [2009] pp. 296. A$34.95 ISBN 9 7807 0223 6624.

Rüdiger, Petra, and Konrad Gross, eds. *Translation of Cultures*. Rodopi. [2009] pp. xiv + 306. €64 ISBN 9 7890 4202 5967.

Salter, Brent. *Copyright, Collaboration and the Future of Dramatic Authorship*. Currency. [2009] pp. 72. A$13.95 ISBN 9 7809 8056 3245.

Sarwal, Amit, and Reema Sarwal, eds. *Reading Down Under: Australian Literary Studies Reader*. SSSPub. [2009] pp. lxxv + 633. Rs995/A$65 ISBN 9788 1902 2821 8.

Schulze-Engler, Frank, and Sissy Helff, eds. *Transcultural English Studies: Theories, Fictions, Realities*. Rodopi. [2009] pp. xvi + 469. €97 ISBN 9 7890 4202 5639.

Singh, Jaspal K., and Rajendra Chetty, eds. *Indian Writers: Transnationalisms and Diasporas*. Lang. [2010] pp. 186. $76.95 ISBN 9 7814 3310 6316.

Stachurski, Christina. *Reading Pakeha? Fiction and Identity in Aotearoa New Zealand*. Rodopi. [2009] pp. 207. €50 ISBN 9 7890 4202 6445.

Steggall, Stephany. *Bruce Dawe: Life Cycle*. Ginninderra. [2009] pp. 367. A$30 ISBN 9 7817 4027 5675.

Summo-O'Connell, Renata, ed. *Imagined Australia: Reflections around the Reciprocal Construction of Identity between Australia and Europe*. Lang. [2009] pp. x + 401. £55.70 ISBN 9 7830 3430 0087.

Theile, Verena, and Marie Drews, eds. *Reclaiming Home, Remembering Motherhood, Rewriting History: African American and Afro-Caribbean Women's Literature in the Twentieth Century*. CambridgeSP. [2009] pp. xxi + 305. £44.99 ISBN 9 7814 4380 9627.

Thiara, Nicole Weickgenannt. *Salman Rushdie and Indian Historiography: Writing the Nation into Being*. Palgrave. [2009] pp. 226. £52 ISBN 9 7802 3020 5482.

Toyin, Falola, and Ngom Fallou, eds. *Oral and Written Expressions of African Cultures*. CarolinaAc. [2009] pp. xxxviii + 223. $28 ISBN 9 7815 9460 6472.

Uhlmann, Anthony, Helen Groth, Paul Sheehan, and Stephen McLaren, eds. *Literature and Sensation*. CambridgeSP. [2009] pp. xxii + 322. $69.99 ISBN 9 7814 4380 1164.

Vanden Driesen, Cynthia. *Writing the Nation: Patrick White and the Indigene*. Rodopi. [2009] pp. xxxvi + 207. A$97.95 ISBN 9 7890 4202 5165.

Winks, Christopher. *Symbolic Cities in Caribbean Literature*. Palgrave Macmillan. [2009] pp. xvii + 194. $124 ISBN 9 7802 3061 2181.

Yerima, Ahmed, Bakare Ojo-Rasaki, and Arnold Udoka, eds. *Critical Perspectives on Dance in Nigeria*. Kraft. [2009] pp. 3228. €19.95 ISBN 9 7803 9169 X.

XVIII

Bibliography and Textual Criticism

WILLIAM BAKER

Last year's survey began with a lament for the absence of *Studies in Bibliography*. Volume 58 (*SB* 58[2007–8]) was published in September 2010. The question is, was it worth waiting for? It has eight articles, but no apology for its lateness in appearing. It opens with Richard Bucci's 'Mind and Textual Matter' (*SB* 58[2007–8] 1–47). Bucci's is an extensive consideration of 'the critical editorial approach to Anglophone literary works which arose alongside the "new bibliography"' (p. 4). Amongst texts and theories about them, considered are essays in Stephen Orgel's *The Authentic Shakespeare and other problems of the Early Modern Stage* [2002], Paul Werstine's writings in *Shakespeare Quarterly*, Text and elsewhere. Interestingly, some of Bucci's text is concerned with responses to W.W. Greg's 'The Rationale of Copy-Text' (pp. 11ff.) and McKerrow, Bowers, Tanselle, and McGann's reactions to it, see for instance specifically p. 18 n. 25. For Bucci, there was 'an initial lack of clarity on the part of some author-focused editors about the need to deepen the definition of their editorial goal'. Additionally, with the exception of Bowers and Tanselle, 'few contributions to the scholarly journals published little in the way of meaningful assessments of the editions' (p. 21). He finds, however, Hans Zeller's 'A New Approach to the Critical Constitution of Literary Texts' (*SB* 28[1975] 231–64) 'provocative and helpful' and also the work of the 'learned German Jewish philologist Ernst Grumach (1902–67)' who was the first editor of 'the edition of Goethe's works prepared by the Deutsche Akademie der Wissenschaften zu Berlin (DDR), from 1949' (p. 22).

Bucci's essay is particularly interesting as it is the work of a scholar who is aware of distinguished editions outside of the Anglo-American editorial tradition. A detailed discussion of Zeller (pp. 22–6), is followed by a consideration of David Greetham's *Theories of the Text* [1999] and return to a consideration of Bowers, McKerrow, and Tanselle. In his closing pages, Bucci, an editor with the University of California's Mark Twain Project, turns to the editing of American texts, the Northwestern-Newbury edition of Melville's *Typee* [1968] and the University of California Press's Mark Twain's *A Connecticut Yankee in King Arthur's Court* [1979]. For Bucci, 'The American experience has confirmed much past editorial wisdom, but also demonstrated that in the approach to works represented by abundant original textual

The Year's Work in English Studies, Volume 90 (2011)
doi:10.1093/ywes/mar006

evidence, scholarly attention shifts' (p. 46). Bucci's article has covered largely known territory and familiar ground from an interesting perspective: it is pleasing to see a reawakening of interest in Hans Zeller's work, and moving to learn of the experience and significance of the work of Ernst Grumach.

John Ivor Carlson's 'Scribal Intentions in Medieval Romance: A Case Study of Robert Thornton' (*SB* 58[2007–8] 49–71) focuses upon the work of Robert Thornton, described by Carlson as 'otherwise an unremarkable member of the fifteenth-century English gentry [who] created two miscellanies intended for his family's private edification: Lincoln Cathedra MS 91 (olim Lincoln Cathedral A.5.2) and British Library MS Add. 31042'. In Thornton's manuscripts and their examination, the 'providential combination of scribal independence with textual merit makes tenable an investigation into one copyist's compilation methods that could reshape widely-accepted notions about an important source of medieval literature' (p. 51). Carlson's essay is divided into six sections: 'A Rationale of "Scribal Corruption"?' (*SB* 58[2007–8] 49–51); 'Past Assessments of Robert Thornton' (*SB* 58[2007–8] 51–3); 'The Methodology of Reassessment' (*SB* 58[2007–8] 53–5); 'Constructing Thornton's Scribal Profile' (*SB* 58[2007–8] 55–62); 'Form Profile to Rationale' (*SB* 58[2007–8] 62–6), and 'Conclusions and Application' (*SB* 58[2007–8] 66–8). There are two appendices: 'Appendix 1: Manuscripts and Lines Collated and Critical Editions Covered' (*SB* 58[2007–8] 68–9) and 'Appendix 2: Examples of Scribal Habits' (*SB* 58[2007–8] 69–71).

S.W. Reid (1943–2010) taught at Kent State University and founded the university's Institute for Bibliography and Editing. In addition to being textual editor of *The Novels and Related Works of Charles Brockden Brown: Bicentennial Edition*, he was the chief executive editor of the *Cambridge Edition of the Works of Joseph Conrad*. David L. Vander Meulen in his 'Notes on Contributors' adds that the 'present article, in the journal that was the venue for his first publication in 1971, is an outgrowth of his doctoral work at the University of Virginia, where he was the last dissertation student of Fredson Bowers and received his PhD in 1972' (p. 305). Reid writes on 'Compositor of B's Speech-Prefixes in the First Folio of Shakespeare and the Question of Copy for *2 Henry IV*' (*SB* 58[2007–8] 73–108). There is an appendix containing 'Compositor B's speech-prefixes in the seven Folio plays set from known quarto copy: *Much Ado About Nothing*, *Love's Labour's Lost*, *A Midsummer Night's Dream*, *The Merchant of Venice*, *1 Henry IV*, *Titus Andronicus*, and *Romeo and Juliet* (pp. 103–8).

Gerald E. Downs's 'Memorial Transmission and Shorthand, and *John of Bordeaux*' (*SB* 58[2007–8] 109–34), is an 'analysis of the manuscript playtext *John of Bordeaux*', now at the 'Estates Office, Alnwick Castle, Northumberland'. Downs 'indicates that it is transcribed from the stenographic recording of a stage performance'. He compares 'this inference to prior scholarly opinion that the text is either a memorial reconstruction or a descendent transcription of authorized text and' discusses 'the implications' of his findings (p. 109). Downs concludes that 'Theatrical reporting may account for a wide range of printed plays, but memorial reconstruction should be recognized as a viable explanation for only a few special cases' (p. 134). Alan D. Boehm contributes 'The Bagford Chapel Rules: A Set of English Printing

House Regulations, *circa* 1686–1707' (*SB* 58[2007–8] 135–43). It is known that 'three sets of chapel rules' survive. Boehm's is an account and analysis of 'a fourth and practically unknown set of chapel rules from the period-preserved in the British Library's Department of Printed Books... the document is part of the Bagford Title-pages Collection, which was assembled during the late 1600s and early 1700s by John Bagford (1650–1716), a London book dealer and an antiquarian with a keen interest in bibliography' (pp. 135–6). Following his description and analysis, Boehm provides an 'Appendix' (pp. 142–3) printing the discovery.

Michael Winship's '"The Tragedy of the Book Industry"? Bookstores and Book Distribution in the United States to 1950' (*SB* 58[2007–8] 145–84), is indebted, as Winship acknowledges, to O.H. Cheney's *Economic Survey of the Book Industry* [1931]. Winship echoes Cheney and suggests 'that it is the *study* of book distribution that may well be the "tragedy" of American book history' (p. 145). The lack of such a 'study' means that 'virtually every argument that historians of the American book have made over the past decades—about authorship, publishing, audiences, reader response, and innumerable other topics—must remain provisional'. Winship adds, 'Each of these arguments relies on untested assumptions about the connections between authors, publishers, and readers, for these connections depend upon the mechanisms of distribution.' Following a consideration of the 'failure of book historians' (pp. 145–6), Winship attempts to redress the balance and provides a checklist of 'Directories of American Bookstores to 1950' (pp. 154–84). This is divided into '1. General Bookstores', sixty-two of these are listed with additional information (pp. 157–79), and 'II. Second-Hand and Antiquarian Bookstores', also containing additional information (pp. 179–84). There are two accompanying tables: 'Directories of General Bookstores' with selected years from 1854 to 1950, and 'Directories of Second-Hand and Antiquarian Bookstores' with selected years from 1885 to 1949 (pp. 183–4).

Of interest is Christian Y. Dupont's 'Collecting Dante from Tuscany: The Formation of the Fiske Dante Collection at Cornell University' (*SB* 58[2007–8] 185–210), describing the collection obsession of Dante by Daniel Willard Fiske (1831–1904). A volume of *SB* wouldn't be complete without an essay by G. Thomas Tanselle. On this occasion, he writes on 'Book-Jackets of the 1890s' (*SB* 58[2007–8] 211–304). Tanselle notes, 'For about forty years I have been interested in documenting the growth in the use of book-jackets (and other detachable coverings of books) by publishers and have made notes on every pre-1901 example that came to my attention.' Tanselle is adding to his previous explorations in the field and 'presenting entries, prefaced by a brief account of recent book-jacket news and a summary of some of the information revealed by the 1890s list' (p. 211). Tanselle's commentary (pp. 211–23) is followed by 'A List of Examples, 1891–1900, of British and American Publishers' Printed Book-Jackets, Boxes, and Other Detachable Coverings' (pp. 224–86) and a very useful 'Index to the List' divided into '(1) Authors, Editors, Illustrators, Translators (plus personal-name subjects, and titles without named authors)' (pp. 287–95), '(2) Publishers and Series' (pp. 295–9), '(3) Libraries' (pp. 299–300), '(4) Collectors' (pp. 300–1), '(5) Dealers and Auction Houses' (pp. 301–3), and '(6) Scholars (and other persons who have provided information, not covered under previous headings, in published or unpublished form)' (pp. 303–4).

Well, is this issue of *SB* worth waiting for? The eight articles cover textual theory, manuscript findings, the study of Shakespeare's compositors, the complex questions of textual transmission, the book industry during the first half of the twentieth century in the United States, the formation of a Dante collection at Cornell University, and 1890s dust-jackets. Clearly, many of these articles will be cited in the future. They are replete with erudition, authoritative, and on the whole well written. There is inevitably a caveat. Many fields of learned endeavour are beset by the acceptance of recognized authority figures and this issue of *SB* is no exception. Articles by Michael Winship and others are refreshing in that they do call into question previously received wisdom. Michael Winship is the holder of an Endowed Chair and is in a position to question those perceived to be in authority. Scholarly endeavour can only proceed through a process of continuing questioning. In a rapidly diminishing job market, and with the pressures to gain appointments and tenure—then what is new?—it is a consummation devoutly to be wished that questioning of the work of those perceived to be in positions of authority and in prestigious university departments will not diminish.

The Papers of the Bibliographical Society of America (*PBSA* 103[2009]) yet again contain highly readable and important contributions. Nicholas D. Nace's 'The Publication of Urania Johnson's "Unpublishable" *Amira*' (*PBSA* 103:i[2009] 5–18) takes up where Samuel Richardson left off and follows the fortunes of Urania Johnson's *Almira*: 'Urania took the occasion of Richardson's death to actively begin promoting her own work with those who had previously published her poetry and had publicly advocated women's writing' (p. 18). Alan R. Young's 'Charles Knight and the Nineteenth-Century Market for Shakespeare' (*PBSA* 103:i[2009] 19–41) concludes with a detailed tabulation of 'Charles Knight's Early Editions of Shakespeare' (pp. 37–41). Young discusses in detail 'a remarkable commercial publishing venture... Charles Knight's *Pictorial Edition of the Works of Shakspere*'. Knight's work tapped a market that 'was inextricably linked to the ever expanding Victorian cult of Shakespeare among all social classes that derived from the growing knowledge of and veneration for Shakespeare'. Knight's edition plus a 'newly researched biography of Shakespeare, appeared in 55 parts between 1838 and 1843. (It was also published in eight volumes between 1839 and 1843 as material became available)' (p. 19). Young illuminates 'the diffusion of Shakespeare's texts... the interpretive commentary concerning them... the understanding and knowledge concerning the chronology of Shakespeare's plays and the biography of Shakespeare'. Consequently, Young argues 'that single-handedly as publisher, editor, commentator, and researcher Knight made an enormous contribution to Victorian awareness of Shakespeare' (p. 36).

David Stoker's 'Establishing Lady Fenn's Canon' (*PBSA* 103:i[2009] 43–72) is a continuation of Stoker's previous work. He wrote 'the [*ODNB*] entry for Sir John Fenn (1739–4), the English antiquary' (p. 43). In this *PBSA* article, Stoker investigates the activities of Sir John Fenn's wife Lady Ellenor Fenn. He concludes that 'The case of Lady Ellenor Fenn and the large number of incorrect attributions associated with her highlights some of the difficulties encountered in the bibliographical study of early children's books' (p. 63). Stoker's detective work contains an 'Appendix: A Checklist of Books and Teaching Schemes Believed to Have Been Written or Compiled by Lady Fenn' (pp. 64–72). Brian Parker's 'Six Precursors for *Sweet Bird of Youth*' (*PBSA* 103:i[2009] 73–88) identifies precursors for Tennessee Williams's great drama and his deep indebtedness to his director Elia Kazan. In a 'Bibliographical Note' Alan D. Boehm writes at some length on '"The Well and Good Government of the *Chappel*": A Note on Printing-house Customs, c.1680–1750' (*PBSA* 103:i[2009] 89–97). Boehm illuminates late seventeenth-century and eighteenth-century English printing house activities. The June 2009 issue of *PBSA* contains one item of direct relevance to *YWES* readers, Ross Alloway's 'The Sequestration of Archibald Constable and Company' (*PBSA* 103:ii[2009] 224–43). Alloway throws light upon Archibald Constable and Company's bankruptcy, and there are tables illustrating the 'Depreciation of Assets, March 1826 through September 1827' (p. 234) and of 'Estimated debt May 1826 through November 1831' (p. 238). Alloway concludes that 'by the time of his sequestration, Constable was 52 years old and in too poor health to make a financial recovery. He died an undischarged bankrupt one year after proceedings had begun.' This is in stark contrast to the other main player. For Cadell 'the sequestration emancipated [him] from the insurmountable debt'. Furthermore, 'though he was not discharged until April 1829, with financial help from his family and, most importantly, the favor of Scott, the sequestration set him on course to become a wealthy, if somewhat predictable, publisher' (p. 243).

The September 2009 *PBSA* opens with Roy Bearden-White's 'A History of Guilty Pleasure: Chapbooks and the Lemoines' (*PBSA* 103:iii[2009] 284–318). This is accompanied by illustrations from drawing chapbook compilations (pp. 284, 304, 312). Bearden-White's article describes the activities of Ann and Henry Lemoine both of whom published chapbooks, that is 'small, paper bound books sold by peddlers, itinerant salesman, and chapmen during the eighteenth and early nineteenth centuries' (p. 284). Bearden-White provides a fascinating glimpse into a hitherto relatively neglected area of printing and publishing history. So does Frank Brannon in his 'Metal Type from the Print Shop of the Historical *Cherokee Phoenix* Newspaper' (*PBSA* 103:iii[2009] 319–35) concerning publication and printing in another country, another period, and another civilization. Brannon's account also contains fascinating illustrative material and tabulations. Specific author and text is the subject of Patrick Denman Flanery's 'Readership, Authority, and Identity: Some Competing Texts of Evelyn Waugh's *A Handful of Dust*' (*PBSA* 103:iii[2009] 337–56), which utilizes the material 'in Waugh's library housed at the Harry Ransom Humanities Research Institute at the University of Texas' (p. 343) and illustrates what a complex textual history Waugh's novel had, especially in relation to a similar serialization under his name in *Harper's Bazaar*. Flanery concludes that 'literature is always marked by its material instantiations' (p. 356). Textual variations also preoccupy Brian Parker's 'A Provisional Stemma of Drafts and Revisions for Tennessee Williams's *Sweet Bird of Youth* (1959)' (*PBSA* 103:iii[2009] 357–90). Parker draws upon Williams's various drafts and revisions found in eleven libraries. As Parker observes, 'A problem common to all Williams's work was his frantic, improvisational method of composition' (p. 358). His article describes eight drafts of *Sweet Bird of Youth*, the film version, subsequent revivals of the work, and a listing of 'Archival Materials Mentioned' (pp. 385–90).

The December issue also contains some fascinating materials. Terry Belanger's BSA Annual Address, 'A View from the Bridge: Further Meditations by the Captain of the Iceberg' (*PBSA* 103:iv[2009] 421–33), uses the analogy of the *Titanic* to describe what he perceives as happening. In his concluding paragraph Belanger comments: 'Today's great research libraries seem on the whole to be less interested in collecting and preserving new printed books than at any time since the later fifteenth century.' Further, 'No doubt the good ship will go down, sooner or later, but meanwhile we can all help preserve the physical—the bibliographical—evidence that defines and illuminates our time, and that of the recent past' (p. 432). Timothy L. Stinson's 'Knowledge of the Flesh: Using DNA Analysis to Unlock Bibliographical Secrets of Medieval Parchment' (*PBSA* 103:iv[2009] 435–53) is also fascinating. He begins by amplifying what is meant by 'DNA' (pp. 436–8), gives an account of 'Background of Studies to Date' (pp. 439–41) and then proceeds to describe 'New Investigations' (pp. 441–6), 'Interpretation of Data' (pp. 446–8), and the 'Relationship to Bibliography/Potential Benefits' (pp. 448–51), and concludes on pp. 451–3. What Stinson analyses is by no means limited in its implications to medieval parchments. There are exciting possibilities here, if, of course, we had world enough and time—and the money.

Mark Towsey's 'First Steps in Associational Reading: Book Use and Sociability at the Wigtown Subscription Library, 1795–9' (*PBSA* 103:iv[2009] 455–95) provides an account of two years in the late eighteenth century of activities in a library in 'A small and sleepy former market town in the southwest corner of Scotland [that] proudly claims today to be home to 900 people, a malt whiskey distillery, nineteen bookshops, and a quarter of a million books' (p. 455). There is a detailed appendix tabulating 'Books Borrowed from the Wigtown Subscription Library, 1796–9' (pp. 482–90), and a second appendix tabulating 'Borrowers from the Wigtown Subscription Library, 1796–9' (pp. 491–5). Amy Root's 'Designing the Borzoi: Alfred A. Knopf, Inc., Creates a Brand of Excellence, 1915–29' (*PBSA* 103:iv[2009] 497–513) is an account of a distinguished publisher's 'branding strategy' (p. 513), during the years 1915–29. Naomi Stubbs's 'The Final Revisions to David Garrick's First Play' (*PBSA* 103:iv[2009] 515–32) describes his revisions to *Lethe*, drawing upon materials at the Folger Shakespeare Library, Washington, DC, and the John Rylands Library at the University of Manchester. Stubbs's article is followed by a review essay by David McKitterick, 'Harvesting the British Book Trade' (*PBSA* 103:iv[2009] 533–8), a review of Trevor Howard-Hill's *The British Book Trade, 1475–1890: A Bibliography*. The four issues of *PBSA* contain succinct reviews of recent pertinent work and short, incisive reviews penned by its indefatigable editor, Trevor Howard-Hill.

The two-volume *The British Book Trade, 1475–1890: A Bibliography* complements the doyen of bibliographers Trevor Howard-Hill's great nine-volume *Index to British Literary Bibliography* [1969–] and his *British Book Trade Dissertations to 1980* [1998]. The volumes provide 'for the first time a bibliographical conspectus of the history of the British book trade and books from the beginning of printing in Britain to 1890, the date at which the coverage of the *Index* begins. A clearly written explanatory introduction (p. xxiii) encompasses the 'Scope' (pp. xxiii–lxxi), 'Style of Entry' (pp. xxxix–xxxvi), their arrangement (pp. xxxvi–xlviii), indexes (pp. xlix–liii), and 'Index to topics mentioned in the Introduction' (pp. liv–lxv). There is an abbreviations table and listing of bibliographical references (pp. lxvii–lxxi). Contents range from book production and distribution, regulation, censorship, trials, individual publishers and printers, typographers, paper and paper-making, to illustration processes, presses and machines, prices and wages, bookbinding, copyright, collections and sales, libraries, and a myriad of other topics. The first volume covers nos. 1–11120, and the second nos. 11121–24567. An accompanying CD-ROM contains a comprehensive author and subject index revealing the eclectic coverage of this monumental work. There are brief descriptive notes based on Trevor Howard-Hill's personal inspection of each item. For instance, item 786 under *The Winter's Tale*, Cecil Harbottle's 'The old corrector on The winter's tale' published in 'N&Q ser. 1 8 no. 196: 95–7' in 1853 'Disputes Collier's adoption of Perkins F2 readings' (p. 70). To take just one more example from many, item 1745 for Charles Reade his 'The course of true love never did run smooth' appearing in the 'Our weekly gossip' columns of the *Athenaeum* in October 1857 refers to Reade's 'Clouds and Sunshine'. This contains the comment 'Reade's story "anticipated" by George Sand' (p. 143)! Composed in clear computer-generated typeface and firmly bound, the entry numbers and names are in bold followed by title and, if required, journal pagination and dating. In short, this is a great work of bibliographical reference that should be in all libraries and will be of service to scholars for generations to come.

The twelfth volume of *Book History*, edited by Ezra Greenspan and Jonathan Rose, contains much of interest to *YWES* readers. The extensive opening essay by Elizabeth Yale focuses on 'With Slips and Scraps: How Early Modern Naturalists Invented the Archive' (*BH* 12[2009] 1–36). Yale's attention is mainly on seventeenth-century English antiquaries and natural historians, although she refers to earlier periods and later ones. A good deal of attention is devoted to the founding of the Ashmolean Museum. Yale's conclusion is somewhat startling. She writes, 'In some ways, the situation facing seventeenth-century naturalists and antiquaries was not unlike that faced now by archivists, librarians, historians and scientists. New forms of information, and ways of communicating it, proliferate.' After outlining these, she observes: 'some of the issues at play are similar, and the seventeenth-century experience may inform our own' (p. 22). There are 115 notes to Yale's contribution (pp. 24–36).

Jeffrey Todd Knight's '"Furnished" for Action: Renaissance Books as Furniture' (*BH* 12[2009] 37–73) draws upon various materials including illustrations to illuminate the subject of books as furniture in Renaissance libraries. Sharon Murphy's 'Imperial Reading: The East India Company's Lending Libraries for Soldiers, c.1819–1834' (*BH* 12[2009] 74–99) examines 'the East India Company's decision to establish lending libraries for soldiers at its stations in India during the early 1820s and 1830s' (p. 75). Amongst the issues examined are the criteria the company followed when supplying books to its forces. Murphy draws upon East India Company records. She concludes with the comment, 'the larger question of whether the books supplied to European soldiers in the colonies facilitated the imperial enterprise is clearly worthy of further study' (p. 91). Emily B. Todd's 'Establishing Routes for Fiction in the United States: Walter Scott's Novels and the Early Nineteenth-Century American Publishing Industry' (*BH* 12[2009] 100–28), demonstrates that Scott's 'novels gave publishers what they had been looking for: the certainty that novels could sell throughout the United States, and in the process, I would argue, American publishers and readers came to regard the novels as their own' (p. 123). There are two full-page, black and white figures accompanying Todd's contribution (pp. 108, 122). The latter contains an illustration of marginalia from what is assumed to be a front paper of the second volume of *Tales of My Landlord First Series*, published in Philadelphia in 1817 by Moses Thomas and now at the Library Company of Philadelphia. The marginalia dating from the late 1820s contain the clearly visible comment: 'Is it not a pity that the great Philadelphia Library cannot afford a complete edition of the marvelous novels'.

Teresa A. Goddu writes on 'The Antislavery Almanac and the Discourse of Numeracy' (*BH* 12[2009] 129–55). Goddu argues that 'Numeracy and its attendant print form, the almanac, were instrumental to the creation of anti-slavery's rationalized print system and, hence, foundational to its success' (p. 150). Mike Esbester's fully illustrated contribution tackles the fascinating subject of 'Nineteenth-Century Timetables and the History of Reading' (*BH* 12[2009] 156–85). Michael Anesko writes on 'Collected Editions and the Consolidation of Cultural Authority: The Case of Henry James' (*BH* 12[2009] 186–208). He concludes that 'Through all of its paradoxes and vicissitudes, the history of Henry James's collected editions reveals to us the complex process by which an author and his works become invested with cultural authority' (p. 203). Jennifer J. Connor writes on the subject of 'Stalwart Giants: Medical Cosmopolitanism, Canadian Authorship, and American Publishers' (*BH* 12[2009] 209–39).

Kathleen McDowell tackles the subject of 'Toward a History of Children as Readers, 1890–1930' (*BH* 12[2009] 240–65). Her subject 'is to outline some of the basic issues in writing a history of children as readers, particularly in relation to the fields of the history of childhood and children's literature' (p. 241). Claire Parfait is interested in 'Rewriting History: The Publication of W.E.B. Du Bois's *Black Reconstruction in America* (1935)' (*BH* 12[2009] 266–94). Alice Staveley in the penultimate essay discourses on 'Marketing Virginia Woolf: Women, War, and Public Relations in *Three Guineas*' (*BH* 12[2009] 295–339), drawing upon various archival materials. In the final essay in this most useful collection, Ben Kafka writes on 'Paperwork: The State of the Discipline' (*BH* 12[2009] 340–53). For Kafka, although there are 'similarities between book history and the history of paperwork', there are essential differences. 'While the future of the book is uncertain, the future of paperwork is clear. Greater and greater proportions of what Vismann calls its "transfer operations" till take place electronically' (p. 351).

The Book Collector volume 58 for 2009 contains much that is fascinating and useful; in fact the present writer confesses that it is one of his favourite reads. Nicolas Barker's 'The History of Libraries in Britain' (*BC* 58:i[2009] 11–28), is a detailed and thoughtful review of the three-volume *Cambridge History of Libraries in Britain and Ireland* published by the Cambridge University Press in 2006. Each *BC* issue contains 'News & Comments' replete with fascinating items. For instance the spring issue contains bibliographical and biographical information on T.S. Eliot (p. 34), Graham Greene (p. 36), and, to mention one other, Edward Lear (p. 38), not to forget Algernon Charles Swinburne and contributions on Swinburne in *The Book Collector* (pp. 42–3). Accompanied by six black and white illustrations, Felicity Simpson's 'The Library at Wallington' (*BC* 58:i[2009] 45–71) describes the now National Trust Library at Wallington Hall, 'situated twenty miles north-west of Newcastle-upon-Tyne' (p. 45). The library 'contains approximately 3,500 titles, but the total number of volumes is close to 6,000' (p. 46), and it is closely associated with the great Trevelyan family, many of whom were avid bibliophiles. 'The oldest book in the house, Polydore Vergil's *Anglicae Historiae*, was bought by Sir Walter [Caverly Blackett] while in Rome in 1837' (p. 53). However, many interesting items belonged to Thomas Babington Macaulay (1800–59), whose sister Hannah married Sir Charles Edward Trevelyan, a colonial civil servant. Many of the great Macaulay's books passed to his sister and then to the library at Wallington. Many of these volumes contain his marginalia: Thomas Babington Macaulay was a copious annotator. Simpson writes that in addition to classical authors 'Other authors represented at Wallington include Defoe, Voltaire, Massinger, Coleridge, James Shirley, Shakespeare (whose editors' interpretations Macaulay often objected to strongly), Fielding, Goldsmith and many others' (p. 56).

John Saumarez Smith's 'Destruction of the Country House Library' (*BC* 58:i[2009] 73–8) continues the work of the late, great A.N.L. Munby. Smith studies the catalogues revealed in the collection of Norman Norris (1917–91), who had 'retained at least 200 catalogues' (p. 74). From these, he focuses upon 'two country house sales that took place within two months of each other in 1939: Dropmore House in February and Hampden House in April. The first was the home of the Grenvilles, the second of the Hampdens.' Smith's account is somewhat confusing as following his description of the Dropmore House February 1939 sale he then diverts to 'the Kemsley auction at Dropmore [that] happened thirty years later in March 1969' (p. 77). Somewhat revealingly in his final paragraph Smith observes that 'the ring in 1939 would have had a field day' (p. 78). James Fergusson writes on 'The Siegfried Sassoon Fellowship' (*BC* 58:i[2009] 79–81), especially upon the contents of its newsletter, *Siegfried's Journal*, and the recent issues. He also describes its annual one-day conference and annual cricket match. At the end of his succinct account may be found details of 'The Siegfried Sassoon Fellowship' (p. 81).Obituaries in this 2009 spring issue include that by Nicolas Barker of Vivian Ridler (1913–2009), the distinguished Oxford University printer, reprinted from *The Independent*.

The summer 2009 issue opens with Nicolas Barker's review (*BC* 58:ii[2009] 167–82), of *The British Book Trade: An Oral History*, edited by Sue Bradley, published by the British Library in 2008, and which was curiously omitted from last year's *YWES* assessment. As is to be expected, Barker's review is judicious and he points out the strengths and the weaknesses of the work, including the omission of 'the third main element of the book trade, manufacturing' (p. 177). Edward H. Cohen's 'The 1918 *Poems of Gerard Manley Hopkins*' (*BC* 58:ii[2009] 199–218) contains a descriptive and historical bibliography of 'the *Poems of Gerard Manley Hopkins* edited by Robert Bridges and published in London in 1918 by Humphrey Milford for the Oxford University Press'. As Cohen points out, 'Few books are as highly prized by collectors of modern poetry' as this volume (p. 199). The present writer must confess to having once possessed a copy and thinking that it was of little significance, writing in it in biro and then disposing of it. Cohen's article reveals what a foolish deed this was and why the book is highly prized. He also discusses Hopkins's manuscripts and the role Robert Bridges played in the publication of Hopkins's 1918 *Poems*, plus describing the various binding states, and the circumstances leading up to its publication. In short, a fascinating article from which much is gleaned. Thomas McGeary's 'John Brindley's Bookbindings for Frederick, Prince of Wales' (*BC* 58:ii[2009] 219–40) provides six figures illustrating Brindley's bindings (pp. 234–40), a table showing 'John Brindley Tools Used on Books Bound for Frederick, Prince of Wales' (p. 233), and draws upon 'several bills by Brindley for binding books' for his patron that have recently come to light at the Houghton Library, Harvard University (pp. 219–24). McGeary also draws upon the 'British Library, Register of Warrants for Payments of Tradesmen' (pp. 225–32) to illuminate Brindley's activities.

Stephen Clarke's '"I fear I am altogether done for": H. Maynard Smith and the Tribulations of Editing Evelyn's *Diary*' (*BC* 58:ii[2009] 241–54), throws light upon H. Maynard Smith's (1869–1949) trials and tribulations in editing John Evelyn's diary. Clarke notes that when 'in 1955 de Beer's still standard edition of Evelyn's *Diary* was published to great and lasting acclaim', in his introduction de Beer 'noted that Maynard Smith had produced the first and only important analysis of Evelyn's text' (pp. 251–2). John Saumarez Smith's 'Salesman to the Last Literary Salon' (*BC* 58:ii[2009] 255–9) illuminates a section of the upscale London booktrade in the post-Second World War era. James Fergusson writes on 'The Powys Society' in 'Author Societies 2' (*BC* 58:ii[2009] 263–5).

The autumn issue of *BC* opens with a review by Nicolas Barker of David Pearson's important *Books as History* published by the British Library and Oak Knoll Press in 2008 (*BC* 58:iii[2009] 333–4). As Barker writes, '*Books as History* will help anyone, but especially the beginner, find out how much more there is to be learned from any book' (p. 334). Richard Garnett's fascinating 'A Victorian Album' (*BC* 58:iii[2009] 345–60) is accompanied by three figurative illustrations (pp. 358–60). Garnett describes 'a chunky volume of 187 somewhat casually numbered leaves . . . bound in dark green leather' which he inherited in 1975 from his father's cousin. Inspection revealed that 'Among much else it had, pasted in, 76 letters and 63 cut-off signatures, many from well-known people.' The album had belonged to Garnett's great-grandmother. 'It had been given to Olivia Narney Singleton, as she then was, at Christmas 1859, when she was seventeen, by her uncle John Westland Marston. He was a minor poet, who enjoyed the company of his betters, and, like Dickens and Wilkie Collins, was much attracted to the stage' (p. 345). For further information and details concerning its treasures, the reader's attention is drawn to Garnett's wonderful article! A.S.G. Edwards performs a valuable service by contributing 'The Published Writings of A.N.L. Munby: A Supplement' (*BC* 58:iii[2009] 377–82), and 'supplements the list of writings by A.N.L. Munby' that Nicolas Barker included in his edition of Munby's *Essays and Papers* (London: Scolar Press [1977], pp. 235–41). As Edwards indicates, 'many of the items . . . are recorded in the on-line *TLS Centenary Archive* (Primary Resource Media), not, of course, available to Barker' (p. 377).

Ian Christie-Miller's 'New Tools for Old Paper' (*BC* 58:iii[2009] 383–7), replete with four illustrative figures, draws upon 'the advent of digital imaging, image processing, archiving and dissemination' in order 'to sketch out some of the ways in which backlighting of paper with digitization is now being harnessed' to reveal much about 'the potential value of paper and watermark research' (p. 383). Christie-Miller discusses the significance of the fact that 'for the unicorns some watermarks are found more often than others in a 1526 book of herbals' (p. 384) and the fact that 'sensitivity to religious symbolism is evident from' watermarks (p. 387). Clearly much more should be written on the subject and hopefully the new methods associated with digitization will help in this process. Images found in watermarks from 'the records of one of the bastions of the old religious regime—Battle Abbey . . . [an] image . . . a vestige of that old order', in other words before the destruction of the monasteries' (p. 387), are in themselves revealing (see p. 388). John Saumarez Smith writes on a different period and a different subject in his 'Anthony Trollope and the Man from Wall Street' (*BC* 58:iii[2009] 391–5). Saumarez Smith draws upon his days as a bookseller at Heywood Hill in London and his meetings with Albert H. Gordon, the eminent Wall Street businessman. Gordon collected books, and especially Anthony Trollope. He seriously began collecting at Trollope at the age of 70. Al Gordon died in 2009, aged 107. The third article in the 'Author Societies' series is Alan Bell's 'The Sydney Smith Association' (*BC* 58:iii[2009] 399–401). This was founded in 1996 with its aims 'To advance the education of the public in the life and works of Sydney Smith' and also 'To advance the Christian religion by the preservation and upkeep of churches connected with Sydney Smith' (p. 401). Sydney Smith (1771–1845) 'was a working clergyman, and an accomplished reviewer for one of the main quarterly journals of the day' (p. 399). He was Canon of St Paul's and also a Yorkshire country parson.

The winter *BC* contains several items of interest including another valuable contribution from A.S.G. Edwards, a member of the *BC*'s editorial board. In his 'T.S. Eliot and Friends: *Noctes Binanianae* (1939)' (*BC* 58:iv[2009] 503–9) Edwards writes, 'in spite of Eliot's association with it, the circumstances of *Noctes*' only printing and of its subsequent circulation seem never to have been clearly described' (p. 503). The analysis reveals that 'Eliot himself was responsible for the greatest number of these verses, eight' that is, 'self-consciously coterie verse, full of private allusions' (p. 504). The whereabouts of four proof copies are described, plus the whereabouts of nineteen extant copies. In an appendix Edwards describes 'The contents and authorship of the final published edition of *Noctes Binanianae*' (pp. 509–10). John Saumarez Smith's 'The London Telephone Directory in a White Chemise' (*BC* 58:iv[2009] 511–15) describes his amusing visit in the early 1990s to the collection of books of the late Dowager Marchioness of Cholmondeley. Roger Eliot Stoddard's 'Uncollected Authors LXX: W.G. Sebald' (*BC* 58:iv[2009] 517–42) contains 'A Checklist of Books Published by W.G. Sebald' (1944–2001) (pp. 521–36). This is more than a checklist and contains detailed descriptions that are accompanied by six illustrative figures. A *BC* tradition is continued in the comic 'Christmas Catalogue No. 13' (*BC* 58:iv[2009] 551–62), containing 'the wells of error' (p. 551) to be found in bookseller's catalogues. James Fergusson writes on 'The Anthony Powell Society: Author Societies 4' (*BC* 58:iv[2009] 563–482).

Each issue of *BC* contains an interesting 'News & Comments' feature, lists of sales, of catalogues, of exhibitions, book reviews, and obituaries, usually reprinted from *The Independent* and invariably authored by Nicolas Barker. Special mention should be made of Nicolas Barker's obituary of the late Marjorie Wynne (1917–2009), who 'was the first person that any visitor to Yale's Rare Book Room (as it then was) met (*BC* 58:iii[2009] 439–40). The welcome that she instantly extended was not to be forgotten' (p. 439). Although retired from the Beinecke in 1987, this did not stop her active attendance at Grolier Club tours and at conferences. She was, as the present writer can attest, a great help to scholars, and will be sadly missed.

The Library: The Transactions of the Bibliographical Society [2009] maintains on a quarterly basis its very high standards. Markman Ellis's 'Coffee-House Libraries in Mid-Eighteenth Century London' (*Library* 10:i[2009] 3–40), using provenance documents, reconstructs some of the most important mid-eighteenth-century London coffee-houses. Ellis provides information on the books found in the coffee-house collections and their accession. Sharon Ragaz's 'The Spurious *Tales of My Landlord*' (*Library* 10:i[2009] 41–56), explores the complex publishing history of two titles published in 1819 and 1820 claiming to be additions to Walter Scott's *Tales of my Landlord*. Three series of these tales had already appeared by then, and Ragaz illuminates the publishing activities of the time and Walter Scott's relationship with the market at this stage in his career. B.J. McMullin's 'Early "Secular" Press Figures' (*Library* 10:i[2009] 57–65) continues McMullin's exploration of the early years of press figures in secular publishing and finds probable illustrations of their use earlier than had previously been thought in volumes printed by John Streater in the late 1660s.

Richard Serjeantson and Thomas Woolford's 'The Scribal Publication of a Printed Book: Francis Bacon's *Certaine Considerations Touching . . . the Church of England (1604)*' (*Library* 10:ii[2009] 119–56) examines the publication history of the first printing of Francis Bacon's *Certaine Considerations Touching the Better Pacification and Edification of the Church of England* [1604]. The authors show that Thomas Purfoot, Jr., the printer, experienced problems resulting largely from the fact that the bishop of London Richard Bancroft was involved with the early printing. However, some of the printed sheets evaded Bancroft's delaying tactics and half of the book became available to readers through copies made by professional scribes in manuscripts. Serjeantson and Woolford unravel the complex political and ecclesiological background to the writing of Bacon's work and printing. They also reveal Bacon's role in the printing and partial suppression of his own book. Nancy A. Mace's 'The Market for Music in the Late Eighteenth Century and the Entry Books of the Stationers' Company' (*Library* 10:ii[2009] 157–87) is of interest to *YWES* readers largely because she examines the reasons for an increase in demand for printed music in the last half of the eighteenth century and also throws further light upon the activities of the Stationers' Company.

Kirk Melnikoff's interesting article, 'Thomas Hacket and the Ventures of an Elizabethan Publisher' (*Library* 10:iii[2009] 257–71), throws light upon the London publishing world of the late sixteenth century, and in particular the life and career of Thomas Hacket, a bookseller working in London between 1556 and 1590. In addition to Hacket's own translations, he put up the money while a stationer for many important texts, including the first English translation of Ovid's Narcissus myth, Thomas Nash's first venture into printing, and some of the earliest descriptions of the Americas to appear in England. Melnikoff also assesses Hacket's significance in the book trade. In his 'Nathaniel Mist, Daniel Defoe, and the Perils of Publishing' (*Library* 10:iii[2009] 298–313), the eminent eighteenth-century scholar and critic Pat Rogers throws further light upon Daniel Defoe, pirated editions, and early eighteenth-century publishing. Rogers's focus is Nathaniel Mist (d. 1737), Jacobean printer and newspaper proprietor. Rogers throws doubt upon the idea, primarily based on press advertisements, that Mist was the begetter of a pirated edition of Defoe's *Captain Singleton* in 1721. Rogers draws upon unpublished documents in the National Archives in addition to comprehensive newspaper coverage of Mist's trials for seditious libel in his newspaper *The Weekly Journal; or Saturday's Post*. Mist was prosecuted on two distinct seditious libel charges. On one, in February 1721 he received a sentence that involved some time in the pillory. Consequently, his Jacobite supporters regarded him as a hero. The second charge was dropped, but the authorities pursued him relentlessly and Mist disappeared. Rogers's brilliant Sherlock Holmes-type unravelling reveals the ways in which the book trade was regulated by the authorities at the time and some of the ways in which the publishing trade, publishers, journalists, and printers, evaded the authorities.

Nicholas Seager's 'Prudence and Plagiarism in the 1740 Continuation of Defoe's *Roxana*' (*Library* 10:iv[2009] 357–71) focuses upon Elizabeth Applebee's 1740 spurious continuation of Daniel Defoe's *Roxana* [1724]. Her continuation contained at least seven different texts, although it largely drew upon the seventeenth-century conduct manual, *Humane Prudence* by William de Britaine. Seager digs up the very complex publication history of Applebee's work post-1740, and speculates why there has been neglect of the continuations of Defoe's *Roxana*. Hao Tianhu's '*Hesperides, or the Muse's Garden* and its Manuscript History' (*Library* 10:iv[2009] 372–404) provides an analysis of a seventeenth-century manuscript commonplace book. Hao Tianhu presents a comparison of the different versions and sheds light upon their probable production and dating. Humphrey Moseley initially entered *Hesperides* in the Stationers' Register, and Tianhu discusses his role in the history of the commonplace book. This interesting article concludes with transcriptions of the catalogues from the two Folger manuscripts in which they are found. Anthony James West's 'Ownership of Shakespeare's First Folios over Four Centuries' (*Library* 10:iv[2009] 405–8), continues West's outstanding work on Shakespeare's First Folio by providing an account of the provenance, that is who bought, sold, owned, and received a copy or copies of the First Folio from 1623 to the present. Notable is the fact that few institutions in the seventeenth and eighteenth centuries owned a First Folio; however, the situation changed in the nineteenth century. In short, yet again *The Library* provides excellent articles, comprehensive book reviews, and accounts of recent books published in the field.

The title of *Library History* is now *Library & Information History* but we will still be using the same abbreviation (*LH*) for it. It usually contains some items of interest to *YWES* readers, and volume 25 is no exception. The March 2009 issue contains Edward Potten's '"A great number of Usefull [*sic*] books": The Hidden Library of Henry Booth, 1st Earl of Warrington (1652–1694)' (*LH* 25:i[2009] 33–49). This illuminates seventeenth-century and earlier collections, and provides 'a rare insight into the influences, reading habits, and development of a character [Henry Booth] who played an active role in both the local and national stages throughout the tumultuous latter half of the seventeenth century' (p. 46). Linda J. Parr's 'Sunday School Libraries in Halifax and Huddersfield before Public Libraries' (*LH* 25:i[2009] 50–67), edited by K.A. Manley, sheds light upon what was available for working-class children in Halifax and Huddersfield before the emergence of public libraries. The late Linda J. Parr focuses upon the middle of the nineteenth century, as this is a period in which library catalogues became available.

The June 2009 *LH* has three articles of relevance. Heather Gaunt's 'Social Memory in the Public Historical Sphere: Henry Savery's *The Hermit in Van Diemen's Land* and the Tasmanian Public Library' (*LH* 25:ii[2009] 79–96) assesses the consequences of the publication of convict author Henry Savery's *The Hermit in Van Diemen's Land: From the Colonial Times*, published in 1829. Gaunt's concern is from a specific instance of the development of a colonial public library to enrich the study of 'the ways in which social memory is formed, disseminated, institutionalized and negotiated through artifact and text' (p. 79). Hers is 'the study of the formation of collective memory' (pp. 79–80), with specific reference to a text, *The Hermit in Van Diemen's Land*, and a specific institution, the Tasmanian Public Library. K.E. Attar's 'Incunabula at Senate House Library: Growth of a Collection' (*LH* 25:ii[2009] 97–116) answers the question 'How does a University library established in the late nineteenth century and donation-driven into the twentieth acquire a collection of incunabula?' His article 'examines the growth of the incunabula collection at Senate House Library, University of London (formerly known as the University of London Library), from the twenty-two fifteenth-century books in the foundation collection of Augustus De Morgan, given in 1871, to the twenty-first century' (p. 97). Hopefully, Attar's article will draw attention to a rich repository of literary and historical materials at the Senate House Library. Focus has been on the incredible collections, especially of incunabula, at the Bodleian Library, Oxford, and at Cambridge University Library. Not all treasures are the exclusive domain of the city of dreaming spires and East Anglian technological development: much may be found in the centre of the UK's capital city!

Brendan Luyt's 'The Importance of Fiction to the Raffles Library, Singapore, during the Long Nineteenth-Century' (*LH* 25:ii[2009] 117–31) 'explores, from the available evidence, the attitudes towards fiction held by officials of the Raffles Library, Singapore' (p. 117). The library collected fiction, and the article contains six tabulated appendices. The first contains the 'Results of the 1881 ALA Survey of Potentially Objectionable Books' (pp. 126–7), revealing that at the top of the list was G.W.M. Reynolds and at the bottom of the list were Wilkie Collins and Bulwer Lytton. A second appendix lists 'Top banned UK authors (taken from the 1881 ALA Survey of Potentially Objectionable Books)'. These were, in order of banning: G.W.M. Reynolds, Helen Mathers, E.C.G. Murray, Ouida, Mrs Forrester, Braddon, and Rhoda Broughton. Incidentally, Mrs Forrester does not appear in either the first edition or second edition of John Sutherland's exceedingly comprehensive *The Longman Companion to Victorian Fiction* [1988, 2009]. The third appendix lists 'Works of authors used by Ernest Baker as examples of his fiction classification scheme found in the Raffles Library as of 1901'. Of the so-called 'First Rank' (Baker's classification), there were twenty Henry James and seventeen George Merediths. Of 'Popular Mediocrities' Mrs Braddon leads the list with fifty-five works, with Mrs Henry Wood on thirty-four and Ouida on twenty-nine. Described as 'Below the Standard' Captain Marryat is far ahead with thirty-eight works (pp. 127–8). The remaining appendices contain: 'Number of fiction titles acquired by the Raffles Library as percentage of total titles acquired (no data available for blank years)' (the blank years are 1879 through to 1885, 1891, and 1893); 'Fiction as percentage of total circulation of the Raffles Library for available years'; and 'Subscription revenue versus book and magazine purchases, 1877–1912' (pp. 129–30). There is much food for further research here, especially in the area of what were considered 'First Rank', 'Popular Mediocrities', and 'Below the Standard'. Luyt demonstrates 'that those responsible for the fiction collection in the Raffles Library were liberal in their selection of titles' (p. 126).

The September issue contains interesting articles but little of direct relevance for our purposes. However, the December 2009 issue contains articles that illuminate the study of Victorian England, and, once again, the Raffles Library. 'Libraries and the Victoria County History' (*LH* 25:iv[2009] 217–26) provides a guide by J.V. Beckett, the current Victoria County History director, to the great project's 'background, the way in which county editors handle libraries within the ongoing research work, and the use that local historians more generally make of libraries, particularly those which contain contemporary printed material and archives' (p. 217). Agnese Galeffi's 'Biographical and Cataloguing Common Ground: Panizzi and Lubetzky, Kindred Spirits Separated by a Century' (*LH* 25:iv[2009] 227–46) is not only of interest for students of cataloguing history, rules, and theory, but also sheds light upon the work of Antonio Panizzi (1797–1879), the British Museum's librarian, who spent almost 'thirty-five years of his life, from 1831 to 1865, at the British Museum Library, where he was ultimately appointed Principal Librarian' (p. 240), and Seymour Lubetzky (1898–2003), who lived to a very advanced old age. Lubetzky settled in southern California, and was the author of the *Code of Cataloguing Rules* [1960]. As Galeffi writes, they 'were both exiles, both foreigners in English speaking countries; both were originally scholars of literature, and both found themselves immersed in the world of librarianship, encouraged by mentors' (pp. 227–8).

A different world is described in Audrey M. Cairns and Peter H. Reid's 'The Historical Development of the Library of St Mary's College, Blairs, Aberdeen, 1829–1986' (*LH* 25:iv[2009] 247–64). As Cairns and Reid indicate, 'Catholic libraries are an under-researched area in library history' (p. 247). To return to the Raffles Library, Lim Peng Han writes on 'The Beginning and Development of the Raffles Library in Singapore, 1823–1941: A Nineteenth-Century and Early Twentieth-Century British Colonial Enclave' (*LH* 25:iv[2009] 265–78). Peng Han writes, 'Throughout the period 1904 to 1938 about 80 per cent of the library's subscribers were Europeans, mostly of British descent, since the book collection consisted of English books. The article will show how the Raffles Library became a colonial enclave, a reading club, or research library for the elite European community and had an impact on the lives of the British colonies in Singapore' (p. 265). Each issue of *LH* contains most useful reviews by eminent authorities bringing a different perspective to bear upon the volumes reviewed. For instance, John Feather's assessment of T.H. Howard-Hill's two-volume *The British Book Trade, 1475–1890: A Bibliography* (reviewed elsewhere in this essay) (*LH* 25:iv[2009] 281–2), concludes with the true words that Howard-Hill 'has done more than enough to earn . . . a comfortable retirement, safe in the knowledge that generations of scholars will benefit from his efforts' (p. 282).

Only one issue of *Publishing History* seems to have been published in 2009. John Issitt's 'From *Gregory's Dictionary* to *Nicholson's Encyclopedia*: Intrigue and Literary Craft in the Reshaping of Knowledge' (*PubH* 65[2009] 5–40), is a lengthy illustrative account focusing upon the two illustrations from the 'the opening of the nineteenth century' expanding 'market for encyclopedic dictionaries', *Gregory's Dictionary of Arts and Sciences* and *Nicholson's British Encyclopedia.* Issitt traces 'how one such product, *Gregory's Dictionary* . . . issued by Sir Richard Phillips in 1807' and initially aimed 'for the market of the gentleman-scholar, was reformulated into a product designed for a more eclectic, lower-class audience' (p. 5). Edward Jacobs's 'The Pursuit of an Unstamped Newspaper: Interactions between prosecution and the evolving form, politics, and business practices of John Cleave's *Weekly Police Gazette* (1834–36)' (*PubH* 65[2009] 41–70), explores 'how the prosecutions of *WPG* [*Weekly Police Gazette*] interacted with the significant changes in content and format that it manifested during its two-year run and with the practicalities of Cleave's business as publisher of an illegal unstamped paper' (p. 41). Jacobs's article contains forty-four detailed notations. Kate Macdonald's 'The Diversification of Thomas Nelson & Sons: John Buchan and the Nelson Archive, 1909–1911' (*PubH* 65[2009] 71–97) focuses upon the activities of John Buchan and the firm of Thomas Nelson and Sons. Buchan started working in 1907 for 'the Edinburgh publishing house with whom he was to be identified, as both an associate employee and an author, for the next twenty-two years' (p. 71). In her account, Kate Macdonald utilizes the papers of Thomas Nelson and Sons deposited at Edinburgh University Library and its Special Collections. Her article is accompanied by 117 notes.

In the final essay of this issue of *PubH*, Iain Stevenson writes on 'Robert Maxwell and the Invention of Modern Scientific Publishing' (*PubH* 65[2009] 97–113). For Stevenson, Maxwell was 'arguably both one of the most brilliant and the most villainous characters ever to grace or disgrace British publishing' (p. 97). Stevenson admits that 'Maxwell's journals did, it must be said, genuinely advance science and human knowledge enormously and led (particularly in the medical and life sciences) to important breakthroughs that alleviated human suffering.' He adds, 'Maxwell was proud of what he was doing for science and somewhere there was (or had once been) a spark of idealism' (p. 105). Stevenson casts doubt upon conspiracy theories that Maxwell's death was the result of activities by various intelligence operations and concludes that 'After almost forty-five years of dubious dealings, duplicity, fraud and sharp practice (along with, let it be said, brilliant publishing, tremendous vision and entrepreneurship), he quite simply had nowhere else to go, and took what must have seemed the only course left open to him' (p. 110). In a footnote, Stevenson adds that he suspects that Maxwell 'would by now be garlanded with honours, including a peerage and chancellorship of a major university'. He appositely adds, 'To do it justice, his story deserves the creative attention of a great operatic composer' (p. 113).

It would be misleading to overlook useful materials in the *Harvard Library Bulletin*. The first two numbers of volume 19 [Spring/Summer 2008], although published in February 2010, will be covered in this review. They consist of William H. Bond's '"From the great desire of promoting learning": Thomas Hollis's Gifts to the Harvard College Library' (*HLB* 19:i–ii[2008] viii–206). This has an introduction by Allen Reddick (pp. 1–31) and a brief preface by William P. Stoneman (pp. vi–viii). In his preface Stoneman pays tribute to the work of William Henry Bond, who was the librarian of the Houghton Library at Harvard from 1965 to 1982 and whose 'Sandars Lectures in Bibliography at Cambridge University in 1982 became the basis of his well-received monograph, *Thomas Hollis of Lincoln's Inn: A Whig and His Books* (1990). He also edited "Letters from Thomas Hollis of Lincoln's Inn to Andrew Eliot" for *Proceedings of the Massachusetts Historical Society* [1988]' (p. 206). Allen Reddick's extensive introduction explains the background to Hollis's (1659–1731) gift to the New World, which Reddick divides into thirty-one categories of significance (pp. 23–6). As Reddick observes, 'Thomas Hollis's importance to eighteenth-century British culture and the dissemination of "liberty" throughout the world is being uncovered to an extent never before possible, even in his own lifetime. This checklist is a crucial step in the process of discovery' (p. 30). Bond's 'Checklist of Thomas Hollis's Gifts to the Harvard College Library' is alphabetically arranged and contains some descriptions, so it would be misleading to describe it as enumerative: see for instance his comments on the editions of John Locke (p. 122) and John Milton (pp. 132–6). The first author listed is 'Abbati Oliveri-Giordani, Annibale degli, 1708–1789' (p. 35) and the last author listed is 'Zurita, Jeronimo, 1512–1580' (p. 204). There are eight coloured illustrations containing Hollis's comments, sometimes on the acquisitions of his books: see for instance p. 177, his recounting of 'the complicated history of this damaged gift', that is, the copy of William Prynne's *An Exact Chronological Vindication* (London [1666]). The *Harvard Library Bulletin* (19:iii–iv [Fall/Winter 2008], published in April 2009, is devoted to 'Harvard's Lincoln' (*HLB* 19:iii–iv[2008] vii–80). In other words, the Abraham Lincoln collection of Thomas A. Horrocks. In effect, this is 'A Catalogue of an Exhibition at Houghton Library, 20 January–25 April 2009', curated by Thomas A. Horrocks (pp. 15–80). There is an interesting introduction by Horrocks (pp. 1–11), and a foreword by Harold Holzer (pp. v–vii). The issue contains twenty-one coloured accompanying illustrations.

The first issue of *The Huntington Library Quarterly* contains Philip Connell's 'Newtonian Physico-Theology and the Varieties of Whiggism in James Thomson's "The Seasons"' (*HLQ* 72:i[2009]) 1–28). Connell concentrates on the political, religious, and philosophical meanings of Thomson's poem. For Connell, the poem 'offers a supple and sophisticated commentary on the shifting politico-religious contexts of Newtonian natural philosophy in early Hanoverian England' (p. 1). Mark Crosby's '"A Fabricated Perjury": The [Mis]Trial of William Blake' (*HLQ* 72:i[2009] 29–47) examines the trial of William Blake, who, on 22 January 1804 was tried at the Chichester quarter sessions on charges of sedition. Crosby places this trial, Rex *v*. Blake, in its historical and legal context in order to examine William Blake's perception that 'the charges against him were "a Fabricated Perjury"'. Interestingly, Crosby 'reveals that the local justices of the peace misinterpreted the legislation governing the offenses that was used to try Blake'. For Crosby, the suggestion is 'that the Sussex authorities were prepared to misuse the law of sedition in order to set an example for the local populace as Britain mustered her defenses for the expected landing of Napoleon's Imperial Army' (p. 29). As with the other contributions to *HLQ*, Elizabeth Heckendorn Cook's 'Charlotte Smith and "The Swallow": Migration and Romantic Authorship' (*HLQ* 72:i[2009] 48–67), draws upon printed and manuscript materials at the Huntington Library. Cook examines the significance of the swallow in the work of Charlotte Smith, with especial focus upon her 'ornithological handbook for children and her posthumous "Beachy Head and Other Poems" (1807)'. For Cook, Smith rewrites, using 'the figure of the swallow, the traditional association of female art with the pathos of the Philomela-as-nightingale story'. Further, 'Signifying through its natural-historical associations simultaneously the domestic and the mysterious, the maternal and the exotic, the swallow offers Smith a complex and personally appropriate emblem of female Romantic authorship' (p. 48). Although this may sound rather pretentious, in fact the article contains interesting revelations about the use of birds as images in the work of a Romantic author such Charlotte Smith.

The great William Blake scholar G.E. Bentley, Jr., in his 'Blake's Murderesses: Visionary Heads of Wickedness' (*HLQ* 72:i[2009] 69–105), focuses upon four of Blake's portraits drawn between 1819 and 1825. These four 'depicted common murderesses, three of them from the eighteenth century'. Bentley is concerned with the sources of Blake's information, arguing that they came 'from the gutter press of contemporary pamphlets or compendia such as the "Newgate Calendar"'. Bentley reveals that 'Some of these bear inscribed portraits which Blake's Visionary Heads seem to echo. Blake's purpose may have been to discover whether the physiognomies of such moral monsters revealed their character. The banal portraits of Blake's murderous women suggest that the answer is no' (p. 69). Another eminent Blake scholar, Morton D. Paley, in his '"A Virgin of Twelve Years": Ololon in Blake's Milton' (*HLQ* 72:i[2009] 106–12), considers the significance of the age of 12 for the virgin in Blake's garden in his *Milton*. The expression 'as a Virgin of twelve years' does not have a biblical foundation, 'but occurs in the apocryphal Protoevangelium Jacobi, or "Infancy Gospel of James"' (p. 106). This first *HLQ* issue contains Philip J. Stern's review article, 'Neither East nor West, Border, nor Breed, nor Birth: Early Modern Empire and Global History' (*HLQ* 72:i[2009] 113–26). Stern considers four recently published works: Miles Ogborn's *Indian Ink: Script and Print in the Making of the English East India Company*; Alison Games's *The Web of Empire: English Cosmopolitans in an Age of Expansion, 1560–1660*; Linda Colley's *The Ordeal of Elizabeth Marsh: A Woman in World History*; and Miles Ogborn's *Global Lives: Britain and the World, 1550–1800*.

HLQ (72:ii[2009]) focuses on prison writings in early modern England. The context is set by John Taylor, William H. Sherman, and William J. Sheils in their preface (*HLQ* 72:ii[2009] 127–32). Thomas S. Freeman in his 'Introduction: The Rise of Prison Literature' (*HLQ* 72:ii[2009] 133–46), argues that 'prison writing became a characteristic cultural form of early modern England'. The seeds of its appeal are to be found in the increase in the prison population, especially amongst the educated elites who were incarcerated on political and religious grounds or for reasons of debt. There was also an increased audience of religious and political sympathizers and a growth in the book trade. However, 'prison was humiliating, injurious to reputation and dangerous to health'. As Freeman points out, 'Many questions about the causes and effects of this form of writing remain; it is nevertheless essential to an understanding of early modern culture, including the nature of crime and punishment and the history of the Reformation' (p. 133). His introduction is accompanied by forty-one references that provide a secondary bibliography of studies in prison literature.

Molly Murray, in her 'Measured Sentences: Forming Literature in the Early Modern Prison' (*HLQ* 72:ii[2009] 147–67), describes 'the early modern English prison [as] porous, unsystematic, and contingent, governed by particular and shifting relationships'. She 'recovers this vibrantly irregular prison world as an important site of textual production'. Using a neglected manuscript psalter that was produced in the Tower of London, Murray suggests a fresh manner of perceiving 'both the conditions and consolations of prison writing—especially prison poetry' (p. 147). Ruth Ahnert, in her 'Writing in the Tower of London during the Reformation, ca. 1530–1558' (*HLQ* 72:ii[2009] 168–92), specifically focuses on the Tower during the periods of Henry VIII,

Edward VI, and Mary I. Ahnert, and utilizes 'acts of graffiti, marginal annotations by Edward Seymour and Lady Jane Grey, and more canonical works of prison literature by Thomas More in order to suggest that, by writing, prisoners can assert themselves, create community, re-present their imprisonment as a pious retreat, or—in the case of More—transcend the penal system by eschewing the particularity of prison production' (p. 168). Ahnert's article is accompanied by fifty-five extensive footnote references. Jerome de Groot's 'Prison Writing, Writing Prison during the 1640s and 1650s' (*HLQ* 72:ii[2009] 193–215), examines the manner in which prison was perceived in the writings of those royalists who were imprisoned during the 1640s and 1650s. For de Groot, 'Prison writing shows us not simply the models that royalism deployed to represent itself but also how it understood and engaged with multiple other discourses, including law, religion, and dissidence'. (p. 193). De Groot's analysis is accompanied by eighty-eight references providing a guide to primary and secondary resources dealing with royalists during that period.

Robyn Adams's '"The service I am here for": William Herle in the Marshalsea Prison, 1571' (*HLQ* 72:ii[2009] 217–38), centres upon the letters the Elizabethan intelligence officer and agent provocateur William Herle (d. 1588/9) wrote to William Cecil, Lord Burghley. During the unfolding of the spring 1571 Ridolfi plot, Herle was incarcerated in the Marshalsea Prison on a piracy charge. He became a prison spy under the direction of the authorities, and his letters contain a rich documentation of Tudor prison life affording 'a glimpse of the conditions and layout of the ramshackle Marshalsea'. They also illuminate 'the prisoners' efforts to circumvent the restrictions of prison life by smuggling letters and objects through the porous membrane of the prison walls' (p. 217). This is fascinating stuff, perhaps providing raw material for a film or TV Sunday night drama. More pragmatic is William H. Sherman's 'Patents and Prisons: Simon Sturtevant and the Death of the Renaissance Inventor' (*HLQ* 72:ii[2009] 239–56). Simon Sturtevant (*c.*1570–1624?) was an eclectic author who wrote on subjects as diverse as lexicography and military technology. He also 'secured patents in the fields of hydraulic engineering, metallurgy, and book production'. However, in common with many other speculators, he ended up in the debtor's prison: 'his fate is a painful reminder of the epidemic of debt that swept through Elizabethan and Jacobean London, and he has much to teach us about those who made their livings—and sometimes lost their lives—during what Defoe would later call the first Age of Projects' (p. 239). Sherman's delving into an extremely obscure but fascinating life is documented by fifty-six references, including citations from Sturtevant's writings.

Catie Gills, 'Evans and Cheevers's "A Short Relation" in Context: Flesh, Spirit, and Authority in Quaker Prison Writings, 1650–1662' (*HLQ* 72:ii[2009] 257–72), focuses upon the English Quaker authors Catherine Evans and Sarah Cheevers's '"This is a Short Relation of Some of the Cruel Sufferings"...in the "Inquisition in the Island of Malta"' [1662]. This was written from a Maltese prison where they were incarcerated by a section of the Roman Inquisition. Their work is compared and contrasted with previous accounts of imprisonment written by Quakers. Gill focuses upon the manner in which the authors' gender affected both their experience and the way they wrote about it.

Gill highlights Evans and Cheevers's 'forthright resolve in denying their imprisoners' authority, their foregrounding of bodily suffering, and their evocation of Quaker antinomian and martyrological traditions' (p. 257). It hardly surprising that John Bunyan appears in this special issue of *HLQ* devoted to early modern prison literature. Kathleen Lynch's 'Into Jail and into Print: John Bunyan Writes the Godly Self' (*HLQ* 72:ii[2009] 273–90) concentrates on the impact of imprisonment upon his writing and the way in which the writing changed over time. For instance, *Grace Abounding* [1666] 'elaborated the oral testimony delivered to join a gathered church... with his lengthening imprisonment confirming the durability of his spiritual assurance'. Lynch argues that Bunyan in his other works perceives his time in prison as 'experienced variously as a suspension from his polemical work and as a repetitive framework to be filled with episodic narrative' (p. 273). Rivkah Zim's 'Afterword. Writing behind Bars: Literary Contexts and the Authority of Carceral Experience' (*HLQ* 72:ii[2009] 291–311) draws upon the testimony of Boethius, a sixteenth-century prisoner, and early modern examples of prisoners' writings, including works by Thomas More and John Bunyan, to illustrate 'how adversity was exploited to promote political strategies'. In addition, Zim 'considers some modern critical approaches to prison writing and proposes a conceptual framework for what we might call a politics of prison writing' (p. 291).

Debora Shuger's 'St Mary the Virgin and the Birth of the Public Sphere' (*HLQ* 72:iii[2009] 313–46) is concerned with Latin disputations in Elizabethan universities. These were necessary for the majority of university degrees. Interestingly, many of the disputations concerned complex current issues of a political and religious nature. J. Sears McGee's 'A "Carkass" of "Mere Dead Paper": The Polemical Career of Francis Rous, Puritan MP' (*HLQ* 72:iii[2009] 374–371), examines the prolific writings of Francis Rous (1581–1659), who was John Pym's stepbrother. For McGee, such a study 'can deepen our understanding of the development of Pym's ideology' and, furthermore, McGee 'examines a sharp polemical exchange between the Catholic Sir Tobie Mathew, the Laudian Christopher Potter, and the Puritan Rous that began in the early 1630s and analyzes Rous's writings up to the time he wrote his answer to Mathew' (p. 374). Andrea Brady's '"Without welt, gard, or embrodery": A Funeral Elegy for Cicely Ridgeway, Countess of Londonderry (1628)' (*HLQ* 72:iii[2009] 373–95) presents a previously unpublished and undiscovered seventeenth-century manuscript elegy. The poem 'written in tribute to one of Elizabeth's maids of honour, is unusual in the extensive biographical details it provides and in its depiction of an early modern woman's domestic life'. It reveals much about Cicely Ridgeway's character, 'including her resistance to the norms of "obedience" and her independence within marriage. Although the hypermetrical elegy may lack literary quality, it offers significant insights into the life of a seventeenth-century noblewoman' (p. 373). This issue of *HLQ* also includes detailed reviews of recent works dealing with the personalities and concerns of early modern England. These issues contain excellent illustrations taken from the Huntington's exceedingly rich and eclectic collections.

The entire December 2009 issue (*HLQ* 72:iv[2009] 1–101) is devoted to Peter Kidd's *Guide to Medieval and Renaissance Manuscripts in the Huntington Library*. Kidd's is a supplement to C.W. Dutschke's *Guide*, published in 1989, in two volumes. In acknowledgement of the twentieth anniversary of the *Guide*'s appearance, Kidd's supplement describes manuscripts acquired by the Huntington between 1988 and January 2009 as well as previously acquired fragments not described in the *Guide*. It should be added that most issues of *HLQ* contain regular reports on its recent acquisitions in the 'Intramuralia' section of the journal, and Kidd's supplement considerably amplifies these regular updatings. *YWES* readers hardly need reminding that each issue of *HLQ* also contains most useful book reviews.

The Eighteenth-Century Intelligencer, the bibliographically inclined bulletin of the East-Central American Society for Eighteenth-Century Studies, appeared in three numbers for 2009, new series, volume 23 (January, May, September, separately paginated). The January number begins with David Wallace Spielman's 'Bibliographic Information for Fifty-Three Unlocated Eighteenth-Century Items in [James Fullarton] Arnott and [John William] Robinson's *English Theatrical Literature, 1559–1900* [1970]' (*ECIntell* 23:i[2009] 1–16). Arnott and Robinson, though they normally examined the entries for their bibliography, entered some on the word of others, without having seen them. Spielman, taking advantage of the text-based Eighteenth Century Collections Online (ECCO), provides further references and describes the contents of these brief references. Organizing his augmented entries by Arnot and Robinson's reference numbers, Spielman provides author, title, imprint information, sale price if known, ECCO number (with library source for copy reproduced on ECCO), ESTC number (with number of copies recorded by the ESTC), pagination, and additional descriptive information, including summary. Some of these eighteenth-century publications on theatre prove important to theatre historians, and these are described at greater length. For instance, the *Petition of Stephen Kemble, Manager of New Theatre of Edinburgh* [1793], A&R #1957, is located in two copies; the discussion of Kemble's petition leads to the description of a related *Memorial for Stephen Kemble* [1793], which is not in Arnott and Robinson and is available on ECCO. Spielman subsequently revised this article and posted it at the Bibliographical Society of America's electronic internet archive, BibSite.

Also in the January issue is James E. May's 'Some Problems in ECCO (and ESTC)' (*ECIntell* 23:i[2009] 20–30), which surveys shortcomings in the search tool employed by Spielman that, according to some, is revolutionizing eighteenth-century studies. May identifies problems involving the digitized images, often arising from the microfilm on which they are based, and he notes the high error rate in searches. ECCO relies almost entirely on the ESTC for its bibliographical information; thus, the ESTC's errors for authorship, format, and relationship to other editions and issues are repeated in the ECCO citation page and also in the database's headings (errors are especially common in multi-volume works). Many of ECCO's flaws arise from the absence of any editorial expertise. The Gale Corporation producing the work had no staff to note such needed information as imperfections in the copy reproduced, differences between copies of the same edition when multiple copies in varying states were digitized, or misinformation on the title pages of works reproduced. May illustrates the sort of searches that have the highest error rates. He also warns readers that many editions recorded by the ESTC are not reproduced in ECCO and that many corrections and additions to the ESTC are not reflected in ECCO's reproduction of dated ESTC information (and, while the ESTC tends to indicate what editions are digitized on ECCO, ESTC fails to note many texts that have been reproduced on ECCO). The issue also includes Robert G. Walker's 'Hyenas and Black Swans: Notes on Annotating Richardson's *Grandison*' (*ECIntell* 23:i[2009] 17–20), reviews of over half a dozen books, a memorial tribute to the late J.A. Leo Lemay by Susan C. Imbarrato (*ECIntell* 23:i[2009] 55–7), accounts of tercentenary events for Samuel Johnson, and the note "Cover Illustration [for this *Intelligencer*]: Dr. Samuel Johnson Depicted in "Emblematical Frontispiece" from the *Gentleman's Magazine* 1747' by O.M. Brack, Jr. (*ECIntell* 23:i[2009] 59).

The May 2009 *Intelligencer* includes two articles related to periodicals of the long eighteenth century. In 'An Introduction to "The Newdigate Newsletters" (13 January 1674 through 29 September 1715)' (*ECIntell* 23:ii[2009] 7–18), Philip Hines, Jr., shares material from an early draft of his forthcoming transcription, or edition, of the 3,940 manuscript newsletters held by the Folger Shakespeare Library, most received by Sir Richard Newdigate, of Arbury, Warwickshire. Hines, who has been transcribing the newsletters for several decades, reported on the newsletters previously in three articles demonstrating their relevance to scholars (*Theatre Notebook*, in 1985, 1995, and 2002). Here he provides an overview of the manuscript cache (such as where there are gaps), a short account of their origins (in the Secretary of State's office), and some comparisons to the same day's texts in the Newdigate and other manuscript newsletters sent out from London (such as those to Greenwich Hospital). The other article on serials is by James E. May, much in the spirit of his critique of ECCO: 'Assessing the Inclusiveness of Searches in the Online Burney Newspaper Collection' (*ECIntell* 23:ii[2009] 28–34). The British Library digitized microfilm of newspapers, magazines, and tracts in its Burney Collection (the microfilm produced by Research Publications beginning in the 1970s); this product was then distributed by Gale Corporation, which had successfully distributed ECCO, another expensive subscription text-base. The online Burney Collection can be searched much as ECCO can, though the search engine is not quite as accurate and there are more difficulties showing the results. (The reproduced issues can also be browsed by title.) May reports on searches for the names of authors, titles, publishers, keywords in mottos, and the like in newspaper advertisements; he compares the results with advertisements known to be in the Burney collection from his earlier search of microfilm (much is missed, including entire editions repeatedly advertised, and much erroneous junk is caught in the nets). The issue also contains Hermann Josef Real's 'Paraklausithyron: Some Vestiges of a Forgotten Literary Genre in Seventeenth- and Eighteenth-Century Poetry', a note tracing from Theocritus to Matthew Prior a formulaic lament of the lover outside the beloved's locked door (*ECIntell* 23:ii[2009] 18–28).

The September *Intelligencer* offers a forum of compressed conference presentations by teachers and some students on their classroom experiences employing ECCO and EEBO. The latter is the searchable text-base Early English Books Online, which contains digitized seventeenth-century texts. The papers, from the East-Central American Society for Eighteenth-Century Studies meeting in autumn 2008, are assembled as 'Papers on Teaching with ECCO and EBBO', with a short introduction by Linda V. Troost (*ECIntell* 23:iii[2009] 3–29). The papers, some with tables and illustrations, are Nancy Mace's 'Using *ECCO* in Undergraduate Survey Courses' (*ECIntell* 23:iii[2009] 2–4); Eleanor F. Shevlin's 'Exploring Context and Canonicity: Lessons from the *ECCO* and *EEBO* Databases' (*ECIntell* 23:iii[2009] 4–13), with appendices offering sample search results and selected entries from a glossary distributed to students; Sayre N. Greenfield's 'Undergraduate Use of Search Engines in *EEBO* and *ECCO*' (*ECIntell* 23:iii[2009] 13–16); Michelle Sarver's 'Star: A Survey and Analysis of Linguistic Changes' involving the word 'star' (*ECIntell* 23:iii[2009] 16–21); Brian Glover's '*EEBO*, *ECCO*, and the Eighteenth-Century Novel Course' (*ECIntell* 23:iii[2009] 21–4); and Rachael Federico's Self-Help for Better Conduct (*ECIntell* 23:iii[2009] 24–9), which discusses conduct books as a context for Samuel Richardson's *Pamela*. The issue includes an exhibition review of a major eighteenth-century botanical artist and illustrator: 'Georg Dionysius Ehret at the New York Botanical Gardens', by Brijraj Singh (*ECIntell* 23:iii[2009] 30–2), as well as reviews and announcements relevant to scholars of eighteenth-century studies.

The Journal of Scholarly Publishing (*JScholP* 40:1[2009]) also continues to publish materials of interest. The second issue of volume 40 opens with an edited version of Lindsay Waters's keynote address to the Council of Editors of Learned Journals at the 2007 MLA Convention. Written with Jana L. Argersinger, it is entitled 'Slow Writing; or Getting off the Book Standard: What Can Journal Editors Do?' (*JScholP* 40:ii[2009] 129–43). Waters and Argersinger focus upon the journal editor's role in the essay form, which they argue 'is poised to take the ascendant' (p. 129). Jana L. Argersinger's 'Inside the Journal Editor's Office: A 2007 CELJ Roundtable' (*JScholP* 40:ii[2009] 144–83) provides information about papers 'discussed at the 2007 Modern Language Association (MLA) convention in Chicago' (p. 144), and also the essays presented at the Council of Editors of Learned Journals (CELJ) roundtable. Wendy Laura Belcher, in her 'Reflections on Ten Years of Teaching Writing to Graduate Students and Junior Faculty' (*JScholP* 40:ii[2009] 184–99), 'reports on the origins, pedagogy, structure, and limitations of a writing workshop the author devised for graduate students and faculty to aid them in publishing articles in peer-reviewed journals' (p. 184). An interesting topical concern is the subject of Stephen K. Donovan's 'A Tax on Productivity?' (*JScholP* 40:ii[2009] 201–5). Donovan focuses upon the implications of the PDF, which he argues 'has seen a revitalization of the offprint, reducing authors' costs and making papers widely available from multiple sources on the World Wide Web' (p. 201). William W. Savage tackles pertinent concerns that others may be fearful of tackling. His 'The Transom End Runs and End Runners' (*JScholP* 40:ii[2009] 206–11) is no exception. Savage 'reflects on responsible scholarly publication' and 'discusses how people with higher positions used their connections and superiority to publish papers without taking in consideration the quality' (p. 206).

JScholP 40:iii[2009] has interesting articles of relevance to *YWES* readers. Joan F. Cheverie, Jennifer Boettcher, and John Buschman, in their 'Digital Scholarship in the University Tenure and Promotion Process' (*JScholP* 40:iii[2009] 219–30), consider various perceptions of digital scholarship, especially in terms of promotion and tenure in North American university settings. Allan H. Pasco's 'Should Graduate Students Publish?' (*JScholP* 40:iii[2009] 231–40) considers the pros and cons of the question. He concludes that 'While the process of turning papers into first-rate publications can be a wonderfully useful experience, it can also take more time than students can afford and be undeservedly damaging to their self-confidence' (p. 231). However, his interesting article fails to consider pressures produced by the diminishing job market on both sides of the Atlantic and elsewhere. These days a well-placed, refereed article or articles may well make the difference between a job interview and not being called for the final cut. Victor N. Shaw's 'Scholarly Publishing: Reforms for User Friendliness and System Efficiency' (*JScholP* 40:iii[2009] 241–62), examines the complex interrelationships between editors, publishers, authors, and scholars. Shaw writes, 'In academic publishing, editors and publishers may think that they give too much leeway to authors and scholars in terms of content, quality control, and scheduling of production, while academic contributors grumble that they are cold-shouldered, pushed around, manipulated, and even abused by the publisher and the printing establishment' (p. 241). Marianne Cotugno's 'A Benevolent Conspiracy: Conrad Richter, Paul Reynolds, Jr. and Alfred A. Knopf' (*JScholP* 40:iii[2009] 263–86) examines the relationship between the author Conrad Richter, his agent, Paul Reynolds, Jr., and Alfred A. Knopf, the publisher. Richter (1890–1968), a now forgotten novelist, won the Pulitzer Prize in 1951 for *The Town* and the American National Book Award in 1961 for *The Waters of Kronos*.

The pre-eminent antipodean bibliographical journal *Script & Print* (*BSANZB*) volume 33, numbers i–iv [2009], edited by Meredith Sherlock, Brian McMullin, and Wallace Kirsop, is entitled *Superior in his Profession: Essays in Memory of Harold Love*. It is devoted to recording the life and achievements of probably the most distinguished Australian bibliographer and textual editor of the twentieth century. Meredith Sherlock's preface (*BSANZB* 33:i–iv[2009] 7–8) outlines briefly Love's career and achievements, mentioning something that may be forgotten: his great love of music. Brian McMullin and Meredith Sherlock's 'Harold Love—A Bibliography' (*BSANZB* 33:i–iv[2009] 9–27) records its subject's accomplishments starting in 1965 and concluding with three items in press. Lurline Stuart's 'Harold Love: A Personal Memoir' (*BSANZB* 33:i–iv[2009] 28–31) is the memoir of a mature student who studied with Love at Monash University in the late 1960s. B.J. McMullin's '"Queen Mab what's she?"' (*BSANZB* 33:i–iv[2009] 32–44) considers Mercutio's 'Queen Mab' speech in the fourth scene of the first act of Shakespeare's *Romeo and Juliet* that 'has long been identified by editor's of the play as being problematic, particularly in its repetitions and in the ordering of its lines in what is accepted as the most authoritative early text, the text used as the basis for modern editions' (p. 32). John Emmerson's 'The English Pamphlet Trade in 1642' (*BSANZB* 33:i–iv[2009] 45–60) is accompanied by eight full-page black and white reproductions and considers another field that interested Harold Love. Nicholas Fisher's 'Mending What Fletcher Wrote: Rochester's Reworking of Fletcher's *Valentinian*' (*BSANZB* 33:i–iv[2009] 61–75) is a clear account of Rochester's reworking, and John Burrows's 'Mulgrave, Dryden, and *An Essay upon Satire*' (*BSANZB* 33:i–iv[2009] 76–91) considers an issue drawn to Burrows's 'attention by Harold Love early in 2005' (p. 76) relating to the complex relationship between the work of John Sheffield, third earl of Mulgrave, and John Dryden. Burrows's essay is accompanied by three statistical tables and two figures drawn from computer-generated texts.

Felicity Henderson, in her 'Robert Hooke's Archive' (*BSANZB* 33:i–iv[2009] 92–108), following 'a brief survey of the archive reveals dimensions to Hooke's work that had not previously been given much thought' (p. 107). Clive Probyn's '"Players and Scrapers": Dean Swift Goes Shopping, for Music' (*BSANZB* 33:i–iv[2009] 109–24) examines the issue of Jonathan Swift's relationship to music and concludes with an 'Appendix: Swift's "Shopping List" in Forster MS 519' (p. 124) revealing Swift's search for books of anthems. Judith Milhous and Robert D. Hume write on 'Theatre Account Books in Eighteenth-Century London' (*BSANZB* 33:i–iv[2009] 125–35). Patrick Spedding's 'Lady Mary Wortley Montagu, Manuscript Publication and the Vanity of Popular Applause' (*BSANZB* 33:i–iv[2009] 136–60) examines 'Montagu's letters to her daughter and explain[s] how these may reflect her attitudes to authorship, writing and publishing'. He also looks at 'the evidence for Montagu's publishing activities in manuscript and in print, and consider[s] why it may be that Montagu's words and actions have been so often misunderstood' (p. 136). Peter Shillingsburg's 'Editing Lectures as Performances or Publication: Thackeray's *The Four Georges*' (*BSANZB* 33:i–iv[2009] 161–75) reveals the complications involved in preparing an edition of Thackeray's lectures. Shillingsburg concludes by providing an 'Appendix of Examples' that 'will suffice to demonstrate that sorting out the motives for changes and distinguishing the deliberate from the inadvertent [is] not easy' (p. 171). Elizabeth Webby's 'Harlequin in Van Diemen's Land' (*BSANZB* 33:i–iv[2009] 176–84) opens with an account of her initial meeting with Harold Love in the late 1970s and then proceeds to discuss his encouragement of her work on nineteenth-century Australian pantomime. Robert Jordan's 'Australia's Worst Actor? The Life, Art, and Business Practices of Mr. Henry Kemble of Drury Lane, Monopolylogist' (*BSANZB* 33:i–iv[2009] 185–217) is an account of Henry Kemble's relationship with Australia and reveals much about the state of the Sydney theatre in the middle of the nineteenth century.

Wallace Kirsop's '"Romancing the Stone": R.H. Horne, Daniel Deniehy and Lithography' (*BSANZB* 33:i–iv[2009] 217–21) is a short account of a copy of R.H. Horne's *Exposition of the False Medium and Barriers Excluding Men of Genius from the Public* [1832–3] that emerged in a March 2009 Australian book auction. The work 'has a reputation of being the first . . . to reveal the existence of publishers' readers to the world at large' (p. 217). Kirsop also contributes 'Adelaide Ristori's Friends and Admirers in Sydney in 1875: The Story of an Illuminated Address' (*BSANZB* 33:i–iv[2009] 222–33). This is a record of a purchase made in 1961 from Tyrrell's Bookshop in George Street,

Sydney. Mary Jane Edwards's 'William Kirby's *The Chien D'Or/The Golden Dog/A Legend of Quebec*: Translation and Transformation' (*BSANZB* 33:i–iv[2009] 234–50) is a 'much revised version' of a paper she gave in 2004. Harold Love was in the audience and greatly encouraged her, so she dedicates 'this much revised version of my Vancouver talk to the memory of Harold Love' (p. 234). In the final contribution, Paul Eggert, in his 'Advice for Scholarly Editors of Australian Literature: "Just Push On"' (*BSANZB* 33:i–iv[2009] 251–63), focuses 'on the activity of scholarly editing in Australia' and Harold Love's involvement with the 'Academy Editions of Australian Literature' (p. 251).

This seems the appropriate place to mention John Arnold and John Hay's *The Bibliography of Australian Literature, P–Z*, that 'completes the alphabetical listing of the creative output in book form by Australian authors since the beginning of European settlement in Australia to the year 2000'. In their introduction Arnold and Hay remind their readers that '*BAL* focuses on creative literature in its narrower definition. The genres covered are drama, poetry and fiction (including collections of short stories by a single author)'. In addition, 'Works for children in these genres are also included and listed under the encompassing heading Children's Books Include' (p. 9). There are three appendices: 'Excluded and Relocated Authors and Titles (P–Z)' (pp. 795–8), 'Index of Pseudonyms and Variant Names' (pp. 799–870), and 'Index of Titles' (pp. 871–993). *BAL* is a great work and record of centuries of creative achievement.

The *Book and Magazine Collector* has been arriving irregularly, so assessment here will not be as comprehensive as one would wish. The March 2009 issue contains, replete with illustrations, an article by Richard Dalby on the illustrations for A.A. Milne's *Winnie-the-Pooh* (*BMC* 305[2009] 12–19). Crispin Jackson's 'Saints, Singers and L. Ron Hubbard' (*BMC* 305[2009] 23–9) reflects upon his thirteen years as *BMC*'s editor and the fashions in the book trade, as does Jonathan Scott in his 'The Secret Collector' (*BMC* 305[2009] 33–5). Richard Dalby, a contributor and adviser to *BMC* since its initial issue 'looks back over the trends of a quarter century' (p. 36) in British-based book collecting and selling activity in his 'The First Twenty-Five Years' (*BMC* 305[2009] 36–9). Jonathan Scott, in 'Gilt-Edged Bonds' (*BMC* 305[2009] 42–53), naturally replete with glossy illustrations, 'gauges the recession-proof market in Ian Fleming's James Bond books' (p. 42). This is accompanied with a price listing of 'James Bond—the US First Editions' (p. 52). Rod Collins's 'How to Spot a Fake Spy' (*BMC* 305[2009] 54–5) examines the issue of 'faked Fleming signatures [and] has put together some tips for the wary' (p. 54). Mark Valentine's 'Saki—Edwardian Satirist' (*BMC* 305[2009] 58–66) is a detailed account of the life and writings of Hector Hugh Munro (1870–1916), otherwise known as Saki, followed by 'Saki (H.H. Munro)—Complete UK Bibliography' (p. 66). Mark Valentine's 'The Lost Saki Satire' (*BMC* 305[2009] 68–76) contains Saki's contributions to '*The House Annual*, a Christmas charity anthology in 1902' (p. 68), and contains the accompanying illustrations (pp. 70–6). David Howard writes on 'The Books of V.S. Naipaul' (*BMC* 305[2009] 78–88), and concludes with 'V.S. Naipaul—UK Bibliography' (pp. 88–9). It should be said that the *BMC* bibliographies are very basic listings in date order of first appearance, containing title, publisher, date of publication, and a 'Priceguide to current values of first editions in fine condition without (and with) dustjackets' (p. 88). In the instance of Naipul, there is also a listing of 'Essential Reading' (p. 89). Rosalind Parker writes a short but interesting article on the largely neglected 'Harry Crosby' (*BMC* 305[2009] 92–8), 'experimental poet, photographer, pilot and co-proprietor of the Black Sun Press [who] died by his own hand at the age of 31 on 10 December 1929' (p. 93). Rosalind Parker's account concludes with 'Harry Crosby—Bibliography' (p. 99), some of the titles being expensive. The final contribution to this March 2009 issue is by David Ashford, who 'celebrates Fenimore Cooper's classic American novel and all its many appearances in films, illustrations and picture strips' (p. 102). Ashford's appropriately illustrated 'The Last of the Mohicans' (*BMC* 305[2009] 102–14) concludes with 'The Last of the Mohicans Price Guide' (p. 115).

The April issue of *BMC*, in addition to the usual guide to auctions and prices realized, contains Mike Ashley's 'Churchill in the Strand' (*BMC* 306[2009] 30–9), and Ashley's 'Churchill in the Strand—Price Guide' (*BMC* 306[2009] 40–1), which 'lists all of Sir Winston Churchill's contribution to the English edition of *The Strand* grouped by volume with individual issues cited. It also lists important items about Churchill' (p. 40). Crispin Jackson's 'Welcome to Hard Times' (*BMC* 306[2009] 60–9) is concerned with answering the questions 'which books should we turn to make sense of the current debacle, and to answer the three basic questions which must exercise the minds of all serious people at this dark time: how did we get here? Where are we heading? And where do we look for salvation?' (p. 61). So Jackson describes books on 'greed' (p. 61), ranging from Dickens's *Little Dorrit* to Trollope's *The Way We Live Now*. The second question contains comments on 'Richard Jefferies' apocalyptic novel *After London or, Wild England* (1885)' and H.G. Wells's *The Time Machine* [1895]. John Kenneth Galbraith's *The Affluent Society* [1958] is singled out as 'Probably the most widely-read modern work of economics' (p. 67). The article concludes with '*David Copperfield* and a man whose life has been one long credit crisis: Wilkins Micawber' (p. 70). Jackson's timely article concludes with 'Surviving the Crash—Price Guide to Key Titles', the most expensive item listed being Adam Smith's *An Enquiry into the Nature and Causes of the Wealth of Nations*, published in two volumes by Strahan & Cadell in 1776. Even a re-bound set is priced between £30,000 and £50,000 and more (p. 71).

Mike Gent writes on 'Alan Moore: Fearful Symmetry' (*BMC* 306[2009] 76–87), the American comic 'medium's first superstar writer [who] emerged from the unlikely setting of Northampton, England' (p. 77). Apart from rather garish illustrations there is an 'Alan Moore Bibliography' (pp. 88–93). Incidentally, no item seems to be highly priced; most may be found for no more than £20, although the 1991 paperback *Miracleman Book Three: Olympus* published by Eclipse may well cost over £200! Sean Egan writes about and interviews the American Midwest novelist William Goldman (*BMC* 306[2009] 94–103). Curiously, no price listing accompanies the interview. In 'Algernon Charles Swinburne' (*BMC* 306[2009] 104–11), 'on the centenary of his death on 10 April 1909, Rikky Rooksby assesses recent additions to the

Swinburne shelf' (p. 104). Rooksby also contributes 'Algernon Charles Swinburne: Select UK Bibliography' (*BMC* 306[2009] 112–13).

The May issue leads with Richard Dalby's 'Dracula: A Special Report, and some New Collectables' (*BMC* 307[2009] 10–13). Dalby gives an account of Dublin City Council's ' "One City One Book" project' which in April 2009 was 'devoted to Bram Stoker and his classic novel *Dracula* (1897)' (p. 10). Nick Hogarth's 'Shakespeare' (*BMC* 307[2009] 24–33) is an account of the 'booming... Shakespeare industry' (p. 25). There is an accompanying 'Shakespeare: A Select Bibliography' (*BMC* 307[2009] 34–7), although the present writer is not too convinced of the necessity to include brief details of the First Folio with its price indication of £2.5–£3.5 million (p. 34). Richard Dalby presents a very readable account of 'The Campaigns of Arthur Conan Doyle: His Non-Fiction, Plays and Poetry' (*BMC* 307[2009] 40–9), followed by 'Arthur Conan Doyle—UK/US Bibliography' (*BMC* 307[2009] 50–1). This is followed by David Blake's 'The Detective Novels of Phoebe Atwood Taylor: A Centenary Tribute' (*BMC* 307[2009] 54–64), and his 'Phoebe Atwood Taylor—US/UK Bibliography' (*BMC* 307[2009] 64–5). Mark Baldwin writes a fascinating account of 'Behind Enemy Lines: The Literature of the Special Operations Executive' (*BMC* 307[2009] 71–83), and 'The Special Operations Executive –UK Bibliography' (*BMC* 307[2009] 84–5). Mike Ashley's 'The Passing Show' (*BMC* 307[2009] 86–98) is an account of '*The Passing Show*... a weekly paper of humour and short fiction'. This had two incarnations. In its first it 'ran from 20 March 1915 to 19 March 1932, a total of 918 issues'. The second incarnation saw a total revamping and continuation 'as *The New Passing Show* (though the title soon reverted) from 26 March 1932 to 25 February 1939, a further 362 issues'. Ashley's article focuses upon the second incarnation, and the contributors and cartoonists, who included Charles Crombie, Owen Aves, Barry Pain, W.A. Darlington, and others (p. 87). P.J. Wodehouse's serial *The Luck of the Bodkins* started in the issue of 21 September 1935 and was illustrated by Illingworth (p. 90). This fascinating account is accompanied by a price guide; a complete run from the 26 March 1932 to 25 February 1939 with 362 issues is estimated to cost around £3,000. Contributors include Edgar Rice Burroughs, Dorothy L. Sayers, John Dickson Carr, Bruce Bairnsfather, W. Heath Robinson, and others (p. 98). 'Fritz Leiber [1910–92], one of the most versatile and unorthodox writers of science fiction, fantasy and horror ever' (p. 101) is the focus of John Howards's 'Fritz Leiber' (*BMC* 307[2009] 100–11). The tribute to this Chicago-born fantasist inevitably contains some suitably gory illustrations and is accompanied by 'Fritz Leiber—US/UK Bibliography' (*BMC* 307[2009] 111–13).

The October issue, in addition to Andrew Thomas's 'Unidentified Flying Objects' (*BMC* 312[2009] 28–42), with 'Unidentified Flying Objects US & UK Bibliography' (*BMC* 312[2009] 43–5), contains the second part of Rupert Neelands's 'Dr. Samuel Johnson' (*BMC* 312[2009] 48–63). The first part was published in issue 311, which was not sent to the present reviewer. Neelands, an eminent London bookman, focuses in this part on *Rasselas*, and concludes with a selected bibliography of Samuel Johnson (pp. 61–3). The collecting of Johnson is an expensive business. Mark Warby writes on 'Bruce Bairnsfather in Magazines' (*BMC* 312[2009] 67–79), and contributes 'Bruce Bairnsfather UK & US Magazine Bibliography 1915–1959' (*BMC* 312[2009] 80–3). The Bairnsfather collector need not expend even three-quarters of what would be needed for the Samuel Johnson collector. Mike Ashley writes on 'Wodehouse in the Strand' (*BMC* 312[2009] 88–98), followed by 'Wodehouse in the Strand—Price Guide' (*BMC* 312[2009] 98–103), and James Doig writes on 'R.R. Ryan' (*BMC* 312[2009] 104–12), 'one of the most collectible twentieth-century thriller writers' (p. 105). The article concludes with 'R.R. Ryan Bibliography' (p. 112). There is a brief, informative 'Note on Late Issue Dustjackets' (*BMC* 312[2009] 104), by Richard Dalby, focusing upon Agatha Christie and Ryan.

The December issue contains Nick Hogarth's 'The Wasp in a Wig' (*BMC* 314[2009] 26–39), focusing upon Lewis Carroll hoaxes, and is accompanied by 'Collecting Carrolliana: The Missing Episode of Alice: A Select Bibliography' (pp. 41–2). Richard Dalby's 'Edward Fitzgerald's *Rubáiyát of Omar Khayyam*: A 150th Anniversary Celebration' (*BMC* 314[2009] 44–59), contains glossy pictures and 'Edward Fitzgerald's *Rubáiyát of Omar Khayyam* UK/US Bibliography' (*BMC* 314[2009] 59–61). David Howard contributes 'The Books of Elizabeth Jenkins' (*BMC* 314[2009] 66–77), accompanied by embarrassing pink and concluding with 'Elizabeth Jenkins UK Bibliography' (p. 77). Vic Pratt's 'Robert Crumb: Keep on Trucking' (*BMC* 314[2009] 82–94), centres upon underground comics and concludes with a detailed 'Robert Crumb—Bibliography and Price Guide' (*BMC* 314[2009] 95–9). Barry Forshaw's 'James Crumley' (*BMC* 314[2009] 100–9), is aimed at 'Aficionados of the best American crime writing' (p. 101): there is even a 'James Crumley—US/UK Bibliography' (p. 109). Stephen Honey hones in on 'Jeff Clements: Designer, Bookbinder: Part I' (*BMC* 314[2009] 110–13). The contents of the December issue, ranging from Lewis Carroll hoaxes to Edward Fitzgerald and San Francisco comics, reveal that *BMC* appeals to an eclectic range of readers with eclectic reservoirs of pocket money. There is always something interesting to be found in the illustrated issues and in the prefatory short items describing book chat, new collectibles, and even providing 'Haggling: A Beginners Guide' by Stephen Honey (*BMC* 314[2009] 20–3).

In a highly interesting article, Russell McDonald focuses on 'Revision and Competing Voices in D.H. Lawrence's Collaborations with Women' (*Textual Cultures* 4:i[Spring 2009] 1–25), in which McDonald focuses on D.H. Lawrence's working relationships with Louie Burrows on his short story 'Goose Fair', Jesse Chambers on *Sons and Lovers*, and Mollie Skinner, the Australian novelist, on his late novel *The Boy in the Bush*. McDonald observes that 'The vibrant interplay of male and female voices that animates many of the drafts, fragments, and published versions of these works reveals' their author's 'desire to preserve his disagreements with women by letting their contributions stand in unresolved dialogue with his own.' Further, McDonald 'examines some uses and limitations of the *Cambridge Edition of the Works of D.H. Lawrence*, which too often misrepresents Lawrence's literary-cultural contexts of production by codifying works he wrote with others as products of his genius alone'. Most interestingly, McDonald notes that Lawrence 'repeatedly invited and often depended on women to help share the texts "he would have wished to see printed"' (p. 1).

Maura Ives, in another informative essay, 'Teaching Women's Art in America: Alice Donlevy's Designs for Christina Rossetti's *Consider*' (*Textual Cultures* 4:i[Spring 2009] 26–54), contextualizes Alice Donlevy's *Practical Hints on the Art of Illumination* [1867]. Ives reveals that Donlevy's poem *Consider* and her book were published 'not only as a tribute to [Christina] Rossetti, but as a demonstration of her own knowledge, talent, and authority'. According to Ives's account, 'Donlevy incorporated and revised Rossetti's poem as well as the poetry of Adelaide Procter within *Practical Hints* as part of her effort to formulate a model and establish a collaborative artistic process for her readers' (p. 26).

Linda Charnes's 'Anticipating Nostalgia: Finding Temporal Logic in a Textual Anomaly' (*Textual Cultures* 4:i[Spring 2009] 72–83), in spite of its slightly off-putting title 'proposes new ways of imagining textual history by exploring radically diverse cultural relationships to time'. Charnes discusses Lewis Theobald's 1733 emendation of the Folio text of *Henry V*, 'a Table of green fields' to '[a] babled of green fields'. In this way, Theobald laid 'the affective and interpretive groundwork for what would become, in successive centuries, a sentimentalized version both of Falstaff as a character and of England's empire-building as a nation'. Charnes cleverly utilizes what she refers to as 'this extraordinary textual *crux*' in order to comprehend the manner in which 'an eighteenth-century medical term, "nostalgia," which was originally conceived as a disease involving a disordered relationship to place, evolved into a more generalized term involving a longing to return to a glorious, and misrecognized, past' (p. 72).

David L. Vander Meulen's 'Bibliography and Other History' (*Textual Cultures* 4:i[Spring 2009] 113–28) distinguishes and relates 'three forms of intellectual activity: bibliography, textual criticism, and book history' (p. 113). Vander Meulen's essay is divided into three parts. In the first, he considers 'Definitions' (pp. 114–18). In the second he considers 'Relations' between the three approaches (pp. 118–21), and in the third, 'Conclusion' (pp. 121–6), he attempts to wrestle with the question, 'How *do* these three subjects relate?' For Vander Meulen, the 'approaches intersect... when they deal with physical books' (p. 121). Vander Meulen writes that 'ignoring other scholarship impedes the growth of understanding' (p. 126). Somewhat curiously, his listing of 'Works Cited' finds some eminent authors such as Fredson Bowers and G. Thomas Tanselle quoted much more extensively than any others, leading to the conclusion, perhaps a not altogether healthy one, that many fields of intellectual endeavour—and bibliography appears to be no exception—have their role models or authorities! Vander Meulen's is a well-written and well-argued account of the state of play as it exists in the three interrelated fields, 'bibliography, textual criticism, and book history'.

H. Wayne Storey's 'Interpretative Mechanisms in the Textual Cultures of Scholarly Editing' (*Textual Cultures* 4:i[Spring 2009] 129–47) is a companion piece to Vander Meulen's article. Both originated in talks given at the Fourteenth Biennial International Interdisciplinary Conference of the Society for Textual Scholarship held in New York in March 2007. Vander Meulen's essay is historically based; Wayne Storey's, on the other hand, 'examines recent questions in the field of textual criticism and its relations to book history, historical linguistics, bibliography, codicology, and literary criticism'. Wayne Storey is far less Anglo-American-orientated in his references than Vander Meulen, and 'investigates the place of material philology and the thorny questions of interpretation, the stemma codicum, and the textus receptus as—for better or worse—essential parts of scholarly editing' (p. 129). The Spring 2009 issue of *Textual Cultures* concludes with reviews including Peter P. Reed's 'Anglo-American Review Essay' focusing on 'Book Objects, Archives, and Ritual Repertoires in Colonial New England' (*Textual Cultures* 4:i[Spring 2009] 148–50).

There are three references to the work of the great W.W. Greg (1857–1959) in Vander Meulen's listing of 'Works Cited' (p. 127), demonstrating that some of Greg's work has stood the test of time. The Autumn 2009 *Textual Cultures* is devoted to assessments of W.W. Greg and his relevance today. A.S.G. Edwards's 'W.W. Greg Fifty Years On' (*Textual Cultures* 4:ii[Spring 2009] 1–2), deals with the genesis for the present tribute to Greg, explaining that the papers 'were all originally delivered at a conference, "W.W. Greg: Aspects of a Life" held at Trinity College, Cambridge on 14 March 2009' (p. 1). In effect, this marked the fiftieth anniversary of Greg's death. Michael Caines's 'W.W. Greg Beyond Bibliography' (*Textual Cultures* 4:ii[Spring 2009] 3–20) examines the non-bibliographical side of Greg, including his 'interests in poetry and mountaineering, his personal association with *The Economist* and study of economics, his childhood and his responses to the First and Second World Wars'. Caines's intention is 'to discern something of the man behind the "remote, Olympian figure" of New Bibliography (as F.C. Francis saw him)'. Furthermore, Caines's paper 'suggests that both the systematic mind and the literary sensibility that inform Greg's writings on bibliographical matters are present in these non-bibliographical aspects of his life' (p. 3).

David McKitterick's 'W.W. Greg, the Scholar-Librarian' (*Textual Cultures* 4:ii[Spring 2009] 21–30) places Greg's work within the context of the library at Trinity College, Cambridge: Greg was appointed its librarian in 1907 at the age of 32, but did not stay very long. McKitterick considers the impact of the library's 'Capell collection of Shakespeareana'. This became 'an ideal resource with which to pursue his discussions on editorial matters with A.W. Pollard, R.B. McKerrow, and others'. Part of this discourse is revealed in Greg's 'annotated copy of Pollard's study of the Shakespeare folios and quartos (1909), and while Librarian he also wrote his pioneering account of the Pavier quartos. At the same time he was modernizing the college library' (p. 21).

A.C. Green's 'The Difference Between McKerrow and Greg' (*Textual Cultures* 4:ii[Spring 2009] 31–53) compares and contrasts the work of the two, paying particular attention to *The Editorial Problem in Shakespeare* [1942], and *Prolegomena for the Oxford Shakespeare* [1939], respectively. Green utilizes unpublished correspondence and 'also considers the genesis of Greg's views on the "rationale of copy-text"' (p. 31). A.S.G. Edward's 'W.W. Greg and Medieval English Literature' (*Textual Cultures* 4:ii[Spring 2009] 54–62) examines a neglected area of Greg's work, his 'writings on palaeography and codicology, the Middle English lyric, Chaucer, alliterative poetry, and medieval drama' (p. 54). As Edwards concludes, these writings 'provides us, at the very least, with a further reminder of the multi-facetedness of Greg's rich intellectual life' (p. 61). T.H. Howard-Hill's 'W.W. Greg as Bibliographer' (*Textual Cultures* 4:ii[Spring 2009] 63–75), a well-written account, discusses Greg's perception of bibliography and bibliographical investigation and pays particular attention to what 'is widely regarded as a monument of descriptive bibliography', Greg's 'monumental' (p. 63) *A Bibliography of the English Printed Drama to the Restoration* (4 vols.; London: Bibliographical Society [1939–59]). Laurie Maguire's 'W.W. Greg as Literary Critic' (*Textual Cultures* 4:ii[Spring 2009] 76–87) considers Greg's 'three forays into interpretive literary criticism', his 'articles on *Dr. Faustus*, *Hamlet*, and *King Lear*' (p. 76). Gary Taylor's '*In Media Res*: From Jerome through Greg to Jerome (McGann)' (*Textual Cultures* 4:ii[Spring 2009] 88–101) considers the reasons for 'Greg's neglect of Jerome, the most influential editor in the Western tradition' (p. 88). For McGann, Greg 'transcribed, he did not translate'. Taylor writes that both Greg and Jerome 'belong to the larger field of transmediation, a practical and conceptual category that links the work of editors as different as Jerome, Greg, and McGann' (p. 88). In the final essay of this fascinating and informative issue, Sukanta Chaudhuri considers 'W.W. Greg, Postmodernist' (*Textual Cultures* 4:ii[Spring 2009] 102–10). For Chaudhuri, 'Authenticating new editorial practices like the validation of parallel or alternative texts of the same work, Greg's contributions to editorial theory anticipate many premises of contemporary postmodern thought' (p. 102).

This assessment of a special issue devoted to Greg, and we are much indebted to A.S.G. Edwards for seeing it through to fruition, should not conclude without two personal reminiscences. Firstly, the present writer wished some years ago to write a monograph on Greg. He decided to go to the Yale Elizabethan Collection to examine Greg's personal copies, for instance his copy of *Hamlet*. Greg, the present audience hardly needs telling, wrote much and expended much time on the editorial problems involved with *Hamlet*. His copy of the work at the Yale Elizabeth Collection was, surprisingly, more or less unannotated. The same was true of copies of the other texts which he'd spent so much time writing about. Further, a letter to his daughter, then getting on in years, received the reply that her memories of her father were not terribly positive and that I could use what I liked of unpublished materials relating to him. The letter contained an anecdote concerning a visit to an Old Vic production of *Hamlet* which her mother had forced her father to attend with his daughter and wife. According to the daughter's recollections, the unwilling W.W. Greg went to the theatre and promptly fell asleep, snoring rather loudly. As soon as the intervals occurred, he automatically woke up! Needless to say, somehow the letter put me off writing about W.W. Greg and I passed the work on to Joseph Rosenbaum, who produced *Sir Walter William Greg* [1998], a collection of his writings and articles on Greg: some of these are curiously neglected in this issue of *Textual Cultures*.

James G. Buickerood's edited *Eighteenth-Century Thought*, volume 4, contains several essays and a review essay of interest to *YWES* readers. John Locke seems to be the main focus. Essays include: J.C. Walmsley and

E. Meyer's 'John Locke's "Respirationis usus": Text and Translation' (pp. 1–28); Philip Milton's 'John Locke's Expulsion from Christ Church in 1684' (pp. 29–65); Nathaniel Wolloch's '*The Turkish Spy* and Eighteenth-Century British Theriophily' (pp. 67–85), in which Wolloch 'examines the importance of *The Turkish Spy*, a popular literary work in eighteenth-century Britain, for understanding early modern theriophilic argumentation in favor of animals' (p. 67); Peter R. Anstey's 'The Experimental History of the Understanding from Locke to Sterne' (pp. 143–69); Lorne Falkenstein's 'Hume on "Genuine," "True," and "Rational" Religion' (pp. 171–201); James A. Harris's 'Innateness in British Philosophy, *c.*1750–1820' (pp. 203–27); Anthony J. Di Lorenzo's 'Dissenting Protestantism as a Language of Revolution in Thomas Paine's *Common Sense*' (pp. 229–83); and Judith C. Mueller's 'Animal Ascension in the Long Eighteenth Century: The Contested "Creature" of Romans 8' (pp. 285–310). For Mueller, 'The debate about Romans 8 reflects a range of beliefs among eighteenth-century British Christians about the value inherent in the nonhuman world' (p. 285). The volume concludes with Mark Goldie's 'Review Essay' on 'The Present State of Locke Biography' (pp. 373–96). There is a name-based index (pp. 399–410).

Kathryn Duncan's edited collection, *Religion in the Age of Reason: A Transatlantic Study of the Long Eighteenth Century*, is part of AMS Studies in the Eighteenth Century. Twelve scholars, Anne Barbeau Gardiner, Kevin L. Cope, Patricia C. Brückmann, Gary Kuchar, Michael Austin, Bob Tennant, Harry Clark Maddux, Katherine M. Quinsey, Michael Rotenberg-Schwartz, Brian Fehler, Brett C. McInelly, and Peter Nockles analyse the role played by religion during the seventeenth and eighteenth centuries. Subjects range from 'Fading Fast but Still in Print: The Brink of Visibility and the Form of Religious Experience, Spinoza to Cowper' (Kevin L. Cope; pp. 19–42) to Brett C. McInelly's 'Method or Madness: Methodist Devotion and the Anti-Methodist Response' (pp. 195–210). The volume is nicely produced, the binding is firm, and the notes are not relegated to the end of the text of individual essays but found at the foot of the page. Some essays are denser than others, but it would be invidious to single these out. The detailed index'(pp. 227–33) is most welcome.

Jean-François Kosta-Théfaine's edited *Travels and Travelogues in the Middle Ages* is part of the AMS series Studies in the Middle Ages (p. iv). It is divided into three sections. The first 'The Composition, Rewriting, Translation, and Iconographical Representation of Medieval Travelogues' (pp. 3–154), has four essays. Ana Pinto writes on '*Mandeville's Travels*: A *Rihla* in Disguise' (pp. 3–57); Marianne O'Doherty writes on '"They are like beasts, for they have no law": Ethnography and Constructions of Human Difference in Late-Medieval Translations of Marco Polo's *Book*' (pp. 59–93); Richard Maber and Angela Tregoning write on 'Conveying the Unimaginable: Odoric of Pordenone's Travels and their Vernacular Translations' (pp. 95–134); and Jean-François Kosta-Théfaine writes on 'The Pierpont Morgan Library Manuscript M.723: Illustrations of Hayton's *La Fleur des histoires d'Orient*' (pp. 135–54). The second section, 'Discovery of the Other—Discovery of the Elsewhere' (pp. 157–230), has three essays. In the first,

Christopher Roman considers 'Margery Kempe and Italy: Sacred Space and the Community in her Soul' (pp. 157–88); in the second, Katrin Rupp considers 'Stairway to Hell: Infernal Journeys in Some Old and Middle English Texts' (pp. 189–204); and Cong Ellen Zhang writes on 'Sties, Places, and the Empire: Lu You's Travel on the Yangzi River in Southern Song China' (pp. 205–30). The third and final section focuses upon 'Travels in Literary Texts' (pp. 233–61). There are two contributions. Adriano Duque writes on 'The Text as Map: Benedict the Pole's Account of the Carpine Mission to Mongolia (1246–1247)' (pp. 233–48), and Wisam Mansour illuminates 'Desert Traveling in al-Shanfara's "Lamiyyatu'l Arab"' (pp. 249–61). The volume concludes with a alphabetically arranged bibliography (pp. 263–90). This is followed by 'Notes on Contributors' (pp. 291–3) and a name-based index (pp. 295–8).

Matthew Wynn Sivils and Jeffrey Walker's *Literature in the Early American Republic: Annual Studies on Cooper and his Contemporaries* is 'the inaugural volume of the new annual'. This is a 'peer-reviewed scholarly journal [that] welcomes a wide range of submissions on the literary culture of the United States from the adoption of the Constitution in 1789 to the death of James Fenimore Cooper in 1851'. The preface adds that this is 'an era covering seven decades too often ignored in American literary scholarship' (p. vii). James D. Wallace's 'Yellow Fever, Race, the Constitution, Nullification: Philip Freneau's *National Gazette* in Philadelphia, 1793' (pp. 1–28) focuses on the *National Gazette's* issue of 11 September and its contents. These encompass information concerning 'the President fleeing the Yellow Fever; a public service message asking for African American Volunteers; a short reprint from a South Carolina Newspaper regarding the politics of race; and an editorial comment titled "Reflections on Several Subjects" concerning the debate over "nullification," the putative power of individual states to "nullify federal laws"' (p. xi). William Merrill Decker's '"Who Ain't a Slave?" *Moby-Dick* and the Slave Narrative Tradition' (pp. 29–55) focuses upon '*Moby-Dick* as an antebellum sea tale that pays cautious tribute to the slave narrative tradition' (p. xi).

Rochelle Raineri Zuck's 'Cultivation, Commerce, and Cupidity: Late-Jacksonian Virtue in James Fenimore Cooper's *The Crater*' (pp. 57–88) is an exploration of James Fenimore Cooper's 1851 novel *The Crater* 'through the lens of its economic and political context to explore the novel's argument about the fate of virtue in Jacksonian America' (p. xii). Lance Schachterle's 'The Themes of Land and Leadership in "The Littlepage Manuscripts"' (pp. 89–131) again focuses on work by Fenimore Cooper, his 'The Littlepage Manuscripts... the largest scale work of fiction [that he] ever conceived' (p. 89). Cooper is the focus of another essay, Allan M. Axelrad's 'Cooper's Literary Landscape Art and American Landscape Painting: From Mountain Gothic to Forest Gothic and Luminism' (pp. 133–68). David Cody's 'Hawthorne as Borrower' (pp. 169–96) traces Hawthorne's indebtedness to other sources, especially 'volume 1 of *The American Magazine of Useful and Entertaining Knowledge*' (p. 172). Cody's essay contains an enumerative, alphabetically arranged listing of '*American Magazine Sources* Unmentioned by Turner' in his 1941 *Hawthorne as Editor* (pp. 173–87). Cody draws upon

Hawthorne's *Lost Notebook* entries (p. 170), and discusses their significance (pp. 187–94). Leland S. Person's '*The Ways of the Hour*: Cooper's Scarlet Letter' (pp. 197–220), draws attention to 'the interesting similarities' between two novels published in the same year, 1850, *The Scarlet Letter* and Cooper's *The Ways of the Hour*. Barbara Alice Mann clearly discusses influence in her 'Aunt Jane and Father Fenimore: The Influence of Jane Austen on James Fenimore Cooper' (pp. 221–53).

In the same volume, John C. Havard's 'The Ideological Significance of Dualistic Native American Characterization in James Fenimore Cooper's *The Last of the Mohicans* and Juan León Mera's *Cumandá*' (pp. 255–78) assesses the impact of Cooper's work upon 'the Ecuadorian novelist and politician Juan León Mera's *Cumandá*' published in 1879 (p. 255). The final essay in this most interesting first volume is on 'Come, All You Sons of Liberty: The American Naval Ballad in the Early 1840s' by R.D. Madison and Karen Lentz Madison (pp. 279–92), and demonstrates that 'a close examination of' naval songsters of the period 'reveals both national and self-awareness of the role of the navy in the identity of the early republic' (p. xv). Each essay is followed by extensive notation and detailed, enumerative, alphabetically listed bibliographies. There is a note on contributors and a useful name-based index (pp. 293–308).

The James Fenimore Cooper revival witnesses an edition of his *Ned Meyers; or, a Life Before the Mast*, with a historical introduction and preface by William S. Dudley and Hugh Egan (pp. xiii–liii, 1–3) followed by the text edited by Karen Lentz Madison and R.D. Madison (pp. 5–217). There is then a 'Textual Commentary' (pp. 219–27), and a 'Note on the Manuscript', now at Yale University Library (pp. 229–30). This fine addition to 'the AMS Press Editions of the Writings of James Fenimore Cooper' (p. ii) concludes with 'Textual Notes', 'Emendations', 'Rejected Readings', and a listing of 'Word-Divisions' (pp. 231–52). The text is accompanied by five black and white full-page illustrations. *Ned Meyers; or, a Life Before the Mast* was published in 1843 and is a celebration of the maritime activities of a Nova Scotia runaway who became a Yankee sailor. As the editors point out, 'Cooper wrote more authentically than most authors about the sea and seafaring men. He knew them well; he had been one of them' (p. xiii).

Jackson R. Bryer and Richard Kopley edited *Resources for American Literary Study*. Volume 32, opens with Kevin J. Hayes's moving 'Remembering Leo: A Tribute to J.A. Leo Lemay (1935–2008)' (pp. 1–7)—'the distinguished scholar of early American literature, especially Benjamin Franklin' (pp. x). Robert DeMott and Brian Railsback's 'Prospects for the Study of John Steinbeck' (pp. 9–47) is in effect a review of the state of Steinbeck studies today. The notes following their essay are detailed (pp. 35–9), and there is a lengthy alphabetically arranged listing of works cited (pp. 39–47). Carol DeBoer-Langworthy's 'Not a Bourgeois Project: Neith Boyce's *The Story of an American Family*' (pp. 49–83) is a study of the work of the neglected writer Neith Boyce (1872–1951) and is based upon an analysis of her 'working typescripts in the Hapgood Family Papers in the American Literature Collection at Yale's Beinecke Rare Book and Manuscript Library' (p. 49). Jessie Bray's '"Not a *pure* idealist": Ralph Waldo Emerson, Edward

Waldo Emerson, and the Civil War' (pp. 85–97), largely focuses upon Emerson's 12 November 1863 letter to Colonel E.N. Hallowell (1836–71), who commanded 'the Fifty-Fourth Massachusetts Volunteers'. As Bray explains, this was 'the first federally-funded, all-black infantry'. Hallowell was hoping that Emerson, who 'numbered among the Fifty-Fourth's financial supporters', would assist in enlisting Hallowell's son Edward (1844–1930) for the war effort. Emerson's letter asks Hallowell not to persuade his son to enlist, and Bray considers the reasons underlying Emerson's apparent negative attitude.

Michael Anesko and N. Christine Brookes's 'Ancestral Footsteps: Montégut on Monte-Beni' (in Bryer and Kopley, eds., pp. 109–40) considers the background for Henry James's 'concise, critical biography of Nathaniel Hawthorne (1804–64)', which he wrote 'for Macmillan's English Men of Letters series' (p. 109). Keith Newlan's 'Unwitting Provocateur: Mary Wilkins Freeman and the American Academy of Arts and Letters' (pp. 141–61) is an account of the recognition which came to the now neglected writer Mary Wilkins Freeman (1852–1930). In 1925 she 'was honored by the American Academy of Arts and Letters as the first recipient of the William Dean Howells Medal for distinction in fiction, an honor awarded every five years' (p. 141). Pamela R. Matthews's 'Reimagining *The Sheltered Life*: Catherine Turney Adapts Ellen Glasgow' (pp. 163–239) is an extended account with text of the 'screenwriter and playwright Catherine Turney['s] (1905–98)... dramatic adaptation of *The Sheltered Life*'. This is an adaptation of Ellen Glasgow's (1873–1945) 1932 novel of the same name (p. 163). In addition to providing the background to the work and an analysis (pp. 163–76), Matthews provides a 'Note on the Text of Turney's *The Sheltered Life*' (p. 176) and the text (pp. 176–236). This is then followed by 'Notes' (pp. 236–7) and 'Works Cited' (pp. 237–9).

In the same volume, Nicholas Moschovakis and David Roessel give an account with the text of '*Jungle, or Walter Find the Pearl*: A Previously Unpublished One-Act Play by Tennessee Williams' (pp. 241–66). They provide an introduction (pp. 241–4), the text (pp. 244–63), 'Notes' (pp. 263–5), and 'Works Cited' (pp. 265–6). Gretchen Comba's 'William Maxwell: A Checklist of the Primary Sources' (pp. 267–96) 'categorizes the complicated body of Maxwell's work'. Her intention 'is to provide the primary source foundation that will allow others to examine, in the words of Ellen Bryant Voight, '"Maxwell's growth as a writer, the deepening complexity of what he wrote... through the structure used and the choice of a writing style"' (p. 267). The checklist is enumerated and divided into 'Publications in Periodicals' (pp. 269–75), 'Nonfiction' (pp. 275–7), 'Poetry' (p. 277), 'Book Reviews' (pp. 277–80), and then 'Published Books and Portions of Books (First American Editions)'. These are divided into genres such as 'Short Story Collections', 'Novels', and so on (pp. 280–92). There is a section too on 'Publications and Anthologies' (pp. 292–5). The remainder of volume 32 of *Resources for American Literary Studies* consists of valuable, detailed reviews (pp. 297–365), and this most useful volume concludes with an 'Index of Authors', 'Index of Subjects', and 'Index of Books Reviewed' (pp. 367–72).

Richard Kopley and Barbara Cantalupo's *Prospects for the Study of American Literature II* is the second in a reference-book series that aims at 'the need for a regular assessment for the future of American literary study' (p. xv). Lance Schachterle's 'James Fenimore Cooper' (pp. 1–25); Leland S. Person's 'Nathaniel Hawthorne' (pp. 26–49); Larry J. Reynold's 'Margaret Fuller' (pp. 50–71); Mary Loeffelholz's 'Emily Dickinson' (pp. 72–96); Daniel Shealy's 'Louisa May Alcott' (pp. 97–118); Sarah B. Daughtery's 'William Dean Howells' (pp. 119–36); Eric Carl Link's 'Frank Norris' (pp. 137–50); Jeanne Campbell Reesman's 'Jack London' (pp. 151–89); Paul A. Orlov's 'Theodore Dreiser' (pp. 190–215); James L.W. West III's 'F. Scott Fitzgerald' (pp. 216–34); Madeline C. Smith and Richard Eaton's 'Eugene O'Neill' (pp. 235–58); Robin G. Schulze's 'Marianne Moore' (pp. 259–74); Maurice Wallace's 'James Baldwin' (pp. 275–88); Gayle Pemberton's 'Ralph Ellison' (pp. 289–303); and Pearl Amelia McHaney's 'Eudora Welty' (pp. 304–23) are all clear accounts of the critical and textual state of play relating to their chosen authors. Each essay is accompanied by an extensive, enumerative, alphabetically arranged listing of works cited. The useful reference work concludes with an extensive index (pp. 325–55).

Serge Soupel, Kevin L. Cope, and Alexander Pettit, with editorial contributions by Laura Thomason Wood, have compiled a collection of sixteen essays revolving around the broad subject of 'adventure during the "long" eighteenth century' (pp. xi–xii) in their *Adventure: An Eighteenth-Century Idiom. Essays on the Daring and the Bold as a Pre-Modern Medium*. The book is divided into four parts. In the first part, 'Adventures of the Mind', the essays include Alan Ingram on 'Boswell's Big Adventures: London, Scotland, London' (pp. 3–22); Elizabeth Soubrenie, 'Chance, Providence and Fate: The Spiritual Adventures of John Bunyan and William Cowper' (pp. 23–39); Hélène Dachez on 'The Adventure of Sense(s) in Richardson's *Clarissa*' (pp. 41–62); and John A. Baker on 'Venture and Adventure in Edward Young's *Night Thoughts* (1742–1746)' (pp. 63–87). Baker's essay rather interestingly begins with a discussion (pp. 63–6) of Philip Larkin's 'treatment of daytime and its implication in his poem "Days"' (p. 63) before he discusses Edward Young! The second part of the volume, 'Adventures in Genre' (p. 89), contains four essays: Gerald J. Butler writes on 'Defoe and the End of Epic Adventure: The Example of *Roxana*' (pp. 91–109); Jean Dixsaut writes on 'Adventure in Lilliput: Gulliver the Doomed Fire Fighter' (pp. 111–24); Victoria Bridges Moussaron writes on 'The Adventure of a "Sublime Subject": *The Shipwreck* (1762) by William Falconer' (pp. 125–43); and Guyonne Leduc, in one of the more amusing titles in the volume, discourses on 'The Adventure of Cross-Dressing: Hannah Snell (1723–92), a Woman Soldier' (pp. 145–67). The third part is devoted to 'The Places of Adventure' (p. 169): William Roberts writes on 'Thomas Gray's Adventures in Scotland and the English Lake District' (pp. 171–88), Yannick Deschamps writes on 'The Adventures of Daniel Defoe in Scotland (1706–07): Secret Agent, Propagandist, and Entrepreneur' (pp. 189–209); Pierre Carboni writes on 'Boswell and the Extraordinary Adventures of Prince Charles Edward Stuart in the Hebrides' (pp. 211–20); and Andrew Varney writes on 'Fielding's Last Adventure: *The Journal of a Voyage to Lisbon*' (pp. 221–32). The fourth part is concerned with 'Adventure as Social Process' (p. 233) and contains four essays on the subject: Norbert Col's 'The Moralist's Adventure: Rewriting

History in *Gulliver's Travels*' (pp. 235–50); H.J.K. Jenkins's 'A Looking-Glass Adventure: Lord Orford's Fenland Cruise' (pp. 251–73); Habib Arjoud's 'The Economy of Adventure in Defoe's Novels' (pp. 275–303); and James P. Carson's 'Interracial Adventures: The Black Caribs of St. Vincent' (pp. 305–24). Serge Soupel's brief 'Afterword' (pp. 325–7) sums up the essays in the volume. There are 'Abstracts' (pp. 329–34), and a helpful, author-based index (pp. 335–43). Clearly, in such a diverse volume, some essays are less opaque than others, and some will be of greater interest than others depending on the individual reader. The binding is sturdy and AMS Press has produced yet another useful volume in the AMS Studies in the Eighteenth Century series.

Emblematica 17[2009] witnesses a change in typeface from previous issues. It has moved from 'a variant of Garamond' to 'a variant of Palatino' (p. xi). There is an 'In Memoriam' (*Embl* 17[2009] xv–xvi) to Egon Verheyen who was on *Emblematica*'s editorial board, and to John F. Moffitt, whose contribution 'An Emblematic Source for Goya's Engraving of a Syphilitic "Matrimonial Blunder"' is in this volume (*Embl* 17[2009] 257–70). Contributions of interest to *YWES* readers include Daniel Russell's 'Emblems, Frames, and Other Marginalia: Defining the Emblematic' (*Embl* 17[2009] 1–40). Russell's is a most useful and clearly written account of what emblem studies are and their history. Gerard Kilroy's 'Sir Thomas Tresham: His Emblem' (*Embl* 17[2009] 149–80) focuses upon 'the existence of an emblem of Sir Thomas Tresham (1543–1605) by Remigius Hogenberg (1536–88)'. Today, Tresham 'is probably best known today for the buildings and gardens he left behind in Northamptonshire' (p. 149) and the recent discovery by Hogenberg has just come to light. Michael Bath's 'An Emblematic Embroidery in the Burrell Collection' (*Embl* 17[2009] 181–90) describes five embroideries in the historical embroidery collection of the 'Glasgow ship owner Sir William Burrell (1861–1958)... now held at the city's Burrell Collection'. These five emblems are 'worked in wool on linen in cross-stitch and without lines worked with silver or gold in chain stitch' (p. 181). Averill Lukic's 'The Same Anticipation of Resurrection: Paradin in North Wales?' (*Embl* 17[2009] 229–38) is concerned with some of the 'few recorded instances of the use of emblem books as sources for funeral monuments' (p. 229). Kristen L. Olson's 'Picture—Pattern—Poesis: Visuality, the Emblem, and Seventeenth-Century English Religious Lyric' (*Embl* 17[2009] 271–98) 'examines visual representation in English religious lyrics of the seventeenth century, clarifying the influence of emblem poetics on that genre'. Olson focuses upon 'a comparison of poems by Richard Crashaw, Francis Quarles, Christopher Harvey, and George Herbert' (p. 271). Sarah Howe's '"Silent Parables": Making Pictures Speak in Quarles's *Emblemes*' (*Embl* 17[2009] 299–318) 'investigates how voice is produced in the "silent parables" of Francis Quarles's emblems' (p. 299).

Rüdiger Ahrens and Klaus Stierstorfer's edited *Symbolism: An International Annual of Critical Aesthetics*. Volume 9, with its special focus on 'Literature and Circularity', contains Christoph Henke and Martin Middeke's 'Literature and Circularity: An Introduction' (pp. 1–12). Amongst the writers considered are T.S. Eliot, Northrop Frye, William Blake and others. Verena O. Lobsien, in her 'Squaring the Circle: Neoplatonic Versions of the Self in Early Modern

Poetry' (pp. 13–39), 'attempts to show how circular figures of thought are realized, modified, and sometimes radically re-structured in poetic texts by Sydney, Wyatt, Donne, and Marvell' (p. 13). Helga Schwalm's 'Circularity and Subjectivity in Autobiography: Conversion, Closure, Hermeneutics, and Beyond' (pp. 41–65) 'argues that... structures of closure are interwoven with and undercut by structures of doubling and repetition'. She traces 'the historical development of such increasingly destabilized and spiral autobiographical circularities from Augustinian spiritual autobiography to De Quincey's plural Romantic autobiography' (p. 41). In fact, there is a quite detailed discussion of De Quincey's *Autobiographical Sketches* (pp. 61–5). Christoph Henke writes on 'Life Spirals and Commonsense Aporias: Samuel Johnson's *Rasselas* Revisited' (pp. 67–84). Drawing upon William Blake, Emerson, De Quincey, and others, Aleida Assmann writes on 'Circle and Line: Cultural Constructions of Time Between History and Memory' (pp. 85–101). She 'reflects upon the complex relationship between the cultural images of circle and [the] straight line' (p. 85). Martin Middeke's 'On Circles and Spirals: Time, Repetition, and Meta-Hermeneutics in Literature' (pp. 103–28), replete with images (see pp. 106–7), 'traces the spiral or looping movement of the hermeneutic circle in literature of the late-nineteenth and twentieth century' (p. 103). Middeke draws upon the writings of Thomas Hardy, Joseph Conrad, H.G. Wells, and Samuel Beckett.

In the same volume, Poems by Edward Thomas and W.H. Auden's villanelle 'If I Could Tell You' are the central texts drawn upon by Hans Ulrich Seeber, in his 'Organic and Textual Circularity in Poems by Edward Thomas and W.H. Auden' (pp. 129–40). The eminent J. Hillis Miller contributes 'The Circle and the Straight Line in William Faulkner's *Light in August*' (pp. 141–60). Miller's analysis concludes that in *Light in August* 'Faulkner's genius... can at least partly be defined as the ability to appropriate the more or less universal, even banal, image of human life as a journey along a road, straight or circular.' Miller continues, 'With an almost uniquely powerful and moving narrative eloquence, he then dramatizes and creatively transforms that figure in one of the greatest United States modernist novels' (p. 160). Albert Kümmel-Schnur's 'Fake Resurrections: On the Motif of Recurrence in Philip K. Dick' (pp. 161–80) contains a close analysis of three Dick short stories, 'Stability' [1947], 'The Skull' [1952], and 'Exhibit Piece' [1954], that reveal 'different modes of circular time structures' (p. 161). Julian Wolfreys, in his 'The Unbearable Circularity of Being' (pp. 181–92), draws upon 'the philosophy of Immanuel Kant, and the poetry of Michel Deguy and Paul Celan' (p. 181), in addition to the references to Derrida, which we've come to expect from Wolfreys. Susana Onega's 'Circularity and the Quest in the Novels of Jeanette Winterson' (pp. 193–216) contains a thorough analysis of the motifs of 'love and the relation of self and other' (p. 193) in Winterson's work. Christina Wald writes on 'Second Selves, Second Stories: Unreliable Narration and the Circularity of Reading in Ford Madox Ford's *The Good Soldier* and Chuck Palahniuk's/David Fincher's *Fight Club*' (pp. 217–41).

Barbara Puschmann-Nalenz's 'The Disturbed Image: (Re)Visions of Space and Englishness in Contemporary British Fiction' (pp. 267–83) 'explores the concepts of space, representation, and Englishness in two postmodern novels that have frequently been examined for their concern with time and history: John Fowles's *The French Lieutenant's Woman* and Peter Ackroyd's *The Great Fire of London*' (p. 267). Daniela Carpi writes on '*Prospero's Books* by Peter Greenaway and *The Tempest* by William Shakespeare: Science, Magic and Painting' (pp. 285–93). Also of relevance to *YWES* readers in *Symbolism*, volume 9, is Jana Gohrisch's 'The White Man's Descent into Hell: J.M. Coetzee's Novel *Disgrace* and the Political Uses of Transculturality' (pp. 295–311). The volume concludes with book reviews, a listing of contributors, and an author-orientated index (pp. 369–400). Obviously, in such an eclectic collection, some essays are less pretentious and better written than others.

An addition to the ongoing Chaucer Bibliographies series under the general editorship of Thomas Hahn and published by the University of Toronto Press in association with the University of Rochester, is Peter Goodall's important *Chaucer's Monk's Tale and Nun's Priest's Tale: An Annotated Bibliography 1900–2000*. There are 1,078 items annotated. Goodall's work is divided into nine sections: 'Editions, Translations, Modernizations, and Retellings' (pp. 3–51); 'Bibliographies, Handbooks, and Indexes' (pp. 52–62); 'Manuscript and Textual Studies' (pp. 63–81); 'Prosody, Linguistic, and Lexical Studies' (pp. 82–100); 'Sources, Analogues, and Allusions' (pp. 101–48); 'The Narrators of the Tales Considered as Characters' (pp. 149–66); 'The Tales Considered Together' (pp. 166–201); '*The Monk's Tale*' (pp. 201–24); and '*The Nun's Priest's Tale*' (pp. 225–303). Each section contains Goodall's expository introduction. There is a listing of 'Abbreviations and Works Cited' (pp. xv–xviii), and a most helpful, clearly written introduction (pp. xix–xlviii). The index (pp. 304–38) is indispensable. However, a production problem is indicated in an inserted slip on p. 201 following the section on 'The Tales Together' and the detailed annotation of item 690, David Aers's *Chaucer*, published by Harvester in 1986. The printed slip points out that 'The end of entry 690 and the entries numbered 691–722i (following p. 200) are missing from the printed book. The complete text of these entries is available at www.utparchives.com/archive/Goodall691–722.pdf' (p. 201). It can only be hoped that the University of Toronto Press will maintain this weblink and that it will not disappear into the ether in the manner of so many other weblinks.

William M. Robbins's *Stanley Elkin: A Comprehensive Bibliography* consists of two parts. The first part, 'Primary Works', is divided into thirteen sections (pp. 31–263). The second part is 'Secondary Works Dealing with Stanley Elkin' and consists of fifteen sections (pp. 265–456). Of particular interest are the descriptions of Elkin's novels which are 'listed chronologically, with full descriptions for American and British First Editions and Important Variants. Subsequent editions, usually paperback, have brief descriptions that include pagination, size and price, though other distinguishing characteristics, such as number of copies when known, are also noted' (p. 2). There is also a listing of Elkin's 'Chronology, Honors, and Awards' (pp. xiv–l) and a worthwhile 'overview of how Elkin was received, reviewed, pigeonholed, extolled, and occasionally misunderstood and dismissed' (p. 2: 7–25). Robbins's fascinating and important work also includes 'How Bill Danforth Saved Me from My

Darker Nature', described by Robbins as 'An original piece that Stanley Elkin kindly granted [him] the right to publish' (pp. 2: 26–7). *Stanley Elkin: A Comprehensive Bibliography* will remain the definitive record for further research and investigation on Stanley Elkin (1930–95).

John E. Bassett's *William Faulkner: An Annotated Bibliography of Criticism since 1988* is exactly what it says it is and 'brings up through 2007 the listings of Faulkner criticisms and scholarship' (p. vii) covered in earlier works. The annotations are very detailed and useful. The work is divided into six sections. Following a clear introduction (pp. 1–10), there are 'Books on Faulkner' (pp. 11–50) and 'Studies of Individual Novels' (pp. 51–310), followed by 'Studies of Short Stories, Poetry, and Miscellaneous Prose' (pp. 311–48). There is a section on 'Topical Studies' (pp. 349–444) encompassing 'Commentaries Covering Several Works' (pp. 349–422); 'Biographies and Commentary on Faulkner's Life' (pp. 423–34), and 'Checklists and Bibliographical Materials' (pp. 435–44). Section IV, 'Other Materials', encompasses 'Reviews of Books about Falkner' (pp. 445–66); 'Magazine and Journal Articles' (pp. 467–77); 'Newspaper Articles' (pp. 478–82); 'Books' (pp. 483–90); 'Doctoral Dissertations' (pp. 491–519); 'Selected Criticism Prior to 1988)' (pp. 520–2); and 'Late Additions' (pp. 523–50). There is also an 'Index of Critics' (pp. 551–92) to conclude, this most useful work.

Jack W.C. Hagstrom and Bill Morgan's *James Ingram Merrill: A Descriptive Bibliography*, is a tribute to the Pulitzer Prize-winning poet James Merrill (1926–95). Prepared with the co-operation of the poet himself, it is divided into ten sections and four appendices. The ten sections record: 'Books, Pamphlets and Broadsides' (pp. 1–150); 'Books and Pamphlets Containing Original Contributions of First Book Appearances of Poems, Translations, or Prose' (pp. 151–82); 'First Periodical and Newspaper Appearances of Poems and Prose' (pp. 183–228); 'Translations of Poems and Prose' (pp. 229–36); 'Interviews with James Merrill' (pp. 237–40); 'Recordings of Poems and Prose' (pp. 241–6); 'Musical Settings of Poems and Prose' (pp. 247–52); 'Statements/Endorsements of Dust Jackets and Wrappers, etc.' (pp. 253–76); 'Miscellany' (pp. 277–86); and 'Inscriptions in Books Recorded in Book Dealers' or Auction Catalogues' (pp. 287–312). The four appendices contain: 'Reviews, by Others, of Books by James Merrill' (pp. 313–48); 'Critical Articles on James Merrill's Works' (pp. 349–70); 'Obituaries, Tributes, and Reminiscences of James Merrill' (pp. 371–6); and 'Dedications of Poems, Prose, or Books to James Merrill' (pp. 377–82). There is an extensive index (pp. 383–421) to this excellent work which contains all you need to know about a very interesting poet.

The first volume of Steven Abbott's two-volume *Gore Vidal: A Bibliography, 1940–2009*, in addition to an introduction (pp. xi–xvi), contains Section A, 'Books and Pamphlets by Gore Vidal' (pp. 15–182). This is followed by 'Grayscale Images: Selected Dust Jackets, Covers of Paperbound Editions, Covers of Proof Copies, and Title Pages' (pp. 183–258). Section B contains 'Books and Pamphlets with Contributions by Gore Vidal' (pp. 271–344). Section C contains 'Contributions to Periodicals: Essays, Reviews, Comments, Speeches, Poetry, Short Stories, Published Letters to the Editor, and Excerpts from Vidal's Books' (pp. 345–84). This is followed by an

'Introduction to the Foreign Editions by Professor Harry Kloman' (pp. 385–6), and Section D, 'Translations into Foreign Languages of Books by Gore Vidal, by Language' (pp. 387–416). There are two appendices to the first volume: 'Appendix I: A Chronology of Selected Highlights of Vidal's Life (1925–2009)' (pp. 417–36); and 'Appendix II: A Table of Vidal's Essays, Plays and Short Stories' (pp. 437–58). There is also an index to this volume (pp. 459–500).

The second volume is on CD-ROM and begins with a continuation of Section D: 'Da. Foreign Editions by Title' (pp. 501–28) and 'Db. Foreign Editions with Full Bibliographic Citations: French, Italian, Spanish' (pp. 529–84). Section E is devoted to 'Audio-Visual Media: Television and Film' (pp. 585–8), Section Ea to 'Audio-Visual Media: Audio Recordings, Film and TV Mountings, and Electronic Editions of Vidal's Books, Plays, and Essays' (pp. 589–92) and Section Eb to 'Audio-Visual Media: On-Line Periodicals: Essays, Comments, Excerpts, and Reviews' (pp. 593–4). Section F is devoted to 'Interviews: Selected Appearances in Periodicals and Books' (pp. 595–604), with Fa, 'Interviews and Commentary: Selected Appearances in Audio-Visual Media' (pp. 605–8). There are four more appendices: 'Appendix III: A Selection of Vidal's Small Press Appearances' (pp. 609–12); 'Appendix IV: A Selection of Critical Studies of Vidal's Oeuvre (1951–2009)' (pp. 613–16); 'Appendix V: A Selected Listing of Vidal's Film and Television Work as an Actor, Including as a Narrator (1946–2009)' (pp. 617–18), and 'Appendix VI: A Table of Vidal's Afterwords, Epilogues, Forewords, Introductions, Notes, and Prefaces' (pp. 619–36).

Many of the sections contain extensive bibliographical descriptions. The final section of the second volume on CD-ROM, entitled 'Color Images: Selected Dust Jackets, Covers of Paper Bound Editions, Covers of Proof Copies, Title Pages, and Packaging of Audio-Visual Appearances' (pp. 637–757) has over 1,000 images. The first volume contains over 650 grayscale images. Abbott's work will remain the definitive record of this fascinating author's achievement and it is based upon Vidal's literary archives, evidence provided by his agents and publishers, and his personal library located in Ravello, Italy. It clearly is a labour of love and devotion by Steven Abbott. His *Gore Vidal: A Bibliography, 1940–2009* is a must for anyone interested in its subject.

G. Thomas Tanselle's *Bibliographical Analysis: A Historical Introduction* is based upon his Sandars Lectures given at the University of Cambridge in May 1997. The work is divided into three sections: firstly, the 'Foundations' (pp. 6–30), secondly, 'Analysis of Manufacturing Clues' (pp. 31–60), and thirdly, 'Analysis of Design Features' (pp. 61–88). Notes are at the back of the text (pp. 89–116) and there is an alphabetical list of 'Further Reading: Works Cited' (pp. 117–47), followed by a 'Chronological Index' (pp. 147–51), a 'Subject Guide' (pp. 151–60), and an index (pp. 161–7). The first chapter, 'Foundations', consists of four sections: 'To 1908' (pp. 6–14), '1908–1945' (pp. 14–22), '1945–1969' (pp. 22–5), and 'Since 1969' (pp. 25–30). The second chapter also has four sections: 'Compositor Study of Sixteenth- and Seventeenth-Century Books' (pp. 31–42), 'Presswork Study of Sixteenth- and Seventeenth-Century Books' (pp. 43–7), 'Study of Fifteenth-Century

Books' (pp. 48–52), and 'Study of Eighteenth-, Nineteenth-, and Twentieth-Century Books' (pp. 52–60). The final chapter has a similar number of sections, beginning with 'Basic Considerations' (pp. 61–9), then 'Psychological Study' (pp. 69–75), followed by 'Cultural Study' (pp. 75–81), and concluding with 'Aesthetic Study' (pp. 81–8).

Unfortunately, Tanselle's bibliographical analysis is not illustrated. Tanselle writes authoritatively and clearly. There is some confusion between analytical bibliography and descriptive bibliography, with insufficient attention paid to the latter. Inevitably, there are some omissions. However, *Bibliographical Analysis: A Historical Introduction* is yet another definitive work by G. Thomas Tanselle. Of especial interest is his fourth chapter, which considers various approaches to bibliographical study and its proponents. For instance, what he refers to as 'the "cultural" approach to the analysis of book design can be illustrated by a teaching exercise used by D.F. McKenzie' (p. 75). Other names appearing in the 'Cultural Study' section include Stanley Morison, Bertrand H. Bronson, Nicolas Barker, and David McKitterick: names which appear elsewhere in Tanselle's book. The 'Notes' at the end of the text are not limited to their immediate context but are most informative relating to their subject: see for instance note 32, pp. 94–5, concerning Fredson Bower's 'substantial criticism of analytical bibliography' (p. 25). In short, this is an important work, and an interesting review of it by Nicolas Barker may be found in *The Library* (11:ii[2010] 232–4).

Nigel Alderman and C.D. Blanton's edited *A Concise Companion to Postwar British and Irish Poetry* is a useful reference work. In addition to the editors' introduction (pp. 1–10), there are entries by: Vincent Sherry on 'Poetic Modernism and the Century's Wars' (pp. 11–31); Stephen Burt on 'The Movement and the Mainstream' (pp. 32–50); Nigel Alderman on 'Myth, History, and *The New Poetry*' (pp. 51–71); Michael Thurston on 'Region and Nation in Britain and Ireland' (pp. 72–91); John P. Waters on 'Form and Identity in Northern Irish Poetry' (pp. 92–110); Jahan Ramazani on 'Poetry and Decolonization' (pp. 111–33); C.D. Blanton on 'Transatlantic Currents' (pp. 134–54); Drew Milne on 'Neo-Modernism and Avant-Garde Orientations' (pp. 155–75); Linda A. Kinnahan on 'Contemporary British Women Poets and the Lyric Subject' (pp. 176–99); Erica Falci on 'Place, Space, and Landscape' (pp. 200–20); Romana Huk on 'Poetry and Religion' (pp. 221–42); and Peter Middleton on 'Institutions of Poetry in Postwar Britain' (pp. 243–63). The volume contains a detailed index (pp. 285–97). Clearly, some of the articles are less opaque and interesting than others, but on the whole, this is a valuable addition to individual and library reference shelves.

Rebecca Lemon, Emma Mason, Jonathan Roberts, and Christopher Rowland's edited *The Blackwell Companion to the Bible in English Literature*, an extremely useful volume, is offered 'as an aid in understanding the vast influence of the Bible on English literature, rather than as a definitive and exhaustive study of the topic' (p. 6). It is divided into six parts. The first part, 'Introduction', contains, in addition to a 'General Introduction' (pp. 3–9), Christopher Rowland on 'The Literature of the Bible' (pp. 10–21) and David Jasper on 'Biblical Hermeneutics and Literary Theory' (pp. 22–38).

The second part, on 'Medieval', in addition to Daniel Anlezark's introduction (pp. 39–40), contains six essays ranging from Catherine A.M. Clarke's 'Old English Poetry' (pp. 61–75), and Douglas Gray on 'The Medieval Religious Lyric' (pp. 76–84), to Christina Whitehead on 'Geoffrey Chaucer' (pp. 134–52). The third part, 'Early Modern', in addition to Roger Poley's introduction (pp. 153–4), contains ten essays, beginning with Elizabeth Clarke on 'Early Modern Women' (pp. 155–68), running through Rivkah Zim on 'Mary Sidney' (pp. 211–24), Hannibal Hamlin on 'William Shakespeare' (pp. 225–38), to Gerard Reedy, S.J. on 'John Dryden' (pp. 297–310).

Part IV, devoted to 'Eighteenth Century and Romantic', in addition to Stephen Prickett's introduction (pp. 313–28), contains J.R. Watson on 'Eighteenth-Century Hymn Writers' (pp. 329–44) through to Bernard Beatty on 'P.B. Shelley' (pp. 451–62). Elisabeth Jay introduces the fifth part, devoted to Victorians (pp. 463–4), containing nine essays. These range from Kirstie Blair on 'Alfred Tennyson' (pp. 496–511) and Charles LaPorte on 'George Eliot' (pp. 536–50), to Andrew Tate on 'Decadence' (pp. 587–600). The final part of this valuable work is devoted to the 'Modernists'. Following Ward Blanton's introduction (pp. 601–2), there are essays ranging from Edward Larrisy on 'W.B. Yeats' (pp. 617–28), to David Fuller on T.S. Eliot' (pp. 667–80), and Jane Potter on 'The Great War Poets' (pp. 681–95). The volume concludes with an index (pp. 696–702).

Soko Tomita writes, in her introduction to her *A Bibliographical Catalogue of Italian Books Printed in England 1558–1603*, 'This is a bibliographical catalogue of 291 Italian books (451 editions) published in England during the reign of Queen Elizabeth I, covering the years from 1558 to 1603. It is a work of reference which summarizes knowledge to date and provides foundations for new work on subject of Anglo-Italian transactions in Elizabethan literature' (p. 1). The introduction (pp. 1–80) contains an account of criticism (pp. 1–10), and a most comprehensive discussion of the catalogue itself (pp. 11–80). It is followed by the bibliographical catalogue which is replete with detail and useful information (pp. 81–450). There are seven appendices to this important work of scholarship: 'List of Books Excluded from Scott's [Mary August Scott, *Elizabethan Translations from the Italian*, 1916] Listings' (pp. 451–6); 'Title-Pages with Compartments or Devices Not Included in "McKerrow" [Ronald B. McKerrow, *Printers' and Publishers' Devices in England and Scotland 1485–1640*, 1913] or "McKerrow and Ferguson" [Ronald B. McKerrow and F.S. Ferguson, *Title-Page Borders Used in England and Scotland, 1485–1640*, 1932]' (pp. 457–82); 'Graphs of Italian Books in England According to their Genre 1558–1603' (pp. 483–90); 'Table of Italian Books in Latin in England 1558–1603' (pp. 491–6); 'Table of Printers and Publishers of Italian Books in England 1558–1603' (pp. 497–530); 'Table of Source Texts of Italian Books in England' (pp. 531–49); and 'Table of Printers and Publishers of Source Texts' (pp. 549–60). There is no doubt that this is a most important work which concludes with the very helpful 'Bibliography of Other Works Cited' (pp. 561–76); a 'General Index' (pp. 575–94), and a 'Title Index' (pp. 595–606).

Kathleen A. Johnson and Steven R. Harris's *Teaching Literary Research: Challenges in a Changing Environment* is largely the product of librarians with some input from English professors and is largely North American, primarily United States-based. The book is divided into three sections. The first four chapters 'address questions of how information literacy might advance the goals of the undergraduate literature curriculum' (p. 3). These are followed by four essays on 'the question of research within specific literary methodologies or genres. These include approaches to teaching non-majors and non-native English speaking populations' (p. 4). In the third section, seven chapters 'illustrate various experiences of librarians in teaching literary research' (p. 5)—it must be stressed that the context is North America. Contents include: Van E. Hillard's 'Information Literacy as Situated Literacy' (pp. 11–21); John C. Bean and Nalini Iyer's '"I couldn't find an article that answered my question:" Teaching the Construction of Meaning in Undergraduate Literary Research' (pp. 22–40); Kate Koppelman's 'Literary Eavesdropping and the Socially Graceful Critic' (pp. 41–60); Elizabeth M. Williams's 'The Printing Press and the Web: Modernists Teaching Postmodernists' (pp. 61–80); Kate Manuel's 'Researching Southwestern Literature: Challenges and Strategies' (pp. 83–108); Miriam Laskin and José Diaz's 'Literary Research in a Bilingual Environment: Information Literacy as a Language-Learning Tool' (pp. 109–28); Vickery Lebbin and Kristin M. McAndrews's 'Ways of Knowing: Integrating Folklore Studies with Composition and Information Literacy through a Learning Community' (pp. 129–42); Austin Booth and Laura Taddeo's 'The Changing Nature of the Book: Literary Research, Cultural Studies, and the Digital Age' (pp. 143–65); Meg Meiman's 'Through the Eyes of Picasso: Literary Research from the Best of Both Worlds' (pp. 169–81); William A. Wortman's 'Libraries, Librarians, and the Resources of Literary Study' (pp. 182–201); Sheril J. Hook and Veronica Reyes-Escudero's 'Librarians Influencing the Literature Core Curriculum' (pp. 202–15); Helen C. Williams's 'Training Librarians for Teaching Literary Research Methods' (pp. 216–20); Daniel Coffey's 'Work in Progress: A Review of the Literature of Literary Research Instruction 1978–2003' (pp. 227–46); and Kathleen A. Johnson's 'Work in Progress; A Review of the Literature of Literary Research Instruction 2002–2008' (pp. 247–56). There is an 'Appendix: Research Competency Guidelines for Literatures in English' (pp. 257–61). The book concludes with a listing of contributors (pp. 262–6) and a detailed index (pp. 267–74). Each chapter of this useful volume is followed by at times extensive notation.

A.P. Cowie has edited a series of essays presenting an extensive account of English lexicography from its beginnings in medieval glosses, through its extensive developments in the eighteenth century, to its present computer-based status, in his *The Oxford History of English Lexicography*, volume 1: *General-Purpose Dictionaries* and volume 2: *Specialized Dictionaries*. The two volumes encompass dictionaries of English and other varieties as well as American English and developments elsewhere. The first volume, in addition to notes on contributors and lists of illustrations and abbreviations, contains the editor's clear introduction (pp. 1–16) and is divided into two sections. The first focuses upon 'Early Glossaries; Bilingual and Multilingual Dictionaries', and has six essays: Hans Sauer's 'Glosses, Glossaries, and Dictionaries in the Medieval Period' (pp. 17–40); Janet Bately's 'Bilingual and

Multilingual Dictionaries of the Renaissance and Early Seventeenth Century' (pp. 41–64); Monique C. Cormier's 'Bilingual Dictionaries of the Late Seventeenth and Eighteenth Centuries' (pp. 65–85); Carla Marello's 'Bilingual Dictionaries of the Nineteenth and Twentieth Centuries' (pp. 86–104), and Donna M.T. Cr. Farina and George Durman's 'Bilingual Dictionaries of English and Russian in the Eighteenth to the Twentieth Centuries' (pp. 105–30). The second part focuses upon 'The History of English Monolingual Dictionaries' and consists of ten entries: N.E. Osselton's 'The Early Development of the English Monolingual Dictionary (Seventeenth and Early Eighteenth Centuries)' (pp. 131–54); Allen Reddick's 'Johnson and Richardson' (pp. 155–81); Sidney I. Landau's 'Major American Dictionaries' (pp. 182–229); Lynda Mugglestone's 'The *Oxford English Dictionary*' (pp. 230–59); Charlotte Brewer's 'The *OED* Supplements' (pp. 260–78); Richard W. Bailey's 'National and Regional Dictionaries of English' (pp. 279–301); Margaret Dareau and Iseabail Macleod's 'Dictionaries of Scots' (pp. 302–25); Michael Adams's 'The Period Dictionaries' (pp. 326–52); Jeannette Allsopp's 'Dictionaries of Caribbean English' (pp. 353–77); and Edmund Weiner's 'The Electronic *OED*: The Computerization of a Historical Dictionary' (pp. 378–409). This first volume concludes with references and an index.

The second volume is divided into two parts. In the first part, 'Dictionaries Specialized According to Ordering of Entries, Topical or Linguistic Content, or Speech Community', essays include Werner Hüllen's 'Dictionaries of Synonyms and Thesauri', (pp. 25–46); Michael Rand Hoare's 'Scientific and Technical Dictionaries', (pp. 47–93); Carole Hough's 'Dictionaries of Place-Names' (pp. 94–121); Patrick Hanks's 'Dictionaries of Personal Names' (pp. 122–48); Joan C. Beal's 'Pronouncing Dictionaries—I. Eighteenth and Early Nineteenth Centuries' (pp. 149–75); Beverly Collins and Inger M. Mees's 'Pronouncing Dictionaries—II. Mid-Nineteenth Century to the Present Day' (pp. 176–218); Thomas Herbst and Michael Klotz's 'Syntagmatic and Phraseological Dictionaries' (pp. 219–44); Elizabeth Knowles's 'Dictionaries of Quotations' (pp. 245–68); Anatoly Liberman's 'English Etymological Dictionaries' (pp. 269–89); Robert Penhallurick's 'Dialect Dictionaries' (pp. 290–313); and Julie Coleman's 'Slang and Cant Dictionaries' (pp. 314–38). The second part focuses upon 'Dictionaries Specialized According to Uses and Users'. There are six entries: Robert Allen's 'Dictionaries of Usage' (pp. 339–60); Sidney I. Landau's 'The American Collegiate Dictionaries' (pp. 361–84); A.P. Cowie's 'The Earliest Foreign Learners' Dictionaries' (pp. 385–411); Thierry Fontenelle's 'Linguistic Research and Learners' Dictionaries: the *Longman Dictionary of Contemporary English*' (pp. 412–35); Rosamund Moon's 'The Cobuild Project' (pp. 436–57); and Hilary Nesi's 'Dictionaries in Electronic Form' (pp. 458–78). The second volume concludes with a listing of references and an index.

R.M. Thomson's *A Descriptive Catalogue of the Medieval Manuscripts of Merton College, Oxford*, with a description of the Greek manuscripts by N.G. Wilson, comes with black and white and colour illustrations in a very handsome quarto volume. The front panel of the jacket contains an illustration of a 'Historiated initial showing two philosophers engaged in disputation. Merton College MS 269, fol. 132r'. In addition to the usual prefatory materials including lists of illustrations, acknowledgements, abbreviations, introduction, and editorial conventions, and the catalogue itself, there are four appendices: 'Appendix A: The Greek Manuscripts' (pp. 267–8); 'Appendix B: Extracts from the Merton Account Rolls Relating to Books and the Library' (pp. 269–81); 'Appendix C: Merton College Books in John Bale's Index' (pp. 282–6); and 'Appendix D: The Section on Merton Manuscripts in Thomas James' Ecloga' (pp. 287–96). There is an 'Index of Manuscripts, Early Printed Books, and Records' (pp. 297–305), a useful, detailed 'General Index' (pp. 306–30), and an extensive listing of plates (pp. 331–440). Thomson's catalogue is an invaluable guide to the intellectual activities at Oxford University in the period extending from the thirteenth to the sixteenth centuries, and on the acquisition, manufacture, and use of books at that time.

English literary studies emanating from the Department of English at the University of Victoria, British Columbia, continues to produce valuable monographs. The familiar brownish covers have now been replaced with more decorative ones and the presentation has been spruced up. This in no way detracts from the quality that has come to be expected from this distinguished series. Two recent volumes to appear are Lisa Narbeshuber's *Confessing Cultures: Politics and the Self in the Poetry of Sylvia Plath* and Kathryn Kerby-Fulton's edited *Women and the Divine in Literature before 1700: Essays in Memory of Margot Louis*. Narbeshuber's well-written study of Plath focuses upon the late poems and the question of whether their author adopted a fresh attitude towards her poetry and technique in general. Narbeshuber believes that 'the progression of Sylvia Plath's art mirrors the shift from a certain Anglo-modernism to postmodernism' (p. vii). Narbeshuber concludes that ultimately 'almost in spite of herself [Plath] remains an eternally open eye, regarding her world' (p. 90). The monograph contains particularly fine analysis and close readings of late poems such as 'Face Lift', 'Tulips', and 'In Plaster', amongst others.

Kathryn Kerby-Fulton's edited *Women and the Divine in Literature before 1700* is a series of ten essays by diverse hands and the editor's introduction published as a tribute to Margot Kathleen Louis (1954–2007), 'a scholar of Victorian poetry', whose first love was medieval literature. She was, to quote from Patricia Young's obituary in the *Times Colonist* and *Globe and Mail* in September 2007, a 'champion of feminist causes and writing, and a passionate student of the feminine divine' (p. [i]). In her introduction Kerby-Fulton writes on 'Skepticism, Agnosticism and Belief: The Spectrum of Attitudes Towards Women's Vision in Medieval England' (pp. 1–17). Other chapters include Linda Olson on 'Mother and More for the Middle Ages: Monica as Teacher, Visionary, Philosopher and Mystic' (pp. 19–42). Olson's contribution has three appendices: '*Capitula* Concerning Monica in Robert Kilwardby's Summary of the *Confessiones* (Bibliothèque Nationale MS lat. 2117)'; 'Marginalia Annotations Concerning Monica in Master John Malberthorp's *Confessiones* (Eton College MS 47); and 'Depicting Monica in Jacques Legrand's Illustrative Program for the Vita Augustini' (pp. 43–7). Thea Todd writes on 'Revisiting Christina's Vow of Virginity: The Influence of

Developing Marriage Law on Christina of Markyate's *Life*' (pp. 49–63). Julianne Bruneau discusses 'Truth, Sex, and Divine Poetics in Alan of Lille's *De Planctu Naturae*' (pp. 65–86). Adrienne Williams Boyarin discusses 'Sealed Flesh, Book-Skin: How to Read the Female Body in the Early Middle English *Seinte Margarete*' (pp. 87–106). Maidie Hilmo focuses upon 'Iconic Representations of Chaucer's Two Nuns and their Tales from Manuscript to Print' (pp. 107–35). The remaining five contributions are: Heather Reid's 'Female Initiation Rites and Women Visionaries: Mystical Marriage in the Middle English Translation of *The Storie of Asneth*' (pp. 137–52); Johanne Paquette's 'Male Approbation in the Extant Glosses to the *Book of Margery Kempe*' (pp. 153–69); Jonathan Juilfs's '*This boke is begonne . . . but it is nott yet performyd*: Compilations of Julian of Norwich's *A Revelation of Love*, 1413–1670' (pp. 171–84); Jennifer Morrish's 'Susanna Elisabeth Prasch, Neo-Latin Novels, and Female Characters in *Psyche Cretica* (Regensburg, 1685)' (pp. 185–201); and Rosalynn Voaden's '*Epilogue*: A Catena of Women' (pp. 203–9). The volume contains extensive footnote documentation (pp. 211–76) and biographical notes on the contributors (pp. 277–9). The book is very well designed with Minion Pro text face; there are also accompanying black and white illustrations and tabulations.

Oak Knoll Press and the Center for the Book in the Library of Congress have collaborated to publish *Series Americana: Post Depression-Era Regional Literature, 1938–1980. A Descriptive Bibliography*, Carol Fitzgerald's detailed descriptions of books published during the years 1938 to 1980 that 'described American culture and society and the nation's natural resources' (p. xii). It is based upon an exhibition held on 25 October 2007 at the Bienes Museum of the Modern Book at the Broward County Library in Fort Lauderdale, Florida. 'The series featured in this book . . . comprise 163 titles and the work of 237 authors and 19 editors, providing a broad representation of the Series Americana published in the post-Depression era and the following decades' (p. xvii). Following an introduction (pp. xxiii–xxx), information on 'Series Americana' (pp. xxxi–xxxvi), the main entries consist of essays on publishing history, including the dust-jacket and the photographer involved, with black and white illustrations of each dust-jacket and detailed descriptive bibliographical data. These are followed by notes on 'Reprints and Reproductions', notes on the historical place if necessary, reviews, and the sources used for the description (see for instance pp. 8–9). The descriptions are itemized AL1, that is 'American Landmarks' (p. 8) through to the final item in volume 2, 'The American Forts Series', 'AFT9' (p. 932)—the pagination is continuous in the two volumes. There are three appendices: 'Imprints, Colophons, and Series Devices' (pp. 941–7) that include illustrations of bindings and publishers' devices; 'An Alphabetical Listing of the Authors by Series' (pp. 948–51); 'Citations and Abbreviations' (pp. 952–3), followed by an extensive index (pp. 955–78). Sturdily bound and designed with attractive typography by Scott James Vile, these volumes are a most impressive and definitive addition to twentieth-century American bibliography.

James Kearney's *The Incarnate in Text: Imagining the Book in Reformation England* is an 'exploration of the way that the book was imagined in Reformation England' (p. 3). Kearney's focus is upon the post-Reformation book as 'an object in crisis'. This crisis 'occasioned many attacks on artistic representation. Paintings, statues, entire buildings were destroyed, music was forbidden, theater and poetry were denounced—all in the name of eradicating superstition and idolatry' (p. 4). An extensive, closely argued introduction (pp. 1–41), is followed by chapters on 'Relics of the Mind: Erasmian Humanism and Textual Presence' (pp. 42–84); 'Rewriting the Letter: Textual Icons and Linguistic Artifacts in Book I of *The Faerie Queene*' (pp. 85–139); 'The Reading of the Damned: *Doctor Faustus* and Textual Conversion' (pp. 140–77); 'Book, Trinket, Fetish: Letters and Mastery in *The Tempest*' (pp. 178–23); and an 'Epilogue' focusing upon 'Bacons' Impossible Book', *New Atlantis* (pp. 224–39).There are extensive notes following the chapters (pp. 241–79), an alphabetically arranged, enumerative bibliography (pp. 282–304), and a detailed index (pp. 305–9). This deeply learned book is accompanied by twenty-one helpful illustrations.

Sarah Ellenzweig's *The Fringes of Belief: English Literature, Ancient Heresy, and the Politics of Freethinking, 1660–1760* consists of an 'investigation of English freethinking' (p. 28), concluding 'with an examination of Pope's *Essay on Man*' (p. 28). Following a detailed 'Introduction: Literary Culture, the Classical Past, and the Rise of Restoration Freethinking' (pp. 1–28), the book is divided into two parts: 'Libertine Precursors' (pp. 31–79) and 'Skepticism and Piety' (pp. 83–131). Part I consists of two chapters, one on 'Rochester, Blount, and the Faith of Unbelief' (pp. 31–51) and one on 'Behn, Fontenelle, and the Cheats of Revealed Religion' (pp. 53–79). The second part also has two chapters, the first on 'Swift's *Tale of a Tub* and the Anthropology of Religion' (pp. 83–109), and the second on 'Suspending Disbelief: *Swift, Credulity, and the Pious Fraud*' (pp. 111–31). In her 'Conclusion' Ellenzweig writes on 'Pope's *Essay on Man* and the Afterlife of English Freethinking' (pp. 133–52). The text of what is not a lengthy monograph is followed by detailed notes (pp. 153–207), and an alphabetically based, enumerative bibliography (pp. 209–27). There is in addition a detailed and useful index (pp. 229–40). This is a learned monograph; however, one could only wish that the sentences were slightly shorter!

Peter McDonald's provocatively entitled and important *The Literature Police: Apartheid Censorship and its Cultural Consequences* draws upon his knowledge of South Africa. As McDonald notes, 'Writing about apartheid South Africa inevitably involves negotiating a complex and highly contested array of names for various collective identities, which, in the case of the state's own official lexicon, were part of the apparatus of racist repression' (p. xv). In the detailed first part, 'Creating Spaces/Guarding Borders' (pp. 21–216), McDonald writes on 'Censors' (pp. 21–82); 'Publishers' (pp. 83–157), and 'Writers' (pp. 158–216). The second part focuses upon 'Singular Situations/ Disruptive Moments' (pp. 219–341). There are chapters on 'Nadine Gordimer and the Strength of the African Novel' (pp. 219–40); 'African versus *Volks* Humanism: Es'Kia Mphahlele's Worldly Music and the Transcendent Space of Culture' (pp. 241–57); 'Connected Versus Internal Critics: Breytenbach, Leroux, and the *Volk* Avant-Garde' (pp. 258–78); 'Black Books, Black (Anti–)Poetics' (pp. 279–302); 'J.M. Coetzee: The Provincial Storyteller' (pp. 303–20); and 'Protest and Beyond: Third World People's Stories in the

Staffrider Series' (pp. 321–41). Each of these chapter headings for these two parts is highlighted by the startling visual image of bold, black typesetting. There is a 'Postscript' (pp. 343–53) focusing upon Albie Sachs's activities. This is followed by a helpful 'Chronology' (pp. 355–63) and 'Notes to the Text' (pp. 365–89). There is an enumerative 'Select Bibliography' (pp. 391–9) usefully divided into 'Archival Sources' (p. 391), 'Digital Sources' (pp. 391–2), 'Oral Sources' (largely personal interviews) (pp. 392), and 'Published Sources' divided into 'Government Documents' and 'Other' (pp. 392–9). The final three theses are cited at the end (p. 399). McDonald's acknowledgements (pp. 401–2), too, are not without interest and are followed by a name-orientated index (pp. 403–16). The text contains a number of illustrations, some of which are fairly startling: see for instance 'The front and back cover of James Matthews's *pass me a meat-ball, Jones* (1977)' (p. 294). In short, Peter McDonald's *The Literature Police* is, to repeat, a very important work.

An important and interesting work is Hazard Adams's *Blake's Margins: An Interpretive Study of the Annotations*. This is the first critical work to consider William Blake's annotations in their entirety. Hazard Adams discusses Blake's annotations to 'Johann Caspar Lavater's *Aphorisms on Man*' (pp. 7–27); to 'Emanuel Swedenborg's *Heaven and Hell, Divine Love and Divine Wisdom*, and *Divine Providence*' (pp. 28–60); to 'Bishop Richard Watson's *An Apology for the Bible*' (pp. 61–80); to 'Sir Francis Bacon's *Essays Moral, Economical and Political*' (pp. 81–96); to 'Henry Boyd's *A Translation of the Inferno* of Dante Alighieri' (pp. 97–108); to 'Sir Joshua Reynolds's *Discourses on Art*' (pp. 109–38); to 'J.C. Spurzheim's *Observations on the Deranged Manifestations the Mind, or Insanity*' (pp. 139–49); to 'Bishop George Berkeley's *Siris*' (pp. 150–9); to 'William Wordsworth's *Poems* and Preface to *The Excursion*' (pp. 160–76); and to 'Robert John Thornton's *The Lord's Prayer, Newly Translated*' (pp. 177–94). There is a clear introduction (pp. 3–6) explaining Adams's intentions, and a final 'Note on Blake's Reading' (pp. 195–7). Adams's study reveals that 'Blake was an avid critic and commentator' (p. 197). This very useful book for students of Blake, intellectual history, and marginalia; it also has a helpful index (pp. 199–204).

Brief mention should be made of the influential Anthony Grafton's widely reviewed *Worlds Made by Words: Scholarship and Community in the Modern West*. The book consists mostly of previously published essays that have appeared in journals, such as the *New York Review of Books*, the *American Scholar*, and the *London Review of Books*. In his final three chapters, which focus upon prominent twentieth-century American intellectuals, Grafton argues 'that even in the age of mass media, electronic databases, and search engines, local conditions still enable us to know certain things—and prevent us from knowing others' (p. 7). The initial nine chapters in *Worlds Made by Words* 'concern themselves with the particular mosaic of scholarly communities' studied by Grafton 'since the early 1970s: the early modern republic of letters' (p. 6). Chapters 5 and 11 may be of particular interest to *YWES* readers as they focus upon, in the first instance, 'The Intellectual Origins of Bacon's *New Atlantis*' (pp. 98–113), and, in chapter 11, 'The Messrs. Casaubon: Isaac Casaubon and Mark Pattison' (pp. 216–30).

The third edition of Frederick G. Ruffner, Jr., and Laurence Urdang's *Ruffner's Allusions, Cultural, Literary and Historical: A Thematic Dictionary*, first published in 1982, increases 'the number of entries, from 8,700 in the Second Edition, to nearly 13,000 in the Third' (p. vii). It is 'Dedicated to the Memory of Laurence Urdang, March 21, 1927–August 21, 2008', described as 'one of the greatest lexicographers of the modern era' (p. vi). The volume explicates the meaning of the innumerable allusions found in everyday reading and speech. It is divided into 734 thematic categories beginning with 'Abandonment' and concluding with 'Zodiac' (pp. xvii, xxx). To take a few instances of what the reader will find in the volume: 'Virginia Slims cigarette trademark marketed to "independent women." "You've come a long way, baby" as a slogan. [Trademarks: Crowley *Trad*, 630]' followed by 'Wisk, Miss lady with a mission. [Br. Lit.: *Bleak House*]' (p. 652); the twelfth explanation under 'Zodiac' reads, 'Virgo virgin (Aug. 23–Sept. 22). [Astrology: Hall, 315]' (p. 817). There is an extensive bibliography of sources used (pp. 821–66) and an index (pp. 869–969).

Ted Striphas, in his *The Late Age of Print: Everyday Book Culture from Consumerism to Control*, argues that in spite of the transformations in textual communications during the last decade or so of the twentieth century and the start of the twenty-first, traditional print forms represented by books are still around and flourishing. Striphas writes, 'The sooner we come to grips with the vitality of books in the late age of print, the sooner we'll be able to explore even more meaningfully how, through the growing prevalence of books in everyday life, present conditions are opening out onto emergent futures' (p. 188).

Amanda Vickery's superbly illustrated, both in colour and black and white, *Behind Closed Doors: At Home in Georgian England* has been well served by its publishers Yale University Press. Vickery draws upon diverse sources to give an account of the lives and activities of the human beings who lived in the homes of Georgian England. There is the gentlewoman Anne Dormer living in a stately Oxfordshire mansion, the future novelist Anthony Trollope trying to write himself out of his depressing London lodgings, those who keep up appearances in small rooms with yellow wallpaper and servants lucky to possesses a locking box. Vickery writes movingly of 'spinsters . . . ready to pack up their things and move on, insinuating themselves into another household as circumstances demanded. Any permanence lay with her chattels, the tea set and bed curtains, not in a static residence. The comfort of home inhered in her movables' (p. 307). The well-written text is followed by extensive documentation (pp. 308–49), a listing of 'Manuscript Collections' drawn upon (pp. 350–8) and a 'Select Bibliography' of printed primary and secondary sources (pp. 359–67). There is a very helpful index too (pp. 368–82). The dust-jacket, which no doubt will be unfortunately removed in libraries, is also worth preserving.

Philip Ford and Roger P.H. Green's *George Buchanan: Poet and Dramatist* is a welcome addition to our knowledge and perceptions of this neglected Scottish-French sixteenth-century neo-Latinist. The sixteen essays written by diverse hands encompass 'Buchanan's Secular Poetry' (pp. 3–71), 'Buchanan's Poetic Psalm Paraphrases and their Music' (pp. 75–160), 'The Dramas of

George Buchanan' (pp. 163–95), and 'The Reception of Buchanan's Poetry and Drama' (pp. 217–312). There is a detailed index (pp. 313–22). This exceptionally well produced and illustrated volume with contributions from Elwira Buszewicz, Giacomo Dardinali, Nathalie Catellani-Dufrêne, Jean-Frédéric Chevalier, Robert Crawford, Robert Cummings, Margaret Duncumb, Carine Ferradou, Philip Ford, Emma Gee, Roger Green, R.D.S. Jack, John MacQueen, James Porter, and Jamie Reid Baxter is the definitive critical scholarly work on its subject.

The great 'Cornell Yeats' continues with an edition of *'The Golden Helmet' and 'The Green Helmet' Manuscript Materials by W.B. Yeats*, edited by William P. Hogan. The erudite introduction (pp. xvii–xxix) is followed by a clear statement of 'Transcription Principles and Procedures' (pp. xxx–xxxi), and is the text of the 'Galley Proof of the Quinn Edition' at the New York Public Library (pp. 2–15). The rest of the volume consists of recto transcription and verso reproduction of the late 1909 holograph draft now at the National Library of Ireland. 'Variants between this and *The Green Helmet*'s first book printing in *The Green Helmet and Other Poems* (Dundrum: Cuala Press, 1910)' (p. 17) are collated below the transcriptions. There are two appendices: 'Transcription of Yeats's Note to the Play. NLI [National Library of Ireland] 13,571' (p. 143), and two 'Cast Photographs. NLI 1731' from the first production at the Abbey Theatre (pp. 146–7).

Bertram Brooker (1888–1955) is now unfortunately a forgotten figure. He was the first Canadian to have an exhibition of abstract art and he was the first winner of the Canadian Governor General's Award for Literature. Hopefully Gregory Betts's edited *The Wrong World: Selected Stories and Essays of Bertram Brooker* will lead to a revival of interest in his life, work, and achievements. Betts's introduction (pp. xi–xlix) gives a clear, detailed account of Brooker. The texts of eight of his short fictions (pp. 3–79), are followed by the text of 'Brooker's expansive mystical romance, the novella *The Wrong World* [which] presents an intriguing reversal of the recurring narrative of Canadian naturalization explored in the other texts' (p. xxxvii), and the text is found on pp. 83–150. This is followed by selections from Brooker's 'Essays and Polemics' (pp. 153–216). Betts provides a most detailed account of 'Textual Chronology and Editorial Procedures' (pp. 217–20), 'Explanatory Notes' (pp. 221–44), and 'Textual Emendations and Revisions' (pp. 245–80), followed by an enumerative, alphabetically arranged 'Works Cited' (pp. 281–8).

Brian Dibble's *Doing Life: A Biography of Elizabeth Jolley* records the life and publishing career of a fine Australian writer who began her career when she was in her fifties in Australia. Dibble draws upon his subject's private papers and has travelled the world to follow connections in Elizabeth Jolley's (1923–2007) stories. The focus is Australia but there are also sections dealing with Austria, various parts of England, and Scotland. The work concludes with an extensive listing of 'Works Cited' (pp. 309–33). The first part is 'Elizabeth Jolley—Novels and Collections' (pp. 309–16), followed by 'Elizabeth Jolley—Archival Material' including letters and notebooks (pp. 316–19). Dibble clearly acknowledges his debt to his and Barbara Milech's *Elizabeth Jolley—A Bibliography, 1965–2007*, 'published online through the Elizabeth Jolley Research Collection, John Curtin Prime Ministerial Library, Curtin University of Technology, Perth, WA, at http://john.curtin.edu.au/jolley' (p. 309). There is also a list of 'Works on Elizabeth Jolley' alphabetically arranged by authors (pp. 319–33).

The Voltaire Foundation at Oxford published a collection of essays edited by Frank A. Kafker and Jeff Loveland on *The Early Britannica: The Growth of an Outstanding Encyclopedia*. The editors' introduction (pp. 1–9) is followed by their detailed 'William Smellie's edition (1768–71): A Modest Start' (pp. 11–67). Kathleen Hardesty Doig, Frank A. Kafker, Jeff Loveland, and Dennis A. Trinkle write on 'James Tytler's Edition (1777–84): A Vast Expansion and Improvement' (pp. 69–155). Kathleen Hardesty Doig, Frank A. Kafker, and William E. Morris write, with the assistance of Marion A. Brown and Jeff Loveland, on 'Colin MacFarquhar, George Gleig and Possibly James Tytler's Edition (1788–97): The Attainment of Recognition and Eminence' (pp. 157–251). 'George Gleig's *Supplement* to the Third Edition (1801–3): Learned and Combative' is the subject of an essay by Kathleen Hardesty Doig, Frank A. Kafker, and Jeff Loveland (pp. 252–97). Frank A. Kafker contributes 'Epilogue: The Tortoise and the Hare: The Longevity of the *Encyclopedia Britannica* and the *Encyclopédie* Compared' (pp. 299–307). There is an extensive bibliography consisting of a description of 'Manuscripts' (pp. 309–10), 'Editions and Prospectuses of the *Encyclopedia Britannica* (1768–1803)' (pp. 310–11), and 'Other Published Works and Dissertations Cited' (pp. 311–33). The volume concludes with a detailed index (pp. 335–49). There are thirteen full-page, black and white illustrations.

John Wilson Foster's *Between Shadows: Modern Irish Writing and Culture* is a sequel to the author's *Colonial Consequences* [1991], and is similarly preoccupied with late nineteenth-century and twentieth-century Irish writers. Foster places writers such as Wilde, Yeats, Joyce, Trevor, Heaney, and Sebastian Barry, amongst others, within their social, political, and economic context. There is interesting material on Ulster and its literary scene during the Second World War, the Irish Nationalist movements, and the First World War. Somewhat curiously, the computer-generated typesetting is in bold, which is rather startling to the eye. The volume lacks a bibliography, although notes are to be found at the end of each of the sixteen chapters, and there is an author-based index (pp. 253–7).

Brief mention should be made of Debra Marmor and Herbert Danner's translation of Rüdiger Görner's *London Fragments: A Literary Expedition*, which was originally published in German in 2003. Görner, the chair of the Department of German at Queen Mary College, University of London, writes an unashamed travel guide and celebration of the city that he loves. Unlike other recent books on London, this one is unpretentious and clearly written, and revolves around the great city's writers who recreated London. These range from Thomas Carlyle, Shakespeare, and Keats to Pinter and Hanif Kureishi. There is a useful biographical index (pp. 119–28) and bibliography (pp. 129–31), followed by seven full-page, black and white portraits of writers, ranging from Anthony Trollope to T.S. Eliot.

Mention too should be made of Sue Brown's *Joseph Severn, A Life: The Rewards of Friendship*. Severn was close to Keats and an artist of considerable contemporary repute. He may be neglected as his long life (he lived from 1793 to 1879) spans the Romantics and the Victorians. In addition to pressing for an early biography and a fitting memorial for Keats in the Protestant cemetery in Rome, he lived on as an advocate of Keats and was reburied in 1882 next to the poet. However, twentieth-century biographers tended to denigrate him as unreliable and self-promoting regarding Keats. Sue Brown draws upon unpublished documents to reassess his achievements and his period as British consul in Rome from 1861 to 1872. In addition to long friendships with Leigh Hunt, Mary Shelley, Charles Eastlake, Richard Monkton Milnes, and others, Severn, while in Rome, welcomed Gladstone (who became his patron), Ruskin, Walter Scott, Wordsworth, Turner, Samuel Palmer, David Wilkie, and many others. Brown's well-written, readable life is accompanied by twenty illustrations, and there are nine plates. Inevitably when this book enters libraries as it should, the dust-wrapper will be thrown away. This is a pity, as it contains a jacket illustration, a portrait of Joseph Severn, by Seymour Kirkup dated 1822.

One of the pre-eminent late twentieth-century and early twenty-first-century bibliographers who traverses the move from the printed word to electronic formats, Jerome McGann has produced a learned but amusing little book, *Are the Humanities Inconsequent? Interpreting Marx's Riddle of the Dog*. According to the description on the publisher's website (the Prickly Paradigm Press, Chicago; www.prickly-paradigm.com), 'Adapting the discontinuous and multi-tonal critical procedures of works like Carlyle's *Sartor Resartus* and Laura Riding's *Anarchism Is Not Enough*, Jerome McGann subjects current literary studies to a patacritical investigation. The investigation centers in the interpretation of a notorious modern riddle.' The website then quotes from the opening of McGann's book: 'Outside of a dog, a book is a man's best friend. Inside of a dog, it's too dark to read' (p. i). McGann then works by indirection and uses multiple points of view to argue that 'aesthetics is always a science of exceptions, and that any given critical practice is also always an exception from itself'. His work is based upon two assumptions: first 'that the riddle of the dog conceals an allegory about book culture and is addressed to the academic custodians of book culture' and secondly, 'that any explanation of the riddle is necessarily implicated in the problem posed by the riddle of the dog. It therefore remains to be seen—it is the reader's part to decide—whether the book is a friend to man or—perhaps like Marx's riddle, too dark to read' (p. i). This is clever, almost Thomist!

A recent addition to the wonderful Juvenilia Press Editions devoted 'to the recovery, publication, and critical exploration of childhood writings' (p. ii) is Annette Upfal and Christine Alexander's splendid *Jane Austen's The History of England & Cassandra's Portraits*. Founded in 1994 by the eminent critic and scholar Juliet McMaster at the University of Alberta in Edmonton, since 2001 the press has been located at the University of New South Wales in Sydney. Its presiding general editor and director is the doyenne of juvenilia studies and the world authority on the Brontës, Professor Christine Alexander. Annette Upfal's edition of *Jane Austen's The History of England* comes replete with ten illustrations, some of them in colour. There is an extensive, most informative introduction (pp. xiv–liii) encompassing 'The *History* as Parody' (pp. xv–xxii),

'The *History* and the Austen Family' (pp. xxiii–xxiv), 'A Room of Their Own' (pp. xxv–xxvii), 'Creating the Images' (pp. xxvii–xxxvii), 'Cassandra's Images and the Hidden Narrative' (pp. xxxvii–xl), 'The *History* as Autobiography' (pp. xl–xlii), and 'Cassandra's Images and Jane Austen's Text: An Autobiographical Reading' (pp. xlii–li). This is followed by 'A Note on the Text' (p. lv) and the text itself (pp. 1–19). There are 137 most helpful 'Explanatory Notes' (pp. 20–49), a listing of 'Textual Notes' (p. 50), and three appendices. The first, 'Appendix A: Why Didn't Family Members Recognize the Images in the *History?*' (pp. 51–4), the second, 'Appendix B: Costume Evidence in Cassandra's Portraits of the Three Queens: Mary, Queen of Scots, Elizabeth and Mary' (pp. 55–65), and 'Appendix C: Dr. Pamela Craig's Report on the Images in *The History of England*' (pp. 66–8). This wonderful volume concludes with an alphabetically arranged, enumerative 'Works Cited and Consulted' (pp. 69–73). This latest edition to the Juvenilia Press series is splendidly designed by 'Winston Pei, Black Riders Design' (p. iv) and is an indispensable contribution to Jane Austen studies as well as to juvenilia studies and textual editing.

Mention should be made of Dinah Hazell's *Poverty in Late Middle English Literature: The Meene and the Riche*. This most useful study hopefully will not be neglected. It draws upon *Piers Plowman* and other texts to present a picture of fourteenth-century poverty, ranging from the aristocrat to the pauper. The author's concern is also to explore the ways in which poverty is utilized as a basic theme and concern in the literature of the period. Texts studied include *Havelok*, *The Prioress's Tale*, and other Chaucerian works, *The Corpus Christi Shepherd's Plays* and Capgrave's *Life of Gilbert*. Hazell writes clearly and with considerable insight. The book is well designed with most useful notation at the foot of the page. In addition, there are most useful alphabetically arranged, enumerative bibliographies of 'Primary Sources' (pp. 213–16) and 'Secondary Sources' (pp. 216–22), and a useful index (pp. 223–33) to this important study.

It would be wrong to ignore Laurence Lerner's latest book, *Reading Women's Poetry*, which attempts to overturn what its author regards as 'something inherently patriarchal about what we have traditionally expected of poems'. He calls 'for an alternative canon, judged by different criteria'. The creation of such a canon faces 'two important and fascinating questions. First, what will it say about the female writers already accepted into the traditional canon?' These writers include Jane Austen, Charlotte Brontë, George Eliot, Elizabeth Browning, Christina Rossetti, Emily Dickinson, and others. The second question is: 'Since an alternative canon implies alternative criteria, what are the patriarchal criteria for judging poetry, and what would the alternative, feminist criteria be?' (pp. 4–5). These and others are the issues Lerner investigates in his clearly written study. There are chapters on the Augustans and Romantics, and on the nineteenth and twentieth centuries, and the book concludes with 'Aurora Leigh, or What Is It Like To Be a Woman Poet?' (pp. 177–88), and 'A Name of One's Own' (pp. 189–92). There is an index of poets divided by gender (pp. 193–4). Lerner's readings of poems are remarkably astute. He certainly has interesting comments to make.

Occasionally this chapter draws its readers' attention book dealers' and auctioneers' catalogues that may be of interest and should be recorded. Joshua

Heller, *Classic Examples of the Art of the Book: Catalogue Thirty Seven, Summer 2009* is one instance. It is illustrated with magnificent colour illustrations providing examples for sale of the art of the book focusing primarily upon recent American private press productions, although it is not exclusively American-based. For example, there is described the Circle Press's '*Bluebeard's Castle*. [Poetry by] Roy Fisher for 9 3-dimensional pop-up designs by Ron King'. This was published in Guildford, Surrey, in 1972. It was limited to 157 of 175 copies plus fifteen proofs with prospectuses and related ephemera. The poetry and the design are based upon Bartok's opera. This item is priced at $3,000 (see pp. 9–10). There are in fact five Circle Press items listed (items 9–13) including 'Ron King's *Tabernacle*—The King Family History of Seven Generations of Printers' with verse by Roy Fisher published in London in 2001 in a limited edition of fifty-six sets. This is priced at $4,500. Heller's catalogue with its coloured illustrations of each of the 115 items for sale constitutes a documentary history of very modern fine press printing and illuminates not only contemporary printing and private press history but also the accomplishments of poets and book design artists such as Roy Fisher, Paul Johnson, and Ron King, amongst others.

Allison Hoover Bartlett's *The Man Who Loved Books Too Much: The True Story of a Thief, a Detective, and a World of Literary Obsession*, is a true tale of book theft and detection. The story of a Californian book dealer and his nefarious activities is interwoven with that of a Salt Lake City book dealer who becomes obsessed with the aim of tracking down and exposing the former. Their story is interwoven with the history of book theft and obsession throughout the ages. Bartlett has certainly done her research. She writes well with a narrative sense of flow and illuminates the rare book world of modern America and human motivation, which does not change much throughout the ages.

A semi-autobiographical memoir with a title taken from Groucho Marx by self-confessed rogue Rick Gekoski is not without interest to *YWES* readers. Gekoski gained a D.Phil. at Oxford on Joseph Conrad and taught English at the University of Warwick until 1987. Five years earlier, he had begun his own business dealing in rare books and manuscripts. Gekoski, in his *Outside of a Dog: A Bibliomemoir*, writes with zest and verve on the various characters he has met in the world of book dealing. He specializes in modern first editions and manuscripts, and so his bibliomemoir is full of anecdotes about contemporary writers and their archives. Regrettably there is no index, but the short chapters move effortlessly from auctions in Leamington Spa, to the objections of the author's first wife, to his purchasing obsessions, courses on Yeats and the University of Pennsylvania, to Oxford, Matthew Arnold, Alan Ginsberg, and so much more. In short, Gekoski's *Outside of a Dog* is fascinating and highly recommended. Certainly its author has made considerably more money, than if he had remained teaching at the University of Warwick. Whether he is any happier must remain in a world of speculation.

James Vigus's *Platonic Coleridge* is part of Legenda's excellent Studies in Comparative Literature series published by the Modern Humanities Research Association and Maney Publishing. As Vigus says upfront, 'This book examines the philosophical writing of Samuel Taylor Coleridge, in the light of his relationship to Plato.' Vigus documents 'as far as possible, when and via which texts and commentaries Coleridge read Plato'. He also argues 'that the form and content of Coleridge's writing, mainly but not exclusively his later prose, can be usefully interpreted with reference to Plato's thought' (p. 1). Inevitably, Coleridge's reading of Plato is the central focus of the book and Vigus draws upon Coleridge's notebooks, annotations, and copious marginalia in his copies of Plato, drawing upon Ralph J. Coffman's *Coleridge's Library: A Bibliography of Books Owned or Read by Samuel Taylor Coleridge* [1987], and work on Coleridge's marginalia, especially by George Whalley and H.J. Jackson (1980–2001). Of considerable importance for Coleridge's reading were Thomas Taylor's translations, published in five volumes in 1804. Coleridge's response to his readings is clearly described and analysed in this well-written monograph, which should be of interest to all students of Coleridge and the reception of Platonic ideas in English literature.

Marilyn Deegan and Kathryn Sutherland's *Transferred Illusions: Digital Technology and the Forms of Print* places the early twenty-first-century revolution in the manner of reading, witnessed by the internet and its implications, in historical context. The authors draw parallels between recent ways of reading and earlier ones. For them, the new modes of publishing are not necessarily as revolutionary as may be perceived. In short, Deegan and Sutherland have very interesting things to say about recurrent patterns in the transmission of forms of print. There are chapters on 'After Print?' (pp. 1–28), 'A Future and a Past for Newsprint' (pp. 29–58), 'The Cultural Work of Editing' (pp. 59–88), 'New Modes of Publishing' (pp. 89–118), 'The Universal Library' (pp. 119–54), and 'Durable Futures' (pp. 155–82). The fifth chapter, on 'The Universal Library', contains material on 'A Brief History of Libraries' (pp. 120–6), 'Computerization in Libraries', (pp. 126–32), 'Digitization and Scholarship' (pp. 132–5), and 'Digital Libraries and Mass Digitizaiton' (pp. 135–54), providing much food for thought.

Marilyn Deegan and Kathryn Sutherland's *Text Editing, Print and the Digital Word* is divided into two parts. Following the editors' succinct introduction (pp. 1–12), the first part, 'In Theory', contains Kathryn Sutherland's 'Being Critical: Paper-Based Editing and the Digital Environment' (pp. 13–26); Mats Dahlström's 'The Compleat Edition' (pp. 27–44); Dino Buzzetti's 'Digital Editions and Text Processing' (pp. 45–62); Paul Eggert's 'The Book, the E-Text and the "Work-Site"' (pp. 63–82); Gabriel Bodard and Juan Garcés' 'Open Source Critical Editions: A Rationale' (pp. 83–98); and Edward Vanhoutte's 'Every Reader his own Bibliographer—An Absurdity?' (pp. 99–112). The second part, 'In Practice', contains five essays: Espen S. Ore's '"...They Hid their Books Underground"' (pp. 113–26); Linda Bree and James McLaverty's 'The Cambridge Edition of the Works of Jonathan Swift and the Future of the Scholarly Edition' (pp. 127–36); James Mussell and Suzanne Paylor's 'Editions and Archives: Textual Editing and the Nineteenth-Century Serials Edition (ncse)' (pp. 137–58); Charlotte Roueché's 'Digitizing Inscribed Texts' (pp. 159–68); and Elena Pierazzo's 'Digital Genetic Editions: The Encoding of Time in Manuscript Transcription' (pp. 169–86). There is an extensive bibliography (pp. 187–98) and a useful index (pp. 199–223).

Peter Brooker and Andrew Thacker's edited *The Oxford Critical and Cultural History of Modernist Magazines*, volume 1: *Britain and Ireland 1880–1955* is divided into ten parts each with an introduction written by the editors explaining and reviewing what is to follow. Thirty-eight contributing scholars write on 'Victorian Precursors' (pp. 33–65), '*Fin-de-Siècle* Ventures (1884–1906)' (pp. 76–141), 'Early Statements (1899–1915)' (pp. 152–96), 'Transitions' (pp. 205–59), 'Interventions' (pp. 269–336), 'Editors and Programmes' (pp. 340–451), 'Into the 1920s: Dispersal and Difference' (pp. 462–588), 'Commitment to the New' (pp. 599–703), 'Beyond the Metropolis' (pp. 714–824), and 'The Call to Criticism and Modernist Destinies' (pp. 833–97). These ten sections concentrate on eighty-four magazines, although of course other ones are mentioned and on occasion discussed. There are notable exclusions. *Life and Letters*, which ran from 1928 to 1935, is discussed (see pp. 428–51), but not the *Bookman* (1891–1935), with which the former subsequently merged.

It would be inappropriate to single out for especial attention one contribution or contributor rather than another in such a collaborative undertaking. Clearly, some chapters are less opaque than others and have lengthy footnote documentation that can detract from the text. It is pleasing to find discussion and analysis of financial records, editorial policy and selection criteria, the underlying agendas for the magazines, in many instances the careers and motives of their editors in the founding of them, the contributions and contributors, circulation, and distribution. There could be more on layout, on individual magazine design, typography, and binding, and their significance.

This admirable addition to the reference shelves has 102 black and white illustrations, mostly of covers. The aim of these, presumably, is to assist in the visualization of the physicality of the magazine. Unfortunately, however, many of the illustrations are far too small to serve this function (see for instance the cover of *Form* for April 1916, illustrated on p. 572). There are two tabular lists: 'Timeline for Selected Periodicals, 1908–19', and 'Prices of Selected Periodicals c.1850–1950' (pp. 22, 24–5). The enumerative alphabetically arranged bibliography is extensive (pp. 899–930), and the index is detailed and helpful (pp. 931–55). The volume seems to be well bound to survive continuous library usage. In short, despite some caveats, *The Oxford Critical and Cultural History of Modernist Magazines*, volume 1: *Britain and Ireland 1880–1955* is an indispensible library purchase. It is an important reference work for all students of, to use the general catchall expression, 'modernism'.

Barry Forshaw's two-volume *British Crime Writing: An Encyclopedia* contains alphabetically listed accounts of British crime writers and writing. It is replete with very interesting information, giving a biographical account as well as an account of work. To take one example, Philip Gooden's entry on the now largely forgotten but fine writer 'Bonfiglioli, Kyril (1928–1985)' opens with the comment that 'Crime fiction, like other branches of literature, has its maverick writers, and Kiryl Bonfiglioli was an outstanding example of the category'. Gooden's last sentence of his first paragraph reads: 'No one else, however, has provided quite the stylized exuberance and absurd tone of

Bonfiglioli's novels featuring Charlie Mortdecai.' Bonfiglioli's *Don't Point That Thing at Me* [1972] won the John Creasey Memorial Dagger awarded to 'the best first crime novel'. He subsequently produced four additional novels before dying from cirrhosis in 1985: 'his final decade was dogged by poverty and alcoholism'. As Gooden comments, few 'read Bonfiglioli for his plotting or for the traditional pleasures of suspense and mystery'. Gooden adds, that Bonfiglioli's 'attraction lies in the highly distinctive tone adopted by Mortdecai—a snobbish tone which is discursive—and often being Wodehousian in phrasing: gamey and rich' (pp. 71–2). Each entry in the encyclopedia is followed by a listing of the individual author's selected works. Forshaw's *British Crime Writing: A Encyclopedia* is highly recommended, although of course, individual entries may vary.

Chris Gostick's *T.F. Powys's Favourite Bookseller: The Story of Charles Lahr* is a delightfully produced and illustrated pamphlet retelling the story of Charles Lahr (1885–1971), whose friendship the Powys family cultivated. Indeed, Lahr 'appears in a great many of the literary memoirs of the years 1920 to 1950. He was an unusually eccentric and larger than life character at a time when London had many such individuals—something which sadly is no longer the case' (p. 3). He was also know to H.E. Bates, D.H. Lawrence, Emanuel Litvinoff, and others. Although Lahr was associated with anarchists, Gostick focuses instead upon Lahr's bookselling, bookshop, and magazine activity, especially *The New Coterie*, which he began to publish in the summer of 1925. He and K.S. Bhat, 'a radical Indian doctor with a taste for mystical literature and a medical practice in East London', had 'a good eye for emerging literary talent, and many young writers were first published in the magazine, but it attracted heavyweights too, such as D.H. Lawrence, Aldous Huxley, Nancy Cunard, and Liam O'Flaherty together with the illustrator William Roberts' (p. 9). Gostick's focus is Lahr's Red Lion bookshop run by himself and his wife Esther, and their activities, including Charles Lahr's arrest in January 1935 'on a charge of receiving stolen property' (p. 23). Gostick, an authority on the Powys family and James Handley, focuses upon the latter's attempts to assist Lahr and his family during the difficult period in which Lahr served six months in Wormwood Scrubs. Gostick concludes that it was his 'absolute commitment to the importance of ideas and imagination, at a time when this was far from easy, which singled out Charles Lahr as a special and unique individual' (p. 30).

Mention should be made of the issue of *The Hollins Critic* 46:iii containing reminiscences of the American poet and critic Donald Hall (b. 1928), who spent some time in Britain. The issue contains reminiscences of Donald Hall (pp. 1–16) by Lewis Turco and contains an enumerative listing with publishers and prices of 'Books by Donald Hall' divided into poetry, non-fiction, plays, and children's books (pp. 12–13). The July/September issue of *Études Anglaises* (*EA* 62–3[2009]) is devoted to Indian writing in English and contains Alexis Tadié's most useful enumerative 'Bibliography of Indian Writing in English' (*EA* 62–3[2009] 379–84), which follows Vanessa Guignery and Alexis Tadié's 'In Custody and Beyond: A Conversation with Anita Desai' (*EA* 62–3[2009] 370–8). Tadié's bibliography is divided into four alphabetically arranged sections: 'Novels and Short Stories in English' (pp. 379–82); 'Poetry' (pp. 382–3); 'Anthologies' (pp. 383–4); and 'Novels in Other Indian Languages Cited in the Essay' (p. 384). *The Journal of Commonwealth Literature* (*JCL* 44:iv[2009]) is devoted to the 'Annual Bibliography of Commonwealth Literature'. There are sections on Australia, Canada, the Caribbean, East and Central Africa, India, Malaysia, Singapore, New Zealand, Pakistan, South Africa, Sri Lanka, and West Africa. All in all, most welcome.

There has been recent controversy over Wikipedia, its contributors and its reliability. Dan O'Sullivan's *Wikipedia: A New Community of Practice?* is an 'attempt to map out and weigh up the implications of a means of knowledge dissemination, but also production, that is the most far-reaching of any in existence today'. The second half of the book focuses predominantly on Wikipedia itself. O'Sullivan's conclusion has been seriously questioned. He writes that 'Every article in Wikipedia, even when predominantly written by one person, has in all probability been copy-edited, peer-reviewed, argued over or had images added to it by many others.' Further, 'A culture of sharing and participation is the most radical feature of the entire project, and the most promising for the future of the Internet, and hence for our way of life' (pp. 185–6). There is a useful index to this well-written work. Maybe O'Sullivan's study will be seen as an analysis of an ephemeral fad of the first decade or so of the twenty-first century; maybe not. Only time will tell.

The distinguished Japanese Shakespearian and Renaissance scholar Akihiro Yamada, in his *Secrets of the Printed Page in the Age of Shakespeare: Bibliographical Studies in the Plays of Beaumont, Chapman, Dekker, Fletcher, Ford, Marston, Shakespeare, Shirley and the Text of King James I's The True Lawe of Free Monarchies*, argues that, while Shakespeare and his contemporaries wrote for audiences, they also had in their minds potential readers. For Yamada, textual criticism should aim to restore texts to the versions their authors may have intended in the belief that they were creating works that would survive the ravages of time. So Yamada presents studies of books printed by Thomas Creede and Peter Short, who also printed Shakespeare. Yamada also presents exact bibliographical analyses of all the known extant copies of the very earliest editions of plays by George Chapman, John Ford, and John Marston. Such studies are placed alongside much shorter general essays that interest textual bibliographers and also critics of the Renaissance. In addition, *Secrets of the Printed Page in the Age of Shakespeare* presents the first original-spelling edition of an untitled seventeenth-century drama found in Edgerton MS 1994, folios 212–23 in the British Library. This is called *Arcadia Restored*. Yamada also prepared a modern-spelling edition of this that was published as AMS Studies in the Renaissance 47. There are appendices, the first on 'Press Variants in Early Quartos of Alphonsus, The Ball, *Bussy D'Ambois* (Q7), Chabot, and *Two Wise Men*' and secondly, 'A List of Akihiro Yamada's Bibliographical Papers in Japanese Journals on Early Quartos of Chapman, Ford and Marston'. These are followed by listings of 'Lineation in *Arcadia Restored*' and a 'Glossary to *Arcadia Restored*'. This most interesting book concludes with a very helpful index (pp. 261–89).

Janel Mueller and Joshua Scodel's *Elizabeth I: Translations* is a nicely produced two-volume work presenting original and modernized spellings in a facing-page format in an attempt to make all of Elizabeth I's writings available. It includes the body of translations she made over the course of her lifetime from and into Latin, French, and Italian. The first volume consists of 'Translations 1554–1589' and the second volume, 'Translations, 1592–1598'. There is an extensive introduction and of course 'Commentary' with five illustrations in the first volume and five in the second. All in all, this is a very valuable work of scholarly achievement and reference.

The present writer is reluctant to include online databases as they are subject to frequent migration or simply disappear somewhere into the ether! However, it is to be assumed that the Gladstone database (GladCAT) will not be ephemeral. This database claims to give fully searchable details on Gladstone's annotations and marginalia and aims to identify and create a catalogue of the books personally owned by William Ewart Gladstone and his annotations to these books. It is a product of a three-year AHRC-funded research project undertaken by St Deiniol's Library and the University of Liverpool. Further information may be found at http://www.st-deiniols.com/the-library/gladcat.htm. Pierre A. Walker and Greg W. Zacharias continue their great *Complete Letters of Henry James, 1872–1876*, volume 2. This volume covers letters from 15 July 1873 to 15 October 1875. There are letters to his father, his sister, his brother, and other members of the family, plus his publishers. Carefully edited and transcribed, they are accompanied by detailed annotations and as usual a very helpful 'Chronology' (pp. xix–xxxiv). This is textual annotation and editing at its finest.

A book which may otherwise get overlooked and slip between various periods' stalls, Margery Palmer McCulloch's *Scottish Modernism and its Contexts 1918–1959: Literature, National Identity and Cultural Exchange* is a study of Scottish literature in the period after 1918. McCulloch argues that in this period there was 'a Scottish literary modernism drawing on artistic influences from European modernism and rooted in the desire to recover a self-determining identity for Scotland both culturally and politically' (p. 1). Amongst the authors considered are C.M. Grieve (Hugh MacDiarmid), Neil M. Gunn, and Edwin Muir. In the first part, 'Transforming Traditions' (pp. 11–92), the focus is on C.M. Grieve (Hugh MacDiarmid), and there is an interesting chapter focusing upon 'Women, Modernism and the Modern World' (pp. 68–92). The second section, entitled 'Ideology and Literature', moves from a consideration of the question 'Whither Scotland? Politics and Society between the Wars' (pp. 93–112) to a consideration of Neil M. Gunn entitled 'Re-imagining the Highlands' (pp. 113–30), and then to '*A Scots Quair*' (pp. 131–54) and 'Poetry and Politics' (pp. 154–68). The third part, 'World War Two and its Aftermath', has two sections: 'Visionaries and Revisionaries: Late Muir and MacDiarmid' (pp. 169–98) and 'Continuities and New Voices' (pp. 198–215). The book concludes with a very useful bibliography of works cited (pp. 216–22) and an index (pp. 223–9).

A useful addition to the MLA series Options for Teaching is Stephen E. Tabachnick's edited *Teaching the Graphic Novel*. In addition to a clearly written introduction (pp. 1–18), there are five parts by various hands. The first is on 'Theoretical and Aesthetic Issues' (pp. 19–68); the second on 'Social Issues' (pp. 68–110), the third on 'Individual Creators' (pp. 111–216), the fourth on 'Courses and Contexts' (pp. 217–326), and the fifth on 'Resources' (pp. 327–40). Clearly with so many contributors there is a considerable amount of unevenness. Part III, on 'Individual Creators', contains some particularly interesting accounts, including Mark Feldman's 'The Urban Studies of Ben Katchor' (pp. 129–36), J. Caitlin Finlayson's 'The Boundaries of Genre: Translating Shakespeare in Anthony Johnston and Brett Welde's *Julius*' (pp. 188–99), and Christine Ferguson's 'Steam Punk and the Visualization of the Victorian: Teaching Alan Moore's *The League of Extraordinary Gentleman* and *From Hell*' (pp. 200–7), to name but three from many. The two essays in 'Resources' are of particular value, constituting in a sense a bibliography of the field. They include Chris Matz's 'Supporting the Teaching of the Graphic Novel: The Role of the Academic Library' (pp. 327–32)—North American-based but still very useful, and, curiously unattributed but nevertheless one of the most informative contributions to the whole book, 'A Selected Bibliography of the Graphic Novel and Sequential Art' (pp. 333–41). This is alphabetically arranged. In addition, there is a useful but limited index (pp. 345–51).

Katherine Forsyth's seemingly expensive *Studies of the Book of Deer* contains some fascinating illustrations and focuses upon an interesting text. The volume is divided into three sections by diverse hands. The first, focusing on 'The Gospel Book' (pp. 3–118), consists of four essays including Patrick Zutshi's 'The Book of Deer after *c.*1150. Appendix: Unpublished Writings by Henry Bradshaw Concerning the Book of Deer' (pp. 98–118). The second contains seven essays on 'The Property Records' (pp. 119–362). There essays ranging from Roibeard Ó Maolalaigh's 'The Property Records: Diplomatic Edition Including Accents' (pp. 119–30), and Katherine Forsyth, Dauvit Broun, and Thomas Clancy's 'The property records: text and translation' (pp. 131–44), and concluding with Dauvit Broun's 'The Property Records in the Book of Deer as a Source for Early Scottish Society' (pp. 313–62). The final section, 'Deer in Context', has four contributions: Thomas Clancy's 'Deer and the Early Church in North-Eastern Scotland' (pp. 363–97); Katherine Forsyth's 'The Stones of Deer' (pp. 398–438); Richard Fawcett's 'The Cistercian Abbey of Deer. Appendix: Old Deer Parish Church' (pp. 439–62); and 'Mark Dilworth's 'Deer and its Abbots in the Late Middle Ages' (pp. 463–74). There is a short index (pp. 475–80).

Robert Darnton's *The Case for Books: Past, Present, and Future* is just one of many current publications defending the book against perceived current threats. Darnton writes in his introduction that 'This is a book about books, an unashamed apology for the printed word, past, present, and future. It is also an argument about the place of books in the digital environment that has now become a fundamental fact of life for millions of human beings.' He continues, 'Far from deploring electronic modes of communication, I want to explore the possibilities of aligning them with the power that Johannes Guttenberg unleashed more than five centuries ago. What common ground exists between old books and e-books?' (p. 7). This clearly written book is divided into three parts: 'Future' (pp. 3–66), 'Present' (pp. 67–108), and 'Past' (pp. 109–206). The opening of Part III consists of a chapter headed 'A Paean to Paper' (pp. 109–30). There is a bibliography and an index (pp. 207–18). The present reviewer is collecting such books defending the book.

Volume 4 of the great edition of *The Works of Thomas Traherne*, edited by Jan Ross, contains the first definitive printed edition of Traherne's notebooks, and also a previously unpublished manuscript book found at the Bodleian Library, *Church's Year Book* (pp. 1–261). In addition, there is *A Serious and Pathetical Contemplation of the Mercies of GOD, in Several Most Devout and Sublime Thanksgivings for the Same*, initially printed in 1699 (pp. 313–434). The appendix contains *Meditations on the Six Days of Creation* (pp. 437–500), a work of questionable attribution, Nathaniel Spinckes's 'The Preface to *A Collection of Meditations and Devotions*' (pp. 501–10), and passages from George Hicks, *A Second Collection of Controversial Letters Relating to the Church of England, and the Church of Rome* (pp. 511–12). In addition, there is 'William T. Brooke's Account of the Discovery of Thomas Traherne's Manuscripts: "The Story of the Traherne MSS. by their Finder" '(pp. 513–16). This is at the Bodleian Library and published here from the manuscript for the first time. The appendix concludes with '*Church's Year-Book*: Manuscript Foliation' (pp. 517–18). There is also a most useful glossary (pp. 519–22) and in common with the other volumes in *The Works of Thomas Traherne* there is an extremely detailed, helpful introduction (pp. xvii–liv). The editor Jan Ross includes with each section clear, detailed textual emendations and notes.

Ian Norrie ran the High Hill Bookshop in the fashionable Hampstead High Street in London. His *The Business of Lunch: A Bookman's Life and Travels* is his colourful account of his customers, of whom one would have liked more, and his reflections on the traditions of bookselling and publishing. In short, this is a memoir which will be a useful addition to studies of the book business in London in the period following the Second World War. In addition there is a delightful dust-jacket by Sydney Arrobus illustrating the old High Hill Bookshop, 11–12 Hampstead High Street.

The Butler Library at Columbia University, 18 February–29 May 2009, gave an exhibition in honour of the collector and his books. *Imprints from the '90s: Selections from the Library of James G. Nelson: An Exhibition in Honor of the Collector & his Books* consists of lectures given on 18 February 2009. In addition to G. Thomas Tanselle's introductory remarks, Sharon Marcus spoke on 'The Art of the Book' and Erik Gray spoke on 'Distractingly Beautiful Books of Poetry from the Late 19th Century'. These talks are a tribute to the magnificent library of James G. Nelson, consisting of exceedingly fine collections of major and minor figures of late nineteenth- and early twentieth-century British literature and the arts. Authors collected range from Aubrey Beardsley, Walter Crane, and Ernest Dowson to William Watson, Oscar Wilde, and William Butler Yeats. The Butler Library is exceedingly fortunate.

The first volume of the two-volume *Cultural History of Reading* is edited by Gabrielle Watling and focuses on 'World Literature'. The second volume is edited by Sara E. Quay and focuses on 'American Literature'. The first volume is divided into five parts. The first focuses on 'The Americas' and contains three chapters (pp. 3–60); the second on 'Europe and Britain' with nine chapters (pp. 61–286); the third on 'Asia and the Pacific' with seven chapters (pp. 287–422); the fourth on 'South Asia and the Indian Sub-Continent (India, Pakistan, Bangladesh, Sri Lanka)' with four chapters (pp. 423–520); and the fifth on 'Africa and the Middle East' with four chapters (pp. 521–610). There is an 'Appendix—Representative Bibliographies for Other Reading Areas' (pp. 611–14), followed by an extensive index (pp. 615–50). The various contributors to these volumes explore thoroughly 'what people have read and why they have read it, at different times and in different places in America and around the world . . . the project links key cultural changes and events to the reading material of the period' (p. ix). The second volume is not dissimilar to the first, although it only has eleven chapters by various hands and is much shorter. The first chapter is devoted to 'Reading in the Era of Discovery and Exploration: Prior to 1700' (pp. 1–28), and the eleventh chapter is on 'Reading in the Twenty-First Century: 2000–2007' (pp. 349–76). There is a list of 'Recommended Readings' (pp. 377–8) and a useful index (pp. 379–404).

The fourth volume of *A History of the Book in America, Print in Motion, The Expansion of Publishing and Reading in the United States, 1880–1940*, edited by Carl F. Kaestle and Janice A. Radway, is divided into four sections, followed by an epilogue. There is also a 'Prologue' by the editors (pp. 1–6). This fourth volume is concerned with a period of change and rapid expansion, a print boom. The first section, entitled 'Print in Motion', contains the editor's 'A Framework for the History of Publishing and Reading in the United States, 1880–1940' (pp. 7–21) and the second chapter, Carl F. Kaestle's 'Seeing the Sites: Readers, Publishers, and Local Print Cultures in 1880' (pp. 22–48). The second section is concerned with 'The Publishing Trades' and in addition to the editor's introduction (pp. 49–55), contains eight chapters. Distinguished contributors include Michael Winship on 'The Rise of a National Book Trade System in the United States' (pp. 56–77), and James L.W. West III on 'The Expansion of the National Book Trade System' (pp. 78–89). The third section, on 'The Social Uses of Print', in addition to the editors' introduction (pp. 193–6), contains ten again fascinating chapters, as does the fourth section, 'Readers and Reading'. This is divided into two. In the first part, on 'Institutions' (pp. 411–70), in addition to the editors' introduction (pp. 411–14)—they also write an introduction (pp. 471–5) to the second part—there are three chapters. The second part, 'Reading in Situ' (pp. 471–527), also has three chapters. The editors contribute an 'Epilogue' (pp. 528–36). There is a very valuable 'Bibliographical Essay' (pp. 623–48), and an index (pp. 649–68). This excellent volume is accompanied by twenty-one figures and tables.

Leslie Mitchell's *Maurice Bowra: A Life* recounts the life and work of an extremely powerful figure in Oxford and in the British academic establishment, Sir Maurice Bowra (1898–1971). A classicist who did not produce as much as he promised, a poet, a wit, and a raconteur extraordinary, he served on the Western Front in the First World War, became a Fellow of Wadham College for sixteen years, was Warden of the college for thirty-two years, and Vice Chancellor of Oxford University from 1951 to 1954. Born into the British colonial elite, his father was a high-ranking administrator serving in China; his childhood was not without incident. He rode on his pony to the tunes of the emperors, narrowly escaped with his life during the Boxer Rebellion, and was in San Francisco prior to the great earthquake. His twelfth birthday was celebrated in Algiers. The Great Depression began when he was sent to boarding school in Cheltenham, and his experiences on the Western Front never left him. Bowra was a paradox, as Mitchell reveals. He was a cosmopolitan and yet could be extremely parochial. His scholarship was far from distinguished and his mentor Gilbert Murray was influential in denying him the Oxford Chair of Greek. Mitchell's life not only reveals much about Oxford and the academic establishment of the first half of the twentieth century, but is also a personal biography revealing a man haunted by many demons, including his own sexuality and fear of scandal. Literary figures bound in and out of the highly readable *Maurice Bowra: A Life*.

Last but by no means least in this survey, Stephen Knight's *Merlin: Knowledge and Power through the Ages* is a study of the Merlin myth and contains an extensive primary bibliography (pp. 231–44) and secondary bibliography (pp. 245–62) of the subject. There is also a very detailed index (pp. 263–75). An article which may not be noticed elsewhere is Ina Ferris's 'Book Fancy: Bibliomania and the Literary World' (*KSJ* 57[2009] 33–52). In an interesting review assessment of recent work, Ina Ferris considers the implications of the fact that recently 'bibliomania has received wider and more serious critical attention in Romantic studies' (p. 33). She concludes that 'A period figure like the book-man opens up to view an often occluded disjunction, one that defined the contest between outward and inward book, and which rendered the printed book itself an important if paradoxical sense literature's problem' (p. 52).

Note

The writer wishes to thank Jayne Crosby-Lindner, Professor James E. May, and Professor David L. Vander Meulen for their help with this chapter.

Books Reviewed

Abbott, Steven. *Gore Vidal: A Bibliography, 1940–2009*. OakK. [2009] pp. 637 + 120. CD-ROM. $195 ISBN 9 7815 8456 2207.

Adams, Hazard. *Blake's Margins: An Interpretive Study of the Annotations*. McFarland. [2009] pp. 212. $39.95 ISBN 9 7807 8644 5363.

Ahrens, Rudiger, and Klaus Stierstorfer. *Symbolism: An International Annual of Critical Aesthetics*, vol. 9. AMS. [2009] pp. xiii + 392. $157.50 ISBN 9 7804 0463 5695.

Alderman, Nigel, and C.D. Blanton, eds. *A Concise Companion to Postwar British and Irish Poetry*. Blackwell. [2009] pp. xxviii + 298. $104.95 ISBN 9 7814 0512 9244.

Arnold, John, and John Hay. *The Bibliography of Australian Literature, P–Z*. UQP. [2009] pp. 995. $130 ISBN 9 7807 0223 6891.

Bartlett, Allison Hoover. *The Man who Loved Books Too Much: The True Story of a Thief, a Detective, and a World of Literary Obsession*. Riverhead. [2009] pp. 288. $24.59 ISBN 9 7815 9448 8917.

Bassett, John E. *William Faulkner: An Annotated Bibliography of Criticism since 1988*. Scarecrow. [2009] pp. vi + 594. $100 ISBN 9 7808 1086 7413.

Betts, Gregory, ed. *The Wrong World: Selected Stories and Essays of Bertram Brooker*. UOttawaP. [2009] pp. xlix + 288. $30 ISBN 9 7807 7660 6965.

Brooker, Peter, and Andrew Thacker, eds. *The Oxford Critical and Cultural History of Modernist Magazines*. OUP. [2009] pp. xvii + 955. $180 ISBN 9 7801 9921 1159.

Brown, Sue. *Joseph Severn, a Life: The Rewards of Friendship*. OUP. [2009] pp. 432. £30 ISBN 9 7801 9956 5023.

Bryer, Jackson R., and Richard Kopley, eds. *Resources for American Literary Study*, vol. 32. AMS. [2009] pp. xii + 373. $187.50 ISBN 9 7804 0464 6325.

Buickerood, James G. *Eighteenth-Century Thought*, vol. 4. AMS. [2009] pp. 410. $137.50 ISBN 9 7804 0463 7644.

Cooper, James Fenimore. *Ned Meyers; or, A Life before the Mast*. Karen Lentz Madison and R.D. Madison, historical introd. William S. Dudley and Hugh Egan. AMS. [2009] pp. liv+252. $125 ISBN 9 7804 0464 4673.

Cowie, A.P., ed. The Oxford History of English Lexicography, *vol. 1*: General-Purpose Dictionaries, *vol. 2*: Specialized Dictionaries. Clarendon. [2009] vol. 1: pp. xviii + 467 ISBN 9 7801 9928 5600, vol. 2: pp. xix + 551 ISBN 9 7801 9928 5617, 2-vol set £175 ISBN 9 7801 9928 5624.

Darnton, Robert. *The Case for Books: Past, Present, and Future*. Public Affairs. [2009] pp. 219. $23.95 ISBN 9 7815 8648 8260.

Deegan, Marilyn, and Kathryn Sutherland, eds. *Text Editing, Print, and the Digital Word*. Ashgate. [2009] pp. xvi + 224. $99.95 ISBN 9 7807 5467 3071.

Deegan, Marilyn, and Kathryn Sutherland. *Transferred Illusions: Digital Technology and the Forms of Print*. Ashgate. [2009] pp. 218. £55 ISBN 9 7807 5467 0162.

Dibble, Brian. *Doing Life: A Biography of Elizabeth Jolley*. UWAP. [2008] pp. 352. $32 ISBN 9 7819 2140 1060.

Duncan, Kathryn, ed. *Religion in the Age of Reason: A Transatlantic Study of the Long Eighteenth Century*. AMS. [2009] pp. xx + 234. $84.50 ISBN 9 7804 0464 8534.

Ellenzweig, Sarah. *The Fringes of Belief: English Literature, Ancient Heresy, and the Politics of Freethinking, 1660–1760*. StanfordUP. [2009] pp. xii + 240. $60 ISBN 9 7808 0475 8772.

Fitzgerald, Carol. *Series Americana: Post Depression-Era Regional Literature, 1938–1980. A Descriptive Bibliography*, 2 vols. OakK/Center for the Book in the Library of Congress. [2009] pp. xxxvi + 978. $125 ISBN 9 7815 8456 2528.

Ford, Philip, and Roger P.H. Green, eds. *George Buchanan: Poet and Dramatist*. Classical Press of Wales. [2009] pp. xxxiii + 322. $100 ISBN 9 7819 0512 5364.

Forshaw, Barry. *British Crime Writing: An Encyclopedia*, 2 vols. Greenwood. [2009] pp. xxiv + 419. $149 ISBN 9 7818 4645 0228.

Forsyth, Katherine. *Studies of the Book of Deer*. FCP. [2009] pp. xvii + 481. $120 ISBN 9 7818 5182 5691.

Foster, John Wilson. *Between Shadows: Modern Irish Writing and Culture*. Foreword by Edna Longley. IAP. [2009] pp. x + 257. $69.95 ISBN 9 7807 1653 0053.

Gekoski, Rick. *Outside of a Dog: A Bibliomemoir*. Constable. [2009] pp. x + 278. $14.99 ISBN 9 7818 4529 8838.

Gladstone Database. [GladCAT]. http://www.st-deiniols.com/the-library/gladcat.htm.

Goodall, Peter. *Chaucer's Monk's Tale and Nun's Priest's Tale: An Annotated Bibliography 1900–2000*. UTorP. [2009] pp. xlvii + 338. $110 ISBN 9 7808 0209 3202.

Görner, Rüdiger. *London Fragments: A Literary Expedition*. Trans. Debra Marmor and Herbert Danner. ArmchairTraveller. [2007] pp. xiv+132+7 illustrations. £7.95 ($11.95) ISBN 9 7819 0659 8730.

Gostick, Chris. T.F. *Powys's Favourite Bookseller: The Story of Charles Lahr*. Cecil Woolf. [2009] pp. 33. n.p. ISBN 9 7819 0728 6218.

Grafton, Anthony. *Worlds Made by Words: Scholarship and Community in the Modern West*. HarvardUP. [2009] pp. 422. $29.95 ISBN 9 7806 7403 2576.

Hagstrom, Jack W.C., and Bill Morgan. *James Ingram Merrill: A Descriptive Bibliography*. OakK. [2009] pp. 496. $95 ISBN 9 7815 8456 2641.

Hazell, Dinah. *Poverty in Late Middle English Literature: The Meene and the Riche*. FCP. [2009] pp. 234. $65 ISBN 9 7818 4682 1554.

Heller, Joshua. *Classic Examples of the Art of the Book: Catalogue Thirty Seven, Summer 2009*. [2009] pp. 90. Available from joshuahellerrarebooks.com.

Hogan, William P. *'The Golden Helmet' and 'The Green Helmet' Manuscript Materials by W.B. Yeats*. CornUP. [2009] pp. xxxii + 147. $69.90 ISBN 9 7808 0144 7044.

Howard-Hill, T.H. *The British Book Trade, 1475–1890: A Bibliography*, 2 vols. BL/OakK. [2009] pp. lxii + 1,776. $175 ISBN 9 7807 1235 0594.

Imprints from the '90s: Selections from the Library of James G. Nelson: An Exhibition in Honor of the Collector & his Books, February 18–May 29, 2009. [2009] pagination and price unavailable.

Johnson, Kathleen A., and Steven R. Harris, eds. *Teaching Literary Research: Challenges in a Changing Environment*. ACRL Publications Librarianship 60. [2009] pp. 274. $55 ISBN 9 7808 3898 5090.

Kaestle, Carl F., and Janice A. Radway, eds. *A History of the Book in America, vol. 4: Print in Motion: The Expansion of Publishing and Reading in the United States, 1880–1940*. American Antiquarian Society/UNCP. [2009] pp. 669. $60 ISBN 9 7808 0783 1861.

Kafker, Frank A., and Jeff Loveland, eds. *The Early Britannica: The Growth of an Outstanding Encyclopedia*. SVEC. [2009] pp. xiii + 349. $115 ISBN 9 7807 2940 9810.

Kearney, James. *The Incarnate in Text: Imagining the Book in Reformation England*. UPennP. [2009] pp. 336. $65 ISBN 9 7808 1224 1587.

Kerby-Fulton, Kathryn, ed. *Women and the Divine in Literature before 1700: Essays in Memory of Margot Louis*. ELS Editions. [2009] pp. 333. $30 ISBN 9 7815 5052 3830.

Knight, Stephen. *Merlin: Knowledge and Power through the Ages*. CornUP. [2009] pp. xx + 276. $27.95 ISBN 9 7808 0144 3657.

Kopley, Richard, and Barbara Cantalupo. *Prospects for the Study of American Literature II*. AMS. [2009] pp. xx + 355. $122.50 ISBN 9 7804 0461 5987.

Kosta-Théfaine, Jean-François. *Travels and Travelogues in the Middle Ages*. AMS. [2009] pp. vii + 298. $96.50 ISBN 9 7804 0464 1689.

Lemon, Rebecca, Emma Mason, Jonathan Roberts, and Christopher Rowland, eds. *The Blackwell Companion to the Bible in English Literature*. Blackwell. [2009] pp. x + 703. $199.95 ISBN 9 7814 0513 1605.

Lerner, Laurence. *Reading Women's Poetry*. SussexAP. [2009] pp. 194. $34.95 ISBN 9 7818 4519 3348.

McCulloch, Margery Palmer. *Scottish Modernism and its Contexts 1918–1959: Literature, National Identity and Cultural Exchange*. EdinUP. [2009] pp. 230. $110 ISBN 9 7807 4863 4743.

McDonald, Peter. *The Literature Police: Apartheid Censorship and its Cultural Consequences*. OUP. [2009] pp. xvi + 416. £25 ISBN 9 7801 9928 3347.

McGann, Jerome. *Are the Humanities Inconsequent? Interpreting Marx's Riddle of the Dog*. Prickly Paradigm Press. [2009] pp. x + 100. $12.95 ISBN 9 7809 7940 5761.

Mitchell, Leslie. *Maurice Bowra: A Life*. OUP. [2009] pp. xii + 386. $50 ISBN 9 7801 9929 5845.

Mueller, Janel, and Joshua Scodel. *Elizabeth I: Translations*. UChicP. [2009] vol. 1: pp. 504, ISBN 9 7802 2620 1313, vol. 2: pp. 512, ISBN 9 7802 2620 1320. $50 the set.

Narbeshuber, Lisa. *Confessing Cultures: Politics and the Self in the Poetry of Sylvia Plath*. ELS Editions. [2009] pp. xxiii + 103. $18 ISBN 9 7805 5058 3854.

Norrie, Ian. *The Business of Lunch: A Bookman's Life and Travels*. Quartet. [2009] pp. 352. £20 ISBN 9 7807 0437 1507.

O'Sullivan, Dan. *Wikipedia: A New Community of Practice?* Ashgate. [2009] pp. xiii + 192. $79.95 ISBN 9 7807 5467 4337.

Robbins, William. *Stanley Elkin: A Comprehensive Bibliography*. Scarecrow. [2009] pp. xviii + 488. $110 ISBN 9 7808 1086 9561.

Ross, Jan, ed. *The Works of Thomas Traherne*, vol. 4. Brewer. [2009] pp. liv + 523. $145 ISBN 9 7818 4384 1968.

Ruffner, Frederick G.Jr., and Laurence Urdang. *Ruffner's Allusions, Cultural, Literary and Historical: A Thematic Dictionary*. Omnigraphics. [2009] pp. xxix + 969. $70 ISBN 9 7807 8081 1225.

Sivils, Matthew Wynn, and Jeffrey Walker. *Literature in the Early American Republic: Annual Studies on Cooper and his Contemporaries*. AMS. [2009] pp. xv + 308. $125 ISBN 9 7804 0463 9112.

Soupel, Serge, Kevin L. Cope, and Alexander Pettit. *Adventure: An Eighteenth-Century Idiom. Essays on the Daring and the Bold as a Pre-Modern Medium*. AMS. [2009] pp. xx + 343. $145 ISBN 9 7804 0464 8589.

Striphas, Ted. *The Late Age of Print: Everyday Book Culture from Consumerism to Control*. ColUP. [2009] pp. vii + 242. $27.50 ISBN 9 7802 3114 8146.

Tabachnick, Stephen E. *Teaching the Graphic Novel*. MLA. [2009] pp. 352. $40 ISBN 9 7816 0329 0616.

Tanselle, G. Thomas. *Bibliographical Analysis: A Historical Introduction*. CUP. [2009] pp. 167. £45 ISBN 9 7805 2176 0348.

Thomson, R.M. *A Descriptive Catalogue of the Medieval Manuscripts of Merton College, Oxford*. with a description of the Greek Manuscripts by N.G. Wilson. Brewer. [2009] pp. xlv+440. £180 ISBN 9 7818 4384 1883.

Tomita, Soko. *A Bibliographical Catalogue of Italian Books Printed in England 1558–1603*. Ashgate. [2009] pp. xx + 607. $124.99 ISBN 9 7807 5466 3736.

Upfal, Annette, and Christine Alexander, eds. *Jane Austen's The History of England & Cassandra's Portraits*. Juvenilia Press. [2009] pp. lvi + 78. A$15 ISBN 9 7807 3342 7800.

Vickery, Amanda. *Behind Closed Doors: At Home in Georgian England*. YaleUP. [2009] pp. 368. $45 ISBN 9 7803 0015 4535.

Vigus, James. *Platonic Coleridge*. Legenda. [2009] pp. xii + 188. $89.50 ISBN 9 7819 0654 0067.

Walker, Pierre A., and Greg W. Zacharias. *The Complete Letters of Henry James, 1872–1876*, vol. 2. UNebP. [2009] pp. 342. $130 ISBN 9 7808 0322 2977.

Watling, Gabrielle, and Sara E. Quay, eds. *Cultural History of Reading*, 2 vols. Greenwood. [2009] vol. 1: pp. x+654, vol. 2: pp. xii+406. $199.95 ISBN 9 7803 1333 7444.

Yamada, Akihiro. *Secrets of the Printed Page in the Age of Shakespeare: Bibliographical Studies in the Plays of Beaumont, Chapman, Dekker, Fletcher, Ford, Marston, Shakespeare, Shirley and the Text of King James I's The True Lawe of Free Monarchies*. AMS. [2009] pp. 290. $137.50 ISBN 9 7804 0462 3463.

YWES Index of Critics

The Year's Work in English Studies, Volume 90 (2011)
doi:10.1093/ywes/mar021

YWES Index of Author and Subjects

Notes

(1) Material which has not been seen by contributors is not indexed.
(2) Authors such a A.S. Byatt, who are both authors of criticism and subjects of discussion, are listed in whichever index is appropriate for each reference.
(3) Author entries have subdivisions listed in the following order:
  (a) author's relationship with other author's
  (b) author's relationship with other subjects
  (c) author's characteristics
  (d) author's works (listed alphabetically)
(4) A page reference in **bold** represents a main entry for that particular subject.